Zac Conway
PRESENTED TO
Show of friendship
ON THE OCCASION OF
Frances Garrett
BY
May 22, 2008
DATE

OLD TESTAMENT

NEW TESTAMENT

THE GOSPELS

PAUL'S LETTERS

GENERAL LETTERS

PROPHECY

JANUARY

DAILY TREASURES FROM GOD
A Daily Reading Guide

ME

1 ❑ What is the best way to get my day off to a good start? . . . . Psalm 119:147
2 ❑ How can I be pure? . . . . Psalm 119:9
3 ❑ Why should I take care of my body if it isn't going to last forever? 1 Corinthians 6:15
4 ❑ How do I know if I'm a hypocrite? . . . . Matthew 23:28
5 ❑ How can I make my life count for something? . . . . 1 Corinthians 13:13
6 ❑ How does God feel when he thinks about me? . . . . Ephesians 1:5
7 ❑ What does God give me? . . . . John 10:28

If you would like to read more about *ME,* go to the Treasure Map and see:
Your Body, Self-examination, Be Fair, Gifts from God.

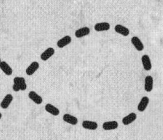

Find today's date, read the question, and look up the answer.

GOD

8 ❑ How can God be everywhere at once? . . . . Psalm 139:8
9 ❑ What does nature tell us about God? . . . . Psalm 19:1
10 ❑ Does God ever give up on people? . . . . Ezra 5:12
11 ❑ How much control does God have over the world? . . . Psalm 135:6
12 ❑ How can God live inside me? . . . . John 14:17
13 ❑ Does God see every little thing I think and do? . . . . . . Ezekiel 11:5
14 ❑ What does the Holy Spirit do? . . . . John 14:26
15 ❑ What does it mean that God is jealous? . . . . Exodus 34:14
16 ❑ How can I know that God will keep his word? . . . . Deuteronomy 32:4
17 ❑ How powerful is God? . . . . Luke 1:37

If you would like to read more about *GOD,* go to the Treasure Map and see:
Nature's Praise, God at Work, Dishonest People, Guidance, The Holy Spirit.

WORK

18 ❑ Why should I do my best even when no one is looking? . . . . Colossians 3:24
19 ❑ Does God expect us to work all the time? . . . . Exodus 34:21
20 ❑ Does God ever use young people to do important work for him? . . . 1 Samuel 17:33
21 ❑ Why should I work hard? . . . . Proverbs 13:4

If you would like to read more about *WORK,* go to the Treasure Map and see:
"It's Her Fault!", Working with God, Work.

ADULTS

22 ❑ Why should we respect authority? . . . . Romans 13:2
23 ❑ How should we act toward government leaders? . . . . . Romans 13:1
24 ❑ How should I treat old people? . . . . 1 Timothy 5:1-2

If you would like to read more about *ADULTS,* go to the Treasure Map and see:
Respecting Adults.

PRIDE

25 ❑ Why does God want us to be humble? . . . . Psalm 119:21
26 ❑ What's wrong with pride? . . . . Proverbs 11:2
27 ❑ If I do something really well, should I be proud of myself? . . . Romans 12:16
28 ❑ What does the Bible say to arrogant people? . . . . Psalm 138:6

If you would like to read more about *PRIDE,* go to the Treasure Map and see:
Meekness, Modesty, Good Looks.

ANGER

29 ❑ Is it OK to lose your temper once in awhile? . . . . Proverbs 16:32
30 ❑ What should I do when I get really angry with someone? . . . Ephesians 4:31
31 ❑ Is it ever good to get angry? . . . . 1 Samuel 11:6

If you would like to read more about *ANGER,* go to the Treasure Map and see:
Temper, Mad.

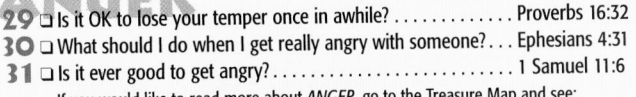

DAILY TREASURES FROM GOD

A Daily Reading Guide

FEBRUARY

FRIENDS

1 ❑ How can I get other kids to respect me? . . . . 1 Thessalonians 4:12
2 ❑ How can I be a good friend? . . . . 2 Corinthians 12:15
3 ❑ What can I do when a friend gets angry at me? . . . . Romans 12:18
4 ❑ Does God care what kind of friend I am? . . . . Proverbs 27:10
5 ❑ How can I be a better friend? . . . . Titus 2:7
6 ❑ Is it normal for my friends to let me down sometimes? . . . . Psalm 38:11
7 ❑ Is it OK for me to be around evil people as long as I'm careful not to do evil? . . . . 2 Peter 3:17
8 ❑ When one of my friends is being treated unfairly, when should I speak up? . . . . 1 Samuel 19:4
9 ❑ What are some examples of friendship? . . . . 1 Samuel 18:1
10 ❑ How can I get people to like me? . . . . Titus 3:2
11 ❑ What does it mean to be a loyal friend? . . . . 1 Samuel 20:17

If you would like to read more about *FRIENDS*, go to the Treasure Map and see:
Being Friendless, "Thank You", Trusting in People, Bad Friends.

GIVING

12 ❑ What does it mean to be generous? . . . . Luke 3:11
13 ❑ What do I get out of giving? . . . . Proverbs 3:9-10
14 ❑ Why do we give money to the church? . . . . Proverbs 3:9
15 ❑ How is it more blessed to give than to receive? . . . . 2 Corinthians 8:9
16 ❑ Does it really matter whether I give money or food to help people? . . . James 2:16
17 ❑ What is generosity? . . . . 2 Corinthians 8:2

If you would like to read more about *GIVING*, go to the Treasure Map and see:
How to Give.

Find today's date, read the question, and look up the answer.

SELF-CONFIDENCE

18 ❑ Is it OK for me to believe in myself? . . . . 1 Corinthians 10:12
19 ❑ What's wrong with trying to do everything on my own? . . . . Matthew 18:19
20 ❑ Is it OK to believe you're better than everyone else if you are better than everyone else? . . . Proverbs 16:2

CHRISTIAN LIFE

21 ❑ What should I do if kids make fun of me for being a Christian? . . 1 Peter 4:16
22 ❑ How can I get closer to God? . . . . Jeremiah 29:13
23 ❑ How can I become a stronger Christian? . . . . 2 Thessalonians 2:15
24 ❑ How long can I wait before deciding to follow God? . . . . Joshua 24:15
25 ❑ What kind of commitment does God want from me? . . . . Romans 12:1
26 ❑ What are my Christian duties? . . . . Ephesians 5:8
27 ❑ How should I be different now that I'm a Christian? . . . . Romans 6:7
28 ❑ What have I got to brag about? . . . . 1 Corinthians 1:31

If you would like to read more about *CHRISTIAN LIFE*, go to the Treasure Map and see:
Remember..., The Time Is Now, Loving Jesus, Talents, Who Is Religious?

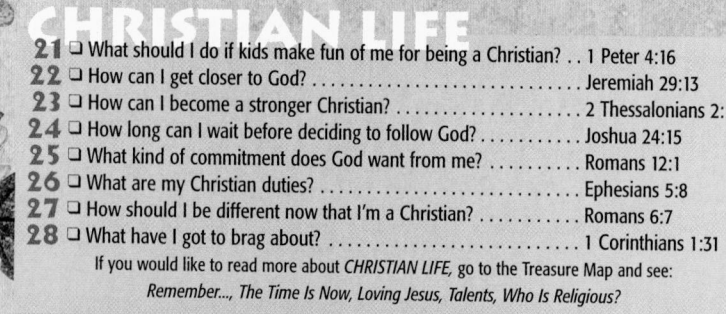

MARCH

DAILY TREASURES FROM GOD
A Daily Reading Guide

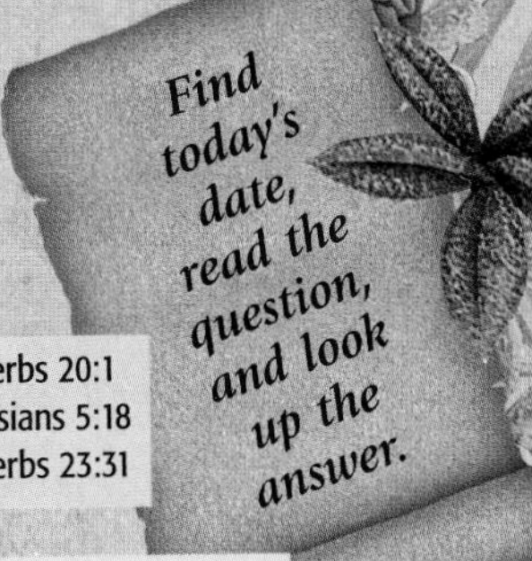
Find today's date, read the question, and look up the answer.

BAD PEOPLE

1 ❑ Why do people do bad things? . . . . Mark 7:21
2 ❑ What does God think of people who do really bad things? . . Isaiah 9:17
3 ❑ Are some people too bad for God to save? . . . . 1 John 2:2

If you would like to read more about *BAD PEOPLE,* go to the Treasure Map and see: *Procrastination, Friend of Jesus.*

ANGELS

4 ❑ What do angels do? . . . . Hebrews 1:14
5 ❑ Does each person have a guardian angel? . . . Psalm 34:7
6 ❑ Do I have a guardian angel? . . . . Psalm 91:11

DRINKING

7 ❑ What does the Bible say about drinking? . . . . Proverbs 20:1
8 ❑ What's wrong with getting drunk? . . . . Ephesians 5:18
9 ❑ What should I do if a friend offers me a sip of beer? . . . Proverbs 23:31

ATTITUDES

10 ❑ What sort of attitudes can get me in trouble? . . . . Psalm 50:17
11 ❑ What is the fear of the Lord? . . . . Proverbs 3:7
12 ❑ What's wrong with being stubborn? . . . . Proverbs 28:14

If you would like to read more about *ATTITUDES,* go to the Treasure Map and see: *Willingness to Learn, Stubborn People.*

BIBLE

13 ❑ What's so special about the Bible? . . . . Hebrews 4:12
14 ❑ Why did God give us the Bible? . . . . John 20:31
15 ❑ What can the Bible do for me? . . . . Psalm 19:8
16 ❑ Why do my parents and Sunday School teachers spend so much time teaching me the Bible? . . Psalm 119:72
17 ❑ What should I do with all the Bible lessons I hear? . . . . James 1:23-24
18 ❑ Why should I read the Bible? . . . . Matthew 13:23

If you would like to read more about *BIBLE,* go to the Treasure Map and see: *Instruction, Reading the Bible, Ignorance.*

PROBLEMS

19 ❑ What should I do when I'm feeling stressed out? . . . . James 1:12
20 ❑ How can the Bible help me understand my problems? . . . . Proverbs 2:6
21 ❑ Does God know what I'm going through? . . . . 1 John 3:20
22 ❑ How can I feel peaceful when there is so much wrong with the world? . . John 16:33
23 ❑ From what kinds of situations is God willing to rescue me? . . . . 2 Timothy 4:18
24 ❑ Everything's going wrong–what am I going to do? . . . . Matthew 6:25
25 ❑ Are my problems too big for God? . . . . Matthew 4:24

If you would like to read more about *PROBLEMS,* go to the Treasure Map and see: *Weakness, Seeking Peace.*

WORSHIP

26 ❑ Why doesn't God want us to worship idols? . . . . Deuteronomy 6:4
27 ❑ If I respect and worship God, does that mean I always act serious when I talk about him? . . Psalm 33:8
28 ❑ Why should I worship God? . . . . 1 Chronicles 16:29

If you would like to read more about *WORSHIP,* go to the Treasure Map and see: *Don't Forget... , Names of God.*

GOD'S WILL

29 ❑ Is it possible to do what God wants but do it the wrong way? . . Matthew 6:2
30 ❑ What does God expect of me? . . . . Leviticus 11:45
31 ❑ How do I know what God wants me to do? . . . . Isaiah 30:21

If you would like to read more about *GOD'S WILL,* go to the Treasure Map and see: *Fanatics, Honesty.*

DAILY TREASURES FROM GOD
A Daily Reading Guide

APRIL

Find today's date, read the question, and look up the answer.

DANGERS

1 ❑ What does God want me to watch out for? . . . . Mark 13:33
2 ❑ What should I watch out for? . . . . Matthew 26:41

If you would like to read more about *DANGERS,* go to the Treasure Map and see: *"Dangerous Kisses."*

THOUGHTS

3 ❑ Does God care what I think about? . . . . Romans 8:7
4 ❑ How can I clean up my mind? . . . . Philippians 4:8
5 ❑ Are dirty thoughts bad if you don't do what you think about? . . . Matthew 15:19

If you would like to read more about *THOUGHTS,* go to the Treasure Map and see: *Heart.*

GOD'S ANGER

6 ❑ Is God really angry all the time? . . . . Psalm 86:5
7 ❑ What makes God angry? . . . . Romans 1:18
8 ❑ Does God get angry when people are mean to weaker people? . . Psalm 82:3
9 ❑ Is God always angry at me? . . . . Nehemiah 9:17
10 ❑ How do I know God isn't angry with me? . . . . Luke 6:37
11 ❑ When does God say, "Enough is enough"? . . . . Matthew 11:20
12 ❑ What kind of kids really make God upset? . . . . Proverbs 30:17

If you would like to read more about *GOD'S ANGER,* go to the Treasure Map and see: *Helping Weak People, Sin (Warnings).*

VALUE OF PEOPLE

13 ❑ Am I really that important to God? . . . . 1 Peter 1:18-19
14 ❑ What does "made in God's image" mean? . . . . Genesis 1:26-27

KINDNESS

15 ❑ Am I supposed to be nice to that kid in school who drives everybody crazy? . . John 8:7
16 ❑ If a kid is mean to me, why should I be nice to him? . . . . Luke 6:35
17 ❑ Why should I be kind to people who are not kind? . . . . James 4:17

PLEASING GOD

18 ❑ What kind of service does God like best? . . . . Acts 20:18-19
19 ❑ Who does God like best? . . . . Acts 10:35
20 ❑ What kinds of deeds please God? . . . . Hebrews 13:16
21 ❑ Do I have to be good before God will love me? . . . . Romans 3:24

If you would like to read more about *PLEASING GOD,* go to the Treasure Map and see: *God's Friends, Sympathy, Who Deserves Christ?*

CHANGE

22 What does God want to change in me when I become a Christian? . . Ephesians 4:22
23 How can I be more like God? . . . . Ephesians 4:32
24 How is God changing me? . . . . Romans 12:2
25 How can I become a better person? . . . . Hebrews 12:1
26 What does it mean to repent? . . . . 2 Corinthians 5:20

If you would like to read more about *CHANGE,* go to the Treasure Map and see: *Walking with God.*

OBEDIENCE

27 ❑ What does obedience mean? . . . . Ephesians 6:6
28 ❑ What if I'm tired of doing good? . . . . Galatians 6:9
29 ❑ What happens if I just decide not to listen to God? . . . Isaiah 42:25
30 ❑ What happens when I live God's way? . . . . Isaiah 26:7

If you would like to read more about *OBEDIENCE,* go to the Treasure Map and see: *Obeying Christ, Double Life, Salvation.*

MAY

DAILY TREASURES FROM GOD
A Daily Reading Guide

TEMPTATION

1 ❑ What can I do when I feel like giving in to temptation? . . . . . . Proverbs 4:14
2 ❑ What should I do when I feel tempted? . . . . James 4:7
3 ❑ Does God know how hard it is for me to resist temptation? . . 1 Corinthians 10:13
4 ❑ How can Jesus help me say no to temptation? . . . . John 15:5

REWARDS

5 ❑ What reward is there in being good? . . . . Proverbs 12:13
6 ❑ What rewards does God give to people who obey him? . . . . Revelation 5:10
7 ❑ Will I get a reward when Jesus comes back? . . . . 1 Peter 5:4
8 ❑ Will I be rewarded for something good I did even if no one else saw it? . . Matthew 10:42

If you would like to read more about *REWARDS*, go to the Treasure Map and see:
Suffering Rewarded, Serving.

SATAN AND DEMONS

9 ❑ What kind of power does Satan have? . . . . Ephesians 6:12
10 ❑ Should I be afraid of Satan? . . . . Romans 16:20
11 ❑ Can demons hurt me? . . . . Ephesians 6:12
12 ❑ Is it true that "the devil made me do it"? . . . . 1 John 4:4
13 ❑ What is the antichrist? . . . . 1 John 4:3
14 ❑ What will happen to Satan? . . . . Revelation 20:10

JUSTICE

15 ❑ How do we know God is fair? . . . . Proverbs 16:11
16 ❑ Why do some kids get caught and others don't? . . . . Psalm 37:35
17 ❑ Why do some people do good and it seems like they don't get rewarded? . . Ezekiel 18:25
18 ❑ Why do some kids seem to get away with anything? . . . . Matthew 12:36

If you would like to read more about *JUSTICE*, go to the Treasure Map and see: *Blame, Faith Tested.*

Find today's date, read the question, and look up the answer.

SERVING

19 ❑ Should I tell people about how I serve God? . . . . Matthew 6:16
20 ❑ Why does God want us to work so hard serving people? . . John 13:14

If you would like to read more about *SERVING*, go to the Treasure Map and see:
Work that Helps Others.

SALVATION

21 ❑ What do I have to do to become a Christian? . . . . John 3:16
22 ❑ What happens to me when I become a Christian? . . . . 2 Corinthians 5:17
23 ❑ Will I go to heaven if I'm really good? . . . . Romans 9:32
24 ❑ Does everyone have a chance to become a Christian? . . . . Titus 2:11-12
25 ❑ Is Jesus really the only way to heaven? . . . . Acts 4:12
26 ❑ Is there anybody God does not want to become a Christian? . . 1 Timothy 2:4
27 ❑ I want to become a Christian. How can I? . . . . Romans 10:9

If you would like to read more about *SALVATION*, go to the Treasure Map and see:
Salvation by Faith, Why Jesus Came, Heaven.

PARENTS

28 ❑ Why did God give me my parents? . . . . Proverbs 6:23
29 ❑ Why do my parents say they discipline me "for my own good"? . . Proverbs 22:15
30 ❑ Why do my parents always want to know where I am? . . . . 1 Samuel 10:2
31 ❑ Why does God let my parents discipline me? . . . . Proverbs 13:24

DAILY TREASURES FROM GOD
A Daily Reading Guide

JUNE

SUCCESS

1 ❑ What can go wrong when everything's going right? . . Proverbs 30:9
2 ❑ How can I get God to bless me? . . . . Matthew 6:33

JUDGMENT

3 ❑ What does it mean that God is a judge? . . . . Psalm 75:7
4 ❑ Why doesn't God just destroy all the bad people right now? . . 2 Peter 3:9
5 ❑ Will God really judge everything we do? . . . . 2 Corinthians 5:10
6 ❑ Will sinners ever get what they deserve? . . . . 2 Thessalonians 1:9

If you would like to read more about *JUDGMENT,* go to the Treasure Map and see: *Bad People.*

GOD'S CARE

7 ❑ How can I get God to help me? . . . . Luke 6:38
8 ❑ How is God like a father? . . . . Deuteronomy 10:18
9 ❑ How can I be sure God is watching over me? . . . . Psalm 37:28
10 ❑ How can I know God will always be there when I need him? . . Isaiah 63:16
11 ❑ Does God really care about me? . . . . 1 Peter 5:7
12 ❑ Where can I go when I feel down? . . . . 2 Corinthians 1:3

If you would like to read more about *GOD'S CARE,* go to the Treasure Map and see:
God's Promises, God's Love, Grief.

Find today's date, read the question, and look up the answer.

OTHERS

13 ❑ Which is more important, to love God or to love people? . . . . . 1 John 4:7
14 ❑ Why should I be friends with the kids that no one else likes? . . Matthew 9:10
15 ❑ What is the Golden Rule? . . . . Matthew 7:12
16 ❑ What does hospitality mean? . . . . Romans 12:13
17 ❑ What should I do if I can't stand somebody? . . . . Leviticus 19:17

If you would like to read more about *OTHERS,* go to the Treasure Map and see:
Cold Shoulder, New Kids.

PRIORITIES

18 ❑ What is my most important job? . . . . Matthew 6:33
19 ❑ What is the most important trait to have? . . . . 1 Corinthians 13:13
20 ❑ What does God want most out of us? . . . . Micah 6:8
21 ❑ What does God most want from me? . . . . Matthew 22:37
22 ❑ What's the number one goal I can have for my life? . . Deuteronomy 5:32

If you would like to read more about *PRIORITIES,* go to the Treasure Map and see:
Seeking God.

MONEY

23 ❑ Why doesn't God just give me more money? I sure could use it. . . 1 Timothy 6:17
24 ❑ Why does the Bible tell me not to trust in riches? . . . . Proverbs 11:4
25 ❑ Why doesn't God make me rich? . . . . 1 Timothy 6:9
26 ❑ What's wrong with being stingy? . . . . Proverbs 21:13
27 ❑ What's good about not being rich? . . . . James 2:5
28 ❑ Is there anything wrong with being successful? . . . . Luke 11:43

If you would like to read more about *MONEY,* go to the Treasure Map and see: *Soon Gone.*

GROWING UP

29 ❑ What does it mean to grow up? . . . . 2 Peter 1:5-6
30 ❑ Is making a decision by myself the grown-up thing to do? . . Proverbs 15:22

If you would like to read more about *GROWING UP,* go to the Treasure Map and see:
Making Progress.

JULY

DAILY TREASURES FROM GOD
A Daily Reading Guide

TIME

1 ❑ What are God's instructions about how I use my time? . . Ephesians 5:15-16
2 ❑ What's wrong with wasting time? . . . . Psalm 39:5
3 ❑ When is it good to hurry? . . . . Psalm 119:60
4 ❑ What should I do when I'm bored? . . . . 1 Timothy 5:13

If you would like to read more about *TIME,* go to the Treasure Map and see:
Waste, Serving Quickly, Willingness to Work.

FAMILY LIFE

5 ❑ How does God want me to treat my family? . . . . Romans 14:13
6 ❑ Is it ever OK to argue with my brother or sister? . . . . Proverbs 18:19
7 ❑ What can I do when my brother or sister drives me crazy? . . Ephesians 4:2
8 ❑ What should I do to keep the peace in my family? . . . . Romans 14:19

FORGIVENESS

9 ❑ Will God forgive me even if I do something really bad? . . . . 1 John 1:9
10 ❑ If God can't stand sin, and I sin sometimes, how can God stand me? . . . . Romans 5:1
11 ❑ Why did I get in trouble if God forgave me? . . . . Ephesians 5:6
12 ❑ Why should I forgive others? . . . . Matthew 6:15
13 ❑ If someone makes fun of me at school, does God expect me to forgive the person? . . Luke 11:4
14 ❑ How can I be forgiven? . . . . Romans 3:25

If you would like to read more about *FORGIVENESS,* go to the Treasure Map and see: *Feeling Sorry.*

Find today's date, read the question, and look up the answer.

LYING

15 ❑ My friends say it's OK to lie if it doesn't hurt anyone. Is that true? . . Proverbs 12:22
16 ❑ Should I tell the truth even if I know it will get a friend in trouble? . . Exodus 23:1
17 ❑ What happens to liars? . . . . Proverbs 19:5

If you would like to read more about *LYING,* go to the Treasure Map and see:
Lying to Yourself, Telling the Truth, Perjury.

FUTURE

18 ❑ What's the best way to prepare for the future? . . . . Matthew 24:44
19 ❑ What kind of future has God planned for me? . . . . 2 Corinthians 5:1

If you would like to read more about *FUTURE,* go to the Treasure Map and see: *The Future.*

FAITH

20 ❑ Why is faith important? . . . . Hebrews 11:6
21 ❑ What difference does it make in my everyday life that I have faith in God? . . Romans 10:11

If you would like to read more about *FAITH,* go to the Treasure Map and see: *Trusting God, God's Response.*

SIN

22 ❑ Why shouldn't we sin? . . . . Proverbs 11:19
23 ❑ Why should I take sin seriously? . . . . Psalm 7:12
24 ❑ Are there people who don't sin? . . . . Romans 3:23
25 ❑ Does sin always have consequences? . . . . Ecclesiastes 11:9
26 ❑ Why should I confess my sins to God if he already knows about them? . . Psalm 38:4
27 ❑ What happens when I give in to sin? . . . . Genesis 25:29-30, 33
28 ❑ Does Jesus ever punish people for their sin? . . . . John 5:22

If you would like to read more about *SIN,* go to the Treasure Map and see:
Disappointment, Blinded by Sin, Confession, Cost of Sin.

FUN

29 ❑ How does God want me to act at parties? . . . . Galatians 5:21
30 ❑ Is there anything bad about laughing? . . . . Luke 6:25
31 ❑ Why doesn't God want us to have fun? . . . . Nehemiah 8:10

If you would like to read more about *FUN,* go to the Treasure Map and see: *Happiness.*

DAILY TREASURES FROM GOD
A Daily Reading Guide

AUGUST

JESUS

1 ❑ Why does the Bible call Jesus a Savior? .... John 6:67-68
2 ❑ What can I learn about God by learning about Jesus? .... Hebrews 1:3
3 ❑ What's so special about Jesus? .... Acts 4:12
4 ❑ Was Jesus really a man? .... Luke 1:31
5 ❑ Where does Jesus live? .... Romans 8:10
6 ❑ If Jesus is king, why are there so many problems in the world? .... 1 Corinthians 15:25
7 ❑ When Jesus was on earth, did he have good days and bad days like I do? .... Hebrews 12:2
8 ❑ Why did Jesus have to die? .... 1 Peter 2:24
9 ❑ Why does the Bible call Jesus the "Lamb of God"? .... John 1:29

If you would like to read more about *JESUS,* go to the Treasure Map and see:
The Teacher, The Ultimate, Jesus' Friends, God's Presence, Violence, Unhappiness.

SUFFERING

10 ❑ Why do bad things happen to good kids? .... Hebrews 12:7
11 ❑ Why do I have to suffer? .... 1 Peter 1:7
12 ❑ How can I feel better when I'm hurting? .... Romans 5:3
13 ❑ Why should I "count it all joy" when things go wrong? .. Hebrews 12:11
14 ❑ Why are some lessons so hard to learn? .... Psalm 119:71
15 ❑ Why do Christians have to suffer for their faith? .... John 15:20
16 ❑ Why do bad things happen to me? .... Proverbs 3:11-12
17 ❑ If God loves me, why isn't life easier? .... Matthew 16:24

If you would like to read more about *SUFFERING,* go to the Treasure Map and see:
Being Smart, Why Suffer?

Find today's date, read the question, and look up the answer.

PRAYER

18 ❑ Why are we supposed to pray? .... Matthew 26:41
19 ❑ Does God listen when I pray? .... Hebrews 4:16
20 ❑ What can I do when I feel like giving up praying about something? .. James 5:7
21 ❑ Does God want me to ask him for things, or does he get tired of it? .. Jeremiah 10:21
22 ❑ How should I pray? .... 1 John 5:14
23 ❑ Will God answer my prayers? .... John 14:13
24 ❑ What difference does it make if I pray for someone? .... Psalm 106:23
25 ❑ Should I keep praying even if it seems God isn't answering? .... Romans 12:12
26 ❑ How can I tell if God is listening when I pray? .... Psalm 5:3
27 ❑ Why does my pastor talk about a "prayer closet"? .... Matthew 6:6
28 ❑ Does God always answer prayer? .... Luke 11:9
29 ❑ What should I do if God doesn't answer my prayers right away? ..... Psalm 37:7
30 ❑ When should I pray? .... 1 Thessalonians 5:17
31 ❑ Are there times when God does not answer prayer? .... Isaiah 59:2

If you would like to read more about *PRAYER,* go to the Treasure Map and see:
Waiting for God, Being Hasty.

SEPTEMBER

DAILY TREASURES FROM GOD
A Daily Reading Guide

LEARNING

1 ❑ What does God want to teach me? . . . . Psalm 32:8
2 ❑ Ignorance is bliss, right? . . . . Proverbs 8:5
3 ❑ What's the best reason for trying hard in school? . . . . . . Proverbs 14:23
4 ❑ How can I learn from Jesus the way the disciples did? . . Matthew 13:36

If you would like to read more about *LEARNING,* go to the Treasure Map and see: *Unknown Sins, Study.*

DEATH

5 ❑ Does our spirit live in heaven after we die, or do we come back as someone else? . . 2 Corinthians 4:14
6 ❑ What happens to my spirit after I die? . . . . Luke 20:36
7 ❑ What is spiritual death? . . . . Revelation 21:8

If you would like to read more about *DEATH,* go to the Treasure Map and see: *Mortality, Death.*

Find today's date, read the question, and look up the answer.

LAZINESS

8 ❑ Am I lazy just because I don't want to do boring chores? . . Proverbs 18:9
9 ❑ What advice does the Bible give to lazy people? . . . . Proverbs 6:6

If you would like to read more about *LAZINESS,* go to the Treasure Map and see: *Helping at Home, Sleep.*

FEAR/COURAGE

10 ❑ Why does the Bible tell us to fear God? . . . . Proverbs 1:7
11 ❑ Is it wrong to be superstitious? . . . . Jeremiah 10:2
12 ❑ Can God protect me from bullies? . . . . 1 Chronicles 29:12
13 ❑ Are God's people safe from crime? . . . . Psalm 27:12
14 ❑ What can I do when I feel weak and scared? . . . . Psalm 73:26
15 ❑ What can keep me from being afraid? . . . . Proverbs 1:33

If you would like to read more about *FEAR AND COURAGE,* go to the Treasure Map and see: *Earth.*

REPENTANCE

16 ❑ What does "repentance" mean? . . . . Luke 13:2-3
17 ❑ What is remorse? . . . . Matthew 26:75
18 ❑ What will happen if I tell God I'm sorry for my sins? . . Acts 3:19

If you would like to read more about *REPENTANCE,* go to the Treasure Map and see: *Feeling Guilty, What Jesus Did.*

FOOD

19 ❑ Why should I thank God for my food? . . . . Luke 17:17-18
20 ❑ What's wrong with eating as much as I want? . . . . Proverbs 23:20
21 ❑ Is it OK to eat and eat and eat and eat and eat and eat? . . . . . Proverbs 25:16

If you would like to read more about *FOOD,* go to the Treasure Map and see: *Saying Thank You.*

LEADERSHIP

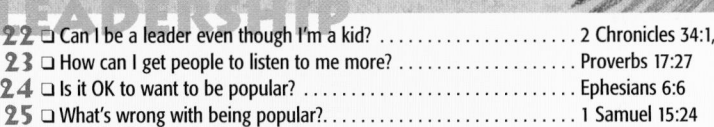

22 ❑ Can I be a leader even though I'm a kid? . . . . 2 Chronicles 34:1,3
23 ❑ How can I get people to listen to me more? . . . . Proverbs 17:27
24 ❑ Is it OK to want to be popular? . . . . Ephesians 6:6
25 ❑ What's wrong with being popular? . . . . 1 Samuel 15:24
26 ❑ Does being a leader mean you get to push other people around? . . Psalm 2:10-11

If you would like to read more about *LEADERSHIP,* go to the Treasure Map and see: *Favoritism.*

WISDOM

27 ❑ Does God give kids wisdom? . . . . Proverbs 2:3
28 ❑ How is God's wisdom different from the world's wisdom? . . . . James 3:17
29 ❑ Why do some people say, "Don't believe everything you hear"? . . Matthew 24:4
30 ❑ Why does God give wisdom to some people but not to others? . . . James 1:5

If you would like to read more about *WISDOM,* go to the Treasure Map and see: *Discretion.*

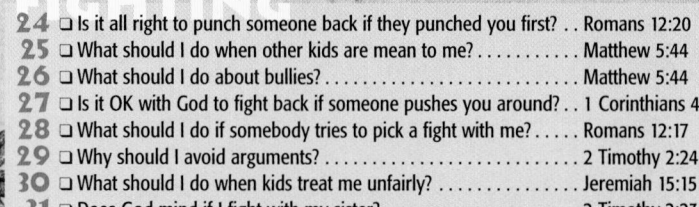

DAILY TREASURES FROM GOD
A Daily Reading Guide

OCTOBER

Find today's date, read the question, and look up the answer.

WITNESSING

1 ❑ What is witnessing? . . . . Acts 1:8
2 ❑ How can I show my friends that I'm a Christian? . . . . . . John 13:35
3 ❑ Do I have to tell others what I know about God? . . . . . . 1 Corinthians 9:17
4 ❑ What can I say to my friends about Jesus? . . . . 1 Peter 3:15
5 ❑ How can I lead others to Christ? . . . . Matthew 5:16

If you would like to read more about *WITNESSING,* go to the Treasure Map and see: *Publicly Christian.*

ANIMALS

6 ❑ Does God care how we treat animals? . . . . Proverbs 12:10
7 ❑ Does God care about animals? . . . . Deuteronomy 22:6
8 ❑ Are people more important than animals, or just the same? . . Matthew 6:26

RIGHT AND WRONG

9 ❑ Is it OK just to be mostly good? . . . . Matthew 5:20
10 ❑ What will happen if I ignore my conscience? . . . . Matthew 13:15
11 ❑ What should I do if my friends tell me to do one thing, but it goes against something God tells me to do? . . . . Acts 5:29
12 ❑ Is it OK for me to do some of the bad stuff my friends do so they'll like me more? . . . . 1 Thessalonians 5:22
13 ❑ What harm can it do to be a little naughty? . . . . Proverbs 11:3
14 ❑ Is stealing always wrong? . . . . Exodus 20:15
15 ❑ Does God care whether people speed when they're driving? . . 1 Peter 2:13-14
16 ❑ Does God keep track of all the things I've done wrong? . . . . . . Isaiah 44:22
17 ❑ Are God's ways really best? . . . . Psalm 18:30
18 ❑ Why should I keep a clear conscience? . . . . 1 Peter 3:16
19 ❑ I can do whatever I want, right? . . . . Galatians 5:13

If you would like to read more about *RIGHT AND WRONG,* go to the Treasure Map and see: *Guilty Conscience, Excusing Sin, Sin Hurts, Impatience, Guilty Fear, Getting Ahead.*

LIVING IN THE WORLD

20 ❑ How does God want me to treat my neighbors? . . . . Leviticus 19:18
21 ❑ How can I make a difference in people's lives? . . . . Proverbs 15:23
22 ❑ What's wrong with racism? . . . . Romans 10:12
23 ❑ How can I make my neighborhood a better place? . . . . Isaiah 54:14

If you would like to read more about *LIVING IN THE WORLD,* go to the Treasure Map and see: *Young Women.*

FIGHTING

24 ❑ Is it all right to punch someone back if they punched you first? . . Romans 12:20
25 ❑ What should I do when other kids are mean to me? . . . . Matthew 5:44
26 ❑ What should I do about bullies? . . . . Matthew 5:44
27 ❑ Is it OK with God to fight back if someone pushes you around? . . 1 Corinthians 4:12
28 ❑ What should I do if somebody tries to pick a fight with me? . . . . . Romans 12:17
29 ❑ Why should I avoid arguments? . . . . 2 Timothy 2:24
30 ❑ What should I do when kids treat me unfairly? . . . . Jeremiah 15:15
31 ❑ Does God mind if I fight with my sister? . . . . 2 Timothy 2:23

If you would like to read more about *FIGHTING,* go to the Treasure Map and see: *Examples of Revenge, Getting Along, Suing People, Whom Can You Trust?*

NOVEMBER

DAILY TREASURES FROM GOD
A Daily Reading Guide

TRUSTING GOD

1 ❑ Why should I trust God? . . . . Deuteronomy 32:4
2 ❑ Why do some people say, "Lord willing"? . . . . Proverbs 19:21
3 ❑ Why should I depend on God when I can take care of myself? . . John 3:27

SPEECH

4 ❑ Is it possible to talk too much? . . . . Proverbs 10:19
5 ❑ What's wrong with telling people off when they deserve it?. . . . . Matthew 5:7
6 ❑ Why is it wrong to spread rumors? . . . . Proverbs 20:19
7 ❑ As long as I don't say anything wrong, does it matter how I say it? . . Titus 3:1-2
8 ❑ Does anything I say make a difference? . . . . 2 Chronicles 35:2
9 ❑ Is it OK to call someone a name? . . . . Ecclesiastes 10:20

If you would like to read more about *SPEECH,* go to the Treasure Map and see:
Foolish Promises, Swearing, Legalism, Embarrassing God.

FOLLOWING CHRIST

10 ❑ Is it really worth it to follow Jesus? . . . . Luke 18:29-30
11 ❑ Will I really be happy if I live God's way? . . . . Psalm 32:11
12 ❑ What difference does it make in my life whether I follow Jesus? . . Matthew 7:26-27

If you would like to read more about *FOLLOWING CHRIST,* go to the Treasure Map and see:
Sacrifice, Gladness.

Find today's date, read the question, and look up the answer.

CHURCH

13 ❑ Why should I go to church? . . . . Romans 12:6
14 ❑ Do kids matter in church? . . . . 1 Corinthians 12:27
15 ❑ What's my role in church? . . . . 1 Thessalonians 3:10
16 ❑ Why do some people raise their hands in church? . . . Psalm 143:6
17 ❑ Why is it important that I be baptized? . . . . Acts 2:38
18 ❑ Why do we have Sunday School? . . . . Ezra 7:10
19 ❑ What can I do if I don't get anything out of church? . . Hebrews 10:25
20 ❑ How am I supposed to act toward the pastor? . . . . . . 1 Timothy 5:17
21 ❑ Why do people insist on quiet in church? . . . . Ecclesiastes 3:7

If you would like to read more about *CHURCH,* go to the Treasure Map and see:
Friends and Church.

JOKING AND TEASING

22 ❑ What if I do something mean but I'm just joking–is that bad? . . . . Proverbs 4:16
23 ❑ What's wrong with picking on kids who are weird?. Amos 1:11
24 ❑ Is it OK to make jokes about people who are different? . . . . Acts 10:28

If you would like to read more about *JOKING AND TEASING,* go to the Treasure Map and see:
Teasing and Joking, Mocking.

THANKFULNESS

25 ❑ What do I have to be thankful for? . . . . Psalm 68:19
26 ❑ What should I thank God for? . . . . 1 Thessalonians 5:18
27 ❑ Why should I thank God for things that my parents bought me? . . Deuteronomy 8:18

If you would like to read more about *THANKFULNESS,* go to the Treasure Map and see:
Using What You Have, Unthankfulness to People.

ADVICE

28 ❑ How many people should I ask for advice?. . . . . Proverbs 15:22
29 ❑ What advice does God have for me?. . . . . 1 Timothy 4:12
30 ❑ Is there a right and wrong way to give advice? . . 1 Thessalonians 5:14

If you would like to read more about *ADVICE,* go to the Treasure Map and see:
Taking Advice, Free Samples.

DAILY TREASURES FROM GOD
A Daily Reading Guide

DECEMBER

THINGS

1 ☐ What's so bad about wanting things? . . . . . Ecclesiastes 5:10
2 ☐ If someone asks me to borrow something, is it wrong to say no? . . . . . Matthew 5:42
3 ☐ What's wrong with spending all your money on the things you want? . . Proverbs 21:17
4 ☐ Does God mind if I want something like somebody else has? . . . . . Romans 13:13
5 ☐ Is it a sin not to share your toys? . . . . . Matthew 5:42
6 ☐ What does God want me to do with my stuff? . . . . . Luke 12:33
7 ☐ What does contentment have to do with wanting something new? . . . . 1 Timothy 6:6, 8

If you would like to read more about *THINGS,* go to the Treasure Map and see:
Worshiping Things, Discontentment, Showing Off Stuff, Being Frugal.

POOR PEOPLE

8 ☐ How does God feel about poor people? . . . . . Proverbs 19:17
9 ☐ How should I treat the poor kids at school? . . . . . Deuteronomy 16:19
10 ☐ What does God do for poor people? . . . . . Psalm 12:5

If you would like to read more about *POOR PEOPLE,* go to the Treasure Map and see:
Bribery.

Find today's date, read the question, and look up the answer.

HAPPINESS

11 ☐ Why should I look on the bright side? . . . . . Habakkuk 3:17-18
12 ☐ What should I do if I don't feel joyful? . . . . . Philippians 4:4
13 ☐ Is it really true that money won't make you happy? . . Revelation 3:17
14 ☐ What really makes a person happy? . . . . . Psalm 144:15

If you would like to read more about *HAPPINESS,* go to the Treasure Map and see:
Praising God, Hoarding, Satisfaction.

HELPING PEOPLE

15 ☐ Is it a sin not to help someone who needs help? . . . . . James 1:27
16 ☐ How can I help a sick friend? . . . . . 2 Kings 13:14
17 ☐ What should I do for someone who is discouraged? . . 1 Thessalonians 5:11
18 ☐ What does it mean to show compassion? . . . . . Luke 10:33-34

RETURN OF CHRIST

19 ☐ Why is Jesus coming to earth a second time? . . . . . Jude 1:14-15
20 ☐ How do we know Jesus will come back? . . . . . Matthew 26:64
21 ☐ When will Jesus come back? . . . . . Matthew 24:36
22 ☐ What will happen when Jesus comes back? . . . . . Revelation 20:13
23 ☐ How can I know if I'm ready for Jesus to come back? . . 1 Thessalonians 5:5-6
24 ☐ What can I do to get ready for Jesus' return? . . . . . Philippians 4:5
25 ☐ Will people really get punished when Jesus returns? . . . 2 Thessalonians 1:7-8

If you would like to read more about *RETURN OF CHRIST,* go to the Treasure Map and see:
Watching for Jesus' Return.

FAILURE

26 ☐ Does God expect me to be perfect? . . . . . 2 Corinthians 13:11
27 ☐ How can I stop making the same mistake again and again? . . . . . Deuteronomy 9:7
28 ☐ Did people in the Bible like Moses and the disciples ever mess up? . . . . . Numbers 20:12
29 ☐ If I went to God five times to ask forgiveness for getting angry at my step-sister, but I did it again today, will God still be kind to me and forgive me? . . . Isaiah 55:7
30 ☐ What can I do about my bad habits? . . . . . Romans 6:16
31 ☐ How can I be sure God will not punish me for being bad? . . . . . Luke 18:13

THE TREASURE STUDY BIBLE

THE TREASURE STUDY BIBLE

THOMPSON STUDY SYSTEM™

WRITERS:
BETSY ROSSEN ELLIOT
CAROL SMITH &
VALERIE WEIDEMANN

EDITOR:
DARYL LUCAS

B. B. KIRKBRIDE BIBLE CO., INC.
INDIANAPOLIS, INDIANA

This Bible has been developed and produced by The Livingstone Corporation. Project staff include Dr. James Galvin, Daryl Lucas, Valerie Weidemann, Carol Smith, Christopher D. Hudson, Collette Placek, Laura M. Lyons, Kathleen Ristow, and Thomas Ristow.

Printed in the United States of America

98 99 00 01 02 10 9 8 7 6 5 4 3 2 1

Table of Contents

THE OLD TESTAMENT

THE NEW TESTAMENT

BOOKS OF THE BIBLE ALPHABETICALLY

Introduction to the Treasure Study Bible

What comes to mind when you think of treasure? Imagine hundreds of solid gold and silver coins . . . dozens of diamonds, rubies, emeralds, and sapphires . . . rings, necklaces, circlets, and daggers encrusted with gems. Imagine them all jammed into a huge wooden chest, wrapped with iron bands and bolted with the heaviest lock. Imagine the chest buried beneath the sand somewhere on a deserted island, out of reach to all . . . but the holder of an old, dirty map and a sense of adventure.

What could be better than a hunt for a treasure chest like *that?*

How about a hunt for God's instructions? The commands and words of God are so valuable they're priceless. Psalm 19:10 puts it this way:

> More to be desired *are they* than gold, yea, than much fine gold: sweeter also than honey and the honeycomb.

The Bible is a treasure chest like none you've ever seen or imagined before. That is because God's instructions make you rich in ways you can't put in a bank. They give you priceless advice on money, school, and planning. They tell you how to get along with friends, brothers, sisters, parents, and enemies. They tell you what is important and what is a waste of time. They tell you what you need to know about the future. And they help you understand what is going on today.

So if you want to go hunting for treasure, you can do no better than to start right here. "In [Christ] are hid all the treasures of wisdom and knowledge." (Colossians 2:3), buried in the many pages of your Bible. All you have to do is follow the map.

> My son, if thou wilt receive my words, and hide my commandments with thee;
> So that thou incline thine ear unto wisdom, *and* apply thine heart to understanding;
> Yea, if thou criest after knowledge, *and* liftest up thy voice for understanding;
> If thou seekest her as silver, and searchest for her as *for* hid treasures;
> Then shalt thou understand the fear of the LORD, and find the knowledge of God.
>
> (Proverbs 2:1–5)

So dust off your compass and turn the page. Your adventures are about to begin . . .

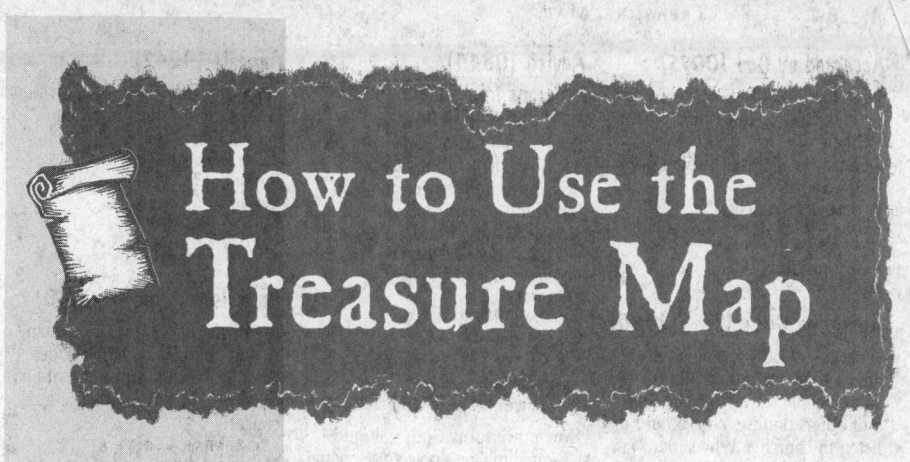

How to Use the Treasure Map

Welcome to the Treasure Map! Every chain in the *Treasure Study Bible* starts here. More than 500 treasure hunts are listed alphabetically. Whenever you want to study the Scriptures, this is the place to begin.

Each Topical Entry has five parts: (1) the treasure hunt's **title**, (2) the official Thompson Chain-Reference® **number**, (3) a list of **questions**, (4) the starting Bible **reference**, and (5) a short list of **related treasure hunts**.

The **title** is the same one you will find in the Treasure Chest and at every stop along that treasure hunt.

The **number** is the treasure hunt's official Thompson Chain-Reference® number. It's the same one you'll find in a Thompson Chain-Reference® Study Bible.

Under the title and number are **questions** about God, life, and getting along with others. You'll find the answers to these questions in the treasure hunt. Check out this list to help you decide if the hunt is of interest to you. You can even check off the questions as you find the answers.

The starting Bible **reference** tells you where the hunt begins. Just go to the appropriate Bible book, chapter, and verse and look for the treasure hunt **title** with the symbol. Then follow the arrows to the next stop (and so on, and so on, and so on) until you get to the symbol. That's your cue to zip to the Treasure Chest in the back (page CHEST 1).

Finally, **related treasure hunts** point to other hunts in the *Treasure Bible* that may interest you. They're listed alphabetically here in the Treasure Map so you can find them just like in a dictionary.

Every treasure hunt in the *Treasure Bible* has something for you to discover. Flip through the pages and look for hunts that interest you. Check out the questions for mysteries you'd like to solve. Then go digging through the Bible and see how much treasure you can find!

Accepted by God (0025)

Who does God like best? • How can I please God? • How can I get God to like me? • How do I know God isn't mad at me? • Who does God accept?

THE SEARCH BEGINS AT
EXODUS 28:38

SEE ALSO
PLEASING GOD
WALKING WITH GOD

Accepting God's Word (2960)

What does God want me to do after I hear a sermon? • Why do some people learn from the Bible and others don't? • Why should I listen in church? • Why should I read the Bible?

THE SEARCH BEGINS AT
MATTHEW 13:23

SEE ALSO
LEARNING FROM JESUS
LISTENING AND DOING

Accepting People (4119)

Is it OK to be popular at school? • Do I have to be friends with everyone? • Is it OK to make fun of kids who are different? • Why should I be friends with the kids that no one else likes?

THE SEARCH BEGINS AT
MATTHEW 9:10

SEE ALSO
BEING A FRIEND
DIFFERENT PEOPLE
HOSPITALITY
POPULARITY

Actions Judged (1353)

How God will judge all we do

If I do something mean but no one sees, will God judge me? • What does it mean that God is a judge? • Which matters more to God—my actions or my words? • What will God judge? • Will God really judge EVERYTHING we do?

THE SEARCH BEGINS AT
PSALM 62:12

SEE ALSO
GETTING CAUGHT
GOD AS JUDGE

Adopted by God (0739)

How does God feel when he thinks about me? • Is God like a parent? • Does God think of me as a servant, a royal subject, a kid, or something else?

THE SEARCH BEGINS AT
DEUTERONOMY 14:2

SEE ALSO
ACCEPTED BY GOD
FAMILY

Advice (0844)

Opinions from others about what you should do

People say to me: "Make your own decision." Is it still my own decision if I ask advice about it? • Is making a decision by myself the grown-up thing to do?

THE SEARCH BEGINS AT
PROVERBS 11:14

SEE ALSO
GETTING OPINIONS
GIVING ADVICE
TAKING ADVICE

All-powerful (3809)

How powerful is God? • Should I be scared of God's power? • How can I feel God's power? • If God can do anything, why doesn't he solve all of my problems?

THE SEARCH BEGINS AT
JOB 42:2

SEE ALSO
GOD'S POWER
SELF-CONFIDENCE
WHOM CAN YOU TRUST?

Ambition (3195)

Can I try too hard? • Is there anything wrong with being successful? • Can I be a success and a failure at the same time?

THE SEARCH BEGINS AT
GENESIS 11:4

SEE ALSO
GETTING AHEAD
SUCCESS
TEAMWORK

Angels (0143)

God's messengers

Does every person have a guardian angel? • What do angels do?

THE SEARCH BEGINS AT
EXODUS 14:19

SEE ALSO
DEMONS
RESISTING SATAN
SATAN'S WEAKNESS
TEMPTATION
TEMPTED BY SATAN

Anger (3959)

Is it ever good to get angry? • Does God ever get angry? • When does God want me to get angry? • How can I know if I'm angry for the right reasons?

THE SEARCH BEGINS AT
EXODUS 32:19

SEE ALSO
MAD
TEMPER

Animals (4042)

Does God care about animals? • What should I do if I find an animal that is hurt?

THE SEARCH BEGINS AT
EXODUS 23:5

SEE ALSO
CRUELTY TO ANIMALS
EARTH
NICE

Animals vs. People (2240)

Are people more important than animals, or just the same? • Does God think us of as just one of his creatures, such as a whale or a cougar?

THE SEARCH BEGINS AT
GENESIS 1:28

SEE ALSO
ANIMALS
CRUELTY TO ANIMALS
EARTH
VALUE OF PEOPLE

Answers to Prayer (2819)

Does God always answer prayer?

THE SEARCH BEGINS AT
PSALM 91:15

SEE ALSO
DUTY TO PRAY
UNANSWERED PRAYER

Apathy (1083)

Not caring; being indifferent

What does it mean when I feel like I just don't care even though I want to care? • What's the danger in not caring—someone else will, won't they?

THE SEARCH BEGINS AT
PSALM 123:4

SEE ALSO
LAZINESS
NICE
NOT PRAYING

Approaching God (0522)

Coming to God in prayer

Will God get angry if I pray after I sin? • Is God angry at me? • Does God listen when I pray?

THE SEARCH BEGINS AT
EPHESIANS 3:12

SEE ALSO
ACCEPTED BY GOD
PLEASING GOD
PRAYER
PRAYING

Arguing (3732)

Why should I avoid arguments? • What can I do to avoid arguments? • When is it OK to try to prove that I am right?

THE SEARCH BEGINS AT
Proverbs 3:30
SEE ALSO
Argument Avoidance
Fighting
Teamwork

Argument Avoidance (1183)

Does God care if I get in a fight at school? • Does God mind if I fight with my sister?
THE SEARCH BEGINS AT
Proverbs 4:15
SEE ALSO
Arguing
Fighting
Stay Away

Arrogance (1722)

Warnings against pride

Why does God want us to be humble? • What's wrong with pride?
THE SEARCH BEGINS AT
Psalm 10:2
SEE ALSO
Conceit
Proud People

Bad Examples (1176)

Is it OK for me to be around evil people as long as I'm careful not to do evil? • Can God give me the strength to be around wrong stuff without doing it?
THE SEARCH BEGINS AT
Leviticus 20:23
SEE ALSO
Friendship
Warning!

Bad Friends (0276)

Friends who have a bad influence on you

How can I choose good friends? • If I'm supposed to love everybody, why am I supposed to stay away from certain kids?
THE SEARCH BEGINS AT
Exodus 23:2
SEE ALSO
Friendship
Good Friends
Whom Can You Trust?

Bad Habits (2139)

What can I do about my bad habits? • If I REALLY wanted to stop sinning, I could, couldn't I?
THE SEARCH BEGINS AT
Proverbs 5:22
SEE ALSO
Change
Freedom
Old Life

Bad News (1350)

Who will be crying—and why—when Jesus returns

Will people really get punished when Jesus returns? • What will make people unhappy when Jesus returns?
THE SEARCH BEGINS AT
Matthew 24:30
SEE ALSO
End Times
Good News
Ouch!

Bad People (0031)

People who love evil and do it

Why do some people do bad things? • Am I a bad person if I did something wrong?
THE SEARCH BEGINS AT
Proverbs 1:16
SEE ALSO
Bad Friends
Evildoers

Bad Thoughts (2352)

Does God care what I think about? • Are dirty thoughts bad if you don't do what you think about? • If I don't DO sin and I only THINK it, is it still sin?
THE SEARCH BEGINS AT
Deuteronomy 15:9
SEE ALSO
Brain Power
Source of Evil

Baptism (0756)

Why is it important that I be baptized? • What exactly does it mean to be baptized? • Is baptism like having a bath?
THE SEARCH BEGINS AT
Matthew 28:19
SEE ALSO
Church
Going to Church
Worship

Be Fair (1976)

What can I do about injustice? • Why should I be fair to others when they aren't fair to me? • If I don't like somebody, do I still have to treat the person fairly?
THE SEARCH BEGINS AT
Deuteronomy 16:20
SEE ALSO
Fair to the Poor
Leaders Should…

Being a Friend (1324)

Did the people I read about in the Bible hang around together? • When my friends go through a hard time, should I try to help or leave them alone?
THE SEARCH BEGINS AT
Ruth 1:16
SEE ALSO
Cold Shoulder
Friendship
Helping Friends
Praying for Others

Being Friendless (1329)

Does God care if I don't have any friends? • What sort of trouble did Bible people have with friendships?
THE SEARCH BEGINS AT
Psalm 31:11
SEE ALSO
Being a Friend
Friendship
Good Friends

Being Frugal (1334)

Using leftovers

Does God care whether I save money? • What does it mean to be frugal? • Why shouldn't we waste things? • What does God think about wasting things?
THE SEARCH BEGINS AT
Genesis 41:35-36
SEE ALSO
Luxury
Planning
Ready for the Future
Waste

Being Hasty (2919)

Making decisions thoughtlessly or too fast

When should I go slow instead of fast? • What's wrong with being hasty?
THE SEARCH BEGINS AT
Proverbs 19:2
SEE ALSO
Hurrying
Making Progress
The Time Is Now

Being Quiet (3290)

Not talking or making noise

Why do people insist on quiet in church? • What's wrong with a little noise in church? • Does God think kids should always be quiet?
THE SEARCH BEGINS AT
Joshua 6:10
SEE ALSO
Gossiping
Restraint
Talking
Wise Words

Being Smart (2021)

What do I have to offer if I'm not that smart? • If I hang around with the smartest kids in school, will that help me be the smartest? • When God talks about knowledge, does he mean the brainy kind of knowledge?

THE SEARCH BEGINS AT
Isaiah 44:25
SEE ALSO
Study
Willingness to Learn

Being Stingy (2127)

Not giving; keeping everything to yourself

Will people dislike me if I'm stingy? • What's wrong with being stingy? • Why should I be generous with my stuff? • I give to God, but I enjoy saving my money. Does that make me stingy?

THE SEARCH BEGINS AT
Proverbs 11:24
SEE ALSO
Generosity
Giving
Money's Dangers

Believer Be Glad (3719)

If you're a Christian, you can count on these seven things

Can I count on God to come through for me when I need him? • Is it really worth it to be a Christian? • What kind of future has God planned for me?

THE SEARCH BEGINS AT
1 Kings 8:56
SEE ALSO
Rewards
Sacrifice
Why Do Right?

Benefits of Faith (1208)

What are the rewards for believing in God? • What difference does it make in my everyday life that I have faith in God?

THE SEARCH BEGINS AT
Matthew 21:22
SEE ALSO
Eternal Life
Gifts from God
God's Love
Heaven
No Condemnation

Better Neighborhoods (2527)

How can I make my neighborhood a better place? • If there are a lot of Christians living in town, does that make it better?

THE SEARCH BEGINS AT
Proverbs 11:11
SEE ALSO
Crime
Obeying the Law
Safety
Violence

Blame (3453)

Who is responsible when you do something wrong; "It's not my fault!"

Does God blame my parents when I mess up? • Will God ever punish me for my friends' mistakes? • Will God let me into heaven because my parents are Christians?

THE SEARCH BEGINS AT
Deuteronomy 24:16
SEE ALSO
Confession
"It's Her Fault!"

Blessing (0481)

How can I get God to bless me? • Whom does God bless?

THE SEARCH BEGINS AT
Exodus 23:25
SEE ALSO
Answers to Prayer
Benefits of Faith

Blessings (0480)

Good things that God does for you; good things that God gives you

What do I have to be thankful for • Why should I be thankful?

THE SEARCH BEGINS AT
Genesis 24:35
SEE ALSO
Gifts from God
God's Care for Kids
God's Care for You

Blinded by Sin (4171)

Why is it so hard to do what's right? • Why do I sometimes make bad choices? • How can sin affect my common sense?

THE SEARCH BEGINS AT
Ecclesiastes 9:3
SEE ALSO
Callousness
Discretion
Doing Good

Boasting (0519)

What's the best thing about being a Christian? • What have Christians got? • What have I got? • What have I got to brag about?

THE SEARCH BEGINS AT
Psalm 34:2
SEE ALSO
Arrogance
Conceit
Proud People
Showing Off
Talking
Wise Words

Boredom (0033)

Being a busybody; hanging out; bumming around; spending time doing nothing

What should I do when I'm bored? • Is it OK to be a couch potato? • What if I have nothing to do? • If I have nothing to do, is it OK to bug my sister?

THE SEARCH BEGINS AT
2 Thessalonians 3:11
SEE ALSO
Gossiping
Lazy People
Rest
Sleep
Working Hard

Borrowing (0582)

Using something that belongs to someone else

If I borrow my friend's glove and my dog chews it up, what should I do? • If someone asks me to borrow something, is it wrong to say no? • What does God think about people borrowing something and never returning it?

THE SEARCH BEGINS AT
Exodus 22:14
SEE ALSO
Golden Rule
Greed

Brain Power (2351)

Does God care what I think about? • Are dirty thoughts bad if you don't do what you think about? • Is it all right to laugh at dirty jokes?

THE SEARCH BEGINS AT
Romans 1:28
SEE ALSO
Bad Thoughts
Old Life
Source of Evil

Bribery (2548)

Paying someone in authority to break the rules for you

Why does God hate bribery? • If my friend bribes me with candy (instead of money) is it still wrong?

THE SEARCH BEGINS AT
Exodus 23:8
SEE ALSO
Greed
Money's Dangers

Bullies (3484)

Being picked on; unfair treatment

Why do other kids pick on me for no reason? • What should I do when kids treat me unfairly? •

What's wrong with getting back at kids who hurt me?

THE SEARCH BEGINS AT
Psalm 7:1

SEE ALSO
Injustice
Revenge
Suffering for Jesus

Callousness (4205)

How sin can wear down your conscience and make things worse

Why don't I feel rotten when I do something wrong? • What will happen if I ignore my conscience? • What should I do if I don't feel guilty about sinning?

THE SEARCH BEGINS AT
Ezra 9:6

SEE ALSO
Guilty Conscience
Ouch!
Sin Hurts

Caring for Church (0732)

How can I help out at church? • What's my role in church?

THE SEARCH BEGINS AT
Acts 20:31

SEE ALSO
Church
God's Body
Going to Church

Change (1789)

Everybody sins sometimes, so why should I try not to sin? • What does it mean to repent? •What is repentance?

THE SEARCH BEGINS AT
Jeremiah 35:15

SEE ALSO
Old Life
Repent!

Christ as Judge (1355)

Does Jesus ever punish people for their sin? • What does Jesus think about the people he punishes? • Can I tell by looking at people if they are pleasing God?

THE SEARCH BEGINS AT
Matthew 25:32

SEE ALSO
Actions Judged
God as Judge

Christian Duties (2171)

I have chores to do in my family. Are there chores in the family of God? • What are my Christian duties?

THE SEARCH BEGINS AT
2 Chronicles 5:13-14

SEE ALSO
Golden Rule
Job One
The Ultimate

Christmas (0720)

Was Jesus really God? • Was Jesus really a man? • Why did God send Jesus?

THE SEARCH BEGINS AT
Isaiah 7:14

SEE ALSO
God on Earth
Jesus' Return
What Jesus Did

Church (0485)

Why should I go to church? • How can I get more out of church?

THE SEARCH BEGINS AT
Matthew 25:15

SEE ALSO
Desire for God
Praising God
Worship

Clear Conscience (0825)

When you know you've done nothing wrong

Why does it feel SO good to have a clear conscience? • If I haven't done anything wrong, am I better than other people? • How will I know if my conscience is clear?

THE SEARCH BEGINS AT
Acts 24:16

SEE ALSO
Feeling Guilty
Guilty Fear

Cold Shoulder (3401)

How not to treat strangers

Is it OK to hang out with the same group of friends all the time? • If I see a new kid at school, do I HAVE to talk to him? • What's wrong with ignoring new kids? • How does God want me to treat new kids?

THE SEARCH BEGINS AT
Numbers 20:18

SEE ALSO
Comforting Others
Hospitality

Comforting Others (0785)

How can I help someone who is hurting? • What should I do for someone who is discouraged? • Does it really make a difference to say something positive?

THE SEARCH BEGINS AT
Isaiah 40:1

SEE ALSO
Compassion
Encouraging People
Sympathy

Commitment (3508)

A promise to do something

What kind of commitment does God want from me? • Is it OK to hold some things back from God? • What does God want most from me? • How can I please God?

THE SEARCH BEGINS AT
Exodus 32:29

SEE ALSO
Obeying Christ
Obeying God
The Time Is Now

Compassion (3519)

Feeling sorrow for others who hurt

What does it mean to show compassion? • Is compassion more than feeling sorry for people? • What can I do if I don't feel any compassion? • Who am I supposed to help out?

THE SEARCH BEGINS AT
Exodus 2:6

SEE ALSO
Examples of Mercy
Work that Helps Others

Conceit (1728)

When you think you're better than other people

If I do something really well, should I be proud of myself? • What is conceit? • Does God mind if I hang out only with rich kids?

THE SEARCH BEGINS AT
Proverbs 3:7

SEE ALSO
Arrogance
Boasting
Humility
Proud People

Confession (0816)

Admitting your sin; telling God you're sorry for doing something wrong

Will God forgive my sin even if I don't pray? • Do I have to admit it when I'm wrong? (it feels yucky) • What do I have to do to have my sin forgiven and forgotten?

THE SEARCH BEGINS AT
Leviticus 16:21

SEE ALSO
God Sees Sin
Not Confessing

Contentment (0829)

Being happy with what you have, even if it isn't very much

What does contentment have to do with wanting something new? • My uncle just sits around all day watching TV. Is that contentment?

THE SEARCH BEGINS AT
Proverbs 15:16

SEE ALSO
Apathy
Discontentment
Envy
Greed

Controlling Yourself (3205)

If God loves me, why isn't life easier? • Why is the Christian life so hard? • What does it mean to "deny yourself"?

THE SEARCH BEGINS AT
Matthew 16:24

SEE ALSO
Drinking
Moderation
Restraint

Cost of Sin (3801)

Why is it so hard to stand up for what is right? • Why do I feel so scared to tell other kids that I'm a Christian? • How can I get stronger in my faith?

THE SEARCH BEGINS AT
Leviticus 26:37

SEE ALSO
Feeling Helpless
Ouch!
Sinner Beware

Crime (2000)

What does God think about crime? • Is it OK to watch violence on TV?

THE SEARCH BEGINS AT
Genesis 49:5

SEE ALSO
Cruel Talk
Violence

The Crowd (2924)

Popular opinion

Should I try to be part of the crowd or not? • Should I try to influence the crowd or not? • Is it always wrong to go along with the crowd?

THE SEARCH BEGINS AT
1 Samuel 14:45

SEE ALSO
Popularity
Standing Strong
Why Do Right?

Cruel Talk (3304)

Using words in a cruel or destructive way

As long as I don't say anything wrong, does it matter how I say it?

THE SEARCH BEGINS AT
Ephesians 4:31

SEE ALSO
Talking
Wise Words

Cruelty (3520)

Is it OK to be mean to kids who are mean to me? • What's wrong with picking on kids who are weird? • Is it OK to ignore kids I don't like?

THE SEARCH BEGINS AT
Job 24:9

SEE ALSO
Crime
Cruelty to Animals
Mercy

Cruelty to Animals (2002)

Does God care how we treat animals? • Is it wrong to be mean to a pet?

THE SEARCH BEGINS AT
Numbers 22:27

SEE ALSO
Animals
Compassion

Cursing (0479)

Is it OK to call someone a name? • Is it OK to hate someone if he deserves it?

THE SEARCH BEGINS AT
Ecclesiastes 10:20

SEE ALSO
Cruel Talk
Lying
Swearing
Talking

"Dangerous Kisses" (3661)

Flattery and other false forms of friendship

How can a kiss be dangerous? • Is it OK to trust people who are nice to me? • What's wrong with trusting everyone? • Why do some kids say things they don't mean?

THE SEARCH BEGINS AT
2 Samuel 15:5

SEE ALSO
Bad Friends
Deception

Death (2158)

Is there anything in the world that won't die? • Why should I be careful? • Do we really die or do we just sort of sleep?

THE SEARCH BEGINS AT
2 Samuel 14:14

SEE ALSO
Mortality
Your Body

Deception (1796)

How can I know the good from the bad? • Why do some people say, "Don't believe everything you hear"? • When a person says something I think is a lie, how should I question it?

THE SEARCH BEGINS AT
Matthew 24:4

SEE ALSO
Ignorance
Naiveté

Defeat of Satan (3149)

Is Jesus at war with Satan? • What will happen to Satan?

THE SEARCH BEGINS AT
Genesis 3:15

SEE ALSO
Satan's Power
Satan's Weakness

Demons (3156)

The devil's angels

What are demons? • Can demons hurt me?

THE SEARCH BEGINS AT
Matthew 12:45

SEE ALSO
Angels
Satan's Power
Satan's Weakness

Desire for God (0983)

Wanting to feel God's presence

Why do some people raise their hands in church? • How can I feel close to God?

THE SEARCH BEGINS AT
Psalm 42:2

SEE ALSO
God's Presence
Praising God
Worship

Determination (3441)

Perseverance

What should I do when I feel like giving up on God? • What if I'm tired of doing good? • Why do I need perseverance? • How can I win more?

THE SEARCH BEGINS AT
Job 17:9

SEE ALSO
Commitment
Quitting

Devotions (1002)

Reading the Bible and praying each day

What kinds of things should I do first thing in the morning? • What is the best way to get my day off to a good start? • Does God care how I start my day?

THE SEARCH BEGINS AT
Genesis 28:16

SEE ALSO
Finding God
Prayer
Praying

Different People (4083)

Is it OK to make jokes about people who are different? • Why do some kids make fun of others who are a different color? • If a person doesn't speak English, does that mean he's dumb? • Why should I reach out to different kids when it's easier to be friends with kids who are just like me?

THE SEARCH BEGINS AT
Luke 9:53
SEE ALSO
Accepting People
Hate
Importance of Love
Loving Others

Difficulties (0497)

Why are some things so hard to do? • Why do bad things happen to me?

THE SEARCH BEGINS AT
Deuteronomy 8:5
SEE ALSO
Endurance
God's Promises
Hardship
Pain

Diligence (0564)

Does God notice if I do my chores without being asked? • Why should I work hard?

THE SEARCH BEGINS AT
Proverbs 10:4
SEE ALSO
Work
Working Hard

Disappointment (1190)

Is it possible to keep myself from ever being disappointed? • When I am disappointed, is it my fault?

THE SEARCH BEGINS AT
Deuteronomy 28:39
SEE ALSO
Contentment
Mockers
Satisfaction

Discipline (1630)

When parents crack the whip

Why does God let my parents discipline me? • What does God think of parents who punish their kids?

THE SEARCH BEGINS AT
Proverbs 13:24
SEE ALSO
Getting Caught
Quitting

Discontentment (1121)

Always wanting more; never being happy with what you have

Why do I always want something else right after I just got something I wanted? • Why does it feel so good to get something new? • Is there a way to stop wanting more stuff?

THE SEARCH BEGINS AT
Ecclesiastes 1:8
SEE ALSO
Contentment
Envy

Discretion (2916)

Knowing what to say and when to say it

Is there ever a time when I should be quiet even when I have something to say? • How can I learn discretion?

THE SEARCH BEGINS AT
Genesis 41:39
SEE ALSO
Getting Wisdom
True Wisdom

Dishonest People (3705)

People who try to deceive others

How can I tell if a person is deceitful? • If God loves everyone, why should I avoid certain people? • Is it OK to make friends with someone who is dishonest?

THE SEARCH BEGINS AT
Psalm 36:3
SEE ALSO
Honesty
Liars

Doing Good (3905)

Is it enough to do nice things for my friends? • Who does God want me to help? • If a kid is mean to me, why should I be nice to him?

THE SEARCH BEGINS AT
Psalm 34:14
SEE ALSO
Good Works
Righteousness

Don't Be Unfair (1982)

How should I treat the poor kids at school? • If I give that poor kid in school the messed up book, he won't notice cause he's not used to nice things. Is that unfair? • If I'm unfair but nobody notices, is it still wrong?

THE SEARCH BEGINS AT
Deuteronomy 16:19
SEE ALSO
Bullies
Fair to the Poor
Luxury
Sympathy

Don't Forget... (3003)

I forgot something important. What was it? • Is it possible to forget about God?

THE SEARCH BEGINS AT
Deuteronomy 4:9
SEE ALSO
Commitment
Gratitude
Thankfulness

Double Life (3445)

Will God be happy with me if I just go to church on Sundays? • Should I act better on Sundays than I do the rest of the week? • Can I live for God and myself at the same time?

THE SEARCH BEGINS AT
2 Kings 17:33
SEE ALSO
Commitment
Hypocrisy

Drinking (3568)

Is it right or wrong to drink? • Is it OK to drink if no one sees you do it? • What does the Bible say about drinking?

THE SEARCH BEGINS AT
Leviticus 10:9
SEE ALSO
Drinking Too Much
Getting Drunk
Weakness

Drinking Too Much (3575)

What should I do if a friend offers me a sip of beer? • Is it OK to drink sometimes? • What happens when people drink too much? • Is it OK to drink a lot to celebrate something?

THE SEARCH BEGINS AT
Proverbs 20:1
SEE ALSO
Drinking
Getting Drunk
Moderation
Self-control

Duty to Pray (2817)

When should I pray? • Why are we supposed to pray? • Does God really require us to pray?

THE SEARCH BEGINS AT
1 Chronicles 16:11
SEE ALSO
Seeking God
Waiting for God

Earning Heaven (4120)

Trying to earn a place in heaven; doing good deeds to earn salvation

Will I go to heaven if I'm really good? • If I sin right before I die, will I still go to heaven? • If I can't earn my way to heaven, why should I try to be good?
THE SEARCH BEGINS AT
Luke 18:12
SEE ALSO
Salvation
Trusting in People
Wealth

Earth (3455)

How does God want us to care for the earth? • How does God feel about the way we treat the earth? • In what ways do we mistreat the earth? • What things can I do to take better care of the earth?
THE SEARCH BEGINS AT
Exodus 19:5
SEE ALSO
Cruelty to Animals
Your Body

Embarrassing God (2997)

How can a person embarrass God? • What difference does it make if I rebel against God—aren't I only hurting myself?
THE SEARCH BEGINS AT
2 Samuel 12:14
SEE ALSO
Pleasing God
Rebellion

Encouraging People (1019)

Supporting people with your words and actions

Does anything I say make a difference? • When will I be old enough to help people the way Jesus did?
THE SEARCH BEGINS AT
Exodus 14:13
SEE ALSO
Cruel Talk
Saying Thank You
Wise Words

End Times (0196)

What will happen before Jesus comes back?

What are the end times? • What is the antichrist? • How can I tell a good spiritual teacher from a bad one?
THE SEARCH BEGINS AT
1 John 2:18
SEE ALSO
Bad News
Good News
Watching for Jesus' Return

Endurance (3440)

Having courage to keep going; not giving up

Why do bad things happen to good kids? • What should I do when bad things happen to me? • Is it best just to "grin and bear it" when things get bad? • How can God help me endure pain and problems?
THE SEARCH BEGINS AT
Matthew 10:22
SEE ALSO
Determination
Disappointment
One Goal
Quitting
Suffering

Enemies (4082)

What should I do when other kids are mean to me? • Is it OK to fight back when someone hurts me? • Why should I pray for kids I don't even like? • How can praying for my enemies help me?
THE SEARCH BEGINS AT
Matthew 5:44
SEE ALSO
Loving Enemies
Nice
Revenge

Envy (1137)

Wishing you had what someone else has

Does God mind if I want something like somebody else has? • Is it wrong to feel bad if somebody has nicer stuff than I do?
THE SEARCH BEGINS AT
Psalm 37:1
SEE ALSO
Contentment
Discontentment
God Is Jealous
Greed

Equality (2238)

What's wrong with racism? • Are we really all equal in God's sight? • Are there certain kinds of people that God likes better than others?
THE SEARCH BEGINS AT
Proverbs 22:2
SEE ALSO
Be Fair
Favoritism

Eternal Life (2405)

Life that lasts forever

What happens to my spirit after I die? • Does my spirit die when my body does? • Does my spirit ever die?
THE SEARCH BEGINS AT
Luke 20:36
SEE ALSO
Life After Death
Resurrection
Salvation

Everyone Sins (3340)

Are there people who don't sin? • What does God do for people who never do anything bad?
THE SEARCH BEGINS AT
Genesis 6:5
SEE ALSO
Feeling Guilty
Feeling Helpless

Evil Attacks (0970)

Attacks on your faith—temptation, lies about you, and other attacks on your faith

Where can I go for help when someone makes fun of me for being a Christian? • From what kinds of situations is God willing to rescue me? • Does God help me resist temptation?
THE SEARCH BEGINS AT
Job 5:19
SEE ALSO
Promises to the Poor
Temptation
Tempted by Satan

Evildoers (1161)

People who do evil; people who deliberately do bad things whenever they can

What does God think of people who do really bad things? • Is there any kind of person God wants me to stay away from?
THE SEARCH BEGINS AT
Psalm 34:16
SEE ALSO
Bad News
Bad People
Doing Good

Examples of Generosity (2115)

People who gave more than expected

What is generosity? • If I'm angry about giving up something but I gave it up anyway, am I generous? • What difference does it make whether I'm generous? • What happens when people are generous?
THE SEARCH BEGINS AT
Exodus 35:22
SEE ALSO
Being Stingy
Giving
Promises to Givers

Examples of Mercy (2296)

Am I supposed to be nice to that kid in school who drives everybody crazy?

THE SEARCH BEGINS AT
1 Samuel 11:13
SEE ALSO
Compassion
Gentleness
Kindness
Mercy

Examples of Revenge (2281)

Does God want me to take care of myself when someone is mean to me? • What should I do if somebody tries to pick a fight with me?
THE SEARCH BEGINS AT
1 Kings 19:2
SEE ALSO
Bullies
Expecting Pain

Excusing Sin (2670)

Pretending that sin is not wrong; approving of wrong; doing bad things and calling them good

Is it OK to do something bad as long as you don't get caught? • If I take something but pretend like I'm borrowing it, is it stealing?
THE SEARCH BEGINS AT
Proverbs 17:15
SEE ALSO
Holiness
Ouch!
Repent!
Used to Sin

Expecting Pain (3483)

Why do Christians have to suffer for their faith? • Jesus said he would give us "abundant life." Does that mean everything gets better after you become a Christian? • Should Christians expect pain?
THE SEARCH BEGINS AT
Matthew 10:17
SEE ALSO
Suffering for Jesus
Why Suffer?

Fair to the Poor (2801)

Does God get angry when people are mean to weaker people? • How can I please God? • At school kids make fun of other kids who don't have name brand stuff. Does God have anything to say about that?
THE SEARCH BEGINS AT
Psalm 82:3
SEE ALSO
Be Fair
Don't Be Unfair
Favoritism

Faith (1202)

What is the greatest gift I can give to God? • Why is faith important?
THE SEARCH BEGINS AT
2 Chronicles 20:20
SEE ALSO
Forgiveness
Justification by Faith
Salvation by Faith
Trusting God

Faith Tested (1213)

Why do I sometimes doubt my faith? • Why is it hard to believe sometimes?
THE SEARCH BEGINS AT
Matthew 15:23
SEE ALSO
Being Friendless
Hardship
Popularity
Suffering for Jesus

Family (3393)

How does God want me to treat my family? • Does God want me to treat others just as well as I treat my family? • If God is our Father, does that mean I'm related to everyone in the whole world?
THE SEARCH BEGINS AT
Proverbs 22:2
SEE ALSO
Fair to the Poor
Giving
Kindness
Love for Friends
Loving Others

Fanatics (1241)

Is there anything wrong with going crazy at a ball game? • Is there anything wrong with getting out-of-your-head excited?
THE SEARCH BEGINS AT
1 Kings 18:28
SEE ALSO
Self-control
Superstition

Favoritism (1984)

When enforcing the rules: treating one person better than another; being nice to people you like and cruel to people you don't like

Is it OK that I like some people better than others? • If I'm team captain, can I do whatever I want? • What should I do if I'm in charge and my friends want me to do them a favor?
THE SEARCH BEGINS AT
Leviticus 19:15
SEE ALSO
Don't Be Unfair
Fair to the Poor
Poverty

Fearing God (3034)

Having respect for God; respecting God's awesomeness

Why does the Bible say we should fear God? • What is the fear of the Lord?
THE SEARCH BEGINS AT
Deuteronomy 10:12
SEE ALSO
Humility
Respecting God

Feeling Guilty (1763)

What should I feel guilty about? • What should I do when I feel guilty? • Do guilty feelings go away after a while?
THE SEARCH BEGINS AT
Genesis 42:21
SEE ALSO
Clear Conscience
Feeling Helpless
Feeling Sorry
Guilty Conscience
Guilty Fear

Feeling Helpless (3799)

What can I do when I feel helpless? • I know what is right—why can't I just do it? • Why can't I have more control over myself? • How can Jesus help me say no to temptation?
THE SEARCH BEGINS AT
Luke 13:11
SEE ALSO
Finding Strength
God's Role

Feeling Sorry (2712)

A good kind of sadness

What should I do when I feel guilty? • Should I feel bad when I sin?
THE SEARCH BEGINS AT
Psalm 34:18
SEE ALSO
Confession
Not Confessing

Fighting (3733)

What can I do if my brother picks a fight with me? • Is it ever OK to argue with my brother or sister? • How can I fix problems in my family without fighting?
THE SEARCH BEGINS AT
Genesis 21:10
SEE ALSO
Arguing
Argument Avoidance
Teamwork

Finding God (4100)

Why does God seem so far away? • What can I do when I feel lonely?

• How can I get closer to God? • Can I find God in nature?
THE SEARCH BEGINS AT
JOB 23:3
SEE ALSO
ADOPTED BY GOD
APPROACHING GOD
LOVE FOR GOD

Finding Strength (3806)
The world is scary—can God protect me? • What can I do when I feel weak and scared? • Why should I go to God? • How can God protect me?
THE SEARCH BEGINS AT
EXODUS 15:2
SEE ALSO
FEELING HELPLESS
GOD'S POWER
GOD'S ROLE
THE HOLY SPIRIT
WEAKNESS

Following God (1793)
Sometimes I feel like I don't say no to God, but I don't say yes either. Is that possible? • How long can I wait before deciding to follow God? • If I just stay out of trouble, is that the same as following God?
THE SEARCH BEGINS AT
DEUTERONOMY 30:15
SEE ALSO
OBEYING GOD
PLEASING GOD
SERVING JESUS

Foolish Promises (2610)
Making a promise you shouldn't
Am I supposed to keep EVERY promise I make? • Am I supposed to keep the promises I wish I hadn't made?
THE SEARCH BEGINS AT
GENESIS 25:33
SEE ALSO
GOD'S WORD
SEEKING PEACE
TALKING

For Kids Only (3964)
Advice in the Bible that is just for young people
When I have a problem, where can I go for advice? • How can I know whose advice to follow? • What advice does God have for me? • How can I know how God wants me to live?
THE SEARCH BEGINS AT
PSALM 119:9
SEE ALSO
GROWING UP
RESPECTING ADULTS

Forgiveness (1314)
Does God love me enough to forgive me when I mess up? • Will God forgive me even if I do something really bad? • How do I know God has forgiven me? • If God forgives my sin, does it matter that I sin?
THE SEARCH BEGINS AT
LEVITICUS 5:10
SEE ALSO
GOD'S FORGIVENESS
REPENT!
REPENTANCE

Forgiveness of Sin (3127)
Can God really forgive AND forget? • How can I be forgiven?
THE SEARCH BEGINS AT
MATTHEW 26:28
SEE ALSO
CONFESSION
FORGIVENESS
NOT CONFESSING

Forgiving Others (1315)
If someone makes fun of me at school, does God expect me to forgive the person? • If I forgive people, will they think they can run all over me?
THE SEARCH BEGINS AT
MARK 11:25
SEE ALSO
LOVING ENEMIES
REVENGE
SHOWING MERCY
VENGEANCE

Free Samples (1177)
Is it OK to try to be like a person you respect? • When I try to be like someone I respect, does that make God feel left out?
THE SEARCH BEGINS AT
JOHN 13:15
SEE ALSO
FRIENDSHIP
GOOD FRIENDS

Free to... (2136)
Proper use of freedom
Why should I care about other people watching me? • I can do whatever I want, right?
THE SEARCH BEGINS AT
1 CORINTHIANS 8:9
SEE ALSO
FREE SAMPLES
GOODNESS REWARDED
LEADERS SHOULD...
THIS FOR THAT

Freedom (3503)
Being able to say no to bad habits
How should I be different now that I'm a Christian? • What do I have to stop doing? • Why is it so hard to stop doing all the bad things I did before I became a Christian? • Can Jesus help me break my bad habits?
THE SEARCH BEGINS AT
ROMANS 6:2
SEE ALSO
BAD HABITS
CHANGE

Friend of Jesus (4104)
If I do something really bad, will Jesus stop being my friend? • I know I've let Jesus down—what should I do? • How did Jesus choose his friends? • Why does Jesus want to be my friend?
THE SEARCH BEGINS AT
MATTHEW 11:19
SEE ALSO
FORGIVENESS OF SIN
GOD'S FRIENDS

Friends and Church (3924)
How can I tell my friends about Jesus? • Why should I invite my friends to church? • Why is it important to go to church? • How can I get more out of church?
THE SEARCH BEGINS AT
2 CHRONICLES 30:1
SEE ALSO
CHURCH
FRIENDSHIP
WITNESSING
WORSHIP

Friendship (1322)
Does God care what kind of friend I am? • What does God think when I spend time with my friends? • What does God think of friendship?
THE SEARCH BEGINS AT
PROVERBS 17:17
SEE ALSO
BAD FRIENDS
BEING A FRIEND
BEING FRIENDLESS
FRIENDS AND CHURCH
GOOD FRIENDS
HELPING FRIENDS
LOVE FOR FRIENDS
NEIGHBORS

The Future (2492)
Can crystal balls and fortune tellers let you see into the future?
THE SEARCH BEGINS AT
PROVERBS 27:1
SEE ALSO
PLANNING
READY FOR THE FUTURE

Generosity (2126)

Giving more than expected

Am I generous if I gladly give what God asks of me? • Does God expect me to be generous, or is it enough for me just to give a little? • What does God want me to do with my stuff? • What should I do if someone asks me for something?

THE SEARCH BEGINS AT
Leviticus 25:35
SEE ALSO
Kind to the Poor
Loving Others
Promises to Givers
Sympathy

Gentleness (2276)

Is there anything wrong with being rowdy? • How can I get people to like me?

THE SEARCH BEGINS AT
1 Thessalonians 2:7
SEE ALSO
Being a Friend
Getting Along
Kindness
Meekness

Getting Ahead (0580)

Sometimes I feel bad when I win, because someone else loses. Should I feel bad? • Is it OK to want to win real bad? • What are the limits on getting ahead?

THE SEARCH BEGINS AT
Proverbs 16:8
SEE ALSO
Ambition
Success
Working Hard

Getting Along (3725)

Why is it important for me to get along with other Christians? • Why do some Christians fight? • Do I have to agree with everything Christians say? • What should I do if I disagree with a Christian friend?

THE SEARCH BEGINS AT
1 Corinthians 1:10
SEE ALSO
Love for Friends
Loving Others

Getting Caught (3452)

Why do some kids seem to get away with anything? • Does God keep track of everything I do? • Do I have to pay for my mistakes? • Can a person hide from God?

THE SEARCH BEGINS AT
Matthew 12:36
SEE ALSO
Discipline
Obeying the Law

Getting Drunk (3571)

Drinking too much alcohol

What's wrong with getting drunk? • Why do some people try to get drunk? • Is it OK to drink as long as you don't get drunk? • What does the Bible say about drinking?

THE SEARCH BEGINS AT
Deuteronomy 21:20
SEE ALSO
Drinking
Drinking Too Much

Getting Opinions (0848)

What do I do if I ask two people's advice and they have different opinions? • How many people should I ask for advice?

THE SEARCH BEGINS AT
Proverbs 11:14
SEE ALSO
Advice
Giving Advice
God's Guidance

Getting Wisdom (3843)

Why do people need wisdom? • Where can I get wisdom? • Can God make me wise even though I'm a kid? • Why does God give wisdom to some people but not to others?

THE SEARCH BEGINS AT
Proverbs 2:6
SEE ALSO
Praying for Wisdom
True Wisdom

Gifts from God (4157)

What has God given me? • Why did God give me some talents but not others? • How am I supposed to use the gifts God gives me?

THE SEARCH BEGINS AT
Job 32:8
SEE ALSO
Church
Talents

Giving (2117)

Does God expect me to give away everything I have, even my birthday presents? • What does it mean to be generous? • What happens to people who are generous?

THE SEARCH BEGINS AT
Deuteronomy 15:12-14
SEE ALSO
Being Stingy
Kind to the Needy
Kind to the Poor
Love for Friends
Loving Others
New Kids

Giving Advice (0799)

Why do people get mad when I give them advice? • Is there a right and wrong way to give advice? • Should it be fun to give advice?

THE SEARCH BEGINS AT
Romans 15:14
SEE ALSO
Advice
Guidance
Wise Words

Giving In (3588)

Why people give in to temptation

Why does sin look so good? • What happens when I give in to sin? • How can I learn to resist temptation?

THE SEARCH BEGINS AT
Genesis 3:6
SEE ALSO
Restraint
Saying No
Temptation

Gladness (1936)

Happiness; being glad

What kind of things made the people in the Bible glad?

THE SEARCH BEGINS AT
2 Chronicles 30:21
SEE ALSO
Positive Attitude
Rejoicing

God as Judge (1354)

When will evil people get their punishment? • What does it mean that God is a judge? • Why does it seem like some people don't care about God but don't ever get punished for it?

THE SEARCH BEGINS AT
Genesis 18:25
SEE ALSO
Actions Judged
Blame
Christ as Judge

God as Teacher (3556)

What does God want to teach me? • What does God want to do for me? • Does God really know what is best for me? • How can I learn the lessons God has for me?

THE SEARCH BEGINS AT
Exodus 4:15
SEE ALSO
Sunday School

God at Work (1166)

Does God just sit back and watch us from Heaven? • What does God

have to do with what happens in the news? • What influence does God have on the world?
THE SEARCH BEGINS AT
Genesis 45:8
SEE ALSO
God's Role
Rulers
Working with God

God Calls You (1791)

Is God just sitting up in heaven and waiting for me to decide to follow him? • Is there anybody God does NOT want to become a Christian?
THE SEARCH BEGINS AT
Isaiah 45:22
SEE ALSO
Forgiveness of Sin
Salvation for Anyone

God Is Jealous (1850)

Can jealousy ever be a good thing? • If God is good and God is jealous, then is jealousy good or bad? • What does it mean that God is jealous?
THE SEARCH BEGINS AT
Exodus 20:5
SEE ALSO
Friend of Jesus
Why Not Sin?

God on Earth (4044)

What is God like? • How can I learn more about God? • Why did God become a man? • What can I learn about God by learning about Jesus?
THE SEARCH BEGINS AT
2 Corinthians 4:4
SEE ALSO
Friend of Jesus
Jesus
Names of God

God Sees Sin (0804)

Is there ANY way to keep something we've done wrong from God? • Does God see every little thing I think and do? • Is it crazy to hide something from God?
THE SEARCH BEGINS AT
Job 10:14
SEE ALSO
Confession
Not Confessing
What God Knows

God's Anger (3132)

Does God get angry? • When does God get angry? • What makes God angry?
THE SEARCH BEGINS AT
2 Kings 22:13
SEE ALSO
Losers
Sinner Beware
Used to Sin

God's Body (0726)

The church; all Christians everywhere

Do kids matter in church? • What is church for? • What can I do in the church?
THE SEARCH BEGINS AT
Romans 12:5
SEE ALSO
Caring for Church
Church

God's Care for Kids (3830)

How is God like a father? • What can I do when I have problems at home? • Does God care about my family problems? • How can I be sure God cares about me?
THE SEARCH BEGINS AT
Deuteronomy 10:18
SEE ALSO
Fair to the Poor
Kind to the Poor

God's Care for You (2911)

God has so many people to listen to. How can he hear me? • Does God really care about me?
THE SEARCH BEGINS AT
Psalm 115:12
SEE ALSO
God's Comfort
Value of People

God's Comfort (0783)

Where can I go when I feel down? • How does God help me? • What should I do when I feel sad?
THE SEARCH BEGINS AT
Psalm 71:21
SEE ALSO
Comforting Others
Suffering

God's Control (3415)

The extent of God's power in the world

How much control does God have over the world? • After God made the world, did he just leave it to run by itself? • Is there anything that God can't control? • What should I do if I think God has made a mistake?
THE SEARCH BEGINS AT
Deuteronomy 4:39
SEE ALSO
God's Power
Help!

God's Forgiveness (3125)

Does God want me to say I'm sorry over and over again? • Does God keep track of all the things I've done wrong?
THE SEARCH BEGINS AT
Isaiah 43:25
SEE ALSO
Forgiveness
Promise of Mercy

God's Friends (1327)

Does God consider me his friend? • Who are God's friends? • Does God want to be my friend even if I sin sometimes? • How can I be God's friend?
THE SEARCH BEGINS AT
Exodus 33:11
SEE ALSO
Approaching God
Lying
Seeking God

God's Guidance (1465)

God's leading

How can I hear God speak to me? • How do I know what God wants me to do?
THE SEARCH BEGINS AT
Psalm 23:2
SEE ALSO
Getting Wisdom
God's Teaching

God's Justice (1975)

How do we know God is fair? • Can a person ever be completely fair?
THE SEARCH BEGINS AT
Deuteronomy 32:4
SEE ALSO
Be Fair
Don't Be Unfair
God as Judge

God's Love (2206)

If I show my love for God by obeying him, how does he show his love for me? • How does God love me? • Why does God care about us?
THE SEARCH BEGINS AT
Deuteronomy 7:8
SEE ALSO
Mercy from God
Promise of Mercy

God's Mercy (2297)

If God wanted to, could he be mean? • Is God really angry all the time? • What should I do if I really mess up?
THE SEARCH BEGINS AT
Deuteronomy 4:31
SEE ALSO
Forgiveness

Grace
Mercy
Mercy from God

God's Patience (2277)

Why doesn't God just destroy all the bad people right now? • Why does God get so angry? • Does God ever get tired of waiting for me to get it right?

THE SEARCH BEGINS AT
Numbers 14:18
SEE ALSO
Forgiveness
God's Mercy

God's Perfection (2730)

Why should I trust God? • What is God like?

THE SEARCH BEGINS AT
Deuteronomy 32:4
SEE ALSO
God's Promises
God's Word
Perfect Father

God's Power (3808)

Can God protect me from bullies? • Does God ever give power to kids? • How can I understand God's power? • Why should I learn about God's power?

THE SEARCH BEGINS AT
1 Chronicles 29:12
SEE ALSO
All-powerful
Finding Strength
Jesus the King

God's Presence (0038)

Being in God's presence; getting close to God

How can I get closer to God? • Am I allowed in God's presence, or do I have to have a priest help me?

THE SEARCH BEGINS AT
Psalm 24:3-4
SEE ALSO
Accepted by God
Praying

God's Promises (2878)

Does God ever break a promise? • How do God's promises affect me? • What's so special about the promises of God?

THE SEARCH BEGINS AT
1 Kings 8:56
SEE ALSO
Faith Tested
Meekness
Promises to Givers
Promises to the Poor
Repentance
Resurrection
Why Fear God

God's Response (1211)

How does my faith affect God? • Does God like it when I ask him for help?

THE SEARCH BEGINS AT
Mark 1:41
SEE ALSO
Faith
Pleasing God

God's Role (3798)

What do we need God for? • How does God affect my life? • What difference does it make that God is in my life? • Why should I depend on God when I can take care of myself? • What's wrong with depending on my brains and talent to get me through life?

THE SEARCH BEGINS AT
2 Chronicles 20:12
SEE ALSO
Feeling Helpless
Humility

God's Teaching (1607)

Do I know everything I need to know when I become a Christian? • What does the Holy Spirit do? • Are teachers and books the only way I can learn about God?

THE SEARCH BEGINS AT
Nehemiah 9:20
SEE ALSO
God's Guidance
Learning from Jesus

God's Ways (4160)

What is so special about God's ways? • How can I find out God's will for me?

THE SEARCH BEGINS AT
Psalm 18:30
SEE ALSO
Obeying God
Trusting God

God's Word (3700)

The Bible

Why should I believe God's promises? • Has God ever lied? • How can I know that God will keep his word? • How can I have more faith in God's promises?

THE SEARCH BEGINS AT
Deuteronomy 32:4
SEE ALSO
Honesty
Lying
Sincerity

Going to Church (3523)

Why do people go to church? • Why do my parents make me go to church? • What can I do if I don't get anything out of church? • Does God want me to go to church even if it's boring? • Is it ever OK to skip church?

THE SEARCH BEGINS AT
Matthew 12:9
SEE ALSO
Christian Duties
Worship

Golden Rule (1433)

The most important people-rule of all

What is the Golden Rule? • What's God's most important rule of all? • How can I get along with others? • What are God's rules for getting along?

THE SEARCH BEGINS AT
Matthew 7:12
SEE ALSO
Hate
Job One
Love
The Ultimate

Good Friends (1323)

Did people in the Bible have friends and hang around together? • What does the Bible say about good friendships? • How can I be a good friend? • What are some good examples of good friends?

THE SEARCH BEGINS AT
1 Samuel 18:1
SEE ALSO
Being a Friend
Being Friendless
Friendship

Good Looks (0205)

Why do my parents say, "It's what's on the inside that counts"? • If the inside counts most, why do kids make fun of me for the way I look? • Is it OK to pick on ugly kids? • What's so bad about wanting to wear clothes that are in style?

THE SEARCH BEGINS AT
1 Samuel 16:7
SEE ALSO
Arrogance
Boasting
Modesty

Good News (1349)

Who will be celebrating—and why—when Jesus returns

Will I get a reward when Jesus comes back? • What kind of rewards does Jesus give?

THE SEARCH BEGINS AT
Luke 12:37
SEE ALSO
Bad News
End Times

Jesus' Return: When?
Jesus' Return: Why?

Good Rewarded (1165)

Is God keeping track of my good deeds? • Does God notice when I'm obeying him? • What rewards does God give to people who obey him?

THE SEARCH BEGINS AT
Psalm 91:14

SEE ALSO
Bad News
Good News
Jesus' Return: Why?
Ready for Jesus' Return
Second Coming
Suffering Rewarded

Good Works (3902)

Doing good

How can I show God that I love him? • If faith is all I need to get to heaven, why should I do good works? • Why are good works important? • How can I lead others to Christ?

THE SEARCH BEGINS AT
Matthew 5:16

SEE ALSO
Doing Good
Righteousness

Goodness Rewarded (1364)

Will I be rewarded for something good I did even if no one else saw it? • Why does God reward us?

THE SEARCH BEGINS AT
Daniel 12:3

SEE ALSO
Christ as Judge
Heaven

The Gospel (3461)

The truth about Jesus; the news that he wants to forgive our sins and run our lives

Why doesn't everyone understand the gospel? • What can I do to understand the gospel better? • Do I have to tell others what I know about God? • Whose job is it to tell others about Jesus?

THE SEARCH BEGINS AT
1 Corinthians 9:17

SEE ALSO
Good News
Witnessing

Gossiping (3307)

Telling people secrets that you don't have a right to tell

Why is it wrong to spread rumors? • What's wrong with gossip?

THE SEARCH BEGINS AT
Leviticus 19:16

SEE ALSO
Boredom
Talking
Teasing and Joking

Grace (1447)

God's favor

Do I have to be good before God will love me? • If God forgives my sin today, will he hold it against me tomorrow?

THE SEARCH BEGINS AT
Acts 15:11

SEE ALSO
Good Works
Justification by Faith

Gratitude (1458)

What difference does it make whether I thank God for things? • What should I thank God for? • What happens to people who don't say thank you to God? • Why should I thank God for my food?

THE SEARCH BEGINS AT
Deuteronomy 32:6

SEE ALSO
Thankfulness
"Thank You"
Saying Thank You

A Great Gift (3123)

What do I have to do to become a Christian? • Is salvation really free?

THE SEARCH BEGINS AT
John 3:16

SEE ALSO
Believer Be Glad
Benefits of Faith
Salvation

Greed (4070)

Is it OK to want the stuff my friends have? • What's so bad about wanting things? • Why does the thrill of getting new things wear off so fast?

THE SEARCH BEGINS AT
Proverbs 1:19

SEE ALSO
Contentment
Hoarding

Grief (1948)

Sorrow; sadness

Why do people feel sad at funerals? • Is it normal to cry if you feel sad?

THE SEARCH BEGINS AT
Genesis 23:2

SEE ALSO
Positive Attitude
Rejoicing

Growing Spiritually (0995)

Changing from a baby Christian into a grown-up Christian

What does it mean to grow up? • How does God help me grow up? • Does my spirit grow like my body does? • What helps my spirit grow?

THE SEARCH BEGINS AT
2 Corinthians 9:10

SEE ALSO
Change
God's Perfection
Perfection

Growing Up (4006)

What can I do to make growing up easier? • How can my parents help me grow up? • Why do my parents say they discipline me "for my own good"?

THE SEARCH BEGINS AT
Proverbs 22:15

SEE ALSO
Young Men
Young Women

Guidance (1611)

How does God help me? • Sometimes I can't decide what to do. How do I know what God wants? • When I have to make a choice is there always a right one and a wrong one?

THE SEARCH BEGINS AT
John 16:13

SEE ALSO
Advice
God's Guidance

The Guide (0419)

Using the Bible to help you make decisions

What can the Bible do for me? • What should I do if I need some advice? • Why should I read the Bible?

THE SEARCH BEGINS AT
Psalm 19:8

SEE ALSO
Being Smart
Power of the Bible
Purity
Reading the Bible
Valuing the Bible
Why the Bible?

Guilty Conscience (0826)

When you feel guilty for something you did

Why do I feel bad inside when I do something wrong? • Will saying I'm sorry make the guilt go away? • Does God make me feel guilty?

THE SEARCH BEGINS AT
Genesis 42:21

SEE ALSO
Clear Conscience
Feeling Guilty
God Sees Sin

Guilty Fear (0856)

When you're afraid because you did something wrong

Why do I feel afraid after I do something wrong? • Is there a way not to feel afraid?

THE SEARCH BEGINS AT

Genesis 3:8

SEE ALSO

Clear Conscience
Guilty Conscience
Remorse

Happiness (1940)

Why doesn't God just give me things that make me happy? • If I try really hard, could I be happy every minute of every day?

THE SEARCH BEGINS AT

Job 20:5

SEE ALSO

Satisfaction
Source of Happiness

Hard-heart Aches (2716)

Consequences of hardening your heart against God

What's wrong with being stubborn? • What happens to people who harden their hearts against God? • Can I ignore God when he's trying to tell me something?

THE SEARCH BEGINS AT

Psalm 95:8

SEE ALSO

Refusing Correction
Stubborn People

Hard-hearted (2713)

When you become stubborn and refuse to stop doing wrong

What does God do if a person keeps on disobeying him? • Does God ever get impatient with people? • When does God say, "Enough is enough"?

THE SEARCH BEGINS AT

Leviticus 26:23

SEE ALSO

Feeling Sorry
Rebellion
Repent!
Stubborn People

Hardship (0490)

Breakdowns, inconvenience, mistakes, troubles, and problems

How can good come from suffering? • Why should I "count it all joy" when things go wrong?

THE SEARCH BEGINS AT

Job 5:17

SEE ALSO

Expecting Pain
Life Tests
Pain

Hate (2210)

Is hate the opposite of love? • Is it ever right to hate? • God wants me to hate bad people . . . doesn't he? • What should I do if I can't stand somebody?

THE SEARCH BEGINS AT

Leviticus 19:17

SEE ALSO

Envy
Malice

Heart (4162)

How can watching TV affect me? • Is it OK to listen to popular music? • If reading is good for me, why should I avoid certain books and magazines?

THE SEARCH BEGINS AT

Proverbs 4:23

SEE ALSO

Swearing
Talking
Teasing and Joking
Used to Sin

Heaven (1359)

Will I cry if I fall down in heaven? • Will I be scared of the dark in heaven?

THE SEARCH BEGINS AT

Revelation 21:1, 4

SEE ALSO

Good News
Goodness Rewarded
Resurrection

Help! (4134)

What should I do when I've really messed up? • Are my problems too big for God? • Has God given up on me? • If my problems are my own fault, will God still help me?

THE SEARCH BEGINS AT

Matthew 4:24

SEE ALSO

All-powerful
God's Power
The Holy Spirit
Not Praying
Prayer

Helping at Home (4041)

What should I do if I don't feel like helping around the house? • What's wrong with having a messy room? • Why should I help my parents take care of our home?

THE SEARCH BEGINS AT

Mark 5:19

SEE ALSO

Fighting
Humility
Serving Jesus
Serving People
Teamwork
Willingness to Work
Work
Work that Helps Others
Working Hard
Working with God

Helping Friends (1784)

Speaking up for someone else

When one of my friends is afraid to ask a question, should I ask it for her or make her ask on her own? • When one of my friends is being treated unfairly, when should I speak up?

THE SEARCH BEGINS AT

Genesis 37:21

SEE ALSO

Giving
Good Works
Humility
Serving

Helping Weak People (1061)

Does helping the weak mean my little brother and sister, too? • Would God want me to risk my reputation at school by hanging around with some un-cool kids to help them?

THE SEARCH BEGINS AT

Matthew 25:35-36

SEE ALSO

Compassion
Nice
Sympathy
Work that Helps Others

Hoarding (2811)

Saving money just to have a lot of it

If I save a lot of money, will that make me secure? • Should I save up my money?

THE SEARCH BEGINS AT

Job 27:16-17

SEE ALSO

Generosity
Wealth

Holiness (1598)

What is holiness? • If I try to be holy, does that mean I can never have fun? • If something is holy, does that mean I can't touch it? • What does God expect of me?

THE SEARCH BEGINS AT

Exodus 19:6

SEE ALSO

Perfection
Righteousness

The Holy Spirit (3803)

How does the Holy Spirit work? • Does the Holy Spirit ever help kids? • Can God's Spirit give me courage?

THE SEARCH BEGINS AT
Micah 3:8
SEE ALSO
God's Teaching
Guidance
The Spirit in You

Honesty (3701)

Do I have to tell the truth if I know it will get me or my friends in trouble? • Should I tell the truth even if people don't want to hear it? • Is it ever OK to keep the truth to myself?

THE SEARCH BEGINS AT
Proverbs 12:19
SEE ALSO
Lying
Sincerity

Hospitality (3398)

Showing kindness to people who are "just passing through"

Do I have to have a big house and my own room to be hospitable? • Is hospitality more than inviting my friends over to my house? • How can I make people feel welcome at my house? • What can I do if my parents don't want me to invite kids over to our house? • What does hospitality mean?

THE SEARCH BEGINS AT
Romans 12:13
SEE ALSO
Love for Friends
Loving Others

How to Be Saved (3118)

What you must do to be saved from your sins; how to receive God's forgiveness; how to get to heaven

I want to become a Christian. How can I? • I've just become a Christian. Now what? • What does God expect of us?

THE SEARCH BEGINS AT
Matthew 10:22
SEE ALSO
Justification by Faith
Only One Savior
Salvation by Faith

How to Give (2121)

How does God want me to give? • What do I have to offer when I don't have very much in the first place? • What should I do if I don't FEEL like giving?

THE SEARCH BEGINS AT
Deuteronomy 16:17
SEE ALSO
Fair to the Poor
Kind to the Poor
Generosity

How to Pray (2824)

How should I pray? • How does God want us to pray?

THE SEARCH BEGINS AT
2 Chronicles 7:14
SEE ALSO
Prayer
Seeking God

Humility (3897)

What kind of service does God like best? • Is it OK to want to impress others with my service? • If God thinks I'm great, why should I be humble?

THE SEARCH BEGINS AT
Matthew 10:42
SEE ALSO
Modesty
Serving People

Hurrying (1498)

If "haste makes waste," is it ever good to hurry? • When is it good to hurry? • What does God think about people who hurry? • Did people in the Bible ever have to hurry like I do getting ready for school sometimes?

THE SEARCH BEGINS AT
1 Samuel 21:8
SEE ALSO
Being Hasty
Life Is Short
Time

Hurtful Lying (3856)

Lies that hurt and destroy

How can lying hurt people? • Is it OK to listen to rumors as long as I don't spread them? • Should I tell the truth even if I know it will get a friend in trouble?

THE SEARCH BEGINS AT
Exodus 20:16
SEE ALSO
Honesty
Lying

Hurting Yourself (0521)

What does the Bible say about my body? • Why should I take care of my body if it isn't going to last forever?

THE SEARCH BEGINS AT
Leviticus 19:28
SEE ALSO
Jesus' Home
Your Body

Hypocrisy (2994)

Saying one thing and doing another

How can I spot a hypocrite? • How do I know if I'm a hypocrite?

THE SEARCH BEGINS AT
Proverbs 23:7
SEE ALSO
Dishonest People
Lying
Phonies

Idle Talk (3306)

Talking too much

Is it OK to talk and talk and talk and talk and talk and talk? • Is it possible to talk too much? • My friend says, "You talk too much!" Is he right?

THE SEARCH BEGINS AT
Job 11:12
SEE ALSO
Cruel Talk
Talking
Wise Words

Ignorance (2036)

Facts we don't know

Is ignorance the same as being dumb? • Do I have to understand God completely to have faith in him?

THE SEARCH BEGINS AT
Job 8:9
SEE ALSO
The Future
Naiveté
Study

Impatience (2694)

How can I learn to be patient? • Does patience come naturally or do I have to work at it? • Does God understand when I become impatient?

THE SEARCH BEGINS AT
Numbers 20:10
SEE ALSO
Patience
Waiting

Importance of Love (2209)

Which is the most important trait to have?

THE SEARCH BEGINS AT
1 Corinthians 13:13
SEE ALSO
God's Love
Golden Rule
Love

Injustice (1981)

Why do some people do good and it seems like they don't get rewarded? • Why do some people do wrong and it seems like they don't get punished?

THE SEARCH BEGINS AT
Job 12:6

SEE ALSO
Be Fair
Don't Be Unfair
Just You Wait

Instruction (1782)

Who is supposed to teach me about God? • What does God want my parents to teach me?

THE SEARCH BEGINS AT
Leviticus 10:11

SEE ALSO
Learning from Jesus
Rejecting God's Word

Invisible Gifts (0486)

The way in which God has "gifted" you

What does God give me? • What do I have?

THE SEARCH BEGINS AT
Isaiah 56:4-5

SEE ALSO
Gifts from God
Talents

Invisible Wealth (2812)

Being rich in things besides money

What could be better than being rich? • What does it mean to be really rich? • What's good about not being rich?

THE SEARCH BEGINS AT
Proverbs 8:18

SEE ALSO
Gifts from God
Greed
Heaven
Money's Limits
The Ultimate

"It's Her Fault!" (3454)

Facing your mistakes

When I've done something wrong, do I HAVE to confess? • Why should I admit my mistakes? • What's wrong with trying to cover up mistakes?

THE SEARCH BEGINS AT
Genesis 3:13

SEE ALSO
Confession
Remorse
Willingness to Work

Jesus (4188)

Why should I believe in Jesus? • What's so special about Jesus? • Will my friends go to heaven if they're good but don't believe in Jesus?

THE SEARCH BEGINS AT
John 3:16

SEE ALSO
Only One Savior

Jesus' Friends (1326)

What kind of friends did Jesus have? • What kind of stuff did Jesus do with his friends?

THE SEARCH BEGINS AT
John 11:5

SEE ALSO
Friendship
God on Earth
God's Friends

Jesus' Home (3583)

Christ in you

Where is Jesus' home? • Where does Jesus live? • How can we know where Jesus lives?

THE SEARCH BEGINS AT
John 14:20

SEE ALSO
Hurting Yourself
The Spirit in You

Jesus' Joy (1926)

Was Jesus ever happy? • When Jesus was on earth, did he have good days and bad days like I do?

THE SEARCH BEGINS AT
Luke 10:21

SEE ALSO
Disappointment
Happiness
Joy

Jesus' Return (3784)

When will Jesus come back? • Why didn't Jesus tell us more about his return? • How can I know if I'm ready for Jesus to come back?

THE SEARCH BEGINS AT
Matthew 25:13

SEE ALSO
Bad News
Good News
Jesus' Return: When?
Jesus' Return: Why?
Ready for Jesus' Return
Second Coming
Watching for Jesus' Return

Jesus' Return: When? (1345)

The timing of Jesus' return

I've heard there's a book that gives the very day when Jesus is coming back. Could it be right? • When will Jesus come back?

THE SEARCH BEGINS AT
Matthew 24:27

SEE ALSO
Jesus' Return: Why?
Ready for the Future
Second Coming

Jesus' Return: Why? (1347)

The reason for Jesus' return

Why is Jesus coming to earth a second time? • Whenever I sin I go to God and admit it—when do the people who don't do that have to admit their sin?

THE SEARCH BEGINS AT
Matthew 16:27

SEE ALSO
Defeat of Satan
Heaven
Jesus' Return: When?

Jesus the King (3421)

Is Jesus the king of the world? • If Jesus is king, why are there so many problems in the world? • Why doesn't Jesus fix all of our problems? • Will Jesus' rule change in the future?

THE SEARCH BEGINS AT
Psalm 2:6

SEE ALSO
God's Control
God's Justice
The Teacher

Jesus the Lamb (3365)

Why the Bible calls Jesus the "Lamb of God"

Why does the Bible call Jesus the "Lamb of God"? • How is Jesus like a lamb? • How can the name "Lamb of God" help me under-stand Jesus? • How does God forgive me?

THE SEARCH BEGINS AT
Isaiah 53:7

SEE ALSO
Forgiveness of Sin
Freedom
Jesus

Job One (4181)

Your most important job

What is my most important job? • What does God want most from me? • How can I know if God is happy with me?

THE SEARCH BEGINS AT
Joshua 24:15

SEE ALSO
Golden Rule
Importance of Love

Joy (1928)

What is joy? • Why doesn't God want us to have fun? • Everyone in church looks so serious. Is God more pleased when we are serious than when we are laughing?

THE SEARCH BEGINS AT
Nehemiah 8:10

SEE ALSO
Mischief
Source of Happiness

Just You Wait (2897)

Why some kids seem to get away with everything

Why do some kids get caught and others don't? • Why do some kids get away with doing bad things?
THE SEARCH BEGINS AT
Job 12:6
SEE ALSO
God as Judge
God's Justice
Injustice

Justification by Faith (1203)
If God can't stand sin, and I sin sometimes, how can God stand me? • Does Jesus' death make a difference in my life even if I don't believe it?
THE SEARCH BEGINS AT
Habakkuk 2:4
SEE ALSO
Forgiveness of Sin
Only One Savior
Salvation by Faith

Kind to the Needy (3829)
Is it a sin not to help someone who needs help? • How can I find out who needs help? • What can I do if I don't know how to help someone?
THE SEARCH BEGINS AT
Exodus 22:22
SEE ALSO
Fair to the Poor
Giving
Kind to the Poor

Kind to the Poor (2802)
How does God feel about poor people? • What can I do about poverty?
THE SEARCH BEGINS AT
Exodus 23:11
SEE ALSO
Giving
God's Care for Kids
Kind to the Needy
Kindness

Kindness (1998)
How can I be more like God? • Does God want me to be kind even to my brothers and sisters? • What should I do when I get angry at somebody?
THE SEARCH BEGINS AT
Romans 12:10
SEE ALSO
Kind to the Needy
Kind to the Poor
New Kids
Sympathy

Laughter (1942)
Is there anything bad about laughing?
THE SEARCH BEGINS AT
Proverbs 14:13
SEE ALSO
Happiness
Teasing and Joking

Laziness (0581)
Not working when you should be working; avoiding work for no good reason
Am I lazy just because I don't want to clean my room? • Am I lazy just because I don't want to do boring chores? • Is it wrong to want just to hang around with your friends?
THE SEARCH BEGINS AT
Proverbs 18:9
SEE ALSO
Lazy People
Work
Working Hard

Lazy People (3384)
People who don't do their fair share of work
What's wrong with being lazy? • What happens to lazy people? • What can lazy people do to change? • What advice does the Bible give to lazy people?
THE SEARCH BEGINS AT
Proverbs 6:6
SEE ALSO
Laziness
Sleep

Leaders Should... (2541)
Duties of leaders and rulers
What special duties does a leader have? • Does being a leader mean you get to push other people around?
THE SEARCH BEGINS AT
Deuteronomy 17:16
SEE ALSO
Be Fair
Rulers

Learning from Jesus (2963)
How can I learn from Jesus the way the disciples did?
THE SEARCH BEGINS AT
Matthew 13:36
SEE ALSO
Seeking God
The Teacher

Legalism (2990)
Being proud of yourself for keeping the rules
Is it possible to displease God when I'm following the rules?
THE SEARCH BEGINS AT
Mark 2:24
SEE ALSO
Phonies
Self-righteousness

Lessons of Life (4179)
How can I learn to do what is right? • What does God want to teach me? • Why are some lessons so hard to learn?
THE SEARCH BEGINS AT
Psalm 119:71
SEE ALSO
Parents
Understanding
Willingness to Learn

Liars (3703)
People who lie; who don't tell the truth
What does God think of liars? • Is it OK to lie if I know I'll never get caught? • What happens to liars?
THE SEARCH BEGINS AT
Psalm 63:11
SEE ALSO
Dishonest People
Honesty

Life After Death (2416)
What will happen when Jesus comes back? • When Jesus comes again, will just the Christians be resurrected or everyone? • When Jesus comes back, what will happen to people who weren't saved?
THE SEARCH BEGINS AT
Daniel 12:2
SEE ALSO
Death
End Times
Ready for the Future

Life Is Short (2147)
Why do adults say, "You've grown so fast!" • What's wrong with wasting time? • Why does my mom think summer goes so slow when I think it goes so fast?
THE SEARCH BEGINS AT
Genesis 47:9
SEE ALSO
Death
Mortality
Your Body

Life Tests (2149)
In what ways does life test me? • Why should I welcome problems? • What should I do when I'm feeling stressed out?
THE SEARCH BEGINS AT
Psalm 17:3
SEE ALSO
Faith Tested
Pain
Tempted by Satan

Listening and Doing (0943)

What you do about it when you find out what God wants you to do

Why do I sometimes fail to do what I know God wants me to do? • What should I do with all the Bible lessons I hear?

THE SEARCH BEGINS AT
Ezekiel 33:32

SEE ALSO
Apathy
Hard-heart Aches

Living for God (4014)

How can I get other kids to respect me? • Why does the Bible have so many rules about how to live? • If I live by God's rules, will I miss a lot of fun? • What will other kids think of me if I live by the Bible's rules?

THE SEARCH BEGINS AT
Philippians 1:27

SEE ALSO
Commitment
Following God

Loneliness (1331)

Why do I feel lonely if I have friends? • Is it normal for my friends to let me down sometimes?

THE SEARCH BEGINS AT
Psalm 38:11

SEE ALSO
Being Friendless
Cold Shoulder
God's Care for You

Losers (2914)

What does God get angry about? • What does God think about the evil in the world? • Does God ever get annoyed with me? • Does God ever give up on people?

THE SEARCH BEGINS AT
Numbers 14:11

SEE ALSO
Christ as Judge
Rebellion

Love (4183)

How can I show my friends that I'm a Christian? • Do I have to love everybody? • Why should I love kids who are mean to me?

THE SEARCH BEGINS AT
John 13:35

SEE ALSO
Golden Rule
Hate
Importance of Love
Love for Friends
Loving Others
Nice

Love for Friends (2202)

How can I be a good friend? • How did friends in the Bible treat each other? • What makes the difference between friends and strangers?

THE SEARCH BEGINS AT
1 Samuel 18:3

SEE ALSO
Being a Friend
Compassion
Friendship
Good Friends

Love for God (2207)

How can I show God how much I love him? • What does God most want from me?

THE SEARCH BEGINS AT
Deuteronomy 6:5

SEE ALSO
Loving Others
Pleasing God

Loving Enemies (3395)

What should I do about bullies? • What's the best way to get back at somebody? • How can I love my enemies?

THE SEARCH BEGINS AT
Exodus 23:4

SEE ALSO
Family
Neighbors

Loving Jesus (2205)

Did Jesus have friends? • How did the people who lived around Jesus show they loved him?

THE SEARCH BEGINS AT
Luke 7:47

SEE ALSO
Suffering for Jesus
Why Suffer?

Loving Others (2201)

What's the most important rule of all? • Which is more important, to love God or to love people? • Do I really have to love EVERYBODY?

THE SEARCH BEGINS AT
Deuteronomy 10:19

SEE ALSO
Giving
Kind to the Poor
Neighbors
New Kids
Sympathy
Work that Helps Others

Luxury (3200)

Living for pleasure; indulgence; always buying what will taste good, feel good, and make you look good

Why should I wait for what I want? • What's wrong with spending all your money on the things you want?

THE SEARCH BEGINS AT
Proverbs 21:17

SEE ALSO
Being Frugal
Greed
Parties
Poverty
Restraint

Lying (3702)

What's wrong with telling "little white lies"? • My friends say it's OK to lie if it doesn't hurt anyone. Is that true? • How can I get out of the habit of lying?

THE SEARCH BEGINS AT
Leviticus 19:11

SEE ALSO
Dishonest People
Honesty
Hurtful Lying
Liars
Perjury

Lying to Yourself (3196)

What's wrong with a little white lie? • Is it possible to believe my own lies?

THE SEARCH BEGINS AT
Psalm 36:2

SEE ALSO
Honesty
Hurtful Lying

Mad (3953)

Is it OK to get angry if someone puts me down? • When is it wrong to get angry? • What can I do when I feel really angry?

THE SEARCH BEGINS AT
Genesis 4:5

SEE ALSO
Anger
Temper

Made in God's Image (2239)

Do people look like God? • Does God look like a person? • What does "made in God's image" mean?

THE SEARCH BEGINS AT
Genesis 1:26-27

SEE ALSO
Hurting Yourself
Value of People
Your Body

Making Progress (0999)

How to know if you're growing spiritually

How can I tell if my spirit is growing stronger? • Can other people tell if my spirit has grown?

THE SEARCH BEGINS AT
Job 17:9

SEE ALSO
Change
Growing Spiritually
Perfection

Malice (2003)

A mean, cruel, angry, or hateful attitude; ill will; meanness

Sometimes when I'm angry with people I hope something bad will happen to them. Is that OK as long as I don't do anything about it? • What should I do if I want to hurt somebody? • What should I do when I get REALLY angry with someone?

THE SEARCH BEGINS AT
1 Corinthians 5:8
SEE ALSO
Compassion
Hate

Meekness (2271)

Being reserved and calm instead of aggressive and pushy

Is it wrong to be obnoxious? • People ignore quiet kids. Does God ignore them too? • I notice loud people more than quiet people. Is that how God is too?

THE SEARCH BEGINS AT
Psalm 22:26
SEE ALSO
Gentleness
Self-control

Mercy (1086)

Why should I be kind to people who are not kind? • Isn't it my job to call people jerks if they're acting like jerks?

THE SEARCH BEGINS AT
Psalm 109:16
SEE ALSO
Cold Shoulder
God's Mercy
Nice

Mercy from God (2300)

Times when God was merciful (kind) to people who deserved to be punished

Does God look for chances to catch me doing wrong? • Will God punish me whenever I do something bad? • Is God always angry at me?

THE SEARCH BEGINS AT
Genesis 18:26
SEE ALSO
God's Mercy
The Teacher

Mischief (2377)

Planning to make trouble; plotting against someone; playing practical jokes on people

Does God think it's sin when I play a practical joke? • What if I do something mean but I'm just joking—is that bad?

THE SEARCH BEGINS AT
1 Samuel 23:9
SEE ALSO
Talking
Teasing and Joking

Mistakes (4064)

I've messed up. What should I do now? • How long should I feel bad about making a mistake? • How can thinking about my mistakes help me? • How can I stop making the same mistake again and again?

THE SEARCH BEGINS AT
Genesis 41:9
SEE ALSO
Lessons of Life
Remorse

Mockers (2393)

People who insult others; people who make fun of others, call them names, and cut them down

What kinds of kids should I stay away from? • What kind of kids really make God upset? • What does God think of the kid who makes fun of the girls at the bus stop?

THE SEARCH BEGINS AT
Proverbs 17:5
SEE ALSO
Mocking
Teasing and Joking

Mocking (2394)

Making fun of people; cutting people down

How does God want us to treat people? • Is it OK to make fun of people? • Does God care if I make faces at someone?

THE SEARCH BEGINS AT
2 Kings 2:23
SEE ALSO
Accepting People
Bullies
Expecting Pain
Mockers

Moderation (3574)

What's wrong with eating as much as I want? • Is it OK to spend all the money I have? • Is it possible to have too much fun?

THE SEARCH BEGINS AT
Proverbs 23:20
SEE ALSO
Parties
Restraint
Self-control

Modesty (3875)

Does God care what kind of clothes I wear? • What's wrong with wanting the best-looking clothes? • Is it OK for girls to wear as much makeup and jewelry as they want?

THE SEARCH BEGINS AT
Genesis 24:65
SEE ALSO
Conceit
Humility
Showing Off
Showing Off Stuff

Money's Dangers (2806)

Why doesn't God make me rich? • Could there be anything bad about having as much money as you want?

THE SEARCH BEGINS AT
Deuteronomy 8:13-14
SEE ALSO
Just You Wait
Success
Wealth

Money's Limits (2807)

Why does the Bible tell me not to trust in riches?

THE SEARCH BEGINS AT
Proverbs 11:4
SEE ALSO
Being Frugal
Greed
Money's Dangers

Mortality (2403)

The fact that everyone dies and that life on earth is temporary

If I take good enough care of myself, can I live forever?

THE SEARCH BEGINS AT
Job 4:19
SEE ALSO
Death
Life After Death

Naiveté (3854)

Is it wrong to be naive? • Ignorance is bliss, right?

THE SEARCH BEGINS AT
Proverbs 1:22
SEE ALSO
Deception
Ignorance

Names of God (3633)

The names that the Bible uses for God

Why do people use different names for God when they pray? • Are some of the names of God better than others? • How can I decide which names I should use for God? • What names does God have?

THE SEARCH BEGINS AT
Genesis 17:1
SEE ALSO
Finding Strength
God as Judge
Perfect Father

Nature Teaches Us (2498)

Where can I learn about God? • Is church the only place I learn about God? • What does nature tell us about God?

THE SEARCH BEGINS AT
Psalm 19:1
SEE ALSO
Christmas
God's Teaching
The Guide

Nature's Praise (2569)

The way nature praises God

Does nature obey God?

THE SEARCH BEGINS AT
Psalm 65:13
SEE ALSO
Nature Teaches Us
Praising God

Neighbors (3394)

People you come in contact with

How does God want me to treat my neighbors? • Is it OK to treat others the same way they treat me? • How can I be nice to people who are mean to me?

THE SEARCH BEGINS AT
Leviticus 19:18
SEE ALSO
Forgiving Others
Kindness
Love for Friends
Loving Enemies
Loving Others
Patience
Sympathy

New Kids (3396)

Helping and welcoming kids you don't know; showing hospitality

How does God want me to treat kids I don't know? • Is it safe to try to help people I don't know? • How can I help strangers if my parents tell me not to talk to them? • When should I stay away from strangers?

THE SEARCH BEGINS AT
Exodus 22:21
SEE ALSO
Cold Shoulder
Kindness
Sympathy

New Life (2582)

How can I change the kind of person I am? • How can I become a better person? • Can God really change me? • What happens to me when I become a Christian? • Does God remember all my old sins even after I confess them?

THE SEARCH BEGINS AT
Psalm 40:3
SEE ALSO
Bad Habits
Change
Friend of Jesus
New Person
Old Life
Power of the Bible
Repent!
Who Deserves Christ?

New Person (2584)

How is God changing me? • What does the Holy Spirit do? • What difference does it make that God lives in me?

THE SEARCH BEGINS AT
Psalm 51:10
SEE ALSO
Change
Holiness
God's Forgiveness
God's Teaching
Guidance

Nice (1436)

When someone is just plain mean, can I go ahead and let them have it? • Is it OK with God to fight back if someone pushes you around? • What good does it do to be nice to someone who is NEVER nice?

THE SEARCH BEGINS AT
Genesis 45:15
SEE ALSO
Love
Vengeance

No Condemnation (3124)

How do I know God isn't angry with me?

THE SEARCH BEGINS AT
Isaiah 50:9
SEE ALSO
Forgiveness of Sin
God's Forgiveness

No Mercy (2302)

Withholding mercy from others

Why should I forgive others? • Is there anyone God will NOT be merciful to?

THE SEARCH BEGINS AT
Matthew 6:15
SEE ALSO
Forgiving Others
Grace
Mercy

Not Caring (4163)

What does it mean to be a "Good Samaritan"? • Does it really matter whether I give money or food to help people? • Why are some people afraid of helping others?

THE SEARCH BEGINS AT
Genesis 4:9
SEE ALSO
Apathy
Cruelty
Loving Others
Nice
Sympathy

Not Confessing (1764)

Not telling God you're sorry for doing something wrong

What happens if I don't confess my sin? • Why should I confess my sins to God if he already knows about them?

THE SEARCH BEGINS AT
Psalm 32:3
SEE ALSO
Confession
Feeling Sorry

Not Praying (1089)

Does God want me to ask him for things, or does he get tired of it? • Is it important to God that I tell him about the things I need even though he knows everything?

THE SEARCH BEGINS AT
Psalm 53:4
SEE ALSO
Help!
Praying
The Time Is Now

Obeying Christ (2619)

Did people in the Bible obey Jesus? • What examples does the Bible give of obeying Jesus?

THE SEARCH BEGINS AT
Matthew 4:20
SEE ALSO
Commitment
Following God

Obeying God (2614)

What should I do if my friends tell me to do one thing, but it goes against something God tells me to do?

THE SEARCH BEGINS AT
Deuteronomy 26:16
SEE ALSO
Following God
Obeying the Law

Obeying the Law (2525)

Can I do whatever I want when I'm older? • Does God care whether people speed when they're driving?

THE SEARCH BEGINS AT
Ezra 7:26
SEE ALSO
Crime
Free to...
Rulers
Violence

Old Life (2642)

When I become a Christian do I become a different person? • What does God want to change in me when I become a Christian?
THE SEARCH BEGINS AT
Romans 6:6
SEE ALSO
Bad Habits
Growing Spiritually
Making Progress

Old People (3976)

How should I treat old people? • What can I learn from my grandparents? • What's wrong with making fun of old people? • What do old people have to offer?
THE SEARCH BEGINS AT
2 Kings 2:23
SEE ALSO
Respecting Adults
Respecting God's People
Rulers

One Goal (3442)

Staying focused on serving God; having one ultimate goal for your life and sticking to it

What goals does God want me to have? • What's the number one goal I can have for my life? • What can distract me from God's goals for me? • How can I stay focused on living God's way?
THE SEARCH BEGINS AT
Deuteronomy 5:32
SEE ALSO
Job One
Perfection
Planning

Only Human (2734)

Did people in the Bible like Moses and the disciples ever mess up? • Does God expect me to be perfect?
THE SEARCH BEGINS AT
Genesis 20:2
SEE ALSO
Mistakes
Perfection
Weakness

Only One God (2649)

Why do we worship God? • Why doesn't God want us to worship idols? • Are there other gods besides the one I hear about at church?
THE SEARCH BEGINS AT
Deuteronomy 4:35
SEE ALSO
Going to Church
Only One Savior
Worshiping Things

Only One Savior (3117)

Is there really only one way to heaven? • Did God provide more than one way for our sins to be forgiven? • Is Jesus really the only way to heaven?
THE SEARCH BEGINS AT
Luke 1:69
SEE ALSO
Jesus the Lamb
Our Savior
Salvation by Faith
What Jesus Did
Why Jesus Came
Why Jesus Died

Ouch! (2620)

Why did I get in trouble if God forgave me? • If God loves me, does that mean I won't be punished when I do wrong?
THE SEARCH BEGINS AT
Deuteronomy 11:28
SEE ALSO
Sinner Beware
Warning!

Our Savior (3368)

Jesus Christ

Why does the Bible call Jesus a Savior? • Why do I need a Savior? • What can Jesus save me from? • Can anyone else save me besides Jesus?
THE SEARCH BEGINS AT
Isaiah 59:16
SEE ALSO
Only One Savior
Salvation by Faith

Pain (0496)

Hurts; suffering

Why do bad things happen? • Why do I have to suffer?
THE SEARCH BEGINS AT
Job 23:10
SEE ALSO
Difficulties
Expecting Pain
Life Tests

Parents (1778)

Being teachable; knowing the value of education

Why did God give me my parents? • Does God care how I do in school? • What should I do if I don't understand why my parents want me to do something? • Do I really have to obey my parents?
THE SEARCH BEGINS AT
Proverbs 1:8
SEE ALSO
Parents Care
The Teacher
Willingness to Learn
Wise Thoughts

Parents Care (1642)

Why do my parents always want to know where I am? • Do parents care just because they are parents and they have to? • Is it my parents' job to care about me?
THE SEARCH BEGINS AT
Genesis 37:14
SEE ALSO
Family
Respecting Adults

Parties (3408)

Does God mind if I have fun at parties? • How does God want me to act at parties? • What kind of parties should I avoid?
THE SEARCH BEGINS AT
Exodus 32:6
SEE ALSO
Guilty Fear
Holiness
Joy
Laziness
Mischief
Moderation
Procrastination

Patience (2275)

What can I do when my brother or sister drives me crazy? • Does my little brother irritate God as much as he does me? • Do I HAVE to be patient? • Does God expect me to be patient even with my sister?
THE SEARCH BEGINS AT
1 Corinthians 13:7
SEE ALSO
Quitting
Showing Mercy
Vengeance

Peace (3777)

Is it OK to stay angry at a friend for a little while? • What can I do when a friend gets angry at me? • If I didn't do anything wrong, do I HAVE to say I'm sorry?
THE SEARCH BEGINS AT
Ecclesiastes 10:4
SEE ALSO
Patience
Peacemaking

Peace of Mind (3013)

How can I feel peaceful when there is so much wrong with the world? • How can I stop being so upset? •

What should I do whenever I feel upset or afraid?
THE SEARCH BEGINS AT
Psalm 29:11
SEE ALSO
Guilty Fear
Joy
Mischief

Peacemaking (3778)

If my sister picks a fight with me, is it OK to fight back? • What's wrong with arguing as long as we don't hurt each other? • What should I do to keep the peace in my family?
THE SEARCH BEGINS AT
Proverbs 12:20
SEE ALSO
Arguing
Fighting
Peace

Perfect Father (1246)

How is God like a father? • How can I know God will always be there when I need him?
THE SEARCH BEGINS AT
1 Chronicles 29:10
SEE ALSO
God's Care for Kids
Jesus

Perfection (2729)

Even though God will forgive, should I still try not to sin at all? • Does God expect me to be PERFECT?
THE SEARCH BEGINS AT
Genesis 17:1
SEE ALSO
Change
Growing Spiritually
Holiness

Perjury (0871)

Lying under oath; lying in court; giving false testimony

Is it ever against the law to break a promise? • What does it mean to take an oath? • How can lying hurt you? • What does perjury mean?
THE SEARCH BEGINS AT
Leviticus 6:3
SEE ALSO
Crime
Honesty
Hurtful Lying

Phonies (2750)

Hypocrites; fakes

Is it possible to do what God wants but do it the wrong way? • Is it possible to be a good person on the outside but a bad person on the inside?
THE SEARCH BEGINS AT
Matthew 6:2
SEE ALSO
Bad News
Liars

Pitfalls (3785)

Dangers along the way

Can giving in to temptation really hurt me? • What should I watch out for? • What should I be careful about? • What's wrong with being smug if you're better than others?
THE SEARCH BEGINS AT
Deuteronomy 4:9
SEE ALSO
Getting Along
Sinner Beware
Warning!

Planning (2774)

How to make the best plans

What kind of plans should I make for the future? • Why do some people say, "Lord willing"?
THE SEARCH BEGINS AT
Genesis 11:4
SEE ALSO
The Future
One Goal
Procrastination
Ready for the Future

Pleasing God (1253)

What kinds of deeds please God? • Is pleasing God more important than pleasing parents?
THE SEARCH BEGINS AT
Proverbs 16:7
SEE ALSO
Accepted by God
Who Is Religious?

Popularity (2789)

Doing something just to please a crowd

Why should I make up my own mind when my friends tell me what to do? • Is it OK to want to be popular? • What's wrong with doing what everybody else is doing?
THE SEARCH BEGINS AT
John 12:43
SEE ALSO
Bad Friends
Being Friendless
The Crowd
Standing Strong

Positive Attitude (1934)

Looking on the bright side

Why should I look on the bright side? • What is there to be happy about when everything is going wrong?
THE SEARCH BEGINS AT
Habakkuk 3:17-18
SEE ALSO
Endurance
Hardship

Poverty (2798)

Is it really true that money won't make you happy? • What makes people happy with their lives?
THE SEARCH BEGINS AT
Jeremiah 5:4
SEE ALSO
Being Frugal
Money's Dangers
Money's Limits
Wealth

Power of the Bible (0421)

What's so special about the Bible? • What good does it do to read the Bible? • What can the Bible do for me?
THE SEARCH BEGINS AT
Jeremiah 5:14
SEE ALSO
Being Smart
Purity
Reading the Bible
Valuing the Bible
Why the Bible?

Praising God (1451)

Why do some people say, "Praise the Lord!"? • How can I praise God if I don't like to sing?
THE SEARCH BEGINS AT
Psalm 9:11
SEE ALSO
Going to Church
Worship

Pray and Wait (3607)

Waiting for God's answers to our prayers

Why doesn't God answer my prayers right away? • What can I do when I feel like giving up praying about something? • How can waiting for God be good for me?
THE SEARCH BEGINS AT
Psalm 13:1
SEE ALSO
Praying
Waiting

Prayer (4193)

Why should I pray? • What should I pray for? • Is there a right or wrong way to pray? • Will God answer my prayers?
THE SEARCH BEGINS AT
Matthew 21:22
SEE ALSO
Answers to Prayer
Duty to Pray
How to Pray
Not Praying
Praying
Praying for Others
Unanswered Prayer

Praying (1003)

Talking to God and inviting him to talk to you through your thoughts

Should praying be easy? • How can I tell if God is listening when I pray? • How can I listen for God to speak to me?

THE SEARCH BEGINS AT
Psalm 5:3
SEE ALSO
Approaching God
Devotions
God's Friends
Prayer

Praying Alone (2833)

How does God want us to pray? • Should I tell the person I'm praying for that I'm praying for her? • Do I have to show it when I pray? • How should I pray? • Why does my pastor talk about a "prayer closet"?

THE SEARCH BEGINS AT
Deuteronomy 9:25
SEE ALSO
Phonies
Praying

Praying for Mercy (2301)

Do I need to ask for God's mercy in order to get it? • How can I be sure God will not punish me for being bad? • What should I pray about?

THE SEARCH BEGINS AT
Deuteronomy 21:8
SEE ALSO
Forgiveness of Sin
God's Mercy
Mercy from God
Promise of Mercy

Praying for Others (1785)

What difference does it make if I pray for someone? • Praying seems like such a small thing to do. Aren't there bigger, more helpful things I can do for someone? • What should I pray for?

THE SEARCH BEGINS AT
Exodus 32:32
SEE ALSO
Answers to Prayer
Enemies
Helping Weak People

Praying for Wisdom (3841)

Does God give kids wisdom? • Can God make a kid wiser than an adult? • When should I ask God for wisdom? • Can praying for wisdom really help? • What should I pray for? • How can I know if God hears my prayers?

THE SEARCH BEGINS AT
2 Chronicles 1:10
SEE ALSO
Getting Wisdom
True Wisdom

Procrastination (1500)

Putting something off till later when you can do it now

Did people in the Bible ever put off what they needed to do? • Why should I do my chores before I have fun? • Why shouldn't I do what I WANT to do before I do what I HAVE to do?

THE SEARCH BEGINS AT
Genesis 19:16
SEE ALSO
Laziness
Life Is Short

Promise of Mercy (2299)

If I went to God 5 times to ask forgiveness for getting angry at my step-sister, but I did it again today, will God still be kind to me and forgive me?

THE SEARCH BEGINS AT
Exodus 34:7
SEE ALSO
Forgiveness
God's Forgiveness

Promises to Givers (2882)

If I'm generous, how do I know I won't lose everything I have? • What do I get out of giving? • Why should I be generous?

THE SEARCH BEGINS AT
Psalm 41:1
SEE ALSO
Generosity
Giving

Promises to the Poor (2885)

Does God look down on poor people? • What does God do for poor people?

THE SEARCH BEGINS AT
Job 5:15
SEE ALSO
God's Care for Kids
Kind to the Needy

Protection (0364)

Does each person have a guardian angel? • What should I do when I'm scared? • Can God protect me?

THE SEARCH BEGINS AT
2 Chronicles 16:9
SEE ALSO
Safety
Security

Proud People (1726)

People who are arrogant or haughty

What does the Bible say to arrogant people? • Is pride a sin? • Will God judge people for being conceited?

THE SEARCH BEGINS AT
Psalm 40:4
SEE ALSO
Arrogance
Boasting

Publicly Christian (1016)

Letting others know you are a Christian

Do I need to share my faith with every person I pass on the bus? • Why do I feel embarrassed sometimes to admit that I'm a Christian? • Does God want me to share my faith even if people don't want to hear it?

THE SEARCH BEGINS AT
John 3:1-2
SEE ALSO
The Gospel
Witnessing

Purity (0423)

What can the Bible do for me? • How can I be pure? • Why should I read the Bible? • How does it help me to read the Bible?

THE SEARCH BEGINS AT
Psalm 119:9
SEE ALSO
Being Smart
The Guide
Power of the Bible
Reading the Bible
Valuing the Bible
Why the Bible?

Quitting (2691)

Determination; sticking to it; not giving up

Should I keep trying to obey God even if I keep messing up? • Should I keep praying even if it seems God isn't answering?

THE SEARCH BEGINS AT
Ecclesiastes 7:8
SEE ALSO
Endurance
Holiness
Standing Strong

Reading the Bible (0428)

What am I supposed to do with the Bible? • What if I don't understand the Bible?

THE SEARCH BEGINS AT
Deuteronomy 17:19
SEE ALSO
Being Smart
Power of the Bible
Valuing the Bible
Why the Bible?

Ready for Jesus' Return (1346)

Being ready for Christ's second coming

What can I do to get ready for Jesus' return? • Who will be surprised when Jesus returns?

THE SEARCH BEGINS AT
Philippians 4:5

SEE ALSO
Procrastination
Second Coming

Ready for the Future (2951)

If I don't know the future, how can I prepare for it? • What's the best way to prepare for the future?

THE SEARCH BEGINS AT
2 Kings 20:1

SEE ALSO
Jesus' Return
Pitfalls
Watching for Jesus' Return

Rebellion (2551)

Why do we have so much crime? • What can I do about crime? • Why should we respect authority?

THE SEARCH BEGINS AT
Deuteronomy 17:12

SEE ALSO
Crime
Hard-hearted
Obeying the Law
Peacemaking

Refusing Correction (2715)

What happens if I just decide not to listen to God? • Why do bad things happen to me? • How does God respond if people just ignore him?

THE SEARCH BEGINS AT
Isaiah 1:5

SEE ALSO
Rebellion
Used to Sin

Rejecting God's Word (2967)

How can it hurt a person to reject the Bible? • What sort of attitudes can get me in trouble?

THE SEARCH BEGINS AT
2 Chronicles 30:10

SEE ALSO
Discipline
Gratitude
Learning from Jesus
Parents
Stubborn People

Rejoicing (1932)

Am I supposed to be able to MAKE myself be happy? • What should I do if I don't feel joyful? • Does God want us to be happy? • Why does God tell us to rejoice?

THE SEARCH BEGINS AT
Deuteronomy 12:7

SEE ALSO
Happiness
Source of Happiness

Religious People (2985)

What does God want most out of us?

THE SEARCH BEGINS AT
Deuteronomy 10:12

SEE ALSO
Phonies
The Ultimate
Who Is Religious?

Remember... (2999)

When does God want me to think about him? • What was I supposed to remember?

THE SEARCH BEGINS AT
Nehemiah 4:14

SEE ALSO
Don't Forget...
Self-confidence

Remorse (1765)

Feeling sorry

If I tell God I'm sorry for my sin, is that enough? • What is remorse?

THE SEARCH BEGINS AT
Numbers 14:39

SEE ALSO
Feeling Guilty
Not Confessing
Repentance

Repent! (2706)

Turning away from your sin

How do you get Jesus to forgive you? • What does "repentance" mean? • Do people ever get too old to repent of their sins? • Will God forgive me if I tell him I'm sorry?

THE SEARCH BEGINS AT
2 Kings 17:13

SEE ALSO
Change
Confession
Not Confessing

Repentance (2884)

What will happen if I tell God I'm sorry for my sins?

THE SEARCH BEGINS AT
Psalm 34:18

SEE ALSO
Feeling Sorry
Forgiveness

Resisting Satan (3154)

What should I do when I feel tempted? • How can I escape the devil's power? • How can I be strong when I am tempted to do something wrong?

THE SEARCH BEGINS AT
Ephesians 4:26-27

SEE ALSO
Defeat of Satan
Satan's Power
Satan's Weakness
Saying No

Respecting Adults (3974)

Why should I respect my elders? • How can kids show respect for adults? • If I show respect for my parents, should they show respect for me? • If my parents don't understand me, why should I listen to their advice?

THE SEARCH BEGINS AT
Leviticus 19:32

SEE ALSO
Giving Advice
Rulers
Taking Advice

Respecting God (3030)

If I respect and worship God, does that mean I always act serious when I talk about him?

THE SEARCH BEGINS AT
Exodus 3:5

SEE ALSO
Respecting Adults
Why Fear God

Respecting God's People (3032)

How am I supposed to act toward the pastor? • Why shouldn't I make fun of my Sunday School teacher? He dresses funny.

THE SEARCH BEGINS AT
Exodus 33:8

SEE ALSO
Golden Rule
Serving People

Rest (3010)

Relaxation

Is it OK just to relax sometimes? • Does God expect us to work all the time?

THE SEARCH BEGINS AT
Exodus 23:12

SEE ALSO
Moderation
Sleep
Work

Restraint (3207)

Having control of your appetites; not giving in to every urge

Is it OK to eat and eat and eat and eat and eat and eat? • What does the Bible have to say to couch potatoes?

THE SEARCH BEGINS AT
Proverbs 23:1-2
SEE ALSO
Discipline
Moderation
Self-control

Results of Sin (3975)

Does God punish people for their mistakes? • Does sin always have consequences? • Is it OK to do something wrong if I know I can get away with it?
THE SEARCH BEGINS AT
Job 13:26
SEE ALSO
Blinded by Sin
Ouch!

Resurrection (2407)

What life is like after we die

Does our spirit live in heaven after we die, or do we come back as someone else? • When Jesus comes back, what will happen to the Christians?
THE SEARCH BEGINS AT
Psalm 49:15
SEE ALSO
End Times
Life After Death
Second Coming

Revenge (2279)

Getting back at someone; holding a grudge; retaliating

If someone does something mean to me should I do something mean back? • What should I do if somebody tries to pick a fight with me? • Will people respect me more if I fight tough?
THE SEARCH BEGINS AT
Leviticus 19:18
SEE ALSO
Hate
Loving Enemies
Showing Mercy
Vengeance

Rewarded Goodness (3054)

How does it help me to be good? • How does God reward righteous people? • What reward is there in being good?
THE SEARCH BEGINS AT
Job 36:7
SEE ALSO
Blessing
Blessings
Goodness Rewarded
Suffering Rewarded

Rewards (4086)

How can I get God to help me? • Why does God bless some people and not others? • What kind of people does God want me to help? • Why should I bother helping kids who can't pay me back?
THE SEARCH BEGINS AT
Psalm 41:3
SEE ALSO
Apathy
Helping Weak People
Mercy
Nice
Sympathy
Work that Helps Others

Right Paths (2688)

What does it mean to live rightly? • How can I know what is right? • What happens when I live God's way?
THE SEARCH BEGINS AT
Psalm 16:11
SEE ALSO
Doing Good
Holiness
The Time Is Now

Righteousness (3080)

Goodness; always doing right

Does God really expect me to try not to sin AT ALL? • Is it OK just to be mostly good?
THE SEARCH BEGINS AT
Daniel 4:27
SEE ALSO
Doing Good
Holiness
Obeying God
Who Is Religious?

Rulers (2526)

How should we act toward government leaders? • Is obeying the law the same as obeying God?
THE SEARCH BEGINS AT
Exodus 22:28
SEE ALSO
Obeying the Law
Rebellion

Sacrifice (4156)

Why is it so hard to be a Christian? • Why are there so many "Don'ts" in the Bible? • What does God want me to give up? • What will I get in return for the sacrifices I make for God?
THE SEARCH BEGINS AT
Matthew 19:21
SEE ALSO
Believer Be Glad
Rewards

Safety (2913)

God's protection

How can I be sure God is watching over me? • How can I stop feeling so afraid?
THE SEARCH BEGINS AT
Deuteronomy 6:24
SEE ALSO
Evil Attacks
Security

Salvation (1087)

When God forgives your sins

If being a Christian is so great, why do some people just walk away from it? • How can I know I'm ready to be a Christian?
THE SEARCH BEGINS AT
Ezekiel 33:9
SEE ALSO
Earning Heaven
Forgiveness of Sin

Salvation by Faith (1206)

I know that Jesus died. Is that all it takes to be saved? • From what does God save me?
THE SEARCH BEGINS AT
John 3:15
SEE ALSO
Faith
Justification by Faith
Salvation

Salvation for Anyone (3119)

Does everyone have a chance to become a Christian?
THE SEARCH BEGINS AT
Luke 3:6
SEE ALSO
God Calls You
God's Care for You
Only One Savior

Satan's Power (3150)

What kind of power does Satan have? • Is Jesus more powerful than Satan? • Can Satan hurt me? • Is Satan real?
THE SEARCH BEGINS AT
Job 1:12
SEE ALSO
Defeat of Satan
Satan's Weakness

Satan's Weakness (4199)

Limits on Satan's power

Should I be afraid of Satan? • How much power does Satan have? • Why does God let Satan tempt us?
THE SEARCH BEGINS AT
Job 1:12
SEE ALSO
Power of the Bible
Resisting Satan
Satan's Power

Satisfaction (0984)

How can I be satisfied? • What should I do when I feel lonely?
THE SEARCH BEGINS AT
Psalm 17:15

SEE ALSO
Apathy
Contentment
Discontentment
Envy

Saying No (3590)

Why is it so hard to say no to sin? • What can I do when I feel like giving in to temptation? • How can God help me say no to sin?

THE SEARCH BEGINS AT
Proverbs 1:10

SEE ALSO
Giving In
Resisting Satan

Saying Thank You (4116)

What has God done for me? • Why is it important to be thankful? • How does God feel when I forget to say thank you? • How can I learn to be thankful?

THE SEARCH BEGINS AT
Isaiah 43:24

SEE ALSO
Gifts from God
Unthankfulness to People

Second Coming (1344)

The Bible says that Jesus will return some day

Does the Bible really say that Jesus will come back? • How do we know Jesus will come back? • When will Jesus come back? • How will Jesus come back?

THE SEARCH BEGINS AT
Matthew 26:64

SEE ALSO
Bad News
Good News
Jesus' Return

Security (3174)

Safety; confidence

What can I do when I feel afraid? • What can keep me from being afraid?

THE SEARCH BEGINS AT
Job 11:18

SEE ALSO
God's Control
God's Power
Safety
Trusting God
Value of People

Seeking God (3191)

How can I get to know God more?

THE SEARCH BEGINS AT
Deuteronomy 4:29

SEE ALSO
Answers to Prayer
Duty to Pray
How to Pray
Praying Alone
Waiting for God

Seeking Peace (3015)

Not conflict

Can I do something to help myself feel peaceful?

THE SEARCH BEGINS AT
Job 22:21

SEE ALSO
Fighting
Peacemaking

Self-confidence (3188)

Is it OK for me to believe in myself?

THE SEARCH BEGINS AT
Proverbs 28:26

SEE ALSO
Don't Forget...
Remember...
Success

Self-control (3569)

Being able to say no to your desires; doing what you SHOULD do no matter how you feel about it

Is it OK to eat like a pig if you're really hungry? • Why should I "bite my tongue"? • Is it OK to lose your temper once in awhile? • Is it OK to do whatever feels good? • How can I learn self-control?

THE SEARCH BEGINS AT
Proverbs 16:32

SEE ALSO
Temper

Self-examination (3197)

Honesty with yourself

How can I be honest with myself?

THE SEARCH BEGINS AT
Lamentations 3:40

SEE ALSO
Lying
Lying to Yourself
What God Knows

Self-righteousness (3219)

Thinking you are always right and good

Do I have to admit it every time I do something wrong? • Is it OK to believe you're better than everyone else if you ARE better than everyone else?

THE SEARCH BEGINS AT
Deuteronomy 9:4

SEE ALSO
Arrogance
Conceit
Hypocrisy
Phonies
Showing Off

Serving (3900)

Is it OK to complain about the jobs my parents give me as long as I get the work done? • Is there a way to make my work more fun? • What kind of service does God want from me?

THE SEARCH BEGINS AT
Nehemiah 12:43

SEE ALSO
Humility
Serving Quickly

Serving Jesus (3895)

Why should I do my best even when no one is looking? • How can I do my best ALL the time? • What does it mean to serve Jesus?

THE SEARCH BEGINS AT
John 12:26

SEE ALSO
Serving People
Work
Working with God

Serving People (3896)

Why does God want us to work so hard serving people? • What should I do if I don't feel like serving? • If I spend all my time serving others, who will look out for me? • How can I be more like Jesus?

THE SEARCH BEGINS AT
Mark 10:43-44

SEE ALSO
Serving Jesus
Work
Working with God

Serving Quickly (3899)

How can I know how God wants me to serve? • Is it OK to wait until I get older to serve God? • I don't know how to serve God—what should I do?

THE SEARCH BEGINS AT
1 Kings 19:20

SEE ALSO
Hurrying
Lazy People
Willingness to Work

Sharing (0583)

What should I do if someone wants to borrow lunch money? • How can I serve God with my stuff? • Do I HAVE to share my stuff? • Is it a sin not to share your toys?

THE SEARCH BEGINS AT
Deuteronomy 15:8

SEE ALSO
Serving
Showing Off Stuff

Showing Mercy (2298)
Why do I feel bad when I see kids make fun of someone? • What's wrong with telling people off when they deserve it?
THE SEARCH BEGINS AT
Proverbs 3:3
SEE ALSO
Loving Others
Patience
Revenge

Showing Off (1026)
Trying to impress people with what you can do
What is it that turns me off about people showing off in church? • Should I tell people about how I serve God?
THE SEARCH BEGINS AT
2 Kings 10:16
SEE ALSO
Boasting
Proud People
Showing Off Stuff

Showing Off Stuff (1025)
Trying to impress others with what you have
Is it OK to show off my new clothes? • Is there anything wrong with always wanting to be at the head of the line?
THE SEARCH BEGINS AT
Esther 1:4
SEE ALSO
Boasting
Proud People
Showing Off

Sick People (3397)
How can I help a sick friend? • What do sick people need? • Why should I visit sick people? • What kind of help do sick people want from me?
THE SEARCH BEGINS AT
2 Kings 8:29
SEE ALSO
Being a Friend
Comforting Others
Compassion
Serving People

Sin Hurts (0383)
Can sinning hurt you? • What can sinning do to you?
THE SEARCH BEGINS AT
Proverbs 6:33
SEE ALSO
Bad Thoughts
Confession
Not Confessing
Ouch!
Remorse
Sin (Warnings)

Sin (Warnings) (1795)
Warnings for those who insist on living their own way instead of God's
How angry does God get at sin? • What sort of things would make God angry at me? • Does God ever run out of patience?
THE SEARCH BEGINS AT
Genesis 19:17
SEE ALSO
Warning!
Watch Out!

Sincerity (2987)
How can I be a better friend? • Why don't people trust me?
THE SEARCH BEGINS AT
Joshua 24:14
SEE ALSO
Hypocrisy
Lying to Yourself
Phonies

Sinner Beware (3720)
If you go on rebelling against God, you can count on these seven things.
Why does God let sinners get away with so much? • Will sinners ever get what they deserve? • What will the future be like for sinners?
THE SEARCH BEGINS AT
Numbers 32:23
SEE ALSO
Believer Be Glad
Sacrifice

Sleep (3377)
Is it OK to sleep in on weekends? • What does the Bible say about sleep? • Does God care how much sleep I get? • When is it bad to sleep in?
THE SEARCH BEGINS AT
Proverbs 6:4
SEE ALSO
Laziness
Lazy People
Rest

Soon Gone (2809)
Is there money in heaven?
THE SEARCH BEGINS AT
Job 20:28
SEE ALSO
Source of Wealth
Things That Last

Source of Evil (1545)
Why people do bad things
Why do people do bad things? • What makes a person evil? • Why is it sometimes exciting to be around people who do bad things? • If I sin, does that make me an evil person? • Is there a difference between sinning and being evil?
THE SEARCH BEGINS AT
Ecclesiastes 8:11
SEE ALSO
Bad Thoughts
Evildoers
Forgiveness of Sin

Source of Happiness (1937)
Where happiness comes from
How can I be happy? • What really makes a person happy? • Is happiness a mood that comes and goes, or do I have some control over it?
THE SEARCH BEGINS AT
Psalm 128:2
SEE ALSO
Positive Attitude
Rejoicing

Source of Wealth (2805)
Why should I thank God for things that my parents bought me?
THE SEARCH BEGINS AT
Deuteronomy 8:18
SEE ALSO
Gifts from God
Thankfulness

The Spirit in You (1602)
How can God live inside me? • Is God with me all the time?
THE SEARCH BEGINS AT
Ezekiel 36:27
SEE ALSO
God's Presence
Jesus' Home

Spiritual Death (2163)
Can my spirit die? • What is spiritual death?
THE SEARCH BEGINS AT
Genesis 2:17
SEE ALSO
Bad News
Death
Mortality

Standing Strong (3438)
Holding on to your faith
If I believe in Jesus, do I have to do anything else? • What can weaken my faith? • What can make my faith stronger? • How can I become a stronger Christian?
THE SEARCH BEGINS AT
Joshua 23:7-8
SEE ALSO
Commitment
This for That

Starting Over (3346)
What can I do about my sin? • How can I become a better person?

• It's hard to stop sinning. Is it worth it?
THE SEARCH BEGINS AT
Job 11:14
SEE ALSO
Confession
Stay Away

Stay Away! (1798)

Is it OK for me to do some of the bad stuff my friends do so they'll like me more? • What should I do when I find out something bad is going on? • How much does God want us to avoid evil?
THE SEARCH BEGINS AT
Job 28:28
SEE ALSO
Evildoers
Sin Hurts
Warning!
Watch Out!

Stealing (3447)

Taking what does not belong to you

Is stealing always wrong? • Sometimes stealing small things is easy—what's so bad about it? • Should I feel guilty if I stole something a long time ago?
THE SEARCH BEGINS AT
Exodus 20:15
SEE ALSO
Honesty
Love
Lying

Stubborn People (2714)

People who won't listen to correction

What if I don't WANT to say I'm sorry? • Will God make me say I'm sorry for my sin? • What should I do when I realize I've done something wrong?
THE SEARCH BEGINS AT
2 Kings 17:14
SEE ALSO
Discipline
Hard-hearted
Rebellion
Used to Sin

Study (2028)

What's important about education and training

Does God want me to learn, or is school just something my parents care about? • What does God think of school? • Does God care how I do in school? • Why do my parents want me to do well in school when the Bible says that knowledge makes people proud?
THE SEARCH BEGINS AT
Daniel 1:17
SEE ALSO
Being Smart
Ignorance
Naiveté

Submitting to God (3507)

Doing whatever God wants

What's wrong with wanting my own way? • Can I submit to God and still get my own way? • What do I have to give up to submit to God? • Why should I do God's will? • How can I please God? • What does obedience mean?
THE SEARCH BEGINS AT
Psalm 40:8
SEE ALSO
Obeying God
Pleasing God

Success (2898)

Traps that go with being successful

Why do adults sometimes say, "Don't let it go to your head"? • What can go wrong when everything's going right? • What's wrong with success? • What does success do to my relationship with God?
THE SEARCH BEGINS AT
Deuteronomy 6:10-12
SEE ALSO
Arrogance
Money's Dangers

Suffering (0499)

How can I feel better when I'm hurting? • Why do bad things happen? • Why do people suffer? • Why am I suffering?
THE SEARCH BEGINS AT
Deuteronomy 4:30
SEE ALSO
Endurance
God's Comfort
God's Promises
Hardship
Pain

Suffering for Jesus (3474)

When people abuse you for your Christian beliefs

What's wrong with keeping my faith to myself? • Will other kids make fun of me if I tell them I'm a Christian? • Why do some people want to see Christians suffer?
THE SEARCH BEGINS AT
Acts 5:41
SEE ALSO
Expecting Pain
Why Suffer?

Suffering Rewarded (1365)

Why does God let my family go through a hard time? Has he forgotten to take care of us? • How long should I wait for God to help me out of a bad time?
THE SEARCH BEGINS AT
Matthew 5:11-12
SEE ALSO
Expecting Pain
Goodness Rewarded
Heaven

Suing People (0870)

Taking someone to court to settle a disagreement

What does it mean to take someone to court or to sue them? • How does God feel about one person suing another person? • What is a better way to settle a disagreement?
THE SEARCH BEGINS AT
Proverbs 25:8
SEE ALSO
Arguing
Fighting

Sunday School (1779)

Any place where others teach you about God and living God's way

Who can teach me to pray or to have more faith? • How can I learn more about living the Christian life? • Why do we have Sunday School?
THE SEARCH BEGINS AT
1 Samuel 9:27
SEE ALSO
The Teacher
Willingness to Learn

Superstition (2998)

Belief in luck; belief in a "force"

Is there such a thing as luck? • Will I have bad luck if I walk under a ladder? • Is it wrong to be superstitious? • Is it OK to have a good luck charm?
THE SEARCH BEGINS AT
1 Samuel 4:3
SEE ALSO
Demons
God at Work

Swearing (0475)

Cussing; using profanity

What's wrong with cussing? • What's wrong with swearing? • If you say Jesus when you're mad, isn't that like praying? • Is it all right to say bad things if there is no one there to hear you?

THE SEARCH BEGINS AT
Exodus 20:7
SEE ALSO
Cursing
Names of God
Talking

Sympathy (3515)
Feeling what someone else feels
Who needs sympathy? • What can I do if I don't feel sorry for people? • Can God help me have more sympathy for others?
THE SEARCH BEGINS AT
Isaiah 58:7
SEE ALSO
God's Care for Kids
Kind to the Needy
Kind to the Poor
Kindness
Love for Friends
Loving Others

Taking Advice (0795)
What to do when people give you suggestions
Do I have to accept help? • If someone gives me advice does it mean I wasn't doing a good job?
THE SEARCH BEGINS AT
Psalm 141:5
SEE ALSO
Giving Advice
Parents
Respecting Adults

Talents (4016)
How can I use my talents best? • Is it OK to be proud of the talents God gave me? • How can I know if I'm using my talents in the right way?
THE SEARCH BEGINS AT
Matthew 25:20
SEE ALSO
Ambition
Gifts from God

Talking (3295)
How can I get people to listen to me more? • If "talk is cheap," why do my parents tell me not to swear?
THE SEARCH BEGINS AT
Proverbs 17:27
SEE ALSO
Being Quiet
Cruel Talk
Encouraging People
Foolish Promises
Gossiping
Saying Thank You
Swearing
Teasing and Joking
Wise Words

The Teacher (3555)
What kind of teacher was Jesus? • Why did people listen to Jesus? • What does Jesus want to teach me? • How can I become a student of Jesus? • What did Jesus do while he was on earth?
THE SEARCH BEGINS AT
Matthew 4:23
SEE ALSO
Jesus the King
Learning from Jesus
Sunday School

Teamwork (3728)
How can other Christian kids help me? • What's wrong with trying to do everything on my own? • Why should Christians work together?
THE SEARCH BEGINS AT
Exodus 17:12
SEE ALSO
Advice
Getting Along
Getting Opinions
Work

Teasing and Joking (1890)
Why do people say mean things and then say they're just joking? • Why do people get angry when I'm just teasing them? • What's wrong with teasing and joking?
THE SEARCH BEGINS AT
Proverbs 26:19
SEE ALSO
Getting Drunk
Parties

Telling the Truth (4081)
Why is it so important to tell the truth? • Is it OK to lie sometimes? • What should I do if I know I'll get in big trouble if I tell the truth?
THE SEARCH BEGINS AT
Matthew 3:7
SEE ALSO
Dishonest People
Honesty
Liars
Lying

Temper (3957)
What's wrong with losing my temper once in awhile? • How can I stop losing my temper? • Can God help me control my temper?
THE SEARCH BEGINS AT
2 Chronicles 28:9
SEE ALSO
Anger
Mad

Temptation (3586)
An urge or desire to do something wrong
Why does God let Satan tempt me? • Does God know how hard it is for me to resist temptation? • How can God help me when I'm tempted to sin?
THE SEARCH BEGINS AT
1 Corinthians 10:13
SEE ALSO
Controlling Yourself
Restraint
Tempted by Satan

Tempted by Satan (2887)
Temptations that come from the devil
Why do I fight temptation? • If I give in to temptation, will it go away? • Is it true that "the devil made me do it"?
THE SEARCH BEGINS AT
Luke 10:19
SEE ALSO
Demons
Evil Attacks
Stay Away
Temptation

"Thank You" (1450)
Is it important to God that I say thank you? • What difference does it make whether I say thank you? • Did people in the Bible thank each other?
THE SEARCH BEGINS AT
Ruth 2:10
SEE ALSO
Saying Thank You
Thankfulness

Thankfulness (1455)
What is the best way to be "thankful"? • Does God want me to TELL him I'm thankful or SHOW him? • What should I thank God for?
THE SEARCH BEGINS AT
Deuteronomy 8:10
SEE ALSO
Gratitude
Saying Thank You
"Thank You"

Things That Last (3657)
How can kids make a difference in the world? • How can I make my life count for something? • How does God want me to spend my time?
THE SEARCH BEGINS AT
1 Kings 19:8
SEE ALSO
Life Is Short
Value of People
Worshiping Things

This for That (3206)
Giving up something that is important to you to gain something even more important

What do I give up to follow Jesus? • Is it really worth it to follow Jesus?
THE SEARCH BEGINS AT
MARK 10:28
SEE ALSO
COMMITMENT
FREEDOM
SACRIFICE
SUBMITTING TO GOD

Time (3626)
The way we use it

What's wrong with putting things off until later? • Is it OK to wait until I'm older to live for God? • What are God's instructions about how I use my time?
THE SEARCH BEGINS AT
PSALM 90:12
SEE ALSO
BEING HASTY
LIFE IS SHORT
PROCRASTINATION

The Time Is Now (3446)

Is it OK to wait until I'm older to decide whether to follow God? • I really don't know what to believe—how can I make up my mind about God? • Is it ever too late to believe in Jesus?
THE SEARCH BEGINS AT
1 KINGS 18:21
SEE ALSO
DEATH
READY FOR THE FUTURE

Tithing (2120)
Giving to God

Why does God want me to give to him when he has all he needs? • Why do we give money to the church?
THE SEARCH BEGINS AT
EXODUS 25:2
SEE ALSO
BEING STINGY
EXAMPLES OF GENEROSITY

True Wisdom (3840)

What is wisdom? • What's the best source of advice? • How can the Bible help me? • Are there different kinds of wisdom? • How is God's wisdom different from the world's wisdom?
THE SEARCH BEGINS AT
JOB 28:28
SEE ALSO
PRAYING FOR WISDOM
UNDERSTANDING

Trusting God (1214)

How do I know if God can be trusted? • Is it possible for a person never to learn to trust God?
THE SEARCH BEGINS AT
PSALM 37:3, 5
SEE ALSO
FAITH
GOD'S PROMISES

Trusting in People (3184)

Will the people who love me ever let me down? • Whom should I trust?
THE SEARCH BEGINS AT
PSALM 118:9
SEE ALSO
GOD'S CARE FOR YOU
GOD'S ROLE

The Ultimate (3179)

What's the ultimate? • How important is Jesus? • Why is Jesus important?
THE SEARCH BEGINS AT
PSALM 118:22
SEE ALSO
GOLDEN RULE
IMPORTANCE OF LOVE
JOB ONE

Unanswered Prayer (2820)

Why won't God answer my prayer? • Are there times when God does not answer prayer?
THE SEARCH BEGINS AT
DEUTERONOMY 1:45
SEE ALSO
PRAYING
SEEKING GOD

Understanding (3848)

The Bible doesn't make sense to me—how can I understand it better? • How can the Bible help me understand my problems? • How can the Bible protect me from sin?
THE SEARCH BEGINS AT
DEUTERONOMY 4:6
SEE ALSO
GETTING WISDOM
TRUE WISDOM

Unhappiness (0669)

If I am a Christian will I ever be unhappy? • Did people in the Bible have bad days?
THE SEARCH BEGINS AT
NUMBERS 11:15
SEE ALSO
CONTENTMENT
DISCONTENTMENT
JOY
SOURCE OF HAPPINESS

Unknown Sins (3357)
Sins you commit without knowing it

Can I sin without knowing it? • If I don't feel guilty, does that mean I haven't sinned? • Am I responsible for sins I don't know about? • Will God punish me for sins I don't know I've done?
THE SEARCH BEGINS AT
LEVITICUS 4:2
SEE ALSO
HELP!
USED TO SIN
WHY DO RIGHT?
WHY NOT SIN?

Unselfishness (3227)

Is it really more blessed to give than to receive? • Is it ever fun to be unselfish?
THE SEARCH BEGINS AT
GENESIS 13:9
SEE ALSO
COMPASSION
EXAMPLES OF GENEROSITY
FRIENDSHIP
GIVING
GOOD FRIENDS
LOVE FOR FRIENDS
SERVING
WORK THAT HELPS OTHERS

Unthankfulness to People (1459)

Why does God want us to say thank you? • What should I do if I don't FEEL thankful—should I still say thank you? • Does God care whether I'm polite?
THE SEARCH BEGINS AT
GENESIS 40:23
SEE ALSO
"THANK YOU"
THANKFULNESS

Used to Sin (2745)

What harm can it do to be a little naughty? • Can a person get so used to evil that he doesn't even notice it? • How bad can things get? • How bad can people be?
THE SEARCH BEGINS AT
PROVERBS 11:3
SEE ALSO
CALLOUSNESS
REMORSE

Using What You Have (3451)
Your job; why you are here

What happens when people don't use what they have? • What has God given me? • How can I figure out what talents I have? • How does God want to use me?
THE SEARCH BEGINS AT
MATTHEW 25:14-15
SEE ALSO
SOURCE OF WEALTH
TALENTS

Value of People (2243)

How can I be important to God if there are so many people in the world? • Am I really that important to God?

THE SEARCH BEGINS AT
John 3:16

SEE ALSO
Hurting Yourself
Why Jesus Came
Your Body

Valuing the Bible (3697)

Why do my parents and Sunday School teachers spend so much time teaching me the Bible? • Why should I try to learn Bible stories and verses? • How can the truth help me?

THE SEARCH BEGINS AT
Psalm 119:72

SEE ALSO
Getting Wisdom
God's Word
Praying for Wisdom
True Wisdom

Vengeance (1437)

Getting back at someone

What should I do when someone picks on me? • Is it OK to tell people to shut up if they're being jerks? • Is it all right to throw rocks at someone who threw rocks at you?

THE SEARCH BEGINS AT
Exodus 23:5

SEE ALSO
Enemies
Nice
Revenge

Violence (2547)

Are things better or worse than they used to be? • Was there as much violence in Bible times as there is today? • What can we do about the violence in the world?

THE SEARCH BEGINS AT
Genesis 6:13

SEE ALSO
Crime
Gentleness
Safety

Waiting (2693)

Waiting for God to rescue, help, or do a miracle

What should I do if God doesn't answer my prayers right away? • Why does it sometimes seem like God isn't doing anything?

THE SEARCH BEGINS AT
Genesis 49:18

SEE ALSO
Praying
Time
Unanswered Prayer

Waiting for God (3762)

Why does God take so long to act? • Why does God want me to wait for him? • How long do I have to wait for God?

THE SEARCH BEGINS AT
Psalm 25:5

SEE ALSO
Answers to Prayer
Duty to Pray
How to Pray
Praying Alone

Walking with God (1267)

Living every day in a relationship with God

I can't even see God; how can I live with him? • Why does God want to be with me all the time? • Does God want to be with me all the time because he is pleased with me, or because I'm in trouble and he wants to keep an eye on me?

THE SEARCH BEGINS AT
Genesis 5:22-24

SEE ALSO
Devotions
Pleasing God
Praying

Warning! (3618)

Warnings from God

What warnings has God given? • Why should I take sin seriously? • What will happen to people who ignore God's rules?

THE SEARCH BEGINS AT
Leviticus 26:16

SEE ALSO
Getting Along
Pitfalls
Sinner Beware

Waste (1335)

What's wrong with littering? • Why is it wrong to waste stuff?

THE SEARCH BEGINS AT
Proverbs 12:27

SEE ALSO
Being Frugal
Earth

Watch Out! (1799)

Scriptures that say, "Be careful! Hazard ahead!"

What Scriptures beside the Ten Commandments tell me how to act? • How can I please God? • What does God want me to watch out for?

THE SEARCH BEGINS AT
Matthew 6:1

SEE ALSO
Pitfalls
Warning!

Watching for Jesus' Return (1348)

What you can do to be ready for Jesus' return

What does it mean to "watch for Jesus' return"? • Does God want me to watch for his coming every minute of the day? • Does God want me to quit playing ball so that I can watch for his coming?

THE SEARCH BEGINS AT
Matthew 24:44

SEE ALSO
Jesus' Return
Jesus' Return: When?
Ready for the Future

Weakness (3805)

What should I do about my weaknesses? • How can God use my weaknesses? • Why should I admit my weaknesses? • What's wrong with trying to hide my weak spots?

THE SEARCH BEGINS AT
Psalm 8:2

SEE ALSO
Feeling Helpless
God's Role
The Holy Spirit

Wealth (3185)

What are the down sides to having money? • Why doesn't God just give me more money? I sure could use it. • Does money take care of everything? • Can money make me happy?

THE SEARCH BEGINS AT
Job 31:24-25, 28

SEE ALSO
Money's Limits
Soon Gone

What God Knows (3850)

Does God know what I'm going through? • Why should I be honest with God about my problems? • Is it possible to hide from God?

THE SEARCH BEGINS AT
Job 26:6

SEE ALSO
Everyone Sins
Fearing God
God Sees Sin
God's Mercy
God's Patience

What Jesus Did (3362)

What Jesus accomplished when he came to earth as a man

What should I do when I do something wrong? • How long should I feel guilty? • How can I know whether God will forgive me?

• How does Jesus take away sin? • What did Jesus do with our sin? • How does Jesus save us? • What does Jesus do with our sins?

THE SEARCH BEGINS AT
Isaiah 53:12

SEE ALSO
Forgiveness of Sin
Jesus the Lamb

Where Is God? (2645)

How can God be everywhere at once? • When God is helping someone in the hospital, does he leave me to go do that?

THE SEARCH BEGINS AT
Deuteronomy 4:39

SEE ALSO
God's Presence
God's Teaching
Guidance
Names of God

Who Can Be Saved? (3359)

Who gets to go to heaven

Are some people too bad for God to save? • Why do I need to be saved? • How can I get saved? • What will happen if I ask Jesus to save me from my sins?

THE SEARCH BEGINS AT
1 Corinthians 15:3

SEE ALSO
A Great Gift
Justification by Faith
Results of Sin
Salvation
Salvation by Faith
Salvation for Anyone

Who Deserves Christ? (3736)

Who deserves to be in God's family? • What does it take to get into God's family? • Do I deserve to be part of God's family? • Do I need to make any changes in my life?

THE SEARCH BEGINS AT
Matthew 10:37

SEE ALSO
Accepted by God
Commitment

Who Is Religious? (2986)

Who are some good people to copy? • Where can I get good role models?

THE SEARCH BEGINS AT
Genesis 5:24

SEE ALSO
Praying Alone
Religious People
Young Men

Whom Can You Trust? (1330)

How can I spot bad friends? • What should I do if my friend lets me down?

THE SEARCH BEGINS AT
Job 16:20

SEE ALSO
Bad Friends
"Dangerous Kisses"

Why Do Right? (3737)

Rewards to those who do what is right

What are the rewards of doing what is right? • Is it more fun to do your own thing or to follow God? • Will I really be happy if I live God's way?

THE SEARCH BEGINS AT
Psalm 7:10

SEE ALSO
Benefits of Faith
Goodness Rewarded
Obeying God
Sinner Beware

Why Fear God? (3035)

Why does the Bible tell us to fear God? • Does God want me to be afraid of him? • How can I fear God?

THE SEARCH BEGINS AT
1 Samuel 12:14

SEE ALSO
Blessing
God's Promises
Obeying God

Why Jesus Came (3360)

The reason Jesus came to earth

Why was Jesus born? • Why did Jesus have to leave heaven? • What would have happened if Jesus had not come to earth?

THE SEARCH BEGINS AT
Luke 2:11

SEE ALSO
Only One Savior
Ouch!

Why Jesus Died (3361)

The reason Jesus died on the cross

Why did Jesus have to die? • Where would I be without Jesus? • What price should I pay for my sin? • How can I get out of paying the price for my sin?

THE SEARCH BEGINS AT
Psalm 69:9

SEE ALSO
How to Be Saved
Jesus
Jesus the Lamb
Second Coming

Why Not Sin? (3352)

Reasons for not sinning

Why shouldn't I sin?

THE SEARCH BEGINS AT
Genesis 2:17

SEE ALSO
Blinded by Sin
Spiritual Death

Why Suffer? (3476)

Reasons to be glad when you take heat for being a Christian

Is it OK to try to avoid suffering for Christ? • What should I do when kids are mean to me because I'm a Christian? • What will happen to people who suffer for Jesus? • How is it possible to be happy when you're hurting?

THE SEARCH BEGINS AT
Luke 6:22

SEE ALSO
Expecting Pain
Positive Attitude

Why the Bible? (0424)

Why God gave us the Bible

Why did God give us the Bible? • Why do we have the Bible? • Why should I read the Bible?

THE SEARCH BEGINS AT
John 20:31

SEE ALSO
Being Smart
The Guide
Power of the Bible
Purity
Reading the Bible
Valuing the Bible

Wicked Insecurity (3180)

What difference does it make in my life whether I follow Jesus? • What risks do I take if I ignore God?

THE SEARCH BEGINS AT
Psalm 73:18

SEE ALSO
Guilty Conscience
Guilty Fear
Why Not Sin?

Willingness to Learn (2962)

How can I be smarter? • What can keep people from learning about God? • Why is it important to be teachable?

THE SEARCH BEGINS AT
Ezra 8:21

SEE ALSO
Lessons of Life
Parents
The Teacher

Willingness to Work (3892)

Is it OK to be lazy once in awhile? • What's wrong with putting off my work to the last minute? • As long as I get my work done, does my attitude matter?

THE SEARCH BEGINS AT
Judges 5:2

THE SEARCH BEGINS AT
Proverbs 6:6
SEE ALSO
Laziness
Work
Work that Helps Others
Working with God

Wise Thoughts (2356)

How can I clean up my mind? • Do I have control over my thoughts or do they just pop in and out of my head? • What are some good thoughts to have? • What does God want me to think about?

THE SEARCH BEGINS AT
Psalm 48:9
SEE ALSO
Bad Thoughts
Willingness to Learn

Wise Words (3297)

How can I make a difference in people's lives?

THE SEARCH BEGINS AT
Job 6:25
SEE ALSO
Cruel Talk
Idle Talk
Talking

Witnessing (3603)

Telling others what you know about God

Shouldn't I wait to learn more before I start telling my friends about Christ? • Why should I tell others what I know about God? • What's wrong with keeping my faith a secret? • What is witnessing?

THE SEARCH BEGINS AT
Isaiah 43:10
SEE ALSO
Good News
Who Can Be Saved
Your Testimony

Work (3890)

What kind of work has God given me? • Does God expect too much from me? • Who can I go to for help when my work seems too hard?

THE SEARCH BEGINS AT
Matthew 25:22-23
SEE ALSO
Finding Strength
Laziness
Rest
Teamwork
Work that Helps Others
Working Hard
Working with God

Work that Helps Others (3888)

What should I do when I grow up? • Are some kinds of work better than others? • What kind of work does God want me to do?

THE SEARCH BEGINS AT
2 Chronicles 28:15
SEE ALSO
Helping at Home
Helping Friends
Helping Weak People
Work

Working Hard (0605)

Is it OK just to hang out? • What's the best reason for trying hard in school?

THE SEARCH BEGINS AT
Genesis 2:15
SEE ALSO
Laziness
Rest
Work

Working with God (3891)

Can God really help me with the stuff I have to do today? • How can I get God to help me? • What does it mean to work with God?

THE SEARCH BEGINS AT
1 Samuel 14:45
SEE ALSO
Work
Work that Helps Others

Worry (3022)

Anxiety

How can I stop worrying? My mind just keeps on doing it. • Everything's going wrong—what am I going to do? • What should I do when everything goes crazy?

THE SEARCH BEGINS AT
Psalm 127:2
SEE ALSO
God's Care for You
Parents Care

Worship (3921)

What is worship? • Why should I worship God? • What can I do if the worship services at my church are boring? • What am I supposed to get out of worship?

THE SEARCH BEGINS AT
Deuteronomy 26:10
SEE ALSO
Fearing God
Respecting God
Why Fear God

Worshiping Things (3748)

What is idol worship? • Why should I worry about idol worship? • What things could I be tempted to worship besides God?

THE SEARCH BEGINS AT
Deuteronomy 32:21
SEE ALSO
Church
Only One God
Praying

Young Leaders (3965)

Can I be a leader even though I'm a kid? • Why should I want to be a leader? • What do I have to do to become a leader? • What kind of leader does God want me to be?

THE SEARCH BEGINS AT
Genesis 41:46
SEE ALSO
For Kids Only
Growing Up
Young Men
Young Women

Young Men (3966)

Does God ever use young people to do important work for him? • I'm just a kid—what can I do for God? • How can I know if God wants to use me? • What can I learn from stories of other young people in the Bible?

THE SEARCH BEGINS AT
Genesis 41:38
SEE ALSO
For Kids Only
Growing Up
Young Women

Young Women (3968)

What can I learn from women in the Bible? • Was it easier to be a Christian in Bible times?

THE SEARCH BEGINS AT
Judges 11:36
SEE ALSO
For Kids Only
Growing Up
Young Men

Your Body (3656)

Is it OK to try to make my body look as good as possible? • Why didn't God give me a better-looking body? • Why doesn't God make our bodies last forever?

THE SEARCH BEGINS AT
1 Samuel 20:3
SEE ALSO
Life Is Short
Mortality

Your Testimony (3600)

Telling others what God has done for you

What can I say to my friends about Jesus? • How can I tell others about God when I don't know much myself? • I'm too scared to tell my friends about God—what can I do? • Is it OK not to tell my friends I'm a Christian as long as I act like one?

THE SEARCH BEGINS AT
1 Chronicles 16:8
SEE ALSO
Publicly Christian
Witnessing

Old Testament

Genesis

Moses

God made the world and started a plan to save people from sin.

Around 1450 B.C.

MAIN PEOPLE

Adam, Eve, Noah, Abram (later named Abraham), Sarai (Sarah), Isaac, Rebekah, Jacob, Rachel, Joseph

SPECIAL FEATURES

- *Tells the creation story not once, but twice*
- *Describes how the first family got along . . . and didn't get along, as sin creeps into the picture*
- *Explains in detail how Noah built the ark and organized all those animals*
- *Introduces a dreamer with a great-looking robe, whose life was a showcase for God's faithfulness*
- *First book of Law*

HOW THE BOOK GOT ITS NAME

The word genesis means "beginnings." Here you'll find the opening chapters of the story of the earth and its creatures, people, sin, different languages and nations, and of God's plan to make it all turn out OK.

1

1 In the beginning God created the
heaven and the earth.
2 And the earth was without form, and
void; and darkness *was* upon the face of
the deep. And the Spirit of God moved
upon the face of the waters.
3 And God said, Let there be light: and
there was light.
4 And God saw the light, that *it was* good:
and God divided the light from the darkness.
5 And God called the light Day, and the
darkness he called Night. And the evening
and the morning were the first day.
6 And God said, Let there be a firmament
in the midst of the waters, and let it divide
the waters from the waters.
7 And God made the firmament, and divided the waters which *were* under the firmament from the waters which *were* above
the firmament: and it was so.
8 And God called the firmament Heaven.
And the evening and the morning were the
second day.
9 And God said, Let the waters under the
heaven be gathered together unto one
place, and let the dry *land* appear: and it
was so.
10 And God called the dry *land* Earth; and
the gathering together of the waters called
he Seas: and God saw that *it was* good.
11 And God said, Let the earth bring forth
grass, the herb yielding seed, *and* the fruit
tree yielding fruit after his kind, whose

seed *is* in itself, upon the earth: and it was so.

12 And the earth brought forth grass, *and* herb yielding seed after his kind, and the tree yielding fruit, whose seed *was* in itself, after his kind: and God saw that *it was* good.

13 And the evening and the morning were the third day.

14 And God said, Let there be lights in the firmament of the heaven to divide the day from the night; and let them be for signs, and for seasons, and for days, and years:

15 And let them be for lights in the firmament of the heaven to give light upon the earth: and it was so.

16 And God made two great lights; the greater light to rule the day, and the lesser light to rule the night: *he made* the stars also.

17 And God set them in the firmament of the heaven to give light upon the earth,

18 And to rule over the day and over the night, and to divide the light from the darkness: and God saw that *it was* good.

19 And the evening and the morning were the fourth day.

20 And God said, Let the waters bring forth abundantly the moving creature that hath life, and fowl *that* may fly above the earth in the open firmament of heaven.

21 And God created great whales, and every living creature that moveth, which the waters brought forth abundantly, after their kind, and every winged fowl after his kind: and God saw that *it was* good.

22 And God blessed them, saying, Be fruitful, and multiply, and fill the waters in the seas, and let fowl multiply in the earth.

23 And the evening and the morning were the fifth day.

24 And God said, Let the earth bring forth the living creature after his kind, cattle, and creeping thing, and beast of the earth after his kind: and it was so.

25 And God made the beast of the earth after his kind, and cattle after their kind, and every thing that creepeth upon the earth after his kind: and God saw that *it was* good.

26 And God said, Let us make man in our image, after our likeness: and let them have dominion over the fish of the sea, and over the fowl of the air, and over the cattle, and over all the earth, and over every creeping thing that creepeth upon the earth.

1:26-27
Made in God's Image
◄ Genesis 5:1 ►

27 So God created man in his *own* image, in the image of God created he him; male and female created he them.

28 And God blessed them, and God said unto them, Be fruitful, and multiply, and replenish the earth, and subdue it: and have dominion over the fish of the sea, and over the fowl of the air, and over every living thing that moveth upon the earth.

1:28
Animals vs. People
◄ Psalm 8:6 ►

29 And God said, Behold, I have given you every herb bearing seed, which *is* upon the face of all the earth, and every tree, in the which *is* the fruit of a tree yielding seed; to you it shall be for meat.

30 And to every beast of the earth, and to every fowl of the air, and to every thing that creepeth upon the earth, wherein *there is* life, *I have given* every green herb for meat: and it was so.

31 And God saw every thing that he had made, and, behold, *it was* very good. And the evening and the morning were the sixth day.

2

1 Thus the heavens and the earth were finished, and all the host of them.

2 And on the seventh day God ended his work which he had made; and he rested on the seventh day from all his work which he had made.

3 And God blessed the seventh day, and sanctified it: because that in it he had rested from all his work which God created and made.

4 These *are* the generations of the heavens and of the earth when they were created, in the day that the LORD God made the earth and the heavens,

5 And every plant of the field before it was in the earth, and every herb of the field before it grew: for the LORD God had not caused it to rain upon the earth, and *there was* not a man to till the ground.

6 But there went up a mist from the earth, and watered the whole face of the ground.

7 And the LORD God formed man *of* the dust of the ground, and breathed into his nostrils the breath of life; and man became a living soul.

8 And the LORD God planted a garden eastward in Eden; and there he put the man whom he had formed.

9 And out of the ground made the LORD God to grow every tree that is pleasant to the sight, and good for food; the tree of life also in the midst of the garden, and the tree of knowledge of good and evil.

10 And a river went out of Eden to water the garden; and from thence it was parted, and became into four heads.

11 The name of the first *is* Pison: that *is* it which compasseth the whole land of Havilah, where *there is* gold;

12 And the gold of that land *is* good: there *is* bdellium and the onyx stone.

13 And the name of the second river *is* Gihon: the same *is* it that compasseth the whole land of Ethiopia.

14 And the name of the third river *is* Hiddekel: that *is* it which goeth toward the east of Assyria. And the fourth river *is* Euphrates.

15 And the LORD God took the man, and put him into the garden of Eden to dress it and to keep it.

> 2:15
> Working Hard
> ◄ Genesis 3:19 ►

16 And the LORD God commanded the man, saying, Of every tree of the garden thou mayest freely eat:

17 But of the tree of the knowledge of good and evil, thou shalt not eat of it: for in the day that thou eatest thereof thou shalt surely die.

> 2:17
> Spiritual Death
> ◄ Proverbs 8:36 ►

> 2:17
> Why Not Sin?
> ◄ Genesis 3:19 ►

18 And the LORD God said, *It is* not good that the man should be alone; I will make him an help meet for him.

19 And out of the ground the LORD God formed every beast of the field, and every fowl of the air; and brought *them* unto Adam to see what he would call them: and whatsoever Adam called every living creature, that *was* the name thereof.

20 And Adam gave names to all cattle, and to the fowl of the air, and to every beast of the field; but for Adam there was not found an help meet for him.

21 And the LORD God caused a deep sleep to fall upon Adam and he slept: and he took one of his ribs, and closed up the flesh instead thereof;

22 And the rib, which the LORD God had taken from man, made he a woman, and brought her unto the man.

23 And Adam said, This *is* now bone of my bones, and flesh of my flesh: she shall be called Woman, because she was taken out of Man.

24 Therefore shall a man leave his father and his mother, and shall cleave unto his wife: and they shall be one flesh.

25 And they were both naked, the man and his wife, and were not ashamed.

3

1 Now the serpent was more subtil than any beast of the field which the LORD God had made. And he said unto the woman, Yea, hath God said, Ye shall not eat of every tree of the garden?

2 And the woman said unto the serpent, We may eat of the fruit of the trees of the garden:

3 But of the fruit of the tree which *is* in the midst of the garden, God hath said, Ye shall not eat of it, neither shall ye touch it, lest ye die.

4 And the serpent said unto the woman, Ye shall not surely die:

5 For God doth know that in the day ye eat thereof, then your eyes shall be opened, and ye shall be as gods, knowing good and evil.

6 And when the woman saw that the tree *was* good for food, and that it *was* pleasant to the eyes, and a tree to be desired to make *one* wise, she took of the fruit thereof, and did eat, and gave also unto her husband with her; and he did eat.

> 3:6 Giving In
> ◄ Genesis 13:10-11, 13 ►

7 And the eyes of them both were opened, and they knew that they *were* naked; and they sewed fig leaves together, and made themselves aprons.

8 And they heard the voice of the LORD God walking in the garden in the cool of the day: and Adam and his wife hid themselves from the presence of the LORD God

Turn to the next page for more . . .

amongst the trees of the garden.

9 And the LORD God called unto Adam, and said unto him, Where *art* thou?

> **3:8**
> **Guilty Fear**
> ◄ Genesis 45:3 ►

10 And he said, I heard thy voice in the garden, and I was afraid, because I *was* naked; and I hid myself.

11 And he said, Who told thee that thou *wast* naked? Hast thou eaten of the tree, whereof I commanded thee that thou shouldest not eat?

12 And the man said, The woman whom thou gavest *to be* with me, she gave me of the tree, and I did eat.

13 And the LORD God said unto the woman, What *is* this *that* thou hast done? And the woman said, The serpent beguiled me, and I did eat.

> **3:13**
> **"It's Her Fault!"**
> ◄ Genesis 16:5 ►

14 And the LORD God said unto the serpent, Because thou hast done this, thou *art* cursed above all cattle, and above every beast of the field; upon thy belly shalt thou go, and dust shalt thou eat all the days of thy life:

15 And I will put enmity between thee and the woman, and between thy seed and her seed; it shall bruise thy head, and thou shalt bruise his heel.

> **3:15**
> **Defeat of Satan**
> ◄ Luke 4:13 ►

16 Unto the woman he said, I will greatly multiply thy sorrow and thy conception; in sorrow thou shalt bring forth children; and thy desire *shall be* to thy husband, and he shall rule over thee.

17 And unto Adam he said, Because thou hast hearkened unto the voice of thy wife, and hast eaten of the tree, of which I commanded thee, saying, Thou shalt not eat of it: cursed *is* the ground for thy sake; in sorrow shalt thou eat *of* it all the days of thy life;

18 Thorns also and thistles shall it bring forth to thee; and thou shalt eat the herb of the field;

19 In the sweat of thy face shalt thou eat bread, till thou return unto the ground; for out of it wast thou taken: for dust thou *art*, and unto dust shalt thou return.

> **3:19 Why Not Sin?**
> ◄ Genesis 2:17
> Deuteronomy 32:51 ►

20 And Adam called his wife's name Eve; because she was the mother of all living.

> **3:19 Working Hard**
> ◄ Genesis 2:15
> Leviticus 23:3 ►

21 Unto Adam also and to his wife did the LORD God make coats of skins, and clothed them.

22 And the LORD God said, Behold, the man is become as one of us, to know good and evil: and now, lest he put forth his hand, and take also of the tree of life, and eat, and live for ever:

23 Therefore the LORD God sent him forth from the garden of Eden, to till the ground from whence he was taken.

24 So he drove out the man; and he placed at the east of the garden of Eden Cherubim, and a flaming sword which turned every way, to keep the way of the tree of life.

4

1 And Adam knew Eve his wife; and she conceived, and bare Cain, and said, I have gotten a man from the LORD.

2 And she again bare his brother Abel. And Abel was a keeper of sheep, but Cain was a tiller of the ground.

3 And in process of time it came to pass, that Cain brought of the fruit of the ground an offering unto the LORD.

4 And Abel, he also brought of the firstlings of his flock and of the fat thereof. And the LORD had respect unto Abel and to his offering:

5 But unto Cain and to his offering he had not respect. And Cain was very wroth, and his countenance fell.

> **4:5**
> **Mad**
> ◄ 1 Samuel 18:8 ►

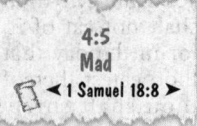

6 And the LORD said unto Cain, Why art thou wroth? and why is thy countenance fallen?

7 If thou doest well, shalt thou not be accepted? and if thou doest not well, sin lieth at the door. And unto thee *shall be* his desire, and thou shalt rule over him.

8 And Cain talked with Abel his brother: and it came to pass, when they were in the field, that Cain rose up against Abel his brother, and slew him.

9And the LORD
said unto Cain,
Where *is* Abel thy
brother? And he
said, I know not:
Am I my brother's
keeper?

4:9
Not Caring
◄ Matthew 15:23 ►

10And he said, What hast thou done? the
voice of thy brother's blood crieth unto me
from the ground.
11And now *art* thou cursed from the
earth, which hath opened her mouth to
receive thy brother's blood from thy hand;
12When thou tillest the ground, it shall
not henceforth yield unto thee her
strength; a fugitive and a vagabond shalt
thou be in the earth.
13And Cain said unto the LORD, My punishment *is* greater than I can bear.
14Behold, thou hast driven me out this
day from the face of the earth; and from
thy face shall I be hid; and I shall be a fugitive and a vagabond in the earth; and it
shall come to pass, *that* every one that
findeth me shall slay me.
15And the LORD said unto him, Therefore whosoever slayeth Cain, vengeance
shall be taken on him sevenfold. And the
LORD set a mark upon Cain, lest any finding him should kill him.
16And Cain went out from the presence
of the LORD, and dwelt in the land of Nod,
on the east of Eden.
17And Cain knew his wife; and she conceived, and bare Enoch: and he builded a
city, and called the name of the city, after
the name of his son, Enoch.
18And unto Enoch was born Irad: and
Irad begat Mehujael: and Mehujael begat
Methusael: and Methusael begat Lamech.
19And Lamech took unto him two wives:
the name of the one *was* Adah, and the
name of the other Zillah.
20And Adah bare Jabal: he was the father of such as dwell in tents, and *of such
as have* cattle.
21And his brother's name *was* Jubal: he
was the father of all such as handle the
harp and organ.
22And Zillah, she also bare Tubal-cain,
an instructer of every artificer in brass and
iron: and the sister of Tubal-cain *was*
Naamah.
23And Lamech said unto his wives, Adah
and Zillah, Hear my voice; ye wives of Lamech, hearken unto my speech: for I have
slain a man to my wounding, and a young
man to my hurt.
24If Cain shall be avenged sevenfold,
truly Lamech seventy and sevenfold.
25And Adam knew his wife again; and
she bare a son, and called his name Seth:
For God, *said she,* hath appointed me another seed instead of Abel, whom Cain
slew.
26And to Seth, to him also there was
born a son; and he called his name Enos:
then began men to call upon the name of
the LORD.

5
1This *is* the book
of the generations
of Adam. In the day
that God created
man, in the likeness
of God made he
him;

5:1 Made in God's Image
◄ Genesis 1:26-27
Genesis 9:6 ►

2Male and female created he them; and
blessed them, and called their name Adam,
in the day when they were created.
3And Adam lived an hundred and thirty
years, and begat *a son* in his own likeness,
after his image; and called his name Seth:
4And the days of Adam after he had begotten Seth were eight hundred years: and
he begat sons and daughters:
5And all the days that Adam lived were
nine hundred and thirty years: and he died.
6And Seth lived an hundred and five
years, and begat Enos:
7And Seth lived after he begat Enos eight
hundred and seven years, and begat sons
and daughters:
8And all the days of Seth were nine hundred and twelve years: and he died.
9And Enos lived ninety years, and begat
Cainan:
10And Enos lived after he begat Cainan
eight hundred and fifteen years, and begat
sons and daughters:
11And all the days of Enos were nine
hundred and five years: and he died.
12And Cainan lived seventy years, and
begat Mahalaleel:
13And Cainan lived after he begat
Mahalaleel eight hundred and forty years,
and begat sons and daughters:
14And all the days of Cainan were nine
hundred and ten years: and he died.
15And Mahalaleel lived sixty and five
years, and begat Jared:

16And Mahalaleel lived after he begat
Jared eight hundred and thirty years, and
begat sons and daughters:
17And all the days of Mahalaleel were
eight hundred ninety and five years: and
he died.
18And Jared lived an hundred sixty and
two years, and he begat Enoch:
19And Jared lived after he begat Enoch
eight hundred years, and begat sons and
daughters:
20And all the days of Jared were nine
hundred sixty and two years: and he died.
21And Enoch lived sixty and five years,
and begat Methuselah:
22And Enoch
walked with God
after he begat
Methuselah three
hundred years, and
begat sons and
daughters:

5:22-24
Walking with God
◄ Genesis 6:9 ►

23And all the days of Enoch were three
hundred sixty and five years:
24And Enoch
walked with God:
and he *was* not; for
God took him.
25And Methuse-
lah lived an hun-
dred eighty and seven years, and begat
Lamech:

5:24
Who Is Religious?
◄ Genesis 6:9 ►

26And Methuselah lived after he begat
Lamech seven hundred eighty and two
years, and begat sons and daughters:
27And all the days of Methuselah were
nine hundred sixty and nine years: and he
died.
28And Lamech lived an hundred eighty
and two years, and begat a son:
29And he called his name Noah, saying,
This *same* shall comfort us concerning our
work and toil of our hands, because of the
ground which the LORD hath cursed.
30And Lamech lived after he begat Noah
five hundred ninety and five years, and
begat sons and daughters:
31And all the days of Lamech were seven
hundred seventy and seven years: and he
died.
32And Noah was five hundred years old:
and Noah begat Shem, Ham, and Japheth.

6

1And it came to pass, when men began
to multiply on the face of the earth, and
daughters were born unto them,
2That the sons of God saw the daughters of men that they *were* fair; and they
took them wives of all which they chose.
3And the LORD said, My spirit shall not
always strive with man, for that he also *is*
flesh: yet his days shall be an hundred and
twenty years.
4There were giants in the earth in those
days; and also after that, when the sons of
God came in unto the daughters of men,
and they bare *children* to them, the same
became mighty men which *were* of old, men
of renown.
5And GOD saw
that the wickedness
of man *was* great in
the earth, and *that*
every imagination
of the thoughts of
his heart *was* only evil continually.

6:5
Everyone Sins
◄ 1 Kings 8:46 ►

6And it repented the LORD that he had
made man on the earth, and it grieved him
at his heart.
7And the LORD said, I will destroy man
whom I have created from the face of the
earth; both man, and beast, and the creeping thing, and the fowls of the air; for it
repenteth me that I have made them.
8But Noah found grace in the eyes of
the LORD.
9These *are* the gen-
erations of Noah:
Noah was a just
man *and* perfect in
his generations, *and*
Noah walked with
God.
10And Noah be-
gat three sons,
Shem, Ham, and
Japheth.
11The earth also
was corrupt before God, and the earth was
filled with violence.

6:9 Walking with God
◄ Genesis 5:22-24
2 Kings 23:3 ►

6:9 Who Is Religious?
◄ Genesis 5:24
1 Chronicles 4:10 ►

12And God looked upon the earth, and,
behold, it was corrupt; for all flesh had
corrupted his way upon the earth.
13And God said
unto Noah, The
end of all flesh is
come before me;
for the earth is
filled with violence
through them; and, behold, I will destroy
them with the earth.

6:13
Violence
◄ Job 24:2 ►

14Make thee an ark of gopher wood;
rooms shalt thou make in the ark, and
shalt pitch it within and without with
pitch.
15And this *is the fashion* which thou shalt
make it *of:* The length of the ark *shall be*
three hundred cubits, the breadth of it fifty cubits, and the height of it thirty cubits.
16A window shalt thou make to the ark,
and in a cubit shalt thou finish it above;
and the door of the ark shalt thou set in
the side thereof; *with* lower, second, and
third *stories* shalt thou make it.
17And, behold, I, even I, do bring a flood
of waters upon the earth, to destroy all
flesh, wherein *is* the breath of life, from
under heaven; *and* every thing that *is* in
the earth shall die.
18But with thee will I establish my covenant; and thou shalt come into the ark,
thou, and thy sons, and thy wife, and thy
sons' wives with thee.
19And of every living thing of all flesh,
two of every *sort* shalt thou bring into the
ark, to keep *them* alive with thee; they shall
be male and female.
20Of fowls after their kind, and of cattle
after their kind, of every creeping thing of
the earth after his kind, two of every *sort*
shall come unto thee, to keep *them* alive.
21And take thou unto thee of all food
that is eaten, and thou shalt gather *it* to
thee; and it shall be for food for thee, and
for them.
22Thus did Noah; according to all that
God commanded him, so did he.

7

1And the LORD said unto Noah, Come
thou and all thy house into the ark; for
thee have I seen righteous before me in
this generation.
2Of every clean beast thou shalt take to
thee by sevens, the male and his female:
and of beasts that *are* not clean by two,
the male and his female.
3Of fowls also of the air by sevens, the
male and the female; to keep seed alive
upon the face of all the earth.
4For yet seven days, and I will cause it
to rain upon the earth forty days and forty
nights; and every living substance that I
have made will I destroy from off the face
of the earth.
5And Noah did according unto all that
the LORD commanded him.
6And Noah *was* six hundred years old
when the flood of waters was upon the
earth.
7And Noah went in, and his sons, and
his wife, and his sons' wives with him, into
the ark, because of the waters of the flood.
8Of clean beasts, and of beasts that *are*
not clean, and of fowls, and of every thing
that creepeth upon the earth,
9There went in two and two unto Noah
into the ark, the male and the female, as
God had commanded Noah.
10And it came to pass after seven days,
that the waters of the flood were upon the
earth.
11In the six hundredth year of Noah's
life, in the second month, the seventeenth
day of the month, the same day were all
the fountains of the great deep broken up,
and the windows of heaven were opened.
12And the rain was upon the earth forty
days and forty nights.
13In the selfsame day entered Noah, and
Shem, and Ham, and Japheth, the sons of
Noah, and Noah's wife, and the three wives
of his sons with them, into the ark;
14They, and every beast after his kind,
and all the cattle after their kind, and every
creeping thing that creepeth upon the earth
after his kind, and every fowl after his kind,
every bird of every sort.
15And they went in unto Noah into the
ark, two and two of all flesh, wherein *is*
the breath of life.
16And they that went in, went in male
and female of all flesh, as God had commanded him: and the LORD shut him in.
17And the flood was forty days upon the
earth; and the waters increased, and bare
up the ark, and it was lift up above the
earth.
18And the waters prevailed, and were
increased greatly upon the earth; and the
ark went upon the face of the waters.
19And the waters prevailed exceedingly
upon the earth; and all the high hills, that
were under the whole heaven, were covered.
20Fifteen cubits upward did the waters
prevail; and the mountains were covered.
21And all flesh died that moved upon
the earth, both of fowl, and of cattle, and
of beast, and of every creeping thing that
creepeth upon the earth, and every man:
22All in whose nostrils *was* the breath
of life, of all that *was* in the dry *land*, died.

23 And every living substance was destroyed which was upon the face of the ground, both man, and cattle, and the creeping things, and the fowl of the heaven; and they were destroyed from the earth: and Noah only remained *alive*, and they that *were* with him in the ark.

24 And the waters prevailed upon the earth an hundred and fifty days.

8

1 And God remembered Noah, and every living thing, and all the cattle that *was* with him in the ark: and God made a wind to pass over the earth, and the waters asswaged;

2 The fountains also of the deep and the windows of heaven were stopped, and the rain from heaven was restrained;

3 And the waters returned from off the earth continually: and after the end of the hundred and fifty days the waters were abated.

4 And the ark rested in the seventh month, on the seventeenth day of the month, upon the mountains of Ararat.

5 And the waters decreased continually until the tenth month: in the tenth *month*, on the first *day* of the month, were the tops of the mountains seen.

6 And it came to pass at the end of forty days, that Noah opened the window of the ark which he had made:

7 And he sent forth a raven, which went forth to and fro, until the waters were dried up from off the earth.

8 Also he sent forth a dove from him, to see if the waters were abated from off the face of the ground;

9 But the dove found no rest for the sole of her foot, and she returned unto him into the ark, for the waters *were* on the face of the whole earth: then he put forth his hand, and took her, and pulled her in unto him into the ark.

10 And he stayed yet other seven days; and again he sent forth the dove out of the ark;

11 And the dove came in to him in the evening; and, lo, in her mouth *was* an olive leaf pluckt off: so Noah knew that the waters were abated from off the earth.

12 And he stayed yet other seven days; and sent forth the dove; which returned not again unto him any more.

13 And it came to pass in the six hundredth and first year, in the first *month*, the first *day* of the month, the waters were dried up from off the earth: and Noah removed the covering of the ark, and looked, and, behold, the face of the ground was dry.

14 And in the second month, on the seven and twentieth day of the month, was the earth dried.

15 And God spake unto Noah, saying,

16 Go forth of the ark, thou, and thy wife, and thy sons, and thy sons' wives with thee.

17 Bring forth with thee every living thing that *is* with thee, of all flesh, *both* of fowl, and of cattle, and of every creeping thing that creepeth upon the earth; that they may breed abundantly in the earth, and be fruitful, and multiply upon the earth.

18 And Noah went forth, and his sons, and his wife, and his sons' wives with him:

19 Every beast, every creeping thing, and every fowl, *and* whatsoever creepeth upon the earth, after their kinds, went forth out of the ark.

20 And Noah builded an altar unto the LORD; and took of every clean beast, and of every clean fowl, and offered burnt offerings on the altar.

21 And the LORD smelled a sweet savour; and the LORD said in his heart, I will not again curse the ground any more for man's sake; for the imagination of man's heart *is* evil from his youth; neither will I again smite any more every thing living, as I have done.

22 While the earth remaineth, seedtime and harvest, and cold and heat, and summer and winter, and day and night shall not cease.

9

1 And God blessed Noah and his sons, and said unto them, Be fruitful, and multiply, and replenish the earth.

2 And the fear of you and the dread of you shall be upon every beast of the earth, and upon every fowl of the air, upon all that moveth *upon* the earth, and upon all the fishes of the sea; into your hand are they delivered.

3 Every moving thing that liveth shall be meat for you; even as the green herb have I given you all things.

4 But flesh with the life thereof, *which is* the blood thereof, shall ye not eat.

5 And surely your blood of your lives will I require; at the hand of every beast will I require it, and at the hand of man; at the hand of every man's brother will I require the life of man.

6 Whoso sheddeth man's blood, by man shall his blood be shed: for in the image of God made he man.

9:6 Made in God's Image
◄ Genesis 5:1
1 Corinthians 11:7 ►

7 And you, be ye fruitful, and multiply; bring forth abundantly in the earth, and multiply therein.

8 And God spake unto Noah, and to his sons with him, saying,

9 And I, behold, I establish my covenant with you, and with your seed after you;

10 And with every living creature that *is* with you, of the fowl, of the cattle, and of every beast of the earth with you; from all that go out of the ark, to every beast of the earth.

11 And I will establish my covenant with you; neither shall all flesh be cut off any more by the waters of a flood; neither shall there any more be a flood to destroy the earth.

12 And God said, This *is* the token of the covenant which I make between me and you and every living creature that *is* with you, for perpetual generations:

13 I do set my bow in the cloud, and it shall be for a token of a covenant between me and the earth.

14 And it shall come to pass, when I bring a cloud over the earth, that the bow shall be seen in the cloud:

15 And I will remember my covenant, which *is* between me and you and every living creature of all flesh; and the waters shall no more become a flood to destroy all flesh.

16 And the bow shall be in the cloud; and I will look upon it, that I may remember the everlasting covenant between God and every living creature of all flesh that *is* upon the earth.

17 And God said unto Noah, This *is* the token of the covenant, which I have established between me and all flesh that *is* upon the earth.

18 And the sons of Noah, that went forth of the ark, were Shem, and Ham, and Japheth: and Ham *is* the father of Canaan.

19 These *are* the three sons of Noah: and of them was the whole earth overspread.

20 And Noah began *to be* an husbandman, and he planted a vineyard:

21 And he drank of the wine, and was drunken; and he was uncovered within his tent.

22 And Ham, the father of Canaan, saw the nakedness of his father, and told his two brethren without.

23 And Shem and Japheth took a garment, and laid *it* upon both their shoulders, and went backward, and covered the nakedness of their father; and their faces *were* backward, and they saw not their father's nakedness.

24 And Noah awoke from his wine, and knew what his younger son had done unto him.

25 And he said, Cursed *be* Canaan; a servant of servants shall he be unto his brethren.

26 And he said, Blessed *be* the LORD God of Shem; and Canaan shall be his servant.

27 God shall enlarge Japheth, and he shall dwell in the tents of Shem; and Canaan shall be his servant.

28 And Noah lived after the flood three hundred and fifty years.

29 And all the days of Noah were nine hundred and fifty years: and he died.

10

1 Now these *are* the generations of the sons of Noah, Shem, Ham, and Japheth: and unto them were sons born after the flood.

2 The sons of Japheth; Gomer, and Magog, and Madai, and Javan, and Tubal, and Meshech, and Tiras.

3 And the sons of Gomer; Ashkenaz, and Riphath, and Togarmah.

4 And the sons of Javan; Elishah, and Tarshish, Kittim, and Dodanim.

5 By these were the isles of the Gentiles divided in their lands; every one after his tongue, after their families, in their nations.

6 And the sons of Ham; Cush, and Mizraim, and Phut, and Canaan.

7 And the sons of Cush; Seba, and Havilah, and Sabtah, and Raamah, and Sabtechah: and the sons of Raamah; Sheba, and Dedan.

8 And Cush begat Nimrod: he began to be a mighty one in the earth.

9 He was a mighty hunter before the LORD: wherefore it is said, Even as Nimrod the mighty hunter before the LORD.

10 And the beginning of his kingdom was Babel, and Erech, and Accad, and Calneh, in the land of Shinar.

11Out of that land went forth Asshur,
and builded Nineveh, and the city Rehoboth, and Calah,
12And Resen between Nineveh and Calah: the same *is* a great city.
13And Mizraim begat Ludim, and
Anamim, and Lehabim, and Naphtuhim,
14And Pathrusim, and Casluhim, (out
of whom came Philistim,) and Caphtorim.
15And Canaan begat Sidon his firstborn,
and Heth,
16And the Jebusite, and the Amorite, and
the Girgasite,
17And the Hivite, and the Arkite, and the
Sinite,
18And the Arvadite, and the Zemarite,
and the Hamathite: and afterward were the
families of the Canaanites spread abroad.
19And the border of the Canaanites was
from Sidon, as thou comest to Gerar, unto
Gaza; as thou goest, unto Sodom, and
Gomorrah, and Admah, and Zeboim, even
unto Lasha.
20These *are* the sons of Ham, after their
families, after their tongues, in their countries, *and* in their nations.
21Unto Shem also, the father of all the
children of Eber, the brother of Japheth
the elder, even to him were *children* born.
22The children of Shem; Elam, and Asshur, and Arphaxad, and Lud, and Aram.
23And the children of Aram; Uz, and
Hul, and Gether, and Mash.
24And Arphaxad begat Salah; and Salah
begat Eber.
25And unto Eber were born two sons:
the name of one *was* Peleg; for in his days
was the earth divided; and his brother's
name *was* Joktan.
26And Joktan begat Almodad, and She-
leph, and Hazar-maveth, and Jerah,
27And Hadoram, and Uzal, and Diklah,
28And Obal, and Abimael, and Sheba,
29And Ophir, and Havilah, and Jobab:
all these *were* the sons of Joktan.
30And their dwelling was from Mesha,
as thou goest unto Sephar a mount of the
east.
31These *are* the sons of Shem, after their
families, after their tongues, in their lands,
after their nations.
32These *are* the families of the sons of
Noah, after their generations, in their nations: and by these were the nations divided in the earth after the flood.

11
1And the whole earth was of one language, and of one speech.
2And it came to pass, as they journeyed
from the east, that they found a plain in
the land of Shinar; and they dwelt there.
3And they said one to another, Go to,
let us make brick, and burn them
throughly. And they had brick for stone,
and slime had they for morter.
4And they said,
Go to, let us build
us a city and a tow-
er, whose top *may
reach* unto heaven;
and let us make us
a name, lest we be
scattered abroad
upon the face of the
whole earth.
5And the LORD
came down to see
the city and the tower, which the children
of men builded.

11:4 Ambition
2 Samuel 15:1-2, 4 ➤

11:4 Planning
◄ Proverbs 19:21 ➤

6And the LORD said, Behold, the people
is one, and they have all one language; and
this they begin to do: and now nothing
will be restrained from them, which they
have imagined to do.
7Go to, let us go down, and there confound their language, that they may not
understand one another's speech.
8So the LORD scattered them abroad
from thence upon the face of all the earth:
and they left off to build the city.
9Therefore is the name of it called Babel; because the LORD did there confound
the language of all the earth: and from
thence did the LORD scatter them abroad
upon the face of all the earth.
10These *are* the generations of Shem:
Shem *was* an hundred years old, and begat
Arphaxad two years after the flood:
11And Shem lived after he begat Arphaxad five hundred years, and begat sons and
daughters.
12And Arphaxad lived five and thirty
years, and begat Salah:
13And Arphaxad lived after he begat
Salah four hundred and three years, and
begat sons and daughters.
14And Salah lived thirty years, and begat
Eber:
15And Salah lived after he begat Eber
four hundred and three years, and begat
sons and daughters.

16And Eber lived four and thirty years, and begat Peleg:

17And Eber lived after he begat Peleg four hundred and thirty years, and begat sons and daughters.

18And Peleg lived thirty years, and begat Reu:

19And Peleg lived after he begat Reu two hundred and nine years, and begat sons and daughters.

20And Reu lived two and thirty years, and begat Serug:

21And Reu lived after he begat Serug two hundred and seven years, and begat sons and daughters.

22And Serug lived thirty years, and begat Nahor:

23And Serug lived after he begat Nahor two hundred years, and begat sons and daughters.

24And Nahor lived nine and twenty years, and begat Terah:

25And Nahor lived after he begat Terah an hundred and nineteen years, and begat sons and daughters.

26And Terah lived seventy years, and begat Abram, Nahor, and Haran.

27Now these *are* the generations of Terah: Terah begat Abram, Nahor, and Haran; and Haran begat Lot.

28And Haran died before his father Terah in the land of his nativity, in Ur of the Chaldees.

29And Abram and Nahor took them wives: the name of Abram's wife *was* Sarai; and the name of Nahor's wife, Milcah, the daughter of Haran, the father of Milcah, and the father of Iscah.

30But Sarai was barren; she *had* no child.

31And Terah took Abram his son, and Lot the son of Haran his son's son, and Sarai his daughter in law, his son Abram's wife; and they went forth with them from Ur of the Chaldees, to go into the land of Canaan; and they came unto Haran, and dwelt there.

32And the days of Terah were two hundred and five years: and Terah died in Haran.

12

1Now the LORD had said unto Abram, Get thee out of thy country, and from thy kindred, and from thy father's house, unto a land that I will shew thee:

2And I will make of thee a great nation, and I will bless thee, and make thy name great; and thou shalt be a blessing:

3And I will bless them that bless thee, and curse him that curseth thee: and in thee shall all families of the earth be blessed.

4So Abram departed, as the LORD had spoken unto him; and Lot went with him: and Abram *was* seventy and five years old when he departed out of Haran.

5And Abram took Sarai his wife, and Lot his brother's son, and all their substance that they had gathered, and the souls that they had gotten in Haran; and they went forth to go into the land of Canaan; and into the land of Canaan they came.

6And Abram passed through the land unto the place of Sichem, unto the plain of Moreh. And the Canaanite *was* then in the land.

7And the LORD appeared unto Abram, and said, Unto thy seed will I give this land: and there builded he an altar unto the LORD, who appeared unto him.

8And he removed from thence unto a mountain on the east of Bethel, and pitched his tent, *having* Bethel on the west, and Hai on the east: and there he builded an altar unto the LORD, and called upon the name of the LORD.

9And Abram journeyed, going on still toward the south.

10And there was a famine in the land: and Abram went down into Egypt to sojourn there; for the famine *was* grievous in the land.

11And it came to pass, when he was come near to enter into Egypt, that he said unto Sarai his wife, Behold now, I know that thou *art* a fair woman to look upon:

12Therefore it shall come to pass, when the Egyptians shall see thee, that they shall say, This *is* his wife: and they will kill me, but they will save thee alive.

13Say, I pray thee, thou *art* my sister: that it may be well with me for thy sake; and my soul shall live because of thee.

14And it came to pass, that, when Abram was come into Egypt, the Egyptians beheld the woman that she *was* very fair.

15The princes also of Pharaoh saw her, and commended her before Pharaoh: and the woman was taken into Pharaoh's house.

16And he entreated Abram well for her

sake: and he had sheep, and oxen, and he
asses, and menservants, and maidservants,
and she asses, and camels.
17And the LORD plagued Pharaoh and
his house with great plagues because of
Sarai Abram's wife.
18And Pharaoh called Abram, and said,
What *is* this *that* thou hast done unto me?
why didst thou not tell me that she *was*
thy wife?
19Why saidst thou, She *is* my sister? so I
might have taken her to me to wife: now
therefore behold thy wife, take *her,* and go
thy way.
20And Pharaoh commanded *his* men
concerning him: and they sent him away,
and his wife, and all that he had.

13

1And Abram went up out of Egypt, he,
and his wife, and all that he had, and Lot
with him, into the south.
2And Abram *was* very rich in cattle, in
silver, and in gold.
3And he went on his journeys from the
south even to Bethel, unto the place where
his tent had been at the beginning, between Bethel and Hai;
4Unto the place of the altar, which he
had made there at the first: and there
Abram called on the name of the LORD.
5And Lot also, which went with Abram,
had flocks, and herds, and tents.
6And the land was not able to bear them,
that they might dwell together: for their
substance was great, so that they could not
dwell together.
7And there was a strife between the herdmen of Abram's cattle and the herdmen
of Lot's cattle: and the Canaanite and the
Perizzite dwelled then in the land.
8And Abram said unto Lot, Let there be
no strife, I pray thee, between me and thee,
and between my herdmen and thy herdmen; for we *be* brethren.
9*Is* not the whole
land before thee?
separate thyself, I
pray thee, from me:
if *thou wilt take* the
left hand, then I
will go to the right;
or if *thou depart* to
the right hand, then
I will go to the left.
10And Lot lifted
up his eyes, and be-
held all the plain of Jordan, that it *was*
well watered every where, before the LORD
destroyed Sodom and Gomorrah, *even* as
the garden of the LORD, like the land of
Egypt, as thou comest unto Zoar.
11Then Lot chose him all the plain of
Jordan; and Lot journeyed east: and they
separated themselves the one from the
other.
12Abram dwelled in the land of Canaan,
and Lot dwelled in the cities of the plain,
and pitched *his* tent toward Sodom.
13But the men of Sodom *were* wicked
and sinners before the LORD exceedingly.
14And the LORD said unto Abram, after
that Lot was separated from him, Lift up
now thine eyes, and look from the place
where thou art northward, and southward,
and eastward, and westward:
15For all the land which thou seest, to
thee will I give it, and to thy seed for ever.
16And I will make thy seed as the dust
of the earth: so that if a man can number
the dust of the earth, *then* shall thy seed
also be numbered.
17Arise, walk through the land in the
length of it and in the breadth of it; for I
will give it unto thee.
18Then Abram removed *his* tent, and
came and dwelt in the plain of Mamre,
which *is* in Hebron, and built there an altar unto the LORD.

14

1And it came to pass in the days of Amraphel king of Shinar, Arioch king of Ellasar, Chedorlaomer king of Elam, and Tidal
king of nations;
2*That these* made war with Bera king of
Sodom, and with Birsha king of Gomorrah, Shinab king of Admah, and Sheme-
ber king of Zeboiim, and the king of Bela,
which is Zoar.
3All these were joined together in the
vale of Siddim, which is the salt sea.
4Twelve years they served Chedorlaomer,
and in the thirteenth year they rebelled.
5And in the fourteenth year came Chedorlaomer, and the kings that *were* with him,
and smote the Rephaims in Ashteroth
Karnaim, and the Zuzims in Ham, and the
Emims in Shaveh Kiriathaim,
6And the Horites in their mount
Seir, unto El-paran, which *is* by the wilderness.
7And they returned, and came to En-
mishpat, which *is* Kadesh, and smote all

13:9
Unselfishness
◄ Genesis 14:23 ►

13:10-11, 13 Giving In
◄ Genesis 3:6
Genesis 25:29-30 ►

the country of the Amalekites, and also the Amorites that dwelt in Hazezon-tamar.

8 And there went out the king of Sodom, and the king of Gomorrah, and the king of Admah, and the king of Zeboiim, and the king of Bela (the same *is* Zoar;) and they joined battle with them in the vale of Siddim;

9 With Chedorlaomer the king of Elam, and with Tidal king of nations, and Amraphel king of Shinar, and Arioch king of Ellasar; four kings with five.

10 And the vale of Siddim *was full of* slimepits; and the kings of Sodom and Gomorrah fled, and fell there; and they that remained fled to the mountain.

11 And they took all the goods of Sodom and Gomorrah, and all their victuals, and went their way.

12 And they took Lot, Abram's brother's son, who dwelt in Sodom, and his goods, and departed.

13 And there came one that had escaped, and told Abram the Hebrew; for he dwelt in the plain of Mamre the Amorite, brother of Eshcol, and brother of Aner: and these *were* confederate with Abram.

14 And when Abram heard that his brother was taken captive, he armed his trained *servants,* born in his own house, three hundred and eighteen, and pursued *them* unto Dan.

15 And he divided himself against them, he and his servants, by night, and smote them, and pursued them unto Hobah, which *is* on the left hand of Damascus.

16 And he brought back all the goods, and also brought again his brother Lot, and his goods, and the women also, and the people.

17 And the king of Sodom went out to meet him after his return from the slaughter of Chedorlaomer, and of the kings that *were* with him, at the valley of Shaveh, which *is* the king's dale.

18 And Melchizedek king of Salem brought forth bread and wine: and he *was* the priest of the most high God.

19 And he blessed him, and said, Blessed *be* Abram of the most high God, possessor of heaven and earth:

20 And blessed be the most high God, which hath delivered thine enemies into thy hand. And he gave him tithes of all.

21 And the king of Sodom said unto Abram, Give me the persons, and take the goods to thyself.

22 And Abram said to the king of Sodom, I have lift up mine hand unto the LORD, the most high God, the possessor of heaven and earth,

23 That I will not *take* from a thread even to a shoelatchet, and that I will not take any thing that *is* thine, lest thou shouldest say, I have made Abram rich:

14:23 Unselfishness
◄ Genesis 13:9
Genesis 50:21 ►

24 Save only that which the young men have eaten, and the portion of the men which went with me, Aner, Eshcol, and Mamre; let them take their portion.

15

1 After these things the word of the LORD came unto Abram in a vision, saying, Fear not, Abram: I *am* thy shield, *and* thy exceeding great reward.

2 And Abram said, Lord GOD, what wilt thou give me, seeing I go childless, and the steward of my house is this Eliezer of Damascus?

3 And Abram said, Behold, to me thou hast given no seed: and, lo, one born in my house is mine heir.

4 And, behold, the word of the LORD *came* unto him, saying, This shall not be thine heir; but he that shall come forth out of thine own bowels shall be thine heir.

5 And he brought him forth abroad, and said, Look now toward heaven, and tell the stars, if thou be able to number them: and he said unto him, So shall thy seed be.

6 And he believed in the LORD; and he counted it to him for righteousness.

7 And he said unto him, I *am* the LORD that brought thee out of Ur of the Chaldees, to give thee this land to inherit it.

8 And he said, Lord GOD, whereby shall I know that I shall inherit it?

9 And he said unto him, Take me an heifer of three years old, and a she goat of three years old, and a ram of three years old, and a turtledove, and a young pigeon.

10 And he took unto him all these, and divided them in the midst, and laid each piece one against another: but the birds divided he not.

11 And when the fowls came down upon the carcases, Abram drove them away.

12 And when the sun was going down, a

deep sleep fell upon Abram; and, lo, an horror of great darkness fell upon him.

13 And he said unto Abram, Know of a surety that thy seed shall be a stranger in a land *that is* not theirs, and shall serve them; and they shall afflict them four hundred years;

14 And also that nation, whom they shall serve, will I judge: and afterward shall they come out with great substance.

15 And thou shalt go to thy fathers in peace; thou shalt be buried in a good old age.

16 But in the fourth generation they shall come hither again: for the iniquity of the Amorites *is* not yet full.

17 And it came to pass, that, when the sun went down, and it was dark, behold a smoking furnace, and a burning lamp that passed between those pieces.

18 In the same day the LORD made a covenant with Abram, saying, Unto thy seed have I given this land, from the river of Egypt unto the great river, the river Euphrates:

19 The Kenites, and the Kenizzites, and the Kadmonites,

20 And the Hittites, and the Perizzites, and the Rephaims,

21 And the Amorites, and the Canaanites, and the Girgashites, and the Jebusites.

16

1 Now Sarai Abram's wife bare him no children: and she had an handmaid, an Egyptian, whose name *was* Hagar.

2 And Sarai said unto Abram, Behold now, the LORD hath restrained me from bearing: I pray thee, go in unto my maid; it may be that I may obtain children by her. And Abram hearkened to the voice of Sarai.

3 And Sarai Abram's wife took Hagar her maid the Egyptian, after Abram had dwelt ten years in the land of Canaan, and gave her to her husband Abram to be his wife.

4 And he went in unto Hagar, and she conceived: and when she saw that she had conceived, her mistress was despised in her eyes.

5 And Sarai said unto Abram, My wrong *be* upon thee: I have given my maid into thy bosom; and when she saw that she had conceived, I was despised in her eyes: the LORD judge between me and thee.

16:5 "It's Her Fault!"
◄ Genesis 3:13
Genesis 27:36 ►

6 But Abram said unto Sarai, Behold, thy maid *is* in thy hand; do to her as it pleaseth thee. And when Sarai dealt hardly with her, she fled from her face.

7 And the angel of the LORD found her by a fountain of water in the wilderness, by the fountain in the way to Shur.

8 And he said, Hagar, Sarai's maid, whence camest thou? and whither wilt thou go? And she said, I flee from the face of my mistress Sarai.

9 And the angel of the LORD said unto her, Return to thy mistress, and submit thyself under her hands.

10 And the angel of the LORD said unto her, I will multiply thy seed exceedingly, that it shall not be numbered for multitude.

11 And the angel of the LORD said unto her, Behold, thou *art* with child, and shalt bear a son, and shalt call his name Ishmael; because the LORD hath heard thy affliction.

12 And he will be a wild man; his hand *will be* against every man, and every man's hand against him; and he shall dwell in the presence of all his brethren.

13 And she called the name of the LORD that spake unto her, Thou God seest me: for she said, Have I also here looked after him that seeth me?

14 Wherefore the well was called Beer-lahai-roi; behold, *it is* between Kadesh and Bered.

15 And Hagar bare Abram a son: and Abram called his son's name, which Hagar bare, Ishmael.

16 And Abram *was* fourscore and six years old, when Hagar bare Ishmael to Abram.

17

1 And when Abram was ninety years old and nine, the LORD appeared to Abram, and said unto him, I *am* the Almighty God; walk before me, and be thou perfect.

2 And I will make my covenant between me and thee, and will multiply thee exceedingly.

17:1
Names of God
◄ Genesis 18:25 ►

17:1 Perfection
◄
Deuteronomy 18:13 ►

3 And Abram fell on his face: and God
talked with him, saying,
4 As for me, behold, my covenant *is* with
thee, and thou shalt be a father of many
nations.
5 Neither shall thy name any more be
called Abram, but thy name shall be Abraham; for a father of many nations have I
made thee.
6 And I will make thee exceeding fruitful, and I will make nations of thee, and
kings shall come out of thee.
7 And I will establish my covenant between me and thee and thy seed after thee
in their generations for an everlasting covenant, to be a God unto thee, and to thy
seed after thee.
8 And I will give unto thee, and to thy
seed after thee, the land wherein thou art
a stranger, all the land of Canaan, for an
everlasting possession; and I will be their
God.
9 And God said unto Abraham, Thou
shalt keep my covenant therefore, thou,
and thy seed after thee in their generations.
10 This *is* my covenant, which ye shall
keep, between me and you and thy seed
after thee; Every man child among you
shall be circumcised.
11 And ye shall circumcise the flesh of
your foreskin; and it shall be a token of
the covenant betwixt me and you.
12 And he that is eight days old shall be
circumcised among you, every man child
in your generations, he that is born in the
house, or bought with money of any
stranger, which *is* not of thy seed.
13 He that is born in thy house, and he
that is bought with thy money, must needs
be circumcised: and my covenant shall be
in your flesh for an everlasting covenant.
14 And the uncircumcised man child
whose flesh of his foreskin is not circumcised, that soul shall be cut off from his
people; he hath broken my covenant.
15 And God said unto Abraham, As for
Sarai thy wife, thou shalt not call her name
Sarai, but Sarah *shall* her name *be.*
16 And I will bless her, and give thee a
son also of her: yea, I will bless her, and
she shall be *a mother* of nations; kings of
people shall be of her.
17 Then Abraham fell upon his face, and
laughed, and said in his heart, Shall *a child*
be born unto him that is an hundred years
old? and shall Sarah, that is ninety years
old, bear?
18 And Abraham said unto God, O that
Ishmael might live before thee!
19 And God said, Sarah thy wife shall
bear thee a son indeed; and thou shalt
call his name Isaac: and I will establish my
covenant with him for an everlasting covenant, *and* with his seed after him.
20 And as for Ishmael, I have heard thee:
Behold, I have blessed him, and will make
him fruitful, and will multiply him exceedingly; twelve princes shall he beget, and I
will make him a great nation.
21 But my covenant will I establish with
Isaac, which Sarah shall bear unto thee at
this set time in the next year.
22 And he left off talking with him, and
God went up from Abraham.
23 And Abraham took Ishmael his son,
and all that were born in his house, and
all that were bought with his money, every
male among the men of Abraham's house;
and circumcised the flesh of their foreskin
in the selfsame day, as God had said unto
him.
24 And Abraham *was* ninety years old and
nine, when he was circumcised in the flesh
of his foreskin.
25 And Ishmael his son *was* thirteen years
old, when he was circumcised in the flesh
of his foreskin.
26 In the selfsame day was Abraham circumcised, and Ishmael his son.
27 And all the men of his house, born in
the house, and bought with money of the
stranger, were circumcised with him.

18

1 And the LORD appeared unto him in
the plains of Mamre: and he sat in the tent
door in the heat of the day;
2 And he lift up his eyes and looked, and,
lo, three men stood by him: and when he
saw *them,* he ran to meet them from the
tent door, and bowed himself toward the
ground,
3 And said, My Lord, if now I have found
favour in thy sight, pass not away, I pray
thee, from thy servant:
4 Let a little water, I pray you, be fetched,
and wash your feet, and rest yourselves
under the tree:
5 And I will fetch a morsel of bread, and
comfort ye your hearts; after that ye shall
pass on: for therefore are ye come to your

servant. And they said, So do, as thou hast
said.
6 And Abraham hastened into the tent
unto Sarah, and said, Make ready quickly
three measures of fine meal, knead *it*, and
make cakes upon the hearth.
7 And Abraham ran unto the herd, and
fetcht a calf tender and good, and gave
it unto a young man; and he hasted to
dress it.
8 And he took butter, and milk, and the
calf which he had dressed, and set *it* before them; and he stood by them under
the tree, and they did eat.
9 And they said unto him, Where *is* Sarah
thy wife? And he said, Behold, in the tent.
10 And he said, I will certainly return
unto thee according to the time of life; and,
lo, Sarah thy wife shall have a son. And
Sarah heard *it* in the tent door, which *was*
behind him.
11 Now Abraham and Sarah *were* old *and*
well stricken in age; *and* it ceased to be with
Sarah after the manner of women.
12 Therefore Sarah laughed within herself, saying, After I am waxed old shall I
have pleasure, my lord being old also?
13 And the LORD said unto Abraham,
Wherefore did Sarah laugh, saying, Shall I
of a surety bear a child, which am old?
14 Is any thing too hard for the LORD? At
the time appointed I will return unto thee,
according to the time of life, and Sarah
shall have a son.
15 Then Sarah denied, saying, I laughed
not; for she was afraid. And he said, Nay;
but thou didst laugh.
16 And the men rose up from thence, and
looked toward Sodom: and Abraham went
with them to bring them on the way.
17 And the LORD said, Shall I hide from
Abraham that thing which I do;
18 Seeing that Abraham shall surely become a great and mighty nation, and all
the nations of the earth shall be blessed in
him?
19 For I know him, that he will command
his children and his household after him,
and they shall keep the way of the LORD,
to do justice and judgment; that the LORD
may bring upon Abraham that which he
hath spoken of him.
20 And the LORD said, Because the cry of
Sodom and Gomorrah is great, and because their sin is very grievous;
21 I will go down now, and see whether
they have done altogether according to the
cry of it, which is come unto me; and if
not, I will know.
22 And the men turned their faces from
thence, and went toward Sodom: but Abraham stood yet before the LORD.
23 And Abraham drew near, and said,
Wilt thou also destroy the righteous with
the wicked?
24 Peradventure there be fifty righteous
within the city: wilt thou also destroy and
not spare the place for the fifty righteous
that *are* therein?
25 That be far
from thee to do af-
ter this manner, to
slay the righteous
with the wicked:
and that the righ-
teous should be as
the wicked, that be
far from thee: Shall
not the Judge of all
the earth do right?
26 And the LORD
said, If I find in
Sodom fifty righ-
teous within the
city, then I will
spare all the place
for their sakes.

18:25
God as Judge
◄ Psalm 58:11 ►

18:25 Names of God
◄ Genesis 17:1
Exodus 3:14 ►

18:26
Mercy from God
◄ Genesis 19:16 ►

27 And Abraham answered and said, Behold now, I have taken upon me to speak
unto the Lord, which *am but* dust and
ashes:
28 Peradventure there shall lack five of
the fifty righteous: wilt thou destroy all the
city for *lack of* five? And he said, If I find
there forty and five, I will not destroy *it*.
29 And he spake unto him yet again, and
said, Peradventure there shall be forty
found there. And he said, I will not do *it*
for forty's sake.
30 And he said *unto him*, Oh let not the
Lord be angry, and I will speak: Peradventure there shall thirty be found there.
And he said, I will not do *it*, if I find thirty
there.
31 And he said, Behold now, I have tak-
en upon me to speak unto the Lord: Peradventure there shall be twenty found there.
And he said, I will not destroy *it* for
twenty's sake.
32 And he said, Oh let not the Lord be

angry, and I will speak yet but this once:
Peradventure ten shall be found there. And
he said, I will not destroy *it* for ten's sake.
33 And the LORD went his way, as soon
as he had left communing with Abraham:
and Abraham returned unto his place.

19

1 And there came two angels to Sodom
at even; and Lot sat in the gate of Sodom:
and Lot seeing *them* rose up to meet them;
and he bowed himself with his face toward
the ground;
2 And he said, Behold now, my lords,
turn in, I pray you, into your servant's
house, and tarry all night, and wash your
feet, and ye shall rise up early, and go on
your ways. And they said, Nay; but we will
abide in the street all night.
3 And he pressed upon them greatly;
and they turned in unto him, and entered
into his house; and he made them a feast,
and did bake unleavened bread, and they
did eat.
4 But before they lay down, the men of
the city, *even* the men of Sodom, compassed the house round, both old and
young, all the people from every quarter:
5 And they called unto Lot, and said unto
him, Where *are* the men which came in to
thee this night? bring them out unto us,
that we may know them.
6 And Lot went out at the door unto
them, and shut the door after him,
7 And said, I pray you, brethren, do not
so wickedly.
8 Behold now, I have two daughters
which have not known man; let me, I pray
you, bring them out unto you, and do ye
to them as *is* good in your eyes: only unto
these men do nothing; for therefore came
they under the shadow of my roof.
9 And they said, Stand back. And they
said *again*, This one *fellow* came in to sojourn, and he will needs be a judge: now
will we deal worse with thee, than with
them. And they pressed sore upon the
man, *even* Lot, and came near to break the
door.
10 But the men put forth their hand, and
pulled Lot into the house to them, and
shut to the door.
11 And they smote the men that *were* at
the door of the house with blindness, both
small and great: so that they wearied themselves to find the door.
12 And the men said unto Lot, Hast thou
here any besides? son in law, and thy sons,
and thy daughters, and whatsoever thou
hast in the city, bring *them* out of this place:
13 For we will destroy this place, because
the cry of them is waxen great before the
face of the LORD; and the LORD hath sent
us to destroy it.
14 And Lot went out, and spake unto his
sons in law, which married his daughters,
and said, Up, get you out of this place; for
the LORD will destroy this city. But he
seemed as one that mocked unto his sons
in law.
15 And when the morning arose, then the
angels hastened Lot, saying, Arise, take thy
wife, and thy two daughters, which are
here; lest thou be consumed in the iniquity of the city.
16 And while he
lingered, the men
laid hold upon his
hand, and upon the
hand of his wife,
and upon the hand
of his two daugh-
ters; the LORD being
merciful unto him:
and they brought
him forth, and set
him without the
city.
17 And it came to
pass, when they
had brought them
forth abroad, that
he said, Escape for
thy life; look not behind thee, neither stay
thou in all the plain; escape to the mountain, lest thou be consumed.

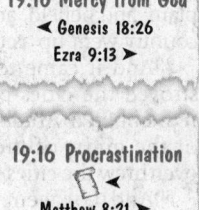

19:16 Mercy from God
◄ Genesis 18:26
Ezra 9:13 ►

19:16 Procrastination
◄
Matthew 8:21 ►

19:17 Sin (Warnings)
◄
Deuteronomy 29:20 ►

18 And Lot said unto them, Oh, not so,
my Lord:
19 Behold now, thy servant hath found
grace in thy sight, and thou hast magnified thy mercy, which thou hast shewed
unto me in saving my life; and I cannot
escape to the mountain, lest some evil take
me, and I die:
20 Behold now, this city *is* near to flee
unto, and it *is* a little one: Oh, let me escape thither, (*is* it not a little one?) and
my soul shall live.
21 And he said unto him, See, I have accepted thee concerning this thing also, that
I will not overthrow this city, for the which
thou hast spoken.

22 Haste thee, escape thither; for I cannot do any thing till thou be come thither. Therefore the name of the city was called Zoar.

23 The sun was risen upon the earth when Lot entered into Zoar.

24 Then the LORD rained upon Sodom and upon Gomorrah brimstone and fire from the LORD out of heaven;

25 And he overthrew those cities, and all the plain, and all the inhabitants of the cities, and that which grew upon the ground.

26 But his wife looked back from behind him, and she became a pillar of salt.

27 And Abraham gat up early in the morning to the place where he stood before the LORD:

28 And he looked toward Sodom and Gomorrah, and toward all the land of the plain, and beheld, and, lo, the smoke of the country went up as the smoke of a furnace.

29 And it came to pass, when God destroyed the cities of the plain, that God remembered Abraham, and sent Lot out of the midst of the overthrow, when he overthrew the cities in the which Lot dwelt.

30 And Lot went up out of Zoar, and dwelt in the mountain, and his two daughters with him; for he feared to dwell in Zoar: and he dwelt in a cave, he and his two daughters.

31 And the firstborn said unto the younger, Our father *is* old, and *there is* not a man in the earth to come in unto us after the manner of all the earth:

32 Come, let us make our father drink wine, and we will lie with him, that we may preserve seed of our father.

33 And they made their father drink wine that night: and the firstborn went in, and lay with her father; and he perceived not when she lay down, nor when she arose.

34 And it came to pass on the morrow, that the firstborn said unto the younger, Behold, I lay yesternight with my father: let us make him drink wine this night also; and go thou in, *and* lie with him, that we may preserve seed of our father.

35 And they made their father drink wine that night also: and the younger arose, and lay with him; and he perceived not when she lay down, nor when she arose.

36 Thus were both the daughters of Lot with child by their father.

37 And the firstborn bare a son, and called his name Moab: the same *is* the father of the Moabites unto this day.

38 And the younger, she also bare a son, and called his name Benammi: the same *is* the father of the children of Ammon unto this day.

20

1 And Abraham journeyed from thence toward the south country, and dwelled between Kadesh and Shur, and sojourned in Gerar.

2 And Abraham said of Sarah his wife, She *is* my sister: and Abimelech king of Gerar sent, and took Sarah.

20:2
Only Human
◄ Numbers 20:12 ►

3 But God came to Abimelech in a dream by night, and said to him, Behold, thou *art but* a dead man, for the woman which thou hast taken; for she *is* a man's wife.

4 But Abimelech had not come near her: and he said, Lord, wilt thou slay also a righteous nation?

5 Said he not unto me, She *is* my sister? and she, even she herself said, He *is* my brother: in the integrity of my heart and innocency of my hands have I done this.

6 And God said unto him in a dream, Yea, I know that thou didst this in the integrity of thy heart; for I also withheld thee from sinning against me: therefore suffered I thee not to touch her.

7 Now therefore restore the man *his* wife; for he *is* a prophet, and he shall pray for thee, and thou shalt live: and if thou restore *her* not, know thou that thou shalt surely die, thou, and all that *are* thine.

8 Therefore Abimelech rose early in the morning, and called all his servants, and told all these things in their ears: and the men were sore afraid.

9 Then Abimelech called Abraham, and said unto him, What hast thou done unto us? and what have I offended thee, that thou hast brought on me and on my kingdom a great sin? thou hast done deeds unto me that ought not to be done.

10 And Abimelech said unto Abraham, What sawest thou, that thou hast done this thing?

11 And Abraham said, Because I thought, Surely the fear of God *is* not in this place; and they will slay me for my wife's sake.

12 And yet indeed *she is* my sister; she *is*

the daughter of my father, but not the
daughter of my mother; and she became
my wife.
13 And it came to pass, when God caused
me to wander from my father's house, that
I said unto her, This *is* thy kindness which
thou shalt shew unto me; at every place
whither we shall come, say of me, He *is*
my brother.
14 And Abimelech took sheep, and oxen,
and menservants, and womenservants, and
gave *them* unto Abraham, and restored him
Sarah his wife.
15 And Abimelech said, Behold, my land
is before thee: dwell where it pleaseth thee.
16 And unto Sarah he said, Behold, I have
given thy brother a thousand *pieces* of silver: behold, he *is* to thee a covering of the
eyes, unto all that *are* with thee, and with
all *other*: thus she was reproved.
17 So Abraham prayed unto God: and
God healed Abimelech, and his wife, and
his maidservants; and they bare *children*.
18 For the LORD had fast closed up all the
wombs of the house of Abimelech, because of Sarah Abraham's wife.

21

1 And the LORD visited Sarah as he had
said, and the LORD did unto Sarah as he
had spoken.
2 For Sarah conceived, and bare Abraham a son in his old age, at the set time of
which God had spoken to him.
3 And Abraham called the name of his
son that was born unto him, whom Sarah
bare to him, Isaac.
4 And Abraham circumcised his son Isaac
being eight days old, as God had commanded him.
5 And Abraham was an hundred years
old, when his son Isaac was born unto
him.
6 And Sarah said, God hath made me to
laugh, *so that* all that hear will laugh with
me.
7 And she said, Who would have said
unto Abraham, that Sarah should have
given children suck? for I have born *him* a
son in his old age.
8 And the child grew, and was weaned:
and Abraham made a great feast the *same*
day that Isaac was weaned.
9 And Sarah saw the son of Hagar the
Egyptian, which she had born unto Abraham, mocking.
10 Wherefore she said unto Abraham,
Cast out this bond-
woman and her
son: for the son of
this bondwoman
shall not be heir
with my son, *even*
with Isaac.

21:10
Fighting
◄ Proverbs 18:19 ►

11 And the thing was very grievous in
Abraham's sight because of his son.
12 And God said unto Abraham, Let it
not be grievous in thy sight because of the
lad, and because of thy bondwoman; in
all that Sarah hath said unto thee, hearken unto her voice; for in Isaac shall thy
seed be called.
13 And also of the son of the bondwoman will I make a nation, because he *is*
thy seed.
14 And Abraham rose up early in the
morning, and took bread, and a bottle of
water, and gave *it* unto Hagar, putting *it*
on her shoulder, and the child, and sent
her away: and she departed, and wandered
in the wilderness of Beer-sheba.
15 And the water was spent in the bottle,
and she cast the child under one of the
shrubs.
16 And she went, and sat her down over
against *him* a good way off, as it were a
bowshot: for she said, Let me not see the
death of the child. And she sat over against
him, and lift up her voice, and wept.
17 And God heard the voice of the lad;
and the angel of God called to Hagar out
of heaven, and said unto her, What aileth
thee, Hagar? fear not; for God hath heard
the voice of the lad where he *is*.
18 Arise, lift up the lad, and hold him in
thine hand; for I will make him a great
nation.
19 And God opened her eyes, and she saw
a well of water; and she went, and filled
the bottle with water, and gave the lad
drink.
20 And God was with the lad; and he
grew, and dwelt in the wilderness, and
became an archer.
21 And he dwelt in the wilderness of Paran: and his mother took him a wife out
of the land of Egypt.
22 And it came to pass at that time, that
Abimelech and Phichol the chief captain
of his host spake unto Abraham, saying,
God *is* with thee in all that thou doest:
23 Now therefore swear unto me here by

God that thou wilt not deal falsely with me, nor with my son, nor with my son's son: *but* according to the kindness that I have done unto thee, thou shalt do unto me, and to the land wherein thou hast sojourned.

24 And Abraham said, I will swear.

25 And Abraham reproved Abimelech because of a well of water, which Abimelech's servants had violently taken away.

26 And Abimelech said, I wot not who hath done this thing: neither didst thou tell me, neither yet heard I *of it,* but to day.

27 And Abraham took sheep and oxen, and gave them unto Abimelech; and both of them made a covenant.

28 And Abraham set seven ewe lambs of the flock by themselves.

29 And Abimelech said unto Abraham, What *mean* these seven ewe lambs which thou hast set by themselves?

30 And he said, For *these* seven ewe lambs shalt thou take of my hand, that they may be a witness unto me, that I have digged this well.

31 Wherefore he called that place Beer-sheba; because there they sware both of them.

32 Thus they made a covenant at Beer-sheba: then Abimelech rose up, and Phichol the chief captain of his host, and they returned into the land of the Philistines.

33 And *Abraham* planted a grove in Beer-sheba, and called there on the name of the LORD, the everlasting God.

34 And Abraham sojourned in the Philistines' land many days.

22

1 And it came to pass after these things, that God did tempt Abraham, and said unto him, Abraham: and he said, Behold, *here I am.*

2 And he said, Take now thy son, thine only *son* Isaac, whom thou lovest, and get thee into the land of Moriah; and offer him there for a burnt offering upon one of the mountains which I will tell thee of.

3 And Abraham rose up early in the morning, and saddled his ass, and took two of his young men with him, and Isaac his son, and clave the wood for the burnt offering, and rose up, and went unto the place of which God had told him.

4 Then on the third day Abraham lifted up his eyes, and saw the place afar off.

5 And Abraham said unto his young men, Abide ye here with the ass; and I and the lad will go yonder and worship, and come again to you,

6 And Abraham took the wood of the burnt offering, and laid *it* upon Isaac his son; and he took the fire in his hand, and a knife; and they went both of them together.

7 And Isaac spake unto Abraham his father, and said, My father: and he said, Here *am* I, my son. And he said, Behold the fire and the wood: but where *is* the lamb for a burnt offering?

8 And Abraham said, My son, God will provide himself a lamb for a burnt offering: so they went both of them together.

9 And they came to the place which God had told him of; and Abraham built an altar there, and laid the wood in order, and bound Isaac his son, and laid him on the altar upon the wood.

10 And Abraham stretched forth his hand, and took the knife to slay his son.

11 And the angel of the LORD called unto him out of heaven, and said, Abraham, Abraham: and he said, Here *am* I.

12 And he said, Lay not thine hand upon the lad, neither do thou any thing unto him: for now I know that thou fearest God, seeing thou hast not withheld thy son, thine only *son* from me.

13 And Abraham lifted up his eyes, and looked, and behold behind *him* a ram caught in a thicket by his horns: and Abraham went and took the ram, and offered him up for a burnt offering in the stead of his son.

14 And Abraham called the name of that place Jehovah-jireh: as it is said *to* this day, In the mount of the LORD it shall be seen.

15 And the angel of the LORD called unto Abraham out of heaven the second time,

16 And said, By myself have I sworn, saith the LORD, for because thou hast done this thing, and hast not withheld thy son, thine only *son:*

17 That in blessing I will bless thee, and in multiplying I will multiply thy seed as the stars of the heaven, and as the sand which *is* upon the sea shore; and thy seed shall possess the gate of his enemies;

18 And in thy seed shall all the nations of the earth be blessed; because thou hast obeyed my voice.

19 So Abraham returned unto his young men, and they rose up and went together to Beer-sheba; and Abraham dwelt at Beer-sheba.

20 And it came to pass after these things, that it was told Abraham, saying, Behold, Milcah, she hath also born children unto thy brother Nahor;

21 Huz his firstborn, and Buz his brother, and Kemuel the father of Aram,

22 And Chesed, and Hazo, and Pildash, and Jidlaph, and Bethuel.

23 And Bethuel begat Rebekah: these eight Milcah did bear to Nahor, Abraham's brother.

24 And his concubine, whose name *was* Reumah, she bare also Tebah, and Gaham, and Thahash, and Maachah.

23

1 And Sarah was an hundred and seven and twenty years old: *these were* the years of the life of Sarah.

2 And Sarah died in Kirjath-arba; the same *is* Hebron in the land of Canaan: and Abraham came to mourn for Sarah, and to weep for her.

23:2
Grief
◄ Genesis 37:35 ►

3 And Abraham stood up from before his dead, and spake unto the sons of Heth, saying,

4 I *am* a stranger and a sojourner with you: give me a possession of a buryingplace with you, that I may bury my dead out of my sight.

5 And the children of Heth answered Abraham, saying unto him,

6 Hear us, my lord: thou *art* a mighty prince among us: in the choice of our sepulchres bury thy dead; none of us shall withhold from thee his sepulchre, but that thou mayest bury thy dead.

7 And Abraham stood up, and bowed himself to the people of the land, *even* to the children of Heth.

8 And he communed with them, saying, If it be your mind that I should bury my dead out of my sight; hear me, and intreat for me to Ephron the son of Zohar,

9 That he may give me the cave of Machpelah, which he hath, which *is* in the end of his field; for as much money as it is worth he shall give it me for a possession of a buryingplace amongst you.

10 And Ephron dwelt among the children of Heth: and Ephron the Hittite answered Abraham in the audience of the children of Heth, *even* of all that went in at the gate of his city, saying,

11 Nay, my lord, hear me: the field give I thee, and the cave that *is* therein, I give it thee; in the presence of the sons of my people give I it thee: bury thy dead.

12 And Abraham bowed down himself before the people of the land.

13 And he spake unto Ephron in the audience of the people of the land, saying, But if thou *wilt give it,* I pray thee, hear me: I will give thee money for the field; take *it* of me, and I will bury my dead there.

14 And Ephron answered Abraham, saying unto him,

15 My lord, hearken unto me: the land *is worth* four hundred shekels of silver; what *is* that betwixt me and thee? bury therefore thy dead.

16 And Abraham hearkened unto Ephron; and Abraham weighed to Ephron the silver, which he had named in the audience of the sons of Heth, four hundred shekels of silver, current *money* with the merchant.

17 And the field of Ephron, which *was* in Machpelah, which *was* before Mamre, the field, and the cave which *was* therein, and all the trees that *were* in the field, that *were* in all the borders round about, were made sure

18 Unto Abraham for a possession in the presence of the children of Heth, before all that went in at the gate of his city.

19 And after this, Abraham buried Sarah his wife in the cave of the field of Machpelah before Mamre: the same *is* Hebron in the land of Canaan.

20 And the field, and the cave that *is* therein, were made sure unto Abraham for a possession of a buryingplace by the sons of Heth.

24

1 And Abraham was old, *and* well stricken in age: and the LORD had blessed Abraham in all things.

2 And Abraham said unto his eldest servant of his house, that ruled over all that he had, Put, I pray thee, thy hand under my thigh:

3 And I will make thee swear by the LORD, the God of heaven, and the God of the earth, that thou shalt not take a wife unto

my son of the daughters of the Canaanites, among whom I dwell:
4 But thou shalt go unto my country, and
to my kindred, and take a wife unto my
son Isaac.
5 And the servant said unto him, Peradventure the woman will not be willing to
follow me unto this land: must I needs
bring thy son again unto the land from
whence thou camest?
6 And Abraham said unto him, Beware
thou that thou bring not my son thither
again.
7 The LORD God of heaven, which took
me from my father's house, and from the
land of my kindred, and which spake unto
me, and that sware unto me, saying, Unto
thy seed will I give this land; he shall send
his angel before thee, and thou shalt take
a wife unto my son from thence.
8 And if the woman will not be willing
to follow thee, then thou shalt be clear
from this my oath: only bring not my son
thither again.
9 And the servant put his hand under the
thigh of Abraham his master, and sware
to him concerning that matter.
10 And the servant took ten camels of the
camels of his master, and departed; for all
the goods of his master *were* in his hand:
and he arose, and went to Mesopotamia,
unto the city of Nahor.
11 And he made his camels to kneel down
without the city by a well of water at the
time of the evening, *even* the time that
women go out to draw *water*.
12 And he said, O LORD God of my master Abraham, I pray thee, send me good
speed this day, and shew kindness unto
my master Abraham.
13 Behold, I stand *here* by the well of
water; and the daughters of the men of the
city come out to draw water:
14 And let it come to pass, that the damsel to whom I shall say, Let down thy pitcher, I pray thee, that I may drink; and she
shall say, Drink, and I will give thy camels
drink also: *let the same be* she *that* thou hast
appointed for thy servant Isaac; and thereby shall I know that thou hast shewed
kindness unto my master.
15 And it came to pass, before he had
done speaking, that, behold, Rebekah
came out, who was born to Bethuel, son
of Milcah, the wife of Nahor, Abraham's
brother, with her pitcher upon her shoulder.
16 And the damsel *was* very fair to look
upon, a virgin, neither had any man
known her: and she went down to the well,
and filled her pitcher, and came up.
17 And the servant ran to meet her, and
said, Let me, I pray thee, drink a little water of thy pitcher.
18 And she said, Drink, my lord: and she
hasted, and let down her pitcher upon her
hand, and gave him drink.
19 And when she had done giving him
drink, she said, I will draw *water* for thy
camels also, until they have done drinking.
20 And she hasted, and emptied her
pitcher into the trough, and ran again unto
the well to draw *water*, and drew for all his
camels.
21 And the man wondering at her held
his peace, to wit whether the LORD had
made his journey prosperous or not.
22 And it came to pass, as the camels had
done drinking, that the man took a gold-
en earring of half a shekel weight, and two
bracelets for her hands of ten *shekels* weight
of gold;
23 And said, Whose daughter *art* thou?
tell me, I pray thee: is there room *in* thy
father's house for us to lodge in?
24 And she said unto him, I *am* the
daughter of Bethuel the son of Milcah,
which she bare unto Nahor.
25 She said moreover unto him, We have
both straw and provender enough, and
room to lodge in.
26 And the man bowed down his head,
and worshipped the LORD.
27 And he said, Blessed *be* the LORD God
of my master Abraham, who hath not left
destitute my master of his mercy and his
truth: I *being* in the way, the LORD led me
to the house of my master's brethren.
28 And the damsel ran, and told *them of*
her mother's house these things.
29 And Rebekah had a brother, and his
name *was* Laban: and Laban ran out unto
the man, unto the well.
30 And it came to pass, when he saw the
earring and bracelets upon his sister's
hands, and when he heard the words of
Rebekah his sister, saying, Thus spake the
man unto me; that he came unto the man;
and, behold, he stood by the camels at the
well.

31 And he said, Come in, thou blessed of the LORD; wherefore standest thou without? for I have prepared the house, and room for the camels.

32 And the man came into the house: and he ungirded his camels, and gave straw and provender for the camels, and water to wash his feet, and the men's feet that *were* with him.

33 And there was set *meat* before him to eat: but he said, I will not eat, until I have told mine errand. And he said, Speak on.

34 And he said, I *am* Abraham's servant.

35 And the LORD hath blessed my master greatly; and he is become great: and he hath given him flocks, and herds, and silver, and gold, and menservants, and maidservants, and camels, and asses.

24:35
Blessings
◄ 2 Samuel 6:11 ►

36 And Sarah my master's wife bare a son to my master when she was old: and unto him hath he given all that he hath.

37 And my master made me swear, saying, Thou shalt not take a wife to my son of the daughters of the Canaanites, in whose land I dwell:

38 But thou shalt go unto my father's house, and to my kindred, and take a wife unto my son.

39 And I said unto my master, Peradventure the woman will not follow me.

40 And he said unto me, The LORD, before whom I walk, will send his angel with thee, and prosper thy way; and thou shalt take a wife for my son of my kindred, and of my father's house:

41 Then shalt thou be clear from *this* my oath, when thou comest to my kindred; and if they give not thee *one,* thou shalt be clear from my oath.

42 And I came this day unto the well, and said, O LORD God of my master Abraham, if now thou do prosper my way which I go;

43 Behold, I stand by the well of water; and it shall come to pass, that when the virgin cometh forth to draw *water,* and I say to her, Give me, I pray thee, a little water of thy pitcher to drink;

44 And she say to me, Both drink thou, and I will also draw for thy camels: *let* the same *be* the woman whom the LORD hath appointed out for my master's son.

45 And before I had done speaking in mine heart, behold, Rebekah came forth with her pitcher on her shoulder; and she went down unto the well, and drew *water:* and I said unto her, Let me drink, I pray thee.

46 And she made haste, and let down her pitcher from her *shoulder,* and said, Drink, and I will give thy camels drink also: so I drank, and she made the camels drink also.

47 And I asked her, and said, Whose daughter *art* thou? And she said, The daughter of Bethuel, Nahor's son, whom Milcah bare unto him: and I put the earring upon her face, and the bracelets upon her hands.

48 And I bowed down my head, and worshipped the LORD, and blessed the LORD God of my master Abraham, which had led me in the right way to take my master's brother's daughter unto his son.

49 And now if ye will deal kindly and truly with my master, tell me: and if not, tell me; that I may turn to the right hand, or to the left.

50 Then Laban and Bethuel answered and said, The thing proceedeth from the LORD: we cannot speak unto thee bad or good.

51 Behold, Rebekah *is* before thee, take *her,* and go, and let her be thy master's son's wife, as the LORD hath spoken.

52 And it came to pass, that, when Abraham's servant heard their words, he worshipped the LORD, *bowing himself* to the earth.

53 And the servant brought forth jewels of silver, and jewels of gold, and raiment, and gave *them* to Rebekah: he gave also to her brother and to her mother precious things.

54 And they did eat and drink, he and the men that *were* with him, and tarried all night; and they rose up in the morning, and he said, Send me away unto my master.

55 And her brother and her mother said, Let the damsel abide with us *a few* days, at the least ten; after that she shall go.

56 And he said unto them, Hinder me not, seeing the LORD hath prospered my way; send me away that I may go to my master.

57 And they said, We will call the damsel, and enquire at her mouth.

58 And they called Rebekah, and said

unto her, Wilt thou go with this man? And
she said, I will go.
59And they sent away Rebekah their sister, and her nurse, and Abraham's servant,
and his men.
60And they blessed Rebekah, and said
unto her, Thou *art* our sister, be thou *the
mother* of thousands of millions, and let
thy seed possess the gate of those which
hate them.
61And Rebekah arose, and her damsels,
and they rode upon the camels, and followed the man: and the servant took Rebekah, and went his way.
62And Isaac came from the way of the
well Lahai-roi; for he dwelt in the south
country.
63And Isaac went out to meditate in the
field at the eventide: and he lifted up his
eyes, and saw, and, behold, the camels *were*
coming.
64And Rebekah lifted up her eyes, and
when she saw Isaac, she lighted off the
camel.
65For she *had*
said unto the ser-
vant, What man *is*
this that walketh in
the field to meet us?
And the servant *had*
said, It *is* my master: therefore she took a
vail, and covered herself.

24:65
Modesty
◄ 1 Timothy 2:9-10 ►

66And the servant told Isaac all things
that he had done.
67And Isaac brought her into his mother Sarah's tent, and took Rebekah, and she
became his wife; and he loved her: and
Isaac was comforted after his mother's
death.

25

1Then again Abraham took a wife, and
her name *was* Keturah.
2And she bare him Zimran, and Jokshan, and Medan, and Midian, and Ishbak, and Shuah.
3And Jokshan begat Sheba, and Dedan.
And the sons of Dedan were Asshurim, and
Letushim, and Leummim.
4And the sons of Midian; Ephah, and
Epher, and Hanoch, and Abidah, and
Eldaah. All these *were* the children of Keturah.
5And Abraham gave all that he had unto
Isaac.
6But unto the sons of the concubines,
which Abraham had, Abraham gave gifts,
and sent them away from Isaac his son,
while he yet lived, eastward, unto the east
country.
7And these *are* the days of the years of
Abraham's life which he lived, an hundred
threescore and fifteen years.
8Then Abraham gave up the ghost, and
died in a good old age, an old man,
and full *of years;* and was gathered to his
people.
9And his sons Isaac and Ishmael buried
him in the cave of Machpelah, in the field
of Ephron the son of Zohar the Hittite,
which *is* before Mamre;
10The field which Abraham purchased
of the sons of Heth: there was Abraham
buried, and Sarah his wife.
11And it came to pass after the death of
Abraham, that God blessed his son Isaac;
and Isaac dwelt by the well Lahai-roi.
12Now these *are* the generations of Ishmael, Abraham's son, whom Hagar the
Egyptian, Sarah's handmaid, bare unto
Abraham:
13And these *are* the names of the sons
of Ishmael, by their names, according to
their generations: the firstborn of Ishmael,
Nebajoth; and Kedar, and Adbeel, and
Mibsam,
14And Mishma, and Dumah, and Massa,
15Hadar, and Tema, Jetur, Naphish, and
Kedemah:
16These *are* the sons of Ishmael, and
these *are* their names, by their towns,
and by their castles; twelve princes according to their nations.
17And these *are* the years of the life of
Ishmael, an hundred and thirty and seven
years: and he gave up the ghost and died;
and was gathered unto his people.
18And they dwelt from Havilah unto
Shur, that *is* before Egypt, as thou goest
toward Assyria: *and* he died in the presence of all his brethren.
19And these *are* the generations of Isaac,
Abraham's son: Abraham begat Isaac:
20And Isaac was forty years old when he
took Rebekah to wife, the daughter of Bethuel the Syrian of Padan-aram, the sister
to Laban the Syrian.
21And Isaac intreated the LORD for his
wife, because she *was* barren: and the LORD
was intreated of him, and Rebekah his wife
conceived.
22And the children struggled together

within her; and she said, If *it be* so, why
am I thus? And she went to enquire of the
LORD.
23 And the LORD said unto her, Two nations *are* in thy womb, and two manner of
people shall be separated from thy bowels; and *the one* people shall be stronger
than *the other* people; and the elder shall
serve the younger.
24 And when her days to be delivered
were fulfilled, behold, *there were* twins in
her womb.
25 And the first came out red, all over like
an hairy garment; and they called his name
Esau.
26 And after that came his brother out,
and his hand took hold on Esau's heel; and
his name was called Jacob: and Isaac *was*
threescore years old when she bare them.
27 And the boys grew: and Esau was a
cunning hunter, a man of the field; and
Jacob *was* a plain man, dwelling in tents.
28 And Isaac loved Esau, because he did
eat of *his* venison: but Rebekah loved
Jacob.
29 And Jacob sod
pottage: and Esau
came from the
field, and he *was*
faint:
30 And Esau said
to Jacob, Feed me, I pray thee, with that
same red *pottage;* for I *am* faint: therefore
was his name called Edom.

25:29-30 Giving In
◄ Genesis 13:10-11, 13
Genesis 25:33 ►

31 And Jacob said, Sell me this day thy
birthright.
32 And Esau said, Behold, I *am* at the
point to die: and what profit shall this
birthright do to me?
33 And Jacob said,
Swear to me this
day; and he sware
unto him: and he
sold his birthright
unto Jacob.

25:33 Giving In
◄ Genesis 25:29-30
Joshua 7:21 ►

34 Then Jacob gave
Esau bread and pot-
tage of lentiles; and
he did eat and drink,
and rose up, and
went his way: thus
Esau despised *his* birthright.

25:33
Foolish Promises
◄ Joshua 9:19 ►

26

1 And there was a famine in the land,
beside the first famine that was in the
days of Abraham. And Isaac went unto
Abimelech king of the Philistines unto
Gerar.
2 And the LORD appeared unto him, and
said, Go not down into Egypt; dwell in the
land which I shall tell thee of:
3 Sojourn in this land, and I will be with
thee, and will bless thee; for unto thee, and
unto thy seed, I will give all these countries, and I will perform the oath which I
sware unto Abraham thy father;
4 And I will make thy seed to multiply
as the stars of heaven, and will give unto
thy seed all these countries; and in thy seed
shall all the nations of the earth be blessed;
5 Because that Abraham obeyed my
voice, and kept my charge, my commandments, my statutes, and my laws.
6 And Isaac dwelt in Gerar:
7 And the men of the place asked *him* of
his wife; and he said, She *is* my sister: for
he feared to say, *She is* my wife; lest, *said
he,* the men of the place should kill me for
Rebekah; because she *was* fair to look
upon.
8 And it came to pass, when he had been
there a long time, that Abimelech king of
the Philistines looked out at a window, and
saw, and, behold, Isaac *was* sporting with
Rebekah his wife.
9 And Abimelech called Isaac, and said,
Behold, of a surety she *is* thy wife: and how
saidst thou, She *is* my sister? And Isaac said
unto him, Because I said, Lest I die for her.
10 And Abimelech said, What *is* this thou
hast done unto us? one of the people
might lightly have lien with thy wife, and
thou shouldest have brought guiltiness
upon us.
11 And Abimelech charged all *his* people,
saying, He that toucheth this man or his
wife shall surely be put to death.
12 Then Isaac sowed in that land, and
received in the same year an hundredfold:
and the LORD blessed him.
13 And the man waxed great, and went
forward, and grew until he became very
great:
14 For he had possession of flocks, and
possession of herds, and great store of servants: and the Philistines envied him.
15 For all the wells which his father's servants had digged in the days of Abraham
his father, the Philistines had stopped
them, and filled them with earth.
16 And Abimelech said unto Isaac, Go

from us; for thou art much mightier
than we.
17And Isaac departed thence, and
pitched his tent in the valley of Gerar, and
dwelt there.
18And Isaac digged again the wells of
water, which they had digged in the days
of Abraham his father; for the Philistines
had stopped them after the death of Abraham: and he called their names after the
names by which his father had called
them.
19And Isaac's servants digged in the valley, and found there a well of springing
water.
20And the herdmen of Gerar did strive
with Isaac's herdmen, saying, The water *is*
ours: and he called the name of the well
Esek; because they strove with him.
21And they digged another well, and
strove for that also: and he called the name
of it Sitnah.
22And he removed from thence, and
digged another well; and for that they
strove not: and he called the name of it
Rehoboth; and he said, For now the LORD
hath made room for us, and we shall be
fruitful in the land.
23And he went up from thence to Beer-
sheba.
24And the LORD appeared unto him the
same night, and said, I *am* the God of Abraham thy father: fear not, for I *am* with thee,
and will bless thee, and multiply thy seed
for my servant Abraham's sake.
25And he builded an altar there, and
called upon the name of the LORD and
pitched his tent there: and there Isaac's
servants digged a well.
26Then Abimelech went to him from
Gerar, and Ahuzzath one of his friends,
and Phichol the chief captain of his army.
27And Isaac said unto them, Wherefore
come ye to me, seeing ye hate me, and have
sent me away from you?
28And they said, We saw certainly that
the LORD was with thee: and we said, Let
there be now an oath betwixt us, *even*
betwixt us and thee, and let us make a covenant with thee;
29That thou wilt do us no hurt, as we
have not touched thee, and as we have
done unto thee nothing but good, and
have sent thee away in peace: thou *art* now
the blessed of the LORD.
30And he made them a feast, and they
did eat and drink.
31And they rose up betimes in the morning, and sware one to another: and Isaac
sent them away, and they departed from
him in peace.
32And it came to pass the same day, that
Isaac's servants came, and told him concerning the well which they had digged,
and said unto him, We have found water.
33And he called it Shebah: therefore
the name of the city *is* Beer-sheba unto
this day.
34And Esau was forty years old when he
took to wife Judith the daughter of Beeri
the Hittite, and Bashemath the daughter
of Elon the Hittite:
35Which were a grief of mind unto Isaac
and to Rebekah.

27

1And it came to pass, that when Isaac
was old, and his eyes were dim, so that he
could not see, he called Esau his eldest son,
and said unto him, My son: and he said
unto him, Behold, *here am* I.
2And he said, Behold now, I am old, I
know not the day of my death:
3Now therefore take, I pray thee, thy
weapons, thy quiver and thy bow, and go
out to the field, and take me *some* venison;
4And make me savoury meat, such as I
love, and bring *it* to me, that I may eat;
that my soul may bless thee before I die.
5And Rebekah heard when Isaac spake
to Esau his son. And Esau went to the field
to hunt *for* venison, *and* to bring *it*.
6And Rebekah spake unto Jacob her son,
saying, Behold, I heard thy father speak
unto Esau thy brother, saying,
7Bring me venison, and make me
savoury meat, that I may eat, and bless thee
before the LORD before my death.
8Now therefore, my son, obey my voice
according to that which I command thee.
9Go now to the flock, and fetch me from
thence two good kids of the goats; and I
will make them savoury meat for thy father, such as he loveth:
10And thou shalt bring *it* to thy father,
that he may eat, and that he may bless thee
before his death.
11And Jacob said to Rebekah his mother, Behold, Esau my brother *is* a hairy man,
and I *am* a smooth man:
12My father peradventure will feel me,

and I shall seem to him as a deceiver; and
I shall bring a curse upon me, and not a
blessing.
13 And his mother said unto him, Upon
me *be* thy curse, my son: only obey my
voice, and go fetch me *them*.
14 And he went, and fetched, and brought
them to his mother: and his mother made
savoury meat, such as his father loved.
15 And Rebekah took goodly raiment of
her eldest son Esau, which *were* with her
in the house, and put them upon Jacob
her younger son:
16 And she put the skins of the kids of
the goats upon his hands, and upon the
smooth of his neck:
17 And she gave the savoury meat and the
bread, which she had prepared, into the
hand of her son Jacob.
18 And he came unto his father, and said,
My father: and he said, Here *am* I; who *art*
thou, my son?
19 And Jacob said unto his father, I *am*
Esau thy firstborn; I have done according
as thou badest me: arise, I pray thee, sit
and eat of my venison, that thy soul may
bless me.
20 And Isaac said unto his son, How *is it*
that thou hast found *it* so quickly, my son?
And he said, Because the LORD thy God
brought *it* to me.
21 And Isaac said unto Jacob, Come near,
I pray thee, that I may feel thee, my son,
whether thou *be* my very son Esau or not.
22 And Jacob went near unto Isaac his
father; and he felt him, and said, The voice
is Jacob's voice, but the hands *are* the hands
of Esau.
23 And he discerned him not, because his
hands were hairy, as his brother Esau's
hands: so he blessed him.
24 And he said, *Art* thou my very son
Esau? And he said, I *am*.
25 And he said, Bring *it* near to me, and I
will eat of my son's venison, that my soul
may bless thee. And he brought *it* near to
him, and he did eat: and he brought him
wine, and he drank.
26 And his father Isaac said unto him,
Come near now, and kiss me, my son.
27 And he came near, and kissed him:
and he smelled the smell of his raiment,
and blessed him, and said, See, the smell
of my son *is* as the smell of a field which
the LORD hath blessed:
28 Therefore God give thee of the dew
of heaven, and the fatness of the earth,
and plenty of corn and wine:
29 Let people serve thee, and nations bow
down to thee: be lord over thy brethren,
and let thy mother's sons bow down to
thee: cursed *be* every one that curseth thee,
and blessed *be* he that blesseth thee.
30 And it came to pass, as soon as Isaac
had made an end of blessing Jacob, and
Jacob was yet scarce gone out from the
presence of Isaac his father, that Esau his
brother came in from his hunting.
31 And he also had made savoury meat,
and brought it unto his father, and said
unto his father, Let my father arise, and
eat of his son's venison, that thy soul may
bless me.
32 And Isaac his father said unto him,
Who *art* thou? And he said, I *am* thy son,
thy firstborn Esau.
33 And Isaac trembled very exceedingly,
and said, Who? where *is* he that hath tak-
en venison, and brought *it* me, and I have
eaten of all before thou camest, and have
blessed him? yea, *and* he shall be blessed.
34 And when Esau heard the words of his
father, he cried with a great and exceeding
bitter cry, and said unto his father, Bless
me, *even* me also, O my father.
35 And he said, Thy brother came with
subtilty, and hath taken away thy blessing.
36 And he said,
Is not he rightly
named Jacob? for
he hath supplanted
me these two times:
he took away my
birthright; and, behold, now he hath taken
away my blessing. And he said, Hast thou
not reserved a blessing for me?

27:36 "It's Her Fault!"
◄ Genesis 16:5
Exodus 32:22 ►

37 And Isaac answered and said unto
Esau, Behold, I have made him thy lord,
and all his brethren have I given to him
for servants; and with corn and wine have
I sustained him: and what shall I do now
unto thee, my son?
38 And Esau said unto his father, Hast
thou but one blessing, my father? bless me,
even me also, O my father. And Esau lifted
up his voice, and wept.
39 And Isaac his father answered and said
unto him, Behold, thy dwelling shall be
the fatness of the earth, and of the dew of
heaven from above;

40 And by thy sword shalt thou live, and
shalt serve thy brother; and it shall come
to pass when thou shalt have the dominion, that thou shalt break his yoke from
off thy neck.
41 And Esau hated Jacob because of the
blessing wherewith his father blessed him:
and Esau said in his heart, The days of
mourning for my father are at hand; then
will I slay my brother Jacob.
42 And these words of Esau her elder son
were told to Rebekah: and she sent and
called Jacob her younger son, and said
unto him, Behold, thy brother Esau, as
touching thee, doth comfort himself, *pur-
posing* to kill thee.
43 Now therefore, my son, obey my
voice; and arise, flee thou to Laban my
brother to Haran;
44 And tarry with him a few days, until
thy brother's fury turn away;
45 Until thy brother's anger turn away
from thee, and he forget *that* which thou
hast done to him: then I will send, and
fetch thee from thence: why should I be
deprived also of you both in one day?
46 And Rebekah said to Isaac, I am weary of my life because of the daughters of
Heth: if Jacob take a wife of the daughters
of Heth, such as these *which are* of the
daughters of the land, what good shall my
life do me?

28

1 And Isaac called Jacob, and blessed
him, and charged him, and said unto him,
Thou shalt not take a wife of the daughters of Canaan.
2 Arise, go to Padan-aram, to the house
of Bethuel thy mother's father; and take
thee a wife from thence of the daughters
of Laban thy mother's brother.
3 And God Almighty bless thee, and
make thee fruitful, and multiply thee, that
thou mayest be a multitude of people;
4 And give thee the blessing of Abraham,
to thee, and to thy seed with thee; that thou
mayest inherit the land wherein thou art a
stranger, which God gave unto Abraham.
5 And Isaac sent away Jacob: and he went
to Padan-aram unto Laban, son of Bethuel
the Syrian, the brother of Rebekah, Jacob's
and Esau's mother.
6 When Esau saw that Isaac had blessed
Jacob, and sent him away to Padan-aram,
to take him a wife from thence; and that
as he blessed him he gave him a charge,
saying, Thou shalt not take a wife of the
daughters of Canaan;
7 And that Jacob obeyed his father and
his mother, and was gone to Padan-aram;
8 And Esau seeing that the daughters of
Canaan pleased not Isaac his father;
9 Then went Esau unto Ishmael, and took
unto the wives which he had Mahalath the
daughter of Ishmael Abraham's son, the
sister of Nebajoth, to be his wife.
10 And Jacob went out from Beer-sheba,
and went toward Haran.
11 And he lighted upon a certain place,
and tarried there all night, because the sun
was set; and he took of the stones of that
place, and put *them for* his pillows, and lay
down in that place to sleep.
12 And he dreamed, and behold a ladder set up on the earth, and the top of it
reached to heaven: and behold the angels
of God ascending and descending on it.
13 And, behold, the LORD stood above
it, and said, I *am* the LORD God of Abraham thy father, and the God of Isaac: the
land whereon thou liest, to thee will I give
it, and to thy seed;
14 And thy seed shall be as the dust of
the earth, and thou shalt spread abroad to
the west, and to the east, and to the north,
and to the south: and in thee and in thy
seed shall all the families of the earth be
blessed.
15 And, behold, I *am* with thee, and will
keep thee in all *places* whither thou goest,
and will bring thee again into this land;
for I will not leave thee, until I have done
that which I have spoken to thee of.
16 And Jacob
awaked out of his
sleep, and he said,
Surely the LORD is
in this place; and I
knew *it* not.
17 And he was
afraid, and said,
How dreadful *is*
this place! this *is*
none other but the
house of God, and
this *is* the gate of heaven.

28:16
Devotions
◄ Genesis 28:17-18 ►

28:17-18 Devotions
◄ Genesis 28:16
Exodus 24:4 ►

18 And Jacob rose up early in the morning, and took the stone that he had put *for*
his pillows, and set it up *for* a pillar, and
poured oil upon the top of it.
19 And he called the name of that place

Bethel: but the name of that city *was called*
Luz at the first.
20And Jacob vowed a vow, saying, If God
will be with me, and will keep me in this
way that I go, and will give me bread to
eat, and raiment to put on,
21So that I come again to my father's
house in peace; then shall the LORD be my
God:
22And this stone, which I have set *for* a
pillar, shall be God's house: and of all that
thou shalt give me I will surely give the
tenth unto thee.

29

1Then Jacob went on his journey, and
came into the land of the people of the
east.
2And he looked, and behold a well in
the field, and, lo, there *were* three flocks
of sheep lying by it; for out of that well
they watered the flocks: and a great stone
was upon the well's mouth.
3And thither were all the flocks gathered:
and they rolled the stone from the well's
mouth, and watered the sheep, and put the
stone again upon the well's mouth in his
place.
4And Jacob said unto them, My brethren, whence *be* ye? And they said, Of Haran *are* we.
5And he said unto them, Know ye Laban the son of Nahor? And they said, We
know *him*.
6And he said unto them, *Is* he well? And
they said, *He is* well: and, behold, Rachel
his daughter cometh with the sheep.
7And he said, Lo, *it is* yet high day, neither *is it* time that the cattle should be gathered together: water ye the sheep, and go
and feed *them*.
8And they said, We cannot, until all the
flocks be gathered together, and *till* they
roll the stone from the well's mouth; then
we water the sheep.
9And while he yet spake with them, Rachel came with her father's sheep: for she
kept them.
10And it came to pass, when Jacob saw
Rachel the daughter of Laban his mother's
brother, and the sheep of Laban his
mother's brother, that Jacob went near, and
rolled the stone from the well's mouth,
and watered the flock of Laban his
mother's brother.
11And Jacob kissed Rachel, and lifted up
his voice, and wept.
12And Jacob told Rachel that he *was* her
father's brother, and that he *was* Rebekah's
son: and she ran and told her father.
13And it came to pass, when Laban
heard the tidings of Jacob his sister's son,
that he ran to meet him, and embraced
him, and kissed him, and brought him to
his house. And he told Laban all these
things.
14And Laban said to him, Surely thou
art my bone and my flesh. And he abode
with him the space of a month.
15And Laban said unto Jacob, Because
thou *art* my brother, shouldest thou therefore serve me for nought? tell me, what
shall thy wages *be*?
16And Laban had two daughters: the
name of the elder *was* Leah, and the name
of the younger *was* Rachel.
17Leah *was* tender eyed; but Rachel was
beautiful and well favoured.
18And Jacob loved Rachel; and said, I
will serve thee seven years for Rachel thy
younger daughter.
19And Laban said, *It is* better that I give
her to thee, than that I should give her to
another man: abide with me.
20And Jacob served seven years for Rachel; and they seemed unto him *but* a few
days, for the love he had to her.
21And Jacob said unto Laban, Give *me*
my wife, for my days are fulfilled, that I
may go in unto her.
22And Laban gathered together all the
men of the place, and made a feast.
23And it came to pass in the evening,
that he took Leah his daughter, and
brought her to him; and he went in unto
her.
24And Laban gave unto his daughter
Leah Zilpah his maid *for* an handmaid.
25And it came to pass, that in the morning, behold, it *was* Leah: and he said to
Laban, What *is* this thou hast done unto
me? did not I serve with thee for Rachel?
wherefore then hast thou beguiled me?
26And Laban said, It must not be so
done in our country, to give the younger
before the firstborn.
27Fulfil her week, and we will give thee
this also for the service which thou shalt
serve with me yet seven other years.
28And Jacob did so, and fulfilled her
week: and he gave him Rachel his daughter to wife also.

29 And Laban gave to Rachel his daughter Bilhah his handmaid to be her maid.

30 And he went in also unto Rachel, and he loved also Rachel more than Leah, and served with him yet seven other years.

31 And when the LORD saw that Leah *was* hated, he opened her womb: but Rachel *was* barren.

32 And Leah conceived, and bare a son, and she called his name Reuben: for she said, Surely the LORD hath looked upon my affliction; now therefore my husband will love me.

33 And she conceived again, and bare a son; and said, Because the LORD hath heard that I *was* hated, he hath therefore given me this *son* also: and she called his name Simeon.

34 And she conceived again, and bare a son; and said, Now this time will my husband be joined unto me, because I have born him three sons: therefore was his name called Levi.

35 And she conceived again, and bare a son: and she said, Now will I praise the LORD: therefore she called his name Judah; and left bearing.

30

1 And when Rachel saw that she bare Jacob no children, Rachel envied her sister; and said unto Jacob, Give me children, or else I die.

2 And Jacob's anger was kindled against Rachel: and he said, *Am* I in God's stead, who hath withheld from thee the fruit of the womb?

3 And she said, Behold my maid Bilhah, go in unto her; and she shall bear upon my knees that I may also have children by her.

4 And she gave him Bilhah her handmaid to wife: and Jacob went in unto her.

5 And Bilhah conceived, and bare Jacob a son.

6 And Rachel said, God hath judged me, and hath also heard my voice, and hath given me a son: therefore called she his name Dan.

7 And Bilhah Rachel's maid conceived again, and bare Jacob a second son.

8 And Rachel said, With great wrestlings have I wrestled with my sister, and I have prevailed: and she called his name Naphtali.

9 When Leah saw that she had left bearing, she took Zilpah her maid, and gave her Jacob to wife.

10 And Zilpah Leah's maid bare Jacob a son.

11 And Leah said, A troop cometh: and she called his name Gad.

12 And Zilpah Leah's maid bare Jacob a second son.

13 And Leah said, Happy am I, for the daughters will call me blessed: and she called his name Asher.

14 And Reuben went in the days of wheat harvest, and found mandrakes in the field, and brought them unto his mother Leah. Then Rachel said to Leah, Give me, I pray thee, of thy son's mandrakes.

15 And she said unto her, *Is it* a small matter that thou hast taken my husband? and wouldest thou take away my son's mandrakes also? And Rachel said, Therefore he shall lie with thee to night for thy son's mandrakes.

16 And Jacob came out of the field in the evening, and Leah went out to meet him, and said, Thou must come in unto me; for surely I have hired thee with my son's mandrakes. And he lay with her that night.

17 And God hearkened unto Leah, and she conceived, and bare Jacob the fifth son.

18 And Leah said, God hath given me my hire, because I have given my maiden to my husband: and she called his name Issachar.

19 And Leah conceived again, and bare Jacob the sixth son.

20 And Leah said, God hath endued me *with* a good dowry; now will my husband dwell with me, because I have born him six sons: and she called his name Zebulun.

21 And afterwards she bare a daughter, and called her name Dinah.

22 And God remembered Rachel, and God hearkened to her, and opened her womb.

23 And she conceived, and bare a son; and said, God hath taken away my reproach:

24 And she called his name Joseph; and said, The LORD shall add to me another son.

25 And it came to pass, when Rachel had born Joseph, that Jacob said unto Laban, Send me away, that I may go unto mine own place, and to my country.

26 Give *me* my wives and my children, for whom I have served thee, and let me

go: for thou knowest my service which I have done thee.

27 And Laban said unto him, I pray thee, if I have found favour in thine eyes, *tarry: for* I have learned by experience that the LORD hath blessed me for thy sake.

28 And he said, Appoint me thy wages, and I will give *it.*

29 And he said unto him, Thou knowest how I have served thee, and how thy cattle was with me.

30 For *it was* little which thou hadst before I *came,* and it is *now* increased unto a multitude; and the LORD hath blessed thee since my coming: and now when shall I provide for mine own house also?

31 And he said, What shall I give thee? And Jacob said, Thou shalt not give me any thing: if thou wilt do this thing for me, I will again feed *and* keep thy flock:

32 I will pass through all thy flock to day, removing from thence all the speckled and spotted cattle, and all the brown cattle among the sheep, and the spotted and speckled among the goats: and *of such* shall be my hire.

33 So shall my righteousness answer for me in time to come, when it shall come for my hire before thy face: every one that *is* not speckled and spotted among the goats, and brown among the sheep, that shall be counted stolen with me.

34 And Laban said, Behold, I would it might be according to thy word.

35 And he removed that day the he goats that were ringstraked and spotted, and all the she goats that were speckled and spotted, *and* every one that had *some* white in it, and all the brown among the sheep, and gave *them* into the hand of his sons.

36 And he set three days' journey betwixt himself and Jacob: and Jacob fed the rest of Laban's flocks.

37 And Jacob took him rods of green poplar, and of the hazel and chesnut tree; and pilled white strakes in them, and made the white appear which *was* in the rods.

38 And he set the rods which he had pilled before the flocks in the gutters in the watering troughs when the flocks came to drink, that they should conceive when they came to drink.

39 And the flocks conceived before the rods, and brought forth cattle ringstraked, speckled, and spotted.

40 And Jacob did separate the lambs, and set the faces of the flocks toward the ringstraked, and all the brown in the flock of Laban; and he put his own flocks by themselves, and put them not unto Laban's cattle.

41 And it came to pass, whensoever the stronger cattle did conceive, that Jacob laid the rods before the eyes of the cattle in the gutters, that they might conceive among the rods.

42 But when the cattle were feeble, he put *them* not in: so the feebler were Laban's, and the stronger Jacob's.

43 And the man increased exceedingly, and had much cattle, and maidservants, and menservants, and camels, and asses.

31

1 And he heard the words of Laban's sons, saying, Jacob hath taken away all that *was* our father's; and of *that* which *was* our father's hath he gotten all this glory.

2 And Jacob beheld the countenance of Laban, and, behold, it *was* not toward him as before.

3 And the LORD said unto Jacob, Return unto the land of thy fathers, and to thy kindred; and I will be with thee.

4 And Jacob sent and called Rachel and Leah to the field unto his flock,

5 And said unto them, I see your father's countenance, that it *is* not toward me as before; but the God of my father hath been with me.

6 And ye know that with all my power I have served your father.

7 And your father hath deceived me, and changed my wages ten times; but God suffered him not to hurt me.

8 If he said thus, The speckled shall be thy wages; then all the cattle bare speckled: and if he said thus, The ringstraked shall be thy hire; then bare all the cattle ringstraked.

9 Thus God hath taken away the cattle of your father, and given *them* to me.

10 And it came to pass at the time that the cattle conceived, that I lifted up mine eyes, and saw in a dream, and, behold, the rams which leaped upon the cattle *were* ringstraked, speckled, and grisled.

11 And the angel of God spake unto me in a dream, *saying,* Jacob: And I said, Here *am* I.

12 And he said, Lift up now thine eyes, and see, all the rams which leap upon the

cattle *are* ringstraked, speckled, and grisled: for I have seen all that Laban doeth unto thee.

13 I *am* the God of Bethel, where thou anointedst the pillar, *and* where thou vowedst a vow unto me: now arise, get thee out from this land, and return unto the land of thy kindred.

14 And Rachel and Leah answered and said unto him, *Is there* yet any portion or inheritance for us in our father's house?

15 Are we not counted of him strangers? for he hath sold us, and hath quite devoured also our money.

16 For all the riches which God hath taken from our father, that *is* ours, and our children's: now then, whatsoever God hath said unto thee, do.

17 Then Jacob rose up, and set his sons and his wives upon camels;

18 And he carried away all his cattle, and all his goods which he had gotten, the cattle of his getting, which he had gotten in Padan-aram, for to go to Isaac his father in the land of Canaan.

19 And Laban went to shear his sheep: and Rachel had stolen the images that *were* her father's.

20 And Jacob stole away unawares to Laban the Syrian, in that he told him not that he fled.

21 So he fled with all that he had; and he rose up, and passed over the river, and set his face *toward* the mount Gilead.

22 And it was told Laban on the third day that Jacob was fled.

23 And he took his brethren with him, and pursued after him seven days' journey; and they overtook him in the mount Gilead.

24 And God came to Laban the Syrian in a dream by night, and said unto him, Take heed that thou speak not to Jacob either good or bad.

25 Then Laban overtook Jacob. Now Jacob had pitched his tent in the mount: and Laban with his brethren pitched in the mount of Gilead.

26 And Laban said to Jacob, What hast thou done, that thou hast stolen away unawares to me, and carried away my daughters, as captives *taken* with the sword?

27 Wherefore didst thou flee away secretly, and steal away from me; and didst not tell me, that I might have sent thee away with mirth, and with songs, with tabret, and with harp?

28 And hast not suffered me to kiss my sons and my daughters? thou hast now done foolishly in *so* doing.

29 It is in the power of my hand to do you hurt: but the God of your father spake unto me yesternight, saying, Take thou heed that thou speak not to Jacob either good or bad.

30 And now, *though* thou wouldest needs be gone, because thou sore longedst after thy father's house, *yet* wherefore hast thou stolen my gods?

31 And Jacob answered and said to Laban, Because I was afraid: for I said, Peradventure thou wouldest take by force thy daughters from me.

32 With whomsoever thou findest thy gods, let him not live: before our brethren discern thou what *is* thine with me, and take *it* to thee. For Jacob knew not that Rachel had stolen them.

33 And Laban went into Jacob's tent, and into Leah's tent, and into the two maidservants' tents; but he found *them* not. Then went he out of Leah's tent, and entered into Rachel's tent.

34 Now Rachel had taken the images, and put them in the camel's furniture, and sat upon them. And Laban searched all the tent, but found *them* not.

35 And she said to her father, Let it not displease my lord that I cannot rise up before thee; for the custom of women *is* upon me. And he searched, but found not the images.

36 And Jacob was wroth, and chode with Laban: and Jacob answered and said to Laban, What *is* my trespass? what *is* my sin, that thou hast so hotly pursued after me?

37 Whereas thou hast searched all my stuff, what hast thou found of all thy household stuff? set *it* here before my brethren and thy brethren, that they may judge betwixt us both.

38 This twenty years *have* I *been* with thee; thy ewes and thy she goats have not cast their young, and the rams of thy flock have I not eaten.

39 That which was torn *of beasts* I brought not unto thee; I bare the loss of it; of my hand didst thou require it, *whether* stolen by day, or stolen by night.

40 *Thus* I was; in the day the drought con-

sumed me, and the frost by night; and my
sleep departed from mine eyes.
41 Thus have I been twenty years in thy
house; I served thee fourteen years for thy
two daughters, and six years for thy cattle:
and thou hast changed my wages ten times.
42 Except the God of my father, the God
of Abraham, and the fear of Isaac, had
been with me, surely thou hadst sent me
away now empty. God hath seen mine affliction and the labour of my hands, and
rebuked *thee* yesternight.
43 And Laban answered and said unto
Jacob, *These* daughters *are* my daughters,
and *these* children *are* my children, and
these cattle *are* my cattle, and all that thou
seest *is* mine: and what can I do this day
unto these my daughters, or unto their
children which they have born?
44 Now therefore come thou, let us make
a covenant, I and thou; and let it be for a
witness between me and thee.
45 And Jacob took a stone, and set it up
for a pillar.
46 And Jacob said unto his brethren,
Gather stones; and they took stones, and
made an heap: and they did eat there upon
the heap.
47 And Laban called it Jegar-sahadutha:
but Jacob called it Galeed.
48 And Laban said, This heap *is* a witness
between me and thee this day. Therefore
was the name of it called Galeed;
49 And Mizpah; for he said, The LORD
watch between me and thee, when we are
absent one from another.
50 If thou shalt afflict my daughters, or
if thou shalt take *other* wives beside my
daughters, no man *is* with us; see, God *is*
witness betwixt me and thee.
51 And Laban said to Jacob, Behold this
heap, and behold *this* pillar, which I have
cast betwixt me and thee;
52 This heap *be* witness, and *this* pillar *be*
witness, that I will not pass over this heap
to thee, and that thou shalt not pass over
this heap and this pillar unto me, for harm.
53 The God of Abraham, and the God of
Nahor, the God of their father, judge betwixt us. And Jacob sware by the fear of
his father Isaac.
54 Then Jacob offered sacrifice upon the
mount, and called his brethren to eat
bread: and they did eat bread, and tarried
all night in the mount.
55 And early in the morning Laban rose
up, and kissed his sons and his daughters,
and blessed them: and Laban departed,
and returned unto his place.

32

1 And Jacob went on his way, and the
angels of God met him.
2 And when Jacob saw them, he said,
This *is* God's host: and he called the name
of that place Mahanaim.
3 And Jacob sent messengers before him
to Esau his brother unto the land of Seir,
the country of Edom.
4 And he commanded them, saying, Thus
shall ye speak unto my lord Esau; Thy servant Jacob saith thus, I have sojourned
with Laban, and stayed there until now:
5 And I have oxen, and asses, flocks, and
menservants, and womenservants: and I
have sent to tell my lord, that I may find
grace in thy sight.
6 And the messengers returned to Jacob,
saying, We came to thy brother Esau, and
also he cometh to meet thee, and four
hundred men with him.
7 Then Jacob was greatly afraid and distressed: and he divided the people that *was*
with him, and the flocks, and herds, and
the camels, into two bands;
8 And said, If Esau come to the one company, and smite it, then the other company which is left shall escape.
9 And Jacob said, O God of my father
Abraham, and God of my father Isaac, the
LORD which saidst unto me, Return unto
thy country, and to thy kindred, and I will
deal well with thee:
10 I am not worthy of the least of all the
mercies, and of all the truth, which thou
hast shewed unto thy servant; for with my
staff I passed over this Jordan; and now I
am become two bands.
11 Deliver me, I pray thee, from the hand
of my brother, from the hand of Esau: for
I fear him, lest he will come and smite me,
and the mother with the children.
12 And thou saidst, I will surely do thee
good, and make thy seed as the sand of
the sea, which cannot be numbered for
multitude.
13 And he lodged there that same night;
and took of that which came to his hand a
present for Esau his brother;
14 Two hundred she goats, and twenty
he goats, two hundred ewes, and twenty
rams,

15 Thirty milch camels with their colts, forty kine, and ten bulls, twenty she asses, and ten foals.

16 And he delivered *them* into the hand of his servants, every drove by themselves; and said unto his servants, Pass over before me, and put a space betwixt drove and drove.

17 And he commanded the foremost, saying, When Esau my brother meeteth thee, and asketh thee, saying, Whose *art* thou? and whither goest thou? and whose *are* these before thee?

18 Then thou shalt say, *They be* thy servant Jacob's; it *is* a present sent unto my lord Esau: and, behold, also he *is* behind us.

19 And so commanded he the second, and the third, and all that followed the droves, saying, On this manner shall ye speak unto Esau, when ye find him.

20 And say ye moreover, Behold, thy servant Jacob *is* behind us. For he said, I will appease him with the present that goeth before me, and afterward I will see his face; peradventure he will accept of me.

21 So went the present over before him: and himself lodged that night in the company.

22 And he rose up that night, and took his two wives, and his two womenservants, and his eleven sons, and passed over the ford Jabbok.

23 And he took them, and sent them over the brook, and sent over that he had.

24 And Jacob was left alone; and there wrestled a man with him until the breaking of the day.

25 And when he saw that he prevailed not against him, he touched the hollow of his thigh; and the hollow of Jacob's thigh was out of joint, as he wrestled with him.

26 And he said, Let me go, for the day breaketh. And he said, I will not let thee go, except thou bless me.

27 And he said unto him, What *is* thy name? And he said, Jacob.

28 And he said, Thy name shall be called no more Jacob, but Israel: for as a prince hast thou power with God and with men, and hast prevailed.

29 And Jacob asked *him,* and said, Tell *me,* I pray thee, thy name. And he said, Wherefore *is* it *that* thou dost ask after my name? And he blessed him there.

30 And Jacob called the name of the place Peniel: for I have seen God face to face, and my life is preserved.

31 And as he passed over Penuel the sun rose upon him, and he halted upon his thigh.

32 Therefore the children of Israel eat not *of* the sinew which shrank, which *is* upon the hollow of the thigh, unto this day: because he touched the hollow of Jacob's thigh in the sinew that shrank.

33

1 And Jacob lifted up his eyes, and looked, and, behold, Esau came, and with him four hundred men. And he divided the children unto Leah, and unto Rachel, and unto the two handmaids.

2 And he put the handmaids and their children foremost, and Leah and her children after, and Rachel and Joseph hindermost.

3 And he passed over before them, and bowed himself to the ground seven times, until he came near to his brother.

4 And Esau ran to meet him, and embraced him, and fell on his neck, and kissed him: and they wept.

5 And he lifted up his eyes, and saw the women and the children; and said, Who *are* those with thee? And he said, The children which God hath graciously given thy servant.

6 Then the handmaidens came near, they and their children, and they bowed themselves.

7 And Leah also with her children came near, and bowed themselves: and after came Joseph near and Rachel, and they bowed themselves.

8 And he said, What *meanest* thou by all this drove which I met? And he said, *These are* to find grace in the sight of my lord.

9 And Esau said, I have enough, my brother; keep that thou hast unto thyself.

10 And Jacob said, Nay, I pray thee, if now I have found grace in thy sight, then receive my present at my hand: for therefore I have seen thy face, as though I had seen the face of God, and thou wast pleased with me.

11 Take, I pray thee, my blessing that is brought to thee; because God hath dealt graciously with me, and because I have enough. And he urged him, and he took *it.*

12 And he said, Let us take our journey, and let us go, and I will go before thee.

13 And he said unto him, My lord

knoweth that the children *are* tender, and
the flocks and herds with young *are* with
me: and if men should overdrive them one
day, all the flock will die.
14Let my lord, I pray thee, pass over before his servant: and I will lead on softly,
according as the cattle that goeth before
me and the children be able to endure,
until I come unto my lord unto Seir.
15And Esau said, Let me now leave with
thee *some* of the folk that *are* with me. And
he said, What needeth it? let me find grace
in the sight of my lord.
16So Esau returned that day on his way
unto Seir.
17And Jacob journeyed to Succoth, and
built him an house, and made booths for
his cattle: therefore the name of the place
is called Succoth.
18And Jacob came to Shalem, a city of
Shechem, which *is* in the land of Canaan,
when he came from Padan-aram; and
pitched his tent before the city.
19And he bought a parcel of a field,
where he had spread his tent, at the hand
of the children of Hamor, Shechem's father, for an hundred pieces of money.
20And he erected there an altar, and
called it El-elohe-Israel.

34

1And Dinah the daughter of Leah, which
she bare unto Jacob, went out to see the
daughters of the land.
2And when Shechem the son of Hamor
the Hivite, prince of the country, saw her,
he took her, and lay with her, and defiled
her.
3And his soul clave unto Dinah the
daughter of Jacob, and he loved the damsel, and spake kindly unto the damsel.
4And Shechem spake unto his father
Hamor, saying, Get me this damsel to wife.
5And Jacob heard that he had defiled
Dinah his daughter: now his sons were
with his cattle in the field: and Jacob held
his peace until they were come.
6And Hamor the father of Shechem went
out unto Jacob to commune with him.
7And the sons of Jacob came out of the
field when they heard *it*: and the men were
grieved, and they were very wroth, because
he had wrought folly in Israel in lying with
Jacob's daughter; which thing ought not
to be done.
8And Hamor communed with them,
saying, The soul of my son Shechem
longeth for your daughter: I pray you give
her him to wife.
9And make ye marriages with us, *and*
give your daughters unto us, and take our
daughters unto you.
10And ye shall dwell with us: and the
land shall be before you; dwell and trade
ye therein, and get you possessions therein.
11And Shechem said unto her father and
unto her brethren, Let me find grace in
your eyes, and what ye shall say unto me I
will give.
12Ask me never so much dowry and gift,
and I will give according as ye shall say
unto me: but give me the damsel to wife.
13And the sons of Jacob answered Shechem and Hamor his father deceitfully,
and said, because he had defiled Dinah
their sister:
14And they said unto them, We cannot
do this thing, to give our sister to one that
is uncircumcised; for that *were* a reproach
unto us:
15But in this will we consent unto you:
If ye will be as we *be*, that every male of
you be circumcised;
16Then will we give our daughters unto
you, and we will take your daughters to
us, and we will dwell with you, and we
will become one people.
17But if ye will not hearken unto us, to
be circumcised; then will we take our
daughter, and we will be gone.
18And their words pleased Hamor, and
Shechem Hamor's son.
19And the young man deferred not to
do the thing, because he had delight
in Jacob's daughter: and he *was* more
honourable than all the house of his father.
20And Hamor and Shechem his son
came unto the gate of their city, and communed with the men of their city, saying,
21These men *are* peaceable with us;
therefore let them dwell in the land, and
trade therein; for the land, behold, *it is*
large enough for them; let us take their
daughters to us for wives, and let us give
them our daughters.
22Only herein will the men consent
unto us for to dwell with us, to be one
people, if every male among us be circumcised, as they *are* circumcised.
23*Shall* not their cattle and their substance and every beast of their *be* ours?

only let us consent unto them, and they will dwell with us.

24 And unto Hamor and unto Shechem his son hearkened all that went out of the gate of his city; and every male was circumcised, all that went out of the gate of his city.

25 And it came to pass on the third day, when they were sore, that two of the sons of Jacob, Simeon and Levi, Dinah's brethren, took each man his sword, and came upon the city boldly, and slew all the males.

26 And they slew Hamor and Shechem his son with the edge of the sword, and took Dinah out of Shechem's house, and went out.

27 The sons of Jacob came upon the slain, and spoiled the city, because they had defiled their sister.

28 They took their sheep, and their oxen, and their asses, and that which *was* in the city, and that which *was* in the field,

29 And all their wealth, and all their little ones, and their wives took they captive, and spoiled even all that *was* in the house.

30 And Jacob said to Simeon and Levi, Ye have troubled me to make me to stink among the inhabitants of the land, among the Canaanites and the Perizzites: and I *being* few in number, they shall gather themselves together against me, and slay me; and I shall be destroyed, I and my house.

31 And they said, Should he deal with our sister as with an harlot?

35

1 And God said unto Jacob, Arise, go up to Bethel, and dwell there: and make there an altar unto God, that appeared unto thee when thou fleddest from the face of Esau thy brother.

2 Then Jacob said unto his household, and to all that *were* with him, Put away the strange gods that *are* among you, and be clean, and change your garments:

3 And let us arise, and go up to Bethel; and I will make there an altar unto God, who answered me in the day of my distress, and was with me in the way which I went.

4 And they gave unto Jacob all the strange gods which *were* in their hand, and *all their* earrings which *were* in their ears; and Jacob hid them under the oak which *was* by Shechem.

5 And they journeyed: and the terror of God was upon the cities that *were* round about them, and they did not pursue after the sons of Jacob.

6 So Jacob came to Luz, which *is* in the land of Canaan, that *is*, Bethel, he and all the people that *were* with him.

7 And he built there an altar, and called the place El-beth-el: because there God appeared unto him, when he fled from the face of his brother.

8 But Deborah Rebekah's nurse died, and she was buried beneath Bethel under an oak: and the name of it was called Allon-bachuth.

9 And God appeared unto Jacob again, when he came out of Padan-aram, and blessed him.

10 And God said unto him, Thy name *is* Jacob: thy name shall not be called any more Jacob, but Israel shall be thy name: and he called his name Israel.

11 And God said unto him, I *am* God Almighty: be fruitful and multiply; a nation and a company of nations shall be of thee, and kings shall come out of thy loins;

12 And the land which I gave Abraham and Isaac, to thee I will give it, and to thy seed after thee will I give the land.

13 And God went up from him in the place where he talked with him.

14 And Jacob set up a pillar in the place where he talked with him, *even* a pillar of stone: and he poured a drink offering thereon, and he poured oil thereon.

15 And Jacob called the name of the place where God spake with him, Bethel.

16 And they journeyed from Bethel; and there was but a little way to come to Ephrath: and Rachel travailed, and she had hard labour.

17 And it came to pass, when she was in hard labour, that the midwife said unto her, Fear not; thou shalt have this son also.

18 And it came to pass, as her soul was in departing, (for she died) that she called his name Ben-oni: but his father called him Benjamin.

19 And Rachel died, and was buried in the way to Ephrath, which *is* Bethlehem.

20 And Jacob set a pillar upon her grave: that *is* the pillar of Rachel's grave unto this day.

21 And Israel journeyed, and spread his tent beyond the tower of Edar.

22 And it came to pass, when Israel dwelt in that land, that Reuben went and lay with Bilhah his father's concubine: and Israel heard *it.* Now the sons of Jacob were twelve:

23 The sons of Leah; Reuben, Jacob's firstborn, and Simeon, and Levi, and Judah, and Issachar, and Zebulun:

24 The sons of Rachel; Joseph, and Benjamin:

25 And the sons of Bilhah, Rachel's handmaid; Dan, and Naphtali:

26 And the sons of Zilpah, Leah's handmaid; Gad, and Asher: these *are* the sons of Jacob, which were born to him in Padan-aram.

27 And Jacob came unto Isaac his father unto Mamre, unto the city of Arbah, which *is* Hebron, where Abraham and Isaac sojourned.

28 And the days of Isaac were an hundred and fourscore years.

29 And Isaac gave up the ghost, and died, and was gathered unto his people, *being* old and full of days: and his sons Esau and Jacob buried him.

36

1 Now these *are* the generations of Esau, who *is* Edom.

2 Esau took his wives of the daughters of Canaan; Adah the daughter of Elon the Hittite, and Aholibamah the daughter of Anah the daughter of Zibeon the Hivite;

3 And Bashemath Ishmael's daughter, sister of Nebajoth.

4 And Adah bare to Esau Eliphaz; and Bashemath bare Reuel;

5 And Aholibamah bare Jeush, and Jaalam, and Korah: these *are* the sons of Esau, which were born unto him in the land of Canaan.

6 And Esau took his wives, and his sons, and his daughters, and all the persons of his house, and his cattle, and all his beasts, and all his substance, which he had got in the land of Canaan; and went into the country from the face of his brother Jacob.

7 For their riches were more than that they might dwell together; and the land wherein they were strangers could not bear them because of their cattle.

8 Thus dwelt Esau in mount Seir: Esau *is* Edom.

9 And these *are* the generations of Esau the father of the Edomites in mount Seir:

10 These *are* the names of Esau's sons; Eliphaz the son of Adah the wife of Esau, Reuel the son of Bashemath the wife of Esau.

11 And the sons of Eliphaz were Teman, Omar, Zepho, and Gatam, and Kenaz.

12 And Timna was concubine to Eliphaz Esau's son; and she bare to Eliphaz Amalek: these *were* the sons of Adah Esau's wife.

13 And these *are* the sons of Reuel; Nahath, and Zerah, Shammah, and Mizzah: these were the sons of Bashemath Esau's wife.

14 And these were the sons of Aholibamah, the daughter of Anah the daughter of Zibeon, Esau's wife: and she bare to Esau Jeush, and Jaalam, and Korah.

15 These *were* dukes of the sons of Esau: the sons of Eliphaz the firstborn *son* of Esau; duke Teman, duke Omar, duke Zepho, duke Kenaz,

16 Duke Korah, duke Gatam, *and* duke Amalek: these *are* the dukes *that came* of Eliphaz in the land of Edom; these *were* the sons of Adah.

17 And these *are* the sons of Reuel Esau's son; duke Nahath, duke Zerah, duke Shammah, duke Mizzah: these *are* the dukes *that came* of Reuel in the land of Edom; these *are* the sons of Bashemath Esau's wife.

18 And these *are* the sons of Aholibamah Esau's wife; duke Jeush, duke Jaalam, duke Korah: these *were* the dukes *that came* of Aholibamah the daughter of Anah, Esau's wife.

19 These *are* the sons of Esau, who *is* Edom, and these *are* their dukes.

20 These *are* the sons of Seir the Horite, who inhabited the land; Lotan, and Shobal, and Zibeon, and Anah,

21 And Dishon, and Ezer, and Dishan: these *are* the dukes of the Horites, the children of Seir in the land of Edom.

22 And the children of Lotan were Hori and Hemam; and Lotan's sister *was* Timna.

23 And the children of Shobal *were* these; Alvan, and Manahath, and Ebal, Shepho, and Onam.

24 And these *are* the children of Zibeon; both Ajah, and Anah: this *was that* Anah that found the mules in the wilderness, as he fed the asses of Zibeon his father.

25 And the children of Anah *were* these; Dishon, and Aholibamah the daughter of Anah.

26 And these *are* the children of Dishon; Hemdan, and Eshban, and Ithran, and Cheran.

27 The children of Ezer *are* these; Bilhan, and Zaavan, and Akan.

28 The children of Dishan *are* these: Uz, and Aran.

29 These *are* the dukes *that came* of the Horites; duke Lotan, duke Shobal, duke Zibeon, duke Anah,

30 Duke Dishon, duke Ezer, duke Dishan: these *are* the dukes *that came* of Hori, among their dukes in the land of Seir.

31 And these *are* the kings that reigned in the land of Edom, before there reigned any king over the children of Israel.

32 And Bela the son of Beor reigned in Edom: and the name of his city *was* Dinhabah.

33 And Bela died, and Jobab the son of Zerah of Bozrah reigned in his stead.

34 And Jobab died, and Husham of the land of Temani reigned in his stead.

35 And Husham died, and Hadad the son of Bedad, who smote Midian in the field of Moab, reigned in his stead: and the name of his city *was* Avith.

36 And Hadad died, and Samlah of Masrekah reigned in his stead.

37 And Samlah died, and Saul of Rehoboth *by* the river reigned in his stead.

38 And Saul died, and Baal-hanan the son of Achbor reigned in his stead.

39 And Baal-hanan the son of Achbor died, and Hadar reigned in his stead: and the name of his city *was* Pau; and his wife's name *was* Mehetabel, the daughter of Matred, the daughter of Mezahab.

40 And these *are* the names of the dukes *that came* of Esau, according to their families, after their places, by their names; duke Timnah, duke Alvah, duke Jetheth,

41 Duke Aholibamah, duke Elah, duke Pinon,

42 Duke Kenaz, duke Teman, duke Mibzar,

43 Duke Magdiel, duke Iram: these *be* the dukes of Edom, according to their habitations in the land of their possession: he *is* Esau the father of the Edomites.

37

1 And Jacob dwelt in the land wherein his father was a stranger, in the land of Canaan.

2 These *are* the generations of Jacob. Joseph, *being* seventeen years old, was feeding the flock with his brethren; and the lad *was* with the sons of Bilhah, and with the sons of Zilpah, his father's wives: and Joseph brought unto his father their evil report.

3 Now Israel loved Joseph more than all his children, because he *was* the son of his old age: and he made him a coat of *many* colours.

4 And when his brethren saw that their father loved him more than all his brethren, they hated him, and could not speak peaceably unto him.

5 And Joseph dreamed a dream, and he told *it* his brethren: and they hated him yet the more.

6 And he said unto them, Hear, I pray you, this dream which I have dreamed:

7 For, behold, we *were* binding sheaves in the field, and, lo, my sheaf arose, and also stood upright; and, behold, your sheaves stood round about, and made obeisance to my sheaf.

8 And his brethren said to him, Shalt thou indeed reign over us? or shalt thou indeed have dominion over us? And they hated him yet the more for his dreams, and for his words.

9 And he dreamed yet another dream, and told it his brethren, and said, Behold, I have dreamed a dream more; and, behold, the sun and the moon and the eleven stars made obeisance to me.

10 And he told *it* to his father, and to his brethren: and his father rebuked him, and said unto him, What *is* this dream that thou hast dreamed? Shall I and thy mother and thy brethren indeed come to bow down ourselves to thee to the earth?

11 And his brethren envied him; but his father observed the saying.

12 And his brethren went to feed their father's flock in Shechem.

13 And Israel said unto Joseph, Do not thy brethren feed *the flock* in Shechem? come, and I will send thee unto them. And he said to him, Here *am* I.

14 And he said to him, Go, I pray thee, see whether it be well with thy brethren, and well with the flocks; and bring me word again. So he sent him out of the vale of Hebron, and he came to Shechem.

37:14
Parents Care
◄ 1 Samuel 10:2 ►

15 And a certain man found him, and, behold, *he was* wandering in the field: and the man asked him, saying, What seekest thou?

16 And he said, I seek my brethren: tell me, I pray thee, where they feed *their flocks.*

17 And the man said, They are departed hence; for I heard them say, Let us go to Dothan. And Joseph went after his brethren, and found them in Dothan.

18 And when they saw him afar off, even before he came near unto them, they conspired against him to slay him.

19 And they said one to another, Behold, this dreamer cometh.

20 Come now therefore, and let us slay him, and cast him into some pit, and we will say, Some evil beast hath devoured him: and we shall see what will become of his dreams.

21 And Reuben heard *it,* and he delivered him out of their hands; and said, Let us not kill him.

37:21
Helping Friends
◄ Genesis 37:26 ►

22 And Reuben said unto them, Shed no blood, *but* cast him into this pit that *is* in the wilderness, and lay no hand upon him; that he might rid him out of their hands, to deliver him to his father again.

23 And it came to pass, when Joseph was come unto his brethren, that they stript Joseph out of his coat, *his* coat of *many* colours that *was* on him;

24 And they took him, and cast him into a pit: and the pit *was* empty, *there was* no water in it.

25 And they sat down to eat bread: and they lifted up their eyes and looked, and, behold, a company of Ishmeelites came from Gilead with their camels bearing spicery and balm and myrrh, going to carry *it* down to Egypt.

26 And Judah said unto his brethren, What profit *is it* if we slay our brother, and conceal his blood?

37:26 Helping Friends
◄ Genesis 37:21
Genesis 44:33 ►

27 Come, and let us sell him to the Ishmeelites, and let not our hand be upon him; for he *is* our brother *and* our flesh. And his brethren were content.

28 Then there passed by Midianites merchantmen; and they drew and lifted up Joseph out of the pit, and sold Joseph to the Ishmeelites for twenty *pieces* of silver: and they brought Joseph into Egypt.

29 And Reuben returned unto the pit; and, behold, Joseph *was* not in the pit; and he rent his clothes.

30 And he returned unto his brethren, and said, The child *is* not; and I, whither shall I go?

31 And they took Joseph's coat, and killed a kid of the goats, and dipped the coat in the blood;

32 And they sent the coat of *many* colours, and they brought *it* to their father; and said, This have we found: know now whether it *be* thy son's coat or no.

33 And he knew it, and said, *It is* my son's coat; an evil beast hath devoured him; Joseph is without doubt rent in pieces.

34 And Jacob rent his clothes, and put sackcloth upon his loins, and mourned for his son many days.

35 And all his sons and all his daughters rose up to comfort him; but he refused to be comforted; and he said, For I will go down into the grave unto my son mourning. Thus his father wept for him.

37:35 Grief
◄ Genesis 23:2
Genesis 42:38 ►

36 And the Midianites sold him into Egypt unto Potiphar, an officer of Pharaoh's, *and* captain of the guard.

38

1 And it came to pass at that time, that Judah went down from his brethren, and turned in to a certain Adullamite, whose name *was* Hirah.

2 And Judah saw there a daughter of a certain Canaanite, whose name *was* Shuah; and he took her, and went in unto her.

3 And she conceived, and bare a son; and he called his name Er.

4 And she conceived again, and bare a son; and she called his name Onan.

5 And she yet again conceived, and bare a son; and called his name Shelah: and he was at Chezib, when she bare him.

6 And Judah took a wife for Er his firstborn, whose name *was* Tamar.

7 And Er, Judah's firstborn, was wicked in the sight of the LORD; and the LORD slew him.

8 And Judah said unto Onan, Go in unto

thy brother's wife, and marry her, and raise up seed to thy brother.

9 And Onan knew that the seed should not be his; and it came to pass, when he went in unto his brother's wife, that he spilled *it* on the ground, lest that he should give seed to his brother.

10 And the thing which he did displeased the LORD: wherefore he slew him also.

11 Then said Judah to Tamar his daughter in law, Remain a widow at thy father's house, till Shelah my son be grown: for he said, Lest peradventure he die also, as his brethren *did*. And Tamar went and dwelt in her father's house.

12 And in process of time the daughter of Shuah Judah's wife died; and Judah was comforted, and went up unto his sheepshearers to Timnath, he and his friend Hirah the Adullamite.

13 And it was told Tamar, saying, Behold thy father in law goeth up to Timnath to shear his sheep.

14 And she put her widow's garments off from her, and covered her with a vail, and wrapped herself, and sat in an open place, which *is* by the way to Timnath; for she saw that Shelah was grown, and she was not given unto him to wife.

15 When Judah saw her, he thought her *to be* an harlot; because she had covered her face.

16 And he turned unto her by the way, and said, Go to, I pray thee, let me come in unto thee; (for he knew not that she *was* his daughter in law.) And she said, What wilt thou give me, that thou mayest come in unto me?

17 And he said, I will send *thee* a kid from the flock. And she said, Wilt thou give *me* a pledge, till thou send *it*?

18 And he said, What pledge shall I give thee? And she said, Thy signet, and thy bracelets, and thy staff that *is* in thine hand. And he gave *it* her, and came in unto her, and she conceived by him.

19 And she arose, and went away, and laid by her vail from her, and put on the garments of her widowhood.

20 And Judah sent the kid by the hand of his friend the Adullamite, to receive *his* pledge from the woman's hand: but he found her not.

21 Then he asked the men of that place, saying, Where *is* the harlot, that *was* openly by the way side? And they said, There was no harlot in this *place*.

22 And he returned to Judah, and said, I cannot find her; and also the men of the place said, *that* there was no harlot in this *place*.

23 And Judah said, Let her take *it* to her, lest we be shamed: behold, I sent this kid, and thou hast not found her.

24 And it came to pass about three months after, that it was told Judah, saying, Tamar thy daughter in law hath played the harlot; and also, behold, she *is* with child by whoredom. And Judah said, Bring her forth, and let her be burnt.

25 When she *was* brought forth, she sent to her father in law, saying, By the man, whose these *are*, *am* I with child: and she said, Discern, I pray thee, whose *are* these, the signet, and bracelets, and staff.

26 And Judah acknowledged *them*, and said, She hath been more righteous than I; because that I gave her not to Shelah my son. And he knew her again no more.

27 And it came to pass in the time of her travail, that, behold, twins *were* in her womb.

28 And it came to pass, when she travailed, that *the one* put out *his* hand: and the midwife took and bound upon his hand a scarlet thread, saying, This came out first.

29 And it came to pass, as he drew back his hand, that, behold, his brother came out: and she said, How hast thou broken forth? *this* breach *be* upon thee: therefore his name was called Pharez.

30 And afterward came out his brother, that had the scarlet thread upon his hand: and his name was called Zarah.

39

1 And Joseph was brought down to Egypt; and Potiphar, an officer of Pharaoh, captain of the guard, an Egyptian, bought him of the hands of the Ishmeelites, which had brought him down thither.

2 And the LORD was with Joseph, and he was a prosperous man; and he was in the house of his master the Egyptian.

3 And his master saw that the LORD *was* with him, and that the LORD made all that he did to prosper in his hand.

4 And Joseph found grace in his sight, and he served him: and he made him overseer over his house, and all *that* he had he put into his hand.

5 And it came to pass from the time *that* he had made him overseer in his house, and over all that he had, that the LORD blessed the Egyptian's house for Joseph's sake; and the blessing of the LORD was upon all that he had in the house, and in the field.

6 And he left all that he had in Joseph's hand; and he knew not ought he had, save the bread which he did eat. And Joseph was *a* goodly *person,* and well favoured.

7 And it came to pass after these things, that his master's wife cast her eyes upon Joseph; and she said, Lie with me.

8 But he refused, and said unto his master's wife, Behold, my master wotteth not what *is* with me in the house, and he hath committed all that he hath to my hand;

9 *There is* none greater in this house than I; neither hath he kept back any thing from me but thee, because thou *art* his wife: how then can I do this great wickedness, and sin against God?

10 And it came to pass, as she spake to Joseph day by day, that he hearkened not unto her, to lie by her, *or* to be with her.

11 And it came to pass about this time, that *Joseph* went into the house to do his business; and *there was* none of the men of the house there within.

12 And she caught him by his garment, saying, Lie with me: and he left his garment in her hand, and fled, and got him out.

13 And it came to pass, when she saw that he had left his garment in her hand, and was fled forth,

14 That she called unto the men of her house, and spake unto them, saying, See, he hath brought in an Hebrew unto us to mock us; he came in unto me to lie with me, and I cried with a loud voice:

15 And it came to pass, when he heard that I lifted up my voice and cried, that he left his garment with me, and fled, and got him out.

16 And she laid up his garment by her, until his lord came home.

17 And she spake unto him according to these words, saying, The Hebrew servant, which thou hast brought unto us, came in unto me to mock me:

18 And it came to pass, as I lifted up my voice and cried, that he left his garment with me, and fled out.

19 And it came to pass, when his master heard the words of his wife, which she spake unto him, saying, After this manner did thy servant to me; that his wrath was kindled.

20 And Joseph's master took him, and put him into the prison, a place where the king's prisoners *were* bound: and he was there in the prison.

21 But the LORD was with Joseph, and shewed him mercy, and gave him favour in the sight of the keeper of the prison.

22 And the keeper of the prison committed to Joseph's hand all the prisoners that *were* in the prison; and whatsoever they did there, he was the doer *of it.*

23 The keeper of the prison looked not to any thing *that was* under his hand; because the LORD was with him, and *that* which he did, the LORD made *it* to prosper.

40

1 And it came to pass after these things, *that* the butler of the king of Egypt and *his* baker had offended their lord the king of Egypt.

2 And Pharaoh was wroth against two *of* his officers, against the chief of the butlers, and against the chief of the bakers.

3 And he put them in ward in the house of the captain of the guard, into the prison, the place where Joseph *was* bound.

4 And the captain of the guard charged Joseph with them, and he served them: and they continued a season in ward.

5 And they dreamed a dream both of them, each man his dream in one night, each man according to the interpretation of his dream, the butler and the baker of the king of Egypt, which *were* bound in the prison.

6 And Joseph came in unto them in the morning, and looked upon them, and, behold, they *were* sad.

7 And he asked Pharaoh's officers that *were* with him in the ward of his lord's house, saying, Wherefore look ye *so* sadly to day?

8 And they said unto him, We have dreamed a dream, and *there is* no interpreter of it. And Joseph said unto them, *Do* not interpretations *belong* to God? tell me *them,* I pray you.

9 And the chief butler told his dream to Joseph, and said to him, In my dream, behold, a vine *was* before me;

10And in the vine *were* three branches:
and it *was* as though it budded, *and* her
blossoms shot forth; and the clusters
thereof brought forth ripe grapes:
11And Pharaoh's cup *was* in my hand:
and I took the grapes, and pressed them
into Pharaoh's cup, and I gave the cup into
Pharaoh's hand.
12And Joseph said unto him, This *is* the
interpretation of it: The three branches *are*
three days:
13Yet within three days shall Pharaoh lift
up thine head, and restore thee unto thy
place: and thou shalt deliver Pharaoh's cup
into his hand, after the former manner
when thou wast his butler.
14But think on me when it shall be well
with thee, and shew kindness, I pray
thee, unto me, and make mention of me
unto Pharaoh, and bring me out of this
house:
15For indeed I was stolen away out of
the land of the Hebrews: and here also
have I done nothing that they should put
me into the dungeon.
16When the chief baker saw that the interpretation was good, he said unto Joseph, I also *was* in my dream, and, behold,
I had three white baskets on my head:
17And in the uppermost basket *there was*
of all manner of bakemeats for Pharaoh;
and the birds did eat them out of the basket upon my head.
18And Joseph answered and said, This
is the interpretation thereof: The three baskets *are* three days:
19Yet within three days shall Pharaoh lift
up thy head from off thee, and shall hang
thee on a tree; and the birds shall eat thy
flesh from off thee.
20And it came to pass the third day,
which was Pharaoh's birthday, that he made
a feast unto all his servants: and he lifted
up the head of the chief butler and of the
chief baker among his servants.
21And he restored the chief butler unto
his butlership again; and he gave the cup
into Pharaoh's hand:
22But he hanged the chief baker: as
Joseph had inter-
preted to them.
23Yet did not the
chief butler remem-
ber Joseph, but for-
gat him.

40:23 Unthankfulness to People
◄ Numbers 16:13 ►

41

1And it came to pass at the end of two
full years, that Pharaoh dreamed: and,
behold, he stood by the river.
2And, behold, there came up out of the
river seven well favoured kine and fatfleshed; and they fed in a meadow.
3And, behold, seven other kine came up
after them out of the river, ill favoured and
leanfleshed; and stood by the *other* kine
upon the brink of the river.
4And the ill favoured and leanfleshed
kine did eat up the seven well favoured and
fat kine. So Pharaoh awoke.
5And he slept and dreamed the second
time: and, behold, seven ears of corn came
up upon one stalk, rank and good.
6And, behold, seven thin ears and
blasted with the east wind sprung up after
them.
7And the seven thin ears devoured the
seven rank and full ears. And Pharaoh
awoke, and, behold, *it was* a dream.
8And it came to pass in the morning that
his spirit was troubled; and he sent and
called for all the magicians of Egypt, and
all the wise men thereof: and Pharaoh told
them his dream; but *there was* none that
could interpret them unto Pharaoh.
9Then spake the
chief butler unto
Pharaoh, saying, I
do remember my
faults this day:
10Pharaoh was
wroth with his servants, and put me in
ward in the captain of the guard's house,
both me and the chief baker:
11And we dreamed a dream in one night,
I and he; we dreamed each man according
to the interpretation of his dream.
12And *there was* there with us a young
man, an Hebrew, servant to the captain of
the guard; and we told him, and he interpreted to us our dreams; to each man according to his dream he did interpret.
13And it came to pass, as he interpreted
to us, so it was; me he restored unto mine
office, and him he hanged.
14Then Pharaoh sent and called Joseph,
and they brought him hastily out of the
dungeon: and he shaved *himself*, and
changed his raiment, and came in unto
Pharaoh.
15And Pharaoh said unto Joseph, I have
dreamed a dream, and *there is* none that

41:9 Mistakes
◄
Deuteronomy 9:7 ►

can interpret it: and I have heard say of
thee, *that* thou canst understand a dream
to interpret it.
16And Joseph answered Pharaoh, saying,
It is not in me: God shall give Pharaoh an
answer of peace.
17And Pharaoh said unto Joseph, In my
dream, behold, I stood upon the bank of
the river:
18And, behold, there came up out of
the river seven kine, fatfleshed and well
favoured; and they fed in a meadow:
19And, behold, seven other kine came
up after them, poor and very ill favoured
and leanfleshed, such as I never saw in all
the land of Egypt for badness:
20And the lean and the ill favoured kine
did eat up the first seven fat kine:
21And when they had eaten them up, it
could not be known that they had eaten
them; but they *were* still ill favoured, as at
the beginning. So I awoke.
22And I saw in my dream, and, behold,
seven ears came up in one stalk, full and
good:
23And, behold, seven ears, withered,
thin, *and* blasted with the east wind,
sprung up after them:
24And the thin ears devoured the seven
good ears: and I told *this* unto the magicians; but *there was* none that could declare *it* to me.
25And Joseph said unto Pharaoh, The
dream of Pharaoh *is* one: God hath shewed
Pharaoh what he *is* about to do.
26The seven good kine *are* seven years;
and the seven good ears *are* seven years:
the dream *is* one.
27And the seven thin and ill favoured
kine that came up after them *are* seven
years; and the seven empty ears blasted
with the east wind shall be seven years of
famine.
28This *is* the thing which I have spoken
unto Pharaoh: What God *is* about to do
he sheweth unto Pharaoh.
29Behold, there come seven years of great
plenty throughout all the land of Egypt:
30And there shall arise after them seven
years of famine; and all the plenty shall
be forgotten in the land of Egypt; and the
famine shall consume the land;
31And the plenty shall not be known in
the land by reason of that famine following; for it *shall be* very grievous.
32And for that the dream was doubled
unto Pharaoh twice; *it is* because the thing
is established by God, and God will shortly bring it to pass.
33Now therefore let Pharaoh look out a
man discreet and wise, and set him over
the land of Egypt.
34Let Pharaoh do *this*, and let him appoint officers over the land, and take up
the fifth part of the land of Egypt in the
seven plenteous years.
35And let them
gather all the food
of those good years
that come, and lay
up corn under the
hand of Pharaoh,
and let them keep food in the cities.

41:35-36
Being Frugal
◄ Proverbs 21:20 ►

36And that food shall be for store to the
land against the seven years of famine,
which shall be in the land of Egypt; that
the land perish not through the famine.
37And the thing was good in the eyes of
Pharaoh, and in the eyes of all his servants.
38And Pharaoh
said unto his ser-
vants, Can we find
such a one as this *is*,
a man in whom the
Spirit of God *is*?

41:38
Young Men
◄ Genesis 41:46 ►

39And Pharaoh
said unto Joseph,
Forasmuch as God
hath shewed thee
all this, *there is* none
so discreet and wise
as thou *art*:

41:39
Discretion
◄ Proverbs 2:11 ►

40Thou shalt be over my house, and according unto thy word shall all my people
be ruled: only in the throne will I be greater
than thou.
41And Pharaoh said unto Joseph, See, I
have set thee over all the land of Egypt.
42And Pharaoh took off his ring from
his hand, and put it upon Joseph's hand,
and arrayed him in vestures of fine linen,
and put a gold chain about his neck;
43And he made him to ride in the second chariot which he had; and they cried
before him, Bow the knee: and he made
him *ruler* over all the land of Egypt.
44And Pharaoh said unto Joseph, I *am*
Pharaoh, and without thee shall no man
lift up his hand or foot in all the land of
Egypt.

45 And Pharaoh called Joseph's name Zaphnath-paaneah; and he gave him to wife Asenath the daughter of Poti-pherah priest of On. And Joseph went out over *all* the land of Egypt.

46 And Joseph *was* thirty years old when he stood before Pharaoh king of Egypt. And Joseph went out from the presence of Pharaoh, and went throughout all the land of Egypt.

41:46
Young Leaders
◄ 1 Samuel 17:33 ►

41:46 Young Men
◄ Genesis 41:38
1 Samuel 2:26 ►

47 And in the seven plenteous years the earth brought forth by handfuls.

48 And he gathered up all the food of the seven years, which were in the land of Egypt, and laid up the food in the cities: the food of the field, which *was* round about every city, laid he up in the same.

49 And Joseph gathered corn as the sand of the sea, very much, until he left numbering; for *it was* without number.

50 And unto Joseph were born two sons before the years of famine came, which Asenath the daughter of Poti-pherah priest of On bare unto him.

51 And Joseph called the name of the firstborn Manasseh: For God, *said he,* hath made me forget all my toil, and all my father's house.

52 And the name of the second called he Ephraim: For God hath caused me to be fruitful in the land of my affliction.

53 And the seven years of plenteousness, that was in the land of Egypt, were ended.

54 And the seven years of dearth began to come, according as Joseph had said: and the dearth was in all lands; but in all the land of Egypt there was bread.

55 And when all the land of Egypt was famished, the people cried to Pharaoh for bread: and Pharaoh said unto all the Egyptians, Go unto Joseph; what he saith to you, do.

56 And the famine was over all the face of the earth: and Joseph opened all the storehouses, and sold unto the Egyptians; and the famine waxed sore in the land of Egypt.

57 And all countries came into Egypt to Joseph for to buy *corn;* because that the famine was so sore in all lands.

42

1 Now when Jacob saw that there was corn in Egypt, Jacob said unto his sons, Why do ye look one upon another?

2 And he said, Behold, I have heard that there is corn in Egypt: get you down thither, and buy for us from thence; that we may live, and not die.

3 And Joseph's ten brethren went down to buy corn in Egypt.

4 But Benjamin, Joseph's brother, Jacob sent not with his brethren; for he said, Lest peradventure mischief befall him.

5 And the sons of Israel came to buy *corn* among those that came: for the famine was in the land of Canaan.

6 And Joseph *was* the governor over the land, *and* he *it was* that sold to all the people of the land: and Joseph's brethren came, and bowed down themselves before him *with* their faces to the earth.

7 And Joseph saw his brethren, and he knew them, but made himself strange unto them, and spake roughly unto them; and he said unto them, Whence come ye? And they said, From the land of Canaan to buy food.

8 And Joseph knew his brethren, but they knew not him.

9 And Joseph remembered the dreams which he dreamed of them, and said unto them, Ye *are* spies; to see the nakedness of the land ye are come.

10 And they said unto him, Nay, my lord, but to buy food are thy servants come.

11 We *are* all one man's sons; we *are* true *men,* thy servants are no spies.

12 And he said unto them, Nay, but to see the nakedness of the land ye are come.

13 And they said, Thy servants *are* twelve brethren, the sons of one man in the land of Canaan; and, behold, the youngest *is* this day with our father, and one *is* not.

14 And Joseph said unto them, That *is it* that I spake unto you, saying, Ye *are* spies:

15 Hereby ye shall be proved: By the life of Pharaoh ye shall not go forth hence, except your youngest brother come hither.

16 Send one of you, and let him fetch your brother, and ye shall be kept in prison, that your words may be proved, whether *there be any* truth in you: or else by the life of Pharaoh surely ye *are* spies.

17And he put them all together into ward three days.

18And Joseph said unto them the third day, This do, and live; *for* I fear God:

19If ye *be* true *men,* let one of your brethren be bound in the house of your prison: go ye, carry corn for the famine of your houses:

20But bring your youngest brother unto me; so shall your words be verified, and ye shall not die. And they did so.

21And they said one to another, We *are* verily guilty concerning our brother, in that we saw the anguish of his soul, when he besought us, and we would not hear; therefore is this distress come upon us.

> **42:21**
> **Feeling Guilty**
> ◄ Exodus 9:27 ►

> **42:21**
> **Guilty Conscience**
> ◄ Exodus 9:27 ►

22And Reuben answered them, saying, Spake I not unto you, saying, Do not sin against the child; and ye would not hear? therefore, behold, also his blood is required.

23And they knew not that Joseph understood *them;* for he spake unto them by an interpreter.

24And he turned himself about from them, and wept; and returned to them again, and communed with them, and took from them Simeon, and bound him before their eyes.

25Then Joseph commanded to fill their sacks with corn, and to restore every man's money into his sack, and to give them provision for the way: and thus did he unto them.

26And they laded their asses with the corn, and departed thence.

27And as one of them opened his sack to give his ass provender in the inn, he espied his money; for, behold, it *was* in his sack's mouth.

28And he said unto his brethren, My money is restored; and, lo, *it is* even in my sack: and their heart failed *them,* and they were afraid, saying one to another, What *is* this *that* God hath done unto us?

29And they came unto Jacob their father unto the land of Canaan, and told him all that befell unto them; saying,

30The man, *who is* the lord of the land, spake roughly to us, and took us for spies of the country.

31And we said unto him, We *are* true *men;* we are no spies:

32We *be* twelve brethren, sons of our father; one *is* not, and the youngest *is* this day with our father in the land of Canaan.

33And the man, the lord of the country, said unto us, Hereby shall I know that ye *are* true *men;* leave one of your brethren *here* with me, and take *food for* the famine of your households, and be gone:

34And bring your youngest brother unto me: then shall I know that ye *are* no spies, but *that* ye *are* true *men: so* will I deliver you your brother, and ye shall traffick in the land.

35And it came to pass as they emptied their sacks, that, behold, every man's bundle of money *was* in his sack: and when *both* they and their father saw the bundles of money, they were afraid.

36And Jacob their father said unto them, Me have ye bereaved *of my children:* Joseph *is* not, and Simeon *is* not, and ye will take Benjamin *away:* all these things are against me.

37And Reuben spake unto his father, saying, Slay my two sons, if I bring him not to thee: deliver him into my hand, and I will bring him to thee again.

38And he said, My son shall not go down with you; for his brother is dead, and he is left alone: if mischief befall him by the way in the which ye go, then shall ye bring down my gray hairs with sorrow to the grave.

> **42:38 Grief**
> ◄ Genesis 37:35
> Judges 21:2 ►

43

1And the famine *was* sore in the land.

2And it came to pass, when they had eaten up the corn which they had brought out of Egypt, their father said unto them, Go again, buy us a little food.

3And Judah spake unto him, saying, The man did solemnly protest unto us, saying, Ye shall not see my face, except your brother *be* with you.

4If thou wilt send our brother with us, we will go down and buy thee food:

5But if thou wilt not send *him,* we will not go down: for the man said unto us, Ye shall not see my face, except your brother *be* with you.

6And Israel said, Wherefore dealt ye *so*
ill with me, *as* to tell the man whether ye
had yet a brother?
7And they said, The man asked us straitly
of our state, and of our kindred, saying, *Is*
your father yet alive? have ye *another*
brother? and we told him according to the
tenor of these words: could we certainly
know that he would say, Bring your
brother down?
8And Judah said unto Israel his father,
Send the lad with me, and we will arise
and go; that we may live, and not die, both
we, and thou, *and* also our little ones.
9I will be surety for him; of my hand
shalt thou require him: if I bring him not
unto thee, and set him before thee, then
let me bear the blame for ever:
10For except we had lingered, surely now
we had returned this second time.
11And their father Israel said unto them,
If *it must be* so now, do this; take of the
best fruits in the land in your vessels, and
carry down the man a present, a little balm,
and a little honey, spices, and myrrh, nuts,
and almonds:
12And take double money in your hand;
and the money that was brought again in
the mouth of your sacks, carry *it* again in
your hand; peradventure it *was* an oversight:
13Take also your brother, and arise, go
again unto the man:
14And God Almighty give you mercy
before the man, that he may send away
your other brother, and Benjamin. If I be
bereaved *of my children,* I am bereaved.
15And the men took that present, and
they took double money in their hand, and
Benjamin; and rose up, and went down to
Egypt, and stood before Joseph.
16And when Joseph saw Benjamin with
them, he said to the ruler of his house,
Bring *these* men home, and slay, and make
ready; for *these* men shall dine with me at
noon.
17And the man did as Joseph bade; and
the man brought the men into Joseph's
house.
18And the men were afraid, because they
were brought into Joseph's house; and they
said, Because of the money that was returned in our sacks at the first time are we
brought in; that he may seek occasion
against us, and fall upon us, and take us
for bondmen, and our asses.
19And they came near to the steward of
Joseph's house, and they communed with
him at the door of the house,
20And said, O sir, we came indeed down
at the first time to buy food:
21And it came to pass, when we came to
the inn, that we opened our sacks, and,
behold, *every* man's money *was* in the
mouth of his sack, our money in full
weight: and we have brought it again in
our hand.
22And other money have we brought
down in our hands to buy food: we cannot tell who put our money in our sacks.
23And he said, Peace *be* to you, fear not:
your God, and the God of your father, hath
given you treasure in your sacks: I had your
money. And he brought Simeon out unto
them.
24And the man brought the men into
Joseph's house, and gave *them* water, and
they washed their feet; and he gave their
asses provender.
25And they made ready the present
against Joseph came at noon: for they
heard that they should eat bread there.
26And when Joseph came home, they
brought him the present which *was* in their
hand into the house, and bowed themselves to him to the earth.
27And he asked them of *their* welfare,
and said, *Is* your father well, the old man
of whom ye spake? *Is* he yet alive?
28And they answered, Thy servant our
father *is* in good health, he *is* yet alive. And
they bowed down their heads, and made
obeisance.
29And he lifted up his eyes, and saw his
brother Benjamin, his mother's son, and
said, *Is* this your younger brother, of whom
ye spake unto me? And he said, God be
gracious unto thee, my son.
30And Joseph made haste; for his bowels did yearn upon his brother: and he
sought *where* to weep; and he entered into
his chamber, and wept there.
31And he washed his face, and went out,
and refrained himself, and said, Set on
bread.
32And they set on for him by himself,
and for them by themselves, and for the
Egyptians, which did eat with him, by
themselves: because the Egyptians might
not eat bread with the Hebrews; for that *is*
an abomination unto the Egyptians.

33 And they sat before him, the firstborn according to his birthright, and the youngest according to his youth: and the men marvelled one at another.

34 And he took *and sent* messes unto them from before him: but Benjamin's mess was five times so much as any of theirs. And they drank, and were merry with him.

44

1 And he commanded the steward of his house, saying, Fill the men's sacks *with* food, as much as they can carry, and put every man's money in his sack's mouth.

2 And put my cup, the silver cup, in the sack's mouth of the youngest, and his corn money. And he did according to the word that Joseph had spoken.

3 As soon as the morning was light, the men were sent away, they and their asses.

4 *And* when they were gone out of the city, *and* not *yet* far off, Joseph said unto his steward, Up, follow after the men; and when thou dost overtake them, say unto them, Wherefore have ye rewarded evil for good?

5 *Is* not this *it* in which my lord drinketh, and whereby indeed he divineth? ye have done evil in so doing.

6 And he overtook them, and he spake unto them these same words.

7 And they said unto him, Wherefore saith my lord these words? God forbid that thy servants should do according to this thing:

8 Behold, the money, which we found in our sacks' mouths, we brought again unto thee out of the land of Canaan: how then should we steal out of thy lord's house silver or gold?

9 With whomsoever of thy servants it be found, both let him die, and we also will be my lord's bondmen.

10 And he said, Now also *let* it *be* according unto your words; he with whom it is found shall be my servant; and ye shall be blameless.

11 Then they speedily took down every man his sack to the ground, and opened every man his sack.

12 And he searched, *and* began at the eldest, and left at the youngest: and the cup was found in Benjamin's sack.

13 Then they rent their clothes, and laded every man his ass, and returned to the city.

14 And Judah and his brethren came to Joseph's house; for he *was* yet there: and they fell before him on the ground.

15 And Joseph said unto them, What deed *is* this that ye have done? wot ye not that such a man as I can certainly divine?

16 And Judah said, What shall we say unto my lord? what shall we speak? or how shall we clear ourselves? God hath found out the iniquity of thy servants: behold, we *are* my lord's servants, both we, and *he* also with whom the cup is found.

17 And he said, God forbid that I should do so: *but* the man in whose hand the cup is found, he shall be my servant; and as for you, get you up in peace unto your father.

18 Then Judah came near unto him, and said, Oh my lord, let thy servant, I pray thee, speak a word in my lord's ears, and let not thine anger burn against thy servant: for thou *art* even as Pharaoh.

19 My lord asked his servants, saying, Have ye a father, or a brother?

20 And we said unto my lord, We have a father, an old man, and a child of his old age, a little one; and his brother is dead, and he alone is left of his mother, and his father loveth him.

21 And thou saidst unto thy servants, Bring him down unto me, that I may set mine eyes upon him.

22 And we said unto my lord, The lad cannot leave his father: for *if* he should leave his father, *his father* would die.

23 And thou saidst unto thy servants, Except your youngest brother come down with you, ye shall see my face no more.

24 And it came to pass when we came up unto thy servant my father, we told him the words of my lord.

25 And our father said, Go again, *and* buy us a little food.

26 And we said, We cannot go down: if our youngest brother be with us, then will we go down: for we may not see the man's face, except our youngest brother *be* with us.

27 And thy servant my father said unto us, Ye know that my wife bare me two *sons:*

28 And the one went out from me, and I said, Surely he is torn in pieces; and I saw him not since:

29 And if ye take this also from me, and mischief befall him, ye shall bring down my gray hairs with sorrow to the grave.

30Now therefore when I come to thy
servant my father, and the lad *be* not with
us; seeing that his life is bound up in the
lad's life;
31It shall come to pass, when he seeth
that the lad *is* not *with us,* that he will die:
and thy servants shall bring down the gray
hairs of thy servant our father with sorrow
to the grave.
32For thy servant became surety for the
lad unto my father, saying, If I bring him
not unto thee, then I shall bear the blame
to my father for ever.
33Now therefore,
I pray thee, let thy
servant abide in-
stead of the lad a
bondman to my
lord; and let the lad
go up with his brethren.

44:33 Helping Friends
◄ Genesis 37:26
1 Samuel 19:4 ►

34For how shall I go up to my father,
and the lad *be* not with me? lest peradventure I see the evil that shall come on
my father.

45

1Then Joseph could not refrain himself
before all them that stood by him; and he
cried, Cause every man to go out from me.
And there stood no man with him, while
Joseph made himself known unto his
brethren.
2And he wept aloud: and the Egyptians
and the house of Pharaoh heard.
3And Joseph said
unto his brethren, I
am Joseph; doth my
father yet live? And
his brethren could
not answer him; for
they were troubled at his presence.

45:3 Guilty Fear
◄ Genesis 3:8
Leviticus 26:17 ►

4And Joseph said unto his brethren,
Come near to me, I pray you. And they
came near. And he said, I *am* Joseph your
brother, whom ye sold into Egypt.
5Now therefore be not grieved, nor angry with yourselves, that ye sold me hither:
for God did send me before you to preserve life.
6For these two years *hath* the famine *been*
in the land: and yet *there are* five years, in
the which *there shall* neither *be* earing nor
harvest.
7And God sent me before you to preserve you a posterity in the earth, and to
save your lives by a great deliverance.
8So now *it was* not you *that* sent me
hither, but God:
and he hath made
me a father to Phar-
aoh, and lord of all
his house, and a rul-
er throughout all
the land of Egypt.

45:8
God at Work
◄ 1 Samuel 2:7 ►

9Haste ye, and go up to my father, and
say unto him, Thus saith thy son Joseph,
God hath made me lord of all Egypt: come
down unto me, tarry not:
10And thou shalt dwell in the land of
Goshen, and thou shalt be near unto me,
thou, and thy children, and thy children's
children, and thy flocks, and thy herds, and
all that thou hast:
11And there will I nourish thee; for yet
there are five years of famine; lest thou, and
thy household, and all that thou hast,
come to poverty.
12And, behold, your eyes see, and the
eyes of my brother Benjamin, that *it is* my
mouth that speaketh unto you.
13And ye shall tell my father of all my
glory in Egypt, and of all that ye have seen;
and ye shall haste and bring down my father hither.
14And he fell upon his brother Benjamin's neck, and wept; and Benjamin
wept upon his neck.
15Moreover he
kissed all his breth-
ren, and wept upon
them: and after that
his brethren talked
with him.

45:15 Nice
◄
Numbers 12:13 ►

16And the fame thereof was heard in
Pharaoh's house, saying, Joseph's brethren
are come: and it pleased Pharaoh well, and
his servants.
17And Pharaoh said unto Joseph, Say
unto thy brethren, This do ye; lade your
beasts, and go, get you unto the land of
Canaan;
18And take your father and your households, and come unto me: and I will give
you the good of the land of Egypt, and ye
shall eat the fat of the land.
19Now thou art commanded, this do ye;
take you wagons out of the land of Egypt
for your little ones, and for your wives, and
bring your father, and come.
20Also regard not your stuff; for the good
of all the land of Egypt *is* yours.
21And the children of Israel did so: and

Joseph gave them wagons, according to the commandment of Pharaoh, and gave them provision for the way.

22 To all of them he gave each man changes of raiment; but to Benjamin he gave three hundred *pieces* of silver, and five changes of raiment.

23 And to his father he sent after this *manner;* ten asses laden with the good things of Egypt, and ten she asses laden with corn and bread and meat for his father by the way.

24 So he sent his brethren away, and they departed: and he said unto them, See that ye fall not out by the way.

25 And they went up out of Egypt, and came into the land of Canaan unto Jacob their father,

26 And told him, saying, Joseph *is* yet alive, and he *is* governor over all the land of Egypt. And Jacob's heart fainted, for he believed them not.

27 And they told him all the words of Joseph, which he had said unto them: and when he saw the wagons which Joseph had sent to carry him, the spirit of Jacob their father revived:

28 And Israel said, *It is* enough; Joseph my son *is* yet alive: I will go and see him before I die.

46

1 And Israel took his journey with all that he had, and came to Beer-sheba, and offered sacrifices unto the God of his father Isaac.

2 And God spake unto Israel in the visions of the night, and said, Jacob, Jacob. And he said, Here *am* I.

3 And he said, I *am* God, the God of thy father: fear not to go down into Egypt; for I will there make of thee a great nation:

4 I will go down with thee into Egypt; and I will also surely bring thee up *again:* and Joseph shall put his hand upon thine eyes.

5 And Jacob rose up from Beer-sheba: and the sons of Israel carried Jacob their father, and their little ones, and their wives, in the wagons which Pharaoh had sent to carry him.

6 And they took their cattle, and their goods, which they had gotten in the land of Canaan, and came into Egypt, Jacob, and all his seed with him:

7 His sons, and his sons' sons with him, his daughters, and his sons' daughters, and all his seed brought he with him into Egypt.

8 And these *are* the names of the children of Israel, which came into Egypt, Jacob and his sons: Reuben, Jacob's firstborn.

9 And the sons of Reuben; Hanoch, and Phallu, and Hezron, and Carmi.

10 And the sons of Simeon; Jemuel, and Jamin, and Ohad, and Jachin, and Zohar, and Shaul the son of a Canaanitish woman.

11 And the sons of Levi; Gershon, Kohath, and Merari.

12 And the sons of Judah; Er, and Onan, and Shelah, and Pharez, and Zarah: but Er and Onan died in the land of Canaan. And the sons of Pharez were Hezron and Hamul.

13 And the sons of Issachar; Tola, and Phuvah, and Job, and Shimron.

14 And the sons of Zebulun; Sered, and Elon, and Jahleel.

15 These *be* the sons of Leah, which she bare unto Jacob in Padan-aram, with his daughter Dinah: all the souls of his sons and his daughters *were* thirty and three.

16 And the sons of Gad; Ziphion, and Haggi, Shuni, and Ezbon, Eri, and Arodi, and Areli.

17 And the sons of Asher; Jimnah, and Ishuah, and Isui, and Beriah, and Serah their sister: and the sons of Beriah; Heber, and Malchiel.

18 These *are* the sons of Zilpah, whom Laban gave to Leah his daughter, and these she bare unto Jacob, *even* sixteen souls.

19 The sons of Rachel Jacob's wife; Joseph, and Benjamin.

20 And unto Joseph in the land of Egypt were born Manasseh and Ephraim, which Asenath the daughter of Poti-pherah priest of On bare unto him.

21 And the sons of Benjamin *were* Belah, and Becher, and Ashbel, Gera, and Naaman, Ehi, and Rosh, Muppim, and Huppim, and Ard.

22 These *are* the sons of Rachel, which were born to Jacob: all the souls *were* fourteen.

23 And the sons of Dan; Hushim.

24 And the sons of Naphtali; Jahzeel, and Guni, and Jezer, and Shillem.

25 These *are* the sons of Bilhah, which Laban gave unto Rachel his daughter, and she bare these unto Jacob: all the souls *were* seven.

26All the souls that came with Jacob into Egypt, which came out of his loins, besides Jacob's sons' wives, all the souls *were* threescore and six;

27And the sons of Joseph, which were born him in Egypt, *were* two souls: all the souls of the house of Jacob, which came into Egypt, *were* threescore and ten.

28And he sent Judah before him unto Joseph, to direct his face unto Goshen; and they came into the land of Goshen.

29And Joseph made ready his chariot, and went up to meet Israel his father, to Goshen, and presented himself unto him; and he fell on his neck, and wept on his neck a good while.

30And Israel said unto Joseph, Now let me die, since I have seen thy face, because thou *art* yet alive.

31And Joseph said unto his brethren, and unto his father's house, I will go up, and shew Pharaoh, and say unto him, My brethren, and my father's house, which *were* in the land of Canaan, are come unto me;

32And the men *are* shepherds, for their trade hath been to feed cattle; and they have brought their flocks, and their herds, and all that they have.

33And it shall come to pass, when Pharaoh shall call you, and shall say, What *is* your occupation?

34That ye shall say, Thy servants' trade hath been about cattle from our youth even until now, both we, *and* also our fathers: that ye may dwell in the land of Goshen; for every shepherd *is* an abomination unto the Egyptians.

47

1Then Joseph came and told Pharaoh, and said, My father and my brethren, and their flocks, and their herds, and all that they have, are come out of the land of Canaan; and, behold, they *are* in the land of Goshen.

2And he took some of his brethren, *even* five men, and presented them unto Pharaoh.

3And Pharaoh said unto his brethren, What *is* your occupation? And they said unto Pharaoh, Thy servants *are* shepherds, both we, *and* also our fathers.

4They said moreover unto Pharaoh, For to sojourn in the land are we come; for thy servants have no pasture for their flocks; for the famine *is* sore in the land of Canaan: now therefore, we pray thee, let thy servants dwell in the land of Goshen.

5And Pharaoh spake unto Joseph, saying, Thy father and thy brethren are come unto thee:

6The land of Egypt *is* before thee; in the best of the land make thy father and brethren to dwell; in the land of Goshen let them dwell: and if thou knowest *any* men of activity among them, then make them rulers over my cattle.

7And Joseph brought in Jacob his father, and set him before Pharaoh: and Jacob blessed Pharaoh.

8And Pharaoh said unto Jacob, How old *art* thou?

9And Jacob said unto Pharaoh, The days of the years of my pilgrimage *are* an hundred and thirty years: few and evil have the days of the years of my life been, and have not attained unto the days of the years of the life of my fathers in the days of their pilgrimage.

47:9 Life Is Short
1 Chronicles 29:15 ➤

10And Jacob blessed Pharaoh, and went out from before Pharaoh.

11And Joseph placed his father and his brethren, and gave them a possession in the land of Egypt, in the best of the land, in the land of Rameses, as Pharaoh had commanded.

12And Joseph nourished his father, and his brethren, and all his father's household, with bread, according to *their* families.

13And *there was* no bread in all the land; for the famine *was* very sore, so that the land of Egypt and *all* the land of Canaan fainted by reason of the famine.

14And Joseph gathered up all the money that was found in the land of Egypt, and in the land of Canaan, for the corn which they bought: and Joseph brought the money into Pharaoh's house.

15And when money failed in the land of Egypt, and in the land of Canaan, all the Egyptians came unto Joseph, and said, Give us bread: for why should we die in thy presence? for the money faileth.

16And Joseph said, Give your cattle; and I will give you for your cattle, if money fail.

17And they brought their cattle unto Joseph: and Joseph gave them bread *in exchange* for horses, and for the flocks, and for the cattle of the herds, and for the asses: and he fed them with bread for all their cattle for that year.

18 When that year was ended, they came unto him the second year, and said unto him, We will not hide *it* from my lord, how that our money is spent; my lord also hath our herds of cattle; there is not ought left in the sight of my lord, but our bodies, and our lands:

19 Wherefore shall we die before thine eyes, both we and our land? buy us and our land for bread, and we and our land will be servants unto Pharaoh: and give *us* seed, that we may live, and not die, that the land be not desolate.

20 And Joseph bought all the land of Egypt for Pharaoh; for the Egyptians sold every man his field, because the famine prevailed over them: so the land became Pharaoh's.

21 And as for the people, he removed them to cities from *one* end of the borders of Egypt even to the *other* end thereof.

22 Only the land of the priests bought he not; for the priests had a portion *assigned them* of Pharaoh, and did eat their portion which Pharaoh gave them: wherefore they sold not their lands.

23 Then Joseph said unto the people, Behold, I have bought you this day and your land for Pharaoh: lo, *here is* seed for you, and ye shall sow the land.

24 And it shall come to pass in the increase, that ye shall give the fifth *part* unto Pharaoh, and four parts shall be your own, for seed of the field, and for your food, and for them of your households, and for food for your little ones.

25 And they said, Thou hast saved our lives: let us find grace in the sight of my lord, and we will be Pharaoh's servants.

26 And Joseph made it a law over the land of Egypt unto this day, *that* Pharaoh should have the fifth *part;* except the land of the priests only, *which* became not Pharaoh's.

27 And Israel dwelt in the land of Egypt, in the country of Goshen; and they had possessions therein, and grew, and multiplied exceedingly.

28 And Jacob lived in the land of Egypt seventeen years: so the whole age of Jacob was an hundred forty and seven years.

29 And the time drew nigh that Israel must die: and he called his son Joseph, and said unto him, If now I have found grace in thy sight, put, I pray thee, thy hand under my thigh, and deal kindly and truly with me; bury me not, I pray thee, in Egypt:

30 But I will lie with my fathers, and thou shalt carry me out of Egypt, and bury me in their buryingplace. And he said, I will do as thou hast said.

31 And he said, Swear unto me. And he sware unto him. And Israel bowed himself upon the bed's head.

48

1 And it came to pass after these things, that *one* told Joseph, Behold, thy father *is* sick: and he took with him his two sons, Manasseh and Ephraim.

2 And *one* told Jacob, and said, Behold, thy son Joseph cometh unto thee: and Israel strengthened himself, and sat upon the bed.

3 And Jacob said unto Joseph, God Almighty appeared unto me at Luz in the land of Canaan, and blessed me,

4 And said unto me, Behold, I will make thee fruitful, and multiply thee, and I will make of thee a multitude of people; and will give this land to thy seed after thee *for* an everlasting possession.

5 And now thy two sons, Ephraim and Manasseh, which were born unto thee in the land of Egypt before I came unto thee into Egypt, *are* mine; as Reuben and Simeon, they shall be mine.

6 And thy issue, which thou begettest after them, shall be thine, *and* shall be called after the name of their brethren in their inheritance.

7 And as for me, when I came from Padan, Rachel died by me in the land of Canaan in the way, when yet *there was* but a little way to come unto Ephrath: and I buried her there in the way of Ephrath; the same *is* Bethlehem.

8 And Israel beheld Joseph's sons, and said, Who *are* these?

9 And Joseph said unto his father, They *are* my sons, whom God hath given me in this *place.* And he said, Bring them, I pray thee, unto me, and I will bless them.

10 Now the eyes of Israel were dim for age, *so that* he could not see. And he brought them near unto him; and he kissed them, and embraced them.

11 And Israel said unto Joseph, I had not

thought to see thy face: and, lo, God hath shewed me also thy seed.

12 And Joseph brought them out from between his knees, and he bowed himself with his face to the earth.

13 And Joseph took them both, Ephraim in his right hand toward Israel's left hand, and Manasseh in his left hand toward Israel's right hand, and brought *them* near unto him.

14 And Israel stretched out his right hand, and laid *it* upon Ephraim's head, who *was* the younger, and his left hand upon Manasseh's head, guiding his hands wittingly; for Manasseh *was* the firstborn.

15 And he blessed Joseph, and said, God, before whom my fathers Abraham and Isaac did walk, the God which fed me all my life long unto this day,

16 The Angel which redeemed me from all evil, bless the lads; and let my name be named on them, and the name of my fathers Abraham and Isaac; and let them grow into a multitude in the midst of the earth.

17 And when Joseph saw that his father laid his right hand upon the head of Ephraim, it displeased him: and he held up his father's hand, to remove it from Ephraim's head unto Manasseh's head.

18 And Joseph said unto his father, Not so, my father: for this *is* the firstborn; put thy right hand upon his head.

19 And his father refused, and said, I know *it,* my son, I know *it:* he also shall become a people, and he also shall be great: but truly his younger brother shall be greater than he, and his seed shall become a multitude of nations.

20 And he blessed them that day, saying, In thee shall Israel bless, saying, God make thee as Ephraim and as Manasseh: and he set Ephraim before Manasseh.

21 And Israel said unto Joseph, Behold, I die: but God shall be with you, and bring you again unto the land of your fathers.

22 Moreover I have given to thee one portion above thy brethren, which I took out of the hand of the Amorite with my sword and with my bow.

49

1 And Jacob called unto his sons, and said, Gather yourselves together, that I may tell you *that* which shall befall you in the last days.

2 Gather yourselves together, and hear, ye sons of Jacob; and hearken unto Israel your father.

3 Reuben, thou *art* my firstborn, my might, and the beginning of my strength, the excellency of dignity, and the excellency of power:

4 Unstable as water, thou shalt not excel; because thou wentest up to thy father's bed; then defiledst thou *it:* he went up to my couch.

5 Simeon and Levi *are* brethren; instruments of cruelty *are in* their habitations.

49:5
Crime
◄ Psalm 27:12 ►

6 O my soul, come not thou into their secret; unto their assembly, mine honour, be not thou united: for in their anger they slew a man, and in their selfwill they digged down a wall.

7 Cursed *be* their anger, for *it was* fierce; and their wrath, for it was cruel: I will divide them in Jacob, and scatter them in Israel.

8 Judah, thou *art he* whom thy brethren shall praise: thy hand *shall be* in the neck of thine enemies; thy father's children shall bow down before thee.

9 Judah *is* a lion's whelp: from the prey, my son, thou art gone up: he stooped down, he couched as a lion, and as an old lion; who shall rouse him up?

10 The sceptre shall not depart from Judah, nor a lawgiver from between his feet, until Shiloh come; and unto him *shall* the gathering of the people *be.*

11 Binding his foal unto the vine, and his ass's colt unto the choice vine; he washed his garments in wine, and his clothes in the blood of grapes:

12 His eyes *shall be* red with wine, and his teeth white with milk.

13 Zebulun shall dwell at the haven of the sea; and he *shall be* for an haven of ships; and his border *shall be* unto Zidon.

14 Issachar *is* a strong ass couching down between two burdens:

15 And he saw that rest *was* good, and the land that *it was* pleasant; and bowed his shoulder to bear, and became a servant unto tribute.

16 Dan shall judge his people, as one of the tribes of Israel.

17 Dan shall be a serpent by the way, an adder in the path, that biteth the horse

heels, so that his rider shall fall backward.

18 I have waited for thy salvation, O LORD.

49:18
Waiting
◄ Psalm 33:20 ►

19 Gad, a troop shall overcome him: but he shall overcome at the last.

20 Out of Asher his bread *shall be* fat, and he shall yield royal dainties.

21 Naphtali *is* a hind let loose: he giveth goodly words.

22 Joseph *is* a fruitful bough, *even* a fruitful bough by a well; *whose* branches run over the wall:

23 The archers have sorely grieved him, and shot *at him,* and hated him:

24 But his bow abode in strength, and the arms of his hands were made strong by the hands of the mighty *God* of Jacob; (from thence *is* the shepherd, the stone of Israel:)

25 *Even* by the God of thy father, who shall help thee; and by the Almighty, who shall bless thee with blessings of heaven above, blessings of the deep that lieth under, blessings of the breasts, and of the womb:

26 The blessings of thy father have prevailed above the blessings of my progenitors unto the utmost bound of the everlasting hills: they shall be on the head of Joseph, and on the crown of the head of him that was separate from his brethren.

27 Benjamin shall ravin *as* a wolf: in the morning he shall devour the prey, and at night he shall divide the spoil.

28 All these *are* the twelve tribes of Israel: and this *is it* that their father spake unto them, and blessed them; every one according to his blessing he blessed them.

29 And he charged them, and said unto them, I am to be gathered unto my people: bury me with my fathers in the cave that *is* in the field of Ephron the Hittite,

30 In the cave that *is* in the field of Machpelah, which *is* before Mamre, in the land of Canaan, which Abraham bought with the field of Ephron the Hittite for a possession of a buryingplace.

31 There they buried Abraham and Sarah his wife; there they buried Isaac and Rebekah his wife; and there I buried Leah.

32 The purchase of the field and of the cave that *is* therein *was* from the children of Heth.

33 And when Jacob had made an end of commanding his sons, he gathered up his feet into the bed, and yielded up the ghost, and was gathered unto his people.

50

1 And Joseph fell upon his father's face, and wept upon him, and kissed him.

2 And Joseph commanded his servants the physicians to embalm his father: and the physicians embalmed Israel.

3 And forty days were fulfilled for him; for so are fulfilled the days of those which are embalmed: and the Egyptians mourned for him threescore and ten days.

4 And when the days of his mourning were past, Joseph spake unto the house of Pharaoh, saying, If now I have found grace in your eyes, speak, I pray you, in the ears of Pharaoh, saying,

5 My father made me swear, saying, Lo, I die: in my grave which I have digged for me in the land of Canaan, there shalt thou bury me. Now therefore let me go up, I pray thee, and bury my father, and I will come again.

6 And Pharaoh said, Go up, and bury thy father, according as he made thee swear.

7 And Joseph went up to bury his father: and with him went up all the servants of Pharaoh, the elders of his house, and all the elders of the land of Egypt,

8 And all the house of Joseph, and his brethren, and his father's house: only their little ones, and their flocks, and their herds, they left in the land of Goshen.

9 And there went up with him both chariots and horsemen: and it was a very great company.

10 And they came to the threshingfloor of Atad, which *is* beyond Jordan, and there they mourned with a great and very sore lamentation: and he made a mourning for his father seven days.

11 And when the inhabitants of the land, the Canaanites, saw the mourning in the floor of Atad, they said, This *is* a grievous mourning to the Egyptians: wherefore the name of it was called Abel-mizraim, which *is* beyond Jordan.

12 And his sons did unto him according as he commanded them:

13 For his sons carried him into the land of Canaan, and buried him in the cave of the field of Machpelah, which Abraham

bought with the field for a possession of a buryingplace of Ephron the Hittite, before Mamre.

14 And Joseph returned into Egypt, he, and his brethren, and all that went up with him to bury his father, after he had buried his father.

15 And when Joseph's brethren saw that their father was dead, they said, Joseph will peradventure hate us, and will certainly requite us all the evil which we did unto him.

16 And they sent a messenger unto Joseph, saying, Thy father did command before he died, saying,

17 So shall ye say unto Joseph, Forgive, I pray thee now, the trespass of thy brethren, and their sin; for they did unto thee evil: and now, we pray thee, forgive the trespass of the servants of the God of thy father. And Joseph wept when they spake unto him.

18 And his brethren also went and fell down before his face; and they said, Behold, we *be* thy servants.

19 And Joseph said unto them, Fear not: for *am* I in the place of God?

20 But as for you, ye thought evil against me; *but* God meant it unto good, to bring to pass, as *it is* this day, to save much people alive.

21 Now therefore fear ye not: I will nourish you, and your little ones. And he comforted them, and spake kindly unto them.

50:21 Unselfishness
◄ Genesis 14:23
Numbers 11:29 ►

22 And Joseph dwelt in Egypt, he, and his father's house: and Joseph lived an hundred and ten years.

23 And Joseph saw Ephraim's children of the third *generation:* the children also of Machir the son Manasseh were brought up upon Joseph's knees.

24 And Joseph said unto his brethren, I die: and God will surely visit you, and bring you out of this land unto the land which he sware to Abraham, to Isaac, and to Jacob.

25 And Joseph took an oath of the children of Israel, saying, God will surely visit you, and ye shall carry up my bones from hence.

26 So Joseph died, *being* an hundred and ten years old: and they embalmed him, and he was put in a coffin in Egypt.

Exodus

AUTHOR
Moses

MAIN POINT
God heard the cry of his people, Israel, and rescued them from slavery in Egypt.

DATE WRITTEN
Around 1450 B.C. (same time as Genesis)

40 CHAPTERS

MAIN PEOPLE

Moses, Pharaoh, Pharaoh's daughter, Miriam, Aaron, Joshua, Caleb

SPECIAL FEATURES

- *Tells the story of Moses, a baby who rode a river in a basket and grew up to lead God's people out of slavery*
- *Describes some gross plagues, such as the Nile River turning into blood and hordes of frogs*
- *Includes the story of God opening up the Red Sea for his people and then closing it up to crash upon Pharaoh's army*
- *Explains how God gave Moses the Ten Commandments and then had to give them again because Moses got mad and broke the tablets on which they were written*
- *Second book of Law*

HOW THE BOOK GOT ITS NAME

The word exodus means "getting outta here," like the word exit. This second book written by Moses tells the story of how God got his people out of slavery in Egypt.

1 1Now these *are* the names of the children of Israel, which came into Egypt;
every man and his household came with
Jacob.
2Reuben, Simeon, Levi, and Judah,
3Issachar, Zebulun, and Benjamin,
4Dan, and Naphtali, Gad, and Asher.
5And all the souls that came out of the
loins of Jacob were seventy souls: for Joseph was in Egypt *already.*
6And Joseph died, and all his brethren,
and all that generation.
7And the children of Israel were fruitful, and increased abundantly, and multiplied, and waxed exceeding mighty; and
the land was filled with them.
8Now there arose up a new king over
Egypt, which knew not Joseph.
9And he said unto his people, Behold,
the people of the children of Israel *are*
more and mightier than we:
10Come on, let us deal wisely with them;
lest they multiply, and it come to pass, that,
when there falleth out any war, they join

also unto our enemies, and fight against
us, and *so* get them up out of the land.
11 Therefore they did set over them taskmasters to afflict them with their burdens.
And they built for Pharaoh treasure cities,
Pithom and Raamses.
12 But the more they afflicted them, the
more they multiplied and grew. And they
were grieved because of the children of
Israel.
13 And the Egyptians made the children
of Israel to serve with rigour:
14 And they made their lives bitter with
hard bondage, in morter, and in brick, and
in all manner of service in the field: all
their service, wherein they made them
serve, *was* with rigour.
15 And the king of Egypt spake to the
Hebrew midwives, of which the name of
the one *was* Shiphrah, and the name of the
other Puah:
16 And he said, When ye do the office of
a midwife to the Hebrew women, and see
them upon the stools; if it *be* a son, then ye
shall kill him: but if it *be* a daughter, then
she shall live.
17 But the midwives feared God, and did
not as the king of Egypt commanded them,
but saved the men children alive.
18 And the king of Egypt called for the
midwives, and said unto them, Why have
ye done this thing, and have saved the men
children alive?
19 And the midwives said unto Pharaoh,
Because the Hebrew women *are* not as the
Egyptian women; for they *are* lively, and
are delivered ere the midwives come in
unto them.
20 Therefore God dealt well with the
midwives: and the people multiplied, and
waxed very mighty.
21 And it came to pass, because the midwives feared God, that he made them
houses.
22 And Pharaoh charged all his people,
saying, Every son that is born ye shall cast
into the river, and every daughter ye shall
save alive.

2

1 And there went a man of the house of
Levi, and took *to wife* a daughter of Levi.
2 And the woman conceived, and bare a
son: and when she saw him that he *was a*
goodly *child*, she hid him three months.
3 And when she could not longer hide
him, she took for him an ark of bulrushes,
and daubed it with slime and with pitch,
and put the child therein; and she laid *it*
in the flags by the river's brink.
4 And his sister stood afar off, to wit what
would be done to him.
5 And the daughter of Pharaoh came
down to wash *herself* at the river; and her
maidens walked along by the river's side;
and when she saw the ark among the flags,
she sent her maid to fetch it.
6 And when she
had opened *it*, she
saw the child: and,
behold, the babe
wept. And she had
compassion on him,
and said, This *is one* of the Hebrews' children.

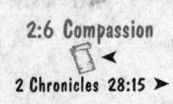

2:6 Compassion
◄
2 Chronicles 28:15 ➤

7 Then said his sister to Pharaoh's daughter, Shall I go and call to thee a nurse of
the Hebrew women, that she may nurse
the child for thee?
8 And Pharaoh's daughter said to her, Go.
And the maid went and called the child's
mother.
9 And Pharaoh's daughter said unto her,
Take this child away, and nurse it for me,
and I will give *thee* thy wages. And the
woman took the child, and nursed it.
10 And the child grew, and she brought
him unto Pharaoh's daughter, and he became her son. And she called his name
Moses: and she said, Because I drew him
out of the water.
11 And it came to pass in those days,
when Moses was grown, that he went out
unto his brethren, and looked on their
burdens: and he spied an Egyptian smiting an Hebrew, one of his brethren.
12 And he looked this way and that way,
and when he saw that *there was* no man,
he slew the Egyptian, and hid him in the
sand.
13 And when he went out the second day,
behold, two men of the Hebrews strove
together: and he said to him that did
the wrong, Wherefore smitest thou thy
fellow?
14 And he said, Who made thee a prince
and a judge over us? intendest thou to kill
me, as thou killedst the Egyptian? And
Moses feared, and said, Surely this thing
is known.
15 Now when Pharaoh heard this thing,
he sought to slay Moses. But Moses fled

from the face of Pharaoh, and dwelt in
the land of Midian: and he sat down by a
well.
16Now the priest of Midian had seven
daughters: and they came and drew *water*,
and filled the troughs to water their father's
flock.
17And the shepherds came and drove
them away: but Moses stood up and
helped them, and watered their flock.
18And when they came to Reuel their
father, he said, How *is it that* ye are come
so soon to day?
19And they said, An Egyptian delivered
us out of the hand of the shepherds, and
also drew *water* enough for us, and watered
the flock.
20And he said unto his daughters, And
where *is* he? why *is* it *that* ye have left the
man? call him, that he may eat bread.
21And Moses was content to dwell with
the man: and he gave Moses Zipporah his
daughter.
22And she bare *him* a son, and he called
his name Gershom: for he said, I have been
a stranger in a strange land.
23And it came to pass in process of time,
that the king of Egypt died: and the
children of Israel sighed by reason of
the bondage, and they cried, and their
cry came up unto God by reason of the
bondage.
24And God heard their groaning, and
God remembered his covenant with Abraham, with Isaac, and with Jacob.
25And God looked upon the children of
Israel, and God had respect unto *them*.

3

1Now Moses kept the flock of Jethro his
father in law, the priest of Midian: and he
led the flock to the backside of the desert,
and came to the mountain of God, *even* to
Horeb.
2And the angel of the LORD appeared
unto him in a flame of fire out of the midst
of a bush: and he looked, and, behold, the
bush burned with fire, and the bush *was*
not consumed.
3And Moses said, I will now turn aside,
and see this great sight, why the bush is
not burnt.
4And when the LORD saw that he turned
aside to see, God called unto him out of
the midst of the bush, and said, Moses,
Moses. And he said, Here *am* I.
5And he said, Draw not nigh hither: put
off thy shoes from
off thy feet, for
the place whereon
thou standest *is*
holy ground.

3:5
Respecting God
◄ Joshua 5:15 ►

6Moreover he
said, I *am* the God of thy father, the God
of Abraham, the God of Isaac, and the God
of Jacob. And Moses hid his face; for he
was afraid to look upon God.
7And the LORD said, I have surely seen
the affliction of my people which *are* in
Egypt, and have heard their cry by reason
of their taskmasters; for I know their sorrows;
8And I am come down to deliver them
out of the hand of the Egyptians, and to
bring them up out of that land unto a good
land and a large, unto a land flowing with
milk and honey; unto the place of the Canaanites, and the Hittites, and the Amorites, and the Perizzites, and the Hivites,
and the Jebusites.
9Now therefore, behold, the cry of the
children of Israel is come unto me: and I
have also seen the oppression wherewith
the Egyptians oppress them.
10Come now therefore, and I will send
thee unto Pharaoh, that thou mayest bring
forth my people the children of Israel out
of Egypt.
11And Moses said unto God, Who *am* I,
that I should go unto Pharaoh, and that I
should bring forth the children of Israel
out of Egypt?
12And he said, Certainly I will be with
thee; and this *shall be* a token unto thee,
that I have sent thee: When thou hast
brought forth the people out of Egypt, ye
shall serve God upon this mountain.
13And Moses said unto God, Behold,
when I come unto the children of Israel,
and shall say unto them, The God of your
fathers hath sent me unto you; and they
shall say to me, What *is* his name? what
shall I say unto them?
14And God said
unto Moses, I AM
THAT I AM: and he
said, Thus shalt
thou say unto the
children of Israel, I
AM hath sent me unto you.

3:14 Names of God
◄ Genesis 18:25
Exodus 6:3 ►

15And God said moreover unto Moses,
Thus shalt thou say unto the children of

Israel, The LORD God of your fathers, the
God of Abraham, the God of Isaac, and
the God of Jacob, hath sent me unto you:
this *is* my name for ever, and this *is* my
memorial unto all generations.
16Go, and gather the elders of Israel together, and say unto them, The LORD God
of your fathers, the God of Abraham, of
Isaac, and of Jacob, appeared unto me,
saying, I have surely visited you, and *seen*
that which is done to you in Egypt:
17And I have said, I will bring you up
out of the affliction of Egypt unto the land
of the Canaanites, and the Hittites, and the
Amorites, and the Perizzites, and the Hivites, and the Jebusites, unto a land flowing with milk and honey.
18And they shall hearken to thy voice:
and thou shalt come, thou and the elders
of Israel, unto the king of Egypt, and ye
shall say unto him, The LORD God of the
Hebrews hath met with us: and now let us
go, we beseech thee, three days' journey
into the wilderness, that we may sacrifice
to the LORD our God.
19And I am sure that the king of Egypt
will not let you go, no, not by a mighty
hand.
20And I will stretch out my hand, and
smite Egypt with all my wonders which I
will do in the midst thereof: and after that
he will let you go.
21And I will give this people favour in
the sight of the Egyptians: and it shall
come to pass, that, when ye go, ye shall
not go empty:
22But every woman shall borrow of her
neighbour, and of her that sojourneth in
her house, jewels of silver, and jewels of
gold, and raiment: and ye shall put *them*
upon your sons, and upon your daughters;
and ye shall spoil the Egyptians.

4

1And Moses answered and said, But,
behold, they will not believe me, nor hearken unto my voice: for they will say, The
LORD hath not appeared unto thee.
2And the LORD said unto him, What *is*
that in thine hand? And he said, A rod.
3And he said, Cast it on the ground. And
he cast it on the ground, and it became a
serpent; and Moses fled from before it.
4And the LORD said unto Moses, Put
forth thine hand, and take it by the tail.
And he put forth his hand, and caught it,
and it became a rod in his hand:
5That they may believe that the LORD
God of their fathers, the God of Abraham,
the God of Isaac, and the God of Jacob,
hath appeared unto thee.
6And the LORD said furthermore unto
him, Put now thine hand into thy bosom.
And he put his hand into his bosom: and
when he took it out, behold, his hand *was*
leprous as snow.
7And he said, Put thine hand into thy
bosom again. And he put his hand into
his bosom again; and plucked it out of his
bosom, and, behold, it was turned again
as his *other* flesh.
8And it shall come to pass, if they will
not believe thee, neither hearken to the
voice of the first sign, that they will believe the voice of the latter sign.
9And it shall come to pass, if they will
not believe also these two signs, neither
hearken unto thy voice, that thou shalt take
of the water of the river, and pour *it* upon
the dry *land:* and the water which thou
takest out of the river shall become blood
upon the dry *land.*
10And Moses said unto the LORD, O my
Lord, I *am* not eloquent, neither heretofore, nor since thou hast spoken unto thy
servant: but I *am* slow of speech, and of a
slow tongue.
11And the LORD said unto him, Who
hath made man's mouth? or who maketh
the dumb, or deaf, or the seeing, or the
blind? have not I the LORD?
12Now therefore go, and I will be with
thy mouth, and teach thee what thou
shalt say.
13And he said, O my Lord, send, I pray
thee, by the hand *of him whom* thou wilt
send.
14And the anger of the LORD was kindled against Moses, and he said, *Is* not
Aaron the Levite thy brother? I know that
he can speak well. And also, behold, he
cometh forth to meet thee: and when he
seeth thee, he will be glad in his heart.
15And thou shalt
speak unto him, and
put words in his
mouth: and I will
be with thy mouth,
and with his mouth,
and will teach you what ye shall do.

4:15
God as Teacher
◄ Deuteronomy 4:36 ►

16And he shall be thy spokesman unto
the people: and he shall be, *even* he shall

be to thee instead of a mouth, and thou
shalt be to him instead of God.
17 And thou shalt take this rod in thine
hand, wherewith thou shalt do signs.
18 And Moses went and returned to Jethro his father in law, and said unto him,
Let me go, I pray thee, and return unto my
brethren which *are* in Egypt, and see
whether they be yet alive. And Jethro said
to Moses, Go in peace.
19 And the LORD said unto Moses in Midian, Go, return into Egypt: for all the men
are dead which sought thy life.
20 And Moses took his wife and his sons,
and set them upon an ass, and he returned
to the land of Egypt: and Moses took the
rod of God in his hand.
21 And the LORD said unto Moses, When
thou goest to return into Egypt, see that
thou do all those wonders before Pharaoh,
which I have put in thine hand: but I will
harden his heart, that he shall not let the
people go.
22 And thou shalt say unto Pharaoh,
Thus saith the LORD, Israel *is* my son, *even*
my firstborn:
23 And I say unto thee, Let my son go,
that he may serve me: and if thou refuse
to let him go, behold, I will slay thy son,
even thy firstborn.
24 And it came to pass by the way in the
inn, that the LORD met him, and sought
to kill him.
25 Then Zipporah took a sharp stone,
and cut off the foreskin of her son, and
cast *it* at his feet, and said, Surely a bloody
husband *art* thou to me.
26 So he let him go: then she said, A
bloody husband *thou art*, because of the
circumcision.
27 And the LORD said to Aaron, Go into
the wilderness to meet Moses. And he
went, and met him in the mount of God,
and kissed him.
28 And Moses told Aaron all the words
of the LORD who had sent him, and all the
signs which he had commanded him.
29 And Moses and Aaron went and gathered together all the elders of the children
of Israel:
30 And Aaron spake all the words which
the LORD had spoken unto Moses, and did
the signs in the sight of the people.
31 And the people believed: and when
they heard that the LORD had visited the
children of Israel, and that he had looked
upon their affliction, then they bowed
their heads and worshipped.

5

1 And afterward Moses and Aaron went
in, and told Pharaoh, Thus saith the LORD
God of Israel, Let my people go, that they
may hold a feast unto me in the wilderness.
2 And Pharaoh said, Who *is* the LORD,
that I should obey his voice to let Israel
go? I know not the LORD, neither will I let
Israel go.
3 And they said, The God of the Hebrews
hath met with us: let us go, we pray thee,
three days' journey into the desert, and
sacrifice unto the LORD our God; lest he
fall upon us with pestilence, or with the
sword.
4 And the king of Egypt said unto them,
Wherefore do ye, Moses and Aaron, let the
people from their works? get you unto
your burdens.
5 And Pharaoh said, Behold, the people
of the land now *are* many, and ye make
them rest from their burdens.
6 And Pharaoh commanded the same
day the taskmasters of the people, and their
officers, saying,
7 Ye shall no more give the people straw
to make brick, as heretofore: let them go
and gather straw for themselves.
8 And the tale of the bricks, which they
did make heretofore, ye shall lay upon
them; ye shall not diminish *ought* thereof:
for they *be* idle; therefore they cry, saying,
Let us go *and* sacrifice to our God.
9 Let there more work be laid upon the
men, that they may labour therein; and let
them not regard vain words.
10 And the taskmasters of the people
went out, and their officers, and they spake
to the people, saying, Thus saith Pharaoh,
I will not give you straw.
11 Go ye, get you straw where ye can find
it: yet not ought of your work shall be diminished.
12 So the people were scattered abroad
throughout all the land of Egypt to gather
stubble instead of straw.
13 And the taskmasters hasted *them*, saying, Fulfil your works, *your* daily tasks, as
when there was straw.
14 And the officers of the children of Israel, which Pharaoh's taskmasters had set
over them, were beaten, *and* demanded,

Wherefore have ye not fulfilled your task in making brick both yesterday and to day, as heretofore?

15 Then the officers of the children of Israel came and cried unto Pharaoh, saying, Wherefore dealest thou thus with thy servants?

16 There is no straw given unto thy servants, and they say to us, Make brick: and, behold, thy servants *are* beaten; but the fault *is* in thine own people.

17 But he said, Ye *are* idle, *ye are* idle: therefore ye say, Let us go *and* do sacrifice to the LORD.

18 Go therefore now, *and* work; for there shall no straw be given you, yet shall ye deliver the tale of bricks.

19 And the officers of the children of Israel did see *that* they *were* in evil *case*, after it was said, Ye shall not minish *ought* from your bricks of your daily task.

20 And they met Moses and Aaron, who stood in the way, as they came forth from Pharaoh:

21 And they said unto them, The LORD look upon you, and judge; because ye have made our savour to be abhorred in the eyes of Pharaoh, and in the eyes of his servants, to put a sword in their hand to slay us.

22 And Moses returned unto the LORD, and said, Lord, wherefore hast thou *so* evil entreated this people? why *is* it *that* thou hast sent me?

23 For since I came to Pharaoh to speak in thy name, he hath done evil to this people; neither hast thou delivered thy people at all.

6

1 Then the LORD said unto Moses, Now shalt thou see what I will do to Pharaoh: for with a strong hand shall he let them go, and with a strong hand shall he drive them out of his land.

2 And God spake unto Moses, and said unto him, I *am* the LORD:

3 And I appeared unto Abraham, unto Isaac, and unto Jacob, by *the name of* God Almighty, but by my name JEHOVAH was I not known to them.

6:3 Names of God
◄ Exodus 3:14
Exodus 15:2 ►

4 And I have also established my covenant with them, to give them the land of Canaan, the land of their pilgrimage, wherein they were strangers.

5 And I have also heard the groaning of the children of Israel, whom the Egyptians keep in bondage; and I have remembered my covenant.

6 Wherefore say unto the children of Israel, I *am* the LORD, and I will bring you out from under the burdens of the Egyptians, and I will rid you out of their bondage, and I will redeem you with a stretched out arm, and with great judgments:

7 And I will take you to me for a people, and I will be to you a God: and ye shall know that I *am* the LORD your God, which bringeth you out from under the burdens of the Egyptians.

8 And I will bring you in unto the land, concerning the which I did swear to give it to Abraham, to Isaac, and to Jacob; and I will give it you for an heritage: I *am* the LORD.

9 And Moses spake so unto the children of Israel: but they hearkened not unto Moses for anguish of spirit, and for cruel bondage.

10 And the LORD spake unto Moses, saying,

11 Go in, speak unto Pharaoh king of Egypt, that he let the children of Israel go out of his land.

12 And Moses spake before the LORD, saying, Behold, the children of Israel have not hearkened unto me; how then shall Pharaoh hear me, who *am* of uncircumcised lips?

13 And the LORD spake unto Moses and unto Aaron, and gave them a charge unto the children of Israel, and unto Pharaoh king of Egypt, to bring the children of Israel out of the land of Egypt.

14 These *be* the heads of their fathers' houses: The sons of Reuben the firstborn of Israel; Hanoch, and Pallu, Hezron, and Carmi: these *be* the families of Reuben.

15 And the sons of Simeon; Jemuel, and Jamin, and Ohad, and Jachin, and Zohar, and Shaul the son of a Canaanitish woman: these *are* the families of Simeon.

16 And these *are* the names of the sons of Levi according to their generations; Gershon, and Kohath, and Merari: and the years of the life of Levi *were* an hundred thirty and seven years.

17 The sons of Gershon; Libni, and Shimi, according to their families.

18 And the sons of Kohath; Amram, and

Izhar, and Hebron, and Uzziel: and the years of the life of Kohath *were* an hundred thirty and three years.

19 And the sons of Merari; Mahali and Mushi: these *are* the families of Levi according to their generations.

20 And Amram took him Jochebed his father's sister to wife; and she bare him Aaron and Moses: and the years of the life of Amram *were* an hundred and thirty and seven years.

21 And the sons of Izhar; Korah, and Nepheg, and Zichri.

22 And the sons of Uzziel; Mishael, and Elzaphan, and Zithri.

23 And Aaron took him Elisheba, daughter of Amminadab, sister of Naashon, to wife; and she bare him Nadab, and Abihu, Eleazar, and Ithamar.

24 And the sons of Korah; Assir, and Elkanah, and Abiasaph: these *are* the families of the Korhites.

25 And Eleazar Aaron's son took him *one* of the daughters of Putiel to wife; and she bare him Phinehas: these *are* the heads of the fathers of the Levites according to their families.

26 These *are* that Aaron and Moses, to whom the LORD said, Bring out the children of Israel from the land of Egypt according to their armies.

27 These *are* they which spake to Pharaoh king of Egypt, to bring out the children of Israel from Egypt: these *are* that Moses and Aaron.

28 And it came to pass on the day *when* the LORD spake unto Moses in the land of Egypt,

29 That the LORD spake unto Moses, saying, I *am* the LORD: speak thou unto Pharaoh king of Egypt all that I say unto thee.

30 And Moses said before the LORD, Behold, I *am* of uncircumcised lips, and how shall Pharaoh hearken unto me?

7

1 And the LORD said unto Moses, See, I have made thee a god to Pharaoh: and Aaron thy brother shall be thy prophet.

2 Thou shalt speak all that I command thee: and Aaron thy brother shall speak unto Pharaoh, that he send the children of Israel out of his land.

3 And I will harden Pharaoh's heart, and multiply my signs and my wonders in the land of Egypt.

4 But Pharaoh shall not hearken unto you, that I may lay my hand upon Egypt, and bring forth mine armies, *and* my people the children of Israel, out of the land of Egypt by great judgments.

5 And the Egyptians shall know that I *am* the LORD, when I stretch forth mine hand upon Egypt, and bring out the children of Israel from among them.

6 And Moses and Aaron did as the LORD commanded them, so did they.

7 And Moses *was* fourscore years old, and Aaron fourscore and three years old, when they spake unto Pharaoh.

8 And the LORD spake unto Moses and unto Aaron, saying,

9 When Pharaoh shall speak unto you, saying, Shew a miracle for you: then thou shalt say unto Aaron, Take thy rod, and cast *it* before Pharaoh, *and* it shall become a serpent.

10 And Moses and Aaron went in unto Pharaoh, and they did so as the LORD had commanded: and Aaron cast down his rod before Pharaoh, and before his servants, and it became a serpent.

11 Then Pharaoh also called the wise men and the sorcerers: now the magicians of Egypt, they also did in like manner with their enchantments.

12 For they cast down every man his rod, and they became serpents: but Aaron's rod swallowed up their rods.

13 And he hardened Pharaoh's heart, that he hearkened not unto them; as the LORD had said.

14 And the LORD said unto Moses, Pharaoh's heart *is* hardened, he refuseth to let the people go.

15 Get thee unto Pharaoh in the morning; lo, he goeth out unto the water; and thou shalt stand by the river's brink against he come; and the rod which was turned to a serpent shalt thou take in thine hand.

16 And thou shalt say unto him, The LORD God of the Hebrews hath sent me unto thee, saying, Let my people go, that they may serve me in the wilderness: and, behold, hitherto thou wouldest not hear.

17 Thus saith the LORD, In this thou shalt know that I *am* the LORD: behold, I will smite with the rod that *is* in mine hand upon the waters which *are* in the river, and they shall be turned to blood.

18 And the fish that *is* in the river shall die, and the river shall stink; and the

Egyptians shall lothe to drink of the water
of the river.
19 And the LORD spake unto Moses, Say
unto Aaron, Take thy rod, and stretch out
thine hand upon the waters of Egypt, upon
their streams, upon their rivers, and upon
their ponds, and upon all their pools of
water, that they may become blood; and
that there may be blood throughout all the
land of Egypt, both in *vessels of* wood, and
in *vessels of* stone.
20 And Moses and Aaron did so, as the
LORD commanded; and he lifted up the
rod, and smote the waters that *were* in
the river, in the sight of Pharaoh, and in
the sight of his servants; and all the waters
that *were* in the river were turned to blood.
21 And the fish that *was* in the river died;
and the river stank, and the Egyptians
could not drink of the water of the river;
and there was blood throughout all the
land of Egypt.
22 And the magicians of Egypt did so
with their enchantments: and Pharaoh's
heart was hardened, neither did he hearken unto them; as the LORD had said.
23 And Pharaoh turned and went into his
house, neither did he set his heart to this
also.
24 And all the Egyptians digged round
about the river for water to drink; for they
could not drink of the water of the river.
25 And seven days were fulfilled, after
that the LORD had smitten the river.

8

1 And the LORD spake unto Moses, Go
unto Pharaoh, and say unto him, Thus
saith the LORD, Let my people go, that they
may serve me.
2 And if thou refuse to let *them* go, behold, I will smite all thy borders with frogs:
3 And the river shall bring forth frogs
abundantly, which shall go up and come
into thine house, and into thy bedchamber, and upon thy bed, and into the
house of thy servants, and upon thy people, and into thine ovens, and into thy
kneadingtroughs:
4 And the frogs shall come up both on
thee, and upon thy people, and upon all
thy servants.
5 And the LORD spake unto Moses, Say
unto Aaron, Stretch forth thine hand with
thy rod over the streams, over the rivers,
and over the ponds, and cause frogs to
come up upon the land of Egypt.
6 And Aaron stretched out his hand over
the waters of Egypt; and the frogs came up,
and covered the land of Egypt.
7 And the magicians did so with their
enchantments, and brought up frogs upon
the land of Egypt.
8 Then Pharaoh called for Moses and
Aaron, and said, Intreat the LORD, that
he may take away the frogs from me, and
from my people; and I will let the people
go, that they may do sacrifice unto the
LORD.
9 And Moses said unto Pharaoh, Glory
over me: when shall I intreat for thee, and
for thy servants, and for thy people, to destroy the frogs from thee and thy houses,
that they may remain in the river only?
10 And he said, To morrow. And he said,
Be it according to thy word: that thou
mayest know that *there is* none like unto
the LORD our God.
11 And the frogs shall depart from thee,
and from thy houses, and from thy servants, and from thy people; they shall remain in the river only.
12 And Moses and Aaron went out from
Pharaoh: and Moses cried unto the LORD
because of the frogs which he had brought
against Pharaoh.
13 And the LORD did according to the
word of Moses; and the frogs died out of
the houses, out of the villages, and out of
the fields.
14 And they gathered them together
upon heaps: and the land stank.
15 But when Pharaoh saw that there was
respite, he hardened his heart, and hearkened not unto them; as the LORD had
said.
16 And the LORD said unto Moses, Say
unto Aaron, Stretch out thy rod, and smite
the dust of the land, that it may become
lice throughout all the land of Egypt.
17 And they did so; for Aaron stretched
out his hand with his rod, and smote the
dust of the earth, and it became lice in
man, and in beast; all the dust of the land
became lice throughout all the land of
Egypt.
18 And the magicians did so with their
enchantments to bring forth lice, but they
could not: so there were lice upon man,
and upon beast.
19 Then the magicians said unto Pharaoh, This *is* the finger of God: and

Pharaoh's heart was hardened, and he hearkened not unto them; as the LORD had said.

20 And the LORD said unto Moses, Rise up early in the morning, and stand before Pharaoh; lo, he cometh forth to the water; and say unto him, Thus saith the LORD, Let my people go, that they may serve me.

21 Else, if thou wilt not let my people go, behold, I will send swarms *of flies* upon thee, and upon thy servants, and upon thy people, and into thy houses: and the houses of the Egyptians shall be full of swarms *of flies*, and also the ground whereon they *are*.

22 And I will sever in that day the land of Goshen, in which my people dwell, that no swarms *of flies* shall be there; to the end thou mayest know that I *am* the LORD in the midst of the earth.

23 And I will put a division between my people and thy people: to morrow shall this sign be.

24 And the LORD did so; and there came a grievous swarm *of flies* into the house of Pharaoh, and *into* his servants' houses, and into all the land of Egypt: the land was corrupted by reason of the swarm *of flies*.

25 And Pharaoh called for Moses and for Aaron, and said, Go ye, sacrifice to your God in the land.

26 And Moses said, It is not meet so to do; for we shall sacrifice the abomination of the Egyptians to the LORD our God: lo, shall we sacrifice the abomination of the Egyptians before their eyes, and will they not stone us?

27 We will go three days' journey into the wilderness, and sacrifice to the LORD our God, as he shall command us.

28 And Pharaoh said, I will let you go, that ye may sacrifice to the LORD your God in the wilderness; only ye shall not go very far away: intreat for me.

29 And Moses said, Behold, I go out from thee, and I will intreat the LORD that the swarms *of flies* may depart from Pharaoh, from his servants, and from his people, to morrow: but let not Pharaoh deal deceitfully any more in not letting the people go to sacrifice to the LORD.

30 And Moses went out from Pharaoh, and intreated the LORD.

31 And the LORD did according to the word of Moses; and he removed the swarms *of flies* from Pharaoh, from his servants, and from his people; there remained not one.

32 And Pharaoh hardened his heart at this time also, neither would he let the people go.

9

1 Then the LORD said unto Moses, Go in unto Pharaoh, and tell him, Thus saith the LORD God of the Hebrews, Let my people go, that they may serve me.

2 For if thou refuse to let *them* go, and wilt hold them still,

3 Behold, the hand of the LORD is upon thy cattle which *is* in the field, upon the horses, upon the asses, upon the camels, upon the oxen, and upon the sheep: *there shall be* a very grievous murrain.

4 And the LORD shall sever between the cattle of Israel and the cattle of Egypt: and there shall nothing die of all *that is* the children's of Israel.

5 And the LORD appointed a set time, saying, To morrow the LORD shall do this thing in the land.

6 And the LORD did that thing on the morrow, and all the cattle of Egypt died: but of the cattle of the children of Israel died not one.

7 And Pharaoh sent, and, behold, there was not one of the cattle of the Israelites dead. And the heart of Pharaoh was hardened, and he did not let the people go.

8 And the LORD said unto Moses and unto Aaron, Take to you handfuls of ashes of the furnace, and let Moses sprinkle it toward the heaven in the sight of Pharaoh.

9 And it shall become small dust in all the land of Egypt, and shall be a boil breaking forth *with* blains upon man, and upon beast, throughout all the land of Egypt.

10 And they took ashes of the furnace, and stood before Pharaoh; and Moses sprinkled it up toward heaven; and it became a boil breaking forth *with* blains upon man, and upon beast.

11 And the magicians could not stand before Moses because of the boils; for the boil was upon the magicians, and upon all the Egyptians.

12 And the LORD hardened the heart of Pharaoh, and he hearkened not unto them; as the LORD had spoken unto Moses.

13 And the LORD said unto Moses, Rise up early in the morning, and stand before Pharaoh, and say unto him, Thus saith the

LORD God of the Hebrews, Let my people
go, that they may serve me.
14For I will at this time send all my
plagues upon thine heart, and upon thy
servants, and upon thy people; that thou
mayest know that *there is* none like me in
all the earth.
15For now I will stretch out my hand,
that I may smite thee and thy people with
pestilence; and thou shalt be cut off from
the earth.
16And in very deed for this *cause* have I
raised thee up, for to shew *in* thee my power; and that my name may be declared
throughout all the earth.
17As yet exaltest thou thyself against my
people, that thou wilt not let them go?
18Behold, to morrow about this time I
will cause it to rain a very grievous hail,
such as hath not been in Egypt since the
foundation thereof even until now.
19Send therefore now, *and* gather thy
cattle, and all that thou hast in the field;
for upon every man and beast which shall
be found in the field, and shall not be
brought home, the hail shall come down
upon them, and they shall die.
20He that feared the word of the LORD
among the servants of Pharaoh made his
servants and his cattle flee into the houses:
21And he that regarded not the word of
the LORD left his servants and his cattle in
the field.
22And the LORD said unto Moses, Stretch
forth thine hand toward heaven, that there
may be hail in all the land of Egypt, upon
man, and upon beast, and upon every herb
of the field, throughout the land of Egypt.
23And Moses stretched forth his rod toward heaven: and the LORD sent thunder
and hail, and the fire ran along upon the
ground; and the LORD rained hail upon the
land of Egypt.
24So there was hail, and fire mingled
with the hail, very grievous, such as there
was none like it in all the land of Egypt
since it became a nation.
25And the hail smote throughout all the
land of Egypt all that *was* in the field, both
man and beast; and the hail smote every
herb of the field, and brake every tree of
the field.
26Only in the land of Goshen, where the
children of Israel *were,* was there no hail.
27And Pharaoh sent, and called for Moses and Aaron, and
said unto them, I
have sinned this
time: the LORD *is*
righteous, and I
and my people *are*
wicked.
28Intreat the
LORD (for *it is*
enough) that there
be no *more* mighty
thunderings and
hail; and I will let you go, and ye shall stay
no longer.
29And Moses said unto him, As soon as
I am gone out of the city, I will spread
abroad my hands unto the LORD; *and* the
thunder shall cease, neither shall there be
any more hail; that thou mayest know how
that the earth *is* the LORD'S.
30But as for thee and thy servants, I know
that ye will not yet fear the LORD God.
31And the flax and the barley was smitten: for the barley *was* in the ear, and the
flax *was* bolled.
32But the wheat and the rie were not
smitten: for they *were* not grown up.
33And Moses went out of the city from
Pharaoh, and spread abroad his hands
unto the LORD: and the thunders and hail
ceased, and the rain was not poured upon
the earth.
34And when Pharaoh saw that the rain
and the hail and the thunders were ceased,
he sinned yet more, and hardened his
heart, he and his servants.
35And the heart of Pharaoh was hardened, neither would he let the children
of Israel go; as the LORD had spoken by
Moses.

10

1And the LORD said unto Moses, Go in
unto Pharaoh: for I have hardened his
heart, and the heart of his servants, that I
might shew these my signs before him:
2And that thou mayest tell in the ears of
thy son, and of thy son's son, what things
I have wrought in Egypt, and my signs
which I have done among them; that ye
may know how that I *am* the LORD.
3And Moses and Aaron came in unto
Pharaoh, and said unto him, Thus saith
the LORD God of the Hebrews, How long
wilt thou refuse to humble thyself before
me? let my people go, that they may
serve me.

9:27 Feeling Guilty
◄ Genesis 42:21
Numbers 21:7 ►

9:27 Guilty Conscience
◄ Genesis 42:21
Ezra 9:6 ►

4 Else, if thou refuse to let my people go,
behold, to morrow will I bring the locusts
into thy coast:
5 And they shall cover the face of the
earth, that one cannot be able to see the
earth: and they shall eat the residue of that
which is escaped, which remaineth unto
you from the hail, and shall eat every tree
which groweth for you out of the field:
6 And they shall fill thy houses, and the
houses of all thy servants, and the houses
of all the Egyptians; which neither thy fathers, nor thy fathers' fathers have seen,
since the day that they were upon the earth
unto this day. And he turned himself, and
went out from Pharaoh.
7 And Pharaoh's servants said unto him,
How long shall this man be a snare unto
us? let the men go, that they may serve the
LORD their God: knowest thou not yet that
Egypt is destroyed?
8 And Moses and Aaron were brought
again unto Pharaoh: and he said unto
them, Go, serve the LORD your God: *but*
who *are* they that shall go?
9 And Moses said, We will go with our
young and with our old, with our sons and
with our daughters, with our flocks and
with our herds will we go; for we *must hold*
a feast unto the LORD.
10 And he said unto them, Let the
LORD be so with you, as I will let you go,
and your little ones: look *to it;* for evil *is*
before you.
11 Not so: go now ye *that are* men, and
serve the LORD; for that ye did desire.
And they were driven out from Pharaoh's
presence.
12 And the LORD said unto Moses, Stretch
out thine hand over the land of Egypt
for the locusts, that they may come up
upon the land of Egypt, and eat every herb
of the land, *even* all that the hail hath
left.
13 And Moses stretched forth his rod over
the land of Egypt, and the LORD brought
an east wind upon the land all that day,
and all *that* night; *and* when it was morning, the east wind brought the locusts.
14 And the locusts went up over all the
land of Egypt, and rested in all the coasts
of Egypt: very grievous *were they;* before
them there were no such locusts as they,
neither after them shall be such.
15 For they covered the face of the whole
earth, so that the land was darkened; and
they did eat every herb of the land, and all
the fruit of the trees which the hail had
left: and there remained not any green
thing in the trees, or in the herbs of the
field, through all the land of Egypt.
16 Then Pharaoh called for Moses and
Aaron in haste; and he said, I have sinned
against the LORD your God, and against
you.
17 Now therefore forgive, I pray thee, my
sin only this once, and intreat the LORD
your God, that he may take away from me
this death only.
18 And he went out from Pharaoh, and
intreated the LORD.
19 And the LORD turned a mighty strong
west wind, which took away the locusts,
and cast them into the Red sea; there remained not one locust in all the coasts of
Egypt.
20 But the LORD hardened Pharaoh's
heart, so that he would not let the children of Israel go.
21 And the LORD said unto Moses, Stretch
out thine hand toward heaven, that there
may be darkness over the land of Egypt,
even darkness *which* may be felt.
22 And Moses stretched forth his hand
toward heaven; and there was a thick darkness in all the land of Egypt three days:
23 They saw not one another, neither rose
any from his place for three days: but all
the children of Israel had light in their
dwellings.
24 And Pharaoh called unto Moses, and
said, Go ye, serve the LORD; only let your
flocks and your herds be stayed: let your
little ones also go with you.
25 And Moses said, Thou must give us
also sacrifices and burnt offerings, that we
may sacrifice unto the LORD our God.
26 Our cattle also shall go with us; there
shall not an hoof be left behind; for thereof
must we take to serve the LORD our God;
and we know not with what we must serve
the LORD, until we come thither.
27 But the LORD hardened Pharaoh's
heart, and he would not let them go.
28 And Pharaoh said unto him, Get thee
from me, take heed to thyself, see my face
no more; for in *that* day thou seest my face
thou shalt die.
29 And Moses said, Thou hast spoken
well, I will see thy face again no more.

11 1 And the LORD said unto Moses, Yet will I bring one plague *more* upon Pharaoh, and upon Egypt; afterwards he will let you go hence: when he shall let *you* go, he shall surely thrust you out hence altogether.

2 Speak now in the ears of the people, and let every man borrow of his neighbour, and every woman of her neighbour, jewels of silver, and jewels of gold.

3 And the LORD gave the people favour in the sight of the Egyptians. Moreover the man Moses *was* very great in the land of Egypt, in the sight of Pharaoh's servants, and in the sight of the people.

4 And Moses said, Thus saith the LORD, About midnight will I go out into the midst of Egypt:

5 And all the firstborn in the land of Egypt shall die, from the firstborn of Pharaoh that sitteth upon his throne, even unto the firstborn of the maidservant that *is* behind the mill; and all the firstborn of beasts.

6 And there shall be a great cry throughout all the land of Egypt, such as there was none like it, nor shall be like it any more.

7 But against any of the children of Israel shall not a dog move his tongue, against man or beast: that ye may know how that the LORD doth put a difference between the Egyptians and Israel.

8 And all these thy servants shall come down unto me, and bow down themselves unto me, saying, Get thee out, and all the people that follow thee: and after that I will go out. And he went out from Pharaoh in a great anger.

9 And the LORD said unto Moses, Pharaoh shall not hearken unto you; that my wonders may be multiplied in the land of Egypt.

10 And Moses and Aaron did all these wonders before Pharaoh: and the LORD hardened Pharaoh's heart, so that he would not let the children of Israel go out of his land.

12 1 And the LORD spake unto Moses and Aaron in the land of Egypt, saying,

2 This month *shall be* unto you the beginning of months: it *shall be* the first month of the year to you.

3 Speak ye unto all the congregation of Israel, saying, In the tenth *day* of this month they shall take to them every man a lamb, according to the house of *their* fathers, a lamb for an house:

4 And if the household be too little for the lamb, let him and his neighbour next unto his house take *it* according to the number of the souls; every man according to his eating shall make your count for the lamb.

5 Your lamb shall be without blemish, a male of the first year: ye shall take *it* out from the sheep, or from the goats:

6 And ye shall keep it up until the fourteenth day of the same month: and the whole assembly of the congregation of Israel shall kill it in the evening.

7 And they shall take of the blood, and strike *it* on the two side posts and on the upper door post of the houses, wherein they shall eat it.

8 And they shall eat the flesh in that night, roast with fire, and unleavened bread; *and* with bitter *herbs* they shall eat it.

9 Eat not of it raw, nor sodden at all with water, but roast *with* fire; his head with his legs, and with the purtenance thereof.

10 And ye shall let nothing of it remain until the morning; and that which remaineth of it until the morning ye shall burn with fire.

11 And thus shall ye eat it; *with* your loins girded, your shoes on your feet, and your staff in your hand; and ye shall eat it in haste: it *is* the LORD'S passover.

12 For I will pass through the land of Egypt this night, and will smite all the firstborn in the land of Egypt, both man and beast; and against all the gods of Egypt I will execute judgment: I *am* the LORD.

13 And the blood shall be to you for a token upon the houses where ye *are*: and when I see the blood, I will pass over you, and the plague shall not be upon you to destroy *you*, when I smite the land of Egypt.

14 And this day shall be unto you for a memorial; and ye shall keep it a feast to the LORD throughout your generations; ye shall keep it a feast by an ordinance for ever.

15 Seven days shall ye eat unleavened bread; even the first day ye shall put away leaven out of your houses: for whosoever eateth leavened bread from the first day until the seventh day, that soul shall be cut off from Israel.

16 And in the first day *there shall be* an

holy convocation, and in the seventh day there shall be an holy convocation to you; no manner of work shall be done in them, save *that* which every man must eat, that only may be done of you.

17 And ye shall observe *the feast of* unleavened bread; for in this selfsame day have I brought your armies out of the land of Egypt: therefore shall ye observe this day in your generations by an ordinance for ever.

18 In the first *month,* on the fourteenth day of the month at even, ye shall eat unleavened bread, until the one and twentieth day of the month at even.

19 Seven days shall there be no leaven found in your houses: for whosoever eateth that which is leavened, even that soul shall be cut off from the congregation of Israel, whether he be a stranger, or born in the land.

20 Ye shall eat nothing leavened; in all your habitations shall ye eat unleavened bread.

21 Then Moses called for all the elders of Israel, and said unto them, Draw out and take you a lamb according to your families, and kill the passover.

22 And ye shall take a bunch of hyssop, and dip *it* in the blood that *is* in the bason, and strike the lintel and the two side posts with the blood that *is* in the bason; and none of you shall go out at the door of his house until the morning.

23 For the LORD will pass through to smite the Egyptians; and when he seeth the blood upon the lintel, and on the two side posts, the LORD will pass over the door, and will not suffer the destroyer to come in unto your houses to smite *you.*

24 And ye shall observe this thing for an ordinance to thee and to thy sons for ever.

25 And it shall come to pass, when ye be come to the land which the LORD will give you, according as he hath promised, that ye shall keep this service.

26 And it shall come to pass, when your children shall say unto you, What mean ye by this service?

27 That ye shall say, It *is* the sacrifice of the LORD'S passover, who passed over the houses of the children of Israel in Egypt, when he smote the Egyptians, and delivered our houses. And the people bowed the head and worshipped.

28 And the children of Israel went away, and did as the LORD had commanded Moses and Aaron, so did they.

29 And it came to pass, that at midnight the LORD smote all the firstborn in the land of Egypt, from the firstborn of Pharaoh that sat on his throne unto the firstborn of the captive that *was* in the dungeon; and all the firstborn of cattle.

30 And Pharaoh rose up in the night, he, and all his servants, and all the Egyptians; and there was a great cry in Egypt; for *there was* not a house where *there was* not one dead.

31 And he called for Moses and Aaron by night, and said, Rise up, *and* get you forth from among my people, both ye and the children of Israel; and go, serve the LORD, as ye have said.

32 Also take your flocks and your herds, as ye have said, and be gone; and bless me also.

33 And the Egyptians were urgent upon the people, that they might send them out of the land in haste; for they said, We *be* all dead *men.*

34 And the people took their dough before it was leavened, their kneadingtroughs being bound up in their clothes upon their shoulders.

35 And the children of Israel did according to the word of Moses; and they borrowed of the Egyptians jewels of silver, and jewels of gold, and raiment:

36 And the LORD gave the people favour in the sight of the Egyptians, so that they lent unto them *such things as they required.* And they spoiled the Egyptians.

37 And the children of Israel journeyed from Rameses to Succoth, about six hundred thousand on foot *that were* men, beside children.

38 And a mixed multitude went up also with them; and flocks, and herds, *even* very much cattle.

39 And they baked unleavened cakes of the dough which they brought forth out of Egypt, for it was not leavened; because they were thrust out of Egypt, and could not tarry, neither had they prepared for themselves any victual.

40 Now the sojourning of the children of Israel, who dwelt in Egypt, *was* four hundred and thirty years.

41 And it came to pass at the end of the

four hundred and thirty years, even the
selfsame day it came to pass, that all the
hosts of the LORD went out from the land
of Egypt.
42 It *is* a night to be much observed unto
the LORD for bringing them out from the
land of Egypt: this *is* that night of the LORD
to be observed of all the children of Israel
in their generations.
43 And the LORD said unto Moses and
Aaron, This *is* the ordinance of the passover: There shall no stranger eat thereof:
44 But every man's servant that is bought
for money, when thou hast circumcised
him, then shall he eat thereof.
45 A foreigner and an hired servant shall
not eat thereof.
46 In one house shall it be eaten; thou
shalt not carry forth ought of the flesh
abroad out of the house; neither shall ye
break a bone thereof.
47 All the congregation of Israel shall
keep it.
48 And when a stranger shall sojourn
with thee, and will keep the passover to
the LORD, let all his males be circumcised,
and then let him come near and keep it;
and he shall be as one that is born in the
land: for no uncircumcised person shall
eat thereof.
49 One law shall be to him that is
homeborn, and unto the stranger that
sojourneth among you.
50 Thus did all the children of Israel; as
the LORD commanded Moses and Aaron,
so did they.
51 And it came to pass the selfsame day,
that the LORD did bring the children of
Israel out of the land of Egypt by their
armies.

13

1 And the LORD spake unto Moses,
saying,
2 Sanctify unto me all the firstborn,
whatsoever openeth the womb among the
children of Israel, *both* of man and of beast:
it *is* mine.
3 And Moses said unto the people, Remember this day, in which ye came out
from Egypt, out of the house of bondage;
for by strength of hand the LORD brought
you out from this *place:* there shall no leavened bread be eaten.
4 This day came ye out in the month
Abib.
5 And it shall be when the LORD shall
bring thee into the land of the Canaanites, and the Hittites, and the Amorites, and
the Hivites, and the Jebusites, which he
sware unto thy fathers to give thee, a land
flowing with milk and honey, that thou
shalt keep this service in this month.
6 Seven days thou shalt eat unleavened
bread, and in the seventh day *shall be* a feast
to the LORD.
7 Unleavened bread shall be eaten seven
days; and there shall no leavened bread be
seen with thee, neither shall there be
leaven seen with thee in all thy quarters.
8 And thou shalt shew thy son in that
day, saying, *This is done* because of that
which the LORD did unto me when I came
forth out of Egypt.
9 And it shall be for a sign unto thee
upon thine hand, and for a memorial between thine eyes, that the LORD'S law may
be in thy mouth: for with a strong hand
hath the LORD brought thee out of Egypt.
10 Thou shalt therefore keep this ordinance in his season from year to year.
11 And it shall be when the LORD shall
bring thee into the land of the Canaanites, as he sware unto thee and to thy fathers, and shall give it thee,
12 That thou shalt set apart unto the
LORD all that openeth the matrix, and every
firstling that cometh of a beast which thou
hast; the males *shall be* the LORD'S.
13 And every firstling of an ass thou shalt
redeem with a lamb; and if thou wilt not
redeem it, then thou shalt break his neck:
and all the firstborn of man among thy
children shalt thou redeem.
14 And it shall be when thy son asketh
thee in time to come, saying, What *is* this?
that thou shalt say unto him, By strength
of hand the LORD brought us out from
Egypt, from the house of bondage:
15 And it came to pass, when Pharaoh
would hardly let us go, that the LORD slew
all the firstborn in the land of Egypt, both
the firstborn of man, and the firstborn of
beast: therefore I sacrifice to the LORD all
that openeth the matrix, being males; but
all the firstborn of my children I redeem.
16 And it shall be for a token upon thine
hand, and for frontlets between thine eyes:
for by strength of hand the LORD brought
us forth out of Egypt.
17 And it came to pass, when Pharaoh
had let the people go, that God led them

not *through* the way of the land of the Philistines, although that *was* near; for God said, Lest peradventure the people repent when they see war, and they return to Egypt:

18 But God led the people about, *through* the way of the wilderness of the Red sea: and the children of Israel went up harnessed out of the land of Egypt.

19 And Moses took the bones of Joseph with him: for he had straitly sworn the children of Israel, saying, God will surely visit you; and ye shall carry up my bones away hence with you.

20 And they took their journey from Succoth, and encamped in Etham, in the edge of the wilderness.

21 And the LORD went before them by day in a pillar of a cloud, to lead them the way; and by night in a pillar of fire, to give them light; to go by day and night:

22 He took not away the pillar of the cloud by day, nor the pillar of fire by night, *from* before the people.

14

1 And the LORD spake unto Moses, saying,

2 Speak unto the children of Israel, that they turn and encamp before Pi-hahiroth, between Migdol and the sea, over against Baal-zephon: before it shall ye encamp by the sea.

3 For Pharaoh will say of the children of Israel, They *are* entangled in the land, the wilderness hath shut them in.

4 And I will harden Pharaoh's heart, that he shall follow after them; and I will be honoured upon Pharaoh, and upon all his host; that the Egyptians may know that I *am* the LORD. And they did so.

5 And it was told the king of Egypt that the people fled: and the heart of Pharaoh and of his servants was turned against the people, and they said, Why have we done this, that we have let Israel go from serving us?

6 And he made ready his chariot, and took his people with him:

7 And he took six hundred chosen chariots, and all the chariots of Egypt, and captains over every one of them.

8 And the LORD hardened the heart of Pharaoh king of Egypt, and he pursued after the children of Israel: and the children of Israel went out with an high hand.

9 But the Egyptians pursued after them, all the horses *and* chariots of Pharaoh, and his horsemen, and his army, and overtook them encamping by the sea, beside Pi-hahiroth, before Baal-zephon.

10 And when Pharaoh drew nigh, the children of Israel lifted up their eyes, and, behold, the Egyptians marched after them; and they were sore afraid: and the children of Israel cried out unto the LORD.

11 And they said unto Moses, Because *there were* no graves in Egypt, hast thou taken us away to die in the wilderness? wherefore hast thou dealt thus with us, to carry us forth out of Egypt?

12 *Is* not this the word that we did tell thee in Egypt, saying, Let us alone, that we may serve the Egyptians? For *it had been* better for us to serve the Egyptians, than that we should die in the wilderness.

13 And Moses said unto the people, Fear ye not, stand still, and see the salvation of the LORD, which he will shew to you to day: for the Egyptians whom ye have seen to day, ye shall see them again no more for ever.

> **14:13**
> **Encouraging People**
> ◄ 2 Chronicles 35:2 ►

14 The LORD shall fight for you, and ye shall hold your peace.

15 And the LORD said unto Moses, Wherefore criest thou unto me? speak unto the children of Israel, that they go forward:

16 But lift thou up thy rod, and stretch out thine hand over the sea, and divide it: and the children of Israel shall go on dry *ground* through the midst of the sea.

17 And I, behold, I will harden the hearts of the Egyptians, and they shall follow them: and I will get me honour upon Pharaoh, and upon all his host, upon his chariots, and upon his horsemen.

18 And the Egyptians shall know that I *am* the LORD, when I have gotten me honour upon Pharaoh, upon his chariots, and upon his horsemen.

19 And the angel of God, which went before the camp of Israel, removed and went behind them; and the pillar of the cloud went from before their face, and stood behind them:

> **14:19**
> **Angels**
> ◄ Psalm 91:11 ►

20 And it came between the camp of the

Egyptians and the camp of Israel; and it was a cloud and darkness *to them,* but it gave light by night *to these:* so that the one came not near the other all the night.

21 And Moses stretched out his hand over the sea; and the LORD caused the sea to go *back* by a strong east wind all that night, and made the sea dry *land,* and the waters were divided.

22 And the children of Israel went into the midst of the sea upon the dry *ground:* and the waters *were* a wall unto them on their right hand, and on their left.

23 And the Egyptians pursued, and went in after them to the midst of the sea, *even* all Pharaoh's horses, his chariots, and his horsemen.

24 And it came to pass, that in the morning watch the LORD looked unto the host of the Egyptians through the pillar of fire and of the cloud, and troubled the host of the Egyptians,

25 And took off their chariot wheels, that they drave them heavily: so that the Egyptians said, Let us flee from the face of Israel; for the LORD fighteth for them against the Egyptians.

26 And the LORD said unto Moses, Stretch out thine hand over the sea, that the waters may come again upon the Egyptians, upon their chariots, and upon their horsemen.

27 And Moses stretched forth his hand over the sea, and the sea returned to his strength when the morning appeared; and the Egyptians fled against it; and the LORD overthrew the Egyptians in the midst of the sea.

28 And the waters returned, and covered the chariots, and the horsemen, *and* all the host of Pharaoh that came into the sea after them; there remained not so much as one of them.

29 But the children of Israel walked upon dry *land* in the midst of the sea; and the waters *were* a wall unto them on their right hand, and on their left.

30 Thus the LORD saved Israel that day out of the hand of the Egyptians; and Israel saw the Egyptians dead upon the sea shore.

31 And Israel saw that great work which the LORD did upon the Egyptians: and the people feared the LORD, and believed the LORD, and his servant Moses.

15

1 Then sang Moses and the children of Israel this song unto the LORD, and spake, saying, I will sing unto the LORD, for he hath triumphed gloriously: the horse and his rider hath he thrown into the sea.

15:2
Finding Strength
◄ 2 Samuel 22:33 ►

15:2 Names of God
◄ Exodus 6:3
Deuteronomy 10:17 ►

2 The LORD *is* my strength and song, and he is become my salvation: he *is* my God, and I will prepare him an habitation; my father's God, and I will exalt him.

3 The LORD *is* a man of war: the LORD *is* his name.

4 Pharaoh's chariots and his host hath he cast into the sea: his chosen captains also are drowned in the Red sea.

5 The depths have covered them: they sank into the bottom as a stone.

6 Thy right hand, O LORD, is become glorious in power: thy right hand, O LORD, hath dashed in pieces the enemy.

7 And in the greatness of thine excellency thou hast overthrown them that rose up against thee: thou sentest forth thy wrath, *which* consumed them as stubble.

8 And with the blast of thy nostrils the waters were gathered together, the floods stood upright as an heap, *and* the depths were congealed in the heart of the sea.

9 The enemy said, I will pursue, I will overtake, I will divide the spoil; my lust shall be satisfied upon them; I will draw my sword, my hand shall destroy them.

10 Thou didst blow with thy wind, the sea covered them: they sank as lead in the mighty waters.

11 Who *is* like unto thee, O LORD, among the gods? who *is* like thee, glorious in holiness, fearful *in* praises, doing wonders?

12 Thou stretchedst out thy right hand, the earth swallowed them.

13 Thou in thy mercy hast led forth the people *which* thou hast redeemed: thou hast guided *them* in thy strength unto thy holy habitation.

14 The people shall hear, *and* be afraid: sorrow shall take hold on the inhabitants of Palestina.

15 Then the dukes of Edom shall be amazed; the mighty men of Moab, trem-

bling shall take hold upon them; all the inhabitants of Canaan shall melt away.

16 Fear and dread shall fall upon them; by the greatness of thine arm they shall be *as* still as a stone; till thy people pass over, O LORD, till the people pass over, *which* thou hast purchased.

17 Thou shalt bring them in, and plant them in the mountain of thine inheritance, *in* the place, O LORD, *which* thou hast made for thee to dwell in, *in* the Sanctuary, O Lord, *which* thy hands have established.

18 The LORD shall reign for ever and ever.

19 For the horse of Pharaoh went in with his chariots and with his horsemen into the sea, and the LORD brought again the waters of the sea upon them; but the children of Israel went on dry *land* in the midst of the sea.

20 And Miriam the prophetess, the sister of Aaron, took a timbrel in her hand; and all the women went out after her with timbrels and with dances.

21 And Miriam answered them, Sing ye to the LORD, for he hath triumphed gloriously; the horse and his rider hath he thrown into the sea.

22 So Moses brought Israel from the Red sea, and they went out into the wilderness of Shur; and they went three days in the wilderness, and found no water.

23 And when they came to Marah, they could not drink of the waters of Marah, for they *were* bitter: therefore the name of it was called Marah.

24 And the people murmured against Moses, saying, What shall we drink?

25 And he cried unto the LORD; and the LORD shewed him a tree, *which* when he had cast into the waters, the waters were made sweet: there he made for them a statute and an ordinance, and there he proved them,

26 And said, If thou wilt diligently hearken to the voice of the LORD thy God, and wilt do that which is right in his sight, and wilt give ear to his commandments, and keep all his statutes, I will put none of these diseases upon thee, which I have brought upon the Egyptians: for I *am* the LORD that healeth thee.

27 And they came to Elim, where *were* twelve wells of water, and threescore and ten palm trees: and they encamped there by the waters.

16

1 And they took their journey from Elim, and all the congregation of the children of Israel came unto the wilderness of Sin, which *is* between Elim and Sinai, on the fifteenth day of the second month after their departing out of the land of Egypt.

2 And the whole congregation of the children of Israel murmured against Moses and Aaron in the wilderness:

3 And the children of Israel said unto them, Would to God we had died by the hand of the LORD in the land of Egypt, when we sat by the flesh pots, *and* when we did eat bread to the full; for ye have brought us forth into this wilderness, to kill this whole assembly with hunger.

4 Then said the LORD unto Moses, Behold, I will rain bread from heaven for you; and the people shall go out and gather a certain rate every day, that I may prove them, whether they will walk in my law, or no.

5 And it shall come to pass, that on the sixth day they shall prepare *that* which they bring in; and it shall be twice as much as they gather daily.

6 And Moses and Aaron said unto all the children of Israel, At even, then ye shall know that the LORD hath brought you out from the land of Egypt:

7 And in the morning, then ye shall see the glory of the LORD; for that he heareth your murmurings against the LORD: and what *are* we, that ye murmur against us?

8 And Moses said, *This shall be,* when the LORD shall give you in the evening flesh to eat, and in the morning bread to the full; for that the LORD heareth your murmurings which ye murmur against him: and what *are* we? your murmurings *are* not against us, but against the LORD.

9 And Moses spake unto Aaron, Say unto all the congregation of the children of Israel, Come near before the LORD: for he hath heard your murmurings.

10 And it came to pass, as Aaron spake unto the whole congregation of the children of Israel, that they looked toward the wilderness, and, behold, the glory of the LORD appeared in the cloud.

11 And the LORD spake unto Moses, saying,

12 I have heard the murmurings of the children of Israel: speak unto them, saying, At even ye shall eat flesh, and in the

morning ye shall be filled with bread; and ye shall know that I *am* the LORD your God.

13 And it came to pass, that at even the quails came up, and covered the camp: and in the morning the dew lay round about the host.

14 And when the dew that lay was gone up, behold, upon the face of the wilderness *there lay* a small round thing, *as* small as the hoar frost on the ground.

15 And when the children of Israel saw *it,* they said one to another, It *is* manna: for they wist not what it *was.* And Moses said unto them, This *is* the bread which the LORD hath given you to eat.

16 This *is* the thing which the LORD hath commanded, Gather of it every man *according to* his eating, an omer for every man, according to the number of your persons; take ye every man for *them* which *are* in his tents.

17 And the children of Israel did so, and gathered, some more, some less.

18 And when they did mete *it* with an omer, he that gathered much had nothing over, and he that gathered little had no lack; they gathered every man according to his eating.

19 And Moses said, Let no man leave of it till the morning.

20 Notwithstanding they hearkened not unto Moses; but some of them left of it until the morning, and it bred worms, and stank: and Moses was wroth with them.

21 And they gathered it every morning, every man according to his eating: and when the sun waxed hot, it melted.

22 And it came to pass, *that* on the sixth day they gathered twice as much bread, two omers for one *man:* and all the rulers of the congregation came and told Moses.

23 And he said unto them, This *is that* which the LORD hath said, To morrow *is* the rest of the holy sabbath unto the LORD: bake *that* which ye will bake *to day,* and seethe that ye will seethe; and that which remaineth over lay up for you to be kept until the morning.

24 And they laid it up till the morning, as Moses bade: and it did not stink, neither was there any worm therein.

25 And Moses said, Eat that to day; for to day *is* a sabbath unto the LORD: to day ye shall not find it in the field.

26 Six days ye shall gather it; but on the seventh day, *which is* the sabbath, in it there shall be none.

27 And it came to pass, *that* there went out *some* of the people on the seventh day for to gather, and they found none.

28 And the LORD said unto Moses, How long refuse ye to keep my commandments and my laws?

29 See, for that the LORD hath given you the sabbath, therefore he giveth you on the sixth day the bread of two days; abide ye every man in his place, let no man go out of his place on the seventh day.

30 So the people rested on the seventh day.

31 And the house of Israel called the name thereof Manna: and it *was* like coriander seed, white; and the taste of it *was* like wafers *made* with honey.

32 And Moses said, This *is* the thing which the LORD commandeth, Fill an omer of it to be kept for your generations; that they may see the bread wherewith I have fed you in the wilderness, when I brought you forth from the land of Egypt.

33 And Moses said unto Aaron, Take a pot, and put an omer full of manna therein, and lay it up before the LORD, to be kept for your generations.

34 As the LORD commanded Moses, so Aaron laid it up before the Testimony, to be kept.

35 And the children of Israel did eat manna forty years, until they came to a land inhabited; they did eat manna, until they came unto the borders of the land of Canaan.

36 Now an omer *is* the tenth *part* of an ephah.

17

1 And all the congregation of the children of Israel journeyed from the wilderness of Sin, after their journeys, according to the commandment of the LORD, and pitched in Rephidim: and *there was* no water for the people to drink.

2 Wherefore the people did chide with Moses, and said, Give us water that we may drink. And Moses said unto them, Why chide ye with me? wherefore do ye tempt the LORD?

3 And the people thirsted there for water; and the people murmured against Moses, and said, Wherefore *is* this *that* thou hast brought us up out of Egypt, to kill us and our children and our cattle with thirst?

4 And Moses cried unto the LORD, saying, What shall I do unto this people? they
be almost ready to stone me.
5 And the LORD said unto Moses, Go on
before the people, and take with thee of
the elders of Israel; and thy rod, wherewith thou smotest the river, take in thine
hand, and go.
6 Behold, I will stand before thee there
upon the rock in Horeb; and thou shalt
smite the rock, and there shall come water out of it, that the people may drink.
And Moses did so in the sight of the elders of Israel.
7 And he called the name of the place
Massah, and Meribah, because of the chid-
ing of the children of Israel, and because
they tempted the LORD, saying, Is the LORD
among us, or not?
8 Then came Amalek, and fought with
Israel in Rephidim.
9 And Moses said unto Joshua, Choose
us out men, and go out, fight with Amalek: to morrow I will stand on the top of
the hill with the rod of God in mine hand.
10 So Joshua did as Moses had said to
him, and fought with Amalek: and Moses,
Aaron, and Hur went up to the top of the
hill.
11 And it came to pass, when Moses held
up his hand, that Israel prevailed: and
when he let down his hand, Amalek prevailed.
12 But Moses'
hands *were* heavy;
and they took a
stone, and put *it*
under him, and he
sat thereon; and
Aaron and Hur stayed up his hands, the
one on the one side, and the other on the
other side; and his hands were steady until the going down of the sun.

17:12
Teamwork
◄ Judges 20:11 ►

13 And Joshua discomfited Amalek and
his people with the edge of the sword.
14 And the LORD said unto Moses, Write
this *for* a memorial in a book, and rehearse
it in the ears of Joshua: for I will utterly
put out the remembrance of Amalek from
under heaven.
15 And Moses built an altar, and called
the name of it Jehovah-nissi:
16 For he said, Because the LORD hath
sworn *that* the LORD *will have* war with
Amalek from generation to generation.

18

1 When Jethro, the priest of Midian,
Moses' father in law, heard of all that God
had done for Moses, and for Israel his people, *and* that the LORD had brought Israel
out of Egypt;
2 Then Jethro, Moses' father in law, took
Zipporah, Moses' wife, after he had sent
her back,
3 And her two sons; of which the name
of the one *was* Gershom; for he said, I have
been an alien in a strange land:
4 And the name of the other *was* Eliezer;
for the God of my father, *said he, was* mine
help, and delivered me from the sword of
Pharaoh:
5 And Jethro, Moses' father in law, came
with his sons and his wife unto Moses into
the wilderness, where he encamped at the
mount of God:
6 And he said unto Moses, I thy father in
law Jethro am come unto thee, and thy
wife, and her two sons with her.
7 And Moses went out to meet his father
in law, and did obeisance, and kissed him;
and they asked each other of *their* welfare;
and they came into the tent.
8 And Moses told his father in law all that
the LORD had done unto Pharaoh and to
the Egyptians for Israel's sake, *and* all the
travail that had come upon them by the
way, and *how* the LORD delivered them.
9 And Jethro rejoiced for all the goodness which the LORD had done to Israel,
whom he had delivered out of the hand
of the Egyptians.
10 And Jethro said, Blessed *be* the LORD,
who hath delivered you out of the hand
of the Egyptians, and out of the hand of
Pharaoh, who hath delivered the people
from under the hand of the Egyptians.
11 Now I know that the LORD *is* greater
than all gods: for in the thing wherein they
dealt proudly *he was* above them.
12 And Jethro, Moses' father in law, took
a burnt offering and sacrifices for God: and
Aaron came, and all the elders of Israel, to
eat bread with Moses' father in law before
God.
13 And it came to pass on the morrow,
that Moses sat to judge the people: and
the people stood by Moses from the morning unto the evening.
14 And when Moses' father in law saw
all that he did to the people, he said, What
is this thing that thou doest to the people?

why sittest thou thyself alone, and all the
people stand by thee from morning unto
even?
15 And Moses said unto his father in law,
Because the people come unto me to enquire of God:
16 When they have a matter, they come
unto me; and I judge between one and
another, and I do make *them* know the statutes of God, and his laws.
17 And Moses' father in law said unto
him, The thing that thou doest *is* not good.
18 Thou wilt surely wear away, both thou,
and this people that *is* with thee: for this
thing *is* too heavy for thee; thou art not
able to perform it thyself alone.
19 Hearken now unto my voice, I will
give thee counsel, and God shall be with
thee: Be thou for the people to God-ward,
that thou mayest bring the causes unto
God:
20 And thou shalt teach them ordinances
and laws, and shalt shew them the way
wherein they must walk, and the work that
they must do.
21 Moreover thou shalt provide out of all
the people able men, such as fear God,
men of truth, hating covetousness; and
place *such* over them, *to be* rulers of thousands, *and* rulers of hundreds, rulers of fifties, and rulers of tens:
22 And let them judge the people at all
seasons: and it shall be, *that* every great
matter they shall bring unto thee, but every
small matter they shall judge: so shall it
be easier for thyself, and they shall bear
the burden with thee.
23 If thou shalt do this thing, and God
command thee *so*, then thou shalt be able
to endure, and all this people shall also
go to their place in peace.
24 So Moses hearkened to the voice of
his father in law, and did all that he had
said.
25 And Moses chose able men out of all
Israel, and made them heads over the
people, rulers of thousands, rulers of
hundreds, rulers of fifties, and rulers of
tens.
26 And they judged the people at all seasons: the hard causes they brought unto
Moses, but every small matter they judged
themselves.
27 And Moses let his father in law depart;
and he went his way into his own land.

19

1 In the third month, when the children
of Israel were gone forth out of the land
of Egypt, the same day came they *into* the
wilderness of Sinai.
2 For they were departed from Rephidim,
and were come *to* the desert of Sinai, and
had pitched in the wilderness; and there
Israel camped before the mount.
3 And Moses went up unto God, and the
LORD called unto him out of the mountain, saying, Thus shalt thou say to the
house of Jacob, and tell the children of
Israel;
4 Ye have seen what I did unto the Egyptians, and *how* I bare you on eagles' wings,
and brought you unto myself.
5 Now therefore,
if ye will obey my
voice indeed, and
keep my covenant,
then ye shall be a
peculiar treasure
unto me above all
people: for all the
earth *is* mine:
6 And ye shall be
unto me a kingdom
of priests, and an
holy nation. These *are* the words which
thou shalt speak unto the children of
Israel.

19:5
Earth
◄ Leviticus 25:23 ►

19:6
Holiness
◄ Leviticus 11:45 ►

7 And Moses came and called for the elders of the people, and laid before their
faces all these words which the LORD commanded him.
8 And all the people answered together,
and said, All that the LORD hath spoken
we will do. And Moses returned the words
of the people unto the LORD.
9 And the LORD said unto Moses, Lo, I
come unto thee in a thick cloud, that the
people may hear when I speak with thee,
and believe thee for ever. And Moses told
the words of the people unto the LORD.
10 And the LORD said unto Moses, Go
unto the people, and sanctify them to day
and to morrow, and let them wash their
clothes,
11 And be ready against the third day: for
the third day the LORD will come down in
the sight of all the people upon mount
Sinai.
12 And thou shalt set bounds unto the
people round about, saying, Take heed to
yourselves, *that ye* go *not* up into the

mount, or touch the border of it: whosoever toucheth the mount shall be surely
put to death:
13 There shall not an hand touch it, but
he shall surely be stoned, or shot through;
whether *it be* beast or man, it shall not live:
when the trumpet soundeth long, they
shall come up to the mount.
14 And Moses went down from the
mount unto the people, and sanctified the
people; and they washed their clothes.
15 And he said unto the people, Be ready
against the third day: come not at *your*
wives.
16 And it came to pass on the third day
in the morning, that there were thunders
and lightnings, and a thick cloud upon the
mount, and the voice of the trumpet exceeding loud; so that all the people that
was in the camp trembled.
17 And Moses brought forth the people
out of the camp to meet with God; and
they stood at the nether part of the mount.
18 And mount Sinai was altogether on a
smoke, because the LORD descended upon
it in fire: and the smoke thereof ascended
as the smoke of a furnace, and the whole
mount quaked greatly.
19 And when the voice of the trumpet
sounded long, and waxed louder and louder, Moses spake, and God answered him
by a voice.
20 And the LORD came down upon
mount Sinai, on the top of the mount: and
the LORD called Moses *up* to the top of the
mount; and Moses went up.
21 And the LORD said unto Moses, Go
down, charge the people, lest they break
through unto the LORD to gaze, and many
of them perish.
22 And let the priests also, which come
near to the LORD, sanctify themselves, lest
the LORD break forth upon them.
23 And Moses said unto the LORD, The
people cannot come up to mount Sinai:
for thou chargedst us, saying, Set bounds
about the mount, and sanctify it.
24 And the LORD said unto him, Away,
get thee down, and thou shalt come up,
thou, and Aaron with thee: but let not the
priests and the people break through to
come up unto the LORD, lest he break forth
upon them.
25 So Moses went down unto the people, and spake unto them.

20

1 And God spake all these words, saying,
2 I *am* the LORD thy God, which have
brought thee out of the land of Egypt, out
of the house of bondage.
3 Thou shalt have no other gods before me.
4 Thou shalt not make unto thee any
graven image, or any likeness *of any thing*
that *is* in heaven above, or that *is* in the
earth beneath, or that *is* in the water under the earth:
5 Thou shalt not
bow down thyself
to them, nor serve
them: for I the LORD
thy God *am* a jeal-
ous God, visiting the
iniquity of the fa-
thers upon the chil-
dren unto the third
and fourth *genera-
tion* of them that
hate me;
6 And shewing mercy unto thousands of
them that love me, and keep my commandments.
7 Thou shalt not take the name of the
LORD thy God in vain; for the LORD will
not hold him guiltless that taketh his name
in vain.
8 Remember the sabbath day, to keep it
holy.
9 Six days shalt thou labour, and do all
thy work:
10 But the seventh day *is* the sabbath of
the LORD thy God: *in it* thou shalt not do
any work, thou, nor thy son, nor thy
daughter, thy manservant, nor thy maidservant, nor thy cattle, nor thy stranger that
is within thy gates:
11 For *in* six days the LORD made heaven
and earth, the sea, and all that in them *is*,
and rested the seventh day: wherefore the
LORD blessed the sabbath day, and hallowed it.
12 Honour thy father and thy mother:
that thy days may be long upon the land
which the LORD thy God giveth thee.
13 Thou shalt not kill.
14 Thou shalt not
commit adultery.
15 Thou shalt not
steal.
16 Thou shalt not
bear false witness

20:5
God Is Jealous
◄ Exodus 34:14 ►

20:7
Swearing
◄ Leviticus 19:12 ►

20:15 Stealing
◄ Deuteronomy 23:24 ►

Turn to the next page for more . . .

against thy neigh-
bour.
17 Thou shalt not
covet thy neigh-
bour's house, thou
shalt not covet thy
neighbour's wife, nor his manservant,
nor his maidservant, nor his ox, nor
his ass, nor any thing that *is* thy neighbour's.

20:16
Hurtful Lying
◄ Exodus 23:1 ►

18 And all the people saw the thunderings, and the lightnings, and the noise
of the trumpet, and the mountain smoking: and when the people saw *it*, they removed, and stood afar off.
19 And they said unto Moses, Speak thou
with us, and we will hear: but let not God
speak with us, lest we die.
20 And Moses said unto the people, Fear
not: for God is come to prove you, and
that his fear may be before your faces, that
ye sin not.
21 And the people stood afar off, and
Moses drew near unto the thick darkness
where God *was*.
22 And the LORD said unto Moses, Thus
thou shalt say unto the children of Israel,
Ye have seen that I have talked with you
from heaven.
23 Ye shall not make with me gods of silver, neither shall ye make unto you gods
of gold.
24 An altar of earth thou shalt make unto
me, and shalt sacrifice thereon thy burnt
offerings, and thy peace offerings, thy
sheep, and thine oxen: in all places where
I record my name I will come unto thee,
and I will bless thee.
25 And if thou wilt make me an altar of
stone, thou shalt not build it of hewn
stone: for if thou lift up thy tool upon it,
thou hast polluted it.
26 Neither shalt thou go up by steps unto
mine altar, that thy nakedness be not discovered thereon.

21

1 Now these *are* the judgments which
thou shalt set before them.
2 If thou buy an Hebrew servant, six years
he shall serve: and in the seventh he shall
go out free for nothing.
3 If he came in by himself, he shall go
out by himself: if he were married, then
his wife shall go out with him.
4 If his master have given him a wife, and
she have born him sons or daughters; the
wife and her children shall be her master's,
and he shall go out by himself.
5 And if the servant shall plainly say, I
love my master, my wife, and my children;
I will not go out free:
6 Then his master shall bring him unto
the judges; he shall also bring him to the
door, or unto the door post; and his master shall bore his ear through with an aul;
and he shall serve him for ever.
7 And if a man sell his daughter to be a
maidservant, she shall not go out as the
menservants do.
8 If she please not her master, who hath
betrothed her to himself, then shall he let
her be redeemed: to sell her unto a strange
nation he shall have no power, seeing he
hath dealt deceitfully with her.
9 And if he have betrothed her unto his
son, he shall deal with her after the manner of daughters.
10 If he take him another *wife*; her food,
her raiment, and her duty of marriage,
shall he not diminish.
11 And if he do not these three unto her,
then shall she go out free without money.
12 He that smiteth a man, so that he die,
shall be surely put to death.
13 And if a man lie not in wait, but God
deliver *him* into his hand; then I will
appoint thee a place whither he shall
flee.
14 But if a man come presumptuously
upon his neighbour, to slay him with guile;
thou shalt take him from mine altar, that
he may die.
15 And he that smiteth his father, or his
mother, shall be surely put to death.
16 And he that stealeth a man, and selleth
him, or if he be found in his hand, he shall
surely be put to death.
17 And he that curseth his father, or his
mother, shall surely be put to death.
18 And if men strive together, and one
smite another with a stone, or with *his* fist,
and he die not, but keepeth *his* bed:
19 If he rise again, and walk abroad upon
his staff, then shall he that smote *him* be
quit: only he shall pay *for* the loss of his
time, and shall cause *him* to be thoroughly healed.
20 And if a man smite his servant, or his
maid, with a rod, and he die under his
hand; he shall be surely punished.
21 Notwithstanding, if he continue a day

or two, he shall not be punished: for he *is* his money.

22 If men strive, and hurt a woman with child, so that her fruit depart *from her,* and yet no mischief follow: he shall be surely punished, according as the woman's husband will lay upon him; and he shall pay as the judges *determine.*

23 And if *any* mischief follow, then thou shalt give life for life,

24 Eye for eye, tooth for tooth, hand for hand, foot for foot,

25 Burning for burning, wound for wound, stripe for stripe.

26 And if a man smite the eye of his servant, or the eye of his maid, that it perish; he shall let him go free for his eye's sake.

27 And if he smite out his manservant's tooth, or his maidservant's tooth; he shall let him go free for his tooth's sake.

28 If an ox gore a man or a woman, that they die: then the ox shall be surely stoned, and his flesh shall not be eaten; but the owner of the ox *shall be* quit.

29 But if the ox were wont to push with his horn in time past, and it hath been testified to his owner, and he hath not kept him in, but that he hath killed a man or a woman; the ox shall be stoned, and his owner also shall be put to death.

30 If there be laid on him a sum of money, then he shall give for the ransom of his life whatsoever is laid upon him.

31 Whether he have gored a son, or have gored a daughter, according to this judgment shall it be done unto him.

32 If the ox shall push a manservant or a maidservant; he shall give unto their master thirty shekels of silver, and the ox shall be stoned.

33 And if a man shall open a pit, or if a man shall dig a pit, and not cover it, and an ox or an ass fall therein;

34 The owner of the pit shall make *it* good, *and* give money unto the owner of them; and the dead *beast* shall be his.

35 And if one man's ox hurt another's, that he die; then they shall sell the live ox, and divide the money of it; and the dead *ox* also they shall divide.

36 Or if it be known that the ox hath used to push in time past, and his owner hath not kept him in; he shall surely pay ox for ox; and the dead shall be his own.

22

1 If a man shall steal an ox, or a sheep, and kill it, or sell it; he shall restore five oxen for an ox, and four sheep for a sheep.

2 If a thief be found breaking up, and be smitten that he die, *there shall* no blood *be shed* for him.

3 If the sun be risen upon him, *there shall be* blood *shed* for him; *for* he should make full restitution; if he have nothing, then he shall be sold for his theft.

4 If the theft be certainly found in his hand alive, whether it be ox, or ass, or sheep; he shall restore double.

5 If a man shall cause a field or vineyard to be eaten, and shall put in his beast, and shall feed in another man's field; of the best of his own field, and of the best of his own vineyard, shall he make restitution.

6 If fire break out, and catch in thorns, so that the stacks of corn, or the standing corn, or the field, be consumed *therewith;* he that kindled the fire shall surely make restitution.

7 If a man shall deliver unto his neighbour money or stuff to keep, and it be stolen out of the man's house; if the thief be found, let him pay double.

8 If the thief be not found, then the master of the house shall be brought unto the judges, *to see* whether he have put his hand unto his neighbour's goods.

9 For all manner of trespass, *whether it be* for ox, for ass, for sheep, for raiment, *or* for any manner of lost thing, which *another* challengeth to be his, the cause of both parties shall come before the judges; *and* whom the judges shall condemn, he shall pay double unto his neighbour.

10 If a man deliver unto his neighbour an ass, or an ox, or a sheep, or any beast, to keep; and it die, or be hurt, or driven away, no man seeing *it:*

11 *Then* shall an oath of the LORD be between them both, that he hath not put his hand unto his neighbour's goods; and the owner of it shall accept *thereof,* and he shall not make *it* good.

12 And if it be stolen from him, he shall make restitution unto the owner thereof.

13 If it be torn in pieces, *then* let him bring it *for* witness, *and* he shall not make good that which was torn.

14 And if a man borrow *ought* of his neighbour, and it be hurt, or die, the owner

Turn to the next page for more . . .

thereof *being* not
with it, he shall
surely make *it*
good.
15 *But* if the own-
er thereof *be* with it,
he shall not make *it* good: if it *be* an hired
thing, it came for his hire.

> **22:14 Borrowing** ◄ 2 Kings 6:5 ►

16 And if a man entice a maid that is not
betrothed, and lie with her, he shall surely endow her to be his wife.
17 If her father utterly refuse to give her
unto him, he shall pay money according
to the dowry of virgins.
18 Thou shalt not suffer a witch to live.
19 Whosoever lieth with a beast shall
surely be put to death.
20 He that sacrificeth unto *any* god, save
unto the LORD only, he shall be utterly destroyed.
21 Thou shalt nei-
ther vex a stranger,
nor oppress him:
for ye were strang-
ers in the land of
Egypt.

> **22:21 New Kids** ◄ Exodus 23:9 ►

22 Ye shall not af-
flict any widow, or
fatherless child.
23 If thou afflict
them in any wise,
and they cry at all
unto me, I will surely hear their cry;

> **22:22 Kind to the Needy** ◄ Deuteronomy 14:29 ►

24 And my wrath shall wax hot, and I will
kill you with the sword; and your wives
shall be widows, and your children fatherless.
25 If thou lend money to *any of* my people *that is* poor by thee, thou shalt not be
to him as an usurer, neither shalt thou lay
upon him usury.
26 If thou at all take thy neighbour's raiment to pledge, thou shalt deliver it unto
him by that the sun goeth down:
27 For that *is* his covering only, it *is* his
raiment for his skin: wherein shall he
sleep? and it shall come to pass, when he
crieth unto me, that I will hear; for I *am*
gracious.
28 Thou shalt not
revile the gods, nor
curse the ruler of
thy people.
29 Thou shalt not
delay *to offer* the
first of thy ripe fruits, and of thy liquors:
the firstborn of thy sons shalt thou give
unto me.

> **22:28 Rulers** ◄ 1 Samuel 24:6 ►

30 Likewise shalt thou do with thine
oxen, *and* with thy sheep: seven days it
shall be with his dam; on the eighth day
thou shalt give it me.
31 And ye shall be holy men unto me:
neither shall ye eat *any* flesh *that is* torn of
beasts in the field; ye shall cast it to the
dogs.

23

1 Thou shalt not
raise a false report:
put not thine hand
with the wicked to
be an unrighteous
witness.

> **23:1 Hurtful Lying** ◄ Exodus 20:16 Deuteronomy 19:16 ►

2 Thou shalt not
follow a multitude
to *do* evil; neither
shalt thou speak in
a cause to decline
after many to wrest
judgment:

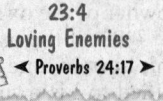

> **23:2 Bad Friends** ◄ Exodus 23:33 ►

3 Neither shalt
thou countenance a
poor man in his
cause.

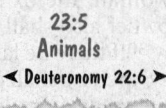

> **23:4 Loving Enemies** ◄ Proverbs 24:17 ►

4 If thou meet
thine enemy's ox or
his ass going astray,
thou shalt surely
bring it back to him
again.

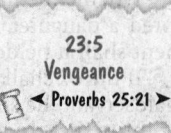

> **23:5 Animals** ◄ Deuteronomy 22:6 ►

5 If thou see the
ass of him that
hateth thee lying
under his burden,
and wouldest for-
bear to help him,
thou shalt surely help with him.

> **23:5 Vengeance** ◄ Proverbs 25:21 ►

6 Thou shalt not wrest the judgment of
thy poor in his cause.
7 Keep thee far from a false matter; and
the innocent and righteous slay thou not:
for I will not justify the wicked.
8 And thou shalt
take no gift: for the
gift blindeth the
wise, and pervert-
eth the words of the
righteous.

> **23:8 Bribery** ◄ Psalm 26:10 ►

9 Also thou shalt not oppress a stranger:
for ye know the heart of a stranger, seeing
ye were strangers in the land of Egypt.

10And six years thou shalt sow thy land, and shalt gather in the fruits thereof:

23:9 New Kids
◄ Exodus 22:21
Leviticus 19:34 ►

11But the seventh *year* thou shalt let it rest and lie still; that the poor of thy people may eat: and what they leave the beasts of the field shall eat. In like manner thou shalt deal with thy vineyard, *and* with thy oliveyard.

23:11 Kind to the Poor
◄ Leviticus 25:25 ►

12Six days thou shalt do thy work, and on the seventh day thou shalt rest: that thine ox and thine ass may rest, and the son of thy handmaid, and the stranger, may be refreshed.

23:12 Rest
◄ Exodus 31:15 ►

13And in all *things* that I have said unto you be circumspect: and make no mention of the name of other gods, neither let it be heard out of thy mouth.

14Three times thou shalt keep a feast unto me in the year.

15Thou shalt keep the feast of unleavened bread: (thou shalt eat unleavened bread seven days, as I commanded thee, in the time appointed of the month Abib; for in it thou camest out from Egypt: and none shall appear before me empty:)

16And the feast of harvest, the firstfruits of thy labours, which thou hast sown in the field: and the feast of ingathering, *which is* in the end of the year, when thou hast gathered in thy labours out of the field.

17Three times in the year all thy males shall appear before the Lord GOD.

18Thou shalt not offer the blood of my sacrifice with leavened bread; neither shall the fat of my sacrifice remain until the morning.

19The first of the firstfruits of thy land thou shalt bring into the house of the LORD thy God. Thou shalt not seethe a kid in his mother's milk.

20Behold, I send an Angel before thee, to keep thee in the way, and to bring thee into the place which I have prepared.

21Beware of him, and obey his voice, provoke him not; for he will not pardon your transgressions: for my name *is* in him.

22But if thou shalt indeed obey his voice, and do all that I speak; then I will be an enemy unto thine enemies, and an adversary unto thine adversaries.

23For mine Angel shall go before thee, and bring thee in unto the Amorites, and the Hittites, and the Perizzites, and the Canaanites, and the Hivites, and the Jebusites: and I will cut them off.

24Thou shalt not bow down to their gods, nor serve them, nor do after their works: but thou shalt utterly overthrow them, and quite break down their images.

25And ye shall serve the LORD your God, and he shall bless thy bread, and thy water; and I will take sickness away from the midst of thee.

23:25 Blessing
◄ Psalm 81:16 ►

26There shall nothing cast their young, nor be barren, in thy land: the number of thy days I will fulfil.

27I will send my fear before thee, and will destroy all the people to whom thou shalt come, and I will make all thine enemies turn their backs unto thee.

28And I will send hornets before thee, which shall drive out the Hivite, the Canaanite, and the Hittite, from before thee.

29I will not drive them out from before thee in one year; lest the land become desolate, and the beast of the field multiply against thee.

30By little and little I will drive them out from before thee, until thou be increased, and inherit the land.

31And I will set thy bounds from the Red sea even unto the sea of the Philistines, and from the desert unto the river: for I will deliver the inhabitants of the land into your hand; and thou shalt drive them out before thee.

32Thou shalt make no covenant with them, nor with their gods.

33They shall not dwell in thy land, lest they make thee sin against me: for if thou serve their gods, it will surely be a snare unto thee.

23:33 Bad Friends
◄ Exodus 23:2
Exodus 34:12 ►

24

1 And he said unto Moses, Come up unto the LORD, thou, and Aaron, Nadab, and Abihu, and seventy of the elders of Israel; and worship ye afar off.

2 And Moses alone shall come near the LORD: but they shall not come nigh; neither shall the people go up with him.

3 And Moses came and told the people all the words of the LORD, and all the judgments: and all the people answered with one voice, and said, All the words which the LORD hath said will we do.

4 And Moses wrote all the words of the LORD, and rose up early in the morning, and builded an altar under the hill, and twelve pillars, according to the twelve tribes of Israel.

24:4 Devotions
◄ Genesis 28:17-18
1 Samuel 1:19 ►

5 And he sent young men of the children of Israel, which offered burnt offerings, and sacrificed peace offerings of oxen unto the LORD.

6 And Moses took half of the blood, and put *it* in basons; and half of the blood he sprinkled on the altar.

7 And he took the book of the covenant, and read in the audience of the people: and they said, All that the LORD hath said will we do, and be obedient.

8 And Moses took the blood, and sprinkled *it* on the people, and said, Behold the blood of the covenant, which the LORD hath made with you concerning all these words.

9 Then went up Moses, and Aaron, Nadab, and Abihu, and seventy of the elders of Israel:

10 And they saw the God of Israel: and *there was* under his feet as it were a paved work of a sapphire stone, and as it were the body of heaven in *his* clearness.

11 And upon the nobles of the children of Israel he laid not his hand: also they saw God, and did eat and drink.

12 And the LORD said unto Moses, Come up to me into the mount, and be there: and I will give thee tables of stone, and a law, and commandments which I have written; that thou mayest teach them.

13 And Moses rose up, and his minister Joshua: and Moses went up into the mount of God.

14 And he said unto the elders, Tarry ye here for us, until we come again unto you: and, behold, Aaron and Hur *are* with you: if any man have any matters to do, let him come unto them.

15 And Moses went up into the mount, and a cloud covered the mount.

16 And the glory of the LORD abode upon mount Sinai, and the cloud covered it six days: and the seventh day he called unto Moses out of the midst of the cloud.

17 And the sight of the glory of the LORD *was* like devouring fire on the top of the mount in the eyes of the children of Israel.

18 And Moses went into the midst of the cloud, and gat him up into the mount: and Moses was in the mount forty days and forty nights.

25

1 And the LORD spake unto Moses, saying,

2 Speak unto the children of Israel, that they bring me an offering: of every man that giveth it willingly with his heart ye shall take my offering.

25:2
Tithing
◄ Exodus 35:5 ►

3 And this *is* the offering which ye shall take of them; gold, and silver, and brass,

4 And blue, and purple, and scarlet, and fine linen, and goats' *hair,*

5 And rams' skins dyed red, and badgers' skins, and shittim wood,

6 Oil for the light, spices for anointing oil, and for sweet incense,

7 Onyx stones, and stones to be set in the ephod, and in the breastplate.

8 And let them make me a sanctuary; that I may dwell among them.

9 According to all that I shew thee, *after* the pattern of the tabernacle, and the pattern of all the instruments thereof, even so shall ye make *it.*

10 And they shall make an ark *of* shittim wood: two cubits and a half *shall be* the length thereof, and a cubit and a half the breadth thereof, and a cubit and a half the height thereof.

11 And thou shalt overlay it with pure gold, within and without shalt thou overlay it, and shalt make upon it a crown of gold round about.

12 And thou shalt cast four rings of gold for it, and put *them* in the four corners thereof; and two rings *shall be* in the one

side of it, and two rings in the other side of it.

13 And thou shalt make staves *of* shittim wood, and overlay them with gold.

14 And thou shalt put the staves into the rings by the sides of the ark, that the ark may be borne with them.

15 The staves shall be in the rings of the ark: they shall not be taken from it.

16 And thou shalt put into the ark the testimony which I shall give thee.

17 And thou shalt make a mercy seat *of* pure gold: two cubits and a half *shall be* the length thereof, and a cubit and a half the breadth thereof.

18 And thou shalt make two cherubims *of* gold, *of* beaten work shalt thou make them, in the two ends of the mercy seat.

19 And make one cherub on the one end, and the other cherub on the other end: *even* of the mercy seat shall ye make the cherubims on the two ends thereof.

20 And the cherubim shall stretch forth *their* wings on high, covering the mercy seat with their wings, and their faces *shall look* one to another; toward the mercy seat shall the faces of the cherubims be.

21 And thou shalt put the mercy seat above upon the ark; and in the ark thou shalt put the testimony that I shall give thee.

22 And there I will meet with thee, and I will commune with thee from above the mercy seat, from between the two cherubims which *are* upon the ark of the testimony, of all *things* which I will give thee in commandment unto the children of Israel.

23 Thou shalt also make a table *of* shittim wood: two cubits *shall be* the length thereof, and a cubit the breadth thereof, and a cubit and a half the height thereof.

24 And thou shalt overlay it with pure gold, and make thereto a crown of gold round about.

25 And thou shalt make unto it a border of an hand breadth round about, and thou shalt make a golden crown to the border thereof round about.

26 And thou shalt make for it four rings of gold, and put the rings in the four corners that *are* on the four feet thereof.

27 Over against the border shall the rings be for places of the staves to bear the table.

28 And thou shalt make the staves *of* shittim wood, and overlay them with gold, that the table may be borne with them.

29 And thou shalt make the dishes thereof, and spoons thereof, and covers thereof, and bowls thereof, to cover withal: *of* pure gold shalt thou make them.

30 And thou shalt set upon the table shewbread before me alway.

31 And thou shalt make a candlestick *of* pure gold: *of* beaten work shall the candlestick be made: his shaft, and his branches, his bowls, his knops, and his flowers, shall be of the same.

32 And six branches shall come out of the sides of it; three branches of the candlestick out of the one side, and three branches of the candlestick out of the other side:

33 Three bowls made like unto almonds, *with* a knop and a flower in one branch; and three bowls made like almonds in the other branch, *with* a knop and a flower: so in the six branches that come out of the candlestick.

34 And in the candlestick *shall be* four bowls made like unto almonds, *with* their knops and their flowers.

35 And *there shall be* a knop under two branches of the same, and a knop under two branches of the same, and a knop under two branches of the same, according to the six branches that proceed out of the candlestick.

36 Their knops and their branches shall be of the same: all it *shall be* one beaten work *of* pure gold.

37 And thou shalt make the seven lamps thereof: and they shall light the lamps thereof, that they may give light over against it.

38 And the tongs thereof, and the snuffdishes thereof, *shall be of* pure gold.

39 *Of* a talent of pure gold shall he make it, with all these vessels.

40 And look that thou make *them* after their pattern, which was shewed thee in the mount.

26

1 Moreover thou shalt make the tabernacle *with* ten curtains *of* fine twined linen, and blue, and purple, and scarlet: *with* cherubims of cunning work shalt thou make them.

2 The length of one curtain *shall be* eight and twenty cubits, and the breadth of one

curtain four cubits: and every one of the curtains shall have one measure.

3 The five curtains shall be coupled together one to another; and *other* five curtains *shall be* coupled one to another.

4 And thou shalt make loops of blue upon the edge of the one curtain from the selvedge in the coupling; and likewise shalt thou make in the uttermost edge of *another* curtain, in the coupling of the second.

5 Fifty loops shalt thou make in the one curtain, and fifty loops shalt thou make in the edge of the curtain that *is* in the coupling of the second; that the loops may take hold one of another.

6 And thou shalt make fifty taches of gold, and couple the curtains together with the taches: and it shall be one tabernacle.

7 And thou shalt make curtains *of* goats' *hair* to be a covering upon the tabernacle: eleven curtains shalt thou make.

8 The length of one curtain *shall be* thirty cubits, and the breadth of one curtain four cubits: and the eleven curtains *shall be all* of one measure.

9 And thou shalt couple five curtains by themselves, and six curtains by themselves, and shalt double the sixth curtain in the forefront of the tabernacle.

10 And thou shalt make fifty loops on the edge of the one curtain *that is* outmost in the coupling, and fifty loops in the edge of the curtain which coupleth the second.

11 And thou shalt make fifty taches of brass, and put the taches into the loops, and couple the tent together, that it may be one.

12 And the remnant that remaineth of the curtains of the tent, the half curtain that remaineth, shall hang over the backside of the tabernacle.

13 And a cubit on the one side, and a cubit on the other side of that which remaineth in the length of the curtains of the tent, it shall hang over the sides of the tabernacle on this side and on that side, to cover it.

14 And thou shalt make a covering for the tent *of* rams' skins dyed red, and a covering above *of* badgers' skins.

15 And thou shalt make boards for the tabernacle *of* shittim wood standing up.

16 Ten cubits *shall be* the length of a board, and a cubit and a half *shall be* the breadth of one board.

17 Two tenons *shall there be* in one board, set in order one against another: thus shalt thou make for all the boards of the tabernacle.

18 And thou shalt make the boards for the tabernacle, twenty boards on the south side southward.

19 And thou shalt make forty sockets of silver under the twenty boards; two sockets under one board for his two tenons, and two sockets under another board for his two tenons.

20 And for the second side of the tabernacle on the north side *there shall be* twenty boards:

21 And their forty sockets *of* silver; two sockets under one board, and two sockets under another board.

22 And for the sides of the tabernacle westward thou shalt make six boards.

23 And two boards shalt thou make for the corners of the tabernacle in the two sides.

24 And they shall be coupled together beneath, and they shall be coupled together above the head of it unto one ring: thus shall it be for them both; they shall be for the two corners.

25 And they shall be eight boards, and their sockets *of* silver, sixteen sockets; two sockets under one board, and two sockets under another board.

26 And thou shalt make bars *of* shittim wood; five for the boards of the one side of the tabernacle,

27 And five bars for the boards of the other side of the tabernacle, and five bars for the boards of the side of the tabernacle, for the two sides westward.

28 And the middle bar in the midst of the boards shall reach from end to end.

29 And thou shalt overlay the boards with gold, and make their rings *of* gold *for* places for the bars: and thou shalt overlay the bars with gold.

30 And thou shalt rear up the tabernacle according to the fashion thereof which was shewed thee in the mount.

31 And thou shalt make a vail *of* blue, and purple, and scarlet, and fine twined linen of cunning work: with cherubims shall it be made:

32 And thou shalt hang it upon four pillars of shittim *wood* overlaid with gold: their hooks *shall be of* gold, upon the four sockets of silver.

33And thou shalt hang up the vail under the taches, that thou mayest bring in thither within the vail the ark of the testimony: and the vail shall divide unto you between the holy *place* and the most holy.

34And thou shalt put the mercy seat upon the ark of the testimony in the most holy *place.*

35And thou shalt set the table without the vail, and the candlestick over against the table on the side of the tabernacle toward the south: and thou shalt put the table on the north side.

36And thou shalt make an hanging for the door of the tent, *of* blue, and purple, and scarlet, and fine twined linen, wrought with needlework.

37And thou shalt make for the hanging five pillars *of* shittim *wood,* and overlay them with gold, *and* their hooks *shall be of* gold: and thou shalt cast five sockets of brass for them.

27

1And thou shalt make an altar *of* shittim wood, five cubits long, and five cubits broad; the altar shall be foursquare: and the height thereof *shall be* three cubits.

2And thou shalt make the horns of it upon the four corners thereof: his horns shall be of the same: and thou shalt overlay it with brass.

3And thou shalt make his pans to receive his ashes, and his shovels, and his basons, and his fleshhooks, and his firepans: all the vessels thereof thou shalt make *of* brass.

4And thou shalt make for it a grate of network *of* brass; and upon the net shalt thou make four brasen rings in the four corners thereof.

5And thou shalt put it under the compass of the altar beneath, that the net may be even to the midst of the altar.

6And thou shalt make staves for the altar, staves *of* shittim wood, and overlay them with brass.

7And the staves shall be put into the rings, and the staves shall be upon the two sides of the altar, to bear it.

8Hollow with boards shalt thou make it: as it was shewed thee in the mount, so shall they make *it.*

9And thou shalt make the court of the tabernacle: for the south side southward *there shall be* hangings for the court *of* fine twined linen of an hundred cubits long for one side:

10And the twenty pillars thereof and their twenty sockets *shall be of* brass; the hooks of the pillars and their fillets *shall be of* silver.

11And likewise for the north side in length *there shall be* hangings of an hundred *cubits* long, and his twenty pillars and their twenty sockets *of* brass; the hooks of the pillars and their fillets *of* silver.

12And *for* the breadth of the court on the west side *shall be* hangings of fifty cubits: their pillars ten, and their sockets ten.

13And the breadth of the court on the east side eastward *shall be* fifty cubits.

14The hangings of one side *of the gate shall be* fifteen cubits: their pillars three, and their sockets three.

15And on the other side *shall be* hangings fifteen *cubits:* their pillars three, and their sockets three.

16And for the gate of the court *shall be* an hanging of twenty cubits, *of* blue, and purple, and scarlet, and fine twined linen, wrought with needlework: *and* their pillars *shall be* four, and their sockets four.

17All the pillars round about the court *shall be* filleted with silver; their hooks *shall be of* silver, and their sockets of brass.

18The length of the court *shall be* an hundred cubits, and the breadth fifty every where, and the height five cubits *of* fine twined linen, and their sockets *of* brass.

19All the vessels of the tabernacle in all the service thereof, and all the pins thereof, and all the pins of the court, *shall be of* brass.

20And thou shalt command the children of Israel, that they bring thee pure oil olive beaten for the light, to cause the lamp to burn always.

21In the tabernacle of the congregation without the vail, which *is* before the testimony, Aaron and his sons shall order it from evening to morning before the LORD: *it shall be* a statute for ever unto their generations on the behalf of the children of Israel.

28

1And take thou unto thee Aaron thy brother, and his sons with him, from among the children of Israel, that he may minister unto me in the priest's office, *even* Aaron, Nadab and Abihu, Eleazar and Ithamar, Aaron's sons.

2And thou shalt make holy garments for Aaron thy brother for glory and for beauty.

3And thou shalt speak unto all *that are* wise hearted, whom I have filled with the spirit of wisdom, that they may make Aaron's garments to consecrate him, that he may minister unto me in the priest's office.

4And these *are* the garments which they shall make; a breastplate, and an ephod, and a robe, and a broidered coat, a mitre, and a girdle: and they shall make holy garments for Aaron thy brother, and his sons, that he may minister unto me in the priest's office.

5And they shall take gold, and blue, and purple, and scarlet, and fine linen.

6And they shall make the ephod *of* gold, *of* blue, and *of* purple, *of* scarlet, and fine twined linen, with cunning work.

7It shall have the two shoulderpieces thereof joined at the two edges thereof; and *so* it shall be joined together.

8And the curious girdle of the ephod, which *is* upon it, shall be of the same, according to the work thereof; *even of* gold, *of* blue, and purple, and scarlet, and fine twined linen.

9And thou shalt take two onyx stones, and grave on them the names of the children of Israel:

10Six of their names on one stone, and *the other* six names of the rest on the other stone, according to their birth.

11With the work of an engraver in stone, *like* the engravings of a signet, shalt thou engrave the two stones with the names of the children of Israel: thou shalt make them to be set in ouches of gold.

12And thou shalt put the two stones upon the shoulders of the ephod *for* stones of memorial unto the children of Israel: and Aaron shall bear their names before the LORD upon his two shoulders for a memorial.

13And thou shalt make ouches *of* gold;

14And two chains *of* pure gold at the ends; *of* wreathen work shalt thou make them, and fasten the wreathen chains to the ouches.

15And thou shalt make the breastplate of judgment with cunning work; after the work of the ephod thou shalt make it; *of* gold, *of* blue, and *of* purple, and *of* scarlet, and *of* fine twined linen, shalt thou make it.

16Foursquare it shall be *being* doubled; a span *shall be* the length thereof, and a span *shall be* the breadth thereof.

17And thou shalt set in it settings of stones, *even* four rows of stones: *the first* row *shall be* a sardius, a topaz, and a carbuncle: *this shall be* the first row.

18And the second row *shall be* an emerald, a sapphire, and a diamond.

19And the third row a ligure, an agate, and an amethyst.

20And the fourth row a beryl, and an onyx, and a jasper: they shall be set in gold in their inclosings.

21And the stones shall be with the names of the children of Israel, twelve, according to their names, *like* the engravings of a signet; every one with his name shall they be according to the twelve tribes.

22And thou shalt make upon the breastplate chains at the ends *of* wreathen work *of* pure gold.

23And thou shalt make upon the breastplate two rings of gold, and shalt put the two rings on the two ends of the breastplate.

24And thou shalt put the two wreathen *chains* of gold in the two rings *which are* on the ends of the breastplate.

25And *the other* two ends of the two wreathen *chains* thou shalt fasten in the two ouches, and put *them* on the shoulderpieces of the ephod before it.

26And thou shalt make two rings of gold, and thou shalt put them upon the two ends of the breastplate in the border thereof, which *is* in the side of the ephod inward.

27And two *other* rings of gold thou shalt make, and shalt put them on the two sides of the ephod underneath, toward the forepart thereof, over against the *other* coupling thereof, above the curious girdle of the ephod.

28And they shall bind the breastplate by the rings thereof unto the rings of the ephod with a lace of blue, that *it* may be above the curious girdle of the ephod, and that the breastplate be not loosed from the ephod.

29And Aaron shall bear the names of the children of Israel in the breastplate of judgment upon his heart, when he goeth in unto the holy *place,* for a memorial before the LORD continually.

30And thou shalt put in the breastplate

of judgment the Urim and the Thummim; and they shall be upon Aaron's heart, when he goeth in before the LORD: and Aaron shall bear the judgment of the children of Israel upon his heart before the LORD continually.

31 And thou shalt make the robe of the ephod all *of* blue.

32 And there shall be an hole in the top of it, in the midst thereof: it shall have a binding of woven work round about the hole of it, as it were the hole of an habergeon, that it be not rent.

33 And *beneath* upon the hem of it thou shalt make pomegranates *of* blue, and *of* purple, and *of* scarlet, round about the hem thereof; and bells of gold between them round about:

34 A golden bell and a pomegranate, a golden bell and a pomegranate, upon the hem of the robe round about.

35 And it shall be upon Aaron to minister: and his sound shall be heard when he goeth in unto the holy *place* before the LORD, and when he cometh out, that he die not.

36 And thou shalt make a plate *of* pure gold, and grave upon it, *like* the engravings of a signet, HOLINESS TO THE LORD.

37 And thou shalt put it on a blue lace, that it may be upon the mitre; upon the forefront of the mitre it shall be.

38 And it shall be upon Aaron's forehead, that Aaron may bear the iniquity of the holy things, which the children of Israel shall hallow in all their holy gifts; and it shall be always upon his forehead, that they may be accepted before the LORD.

28:38
Accepted by God
◄ 2 Samuel 24:23 ►

39 And thou shalt embroider the coat of fine linen, and thou shalt make the mitre *of* fine linen, and thou shalt make the girdle *of* needlework.

40 And for Aaron's sons thou shalt make coats, and thou shalt make for them girdles, and bonnets shalt thou make for them, for glory and for beauty.

41 And thou shalt put them upon Aaron thy brother, and his sons with him; and shalt anoint them, and consecrate them, and sanctify them, that they may minister unto me in the priest's office.

42 And thou shalt make them linen breeches to cover their nakedness; from the loins even unto the thighs they shall reach:

43 And they shall be upon Aaron, and upon his sons, when they come in unto the tabernacle of the congregation, or when they come near unto the altar to minister in the holy *place;* that they bear not iniquity, and die: *it shall be* a statute for ever unto him and his seed after him.

29

1 And this *is* the thing that thou shalt do unto them to hallow them, to minister unto me in the priest's office: Take one young bullock, and two rams without blemish,

2 And unleavened bread, and cakes unleavened tempered with oil, and wafers unleavened anointed with oil: *of* wheaten flour shalt thou make them.

3 And thou shalt put them into one basket, and bring them in the basket, with the bullock and the two rams.

4 And Aaron and his sons thou shalt bring unto the door of the tabernacle of the congregation, and shalt wash them with water.

5 And thou shalt take the garments, and put upon Aaron the coat, and the robe of the ephod, and the ephod, and the breastplate, and gird him with the curious girdle of the ephod:

6 And thou shalt put the mitre upon his head, and put the holy crown upon the mitre.

7 Then shalt thou take the anointing oil, and pour *it* upon his head, and anoint him.

8 And thou shalt bring his sons, and put coats upon them.

9 And thou shalt gird them with girdles, Aaron and his sons, and put the bonnets on them: and the priest's office shall be theirs for a perpetual statute: and thou shalt consecrate Aaron and his sons.

10 And thou shalt cause a bullock to be brought before the tabernacle of the congregation: and Aaron and his sons shall put their hands upon the head of the bullock.

11 And thou shalt kill the bullock before the LORD, *by* the door of the tabernacle of the congregation.

12 And thou shalt take of the blood of the bullock, and put *it* upon the horns

of the altar with thy finger, and pour all the blood beside the bottom of the altar.

13 And thou shalt take all the fat that covereth the inwards, and the caul *that is* above the liver, and the two kidneys, and the fat that *is* upon them, and burn *them* upon the altar.

14 But the flesh of the bullock, and his skin, and his dung, shalt thou burn with fire without the camp: it *is* a sin offering.

15 Thou shalt also take one ram; and Aaron and his sons shall put their hands upon the head of the ram.

16 And thou shalt slay the ram, and thou shalt take his blood, and sprinkle *it* round about upon the altar.

17 And thou shalt cut the ram in pieces, and wash the inwards of him, and his legs, and put *them* unto his pieces, and unto his head.

18 And thou shalt burn the whole ram upon the altar: it *is* a burnt offering unto the LORD: it *is* a sweet savour, an offering made by fire unto the LORD.

19 And thou shalt take the other ram; and Aaron and his sons shall put their hands upon the head of the ram.

20 Then shalt thou kill the ram, and take of his blood, and put *it* upon the tip of the right ear of Aaron, and upon the tip of the right ear of his sons, and upon the thumb of their right hand, and upon the great toe of their right foot, and sprinkle the blood upon the altar round about.

21 And thou shalt take of the blood that *is* upon the altar, and of the anointing oil, and sprinkle *it* upon Aaron, and upon his garments, and upon his sons, and upon the garments of his sons with him: and he shall be hallowed, and his garments, and his sons, and his sons' garments with him.

22 Also thou shalt take of the ram the fat and the rump, and the fat that covereth the inwards, and the caul *above* the liver, and the two kidneys, and the fat that *is* upon them, and the right shoulder; for it *is* a ram of consecration:

23 And one loaf of bread, and one cake of oiled bread, and one wafer out of the basket of the unleavened bread that *is* before the LORD:

24 And thou shalt put all in the hands of Aaron, and in the hands of his sons; and shalt wave them *for* a wave offering before the LORD.

25 And thou shalt receive them of their hands, and burn *them* upon the altar for a burnt offering, for a sweet savour before the LORD: it *is* an offering made by fire unto the LORD.

26 And thou shalt take the breast of the ram of Aaron's consecration, and wave it *for* a wave offering before the LORD: and it shall be thy part.

27 And thou shalt sanctify the breast of the wave offering, and the shoulder of the heave offering, which is waved, and which is heaved up, of the ram of the consecration, *even* of *that* which *is* for Aaron, and of *that* which is for his sons:

28 And it shall be Aaron's and his sons' by a statute for ever from the children of Israel: for it *is* an heave offering: and it shall be an heave offering from the children of Israel of the sacrifice of their peace offerings, *even* their heave offering unto the LORD.

29 And the holy garments of Aaron shall be his sons' after him, to be anointed therein, and to be consecrated in them.

30 *And* that son that is priest in his stead shall put them on seven days, when he cometh into the tabernacle of the congregation to minister in the holy *place*.

31 And thou shalt take the ram of the consecration, and seethe his flesh in the holy place.

32 And Aaron and his sons shall eat the flesh of the ram, and the bread that *is* in the basket, *by* the door of the tabernacle of the congregation.

33 And they shall eat those things wherewith the atonement was made, to consecrate *and* to sanctify them: but a stranger shall not eat *thereof*, because they *are* holy.

34 And if ought of the flesh of the consecrations, or of the bread, remain unto the morning, then thou shalt burn the remainder with fire: it shall not be eaten, because it *is* holy.

35 And thus shalt thou do unto Aaron, and to his sons, according to all *things* which I have commanded thee: seven days shalt thou consecrate them.

36 And thou shalt offer every day a bullock *for* a sin offering for atonement: and thou shalt cleanse the altar, when thou hast made an atonement for it, and thou shalt anoint it, to sanctify it.

37 Seven days thou shalt make an atone-

ment for the altar, and sanctify it; and it shall be an altar most holy: whatsoever toucheth the altar shall be holy.

38 Now this *is that* which thou shalt offer upon the altar; two lambs of the first year day by day continually.

39 The one lamb thou shalt offer in the morning; and the other lamb thou shalt offer at even:

40 And with the one lamb a tenth deal of flour mingled with the fourth part of an hin of beaten oil; and the fourth part of an hin of wine *for* a drink offering.

41 And the other lamb thou shalt offer at even, and shalt do thereto according to the meat offering of the morning, and according to the drink offering thereof, for a sweet savour, an offering made by fire unto the LORD.

42 *This shall be* a continual burnt offering throughout your generations *at* the door of the tabernacle of the congregation before the LORD: where I will meet you, to speak there unto thee.

43 And there I will meet with the children of Israel, and *the tabernacle* shall be sanctified by my glory.

44 And I will sanctify the tabernacle of the congregation, and the altar: I will sanctify also both Aaron and his sons, to minister to me in the priest's office.

45 And I will dwell among the children of Israel, and will be their God.

46 And they shall know that I *am* the LORD their God, that brought them forth out of the land of Egypt, that I may dwell among them: I *am* the LORD their God.

30

1 And thou shalt make an altar to burn incense upon: *of* shittim wood shalt thou make it.

2 A cubit *shall be* the length thereof, and a cubit the breadth thereof; foursquare shall it be: and two cubits *shall be* the height thereof: the horns thereof *shall be* of the same.

3 And thou shalt overlay it with pure gold, the top thereof, and the sides thereof round about, and the horns thereof; and thou shalt make unto it a crown of gold round about.

4 And two golden rings shalt thou make to it under the crown of it, by the two corners thereof, upon the two sides of it shalt thou make *it;* and they shall be for places for the staves to bear it withal.

5 And thou shalt make the staves *of* shittim wood, and overlay them with gold.

6 And thou shalt put it before the vail that *is* by the ark of the testimony, before the mercy seat that *is* over the testimony, where I will meet with thee.

7 And Aaron shall burn thereon sweet incense every morning: when he dresseth the lamps, he shall burn incense upon it.

8 And when Aaron lighteth the lamps at even, he shall burn incense upon it, a perpetual incense before the LORD throughout your generations.

9 Ye shall offer no strange incense thereon, nor burnt sacrifice, nor meat offering; neither shall ye pour drink offering thereon.

10 And Aaron shall make an atonement upon the horns of it once in a year with the blood of the sin offering of atonements: once in the year shall he make atonement upon it throughout your generations: it *is* most holy unto the LORD.

11 And the LORD spake unto Moses, saying,

12 When thou takest the sum of the children of Israel after their number, then shall they give every man a ransom for his soul unto the LORD, when thou numberest them; that there be no plague among them, when *thou* numberest them.

13 This they shall give, every one that passeth among them that are numbered, half a shekel after the shekel of the sanctuary: (a shekel *is* twenty gerahs:) an half shekel *shall be* the offering of the LORD.

14 Every one that passeth among them that are numbered, from twenty years old and above, shall give an offering unto the LORD.

15 The rich shall not give more, and the poor shall not give less than half a shekel, when *they* give an offering unto the LORD, to make an atonement for your souls.

16 And thou shalt take the atonement money of the children of Israel, and shalt appoint it for the service of the tabernacle of the congregation; that it may be a memorial unto the children of Israel before the LORD, to make an atonement for your souls.

17 And the LORD spake unto Moses, saying,

18 Thou shalt also make a laver *of* brass, and his foot *also of* brass, to wash *withal:*

and thou shalt put it between the tabernacle of the congregation and the altar, and thou shalt put water therein.

19 For Aaron and his sons shall wash their hands and their feet thereat:

20 When they go into the tabernacle of the congregation, they shall wash with water, that they die not; or when they come near to the altar to minister, to burn offering made by fire unto the LORD:

21 So they shall wash their hands and their feet, that they die not: and it shall be a statute for ever to them, *even* to him and to his seed throughout their generations.

22 Moreover the LORD spake unto Moses, saying,

23 Take thou also unto thee principal spices, of pure myrrh five hundred *shekels,* and of sweet cinnamon half so much, *even* two hundred and fifty *shekels,* and of sweet calamus two hundred and fifty *shekels,*

24 And of cassia five hundred *shekels,* after the shekel of the sanctuary, and of oil olive an hin:

25 And thou shalt make it an oil of holy ointment, an ointment compound after the art of the apothecary: it shall be an holy anointing oil.

26 And thou shalt anoint the tabernacle of the congregation therewith, and the ark of the testimony,

27 And the table and all his vessels, and the candlestick and his vessels, and the altar of incense,

28 And the altar of burnt offering with all his vessels, and the laver and his foot.

29 And thou shalt sanctify them, that they may be most holy: whatsoever toucheth them shall be holy.

30 And thou shalt anoint Aaron and his sons, and consecrate them, that *they* may minister unto me in the priest's office.

31 And thou shalt speak unto the children of Israel, saying, This shall be an holy anointing oil unto me throughout your generations.

32 Upon man's flesh shall it not be poured, neither shall ye make *any other* like it, after the composition of it: it *is* holy, *and* it shall be holy unto you.

33 Whosoever compoundeth *any* like it, or whosoever putteth *any* of it upon a stranger, shall even be cut off from his people.

34 And the LORD said unto Moses, Take unto thee sweet spices, stacte, and onycha, and galbanum; *these* sweet spices with pure frankincense: of each shall there be a like *weight:*

35 And thou shalt make it a perfume, a confection after the art of the apothecary, tempered together, pure *and* holy:

36 And thou shalt beat *some* of it very small, and put of it before the testimony in the tabernacle of the congregation, where I will meet with thee: it shall be unto you most holy.

37 And *as for* the perfume which thou shalt make, ye shall not make to yourselves according to the composition thereof: it shall be unto thee holy for the LORD.

38 Whosoever shall make like unto that, to smell thereto, shall even be cut off from his people.

31

1 And the LORD spake unto Moses, saying,

2 See, I have called by name Bezaleel the son of Uri, the son of Hur, of the tribe of Judah:

3 And I have filled him with the spirit of God, in wisdom, and in understanding, and in knowledge, and in all manner of workmanship,

4 To devise cunning works, to work in gold, and in silver, and in brass,

5 And in cutting of stones, to set *them,* and in carving of timber, to work in all manner of workmanship.

6 And I, behold, I have given with him Aholiab, the son of Ahisamach, of the tribe of Dan: and in the hearts of all that are wise hearted I have put wisdom, that they may make all that I have commanded thee;

7 The tabernacle of the congregation, and the ark of the testimony, and the mercy seat that *is* thereupon, and all the furniture of the tabernacle,

8 And the table and his furniture, and the pure candlestick with all his furniture, and the altar of incense,

9 And the altar of burnt offering with all his furniture, and the laver and his foot,

10 And the cloths of service, and the holy garments for Aaron the priest, and the garments of his sons, to minister in the priest's office,

11 And the anointing oil, and sweet incense for the holy *place:* according to all that I have commanded thee shall they do.

12 And the LORD spake unto Moses,
saying,
13 Speak thou also unto the children of
Israel, saying, Verily my sabbaths ye shall
keep: for it *is* a sign between me and you
throughout your generations; that *ye* may
know that I *am* the LORD that doth sanctify you.
14 Ye shall keep the sabbath therefore; for
it *is* holy unto you: every one that defileth
it shall surely be put to death: for whosoever doeth *any* work therein, that soul shall
be cut off from among his people.
15 Six days may
work be done; but
in the seventh *is*
the sabbath of rest,
holy to the LORD:
whosoever doeth
any work in the sabbath day, he shall surely be put to death.

31:15 Rest
◄ Exodus 23:12
Exodus 34:21 ►

16 Wherefore the children of Israel shall
keep the sabbath, to observe the sabbath
throughout their generations, *for* a perpetual covenant.
17 It *is* a sign between me and the children of Israel for ever: for *in* six days the
LORD made heaven and earth, and on the
seventh day he rested, and was refreshed.
18 And he gave unto Moses, when he had
made an end of communing with him
upon mount Sinai, two tables of testimony, tables of stone, written with the finger
of God.

32

1 And when the people saw that Moses
delayed to come down out of the mount,
the people gathered themselves together
unto Aaron, and said unto him, Up, make
us gods, which shall go before us; for *as
for* this Moses, the man that brought us
up out of the land of Egypt, we wot not
what is become of him.
2 And Aaron said unto them, Break off
the golden earrings, which *are* in the ears
of your wives, of your sons, and of your
daughters, and bring *them* unto me.
3 And all the people brake off the gold-
en earrings which *were* in their ears, and
brought *them* unto Aaron.
4 And he received *them* at their hand, and
fashioned it with a graving tool, after he
had made it a molten calf: and they said,
These *be* thy gods, O Israel, which brought
thee up out of the land of Egypt.
5 And when Aaron saw *it,* he built an altar before it; and Aaron made proclamation, and said, To morrow *is* a feast to the
LORD.
6 And they rose
up early on the
morrow, and of-
fered burnt offer-
ings, and brought
peace offerings; and
the people sat down to eat and to drink,
and rose up to play.

32:6
Parties
◄ Judges 9:27 ►

7 And the LORD said unto Moses, Go, get
thee down; for thy people, which thou
broughtest out of the land of Egypt, have
corrupted *themselves:*
8 They have turned aside quickly out of
the way which I commanded them: they
have made them a molten calf, and have
worshipped it, and have sacrificed thereunto, and said, These *be* thy gods, O Israel,
which have brought thee up out of the land
of Egypt.
9 And the LORD said unto Moses, I have
seen this people, and, behold, it *is* a
stiffnecked people:
10 Now therefore let me alone, that my
wrath may wax hot against them, and that
I may consume them: and I will make of
thee a great nation.
11 And Moses besought the LORD his
God, and said, LORD, why doth thy wrath
wax hot against thy people, which thou
hast brought forth out of the land of Egypt
with great power, and with a mighty hand?
12 Wherefore should the Egyptians
speak, and say, For mischief did he bring
them out, to slay them in the mountains,
and to consume them from the face of the
earth? Turn from thy fierce wrath, and repent of this evil against thy people.
13 Remember Abraham, Isaac, and Israel,
thy servants, to whom thou swarest by
thine own self, and saidst unto them, I will
multiply your seed as the stars of heaven,
and all this land that I have spoken of will
I give unto your seed, and they shall inherit *it* for ever.
14 And the LORD repented of the evil
which he thought to do unto his people.
15 And Moses turned, and went down
from the mount, and the two tables of the
testimony *were* in his hand: the tables *were*
written on both their sides; on the one side
and on the other *were* they written.
16 And the tables *were* the work of God,

and the writing *was* the writing of God, graven upon the tables.

17And when Joshua heard the noise of the people as they shouted, he said unto Moses, *There is* a noise of war in the camp.

18And he said, *It is* not the voice of *them that* shout for mastery, neither *is it* the voice of *them that* cry for being overcome: *but* the noise of *them that* sing do I hear.

19And it came to pass, as soon as he came nigh unto the camp, that he saw the calf, and the dancing: and Moses' anger waxed hot, and he cast the tables out of his hands, and brake them beneath the mount.

32:19
Anger
◄ Leviticus 10:16 ►

20And he took the calf which they had made, and burnt *it* in the fire, and ground *it* to powder, and strawed *it* upon the water, and made the children of Israel drink *of it*.

21And Moses said unto Aaron, What did this people unto thee, that thou hast brought so great a sin upon them?

22And Aaron said, Let not the anger of my lord wax hot: thou knowest the people, that they *are set* on mischief.

32:22 "It's Her Fault!"
◄ Genesis 27:36
1 Samuel 15:21 ►

23For they said unto me, Make us gods, which shall go before us: for *as for* this Moses, the man that brought us up out of the land of Egypt, we wot not what is become of him.

24And I said unto them, Whosoever hath any gold, let them break *it* off. So they gave *it* me: then I cast it into the fire, and there came out this calf.

25And when Moses saw that the people *were* naked; (for Aaron had made them naked unto *their* shame among their enemies:)

26Then Moses stood in the gate of the camp, and said, Who *is* on the LORD'S side? *let him come* unto me. And all the sons of Levi gathered themselves together unto him.

27And he said unto them, Thus saith the LORD God of Israel, Put every man his sword by his side, *and* go in and out from gate to gate throughout the camp, and slay every man his brother, and every man his companion, and every man his neighbour.

28And the children of Levi did according to the word of Moses: and there fell of the people that day about three thousand men.

29For Moses had said, Consecrate yourselves to day to the LORD, even every man upon his son, and upon his brother; that he may bestow upon you a blessing this day.

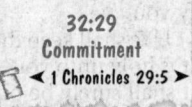

32:29
Commitment
◄ 1 Chronicles 29:5 ►

30And it came to pass on the morrow, that Moses said unto the people, Ye have sinned a great sin: and now I will go up unto the LORD; peradventure I shall make an atonement for your sin.

31And Moses returned unto the LORD, and said, Oh, this people have sinned a great sin, and have made them gods of gold.

32Yet now, if thou wilt forgive their sin—; and if not, blot me, I pray thee, out of thy book which thou hast written.

32:32
Praying for Others
◄ Numbers 12:13 ►

33And the LORD said unto Moses, Whosoever hath sinned against me, him will I blot out of my book.

34Therefore now go, lead the people unto *the place* of which I have spoken unto thee: behold, mine Angel shall go before thee: nevertheless in the day when I visit I will visit their sin upon them.

35And the LORD plagued the people, because they made the calf, which Aaron made.

33

1And the LORD said unto Moses, Depart, *and* go up hence, thou and the people which thou hast brought up out of the land of Egypt, unto the land which I sware unto Abraham, to Isaac, and to Jacob, saying, Unto thy seed will I give it:

2And I will send an angel before thee; and I will drive out the Canaanite, the Amorite, and the Hittite, and the Perizzite, the Hivite, and the Jebusite:

3Unto a land flowing with milk and honey: for I will not go up in the midst of thee; for thou *art* a stiffnecked people: lest I consume thee in the way.

4 And when the people heard these evil
tidings, they mourned: and no man did
put on him his ornaments.
5 For the LORD had said unto Moses, Say
unto the children of Israel, Ye *are* a
stiffnecked people: I will come up into the
midst of thee in a moment, and consume
thee: therefore now put off thy ornaments
from thee, that I may know what to do
unto thee.
6 And the children of Israel stripped
themselves of their ornaments by the
mount Horeb.
7 And Moses took the tabernacle, and
pitched it without the camp, afar off from
the camp, and called it the Tabernacle of
the congregation. And it came to pass, *that*
every one which sought the LORD went out
unto the tabernacle of the congregation,
which *was* without the camp.
8 And it came to
pass, when Moses
went out unto the
tabernacle, *that* all
the people rose up,
and stood every
man *at* his tent door, and looked after
Moses, until he was gone into the tabernacle.

33:8
Respecting God's People
◄ Acts 28:10 ►

9 And it came to pass, as Moses entered
into the tabernacle, the cloudy pillar
descended, and stood *at* the door of the
tabernacle, and *the LORD* talked with
Moses.
10 And all the people saw the cloudy pillar stand *at* the tabernacle door: and all
the people rose up and worshipped, every
man *in* his tent door.
11 And the LORD
spake unto Moses
face to face, as a
man speaketh unto
his friend. And he
turned again into
the camp: but his servant Joshua, the son
of Nun, a young man, departed not out of
the tabernacle.

33:11
God's Friends
◄ Numbers 12:8 ►

12 And Moses said unto the LORD, See,
thou sayest unto me, Bring up this people: and thou hast not let me know whom
thou wilt send with me. Yet thou hast said,
I know thee by name, and thou hast also
found grace in my sight.
13 Now therefore, I pray thee, if I have
found grace in thy sight, shew me now thy
way, that I may know thee, that I may find
grace in thy sight: and consider that this
nation *is* thy people.
14 And he said, My presence shall go *with*
thee, and I will give thee rest.
15 And he said unto him, If thy presence
go not *with me,* carry us not up hence.
16 For wherein shall it be known here
that I and thy people have found grace in
thy sight? *is it* not in that thou goest with
us? so shall we be separated, I and thy people, from all the people that *are* upon the
face of the earth.
17 And the LORD said unto Moses, I will
do this thing also that thou hast spoken:
for thou hast found grace in my sight, and
I know thee by name.
18 And he said, I beseech thee, shew me
thy glory.
19 And he said, I will make all my goodness pass before thee, and I will proclaim
the name of the LORD before thee; and will
be gracious to whom I will be gracious,
and will shew mercy on whom I will shew
mercy.
20 And he said, Thou canst not see my
face: for there shall no man see me, and
live.
21 And the LORD said, Behold, *there is* a
place by me, and thou shalt stand upon a
rock:
22 And it shall come to pass, while my
glory passeth by, that I will put thee in a
clift of the rock, and will cover thee with
my hand while I pass by:
23 And I will take away mine hand, and
thou shalt see my back parts: but my face
shall not be seen.

34

1 And the LORD said unto Moses, Hew
thee two tables of stone like unto the first:
and I will write upon *these* tables the words
that were in the first tables, which thou
brakest.
2 And be ready in the morning, and come
up in the morning unto mount Sinai, and
present thyself there to me in the top of
the mount.
3 And no man shall come up with thee,
neither let any man be seen throughout
all the mount; neither let the flocks nor
herds feed before that mount.
4 And he hewed two tables of stone like
unto the first; and Moses rose up early in
the morning, and went up unto mount
Sinai, as the LORD had commanded him,

and took in his hand the two tables of
stone.
5And the LORD descended in the cloud,
and stood with him there, and proclaimed
the name of the LORD.
6And the LORD passed by before him,
and proclaimed, The LORD, The LORD God,
merciful and gracious, longsuffering, and
abundant in goodness and truth,
7Keeping mercy
for thousands, for-
giving iniquity and
transgression and
sin, and that will by
no means clear *the*
guilty; visiting the iniquity of the fathers
upon the children, and upon the children's
children, unto the third and to the fourth
generation.

34:7
Promise of Mercy
◄ 2 Samuel 22:26 ►

8And Moses made haste, and bowed his
head toward the earth, and worshipped.
9And he said, If now I have found grace
in thy sight, O Lord, let my Lord, I pray
thee, go among us; for it *is* a stiffnecked
people; and pardon our iniquity and our
sin, and take us for thine inheritance.
10And he said, Behold, I make a covenant: before all thy people I will do mar-
vels, such as have not been done in all the
earth, nor in any nation: and all the people among which thou *art* shall see the
work of the LORD: for it *is* a terrible thing
that I will do with thee.
11Observe thou that which I command
thee this day: behold, I drive out before
thee the Amorite, and the Canaanite, and
the Hittite, and the Perizzite, and the Hivite, and the Jebusite.
12Take heed to
thyself, lest thou
make a covenant
with the inhabi-
tants of the land
whither thou goest,
lest it be for a snare in the midst of thee:

34:12 Bad Friends
◄ Exodus 23:33
Psalm 1:1 ►

13But ye shall destroy their altars, break
their images, and cut down their groves:
14For thou shalt
worship no other
god: for the LORD,
whose name *is* Jeal-
ous, *is* a jealous God:

34:14 God Is Jealous
◄ Exodus 20:5
Deuteronomy 4:24 ►

15Lest thou make
a covenant with the inhabitants of the
land, and they go a whoring after their
gods, and do sacrifice unto their gods, and
one call thee, and thou eat of his sacrifice;
16And thou take of their daughters unto
thy sons, and their daughters go a whoring after their gods, and make thy sons go
a whoring after their gods.
17Thou shalt make thee no molten gods.
18The feast of unleavened bread shalt
thou keep. Seven days thou shalt eat unleavened bread, as I commanded thee, in
the time of the month Abib: for in the
month Abib thou camest out from Egypt.
19All that openeth the matrix *is* mine;
and every firstling among thy cattle, *wheth-*
er ox or sheep, *that is male.*
20But the firstling of an ass thou shalt
redeem with a lamb: and if thou redeem
him not, then shalt thou break his neck.
All the firstborn of thy sons thou shalt redeem. And none shall appear before me
empty.
21Six days thou
shalt work, but on
the seventh day
thou shalt rest: in
earing time and in
harvest thou shalt
rest.

34:21 Rest
◄ Exodus 31:15
Exodus 35:2 ►

22And thou shalt observe the feast of
weeks, of the firstfruits of wheat harvest,
and the feast of ingathering at the year's
end.
23Thrice in the year shall all your men
children appear before the Lord GOD, the
God of Israel.
24For I will cast out the nations before
thee, and enlarge thy borders: neither shall
any man desire thy land, when thou shalt
go up to appear before the LORD thy God
thrice in the year.
25Thou shalt not offer the blood of my
sacrifice with leaven; neither shall the sacrifice of the feast of the passover be left
unto the morning.
26The first of the firstfruits of thy land
thou shalt bring unto the house of the
LORD thy God. Thou shalt not seethe a kid
in his mother's milk.
27And the LORD said unto Moses, Write
thou these words: for after the tenor of
these words I have made a covenant with
thee and with Israel.
28And he was there with the LORD forty
days and forty nights; he did neither eat
bread, nor drink water. And he wrote upon

the tables the words of the covenant, the ten commandments.

29 And it came to pass, when Moses came down from mount Sinai with the two tables of testimony in Moses' hand, when he came down from the mount, that Moses wist not that the skin of his face shone while he talked with him.

30 And when Aaron and all the children of Israel saw Moses, behold, the skin of his face shone; and they were afraid to come nigh him.

31 And Moses called unto them; and Aaron and all the rulers of the congregation returned unto him: and Moses talked with them.

32 And afterward all the children of Israel came nigh: and he gave them in commandment all that the LORD had spoken with him in mount Sinai.

33 And *till* Moses had done speaking with them, he put a vail on his face.

34 But when Moses went in before the LORD to speak with him, he took the vail off, until he came out. And he came out, and spake unto the children of Israel *that* which he was commanded.

35 And the children of Israel saw the face of Moses, that the skin of Moses' face shone: and Moses put the vail upon his face again, until he went in to speak with him.

35

1 And Moses gathered all the congregation of the children of Israel together, and said unto them, These *are* the words which the LORD hath commanded, that *ye* should do them.

2 Six days shall work be done, but on the seventh day there shall be to you an holy day, a sabbath of rest to the LORD: whosoever doeth work therein shall be put to death.

35:2 Rest
◄ Exodus 34:21
Leviticus 23:3 ►

3 Ye shall kindle no fire throughout your habitations upon the sabbath day.

4 And Moses spake unto all the congregation of the children of Israel, saying, This *is* the thing which the LORD commanded, saying,

5 Take ye from among you an offering unto the LORD: whosoever *is* of a willing heart, let him bring it, an offering of the LORD; gold, and silver, and brass,

35:5 Tithing
◄ Exodus 25:2
Numbers 31:50 ►

6 And blue, and purple, and scarlet, and fine linen, and goats' *hair*,

7 And rams' skins dyed red, and badgers' skins, and shittim wood,

8 And oil for the light, and spices for anointing oil, and for the sweet incense,

9 And onyx stones, and stones to be set for the ephod, and for the breastplate.

10 And every wise hearted among you shall come, and make all that the LORD hath commanded;

11 The tabernacle, his tent, and his covering, his taches, and his boards, his bars, his pillars, and his sockets,

12 The ark, and the staves thereof, *with* the mercy seat, and the vail of the covering,

13 The table, and his staves, and all his vessels, and the shewbread,

14 The candlestick also for the light, and his furniture, and his lamps, with the oil for the light,

15 And the incense altar, and his staves, and the anointing oil, and the sweet incense, and the hanging for the door at the entering in of the tabernacle,

16 The altar of burnt offering, with his brasen grate, his staves, and all his vessels, the laver and his foot,

17 The hangings of the court, his pillars, and their sockets, and the hanging for the door of the court,

18 The pins of the tabernacle, and the pins of the court, and their cords,

19 The cloths of service, to do service in the holy *place*, the holy garments for Aaron the priest, and the garments of his sons, to minister in the priest's office.

20 And all the congregation of the children of Israel departed from the presence of Moses.

21 And they came, every one whose heart stirred him up, and every one whom his spirit made willing, *and* they brought the LORD'S offering to the work of the tabernacle of the congregation, and for all his service, and for the holy garments.

22 And they came, both men and women, as many as were willing hearted, *and* brought bracelets, and earrings, and

35:22 Examples of Generosity
◄ Exodus 36:5 ►

rings, and tablets, all jewels of gold: and every man that offered *offered* an offering of gold unto the LORD.

23 And every man, with whom was found blue, and purple, and scarlet, and fine linen, and goats' *hair,* and red skins of rams, and badgers' skins, brought *them.*

24 Every one that did offer an offering of silver and brass brought the LORD'S offering: and every man, with whom was found shittim wood for any work of the service, brought *it.*

25 And all the women that were wise hearted did spin with their hands, and brought that which they had spun, *both* of blue, and of purple, *and* of scarlet, and of fine linen.

26 And all the women whose heart stirred them up in wisdom spun goats' *hair.*

27 And the rulers brought onyx stones, and stones to be set, for the ephod, and for the breastplate;

28 And spice, and oil for the light, and for the anointing oil, and for the sweet incense.

29 The children of Israel brought a willing offering unto the LORD, every man and woman, whose heart made them willing to bring for all manner of work, which the LORD had commanded to be made by the hand of Moses.

30 And Moses said unto the children of Israel, See, the LORD hath called by name Bezaleel the son of Uri, the son of Hur, of the tribe of Judah;

31 And he hath filled him with the spirit of God, in wisdom, in understanding, and in knowledge, and in all manner of workmanship;

32 And to devise curious works, to work in gold, and in silver, and in brass,

33 And in the cutting of stones, to set *them,* and in carving of wood, to make any manner of cunning work.

34 And he hath put in his heart that he may teach, *both* he, and Aholiab, the son of Ahisamach, of the tribe of Dan.

35 Them hath he filled with wisdom of heart, to work all manner of work, of the engraver, and of the cunning workman, and of the embroiderer, in blue, and in purple, in scarlet, and in fine linen, and of the weaver, *even* of them that do any work, and of those that devise cunning work.

36

1 Then wrought Bezaleel and Aholiab, and every wise hearted man, in whom the LORD put wisdom and understanding to know how to work all manner of work for the service of the sanctuary, according to all that the LORD had commanded.

2 And Moses called Bezaleel and Aholiab, and every wise hearted man, in whose heart the LORD had put wisdom, *even* every one whose heart stirred him up to come unto the work to do it:

3 And they received of Moses all the offering, which the children of Israel had brought for the work of the service of the sanctuary, to make it *withal.* And they brought yet unto him free offerings every morning.

4 And all the wise men, that wrought all the work of the sanctuary, came every man from his work which they made;

5 And they spake unto Moses, saying, The people bring much more than enough for the service of the work, which the LORD commanded to make.

36:5
Examples of Generosity
◄ Exodus 35:22
Numbers 7:3 ►

6 And Moses gave commandment, and they caused it to be proclaimed throughout the camp, saying, Let neither man nor woman make any more work for the offering of the sanctuary. So the people were restrained from bringing.

7 For the stuff they had was sufficient for all the work to make it, and too much.

8 And every wise hearted man among them that wrought the work of the tabernacle made ten curtains *of* fine twined linen, and blue, and purple, and scarlet: *with* cherubims of cunning work made he them.

9 The length of one curtain *was* twenty and eight cubits, and the breadth of one curtain four cubits: the curtains *were* all of one size.

10 And he coupled the five curtains one unto another: and *the other* five curtains he coupled one unto another.

11 And he made loops of blue on the edge of one curtain from the selvedge in the coupling: likewise he made in the uttermost side of *another* curtain, in the coupling of the second.

12 Fifty loops made he in one curtain, and fifty loops made he in the edge of the curtain which *was* in the coupling of the

second: the loops held one *curtain* to another.

13And he made fifty taches of gold, and coupled the curtains one unto another with the taches: so it became one tabernacle.

14And he made curtains *of* goats' *hair* for the tent over the tabernacle: eleven curtains he made them.

15The length of one curtain *was* thirty cubits, and four cubits *was* the breadth of one curtain: the eleven curtains *were* of one size.

16And he coupled five curtains by themselves, and six curtains by themselves.

17And he made fifty loops upon the uttermost edge of the curtain in the coupling, and fifty loops made he upon the edge of the curtain which coupleth the second.

18And he made fifty taches *of* brass to couple the tent together, that it might be one.

19And he made a covering for the tent *of* rams' skins dyed red, and a covering *of* badgers' skins above *that.*

20And he made boards for the tabernacle *of* shittim wood, standing up.

21The length of a board *was* ten cubits, and the breadth of a board one cubit and a half.

22One board had two tenons, equally distant one from another: thus did he make for all the boards of the tabernacle.

23And he made boards for the tabernacle; twenty boards for the south side southward:

24And forty sockets of silver he made under the twenty boards; two sockets under one board for his two tenons, and two sockets under another board for his two tenons.

25And for the other side of the tabernacle, *which is* toward the north corner, he made twenty boards,

26And their forty sockets of silver; two sockets under one board, and two sockets under another board.

27And for the sides of the tabernacle westward he made six boards.

28And two boards made he for the corners of the tabernacle in the two sides.

29And they were coupled beneath, and coupled together at the head thereof, to one ring: thus he did to both of them in both the corners.

30And there were eight boards; and their sockets *were* sixteen sockets of silver, under every board two sockets.

31And he made bars of shittim wood; five for the boards of the one side of the tabernacle,

32And five bars for the boards of the other side of the tabernacle, and five bars for the boards of the tabernacle for the sides westward.

33And he made the middle bar to shoot through the boards from the one end to the other.

34And he overlaid the boards with gold, and made their rings *of* gold *to be* places for the bars, and overlaid the bars with gold.

35And he made a vail *of* blue, and purple, and scarlet, and fine twined linen: *with* cherubims made he it of cunning work.

36And he made thereunto four pillars *of* shittim *wood,* and overlaid them with gold: their hooks *were of* gold; and he cast for them four sockets of silver.

37And he made an hanging for the tabernacle door *of* blue, and purple, and scarlet, and fine twined linen, of needlework;

38And the five pillars of it with their hooks: and he overlaid their chapiters and their fillets with gold: but their five sockets *were of* brass.

37

1And Bezaleel made the ark *of* shittim wood: two cubits and a half *was* the length of it, and a cubit and a half the breadth of it, and a cubit and a half the height of it:

2And he overlaid it with pure gold within and without, and made a crown of gold to it round about.

3And he cast for it four rings of gold, *to be set* by the four corners of it; even two rings upon the one side of it, and two rings upon the other side of it.

4And he made staves *of* shittim wood, and overlaid them with gold.

5And he put the staves into the rings by the sides of the ark, to bear the ark.

6And he made the mercy seat *of* pure gold: two cubits and a half *was* the length thereof, and one cubit and a half the breadth thereof.

7And he made two cherubims *of* gold, beaten out of one piece made he them, on the two ends of the mercy seat;

8One cherub on the end on this side, and another cherub on the *other* end on

that side: out of the mercy seat made he
the cherubims on the two ends thereof.
9 And the cherubims spread out *their*
wings on high, *and* covered with their
wings over the mercy seat, with their faces
one to another; *even* to the mercy seatward
were the faces of the cherubims.
10 And he made the table *of* shittim
wood: two cubits *was* the length thereof,
and a cubit the breadth thereof, and a cubit and a half the height thereof:
11 And he overlaid it with pure gold, and
made thereunto a crown of gold round
about.
12 Also he made thereunto a border of
an handbreadth round about; and made
a crown of gold for the border thereof
round about.
13 And he cast for it four rings of gold,
and put the rings upon the four corners
that *were* in the four feet thereof.
14 Over against the border were the rings,
the places for the staves to bear the table.
15 And he made the staves *of* shittim
wood, and overlaid them with gold, to
bear the table.
16 And he made the vessels which *were*
upon the table, his dishes, and his spoons,
and his bowls, and his covers to cover
withal, *of* pure gold.
17 And he made the candlestick *of* pure
gold: *of* beaten work made he the candlestick; his shaft, and his branch, his bowls,
his knops, and his flowers, were of the
same:
18 And six branches going out of the sides
thereof; three branches of the candlestick
out of the one side thereof, and three
branches of the candlestick out of the other
side thereof:
19 Three bowls made after the fashion of
almonds in one branch, a knop and a flower; and three bowls made like almonds in
another branch, a knop and a flower: so
throughout the six branches going out of
the candlestick.
20 And in the candlestick *were* four bowls
made like almonds, his knops, and his
flowers:
21 And a knop under two branches of the
same, and a knop under two branches of
the same, and a knop under two branches
of the same, according to the six branches
going out of it.
22 Their knops and their branches were
of the same: all of it *was* one beaten work
of pure gold.
23 And he made his seven lamps, and his
snuffers, and his snuffdishes, *of* pure gold.
24 *Of* a talent of pure gold made he it,
and all the vessels thereof.
25 And he made the incense altar *of*
shittim wood: the length of *it was* a cubit,
and the breadth of it a cubit; it *was* foursquare; and two cubits *was* the height of
it; the horns thereof were of the same.
26 And he overlaid it with pure gold, *both*
the top of it, and the sides thereof round
about, and the horns of it: also he made
unto it a crown of gold round about.
27 And he made two rings of gold for it
under the crown thereof, by the two corners of it, upon the two sides thereof, to
be places for the staves to bear it withal.
28 And he made the staves *of* shittim
wood, and overlaid them with gold.
29 And he made the holy anointing oil,
and the pure incense of sweet spices, according to the work of the apothecary.

38

1 And he made the altar of burnt offering *of* shittim wood: five cubits *was* the
length thereof, and five cubits the breadth
thereof; *it was* foursquare; and three cubits the height thereof.
2 And he made the horns thereof on the
four corners of it; the horns thereof were
of the same: and he overlaid it with brass.
3 And he made all the vessels of the altar, the pots, and the shovels, and the
basons, *and* the fleshhooks, and the firepans: all the vessels thereof made he *of*
brass.
4 And he made for the altar a brasen grate
of network under the compass thereof beneath unto the midst of it.
5 And he cast four rings for the four ends
of the grate of brass, *to be* places for the
staves.
6 And he made the staves *of* shittim
wood, and overlaid them with brass.
7 And he put the staves into the rings on
the sides of the altar, to bear it withal; he
made the altar hollow with boards.
8 And he made the laver *of* brass, and the
foot of it *of* brass, of the lookingglasses of
the women assembling, which assembled
at the door of the tabernacle of the congregation.
9 And he made the court: on the south
side southward the hangings of the court

were of fine twined linen, an hundred cubits:

10 Their pillars *were* twenty, and their brasen sockets twenty; the hooks of the pillars and their fillets *were of* silver.

11 And for the north side *the hangings were* an hundred cubits, their pillars *were* twenty, and their sockets of brass twenty; the hooks of the pillars and their fillets *of* silver.

12 And for the west side *were* hangings of fifty cubits, their pillars ten, and their sockets ten; the hooks of the pillars and their fillets *of* silver.

13 And for the east side eastward fifty cubits.

14 The hangings of the one side *of the gate were* fifteen cubits; their pillars three, and their sockets three.

15 And for the other side of the court gate, on this hand and that hand, *were* hangings of fifteen cubits; their pillars three, and their sockets three.

16 All the hangings of the court round about *were* of fine twined linen.

17 And the sockets for the pillars *were of* brass; the hooks of the pillars and their fillets *of* silver; and the overlaying of their chapiters *of* silver; and all the pillars of the court *were* filleted with silver.

18 And the hanging for the gate of the court *was* needlework, *of* blue, and purple, and scarlet, and fine twined linen: and twenty cubits *was* the length, and the height in the breadth *was* five cubits, answerable to the hangings of the court.

19 And their pillars *were* four, and their sockets *of* brass four; their hooks *of* silver, and the overlaying of their chapiters and their fillets *of* silver.

20 And all the pins of the tabernacle, and of the court round about, *were of* brass.

21 This is the sum of the tabernacle, *even* of the tabernacle of testimony, as it was counted, according to the commandment of Moses, *for* the service of the Levites, by the hand of Ithamar, son to Aaron the priest.

22 And Bezaleel the son of Uri, the son of Hur, of the tribe of Judah, made all that the LORD commanded Moses.

23 And with him *was* Aholiab, son of Ahisamach, of the tribe of Dan, an engraver, and a cunning workman, and an embroiderer in blue, and in purple, and in scarlet, and fine linen.

24 All the gold that was occupied for the work in all the work of the holy *place,* even the gold of the offering, was twenty and nine talents, and seven hundred and thirty shekels, after the shekel of the sanctuary.

25 And the silver of them that were numbered of the congregation *was* an hundred talents, and a thousand seven hundred and threescore and fifteen shekels, after the shekel of the sanctuary:

26 A bekah for every man, *that is,* half a shekel, after the shekel of the sanctuary, for every one that went to be numbered, from twenty years old and upward, for six hundred thousand and three thousand and five hundred and fifty *men.*

27 And of the hundred talents of silver were cast the sockets of the sanctuary, and the sockets of the vail; an hundred sockets of the hundred talents, a talent for a socket.

28 And of the thousand seven hundred seventy and five *shekels* he made hooks for the pillars, and overlaid their chapiters, and filleted them.

29 And the brass of the offering *was* seventy talents, and two thousand and four hundred shekels.

30 And therewith he made the sockets to the door of the tabernacle of the congregation, and the brasen altar, and the brasen grate for it, and all the vessels of the altar,

31 And the sockets of the court round about, and the sockets of the court gate, and all the pins of the tabernacle, and all the pins of the court round about.

39

1 And of the blue, and purple, and scarlet, they made cloths of service, to do service in the holy *place,* and made the holy garments for Aaron; as the LORD commanded Moses.

2 And he made the ephod *of* gold, blue, and purple, and scarlet, and fine twined linen.

3 And they did beat the gold into thin plates, and cut *it into* wires, to work *it* in the blue, and in the purple, and in the scarlet, and in the fine linen, *with* cunning work.

4 They made shoulderpieces for it, to couple *it* together: by the two edges was it coupled together.

5 And the curious girdle of his ephod, that *was* upon it, *was* of the same, according to the work thereof; *of* gold, blue, and

purple, and scarlet, and fine twined linen; as the LORD commanded Moses.

6And they wrought onyx stones inclosed in ouches of gold, graven, as signets are graven, with the names of the children of Israel.

7And he put them on the shoulders of the ephod, *that they should be* stones for a memorial to the children of Israel; as the LORD commanded Moses.

8And he made the breastplate *of* cunning work, like the work of the ephod; *of* gold, blue, and purple, and scarlet, and fine twined linen.

9It was foursquare; they made the breastplate double: a span *was* the length thereof, and a span the breadth thereof, *being* doubled.

10And they set in it four rows of stones: *the first* row *was* a sardius, a topaz, and a carbuncle: this *was* the first row.

11And the second row, an emerald, a sapphire, and a diamond.

12And the third row, a ligure, an agate, and an amethyst.

13And the fourth row, a beryl, an onyx, and a jasper: *they were* inclosed in ouches of gold in their inclosings.

14And the stones *were* according to the names of the children of Israel, twelve, according to their names, *like* the engravings of a signet, every one with his name, according to the twelve tribes.

15And they made upon the breastplate chains at the ends, *of* wreathen work *of* pure gold.

16And they made two ouches *of* gold, and two gold rings; and put the two rings in the two ends of the breastplate.

17And they put the two wreathen chains of gold in the two rings on the ends of the breastplate.

18And the two ends of the two wreathen chains they fastened in the two ouches, and put them on the shoulderpieces of the ephod, before it.

19And they made two rings of gold, and put *them* on the two ends of the breastplate, upon the border of it, which *was* on the side of the ephod inward.

20And they made two *other* golden rings, and put them on the two sides of the ephod underneath, toward the forepart of it, over against the *other* coupling thereof, above the curious girdle of the ephod.

21And they did bind the breastplate by his rings unto the rings of the ephod with a lace of blue, that it might be above the curious girdle of the ephod, and that the breastplate might not be loosed from the ephod; as the LORD commanded Moses.

22And he made the robe of the ephod *of* woven work, all *of* blue.

23And *there was* an hole in the midst of the robe, as the hole of an habergeon, *with* a band round about the hole, that it should not rend.

24And they made upon the hems of the robe pomegranates *of* blue, and purple, and scarlet, *and* twined *linen.*

25And they made bells *of* pure gold, and put the bells between the pomegranates upon the hem of the robe, round about between the pomegranates;

26A bell and a pomegranate, a bell and a pomegranate, round about the hem of the robe to minister *in;* as the LORD commanded Moses.

27And they made coats *of* fine linen *of* woven work for Aaron, and for his sons,

28And a mitre *of* fine linen, and goodly bonnets *of* fine linen, and linen breeches *of* fine twined linen,

29And a girdle *of* fine twined linen, and blue, and purple, and scarlet, *of* needlework; as the LORD commanded Moses.

30And they made the plate of the holy crown *of* pure gold, and wrote upon it a writing, *like to* the engravings of a signet, HOLINESS TO THE LORD.

31And they tied unto it a lace of blue, to fasten *it* on high upon the mitre; as the LORD commanded Moses.

32Thus was all the work of the tabernacle of the tent of the congregation finished: and the children of Israel did according to all that the LORD commanded Moses, so did they.

33And they brought the tabernacle unto Moses, the tent, and all his furniture, his taches, his boards, his bars, and his pillars, and his sockets,

34And the covering of rams' skins dyed red, and the covering of badgers' skins, and the vail of the covering,

35The ark of the testimony, and the staves thereof, and the mercy seat,

36The table, *and* all the vessels thereof, and the shewbread,

37The pure candlestick, *with* the lamps

thereof, *even with* the lamps to be set in order, and all the vessels thereof, and the oil for light,

38 And the golden altar, and the anointing oil, and the sweet incense, and the hanging for the tabernacle door,

39 The brasen altar, and his grate of brass, his staves, and all his vessels, the laver and his foot,

40 The hangings of the court, his pillars, and his sockets, and the hanging for the court gate, his cords, and his pins, and all the vessels of the service of the tabernacle, for the tent of the congregation,

41 The cloths of service to do service in the holy *place,* and the holy garments for Aaron the priest, and his sons' garments, to minister in the priest's office.

42 According to all that the LORD commanded Moses, so the children of Israel made all the work.

43 And Moses did look upon all the work, and, behold, they have done it as the LORD had commanded, even so had they done it: and Moses blessed them.

40

1 And the LORD spake unto Moses, saying,

2 On the first day of the first month shalt thou set up the tabernacle of the tent of the congregation.

3 And thou shalt put therein the ark of the testimony, and cover the ark with the vail.

4 And thou shalt bring in the table, and set in order the things that are to be set in order upon it; and thou shalt bring in the candlestick, and light the lamps thereof.

5 And thou shalt set the altar of gold for the incense before the ark of the testimony, and put the hanging of the door to the tabernacle.

6 And thou shalt set the altar of the burnt offering before the door of the tabernacle of the tent of the congregation.

7 And thou shalt set the laver between the tent of the congregation and the altar, and shalt put water therein.

8 And thou shalt set up the court round about, and hang up the hanging at the court gate.

9 And thou shalt take the anointing oil, and anoint the tabernacle, and all that *is* therein, and shalt hallow it, and all the vessels thereof: and it shall be holy.

10 And thou shalt anoint the altar of the burnt offering, and all his vessels, and sanctify the altar: and it shall be an altar most holy.

11 And thou shalt anoint the laver and his foot, and sanctify it.

12 And thou shalt bring Aaron and his sons unto the door of the tabernacle of the congregation, and wash them with water.

13 And thou shalt put upon Aaron the holy garments, and anoint him, and sanctify him; that he may minister unto me in the priest's office.

14 And thou shalt bring his sons, and clothe them with coats:

15 And thou shalt anoint them, as thou didst anoint their father, that they may minister unto me in the priest's office: for their anointing shall surely be an everlasting priesthood throughout their generations.

16 Thus did Moses: according to all that the LORD commanded him, so did he.

17 And it came to pass in the first month in the second year, on the first *day* of the month, *that* the tabernacle was reared up.

18 And Moses reared up the tabernacle, and fastened his sockets, and set up the boards thereof, and put in the bars thereof, and reared up his pillars.

19 And he spread abroad the tent over the tabernacle, and put the covering of the tent above upon it; as the LORD commanded Moses.

20 And he took and put the testimony into the ark, and set the staves on the ark, and put the mercy seat above upon the ark:

21 And he brought the ark into the tabernacle, and set up the vail of the covering, and covered the ark of the testimony; as the LORD commanded Moses.

22 And he put the table in the tent of the congregation, upon the side of the tabernacle northward, without the vail.

23 And he set the bread in order upon it before the LORD; as the LORD had commanded Moses.

24 And he put the candlestick in the tent of the congregation, over against the table, on the side of the tabernacle southward.

25 And he lighted the lamps before the LORD; as the LORD commanded Moses.

26 And he put the golden altar in the tent of the congregation before the vail:

27And he burnt sweet incense thereon; as the LORD commanded Moses.

28And he set up the hanging *at* the door of the tabernacle.

29And he put the altar of burnt offering *by* the door of the tabernacle of the tent of the congregation, and offered upon it the burnt offering and the meat offering; as the LORD commanded Moses.

30And he set the laver between the tent of the congregation and the altar, and put water there, to wash *withal*.

31And Moses and Aaron and his sons washed their hands and their feet thereat:

32When they went into the tent of the congregation, and when they came near unto the altar, they washed; as the LORD commanded Moses.

33And he reared up the court round about the tabernacle and the altar, and set up the hanging of the court gate. So Moses finished the work.

34Then a cloud covered the tent of the congregation, and the glory of the LORD filled the tabernacle.

35And Moses was not able to enter into the tent of the congregation, because the cloud abode thereon, and the glory of the LORD filled the tabernacle.

36And when the cloud was taken up from over the tabernacle, the children of Israel went onward in all their journeys:

37But if the cloud were not taken up, then they journeyed not till the day that it was taken up.

38For the cloud of the LORD *was* upon the tabernacle by day, and fire was on it by night, in the sight of all the house of Israel, throughout all their journeys.

Leviticus

AUTHOR
Moses

MAIN POINT
God gave laws to his people so that they would honor him and live healthy lives.

DATE WRITTEN
1445-1444 B.C.

27 CHAPTERS

MAIN PEOPLE

Moses, Aaron, Aaron's sons

SPECIAL FEATURES

- *Describes several kinds of offerings, including those for guilt, grain, sin, and fellowship*
- *Explains why two of Aaron's sons were burned to death when they did a burnt offering wrong*
- *Tells what God has to say about getting rid of mildew, growing crops, and personal hygiene*
- *Gives instructions for the first Day of Atonement—still a major Jewish holiday*
- *Shows that God loves celebrations as much as laws when he called for various feasts*
- *Third book of Law*

HOW THE BOOK GOT ITS NAME

The word leviticus indicates that the book is a handbook for the Levites, the priests of God's people.

1
1And the LORD called unto Moses, and
spake unto him out of the tabernacle of
the congregation, saying,
2Speak unto the children of Israel, and
say unto them, If any man of you bring an
offering unto the LORD, ye shall bring your
offering of the cattle, *even* of the herd, and
of the flock.
3If his offering *be* a burnt sacrifice of the
herd, let him offer a male without blemish: he shall offer it of his own voluntary
will at the door of the tabernacle of the
congregation before the LORD.
4And he shall put his hand upon the
head of the burnt offering; and it shall
be accepted for him to make atonement
for him.
5And he shall kill the bullock before the
LORD: and the priests, Aaron's sons, shall
bring the blood, and sprinkle the blood
round about upon the altar that *is by* the
door of the tabernacle of the congregation.
6And he shall flay the burnt offering,
and cut it into his pieces.
7And the sons of Aaron the priest shall
put fire upon the altar, and lay the wood
in order upon the fire:
8And the priests, Aaron's sons, shall lay
the parts, the head, and the fat, in order
upon the wood that *is* on the fire which *is*
upon the altar:
9But his inwards and his legs shall he
wash in water: and the priest shall burn
all on the altar, *to be* a burnt sacrifice, an

offering made by fire, of a sweet savour
unto the LORD.
10 And if his offering *be* of the flocks,
namely, of the sheep, or of the goats, for a
burnt sacrifice; he shall bring it a male
without blemish.
11 And he shall kill it on the side of the
altar northward before the LORD: and the
priests, Aaron's sons, shall sprinkle his
blood round about upon the altar.
12 And he shall cut it into his pieces, with
his head and his fat: and the priest shall
lay them in order on the wood that *is* on
the fire which *is* upon the altar:
13 But he shall wash the inwards and the
legs with water: and the priest shall bring
it all, and burn *it* upon the altar: it *is* a burnt
sacrifice, an offering made by fire, of a
sweet savour unto the LORD.
14 And if the burnt sacrifice for his offering to the LORD *be* of fowls, then he shall
bring his offering of turtledoves, or of
young pigeons.
15 And the priest shall bring it unto the
altar, and wring off his head, and burn *it*
on the altar; and the blood thereof shall
be wrung out at the side of the altar:
16 And he shall pluck away his crop with
his feathers, and cast it beside the altar on
the east part, by the place of the ashes:
17 And he shall cleave it with the wings
thereof, *but* shall not divide *it* asunder: and
the priest shall burn it upon the altar, upon
the wood that *is* upon the fire: it *is* a burnt
sacrifice, an offering made by fire, of a
sweet savour unto the LORD.

2

1 And when any will offer a meat offering unto the LORD, his offering shall be *of*
fine flour; and he shall pour oil upon it,
and put frankincense thereon:
2 And he shall bring it to Aaron's sons
the priests: and he shall take thereout his
handful of the flour thereof, and of the
oil thereof, with all the frankincense
thereof; and the priest shall burn the memorial of it upon the altar, *to be* an offering made by fire, of a sweet savour unto
the LORD:
3 And the remnant of the meat offerings
shall be Aaron's and his sons': *it is* a thing
most holy of the offerings of the LORD
made by fire.
4 And if thou bring an oblation of a meat
offering baken in the oven, *it shall be*
unleavened cakes of fine flour mingled
with oil, or unleavened wafers anointed
with oil.
5 And if thy oblation *be* a meat offering
baken in a pan, it shall be *of* fine flour unleavened, mingled with oil.
6 Thou shalt part it in pieces, and pour
oil thereon: it *is* a meat offering.
7 And if thy oblation *be* a meat offering
baken in the frying pan, it shall be made *of*
fine flour with oil.
8 And thou shalt bring the meat offering
that is made of these things unto the LORD:
and when it is presented unto the priest,
he shall bring it unto the altar.
9 And the priest shall take from the meat
offering a memorial thereof, and shall
burn *it* upon the altar: *it is* an offering
made by fire, of a sweet savour unto the
LORD.
10 And that which is left of the meat offering *shall be* Aaron's and his sons': *it is* a
thing most holy of the offerings of the
LORD made by fire.
11 No meat offering, which ye shall bring
unto the LORD, shall be made with leaven:
for ye shall burn no leaven, nor any honey,
in any offering of the LORD made by fire.
12 As for the oblation of the firstfruits,
ye shall offer them unto the LORD: but they
shall not be burnt on the altar for a sweet
savour.
13 And every oblation of thy meat offering shalt thou season with salt; neither
shalt thou suffer the salt of the covenant
of thy God to be lacking from thy meat
offering: with all thine offerings thou shalt
offer salt.
14 And if thou offer a meat offering of
thy firstfruits unto the LORD, thou shalt
offer for the meat offering of thy firstfruits
green ears of corn dried by the fire, *even*
corn beaten out of full ears.
15 And thou shalt put oil upon it, and
lay frankincense thereon: it *is* a meat offering.
16 And the priest shall burn the memorial of it, *part* of the beaten corn thereof,
and *part* of the oil thereof, with all the
frankincense thereof: *it is* an offering made
by fire unto the LORD.

3

1 And if his oblation *be* a sacrifice of
peace offering, if he offer *it* of the herd;
whether *it be* a male or female, he shall
offer it without blemish before the LORD.
2 And he shall lay his hand upon the

head of his offering, and kill it *at* the door of the tabernacle of the congregation: and Aaron's sons the priests shall sprinkle the blood upon the altar round about.

3 And he shall offer of the sacrifice of the peace offering an offering made by fire unto the LORD; the fat that covereth the inwards, and all the fat that *is* upon the inwards,

4 And the two kidneys, and the fat that *is* on them, which *is* by the flanks, and the caul above the liver, with the kidneys, it shall he take away.

5 And Aaron's sons shall burn it on the altar upon the burnt sacrifice, which *is* upon the wood that *is* on the fire: *it is* an offering made by fire, of a sweet savour unto the LORD.

6 And if his offering for a sacrifice of peace offering unto the LORD *be* of the flock; male or female, he shall offer it without blemish.

7 If he offer a lamb for his offering, then shall he offer it before the LORD.

8 And he shall lay his hand upon the head of his offering, and kill it before the tabernacle of the congregation: and Aaron's sons shall sprinkle the blood thereof round about upon the altar.

9 And he shall offer of the sacrifice of the peace offering an offering made by fire unto the LORD; the fat thereof, *and* the whole rump, it shall he take off hard by the backbone; and the fat that covereth the inwards, and all the fat that *is* upon the inwards,

10 And the two kidneys, and the fat that *is* upon them, which *is* by the flanks, and the caul above the liver, with the kidneys, it shall he take away.

11 And the priest shall burn it upon the altar: *it is* the food of the offering made by fire unto the LORD.

12 And if his offering *be* a goat, then he shall offer it before the LORD.

13 And he shall lay his hand upon the head of it, and kill it before the tabernacle of the congregation: and the sons of Aaron shall sprinkle the blood thereof upon the altar round about.

14 And he shall offer thereof his offering, *even* an offering made by fire unto the LORD; the fat that covereth the inwards, and all the fat that *is* upon the inwards,

15 And the two kidneys, and the fat that *is* upon them, which *is* by the flanks, and the caul above the liver, with the kidneys, it shall he take away.

16 And the priest shall burn them upon the altar: *it is* the food of the offering made by fire for a sweet savour: all the fat *is* the LORD'S.

17 *It shall be* a perpetual statute for your generations throughout all your dwellings, that ye eat neither fat nor blood.

4

1 And the LORD spake unto Moses, saying,

2 Speak unto the children of Israel, saying, If a soul shall sin through ignorance against any of the commandments of the LORD *concerning things* which ought not to be done, and shall do against any of them:

4:2
Unknown Sins
◄ Leviticus 5:17 ►

3 If the priest that is anointed do sin according to the sin of the people; then let him bring for his sin, which he hath sinned, a young bullock without blemish unto the LORD for a sin offering.

4 And he shall bring the bullock unto the door of the tabernacle of the congregation before the LORD; and shall lay his hand upon the bullock's head, and kill the bullock before the LORD.

5 And the priest that is anointed shall take of the bullock's blood, and bring it to the tabernacle of the congregation:

6 And the priest shall dip his finger in the blood, and sprinkle of the blood seven times before the LORD, before the vail of the sanctuary.

7 And the priest shall put *some* of the blood upon the horns of the altar of sweet incense before the LORD, which *is* in the tabernacle of the congregation: and shall pour all the blood of the bullock at the bottom of the altar of the burnt offering, which *is at* the door of the tabernacle of the congregation.

8 And he shall take off from it all the fat of the bullock for the sin offering; the fat that covereth the inwards, and all the fat that *is* upon the inwards,

9 And the two kidneys, and the fat that *is* upon them, which *is* by the flanks, and the caul above the liver, with the kidneys, it shall he take away,

10 As it was taken off from the bullock

of the sacrifice of peace offerings: and the priest shall burn them upon the altar of the burnt offering.

11 And the skin of the bullock, and all his flesh, with his head, and with his legs, and his inwards, and his dung,

12 Even the whole bullock shall he carry forth without the camp unto a clean place, where the ashes are poured out, and burn him on the wood with fire: where the ashes are poured out shall he be burnt.

13 And if the whole congregation of Israel sin through ignorance, and the thing be hid from the eyes of the assembly, and they have done *somewhat against* any of the commandments of the LORD *concerning things* which should not be done, and are guilty;

14 When the sin, which they have sinned against it, is known, then the congregation shall offer a young bullock for the sin, and bring him before the tabernacle of the congregation.

15 And the elders of the congregation shall lay their hands upon the head of the bullock before the LORD: and the bullock shall be killed before the LORD.

16 And the priest that is anointed shall bring of the bullock's blood to the tabernacle of the congregation:

17 And the priest shall dip his finger *in some* of the blood, and sprinkle *it* seven times before the LORD, *even* before the vail.

18 And he shall put *some* of the blood upon the horns of the altar which *is* before the LORD, that *is* in the tabernacle of the congregation, and shall pour out all the blood at the bottom of the altar of the burnt offering, which *is at* the door of the tabernacle of the congregation.

19 And he shall take all his fat from him, and burn *it* upon the altar.

20 And he shall do with the bullock as he did with the bullock for a sin offering, so shall he do with this: and the priest shall make an atonement for them, and it shall be forgiven them.

21 And he shall carry forth the bullock without the camp, and burn him as he burned the first bullock: it *is* a sin offering for the congregation.

22 When a ruler hath sinned, and done *somewhat* through ignorance *against* any of the commandments of the LORD his God *concerning things* which should not be done, and is guilty;

23 Or if his sin, wherein he hath sinned, come to his knowledge; he shall bring his offering, a kid of the goats, a male without blemish:

24 And he shall lay his hand upon the head of the goat, and kill it in the place where they kill the burnt offering before the LORD: it *is* a sin offering.

25 And the priest shall take of the blood of the sin offering with his finger, and put *it* upon the horns of the altar of burnt offering, and shall pour out his blood at the bottom of the altar of burnt offering.

26 And he shall burn all his fat upon the altar, as the fat of the sacrifice of peace offerings: and the priest shall make an atonement for him as concerning his sin, and it shall be forgiven him.

27 And if any one of the common people sin through ignorance, while he doeth *somewhat against* any of the commandments of the LORD *concerning things* which ought not to be done, and be guilty;

28 Or if his sin, which he hath sinned, come to his knowledge: then he shall bring his offering, a kid of the goats, a female without blemish, for his sin which he hath sinned.

29 And he shall lay his hand upon the head of the sin offering, and slay the sin offering in the place of the burnt offering.

30 And the priest shall take of the blood thereof with his finger, and put *it* upon the horns of the altar of burnt offering, and shall pour out all the blood thereof at the bottom of the altar.

31 And he shall take away all the fat thereof, as the fat is taken away from off the sacrifice of peace offerings; and the priest shall burn *it* upon the altar for a sweet savour unto the LORD; and the priest shall make an atonement for him, and it shall be forgiven him.

32 And if he bring a lamb for a sin offering, he shall bring it a female without blemish.

33 And he shall lay his hand upon the head of the sin offering, and slay it for a sin offering in the place where they kill the burnt offering

34 And the priest shall take of the blood of the sin offering with his finger, and put *it* upon the horns of the altar of burnt of-

fering, and shall pour out all the blood thereof at the bottom of the altar:

35 And he shall take away all the fat thereof, as the fat of the lamb is taken away from the sacrifice of the peace offerings; and the priest shall burn them upon the altar, according to the offerings made by fire unto the LORD: and the priest shall make an atonement for his sin that he hath committed, and it shall be forgiven him.

5

1 And if a soul sin, and hear the voice of swearing, and *is* a witness, whether he hath seen or known *of it;* if he do not utter *it,* then he shall bear his iniquity.

2 Or if a soul touch any unclean thing, whether *it be* a carcase of an unclean beast, or a carcase of unclean cattle, or the carcase of unclean creeping things, and *if* it be hidden from him; he also shall be unclean, and guilty.

3 Or if he touch the uncleanness of man, whatsoever uncleanness *it be* that a man shall be defiled withal, and it be hid from him; when he knoweth *of it,* then he shall be guilty.

4 Or if a soul swear, pronouncing with *his* lips to do evil, or to do good, whatsoever *it be* that a man shall pronounce with an oath, and it be hid from him; when he knoweth *of it,* then he shall be guilty in one of these.

5 And it shall be, when he shall be guilty in one of these *things,* that he shall confess that he hath sinned in that *thing:*

6 And he shall bring his trespass offering unto the LORD for his sin which he hath sinned, a female from the flock, a lamb or a kid of the goats, for a sin offering; and the priest shall make an atonement for him concerning his sin.

7 And if he be not able to bring a lamb, then he shall bring for his trespass, which he hath committed, two turtledoves, or two young pigeons, unto the LORD; one for a sin offering, and the other for a burnt offering.

8 And he shall bring them unto the priest, who shall offer *that* which *is* for the sin offering first, and wring off his head from his neck, but shall not divide *it* asunder:

9 And he shall sprinkle of the blood of the sin offering upon the side of the altar; and the rest of the blood shall be wrung out at the bottom of the altar: it *is* a sin offering.

10 And he shall offer the second *for* a burnt offering, according to the manner: and the priest shall make an atonement for him for his sin which he hath sinned, and it shall be forgiven him.

5:10 Forgiveness
◄ Psalm 103:3 ►

11 But if he be not able to bring two turtledoves, or two young pigeons, then he that sinned shall bring for his offering the tenth part of an ephah of fine flour for a sin offering; he shall put no oil upon it, neither shall he put *any* frankincense thereon: for it *is* a sin offering.

12 Then shall he bring it to the priest, and the priest shall take his handful of it, *even* a memorial thereof, and burn *it* on the altar, according to the offerings made by fire unto the LORD: it *is* a sin offering.

13 And the priest shall make an atonement for him as touching his sin that he hath sinned in one of these, and it shall be forgiven him: and *the remnant* shall be the priest's, as a meat offering.

14 And the LORD spake unto Moses, saying,

15 If a soul commit a trespass, and sin through ignorance, in the holy things of the LORD; then he shall bring for his trespass unto the LORD a ram without blemish out of the flocks, with thy estimation by shekels of silver, after the shekel of the sanctuary, for a trespass offering:

16 And he shall make amends for the harm that he hath done in the holy thing, and shall add the fifth part thereto, and give it unto the priest: and the priest shall make an atonement for him with the ram of the trespass offering, and it shall be forgiven him.

17 And if a soul sin, and commit any of these things which are forbidden to be done by the commandments of the LORD; though he wist *it* not, yet is he guilty, and shall bear his iniquity.

5:17 Unknown Sins
◄ Leviticus 4:2
Luke 12:48 ►

18 And he shall bring a ram without blemish out of the flock, with thy estimation, for a trespass offering, unto the priest: and the priest shall make an atonement for him concerning his ignorance wherein

he erred and wist *it* not, and it shall be
forgiven him.
19It *is* a trespass offering: he hath certainly trespassed against the LORD.

6

1And the LORD spake unto Moses,
saying,
2If a soul sin, and commit a trespass
against the LORD, and lie unto his neighbour in that which was delivered him to
keep, or in fellowship, or in a thing taken
away by violence, or hath deceived his
neighbour;
3Or have found
that which was
lost, and lieth con-
cerning it, and
sweareth falsely; in
any of all these that
a man doeth, sinning therein:

6:3
Perjury
◄ Leviticus 19:12 ►

4Then it shall be, because he hath
sinned, and is guilty, that he shall restore
that which he took violently away, or the
thing which he hath deceitfully gotten, or
that which was delivered him to keep, or
the lost thing which he found,
5Or all that about which he hath sworn
falsely; he shall even restore it in the principal, and shall add the fifth part more
thereto, *and* give it unto him to whom it
appertaineth, in the day of his trespass
offering.
6And he shall bring his trespass offering unto the LORD, a ram without blemish out of the flock, with thy estimation,
for a trespass offering, unto the priest:
7And the priest shall make an atonement for him before the LORD: and it shall
be forgiven him for any thing of all that
he hath done in trespassing therein.
8And the LORD spake unto Moses,
saying,
9Command Aaron and his sons, saying,
This *is* the law of the burnt offering: It *is*
the burnt offering, because of the burning
upon the altar all night unto the morning, and the fire of the altar shall be burning in it.
10And the priest shall put on his linen
garment, and his linen breeches shall he
put upon his flesh, and take up the ashes
which the fire hath consumed with the
burnt offering on the altar, and he shall
put them beside the altar.
11And he shall put off his garments, and
put on other garments, and carry forth the
ashes without the camp unto a clean place.
12And the fire upon the altar shall be
burning in it; it shall not be put out: and
the priest shall burn wood on it every
morning, and lay the burnt offering in order upon it; and he shall burn thereon the
fat of the peace offerings.
13The fire shall ever be burning upon
the altar; it shall never go out.
14And this *is* the law of the meat offering: the sons of Aaron shall offer it before
the LORD, before the altar.
15And he shall take of it his handful, of
the flour of the meat offering, and of the
oil thereof, and all the frankincense which
is upon the meat offering, and shall burn
it upon the altar *for* a sweet savour, *even*
the memorial of it, unto the LORD.
16And the remainder thereof shall Aaron
and his sons eat: with unleavened bread
shall it be eaten in the holy place; in the
court of the tabernacle of the congregation
they shall eat it.
17It shall not be baken with leaven. I
have given it *unto them for* their portion of
my offerings made by fire; it *is* most holy,
as *is* the sin offering, and as the trespass
offering.
18All the males among the children of
Aaron shall eat of it. *It shall be* a statute for
ever in your generations concerning the
offerings of the LORD made by fire: every
one that toucheth them shall be holy.
19And the LORD spake unto Moses,
saying,
20This *is* the offering of Aaron and of
his sons, which they shall offer unto the
LORD in the day when he is anointed; the
tenth part of an ephah of fine flour for a
meat offering perpetual, half of it in the
morning, and half thereof at night.
21In a pan it shall be made with oil; *and
when it is* baken, thou shalt bring it in: *and*
the baken pieces of the meat offering shalt
thou offer *for* a sweet savour unto the LORD.
22And the priest of his sons that is
anointed in his stead shall offer it: *it is* a
statute for ever unto the LORD, it shall be
wholly burnt.
23For every meat offering for the priest
shall be wholly burnt: it shall not be eaten.
24And the LORD spake unto Moses,
saying,
25Speak unto Aaron and to his sons, saying, This *is* the law of the sin offering: In

the place where the burnt offering is killed
shall the sin offering be killed before the
LORD: it *is* most holy.
26 The priest that offereth it for sin shall
eat it: in the holy place shall it be eaten, in
the court of the tabernacle of the congregation.
27 Whatsoever shall touch the flesh
thereof shall be holy: and when there is
sprinkled of the blood thereof upon any
garment, thou shalt wash that whereon it
was sprinkled in the holy place.
28 But the earthen vessel wherein it is
sodden shall be broken: and if it be sodden
in a brasen pot, it shall be both scoured,
and rinsed in water.
29 All the males among the priests shall
eat thereof: it *is* most holy.
30 And no sin offering, whereof *any* of
the blood is brought into the tabernacle
of the congregation to reconcile *withal* in
the holy *place,* shall be eaten: it shall be
burnt in the fire.

7

1 Likewise this *is* the law of the trespass
offering: it *is* most holy.
2 In the place where they kill the burnt
offering shall they kill the trespass offering: and the blood thereof shall he sprinkle round about upon the altar.
3 And he shall offer of it all the fat
thereof; the rump, and the fat that covereth
the inwards,
4 And the two kidneys, and the fat that *is*
on them, which *is* by the flanks, and the
caul *that is* above the liver, with the kidneys, it shall he take away:
5 And the priest shall burn them upon
the altar *for* an offering made by fire unto
the LORD: it *is* a trespass offering.
6 Every male among the priests shall eat
thereof: it shall be eaten in the holy place:
it *is* most holy.
7 As the sin offering *is,* so *is* the trespass
offering: *there is* one law for them: the
priest that maketh atonement therewith
shall have *it.*
8 And the priest that offereth any man's
burnt offering, *even* the priest shall have
to himself the skin of the burnt offering
which he hath offered.
9 And all the meat offering that is baken
in the oven, and all that is dressed in the
fryingpan, and in the pan, shall be the
priest's that offereth it.
10 And every meat offering, mingled with
oil, and dry, shall all the sons of Aaron
have, one *as much* as another.
11 And this *is* the law of the sacrifice of
peace offerings, which he shall offer unto
the LORD.
12 If he offer it for a thanksgiving, then
he shall offer with the sacrifice of thanksgiving unleavened cakes mingled with oil,
and unleavened wafers anointed with oil,
and cakes mingled with oil, of fine flour,
fried.
13 Besides the cakes, he shall offer *for* his
offering leavened bread with the sacrifice
of thanksgiving of his peace offerings.
14 And of it he shall offer one out of the
whole oblation *for* an heave offering unto
the LORD, *and* it shall be the priest's that
sprinkleth the blood of the peace offerings.
15 And the flesh of the sacrifice of his
peace offerings for thanksgiving shall be
eaten the same day that it is offered; he
shall not leave any of it until the morning.
16 But if the sacrifice of his offering *be* a
vow, or a voluntary offering, it shall be
eaten the same day that he offereth his
sacrifice: and on the morrow also the remainder of it shall be eaten:
17 But the remainder of the flesh of the
sacrifice on the third day shall be burnt
with fire.
18 And if *any* of the flesh of the sacrifice
of his peace offerings be eaten at all on
the third day, it shall not be accepted, neither shall it be imputed unto him that
offereth it: it shall be an abomination, and
the soul that eateth of it shall bear his iniquity.
19 And the flesh that toucheth any unclean *thing* shall not be eaten; it shall be
burnt with fire: and as for the flesh, all that
be clean shall eat thereof.
20 But the soul that eateth *of* the flesh of
the sacrifice of peace offerings, that *pertain*
unto the LORD, having his uncleanness
upon him, even that soul shall be cut off
from his people.
21 Moreover the soul that shall touch any
unclean *thing, as* the uncleanness of man,
or *any* unclean beast, or any abominable
unclean *thing,* and eat of the flesh of the
sacrifice of peace offerings, which *pertain*
unto the LORD, even that soul shall be cut
off from his people.
22 And the LORD spake unto Moses,
saying,

23 Speak unto the children of Israel, saying, Ye shall eat no manner of fat, of ox, or of sheep, or of goat.

24 And the fat of the beast that dieth of itself, and the fat of that which is torn with beasts, may be used in any other use: but ye shall in no wise eat of it.

25 For whosoever eateth the fat of the beast, of which men offer an offering made by fire unto the LORD, even the soul that eateth *it* shall be cut off from his people.

26 Moreover ye shall eat no manner of blood, *whether it be* of fowl or of beast, in any of your dwellings.

27 Whatsoever soul *it be* that eateth any manner of blood, even that soul shall be cut off from his people.

28 And the LORD spake unto Moses, saying,

29 Speak unto the children of Israel, saying, He that offereth the sacrifice of his peace offerings unto the LORD shall bring his oblation unto the LORD of the sacrifice of his peace offerings.

30 His own hands shall bring the offerings of the LORD made by fire, the fat with the breast, it shall he bring, that the breast may be waved *for* a wave offering before the LORD.

31 And the priest shall burn the fat upon the altar: but the breast shall be Aaron's and his sons'.

32 And the right shoulder shall ye give unto the priest *for* an heave offering of the sacrifices of your peace offerings.

33 He among the sons of Aaron, that offereth the blood of the peace offerings, and the fat, shall have the right shoulder for *his* part.

34 For the wave breast and the heave shoulder have I taken of the children of Israel from off the sacrifices of their peace offerings, and have given them unto Aaron the priest and unto his sons by a statute for ever from among the children of Israel.

35 This *is the portion* of the anointing of Aaron, and of the anointing of his sons, out of the offerings of the LORD made by fire, in the day *when* he presented them to minister unto the LORD in the priest's office;

36 Which the LORD commanded to be given them of the children of Israel, in the day that he anointed them, *by* a statute for ever throughout their generations.

37 This *is* the law of the burnt offering, of the meat offering, and of the sin offering, and of the trespass offering, and of the consecrations, and of the sacrifice of the peace offerings;

38 Which the LORD commanded Moses in mount Sinai, in the day that he commanded the children of Israel to offer their oblations unto the LORD, in the wilderness of Sinai.

8

1 And the LORD spake unto Moses, saying,

2 Take Aaron and his sons with him, and the garments, and the anointing oil, and a bullock for the sin offering, and two rams, and a basket of unleavened bread;

3 And gather thou all the congregation together unto the door of the tabernacle of the congregation.

4 And Moses did as the LORD commanded him; and the assembly was gathered together unto the door of the tabernacle of the congregation.

5 And Moses said unto the congregation, This *is* the thing which the LORD commanded to be done.

6 And Moses brought Aaron and his sons, and washed them with water.

7 And he put upon him the coat, and girded him with the girdle, and clothed him with the robe, and put the ephod upon him, and he girded him with the curious girdle of the ephod, and bound *it* unto him therewith.

8 And he put the breastplate upon him: also he put in the breastplate the Urim and the Thummim.

9 And he put the mitre upon his head; also upon the mitre, *even* upon his forefront, did he put the golden plate, the holy crown; as the LORD commanded Moses.

10 And Moses took the anointing oil, and anointed the tabernacle and all that *was* therein, and sanctified them.

11 And he sprinkled thereof upon the altar seven times, and anointed the altar and all his vessels, both the laver and his foot, to sanctify them.

12 And he poured of the anointing oil upon Aaron's head, and anointed him, to sanctify him.

13 And Moses brought Aaron's sons, and put coats upon them, and girded them with girdles, and put bonnets upon them; as the LORD commanded Moses.

14 And he brought the bullock for the sin offering: and Aaron and his sons laid their hands upon the head of the bullock for the sin offering.

15 And he slew *it;* and Moses took the blood, and put *it* upon the horns of the altar round about with his finger, and purified the altar, and poured the blood at the bottom of the altar, and sanctified it, to make reconciliation upon it.

16 And he took all the fat that *was* upon the inwards, and caul *above* the liver, and the two kidneys, and their fat, and Moses burned *it* upon the altar.

17 But the bullock, and his hide, his flesh, and his dung, he burnt with fire without the camp; as the LORD commanded Moses.

18 And he brought the ram for the burnt offering: and Aaron and his sons laid their hands upon the head of the ram.

19 And he killed *it;* and Moses sprinkled the blood upon the altar round about.

20 And he cut the ram into pieces; and Moses burnt the head, and the pieces, and the fat.

21 And he washed the inwards and the legs in water; and Moses burnt the whole ram upon the altar: it *was* a burnt sacrifice for a sweet savour, *and* an offering made by fire unto the LORD; as the LORD commanded Moses.

22 And he brought the other ram, the ram of consecration: and Aaron and his sons laid their hands upon the head of the ram.

23 And he slew *it;* and Moses took of the blood of it, and put *it* upon the tip of Aaron's right ear, and upon the thumb of his right hand, and upon the great toe of his right foot.

24 And he brought Aaron's sons, and Moses put of the blood upon the tip of their right ear, and upon the thumbs of their right hands, and upon the great toes of their right feet: and Moses sprinkled the blood upon the altar round about.

25 And he took the fat, and the rump, and all the fat that *was* upon the inwards, and the caul *above* the liver, and the two kidneys, and their fat, and the right shoulder:

26 And out of the basket of unleavened bread, that *was* before the LORD, he took one unleavened cake, and a cake of oiled bread, and one wafer, and put *them* on the fat, and upon the right shoulder:

27 And he put all upon Aaron's hands, and upon his sons' hands, and waved them *for* a wave offering before the LORD.

28 And Moses took them from off their hands, and burnt *them* on the altar upon the burnt offering: they *were* consecrations for a sweet savour: it *is* an offering made by fire unto the LORD.

29 And Moses took the breast, and waved it *for* a wave offering before the LORD: *for* of the ram of consecration it was Moses' part; as the LORD commanded Moses.

30 And Moses took of the anointing oil, and of the blood which *was* upon the altar, and sprinkled *it* upon Aaron, *and* upon his garments, and upon his sons, and upon his sons' garments with him; and sanctified Aaron, *and* his garments, and his sons, and his sons' garments with him.

31 And Moses said unto Aaron and to his sons, Boil the flesh *at* the door of the tabernacle of the congregation: and there eat it with the bread that *is* in the basket of consecrations, as I commanded, saying, Aaron and his sons shall eat it.

32 And that which remaineth of the flesh and of the bread shall ye burn with fire.

33 And ye shall not go out of the door of the tabernacle of the congregation *in* seven days, until the days of your consecration be at an end: for seven days shall he consecrate you.

34 As he hath done this day, *so* the LORD hath commanded to do, to make an atonement for you.

35 Therefore shall ye abide *at* the door of the tabernacle of the congregation day and night seven days, and keep the charge of the LORD, that ye die not: for so I am commanded.

36 So Aaron and his sons did all things which the LORD commanded by the hand of Moses.

9

1 And it came to pass on the eighth day, *that* Moses called Aaron and his sons, and the elders of Israel;

2 And he said unto Aaron, Take thee a young calf for a sin offering, and a ram for a burnt offering, without blemish, and offer *them* before the LORD.

3 And unto the children of Israel thou shalt speak, saying, Take ye a kid of the goats for a sin offering; and a calf and a lamb, *both* of the first year, without blemish, for a burnt offering;

4 Also a bullock and a ram for peace offerings, to sacrifice before the LORD; and a meat offering mingled with oil: for to day the LORD will appear unto you.

5 And they brought *that* which Moses commanded before the tabernacle of the congregation: and all the congregation drew near and stood before the LORD.

6 And Moses said, This *is* the thing which the LORD commanded that ye should do: and the glory of the LORD shall appear unto you.

7 And Moses said unto Aaron, Go unto the altar, and offer thy sin offering, and thy burnt offering, and make an atonement for thyself, and for the people: and offer the offering of the people, and make an atonement for them; as the LORD commanded.

8 Aaron therefore went unto the altar, and slew the calf of the sin offering, which *was* for himself.

9 And the sons of Aaron brought the blood unto him: and he dipped his finger in the blood, and put *it* upon the horns of the altar, and poured out the blood at the bottom of the altar:

10 But the fat, and the kidneys, and the caul above the liver of the sin offering, he burnt upon the altar; as the LORD commanded Moses.

11 And the flesh and the hide he burnt with fire without the camp.

12 And he slew the burnt offering; and Aaron's sons presented unto him the blood, which he sprinkled round about upon the altar.

13 And they presented the burnt offering unto him, with the pieces thereof, and the head: and he burnt *them* upon the altar.

14 And he did wash the inwards and the legs, and burnt *them* upon the burnt offering on the altar.

15 And he brought the people's offering, and took the goat, which *was* the sin offering for the people, and slew it, and offered it for sin, as the first.

16 And he brought the burnt offering, and offered it according to the manner.

17 And he brought the meat offering, and took an handful thereof, and burnt *it* upon the altar, beside the burnt sacrifice of the morning.

18 He slew also the bullock and the ram *for* a sacrifice of peace offerings, which *was* for the people: and Aaron's sons presented unto him the blood, which he sprinkled upon the altar round about,

19 And the fat of the bullock and of the ram, the rump, and that which covereth *the inwards,* and the kidneys, and the caul *above* the liver:

20 And they put the fat upon the breasts, and he burnt the fat upon the altar:

21 And the breasts and the right shoulder Aaron waved *for* a wave offering before the LORD; as Moses commanded.

22 And Aaron lifted up his hand toward the people, and blessed them, and came down from offering of the sin offering, and the burnt offering, and peace offerings.

23 And Moses and Aaron went into the tabernacle of the congregation, and came out, and blessed the people: and the glory of the LORD appeared unto all the people.

24 And there came a fire out from before the LORD, and consumed upon the altar the burnt offering and the fat: *which* when all the people saw, they shouted, and fell on their faces.

10

1 And Nadab and Abihu, the sons of Aaron, took either of them his censer, and put fire therein, and put incense thereon, and offered strange fire before the LORD, which he commanded them not.

2 And there went out fire from the LORD, and devoured them, and they died before the LORD.

3 Then Moses said unto Aaron, This *is it* that the LORD spake, saying, I will be sanctified in them that come nigh me, and before all the people I will be glorified. And Aaron held his peace.

4 And Moses called Mishael and Elzaphan, the sons of Uzziel the uncle of Aaron, and said unto them, Come near, carry your brethren from before the sanctuary out of the camp.

5 So they went near, and carried them in their coats out of the camp; as Moses had said.

6 And Moses said unto Aaron, and unto Eleazar and unto Ithamar, his sons, Uncover not your heads, neither rend your clothes; lest ye die, and lest wrath come upon all the people: but let your brethren, the whole house of Israel, bewail the burning which the LORD hath kindled.

7 And ye shall not go out from the door of the tabernacle of the congregation, lest

ye die: for the anointing oil of the LORD *is* upon you. And they did according to the word of Moses.

8 And the LORD spake unto Aaron, saying,

9 Do not drink wine nor strong drink, thou, nor thy sons with thee, when ye go into the tabernacle of the congregation, lest ye die: *it shall be* a statute for ever throughout your generations:

> **10:9 Drinking**
> ◄ Numbers 6:3 ►

10 And that ye may put difference between holy and unholy, and between unclean and clean;

11 And that ye may teach the children of Israel all the statutes which the LORD hath spoken unto them by the hand of Moses.

> **10:11 Instruction**
> ◄ Deuteronomy 6:7 ►

12 And Moses spake unto Aaron, and unto Eleazar and unto Ithamar, his sons that were left, Take the meat offering that remaineth of the offerings of the LORD made by fire, and eat it without leaven beside the altar: for it *is* most holy:

13 And ye shall eat it in the holy place, because it *is* thy due, and thy sons' due, of the sacrifices of the LORD made by fire: for so I am commanded.

14 And the wave breast and heave shoulder shall ye eat in a clean place; thou, and thy sons, and thy daughters with thee: for *they be* thy due, and thy sons' due, *which* are given out of the sacrifices of peace offerings of the children of Israel.

15 The heave shoulder and the wave breast shall they bring with the offerings made by fire of the fat, to wave *it for* a wave offering before the LORD; and it shall be thine, and thy sons' with thee, by a statute for ever; as the LORD hath commanded.

16 And Moses diligently sought the goat of the sin offering, and, behold, it was burnt: and he was angry with Eleazar and Ithamar, the sons of Aaron *which were* left *alive,* saying,

> **10:16 Anger**
> ◄ Exodus 32:19
> Numbers 16:15 ►

17 Wherefore have ye not eaten the sin offering in the holy place, seeing it *is* most holy, and *God* hath given it you to bear the iniquity of the congregation, to make atonement for them before the LORD?

18 Behold, the blood of it was not brought in within the holy *place:* ye should indeed have eaten it in the holy *place,* as I commanded.

19 And Aaron said unto Moses, Behold, this day have they offered their sin offering and their burnt offering before the LORD; and such things have befallen me: and *if* I had eaten the sin offering to day, should it have been accepted in the sight of the LORD?

20 And when Moses heard *that,* he was content.

11

1 And the LORD spake unto Moses and to Aaron, saying unto them,

2 Speak unto the children of Israel, saying, These *are* the beasts which ye shall eat among all the beasts that *are* on the earth.

3 Whatsoever parteth the hoof, and is clovenfooted, *and* cheweth the cud, among the beasts, that shall ye eat.

4 Nevertheless these shall ye not eat of them that chew the cud, or of them that divide the hoof: *as* the camel, because he cheweth the cud, but divideth not the hoof; he *is* unclean unto you.

5 And the coney, because he cheweth the cud, but divideth not the hoof; he *is* unclean unto you.

6 And the hare, because he cheweth the cud, but divideth not the hoof; he *is* unclean unto you.

7 And the swine, though he divide the hoof, and be clovenfooted, yet he cheweth not the cud; he *is* unclean to you.

8 Of their flesh shall ye not eat, and their carcase shall ye not touch; they *are* unclean to you.

9 These shall ye eat of all that *are* in the waters: whatsoever hath fins and scales in the waters, in the seas, and in the rivers, them shall ye eat.

10 And all that have not fins and scales in the seas, and in the rivers, of all that move in the waters, and of any living thing which *is* in the waters, they *shall be* an abomination unto you:

11 They shall be even an abomination unto you; ye shall not eat of their flesh, but ye shall have their carcases in abomination.

12 Whatsoever hath no fins nor scales in the waters, that *shall be* an abomination unto you.

13 And these *are they which* ye shall have in abomination among the fowls; they shall not be eaten, they *are* an abomination: the eagle, and the ossifrage, and the ospray,

14 And the vulture, and the kite after his kind;

15 Every raven after his kind;

16 And the owl, and the night hawk, and the cuckow, and the hawk after his kind,

17 And the little owl, and the cormorant, and the great owl,

18 And the swan, and the pelican, and the gier eagle,

19 And the stork, the heron after her kind, and the lapwing, and the bat.

20 All fowls that creep, going upon *all* four, *shall be* an abomination unto you.

21 Yet these may ye eat of every flying creeping thing that goeth upon *all* four, which have legs above their feet, to leap withal upon the earth;

22 *Even* these of them ye may eat; the locust after his kind, and the bald locust after his kind, and the beetle after his kind, and the grasshopper after his kind.

23 But all *other* flying creeping things, which have four feet, *shall be* an abomination unto you.

24 And for these ye shall be unclean: whosoever toucheth the carcase of them shall be unclean until the even.

25 And whosoever beareth *ought* of the carcase of them shall wash his clothes, and be unclean until the even.

26 *The carcases* of every beast which divideth the hoof, and *is* not clovenfooted, nor cheweth the cud, *are* unclean unto you: every one that toucheth them shall be unclean.

27 And whatsoever goeth upon his paws, among all manner of beasts that go on *all* four, those *are* unclean unto you: whoso toucheth their carcase shall be unclean until the even.

28 And he that beareth the carcase of them shall wash his clothes, and be unclean until the even: they *are* unclean unto you.

29 These also *shall be* unclean unto you among the creeping things that creep upon the earth; the weasel, and the mouse, and the tortoise after his kind,

30 And the ferret, and the chameleon, and the lizard, and the snail, and the mole.

31 These *are* unclean to you among all that creep: whosoever doth touch them, when they be dead, shall be unclean until the even.

32 And upon whatsoever *any* of them, when they are dead, doth fall, it shall be unclean; whether *it be* any vessel of wood, or raiment, or skin, or sack, whatsoever vessel *it be,* wherein *any* work is done, it must be put into water, and it shall be unclean until the even; so it shall be cleansed.

33 And every earthen vessel, whereinto *any* of them falleth, whatsoever *is* in it shall be unclean; and ye shall break it.

34 Of all meat which may be eaten, *that* on which *such* water cometh shall be unclean: and all drink that may be drunk in every *such* vessel shall be unclean.

35 And every *thing* whereupon *any part* of their carcase falleth shall be unclean; *whether it be* oven, or ranges for pots, they shall be broken down: *for* they *are* unclean, and shall be unclean unto you.

36 Nevertheless a fountain or pit, *wherein there is* plenty of water, shall be clean: but that which toucheth their carcase shall be unclean.

37 And if *any part* of their carcase fall upon any sowing seed which is to be sown, it *shall be* clean.

38 But if *any* water be put upon the seed, and *any part* of their carcase fall thereon, it *shall be* unclean unto you.

39 And if any beast, of which ye may eat, die; he that toucheth the carcase thereof shall be unclean until the even.

40 And he that eateth of the carcase of it shall wash his clothes, and be unclean until the even: he also that beareth the carcase of it shall wash his clothes, and be unclean until the even.

41 And every creeping thing that creepeth upon the earth *shall be* an abomination; it shall not be eaten.

42 Whatsoever goeth upon the belly, and whatsoever goeth upon *all* four, or whatsoever hath more feet among all creeping things that creep upon the earth, them ye shall not eat; for they *are* an abomination.

43 Ye shall not make yourselves abominable with any creeping thing that creepeth, neither shall ye make yourselves

unclean with them, that ye should be defiled thereby.
44 For I *am* the LORD your God: ye shall
therefore sanctify yourselves, and ye shall
be holy; for I *am* holy: neither shall ye defile yourselves with any manner of creeping thing that creepeth upon the earth.
45 For I *am* the
LORD that bringeth
you up out of the
land of Egypt, to be
your God: ye shall
therefore be holy,
for I *am* holy.

11:45 Holiness
◄ Exodus 19:6
Leviticus 19:2 ►

46 This *is* the law of the beasts, and of
the fowl, and of every living creature that
moveth in the waters, and of every creature that creepeth upon the earth:
47 To make a difference between the unclean and the clean, and between the beast
that may be eaten and the beast that may
not be eaten.

12

1 And the LORD spake unto Moses,
saying,
2 Speak unto the children of Israel, saying, If a woman have conceived seed, and
born a man child: then she shall be unclean seven days; according to the days of
the separation for her infirmity shall she
be unclean.
3 And in the eighth day the flesh of his
foreskin shall be circumcised.
4 And she shall then continue in the
blood of her purifying three and thirty
days; she shall touch no hallowed thing,
nor come into the sanctuary, until the days
of her purifying be fulfilled.
5 But if she bear a maid child, then she
shall be unclean two weeks, as in her separation: and she shall continue in the
blood of her purifying threescore and six
days.
6 And when the days of her purifying are
fulfilled, for a son, or for a daughter, she
shall bring a lamb of the first year for a
burnt offering, and a young pigeon, or a
turtledove, for a sin offering, unto the door
of the tabernacle of the congregation, unto
the priest:
7 Who shall offer it before the LORD, and
make an atonement for her; and she shall
be cleansed from the issue of her blood.
This *is* the law for her that hath born a male
or a female.
8 And if she be not able to bring a lamb,
then she shall bring two turtles, or two
young pigeons; the one for the burnt offering, and the other for a sin offering: and
the priest shall make an atonement for her,
and she shall be clean.

13

1 And the LORD spake unto Moses and
Aaron, saying,
2 When a man shall have in the skin of
his flesh a rising, a scab, or a bright spot,
and it be in the skin of his flesh *like* the
plague of leprosy; then he shall be brought
unto Aaron the priest, or unto one of his
sons the priests:
3 And the priest shall look on the plague
in the skin of the flesh: and *when* the hair
in the plague is turned white, and the
plague in sight *be* deeper than the skin of
his flesh, it *is* a plague of leprosy: and the
priest shall look on him, and pronounce
him unclean.
4 If the bright spot *be* white in the skin
of his flesh, and in sight *be* not deeper than
the skin, and the hair thereof be not turned
white; then the priest shall shut up *him
that hath* the plague seven days:
5 And the priest shall look on him the
seventh day: and, behold, *if* the plague in
his sight be at a stay, *and* the plague spread
not in the skin; then the priest shall shut
him up seven days more:
6 And the priest shall look on him again
the seventh day: and, behold, *if* the plague
be somewhat dark, *and* the plague spread
not in the skin, the priest shall pronounce
him clean: it *is but* a scab: and he shall wash
his clothes, and be clean.
7 But if the scab spread much abroad in
the skin, after that he hath been seen of
the priest for his cleansing, he shall be seen
of the priest again:
8 And *if* the priest see that, behold, the
scab spreadeth in the skin, then the priest
shall pronounce him unclean: it *is* a leprosy.
9 When the plague of leprosy is in a man,
then he shall be brought unto the priest;
10 And the priest shall see *him:* and, behold, *if* the rising *be* white in the skin, and
it have turned the hair white, and *there be*
quick raw flesh in the rising;
11 It *is* an old leprosy in the skin of his
flesh, and the priest shall pronounce him
unclean, and shall not shut him up: for
he *is* unclean.
12 And if a leprosy break out abroad in

the skin, and the leprosy cover all the skin of *him that hath* the plague from his head even to his foot, wheresoever the priest looketh;

13 Then the priest shall consider: and, behold, *if* the leprosy have covered all his flesh, he shall pronounce *him* clean *that hath* the plague: it is all turned white: he *is* clean.

14 But when raw flesh appeareth in him, he shall be unclean.

15 And the priest shall see the raw flesh, and pronounce him to be unclean: *for* the raw flesh *is* unclean: it *is* a leprosy.

16 Or if the raw flesh turn again, and be changed unto white, he shall come unto the priest;

17 And the priest shall see him: and, behold, *if* the plague be turned into white; then the priest shall pronounce *him* clean *that hath* the plague: he *is* clean.

18 The flesh also, in which, *even* in the skin thereof, was a boil, and is healed,

19 And in the place of the boil there be a white rising, or a bright spot, white, and somewhat reddish, and it be shewed to the priest;

20 And if, when the priest seeth it, behold, it *be* in sight lower than the skin, and the hair thereof be turned white; the priest shall pronounce him unclean: it *is* a plague of leprosy broken out of the boil.

21 But if the priest look on it, and, behold, *there be* no white hairs therein, and *if* it *be* not lower than the skin, but *be* somewhat dark; then the priest shall shut him up seven days:

22 And if it spread much abroad in the skin, then the priest shall pronounce him unclean: it *is* a plague.

23 But if the bright spot stay in his place, *and* spread not, it *is* a burning boil; and the priest shall pronounce him clean.

24 Or if there be *any* flesh, in the skin whereof *there is* a hot burning, and the quick *flesh* that burneth have a white bright spot, somewhat reddish, or white;

25 Then the priest shall look upon it: and, behold, *if* the hair in the bright spot be turned white, and it *be in* sight deeper than the skin; it *is* a leprosy broken out of the burning: wherefore the priest shall pronounce him unclean: it *is* the plague of leprosy.

26 But if the priest look on it, and, behold, *there be* no white hair in the bright spot, and it *be* no lower than the *other* skin, but *be* somewhat dark; then the priest shall shut him up seven days:

27 And the priest shall look upon him the seventh day: *and* if it be spread much abroad in the skin, then the priest shall pronounce him unclean: it *is* the plague of leprosy.

28 And if the bright spot stay in his place, *and* spread not in the skin, but it *be* somewhat dark; it *is* a rising of the burning, and the priest shall pronounce him clean: for it *is* an inflammation of the burning.

29 If a man or woman have a plague upon the head or the beard;

30 Then the priest shall see the plague: and, behold, if it *be* in sight deeper than the skin; *and there be* in it a yellow thin hair; then the priest shall pronounce him unclean: it *is* a dry scall, *even* a leprosy upon the head or beard.

31 And if the priest look on the plague of the scall, and, behold, it *be* not in sight deeper than the skin, and *that there is* no black hair in it; then the priest shall shut up *him that hath* the plague of the scall seven days:

32 And in the seventh day the priest shall look on the plague: and, behold, *if* the scall spread not, and there be in it no yellow hair, and the scall *be* not in sight deeper than the skin;

33 He shall be shaven, but the scall shall he not shave; and the priest shall shut up *him that hath* the scall seven days more:

34 And in the seventh day the priest shall look on the scall: and, behold, *if* the scall be not spread in the skin, nor *be* in sight deeper than the skin; then the priest shall pronounce him clean: and he shall wash his clothes, and be clean.

35 But if the scall spread much in the skin after his cleansing;

36 Then the priest shall look on him: and, behold, if the scall be spread in the skin, the priest shall not seek for yellow hair; he *is* unclean.

37 But if the scall be in his sight at a stay, and *that* there is black hair grown up therein; the scall is healed, he *is* clean: and the priest shall pronounce him clean.

38 If a man also or a woman have in the skin of their flesh bright spots, *even* white bright spots;

39 Then the priest shall look: and, behold, *if* the bright spots in the skin of their flesh *be* darkish white; it *is* a freckled spot *that* groweth in the skin; he *is* clean.

40 And the man whose hair is fallen off his head, he *is* bald; *yet is* he clean.

41 And he that hath his hair fallen off from the part of his head toward his face, he *is* forehead bald: *yet is* he clean.

42 And if there be in the bald head, or bald forehead, a white reddish sore; it *is* a leprosy sprung up in his bald head, or his bald forehead.

43 Then the priest shall look upon it: and, behold, *if* the rising of the sore *be* white reddish in his bald head, or in his bald forehead, as the leprosy appeareth in the skin of the flesh;

44 He is a leprous man, he *is* unclean: the priest shall pronounce him utterly unclean; his plague *is* in his head.

45 And the leper in whom the plague *is*, his clothes shall be rent, and his head bare, and he shall put a covering upon his upper lip, and shall cry, Unclean, unclean.

46 All the days wherein the plague *shall be* in him he shall be defiled; he *is* unclean: he shall dwell alone; without the camp *shall* his habitation *be*.

47 The garment also that the plague of leprosy is in, *whether it be* a woollen garment, or a linen garment;

48 Whether *it be* in the warp, or woof; of linen, or of woollen; whether in a skin, or in any thing made of skin;

49 And if the plague be greenish or reddish in the garment, or in the skin, either in the warp, or in the woof, or in any thing of skin; it *is* a plague of leprosy, and shall be shewed unto the priest:

50 And the priest shall look upon the plague, and shut up *it that hath* the plague seven days:

51 And he shall look on the plague on the seventh day: if the plague be spread in the garment, either in the warp, or in the woof, or in a skin, *or* in any work that is made of skin; the plague *is* a fretting leprosy; it *is* unclean.

52 He shall therefore burn that garment, whether warp or woof, in woollen or in linen, or any thing of skin, wherein the plague is: for it *is* a fretting leprosy; it shall be burnt in the fire.

53 And if the priest shall look, and, behold, the plague be not spread in the garment, either in the warp, or in the woof, or in any thing of skin;

54 Then the priest shall command that they wash *the thing* wherein the plague *is*, and he shall shut it up seven days more:

55 And the priest shall look on the plague, after that it is washed: and, behold, *if* the plague have not changed his colour, and the plague be not spread; it *is* unclean; thou shalt burn it in the fire; it *is* fret inward, *whether* it *be* bare within or without.

56 And if the priest look, and, behold, the plague *be* somewhat dark after the washing of it; then he shall rend it out of the garment, or out of the skin, or out of the warp, or out of the woof:

57 And if it appear still in the garment, either in the warp, or in the woof, or in any thing of skin; it *is* a spreading *plague*: thou shalt burn that wherein the plague *is* with fire.

58 And the garment, either warp, or woof, or whatsoever thing of skin *it be*, which thou shalt wash, if the plague be departed from them, then it shall be washed the second time, and shall be clean.

59 This *is* the law of the plague of leprosy in a garment of woollen or linen, either in the warp, or woof, or any thing of skins, to pronounce it clean, or to pronounce it unclean.

14

1 And the LORD spake unto Moses, saying,

2 This shall be the law of the leper in the day of his cleansing: He shall be brought unto the priest:

3 And the priest shall go forth out of the camp; and the priest shall look, and, behold, *if* the plague of leprosy be healed in the leper;

4 Then shall the priest command to take for him that is to be cleansed two birds alive *and* clean, and cedar wood, and scarlet, and hyssop:

5 And the priest shall command that one of the birds be killed in an earthen vessel over running water:

6 As for the living bird, he shall take it, and the cedar wood, and the scarlet, and the hyssop, and shall dip them and the living bird in the blood of the bird *that was* killed over the running water:

7 And he shall sprinkle upon him that is to be cleansed from the leprosy seven times, and shall pronounce him clean, and

shall let the living bird loose into the open field.

8 And he that is to be cleansed shall wash his clothes, and shave off all his hair, and wash himself in water, that he may be clean: and after that he shall come into the camp, and shall tarry abroad out of his tent seven days.

9 But it shall be on the seventh day, that he shall shave all his hair off his head and his beard and his eyebrows, even all his hair he shall shave off: and he shall wash his clothes, also he shall wash his flesh in water, and he shall be clean.

10 And on the eighth day he shall take two he lambs without blemish, and one ewe lamb of the first year without blemish, and three tenth deals of fine flour *for* a meat offering, mingled with oil, and one log of oil.

11 And the priest that maketh *him* clean shall present the man that is to be made clean, and those things, before the LORD, *at* the door of the tabernacle of the congregation:

12 And the priest shall take one he lamb, and offer him for a trespass offering, and the log of oil, and wave them *for* a wave offering before the LORD:

13 And he shall slay the lamb in the place where he shall kill the sin offering and the burnt offering, in the holy place: for as the sin offering *is* the priest's, *so is* the trespass offering: it *is* most holy:

14 And the priest shall take *some* of the blood of the trespass offering, and the priest shall put *it* upon the tip of the right ear of him that is to be cleansed, and upon the thumb of his right hand, and upon the great toe of his right foot:

15 And the priest shall take *some* of the log of oil, and pour *it* into the palm of his own left hand:

16 And the priest shall dip his right finger in the oil that *is* in his left hand, and shall sprinkle of the oil with his finger seven times before the LORD:

17 And of the rest of the oil that *is* in his hand shall the priest put upon the tip of the right ear of him that is to be cleansed, and upon the thumb of his right hand, and upon the great toe of his right foot, upon the blood of the trespass offering:

18 And the remnant of the oil that *is* in the priest's hand he shall pour upon the head of him that is to be cleansed: and the priest shall make an atonement for him before the LORD.

19 And the priest shall offer the sin offering, and make an atonement for him that is to be cleansed from his uncleanness; and afterward he shall kill the burnt offering:

20 And the priest shall offer the burnt offering and the meat offering upon the altar: and the priest shall make an atonement for him, and he shall be clean.

21 And if he *be* poor, and cannot get so much; then he shall take one lamb *for* a trespass offering to be waved, to make an atonement for him, and one tenth deal of fine flour mingled with oil for a meat offering, and a log of oil;

22 And two turtledoves, or two young pigeons, such as he is able to get; and the one shall be a sin offering, and the other a burnt offering.

23 And he shall bring them on the eighth day for his cleansing unto the priest, unto the door of the tabernacle of the congregation, before the LORD.

24 And the priest shall take the lamb of the trespass offering, and the log of oil, and the priest shall wave them *for* a wave offering before the LORD:

25 And he shall kill the lamb of the trespass offering, and the priest shall take *some* of the blood of the trespass offering, and put *it* upon the tip of the right ear of him that is to be cleansed, and upon the thumb of his right hand, and upon the great toe of his right foot:

26 And the priest shall pour of the oil into the palm of his own left hand:

27 And the priest shall sprinkle with his right finger *some* of the oil that *is* in his left hand seven times before the LORD:

28 And the priest shall put of the oil that *is* in his hand upon the tip of the right ear of him that is to be cleansed, and upon the thumb of his right hand, and upon the great toe of his right foot, upon the place of the blood of the trespass offering:

29 And the rest of the oil that *is* in the priest's hand he shall put upon the head of him that is to be cleansed, to make an atonement for him before the LORD.

30 And he shall offer the one of the turtledoves, or of the young pigeons, such as he can get;

31 *Even* such as he is able to get, the one *for* a sin offering, and the other *for* a burnt offering, with the meat offering: and the priest shall make an atonement for him that is to be cleansed before the LORD.

32 This *is* the law *of him* in whom *is* the plague of leprosy, whose hand is not able to get *that which pertaineth* to his cleansing.

33 And the LORD spake unto Moses and unto Aaron, saying,

34 When ye be come into the land of Canaan, which I give to you for a possession, and I put the plague of leprosy in a house of the land of your possession;

35 And he that owneth the house shall come and tell the priest, saying, It seemeth to me *there is* as it were a plague in the house:

36 Then the priest shall command that they empty the house, before the priest go *into it* to see the plague, that all that *is* in the house be not made unclean: and afterward the priest shall go in to see the house:

37 And he shall look on the plague, and, behold, *if* the plague *be* in the walls of the house with hollow strakes, greenish or reddish, which in sight *are* lower than the wall;

38 Then the priest shall go out of the house to the door of the house, and shut up the house seven days:

39 And the priest shall come again the seventh day, and shall look: and, behold, *if* the plague be spread in the walls of the house;

40 Then the priest shall command that they take away the stones in which the plague *is*, and they shall cast them into an unclean place without the city:

41 And he shall cause the house to be scraped within round about, and they shall pour out the dust that they scrape off without the city into an unclean place:

42 And they shall take other stones, and put *them* in the place of those stones; and he shall take other morter, and shall plaister the house.

43 And if the plague come again, and break out in the house, after that he hath taken away the stones, and after he hath scraped the house, and after it is plaistered;

44 Then the priest shall come and look, and, behold, *if* the plague be spread in the house, it *is* a fretting leprosy in the house: it *is* unclean.

45 And he shall break down the house, the stones of it, and the timber thereof, and all the morter of the house; and he shall carry *them* forth out of the city into an unclean place.

46 Moreover he that goeth into the house all the while that it is shut up shall be unclean until the even.

47 And he that lieth in the house shall wash his clothes; and he that eateth in the house shall wash his clothes.

48 And if the priest shall come in, and look *upon it*, and, behold, the plague hath not spread in the house, after the house was plaistered: then the priest shall pronounce the house clean, because the plague is healed.

49 And he shall take to cleanse the house two birds, and cedar wood, and scarlet, and hyssop:

50 And he shall kill the one of the birds in an earthen vessel over running water:

51 And he shall take the cedar wood, and the hyssop, and the scarlet, and the living bird, and dip them in the blood of the slain bird, and in the running water, and sprinkle the house seven times:

52 And he shall cleanse the house with the blood of the bird, and with the running water, and with the living bird, and with the cedar wood, and with the hyssop, and with the scarlet:

53 But he shall let go the living bird out of the city into the open fields, and make an atonement for the house: and it shall be clean.

54 This *is* the law for all manner of plague of leprosy, and scall,

55 And for the leprosy of a garment, and of a house,

56 And for a rising, and for a scab, and for a bright spot:

57 To teach when *it is* unclean, and when *it is* clean: this *is* the law of leprosy.

15

1 And the LORD spake unto Moses and to Aaron, saying,

2 Speak unto the children of Israel, and say unto them, When any man hath a running issue out of his flesh, *because of* his issue he *is* unclean.

3 And this shall be his uncleanness in his issue: whether his flesh run with his issue, or his flesh be stopped from his issue, it *is* his uncleanness.

4 Every bed, whereon he lieth that hath

the issue, is unclean: and every thing, whereon he sitteth, shall be unclean.

5 And whosoever toucheth his bed shall wash his clothes, and bathe *himself* in water, and be unclean until the even.

6 And he that sitteth on *any* thing whereon he sat that hath the issue shall wash his clothes, and bathe *himself* in water, and be unclean until the even.

7 And he that toucheth the flesh of him that hath the issue shall wash his clothes, and bathe *himself* in water, and be unclean until the even.

8 And if he that hath the issue spit upon him that is clean; then he shall wash his clothes, and bathe *himself* in water, and be unclean until the even.

9 And what saddle soever he rideth upon that hath the issue shall be unclean.

10 And whosoever toucheth any thing that was under him shall be unclean until the even: and he that beareth *any of* those things shall wash his clothes, and bathe *himself* in water, and be unclean until the even.

11 And whomsoever he toucheth that hath the issue, and hath not rinsed his hands in water, he shall wash his clothes, and bathe *himself* in water, and be unclean until the even.

12 And the vessel of earth, that he toucheth which hath the issue, shall be broken: and every vessel of wood shall be rinsed in water.

13 And when he that hath an issue is cleansed of his issue; then he shall number to himself seven days for his cleansing, and wash his clothes, and bathe his flesh in running water, and shall be clean.

14 And on the eighth day he shall take to him two turtledoves, or two young pigeons, and come before the LORD unto the door of the tabernacle of the congregation, and give them unto the priest:

15 And the priest shall offer them, the one *for* a sin offering, and the other *for* a burnt offering; and the priest shall make an atonement for him before the LORD for his issue.

16 And if any man's seed of copulation go out from him, then he shall wash all his flesh in water, and be unclean until the even.

17 And every garment, and every skin, whereon is the seed of copulation, shall be washed with water, and be unclean until the even.

18 The woman also with whom man shall lie *with* seed of copulation, they shall *both* bathe *themselves* in water, and be unclean until the even.

19 And if a woman have an issue, *and* her issue in her flesh be blood, she shall be put apart seven days: and whosoever toucheth her shall be unclean until the even.

20 And every thing that she lieth upon in her separation shall be unclean: every thing also that she sitteth upon shall be unclean.

21 And whosoever toucheth her bed shall wash his clothes, and bathe *himself* in water, and be unclean until the even.

22 And whosoever toucheth any thing that she sat upon shall wash his clothes, and bathe *himself* in water, and be unclean until the even.

23 And if it *be* on *her* bed, or on any thing whereon she sitteth, when he toucheth it, he shall be unclean until the even.

24 And if any man lie with her at all, and her flowers be upon him, he shall be unclean seven days; and all the bed whereon he lieth *shall be* unclean.

25 And if a woman have an issue of her blood many days out of the time of her separation, or if it run beyond the time of her separation; all the days of the issue of her uncleanness shall be as the days of her separation: she *shall be* unclean.

26 Every bed whereon she lieth all the days of her issue shall be unto her as the bed of her separation: and whatsoever she sitteth upon shall be unclean, as the uncleanness of her separation.

27 And whosoever toucheth those things shall be unclean, and shall wash his clothes, and bathe *himself* in water, and be unclean until the even.

28 But if she be cleansed of her issue, then she shall number to herself seven days, and after that she shall be clean.

29 And on the eighth day she shall take unto her two turtles, or two young pigeons, and bring them unto the priest, to the door of the tabernacle of the congregation.

30 And the priest shall offer the one *for* a sin offering, and the other *for* a burnt offering; and the priest shall make an atonement for her before the LORD for the issue of her uncleanness.

31 Thus shall ye separate the children of
Israel from their uncleanness; that they die
not in their uncleanness, when they defile
my tabernacle that *is* among them.
32 This *is* the law of him that hath an issue, and *of him* whose seed goeth from
him, and is defiled therewith;
33 And of her that is sick of her flowers,
and of him that hath an issue, of the man,
and of the woman, and of him that lieth
with her that is unclean.

16

1 And the LORD spake unto Moses after
the death of the two sons of Aaron, when
they offered before the LORD, and died;
2 And the LORD said unto Moses, Speak
unto Aaron thy brother, that he come not
at all times into the holy *place* within the
vail before the mercy seat, which *is* upon
the ark; that he die not: for I will appear
in the cloud upon the mercy seat.
3 Thus shall Aaron come into the holy
place: with a young bullock for a sin offering, and a ram for a burnt offering.
4 He shall put on the holy linen coat, and
he shall have the linen breeches upon his
flesh, and shall be girded with a linen
girdle, and with the linen mitre shall he
be attired: these *are* holy garments; therefore shall he wash his flesh in water, and
so put them on.
5 And he shall take of the congregation
of the children of Israel two kids of the
goats for a sin offering, and one ram for a
burnt offering.
6 And Aaron shall offer his bullock of the
sin offering, which *is* for himself, and make
an atonement for himself, and for his
house.
7 And he shall take the two goats, and
present them before the LORD *at* the door
of the tabernacle of the congregation.
8 And Aaron shall cast lots upon the two
goats; one lot for the LORD, and the other
lot for the scapegoat.
9 And Aaron shall bring the goat upon
which the LORD'S lot fell, and offer him
for a sin offering.
10 But the goat, on which the lot fell to
be the scapegoat, shall be presented alive
before the LORD, to make an atonement
with him, *and* to let him go for a scapegoat into the wilderness.
11 And Aaron shall bring the bullock of
the sin offering, which *is* for himself, and
shall make an atonement for himself, and
for his house, and shall kill the bullock of
the sin offering which *is* for himself:
12 And he shall take a censer full of burning coals of fire from off the altar before
the LORD, and his hands full of sweet incense beaten small, and bring *it* within the
vail:
13 And he shall put the incense upon the
fire before the LORD, that the cloud of the
incense may cover the mercy seat that *is*
upon the testimony, that he die not:
14 And he shall take of the blood of the
bullock, and sprinkle *it* with his finger
upon the mercy seat eastward; and before
the mercy seat shall he sprinkle of the
blood with his finger seven times.
15 Then shall he kill the goat of the sin
offering, that *is* for the people, and bring
his blood within the vail, and do with that
blood as he did with the blood of the bullock, and sprinkle it upon the mercy seat,
and before the mercy seat:
16 And he shall make an atonement for
the holy *place,* because of the uncleanness
of the children of Israel, and because of
their transgressions in all their sins: and
so shall he do for the tabernacle of the
congregation, that remaineth among them
in the midst of their uncleanness.
17 And there shall be no man in the tabernacle of the congregation when he goeth
in to make an atonement in the holy *place,*
until he come out, and have made an
atonement for himself, and for his household, and for all the congregation of Israel.
18 And he shall go out unto the altar that
is before the LORD, and make an atonement for it; and shall take of the blood of
the bullock, and of the blood of the goat,
and put *it* upon the horns of the altar
round about.
19 And he shall sprinkle of the blood
upon it with his finger seven times, and
cleanse it, and hallow it from the uncleanness of the children of Israel.
20 And when he hath made an end of
reconciling the holy *place,* and the tabernacle of the congregation, and the altar,
he shall bring the
live goat:
21 And Aaron
shall lay both his
hands upon the
head of the live

16:21
Confession
◄ Leviticus 26:40 ►

goat, and confess over him all the iniquities of the children of Israel, and all their transgressions in all their sins, putting them upon the head of the goat, and shall send *him* away by the hand of a fit man into the wilderness:

22 And the goat shall bear upon him all their iniquities unto a land not inhabited: and he shall let go the goat in the wilderness.

23 And Aaron shall come into the tabernacle of the congregation, and shall put off the linen garments, which he put on when he went into the holy *place*, and shall leave them there:

24 And he shall wash his flesh with water in the holy place, and put on his garments, and come forth, and offer his burnt offering, and the burnt offering of the people, and make an atonement for himself, and for the people.

25 And the fat of the sin offering shall he burn upon the altar.

26 And he that let go the goat for the scapegoat shall wash his clothes, and bathe his flesh in water, and afterward come into the camp.

27 And the bullock *for* the sin offering, and the goat *for* the sin offering, whose blood was brought in to make atonement in the holy *place*, shall *one* carry forth without the camp; and they shall burn in the fire their skins, and their flesh, and their dung.

28 And he that burneth them shall wash his clothes, and bathe his flesh in water, and afterward he shall come into the camp.

29 And *this* shall be a statute for ever unto you: *that* in the seventh month, on the tenth *day* of the month, ye shall afflict your souls, and do no work at all, *whether it be* one of your own country, or a stranger that sojourneth among you:

30 For on that day shall *the priest* make an atonement for you, to cleanse you, *that* ye may be clean from all your sins before the LORD.

31 It *shall be* a sabbath of rest unto you, and ye shall afflict your souls, by a statute for ever.

32 And the priest, whom he shall anoint, and whom he shall consecrate to minister in the priest's office in his father's stead, shall make the atonement, and shall put on the linen clothes, *even* the holy garments:

33 And he shall make an atonement for the holy sanctuary, and he shall make an atonement for the tabernacle of the congregation, and for the altar, and he shall make an atonement for the priests, and for all the people of the congregation.

34 And this shall be an everlasting statute unto you, to make an atonement for the children of Israel for all their sins once a year. And he did as the LORD commanded Moses.

17

1 And the LORD spake unto Moses, saying,

2 Speak unto Aaron, and unto his sons, and unto all the children of Israel, and say unto them; This *is* the thing which the LORD hath commanded, saying,

3 What man soever *there be* of the house of Israel, that killeth an ox, or lamb, or goat, in the camp, or that killeth *it* out of the camp,

4 And bringeth it not unto the door of the tabernacle of the congregation, to offer an offering unto the LORD before the tabernacle of the LORD; blood shall be imputed unto that man; he hath shed blood; and that man shall be cut off from among his people:

5 To the end that the children of Israel may bring their sacrifices, which they offer in the open field, even that they may bring them unto the LORD, unto the door of the tabernacle of the congregation, unto the priest, and offer them *for* peace offerings unto the LORD.

6 And the priest shall sprinkle the blood upon the altar of the LORD *at* the door of the tabernacle of the congregation, and burn the fat for a sweet savour unto the LORD.

7 And they shall no more offer their sacrifices unto devils, after whom they have gone a whoring. This shall be a statute for ever unto them throughout their generations.

8 And thou shalt say unto them, Whatsoever man *there be* of the house of Israel, or of the strangers which sojourn among you, that offereth a burnt offering of sacrifice,

9 And bringeth it not unto the door of the tabernacle of the congregation, to offer it unto the LORD; even that man shall be cut off from among his people.

10And whatsoever man *there be* of the
house of Israel, or of the strangers that
sojourn among you, that eateth any manner of blood; I will even set my face against
that soul that eateth blood, and will cut
him off from among his people.
11For the life of the flesh *is* in the blood:
and I have given it to you upon the altar
to make an atonement for your souls: for
it *is* the blood *that* maketh an atonement
for the soul.
12Therefore I said unto the children of
Israel, No soul of you shall eat blood, neither shall any stranger that sojourneth
among you eat blood.
13And whatsoever man *there be* of the
children of Israel, or of the strangers that
sojourn among you, which hunteth and
catcheth any beast or fowl that may be
eaten; he shall even pour out the blood
thereof, and cover it with dust.
14For *it is* the life of all flesh; the blood
of it *is* for the life thereof: therefore I said
unto the children of Israel, Ye shall eat the
blood of no manner of flesh: for the life
of all flesh *is* the blood thereof: whosoever eateth it shall be cut off.
15And every soul that eateth that which
died *of itself,* or that which was torn *with
beasts, whether it be* one of your own country, or a stranger, he shall both wash his
clothes, and bathe *himself* in water, and be
unclean until the even: then shall he be
clean.
16But if he wash *them* not, nor bathe his
flesh; then he shall bear his iniquity.

18

1And the LORD spake unto Moses,
saying,
2Speak unto the children of Israel, and
say unto them, I am the LORD your God.
3After the doings of the land of Egypt,
wherein ye dwelt, shall ye not do: and after the doings of the land of Canaan,
whither I bring you, shall ye not do: neither shall ye walk in their ordinances.
4Ye shall do my judgments, and keep
mine ordinances, to walk therein: I *am* the
LORD your God.
5Ye shall therefore keep my statutes, and
my judgments: which if a man do, he shall
live in them: I *am* the LORD.
6None of you shall approach to any that
is near of kin to him, to uncover *their* nakedness: I *am* the LORD.
7The nakedness of thy father, or the nakedness of thy mother, shalt thou not uncover: she *is* thy mother; thou shalt not
uncover her nakedness.
8The nakedness of thy father's wife shalt
thou not uncover: it *is* thy father's nakedness.
9The nakedness of thy sister, the daughter of thy father, or daughter of thy mother, *whether she be* born at home, or born
abroad, *even* their nakedness thou shalt
not uncover.
10The nakedness of thy son's daughter,
or of thy daughter's daughter, *even* their
nakedness thou shalt not uncover: for
theirs *is* thine own nakedness.
11The nakedness of thy father's wife's
daughter, begotten of thy father, she *is* thy
sister, thou shalt not uncover her nakedness.
12Thou shalt not uncover the nakedness
of thy father's sister: she *is* thy father's near
kinswoman.
13Thou shalt not uncover the nakedness
of thy mother's sister: for she *is* thy mother's near kinswoman.
14Thou shalt not uncover the nakedness
of thy father's brother, thou shalt not approach to his wife: she *is* thine aunt.
15Thou shalt not uncover the nakedness
of thy daughter in law: she *is* thy son's wife;
thou shalt not uncover her nakedness.
16Thou shalt not uncover the nakedness
of thy brother's wife: it *is* thy brother's nakedness.
17Thou shalt not uncover the nakedness
of a woman and her daughter, neither shalt
thou take her son's daughter, or her
daughter's daughter, to uncover her nakedness; *for* they *are* her near kinswomen: it *is*
wickedness.
18Neither shalt thou take a wife to her
sister, to vex *her,* to uncover her nakedness,
beside the other in her life *time.*
19Also thou shalt not approach unto a
woman to uncover her nakedness, as long
as she is put apart for her uncleanness.
20Moreover thou shalt not lie carnally
with thy neighbour's wife, to defile thyself
with her.
21And thou shalt not let any of thy seed
pass through *the fire* to Molech, neither
shalt thou profane the name of thy God: I
am the LORD.
22Thou shalt not lie with mankind, as
with womankind: it *is* abomination.

23 Neither shalt thou lie with any beast to defile thyself therewith: neither shall any woman stand before a beast to lie down thereto: it *is* confusion.

24 Defile not ye yourselves in any of these things: for in all these the nations are defiled which I cast out before you:

25 And the land is defiled: therefore I do visit the iniquity thereof upon it, and the land itself vomiteth out her inhabitants.

26 Ye shall therefore keep my statutes and my judgments, and shall not commit *any* of these abominations; *neither* any of your own nation, nor any stranger that sojourneth among you:

27 (For all these abominations have the men of the land done, which *were* before you, and the land is defiled;)

28 That the land spue not you out also, when ye defile it, as it spued out the nations that *were* before you.

29 For whosoever shall commit any of these abominations, even the souls that commit *them* shall be cut off from among their people.

30 Therefore shall ye keep mine ordinance, that *ye* commit not *any one* of these abominable customs, which were committed before you, and that ye defile not yourselves therein: I *am* the LORD your God.

19

1 And the LORD spake unto Moses, saying,

2 Speak unto all the congregation of the children of Israel, and say unto them, Ye shall be holy: for I the LORD your God *am* holy.

19:2 Holiness
◄ Leviticus 11:45
1 Chronicles 16:29 ►

3 Ye shall fear every man his mother, and his father, and keep my sabbaths: I *am* the LORD your God.

4 Turn ye not unto idols, nor make to yourselves molten gods: I *am* the LORD your God.

5 And if ye offer a sacrifice of peace offerings unto the LORD, ye shall offer it at your own will.

6 It shall be eaten the same day ye offer it, and on the morrow: and if ought remain until the third day, it shall be burnt in the fire.

7 And if it be eaten at all on the third day, it *is* abominable; it shall not be accepted.

8 Therefore *every one* that eateth it shall bear his iniquity, because he hath profaned the hallowed thing of the LORD: and that soul shall be cut off from among his people.

9 And when ye reap the harvest of your land, thou shalt not wholly reap the corners of thy field, neither shalt thou gather the gleanings of thy harvest.

10 And thou shalt not glean thy vineyard, neither shalt thou gather *every* grape of thy vineyard; thou shalt leave them for the poor and stranger: I *am* the LORD your God.

11 Ye shall not steal, neither deal falsely, neither lie one to another.

19:11 Lying
◄ Psalm 5:6 ►

12 And ye shall not swear by my name falsely, neither shalt thou profane the name of thy God: I *am* the LORD.

19:12 Perjury
◄ Leviticus 6:3
Zechariah 5:4 ►

19:12 Swearing
◄ Exodus 20:7
Matthew 5:34 ►

13 Thou shalt not defraud thy neighbour, neither rob *him:* the wages of him that is hired shall not abide with thee all night until the morning.

14 Thou shalt not curse the deaf, nor put a stumblingblock before the blind, but shalt fear thy God: I *am* the LORD.

15 Ye shall do no unrighteousness in judgment: thou shalt not respect the person of the poor, nor honour the person of the mighty: *but* in righteousness shalt thou judge thy neighbour.

19:15 Favoritism
◄ Deuteronomy 1:17 ►

16 Thou shalt not go up and down *as* a talebearer among thy people: neither shalt thou stand against the blood of thy neighbour: I *am* the LORD.

19:16 Gossiping
◄ Proverbs 11:13 ►

17 Thou shalt not hate thy brother in thine heart: thou shalt in any wise

19:17 Hate
◄ Proverbs 10:12 ►

rebuke thy neighbour, and not suffer sin
upon him.
18Thou shalt not
avenge, nor bear
any grudge against
the children of thy
people, but thou
shalt love thy neigh-
bour as thyself: I *am*
the LORD.
19Ye shall keep
my statutes. Thou
shalt not let thy cat-
tle gender with a
diverse kind: thou shalt not sow thy field
with mingled seed: neither shall a garment
mingled of linen and woollen come upon
thee.
20And whosoever lieth carnally with a
woman, that *is* a bondmaid, betrothed to
an husband, and not at all redeemed, nor
freedom given her; she shall be scourged;
they shall not be put to death, because she
was not free.
21And he shall bring his trespass offering unto the LORD, unto the door of the
tabernacle of the congregation, *even* a ram
for a trespass offering.
22And the priest shall make an atonement for him with the ram of the trespass
offering before the LORD for his sin which
he hath done: and the sin which he hath
done shall be forgiven him.
23And when ye shall come into the land,
and shall have planted all manner of trees
for food, then ye shall count the fruit
thereof as uncircumcised: three years shall
it be as uncircumcised unto you: it shall
not be eaten of.
24But in the fourth year all the fruit
thereof shall be holy to praise the LORD
withal.
25And in the fifth year shall ye eat of
the fruit thereof, that it may yield unto you
the increase thereof: I *am* the LORD your
God.
26Ye shall not eat *any thing* with the
blood: neither shall ye use enchantment,
nor observe times.
27Ye shall not round the corners of your
heads, neither shalt thou mar the corners
of thy beard.
28Ye shall not make any cuttings in your
flesh for the dead, nor print any marks
upon you: I *am* the LORD.

19:18
Neighbors
◄ Mark 12:31 ►

19:18
Revenge
◄ Proverbs 20:22 ►

29Do not prosti-
tute thy daughter,
to cause her to be a
whore; lest the land
fall to whoredom,
and the land be-
come full of wickedness.
30Ye shall keep my sabbaths, and reverence my sanctuary: I *am* the LORD.
31Regard not them that have familiar
spirits, neither seek after wizards, to be
defiled by them: I *am* the LORD your God.
32Thou shalt rise
up before the hoary
head, and honour
the face of the old
man, and fear thy
God: I *am* the LORD.
33And if a stranger sojourn with thee in
your land, ye shall not vex him.
34*But* the strang-
er that dwelleth
with you shall be
unto you as one
born among you,
and thou shalt love
him as thyself; for ye were strangers in
the land of Egypt: I *am* the LORD your
God.
35Ye shall do no unrighteousness in
judgment, in meteyard, in weight, or in
measure.
36Just balances, just weights, a just
ephah, and a just hin, shall ye have: I *am*
the LORD your God, which brought you
out of the land of Egypt.
37Therefore shall ye observe all my statutes, and all my judgments, and do them:
I *am* the LORD.

19:28
Hurting Yourself
◄ Leviticus 21:5 ►

19:32
Respecting Adults
◄ Job 32:6 ►

19:34 New Kids
◄ Exodus 23:9
Leviticus 25:35 ►

20

1And the LORD spake unto Moses,
saying,
2Again, thou shalt say to the children of
Israel, Whosoever *he be* of the children
of Israel, or of the strangers that sojourn
in Israel, that giveth *any* of his seed unto
Molech; he shall surely be put to death:
the people of the land shall stone him with
stones.
3And I will set my face against that man,
and will cut him off from among his people; because he hath given of his seed unto
Molech, to defile my sanctuary, and to profane my holy name.
4And if the people of the land do any
ways hide their eyes from the man, when

he giveth of his seed unto Molech, and kill him not:

5 Then I will set my face against that man, and against his family, and will cut him off, and all that go a whoring after him, to commit whoredom with Molech, from among their people.

6 And the soul that turneth after such as have familiar spirits, and after wizards, to go a whoring after them, I will even set my face against that soul, and will cut him off from among his people.

7 Sanctify yourselves therefore, and be ye holy: for I *am* the LORD your God.

8 And ye shall keep my statutes, and do them: I *am* the LORD which sanctify you.

9 For every one that curseth his father or his mother shall be surely put to death: he hath cursed his father or his mother; his blood *shall be* upon him.

10 And the man that committeth adultery with *another* man's wife, *even he* that committeth adultery with his neighbour's wife, the adulterer and the adulteress shall surely be put to death.

11 And the man that lieth with his father's wife hath uncovered his father's nakedness: both of them shall surely be put to death; their blood *shall be* upon them.

12 And if a man lie with his daughter in law, both of them shall surely be put to death: they have wrought confusion; their blood *shall be* upon them.

13 If a man also lie with mankind, as he lieth with a woman, both of them have committed an abomination: they shall surely be put to death; their blood *shall be* upon them.

14 And if a man take a wife and her mother, it *is* wickedness: they shall be burnt with fire, both he and they; that there be no wickedness among you.

15 And if a man lie with a beast, he shall surely be put to death: and ye shall slay the beast.

16 And if a woman approach unto any beast, and lie down thereto, thou shalt kill the woman, and the beast: they shall surely be put to death; their blood *shall be* upon them.

17 And if a man shall take his sister, his father's daughter, or his mother's daughter, and see her nakedness, and she see his nakedness; it *is* a wicked thing; and they shall be cut off in the sight of their people: he hath uncovered his sister's nakedness; he shall bear his iniquity.

18 And if a man shall lie with a woman having her sickness, and shall uncover her nakedness; he hath discovered her fountain, and she hath uncovered the fountain of her blood: and both of them shall be cut off from among their people.

19 And thou shalt not uncover the nakedness of thy mother's sister, nor of thy father's sister: for he uncovereth his near kin: they shall bear their iniquity.

20 And if a man shall lie with his uncle's wife, he hath uncovered his uncle's nakedness: they shall bear their sin; they shall die childless.

21 And if a man shall take his brother's wife, it *is* an unclean thing: he hath uncovered his brother's nakedness; they shall be childless.

22 Ye shall therefore keep all my statutes, and all my judgments, and do them: that the land, whither I bring you to dwell therein, spue you not out.

23 And ye shall not walk in the manners of the nation, which I cast out before you: for they committed all these things, and therefore I abhorred them.

20:23
Bad Examples
◄ Deuteronomy 18:9 ►

24 But I have said unto you, Ye shall inherit their land, and I will give it unto you to possess it, a land that floweth with milk and honey: I *am* the LORD your God, which have separated you from *other* people.

25 Ye shall therefore put difference between clean beasts and unclean, and between unclean fowls and clean: and ye shall not make your souls abominable by beast, or by fowl, or by any manner of living thing that creepeth on the ground, which I have separated from you as unclean.

26 And ye shall be holy unto me: for I the LORD *am* holy, and have severed you from *other* people, that ye should be mine.

27 A man also or woman that hath a familiar spirit, or that is a wizard, shall surely be put to death: they shall stone them with stones: their blood *shall be* upon them.

21

1 And the LORD said unto Moses, Speak unto the priests the sons of Aaron, and say unto them, There shall none be defiled for the dead among his people:

2 But for his kin, that is near unto him, *that is,* for his mother, and for his father, and for his son, and for his daughter, and for his brother,

3 And for his sister a virgin, that is nigh unto him, which hath had no husband; for her may he be defiled.

4 *But* he shall not defile himself, *being* a chief man among his people, to profane himself.

5 They shall not make baldness upon their head, neither shall they shave off the corner of their beard, nor make any cuttings in their flesh.

21:5 Hurting Yourself
◄ Leviticus 19:28
1 Corinthians 6:15 ►

6 They shall be holy unto their God, and not profane the name of their God: for the offerings of the LORD made by fire, *and* the bread of their God, they do offer: therefore they shall be holy.

7 They shall not take a wife *that is* a whore, or profane; neither shall they take a woman put away from her husband: for he *is* holy unto his God.

8 Thou shalt sanctify him therefore; for he offereth the bread of thy God: he shall be holy unto thee: for I the LORD, which sanctify you, *am* holy.

9 And the daughter of any priest, if she profane herself by playing the whore, she profaneth her father: she shall be burnt with fire.

10 And *he that is* the high priest among his brethren, upon whose head the anointing oil was poured, and that is consecrated to put on the garments, shall not uncover his head, nor rend his clothes;

11 Neither shall he go in to any dead body, nor defile himself for his father, or for his mother;

12 Neither shall he go out of the sanctuary, nor profane the sanctuary of his God; for the crown of the anointing oil of his God *is* upon him: I *am* the LORD.

13 And he shall take a wife in her virginity.

14 A widow, or a divorced woman, or profane, *or* an harlot, these shall he not take: but he shall take a virgin of his own people to wife.

15 Neither shall he profane his seed among his people: for I the LORD do sanctify him.

16 And the LORD spake unto Moses, saying,

17 Speak unto Aaron, saying, Whosoever *he be* of thy seed in their generations that hath *any* blemish, let him not approach to offer the bread of his God.

18 For whatsoever man *he be* that hath a blemish, he shall not approach: a blind man, or a lame, or he that hath a flat nose, or any thing superfluous,

19 Or a man that is brokenfooted, or brokenhanded,

20 Or crookbackt, or a dwarf, or that hath a blemish in his eye, or be scurvy, or scabbed, or hath his stones broken;

21 No man that hath a blemish of the seed of Aaron the priest shall come nigh to offer the offerings of the LORD made by fire: he hath a blemish; he shall not come nigh to offer the bread of his God.

22 He shall eat the bread of his God, *both* of the most holy, and of the holy.

23 Only he shall not go in unto the vail, nor come nigh unto the altar, because he hath a blemish; that he profane not my sanctuaries: for I the LORD do sanctify them.

24 And Moses told *it* unto Aaron, and to his sons, and unto all the children of Israel.

22

1 And the LORD spake unto Moses, saying,

2 Speak unto Aaron and to his sons, that they separate themselves from the holy things of the children of Israel, and that they profane not my holy name *in those things* which they hallow unto me: I *am* the LORD.

3 Say unto them, Whosoever *he be* of all your seed among your generations, that goeth unto the holy things, which the children of Israel hallow unto the LORD, having his uncleanness upon him, that soul shall be cut off from my presence: I *am* the LORD.

4 What man soever of the seed of Aaron *is* a leper, or hath a running issue; he shall not eat of the holy things, until he be clean. And whoso toucheth any thing *that is* unclean *by* the dead, or a man whose seed goeth from him;

5 Or whosoever toucheth any creeping thing, whereby he may be made unclean, or a man of whom he may take uncleanness, whatsoever uncleanness he hath;

6 The soul which hath touched any such shall be unclean until even, and shall not eat of the holy things, unless he wash his flesh with water.

7 And when the sun is down, he shall be clean, and shall afterward eat of the holy things; because it *is* his food.

8 That which dieth of itself, or is torn *with beasts,* he shall not eat to defile himself therewith: I *am* the LORD.

9 They shall therefore keep mine ordinance, lest they bear sin for it, and die therefore, if they profane it: I the LORD do sanctify them.

10 There shall no stranger eat *of* the holy thing: a sojourner of the priest, or an hired servant, shall not eat *of* the holy thing.

11 But if the priest buy *any* soul with his money, he shall eat of it, and he that is born in his house: they shall eat of his meat.

12 If the priest's daughter also be *married* unto a stranger, she may not eat of an offering of the holy things.

13 But if the priest's daughter be a widow, or divorced, and have no child, and is returned unto her father's house, as in her youth, she shall eat of her father's meat: but there shall no stranger eat thereof.

14 And if a man eat *of* the holy thing unwittingly, then he shall put the fifth *part* thereof unto it, and shall give *it* unto the priest with the holy thing.

15 And they shall not profane the holy things of the children of Israel, which they offer unto the LORD;

16 Or suffer them to bear the iniquity of trespass, when they eat their holy things: for I the LORD do sanctify them.

17 And the LORD spake unto Moses, saying,

18 Speak unto Aaron, and to his sons, and unto all the children of Israel, and say unto them, Whatsoever *he be* of the house of Israel, or of the strangers in Israel, that will offer his oblation for all his vows, and for all his freewill offerings, which they will offer unto the LORD for a burnt offering;

19 *Ye shall offer* at your own will a male without blemish, of the beeves, of the sheep, or of the goats.

20 *But* whatsoever hath a blemish, *that* shall ye not offer: for it shall not be acceptable for you.

21 And whosoever offereth a sacrifice of peace offerings unto the LORD to accomplish *his* vow, or a freewill offering in beeves or sheep, it shall be perfect to be accepted; there shall be no blemish therein.

22 Blind, or broken, or maimed, or having a wen, or scurvy, or scabbed, ye shall not offer these unto the LORD, nor make an offering by fire of them upon the altar unto the LORD.

23 Either a bullock or a lamb that hath any thing superfluous or lacking in his parts, that mayest thou offer *for* a freewill offering; but for a vow it shall not be accepted.

24 Ye shall not offer unto the LORD that which is bruised, or crushed, or broken, or cut; neither shall ye make *any offering thereof* in your land.

25 Neither from a stranger's hand shall ye offer the bread of your God of any of these; because their corruption *is* in them, *and* blemishes *be* in them: they shall not be accepted for you.

26 And the LORD spake unto Moses, saying,

27 When a bullock, or a sheep, or a goat, is brought forth, then it shall be seven days under the dam; and from the eighth day and thenceforth it shall be accepted for an offering made by fire unto the LORD.

28 And *whether it be* cow or ewe, ye shall not kill it and her young both in one day.

29 And when ye will offer a sacrifice of thanksgiving unto the LORD, offer *it* at your own will.

30 On the same day it shall be eaten up; ye shall leave none of it until the morrow: I *am* the LORD.

31 Therefore shall ye keep my commandments, and do them: I *am* the LORD.

32 Neither shall ye profane my holy name; but I will be hallowed among the children of Israel: I *am* the LORD which hallow you,

33 That brought you out of the land of Egypt, to be your God: I *am* the LORD.

23

1 And the LORD spake unto Moses, saying,

2 Speak unto the children of Israel, and say unto them, *Concerning* the feasts of the LORD, which ye shall proclaim *to be* holy convocations, *even* these *are* my feasts.

3 Six days shall work be done: but the

seventh day *is* the sabbath of rest, an holy convocation; ye shall do no work *therein:* it *is* the sabbath of the LORD in all your dwellings.

23:3 Rest
◄ Exodus 35:2
Mark 6:31 ►

23:3 Working Hard
◄ Genesis 3:19
Proverbs 13:11 ►

4 These *are* the feasts of the LORD, *even* holy convocations, which ye shall proclaim in their seasons.

5 In the fourteenth *day* of the first month at even *is* the LORD'S passover.

6 And on the fifteenth day of the same month *is* the feast of unleavened bread unto the LORD: seven days ye must eat unleavened bread.

7 In the first day ye shall have an holy convocation: ye shall do no servile work therein.

8 But ye shall offer an offering made by fire unto the LORD seven days: in the seventh day *is* an holy convocation: ye shall do no servile work *therein.*

9 And the LORD spake unto Moses, saying,

10 Speak unto the children of Israel, and say unto them, When ye be come into the land which I give unto you, and shall reap the harvest thereof, then ye shall bring a sheaf of the firstfruits of your harvest unto the priest:

11 And he shall wave the sheaf before the LORD, to be accepted for you: on the morrow after the sabbath the priest shall wave it.

12 And ye shall offer that day when ye wave the sheaf an he lamb without blemish of the first year for a burnt offering unto the LORD.

13 And the meat offering thereof *shall be* two tenth deals of fine flour mingled with oil, an offering made by fire unto the LORD *for* a sweet savour: and the drink offering thereof *shall be* of wine, the fourth *part* of an hin.

14 And ye shall eat neither bread, nor parched corn, nor green ears, until the selfsame day that ye have brought an offering unto your God: *it shall be* a statute for ever throughout your generations in all your dwellings.

15 And ye shall count unto you from the morrow after the sabbath, from the day that ye brought the sheaf of the wave offering; seven sabbaths shall be complete:

16 Even unto the morrow after the seventh sabbath shall ye number fifty days; and ye shall offer a new meat offering unto the LORD.

17 Ye shall bring out of your habitations two wave loaves of two tenth deals: they shall be of fine flour; they shall be baken with leaven; *they are* the firstfruits unto the LORD.

18 And ye shall offer with the bread seven lambs without blemish of the first year, and one young bullock, and two rams: they shall be *for* a burnt offering unto the LORD, with their meat offering, and their drink offerings, *even* an offering made by fire, of sweet savour unto the LORD.

19 Then ye shall sacrifice one kid of the goats for a sin offering, and two lambs of the first year for a sacrifice of peace offerings.

20 And the priest shall wave them with the bread of the first fruits *for* a wave offering before the LORD, with the two lambs: they shall be holy to the LORD for the priest.

21 And ye shall proclaim on the selfsame day, *that* it may be an holy convocation unto you: ye shall do no servile work *therein: it shall be* a statute for ever in all your dwellings throughout your generations.

22 And when ye reap the harvest of your land, thou shalt not make clean riddance of the corners of thy field when thou reapest, neither shalt thou gather any gleaning of thy harvest: thou shalt leave them unto the poor, and to the stranger: I *am* the LORD your God.

23 And the LORD spake unto Moses, saying,

24 Speak unto the children of Israel, saying, In the seventh month, in the first *day* of the month, shall ye have a sabbath, a memorial of blowing of trumpets, an holy convocation.

25 Ye shall do no servile work *therein:* but ye shall offer an offering made by fire unto the LORD.

26 And the LORD spake unto Moses, saying,

27 Also on the tenth *day* of this seventh month *there shall be* a day of atonement:

it shall be an holy convocation unto you; and ye shall afflict your souls, and offer an offering made by fire unto the LORD.

28 And ye shall do no work in that same day: for it *is* a day of atonement, to make an atonement for you before the LORD your God.

29 For whatsoever soul *it be* that shall not be afflicted in that same day, he shall be cut off from among his people.

30 And whatsoever soul *it be* that doeth any work in that same day, the same soul will I destroy from among his people.

31 Ye shall do no manner of work: *it shall be* a statute for ever throughout your generations in all your dwellings.

32 It *shall be* unto you a sabbath of rest, and ye shall afflict your souls: in the ninth *day* of the month at even, from even unto even, shall ye celebrate your sabbath.

33 And the LORD spake unto Moses, saying,

34 Speak unto the children of Israel, saying, The fifteenth day of this seventh month *shall be* the feast of tabernacles *for* seven days unto the LORD.

35 On the first day *shall be* an holy convocation: ye shall do no servile work *therein*.

36 Seven days ye shall offer an offering made by fire unto the LORD: on the eighth day shall be an holy convocation unto you; and ye shall offer an offering made by fire unto the LORD: it *is* a solemn assembly; *and* ye shall do no servile work *therein*.

37 These *are* the feasts of the LORD, which ye shall proclaim *to be* holy convocations, to offer an offering made by fire unto the LORD, a burnt offering, and a meat offering, a sacrifice, and drink offerings, every thing upon his day:

38 Beside the sabbaths of the LORD, and beside your gifts, and beside all your vows, and beside all your freewill offerings, which ye give unto the LORD.

39 Also in the fifteenth day of the seventh month, when ye have gathered in the fruit of the land, ye shall keep a feast unto the LORD seven days: on the first day *shall be* a sabbath, and on the eighth day *shall be* a sabbath.

40 And ye shall take you on the first day the boughs of goodly trees, branches of palm trees, and the boughs of thick trees, and willows of the brook; and ye shall rejoice before the LORD your God seven days.

41 And ye shall keep it a feast unto the LORD seven days in the year. *It shall be* a statute for ever in your generations: ye shall celebrate it in the seventh month.

42 Ye shall dwell in booths seven days; all that are Israelites born shall dwell in booths:

43 That your generations may know that I made the children of Israel to dwell in booths, when I brought them out of the land of Egypt: I *am* the LORD your God.

44 And Moses declared unto the children of Israel the feasts of the LORD.

24

1 And the LORD spake unto Moses, saying,

2 Command the children of Israel, that they bring unto thee pure oil olive beaten for the light, to cause the lamps to burn continually.

3 Without the vail of the testimony, in the tabernacle of the congregation, shall Aaron order it from the evening unto the morning before the LORD continually: *it shall be* a statute for ever in your generations.

4 He shall order the lamps upon the pure candlestick before the LORD continually.

5 And thou shalt take fine flour, and bake twelve cakes thereof: two tenth deals shall be in one cake.

6 And thou shalt set them in two rows, six on a row, upon the pure table before the LORD.

7 And thou shalt put pure frankincense upon *each* row, that it may be on the bread for a memorial, *even* an offering made by fire unto the LORD.

8 Every sabbath he shall set it in order before the LORD continually, *being taken* from the children of Israel by an everlasting covenant.

9 And it shall be Aaron's and his sons'; and they shall eat it in the holy place: for it *is* most holy unto him of the offerings of the LORD made by fire by a perpetual statute.

10 And the son of an Israelitish woman, whose father *was* an Egyptian, went out among the children of Israel: and this son of the Israelitish *woman* and a man of Israel strove together in the camp;

11 And the Israelitish woman's son blasphemed the name *of the LORD*, and cursed.

And they brought him unto Moses: (and his mother's name *was* Shelomith, the daughter of Dibri, of the tribe of Dan:)

12 And they put him in ward, that the mind of the LORD might be shewed them.

13 And the LORD spake unto Moses, saying,

14 Bring forth him that hath cursed without the camp; and let all that heard *him* lay their hands upon his head, and let all the congregation stone him.

15 And thou shalt speak unto the children of Israel, saying, Whosoever curseth his God shall bear his sin.

16 And he that blasphemeth the name of the LORD, he shall surely be put to death, *and* all the congregation shall certainly stone him: as well the stranger, as he that is born in the land, when he blasphemeth the name *of the LORD*, shall be put to death.

17 And he that killeth any man shall surely be put to death.

18 And he that killeth a beast shall make it good; beast for beast.

19 And if a man cause a blemish in his neighbour; as he hath done, so shall it be done to him;

20 Breach for breach, eye for eye, tooth for tooth: as he hath caused a blemish in a man, so shall it be done to him *again*.

21 And he that killeth a beast, he shall restore it: and he that killeth a man, he shall be put to death.

22 Ye shall have one manner of law, as well for the stranger, as for one of your own country: for I *am* the LORD your God.

23 And Moses spake to the children of Israel, that they should bring forth him that had cursed out of the camp, and stone him with stones. And the children of Israel did as the LORD commanded Moses.

25

1 And the LORD spake unto Moses in mount Sinai, saying,

2 Speak unto the children of Israel, and say unto them, When ye come into the land which I give you, then shall the land keep a sabbath unto the LORD.

3 Six years thou shalt sow thy field, and six years thou shalt prune thy vineyard, and gather in the fruit thereof;

4 But in the seventh year shall be a sabbath of rest unto the land, a sabbath for the LORD: thou shalt neither sow thy field, nor prune thy vineyard.

5 That which groweth of its own accord of thy harvest thou shalt not reap, neither gather the grapes of thy vine undressed: *for* it is a year of rest unto the land.

6 And the sabbath of the land shall be meat for you; for thee, and for thy servant, and for thy maid, and for thy hired servant, and for thy stranger that sojourneth with thee,

7 And for thy cattle, and for the beast that *are* in thy land, shall all the increase thereof be meat.

8 And thou shalt number seven sabbaths of years unto thee, seven times seven years; and the space of the seven sabbaths of years shall be unto thee forty and nine years.

9 Then shalt thou cause the trumpet of the jubile to sound on the tenth *day* of the seventh month, in the day of atonement shall ye make the trumpet sound throughout all your land.

10 And ye shall hallow the fiftieth year, and proclaim liberty throughout *all* the land unto all the inhabitants thereof: it shall be a jubile unto you; and ye shall return every man unto his possession, and ye shall return every man unto his family.

11 A jubile shall that fiftieth year be unto you: ye shall not sow, neither reap that which groweth of itself in it, nor gather *the grapes* in it of thy vine undressed.

12 For it *is* the jubile; it shall be holy unto you: ye shall eat the increase thereof out of the field.

13 In the year of this jubile ye shall return every man unto his possession.

14 And if thou sell ought unto thy neighbour, or buyest *ought* of thy neighbour's hand, ye shall not oppress one another:

15 According to the number of years after the jubile thou shalt buy of thy neighbour, *and* according unto the number of years of the fruits he shall sell unto thee:

16 According to the multitude of years thou shalt increase the price thereof, and according to the fewness of years thou shalt diminish the price of it: for *according* to the number *of the years* of the fruits doth he sell unto thee.

17 Ye shall not therefore oppress one another; but thou shalt fear thy God: for I *am* the LORD your God.

18 Wherefore ye shall do my statutes, and

keep my judgments, and do them; and ye shall dwell in the land in safety.

19 And the land shall yield her fruit, and ye shall eat your fill, and dwell therein in safety.

20 And if ye shall say, What shall we eat the seventh year? behold, we shall not sow, nor gather in our increase:

21 Then I will command my blessing upon you in the sixth year, and it shall bring forth fruit for three years.

22 And ye shall sow the eighth year, and eat *yet* of old fruit until the ninth year; until her fruits come in ye shall eat *of* the old *store.*

23 The land shall not be sold for ever: for the land *is* mine; for ye *are* strangers and sojourners with me.

25:23 Earth
◄ Exodus 19:5
1 Chronicles 29:14 ►

24 And in all the land of your possession ye shall grant a redemption for the land.

25 If thy brother be waxen poor, and hath sold away *some* of his possession, and if any of his kin come to redeem it, then shall he redeem that which his brother sold.

25:25 Kind to the Poor
◄ Exodus 23:11
Deuteronomy 15:7 ►

26 And if the man have none to redeem it, and himself be able to redeem it;

27 Then let him count the years of the sale thereof, and restore the overplus unto the man to whom he sold it; that he may return unto his possession.

28 But if he be not able to restore *it* to him, then that which is sold shall remain in the hand of him that hath bought it until the year of jubile: and in the jubile it shall go out, and he shall return unto his possession.

29 And if a man sell a dwelling house in a walled city, then he may redeem it within a whole year after it is sold; *within* a full year may he redeem it.

30 And if it be not redeemed within the space of a full year, then the house that *is* in the walled city shall be established for ever to him that bought it throughout his generations: it shall not go out in the jubile.

31 But the houses of the villages which have no wall round about them shall be counted as the fields of the country: they may be redeemed, and they shall go out in the jubile.

32 Notwithstanding the cities of the Levites, *and* the houses of the cities of their possession, may the Levites redeem at any time.

33 And if a man purchase of the Levites, then the house that was sold, and the city of his possession, shall go out in *the year of* jubile: for the houses of the cities of the Levites *are* their possession among the children of Israel.

34 But the field of the suburbs of their cities may not be sold; for it *is* their perpetual possession.

35 And if thy brother be waxen poor, and fallen in decay with thee; then thou shalt relieve him: *yea, though he be* a stranger, or a sojourner; that he may live with thee.

25:35 Generosity
◄ Deuteronomy 15:7 ►

25:35 New Kids
◄ Leviticus 19:34
Numbers 35:15 ►

36 Take thou no usury of him, or increase: but fear thy God; that thy brother may live with thee.

37 Thou shalt not give him thy money upon usury, nor lend him thy victuals for increase.

38 I *am* the LORD your God, which brought you forth out of the land of Egypt, to give you the land of Canaan, *and* to be your God.

39 And if thy brother *that dwelleth* by thee be waxen poor, and be sold unto thee; thou shalt not compel him to serve as a bondservant:

40 *But* as an hired servant, *and* as a sojourner, he shall be with thee, *and* shall serve thee unto the year of jubile:

41 And *then* shall he depart from thee, *both* he and his children with him, and shall return unto his own family, and unto the possession of his fathers shall he return.

42 For they *are* my servants, which I brought forth out of the land of Egypt: they shall not be sold as bondmen.

43 Thou shalt not rule over him with rigour; but shalt fear thy God.

44 Both thy bondmen, and thy bond-

maids, which thou shalt have, *shall be* of the heathen that are round about you; of them shall ye buy bondmen and bondmaids.

45 Moreover of the children of the strangers that do sojourn among you, of them shall ye buy, and of their families that *are* with you, which they begat in your land: and they shall be your possession.

46 And ye shall take them as an inheritance for your children after you, to inherit *them for* a possession; they shall be your bondmen for ever: but over your brethren the children of Israel, ye shall not rule one over another with rigour.

47 And if a sojourner or stranger wax rich by thee, and thy brother *that dwelleth* by him wax poor, and sell himself unto the stranger *or* sojourner by thee, or to the stock of the stranger's family:

48 After that he is sold he may be redeemed again; one of his brethren may redeem him:

49 Either his uncle, or his uncle's son, may redeem him, or *any* that is nigh of kin unto him of his family may redeem him; or if he be able, he may redeem himself.

50 And he shall reckon with him that bought him from the year that he was sold to him unto the year of jubile: and the price of his sale shall be according unto the number of years, according to the time of an hired servant shall it be with him.

51 If *there be* yet many years *behind*, according unto them he shall give again the price of his redemption out of the money that he was bought for.

52 And if there remain but few years unto the year of jubile, then he shall count with him, *and* according unto his years shall he give him again the price of his redemption.

53 *And* as a yearly hired servant shall he be with him: *and the other* shall not rule with rigour over him in thy sight.

54 And if he be not redeemed in these *years*, then he shall go out in the year of jubile, *both* he, and his children with him.

55 For unto me the children of Israel *are* servants; they *are* my servants whom I brought forth out of the land of Egypt: I *am* the LORD your God.

26

1 Ye shall make you no idols nor graven image, neither rear you up a standing image, neither shall ye set up *any* image of stone in your land, to bow down unto it: for I *am* the LORD your God.

2 Ye shall keep my sabbaths, and reverence my sanctuary: I *am* the LORD.

3 If ye walk in my statutes, and keep my commandments, and do them;

4 Then I will give you rain in due season, and the land shall yield her increase, and the trees of the field shall yield their fruit.

5 And your threshing shall reach unto the vintage, and the vintage shall reach unto the sowing time: and ye shall eat your bread to the full, and dwell in your land safely.

6 And I will give peace in the land, and ye shall lie down, and none shall make *you* afraid: and I will rid evil beasts out of the land, neither shall the sword go through your land.

7 And ye shall chase your enemies, and they shall fall before you by the sword.

8 And five of you shall chase an hundred, and an hundred of you shall put ten thousand to flight: and your enemies shall fall before you by the sword.

9 For I will have respect unto you, and make you fruitful, and multiply you, and establish my covenant with you.

10 And ye shall eat old store, and bring forth the old because of the new.

11 And I will set my tabernacle among you: and my soul shall not abhor you.

12 And I will walk among you, and will be your God, and ye shall be my people.

13 I *am* the LORD your God, which brought you forth out of the land of Egypt, that ye should not be their bondmen; and I have broken the bands of your yoke, and made you go upright.

14 But if ye will not hearken unto me, and will not do all these commandments;

15 And if ye shall despise my statutes, or if your soul abhor my judgments, so that ye will not do all my commandments, *but* that ye break my covenant:

16 I also will do this unto you; I will even appoint over you terror, consumption, and the burning ague, that shall consume the eyes, and cause sorrow of heart: and ye shall sow your seed in vain, for your enemies shall eat it.

26:16
Warning!
◄ Joshua 23:15 ►

17 And I will set my face against you, and ye shall be slain before your enemies: they that hate you shall reign over you; and ye shall flee when none pursueth you.

26:17 Guilty Fear
◄ Genesis 45:3
Psalm 53:5 ►

18 And if ye will not yet for all this hearken unto me, then I will punish you seven times more for your sins.

19 And I will break the pride of your power; and I will make your heaven as iron, and your earth as brass:

20 And your strength shall be spent in vain: for your land shall not yield her increase, neither shall the trees of the land yield their fruits.

21 And if ye walk contrary unto me, and will not hearken unto me; I will bring seven times more plagues upon you according to your sins.

22 I will also send wild beasts among you, which shall rob you of your children, and destroy your cattle, and make you few in number; and your *high* ways shall be desolate.

23 And if ye will not be reformed by me by these things, but will walk contrary unto me;

26:23
Hard-hearted
◄ Proverbs 1:24 ►

24 Then will I also walk contrary unto you, and will punish you yet seven times for your sins.

25 And I will bring a sword upon you, that shall avenge the quarrel of *my* covenant: and when ye are gathered together within your cities, I will send the pestilence among you; and ye shall be delivered into the hand of the enemy.

26 *And* when I have broken the staff of your bread, ten women shall bake your bread in one oven, and they shall deliver *you* your bread again by weight: and ye shall eat, and not be satisfied.

27 And if ye will not for all this hearken unto me, but walk contrary unto me;

28 Then I will walk contrary unto you also in fury; and I, even I, will chastise you seven times for your sins.

29 And ye shall eat the flesh of your sons, and the flesh of your daughters shall ye eat.

30 And I will destroy your high places, and cut down your images, and cast your carcases upon the carcases of your idols, and my soul shall abhor you.

31 And I will make your cities waste, and bring your sanctuaries unto desolation, and I will not smell the savour of your sweet odours.

32 And I will bring the land into desolation: and your enemies which dwell therein shall be astonished at it.

33 And I will scatter you among the heathen, and will draw out a sword after you: and your land shall be desolate, and your cities waste.

34 Then shall the land enjoy her sabbaths, as long as it lieth desolate, and ye *be* in your enemies' land; *even* then shall the land rest, and enjoy her sabbaths.

35 As long as it lieth desolate it shall rest; because it did not rest in your sabbaths, when ye dwelt upon it.

36 And upon them that are left *alive* of you I will send a faintness into their hearts in the lands of their enemies; and the sound of a shaken leaf shall chase them; and they shall flee, as fleeing from a sword; and they shall fall when none pursueth.

37 And they shall fall one upon another, as it were before a sword, when none pursueth: and ye shall have no power to stand before your enemies.

26:37 Cost of Sin
◄
Deuteronomy 28:32 ►

38 And ye shall perish among the heathen, and the land of your enemies shall eat you up.

39 And they that are left of you shall pine away in their iniquity in your enemies' lands; and also in the iniquities of their fathers shall they pine away with them.

40 If they shall confess their iniquity, and the iniquity of their fathers, with their trespass which they trespassed against me, and that also they have walked contrary unto me;

26:40 Confession
◄ Leviticus 16:21
Numbers 5:7 ►

41 And *that* I also have walked contrary unto them, and have brought them into the land of their enemies; if then their uncircumcised hearts be humbled, and they then accept of the punishment of their iniquity:

42 Then will I remember my covenant with Jacob, and also my covenant with Isaac, and also my covenant with Abraham will I remember; and I will remember the land.

43 The land also shall be left of them, and shall enjoy her sabbaths, while she lieth desolate without them: and they shall accept of the punishment of their iniquity: because, even because they despised my judgments, and because their soul abhorred my statutes.

44 And yet for all that, when they be in the land of their enemies, I will not cast them away, neither will I abhor them, to destroy them utterly, and to break my covenant with them: for I *am* the LORD their God.

45 But I will for their sakes remember the covenant of their ancestors, whom I brought forth out of the land of Egypt in the sight of the heathen, that I might be their God: I *am* the LORD.

46 These *are* the statutes and judgments and laws, which the LORD made between him and the children of Israel in mount Sinai by the hand of Moses.

27

1 And the LORD spake unto Moses, saying,

2 Speak unto the children of Israel, and say unto them, When a man shall make a singular vow, the persons *shall be* for the LORD by thy estimation.

3 And thy estimation shall be of the male from twenty years old even unto sixty years old, even thy estimation shall be fifty shekels of silver, after the shekel of the sanctuary.

4 And if it *be* a female, then thy estimation shall be thirty shekels.

5 And if *it be* from five years old even unto twenty years old, then thy estimation shall be of the male twenty shekels, and for the female ten shekels.

6 And if *it be* from a month old even unto five years old, then thy estimation shall be of the male five shekels of silver, and for the female thy estimation *shall be* three shekels of silver.

7 And if *it be* from sixty years old and above; if *it be* a male, then thy estimation shall be fifteen shekels, and for the female ten shekels.

8 But if he be poorer than thy estimation, then he shall present himself before the priest, and the priest shall value him; according to his ability that vowed shall the priest value him.

9 And if *it be* a beast, whereof men bring an offering unto the LORD, all that *any man* giveth of such unto the LORD shall be holy.

10 He shall not alter it, nor change it, a good for a bad, or a bad for a good: and if he shall at all change beast for beast, then it and the exchange thereof shall be holy.

11 And if *it be* any unclean beast, of which they do not offer a sacrifice unto the LORD, then he shall present the beast before the priest:

12 And the priest shall value it, whether it be good or bad: as thou valuest it, *who art* the priest, so shall it be.

13 But if he will at all redeem it, then he shall add a fifth *part* thereof unto thy estimation.

14 And when a man shall sanctify his house *to be* holy unto the LORD, then the priest shall estimate it, whether it be good or bad: as the priest shall estimate it, so shall it stand.

15 And if he that sanctified it will redeem his house, then he shall add the fifth *part* of the money of thy estimation unto it, and it shall be his.

16 And if a man shall sanctify unto the LORD *some part* of a field of his possession, then thy estimation shall be according to the seed thereof: an homer of barley seed *shall be valued* at fifty shekels of silver.

17 If he sanctify his field from the year of jubile, according to thy estimation it shall stand.

18 But if he sanctify his field after the jubile, then the priest shall reckon unto him the money according to the years that remain, even unto the year of the jubile, and it shall be abated from thy estimation.

19 And if he that sanctified the field will in any wise redeem it, then he shall add the fifth *part* of the money of thy estimation unto it, and it shall be assured to him.

20 And if he will not redeem the field, or if he have sold the field to another man, it shall not be redeemed any more.

21 But the field, when it goeth out in the jubile, shall be holy unto the LORD, as a field devoted; the possession thereof shall be the priest's.

22 And if *a man* sanctify unto the LORD a

field which he hath bought, which *is* not of the fields of his possession;

23 Then the priest shall reckon unto him the worth of thy estimation, *even* unto the year of the jubile: and he shall give thine estimation in that day, *as* a holy thing unto the LORD.

24 In the year of the jubile the field shall return unto him of whom it was bought, *even* to him to whom the possession of the land *did belong*.

25 And all thy estimations shall be according to the shekel of the sanctuary: twenty gerahs shall be the shekel.

26 Only the firstling of the beasts, which should be the LORD'S firstling, no man shall sanctify it; whether *it be* ox, or sheep: it *is* the LORD'S.

27 And if *it be* of an unclean beast, then he shall redeem *it* according to thine estimation, and shall add a fifth *part* of it thereto: or if it be not redeemed, then it shall be sold according to thy estimation.

28 Notwithstanding no devoted thing, that a man shall devote unto the LORD of all that he hath, *both* of man and beast, and of the field of his possession, shall be sold or redeemed: every devoted thing *is* most holy unto the LORD.

29 None devoted, which shall be devoted of men, shall be redeemed; *but* shall surely be put to death.

30 And all the tithe of the land, *whether* of the seed of the land, *or* of the fruit of the tree, *is* the LORD'S: *it is* holy unto the LORD.

31 And if a man will at all redeem *ought* of his tithes, he shall add thereto the fifth *part* thereof.

32 And concerning the tithe of the herd, or of the flock, *even* of whatsoever passeth under the rod, the tenth shall be holy unto the LORD.

33 He shall not search whether it be good or bad, neither shall he change it: and if he change it at all, then both it and the change thereof shall be holy; it shall not be redeemed.

34 These *are* the commandments, which the LORD commanded Moses for the children of Israel in mount Sinai.

Numbers

AUTHOR
Moses

MAIN POINT
The people of Israel had the chance to enter the Promised Land and blew it, but God showed them how to try again.

DATE WRITTEN
1450-1410 B.C.

36 CHAPTERS

MAIN PEOPLE

Moses, Aaron, Miriam, Joshua, Caleb, Eleazar, Balaam, Balak

SPECIAL FEATURES

- ✖ *Gives an amazing account of Moses' well-organized census. The number of Israelites out wandering may surprise you*
- ✖ *Describes how men could become Nazirites, one of the most famous of whom was strong-man Samson (see Judges 13–16)*
- ✖ *Explains how folks in trouble could flee to one of the cities of refuge*
- ✖ *Unravels the tale of the first spy mission in the Bible*
- ✖ *Fourth book of Law*

HOW THE BOOK GOT ITS NAME

The word numbers refers to the number of Israelites counted during the census that Moses did.

1
1And the LORD spake unto Moses in the
wilderness of Sinai, in the tabernacle of
the congregation, on the first *day* of the
second month, in the second year after
they were come out of the land of Egypt,
saying,
2Take ye the sum of all the congregation
of the children of Israel, after their families, by the house of their fathers, with the
number of *their* names, every male by their
polls;
3From twenty years old and upward, all
that are able to go forth to war in Israel:
thou and Aaron shall number them by
their armies.
4And with you there shall be a man of
every tribe; every one head of the house of
his fathers.
5And these *are* the names of the men that
shall stand with you: of *the tribe of* Reuben; Elizur the son of Shedeur.
6Of Simeon; Shelumiel the son of Zurishaddai.
7Of Judah; Nahshon the son of Amminadab.
8Of Issachar; Nethaneel the son of Zuar.

9Of Zebulun; Eliab the son of Helon.
10Of the children of Joseph: of Ephraim; Elishama the son of Ammihud: of
Manasseh; Gamaliel the son of Pedahzur.
11Of Benjamin; Abidan the son of Gideoni.
12Of Dan; Ahiezer the son of Ammishaddai.
13Of Asher; Pagiel the son of Ocran.
14Of Gad; Eliasaph the son of Deuel.
15Of Naphtali; Ahira the son of Enan.
16These *were* the renowned of the congregation, princes of the tribes of their fathers, heads of thousands in Israel.
17And Moses and Aaron took these men
which are expressed by *their* names:
18And they assembled all the congregation together on the first *day* of the second
month, and they declared their pedigrees
after their families, by the house of their
fathers, according to the number of the
names, from twenty years old and upward,
by their polls.
19As the LORD commanded Moses, so
he numbered them in the wilderness of
Sinai.
20And the children of Reuben, Israel's
eldest son, by their generations, after their
families, by the house of their fathers, according to the number of the names, by
their polls, every male from twenty years
old and upward, all that were able to go
forth to war;
21Those that were numbered of them,
even of the tribe of Reuben, *were* forty and
six thousand and five hundred.
22Of the children of Simeon, by their
generations, after their families, by the
house of their fathers, those that were
numbered of them, according to the number of the names, by their polls, every male
from twenty years old and upward, all that
were able to go forth to war;
23Those that were numbered of them,
even of the tribe of Simeon, *were* fifty and
nine thousand and three hundred.
24Of the children of Gad, by their generations, after their families, by the house
of their fathers, according to the number
of the names, from twenty years old
and upward, all that were able to go forth
to war;
25Those that were numbered of them,
even of the tribe of Gad, *were* forty and five
thousand six hundred and fifty.
26Of the children of Judah, by their generations, after their families, by the house
of their fathers, according to the number
of the names, from twenty years old
and upward, all that were able to go forth
to war;
27Those that were numbered of them,
even of the tribe of Judah, *were* threescore
and fourteen thousand and six hundred.
28Of the children of Issachar, by their
generations, after their families, by the
house of their fathers, according to the
number of the names, from twenty years
old and upward, all that were able to go
forth to war;
29Those that were numbered of them,
even of the tribe of Issachar, *were* fifty and
four thousand and four hundred.
30Of the children of Zebulun, by their
generations, after their families, by the
house of their fathers, according to the
number of the names, from twenty years
old and upward, all that were able to go
forth to war;
31Those that were numbered of them,
even of the tribe of Zebulun, *were* fifty and
seven thousand and four hundred.
32Of the children of Joseph, *namely,* of
the children of Ephraim, by their generations, after their families, by the house of
their fathers, according to the number of
the names, from twenty years old and upward, all that were able to go forth to war;
33Those that were numbered of them,
even of the tribe of Ephraim, *were* forty
thousand and five hundred.
34Of the children of Manasseh, by their
generations, after their families, by the
house of their fathers, according to the
number of the names, from twenty years
old and upward, all that were able to go
forth to war;
35Those that were numbered of them,
even of the tribe of Manasseh, *were* thirty
and two thousand and two hundred.
36Of the children of Benjamin, by their
generations, after their families, by the
house of their fathers, according to the
number of the names, from twenty years
old and upward, all that were able to go
forth to war;
37Those that were numbered of them,
even of the tribe of Benjamin, *were* thirty
and five thousand and four hundred.
38Of the children of Dan, by their gen-

erations, after their families, by the house
of their fathers, according to the number of
the names, from twenty years old and upward, all that were able to go forth to war;
39Those that were numbered of them,
even of the tribe of Dan, *were* threescore
and two thousand and seven hundred.
40Of the children of Asher, by their generations, after their families, by the house
of their fathers, according to the number of
the names, from twenty years old and upward, all that were able to go forth to war;
41Those that were numbered of them,
even of the tribe of Asher, *were* forty and
one thousand and five hundred.
42Of the children of Naphtali, throughout their generations, after their families,
by the house of their fathers, according to
the number of the names, from twenty
years old and upward, all that were able
to go forth to war;
43Those that were numbered of them,
even of the tribe of Naphtali, *were* fifty and
three thousand and four hundred.
44These *are* those that were numbered,
which Moses and Aaron numbered, and
the princes of Israel, *being* twelve men: each
one was for the house of his fathers.
45So were all those that were numbered
of the children of Israel, by the house of
their fathers, from twenty years old and
upward, all that were able to go forth to
war in Israel;
46Even all they that were numbered were
six hundred thousand and three thousand
and five hundred and fifty.
47But the Levites after the tribe of their
fathers were not numbered among them.
48For the LORD had spoken unto Moses, saying,
49Only thou shalt not number the tribe
of Levi, neither take the sum of them
among the children of Israel:
50But thou shalt appoint the Levites over
the tabernacle of testimony, and over all
the vessels thereof, and over all things that
belong to it: they shall bear the tabernacle,
and all the vessels thereof; and they shall
minister unto it, and shall encamp round
about the tabernacle.
51And when the tabernacle setteth forward, the Levites shall take it down: and
when the tabernacle is to be pitched, the
Levites shall set it up: and the stranger that
cometh nigh shall be put to death.
52And the children of Israel shall pitch
their tents, every man by his own camp,
and every man by his own standard,
throughout their hosts.
53But the Levites shall pitch round about
the tabernacle of testimony, that there be
no wrath upon the congregation of the
children of Israel: and the Levites shall
keep the charge of the tabernacle of testimony.
54And the children of Israel did according to all that the LORD commanded Moses, so did they.

2

1And the LORD spake unto Moses and
unto Aaron, saying,
2Every man of the children of Israel shall
pitch by his own standard, with the ensign of their father's house: far off about
the tabernacle of the congregation shall
they pitch.
3And on the east side toward the rising
of the sun shall they of the standard of the
camp of Judah pitch throughout their armies: and Nahshon the son of Amminadab *shall be* captain of the children of
Judah.
4And his host, and those that were numbered of them, *were* threescore and fourteen thousand and six hundred.
5And those that do pitch next unto him
shall be the tribe of Issachar: and Nethaneel
the son of Zuar *shall be* captain of the children of Issachar.
6And his host, and those that were numbered thereof, *were* fifty and four thousand
and four hundred.
7*Then* the tribe of Zebulun: and Eliab
the son of Helon *shall be* captain of the
children of Zebulun.
8And his host, and those that were numbered thereof, *were* fifty and seven thousand and four hundred.
9All that were numbered in the camp of
Judah *were* an hundred thousand and fourscore thousand and six thousand and four
hundred, throughout their armies. These
shall first set forth.
10On the south side *shall be* the standard
of the camp of Reuben according to their
armies: and the captain of the children of
Reuben *shall be* Elizur the son of Shedeur.
11And his host, and those that were
numbered thereof, *were* forty and six thousand and five hundred.
12And those which pitch by him *shall be*

the tribe of Simeon: and the captain of the children of Simeon *shall be* Shelumiel the son of Zurishaddai.

13 And his host, and those that were numbered of them, *were* fifty and nine thousand and three hundred.

14 Then the tribe of Gad: and the captain of the sons of Gad *shall be* Eliasaph the son of Reuel.

15 And his host, and those that were numbered of them, *were* forty and five thousand and six hundred and fifty.

16 All that were numbered in the camp of Reuben *were* an hundred thousand and fifty and one thousand and four hundred and fifty, throughout their armies. And they shall set forth in the second rank.

17 Then the tabernacle of the congregation shall set forward with the camp of the Levites in the midst of the camp: as they encamp, so shall they set forward, every man in his place by their standards.

18 On the west side *shall be* the standard of the camp of Ephraim according to their armies: and the captain of the sons of Ephraim *shall be* Elishama the son of Ammihud.

19 And his host, and those that were numbered of them, *were* forty thousand and five hundred.

20 And by him *shall be* the tribe of Manasseh: and the captain of the children of Manasseh *shall be* Gamaliel the son of Pedahzur.

21 And his host, and those that were numbered of them, *were* thirty and two thousand and two hundred.

22 Then the tribe of Benjamin: and the captain of the sons of Benjamin *shall be* Abidan the son of Gideoni.

23 And his host, and those that were numbered of them, *were* thirty and five thousand and four hundred.

24 All that were numbered of the camp of Ephraim *were* an hundred thousand and eight thousand and an hundred, throughout their armies. And they shall go forward in the third rank.

25 The standard of the camp of Dan *shall be* on the north side by their armies: and the captain of the children of Dan *shall be* Ahiezer the son of Ammishaddai.

26 And his host, and those that were numbered of them, *were* threescore and two thousand and seven hundred.

27 And those that encamp by him *shall be* the tribe of Asher: and the captain of the children of Asher *shall be* Pagiel the son of Ocran.

28 And his host, and those that were numbered of them, *were* forty and one thousand and five hundred.

29 Then the tribe of Naphtali: and the captain of the children of Naphtali *shall be* Ahira the son of Enan.

30 And his host, and those that were numbered of them, *were* fifty and three thousand and four hundred.

31 All they that were numbered in the camp of Dan *were* an hundred thousand and fifty and seven thousand and six hundred. They shall go hindmost with their standards.

32 These *are* those which were numbered of the children of Israel by the house of their fathers: all those that were numbered of the camps throughout their hosts *were* six hundred thousand and three thousand and five hundred and fifty.

33 But the Levites were not numbered among the children of Israel; as the LORD commanded Moses.

34 And the children of Israel did according to all that the LORD commanded Moses: so they pitched by their standards, and so they set forward, every one after their families, according to the house of their fathers.

3

1 These also *are* the generations of Aaron and Moses in the day *that* the LORD spake with Moses in mount Sinai.

2 And these *are* the names of the sons of Aaron; Nadab the firstborn, and Abihu, Eleazar, and Ithamar.

3 These *are* the names of the sons of Aaron, the priests which were anointed, whom he consecrated to minister in the priest's office.

4 And Nadab and Abihu died before the LORD, when they offered strange fire before the LORD, in the wilderness of Sinai, and they had no children: and Eleazar and Ithamar ministered in the priest's office in the sight of Aaron their father.

5 And the LORD spake unto Moses, saying,

6 Bring the tribe of Levi near, and present them before Aaron the priest, that they may minister unto him.

7 And they shall keep his charge, and the

charge of the whole congregation before the tabernacle of the congregation, to do the service of the tabernacle.

8 And they shall keep all the instruments of the tabernacle of the congregation, and the charge of the children of Israel, to do the service of the tabernacle.

9 And thou shalt give the Levites unto Aaron and to his sons: they *are* wholly given unto him out of the children of Israel.

10 And thou shalt appoint Aaron and his sons, and they shall wait on their priest's office: and the stranger that cometh nigh shall be put to death.

11 And the LORD spake unto Moses, saying,

12 And I, behold, I have taken the Levites from among the children of Israel instead of all the firstborn that openeth the matrix among the children of Israel: therefore the Levites shall be mine;

13 Because all the firstborn *are* mine; *for* on the day that I smote all the firstborn in the land of Egypt I hallowed unto me all the firstborn in Israel, both man and beast: mine shall they be: I *am* the LORD.

14 And the LORD spake unto Moses in the wilderness of Sinai, saying,

15 Number the children of Levi after the house of their fathers, by their families: every male from a month old and upward shalt thou number them.

16 And Moses numbered them according to the word of the LORD, as he was commanded.

17 And these were the sons of Levi by their names; Gershon, and Kohath, and Merari.

18 And these *are* the names of the sons of Gershon by their families; Libni, and Shimei.

19 And the sons of Kohath by their families; Amram, and Izehar, Hebron, and Uzziel.

20 And the sons of Merari by their families; Mahli, and Mushi. These *are* the families of the Levites according to the house of their fathers.

21 Of Gershon *was* the family of the Libnites, and the family of the Shimites: these *are* the families of the Gershonites.

22 Those that were numbered of them, according to the number of all the males, from a month old and upward, *even* those that were numbered of them *were* seven thousand and five hundred.

23 The families of the Gershonites shall pitch behind the tabernacle westward.

24 And the chief of the house of the father of the Gershonites *shall be* Eliasaph the son of Lael.

25 And the charge of the sons of Gershon in the tabernacle of the congregation *shall be* the tabernacle, and the tent, the covering thereof, and the hanging for the door of the tabernacle of the congregation,

26 And the hangings of the court, and the curtain for the door of the court, which *is* by the tabernacle, and by the altar round about, and the cords of it for all the service thereof.

27 And of Kohath *was* the family of the Amramites, and the family of the Izeharites, and the family of the Hebronites, and the family of the Uzzielites: these *are* the families of the Kohathites.

28 In the number of all the males, from a month old and upward, *were* eight thousand and six hundred, keeping the charge of the sanctuary.

29 The families of the sons of Kohath shall pitch on the side of the tabernacle southward.

30 And the chief of the house of the father of the families of the Kohathites *shall be* Elizaphan the son of Uzziel.

31 And their charge *shall be* the ark, and the table, and the candlestick, and the altars, and the vessels of the sanctuary wherewith they minister, and the hanging, and all the service thereof.

32 And Eleazar the son of Aaron the priest *shall be* chief over the chief of the Levites, *and have* the oversight of them that keep the charge of the sanctuary.

33 Of Merari *was* the family of the Mahlites, and the family of the Mushites: these *are* the families of Merari.

34 And those that were numbered of them, according to the number of all the males, from a month old and upward, *were* six thousand and two hundred.

35 And the chief of the house of the father of the families of Merari *was* Zuriel the son of Abihail: *these* shall pitch on the side of the tabernacle northward.

36 And *under* the custody and charge of the sons of Merari *shall be* the boards of the tabernacle, and the bars thereof, and

the pillars thereof, and the sockets thereof, and all the vessels thereof, and all that serveth thereto,

37 And the pillars of the court round about, and their sockets, and their pins, and their cords.

38 But those that encamp before the tabernacle toward the east, *even* before the tabernacle of the congregation eastward, *shall be* Moses, and Aaron and his sons, keeping the charge of the sanctuary for the charge of the children of Israel; and the stranger that cometh nigh shall be put to death.

39 All that were numbered of the Levites, which Moses and Aaron numbered at the commandment of the LORD, throughout their families, all the males from a month old and upward, *were* twenty and two thousand.

40 And the LORD said unto Moses, Number all the firstborn of the males of the children of Israel from a month old and upward, and take the number of their names.

41 And thou shalt take the Levites for me (I *am* the LORD) instead of all the firstborn among the children of Israel; and the cattle of the Levites instead of all the firstlings among the cattle of the children of Israel.

42 And Moses numbered, as the LORD commanded him, all the firstborn among the children of Israel.

43 And all the firstborn males by the number of names, from a month old and upward, of those that were numbered of them, were twenty and two thousand two hundred and threescore and thirteen.

44 And the LORD spake unto Moses, saying,

45 Take the Levites instead of all the firstborn among the children of Israel, and the cattle of the Levites instead of their cattle; and the Levites shall be mine: I *am* the LORD.

46 And for those that are to be redeemed of the two hundred and threescore and thirteen of the firstborn of the children of Israel, which are more than the Levites;

47 Thou shalt even take five shekels apiece by the poll, after the shekel of the sanctuary shalt thou take *them:* (the shekel *is* twenty gerahs:)

48 And thou shalt give the money, wherewith the odd number of them is to be redeemed, unto Aaron and to his sons.

49 And Moses took the redemption money of them that were over and above them that were redeemed by the Levites:

50 Of the firstborn of the children of Israel took he the money; a thousand three hundred and threescore and five *shekels,* after the shekel of the sanctuary:

51 And Moses gave the money of them that were redeemed unto Aaron and to his sons, according to the word of the LORD, as the LORD commanded Moses.

4

1 And the LORD spake unto Moses and unto Aaron, saying,

2 Take the sum of the sons of Kohath from among the sons of Levi, after their families, by the house of their fathers,

3 From thirty years old and upward even until fifty years old, all that enter into the host, to do the work in the tabernacle of the congregation.

4 This *shall be* the service of the sons of Kohath in the tabernacle of the congregation, *about* the most holy things:

5 And when the camp setteth forward, Aaron shall come, and his sons, and they shall take down the covering vail, and cover the ark of testimony with it:

6 And shall put thereon the covering of badgers' skins, and shall spread over *it* a cloth wholly of blue, and shall put in the staves thereof.

7 And upon the table of shewbread they shall spread a cloth of blue, and put thereon the dishes, and the spoons, and the bowls, and covers to cover withal: and the continual bread shall be thereon:

8 And they shall spread upon them a cloth of scarlet, and cover the same with a covering of badgers' skins, and shall put in the staves thereof.

9 And they shall take a cloth of blue, and cover the candlestick of the light, and his lamps, and his tongs, and his snuffdishes, and all the oil vessels thereof, wherewith they minister unto it:

10 And they shall put it and all the vessels thereof within a covering of badgers' skins, and shall put *it* upon a bar.

11 And upon the golden altar they shall spread a cloth of blue, and cover it with a covering of badgers' skins, and shall put to the staves thereof:

12 And they shall take all the instruments of ministry, wherewith they minister in the sanctuary, and put *them* in a cloth of blue, and cover them with a covering of badgers' skins, and shall put *them* on a bar:

13 And they shall take away the ashes from the altar, and spread a purple cloth thereon:

14 And they shall put upon it all the vessels thereof, wherewith they minister about it, *even* the censers, the fleshhooks, and the shovels, and the basons, all the vessels of the altar; and they shall spread upon it a covering of badgers' skins, and put to the staves of it.

15 And when Aaron and his sons have made an end of covering the sanctuary, and all the vessels of the sanctuary, as the camp is to set forward; after that, the sons of Kohath shall come to bear *it:* but they shall not touch *any* holy thing, lest they die. These *things are* the burden of the sons of Kohath in the tabernacle of the congregation.

16 And to the office of Eleazar the son of Aaron the priest *pertaineth* the oil for the light, and the sweet incense, and the daily meat offering, and the anointing oil, *and* the oversight of all the tabernacle, and of all that therein *is,* in the sanctuary, and in the vessels thereof.

17 And the LORD spake unto Moses and unto Aaron, saying,

18 Cut ye not off the tribe of the families of the Kohathites from among the Levites:

19 But thus do unto them, that they may live, and not die, when they approach unto the most holy things: Aaron and his sons shall go in, and appoint them every one to his service and to his burden:

20 But they shall not go in to see when the holy things are covered, lest they die.

21 And the LORD spake unto Moses, saying,

22 Take also the sum of the sons of Gershon, throughout the houses of their fathers, by their families;

23 From thirty years old and upward until fifty years old shalt thou number them; all that enter in to perform the service, to do the work in the tabernacle of the congregation.

24 This *is* the service of the families of the Gershonites, to serve, and for burdens:

25 And they shall bear the curtains of the tabernacle, and the tabernacle of the congregation, his covering, and the covering of the badgers' skins that *is* above upon it, and the hanging for the door of the tabernacle of the congregation,

26 And the hangings of the court, and the hanging for the door of the gate of the court, which *is* by the tabernacle and by the altar round about, and their cords, and all the instruments of their service, and all that is made for them: so shall they serve.

27 At the appointment of Aaron and his sons shall be all the service of the sons of the Gershonites, in all their burdens, and in all their service: and ye shall appoint unto them in charge all their burdens.

28 This *is* the service of the families of the sons of Gershon in the tabernacle of the congregation: and their charge *shall be* under the hand of Ithamar the son of Aaron the priest.

29 As for the sons of Merari, thou shalt number them after their families, by the house of their fathers;

30 From thirty years old and upward even unto fifty years old shalt thou number them, every one that entereth into the service, to do the work of the tabernacle of the congregation.

31 And this *is* the charge of their burden, according to all their service in the tabernacle of the congregation; the boards of the tabernacle, and the bars thereof, and the pillars thereof, and sockets thereof,

32 And the pillars of the court round about, and their sockets, and their pins, and their cords, with all their instruments, and with all their service: and by name ye shall reckon the instruments of the charge of their burden.

33 This *is* the service of the families of the sons of Merari, according to all their service, in the tabernacle of the congregation, under the hand of Ithamar the son of Aaron the priest.

34 And Moses and Aaron and the chief of the congregation numbered the sons of the Kohathites after their families, and after the house of their fathers,

35 From thirty years old and upward even unto fifty years old, every one that entereth into the service, for the work in the tabernacle of the congregation:

36 And those that were numbered of

them by their families were two thousand seven hundred and fifty.

37 These *were* they that were numbered of the families of the Kohathites, all that might do service in the tabernacle of the congregation, which Moses and Aaron did number according to the commandment of the LORD by the hand of Moses.

38 And those that were numbered of the sons of Gershon, throughout their families, and by the house of their fathers,

39 From thirty years old and upward even unto fifty years old, every one that entereth into the service, for the work in the tabernacle of the congregation,

40 Even those that were numbered of them, throughout their families, by the house of their fathers, were two thousand and six hundred and thirty.

41 These *are* they that were numbered of the families of the sons of Gershon, of all that might do service in the tabernacle of the congregation, whom Moses and Aaron did number according to the commandment of the LORD.

42 And those that were numbered of the families of the sons of Merari, throughout their families, by the house of their fathers,

43 From thirty years old and upward even unto fifty years old, every one that entereth into the service, for the work in the tabernacle of the congregation,

44 Even those that were numbered of them after their families, were three thousand and two hundred.

45 These *be* those that were numbered of the families of the sons of Merari, whom Moses and Aaron numbered according to the word of the LORD by the hand of Moses.

46 All those that were numbered of the Levites, whom Moses and Aaron and the chief of Israel numbered, after their families, and after the house of their fathers,

47 From thirty years old and upward even unto fifty years old, every one that came to do the service of the ministry, and the service of the burden in the tabernacle of the congregation,

48 Even those that were numbered of them, were eight thousand and five hundred and fourscore.

49 According to the commandment of the LORD they were numbered by the hand of Moses, every one according to his service, and according to his burden: thus were they numbered of him, as the LORD commanded Moses.

5

1 And the LORD spake unto Moses, saying,

2 Command the children of Israel, that they put out of the camp every leper, and every one that hath an issue, and whosoever is defiled by the dead:

3 Both male and female shall ye put out, without the camp shall ye put them; that they defile not their camps, in the midst whereof I dwell.

4 And the children of Israel did so, and put them out without the camp: as the LORD spake unto Moses, so did the children of Israel.

5 And the LORD spake unto Moses, saying,

6 Speak unto the children of Israel, When a man or woman shall commit any sin that men commit, to do a trespass against the LORD, and that person be guilty;

7 Then they shall confess their sin which they have done: and he shall recompense his trespass with the principal thereof, and add unto it the fifth *part* thereof, and give *it* unto *him* against whom he hath trespassed.

5:7 Confession
◄ Leviticus 26:40
Ezra 10:11 ►

8 But if the man have no kinsman to recompense the trespass unto, let the trespass be recompensed unto the LORD, *even* to the priest; beside the ram of the atonement, whereby an atonement shall be made for him.

9 And every offering of all the holy things of the children of Israel, which they bring unto the priest, shall be his.

10 And every man's hallowed things shall be his: whatsoever any man giveth the priest, it shall be his.

11 And the LORD spake unto Moses, saying,

12 Speak unto the children of Israel, and say unto them, If any man's wife go aside, and commit a trespass against him,

13 And a man lie with her carnally, and it be hid from the eyes of her husband, and be kept close, and she be defiled, and *there be* no witness against her, neither she be taken *with the manner;*

14 And the spirit of jealousy come upon

him, and he be jealous of his wife, and
she be defiled: or if the spirit of jealousy
come upon him, and he be jealous of his
wife, and she be not defiled:
15 Then shall the man bring his wife unto
the priest, and he shall bring her offering
for her, the tenth *part* of an ephah of barley meal; he shall pour no oil upon it, nor
put frankincense thereon; for it *is* an offering of jealousy, an offering of memorial, bringing iniquity to remembrance.
16 And the priest shall bring her near, and
set her before the LORD:
17 And the priest shall take holy water
in an earthen vessel; and of the dust that
is in the floor of the tabernacle the priest
shall take, and put *it* into the water:
18 And the priest shall set the woman
before the LORD, and uncover the woman's
head, and put the offering of memorial in
her hands, which *is* the jealousy offering:
and the priest shall have in his hand the
bitter water that causeth the curse:
19 And the priest shall charge her by an
oath, and say unto the woman, If no man
have lain with thee, and if thou hast not
gone aside to uncleanness *with another* instead of thy husband, be thou free from
this bitter water that causeth the curse:
20 But if thou hast gone aside *to another*
instead of thy husband, and if thou be
defiled, and some man have lain with thee
beside thine husband:
21 Then the priest shall charge the woman with an oath of cursing, and the priest
shall say unto the woman, The LORD make
thee a curse and an oath among thy people, when the LORD doth make thy thigh
to rot, and thy belly to swell;
22 And this water that causeth the curse
shall go into thy bowels, to make *thy* belly
to swell, and *thy* thigh to rot: And the woman shall say, Amen, amen.
23 And the priest shall write these curses
in a book, and he shall blot *them* out with
the bitter water:
24 And he shall cause the woman to
drink the bitter water that causeth the
curse: and the water that causeth the curse
shall enter into her, *and become* bitter.
25 Then the priest shall take the jealousy
offering out of the woman's hand, and
shall wave the offering before the LORD,
and offer it upon the altar:
26 And the priest shall take an handful
of the offering, *even* the memorial thereof,
and burn *it* upon the altar, and afterward
shall cause the woman to drink the water.
27 And when he hath made her to drink
the water, then it shall come to pass, *that*,
if she be defiled, and have done trespass
against her husband, that the water that
causeth the curse shall enter into her, *and
become* bitter, and her belly shall swell, and
her thigh shall rot: and the woman shall
be a curse among her people.
28 And if the woman be not defiled, but
be clean; then she shall be free, and shall
conceive seed.
29 This *is* the law of jealousies, when a
wife goeth aside *to another* instead of her
husband, and is defiled;
30 Or when the spirit of jealousy cometh
upon him, and he be jealous over his wife,
and shall set the woman before the LORD,
and the priest shall execute upon her all
this law.
31 Then shall the man be guiltless from
iniquity, and this woman shall bear her
iniquity.

6

1 And the LORD spake unto Moses,
saying,
2 Speak unto the children of Israel, and
say unto them, When either man or woman shall separate *themselves* to vow a vow
of a Nazarite, to separate *themselves* unto
the LORD:
3 He shall sepa-
rate *himself* from
wine and strong
drink, and shall
drink no vinegar of
wine, or vinegar of
strong drink, neither shall he drink any
liquor of grapes, nor eat moist grapes, or
dried.

6:3 Drinking
◄ Leviticus 10:9
Deuteronomy 29:6 ►

4 All the days of his separation shall he
eat nothing that is made of the vine tree,
from the kernels even to the husk.
5 All the days of the vow of his separation there shall no razor come upon his
head: until the days be fulfilled, in the
which he separateth *himself* unto the LORD,
he shall be holy, *and* shall let the locks of
the hair of his head grow.
6 All the days that he separateth *himself*
unto the LORD he shall come at no dead
body.
7 He shall not make himself unclean
for his father, or for his mother, for his

brother, or for his sister, when they die: because the consecration of his God *is* upon his head.

8 All the days of his separation he *is* holy unto the LORD.

9 And if any man die very suddenly by him, and he hath defiled the head of his consecration; then he shall shave his head in the day of his cleansing, on the seventh day shall he shave it.

10 And on the eighth day he shall bring two turtles, or two young pigeons, to the priest, to the door of the tabernacle of the congregation:

11 And the priest shall offer the one for a sin offering, and the other for a burnt offering, and make an atonement for him, for that he sinned by the dead, and shall hallow his head that same day.

12 And he shall consecrate unto the LORD the days of his separation, and shall bring a lamb of the first year for a trespass offering: but the days that were before shall be lost, because his separation was defiled.

13 And this *is* the law of the Nazarite, when the days of his separation are fulfilled: he shall be brought unto the door of the tabernacle of the congregation:

14 And he shall offer his offering unto the LORD, one he lamb of the first year without blemish for a burnt offering, and one ewe lamb of the first year without blemish for a sin offering, and one ram without blemish for peace offerings,

15 And a basket of unleavened bread, cakes of fine flour mingled with oil, and wafers of unleavened bread anointed with oil, and their meat offering, and their drink offerings.

16 And the priest shall bring *them* before the LORD, and shall offer his sin offering, and his burnt offering:

17 And he shall offer the ram *for* a sacrifice of peace offerings unto the LORD, with the basket of unleavened bread: the priest shall offer also his meat offering, and his drink offering.

18 And the Nazarite shall shave the head of his separation *at* the door of the tabernacle of the congregation, and shall take the hair of the head of his separation, and put *it* in the fire which *is* under the sacrifice of the peace offerings.

19 And the priest shall take the sodden shoulder of the ram, and one unleavened cake out of the basket, and one unleavened wafer, and shall put *them* upon the hands of the Nazarite, after *the hair of* his separation is shaven:

20 And the priest shall wave them *for* a wave offering before the LORD: this *is* holy for the priest, with the wave breast and heave shoulder: and after that the Nazarite may drink wine.

21 This *is* the law of the Nazarite who hath vowed, *and of* his offering unto the LORD for his separation, beside that *that* his hand shall get: according to the vow which he vowed, so he must do after the law of his separation.

22 And the LORD spake unto Moses, saying,

23 Speak unto Aaron and unto his sons, saying, On this wise ye shall bless the children of Israel, saying unto them,

24 The LORD bless thee, and keep thee:

25 The LORD make his face shine upon thee, and be gracious unto thee:

26 The LORD lift up his countenance upon thee, and give thee peace.

27 And they shall put my name upon the children of Israel; and I will bless them.

7

1 And it came to pass on the day that Moses had fully set up the tabernacle, and had anointed it, and sanctified it, and all the instruments thereof, both the altar and all the vessels thereof, and had anointed them, and sanctified them;

2 That the princes of Israel, heads of the house of their fathers, who *were* the princes of the tribes, and were over them that were numbered, offered:

3 And they brought their offering before the LORD, six covered wagons, and twelve oxen; a wagon for two of the princes, and for each one an ox: and they brought them before the tabernacle.

7:3
Examples of Generosity
◄ Exodus 36:5
1 Chronicles 29:3-4 ►

4 And the LORD spake unto Moses, saying,

5 Take *it* of them, that they may be to do the service of the tabernacle of the congregation; and thou shalt give them unto the Levites, to every man according to his service.

6 And Moses took the wagons and the oxen, and gave them unto the Levites.

7Two wagons and four oxen he gave
unto the sons of Gershon, according to
their service:
8And four wagons and eight oxen he
gave unto the sons of Merari, according
unto their service, under the hand of Ithamar the son of Aaron the priest.
9But unto the sons of Kohath he gave
none: because the service of the sanctuary
belonging unto them *was that* they should
bear upon their shoulders.
10And the princes offered for dedicating
of the altar in the day that it was anointed, even the princes offered their offering
before the altar.
11And the LORD said unto Moses, They
shall offer their offering, each prince on
his day, for the dedicating of the altar.
12And he that offered his offering the
first day was Nahshon the son of Amminadab, of the tribe of Judah:
13And his offering *was* one silver charger,
the weight thereof *was* an hundred and
thirty *shekels,* one silver bowl of seventy
shekels, after the shekel of the sanctuary;
both of them *were* full of fine flour mingled with oil for a meat offering:
14One spoon of ten *shekels* of gold, full
of incense:
15One young bullock, one ram, one
lamb of the first year, for a burnt offering:
16One kid of the goats for a sin offering:
17And for a sacrifice of peace offerings,
two oxen, five rams, five he goats, five
lambs of the first year: this *was* the offering of Nahshon the son of Amminadab.
18On the second day Nethaneel the son
of Zuar, prince of Issachar, did offer:
19He offered *for* his offering one silver
charger, the weight whereof *was* an hundred and thirty *shekels,* one silver bowl of
seventy shekels, after the shekel of the sanctuary; both of them full of fine flour mingled with oil for a meat offering:
20One spoon of gold of ten *shekels,* full
of incense:
21One young bullock, one ram, one
lamb of the first year, for a burnt offering:
22One kid of the goats for a sin offering:
23And for a sacrifice of peace offerings,
two oxen, five rams, five he goats, five
lambs of the first year: this *was* the offering of Nethaneel the son of Zuar.
24On the third day Eliab the son of Helon, prince of the children of Zebulun, *did
offer:*
25His offering *was* one silver charger, the
weight whereof *was* an hundred and thirty *shekels,* one silver bowl of seventy shekels, after the shekel of the sanctuary; both
of them full of fine flour mingled with oil
for a meat offering:
26One golden spoon of ten *shekels,* full
of incense:
27One young bullock, one ram, one
lamb of the first year, for a burnt offering:
28One kid of the goats for a sin offering:
29And for a sacrifice of peace offerings,
two oxen, five rams, five he goats, five
lambs of the first year: this *was* the offering of Eliab the son of Helon.
30On the fourth day Elizur the son of
Shedeur, prince of the children of Reuben,
did offer:
31His offering *was* one silver charger of
the weight of an hundred and thirty *shekels,* one silver bowl of seventy shekels, after the shekel of the sanctuary; both of
them full of fine flour mingled with oil
for a meat offering:
32One golden spoon of ten *shekels,* full
of incense:
33One young bullock, one ram, one
lamb of the first year, for a burnt offering:
34One kid of the goats for a sin offering:
35And for a sacrifice of peace offerings,
two oxen, five rams, five he goats, five
lambs of the first year: this *was* the offering of Elizur the son of Shedeur.
36On the fifth day Shelumiel the son of
Zurishaddai, prince of the children of Simeon, *did offer:*
37His offering *was* one silver charger, the
weight whereof *was* an hundred and thirty
shekels, one silver bowl of seventy shekels,
after the shekel of the sanctuary; both of
them full of fine flour mingled with oil
for a meat offering:
38One golden spoon of ten *shekels,* full
of incense:
39One young bullock, one ram, one
lamb of the first year, for a burnt offering:
40One kid of the goats for a sin offering:
41And for a sacrifice of peace offerings,
two oxen, five rams, five he goats, five
lambs of the first year: this *was* the offering of Shelumiel the son of Zurishaddai.

42 On the sixth day Eliasaph the son of Deuel, prince of the children of Gad, *offered:*

43 His offering *was* one silver charger of the weight of an hundred and thirty *shekels,* a silver bowl of seventy shekels, after the shekel of the sanctuary; both of them full of fine flour mingled with oil for a meat offering:

44 One golden spoon of ten *shekels,* full of incense:

45 One young bullock, one ram, one lamb of the first year, for a burnt offering:

46 One kid of the goats for a sin offering:

47 And for a sacrifice of peace offerings, two oxen, five rams, five he goats, five lambs of the first year: this *was* the offering of Eliasaph the son of Deuel.

48 On the seventh day Elishama the son of Ammihud, prince of the children of Ephraim, *offered:*

49 His offering *was* one silver charger, the weight whereof *was* an hundred and thirty *shekels,* one silver bowl of seventy shekels, after the shekel of the sanctuary; both of them full of fine flour mingled with oil for a meat offering:

50 One golden spoon of ten *shekels,* full of incense:

51 One young bullock, one ram, one lamb of the first year, for a burnt offering:

52 one kid of the goats for a sin offering:

53 And for a sacrifice of peace offerings, two oxen, five rams, five he goats, five lambs of the first year: this *was* the offering of Elishama the son of Ammihud.

54 On the eighth day *offered* Gamaliel the son of Pedahzur, prince of the children of Manasseh:

55 His offering *was* one silver charger of the weight of an hundred and thirty *shekels,* one silver bowl of seventy shekels, after the shekel of the sanctuary; both of them full of fine flour mingled with oil for a meat offering:

56 One golden spoon of ten *shekels,* full of incense:

57 One young bullock, one ram, one lamb of the first year, for a burnt offering:

58 One kid of the goats for a sin offering:

59 And for a sacrifice of peace offerings, two oxen, five rams, five he goats, five lambs of the first year: this *was* the offering of Gamaliel the son of Pedahzur.

60 On the ninth day Abidan the son of Gideoni, prince of the children of Benjamin, *offered:*

61 His offering *was* one silver charger, the weight whereof *was* an hundred and thirty *shekels,* one silver bowl of seventy shekels, after the shekel of the sanctuary; both of them full of fine flour mingled with oil for a meat offering:

62 One golden spoon of ten *shekels,* full of incense:

63 One young bullock, one ram, one lamb of the first year, for a burnt offering:

64 One kid of the goats for a sin offering:

65 And for a sacrifice of peace offerings, two oxen, five rams, five he goats, five lambs of the first year: this *was* the offering of Abidan the son of Gideoni.

66 On the tenth day Ahiezer the son of Ammishaddai, prince of the children of Dan, *offered:*

67 His offering *was* one silver charger, the weight whereof *was* an hundred and thirty *shekels,* one silver bowl of seventy shekels, after the shekel of the sanctuary; both of them full of fine flour mingled with oil for a meat offering:

68 One golden spoon of ten *shekels,* full of incense:

69 One young bullock, one ram, one lamb of the first year, for a burnt offering:

70 One kid of the goats for a sin offering:

71 And for a sacrifice of peace offerings, two oxen, five rams, five he goats, five lambs of the first year: this *was* the offering of Ahiezer the son of Ammishaddai.

72 On the eleventh day Pagiel the son of Ocran, prince of the children of Asher, *offered:*

73 His offering *was* one silver charger, the weight whereof *was* an hundred and thirty *shekels,* one silver bowl of seventy shekels, after the shekel of the sanctuary; both of them full of fine flour mingled with oil for a meat offering:

74 One golden spoon of ten *shekels,* full of incense:

75 One young bullock, one ram, one lamb of the first year, for a burnt offering:

76 One kid of the goats for a sin offering:

77 And for a sacrifice of peace offerings, two oxen, five rams, five he goats, five lambs of the first year: this *was* the offering of Pagiel the son of Ocran.

78 On the twelfth day Ahira the son of

Enan, prince of the children of Naphtali, *offered:*

79 His offering *was* one silver charger, the weight whereof *was* an hundred and thirty *shekels,* one silver bowl of seventy shekels, after the shekel of the sanctuary; both of them full of fine flour mingled with oil for a meat offering:

80 One golden spoon of ten *shekels,* full of incense:

81 One young bullock, one ram, one lamb of the first year, for a burnt offering:

82 One kid of the goats for a sin offering:

83 And for a sacrifice of peace offerings, two oxen, five rams, five he goats, five lambs of the first year: this *was* the offering of Ahira the son of Enan.

84 This *was* the dedication of the altar, in the day when it was anointed, by the princes of Israel: twelve chargers of silver, twelve silver bowls, twelve spoons of gold:

85 Each charger of silver *weighing* an hundred and thirty *shekels,* each bowl seventy: all the silver vessels *weighed* two thousand and four hundred *shekels,* after the shekel of the sanctuary:

86 The golden spoons *were* twelve, full of incense, *weighing* ten *shekels* apiece, after the shekel of the sanctuary: all the gold of the spoons *was* an hundred and twenty *shekels.*

87 All the oxen for the burnt offering *were* twelve bullocks, the rams twelve, the lambs of the first year twelve, with their meat offering: and the kids of the goats for sin offering twelve.

88 And all the oxen for the sacrifice of the peace offerings *were* twenty and four bullocks, the rams sixty, the he goats sixty, the lambs of the first year sixty. This *was* the dedication of the altar, after that it was anointed.

89 And when Moses was gone into the tabernacle of the congregation to speak with him, then he heard the voice of one speaking unto him from off the mercy seat that *was* upon the ark of testimony, from between the two cherubims: and he spake unto him.

8

1 And the LORD spake unto Moses, saying,

2 Speak unto Aaron, and say unto him, When thou lightest the lamps, the seven lamps shall give light over against the candlestick.

3 And Aaron did so; he lighted the lamps thereof over against the candlestick, as the LORD commanded Moses.

4 And this work of the candlestick *was of* beaten gold, unto the shaft thereof, unto the flowers thereof, *was* beaten work: according unto the pattern which the LORD had shewed Moses, so he made the candlestick.

5 And the LORD spake unto Moses, saying,

6 Take the Levites from among the children of Israel, and cleanse them.

7 And thus shalt thou do unto them, to cleanse them: Sprinkle water of purifying upon them, and let them shave all their flesh, and let them wash their clothes, and *so* make themselves clean.

8 Then let them take a young bullock with his meat offering, *even* fine flour mingled with oil, and another young bullock shalt thou take for a sin offering.

9 And thou shalt bring the Levites before the tabernacle of the congregation: and thou shalt gather the whole assembly of the children of Israel together:

10 And thou shalt bring the Levites before the LORD: and the children of Israel shall put their hands upon the Levites:

11 And Aaron shall offer the Levites before the LORD *for* an offering of the children of Israel, that they may execute the service of the LORD.

12 And the Levites shall lay their hands upon the heads of the bullocks: and thou shalt offer the one *for* a sin offering, and the other *for* a burnt offering, unto the LORD, to make an atonement for the Levites.

13 And thou shalt set the Levites before Aaron, and before his sons, and offer them *for* an offering unto the LORD.

14 Thus shalt thou separate the Levites from among the children of Israel: and the Levites shall be mine.

15 And after that shall the Levites go in to do the service of the tabernacle of the congregation: and thou shalt cleanse them, and offer them *for* an offering.

16 For they *are* wholly given unto me from among the children of Israel; instead of such as open every womb, *even instead of* the firstborn of all the children of Israel, have I taken them unto me.

17 For all the firstborn of the children of

Israel *are* mine, *both* man and beast: on the
day that I smote every firstborn in the land
of Egypt I sanctified them for myself.
18 And I have taken the Levites for all the
firstborn of the children of Israel.
19 And I have given the Levites *as* a gift
to Aaron and to his sons from among the
children of Israel, to do the service of
the children of Israel in the tabernacle of
the congregation, and to make an atonement for the children of Israel: that there
be no plague among the children of Israel,
when the children of Israel come nigh unto
the sanctuary.
20 And Moses, and Aaron, and all the
congregation of the children of Israel, did
to the Levites according unto all that
the LORD commanded Moses concerning
the Levites, so did the children of Israel
unto them.
21 And the Levites were purified, and they
washed their clothes; and Aaron offered
them *as* an offering before the LORD; and
Aaron made an atonement for them to
cleanse them.
22 And after that went the Levites in to
do their service in the tabernacle of the
congregation before Aaron, and before his
sons: as the LORD had commanded Moses
concerning the Levites, so did they unto
them.
23 And the LORD spake unto Moses,
saying,
24 This *is it* that *belongeth* unto the Levites: from twenty and five years old and
upward they shall go in to wait upon the
service of the tabernacle of the congregation:
25 And from the age of fifty years they
shall cease waiting upon the service *thereof,*
and shall serve no more:
26 But shall minister with their brethren
in the tabernacle of the congregation, to
keep the charge, and shall do no service.
Thus shalt thou do unto the Levites touching their charge.

9

1 And the LORD spake unto Moses in the
wilderness of Sinai, in the first month of
the second year after they were come out
of the land of Egypt, saying,
2 Let the children of Israel also keep the
passover at his appointed season.
3 In the fourteenth day of this month, at
even, ye shall keep it in his appointed season: according to all the rites of it, and
according to all the ceremonies thereof,
shall ye keep it.
4 And Moses spake unto the children
of Israel, that they should keep the passover.
5 And they kept the passover on the fourteenth day of the first month at even in
the wilderness of Sinai: according to all
that the LORD commanded Moses, so did
the children of Israel.
6 And there were certain men, who were
defiled by the dead body of a man, that
they could not keep the passover on that
day: and they came before Moses and before Aaron on that day:
7 And those men said unto him, We *are*
defiled by the dead body of a man: wherefore are we kept back, that we may not offer an offering of the LORD in his appointed
season among the children of Israel?
8 And Moses said unto them, Stand still,
and I will hear what the LORD will command concerning you.
9 And the LORD spake unto Moses,
saying,
10 Speak unto the children of Israel, saying, If any man of you or of your posterity
shall be unclean by reason of a dead body,
or *be* in a journey afar off, yet he shall keep
the passover unto the LORD.
11 The fourteenth day of the second
month at even they shall keep it, *and* eat it
with unleavened bread and bitter *herbs.*
12 They shall leave none of it unto the
morning, nor break any bone of it: according to all the ordinances of the passover
they shall keep it.
13 But the man that *is* clean, and is not
in a journey, and forbeareth to keep the
passover, even the same soul shall be cut
off from among his people: because he
brought not the offering of the LORD in
his appointed season, that man shall bear
his sin.
14 And if a stranger shall sojourn among
you, and will keep the passover unto the
LORD; according to the ordinance of the
passover, and according to the manner
thereof, so shall he do: ye shall have one
ordinance, both for the stranger, and for
him that was born in the land.
15 And on the day that the tabernacle was
reared up the cloud covered the tabernacle,
namely, the tent of the testimony: and at
even there was upon the tabernacle as

it were the appearance of fire, until the
morning.
16 So it was alway: the cloud covered it
by day, and the appearance of fire by night.
17 And when the cloud was taken up
from the tabernacle, then after that the
children of Israel journeyed: and in
the place where the cloud abode, there the
children of Israel pitched their tents.
18 At the commandment of the LORD
the children of Israel journeyed, and at the
commandment of the LORD they pitched:
as long as the cloud abode upon the tabernacle they rested in their tents.
19 And when the cloud tarried long upon
the tabernacle many days, then the children of Israel kept the charge of the LORD,
and journeyed not.
20 And *so* it was, when the cloud was a
few days upon the tabernacle; according
to the commandment of the LORD they
abode in their tents, and according to the
commandment of the LORD they journeyed.
21 And *so* it was, when the cloud abode
from even unto the morning, and *that* the
cloud was taken up in the morning, then
they journeyed: whether *it was* by day or
by night that the cloud was taken up, they
journeyed.
22 Or *whether it were* two days, or a
month, or a year, that the cloud tarried
upon the tabernacle, remaining thereon,
the children of Israel abode in their tents,
and journeyed not: but when it was taken
up, they journeyed.
23 At the commandment of the LORD
they rested in the tents, and at the commandment of the LORD they journeyed:
they kept the charge of the LORD, at the
commandment of the LORD by the hand
of Moses.

10

1 And the LORD spake unto Moses,
saying,
2 Make thee two trumpets of silver; of a
whole piece shalt thou make them: that
thou mayest use them for the calling of
the assembly, and for the journeying of the
camps.
3 And when they shall blow with them,
all the assembly shall assemble themselves
to thee at the door of the tabernacle of the
congregation.
4 And if they blow *but* with one *trumpet,*
then the princes, *which are* heads of the
thousands of Israel, shall gather themselves unto thee.
5 When ye blow an alarm, then the
camps that lie on the east parts shall go
forward.
6 When ye blow an alarm the second
time, then the camps that lie on the south
side shall take their journey: they shall
blow an alarm for their journeys.
7 But when the congregation is to be
gathered together, ye shall blow, but ye
shall not sound an alarm.
8 And the sons of Aaron, the priests, shall
blow with the trumpets; and they shall be
to you for an ordinance for ever throughout your generations.
9 And if ye go to war in your land against
the enemy that oppresseth you, then ye
shall blow an alarm with the trumpets; and
ye shall be remembered before the LORD
your God, and ye shall be saved from your
enemies.
10 Also in the day of your gladness, and
in your solemn days, and in the beginnings
of your months, ye shall blow with the
trumpets over your burnt offerings, and
over the sacrifices of your peace offerings;
that they may be to you for a memorial
before your God: I *am* the LORD your God.
11 And it came to pass on the twentieth
day of the second month, in the second
year, that the cloud was taken up from off
the tabernacle of the testimony.
12 And the children of Israel took their
journeys out of the wilderness of Sinai;
and the cloud rested in the wilderness of
Paran.
13 And they first took their journey according to the commandment of the LORD
by the hand of Moses.
14 In the first *place* went the standard of
the camp of the children of Judah according to their armies: and over his host *was*
Nahshon the son of Amminadab.
15 And over the host of the tribe of the
children of Issachar *was* Nethaneel the son
of Zuar.
16 And over the host of the tribe of the
children of Zebulun *was* Eliab the son of
Helon.
17 And the tabernacle was taken down;
and the sons of Gershon and the sons of
Merari set forward, bearing the tabernacle.
18 And the standard of the camp of Reuben set forward according to their armies:

and over his host *was* Elizur the son of Shedeur.

19 And over the host of the tribe of the children of Simeon *was* Shelumiel the son of Zurishaddai.

20 And over the host of the tribe of the children of Gad was Eliasaph the son of Deuel.

21 And the Kohathites set forward, bearing the sanctuary: and *the other* did set up the tabernacle against they came.

22 And the standard of the camp of the children of Ephraim set forward according to their armies: and over his host *was* Elishama the son of Ammihud.

23 And over the host of the tribe of the children of Manasseh *was* Gamaliel the son of Pedahzur.

24 And over the host of the tribe of the children of Benjamin *was* Abidan the son of Gideoni.

25 And the standard of the camp of the children of Dan set forward, *which was* the rereward of all the camps throughout their hosts: and over his host *was* Ahiezer the son of Ammishaddai.

26 And over the host of the tribe of the children of Asher *was* Pagiel the son of Ocran.

27 And over the host of the tribe of the children of Naphtali *was* Ahira the son of Enan.

28 Thus *were* the journeyings of the children of Israel according to their armies, when they set forward.

29 And Moses said unto Hobab, the son of Raguel the Midianite, Moses' father in law, We are journeying unto the place of which the LORD said, I will give it you: come thou with us, and we will do thee good: for the LORD hath spoken good concerning Israel.

30 And he said unto him, I will not go; but I will depart to mine own land, and to my kindred.

31 And he said, Leave us not, I pray thee; forasmuch as thou knowest how we are to encamp in the wilderness, and thou mayest be to us instead of eyes.

32 And it shall be, if thou go with us, yea, it shall be, that what goodness the LORD shall do unto us, the same will we do unto thee.

33 And they departed from the mount of the LORD three days' journey: and the ark of the covenant of the LORD went before them in the three days' journey, to search out a resting place for them.

34 And the cloud of the LORD *was* upon them by day, when they went out of the camp.

35 And it came to pass, when the ark set forward, that Moses said, Rise up, LORD, and let thine enemies be scattered; and let them that hate thee flee before thee.

36 And when it rested, he said, Return, O LORD, unto the many thousands of Israel.

11

1 And *when* the people complained, it displeased the LORD: and the LORD heard *it*; and his anger was kindled; and the fire of the LORD burnt among them, and consumed *them that were* in the uttermost parts of the camp.

2 And the people cried unto Moses; and when Moses prayed unto the LORD, the fire was quenched.

3 And he called the name of the place Taberah: because the fire of the LORD burnt among them.

4 And the mixt multitude that *was* among them fell a lusting: and the children of Israel also wept again, and said, Who shall give us flesh to eat?

5 We remember the fish, which we did eat in Egypt freely; the cucumbers, and the melons, and the leeks, and the onions, and the garlick:

6 But now our soul *is* dried away: *there is* nothing at all, beside this manna, *before* our eyes.

7 And the manna *was* as coriander seed, and the colour thereof as the colour of bdellium.

8 *And* the people went about, and gathered *it*, and ground *it* in mills, or beat *it* in a mortar, and baked *it* in pans, and made cakes of it: and the taste of it was as the taste of fresh oil.

9 And when the dew fell upon the camp in the night, the manna fell upon it.

10 Then Moses heard the people weep throughout their families, every man in the door of his tent: and the anger of the LORD was kindled greatly; Moses also was displeased.

11 And Moses said unto the LORD, Wherefore hast thou afflicted thy servant? and wherefore have I not found favour in thy sight, that thou layest the burden of all this people upon me?

12 Have I conceived all this people? have I begotten them, that thou shouldest say unto me, Carry them in thy bosom, as a nursing father beareth the sucking child, unto the land which thou swarest unto their fathers?

13 Whence should I have flesh to give unto all this people? for they weep unto me, saying, Give us flesh, that we may eat.

14 I am not able to bear all this people alone, because *it is* too heavy for me.

15 And if thou deal thus with me, kill me, I pray thee, out of hand, if I have found favour in thy sight; and let me not see my wretchedness.

11:15 Unhappiness
◄ Joshua 7:7 ►

16 And the LORD said unto Moses, Gather unto me seventy men of the elders of Israel, whom thou knowest to be the elders of the people, and officers over them; and bring them unto the tabernacle of the congregation, that they may stand there with thee.

17 And I will come down and talk with thee there: and I will take of the spirit which *is* upon thee, and will put *it* upon them; and they shall bear the burden of the people with thee, that thou bear *it* not thyself alone.

18 And say thou unto the people, Sanctify yourselves against to morrow, and ye shall eat flesh: for ye have wept in the ears of the LORD, saying, Who shall give us flesh to eat? for *it was* well with us in Egypt: therefore the LORD will give you flesh, and ye shall eat.

19 Ye shall not eat one day, nor two days, nor five days, neither ten days, nor twenty days;

20 *But* even a whole month, until it come out at your nostrils, and it be loathsome unto you: because that ye have despised the LORD which *is* among you, and have wept before him, saying, Why came we forth out of Egypt?

21 And Moses said, The people, among whom I *am, are* six hundred thousand footmen; and thou hast said, I will give them flesh, that they may eat a whole month.

22 Shall the flocks and the herds be slain for them, to suffice them? or shall all the fish of the sea be gathered together for them, to suffice them?

23 And the LORD said unto Moses, Is the LORD'S hand waxed short? thou shalt see now whether my word shall come to pass unto thee or not.

24 And Moses went out, and told the people the words of the LORD, and gathered the seventy men of the elders of the people, and set them round about the tabernacle.

25 And the LORD came down in a cloud, and spake unto him, and took of the spirit that *was* upon him, and gave *it* unto the seventy elders: and it came to pass, *that,* when the spirit rested upon them, they prophesied, and did not cease.

26 But there remained two *of the* men in the camp, the name of the one *was* Eldad, and the name of the other Medad: and the spirit rested upon them; and they *were* of them that were written, but went not out unto the tabernacle: and they prophesied in the camp.

27 And there ran a young man, and told Moses, and said, Eldad and Medad do prophesy in the camp.

28 And Joshua the son of Nun, the servant of Moses, *one* of his young men, answered and said, My lord Moses, forbid them.

29 And Moses said unto him, Enviest thou for my sake? would God that all the LORD'S people were prophets, *and* that the LORD would put his spirit upon them!

11:29 Unselfishness
◄ Genesis 50:21
1 Samuel 18:4 ►

30 And Moses gat him into the camp, he and the elders of Israel.

31 And there went forth a wind from the LORD, and brought quails from the sea, and let *them* fall by the camp, as it were a day's journey on this side, and as it were a day's journey on the other side, round about the camp, and as it were two cubits *high* upon the face of the earth.

32 And the people stood up all that day, and all *that* night, and all the next day, and they gathered the quails: he that gathered least gathered ten homers: and they spread *them* all abroad for themselves round about the camp.

33 And while the flesh *was* yet between

their teeth, ere it was chewed, the wrath of
the LORD was kindled against the people,
and the LORD smote the people with a very
great plague.
34And he called the name of that place
Kibroth-hattaavah: because there they buried the people that lusted.
35*And* the people journeyed from Kibroth-hattaavah unto Hazeroth; and abode
at Hazeroth.

12

1And Miriam and Aaron spake against
Moses because of the Ethiopian woman
whom he had married: for he had married an Ethiopian woman.
2And they said, Hath the LORD indeed
spoken only by Moses? hath he not spoken also by us? And the LORD heard *it*.
3(Now the man Moses *was* very meek,
above all the men which *were* upon the
face of the earth.)
4And the LORD spake suddenly unto
Moses, and unto Aaron, and unto Miriam,
Come out ye three unto the tabernacle
of the congregation. And they three came
out.
5And the LORD came down in the pillar
of the cloud, and stood *in* the door of the
tabernacle, and called Aaron and Miriam:
and they both came forth.
6And he said, Hear now my words: If
there be a prophet among you, *I* the LORD
will make myself known unto him in a
vision, *and* will speak unto him in a dream.
7My servant Moses *is* not so, who *is* faithful in all mine house.
8With him will I
speak mouth to
mouth, even appar-
ently, and not in
dark speeches; and
the similitude of
the LORD shall he
behold: wherefore then were ye not afraid
to speak against my servant Moses?

12:8 God's Friends
◄ Exodus 33:11
Deuteronomy 34:10 ►

9And the anger of the LORD was kindled
against them; and he departed.
10And the cloud departed from off the
tabernacle; and, behold, Miriam *became*
leprous, *white* as snow: and Aaron looked
upon Miriam, and, behold, *she was* leprous.
11And Aaron said unto Moses, Alas, my
lord, I beseech thee, lay not the sin upon
us, wherein we have done foolishly, and
wherein we have sinned.
12Let her not be as one dead, of whom
the flesh is half consumed when he
cometh out of his mother's womb.
13And Moses
cried unto the
LORD, saying, Heal
her now, O God, I
beseech thee.

12:13 Nice
◄ Genesis 45:15
1 Samuel 24:17 ►

14And the LORD
said unto Moses,
If her father had
but spit in her face,
should she not be
ashamed seven
days? let her be shut
out from the camp
seven days, and after that let her be received in *again*.

12:13 Praying for Others
◄ Exodus 32:32
Numbers 14:17 ►

15And Miriam was shut out from the
camp seven days: and the people journeyed not till Miriam was brought in *again*.
16And afterward the people removed
from Hazeroth, and pitched in the wilderness of Paran.

13

1And the LORD spake unto Moses,
saying,
2Send thou men, that they may search
the land of Canaan, which I give unto the
children of Israel: of every tribe of their
fathers shall ye send a man, every one a
ruler among them.
3And Moses by the commandment of
the LORD sent them from the wilderness
of Paran: all those men *were* heads of the
children of Israel.
4And these *were* their names: of the tribe
of Reuben, Shammua the son of Zaccur.
5Of the tribe of Simeon, Shaphat the son
of Hori.
6Of the tribe of Judah, Caleb the son of
Jephunneh.
7Of the tribe of Issachar, Igal the son of
Joseph.
8Of the tribe of Ephraim, Oshea the son
of Nun.
9Of the tribe of Benjamin, Palti the son
of Raphu.
10Of the tribe of Zebulun, Gaddiel the
son of Sodi.
11Of the tribe of Joseph, *namely*, of the
tribe of Manasseh, Gaddi the son of Susi.
12Of the tribe of Dan, Ammiel the son
of Gemalli.
13Of the tribe of Asher, Sethur the son
of Michael.

14 Of the tribe of Naphtali, Nahbi the son of Vophsi.

15 Of the tribe of Gad, Geuel the son of Machi.

16 These *are* the names of the men which Moses sent to spy out the land. And Moses called Oshea the son of Nun Jehoshua.

17 And Moses sent them to spy out the land of Canaan, and said unto them, Get you up this *way* southward, and go up into the mountain:

18 And see the land, what it *is;* and the people that dwelleth therein, whether they *be* strong or weak, few or many;

19 And what the land *is* that they dwell in, whether it *be* good or bad; and what cities *they be* that they dwell in, whether in tents, or in strong holds;

20 And what the land *is,* whether it *be* fat or lean, whether there be wood therein, or not. And be ye of good courage, and bring of the fruit of the land. Now the time *was* the time of the firstripe grapes.

21 So they went up, and searched the land from the wilderness of Zin unto Rehob, as men come to Hamath.

22 And they ascended by the south, and came unto Hebron; where Ahiman, Sheshai, and Talmai, the children of Anak, *were.* (Now Hebron was built seven years before Zoan in Egypt.)

23 And they came unto the brook of Eshcol, and cut down from thence a branch with one cluster of grapes, and they bare it between two upon a staff; and *they brought* of the pomegranates, and of the figs.

24 The place was called the brook Eshcol, because of the cluster of grapes which the children of Israel cut down from thence.

25 And they returned from searching of the land after forty days.

26 And they went and came to Moses, and to Aaron, and to all the congregation of the children of Israel, unto the wilderness of Paran, to Kadesh; and brought back word unto them, and unto all the congregation, and shewed them the fruit of the land.

27 And they told him, and said, We came unto the land whither thou sentest us, and surely it floweth with milk and honey; and this *is* the fruit of it.

28 Nevertheless the people *be* strong that dwell in the land, and the cities *are* walled, *and* very great: and moreover we saw the children of Anak there.

29 The Amalekites dwell in the land of the south: and the Hittites, and the Jebusites, and the Amorites, dwell in the mountains: and the Canaanites dwell by the sea, and by the coast of Jordan.

30 And Caleb stilled the people before Moses, and said, Let us go up at once, and possess it; for we are well able to overcome it.

31 But the men that went up with him said, We be not able to go up against the people; for they *are* stronger than we.

32 And they brought up an evil report of the land which they had searched unto the children of Israel, saying, The land, through which we have gone to search it, is a land that eateth up the inhabitants thereof; and all the people that we saw in it *are* men of a great stature.

33 And there we saw the giants, the sons of Anak, *which come* of the giants: and we were in our own sight as grasshoppers, and so we were in their sight.

14

1 And all the congregation lifted up their voice, and cried; and the people wept that night.

2 And all the children of Israel murmured against Moses and against Aaron: and the whole congregation said unto them, Would God that we had died in the land of Egypt! or would God we had died in this wilderness!

3 And wherefore hath the LORD brought us unto this land, to fall by the sword, that our wives and our children should be a prey? were it not better for us to return into Egypt?

4 And they said one to another, Let us make a captain, and let us return into Egypt.

5 Then Moses and Aaron fell on their faces before all the assembly of the congregation of the children of Israel.

6 And Joshua the son of Nun, and Caleb the son of Jephunneh, *which were* of them that searched the land, rent their clothes:

7 And they spake unto all the company of the children of Israel, saying, The land, which we passed through to search it, *is* an exceeding good land.

8 If the LORD delight in us, then he will bring us into this land, and give it us; a land which floweth with milk and honey.

9Only rebel not ye against the LORD, neither fear ye the people of the land; for they *are* bread for us: their defence is departed from them, and the LORD *is* with us: fear them not.

10But all the congregation bade stone them with stones. And the glory of the LORD appeared in the tabernacle of the congregation before all the children of Israel.

11And the LORD said unto Moses, How long will this people provoke me? and how long will it be ere they believe me, for all the signs which I have shewed among them?

14:11
Losers
◄ Numbers 14:23 ►

12I will smite them with the pestilence, and disinherit them, and will make of thee a greater nation and mightier than they.

13And Moses said unto the LORD, Then the Egyptians shall hear *it*, (for thou broughtest up this people in thy might from among them;)

14And they will tell *it* to the inhabitants of this land: *for* they have heard that thou LORD *art* among this people, that thou LORD art seen face to face, and *that* thy cloud standeth over them, and *that* thou goest before them, by daytime in a pillar of a cloud, and in a pillar of fire by night.

15Now *if* thou shalt kill *all* this people as one man, then the nations which have heard the fame of thee will speak, saying,

16Because the LORD was not able to bring this people into the land which he sware unto them, therefore he hath slain them in the wilderness.

17And now, I beseech thee, let the power of my Lord be great, according as thou hast spoken, saying,

14:17 Praying for Others
◄ Numbers 12:13
Deuteronomy 9:26 ►

18The LORD *is* longsuffering, and of great mercy, forgiving iniquity and transgression, and by no means clearing *the guilty,* visiting the iniquity of the fathers upon the children unto the third and fourth *generation.*

14:18
God's Patience
◄ Isaiah 48:9 ►

19Pardon, I beseech thee, the iniquity of this people according unto the greatness of thy mercy, and as thou hast forgiven this people, from Egypt even until now.

20And the LORD said, I have pardoned according to thy word:

21But *as* truly *as* I live, all the earth shall be filled with the glory of the LORD.

22Because all those men which have seen my glory, and my miracles, which I did in Egypt and in the wilderness, and have tempted me now these ten times, and have not hearkened to my voice;

23Surely they shall not see the land which I sware unto their fathers, neither shall any of them that provoked me see it:

14:23 Losers
◄ Numbers 14:11
Numbers 16:30 ►

24But my servant Caleb, because he had another spirit with him, and hath followed me fully, him will I bring into the land whereinto he went; and his seed shall possess it.

25(Now the Amalekites and the Canaanites dwelt in the valley.) To morrow turn you, and get you into the wilderness by the way of the Red sea.

26And the LORD spake unto Moses and unto Aaron, saying,

27How long *shall I bear with* this evil congregation, which murmur against me? I have heard the murmurings of the children of Israel, which they murmur against me.

28Say unto them, *As truly as* I live, saith the LORD, as ye have spoken in mine ears, so will I do to you:

29Your carcases shall fall in this wilderness; and all that were numbered of you, according to your whole number, from twenty years old and upward, which have murmured against me,

30Doubtless ye shall not come into the land, *concerning* which I sware to make you dwell therein, save Caleb the son of Jephunneh, and Joshua the son of Nun.

31But your little ones, which ye said should be a prey, them will I bring in, and they shall know the land which ye have despised.

32But *as for* you, your carcases, they shall fall in this wilderness.

33And your children shall wander in the wilderness forty years, and bear your

whoredoms, until your carcases be wasted in the wilderness.
34 After the number of the days in which
ye searched the land, *even* forty days, each
day for a year, shall ye bear your iniquities, *even* forty years, and ye shall know my
breach of promise.
35 I the LORD have said, I will surely do
it unto all this evil congregation, that are
gathered together against me: in this wilderness they shall be consumed, and there
they shall die.
36 And the men, which Moses sent to
search the land, who returned, and made all
the congregation to murmur against him,
by bringing up a slander upon the land,
37 Even those men that did bring up the
evil report upon the land, died by the
plague before the LORD.
38 But Joshua the son of Nun, and Caleb
the son of Jephunneh, *which were* of the
men that went to search the land, lived *still*.
39 And Moses told
these sayings unto
all the children
of Israel: and the
people mourned
greatly.

14:39
Remorse
◄ 1 Chronicles 21:17 ►

40 And they rose up early in the morning, and gat them up into the top of the
mountain, saying, Lo, we *be here*, and will
go up unto the place which the LORD hath
promised: for we have sinned.
41 And Moses said, Wherefore now do ye
transgress the commandment of the LORD?
but it shall not prosper.
42 Go not up, for the LORD *is* not among
you; that ye be not smitten before your
enemies.
43 For the Amalekites and the Canaanites *are* there before you, and ye shall fall
by the sword: because ye are turned away
from the LORD, therefore the LORD will not
be with you.
44 But they presumed to go up unto the
hill top: nevertheless the ark of the covenant of the LORD, and Moses, departed
not out of the camp.
45 Then the Amalekites came down, and
the Canaanites which dwelt in that hill,
and smote them, and discomfited them,
even unto Hormah.

15

1 And the LORD spake unto Moses,
saying,
2 Speak unto the children of Israel, and
say unto them, When ye be come into
the land of your habitations, which I give
unto you,
3 And will make an offering by fire unto
the LORD, a burnt offering, or a sacrifice in
performing a vow, or in a freewill offering, or in your solemn feasts, to make a
sweet savour unto the LORD, of the herd,
or of the flock:
4 Then shall he that offereth his offering
unto the LORD bring a meat offering of a
tenth deal of flour mingled with the fourth
part of an hin of oil.
5 And the fourth *part* of an hin of wine
for a drink offering shalt thou prepare with
the burnt offering or sacrifice, for one
lamb.
6 Or for a ram, thou shalt prepare *for*
a meat offering two tenth deals of flour
mingled with the third *part* of an hin
of oil.
7 And for a drink offering thou shalt offer the third *part* of an hin of wine, *for* a
sweet savour unto the LORD.
8 And when thou preparest a bullock *for*
a burnt offering, or *for* a sacrifice in performing a vow, or peace offerings unto the
LORD:
9 Then shall he bring with a bullock a
meat offering of three tenth deals of flour
mingled with half an hin of oil.
10 And thou shalt bring for a drink offering half an hin of wine, *for* an offering
made by fire, of a sweet savour unto the
LORD.
11 Thus shall it be done for one bullock,
or for one ram, or for a lamb, or a kid.
12 According to the number that ye shall
prepare, so shall ye do to every one according to their number.
13 All that are born of the country shall
do these things after this manner, in offering an offering made by fire, of a sweet
savour unto the LORD.
14 And if a stranger sojourn with you, or
whosoever *be* among you in your generations, and will offer an offering made by
fire, of a sweet savour unto the LORD; as ye
do, so he shall do.
15 One ordinance *shall be both* for you of
the congregation, and also for the stranger that sojourneth *with you*, an ordinance
for ever in your generations: as ye *are*, so
shall the stranger be before the LORD.
16 One law and one manner shall be for

you, and for the stranger that sojourneth with you.

17 And the LORD spake unto Moses, saying,

18 Speak unto the children of Israel, and say unto them, When ye come into the land whither I bring you,

19 Then it shall be, that, when ye eat of the bread of the land, ye shall offer up an heave offering unto the LORD.

20 Ye shall offer up a cake of the first of your dough *for* an heave offering: as *ye do* the heave offering of the threshingfloor, so shall ye heave it.

21 Of the first of your dough ye shall give unto the LORD an heave offering in your generations.

22 And if ye have erred, and not observed all these commandments, which the LORD hath spoken unto Moses,

23 *Even* all that the LORD hath commanded you by the hand of Moses, from the day that the LORD commanded *Moses,* and henceforward among your generations;

24 Then it shall be, if *ought* be committed by ignorance without the knowledge of the congregation, that all the congregation shall offer one young bullock for a burnt offering, for a sweet savour unto the LORD, with his meat offering, and his drink offering, according to the manner, and one kid of the goats for a sin offering.

25 And the priest shall make an atonement for all the congregation of the children of Israel, and it shall be forgiven them; for it is ignorance: and they shall bring their offering, a sacrifice made by fire unto the LORD, and their sin offering before the LORD, for their ignorance:

26 And it shall be forgiven all the congregation of the children of Israel, and the stranger that sojourneth among them; seeing all the people *were* in ignorance.

27 And if any soul sin through ignorance, then he shall bring a she goat of the first year for a sin offering.

28 And the priest shall make an atonement for the soul that sinneth ignorantly, when he sinneth by ignorance before the LORD, to make an atonement for him; and it shall be forgiven him.

29 Ye shall have one law for him that sinneth through ignorance, *both for* him that is born among the children of Israel, and for the stranger that sojourneth among them.

30 But the soul that doeth *ought* presumptuously, *whether he be* born in the land, or a stranger, the same reproacheth the LORD; and that soul shall be cut off from among his people.

31 Because he hath despised the word of the LORD, and hath broken his commandment, that soul shall utterly be cut off; his iniquity *shall be* upon him.

32 And while the children of Israel were in the wilderness, they found a man that gathered sticks upon the sabbath day.

33 And they that found him gathering sticks brought him unto Moses and Aaron, and unto all the congregation.

34 And they put him in ward, because it was not declared what should be done to him.

35 And the LORD said unto Moses, The man shall be surely put to death: all the congregation shall stone him with stones without the camp.

36 And all the congregation brought him without the camp, and stoned him with stones, and he died; as the LORD commanded Moses.

37 And the LORD spake unto Moses, saying,

38 Speak unto the children of Israel, and bid them that they make them fringes in the borders of their garments throughout their generations, and that they put upon the fringe of the borders a ribband of blue:

39 And it shall be unto you for a fringe, that ye may look upon it, and remember all the commandments of the LORD, and do them; and that ye seek not after your own heart and your own eyes, after which ye use to go a whoring:

40 That ye may remember, and do all my commandments, and be holy unto your God.

41 I *am* the LORD your God, which brought you out of the land of Egypt, to be your God: I *am* the LORD your God.

16

1 Now Korah, the son of Izhar, the son of Kohath, the son of Levi, and Dathan and Abiram, the sons of Eliab, and On, the son of Peleth, sons of Reuben, took *men:*

2 And they rose up before Moses, with certain of the children of Israel, two hundred and fifty princes of the assembly, famous in the congregation, men of renown:

3 And they gathered themselves together against Moses and against Aaron, and
said unto them, *Ye take* too much upon
you, seeing all the congregation *are* holy,
every one of them, and the LORD *is* among
them: wherefore then lift ye up yourselves
above the congregation of the LORD?
4 And when Moses heard *it*, he fell upon
his face:
5 And he spake unto Korah and unto all
his company, saying, Even to morrow the
LORD will shew who *are* his, and *who is*
holy; and will cause *him* to come near unto
him: even *him* whom he hath chosen will
he cause to come near unto him.
6 This do; Take you censers, Korah, and
all his company;
7 And put fire therein, and put incense
in them before the LORD to morrow: and
it shall be *that* the man whom the LORD
doth choose, he *shall be* holy: *ye take* too
much upon you, ye sons of Levi.
8 And Moses said unto Korah, Hear, I
pray you, ye sons of Levi:
9 *Seemeth it but* a small thing unto you,
that the God of Israel hath separated you
from the congregation of Israel, to bring
you near to himself to do the service of
the tabernacle of the LORD, and to stand
before the congregation to minister unto
them?
10 And he hath brought thee near *to him*,
and all thy brethren the sons of Levi with
thee: and seek ye the priesthood also?
11 For which cause *both* thou and all thy
company *are* gathered together against the
LORD: and what *is* Aaron, that ye murmur
against him?
12 And Moses sent to call Dathan and
Abiram, the sons of Eliab: which said, We
will not come up:
13 *Is it* a small
thing that thou hast
brought us up out
of a land that
floweth with milk
and honey, to kill
us in the wilderness, except thou make
thyself altogether a prince over us?

16:13 Unthankfulness to People
◄ Genesis 40:23
Judges 8:35 ►

14 Moreover thou hast not brought us
into a land that floweth with milk and
honey, or given us inheritance of fields and
vineyards: wilt thou put out the eyes of
these men? we will not come up.
15 And Moses was very wroth, and said
unto the LORD, Re-
spect not thou their
offering: I have not
taken one ass from
them, neither have
I hurt one of them.

16:15 Anger
◄ Leviticus 10:16
Judges 14:19 ►

16 And Moses said unto Korah, Be thou
and all thy company before the LORD,
thou, and they, and Aaron, to morrow:
17 And take every man his censer, and put
incense in them, and bring ye before the
LORD every man his censer, two hundred
and fifty censers; thou also, and Aaron,
each *of you* his censer.
18 And they took every man his censer,
and put fire in them, and laid incense
thereon, and stood in the door of the tabernacle of the congregation with Moses
and Aaron.
19 And Korah gathered all the congregation against them unto the door of the tabernacle of the congregation: and the glory
of the LORD appeared unto all the congregation.
20 And the LORD spake unto Moses and
unto Aaron, saying,
21 Separate yourselves from among this
congregation, that I may consume them
in a moment.
22 And they fell upon their faces, and
said, O God, the God of the spirits of all
flesh, shall one man sin, and wilt thou be
wroth with all the congregation?
23 And the LORD spake unto Moses,
saying,
24 Speak unto the congregation, saying,
Get you up from about the tabernacle of
Korah, Dathan, and Abiram.
25 And Moses rose up and went unto
Dathan and Abiram; and the elders of Israel followed him.
26 And he spake unto the congregation,
saying, Depart, I pray you, from the tents of
these wicked men, and touch nothing of
theirs, lest ye be consumed in all their sins.
27 So they gat up from the tabernacle of
Korah, Dathan, and Abiram, on every side:
and Dathan and Abiram came out, and
stood in the door of their tents, and their
wives, and their sons, and their little children.
28 And Moses said, Hereby ye shall know
that the LORD hath sent me to do all these
works; for *I have* not *done them* of mine
own mind.

29 If these men die the common death of all men, or if they be visited after the visitation of all men; *then* the LORD hath not sent me.

30 But if the LORD make a new thing, and the earth open her mouth, and swallow them up, with all that *appertain* unto them, and they go down quick into the pit; then ye shall understand that these men have provoked the LORD.

16:30 Losers
◄ Numbers 14:23
Deuteronomy 9:7 ►

31 And it came to pass, as he had made an end of speaking all these words, that the ground clave asunder that *was* under them:

32 And the earth opened her mouth, and swallowed them up, and their houses, and all the men that *appertained* unto Korah, and all *their* goods.

33 They, and all that *appertained* to them, went down alive into the pit, and the earth closed upon them: and they perished from among the congregation.

34 And all Israel that *were* round about them fled at the cry of them: for they said, Lest the earth swallow us up *also*.

35 And there came out a fire from the LORD, and consumed the two hundred and fifty men that offered incense.

36 And the LORD spake unto Moses, saying,

37 Speak unto Eleazar the son of Aaron the priest, that he take up the censers out of the burning, and scatter thou the fire yonder; for they are hallowed.

38 The censers of these sinners against their own souls, let them make them broad plates *for* a covering of the altar: for they offered them before the LORD, therefore they are hallowed: and they shall be a sign unto the children of Israel.

39 And Eleazar the priest took the brasen censers, wherewith they that were burnt had offered; and they were made broad *plates for* a covering of the altar:

40 *To be* a memorial unto the children of Israel, that no stranger, which is not of the seed of Aaron, come near to offer incense before the LORD; that he be not as Korah, and as his company: as the LORD said to him by the hand of Moses.

41 But on the morrow all the congregation of the children of Israel murmured against Moses and against Aaron, saying, Ye have killed the people of the LORD.

42 And it came to pass, when the congregation was gathered against Moses and against Aaron, that they looked toward the tabernacle of the congregation: and, behold, the cloud covered it, and the glory of the LORD appeared.

43 And Moses and Aaron came before the tabernacle of the congregation.

44 And the LORD spake unto Moses, saying,

45 Get you up from among this congregation, that I may consume them as in a moment. And they fell upon their faces.

46 And Moses said unto Aaron, Take a censer, and put fire therein from off the altar, and put on incense, and go quickly unto the congregation, and make an atonement for them: for there is wrath gone out from the LORD; the plague is begun.

47 And Aaron took as Moses commanded, and ran into the midst of the congregation; and, behold, the plague was begun among the people: and he put on incense, and made an atonement for the people.

48 And he stood between the dead and the living; and the plague was stayed.

49 Now they that died in the plague were fourteen thousand and seven hundred, beside them that died about the matter of Korah.

50 And Aaron returned unto Moses unto the door of the tabernacle of the congregation: and the plague was stayed.

17

1 And the LORD spake unto Moses, saying,

2 Speak unto the children of Israel, and take of every one of them a rod according to the house of *their* fathers, of all their princes according to the house of their fathers twelve rods: write thou every man's name upon his rod.

3 And thou shalt write Aaron's name upon the rod of Levi: for one rod *shall be* for the head of the house of their fathers.

4 And thou shalt lay them up in the tabernacle of the congregation before the testimony, where I will meet with you.

5 And it shall come to pass, *that* the man's rod, whom I shall choose, shall blossom: and I will make to cease from me the murmurings of the children of Israel, whereby they murmur against you.

6 And Moses spake unto the children of

Israel, and every one of their princes gave him a rod apiece, for each prince one, according to their fathers' houses, *even* twelve rods: and the rod of Aaron *was* among their rods.

7 And Moses laid up the rods before the LORD in the tabernacle of witness.

8 And it came to pass, that on the morrow Moses went into the tabernacle of witness; and, behold, the rod of Aaron for the house of Levi was budded, and brought forth buds, and bloomed blossoms, and yielded almonds.

9 And Moses brought out all the rods from before the LORD unto all the children of Israel: and they looked, and took every man his rod.

10 And the LORD said unto Moses, Bring Aaron's rod again before the testimony, to be kept for a token against the rebels; and thou shalt quite take away their murmurings from me, that they die not.

11 And Moses did *so:* as the LORD commanded him, so did he.

12 And the children of Israel spake unto Moses, saying, Behold, we die, we perish, we all perish.

13 Whosoever cometh any thing near unto the tabernacle of the LORD shall die: shall we be consumed with dying?

18

1 And the LORD said unto Aaron, Thou and thy sons and thy father's house with thee shall bear the iniquity of the sanctuary: and thou and thy sons with thee shall bear the iniquity of your priesthood.

2 And thy brethren also of the tribe of Levi, the tribe of thy father, bring thou with thee, that they may be joined unto thee, and minister unto thee: but thou and thy sons with thee *shall minister* before the tabernacle of witness.

3 And they shall keep thy charge, and the charge of all the tabernacle: only they shall not come nigh the vessels of the sanctuary and the altar, that neither they, nor ye also, die.

4 And they shall be joined unto thee, and keep the charge of the tabernacle of the congregation, for all the service of the tabernacle: and a stranger shall not come nigh unto you.

5 And ye shall keep the charge of the sanctuary, and the charge of the altar: that there be no wrath any more upon the children of Israel.

6 And I, behold, I have taken your brethren the Levites from among the children of Israel: to you *they are* given *as* a gift for the LORD, to do the service of the tabernacle of the congregation.

7 Therefore thou and thy sons with thee shall keep your priest's office for every thing of the altar, and within the vail; and ye shall serve: I have given your priest's office *unto you as* a service of gift: and the stranger that cometh nigh shall be put to death.

8 And the LORD spake unto Aaron, Behold, I also have given thee the charge of mine heave offerings of all the hallowed things of the children of Israel; unto thee have I given them by reason of the anointing, and to thy sons, by an ordinance for ever.

9 This shall be thine of the most holy things, *reserved* from the fire: every oblation of theirs, every meat offering of theirs, and every sin offering of theirs, and every trespass offering of theirs, which they shall render unto me, *shall be* most holy for thee and for thy sons.

10 In the most holy *place* shalt thou eat it; every male shall eat it: it shall be holy unto thee.

11 And this *is* thine; the heave offering of their gift, with all the wave offerings of the children of Israel: I have given them unto thee, and to thy sons and to thy daughters with thee, by a statute for ever: every one that is clean in thy house shall eat of it.

12 All the best of the oil, and all the best of the wine, and of the wheat, the firstfruits of them which they shall offer unto the LORD, them have I given thee.

13 *And* whatsoever is first ripe in the land, which they shall bring unto the LORD, shall be thine; every one that is clean in thine house shall eat *of* it.

14 Every thing devoted in Israel shall be thine.

15 Every thing that openeth the matrix in all flesh, which they bring unto the LORD, *whether it be* of men or beasts, shall be thine: nevertheless the firstborn of man shalt thou surely redeem, and the firstling of unclean beasts shalt thou redeem.

16 And those that are to be redeemed from a month old shalt thou redeem, according to thine estimation, for the money

of five shekels, after the shekel of the sanctuary, which *is* twenty gerahs.

17 But the firstling of a cow, or the firstling of a sheep, or the firstling of a goat, thou shalt not redeem; they *are* holy: thou shalt sprinkle their blood upon the altar, and shalt burn their fat *for* an offering made by fire, for a sweet savour unto the LORD.

18 And the flesh of them shall be thine, as the wave breast and as the right shoulder are thine.

19 All the heave offerings of the holy things, which the children of Israel offer unto the LORD, have I given thee, and thy sons and thy daughters with thee, by a statute for ever: it *is* a covenant of salt for ever before the LORD unto thee and to thy seed with thee.

20 And the LORD spake unto Aaron, Thou shalt have no inheritance in their land, neither shalt thou have any part among them: I *am* thy part and thine inheritance among the children of Israel.

21 And, behold, I have given the children of Levi all the tenth in Israel for an inheritance, for their service which they serve, *even* the service of the tabernacle of the congregation.

22 Neither must the children of Israel henceforth come nigh the tabernacle of the congregation, lest they bear sin, and die.

23 But the Levites shall do the service of the tabernacle of the congregation, and they shall bear their iniquity: *it shall be* a statute for ever throughout your generations, that among the children of Israel they have no inheritance.

24 But the tithes of the children of Israel, which they offer *as* an heave offering unto the LORD, I have given to the Levites to inherit: therefore I have said unto them, Among the children of Israel they shall have no inheritance.

25 And the LORD spake unto Moses, saying,

26 Thus speak unto the Levites, and say unto them, When ye take of the children of Israel the tithes which I have given you from them for your inheritance, then ye shall offer up an heave offering of it for the LORD, *even* a tenth *part* of the tithe.

27 And *this* your heave offering shall be reckoned unto you, as though *it were* the corn of the threshingfloor, and as the fulness of the winepress.

28 Thus ye also shall offer an heave offering unto the LORD of all your tithes, which ye receive of the children of Israel; and ye shall give thereof the LORD'S heave offering to Aaron the priest.

29 Out of all your gifts ye shall offer every heave offering of the LORD, of all the best thereof, *even* the hallowed part thereof out of it.

30 Therefore thou shalt say unto them, When ye have heaved the best thereof from it, then it shall be counted unto the Levites as the increase of the threshingfloor, and as the increase of the winepress.

31 And ye shall eat it in every place, ye and your households: for it *is* your reward for your service in the tabernacle of the congregation.

32 And ye shall bear no sin by reason of it, when ye have heaved from it the best of it: neither shall ye pollute the holy things of the children of Israel, lest ye die.

19

1 And the LORD spake unto Moses and unto Aaron, saying,

2 This *is* the ordinance of the law which the LORD hath commanded, saying, Speak unto the children of Israel, that they bring thee a red heifer without spot, wherein *is* no blemish, *and* upon which never came yoke:

3 And ye shall give her unto Eleazar the priest, that he may bring her forth without the camp, and *one* shall slay her before his face:

4 And Eleazar the priest shall take of her blood with his finger, and sprinkle of her blood directly before the tabernacle of the congregation seven times:

5 And *one* shall burn the heifer in his sight; her skin, and her flesh, and her blood, with her dung, shall he burn:

6 And the priest shall take cedar wood, and hyssop, and scarlet, and cast *it* into the midst of the burning of the heifer.

7 Then the priest shall wash his clothes, and he shall bathe his flesh in water, and afterward he shall come into the camp, and the priest shall be unclean until the even.

8 And he that burneth her shall wash his clothes in water, and bathe his flesh in water, and shall be unclean until the even.

9 And a man *that is* clean shall gather up the ashes of the heifer, and lay *them* up without the camp in a clean place, and it

shall be kept for the congregation of the children of Israel for a water of separation: it *is* a purification for sin.

10 And he that gathereth the ashes of the heifer shall wash his clothes, and be unclean until the even: and it shall be unto the children of Israel, and unto the stranger that sojourneth among them, for a statute for ever.

11 He that toucheth the dead body of any man shall be unclean seven days.

12 He shall purify himself with it on the third day, and on the seventh day he shall be clean: but if he purify not himself the third day, then the seventh day he shall not be clean.

13 Whosoever toucheth the dead body of any man that is dead, and purifieth not himself, defileth the tabernacle of the LORD; and that soul shall be cut off from Israel: because the water of separation was not sprinkled upon him, he shall be unclean; his uncleanness *is* yet upon him.

14 This *is* the law, when a man dieth in a tent: all that come into the tent, and all that *is* in the tent, shall be unclean seven days.

15 And every open vessel, which hath no covering bound upon it, *is* unclean.

16 And whosoever toucheth one that is slain with a sword in the open fields, or a dead body, or a bone of a man, or a grave, shall be unclean seven days.

17 And for an unclean *person* they shall take of the ashes of the burnt heifer of purification for sin, and running water shall be put thereto in a vessel:

18 And a clean person shall take hyssop, and dip *it* in the water, and sprinkle *it* upon the tent, and upon all the vessels, and upon the persons that were there, and upon him that touched a bone, or one slain, or one dead, or a grave:

19 And the clean *person* shall sprinkle upon the unclean on the third day, and on the seventh day: and on the seventh day he shall purify himself, and wash his clothes, and bathe himself in water, and shall be clean at even.

20 But the man that shall be unclean, and shall not purify himself, that soul shall be cut off from among the congregation, because he hath defiled the sanctuary of the LORD: the water of separation hath not been sprinkled upon him; he *is* unclean.

21 And it shall be a perpetual statute unto them, that he that sprinkleth the water of separation shall wash his clothes; and he that toucheth the water of separation shall be unclean until even.

22 And whatsoever the unclean *person* toucheth shall be unclean; and the soul that toucheth *it* shall be unclean until even.

20

1 Then came the children of Israel, *even* the whole congregation, into the desert of Zin in the first month: and the people abode in Kadesh; and Miriam died there, and was buried there.

2 And there was no water for the congregation: and they gathered themselves together against Moses and against Aaron.

3 And the people chode with Moses, and spake, saying, Would God that we had died when our brethren died before the LORD!

4 And why have ye brought up the congregation of the LORD into this wilderness, that we and our cattle should die there?

5 And wherefore have ye made us to come up out of Egypt, to bring us in unto this evil place? it *is* no place of seed, or of figs, or of vines, or of pomegranates; neither *is* there any water to drink.

6 And Moses and Aaron went from the presence of the assembly unto the door of the tabernacle of the congregation, and they fell upon their faces: and the glory of the LORD appeared unto them.

7 And the LORD spake unto Moses, saying,

8 Take the rod, and gather thou the assembly together, thou, and Aaron thy brother, and speak ye unto the rock before their eyes; and it shall give forth his water, and thou shalt bring forth to them water out of the rock: so thou shalt give the congregation and their beasts drink.

9 And Moses took the rod from before the LORD, as he commanded him.

10 And Moses and Aaron gathered the congregation together before the rock, and he said unto them, Hear now, ye rebels; must we fetch you water out of this rock?

20:10
Impatience
◄ 2 Kings 5:11-12 ►

11 And Moses lifted up his hand, and with his rod he smote the rock twice: and the water came out abundantly, and the congregation drank, and their beasts *also*.

12 And the LORD spake unto Moses and Aaron, Because ye believed me not, to sanctify me in the eyes of the children of Israel, therefore ye shall not bring this congregation into the land which I have given them.

20:12 Only Human
◄ Genesis 20:2
1 Kings 3:3 ►

13 This *is* the water of Meribah; because the children of Israel strove with the LORD, and he was sanctified in them.

14 And Moses sent messengers from Kadesh unto the king of Edom, Thus saith thy brother Israel, Thou knowest all the travail that hath befallen us:

15 How our fathers went down into Egypt, and we have dwelt in Egypt a long time; and the Egyptians vexed us, and our fathers:

16 And when we cried unto the LORD, he heard our voice, and sent an angel, and hath brought us forth out of Egypt: and, behold, we *are* in Kadesh, a city in the uttermost of thy border:

17 Let us pass, I pray thee, through thy country: we will not pass through the fields, or through the vineyards, neither will we drink *of* the water of the wells: we will go by the king's *high* way, we will not turn to the right hand nor to the left, until we have passed thy borders.

18 And Edom said unto him, Thou shalt not pass by me, lest I come out against thee with the sword.

20:18 Cold Shoulder
◄ Numbers 21:23 ►

19 And the children of Israel said unto him, We will go by the high way: and if I and my cattle drink of thy water, then I will pay for it: I will only, without *doing* any thing *else,* go through on my feet.

20 And he said, Thou shalt not go through. And Edom came out against him with much people, and with a strong hand.

21 Thus Edom refused to give Israel passage through his border: wherefore Israel turned away from him.

22 And the children of Israel, *even* the whole congregation, journeyed from Kadesh, and came unto mount Hor.

23 And the LORD spake unto Moses and Aaron in mount Hor, by the coast of the land of Edom, saying,

24 Aaron shall be gathered unto his people: for he shall not enter into the land which I have given unto the children of Israel, because ye rebelled against my word at the water of Meribah.

25 Take Aaron and Eleazar his son, and bring them up unto mount Hor:

26 And strip Aaron of his garments, and put them upon Eleazar his son: and Aaron shall be gathered *unto his people,* and shall die there.

27 And Moses did as the LORD commanded: and they went up into mount Hor in the sight of all the congregation.

28 And Moses stripped Aaron of his garments, and put them upon Eleazar his son; and Aaron died there in the top of the mount: and Moses and Eleazar came down from the mount.

29 And when all the congregation saw that Aaron was dead, they mourned for Aaron thirty days, *even* all the house of Israel.

21

1 And *when* king Arad the Canaanite, which dwelt in the south, heard tell that Israel came by the way of the spies; then he fought against Israel, and took *some* of them prisoners.

2 And Israel vowed a vow unto the LORD, and said, If thou wilt indeed deliver this people into my hand, then I will utterly destroy their cities.

3 And the LORD hearkened to the voice of Israel, and delivered up the Canaanites; and they utterly destroyed them and their cities: and he called the name of the place Hormah.

4 And they journeyed from mount Hor by the way of the Red sea, to compass the land of Edom: and the soul of the people was much discouraged because of the way.

5 And the people spake against God, and against Moses, Wherefore have ye brought us up out of Egypt to die in the wilderness? for *there is* no bread, neither *is there any* water; and our soul loatheth this light bread.

6 And the LORD sent fiery serpents among the people, and they bit the people; and much people of Israel died.

7 Therefore the people came to Moses, and said, We have sinned, for

21:7 Feeling Guilty
◄ Exodus 9:27
Ezra 9:6 ►

we have spoken against the LORD, and against thee; pray unto the LORD, that he take away the serpents from us. And Moses prayed for the people.

8 And the LORD said unto Moses, Make thee a fiery serpent, and set it upon a pole: and it shall come to pass, that every one that is bitten, when he looketh upon it, shall live.

9 And Moses made a serpent of brass, and put it upon a pole, and it came to pass, that if a serpent had bitten any man, when he beheld the serpent of brass, he lived.

10 And the children of Israel set forward, and pitched in Oboth.

11 And they journeyed from Oboth, and pitched at Ije-abarim, in the wilderness which *is* before Moab, toward the sunrising.

12 From thence they removed, and pitched in the valley of Zared.

13 From thence they removed, and pitched on the other side of Arnon, which *is* in the wilderness that cometh out of the coasts of the Amorites: for Arnon *is* the border of Moab, between Moab and the Amorites.

14 Wherefore it is said in the book of the wars of the LORD, What he did in the Red sea, and in the brooks of Arnon,

15 And at the stream of the brooks that goeth down to the dwelling of Ar, and lieth upon the border of Moab.

16 And from thence *they went* to Beer: that *is* the well whereof the LORD spake unto Moses, Gather the people together, and I will give them water.

17 Then Israel sang this song, Spring up, O well; sing ye unto it:

18 The princes digged the well, the nobles of the people digged it, by *the direction of* the lawgiver, with their staves. And from the wilderness *they went* to Mattanah:

19 And from Mattanah to Nahaliel: and from Nahaliel to Bamoth:

20 And from Bamoth *in* the valley, that *is* in the country of Moab, to the top of Pisgah, which looketh toward Jeshimon.

21 And Israel sent messengers unto Sihon king of the Amorites, saying,

22 Let me pass through thy land: we will not turn into the fields, or into the vineyards; we will not drink *of* the waters of the well: *but* we will go along by the king's *high* way, until we be past thy borders.

23 And Sihon would not suffer Israel to pass through his border: but Sihon gathered all his people together, and went out against Israel into the wilderness: and he came to Jahaz, and fought against Israel.

21:23 Cold Shoulder
◄ Numbers 20:18
Deuteronomy 23:4 ►

24 And Israel smote him with the edge of the sword, and possessed his land from Arnon unto Jabbok, even unto the children of Ammon: for the border of the children of Ammon *was* strong.

25 And Israel took all these cities: and Israel dwelt in all the cities of the Amorites, in Heshbon, and in all the villages thereof.

26 For Heshbon *was* the city of Sihon the king of the Amorites, who had fought against the former king of Moab, and taken all his land out of his hand, even unto Arnon.

27 Wherefore they that speak in proverbs say, Come into Heshbon, let the city of Sihon be built and prepared:

28 For there is a fire gone out of Heshbon, a flame from the city of Sihon: it hath consumed Ar of Moab, *and* the lords of the high places of Arnon.

29 Woe to thee, Moab! thou art undone, O people of Chemosh: he hath given his sons that escaped, and his daughters, into captivity unto Sihon king of the Amorites.

30 We have shot at them; Heshbon is perished even unto Dibon, and we have laid them waste even unto Nophah, which *reacheth* unto Medeba.

31 Thus Israel dwelt in the land of the Amorites.

32 And Moses sent to spy out Jaazer, and they took the villages thereof, and drove out the Amorites that *were* there.

33 And they turned and went up by the way of Bashan: and Og the king of Bashan went out against them, he, and all his people, to the battle at Edrei.

34 And the LORD said unto Moses, Fear him not: for I have delivered him into thy hand, and all his people, and his land; and thou shalt do to him as thou didst unto Sihon king of the Amorites, which dwelt at Heshbon.

35 So they smote him, and his sons, and

all his people, until there was none left
him alive: and they possessed his land.

22

1And the children of Israel set forward,
and pitched in the plains of Moab on this
side Jordan *by* Jericho.

2And Balak the son of Zippor saw all
that Israel had done to the Amorites.

3And Moab was sore afraid of the people, because they *were* many: and Moab
was distressed because of the children of
Israel.

4And Moab said unto the elders of Midian, Now shall this company lick up all
that are round about us, as the ox licketh
up the grass of the field. And Balak the son
of Zippor *was* king of the Moabites at that
time.

5He sent messengers therefore unto Balaam the son of Beor to Pethor, which *is*
by the river of the land of the children of
his people, to call him, saying, Behold,
there is a people come out from Egypt:
behold, they cover the face of the earth,
and they abide over against me:

6Come now therefore, I pray thee, curse
me this people; for they *are* too mighty for
me: peradventure I shall prevail, *that* we
may smite them, and *that* I may drive them
out of the land: for I wot that he whom
thou blessest *is* blessed, and he whom thou
cursest is cursed.

7And the elders of Moab and the elders
of Midian departed with the rewards of
divination in their hand; and they came
unto Balaam, and spake unto him the
words of Balak.

8And he said unto them, Lodge here this
night, and I will bring you word again, as
the LORD shall speak unto me: and the
princes of Moab abode with Balaam.

9And God came unto Balaam, and said,
What men *are* these with thee?

10And Balaam said unto God, Balak the
son of Zippor, king of Moab, hath sent
unto me, *saying,*

11Behold, *there is* a people come out of
Egypt, which covereth the face of the earth:
come now, curse me them; peradventure I
shall be able to overcome them, and drive
them out.

12And God said unto Balaam, Thou
shalt not go with them; thou shalt not
curse the people: for they *are* blessed.

13And Balaam rose up in the morning,
and said unto the princes of Balak, Get you
into your land: for the LORD refuseth to
give me leave to go with you.

14And the princes of Moab rose up, and
they went unto Balak, and said, Balaam
refuseth to come with us.

15And Balak sent yet again princes,
more, and more honourable than they.

16And they came to Balaam, and said to
him, Thus saith Balak the son of Zippor,
Let nothing, I pray thee, hinder thee from
coming unto me:

17For I will promote thee unto very great
honour, and I will do whatsoever thou
sayest unto me: come therefore, I pray thee,
curse me this people.

18And Balaam answered and said unto
the servants of Balak, If Balak would give
me his house full of silver and gold, I cannot go beyond the word of the LORD my
God, to do less or more.

19Now therefore, I pray you, tarry ye also
here this night, that I may know what the
LORD will say unto me more.

20And God came unto Balaam at night,
and said unto him, If the men come to
call thee, rise up, *and* go with them; but
yet the word which I shall say unto thee,
that shalt thou do.

21And Balaam rose up in the morning,
and saddled his ass, and went with the
princes of Moab.

22And God's anger was kindled because
he went: and the angel of the LORD stood
in the way for an adversary against him.
Now he was riding upon his ass, and his
two servants *were* with him.

23And the ass saw the angel of the LORD
standing in the way, and his sword drawn
in his hand: and the ass turned aside out
of the way, and went into the field: and
Balaam smote the ass, to turn her into the
way.

24But the angel of the LORD stood in a
path of the vineyards, a wall *being* on this
side, and a wall on that side.

25And when the ass saw the angel of the
LORD, she thrust herself unto the wall, and
crushed Balaam's foot against the wall: and
he smote her again.

26And the angel of the LORD went further, and stood in a narrow place, where
was no way to turn either to the right hand
or to the left.

27And when the ass saw the angel of the
LORD, she fell down under Balaam: and

Balaam's anger was
kindled, and he
smote the ass with
a staff.
28And the LORD
opened the mouth
of the ass, and she said unto Balaam, What
have I done unto thee, that thou hast smitten me these three times?
29And Balaam said unto the ass, Because
thou hast mocked me: I would there were
a sword in mine hand, for now would I
kill thee.
30And the ass said unto Balaam, *Am* not
I thine ass, upon which thou hast ridden
ever since *I was* thine unto this day? was
I ever wont to do so unto thee? And he
said, Nay.
31Then the LORD opened the eyes of Balaam, and he saw the angel of the LORD
standing in the way, and his sword drawn
in his hand: and he bowed down his head,
and fell flat on his face.
32And the angel of the LORD said unto
him, Wherefore hast thou smitten thine
ass these three times? behold, I went out
to withstand thee, because *thy* way is perverse before me:
33And the ass saw me, and turned from
me these three times: unless she had
turned from me, surely now also I had
slain thee, and saved her alive.
34And Balaam said unto the angel of the
LORD, I have sinned; for I knew not that
thou stoodest in the way against me: now
therefore, if it displease thee, I will get me
back again.
35And the angel of the LORD said unto
Balaam, Go with the men: but only the
word that I shall speak unto thee, that thou
shalt speak. So Balaam went with the
princes of Balak.
36And when Balak heard that Balaam
was come, he went out to meet him unto
a city of Moab, which *is* in the border of
Arnon, which *is* in the utmost coast.
37And Balak said unto Balaam, Did I not
earnestly send unto thee to call thee?
wherefore camest thou not unto me? am
I not able indeed to promote thee to
honour?
38And Balaam said unto Balak, Lo, I am
come unto thee: have I now any power at
all to say any thing? the word that God
putteth in my mouth, that shall I speak.

22:27
Cruelty to Animals
◄ 2 Samuel 8:4 ►

39And Balaam went with Balak, and they
came unto Kirjath-huzoth.
40And Balak offered oxen and sheep,
and sent to Balaam, and to the princes that
were with him.
41And it came to pass on the morrow,
that Balak took Balaam, and brought him
up into the high places of Baal, that thence
he might see the utmost *part* of the people.

23

1And Balaam said unto Balak, Build me
here seven altars, and prepare me here
seven oxen and seven rams.
2And Balak did as Balaam had spoken;
and Balak and Balaam offered on *every* altar a bullock and a ram.
3And Balaam said unto Balak, Stand by
thy burnt offering, and I will go: peradventure the LORD will come to meet me:
and whatsoever he sheweth me I will tell
thee. And he went to an high place.
4And God met Balaam: and he said unto
him, I have prepared seven altars, and I
have offered upon *every* altar a bullock and
a ram.
5And the LORD put a word in Balaam's
mouth, and said, Return unto Balak, and
thus thou shalt speak.
6And he returned unto him, and, lo, he
stood by his burnt sacrifice, he, and all the
princes of Moab.
7And he took up his parable, and said,
Balak the king of Moab hath brought me
from Aram, out of the mountains of the
east, *saying,* Come, curse me Jacob, and
come, defy Israel.
8How shall I curse, whom God hath not
cursed? or how shall I defy, *whom* the LORD
hath not defied?
9For from the top of the rocks I see him,
and from the hills I behold him: lo, the
people shall dwell alone, and shall not be
reckoned among the nations.
10Who can count the dust of Jacob, and
the number of the fourth *part* of Israel? Let
me die the death of the righteous, and let
my last end be like his!
11And Balak said unto Balaam, What
hast thou done unto me? I took thee to
curse mine enemies, and, behold, thou
hast blessed *them* altogether.
12And he answered and said, Must I not
take heed to speak that which the LORD
hath put in my mouth?
13And Balak said unto him, Come, I pray
thee, with me unto another place, from

whence thou mayest see them: thou shalt see but the utmost part of them, and shalt not see them all: and curse me them from thence.

14 And he brought him into the field of Zophim, to the top of Pisgah, and built seven altars, and offered a bullock and a ram on *every* altar.

15 And he said unto Balak, Stand here by thy burnt offering, while I meet *the LORD* yonder.

16 And the LORD met Balaam, and put a word in his mouth, and said, Go again unto Balak, and say thus.

17 And when he came to him, behold, he stood by his burnt offering, and the princes of Moab with him. And Balak said unto him, What hath the LORD spoken?

18 And he took up his parable, and said, Rise up, Balak, and hear; hearken unto me, thou son of Zippor:

19 God *is* not a man, that he should lie; neither the son of man, that he should repent: hath he said, and shall he not do *it*? or hath he spoken, and shall he not make it good?

20 Behold, I have received *commandment* to bless: and he hath blessed; and I cannot reverse it.

21 He hath not beheld iniquity in Jacob, neither hath he seen perverseness in Israel: the LORD his God *is* with him, and the shout of a king *is* among them.

22 God brought them out of Egypt; he hath as it were the strength of an unicorn.

23 Surely *there is* no enchantment against Jacob, neither *is there* any divination against Israel: according to this time it shall be said of Jacob and of Israel, What hath God wrought!

24 Behold, the people shall rise up as a great lion, and lift up himself as a young lion: he shall not lie down until he eat *of* the prey, and drink the blood of the slain.

25 And Balak said unto Balaam, Neither curse them at all, nor bless them at all.

26 But Balaam answered and said unto Balak, Told not I thee, saying, All that the LORD speaketh, that I must do?

27 And Balak said unto Balaam, Come, I pray thee, I will bring thee unto another place; peradventure it will please God that thou mayest curse me them from thence.

28 And Balak brought Balaam unto the top of Peor, that looketh toward Jeshimon.

29 And Balaam said unto Balak, Build me here seven altars, and prepare me here seven bullocks and seven rams.

30 And Balak did as Balaam had said, and offered a bullock and a ram on *every* altar.

24

1 And when Balaam saw that it pleased the LORD to bless Israel, he went not, as at other times, to seek for enchantments, but he set his face toward the wilderness.

2 And Balaam lifted up his eyes, and he saw Israel abiding *in his tents* according to their tribes; and the spirit of God came upon him.

3 And he took up his parable, and said, Balaam the son of Beor hath said, and the man whose eyes are open hath said:

4 He hath said, which heard the words of God, which saw the vision of the Almighty, falling *into a trance*, but having his eyes open:

5 How goodly are thy tents, O Jacob, *and* thy tabernacles, O Israel!

6 As the valleys are they spread forth, as gardens by the river's side, as the trees of lign aloes which the LORD hath planted, *and* as cedar trees beside the waters.

7 He shall pour the water out of his buckets, and his seed *shall be* in many waters, and his king shall be higher than Agag, and his kingdom shall be exalted.

8 God brought him forth out of Egypt; he hath as it were the strength of an unicorn: he shall eat up the nations his enemies, and shall break their bones, and pierce *them* through with his arrows.

9 He couched, he lay down as a lion, and as a great lion: who shall stir him up? Blessed *is* he that blesseth thee, and cursed *is* he that curseth thee.

10 And Balak's anger was kindled against Balaam, and he smote his hands together: and Balak said unto Balaam, I called thee to curse mine enemies, and, behold, thou hast altogether blessed *them* these three times.

11 Therefore now flee thou to thy place: I thought to promote thee unto great honour; but, lo, the LORD hath kept thee back from honour.

12 And Balaam said unto Balak, Spake I not also to thy messengers which thou sentest unto me, saying,

13 If Balak would give me his house full of silver and gold, I cannot go beyond the commandment of the LORD, to do *either*

good or bad of mine own mind; *but* what
the LORD saith, that will I speak?
14And now, behold, I go unto my peo-
ple: come *therefore, and* I will advertise thee
what this people shall do to thy people in
the latter days.
15And he took up his parable, and said,
Balaam the son of Beor hath said, and the
man whose eyes are open hath said:
16He hath said, which heard the words
of God, and knew the knowledge of the
most High, *which* saw the vision of the
Almighty, falling *into a trance,* but having
his eyes open:
17I shall see him, but not now: I shall
behold him, but not nigh: there shall come
a Star out of Jacob, and a Sceptre shall rise
out of Israel, and shall smite the corners
of Moab, and destroy all the children of
Sheth.
18And Edom shall be a possession, Seir
also shall be a possession for his enemies;
and Israel shall do valiantly.
19Out of Jacob shall come he that shall
have dominion, and shall destroy him that
remaineth of the city.
20And when he looked on Amalek, he
took up his parable, and said, Amalek *was*
the first of the nations; but his latter end
shall be that he perish for ever.
21And he looked on the Kenites, and
took up his parable, and said, Strong is thy
dwellingplace, and thou puttest thy nest
in a rock.
22Nevertheless the Kenite shall be wasted, until Asshur shall carry thee away captive.
23And he took up his parable, and said,
Alas, who shall live when God doeth this!
24And ships *shall come* from the coast of
Chittim, and shall afflict Asshur, and shall
afflict Eber, and he also shall perish for
ever.
25And Balaam rose up, and went and
returned to his place: and Balak also went
his way.

25

1And Israel abode in Shittim, and the
people began to commit whoredom with
the daughters of Moab.
2And they called the people unto the
sacrifices of their gods: and the people did
eat, and bowed down to their gods.
3And Israel joined himself unto Baal-
peor: and the anger of the LORD was kindled against Israel.
4And the LORD said unto Moses, Take
all the heads of the people, and hang them
up before the LORD against the sun, that
the fierce anger of the LORD may be turned
away from Israel.
5And Moses said unto the judges of Israel, Slay ye every one his men that were
joined unto Baal-peor.
6And, behold, one of the children of Israel came and brought unto his brethren
a Midianitish woman in the sight of Moses, and in the sight of all the congregation of the children of Israel, who *were*
weeping *before* the door of the tabernacle
of the congregation.
7And when Phinehas, the son of Eleazar, the son of Aaron the priest, saw *it,* he
rose up from among the congregation, and
took a javelin in his hand;
8And he went after the man of Israel into
the tent, and thrust both of them through,
the man of Israel, and the woman through
her belly. So the plague was stayed from
the children of Israel.
9And those that died in the plague were
twenty and four thousand.
10And the LORD spake unto Moses,
saying,
11Phinehas, the son of Eleazar, the son
of Aaron the priest, hath turned my wrath
away from the children of Israel, while he
was zealous for my sake among them, that
I consumed not the children of Israel in
my jealousy.
12Wherefore say, Behold, I give unto him
my covenant of peace:
13And he shall have it, and his seed after him, *even* the covenant of an everlasting priesthood; because he was zealous for
his God, and made an atonement for the
children of Israel.
14Now the name of the Israelite that was
slain, *even* that was slain with the Midianitish woman, *was* Zimri, the son of Salu, a
prince of a chief house among the Simeonites.
15And the name of the Midianitish
woman that was slain *was* Cozbi, the
daughter of Zur; he *was* head over a people, *and* of a chief house in Midian.
16And the LORD spake unto Moses,
saying,
17Vex the Midianites, and smite them:
18For they vex you with their wiles,
wherewith they have beguiled you in the

matter of Peor, and in the matter of Cozbi, the daughter of a prince of Midian, their sister, which was slain in the day of the plague for Peor's sake.

26

1 And it came to pass after the plague, that the LORD spake unto Moses and unto Eleazar the son of Aaron the priest, saying,

2 Take the sum of all the congregation of the children of Israel, from twenty years old and upward, throughout their fathers' house, all that are able to go to war in Israel.

3 And Moses and Eleazar the priest spake with them in the plains of Moab by Jordan *near* Jericho, saying,

4 *Take the sum of the people,* from twenty years old and upward; as the LORD commanded Moses and the children of Israel, which went forth out of the land of Egypt.

5 Reuben, the eldest son of Israel: the children of Reuben; Hanoch, *of whom cometh* the family of the Hanochites: of Pallu, the family of the Palluites:

6 Of Hezron, the family of the Hezronites: of Carmi, the family of the Carmites.

7 These *are* the families of the Reubenites: and they that were numbered of them were forty and three thousand and seven hundred and thirty.

8 And the sons of Pallu; Eliab.

9 And the sons of Eliab; Nemuel, and Dathan, and Abiram. This *is that* Dathan and Abiram, *which were* famous in the congregation, who strove against Moses and against Aaron in the company of Korah, when they strove against the LORD:

10 And the earth opened her mouth, and swallowed them up together with Korah, when that company died, what time the fire devoured two hundred and fifty men: and they became a sign.

11 Notwithstanding the children of Korah died not.

12 The sons of Simeon after their families: of Nemuel, the family of the Nemuelites: of Jamin, the family of the Jaminites: of Jachin, the family of the Jachinites:

13 Of Zerah, the family of the Zarhites: of Shaul, the family of the Shaulites.

14 These *are* the families of the Simeonites, twenty and two thousand and two hundred.

15 The children of Gad after their families: of Zephon, the family of the Zephonites: of Haggi, the family of the Haggites: of Shuni, the family of the Shunites:

16 Of Ozni, the family of the Oznites: of Eri, the family of the Erites:

17 Of Arod, the family of the Arodites: of Areli, the family of the Arelites.

18 These *are* the families of the children of Gad according to those that were numbered of them, forty thousand and five hundred.

19 The sons of Judah *were* Er and Onan: and Er and Onan died in the land of Canaan.

20 And the sons of Judah after their families were; of Shelah, the family of the Shelanites: of Pharez, the family of the Pharzites: of Zerah, the family of the Zarhites.

21 And the sons of Pharez were; of Hezron, the family of the Hezronites: of Hamul, the family of the Hamulites.

22 These *are* the families of Judah according to those that were numbered of them, threescore and sixteen thousand and five hundred.

23 *Of* the sons of Issachar after their families: *of* Tola, the family of the Tolaites: of Pua, the family of the Punites:

24 Of Jashub, the family of the Jashubites: of Shimron, the family of the Shimronites.

25 These *are* the families of Issachar according to those that were numbered of them, threescore and four thousand and three hundred.

26 *Of* the sons of Zebulun after their families: of Sered, the family of the Sardites: of Elon, the family of the Elonites: of Jahleel, the family of the Jahleelites.

27 These *are* the families of the Zebulunites according to those that were numbered of them, threescore thousand and five hundred.

28 The sons of Joseph after their families *were* Manasseh and Ephraim.

29 Of the sons of Manasseh: of Machir, the family of the Machirites: and Machir begat Gilead: of Gilead *come* the family of the Gileadites.

30 These *are* the sons of Gilead: *of* Jeezer, the family of the Jeezerites: of Helek, the family of the Helekites:

31 And *of* Asriel, the family of the Asrielites: and *of* Shechem, the family of the Shechemites:

32 And *of* Shemida, the family of the Shemidaites: and *of* Hepher, the family of the Hepherites.

33 And Zelophehad the son of Hepher had no sons, but daughters: and the names of the daughters of Zelophehad *were* Mahlah, and Noah, Hoglah, Milcah, and Tirzah.

34 These *are* the families of Manasseh, and those that were numbered of them, fifty and two thousand and seven hundred.

35 These *are* the sons of Ephraim after their families: of Shuthelah, the family of the Shuthalhites: of Becher, the family of the Bachrites: of Tahan, the family of the Tahanites.

36 And these *are* the sons of Shuthelah: of Eran, the family of the Eranites.

37 These *are* the families of the sons of Ephraim according to those that were numbered of them, thirty and two thousand and five hundred. These *are* the sons of Joseph after their families.

38 The sons of Benjamin after their families: of Bela, the family of the Belaites: of Ashbel, the family of the Ashbelites: of Ahiram, the family of the Ahiramites:

39 Of Shupham, the family of the Shuphamites: of Hupham, the family of the Huphamites.

40 And the sons of Bela were Ard and Naaman: *of Ard,* the family of the Ardites: *and* of Naaman, the family of the Naamites.

41 These *are* the sons of Benjamin after their families: and they that were numbered of them *were* forty and five thousand and six hundred.

42 These *are* the sons of Dan after their families: of Shuham, the family of the Shuhamites. These *are* the families of Dan after their families.

43 All the families of the Shuhamites, according to those that were numbered of them, *were* threescore and four thousand and four hundred.

44 *Of* the children of Asher after their families: of Jimna, the family of the Jimnites: of Jesui, the family of the Jesuites: of Beriah, the family of the Beriites.

45 Of the sons of Beriah: of Heber, the family of the Heberites: of Malchiel, the family of the Malchielites.

46 And the name of the daughter of Asher *was* Sarah.

47 These *are* the families of the sons of Asher according to those that were numbered of them; *who were* fifty and three thousand and four hundred.

48 *Of* the sons of Naphtali after their families: of Jahzeel, the family of the Jahzeelites: of Guni, the family of the Gunites:

49 Of Jezer, the family of the Jezerites: of Shillem, the family of the Shillemites.

50 These *are* the families of Naphtali according to their families: and they that were numbered of them *were* forty and five thousand and four hundred.

51 These *were* the numbered of the children of Israel, six hundred thousand and a thousand seven hundred and thirty.

52 And the LORD spake unto Moses, saying,

53 Unto these the land shall be divided for an inheritance according to the number of names.

54 To many thou shalt give the more inheritance, and to few thou shalt give the less inheritance: to every one shall his inheritance be given according to those that were numbered of him.

55 Notwithstanding the land shall be divided by lot: according to the names of the tribes of their fathers they shall inherit.

56 According to the lot shall the possession thereof be divided between many and few.

57 And these *are* they that were numbered of the Levites after their families: of Gershon, the family of the Gershonites: of Kohath, the family of the Kohathites: of Merari, the family of the Merarites.

58 These *are* the families of the Levites: the family of the Libnites, the family of the Hebronites, the family of the Mahlites, the family of the Mushites, the family of the Korathites. And Kohath begat Amram.

59 And the name of Amram's wife *was* Jochebed, the daughter of Levi, whom *her mother* bare to Levi in Egypt: and she bare unto Amram Aaron and Moses, and Miriam their sister.

60 And unto Aaron was born Nadab, and Abihu, Eleazar, and Ithamar.

61 And Nadab and Abihu died, when they offered strange fire before the LORD.

62 And those that were numbered of them were twenty and three thousand, all males from a month old and upward: for they were not numbered among the chil-

dren of Israel, because there was no inheritance given them among the children of Israel.

63These *are* they that were numbered by Moses and Eleazar the priest, who numbered the children of Israel in the plains of Moab by Jordan *near* Jericho.

64But among these there was not a man of them whom Moses and Aaron the priest numbered, when they numbered the children of Israel in the wilderness of Sinai.

65For the LORD had said of them, They shall surely die in the wilderness. And there was not left a man of them, save Caleb the son of Jephunneh, and Joshua the son of Nun.

27

1Then came the daughters of Zelophehad, the son of Hepher, the son of Gilead, the son of Machir, the son of Manasseh, of the families of Manasseh the son of Joseph: and these *are* the names of his daughters; Mahlah, Noah, and Hoglah, and Milcah, and Tirzah.

2And they stood before Moses, and before Eleazar the priest, and before the princes and all the congregation, *by* the door of the tabernacle of the congregation, saying,

3Our father died in the wilderness, and he was not in the company of them that gathered themselves together against the LORD in the company of Korah; but died in his own sin, and had no sons.

4Why should the name of our father be done away from among his family, because he hath no son? Give unto us *therefore* a possession among the brethren of our father.

5And Moses brought their cause before the LORD.

6And the LORD spake unto Moses, saying,

7The daughters of Zelophehad speak right: thou shalt surely give them a possession of an inheritance among their father's brethren; and thou shalt cause the inheritance of their father to pass unto them.

8And thou shalt speak unto the children of Israel, saying, If a man die, and have no son, then ye shall cause his inheritance to pass unto his daughter.

9And if he have no daughter, then ye shall give his inheritance unto his brethren.

10And if he have no brethren, then ye shall give his inheritance unto his father's brethren.

11And if his father have no brethren, then ye shall give his inheritance unto his kinsman that is next to him of his family, and he shall possess it: and it shall be unto the children of Israel a statute of judgment, as the LORD commanded Moses.

12And the LORD said unto Moses, Get thee up into this mount Abarim, and see the land which I have given unto the children of Israel.

13And when thou hast seen it, thou also shalt be gathered unto thy people, as Aaron thy brother was gathered.

14For ye rebelled against my commandment in the desert of Zin, in the strife of the congregation, to sanctify me at the water before their eyes: that *is* the water of Meribah in Kadesh in the wilderness of Zin.

15And Moses spake unto the LORD, saying,

16Let the LORD, the God of the spirits of all flesh, set a man over the congregation,

17Which may go out before them, and which may go in before them, and which may lead them out, and which may bring them in; that the congregation of the LORD be not as sheep which have no shepherd.

18And the LORD said unto Moses, Take thee Joshua the son of Nun, a man in whom *is* the spirit, and lay thine hand upon him;

19And set him before Eleazar the priest, and before all the congregation; and give him a charge in their sight.

20And thou shalt put *some* of thine honour upon him, that all the congregation of the children of Israel may be obedient.

21And he shall stand before Eleazar the priest, who shall ask *counsel* for him after the judgment of Urim before the LORD: at his word shall they go out, and at his word they shall come in, *both* he, and all the children of Israel with him, even all the congregation.

22And Moses did as the LORD commanded him: and he took Joshua, and set him before Eleazar the priest, and before all the congregation:

23And he laid his hands upon him, and gave him a charge, as the LORD commanded by the hand of Moses.

28

1 And the LORD spake unto Moses, saying,

2 Command the children of Israel, and say unto them, My offering, *and* my bread for my sacrifices made by fire, *for* a sweet savour unto me, shall ye observe to offer unto me in their due season.

3 And thou shalt say unto them, This *is* the offering made by fire which ye shall offer unto the LORD; two lambs of the first year without spot day by day, *for* a continual burnt offering.

4 The one lamb shalt thou offer in the morning, and the other lamb shalt thou offer at even;

5 And a tenth *part* of an ephah of flour for a meat offering, mingled with the fourth *part* of an hin of beaten oil.

6 *It is* a continual burnt offering, which was ordained in mount Sinai for a sweet savour, a sacrifice made by fire unto the LORD.

7 And the drink offering thereof *shall be* the fourth *part* of an hin for the one lamb: in the holy *place* shalt thou cause the strong wine to be poured unto the LORD *for* a drink offering.

8 And the other lamb shalt thou offer at even: as the meat offering of the morning, and as the drink offering thereof, thou shalt offer *it,* a sacrifice made by fire, of a sweet savour unto the LORD.

9 And on the sabbath day two lambs of the first year without spot, and two tenth deals of flour *for* a meat offering, mingled with oil, and the drink offering thereof:

10 *This is* the burnt offering of every sabbath, beside the continual burnt offering, and his drink offering.

11 And in the beginnings of your months ye shall offer a burnt offering unto the LORD; two young bullocks, and one ram, seven lambs of the first year without spot;

12 And three tenth deals of flour *for* a meat offering, mingled with oil, for one bullock; and two tenth deals of flour *for* a meat offering, mingled with oil, for one ram;

13 And a several tenth deal of flour mingled with oil *for* a meat offering unto one lamb; *for* a burnt offering of a sweet savour, a sacrifice made by fire unto the LORD.

14 And their drink offerings shall be half an hin of wine unto a bullock, and the third *part* of an hin unto a ram, and a fourth *part* of an hin unto a lamb: this *is* the burnt offering of every month throughout the months of the year.

15 And one kid of the goats for a sin offering unto the LORD shall be offered, beside the continual burnt offering, and his drink offering.

16 And in the fourteenth day of the first month *is* the passover of the LORD.

17 And in the fifteenth day of this month *is* the feast: seven days shall unleavened bread be eaten.

18 In the first day *shall be* an holy convocation; ye shall do no manner of servile work *therein:*

19 But ye shall offer a sacrifice made by fire *for* a burnt offering unto the LORD; two young bullocks, and one ram, and seven lambs of the first year: they shall be unto you without blemish:

20 And their meat offering *shall be of* flour mingled with oil: three tenth deals shall ye offer for a bullock, and two tenth deals for a ram;

21 A several tenth deal shalt thou offer for every lamb, throughout the seven lambs:

22 And one goat *for* a sin offering, to make an atonement for you.

23 Ye shall offer these beside the burnt offering in the morning, which *is* for a continual burnt offering.

24 After this manner ye shall offer daily, throughout the seven days, the meat of the sacrifice made by fire, of a sweet savour unto the LORD: it shall be offered beside the continual burnt offering, and his drink offering.

25 And on the seventh day ye shall have an holy convocation; ye shall do no servile work.

26 Also in the day of the firstfruits, when ye bring a new meat offering unto the LORD, after your weeks *be out,* ye shall have an holy convocation; ye shall do no servile work:

27 But ye shall offer the burnt offering for a sweet savour unto the LORD; two young bullocks, one ram, seven lambs of the first year;

28 And their meat offering of flour mingled with oil, three tenth deals unto one bullock, two tenth deals unto one ram,

29 A several tenth deal unto one lamb, throughout the seven lambs;

30 *And* one kid of the goats, to make an atonement for you.

31 Ye shall offer *them* beside the continual burnt offering, and his meat offering, (they shall be unto you without blemish) and their drink offerings.

29

1 And in the seventh month, on the first *day* of the month, ye shall have an holy convocation; ye shall do no servile work: it is a day of blowing the trumpets unto you.

2 And ye shall offer a burnt offering for a sweet savour unto the LORD; one young bullock, one ram, *and* seven lambs of the first year without blemish:

3 And their meat offering *shall be of* flour mingled with oil, three tenth deals for a bullock, *and* two tenth deals for a ram,

4 And one tenth deal for one lamb, throughout the seven lambs:

5 And one kid of the goats *for* a sin offering, to make an atonement for you:

6 Beside the burnt offering of the month, and his meat offering, and the daily burnt offering, and his meat offering, and their drink offerings, according unto their manner, for a sweet savour, a sacrifice made by fire unto the LORD.

7 And ye shall have on the tenth *day* of this seventh month an holy convocation; and ye shall afflict your souls: ye shall not do any work *therein:*

8 But ye shall offer a burnt offering unto the LORD *for* a sweet savour; one young bullock, one ram, *and* seven lambs of the first year; they shall be unto you without blemish:

9 And their meat offering *shall be of* flour mingled with oil, three tenth deals to a bullock, *and* two tenth deals to one ram,

10 A several tenth deal for one lamb, throughout the seven lambs:

11 One kid of the goats *for* a sin offering; beside the sin offering of atonement, and the continual burnt offering, and the meat offering of it, and their drink offerings.

12 And on the fifteenth day of the seventh month ye shall have an holy convocation; ye shall do no servile work, and ye shall keep a feast unto the LORD seven days:

13 And ye shall offer a burnt offering, a sacrifice made by fire, of a sweet savour unto the LORD; thirteen young bullocks, two rams, *and* fourteen lambs of the first year; they shall be without blemish:

14 And their meat offering *shall be of* flour mingled with oil, three tenth deals unto every bullock of the thirteen bullocks, two tenth deals to each ram of the two rams,

15 And a several tenth deal to each lamb of the fourteen lambs:

16 And one kid of the goats *for* a sin offering; beside the continual burnt offering, his meat offering, and his drink offering.

17 And on the second day *ye shall offer* twelve young bullocks, two rams, fourteen lambs of the first year without spot:

18 And their meat offering and their drink offerings for the bullocks, for the rams, and for the lambs, *shall be* according to their number, after the manner:

19 And one kid of the goats *for* a sin offering; beside the continual burnt offering, and the meat offering thereof, and their drink offerings.

20 And on the third day eleven bullocks, two rams, fourteen lambs of the first year without blemish;

21 And their meat offering and their drink offerings for the bullocks, for the rams, and for the lambs, *shall be* according to their number, after the manner:

22 And one goat *for* a sin offering; beside the continual burnt offering, and his meat offering, and his drink offering.

23 And on the fourth day ten bullocks, two rams, *and* fourteen lambs of the first year without blemish:

24 Their meat offering and their drink offerings for the bullocks, for the rams, and for the lambs, *shall be* according to their number, after the manner:

25 And one kid of the goats *for* a sin offering; beside the continual burnt offering, his meat offering, and his drink offering.

26 And on the fifth day nine bullocks, two rams, *and* fourteen lambs of the first year without spot:

27 And their meat offering and their drink offerings for the bullocks, for the rams, and for the lambs, *shall be* according to their number, after the manner:

28 And one goat *for* a sin offering; beside the continual burnt offering, and his meat offering, and his drink offering.

29 And on the sixth day eight bullocks, two rams, *and* fourteen lambs of the first year without blemish:

30 And their meat offering and their drink offerings for the bullocks, for the

rams, and for the lambs, *shall be* according to their number, after the manner:
31 And one goat *for* a sin offering; beside
the continual burnt offering, his meat offering, and his drink offering.
32 And on the seventh day seven bullocks, two rams, *and* fourteen lambs of the
first year without blemish:
33 And their meat offering and their
drink offerings for the bullocks, for the
rams, and for the lambs, *shall be* according to their number, after the manner:
34 And one goat *for* a sin offering; beside
the continual burnt offering, his meat offering, and his drink offering.
35 On the eighth day ye shall have a solemn assembly: ye shall do no servile work
therein:
36 But ye shall offer a burnt offering, a
sacrifice made by fire, of a sweet savour
unto the LORD: one bullock, one ram,
seven lambs of the first year without
blemish:
37 Their meat offering and their drink
offerings for the bullock, for the ram, and
for the lambs, *shall be* according to their
number, after the manner:
38 And one goat *for* a sin offering; beside
the continual burnt offering, and his meat
offering, and his drink offering.
39 These *things* ye shall do unto the LORD
in your set feasts, beside your vows, and
your freewill offerings, for your burnt offerings, and for your meat offerings, and
for your drink offerings, and for your peace
offerings.
40 And Moses told the children of Israel
according to all that the LORD commanded Moses.

30
1 And Moses spake unto the heads of the
tribes concerning the children of Israel,
saying, This *is* the thing which the LORD
hath commanded.
2 If a man vow a vow unto the LORD, or
swear an oath to bind his soul with a bond;
he shall not break his word, he shall do
according to all that proceedeth out of his
mouth.
3 If a woman also vow a vow unto the
LORD, and bind *herself* by a bond, *being* in
her father's house in her youth;
4 And her father hear her vow, and her
bond wherewith she hath bound her soul,
and her father shall hold his peace at her:
then all her vows shall stand, and every
bond wherewith she hath bound her soul
shall stand.
5 But if her father disallow her in the day
that he heareth; not any of her vows, or of
her bonds wherewith she hath bound her
soul, shall stand: and the LORD shall forgive her, because her father disallowed her.
6 And if she had at all an husband, when
she vowed, or uttered ought out of her lips,
wherewith she bound her soul;
7 And her husband heard *it,* and held his
peace at her in the day that he heard *it:*
then her vows shall stand, and her bonds
wherewith she bound her soul shall stand.
8 But if her husband disallowed her on
the day that he heard *it;* then he shall make
her vow which she vowed, and that which
she uttered with her lips, wherewith she
bound her soul, of none effect: and the
LORD shall forgive her.
9 But every vow of a widow, and of her
that is divorced, wherewith they have
bound their souls, shall stand against her.
10 And if she vowed in her husband's
house, or bound her soul by a bond with
an oath;
11 And her husband heard *it,* and held
his peace at her, *and* disallowed her not:
then all her vows shall stand, and every
bond wherewith she bound her soul shall
stand.
12 But if her husband hath utterly made
them void on the day he heard *them; then*
whatsoever proceeded out of her lips concerning her vows, or concerning the bond
of her soul, shall not stand: her husband
hath made them void; and the LORD shall
forgive her.
13 Every vow, and every binding oath to
afflict the soul, her husband may establish it, or her husband may make it void.
14 But if her husband altogether hold his
peace at her from day to day; then he
establisheth all her vows, or all her bonds,
which *are* upon her: he confirmeth them,
because he held his peace at her in the day
that he heard *them.*
15 But if he shall any ways make them
void after that he hath heard *them;* then
he shall bear her iniquity.
16 These *are* the statutes, which the LORD
commanded Moses, between a man and
his wife, between the father and his daughter, *being yet* in her youth in her father's
house.

31

1And the LORD spake unto Moses,
saying,
2Avenge the children of Israel of the
Midianites: afterward shalt thou be gathered unto thy people.
3And Moses spake unto the people, saying, Arm some of yourselves unto the war,
and let them go against the Midianites, and
avenge the LORD of Midian.
4Of every tribe a thousand, throughout
all the tribes of Israel, shall ye send to
the war.
5So there were delivered out of the thousands of Israel, a thousand of *every* tribe,
twelve thousand armed for war.
6And Moses sent them to the war, a
thousand of *every* tribe, them and Phinehas the son of Eleazar the priest, to the
war, with the holy instruments, and the
trumpets to blow in his hand.
7And they warred against the Midianites, as the LORD commanded Moses; and
they slew all the males.
8And they slew the kings of Midian, beside the rest of them that were slain; *namely*, Evi, and Rekem, and Zur, and Hur, and
Reba, five kings of Midian: Balaam also the
son of Beor they slew with the sword.
9And the children of Israel took *all* the
women of Midian captives, and their little
ones, and took the spoil of all their cattle,
and all their flocks, and all their goods.
10And they burnt all their cities wherein
they dwelt, and all their goodly castles,
with fire.
11And they took all the spoil, and all the
prey, *both* of men and of beasts.
12And they brought the captives, and the
prey, and the spoil, unto Moses, and Eleazar the priest, and unto the congregation
of the children of Israel, unto the camp at
the plains of Moab, which *are* by Jordan
near Jericho.
13And Moses, and Eleazar the priest, and
all the princes of the congregation, went
forth to meet them without the camp.
14And Moses was wroth with the officers of the host, *with* the captains over
thousands, and captains over hundreds,
which came from the battle.
15And Moses said unto them, Have ye
saved all the women alive?
16Behold, these caused the children
of Israel, through the counsel of Balaam,
to commit trespass against the LORD in
the matter of Peor, and there was a plague
among the congregation of the LORD.
17Now therefore kill every male among
the little ones, and kill every woman that
hath known man by lying with him.
18But all the women children, that have
not known a man by lying with him, keep
alive for yourselves.
19And do ye abide without the camp
seven days: whosoever hath killed any
person, and whosoever hath touched any
slain, purify *both* yourselves and your
captives on the third day, and on the seventh day.
20And purify all *your* raiment, and all
that is made of skins, and all work of goats'
hair, and all things made of wood.
21And Eleazar the priest said unto the
men of war which went to the battle, This
is the ordinance of the law which the LORD
commanded Moses;
22Only the gold, and the silver, the brass,
the iron, the tin, and the lead,
23Every thing that may abide the fire, ye
shall make *it* go through the fire, and it
shall be clean: nevertheless it shall be purified with the water of separation: and all
that abideth not the fire ye shall make go
through the water.
24And ye shall wash your clothes on the
seventh day, and ye shall be clean, and afterward ye shall come into the camp.
25And the LORD spake unto Moses,
saying,
26Take the sum of the prey that was tak-
en, *both* of man and of beast, thou, and
Eleazar the priest, and the chief fathers of
the congregation:
27And divide the prey into two parts;
between them that took the war upon
them, who went out to battle, and between
all the congregation:
28And levy a tribute unto the LORD of
the men of war which went out to battle:
one soul of five hundred, *both* of the persons, and of the beeves, and of the asses,
and of the sheep:
29Take *it* of their half, and give *it* unto
Eleazar the priest, *for* an heave offering of
the LORD.
30And of the children of Israel's half,
thou shalt take one portion of fifty, of
the persons, of the beeves, of the asses,
and of the flocks, of all manner of beasts,
and give them unto the Levites, which

keep the charge of the tabernacle of the LORD.

31 And Moses and Eleazar the priest did as the LORD commanded Moses.

32 And the booty, *being* the rest of the prey which the men of war had caught, was six hundred thousand and seventy thousand and five thousand sheep,

33 And threescore and twelve thousand beeves,

34 And threescore and one thousand asses,

35 And thirty and two thousand persons in all, of women that had not known man by lying with him.

36 And the half, *which was* the portion of them that went out to war, was in number three hundred thousand and seven and thirty thousand and five hundred sheep:

37 And the LORD'S tribute of the sheep was six hundred and threescore and fifteen.

38 And the beeves *were* thirty and six thousand; of which the LORD'S tribute *was* threescore and twelve.

39 And the asses *were* thirty thousand and five hundred; of which the LORD'S tribute *was* threescore and one.

40 And the persons *were* sixteen thousand; of which the LORD'S tribute *was* thirty and two persons.

41 And Moses gave the tribute, *which was* the LORD'S heave offering, unto Eleazar the priest, as the LORD commanded Moses.

42 And of the children of Israel's half, which Moses divided from the men that warred,

43 (Now the half *that pertained unto* the congregation was three hundred thousand and thirty thousand *and* seven thousand and five hundred sheep,

44 And thirty and six thousand beeves,

45 And thirty thousand asses and five hundred,

46 And sixteen thousand persons;)

47 Even of the children of Israel's half, Moses took one portion of fifty, *both* of man and of beast, and gave them unto the Levites, which kept the charge of the tabernacle of the LORD; as the LORD commanded Moses.

48 And the officers which *were* over thousands of the host, the captains of thousands, and captains of hundreds, came near unto Moses:

49 And they said unto Moses, Thy servants have taken the sum of the men of war which *are* under our charge, and there lacketh not one man of us.

50 We have therefore brought an oblation for the LORD, what every man hath gotten, of jewels of gold, chains, and bracelets, rings, earrings, and tablets, to make an atonement for our souls before the LORD.

31:50 Tithing
◄ Exodus 35:5
2 Samuel 8:10-11 ►

51 And Moses and Eleazar the priest took the gold of them, *even* all wrought jewels.

52 And all the gold of the offering that they offered up to the LORD, of the captains of thousands, and of the captains of hundreds, was sixteen thousand seven hundred and fifty shekels.

53 (*For* the men of war had taken spoil, every man for himself.)

54 And Moses and Eleazar the priest took the gold of the captains of thousands and of hundreds, and brought it into the tabernacle of the congregation, *for* a memorial for the children of Israel before the LORD.

32

1 Now the children of Reuben and the children of Gad had a very great multitude of cattle: and when they saw the land of Jazer, and the land of Gilead, that, behold, the place *was* a place for cattle;

2 The children of Gad and the children of Reuben came and spake unto Moses, and to Eleazar the priest, and unto the princes of the congregation, saying,

3 Ataroth, and Dibon, and Jazer, and Nimrah, and Heshbon, and Elealeh, and Shebam, and Nebo, and Beon,

4 *Even* the country which the LORD smote before the congregation of Israel, *is* a land for cattle, and thy servants have cattle:

5 Wherefore, said they, if we have found grace in thy sight, let this land be given unto thy servants for a possession, *and* bring us not over Jordan.

6 And Moses said unto the children of Gad and to the children of Reuben, Shall your brethren go to war, and shall ye sit here?

7 And wherefore discourage ye the heart of the children of Israel from going over into the land which the LORD hath given them?

8 Thus did your fathers, when I sent them from Kadesh-barnea to see the land.

9 For when they went up unto the valley of Eshcol, and saw the land, they discouraged the heart of the children of Israel, that they should not go into the land which the LORD had given them.

10 And the LORD'S anger was kindled the same time, and he sware, saying,

11 Surely none of the men that came up out of Egypt, from twenty years old and upward, shall see the land which I sware unto Abraham, unto Isaac, and unto Jacob; because they have not wholly followed me:

12 Save Caleb the son of Jephunneh the Kenezite, and Joshua the son of Nun: for they have wholly followed the LORD.

13 And the LORD'S anger was kindled against Israel, and he made them wander in the wilderness forty years, until all the generation, that had done evil in the sight of the LORD, was consumed.

14 And, behold, ye are risen up in your fathers' stead, an increase of sinful men, to augment yet the fierce anger of the LORD toward Israel.

15 For if ye turn away from after him, he will yet again leave them in the wilderness; and ye shall destroy all this people.

16 And they came near unto him, and said, We will build sheepfolds here for our cattle, and cities for our little ones:

17 But we ourselves will go ready armed before the children of Israel, until we have brought them unto their place: and our little ones shall dwell in the fenced cities because of the inhabitants of the land.

18 We will not return unto our houses, until the children of Israel have inherited every man his inheritance.

19 For we will not inherit with them on yonder side Jordan, or forward; because our inheritance is fallen to us on this side Jordan eastward.

20 And Moses said unto them, If ye will do this thing, if ye will go armed before the LORD to war,

21 And will go all of you armed over Jordan before the LORD, until he hath driven out his enemies from before him,

22 And the land be subdued before the LORD: then afterward ye shall return, and be guiltless before the LORD, and before Israel; and this land shall be your possession before the LORD.

23 But if ye will not do so, behold, ye have sinned against the LORD: and be sure your sin will find you out.

32:23 Sinner Beware ◄
Deuteronomy 32:32 ➤

24 Build you cities for your little ones, and folds for your sheep; and do that which hath proceeded out of your mouth.

25 And the children of Gad and the children of Reuben spake unto Moses, saying, Thy servants will do as my lord commandeth.

26 Our little ones, our wives, our flocks, and all our cattle, shall be there in the cities of Gilead:

27 But thy servants will pass over, every man armed for war, before the LORD to battle, as my lord saith.

28 So concerning them Moses commanded Eleazar the priest, and Joshua the son of Nun, and the chief fathers of the tribes of the children of Israel:

29 And Moses said unto them, If the children of Gad and the children of Reuben will pass with you over Jordan, every man armed to battle, before the LORD, and the land shall be subdued before you; then ye shall give them the land of Gilead for a possession:

30 But if they will not pass over with you armed, they shall have possessions among you in the land of Canaan.

31 And the children of Gad and the children of Reuben answered, saying, As the LORD hath said unto thy servants, so will we do.

32 We will pass over armed before the LORD into the land of Canaan, that the possession of our inheritance on this side Jordan *may be* ours.

33 And Moses gave unto them, *even* to the children of Gad, and to the children of Reuben, and unto half the tribe of Manasseh the son of Joseph, the kingdom of Sihon king of the Amorites, and the kingdom of Og king of Bashan, the land, with the cities thereof in the coasts, *even* the cities of the country round about.

34 And the children of Gad built Dibon, and Ataroth, and Aroer,

35 And Atroth, Shophan, and Jaazer, and Jogbehah,

36 And Beth-nimrah, and Beth-haran, fenced cities: and folds for sheep.

37 And the children of Reuben built Heshbon, and Elealeh, and Kirjathaim,

38 And Nebo, and Baal-meon, (their
names being changed,) and Shibmah: and
gave other names unto the cities which
they builded.
39 And the children of Machir the son of
Manasseh went to Gilead, and took it, and
dispossessed the Amorite which *was* in it.
40 And Moses gave Gilead unto Machir
the son of Manasseh; and he dwelt therein.
41 And Jair the son of Manasseh went and
took the small towns thereof, and called
them Havoth-jair.
42 And Nobah went and took Kenath,
and the villages thereof, and called it Nobah, after his own name.

33

1 These *are* the journeys of the children
of Israel, which went forth out of the land of
Egypt with their armies under the hand of
Moses and Aaron.
2 And Moses wrote their goings out according to their journeys by the commandment of the LORD: and these *are* their
journeys according to their goings out.
3 And they departed from Rameses in the
first month, on the fifteenth day of the first
month; on the morrow after the passover
the children of Israel went out with an high
hand in the sight of all the Egyptians.
4 For the Egyptians buried all *their* firstborn, which the LORD had smitten among
them: upon their gods also the LORD executed judgments.
5 And the children of Israel removed
from Rameses, and pitched in Succoth.
6 And they departed from Succoth, and
pitched in Etham, which *is* in the edge of
the wilderness.
7 And they removed from Etham, and
turned again unto Pi-hahiroth, which *is*
before Baal-zephon: and they pitched before Migdol.
8 And they departed from before Pi-
hahiroth, and passed through the midst
of the sea into the wilderness, and went
three days' journey in the wilderness of
Etham, and pitched in Marah.
9 And they removed from Marah, and
came unto Elim: and in Elim *were* twelve
fountains of water, and threescore and ten
palm trees; and they pitched there.
10 And they removed from Elim, and
encamped by the Red sea.
11 And they removed from the Red sea,
and encamped in the wilderness of Sin.
12 And they took their journey out of
the wilderness of Sin, and encamped in
Dophkah.
13 And they departed from Dophkah,
and encamped in Alush.
14 And they removed from Alush, and
encamped at Rephidim, where was no
water for the people to drink.
15 And they departed from Rephidim,
and pitched in the wilderness of Sinai.
16 And they removed from the desert of
Sinai, and pitched at Kibroth-hattaavah.
17 And they departed from Kibroth-
hattaavah, and encamped at Hazeroth.
18 And they departed from Hazeroth,
and pitched in Rithmah.
19 And they departed from Rithmah, and
pitched at Rimmon-parez.
20 And they departed from Rimmon-
parez, and pitched in Libnah.
21 And they removed from Libnah, and
pitched at Rissah.
22 And they journeyed from Rissah, and
pitched in Kehelathah.
23 And they went from Kehelathah, and
pitched in mount Shapher.
24 And they removed from mount Shapher, and encamped in Haradah.
25 And they removed from Haradah, and
pitched in Makheloth.
26 And they removed from Makheloth,
and encamped at Tahath.
27 And they departed from Tahath, and
pitched at Tarah.
28 And they removed from Tarah, and
pitched in Mithcah.
29 And they went from Mithcah, and
pitched in Hashmonah.
30 And they departed from Hashmonah,
and encamped at Moseroth.
31 And they departed from Moseroth,
and pitched in Bene-jaakan.
32 And they removed from Bene-jaakan,
and encamped at Hor-hagidgad.
33 And they went from Hor-hagidgad,
and pitched in Jotbathah.
34 And they removed from Jotbathah,
and encamped at Ebronah.
35 And they departed from Ebronah, and
encamped at Ezion-gaber.
36 And they removed from Ezion-gaber,
and pitched in the wilderness of Zin,
which *is* Kadesh.
37 And they removed from Kadesh, and
pitched in mount Hor, in the edge of the
land of Edom.

38 And Aaron the priest went up into mount Hor at the commandment of the LORD, and died there, in the fortieth year after the children of Israel were come out of the land of Egypt, in the first *day* of the fifth month.

39 And Aaron *was* an hundred and twenty and three years old when he died in mount Hor.

40 And king Arad the Canaanite, which dwelt in the south in the land of Canaan, heard of the coming of the children of Israel.

41 And they departed from mount Hor, and pitched in Zalmonah.

42 And they departed from Zalmonah, and pitched in Punon.

43 And they departed from Punon, and pitched in Oboth.

44 And they departed from Oboth, and pitched in Ije-abarim, in the border of Moab.

45 And they departed from Iim, and pitched in Dibon-gad.

46 And they removed from Dibon-gad, and encamped in Almon-diblathaim.

47 And they removed from Almon-diblathaim, and pitched in the mountains of Abarim, before Nebo.

48 And they departed from the mountains of Abarim, and pitched in the plains of Moab by Jordan *near* Jericho.

49 And they pitched by Jordan, from Beth-jesimoth *even* unto Abel-shittim in the plains of Moab.

50 And the LORD spake unto Moses in the plains of Moab by Jordan *near* Jericho, saying,

51 Speak unto the children of Israel, and say unto them, When ye are passed over Jordan into the land of Canaan;

52 Then ye shall drive out all the inhabitants of the land from before you, and destroy all their pictures, and destroy all their molten images, and quite pluck down all their high places:

53 And ye shall dispossess *the inhabitants* of the land, and dwell therein: for I have given you the land to possess it.

54 And ye shall divide the land by lot for an inheritance among your families: *and* to the more ye shall give the more inheritance, and to the fewer ye shall give the less inheritance: every man's *inheritance* shall be in the place where his lot falleth; according to the tribes of your fathers ye shall inherit.

55 But if ye will not drive out the inhabitants of the land from before you; then it shall come to pass, that those which ye let remain of them *shall be* pricks in your eyes, and thorns in your sides, and shall vex you in the land wherein ye dwell.

56 Moreover it shall come to pass, *that* I shall do unto you, as I thought to do unto them.

34

1 And the LORD spake unto Moses, saying,

2 Command the children of Israel, and say unto them, When ye come into the land of Canaan; (this *is* the land that shall fall unto you for an inheritance, *even* the land of Canaan with the coasts thereof:)

3 Then your south quarter shall be from the wilderness of Zin along by the coast of Edom, and your south border shall be the outmost coast of the salt sea eastward:

4 And your border shall turn from the south to the ascent of Akrabbim, and pass on to Zin: and the going forth thereof shall be from the south to Kadesh-barnea, and shall go on to Hazar-addar, and pass on to Azmon:

5 And the border shall fetch a compass from Azmon unto the river of Egypt, and the goings out of it shall be at the sea.

6 And *as for* the western border, ye shall even have the great sea for a border: this shall be your west border.

7 And this shall be your north border: from the great sea ye shall point out for you mount Hor:

8 From mount Hor ye shall point out *your border* unto the entrance of Hamath; and the goings forth of the border shall be to Zedad:

9 And the border shall go on to Ziphron, and the goings out of it shall be at Hazar-enan: this shall be your north border.

10 And ye shall point out your east border from Hazar-enan to Shepham:

11 And the coast shall go down from Shepham to Riblah, on the east side of Ain; and the border shall descend, and shall reach unto the side of the sea of Chinnereth eastward:

12 And the border shall go down to Jordan, and the goings out of it shall be at the salt sea: this shall be your land with the coasts thereof round about.

13 And Moses commanded the children of Israel, saying, This *is* the land which ye shall inherit by lot, which the LORD commanded to give unto the nine tribes, and to the half tribe:

14 For the tribe of the children of Reuben according to the house of their fathers, and the tribe of the children of Gad according to the house of their fathers, have received *their inheritance;* and half the tribe of Manasseh have received their inheritance:

15 The two tribes and the half tribe have received their inheritance on this side Jordan *near* Jericho eastward, toward the sunrising.

16 And the LORD spake unto Moses, saying,

17 These *are* the names of the men which shall divide the land unto you: Eleazar the priest, and Joshua the son of Nun.

18 And ye shall take one prince of every tribe, to divide the land by inheritance.

19 And the names of the men *are* these: Of the tribe of Judah, Caleb the son of Jephunneh.

20 And of the tribe of the children of Simeon, Shemuel the son of Ammihud.

21 Of the tribe of Benjamin, Elidad the son of Chislon.

22 And the prince of the tribe of the children of Dan, Bukki the son of Jogli.

23 The prince of the children of Joseph, for the tribe of the children of Manasseh, Hanniel the son of Ephod.

24 And the prince of the tribe of the children of Ephraim, Kemuel the son of Shiphtan.

25 And the prince of the tribe of the children of Zebulun, Elizaphan the son of Parnach.

26 And the prince of the tribe of the children of Issachar, Paltiel the son of Azzan.

27 And the prince of the tribe of the children of Asher, Ahihud the son of Shelomi.

28 And the prince of the tribe of the children of Naphtali, Pedahel the son of Ammihud.

29 These *are they* whom the LORD commanded to divide the inheritance unto the children of Israel in the land of Canaan.

35

1 And the LORD spake unto Moses in the plains of Moab by Jordan *near* Jericho, saying,

2 Command the children of Israel, that they give unto the Levites of the inheritance of their possession cities to dwell in; and ye shall give *also* unto the Levites suburbs for the cities round about them.

3 And the cities shall they have to dwell in; and the suburbs of them shall be for their cattle, and for their goods, and for all their beasts.

4 And the suburbs of the cities, which ye shall give unto the Levites, *shall reach* from the wall of the city and outward a thousand cubits round about.

5 And ye shall measure from without the city on the east side two thousand cubits, and on the south side two thousand cubits, and on the west side two thousand cubits, and on the north side two thousand cubits and the city *shall be* in the midst: this shall be to them the suburbs of the cities.

6 And among the cities which ye shall give unto the Levites *there shall be* six cities for refuge, which ye shall appoint for the manslayer, that he may flee thither: and to them ye shall add forty and two cities.

7 *So* all the cities which ye shall give to the Levites *shall be* forty and eight cities: them *shall ye give* with their suburbs.

8 And the cities which ye shall give *shall be* of the possession of the children of Israel: from *them that have* many ye shall give many; but from *them that have* few ye shall give few: every one shall give of his cities unto the Levites according to his inheritance which he inheriteth.

9 And the LORD spake unto Moses, saying,

10 Speak unto the children of Israel, and say unto them, When ye be come over Jordan into the land of Canaan;

11 Then ye shall appoint you cities to be cities of refuge for you; that the slayer may flee thither, which killeth any person at unawares.

12 And they shall be unto you cities for refuge from the avenger; that the manslayer die not, until he stand before the congregation in judgment.

13 And of these cities which ye shall give six cities shall ye have for refuge.

14 Ye shall give three cities on this side Jordan, and three cities shall ye give in the land of Canaan, *which* shall be cities of refuge.

15 These six cities shall be a refuge, *both* for the children of Israel, and for the stranger, and for the sojourner among them: that every one that killeth any person unawares may flee thither.

35:15 New Kids
◄ Leviticus 25:35
Deuteronomy 10:19 ►

16 And if he smite him with an instrument of iron, so that he die, he *is* a murderer: the murderer shall surely be put to death.

17 And if he smite him with throwing a stone, wherewith he may die, and he die, he *is* a murderer: the murderer shall surely be put to death.

18 Or *if* he smite him with an hand weapon of wood, wherewith he may die, and he die, he *is* a murderer: the murderer shall surely be put to death.

19 The revenger of blood himself shall slay the murderer: when he meeteth him, he shall slay him.

20 But if he thrust him of hatred, or hurl at him by laying of wait, that he die;

21 Or in enmity smite him with his hand, that he die: he that smote *him* shall surely be put to death; *for* he *is* a murderer: the revenger of blood shall slay the murderer, when he meeteth him.

22 But if he thrust him suddenly without enmity, or have cast upon him any thing without laying of wait,

23 Or with any stone, wherewith a man may die, seeing *him* not, and cast *it* upon him, that he die, and *was* not his enemy, neither sought his harm:

24 Then the congregation shall judge between the slayer and the revenger of blood according to these judgments:

25 And the congregation shall deliver the slayer out of the hand of the revenger of blood, and the congregation shall restore him to the city of his refuge, whither he was fled: and he shall abide in it unto the death of the high priest, which was anointed with the holy oil.

26 But if the slayer shall at any time come without the border of the city of his refuge, whither he was fled;

27 And the revenger of blood find him without the borders of the city of his refuge, and the revenger of blood kill the slayer; he shall not be guilty of blood:

28 Because he should have remained in the city of his refuge until the death of the high priest: but after the death of the high priest the slayer shall return into the land of his possession.

29 So these *things* shall be for a statute of judgment unto you throughout your generations in all your dwellings.

30 Whoso killeth any person, the murderer shall be put to death by the mouth of witnesses: but one witness shall not testify against any person *to cause him* to die.

31 Moreover ye shall take no satisfaction for the life of a murderer, which *is* guilty of death: but he shall be surely put to death.

32 And ye shall take no satisfaction for him that is fled to the city of his refuge, that he should come again to dwell in the land, until the death of the priest.

33 So ye shall not pollute the land wherein ye *are:* for blood it defileth the land: and the land cannot be cleansed of the blood that is shed therein, but by the blood of him that shed it.

34 Defile not therefore the land which ye shall inhabit, wherein I dwell: for I the LORD dwell among the children of Israel.

36

1 And the chief fathers of the families of the children of Gilead, the son of Machir, the son of Manasseh, of the families of the sons of Joseph, came near, and spake before Moses, and before the princes, the chief fathers of the children of Israel:

2 And they said, The LORD commanded my lord to give the land for an inheritance by lot to the children of Israel: and my lord was commanded by the LORD to give the inheritance of Zelophehad our brother unto his daughters.

3 And if they be married to any of the sons of the *other* tribes of the children of Israel, then shall their inheritance be taken from the inheritance of our fathers, and shall be put to the inheritance of the tribe whereunto they are received: so shall it be taken from the lot of our inheritance.

4 And when the jubile of the children of Israel shall be, then shall their inheritance be put unto the inheritance of the tribe whereunto they are received: so shall their inheritance be taken away from the inheritance of the tribe of our fathers.

5 And Moses commanded the children of Israel according to the word of the LORD,

saying, The tribe of the sons of Joseph hath said well.

6 This *is* the thing which the LORD doth command concerning the daughters of Zelophehad, saying, Let them marry to whom they think best; only to the family of the tribe of their father shall they marry.

7 So shall not the inheritance of the children of Israel remove from tribe to tribe: for every one of the children of Israel shall keep himself to the inheritance of the tribe of his fathers.

8 And every daughter, that possesseth an inheritance in any tribe of the children of Israel, shall be wife unto one of the family of the tribe of her father, that the children of Israel may enjoy every man the inheritance of his fathers.

9 Neither shall the inheritance remove from *one* tribe to another tribe; but every one of the tribes of the children of Israel shall keep himself to his own inheritance.

10 Even as the LORD commanded Moses, so did the daughters of Zelophehad:

11 For Mahlah, Tirzah, and Hoglah, and Milcah, and Noah, the daughters of Zelophehad, were married unto their father's brothers' sons:

12 *And* they were married into the families of the sons of Manasseh the son of Joseph, and their inheritance remained in the tribe of the family of their father.

13 These *are* the commandments and the judgments, which the LORD commanded by the hand of Moses unto the children of Israel in the plains of Moab by Jordan *near* Jericho.

Deuteronomy

AUTHOR
Moses; final summary probably by Joshua

MAIN POINT
God did many wonders for his people and promised to do more for those who are faithful to him.

DATE WRITTEN
1407 or 1406 B.C.

34 CHAPTERS

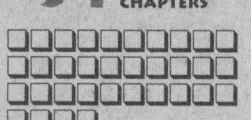

MAIN PEOPLE
Moses, Joshua

SPECIAL FEATURES

- *Comes at the end of 40 years' traveling in the wilderness, at the edge of the Promised Land*
- *Includes three different speeches by Moses, reviewing their history and laws*
- *Is written in the form of a treaty between a king and his subjects, typical for the times*
- *Concludes with the death of Moses*
- *Fifth book of Law*

HOW THE BOOK GOT ITS NAME
The word deuteronomy means "second law," from a Greek mistranslation of chapter 17, verse 18. This book is actually a new application of the first four books of the Bible.

1

1 These *be* the words which Moses spake
unto all Israel on this side Jordan in the
wilderness, in the plain over against the
Red *sea*, between Paran, and Tophel, and
Laban, and Hazeroth, and Dizahab.
2 (*There are* eleven days' *journey* from
Horeb by the way of mount Seir unto
Kadesh-barnea.)
3 And it came to pass in the fortieth year,
in the eleventh month, on the first *day* of
the month, *that* Moses spake unto the children of Israel, according unto all that the
LORD had given him in commandment
unto them;
4 After he had slain Sihon the king of the
Amorites, which dwelt in Heshbon, and
Og the king of Bashan, which dwelt at
Astaroth in Edrei:
5 On this side Jordan, in the land of
Moab, began Moses to declare this law,
saying,
6 The LORD our God spake unto us in
Horeb, saying, Ye have dwelt long enough
in this mount:
7 Turn you, and take your journey, and
go to the mount of the Amorites, and unto
all *the places* nigh thereunto, in the plain,
in the hills, and in the vale, and in the
south, and by the sea side, to the land of
the Canaanites, and unto Lebanon, unto
the great river, the river Euphrates.
8 Behold, I have set the land before you:

go in and possess the land which the LORD
sware unto your fathers, Abraham, Isaac,
and Jacob, to give unto them and to their
seed after them.
9And I spake unto you at that time, saying, I am not able to bear you myself alone:
10The LORD your God hath multiplied
you, and, behold, ye *are* this day as the stars
of heaven for multitude.
11(The LORD God of your fathers make
you a thousand times so many more as ye
are, and bless you, as he hath promised
you!)
12How can I myself alone bear your
cumbrance, and your burden, and your
strife?
13Take you wise men, and understanding, and known among your tribes, and I
will make them rulers over you.
14And ye answered me, and said, The
thing which thou hast spoken *is* good *for*
us to do.
15So I took the chief of your tribes, wise
men, and known, and made them heads
over you, captains over thousands, and
captains over hundreds, and captains over
fifties, and captains over tens, and officers
among your tribes.
16And I charged your judges at that time,
saying, Hear *the causes* between your brethren, and judge righteously between *every*
man and his brother, and the stranger *that*
is with him.
17Ye shall not
respect persons in
judgment; *but* ye
shall hear the small
as well as the great;
ye shall not be afraid
of the face of man; for the judgment *is*
God's: and the cause that is too hard for
you, bring *it* unto me, and I will hear it.

1:17 Favoritism
◄ Leviticus 19:15
Job 13:10 ►

18And I commanded you at that time
all the things which ye should do.
19And when we departed from Horeb,
we went through all that great and terrible
wilderness, which ye saw by the way of
the mountain of the Amorites, as the LORD
our God commanded us; and we came to
Kadesh-barnea.
20And I said unto you, Ye are come unto
the mountain of the Amorites, which the
LORD our God doth give unto us.
21Behold, the LORD thy God hath set the
land before thee: go up *and* possess *it,* as
the LORD God of thy fathers hath said unto
thee; fear not, neither be discouraged.
22And ye came near unto me every one
of you, and said, We will send men before
us, and they shall search us out the land,
and bring us word again by what way we
must go up, and into what cities we shall
come.
23And the saying pleased me well: and I
took twelve men of you, one of a tribe:
24And they turned and went up into the
mountain, and came unto the valley of
Eshcol, and searched it out.
25And they took of the fruit of the land
in their hands, and brought *it* down unto
us, and brought us word again, and said,
It is a good land which the LORD our God
doth give us.
26Notwithstanding ye would not go up,
but rebelled against the commandment of
the LORD your God:
27And ye murmured in your tents, and
said, Because the LORD hated us, he hath
brought us forth out of the land of Egypt,
to deliver us into the hand of the Amorites, to destroy us.
28Whither shall we go up? our brethren
have discouraged our heart, saying, The
people *is* greater and taller than we; the
cities *are* great and walled up to heaven;
and moreover we have seen the sons of the
Anakims there.
29Then I said unto you, Dread not, neither be afraid of them.
30The LORD your God which goeth before you, he shall fight for you, according
to all that he did for you in Egypt before
your eyes;
31And in the wilderness, where thou hast
seen how that the LORD thy God bare thee,
as a man doth bear his son, in all the way
that ye went, until ye came into this place.
32Yet in this thing ye did not believe the
LORD your God,
33Who went in the way before you, to
search you out a place to pitch your tents
in, in fire by night, to shew you by what
way ye should go, and in a cloud by day.
34And the LORD heard the voice of your
words, and was wroth, and sware, saying,
35Surely there shall not one of these men
of this evil generation see that good land,
which I sware to give unto your fathers,
36Save Caleb the son of Jephunneh; he
shall see it, and to him will I give the land

that he hath trodden upon, and to his children, because he hath wholly followed the
LORD.
37 Also the LORD was angry with me for
your sakes, saying, Thou also shalt not go
in thither.
38 *But* Joshua the son of Nun, which
standeth before thee, he shall go in thither:
encourage him: for he shall cause Israel to
inherit it.
39 Moreover your little ones, which ye
said should be a prey, and your children,
which in that day had no knowledge between good and evil, they shall go in
thither, and unto them will I give it, and
they shall possess it.
40 But *as for* you, turn you, and take your
journey into the wilderness by the way of
the Red sea.
41 Then ye answered and said unto me,
We have sinned against the LORD, we will
go up and fight, according to all that the
LORD our God commanded us. And when
ye had girded on every man his weapons
of war, ye were ready to go up into the hill.
42 And the LORD said unto me, Say unto
them, Go not up, neither fight; for I *am*
not among you; lest ye be smitten before
your enemies.
43 So I spake unto you; and ye would not
hear, but rebelled against the commandment of the LORD, and went presumptuously up into the hill.
44 And the Amorites, which dwelt in that
mountain, came out against you, and
chased you, as bees do, and destroyed you
in Seir, *even* unto Hormah.
45 And ye returned
and wept before
the LORD; but the
LORD would not
hearken to your
voice, nor give ear
unto you.

1:45
Unanswered Prayer
◄ 1 Samuel 14:37 ►

46 So ye abode in Kadesh many days, according unto the days that ye abode *there.*

2

1 Then we turned, and took our journey
into the wilderness by the way of the Red
sea, as the LORD spake unto me: and we
compassed mount Seir many days.
2 And the LORD spake unto me, saying,
3 Ye have compassed this mountain long
enough: turn you northward.
4 And command thou the people, say-
ing, Ye *are* to pass through the coast of your
brethren the children of Esau, which dwell
in Seir; and they shall be afraid of you: take
ye good heed unto yourselves therefore:
5 Meddle not with them; for I will not
give you of their land, no, not so much as
a footbreadth; because I have given mount
Seir unto Esau *for* a possession.
6 Ye shall buy meat of them for money,
that ye may eat; and ye shall also buy water of them for money, that ye may drink.
7 For the LORD thy God hath blessed thee
in all the works of thy hand: he knoweth
thy walking through this great wilderness:
these forty years the LORD thy God *hath
been* with thee; thou hast lacked nothing.
8 And when we passed by from our
brethren the children of Esau, which dwelt
in Seir, through the way of the plain from
Elath, and from Ezion-gaber, we turned
and passed by the way of the wilderness
of Moab.
9 And the LORD said unto me, Distress
not the Moabites, neither contend with
them in battle: for I will not give thee of
their land *for* a possession; because I have
given Ar unto the children of Lot *for* a possession.
10 The Emims dwelt therein in times past,
a people great, and many, and tall, as the
Anakims;
11 Which also were accounted giants, as
the Anakims; but the Moabites call them
Emims.
12 The Horims also dwelt in Seir beforetime; but the children of Esau succeeded them, when they had destroyed
them from before them, and dwelt in their
stead; as Israel did unto the land of his
possession, which the LORD gave unto
them.
13 Now rise up, *said I,* and get you over
the brook Zered. And we went over the
brook Zered.
14 And the space in which we came from
Kadesh-barnea, until we were come over
the brook Zered, *was* thirty and eight years;
until all the generation of the men of war
were wasted out from among the host, as
the LORD sware unto them.
15 For indeed the hand of the LORD was
against them, to destroy them from among
the host, until they were consumed.
16 So it came to pass, when all the men
of war were consumed and dead from
among the people,

17 That the LORD spake unto me, saying,

18 Thou art to pass over through Ar, the coast of Moab, this day:

19 And *when* thou comest nigh over against the children of Ammon, distress them not, nor meddle with them: for I will not give thee of the land of the children of Ammon *any* possession; because I have given it unto the children of Lot *for* a possession.

20 (That also was accounted a land of giants: giants dwelt therein in old time; and the Ammonites call them Zamzummims;

21 A people great, and many, and tall, as the Anakims; but the LORD destroyed them before them; and they succeeded them, and dwelt in their stead:

22 As he did to the children of Esau, which dwelt in Seir, when he destroyed the Horims from before them; and they succeeded them, and dwelt in their stead even unto this day:

23 And the Avims which dwelt in Hazerim, *even* unto Azzah, the Caphtorims, which came forth out of Caphtor, destroyed them, and dwelt in their stead.)

24 Rise ye up, take your journey, and pass over the river Arnon: behold, I have given into thine hand Sihon the Amorite, king of Heshbon, and his land: begin to possess *it*, and contend with him in battle.

25 This day will I begin to put the dread of thee and the fear of thee upon the nations *that are* under the whole heaven, who shall hear report of thee, and shall tremble, and be in anguish because of thee.

26 And I sent messengers out of the wilderness of Kedemoth unto Sihon king of Heshbon with words of peace, saying,

27 Let me pass through thy land: I will go along by the high way, I will neither turn unto the right hand nor to the left.

28 Thou shalt sell me meat for money, that I may eat; and give me water for money, that I may drink: only I will pass through on my feet;

29 (As the children of Esau which dwell in Seir, and the Moabites which dwell in Ar, did unto me;) until I shall pass over Jordan into the land which the LORD our God giveth us.

30 But Sihon king of Heshbon would not let us pass by him: for the LORD thy God hardened his spirit, and made his heart obstinate, that he might deliver him into thy hand, as *appeareth* this day.

31 And the LORD said unto me, Behold, I have begun to give Sihon and his land before thee: begin to possess, that thou mayest inherit his land.

32 Then Sihon came out against us, he and all his people, to fight at Jahaz.

33 And the LORD our God delivered him before us; and we smote him, and his sons, and all his people.

34 And we took all his cities at that time, and utterly destroyed the men, and the women, and the little ones, of every city, we left none to remain:

35 Only the cattle we took for a prey unto ourselves, and the spoil of the cities which we took.

36 From Aroer, which *is* by the brink of the river of Arnon, and *from* the city that *is* by the river, even unto Gilead, there was not one city too strong for us: the LORD our God delivered all unto us:

37 Only unto the land of the children of Ammon thou camest not, nor unto any place of the river Jabbok, *nor* unto the cities in the mountains, nor unto whatsoever the LORD our God forbad us.

3

1 Then we turned, and went up the way to Bashan: and Og the king of Bashan came out against us, he and all his people, to battle at Edrei.

2 And the LORD said unto me, Fear him not: for I will deliver him, and all his people, and his land, into thy hand; and thou shalt do unto him as thou didst unto Sihon king of the Amorites, which dwelt at Heshbon.

3 So the LORD our God delivered into our hands Og also, the king of Bashan, and all his people: and we smote him until none was left to him remaining.

4 And we took all his cities at that time, there was not a city which we took not from them, threescore cities, all the region of Argob, the kingdom of Og in Bashan.

5 All these cities *were* fenced with high walls, gates, and bars; beside unwalled towns a great many.

6 And we utterly destroyed them, as we did unto Sihon king of Heshbon, utterly destroying the men, women, and children, of every city.

7 But all the cattle, and the spoil of the cities, we took for a prey to ourselves.

8And we took at that time out of the
hand of the two kings of the Amorites the
land that *was* on this side Jordan, from the
river of Arnon unto mount Hermon;
9(*Which* Hermon the Sidonians call Sirion; and the Amorites call it Shenir;)
10All the cities of the plain, and all Gilead, and all Bashan, unto Salchah and Edrei, cities of the kingdom of Og in Bashan.
11For only Og king of Bashan remained
of the remnant of giants; behold, his bedstead *was* a bedstead of iron; *is* it not in
Rabbath of the children of Ammon? nine
cubits *was* the length thereof, and four
cubits the breadth of it, after the cubit of
a man.
12And this land, *which* we possessed at
that time, from Aroer, which *is* by the river
Arnon, and half mount Gilead, and the
cities thereof, gave I unto the Reubenites
and to the Gadites.
13And the rest of Gilead, and all Bashan,
being the kingdom of Og, gave I unto the
half tribe of Manasseh; all the region of
Argob, with all Bashan, which was called
the land of giants.
14Jair the son of Manasseh took all the
country of Argob unto the coasts of
Geshuri and Maachathi; and called them
after his own name, Bashan-havoth-jair,
unto this day.
15And I gave Gilead unto Machir.
16And unto the Reubenites and unto the
Gadites I gave from Gilead even unto the
river Arnon half the valley, and the border
even unto the river Jabbok, *which is* the
border of the children of Ammon;
17The plain also, and Jordan, and the
coast *thereof,* from Chinnereth even unto
the sea of the plain, *even* the salt sea, under Ashdoth-pisgah eastward.
18And I commanded you at that time,
saying, The LORD your God hath given you
this land to possess it: ye shall pass over
armed before your brethren the children
of Israel, all *that are* meet for the war.
19But your wives, and your little ones,
and your cattle, (*for* I know that ye have
much cattle,) shall abide in your cities
which I have given you;
20Until the LORD have given rest unto
your brethren, as well as unto you, and
until they also possess the land which the
LORD your God hath given them beyond
Jordan: and *then* shall ye return every
man unto his possession, which I have
given you.
21And I commanded Joshua at that time,
saying, Thine eyes have seen all that the
LORD your God hath done unto these two
kings: so shall the LORD do unto all the
kingdoms whither thou passest.
22Ye shall not fear them: for the LORD
your God he shall fight for you.
23And I besought the LORD at that time,
saying,
24O Lord GOD, thou hast begun to shew
thy servant thy greatness, and thy mighty
hand: for what God *is there* in heaven or
in earth, that can do according to thy
works, and according to thy might?
25I pray thee, let me go over, and see the
good land that *is* beyond Jordan, that
goodly mountain, and Lebanon.
26But the LORD was wroth with me for
your sakes, and would not hear me: and
the LORD said unto me, Let it suffice thee;
speak no more unto me of this matter.
27Get thee up into the top of Pisgah, and
lift up thine eyes westward, and northward, and southward, and eastward, and
behold *it* with thine eyes: for thou shalt
not go over this Jordan.
28But charge Joshua, and encourage him,
and strengthen him: for he shall go over
before this people, and he shall cause them
to inherit the land which thou shalt see.
29So we abode in the valley over against
Beth-peor.

4

1Now therefore hearken, O Israel, unto
the statutes and unto the judgments, which
I teach you, for to do *them,* that ye may
live, and go in and possess the land which
the LORD God of your fathers giveth you.
2Ye shall not add unto the word which I
command you, neither shall ye diminish
ought from it, that ye may keep the commandments of the LORD your God which
I command you.
3Your eyes have seen what the LORD did
because of Baal-peor: for all the men that
followed Baal-peor, the LORD thy God hath
destroyed them from among you.
4But ye that did cleave unto the LORD
your God *are* alive every one of you this
day.
5Behold, I have taught you statutes and
judgments, even as the LORD my God commanded me, that ye should do so in the
land whither ye go to possess it.

land of Og king of Bashan, two kings of the Amorites, which *were* on this side Jordan toward the sunrising;

48 From Aroer, which *is* by the bank of the river Arnon, even unto mount Sion, which *is* Hermon,

49 And all the plain on this side Jordan eastward, even unto the sea of the plain, under the springs of Pisgah.

5

1 And Moses called all Israel, and said unto them, Hear, O Israel, the statutes and judgments which I speak in your ears this day, that ye may learn them, and keep, and do them.

2 The LORD our God made a covenant with us in Horeb.

3 The LORD made not this covenant with our fathers, but with us, *even* us, who *are* all of us here alive this day.

4 The LORD talked with you face to face in the mount out of the midst of the fire,

5 (I stood between the LORD and you at that time, to shew you the word of the LORD: for ye were afraid by reason of the fire, and went not up into the mount;) saying,

6 I *am* the LORD thy God, which brought thee out of the land of Egypt, from the house of bondage.

7 Thou shalt have none other gods before me.

8 Thou shalt not make thee *any* graven image, *or* any likeness *of any thing* that *is* in heaven above, or that *is* in the earth beneath, or that *is* in the waters beneath the earth:

9 Thou shalt not bow down thyself unto them, nor serve them: for I the LORD thy God *am* a jealous God, visiting the iniquity of the fathers upon the children unto the third and fourth *generation* of them that hate me,

10 And shewing mercy unto thousands of them that love me and keep my commandments.

11 Thou shalt not take the name of the LORD thy God in vain: for the LORD will not hold *him* guiltless that taketh his name in vain.

12 Keep the sabbath day to sanctify it, as the LORD thy God hath commanded thee.

13 Six days thou shalt labour, and do all thy work:

14 But the seventh day *is* the sabbath of the LORD thy God: *in it* thou shalt not do any work, thou, nor thy son, nor thy daughter, nor thy manservant, nor thy maidservant, nor thine ox, nor thine ass, nor any of thy cattle, nor thy stranger that *is* within thy gates; that thy manservant and thy maidservant may rest as well as thou.

15 And remember that thou wast a servant in the land of Egypt, and *that* the LORD thy God brought thee out thence through a mighty hand and by a stretched out arm: therefore the LORD thy God commanded thee to keep the sabbath day.

16 Honour thy father and thy mother, as the LORD thy God hath commanded thee; that thy days may be prolonged, and that it may go well with thee, in the land which the LORD thy God giveth thee.

17 Thou shalt not kill.

18 Neither shalt thou commit adultery.

19 Neither shalt thou steal.

20 Neither shalt thou bear false witness against thy neighbour.

21 Neither shalt thou desire thy neighbour's wife, neither shalt thou covet thy neighbour's house, his field, or his manservant, or his maidservant, his ox, or his ass, or any *thing* that *is* thy neighbour's.

22 These words the LORD spake unto all your assembly in the mount out of the midst of the fire, of the cloud, and of the thick darkness, with a great voice: and he added no more. And he wrote them in two tables of stone, and delivered them unto me.

23 And it came to pass, when ye heard the voice out of the midst of the darkness, (for the mountain did burn with fire,) that ye came near unto me, *even* all the heads of your tribes, and your elders;

24 And ye said, Behold, the LORD our God hath shewed us his glory and his greatness, and we have heard his voice out of the midst of the fire: we have seen this day that God doth talk with man, and he liveth.

25 Now therefore why should we die? for this great fire will consume us: if we hear the voice of the LORD our God any more, then we shall die.

26 For who *is there of* all flesh, that hath heard the voice of the living God speaking out of the midst of the fire, as we *have*, and lived?

27 Go thou near, and hear all that the LORD our God shall say: and speak thou

unto us all that the LORD our God shall speak unto thee; and we will hear *it,* and do *it.*

28 And the LORD heard the voice of your words, when ye spake unto me; and the LORD said unto me, I have heard the voice of the words of this people, which they have spoken unto thee: they have well said all that they have spoken.

29 O that there were such an heart in them, that they would fear me, and keep all my commandments always, that it might be well with them, and with their children for ever!

30 Go say to them, Get you into your tents again.

31 But as for thee, stand thou here by me, and I will speak unto thee all the commandments, and the statutes, and the judgments, which thou shalt teach them, that they may do *them* in the land which I give them to possess it.

32 Ye shall observe to do therefore as the LORD your God hath commanded you: ye shall not turn aside to the right hand or to the left.

5:32 One Goal
◄ Joshua 1:7 ►

33 Ye shall walk in all the ways which the LORD your God hath commanded you, that ye may live, and *that it may be* well with you, and *that* ye may prolong *your* days in the land which ye shall possess.

6

1 Now these *are* the commandments, the statutes, and the judgments, which the LORD your God commanded to teach you, that ye might do *them* in the land whither ye go to possess it:

2 That thou mightest fear the LORD thy God, to keep all his statutes and his commandments, which I command thee, thou, and thy son, and thy son's son, all the days of thy life; and that thy days may be prolonged.

3 Hear therefore, O Israel, and observe to do *it;* that it may be well with thee, and that ye may increase mightily, as the LORD God of thy fathers hath promised thee, in the land that floweth with milk and honey.

4 Hear, O Israel: The LORD our God *is* one LORD:

6:4 Only One God
◄ Deuteronomy 4:35
Deuteronomy 32:39 ►

5 And thou shalt love the LORD thy God with all thine heart, and with all thy soul, and with all thy might.

6:5 Love for God
◄ Deuteronomy 10:12 ►

6 And these words, which I command thee this day, shall be in thine heart:

7 And thou shalt teach them diligently unto thy children, and shalt talk of them when thou sittest in thine house, and when thou walkest by the way, and when thou liest down, and when thou risest up.

6:7 Instruction
◄ Leviticus 10:11
Psalm 78:6 ►

8 And thou shalt bind them for a sign upon thine hand, and they shall be as frontlets between thine eyes.

9 And thou shalt write them upon the posts of thy house, and on thy gates.

10 And it shall be, when the LORD thy God shall have brought thee into the land which he sware unto thy fathers, to Abraham, to Isaac, and to Jacob, to give thee great and goodly cities, which thou buildedst not,

6:10-12 Don't Forget...
◄ Deuteronomy 4:9
Deuteronomy 8:11 ►

6:10-12 Success
◄ Deuteronomy 32:15 ►

11 And houses full of all good *things,* which thou filledst not, and wells digged, which thou diggedst not, vineyards and olive trees, which thou plantedst not; when thou shalt have eaten and be full;

12 *Then* beware lest thou forget the LORD, which brought thee forth out of the land of Egypt, from the house of bondage.

13 Thou shalt fear the LORD thy God, and serve him, and shalt swear by his name.

14 Ye shall not go after other gods, of the gods of the people which *are* round about you;

15 (For the LORD thy God *is* a jealous God among you) lest the anger of the LORD thy God be kindled against thee, and destroy thee from off the face of the earth.

16 Ye shall not tempt the LORD your God, as ye tempted *him* in Massah.

17 Ye shall diligently keep the commandments of the LORD your God, and his tes-

timonies, and his statutes, which he hath
commanded thee.
18And thou shalt do *that which is* right
and good in the sight of the LORD: that it
may be well with thee, and that thou
mayest go in and possess the good land
which the LORD sware unto thy fathers,
19To cast out all thine enemies from before thee, as the LORD hath spoken.
20*And* when thy son asketh thee in time
to come, saying, What *mean* the testimonies, and the statutes, and the judgments,
which the LORD our God hath commanded you?
21Then thou shalt say unto thy son, We
were Pharaoh's bondmen in Egypt; and the
LORD brought us out of Egypt with a
mighty hand:
22And the LORD shewed signs and wonders, great and sore, upon Egypt, upon
Pharaoh, and upon all his household, before our eyes:
23And he brought us out from thence,
that he might bring us in, to give us the
land which he sware unto our fathers.
24And the LORD
commanded us to
do all these statutes,
to fear the LORD our
God, for our good
always, that he
might preserve us alive, as *it is* at this day.

6:24
Safety
◄ Joshua 24:17 ►

25And it shall be our righteousness, if
we observe to do all these commandments
before the LORD our God, as he hath commanded us.

7

1When the LORD thy God shall bring
thee into the land whither thou goest to
possess it, and hath cast out many nations
before thee, the Hittites, and the Girgashites, and the Amorites, and the Canaanites, and the Perizzites, and the Hivites, and
the Jebusites, seven nations greater and
mightier than thou;
2And when the LORD thy God shall deliver them before thee; thou shalt smite
them, *and* utterly destroy them; thou shalt
make no covenant with them, nor shew
mercy unto them:
3Neither shalt thou make marriages with
them; thy daughter thou shalt not give
unto his son, nor his daughter shalt thou
take unto thy son.
4For they will turn away thy son from
following me, that they may serve other
gods: so will the anger of the LORD be kindled against you, and destroy thee suddenly.
5But thus shall ye deal with them; ye
shall destroy their altars, and break down
their images, and cut down their groves,
and burn their graven images with fire.
6For thou *art* an holy people unto the
LORD thy God: the LORD thy God hath chosen thee to be a special people unto himself, above all people that *are* upon the face
of the earth.
7The LORD did not set his love upon you,
nor choose you, because ye were more in
number than any people; for ye *were* the
fewest of all people:
8But because the
LORD loved you,
and because he
would keep the
oath which he had
sworn unto your
fathers, hath the LORD brought you out
with a mighty hand, and redeemed you
out of the house of bondmen, from the
hand of Pharaoh king of Egypt.

7:8
God's Love
◄ Psalm 146:8 ►

9Know therefore that the LORD thy God,
he *is* God, the faithful God, which keepeth
covenant and mercy with them that love
him and keep his commandments to a
thousand generations;
10And repayeth them that hate him to
their face, to destroy them: he will not be
slack to him that hateth him, he will repay him to his face.
11Thou shalt therefore keep the commandments, and the statutes, and the judgments, which I command thee this day, to
do them.
12Wherefore it shall come to pass, if ye
hearken to these judgments, and keep, and
do them, that the LORD thy God shall keep
unto thee the covenant and the mercy
which he sware unto thy fathers:
13And he will love thee, and bless thee,
and multiply thee: he will also bless the
fruit of thy womb, and the fruit of thy land,
thy corn, and thy wine, and thine oil, the
increase of thy kine, and the flocks of thy
sheep, in the land which he sware unto
thy fathers to give thee.
14Thou shalt be blessed above all people: there shall not be male or female barren among you, or among your cattle.
15And the LORD will take away from thee
all sickness, and will put none of the evil

diseases of Egypt, which thou knowest, upon thee; but will lay them upon all *them* that hate thee.

16And thou shalt consume all the people which the LORD thy God shall deliver thee; thine eye shall have no pity upon them: neither shalt thou serve their gods; for that *will be* a snare unto thee.

17If thou shalt say in thine heart, These nations *are* more than I; how can I dispossess them?

18Thou shalt not be afraid of them: *but* shalt well remember what the LORD thy God did unto Pharaoh, and unto all Egypt;

19The great temptations which thine eyes saw, and the signs, and the wonders, and the mighty hand, and the stretched out arm, whereby the LORD thy God brought thee out: so shall the LORD thy God do unto all the people of whom thou art afraid.

20Moreover the LORD thy God will send the hornet among them, until they that are left, and hide themselves from thee, be destroyed.

21Thou shalt not be affrighted at them: for the LORD thy God *is* among you, a mighty God and terrible.

22And the LORD thy God will put out those nations before thee by little and little: thou mayest not consume them at once, lest the beasts of the field increase upon thee.

23But the LORD thy God shall deliver them unto thee, and shall destroy them with a mighty destruction, until they be destroyed.

24And he shall deliver their kings into thine hand, and thou shalt destroy their name from under heaven: there shall no man be able to stand before thee, until thou have destroyed them.

25The graven images of their gods shall ye burn with fire: thou shalt not desire the silver or gold *that is* on them, nor take *it* unto thee, lest thou be snared therein: for it *is* an abomination to the LORD thy God.

26Neither shalt thou bring an abomination into thine house, lest thou be a cursed thing like it: *but* thou shalt utterly detest it, and thou shalt utterly abhor it; for it *is* a cursed thing.

8

1All the commandments which I command thee this day shall ye observe to do, that ye may live, and multiply, and go in and possess the land which the LORD sware unto your fathers.

2And thou shalt remember all the way which the LORD thy God led thee these forty years in the wilderness, to humble thee, *and* to prove thee, to know what *was* in thine heart, whether thou wouldest keep his commandments, or no.

3And he humbled thee, and suffered thee to hunger, and fed thee with manna, which thou knewest not, neither did thy fathers know; that he might make thee know that man doth not live by bread only, but by every *word* that proceedeth out of the mouth of the LORD doth man live.

4Thy raiment waxed not old upon thee, neither did thy foot swell, these forty years.

5Thou shalt also consider in thine heart, that, as a man chasteneth his son, *so* the LORD thy God chasteneth thee.

8:5
Difficulties
◄ Psalm 94:12 ►

6Therefore thou shalt keep the commandments of the LORD thy God, to walk in his ways, and to fear him.

7For the LORD thy God bringeth thee into a good land, a land of brooks of water, of fountains and depths that spring out of valleys and hills;

8A land of wheat, and barley, and vines, and fig trees, and pomegranates; a land of oil olive, and honey;

9A land wherein thou shalt eat bread without scarceness, thou shalt not lack any *thing* in it; a land whose stones *are* iron, and out of whose hills thou mayest dig brass.

10When thou hast eaten and art full, then thou shalt bless the LORD thy God for the good land which he hath given thee.

8:10
Thankfulness
◄ Psalm 100:4 ►

11Beware that thou forget not the LORD thy God, in not keeping his commandments, and his judgments, and his statutes, which I command thee this day:

8:11 Don't Forget...
◄ Deuteronomy 6:10-12
Judges 8:34 ►

12Lest *when* thou hast eaten and art full, and hast built goodly houses, and dwelt *therein;*

13 And *when* thy herds and thy flocks multiply, and thy silver and thy gold is multiplied, and all that thou hast is multiplied;

> **8:13-14**
> **Money's Dangers**
> ◄ Psalm 62:10 ►

14 Then thine heart be lifted up, and thou forget the LORD thy God, which brought thee forth out of the land of Egypt, from the house of bondage;

15 Who led thee through that great and terrible wilderness, *wherein were* fiery serpents, and scorpions, and drought, where *there was* no water; who brought thee forth water out of the rock of flint;

16 Who fed thee in the wilderness with manna, which thy fathers knew not, that he might humble thee, and that he might prove thee, to do thee good at thy latter end;

17 And thou say in thine heart, My power and the might of *mine* hand hath gotten me this wealth.

18 But thou shalt remember the LORD thy God: for *it is* he that giveth thee power to get wealth, that he may establish his covenant which he sware unto thy fathers, as *it is* this day.

> **8:18**
> **Source of Wealth**
> ◄ 1 Chronicles 29:12 ►

19 And it shall be, if thou do at all forget the LORD thy God, and walk after other gods, and serve them, and worship them, I testify against you this day that ye shall surely perish.

20 As the nations which the LORD destroyeth before your face, so shall ye perish; because ye would not be obedient unto the voice of the LORD your God.

9

1 Hear, O Israel: Thou *art* to pass over Jordan this day, to go in to possess nations greater and mightier than thyself, cities great and fenced up to heaven,

2 A people great and tall, the children of the Anakims, whom thou knowest, and *of whom* thou hast heard *say,* Who can stand before the children of Anak!

3 Understand therefore this day, that the LORD thy God *is* he which goeth over before thee; *as* a consuming fire he shall destroy them, and he shall bring them down before thy face: so shalt thou drive them out, and destroy them quickly, as the LORD hath said unto thee.

4 Speak not thou in thine heart, after that the LORD thy God hath cast them out from before thee, saying, For my righteousness the LORD hath brought me in to possess this land: but for the wickedness of these nations the LORD doth drive them out from before thee.

> **9:4**
> **Self-righteousness**
> ◄ Job 9:20 ►

5 Not for thy righteousness, or for the uprightness of thine heart, dost thou go to possess their land: but for the wickedness of these nations the LORD thy God doth drive them out from before thee, and that he may perform the word which the LORD sware unto thy fathers, Abraham, Isaac, and Jacob.

6 Understand therefore, that the LORD thy God giveth thee not this good land to possess it for thy righteousness; for thou *art* a stiffnecked people.

7 Remember, *and* forget not, how thou provokedst the LORD thy God to wrath in the wilderness: from the day that thou didst depart out of the land of Egypt, until ye came unto this place, ye have been rebellious against the LORD.

> **9:7 Losers**
> ◄ Numbers 16:30
> Deuteronomy 31:20 ►

> **9:7 Mistakes**
> ◄ Genesis 41:9
> Psalm 51:3 ►

8 Also in Horeb ye provoked the LORD to wrath, so that the LORD was angry with you to have destroyed you.

9 When I was gone up into the mount to receive the tables of stone, *even* the tables of the covenant which the LORD made with you, then I abode in the mount forty days and forty nights, I neither did eat bread nor drink water:

10 And the LORD delivered unto me two tables of stone written with the finger of God; and on them *was written* according to all the words, which the LORD spake with you in the mount out of the midst of the fire in the day of the assembly.

11 And it came to pass at the end of forty days and forty nights, *that* the LORD gave me the two tables of stone, *even* the tables of the covenant.

12 And the LORD said unto me, Arise, get

thee down quickly from hence; for thy people which thou hast brought forth out of Egypt have corrupted *themselves;* they are quickly turned aside out of the way which I commanded them; they have made them a molten image.

13 Furthermore the LORD spake unto me, saying, I have seen this people, and, behold, it *is* a stiffnecked people:

14 Let me alone, that I may destroy them, and blot out their name from under heaven: and I will make of thee a nation mightier and greater than they.

15 So I turned and came down from the mount, and the mount burned with fire: and the two tables of the covenant *were* in my two hands.

16 And I looked, and, behold, ye had sinned against the LORD your God, *and* had made you a molten calf: ye had turned aside quickly out of the way which the LORD had commanded you.

17 And I took the two tables, and cast them out of my two hands, and brake them before your eyes.

18 And I fell down before the LORD, as at the first, forty days and forty nights: I did neither eat bread, nor drink water, because of all your sins which ye sinned, in doing wickedly in the sight of the LORD, to provoke him to anger.

19 For I was afraid of the anger and hot displeasure, wherewith the LORD was wroth against you to destroy you. But the LORD hearkened unto me at that time also.

20 And the LORD was very angry with Aaron to have destroyed him: and I prayed for Aaron also the same time.

21 And I took your sin, the calf which ye had made, and burnt it with fire, and stamped it, *and* ground *it* very small, *even* until it was as small as dust: and I cast the dust thereof into the brook that descended out of the mount.

22 And at Taberah, and at Massah, and at Kibroth-hattaavah, ye provoked the LORD to wrath.

23 Likewise when the LORD sent you from Kadesh-barnea, saying, Go up and possess the land which I have given you; then ye rebelled against the commandment of the LORD your God, and ye believed him not, nor hearkened to his voice.

24 Ye have been rebellious against the LORD from the day that I knew you.

25 Thus I fell down before the LORD forty days and forty nights, as I fell down *at the first;* because the LORD had said he would destroy you.

9:25
Praying Alone
◄ 1 Samuel 15:11 ►

26 I prayed therefore unto the LORD, and said, O Lord GOD, destroy not thy people and thine inheritance, which thou hast redeemed through thy greatness, which thou hast brought forth out of Egypt with a mighty hand.

9:26 Praying for Others
◄ Numbers 14:17
1 Samuel 7:5 ►

27 Remember thy servants, Abraham, Isaac, and Jacob; look not unto the stubbornness of this people, nor to their wickedness, nor to their sin:

28 Lest the land whence thou broughtest us out say, Because the LORD was not able to bring them into the land which he promised them, and because he hated them, he hath brought them out to slay them in the wilderness.

29 Yet they *are* thy people and thine inheritance, which thou broughtest out by thy mighty power and by thy stretched out arm.

10

1 At that time the LORD said unto me, Hew thee two tables of stone like unto the first, and come up unto me into the mount, and make thee an ark of wood.

2 And I will write on the tables the words that were in the first tables which thou brakest, and thou shalt put them in the ark.

3 And I made an ark *of* shittim wood, and hewed two tables of stone like unto the first, and went up into the mount, having the two tables in mine hand.

4 And he wrote on the tables, according to the first writing, the ten commandments, which the LORD spake unto you in the mount out of the midst of the fire in the day of the assembly: and the LORD gave them unto me.

5 And I turned myself and came down from the mount, and put the tables in the ark which I had made; and there they be, as the LORD commanded me.

6 And the children of Israel took their journey from Beeroth of the children of Jaakan to Mosera: there Aaron died, and

there he was buried; and Eleazar his son
ministered in the priest's office in his stead.
7 From thence they journeyed unto Gudgodah; and from Gudgodah to Jotbath, a
land of rivers of waters.
8 At that time the LORD separated the
tribe of Levi, to bear the ark of the covenant of the LORD, to stand before the
LORD to minister unto him, and to bless
in his name, unto this day.
9 Wherefore Levi hath no part nor inheritance with his brethren; the LORD *is* his
inheritance, according as the LORD thy God
promised him.
10 And I stayed in the mount, according
to the first time, forty days and forty nights;
and the LORD hearkened unto me at that
time also, *and* the LORD would not destroy
thee.
11 And the LORD said unto me, Arise, take
thy journey before the people, that they
may go in and possess the land, which I
sware unto their fathers to give unto them.
12 And now, Is-
rael, what doth the
LORD thy God re-
quire of thee, but to
fear the LORD thy
God, to walk in all
his ways, and to
love him, and to
serve the LORD thy
God with all thy
heart and with all
thy soul,
13 To keep the
commandments of
the LORD, and his
statutes, which I
command thee this
day for thy good?
14 Behold, the
heaven and the heaven of heavens *is* the
LORD'S thy God, the earth *also,* with all that
therein *is.*
15 Only the LORD had a delight in thy
fathers to love them, and he chose their
seed after them, *even* you above all people, as *it is* this day.
16 Circumcise
therefore the fore-
skin of your heart,
and be no more
stiffnecked.
17 For the LORD

10:12
Fearing God
◄ Deuteronomy 13:4 ►

10:12 Love for God
◄ Deuteronomy 6:5
Deuteronomy 11:1 ►

10:12
Religious People
◄ Ecclesiastes 12:13 ►

10:17 Names of God
◄ Exodus 15:2
Deuteronomy 32:8 ►

your God *is* God of gods, and Lord of lords,
a great God, a mighty, and a terrible, which
regardeth not persons, nor taketh reward:
18 He doth exe-
cute the judgment
of the fatherless and
widow, and loveth
the stranger, in giv-
ing him food and
raiment.
19 Love ye there-
fore the stranger:
for ye were strang-
ers in the land of
Egypt.
20 Thou shalt fear
the LORD thy God;
him shalt thou
serve, and to him
shalt thou cleave,
and swear by his
name.
21 He *is* thy praise, and he *is* thy God, that
hath done for thee these great and terrible
things, which thine eyes have seen.
22 Thy fathers went down into Egypt with
threescore and ten persons; and now the
LORD thy God hath made thee as the stars
of heaven for multitude.

10:18
God's Care for Kids
◄ Psalm 10:14 ►

10:19
Loving Others
◄ Matthew 22:39 ►

10:19 New Kids
◄ Numbers 35:15
Deuteronomy 27:19 ►

11

1 Therefore thou
shalt love the LORD
thy God, and keep
his charge, and his
statutes, and his
judgments, and his
commandments, alway.
2 And know ye this day: for *I speak* not
with your children which have not known,
and which have not seen the chastisement
of the LORD your God, his greatness, his
mighty hand, and his stretched out arm,
3 And his miracles, and his acts, which
he did in the midst of Egypt unto Pharaoh
the king of Egypt, and unto all his land;
4 And what he did unto the army of
Egypt, unto their horses, and to their chariots; how he made the water of the Red
sea to overflow them as they pursued after
you, and *how* the LORD hath destroyed
them unto this day;
5 And what he did unto you in the wilderness, until ye came into this place;
6 And what he did unto Dathan and
Abiram, the sons of Eliab, the son of Reuben: how the earth opened her mouth, and

11:1 Love for God
◄ Deuteronomy 10:12
Joshua 22:5 ►

swallowed them up, and their households, and their tents, and all the substance that *was* in their possession, in the midst of all Israel:

7 But your eyes have seen all the great acts of the LORD which he did.

8 Therefore shall ye keep all the commandments which I command you this day, that ye may be strong, and go in and possess the land, whither ye go to possess it;

9 And that ye may prolong *your* days in the land, which the LORD sware unto your fathers to give unto them and to their seed, a land that floweth with milk and honey.

10 For the land, whither thou goest in to possess it, *is* not as the land of Egypt, from whence ye came out, where thou sowedst thy seed, and wateredst *it* with thy foot, as a garden of herbs:

11 But the land, whither ye go to possess it, *is* a land of hills *and* valleys, and drinketh water of the rain of heaven:

12 A land which the LORD thy God careth for: the eyes of the LORD thy God *are* always upon it, from the beginning of the year even unto the end of the year.

13 And it shall come to pass, if ye shall hearken diligently unto my commandments which I command you this day, to love the LORD your God, and to serve him with all your heart and with all your soul,

14 That I will give *you* the rain of your land in his due season, the first rain and the latter rain, that thou mayest gather in thy corn, and thy wine, and thine oil.

15 And I will send grass in thy fields for thy cattle, that thou mayest eat and be full.

16 Take heed to yourselves, that your heart be not deceived, and ye turn aside, and serve other gods, and worship them;

17 And *then* the LORD'S wrath be kindled against you, and he shut up the heaven, that there be no rain, and that the land yield not her fruit; and *lest* ye perish quickly from off the good land which the LORD giveth you.

18 Therefore shall ye lay up these my words in your heart and in your soul, and bind them for a sign upon your hand, that they may be as frontlets between your eyes.

19 And ye shall teach them your children, speaking of them when thou sittest in thine house, and when thou walkest by the way, when thou liest down, and when thou risest up.

20 And thou shalt write them upon the door posts of thine house, and upon thy gates:

21 That your days may be multiplied, and the days of your children, in the land which the LORD sware unto your fathers to give them, as the days of heaven upon the earth.

22 For if ye shall diligently keep all these commandments which I command you, to do them, to love the LORD your God, to walk in all his ways, and to cleave unto him;

23 Then will the LORD drive out all these nations from before you, and ye shall possess greater nations and mightier than yourselves.

24 Every place whereon the soles of your feet shall tread shall be yours: from the wilderness and Lebanon, from the river, the river Euphrates, even unto the uttermost sea shall your coast be.

25 There shall no man be able to stand before you: *for* the LORD your God shall lay the fear of you and the dread of you upon all the land that ye shall tread upon, as he hath said unto you.

26 Behold, I set before you this day a blessing and a curse;

27 A blessing, if ye obey the commandments of the LORD your God, which I command you this day:

28 And a curse, if ye will not obey the commandments of the LORD your God, but turn aside out of the way which I command you this day, to go after other gods, which ye have not known.

11:28
Ouch!
◄ Deuteronomy 28:15 ►

29 And it shall come to pass, when the LORD thy God hath brought thee in unto the land whither thou goest to possess it, that thou shalt put the blessing upon mount Gerizim, and the curse upon mount Ebal.

30 *Are* they not on the other side Jordan, by the way where the sun goeth down, in the land of the Canaanites, which dwell in the champaign over against Gilgal, beside the plains of Moreh?

31 For ye shall pass over Jordan to go in

to possess the land which the LORD your
God giveth you, and ye shall possess it,
and dwell therein.
32 And ye shall observe to do all the statutes and judgments which I set before you
this day.

12

1 These *are* the statutes and judgments,
which ye shall observe to do in the land,
which the LORD God of thy fathers giveth
thee to possess it, all the days that ye live
upon the earth.
2 Ye shall utterly destroy all the places,
wherein the nations which ye shall possess served their gods, upon the high
mountains, and upon the hills, and under
every green tree:
3 And ye shall overthrow their altars, and
break their pillars, and burn their groves
with fire; and ye shall hew down the graven
images of their gods, and destroy the
names of them out of that place.
4 Ye shall not do so unto the LORD your
God.
5 But unto the place which the LORD your
God shall choose out of all your tribes to
put his name there, *even* unto his habitation shall ye seek, and thither thou shalt
come:
6 And thither ye shall bring your burnt
offerings, and your sacrifices, and your
tithes, and heave offerings of your hand,
and your vows, and your freewill offerings,
and the firstlings of your herds and of your
flocks:
7 And there ye
shall eat before the
LORD your God,
and ye shall rejoice
in all that ye put
your hand unto, ye
and your households, wherein the LORD
thy God hath blessed thee.

> **12:7**
> **Rejoicing**
> ◄ Deuteronomy 16:11 ►

8 Ye shall not do after all *the things* that
we do here this day, every man whatsoever *is* right in his own eyes.
9 For ye are not as yet come to the rest
and to the inheritance, which the LORD
your God giveth you.
10 But *when* ye go over Jordan, and dwell
in the land which the LORD your God
giveth you to inherit, and *when* he giveth
you rest from all your enemies round
about, so that ye dwell in safety;
11 Then there shall be a place which the
LORD your God shall choose to cause his
name to dwell there; thither shall ye bring
all that I command you; your burnt offerings, and your sacrifices, your tithes, and
the heave offering of your hand, and all
your choice vows which ye vow unto the
LORD:
12 And ye shall rejoice before the LORD
your God, ye, and your sons, and your
daughters, and your menservants, and your
maidservants, and the Levite that *is* within your gates; forasmuch as he hath no part
nor inheritance with you.
13 Take heed to thyself that thou offer not
thy burnt offerings in every place that thou
seest:
14 But in the place which the LORD shall
choose in one of thy tribes, there thou shalt
offer thy burnt offerings, and there thou
shalt do all that I command thee.
15 Notwithstanding thou mayest kill and
eat flesh in all thy gates, whatsoever thy
soul lusteth after, according to the blessing of the LORD thy God which he hath
given thee: the unclean and the clean may
eat thereof, as of the roebuck, and as of
the hart.
16 Only ye shall not eat the blood; ye
shall pour it upon the earth as water.
17 Thou mayest not eat within thy gates
the tithe of thy corn, or of thy wine, or of
thy oil, or the firstlings of thy herds or of
thy flock, nor any of thy vows which thou
vowest, nor thy freewill offerings, or heave
offering of thine hand:
18 But thou must eat them before the
LORD thy God in the place which the LORD
thy God shall choose, thou, and thy son,
and thy daughter, and thy manservant, and
thy maidservant, and the Levite that *is*
within thy gates: and thou shalt rejoice
before the LORD thy God in all that thou
puttest thine hands unto.
19 Take heed to thyself that thou forsake
not the Levite as long as thou livest upon
the earth.
20 When the LORD thy God shall enlarge
thy border, as he hath promised thee, and
thou shalt say, I will eat flesh, because thy
soul longeth to eat flesh; thou mayest eat
flesh, whatsoever thy soul lusteth after.
21 If the place which the LORD thy God
hath chosen to put his name there be too
far from thee, then thou shalt kill of thy
herd and of thy flock, which the LORD hath
given thee, as I have commanded thee, and

thou shalt eat in thy gates whatsoever thy soul lusteth after.

22 Even as the roebuck and the hart is eaten, so thou shalt eat them: the unclean and the clean shall eat *of* them alike.

23 Only be sure that thou eat not the blood: for the blood *is* the life; and thou mayest not eat the life with the flesh.

24 Thou shalt not eat it; thou shalt pour it upon the earth as water.

25 Thou shalt not eat it; that it may go well with thee, and with thy children after thee, when thou shalt do *that which is* right in the sight of the LORD.

26 Only thy holy things which thou hast, and thy vows, thou shalt take, and go unto the place which the LORD shall choose:

27 And thou shalt offer thy burnt offerings, the flesh and the blood, upon the altar of the LORD thy God: and the blood of thy sacrifices shall be poured out upon the altar of the LORD thy God, and thou shalt eat the flesh.

28 Observe and hear all these words which I command thee, that it may go well with thee, and with thy children after thee for ever, when thou doest *that which is* good and right in the sight of the LORD thy God.

29 When the LORD thy God shall cut off the nations from before thee, whither thou goest to possess them, and thou succeedest them, and dwellest in their land;

30 Take heed to thyself that thou be not snared by following them, after that they be destroyed from before thee; and that thou enquire not after their gods, saying, How did these nations serve their gods? even so will I do likewise.

31 Thou shalt not do so unto the LORD thy God: for every abomination to the LORD, which he hateth, have they done unto their gods; for even their sons and their daughters they have burnt in the fire to their gods.

32 What thing soever I command you, observe to do it: thou shalt not add thereto, nor diminish from it.

13

1 If there arise among you a prophet, or a dreamer of dreams, and giveth thee a sign or a wonder,

2 And the sign or the wonder come to pass, whereof he spake unto thee, saying, Let us go after other gods, which thou hast not known, and let us serve them;

3 Thou shalt not hearken unto the words of that prophet, or that dreamer of dreams: for the LORD your God proveth you, to know whether ye love the LORD your God with all your heart and with all your soul.

4 Ye shall walk after the LORD your God, and fear him, and keep his commandments, and obey his voice, and ye shall serve him, and cleave unto him.

13:4 Fearing God
◄ Deuteronomy 10:12
Joshua 4:24 ►

5 And that prophet, or that dreamer of dreams, shall be put to death; because he hath spoken to turn *you* away from the LORD your God, which brought you out of the land of Egypt, and redeemed you out of the house of bondage, to thrust thee out of the way which the LORD thy God commanded thee to walk in. So shalt thou put the evil away from the midst of thee.

6 If thy brother, the son of thy mother, or thy son, or thy daughter, or the wife of thy bosom, or thy friend, which *is* as thine own soul, entice thee secretly, saying, Let us go and serve other gods, which thou hast not known, thou, nor thy fathers;

7 *Namely,* of the gods of the people which *are* round about you, nigh unto thee, or far off from thee, from the *one* end of the earth even unto the *other* end of the earth;

8 Thou shalt not consent unto him, nor hearken unto him; neither shall thine eye pity him, neither shalt thou spare, neither shalt thou conceal him:

9 But thou shalt surely kill him; thine hand shall be first upon him to put him to death, and afterwards the hand of all the people.

10 And thou shalt stone him with stones, that he die; because he hath sought to thrust thee away from the LORD thy God, which brought thee out of the land of Egypt, from the house of bondage.

11 And all Israel shall hear, and fear, and shall do no more any such wickedness as this is among you.

12 If thou shalt hear *say* in one of thy cities, which the LORD thy God hath given thee to dwell there, saying,

13 *Certain* men, the children of Belial, are gone out from among you, and have withdrawn the inhabitants of their city, saying, Let us go and serve other gods, which ye have not known;

14 Then shalt thou enquire, and make

search, and ask diligently; and, behold, *if it be* truth, *and* the thing certain, *that* such abomination is wrought among you;

15 Thou shalt surely smite the inhabitants of that city with the edge of the sword, destroying it utterly, and all that *is* therein, and the cattle thereof, with the edge of the sword.

16 And thou shalt gather all the spoil of it into the midst of the street thereof, and shalt burn with fire the city, and all the spoil thereof every whit, for the LORD thy God: and it shall be an heap for ever; it shall not be built again.

17 And there shall cleave nought of the cursed thing to thine hand: that the LORD may turn from the fierceness of his anger, and shew thee mercy, and have compassion upon thee, and multiply thee, as he hath sworn unto thy fathers;

18 When thou shalt hearken to the voice of the LORD thy God, to keep all his commandments which I command thee this day, to do *that which is* right in the eyes of the LORD thy God.

14

1 Ye *are* the children of the LORD your God: ye shall not cut yourselves, nor make any baldness between your eyes for the dead.

2 For thou *art* an holy people unto the LORD thy God, and the LORD hath chosen thee to be a peculiar people unto himself, above all the nations that *are* upon the earth.

14:2
Adopted by God
➤ Isaiah 43:1 ➤

3 Thou shalt not eat any abominable thing.

4 These *are* the beasts which ye shall eat: the ox, the sheep, and the goat,

5 The hart, and the roebuck, and the fallow deer, and the wild goat, and the pygarg, and the wild ox, and the chamois.

6 And every beast that parteth the hoof, and cleaveth the cleft into two claws, *and* cheweth the cud among the beasts, that ye shall eat.

7 Nevertheless these ye shall not eat of them that chew the cud, or of them that divide the cloven hoof; *as* the camel, and the hare, and the coney: for they chew the cud, but divide not the hoof; *therefore* they *are* unclean unto you.

8 And the swine, because it divideth the hoof, yet cheweth not the cud, it *is* unclean unto you: ye shall not eat of their flesh, nor touch their dead carcase.

9 These ye shall eat of all that *are* in the waters: all that have fins and scales shall ye eat:

10 And whatsoever hath not fins and scales ye may not eat; it *is* unclean unto you.

11 *Of* all clean birds ye shall eat.

12 But these *are they* of which ye shall not eat: the eagle, and ossifrage, and the ospray,

13 And the glede, and the kite, and the vulture after his kind,

14 And every raven after his kind,

15 And the owl, and the night hawk, and the cuckow, and the hawk after his kind,

16 The little owl, and the great owl, and the swan,

17 And the pelican, and the gier eagle, and the cormorant,

18 And the stork, and the heron after her kind, and the lapwing, and the bat.

19 And every creeping thing that flieth *is* unclean unto you: they shall not be eaten.

20 *But of* all clean fowls ye may eat.

21 Ye shall not eat *of* any thing that dieth of itself: thou shalt give it unto the stranger that *is* in thy gates, that he may eat it; or thou mayest sell it unto an alien: for thou *art* an holy people unto the LORD thy God. Thou shalt not seethe a kid in his mother's milk.

22 Thou shalt truly tithe all the increase of thy seed, that the field bringeth forth year by year.

23 And thou shalt eat before the LORD thy God, in the place which he shall choose to place his name there, the tithe of thy corn, of thy wine, and of thine oil, and the firstlings of thy herds and of thy flocks; that thou mayest learn to fear the LORD thy God always.

24 And if the way be too long for thee, so that thou art not able to carry it; *or* if the place be too far from thee, which the LORD thy God shall choose to set his name there, when the LORD thy God hath blessed thee:

25 Then shalt thou turn *it* into money, and bind up the money in thine hand, and shalt go unto the place which the LORD thy God shall choose:

26 And thou shalt bestow that money for whatsoever thy soul lusteth after, for oxen,

or for sheep, or for wine, or for strong drink, or for whatsoever thy soul desireth: and thou shalt eat there before the LORD thy God, and thou shalt rejoice, thou, and thine household,

27 And the Levite that *is* within thy gates; thou shalt not forsake him; for he hath no part nor inheritance with thee.

28 At the end of three years thou shalt bring forth all the tithe of thine increase the same year, and shalt lay *it* up within thy gates:

29 And the Levite, (because he hath no part nor inheritance with thee,) and the stranger, and the fatherless, and the widow, which *are* within thy gates, shall come, and shall eat and be satisfied; that the LORD thy God may bless thee in all the work of thine hand which thou doest.

> **14:29 Kind to the Needy**
> ◄ Exodus 22:22
> Deuteronomy 24:17 ►

15

1 At the end of *every* seven years thou shalt make a release.

2 And this *is* the manner of the release: Every creditor that lendeth *ought* unto his neighbour shall release *it;* he shall not exact *it* of his neighbour, or of his brother; because it is called the LORD'S release.

3 Of a foreigner thou mayest exact *it again:* but *that* which is thine with thy brother thine hand shall release;

4 Save when there shall be no poor among you; for the LORD shall greatly bless thee in the land which the LORD thy God giveth thee *for* an inheritance to possess it:

5 Only if thou carefully hearken unto the voice of the LORD thy God, to observe to do all these commandments which I command thee this day.

6 For the LORD thy God blesseth thee, as he promised thee: and thou shalt lend unto many nations, but thou shalt not borrow; and thou shalt reign over many nations, but they shall not reign over thee.

> **15:7 Generosity**
> ◄ Leviticus 25:35
> Proverbs 31:20 ►

7 If there be among you a poor man of one of thy brethren within any of thy gates in thy land which the LORD thy God giveth thee, thou shalt not harden thine heart, nor shut thine hand from thy poor brother:

> **15:7 Kind to the Poor**
> ◄ Leviticus 25:25
> Deuteronomy 24:12 ►

8 But thou shalt open thine hand wide unto him, and shalt surely lend him sufficient for his need, *in that* which he wanteth.

> **15:8**
> **Sharing**
> ◄ Psalm 37:26 ►

9 Beware that there be not a thought in thy wicked heart, saying, The seventh year, the year of release, is at hand; and thine eye be evil against thy poor brother, and thou givest him nought; and he cry unto the LORD against thee, and it be sin unto thee.

> **15:9**
> **Bad Thoughts**
> ◄ Psalm 64:6 ►

10 Thou shalt surely give him, and thine heart shall not be grieved when thou givest unto him: because that for this thing the LORD thy God shall bless thee in all thy works, and in all that thou puttest thine hand unto.

11 For the poor shall never cease out of the land: therefore I command thee, saying, Thou shalt open thine hand wide unto thy brother, to thy poor, and to thy needy, in thy land.

12 *And* if thy brother, an Hebrew man, or an Hebrew woman, be sold unto thee, and serve thee six years; then in the seventh year thou shalt let him go free from thee.

> **15:12-14**
> **Giving**
> ◄ Nehemiah 8:10 ►

13 And when thou sendest him out free from thee, thou shalt not let him go away empty:

14 Thou shalt furnish him liberally out of thy flock, and out of thy floor, and out of thy winepress: *of that* wherewith the LORD thy God hath blessed thee thou shalt give unto him.

15 And thou shalt remember that thou wast a bondman in the land of Egypt, and the LORD thy God redeemed thee: therefore I command thee this thing to day.

16 And it shall be, if he say unto thee, I will not go away from thee; because he loveth thee and thine house, because he is well with thee;

17 Then thou shalt take an aul, and thrust *it* through his ear unto the door, and he

shall be thy servant for ever. And also unto thy maidservant thou shalt do likewise.

18 It shall not seem hard unto thee, when thou sendest him away free from thee; for he hath been worth a double hired servant *to thee,* in serving thee six years: and the LORD thy God shall bless thee in all that thou doest.

19 All the firstling males that come of thy herd and of thy flock thou shalt sanctify unto the LORD thy God: thou shalt do no work with the firstling of thy bullock, nor shear the firstling of thy sheep.

20 Thou shalt eat *it* before the LORD thy God year by year in the place which the LORD shall choose, thou and thy household.

21 And if there be *any* blemish therein, *as if it be* lame, or blind, *or have* any ill blemish, thou shalt not sacrifice it unto the LORD thy God.

22 Thou shalt eat it within thy gates: the unclean and the clean *person shall eat it* alike, as the roebuck, and as the hart.

23 Only thou shalt not eat the blood thereof; thou shalt pour it upon the ground as water.

16

1 Observe the month of Abib, and keep the passover unto the LORD thy God: for in the month of Abib the LORD thy God brought thee forth out of Egypt by night.

2 Thou shalt therefore sacrifice the passover unto the LORD thy God, of the flock and the herd, in the place which the LORD shall choose to place his name there.

3 Thou shalt eat no leavened bread with it; seven days shalt thou eat unleavened bread therewith, *even* the bread of affliction; for thou camest forth out of the land of Egypt in haste: that thou mayest remember the day when thou camest forth out of the land of Egypt all the days of thy life.

4 And there shall be no leavened bread seen with thee in all thy coast seven days; neither shall there *any thing* of the flesh, which thou sacrificedst the first day at even, remain all night until the morning.

5 Thou mayest not sacrifice the passover within any of thy gates, which the LORD thy God giveth thee:

6 But at the place which the LORD thy God shall choose to place his name in, there thou shalt sacrifice the passover at even, at the going down of the sun, at the season that thou camest forth out of Egypt.

7 And thou shalt roast and eat *it* in the place which the LORD thy God shall choose: and thou shalt turn in the morning, and go unto thy tents.

8 Six days thou shalt eat unleavened bread: and on the seventh day *shall be* a solemn assembly to the LORD thy God: thou shalt do no work *therein.*

9 Seven weeks shalt thou number unto thee: begin to number the seven weeks from *such time as* thou beginnest *to put* the sickle to the corn.

10 And thou shalt keep the feast of weeks unto the LORD thy God with a tribute of a freewill offering of thine hand, which thou shalt give *unto the LORD thy God,* according as the LORD thy God hath blessed thee:

11 And thou shalt rejoice before the LORD thy God, thou, and thy son, and thy daughter, and thy manservant, and thy maidservant, and the Levite that *is* within thy gates, and the stranger, and the fatherless, and the widow, that *are* among you, in the place which the LORD thy God hath chosen to place his name there.

16:11 Rejoicing
◄ Deuteronomy 12:7
Psalm 5:11 ►

12 And thou shalt remember that thou wast a bondman in Egypt: and thou shalt observe and do these statutes.

13 Thou shalt observe the feast of tabernacles seven days, after that thou hast gathered in thy corn and thy wine:

14 And thou shalt rejoice in thy feast, thou, and thy son, and thy daughter, and thy manservant, and thy maidservant, and the Levite, the stranger, and the fatherless, and the widow, that *are* within thy gates.

15 Seven days shalt thou keep a solemn feast unto the LORD thy God in the place which the LORD shall choose: because the LORD thy God shall bless thee in all thine increase, and in all the works of thine hands, therefore thou shalt surely rejoice.

16 Three times in a year shall all thy males appear before the LORD thy God in the place which he shall choose; in the feast of unleavened bread, and in the feast of weeks, and in the feast of tabernacles: and they shall not appear before the LORD empty:

17 Every man *shall give* as he is able,

Turn to the next page for more . . .

according to the
blessing of the LORD
thy God which he
hath given thee.
18 Judges and of-
ficers shalt thou
make thee in all thy gates, which the LORD
thy God giveth thee, throughout thy tribes:
and they shall judge the people with just
judgment.

16:17
How to Give
◄ Matthew 5:42 ►

19 Thou shalt not
wrest judgment;
thou shalt not re-
spect persons, nei-
ther take a gift: for
a gift doth blind
the eyes of the wise,
and pervert the
words of the righ-
teous.

16:19
Don't Be Unfair
◄ Deuteronomy 24:17 ►

16:20
Be Fair
◄ Psalm 82:3 ►

20 That which is
altogether just shalt
thou follow, that thou mayest live, and
inherit the land which the LORD thy God
giveth thee.
21 Thou shalt not plant thee a grove of
any trees near unto the altar of the LORD
thy God, which thou shalt make thee.
22 Neither shalt thou set thee up *any* image; which the LORD thy God hateth.

17

1 Thou shalt not sacrifice unto the LORD
thy God *any* bullock, or sheep, wherein is
blemish, *or* any evilfavouredness: for that
is an abomination unto the LORD thy God.
2 If there be found among you, within
any of thy gates which the LORD thy God
giveth thee, man or woman, that hath
wrought wickedness in the sight of the
LORD thy God, in transgressing his covenant,
3 And hath gone and served other gods,
and worshipped them, either the sun, or
moon, or any of the host of heaven, which
I have not commanded;
4 And it be told thee, and thou hast heard
of it, and enquired diligently, and, behold,
it be true, *and* the thing certain, *that* such
abomination is wrought in Israel:
5 Then shalt thou bring forth that man
or that woman, which have committed
that wicked thing, unto thy gates, *even* that
man or that woman, and shalt stone them
with stones, till they die.
6 At the mouth of two witnesses, or three
witnesses, shall he that is worthy of death
be put to death; *but* at the mouth of one
witness he shall not be put to death.
7 The hands of the witnesses shall be first
upon him to put him to death, and afterward the hands of all the people. So thou
shalt put the evil away from among you.
8 If there arise a matter too hard for thee
in judgment, between blood and blood,
between plea and plea, and between stroke
and stroke, *being* matters of controversy
within thy gates: then shalt thou arise, and
get thee up into the place which the LORD
thy God shall choose;
9 And thou shalt come unto the priests
the Levites, and unto the judge that shall
be in those days, and enquire; and they
shall shew thee the sentence of judgment:
10 And thou shalt do according to the
sentence, which they of that place which
the LORD shall choose shall shew thee; and
thou shalt observe to do according to all
that they inform thee:
11 According to the sentence of the law
which they shall teach thee, and according to the judgment which they shall tell
thee, thou shalt do: thou shalt not decline
from the sentence which they shall shew
thee, *to* the right hand, nor *to* the left.
12 And the man
that will do pre-
sumptuously, and
will not hearken
unto the priest that
standeth to minis-
ter there before the LORD thy God, or unto
the judge, even that man shall die: and
thou shalt put away the evil from Israel.

17:12
Rebellion
◄ Ezra 7:26 ►

13 And all the people shall hear, and fear,
and do no more presumptuously.
14 When thou art come unto the land
which the LORD thy God giveth thee, and
shalt possess it, and shalt dwell therein,
and shalt say, I will set a king over me, like
as all the nations that *are* about me;
15 Thou shalt in any wise set *him* king
over thee, whom the LORD thy God shall
choose: *one* from among thy brethren shalt
thou set king over thee: thou mayest not
set a stranger over thee, which *is* not thy
brother.
16 But he shall
not multiply horses
to himself, nor
cause the people to
return to Egypt, to

17:16
Leaders Should...
◄ 2 Samuel 23:3 ►

the end that he should multiply horses: forasmuch as the LORD hath said unto you, Ye shall henceforth return no more that way.

17 Neither shall he multiply wives to himself, that his heart turn not away: neither shall he greatly multiply to himself silver and gold.

18 And it shall be, when he sitteth upon the throne of his kingdom, that he shall write him a copy of this law in a book out of *that which is* before the priests the Levites:

19 And it shall be with him, and he shall read therein all the days of his life: that he may learn to fear the LORD his God, to keep all the words of this law and these statutes, to do them:

> **17:19**
> **Reading the Bible**
> ◄ Isaiah 34:16 ►

20 That his heart be not lifted up above his brethren, and that he turn not aside from the commandment, *to* the right hand, or *to* the left: to the end that he may prolong *his* days in his kingdom, he, and his children, in the midst of Israel.

18

1 The priests the Levites, *and* all the tribe of Levi, shall have no part nor inheritance with Israel: they shall eat the offerings of the LORD made by fire, and his inheritance.

2 Therefore shall they have no inheritance among their brethren: the LORD *is* their inheritance, as he hath said unto them.

3 And this shall be the priest's due from the people, from them that offer a sacrifice, whether *it be* ox or sheep; and they shall give unto the priest the shoulder, and the two cheeks, and the maw.

4 The firstfruit *also* of thy corn, of thy wine, and of thine oil, and the first of the fleece of thy sheep, shalt thou give him.

5 For the LORD thy God hath chosen him out of all thy tribes, to stand to minister in the name of the LORD, him and his sons for ever.

6 And if a Levite come from any of thy gates out of all Israel, where he sojourned, and come with all the desire of his mind unto the place which the LORD shall choose;

7 Then he shall minister in the name of the LORD his God, as all his brethren the Levites *do*, which stand there before the LORD.

8 They shall have like portions to eat, beside that which cometh of the sale of his patrimony.

9 When thou art come into the land which the LORD thy God giveth thee, thou shalt not learn to do after the abominations of those nations.

> **18:9 Bad Examples**
> ◄ Leviticus 20:23
> Proverbs 22:24-25 ►

10 There shall not be found among you *any one* that maketh his son or his daughter to pass through the fire, or that useth divination, *or* an observer of times, or an enchanter, or a witch,

11 Or a charmer, or a consulter with familiar spirits, or a wizard, or a necromancer.

12 For all that do these things *are* an abomination unto the LORD: and because of these abominations the LORD thy God doth drive them out from before thee.

13 Thou shalt be perfect with the LORD thy God.

> **18:13 Perfection**
> ◄ Genesis 17:1
> 1 Kings 8:61 ►

14 For these nations, which thou shalt possess, hearkened unto observers of times, and unto diviners: but as for thee, the LORD thy God hath not suffered thee so *to do*.

15 The LORD thy God will raise up unto thee a Prophet from the midst of thee, of thy brethren, like unto me; unto him ye shall hearken;

16 According to all that thou desiredst of the LORD thy God in Horeb in the day of the assembly, saying, Let me not hear again the voice of the LORD my God, neither let me see this great fire any more, that I die not.

17 And the LORD said unto me, They have well *spoken that* which they have spoken.

18 I will raise them up a Prophet from among their brethren, like unto thee, and will put my words in his mouth; and he shall speak unto them all that I shall command him.

19 And it shall come to pass, *that* whosoever will not hearken unto my words which he shall speak in my name, I will require *it* of him.

20 But the prophet, which shall presume to speak a word in my name, which I have not commanded him to speak, or that

shall speak in the name of other gods, even
that prophet shall die.
21 And if thou say in thine heart, How
shall we know the word which the LORD
hath not spoken?
22 When a prophet speaketh in the name
of the LORD, if the thing follow not, nor
come to pass, that *is* the thing which the
LORD hath not spoken, *but* the prophet
hath spoken it presumptuously: thou shalt
not be afraid of him.

19

1 When the LORD thy God hath cut off
the nations, whose land the LORD thy God
giveth thee, and thou succeedest them, and
dwellest in their cities, and in their houses;
2 Thou shalt separate three cities for thee
in the midst of thy land, which the LORD
thy God giveth thee to possess it.
3 Thou shalt prepare thee a way, and divide the coasts of thy land, which the LORD
thy God giveth thee to inherit, into three
parts, that every slayer may flee thither.
4 And this *is* the case of the slayer, which
shall flee thither, that he may live: Whoso
killeth his neighbour ignorantly, whom he
hated not in time past;
5 As when a man goeth into the wood
with his neighbour to hew wood, and his
hand fetcheth a stroke with the axe to cut
down the tree, and the head slippeth from
the helve, and lighteth upon his neighbour, that he die; he shall flee unto one of
those cities, and live:
6 Lest the avenger of the blood pursue
the slayer, while his heart is hot, and overtake him, because the way is long, and slay
him; whereas he *was* not worthy of death,
inasmuch as he hated him not in time past.
7 Wherefore I command thee, saying,
Thou shalt separate three cities for thee.
8 And if the LORD thy God enlarge thy
coast, as he hath sworn unto thy fathers,
and give thee all the land which he promised to give unto thy fathers;
9 If thou shalt keep all these commandments to do them, which I command thee
this day, to love the LORD thy God, and to
walk ever in his ways; then shalt thou add
three cities more for thee, beside these
three:
10 That innocent blood be not shed in
thy land, which the LORD thy God giveth
thee *for* an inheritance, and *so* blood be
upon thee.
11 But if any man hate his neighbour, and
lie in wait for him, and rise up against him,
and smite him mortally that he die, and
fleeth into one of these cities:
12 Then the elders of his city shall send
and fetch him thence, and deliver him into
the hand of the avenger of blood, that he
may die.
13 Thine eye shall not pity him, but thou
shalt put away *the guilt of* innocent blood
from Israel, that it may go well with thee.
14 Thou shalt not remove thy neighbour's landmark, which they of old time
have set in thine inheritance, which thou
shalt inherit in the land that the LORD thy
God giveth thee to possess it.
15 One witness shall not rise up against
a man for any iniquity, or for any sin, in
any sin that he sinneth: at the mouth of
two witnesses, or at the mouth of three
witnesses, shall the matter be established.
16 If a false wit-
ness rise up against
any man to testify
against him *that*
which is wrong;
17 Then both the
men, between whom the controversy *is*,
shall stand before the LORD, before the
priests and the judges, which shall be in
those days;
18 And the judges shall make diligent
inquisition: and, behold, *if* the witness *be*
a false witness, *and* hath testified falsely
against his brother;
19 Then shall ye do unto him, as he had
thought to have done unto his brother: so
shalt thou put the evil away from among
you.
20 And those which remain shall hear,
and fear, and shall henceforth commit no
more any such evil among you.
21 And thine eye shall not pity; *but* life
shall go for life, eye for eye, tooth for tooth,
hand for hand, foot for foot.

19:16 Hurtful Lying
◄ Exodus 23:1
Proverbs 6:19 ►

20

1 When thou goest out to battle against
thine enemies, and seest horses, and chariots, *and* a people more than thou, be not
afraid of them: for the LORD thy God *is*
with thee, which brought thee up out of
the land of Egypt.
2 And it shall be, when ye are come nigh
unto the battle, that the priest shall approach and speak unto the people,
3 And shall say unto them, Hear, O Israel,
ye approach this day unto battle against

your enemies: let not your hearts faint, fear
not, and do not tremble, neither be ye terrified because of them;
4 For the LORD your God *is* he that goeth
with you, to fight for you against your enemies, to save you.
5 And the officers shall speak unto the
people, saying, What man *is there* that hath
built a new house, and hath not dedicated it? let him go and return to his house,
lest he die in the battle, and another man
dedicate it.
6 And what man *is he* that hath planted
a vineyard, and hath not *yet* eaten of it? let
him *also* go and return unto his house, lest
he die in the battle, and another man eat
of it.
7 And what man *is there* that hath betrothed a wife, and hath not taken her? let
him go and return unto his house, lest he
die in the battle, and another man take her.
8 And the officers shall speak further
unto the people, and they shall say, What
man *is there that is* fearful and fainthearted? let him go and return unto his house,
lest his brethren's heart faint as well as his
heart.
9 And it shall be, when the officers have
made an end of speaking unto the people,
that they shall make captains of the armies
to lead the people.
10 When thou comest nigh unto a city
to fight against it, then proclaim peace
unto it.
11 And it shall be, if it make thee answer
of peace, and open unto thee, then it shall
be, *that* all the people *that is* found therein
shall be tributaries unto thee, and they
shall serve thee.
12 And if it will make no peace with thee,
but will make war against thee, then thou
shalt besiege it:
13 And when the LORD thy God hath delivered it into thine hands, thou shalt smite
every male thereof with the edge of the
sword:
14 But the women, and the little ones,
and the cattle, and all that is in the city,
even all the spoil thereof, shalt thou take
unto thyself; and thou shalt eat the spoil
of thine enemies, which the LORD thy God
hath given thee.
15 Thus shalt thou do unto all the cities
which are very far off from thee, which *are*
not of the cities of these nations.
16 But of the cities of these people, which
the LORD thy God doth give thee *for* an
inheritance, thou shalt save alive nothing
that breatheth:
17 But thou shalt utterly destroy them;
namely, the Hittites, and the Amorites, the
Canaanites, and the Perizzites, the Hivites,
and the Jebusites; as the LORD thy God
hath commanded thee:
18 That they teach you not to do after all
their abominations, which they have done
unto their gods; so should ye sin against
the LORD your God.
19 When thou shalt besiege a city a long
time, in making war against it to take it,
thou shalt not destroy the trees thereof by
forcing an axe against them: for thou
mayest eat of them, and thou shalt not cut
them down (for the tree of the field *is*
man's *life*) to employ *them* in the siege:
20 Only the trees which thou knowest
that they *be* not trees for meat, thou shalt
destroy and cut them down; and thou shalt
build bulwarks against the city that maketh
war with thee, until it be subdued.

21

1 If *one* be found slain in the land which
the LORD thy God giveth thee to possess
it, lying in the field, *and* it be not known
who hath slain him:
2 Then thy elders and thy judges shall
come forth, and they shall measure unto
the cities which *are* round about him that
is slain:
3 And it shall be, *that* the city *which is*
next unto the slain man, even the elders
of that city shall take an heifer, which hath
not been wrought with, *and* which hath
not drawn in the yoke;
4 And the elders of that city shall bring
down the heifer unto a rough valley, which
is neither eared nor sown, and shall strike
off the heifer's neck there in the valley:
5 And the priests the sons of Levi shall
come near; for them the LORD thy God
hath chosen to minister unto him, and to
bless in the name of the LORD; and by their
word shall every controversy and every
stroke be *tried:*
6 And all the elders of that city, *that are*
next unto the slain *man,* shall wash their
hands over the heifer that is beheaded in
the valley:
7 And they shall answer and say, Our
hands have not shed this blood, neither
have our eyes seen *it.*

8 Be merciful, O LORD, unto thy people Israel, whom thou hast redeemed, and lay not innocent blood unto thy people of Israel's charge. And the blood shall be forgiven them.

21:8
Praying for Mercy
◄ 1 Kings 8:30 ►

9 So shalt thou put away the *guilt of* innocent blood from among you, when thou shalt do *that which is* right in the sight of the LORD.

10 When thou goest forth to war against thine enemies, and the LORD thy God hath delivered them into thine hands, and thou hast taken them captive,

11 And seest among the captives a beautiful woman, and hast a desire unto her, that thou wouldest have her to thy wife;

12 Then thou shalt bring her home to thine house; and she shall shave her head, and pare her nails;

13 And she shall put the raiment of her captivity from off her, and shall remain in thine house, and bewail her father and her mother a full month: and after that thou shalt go in unto her, and be her husband, and she shall be thy wife.

14 And it shall be, if thou have no delight in her, then thou shalt let her go whither she will; but thou shalt not sell her at all for money, thou shalt not make merchandise of her, because thou hast humbled her.

15 If a man have two wives, one beloved, and another hated, and they have born him children, *both* the beloved and the hated; and *if* the firstborn son be hers that was hated:

16 Then it shall be, when he maketh his sons to inherit *that* which he hath, *that* he may not make the son of the beloved firstborn before the son of the hated, *which is indeed* the firstborn:

17 But he shall acknowledge the son of the hated *for* the firstborn, by giving him a double portion of all that he hath: for he *is* the beginning of his strength; the right of the firstborn *is* his.

18 If a man have a stubborn and rebellious son, which will not obey the voice of his father, or the voice of his mother, and *that,* when they have chastened him, will not hearken unto them:

19 Then shall his father and his mother lay hold on him, and bring him out unto the elders of his city, and unto the gate of his place;

20 And they shall say unto the elders of his city, This our son *is* stubborn and rebellious, he will not obey our voice; *he is* a glutton, and a drunkard.

21:20
Getting Drunk
◄ Proverbs 20:1 ►

21 And all the men of his city shall stone him with stones, that he die: so shalt thou put evil away from among you; and all Israel shall hear, and fear.

22 And if a man have committed a sin worthy of death, and he be to be put to death, and thou hang him on a tree:

23 His body shall not remain all night upon the tree, but thou shalt in any wise bury him that day; (for he that *is* hanged *is* accursed of God;) that thy land be not defiled, which the LORD thy God giveth thee *for* an inheritance.

22

1 Thou shalt not see the brother's ox or his sheep go astray, and hide thyself from them: thou shalt in any case bring them again unto thy brother.

2 And if thy brother *be* not nigh unto thee, or if thou know him not, then thou shalt bring it unto thine own house, and it shall be with thee until thy brother seek after it, and thou shalt restore it to him again.

3 In like manner shalt thou do with his ass; and so shalt thou do with his raiment; and with all lost things of thy brother's, which he hath lost, and thou hast found, shalt thou do likewise: thou mayest not hide thyself.

4 Thou shalt not see thy brother's ass or his ox fall down by the way, and hide thyself from them: thou shalt surely help him to lift *them* up again.

5 The woman shall not wear that which pertaineth unto a man, neither shall a man put on a woman's garment: for all that do so *are* abomination unto the LORD thy God.

6 If a bird's nest chance to be before thee in the way in any tree, or on the ground, *whether they be* young ones, or eggs, and the dam sitting upon

22:6 Animals
◄ Exodus 23:5
Luke 14:5 ►

the young, or upon the eggs, thou shalt
not take the dam with the young:
7*But* thou shalt in any wise let the dam
go, and take the young to thee; that it may
be well with thee, and *that* thou mayest
prolong *thy* days.
8When thou buildest a new house, then
thou shalt make a battlement for thy roof,
that thou bring not blood upon thine
house, if any man fall from thence.
9Thou shalt not sow thy vineyard with
divers seeds: lest the fruit of thy seed which
thou hast sown, and the fruit of thy vineyard, be defiled.
10Thou shalt not plow with an ox and
an ass together.
11Thou shalt not wear a garment of
divers sorts, *as* of woollen and linen together.
12Thou shalt make thee fringes upon the
four quarters of thy vesture, wherewith
thou coverest *thyself.*
13If any man take a wife, and go in unto
her, and hate her,
14And give occasions of speech against
her, and bring up an evil name upon her,
and say, I took this woman, and when I
came to her, I found her not a maid:
15Then shall the father of the damsel,
and her mother, take and bring forth *the
tokens of* the damsel's virginity unto the
elders of the city in the gate:
16And the damsel's father shall say unto
the elders, I gave my daughter unto this
man to wife, and he hateth her;
17And, lo, he hath given occasions of
speech *against her,* saying, I found not thy
daughter a maid; and yet these *are the tokens of* my daughter's virginity. And they
shall spread the cloth before the elders of
the city.
18And the elders of that city shall take
that man and chastise him;
19And they shall amerce him in an hundred *shekels* of silver, and give *them* unto
the father of the damsel, because he hath
brought up an evil name upon a virgin of
Israel: and she shall be his wife; he may
not put her away all his days.
20But if this thing be true, *and the tokens
of* virginity be not found for the damsel:
21Then they shall bring out the damsel
to the door of her father's house, and the
men of her city shall stone her with stones
that she die: because she hath wrought
folly in Israel, to play the whore in her
father's house: so shalt thou put evil away
from among you.
22If a man be found lying with a woman married to an husband, then they shall
both of them die, *both* the man that lay
with the woman, and the woman: so shalt
thou put away evil from Israel.
23If a damsel *that is* a virgin be betrothed
unto an husband, and a man find her in
the city, and lie with her;
24Then ye shall bring them both out
unto the gate of that city, and ye shall stone
them with stones that they die; the damsel, because she cried not, *being* in the city;
and the man, because he hath humbled
his neighbour's wife: so thou shalt put
away evil from among you.
25But if a man find a betrothed damsel
in the field, and the man force her, and lie
with her: then the man only that lay with
her shall die:
26But unto the damsel thou shalt do
nothing; *there is* in the damsel no sin *worthy* of death: for as when a man riseth
against his neighbour, and slayeth him,
even so *is* this matter:
27For he found her in the field, *and* the
betrothed damsel cried, and *there was* none
to save her.
28If a man find a damsel *that is* a virgin,
which is not betrothed, and lay hold on
her, and lie with her, and they be found;
29Then the man that lay with her shall
give unto the damsel's father fifty *shekels*
of silver, and she shall be his wife; because
he hath humbled her, he may not put her
away all his days.
30A man shall not take his father's wife,
nor discover his father's skirt.

23

1He that is wounded in the stones, or
hath his privy member cut off, shall not
enter into the congregation of the LORD.
2A bastard shall not enter into the congregation of the LORD; even to his tenth
generation shall he not enter into the congregation of the LORD.
3An Ammonite or Moabite shall not
enter into the congregation of the LORD;
even to their tenth
generation shall
they not enter into
the congregation of
the LORD for ever:
4Because they

23:4 Cold Shoulder
◄ Numbers 21:23
Judges 19:15 ►

met you not with bread and with water in the way, when ye came forth out of Egypt; and because they hired against thee Balaam the son of Beor of Pethor of Mesopotamia, to curse thee.

5Nevertheless the LORD thy God would not hearken unto Balaam; but the LORD thy God turned the curse into a blessing unto thee, because the LORD thy God loved thee.

6Thou shalt not seek their peace nor their prosperity all thy days for ever.

7Thou shalt not abhor an Edomite; for he *is* thy brother: thou shalt not abhor an Egyptian; because thou wast a stranger in his land.

8The children that are begotten of them shall enter into the congregation of the LORD in their third generation.

9When the host goeth forth against thine enemies, then keep thee from every wicked thing.

10If there be among you any man, that is not clean by reason of uncleanness that chanceth him by night, then shall he go abroad out of the camp, he shall not come within the camp:

11But it shall be, when evening cometh on, he shall wash *himself* with water: and when the sun is down, he shall come into the camp *again*.

12Thou shalt have a place also without the camp, whither thou shalt go forth abroad:

13And thou shalt have a paddle upon thy weapon; and it shall be, when thou wilt ease thyself abroad, thou shalt dig therewith, and shalt turn back and cover that which cometh from thee:

14For the LORD thy God walketh in the midst of thy camp, to deliver thee, and to give up thine enemies before thee; therefore shall thy camp be holy: that he see no unclean thing in thee, and turn away from thee.

15Thou shalt not deliver unto his master the servant which is escaped from his master unto thee:

16He shall dwell with thee, *even* among you, in that place which he shall choose in one of thy gates, where it liketh him best: thou shalt not oppress him.

17There shall be no whore of the daughters of Israel, nor a sodomite of the sons of Israel.

18Thou shalt not bring the hire of a whore, or the price of a dog, into the house of the LORD thy God for any vow: for even both these *are* abomination unto the LORD thy God.

19Thou shalt not lend upon usury to thy brother; usury of money, usury of victuals, usury of any thing that is lent upon usury:

20Unto a stranger thou mayest lend upon usury; but unto thy brother thou shalt not lend upon usury: that the LORD thy God may bless thee in all that thou settest thine hand to in the land whither thou goest to possess it.

21When thou shalt vow a vow unto the LORD thy God, thou shalt not slack to pay it: for the LORD thy God will surely require it of thee; and it would be sin in thee.

22But if thou shalt forbear to vow, it shall be no sin in thee.

23That which is gone out of thy lips thou shalt keep and perform; *even* a freewill offering, according as thou hast vowed unto the LORD thy God, which thou hast promised with thy mouth.

24When thou comest into thy neighbour's vineyard, then thou mayest eat grapes thy fill at thine own pleasure; but thou shalt not put *any* in thy vessel.

23:24 Stealing
◄ Exodus 20:15
Zechariah 5:3 ►

25When thou comest into the standing corn of thy neighbour, then thou mayest pluck the ears with thine hand; but thou shalt not move a sickle unto thy neighbour's standing corn.

24

1When a man hath taken a wife, and married her, and it come to pass that she find no favour in his eyes, because he hath found some uncleanness in her: then let him write her a bill of divorcement, and give *it* in her hand, and send her out of his house.

2And when she is departed out of his house, she may go and be another man's *wife*.

3And *if* the latter husband hate her, and write her a bill of divorcement, and giveth *it* in her hand, and sendeth her out of his house; or if the latter husband die, which took her *to be* his wife;

4Her former husband, which sent her away, may not take her again to be his wife,

after that she is defiled; for that *is* abomination before the LORD: and thou shalt not
cause the land to sin, which the LORD thy
God giveth thee *for* an inheritance.
5 When a man hath taken a new wife, he
shall not go out to war, neither shall he
be charged with any business: *but* he shall
be free at home one year, and shall cheer
up his wife which he hath taken.
6 No man shall take the nether or the
upper millstone to pledge: for he taketh *a*
man's life to pledge.
7 If a man be found stealing any of his
brethren of the children of Israel, and
maketh merchandise of him, or selleth
him; then that thief shall die; and thou
shalt put evil away from among you.
8 Take heed in the plague of leprosy, that
thou observe diligently, and do according
to all that the priests the Levites shall teach
you: as I commanded them, so ye shall
observe to do.
9 Remember what the LORD thy God did
unto Miriam by the way, after that ye were
come forth out of Egypt.
10 When thou dost lend thy brother any
thing, thou shalt not go into his house to
fetch his pledge.
11 Thou shalt stand abroad, and the man
to whom thou dost lend shall bring out
the pledge abroad unto thee.
12 And if the man
be poor, thou shalt
not sleep with his
pledge:
13 In any case
thou shalt deliver
him the pledge again when the sun goeth
down, that he may sleep in his own raiment, and bless thee: and it shall be righteousness unto thee before the LORD thy
God.

24:12 Kind to the Poor
◄ Deuteronomy 15:7
Psalm 41:1 ►

14 Thou shalt not oppress an hired servant *that is* poor and needy, *whether he be*
of thy brethren, or of thy strangers that *are*
in thy land within thy gates:
15 At his day thou shalt give *him* his hire,
neither shall the sun go down upon it; for
he *is* poor, and setteth his heart upon it:
lest he cry against
thee unto the LORD,
and it be sin unto
thee.
16 The fathers
shall not be put to
death for the children, neither shall the
children be put to death for the fathers:
every man shall be put to death for his
own sin.

24:16 Blame
◄ Job 19:4 ►

17 Thou shalt not
pervert the judg-
ment of the strang-
er, *nor* of the father-
less; nor take a
widow's raiment to
pledge:
18 But thou shalt
remember that
thou wast a bond-
man in Egypt, and
the LORD thy God
redeemed thee thence: therefore I command thee to do this thing.

24:17 Don't Be Unfair
◄ Deuteronomy 16:19
Psalm 82:2 ►

24:17 Kind to the Needy
◄ Deuteronomy 14:29
Deuteronomy 26:12 ►

19 When thou cuttest down thine harvest
in thy field, and hast forgot a sheaf in the
field, thou shalt not go again to fetch it: it
shall be for the stranger, for the fatherless,
and for the widow: that the LORD thy God
may bless thee in all the work of thine
hands.
20 When thou beatest thine olive tree,
thou shalt not go over the boughs again:
it shall be for the stranger, for the fatherless, and for the widow.
21 When thou gatherest the grapes of thy
vineyard, thou shalt not glean *it* afterward:
it shall be for the stranger, for the fatherless, and for the widow.
22 And thou shalt remember that thou
wast a bondman in the land of Egypt:
therefore I command thee to do this thing.

25

1 If there be a controversy between men,
and they come unto judgment, that *the*
judges may judge them; then they shall
justify the righteous, and condemn the
wicked.
2 And it shall be, if the wicked man *be*
worthy to be beaten, that the judge shall
cause him to lie down, and to be beaten
before his face, according to his fault, by a
certain number.
3 Forty stripes he may give him, *and* not
exceed: lest, *if* he should exceed, and beat
him above these with many stripes, then
thy brother should seem vile unto thee.
4 Thou shalt not muzzle the ox when he
treadeth out *the corn*.
5 If brethren dwell together, and one of
them die, and have no child, the wife of
the dead shall not marry without unto a

stranger: her husband's brother shall go in
unto her, and take her to him to wife, and
perform the duty of an husband's brother
unto her.
6 And it shall be, *that* the firstborn which
she beareth shall succeed in the name of
his brother *which is* dead, that his name
be not put out of Israel.
7 And if the man like not to take his
brother's wife, then let his brother's wife
go up to the gate unto the elders, and say,
My husband's brother refuseth to raise up
unto his brother a name in Israel, he will
not perform the duty of my husband's
brother.
8 Then the elders of his city shall call
him, and speak unto him: and *if* he stand
to it, and say, I like not to take her;
9 Then shall his brother's wife come unto
him in the presence of the elders, and loose
his shoe from off his foot, and spit in his
face, and shall answer and say, So shall it
be done unto that man that will not build
up his brother's house.
10 And his name shall be called in Israel,
The house of him that hath his shoe
loosed.
11 When men strive together one with
another, and the wife of the one draweth
near for to deliver her husband out of the
hand of him that smiteth him, and putteth
forth her hand, and taketh him by the secrets:
12 Then thou shalt cut off her hand, thine
eye shall not pity *her.*
13 Thou shalt not have in thy bag divers
weights, a great and a small.
14 Thou shalt not have in thine house
divers measures, a great and a small.
15 *But* thou shalt have a perfect and just
weight, a perfect and just measure shalt
thou have: that thy days may be length-
ened in the land which the LORD thy God
giveth thee.
16 For all that do such things, *and* all that
do unrighteously, *are* an abomination unto
the LORD thy God.
17 Remember what Amalek did unto thee
by the way, when ye were come forth out
of Egypt;
18 How he met thee by the way, and
smote the hindmost of thee, *even* all *that*
were feeble behind thee, when thou *wast*
faint and weary; and he feared not God.
19 Therefore it shall be, when the LORD
thy God hath given thee rest from all thine
enemies round about, in the land which
the LORD thy God giveth thee *for* an inheritance to possess it, *that* thou shalt blot out
the remembrance of Amalek from under
heaven; thou shalt not forget *it.*

26

1 And it shall be, when thou *art* come in
unto the land which the LORD thy God
giveth thee *for* an inheritance, and pos-
sessest it, and dwellest therein;
2 That thou shalt take of the first of all
the fruit of the earth, which thou shalt
bring of thy land that the LORD thy God
giveth thee, and shalt put *it* in a basket,
and shalt go unto the place which the LORD
thy God shall choose to place his name
there.
3 And thou shalt go unto the priest that
shall be in those days, and say unto him,
I profess this day unto the LORD thy
God, that I am come unto the country
which the LORD sware unto our fathers for
to give us.
4 And the priest shall take the basket out
of thine hand, and set it down before the
altar of the LORD thy God.
5 And thou shalt speak and say before
the LORD thy God, A Syrian ready to perish *was* my father, and he went down into
Egypt, and sojourned there with a few, and
became there a nation, great, mighty, and
populous:
6 And the Egyptians evil entreated us,
and afflicted us, and laid upon us hard
bondage:
7 And when we cried unto the LORD God
of our fathers, the LORD heard our voice,
and looked on our affliction, and our
labour, and our oppression:
8 And the LORD brought us forth out of
Egypt with a mighty hand, and with an
outstretched arm, and with great terribleness, and with signs, and with wonders:
9 And he hath brought us into this place,
and hath given us this land, *even* a land
that floweth with milk and honey.
10 And now, be-
hold, I have brought
the firstfruits of the
land, which thou,
O LORD, hast given
me. And thou shalt
set it before the LORD thy God, and worship before the LORD thy God:
11 And thou shalt rejoice in every good

26:10
Worship
◄ 2 Kings 17:36 ►

thing which the LORD thy God hath given unto thee, and unto thine house, thou, and the Levite, and the stranger that *is* among you.

12When thou hast made an end of tithing all the tithes of thine increase the third year, *which is* the year of tithing, and hast given *it* unto the Levite, the stranger, the fatherless, and the widow, that they may eat within thy gates, and be filled;

26:12 Kind to the Needy
◄ Deuteronomy 24:17
Proverbs 23:10 ►

13Then thou shalt say before the LORD thy God, I have brought away the hallowed things out of *mine* house, and also have given them unto the Levite, and unto the stranger, to the fatherless, and to the widow, according to all thy commandments which thou hast commanded me: I have not transgressed thy commandments, neither have I forgotten *them:*

14I have not eaten thereof in my mourning, neither have I taken away *ought* thereof for *any* unclean *use,* nor given *ought* thereof for the dead: *but* I have hearkened to the voice of the LORD my God, *and* have done according to all that thou hast commanded me.

15Look down from thy holy habitation, from heaven, and bless thy people Israel, and the land which thou hast given us, as thou swarest unto our fathers, a land that floweth with milk and honey.

16This day the LORD thy God hath commanded thee to do these statutes and judgments: thou shalt therefore keep and do them with all thine heart, and with all thy soul.

26:16
Obeying God
◄ Deuteronomy 32:46 ►

17Thou hast avouched the LORD this day to be thy God, and to walk in his ways, and to keep his statutes, and his commandments, and his judgments, and to hearken unto his voice:

18And the LORD hath avouched thee this day to be his peculiar people, as he hath promised thee, and that *thou* shouldest keep all his commandments;

19And to make thee high above all nations which he hath made, in praise, and in name, and in honour; and that thou mayest be an holy people unto the LORD thy God, as he hath spoken.

27

1And Moses with the elders of Israel commanded the people, saying, Keep all the commandments which I command you this day.

2And it shall be on the day when ye shall pass over Jordan unto the land which the LORD thy God giveth thee, that thou shalt set thee up great stones, and plaister them with plaister:

3And thou shalt write upon them all the words of this law, when thou art passed over, that thou mayest go in unto the land which the LORD thy God giveth thee, a land that floweth with milk and honey; as the LORD God of thy fathers hath promised thee.

4Therefore it shall be when ye be gone over Jordan, *that* ye shall set up these stones, which I command you this day, in mount Ebal, and thou shalt plaister them with plaister.

5And there shalt thou build an altar unto the LORD thy God, an altar of stones: thou shalt not lift up *any* iron *tool* upon them.

6Thou shalt build the altar of the LORD thy God of whole stones: and thou shalt offer burnt offerings thereon unto the LORD thy God:

7And thou shalt offer peace offerings, and shalt eat there, and rejoice before the LORD thy God.

8And thou shalt write upon the stones all the words of this law very plainly.

9And Moses and the priests the Levites spake unto all Israel, saying, Take heed, and hearken, O Israel; this day thou art become the people of the LORD thy God.

10Thou shalt therefore obey the voice of the LORD thy God, and do his commandments and his statutes, which I command thee this day.

11And Moses charged the people the same day, saying,

12These shall stand upon mount Gerizim to bless the people, when ye are come over Jordan; Simeon, and Levi, and Judah, and Issachar, and Joseph, and Benjamin:

13And these shall stand upon mount Ebal to curse; Reuben, Gad, and Asher, and Zebulun, Dan, and Naphtali.

14And the Levites shall speak, and say unto all the men of Israel with a loud voice,

15 Cursed *be* the man that maketh *any* graven or molten image, an abomination unto the LORD, the work of the hands of the craftsman, and putteth *it* in *a* secret *place.* And all the people shall answer and say, Amen.

16 Cursed *be* he that setteth light by his father or his mother. And all the people shall say, Amen.

17 Cursed *be* he that removeth his neighbour's landmark. And all the people shall say, Amen.

18 Cursed *be* he that maketh the blind to wander out of the way. And all the people shall say, Amen.

19 Cursed *be* he that perverteth the judgment of the stranger, fatherless, and widow. And all the people shall say, Amen.

27:19 New Kids

◄ Deuteronomy 10:19
Deuteronomy 31:12 ►

20 Cursed *be* he that lieth with his father's wife; because he uncovereth his father's skirt. And all the people shall say, Amen.

21 Cursed *be* he that lieth with any manner of beast. And all the people shall say, Amen.

22 Cursed *be* he that lieth with his sister, the daughter of his father, or the daughter of his mother. And all the people shall say, Amen.

23 Cursed *be* he that lieth with his mother in law. And all the people shall say, Amen.

24 Cursed *be* he that smiteth his neighbour secretly. And all the people shall say, Amen.

25 Cursed *be* he that taketh reward to slay an innocent person. And all the people shall say, Amen.

26 Cursed *be* he that confirmeth not *all* the words of this law to do them. And all the people shall say, Amen.

28

1 And it shall come to pass, if thou shalt hearken diligently unto the voice of the LORD thy God, to observe *and* to do all his commandments which I command thee this day, that the LORD thy God will set thee on high above all nations of the earth:

2 And all these blessings shall come on thee, and overtake thee, if thou shalt hearken unto the voice of the LORD thy God.

3 Blessed *shalt* thou *be* in the city, and blessed *shalt* thou *be* in the field.

4 Blessed *shall be* the fruit of thy body, and the fruit of thy ground, and the fruit of thy cattle, the increase of thy kine, and the flocks of thy sheep.

5 Blessed *shall be* thy basket and thy store.

6 Blessed *shalt* thou *be* when thou comest in, and blessed *shalt* thou *be* when thou goest out.

7 The LORD shall cause thine enemies that rise up against thee to be smitten before thy face: they shall come out against thee one way, and flee before thee seven ways.

8 The LORD shall command the blessing upon thee in thy storehouses, and in all that thou settest thine hand unto; and he shall bless thee in the land which the LORD thy God giveth thee.

9 The LORD shall establish thee an holy people unto himself, as he hath sworn unto thee, if thou shalt keep the commandments of the LORD thy God, and walk in his ways.

10 And all people of the earth shall see that thou art called by the name of the LORD; and they shall be afraid of thee.

11 And the LORD shall make thee plenteous in goods, in the fruit of thy body, and in the fruit of thy cattle, and in the fruit of thy ground, in the land which the LORD sware unto thy fathers to give thee.

12 The LORD shall open unto thee his good treasure, the heaven to give the rain unto thy land in his season, and to bless all the work of thine hand: and thou shalt lend unto many nations, and thou shalt not borrow.

13 And the LORD shall make thee the head, and not the tail; and thou shalt be above only, and thou shalt not be beneath; if that thou hearken unto the commandments of the LORD thy God, which I command thee this day, to observe and to do *them:*

14 And thou shalt not go aside from any of the words which I command thee this day, *to* the right hand, or *to* the left, to go after other gods to serve them.

15 But it shall come to pass, if thou wilt not hearken unto the voice of the LORD thy God, to observe to do all his commandments and his statutes

28:15 Ouch!

◄ Deuteronomy 11:28
1 Samuel 12:15 ►

which I command thee this day; that all
these curses shall come upon thee, and
overtake thee:
[16]Cursed *shalt* thou *be* in the city, and
cursed *shalt* thou *be* in the field.
[17]Cursed *shall be* thy basket and thy
store.
[18]Cursed *shall be* the fruit of thy body,
and the fruit of thy land, the increase of
thy kine, and the flocks of thy sheep.
[19]Cursed *shalt* thou *be* when thou
comest in, and cursed *shalt* thou *be* when
thou goest out.
[20]The LORD shall send upon thee cursing, vexation, and rebuke, in all that thou
settest thine hand unto for to do, until
thou be destroyed, and until thou perish
quickly; because of the wickedness of thy
doings, whereby thou hast forsaken me.
[21]The LORD shall make the pestilence
cleave unto thee, until he have consumed
thee from off the land, whither thou goest
to possess it.
[22]The LORD shall smite thee with a consumption, and with a fever, and with an
inflammation, and with an extreme burning, and with the sword, and with blasting, and with mildew; and they shall
pursue thee until thou perish.
[23]And thy heaven that *is* over thy head
shall be brass, and the earth that is under
thee *shall be* iron.
[24]The LORD shall make the rain of thy
land powder and dust: from heaven shall
it come down upon thee, until thou be
destroyed.
[25]The LORD shall cause thee to be smitten before thine enemies: thou shalt go out
one way against them, and flee seven ways
before them: and shalt be removed into
all the kingdoms of the earth.
[26]And thy carcase shall be meat unto
all fowls of the air, and unto the beasts of
the earth, and no man shall fray *them*
away.
[27]The LORD will smite thee with the
botch of Egypt, and with the emerods, and
with the scab, and with the itch, whereof
thou canst not be healed.
[28]The LORD shall smite thee with madness, and blindness, and astonishment of
heart:
[29]And thou shalt grope at noonday, as
the blind gropeth in darkness, and thou
shalt not prosper in thy ways: and thou
shalt be only oppressed and spoiled evermore, and no man shall save *thee.*
[30]Thou shalt betroth a wife, and another
man shall lie with her: thou shalt build
an house, and thou shalt not dwell therein:
thou shalt plant a vineyard, and shalt not
gather the grapes thereof.
[31]Thine ox *shall be* slain before thine
eyes, and thou shalt not eat thereof: thine
ass *shall be* violently taken away from before thy face, and shall not be restored to
thee: thy sheep *shall be* given unto thine
enemies, and thou shalt have none to rescue *them.*
[32]Thy sons and
thy daughters *shall*
be given unto an-
other people, and
thine eyes shall
look, and fail *with*
longing for them all the day long: and *there*
shall be no might in thine hand.

28:32 Cost of Sin
◄ Leviticus 26:37
Joshua 7:12 ►

[33]The fruit of thy land, and all thy
labours, shall a nation which thou knowest
not eat up; and thou shalt be only oppressed and crushed alway:
[34]So that thou shalt be mad for the sight
of thine eyes which thou shalt see.
[35]The LORD shall smite thee in the knees,
and in the legs, with a sore botch that cannot be healed, from the sole of thy foot
unto the top of thy head.
[36]The LORD shall bring thee, and thy
king which thou shalt set over thee, unto
a nation which neither thou nor thy fathers have known; and there shalt thou
serve other gods, wood and stone.
[37]And thou shalt become an astonishment, a proverb, and a byword, among all
nations whither the LORD shall lead thee.
[38]Thou shalt carry much seed out into
the field, and shalt gather *but* little in; for
the locust shall consume it.
[39]Thou shalt
plant vineyards,
and dress *them,* but
shalt neither drink
of the wine, nor
gather *the grapes;* for
the worms shall eat them.

28:39 Disappointment
◄ Job 11:20 ►

[40]Thou shalt have olive trees throughout all thy coasts, but thou shalt not anoint
thyself with the oil; for thine olive shall cast
his fruit.
[41]Thou shalt beget sons and daughters,

but thou shalt not enjoy them; for they shall go into captivity.

42 All thy trees and fruit of thy land shall the locust consume.

43 The stranger that *is* within thee shall get up above thee very high; and thou shalt come down very low.

44 He shall lend to thee, and thou shalt not lend to him: he shall be the head, and thou shalt be the tail.

45 Moreover all these curses shall come upon thee, and shall pursue thee, and overtake thee, till thou be destroyed; because thou hearkenedst not unto the voice of the LORD thy God, to keep his commandments and his statutes which he commanded thee:

46 And they shall be upon thee for a sign and for a wonder, and upon thy seed for ever.

47 Because thou servedst not the LORD thy God with joyfulness, and with gladness of heart, for the abundance of all *things;*

48 Therefore shalt thou serve thine enemies which the LORD shall send against thee, in hunger, and in thirst, and in nakedness, and in want of all *things:* and he shall put a yoke of iron upon thy neck, until he have destroyed thee.

49 The LORD shall bring a nation against thee from far, from the end of the earth, *as swift* as the eagle flieth; a nation whose tongue thou shalt not understand;

50 A nation of fierce countenance, which shall not regard the person of the old, nor shew favour to the young:

51 And he shall eat the fruit of thy cattle, and the fruit of thy land, until thou be destroyed: which *also* shall not leave thee *either* corn, wine, or oil, *or* the increase of thy kine, or flocks of thy sheep, until he have destroyed thee.

52 And he shall besiege thee in all thy gates, until thy high and fenced walls come down, wherein thou trustedst, throughout all thy land: and he shall besiege thee in all thy gates throughout all thy land, which the LORD thy God hath given thee.

53 And thou shalt eat the fruit of thine own body, the flesh of thy sons and of thy daughters, which the LORD thy God hath given thee, in the siege, and in the straitness, wherewith thine enemies shall distress thee:

54 *So that* the man *that is* tender among you, and very delicate, his eye shall be evil toward his brother, and toward the wife of his bosom, and toward the remnant of his children which he shall leave:

55 So that he will not give to any of them of the flesh of his children whom he shall eat: because he hath nothing left him in the siege, and in the straitness, wherewith thine enemies shall distress thee in all thy gates.

56 The tender and delicate woman among you, which would not adventure to set the sole of her foot upon the ground for delicateness and tenderness, her eye shall be evil toward the husband of her bosom, and toward her son, and toward her daughter,

57 And toward her young one that cometh out from between her feet, and toward her children which she shall bear: for she shall eat them for want of all *things* secretly in the siege and straitness, wherewith thine enemy shall distress thee in thy gates.

58 If thou wilt not observe to do all the words of this law that are written in this book, that thou mayest fear this glorious and fearful name, THE LORD THY GOD;

59 Then the LORD will make thy plagues wonderful, and the plagues of thy seed, *even* great plagues, and of long continuance, and sore sicknesses, and of long continuance.

60 Moreover he will bring upon thee all the diseases of Egypt, which thou wast afraid of; and they shall cleave unto thee.

61 Also every sickness, and every plague, which *is* not written in the book of this law, them will the LORD bring upon thee, until thou be destroyed.

62 And ye shall be left few in number, whereas ye were as the stars of heaven for multitude; because thou wouldest not obey the voice of the LORD thy God.

63 And it shall come to pass, *that* as the LORD rejoiced over you to do you good, and to multiply you; so the LORD will rejoice over you to destroy you, and to bring you to nought; and ye shall be plucked from off the land whither thou goest to possess it.

64 And the LORD shall scatter thee among all people, from the one end of the earth even unto the other; and there thou shalt

serve other gods, which neither thou nor thy fathers have known, *even* wood and stone.

65 And among these nations shalt thou find no ease, neither shall the sole of thy foot have rest: but the LORD shall give thee there a trembling heart, and failing of eyes, and sorrow of mind:

66 And thy life shall hang in doubt before thee; and thou shalt fear day and night, and shalt have none assurance of thy life:

67 In the morning thou shalt say, Would God it were even! and at even thou shalt say, Would God it were morning! for the fear of thine heart wherewith thou shalt fear, and for the sight of thine eyes which thou shalt see.

68 And the LORD shall bring thee into Egypt again with ships, by the way whereof I spake unto thee, Thou shalt see it no more again: and there ye shall be sold unto your enemies for bondmen and bondwomen, and no man shall buy *you.*

29

1 These *are* the words of the covenant, which the LORD commanded Moses to make with the children of Israel in the land of Moab, beside the covenant which he made with them in Horeb.

2 And Moses called unto all Israel, and said unto them, Ye have seen all that the LORD did before your eyes in the land of Egypt unto Pharaoh, and unto all his servants, and unto all his land;

3 The great temptations which thine eyes have seen, the signs, and those great miracles:

4 Yet the LORD hath not given you an heart to perceive, and eyes to see, and ears to hear, unto this day.

5 And I have led you forty years in the wilderness: your clothes are not waxen old upon you, and thy shoe is not waxen old upon thy foot.

6 Ye have not eaten bread, neither have ye drunk wine or strong drink: that ye might know that I *am* the LORD your God.

29:6 Drinking
◄ Numbers 6:3
Judges 13:4 ►

7 And when ye came unto this place, Sihon the king of Heshbon, and Og the king of Bashan, came out against us unto battle, and we smote them:

8 And we took their land, and gave it for an inheritance unto the Reubenites, and to the Gadites, and to the half tribe of Manasseh.

9 Keep therefore the words of this covenant, and do them, that ye may prosper in all that ye do.

10 Ye stand this day all of you before the LORD your God; your captains of your tribes, your elders, and your officers, *with* all the men of Israel,

11 Your little ones, your wives, and thy stranger that *is* in thy camp, from the hewer of thy wood unto the drawer of thy water:

12 That thou shouldest enter into covenant with the LORD thy God, and into his oath, which the LORD thy God maketh with thee this day:

13 That he may establish thee to day for a people unto himself, and *that* he may be unto thee a God, as he hath said unto thee, and as he hath sworn unto thy fathers, to Abraham, to Isaac, and to Jacob.

14 Neither with you only do I make this covenant and this oath;

15 But with *him* that standeth here with us this day before the LORD our God, and also with *him* that *is* not here with us this day:

16 (For ye know how we have dwelt in the land of Egypt; and how we came through the nations which ye passed by;

17 And ye have seen their abominations, and their idols, wood and stone, silver and gold, which *were* among them:)

18 Lest there should be among you man, or woman, or family, or tribe, whose heart turneth away this day from the LORD our God, to go *and* serve the gods of these nations; lest there should be among you a root that beareth gall and wormwood;

19 And it come to pass, when he heareth the words of this curse, that he bless himself in his heart, saying, I shall have peace, though I walk in the imagination of mine heart, to add drunkenness to thirst:

29:20 God Is Jealous
◄ Deuteronomy 4:24
Joshua 24:19 ►

20 The LORD will not spare him, but then the anger of the LORD and his jealousy shall smoke

29:20 Sin (Warnings)
◄ Genesis 19:17
Joshua 24:20 ►

against that man, and all the curses that are written in this book shall lie upon him, and the LORD shall blot out his name from under heaven.

21 And the LORD shall separate him unto evil out of all the tribes of Israel, according to all the curses of the covenant that are written in this book of the law:

22 So that the generation to come of your children that shall rise up after you, and the stranger that shall come from a far land, shall say, when they see the plagues of that land, and the sicknesses which the LORD hath laid upon it;

23 *And that* the whole land thereof *is* brimstone, and salt, *and* burning, *that* it is not sown, nor beareth, nor any grass groweth therein, like the overthrow of Sodom, and Gomorrah, Admah, and Zeboim, which the LORD overthrew in his anger, and in his wrath:

24 Even all nations shall say, Wherefore hath the LORD done thus unto this land? what *meaneth* the heat of this great anger?

25 Then men shall say, Because they have forsaken the covenant of the LORD God of their fathers, which he made with them when he brought them forth out of the land of Egypt:

26 For they went and served other gods, and worshipped them, gods whom they knew not, and *whom* he had not given unto them:

27 And the anger of the LORD was kindled against this land, to bring upon it all the curses that are written in this book:

28 And the LORD rooted them out of their land in anger, and in wrath, and in great indignation, and cast them into another land, as *it is* this day.

29 The secret *things belong* unto the LORD our God: but those *things which are* revealed *belong* unto us and to our children for ever, that *we* may do all the words of this law.

30

1 And it shall come to pass, when all these things are come upon thee, the blessing and the curse, which I have set before thee, and thou shalt call *them* to mind among all the nations, whither the LORD thy God hath driven thee,

2 And shalt return unto the LORD thy God, and shalt obey his voice according to all that I command thee this day, thou and thy children, with all thine heart, and with all thy soul;

3 That then the LORD thy God will turn thy captivity, and have compassion upon thee, and will return and gather thee from all the nations, whither the LORD thy God hath scattered thee.

4 If *any* of thine be driven out unto the outmost *parts* of heaven, from thence will the LORD thy God gather thee, and from thence will he fetch thee:

5 And the LORD thy God will bring thee into the land which thy fathers possessed, and thou shalt possess it; and he will do thee good, and multiply thee above thy fathers.

6 And the LORD thy God will circumcise thine heart, and the heart of thy seed, to love the LORD thy God with all thine heart, and with all thy soul, that thou mayest live.

7 And the LORD thy God will put all these curses upon thine enemies, and on them that hate thee, which persecuted thee.

8 And thou shalt return and obey the voice of the LORD, and do all his commandments which I command thee this day.

9 And the LORD thy God will make thee plenteous in every work of thine hand, in the fruit of thy body, and in the fruit of thy cattle, and in the fruit of thy land, for good: for the LORD will again rejoice over thee for good, as he rejoiced over thy fathers:

10 If thou shalt hearken unto the voice of the LORD thy God, to keep his commandments and his statutes which are written in this book of the law, *and* if thou turn unto the LORD thy God with all thine heart, and with all thy soul.

11 For this commandment which I command thee this day, it *is* not hidden from thee, neither *is* it far off.

12 It *is* not in heaven, that thou shouldest say, Who shall go up for us to heaven, and bring it unto us, that we may hear it, and do it?

13 Neither *is* it beyond the sea, that thou shouldest say, Who shall go over the sea for us, and bring it unto us, that we may hear it, and do it?

14 But the word *is* very nigh unto thee, in thy mouth, and in thy heart, that thou mayest do it.

15 See, I have set

30:15
Following God
◄ Joshua 24:15 ►

before thee this day life and good, and
death and evil;
16 In that I command thee this day to
love the LORD thy God, to walk in his ways,
and to keep his commandments and his
statutes and his judgments, that thou
mayest live and multiply: and the LORD thy
God shall bless thee in the land whither
thou goest to possess it.
17 But if thine heart turn away, so that
thou wilt not hear, but shalt be drawn
away, and worship other gods, and serve
them;
18 I denounce unto you this day, that ye
shall surely perish, *and that* ye shall not
prolong *your* days upon the land, whither
thou passest over Jordan to go to possess it.
19 I call heaven and earth to record this
day against you, *that* I have set before you
life and death, blessing and cursing: therefore choose life, that both thou and thy
seed may live:
20 That thou mayest love the LORD thy
God, *and* that thou mayest obey his voice,
and that thou mayest cleave unto him: for
he *is* thy life, and the length of thy days:
that thou mayest dwell in the land which
the LORD sware unto thy fathers, to Abraham, to Isaac, and to Jacob, to give them.

31

1 And Moses went and spake these words
unto all Israel.
2 And he said unto them, I *am* an hundred and twenty years old this day; I can
no more go out and come in: also the LORD
hath said unto me, Thou shalt not go over
this Jordan.
3 The LORD thy God, he will go over before thee, *and* he will destroy these nations
from before thee, and thou shalt possess
them: *and* Joshua, he shall go over before
thee, as the LORD hath said.
4 And the LORD shall do unto them as
he did to Sihon and to Og, kings of the
Amorites, and unto the land of them,
whom he destroyed.
5 And the LORD shall give them up before your face, that ye may do unto them
according unto all the commandments
which I have commanded you.
6 Be strong and of a good courage, fear
not, nor be afraid of them: for the LORD
thy God, he *it is* that doth go with thee; he
will not fail thee, nor forsake thee.
7 And Moses called unto Joshua, and said
unto him in the sight of all Israel, Be strong
and of a good courage: for thou must go
with this people unto the land which the
LORD hath sworn unto their fathers to give
them; and thou shalt cause them to inherit it.
8 And the LORD, he *it is* that doth go before thee; he will be with thee, he will not
fail thee, neither forsake thee: fear not,
neither be dismayed.
9 And Moses wrote this law, and delivered it unto the priests the sons of Levi,
which bare the ark of the covenant of the
LORD, and unto all the elders of Israel.
10 And Moses commanded them, saying,
At the end of *every* seven years, in the solemnity of the year of release, in the feast
of tabernacles,
11 When all Israel is come to appear before the LORD thy God in the place which
he shall choose, thou shalt read this law
before all Israel in their hearing.
12 Gather the peo-
ple together, men,
and women, and
children, and thy
stranger that *is*
within thy gates,
that they may hear, and that they may
learn, and fear the LORD your God, and
observe to do all the words of this law:

31:12 New Kids
◄ Deuteronomy 27:19
Jeremiah 7:6 ►

13 And *that* their children, which have
not known *any thing*, may hear, and learn
to fear the LORD your God, as long as ye
live in the land whither ye go over Jordan
to possess it.
14 And the LORD said unto Moses, Behold, thy days approach that thou must
die: call Joshua, and present yourselves in
the tabernacle of the congregation, that I
may give him a charge. And Moses and
Joshua went, and presented themselves in
the tabernacle of the congregation.
15 And the LORD appeared in the tabernacle in a pillar of a cloud: and the pillar
of the cloud stood over the door of the
tabernacle.
16 And the LORD said unto Moses, Behold, thou shalt sleep with thy fathers; and
this people will rise up, and go a whoring
after the gods of the strangers of the land,
whither they go *to be* among them, and
will forsake me, and break my covenant
which I have made with them.
17 Then my anger shall be kindled
against them in that day, and I will forsake

them, and I will hide my face from them, and they shall be devoured, and many evils and troubles shall befall them; so that they will say in that day, Are not these evils come upon us, because our God *is* not among us?

18 And I will surely hide my face in that day for all the evils which they shall have wrought, in that they are turned unto other gods.

19 Now therefore write ye this song for you, and teach it the children of Israel: put it in their mouths, that this song may be a witness for me against the children of Israel.

20 For when I shall have brought them into the land which I sware unto their fathers, that floweth with milk and honey; and they shall have eaten and filled themselves, and waxen fat; then will they turn unto other gods, and serve them, and provoke me, and break my covenant.

31:20 Losers
◄ Deuteronomy 9:7
Ezra 5:12 ►

21 And it shall come to pass, when many evils and troubles are befallen them, that this song shall testify against them as a witness; for it shall not be forgotten out of the mouths of their seed: for I know their imagination which they go about, even now, before I have brought them into the land which I sware.

22 Moses therefore wrote this song the same day, and taught it the children of Israel.

23 And he gave Joshua the son of Nun a charge, and said, Be strong and of a good courage: for thou shalt bring the children of Israel into the land which I sware unto them: and I will be with thee.

24 And it came to pass, when Moses had made an end of writing the words of this law in a book, until they were finished,

25 That Moses commanded the Levites, which bare the ark of the covenant of the LORD, saying,

26 Take this book of the law, and put it in the side of the ark of the covenant of the LORD your God, that it may be there for a witness against thee.

27 For I know thy rebellion, and thy stiff neck: behold, while I am yet alive with you this day, ye have been rebellious against the LORD; and how much more after my death?

28 Gather unto me all the elders of your tribes, and your officers, that I may speak these words in their ears, and call heaven and earth to record against them.

29 For I know that after my death ye will utterly corrupt *yourselves*, and turn aside from the way which I have commanded you; and evil will befall you in the latter days; because ye will do evil in the sight of the LORD, to provoke him to anger through the work of your hands.

30 And Moses spake in the ears of all the congregation of Israel the words of this song, until they were ended.

32

1 Give ear, O ye heavens, and I will speak; and hear, O earth, the words of my mouth.

2 My doctrine shall drop as the rain, my speech shall distil as the dew, as the small rain upon the tender herb, and as the showers upon the grass:

3 Because I will publish the name of the LORD: ascribe ye greatness unto our God.

4 *He is* the Rock, his work *is* perfect: for all his ways *are* judgment: a God of truth and without iniquity, just and right *is* he.

5 They have corrupted themselves, their spot *is* not *the spot* of his children: *they are* a perverse and crooked generation.

6 Do ye thus requite the LORD, O foolish people and unwise? *is* not he thy father *that* hath bought thee? hath he not made thee, and established thee?

7 Remember the days of old, consider the years of many generations: ask thy father, and he will shew thee; thy elders, and they will tell thee.

8 When the most High divided to the nations their inheritance, when he separated the sons of Adam, he set the bounds

32:4
God's Justice
◄ Psalm 103:6 ►

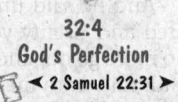

32:4
God's Perfection
◄ 2 Samuel 22:31 ►

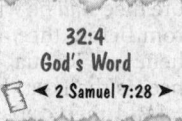

32:4
God's Word
◄ 2 Samuel 7:28 ►

32:6
Gratitude
◄ Nehemiah 9:26 ►

of the people according to the number of the children of Israel.

9 For the LORD'S portion *is* his people; Jacob *is* the lot of his inheritance.

> **32:8 Names of God**
> ◄ Deuteronomy 10:17
> Deuteronomy 33:27 ►

10 He found him in a desert land, and in the waste howling wilderness; he led him about, he instructed him, he kept him as the apple of his eye.

11 As an eagle stirreth up her nest, fluttereth over her young, spreadeth abroad her wings, taketh them, beareth them on her wings:

12 *So* the LORD alone did lead him, and *there was* no strange god with him.

13 He made him ride on the high places of the earth, that he might eat the increase of the fields; and he made him to suck honey out of the rock, and oil out of the flinty rock;

14 Butter of kine, and milk of sheep, with fat of lambs, and rams of the breed of Bashan, and goats, with the fat of kidneys of wheat; and thou didst drink the pure blood of the grape.

15 But Jeshurun waxed fat, and kicked: thou art waxen fat, thou art grown thick, thou art covered *with fatness;* then he forsook God *which* made him, and lightly esteemed the Rock of his salvation.

> **32:15 Success**
> ◄ Deuteronomy 6:10-12
> Proverbs 1:32 ►

16 They provoked him to jealousy with strange *gods,* with abominations provoked they him to anger.

17 They sacrificed unto devils, not to God; to gods whom they knew not, to new *gods that* came newly up, whom your fathers feared not.

18 Of the Rock *that* begat thee thou art unmindful, and hast forgotten God that formed thee.

19 And when the LORD saw *it,* he abhorred *them,* because of the provoking of his sons, and of his daughters.

20 And he said, I will hide my face from them, I will see what their end *shall be:* for they *are* a very froward generation, children in whom *is* no faith.

21 They have moved me to jealousy with *that which is* not God; they have provoked me to anger with their vanities: and I will move them to jealousy with *those which are* not a people; I will provoke them to anger with a foolish nation.

> **32:21 Worshiping Things**
> ◄ 1 Kings 16:13 ►

22 For a fire is kindled in mine anger, and shall burn unto the lowest hell, and shall consume the earth with her increase, and set on fire the foundations of the mountains.

23 I will heap mischiefs upon them; I will spend mine arrows upon them.

24 *They shall be* burnt with hunger, and devoured with burning heat, and with bitter destruction: I will also send the teeth of beasts upon them, with the poison of serpents of the dust.

25 The sword without, and terror within, shall destroy both the young man and the virgin, the suckling *also* with the man of gray hairs.

26 I said, I would scatter them into corners, I would make the remembrance of them to cease from among men:

27 Were it not that I feared the wrath of the enemy, lest their adversaries should behave themselves strangely, *and* lest they should say, Our hand *is* high, and the LORD hath not done all this.

28 For they *are* a nation void of counsel, neither *is there any* understanding in them.

29 O that they were wise, *that* they understood this, *that* they would consider their latter end!

30 How should one chase a thousand, and two put ten thousand to flight, except their Rock had sold them, and the LORD had shut them up?

31 For their rock *is* not as our Rock, even our enemies themselves *being* judges.

32 For their vine *is* of the vine of Sodom, and of the fields of Gomorrah: their grapes *are* grapes of gall, their clusters *are* bitter:

> **32:32 Sinner Beware**
> ◄ Numbers 32:23
> Ecclesiastes 8:8 ►

33 Their wine *is* the poison of dragons, and the cruel venom of asps.

34 *Is* not this laid up in store with me, *and* sealed up among my treasures?

35 To me *belongeth* vengeance, and recompence; their foot shall slide in *due*

time: for the day of their calamity *is* at hand, and the things that shall come upon them make haste.

36 For the LORD shall judge his people, and repent himself for his servants, when he seeth that *their* power is gone, and *there is* none shut up, or left.

37 And he shall say, Where *are* their gods, *their* rock in whom they trusted,

38 Which did eat the fat of their sacrifices, *and* drank the wine of their drink offerings? let them rise up and help you, *and* be your protection.

39 See now that I, *even* I, *am* he, and *there is* no god with me: I kill, and I make alive; I wound, and I heal: neither *is there any* that can deliver out of my hand.

> **32:39 Only One God**
> ◄ Deuteronomy 6:4
> 2 Samuel 7:22 ►

40 For I lift up my hand to heaven, and say, I live for ever.

41 If I whet my glittering sword, and mine hand take hold on judgment; I will render vengeance to mine enemies, and will reward them that hate me.

42 I will make mine arrows drunk with blood, and my sword shall devour flesh; *and that* with the blood of the slain and of the captives, from the beginning of revenges upon the enemy.

43 Rejoice, O ye nations, *with* his people: for he will avenge the blood of his servants, and will render vengeance to his adversaries, and will be merciful unto his land, *and* to his people.

44 And Moses came and spake all the words of this song in the ears of the people, he, and Hoshea the son of Nun.

45 And Moses made an end of speaking all these words to all Israel:

46 And he said unto them, Set your hearts unto all the words which I testify among you this day, which ye shall command your children to observe to do, all the words of this law.

> **32:46 Obeying God**
> ◄ Deuteronomy 26:16
> Joshua 1:8 ►

47 For it *is* not a vain thing for you; because it *is* your life: and through this thing ye shall prolong *your* days in the land, whither ye go over Jordan to possess it.

48 And the LORD spake unto Moses that selfsame day, saying,

49 Get thee up into this mountain Abarim, *unto* mount Nebo, which *is* in the land of Moab, that *is* over against Jericho; and behold the land of Canaan, which I give unto the children of Israel for a possession:

50 And die in the mount whither thou goest up, and be gathered unto thy people; as Aaron thy brother died in mount Hor, and was gathered unto his people:

51 Because ye trespassed against me among the children of Israel at the waters of Meribah-Kadesh, in the wilderness of Zin; because ye sanctified me not in the midst of the children of Israel.

> **32:51 Why Not Sin?**
> ◄ Genesis 3:19
> 1 Chronicles 10:13 ►

52 Yet thou shalt see the land before *thee;* but thou shalt not go thither unto the land which I give the children of Israel.

33

1 And this *is* the blessing, wherewith Moses the man of God blessed the children of Israel before his death.

2 And he said, The LORD came from Sinai, and rose up from Seir unto them; he shined forth from mount Paran, and he came with ten thousands of saints: from his right hand *went* a fiery law for them.

3 Yea, he loved the people; all his saints *are* in thy hand: and they sat down at thy feet; *every one* shall receive of thy words.

4 Moses commanded us a law, *even* the inheritance of the congregation of Jacob.

5 And he was king in Jeshurun, when the heads of the people *and* the tribes of Israel were gathered together.

6 Let Reuben live, and not die; and let *not* his men be few.

7 And this *is the blessing* of Judah: and he said, Hear, LORD, the voice of Judah, and bring him unto his people: let his hands be sufficient for him; and be thou an help *to him* from his enemies.

8 And of Levi he said, *Let* thy Thummim and thy Urim *be* with thy holy one, whom thou didst prove at Massah, *and with* whom thou didst strive at the waters of Meribah;

9 Who said unto his father and to his mother, I have not seen him; neither did he acknowledge his brethren, nor knew his own children: for they have observed thy word, and kept thy covenant.

10 They shall teach Jacob thy judgments,

and Israel thy law: they shall put incense before thee, and whole burnt sacrifice upon thine altar.

11 Bless, LORD, his substance, and accept the work of his hands: smite through the loins of them that rise against him, and of them that hate him, that they rise not again.

12 *And* of Benjamin he said, The beloved of the LORD shall dwell in safety by him; *and the LORD* shall cover him all the day long, and he shall dwell between his shoulders.

13 And of Joseph he said, Blessed of the LORD *be* his land, for the precious things of heaven, for the dew, and for the deep that coucheth beneath,

14 And for the precious fruits *brought forth* by the sun, and for the precious things put forth by the moon,

15 And for the chief things of the ancient mountains, and for the precious things of the lasting hills,

16 And for the precious things of the earth and fulness thereof, and *for* the good will of him that dwelt in the bush: let *the blessing* come upon the head of Joseph, and upon the top of the head of him *that was* separated from his brethren.

17 His glory *is like* the firstling of his bullock, and his horns *are like* the horns of unicorns: with them he shall push the people together to the ends of the earth: and they *are* the ten thousands of Ephraim, and they *are* the thousands of Manasseh.

18 And of Zebulun he said, Rejoice, Zebulun, in thy going out; and, Issachar, in thy tents.

19 They shall call the people unto the mountain; there they shall offer sacrifices of righteousness: for they shall suck *of* the abundance of the seas, and *of* treasures hid in the sand.

20 And of Gad he said, Blessed *be* he that enlargeth Gad: he dwelleth as a lion, and teareth the arm with the crown of the head.

21 And he provided the first part for himself, because there, *in* a portion of the lawgiver, *was he* seated; and he came with the heads of the people, he executed the justice of the LORD, and his judgments with Israel.

22 And of Dan he said, Dan *is* a lion's whelp: he shall leap from Bashan.

23 And of Naphtali he said, O Naphtali, satisfied with favour, and full with the blessing of the LORD: possess thou the west and the south.

24 And of Asher he said, *Let* Asher *be* blessed with children; let him be acceptable to his brethren, and let him dip his foot in oil.

25 Thy shoes *shall be* iron and brass; and as thy days, *so shall* thy strength *be.*

26 *There is* none like unto the God of Jeshurun, *who* rideth upon the heaven in thy help, and in his excellency on the sky.

27 The eternal God *is thy* refuge, and underneath *are* the everlasting arms: and he shall thrust out the enemy from before thee; and shall say, Destroy *them.*

33:27 Names of God
◄ Deuteronomy 32:8
Joshua 3:10 ►

28 Israel then shall dwell in safety alone: the fountain of Jacob *shall be* upon a land of corn and wine; also his heavens shall drop down dew.

29 Happy *art* thou, O Israel: who *is* like unto thee, O people saved by the LORD, the shield of thy help, and who *is* the sword of thy excellency! and thine enemies shall be found liars unto thee; and thou shalt tread upon their high places.

34

1 And Moses went up from the plains of Moab unto the mountain of Nebo, to the top of Pisgah, that *is* over against Jericho. And the LORD shewed him all the land of Gilead, unto Dan,

2 And all Naphtali, and the land of Ephraim, and Manasseh, and all the land of Judah, unto the utmost sea,

3 And the south, and the plain of the valley of Jericho, the city of palm trees, unto Zoar.

4 And the LORD said unto him, This *is* the land which I sware unto Abraham, unto Isaac, and unto Jacob, saying, I will give it unto thy seed: I have caused thee to see *it* with thine eyes, but thou shalt not go over thither.

5 So Moses the servant of the LORD died there in the land of Moab, according to the word of the LORD.

6 And he buried him in a valley in the land of Moab, over against Beth-peor: but no man knoweth of his sepulchre unto this day.

7 And Moses *was* an hundred and twenty

years old when he died: his eye was not dim, nor his natural force abated.

8And the children of Israel wept for Moses in the plains of Moab thirty days: so the days of weeping *and* mourning for Moses were ended.

9And Joshua the son of Nun was full of the spirit of wisdom; for Moses had laid his hands upon him: and the children of Israel hearkened unto him, and did as the LORD commanded Moses.

10And there arose not a prophet since in Israel like unto Moses, whom the LORD knew face to face,

11In all the signs and the wonders, which the LORD sent him to do in the land of Egypt to Pharaoh, and to all his servants, and to all his land,

12And in all that mighty hand, and in all the great terror which Moses shewed in the sight of all Israel.

34:10 God's Friends

◄ Numbers 12:8
2 Chronicles 20:7 ►

Joshua

AUTHOR
Joshua; conclusion possibly written by the high priest Phinehas

MAIN POINT
Success—the amazing history of God's people continues as they finally enter and claim the Promised Land.

DATE WRITTEN
Sometime between 1200 and 550 B.C.

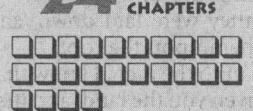

24 CHAPTERS

MAIN PEOPLE

Joshua, Rahab, Achan, Phinehas, Eleazar

SPECIAL FEATURES

- *Discloses how only two of the original million-plus people of the exodus got to enter the Promised Land*
- *Entry begins with a crossing of water, the Jordan River, just as the exodus began with a crossing of the Red Sea*
- *Pays tribute to a sinful woman who saved the lives of Israel's spies*
- *Describes the amazingly musical conquest of the walled town of Jericho*
- *First book of History*

HOW THE BOOK GOT ITS NAME

The book tells the story of the Israelites under Joshua's godly leadership.

1 1Now after the death of Moses the servant of the LORD it came to pass, that the
LORD spake unto Joshua the son of Nun,
Moses' minister, saying,
2Moses my servant is dead; now therefore arise, go over this Jordan, thou, and
all this people, unto the land which I do
give to them, *even* to the children of Israel.
3Every place that the sole of your foot
shall tread upon, that have I given unto
you, as I said unto Moses.
4From the wilderness and this Lebanon
even unto the great river, the river Euphrates, all the land of the Hittites, and unto
the great sea toward the going down of the
sun, shall be your coast.
5There shall not any man be able to
stand before thee all the days of thy life:
as I was with Moses, *so* I will be with thee:
I will not fail thee, nor forsake thee.
6Be strong and of a good courage: for
unto this people shalt thou divide for an
inheritance the land, which I sware unto
their fathers to give them.
7Only be thou
strong and very
courageous, that
thou mayest ob-
serve to do accord-
ing to all the law,
which Moses my servant commanded thee:
turn not from it *to* the right hand or *to* the

1:7 One Goal
◄ Deuteronomy 5:32
Proverbs 4:27 ►

left, that thou mayest prosper whithersoever thou goest.

8 This book of the law shall not depart out of thy mouth; but thou shalt meditate therein day and night, that thou mayest observe to do according to all that is written therein: for then thou shalt make thy way prosperous, and then thou shalt have good success.

1:8 Obeying God
◄ Deuteronomy 32:46
1 Samuel 15:22 ►

9 Have not I commanded thee? Be strong and of a good courage; be not afraid, neither be thou dismayed: for the LORD thy God *is* with thee whithersoever thou goest.

10 Then Joshua commanded the officers of the people, saying,

11 Pass through the host, and command the people, saying, Prepare you victuals; for within three days ye shall pass over this Jordan, to go in to possess the land, which the LORD your God giveth you to possess it.

12 And to the Reubenites, and to the Gadites, and to half the tribe of Manasseh, spake Joshua, saying,

13 Remember the word which Moses the servant of the LORD commanded you, saying, The LORD your God hath given you rest, and hath given you this land.

14 Your wives, your little ones, and your cattle, shall remain in the land which Moses gave you on this side Jordan; but ye shall pass before your brethren armed, all the mighty men of valour, and help them;

15 Until the LORD have given your brethren rest, as *he hath given* you, and they also have possessed the land which the LORD your God giveth them: then ye shall return unto the land of your possession, and enjoy it, which Moses the LORD'S servant gave you on this side Jordan toward the sunrising.

16 And they answered Joshua, saying, All that thou commandest us we will do, and whithersoever thou sendest us, we will go.

17 According as we hearkened unto Moses in all things, so will we hearken unto thee: only the LORD thy God be with thee, as he was with Moses.

18 Whosoever *he be* that doth rebel against thy commandment, and will not hearken unto thy words in all that thou commandest him, he shall be put to death: only be strong and of a good courage.

2

1 And Joshua the son of Nun sent out of Shittim two men to spy secretly, saying, Go view the land, even Jericho. And they went, and came into an harlot's house, named Rahab, and lodged there.

2 And it was told the king of Jericho, saying, Behold, there came men in hither to night of the children of Israel to search out the country.

3 And the king of Jericho sent unto Rahab, saying, Bring forth the men that are come to thee, which are entered into thine house: for they be come to search out all the country.

4 And the woman took the two men, and hid them, and said thus, There came men unto me, but I wist not whence they *were:*

5 And it came to pass *about the time* of shutting of the gate, when it was dark, that the men went out: whither the men went I wot not: pursue after them quickly; for ye shall overtake them.

6 But she had brought them up to the roof of the house, and hid them with the stalks of flax, which she had laid in order upon the roof.

7 And the men pursued after them the way to Jordan unto the fords: and as soon as they which pursued after them were gone out, they shut the gate.

8 And before they were laid down, she came up unto them upon the roof;

9 And she said unto the men, I know that the LORD hath given you the land, and that your terror is fallen upon us, and that all the inhabitants of the land faint because of you.

10 For we have heard how the LORD dried up the water of the Red sea for you, when ye came out of Egypt; and what ye did unto the two kings of the Amorites, that *were* on the other side Jordan, Sihon and Og, whom ye utterly destroyed.

11 And as soon as we had heard *these things,* our hearts did melt, neither did there remain any more courage in any man, because of you: for the LORD your God, he *is* God in heaven above, and in earth beneath.

12 Now therefore, I pray you, swear unto me by the LORD, since I have shewed you kindness, that ye will also shew kindness unto my father's house, and give me a true token:

13 And *that* ye will save alive my father,

and my mother, and my brethren, and my
sisters, and all that they have, and deliver
our lives from death.
14 And the men answered her, Our life
for yours, if ye utter not this our business.
And it shall be, when the LORD hath given
us the land, that we will deal kindly and
truly with thee.
15 Then she let them down by a cord
through the window: for her house *was*
upon the town wall, and she dwelt upon
the wall.
16 And she said unto them, Get you to
the mountain, lest the pursuers meet you;
and hide yourselves there three days, until
the pursuers be returned: and afterward
may ye go your way.
17 And the men said unto her, We *will be*
blameless of this thine oath which thou
hast made us swear.
18 Behold, *when* we come into the land,
thou shalt bind this line of scarlet thread
in the window which thou didst let us
down by: and thou shalt bring thy father,
and thy mother, and thy brethren, and all
thy father's household, home unto thee.
19 And it shall be, *that* whosoever shall
go out of the doors of thy house into the
street, his blood *shall be* upon his head, and
we *will be* guiltless: and whosoever shall
be with thee in the house, his blood *shall
be* on our head, if *any* hand be upon him.
20 And if thou utter this our business,
then we will be quit of thine oath which
thou hast made us to swear.
21 And she said, According unto your
words, so *be* it. And she sent them away,
and they departed: and she bound the scarlet line in the window.
22 And they went, and came unto the
mountain, and abode there three days,
until the pursuers were returned: and the
pursuers sought *them* throughout all the
way, but found *them* not.
23 So the two men returned, and descended from the mountain, and passed
over, and came to Joshua the son of Nun,
and told him all *things* that befell them:
24 And they said unto Joshua, Truly the
LORD hath delivered into our hands all
the land; for even all the inhabitants of
the country do faint because of us.

3

1 And Joshua rose early in the morning;
and they removed from Shittim, and came
to Jordan, he and all the children of Israel, and lodged there before they passed
over.
2 And it came to pass after three days,
that the officers went through the host;
3 And they commanded the people, saying, When ye see the ark of the covenant
of the LORD your God, and the priests the
Levites bearing it, then ye shall remove
from your place, and go after it.
4 Yet there shall be a space between you
and it, about two thousand cubits by measure: come not near unto it, that ye may
know the way by which ye must go: for ye
have not passed *this* way heretofore.
5 And Joshua said unto the people, Sanctify yourselves: for to morrow the LORD will
do wonders among you.
6 And Joshua spake unto the priests, saying, Take up the ark of the covenant, and
pass over before the people. And they took
up the ark of the covenant, and went before the people.
7 And the LORD said unto Joshua, This
day will I begin to magnify thee in the sight
of all Israel, that they may know that, as I
was with Moses, *so* I will be with thee.
8 And thou shalt command the priests
that bear the ark of the covenant, saying,
When ye are come to the brink of the
water of Jordan, ye shall stand still in
Jordan.
9 And Joshua said unto the children of
Israel, Come hither, and hear the words of
the LORD your God.
10 And Joshua
said, Hereby ye
shall know that the
living God *is* among
you, and *that* he
will without fail
drive out from before you the Canaanites,
and the Hittites, and the Hivites, and the
Perizzites, and the Girgashites, and the
Amorites, and the Jebusites.

3:10 Names of God
◄ Deuteronomy 33:27
1 Samuel 1:11 ►

11 Behold, the ark of the covenant of the
Lord of all the earth passeth over before
you into Jordan.
12 Now therefore take you twelve men
out of the tribes of Israel, out of every tribe
a man.
13 And it shall come to pass, as soon as
the soles of the feet of the priests that bear
the ark of the LORD, the Lord of all the
earth, shall rest in the waters of Jordan,
that the waters of Jordan shall be cut off

from the waters that come down from
above; and they shall stand upon an heap.
14 And it came to pass, when the people
removed from their tents, to pass over Jordan, and the priests bearing the ark of the
covenant before the people;
15 And as they that bare the ark were
come unto Jordan, and the feet of the
priests that bare the ark were dipped in the
brim of the water, (for Jordan overfloweth
all his banks all the time of harvest,)
16 That the waters which came down
from above stood *and* rose up upon an
heap very far from the city Adam, that *is*
beside Zaretan: and those that came down
toward the sea of the plain, *even* the salt
sea, failed, *and* were cut off: and the people passed over right against Jericho.
17 And the priests that bare the ark of
the covenant of the LORD stood firm on
dry ground in the midst of Jordan, and all
the Israelites passed over on dry ground,
until all the people were passed clean over
Jordan.

4

1 And it came to pass, when all the people were clean passed over Jordan, that the
LORD spake unto Joshua, saying,
2 Take you twelve men out of the people, out of every tribe a man,
3 And command ye them, saying, Take
you hence out of the midst of Jordan, out
of the place where the priests' feet stood
firm, twelve stones, and ye shall carry them
over with you, and leave them in the lodging place, where ye shall lodge this night.
4 Then Joshua called the twelve men,
whom he had prepared of the children of
Israel, out of every tribe a man:
5 And Joshua said unto them, Pass over
before the ark of the LORD your God into
the midst of Jordan, and take ye up every
man of you a stone upon his shoulder,
according unto the number of the tribes
of the children of Israel:
6 That this may be a sign among you, *that*
when your children ask *their fathers* in time
to come, saying, What *mean* ye by these
stones?
7 Then ye shall answer them, That the
waters of Jordan were cut off before the
ark of the covenant of the LORD; when it
passed over Jordan, the waters of Jordan
were cut off: and these stones shall be for
a memorial unto the children of Israel for
ever.
8 And the children of Israel did so as
Joshua commanded, and took up twelve
stones out of the midst of Jordan, as the
LORD spake unto Joshua, according to the
number of the tribes of the children of Israel, and carried them over with them unto
the place where they lodged, and laid them
down there.
9 And Joshua set up twelve stones in the
midst of Jordan, in the place where the feet
of the priests which bare the ark of the
covenant stood: and they are there unto
this day.
10 For the priests which bare the ark
stood in the midst of Jordan, until every
thing was finished that the LORD commanded Joshua to speak unto the people,
according to all that Moses commanded
Joshua: and the people hasted and passed
over.
11 And it came to pass, when all the people were clean passed over, that the ark of
the LORD passed over, and the priests, in
the presence of the people.
12 And the children of Reuben, and the
children of Gad, and half the tribe of Manasseh, passed over armed before the children of Israel, as Moses spake unto them:
13 About forty thousand prepared for war
passed over before the LORD unto battle,
to the plains of Jericho.
14 On that day the LORD magnified
Joshua in the sight of all Israel; and they
feared him, as they feared Moses, all the
days of his life.
15 And the LORD spake unto Joshua,
saying,
16 Command the priests that bear the ark
of the testimony, that they come up out of
Jordan.
17 Joshua therefore commanded the
priests, saying, Come ye up out of Jordan.
18 And it came to pass, when the priests
that bare the ark of the covenant of the
LORD were come up out of the midst of
Jordan, *and* the soles of the priests' feet
were lifted up unto the dry land, that the
waters of Jordan returned unto their place,
and flowed over all his banks, as *they did*
before.
19 And the people came up out of Jordan on the tenth *day* of the first month,
and encamped in Gilgal, in the east border of Jericho.
20 And those twelve stones, which they

took out of Jordan, did Joshua pitch in
Gilgal.
21And he spake unto the children of Israel, saying, When your children shall ask
their fathers in time to come, saying, What
mean these stones?
22Then ye shall let your children know,
saying, Israel came over this Jordan on dry
land.
23For the LORD your God dried up the
waters of Jordan from before you, until ye
were passed over, as the LORD your God
did to the Red sea, which he dried up from
before us, until we were gone over:
24That all the
people of the earth
might know the
hand of the LORD,
that it *is* mighty:
that ye might fear
the LORD your God for ever.

4:24 Fearing God
◄ Deuteronomy 13:4
Joshua 24:14 ►

5
1And it came to pass, when all the kings
of the Amorites, which *were* on the side
of Jordan westward, and all the kings of
the Canaanites, which *were* by the sea,
heard that the LORD had dried up the waters of Jordan from before the children of
Israel, until we were passed over, that their
heart melted, neither was there spirit in
them any more, because of the children of
Israel.
2At that time the LORD said unto Joshua,
Make thee sharp knives, and circumcise
again the children of Israel the second
time.
3And Joshua made him sharp knives,
and circumcised the children of Israel at
the hill of the foreskins.
4And this *is* the cause why Joshua did
circumcise: All the people that came out
of Egypt, *that were* males, *even* all the men
of war, died in the wilderness by the way,
after they came out of Egypt.
5Now all the people that came out were
circumcised: but all the people *that were*
born in the wilderness by the way as they
came forth out of Egypt, *them* they had not
circumcised.
6For the children of Israel walked forty
years in the wilderness, till all the people
that were men of war, which came out of
Egypt, were consumed, because they
obeyed not the voice of the LORD: unto
whom the LORD sware that he would not
shew them the land, which the LORD sware
unto their fathers that he would give us, a
land that floweth with milk and honey.
7And their children, *whom* he raised up
in their stead, them Joshua circumcised:
for they were uncircumcised, because they
had not circumcised them by the way.
8And it came to pass, when they had
done circumcising all the people, that they
abode in their places in the camp, till they
were whole.
9And the LORD said unto Joshua, This
day have I rolled away the reproach of
Egypt from off you. Wherefore the name
of the place is called Gilgal unto this day.
10And the children of Israel encamped
in Gilgal, and kept the passover on the
fourteenth day of the month at even in the
plains of Jericho.
11And they did eat of the old corn of the
land on the morrow after the passover,
unleavened cakes, and parched *corn* in the
selfsame day.
12And the manna ceased on the morrow after they had eaten of the old corn of
the land; neither had the children of Israel manna any more; but they did eat of
the fruit of the land of Canaan that year.
13And it came to pass, when Joshua was
by Jericho, that he lifted up his eyes and
looked, and, behold, there stood a man
over against him with his sword drawn in
his hand: and Joshua went unto him, and
said unto him, *Art* thou for us, or for our
adversaries?
14And he said, Nay; but *as* captain of the
host of the LORD am I now come. And
Joshua fell on his face to the earth, and
did worship, and said unto him, What
saith my lord unto his servant?
15And the cap-
tain of the LORD'S
host said unto
Joshua, Loose thy
shoe from off thy
foot; for the place
whereon thou standest *is* holy. And Joshua
did so.

5:15 Respecting God
◄ Exodus 3:5
Psalm 4:4 ►

6
1Now Jericho was straitly shut up because of the children of Israel: none went
out, and none came in.
2And the LORD said unto Joshua, See, I
have given into thine hand Jericho, and
the king thereof, *and* the mighty men of
valour.
3And ye shall compass the city, all *ye*

men of war, *and* go round about the city once. Thus shalt thou do six days.

4 And seven priests shall bear before the ark seven trumpets of rams' horns: and the seventh day ye shall compass the city seven times, and the priests shall blow with the trumpets.

5 And it shall come to pass, that when they make a long *blast* with the ram's horn, *and* when ye hear the sound of the trumpet, all the people shall shout with a great shout; and the wall of the city shall fall down flat, and the people shall ascend up every man straight before him.

6 And Joshua the son of Nun called the priests, and said unto them, Take up the ark of the covenant, and let seven priests bear seven trumpets of rams' horns before the ark of the LORD.

7 And he said unto the people, Pass on, and compass the city, and let him that is armed pass on before the ark of the LORD.

8 And it came to pass, when Joshua had spoken unto the people, that the seven priests bearing the seven trumpets of rams' horns passed on before the LORD, and blew with the trumpets: and the ark of the covenant of the LORD followed them.

9 And the armed men went before the priests that blew with the trumpets, and the rereward came after the ark, *the priests* going on, and blowing with the trumpets.

10 And Joshua had commanded the people, saying, Ye shall not shout, nor make any noise with your voice, neither shall *any* word proceed out of your mouth, until the day I bid you shout; then shall ye shout.

6:10
Being Quiet
◄ Ecclesiastes 3:7 ►

11 So the ark of the LORD compassed the city, going about *it* once: and they came into the camp, and lodged in the camp.

12 And Joshua rose early in the morning, and the priests took up the ark of the LORD.

13 And seven priests bearing seven trumpets of rams' horns before the ark of the LORD went on continually, and blew with the trumpets: and the armed men went before them; but the rereward came after the ark of the LORD, *the priests* going on, and blowing with the trumpets.

14 And the second day they compassed the city once, and returned into the camp: so they did six days.

15 And it came to pass on the seventh day, that they rose early about the dawning of the day, and compassed the city after the same manner seven times: only on that day they compassed the city seven times.

16 And it came to pass at the seventh time, when the priests blew with the trumpets, Joshua said unto the people, Shout; for the LORD hath given you the city.

17 And the city shall be accursed, *even* it, and all that *are* therein, to the LORD: only Rahab the harlot shall live, she and all that *are* with her in the house, because she hid the messengers that we sent.

18 And ye, in any wise keep *yourselves* from the accursed thing, lest ye make *yourselves* accursed, when ye take of the accursed thing, and make the camp of Israel a curse, and trouble it.

19 But all the silver, and gold, and vessels of brass and iron, *are* consecrated unto the LORD: they shall come into the treasury of the LORD.

20 So the people shouted when *the priests* blew with the trumpets: and it came to pass, when the people heard the sound of the trumpet, and the people shouted with a great shout, that the wall fell down flat, so that the people went up into the city, every man straight before him, and they took the city.

21 And they utterly destroyed all that *was* in the city, both man and woman, young and old, and ox, and sheep, and ass, with the edge of the sword.

22 But Joshua had said unto the two men that had spied out the country, Go into the harlot's house, and bring out thence the woman, and all that she hath, as ye sware unto her.

23 And the young men that were spies went in, and brought Rahab, and her father, and her mother, and her brethren, and all that she had; and they brought out all her kindred, and left them without the camp of Israel.

24 And they burnt the city with fire, and all that *was* therein: only the silver, and the gold, and the vessels of brass and of iron, they put into the treasury of the house of the LORD.

25 And Joshua saved Rahab the harlot

alive, and her father's household, and all that she had; and she dwelleth in Israel *even* unto this day; because she hid the messengers, which Joshua sent to spy out Jericho.

26 And Joshua adjured *them* at that time, saying, Cursed *be* the man before the LORD, that riseth up and buildeth this city Jericho: he shall lay the foundation thereof in his firstborn, and in his youngest *son* shall he set up the gates of it.

27 So the LORD was with Joshua; and his fame was *noised* throughout all the country.

7

1 But the children of Israel committed a trespass in the accursed thing: for Achan, the son of Carmi, the son of Zabdi, the son of Zerah, of the tribe of Judah, took of the accursed thing: and the anger of the LORD was kindled against the children of Israel.

2 And Joshua sent men from Jericho to Ai, which *is* beside Beth-aven, on the east side of Bethel, and spake unto them, saying, Go up and view the country. And the men went up and viewed Ai.

3 And they returned to Joshua, and said unto him, Let not all the people go up; but let about two or three thousand men go up and smite Ai; *and* make not all the people to labour thither; for they *are but* few.

4 So there went up thither of the people about three thousand men: and they fled before the men of Ai.

5 And the men of Ai smote of them about thirty and six men: for they chased them *from* before the gate *even* unto Shebarim, and smote them in the going down: wherefore the hearts of the people melted, and became as water.

6 And Joshua rent his clothes, and fell to the earth upon his face before the ark of the LORD until the eventide, he and the elders of Israel, and put dust upon their heads.

7 And Joshua said, Alas, O Lord GOD, wherefore hast thou at all brought this people over Jordan, to deliver us into the hand of the Amorites, to destroy us? would to God we had been content, and dwelt on the other side Jordan!

7:7 Unhappiness
◄ Numbers 11:15
1 Kings 19:4 ►

8 O Lord, what shall I say, when Israel turneth their backs before their enemies!

9 For the Canaanites and all the inhabitants of the land shall hear *of it,* and shall environ us round, and cut off our name from the earth: and what wilt thou do unto thy great name?

10 And the LORD said unto Joshua, Get thee up; wherefore liest thou thus upon thy face?

11 Israel hath sinned, and they have also transgressed my covenant which I commanded them: for they have even taken of the accursed thing, and have also stolen, and dissembled also, and they have put *it* even among their own stuff.

12 Therefore the children of Israel could not stand before their enemies, *but* turned *their* backs before their enemies, because they were accursed: neither will I be with you any more, except ye destroy the accursed from among you.

7:12 Cost of Sin
◄ Deuteronomy 28:32
Judges 1:21 ►

13 Up, sanctify the people, and say, Sanctify yourselves against to morrow: for thus saith the LORD God of Israel, *There is* an accursed thing in the midst of thee, O Israel: thou canst not stand before thine enemies, until ye take away the accursed thing from among you.

14 In the morning therefore ye shall be brought according to your tribes: and it shall be, *that* the tribe which the LORD taketh shall come according to the families *thereof;* and the family which the LORD shall take shall come by households; and the household which the LORD shall take shall come man by man.

15 And it shall be, *that* he that is taken with the accursed thing shall be burnt with fire, he and all that he hath: because he hath transgressed the covenant of the LORD, and because he hath wrought folly in Israel.

16 So Joshua rose up early in the morning, and brought Israel by their tribes; and the tribe of Judah was taken:

17 And he brought the family of Judah; and he took the family of the Zarhites: and he brought the family of the Zarhites man by man; and Zabdi was taken:

18 And he brought his household man by man; and Achan, the son of Carmi, the

son of Zabdi, the son of Zerah, of the tribe
of Judah, was taken.
19And Joshua said unto Achan, My son,
give, I pray thee, glory to the LORD God of
Israel, and make confession unto him; and
tell me now what thou hast done; hide *it*
not from me.
20And Achan answered Joshua, and
said, Indeed I have sinned against the
LORD God of Israel, and thus and thus have
I done:
21When I saw
among the spoils a
goodly Babylonish
garment, and two
hundred shekels of
silver, and a wedge
of gold of fifty shekels weight, then I coveted them, and took them; and, behold,
they *are* hid in the earth in the midst of
my tent, and the silver under it.

7:21 Giving In
◄ Genesis 25:33
Judges 14:17 ►

22So Joshua sent messengers, and they
ran unto the tent; and, behold, *it was* hid
in his tent, and the silver under it.
23And they took them out of the midst
of the tent, and brought them unto Joshua,
and unto all the children of Israel, and laid
them out before the LORD.
24And Joshua, and all Israel with him,
took Achan the son of Zerah, and the silver, and the garment, and the wedge of
gold, and his sons, and his daughters, and
his oxen, and his asses, and his sheep, and
his tent, and all that he had: and they
brought them unto the valley of Achor.
25And Joshua said, Why hast thou troubled us? the LORD shall trouble thee this
day. And all Israel stoned him with stones,
and burned them with fire, after they had
stoned them with stones.
26And they raised over him a great heap
of stones unto this day. So the LORD turned
from the fierceness of his anger. Wherefore the name of that place was called, The
valley of Achor, unto this day.

8

1And the LORD said unto Joshua, Fear
not, neither be thou dismayed: take all the
people of war with thee, and arise, go up
to Ai: see, I have given into thy hand the
king of Ai, and his people, and his city,
and his land:
2And thou shalt do to Ai and her king
as thou didst unto Jericho and her king:
only the spoil thereof, and the cattle
thereof, shall ye take for a prey unto yourselves: lay thee an ambush for the city
behind it.
3So Joshua arose, and all the people of
war, to go up against Ai: and Joshua chose
out thirty thousand mighty men of valour,
and sent them away by night.
4And he commanded them, saying, Behold, ye shall lie in wait against the city,
even behind the city: go not very far from
the city, but be ye all ready:
5And I, and all the people that *are* with
me, will approach unto the city: and it shall
come to pass, when they come out against
us, as at the first, that we will flee before
them,
6(For they will come out after us) till
we have drawn them from the city; for they
will say, They flee before us, as at the first:
therefore we will flee before them.
7Then ye shall rise up from the ambush,
and seize upon the city: for the LORD your
God will deliver it into your hand.
8And it shall be, when ye have taken the
city, *that* ye shall set the city on fire: according to the commandment of the LORD
shall ye do. See, I have commanded you.
9Joshua therefore sent them forth: and
they went to lie in ambush, and abode
between Bethel and Ai, on the west side of
Ai: but Joshua lodged that night among
the people.
10And Joshua rose up early in the morning, and numbered the people, and went
up, he and the elders of Israel, before the
people to Ai.
11And all the people, *even the people* of
war that *were* with him, went up, and drew
nigh, and came before the city, and pitched
on the north side of Ai: now *there was* a
valley between them and Ai.
12And he took about five thousand men,
and set them to lie in ambush between
Bethel and Ai, on the west side of the city.
13And when they had set the people,
even all the host that *was* on the north of
the city, and their liers in wait on the west
of the city, Joshua went that night into the
midst of the valley.
14And it came to pass, when the king of
Ai saw *it*, that they hasted and rose up early, and the men of the city went out against
Israel to battle, he and all his people, at a
time appointed, before the plain; but he
wist not that *there were* liers in ambush
against him behind the city.

15 And Joshua and all Israel made as if they were beaten before them, and fled by the way of the wilderness.

16 And all the people that *were* in Ai were called together to pursue after them: and they pursued after Joshua, and were drawn away from the city.

17 And there was not a man left in Ai or Bethel, that went not out after Israel: and they left the city open, and pursued after Israel.

18 And the LORD said unto Joshua, Stretch out the spear that *is* in thy hand toward Ai; for I will give it into thine hand. And Joshua stretched out the spear that *he had* in his hand toward the city.

19 And the ambush arose quickly out of their place, and they ran as soon as he had stretched out his hand: and they entered into the city, and took it, and hasted and set the city on fire.

20 And when the men of Ai looked behind them, they saw, and, behold, the smoke of the city ascended up to heaven, and they had no power to flee this way or that way: and the people that fled to the wilderness turned back upon the pursuers.

21 And when Joshua and all Israel saw that the ambush had taken the city, and that the smoke of the city ascended, then they turned again, and slew the men of Ai.

22 And the other issued out of the city against them; so they were in the midst of Israel, some on this side, and some on that side: and they smote them, so that they let none of them remain or escape.

23 And the king of Ai they took alive, and brought him to Joshua.

24 And it came to pass, when Israel had made an end of slaying all the inhabitants of Ai in the field, in the wilderness wherein they chased them, and when they were all fallen on the edge of the sword, until they were consumed, that all the Israelites returned unto Ai, and smote it with the edge of the sword.

25 And *so* it was, *that* all that fell that day, both of men and women, *were* twelve thousand, *even* all the men of Ai.

26 For Joshua drew not his hand back, wherewith he stretched out the spear, until he had utterly destroyed all the inhabitants of Ai.

27 Only the cattle and the spoil of that city Israel took for a prey unto themselves, according unto the word of the LORD which he commanded Joshua.

28 And Joshua burnt Ai, and made it an heap for ever, *even* a desolation unto this day.

29 And the king of Ai he hanged on a tree until eventide: and as soon as the sun was down, Joshua commanded that they should take his carcase down from the tree, and cast it at the entering of the gate of the city, and raise thereon a great heap of stones, *that remaineth* unto this day.

30 Then Joshua built an altar unto the LORD God of Israel in mount Ebal,

31 As Moses the servant of the LORD commanded the children of Israel, as it is written in the book of the law of Moses, an altar of whole stones, over which no man hath lift up *any* iron: and they offered thereon burnt offerings unto the LORD, and sacrificed peace offerings.

32 And he wrote there upon the stones a copy of the law of Moses, which he wrote in the presence of the children of Israel.

33 And all Israel, and their elders, and officers, and their judges, stood on this side the ark and on that side before the priests the Levites, which bare the ark of the covenant of the LORD, as well the stranger, as he that was born among them; half of them over against mount Gerizim, and half of them over against mount Ebal; as Moses the servant of the LORD had commanded before, that they should bless the people of Israel.

34 And afterward he read all the words of the law, the blessings and cursings, according to all that is written in the book of the law.

35 There was not a word of all that Moses commanded, which Joshua read not before all the congregation of Israel, with the women, and the little ones, and the strangers that were conversant among them.

9

1 And it came to pass, when all the kings which *were* on this side Jordan, in the hills, and in the valleys, and in all the coasts of the great sea over against Lebanon, the Hittite, and the Amorite, the Canaanite, the Perizzite, the Hivite, and the Jebusite, heard *thereof;*

2 That they gathered themselves together, to fight with Joshua and with Israel, with one accord.

3 And when the inhabitants of Gibeon heard what Joshua had done unto Jericho and to Ai,

4 They did work wilily, and went and made as if they had been ambassadors, and took old sacks upon their asses, and wine bottles, old, and rent, and bound up;

5 And old shoes and clouted upon their feet, and old garments upon them; and all the bread of their provision was dry *and* mouldy.

6 And they went to Joshua unto the camp at Gilgal, and said unto him, and to the men of Israel, We be come from a far country: now therefore make ye a league with us.

7 And the men of Israel said unto the Hivites, Peradventure ye dwell among us; and how shall we make a league with you?

8 And they said unto Joshua, We *are* thy servants. And Joshua said unto them, Who *are* ye? and from whence come ye?

9 And they said unto him, From a very far country thy servants are come because of the name of the LORD thy God: for we have heard the fame of him, and all that he did in Egypt,

10 And all that he did to the two kings of the Amorites, that *were* beyond Jordan, to Sihon king of Heshbon, and to Og king of Bashan, which *was* at Ashtaroth.

11 Wherefore our elders and all the inhabitants of our country spake to us, saying, Take victuals with you for the journey, and go to meet them, and say unto them, We *are* your servants: therefore now make ye a league with us.

12 This our bread we took hot *for* our provision out of our houses on the day we came forth to go unto you; but now, behold, it is dry, and it is mouldy:

13 And these bottles of wine, which we filled, *were* new; and, behold, they be rent: and these our garments and our shoes are become old by reason of the very long journey.

14 And the men took of their victuals, and asked not *counsel* at the mouth of the LORD.

15 And Joshua made peace with them, and made a league with them, to let them live: and the princes of the congregation sware unto them.

16 And it came to pass at the end of three days after they had made a league with them, that they heard that they *were* their neighbours, and *that* they dwelt among them.

17 And the children of Israel journeyed, and came unto their cities on the third day. Now their cities *were* Gibeon, and Chephirah, and Beeroth, and Kirjath-jearim.

18 And the children of Israel smote them not, because the princes of the congregation had sworn unto them by the LORD God of Israel. And all the congregation murmured against the princes.

19 But all the princes said unto all the congregation, We have sworn unto them by the LORD God of Israel: now therefore we may not touch them.

9:19 Foolish Promises
◄ Genesis 25:33
Mark 6:23 ►

20 This we will do to them; we will even let them live, lest wrath be upon us, because of the oath which we sware unto them.

21 And the princes said unto them, Let them live; but let them be hewers of wood and drawers of water unto all the congregation; as the princes had promised them.

22 And Joshua called for them, and he spake unto them, saying, Wherefore have ye beguiled us, saying, We *are* very far from you; when ye dwell among us?

23 Now therefore ye *are* cursed, and there shall none of you be freed from being bondmen, and hewers of wood and drawers of water for the house of my God.

24 And they answered Joshua, and said, Because it was certainly told thy servants, how that the LORD thy God commanded his servant Moses to give you all the land, and to destroy all the inhabitants of the land from before you, therefore we were sore afraid of our lives because of you, and have done this thing.

25 And now, behold, we *are* in thine hand: as it seemeth good and right unto thee to do unto us, do.

26 And so did he unto them, and delivered them out of the hand of the children of Israel, that they slew them not.

27 And Joshua made them that day hewers of wood and drawers of water for the congregation, and for the altar of the LORD, even unto this day, in the place which he should choose.

10

1 Now it came to pass, when Adoni-zedek king of Jerusalem had heard how Joshua had taken Ai, and had utterly destroyed it; as he had done to Jericho and her king, so he had done to Ai and her king; and how the inhabitants of Gibeon had made peace with Israel, and were among them;

2 That they feared greatly, because Gibeon *was* a great city, as one of the royal cities, and because it *was* greater than Ai, and all the men thereof *were* mighty.

3 Wherefore Adoni-zedek king of Jerusalem sent unto Hoham king of Hebron, and unto Piram king of Jarmuth, and unto Japhia king of Lachish, and unto Debir king of Eglon, saying,

4 Come up unto me, and help me, that we may smite Gibeon: for it hath made peace with Joshua and with the children of Israel.

5 Therefore the five kings of the Amorites, the king of Jerusalem, the king of Hebron, the king of Jarmuth, the king of Lachish, the king of Eglon, gathered themselves together, and went up, they and all their hosts, and encamped before Gibeon, and made war against it.

6 And the men of Gibeon sent unto Joshua to the camp to Gilgal, saying, Slack not thy hand from thy servants; come up to us quickly, and save us, and help us: for all the kings of the Amorites that dwell in the mountains are gathered together against us.

7 So Joshua ascended from Gilgal, he, and all the people of war with him, and all the mighty men of valour.

8 And the LORD said unto Joshua, Fear them not: for I have delivered them into thine hand; there shall not a man of them stand before thee.

9 Joshua therefore came unto them suddenly, *and* went up from Gilgal all night.

10 And the LORD discomfited them before Israel, and slew them with a great slaughter at Gibeon, and chased them along the way that goeth up to Beth-horon, and smote them to Azekah, and unto Makkedah.

11 And it came to pass, as they fled from before Israel, *and* were in the going down to Beth-horon, that the LORD cast down great stones from heaven upon them unto Azekah, and they died: *they were* more which died with hailstones than *they* whom the children of Israel slew with the sword.

12 Then spake Joshua to the LORD in the day when the LORD delivered up the Amorites before the children of Israel, and he said in the sight of Israel, Sun, stand thou still upon Gibeon; and thou, Moon, in the valley of Ajalon.

13 And the sun stood still, and the moon stayed, until the people had avenged themselves upon their enemies. *Is* not this written in the book of Jasher? So the sun stood still in the midst of heaven, and hasted not to go down about a whole day.

14 And there was no day like that before it or after it, that the LORD hearkened unto the voice of a man: for the LORD fought for Israel.

15 And Joshua returned, and all Israel with him, unto the camp to Gilgal.

16 But these five kings fled, and hid themselves in a cave at Makkedah.

17 And it was told Joshua, saying, The five kings are found hid in a cave at Makkedah.

18 And Joshua said, Roll great stones upon the mouth of the cave, and set men by it for to keep them:

19 And stay ye not, *but* pursue after your enemies, and smite the hindmost of them; suffer them not to enter into their cities: for the LORD your God hath delivered them into your hand.

20 And it came to pass, when Joshua and the children of Israel had made an end of slaying them with a very great slaughter, till they were consumed, that the rest *which* remained of them entered into fenced cities.

21 And all the people returned to the camp to Joshua at Makkedah in peace: none moved his tongue against any of the children of Israel.

22 Then said Joshua, Open the mouth of the cave, and bring out those five kings unto me out of the cave.

23 And they did so, and brought forth those five kings unto him out of the cave, the king of Jerusalem, the king of Hebron, the king of Jarmuth, the king of Lachish, *and* the king of Eglon.

24 And it came to pass, when they brought out those kings unto Joshua, that Joshua called for all the men of Israel, and said unto the captains of the men of war

which went with him, Come near, put your feet upon the necks of these kings. And they came near, and put their feet upon the necks of them.

25 And Joshua said unto them, Fear not, nor be dismayed, be strong and of good courage: for thus shall the LORD do to all your enemies against whom ye fight.

26 And afterward Joshua smote them, and slew them, and hanged them on five trees: and they were hanging upon the trees until the evening.

27 And it came to pass at the time of the going down of the sun, *that* Joshua commanded, and they took them down off the trees, and cast them into the cave wherein they had been hid, and laid great stones in the cave's mouth, *which remain* until this very day.

28 And that day Joshua took Makkedah, and smote it with the edge of the sword, and the king thereof he utterly destroyed, them, and all the souls that *were* therein; he let none remain: and he did to the king of Makkedah as he did unto the king of Jericho.

29 Then Joshua passed from Makkedah, and all Israel with him, unto Libnah, and fought against Libnah:

30 And the LORD delivered it also, and the king thereof, into the hand of Israel; and he smote it with the edge of the sword, and all the souls that *were* therein; he let none remain in it; but did unto the king thereof as he did unto the king of Jericho.

31 And Joshua passed from Libnah, and all Israel with him, unto Lachish, and encamped against it, and fought against it:

32 And the LORD delivered Lachish into the hand of Israel, which took it on the second day, and smote it with the edge of the sword, and all the souls that *were* therein, according to all that he had done to Libnah.

33 Then Horam king of Gezer came up to help Lachish; and Joshua smote him and his people, until he had left him none remaining.

34 And from Lachish Joshua passed unto Eglon, and all Israel with him; and they encamped against it, and fought against it:

35 And they took it on that day, and smote it with the edge of the sword, and all the souls that *were* therein he utterly destroyed that day, according to all that he had done to Lachish.

36 And Joshua went up from Eglon, and all Israel with him, unto Hebron; and they fought against it:

37 And they took it, and smote it with the edge of the sword, and the king thereof, and all the cities thereof, and all the souls that *were* therein; he left none remaining, according to all that he had done to Eglon; but destroyed it utterly, and all the souls that *were* therein.

38 And Joshua returned, and all Israel with him, to Debir; and fought against it:

39 And he took it, and the king thereof, and all the cities thereof; and they smote them with the edge of the sword, and utterly destroyed all the souls that *were* therein; he left none remaining: as he had done to Hebron, so he did to Debir, and to the king thereof; as he had done also to Libnah, and to her king.

40 So Joshua smote all the country of the hills, and of the south, and of the vale, and of the springs, and all their kings: he left none remaining, but utterly destroyed all that breathed, as the LORD God of Israel commanded.

41 And Joshua smote them from Kadesh-barnea even unto Gaza, and all the country of Goshen, even unto Gibeon.

42 And all these kings and their land did Joshua take at one time, because the LORD God of Israel fought for Israel.

43 And Joshua returned, and all Israel with him, unto the camp to Gilgal.

11

1 And it came to pass, when Jabin king of Hazor had heard *those things,* that he sent to Jobab king of Madon, and to the king of Shimron, and to the king of Achshaph,

2 And to the kings that *were* on the north of the mountains, and of the plains south of Chinneroth, and in the valley, and in the borders of Dor on the west,

3 *And to* the Canaanite on the east and on the west, and *to* the Amorite, and the Hittite, and the Perizzite, and the Jebusite in the mountains, and *to* the Hivite under Hermon in the land of Mizpeh.

4 And they went out, they and all their hosts with them, much people, even as the sand that *is* upon the sea shore in multitude, with horses and chariots very many.

5 And when all these kings were met to-

gether, they came and pitched together
at the waters of Merom, to fight against
Israel.
6 And the LORD said unto Joshua, Be not
afraid because of them: for to morrow
about this time will I deliver them up all
slain before Israel: thou shalt hough their
horses, and burn their chariots with fire.
7 So Joshua came, and all the people of
war with him, against them by the waters
of Merom suddenly; and they fell upon
them.
8 And the LORD delivered them into the
hand of Israel, who smote them, and
chased them unto great Zidon, and unto
Misrephoth-maim, and unto the valley of
Mizpeh eastward; and they smote them,
until they left them none remaining.
9 And Joshua did unto them as the LORD
bade him: he houghed their horses, and
burnt their chariots with fire.
10 And Joshua at that time turned back,
and took Hazor, and smote the king
thereof with the sword: for Hazor beforetime was the head of all those kingdoms.
11 And they smote all the souls that *were*
therein with the edge of the sword, utterly
destroying *them:* there was not any left to
breathe: and he burnt Hazor with fire.
12 And all the cities of those kings, and
all the kings of them, did Joshua take, and
smote them with the edge of the sword,
and he utterly destroyed them, as Moses
the servant of the LORD commanded.
13 But *as for* the cities that stood still in
their strength, Israel burned none of them,
save Hazor only; *that* did Joshua burn.
14 And all the spoil of these cities, and
the cattle, the children of Israel took for a
prey unto themselves; but every man they
smote with the edge of the sword, until
they had destroyed them, neither left they
any to breathe.
15 As the LORD commanded Moses his
servant, so did Moses command Joshua,
and so did Joshua; he left nothing undone
of all that the LORD commanded Moses.
16 So Joshua took all that land, the hills,
and all the south country, and all the land
of Goshen, and the valley, and the plain,
and the mountain of Israel, and the valley
of the same;
17 *Even* from the mount Halak, that
goeth up to Seir, even unto Baal-gad in the
valley of Lebanon under mount Hermon:
and all their kings he took, and smote
them, and slew them.
18 Joshua made war a long time with all
those kings.
19 There was not a city that made peace
with the children of Israel, save the Hivites
the inhabitants of Gibeon: all *other* they
took in battle.
20 For it was of the LORD to harden their
hearts, that they should come against Israel in battle, that he might destroy them
utterly, *and* that they might have no favour,
but that he might destroy them, as the
LORD commanded Moses.
21 And at that time came Joshua, and cut
off the Anakims from the mountains, from
Hebron, from Debir, from Anab, and from
all the mountains of Judah, and from all
the mountains of Israel: Joshua destroyed
them utterly with their cities.
22 There was none of the Anakims left in
the land of the children of Israel: only in
Gaza, in Gath, and in Ashdod, there remained.
23 So Joshua took the whole land, according to all that the LORD said unto
Moses; and Joshua gave it for an inheritance unto Israel according to their divisions by their tribes. And the land rested
from war.

12

1 Now these *are* the kings of the land,
which the children of Israel smote, and
possessed their land on the other side Jordan toward the rising of the sun, from the
river Arnon unto mount Hermon, and all
the plain on the east:
2 Sihon king of the Amorites, who dwelt
in Heshbon, *and* ruled from Aroer, which
is upon the bank of the river Arnon, and
from the middle of the river, and from half
Gilead, even unto the river Jabbok, *which*
is the border of the children of Ammon;
3 And from the plain to the sea of
Chinneroth on the east, and unto the sea
of the plain, *even* the salt sea on the east,
the way to Beth-jeshimoth; and from the
south, under Ashdoth-pisgah:
4 And the coast of Og king of Bashan,
which was of the remnant of the giants, that
dwelt at Ashtaroth and at Edrei,
5 And reigned in mount Hermon, and in
Salcah, and in all Bashan, unto the border
of the Geshurites and the Maachathites,
and half Gilead, the border of Sihon king
of Heshbon.

6 Them did Moses the servant of the LORD and the children of Israel smite: and Moses the servant of the LORD gave it *for* a possession unto the Reubenites, and the Gadites, and the half tribe of Manasseh.

7 And these *are* the kings of the country which Joshua and the children of Israel smote on this side Jordan on the west, from Baal-gad in the valley of Lebanon even unto the mount Halak, that goeth up to Seir; which Joshua gave unto the tribes of Israel *for* a possession according to their divisions;

8 In the mountains, and in the valleys, and in the plains, and in the springs, and in the wilderness, and in the south country; the Hittites, the Amorites, and the Canaanites, the Perizzites, the Hivites, and the Jebusites:

9 The king of Jericho, one; the king of Ai, which *is* beside Bethel, one;

10 The king of Jerusalem, one; the king of Hebron, one;

11 The king of Jarmuth, one; the king of Lachish, one;

12 The king of Eglon, one; the king of Gezer, one;

13 The king of Debir, one; the king of Geder, one;

14 The king of Hormah, one; the king of Arad, one;

15 The king of Libnah, one; the king of Adullam, one;

16 The king of Makkedah, one; the king of Bethel, one;

17 The king of Tappuah, one; the king of Hepher, one;

18 The king of Aphek, one; the king of Lasharon, one;

19 The king of Madon, one; the king of Hazor, one;

20 The king of Shimron-meron, one; the king of Achshaph, one;

21 The king of Taanach, one; the king of Megiddo, one;

22 The king of Kedesh, one; the king of Jokneam of Carmel, one;

23 The king of Dor in the coast of Dor, one; the king of the nations of Gilgal, one;

24 The king of Tirzah, one: all the kings thirty and one.

13

1 Now Joshua was old *and* stricken in years; and the LORD said unto him, Thou art old *and* stricken in years, and there remaineth yet very much land to be possessed.

2 This *is* the land that yet remaineth: all the borders of the Philistines, and all Geshuri,

3 From Sihor, which *is* before Egypt, even unto the borders of Ekron northward, *which* is counted to the Canaanite: five lords of the Philistines; the Gazathites, and the Ashdothites, the Eshkalonites, the Gittites, and the Ekronites; also the Avites:

4 From the south, all the land of the Canaanites, and Mearah that *is* beside the Sidonians, unto Aphek, to the borders of the Amorites:

5 And the land of the Giblites, and all Lebanon, toward the sunrising, from Baal-gad under mount Hermon unto the entering into Hamath.

6 All the inhabitants of the hill country from Lebanon unto Misrephoth-maim, *and* all the Sidonians, them will I drive out from before the children of Israel: only divide thou it by lot unto the Israelites for an inheritance, as I have commanded thee.

7 Now therefore divide this land for an inheritance unto the nine tribes, and the half tribe of Manasseh,

8 With whom the Reubenites and the Gadites have received their inheritance, which Moses gave them, beyond Jordan eastward, *even* as Moses the servant of the LORD gave them;

9 From Aroer, that *is* upon the bank of the river Arnon, and the city that *is* in the midst of the river, and all the plain of Medeba unto Dibon;

10 And all the cities of Sihon king of the Amorites, which reigned in Heshbon, unto the border of the children of Ammon;

11 And Gilead, and the border of the Geshurites and Maachathites, and all mount Hermon, and all Bashan unto Salcah;

12 All the kingdom of Og in Bashan, which reigned in Ashtaroth and in Edrei, who remained of the remnant of the giants: for these did Moses smite, and cast them out.

13 Nevertheless the children of Israel expelled not the Geshurites, nor the Maachathites: but the Geshurites and the Maachathites dwell among the Israelites until this day.

14 Only unto the tribe of Levi he gave

none inheritance; the sacrifices of the LORD
God of Israel made by fire *are* their inheritance, as he said unto them.
15 And Moses gave unto the tribe of the
children of Reuben *inheritance* according
to their families.
16 And their coast was from Aroer, that
is on the bank of the river Arnon, and the
city that *is* in the midst of the river, and all
the plain by Medeba;
17 Heshbon, and all her cities that *are* in
the plain; Dibon, and Bamoth-baal, and
Beth-baal-meon,
18 And Jahaza, and Kedemoth, and
Mephaath,
19 And Kirjathaim, and Sibmah, and
Zareth-shahar in the mount of the valley,
20 And Beth-peor, and Ashdoth-pisgah,
and Beth-jeshimoth,
21 And all the cities of the plain, and all
the kingdom of Sihon king of the Amorites, which reigned in Heshbon, whom
Moses smote with the princes of Midian,
Evi, and Rekem, and Zur, and Hur, and
Reba, *which were* dukes of Sihon, dwelling
in the country.
22 Balaam also the son of Beor, the
soothsayer, did the children of Israel slay
with the sword among them that were
slain by them.
23 And the border of the children of Reuben was Jordan, and the border *thereof.*
This *was* the inheritance of the children of
Reuben after their families, the cities and
the villages thereof.
24 And Moses gave *inheritance* unto the
tribe of Gad, *even* unto the children of Gad
according to their families.
25 And their coast was Jazer, and all the
cities of Gilead, and half the land of the
children of Ammon, unto Aroer that *is*
before Rabbah;
26 And from Heshbon unto Ramath-
mizpeh, and Betonim; and from Mahanaim unto the border of Debir;
27 And in the valley, Beth-aram, and
Beth-nimrah, and Succoth, and Zaphon,
the rest of the kingdom of Sihon king of
Heshbon, Jordan and *his* border, *even* unto
the edge of the sea of Chinnereth on the
other side Jordan eastward.
28 This *is* the inheritance of the children
of Gad after their families, the cities, and
their villages.
29 And Moses gave *inheritance* unto the
half tribe of Manasseh: and *this* was *the
possession* of the half tribe of the children
of Manasseh by their families.
30 And their coast was from Mahanaim,
all Bashan, all the kingdom of Og king of
Bashan, and all the towns of Jair, which
are in Bashan, threescore cities:
31 And half Gilead, and Ashtaroth, and
Edrei, cities of the kingdom of Og in Bashan, *were pertaining* unto the children of
Machir the son of Manasseh, *even* to the
one half of the children of Machir by their
families.
32 These *are the countries* which Moses did
distribute for inheritance in the plains of
Moab, on the other side Jordan, by Jericho, eastward.
33 But unto the tribe of Levi Moses gave
not *any* inheritance: the LORD God of Israel *was* their inheritance, as he said unto
them.

14

1 And these *are the countries* which the
children of Israel inherited in the land of
Canaan, which Eleazar the priest, and
Joshua the son of Nun, and the heads of
the fathers of the tribes of the children of
Israel, distributed for inheritance to them.
2 By lot *was* their inheritance, as the LORD
commanded by the hand of Moses, for the
nine tribes, and *for* the half tribe.
3 For Moses had given the inheritance of
two tribes and an half tribe on the other
side Jordan: but unto the Levites he gave
none inheritance among them.
4 For the children of Joseph were two
tribes, Manasseh and Ephraim: therefore
they gave no part unto the Levites in the
land, save cities to dwell *in,* with their suburbs for their cattle and for their substance.
5 As the LORD commanded Moses, so the
children of Israel did, and they divided the
land.
6 Then the children of Judah came unto
Joshua in Gilgal: and Caleb the son of Jephunneh the Kenezite said unto him, Thou
knowest the thing that the LORD said unto
Moses the man of God concerning me and
thee in Kadesh-barnea.
7 Forty years old *was* I when Moses the
servant of the LORD sent me from Kadesh-
barnea to espy out the land; and I brought
him word again as *it was* in mine heart.
8 Nevertheless my brethren that went up
with me made the heart of the people melt:
but I wholly followed the LORD my God.

9And Moses sware on that day, saying,
Surely the land whereon thy feet have trodden shall be thine inheritance, and thy
children's for ever, because thou hast wholly followed the LORD my God.
10And now, behold, the LORD hath kept
me alive, as he said, these forty and five
years, even since the LORD spake this word
unto Moses, while *the children of* Israel
wandered in the wilderness: and now, lo,
I *am* this day fourscore and five years old.
11As yet I *am as* strong this day as *I was* in
the day that Moses sent me: as my strength
was then, even so *is* my strength now, for
war, both to go out, and to come in.
12Now therefore give me this mountain,
whereof the LORD spake in that day; for
thou heardest in that day how the Anakims
were there, and *that* the cities *were* great *and*
fenced: if so be the LORD *will be* with me,
then I shall be able to drive them out, as
the LORD said.
13And Joshua blessed him, and gave
unto Caleb the son of Jephunneh Hebron
for an inheritance.
14Hebron therefore became the inheritance of Caleb the son of Jephunneh the
Kenezite unto this day, because that he
wholly followed the LORD God of Israel.
15And the name of Hebron before *was*
Kirjath-arba; *which Arba was* a great man
among the Anakims. And the land had rest
from war.

15

1*This* then was the lot of the tribe of the
children of Judah by their families; *even*
to the border of Edom the wilderness of
Zin southward *was* the uttermost part of
the south coast.
2And their south border was from the
shore of the salt sea, from the bay that
looketh southward:
3And it went out to the south side to
Maaleh-acrabbim, and passed along to
Zin, and ascended up on the south side
unto Kadesh-barnea, and passed along to
Hezron, and went up to Adar, and fetched
a compass to Karkaa:
4*From thence* it passed toward Azmon,
and went out unto the river of Egypt; and
the goings out of that coast were at the sea:
this shall be your south coast.
5And the east border *was* the salt sea,
even unto the end of Jordan. And *their* border in the north quarter *was* from the bay
of the sea at the uttermost part of Jordan:
6And the border went up to Beth-hogla,
and passed along by the north of Beth-
arabah; and the border went up to the
stone of Bohan the son of Reuben:
7And the border went up toward Debir
from the valley of Achor, and so northward, looking toward Gilgal, that *is* before
the going up to Adummim, which *is* on
the south side of the river: and the border
passed toward the waters of En-shemesh,
and the goings out thereof were at En-
rogel:
8And the border went up by the valley
of the son of Hinnom unto the south side
of the Jebusite; the same *is* Jerusalem: and
the border went up to the top of the mountain that *lieth* before the valley of Hinnom
westward, which *is* at the end of the valley
of the giants northward:
9And the border was drawn from the top
of the hill unto the fountain of the water
of Nephtoah, and went out to the cities of
mount Ephron; and the border was drawn
to Baalah, which *is* Kirjath-jearim:
10And the border compassed from Baalah westward unto mount Seir, and
passed along unto the side of mount Jea-
rim, which *is* Chesalon, on the north side,
and went down to Beth-shemesh, and
passed on to Timnah:
11And the border went out unto the side
of Ekron northward: and the border was
drawn to Shicron, and passed along to
mount Baalah, and went out unto Jabneel; and the goings out of the border were
at the sea.
12And the west border *was* to the great
sea, and the coast *thereof*. This *is* the coast
of the children of Judah round about according to their families.
13And unto Caleb the son of Jephunneh he gave a part among the children of
Judah, according to the commandment of
the LORD to Joshua, *even* the city of Arba
the father of Anak, which *city is* Hebron.
14And Caleb drove thence the three sons
of Anak, Sheshai, and Ahiman, and Talmai, the children of Anak.
15And he went up thence to the inhabitants of Debir: and the name of Debir before *was* Kirjath-sepher.
16And Caleb said, He that smiteth
Kirjath-sepher, and taketh it, to him will I
give Achsah my daughter to wife.
17And Othniel the son of Kenaz, the

brother of Caleb, took it: and he gave him Achsah his daughter to wife.

18 And it came to pass, as she came *unto him*, that she moved him to ask of her father a field: and she lighted off *her* ass; and Caleb said unto her, What wouldest thou?

19 Who answered, Give me a blessing; for thou hast given me a south land; give me also springs of water. And he gave her the upper springs, and the nether springs.

20 This *is* the inheritance of the tribe of the children of Judah according to their families.

21 And the uttermost cities of the tribe of the children of Judah toward the coast of Edom southward were Kabzeel, and Eder, and Jagur,

22 And Kinah, and Dimonah, and Adadah,

23 And Kedesh, and Hazor, and Ithnan,

24 Ziph, and Telem, and Bealoth,

25 And Hazor, Hadattah, and Kerioth, *and* Hezron, which *is* Hazor,

26 Amam, and Shema, and Moladah,

27 And Hazar-gaddah, and Heshmon, and Beth-palet,

28 And Hazar-shual, and Beer-sheba, and Bizjothjah,

29 Baalah, and Iim, and Azem,

30 And Eltolad, and Chesil, and Hormah,

31 And Ziklag, and Madmannah, and Sansannah,

32 And Lebaoth, and Shilhim, and Ain, and Rimmon: all the cities *are* twenty and nine, with their villages:

33 *And* in the valley, Eshtaol, and Zoreah, and Ashnah,

34 And Zanoah, and En-gannim, Tappuah, and Enam,

35 Jarmuth, and Adullam, Socoh, and Azekah,

36 And Sharaim, and Adithaim, and Gederah, and Gederothaim; fourteen cities with their villages:

37 Zenan, and Hadashah, and Migdalgad,

38 And Dilean, and Mizpeh, and Joktheel,

39 Lachish, and Bozkath, and Eglon,

40 And Cabbon, and Lahmam, and Kithlish,

41 And Gederoth, Beth-dagon, and Naamah, and Makkedah; sixteen cities with their villages:

42 Libnah, and Ether, and Ashan,

43 And Jiphtah, and Ashnah, and Nezib,

44 And Keilah, and Achzib, and Mareshah; nine cities with their villages:

45 Ekron, with her towns and her villages:

46 From Ekron even unto the sea, all that *lay* near Ashdod, with their villages:

47 Ashdod with her towns and her villages, Gaza with her towns and her villages, unto the river of Egypt, and the great sea, and the border *thereof*:

48 And in the mountains, Shamir, and Jattir, and Socoh,

49 And Dannah, and Kirjath-sannah, which *is* Debir,

50 And Anab, and Eshtemoh, and Anim,

51 And Goshen, and Holon, and Giloh; eleven cities with their villages:

52 Arab, and Dumah, and Eshean,

53 And Janum, and Beth-tappuah, and Aphekah,

54 And Humtah, and Kirjath-arba, which *is* Hebron, and Zior; nine cities with their villages:

55 Maon, Carmel, and Ziph, and Juttah,

56 And Jezreel, and Jokdeam, and Zanoah,

57 Cain, Gibeah, and Timnah; ten cities with their villages:

58 Halhul, Beth-zur, and Gedor,

59 And Maarath, and Beth-anoth, and Eltekon; six cities with their villages:

60 Kirjath-baal, which *is* Kirjath-jearim, and Rabbah; two cities with their villages:

61 In the wilderness, Beth-arabah, Middin, and Secacah,

62 And Nibshan, and the city of Salt, and En-gedi; six cities with their villages.

63 As for the Jebusites the inhabitants of Jerusalem, the children of Judah could not drive them out: but the Jebusites dwell with the children of Judah at Jerusalem unto this day.

16

1 And the lot of the children of Joseph fell from Jordan by Jericho, unto the water of Jericho on the east, to the wilderness that goeth up from Jericho throughout mount Bethel,

2 And goeth out from Bethel to Luz, and passeth along unto the borders of Archi to Ataroth,

3 And goeth down westward to the coast of Japhleti, unto the coast of Beth-horon the nether, and to Gezer: and the goings out thereof are at the sea.

4 So the children of Joseph, Manasseh
and Ephraim, took their inheritance.
5 And the border of the children of
Ephraim according to their families was
thus: even the border of their inheritance
on the east side was Ataroth-addar, unto
Beth-horon the upper;
6 And the border went out toward the sea
to Michmethah on the north side; and the
border went about eastward unto Taanath-
shiloh, and passed by it on the east to
Janohah;
7 And it went down from Janohah to Ataroth, and to Naarath, and came to Jericho, and went out at Jordan.
8 The border went out from Tappuah
westward unto the river Kanah; and the
goings out thereof were at the sea. This *is*
the inheritance of the tribe of the children
of Ephraim by their families.
9 And the separate cities for the children
of Ephraim *were* among the inheritance of
the children of Manasseh, all the cities with
their villages.
10 And they drave not out the Canaanites that dwelt in Gezer: but the Canaanites dwell among the Ephraimites unto this
day, and serve under tribute.

17

1 There was also a lot for the tribe of
Manasseh; for he *was* the firstborn of Joseph; *to wit,* for Machir the firstborn of
Manasseh, the father of Gilead: because he
was a man of war, therefore he had Gilead
and Bashan.
2 There was also *a lot* for the rest of the
children of Manasseh by their families; for
the children of Abiezer, and for the children of Helek, and for the children of Asriel, and for the children of Shechem, and
for the children of Hepher, and for the
children of Shemida: these *were* the male
children of Manasseh the son of Joseph
by their families.
3 But Zelophehad, the son of Hepher, the
son of Gilead, the son of Machir, the son
of Manasseh, had no sons, but daughters:
and these *are* the names of his daughters,
Mahlah, and Noah, Hoglah, Milcah, and
Tirzah.
4 And they came near before Eleazar the
priest, and before Joshua the son of Nun,
and before the princes, saying, The LORD
commanded Moses to give us an inheritance among our brethren. Therefore according to the commandment of the LORD
he gave them an inheritance among the
brethren of their father.
5 And there fell ten portions to Manasseh, beside the land of Gilead and Bashan,
which *were* on the other side Jordan;
6 Because the daughters of Manasseh had
an inheritance among his sons: and the
rest of Manasseh's sons had the land of
Gilead.
7 And the coast of Manasseh was from
Asher to Michmethah, that *lieth* before
Shechem; and the border went along on
the right hand unto the inhabitants of En-
tappuah.
8 *Now* Manasseh had the land of Tappuah: but Tappuah on the border of Manasseh *belonged* to the children of Ephraim;
9 And the coast descended unto the river
Kanah, southward of the river: these cities
of Ephraim *are* among the cities of Manasseh: the coast of Manasseh also *was* on the
north side of the river, and the outgoings
of it were at the sea:
10 Southward *it was* Ephraim's, and
northward *it was* Manasseh's, and the sea
is his border; and they met together in
Asher on the north, and in Issachar on the
east.
11 And Manasseh had in Issachar and in
Asher Beth-shean and her towns, and Ibleam and her towns, and the inhabitants
of Dor and her towns, and the inhabitants
of Endor and her towns, and the inhabitants of Taanach and her towns, and the
inhabitants of Megiddo and her towns,
even three countries.
12 Yet the children of Manasseh could
not drive out *the inhabitants of* those cities;
but the Canaanites would dwell in that
land.
13 Yet it came to pass, when the children
of Israel were waxen strong, that they put
the Canaanites to tribute; but did not utterly drive them out.
14 And the children of Joseph spake unto
Joshua, saying, Why hast thou given me
but one lot and one portion to inherit, seeing I *am* a great people, forasmuch as the
LORD hath blessed me hitherto?
15 And Joshua answered them, If thou *be*
a great people, *then* get thee up to the wood
country, and cut down for thyself there in
the land of the Perizzites and of the giants,
if mount Ephraim be too narrow for thee.
16 And the children of Joseph said, The

hill is not enough for us: and all the Canaanites that dwell in the land of the valley have chariots of iron, *both they* who *are* of Beth-shean and her towns, and *they* who *are* of the valley of Jezreel.

17 And Joshua spake unto the house of Joseph, *even* to Ephraim and to Manasseh, saying, Thou *art* a great people, and hast great power: thou shalt not have one lot *only:*

18 But the mountain shall be thine; for it *is* a wood, and thou shalt cut it down: and the outgoings of it shall be thine: for thou shalt drive out the Canaanites, though they have iron chariots, *and* though they *be* strong.

18

1 And the whole congregation of the children of Israel assembled together at Shiloh, and set up the tabernacle of the congregation there. And the land was subdued before them.

2 And there remained among the children of Israel seven tribes, which had not yet received their inheritance.

3 And Joshua said unto the children of Israel, How long *are* ye slack to go to possess the land, which the LORD God of your fathers hath given you?

4 Give out from among you three men for *each* tribe: and I will send them, and they shall rise, and go through the land, and describe it according to the inheritance of them; and they shall come *again* to me.

5 And they shall divide it into seven parts: Judah shall abide in their coast on the south, and the house of Joseph shall abide in their coasts on the north.

6 Ye shall therefore describe the land *into* seven parts, and bring *the description* hither to me, that I may cast lots for you here before the LORD our God.

7 But the Levites have no part among you; for the priesthood of the LORD is their inheritance: and Gad, and Reuben, and half the tribe of Manasseh, have received their inheritance beyond Jordan on the east, which Moses the servant of the LORD gave them.

8 And the men arose, and went away: and Joshua charged them that went to describe the land, saying, Go and walk through the land, and describe it, and come again to me, that I may here cast lots for you before the LORD in Shiloh.

9 And the men went and passed through the land, and described it by cities into seven parts in a book, and came *again* to Joshua to the host at Shiloh.

10 And Joshua cast lots for them in Shiloh before the LORD: and there Joshua divided the land unto the children of Israel according to their divisions.

11 And the lot of the tribe of the children of Benjamin came up according to their families: and the coast of their lot came forth between the children of Judah and the children of Joseph.

12 And their border on the north side was from Jordan; and the border went up to the side of Jericho on the north side, and went up through the mountains westward; and the goings out thereof were at the wilderness of Beth-aven.

13 And the border went over from thence toward Luz, to the side of Luz, which *is* Bethel, southward; and the border descended to Ataroth-adar, near the hill that *lieth* on the south side of the nether Beth-horon.

14 And the border was drawn *thence,* and compassed the corner of the sea southward, from the hill that *lieth* before Beth-horon southward; and the goings out thereof were at Kirjath-baal, which *is* Kirjath-jearim, a city of the children of Judah: this *was* the west quarter.

15 And the south quarter *was* from the end of Kirjath-jearim, and the border went out on the west, and went out to the well of waters of Nephtoah:

16 And the border came down to the end of the mountain that *lieth* before the valley of the son of Hinnom, *and* which *is* in the valley of the giants on the north, and descended to the valley of Hinnom, to the side of Jebusi on the south, and descended to En-rogel,

17 And was drawn from the north, and went forth to En-shemesh, and went forth toward Geliloth, which *is* over against the going up of Adummim, and descended to the stone of Bohan the son of Reuben,

18 And passed along toward the side over against Arabah northward, and went down unto Arabah:

19 And the border passed along to the side of Beth-hoglah northward: and the outgoings of the border were at the north bay of the salt sea at the south end of Jordan: this *was* the south coast.

20And Jordan was the border of it on
the east side. This *was* the inheritance of
the children of Benjamin, by the coasts
thereof round about, according to their
families.
21Now the cities of the tribe of the children of Benjamin according to their families were Jericho, and Beth-hoglah, and the
valley of Keziz,
22And Beth-arabah, and Zemaraim, and
Bethel,
23And Avim, and Parah, and Ophrah,
24And Chephar-haammonai, and Oph-
ni, and Gaba; twelve cities with their villages:
25Gibeon, and Ramah, and Beeroth,
26And Mizpeh, and Chephirah, and
Mozah,
27And Rekem, and Irpeel, and Taralah,
28And Zelah, Eleph, and Jebusi, which
is Jerusalem, Gibeath, *and* Kirjath; fourteen
cities with their villages. This *is* the inheritance of the children of Benjamin according to their families.

19

1And the second lot came forth to Simeon, *even* for the tribe of the children of
Simeon according to their families: and
their inheritance was within the inheritance of the children of Judah.
2And they had in their inheritance Beer-
sheba, or Sheba, and Moladah,
3And Hazar-shual, and Balah, and
Azem,
4And Eltolad, and Bethul, and Hormah,
5And Ziklag, and Beth-marcaboth, and
Hazar-susah,
6And Beth-lebaoth, and Sharuhen; thirteen cities and their villages:
7Ain, Remmon, and Ether, and Ashan;
four cities and their villages:
8And all the villages that *were* round
about these cities to Baalath-beer, Ramath
of the south. This is the inheritance of the
tribe of the children of Simeon according
to their families.
9Out of the portion of the children of
Judah *was* the inheritance of the children
of Simeon: for the part of the children of
Judah was too much for them: therefore
the children of Simeon had their inheritance within the inheritance of them.
10And the third lot came up for the children of Zebulun according to their families: and the border of their inheritance
was unto Sarid:
11And their border went up toward the
sea, and Maralah, and reached to Dab-
basheth, and reached to the river that *is*
before Jokneam;
12And turned from Sarid eastward toward the sunrising unto the border of
Chisloth-tabor, and then goeth out to daberath, and goeth up to Japhia,
13And from thence passeth on along on
the east to Gittah-hepher, to Ittah-kazin,
and goeth out to Remmon-methoar to
Neah;
14And the border compasseth it on
the north side to Hannathon: and the
outgoings thereof are in the valley of
Jiphthah-el:
15And Kattath, and Nahallal, and Shimron, and Idalah, and Bethlehem: twelve
cities with their villages.
16This *is* the inheritance of the children
of Zebulun according to their families,
these cities with their villages.
17*And* the fourth lot came out to Issachar, for the children of Issachar according to their families.
18And their border was toward Jezreel,
and Chesulloth, and Shunem,
19And Haphraim, and Shihon, and Ana-
harath,
20And Rabbith, and Kishion, and Abez,
21And Remeth, and En-gannim, and En-
haddah, and Beth-pazzez;
22And the coast reacheth to Tabor, and
Shahazimah, and Beth-shemesh; and the
outgoings of their border were at Jordan:
sixteen cities with their villages.
23This *is* the inheritance of the tribe of
the children of Issachar according to their
families, the cities and their villages.
24And the fifth lot came out for the tribe
of the children of Asher according to their
families.
25And their border was Helkath, and
Hali, and Beten, and Achshaph,
26And Alammelech, and Amad, and
Misheal; and reacheth to Carmel westward,
and to Shihor-libnath;
27And turneth toward the sunrising to
Beth-dagon, and reacheth to Zebulun, and
to the valley of Jiphthah-el toward the
north side of Beth-emek, and Neiel, and
goeth out to Cabul on the left hand,
28And Hebron, and Rehob, and Hammon, and Kanah, *even* unto great Zidon;
29And *then* the coast turneth to Ramah,

and to the strong city Tyre; and the coast
turneth to Hosah; and the outgoings
thereof are at the sea from the coast to
Achzib:
30 Ummah also, and Aphek, and Rehob:
twenty and two cities with their villages.
31 This *is* the inheritance of the tribe of
the children of Asher according to their
families, these cities with their villages.
32 The sixth lot came out to the children
of Naphtali, *even* for the children of Naphtali according to their families.
33 And their coast was from Heleph,
from Allon to Zaanannim, and Adami,
Nekeb, and Jabneel, unto Lakum; and the
outgoings thereof were at Jordan:
34 And *then* the coast turneth westward
to Aznoth-tabor, and goeth out from
thence to Hukkok, and reacheth to Zebulun on the south side, and reacheth to Asher on the west side, and to Judah upon
Jordan toward the sunrising.
35 And the fenced cities *are* Ziddim, Zer,
and Hammath, Rakkath, and Chinnereth,
36 And Adamah, and Ramah, and Hazor,
37 And Kedesh, and Edrei, and En-hazor,
38 And Iron, and Migdal-el, Horem, and
Beth-anath, and Beth-shemesh; nineteen
cities with their villages.
39 This *is* the inheritance of the tribe of
the children of Naphtali according to their
families, the cities and their villages.
40 *And* the seventh lot came out for the
tribe of the children of Dan according to
their families.
41 And the coast of their inheritance was
Zorah, and Eshtaol, and Ir-shemesh,
42 And Shaalabbin, and Ajalon, and
Jethlah,
43 And Elon, and Thimnathah, and
Ekron,
44 And Eltekeh, and Gibbethon, and
Baalath,
45 And Jehud, and Bene-berak, and Gath-
rimmon,
46 And Me-jarkon, and Rakkon, with the
border before Japho.
47 And the coast of the children of Dan
went out *too little* for them: therefore the
children of Dan went up to fight against
Leshem, and took it, and smote it with the
edge of the sword, and possessed it, and
dwelt therein, and called Leshem, Dan,
after the name of Dan their father.
48 This *is* the inheritance of the tribe of
the children of Dan according to their families, these cities with their villages.
49 When they had made an end of dividing the land for inheritance by their
coasts, the children of Israel gave an inheritance to Joshua the son of Nun among
them:
50 According to the word of the LORD
they gave him the city which he asked, *even*
Timnath-serah in mount Ephraim: and he
built the city, and dwelt therein.
51 These *are* the inheritances which Eleazar the priest, and Joshua the son of Nun,
and the heads of the fathers of the tribes
of the children of Israel, divided for an
inheritance by lot in Shiloh before the
LORD, at the door of the tabernacle of
the congregation. So they made an end of
dividing the country.

20

1 The LORD also spake unto Joshua,
saying,
2 Speak to the children of Israel, saying,
Appoint out for you cities of refuge,
whereof I spake unto you by the hand of
Moses:
3 That the slayer that killeth *any* person
unawares *and* unwittingly may flee thither:
and they shall be your refuge from the
avenger of blood.
4 And when he that doth flee unto one
of those cities shall stand at the entering
of the gate of the city, and shall declare
his cause in the ears of the elders of that
city, they shall take him into the city unto
them, and give him a place, that he may
dwell among them.
5 And if the avenger of blood pursue after him, then they shall not deliver the slayer up into his hand; because he smote his
neighbour unwittingly, and hated him not
beforetime.
6 And he shall dwell in that city, until he
stand before the congregation for judgment, *and* until the death of the high priest
that shall be in those days: then shall the
slayer return, and come unto his own city,
and unto his own house, unto the city from
whence he fled.
7 And they appointed Kedesh in Galilee
in mount Naphtali, and Shechem in
mount Ephraim, and Kirjath-arba, which
is Hebron, in the mountain of Judah.
8 And on the other side Jordan by Jericho eastward, they assigned Bezer in the
wilderness upon the plain out of the tribe

of Reuben, and Ramoth in Gilead out of the tribe of Gad, and Golan in Bashan out of the tribe of Manasseh.

9 These were the cities appointed for all the children of Israel, and for the stranger that sojourneth among them, that whosoever killeth *any* person at unawares might flee thither, and not die by the hand of the avenger of blood, until he stood before the congregation.

21

1 Then came near the heads of the fathers of the Levites unto Eleazar the priest, and unto Joshua the son of Nun, and unto the heads of the fathers of the tribes of the children of Israel;

2 And they spake unto them at Shiloh in the land of Canaan, saying, The LORD commanded by the hand of Moses to give us cities to dwell in, with the suburbs thereof for our cattle.

3 And the children of Israel gave unto the Levites out of their inheritance, at the commandment of the LORD, these cities and their suburbs.

4 And the lot came out for the families of the Kohathites: and the children of Aaron the priest, *which were* of the Levites, had by lot out of the tribe of Judah, and out of the tribe of Simeon, and out of the tribe of Benjamin, thirteen cities.

5 And the rest of the children of Kohath *had* by lot out of the families of the tribe of Ephraim, and out of the tribe of Dan, and out of the half tribe of Manasseh, ten cities.

6 And the children of Gershon *had* by lot out of the families of the tribe of Issachar, and out of the tribe of Asher, and out of the tribe of Naphtali, and out of the half tribe of Manasseh in Bashan, thirteen cities.

7 The children of Merari by their families *had* out of the tribe of Reuben, and out of the tribe of Gad, and out of the tribe of Zebulun, twelve cities.

8 And the children of Israel gave by lot unto the Levites these cities with their suburbs, as the LORD commanded by the hand of Moses.

9 And they gave out of the tribe of the children of Judah, and out of the tribe of the children of Simeon, these cities which are *here* mentioned by name,

10 Which the children of Aaron, *being* of the families of the Kohathites, *who were* of the children of Levi, had: for theirs was the first lot.

11 And they gave them the city of Arba the father of Anak, which *city is* Hebron, in the hill *country* of Judah, with the suburbs thereof round about it.

12 But the fields of the city, and the villages thereof, gave they to Caleb the son of Jephunneh for his possession.

13 Thus they gave to the children of Aaron the priest Hebron with her suburbs, *to be* a city of refuge for the slayer; and Libnah with her suburbs,

14 And Jattir with her suburbs, and Eshtemoa with her suburbs,

15 And Holon with her suburbs, and Debir with her suburbs,

16 And Ain with her suburbs, and Juttah with her suburbs, *and* Beth-shemesh with her suburbs; nine cities out of those two tribes.

17 And out of the tribe of Benjamin, Gibeon with her suburbs, Geba with her suburbs,

18 Anathoth with her suburbs, and Almon with her suburbs; four cities.

19 All the cities of the children of Aaron, the priests, *were* thirteen cities with their suburbs.

20 And the families of the children of Kohath, the Levites which remained of the children of Kohath, even they had the cities of their lot out of the tribe of Ephraim.

21 For they gave them Shechem with her suburbs in mount Ephraim, *to be* a city of refuge for the slayer; and Gezer with her suburbs,

22 And Kibzaim with her suburbs, and Beth-horon with her suburbs; four cities.

23 And out of the tribe of Dan, Eltekeh with her suburbs, Gibbethon with her suburbs,

24 Aijalon with her suburbs, Gath-rimmon with her suburbs; four cities.

25 And out of the half tribe of Manasseh, Tanach with her suburbs, and Gath-rimmon with her suburbs; two cities.

26 All the cities *were* ten with their suburbs for the families of the children of Kohath that remained.

27 And unto the children of Gershon, of the families of the Levites, out of the *other* half tribe of Manasseh *they gave* Golan in Bashan with her suburbs, *to be* a city of refuge for the slayer; and Beesh-terah with her suburbs; two cities.

28 And out of the tribe of Issachar, Kishon with her suburbs, Dabareh with her suburbs,

29 Jarmuth with her suburbs, En-gannim with her suburbs; four cities.

30 And out of the tribe of Asher, Mishal with her suburbs, Abdon with her suburbs,

31 Helkath with her suburbs, and Rehob with her suburbs; four cities.

32 And out of the tribe of Naphtali, Kedesh in Galilee with her suburbs, *to be* a city of refuge for the slayer; and Hammoth-dor with her suburbs, and Kartan with her suburbs; three cities.

33 All the cities of the Gershonites according to their families *were* thirteen cities with their suburbs.

34 And unto the families of the children of Merari, the rest of the Levites, out of the tribe of Zebulun, Jokneam with her suburbs, and Kartah with her suburbs,

35 Dimnah with her suburbs, Nahalal with her suburbs; four cities.

36 And out of the tribe of Reuben, Bezer with her suburbs, and Jahazah with her suburbs,

37 Kedemoth with her suburbs, and Mephaath with her suburbs; four cities.

38 And out of the tribe of Gad, Ramoth in Gilead with her suburbs, *to be* a city of refuge for the slayer; and Mahanaim with her suburbs,

39 Heshbon with her suburbs, Jazer with her suburbs; four cities in all.

40 So all the cities for the children of Merari by their families, which were remaining of the families of the Levites, were *by* their lot twelve cities.

41 All the cities of the Levites within the possession of the children of Israel *were* forty and eight cities with their suburbs.

42 These cities were every one with their suburbs round about them: thus *were* all these cities.

43 And the LORD gave unto Israel all the land which he sware to give unto their fathers; and they possessed it, and dwelt therein.

44 And the LORD gave them rest round about, according to all that he sware unto their fathers: and there stood not a man of all their enemies before them; the LORD delivered all their enemies into their hand.

45 There failed not ought of any good thing which the LORD had spoken unto the house of Israel; all came to pass.

22

1 Then Joshua called the Reubenites, and the Gadites, and the half tribe of Manasseh,

2 And said unto them, Ye have kept all that Moses the servant of the LORD commanded you, and have obeyed my voice in all that I commanded you:

3 Ye have not left your brethren these many days unto this day, but have kept the charge of the commandment of the LORD your God.

4 And now the LORD your God hath given rest unto your brethren, as he promised them: therefore now return ye, and get you unto your tents, *and* unto the land of your possession, which Moses the servant of the LORD gave you on the other side Jordan.

5 But take diligent heed to do the commandment and the law, which Moses the servant of the LORD charged you, to love the LORD your God, and to walk in all his ways, and to keep his commandments, and to cleave unto him, and to serve him with all your heart and with all your soul.

22:5 Love for God
◄ Deuteronomy 11:1
Psalm 31:23 ►

6 So Joshua blessed them, and sent them away: and they went unto their tents.

7 Now to the *one* half of the tribe of Manasseh Moses had given *possession* in Bashan: but unto the *other* half thereof gave Joshua among their brethren on this side Jordan westward. And when Joshua sent them away also unto their tents, then he blessed them,

8 And he spake unto them, saying, Return with much riches unto your tents, and with very much cattle, with silver, and with gold, and with brass, and with iron, and with very much raiment: divide the spoil of your enemies with your brethren.

9 And the children of Reuben and the children of Gad and the half tribe of Manasseh returned, and departed from the children of Israel out of Shiloh, which *is* in the land of Canaan, to go unto the country of Gilead, to the land of their possession, whereof they were possessed, according to the word of the LORD by the hand of Moses.

10 And when they came unto the borders

of Jordan, that *are* in the land of Canaan,
the children of Reuben and the children
of Gad and the half tribe of Manasseh built
there an altar by Jordan, a great altar to
see to.
11 And the children of Israel heard say,
Behold, the children of Reuben and the
children of Gad and the half tribe of Manasseh have built an altar over against the
land of Canaan, in the borders of Jordan,
at the passage of the children of Israel.
12 And when the children of Israel heard
of it, the whole congregation of the children of Israel gathered themselves together at Shiloh, to go up to war against them.
13 And the children of Israel sent unto
the children of Reuben, and to the children of Gad, and to the half tribe of Manasseh, into the land of Gilead, Phinehas
the son of Eleazar the priest,
14 And with him ten princes, of each
chief house a prince throughout all the
tribes of Israel; and each one *was* an head
of the house of their fathers among the
thousands of Israel.
15 And they came unto the children of
Reuben, and to the children of Gad, and
to the half tribe of Manasseh, unto the
land of Gilead, and they spake with them,
saying,
16 Thus saith the whole congregation of
the LORD, What trespass *is* this that ye have
committed against the God of Israel, to
turn away this day from following the
LORD, in that ye have builded you an altar,
that ye might rebel this day against the
LORD?
17 *Is* the iniquity of Peor too little for us,
from which we are not cleansed until this
day, although there was a plague in the
congregation of the LORD,
18 But that ye must turn away this day
from following the LORD? and it will be,
seeing ye rebel to day against the LORD, that
to morrow he will be wroth with the whole
congregation of Israel.
19 Notwithstanding, if the land of your
possession *be* unclean, *then* pass ye over
unto the land of the possession of the
LORD, wherein the LORD'S tabernacle
dwelleth, and take possession among us:
but rebel not against the LORD, nor rebel
against us, in building you an altar beside
the altar of the LORD our God.
20 Did not Achan the son of Zerah commit a trespass in the accursed thing, and
wrath fell on all the congregation of Israel? and that man perished not alone in
his iniquity.
21 Then the children of Reuben and the
children of Gad and the half tribe of Manasseh answered, and said unto the heads
of the thousands of Israel,
22 The LORD God of gods, the LORD God
of gods, he knoweth, and Israel he shall
know; if *it be* in rebellion, or if in transgression against the LORD, (save us not this
day,)
23 That we have built us an altar to turn
from following the LORD, or if to offer
thereon burnt offering or meat offering,
or if to offer peace offerings thereon, let
the LORD himself require *it;*
24 And if we have not *rather* done it for
fear of *this* thing, saying, In time to come
your children might speak unto our children, saying, What have ye to do with the
LORD God of Israel?
25 For the LORD hath made Jordan a border between us and you, ye children of
Reuben and children of Gad; ye have no
part in the LORD: so shall your children
make our children cease from fearing the
LORD.
26 Therefore we said, Let us now prepare
to build us an altar, not for burnt offering,
nor for sacrifice:
27 But *that* it *may be* a witness between
us, and you, and our generations after us,
that we might do the service of the LORD
before him with our burnt offerings, and
with our sacrifices, and with our peace offerings; that your children may not say to
our children in time to come, Ye have no
part in the LORD.
28 Therefore said we, that it shall be,
when they should *so* say to us or to our
generations in time to come, that we may
say *again,* Behold the pattern of the altar
of the LORD, which our fathers made, not
for burnt offerings, nor for sacrifices; but
it *is* a witness between us and you.
29 God forbid that we should rebel
against the LORD, and turn this day from
following the LORD, to build an altar for
burnt offerings, for meat offerings, or for
sacrifices, beside the altar of the LORD our
God that *is* before his tabernacle.
30 And when Phinehas the priest, and the
princes of the congregation and heads of

the thousands of Israel which *were* with him, heard the words that the children of Reuben and the children of Gad and the children of Manasseh spake, it pleased them.

31 And Phinehas the son of Eleazar the priest said unto the children of Reuben, and to the children of Gad, and to the children of Manasseh, This day we perceive that the LORD *is* among us, because ye have not committed this trespass against the LORD: now ye have delivered the children of Israel out of the hand of the LORD.

32 And Phinehas the son of Eleazar the priest, and the princes, returned from the children of Reuben, and from the children of Gad, out of the land of Gilead, unto the land of Canaan, to the children of Israel, and brought them word again.

33 And the thing pleased the children of Israel; and the children of Israel blessed God, and did not intend to go up against them in battle, to destroy the land wherein the children of Reuben and Gad dwelt.

34 And the children of Reuben and the children of Gad called the altar *Ed:* for it *shall be* a witness between us that the LORD *is* God.

23

1 And it came to pass a long time after that the LORD had given rest unto Israel from all their enemies round about, that Joshua waxed old *and* stricken in age.

2 And Joshua called for all Israel, *and* for their elders, and for their heads, and for their judges, and for their officers, and said unto them, I am old *and* stricken in age:

3 And ye have seen all that the LORD your God hath done unto all these nations because of you; for the LORD your God *is* he that hath fought for you.

4 Behold, I have divided unto you by lot these nations that remain, to be an inheritance for your tribes, from Jordan, with all the nations that I have cut off, even unto the great sea westward.

5 And the LORD your God, he shall expel them from before you, and drive them from out of your sight; and ye shall possess their land, as the LORD your God hath promised unto you.

6 Be ye therefore very courageous to keep and to do all that is written in the book of the law of Moses, that ye turn not aside therefrom *to* the right hand or *to* the left;

7 That ye come not among these nations, these that remain among you; neither make mention of the names of their gods, nor cause to swear *by them,* neither serve them, nor bow yourselves unto them:

23:7-8
Standing Strong
◄ 1 Samuel 12:21 ►

8 But cleave unto the LORD your God, as ye have done unto this day.

9 For the LORD hath driven out from before you great nations and strong: but *as for* you, no man hath been able to stand before you unto this day.

10 One man of you shall chase a thousand: for the LORD your God, he *it is* that fighteth for you, as he hath promised you.

11 Take good heed therefore unto yourselves, that ye love the LORD your God.

12 Else if ye do in any wise go back, and cleave unto the remnant of these nations, *even* these that remain among you, and shall make marriages with them, and go in unto them, and they to you:

13 Know for a certainty that the LORD your God will no more drive out *any of* these nations from before you; but they shall be snares and traps unto you, and scourges in your sides, and thorns in your eyes, until ye perish from off this good land which the LORD your God hath given you.

14 And, behold, this day I *am* going the way of all the earth: and ye know in all your hearts and in all your souls, that not one thing hath failed of all the good things which the LORD your God spake concerning you; all are come to pass unto you, *and* not one thing hath failed thereof.

15 Therefore it shall come to pass, *that* as all good things are come upon you, which the LORD your God promised you; so shall the LORD bring upon you all evil things, until he have destroyed you from off this good land which the LORD your God hath given you.

23:15 Warning!
◄ Leviticus 26:16
1 Samuel 12:25 ►

16 When ye have transgressed the covenant of the LORD your God, which he commanded you, and have gone and served other gods, and bowed yourselves to them; then shall the anger of the LORD be kindled against you, and ye shall perish

quickly from off the good land which he hath given unto you.

24

1And Joshua gathered all the tribes of Israel to Shechem, and called for the elders of Israel, and for their heads, and for their judges, and for their officers; and they presented themselves before God.

2And Joshua said unto all the people, Thus saith the LORD God of Israel, Your fathers dwelt on the other side of the flood in old time, *even* Terah, the father of Abraham, and the father of Nachor: and they served other gods.

3And I took your father Abraham from the other side of the flood, and led him throughout all the land of Canaan, and multiplied his seed, and gave him Isaac.

4And I gave unto Isaac Jacob and Esau: and I gave unto Esau mount Seir, to possess it; but Jacob and his children went down into Egypt.

5I sent Moses also and Aaron, and I plagued Egypt, according to that which I did among them: and afterward I brought you out.

6And I brought your fathers out of Egypt: and ye came unto the sea; and the Egyptians pursued after your fathers with chariots and horsemen unto the Red sea.

7And when they cried unto the LORD, he put darkness between you and the Egyptians, and brought the sea upon them, and covered them; and your eyes have seen what I have done in Egypt: and ye dwelt in the wilderness a long season.

8And I brought you into the land of the Amorites, which dwelt on the other side Jordan; and they fought with you: and I gave them into your hand, that ye might possess their land; and I destroyed them from before you.

9Then Balak the son of Zippor, king of Moab, arose and warred against Israel, and sent and called Balaam the son of Beor to curse you:

10But I would not hearken unto Balaam; therefore he blessed you still: so I delivered you out of his hand.

11And ye went over Jordan, and came unto Jericho: and the men of Jericho fought against you, the Amorites, and the Perizzites, and the Canaanites, and the Hittites, and the Girgashites, the Hivites, and the Jebusites; and I delivered them into your hand.

12And I sent the hornet before you, which drave them out from before you, *even* the two kings of the Amorites; *but* not with thy sword, nor with thy bow.

13And I have given you a land for which ye did not labour, and cities which ye built not, and ye dwell in them; of the vineyards and oliveyards which ye planted not do ye eat.

14Now therefore fear the LORD, and serve him in sincerity and in truth: and put away the gods which your fathers served on the other side of the flood, and in Egypt; and serve ye the LORD.

24:14 Fearing God
◄ Joshua 4:24
1 Chronicles 16:30 ►

24:14 Sincerity
◄ 1 Corinthians 5:8 ►

15And if it seem evil unto you to serve the LORD, choose you this day whom ye will serve; whether the gods which your fathers served that *were* on the other side of the flood, or the gods of the Amorites, in whose land ye dwell: but as for me and my house, we will serve the LORD.

24:15 Following God
◄ Deuteronomy 30:15
Ruth 1:15 ►

24:15 Job One
◄ Matthew 6:33 ►

16And the people answered and said, God forbid that we should forsake the LORD, to serve other gods;

17For the LORD our God, he *it is* that brought us up and our fathers out of the land of Egypt, from the house of bondage, and which did those great signs in our sight, and preserved us in all the way wherein we went, and among all the people through whom we passed:

24:17 Safety
◄ Deuteronomy 6:24
2 Samuel 8:6 ►

18And the LORD drave out from before us all the people, even the Amorites which dwelt in the land: *therefore* will we also serve the LORD; for he *is* our God.

19And Joshua said unto the peo-

24:19 God Is Jealous
◄ Deuteronomy 29:20
1 Kings 14:22 ►

ple, Ye cannot serve the LORD: for he *is* an
holy God; he *is* a jealous God; he will not
forgive your transgressions nor your sins.
20 If ye forsake
the LORD, and serve
strange gods, then
he will turn and do
you hurt, and con-
sume you, after that
he hath done you good.

24:20 Sin (Warnings)
◄ Deuteronomy 29:20
1 Samuel 12:15 ►

21 And the people said unto Joshua, Nay;
but we will serve the LORD.
22 And Joshua said unto the people, Ye
are witnesses against yourselves that ye
have chosen you the LORD, to serve him.
And they said, *We are* witnesses.
23 Now therefore put away, *said he,* the
strange gods which *are* among you, and
incline your heart unto the LORD God of
Israel.
24 And the people said unto Joshua, The
LORD our God will we serve, and his voice
will we obey.
25 So Joshua made a covenant with the
people that day, and set them a statute and
an ordinance in Shechem.
26 And Joshua wrote these words in the
book of the law of God, and took a great
stone, and set it up there under an oak,
that *was* by the sanctuary of the LORD.
27 And Joshua said unto all the people,
Behold, this stone shall be a witness unto
us; for it hath heard all the words of the
LORD which he spake unto us: it shall be
therefore a witness unto you, lest ye deny
your God.
28 So Joshua let the people depart, every
man unto his inheritance.
29 And it came to pass after these things,
that Joshua the son of Nun, the servant of
the LORD, died, *being* an hundred and ten
years old.
30 And they buried him in the border of
his inheritance in Timnath-serah, which
is in mount Ephraim, on the north side of
the hill of Gaash.
31 And Israel served the LORD all the days
of Joshua, and all the days of the elders
that overlived Joshua, and which had
known all the works of the LORD, that he
had done for Israel.
32 And the bones of Joseph, which the
children of Israel brought up out of Egypt,
buried they in Shechem, in a parcel of
ground which Jacob bought of the sons of
Hamor the father of Shechem for an hundred pieces of silver: and it became the
inheritance of the children of Joseph.
33 And Eleazar the son of Aaron died;
and they buried him in a hill *that pertained
to* Phinehas his son, which was given him
in mount Ephraim.

Judges

AUTHOR
Probably Samuel the judge

MAIN POINT
God can be counted on not only to judge and punish sin but also to forgive and restore those who repent.

DATE WRITTEN
Probably put in its final shape in the sixth century B.C., while the people of Israel were captives in Babylon

21 CHAPTERS

MAIN PEOPLE

Othniel, Ehud, Deborah, Gideon, Abimelech, Jephthah, Samson, Delilah

SPECIAL FEATURES

- *Tells the inspiring yet gory story of two women: judge Deborah and tent-peg-wielding Jael*
- *Describes the military heroics of Gideon*
- *Includes the hair-raising adventure of what happened to Samson's incredible strength*
- *Records Israel's first civil war*
- *Second book of History*

HOW THE BOOK GOT ITS NAME

The word judges refers to the men and women who led the Israelites and saved them from their enemies.

1
1Now after the death of Joshua it came
to pass, that the children of Israel asked
the LORD, saying, Who shall go up for us
against the Canaanites first, to fight against
them?
2And the LORD said, Judah shall go up:
behold, I have delivered the land into his
hand.
3And Judah said unto Simeon his
brother, Come up with me into my lot,
that we may fight against the Canaanites;
and I likewise will go with thee into thy
lot. So Simeon went with him.
4And Judah went up; and the LORD delivered the Canaanites and the Perizzites
into their hand: and they slew of them in
Bezek ten thousand men.
5And they found Adoni-bezek in Bezek:
and they fought against him, and they slew
the Canaanites and the Perizzites.
6But Adoni-bezek fled; and they pursued
after him, and caught him, and cut off his
thumbs and his great toes.
7And Adoni-bezek said, Threescore and
ten kings, having their thumbs and their
great toes cut off, gathered *their meat* under my table: as I have done, so God hath
requited me. And they brought him to Jerusalem, and there he died.
8Now the children of Judah had fought

against Jerusalem, and had taken it, and
smitten it with the edge of the sword, and
set the city on fire.
9 And afterward the children of Judah
went down to fight against the Canaanites, that dwelt in the mountain, and in
the south, and in the valley.
10 And Judah went against the Canaanites that dwelt in Hebron: (now the name
of Hebron before *was* Kirjath-arba:) and
they slew Sheshai, and Ahiman, and Talmai.
11 And from thence he went against the
inhabitants of Debir: and the name of
Debir before *was* Kirjath-sepher:
12 And Caleb said, He that smiteth
Kirjath-sepher, and taketh it, to him will I
give Achsah my daughter to wife.
13 And Othniel the son of Kenaz, Caleb's
younger brother, took it: and he gave him
Achsah his daughter to wife.
14 And it came to pass, when she came
to him, that she moved him to ask of her
father a field: and she lighted from off *her*
ass; and Caleb said unto her, What wilt
thou?
15 And she said unto him, Give me a
blessing: for thou hast given me a south
land; give me also springs of water. And
Caleb gave her the upper springs and the
nether springs.
16 And the children of the Kenite, Moses' father in law, went up out of the city
of palm trees with the children of Judah
into the wilderness of Judah, which *lieth*
in the south of Arad; and they went and
dwelt among the people.
17 And Judah went with Simeon his
brother, and they slew the Canaanites that
inhabited Zephath, and utterly destroyed
it. And the name of the city was called
Hormah.
18 Also Judah took Gaza with the coast
thereof, and Askelon with the coast
thereof, and Ekron with the coast thereof.
19 And the LORD was with Judah; and he
drave out the inhabitants of the mountain;
but could not drive out *the inhabitants of*
the valley, because they had chariots of
iron.
20 And they gave Hebron unto Caleb, as
Moses said: and he expelled thence the
three sons of Anak.
21 And the children of Benjamin did not
drive out the Jebusites that inhabited Jerusalem; but the
Jebusites dwell with
the children of Ben-
jamin in Jerusalem
unto this day.

1:21 Cost of Sin
◄ Joshua 7:12
Judges 2:14 ►

22 And the house
of Joseph, they also went up against Bethel: and the LORD *was* with them.
23 And the house of Joseph sent to de-
scry Bethel. (Now the name of the city
before *was* Luz.)
24 And the spies saw a man come forth
out of the city, and they said unto him,
Shew us, we pray thee, the entrance into
the city, and we will shew thee mercy.
25 And when he shewed them the entrance into the city, they smote the city
with the edge of the sword; but they let go
the man and all his family.
26 And the man went into the land of
the Hittites, and built a city, and called the
name thereof Luz: which *is* the name
thereof unto this day.
27 Neither did Manasseh drive out *the*
inhabitants of Beth-shean and her towns,
nor Taanach and her towns, nor the inhabitants of Dor and her towns, nor the inhabitants of Ibleam and her towns, nor the
inhabitants of Megiddo and her towns: but
the Canaanites would dwell in that land.
28 And it came to pass, when Israel was
strong, that they put the Canaanites to tribute, and did not utterly drive them out.
29 Neither did Ephraim drive out the
Canaanites that dwelt in Gezer; but the
Canaanites dwelt in Gezer among them.
30 Neither did Zebulun drive out the inhabitants of Kitron, nor the inhabitants of
Nahalol; but the Canaanites dwelt among
them, and became tributaries.
31 Neither did Asher drive out the inhabitants of Accho, nor the inhabitants of
Zidon, nor of Ahlab, nor of Achzib, nor of
Helbah, nor of Aphik, nor of Rehob:
32 But the Asherites dwelt among the
Canaanites, the inhabitants of the land: for
they did not drive them out.
33 Neither did Naphtali drive out the inhabitants of Beth-shemesh, nor the inhabitants of Beth-anath; but he dwelt among
the Canaanites, the inhabitants of the land:
nevertheless the inhabitants of Beth-
shemesh and of Beth-anath became tributaries unto them.
34 And the Amorites forced the children

of Dan into the mountain: for they would not suffer them to come down to the valley:

35 But the Amorites would dwell in mount Heres in Aijalon, and in Shaalbim: yet the hand of the house of Joseph prevailed, so that they became tributaries.

36 And the coast of the Amorites *was* from the going up to Akrabbim, from the rock, and upward.

2

1 And an angel of the LORD came up from Gilgal to Bochim, and said, I made you to go up out of Egypt, and have brought you unto the land which I sware unto your fathers; and I said, I will never break my covenant with you.

2 And ye shall make no league with the inhabitants of this land; ye shall throw down their altars: but ye have not obeyed my voice: why have ye done this?

3 Wherefore I also said, I will not drive them out from before you; but they shall be *as thorns* in your sides, and their gods shall be a snare unto you.

4 And it came to pass, when the angel of the LORD spake these words unto all the children of Israel, that the people lifted up their voice, and wept.

5 And they called the name of that place Bochim: and they sacrificed there unto the LORD.

6 And when Joshua had let the people go, the children of Israel went every man unto his inheritance to possess the land.

7 And the people served the LORD all the days of Joshua, and all the days of the elders that outlived Joshua, who had seen all the great works of the LORD, that he did for Israel.

8 And Joshua the son of Nun, the servant of the LORD, died, *being* an hundred and ten years old.

9 And they buried him in the border of his inheritance in Timnath-heres, in the mount of Ephraim, on the north side of the hill Gaash.

10 And also all that generation were gathered unto their fathers: and there arose another generation after them, which knew not the LORD, nor yet the works which he had done for Israel.

11 And the children of Israel did evil in the sight of the LORD, and served Baalim:

12 And they forsook the LORD God of their fathers, which brought them out of the land of Egypt, and followed other gods, of the gods of the people that *were* round about them, and bowed themselves unto them, and provoked the LORD to anger.

13 And they forsook the LORD, and served Baal and Ashtaroth.

14 And the anger of the LORD was hot against Israel, and he delivered them into the hands of spoilers that spoiled them, and he sold them into the hands of their enemies round about, so that they could not any longer stand before their enemies.

2:14 Cost of Sin
◄ Judges 1:21
Judges 16:17 ►

15 Whithersoever they went out, the hand of the LORD was against them for evil, as the LORD had said, and as the LORD had sworn unto them: and they were greatly distressed.

16 Nevertheless the LORD raised up judges, which delivered them out of the hand of those that spoiled them.

17 And yet they would not hearken unto their judges, but they went a whoring after other gods, and bowed themselves unto them: they turned quickly out of the way which their fathers walked in, obeying the commandments of the LORD; *but* they did not so.

18 And when the LORD raised them up judges, then the LORD was with the judge, and delivered them out of the hand of their enemies all the days of the judge: for it repented the LORD because of their groanings by reason of them that oppressed them and vexed them.

19 And it came to pass, when the judge was dead, *that* they returned, and corrupted *themselves* more than their fathers, in following other gods to serve them, and to bow down unto them; they ceased not from their own doings, nor from their stubborn way.

20 And the anger of the LORD was hot against Israel; and he said, Because that this people hath transgressed my covenant which I commanded their fathers, and have not hearkened unto my voice;

21 I also will not henceforth drive out any from before them of the nations which Joshua left when he died:

22 That through them I may prove Israel, whether they will keep the way of the LORD

to walk therein, as their fathers did keep
it, or not.
23Therefore the LORD left those nations,
without driving them out hastily; neither delivered he them into the hand of
Joshua.

3

1Now these *are* the nations which the
LORD left, to prove Israel by them, *even* as
many *of Israel* as had not known all the
wars of Canaan;
2Only that the generations of the children of Israel might know, to teach them
war, at the least such as before knew nothing thereof;
3*Namely*, five lords of the Philistines, and
all the Canaanites, and the Sidonians, and
the Hivites that dwelt in mount Lebanon,
from mount Baal-hermon unto the entering in of Hamath.
4And they were to prove Israel by them,
to know whether they would hearken unto
the commandments of the LORD, which
he commanded their fathers by the hand
of Moses.
5And the children of Israel dwelt among
the Canaanites, Hittites, and Amorites, and
Perizzites, and Hivites, and Jebusites:
6And they took their daughters to be
their wives, and gave their daughters to
their sons, and served their gods.
7And the children of Israel did evil in
the sight of the LORD, and forgat the LORD
their God, and served Baalim and the
groves.
8Therefore the anger of the LORD was hot
against Israel, and he sold them into the
hand of Chushan-rishathaim king of Mesopotamia: and the children of Israel served
Chushan-rishathaim eight years.
9And when the children of Israel cried
unto the LORD, the LORD raised up a deliverer to the children of Israel, who delivered them, *even* Othniel the son of Kenaz,
Caleb's younger brother.
10And the Spirit of the LORD came upon
him, and he judged Israel, and went out
to war: and the LORD delivered Chushan-
rishathaim king of Mesopotamia into his
hand; and his hand prevailed against
Chushan-rishathaim.
11And the land had rest forty years. And
Othniel the son of Kenaz died.
12And the children of Israel did evil
again in the sight of the LORD: and the
LORD strengthened Eglon the king of Moab
against Israel, because they had done evil
in the sight of the LORD.
13And he gathered unto him the children of Ammon and Amalek, and went
and smote Israel, and possessed the city
of palm trees.
14So the children of Israel served Eglon
the king of Moab eighteen years.
15But when the children of Israel cried
unto the LORD, the LORD raised them up a
deliverer, Ehud the son of Gera, a Benjamite, a man lefthanded: and by him the
children of Israel sent a present unto Eglon the king of Moab.
16But Ehud made him a dagger which
had two edges, of a cubit length; and he
did gird it under his raiment upon his right
thigh.
17And he brought the present unto Eglon king of Moab: and Eglon *was* a very fat
man.
18And when he had made an end to offer the present, he sent away the people
that bare the present.
19But he himself turned again from the
quarries that *were* by Gilgal, and said, I
have a secret errand unto thee, O king: who
said, Keep silence. And all that stood by
him went out from him.
20And Ehud came unto him; and he was
sitting in a summer parlour, which he had
for himself alone. And Ehud said, I have a
message from God unto thee. And he arose
out of *his* seat.
21And Ehud put forth his left hand, and
took the dagger from his right thigh, and
thrust it into his belly:
22And the haft also went in after the
blade; and the fat closed upon the blade,
so that he could not draw the dagger out
of his belly; and the dirt came out.
23Then Ehud went forth through the
porch, and shut the doors of the parlour
upon him, and locked them.
24When he was gone out, his servants
came; and when they saw that, behold, the
doors of the parlour *were* locked, they said,
Surely he covereth his feet in his summer
chamber.
25And they tarried till they were ashamed:
and, behold, he opened not the doors of
the parlour; therefore they took a key, and
opened *them*: and, behold, their lord *was*
fallen down dead on the earth.
26And Ehud escaped while they tarried,

and passed beyond the quarries, and escaped unto Seirath.
27 And it came to pass, when he was
come, that he blew a trumpet in the mountain of Ephraim, and the children of Israel
went down with him from the mount, and
he before them.
28 And he said unto them, Follow after
me: for the LORD hath delivered your enemies the Moabites into your hand. And
they went down after him, and took the
fords of Jordan toward Moab, and suffered
not a man to pass over.
29 And they slew of Moab at that time
about ten thousand men, all lusty, and all
men of valour; and there escaped not a man.
30 So Moab was subdued that day under
the hand of Israel. And the land had rest
fourscore years.
31 And after him was Shamgar the son
of Anath, which slew of the Philistines six
hundred men with an ox goad: and he also
delivered Israel.

4

1 And the children of Israel again did evil
in the sight of the LORD, when Ehud was
dead.
2 And the LORD sold them into the hand
of Jabin king of Canaan, that reigned in
Hazor; the captain of whose host *was* Sisera, which dwelt in Harosheth of the Gentiles.
3 And the children of Israel cried unto
the LORD: for he had nine hundred chariots of iron; and twenty years he mightily
oppressed the children of Israel.
4 And Deborah, a prophetess, the wife
of Lapidoth, she judged Israel at that time.
5 And she dwelt under the palm tree of
Deborah between Ramah and Bethel in
mount Ephraim: and the children of Israel came up to her for judgment.
6 And she sent and called Barak the son
of Abinoam out of Kedesh-naphtali, and
said unto him, Hath not the LORD God of
Israel commanded, *saying,* Go and draw
toward mount Tabor, and take with thee
ten thousand men of the children of Naphtali and of the children of Zebulun?
7 And I will draw unto thee to the river
Kishon Sisera, the captain of Jabin's army,
with his chariots and his multitude; and I
will deliver him into thine hand.
8 And Barak said unto her, If thou wilt
go with me, then I will go: but if thou wilt
not go with me, *then* I will not go.
9 And she said, I will surely go with thee:
notwithstanding the journey that thou
takest shall not be for thine honour; for
the LORD shall sell Sisera into the hand of
a woman. And Deborah arose, and went
with Barak to Kedesh.
10 And Barak called Zebulun and Naphtali to Kedesh; and he went up with ten
thousand men at his feet: and Deborah
went up with him.
11 Now Heber the Kenite, *which was* of
the children of Hobab the father in law of
Moses, had severed himself from the Kenites, and pitched his tent unto the plain
of Zaanaim, which *is* by Kedesh.
12 And they shewed Sisera that Barak the
son of Abinoam was gone up to mount
Tabor.
13 And Sisera gathered together all his
chariots, *even* nine hundred chariots of
iron, and all the people that *were* with him,
from Harosheth of the Gentiles unto the
river of Kishon.
14 And Deborah said unto Barak, Up; for
this *is* the day in which the LORD hath delivered Sisera into thine hand: is not the
LORD gone out before thee? So Barak went
down from mount Tabor, and ten thousand men after him.
15 And the LORD discomfited Sisera, and
all *his* chariots, and all *his* host, with the
edge of the sword before Barak; so that
Sisera lighted down off *his* chariot, and fled
away on his feet.
16 But Barak pursued after the chariots,
and after the host, unto Harosheth of the
Gentiles: and all the host of Sisera fell
upon the edge of the sword; *and* there was
not a man left.
17 Howbeit Sisera fled away on his feet
to the tent of Jael the wife of Heber the
Kenite: for *there was* peace between Jabin
the king of Hazor and the house of Heber
the Kenite.
18 And Jael went out to meet Sisera, and
said unto him, Turn in, my lord, turn in
to me; fear not. And when he had turned
in unto her into the tent, she covered him
with a mantle.
19 And he said unto her, Give me, I pray
thee, a little water to drink; for I am thirsty.
And she opened a bottle of milk, and gave
him drink, and covered him.
20 Again he said unto her, Stand in the
door of the tent, and it shall be, when any

man doth come and enquire of thee, and
say, Is there any man here? that thou shalt
say, No.
21Then Jael Heber's wife took a nail of
the tent, and took an hammer in her hand,
and went softly unto him, and smote the
nail into his temples, and fastened it into
the ground: for he was fast asleep and weary. So he died.
22And, behold, as Barak pursued Sisera,
Jael came out to meet him, and said unto
him, Come, and I will shew thee the man
whom thou seekest. And when he came
into her *tent*, behold, Sisera lay dead, and
the nail *was* in his temples.
23So God subdued on that day Jabin the
king of Canaan before the children of Israel.
24And the hand of the children of Israel
prospered, and prevailed against Jabin the
king of Canaan, until they had destroyed
Jabin king of Canaan.

5

1Then sang Deborah and Barak the son
of Abinoam on that day, saying,
2Praise ye the
LORD for the aveng-
ing of Israel, when
the people willingly
offered themselves.

5:2
Willingness to Work
◄ Judges 8:25 ►

3Hear, O ye kings;
give ear, O ye princes; I, *even* I, will sing
unto the LORD; I will sing *praise* to the LORD
God of Israel.
4LORD, when thou wentest out of Seir,
when thou marchedst out of the field of
Edom, the earth trembled, and the heavens dropped, the clouds also dropped
water.
5The mountains melted from before the
LORD, *even* that Sinai from before the LORD
God of Israel.
6In the days of Shamgar the son of
Anath, in the days of Jael, the highways
were unoccupied, and the travelers walked
through byways.
7*The inhabitants of* the villages ceased,
they ceased in Israel, until that I Deborah
arose, that I arose a mother in Israel.
8They chose new gods; then *was* war in
the gates: was there a shield or spear seen
among forty thousand in Israel?
9My heart *is* toward the governors of Israel, that offered themselves willingly
among the people. Bless ye the LORD.
10Speak, ye that ride on white asses,
ye that sit in judgment, and walk by
the way.
11*They that are delivered* from the noise
of archers in the places of drawing water,
there shall they rehearse the righteous acts
of the LORD, *even* the righteous acts *toward
the inhabitants* of his villages in Israel: then
shall the people of the LORD go down to
the gates.
12Awake, awake, Deborah: awake, awake,
utter a song: arise, Barak, and lead thy captivity captive, thou son of Abinoam.
13Then he made him that remaineth
have dominion over the nobles among the
people: the LORD made me have dominion over the mighty.
14Out of Ephraim *was there* a root of
them against Amalek; after thee, Benjamin,
among thy people; out of Machir came
down governors, and out of Zebulun they
that handle the pen of the writer.
15And the princes of Issachar *were* with
Deborah; even Issachar, and also Barak: he
was sent on foot into the valley. For the
divisions of Reuben *there were* great
thoughts of heart.
16Why abodest thou among the sheepfolds, to hear the bleatings of the flocks?
For the divisions of Reuben *there were* great
searchings of heart.
17Gilead abode beyond Jordan: and why
did Dan remain in ships? Asher continued on the sea shore, and abode in his
breaches.
18Zebulun and Naphtali *were* a people
that jeoparded their lives unto the death
in the high places of the field.
19The kings came *and* fought, then
fought the kings of Canaan in Taanach by
the waters of Megiddo; they took no gain
of money.
20They fought from heaven; the stars in
their courses fought against Sisera.
21The river of Kishon swept them away,
that ancient river, the river Kishon. O my
soul, thou hast trodden down strength.
22Then were the horsehoofs broken by
the means of the pransings, the pransings
of their mighty ones.
23Curse ye Meroz, said the angel of the
LORD, curse ye bitterly the inhabitants
thereof; because they came not to the help
of the LORD, to the help of the LORD against
the mighty.
24Blessed above women shall Jael the

wife of Heber the Kenite be, blessed shall she be above women in the tent.

25 He asked water, *and* she gave *him* milk; she brought forth butter in a lordly dish.

26 She put her hand to the nail, and her right hand to the workmen's hammer; and with the hammer she smote Sisera, she smote off his head, when she had pierced and stricken through his temples.

27 At her feet he bowed, he fell, he lay down: at her feet he bowed, he fell: where he bowed, there he fell down dead.

28 The mother of Sisera looked out at a window, and cried through the lattice, Why is his chariot *so* long in coming? why tarry the wheels of his chariots?

29 Her wise ladies answered her, yea, she returned answer to herself,

30 Have they not sped? have they *not* divided the prey; to every man a damsel *or* two; to Sisera a prey of divers colours, a prey of divers colours of needlework, of divers colours of needlework on both sides, *meet* for the necks of *them that take* the spoil?

31 So let all thine enemies perish, O LORD: but *let* them that love him *be* as the sun when he goeth forth in his might. And the land had rest forty years.

6

1 And the children of Israel did evil in the sight of the LORD: and the LORD delivered them into the hand of Midian seven years.

2 And the hand of Midian prevailed against Israel: *and* because of the Midianites the children of Israel made them the dens which *are* in the mountains, and caves, and strong holds.

3 And *so* it was, when Israel had sown, that the Midianites came up, and the Amalekites, and the children of the east, even they came up against them;

4 And they encamped against them, and destroyed the increase of the earth, till thou come unto Gaza, and left no sustenance for Israel, neither sheep, nor ox, nor ass.

5 For they came up with their cattle and their tents, and they came as grasshoppers for multitude; *for* both they and their camels were without number: and they entered into the land to destroy it.

6 And Israel was greatly impoverished because of the Midianites; and the children of Israel cried unto the LORD.

7 And it came to pass, when the children of Israel cried unto the LORD because of the Midianites,

8 That the LORD sent a prophet unto the children of Israel, which said unto them, Thus saith the LORD God of Israel, I brought you up from Egypt, and brought you forth out of the house of bondage;

9 And I delivered you out of the hand of the Egyptians, and out of the hand of all that oppressed you, and drave them out from before you, and gave you their land;

10 And I said unto you, I *am* the LORD your God; fear not the gods of the Amorites, in whose land ye dwell: but ye have not obeyed my voice.

11 And there came an angel of the LORD, and sat under an oak which *was* in Ophrah, that *pertained* unto Joash the Abiezrite: and his son Gideon threshed wheat by the winepress, to hide *it* from the Midianites.

12 And the angel of the LORD appeared unto him, and said unto him, The LORD *is* with thee, thou mighty man of valour.

13 And Gideon said unto him, Oh my Lord, if the LORD be with us, why then is all this befallen us? and where *be* all his miracles which our fathers told us of, saying, Did not the LORD bring us up from Egypt? but now the LORD hath forsaken us, and delivered us into the hands of the Midianites.

14 And the LORD looked upon him, and said, Go in this thy might, and thou shalt save Israel from the hand of the Midianites: have not I sent thee?

15 And he said unto him, Oh my Lord, wherewith shall I save Israel? behold, my family is poor in Manasseh, and I *am* the least in my father's house.

16 And the LORD said unto him, Surely I will be with thee, and thou shalt smite the Midianites as one man.

17 And he said unto him, If now I have found grace in thy sight, then shew me a sign that thou talkest with me.

18 Depart not hence, I pray thee, until I come unto thee, and bring forth my present, and set *it* before thee. And he said, I will tarry until thou come again.

19 And Gideon went in, and made ready a kid, and unleavened cakes of an ephah of flour: the flesh he put in a basket, and he put the broth in a pot, and brought *it*

out unto him under the oak, and presented *it.*
20 And the angel of God said unto him,
Take the flesh and the unleavened cakes,
and lay *them* upon this rock, and pour out
the broth. And he did so.
21 Then the angel of the LORD put forth
the end of the staff that *was* in his hand,
and touched the flesh and the unleavened
cakes; and there rose up fire out of the rock,
and consumed the flesh and the unleavened cakes. Then the angel of the LORD
departed out of his sight.
22 And when Gideon perceived that he
was an angel of the LORD, Gideon said,
Alas, O Lord GOD! for because I have seen
an angel of the LORD face to face.
23 And the LORD said unto him, Peace *be*
unto thee; fear not: thou shalt not die.
24 Then Gideon built an altar there unto
the LORD, and called it Jehovah-shalom:
unto this day it *is* yet in Ophrah of the Abi-
ezrites.
25 And it came to pass the same night,
that the LORD said unto him, Take thy
father's young bullock, even the second
bullock of seven years old, and throw
down the altar of Baal that thy father hath,
and cut down the grove that *is* by it:
26 And build an altar unto the LORD thy
God upon the top of this rock, in the ordered place, and take the second bullock,
and offer a burnt sacrifice with the wood
of the grove which thou shalt cut down.
27 Then Gideon took ten men of his servants, and did as the LORD had said unto
him: and *so* it was, because he feared his
father's household, and the men of the city,
that he could not do *it* by day, that he did
it by night.
28 And when the men of the city arose
early in the morning, behold, the altar of
Baal was cast down, and the grove was cut
down that *was* by it, and the second bullock was offered upon the altar *that was*
built.
29 And they said one to another, Who
hath done this thing? And when they enquired and asked, they said, Gideon the
son of Joash hath done this thing.
30 Then the men of the city said unto Joash, Bring out thy son, that he may die:
because he hath cast down the altar of
Baal, and because he hath cut down the
grove that *was* by it.
31 And Joash said unto all that stood
against him, Will ye plead for Baal? will
ye save him? he that will plead for him,
let him be put to death whilst *it is yet* morning: if he *be* a god, let him plead for himself, because *one* hath cast down his altar.
32 Therefore on that day he called him
Jerubbaal, saying, Let Baal plead against
him, because he hath thrown down his
altar.
33 Then all the Midianites and the Amalekites and the children of the east were
gathered together, and went over, and
pitched in the valley of Jezreel.
34 But the Spirit of the LORD came upon
Gideon, and he blew a trumpet; and Abiezer was gathered after him.
35 And he sent messengers throughout
all Manasseh; who also was gathered after
him: and he sent messengers unto Asher,
and unto Zebulun, and unto Naphtali; and
they came up to meet them.
36 And Gideon said unto God, If thou
wilt save Israel by mine hand, as thou hast
said,
37 Behold, I will put a fleece of wool in
the floor; *and* if the dew be on the fleece
only, and *it be* dry upon all the earth *beside,* then shall I know that thou wilt save
Israel by mine hand, as thou hast said.
38 And it was so: for he rose up early on
the morrow, and thrust the fleece together, and wringed the dew out of the fleece,
a bowl full of water.
39 And Gideon said unto God, Let not
thine anger be hot against me, and I will
speak but this once: let me prove, I pray
thee, but this once with the fleece; let it
now be dry only upon the fleece, and upon
all the ground let there be dew.
40 And God did so that night: for it was
dry upon the fleece only, and there was
dew on all the ground.

7

1 Then Jerubbaal, who *is* Gideon, and all
the people that *were* with him, rose up early, and pitched beside the well of Harod:
so that the host of the Midianites were on
the north side of them, by the hill of Moreh, in the valley.
2 And the LORD said unto Gideon, The
people that *are* with thee *are* too many for
me to give the Midianites into their hands,
lest Israel vaunt themselves against me,
saying, Mine own hand hath saved me.
3 Now therefore go to, proclaim in the

ears of the people, saying, Whosoever *is* fearful and afraid, let him return and depart early from mount Gilead. And there returned of the people twenty and two thousand; and there remained ten thousand.

4 And the LORD said unto Gideon, The people *are* yet *too* many; bring them down unto the water, and I will try them for thee there: and it shall be, *that* of whom I say unto thee, This shall go with thee, the same shall go with thee; and of whomsoever I say unto thee, This shall not go with thee, the same shall not go.

5 So he brought down the people unto the water: and the LORD said unto Gideon, Every one that lappeth of the water with his tongue, as a dog lappeth, him shalt thou set by himself; likewise every one that boweth down upon his knees to drink.

6 And the number of them that lapped, *putting* their hand to their mouth, were three hundred men: but all the rest of the people bowed down upon their knees to drink water.

7 And the LORD said unto Gideon, By the three hundred men that lapped will I save you, and deliver the Midianites into thine hand: and let all the *other* people go every man unto his place.

8 So the people took victuals in their hand, and their trumpets: and he sent all *the rest of* Israel every man unto his tent, and retained those three hundred men: and the host of Midian was beneath him in the valley.

9 And it came to pass the same night, that the LORD said unto him, Arise, get thee down unto the host; for I have delivered it into thine hand.

10 But if thou fear to go down, go thou with Phurah thy servant down to the host:

11 And thou shalt hear what they say; and afterward shall thine hands be strengthened to go down unto the host. Then went he down with Phurah his servant unto the outside of the armed men that *were* in the host.

12 And the Midianites and the Amalekites and all the children of the east lay along in the valley like grasshoppers for multitude; and their camels *were* without number, as the sand by the sea side for multitude.

13 And when Gideon was come, behold, *there was* a man that told a dream unto his fellow, and said, Behold, I dreamed a dream, and, lo, a cake of barley bread tumbled into the host of Midian, and came unto a tent, and smote it that it fell, and overturned it, that the tent lay along.

14 And his fellow answered and said, This *is* nothing else save the sword of Gideon the son of Joash, a man of Israel: *for* into his hand hath God delivered Midian, and all the host.

15 And it was *so,* when Gideon heard the telling of the dream, and the interpretation thereof, that he worshipped, and returned into the host of Israel, and said, Arise; for the LORD hath delivered into your hand the host of Midian.

16 And he divided the three hundred men *into* three companies, and he put a trumpet in every man's hand, with empty pitchers, and lamps within the pitchers.

17 And he said unto them, Look on me, and do likewise: and, behold, when I come to the outside of the camp, it shall be *that,* as I do, so shall ye do.

18 When I blow with a trumpet, I and all that *are* with me, then blow ye the trumpets also on every side of all the camp, and say, *The sword* of the LORD, and of Gideon.

19 So Gideon, and the hundred men that *were* with him, came unto the outside of the camp in the beginning of the middle watch; and they had but newly set the watch: and they blew the trumpets, and brake the pitchers that *were* in their hands.

20 And the three companies blew the trumpets, and brake the pitchers, and held the lamps in their left hands, and the trumpets in their right hands to blow *withal:* and they cried, The sword of the LORD, and of Gideon.

21 And they stood every man in his place round about the camp: and all the host ran, and cried, and fled.

22 And the three hundred blew the trumpets, and the LORD set every man's sword against his fellow, even throughout all the host: and the host fled to Beth-shittah in Zererath, *and* to the border of Abelmeholah, unto Tabbath.

23 And the men of Israel gathered themselves together out of Naphtali, and out of Asher, and out of all Manasseh, and pursued after the Midianites.

24 And Gideon sent messengers throughout all mount Ephraim, saying, Come
down against the Midianites, and take before them the waters unto Beth-barah and
Jordan. Then all the men of Ephraim gathered themselves together, and took the
waters unto Beth-barah and Jordan.
25 And they took two princes of the Midianites, Oreb and Zeeb; and they slew Oreb
upon the rock Oreb, and Zeeb they slew
at the winepress of Zeeb, and pursued Midian, and brought the heads of Oreb and
Zeeb to Gideon on the other side Jordan.

8

1 And the men of Ephraim said unto
him, Why hast thou served us thus, that
thou calledst us not, when thou wentest
to fight with the Midianites? And they did
chide with him sharply.
2 And he said unto them, What have I
done now in comparison of you? *Is* not
the gleaning of the grapes of Ephraim better than the vintage of Abi-ezer?
3 God hath delivered into your hands the
princes of Midian, Oreb and Zeeb: and
what was I able to do in comparison of
you? Then their anger was abated toward
him, when he had said that.
4 And Gideon came to Jordan, *and*
passed over, he, and the three hundred
men that *were* with him, faint, yet pursuing *them*.
5 And he said unto the men of Succoth,
Give, I pray you, loaves of bread unto the
people that follow me; for they *be* faint,
and I am pursuing after Zebah and Zalmunna, kings of Midian.
6 And the princes of Succoth said, *Are* the
hands of Zebah and Zalmunna now in
thine hand, that we should give bread unto
thine army?
7 And Gideon said, Therefore when the
LORD hath delivered Zebah and Zalmunna into mine hand, then I will tear your
flesh with the thorns of the wilderness and
with briers.
8 And he went up thence to Penuel, and
spake unto them likewise: and the men of
Penuel answered him as the men of Succoth had answered *him*.
9 And he spake also unto the men of Penuel, saying, When I come again in peace,
I will break down this tower.
10 Now Zebah and Zalmunna *were* in
Karkor, and their hosts with them, about
fifteen thousand *men*, all that were left of
all the hosts of the children of the east: for
there fell an hundred and twenty thousand
men that drew sword.
11 And Gideon went up by the way of
them that dwelt in tents on the east of
Nobah and Jogbehah, and smote the host:
for the host was secure.
12 And when Zebah and Zalmunna fled,
he pursued after them, and took the two
kings of Midian, Zebah and Zalmunna,
and discomfited all the host.
13 And Gideon the son of Joash returned
from battle before the sun *was up*,
14 And caught a young man of the men
of Succoth, and enquired of him: and he
described unto him the princes of Succoth,
and the elders thereof, *even* threescore and
seventeen men.
15 And he came unto the men of Succoth,
and said, Behold Zebah and Zalmunna,
with whom ye did upbraid me, saying, *Are*
the hands of Zebah and Zalmunna now
in thine hand, that we should give bread
unto thy men *that are* weary?
16 And he took the elders of the city, and
thorns of the wilderness and briers, and
with them he taught the men of Succoth.
17 And he beat down the tower of Penuel, and slew the men of the city.
18 Then said he unto Zebah and Zalmunna, What manner of men *were they* whom
ye slew at Tabor? And they answered, As
thou *art*, so *were* they; each one resembled
the children of a king.
19 And he said, They *were* my brethren,
even the sons of my mother: *as* the LORD
liveth, if ye had saved them alive, I would
not slay you.
20 And he said unto Jether his firstborn,
Up, *and* slay them. But the youth drew not
his sword: for he feared, because he *was*
yet a youth.
21 Then Zebah and Zalmunna said, Rise
thou, and fall upon us: for as the man *is*,
so is his strength. And Gideon arose, and
slew Zebah and Zalmunna, and took away
the ornaments that *were* on their camels'
necks.
22 Then the men of Israel said unto Gideon, Rule thou over us, both thou, and thy
son, and thy son's son also: for thou hast
delivered us from the hand of Midian.
23 And Gideon said unto them, I will not
rule over you, neither shall my son rule
over you: the LORD shall rule over you.

24 And Gideon said unto them, I would desire a request of you, that ye would give me every man the earrings of his prey. (For they had golden earrings, because they *were* Ishmaelites.)

25 And they answered, We will willingly give *them*. And they spread a garment, and did cast therein every man the earrings of his prey.

8:25
Willingness to Work
◄ Judges 5:2
Nehemiah 11:2 ►

26 And the weight of the golden earrings that he requested was a thousand and seven hundred *shekels* of gold; beside ornaments, and collars, and purple raiment that *was* on the kings of Midian, and beside the chains that *were* about their camels' necks.

27 And Gideon made an ephod thereof, and put it in his city, *even* in Ophrah: and all Israel went thither a whoring after it: which thing became a snare unto Gideon, and to his house.

28 Thus was Midian subdued before the children of Israel, so that they lifted up their heads no more. And the country was in quietness forty years in the days of Gideon.

29 And Jerubbaal the son of Joash went and dwelt in his own house.

30 And Gideon had threescore and ten sons of his body begotten: for he had many wives.

31 And his concubine that *was* in Shechem, she also bare him a son, whose name he called Abimelech.

32 And Gideon the son of Joash died in a good old age, and was buried in the sepulchre of Joash his father, in Ophrah of the Abi-ezrites.

33 And it came to pass, as soon as Gideon was dead, that the children of Israel turned again, and went a whoring after Baalim, and made Baal-berith their god.

34 And the children of Israel remembered not the LORD their God, who had delivered them out of the hands of all their enemies on every side:

8:34 Don't Forget...
◄ Deuteronomy 8:11
Psalm 9:17 ►

35 Neither shewed they kindness to the house of Jerubbaal, *namely*, Gideon, according to all the goodness which he had shewed unto Israel.

8:35
Unthankfulness to People
◄ Numbers 16:13
Judges 9:18 ►

9

1 And Abimelech the son of Jerubbaal went to Shechem unto his mother's brethren, and communed with them, and with all the family of the house of his mother's father, saying,

2 Speak, I pray you, in the ears of all the men of Shechem, Whether *is* better for you, either that all the sons of Jerubbaal, *which are* threescore and ten persons, reign over you, or that one reign over you? remember also that I *am* your bone and your flesh.

3 And his mother's brethren spake of him in the ears of all the men of Shechem all these words: and their hearts inclined to follow Abimelech; for they said, He *is* our brother.

4 And they gave him threescore and ten *pieces* of silver out of the house of Baal-berith, wherewith Abimelech hired vain and light persons, which followed him.

5 And he went unto his father's house at Ophrah, and slew his brethren the sons of Jerubbaal, *being* threescore and ten persons, upon one stone: notwithstanding yet Jotham the youngest son of Jerubbaal was left; for he hid himself.

6 And all the men of Shechem gathered together, and all the house of Millo, and went, and made Abimelech king, by the plain of the pillar that *was* in Shechem.

7 And when they told *it* to Jotham, he went and stood in the top of mount Gerizim, and lifted up his voice, and cried, and said unto them, Hearken unto me, ye men of Shechem, that God may hearken unto you.

8 The trees went forth *on a time* to anoint a king over them; and they said unto the olive tree, Reign thou over us.

9 But the olive tree said unto them, Should I leave my fatness, wherewith by me they honour God and man, and go to be promoted over the trees?

10 And the trees said to the fig tree, Come thou, *and* reign over us.

11 But the fig tree said unto them, Should I forsake my sweetness, and my good fruit, and go to be promoted over the trees?

12 Then said the trees unto the vine, Come thou, *and* reign over us.

13 And the vine said unto them, Should I leave my wine, which cheereth God and man, and go to be promoted over the trees?

14 Then said all the trees unto the bramble, Come thou, *and* reign over us.

15 And the bramble said unto the trees, If in truth ye anoint me king over you, *then* come *and* put your trust in my shadow: and if not, let fire come out of the bramble, and devour the cedars of Lebanon.

16 Now therefore, if ye have done truly and sincerely, in that ye have made Abimelech king, and if ye have dealt well with Jerubbaal and his house, and have done unto him according to the deserving of his hands;

17 (For my father fought for you, and adventured his life far, and delivered you out of the hand of Midian:

18 And ye are risen up against my father's house this day, and have slain his sons, threescore and ten persons, upon one stone, and have made Abimelech, the son of his maidservant, king over the men of Shechem, because he *is* your brother;)

9:18
Unthankfulness to People
◄ Judges 8:35
1 Samuel 25:21 ►

19 If ye then have dealt truly and sincerely with Jerubbaal and with his house this day, *then* rejoice ye in Abimelech, and let him also rejoice in you:

20 But if not, let fire come out from Abimelech, and devour the men of Shechem, and the house of Millo; and let fire come out from the men of Shechem, and from the house of Millo, and devour Abimelech.

21 And Jotham ran away, and fled, and went to Beer, and dwelt there, for fear of Abimelech his brother.

22 When Abimelech had reigned three years over Israel,

23 Then God sent an evil spirit between Abimelech and the men of Shechem; and the men of Shechem dealt treacherously with Abimelech:

24 That the cruelty *done* to the threescore and ten sons of Jerubbaal might come, and their blood be laid upon Abimelech their brother, which slew them; and upon the men of Shechem, which aided him in the killing of his brethren.

25 And the men of Shechem set liers in wait for him in the top of the mountains, and they robbed all that came along that way by them: and it was told Abimelech.

26 And Gaal the son of Ebed came with his brethren, and went over to Shechem: and the men of Shechem put their confidence in him.

27 And they went out into the fields, and gathered their vineyards, and trode *the grapes*, and made merry, and went into the house of their god, and did eat and drink, and cursed Abimelech.

9:27 Parties
◄ Exodus 32:6
Judges 16:25 ►

28 And Gaal the son of Ebed said, Who *is* Abimelech, and who *is* Shechem, that we should serve him? *is* not *he* the son of Jerubbaal? and Zebul his officer? serve the men of Hamor the father of Shechem: for why should we serve him?

29 And would to God this people were under my hand! then would I remove Abimelech. And he said to Abimelech, Increase thine army, and come out.

30 And when Zebul the ruler of the city heard the words of Gaal the son of Ebed, his anger was kindled.

31 And he sent messengers unto Abimelech privily, saying, Behold, Gaal the son of Ebed and his brethren be come to Shechem; and, behold, they fortify the city against thee.

32 Now therefore up by night, thou and the people that *is* with thee, and lie in wait in the field:

33 And it shall be, *that* in the morning, as soon as the sun is up, thou shalt rise early, and set upon the city: and, behold, *when* he and the people that *is* with him come out against thee, then mayest thou do to them as thou shalt find occasion.

34 And Abimelech rose up, and all the people that *were* with him, by night, and they laid wait against Shechem in four companies.

35 And Gaal the son of Ebed went out, and stood in the entering of the gate of the city: and Abimelech rose up, and the people that *were* with him, from lying in wait.

36 And when Gaal saw the people, he said to Zebul, Behold, there come people down from the top of the mountains. And

Zebul said unto him, Thou seest the shadow of the mountains as *if they were* men.

37 And Gaal spake again and said, See there come people down by the middle of the land, and another company come along by the plain of Meonenim.

38 Then said Zebul unto him, Where *is* now thy mouth, wherewith thou saidst, Who *is* Abimelech, that we should serve him? *is* not this the people that thou hast despised? go out, I pray now, and fight with them.

39 And Gaal went out before the men of Shechem, and fought with Abimelech.

40 And Abimelech chased him, and he fled before him, and many were overthrown *and* wounded, *even* unto the entering of the gate.

41 And Abimelech dwelt at Arumah: and Zebul thrust out Gaal and his brethren, that they should not dwell in Shechem.

42 And it came to pass on the morrow, that the people went out into the field; and they told Abimelech.

43 And he took the people, and divided them into three companies, and laid wait in the field, and looked, and, behold, the people *were* come forth out of the city; and he rose up against them, and smote them.

44 And Abimelech, and the company that *was* with him, rushed forward, and stood in the entering of the gate of the city: and the two *other* companies ran upon all *the people* that *were* in the fields, and slew them.

45 And Abimelech fought against the city all that day; and he took the city, and slew the people that *was* therein, and beat down the city, and sowed it with salt.

46 And when all the men of the tower of Shechem heard *that*, they entered into an hold of the house of the god Berith.

47 And it was told Abimelech, that all the men of the tower of Shechem were gathered together.

48 And Abimelech gat him up to mount Zalmon, he and all the people that *were* with him; and Abimelech took an axe in his hand, and cut down a bough from the trees, and took it, and laid *it* on his shoulder, and said unto the people that *were* with him, What ye have seen me do, make haste, *and* do as I *have done*.

49 And all the people likewise cut down every man his bough, and followed Abimelech, and put *them* to the hold, and set the hold on fire upon them; so that all the men of the tower of Shechem died also, about a thousand men and women.

50 Then went Abimelech to Thebez, and encamped against Thebez, and took it.

51 But there was a strong tower within the city, and thither fled all the men and women, and all they of the city, and shut *it* to them, and gat them up to the top of the tower.

52 And Abimelech came unto the tower, and fought against it, and went hard unto the door of the tower to burn it with fire.

53 And a certain woman cast a piece of a millstone upon Abimelech's head, and all to brake his skull.

54 Then he called hastily unto the young man his armourbearer, and said unto him, Draw thy sword, and slay me, that men say not of me, A woman slew him. And his young man thrust him through, and he died.

55 And when the men of Israel saw that Abimelech was dead, they departed every man unto his place.

56 Thus God rendered the wickedness of Abimelech, which he did unto his father, in slaying his seventy brethren:

57 And all the evil of the men of Shechem did God render upon their heads: and upon them came the curse of Jotham the son of Jerubbaal.

10

1 And after Abimelech there arose to defend Israel Tola the son of Puah, the son of Dodo, a man of Issachar; and he dwelt in Shamir in mount Ephraim.

2 And he judged Israel twenty and three years, and died, and was buried in Shamir.

3 And after him arose Jair, a Gileadite, and judged Israel twenty and two years.

4 And he had thirty sons that rode on thirty ass colts, and they had thirty cities, which are called Havoth-jair unto this day, which *are* in the land of Gilead.

5 And Jair died, and was buried in Camon.

6 And the children of Israel did evil again in the sight of the LORD, and served Baalim, and Ashtaroth, and the gods of Syria, and the gods of Zidon, and the gods of Moab, and the gods of the children of Ammon, and the gods of the Philistines, and forsook the LORD, and served not him.

7 And the anger of the LORD was hot

against Israel, and he sold them into the
hands of the Philistines, and into the
hands of the children of Ammon.
8And that year they vexed and oppressed
the children of Israel: eighteen years, all
the children of Israel that *were* on the other
side Jordan in the land of the Amorites,
which *is* in Gilead.
9Moreover the children of Ammon
passed over Jordan to fight also against
Judah, and against Benjamin, and against
the house of Ephraim; so that Israel was
sore distressed.
10And the children of Israel cried unto
the LORD, saying, We have sinned against
thee, both because we have forsaken our
God, and also served Baalim.
11And the LORD said unto the children
of Israel, *Did* not *I deliver you* from the
Egyptians, and from the Amorites, from
the children of Ammon, and from the
Philistines?
12The Zidonians also, and the Amalekites, and the Maonites, did oppress you;
and ye cried to me, and I delivered you
out of their hand.
13Yet ye have forsaken me, and served
other gods: wherefore I will deliver you no
more.
14Go and cry unto the gods which ye
have chosen; let them deliver you in the
time of your tribulation.
15And the children of Israel said unto
the LORD, We have sinned: do thou unto
us whatsoever seemeth good unto thee;
deliver us only, we pray thee, this day.
16And they put away the strange gods
from among them, and served the LORD:
and his soul was grieved for the misery of
Israel.
17Then the children of Ammon were
gathered together, and encamped in Gilead. And the children of Israel assembled
themselves together, and encamped in
Mizpeh.
18And the people *and* princes of Gilead
said one to another, What man *is he* that
will begin to fight against the children of
Ammon? he shall be head over all the inhabitants of Gilead.

11

1Now Jephthah the Gileadite was a
mighty man of valour, and he *was* the son
of an harlot: and Gilead begat Jephthah.
2And Gilead's wife bare him sons; and
his wife's sons grew up, and they thrust
out Jephthah, and said unto him, Thou
shalt not inherit in our father's house; for
thou *art* the son of a strange woman.
3Then Jephthah fled from his brethren,
and dwelt in the land of Tob: and there
were gathered vain men to Jephthah, and
went out with him.
4And it came to pass in process of time,
that the children of Ammon made war
against Israel.
5And it was so, that when the children
of Ammon made war against Israel, the
elders of Gilead went to fetch Jephthah out
of the land of Tob:
6And they said unto Jephthah, Come,
and be our captain, that we may fight with
the children of Ammon.
7And Jephthah said unto the elders of
Gilead, Did not ye hate me, and expel me
out of my father's house? and why are ye
come unto me now when ye are in distress?
8And the elders of Gilead said unto
Jephthah, Therefore we turn again to thee
now, that thou mayest go with us, and fight
against the children of Ammon, and be our
head over all the inhabitants of Gilead.
9And Jephthah said unto the elders of
Gilead, If ye bring me home again to fight
against the children of Ammon, and the
LORD deliver them before me, shall I be
your head?
10And the elders of Gilead said unto
Jephthah, The LORD be witness between
us, if we do not so according to thy words.
11Then Jephthah went with the elders of
Gilead, and the people made him head
and captain over them: and Jephthah uttered all his words before the LORD in
Mizpeh.
12And Jephthah sent messengers unto
the king of the children of Ammon, saying, What hast thou to do with me, that
thou art come against me to fight in my
land?
13And the king of the children of Ammon answered unto the messengers of
Jephthah, Because Israel took away my
land, when they came up out of Egypt,
from Arnon even unto Jabbok, and unto
Jordan: now therefore restore those *lands*
again peaceably.
14And Jephthah sent messengers again
unto the king of the children of Ammon:
15And said unto him, Thus saith

Jephthah, Israel took not away the land of Moab, nor the land of the children of Ammon:

16 But when Israel came up from Egypt, and walked through the wilderness unto the Red sea, and came to Kadesh;

17 Then Israel sent messengers unto the king of Edom, saying, Let me, I pray thee, pass through thy land: but the king of Edom would not hearken *thereto*. And in like manner they sent unto the king of Moab: but he would not *consent:* and Israel abode in Kadesh.

18 Then they went along through the wilderness, and compassed the land of Edom, and the land of Moab, and came by the east side of the land of Moab, and pitched on the other side of Arnon, but came not within the border of Moab: for Arnon *was* the border of Moab.

19 And Israel sent messengers unto Sihon king of the Amorites, the king of Heshbon; and Israel said unto him, Let us pass, we pray thee, through thy land into my place.

20 But Sihon trusted not Israel to pass through his coast: but Sihon gathered all his people together, and pitched in Jahaz, and fought against Israel.

21 And the LORD God of Israel delivered Sihon and all his people into the hand of Israel, and they smote them: so Israel possessed all the land of the Amorites, the inhabitants of that country.

22 And they possessed all the coasts of the Amorites, from Arnon even unto Jabbok, and from the wilderness even unto Jordan.

23 So now the LORD God of Israel hath dispossessed the Amorites from before his people Israel, and shouldest thou possess it?

24 Wilt not thou possess that which Chemosh thy god giveth thee to possess? So whomsoever the LORD our God shall drive out from before us, them will we possess.

25 And now *art* thou any thing better than Balak the son of Zippor, king of Moab? did he ever strive against Israel, or did he ever fight against them,

26 While Israel dwelt in Heshbon and her towns, and in Aroer and her towns, and in all the cities that *be* along by the coasts of Arnon, three hundred years? why therefore did ye not recover *them* within that time?

27 Wherefore I have not sinned against thee, but thou doest me wrong to war against me: the LORD the Judge be judge this day between the children of Israel and the children of Ammon.

28 Howbeit the king of the children of Ammon hearkened not unto the words of Jephthah which he sent him.

29 Then the Spirit of the LORD came upon Jephthah, and he passed over Gilead, and Manasseh, and passed over Mizpeh of Gilead, and from Mizpeh of Gilead he passed over *unto* the children of Ammon.

30 And Jephthah vowed a vow unto the LORD, and said, If thou shalt without fail deliver the children of Ammon into mine hands,

31 Then it shall be, that whatsoever cometh forth of the doors of my house to meet me, when I return in peace from the children of Ammon, shall surely be the LORD'S, and I will offer it up for a burnt offering.

32 So Jephthah passed over unto the children of Ammon to fight against them; and the LORD delivered them into his hands.

33 And he smote them from Aroer, even till thou come to Minnith, *even* twenty cities, and unto the plain of the vineyards, with a very great slaughter. Thus the children of Ammon were subdued before the children of Israel.

34 And Jephthah came to Mizpeh unto his house, and, behold, his daughter came out to meet him with timbrels and with dances: and she *was his* only child; beside her he had neither son nor daughter.

35 And it came to pass, when he saw her, that he rent his clothes, and said, Alas, my daughter! thou hast brought me very low, and thou art one of them that trouble me: for I have opened my mouth unto the LORD, and I cannot go back.

36 And she said unto him, My father, *if* thou hast opened thy mouth unto the LORD, do to me according to that which hath proceeded out of thy mouth; forasmuch as the LORD hath taken vengeance for thee of thine enemies, *even* of the children of Ammon.

11:36
Young Women
◄ Ruth 1:16 ►

37 And she said unto her father, Let this thing be done for me: let me alone two months, that I may go up and down upon

the mountains, and bewail my virginity, I
and my fellows.
38 And he said, Go. And he sent her away
for two months: and she went with her
companions, and bewailed her virginity
upon the mountains.
39 And it came to pass at the end of two
months, that she returned unto her father,
who did with her *according* to his vow
which he had vowed: and she knew no
man. And it was a custom in Israel,
40 *That* the daughters of Israel went yearly to lament the daughter of Jephthah the
Gileadite four days in a year.

12

1 And the men of Ephraim gathered
themselves together, and went northward,
and said unto Jephthah, Wherefore pass-
edst thou over to fight against the children
of Ammon, and didst not call us to go with
thee? we will burn thine house upon thee
with fire.
2 And Jephthah said unto them, I and my
people were at great strife with the children of Ammon; and when I called you,
ye delivered me not out of their hands.
3 And when I saw that ye delivered *me*
not, I put my life in my hands, and passed
over against the children of Ammon, and
the LORD delivered them into my hand:
wherefore then are ye come up unto me
this day, to fight against me?
4 Then Jephthah gathered together all the
men of Gilead, and fought with Ephraim:
and the men of Gilead smote Ephraim,
because they said, Ye Gileadites *are* fugitives of Ephraim among the Ephraimites,
and among the Manassites.
5 And the Gileadites took the passages
of Jordan before the Ephraimites: and it
was *so*, that when those Ephraimites which
were escaped said, Let me go over; that the
men of Gilead said unto him, *Art* thou an
Ephraimite? If he said, Nay;
6 Then said they unto him, Say now Shib-
boleth: and he said Sibboleth: for he could
not frame to pronounce *it* right. Then they
took him, and slew him at the passages of
Jordan: and there fell at that time of the
Ephraimites forty and two thousand.
7 And Jephthah judged Israel six years.
Then died Jephthah the Gileadite, and was
buried in *one of* the cities of Gilead.
8 And after him Ibzan of Bethlehem
judged Israel.
9 And he had thirty sons, and thirty
daughters, *whom* he sent abroad, and took
in thirty daughters from abroad for his
sons. And he judged Israel seven years.
10 Then died Ibzan, and was buried at
Bethlehem.
11 And after him Elon, a Zebulonite,
judged Israel; and he judged Israel ten
years.
12 And Elon the Zebulonite died, and
was buried in Aijalon in the country of
Zebulun.
13 And after him Abdon the son of Hillel, a Pirathonite, judged Israel.
14 And he had forty sons and thirty nephews, that rode on threescore and ten ass
colts: and he judged Israel eight years.
15 And Abdon the son of Hillel the Pirathonite died, and was buried in Pirathon
in the land of Ephraim, in the mount of
the Amalekites.

13

1 And the children of Israel did evil again
in the sight of the LORD; and the LORD delivered them into the hand of the Philistines forty years.
2 And there was a certain man of Zorah,
of the family of the Danites, whose name
was Manoah; and his wife *was* barren, and
bare not.
3 And the angel of the LORD appeared
unto the woman, and said unto her,
Behold now, thou *art* barren, and bearest
not: but thou shalt conceive, and bear a
son.
4 Now therefore
beware, I pray thee,
and drink not wine
nor strong drink,
and eat not any un-
clean *thing:*

13:4 Drinking
◄ Deuteronomy 29:6
Proverbs 23:31 ►

5 For, lo, thou shalt conceive, and bear a
son; and no razor shall come on his head:
for the child shall be a Nazarite unto God
from the womb: and he shall begin to deliver Israel out of the hand of the Philistines.
6 Then the woman came and told her
husband, saying, A man of God came unto
me, and his countenance *was* like the countenance of an angel of God, very terrible:
but I asked him not whence he *was*, neither told he me his name:
7 But he said unto me, Behold, thou shalt
conceive, and bear a son; and now drink
no wine nor strong drink, neither eat any
unclean *thing:* for the child shall be a

Nazarite to God from the womb to the day of his death.

8 Then Manoah intreated the LORD, and said, O my Lord, let the man of God which thou didst send come again unto us, and teach us what we shall do unto the child that shall be born.

9 And God hearkened to the voice of Manoah; and the angel of God came again unto the woman as she sat in the field: but Manoah her husband *was* not with her.

10 And the woman made haste, and ran, and shewed her husband, and said unto him, Behold, the man hath appeared unto me, that came unto me the *other* day.

11 And Manoah arose, and went after his wife, and came to the man, and said unto him, *Art* thou the man that spakest unto the woman? And he said, I *am*.

12 And Manoah said, Now let thy words come to pass. How shall we order the child, and *how* shall we do unto him?

13 And the angel of the LORD said unto Manoah, Of all that I said unto the woman let her beware.

14 She may not eat of any *thing* that cometh of the vine, neither let her drink wine or strong drink, nor eat any unclean *thing*: all that I commanded her let her observe.

15 And Manoah said unto the angel of the LORD, I pray thee, let us detain thee, until we shall have made ready a kid for thee.

16 And the angel of the LORD said unto Manoah, Though thou detain me, I will not eat of thy bread: and if thou wilt offer a burnt offering, thou must offer it unto the LORD. For Manoah knew not that he *was* an angel of the LORD.

17 And Manoah said unto the angel of the LORD, What *is* thy name, that when thy sayings come to pass we may do thee honour?

18 And the angel of the LORD said unto him, Why askest thou thus after my name, seeing it *is* secret?

19 So Manoah took a kid with a meat offering, and offered *it* upon a rock unto the LORD: and *the angel* did wonderously; and Manoah and his wife looked on.

20 For it came to pass, when the flame went up toward heaven from off the altar, that the angel of the LORD ascended in the flame of the altar. And Manoah and his wife looked on *it*, and fell on their faces to the ground.

21 But the angel of the LORD did no more appear to Manoah and to his wife. Then Manoah knew that he *was* an angel of the LORD.

22 And Manoah said unto his wife, We shall surely die, because we have seen God.

23 But his wife said unto him, If the LORD were pleased to kill us, he would not have received a burnt offering and a meat offering at our hands, neither would he have shewed us all these *things*, nor would as at this time have told us *such things* as these.

24 And the woman bare a son, and called his name Samson: and the child grew, and the LORD blessed him.

25 And the Spirit of the LORD began to move him at times in the camp of Dan between Zorah and Eshtaol.

14

1 And Samson went down to Timnath, and saw a woman in Timnath of the daughters of the Philistines.

2 And he came up, and told his father and his mother, and said, I have seen a woman in Timnath of the daughters of the Philistines: now therefore get her for me to wife.

3 Then his father and his mother said unto him, *Is there* never a woman among the daughters of thy brethren, or among all my people, that thou goest to take a wife of the uncircumcised Philistines? And Samson said unto his father, Get her for me; for she pleaseth me well.

4 But his father and his mother knew not that it *was* of the LORD, that he sought an occasion against the Philistines: for at that time the Philistines had dominion over Israel.

5 Then went Samson down, and his father and his mother, to Timnath, and came to the vineyards of Timnath: and, behold, a young lion roared against him.

6 And the Spirit of the LORD came mightily upon him, and he rent him as he would have rent a kid, and *he had* nothing in his hand: but he told not his father or his mother what he had done.

7 And he went down, and talked with the woman; and she pleased Samson well.

8 And after a time he returned to take her, and he turned aside to see the carcase of the lion: and, behold, *there was* a swarm of bees and honey in the carcase of the lion.

9 And he took thereof in his hands, and went on eating, and came to his father and mother, and he gave them, and they did eat: but he told not them that he had taken the honey out of the carcase of the lion.

10 So his father went down unto the woman: and Samson made there a feast; for so used the young men to do.

11 And it came to pass, when they saw him, that they brought thirty companions to be with him.

12 And Samson said unto them, I will now put forth a riddle unto you: if ye can certainly declare it me within the seven days of the feast, and find *it* out, then I will give you thirty sheets and thirty change of garments:

13 But if ye cannot declare *it* me, then shall ye give me thirty sheets and thirty change of garments. And they said unto him, Put forth thy riddle, that we may hear it.

14 And he said unto them, Out of the eater came forth meat, and out of the strong came forth sweetness. And they could not in three days expound the riddle.

15 And it came to pass on the seventh day, that they said unto Samson's wife, Entice thy husband, that he may declare unto us the riddle, lest we burn thee and thy father's house with fire: have ye called us to take that we have? *is it* not *so?*

16 And Samson's wife wept before him, and said, Thou dost but hate me, and lovest me not: thou hast put forth a riddle unto the children of my people, and hast not told *it* me. And he said unto her, Behold, I have not told *it* my father nor my mother, and shall I tell *it* thee?

17 And she wept before him the seven days, while their feast lasted: and it came to pass on the seventh day, that he told her, because she lay sore upon him: and she told the riddle to the children of her people.

14:17 Giving In
◄ Joshua 7:21
Judges 16:17 ►

18 And the men of the city said unto him on the seventh day before the sun went down, What *is* sweeter than honey? and what *is* stronger than a lion? And he said unto them, If ye had not plowed with my heifer, ye had not found out my riddle.

19 And the Spirit of the LORD came upon him, and he went down to Ashkelon, and slew thirty men of them, and took their spoil, and gave change of garments unto them which expounded the riddle. And his anger was kindled, and he went up to his father's house.

14:19 Anger
◄ Numbers 16:15
1 Samuel 11:6 ►

20 But Samson's wife was *given* to his companion, whom he had used as his friend.

15

1 But it came to pass within a while after, in the time of wheat harvest, that Samson visited his wife with a kid; and he said, I will go in to my wife into the chamber. But her father would not suffer him to go in.

2 And her father said, I verily thought that thou hadst utterly hated her; therefore I gave her to thy companion: *is* not her younger sister fairer than she? take her, I pray thee, instead of her.

3 And Samson said concerning them, Now shall I be more blameless than the Philistines, though I do them a displeasure.

4 And Samson went and caught three hundred foxes, and took firebrands, and turned tail to tail, and put a firebrand in the midst between two tails.

5 And when he had set the brands on fire, he let *them* go into the standing corn of the Philistines, and burnt up both the shocks, and also the standing corn, with the vineyards *and* olives.

6 Then the Philistines said, Who hath done this? And they answered, Samson, the son in law of the Timnite, because he had taken his wife, and given her to his companion. And the Philistines came up, and burnt her and her father with fire.

7 And Samson said unto them, Though ye have done this, yet will I be avenged of you, and after that I will cease.

8 And he smote them hip and thigh with a great slaughter: and he went down and dwelt in the top of the rock Etam.

9 Then the Philistines went up, and pitched in Judah, and spread themselves in Lehi.

10 And the men of Judah said, Why are ye come up against us? And they answered, To bind Samson are we come up, to do to him as he hath done to us.

11 Then three thousand men of Judah went to the top of the rock Etam, and said to Samson, Knowest thou not that the Philistines *are* rulers over us? what *is* this *that* thou hast done unto us? And he said unto them, As they did unto me, so have I done unto them.

12 And they said unto him, We are come down to bind thee, that we may deliver thee into the hand of the Philistines. And Samson said unto them, Swear unto me, that ye will not fall upon me yourselves.

13 And they spake unto him, saying, No; but we will bind thee fast, and deliver thee into their hand: but surely we will not kill thee. And they bound him with two new cords, and brought him up from the rock.

14 *And* when he came unto Lehi, the Philistines shouted against him: and the Spirit of the LORD came mightily upon him, and the cords that *were* upon his arms became as flax that was burnt with fire, and his bands loosed from off his hands.

15 And he found a new jawbone of an ass, and put forth his hand, and took it, and slew a thousand men therewith.

16 And Samson said, With the jawbone of an ass, heaps upon heaps, with the jaw of an ass have I slain a thousand men.

17 And it came to pass, when he had made an end of speaking, that he cast away the jawbone out of his hand, and called that place Ramath-lehi.

18 And he was sore athirst, and called on the LORD, and said, Thou hast given this great deliverance into the hand of thy servant: and now shall I die for thirst, and fall into the hand of the uncircumcised?

19 But God clave an hollow place that *was* in the jaw, and there came water thereout; and when he had drunk, his spirit came again, and he revived: wherefore he called the name thereof En-hakkore, which *is* in Lehi unto this day.

20 And he judged Israel in the days of the Philistines twenty years.

16

1 Then went Samson to Gaza, and saw there an harlot, and went in unto her.

2 *And it was told* the Gazites, saying, Samson is come hither. And they compassed *him* in, and laid wait for him all night in the gate of the city, and were quiet all the night, saying, In the morning, when it is day, we shall kill him.

3 And Samson lay till midnight, and arose at midnight, and took the doors of the gate of the city, and the two posts, and went away with them, bar and all, and put *them* upon his shoulders, and carried them up to the top of an hill that *is* before Hebron.

4 And it came to pass afterward, that he loved a woman in the valley of Sorek, whose name *was* Delilah.

5 And the lords of the Philistines came up unto her, and said unto her, Entice him, and see wherein his great strength *lieth*, and by what *means* we may prevail against him, that we may bind him to afflict him: and we will give thee every one of us eleven hundred *pieces* of silver.

6 And Delilah said to Samson, Tell me, I pray thee, wherein thy great strength *lieth*, and wherewith thou mightest be bound to afflict thee.

7 And Samson said unto her, If they bind me with seven green withs that were never dried, then shall I be weak, and be as another man.

8 Then the lords of the Philistines brought up to her seven green withs which had not been dried, and she bound him with them.

9 Now *there were* men lying in wait, abiding with her in the chamber. And she said unto him, The Philistines *be* upon thee, Samson. And he brake the withs, as a thread of tow is broken when it toucheth the fire. So his strength was not known.

10 And Delilah said unto Samson, Behold, thou hast mocked me, and told me lies: now tell me, I pray thee, wherewith thou mightest be bound.

11 And he said unto her, If they bind me fast with new ropes that never were occupied, then shall I be weak, and be as another man.

12 Delilah therefore took new ropes, and bound him therewith, and said unto him, The Philistines *be* upon thee, Samson. And *there were* liers in wait abiding in the chamber. And he brake them from off his arms like a thread.

13 And Delilah said unto Samson, Hitherto thou hast mocked me, and told me lies: tell me wherewith thou mightest be bound. And he said unto her, If thou weavest the seven locks of my head with the web.

14 And she fastened *it* with the pin, and

said unto him, The Philistines *be* upon thee, Samson. And he awaked out of his sleep, and went away with the pin of the beam, and with the web.

15And she said unto him, How canst thou say, I love thee, when thine heart *is* not with me? thou hast mocked me these three times, and hast not told me wherein thy great strength *lieth*.

16And it came to pass, when she pressed him daily with her words, and urged him, *so* that his soul was vexed unto death;

17That he told her all his heart, and said unto her, There hath not come a razor upon mine head; for I *have been* a Nazarite unto God from my mother's womb: if I be shaven, then my strength will go from me, and I shall become weak, and be like any *other* man.

16:17 Cost of Sin
◄ Judges 2:14
1 Samuel 17:24 ►

16:17 Giving In
◄ Judges 14:17
1 Samuel 13:12 ►

18And when Delilah saw that he had told her all his heart, she sent and called for the lords of the Philistines, saying, Come up this once, for he hath shewed me all his heart. Then the lords of the Philistines came up unto her, and brought money in their hand.

19And she made him sleep upon her knees; and she called for a man, and she caused him to shave off the seven locks of his head; and she began to afflict him, and his strength went from him.

20And she said, The Philistines *be* upon thee, Samson. And he awoke out of his sleep, and said, I will go out as at other times before, and shake myself. And he wist not that the LORD was departed from him.

21But the Philistines took him, and put out his eyes, and brought him down to Gaza, and bound him with fetters of brass; and he did grind in the prison house.

22Howbeit the hair of his head began to grow again after he was shaven.

23Then the lords of the Philistines gathered them together for to offer a great sacrifice unto Dagon their god, and to rejoice: for they said, Our god hath delivered Samson our enemy into our hand.

24And when the people saw him, they praised their god: for they said, Our god hath delivered into our hands our enemy, and the destroyer of our country, which slew many of us.

25And it came to pass, when their hearts were merry, that they said, Call for Samson, that he may make us sport. And they called for Samson out of the prison house; and he made them sport: and they set him between the pillars.

16:25 Parties
◄ Judges 9:27
1 Samuel 25:36 ►

26And Samson said unto the lad that held him by the hand, Suffer me that I may feel the pillars whereupon the house standeth, that I may lean upon them.

27Now the house was full of men and women; and all the lords of the Philistines *were* there; and *there were* upon the roof about three thousand men and women, that beheld while Samson made sport.

28And Samson called unto the LORD, and said, O Lord GOD, remember me, I pray thee, and strengthen me, I pray thee, only this once, O God, that I may be at once avenged of the Philistines for my two eyes.

29And Samson took hold of the two middle pillars upon which the house stood, and on which it was borne up, of the one with his right hand, and of the other with his left.

30And Samson said, Let me die with the Philistines. And he bowed himself with *all his* might; and the house fell upon the lords, and upon all the people that *were* therein. So the dead which he slew at his death were more than *they* which he slew in his life.

31Then his brethren and all the house of his father came down, and took him, and brought *him* up, and buried him between Zorah and Eshtaol in the buryingplace of Manoah his father. And he judged Israel twenty years.

17

1And there was a man of mount Ephraim, whose name *was* Micah.

2And he said unto his mother, The eleven hundred *shekels* of silver that were taken from thee, about which thou cursedst, and spakest of also in mine ears, behold, the silver *is* with me; I took it. And his mother said, Blessed *be thou* of the LORD, my son.

3And when he had restored the eleven
hundred *shekels* of silver to his mother, his
mother said, I had wholly dedicated the
silver unto the LORD from my hand for my
son, to make a graven image and a molten
image: now therefore I will restore it unto
thee.
4Yet he restored the money unto his
mother; and his mother took two hundred
shekels of silver, and gave them to the
founder, who made thereof a graven image and a molten image: and they were in
the house of Micah.
5And the man Micah had an house of
gods, and made an ephod, and teraphim,
and consecrated one of his sons, who became his priest.
6In those days *there was* no king in Israel, *but* every man did *that which was* right
in his own eyes.
7And there was a young man out of
Bethlehem-judah of the family of Judah,
who *was* a Levite, and he sojourned there.
8And the man departed out of the city
from Bethlehem-judah to sojourn where
he could find *a place:* and he came to
mount Ephraim to the house of Micah, as
he journeyed.
9And Micah said unto him, Whence
comest thou? And he said unto him, I *am*
a Levite of Bethlehem-judah, and I go to
sojourn where I may find *a place.*
10And Micah said unto him, Dwell with
me, and be unto me a father and a priest,
and I will give thee ten *shekels* of silver by
the year, and a suit of apparel, and thy victuals. So the Levite went in.
11And the Levite was content to dwell
with the man; and the young man was
unto him as one of his sons.
12And Micah consecrated the Levite; and
the young man became his priest, and was
in the house of Micah.
13Then said Micah, Now know I that the
LORD will do me good, seeing I have a Levite to *my* priest.

18

1In those days *there was* no king in Israel: and in those days the tribe of the
Danites sought them an inheritance to
dwell in; for unto that day *all their* inheritance had not fallen unto them among the
tribes of Israel.
2And the children of Dan sent of their
family five men from their coasts, men of
valour, from Zorah, and from Eshtaol, to
spy out the land, and to search it; and they
said unto them, Go, search the land: who
when they came to mount Ephraim, to the
house of Micah, they lodged there.
3When they *were* by the house of Micah,
they knew the voice of the young man the
Levite: and they turned in thither, and said
unto him, Who brought thee hither? and
what makest thou in this *place?* and what
hast thou here?
4And he said unto them, Thus and thus
dealeth Micah with me, and hath hired me,
and I am his priest.
5And they said unto him, Ask counsel,
we pray thee, of God, that we may know
whether our way which we go shall be
prosperous.
6And the priest said unto them, Go in
peace: before the LORD *is* your way wherein
ye go.
7Then the five men departed, and came
to Laish, and saw the people that *were*
therein, how they dwelt careless, after the
manner of the Zidonians, quiet and secure;
and *there was* no magistrate in the land,
that might put *them* to shame in *any* thing;
and they *were* far from the Zidonians, and
had no business with *any* man.
8And they came unto their brethren to
Zorah and Eshtaol: and their brethren said
unto them, What *say* ye?
9And they said, Arise, that we may go
up against them: for we have seen the land,
and, behold, it *is* very good: and *are* ye still?
be not slothful to go, *and* to enter to possess the land.
10When ye go, ye shall come unto a people secure, and to a large land: for God
hath given it into your hands; a place
where *there is* no want of any thing that *is*
in the earth.
11And there went from thence of the
family of the Danites, out of Zorah and
out of Eshtaol, six hundred men appointed with weapons of war.
12And they went up, and pitched in
Kirjath-jearim, in Judah: wherefore they
called that place Mahaneh-dan unto this
day: behold, *it is* behind Kirjath-jearim.
13And they passed thence unto mount
Ephraim, and came unto the house of
Micah.
14Then answered the five men that went
to spy out the country of Laish, and said
unto their brethren, Do ye know that there

is in these houses an ephod, and teraphim,
and a graven image, and a molten image?
now therefore consider what ye have to do.
15 And they turned thitherward, and
came to the house of the young man the
Levite, *even* unto the house of Micah, and
saluted him.
16 And the six hundred men appointed
with their weapons of war, which *were* of
the children of Dan, stood by the entering
of the gate.
17 And the five men that went to spy out
the land went up, *and* came in thither, *and*
took the graven image, and the ephod, and
the teraphim, and the molten image:
and the priest stood in the entering of the
gate with the six hundred men *that were*
appointed with weapons of war.
18 And these went into Micah's house,
and fetched the carved image, the ephod,
and the teraphim, and the molten image.
Then said the priest unto them, What
do ye?
19 And they said unto him, Hold thy
peace, lay thine hand upon thy mouth, and
go with us, and be to us a father and a
priest: *is it* better for thee to be a priest unto
the house of one man, or that thou be a
priest unto a tribe and a family in Israel?
20 And the priest's heart was glad, and
he took the ephod, and the teraphim, and
the graven image, and went in the midst
of the people.
21 So they turned and departed, and put
the little ones and the cattle and the carriage before them.
22 *And* when they were a good way from
the house of Micah, the men that *were* in
the houses near to Micah's house were
gathered together, and overtook the children of Dan.
23 And they cried unto the children of
Dan. And they turned their faces, and said
unto Micah, What aileth thee, that thou
comest with such a company?
24 And he said, Ye have taken away my
gods which I made, and the priest, and ye
are gone away: and what have I more? and
what *is* this *that* ye say unto me, What aileth
thee?
25 And the children of Dan said unto
him, Let not thy voice be heard among us,
lest angry fellows run upon thee, and thou
lose thy life, with the lives of thy household.
26 And the children of Dan went their
way: and when Micah saw that they *were*
too strong for him, he turned and went
back unto his house.
27 And they took *the things* which Micah
had made, and the priest which he had,
and came unto Laish, unto a people *that*
were at quiet and secure: and they smote
them with the edge of the sword, and burnt
the city with fire.
28 And *there was* no deliverer, because it
was far from Zidon, and they had no business with *any* man; and it was in the valley
that *lieth* by Beth-rehob. And they built a
city, and dwelt therein.
29 And they called the name of the city
Dan, after the name of Dan their father,
who was born unto Israel: howbeit the
name of the city *was* Laish at the first.
30 And the children of Dan set up the
graven image: and Jonathan, the son of
Gershom, the son of Manasseh, he and his
sons were priests to the tribe of Dan until
the day of the captivity of the land.
31 And they set them up Micah's graven
image, which he made, all the time that
the house of God was in Shiloh.

19

1 And it came to pass in those days, when
there was no king in Israel, that there was a
certain Levite sojourning on the side of
mount Ephraim, who took to him a concubine out of Bethlehem-judah.
2 And his concubine played the whore
against him, and went away from him unto
her father's house to Bethlehem-judah,
and was there four whole months.
3 And her husband arose, and went after
her, to speak friendly unto her, *and* to bring
her again, having his servant with him, and
a couple of asses: and she brought him into
her father's house: and when the father of
the damsel saw him, he rejoiced to meet
him.
4 And his father in law, the damsel's father, retained him; and he abode with him
three days: so they did eat and drink, and
lodged there.
5 And it came to pass on the fourth day,
when they arose early in the morning, that
he rose up to depart: and the damsel's father said unto his son in law, Comfort
thine heart with a morsel of bread, and
afterward go your way.
6 And they sat down, and did eat
and drink both of them together: for the

damsel's father had said unto the man, Be
content, I pray thee, and tarry all night,
and let thine heart be merry.
7 And when the man rose up to depart,
his father in law urged him: therefore he
lodged there again.
8 And he arose early in the morning on
the fifth day to depart: and the damsel's
father said, Comfort thine heart, I pray
thee. And they tarried until afternoon, and
they did eat both of them.
9 And when the man rose up to depart,
he, and his concubine, and his servant, his
father in law, the damsel's father, said unto
him, Behold, now the day draweth toward
evening, I pray you tarry all night: behold,
the day groweth to an end, lodge here, that
thine heart may be merry; and to morrow
get you early on your way, that thou mayest
go home.
10 But the man would not tarry that
night, but he rose up and departed, and
came over against Jebus, which *is* Jerusalem; and *there were* with him two asses saddled, his concubine also *was* with him.
11 *And* when they *were* by Jebus, the day
was far spent; and the servant said unto
his master, Come, I pray thee, and let us
turn in into this city of the Jebusites, and
lodge in it.
12 And his master said unto him, We will
not turn aside hither into the city of a
stranger, that *is* not of the children of Israel; we will pass over to Gibeah.
13 And he said unto his servant, Come,
and let us draw near to one of these places
to lodge all night, in Gibeah, or in Ramah.
14 And they passed on and went their
way; and the sun went down upon them
when they were by Gibeah, which *belongeth*
to Benjamin.
15 And they turned
aside thither, to go
in *and* to lodge in
Gibeah: and when
he went in, he sat
him down in a
street of the city: for *there was* no man that
took them into his house to lodging.

19:15 Cold Shoulder
◄ Deuteronomy 23:4
1 Samuel 25:10 ►

16 And, behold, there came an old man
from his work out of the field at even,
which *was* also of mount Ephraim; and he
sojourned in Gibeah: but the men of the
place *were* Benjamites.
17 And when he had lifted up his eyes,
he saw a wayfaring man in the street of
the city: and the old man said, Whither
goest thou? and whence comest thou?
18 And he said unto him, We *are* passing
from Bethlehem-judah toward the side of
mount Ephraim; from thence *am* I: and I
went to Bethlehem-judah, but I *am now*
going to the house of the LORD; and there
is no man that receiveth me to house.
19 Yet there is both straw and provender
for our asses; and there is bread and wine
also for me, and for thy handmaid, and
for the young man *which is* with thy servants: *there is* no want of any thing.
20 And the old man said, Peace *be* with
thee; howsoever *let* all thy wants *lie* upon
me; only lodge not in the street.
21 So he brought him into his house, and
gave provender unto the asses: and they
washed their feet, and did eat and drink.
22 *Now* as they were making their hearts
merry, behold, the men of the city, certain
sons of Belial, beset the house round
about, *and* beat at the door, and spake to
the master of the house, the old man, saying, Bring forth the man that came into
thine house, that we may know him.
23 And the man, the master of the house,
went out unto them, and said unto them,
Nay, my brethren, *nay,* I pray you, do not
so wickedly; seeing that this man is come
into mine house, do not this folly.
24 Behold, *here is* my daughter a maid-
en, and his concubine; them I will bring
out now, and humble ye them, and do
with them what seemeth good unto you:
but unto this man do not so vile a thing.
25 But the men would not hearken to
him: so the man took his concubine, and
brought her forth unto them; and they
knew her, and abused her all the night
until the morning: and when the day began to spring, they let her go.
26 Then came the woman in the dawning of the day, and fell down at the door
of the man's house where her lord *was,* till
it was light.
27 And her lord rose up in the morning,
and opened the doors of the house, and
went out to go his way: and, behold, the
woman his concubine was fallen down *at*
the door of the house, and her hands *were*
upon the threshold.
28 And he said unto her, Up, and let us
be going. But none answered. Then the

man took her *up* upon an ass, and the man rose up, and gat him unto his place.

29 And when he was come into his house, he took a knife, and laid hold on his concubine, and divided her, *together* with her bones, into twelve pieces, and sent her into all the coasts of Israel.

30 And it was so, that all that saw it said, There was no such deed done nor seen from the day that the children of Israel came up out of the land of Egypt unto this day: consider of it, take advice, and speak *your minds.*

20

1 Then all the children of Israel went out, and the congregation was gathered together as one man, from Dan even to Beersheba, with the land of Gilead, unto the LORD in Mizpeh.

2 And the chief of all the people, *even* of all the tribes of Israel, presented themselves in the assembly of the people of God, four hundred thousand footmen that drew sword.

3 (Now the children of Benjamin heard that the children of Israel were gone up to Mizpeh.) Then said the children of Israel, Tell *us,* how was this wickedness?

4 And the Levite, the husband of the woman that was slain, answered and said, I came into Gibeah that *belongeth* to Benjamin, I and my concubine, to lodge.

5 And the men of Gibeah rose against me, and beset the house round about upon me by night, *and* thought to have slain me: and my concubine have they forced, that she is dead.

6 And I took my concubine, and cut her in pieces, and sent her throughout all the country of the inheritance of Israel: for they have committed lewdness and folly in Israel.

7 Behold, ye *are* all children of Israel; give here your advice and counsel.

8 And all the people arose as one man, saying, We will not any *of us* go to his tent, neither will we any *of us* turn into his house.

9 But now this *shall be* the thing which we will do to Gibeah; *we will go up* by lot against it;

10 And we will take ten men of an hundred throughout all the tribes of Israel, and an hundred of a thousand, and a thousand out of ten thousand, to fetch victual for the people, that they may do, when they come to Gibeah of Benjamin, according to all the folly that they have wrought in Israel.

11 So all the men of Israel were gathered against the city, knit together as one man.

20:11 Teamwork
◄ Exodus 17:12
1 Samuel 14:6-7 ►

12 And the tribes of Israel sent men through all the tribe of Benjamin, saying, What wickedness *is* this that is done among you?

13 Now therefore deliver *us* the men, the children of Belial, which *are* in Gibeah, that we may put them to death, and put away evil from Israel. But the children of Benjamin would not hearken to the voice of their brethren the children of Israel:

14 But the children of Benjamin gathered themselves together out of the cities unto Gibeah, to go out to battle against the children of Israel.

15 And the children of Benjamin were numbered at that time out of the cities twenty and six thousand men that drew sword, beside the inhabitants of Gibeah, which were numbered seven hundred chosen men.

16 Among all this people *there were* seven hundred chosen men lefthanded; every one could sling stones at an hair *breadth,* and not miss.

17 And the men of Israel, beside Benjamin, were numbered four hundred thousand men that drew sword: all these *were* men of war.

18 And the children of Israel arose, and went up to the house of God, and asked counsel of God, and said, Which of us shall go up first to the battle against the children of Benjamin? And the LORD said, Judah *shall go up* first.

19 And the children of Israel rose up in the morning, and encamped against Gibeah.

20 And the men of Israel went out to battle against Benjamin; and the men of Israel put themselves in array to fight against them at Gibeah.

21 And the children of Benjamin came forth out of Gibeah, and destroyed down to the ground of the Israelites that day twenty and two thousand men.

22 And the people the men of Israel encouraged themselves, and set their battle

again in array in the place where they put themselves in array the first day.

23(And the children of Israel went up and wept before the LORD until even, and asked counsel of the LORD, saying, Shall I go up again to battle against the children of Benjamin my brother? And the LORD said, Go up against him.)

24And the children of Israel came near against the children of Benjamin the second day.

25And Benjamin went forth against them out of Gibeah the second day, and destroyed down to the ground of the children of Israel again eighteen thousand men; all these drew the sword.

26Then all the children of Israel, and all the people, went up, and came unto the house of God, and wept, and sat there before the LORD, and fasted that day until even, and offered burnt offerings and peace offerings before the LORD.

27And the children of Israel enquired of the LORD, (for the ark of the covenant of God *was* there in those days,

28And Phinehas, the son of Eleazar, the son of Aaron, stood before it in those days,) saying, Shall I yet again go out to battle against the children of Benjamin my brother, or shall I cease? And the LORD said, Go up; for to morrow I will deliver them into thine hand.

29And Israel set liers in wait round about Gibeah.

30And the children of Israel went up against the children of Benjamin on the third day, and put themselves in array against Gibeah, as at other times.

31And the children of Benjamin went out against the people, *and* were drawn away from the city; and they began to smite of the people, *and* kill, as at other times, in the highways, of which one goeth up to the house of God, and the other to Gibeah in the field, about thirty men of Israel.

32And the children of Benjamin said, They *are* smitten down before us, as at the first. But the children of Israel said, Let us flee, and draw them from the city unto the highways.

33And all the men of Israel rose up out of their place, and put themselves in array at Baal-tamar: and the liers in wait of Israel came forth out of their places, *even* out of the meadows of Gibeah.

34And there came against Gibeah ten thousand chosen men out of all Israel, and the battle was sore: but they knew not that evil *was* near them.

35And the LORD smote Benjamin before Israel: and the children of Israel destroyed of the Benjamites that day twenty and five thousand and an hundred men: all these drew the sword.

36So the children of Benjamin saw that they were smitten: for the men of Israel gave place to the Benjamites, because they trusted unto the liers in wait which they had set beside Gibeah.

37And the liers in wait hasted, and rushed upon Gibeah; and the liers in wait drew *themselves* along, and smote all the city with the edge of the sword.

38Now there was an appointed sign between the men of Israel and the liers in wait, that they should make a great flame with smoke rise up out of the city.

39And when the men of Israel retired in the battle, Benjamin began to smite *and* kill of the men of Israel about thirty persons: for they said, Surely they are smitten down before us, as *in* the first battle.

40But when the flame began to arise up out of the city with a pillar of smoke, the Benjamites looked behind them, and, behold, the flame of the city ascended up to heaven.

41And when the men of Israel turned again, the men of Benjamin were amazed: for they saw that evil was come upon them.

42Therefore they turned *their backs* before the men of Israel unto the way of the wilderness; but the battle overtook them; and them which *came* out of the cities they destroyed in the midst of them.

43*Thus* they inclosed the Benjamites round about, *and* chased them, *and* trode them down with ease over against Gibeah toward the sunrising.

44And there fell of Benjamin eighteen thousand men; all these *were* men of valour.

45And they turned and fled toward the wilderness unto the rock of Rimmon: and they gleaned of them in the highways five thousand men; and pursued hard after them unto Gidom, and slew two thousand men of them.

46So that all which fell that day of Benjamin were twenty and five thousand men that drew the sword; all these *were* men of valour.

47 But six hundred men turned and fled to the wilderness unto the rock Rimmon, and abode in the rock Rimmon four months.

48 And the men of Israel turned again upon the children of Benjamin, and smote them with the edge of the sword, as well the men of *every* city, as the beast, and all that came to hand: also they set on fire all the cities that they came to.

21

1 Now the men of Israel had sworn in Mizpeh, saying, There shall not any of us give his daughter unto Benjamin to wife.

2 And the people came to the house of God, and abode there till even before God, and lifted up their voices, and wept sore;

21:2 Grief
◄ Genesis 42:38
Ruth 1:20 ►

3 And said, O LORD God of Israel, why is this come to pass in Israel, that there should be to day one tribe lacking in Israel?

4 And it came to pass on the morrow, that the people rose early, and built there an altar, and offered burnt offerings and peace offerings.

5 And the children of Israel said, Who *is there* among all the tribes of Israel that came not up with the congregation unto the LORD? For they had made a great oath concerning him that came not up to the LORD to Mizpeh, saying, He shall surely be put to death.

6 And the children of Israel repented them for Benjamin their brother, and said, There is one tribe cut off from Israel this day.

7 How shall we do for wives for them that remain, seeing we have sworn by the LORD that we will not give them of our daughters to wives?

8 And they said, What one *is there* of the tribes of Israel that came not up to Mizpeh to the LORD? And, behold, there came none to the camp from Jabesh-gilead to the assembly.

9 For the people were numbered, and, behold, *there were* none of the inhabitants of Jabesh-gilead there.

10 And the congregation sent thither twelve thousand men of the valiantest, and commanded them, saying, Go and smite the inhabitants of Jabesh-gilead with the edge of the sword, with the women and the children.

11 And this *is* the thing that ye shall do, Ye shall utterly destroy every male, and every woman that hath lain by man.

12 And they found among the inhabitants of Jabesh-gilead four hundred young virgins, that had known no man by lying with any male: and they brought them unto the camp to Shiloh, which *is* in the land of Canaan.

13 And the whole congregation sent *some* to speak to the children of Benjamin that *were* in the rock Rimmon, and to call peaceably unto them.

14 And Benjamin came again at that time; and they gave them wives which they had saved alive of the women of Jabesh-gilead: and yet so they sufficed them not.

15 And the people repented them for Benjamin, because that the LORD had made a breach in the tribes of Israel.

16 Then the elders of the congregation said, How shall we do for wives for them that remain, seeing the women are destroyed out of Benjamin?

17 And they said, *There must be* an inheritance for them that be escaped of Benjamin, that a tribe be not destroyed out of Israel.

18 Howbeit we may not give them wives of our daughters: for the children of Israel have sworn, saying, Cursed *be* he that giveth a wife to Benjamin.

19 Then they said, Behold, *there is* a feast of the LORD in Shiloh yearly *in a place* which *is* on the north side of Bethel, on the east side of the highway that goeth up from Bethel to Shechem, and on the south of Lebonah.

20 Therefore they commanded the children of Benjamin, saying, Go and lie in wait in the vineyards;

21 And see, and, behold, if the daughters of Shiloh come out to dance in dances, then come ye out of the vineyards, and catch you every man his wife of the daughters of Shiloh, and go to the land of Benjamin.

22 And it shall be, when their fathers or their brethren come unto us to complain,

that we will say unto them, Be favourable
unto them for our sakes: because we reserved not to each man his wife in the war:
for ye did not give unto them at this time,
that ye should be guilty.
23And the children of Benjamin did so,
and took *them* wives, according to their
number, of them that danced, whom they
caught: and they went and returned unto
their inheritance, and repaired the cities,
and dwelt in them.
24And the children of Israel departed
thence at that time, every man to his tribe
and to his family, and they went out from
thence every man to his inheritance.
25In those days *there was* no king in Israel: every man did *that which was* right in
his own eyes.

Ruth

AUTHOR
Unknown (some think it was Samuel the judge, but no one knows for sure)

MAIN POINT
Faithfulness to family and to God can have great effects, even if you yourself are not so "great."

DATE WRITTEN
Sometime after the period of the judges (1375-1050 B.C.)

4 CHAPTERS

MAIN PEOPLE

Ruth, Naomi, Boaz

SPECIAL FEATURES

- *Tells a most amazing story of courage and family loyalty*
- *Describes how picking up grain in a field led to a fine marriage for a young widow*
- *Explains an interesting custom concerning sandals*
- *Continues the family line of King David, through whom Jesus would eventually come*
- *Third book of History*

HOW THE BOOK GOT ITS NAME

The title of the book comes from the name of its main character, the young woman from Moab named Ruth.

1
1 Now it came to pass in the days when
the judges ruled, that there was a famine in the land. And a certain man of
Bethlehem-judah went to sojourn in the
country of Moab, he, and his wife, and his
two sons.
2 And the name of the man *was* Elimelech, and the name of his wife Naomi, and
the name of his two sons Mahlon and
Chilion, Ephrathites of Bethlehem-judah.
And they came into the country of Moab,
and continued there.
3 And Elimelech Naomi's husband died;
and she was left, and her two sons.
4 And they took them wives of the wom-
en of Moab; the name of the one *was* Orpah, and the name of the other Ruth: and
they dwelled there about ten years.
5 And Mahlon and Chilion died also
both of them; and the woman was left of
her two sons and her husband.
6 Then she arose with her daughters in
law, that she might return from the country of Moab: for she had heard in the country of Moab how that the LORD had visited
his people in giving them bread.
7 Wherefore she went forth out of the
place where she was, and her two daughters in law with her; and they went on the
way to return unto the land of Judah.
8 And Naomi said unto her two daughters in law, Go, return each to her mother's

house: the LORD deal kindly with you,
as ye have dealt with the dead, and
with me.
9The LORD grant you that ye may find
rest, each *of you* in the house of her husband. Then she kissed them; and they lifted up their voice, and wept.
10And they said unto her, Surely we will
return with thee unto thy people.
11And Naomi said, Turn again, my
daughters: why will ye go with me? *are*
there yet *any more* sons in my womb, that
they may be your husbands?
12Turn again, my daughters, go *your way;*
for I am too old to have an husband. If I
should say, I have hope, *if* I should have
an husband also to night, and should also
bear sons;
13Would ye tarry for them till they were
grown? would ye stay for them from having husbands? nay, my daughters; for it
grieveth me much for your sakes that the
hand of the LORD is gone out against me.
14And they lifted up their voice, and
wept again: and Orpah kissed her mother
in law; but Ruth clave unto her.
15And she said,
Behold, thy sister in
law is gone back
unto her people,
and unto her gods:
return thou after
thy sister in law.
16And Ruth said,
Intreat me not to
leave thee, *or* to re-
turn from follow-
ing after thee: for
whither thou goest,
I will go; and where
thou lodgest, I will
lodge: thy people
shall be my people,
and thy God my
God:
17Where thou diest, will I die, and there
will I be buried: the LORD do so to me,
and more also, *if ought* but death part thee
and me.
18When she saw that she was stedfastly
minded to go with her, then she left speaking unto her.
19So they two went until they came to
Bethlehem. And it came to pass, when they
were come to Bethlehem, that all the city

1:15 Following God
◄ Joshua 24:15
1 Kings 18:21 ►

1:16 Being a Friend
◄ 1 Samuel 20:17 ►

1:16 Young Women
◄ Judges 11:36
Esther 4:16 ►

was moved about them, and they said, *Is*
this Naomi?
20And she said
unto them, Call me
not Naomi, call me
Mara: for the Al-
mighty hath dealt
very bitterly with
me.
21I went out full, and the LORD hath
brought me home again empty: why *then*
call ye me Naomi, seeing the LORD hath
testified against me, and the Almighty hath
afflicted me?
22So Naomi returned, and Ruth the
Moabitess, her daughter in law, with her,
which returned out of the country of
Moab: and they came to Bethlehem in the
beginning of barley harvest.

1:20 Grief
◄ Judges 21:2
2 Samuel 18:33 ►

2

1And Naomi had a kinsman of her
husband's, a mighty man of wealth, of the
family of Elimelech; and his name *was*
Boaz.
2And Ruth the Moabitess said unto Naomi, Let me now go to the field, and glean
ears of corn after *him* in whose sight I shall
find grace. And she said unto her, Go, my
daughter.
3And she went, and came, and gleaned
in the field after the reapers: and her hap
was to light on a part of the field *belonging*
unto Boaz, who *was* of the kindred of Elimelech.
4And behold, Boaz came from Bethlehem, and said unto the reapers, The LORD
be with you. And they answered him, The
LORD bless thee.
5Then said Boaz unto his servant that
was set over the reapers, Whose damsel *is*
this?
6And the servant that was set over the
reapers answered and said, It *is* the
Moabitish damsel that came back with
Naomi out of the country of Moab:
7And she said, I pray you, let me glean
and gather after the reapers among the
sheaves: so she came, and hath continued
even from the morning until now, that she
tarried a little in the house.
8Then said Boaz unto Ruth, Hearest
thou not, my daughter? Go not to glean
in another field, neither go from hence,
but abide here fast by my maidens:
9*Let* thine eyes *be* on the field that they
do reap, and go thou after them: have I

not charged the young men that they shall
not touch thee? and when thou art athirst,
go unto the vessels, and drink of *that* which
the young men have drawn.
10 Then she fell
on her face, and
bowed herself to
the ground, and
said unto him, Why
have I found grace
in thine eyes, that thou shouldest take
knowledge of me, seeing I *am* a stranger?

2:10
"Thank You"
◄ 1 Samuel 14:45 ►

11 And Boaz answered and said unto her,
It hath fully been shewed me, all that thou
hast done unto thy mother in law since
the death of thine husband: and *how* thou
hast left thy father and thy mother, and
the land of thy nativity, and art come unto
a people which thou knewest not heretofore.
12 The LORD recompense thy work, and
a full reward be given thee of the LORD God
of Israel, under whose wings thou art come
to trust.
13 Then she said, Let me find favour in
thy sight, my lord; for that thou hast comforted me, and for that thou hast spoken
friendly unto thine handmaid, though I be
not like unto one of thine handmaidens.
14 And Boaz said unto her, At mealtime
come thou hither, and eat of the bread,
and dip thy morsel in the vinegar. And she
sat beside the reapers: and he reached her
parched *corn,* and she did eat, and was
sufficed, and left.
15 And when she was risen up to glean,
Boaz commanded his young men, saying,
Let her glean even among the sheaves, and
reproach her not:
16 And let fall also *some* of the handfuls
of purpose for her, and leave *them,* that she
may glean *them,* and rebuke her not.
17 So she gleaned in the field until even,
and beat out that she had gleaned: and it
was about an ephah of barley.
18 And she took *it* up, and went into the
city: and her mother in law saw what she
had gleaned: and she brought forth, and
gave to her that she had reserved after she
was sufficed.
19 And her mother in law said unto her,
Where hast thou gleaned to day? and
where wroughtest thou? blessed be he that
did take knowledge of thee. And she
shewed her mother in law with whom she
had wrought, and said, The man's name
with whom I wrought to day *is* Boaz.
20 And Naomi said unto her daughter in
law, Blessed *be* he of the LORD, who hath
not left off his kindness to the living and
to the dead. And Naomi said unto her, The
man *is* near of kin unto us, one of our next
kinsmen.
21 And Ruth the Moabitess said, He said
unto me also, Thou shalt keep fast by my
young men, until they have ended all my
harvest.
22 And Naomi said unto Ruth her daughter in law, *It is* good, my daughter, that thou
go out with his maidens, that they meet
thee not in any other field.
23 So she kept fast by the maidens of
Boaz to glean unto the end of barley harvest and of wheat harvest; and dwelt with
her mother in law.

3

1 Then Naomi her mother in law said
unto her, My daughter, shall I not seek rest
for thee, that it may be well with thee?
2 And now *is* not Boaz of our kindred,
with whose maidens thou wast? Behold,
he winnoweth barley to night in the
threshingfloor.
3 Wash thyself therefore, and anoint thee,
and put thy raiment upon thee, and get
thee down to the floor: *but* make not thyself known unto the man, until he shall
have done eating and drinking.
4 And it shall be, when he lieth down,
that thou shalt mark the place where he
shall lie, and thou shalt go in, and uncover his feet, and lay thee down; and he will
tell thee what thou shalt do.
5 And she said unto her, All that thou
sayest unto me I will do.
6 And she went down unto the floor, and
did according to all that her mother in law
bade her.
7 And when Boaz had eaten and drunk,
and his heart was merry, he went to lie
down at the end of the heap of corn: and
she came softly, and uncovered his feet,
and laid her down.
8 And it came to pass at midnight, that
the man was afraid, and turned himself:
and, behold, a woman lay at his feet.
9 And he said, Who *art* thou? And she
answered, I *am* Ruth thine handmaid:
spread therefore thy skirt over thine
handmaid; for thou *art* a near kinsman.
10 And he said, Blessed *be* thou of the

LORD, my daughter: *for* thou hast shewed
more kindness in the latter end than at the
beginning, inasmuch as thou followedst
not young men, whether poor or rich.
11 And now, my daughter, fear not; I will
do to thee all that thou requirest: for all
the city of my people doth know that thou
art a virtuous woman.
12 And now it is true that I *am thy* near
kinsman: howbeit there is a kinsman nearer than I.
13 Tarry this night, and it shall be in
the morning, *that* if he will perform unto
thee the part of a kinsman, well; let him
do the kinsman's part: but if he will not
do the part of a kinsman to thee, then
will I do the part of a kinsman to thee,
as the LORD liveth: lie down until the
morning.
14 And she lay at his feet until the morning: and she rose up before one could
know another. And he said, Let it not be
known that a woman came into the floor.
15 Also he said, Bring the vail that *thou*
hast upon thee, and hold it. And when she
held it, he measured six *measures* of barley, and laid *it* on her: and she went into
the city.
16 And when she came to her mother in
law, she said, Who *art* thou, my daughter?
And she told her all that the man had done
to her.
17 And she said, These six *measures* of
barley gave he me; for he said to me, Go
not empty unto thy mother in law.
18 Then said she, Sit still, my daughter,
until thou know how the matter will fall:
for the man will not be in rest, until he
have finished the thing this day.

4

1 Then went Boaz up to the gate, and sat
him down there: and, behold, the kinsman
of whom Boaz spake came by; unto whom
he said, Ho, such a one! turn aside, sit
down here. And he turned aside, and sat
down.
2 And he took ten men of the elders of
the city, and said, Sit ye down here. And
they sat down.
3 And he said unto the kinsman, Naomi, that is come again out of the country
of Moab, selleth a parcel of land, which
was our brother Elimelech's:
4 And I thought to advertise thee, saying,
Buy *it* before the inhabitants, and before
the elders of my people. If thou wilt redeem *it,* redeem *it:* but if thou wilt not
redeem *it, then* tell me, that I may know:
for *there is* none to redeem *it* beside thee;
and I *am* after thee. And he said, I will redeem *it.*
5 Then said Boaz, What day thou buyest
the field of the hand of Naomi, thou must
buy *it* also of Ruth the Moabitess, the wife
of the dead, to raise up the name of the
dead upon his inheritance.
6 And the kinsman said, I cannot redeem
it for myself, lest I mar mine own inheritance: redeem thou my right to thyself; for
I cannot redeem *it.*
7 Now this *was the manner* in former time
in Israel concerning redeeming and concerning changing, for to confirm all things;
a man plucked off his shoe, and gave *it* to
his neighbour: and this *was* a testimony
in Israel.
8 Therefore the kinsman said unto Boaz,
Buy *it* for thee. So he drew off his shoe.
9 And Boaz said unto the elders, and *unto*
all the people, Ye *are* witnesses this day,
that I have bought all that *was* Elimelech's,
and all that *was* Chilion's and Mahlon's,
of the hand of Naomi.
10 Moreover Ruth the Moabitess, the wife
of Mahlon, have I purchased to be my wife,
to raise up the name of the dead upon his
inheritance, that the name of the dead be
not cut off from among his brethren, and
from the gate of his place: ye *are* witnesses
this day.
11 And all the people that *were* in the gate,
and the elders, said, *We are* witnesses. The
LORD make the woman that is come into
thine house like Rachel and like Leah,
which two did build the house of Israel:
and do thou worthily in Ephratah, and be
famous in Bethlehem:
12 And let thy house be like the house of
Pharez, whom Tamar bare unto Judah, of
the seed which the LORD shall give thee
of this young woman.
13 So Boaz took Ruth, and she was his
wife: and when he went in unto her, the
LORD gave her conception, and she bare a
son.
14 And the women said unto Naomi,
Blessed *be* the LORD, which hath not left
thee this day without a kinsman, that his
name may be famous in Israel.
15 And he shall be unto thee a restorer
of *thy* life, and a nourisher of thine old age:

for thy daughter in law, which loveth thee,
which is better to thee than seven sons,
hath born him.
16And Naomi took the child, and laid
it in her bosom, and became nurse
unto it.
17And the women her neighbours gave
it a name, saying, There is a son born to
Naomi; and they called his name Obed:
he *is* the father of Jesse, the father of David.

18Now these *are* the generations of
Pharez: Pharez begat Hezron,
19And Hezron begat Ram, and Ram
begat Amminadab,
20And Amminadab begat Nahshon, and
Nahshon begat Salmon,
21And Salmon begat Boaz, and Boaz
begat Obed,
22And Obed begat Jesse, and Jesse begat
David.

1 Samuel

AUTHOR
Unknown (some think it was Samuel the judge, but no one knows for sure)

MAIN POINT
God will not abandon his people, and he honors those who listen and obey him.

DATE WRITTEN
Unknown, though possibly the sixth century B.C., while the people of Israel were captives in Babylon

31 CHAPTERS

MAIN PEOPLE

Eli, Hannah, Samuel, Saul, Jonathan, David, Goliath

SPECIAL FEATURES

- *Describes how the boy Samuel learned to listen to God and then serve him*
- *Tells the sad story of Israel's change from a theocracy (led by God) to a monarchy (led by a king)*
- *Proves that a small shepherd boy with a giant-sized faith has a huge advantage over both his brothers and his enemies*
- *Shows how drooling in your beard can come in handy*
- *Tells the famous story of David and Goliath*
- *Fourth book of History*

HOW THE BOOK GOT ITS NAME

The title of the book refers to its purpose as a record of the life of Samuel, Israel's last judge.

1

1 Now there was a certain man of Rama-
thaim-zophim, of mount Ephraim, and his
name was Elkanah, the son of Jeroham,
the son of Elihu, the son of Tohu, the son
of Zuph, an Ephrathite:
2 And he had two wives; the name of the
one *was* Hannah, and the name of the
other Peninnah: and Peninnah had children, but Hannah had no children.
3 And this man went up out of his city
yearly to worship and to sacrifice unto the
LORD of hosts in Shiloh. And the two sons
of Eli, Hophni and Phinehas, the priests
of the LORD, *were* there.
4 And when the time was that Elkanah
offered, he gave to Peninnah his wife, and
to all her sons and her daughters, portions:
5 But unto Hannah he gave a worthy
portion; for he loved Hannah: but the
LORD had shut up her womb.
6 And her adversary also provoked her
sore, for to make her fret, because the LORD
had shut up her womb.
7 And *as* he did so year by year, when she

went up to the house of the LORD, so she
provoked her; therefore she wept, and did
not eat.
8 Then said Elkanah her husband to her,
Hannah, why weepest thou? and why
eatest thou not? and why is thy heart
grieved? *am* not I better to thee than ten
sons?
9 So Hannah rose up after they had eat-
en in Shiloh, and after they had drunk.
Now Eli the priest sat upon a seat by a post
of the temple of the LORD.
10 And she *was* in bitterness of soul, and
prayed unto the LORD, and wept sore.
11 And she vowed
a vow, and said,
O LORD of hosts, if
thou wilt indeed
look on the afflic-
tion of thine hand-
maid, and remember me, and not forget
thine handmaid, but wilt give unto thine
handmaid a man child, then I will give
him unto the LORD all the days of his life,
and there shall no razor come upon his
head.

1:11 Names of God
◄ Joshua 3:10
2 Samuel 22:2 ►

12 And it came to pass, as she continued
praying before the LORD, that Eli marked
her mouth.
13 Now Hannah, she spake in her heart;
only her lips moved, but her voice was not
heard: therefore Eli thought she had been
drunken.
14 And Eli said unto her, How long wilt
thou be drunken? put away thy wine from
thee.
15 And Hannah answered and said, No,
my lord, I *am* a woman of a sorrowful spirit: I have drunken neither wine nor strong
drink, but have poured out my soul before the LORD.
16 Count not thine handmaid for a
daughter of Belial: for out of the abundance of my complaint and grief have I
spoken hitherto.
17 Then Eli answered and said, Go in
peace: and the God of Israel grant *thee* thy
petition that thou hast asked of him.
18 And she said, Let thine handmaid find
grace in thy sight. So the woman went her
way, and did eat, and her countenance was
no more *sad*.
19 And they rose up in the morning early, and worshipped before the LORD, and
returned, and came to their house to Ramah: and Elkanah
knew Hannah his
wife; and the LORD
remembered her.
20 Wherefore it
came to pass, when
the time was come about after Hannah had
conceived, that she bare a son, and called
his name Samuel, *saying*, Because I have
asked him of the LORD.

1:19 Devotions
◄ Exodus 24:4
2 Chronicles 29:20 ►

21 And the man Elkanah, and all his
house, went up to offer unto the LORD the
yearly sacrifice, and his vow.
22 But Hannah went not up; for she said
unto her husband, *I will not go up* until the
child be weaned, and *then* I will bring him,
that he may appear before the LORD, and
there abide for ever.
23 And Elkanah her husband said unto
her, Do what seemeth thee good; tarry
until thou have weaned him; only the
LORD establish his word. So the woman
abode, and gave her son suck until she
weaned him.
24 And when she had weaned him, she
took him up with her, with three bullocks,
and one ephah of flour, and a bottle of
wine, and brought him unto the house of
the LORD in Shiloh: and the child *was*
young.
25 And they slew a bullock, and brought
the child to Eli.
26 And she said, Oh my lord, *as* thy soul
liveth, my lord, I *am* the woman that stood
by thee here, praying unto the LORD.
27 For this child I prayed; and the LORD
hath given me my petition which I asked
of him:
28 Therefore also I have lent him to the
LORD; as long as he liveth he shall be lent
to the LORD. And he worshipped the LORD
there.

2

1 And Hannah prayed, and said, My
heart rejoiceth in the LORD, mine horn is
exalted in the LORD: my mouth is enlarged
over mine enemies; because I rejoice in thy
salvation.
2 *There is* none holy as the LORD: for *there*
is none beside thee: neither *is there* any rock
like our God.
3 Talk no more so exceeding proudly; let
not arrogancy come out of your mouth:
for the LORD *is* a God of knowledge, and
by him actions are weighed.
4 The bows of the mighty men *are* broken,

and they that stumbled are girded with strength.

5 *They that were* full have hired out themselves for bread; and *they that were* hungry ceased: so that the barren hath born seven; and she that hath many children is waxed feeble.

6 The LORD killeth, and maketh alive: he bringeth down to the grave, and bringeth up.

7 The LORD maketh poor, and maketh rich: he bringeth low, and lifteth up.

2:7 God at Work
◄ Genesis 45:8
2 Samuel 7:8 ►

8 He raiseth up the poor out of the dust, *and* lifteth up the beggar from the dunghill, to set *them* among princes, and to make them inherit the throne of glory: for the pillars of the earth *are* the LORD'S, and he hath set the world upon them.

9 He will keep the feet of his saints, and the wicked shall be silent in darkness; for by strength shall no man prevail.

10 The adversaries of the LORD shall be broken to pieces; out of heaven shall he thunder upon them: the LORD shall judge the ends of the earth; and he shall give strength unto his king, and exalt the horn of his anointed.

11 And Elkanah went to Ramah to his house. And the child did minister unto the LORD before Eli the priest.

12 Now the sons of Eli *were* sons of Belial; they knew not the LORD.

13 And the priest's custom with the people *was, that,* when any man offered sacrifice, the priest's servant came, while the flesh was in seething, with a fleshhook of three teeth in his hand;

14 And he struck *it* into the pan, or kettle, or caldron, or pot; all that the fleshhook brought up the priest took for himself. So they did in Shiloh unto all the Israelites that came thither.

15 Also before they burnt the fat, the priest's servant came, and said to the man that sacrificed, Give flesh to roast for the priest; for he will not have sodden flesh of thee, but raw.

16 And *if* any man said unto him, Let them not fail to burn the fat presently, and *then* take *as much* as thy soul desireth; then he would answer him, *Nay;* but thou shalt give *it me* now: and if not, I will take *it* by force.

17 Wherefore the sin of the young men was very great before the LORD: for men abhorred the offering of the LORD.

18 But Samuel ministered before the LORD, *being* a child, girded with a linen ephod.

19 Moreover his mother made him a little coat, and brought *it* to him from year to year, when she came up with her husband to offer the yearly sacrifice.

20 And Eli blessed Elkanah and his wife, and said, The LORD give thee seed of this woman for the loan which is lent to the LORD. And they went unto their own home.

21 And the LORD visited Hannah, so that she conceived, and bare three sons and two daughters. And the child Samuel grew before the LORD.

22 Now Eli was very old, and heard all that his sons did unto all Israel; and how they lay with the women that assembled *at* the door of the tabernacle of the congregation.

23 And he said unto them, Why do ye such things? for I hear of your evil dealings by all this people.

24 Nay, my sons; for *it is* no good report that I hear: ye make the LORD'S people to transgress.

25 If one man sin against another, the judge shall judge him: but if a man sin against the LORD, who shall intreat for him? Notwithstanding they hearkened not unto the voice of their father, because the LORD would slay them.

26 And the child Samuel grew on, and was in favour both with the LORD, and also with men.

2:26 Young Men
◄ Genesis 41:46
1 Samuel 3:1 ►

27 And there came a man of God unto Eli, and said unto him, Thus saith the LORD, Did I plainly appear unto the house of thy father, when they were in Egypt in Pharaoh's house?

28 And did I choose him out of all the tribes of Israel *to be* my priest, to offer upon mine altar, to burn incense, to wear an ephod before me? and did I give unto the house of thy father all the offerings made by fire of the children of Israel?

29Wherefore kick ye at my sacrifice and at mine offering, which I have commanded *in my* habitation; and honourest thy sons above me, to make yourselves fat with the chiefest of all the offerings of Israel my people?

30Wherefore the LORD God of Israel saith, I said indeed *that* thy house, and the house of thy father, should walk before me for ever: but now the LORD saith, Be it far from me; for them that honour me I will honour, and they that despise me shall be lightly esteemed.

31Behold, the days come, that I will cut off thine arm, and the arm of thy father's house, that there shall not be an old man in thine house.

32And thou shalt see an enemy *in my* habitation, in all *the wealth* which *God* shall give Israel: and there shall not be an old man in thine house for ever.

33And the man of thine, *whom* I shall not cut off from mine altar, *shall be* to consume thine eyes, and to grieve thine heart: and all the increase of thine house shall die in the flower of their age.

34And this *shall be* a sign unto thee, that shall come upon thy two sons, on Hophni and Phinehas; in one day they shall die both of them.

35And I will raise me up a faithful priest, *that* shall do according to *that* which *is* in mine heart and in my mind: and I will build him a sure house; and he shall walk before mine anointed for ever.

36And it shall come to pass, *that* every one that is left in thine house shall come *and* crouch to him for a piece of silver and a morsel of bread, and shall say, Put me, I pray thee, into one of the priests' offices, that I may eat a piece of bread.

3

1And the child Samuel ministered unto the LORD before Eli. And the word of the LORD was precious in those days; *there was* no open vision.

3:1 Young Men
◄ 1 Samuel 2:26
1 Samuel 17:33 ►

2And it came to pass at that time, when Eli *was* laid down in his place, and his eyes began to wax dim, *that* he could not see;

3And ere the lamp of God went out in the temple of the LORD, where the ark of God *was*, and Samuel was laid down *to sleep*;

4That the LORD called Samuel: and he answered, Here *am* I.

5And he ran unto Eli, and said, Here *am* I; for thou calledst me. And he said, I called not; lie down again. And he went and lay down.

6And the LORD called yet again, Samuel. And Samuel arose and went to Eli, and said, Here *am* I; for thou didst call me. And he answered, I called not, my son; lie down again.

7Now Samuel did not yet know the LORD, neither was the word of the LORD yet revealed unto him.

8And the LORD called Samuel again the third time. And he arose and went to Eli, and said, Here *am* I; for thou didst call me. And Eli perceived that the LORD had called the child.

9Therefore Eli said unto Samuel, Go, lie down: and it shall be, if he call thee, that thou shalt say, Speak, LORD; for thy servant heareth. So Samuel went and lay down in his place.

10And the LORD came, and stood, and called as at other times, Samuel, Samuel. Then Samuel answered, Speak; for thy servant heareth.

11And the LORD said to Samuel, Behold, I will do a thing in Israel, at which both the ears of every one that heareth it shall tingle.

12In that day I will perform against Eli all *things* which I have spoken concerning his house: when I begin, I will also make an end.

13For I have told him that I will judge his house for ever for the iniquity which he knoweth; because his sons made themselves vile, and he restrained them not.

14And therefore I have sworn unto the house of Eli, that the iniquity of Eli's house shall not be purged with sacrifice nor offering for ever.

15And Samuel lay until the morning, and opened the doors of the house of the LORD. And Samuel feared to shew Eli the vision.

16Then Eli called Samuel, and said, Samuel, my son. And he answered, Here *am* I.

17And he said, What *is* the thing that *the LORD* hath said unto thee? I pray thee hide *it* not from me: God do so to thee, and more also, if thou hide *any* thing from me of all the things that he said unto thee.

18 And Samuel told him every whit, and hid nothing from him. And he said, It *is* the LORD: let him do what seemeth him good.

19 And Samuel grew, and the LORD was with him, and did let none of his words fall to the ground.

20 And all Israel from Dan even to Beer-sheba knew that Samuel *was* established *to be* a prophet of the LORD.

21 And the LORD appeared again in Shiloh: for the LORD revealed himself to Samuel in Shiloh by the word of the LORD.

4

1 And the word of Samuel came to all Israel. Now Israel went out against the Philistines to battle, and pitched beside Eben-ezer: and the Philistines pitched in Aphek.

2 And the Philistines put themselves in array against Israel: and when they joined battle, Israel was smitten before the Philistines: and they slew of the army in the field about four thousand men.

3 And when the people were come into the camp, the elders of Israel said, Wherefore hath the LORD smitten us to day before the Philistines? Let us fetch the ark of the covenant of the LORD out of Shiloh unto us, that, when it cometh among us, it may save us out of the hand of our enemies.

4:3
Superstition
◄ 1 Kings 20:23 ►

4 So the people sent to Shiloh, that they might bring from thence the ark of the covenant of the LORD of hosts, which dwelleth *between* the cherubims: and the two sons of Eli, Hophni and Phinehas, *were* there with the ark of the covenant of God.

5 And when the ark of the covenant of the LORD came into the camp, all Israel shouted with a great shout, so that the earth rang again.

6 And when the Philistines heard the noise of the shout, they said, What *meaneth* the noise of this great shout in the camp of the Hebrews? And they understood that the ark of the LORD was come into the camp.

7 And the Philistines were afraid, for they said, God is come into the camp. And they said, Woe unto us! for there hath not been such a thing heretofore.

8 Woe unto us! who shall deliver us out of the hand of these mighty Gods? these *are* the Gods that smote the Egyptians with all the plagues in the wilderness.

9 Be strong, and quit yourselves like men, O ye Philistines, that ye be not servants unto the Hebrews, as they have been to you: quit yourselves like men, and fight.

10 And the Philistines fought, and Israel was smitten, and they fled every man into his tent: and there was a very great slaughter; for there fell of Israel thirty thousand footmen.

11 And the ark of God was taken; and the two sons of Eli, Hophni and Phinehas, were slain.

12 And there ran a man of Benjamin out of the army, and came to Shiloh the same day with his clothes rent, and with earth upon his head.

13 And when he came, lo, Eli sat upon a seat by the wayside watching: for his heart trembled for the ark of God. And when the man came into the city, and told *it*, all the city cried out.

14 And when Eli heard the noise of the crying, he said, What *meaneth* the noise of this tumult? And the man came in hastily, and told Eli.

15 Now Eli was ninety and eight years old; and his eyes were dim, that he could not see.

16 And the man said unto Eli, I *am* he that came out of the army, and I fled to day out of the army. And he said, What is there done, my son?

17 And the messenger answered and said, Israel is fled before the Philistines, and there hath been also a great slaughter among the people, and thy two sons also, Hophni and Phinehas, are dead, and the ark of God is taken.

18 And it came to pass, when he made mention of the ark of God, that he fell from off the seat backward by the side of the gate, and his neck brake, and he died: for he was an old man, and heavy. And he had judged Israel forty years.

19 And his daughter in law, Phinehas' wife, was with child, *near* to be delivered: and when she heard the tidings that the ark of God was taken, and that her father in law and her husband were dead, she bowed herself and travailed; for her pains came upon her.

20 And about the time of her death the
women that stood by her said unto her,
Fear not; for thou hast born a son. But she
answered not, neither did she regard *it.*
21 And she named the child I-chabod,
saying, The glory is departed from Israel:
because the ark of God was taken, and
because of her father in law and her husband.
22 And she said, The glory is departed
from Israel: for the ark of God is taken.

5

1 And the Philistines took the ark of God,
and brought it from Eben-ezer unto Ashdod.
2 When the Philistines took the ark of
God, they brought it into the house of
Dagon, and set it by Dagon.
3 And when they of Ashdod arose early
on the morrow, behold, Dagon *was* fallen
upon his face to the earth before the ark
of the LORD. And they took Dagon, and
set him in his place again.
4 And when they arose early on the morrow morning, behold, Dagon *was* fallen
upon his face to the ground before the ark
of the LORD; and the head of Dagon and
both the palms of his hands *were* cut off
upon the threshold; only *the stump of* Dagon was left to him.
5 Therefore neither the priests of Dagon,
nor any that come into Dagon's house,
tread on the threshold of Dagon in Ashdod unto this day.
6 But the hand of the LORD was heavy
upon them of Ashdod, and he destroyed
them, and smote them with emerods, *even*
Ashdod and the coasts thereof.
7 And when the men of Ashdod saw that
it was so, they said, The ark of the God of
Israel shall not abide with us: for his hand
is sore upon us, and upon Dagon our god.
8 They sent therefore and gathered all the
lords of the Philistines unto them, and
said, What shall we do with the ark of the
God of Israel? And they answered, Let the
ark of the God of Israel be carried about
unto Gath. And they carried the ark of the
God of Israel about *thither.*
9 And it was *so,* that, after they had carried it about, the hand of the LORD was
against the city with a very great destruction: and he smote the men of the city,
both small and great, and they had
emerods in their secret parts.
10 Therefore they sent the ark of God to
Ekron. And it came to pass, as the ark of
God came to Ekron, that the Ekronites
cried out, saying, They have brought about
the ark of the God of Israel to us, to slay
us and our people.
11 So they sent and gathered together all
the lords of the Philistines, and said, Send
away the ark of the God of Israel, and let it
go again to his own place, that it slay us
not, and our people: for there was a deadly destruction throughout all the city; the
hand of God was very heavy there.
12 And the men that died not were smitten with the emerods: and the cry of the
city went up to heaven.

6

1 And the ark of the LORD was in the
country of the Philistines seven months.
2 And the Philistines called for the priests
and the diviners, saying, What shall we do
to the ark of the LORD? tell us wherewith
we shall send it to his place.
3 And they said, If ye send away the ark
of the God of Israel, send it not empty;
but in any wise return him a trespass offering: then ye shall be healed, and it shall
be known to you why his hand is not removed from you.
4 Then said they, What *shall be* the trespass offering which we shall return to him?
They answered, Five golden emerods, and
five golden mice, *according to* the number
of the lords of the Philistines: for one
plague *was* on you all, and on your lords.
5 Wherefore ye shall make images of your
emerods, and images of your mice that mar
the land; and ye shall give glory unto the
God of Israel: peradventure he will light-
en his hand from off you, and from off
your gods, and from off your land.
6 Wherefore then do ye harden your
hearts, as the Egyptians and Pharaoh hardened their hearts? when he had wrought
wonderfully among them, did they not let
the people go, and they departed?
7 Now therefore make a new cart, and
take two milch kine, on which there hath
come no yoke, and tie the kine to the cart,
and bring their calves home from them:
8 And take the ark of the LORD, and lay it
upon the cart; and put the jewels of gold,
which ye return him *for* a trespass offering, in a coffer by the side thereof; and send
it away, that it may go.
9 And see, if it goeth up by the way of his
own coast to Beth-shemesh, *then* he hath

done us this great evil: but if not, then we
shall know that *it is* not his hand *that* smote
us; it *was* a chance *that* happened to us.
10And the men did so; and took two
milch kine, and tied them to the cart, and
shut up their calves at home:
11And they laid the ark of the LORD upon
the cart, and the coffer with the mice of
gold and the images of their emerods.
12And the kine took the straight way to
the way of Beth-shemesh, *and* went along
the highway, lowing as they went, and
turned not aside *to* the right hand or *to* the
left; and the lords of the Philistines went
after them unto the border of Beth-shemesh.
13And *they of* Beth-shemesh *were* reaping their wheat harvest in the valley: and
they lifted up their eyes, and saw the ark,
and rejoiced to see *it*.
14And the cart came into the field of
Joshua, a Beth-shemite, and stood there,
where *there was* a great stone: and they
clave the wood of the cart, and offered the
kine a burnt offering unto the LORD.
15And the Levites took down the ark of
the LORD, and the coffer that *was* with it,
wherein the jewels of gold *were,* and put
them on the great stone: and the men of
Beth-shemesh offered burnt offerings and
sacrificed sacrifices the same day unto the
LORD.
16And when the five lords of the Philistines had seen *it,* they returned to Ekron
the same day.
17And these *are* the golden emerods
which the Philistines returned *for* a trespass offering unto the LORD; for Ashdod
one, for Gaza one, for Askelon one, for
Gath one, for Ekron one;
18And the golden mice, *according to* the
number of all the cities of the Philistines
belonging to the five lords, *both* of fenced
cities, and of country villages, even unto
the great *stone of* Abel, whereon they set
down the ark of the LORD: *which stone*
remaineth unto this day in the field of
Joshua, the Beth-shemite.
19And he smote the men of Beth-shemesh, because they had looked into the
ark of the LORD, even he smote of the people fifty thousand and threescore and ten
men: and the people lamented, because
the LORD had smitten *many* of the people
with a great slaughter.
20And the men of Beth-shemesh said,
Who is able to stand before this holy LORD
God? and to whom shall he go up from us?
21And they sent messengers to the inhabitants of Kirjath-jearim, saying, The
Philistines have brought again the ark of
the LORD; come ye down, *and* fetch it up
to you.

7

1And the men of Kirjath-jearim came,
and brought up the ark of the LORD, and
brought it into the house of Abinadab in
the hill, and sanctified Eleazar his son to
keep the ark of the LORD.
2And it came to pass, while the ark
abode in Kirjath-jearim, that the time was
long; for it was twenty years: and all the
house of Israel lamented after the LORD.
3And Samuel spake unto all the house
of Israel, saying, If ye do return unto the
LORD with all your hearts, *then* put away
the strange gods and Ashtaroth from
among you, and prepare your hearts unto
the LORD, and serve him only: and he will
deliver you out of the hand of the Philistines.
4Then the children of Israel did put away
Baalim and Ashtaroth, and served the
LORD only.
5And Samuel
said, Gather all Is-
rael to Mizpeh, and
I will pray for you
unto the LORD.
6And they gath-
ered together to Mizpeh, and drew water,
and poured *it* out before the LORD, and
fasted on that day, and said there, We have
sinned against the LORD. And Samuel
judged the children of Israel in Mizpeh.

7:5 Praying for Others
◄ Deuteronomy 9:26
1 Kings 13:6 ►

7And when the Philistines heard that the
children of Israel were gathered together
to Mizpeh, the lords of the Philistines went
up against Israel. And when the children
of Israel heard *it,* they were afraid of the
Philistines.
8And the children of Israel said to Samuel, Cease not to cry unto the LORD our
God for us, that he will save us out of the
hand of the Philistines.
9And Samuel took a sucking lamb, and
offered *it for* a burnt offering wholly unto
the LORD: and Samuel cried unto the LORD
for Israel; and the LORD heard him.
10And as Samuel was offering up the
burnt offering, the Philistines drew near

to battle against Israel: but the LORD thundered with a great thunder on that day
upon the Philistines, and discomfited
them; and they were smitten before Israel.
11 And the men of Israel went out of
Mizpeh, and pursued the Philistines,
and smote them, until *they came* under
Beth-car.
12 Then Samuel took a stone, and set *it*
between Mizpeh and Shen, and called the
name of it Eben-ezer, saying, Hitherto hath
the LORD helped us.
13 So the Philistines were subdued, and
they came no more into the coast of Israel: and the hand of the LORD was against
the Philistines all the days of Samuel.
14 And the cities which the Philistines
had taken from Israel were restored to Israel, from Ekron even unto Gath; and the
coasts thereof did Israel deliver out of the
hands of the Philistines. And there was
peace between Israel and the Amorites.
15 And Samuel judged Israel all the days
of his life.
16 And he went from year to year in circuit to Bethel, and Gilgal, and Mizpeh, and
judged Israel in all those places.
17 And his return *was* to Ramah; for there
was his house; and there he judged Israel;
and there he built an altar unto the LORD.

8

1 And it came to pass, when Samuel was
old, that he made his sons judges over Israel.
2 Now the name of his firstborn was Joel;
and the name of his second, Abiah: *they
were* judges in Beer-sheba.
3 And his sons walked not in his ways,
but turned aside after lucre, and took
bribes, and perverted judgment.
4 Then all the elders of Israel gathered
themselves together, and came to Samuel
unto Ramah,
5 And said unto him, Behold, thou art
old, and thy sons walk not in thy ways:
now make us a king to judge us like all the
nations.
6 But the thing displeased Samuel, when
they said, Give us a king to judge us. And
Samuel prayed unto the LORD.
7 And the LORD said unto Samuel, Hearken unto the voice of the people in all that
they say unto thee: for they have not rejected thee, but they have rejected me, that
I should not reign over them.
8 According to all the works which they
have done since the day that I brought
them up out of Egypt even unto this day,
wherewith they have forsaken me, and
served other gods, so do they also unto
thee.
9 Now therefore hearken unto their
voice: howbeit yet protest solemnly unto
them, and shew them the manner of the
king that shall reign over them.
10 And Samuel told all the words of the
LORD unto the people that asked of him a
king.
11 And he said, This will be the manner
of the king that shall reign over you: He
will take your sons, and appoint *them*
for himself, for his chariots, and *to be* his
horsemen; and *some* shall run before his
chariots.
12 And he will appoint him captains over
thousands, and captains over fifties; and
will set them to ear his ground, and to reap
his harvest, and to make his instruments
of war, and instruments of his chariots.
13 And he will take your daughters *to be*
confectionaries, and *to be* cooks, and *to be*
bakers.
14 And he will take your fields, and your
vineyards, and your oliveyards, *even* the
best *of them*, and give *them* to his servants.
15 And he will take the tenth of your
seed, and of your vineyards, and give to
his officers, and to his servants.
16 And he will take your menservants,
and your maidservants, and your goodli-
est young men, and your asses, and put
them to his work.
17 He will take the tenth of your sheep:
and ye shall be his servants.
18 And ye shall cry out in that day because of your king which ye shall have
chosen you; and the LORD will not hear
you in that day.
19 Nevertheless the people refused to
obey the voice of Samuel; and they said,
Nay; but we will have a king over us;
20 That we also may be like all the nations; and that our king may judge us, and
go out before us, and fight our battles.
21 And Samuel heard all the words of the
people, and he rehearsed them in the ears
of the LORD.
22 And the LORD said to Samuel, Hearken unto their voice, and make them a
king. And Samuel said unto the men of
Israel, Go ye every man unto his city.

9

1 Now there was a man of Benjamin, whose name *was* Kish, the son of Abiel, the son of Zeror, the son of Bechorath, the son of Aphiah, a Benjamite, a mighty man of power.

2 And he had a son, whose name *was* Saul, a choice young man, and a goodly: and *there was* not among the children of Israel a goodlier person than he: from his shoulders and upward *he was* higher than any of the people.

3 And the asses of Kish Saul's father were lost. And Kish said to Saul his son, Take now one of the servants with thee, and arise, go seek the asses.

4 And he passed through mount Ephraim, and passed through the land of Shalisha, but they found *them* not: then they passed through the land of Shalim, and *there they were* not: and he passed through the land of the Benjamites, but they found *them* not.

5 *And* when they were come to the land of Zuph, Saul said to his servant that *was* with him, Come, and let us return; lest my father leave *caring* for the asses, and take thought for us.

6 And he said unto him, Behold now, *there is* in this city a man of God, and *he is* an honourable man; all that he saith cometh surely to pass: now let us go thither; peradventure he can shew us our way that we should go.

7 Then said Saul to his servant, But, behold, *if* we go, what shall we bring the man? for the bread is spent in our vessels, and *there is* not a present to bring to the man of God: what have we?

8 And the servant answered Saul again, and said, Behold, I have here at hand the fourth part of a shekel of silver: *that* will I give to the man of God, to tell us our way.

9 (Beforetime in Israel, when a man went to enquire of God, thus he spake, Come, and let us go to the seer: for *he that is* now *called* a Prophet was beforetime called a Seer.)

10 Then said Saul to his servant, Well said; come, let us go. So they went unto the city where the man of God *was.*

11 *And* as they went up the hill to the city, they found young maidens going out to draw water, and said unto them, Is the seer here?

12 And they answered them, and said, He is; behold, *he is* before you: make haste now, for he came to day to the city; for *there is* a sacrifice of the people to day in the high place:

13 As soon as ye be come into the city, ye shall straightway find him, before he go up to the high place to eat: for the people will not eat until he come, because he doth bless the sacrifice; *and* afterwards they eat that be bidden. Now therefore get you up; for about this time ye shall find him.

14 And they went up into the city: *and* when they were come into the city, behold, Samuel came out against them, for to go up to the high place.

15 Now the LORD had told Samuel in his ear a day before Saul came, saying,

16 To morrow about this time I will send thee a man out of the land of Benjamin, and thou shalt anoint him *to be* captain over my people Israel, that he may save my people out of the hand of the Philistines: for I have looked upon my people, because their cry is come unto me.

17 And when Samuel saw Saul, the LORD said unto him, Behold the man whom I spake to thee of! this same shall reign over my people.

18 Then Saul drew near to Samuel in the gate, and said, Tell me, I pray thee, where the seer's house *is.*

19 And Samuel answered Saul, and said, I *am* the seer: go up before me unto the high place; for ye shall eat with me to day, and to morrow I will let thee go, and will tell thee all that *is* in thine heart.

20 And as for thine asses that were lost three days ago, set not thy mind on them; for they are found. And on whom *is* all the desire of Israel? *Is it* not on thee, and on all thy father's house?

21 And Saul answered and said, *Am* not I a Benjamite, of the smallest of the tribes of Israel? and my family the least of all the families of the tribe of Benjamin? wherefore then speakest thou so to me?

22 And Samuel took Saul and his servant, and brought them into the parlour, and made them sit in the chiefest place among them that were bidden, which *were* about thirty persons.

23 And Samuel said unto the cook, Bring the portion which I gave thee, of which I said unto thee, Set it by thee.

24 And the cook took up the shoulder,

and *that* which *was* upon it, and set *it* before Saul. And *Samuel* said, Behold that
which is left! set *it* before thee, *and* eat: for
unto this time hath it been kept for thee
since I said, I have invited the people. So
Saul did eat with Samuel that day.
25And when they were come down from
the high place into the city, *Samuel* communed with Saul upon the top of the
house.
26And they arose early: and it came to
pass about the spring of the day, that Samuel called Saul to the top of the house, saying, Up, that I may send thee away. And
Saul arose, and they went out both of
them, he and Samuel, abroad.
27*And* as they
were going down
to the end of the
city, Samuel said to
Saul, Bid the ser-
vant pass on before
us, (and he passed on,) but stand thou
still a while, that I may shew thee the word
of God.

9:27
Sunday School
◄ 2 Kings 17:28 ►

10 1Then Samuel took a vial of oil, and
poured *it* upon his head, and kissed him,
and said, *Is it* not because the LORD hath
anointed thee *to be* captain over his inheritance?
2When thou art
departed from me
to day, then thou
shalt find two men
by Rachel's sepul-
chre in the border
of Benjamin at Zelzah; and they will say
unto thee, The asses which thou wentest
to seek are found: and, lo, thy father hath
left the care of the asses, and sorroweth
for you, saying, What shall I do for my son?

10:2 Parents Care
◄ Genesis 37:14
2 Samuel 18:29 ►

3Then shalt thou go on forward from
thence, and thou shalt come to the plain
of Tabor, and there shall meet thee three
men going up to God to Bethel, one carrying three kids, and another carrying three
loaves of bread, and another carrying a
bottle of wine:
4And they will salute thee, and give thee
two *loaves* of bread; which thou shalt receive of their hands.
5After that thou shalt come to the hill
of God, where *is* the garrison of the Philistines: and it shall come to pass, when thou
art come thither to the city, that thou shalt
meet a company of prophets coming down
from the high place with a psaltery, and a
tabret, and a pipe, and a harp, before them;
and they shall prophesy:
6And the Spirit of the LORD will come
upon thee, and thou shalt prophesy with
them, and shalt be turned into another man.
7And let it be, when these signs are come
unto thee, *that* thou do as occasion serve
thee; for God *is* with thee.
8And thou shalt go down before me to
Gilgal; and, behold, I will come down
unto thee, to offer burnt offerings, *and* to
sacrifice sacrifices of peace offerings: seven
days shalt thou tarry, till I come to thee,
and shew thee what thou shalt do.
9And it was *so*, that when he had turned
his back to go from Samuel, God gave him
another heart: and all those signs came to
pass that day.
10And when they came thither to the
hill, behold, a company of prophets met
him; and the Spirit of God came upon
him, and he prophesied among them.
11And it came to pass, when all that
knew him beforetime saw that, behold, he
prophesied among the prophets, then the
people said one to another, What *is* this
that is come unto the son of Kish? *Is* Saul
also among the prophets?
12And one of the same place answered
and said, But who *is* their father? Therefore it became a proverb, *Is* Saul also
among the prophets?
13And when he had made an end of
prophesying, he came to the high place.
14And Saul's uncle said unto him and
to his servant, Whither went ye? And he
said, To seek the asses: and when we
saw that *they were* no where, we came to
Samuel.
15And Saul's uncle said, Tell me, I pray
thee, what Samuel said unto you.
16And Saul said unto his uncle, He told
us plainly that the asses were found. But
of the matter of the kingdom, whereof
Samuel spake, he told him not.
17And Samuel called the people together unto the LORD to Mizpeh;
18And said unto the children of Israel,
Thus saith the LORD God of Israel, I brought
up Israel out of Egypt, and delivered you
out of the hand of the Egyptians, and out
of the hand of all kingdoms, *and* of them
that oppressed you:

19And ye have this day rejected your
God, who himself saved you out of all your
adversities and your tribulations; and ye
have said unto him, *Nay*, but set a king
over us. Now therefore present yourselves
before the LORD by your tribes, and by your
thousands.
20And when Samuel had caused all the
tribes of Israel to come near, the tribe of
Benjamin was taken.
21When he had caused the tribe of Benjamin to come near by their families, the
family of Matri was taken, and Saul the
son of Kish was taken: and when they
sought him, he could not be found.
22Therefore they enquired of the LORD
further, if the man should yet come thither.
And the LORD answered, Behold, he hath
hid himself among the stuff.
23And they ran and fetched him thence:
and when he stood among the people, he
was higher than any of the people from
his shoulders and upward.
24And Samuel said to all the people, See
ye him whom the LORD hath chosen, that
there is none like him among all the people? And all the people shouted, and said,
God save the king.
25Then Samuel told the people the manner of the kingdom, and wrote *it* in a book,
and laid *it* up before the LORD. And Samuel sent all the people away, every man to
his house.
26And Saul also went home to Gibeah;
and there went with him a band of men,
whose hearts God had touched.
27But the children of Belial said, How
shall this man save us? And they despised
him, and brought him no presents. But he
held his peace.

11

1Then Nahash the Ammonite came up,
and encamped against Jabesh-gilead: and
all the men of Jabesh said unto Nahash,
Make a covenant with us, and we will serve
thee.
2And Nahash the Ammonite answered
them, On this *condition* will I make *a covenant* with you, that I may thrust out all
your right eyes, and lay it *for* a reproach
upon all Israel.
3And the elders of Jabesh said unto him,
Give us seven days' respite, that we may
send messengers unto all the coasts of Israel: and then, if *there be* no man to save
us, we will come out to thee.
4Then came the messengers to Gibeah
of Saul, and told the tidings in the ears of
the people: and all the people lifted up
their voices, and wept.
5And, behold, Saul came after the herd
out of the field; and Saul said, What *aileth*
the people that they weep? And they told
him the tidings of the men of Jabesh.
6And the Spirit of
God came upon
Saul when he heard
those tidings, and
his anger was kin-
dled greatly.

11:6 Anger
◄ Judges 14:19
Nehemiah 5:6 ►

7And he took a yoke of oxen, and hewed
them in pieces, and sent *them* throughout
all the coasts of Israel by the hands of
messengers, saying, Whosoever cometh
not forth after Saul and after Samuel, so
shall it be done unto his oxen. And the
fear of the LORD fell on the people, and
they came out with one consent.
8And when he numbered them in Bezek, the children of Israel were three hundred thousand, and the men of Judah
thirty thousand.
9And they said unto the messengers that
came, Thus shall ye say unto the men of
Jabesh-gilead, To morrow, by *that time* the
sun be hot, ye shall have help. And the
messengers came and shewed *it* to the men
of Jabesh; and they were glad.
10Therefore the men of Jabesh said, To
morrow we will come out unto you, and
ye shall do with us all that seemeth good
unto you.
11And it was *so* on the morrow, that Saul
put the people in three companies; and
they came into the midst of the host in
the morning watch, and slew the Ammonites until the heat of the day: and it came
to pass, that they which remained were
scattered, so that two of them were not left
together.
12And the people said unto Samuel,
Who *is* he that said, Shall Saul reign over
us? bring the men, that we may put them
to death.
13And Saul said,
There shall not a
man be put to
death this day: for
to day the LORD
hath wrought salva-
tion in Israel.

11:13
Examples of Mercy
◄ 1 Samuel 26:9 ►

14 Then said Samuel to the people,
Come, and let us go to Gilgal, and renew
the kingdom there.
15 And all the people went to Gilgal; and
there they made Saul king before the LORD
in Gilgal; and there they sacrificed sacrifices of peace offerings before the LORD;
and there Saul and all the men of Israel
rejoiced greatly.

12

1 And Samuel said unto all Israel, Behold, I have hearkened unto your voice in
all that ye said unto me, and have made a
king over you.
2 And now, behold, the king walketh
before you: and I am old and grayheaded;
and, behold, my sons *are* with you: and I
have walked before you from my childhood unto this day.
3 Behold, here I *am:* witness against me
before the LORD, and before his anointed:
whose ox have I taken? or whose ass have
I taken? or whom have I defrauded? whom
have I oppressed? or of whose hand have I
received *any* bribe to blind mine eyes therewith? and I will restore it you.
4 And they said, Thou hast not defrauded
us, nor oppressed us, neither hast thou
taken ought of any man's hand.
5 And he said unto them, The LORD *is*
witness against you, and his anointed *is*
witness this day, that ye have not found
ought in my hand. And they answered, *He*
is witness.
6 And Samuel said unto the people, *It is*
the LORD that advanced Moses and Aaron,
and that brought your fathers up out of
the land of Egypt.
7 Now therefore stand still, that I may
reason with you before the LORD of all the
righteous acts of the LORD, which he did
to you and to your fathers.
8 When Jacob was come into Egypt, and
your fathers cried unto the LORD, then the
LORD sent Moses and Aaron, which
brought forth your fathers out of Egypt,
and made them dwell in this place.
9 And when they forgat the LORD their
God, he sold them into the hand of Sisera, captain of the host of Hazor, and into
the hand of the Philistines, and into the
hand of the king of Moab, and they fought
against them.
10 And they cried unto the LORD, and
said, We have sinned, because we have forsaken the LORD, and have served Baalim
and Ashtaroth: but now deliver us out of
the hand of our enemies, and we will serve
thee.
11 And the LORD sent Jerubbaal, and Bedan, and Jephthah, and Samuel, and delivered you out of the hand of your
enemies on every side, and ye dwelled safe.
12 And when ye saw that Nahash the king
of the children of Ammon came against
you, ye said unto me, Nay; but a king shall
reign over us: when the LORD your God
was your king.
13 Now therefore behold the king whom
ye have chosen, *and* whom ye have desired!
and, behold, the LORD hath set a king over
you.
14 If ye will fear
the LORD, and serve
him, and obey his
voice, and not rebel
against the com-
mandment of the
LORD, then shall
both ye and also
the king that
reigneth over you
continue following
the LORD your God:
15 But if ye will
not obey the voice
of the LORD, but
rebel against the
commandment of
the LORD, then
shall the hand of
the LORD be against you, as *it was* against
your fathers.

12:14 Why Fear God?
◄ Psalm 25:12 ►

12:15 Ouch!
◄ Deuteronomy 28:15
1 Samuel 28:18 ►

12:15 Sin (Warnings)
◄ Joshua 24:20
Isaiah 28:14 ►

16 Now therefore stand and see this great
thing, which the LORD will do before your
eyes.
17 *Is it* not wheat harvest to day? I will
call unto the LORD, and he shall send thunder and rain; that ye may perceive and see
that your wickedness *is* great, which ye
have done in the sight of the LORD, in asking you a king.
18 So Samuel called unto the LORD; and
the LORD sent thunder and rain that day:
and all the people greatly feared the LORD
and Samuel.
19 And all the people said unto Samuel,
Pray for thy servants unto the LORD thy
God, that we die not: for we have added
unto all our sins *this* evil, to ask us a king.
20 And Samuel said unto the people, Fear

not: ye have done all this wickedness: yet
turn not aside from following the LORD,
but serve the LORD with all your heart;
21And turn ye not
aside: for *then*
should ye go after
vain *things,* which
cannot profit nor
deliver; for they *are*
vain.

12:21 Standing Strong
◄ Joshua 23:7-8
Job 11:14-15 ►

22For the LORD will not forsake his
people for his great name's sake: because
it hath pleased the LORD to make you his
people.
23Moreover as for me, God forbid that I
should sin against the LORD in ceasing to
pray for you: but I will teach you the good
and the right way:
24Only fear the LORD, and serve him in
truth with all your heart: for consider how
great *things* he hath done for you.
25But if ye shall
still do wickedly, ye
shall be consumed,
both ye and your
king.

12:25 Warning!
◄ Joshua 23:15
1 Kings 9:7 ►

13
1Saul reigned one
year; and when he had reigned two years
over Israel,
2Saul chose him three thousand *men* of
Israel; *whereof* two thousand were with Saul
in Michmash and in mount Bethel, and a
thousand were with Jonathan in Gibeah
of Benjamin: and the rest of the people he
sent every man to his tent.
3And Jonathan smote the garrison of the
Philistines that *was* in Geba, and the Philistines heard *of it.* And Saul blew the trumpet throughout all the land, saying, Let the
Hebrews hear.
4And all Israel heard say *that* Saul had
smitten a garrison of the Philistines, and
that Israel also was had in abomination
with the Philistines. And the people were
called together after Saul to Gilgal.
5And the Philistines gathered themselves
together to fight with Israel, thirty thousand chariots, and six thousand horsemen,
and people as the sand which *is* on the sea
shore in multitude: and they came up, and
pitched in Michmash, eastward from Beth-
aven.
6When the men of Israel saw that they
were in a strait, (for the people were distressed,) then the people did hide themselves in caves, and in thickets, and in
rocks, and in high places, and in pits.
7And *some of* the Hebrews went over Jordan to the land of Gad and Gilead. As for
Saul, he *was* yet in Gilgal, and all the people followed him trembling.
8And he tarried seven days, according to
the set time that Samuel *had appointed*: but
Samuel came not to Gilgal; and the people were scattered from him.
9And Saul said, Bring hither a burnt offering to me, and peace offerings. And he
offered the burnt offering.
10And it came to pass, that as soon as
he had made an end of offering the burnt
offering, behold, Samuel came; and Saul
went out to meet him, that he might salute him.
11And Samuel said, What hast thou
done? And Saul said, Because I saw that
the people were scattered from me, and
that thou camest not within the days appointed, and *that* the Philistines gathered
themselves together at Michmash;
12Therefore said
I, The Philistines
will come down
now upon me to
Gilgal, and I have
not made supplica-
tion unto the LORD: I forced myself therefore, and offered a burnt offering.

13:12 Giving In
◄ Judges 16:17
1 Kings 11:1 ►

13And Samuel said to Saul, Thou hast
done foolishly: thou hast not kept the
commandment of the LORD thy God,
which he commanded thee: for now would
the LORD have established thy kingdom
upon Israel for ever.
14But now thy kingdom shall not continue: the LORD hath sought him a man
after his own heart, and the LORD hath
commanded him *to be* captain over his
people, because thou hast not kept *that*
which the LORD commanded thee.
15And Samuel arose, and gat him up
from Gilgal unto Gibeah of Benjamin.
And Saul numbered the people *that*
were present with him, about six hundred
men.
16And Saul, and Jonathan his son, and
the people *that were* present with them,
abode in Gibeah of Benjamin: but the
Philistines encamped in Michmash.
17And the spoilers came out of the camp
of the Philistines in three companies: one

company turned unto the way *that leadeth*
to Ophrah, unto the land of Shual:
18 And another company turned the way
to Beth-horon: and another company
turned *to* the way of the border that
looketh to the valley of Zeboim toward the
wilderness.
19 Now there was no smith found
throughout all the land of Israel: for the
Philistines said, Lest the Hebrews make
them swords or spears:
20 But all the Israelites went down to the
Philistines, to sharpen every man his share,
and his coulter, and his axe, and his mattock.
21 Yet they had a file for the mattocks,
and for the coulters, and for the forks, and
for the axes, and to sharpen the goads.
22 So it came to pass in the day of battle,
that there was neither sword nor spear
found in the hand of any of the people
that *were* with Saul and Jonathan: but with
Saul and with Jonathan his son was there
found.
23 And the garrison of the Philistines
went out to the passage of Michmash.

14

1 Now it came to pass upon a day, that
Jonathan the son of Saul said unto the
young man that bare his armour, Come,
and let us go over to the Philistines' garrison, that *is* on the other side. But he told
not his father.
2 And Saul tarried in the uttermost part
of Gibeah under a pomegranate tree which
is in Migron: and the people that *were* with
him *were* about six hundred men;
3 And Ahiah, the son of Ahitub, I-
chabod's brother, the son of Phinehas, the
son of Eli, the LORD'S priest in Shiloh,
wearing an ephod. And the people knew
not that Jonathan was gone.
4 And between the passages, by which
Jonathan sought to go over unto the Philistines' garrison, *there was* a sharp rock on
the one side and a sharp rock on the other
side: and the name of the one *was* Bozez,
and the name of the other Seneh.
5 The forefront of the one *was* situate
northward over against Michmash, and
the other south-
ward over against
Gibeah.
6 And Jonathan
said to the young
man that bare his
armour, Come, and let us go over unto the
garrison of these uncircumcised: it may be
that the LORD will work for us: for *there is*
no restraint to the LORD to save by many
or by few.
7 And his armourbearer said unto him,
Do all that *is* in thine heart: turn thee; behold, I *am* with thee according to thy heart.
8 Then said Jonathan, Behold, we will
pass over unto *these* men, and we will discover ourselves unto them.
9 If they say thus unto us, Tarry until we
come to you; then we will stand still in
our place, and will not go up unto them.
10 But if they say thus, Come up unto us;
then we will go up: for the LORD hath delivered them into our hand: and this *shall*
be a sign unto us.
11 And both of them discovered themselves unto the garrison of the Philistines:
and the Philistines said, Behold, the Hebrews come forth out of the holes where
they had hid themselves.
12 And the men of the garrison answered
Jonathan and his armourbearer, and said,
Come up to us, and we will shew you a
thing. And Jonathan said unto his armourbearer, Come up after me: for the LORD
hath delivered them into the hand of
Israel.
13 And Jonathan climbed up upon his
hands and upon his feet, and his armourbearer after him: and they fell before
Jonathan; and his armourbearer slew after him.
14 And that first slaughter, which Jonathan and his armourbearer made, was
about twenty men, within as it were an half
acre of land, *which* a yoke *of oxen might*
plow.
15 And there was trembling in the host,
in the field, and among all the people: the
garrison, and the spoilers, they also trembled, and the earth quaked: so it was a very
great trembling.
16 And the watchmen of Saul in Gibeah
of Benjamin looked; and, behold, the
multitude melted away, and they went on
beating down *one another.*
17 Then said Saul unto the people that
were with him, Number now, and see who
is gone from us. And when they had numbered, behold, Jonathan and his armourbearer *were* not *there.*
18 And Saul said unto Ahiah, Bring hither

14:6-7 Teamwork
◄ Judges 20:11
2 Kings 6:1-3 ►

the ark of God. For the ark of God was at that time with the children of Israel.

19 And it came to pass, while Saul talked unto the priest, that the noise that *was* in the host of the Philistines went on and increased: and Saul said unto the priest, Withdraw thine hand.

20 And Saul and all the people that *were* with him assembled themselves, and they came to the battle: and, behold, every man's sword was against his fellow, *and there was* a very great discomfiture.

21 Moreover the Hebrews *that* were with the Philistines before that time, which went up with them into the camp *from the country* round about, even they also *turned* to be with the Israelites that *were* with Saul and Jonathan.

22 Likewise all the men of Israel which had hid themselves in mount Ephraim, *when* they heard that the Philistines fled, even they also followed hard after them in the battle.

23 So the LORD saved Israel that day: and the battle passed over unto Beth-aven.

24 And the men of Israel were distressed that day: for Saul had adjured the people, saying, Cursed *be* the man that eateth *any* food until evening, that I may be avenged on mine enemies. So none of the people tasted *any* food.

25 And all *they of* the land came to a wood; and there was honey upon the ground.

26 And when the people were come into the wood, behold, the honey dropped; but no man put his hand to his mouth: for the people feared the oath.

27 But Jonathan heard not when his father charged the people with the oath: wherefore he put forth the end of the rod that *was* in his hand, and dipped it in an honeycomb, and put his hand to his mouth; and his eyes were enlightened.

28 Then answered one of the people, and said, Thy father straitly charged the people with an oath, saying, Cursed *be* the man that eateth *any* food this day. And the people were faint.

29 Then said Jonathan, My father hath troubled the land: see, I pray you, how mine eyes have been enlightened, because I tasted a little of this honey.

30 How much more, if haply the people had eaten freely to day of the spoil of their enemies which they found? for had there not been now a much greater slaughter among the Philistines?

31 And they smote the Philistines that day from Michmash to Aijalon: and the people were very faint.

32 And the people flew upon the spoil, and took sheep, and oxen, and calves, and slew *them* on the ground: and the people did eat *them* with the blood.

33 Then they told Saul, saying, Behold, the people sin against the LORD, in that they eat with the blood. And he said, Ye have transgressed: roll a great stone unto me this day.

34 And Saul said, Disperse yourselves among the people, and say unto them, Bring me hither every man his ox, and every man his sheep, and slay *them* here, and eat; and sin not against the LORD in eating with the blood. And all the people brought every man his ox with him that night, and slew *them* there.

35 And Saul built an altar unto the LORD: the same was the first altar that he built unto the LORD.

36 And Saul said, Let us go down after the Philistines by night, and spoil them until the morning light, and let us not leave a man of them. And they said, Do whatsoever seemeth good unto thee. Then said the priest, Let us draw near hither unto God.

37 And Saul asked counsel of God, Shall I go down after the Philistines? wilt thou deliver them into the hand of Israel? But he answered him not that day.

14:37
Unanswered Prayer
◄ Deuteronomy 1:45
1 Samuel 28:6 ►

38 And Saul said, Draw ye near hither, all the chief of the people: and know and see wherein this sin hath been this day.

39 For, *as* the LORD liveth, which saveth Israel, though it be in Jonathan my son, he shall surely die. But *there was* not a man among all the people *that* answered him.

40 Then said he unto all Israel, Be ye on one side, and I and Jonathan my son will be on the other side. And the people said unto Saul, Do what seemeth good unto thee.

41 Therefore Saul said unto the LORD God of Israel, Give a perfect *lot*. And Saul and

Jonathan were taken: but the people escaped.
42And Saul said, Cast *lots* between me
and Jonathan my son. And Jonathan was
taken.
43Then Saul said to Jonathan, Tell me
what thou hast done. And Jonathan told
him, and said, I did but taste a little honey with the end of the rod that *was* in mine
hand, *and,* lo, I must die.
44And Saul answered, God do so and
more also: for thou shalt surely die, Jonathan.
45And the people
said unto Saul,
Shall Jonathan die,
who hath wrought
this great salvation
in Israel? God for-
bid: *as* the LORD
liveth, there shall
not one hair of his
head fall to the
ground; for he hath
wrought with God
this day. So the peo-
ple rescued Jona-
than, that he died
not.
46Then Saul went
up from following
the Philistines: and the Philistines went to
their own place.

14:45 "Thank You"
◄ Ruth 2:10
1 Samuel 15:6 ►

14:45
The Crowd
◄ 1 Samuel 15:24 ►

14:45
Working with God
◄ Mark 16:20 ►

47So Saul took the kingdom over Israel,
and fought against all his enemies on every
side, against Moab, and against the children of Ammon, and against Edom, and
against the kings of Zobah, and against the
Philistines: and whithersoever he turned
himself, he vexed *them.*
48And he gathered an host, and smote
the Amalekites, and delivered Israel out of
the hands of them that spoiled them.
49Now the sons of Saul were Jonathan,
and Ishui, and Melchi-shua: and the names
of his two daughters *were these;* the name
of the firstborn Merab, and the name of
the younger Michal:
50And the name of Saul's wife *was* Ahinoam, the daughter of Ahimaaz: and the
name of the captain of his host *was* Abner,
the son of Ner, Saul's uncle.
51And Kish *was* the father of Saul; and
Ner the father of Abner *was* the son of
Abiel.
52And there was sore war against the
Philistines all the days of Saul: and when
Saul saw any strong man, or any valiant
man, he took him unto him.

15

1Samuel also said unto Saul, The LORD
sent me to anoint thee *to be* king over his
people, over Israel: now therefore hearken
thou unto the voice of the words of the
LORD.
2Thus saith the LORD of hosts, I remember *that* which Amalek did to Israel, how
he laid *wait* for him in the way, when he
came up from Egypt.
3Now go and smite Amalek, and utterly
destroy all that they have, and spare them
not; but slay both man and woman, infant and suckling, ox and sheep, camel and
ass.
4And Saul gathered the people together, and numbered them in Telaim, two
hundred thousand footmen, and ten thousand men of Judah.
5And Saul came to a city of Amalek, and
laid wait in the valley.
6And Saul said
unto the Kenites,
Go, depart, get you
down from among
the Amalekites, lest
I destroy you with
them: for ye shewed kindness to all the
children of Israel, when they came up out
of Egypt. So the Kenites departed from
among the Amalekites.

15:6 "Thank You"
◄ 1 Samuel 14:45
2 Samuel 9:1 ►

7And Saul smote the Amalekites from
Havilah *until* thou comest to Shur, that *is*
over against Egypt.
8And he took Agag the king of the Amalekites alive, and utterly destroyed all the
people with the edge of the sword.
9But Saul and the people spared Agag,
and the best of the sheep, and of the oxen,
and of the fatlings, and the lambs, and all
that was good, and would not utterly destroy them: but every thing *that was* vile
and refuse, that they destroyed utterly.
10Then came the word of the LORD unto
Samuel, saying,
11It repenteth me
that I have set up
Saul *to be* king: for
he is turned back
from following me,
and hath not per-
formed my commandments. And it grieved

15:11 Praying Alone
◄ Deuteronomy 9:25
1 Kings 17:19-20 ►

Samuel; and he cried unto the LORD all
night.
12 And when Samuel rose early to meet
Saul in the morning, it was told Samuel,
saying, Saul came to Carmel, and, behold,
he set him up a place, and is gone about,
and passed on, and gone down to Gilgal.
13 And Samuel came to Saul: and Saul
said unto him, Blessed *be* thou of the LORD:
I have performed the commandment of
the LORD.
14 And Samuel said, What *meaneth* then
this bleating of the sheep in mine ears, and
the lowing of the oxen which I hear?
15 And Saul said, They have brought
them from the Amalekites: for the people
spared the best of the sheep and of the
oxen, to sacrifice unto the LORD thy God;
and the rest we have utterly destroyed.
16 Then Samuel said unto Saul, Stay, and
I will tell thee what the LORD hath said
to me this night. And he said unto him,
Say on.
17 And Samuel said, When thou *wast* little in thine own sight, *wast* thou not *made*
the head of the tribes of Israel, and the
LORD anointed thee king over Israel?
18 And the LORD sent thee on a journey,
and said, Go and utterly destroy the sinners the Amalekites, and fight against them
until they be consumed.
19 Wherefore then didst thou not obey
the voice of the LORD, but didst fly upon
the spoil, and didst evil in the sight of the
LORD?
20 And Saul said unto Samuel, Yea, I have
obeyed the voice of the LORD, and have
gone the way which the LORD sent me, and
have brought Agag the king of Amalek, and
have utterly destroyed the Amalekites.
21 But the people
took of the spoil,
sheep and oxen, the
chief of the things
which should have
been utterly de-
stroyed, to sacrifice unto the LORD thy God
in Gilgal.

15:21 "It's Her Fault!"
◄ Exodus 32:22
Matthew 27:24 ►

22 And Samuel
said, Hath the LORD
as great delight in
burnt offerings and
sacrifices, as in
obeying the voice
of the LORD? Behold, to obey *is* better than
sacrifice, *and* to hearken than the fat of
rams.

15:22 Obeying God
◄ Joshua 1:8
Jeremiah 7:23 ►

23 For rebellion *is as* the sin of witchcraft,
and stubbornness *is as* iniquity and idolatry. Because thou hast rejected the word of
the LORD, he hath also rejected thee from
being king.
24 And Saul said
unto Samuel, I have
sinned: for I have
transgressed the
commandment of
the LORD, and thy
words: because I feared the people, and
obeyed their voice.

15:24 The Crowd
◄ 1 Samuel 14:45
Matthew 14:5 ►

25 Now therefore, I pray thee, pardon my
sin, and turn again with me, that I may
worship the LORD.
26 And Samuel said unto Saul, I will not
return with thee: for thou hast rejected the
word of the LORD, and the LORD hath rejected thee from being king over Israel.
27 And as Samuel turned about to go
away, he laid hold upon the skirt of his
mantle, and it rent.
28 And Samuel said unto him, The LORD
hath rent the kingdom of Israel from thee
this day, and hath given it to a neighbour
of thine, *that is* better than thou.
29 And also the Strength of Israel will not
lie nor repent: for he *is* not a man, that he
should repent.
30 Then he said, I have sinned: *yet* honour
me now, I pray thee, before the elders of
my people, and before Israel, and turn
again with me, that I may worship the
LORD thy God.
31 So Samuel turned again after Saul; and
Saul worshipped the LORD.
32 Then said Samuel, Bring ye hither to
me Agag the king of the Amalekites. And
Agag came unto him delicately. And Agag
said, Surely the bitterness of death is past.
33 And Samuel said, As thy sword hath
made women childless, so shall thy mother be childless among women. And Samuel hewed Agag in pieces before the LORD
in Gilgal.
34 Then Samuel went to Ramah; and Saul
went up to his house to Gibeah of Saul.
35 And Samuel came no more to see Saul
until the day of his death: nevertheless
Samuel mourned for Saul: and the LORD
repented that he had made Saul king over
Israel.

16

1 And the LORD said unto Samuel, How long wilt thou mourn for Saul, seeing I have rejected him from reigning over Israel? fill thine horn with oil, and go, I will send thee to Jesse the Bethlehemite: for I have provided me a king among his sons.

2 And Samuel said, How can I go? if Saul hear *it,* he will kill me. And the LORD said, Take an heifer with thee, and say, I am come to sacrifice to the LORD.

3 And call Jesse to the sacrifice, and I will shew thee what thou shalt do: and thou shalt anoint unto me *him* whom I name unto thee.

4 And Samuel did that which the LORD spake, and came to Bethlehem. And the elders of the town trembled at his coming, and said, Comest thou peaceably?

5 And he said, Peaceably: I am come to sacrifice unto the LORD: sanctify yourselves, and come with me to the sacrifice. And he sanctified Jesse and his sons, and called them to the sacrifice.

6 And it came to pass, when they were come, that he looked on Eliab, and said, Surely the LORD'S anointed *is* before him.

7 But the LORD said unto Samuel, Look not on his countenance, or on the height of his stature; because I have refused him: for *the LORD seeth* not as man seeth; for man looketh on the outward appearance, but the LORD looketh on the heart.

16:7
Good Looks
◄ Matthew 23:27 ►

8 Then Jesse called Abinadab, and made him pass before Samuel. And he said, Neither hath the LORD chosen this.

9 Then Jesse made Shammah to pass by. And he said, Neither hath the LORD chosen this.

10 Again, Jesse made seven of his sons to pass before Samuel. And Samuel said unto Jesse, The LORD hath not chosen these.

11 And Samuel said unto Jesse, Are here all *thy* children? And he said, There remaineth yet the youngest, and, behold, he keepeth the sheep. And Samuel said unto Jesse, Send and fetch him: for we will not sit down till he come hither.

12 And he sent, and brought him in. Now he *was* ruddy, *and* withal of a beautiful countenance, and goodly to look to. And the LORD said, Arise, anoint him: for this *is* he.

13 Then Samuel took the horn of oil, and anointed him in the midst of his brethren: and the Spirit of the LORD came upon David from that day forward. So Samuel rose up, and went to Ramah.

14 But the Spirit of the LORD departed from Saul, and an evil spirit from the LORD troubled him.

15 And Saul's servants said unto him, Behold now, an evil spirit from God troubleth thee.

16 Let our lord now command thy servants, *which are* before thee, to seek out a man, *who is* a cunning player on an harp: and it shall come to pass, when the evil spirit from God is upon thee, that he shall play with his hand, and thou shalt be well.

17 And Saul said unto his servants, Provide me now a man that can play well, and bring *him* to me.

18 Then answered one of the servants, and said, Behold, I have seen a son of Jesse the Bethlehemite, *that is* cunning in playing, and a mighty valiant man, and a man of war, and prudent in matters, and a comely person, and the LORD *is* with him.

19 Wherefore Saul sent messengers unto Jesse, and said, Send me David thy son, which *is* with the sheep.

20 And Jesse took an ass *laden* with bread, and a bottle of wine, and a kid, and sent *them* by David his son unto Saul.

21 And David came to Saul, and stood before him: and he loved him greatly; and he became his armourbearer.

22 And Saul sent to Jesse, saying, Let David, I pray thee, stand before me; for he hath found favour in my sight.

23 And it came to pass, when the *evil* spirit from God was upon Saul, that David took an harp, and played with his hand: so Saul was refreshed, and was well, and the evil spirit departed from him.

17

1 Now the Philistines gathered together their armies to battle, and were gathered together at Shochoh, which *belongeth* to Judah, and pitched between Shochoh and Azekah, in Ephes-dammim.

2 And Saul and the men of Israel were gathered together, and pitched by the valley of Elah, and set the battle in array against the Philistines.

3 And the Philistines stood on a mountain

on the one side, and Israel stood on a mountain on the other side: and *there was* a valley between them.

4 And there went out a champion out of the camp of the Philistines, named Goliath, of Gath, whose height *was* six cubits and a span.

5 And *he had* an helmet of brass upon his head, and he *was* armed with a coat of mail; and the weight of the coat *was* five thousand shekels of brass.

6 And *he had* greaves of brass upon his legs, and a target of brass between his shoulders.

7 And the staff of his spear *was* like a weaver's beam; and his spear's head *weighed* six hundred shekels of iron: and one bearing a shield went before him.

8 And he stood and cried unto the armies of Israel, and said unto them, Why are ye come out to set *your* battle in array? *am* not I a Philistine, and ye servants to Saul? choose you a man for you, and let him come down to me.

9 If he be able to fight with me, and to kill me, then will we be your servants: but if I prevail against him, and kill him, then shall ye be our servants, and serve us.

10 And the Philistine said, I defy the armies of Israel this day; give me a man, that we may fight together.

11 When Saul and all Israel heard those words of the Philistine, they were dismayed, and greatly afraid.

12 Now David *was* the son of that Ephrathite of Bethlehemjudah, whose name *was* Jesse; and he had eight sons: and the man went among men *for* an old man in the days of Saul.

13 And the three eldest sons of Jesse went *and* followed Saul to the battle: and the names of his three sons that went to the battle *were* Eliab the first born, and next unto him Abinadab, and the third Shammah.

14 And David *was* the youngest: and the three eldest followed Saul.

15 But David went and returned from Saul to feed his father's sheep at Bethlehem.

16 And the Philistine drew near morning and evening, and presented himself forty days.

17 And Jesse said unto David his son, Take now for thy brethren an ephah of this parched *corn,* and these ten loaves, and run to the camp to thy brethren;

18 And carry these ten cheeses unto the captain of *their* thousand, and look how thy brethren fare, and take their pledge.

19 Now Saul, and they, and all the men of Israel, *were* in the valley of Elah, fighting with the Philistines.

20 And David rose up early in the morning, and left the sheep with a keeper, and took, and went, as Jesse had commanded him; and he came to the trench, as the host was going forth to the fight, and shouted for the battle.

21 For Israel and the Philistines had put the battle in array, army against army.

22 And David left his carriage in the hand of the keeper of the carriage, and ran into the army, and came and saluted his brethren.

23 And as he talked with them, behold, there came up the champion, the Philistine of Gath, Goliath by name, out of the armies of the Philistines, and spake according to the same words: and David heard *them.*

24 And all the men of Israel, when they saw the man, fled from him, and were sore afraid.

17:24 Cost of Sin
◄ Judges 16:17
Jeremiah 51:30 ►

25 And the men of Israel said, Have ye seen this man that is come up? surely to defy Israel is he come up: and it shall be, *that* the man who killeth him, the king will enrich him with great riches, and will give him his daughter, and make his father's house free in Israel.

26 And David spake to the men that stood by him, saying, What shall be done to the man that killeth this Philistine, and taketh away the reproach from Israel? for who *is* this uncircumcised Philistine, that he should defy the armies of the living God?

27 And the people answered him after this manner, saying, So shall it be done to the man that killeth him.

28 And Eliab his eldest brother heard when he spake unto the men; and Eliab's anger was kindled against David, and he said, Why camest thou down hither? and with whom hast thou left those few sheep in the wilderness? I know thy pride, and

the naughtiness of thine heart; for thou
art come down that thou mightest see the
battle.
29 And David said, What have I now
done? *Is there* not a cause?
30 And he turned from him toward another, and spake after the same manner:
and the people answered him again after
the former manner.
31 And when the words were heard which
David spake, they rehearsed *them* before
Saul: and he sent for him.
32 And David said to Saul, Let no man's
heart fail because of him; thy servant will
go and fight with this Philistine.
33 And Saul said
to David, Thou art
not able to go
against this Philis-
tine to fight with
him: for thou *art but*
a youth, and he a
man of war from
his youth.
34 And David said
unto Saul, Thy ser-
vant kept his fa-
ther's sheep, and
there came a lion, and a bear, and took a
lamb out of the flock:

17:33 Young Men
◄ 1 Samuel 3:1
1 Samuel 17:37 ►

17:33 Young Leaders
◄ Genesis 41:46
2 Samuel 5:4 ►

35 And I went out after him, and smote
him, and delivered *it* out of his mouth:
and when he arose against me, I caught
him by his beard, and smote him, and slew
him.
36 Thy servant slew both the lion and the
bear: and this uncircumcised Philistine
shall be as one of them, seeing he hath
defied the armies of the living God.
37 David said
moreover, The LORD
that delivered me
out of the paw of
the lion, and out of
the paw of the bear,
he will deliver me out of the hand of this
Philistine. And Saul said unto David, Go,
and the LORD be with thee.

17:37 Young Men
◄ 1 Samuel 17:33
2 Chronicles 24:1-2 ►

38 And Saul armed David with his
armour, and he put an helmet of brass
upon his head; also he armed him with a
coat of mail.
39 And David girded his sword upon his
armour, and he assayed to go; for he had
not proved *it*. And David said unto Saul, I
cannot go with these; for I have not proved
them. And David put them off him.
40 And he took his staff in his hand, and
chose him five smooth stones out of the
brook, and put them in a shepherd's bag
which he had, even in a scrip; and his sling
was in his hand: and he drew near to the
Philistine.
41 And the Philistine came on and drew
near unto David; and the man that bare
the shield *went* before him.
42 And when the Philistine looked about,
and saw David, he disdained him: for he
was *but* a youth, and ruddy, and of a fair
countenance.
43 And the Philistine said unto David,
Am I a dog, that thou comest to me with
staves? And the Philistine cursed David by
his gods.
44 And the Philistine said to David,
Come to me, and I will give thy flesh unto
the fowls of the air, and to the beasts of
the field.
45 Then said David to the Philistine,
Thou comest to me with a sword, and with
a spear, and with a shield: but I come to
thee in the name of the LORD of hosts, the
God of the armies of Israel, whom thou
hast defied.
46 This day will the LORD deliver thee
into mine hand; and I will smite thee, and
take thine head from thee; and I will give
the carcases of the host of the Philistines
this day unto the fowls of the air, and to
the wild beasts of the earth; that all the
earth may know that there is a God in Israel.
47 And all this assembly shall know that
the LORD saveth not with sword and spear:
for the battle *is* the LORD'S, and he will give
you into our hands.
48 And it came to pass, when the Philistine arose, and came and drew nigh to
meet David, that David hasted, and ran
toward the army to meet the Philistine.
49 And David put his hand in his bag,
and took thence a stone, and slang *it*, and
smote the Philistine in his forehead, that
the stone sunk into his forehead; and he
fell upon his face to the earth.
50 So David prevailed over the Philistine
with a sling and with a stone, and smote
the Philistine, and slew him; but *there was*
no sword in the hand of David.
51 Therefore David ran, and stood upon

the Philistine, and took his sword, and
drew it out of the sheath thereof, and slew
him, and cut off his head therewith. And
when the Philistines saw their champion
was dead, they fled.
52 And the men of Israel and of Judah
arose, and shouted, and pursued the Philistines, until thou come to the valley, and
to the gates of Ekron. And the wounded
of the Philistines fell down by the way
to Shaaraim, even unto Gath, and unto
Ekron.
53 And the children of Israel returned
from chasing after the Philistines, and they
spoiled their tents.
54 And David took the head of the Philistine, and brought it to Jerusalem; but
he put his armour in his tent.
55 And when Saul saw David go forth
against the Philistine, he said unto Abner,
the captain of the host, Abner, whose son
is this youth? And Abner said, *As* thy soul
liveth, O king, I cannot tell.
56 And the king said, Enquire thou
whose son the stripling *is*.
57 And as David returned from the
slaughter of the Philistine, Abner took
him, and brought him before Saul with
the head of the Philistine in his hand.
58 And Saul said to him, Whose son *art*
thou, *thou* young man? And David answered, *I am* the son of thy servant Jesse
the Bethlehemite.

18

1 And it came to
pass, when he had
made an end of
speaking unto Saul,
that the soul of Jon-
athan was knit with
the soul of David, and Jonathan loved him
as his own soul.

> **18:1**
> **Good Friends**
> ◄ 1 Samuel 20:41 ►

2 And Saul took him that day, and would
let him go no more home to his father's
house.
3 Then Jonathan
and David made a
covenant, because
he loved him as his
own soul.

> **18:3**
> **Love for Friends**
> ◄ Acts 20:38 ►

4 And Jonathan
stripped himself of
the robe that *was*
upon him, and gave
it to David, and his
garments, even to
his sword, and to his bow, and to his girdle.

> **18:4 Unselfishness**
> ◄ Numbers 11:29
> 1 Samuel 23:17 ►

5 And David went out whithersoever Saul
sent him, *and* behaved himself wisely: and
Saul set him over the men of war, and he
was accepted in the sight of all the people,
and also in the sight of Saul's servants.
6 And it came to pass as they came, when
David was returned from the slaughter of
the Philistine, that the women came out
of all cities of Israel, singing and dancing,
to meet king Saul, with tabrets, with joy,
and with instruments of musick.
7 And the women answered *one another*
as they played, and said, Saul hath slain
his thousands, and David his ten thousands.
8 And Saul was
very wroth, and the
saying displeased
him; and he said,
They have ascribed
unto David ten
thousands, and to me they have ascribed
but thousands: and *what* can he have more
but the kingdom?

> **18:8 Mad**
> ◄ Genesis 4:5
> 2 Kings 5:12 ►

9 And Saul eyed David from that day and
forward.
10 And it came to pass on the morrow,
that the evil spirit from God came upon
Saul, and he prophesied in the midst of
the house: and David played with his
hand, as at other times: and *there was* a
javelin in Saul's hand.
11 And Saul cast the javelin; for he said, I
will smite David even to the wall *with it*.
And David avoided out of his presence
twice.
12 And Saul was afraid of David, because
the LORD was with him, and was departed
from Saul.
13 Therefore Saul removed him from
him, and made him his captain over a
thousand; and he went out and came in
before the people.
14 And David behaved himself wisely in
all his ways; and the LORD *was* with him.
15 Wherefore when Saul saw that he behaved himself very wisely, he was afraid
of him.
16 But all Israel and Judah loved David,
because he went out and came in before
them.
17 And Saul said to David, Behold my
elder daughter Merab, her will I give thee
to wife: only be thou valiant for me, and

fight the LORD'S battles. For Saul said, Let
not mine hand be upon him, but let the
hand of the Philistines be upon him.
18 And David said unto Saul, Who *am* I?
and what *is* my life, *or* my father's family
in Israel, that I should be son in law to the
king?
19 But it came to pass at the time when
Merab Saul's daughter should have been
given to David, that she was given unto
Adriel the Meholathite to wife.
20 And Michal Saul's daughter loved David: and they told Saul, and the thing
pleased him.
21 And Saul said, I will give him her, that
she may be a snare to him, and that the
hand of the Philistines may be against him.
Wherefore Saul said to David, Thou shalt
this day be my son in law in *the one of* the
twain.
22 And Saul commanded his servants,
saying, Commune with David secretly, and
say, Behold, the king hath delight in thee,
and all his servants love thee: now therefore be the king's son in law.
23 And Saul's servants spake those words
in the ears of David. And David said,
Seemeth it to you *a* light *thing* to be a king's
son in law, seeing that I *am* a poor man,
and lightly esteemed?
24 And the servants of Saul told him, saying, On this manner spake David.
25 And Saul said, Thus shall ye say to
David, The king desireth not any dowry,
but an hundred foreskins of the Philistines, to be avenged of the king's enemies.
But Saul thought to make David fall by
the hand of the Philistines.
26 And when his servants told David
these words, it pleased David well to be
the king's son in law: and the days were
not expired.
27 Wherefore David arose and went, he
and his men, and slew of the Philistines
two hundred men; and David brought
their foreskins, and they gave them in full
tale to the king, that he might be the king's
son in law. And Saul gave him Michal his
daughter to wife.
28 And Saul saw and knew that the LORD
was with David, and *that* Michal Saul's
daughter loved him.
29 And Saul was yet the more afraid of
David; and Saul became David's enemy
continually.
30 Then the princes of the Philistines
went forth: and it came to pass, after they
went forth, *that* David behaved himself
more wisely than all the servants of Saul;
so that his name was much set by.

19

1 And Saul spake to Jonathan his son,
and to all his servants, that they should
kill David.
2 But Jonathan Saul's son delighted
much in David: and Jonathan told David,
saying, Saul my father seeketh to kill thee:
now therefore, I pray thee, take heed to
thyself until the morning, and abide in a
secret *place,* and hide thyself:
3 And I will go out and stand beside my
father in the field where thou *art,* and I
will commune with my father of thee; and
what I see, that I will tell thee.
4 And Jonathan
spake good of Da-
vid unto Saul his
father, and said
unto him, Let not
the king sin against
his servant, against David; because he hath
not sinned against thee, and because his
works *have been* to thee-ward very good:
5 For he did put his life in his hand, and
slew the Philistine, and the LORD wrought
a great salvation for all Israel: thou sawest
it, and didst rejoice: wherefore then wilt
thou sin against innocent blood, to slay
David without a cause?
6 And Saul hearkened unto the voice of
Jonathan: and Saul sware, *As* the LORD
liveth, he shall not be slain.
7 And Jonathan called David, and Jonathan shewed him all those things. And Jonathan brought David to Saul, and he was
in his presence, as in times past.
8 And there was war again: and David
went out, and fought with the Philistines,
and slew them with a great slaughter; and
they fled from him.
9 And the evil spirit from the LORD was
upon Saul, as he sat in his house with his
javelin in his hand: and David played with
his hand.
10 And Saul sought to smite David even
to the wall with the javelin; but he slipped
away out of Saul's presence, and he smote
the javelin into the wall: and David fled,
and escaped that night.
11 Saul also sent messengers unto David's
house, to watch him, and to slay him in

19:4 Helping Friends
◄ Genesis 44:33
1 Samuel 25:24 ►

the morning: and Michal David's wife told
him, saying, If thou save not thy life to
night, to morrow thou shalt be slain.
12 So Michal let David down through a
window: and he went, and fled, and escaped.
13 And Michal took an image, and laid *it*
in the bed, and put a pillow of goats' *hair*
for his bolster, and covered *it* with a cloth.
14 And when Saul sent messengers to
take David, she said, He *is* sick.
15 And Saul sent the messengers *again* to
see David, saying, Bring him up to me in
the bed, that I may slay him.
16 And when the messengers were come
in, behold, *there was* an image in the bed,
with a pillow of goats' *hair* for his bolster.
17 And Saul said unto Michal, Why hast
thou deceived me so, and sent away mine
enemy, that he is escaped? And Michal
answered Saul, He said unto me, Let me
go; why should I kill thee?
18 So David fled, and escaped, and came
to Samuel to Ramah, and told him all that
Saul had done to him. And he and Samuel went and dwelt in Naioth.
19 And it was told Saul, saying, Behold,
David *is* at Naioth in Ramah.
20 And Saul sent messengers to take David: and when they saw the company of
the prophets prophesying, and Samuel
standing *as* appointed over them, the Spirit
of God was upon the messengers of Saul,
and they also prophesied.
21 And when it was told Saul, he sent
other messengers, and they prophesied
likewise. And Saul sent messengers again
the third time, and they prophesied also.
22 Then went he also to Ramah, and
came to a great well that *is* in Sechu: and
he asked and said, Where *are* Samuel and
David? And *one* said, Behold, *they be* at
Naioth in Ramah.
23 And he went thither to Naioth in Ramah: and the Spirit of God was upon him
also, and he went on, and prophesied,
until he came to Naioth in Ramah.
24 And he stript off his clothes also, and
prophesied before Samuel in like manner,
and lay down naked all that day and all
that night. Wherefore they say, *Is* Saul also
among the prophets?

20

1 And David fled from Naioth in Ramah,
and came and said before Jonathan, What
have I done? what *is* mine iniquity? and
what *is* my sin before thy father, that he
seeketh my life?
2 And he said unto him, God forbid;
thou shalt not die: behold, my father will
do nothing either great or small, but that
he will shew it me: and why should my
father hide this thing from me? it *is* not *so*.
3 And David
sware moreover,
and said, Thy father
certainly knoweth
that I have found
grace in thine eyes;
and he saith, Let not Jonathan know this,
lest he be grieved: but truly *as* the LORD
liveth, and *as* thy soul liveth, *there is* but a
step between me and death.

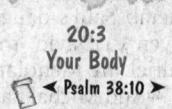

20:3
Your Body
◄ Psalm 38:10 ►

4 Then said Jonathan unto David, Whatsoever thy soul desireth, I will even do *it*
for thee.
5 And David said unto Jonathan, Behold,
to morrow *is* the new moon, and I should
not fail to sit with the king at meat: but let
me go, that I may hide myself in the field
unto the third *day* at even.
6 If thy father at all miss me, then say,
David earnestly asked *leave* of me that he
might run to Bethlehem his city: for *there*
is a yearly sacrifice there for all the family.
7 If he say thus, *It is* well; thy servant shall
have peace: but if he be very wroth, *then*
be sure that evil is determined by him.
8 Therefore thou shalt deal kindly with
thy servant; for thou hast brought thy servant into a covenant of the LORD with thee:
notwithstanding, if there be in me iniquity, slay me thyself; for why shouldest thou
bring me to thy father?
9 And Jonathan said, Far be it from thee:
for if I knew certainly that evil were determined by my father to come upon thee,
then would not I tell it thee?
10 Then said David to Jonathan, Who
shall tell me? or what *if* thy father answer
thee roughly?
11 And Jonathan said unto David, Come,
and let us go out into the field. And they
went out both of them into the field.
12 And Jonathan said unto David,
O LORD God of Israel, when I have sounded my father about to morrow any time,
or the third *day*, and, behold, *if there be*
good toward David, and I then send not
unto thee, and shew it thee;
13 The LORD do so and much more to

Jonathan: but if it please my father *to do* thee evil, then I will shew it thee, and send thee away, that thou mayest go in peace: and the LORD be with thee, as he hath been with my father.

14 And thou shalt not only while yet I live shew me the kindness of the LORD, that I die not:

15 But *also* thou shalt not cut off thy kindness from my house for ever: no, not when the LORD hath cut off the enemies of David every one from the face of the earth.

16 So Jonathan made *a covenant* with the house of David, *saying*, Let the LORD even require *it* at the hand of David's enemies.

17 And Jonathan caused David to swear again, because he loved him: for he loved him as he loved his own soul.

20:17 Being a Friend
◄ Ruth 1:16
2 Kings 2:2 ►

18 Then Jonathan said to David, To morrow *is* the new moon: and thou shalt be missed, because thy seat will be empty.

19 And *when* thou hast stayed three days, *then* thou shalt go down quickly, and come to the place where thou didst hide thyself when the business was *in hand*, and shalt remain by the stone Ezel.

20 And I will shoot three arrows on the side *thereof*, as though I shot at a mark.

21 And, behold, I will send a lad, *saying*, Go, find out the arrows. If I expressly say unto the lad, Behold, the arrows *are* on this side of thee, take them; then come thou: for *there is* peace to thee, and no hurt; *as* the LORD liveth.

22 But if I say thus unto the young man, Behold, the arrows *are* beyond thee; go thy way: for the LORD hath sent thee away.

23 And *as touching* the matter which thou and I have spoken of, behold, the LORD *be* between thee and me for ever.

24 So David hid himself in the field: and when the new moon was come, the king sat him down to eat meat.

25 And the king sat upon his seat, as at other times, *even* upon a seat by the wall: and Jonathan arose, and Abner sat by Saul's side, and David's place was empty.

26 Nevertheless Saul spake not any thing that day: for he thought, Something hath befallen him, he is not clean; surely he *is* not clean.

27 And it came to pass on the morrow, *which was* the second *day* of the month, that David's place was empty: and Saul said unto Jonathan his son, Wherefore cometh not the son of Jesse to meat, neither yesterday, nor to day?

28 And Jonathan answered Saul, David earnestly asked *leave* of me *to go* to Bethlehem:

29 And he said, Let me go, I pray thee; for our family hath a sacrifice in the city; and my brother, he hath commanded me *to be there*: and now, if I have found favour in thine eyes, let me get away, I pray thee, and see my brethren. Therefore he cometh not unto the king's table.

30 Then Saul's anger was kindled against Jonathan, and he said unto him, Thou son of the perverse rebellious *woman*, do not I know that thou hast chosen the son of Jesse to thine own confusion, and unto the confusion of thy mother's nakedness?

31 For as long as the son of Jesse liveth upon the ground, thou shalt not be established, nor thy kingdom. Wherefore now send and fetch him unto me, for he shall surely die.

32 And Jonathan answered Saul his father, and said unto him, Wherefore shall he be slain? what hath he done?

33 And Saul cast a javelin at him to smite him: whereby Jonathan knew that it was determined of his father to slay David.

34 So Jonathan arose from the table in fierce anger, and did eat no meat the second day of the month: for he was grieved for David, because his father had done him shame.

35 And it came to pass in the morning, that Jonathan went out into the field at the time appointed with David, and a little lad with him.

36 And he said unto his lad, Run, find out now the arrows which I shoot. *And* as the lad ran, he shot an arrow beyond him.

37 And when the lad was come to the place of the arrow which Jonathan had shot, Jonathan cried after the lad, and said, *Is* not the arrow beyond thee?

38 And Jonathan cried after the lad, Make speed, haste, stay not. And Jonathan's lad gathered up the arrows, and came to his master.

39 But the lad knew not any thing: only Jonathan and David knew the matter.

40And Jonathan gave his artillery unto his lad, and said unto him, Go, carry *them* to the city.

41*And* as soon as the lad was gone, David arose out of *a place* toward the south, and fell on his face to the ground, and bowed himself three times: and they kissed one another, and wept one with another, until David exceeded.

20:41 Good Friends
◄ 1 Samuel 18:1
2 Samuel 1:26 ►

42And Jonathan said to David, Go in peace, forasmuch as we have sworn both of us in the name of the LORD, saying, The LORD be between me and thee, and between my seed and thy seed for ever. And he arose and departed: and Jonathan went into the city.

21

1Then came David to Nob to Ahimelech the priest: and Ahimelech was afraid at the meeting of David, and said unto him, Why *art* thou alone, and no man with thee?

2And David said unto Ahimelech the priest, The king hath commanded me a business, and hath said unto me, Let no man know any thing of the business whereabout I send thee, and what I have commanded thee: and I have appointed *my* servants to such and such a place.

3Now therefore what is under thine hand? give *me* five *loaves of* bread in mine hand, or what there is present.

4And the priest answered David, and said, *There is* no common bread under mine hand, but there is hallowed bread; if the young men have kept themselves at least from women.

5And David answered the priest, and said unto him, Of a truth women *have been* kept from us about these three days, since I came out, and the vessels of the young men are holy, and *the bread is* in a manner common, yea, though it were sanctified this day in the vessel.

6So the priest gave him hallowed *bread:* for there was no bread there but the shewbread, that was taken from before the LORD, to put hot bread in the day when it was taken away.

7Now a certain man of the servants of Saul *was* there that day, detained before the LORD; and his name *was* Doeg, an Edomite, the chiefest of the herdmen that *belonged* to Saul.

8And David said unto Ahimelech, And is there not here under thine hand spear or sword? for I have neither brought my sword nor my weapons with me, because the king's business required haste.

21:8
Hurrying
◄ 2 Kings 4:29 ►

9And the priest said, The sword of Goliath the Philistine, whom thou slewest in the valley of Elah, behold, it *is here* wrapped in a cloth behind the ephod: if thou wilt take that, take *it:* for *there is* no other save that here. And David said, *There is* none like that; give it me.

10And David arose, and fled that day for fear of Saul, and went to Achish the king of Gath.

11And the servants of Achish said unto him, *Is* not this David the king of the land? did they not sing one to another of him in dances, saying, Saul hath slain his thousands, and David his ten thousands?

12And David laid up these words in his heart, and was sore afraid of Achish the king of Gath.

13And he changed his behaviour before them, and feigned himself mad in their hands, and scrabbled on the doors of the gate, and let his spittle fall down upon his beard.

14Then said Achish unto his servants, Lo, ye see the man is mad: wherefore *then* have ye brought him to me?

15Have I need of mad men, that ye have brought this *fellow* to play the mad man in my presence? shall this *fellow* come into my house?

22

1David therefore departed thence, and escaped to the cave Adullam: and when his brethren and all his father's house heard *it,* they went down thither to him.

2And every one *that was* in distress, and every one that *was* in debt, and every one *that was* discontented, gathered themselves unto him; and he became a captain over them: and there were with him about four hundred men.

3And David went thence to Mizpeh of Moab: and he said unto the king of Moab, Let my father and my mother, I pray thee, come forth, *and be* with you, till I know what God will do for me.

4And he brought them before the king

of Moab: and they dwelt with him all the while that David was in the hold.

5And the prophet Gad said unto David, Abide not in the hold; depart, and get thee into the land of Judah. Then David departed, and came into the forest of Hareth.

6When Saul heard that David was discovered, and the men that *were* with him, (now Saul abode in Gibeah under a tree in Ramah, having his spear in his hand, and all his servants *were* standing about him;)

7Then Saul said unto his servants that stood about him, Hear now, ye Benjamites; will the son of Jesse give every one of you fields and vineyards, *and* make you all captains of thousands, and captains of hundreds;

8That all of you have conspired against me, and *there is* none that sheweth me that my son hath made a league with the son of Jesse, and *there is* none of you that is sorry for me, or sheweth unto me that my son hath stirred up my servant against me, to lie in wait, as at this day?

9Then answered Doeg the Edomite, which was set over the servants of Saul, and said, I saw the son of Jesse coming to Nob, to Ahimelech the son of Ahitub.

10And he enquired of the LORD for him, and gave him victuals, and gave him the sword of Goliath the Philistine.

11Then the king sent to call Ahimelech the priest, the son of Ahitub, and all his father's house, the priests that *were* in Nob: and they came all of them to the king.

12And Saul said, Hear now, thou son of Ahitub. And he answered, Here I *am*, my lord.

13And Saul said unto him, Why have ye conspired against me, thou and the son of Jesse, in that thou hast given him bread, and a sword, and hast enquired of God for him, that he should rise against me, to lie in wait, as at this day?

14Then Ahimelech answered the king, and said, And who *is so* faithful among all thy servants as David, which is the king's son in law, and goeth at thy bidding, and is honourable in thine house?

15Did I then begin to enquire of God for him? be it far from me: let not the king impute *any* thing unto his servant, *nor* to all the house of my father: for thy servant knew nothing of all this, less or more.

16And the king said, Thou shalt surely die, Ahimelech, thou, and all thy father's house.

17And the king said unto the footmen that stood about him, Turn, and slay the priests of the LORD; because their hand also *is* with David, and because they knew when he fled, and did not shew it to me. But the servants of the king would not put forth their hand to fall upon the priests of the LORD.

18And the king said to Doeg, Turn thou, and fall upon the priests. And Doeg the Edomite turned, and he fell upon the priests, and slew on that day fourscore and five persons that did wear a linen ephod.

19And Nob, the city of the priests, smote he with the edge of the sword, both men and women, children and sucklings, and oxen, and asses, and sheep, with the edge of the sword.

20And one of the sons of Ahimelech the son of Ahitub, named Abiathar, escaped, and fled after David.

21And Abiathar shewed David that Saul had slain the LORD'S priests.

22And David said unto Abiathar, I knew *it* that day, when Doeg the Edomite *was* there, that he would surely tell Saul: I have occasioned *the death* of all the persons of thy father's house.

23Abide thou with me, fear not: for he that seeketh my life seeketh thy life: but with me thou *shalt be* in safeguard.

23

1Then they told David, saying, Behold, the Philistines fight against Keilah, and they rob the threshingfloors.

2Therefore David enquired of the LORD, saying, Shall I go and smite these Philistines? And the LORD said unto David, Go, and smite the Philistines, and save Keilah.

3And David's men said unto him, Behold, we be afraid here in Judah: how much more then if we come to Keilah against the armies of the Philistines?

4Then David enquired of the LORD yet again. And the LORD answered him and said, Arise, go down to Keilah; for I will deliver the Philistines into thine hand.

5So David and his men went to Keilah, and fought with the Philistines, and brought away their cattle, and smote them with a great slaughter. So David saved the inhabitants of Keilah.

6And it came to pass, when Abiathar the son of Ahimelech fled to David to Keilah,

that he came down *with* an ephod in his
hand.
7 And it was told Saul that David was
come to Keilah. And Saul said, God hath
delivered him into mine hand; for he is
shut in, by entering into a town that hath
gates and bars.
8 And Saul called all the people together
to war, to go down to Keilah, to besiege
David and his men.
9 And David knew
that Saul secretly
practised mischief
against him; and he
said to Abiathar the
priest, Bring hither
the ephod.

23:9
Mischief
◄ Nehemiah 6:2 ►

10 Then said David, O LORD God of Israel, thy servant hath certainly heard that
Saul seeketh to come to Keilah, to destroy
the city for my sake.
11 Will the men of Keilah deliver me up
into his hand? will Saul come down, as
thy servant hath heard? O LORD God of
Israel, I beseech thee, tell thy servant. And
the LORD said, He will come down.
12 Then said David, Will the men of Keilah deliver me and my men into the hand
of Saul? And the LORD said, They will deliver *thee* up.
13 Then David and his men, *which were*
about six hundred, arose and departed out
of Keilah, and went whithersoever they
could go. And it was told Saul that David
was escaped from Keilah; and he forbare
to go forth.
14 And David abode in the wilderness in
strong holds, and remained in a mountain in the wilderness of Ziph. And Saul
sought him every day, but God delivered
him not into his hand.
15 And David saw that Saul was come out
to seek his life: and David *was* in the wilderness of Ziph in a wood.
16 And Jonathan Saul's son arose, and
went to David into the wood, and strengthened his hand in God.
17 And he said
unto him, Fear not:
for the hand of Saul
my father shall not
find thee; and thou
shalt be king over
Israel, and I shall be next unto thee; and
that also Saul my father knoweth.

23:17 Unselfishness
◄ 1 Samuel 18:4
2 Samuel 23:17 ►

18 And they two made a covenant before
the LORD: and David abode in the wood,
and Jonathan went to his house.
19 Then came up the Ziphites to Saul to
Gibeah, saying, Doth not David hide himself with us in strong holds in the wood,
in the hill of Hachilah, which *is* on the
south of Jeshimon?
20 Now therefore, O king, come down
according to all the desire of thy soul to
come down; and our part *shall be* to deliver him into the king's hand.
21 And Saul said, Blessed *be* ye of the
LORD; for ye have compassion on me.
22 Go, I pray you, prepare yet, and know
and see his place where his haunt is, *and*
who hath seen him there: for it is told me
that he dealeth very subtilly.
23 See therefore, and take knowledge of
all the lurking places where he hideth himself, and come ye again to me with the certainty, and I will go with you: and it shall
come to pass, if he be in the land, that I
will search him out throughout all the
thousands of Judah.
24 And they arose, and went to Ziph before Saul: but David and his men *were* in
the wilderness of Maon, in the plain on
the south of Jeshimon.
25 Saul also and his men went to seek
him. And they told David: wherefore he
came down into a rock, and abode in the
wilderness of Maon. And when Saul heard
that, he pursued after David in the wilderness of Maon.
26 And Saul went on this side of the
mountain, and David and his men on that
side of the mountain: and David made
haste to get away for fear of Saul; for Saul
and his men compassed David and his
men round about to take them.
27 But there came a messenger unto Saul,
saying, Haste thee, and come; for the Philistines have invaded the land.
28 Wherefore Saul returned from pursuing after David, and went against the Philistines: therefore they called that place
Sela-hammahlekoth.
29 And David went up from thence, and
dwelt in strong holds at En-gedi.

24

1 And it came to pass, when Saul was returned from following the Philistines, that
it was told him, saying, Behold, David *is*
in the wilderness of En-gedi.
2 Then Saul took three thousand chosen

men out of all Israel, and went to seek David and his men upon the rocks of the wild goats.

3 And he came to the sheepcotes by the way, where *was* a cave; and Saul went in to cover his feet: and David and his men remained in the sides of the cave.

4 And the men of David said unto him, Behold the day of which the LORD said unto thee, Behold, I will deliver thine enemy into thine hand, that thou mayest do to him as it shall seem good unto thee. Then David arose, and cut off the skirt of Saul's robe privily.

5 And it came to pass afterward, that David's heart smote him, because he had cut off Saul's skirt.

6 And he said unto his men, The LORD forbid that I should do this thing unto my master, the LORD's anointed, to stretch forth mine hand against him, seeing he *is* the anointed of the LORD.

24:6 Rulers
◄ Exodus 22:28
Ecclesiastes 10:20 ►

7 So David stayed his servants with these words, and suffered them not to rise against Saul. But Saul rose up out of the cave, and went on *his* way.

8 David also arose afterward, and went out of the cave, and cried after Saul, saying, My lord the king. And when Saul looked behind him, David stooped with his face to the earth, and bowed himself.

9 And David said to Saul, Wherefore hearest thou men's words, saying, Behold, David seeketh thy hurt?

10 Behold, this day thine eyes have seen how that the LORD had delivered thee to day into mine hand in the cave: and *some* bade *me* kill thee: but *mine eye* spared thee; and I said, I will not put forth mine hand against my lord; for he *is* the LORD's anointed.

11 Moreover, my father, see, yea, see the skirt of thy robe in my hand: for in that I cut off the skirt of thy robe and killed thee not, know thou and see that *there is* neither evil nor transgression in mine hand, and I have not sinned against thee; yet thou huntest my soul to take it.

12 The LORD judge between me and thee, and the LORD avenge me of thee: but mine hand shall not be upon thee.

13 As saith the proverb of the ancients, Wickedness proceedeth from the wicked: but mine hand shall not be upon thee.

14 After whom is the king of Israel come out? after whom dost thou pursue? after a dead dog, after a flea.

15 The LORD therefore be judge, and judge between me and thee, and see, and plead my cause, and deliver me out of thine hand.

16 And it came to pass, when David had made an end of speaking these words unto Saul, that Saul said, *Is* this thy voice, my son David? And Saul lifted up his voice, and wept.

17 And he said to David, Thou *art* more righteous than I: for thou hast rewarded me good, whereas I have rewarded thee evil.

24:17 Nice
◄ Numbers 12:13
1 Samuel 26:11 ►

18 And thou hast shewed this day how that thou hast dealt well with me: forasmuch as when the LORD had delivered me into thine hand, thou killedst me not.

19 For if a man find his enemy, will he let him go well away? wherefore the LORD reward thee good for that thou hast done unto me this day.

20 And now, behold, I know well that thou shalt surely be king, and that the kingdom of Israel shall be established in thine hand.

21 Swear now therefore unto me by the LORD, that thou wilt not cut off my seed after me, and that thou wilt not destroy my name out of my father's house.

22 And David sware unto Saul. And Saul went home; but David and his men gat them up unto the hold.

25

1 And Samuel died; and all the Israelites were gathered together, and lamented him, and buried him in his house at Ramah. And David arose, and went down to the wilderness of Paran.

2 And *there was* a man in Maon, whose possessions *were* in Carmel; and the man *was* very great, and he had three thousand sheep, and a thousand goats: and he was shearing his sheep in Carmel.

3 Now the name of the man *was* Nabal; and the name of his wife Abigail: and *she was* a woman of good understanding, and of a beautiful countenance: but the man

was churlish and evil in his doings; and he *was* of the house of Caleb.

4And David heard in the wilderness that Nabal did shear his sheep.

5And David sent out ten young men, and David said unto the young men, Get you up to Carmel, and go to Nabal, and greet him in my name:

6And thus shall ye say to him that liveth *in prosperity*, Peace *be* both to thee, and peace *be* to thine house, and peace *be* unto all that thou hast.

7And now I have heard that thou hast shearers: now thy shepherds which were with us, we hurt them not, neither was there ought missing unto them, all the while they were in Carmel.

8Ask thy young men, and they will shew thee. Wherefore let the young men find favour in thine eyes: for we come in a good day: give, I pray thee, whatsoever cometh to thine hand unto thy servants, and to thy son David.

9And when David's young men came, they spake to Nabal according to all those words in the name of David, and ceased.

10And Nabal answered David's servants, and said, Who *is* David? and who *is* the son of Jesse? there be many servants now a days that break away every man from his master.

25:10 Cold Shoulder
◄ Judges 19:15
Luke 9:53 ►

11Shall I then take my bread, and my water, and my flesh that I have killed for my shearers, and give *it* unto men, whom I know not whence they *be*?

12So David's young men turned their way, and went again, and came and told him all those sayings.

13And David said unto his men, Gird ye on every man his sword. And they girded on every man his sword; and David also girded on his sword: and there went up after David about four hundred men; and two hundred abode by the stuff.

14But one of the young men told Abigail, Nabal's wife, saying, Behold, David sent messengers out of the wilderness to salute our master; and he railed on them.

15But the men *were* very good unto us, and we were not hurt, neither missed we any thing, as long as we were conversant with them, when we were in the fields:

16They were a wall unto us both by night and day, all the while we were with them keeping the sheep.

17Now therefore know and consider what thou wilt do; for evil is determined against our master, and against all his household: for he *is such* a son of Belial, that *a man* cannot speak to him.

18Then Abigail made haste, and took two hundred loaves, and two bottles of wine, and five sheep ready dressed, and five measures of parched *corn*, and an hundred clusters of raisins, and two hundred cakes of figs, and laid *them* on asses.

19And she said unto her servants, Go on before me; behold, I come after you. But she told not her husband Nabal.

20And it was *so, as* she rode on the ass, that she came down by the covert of the hill, and, behold, David and his men came down against her; and she met them.

21Now David had said, Surely in vain have I kept all that this *fellow* hath in the wilderness, so that nothing was missed of all that *pertained* unto him: and he hath requited me evil for good.

25:21
Unthankfulness to People
◄ Judges 9:18
2 Chronicles 24:22 ►

22So and more also do God unto the enemies of David, if I leave of all that *pertain* to him by the morning light any that pisseth against the wall.

23And when Abigail saw David, she hasted, and lighted off the ass, and fell before David on her face, and bowed herself to the ground,

24And fell at his feet, and said, Upon me, my lord, *upon* me *let this* iniquity *be*: and let thine handmaid, I pray thee, speak in thine audience, and hear the words of thine handmaid.

25:24 Helping Friends
◄ 1 Samuel 19:4
Jeremiah 38:9 ►

25Let not my lord, I pray thee, regard this man of Belial, *even* Nabal: for as his name *is*, so *is* he; Nabal *is* his name, and folly *is* with him: but I thine handmaid saw not the young men of my lord, whom thou didst send.

26Now therefore, my lord, *as* the LORD liveth, and *as* thy soul liveth, seeing the LORD hath withholden thee from coming to *shed* blood, and from avenging thyself

with thine own hand, now let thine enemies, and they that seek evil to my lord,
be as Nabal.
27And now this blessing which thine
handmaid hath brought unto my lord, let
it even be given unto the young men that
follow my lord.
28I pray thee, forgive the trespass of thine
handmaid: for the LORD will certainly
make my lord a sure house; because my
lord fighteth the battles of the LORD, and
evil hath not been found in thee *all* thy
days.
29Yet a man is risen to pursue thee, and
to seek thy soul: but the soul of my lord
shall be bound in the bundle of life with
the LORD thy God; and the souls of thine
enemies, them shall he sling out, *as out* of
the middle of a sling.
30And it shall come to pass, when the
LORD shall have done to my lord according to all the good that he hath spoken
concerning thee, and shall have appointed thee ruler over Israel;
31That this shall be no grief unto thee,
nor offence of heart unto my lord, either
that thou hast shed blood causeless, or that
my lord hath avenged himself: but when
the LORD shall have dealt well with my
lord, then remember thine handmaid.
32And David said to Abigail, Blessed *be*
the LORD God of Israel, which sent thee
this day to meet me:
33And blessed *be* thy advice, and blessed
be thou, which hast kept me this day from
coming to *shed* blood, and from avenging
myself with mine own hand.
34For in very deed, *as* the LORD God of
Israel liveth, which hath kept me back
from hurting thee, except thou hadst
hasted and come to meet me, surely there
had not been left unto Nabal by the morning light any that pisseth against the wall.
35So David received of her hand *that*
which she had brought him, and said unto
her, Go up in peace to thine house; see, I
have hearkened to thy voice, and have accepted thy person.
36And Abigail
came to Nabal; and,
behold, he held a
feast in his house,
like the feast of a
king; and Nabal's
heart *was* merry within him, for he *was* very
drunken: wherefore she told him nothing,
less or more, until the morning light.

25:36 Parties
◄ Judges 16:25
1 Samuel 30:16 ►

37But it came to pass in the morning,
when the wine was gone out of Nabal, and
his wife had told him these things, that
his heart died within him, and he became
as a stone.
38And it came to pass about ten days *after,* that the LORD smote Nabal, that he
died.
39And when David heard that Nabal was
dead, he said, Blessed *be* the LORD, that
hath pleaded the cause of my reproach
from the hand of Nabal, and hath kept his
servant from evil: for the LORD hath returned the wickedness of Nabal upon his
own head. And David sent and communed
with Abigail, to take her to him to wife.
40And when the servants of David were
come to Abigail to Carmel, they spake
unto her, saying, David sent us unto thee
to take thee to him to wife.
41And she arose, and bowed herself on
her face to the earth, and said, Behold, *let*
thine handmaid *be* a servant to wash the
feet of the servants of my lord.
42And Abigail hasted, and arose, and
rode upon an ass, with five damsels of
hers that went after her; and she went after the messengers of David, and became
his wife.
43David also took Ahinoam of Jezreel;
and they were also both of them his wives.
44But Saul had given Michal his daughter, David's wife, to Phalti the son of Laish, which *was* of Gallim.

26

1And the Ziphites came unto Saul to
Gibeah, saying, Doth not David hide himself in the hill of Hachilah, *which is* before
Jeshimon?
2Then Saul arose, and went down to the
wilderness of Ziph, having three thousand
chosen men of Israel with him, to seek
David in the wilderness of Ziph.
3And Saul pitched in the hill of Hachilah, which *is* before Jeshimon, by the way.
But David abode in the wilderness, and
he saw that Saul came after him into the
wilderness.
4David therefore sent out spies, and understood that Saul was come in very deed.
5And David arose, and came to the place
where Saul had pitched: and David beheld
the place where Saul lay, and Abner the
son of Ner, the captain of his host: and

Saul lay in the trench, and the people
pitched round about him.
6 Then answered David and said to
Ahimelech the Hittite, and to Abishai the
son of Zeruiah, brother to Joab, saying,
Who will go down with me to Saul to the
camp? And Abishai said, I will go down
with thee.
7 So David and Abishai came to the people by night: and, behold, Saul lay sleeping within the trench, and his spear stuck
in the ground at his bolster: but Abner and
the people lay round about him.
8 Then said Abishai to David, God hath
delivered thine enemy into thine hand this
day: now therefore let me smite him, I pray
thee, with the spear even to the earth at
once, and I will not *smite* him the second
time.
9 And David said
to Abishai, Destroy
him not: for who
can stretch forth his
hand against the
LORD'S anointed,
and be guiltless?

26:9
Examples of Mercy
◄ 1 Samuel 11:13
2 Samuel 19:22 ►

10 David said furthermore, *As* the LORD
liveth, the LORD shall smite him; or his day
shall come to die; or he shall descend into
battle, and perish.
11 The LORD for-
bid that I should
stretch forth mine
hand against the
LORD'S anointed:
but, I pray thee,
take thou now the spear that *is* at his bolster, and the cruse of water, and let us go.

26:11 Nice
◄ 1 Samuel 24:17
2 Kings 6:22 ►

12 So David took the spear and the cruse
of water from Saul's bolster; and they gat
them away, and no man saw *it,* nor knew
it, neither awaked: for they *were* all asleep;
because a deep sleep from the LORD was
fallen upon them.
13 Then David went over to the other
side, and stood on the top of an hill afar
off; a great space *being* between them:
14 And David cried to the people, and to
Abner the son of Ner, saying, Answerest
thou not, Abner? Then Abner answered
and said, Who *art* thou *that* criest to the
king?
15 And David said to Abner, *Art* not thou
a *valiant* man? and who *is* like to thee in
Israel? wherefore then hast thou not kept
thy lord the king? for there came one
of the people in to destroy the king thy
lord.
16 This thing *is* not good that thou hast
done. *As* the LORD liveth, ye *are* worthy to
die, because ye have not kept your master,
the LORD'S anointed. And now see where
the king's spear is, and the cruse of water
that *was* at his bolster.
17 And Saul knew David's voice, and said,
Is this thy voice, my son David? And David said, *It is* my voice, my lord, O king.
18 And he said, Wherefore doth my lord
thus pursue after his servant? for what have
I done? or what evil *is* in mine hand?
19 Now therefore, I pray thee, let my lord
the king hear the words of his servant.
If the LORD have stirred thee up against me,
let him accept an offering: but if *they be*
the children of men, cursed *be* they before
the LORD; for they have driven me out this
day from abiding in the inheritance of the
LORD, saying, Go, serve other gods.
20 Now therefore, let not my blood fall
to the earth before the face of the LORD:
for the king of Israel is come out to seek a
flea, as when one doth hunt a partridge in
the mountains.
21 Then said Saul, I have sinned: return,
my son David: for I will no more do thee
harm, because my soul was precious in
thine eyes this day: behold, I have played
the fool, and have erred exceedingly.
22 And David answered and said, Behold
the king's spear! and let one of the young
men come over and fetch it.
23 The LORD render to every man his righteousness and his faithfulness: for the
LORD delivered thee into *my* hand to day,
but I would not stretch forth mine hand
against the LORD'S anointed.
24 And, behold, as thy life was much set
by this day in mine eyes, so let my life be
much set by in the eyes of the LORD, and
let him deliver me out of all tribulation.
25 Then Saul said to David, Blessed *be*
thou, my son David: thou shalt both do
great things, and also shalt still prevail. So
David went on his way, and Saul returned
to his place.

27

1 And David said in his heart, I shall now
perish one day by the hand of Saul: *there*
is nothing better for me than that I should
speedily escape into the land of the Philistines; and Saul shall despair of me, to

seek me any more in any coast of Israel: so shall I escape out of his hand.

2 And David arose, and he passed over with the six hundred men that *were* with him unto Achish, the son of Maoch, king of Gath.

3 And David dwelt with Achish at Gath, he and his men, every man with his household, *even* David with his two wives, Ahinoam the Jezreelitess, and Abigail the Carmelitess, Nabal's wife.

4 And it was told Saul that David was fled to Gath: and he sought no more again for him.

5 And David said unto Achish, If I have now found grace in thine eyes, let them give me a place in some town in the country, that I may dwell there: for why should thy servant dwell in the royal city with thee?

6 Then Achish gave him Ziklag that day: wherefore Ziklag pertaineth unto the kings of Judah unto this day.

7 And the time that David dwelt in the country of the Philistines was a full year and four months.

8 And David and his men went up, and invaded the Geshurites, and the Gezrites, and the Amalekites: for those *nations were* of old the inhabitants of the land, as thou goest to Shur, even unto the land of Egypt.

9 And David smote the land, and left neither man nor woman alive, and took away the sheep, and the oxen, and the asses, and the camels, and the apparel, and returned, and came to Achish.

10 And Achish said, Whither have ye made a road to day? And David said, Against the south of Judah, and against the south of the Jerahmeelites, and against the south of the Kenites.

11 And David saved neither man nor woman alive, to bring *tidings* to Gath, saying, Lest they should tell on us, saying, So did David, and so *will be* his manner all the while he dwelleth in the country of the Philistines.

12 And Achish believed David, saying, He hath made his people Israel utterly to abhor him; therefore he shall be my servant for ever.

28

1 And it came to pass in those days, that the Philistines gathered their armies together for warfare, to fight with Israel. And Achish said unto David, Know thou assuredly, that thou shalt go out with me to battle, thou and thy men.

2 And David said to Achish, Surely thou shalt know what thy servant can do. And Achish said to David, Therefore will I make thee keeper of mine head for ever.

3 Now Samuel was dead, and all Israel had lamented him, and buried him in Ramah, even in his own city. And Saul had put away those that had familiar spirits, and the wizards, out of the land.

4 And the Philistines gathered themselves together, and came and pitched in Shunem: and Saul gathered all Israel together, and they pitched in Gilboa.

5 And when Saul saw the host of the Philistines, he was afraid, and his heart greatly trembled.

6 And when Saul enquired of the LORD, the LORD answered him not, neither by dreams nor by Urim, nor by prophets.

28:6 Unanswered Prayer
◄ 1 Samuel 14:37
Psalm 66:18 ►

7 Then said Saul unto his servants, Seek me a woman that hath a familiar spirit, that I may go to her, and enquire of her. And his servants said to him, Behold, *there is* a woman that hath a familiar spirit at Endor.

8 And Saul disguised himself, and put on other raiment, and he went, and two men with him, and they came to the woman by night: and he said, I pray thee, divine unto me by the familiar spirit, and bring me *him* up, whom I shall name unto thee.

9 And the woman said unto him, Behold, thou knowest what Saul hath done, how he hath cut off those that have familiar spirits, and the wizards, out of the land: wherefore then layest thou a snare for my life, to cause me to die?

10 And Saul sware to her by the LORD, saying, *As* the LORD liveth, there shall no punishment happen to thee for this thing.

11 Then said the woman, Whom shall I bring up unto thee? And he said, Bring me up Samuel.

12 And when the woman saw Samuel, she cried with a loud voice: and the woman spake to Saul, saying, Why hast thou deceived me? for thou *art* Saul.

13 And the king said unto her, Be not afraid: for what sawest thou? And the

woman said unto Saul, I saw gods ascending out of the earth.
14And he said unto her, What form *is* he
of? And she said, An old man cometh up;
and he *is* covered with a mantle. And Saul
perceived that it *was* Samuel, and he
stooped with *his* face to the ground, and
bowed himself.
15And Samuel said to Saul, Why hast
thou disquieted me, to bring me up? And
Saul answered, I am sore distressed; for the
Philistines make war against me, and God
is departed from me, and answereth me
no more, neither by prophets, nor by
dreams: therefore I have called thee, that
thou mayest make known unto me what I
shall do.
16Then said Samuel, Wherefore then
dost thou ask of me, seeing the LORD is
departed from thee, and is become thine
enemy?
17And the LORD hath done to him, as
he spake by me: for the LORD hath rent
the kingdom out of thine hand, and given
it to thy neighbour, *even* to David:
18Because thou
obeyedst not the
voice of the LORD,
nor executedst his
fierce wrath upon
Amalek, therefore
hath the LORD done this thing unto thee
this day.

28:18 Ouch!
◄ 1 Samuel 12:15
1 Kings 13:21 ►

19Moreover the LORD will also deliver
Israel with thee into the hand of the Philistines: and to morrow *shalt* thou and thy
sons *be* with me: the LORD also shall deliver the host of Israel into the hand of the
Philistines.
20Then Saul fell straightway all along on
the earth, and was sore afraid, because of
the words of Samuel: and there was no
strength in him; for he had eaten no bread
all the day, nor all the night.
21And the woman came unto Saul, and
saw that he was sore troubled, and said
unto him, Behold, thine handmaid hath
obeyed thy voice, and I have put my life in
my hand, and have hearkened unto thy
words which thou spakest unto me.
22Now therefore, I pray thee, hearken
thou also unto the voice of thine handmaid, and let me set a morsel of bread
before thee; and eat, that thou mayest have
strength, when thou goest on thy way.
23But he refused, and said, I will not eat.
But his servants, together with the woman, compelled him; and he hearkened
unto their voice. So he arose from the
earth, and sat upon the bed.
24And the woman had a fat calf in the
house; and she hasted, and killed it, and
took flour, and kneaded *it*, and did bake
unleavened bread thereof:
25And she brought *it* before Saul, and
before his servants; and they did eat.
Then they rose up, and went away that
night.

29

1Now the Philistines gathered together
all their armies to Aphek: and the Israelites pitched by a fountain which *is* in Jezreel.
2And the lords of the Philistines passed
on by hundreds, and by thousands: but
David and his men passed on in the
rereward with Achish.
3Then said the princes of the Philistines,
What *do* these Hebrews *here*? And Achish
said unto the princes of the Philistines, *Is*
not this David, the servant of Saul the king
of Israel, which hath been with me these
days, or these years, and I have found no
fault in him since he fell *unto me* unto this
day?
4And the princes of the Philistines were
wroth with him; and the princes of the
Philistines said unto him, Make this fellow return, that he may go again to his
place which thou hast appointed him, and
let him not go down with us to battle, lest
in the battle he be an adversary to us: for
wherewith should he reconcile himself
unto his master? *should it* not *be* with the
heads of these men?
5*Is* not this David, of whom they sang
one to another in dances, saying, Saul slew
his thousands, and David his ten thousands?
6Then Achish called David, and said
unto him, Surely, *as* the LORD liveth, thou
hast been upright, and thy going out and
thy coming in with me in the host *is* good
in my sight: for I have not found evil in
thee since the day of thy coming unto me
unto this day: nevertheless the lords favour
thee not.
7Wherefore now return, and go in peace,
that thou displease not the lords of the
Philistines.
8And David said unto Achish, But what

have I done? and what hast thou found in thy servant so long as I have been with thee unto this day, that I may not go fight against the enemies of my lord the king?

9 And Achish answered and said to David, I know that thou *art* good in my sight, as an angel of God: notwithstanding the princes of the Philistines have said, He shall not go up with us to the battle.

10 Wherefore now rise up early in the morning with thy master's servants that are come with thee: and as soon as ye be up early in the morning, and have light, depart.

11 So David and his men rose up early to depart in the morning, to return into the land of the Philistines. And the Philistines went up to Jezreel.

30

1 And it came to pass, when David and his men were come to Ziklag on the third day, that the Amalekites had invaded the south, and Ziklag, and smitten Ziklag, and burned it with fire;

2 And had taken the women captives, that *were* therein: they slew not any, either great or small, but carried *them* away, and went on their way.

3 So David and his men came to the city, and, behold, *it was* burned with fire; and their wives, and their sons, and their daughters, were taken captives.

4 Then David and the people that *were* with him lifted up their voice and wept, until they had no more power to weep.

5 And David's two wives were taken captives, Ahinoam the Jezreelitess, and Abigail the wife of Nabal the Carmelite.

6 And David was greatly distressed; for the people spake of stoning him, because the soul of all the people was grieved, every man for his sons and for his daughters: but David encouraged himself in the LORD his God.

7 And David said to Abiathar the priest, Ahimelech's son, I pray thee, bring me hither the ephod. And Abiathar brought thither the ephod to David.

8 And David enquired at the LORD, saying, Shall I pursue after this troop? shall I overtake them? And he answered him, Pursue: for thou shalt surely overtake *them*, and without fail recover *all*.

9 So David went, he and the six hundred men that *were* with him, and came to the brook Besor, where those that were left behind stayed.

10 But David pursued, he and four hundred men: for two hundred abode behind, which were so faint that they could not go over the brook Besor.

11 And they found an Egyptian in the field, and brought him to David, and gave him bread, and he did eat; and they made him drink water;

12 And they gave him a piece of a cake of figs, and two clusters of raisins: and when he had eaten, his spirit came again to him: for he had eaten no bread, nor drunk *any* water, three days and three nights.

13 And David said unto him, To whom *belongest* thou? and whence *art* thou? And he said, I *am* a young man of Egypt, servant to an Amalekite; and my master left me, because three days agone I fell sick.

14 We made an invasion *upon* the south of the Cherethites, and upon *the coast* which *belongeth* to Judah, and upon the south of Caleb; and we burned Ziklag with fire.

15 And David said to him, Canst thou bring me down to this company? And he said, Swear unto me by God, that thou wilt neither kill me, nor deliver me into the hands of my master, and I will bring thee down to this company.

16 And when he had brought him down, behold, *they were* spread abroad upon all the earth, eating and drinking, and dancing, because of all the great spoil that they had taken out of the land of the Philistines, and out of the land of Judah.

30:16 Parties
◄ 1 Samuel 25:36
Galatians 5:21 ►

17 And David smote them from the twilight even unto the evening of the next day: and there escaped not a man of them, save four hundred young men, which rode upon camels, and fled.

18 And David recovered all that the Amalekites had carried away: and David rescued his two wives.

19 And there was nothing lacking to them, neither small nor great, neither sons nor daughters, neither spoil, nor any *thing* that they had taken to them: David recovered all.

20 And David took all the flocks and the

herds, *which* they drave before those *other* cattle, and said, This *is* David's spoil.

21 And David came to the two hundred men, which were so faint that they could not follow David, whom they had made also to abide at the brook Besor: and they went forth to meet David, and to meet the people that *were* with him: and when David came near to the people, he saluted them.

22 Then answered all the wicked men and *men* of Belial, of those that went with David, and said, Because they went not with us, we will not give them *ought* of the spoil that we have recovered, save to every man his wife and his children, that they may lead *them* away, and depart.

23 Then said David, Ye shall not do so, my brethren, with that which the LORD hath given us, who hath preserved us, and delivered the company that came against us into our hand.

24 For who will hearken unto you in this matter? but as his part *is* that goeth down to the battle, so *shall* his part *be* that tarrieth by the stuff: they shall part alike.

25 And it was *so* from that day forward, that he made it a statute and an ordinance for Israel unto this day.

26 And when David came to Ziklag, he sent of the spoil unto the elders of Judah, *even* to his friends, saying, Behold a present for you of the spoil of the enemies of the LORD;

27 To *them* which *were* in Bethel, and to *them* which *were* in south Ramoth, and to *them* which *were* in Jattir,

28 And to *them* which *were* in Aroer, and to *them* which *were* in Siphmoth, and to *them* which *were* in Eshtemoa,

29 And to *them* which *were* in Rachal, and to *them* which *were* in the cities of the Jerahmeelites, and to *them* which *were* in the cities of the Kenites,

30 And to *them* which *were* in Hormah, and to *them* which *were* in Chor-ashan, and to *them* which *were* in Athach,

31 And to *them* which *were* in Hebron, and to all the places where David himself and his men were wont to haunt.

31

1 Now the Philistines fought against Israel: and the men of Israel fled from before the Philistines, and fell down slain in mount Gilboa.

2 And the Philistines followed hard upon Saul and upon his sons; and the Philistines slew Jonathan, and Abinadab, and Melchi-shua, Saul's sons.

3 And the battle went sore against Saul, and the archers hit him; and he was sore wounded of the archers.

4 Then said Saul unto his armourbearer, Draw thy sword, and thrust me through therewith; lest these uncircumcised come and thrust me through, and abuse me. But his armourbearer would not; for he was sore afraid. Therefore Saul took a sword, and fell upon it.

5 And when his armourbearer saw that Saul was dead, he fell likewise upon his sword, and died with him.

6 So Saul died, and his three sons, and his armourbearer, and all his men, that same day together.

7 And when the men of Israel that *were* on the other side of the valley, and *they* that *were* on the other side Jordan, saw that the men of Israel fled, and that Saul and his sons were dead, they forsook the cities, and fled; and the Philistines came and dwelt in them.

8 And it came to pass on the morrow, when the Philistines came to strip the slain, that they found Saul and his three sons fallen in mount Gilboa.

9 And they cut off his head, and stripped off his armour, and sent into the land of the Philistines round about, to publish *it in* the house of their idols, and among the people.

10 And they put his armour in the house of Ashtaroth: and they fastened his body to the wall of Beth-shan.

11 And when the inhabitants of Jabesh-gilead heard of that which the Philistines had done to Saul;

12 All the valiant men arose, and went all night, and took the body of Saul and the bodies of his sons from the wall of Beth-shan, and came to Jabesh, and burnt them there.

13 And they took their bones, and buried *them* under a tree at Jabesh, and fasted seven days.

2 Samuel

AUTHOR
Unknown (some think it was Samuel the judge, but no one knows for sure)

MAIN POINT
Even imperfect people—if they have a heart for God—can be blessed and be a blessing to many others.

DATE WRITTEN
Unknown, though possibly 930 B.C. or in the sixth century B.C., while the people of Israel were captives in Babylon

24 CHAPTERS

MAIN PEOPLE

David, Abner, Joab, Michal, Ishbaal, Bathsheba, Nathan, Absalom

SPECIAL FEATURES

- *Describes how David mourned for Saul but then, as king of Judah and finally Israel, united the wrecked kingdom left to him*
- *Tells how Jerusalem became the capital of Israel and home of the ark of the covenant*
- *Tells the complete story of David's affair with Bathsheba and reconciliation with God*
- *Lets us see the life of the one who wrote the beautiful hymnbook that we call Psalms*
- *Fifth book of History*

HOW THE BOOK GOT ITS NAME

The title of the book refers to its purpose as a record of the life of Samuel, Israel's last judge.

1
1 Now it came to pass after the death of
Saul, when David was returned from the
slaughter of the Amalekites, and David had
abode two days in Ziklag;
2 It came even to pass on the third day,
that, behold, a man came out of the camp
from Saul with his clothes rent, and earth
upon his head: and *so* it was, when he came
to David, that he fell to the earth, and did
obeisance.
3 And David said unto him, From
whence comest thou? And he said unto
him, Out of the camp of Israel am I escaped.
4 And David said unto him, How went
the matter? I pray thee, tell me. And he
answered, That the people are fled from
the battle, and many of the people also
are fallen and dead; and Saul and Jonathan his son are dead also.

5 And David said unto the young man that told him, How knowest thou that Saul and Jonathan his son be dead?

6 And the young man that told him said, As I happened by chance upon mount Gilboa, behold, Saul leaned upon his spear; and, lo, the chariots and horsemen followed hard after him.

7 And when he looked behind him, he saw me, and called unto me. And I answered, Here *am* I.

8 And he said unto me, Who *art* thou? And I answered him, I *am* an Amalekite.

9 And he said unto me again, Stand, I pray thee, upon me, and slay me: for anguish is come upon me, because my life *is* yet whole in me.

10 So I stood upon him, and slew him, because I was sure that he could not live after that he was fallen: and I took the crown that *was* upon his head, and the bracelet that *was* on his arm, and have brought them hither unto my lord.

11 Then David took hold on his clothes, and rent them; and likewise all the men that *were* with him:

12 And they mourned, and wept, and fasted until even, for Saul, and for Jonathan his son, and for the people of the LORD, and for the house of Israel; because they were fallen by the sword.

13 And David said unto the young man that told him, Whence *art* thou? And he answered, I *am* the son of a stranger, an Amalekite.

14 And David said unto him, How wast thou not afraid to stretch forth thine hand to destroy the LORD'S anointed?

15 And David called one of the young men, and said, Go near, *and* fall upon him. And he smote him that he died.

16 And David said unto him, Thy blood *be* upon thy head; for thy mouth hath testified against thee, saying, I have slain the LORD'S anointed.

17 And David lamented with this lamentation over Saul and over Jonathan his son:

18 (Also he bade them teach the children of Judah *the use of* the bow: behold, *it is* written in the book of Jasher.)

19 The beauty of Israel is slain upon thy high places: how are the mighty fallen!

20 Tell *it* not in Gath, publish *it* not in the streets of Askelon; lest the daughters of the Philistines rejoice, lest the daughters of the uncircumcised triumph.

21 Ye mountains of Gilboa, *let there be* no dew, neither *let there be* rain, upon you, nor fields of offerings: for there the shield of the mighty is vilely cast away, the shield of Saul, *as though he had* not *been* anointed with oil.

22 From the blood of the slain, from the fat of the mighty, the bow of Jonathan turned not back, and the sword of Saul returned not empty.

23 Saul and Jonathan *were* lovely and pleasant in their lives, and in their death they were not divided: they were swifter than eagles, they were stronger than lions.

24 Ye daughters of Israel, weep over Saul, who clothed you in scarlet, with *other* delights, who put on ornaments of gold upon your apparel.

25 How are the mighty fallen in the midst of the battle! O Jonathan, *thou wast* slain in thine high places.

26 I am distressed for thee, my brother Jonathan: very pleasant hast thou been unto me: thy love to me was wonderful, passing the love of women.

1:26 Good Friends
◄ 1 Samuel 20:41
2 Samuel 15:37 ►

27 How are the mighty fallen, and the weapons of war perished!

2

1 And it came to pass after this, that David enquired of the LORD, saying, Shall I go up into any of the cities of Judah? And the LORD said unto him, Go up. And David said, Whither shall I go up? And he said, Unto Hebron.

2 So David went up thither, and his two wives also, Ahinoam the Jezreelitess, and Abigail Nabal's wife the Carmelite.

3 And his men that *were* with him did David bring up, every man with his household: and they dwelt in the cities of Hebron.

4 And the men of Judah came, and there they anointed David king over the house of Judah. And they told David, saying, *That* the men of Jabesh-gilead *were they* that buried Saul.

5 And David sent messengers unto the men of Jabesh-gilead, and said unto them, Blessed *be* ye of the LORD, that ye have shewed this kindness unto your lord, *even* unto Saul, and have buried him.

6And now the LORD shew kindness and truth unto you: and I also will requite you this kindness, because ye have done this thing.

7Therefore now let your hands be strengthened, and be ye valiant: for your master Saul is dead, and also the house of Judah have anointed me king over them.

8But Abner the son of Ner, captain of Saul's host, took Ish-bosheth the son of Saul, and brought him over to Mahanaim;

9And made him king over Gilead, and over the Ashurites, and over Jezreel, and over Ephraim, and over Benjamin, and over all Israel.

10Ish-bosheth Saul's son *was* forty years old when he began to reign over Israel, and reigned two years. But the house of Judah followed David.

11And the time that David was king in Hebron over the house of Judah was seven years and six months.

12And Abner the son of Ner, and the servants of Ish-bosheth the son of Saul, went out from Mahanaim to Gibeon.

13And Joab the son of Zeruiah, and the servants of David, went out, and met together by the pool of Gibeon: and they sat down, the one on the one side of the pool, and the other on the other side of the pool.

14And Abner said to Joab, Let the young men now arise, and play before us. And Joab said, Let them arise.

15Then there arose and went over by number twelve of Benjamin, which *pertained* to Ish-bosheth the son of Saul, and twelve of the servants of David.

16And they caught every one his fellow by the head, and *thrust* his sword in his fellow's side; so they fell down together: wherefore that place was called Helkath-hazzurim, which *is* in Gibeon.

17And there was a very sore battle that day; and Abner was beaten, and the men of Israel, before the servants of David.

18And there were three sons of Zeruiah there, Joab, and Abishai, and Asahel: and Asahel *was as* light of foot as a wild roe.

19And Asahel pursued after Abner; and in going he turned not to the right hand nor to the left from following Abner.

20Then Abner looked behind him, and said, *Art* thou Asahel? And he answered, I *am*.

21And Abner said to him, Turn thee aside to thy right hand or to thy left, and lay thee hold on one of the young men, and take thee his armour. But Asahel would not turn aside from following of him.

22And Abner said again to Asahel, Turn thee aside from following me: wherefore should I smite thee to the ground? how then should I hold up my face to Joab thy brother?

23Howbeit he refused to turn aside: wherefore Abner with the hinder end of the spear smote him under the fifth *rib*, that the spear came out behind him; and he fell down there, and died in the same place: and it came to pass, *that* as many as came to the place where Asahel fell down and died stood still.

24Joab also and Abishai pursued after Abner: and the sun went down when they were come to the hill of Ammah, that *lieth* before Giah by the way of the wilderness of Gibeon.

25And the children of Benjamin gathered themselves together after Abner, and became one troop, and stood on the top of an hill.

26Then Abner called to Joab, and said, Shall the sword devour for ever? knowest thou not that it will be bitterness in the latter end? how long shall it be then, ere thou bid the people return from following their brethren?

27And Joab said, *As* God liveth, unless thou hadst spoken, surely then in the morning the people had gone up every one from following his brother.

28So Joab blew a trumpet, and all the people stood still, and pursued after Israel no more, neither fought they any more.

29And Abner and his men walked all that night through the plain, and passed over Jordan, and went through all Bithron, and they came to Mahanaim.

30And Joab returned from following Abner: and when he had gathered all the people together, there lacked of David's servants nineteen men and Asahel.

31But the servants of David had smitten of Benjamin, and of Abner's men, *so that* three hundred and threescore men died.

32And they took up Asahel, and buried him in the sepulchre of his father, which *was in* Bethlehem. And Joab and his men went all night, and they came to Hebron at break of day.

3

1 Now there was long war between the house of Saul and the house of David: but David waxed stronger and stronger, and the house of Saul waxed weaker and weaker.

2 And unto David were sons born in Hebron: and his firstborn was Amnon, of Ahinoam the Jezreelitess;

3 And his second, Chileab, of Abigail the wife of Nabal the Carmelite; and the third, Absalom the son of Maacah the daughter of Talmai king of Geshur;

4 And the fourth, Adonijah the son of Haggith; and the fifth, Shephatiah the son of Abital;

5 And the sixth, Ithream, by Eglah David's wife. These were born to David in Hebron.

6 And it came to pass, while there was war between the house of Saul and the house of David, that Abner made himself strong for the house of Saul.

7 And Saul had a concubine, whose name *was* Rizpah, the daughter of Aiah: and *Ish-bosheth* said to Abner, Wherefore hast thou gone in unto my father's concubine?

8 Then was Abner very wroth for the words of Ish-bosheth, and said, *Am* I a dog's head, which against Judah do shew kindness this day unto the house of Saul thy father, to his brethren, and to his friends, and have not delivered thee into the hand of David, that thou chargest me to day with a fault concerning this woman?

9 So do God to Abner, and more also, except, as the LORD hath sworn to David, even so I do to him;

10 To translate the kingdom from the house of Saul, and to set up the throne of David over Israel and over Judah, from Dan even to Beer-sheba.

11 And he could not answer Abner a word again, because he feared him.

12 And Abner sent messengers to David on his behalf, saying, Whose *is* the land? saying *also,* Make thy league with me, and, behold, my hand *shall be* with thee, to bring about all Israel unto thee.

13 And he said, Well; I will make a league with thee: but one thing I require of thee, that is, Thou shalt not see my face, except thou first bring Michal Saul's daughter, when thou comest to see my face.

14 And David sent messengers to Ish-bosheth Saul's son, saying, Deliver *me* my wife Michal, which I espoused to me for an hundred foreskins of the Philistines.

15 And Ish-bosheth sent, and took her from *her* husband, *even* from Phaltiel the son of Laish.

16 And her husband went with her along weeping behind her to Bahurim. Then said Abner unto him, Go, return. And he returned.

17 And Abner had communication with the elders of Israel, saying, Ye sought for David in times past *to be* king over you:

18 Now then do *it:* for the LORD hath spoken of David, saying, By the hand of my servant David I will save my people Israel out of the hand of the Philistines, and out of the hand of all their enemies.

19 And Abner also spake in the ears of Benjamin: and Abner went also to speak in the ears of David in Hebron all that seemed good to Israel, and that seemed good to the whole house of Benjamin.

20 So Abner came to David to Hebron, and twenty men with him. And David made Abner and the men that *were* with him a feast.

21 And Abner said unto David, I will arise and go, and will gather all Israel unto my lord the king, that they may make a league with thee, and that thou mayest reign over all that thine heart desireth. And David sent Abner away; and he went in peace.

22 And, Behold, the servants of David and Joab came from *pursuing* a troop, and brought in a great spoil with them: but Abner *was* not with David in Hebron; for he had sent him away, and he was gone in peace.

23 When Joab and all the host that *was* with him were come, they told Joab, saying, Abner the son of Ner came to the king, and he hath sent him away, and he is gone in peace.

24 Then Joab came to the king, and said, What hast thou done? behold, Abner came unto thee; why *is* it *that* thou hast sent him away, and he is quite gone?

25 Thou knowest Abner the son of Ner, that he came to deceive thee, and to know thy going out and thy coming in, and to know all that thou doest.

26 And when Joab was come out from David, he sent messengers after Abner, which brought him again from the well of Sirah: but David knew *it* not.

27 And when Abner was returned to Hebron, Joab took him aside in the gate to speak with him quietly, and smote him there under the fifth *rib,* that he died, for the blood of Asahel his brother.

28 And afterward when David heard *it,* he said, I and my kingdom *are* guiltless before the LORD for ever from the blood of Abner the son of Ner:

29 Let it rest on the head of Joab, and on all his father's house; and let there not fail from the house of Joab one that hath an issue, or that is a leper, or that leaneth on a staff, or that falleth on the sword, or that lacketh bread.

30 So Joab and Abishai his brother slew Abner, because he had slain their brother Asahel at Gibeon in the battle.

31 And David said to Joab, and to all the people that *were* with him, Rend your clothes, and gird you with sackcloth, and mourn before Abner. And king David *himself* followed the bier.

32 And they buried Abner in Hebron: and the king lifted up his voice, and wept at the grave of Abner; and all the people wept.

33 And the king lamented over Abner, and said, Died Abner as a fool dieth?

34 Thy hands *were* not bound, nor thy feet put into fetters: as a man falleth before wicked men, *so* fellest thou. And all the people wept again over him.

35 And when all the people came to cause David to eat meat while it was yet day, David sware, saying, So do God to me, and more also, if I taste bread, or ought else, till the sun be down.

36 And all the people took notice *of it,* and it pleased them: as whatsoever the king did pleased all the people.

37 For all the people and all Israel understood that day that it was not of the king to slay Abner the son of Ner.

38 And the king said unto his servants, Know ye not that there is a prince and a great man fallen this day in Israel?

39 And I *am* this day weak, though anointed king; and these men the sons of Zeruiah *be* too hard for me: the LORD shall reward the doer of evil according to his wickedness.

4

1 And when Saul's son heard that Abner was dead in Hebron, his hands were feeble, and all the Israelites were troubled.

2 And Saul's son had two men *that were* captains of bands: the name of the one *was* Baanah, and the name of the other Rechab, the sons of Rimmon a Beerothite, of the children of Benjamin: (for Beeroth also was reckoned to Benjamin:

3 And the Beerothites fled to Gittaim, and were sojourners there until this day.)

4 And Jonathan, Saul's son, had a son *that was* lame of *his* feet. He was five years old when the tidings came of Saul and Jonathan out of Jezreel, and his nurse took him up, and fled: and it came to pass, as she made haste to flee, that he fell, and became lame. And his name *was* Mephibosheth.

5 And the sons of Rimmon the Beerothite, Rechab and Baanah, went, and came about the heat of the day to the house of Ish-bosheth, who lay on a bed at noon.

6 And they came thither into the midst of the house, *as though* they would have fetched wheat; and they smote him under the fifth *rib:* and Rechab and Baanah his brother escaped.

7 For when they came into the house, he lay on his bed in his bedchamber, and they smote him, and slew him, and beheaded him, and took his head, and gat them away through the plain all night.

8 And they brought the head of Ish-bosheth unto David to Hebron, and said to the king, Behold the head of Ish-bosheth the son of Saul thine enemy, which sought thy life; and the LORD hath avenged my lord the king this day of Saul, and of his seed.

9 And David answered Rechab and Baanah his brother, the sons of Rimmon the Beerothite, and said unto them, As the LORD liveth, who hath redeemed my soul out of all adversity,

10 When one told me, saying, Behold, Saul is dead, thinking to have brought good tidings, I took hold of him, and slew him in Ziklag, who *thought* that I would have given him a reward for his tidings:

11 How much more, when wicked men have slain a righteous person in his own house upon his bed? shall I not therefore now require his blood of your hand, and take you away from the earth?

12And David commanded his young
men, and they slew them, and cut off their
hands and their feet, and hanged *them* up
over the pool in Hebron. But they took
the head of Ish-bosheth, and buried *it* in
the sepulchre of Abner in Hebron.

5

1Then came all the tribes of Israel to
David unto Hebron, and spake, saying,
Behold, we *are* thy bone and thy flesh.
2Also in time past, when Saul was king
over us, thou wast he that leddest out and
broughtest in Israel: and the LORD said to
thee, Thou shalt feed my people Israel, and
thou shalt be a captain over Israel.
3So all the elders of Israel came to the
king to Hebron; and king David made a
league with them in Hebron before the
LORD: and they anointed David king over
Israel.
4David *was* thirty
years old when he
began to reign, *and*
he reigned forty
years.

5:4 Young Leaders
◄ 1 Samuel 17:33
2 Chronicles 24:1 ►

5In Hebron he
reigned over Judah seven years and six
months: and in Jerusalem he reigned
thirty and three years over all Israel and
Judah.
6And the king and his men went to Jerusalem unto the Jebusites, the inhabitants
of the land: which spake unto David, saying, Except thou take away the blind and
the lame, thou shalt not come in hither:
thinking, David cannot come in hither.
7Nevertheless David took the strong
hold of Zion: the same *is* the city of David.
8And David said on that day, Whosoever getteth up to the gutter, and smiteth
the Jebusites, and the lame and the blind,
that are hated of David's soul, *he shall be
chief and captain.* Wherefore they said, The
blind and the lame shall not come into
the house.
9So David dwelt in the fort, and called
it the city of David. And David built round
about from Millo and inward.
10And David went on, and grew great,
and the LORD God of hosts *was* with him.
11And Hiram king of Tyre sent messengers to David, and cedar trees, and carpenters, and masons: and they built David an
house.
12And David perceived that the LORD
had established him king over Israel, and
that he had exalted his kingdom for his
people Israel's sake.
13And David took *him* more concubines
and wives out of Jerusalem, after he was
come from Hebron: and there were yet
sons and daughters born to David.
14And these *be* the names of those that
were born unto him in Jerusalem; Sham-
muah, and Shobab, and Nathan, and Solomon,
15Ibhar also, and Elishua, and Nepheg,
and Japhia,
16And Elishama, and Eliada, and Eliphalet.
17But when the Philistines heard that
they had anointed David king over Israel,
all the Philistines came up to seek David;
and David heard *of it,* and went down to
the hold.
18The Philistines also came and spread
themselves in the valley of Rephaim.
19And David enquired of the LORD, saying, Shall I go up to the Philistines? wilt
thou deliver them into mine hand? And
the LORD said unto David, Go up: for I will
doubtless deliver the Philistines into thine
hand.
20And David came to Baal-perazim, and
David smote them there, and said, The
LORD hath broken forth upon mine enemies before me, as the breach of waters.
Therefore he called the name of that place
Baal-perazim.
21And there they left their images, and
David and his men burned them.
22And the Philistines came up yet again,
and spread themselves in the valley of
Rephaim.
23And when David enquired of the
LORD, he said, Thou shalt not go up; *but*
fetch a compass behind them, and come
upon them over against the mulberry trees.
24And let it be, when thou hearest the
sound of a going in the tops of the mulberry trees, that then thou shalt bestir thyself: for then shall the LORD go out before
thee, to smite the host of the Philistines.
25And David did so, as the LORD had
commanded him; and smote the Philistines from Geba until thou come to Gazer.

6

1Again, David gathered together all *the*
chosen *men* of Israel, thirty thousand.
2And David arose, and went with all the
people that *were* with him from Baale of
Judah, to bring up from thence the ark of

God, whose name is called by the name
of the LORD of hosts that dwelleth *between*
the cherubims.
3 And they set the ark of God upon a new
cart, and brought it out of the house of
Abinadab that *was* in Gibeah: and Uzzah
and Ahio, the sons of Abinadab, drave the
new cart.
4 And they brought it out of the house
of Abinadab which *was* at Gibeah, accom-
panying the ark of God: and Ahio went
before the ark.
5 And David and all the house of Israel
played before the LORD on all manner of
instruments made of fir wood, even on
harps, and on psalteries, and on timbrels,
and on cornets, and on cymbals.
6 And when they came to Nachon's
threshingfloor, Uzzah put forth *his hand*
to the ark of God, and took hold of it; for
the oxen shook *it*.
7 And the anger of the LORD was kindled
against Uzzah; and God smote him there
for *his* error; and there he died by the ark
of God.
8 And David was displeased, because the
LORD had made a breach upon Uzzah: and
he called the name of the place Perez-
uzzah to this day.
9 And David was afraid of the LORD that
day, and said, How shall the ark of the
LORD come to me?
10 So David would not remove the ark
of the LORD unto him into the city of David: but David carried it aside into the
house of Obed-edom the Gittite.
11 And the ark
of the LORD con-
tinued in the
house of Obed-
edom the Gittite
three months: and
the LORD blessed Obed-edom, and all his
household.

6:11 Blessings
◄ Genesis 24:35
1 Kings 3:13 ►

12 And it was told king David, saying,
The LORD hath blessed the house of Obed-
edom, and all that *pertaineth* unto him,
because of the ark of God. So David went
and brought up the ark of God from the
house of Obed-edom into the city of David with gladness.
13 And it was *so*, that when they that bare
the ark of the LORD had gone six paces, he
sacrificed oxen and fatlings.
14 And David danced before the LORD
with all *his* might; and David *was* girded
with a linen ephod.
15 So David and all the house of Israel
brought up the ark of the LORD with shouting, and with the sound of the trumpet.
16 And as the ark of the LORD came into
the city of David, Michal Saul's daughter
looked through a window, and saw king
David leaping and dancing before the
LORD; and she despised him in her heart.
17 And they brought in the ark of the
LORD, and set it in his place, in the midst
of the tabernacle that David had pitched
for it: and David offered burnt offerings
and peace offerings before the LORD.
18 And as soon as David had made an
end of offering burnt offerings and peace
offerings, he blessed the people in the
name of the LORD of hosts.
19 And he dealt among all the people,
even among the whole multitude of Israel,
as well to the women as men, to every one
a cake of bread, and a good piece *of flesh*,
and a flagon *of wine*. So all the people departed every one to his house.
20 Then David returned to bless his
household. And Michal the daughter of
Saul came out to meet David, and said,
How glorious was the king of Israel today,
who uncovered himself to day in the eyes
of the handmaids of his servants, as one
of the vain fellows shamelessly uncovereth
himself!
21 And David said unto Michal, *It was*
before the LORD, which chose me before
thy father, and before all his house, to appoint me ruler over the people of the LORD,
over Israel: therefore will I play before the
LORD.
22 And I will yet be more vile than thus,
and will be base in mine own sight: and
of the maidservants which thou hast spoken of, of them shall I be had in honour.
23 Therefore Michal the daughter of Saul
had no child unto the day of her death.

7

1 And it came to pass, when the king sat
in his house, and the LORD had given him
rest round about from all his enemies;
2 That the king said unto Nathan the
prophet, See now, I dwell in an house of
cedar, but the ark of God dwelleth within
curtains.
3 And Nathan said to the king, Go, do
all that *is* in thine heart; for the LORD *is*
with thee.

4 And it came to pass that night, that the word of the LORD came unto Nathan, saying,

5 Go and tell my servant David, Thus saith the LORD, Shalt thou build me an house for me to dwell in?

6 Whereas I have not dwelt in *any* house since the time that I brought up the children of Israel out of Egypt, even to this day, but have walked in a tent and in a tabernacle.

7 In all *the places* wherein I have walked with all the children of Israel spake I a word with any of the tribes of Israel, whom I commanded to feed my people Israel, saying, Why build ye not me an house of cedar?

8 Now therefore so shalt thou say unto my servant David, Thus saith the LORD of hosts, I took thee from the sheepcote, from following the sheep, to be ruler over my people, over Israel:

7:8 God at Work
◄ 1 Samuel 2:7
1 Kings 14:7 ►

9 And I was with thee whithersoever thou wentest, and have cut off all thine enemies out of thy sight, and have made thee a great name, like unto the name of the great *men* that *are* in the earth.

10 Moreover I will appoint a place for my people Israel, and will plant them, that they may dwell in a place of their own, and move no more; neither shall the children of wickedness afflict them any more, as beforetime,

11 And as since the time that I commanded judges *to be* over my people Israel, and have caused thee to rest from all thine enemies. Also the LORD telleth thee that he will make thee an house.

12 And when thy days be fulfilled, and thou shalt sleep with thy fathers, I will set up thy seed after thee, which shall proceed out of thy bowels, and I will establish his kingdom.

13 He shall build an house for my name, and I will stablish the throne of his kingdom for ever.

14 I will be his father, and he shall be my son. If he commit iniquity, I will chasten him with the rod of men, and with the stripes of the children of men:

15 But my mercy shall not depart away from him, as I took *it* from Saul, whom I put away before thee.

16 And thine house and thy kingdom shall be established for ever before thee: thy throne shall be established for ever.

17 According to all these words, and according to all this vision, so did Nathan speak unto David.

18 Then went king David in, and sat before the LORD, and he said, Who *am* I, O Lord GOD? and what *is* my house, that thou hast brought me hitherto?

19 And this was yet a small thing in thy sight, O Lord GOD; but thou hast spoken also of thy servant's house for a great while to come. And *is* this the manner of man, O Lord GOD?

20 And what can David say more unto thee? for thou, Lord GOD, knowest thy servant.

21 For thy word's sake, and according to thine own heart, hast thou done all these great things, to make thy servant know *them*.

22 Wherefore thou art great, O LORD God: for *there is* none like thee, neither *is there any* God beside thee, according to all that we have heard with our ears.

7:22 Only One God
◄ Deuteronomy 32:39
1 Chronicles 17:20 ►

23 And what one nation in the earth *is* like thy people, *even* like Israel, whom God went to redeem for a people to himself, and to make him a name, and to do for you great things and terrible, for thy land, before thy people, which thou redeemedst to thee from Egypt, *from* the nations and their gods?

24 For thou hast confirmed to thyself thy people Israel *to be* a people unto thee for ever: and thou, LORD, art become their God.

25 And now, O LORD God, the word that thou hast spoken concerning thy servant, and concerning his house, establish *it* for ever, and do as thou hast said.

26 And let thy name be magnified for ever, saying, The LORD of hosts *is* the God over Israel: and let the house of thy servant David be established before thee.

27 For thou, O LORD of hosts, God of Israel, hast revealed to thy servant, saying, I will build thee an house: therefore hath thy servant found in his heart to pray this prayer unto thee.

28 And now, O Lord GOD, thou *art* that

God, and thy words be true, and thou hast promised this goodness unto thy servant:

> **7:28 God's Word**
> ◄ Deuteronomy 32:4
> Psalm 33:4 ►

29 Therefore now let it please thee to bless the house of thy servant, that it may continue for ever before thee: for thou, O Lord GOD, hast spoken *it:* and with thy blessing let the house of thy servant be blessed for ever.

8

1 And after this it came to pass, that David smote the Philistines, and subdued them: and David took Metheg-ammah out of the hand of the Philistines.

2 And he smote Moab, and measured them with a line, casting them down to the ground; even with two lines measured he to put to death, and with one full line to keep alive. And so the Moabites became David's servants, *and* brought gifts.

3 David smote also Hadadezer, the son of Rehob, king of Zobah, as he went to recover his border at the river Euphrates.

4 And David took from him a thousand *chariots,* and seven hundred horsemen, and twenty thousand footmen: and David houghed all the chariot *horses,* but reserved of them *for* an hundred chariots.

> **8:4 Cruelty to Animals**
> ◄ Numbers 22:27
> 1 Chronicles 18:4 ►

5 And when the Syrians of Damascus came to succour Hadadezer king of Zobah, David slew of the Syrians two and twenty thousand men.

6 Then David put garrisons in Syria of Damascus: and the Syrians became servants to David, *and* brought gifts. And the LORD preserved David whithersoever he went.

> **8:6 Safety**
> ◄ Joshua 24:17
> Nehemiah 9:6 ►

7 And David took the shields of gold that were on the servants of Hadadezer, and brought them to Jerusalem.

8 And from Betah, and from Berothai, cities of Hadadezer, king David took exceeding much brass.

9 When Toi king of Hamath heard that David had smitten all the host of Hadadezer,

10 Then Toi sent Joram his son unto king David, to salute him, and to bless him, because he had fought against Hadadezer, and smitten him: for Hadadezer had wars with Toi. And *Joram* brought with him vessels of silver, and vessels of gold, and vessels of brass:

> **8:10-11 Tithing**
> ◄ Numbers 31:50
> 1 Chronicles 29:9 ►

11 Which also king David did dedicate unto the LORD, with the silver and gold that he had dedicated of all nations which he subdued;

12 Of Syria, and of Moab, and of the children of Ammon, and of the Philistines, and of Amalek, and of the spoil of Hadadezer, son of Rehob, king of Zobah.

13 And David gat *him* a name when he returned from smiting of the Syrians in the valley of salt, *being* eighteen thousand *men.*

14 And he put garrisons in Edom; throughout all Edom put he garrisons, and all they of Edom became David's servants. And the LORD preserved David whithersoever he went.

15 And David reigned over all Israel; and David executed judgment and justice unto all his people.

16 And Joab the son of Zeruiah *was* over the host; and Jehoshaphat the son of Ahilud *was* recorder;

17 And Zadok the son of Ahitub, and Ahimelech the son of Abiathar, *were* the priests; and Seraiah *was* the scribe;

18 And Benaiah the son of Jehoiada *was over* both the Cherethites and the Pelethites; and David's sons were chief rulers.

9

1 And David said, Is there yet any that is left of the house of Saul, that I may shew him kindness for Jonathan's sake?

> **9:1 "Thank You"**
> ◄ 1 Samuel 15:6
> 2 Samuel 10:2 ►

2 And *there was* of the house of Saul a servant whose name *was* Ziba. And when they had called him unto David, the king said unto him, *Art* thou Ziba? And he said, Thy servant *is he.*

3 And the king said, *Is* there not yet any of the house of Saul, that I may shew the kindness of God unto him? And Ziba said unto the king, Jonathan hath yet a son, *which is* lame on *his* feet.

4 And the king said unto him, Where *is* he? And Ziba said unto the king, Behold,

he *is* in the house of Machir, the son of Ammiel, in Lo-debar.

5 Then king David sent, and fetched him out of the house of Machir, the son of Ammiel, from Lo-debar.

6 Now when Mephibosheth, the son of Jonathan, the son of Saul, was come unto David, he fell on his face, and did reverence. And David said, Mephibosheth. And he answered, Behold thy servant!

7 And David said unto him, Fear not: for I will surely shew thee kindness for Jonathan thy father's sake, and will restore thee all the land of Saul thy father; and thou shalt eat bread at my table continually.

8 And he bowed himself, and said, What *is* thy servant, that thou shouldest look upon such a dead dog as I *am?*

9 Then the king called to Ziba, Saul's servant, and said unto him, I have given unto thy master's son all that pertained to Saul and to all his house.

10 Thou therefore, and thy sons, and thy servants, shall till the land for him, and thou shalt bring in *the fruits,* that thy master's son may have food to eat: but Mephibosheth thy master's son shall eat bread alway at my table. Now Ziba had fifteen sons and twenty servants.

11 Then said Ziba unto the king, According to all that my lord the king hath commanded his servant, so shall thy servant do. As for Mephibosheth, *said the king,* he shall eat at my table, as one of the king's sons.

12 And Mephibosheth had a young son, whose name *was* Micha. And all that dwelt in the house of Ziba *were* servants unto Mephibosheth.

13 So Mephibosheth dwelt in Jerusalem: for he did eat continually at the king's table; and was lame on both his feet.

10

1 And it came to pass after this, that the king of the children of Ammon died, and Hanun his son reigned in his stead.

2 Then said David, I will shew kindness unto Hanun the son of Nahash, as his father shewed kindness unto me. And David sent to comfort him by the hand of his servants for his father. And David's servants came into the land of the children of Ammon.

10:2 "Thank You"
◄ 2 Samuel 9:1
1 Kings 2:7 ►

3 And the princes of the children of Ammon said unto Hanun their lord, Thinkest thou that David doth honour thy father, that he hath sent comforters unto thee? hath not David *rather* sent his servants unto thee, to search the city, and to spy it out, and to overthrow it?

4 Wherefore Hanun took David's servants, and shaved off the one half of their beards, and cut off their garments in the middle, *even* to their buttocks, and sent them away.

5 When they told *it* unto David, he sent to meet them, because the men were greatly ashamed: and the king said, Tarry at Jericho until your beards be grown, and *then* return.

6 And when the children of Ammon saw that they stank before David, the children of Ammon sent and hired the Syrians of Beth-rehob, and the Syrians of Zoba, twenty thousand footmen, and of king Maacah a thousand men, and of Ish-tob twelve thousand men.

7 And when David heard of *it,* he sent Joab, and all the host of the mighty men.

8 And the children of Ammon came out, and put the battle in array at the entering in of the gate: and the Syrians of Zoba, and of Rehob, and Ish-tob, and Maacah, *were* by themselves in the field.

9 When Joab saw that the front of the battle was against him before and behind, he chose of all the choice *men* of Israel, and put *them* in array against the Syrians:

10 And the rest of the people he delivered into the hand of Abishai his brother, that he might put *them* in array against the children of Ammon.

11 And he said, If the Syrians be too strong for me, then thou shalt help me: but if the children of Ammon be too strong for thee, then I will come and help thee.

12 Be of good courage, and let us play the men for our people, and for the cities of our God: and the LORD do that which seemeth him good.

13 And Joab drew nigh, and the people that *were* with him, unto the battle against the Syrians: and they fled before him.

14 And when the children of Ammon saw that the Syrians were fled, then fled they also before Abishai, and entered into the city. So Joab returned from the children of Ammon, and came to Jerusalem.

15 And when the Syrians saw that they
were smitten before Israel, they gathered
themselves together.
16 And Hadarezer sent, and brought out
the Syrians that *were* beyond the river: and
they came to Helam; and Shobach the captain of the host of Hadarezer *went* before
them.
17 And when it was told David, he gathered all Israel together, and passed over
Jordan, and came to Helam. And the Syrians set themselves in array against David,
and fought with him.
18 And the Syrians fled before Israel; and
David slew *the men of* seven hundred chariots of the Syrians, and forty thousand
horsemen, and smote Shobach the captain
of their host, who died there.
19 And when all the kings *that were* servants to Hadarezer saw that they were
smitten before Israel, they made peace
with Israel, and served them. So the Syrians feared to help the children of Ammon
any more.

11

1 And it came to pass, after the year was
expired, at the time when kings go forth *to
battle*, that David sent Joab, and his servants with him, and all Israel; and they
destroyed the children of Ammon, and
besieged Rabbah. But David tarried still at
Jerusalem.
2 And it came to pass in an eveningtide,
that David arose from off his bed, and
walked upon the roof of the king's house:
and from the roof he saw a woman washing herself; and the woman *was* very beautiful to look upon.
3 And David sent and enquired after the
woman. And *one* said, *Is* not this Bath-
sheba, the daughter of Eliam, the wife of
Uriah the Hittite?
4 And David sent messengers, and took
her; and she came in unto him, and he lay
with her; for she was purified from her
uncleanness: and she returned unto her
house.
5 And the woman conceived, and sent
and told David, and said, I *am* with child.
6 And David sent to Joab, *saying*, Send
me Uriah the Hittite. And Joab sent Uriah
to David.
7 And when Uriah was come unto him,
David demanded *of him* how Joab did, and
how the people did, and how the war prospered.
8 And David said to Uriah, Go down to
thy house, and wash thy feet. And Uriah
departed out of the king's house, and there
followed him a mess *of meat* from the king.
9 But Uriah slept at the door of the king's
house with all the servants of his lord, and
went not down to his house.
10 And when they had told David, saying, Uriah went not down unto his house,
David said unto Uriah, Camest thou not
from *thy* journey? why *then* didst thou not
go down unto thine house?
11 And Uriah said unto David, The ark,
and Israel, and Judah, abide in tents; and
my lord Joab, and the servants of my lord,
are encamped in the open fields; shall I
then go into mine house, to eat and to
drink, and to lie with my wife? *as* thou
livest, and *as* thy soul liveth, I will not do
this thing.
12 And David said to Uriah, Tarry here
to day also, and to morrow I will let thee
depart. So Uriah abode in Jerusalem that
day, and the morrow.
13 And when David had called him, he
did eat and drink before him; and he made
him drunk: and at even he went out to lie
on his bed with the servants of his lord,
but went not down to his house.
14 And it came to pass in the morning,
that David wrote a letter to Joab, and sent
it by the hand of Uriah.
15 And he wrote in the letter, saying, Set
ye Uriah in the forefront of the hottest
battle, and retire ye from him, that he may
be smitten, and die.
16 And it came to pass, when Joab observed the city, that he assigned Uriah unto
a place where he knew that valiant men
were.
17 And the men of the city went out, and
fought with Joab: and there fell *some* of
the people of the servants of David; and
Uriah the Hittite died also.
18 Then Joab sent and told David all the
things concerning the war;
19 And charged the messenger, saying,
When thou hast made an end of telling
the matters of the war unto the king,
20 And if so be that the king's wrath arise,
and he say unto thee, Wherefore approached ye so nigh unto the city when ye
did fight? knew ye not that they would
shoot from the wall?
21 Who smote Abimelech the son of

Jerubbesheth? did not a woman cast a
piece of a millstone upon him from the
wall, that he died in Thebez? why went ye
nigh the wall? then say thou, Thy servant
Uriah the Hittite is dead also.
22So the messenger went, and came and
shewed David all that Joab had sent him
for.
23And the messenger said unto David,
Surely the men prevailed against us, and
came out unto us into the field, and we
were upon them even unto the entering of
the gate.
24And the shooters shot from off the
wall upon thy servants; and *some* of the
king's servants be dead, and thy servant
Uriah the Hittite is dead also.
25Then David said unto the messenger,
Thus shalt thou say unto Joab, Let not this
thing displease thee, for the sword devoureth one as well as another: make thy
battle more strong against the city, and
overthrow it: and encourage thou him.
26And when the wife of Uriah heard that
Uriah her husband was dead, she mourned
for her husband.
27And when the mourning was past,
David sent and fetched her to his house,
and she became his wife, and bare him a
son. But the thing that David had done
displeased the LORD.

12

1And the LORD sent Nathan unto David. And he came unto him, and said unto
him, There were two men in one city; the
one rich, and the other poor.
2The rich *man* had exceeding many
flocks and herds:
3But the poor *man* had nothing, save one
little ewe lamb, which he had bought and
nourished up: and it grew up together with
him, and with his children; it did eat of
his own meat, and drank of his own cup,
and lay in his bosom, and was unto him
as a daughter.
4And there came a traveller unto the rich
man, and he spared to take of his own
flock and of his own herd, to dress for the
wayfaring man that was come unto him;
but took the poor man's lamb, and dressed
it for the man that was come to him.
5And David's anger was greatly kindled
against the man; and he said to Nathan,
As the LORD liveth, the man that hath done
this *thing* shall surely die:
6And he shall restore the lamb fourfold,
because he did this thing, and because he
had no pity.
7And Nathan said to David, Thou *art* the
man. Thus saith the LORD God of Israel, I
anointed thee king over Israel, and I delivered thee out of the hand of Saul;
8And I gave thee thy master's house, and
thy master's wives into thy bosom, and
gave thee the house of Israel and of Judah;
and if *that had been* too little, I would
moreover have given unto thee such and
such things.
9Wherefore hast thou despised the commandment of the LORD, to do evil in his
sight? thou hast killed Uriah the Hittite
with the sword, and hast taken his wife *to
be* thy wife, and hast slain him with the
sword of the children of Ammon.
10Now therefore the sword shall never
depart from thine house; because thou
hast despised me, and hast taken the wife
of Uriah the Hittite to be thy wife.
11Thus saith the LORD, Behold, I will
raise up evil against thee out of thine own
house, and I will take thy wives before
thine eyes, and give *them* unto thy neighbour, and he shall lie with thy wives in
the sight of this sun.
12For thou didst *it* secretly: but I will do
this thing before all Israel, and before the
sun.
13And David said unto Nathan, I have
sinned against the LORD. And Nathan said
unto David, The LORD also hath put away
thy sin; thou shalt not die.
14Howbeit, be-
cause by this deed
thou hast given
great occasion to
the enemies of the
LORD to blaspheme,
the child also *that is* born unto thee shall
surely die.

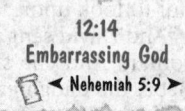

12:14
Embarrassing God
◄ Nehemiah 5:9 ►

15And Nathan departed unto his house.
And the LORD struck the child that Uriah's
wife bare unto David, and it was very sick.
16David therefore besought God for the
child; and David fasted, and went in, and
lay all night upon the earth.
17And the elders of his house arose, *and
went* to him, to raise him up from the
earth: but he would not, neither did he
eat bread with them.
18And it came to pass on the seventh
day, that the child died. And the servants

of David feared to tell him that the child
was dead: for they said, Behold, while the
child was yet alive, we spake unto him, and
he would not hearken unto our voice: how
will he then vex himself, if we tell him that
the child is dead?
19 But when David saw that his servants
whispered, David perceived that the child
was dead: therefore David said unto his
servants, Is the child dead? And they said,
He is dead.
20 Then David arose from the earth,
and washed, and anointed *himself*, and
changed his apparel, and came into the
house of the LORD, and worshipped: then
he came to his own house; and when he
required, they set bread before him, and
he did eat.
21 Then said his servants unto him, What
thing *is* this that thou hast done? thou
didst fast and weep for the child, *while it*
was alive; but when the child was dead,
thou didst rise and eat bread.
22 And he said, While the child was yet
alive, I fasted and wept: for I said, Who
can tell *whether* GOD will be gracious to
me, that the child may live?
23 But now he is dead, wherefore should
I fast? can I bring him back again? I shall
go to him, but he shall not return to me.
24 And David comforted Bath-sheba his
wife, and went in unto her, and lay with
her: and she bare a son, and he called his
name Solomon: and the LORD loved him.
25 And he sent by the hand of Nathan
the prophet; and he called his name Jedi-
diah, because of the LORD.
26 And Joab fought against Rabbah of the
children of Ammon, and took the royal
city.
27 And Joab sent messengers to David,
and said, I have fought against Rabbah,
and have taken the city of waters.
28 Now therefore gather the rest of the
people together, and encamp against the
city, and take it: lest I take the city, and it
be called after my name.
29 And David gathered all the people together, and went to Rabbah, and fought
against it, and took it.
30 And he took their king's crown from
off his head, the weight whereof *was* a talent of gold with the precious stones: and it
was *set* on David's head. And he brought
forth the spoil of the city in great abundance.
31 And he brought forth the people that
were therein, and put *them* under saws, and
under harrows of iron, and under axes of
iron, and made them pass through the
brickkiln: and thus did he unto all the
cities of the children of Ammon. So David and all the people returned unto Jerusalem.

13

1 And it came to pass after this, that Absalom the son of David had a fair sister,
whose name *was* Tamar; and Amnon the
son of David loved her.
2 And Amnon was so vexed, that he fell
sick for his sister Tamar; for she *was* a virgin; and Amnon thought it hard for him
to do any thing to her.
3 But Amnon had a friend, whose name
was Jonadab, the son of Shimeah David's
brother: and Jonadab *was* a very subtil
man.
4 And he said unto him, Why *art* thou,
being the king's son, lean from day to day?
wilt thou not tell me? And Amnon said
unto him, I love Tamar, my brother
Absalom's sister.
5 And Jonadab said unto him, Lay thee
down on thy bed, and make thyself sick:
and when thy father cometh to see thee,
say unto him, I pray thee, let my sister Tamar come, and give me meat, and dress
the meat in my sight, that I may see *it*, and
eat *it* at her hand.
6 So Amnon lay down, and made himself sick: and when the king was come to
see him, Amnon said unto the king, I pray
thee, let Tamar my sister come, and make
me a couple of cakes in my sight, that I
may eat at her hand.
7 Then David sent home to Tamar, saying, Go now to thy brother Amnon's
house, and dress him meat.
8 So Tamar went to her brother Amnon's
house; and he was laid down. And she took
flour, and kneaded *it*, and made cakes in
his sight, and did bake the cakes.
9 And she took a pan, and poured
them out before him; but he refused to eat.
And Amnon said, Have out all men from
me. And they went out every man from
him.
10 And Amnon said unto Tamar, Bring
the meat into the chamber, that I may eat
of thine hand. And Tamar took the cakes
which she had made, and brought *them*
into the chamber to Amnon her brother.

11 And when she had brought *them* unto him to eat, he took hold of her, and said unto her, Come lie with me, my sister.

12 And she answered him, Nay, my brother, do not force me; for no such thing ought to be done in Israel: do not thou this folly.

13 And I, whither shall I cause my shame to go? and as for thee, thou shalt be as one of the fools in Israel. Now therefore, I pray thee, speak unto the king; for he will not withhold me from thee.

14 Howbeit he would not hearken unto her voice: but, being stronger than she, forced her, and lay with her.

15 Then Amnon hated her exceedingly; so that the hatred wherewith he hated her *was* greater than the love wherewith he had loved her. And Amnon said unto her, Arise, be gone.

16 And she said unto him, *There is* no cause: this evil in sending me away *is* greater than the other that thou didst unto me. But he would not hearken unto her.

17 Then he called his servant that ministered unto him, and said, Put now this *woman* out from me, and bolt the door after her.

18 And *she had* a garment of divers colours upon her: for with such robes were the king's daughters *that were* virgins apparelled. Then his servant brought her out, and bolted the door after her.

19 And Tamar put ashes on her head, and rent her garment of divers colours that *was* on her, and laid her hand on her head, and went on crying.

20 And Absalom her brother said unto her, Hath Amnon thy brother been with thee? but hold now thy peace, my sister: he *is* thy brother; regard not this thing. So Tamar remained desolate in her brother Absalom's house.

21 But when king David heard of all these things, he was very wroth.

22 And Absalom spake unto his brother Amnon neither good nor bad: for Absalom hated Amnon, because he had forced his sister Tamar.

23 And it came to pass after two full years, that Absalom had sheepshearers in Baalhazor, which *is* beside Ephraim: and Absalom invited all the king's sons.

24 And Absalom came to the king, and said, Behold now, thy servant hath sheepshearers; let the king, I beseech thee, and his servants go with thy servant.

25 And the king said to Absalom, Nay, my son, let us not all now go, lest we be chargeable unto thee. And he pressed him: howbeit he would not go, but blessed him.

26 Then said Absalom, If not, I pray thee, let my brother Amnon go with us. And the king said unto him, Why should he go with thee?

27 But Absalom pressed him, that he let Amnon and all the king's sons go with him.

28 Now Absalom had commanded his servants, saying, Mark ye now when Amnon's heart is merry with wine, and when I say unto you, Smite Amnon; then kill him, fear not: have not I commanded you? be courageous and be valiant.

29 And the servants of Absalom did unto Amnon as Absalom had commanded. Then all the king's sons arose, and every man gat him up upon his mule, and fled.

30 And it came to pass, while they were in the way, that tidings came to David, saying, Absalom hath slain all the king's sons, and there is not one of them left.

31 Then the king arose, and tare his garments, and lay on the earth; and all his servants stood by with their clothes rent.

32 And Jonadab, the son of Shimeah David's brother, answered and said, Let not my lord suppose *that* they have slain all the young men the king's sons; for Amnon only is dead: for by the appointment of Absalom this hath been determined from the day that he forced his sister Tamar.

33 Now therefore let not my lord the king take the thing to his heart, to think that all the king's sons are dead: for Amnon only is dead.

34 But Absalom fled. And the young man that kept the watch lifted up his eyes, and looked, and, behold, there came much people by the way of the hill side behind him.

35 And Jonadab said unto the king, Behold, the king's sons come: as thy servant said, so it is.

36 And it came to pass, as soon as he had made an end of speaking, that, behold, the king's sons came, and lifted up their voice and wept: and the king also and all his servants wept very sore.

37 But Absalom fled, and went to Talmai, the son of Ammihud, king of Geshur. And *David* mourned for his son every day.

38 So Absalom fled, and went to Geshur, and was there three years.

39 And *the soul of* king David longed to go forth unto Absalom: for he was comforted concerning Amnon, seeing he was dead.

14

1 Now Joab the son of Zeruiah perceived that the king's heart *was* toward Absalom.

2 And Joab sent to Tekoah, and fetched thence a wise woman, and said unto her, I pray thee, feign thyself to be a mourner, and put on now mourning apparel, and anoint not thyself with oil, but be as a woman that had a long time mourned for the dead:

3 And come to the king, and speak on this manner unto him. So Joab put the words in her mouth.

4 And when the woman of Tekoah spake to the king, she fell on her face to the ground, and did obeisance, and said, Help, O king.

5 And the king said unto her, What aileth thee? And she answered, I *am* indeed a widow woman, and mine husband is dead.

6 And thy handmaid had two sons, and they two strove together in the field, and *there was* none to part them, but the one smote the other, and slew him.

7 And, behold, the whole family is risen against thine handmaid, and they said, Deliver him that smote his brother, that we may kill him, for the life of his brother whom he slew; and we will destroy the heir also: and so they shall quench my coal which is left, and shall not leave to my husband *neither* name nor remainder upon the earth.

8 And the king said unto the woman, Go to thine house, and I will give charge concerning thee.

9 And the woman of Tekoah said unto the king, My lord, O king, the iniquity *be* on me, and on my father's house: and the king and his throne *be* guiltless.

10 And the king said, Whosoever saith *ought* unto thee, bring him to me, and he shall not touch thee any more.

11 Then said she, I pray thee, let the king remember the LORD thy God, that thou wouldest not suffer the revengers of blood to destroy any more, lest they destroy my son. And he said, As the LORD liveth, there shall not one hair of thy son fall to the earth.

12 Then the woman said, Let thine handmaid, I pray thee, speak *one* word unto my lord the king. And he said, Say on.

13 And the woman said, Wherefore then hast thou thought such a thing against the people of God? for the king doth speak this thing as one which is faulty, in that the king doth not fetch home again his banished.

14 For we must needs die, and *are* as water spilt on the ground, which cannot be gathered up again; neither doth God respect *any* person: yet doth he devise means, that his banished be not expelled from him.

14:14
Death
◄ Job 30:23 ►

15 Now therefore that I am come to speak of this thing unto my lord the king, *it is* because the people have made me afraid: and thy handmaid said, I will now speak unto the king; it may be that the king will perform the request of his handmaid.

16 For the king will hear, to deliver his handmaid out of the hand of the man *that would* destroy me and my son together out of the inheritance of God.

17 Then thine handmaid said, The word of my lord the king shall now be comfortable: for as an angel of God, so *is* my lord the king to discern good and bad: therefore the LORD thy God will be with thee.

18 Then the king answered and said unto the woman, Hide not from me, I pray thee, the thing that I shall ask thee. And the woman said, Let my lord the king now speak.

19 And the king said, *Is not* the hand of Joab with thee in all this? And the woman answered and said, *As* thy soul liveth, my lord the king, none can turn to the right hand or to the left from ought that my lord the king hath spoken: for thy servant Joab, he bade me, and he put all these words in the mouth of thine handmaid:

20 To fetch about this form of speech hath thy servant Joab done this thing: and my lord *is* wise, according to the wisdom of an angel of God, to know all *things* that *are* in the earth.

21 And the king said unto Joab, Behold
now, I have done this thing: go therefore,
bring the young man Absalom again.
22 And Joab fell to the ground on his face,
and bowed himself, and thanked the king:
and Joab said, Today thy servant knoweth
that I have found grace in thy sight, my
lord, O king, in that the king hath fulfilled
the request of his servant.
23 So Joab arose and went to Geshur, and
brought Absalom to Jerusalem.
24 And the king said, Let him turn to his
own house, and let him not see my face.
So Absalom returned to his own house,
and saw not the king's face.
25 But in all Israel there was none to be
so much praised as Absalom for his beauty: from the sole of his foot even to the
crown of his head there was no blemish
in him.
26 And when he polled his head, (for it
was at every year's end that he polled *it:*
because *the hair* was heavy on him, therefore he polled it:) he weighed the hair of
his head at two hundred shekels after the
king's weight.
27 And unto Absalom there were born
three sons, and one daughter, whose name
was Tamar: she was a woman of a fair countenance.
28 So Absalom dwelt two full years in Jerusalem, and saw not the king's face.
29 Therefore Absalom sent for Joab, to
have sent him to the king; but he would
not come to him: and when he sent again
the second time, he would not come.
30 Therefore he said unto his servants,
See, Joab's field is near mine, and he hath
barley there; go and set it on fire. And
Absalom's servants set the field on fire.
31 Then Joab arose, and came to Absalom unto *his* house, and said unto him,
Wherefore have thy servants set my field
on fire?
32 And Absalom answered Joab, Behold,
I sent unto thee, saying, Come hither, that
I may send thee to the king, to say, Wherefore am I come from Geshur? *it had been*
good for me *to have been* there still: now
therefore let me see the king's face; and
if there be *any* iniquity in me, let him
kill me.
33 So Joab came to the king, and told
him: and when he had called for Absalom,
he came to the king, and bowed himself
on his face to the ground before the king:
and the king kissed Absalom.

15

1 And it came to pass after this, that Absalom prepared him chariots and horses,
and fifty men to run before him.
2 And Absalom
rose up early, and
stood beside the
way of the gate: and
it was *so,* that when
any man that had a
controversy came to the king for judgment,
then Absalom called unto him, and said,
Of what city *art* thou? And he said, Thy
servant *is* of one of the tribes of Israel.

15:1-2, 4 Ambition
◄ Genesis 11:4
1 Kings 1:5 ►

3 And Absalom said unto him, See, thy
matters *are* good and right; but *there is* no
man *deputed* of the king to hear thee.
4 Absalom said moreover, Oh that I were
made judge in the land, that every man
which hath any suit or cause might come
unto me, and I would do him justice!
5 And it was *so,*
that when any man
came nigh *to him* to
do him obeisance,
he put forth his
hand, and took him,
and kissed him.

15:5
"Dangerous Kisses"
◄ 2 Samuel 20:9 ►

6 And on this manner did Absalom to
all Israel that came to the king for judgment: so Absalom stole the hearts of the
men of Israel.
7 And it came to pass after forty years,
that Absalom said unto the king, I pray
thee, let me go and pay my vow, which I
have vowed unto the LORD, in Hebron.
8 For thy servant vowed a vow while I
abode at Geshur in Syria, saying, If the
LORD shall bring me again indeed to Jerusalem, then I will serve the LORD.
9 And the king said unto him, Go in
peace. So he arose, and went to Hebron.
10 But Absalom sent spies throughout all
the tribes of Israel, saying, As soon as ye
hear the sound of the trumpet, then ye
shall say, Absalom reigneth in Hebron.
11 And with Absalom went two hundred
men out of Jerusalem, *that were* called; and
they went in their simplicity, and they
knew not any thing.
12 And Absalom sent for Ahithophel the
Gilonite, David's counsellor, from his city,
even from Giloh, while he offered sacrifices. And the conspiracy was strong; for

the people increased continually with Absalom.

13And there came a messenger to David, saying, The hearts of the men of Israel are after Absalom.

14And David said unto all his servants that *were* with him at Jerusalem, Arise, and let us flee; for we shall not *else* escape from Absalom: make speed to depart, lest he overtake us suddenly, and bring evil upon us, and smite the city with the edge of the sword.

15And the king's servants said unto the king, Behold, thy servants *are ready to do* whatsoever my lord the king shall appoint.

16And the king went forth, and all his household after him. And the king left ten women, *which were* concubines, to keep the house.

17And the king went forth, and all the people after him, and tarried in a place that was far off.

18And all his servants passed on beside him; and all the Cherethites, and all the Pelethites, and all the Gittites, six hundred men which came after him from Gath, passed on before the king.

19Then said the king to Ittai the Gittite, Wherefore goest thou also with us? return to thy place, and abide with the king: for thou *art* a stranger, and also an exile.

20Whereas thou camest *but* yesterday, should I this day make thee go up and down with us? seeing I go whither I may, return thou, and take back thy brethren: mercy and truth *be* with thee.

21And Ittai answered the king, and said, *As* the LORD liveth, and *as* my lord the king liveth, surely in what place my lord the king shall be, whether in death or life, even there also will thy servant be.

22And David said to Ittai, Go and pass over. And Ittai the Gittite passed over, and all his men, and all the little ones that *were* with him.

23And all the country wept with a loud voice, and all the people passed over: the king also himself passed over the brook Kidron, and all the people passed over, toward the way of the wilderness.

24And lo Zadok also, and all the Levites *were* with him, bearing the ark of the covenant of God: and they set down the ark of God; and Abiathar went up, until all the people had done passing out of the city.

25And the king said unto Zadok, Carry back the ark of God into the city: if I shall find favour in the eyes of the LORD, he will bring me again, and shew me *both* it, and his habitation:

26But if he thus say, I have no delight in thee; behold, *here am* I, let him do to me as seemeth good unto him.

27The king said also unto Zadok the priest, *Art not* thou a seer? return into the city in peace, and your two sons with you, Ahimaaz thy son, and Jonathan the son of Abiathar.

28See, I will tarry in the plain of the wilderness, until there come word from you to certify me.

29Zadok therefore and Abiathar carried the ark of God again to Jerusalem: and they tarried there.

30And David went up by the ascent of *mount* Olivet, and wept as he went up, and had his head covered, and he went barefoot: and all the people that *was* with him covered every man his head, and they went up, weeping as they went up.

31And *one* told David, saying, Ahithophel *is* among the conspirators with Absalom. And David said, O LORD, I pray thee, turn the counsel of Ahithophel into foolishness.

32And it came to pass, that *when* David was come to the top *of the mount,* where he worshipped God, behold, Hushai the Archite came to meet him with his coat rent, and earth upon his head:

33Unto whom David said, If thou passest on with me, then thou shalt be a burden unto me:

34But if thou return to the city, and say unto Absalom, I will be thy servant, O king; *as* I *have been* thy father's servant hitherto, so *will* I now also *be* thy servant: then mayest thou for me defeat the counsel of Ahithophel.

35And *hast thou* not there with thee Zadok and Abiathar the priests? therefore it shall be, *that* what thing soever thou shalt hear out of the king's house, thou shalt tell *it* to Zadok and Abiathar the priests.

36Behold, *they have* there with them their two sons, Ahimaaz Zadok's *son,* and Jonathan Abiathar's *son;* and by them ye shall send unto me every thing that ye can hear.

37So Hushai David's friend came into

Turn to the next page for more . . .

the city, and Absa-
lom came into Jeru-
salem.

15:37 Good Friends
◄ 2 Samuel 1:26
1 Kings 5:1 ►

16 1And when Da-
vid was a little past
the top *of the hill,*
behold, Ziba the servant of Mephibosheth
met him, with a couple of asses saddled,
and upon them two hundred *loaves* of
bread, and an hundred bunches of raisins,
and an hundred of summer fruits, and a
bottle of wine.
2And the king said unto Ziba, What
meanest thou by these? And Ziba said, The
asses *be* for the king's household to ride
on; and the bread and summer fruit for
the young men to eat; and the wine, that
such as be faint in the wilderness may
drink.
3And the king said, And where *is* thy
master's son? And Ziba said unto the king,
Behold, he abideth at Jerusalem: for he
said, Today shall the house of Israel restore
me the kingdom of my father.
4Then said the king to Ziba, Behold,
thine *are* all that *pertained* unto Mephibosheth. And Ziba said, I humbly beseech
thee *that* I may find grace in thy sight, my
lord, O king.
5And when king David came to Bahurim, behold, thence came out a man of the
family of the house of Saul, whose name
was Shimei, the son of Gera: he came forth,
and cursed still as he came.
6And he cast stones at David, and at all
the servants of king David: and all the people and all the mighty men *were* on his
right hand and on his left.
7And thus said Shimei when he cursed,
Come out, come out, thou bloody man,
and thou man of Belial:
8The LORD hath returned upon thee all
the blood of the house of Saul, in whose
stead thou hast reigned; and the LORD hath
delivered the kingdom into the hand of
Absalom thy son: and, behold, thou *art*
taken in thy mischief, because thou *art* a
bloody man.
9Then said Abishai the son of Zeruiah
unto the king, Why should this dead dog
curse my lord the king? let me go over, I
pray thee, and take off his head.
10And the king said, What have I to do
with you, ye sons of Zeruiah? so let him
curse, because the LORD hath said unto
him, Curse David. Who shall then say,
Wherefore hast thou done so?
11And David said to Abishai, and to all
his servants, Behold, my son, which came
forth of my bowels, seeketh my life: how
much more now *may this* Benjamite *do it?*
let him alone, and let him curse; for the
LORD hath bidden him.
12It may be that the LORD will look
on mine affliction, and that the LORD
will requite me good for his cursing this
day.
13And as David and his men went by
the way, Shimei went along on the hill's
side over against him, and cursed as he
went, and threw stones at him, and cast
dust.
14And the king, and all the people that
were with him, came weary, and refreshed
themselves there.
15And Absalom, and all the people the
men of Israel, came to Jerusalem, and
Ahithophel with him.
16And it came to pass, when Hushai the
Archite, David's friend, was come unto
Absalom, that Hushai said unto Absalom,
God save the king, God save the king.
17And Absalom said to Hushai, *Is* this
thy kindness to thy friend? why wentest
thou not with thy friend?
18And Hushai said unto Absalom, Nay;
but whom the LORD, and this people, and
all the men of Israel, choose, his will I be,
and with him will I abide.
19And again, whom should I serve?
should I not *serve* in the presence of his son?
as I have served in thy father's presence, so
will I be in thy presence.
20Then said Absalom to Ahithophel,
Give counsel among you what we shall do.
21And Ahithophel said unto Absalom,
Go in unto thy father's concubines, which
he hath left to keep the house; and all
Israel shall hear that thou art abhorred of
thy father: then shall the hands of all that
are with thee be strong.
22So they spread Absalom a tent upon
the top of the house; and Absalom went
in unto his father's concubines in the sight
of all Israel.
23And the counsel of Ahithophel, which
he counselled in those days, *was* as if a man
had enquired at the oracle of God: so *was*
all the counsel of Ahithophel both with
David and with Absalom.

17

1 Moreover Ahithophel said unto Absalom, Let me now choose out twelve thousand men, and I will arise and pursue after David this night:

2 And I will come upon him while he *is* weary and weak handed, and will make him afraid: and all the people that *are* with him shall flee; and I will smite the king only:

3 And I will bring back all the people unto thee: the man whom thou seekest *is* as if all returned: *so* all the people shall be in peace.

4 And the saying pleased Absalom well, and all the elders of Israel.

5 Then said Absalom, Call now Hushai the Archite also, and let us hear likewise what he saith.

6 And when Hushai was come to Absalom, Absalom spake unto him, saying, Ahithophel hath spoken after this manner: shall we do *after* his saying? if not; speak thou.

7 And Hushai said unto Absalom, The counsel that Ahithophel hath given *is* not good at this time.

8 For, said Hushai, thou knowest thy father and his men, that they *be* mighty men, and they *be* chafed in their minds, as a bear robbed of her whelps in the field: and thy father *is* a man of war, and will not lodge with the people.

9 Behold, he is hid now in some pit, or in some *other* place: and it will come to pass, when some of them be overthrown at the first, that whosoever heareth it will say, There is a slaughter among the people that follow Absalom.

10 And he also *that is* valiant, whose heart *is* as the heart of a lion, shall utterly melt: for all Israel knoweth that thy father *is* a mighty man, and *they* which *be* with him *are* valiant men.

11 Therefore I counsel that all Israel be generally gathered unto thee, from Dan even to Beer-sheba, as the sand that *is* by the sea for multitude; and that thou go to battle in thine own person.

12 So shall we come upon him in some place where he shall be found, and we will light upon him as the dew falleth on the ground: and of him and of all the men that *are* with him there shall not be left so much as one.

13 Moreover, if he be gotten into a city, then shall all Israel bring ropes to that city, and we will draw it into the river, until there be not one small stone found there.

14 And Absalom and all the men of Israel said, The counsel of Hushai the Archite *is* better than the counsel of Ahithophel. For the LORD had appointed to defeat the good counsel of Ahithophel, to the intent that the LORD might bring evil upon Absalom.

15 Then said Hushai unto Zadok and to Abiathar the priests, Thus and thus did Ahithophel counsel Absalom and the elders of Israel; and thus and thus have I counselled.

16 Now therefore send quickly, and tell David, saying, Lodge not this night in the plains of the wilderness, but speedily pass over; lest the king be swallowed up, and all the people that *are* with him.

17 Now Jonathan and Ahimaaz stayed by En-rogel; for they might not be seen to come into the city: and a wench went and told them; and they went and told king David.

18 Nevertheless a lad saw them, and told Absalom: but they went both of them away quickly, and came to a man's house in Bahurim, which had a well in his court; whither they went down.

19 And the woman took and spread a covering over the well's mouth, and spread ground corn thereon; and the thing was not known.

20 And when Absalom's servants came to the woman to the house, they said, Where *is* Ahimaaz and Jonathan? And the woman said unto them, They be gone over the brook of water. And when they had sought and could not find *them*, they returned to Jerusalem.

21 And it came to pass, after they were departed, that they came up out of the well, and went and told king David, and said unto David, Arise, and pass quickly over the water: for thus hath Ahithophel counselled against you.

22 Then David arose, and all the people that *were* with him, and they passed over Jordan: by the morning light there lacked not one of them that was not gone over Jordan.

23 And when Ahithophel saw that his counsel was not followed, he saddled *his* ass, and arose, and gat him home to

his house, to his city, and put his household in order, and hanged himself, and died, and was buried in the sepulchre of his father.

24 Then David came to Mahanaim. And Absalom passed over Jordan, he and all the men of Israel with him.

25 And Absalom made Amasa captain of the host instead of Joab: which Amasa *was* a man's son, whose name *was* Ithra an Israelite, that went in to Abigail the daughter of Nahash, sister to Zeruiah Joab's mother.

26 So Israel and Absalom pitched in the land of Gilead.

27 And it came to pass, when David was come to Mahanaim, that Shobi the son of Nahash of Rabbah of the children of Ammon, and Machir the son of Ammiel of Lo-debar, and Barzillai the Gileadite of Rogelim,

28 Brought beds, and basons, and earthen vessels, and wheat, and barley, and flour, and parched *corn,* and beans, and lentiles, and parched *pulse,*

29 And honey, and butter, and sheep, and cheese of kine, for David, and for the people that *were* with him, to eat: for they said, The people *is* hungry, and weary, and thirsty, in the wilderness.

18

1 And David numbered the people that *were* with him, and set captains of thousands and captains of hundreds over them.

2 And David sent forth a third part of the people under the hand of Joab, and a third part under the hand of Abishai the son of Zeruiah, Joab's brother, and a third part under the hand of Ittai the Gittite. And the king said unto the people, I will surely go forth with you myself also.

3 But the people answered, Thou shalt not go forth: for if we flee away, they will not care for us; neither if half of us die, will they care for us: but now *thou art* worth ten thousand of us: therefore now *it is* better that thou succour us out of the city.

4 And the king said unto them, What seemeth you best I will do. And the king stood by the gate side, and all the people came out by hundreds and by thousands.

5 And the king commanded Joab and Abishai and Ittai, saying, *Deal* gently for my sake with the young man, *even* with Absalom. And all the people heard when the king gave all the captains charge concerning Absalom.

6 So the people went out into the field against Israel: and the battle was in the wood of Ephraim;

7 Where the people of Israel were slain before the servants of David, and there was there a great slaughter that day of twenty thousand *men.*

8 For the battle was there scattered over the face of all the country: and the wood devoured more people that day than the sword devoured.

9 And Absalom met the servants of David. And Absalom rode upon a mule, and the mule went under the thick boughs of a great oak, and his head caught hold of the oak, and he was taken up between the heaven and the earth; and the mule that *was* under him went away.

10 And a certain man saw it, and told Joab, and said, Behold, I saw Absalom hanged in an oak.

11 And Joab said unto the man that told him, And, behold, thou sawest *him,* and why didst thou not smite him there to the ground? and I would have given thee ten *shekels* of silver, and a girdle.

12 And the man said unto Joab, Though I should receive a thousand *shekels* of silver in mine hand, *yet* would I not put forth mine hand against the king's son: for in our hearing the king charged thee and Abishai and Ittai, saying, Beware that none *touch* the young man Absalom.

13 Otherwise I should have wrought falsehood against mine own life: for there is no matter hid from the king, and thou thyself wouldest have set thyself against *me.*

14 Then said Joab, I may not tarry thus with thee. And he took three darts in his hand, and thrust them through the heart of Absalom, while he *was* yet alive in the midst of the oak.

15 And ten young men that bare Joab's armour compassed about and smote Absalom, and slew him.

16 And Joab blew the trumpet, and the people returned from pursuing after Israel: for Joab held back the people.

17 And they took Absalom, and cast him into a great pit in the wood, and laid a very great heap of stones upon him: and all Israel fled every one to his tent.

18 Now Absalom in his lifetime had taken

and reared up for himself a pillar, which *is*
in the king's dale: for he said, I have no son
to keep my name in remembrance: and he
called the pillar after his own name: and
it is called unto this day, Absalom's place.
19 Then said Ahimaaz the son of Zadok,
Let me now run, and bear the king tidings,
how that the LORD hath avenged him of
his enemies.
20 And Joab said unto him, Thou shalt
not bear tidings this day, but thou shalt
bear tidings another day: but this day thou
shalt bear no tidings, because the king's
son is dead.
21 Then said Joab to Cushi, Go tell the
king what thou hast seen. And Cushi
bowed himself unto Joab, and ran.
22 Then said Ahimaaz the son of Zadok
yet again to Joab, But howsoever, let me, I
pray thee, also run after Cushi. And Joab
said, Wherefore wilt thou run, my son,
seeing that thou hast no tidings ready?
23 But howsoever, *said he,* let me run. And
he said unto him, Run. Then Ahimaaz ran
by the way of the plain, and overran Cushi.
24 And David sat between the two gates:
and the watchman went up to the roof over
the gate unto the wall, and lifted up his
eyes, and looked, and behold a man running alone.
25 And the watchman cried, and told the
king. And the king said, If he *be* alone, *there*
is tidings in his mouth. And he came apace,
and drew near.
26 And the watchman saw another man
running: and the watchman called unto
the porter, and said, Behold *another* man
running alone. And the king said, He also
bringeth tidings.
27 And the watchman said, Me thinketh
the running of the foremost is like the running of Ahimaaz the son of Zadok. And
the king said, He *is* a good man, and
cometh with good tidings.
28 And Ahimaaz called, and said unto the
king, All is well. And he fell down to the
earth upon his face before the king, and
said, Blessed *be* the LORD thy God, which
hath delivered up the men that lifted up
their hand against
my lord the king.
29 And the king
said, Is the young
man Absalom safe?
And Ahimaaz an-

18:29 Parents Care
◄ 1 Samuel 10:2
Esther 2:11 ►

swered, When Joab sent the king's servant,
and *me* thy servant, I saw a great tumult,
but I knew not what *it was.*
30 And the king said *unto him,* Turn aside,
and stand here. And he turned aside, and
stood still.
31 And, behold, Cushi came; and Cushi
said, Tidings, my lord the king: for the
LORD hath avenged thee this day of all
them that rose up against thee.
32 And the king said unto Cushi, *Is* the
young man Absalom safe? And Cushi answered, The enemies of my lord the king,
and all that rise against thee to do *thee* hurt,
be as *that* young man *is.*
33 And the king
was much moved,
and went up to the
chamber over the
gate, and wept: and
as he went, thus he
said, O my son Absalom, my son, my son
Absalom! would God I had died for thee,
O Absalom, my son, my son!

18:33 Grief
◄ Ruth 1:20
Job 1:20 ►

19
1 And it was told Joab, Behold, the king
weepeth and mourneth for Absalom.
2 And the victory that day was *turned* into
mourning unto all the people: for the people heard say that day how the king was
grieved for his son.
3 And the people gat them by stealth that
day into the city, as people being ashamed
steal away when they flee in battle.
4 But the king covered his face, and the
king cried with a loud voice, O my son
Absalom, O Absalom, my son, my son!
5 And Joab came into the house to the
king, and said, Thou hast shamed this day
the faces of all thy servants, which this day
have saved thy life, and the lives of thy sons
and of thy daughters, and the lives of thy
wives, and the lives of thy concubines;
6 In that thou lovest thine enemies, and
hatest thy friends. For thou hast declared
this day, that thou regardest neither princes
nor servants: for this day I perceive, that if
Absalom had lived, and all we had died
this day, then it had pleased thee well.
7 Now therefore arise, go forth, and speak
comfortably unto thy servants: for I swear
by the LORD, if thou go not forth, there
will not tarry one with thee this night: and
that will be worse unto thee than all the
evil that befell thee from thy youth until
now.

8 Then the king arose, and sat in the gate.
And they told unto all the people, saying,
Behold, the king doth sit in the gate. And
all the people came before the king: for
Israel had fled every man to his tent.
9 And all the people were at strife
throughout all the tribes of Israel, saying,
The king saved us out of the hand of our
enemies, and he delivered us out of the
hand of the Philistines; and now he is fled
out of the land for Absalom.
10 And Absalom, whom we anointed
over us, is dead in battle. Now therefore
why speak ye not a word of bringing the
king back?
11 And king David sent to Zadok and to
Abiathar the priests, saying, Speak unto the
elders of Judah, saying, Why are ye the last
to bring the king back to his house? seeing the speech of all Israel is come to the
king, *even* to his house.
12 Ye *are* my brethren, ye *are* my bones
and my flesh: wherefore then are ye the
last to bring back the king?
13 And say ye to Amasa, *Art* thou not of
my bone, and of my flesh? God do so to
me, and more also, if thou be not captain
of the host before me continually in the
room of Joab.
14 And he bowed the heart of all the men
of Judah, even as *the heart of* one man; so
that they sent *this word* unto the king, Return thou, and all thy servants.
15 So the king returned, and came to Jordan. And Judah came to Gilgal, to go to
meet the king, to conduct the king over
Jordan.
16 And Shimei the son of Gera, a Benjamite, which *was* of Bahurim, hasted and
came down with the men of Judah to meet
king David.
17 And *there were* a thousand men of Benjamin with him, and Ziba the servant of
the house of Saul, and his fifteen sons and
his twenty servants with him; and they
went over Jordan before the king.
18 And there went over a ferry boat to
carry over the king's household, and to do
what he thought good. And Shimei the son
of Gera fell down before the king, as he
was come over Jordan;
19 And said unto the king, Let not my
lord impute iniquity unto me, neither do
thou remember that which thy servant did
perversely the day that my lord the king
went out of Jerusalem, that the king should
take it to his heart.
20 For thy servant doth know that I have
sinned: therefore, behold, I am come the
first this day of all the house of Joseph to
go down to meet my lord the king.
21 But Abishai the son of Zeruiah answered and said, Shall not Shimei be put
to death for this, because he cursed the
LORD'S anointed?
22 And David said,
What have I to do
with you, ye sons
of Zeruiah, that ye
should this day
be adversaries unto
me? shall there any man be put to death
this day in Israel? for do not I know that I
am this day king over Israel?

19:22
Examples of Mercy
◄ 1 Samuel 26:9
1 Kings 1:52 ►

23 Therefore the king said unto Shimei,
Thou shalt not die. And the king sware
unto him.
24 And Mephibosheth the son of Saul
came down to meet the king, and had neither dressed his feet, nor trimmed his
beard, nor washed his clothes, from the
day the king departed until the day he
came *again* in peace.
25 And it came to pass, when he was
come to Jerusalem to meet the king, that
the king said unto him, Wherefore wentest
not thou with me, Mephibosheth?
26 And he answered, My lord, O king, my
servant deceived me: for thy servant said, I
will saddle me an ass, that I may ride
thereon, and go to the king; because thy
servant *is* lame.
27 And he hath slandered thy servant
unto my lord the king; but my lord the
king *is* as an angel of God: do therefore
what is good in thine eyes.
28 For all *of* my father's house were but
dead men before my lord the king: yet
didst thou set thy servant among them that
did eat at thine own table. What right
therefore have I yet to cry any more unto
the king?
29 And the king said unto him, Why
speakest thou any more of thy matters? I
have said, Thou and Ziba divide the land.
30 And Mephibosheth said unto the king,
Yea, let him take all, forasmuch as my lord
the king is come again in peace unto his
own house.
31 And Barzillai the Gileadite came down

and the five sons of Michal the daughter of Saul, whom she brought up for Adriel the son of Barzillai the Meholathite:

9 And he delivered them into the hands of the Gibeonites, and they hanged them in the hill before the LORD: and they fell *all* seven together, and were put to death in the days of harvest, in the first *days,* in the beginning of barley harvest.

10 And Rizpah the daughter of Aiah took sackcloth, and spread it for her upon the rock, from the beginning of harvest until water dropped upon them out of heaven, and suffered neither the birds of the air to rest on them by day, nor the beasts of the field by night.

11 And it was told David what Rizpah the daughter of Aiah, the concubine of Saul, had done.

12 And David went and took the bones of Saul and the bones of Jonathan his son from the men of Jabesh-gilead, which had stolen them from the street of Beth-shan, where the Philistines had hanged them, when the Philistines had slain Saul in Gilboa:

13 And he brought up from thence the bones of Saul and the bones of Jonathan his son; and they gathered the bones of them that were hanged.

14 And the bones of Saul and Jonathan his son buried they in the country of Benjamin in Zelah, in the sepulchre of Kish his father: and they performed all that the king commanded. And after that God was intreated for the land.

15 Moreover the Philistines had yet war again with Israel; and David went down, and his servants with him, and fought against the Philistines: and David waxed faint.

16 And Ishbi-benob, which *was* of the sons of the giant, the weight of whose spear *weighed* three hundred *shekels* of brass in weight, he being girded with a new *sword,* thought to have slain David.

17 But Abishai the son of Zeruiah succoured him, and smote the Philistine, and killed him. Then the men of David sware unto him, saying, Thou shalt go no more out with us to battle, that thou quench not the light of Israel.

18 And it came to pass after this, that there was again a battle with the Philistines at Gob: then Sibbechai the Hushathite slew Saph, which *was* of the sons of the giant.

19 And there was again a battle in Gob with the Philistines, where Elhanan the son of Jaare-oregim, a Bethlehemite, slew *the brother of* Goliath the Gittite, the staff of whose spear *was* like a weaver's beam.

20 And there was yet a battle in Gath, where was a man of *great* stature, that had on every hand six fingers, and on every foot six toes, four and twenty in number; and he also was born to the giant.

21 And when he defied Israel, Jonathan the son of Shimeah the brother of David slew him.

22 These four were born to the giant in Gath, and fell by the hand of David, and by the hand of his servants.

22

1 And David spake unto the LORD the words of this song in the day *that* the LORD had delivered him out of the hand of all his enemies, and out of the hand of Saul:

2 And he said, The LORD *is* my rock, and my fortress, and my deliverer;

22:2 Names of God
◄ 1 Samuel 1:11
1 Chronicles 29:10 ►

3 The God of my rock; in him will I trust: *he is* my shield, and the horn of my salvation, my high tower, and my refuge, my saviour; thou savest me from violence.

4 I will call on the LORD, *who is* worthy to be praised: so shall I be saved from mine enemies.

5 When the waves of death compassed me, the floods of ungodly men made me afraid;

6 The sorrows of hell compassed me about; the snares of death prevented me;

7 In my distress I called upon the LORD, and cried to my God: and he did hear my voice out of his temple, and my cry *did enter* into his ears.

8 Then the earth shook and trembled; the foundations of heaven moved and shook, because he was wroth.

9 There went up a smoke out of his nostrils, and fire out of his mouth devoured: coals were kindled by it.

10 He bowed the heavens also, and came down; and darkness *was* under his feet.

11 And he rode upon a cherub, and did fly: and he was seen upon the wings of the wind.

12 And he made darkness pavilions

round about him, dark waters, *and* thick clouds of the skies.

13 Through the brightness before him were coals of fire kindled.

14 The LORD thundered from heaven, and the most High uttered his voice.

15 And he sent out arrows, and scattered them; lightning, and discomfited them.

16 And the channels of the sea appeared, the foundations of the world were discovered, at the rebuking of the LORD, at the blast of the breath of his nostrils.

17 He sent from above, he took me; he drew me out of many waters;

18 He delivered me from my strong enemy, *and* from them that hated me: for they were too strong for me.

19 They prevented me in the day of my calamity: but the LORD was my stay.

20 He brought me forth also into a large place: he delivered me, because he delighted in me.

21 The LORD rewarded me according to my righteousness: according to the cleanness of my hands hath he recompensed me.

22 For I have kept the ways of the LORD, and have not wickedly departed from my God.

23 For all his judgments *were* before me: and *as for* his statutes, I did not depart from them.

24 I was also upright before him, and have kept myself from mine iniquity.

25 Therefore the LORD hath recompensed me according to my righteousness; according to my cleanness in his eye sight.

26 With the merciful thou wilt shew thyself merciful, *and* with the upright man thou wilt shew thyself upright.

22:26 Promise of Mercy
◄ Exodus 34:7
2 Chronicles 30:9 ►

27 With the pure thou wilt shew thyself pure; and with the froward thou wilt shew thyself unsavoury.

28 And the afflicted people thou wilt save: but thine eyes *are* upon the haughty, *that* thou mayest bring *them* down.

29 For thou *art* my lamp, O LORD: and the LORD will lighten my darkness.

30 For by thee I have run through a troop: by my God have I leaped over a wall.

31 *As for* God, his way *is* perfect; the word of the LORD *is* tried: he *is* a buckler to all them that trust in him.

22:31 God's Perfection
◄ Deuteronomy 32:4
Psalm 18:30 ►

32 For who *is* God, save the LORD? and who *is* a rock, save our God?

33 God *is* my strength *and* power: and he maketh my way perfect.

22:33 Finding Strength
◄ Exodus 15:2
Psalm 28:8 ►

34 He maketh my feet like hinds' *feet*: and setteth me upon my high places.

35 He teacheth my hands to war; so that a bow of steel is broken by mine arms.

36 Thou hast also given me the shield of thy salvation: and thy gentleness hath made me great.

37 Thou hast enlarged my steps under me; so that my feet did not slip.

38 I have pursued mine enemies, and destroyed them; and turned not again until I had consumed them.

39 And I have consumed them, and wounded them, that they could not arise: yea, they are fallen under my feet.

40 For thou hast girded me with strength to battle: them that rose up against me hast thou subdued under me.

41 Thou hast also given me the necks of mine enemies, that I might destroy them that hate me.

42 They looked, but *there was* none to save; *even* unto the LORD, but he answered them not.

43 Then did I beat them as small as the dust of the earth, I did stamp them as the mire of the street, *and* did spread them abroad.

44 Thou also hast delivered me from the strivings of my people, thou hast kept me *to be* head of the heathen: a people *which* I knew not shall serve me.

45 Strangers shall submit themselves unto me: as soon as they hear, they shall be obedient unto me.

46 Strangers shall fade away, and they shall be afraid out of their close places.

47 The LORD liveth; and blessed *be* my rock; and exalted be the God of the rock of my salvation.

48 It *is* God that avengeth me, and that bringeth down the people under me,

49 And that bringeth me forth from mine enemies: thou also hast lifted me up on

high above them that rose up against me:
thou hast delivered me from the violent
man.
50 Therefore I will give thanks unto thee,
O LORD, among the heathen, and I will
sing praises unto thy name.
51 *He is* the tower of salvation for his
king: and sheweth mercy to his anointed,
unto David, and to his seed for evermore.

23

1 Now these *be* the last words of David.
David the son of Jesse said, and the man
who was raised up on high, the anointed
of the God of Jacob, and the sweet psalm-
ist of Israel, said,
2 The Spirit of the LORD spake by me, and
his word *was* in my tongue.
3 The God of Is-
rael said, the Rock
of Israel spake to
me, He that ruleth
over men *must be*
just, ruling in the
fear of God.

23:3 Leaders Should...
◄ Deuteronomy 17:16
2 Chronicles 19:6 ►

4 And *he shall be* as the light of the morning, *when* the sun riseth, *even* a morning
without clouds; *as* the tender grass *spring-*
ing out of the earth by clear shining after
rain.
5 Although my house *be* not so with God;
yet he hath made with me an everlasting
covenant, ordered in all *things,* and sure:
for *this is* all my salvation, and all *my* desire, although he make *it* not to grow.
6 But *the sons* of Belial *shall be* all of them
as thorns thrust away, because they cannot be taken with hands:
7 But the man *that* shall touch them must
be fenced with iron and the staff of a spear;
and they shall be utterly burned with fire
in the *same* place.
8 These *be* the names of the mighty men
whom David had: The Tachmonite that sat
in the seat, chief among the captains; the
same *was* Adino the Eznite: *he lift up his*
spear against eight hundred, whom he slew
at one time.
9 And after him *was* Eleazar the son of
Dodo the Ahohite, *one* of the three mighty
men with David, when they defied the
Philistines *that* were there gathered together to battle, and the men of Israel were
gone away:
10 He arose, and smote the Philistines until his hand was weary, and his hand clave
unto the sword: and the LORD wrought a
great victory that day; and the people returned after him only to spoil.
11 And after him *was* Shammah the son
of Agee the Hararite. And the Philistines
were gathered together into a troop, where
was a piece of ground full of lentiles: and
the people fled from the Philistines.
12 But he stood in the midst of the
ground, and defended it, and slew the Philistines: and the LORD wrought a great victory.
13 And three of the thirty chief went
down, and came to David in the harvest
time unto the cave of Adullam: and the
troop of the Philistines pitched in the valley of Rephaim.
14 And David *was* then in an hold, and
the garrison of the Philistines *was* then *in*
Bethlehem.
15 And David longed, and said, Oh that
one would give me drink of the water of
the well of Bethlehem, which *is* by the gate!
16 And the three mighty men brake
through the host of the Philistines, and
drew water out of the well of Bethlehem,
that *was* by the gate, and took *it,* and
brought *it* to David: nevertheless he would
not drink thereof, but poured it out unto
the LORD.
17 And he said, Be
it far from me,
O LORD, that I
should do this: *is*
not this the blood of
the men that went
in jeopardy of their lives? therefore he
would not drink it. These things did these
three mighty men.

23:17 Unselfishness
◄ 1 Samuel 23:17
Daniel 5:17 ►

18 And Abishai, the brother of Joab, the
son of Zeruiah, was chief among three.
And he lifted up his spear against three
hundred, *and* slew *them,* and had the name
among three.
19 Was he not most honourable of three?
therefore he was their captain: howbeit he
attained not unto the *first* three.
20 And Benaiah the son of Jehoiada, the
son of a valiant man, of Kabzeel, who had
done many acts, he slew two lionlike men
of Moab: he went down also and slew a
lion in the midst of a pit in time of snow:
21 And he slew an Egyptian, a goodly
man: and the Egyptian had a spear in his
hand; but he went down to him with a
staff, and plucked the spear out of the

Egyptian's hand, and slew him with his own spear.

22 These *things* did Benaiah the son of Jehoiada, and had the name among three mighty men.

23 He was more honourable than the thirty, but he attained not to the *first* three. And David set him over his guard.

24 Asahel the brother of Joab *was* one of the thirty; Elhanan the son of Dodo of Bethlehem,

25 Shammah the Harodite, Elika the Harodite,

26 Helez the Paltite, Ira the son of Ikkesh the Tekoite,

27 Abiezer the Anethothite, Mebunnai the Hushathite,

28 Zalmon the Ahohite, Maharai the Netophathite,

29 Heleb the son of Baanah, a Netophathite, Ittai the son of Ribai out of Gibeah of the children of Benjamin,

30 Benaiah the Pirathonite, Hiddai of the brooks of Gaash,

31 Abi-albon the Arbathite, Azmaveth the Barhumite,

32 Eliahba the Shaalbonite, of the sons of Jashen, Jonathan,

33 Shammah the Hararite, Ahiam the son of Sharar the Hararite,

34 Eliphelet the son of Ahasbai, the son of the Maachathite, Eliam the son of Ahithophel the Gilonite,

35 Hezrai the Carmelite, Paarai the Arbite,

36 Igal the son of Nathan of Zobah, Bani the Gadite,

37 Zelek the Ammonite, Nahari the Beerothite, armourbearer to Joab the son of Zeruiah,

38 Ira an Ithrite, Gareb an Ithrite,

39 Uriah the Hittite: thirty and seven in all.

24

1 And again the anger of the LORD was kindled against Israel, and he moved David against them to say, Go, number Israel and Judah.

2 For the king said to Joab the captain of the host, which *was* with him, Go now through all the tribes of Israel, from Dan even to Beer-sheba, and number ye the people, that I may know the number of the people.

3 And Joab said unto the king, Now the LORD thy God add unto the people, how many soever they be, an hundredfold, and that the eyes of my lord the king may see *it:* but why doth my lord the king delight in this thing?

4 Notwithstanding the king's word prevailed against Joab, and against the captains of the host. And Joab and the captains of the host went out from the presence of the king, to number the people of Israel.

5 And they passed over Jordan, and pitched in Aroer, on the right side of the city that *lieth* in the midst of the river of Gad, and toward Jazer:

6 Then they came to Gilead, and to the land of Tahtim-hodshi; and they came to Dan-jaan, and about to Zidon,

7 And came to the strong hold of Tyre, and to all the cities of the Hivites, and of the Canaanites: and they went out to the south of Judah, *even* to Beer-sheba.

8 So when they had gone through all the land, they came to Jerusalem at the end of nine months and twenty days.

9 And Joab gave up the sum of the number of the people unto the king: and there were in Israel eight hundred thousand valiant men that drew the sword; and the men of Judah *were* five hundred thousand men.

10 And David's heart smote him after that he had numbered the people. And David said unto the LORD, I have sinned greatly in that I have done: and now, I beseech thee, O LORD, take away the iniquity of thy servant; for I have done very foolishly.

11 For when David was up in the morning, the word of the LORD came unto the prophet Gad, David's seer, saying,

12 Go and say unto David, Thus saith the LORD, I offer thee three *things;* choose thee one of them, that I may *do it* unto thee.

13 So Gad came to David, and told him, and said unto him, Shall seven years of famine come unto thee in thy land? or wilt thou flee three months before thine enemies, while they pursue thee? or that there be three days' pestilence in thy land? now advise, and see what answer I shall return to him that sent me.

14 And David said unto Gad, I am in a great strait: let us fall now into the hand of the LORD; for his mercies *are*

24:14 God's Mercy
◄ Deuteronomy 4:31
Psalm 86:5 ►

great: and let me not fall into the hand of
man.
15 So the LORD sent a pestilence upon
Israel from the morning even to the time
appointed: and there died of the people
from Dan even to Beer-sheba seventy thousand men.
16 And when the angel stretched out his
hand upon Jerusalem to destroy it, the
LORD repented him of the evil, and said to
the angel that destroyed the people, It is
enough: stay now thine hand. And the
angel of the LORD was by the threshing-
place of Araunah the Jebusite.
17 And David spake unto the LORD when
he saw the angel that smote the people,
and said, Lo, I have sinned, and I have
done wickedly: but these sheep, what have
they done? let thine hand, I pray thee, be
against me, and against my father's house.
18 And Gad came that day to David, and
said unto him, Go up, rear an altar unto
the LORD in the threshingfloor of Araunah
the Jebusite.
19 And David, according to the saying of
Gad, went up as the LORD commanded.
20 And Araunah looked, and saw the king
and his servants coming on toward him:
and Araunah went out, and bowed himself before the king on his face upon the
ground.
21 And Araunah said, Wherefore is my
lord the king come to his servant? And
David said, To buy the threshingfloor of
thee, to build an altar unto the LORD,
that the plague may be stayed from the
people.
22 And Araunah said unto David, Let my
lord the king take and offer up what
seemeth good unto him: behold, *here be*
oxen for burnt sacrifice, and threshing instruments and *other* instruments of the
oxen for wood.
23 All these *things*
did Araunah, *as* a
king, give unto the
king. And Araunah
said unto the king,
The LORD thy God
accept thee.

24:23 Accepted by God
◄ Exodus 28:38
Job 42:9 ►

24 And the king said unto Araunah, Nay;
but I will surely buy *it* of thee at a price:
neither will I offer burnt offerings unto the
LORD my God of that which doth cost me
nothing. So David bought the threshingfloor and the oxen for fifty shekels of
silver.
25 And David built there an altar unto
the LORD, and offered burnt offerings and
peace offerings. So the LORD was intreated
for the land, and the plague was stayed
from Israel.

1 Kings

AUTHOR

Unknown; possibly Jeremiah the prophet or a group of prophets

MAIN POINT

The lives and accomplishments of God's faithful servants stand in remarkable contrast to those who became unfaithful to him.

DATE WRITTEN

Unknown.

22 CHAPTERS

MAIN PEOPLE

David, Solomon, Rehoboam, Jeroboam, the queen of Sheba, Elijah, Ahab, Jezebel

SPECIAL FEATURES

- *Was originally one book with 2 Kings*
- *Describes the reign of Solomon, one of the wisest people in the Bible who did some really stupid things later in life*
- *Explains how the kingdom of Israel split into two nations*
- *Recounts the amazing career of Elijah, prophet and sometime crybaby*
- *Sixth book of History*

HOW THE BOOK GOT ITS NAME

Kings refers to the main characters of the book: the first kings of Israel and Judah.

1

1Now king David was old *and* stricken
in years; and they covered him with
clothes, but he gat no heat.
2Wherefore his servants said unto him,
Let there be sought for my lord the king a
young virgin: and let her stand before the
king, and let her cherish him, and let her
lie in thy bosom, that my lord the king
may get heat.
3So they sought for a fair damsel
throughout all the coasts of Israel, and found
Abishag a Shunammite, and brought her
to the king.
4And the damsel *was* very fair, and cher-
ished the king, and ministered to him: but
the king knew her not.
5Then Adonijah
the son of Haggith
exalted himself,
saying, I will be
king: and he pre-
pared him chariots
and horsemen, and fifty men to run before him.

1:5 Ambition
◄ 2 Samuel 15:1-2, 4
2 Kings 14:10 ►

6And his father had not displeased him
at any time in saying, Why hast thou done
so? and he also *was a* very goodly *man;* and
his mother bare him after Absalom.
7And he conferred with Joab the son of
Zeruiah, and with Abiathar the priest: and
they following Adonijah helped *him.*
8But Zadok the priest, and Benaiah the

son of Jehoiada, and Nathan the prophet,
and Shimei, and Rei, and the mighty men
which *belonged* to David, were not with
Adonijah.
9And Adonijah slew sheep and oxen and
fat cattle by the stone of Zoheleth, which
is by En-rogel, and called all his brethren
the king's sons, and all the men of Judah
the king's servants:
10But Nathan the prophet, and Benaiah,
and the mighty men, and Solomon his
brother, he called not.
11Wherefore Nathan spake unto Bath-
sheba the mother of Solomon, saying, Hast
thou not heard that Adonijah the son of
Haggith doth reign, and David our lord
knoweth *it* not?
12Now therefore come, let me, I pray
thee, give thee counsel, that thou mayest
save thine own life, and the life of thy son
Solomon.
13Go and get thee in unto king David,
and say unto him, Didst not thou, my lord,
O king, swear unto thine handmaid, saying, Assuredly Solomon thy son shall reign
after me, and he shall sit upon my throne?
why then doth Adonijah reign?
14Behold, while thou yet talkest there
with the king, I also will come in after thee,
and confirm thy words.
15And Bath-sheba went in unto the king
into the chamber: and the king was very
old; and Abishag the Shunammite ministered unto the king.
16And Bath-sheba bowed, and did obeisance unto the king. And the king said,
What wouldest thou?
17And she said unto him, My lord, thou
swarest by the LORD thy God unto thine
handmaid, *saying,* Assuredly Solomon thy
son shall reign after me, and he shall sit
upon my throne.
18And now, behold, Adonijah reigneth;
and now, my lord the king, thou knowest
it not:
19And he hath slain oxen and fat cattle
and sheep in abundance, and hath called
all the sons of the king, and Abiathar the
priest, and Joab the captain of the host:
but Solomon thy servant hath he not
called.
20And thou, my lord, O king, the eyes
of all Israel *are* upon thee, that thou
shouldest tell them who shall sit on the
throne of my lord the king after him.
21Otherwise it shall come to pass, when
my lord the king shall sleep with his fathers, that I and my son Solomon shall be
counted offenders.
22And, lo, while she yet talked with the
king, Nathan the prophet also came in.
23And they told the king, saying, Behold
Nathan the prophet. And when he was
come in before the king, he bowed himself before the king with his face to the
ground.
24And Nathan said, My lord, O king,
hast thou said, Adonijah shall reign after
me, and he shall sit upon my throne?
25For he is gone down this day, and hath
slain oxen and fat cattle and sheep in abundance, and hath called all the king's sons,
and the captains of the host, and Abiathar
the priest; and, behold, they eat and drink
before him, and say, God save king Adonijah.
26But me, *even* me thy servant, and Zadok the priest, and Benaiah the son of Jehoiada, and thy servant Solomon, hath he
not called.
27Is this thing done by my lord the king,
and thou hast not shewed *it* unto thy servant, who should sit on the throne of my
lord the king after him?
28Then king David answered and said,
Call me Bath-sheba. And she came into the
king's presence, and stood before the king.
29And the king sware, and said, *As* the
LORD liveth, that hath redeemed my soul
out of all distress,
30Even as I sware unto thee by the LORD
God of Israel, saying, Assuredly Solomon
thy son shall reign after me, and he shall
sit upon my throne in my stead; even so
will I certainly do this day.
31Then Bath-sheba bowed with *her* face
to the earth, and did reverence to the king,
and said, Let my lord king David live for
ever.
32And king David said, Call me Zadok
the priest, and Nathan the prophet, and
Benaiah the son of Jehoiada. And they
came before the king.
33The king also said unto them, Take
with you the servants of your lord,
and cause Solomon my son to ride upon
mine own mule, and bring him down to
Gihon:
34And let Zadok the priest and Nathan
the prophet anoint him there king over

Israel: and blow ye with the trumpet, and say, God save king Solomon.

35Then ye shall come up after him, that he may come and sit upon my throne; for he shall be king in my stead: and I have appointed him to be ruler over Israel and over Judah.

36And Benaiah the son of Jehoiada answered the king, and said, Amen: the LORD God of my lord the king say so *too*.

37As the LORD hath been with my lord the king, *even* so be he with Solomon, and make his throne greater than the throne of my lord king David.

38So Zadok the priest, and Nathan the prophet, and Benaiah the son of Jehoiada, and the Cherethites, and the Pelethites, went down, and caused Solomon to ride upon king David's mule, and brought him to Gihon.

39And Zadok the priest took an horn of oil out of the tabernacle, and anointed Solomon. And they blew the trumpet; and all the people said, God save king Solomon.

40And all the people came up after him, and the people piped with pipes, and rejoiced with great joy, so that the earth rent with the sound of them.

41And Adonijah and all the guests that *were* with him heard *it* as they had made an end of eating. And when Joab heard the sound of the trumpet, he said, Wherefore *is this* noise of the city being in an uproar?

42And while he yet spake, behold, Jonathan the son of Abiathar the priest came: and Adonijah said unto him, Come in; for thou *art* a valiant man, and bringest good tidings.

43And Jonathan answered and said to Adonijah, Verily our lord king David hath made Solomon king.

44And the king hath sent with him Zadok the priest, and Nathan the prophet, and Benaiah the son of Jehoiada, and the Cherethites, and the Pelethites, and they have caused him to ride upon the king's mule:

45And Zadok the priest and Nathan the prophet have anointed him king in Gihon: and they are come up from thence rejoicing, so that the city rang again. This *is* the noise that ye have heard.

46And also Solomon sitteth on the throne of the kingdom.

47And moreover the king's servants came to bless our lord king David, saying, God make the name of Solomon better than thy name, and make his throne greater than thy throne. And the king bowed himself upon the bed.

48And also thus said the king, Blessed *be* the LORD God of Israel, which hath given *one* to sit on my throne this day, mine eyes even seeing *it*.

49And all the guests that *were* with Adonijah were afraid, and rose up, and went every man his way.

50And Adonijah feared because of Solomon, and arose, and went, and caught hold on the horns of the altar.

51And it was told Solomon, saying, Behold, Adonijah feareth king Solomon: for, lo, he hath caught hold on the horns of the altar, saying, Let king Solomon swear unto me to day that he will not slay his servant with the sword.

52And Solomon said, If he will shew himself a worthy man, there shall not an hair of him fall to the earth: but if wickedness shall be found in him, he shall die.

1:52 Examples of Mercy
◄ 2 Samuel 19:22
2 Kings 6:22 ►

53So king Solomon sent, and they brought him down from the altar. And he came and bowed himself to king Solomon: and Solomon said unto him, Go to thine house.

2

1Now the days of David drew nigh that he should die; and he charged Solomon his son, saying,

2I go the way of all the earth: be thou strong therefore, and shew thyself a man;

3And keep the charge of the LORD thy God, to walk in his ways, to keep his statutes, and his commandments, and his judgments, and his testimonies, as it is written in the law of Moses, that thou mayest prosper in all that thou doest, and whithersoever thou turnest thyself:

4That the LORD may continue his word which he spake concerning me, saying, If thy children take heed to their way, to walk before me in truth with all their heart and with all their soul, there shall not fail thee (said he) a man on the throne of Israel.

5Moreover thou knowest also what Joab the son of Zeruiah did to me, *and* what he did to the two captains of the hosts of Israel, unto Abner the son of Ner, and unto Amasa the son of Jether, whom he slew, and shed the blood of war in peace, and put the blood of war upon his girdle that *was* about his loins, and in his shoes that *were* on his feet.

6 Do therefore according to thy wisdom, and let not his hoar head go down to the grave in peace.

7 But shew kindness unto the sons of Barzillai the Gileadite, and let them be of those that eat at thy table: for so they came to me when I fled because of Absalom thy brother.

2:7 "Thank You"
◄ 2 Samuel 10:2
2 Kings 4:13 ►

8 And, behold, *thou hast* with thee Shimei the son of Gera, a Benjamite of Bahurim, which cursed me with a grievous curse in the day when I went to Mahanaim: but he came down to meet me at Jordan, and I sware to him by the LORD, saying, I will not put thee to death with the sword.

9 Now therefore hold him not guiltless: for thou *art* a wise man, and knowest what thou oughtest to do unto him; but his hoar head bring thou down to the grave with blood.

10 So David slept with his fathers, and was buried in the city of David.

11 And the days that David reigned over Israel *were* forty years: seven years reigned he in Hebron, and thirty and three years reigned he in Jerusalem.

12 Then sat Solomon upon the throne of David his father; and his kingdom was established greatly.

13 And Adonijah the son of Haggith came to Bath-sheba the mother of Solomon. And she said, Comest thou peaceably? And he said, Peaceably.

14 He said moreover, I have somewhat to say unto thee. And she said, Say on.

15 And he said, Thou knowest that the kingdom was mine, and *that* all Israel set their faces on me, that I should reign: howbeit the kingdom is turned about, and is become my brother's: for it was his from the LORD.

16 And now I ask one petition of thee, deny me not. And she said unto him, Say on.

17 And he said, Speak, I pray thee, unto Solomon the king, (for he will not say thee nay,) that he give me Abishag the Shunammite to wife.

18 And Bath-sheba said, Well; I will speak for thee unto the king.

19 Bath-sheba therefore went unto king Solomon, to speak unto him for Adonijah. And the king rose up to meet her, and bowed himself unto her, and sat down on his throne, and caused a seat to be set for the king's mother; and she sat on his right hand.

20 Then she said, I desire one small petition of thee; *I pray thee,* say me not nay. And the king said unto her, Ask on, my mother: for I will not say thee nay.

21 And she said, Let Abishag the Shunammite be given to Adonijah thy brother to wife.

22 And king Solomon answered and said unto his mother, And why dost thou ask Abishag the Shunammite for Adonijah? ask for him the kingdom also; for he *is* mine elder brother; even for him, and for Abiathar the priest, and for Joab the son of Zeruiah.

23 Then king Solomon sware by the LORD, saying, God do so to me, and more also, if Adonijah have not spoken this word against his own life.

24 Now therefore, *as* the LORD liveth, which hath established me, and set me on the throne of David my father, and who hath made me an house, as he promised, Adonijah shall be put to death this day.

25 And king Solomon sent by the hand of Benaiah the son of Jehoiada; and he fell upon him that he died.

26 And unto Abiathar the priest said the king, Get thee to Anathoth, unto thine own fields; for thou *art* worthy of death: but I will not at this time put thee to death, because thou barest the ark of the Lord GOD before David my father, and because thou hast been afflicted in all wherein my father was afflicted.

27 So Solomon thrust out Abiathar from being priest unto the LORD; that he might fulfil the word of the LORD, which he spake concerning the house of Eli in Shiloh.

28 Then tidings came to Joab: for Joab had turned after Adonijah, though he turned not after Absalom. And Joab fled unto the tabernacle of the LORD, and caught hold on the horns of the altar.

29 And it was told king Solomon that Joab was fled unto the tabernacle of the LORD; and, behold, *he is* by the altar. Then Solomon sent Benaiah the son of Jehoiada, saying, Go, fall upon him.

30 And Benaiah came to the tabernacle of the LORD, and said unto him, Thus saith the king, Come forth. And he said, Nay; but I will die here. And Benaiah brought the king word again, saying, Thus said Joab, and thus he answered me.

31 And the king said unto him, Do as he hath said, and fall upon him, and bury him; that thou mayest take away the innocent blood, which Joab shed, from me, and from the house of my father.

32 And the LORD shall return his blood upon his own head, who fell upon two men more righteous and better than he, and slew them with the sword, my father David not knowing *thereof, to wit,* Abner the son of Ner, captain of the host of Israel, and Amasa the son of Jether, captain of the host of Judah.

33 Their blood shall therefore return upon the head of Joab, and upon the head of his seed for ever: but upon David, and upon his seed, and upon his house, and upon his throne, shall there be peace for ever from the LORD.

34 So Benaiah the son of Jehoiada went up, and fell upon him, and slew him: and he was buried in his own house in the wilderness.

35 And the king put Benaiah the son of Jehoiada in his room over the host: and Zadok the priest did the king put in the room of Abiathar.

36 And the king sent and called for Shimei, and said unto him, Build thee an house in Jerusalem, and dwell there, and go not forth thence any whither.

37 For it shall be, *that* on the day thou goest out, and passest over the brook Kidron, thou shalt know for certain that thou shalt surely die: thy blood shall be upon thine own head.

38 And Shimei said unto the king, The saying *is* good: as my lord the king hath said, so will thy servant do. And Shimei dwelt in Jerusalem many days.

39 And it came to pass at the end of three years, that two of the servants of Shimei ran away unto Achish son of Maachah king of Gath. And they told Shimei, saying, Behold, thy servants *be* in Gath.

40 And Shimei arose, and saddled his ass, and went to Gath to Achish to seek his servants: and Shimei went, and brought his servants from Gath.

41 And it was told Solomon that Shimei had gone from Jerusalem to Gath, and was come again.

42 And the king sent and called for Shimei, and said unto him, Did I not make thee to swear by the LORD, and protested unto thee, saying, Know for a certain, on the day thou goest out, and walkest abroad any whither, that thou shalt surely die? and thou saidst unto me, The word *that* I have heard *is* good.

43 Why then hast thou not kept the oath of the LORD, and the commandment that I have charged thee with?

44 The king said moreover to Shimei, Thou knowest all the wickedness which thine heart is privy to, that thou didst to David my father: therefore the LORD shall return thy wickedness upon thine own head;

45 And king Solomon *shall be* blessed, and the throne of David shall be established before the LORD for ever.

46 So the king commanded Benaiah the son of Jehoiada; which went out, and fell upon him, that he died. And the kingdom was established in the hand of Solomon.

3

1 And Solomon made affinity with Pharaoh king of Egypt, and took Pharaoh's daughter, and brought her into the city of David, until he had made an end of building his own house, and the house of the LORD, and the wall of Jerusalem round about.

2 Only the people sacrificed in high places, because there was no house built unto the name of the LORD, until those days.

3 And Solomon loved the LORD, walking in the statutes of David his father: only he sacrificed and burnt incense in high places.

3:3 Only Human
◄ Numbers 20:12
1 Kings 22:43 ►

4 And the king went to Gibeon to sacrifice there; for that *was* the great high place: a thousand burnt offerings did Solomon offer upon that altar.

5 In Gibeon the LORD appeared to Solo-

mon in a dream by night: and God said, Ask what I shall give thee.

6 And Solomon said, Thou hast shewed unto thy servant David my father great mercy, according as he walked before thee in truth, and in righteousness, and in uprightness of heart with thee; and thou hast kept for him this great kindness, that thou hast given him a son to sit on his throne, as *it is* this day.

7 And now, O LORD my God, thou hast made thy servant king instead of David my father: and I *am but* a little child: I know not *how* to go out or come in.

8 And thy servant *is* in the midst of thy people which thou hast chosen, a great people, that cannot be numbered nor counted for multitude.

9 Give therefore thy servant an understanding heart to judge thy people, that I may discern between good and bad: for who is able to judge this thy so great a people?

10 And the speech pleased the Lord, that Solomon had asked this thing.

11 And God said unto him, Because thou hast asked this thing, and hast not asked for thyself long life; neither hast asked riches for thyself, nor hast asked the life of thine enemies; but hast asked for thyself understanding to discern judgment;

12 Behold, I have done according to thy words: lo, I have given thee a wise and an understanding heart; so that there was none like thee before thee, neither after thee shall any arise like unto thee.

13 And I have also given thee that which thou hast not asked, both riches, and honour: so that there shall not be any among the kings like unto thee all thy days.

3:13 Blessings
◄ 2 Samuel 6:11
Psalm 65:9 ►

14 And if thou wilt walk in my ways, to keep my statutes and my commandments, as thy father David did walk, then I will lengthen thy days.

15 And Solomon awoke; and, behold, *it was* a dream. And he came to Jerusalem, and stood before the ark of the covenant of the LORD, and offered up burnt offerings, and offered peace offerings, and made a feast to all his servants.

16 Then came there two women, *that were* harlots, unto the king, and stood before him.

17 And the one woman said, O my lord, I and this woman dwell in one house; and I was delivered of a child with her in the house.

18 And it came to pass the third day after that I was delivered, that this woman was delivered also: and we *were* together; *there was* no stranger with us in the house, save we two in the house.

19 And this woman's child died in the night; because she overlaid it.

20 And she arose at midnight, and took my son from beside me, while thine handmaid slept, and laid it in her bosom, and laid her dead child in my bosom.

21 And when I rose in the morning to give my child suck, behold, it was dead: but when I had considered it in the morning, behold, it was not my son, which I did bear.

22 And the other woman said, Nay; but the living *is* my son, and the dead *is* thy son. And this said, No; but the dead *is* thy son, and the living *is* my son. Thus they spake before the king.

23 Then said the king, The one saith, This *is* my son that liveth, and thy son *is* the dead: and the other saith, Nay; but thy son *is* the dead, and my son *is* the living.

24 And the king said, Bring me a sword. And they brought a sword before the king.

25 And the king said, Divide the living child in two, and give half to the one, and half to the other.

26 Then spake the woman whose the living child *was* unto the king, for her bowels yearned upon her son, and she said, O my lord, give her the living child, and in no wise slay it. But the other said, Let it be neither mine nor thine, *but* divide *it*.

27 Then the king answered and said, Give her the living child, and in no wise slay it: she *is* the mother thereof.

28 And all Israel heard of the judgment which the king had judged; and they feared the king: for they saw that the wisdom of God *was* in him, to do judgment.

4

1 So king Solomon was king over all Israel.

2 And these *were* the princes which he had; Azariah the son of Zadok the priest,

3 Elihoreph and Ahiah, the sons of

Shisha, scribes; Jehoshaphat the son of Ahilud, the recorder.

4And Benaiah the son of Jehoiada *was* over the host: and Zadok and Abiathar *were* the priests:

5And Azariah the son of Nathan *was* over the officers: and Zabud the son of Nathan *was* principal officer, *and* the king's friend:

6And Ahishar *was* over the household: and Adoniram the son of Abda *was* over the tribute.

7And Solomon had twelve officers over all Israel, which provided victuals for the king and his household: each man his month in a year made provision.

8And these *are* their names: The son of Hur, in mount Ephraim:

9The son of Dekar, in Makaz, and in Shaalbim, and Beth-shemesh, and Elon-beth-hanan:

10The son of Hesed, in Aruboth; to him *pertained* Sochoh, and all the land of Hepher:

11The son of Abinadab, in all the region of Dor; which had Taphath the daughter of Solomon to wife:

12Baana the son of Ahilud; *to him pertained* Taanach and Megiddo, and all Beth-shean, which is by Zartanah beneath Jezreel, from Beth-shean to Abel-meholah, *even* unto *the place that is* beyond Jokneam:

13The son of Geber, in Ramoth-gilead; to him *pertained* the towns of Jair the son of Manasseh, which *are* in Gilead; to him *also pertained* the region of Argob, which *is* in Bashan, threescore great cities with walls and brasen bars:

14Ahinadab the son of Iddo *had* Mahanaim:

15Ahimaaz *was* in Naphtali; he also took Basmath the daughter of Solomon to wife:

16Baanah the son of Hushai *was* in Asher and in Aloth:

17Jehoshaphat the son of Paruah, in Issachar:

18Shimei the son of Elah, in Benjamin:

19Geber the son of Uri *was* in the country of Gilead, *in* the country of Sihon king of the Amorites, and of Og king of Bashan; and *he was* the only officer which *was* in the land.

20Judah and Israel *were* many, as the sand which *is* by the sea in multitude, eating and drinking, and making merry.

21And Solomon reigned over all kingdoms from the river unto the land of the Philistines, and unto the border of Egypt: they brought presents, and served Solomon all the days of his life.

22And Solomon's provision for one day was thirty measures of fine flour, and threescore measures of meal,

23Ten fat oxen, and twenty oxen out of the pastures, and an hundred sheep, beside harts, and roebucks, and fallowdeer, and fatted fowl.

24For he had dominion over all *the region* on this side the river, from Tiphsah even to Azzah, over all the kings on this side the river: and he had peace on all sides round about him.

25And Judah and Israel dwelt safely, every man under his vine and under his fig tree, from Dan even to Beer-sheba, all the days of Solomon.

26And Solomon had forty thousand stalls of horses for his chariots, and twelve thousand horsemen.

27And those officers provided victual for king Solomon, and for all that came unto king Solomon's table, every man in his month: they lacked nothing.

28Barley also and straw for the horses and dromedaries brought they unto the place where *the officers* were, every man according to his charge.

29And God gave Solomon wisdom and understanding exceeding much, and largeness of heart, even as the sand that *is* on the sea shore.

30And Solomon's wisdom excelled the wisdom of all the children of the east country, and all the wisdom of Egypt.

31For he was wiser than all men; than Ethan the Ezrahite, and Heman, and Chalcol, and Darda, the sons of Mahol: and his fame was in all nations round about.

32And he spake three thousand proverbs: and his songs were a thousand and five.

33And he spake of trees, from the cedar tree that *is* in Lebanon even unto the hyssop that springeth out of the wall: he spake also of beasts, and of fowl, and of creeping things, and of fishes.

34And there came of all people to hear the wisdom of Solomon, from all kings of the earth, which had heard of his wisdom.

5

1 And Hiram king
of Tyre sent his ser-
vants unto Solo-
mon; for he had
heard that they had
anointed him king
in the room of his father: for Hiram was
ever a lover of David.

5:1 Good Friends
◄ 2 Samuel 15:37
2 Corinthians 2:13 ►

2 And Solomon sent to Hiram, saying,
3 Thou knowest how that David my father could not build an house unto the
name of the LORD his God for the wars
which were about him on every side, until
the LORD put them under the soles of his
feet.
4 But now the LORD my God hath given
me rest on every side, *so that there is* neither adversary nor evil occurrent.
5 And, behold, I purpose to build an
house unto the name of the LORD my God,
as the LORD spake unto David my father,
saying, Thy son, whom I will set upon thy
throne in thy room, he shall build an
house unto my name.
6 Now therefore command thou that
they hew me cedar trees out of Lebanon;
and my servants shall be with thy servants:
and unto thee will I give hire for thy servants according to all that thou shalt appoint: for thou knowest that *there is* not
among us any that can skill to hew timber
like unto the Sidonians.
7 And it came to pass, when Hiram heard
the words of Solomon, that he rejoiced
greatly, and said, Blessed *be* the LORD this
day, which hath given unto David a wise
son over this great people.
8 And Hiram sent to Solomon, saying, I
have considered the things which thou
sentest to me for: *and* I will do all thy desire concerning timber of cedar, and concerning timber of fir.
9 My servants shall bring *them* down
from Lebanon unto the sea: and I will convey them by sea in floats unto the place
that thou shalt appoint me, and will cause
them to be discharged there, and thou
shalt receive *them:* and thou shalt accomplish my desire, in giving food for my
household.
10 So Hiram gave Solomon cedar trees
and fir trees *according to* all his desire.
11 And Solomon gave Hiram twenty
thousand measures of wheat *for* food to
his household, and twenty measures of
pure oil: thus gave Solomon to Hiram year
by year.
12 And the LORD gave Solomon wisdom,
as he promised him: and there was peace
between Hiram and Solomon; and they
two made a league together.
13 And king Solomon raised a levy out
of all Israel; and the levy was thirty thousand men.
14 And he sent them to Lebanon ten
thousand a month by courses: a month
they were in Lebanon, *and* two months at
home: and Adoniram *was* over the levy.
15 And Solomon had threescore and ten
thousand that bare burdens, and fourscore
thousand hewers in the mountains;
16 Beside the chief of Solomon's officers
which *were* over the work, three thousand
and three hundred, which ruled over the
people that wrought in the work.
17 And the king commanded, and they
brought great stones, costly stones, *and*
hewed stones, to lay the foundation of the
house.
18 And Solomon's builders and Hiram's
builders did hew *them*, and the stone-
squarers: so they prepared timber and
stones to build the house.

6

1 And it came to pass in the four hundred and eightieth year after the children
of Israel were come out of the land of
Egypt, in the fourth year of Solomon's
reign over Israel, in the month Zif, which
is the second month, that he began to
build the house of the LORD.
2 And the house which king Solomon
built for the LORD, the length thereof *was*
threescore cubits, and the breadth thereof
twenty *cubits*, and the height thereof thirty
cubits.
3 And the porch before the temple of the
house, twenty cubits *was* the length
thereof, according to the breadth of the
house; *and* ten cubits *was* the breadth
thereof before the house.
4 And for the house he made windows
of narrow lights.
5 And against the wall of the house he
built chambers round about, *against* the
walls of the house round about, *both* of
the temple and of the oracle: and he made
chambers round about:
6 The nethermost chamber *was* five cubits broad, and the middle *was* six cubits
broad, and the third *was* seven cubits

broad: for without *in the wall* of the house
he made narrowed rests round about, that
the beams should not be fastened in the
walls of the house.
7And the house, when it was in building, was built of stone made ready before
it was brought thither: so that there was
neither hammer nor axe *nor* any tool of
iron heard in the house, while it was in
building.
8The door for the middle chamber *was*
in the right side of the house: and they
went up with winding stairs into the middle *chamber,* and out of the middle into
the third.
9So he built the house, and finished it;
and covered the house with beams and
boards of cedar.
10And *then* he built chambers against all
the house, five cubits high: and they rested on the house *with* timber of cedar.
11And the word of the LORD came to
Solomon, saying,
12*Concerning* this house which thou art
in building, if thou wilt walk in my statutes, and execute my judgments, and keep
all my commandments to walk in them;
then will I perform my word with thee,
which I spake unto David thy father:
13And I will dwell among the children
of Israel, and will not forsake my people
Israel.
14So Solomon built the house, and finished it.
15And he built the walls of the house
within with boards of cedar, both the floor
of the house, and the walls of the cieling:
and he covered *them* on the inside with
wood, and covered the floor of the house
with planks of fir.
16And he built twenty cubits on the sides
of the house, both the floor and the walls
with boards of cedar: he even built *them*
for it within, *even* for the oracle, *even* for
the most holy *place.*
17And the house, that *is,* the temple before it, was forty cubits *long.*
18And the cedar of the house within *was*
carved with knops and open flowers: all
was cedar; there was no stone seen.
19And the oracle he prepared in the
house within, to set there the ark of the
covenant of the LORD.
20And the oracle in the forepart *was*
twenty cubits in length, and twenty cubits
in breadth, and twenty cubits in the height
thereof: and he overlaid it with pure gold;
and so covered the altar *which was of* cedar.
21So Solomon overlaid the house within with pure gold: and he made a partition by the chains of gold before the oracle;
and he overlaid it with gold.
22And the whole house he overlaid with
gold, until he had finished all the house:
also the whole altar that *was* by the oracle
he overlaid with gold.
23And within the oracle he made two
cherubims *of* olive tree, *each* ten cubits
high.
24And five cubits *was* the one wing of
the cherub, and five cubits the other wing
of the cherub: from the uttermost part of
the one wing unto the uttermost part of
the other *were* ten cubits.
25And the other cherub *was* ten cubits:
both the cherubims *were* of one measure
and one size.
26The height of the one cherub *was* ten
cubits, and so *was it* of the other cherub.
27And he set the cherubims within the
inner house: and they stretched forth the
wings of the cherubims, so that the wing
of the one touched the *one* wall, and the
wing of the other cherub touched the other
wall; and their wings touched one another
in the midst of the house.
28And he overlaid the cherubims with
gold.
29And he carved all the walls of the
house round about with carved figures of
cherubims and palm trees and open flowers, within and without.
30And the floor of the house he overlaid with gold, within and without.
31And for the entering of the oracle he
made doors *of* olive tree: the lintel *and* side
posts *were* a fifth part *of the wall.*
32The two doors also *were of* olive tree;
and he carved upon them carvings of
cherubims and palm trees and open flowers, and overlaid *them* with gold, and
spread gold upon the cherubims, and
upon the palm trees.
33So also made he for the door of the
temple posts *of* olive tree, a fourth part *of
the wall.*
34And the two doors *were of* fir tree: the
two leaves of the one door *were* folding,
and the two leaves of the other door *were*
folding.

35 And he carved *thereon* cherubims and palm trees and open flowers: and covered *them* with gold fitted upon the carved work.

36 And he built the inner court with three rows of hewed stone, and a row of cedar beams.

37 In the fourth year was the foundation of the house of the LORD laid, in the month Zif:

38 And in the eleventh year, in the month Bul, which *is* the eighth month, was the house finished throughout all the parts thereof, and according to all the fashion of it. So was he seven years in building it.

7

1 But Solomon was building his own house thirteen years, and he finished all his house.

2 He built also the house of the forest of Lebanon; the length thereof *was* an hundred cubits, and the breadth thereof fifty cubits, and the height thereof thirty cubits, upon four rows of cedar pillars, with cedar beams upon the pillars.

3 And *it was* covered with cedar above upon the beams, that *lay* on forty five pillars, fifteen *in* a row.

4 And *there were* windows *in* three rows, and light *was* against light *in* three ranks.

5 And all the doors and posts *were* square, with the windows: and light *was* against light *in* three ranks.

6 And he made a porch of pillars; the length thereof *was* fifty cubits, and the breadth thereof thirty cubits: and the porch *was* before them: and the *other* pillars and the thick beam *were* before them.

7 Then he made a porch for the throne where he might judge, *even* the porch of judgment: and *it was* covered with cedar from one side of the floor to the other.

8 And his house where he dwelt *had* another court within the porch, *which* was of the like work. Solomon made also an house for Pharaoh's daughter, whom he had taken *to wife,* like unto this porch.

9 All these *were of* costly stones, according to the measures of hewed stones, sawed with saws, within and without, even from the foundation unto the coping, and *so* on the outside toward the great court.

10 And the foundation *was of* costly stones, even great stones, stones of ten cubits, and stones of eight cubits.

11 And above *were* costly stones, after the measures of hewed stones, and cedars.

12 And the great court round about *was* with three rows of hewed stones, and a row of cedar beams, both for the inner court of the house of the LORD, and for the porch of the house.

13 And king Solomon sent and fetched Hiram out of Tyre.

14 He *was* a widow's son of the tribe of Naphtali, and his father *was* a man of Tyre, a worker in brass: and he was filled with wisdom, and understanding, and cunning to work all works in brass. And he came to king Solomon, and wrought all his work.

15 For he cast two pillars of brass, of eighteen cubits high apiece: and a line of twelve cubits did compass either of them about.

16 And he made two chapiters *of* molten brass, to set upon the tops of the pillars: the height of the one chapiter *was* five cubits, and the height of the other chapiter *was* five cubits:

17 *And* nets of checker work, and wreaths of chain work, for the chapiters which *were* upon the top of the pillars; seven for the one chapiter, and seven for the other chapiter.

18 And he made the pillars, and two rows round about upon the one network, to cover the chapiters that *were* upon the top, with pomegranates: and so did he for the other chapiter.

19 And the chapiters that *were* upon the top of the pillars *were* of lily work in the porch, four cubits.

20 And the chapiters upon the two pillars *had pomegranates* also above, over against the belly which *was* by the network: and the pomegranates *were* two hundred in rows round about upon the other chapiter.

21 And he set up the pillars in the porch of the temple: and he set up the right pillar, and called the name thereof Jachin: and he set up the left pillar, and he called the name thereof Boaz.

22 And upon the top of the pillars *was* lily work: so was the work of the pillars finished.

23 And he made a molten sea, ten cubits from the one brim to the other: *it was* round all about, and his height *was* five cubits: and a line of thirty cubits did compass it round about.

24 And under the brim of it round about
there were knops compassing it, ten in a
cubit, compassing the sea round about: the
knops *were* cast in two rows, when it was
cast.
25 It stood upon twelve oxen, three looking toward the north, and three looking
toward the west, and three looking toward
the south, and three looking toward the
east: and the sea *was set* above upon them,
and all their hinder parts *were* inward.
26 And it *was* an hand breadth thick, and
the brim thereof was wrought like the brim
of a cup, with flowers of lilies: it contained
two thousand baths.
27 And he made ten bases of brass; four
cubits *was* the length of one base, and four
cubits the breadth thereof, and three cubits the height of it.
28 And the work of the bases *was* on this
manner: they had borders, and the borders
were between the ledges:
29 And on the borders that *were* between
the ledges *were* lions, oxen, and cherubims:
and upon the ledges *there was* a base above:
and beneath the lions and oxen *were* certain additions made of thin work.
30 And every base had four brasen
wheels, and plates of brass: and the four
corners thereof had undersetters: under the
laver *were* undersetters molten, at the side
of every addition.
31 And the mouth of it within the
chapiter and above *was* a cubit: but the
mouth thereof *was* round *after* the work
of the base, a cubit and an half: and also
upon the mouth of it *were* gravings with
their borders, foursquare, not round.
32 And under the borders *were* four
wheels; and the axletrees of the wheels *were*
joined to the base: and the height of a wheel
was a cubit and a half a cubit.
33 And the work of the wheels *was* like
the work of a chariot wheel: their axletrees,
and their naves, and their felloes, and their
spokes, *were* all molten.
34 And *there were* four undersetters to the
four corners of one base: *and* the undersetters *were* of the very base itself.
35 And in the top of the base *was there* a
round compass of half a cubit high: and
on the top of the base the ledges thereof
and the borders thereof *were* of the same.
36 For on the plates of the ledges thereof,
and on the borders thereof, he graved
cherubims, lions, and palm trees, according to the proportion of every one, and
additions round about.
37 After this *manner* he made the ten bases: all of them had one casting, one measure, *and* one size.
38 Then made he ten lavers of brass: one
laver contained forty baths: *and* every laver was four cubits: *and* upon every one of
the ten bases one laver.
39 And he put five bases on the right side
of the house, and five on the left side of
the house: and he set the sea on the right
side of the house eastward over against the
south.
40 And Hiram made the lavers, and the
shovels, and the basons. So Hiram made
an end of doing all the work that he made
king Solomon for the house of the LORD:
41 The two pillars, and the *two* bowls of
the chapiters that *were* on the top of the
two pillars; and the two networks, to cover the two bowls of the chapiters which
were upon the top of the pillars;
42 And four hundred pomegranates for
the two networks, *even* two rows of pomegranates for one network, to cover the two
bowls of the chapiters that *were* upon the
pillars;
43 And the ten bases, and ten lavers on
the bases;
44 And one sea, and twelve oxen under
the sea;
45 And the pots, and the shovels, and the
basons: and all these vessels, which Hiram
made to king Solomon for the house of
the LORD, *were of* bright brass.
46 In the plain of Jordan did the king cast
them, in the clay ground between Succoth
and Zarthan.
47 And Solomon left all the vessels *un-*
weighed, because they were exceeding
many: neither was the weight of the brass
found out.
48 And Solomon made all the vessels that
pertained unto the house of the LORD: the
altar of gold, and the table of gold, whereupon the shewbread *was*,
49 And the candlesticks of pure gold, five
on the right *side*, and five on the left, before the oracle, with the flowers, and the
lamps, and the tongs *of* gold,
50 And the bowls, and the snuffers, and
the basons, and the spoons, and the censers *of* pure gold; and the hinges *of* gold,

both for the doors of the inner house, the most holy *place, and* for the doors of the house, *to wit,* of the temple.

51 So was ended all the work that king Solomon made for the house of the LORD. And Solomon brought in the things which David his father had dedicated; *even* the silver, and the gold, and the vessels, did he put among the treasures of the house of the LORD.

8

1 Then Solomon assembled the elders of Israel, and all the heads of the tribes, the chief of the fathers of the children of Israel, unto king Solomon in Jerusalem, that they might bring up the ark of the covenant of the LORD out of the city of David, which *is* Zion.

2 And all the men of Israel assembled themselves unto king Solomon at the feast in the month Ethanim, which *is* the seventh month.

3 And all the elders of Israel came, and the priests took up the ark.

4 And they brought up the ark of the LORD, and the tabernacle of the congregation, and all the holy vessels that *were* in the tabernacle, even those did the priests and the Levites bring up.

5 And king Solomon, and all the congregation of Israel, that *were* assembled unto him, were with him before the ark, sacrificing sheep and oxen, that could not be told nor numbered for multitude.

6 And the priests brought in the ark of the covenant of the LORD unto his place, into the oracle of the house, to the most holy *place, even* under the wings of the cherubims.

7 For the cherubims spread forth *their* two wings over the place of the ark, and the cherubims covered the ark and the staves thereof above.

8 And they drew out the staves, that the ends of the staves were seen out in the holy *place* before the oracle, and they were not seen without: and there they are unto this day.

9 *There was* nothing in the ark save the two tables of stone, which Moses put there at Horeb, when the LORD made *a covenant* with the children of Israel, when they came out of the land of Egypt.

10 And it came to pass, when the priests were come out of the holy *place,* that the cloud filled the house of the LORD,

11 So that the priests could not stand to minister because of the cloud: for the glory of the LORD had filled the house of the LORD.

12 Then spake Solomon, The LORD said that he would dwell in thick darkness.

13 I have surely built thee an house to dwell in, a settled place for thee to abide in for ever.

14 And the king turned his face about, and blessed all the congregation of Israel: (and all the congregation of Israel stood;)

15 And he said, Blessed *be* the LORD God of Israel, which spake with his mouth unto David my father, and hath with his hand fulfilled *it,* saying,

16 Since the day that I brought forth my people Israel out of Egypt, I chose no city out of all the tribes of Israel to build an house, that my name might be therein; but I chose David to be over my people Israel.

17 And it was in the heart of David my father to build an house for the name of the LORD God of Israel.

18 And the LORD said unto David my father, Whereas it was in thine heart to build an house unto my name, thou didst well that it was in thine heart.

19 Nevertheless thou shalt not build the house; but thy son that shall come forth out of thy loins, he shall build the house unto my name.

20 And the LORD hath performed his word that he spake, and I am risen up in the room of David my father, and sit on the throne of Israel, as the LORD promised, and have built an house for the name of the LORD God of Israel.

21 And I have set there a place for the ark, wherein *is* the covenant of the LORD, which he made with our fathers, when he brought them out of the land of Egypt.

22 And Solomon stood before the altar of the LORD in the presence of all the congregation of Israel, and spread forth his hands toward heaven:

23 And he said, LORD God of Israel, *there is* no God like thee, in heaven above, or on earth beneath, who keepest covenant and mercy with thy servants that walk before thee with all their heart:

24 Who hast kept with thy servant David my father that thou promisedst him: thou spakest also with thy mouth, and hast fulfilled *it* with thine hand, as *it is* this day.

25 Therefore now, LORD God of Israel,
keep with thy servant David my father that
thou promisedst him, saying, There shall
not fail thee a man in my sight to sit on
the throne of Israel; so that thy children
take heed to their way, that they walk before me as thou hast walked before me.
26 And now, O God of Israel, let thy
word, I pray thee, be verified, which thou
spakest unto thy servant David my father.
27 But will God indeed dwell on the
earth? behold, the heaven and heaven of
heavens cannot contain thee; how much
less this house that I have builded?
28 Yet have thou respect unto the prayer
of thy servant, and to his supplication,
O LORD my God, to hearken unto the cry
and to the prayer, which thy servant
prayeth before thee to day:
29 That thine eyes may be open toward
this house night and day, *even* toward the
place of which thou hast said, My name
shall be there: that thou mayest hearken
unto the prayer which thy servant shall
make toward this place.
30 And hearken
thou to the suppli-
cation of thy ser-
vant, and of thy
people Israel, when
they shall pray to-
ward this place: and hear thou in heaven
thy dwelling place: and when thou hearest,
forgive.

8:30 Praying for Mercy
◄ Deuteronomy 21:8
Psalm 6:2 ►

31 If any man trespass against his neighbour, and an oath be laid upon him to
cause him to swear, and the oath come
before thine altar in this house:
32 Then hear thou in heaven, and do, and
judge thy servants, condemning the wicked, to bring his way upon his head; and
justifying the righteous, to give him according to his righteousness.
33 When thy people Israel be smitten
down before the enemy, because they have
sinned against thee, and shall turn again
to thee, and confess thy name, and pray,
and make supplication unto thee in this
house:
34 Then hear thou in heaven, and forgive
the sin of thy people Israel, and bring them
again unto the land which thou gavest
unto their fathers.
35 When heaven is shut up, and there is
no rain, because they have sinned against
thee; if they pray toward this place, and
confess thy name, and turn from their sin,
when thou afflictest them:
36 Then hear thou in heaven, and forgive
the sin of thy servants, and of thy people
Israel, that thou teach them the good way
wherein they should walk, and give rain
upon thy land, which thou hast given to
thy people for an inheritance.
37 If there be in the land famine, if there
be pestilence, blasting, mildew, locust, *or*
if there be caterpiller; if their enemy besiege them in the land of their cities; whatsoever plague, whatsoever sickness *there be;*
38 What prayer and supplication soever
be *made* by any man, *or* by all thy people
Israel, which shall know every man the
plague of his own heart, and spread forth
his hands toward this house:
39 Then hear thou in heaven thy dwelling place, and forgive, and do, and give to
every man according to his ways, whose
heart thou knowest; (for thou, *even* thou
only, knowest the hearts of all the children
of men;)
40 That they may fear thee all the days
that they live in the land which thou gavest
unto our fathers.
41 Moreover concerning a stranger, that
is not of thy people Israel, but cometh out
of a far country for thy name's sake;
42 (For they shall hear of thy great name,
and of thy strong hand, and of thy
stretched out arm;) when he shall come
and pray toward this house;
43 Hear thou in heaven thy dwelling
place, and do according to all that the
stranger calleth to thee for: that all people
of the earth may know thy name, to fear
thee, as *do* thy people Israel; and that they
may know that this house, which I have
builded, is called by thy name.
44 If thy people go out to battle against
their enemy, whithersoever thou shalt send
them, and shall pray unto the LORD toward
the city which thou hast chosen, and *toward* the house that I have built for thy
name:
45 Then hear thou in heaven their prayer
and their supplica-
tion, and maintain
their cause.
46 If they sin
against thee, (for
there is no man that

8:46 Everyone Sins
◄ Genesis 6:5
Psalm 14:3 ►

sinneth not,) and thou be angry with them, and deliver them to the enemy, so that they carry them away captives unto the land of the enemy, far or near;

47 *Yet* if they shall bethink themselves in the land whither they were carried captives, and repent, and make supplication unto thee in the land of them that carried them captives, saying, We have sinned, and have done perversely, we have committed wickedness;

48 And *so* return unto thee with all their heart, and with all their soul, in the land of their enemies, which led them away captive, and pray unto thee toward their land, which thou gavest unto their fathers, the city which thou hast chosen, and the house which I have built for thy name:

49 Then hear thou their prayer and their supplication in heaven thy dwelling place, and maintain their cause,

50 And forgive thy people that have sinned against thee and all their transgressions wherein they have transgressed against thee, and give them compassion before them who carried them captive, that they may have compassion on them:

51 For they *be* thy people, and thine inheritance, which thou broughtest forth out of Egypt, from the midst of the furnace of iron:

52 That thine eyes may be open unto the supplication of thy servant, and unto the supplication of thy people Israel, to hearken unto them in all that they call for unto thee.

53 For thou didst separate them from among all the people of the earth, *to be* thine inheritance, as thou spakest by the hand of Moses thy servant, when thou broughtest our fathers out of Egypt, O Lord GOD.

54 And it was *so*, that when Solomon had made an end of praying all this prayer and supplication unto the LORD, he arose from before the altar of the LORD, from kneeling on his knees with his hands spread up to heaven.

55 And he stood, and blessed all the congregation of Israel with a loud voice, saying,

56 Blessed *be* the LORD, that hath given rest unto his people Israel, according to all that he promised: there hath not failed one word of all his good promise, which he promised by the hand of Moses his servant.

8:56
Believer Be Glad
◄ Isaiah 28:16 ►

8:56
God's Promises
◄ Romans 4:21 ►

57 The LORD our God be with us, as he was with our fathers: let him not leave us, nor forsake us:

58 That he may incline our hearts unto him, to walk in all his ways, and to keep his commandments, and his statutes, and his judgments, which he commanded our fathers.

59 And let these my words, wherewith I have made supplication before the LORD, be nigh unto the LORD our God day and night, that he maintain the cause of his servant, and the cause of his people Israel at all times, as the matter shall require:

60 That all the people of the earth may know that the LORD *is* God, *and that there is* none else.

61 Let your heart therefore be perfect with the LORD our God, to walk in his statutes, and to keep his commandments, as at this day.

8:61 Perfection
◄ Deuteronomy 18:13
Matthew 5:48 ►

62 And the king, and all Israel with him, offered sacrifice before the LORD.

63 And Solomon offered a sacrifice of peace offerings, which he offered unto the LORD, two and twenty thousand oxen, and an hundred and twenty thousand sheep. So the king and all the children of Israel dedicated the house of the LORD.

64 The same day did the king hallow the middle of the court that *was* before the house of the LORD: for there he offered burnt offerings, and meat offerings, and the fat of the peace offerings: because the brasen altar that *was* before the LORD *was* too little to receive the burnt offerings, and meat offerings, and the fat of the peace offerings.

65 And at that time Solomon held a feast, and all Israel with him, a great congregation, from the entering in of Hamath unto the river of Egypt, before the LORD our God, seven days and seven days, *even* fourteen days.

66 On the eighth day he sent the people

away: and they blessed the king, and went unto their tents joyful and glad of heart for all the goodness that the LORD had done for David his servant, and for Israel his people.

9

1 And it came to pass, when Solomon had finished the building of the house of the LORD, and the king's house, and all Solomon's desire which he was pleased to do,

2 That the LORD appeared to Solomon the second time, as he had appeared unto him at Gibeon.

3 And the LORD said unto him, I have heard thy prayer and thy supplication, that thou hast made before me: I have hallowed this house, which thou hast built, to put my name there for ever; and mine eyes and mine heart shall be there perpetually.

4 And if thou wilt walk before me, as David thy father walked, in integrity of heart, and in uprightness, to do according to all that I have commanded thee, *and* wilt keep my statutes and my judgments:

5 Then I will establish the throne of thy kingdom upon Israel for ever, as I promised to David thy father, saying, There shall not fail thee a man upon the throne of Israel.

6 *But* if ye shall at all turn from following me, ye or your children, and will not keep my commandments *and* my statutes which I have set before you, but go and serve other gods, and worship them:

7 Then will I cut off Israel out of the land which I have given them; and this house, which I have hallowed for my name, will I cast out of my sight; and Israel shall be a proverb and a byword among all people:

9:7 Warning!
◄ 1 Samuel 12:25
Psalm 7:12 ►

8 And at this house, *which* is high, every one that passeth by it shall be astonished, and shall hiss; and they shall say, Why hath the LORD done thus unto this land, and to this house?

9 And they shall answer, Because they forsook the LORD their God, who brought forth their fathers out of the land of Egypt, and have taken hold upon other gods, and have worshipped them, and served them: therefore hath the LORD brought upon them all this evil.

10 And it came to pass at the end of twenty years, when Solomon had built the two houses, the house of the LORD, and the king's house,

11 (*Now* Hiram the king of Tyre had furnished Solomon with cedar trees and fir trees, and with gold, according to all his desire,) that then king Solomon gave Hiram twenty cities in the land of Galilee.

12 And Hiram came out from Tyre to see the cities which Solomon had given him; and they pleased him not.

13 And he said, What cities *are* these which thou hast given me, my brother? And he called them the land of Cabul unto this day.

14 And Hiram sent to the king sixscore talents of gold.

15 And this *is* the reason of the levy which king Solomon raised; for to build the house of the LORD, and his own house, and Millo, and the wall of Jerusalem, and Hazor, and Megiddo, and Gezer.

16 *For* Pharaoh king of Egypt had gone up, and taken Gezer, and burnt it with fire, and slain the Canaanites that dwelt in the city, and given it *for* a present unto his daughter, Solomon's wife.

17 And Solomon built Gezer, and Bethhoron the nether,

18 and Baalath, and Tadmor in the wilderness, in the land,

19 And all the cities of store that Solomon had, and cities for his chariots, and cities for his horsemen, and that which Solomon desired to build in Jerusalem, and in Lebanon, and in all the land of his dominion.

20 *And* all the people *that were* left of the Amorites, Hittites, Perizzites, Hivites, and Jebusites, which *were* not of the children of Israel,

21 Their children that were left after them in the land, whom the children of Israel also were not able utterly to destroy, upon those did Solomon levy a tribute of bondservice unto this day.

22 But of the children of Israel did Solomon make no bondmen: but they *were* men of war, and his servants, and his princes, and his captains, and rulers of his chariots, and his horsemen.

23 These *were* the chief of the officers that *were* over Solomon's work, five hundred and fifty, which bare rule over the people that wrought in the work.

24 But Pharaoh's daughter came up out of the city of David unto her house which *Solomon* had built for her: then did he build Millo.

25 And three times in a year did Solomon offer burnt offerings and peace offerings upon the altar which he built unto the LORD, and he burnt incense upon the altar that *was* before the LORD. So he finished the house.

26 And king Solomon made a navy of ships in Ezion-geber, which *is* beside Eloth, on the shore of the Red sea, in the land of Edom.

27 And Hiram sent in the navy his servants, shipmen that had knowledge of the sea, with the servants of Solomon.

28 And they came to Ophir, and fetched from thence gold, four hundred and twenty talents, and brought *it* to king Solomon.

10

1 And when the queen of Sheba heard of the fame of Solomon concerning the name of the LORD, she came to prove him with hard questions.

2 And she came to Jerusalem with a very great train, with camels that bare spices, and very much gold, and precious stones: and when she was come to Solomon, she communed with him of all that was in her heart.

3 And Solomon told her all her questions: there was not *any* thing hid from the king, which he told her not.

4 And when the queen of Sheba had seen all Solomon's wisdom, and the house that he had built,

5 And the meat of his table, and the sitting of his servants, and the attendance of his ministers, and their apparel, and his cupbearers, and his ascent by which he went up unto the house of the LORD; there was no more spirit in her.

6 And she said to the king, It was a true report that I heard in mine own land of thy acts and of thy wisdom.

7 Howbeit I believed not the words, until I came, and mine eyes had seen *it*: and, behold, the half was not told me: thy wisdom and prosperity exceedeth the fame which I heard.

8 Happy *are* thy men, happy *are* these thy servants, which stand continually before thee, *and* that hear thy wisdom.

9 Blessed be the LORD thy God, which delighted in thee, to set thee on the throne of Israel: because the LORD loved Israel for ever, therefore made he thee king, to do judgment and justice.

10 And she gave the king an hundred and twenty talents of gold, and of spices very great store, and precious stones: there came no more such abundance of spices as these which the queen of Sheba gave to king Solomon.

11 And the navy also of Hiram, that brought gold from Ophir, brought in from Ophir great plenty of almug trees, and precious stones.

12 And the king made of the almug trees pillars for the house of the LORD, and for the king's house, harps also and psalteries for singers: there came no such almug trees, nor were seen unto this day.

13 And king Solomon gave unto the queen of Sheba all her desire, whatsoever she asked, beside *that* which Solomon gave her of his royal bounty. So she turned and went to her own country, she and her servants.

14 Now the weight of gold that came to Solomon in one year was six hundred threescore and six talents of gold,

15 Beside *that he had* of the merchantmen, and of the traffick of the spice merchants, and of all the kings of Arabia, and of the governors of the country.

16 And king Solomon made two hundred targets *of* beaten gold: six hundred *shekels* of gold went to one target.

17 And *he made* three hundred shields *of* beaten gold; three pound of gold went to one shield: and the king put them in the house of the forest of Lebanon.

18 Moreover the king made a great throne of ivory, and overlaid it with the best gold.

19 The throne had six steps, and the top of the throne *was* round behind: and *there were* stays on either side on the place of the seat, and two lions stood beside the stays.

20 And twelve lions stood there on the one side and on the other upon the six steps: there was not the like made in any kingdom.

21 And all king Solomon's drinking vessels *were of* gold, and all the vessels of the house of the forest of Lebanon *were of* pure gold; none *were of* silver: it was nothing accounted of in the days of Solomon.

22 For the king had at sea a navy of

Tharshish with the navy of Hiram: once in three years came the navy of Tharshish, bringing gold, and silver, ivory, and apes, and peacocks.

23 So king Solomon exceeded all the kings of the earth for riches and for wisdom.

24 And all the earth sought to Solomon, to hear his wisdom, which God had put in his heart.

25 And they brought every man his present, vessels of silver, and vessels of gold, and garments, and armour, and spices, horses, and mules, a rate year by year.

26 And Solomon gathered together chariots and horsemen: and he had a thousand and four hundred chariots, and twelve thousand horsemen, whom he bestowed in the cities for chariots, and with the king at Jerusalem.

27 And the king made silver *to be* in Jerusalem as stones, and cedars made he *to be* as the sycomore trees that *are* in the vale, for abundance.

28 And Solomon had horses brought out of Egypt, and linen yarn: the king's merchants received the linen yarn at a price.

29 And a chariot came up and went out of Egypt for six hundred *shekels* of silver, and an horse for an hundred and fifty: and so for all the kings of the Hittites, and for the kings of Syria, did they bring *them* out by their means.

11

1 But king Solomon loved many strange women, together with the daughter of Pharaoh, women of the Moabites, Ammonites, Edomites, Zidonians, *and* Hittites;

11:1 Giving In
◄ 1 Samuel 13:12
1 Kings 11:4 ►

2 Of the nations *concerning* which the LORD said unto the children of Israel, Ye shall not go in to them, neither shall they come in unto you: *for* surely they will turn away your heart after their gods: Solomon clave unto these in love.

3 And he had seven hundred wives, princesses, and three hundred concubines: and his wives turned away his heart.

11:4 Giving In
◄ 1 Kings 11:1
Mark 10:35-37 ►

4 For it came to pass, when Solomon was old, *that* his wives turned away his heart after other gods: and his heart was not perfect with the LORD his God, as *was* the heart of David his father.

5 For Solomon went after Ashtoreth the goddess of the Zidonians, and after Milcom the abomination of the Ammonites.

6 And Solomon did evil in the sight of the LORD, and went not fully after the LORD, as *did* David his father.

7 Then did Solomon build an high place for Chemosh, the abomination of Moab, in the hill that *is* before Jerusalem, and for Molech, the abomination of the children of Ammon.

8 And likewise did he for all his strange wives, which burnt incense and sacrificed unto their gods.

9 And the LORD was angry with Solomon, because his heart was turned from the LORD God of Israel, which had appeared unto him twice,

10 And had commanded him concerning this thing, that he should not go after other gods: but he kept not that which the LORD commanded.

11 Wherefore the LORD said unto Solomon, Forasmuch as this is done of thee, and thou hast not kept my covenant and my statutes, which I have commanded thee, I will surely rend the kingdom from thee, and will give it to thy servant.

12 Notwithstanding in thy days I will not do it for David thy father's sake: *but* I will rend it out of the hand of thy son.

13 Howbeit I will not rend away all the kingdom; *but* will give one tribe to thy son for David my servant's sake, and for Jerusalem's sake which I have chosen.

14 And the LORD stirred up an adversary unto Solomon, Hadad the Edomite: he *was* of the king's seed in Edom.

15 For it came to pass, when David was in Edom, and Joab the captain of the host was gone up to bury the slain, after he had smitten every male in Edom;

16 (For six months did Joab remain there with all Israel, until he had cut off every male in Edom:)

17 That Hadad fled, he and certain Edomites of his father's servants with him, to go into Egypt; Hadad *being* yet a little child.

18And they arose out of Midian, and came to Paran: and they took men with them out of Paran, and they came to Egypt, unto Pharaoh king of Egypt; which gave him an house, and appointed him victuals, and gave him land.
19And Hadad found great favour in the sight of Pharaoh, so that he gave him to wife the sister of his own wife, the sister of Tahpenes the queen.
20And the sister of Tahpenes bare him Genubath his son, whom Tahpenes weaned in Pharaoh's house: and Genubath was in Pharaoh's household among the sons of Pharaoh.
21And when Hadad heard in Egypt that David slept with his fathers, and that Joab the captain of the host was dead, Hadad said to Pharaoh, Let me depart, that I may go to mine own country.
22Then Pharaoh said unto him, But what hast thou lacked with me, that, behold, thou seekest to go to thine own country? And he answered, Nothing: howbeit let me go in any wise.
23And God stirred him up *another* adversary, Rezon the son of Eliadah, which fled from his lord Hadadezer king of Zobah:
24And he gathered men unto him, and became captain over a band, when David slew them *of Zobah:* and they went to Damascus, and dwelt therein, and reigned in Damascus.
25And he was an adversary to Israel all the days of Solomon, beside the mischief that Hadad *did:* and he abhorred Israel, and reigned over Syria.
26And Jeroboam the son of Nebat, an Ephrathite of Zereda, Solomon's servant, whose mother's name *was* Zeruah, a widow woman, even he lifted up *his* hand against the king.
27And this *was* the cause that he lifted up *his* hand against the king: Solomon built Millo, *and* repaired the breaches of the city of David his father.
28And the man Jeroboam *was* a mighty man of valour: and Solomon seeing the young man that he was industrious, he made him ruler over all the charge of the house of Joseph.
29And it came to pass at that time when Jeroboam went out of Jerusalem, that the prophet Ahijah the Shilonite found him in the way; and he had clad himself with a new garment; and they two *were* alone in the field:
30And Ahijah caught the new garment that *was* on him, and rent it *in* twelve pieces:
31And he said to Jeroboam, Take thee ten pieces: for thus saith the LORD, the God of Israel, Behold, I will rend the kingdom out of the hand of Solomon, and will give ten tribes to thee:
32(But he shall have one tribe for my servant David's sake, and for Jerusalem's sake, the city which I have chosen out of all the tribes of Israel:)
33Because that they have forsaken me, and have worshipped Ashtoreth the goddess of the Zidonians, Chemosh the god of the Moabites, and Milcom the god of the children of Ammon, and have not walked in my ways, to do *that which is* right in mine eyes, and *to keep* my statutes and my judgments, as *did* David his father.
34Howbeit I will not take the whole kingdom out of his hand: but I will make him prince all the days of his life for David my servant's sake, whom I chose, because he kept my commandments and my statutes:
35But I will take the kingdom out of his son's hand, and will give it unto thee, *even* ten tribes.
36And unto his son will I give one tribe, that David my servant may have a light alway before me in Jerusalem, the city which I have chosen me to put my name there.
37And I will take thee, and thou shalt reign according to all that thy soul desireth, and shalt be king over Israel.
38And it shall be, if thou wilt hearken unto all that I command thee, and wilt walk in my ways, and do *that is* right in my sight, to keep my statutes and my commandments, as David my servant did; that I will be with thee, and build thee a sure house, as I built for David, and will give Israel unto thee.
39And I will for this afflict the seed of David, but not for ever.
40Solomon sought therefore to kill Jeroboam. And Jeroboam arose, and fled into Egypt, unto Shishak king of Egypt, and was in Egypt until the death of Solomon.
41And the rest of the acts of Solomon,

and all that he did, and his wisdom, *are* they not written in the book of the acts of Solomon?

42 And the time that Solomon reigned in Jerusalem over all Israel *was* forty years.

43 And Solomon slept with his fathers, and was buried in the city of David his father: and Rehoboam his son reigned in his stead.

12

1 And Rehoboam went to Shechem: for all Israel were come to Shechem to make him king.

2 And it came to pass, when Jeroboam the son of Nebat, who was yet in Egypt, heard *of it,* (for he was fled from the presence of king Solomon, and Jeroboam dwelt in Egypt;)

3 That they sent and called him. And Jeroboam and all the congregation of Israel came, and spake unto Rehoboam, saying,

4 Thy father made our yoke grievous: now therefore make thou the grievous service of thy father, and his heavy yoke which he put upon us, lighter, and we will serve thee.

5 And he said unto them, Depart yet *for* three days, then come again to me. And the people departed.

6 And king Rehoboam consulted with the old men, that stood before Solomon his father while he yet lived, and said, How do ye advise that I may answer this people?

7 And they spake unto him, saying, If thou wilt be a servant unto this people this day, and wilt serve them, and answer them, and speak good words to them, then they will be thy servants for ever.

8 But he forsook the counsel of the old men, which they had given him, and consulted with the young men that were grown up with him, *and* which stood before him:

9 And he said unto them, What counsel give ye that we may answer this people, who have spoken to me, saying, Make the yoke which thy father did put upon us lighter?

10 And the young men that were grown up with him spake unto him, saying, Thus shalt thou speak unto this people that spake unto thee, saying, Thy father made our yoke heavy, but make thou *it* lighter unto us; thus shalt thou say unto them, My little *finger* shall be thicker than my father's loins.

11 And now whereas my father did lade you with a heavy yoke, I will add to your yoke: my father hath chastised you with whips, but I will chastise you with scorpions.

12 So Jeroboam and all the people came to Rehoboam the third day, as the king had appointed, saying, Come to me again the third day.

13 And the king answered the people roughly, and forsook the old men's counsel that they gave him;

14 And spake to them after the counsel of the young men, saying, My father made your yoke heavy, and I will add to your yoke: my father *also* chastised you with whips, but I will chastise you with scorpions.

15 Wherefore the king hearkened not unto the people; for the cause was fromthe LORD, that he might perform his saying, which the LORD spake by Ahijah the Shilonite unto Jeroboam the son of Nebat.

16 So when all Israel saw that the king hearkened not unto them, the people answered the king, saying, What portion have we in David? neither *have we* inheritance in the son of Jesse: to your tents, O Israel: now see to thine own house, David. So Israel departed unto their tents.

17 But *as for* the children of Israel which dwelt in the cities of Judah, Rehoboam reigned over them.

18 Then king Rehoboam sent Adoram, who *was* over the tribute; and all Israel stoned him with stones, that he died. Therefore king Rehoboam made speed to get him up to his chariot, to flee to Jerusalem.

19 So Israel rebelled against the house of David unto this day.

20 And it came to pass, when all Israel heard that Jeroboam was come again, that they sent and called him unto the congregation, and made him king over all Israel: there was none that followed the house of David, but the tribe of Judah only.

21 And when Rehoboam was come to Jerusalem, he assembled all the house of Judah, with the tribe of Benjamin, an hundred and fourscore thousand chosen men, which were warriors, to fight against the house of Israel, to bring the kingdom again to Rehoboam the son of Solomon.

22 But the word of God came unto Shemaiah the man of God, saying,

23 Speak unto Rehoboam, the son of Solomon, king of Judah, and unto all the house of Judah and Benjamin, and to the remnant of the people, saying,

24 Thus saith the LORD, Ye shall not go up, nor fight against your brethren the children of Israel: return every man to his house; for this thing is from me. They hearkened therefore to the word of the LORD, and returned to depart, according to the word of the LORD.

25 Then Jeroboam built Shechem in mount Ephraim, and dwelt therein; and went out from thence, and built Penuel.

26 And Jeroboam said in his heart, Now shall the kingdom return to the house of David:

27 If this people go up to do sacrifice in the house of the LORD at Jerusalem, then shall the heart of this people turn again unto their lord, *even* unto Rehoboam king of Judah, and they shall kill me, and go again to Rehoboam king of Judah.

28 Whereupon the king took counsel, and made two calves *of* gold, and said unto them, It is too much for you to go up to Jerusalem: behold thy gods, O Israel, which brought thee up out of the land of Egypt.

29 And he set the one in Bethel, and the other put he in Dan.

30 And this thing became a sin: for the people went *to worship* before the one, *even* unto Dan.

31 And he made an house of high places, and made priests of the lowest of the people, which were not of the sons of Levi.

32 And Jeroboam ordained a feast in the eighth month, on the fifteenth day of the month, like unto the feast that *is* in Judah, and he offered upon the altar. So did he in Bethel, sacrificing unto the calves that he had made: and he placed in Bethel the priests of the high places which he had made.

33 So he offered upon the altar which he had made in Bethel the fifteenth day of the eighth month, *even* in the month which he had devised of his own heart; and ordained a feast unto the children of Israel: and he offered upon the altar, and burnt incense.

13

1 And, behold, there came a man of God out of Judah by the word of the LORD unto Bethel: and Jeroboam stood by the altar to burn incense.

2 And he cried against the altar in the word of the LORD, and said, O altar, altar, thus saith the LORD; Behold, a child shall be born unto the house of David, Josiah by name; and upon thee shall he offer the priests of the high places that burn incense upon thee, and men's bones shall be burnt upon thee.

3 And he gave a sign the same day, saying, This *is* the sign which the LORD hath spoken; Behold, the altar shall be rent, and the ashes that *are* upon it shall be poured out.

4 And it came to pass, when king Jeroboam heard the saying of the man of God, which had cried against the altar in Bethel, that he put forth his hand from the altar, saying, Lay hold on him. And his hand, which he put forth against him, dried up, so that he could not pull it in again to him.

5 The altar also was rent, and the ashes poured out from the altar, according to the sign which the man of God had given by the word of the LORD.

6 And the king answered and said unto the man of God, Intreat now the face of the LORD thy God, and pray for me, that my hand may be restored me again. And the man of God besought the LORD, and the king's hand was restored him again, and became as *it was* before.

13:6 Praying for Others
◄ 1 Samuel 7:5
1 Chronicles 21:17 ►

7 And the king said unto the man of God, Come home with me, and refresh thyself, and I will give thee a reward.

8 And the man of God said unto the king, If thou wilt give me half thine house, I will not go in with thee, neither will I eat bread nor drink water in this place:

9 For so was it charged me by the word of the LORD, saying, Eat no bread, nor drink water, nor turn again by the same way that thou camest.

10 So he went another way, and returned not by the way that he came to Bethel.

11 Now there dwelt an old prophet in Bethel; and his sons came and told him all the works that the man of God had done that day in Bethel: the words which he had spoken unto the king, them they told also to their father.

12 And their father said unto them, What way went he? For his sons had seen what

way the man of God went, which came from Judah.

13 And he said unto his sons, Saddle me the ass. So they saddled him the ass: and he rode thereon,

14 And went after the man of God, and found him sitting under an oak: and he said unto him, *Art* thou the man of God that camest from Judah? And he said, I *am.*

15 Then he said unto him, Come home with me, and eat bread.

16 And he said, I may not return with thee, nor go in with thee: neither will I eat bread nor drink water with thee in this place:

17 For it was said to me by the word of the LORD, Thou shalt eat no bread nor drink water there, nor turn again to go by the way that thou camest.

18 He said unto him, I *am* a prophet also as thou *art;* and an angel spake unto me by the word of the LORD, saying, Bring him back with thee into thine house, that he may eat bread and drink water. *But* he lied unto him.

19 So he went back with him, and did eat bread in his house, and drank water.

20 And it came to pass, as they sat at the table, that the word of the LORD came unto the prophet that brought him back:

21 And he cried unto the man of God that came from Judah, saying, Thus saith the LORD, Forasmuch as thou hast disobeyed the mouth of the LORD, and hast not kept the commandment which the LORD thy God commanded thee,

13:21 Ouch!
◄ 1 Samuel 28:18
Jeremiah 12:17 ►

22 But camest back, and hast eaten bread and drunk water in the place, of the which *the LORD* did say to thee, Eat no bread, and drink no water; thy carcase shall not come unto the sepulchre of thy fathers.

23 And it came to pass, after he had eaten bread, and after he had drunk, that he saddled for him the ass, *to wit,* for the prophet whom he had brought back.

24 And when he was gone, a lion met him by the way, and slew him: and his carcase was cast in the way, and the ass stood by it, the lion also stood by the carcase.

25 And, behold, men passed by, and saw the carcase cast in the way, and the lion standing by the carcase: and they came and told *it* in the city where the old prophet dwelt.

26 And when the prophet that brought him back from the way heard *thereof,* he said, It *is* the man of God, who was disobedient unto the word of the LORD: therefore the LORD hath delivered him unto the lion, which hath torn him, and slain him, according to the word of the LORD, which he spake unto him.

27 And he spake to his sons, saying, Saddle me the ass. And they saddled *him.*

28 And he went and found his carcase cast in the way, and the ass and the lion standing by the carcase: the lion had not eaten the carcase, nor torn the ass.

29 And the prophet took up the carcase of the man of God, and laid it upon the ass, and brought it back: and the old prophet came to the city, to mourn and to bury him.

30 And he laid his carcase in his own grave; and they mourned over him, *saying,* Alas, my brother!

31 And it came to pass, after he had buried him, that he spake to his sons, saying, When I am dead, then bury me in the sepulchre wherein the man of God *is* buried; lay my bones beside his bones:

32 For the saying which he cried by the word of the LORD against the altar in Bethel, and against all the houses of the high places which *are* in the cities of Samaria, shall surely come to pass.

33 After this thing Jeroboam returned not from his evil way, but made again of the lowest of the people priests of the high places: whosoever would, he consecrated him, and he became *one* of the priests of the high places.

34 And this thing became sin unto the house of Jeroboam, even to cut *it* off, and to destroy *it* from off the face of the earth.

14

1 At that time Abijah the son of Jeroboam fell sick.

2 And Jeroboam said to his wife, Arise, I pray thee, and disguise thyself, that thou be not known to be the wife of Jeroboam; and get thee to Shiloh: behold, there *is* Ahijah the prophet, which told me that *I should be* king over this people.

3 And take with thee ten loaves, and cracknels, and a cruse of honey, and go to him: he shall tell thee what shall become of the child.

4 And Jeroboam's wife did so, and arose, and went to Shiloh, and came to the house of Ahijah. But Ahijah could not see; for his eyes were set by reason of his age.

5 And the LORD said unto Ahijah, Behold, the wife of Jeroboam cometh to ask a thing of thee for her son; for he is sick: thus and thus shalt thou say unto her: for it shall be, when she cometh in, that she shall feign herself *to be* another *woman*.

6 And it was *so*, when Ahijah heard the sound of her feet as she came in at the door, that he said, Come in, thou wife of Jeroboam; why feignest thou thyself *to be* another? for I *am* sent to thee *with* heavy *tidings*.

7 Go, tell Jeroboam, Thus saith the LORD God of Israel, Forasmuch as I exalted thee from among the people, and made thee prince over my people Israel,

14:7 God at Work
◄ 2 Samuel 7:8
Psalm 75:7 ►

8 And rent the kingdom away from the house of David, and gave it thee: and *yet* thou hast not been as my servant David, who kept my commandments, and who followed me with all his heart, to do *that* only *which was* right in mine eyes;

9 But hast done evil above all that were before thee: for thou hast gone and made thee other gods, and molten images, to provoke me to anger, and hast cast me behind thy back:

10 Therefore, behold, I will bring evil upon the house of Jeroboam, and will cut off from Jeroboam him that pisseth against the wall, *and* him that is shut up and left in Israel, and will take away the remnant of the house of Jeroboam, as a man taketh away dung, till it be all gone.

11 Him that dieth of Jeroboam in the city shall the dogs eat; and him that dieth in the field shall the fowls of the air eat: for the LORD hath spoken *it*.

12 Arise thou therefore, get thee to thine own house: *and* when thy feet enter into the city, the child shall die.

13 And all Israel shall mourn for him, and bury him: for he only of Jeroboam shall come to the grave, because in him there is found *some* good thing toward the LORD God of Israel in the house of Jeroboam.

14 Moreover the LORD shall raise him up a king over Israel, who shall cut off the house of Jeroboam that day: but what? even now.

15 For the LORD shall smite Israel, as a reed is shaken in the water, and he shall root up Israel out of this good land, which he gave to their fathers, and shall scatter them beyond the river, because they have made their groves, provoking the LORD to anger.

16 And he shall give Israel up because of the sins of Jeroboam, who did sin, and who made Israel to sin.

17 And Jeroboam's wife arose, and departed, and came to Tirzah: *and* when she came to the threshold of the door, the child died;

18 And they buried him; and all Israel mourned for him, according to the word of the LORD, which he spake by the hand of his servant Ahijah the prophet.

19 And the rest of the acts of Jeroboam, how he warred, and how he reigned, behold, they *are* written in the book of the chronicles of the kings of Israel.

20 And the days which Jeroboam reigned *were* two and twenty years: and he slept with his fathers, and Nadab his son reigned in his stead.

21 And Rehoboam the son of Solomon reigned in Judah. Rehoboam *was* forty and one years old when he began to reign, and he reigned seventeen years in Jerusalem, the city which the LORD did choose out of all the tribes of Israel, to put his name there. And his mother's name *was* Naamah an Ammonitess.

22 And Judah did evil in the sight of the LORD, and they provoked him to jealousy with their sins which they had committed, above all that their fathers had done.

14:22 God Is Jealous
◄ Joshua 24:19
1 Corinthians 10:22 ►

23 For they also built them high places, and images, and groves, on every high hill, and under every green tree.

24 And there were also sodomites in the land: *and* they did according to all the abominations of the nations which the LORD cast out before the children of Israel.

25 And it came to pass in the fifth year of

king Rehoboam, *that* Shishak king of Egypt
came up against Jerusalem:
26 And he took away the treasures of the
house of the LORD, and the treasures of
the king's house; he even took away all:
and he took away all the shields of gold
which Solomon had made.
27 And king Rehoboam made in their
stead brasen shields, and committed *them*
unto the hands of the chief of the guard,
which kept the door of the king's house.
28 And it was *so,* when the king went into
the house of the LORD, that the guard bare
them, and brought them back into the
guard chamber.
29 Now the rest of the acts of Rehoboam, and all that he did, *are* they not written in the book of the chronicles of the
kings of Judah?
30 And there was war between Rehoboam and Jeroboam all *their* days.
31 And Rehoboam slept with his fathers,
and was buried with his fathers in the city
of David. And his mother's name *was* Naamah an Ammonitess. And Abijam his son
reigned in his stead.

15

1 Now in the eighteenth year of king Jeroboam the son of Nebat reigned Abijam
over Judah.
2 Three years reigned he in Jerusalem.
And his mother's name *was* Maachah, the
daughter of Abishalom.
3 And he walked in all the sins of his father, which he had done before him: and
his heart was not perfect with the LORD
his God, as the heart of David his father.
4 Nevertheless for David's sake did the
LORD his God give him a lamp in Jerusalem, to set up his son after him, and to
establish Jerusalem:
5 Because David did *that which was* right
in the eyes of the LORD, and turned not
aside from any *thing* that he commanded
him all the days of his life, save only in
the matter of Uriah the Hittite.
6 And there was war between Rehoboam
and Jeroboam all the days of his life.
7 Now the rest of the acts of Abijam, and
all that he did, *are* they not written in the
book of the chronicles of the kings of Judah? And there was war between Abijam
and Jeroboam.
8 And Abijam slept with his fathers; and
they buried him in the city of David: and
Asa his son reigned in his stead.
9 And in the twentieth year of Jeroboam
king of Israel reigned Asa over Judah.
10 And forty and one years reigned he in
Jerusalem. And his mother's name *was*
Maachah, the daughter of Abishalom.
11 And Asa did *that which was* right in the
eyes of the LORD, as *did* David his father.
12 And he took away the sodomites out
of the land, and removed all the idols that
his fathers had made.
13 And also Maachah his mother, even
her he removed from *being* queen, because
she had made an idol in a grove; and Asa
destroyed her idol, and burnt *it* by the
brook Kidron.
14 But the high places were not removed:
nevertheless Asa's heart was perfect with
the LORD all his days.
15 And he brought in the things which
his father had dedicated, and the things
which himself had dedicated, into the
house of the LORD, silver, and gold, and
vessels.
16 And there was war between Asa and
Baasha king of Israel all their days.
17 And Baasha king of Israel went up
against Judah, and built Ramah, that he
might not suffer any to go out or come in
to Asa king of Judah.
18 Then Asa took all the silver and the
gold *that were* left in the treasures of the
house of the LORD, and the treasures of
the king's house, and delivered them into
the hand of his servants: and king Asa
sent them to Ben-hadad, the son of Tabri-
mon, the son of Hezion, king of Syria, that
dwelt at Damascus, saying,
19 *There is* a league between me and thee,
and between my father and thy father: behold, I have sent unto thee a present of
silver and gold; come and break thy league
with Baasha king of Israel, that he may
depart from me.
20 So Ben-hadad hearkened unto king
Asa, and sent the captains of the hosts
which he had against the cities of Israel,
and smote Ijon, and Dan, and Abel-beth-
maachah, and all Cinneroth, with all the
land of Naphtali.
21 And it came to pass, when Baasha
heard *thereof,* that he left off building of
Ramah, and dwelt in Tirzah.
22 Then king Asa made a proclamation
throughout all Judah; none *was* exempted:
and they took away the stones of Ramah,

and the timber thereof, wherewith Baasha had builded; and king Asa built with them Geba of Benjamin, and Mizpah.

23 The rest of all the acts of Asa, and all his might, and all that he did, and the cities which he built, *are* they not written in the book of the chronicles of the kings of Judah? Nevertheless in the time of his old age he was diseased in his feet.

24 And Asa slept with his fathers, and was buried with his fathers in the city of David his father: and Jehoshaphat his son reigned in his stead.

25 And Nadab the son of Jeroboam began to reign over Israel in the second year of Asa king of Judah, and reigned over Israel two years.

26 And he did evil in the sight of the LORD, and walked in the way of his father, and in his sin wherewith he made Israel to sin.

27 And Baasha the son of Ahijah, of the house of Issachar, conspired against him; and Baasha smote him at Gibbethon, which *belonged* to the Philistines; for Nadab and all Israel laid siege to Gibbethon.

28 Even in the third year of Asa king of Judah did Baasha slay him, and reigned in his stead.

29 And it came to pass, when he reigned, *that* he smote all the house of Jeroboam; he left not to Jeroboam any that breathed, until he had destroyed him, according unto the saying of the LORD, which he spake by his servant Ahijah the Shilonite:

30 Because of the sins of Jeroboam which he sinned, and which he made Israel sin, by his provocation wherewith he provoked the LORD God of Israel to anger.

31 Now the rest of the acts of Nadab, and all that he did, *are* they not written in the book of the chronicles of the kings of Israel?

32 And there was war between Asa and Baasha king of Israel all their days.

33 In the third year of Asa king of Judah began Baasha the son of Ahijah to reign over all Israel in Tirzah, twenty and four years.

34 And he did evil in the sight of the LORD, and walked in the way of Jeroboam, and in his sin wherewith he made Israel to sin.

16

1 Then the word of the LORD came to Jehu the son of Hanani against Baasha, saying,

2 Forasmuch as I exalted thee out of the dust, and made thee prince over my people Israel; and thou hast walked in the way of Jeroboam, and hast made my people Israel to sin, to provoke me to anger with their sins;

3 Behold, I will take away the posterity of Baasha, and the posterity of his house; and will make thy house like the house of Jeroboam the son of Nebat.

4 Him that dieth of Baasha in the city shall the dogs eat; and him that dieth of his in the fields shall the fowls of the air eat.

5 Now the rest of the acts of Baasha, and what he did, and his might, *are* they not written in the book of the chronicles of the kings of Israel?

6 So Baasha slept with his fathers, and was buried in Tirzah: and Elah his son reigned in his stead.

7 And also by the hand of the prophet Jehu the son of Hanani came the word of the LORD against Baasha, and against his house, even for all the evil that he did in the sight of the LORD, in provoking him to anger with the work of his hands, in being like the house of Jeroboam; and because he killed him.

8 In the twenty and sixth year of Asa king of Judah began Elah the son of Baasha to reign over Israel in Tirzah, two years.

9 And his servant Zimri, captain of half *his* chariots, conspired against him, as he was in Tirzah, drinking himself drunk in the house of Arza steward of *his* house in Tirzah.

10 And Zimri went in and smote him, and killed him, in the twenty and seventh year of Asa king of Judah, and reigned in his stead.

11 And it came to pass, when he began to reign, as soon as he sat on his throne, *that* he slew all the house of Baasha: he left him not one that pisseth against a wall, neither of his kinsfolks, nor of his friends.

12 Thus did Zimri destroy all the house of Baasha, according to the word of the LORD, which he spake against Baasha by Jehu the prophet,

13 For all the sins of Baasha, and the sins of Elah his son, by which they sinned, and by

16:13 Worshiping Things
◄ Deuteronomy 32:21
Psalm 31:6 ►

which they made Israel to sin, in provoking the LORD God of Israel to anger with
their vanities.
14 Now the rest of the acts of Elah, and
all that he did, *are* they not written in the
book of the chronicles of the kings of Israel?
15 In the twenty and seventh year of Asa
king of Judah did Zimri reign seven days
in Tirzah. And the people *were* encamped
against Gibbethon, which *belonged* to the
Philistines.
16 And the people *that were* encamped
heard say, Zimri hath conspired, and hath
also slain the king: wherefore all Israel
made Omri, the captain of the host, king
over Israel that day in the camp.
17 And Omri went up from Gibbethon,
and all Israel with him, and they besieged
Tirzah.
18 And it came to pass, when Zimri saw
that the city was taken, that he went into
the palace of the king's house, and burnt
the king's house over him with fire, and
died,
19 For his sins which he sinned in doing
evil in the sight of the LORD, in walking in
the way of Jeroboam, and in his sin which
he did, to make Israel to sin.
20 Now the rest of the acts of Zimri, and
his treason that he wrought, *are* they not
written in the book of the chronicles of
the kings of Israel?
21 Then were the people of Israel divided into two parts: half of the people followed Tibni the son of Ginath, to make
him king; and half followed Omri.
22 But the people that followed Omri
prevailed against the people that followed
Tibni the son of Ginath: so Tibni died, and
Omri reigned.
23 In the thirty and first year of Asa king
of Judah began Omri to reign over Israel,
twelve years: six years reigned he in Tirzah.
24 And he bought the hill Samaria of
Shemer for two talents of silver, and built
on the hill, and called the name of the city
which he built, after the name of Shemer,
owner of the hill, Samaria.
25 But Omri wrought evil in the eyes of
the LORD, and did worse than all that *were*
before him.
26 For he walked in all the way of Jeroboam the son of Nebat, and in his sin
wherewith he made Israel to sin, to provoke the LORD God of Israel to anger with
their vanities.
27 Now the rest of the acts of Omri which
he did, and his might that he shewed, *are*
they not written in the book of the chronicles of the kings of Israel?
28 So Omri slept with his fathers, and
was buried in Samaria: and Ahab his son
reigned in his stead.
29 And in the thirty and eighth year of
Asa king of Judah began Ahab the son of
Omri to reign over Israel: and Ahab the
son of Omri reigned over Israel in Samaria twenty and two years.
30 And Ahab the son of Omri did evil in
the sight of the LORD above all that *were*
before him.
31 And it came to pass, as if it had been a
light thing for him to walk in the sins of
Jeroboam the son of Nebat, that he took
to wife Jezebel the daughter of Ethbaal
king of the Zidonians, and went and served
Baal, and worshipped him.
32 And he reared up an altar for Baal in
the house of Baal, which he had built in
Samaria.
33 And Ahab made a grove; and Ahab did
more to provoke the LORD God of Israel
to anger than all the kings of Israel that
were before him.
34 In his days did Hiel the Bethelite build
Jericho: he laid the foundation thereof in
Abiram his firstborn, and set up the gates
thereof in his youngest *son* Segub, according to the word of the LORD, which he
spake by Joshua the son of Nun.

17

1 And Elijah the Tishbite, *who was* of the
inhabitants of Gilead, said unto Ahab, *As*
the LORD God of Israel liveth, before
whom I stand, there shall not be dew nor
rain these years, but according to my word.
2 And the word of the LORD came unto
him, saying,
3 Get thee hence, and turn thee eastward,
and hide thyself by the brook Cherith, that
is before Jordan.
4 And it shall be, *that* thou shalt drink of
the brook; and I have commanded the ravens to feed thee there.
5 So he went and did according unto the
word of the LORD: for he went and dwelt
by the brook Cherith, that *is* before Jordan.
6 And the ravens brought him bread and
flesh in the morning, and bread and flesh
in the evening; and he drank of the brook.

7 And it came to pass after a while, that the brook dried up, because there had been no rain in the land.

8 And the word of the LORD came unto him, saying,

9 Arise, get thee to Zarephath, which *belongeth* to Zidon, and dwell there: behold, I have commanded a widow woman there to sustain thee.

10 So he arose and went to Zarephath. And when he came to the gate of the city, behold, the widow woman *was* there gathering of sticks: and he called to her, and said, Fetch me, I pray thee, a little water in a vessel, that I may drink.

11 And as she was going to fetch *it,* he called to her, and said, Bring me, I pray thee, a morsel of bread in thine hand.

12 And she said, *As* the LORD thy God liveth, I have not a cake, but an handful of meal in a barrel, and a little oil in a cruse: and, behold, I *am* gathering two sticks, that I may go in and dress it for me and my son, that we may eat it, and die.

13 And Elijah said unto her, Fear not; go *and* do as thou hast said: but make me thereof a little cake first, and bring *it* unto me, and after make for thee and for thy son.

14 For thus saith the LORD God of Israel, The barrel of meal shall not waste, neither shall the cruse of oil fail, until the day *that* the LORD sendeth rain upon the earth.

15 And she went and did according to the saying of Elijah: and she, and he, and her house, did eat *many* days.

16 *And* the barrel of meal wasted not, neither did the cruse of oil fail, according to the word of the LORD, which he spake by Elijah.

17 And it came to pass after these things, *that* the son of the woman, the mistress of the house, fell sick; and his sickness was so sore, that there was no breath left in him.

18 And she said unto Elijah, What have I to do with thee, O thou man of God? art thou come unto me to call my sin to remembrance, and to slay my son?

19 And he said unto her, Give me thy son. And he took him out of her bosom, and carried him up into a loft, where he abode, and laid him upon his own bed.

17:19-20 Praying Alone
◄ 1 Samuel 15:11
Daniel 6:10 ►

20 And he cried unto the LORD, and said, O LORD my God, hast thou also brought evil upon the widow with whom I sojourn, by slaying her son?

21 And he stretched himself upon the child three times, and cried unto the LORD, and said, O LORD my God, I pray thee, let this child's soul come into him again.

22 And the LORD heard the voice of Elijah; and the soul of the child came into him again, and he revived.

23 And Elijah took the child, and brought him down out of the chamber into the house, and delivered him unto his mother: and Elijah said, See, thy son liveth.

24 And the woman said to Elijah, Now by this I know that thou *art* a man of God, *and* that the word of the LORD in thy mouth *is* truth.

18

1 And it came to pass *after* many days, that the word of the LORD came to Elijah in the third year, saying, Go, shew thyself unto Ahab; and I will send rain upon the earth.

2 And Elijah went to shew himself unto Ahab. And *there was* a sore famine in Samaria.

3 And Ahab called Obadiah, which *was* the governor of *his* house. (Now Obadiah feared the LORD greatly:

4 For it was *so,* when Jezebel cut off the prophets of the LORD, that Obadiah took an hundred prophets, and hid them by fifty in a cave, and fed them with bread and water.)

5 And Ahab said unto Obadiah, Go into the land, unto all fountains of water, and unto all brooks: peradventure we may find grass to save the horses and mules alive, that we lose not all the beasts.

6 So they divided the land between them to pass throughout it: Ahab went one way by himself, and Obadiah went another way by himself.

7 And as Obadiah was in the way, behold, Elijah met him: and he knew him, and fell on his face, and said, *Art* thou that my lord Elijah?

8 And he answered him, I *am:* go, tell thy lord, Behold, Elijah *is here.*

9 And he said, What have I sinned, that thou wouldest deliver thy servant into the hand of Ahab, to slay me?

10 *As* the LORD thy God liveth, there is
no nation or kingdom, whither my lord
hath not sent to seek thee: and when they
said, *He is* not *there;* he took an oath of
the kingdom and nation, that they found
thee not.
11 And now thou sayest, Go, tell thy lord,
Behold, Elijah *is here.*
12 And it shall come to pass, *as soon as* I
am gone from thee, that the Spirit of the
LORD shall carry thee whither I know not;
and *so* when I come and tell Ahab, and he
cannot find thee, he shall slay me: but I
thy servant fear the LORD from my youth.
13 Was it not told my lord what I did
when Jezebel slew the prophets of the
LORD, how I hid an hundred men of the
LORD'S prophets by fifty in a cave, and fed
them with bread and water?
14 And now thou sayest, Go, tell thy lord,
Behold, Elijah *is here:* and he shall slay me.
15 And Elijah said, *As* the LORD of hosts
liveth, before whom I stand, I will surely
shew myself unto him to day.
16 So Obadiah went to meet Ahab, and
told him: and Ahab went to meet Elijah.
17 And it came to pass, when Ahab saw
Elijah, that Ahab said unto him, *Art* thou
he that troubleth Israel?
18 And he answered, I have not troubled
Israel; but thou, and thy father's house, in
that ye have forsaken the commandments
of the LORD, and thou hast followed
Baalim.
19 Now therefore send, *and* gather to me
all Israel unto mount Carmel, and the
prophets of Baal four hundred and fifty,
and the prophets of the groves four hundred, which eat at Jezebel's table.
20 So Ahab sent unto all the children of
Israel, and gathered the prophets together
unto mount Carmel.
21 And Elijah came
unto all the people,
and said, How long
halt ye between two
opinions? if the
LORD *be* God, fol-
low him: but if
Baal, *then* follow
him. And the peo-
ple answered him
not a word.

18:21 Following God
◄ Ruth 1:15
Matthew 27:17 ►

18:21
The Time Is Now
◄ 2 Kings 17:41 ►

22 Then said Eli-
jah unto the people, I, *even* I only, remain
a prophet of the LORD; but Baal's prophets *are* four hundred and fifty men.
23 Let them therefore give us two bullocks; and let them choose one bullock for
themselves, and cut it in pieces, and lay *it*
on wood, and put no fire *under:* and I will
dress the other bullock, and lay *it* on wood,
and put no fire *under:*
24 And call ye on the name of your gods,
and I will call on the name of the LORD:
and the God that answereth by fire, let him
be God. And all the people answered and
said, It is well spoken.
25 And Elijah said unto the prophets of
Baal, Choose you one bullock for yourselves, and dress *it* first; for ye *are* many;
and call on the name of your gods, but
put no fire *under.*
26 And they took the bullock which was
given them, and they dressed *it,* and called
on the name of Baal from morning even
until noon, saying, O Baal, hear us. But
there was no voice, nor any that answered.
And they leaped upon the altar which was
made.
27 And it came to pass at noon, that Elijah mocked them, and said, Cry aloud: for
he *is* a god; either he is talking, or he is
pursuing, or he is in a journey, *or* peradventure he sleepeth, and must be awaked.
28 And they cried
aloud, and cut
themselves after
their manner with
knives and lancets,
till the blood gushed
out upon them.

18:28
Fanatics
◄ John 19:15 ►

29 And it came to pass, when midday was
past, and they prophesied until the *time*
of the offering of the *evening* sacrifice, that
there was neither voice, nor any to answer,
nor any that regarded.
30 And Elijah said unto all the people,
Come near unto me. And all the people
came near unto him. And he repaired the
altar of the LORD *that was* broken down.
31 And Elijah took twelve stones, according to the number of the tribes of the sons
of Jacob, unto whom the word of the LORD
came, saying, Israel shall be thy name:
32 And with the stones he built an altar
in the name of the LORD: and he made a
trench about the altar, as great as would
contain two measures of seed.
33 And he put the wood in order, and

cut the bullock in pieces, and laid *him* on the wood, and said, Fill four barrels with water, and pour *it* on the burnt sacrifice, and on the wood.

34 And he said, Do *it* the second time. And they did *it* the second time. And he said, Do *it* the third time. And they did *it* the third time.

35 And the water ran round about the altar; and he filled the trench also with water.

36 And it came to pass at *the time of* the offering of the *evening* sacrifice, that Elijah the prophet came near, and said, LORD God of Abraham, Isaac, and of Israel, let it be known this day that thou *art* God in Israel, and *that* I *am* thy servant, and *that* I have done all these things at thy word.

37 Hear me, O LORD, hear me, that this people may know that thou *art* the LORD God, and *that* thou hast turned their heart back again.

38 Then the fire of the LORD fell, and consumed the burnt sacrifice, and the wood, and the stones, and the dust, and licked up the water that *was* in the trench.

39 And when all the people saw *it*, they fell on their faces: and they said, The LORD, he *is* the God; the LORD, he *is* the God.

40 And Elijah said unto them, Take the prophets of Baal; let not one of them escape. And they took them: and Elijah brought them down to the brook Kishon, and slew them there.

41 And Elijah said unto Ahab, Get thee up, eat and drink; for *there is* a sound of abundance of rain.

42 So Ahab went up to eat and to drink. And Elijah went up to the top of Carmel; and he cast himself down upon the earth, and put his face between his knees,

43 And said to his servant, Go up now, look toward the sea. And he went up, and looked, and said, *There is* nothing. And he said, Go again seven times.

44 And it came to pass at the seventh time, that he said, Behold, there ariseth a little cloud out of the sea, like a man's hand. And he said, Go up, say unto Ahab, Prepare *thy chariot*, and get thee down, that the rain stop thee not.

45 And it came to pass in the mean while, that the heaven was black with clouds and wind, and there was a great rain. And Ahab rode, and went to Jezreel.

46 And the hand of the LORD was on Elijah; and he girded up his loins, and ran before Ahab to the entrance of Jezreel.

19

1 And Ahab told Jezebel all that Elijah had done, and withal how he had slain all the prophets with the sword.

2 Then Jezebel sent a messenger unto Elijah, saying, So let the gods do *to me*, and more also, if I make not thy life as the life of one of them by to morrow about this time.

19:2 Examples of Revenge
◄ 1 Kings 22:27 ►

3 And when he saw *that*, he arose, and went for his life, and came to Beer-sheba, which *belongeth* to Judah, and left his servant there.

4 But he himself went a day's journey into the wilderness, and came and sat down under a juniper tree: and he requested for himself that he might die; and said, It is enough; now, O LORD, take away my life; for I *am* not better than my fathers.

19:4 Unhappiness
◄ Joshua 7:7
Job 10:1 ►

5 And as he lay and slept under a juniper tree, behold, then an angel touched him, and said unto him, Arise *and* eat.

6 And he looked, and, behold, *there was* a cake baken on the coals, and a cruse of water at his head. And he did eat and drink, and laid him down again.

7 And the angel of the LORD came again the second time, and touched him, and said, Arise *and* eat; because the journey *is* too great for thee.

8 And he arose, and did eat and drink, and went in the strength of that meat forty days and forty nights unto Horeb the mount of God.

19:8 Things That Last
◄ John 6:27 ►

9 And he came thither unto a cave, and lodged there; and, behold, the word of the LORD *came* to him, and he said unto him, What doest thou here, Elijah?

10 And he said, I have been very jealous for the LORD God of hosts: for the children of Israel have forsaken thy covenant, thrown down thine altars, and slain thy prophets with the sword; and I, *even* I only,

am left; and they seek my life, to take it
away.
11 And he said, Go forth, and stand upon
the mount before the LORD. And, behold,
the LORD passed by, and a great and strong
wind rent the mountains, and brake in
pieces the rocks before the LORD; *but* the
LORD *was* not in the wind: and after the
wind an earthquake; *but* the LORD *was* not
in the earthquake:
12 And after the earthquake a fire; *but* the
LORD *was* not in the fire: and after the fire
a still small voice.
13 And it was *so*, when Elijah heard *it*,
that he wrapped his face in his mantle, and
went out, and stood in the entering in of
the cave. And, behold, *there came* a voice
unto him, and said, What doest thou here,
Elijah?
14 And he said, I have been very jealous
for the LORD God of hosts: because the
children of Israel have forsaken thy covenant, thrown down thine altars, and slain
thy prophets with the sword; and I, *even* I
only, am left; and they seek my life, to take
it away.
15 And the LORD said unto him, Go, return on thy way to the wilderness of Damascus: and when thou comest, anoint
Hazael *to be* king over Syria:
16 And Jehu the son of Nimshi shalt thou
anoint *to be* king over Israel: and Elisha
the son of Shaphat of Abel-meholah shalt
thou anoint *to be* prophet in thy room.
17 And it shall come to pass, *that* him that
escapeth the sword of Hazael shall Jehu
slay: and him that escapeth from the sword
of Jehu shall Elisha slay.
18 Yet I have left *me* seven thousand in
Israel, all the knees which have not bowed
unto Baal, and every mouth which hath
not kissed him.
19 So he departed thence, and found Elisha the son of Shaphat, who *was* plowing
with twelve yoke *of oxen* before him, and
he with the twelfth: and Elijah passed by
him, and cast his mantle upon him.
20 And he left the
oxen, and ran after
Elijah, and said, Let
me, I pray thee, kiss
my father and my
mother, and *then* I
will follow thee. And he said unto him, Go
back again: for what have I done to thee?

19:20
Serving Quickly
◄ Mark 1:18 ►

21 And he returned back from him, and
took a yoke of oxen, and slew them, and
boiled their flesh with the instruments of
the oxen, and gave unto the people, and
they did eat. Then he arose, and went after
Elijah, and ministered unto him.

20

1 And Ben-hadad the king of Syria gathered all his host together: and *there were*
thirty and two kings with him, and horses,
and chariots: and he went up and besieged
Samaria, and warred against it.
2 And he sent messengers to Ahab king
of Israel into the city, and said unto him,
Thus saith Ben-hadad,
3 Thy silver and thy gold *is* mine; thy
wives also and thy children, *even* the good-
liest, *are* mine.
4 And the king of Israel answered and
said, My lord, O king, according to thy
saying, I *am* thine, and all that I have.
5 And the messengers came again, and
said, Thus speaketh Ben-hadad, saying,
Although I have sent unto thee, saying,
Thou shalt deliver me thy silver, and thy
gold, and thy wives, and thy children;
6 Yet I will send my servants unto thee
to morrow about this time, and they shall
search thine house, and the houses of thy
servants; and it shall be, *that* whatsoever
is pleasant in thine eyes, they shall put *it*
in their hand, and take *it* away.
7 Then the king of Israel called all the
elders of the land, and said, Mark, I pray
you, and see how this *man* seeketh mischief: for he sent unto me for my wives,
and for my children, and for my silver, and
for my gold; and I denied him not.
8 And all the elders and all the people
said unto him, Hearken not *unto him*, nor
consent.
9 Wherefore he said unto the messengers
of Ben-hadad, Tell my lord the king, All
that thou didst send for to thy servant at
the first I will do: but this thing I may not
do. And the messengers departed, and
brought him word again.
10 And Ben-hadad sent unto him, and
said, The gods do so unto me, and more
also, if the dust of Samaria shall suffice for
handfuls for all the people that follow me.
11 And the king of Israel answered and
said, Tell *him*, Let not him that girdeth on
his harness boast himself as he that putteth
it off.
12 And it came to pass, when *Ben-hadad*

heard this message, as he *was* drinking, he
and the kings in the pavilions,that he said
unto his servants, Set *yourselves in array*.
And they set *themselves in array* against the
city.

13 And, behold, there came a prophet
unto Ahab king of Israel, saying, Thus saith
the LORD, Hast thou seen all this great
multitude? behold, I will deliver it into
thine hand this day; and thou shalt know
that I *am* the LORD.

14 And Ahab said, By whom? And he
said, Thus saith the LORD, *Even* by the
young men of the princes of the provinces.
Then he said, Who shall order the battle?
And he answered, Thou.

15 Then he numbered the young men of
the princes of the provinces, and they were
two hundred and thirty two: and after
them he numbered all the people, *even* all
the children of Israel, *being* seven thousand.

16 And they went out at noon. But Ben-
hadad *was* drinking himself drunk in the
pavilions, he and the kings, the thirty and
two kings that helped him.

17 And the young men of the princes of
the provinces went out first; and Ben-
hadad sent out, and they told him, saying, There are men come out of Samaria.

18 And he said, Whether they be come
out for peace, take them alive; or whether
they be come out for war, take them alive.

19 So these young men of the princes of
the provinces came out of the city, and the
army which followed them.

20 And they slew every one his man: and
the Syrians fled; and Israel pursued them:
and Ben-hadad the king of Syria escaped
on an horse with the horsemen.

21 And the king of Israel went out, and
smote the horses and chariots, and slew
the Syrians with a great slaughter.

22 And the prophet came to the king of
Israel, and said unto him, Go, strengthen
thyself, and mark, and see what thou doest:
for at the return of the year the king of Syria
will come up against thee.

23 And the ser-
vants of the king of
Syria said unto
him, Their gods *are*
gods of the hills;
therefore they were
stronger than we; but let us fight against
them in the plain, and surely we shall be
stronger than they.

20:23 Superstition
◄ 1 Samuel 4:3
Jeremiah 10:2 ►

24 And do this thing, Take the kings away,
every man out of his place, and put captains in their rooms:

25 And number thee an army, like the
army that thou hast lost, horse for horse,
and chariot for chariot: and we will fight
against them in the plain, *and* surely we
shall be stronger than they. And he hearkened unto their voice, and did so.

26 And it came to pass at the return of
the year, that Ben-hadad numbered the
Syrians, and went up to Aphek, to fight
against Israel.

27 And the children of Israel were numbered, and were all present, and went
against them: and the children of Israel
pitched before them like two little flocks
of kids; but the Syrians filled the country.

28 And there came a man of God, and
spake unto the king of Israel, and said,
Thus saith the LORD, Because the Syrians
have said, The LORD *is* God of the hills,
but he *is* not God of the valleys, therefore
will I deliver all this great multitude into
thine hand, and ye shall know that I *am*
the LORD.

29 And they pitched one over against the
other seven days. And *so* it was, that in the
seventh day the battle was joined: and the
children of Israel slew of the Syrians an
hundred thousand footmen in one day.

30 But the rest fled to Aphek, into the city;
and *there* a wall fell upon twenty and seven
thousand of the men *that were* left. And
Ben-hadad fled, and came into the city,
into an inner chamber.

31 And his servants said unto him, Behold now, we have heard that the kings of
the house of Israel *are* merciful kings: let
us, I pray thee, put sackcloth on our loins,
and ropes upon our heads, and go out to
the king of Israel: peradventure he will save
thy life.

32 So they girded sackcloth on their
loins, and *put* ropes on their heads, and
came to the king of Israel, and said, Thy
servant Ben-hadad saith, I pray thee, let me
live. And he said, *Is* he yet alive? he *is* my
brother.

33 Now the men did diligently observe
whether *any thing would come* from him,
and did hastily catch *it*: and they said, Thy
brother Ben-hadad. Then he said, Go ye,

bring him. Then Ben-hadad came forth to
him; and he caused him to come up into
the chariot.
34And *Ben-hadad* said unto him, The cities, which my father took from thy father,
I will restore; and thou shalt make streets
for thee in Damascus, as my father made
in Samaria. Then *said Ahab,* I will send thee
away with this covenant. So he made a
covenant with him, and sent him away.
35And a certain man of the sons of the
prophets said unto his neighbour in the
word of the LORD, Smite me, I pray thee.
And the man refused to smite him.
36Then said he unto him, Because thou
hast not obeyed the voice of the LORD,
behold, as soon as thou art departed from
me, a lion shall slay thee. And as soon as
he was departed from him, a lion found
him, and slew him.
37Then he found another man, and said,
Smite me, I pray thee. And the man smote
him, so that in smiting he wounded *him.*
38So the prophet departed, and waited
for the king by the way, and disguised himself with ashes upon his face.
39And as the king passed by, he cried
unto the king: and he said, Thy servant
went out into the midst of the battle; and,
behold, a man turned aside, and brought
a man unto me, and said, Keep this man:
if by any means he be missing, then shall
thy life be for his life, or else thou shalt
pay a talent of silver.
40And as thy servant was busy here and
there, he was gone. And the king of Israel
said unto him, So *shall* thy judgment *be;*
thyself hast decided *it.*
41And he hasted, and took the ashes
away from his face; and the king of Israel discerned him that he *was* of the
prophets.
42And he said unto him, Thus saith the
LORD, Because thou hast let go out of *thy*
hand a man whom I appointed to utter
destruction, therefore thy life shall go for
his life, and thy people for his people.
43And the king of Israel went to his
house heavy and displeased, and came to
Samaria.

21

1And it came to pass after these things,
that Naboth the Jezreelite had a vineyard,
which *was* in Jezreel, hard by the palace of
Ahab king of Samaria.
2And Ahab spake unto Naboth, saying,
Give me thy vineyard, that I may have it
for a garden of herbs, because it *is* near
unto my house: and I will give thee for it a
better vineyard than it; *or,* if it seem good
to thee, I will give thee the worth of it in
money.
3And Naboth said to Ahab, The LORD
forbid it me, that I should give the inheritance of my fathers unto thee.
4And Ahab came into his house heavy
and displeased because of the word which
Naboth the Jezreelite had spoken to him:
for he had said, I will not give thee the
inheritance of my fathers. And he laid him
down upon his bed, and turned away his
face, and would eat no bread.
5But Jezebel his wife came to him, and
said unto him, Why is thy spirit so sad,
that thou eatest no bread?
6And he said unto her, Because I spake
unto Naboth the Jezreelite, and said unto
him, Give me thy vineyard for money; or
else, if it please thee, I will give thee *another* vineyard for it: and he answered, I
will not give thee my vineyard.
7And Jezebel his wife said unto him,
Dost thou now govern the kingdom of Israel? arise, *and* eat bread, and let thine
heart be merry: I will give thee the vineyard of Naboth the Jezreelite.
8So she wrote letters in Ahab's name,
and sealed *them* with his seal, and sent the
letters unto the elders and to the nobles
that *were* in his city, dwelling with Naboth.
9And she wrote in the letters, saying,
Proclaim a fast, and set Naboth on high
among the people:
10And set two men, sons of Belial, before him, to bear witness against him, saying, Thou didst blaspheme God and the
king. And *then* carry him out, and stone
him, that he may die.
11And the men of his city, *even* the elders and the nobles who were the inhabitants in his city, did as Jezebel had sent
unto them, *and* as it *was* written in the
letters which she had sent unto them.
12They proclaimed a fast, and set Naboth on high among the people.
13And there came in two men, children
of Belial, and sat before him: and the men
of Belial witnessed against him, *even*
against Naboth, in the presence of the people, saying, Naboth did blaspheme God
and the king. Then they carried him forth

out of the city, and stoned him with stones, that he died.

14 Then they sent to Jezebel, saying, Naboth is stoned, and is dead.

15 And it came to pass, when Jezebel heard that Naboth was stoned, and was dead, that Jezebel said to Ahab, Arise, take possession of the vineyard of Naboth the Jezreelite, which he refused to give thee for money: for Naboth is not alive, but dead.

16 And it came to pass, when Ahab heard that Naboth was dead, that Ahab rose up to go down to the vineyard of Naboth the Jezreelite, to take possession of it.

17 And the word of the LORD came to Elijah the Tishbite, saying,

18 Arise, go down to meet Ahab king of Israel, which *is* in Samaria: behold, *he is* in the vineyard of Naboth, whither he is gone down to possess it.

19 And thou shalt speak unto him, saying, Thus saith the LORD, Hast thou killed, and also taken possession? And thou shalt speak unto him, saying, Thus saith the LORD, In the place where dogs licked the blood of Naboth shall dogs lick thy blood, even thine.

20 And Ahab said to Elijah, Hast thou found me, O mine enemy? And he answered, I have found *thee*: because thou hast sold thyself to work evil in the sight of the LORD.

21 Behold, I will bring evil upon thee, and will take away thy posterity, and will cut off from Ahab him that pisseth against the wall, and him that is shut up and left in Israel,

22 And will make thine house like the house of Jeroboam the son of Nebat, and like the house of Baasha the son of Ahijah, for the provocation wherewith thou hast provoked *me* to anger, and made Israel to sin.

23 And of Jezebel also spake the LORD, saying, The dogs shall eat Jezebel by the wall of Jezreel.

24 Him that dieth of Ahab in the city the dogs shall eat; and him that dieth in the field shall the fowls of the air eat.

25 But there was none like unto Ahab, which did sell himself to work wickedness in the sight of the LORD, whom Jezebel his wife stirred up.

26 And he did very abominably in following idols, according to all *things* as did the Amorites, whom the LORD cast out before the children of Israel.

27 And it came to pass, when Ahab heard those words, that he rent his clothes, and put sackcloth upon his flesh, and fasted, and lay in sackcloth, and went softly.

28 And the word of the LORD came to Elijah the Tishbite, saying,

29 Seest thou how Ahab humbleth himself before me? because he humbleth himself before me, I will not bring the evil in his days: *but* in his son's days will I bring the evil upon his house.

22

1 And they continued three years without war between Syria and Israel.

2 And it came to pass in the third year, that Jehoshaphat the king of Judah came down to the king of Israel.

3 And the king of Israel said unto his servants, Know ye that Ramoth in Gilead *is* ours, and we *be* still, *and* take it not out of the hand of the king of Syria?

4 And he said unto Jehoshaphat, Wilt thou go with me to battle to Ramoth-gilead? And Jehoshaphat said to the king of Israel, I *am* as thou *art*, my people as thy people, my horses as thy horses.

5 And Jehoshaphat said unto the king of Israel, Enquire, I pray thee, at the word of the LORD to day.

6 Then the king of Israel gathered the prophets together, about four hundred men, and said unto them, Shall I go against Ramoth-gilead to battle, or shall I forbear? And they said, Go up; for the Lord shall deliver *it* into the hand of the king.

7 And Jehoshaphat said, *Is there* not here a prophet of the LORD besides, that we might enquire of him?

8 And the king of Israel said unto Jehoshaphat, *There is* yet one man, Micaiah the son of Imlah, by whom we may enquire of the LORD: but I hate him; for he doth not prophesy good concerning me, but evil. And Jehoshaphat said, Let not the king say so.

9 Then the king of Israel called an officer, and said, Hasten *hither* Micaiah the son of Imlah.

10 And the king of Israel and Jehoshaphat the king of Judah sat each on his throne, having put on their robes, in a void place in the entrance of the gate of Samaria; and all the prophets prophesied before them.

11 And Zedekiah the son of Chenaanah

made him horns of iron: and he said, Thus
saith the LORD, With these shalt thou push
the Syrians, until thou have consumed
them.
12 And all the prophets prophesied so,
saying, Go up to Ramoth-gilead, and prosper: for the LORD shall deliver *it* into the
king's hand.
13 And the messenger that was gone to
call Micaiah spake unto him, saying, Behold now, the words of the prophets *de-*
clare good unto the king with one mouth:
let thy word, I pray thee, be like the word
of one of them, and speak *that which is*
good.
14 And Micaiah said, *As* the LORD liveth,
what the LORD saith unto me, that will I
speak.
15 So he came to the king. And the king
said unto him, Micaiah, shall we go against
Ramoth-gilead to battle, or shall we forbear? And he answered him, Go, and prosper: for the LORD shall deliver *it* into the
hand of the king.
16 And the king said unto him, How
many times shall I adjure thee that thou
tell me nothing but *that which is* true in
the name of the LORD?
17 And he said, I saw all Israel scattered
upon the hills, as sheep that have not a
shepherd: and the LORD said, These have
no master: let them return every man to
his house in peace.
18 And the king of Israel said unto Jehoshaphat, Did I not tell thee that he
would prophesy no good concerning me,
but evil?
19 And he said, Hear thou therefore the
word of the LORD: I saw the LORD sitting
on his throne, and all the host of heaven
standing by him on his right hand and on
his left.
20 And the LORD said, Who shall persuade Ahab, that he may go up and fall at
Ramoth-gilead? And one said on this manner, and another said on that manner.
21 And there came forth a spirit, and
stood before the LORD, and said, I will
persuade him.
22 And the LORD said unto him, Wherewith? And he said, I will go forth, and I
will be a lying spirit in the mouth of all
his prophets. And he said, Thou shalt persuade *him,* and prevail also: go forth, and
do so.
23 Now therefore, behold, the LORD hath
put a lying spirit in the mouth of all these
thy prophets, and the LORD hath spoken
evil concerning thee.
24 But Zedekiah the son of Chenaanah
went near, and smote Micaiah on the
cheek, and said, Which way went the Spirit of the LORD from me to speak unto thee?
25 And Micaiah said, Behold, thou shalt
see in that day, when thou shalt go into
an inner chamber to hide thyself.
26 And the king of Israel said, Take Micaiah, and carry him back unto Amon the
governor of the city, and to Joash the king's
son;
27 And say, Thus
saith the king, Put
this *fellow* in the
prison, and feed
him with bread of
affliction and with
water of affliction, until I come in peace.

22:27
Examples of Revenge
◄ 1 Kings 19:2
Esther 3:6 ►

28 And Micaiah said, If thou return at all
in peace, the LORD hath not spoken by me.
And he said, Hearken, O people, every one
of you.
29 So the king of Israel and Jehoshaphat
the king of Judah went up to Ramoth-
gilead.
30 And the king of Israel said unto Jehoshaphat, I will disguise myself, and enter into the battle; but put thou on thy
robes. And the king of Israel disguised
himself, and went into the battle.
31 But the king of Syria commanded his
thirty and two captains that had rule over
his chariots, saying, Fight neither with
small nor great, save only with the king of
Israel.
32 And it came to pass, when the captains
of the chariots saw Jehoshaphat, that they
said, Surely it *is* the king of Israel. And they
turned aside to fight against him: and Jehoshaphat cried out.
33 And it came to pass, when the captains
of the chariots perceived that it *was* not
the king of Israel, that they turned back
from pursuing him.
34 And a *certain* man drew a bow at a venture, and smote the king of Israel between
the joints of the harness: wherefore he said
unto the driver of his chariot, Turn thine
hand, and carry me out of the host; for I
am wounded.
35 And the battle increased that day: and

the king was stayed up in his chariot
against the Syrians, and died at even: and
the blood ran out of the wound into the
midst of the chariot.
36 And there went a proclamation
throughout the host about the going down
of the sun, saying, Every man to his city,
and every man to his own country.
37 So the king died, and was brought to
Samaria; and they buried the king in Samaria.
38 And *one* washed the chariot in the
pool of Samaria; and the dogs licked up
his blood; and they washed his armour;
according unto the word of the LORD
which he spake.
39 Now the rest of the acts of Ahab, and
all that he did, and the ivory house which
he made, and all the cities that he built,
are they not written in the book of the
chronicles of the kings of Israel?
40 So Ahab slept with his fathers; and
Ahaziah his son reigned in his stead.
41 And Jehoshaphat the son of Asa began to reign over Judah in the fourth year
of Ahab king of Israel.
42 Jehoshaphat *was* thirty and five years
old when he began to reign; and he reigned
twenty and five years in Jerusalem. And his
mother's name *was* Azubah the daughter
of Shilhi.
43 And he walked
in all the ways of
Asa his father; he
turned not aside
from it, doing *that*
which was right in
the eyes of the LORD: nevertheless the high
places were not taken away; *for* the people
offered and burnt incense yet in the high
places.
44 And Jehoshaphat made peace with the
king of Israel.
45 Now the rest of the acts of Jehoshaphat, and his might that he shewed, and
how he warred, *are* they not written in the
book of the chronicles of the kings of Judah?
46 And the remnant of the sodomites,
which remained in the days of his father
Asa, he took out of the land.
47 *There was* then no king in Edom: a deputy *was* king.
48 Jehoshaphat made ships of Tharshish
to go to Ophir for gold: but they went
not; for the ships were broken at Ezion-
geber.
49 Then said Ahaziah the son of Ahab
unto Jehoshaphat, Let my servants go with
thy servants in the ships. But Jehoshaphat
would not.
50 And Jehoshaphat slept with his fathers, and was buried with his fathers in
the city of David his father: and Jehoram
his son reigned in his stead.
51 Ahaziah the son of Ahab began to
reign over Israel in Samaria the seventeenth
year of Jehoshaphat king of Judah, and
reigned two years over Israel.
52 And he did evil in the sight of the
LORD, and walked in the way of his father,
and in the way of his mother, and in the
way of Jeroboam the son of Nebat, who
made Israel to sin:
53 For he served Baal, and worshipped
him, and provoked to anger the LORD God
of Israel, according to all that his father
had done.

22:43 Only Human
◄ 1 Kings 3:3
2 Chronicles 16:12 ►

2 Kings

AUTHOR
Unknown; possibly Jeremiah the prophet or a group of prophets

MAIN POINT
Actions and decisions have consequences, as vividly shown in the lives of the kings of Israel and Judah.

DATE WRITTEN
Unknown

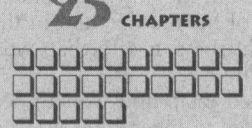

25 CHAPTERS

MAIN PEOPLE
Elijah, Elisha, Shunammite woman, Naaman, Jezebel, Jehu, Joash, Hezekiah, Sennacherib, Isaiah, Manasseh, Josiah, Jehoiakim, Zedekiah, Nebuchadnezzar

SPECIAL FEATURES
- *Was once a part of 1 Kings*
- *Shows why only two of the many kings of Judah and Israel were called good*
- *Shows how the Spirit of God and the tradition of miracles passed from the prophet Elijah to his friend Elisha*
- *Gets our attention with Jezebel's death*
- *Recounts how the Israelites were conquered and taken captive to Assyria—all because they rejected God*
- *Seventh book of History*

HOW THE BOOK GOT ITS NAME
Kings refers to the main characters of the book: the continuing lines of the kings of Israel and Judah.

1 1Then Moab rebelled against Israel after
the death of Ahab.
2And Ahaziah fell down through a
lattice in his upper chamber that *was* in
Samaria, and was sick: and he sent messengers, and said unto them, Go, enquire
of Baal-zebub the god of Ekron whether I
shall recover of this disease.
3But the angel of the LORD said to Elijah the Tishbite, Arise, go up to meet the
messengers of the king of Samaria, and say
unto them, *Is it* not because *there is* not a
God in Israel, *that* ye go to enquire of Baal-
zebub the god of Ekron?
4Now therefore thus saith the LORD,
Thou shalt not come down from that bed
on which thou art gone up, but shalt surely die. And Elijah departed.
5And when the messengers turned back
unto him, he said unto them, Why are ye
now turned back?
6And they said unto him, There came a
man up to meet us, and said unto us, Go,
turn again unto the king that sent you, and
say unto him, Thus saith the LORD, *Is it*
not because *there is* not a God in Israel,
that thou sendest to enquire of Baal-zebub
the god of Ekron? therefore thou shalt not

come down from that bed on which thou
art gone up, but shalt surely die.
7 And he said unto them, What manner
of man *was he* which came up to meet you,
and told you these words?
8 And they answered him, *He was* an
hairy man, and girt with a girdle of leath-
er about his loins. And he said, It *is* Elijah
the Tishbite.
9 Then the king sent unto him a captain
of fifty with his fifty. And he went up to
him: and, behold, he sat on the top of an
hill. And he spake unto him, Thou man
of God, the king hath said, Come down.
10 And Elijah answered and said to the
captain of fifty, If I *be* a man of God, then
let fire come down from heaven, and consume thee and thy fifty. And there came
down fire from heaven, and consumed
him and his fifty.
11 Again also he sent unto him another
captain of fifty with his fifty. And he answered and said unto him, O man of God,
thus hath the king said, Come down
quickly.
12 And Elijah answered and said unto
them, If I *be* a man of God, let fire come
down from heaven, and consume thee and
thy fifty. And the fire of God came down
from heaven, and consumed him and his
fifty.
13 And he sent again a captain of the
third fifty with his fifty. And the third captain of fifty went up, and came and fell on
his knees before Elijah, and besought him,
and said unto him, O man of God, I pray
thee, let my life, and the life of these fifty
thy servants, be precious in thy sight.
14 Behold, there came fire down from
heaven, and burnt up the two captains of
the former fifties with their fifties: therefore let my life now be precious in thy
sight.
15 And the angel of the LORD said unto
Elijah, Go down with him: be not afraid
of him. And he arose, and went down with
him unto the king.
16 And he said unto him, Thus saith the
LORD, Forasmuch as thou hast sent messengers to enquire of Baal-zebub the god
of Ekron, *is it* not because *there is* no God
in Israel to enquire of his word? therefore
thou shalt not come down off that bed
on which thou art gone up, but shalt surely die.
17 So he died according to the word of
the LORD which Elijah had spoken. And
Jehoram reigned in his stead in the second year of Jehoram the son of Jehoshaphat king of Judah; because he had no son.
18 Now the rest of the acts of Ahaziah
which he did, *are* they not written in the
book of the chronicles of the kings of Israel?

2

1 And it came to pass, when the LORD
would take up Elijah into heaven by a
whirlwind, that Elijah went with Elisha
from Gilgal.
2 And Elijah said
unto Elisha, Tarry
here, I pray thee; for
the LORD hath sent
me to Bethel. And
Elisha said *unto*
him, *As* the LORD liveth, and as thy soul
liveth, I will not leave thee. So they went
down to Bethel.

2:2 Being a Friend
◄ 1 Samuel 20:17
Matthew 27:55-56 ►

3 And the sons of the prophets that *were*
at Bethel came forth to Elisha, and said
unto him, Knowest thou that the LORD will
take away thy master from thy head to day?
And he said, Yea, I know *it;* hold ye your
peace.
4 And Elijah said unto him, Elisha, tarry
here, I pray thee; for the LORD hath sent
me to Jericho. And he said, *As* the LORD
liveth, and *as* thy soul liveth, I will not
leave thee. So they came to Jericho.
5 And the sons of the prophets that *were*
at Jericho came to Elisha, and said unto
him, Knowest thou that the LORD will take
away thy master from thy head to day? And
he answered, Yea, I know *it;* hold ye your
peace.
6 And Elijah said unto him, Tarry, I pray
thee, here; for the LORD hath sent me to
Jordan. And he said, *As* the LORD liveth,
and *as* thy soul liveth, I will not leave thee.
And they two went on.
7 And fifty men of the sons of the prophets went, and stood to view afar off: and
they two stood by Jordan.
8 And Elijah took his mantle, and
wrapped *it* together, and smote the waters,
and they were divided hither and thither,
so that they two went over on dry ground.
9 And it came to pass, when they were
gone over, that Elijah said unto Elisha, Ask
what I shall do for thee, before I be taken
away from thee. And Elisha said, I pray

thee, let a double portion of thy spirit be upon me.

10 And he said, Thou hast asked a hard thing: *nevertheless,* if thou see me *when I am* taken from thee, it shall be so unto thee; but if not, it shall not be so.

11 And it came to pass, as they still went on, and talked, that, behold, *there appeared* a chariot of fire, and horses of fire, and parted them both asunder; and Elijah went up by a whirlwind into heaven.

12 And Elisha saw *it,* and he cried, My father, my father, the chariot of Israel, and the horsemen thereof. And he saw him no more: and he took hold of his own clothes, and rent them in two pieces.

13 He took up also the mantle of Elijah that fell from him, and went back, and stood by the bank of Jordan;

14 And he took the mantle of Elijah that fell from him, and smote the waters, and said, Where *is* the LORD God of Elijah? and when he also had smitten the waters, they parted hither and thither: and Elisha went over.

15 And when the sons of the prophets which *were* to view at Jericho saw him, they said, The spirit of Elijah doth rest on Elisha. And they came to meet him, and bowed themselves to the ground before him.

16 And they said unto him, Behold now, there be with thy servants fifty strong men; let them go, we pray thee, and seek thy master: lest peradventure the Spirit of the LORD hath taken him up, and cast him upon some mountain, or into some valley. And he said, Ye shall not send.

17 And when they urged him till he was ashamed, he said, Send. They sent therefore fifty men; and they sought three days, but found him not.

18 And when they came again to him, (for he tarried at Jericho,) he said unto them, Did I not say unto you, Go not?

19 And the men of the city said unto Elisha, Behold, I pray thee, the situation of this city *is* pleasant, as my lord seeth: but the water *is* naught, and the ground barren.

20 And he said, Bring me a new cruse, and put salt therein. And they bring *it* to him.

21 And he went forth unto the spring of the waters, and cast the salt in there, and said, Thus saith the LORD, I have healed these waters; there shall not be from thence any more death or barren *land.*

22 So the waters were healed unto this day, according to the saying of Elisha which he spake.

23 And he went up from thence unto Bethel: and as he was going up by the way, there came forth little children out of the city, and mocked him, and said unto him, Go up, thou bald head; go up, thou bald head.

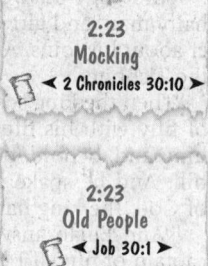

2:23
Mocking
◄ 2 Chronicles 30:10 ►

2:23
Old People
◄ Job 30:1 ►

24 And he turned back, and looked on them, and cursed them in the name of the LORD. And there came forth two she bears out of the wood, and tare forty and two children of them.

25 And he went from thence to mount Carmel, and from thence he returned to Samaria.

3

1 Now Jehoram the son of Ahab began to reign over Israel in Samaria the eighteenth year of Jehoshaphat king of Judah, and reigned twelve years.

2 And he wrought evil in the sight of the LORD; but not like his father, and like his mother: for he put away the image of Baal that his father had made.

3 Nevertheless he cleaved unto the sins of Jeroboam the son of Nebat, which made Israel to sin; he departed not therefrom.

4 And Mesha king of Moab was a sheepmaster, and rendered unto the king of Israel an hundred thousand lambs, and an hundred thousand rams, with the wool.

5 But it came to pass, when Ahab was dead, that the king of Moab rebelled against the king of Israel.

6 And king Jehoram went out of Samaria the same time, and numbered all Israel.

7 And he went and sent to Jehoshaphat the king of Judah, saying, The king of Moab hath rebelled against me: wilt thou go with me against Moab to battle? And he said, I will go up: I *am* as thou *art,* my people as thy people, *and* my horses as thy horses.

8 And he said, Which way shall we go up? And he answered, The way through the wilderness of Edom.

9 So the king of Israel went, and the king of Judah, and the king of Edom: and they fetched a compass of seven days' journey: and there was no water for the host, and for the cattle that followed them.

10 And the king of Israel said, Alas! that the LORD hath called these three kings together, to deliver them into the hand of Moab!

11 But Jehoshaphat said, *Is there* not here a prophet of the LORD, that we may enquire of the LORD by him? And one of the king of Israel's servants answered and said, Here *is* Elisha the son of Shaphat, which poured water on the hands of Elijah.

12 And Jehoshaphat said, The word of the LORD is with him. So the king of Israel and Jehoshaphat and the king of Edom went down to him.

13 And Elisha said unto the king of Israel, What have I to do with thee? get thee to the prophets of thy father, and to the prophets of thy mother. And the king of Israel said unto him, Nay: for the LORD hath called these three kings together, to deliver them into the hand of Moab.

14 And Elisha said, *As* the LORD of hosts liveth, before whom I stand, surely, were it not that I regard the presence of Jehoshaphat the king of Judah, I would not look toward thee, nor see thee.

15 But now bring me a minstrel. And it came to pass, when the minstrel played, that the hand of the LORD came upon him.

16 And he said, Thus saith the LORD, Make this valley full of ditches.

17 For thus saith the LORD, Ye shall not see wind, neither shall ye see rain; yet that valley shall be filled with water, that ye may drink, both ye, and your cattle, and your beasts.

18 And this is *but* a light thing in the sight of the LORD: he will deliver the Moabites also into your hand.

19 And ye shall smite every fenced city, and every choice city, and shall fell every good tree, and stop all wells of water, and mar every good piece of land with stones.

20 And it came to pass in the morning, when the meat offering was offered, that, behold, there came water by the way of Edom, and the country was filled with water.

21 And when all the Moabites heard that the kings were come up to fight against them, they gathered all that were able to put on armour, and upward, and stood in the border.

22 And they rose up early in the morning, and the sun shone upon the water, and the Moabites saw the water on the other side *as* red as blood:

23 And they said, This *is* blood: the kings are surely slain, and they have smitten one another: now therefore, Moab, to the spoil.

24 And when they came to the camp of Israel, the Israelites rose up and smote the Moabites, so that they fled before them: but they went forward smiting the Moabites, even in *their* country.

25 And they beat down the cities, and on every good piece of land cast every man his stone, and filled it; and they stopped all the wells of water, and felled all the good trees: only in Kir-haraseth left they the stones thereof; howbeit the slingers went about *it,* and smote it.

26 And when the king of Moab saw that the battle was too sore for him, he took with him seven hundred men that drew swords, to break through *even* unto the king of Edom: but they could not.

27 Then he took his eldest son that should have reigned in his stead, and offered him *for* a burnt offering upon the wall. And there was great indignation against Israel: and they departed from him, and returned to *their own* land.

4

1 Now there cried a certain woman of the wives of the sons of the prophets unto Elisha, saying, Thy servant my husband is dead; and thou knowest that thy servant did fear the LORD: and the creditor is come to take unto him my two sons to be bondmen.

2 And Elisha said unto her, What shall I do for thee? tell me, what hast thou in the house? And she said, Thine handmaid hath not any thing in the house, save a pot of oil.

3 Then he said, Go, borrow thee vessels abroad of all thy neighbours, *even* empty vessels; borrow not a few.

4 And when thou art come in, thou shalt shut the door upon thee and upon thy sons, and shalt pour out into all those vessels, and thou shalt set aside that which is full.

5 So she went from him, and shut the door upon her and upon her sons, who

brought *the vessels* to her; and she poured out.

6 And it came to pass, when the vessels were full, that she said unto her son, Bring me yet a vessel. And he said unto her, *There is* not a vessel more. And the oil stayed.

7 Then she came and told the man of God. And he said, Go, sell the oil, and pay thy debt, and live thou and thy children of the rest.

8 And it fell on a day, that Elisha passed to Shunem, where *was* a great woman; and she constrained him to eat bread. And so it was, *that* as oft as he passed by, he turned in thither to eat bread.

9 And she said unto her husband, Behold now, I perceive that this *is* an holy man of God, which passeth by us continually.

10 Let us make a little chamber, I pray thee, on the wall; and let us set for him there a bed, and a table, and a stool, and a candlestick: and it shall be, when he cometh to us, that he shall turn in thither.

11 And it fell on a day, that he came thither, and he turned into the chamber, and lay there.

12 And he said to Gehazi his servant, Call this Shunammite. And when he had called her, she stood before him.

13 And he said unto him, Say now unto her, Behold, thou hast been careful for us with all this care; what *is* to be done for thee? wouldest thou be spoken for to the king, or to the captain of the host? And she answered, I dwell among mine own people.

4:13 "Thank You"
◄ 1 Kings 2:7
Acts 28:10 ►

14 And he said, What then *is* to be done for her? And Gehazi answered, Verily she hath no child, and her husband is old.

15 And he said, Call her. And when he had called her, she stood in the door.

16 And he said, About this season, according to the time of life, thou shalt embrace a son. And she said, Nay, my lord, *thou* man of God, do not lie unto thine handmaid.

17 And the woman conceived, and bare a son at that season that Elisha had said unto her, according to the time of life.

18 And when the child was grown, it fell on a day, that he went out to his father to the reapers.

19 And he said unto his father, My head, my head. And he said to a lad, Carry him to his mother.

20 And when he had taken him, and brought him to his mother, he sat on her knees till noon, and *then* died.

21 And she went up, and laid him on the bed of the man of God, and shut *the door* upon him, and went out.

22 And she called unto her husband, and said, Send me, I pray thee, one of the young men, and one of the asses, that I may run to the man of God, and come again.

23 And he said, Wherefore wilt thou go to him to day? *it is* neither new moon, nor sabbath. And she said, *It shall be* well.

24 Then she saddled an ass, and said to her servant, Drive, and go forward; slack not *thy* riding for me, except I bid thee.

25 So she went and came unto the man of God to mount Carmel. And it came to pass, when the man of God saw her afar off, that he said to Gehazi his servant, Behold, *yonder is* that Shunammite:

26 Run now, I pray thee, to meet her, and say unto her, *Is it* well with thee? *is it* well with thy husband? *is it* well with the child? And she answered, *It is* well.

27 And when she came to the man of God to the hill, she caught him by the feet: but Gehazi came near to thrust her away. And the man of God said, Let her alone; for her soul *is* vexed within her: and the LORD hath hid *it* from me, and hath not told me.

28 Then she said, Did I desire a son of my lord? did I not say, Do not deceive me?

29 Then he said to Gehazi, Gird up thy loins, and take my staff in thine hand, and go thy way: if thou meet any man, salute him not; and if any salute thee, answer him not again: and lay my staff upon the face of the child.

4:29 Hurrying
◄ 1 Samuel 21:8
2 Chronicles 24:5 ►

30 And the mother of the child said, *As* the LORD liveth, and *as* thy soul liveth, I will not leave thee. And he arose, and followed her.

31 And Gehazi passed on before them, and laid the staff upon the face of the child; but *there was* neither voice, nor hearing. Wherefore he went again to meet him, and told him, saying, The child is not awaked.

32 And when Elisha was come into the house, behold, the child was dead, *and* laid upon his bed.

33 He went in therefore, and shut the door upon them twain, and prayed unto the LORD.

34 And he went up, and lay upon the child, and put his mouth upon his mouth, and his eyes upon his eyes, and his hands upon his hands: and he stretched himself upon the child; and the flesh of the child waxed warm.

35 Then he returned, and walked in the house to and fro; and went up, and stretched himself upon him: and the child sneezed seven times, and the child opened his eyes.

36 And he called Gehazi, and said, Call this Shunammite. So he called her. And when she was come in unto him, he said, Take up thy son.

37 Then she went in, and fell at his feet, and bowed herself to the ground, and took up her son, and went out.

38 And Elisha came again to Gilgal: and *there was* a dearth in the land; and the sons of the prophets *were* sitting before him: and he said unto his servant, Set on the great pot, and seethe pottage for the sons of the prophets.

39 And one went out into the field to gather herbs, and found a wild vine, and gathered thereof wild gourds his lap full, and came and shred *them* into the pot of pottage: for they knew *them* not.

40 So they poured out for the men to eat. And it came to pass, as they were eating of the pottage, that they cried out, and said, O *thou* man of God, *there is* death in the pot. And they could not eat *thereof.*

41 But he said, Then bring meal. And he cast *it* into the pot; and he said, Pour out for the people, that they may eat. And there was no harm in the pot.

42 And there came a man from Baal-shalisha, and brought the man of God bread of the firstfruits, twenty loaves of barley, and full ears of corn in the husk thereof. And he said, Give unto the people, that they may eat.

43 And his servitor said, What, should I set this before an hundred men? He said again, Give the people, that they may eat: for thus saith the LORD, They shall eat, and shall leave *thereof.*

44 So he set *it* before them, and they did eat, and left *thereof,* according to the word of the LORD.

5

1 Now Naaman, captain of the host of the king of Syria, was a great man with his master, and honourable, because by him the LORD had given deliverance unto Syria: he was also a mighty man in valour, *but he was* a leper.

2 And the Syrians had gone out by companies, and had brought away captive out of the land of Israel a little maid; and she waited on Naaman's wife.

3 And she said unto her mistress, Would God my lord *were* with the prophet that *is* in Samaria! for he would recover him of his leprosy.

4 And *one* went in, and told his lord, saying, Thus and thus said the maid that *is* of the land of Israel.

5 And the king of Syria said, Go to, go, and I will send a letter unto the king of Israel. And he departed, and took with him ten talents of silver, and six thousand *pieces* of gold, and ten changes of raiment.

6 And he brought the letter to the king of Israel, saying, Now when this letter is come unto thee, behold, I have *therewith* sent Naaman my servant to thee, that thou mayest recover him of his leprosy.

7 And it came to pass, when the king of Israel had read the letter, that he rent his clothes, and said, *Am* I God, to kill and to make alive, that this man doth send unto me to recover a man of his leprosy? wherefore consider, I pray you, and see how he seeketh a quarrel against me.

8 And it was *so,* when Elisha the man of God had heard that the king of Israel had rent his clothes, that he sent to the king, saying, Wherefore hast thou rent thy clothes? let him come now to me, and he shall know that there is a prophet in Israel.

9 So Naaman came with his horses and with his chariot, and stood at the door of the house of Elisha.

10 And Elisha sent a messenger unto him, saying, Go and wash in the Jordan seven times, and thy flesh shall come again to thee, and thou shalt be clean.

11 But Naaman was wroth, and went away, and said, Behold, I thought, He

5:11-12 Impatience
◄ Numbers 20:10
Jonah 4:8-9 ►

will surely come out to me, and stand, and call on the name of the LORD his God, and strike his hand over the place, and recover the leper.

12*Are* not Abana and Pharpar, rivers of Damascus, better than all the waters of Israel? may I not wash in them, and be clean? So he turned and went away in a rage.

5:12 Mad
◄ 1 Samuel 18:8
2 Chronicles 16:10 ►

13And his servants came near, and spake unto him, and said, My father, *if* the prophet had bid thee *do some* great thing, wouldest thou not have done *it?* how much rather then, when he saith to thee, Wash, and be clean?

14Then went he down, and dipped himself seven times in Jordan, according to the saying of the man of God: and his flesh came again like unto the flesh of a little child, and he was clean.

15And he returned to the man of God, he and all his company, and came, and stood before him: and he said, Behold, now I know that *there is* no God in all earth, but in Israel: now therefore, I pray thee, take a blessing of thy servant.

16But he said, *As* the LORD liveth, before whom I stand, I will receive none. And he urged him to take *it;* but he refused.

17And Naaman said, Shall there not then, I pray thee, be given to thy servant two mules' burden of earth? for thy servant will henceforth offer neither burnt offering nor sacrifice unto other gods, but unto the LORD.

18In this thing the LORD pardon thy servant, *that* when my master goeth into the house of Rimmon to worship there, and he leaneth on my hand, and I bow myself in the house of Rimmon: when I bow down myself in the house of Rimmon, the LORD pardon thy servant in this thing.

19And he said unto him, Go in peace. So he departed from him a little way.

20But Gehazi, the servant of Elisha the man of God, said, Behold, my master hath spared Naaman this Syrian, in not receiving at his hands that which he brought: but, *as* the LORD liveth, I will run after him, and take somewhat of him.

21So Gehazi followed after Naaman. And when Naaman saw *him* running after him, he lighted down from the chariot to meet him, and said, *Is* all well?

22And he said, All *is* well. My master hath sent me, saying, Behold, even now there be come to me from mount Ephraim two young men of the sons of the prophets: give them, I pray thee, a talent of silver, and two changes of garments.

23And Naaman said, Be content, take two talents. And he urged him, and bound two talents of silver in two bags, with two changes of garments, and laid *them* upon two of his servants; and they bare *them* before him.

24And when he came to the tower, he took *them* from their hand, and bestowed *them* in the house: and he let the men go, and they departed.

25But he went in, and stood before his master. And Elisha said unto him, Whence *comest thou,* Gehazi? And he said, Thy servant went no whither.

26And he said unto him, Went not mine heart *with thee,* when the man turned again from his chariot to meet thee? *Is it* a time to receive money, and to receive garments, and oliveyards, and vineyards, and sheep, and oxen, and menservants, and maidservants?

27The leprosy therefore of Naaman shall cleave unto thee, and unto thy seed for ever. And he went out from his presence a leper *as white* as snow.

6

1And the sons of the prophets said unto Elisha, Behold now, the place where we dwell with thee is too strait for us.

6:1-3 Teamwork
◄ 1 Samuel 14:6-7
1 Chronicles 12:38 ►

2Let us go, we pray thee, unto Jordan, and take thence every man a beam, and let us make us a place there, where we may dwell. And he answered, Go ye.

3And one said, Be content, I pray thee, and go with thy servants. And he answered, I will go.

4So he went with them. And when they came to Jordan, they cut down wood.

5But as one was felling a beam, the axe head fell into the water: and he cried, and said, Alas, master! for it was borrowed.

6:5 Borrowing
◄ Exodus 22:14
Psalm 37:21 ►

6And the man of God said, Where fell
it? And he shewed him the place. And he
cut down a stick, and cast *it* in thither; and
the iron did swim.
7Therefore said he, Take *it* up to thee.
And he put out his hand, and took it.
8Then the king of Syria warred against
Israel, and took counsel with his servants,
saying, In such and such a place *shall be*
my camp.
9And the man of God sent unto the king
of Israel, saying, Beware that thou pass not
such a place; for thither the Syrians are
come down.
10And the king of Israel sent to the place
which the man of God told him and
warned him of, and saved himself there,
not once nor twice.
11Therefore the heart of the king of Syria was sore troubled for this thing; and he
called his servants, and said unto them,
Will ye not shew me which of us *is* for the
king of Israel?
12And one of his servants said, None,
my lord, O king: but Elisha, the prophet
that *is* in Israel, telleth the king of Israel
the words that thou speakest in thy
bedchamber.
13And he said, Go and spy where he *is*,
that I may send and fetch him. And it was
told him, saying, Behold, *he is* in Dothan.
14Therefore sent he thither horses, and
chariots, and a great host: and they came
by night, and compassed the city about.
15And when the servant of the man of
God was risen early, and gone forth, behold, an host compassed the city both with
horses and chariots. And his servant said
unto him, Alas, my master! how shall
we do?
16And he answered, Fear not: for they
that *be* with us *are* more than they that *be*
with them.
17And Elisha prayed, and said, LORD, I
pray thee, open his eyes, that he may see.
And the LORD opened the eyes of the young
man; and he saw: and, behold, the mountain *was* full of horses and chariots of fire
round about Elisha.
18And when they came down to him,
Elisha prayed unto the LORD, and said,
Smite this people, I pray thee, with blindness. And he smote them with blindness
according to the word of Elisha.
19And Elisha said unto them, This *is* not
the way, neither *is* this the city: follow me,
and I will bring you to the man whom ye
seek. But he led them to Samaria.
20And it came to pass, when they were
come into Samaria, that Elisha said, LORD,
open the eyes of these *men*, that they may
see. And the LORD opened their eyes, and
they saw; and, behold, *they were* in the
midst of Samaria.
21And the king of Israel said unto Elisha, when he saw them, My father, shall I
smite *them*? shall I smite *them*?
22And he an-
swered, Thou shalt
not smite *them*:
wouldest thou smite
those whom thou
hast taken captive
with thy sword and
with thy bow? set
bread and water
before them, that
they may eat and
drink, and go to
their master.

6:22 Examples of Mercy
◄ 1 Kings 1:52
Luke 9:55 ►

6:22 Nice
◄ 1 Samuel 26:11
Psalm 35:13 ►

23And he prepared great provision for
them: and when they had eaten and drunk,
he sent them away, and they went to their
master. So the bands of Syria came no
more into the land of Israel.
24And it came to pass after this, that Ben-
hadad king of Syria gathered all his host,
and went up, and besieged Samaria.
25And there was a great famine in Samaria: and, behold, they besieged it, until
an ass's head was *sold* for fourscore *pieces*
of silver, and the fourth part of a cab of
dove's dung for five *pieces* of silver.
26And as the king of Israel was passing
by upon the wall, there cried a woman
unto him, saying, Help, my lord, O king.
27And he said, If the LORD do not help
thee, whence shall I help thee? out of the
barnfloor, or out of the winepress?
28And the king said unto her, What
aileth thee? And she answered, This woman said unto me, Give thy son, that we may
eat him to day, and we will eat my son to
morrow.
29So we boiled my son, and did eat him:
and I said unto her on the next day, Give
thy son, that we may eat him: and she hath
hid her son.
30And it came to pass, when the king
heard the words of the woman, that he rent

his clothes; and he passed by upon the wall, and the people looked, and, behold, *he had* sackcloth within upon his flesh.

31 Then he said, God do so and more also to me, if the head of Elisha the son of Shaphat shall stand on him this day.

32 But Elisha sat in his house, and the elders sat with him; and *the king* sent a man from before him: but ere the messenger came to him, he said to the elders, See ye how this son of a murderer hath sent to take away mine head? look, when the messenger cometh, shut the door, and hold him fast at the door: *is* not the sound of his master's feet behind him?

33 And while he yet talked with them, behold, the messenger came down unto him: and he said, Behold, this evil *is* of the LORD; what should I wait for the LORD any longer?

7

1 Then Elisha said, Hear ye the word of the LORD; Thus saith the LORD, To morrow about this time *shall* a measure of fine flour *be sold* for a shekel, and two measures of barley for a shekel, in the gate of Samaria.

2 Then a lord on whose hand the king leaned answered the man of God, and said, Behold, *if* the LORD would make windows in heaven, might this thing be? And he said, Behold, thou shalt see *it* with thine eyes, but shalt not eat thereof.

3 And there were four leprous men at the entering in of the gate: and they said one to another, Why sit we here until we die?

4 If we say, We will enter into the city, then the famine *is* in the city, and we shall die there: and if we sit still here, we die also. Now therefore come, and let us fall unto the host of the Syrians: if they save us alive, we shall live; and if they kill us, we shall but die.

5 And they rose up in the twilight, to go unto the camp of the Syrians: and when they were come to the uttermost part of the camp of Syria, behold, *there was* no man there.

6 For the Lord had made the host of the Syrians to hear a noise of chariots, and a noise of horses, *even* the noise of a great host: and they said one to another, Lo, the king of Israel hath hired against us the kings of the Hittites, and the kings of the Egyptians, to come upon us.

7 Wherefore they arose and fled in the twilight, and left their tents, and their horses, and their asses, even the camp as it *was,* and fled for their life.

8 And when these lepers came to the uttermost part of the camp, they went into one tent, and did eat and drink, and carried thence silver, and gold, and raiment, and went and hid *it;* and came again, and entered into another tent, and carried thence *also,* and went and hid *it.*

9 Then they said one to another, We do not well: this day *is* a day of good tidings, and we hold our peace: if we tarry till the morning light, some mischief will come upon us: now therefore come, that we may go and tell the king's household.

10 So they came and called unto the porter of the city: and they told them, saying, We came to the camp of the Syrians, and, behold, *there was* no man there, neither voice of man, but horses tied, and asses tied, and the tents as they *were.*

11 And he called the porters; and they told *it* to the king's house within.

12 And the king arose in the night, and said unto his servants, I will now shew you what the Syrians have done to us. They know that we *be* hungry; therefore are they gone out of the camp to hide themselves in the field, saying, When they come out of the city, we shall catch them alive, and get into the city.

13 And one of his servants answered and said, Let *some* take, I pray thee, five of the horses that remain, which are left in the city, (behold, they *are* as all the multitude of Israel that are left in it: behold, *I say,* they *are* even as all the multitude of the Israelites that are consumed:) and let us send and see.

14 They took therefore two chariot horses; and the king sent after the host of the Syrians, saying, Go and see.

15 And they went after them unto Jordan: and, lo, all the way *was* full of garments and vessels, which the Syrians had cast away in their haste. And the messengers returned, and told the king.

16 And the people went out, and spoiled the tents of the Syrians. So a measure of fine flour was *sold* for a shekel, and two measures of barley for a shekel, according to the word of the LORD.

17 And the king appointed the lord on whose hand he leaned to have the charge

of the gate: and the people trode upon him
in the gate, and he died, as the man of God
had said, who spake when the king came
down to him.
18 And it came to pass as the man of God
had spoken to the king, saying, Two measures of barley for a shekel, and a measure
of fine flour for a shekel, shall be to morrow about this time in the gate of Samaria:
19 And that lord answered the man of
God, and said, Now, behold, *if* the LORD
should make windows in heaven, might
such a thing be? And he said, Behold, thou
shalt see it with thine eyes, but shalt not
eat thereof.
20 And so it fell out unto him: for the
people trode upon him in the gate, and
he died.

8

1 Then spake Elisha unto the woman,
whose son he had restored to life, saying,
Arise, and go thou and thine household,
and sojourn wheresoever thou canst sojourn: for the LORD hath called for a famine; and it shall also come upon the land
seven years.
2 And the woman arose, and did after the
saying of the man of God: and she went
with her household, and sojourned in the
land of the Philistines seven years.
3 And it came to pass at the seven years'
end, that the woman returned out of the
land of the Philistines: and she went forth
to cry unto the king for her house and for
her land.
4 And the king talked with Gehazi the
servant of the man of God, saying, Tell me,
I pray thee, all the great things that Elisha
hath done.
5 And it came to pass, as he was telling
the king how he had restored a dead body
to life, that, behold, the woman, whose
son he had restored to life, cried to the king
for her house and for her land. And Gehazi said, My lord, O king, this *is* the woman, and this *is* her son, whom Elisha
restored to life.
6 And when the king asked the woman,
she told him. So the king appointed unto
her a certain officer, saying, Restore all that
was hers, and all the fruits of the field since
the day that she left the land, even until
now.
7 And Elisha came to Damascus; and
Ben-hadad the king of Syria was sick; and
it was told him, saying, The man of God is
come hither.
8 And the king said unto Hazael, Take a
present in thine hand, and go, meet the
man of God, and enquire of the LORD by
him, saying, Shall I recover of this disease?
9 So Hazael went to meet him, and took
a present with him, even of every good
thing of Damascus, forty camels' burden,
and came and stood before him, and said,
Thy son Ben-hadad king of Syria hath sent
me to thee, saying, Shall I recover of this
disease?
10 And Elisha said unto him, Go, say
unto him, Thou mayest certainly recover:
howbeit the LORD hath shewed me that he
shall surely die.
11 And he settled his countenance stedfastly, until he was ashamed: and the man
of God wept.
12 And Hazael said, Why weepeth my
lord? And he answered, Because I know the
evil that thou wilt do unto the children of
Israel: their strong holds wilt thou set on
fire, and their young men wilt thou slay
with the sword, and wilt dash their children, and rip up their women with child.
13 And Hazael said, But what, *is* thy servant a dog, that he should do this great
thing? And Elisha answered, The LORD
hath shewed me that thou *shalt be* king over
Syria.
14 So he departed from Elisha, and came
to his master; who said to him, What said
Elisha to thee? And he answered, He told
me *that* thou shouldest surely recover.
15 And it came to pass on the morrow,
that he took a thick cloth, and dipped *it*
in water, and spread *it* on his face, so that
he died: and Hazael reigned in his stead.
16 And in the fifth year of Joram the son
of Ahab king of Israel, Jehoshaphat *being*
then king of Judah, Jehoram the son of
Jehoshaphat king of Judah began to reign.
17 Thirty and two years old was he when
he began to reign; and he reigned eight
years in Jerusalem.
18 And he walked in the way of the kings
of Israel, as did the house of Ahab: for the
daughter of Ahab was his wife: and he did
evil in the sight of the LORD.
19 Yet the LORD would not destroy Judah
for David his servant's sake, as he promised him to give him alway a light, *and* to
his children.

20 In his days Edom revolted from under the hand of Judah, and made a king
over themselves.
21 So Joram went over to Zair, and all the
chariots with him: and he rose by night,
and smote the Edomites which compassed
him about, and the captains of the chariots: and the people fled into their tents.
22 Yet Edom revolted from under the
hand of Judah unto this day. Then Libnah
revolted at the same time.
23 And the rest of the acts of Joram, and
all that he did, *are* they not written in the
book of the chronicles of the kings of Judah?
24 And Joram slept with his fathers, and
was buried with his fathers in the city of
David: and Ahaziah his son reigned in his
stead.
25 In the twelfth year of Joram the son
of Ahab king of Israel did Ahaziah the son
of Jehoram king of Judah begin to reign.
26 Two and twenty years old *was* Ahaziah when he began to reign; and he reigned
one year in Jerusalem. And his mother's
name *was* Athaliah, the daughter of Omri
king of Israel.
27 And he walked in the way of the house
of Ahab, and did evil in the sight of the
LORD, as *did* the house of Ahab: for he *was*
the son in law of the house of Ahab.
28 And he went with Joram the son of
Ahab to the war against Hazael king of
Syria in Ramoth-gilead; and the Syrians
wounded Joram.
29 And king Jo-
ram went back to be
healed in Jezreel of
the wounds which
the Syrians had
given him at Ra-
mah, when he fought against Hazael king
of Syria. And Ahaziah the son of Jehoram
king of Judah went down to see Joram the
son of Ahab in Jezreel, because he was sick.

8:29
Sick People
◄ 2 Kings 13:14 ►

9

1 And Elisha the prophet called one of
the children of the prophets, and said unto
him, Gird up thy loins, and take this box
of oil in thine hand, and go to Ramoth-
gilead:
2 And when thou comest thither, look
out there Jehu the son of Jehoshaphat the
son of Nimshi, and go in, and make him
arise up from among his brethren, and
carry him to an inner chamber;
3 Then take the box of oil, and pour *it*
on his head, and say, Thus saith the LORD,
I have anointed thee king over Israel. Then
open the door, and flee, and tarry not.
4 So the young man, *even* the young man
the prophet, went to Ramoth-gilead.
5 And when he came, behold, the captains of the host *were* sitting; and he said,
I have an errand to thee, O captain. And
Jehu said, Unto which of all us? And he
said, To thee, O captain.
6 And he arose, and went into the house;
and he poured the oil on his head, and
said unto him, Thus saith the LORD God
of Israel, I have anointed thee king over
the people of the LORD, *even* over Israel.
7 And thou shalt smite the house of Ahab
thy master, that I may avenge the blood of
my servants the prophets, and the blood
of all the servants of the LORD, at the hand
of Jezebel.
8 For the whole house of Ahab shall perish: and I will cut off from Ahab him that
pisseth against the wall, and him that is
shut up and left in Israel:
9 And I will make the house of Ahab like
the house of Jeroboam the son of Nebat,
and like the house of Baasha the son of
Ahijah:
10 And the dogs shall eat Jezebel in the
portion of Jezreel, and *there shall be* none
to bury *her*. And he opened the door, and
fled.
11 Then Jehu came forth to the servants
of his lord: and *one* said unto him, *Is* all
well? wherefore came this mad *fellow* to
thee? And he said unto them, Ye know the
man, and his communication.
12 And they said, *It is* false; tell us now.
And he said, Thus and thus spake he to
me, saying, Thus saith the LORD, I have
anointed thee king over Israel.
13 Then they hasted, and took every man
his garment, and put *it* under him on the
top of the stairs, and blew with trumpets,
saying, Jehu is king.
14 So Jehu the son of Jehoshaphat the
son of Nimshi conspired against Joram.
(Now Joram had kept Ramoth-gilead, he
and all Israel, because of Hazael king of
Syria.
15 But king Joram was returned to be
healed in Jezreel of the wounds which the
Syrians had given him, when he fought
with Hazael king of Syria.) And Jehu said,

If it be your minds, *then* let none go forth
nor escape out of the city to go to tell *it* in
Jezreel.
16 So Jehu rode in a chariot, and went to
Jezreel; for Joram lay there. And Ahaziah
king of Judah was come down to see Joram.
17 And there stood a watchman on the
tower in Jezreel, and he spied the company of Jehu as he came, and said, I see a
company. And Joram said, Take an horseman, and send to meet them, and let him
say, *Is it* peace?
18 So there went one on horseback to
meet him, and said, Thus saith the king, *Is
it* peace? And Jehu said, What hast thou to
do with peace? turn thee behind me. And
the watchman told, saying, The messenger came to them, but he cometh not
again.
19 Then he sent out a second on horseback, which came to them, and said, Thus
saith the king, *Is it* peace? And Jehu answered, What hast thou to do with peace?
turn thee behind me.
20 And the watchman told, saying, He
came even unto them, and cometh not
again: and the driving *is* like the driving
of Jehu the son of Nimshi; for he driveth
furiously.
21 And Joram said, Make ready. And his
chariot was made ready. And Joram king
of Israel and Ahaziah king of Judah went
out, each in his chariot, and they went out
against Jehu, and met him in the portion
of Naboth the Jezreelite.
22 And it came to pass, when Joram saw
Jehu, that he said, *Is it* peace, Jehu? And
he answered, What peace, so long as the
whoredoms of thy mother Jezebel and her
witchcrafts *are so* many?
23 And Joram turned his hands, and fled,
and said to Ahaziah, *There is* treachery,
O Ahaziah.
24 And Jehu drew a bow with his full
strength, and smote Jehoram between his
arms, and the arrow went out at his heart,
and he sunk down in his chariot.
25 Then said *Jehu* to Bidkar his captain,
Take up, *and* cast him in the portion of
the field of Naboth the Jezreelite: for remember how that, when I and thou rode
together after Ahab his father, the LORD
laid this burden upon him;
26 Surely I have seen yesterday the blood
of Naboth, and the blood of his sons, saith
the LORD; and I will requite thee in this
plat, saith the LORD. Now therefore take
and cast him into the plat *of ground,* according to the word of the LORD.
27 But when Ahaziah the king of Judah
saw *this,* he fled by the way of the garden
house. And Jehu followed after him, and
said, Smite him also in the chariot. *And
they did so* at the going up to Gur, which *is*
by Ibleam. And he fled to Megiddo, and
died there.
28 And his servants carried him in a chariot to Jerusalem, and buried him in his
sepulchre with his fathers in the city of
David.
29 And in the eleventh year of Joram the
son of Ahab began Ahaziah to reign over
Judah.
30 And when Jehu was come to Jezreel,
Jezebel heard *of it;* and she painted her
face, and tired her head, and looked out
at a window.
31 And as Jehu entered in at the gate,
she said, *Had* Zimri peace, who slew his
master?
32 And he lifted up his face to the window, and said, Who *is* on my side? who?
And there looked out to him two *or* three
eunuchs.
33 And he said, Throw her down. So they
threw her down: and *some* of her blood
was sprinkled on the wall, and on the
horses: and he trode her under foot.
34 And when he was come in, he did eat
and drink, and said, Go, see now this
cursed *woman,* and bury her: for she *is* a
king's daughter.
35 And they went to bury her: but they
found no more of her than the skull, and
the feet, and the palms of *her* hands.
36 Wherefore they came again, and told
him. And he said, This *is* the word of the
LORD, which he spake by his servant Elijah the Tishbite, saying, In the portion of
Jezreel shall dogs eat the flesh of Jezebel:
37 And the carcase of Jezebel shall be as
dung upon the face of the field in the portion of Jezreel; *so* that they shall not say,
This *is* Jezebel.

10

1 And Ahab had seventy sons in Samaria. And Jehu wrote letters, and sent to Samaria, unto the rulers of Jezreel, to the
elders, and to them that brought up Ahab's
children, saying,

2Now as soon as this letter cometh to you, seeing your master's sons *are* with you, and *there are* with you chariots and horses, a fenced city also, and armour;

3Look even out the best and meetest of your master's sons, and set *him* on his father's throne, and fight for your master's house.

4But they were exceedingly afraid, and said, Behold, two kings stood not before him: how then shall we stand?

5And he that *was* over the house, and he that *was* over the city, the elders also, and the bringers up *of the children*, sent to Jehu, saying, We *are* thy servants, and will do all that thou shalt bid us; we will not make any king: do thou *that which is* good in thine eyes.

6Then he wrote a letter the second time to them, saying, If ye *be* mine, and *if* ye will hearken unto my voice, take ye the heads of the men your master's sons, and come to me to Jezreel by to morrow this time. Now the king's sons, *being* seventy persons, *were* with the great men of the city, which brought them up.

7And it came to pass, when the letter came to them, that they took the king's sons, and slew seventy persons, and put their heads in baskets, and sent him *them* to Jezreel.

8And there came a messenger, and told him, saying, They have brought the heads of the king's sons. And he said, Lay ye them in two heaps at the entering in of the gate until the morning.

9And it came to pass in the morning, that he went out, and stood, and said to all the people, Ye *be* righteous: behold, I conspired against my master, and slew him: but who slew all these?

10Know now that there shall fall unto the earth nothing of the word of the LORD, which the LORD spake concerning the house of Ahab: for the LORD hath done *that* which he spake by his servant Elijah.

11So Jehu slew all that remained of the house of Ahab in Jezreel, and all his great men, and his kinsfolks, and his priests, until he left him none remaining.

12And he arose and departed, and came to Samaria. *And* as he *was* at the shearing house in the way,

13Jehu met with the brethren of Ahaziah king of Judah, and said, Who *are* ye? And they answered, We *are* the brethren of Ahaziah; and we go down to salute the children of the king and the children of the queen.

14And he said, Take them alive. And they took them alive, and slew them at the pit of the shearing house, *even* two and forty men; neither left he any of them.

15And when he was departed thence, he lighted on Jehonadab the son of Rechab *coming* to meet him: and he saluted him, and said to him, Is thine heart right, as my heart *is* with thy heart? And Jehonadab answered, It is. If it be, give *me* thine hand. And he gave *him* his hand; and he took him up to him into the chariot.

16And he said, Come with me, and see my zeal for the LORD. So they made him ride in his chariot.

10:16
Showing Off
◄ Matthew 6:2, 5 ►

17And when he came to Samaria, he slew all that remained unto Ahab in Samaria, till he had destroyed him, according to the saying of the LORD, which he spake to Elijah.

18And Jehu gathered all the people together, and said unto them, Ahab served Baal a little; *but* Jehu shall serve him much.

19Now therefore call unto me all the prophets of Baal, all his servants, and all his priests; let none be wanting: for I have a great sacrifice *to do* to Baal; whosoever shall be wanting, he shall not live. But Jehu did *it* in subtilty, to the intent that he might destroy the worshippers of Baal.

20And Jehu said, Proclaim a solemn assembly for Baal. And they proclaimed *it*.

21And Jehu sent through all Israel: and all the worshippers of Baal came, so that there was not a man left that came not. And they came into the house of Baal; and the house of Baal was full from one end to another.

22And he said unto him that *was* over the vestry, Bring forth vestments for all the worshippers of Baal. And he brought them forth vestments.

23And Jehu went, and Jehonadab the son of Rechab, into the house of Baal, and said unto the worshippers of Baal, Search, and look that there be here with you none of the servants of the LORD, but the worshippers of Baal only.

24 And when they went in to offer sacrifices and burnt offerings, Jehu appointed fourscore men without, and said, *If* any of the men whom I have brought into your hands escape, *he that letteth him go,* his life *shall be* for the life of him.

25 And it came to pass, as soon as he had made an end of offering the burnt offering, that Jehu said to the guard and to the captains, Go in, *and* slay them; let none come forth. And they smote them with the edge of the sword; and the guard and the captains cast *them* out, and went to the city of the house of Baal.

26 And they brought forth the images out of the house of Baal, and burned them.

27 And they brake down the image of Baal, and brake down the house of Baal, and made it a draught house unto this day.

28 Thus Jehu destroyed Baal out of Israel.

29 Howbeit *from* the sins of Jeroboam the son of Nebat, who made Israel to sin, Jehu departed not from after them, *to wit,* the golden calves that *were* in Bethel, and that *were* in Dan.

30 And the LORD said unto Jehu, Because thou hast done well in executing *that which is* right in mine eyes, *and* hast done unto the house of Ahab according to all that *was* in mine heart, thy children of the fourth *generation* shall sit on the throne of Israel.

31 But Jehu took no heed to walk in the law of the LORD God of Israel with all his heart: for he departed not from the sins of Jeroboam, which made Israel to sin.

32 In those days the LORD began to cut Israel short: and Hazael smote them in all the coasts of Israel;

33 From Jordan eastward, all the land of Gilead, the Gadites, and the Reubenites, and the Manassites, from Aroer, which is by the river Arnon, even Gilead and Bashan.

34 Now the rest of the acts of Jehu, and all that he did, and all his might, *are* they not written in the book of the chronicles of the kings of Israel?

35 And Jehu slept with his fathers: and they buried him in Samaria. And Jehoahaz his son reigned in his stead.

36 And the time that Jehu reigned over Israel in Samaria *was* twenty and eight years.

11

1 And when Athaliah the mother of Ahaziah saw that her son was dead, she arose and destroyed all the seed royal.

2 But Jehosheba, the daughter of king Joram, sister of Ahaziah, took Joash the son of Ahaziah and stole him from among the king's sons *which were* slain; and they hid him, *even* him and his nurse, in the bedchamber from Athaliah, so that he was not slain.

3 And he was with her hid in the house of the LORD six years. And Athaliah did reign over the land.

4 And the seventh year Jehoiada sent and fetched the rulers over hundreds, with the captains and the guard, and brought them to him into the house of the LORD, and made a covenant with them, and took an oath of them in the house of the LORD, and shewed them the king's son.

5 And he commanded them, saying, This *is* the thing that ye shall do; A third part of you that enter in on the sabbath shall even be keepers of the watch of the king's house;

6 And a third part *shall be* at the gate of Sur; and a third part at the gate behind the guard: so shall ye keep the watch of the house, that it be not broken down.

7 And two parts of all you that go forth on the sabbath, even they shall keep the watch of the house of the LORD about the king.

8 And ye shall compass the king round about, every man with his weapons in his hand: and he that cometh within the ranges, let him be slain: and be ye with the king as he goeth out and as he cometh in.

9 And the captains over the hundreds did according to all *things* that Jehoiada the priest commanded: and they took every man his men that were to come in on the sabbath, with them that should go out on the sabbath, and came to Jehoiada the priest.

10 And to the captains over hundreds did the priest give king David's spears and shields, that *were* in the temple of the LORD.

11 And the guard stood, every man with his weapons in his hand, round about the king, from the right corner of the temple to the left corner of the temple, *along* by the altar and the temple.

12 And he brought forth the king's son,

and put the crown upon him, and *gave him*
the testimony; and they made him king,
and anointed him; and they clapped their
hands, and said, God save the king.
13 And when Athaliah heard the noise
of the guard *and* of the people, she came
to the people into the temple of the LORD.
14 And when she looked, behold, the
king stood by a pillar, as the manner *was,*
and the princes and the trumpeters by the
king, and all the people of the land rejoiced, and blew with trumpets: and Athaliah rent her clothes, and cried, Treason,
Treason.
15 But Jehoiada the priest commanded
the captains of the hundreds, the officers
of the host, and said unto them, Have her
forth without the ranges: and him that
followeth her kill with the sword. For the
priest had said, Let her not be slain in the
house of the LORD.
16 And they laid hands on her; and she
went by the way by the which the horses
came into the king's house: and there was
she slain.
17 And Jehoiada made a covenant between the LORD and the king and the people that they should be the LORD'S people;
between the king also and the people.
18 And all the people of the land went
into the house of Baal, and brake it down;
his altars and his images brake they in
pieces thoroughly, and slew Mattan the
priest of Baal before the altars. And the
priest appointed officers over the house of
the LORD.
19 And he took the rulers over hundreds,
and the captains, and the guard, and all
the people of the land; and they brought
down the king from the house of the LORD,
and came by the way of the gate of the
guard to the king's house. And he sat on
the throne of the kings.
20 And all the people of the land rejoiced,
and the city was in quiet: and they slew
Athaliah with the sword *beside* the king's
house.
21 Seven years old *was* Jehoash when he
began to reign.

12

1 In the seventh year of Jehu Jehoash
began to reign; and forty years reigned he
in Jerusalem. And his mother's name *was*
Zibiah of Beer-sheba.
2 And Jehoash did *that which was* right
in the sight of the LORD all his days
wherein Jehoiada the priest instructed
him.
3 But the high places were not taken
away: the people still sacrificed and burnt
incense in the high places.
4 And Jehoash said to the priests, All the
money of the dedicated things that is
brought into the house of the LORD, *even*
the money of every one that passeth *the
account,* the money that every man is set
at, *and* all the money that cometh into any
man's heart to bring into the house of the
LORD,
5 Let the priests take *it* to them, every
man of his acquaintance: and let them repair the breaches of the house, wheresoever any breach shall be found.
6 But it was *so, that* in the three and twentieth year of king Jehoash the priests had
not repaired the breaches of the house.
7 Then king Jehoash called for Jehoiada
the priest, and the *other* priests, and said
unto them, Why repair ye not the breaches
of the house? now therefore receive no
more money of your acquaintance, but
deliver it for the breaches of the house.
8 And the priests consented to receive no
more money of the people, neither to repair the breaches of the house.
9 But Jehoiada the priest took a chest,
and bored a hole in the lid of it, and set it
beside the altar, on the right side as one
cometh into the house of the LORD: and
the priests that kept the door put therein
all the money *that was* brought into the
house of the LORD.
10 And it was *so,* when they saw that *there
was* much money in the chest, that the
king's scribe and the high priest came up,
and they put up in bags, and told the money that was found in the house of the LORD.
11 And they gave the money, being told,
into the hands of them that did the work,
that had the oversight of the house of the
LORD: and they laid it out to the carpenters and builders, that wrought upon the
house of the LORD,
12 And to masons, and hewers of stone,
and to buy timber and hewed stone to repair the breaches of the house of the LORD,
and for all that was laid out for the house
to repair *it.*
13 Howbeit there were not made for the
house of the LORD bowls of silver, snuffers, basons, trumpets, any vessels of gold,

or vessels of silver, of the money *that was*
brought into the house of the LORD:
14 But they gave that to the workmen,
and repaired therewith the house of the
LORD.
15 Moreover they reckoned not with the
men, into whose hand they delivered
the money to be bestowed on workmen:
for they dealt faithfully.
16 The trespass money and sin money
was not brought into the house of the
LORD: it was the priests'.
17 Then Hazael king of Syria went up,
and fought against Gath, and took it: and
Hazael set his face to go up to Jerusalem.
18 And Jehoash king of Judah took all
the hallowed things that Jehoshaphat, and
Jehoram, and Ahaziah, his fathers, kings
of Judah, had dedicated, and his own hallowed things, and all the gold *that was*
found in the treasures of the house of the
LORD, and in the king's house, and sent *it*
to Hazael king of Syria: and he went away
from Jerusalem.
19 And the rest of the acts of Joash, and
all that he did, *are* they not written in the
book of the chronicles of the kings of Judah?
20 And his servants arose, and made a
conspiracy, and slew Joash in the house of
Millo, which goeth down to Silla.
21 For Jozachar the son of Shimeath, and
Jehozabad the son of Shomer, his servants,
smote him, and he died; and they buried
him with his fathers in the city of David:
and Amaziah his son reigned in his stead.

13

1 In the three and twentieth year of Joash the son of Ahaziah king of Judah Jehoahaz the son of Jehu began to reign over
Israel in Samaria, *and reigned* seventeen
years.
2 And he did *that which was* evil in the
sight of the LORD, and followed the sins
of Jeroboam the son of Nebat, which made
Israel to sin; he departed not therefrom.
3 And the anger of the LORD was kindled
against Israel, and he delivered them into
the hand of Hazael king of Syria, and into
the hand of Ben-hadad the son of Hazael,
all *their* days.
4 And Jehoahaz besought the LORD, and
the LORD hearkened unto him: for he saw
the oppression of Israel, because the king
of Syria oppressed them.
5 (And the LORD gave Israel a saviour, so
that they went out from under the hand
of the Syrians: and the children of Israel
dwelt in their tents, as beforetime.
6 Nevertheless they departed not from
the sins of the house of Jeroboam, who
made Israel sin, *but* walked therein: and
there remained the grove also in Samaria.)
7 Neither did he leave of the people to
Jehoahaz but fifty horsemen, and ten chariots, and ten thousand footmen; for the
king of Syria had destroyed them, and had
made them like the dust by threshing.
8 Now the rest of the acts of Jehoahaz,
and all that he did, and his might, *are* they
not written in the book of the chronicles
of the kings of Israel?
9 And Jehoahaz slept with his fathers;
and they buried him in Samaria: and Joash his son reigned in his stead.
10 In the thirty and seventh year of Joash
king of Judah began Jehoash the son of
Jehoahaz to reign over Israel in Samaria,
and reigned sixteen years.
11 And he did *that which was* evil in the
sight of the LORD; he departed not from
all the sins of Jeroboam the son of Nebat,
who made Israel sin: *but* he walked therein.
12 And the rest of the acts of Joash, and
all that he did, and his might wherewith
he fought against Amaziah king of Judah,
are they not written in the book of the
chronicles of the kings of Israel?
13 And Joash slept with his fathers; and
Jeroboam sat upon his throne: and Joash
was buried in Samaria with the kings of
Israel.
14 Now Elisha was
fallen sick of his
sickness whereof
he died. And Joash
the king of Israel
came down unto
him, and wept over his face, and said, O my
father, my father, the chariot of Israel, and
the horsemen thereof.

13:14 Sick People
◄ 2 Kings 8:29
Job 2:11 ►

15 And Elisha said unto him, Take bow
and arrows. And he took unto him bow
and arrows.
16 And he said to the king of Israel, Put
thine hand upon the bow. And he put his
hand *upon it:* and Elisha put his hands
upon the king's hands.
17 And he said, Open the window eastward. And he opened *it.* Then Elisha said,
Shoot. And he shot. And he said, The arrow

of the LORD'S deliverance, and the arrow of deliverance from Syria: for thou shalt smite the Syrians in Aphek, till thou have consumed *them.*

18 And he said, Take the arrows. And he took *them.* And he said unto the king of Israel, Smite upon the ground. And he smote thrice, and stayed.

19 And the man of God was wroth with him, and said, Thou shouldest have smitten five or six times; then hadst thou smitten Syria till thou hadst consumed *it:* whereas now thou shalt smite Syria *but* thrice.

20 And Elisha died, and they buried him. And the bands of the Moabites invaded the land at the coming in of the year.

21 And it came to pass, as they were burying a man, that, behold, they spied a band *of men;* and they cast the man into the sepulchre of Elisha: and when the man was let down, and touched the bones of Elisha, he revived, and stood up on his feet.

22 But Hazael king of Syria oppressed Israel all the days of Jehoahaz.

23 And the LORD was gracious unto them, and had compassion on them, and had respect unto them, because of his covenant with Abraham, Isaac, and Jacob, and would not destroy them, neither cast he them from his presence as yet.

24 So Hazael king of Syria died; and Benhadad his son reigned in his stead.

25 And Jehoash the son of Jehoahaz took again out of the hand of Ben-hadad the son of Hazael the cities, which he had taken out of the hand of Jehoahaz his father by war. Three times did Joash beat him, and recovered the cities of Israel.

14

1 In the second year of Joash son of Jehoahaz king of Israel reigned Amaziah the son of Joash king of Judah.

2 He was twenty and five years old when he began to reign, and reigned twenty and nine years in Jerusalem. And his mother's name *was* Jehoaddan of Jerusalem.

3 And he did *that which was* right in the sight of the LORD, yet not like David his father: he did according to all things as Joash his father did.

4 Howbeit the high places were not taken away: as yet the people did sacrifice and burnt incense on the high places.

5 And it came to pass, as soon as the kingdom was confirmed in his hand, that he slew his servants which had slain the king his father.

6 But the children of the murderers he slew not: according unto that which is written in the book of the law of Moses, wherein the LORD commanded, saying, The fathers shall not be put to death for the children, nor the children be put to death for the fathers; but every man shall be put to death for his own sin.

7 He slew of Edom in the valley of salt ten thousand, and took Selah by war, and called the name of it Joktheel unto this day.

8 Then Amaziah sent messengers to Jehoash, the son of Jehoahaz son of Jehu, king of Israel, saying, Come, let us look one another in the face.

9 And Jehoash the king of Israel sent to Amaziah king of Judah, saying, The thistle that *was* in Lebanon sent to the cedar that *was* in Lebanon, saying, Give thy daughter to my son to wife: and there passed by a wild beast that *was* in Lebanon, and trode down the thistle.

10 Thou hast indeed smitten Edom, and thine heart hath lifted thee up: glory *of this,* and tarry at home: for why shouldest thou meddle to *thy* hurt, that thou shouldest fall, *even* thou, and Judah with thee?

14:10 Ambition
◄ 1 Kings 1:5
Psalm 49:11 ►

11 But Amaziah would not hear. Therefore Jehoash king of Israel went up; and he and Amaziah king of Judah looked one another in the face at Beth-shemesh, which *belongeth* to Judah.

12 And Judah was put to the worse before Israel; and they fled every man to their tents.

13 And Jehoash king of Israel took Amaziah king of Judah, the son of Jehoash the son of Ahaziah, at Beth-shemesh, and came to Jerusalem, and brake down the wall of Jerusalem from the gate of Ephraim unto the corner gate, four hundred cubits.

14 And he took all the gold and silver, and all the vessels that were found in the house of the LORD, and in the treasures of the king's house, and hostages, and returned to Samaria.

15 Now the rest of the acts of Jehoash which he did, and his might, and how he

fought with Amaziah king of Judah, *are*
they not written in the book of the chronicles of the kings of Israel?
16And Jehoash slept with his fathers, and
was buried in Samaria with the kings of
Israel; and Jeroboam his son reigned in his
stead.
17And Amaziah the son of Joash king
of Judah lived after the death of Jehoash
son of Jehoahaz king of Israel fifteen years.
18And the rest of the acts of Amaziah,
are they not written in the book of the
chronicles of the kings of Judah?
19Now they made a conspiracy against
him in Jerusalem: and he fled to Lachish;
but they sent after him to Lachish, and slew
him there.
20And they brought him on horses: and
he was buried at Jerusalem with his fathers
in the city of David.
21And all the people of Judah took
Azariah, which *was* sixteen years old, and
made him king instead of his father Amaziah.
22He built Elath, and restored it to Judah, after that the king slept with his
fathers.
23In the fifteenth year of Amaziah the
son of Joash king of Judah Jeroboam the
son of Joash king of Israel began to reign
in Samaria, *and reigned* forty and one years.
24And he did *that which was* evil in the
sight of the LORD: he departed not from
all the sins of Jeroboam the son of Nebat,
who made Israel to sin.
25He restored the coast of Israel from
the entering of Hamath unto the sea of the
plain, according to the word of the LORD
God of Israel, which he spake by the hand
of his servant Jonah, the son of Amittai,
the prophet, which *was* of Gath-hepher.
26For the LORD saw the affliction of Israel, *that it was* very bitter: for *there was* not
any shut up, nor any left, nor any helper
for Israel.
27And the LORD said not that he would
blot out the name of Israel from under
heaven: but he saved them by the hand of
Jeroboam the son of Joash.
28Now the rest of the acts of Jeroboam,
and all that he did, and his might, how he
warred, and how he recovered Damascus,
and Hamath, *which belonged* to Judah, for
Israel, *are* they not written in the book of
the chronicles of the kings of Israel?
29And Jeroboam slept with his fathers,
even with the kings of Israel; and Zachariah
his son reigned in his stead.
15 1In the twenty and seventh year of Jeroboam king of Israel began Azariah son of
Amaziah king of Judah to reign.
2Sixteen years old was he when he began to reign, and he reigned two and fifty
years in Jerusalem. And his mother's name
was Jecholiah of Jerusalem.
3And he did *that which was* right in the
sight of the LORD, according to all that his
father Amaziah had done;
4Save that the high places were not removed: the people sacrificed and burnt
incense still on the high places.
5And the LORD smote the king, so that
he was a leper unto the day of his death,
and dwelt in a several house. And Jotham
the king's son *was* over the house, judging
the people of the land.
6And the rest of the acts of Azariah, and
all that he did, *are* they not written in
the book of the chronicles of the kings of
Judah?
7So Azariah slept with his fathers; and
they buried him with his fathers in the city
of David: and Jotham his son reigned in
his stead.
8In the thirty and eighth year of Azariah
king of Judah did Zachariah the son of Jeroboam reign over Israel in Samaria six
months.
9And he did *that which was* evil in the sight
of the LORD, as his fathers had done: he
departed not from the sins of Jeroboam
the son of Nebat, who made Israel to sin.
10And Shallum the son of Jabesh conspired against him, and smote him before
the people, and slew him, and reigned in
his stead.
11And the rest of the acts of Zachariah,
behold, they *are* written in the book of the
chronicles of the kings of Israel.
12This *was* the word of the LORD which
he spake unto Jehu, saying, Thy sons shall
sit on the throne of Israel unto the fourth
generation. And so it came to pass.
13Shallum the son of Jabesh began to
reign in the nine and thirtieth year of Uzziah king of Judah; and he reigned a full
month in Samaria.
14For Menahem the son of Gadi went
up from Tirzah, and came to Samaria, and
smote Shallum the son of Jabesh in

Samaria, and slew him, and reigned in his stead.

15 And the rest of the acts of Shallum, and his conspiracy which he made, behold, they *are* written in the book of the chronicles of the kings of Israel.

16 Then Menahem smote Tiphsah, and all that *were* therein, and the coasts thereof from Tirzah: because they opened not *to him,* therefore he smote *it; and* all the women therein that were with child he ripped up.

17 In the nine and thirtieth year of Azariah king of Judah began Menahem the son of Gadi to reign over Israel, *and reigned* ten years in Samaria.

18 And he did *that which was* evil in the sight of the LORD: he departed not all his days from the sins of Jeroboam the son of Nebat, who made Israel to sin.

19 *And* Pul the king of Assyria came against the land: and Menahem gave Pul a thousand talents of silver, that his hand might be with him to confirm the kingdom in his hand.

20 And Menahem exacted the money of Israel, *even* of all the mighty men of wealth, of each man fifty shekels of silver, to give to the king of Assyria. So the king of Assyria turned back, and stayed not there in the land.

21 And the rest of the acts of Menahem, and all that he did, *are* they not written in the book of the chronicles of the kings of Israel?

22 And Menahem slept with his fathers; and Pekahiah his son reigned in his stead.

23 In the fiftieth year of Azariah king of Judah Pekahiah the son of Menahem began to reign over Israel in Samaria, *and reigned* two years.

24 And he did *that which was* evil in the sight of the LORD: he departed not from the sins of Jeroboam the son of Nebat, who made Israel to sin.

25 But Pekah the son of Remaliah, a captain of his, conspired against him, and smote him in Samaria, in the palace of the king's house, with Argob and Arieh, and with him fifty men of the Gileadites: and he killed him, and reigned in his room.

26 And the rest of the acts of Pekahiah, and all that he did, behold, they *are* written in the book of the chronicles of the kings of Israel.

27 In the two and fiftieth year of Azariah king of Judah Pekah the son of Remaliah began to reign over Israel in Samaria, *and reigned* twenty years.

28 And he did *that which was* evil in the sight of the LORD: he departed not from the sins of Jeroboam the son of Nebat, who made Israel to sin.

29 In the days of Pekah king of Israel came Tiglath-pileser king of Assyria, and took Ijon, and Abel-beth-maachah, and Janoah, and Kedesh, and Hazor, and Gilead, and Galilee, all the land of Naphtali, and carried them captive to Assyria.

30 And Hoshea the son of Elah made a conspiracy against Pekah the son of Remaliah, and smote him, and slew him, and reigned in his stead, in the twentieth year of Jotham the son of Uzziah.

31 And the rest of the acts of Pekah, and all that he did, behold, they *are* written in the book of the chronicles of the kings of Israel.

32 In the second year of Pekah the son of Remaliah king of Israel began Jotham the son of Uzziah king of Judah to reign.

33 Five and twenty years old was he when he began to reign, and he reigned sixteen years in Jerusalem. And his mother's name *was* Jerusha, the daughter of Zadok.

34 And he did *that which was* right in the sight of the LORD: he did according to all that his father Uzziah had done.

35 Howbeit the high places were not removed: the people sacrificed and burned incense still in the high places. He built the higher gate of the house of the LORD.

36 Now the rest of the acts of Jotham, and all that he did, *are* they not written in the book of the chronicles of the kings of Judah?

37 In those days the LORD began to send against Judah Rezin the king of Syria, and Pekah the son of Remaliah.

38 And Jotham slept with his fathers, and was buried with his fathers in the city of David his father: and Ahaz his son reigned in his stead.

16

1 In the seventeenth year of Pekah the son of Remaliah Ahaz the son of Jotham king of Judah began to reign.

2 Twenty years old *was* Ahaz when he began to reign, and reigned sixteen years in Jerusalem, and did not *that which was* right in the sight of the LORD his God, like David his father.

3 But he walked in the way of the kings of Israel, yea, and made his son to pass through the fire, according to the abominations of the heathen, whom the LORD cast out from before the children of Israel.

4 And he sacrificed and burnt incense in the high places, and on the hills, and under every green tree.

5 Then Rezin king of Syria and Pekah son of Remaliah king of Israel came up to Jerusalem to war: and they besieged Ahaz, but could not overcome *him*.

6 At that time Rezin king of Syria recovered Elath to Syria, and drave the Jews from Elath: and the Syrians came to Elath, and dwelt there unto this day.

7 So Ahaz sent messengers to Tiglath-pileser king of Assyria, saying, I *am* thy servant and thy son: come up, and save me out of the hand of the king of Syria, and out of the hand of the king of Israel, which rise up against me.

8 And Ahaz took the silver and gold that was found in the house of the LORD, and in the treasures of the king's house, and sent *it for* a present to the king of Assyria.

9 And the king of Assyria hearkened unto him: for the king of Assyria went up against Damascus, and took it, and carried *the people of* it captive to Kir, and slew Rezin.

10 And king Ahaz went to Damascus to meet Tiglath-pileser king of Assyria, and saw an altar that *was* at Damascus: and king Ahaz sent to Urijah the priest the fashion of the altar, and the pattern of it, according to all the workmanship thereof.

11 And Urijah the priest built an altar according to all that king Ahaz had sent from Damascus: so Urijah the priest made *it* against king Ahaz came from Damascus.

12 And when the king was come from Damascus, the king saw the altar: and the king approached to the altar, and offered thereon.

13 and he burnt his burnt offering and his meat offering, and poured his drink offering, and sprinkled the blood of his peace offerings, upon the altar.

14 And he brought also the brasen altar, which *was* before the LORD, from the forefront of the house, from between the altar and the house of the LORD, and put it on the north side of the altar.

15 And king Ahaz commanded Urijah the priest, saying, Upon the great altar burn the morning burnt offering, and the evening meat offering, and the king's burnt sacrifice, and his meat offering, with the burnt offering of all the people of the land, and their meat offering, and their drink offerings; and sprinkle upon it all the blood of the burnt offering, and all the blood of the sacrifice: and the brasen altar shall be for me to enquire *by*.

16 Thus did Urijah the priest, according to all that king Ahaz commanded.

17 And king Ahaz cut off the borders of the bases, and removed the laver from off them; and took down the sea from off the brasen oxen that *were* under it, and put it upon a pavement of stones.

18 And the covert for the sabbath that they had built in the house, and the king's entry without, turned he from the house of the LORD for the king of Assyria.

19 Now the rest of the acts of Ahaz which he did, *are* they not written in the book of the chronicles of the kings of Judah?

20 And Ahaz slept with his fathers, and was buried with his fathers in the city of David: and Hezekiah his son reigned in his stead.

17

1 In the twelfth year of Ahaz king of Judah began Hoshea the son of Elah to reign in Samaria over Israel nine years.

2 And he did *that which was* evil in the sight of the LORD, but not as the kings of Israel that were before him.

3 Against him came up Shalmaneser king of Assyria; and Hoshea became his servant, and gave him presents.

4 And the king of Assyria found conspiracy in Hoshea: for he had sent messengers to So king of Egypt, and brought no present to the king of Assyria, as *he had done* year by year: therefore the king of Assyria shut him up, and bound him in prison.

5 Then the king of Assyria came up throughout all the land, and went up to Samaria, and besieged it three years.

6 In the ninth year of Hoshea the king of Assyria took Samaria, and carried Israel away into Assyria, and placed them in Halah and in Habor *by* the river of Gozan, and in the cities of the Medes.

7 For *so* it was, that the children of Israel had sinned against the LORD their God, which had brought them up out of the land of Egypt, from under the hand of

Pharaoh king of Egypt, and had feared
other gods,
8 And walked in the statutes of the heathen, whom the LORD cast out from before the children of Israel, and of the kings
of Israel, which they had made.
9 And the children of Israel did secretly
those things that *were* not right against the
LORD their God, and they built them high
places in all their cities, from the tower of
the watchmen to the fenced city.
10 And they set them up images and
groves in every high hill, and under every
green tree:
11 And there they burnt incense in all the
high places, as *did* the heathen whom the
LORD carried away before them; and
wrought wicked things to provoke the
LORD to anger:
12 For they served idols, whereof the
LORD had said unto them, Ye shall not do
this thing.
13 Yet the LORD
testified against Is-
rael, and against
Judah, by all the
prophets, *and by* all
the seers, saying,
Turn ye from your evil ways, and keep my
commandments *and* my statutes, according to all the law which I commanded your
fathers, and which I sent to you by my servants the prophets.

17:13
Repent!
◄ 2 Chronicles 30:6 ►

14 Notwithstand-
ing they would not
hear, but hardened
their necks, like to
the neck of their fa-
thers, that did not
believe in the LORD their God.

17:14
Stubborn People
◄ 2 Chronicles 28:22 ►

15 And they rejected his statutes, and his
covenant that he made with their fathers,
and his testimonies which he testified
against them; and they followed vanity,
and became vain, and went after the heathen that *were* round about them, *concerning* whom the LORD had charged them, that
they should not do like them.
16 And they left all the commandments
of the LORD their God, and made them
molten images, *even* two calves, and made
a grove, and worshipped all the host of
heaven, and served Baal.
17 And they caused their sons and their
daughters to pass through the fire, and
used divination and enchantments, and
sold themselves to do evil in the sight of
the LORD, to provoke him to anger.
18 Therefore the LORD was very angry
with Israel, and removed them out of his
sight: there was none left but the tribe of
Judah only.
19 Also Judah kept not the commandments of the LORD their God, but walked
in the statutes of Israel which they made.
20 And the LORD rejected all the seed of
Israel, and afflicted them, and delivered
them into the hand of spoilers, until he
had cast them out of his sight.
21 For he rent Israel from the house of
David; and they made Jeroboam the son
of Nebat king: and Jeroboam drave Israel
from following the LORD, and made them
sin a great sin.
22 For the children of Israel walked in all
the sins of Jeroboam which he did; they
departed not from them;
23 Until the LORD removed Israel out of
his sight, as he had said by all his servants
the prophets. So was Israel carried away
out of their own land to Assyria unto this
day.
24 And the king of Assyria brought *men*
from Babylon, and from Cuthah, and from
Ava, and from Hamath, and from Sepharvaim, and placed *them* in the cities of Samaria instead of the children of Israel: and
they possessed Samaria, and dwelt in the
cities thereof.
25 And *so* it was at the beginning of their
dwelling there, *that* they feared not the
LORD: therefore the LORD sent lions among
them, which slew *some* of them.
26 Wherefore they spake to the king of
Assyria, saying, The nations which thou
hast removed, and placed in the cities of
Samaria, know not the manner of the God
of the land: therefore he hath sent lions
among them, and, behold, they slay them,
because they know not the manner of the
God of the land.
27 Then the king of Assyria commanded, saying, Carry thither one of the priests
whom ye brought from thence; and let
them go and dwell
there, and let him
teach them the
manner of the God
of the land.
28 Then one of

17:28 Sunday School
◄ 1 Samuel 9:27
2 Chronicles 17:7 ►

the priests whom they had carried away from Samaria came and dwelt in Bethel, and taught them how they should fear the LORD.

29Howbeit every nation made gods of their own, and put *them* in the houses of the high places which the Samaritans had made, every nation in their cities wherein they dwelt.

30And the men of Babylon made Succoth-benoth, and the men of Cuth made Nergal, and the men of Hamath made Ashima,

31And the Avites made Nibhaz and Tartak, and the Sepharvites burnt their children in fire to Adrammelech and Anammelech, the gods of Sepharvaim.

32So they feared the LORD, and made unto themselves of the lowest of them priests of the high places, which sacrificed for them in the houses of the high places.

33They feared the LORD, and served their own gods, after the manner of the nations whom they carried away from thence.

17:33 Double Life
◄ 1 Chronicles 12:33 ►

34Unto this day they do after the former manners: they fear not the LORD, neither do they after their statutes, or after their ordinances, or after the law and commandment which the LORD commanded the children of Jacob, whom he named Israel;

35With whom the LORD had made a covenant, and charged them saying, Ye shall not fear other gods, nor bow yourselves to them, nor serve them, nor sacrifice to them:

36But the LORD, who brought you up out of the land of Egypt with great power and a stretched out arm, him shall ye fear, and him shall ye worship, and to him shall ye do sacrifice.

17:36 Worship
◄ Deuteronomy 26:10
1 Chronicles 16:29 ►

37And the statutes, and the ordinances, and the law, and the commandment, which he wrote for you, ye shall observe to do for evermore; and ye shall not fear other gods.

38And the covenant that I have made with you ye shall not forget; neither shall ye fear other gods.

39But the LORD your God ye shall fear; and he shall deliver you out of the hand of all your enemies.

40Howbeit they did not hearken, but they did after their former manner.

41So these nations feared the LORD, and served their graven images, both their children, and their children's children: as did their fathers, so do they unto this day.

17:41 The Time Is Now
◄ 1 Kings 18:21
Hosea 10:2 ►

18

1Now it came to pass in the third year of Hoshea son of Elah king of Israel, *that* Hezekiah the son of Ahaz king of Judah began to reign.

2Twenty and five years old was he when he began to reign; and he reigned twenty and nine years in Jerusalem. His mother's name also *was* Abi, the daughter of Zachariah.

3And he did *that which was* right in the sight of the LORD, according to all that David his father did.

4He removed the high places, and brake the images, and cut down the groves, and brake in pieces the brasen serpent that Moses had made: for unto those days the children of Israel did burn incense to it: and he called it Nehushtan.

5He trusted in the LORD God of Israel; so that after him was none like him among all the kings of Judah, nor *any* that were before him.

6For he clave to the LORD, *and* departed not from following him, but kept his commandments, which the LORD commanded Moses.

7And the LORD was with him; *and* he prospered whithersoever he went forth: and he rebelled against the king of Assyria, and served him not.

8He smote the Philistines, *even* unto Gaza, and the borders thereof, from the tower of the watchmen to the fenced city.

9And it came to pass in the fourth year of king Hezekiah, which *was* the seventh year of Hoshea son of Elah king of Israel, *that* Shalmaneser king of Assyria came up against Samaria, and besieged it.

10And at the end of three years they took it: *even* in the sixth year of Hezekiah, that *is* the ninth year of Hoshea king of Israel, Samaria was taken.

11And the king of Assyria did carry away
Israel unto Assyria, and put them in Halah and in Habor *by* the river of Gozan,
and in the cities of the Medes:
12Because they obeyed not the voice of
the LORD their God, but transgressed his
covenant, *and* all that Moses the servant
of the LORD commanded, and would not
hear *them,* nor do *them.*
13Now in the fourteenth year of king
Hezekiah did Sennacherib king of Assyria
come up against all the fenced cities of
Judah, and took them.
14And Hezekiah king of Judah sent to
the king of Assyria to Lachish, saying, I
have offended; return from me: that which
thou puttest on me will I bear. And the
king of Assyria appointed unto Hezekiah
king of Judah three hundred talents of silver and thirty talents of gold.
15And Hezekiah gave *him* all the silver
that was found in the house of the LORD,
and in the treasures of the king's house.
16At that time did Hezekiah cut off *the
gold from* the doors of the temple of the
LORD, and *from* the pillars which Hezekiah king of Judah had overlaid, and gave it
to the king of Assyria.
17And the king of Assyria sent Tartan
and Rabsaris and Rab-shakeh from Lachish
to king Hezekiah with a great host against
Jerusalem. And they went up and came to
Jerusalem. And when they were come up,
they came and stood by the conduit of the
upper pool, which *is* in the highway of the
fuller's field.
18And when they had called to the king,
there came out to them Eliakim the son of
Hilkiah, which *was* over the household,
and Shebna the scribe, and Joah the son
of Asaph the recorder.
19And Rab-shakeh said unto them,
Speak ye now to Hezekiah, Thus saith the
great king, the king of Assyria, What confidence *is* this wherein thou trustest?
20Thou sayest, (but *they are but* vain
words,) *I have* counsel and strength for the
war. Now on whom dost thou trust, that
thou rebellest against me?
21Now, behold, thou trustest upon the
staff of this bruised reed, *even* upon Egypt,
on which if a man lean, it will go into his
hand, and pierce it: so *is* Pharaoh king of
Egypt unto all that trust on him.
22But if ye say unto me, We trust in the
LORD our God: *is* not that he, whose high
places and whose altars Hezekiah hath tak-
en away, and hath said to Judah and Jerusalem, Ye shall worship before this altar
in Jerusalem?
23Now therefore, I pray thee, give
pledges to my lord the king of Assyria, and
I will deliver thee two thousand horses, if
thou be able on thy part to set riders upon
them.
24How then wilt thou turn away the face
of one captain of the least of my master's
servants, and put thy trust on Egypt for
chariots and for horsemen?
25Am I now come up without the LORD
against this place to destroy it? The LORD
said to me, Go up against this land, and
destroy it.
26Then said Eliakim the son of Hilkiah,
and Shebna, and Joah, unto Rab-shakeh,
Speak, I pray thee, to thy servants in the
Syrian language; for we understand *it:* and
talk not with us in the Jews' language in
the ears of the people that *are* on the wall.
27But Rab-shakeh said unto them, Hath
my master sent me to thy master, and to
thee, to speak these words? *hath he* not *sent
me* to the men which sit on the wall, that
they may eat their own dung, and drink
their own piss with you.
28Then Rab-shakeh stood and cried with
a loud voice in the Jews' language, and
spake, saying, Hear the word of the great
king, the king of Assyria:
29Thus saith the king, Let not Hezekiah
deceive you: for he shall not be able to
deliver you out of his hand:
30Neither let Hezekiah make you trust
in the LORD, saying, The LORD will surely
deliver us, and this city shall not be delivered into the hand of the king of Assyria.
31Hearken not to Hezekiah: for thus
saith the king of Assyria, Make *an agreement* with me by a present, and come out
to me, and *then* eat ye every man of his
own vine, and every one of his fig tree, and
drink ye every one the waters of his cistern:
32Until I come and take you away to a
land like your own land, a land of corn
and wine, a land of bread and vineyards, a
land of oil olive and of honey, that ye may
live, and not die: and hearken not unto
Hezekiah, when he persuadeth you, saying, The LORD will deliver us.

33 Hath any of the gods of the nations delivered at all his land out of the hand of the king of Assyria?

34 Where *are* the gods of Hamath, and of Arpad? where *are* the gods of Sepharvaim, Hena, and Ivah? have they delivered Samaria out of mine hand?

35 Who *are* they among all the gods of the countries, that have delivered their country out of mine hand, that the LORD should deliver Jerusalem out of mine hand?

36 But the people held their peace, and answered him not a word: for the king's commandment was, saying, Answer him not.

37 Then came Eliakim the son of Hilkiah, which *was* over the household, and Shebna the scribe, and Joah the son of Asaph the recorder, to Hezekiah with *their* clothes rent, and told him the words of Rab-shakeh.

19

1 And it came to pass, when king Hezekiah heard *it,* that he rent his clothes, and covered himself with sackcloth, and went into the house of the LORD.

2 And he sent Eliakim, which *was* over the household, and Shebna the scribe, and the elders of the priests, covered with sackcloth, to Isaiah the prophet the son of Amoz.

3 And they said unto him, Thus saith Hezekiah, This day *is* a day of trouble, and of rebuke, and blasphemy: for the children are come to the birth, and *there is* not strength to bring forth.

4 It may be the LORD thy God will hear all the words of Rab-shakeh, whom the king of Assyria his master hath sent to reproach the living God; and will reprove the words which the LORD thy God hath heard: wherefore lift up *thy* prayer for the remnant that are left.

5 So the servants of king Hezekiah came to Isaiah.

6 And Isaiah said unto them, Thus shall ye say to your master, Thus saith the LORD, Be not afraid of the words which thou hast heard, with which the servants of the king of Assyria have blasphemed me.

7 Behold, I will send a blast upon him, and he shall hear a rumour, and shall return to his own land; and I will cause him to fall by the sword in his own land.

8 So Rab-shakeh returned, and found the king of Assyria warring against Libnah: for he had heard that he was departed from Lachish.

9 And when he heard say of Tirhakah king of Ethiopia, Behold, he is come out to fight against thee: he sent messengers again unto Hezekiah, saying,

10 Thus shall ye speak to Hezekiah king of Judah, saying, Let not thy God in whom thou trustest deceive thee, saying, Jerusalem shall not be delivered into the hand of the king of Assyria.

11 Behold, thou hast heard what the kings of Assyria have done to all lands, by destroying them utterly: and shalt thou be delivered?

12 Have the gods of the nations delivered them which my fathers have destroyed; *as* Gozan, and Haran, and Rezeph, and the children of Eden which *were* in Thelasar?

13 Where *is* the king of Hamath, and the king of Arpad, and the king of the city of Sepharvaim, of Hena, and Ivah?

14 And Hezekiah received the letter of the hand of the messengers, and read it: and Hezekiah went up into the house of the LORD, and spread it before the LORD.

15 And Hezekiah prayed before the LORD, and said, O LORD God of Israel, which dwellest *between* the cherubims, thou art the God, *even* thou alone, of all the kingdoms of the earth: thou hast made heaven and earth.

16 LORD, bow down thine ear, and hear: open, LORD, thine eyes, and see: and hear the words of Sennacherib, which hath sent him to reproach the living God.

17 Of a truth, LORD, the kings of Assyria have destroyed the nations and their lands,

18 And have cast their gods into the fire: for they *were* no gods, but the work of men's hands, wood and stone: therefore they have destroyed them.

19 Now therefore, O LORD our God, I beseech thee, save thou us out of his hand, that all the kingdoms of the earth may know that thou *art* the LORD God, *even* thou only.

20 Then Isaiah the son of Amoz sent to Hezekiah, saying, Thus saith the LORD God of Israel, *That* which thou hast prayed to me against Sennacherib king of Assyria I have heard.

21 This *is* the word that the LORD hath spoken concerning him; The virgin the

daughter of Zion hath despised thee, *and*
laughed thee to scorn; the daughter of
Jerusalem hath shaken her head at thee.

22 Whom hast thou reproached and
blasphemed? and against whom hast thou
exalted *thy* voice, and lifted up thine eyes
on high? *even* against the Holy *One* of
Israel.

23 By the messengers thou hast reproached the Lord, and hast said, With the
multitude of my chariots I am come up to
the height of the mountains, to the sides
of Lebanon, and will cut down the tall cedar trees thereof, *and* the choice fir trees
thereof: and I will enter into the lodgings
of his borders, *and into* the forest of his
Carmel.

24 I have digged and drunk strange waters, and with the sole of my feet have I
dried up all the rivers of besieged places.

25 Hast thou not heard long ago *how* I
have done it, *and* of ancient times that
I have formed it? now have I brought it to
pass, that thou shouldest be to lay waste
fenced cities *into* ruinous heaps.

26 Therefore their inhabitants were of
small power, they were dismayed and confounded; they were *as* the grass of the field,
and *as* the green herb, *as* the grass on the
house tops, and *as corn* blasted before it
be grown up.

27 But I know thy abode, and thy going
out, and thy coming in, and thy rage
against me.

28 Because thy rage against me and thy
tumult is come up into mine ears, therefore I will put my hook in thy nose,
and my bridle in thy lips, and I will turn
thee back by the way by which thou
camest.

29 And this *shall be* a sign unto thee, Ye
shall eat this year such things as grow of
themselves, and in the second year that
which springeth of the same; and in the
third year sow ye, and reap, and plant vineyards, and eat the fruits thereof.

30 And the remnant that is escaped of the
house of Judah shall yet again take root
downward, and bear fruit upward.

31 For out of Jerusalem shall go forth a
remnant, and they that escape out of
mount Zion: the zeal of the LORD *of hosts*
shall do this.

32 Therefore thus saith the LORD concerning the king of Assyria, He shall not come
into this city, nor shoot an arrow there,
nor come before it with shield, nor cast a
bank against it.

33 By the way that he came, by the same
shall he return, and shall not come into
this city, saith the LORD.

34 For I will defend this city, to save it,
for mine own sake, and for my servant
David's sake.

35 And it came to pass that night, that
the angel of the LORD went out, and smote
in the camp of the Assyrians an hundred
fourscore and five thousand: and when
they arose early in the morning, behold,
they *were* all dead corpses.

36 So Sennacherib king of Assyria departed, and went and returned, and dwelt at
Nineveh.

37 And it came to pass, as he was worshipping in the house of Nisroch his god,
that Adrammelech and Sharezer his sons
smote him with the sword: and they escaped into the land of Armenia. And Esar-
haddon his son reigned in his stead.

20

1 In those days
was Hezekiah sick
unto death. And
the prophet Isaiah
the son of Amoz
came to him, and
said unto him, Thus saith the LORD, Set
thine house in order; for thou shalt die,
and not live.

> **20:1**
> **Ready for the Future**
> ◄ Amos 4:12 ►

2 Then he turned his face to the wall, and
prayed unto the LORD, saying,

3 I beseech thee, O LORD, remember now
how I have walked before thee in truth and
with a perfect heart, and have done *that
which is* good in thy sight. And Hezekiah
wept sore.

4 And it came to pass, afore Isaiah was
gone out into the middle court, that the
word of the LORD came to him, saying,

5 Turn again, and tell Hezekiah the captain of my people, Thus saith the LORD,
the God of David thy father, I have heard
thy prayer, I have seen thy tears: behold, I
will heal thee: on the third day thou shalt
go up unto the house of the LORD.

6 And I will add unto thy days fifteen
years; and I will deliver thee and this city
out of the hand of the king of Assyria; and
I will defend this city for mine own sake,
and for my servant David's sake.

7 And Isaiah said, Take a lump of figs.

And they took and laid *it* on the boil, and
he recovered.
8 And Hezekiah said unto Isaiah, What
shall be the sign that the LORD will heal
me, and that I shall go up into the house
of the LORD the third day?
9 And Isaiah said, This sign shalt thou
have of the LORD, that the LORD will do
the thing that he hath spoken: shall the
shadow go forward ten degrees, or go back
ten degrees?
10 And Hezekiah answered, It is a light
thing for the shadow to go down ten degrees: nay, but let the shadow return backward ten degrees.
11 And Isaiah the prophet cried unto the
LORD: and he brought the shadow ten degrees backward, by which it had gone
down in the dial of Ahaz.
12 At that time Berodach-baladan, the
son of Baladan, king of Babylon, sent letters and a present unto Hezekiah: for he
had heard that Hezekiah had been sick.
13 And Hezekiah hearkened unto them,
and shewed them all the house of his precious things, the silver, and the gold, and
the spices, and the precious ointment, and
all the house of his armour, and all that
was found in his treasures: there was nothing in his house, nor in all his dominion,
that Hezekiah shewed them not.
14 Then came Isaiah the prophet unto
king Hezekiah, and said unto him, What
said these men? and from whence came
they unto thee? And Hezekiah said, They
are come from a far country, *even* from
Babylon.
15 And he said, What have they seen in
thine house? And Hezekiah answered, All
the things that *are* in mine house have they
seen: there is nothing among my treasures
that I have not shewed them.
16 And Isaiah said unto Hezekiah, Hear
the word of the LORD.
17 Behold, the days come, that all that *is*
in thine house,and that which thy fathers
have laid up in store unto this day, shall
be carried into Babylon: nothing shall be
left, saith the LORD.
18 And of thy sons that shall issue from
thee, which thou shalt beget, shall they
take away; and they shall be eunuchs in
the palace of the king of Babylon.
19 Then said Hezekiah unto Isaiah, Good
is the word of the LORD which thou hast
spoken. And he said, *Is it* not *good,* if peace
and truth be in my days?
20 And the rest of the acts of Hezekiah,
and all his might, and how he made a
pool, and a conduit, and brought water
into the city, *are* they not written in the
book of the chronicles of the kings of Judah?
21 And Hezekiah slept with his fathers:
and Manasseh his son reigned in his stead.

21

1 Manasseh *was* twelve years old when
he began to reign, and reigned fifty and
five years in Jerusalem. And his mother's
name *was* Hephzi-bah.
2 And he did *that which was* evil in the
sight of the LORD, after the abominations
of the heathen, whom the LORD cast out
before the children of Israel.
3 For he built up again the high places
which Hezekiah his father had destroyed;
and he reared up altars for Baal, and made
a grove, as did Ahab king of Israel; and
worshipped all the host of heaven, and
served them.
4 And he built altars in the house of the
LORD, of which the LORD said, In Jerusalem will I put my name.
5 And he built altars for all the host of
heaven in the two courts of the house of
the LORD.
6 And he made his son pass through
the fire, and observed times, and used
enchantments, and dealt with familiar
spirits and wizards: he wrought much
wickedness in the sight of the LORD, to provoke *him* to anger.
7 And he set a graven image of the grove
that he had made in the house, of which
the LORD said to David, and to Solomon
his son, In this house, and in Jerusalem,
which I have chosen out of all tribes of
Israel, will I put my name for ever:
8 Neither will I make the feet of Israel
move any more out of the land which I
gave their fathers; only if they will observe
to do according to all that I have commanded them, and according to all the law
that my servant Moses commanded them.
9 But they hearkened not: and Manasseh
seduced them to do more evil than did the
nations whom the LORD destroyed before
the children of Israel.
10 And the LORD spake by his servants the
prophets, saying,
11 Because Manasseh king of Judah hath

done these abominations, *and* hath done wickedly above all that the Amorites did, which *were* before him, and hath made Judah also to sin with his idols:

12 Therefore thus saith the LORD God of Israel, Behold, I *am* bringing *such* evil upon Jerusalem and Judah, that whosoever heareth of it, both his ears shall tingle.

13 And I will stretch over Jerusalem the line of Samaria, and the plummet of the house of Ahab: and I will wipe Jerusalem as *a man* wipeth a dish, wiping *it,* and turning *it* upside down.

14 And I will forsake the remnant of mine inheritance, and deliver them into the hand of their enemies; and they shall become a prey and a spoil to all their enemies;

15 Because they have done *that which was* evil in my sight,and have provoked me to anger, since the day their fathers came forth out of Egypt, even unto this day.

16 Moreover Manasseh shed innocent blood very much, till he had filled Jerusalem from one end to another; beside his sin wherewith he made Judah to sin, in doing *that which was* evil in the sight of the LORD.

17 Now the rest of the acts of Manasseh, and all that he did, and his sin that he sinned, *are* they not written in the book of the chronicles of the kings of Judah?

18 And Manasseh slept with his fathers, and was buried in the garden of his own house, in the garden of Uzza: and Amon his son reigned in his stead.

19 Amon *was* twenty and two years old when he began to reign, and he reigned two years in Jerusalem. And his mother's name *was* Meshullemeth, the daughter of Haruz of Jotbah.

20 And he did *that which was* evil in the sight of the LORD, as his father Manasseh did.

21 And he walked in all the way that his father walked in, and served the idols that his father served, and worshipped them:

22 And he forsook the LORD God of his fathers, and walked not in the way of the LORD.

23 And the servants of Amon conspired against him, and slew the king in his own house.

24 And the people of the land slew all them that had conspired against king Amon; and the people of the land made Josiah his son king in his stead.

25 Now the rest of the acts of Amon which he did, *are* they not written in the book of the chronicles of the kings of Judah?

26 And he was buried in his sepulchre in the garden of Uzza: and Josiah his son reigned in his stead.

22

1 Josiah *was* eight years old when he began to reign, and he reigned thirty and one years in Jerusalem. And his mother's name *was* Jedidah, the daughter of Adaiah of Boscath.

2 And he did *that which was* right in the sight of the LORD, and walked in all the way of David his father, and turned not aside to the right hand or to the left.

3 And it came to pass in the eighteenth year of king Josiah, *that* the king sent Shaphan the son of Azaliah, the son of Meshullam, the scribe, to the house of the LORD, saying,

4 Go up to Hilkiah the high priest, that he may sum the silver which is brought into the house of the LORD, which the keepers of the door have gathered of the people:

5 And let them deliver it into the hand of the doers of the work, that have the oversight of the house of the LORD: and let them give it to the doers of the work which *is* in the house of the LORD, to repair the breaches of the house,

6 Unto carpenters, and builders, and masons, and to buy timber and hewn stone to repair the house.

7 Howbeit there was no reckoning made with them of the money that was delivered into their hand, because they dealt faithfully.

8 And Hilkiah the high priest said unto Shaphan the scribe, I have found the book of the law in the house of the LORD. And Hilkiah gave the book to Shaphan, and he read it.

9 And Shaphan the scribe came to the king, and brought the king word again, and said, Thy servants have gathered the money that was found in the house, and have delivered it into the hand of them that do the work, that have the oversight of the house of the LORD.

10 And Shaphan the scribe shewed the king, saying, Hilkiah the priest hath deliv-

ered me a book. And Shaphan read it before the king.

11 And it came to pass, when the king had heard the words of the book of the law, that he rent his clothes.

12 And the king commanded Hilkiah the priest, and Ahikam the son of Shaphan, and Achbor the son of Michaiah, and Shaphan the scribe, and Asahiah a servant of the king's, saying,

13 Go ye, enquire of the LORD for me, and for the people, and for all Judah, concerning the words of this book that is found: for great *is* the wrath of the LORD that is kindled against us, because our fathers have not hearkened unto the words of this book, to do according unto all that which is written concerning us.

> **22:13**
> **God's Anger**
> ◄ Psalm 2:12 ►

14 So Hilkiah the priest, and Ahikam, and Achbor, and Shaphan, and Asahiah, went unto Huldah the prophetess, the wife of Shallum the son of Tikvah, the son of Harhas, keeper of the wardrobe; (now she dwelt in Jerusalem in the college;) and they communed with her.

15 And she said unto them, Thus saith the LORD God of Israel, Tell the man that sent you to me,

16 Thus saith the LORD, Behold, I will bring evil upon this place, and upon the inhabitants thereof, *even* all the words of the book which the king of Judah hath read:

17 Because they have forsaken me, and have burned incense unto other gods, that they might provoke me to anger with all the works of their hands; therefore my wrath shall be kindled against this place, and shall not be quenched.

18 But to the king of Judah which sent you to enquire of the LORD, thus shall ye say to him, Thus saith the LORD God of Israel, *As touching* the words which thou hast heard;

19 Because thine heart was tender, and thou hast humbled thyself before the LORD, when thou heardest what I spake against this place, and against the inhabitants thereof, that they should become a desolation and a curse, and hast rent thy clothes, and wept before me; I also have heard *thee,* saith the LORD.

20 Behold therefore, I will gather thee unto thy fathers, and thou shalt be gathered into thy grave in peace; and thine eyes shall not see all the evil which I will bring upon this place. And they brought the king word again.

23

1 And the king sent, and they gathered unto him all the elders of Judah and of Jerusalem.

2 And the king went up into the house of the LORD, and all the men of Judah and all the inhabitants of Jerusalem with him, and the priests, and the prophets, and all the people, both small and great: and he read in their ears all the words of the book of the covenant which was found in the house of the LORD.

3 And the king stood by a pillar, and made a covenant before the LORD, to walk after the LORD, and to keep his commandments and his testimonies and his statutes with all *their* heart and all *their* soul, to perform the words of this covenant that were written in this book. And all the people stood to the covenant.

> **23:3 Walking with God**
> ◄ Genesis 6:9
> Micah 4:5 ►

4 And the king commanded Hilkiah the high priest, and the priests of the second order, and the keepers of the door, to bring forth out of the temple of the LORD all the vessels that were made for Baal, and for the grove, and for all the host of heaven: and he burned them without Jerusalem in the fields of Kidron, and carried the ashes of them unto Bethel.

5 And he put down the idolatrous priests, whom the kings of Judah had ordained to burn incense in the high places in the cities of Judah, and in the places round about Jerusalem; them also that burned incense unto Baal, to the sun, and to the moon, and to the planets, and to all the host of heaven.

6 And he brought out the grove from the house of the LORD, without Jerusalem, unto the brook Kidron, and burned it at the brook Kidron, and stamped *it* small to powder, and cast the powder thereof upon the graves of the children of the people.

7 And he brake down the houses of the sodomites, that *were* by the house of the LORD, where the women wove hangings for the grove.

8 And he brought all the priests out of the cities of Judah, and defiled the high places where the priests had burned incense, from Geba to Beer-sheba, and brake down the high places of the gates that *were* in the entering in of the gate of Joshua the governor of the city, which *were* on a man's left hand at the gate of the city.

9 Nevertheless the priests of the high places came not up to the altar of the LORD in Jerusalem, but they did eat of the unleavened bread among their brethren.

10 And he defiled Topheth, which *is* in the valley of the children of Hinnom, that no man might make his son or his daughter to pass through the fire to Molech.

11 And he took away the horses that the kings of Judah had given to the sun, at the entering in of the house of the LORD, by the chamber of Nathan-melech the chamberlain, which *was* in the suburbs, and burned the chariots of the sun with fire.

12 And the altars that *were* on the top of the upper chamber of Ahaz, which the kings of Judah had made, and the altars which Manasseh had made in the two courts of the house of the LORD, did the king beat down, and brake *them* down from thence, and cast the dust of them into the brook Kidron.

13 And the high places that *were* before Jerusalem, which *were* on the right hand of the mount of corruption, which Solomon the king of Israel had builded for Ashtoreth the abomination of the Zidonians, and for Chemosh the abomination of the Moabites, and for Milcom the abomination of the children of Ammon, did the king defile.

14 And he brake in pieces the images, and cut down the groves, and filled their places with the bones of men.

15 Moreover the altar that *was* at Bethel, *and* the high place which Jeroboam the son of Nebat, who made Israel to sin, had made, both that altar and the high place he brake down, and burned the high place, *and* stamped *it* small to powder, and burned the grove.

16 And as Josiah turned himself, he spied the sepulchres that *were* there in the mount, and sent, and took the bones out of the sepulchres, and burned *them* upon the altar, and polluted it, according to the word of the LORD which the man of God proclaimed, who proclaimed these words.

17 Then he said, What title *is* that that I see? And the men of the city told him, *It is* the sepulchre of the man of God, which came from Judah, and proclaimed these things that thou hast done against the altar of Bethel.

18 And he said, Let him alone; let no man move his bones. So they let his bones alone, with the bones of the prophet that came out of Samaria.

19 And all the houses also of the high places that *were* in the cities of Samaria, which the kings of Israel had made to provoke *the* LORD to anger, Josiah took away, and did to them according to all the acts that he had done in Bethel.

20 And he slew all the priests of the high places that *were* there upon the altars, and burned men's bones upon them, and returned to Jerusalem.

21 And the king commanded all the people, saying, Keep the passover unto the LORD your God, as *it is* written in the book of this covenant.

22 Surely there was not holden such a passover from the days of the judges that judged Israel, nor in all the days of the kings of Israel, nor of the kings of Judah;

23 But in the eighteenth year of king Josiah, *wherein* this passover was holden to the LORD in Jerusalem.

24 Moreover the *workers with* familiar spirits, and the wizards, and the images, and the idols, and all the abominations that were spied in the land of Judah and in Jerusalem, did Josiah put away, that he might perform the words of the law which were written in the book that Hilkiah the priest found in the house of the LORD.

25 And like unto him was there no king before him, that turned to the LORD with all his heart, and with all his soul, and with all his might, according to all the law of Moses; neither after him arose there *any* like him.

26 Notwithstanding the LORD turned not from the fierceness of his great wrath, wherewith his anger was kindled against Judah, because of all the provocations that Manasseh had provoked him withal.

27 And the LORD said, I will remove Judah also out of my sight, as I have removed Israel, and will cast off this city Jerusalem

which I have chosen, and the house of
which I said, My name shall be there.
28 Now the rest of the acts of Josiah, and
all that he did, *are* they not written in the
book of the chronicles of the kings of
Judah?
29 In his days Pharaoh-nechoh king of
Egypt went up against the king of Assyria
to the river Euphrates: and king Josiah
went against him; and he slew him at Megiddo, when he had seen him.
30 And his servants carried him in a chariot dead from Megiddo, and brought him
to Jerusalem, and buried him in his own
sepulchre. And the people of the land took
Jehoahaz the son of Josiah, and anointed
him, and made him king in his father's
stead.
31 Jehoahaz *was* twenty and three years
old when he began to reign; and he reigned
three months in Jerusalem. And his
mother's name *was* Hamutal, the daughter of Jeremiah of Libnah.
32 And he did *that which was* evil in the
sight of the LORD, according to all that his
fathers had done.
33 And Pharaoh-nechoh put him in
bands at Riblah in the land of Hamath,
that he might not reign in Jerusalem; and
put the land to a tribute of an hundred
talents of silver, and a talent of gold.
34 And Pharaoh-nechoh made Eliakim
the son of Josiah king in the room of Josiah his father, and turned his name to Jehoiakim, and took Jehoahaz away: and he
came to Egypt, and died there.
35 And Jehoiakim gave the silver and the
gold to Pharaoh; but he taxed the land to
give the money according to the commandment of Pharaoh: he exacted the silver and the gold of the people of the land,
of every one according to his taxation, to
give *it* unto Pharaoh-nechoh.
36 Jehoiakim *was* twenty and five years
old when he began to reign; and he reigned
eleven years in Jerusalem. And his mother's
name *was* Zebudah, the daughter of Pedaiah of Rumah.
37 And he did *that which was* evil in the
sight of the LORD, according to all that his
fathers had done.

24

1 In his days Nebuchadnezzar king of
Babylon came up, and Jehoiakim became
his servant three years: then he turned and
rebelled against him.
2 And the LORD sent against him bands
of the Chaldees, and bands of the Syrians,
and bands of the Moabites, and bands of
the children of Ammon, and sent them
against Judah to destroy it, according to
the word of the LORD, which he spake by
his servants the prophets.
3 Surely at the commandment of the
LORD came *this* upon Judah, to remove
them out of his sight, for the sins of Manasseh, according to all that he did;
4 And also for the innocent blood that
he shed: for he filled Jerusalem with innocent blood; which the LORD would not
pardon.
5 Now the rest of the acts of Jehoiakim,
and all that he did, *are* they not written in
the book of the chronicles of the kings of
Judah?
6 So Jehoiakim slept with his fathers: and
Jehoiachin his son reigned in his stead.
7 And the king of Egypt came not again
any more out of his land: for the king of
Babylon had taken from the river of Egypt
unto the river Euphrates all that pertained
to the king of Egypt.
8 Jehoiachin *was* eighteen years old when
he began to reign, and he reigned in Jerusalem three months. And his mother's
name *was* Nehushta, the daughter of Elnathan of Jerusalem.
9 And he did *that which was* evil in the
sight of the LORD, according to all that his
father had done.
10 At that time the servants of Nebuchadnezzar king of Babylon came up against
Jerusalem, and the city was besieged.
11 And Nebuchadnezzar king of Babylon
came against the city, and his servants did
besiege it.
12 And Jehoiachin the king of Judah went
out to the king of Babylon, he, and his
mother, and his servants, and his princes,
and his officers: and the king of Babylon
took him in the eighth year of his reign.
13 And he carried out thence all the treasures of the house of the LORD, and the
treasures of the king's house, and cut in
pieces all the vessels of gold which Solomon king of Israel had made in the temple of the LORD, as the LORD had said.
14 And he carried away all Jerusalem, and
all the princes, and all the mighty men of
valour, *even* ten thousand captives, and all
the craftsmen and smiths: none remained,

save the poorest sort of the people of the
land.
15And he carried away Jehoiachin to
Babylon, and the king's mother, and the
king's wives, and his officers, and the
mighty of the land, *those* carried he into
captivity from Jerusalem to Babylon.
16And all the men of might, *even* seven
thousand, and craftsmen and smiths a
thousand, all *that were* strong *and* apt for
war, even them the king of Babylon
brought captive to Babylon.
17And the king of Babylon made Mattaniah his father's brother king in his stead,
and changed his name to Zedekiah.
18Zedekiah *was* twenty and one years old
when he began to reign, and he reigned
eleven years in Jerusalem. And his mother's
name *was* Hamutal, the daughter of Jeremiah of Libnah.
19And he did *that which was* evil in the
sight of the LORD, according to all that Jehoiakim had done.
20For through the anger of the LORD it
came to pass in Jerusalem and Judah, until he had cast them out from his presence,
that Zedekiah rebelled against the king of
Babylon.

25

1And it came to pass in the ninth year
of his reign, in the tenth month, in the
tenth *day* of the month, *that* Nebuchadnezzar king of Babylon came, he, and all
his host, against Jerusalem, and pitched
against it; and they built forts against it
round about.
2And the city was besieged unto the eleventh year of king Zedekiah.
3And on the ninth *day* of the *fourth*
month the famine prevailed in the city, and
there was no bread for the people of the
land.
4And the city was broken up, and all the
men of war *fled* by night by the way of
the gate between two walls, which *is* by
the king's garden: (now the Chaldees *were*
against the city round about:) and *the king*
went the way toward the plain.
5And the army of the Chaldees pursued
after the king, and overtook him in the
plains of Jericho: and all his army were
scattered from him.
6So they took the king, and brought him
up to the king of Babylon to Riblah; and
they gave judgment upon him.
7And they slew the sons of Zedekiah
before his eyes, and put out the eyes of
Zedekiah, and bound him with fetters of
brass, and carried him to Babylon.
8And in the fifth month, on the seventh
day of the month, which *is* the nineteenth
year of king Nebuchadnezzar king of Babylon, came Nebuzar-adan, captain of the
guard, a servant of the king of Babylon,
unto Jerusalem:
9And he burnt the house of the LORD,
and the king's house, and all the houses
of Jerusalem, and every great *man's* house
burnt he with fire.
10And all the army of the Chaldees, that
were with the captain of the guard, brake
down the walls of Jerusalem round about.
11Now the rest of the people *that were*
left in the city, and the fugitives that fell
away to the king of Babylon, with the remnant of the multitude, did Nebuzar-adan
the captain of the guard carry away.
12But the captain of the guard left of the
poor of the land *to be* vinedressers and
husbandmen.
13And the pillars of brass that *were* in
the house of the LORD, and the bases,
and the brasen sea that *was* in the house
of the LORD, did the Chaldees break in
pieces, and carried the brass of them to
Babylon.
14And the pots, and the shovels, and the
snuffers, and the spoons, and all the vessels of brass wherewith they ministered,
took they away.
15And the firepans, and the bowls, *and*
such things as *were* of gold, *in* gold, and of
silver, *in* silver, the captain of the guard
took away.
16The two pillars, one sea, and the bases which Solomon had made for the house
of the LORD; the brass of all these vessels
was without weight.
17The height of the one pillar *was* eighteen cubits, and the chapiter upon it *was*
brass: and the height of the chapiter three
cubits; and the wreathen work, and pomegranates upon the chapiter round about,
all of brass: and like unto these had the
second pillar with wreathen work.
18And the captain of the guard took
Seraiah the chief priest, and Zephaniah the
second priest, and the three keepers of the
door:
19And out of the city he took an officer
that was set over the men of war, and five

men of them that were in the king's presence, which were found in the city, and
the principal scribe of the host, which
mustered the people of the land, and threescore men of the people of the land *that*
were found in the city:
20 And Nebuzar-adan captain of the
guard took these, and brought them to the
king of Babylon to Riblah:
21 And the king of Babylon smote them,
and slew them at Riblah in the land of
Hamath. So Judah was carried away out
of their land.
22 And *as for* the people that remained
in the land of Judah, whom Nebuchadnezzar king of Babylon had left, even over
them he made Gedaliah the son of Ahikam, the son of Shaphan, ruler.
23 And when all the captains of the armies, they and their men, heard that the
king of Babylon had made Gedaliah governor, there came to Gedaliah to Mizpah,
even Ishmael the son of Nethaniah, and
Johanan the son of Careah, and Seraiah
the son of Tanhumeth the Netophathite,
and Jaazaniah the son of a Maachathite,
they and their men.
24 And Gedaliah sware to them, and to
their men, and said unto them, Fear not
to be the servants of the Chaldees: dwell
in the land, and serve the king of Babylon;
and it shall be well with you.
25 But it came to pass in the seventh
month, that Ishmael the son of Nethaniah, the son of Elishama, of the seed royal,
came, and ten men with him, and smote
Gedaliah, that he died, and the Jews and
the Chaldees that were with him at Mizpah.
26 And all the people, both small and
great, and the captains of the armies, arose,
and came to Egypt: for they were afraid of
the Chaldees.
27 And it came to pass in the seven and
thirtieth year of the captivity of Jehoiachin
king of Judah, in the twelfth month, on
the seven and twentieth *day* of the month,
that Evil-merodach king of Babylon in the
year that he began to reign did lift up the
head of Jehoiachin king of Judah out of
prison;
28 And he spake kindly to him, and set
his throne above the throne of the kings
that *were* with him in Babylon;
29 And changed his prison garments: and
he did eat bread continually before him
all the days of his life.
30 And his allowance *was* a continual allowance given him of the king, a daily rate
for every day, all the days of his life.

1 Chronicles

AUTHOR
Probably Ezra the scribe

MAIN POINT
There has been one God from the begininning, who established Israel's one true heritage and continued it through David's line.

DATE WRITTEN
Approximately 430 B.C.

29 CHAPTERS

MAIN PEOPLE

David, Solomon

SPECIAL FEATURES

- *Was originally one book with 2 Chronicles*
- *Comments on the events of 1 and 2 Samuel, telling about Israel's faith more than politics*
- *Has the Bible's longest genealogy*
- *Tells how David organized dozens of priests and their duties*
- *Explains why David, who wanted to build a temple to replace the tabernacle, had to let his son Solomon do it*
- *Eighth book of History*

HOW THE BOOK GOT ITS NAME

When Jerome translated the book from Hebrew into Latin, he proclaimed it "the chronicle of the whole of sacred history" (the Hebrew name means "journals").

1

1Adam, Sheth, Enosh,
2Kenan, Mahalaleel, Jered,
3Henoch, Methuselah, Lamech,
4Noah, Shem, Ham, and Japheth.
5The sons of Japheth; Gomer, and Magog, and Madai, and Javan, and Tubal, and
Meshech, and Tiras.
6And the sons of Gomer; Ashchenaz,
and Riphath, and Togarmah.
7And the sons of Javan; Elishah, and Tarshish, Kittim, and Dodanim.
8The sons of Ham; Cush, and Mizraim,
Put, and Canaan.
9And the sons of Cush; Seba, and Havilah, and Sabta, and Raamah, and Sabtecha.
And the sons of Raamah; Sheba, and Dedan.
10And Cush begat Nimrod: he began to
be mighty upon the earth.
11And Mizraim begat Ludim, and Anamim, and Lehabim, and Napthtuhim,
12And Pathrusim, and Casluhim, (of
whom came the Philistines,) and Caph-
thorim.
13And Canaan begat Zidon his firstborn,
and Heth,
14The Jebusite also, and the Amorite,
and the Girgashite,
15And the Hivite, and the Arkite, and the
Sinite,

16 And the Arvadite, and the Zemarite,
and the Hamathite.
17 The sons of Shem; Elam, and Asshur,
and Arphaxad, and Lud, and Aram, and
Uz, and Hul, and Gether, and Meshech.
18 And Arphaxad begat Shelah, and Shelah begat Eber.
19 And unto Eber were born two sons:
the name of the one *was* Peleg; because in
his days the earth was divided: and his
brother's name *was* Joktan.
20 And Joktan begat Almodad, and She-
leph, and Hazarmaveth, and Jerah,
21 Hadoram also, and Uzal, and Diklah,
22 And Ebal, and Abimael, and Sheba,
23 And Ophir, and Havilah, and Jobab.
All these *were* the sons of Joktan.
24 Shem, Arphaxad, Shelah,
25 Eber, Peleg, Reu,
26 Serug, Nahor, Terah,
27 Abram; the same *is* Abraham.
28 The sons of Abraham; Isaac, and Ishmael.
29 These *are* their generations: The firstborn of Ishmael, Nebaioth; then Kedar,
and Adbeel, and Mibsam,
30 Mishma and Dumah, Massa, Hadad,
and Tema,
31 Jetur, Naphish, and Kedemah. These
are the sons of Ishmael.
32 Now the sons of Keturah, Abraham's
concubine: she bare Zimran, and Jokshan,
and Medan, and Midian, and Ishbak, and
Shuah. And the sons of Jokshan; Sheba,
and Dedan.
33 And the sons of Midian; Ephah, and
Epher, and Henoch, and Abida, and Eldaah. All these *are* the sons of Keturah.
34 And Abraham begat Isaac. The sons
of Isaac; Esau and Israel.
35 The sons of Esau; Eliphaz, Reuel, and
Jeush, and Jaalam, and Korah.
36 The sons of Eliphaz; Teman, and
Omar, Zephi, and Gatam, Kenaz, and Timna, and Amalek.
37 The sons of Reuel; Nahath, Zerah,
Shammah, and Mizzah.
38 And the sons of Seir; Lotan, and Shobal, and Zibeon, and Anah, and Dishon,
and Ezar, and Dishan.
39 And the sons of Lotan; Hori, and Ho-
mam: and Timna *was* Lotan's sister.
40 The sons of Shobal; Alian, and Manahath, and Ebal, Shephi, and Onam. And
the sons of Zibeon; Aiah, and Anah.
41 The sons of Anah; Dishon. And the
sons of Dishon; Amram, and Eshban, and
Ithran, and Cheran.
42 The sons of Ezer; Bilhan, and Zavan,
and Jakan. The sons of Dishan; Uz, and
Aran.
43 Now these *are* the kings that reigned
in the land of Edom before *any* king
reigned over the children of Israel; Bela the
son of Beor: and the name of his city *was*
Dinhabah.
44 And when Bela was dead, Jobab the
son of Zerah of Bozrah reigned in his stead.
45 And when Jobab was dead, Husham
of the land of the Temanites reigned in his
stead.
46 And when Husham was dead, Hadad
the son of Bedad, which smote Midian
in the field of Moab, reigned in his stead:
and the name of his city *was* Avith.
47 And when Hadad was dead, Samlah
of Masrekah reigned in his stead.
48 And when Samlah was dead, Shaul of
Rehoboth by the river reigned in his stead.
49 And when Shaul was dead, Baal-hanan
the son of Achbor reigned in his stead.
50 And when Baal-hanan was dead, Hadad reigned in his stead: and the name of
his city *was* Pai; and his wife's name *was*
Mehetabel, the daughter of Matred, the
daughter of Mezahab.
51 Hadad died also. And the dukes of
Edom were; duke Timnah, duke Aliah,
duke Jetheth,
52 Duke Aholibamah, duke Elah, duke
Pinon,
53 Duke Kenaz, duke Teman, duke
Mibzar,
54 Duke Magdiel, duke Iram. These *are*
the dukes of Edom.

2

1 These *are* the sons of Israel; Reuben,
Simeon, Levi, and Judah, Issachar, and
Zebulun,
2 Dan, Joseph, and Benjamin, Naphtali,
Gad, and Asher.
3 The sons of Judah; Er, and Onan, and
Shelah: *which* three were born unto him
of the daughter of Shua the Canaanitess.
And Er, the firstborn of Judah, was evil in
the sight of the LORD; and he slew him.
4 And Tamar his daughter in law bare
him Pharez and Zerah. All the sons of
Judah *were* five.
5 The sons of Pharez; Hezron, and
Hamul.

6 And the sons of Zerah; Zimri, and Ethan, and Heman, and Calcol, and Dara: five of them in all.

7 And the sons of Carmi; Achar, the troubler of Israel, who transgressed in the thing accursed.

8 And the sons of Ethan; Azariah.

9 The sons also of Hezron, that were born unto him; Jerahmeel, and Ram, and Chelubai.

10 And Ram begat Amminadab; and Amminadab begat Nahshon, prince of the children of Judah;

11 And Nahshon begat Salma, and Salma begat Boaz,

12 And Boaz begat Obed, and Obed begat Jesse,

13 And Jesse begat his firstborn Eliab, and Abinadab the second, and Shimma the third,

14 Nethaneel the fourth, Raddai the fifth,

15 Ozem the sixth, David the seventh:

16 Whose sisters *were* Zeruiah, and Abigail. And the sons of Zeruiah; Abishai, and Joab, and Asahel, three.

17 And Abigail bare Amasa: and the father of Amasa *was* Jether the Ishmeelite.

18 And Caleb the son of Hezron begat *children* of Azubah *his* wife, and of Jerioth: her sons *are* these; Jesher, and Shobab, and Ardon.

19 And when Azubah was dead, Caleb took unto him Ephrath, which bare him Hur.

20 And Hur begat Uri, and Uri begat Bezaleel.

21 And afterward Hezron went in to the daughter of Machir the father of Gilead, whom he married when he *was* threescore years old; and she bare him Segub.

22 And Segub begat Jair, who had three and twenty cities in the land of Gilead.

23 And he took Geshur, and Aram, with the towns of Jair, from them, with Kenath, and the towns thereof, *even* threescore cities. All these *belonged to* the sons of Machir the father of Gilead.

24 And after that Hezron was dead in Caleb-ephratah, then Abiah Hezron's wife bare him Ashur the father of Tekoa.

25 And the sons of Jerahmeel the firstborn of Hezron were, Ram the firstborn, and Bunah, and Oren, and Ozem, *and* Ahijah.

26 Jerahmeel had also another wife, whose name *was* Atarah; she *was* the mother of Onam.

27 And the sons of Ram the firstborn of Jerahmeel were, Maaz, and Jamin, and Eker.

28 And the sons of Onam were, Shammai, and Jada. And the sons of Shammai; Nadab, and Abishur.

29 And the name of the wife of Abishur *was* Abihail, and she bare him Ahban, and Molid.

30 And the sons of Nadab; Seled, and Appaim: but Seled died without children.

31 And the sons of Appaim; Ishi. And the sons of Ishi; Sheshan. And the children of Sheshan; Ahlai.

32 And the sons of Jada the brother of Shammai; Jether and Jonathan: and Jether died without children.

33 And the sons of Jonathan; Peleth, and Zaza. These were the sons of Jerahmeel.

34 Now Sheshan had no sons, but daughters. And Sheshan had a servant, an Egyptian, whose name *was* Jarha.

35 And Sheshan gave his daughter to Jarha his servant to wife; and she bare him Attai.

36 And Attai begat Nathan, and Nathan begat Zabad,

37 And Zabad begat Ephlal, and Ephlal begat Obed,

38 And Obed begat Jehu, and Jehu begat Azariah,

39 And Azariah begat Helez, and Helez begat Eleasah,

40 And Eleasah begat Sisamai, and Sisamai begat Shallum,

41 And Shallum begat Jekamiah, and Jekamiah begat Elishama.

42 Now the sons of Caleb the brother of Jerahmeel *were*, Mesha his firstborn, which *was* the father of Ziph; and the sons of Mareshah the father of Hebron.

43 And the sons of Hebron; Korah, and Tappuah, and Rekem, and Shema.

44 And Shema begat Raham, the father of Jorkoam: and Rekem begat Shammai.

45 And the son of Shammai *was* Maon: and Maon *was* the father of Beth-zur.

46 And Ephah, Caleb's concubine, bare Haran, and Moza, and Gazez: and Haran begat Gazez.

47 And the sons of Jahdai; Regem, and Jotham, and Gesham, and Pelet, and Ephah, and Shaaph.

48 Maachah, Caleb's concubine, bare Sheber, and Tirhanah.

49 She bare also Shaaph the father of Madmannah, Sheva the father of Machbenah, and the father of Gibea: and the daughter of Caleb *was* Achsa.

50 These were the sons of Caleb the son of Hur, the firstborn of Ephratah; Shobal the father of Kirjath-jearim,

51 Salma the father of Bethlehem, Hareph the father of Beth-gader.

52 And Shobal the father of Kirjath-jearim had sons; Haroeh, *and* half of the Manahethites.

53 And the families of Kirjath-jearim; the Ithrites, and the Puhites, and the Shumathites, and the Mishraites; of them came the Zareathites, and the Eshtaulites.

54 The sons of Salma; Bethlehem, and the Netophathites, Ataroth, the house of Joab, and half of the Manahethites, the Zorites.

55 And the families of the scribes which dwelt at Jabez; the Tirathites, the Shimeathites, *and* Suchathites. These *are* the Kenites that came of Hemath, the father of the house of Rechab.

3

1 Now these were the sons of David, which were born unto him in Hebron; the firstborn Amnon, of Ahinoam the Jezreelitess; the second Daniel, of Abigail the Carmelitess:

2 The third, Absalom the son of Maachah the daughter of Talmai king of Geshur: the fourth, Adonijah the son of Haggith:

3 The fifth, Shephatiah of Abital: the sixth, Ithream by Eglah his wife.

4 *These* six were born unto him in Hebron; and there he reigned seven years and six months: and in Jerusalem he reigned thirty and three years.

5 And these were born unto him in Jerusalem; Shimea, and Shobab, and Nathan, and Solomon, four, of Bath-shua the daughter of Ammiel:

6 Ibhar also, and Elishama, and Eliphelet,

7 And Nogah, and Nepheg, and Japhia,

8 And Elishama, and Eliada, and Eliphelet, nine.

9 *These were* all the sons of David, beside the sons of the concubines, and Tamar their sister.

10 And Solomon's son *was* Rehoboam, Abia his son, Asa his son, Jehoshaphat his son,

11 Joram his son, Ahaziah his son, Joash his son,

12 Amaziah his son, Azariah his son, Jotham his son,

13 Ahaz his son, Hezekiah his son, Manasseh his son,

14 Amon his son, Josiah his son.

15 And the sons of Josiah *were,* the firstborn Johanan, the second Jehoiakim, the third Zedekiah, the fourth Shallum.

16 And the sons of Jehoiakim: Jeconiah his son, Zedekiah his son.

17 And the sons of Jeconiah; Assir, Salathiel his son,

18 Malchiram also, and Pedaiah, and Shenazar, Jecamiah, Hoshama, and Nedabiah.

19 And the sons of Pedaiah *were,* Zerubbabel, and Shimei: and the sons of Zerubbabel; Meshullam, and Hananiah, and Shelomith their sister:

20 And Hashubah, and Ohel, and Berechiah, and Hasadiah, Jushab-hesed, five.

21 And the sons of Hananiah; Pelatiah, and Jesaiah: the sons of Rephaiah, the sons of Arnan, the sons of Obadiah, the sons of Shechaniah.

22 And the sons of Shechaniah; Shemaiah; and the sons of Shemaiah; Hattush, and Igeal, and Bariah, and Neariah, and Shaphat, six.

23 And the sons of Neariah; Elioenai, and Hezekiah, and Azrikam, three.

24 And the sons of Elioenai *were,* Hodaiah, and Eliashib, and Pelaiah, and Akkub, and Johanan, and Dalaiah, and Anani, seven.

4

1 The sons of Judah; Pharez, Hezron, and Carmi, and Hur, and Shobal.

2 And Reaiah the son of Shobal begat Jahath; and Jahath begat Ahumai and Lahad. These *are* the families of the Zorathites.

3 And these *were of* the father of Etam; Jezreel, and Ishma, and Idbash: and the name of their sister *was* Hazelelponi:

4 And Penuel the father of Gedor and Ezer the father of Hushah. These *are* the sons of Hur, the firstborn of Ephratah, the father of Bethlehem.

5 And Ashur the father of Tekoa had two wives, Helah and Naarah.

6 And Naarah bare him Ahuzam, and Hepher, and Temeni, and Haahashtari. These *were* the sons of Naarah.

7And the sons of Helah *were,* Zereth, and Jezoar, and Ethnan.

8And Coz begat Anub, and Zobebah, and the families of Aharhel the son of Harum.

9And Jabez was more honourable than his brethren: and his mother called his name Jabez, saying, Because I bare him with sorrow.

10And Jabez called on the God of Israel, saying, Oh that thou wouldest bless me indeed, and enlarge my coast, and that thine hand might be with me, and that thou wouldest keep *me* from evil, that it may not grieve me! And God granted him that which he requested.

4:10 Who Is Religious?
◄ Genesis 6:9
2 Chronicles 31:20 ►

11And Chelub the brother of Shuah begat Mehir, which *was* the father of Eshton.

12And Eshton begat Beth-rapha, and Paseah, and Tehinnah the father of Irnahash. These *are* the men of Rechah.

13And the sons of Kenaz; Othniel, and Seraiah: and the sons of Othniel; Hathath.

14And Meonothai begat Ophrah: and Seraiah begat Joab, the father of the valley of Charashim; for they were craftsmen.

15And the sons of Caleb the son of Jephunneh; Iru, Elah, and Naam: and the sons of Elah, even Kenaz.

16And the sons of Jehaleleel; Ziph, and Ziphah, Tiria, and Asareel.

17And the sons of Ezra *were,* Jether, and Mered, and Epher, and Jalon: and she bare Miriam, and Shammai, and Ishbah the father of Eshtemoa.

18And his wife Jehudijah bare Jered the father of Gedor, and Heber the father of Socho, and Jekuthiel the father of Zanoah. And these *are* the sons of Bithiah the daughter of Pharaoh, which Mered took.

19And the sons of *his* wife Hodiah the sister of Naham, the father of Keilah the Garmite, and Eshtemoa the Maachathite.

20And the sons of Shimon *were,* Amnon, and Rinnah, Ben-hanan, and Tilon. And the sons of Ishi *were,* Zoheth, and Benzoheth.

21The sons of Shelah the son of Judah *were,* Er the father of Lecah, and Laadah the father of Mareshah, and the families of the house of them that wrought fine linen, of the house of Ashbea,

22And Jokim, and the men of Chozeba, and Joash, and Saraph, who had the dominion in Moab, and Jashubi-lehem. And *these are* ancient things.

23These *were* the potters, and those that dwelt among plants and hedges: there they dwelt with the king for his work.

24The sons of Simeon *were,* Nemuel, and Jamin, Jarib, Zerah, *and* Shaul:

25Shallum his son, Mibsam his son, Mishma his son.

26And the sons of Mishma; Hamuel his son, Zacchur his son, Shimei his son.

27And Shimei had sixteen sons and six daughters; but his brethren had not many children, neither did all their family multiply, like to the children of Judah.

28And they dwelt at Beer-sheba, and Moladah, and Hazar-shual,

29And at Bilhah, and at Ezem, and at Tolad,

30And at Bethuel, and at Hormah, and at Ziklag,

31And at Beth-marcaboth, and Hazarsusim, and at Beth-birei, and at Shaaraim. These *were* their cities unto the reign of David.

32And their villages *were,* Etam, and Ain, Rimmon, and Tochen, and Ashan, five cities:

33And all their villages that *were* round about the same cities, unto Baal. These *were* their habitations, and their genealogy.

34And Meshobab, and Jamlech, and Joshah the son of Amaziah,

35And Joel, and Jehu the son of Josibiah, the son of Seraiah, the son of Asiel,

36And Elioenai, and Jaakobah, and Jeshohaiah, and Asaiah, and Adiel, and Jesimiel, and Benaiah,

37And Ziza the son of Shiphi, the son of Allon, the son of Jedaiah, the son of Shimri, the son of Shemaiah;

38These mentioned by *their* names *were* princes in their families: and the house of their fathers increased greatly.

39And they went to the entrance of Gedor, *even* unto the east side of the valley, to seek pasture for their flocks.

40And they found fat pasture and good, and the land *was* wide, and quiet, and peaceable; for *they* of Ham had dwelt there of old.

41 And these written by name came in the days of Hezekiah king of Judah, and smote their tents, and the habitations that were found there, and destroyed them utterly unto this day, and dwelt in their rooms: because *there was* pasture there for their flocks.

42 And *some* of them, *even* of the sons of Simeon, five hundred men, went to mount Seir, having for their captains Pelatiah, and Neariah, and Rephaiah, and Uzziel, the sons of Ishi.

43 And they smote the rest of the Amalekites that were escaped, and dwelt there unto this day.

5

1 Now the sons of Reuben the firstborn of Israel, (for he *was* the firstborn; but, forasmuch as he defiled his father's bed, his birthright was given unto the sons of Joseph the son of Israel: and the genealogy is not to be reckoned after the birthright.

2 For Judah prevailed above his brethren, and of him *came* the chief ruler; but the birthright *was* Joseph's:)

3 The sons, *I say,* of Reuben the firstborn of Israel *were,* Hanoch, and Pallu, Hezron, and Carmi.

4 The sons of Joel; Shemaiah his son, Gog his son, Shimei his son,

5 Micah his son, Reaia his son, Baal his son,

6 Beerah his son, whom Tilgath-pilneser king of Assyria carried away *captive:* he *was* prince of the Reubenites.

7 And his brethren by their families, when the genealogy of their generations was reckoned, *were* the chief, Jeiel, and Zechariah,

8 And Bela the son of Azaz, the son of Shema, the son of Joel, who dwelt in Aroer, even unto Nebo and Baal-meon:

9 And eastward he inhabited unto the entering in of the wilderness from the river Euphrates: because their cattle were multiplied in the *land* of Gilead.

10 And in the days of Saul they made war with the Hagarites, who fell by their hand: and they dwelt in their tents throughout all the east *land* of Gilead.

11 And the children of Gad dwelt over against them, in the land of Bashan unto Salchah:

12 Joel the chief, and Shapham the next, and Jaanai, and Shaphat in Bashan.

13 And their brethren of the house of their fathers *were,* Michael, and Meshullam, and Sheba, and Jorai, and Jachan, and Zia, and Heber, seven.

14 These *are* the children of Abihail the son of Huri, the son of Jaroah, the son of Gilead, the son of Michael, the son of Jeshishai, the son of Jahdo, the son of Buz;

15 Ahi the son of Abdiel, the son of Guni, chief of the house of their fathers.

16 And they dwelt in Gilead in Bashan, and in her towns, and in all the suburbs of Sharon, upon their borders.

17 All these were reckoned by genealogies in the days of Jotham king of Judah, and in the days of Jeroboam king of Israel.

18 The sons of Reuben, and the Gadites, and half the tribe of Manasseh, of valiant men, men able to bear buckler and sword, and to shoot with bow, and skilful in war, *were* four and forty thousand seven hundred and threescore, that went out to the war.

19 And they made war with the Hagarites, with Jetur, and Nephish, and Nodab.

20 And they were helped against them, and the Hagarites were delivered into their hand, and all that *were* with them: for they cried to God in the battle, and he was intreated of them; because they put their trust in him.

21 And they took away their cattle; of their camels fifty thousand, and of sheep two hundred and fifty thousand, and of asses two thousand, and of men an hundred thousand.

22 For there fell down many slain, because the war *was* of God. And they dwelt in their steads until the captivity.

23 And the children of the half tribe of Manasseh dwelt in the land: they increased from Bashan unto Baal-hermon and Senir, and unto mount Hermon.

24 And these *were* the heads of the house of their fathers, even Epher, and Ishi, and Eliel, and Azriel, and Jeremiah, and Hodaviah, and Jahdiel, mighty men of valour, famous men, *and* heads of the house of their fathers.

25 And they transgressed against the God of their fathers, and went a whoring after the gods of the people of the land, whom God destroyed before them.

26 And the God of Israel stirred up the spirit of Pul king of Assyria, and the spirit

of Tilgath-pilneser king of Assyria, and he
carried them away, even the Reubenites,
and the Gadites, and the half tribe of Manasseh, and brought them unto Halah,
and Habor, and Hara, and to the river
Gozan, unto this day.

6

1 The sons of Levi; Gershon, Kohath, and
Merari.
2 And the sons of Kohath; Amram, Izhar, and Hebron, and Uzziel.
3 And the children of Amram; Aaron, and
Moses, and Miriam. The sons also of
Aaron; Nadab, and Abihu, Eleazar, and Ithamar.
4 Eleazar begat Phinehas, Phinehas begat
Abishua,
5 And Abishua begat Bukki, and Bukki
begat Uzzi,
6 And Uzzi begat Zerahiah, and Zerahiah begat Meraioth,
7 Meraioth begat Amariah, and Amariah begat Ahitub,
8 And Ahitub begat Zadok, and Zadok
begat Ahimaaz,
9 And Ahimaaz begat Azariah, and Azariah begat Johanan,
10 And Johanan begat Azariah, (he *it is*
that executed the priest's office in the temple that Solomon built in Jerusalem:)
11 And Azariah begat Amariah, and Amariah begat Ahitub,
12 And Ahitub begat Zadok, and Zadok
begat Shallum,
13 And Shallum begat Hilkiah, and Hilkiah begat Azariah,
14 And Azariah begat Seraiah, and Seraiah begat Jehozadak,
15 And Jehozadak went *into captivity*,
when the LORD carried away Judah and
Jerusalem by the hand of Nebuchadnezzar.
16 The sons of Levi; Gershom, Kohath,
and Merari.
17 And these *be* the names of the sons of
Gershom; Libni, and Shimei.
18 And the sons of Kohath *were*, Amram,
and Izhar, and Hebron, and Uzziel.
19 The sons of Merari; Mahli, and Mushi. And these *are* the families of the Levites according to their fathers.
20 Of Gershom; Libni his son, Jahath his
son, Zimmah his son,
21 Joah his son, Iddo his son, Zerah his
son, Jeaterai his son.
22 The sons of Kohath; Amminadab his
son, Korah his son, Assir his son,
23 Elkanah his son, and Ebiasaph his
son, and Assir his son,
24 Tahath his son, Uriel his son, Uzziah
his son, and Shaul his son.
25 And the sons of Elkanah; Amasai, and
Ahimoth.
26 *As for* Elkanah: the sons of Elkanah;
Zophai his son, and Nahath his son,
27 Eliab his son, Jeroham his son, Elkanah his son.
28 And the sons of Samuel; the firstborn
Vashni, and Abiah.
29 The sons of Merari; Mahli, Libni his
son, Shimei his son, Uzza his son,
30 Shimea his son, Haggiah his son, Asaiah his son.
31 And these *are they* whom David set
over the service of song in the house of
the LORD, after that the ark had rest.
32 And they ministered before the dwelling place of the tabernacle of the congregation with singing, until Solomon had
built the house of the LORD in Jerusalem:
and *then* they waited on their office according to their order.
33 And these *are* they that waited with
their children. Of the sons of the Kohathites: Heman a singer, the son of Joel, the
son of Shemuel,
34 The son of Elkanah, the son of Jeroham, the son of Eliel, the son of Toah,
35 The son of Zuph, the son of Elkanah,
the son of Mahath, the son of Amasai,
36 The son of Elkanah, the son of Joel,
the son of Azariah, the son of Zephaniah,
37 The son of Tahath, the son of Assir,
the son of Ebiasaph, the son of Korah,
38 The son of Izhar, the son of Kohath,
the son of Levi, the son of Israel.
39 And his brother Asaph, who stood on
his right hand, *even* Asaph the son of
Berachiah, the son of Shimea,
40 The son of Michael, the son of Baase-
iah, the son of Malchiah,
41 The son of Ethni, the son of Zerah, the
son of Adaiah,
42 The son of Ethan, the son of Zimmah,
the son of Shimei,
43 The son of Jahath, the son of Gershom, the son of Levi.
44 And their brethren the sons of Merari
stood on the left hand: Ethan the son of
Kishi, the son of Abdi, the son of Malluch,
45 The son of Hashabiah, the son of
Amaziah, the son of Hilkiah,

46 The son of Amzi, the son of Bani, the son of Shamer,

47 The son of Mahli, the son of Mushi, the son of Merari, the son of Levi.

48 Their brethren also the Levites *were* appointed unto all manner of service of the tabernacle of the house of God.

49 But Aaron and his sons offered upon the altar of the burnt offering, and on the altar of incense, *and were appointed* for all the work of the *place* most holy, and to make an atonement for Israel, according to all that Moses the servant of God had commanded.

50 And these *are* the sons of Aaron; Eleazar his son, Phinehas his son, Abishua his son,

51 Bukki his son, Uzzi his son, Zerahiah his son,

52 Meraioth his son, Amariah his son, Ahitub his son,

53 Zadok his son, Ahimaaz his son.

54 Now these *are* their dwelling places throughout their castles in their coasts, of the sons of Aaron, of the families of the Kohathites: for theirs was the lot.

55 And they gave them Hebron in the land of Judah, and the suburbs thereof round about it.

56 But the fields of the city, and the villages thereof, they gave to Caleb the son of Jephunneh.

57 And to the sons of Aaron they gave the cities of Judah, *namely,* Hebron, *the city* of refuge, and Libnah with her suburbs, and Jattir, and Eshtemoa, with their suburbs,

58 And Hilen with her suburbs, Debir with her suburbs,

59 And Ashan with her suburbs, and Beth-shemesh with her suburbs:

60 And out of the tribe of Benjamin; Geba with her suburbs, and Alemeth with her suburbs, and Anathoth with her suburbs. All their cities throughout their families *were* thirteen cities.

61 And unto the sons of Kohath, *which were* left of the family of that tribe, *were cities given* out of the half tribe, *namely, out of* the half *tribe* of Manasseh, by lot, ten cities.

62 And to the sons of Gershom throughout their families out of the tribe of Issachar, and out of the tribe of Asher, and out of the tribe of Naphtali, and out of the tribe of Manasseh in Bashan, thirteen cities.

63 Unto the sons of Merari *were given* by lot, throughout their families, out of the tribe of Reuben, and out of the tribe of Gad, and out of the tribe of Zebulun, twelve cities.

64 And the children of Israel gave to the Levites *these* cities with their suburbs.

65 And they gave by lot out of the tribe of the children of Judah, and out of the tribe of the children of Simeon, and out of the tribe of the children of Benjamin, these cities, which are called by *their* names.

66 And *the residue* of the families of the sons of Kohath had cities of their coasts out of the tribe of Ephraim.

67 And they gave unto them, *of* the cities of refuge, Shechem in mount Ephraim with her suburbs; *they gave* also Gezer with her suburbs,

68 And Jokmeam with her suburbs, and Beth-horon with her suburbs,

69 And Aijalon with her suburbs, and Gath-rimmon with her suburbs:

70 And out of the half tribe of Manasseh; Aner with her suburbs, and Bileam with her suburbs, for the family of the remnant of the sons of Kohath.

71 Unto the sons of Gershom *were given* out of the family of the half tribe of Manasseh, Golan in Bashan with her suburbs, and Ashtaroth with her suburbs:

72 And out of the tribe of Issachar; Kedesh with her suburbs, Daberath with her suburbs,

73 And Ramoth with her suburbs, and Anem with her suburbs:

74 And out of the tribe of Asher; Mashal with her suburbs, and Abdon with her suburbs,

75 And Hukok with her suburbs, and Rehob with her suburbs:

76 And out of the tribe of Naphtali; Kedesh in Galilee with her suburbs, and Hammon with her suburbs, and Kirjathaim with her suburbs.

77 Unto the rest of the children of Merari *were given* out of the tribe of Zebulun, Rimmon with her suburbs, Tabor with her suburbs:

78 And on the other side Jordan by Jericho, on the east side of Jordan, *were given them* out of the tribe of Reuben, Bezer in

the wilderness with her suburbs, and Jah-
zah with her suburbs,
79 Kedemoth also with her suburbs, and
Mephaath with her suburbs:
80 And out of the tribe of Gad; Ramoth
in Gilead with her suburbs, and Mahanaim with her suburbs,
81 And Heshbon with her suburbs, and
Jazer with her suburbs.

7

1 Now the sons of Issachar *were,* Tola,
and Puah, Jashub, and Shimrom, four.
2 And the sons of Tola; Uzzi, and Rephaiah, and Jeriel, and Jahmai, and Jibsam,
and Shemuel, heads of their father's house,
to wit, of Tola: *they were* valiant men of
might in their generations; whose number *was* in the days of David two and twenty thousand and six hundred.
3 And the sons of Uzzi; Izrahiah: and the
sons of Izrahiah; Michael, and Obadiah,
and Joel, Ishiah, five: all of them chief
men.
4 And with them, by their generations,
after the house of their fathers, *were* bands
of soldiers for war, six and thirty thousand
men: for they had many wives and sons.
5 And their brethren among all the families of Issachar *were* valiant men of might,
reckoned in all by their genealogies fourscore and seven thousand.
6 *The sons* of Benjamin; Bela, and Becher,
and Jediael, three.
7 And the sons of Bela; Ezbon, and Uzzi,
and Uzziel, and Jerimoth, and Iri, five;
heads of the house of *their* fathers, mighty
men of valour; and were reckoned by their
genealogies twenty and two thousand and
thirty and four.
8 And the sons of Becher; Zemira, and
Joash, and Eliezer, and Elioenai, and Omri,
and Jerimoth, and Abiah, and Anathoth,
and Alameth. All these *are* the sons of
Becher.
9 And the number of them, after their
genealogy by their generations, heads of
the house of the fathers, mighty men of
valour, *was* twenty thousand and two hundred.
10 The sons also of Jediael; Bilhan: and
the sons of Bilhan; Jeush, and Benjamin,
and Ehud, and Chenaanah, and Zethan,
and Tharshish, and Ahishahar.
11 All these the sons of Jediael, by the
heads of their fathers, mighty men of
valour, *were* seventeen thousand and two
hundred *soldiers,* fit to go out for war *and*
battle.
12 Shuppim also, and Huppim, the children of Ir, *and* Hushim, the sons of Aher.
13 The sons of Naphtali; Jahziel, and
Guni, and Jezer, and Shallum, the sons of
Bilhah.
14 The sons of Manasseh; Ashriel, whom
she bare: *(but* his concubine the Aramitess
bare Machir the father of Gilead:
15 And Machir took to wife *the sister* of
Huppim and Shuppim, whose sister's
name *was* Maachah;) and the name of the
second *was* Zelophehad: and Zelophehad
had daughters.
16 And Maachah the wife of Machir bare
a son, and she called his name Peresh; and
the name of his brother *was* Sheresh; and
his sons *were* Ulam and Rakem.
17 And the sons of Ulam; Bedan. These
were the sons of Gilead, the son of Machir,
the son of Manasseh.
18 And his sister Hammoleketh bare
Ishod, and Abiezer, and Mahalah.
19 And the sons of Shemidah were, Ahi-
an, and Shechem, and Likhi, and Aniam.
20 And the sons of Ephraim; Shuthelah,
and Bered his son, and Tahath his son, and
Eladah his son, and Tahath his son,
21 And Zabad his son, and Shuthelah his
son, and Ezer, and Elead, whom the men
of Gath *that were* born in *that* land slew,
because they came down to take away their
cattle.
22 And Ephraim their father mourned
many days, and his brethren came to comfort him.
23 And when he went in to his wife, she
conceived, and bare a son, and he called
his name Beriah, because it went evil with
his house.
24 (And his daughter *was* Sherah, who
built Beth-horon the nether, and the upper, and Uzzen-sherah.)
25 And Rephah *was* his son, also Resheph,
and Telah his son, and Tahan his son,
26 Laadan his son, Ammihud his son,
Elishama his son,
27 Non his son, Jehoshuah his son.
28 And their possessions and habitations
were, Bethel and the towns thereof, and
eastward Naaran, and westward Gezer,
with the towns thereof; Shechem also and
the towns thereof, unto Gaza and the
towns thereof:

29 And by the borders of the children of Manasseh, Beth-shean and her towns, Taanach and her towns, Megiddo and her towns, Dor and her towns. In these dwelt the children of Joseph the son of Israel.

30 The sons of Asher; Imnah, and Isuah, and Ishuai, and Beriah, and Serah their sister.

31 And the sons of Beriah; Heber, and Malchiel, who *is* the father of Birzavith.

32 And Heber begat Japhlet, and Shomer, and Hotham, and Shua their sister.

33 And the sons of Japhlet; Pasach, and Bimhal, and Ashvath. These *are* the children of Japhlet.

34 And the sons of Shamer; Ahi, and Rohgah, Jehubbah, and Aram.

35 And the sons of his brother Helem; Zophah, and Imna, and Shelesh, and Amal.

36 The sons of Zophah; Suah, and Harnepher, and Shual, and Beri, and Imrah,

37 Bezer, and Hod, and Shamma and Shilshah, and Ithran, and Beera.

38 And the sons of Jether; Jephunneh, and Pispah, and Ara.

39 And the sons of Ulla; Arah, and Haniel, and Rezia.

40 All these *were* the children of Asher, heads of *their* father's house, choice *and* mighty men of valour, chief of the princes. And the number throughout the genealogy of them that were apt to the war *and* to battle *was* twenty and six thousand men.

8

1 Now Benjamin begat Bela his firstborn, Ashbel the second, and Aharah the third,

2 Nohah the fourth, and Rapha the fifth.

3 And the sons of Bela were, Addar, and Gera, and Abihud,

4 And Abishua, and Naaman, and Ahoah,

5 And Gera, and Shephuphan, and Huram.

6 And these *are* the sons of Ehud: these are the heads of the fathers of the inhabitants of Geba, and they removed them to Manahath:

7 And Naaman, and Ahiah, and Gera, he removed them, and begat Uzza, and Ahihud.

8 And Shaharaim begat *children* in the country of Moab, after he had sent them away; Hushim and Baara *were* his wives.

9 And he begat of Hodesh his wife, Jobab, and Zibia, and Mesha, and Malcham,

10 And Jeuz, and Shachia, and Mirma. These *were* his sons, heads of the fathers.

11 And of Hushim he begat Abitub, and Elpaal.

12 The sons of Elpaal; Eber, and Misham, and Shamed, who built Ono, and Lod, with the towns thereof:

13 Beriah also, and Shema, who *were* heads of the fathers of the inhabitants of Aijalon, who drove away the inhabitants of Gath:

14 And Ahio, Shashak, and Jeremoth,

15 And Zebadiah, and Arad, and Ader,

16 And Michael, and Ispah, and Joha, the sons of Beriah;

17 And Zebadiah, and Meshullam, and Hezeki, and Heber,

18 Ishmerai also, and Jezliah, and Jobab, the sons of Elpaal;

19 And Jakim, and Zichri, and Zabdi,

20 And Elienai, and Zilthai, and Eliel,

21 And Adaiah, and Beraiah, and Shimrath, the sons of Shimhi;

22 And Ishpan, and Heber, and Eliel,

23 And Abdon, and Zichri, and Hanan,

24 And Hananiah, and Elam, and Antothijah,

25 And Iphedeiah, and Penuel, the sons of Shashak;

26 And Shamsherai, and Shehariah, and Athaliah,

27 And Jaresiah, and Eliah, and Zichri, the sons of Jeroham.

28 These *were* heads of the fathers, by their generations, chief *men*. These dwelt in Jerusalem.

29 And at Gibeon dwelt the father of Gibeon; whose wife's name *was* Maachah:

30 And his firstborn son Abdon, and Zur, and Kish, and Baal, and Nadab,

31 And Gedor, and Ahio, and Zacher.

32 And Mikloth begat Shimeah. And these also dwelt with their brethren in Jerusalem, over against them.

33 And Ner begat Kish, and Kish begat Saul, and Saul begat Jonathan, and Malchishua, and Abinadab, and Esh-baal.

34 And the son of Jonathan *was* Merib-baal; and Merib-baal begat Micah.

35 And the sons of Micah *were*, Pithon, and Melech, and Tarea, and Ahaz.

36 And Ahaz begat Jehoadah; and

Jehoadah begat Alemeth, and Azmaveth,
and Zimri; and Zimri begat Moza,
37 And Moza begat Binea: Rapha *was* his
son, Eleasah his son, Azel his son:
38 And Azel had six sons, whose names
are these, Azrikam, Bocheru, and Ishmael,
and Sheariah, and Obadiah, and Hanan.
All these *were* the sons of Azel.
39 And the sons of Eshek his brother *were,*
Ulam his firstborn, Jehush the second, and
Eliphelet the third.
40 And the sons of Ulam were mighty
men of valour, archers, and had many
sons, and sons' sons, an hundred and fifty.
All these *are* of the sons of Benjamin.

9 1 So all Israel were reckoned by genealogies; and, behold, they *were* written in the
book of the kings of Israel and Judah, *who*
were carried away to Babylon for their
transgression.
2 Now the first inhabitants that *dwelt* in
their possessions in their cities *were,* the
Israelites, the priests, Levites, and the
Nethinims.
3 And in Jerusalem dwelt of the children
of Judah, and of the children of Benjamin,
and of the children of Ephraim, and Manasseh;
4 Uthai the son of Ammihud, the son of
Omri, the son of Imri, the son of Bani, of
the children of Pharez the son of Judah.
5 And of the Shilonites; Asaiah the firstborn, and his sons.
6 And of the sons of Zerah; Jeuel, and
their brethren, six hundred and ninety.
7 And of the sons of Benjamin; Sallu the
son of Meshullam, the son of Hodaviah,
the son of Hasenuah,
8 And Ibneiah the son of Jeroham, and
Elah the son of Uzzi, the son of Michri,
and Meshullam the son of Shephatiah, the
son of Reuel, the son of Ibnijah;
9 And their brethren, according to their
generations, nine hundred and fifty and
six. All these men *were* chief of the fathers
in the house of their fathers.
10 And of the priests; Jedaiah, and Jehoiarib, and Jachin,
11 And Azariah the son of Hilkiah, the
son of Meshullam, the son of Zadok,
the son of Meraioth, the son of Ahitub,
the ruler of the house of God;
12 And Adaiah the son of Jeroham, the
son of Pashur, the son of Malchijah, and
Maasiai the son of Adiel, the son of Jahze-
rah, the son of Meshullam, the son of Me-
shillemith, the son of Immer;
13 And their brethren, heads of the house
of their fathers, a thousand and seven hundred and threescore; very able men for the
work of the service of the house of God.
14 And of the Levites; Shemaiah the son
of Hasshub, the son of Azrikam, the son
of Hashabiah, of the sons of Merari;
15 And Bakbakkar, Heresh, and Galal,
and Mattaniah the son of Micah, the son
of Zichri, the son of Asaph;
16 And Obadiah the son of Shemaiah,
the son of Galal, the son of Jeduthun, and
Berechiah the son of Asa, the son of Elkanah, that dwelt in the villages of the Netophathites.
17 And the porters *were,* Shallum, and
Akkub, and Talmon, and Ahiman, and
their brethren: Shallum *was* the chief;
18 Who hitherto *waited* in the king's gate
eastward: they *were* porters in the companies of the children of Levi.
19 And Shallum the son of Kore, the son
of Ebiasaph, the son of Korah, and his
brethren, of the house of his father, the
Korahites, *were* over the work of the service, keepers of the gates of the tabernacle: and their fathers, *being* over the host
of the Lord, *were* keepers of the entry.
20 And Phinehas the son of Eleazar was
the ruler over them in time past, *and* the
Lord *was* with him.
21 *And* Zechariah the son of Meshelemiah *was* porter of the door of the tabernacle of the congregation.
22 All these *which were* chosen to be porters in the gates *were* two hundred and
twelve. These were reckoned by their genealogy in their villages, whom David and
Samuel the seer did ordain in their set office.
23 So they and their children *had* the
oversight of the gates of the house of the
Lord, *namely,* the house of the tabernacle,
by wards.
24 In four quarters were the porters, toward the east, west, north, and south.
25 And their brethren, *which were* in their
villages, *were* to come after seven days from
time to time with them.
26 For these Levites, the four chief porters, were in *their* set office, and were over
the chambers and treasuries of the house
of God.

27 And they lodged round about the house of God, because the charge *was* upon them, and the opening thereof every morning *pertained* to them.

28 And *certain* of them had the charge of the ministering vessels, that they should bring them in and out by tale.

29 *Some* of them also *were* appointed to oversee the vessels, and all the instruments of the sanctuary, and the fine flour, and the wine, and the oil, and the frankincense, and the spices.

30 And *some* of the sons of the priests made the ointment of the spices.

31 And Mattithiah, *one* of the Levites, who *was* the firstborn of Shallum the Korahite, had the set office over the things that were made in the pans.

32 And *other* of their brethren, of the sons of the Kohathites, *were* over the shewbread, to prepare *it* every sabbath.

33 And these *are* the singers, chief of the fathers of the Levites, *who remaining* in the chambers *were* free: for they were employed in *that* work day and night.

34 These chief fathers of the Levites *were* chief throughout their generations; these dwelt at Jerusalem.

35 And in Gibeon dwelt the father of Gibeon, Jehiel, whose wife's name *was* Maachah:

36 And his firstborn son Abdon, then Zur, and Kish, and Baal, and Ner, and Nadab,

37 And Gedor, and Ahio, and Zechariah, and Mikloth.

38 And Mikloth begat Shimeam. And they also dwelt with their brethren at Jerusalem, over against their brethren.

39 And Ner begat Kish; and Kish begat Saul; and Saul begat Jonathan, and Malchishua, and Abinadab, and Esh-baal.

40 And the son of Jonathan *was* Merib-baal: and Merib-baal begat Micah.

41 And the sons of Micah *were,* Pithon, and Melech, and Tahrea, *and Ahaz.*

42 And Ahaz begat Jarah; and Jarah begat Alemeth, and Azmaveth, and Zimri; and Zimri begat Moza;

43 And Moza begat Binea; and Rephaiah his son, Eleasah his son, Azel his son.

44 And Azel had six sons, whose names *are* these, Azrikam, Bocheru, and Ishmael, and Sheariah, and Obadiah, and Hanan: these *were* the sons of Azel.

10

1 Now the Philistines fought against Israel; and the men of Israel fled from before the Philistines, and fell down slain in mount Gilboa.

2 And the Philistines followed hard after Saul, and after his sons; and the Philistines slew Jonathan, and Abinadab, and Malchi-shua, the sons of Saul.

3 And the battle went sore against Saul, and the archers hit him, and he was wounded of the archers.

4 Then said Saul to his armourbearer, Draw thy sword, and thrust me through therewith; lest these uncircumcised come and abuse me. But his armourbearer would not; for he was sore afraid. So Saul took a sword, and fell upon it.

5 And when his armourbearer saw that Saul was dead, he fell likewise on the sword, and died.

6 So Saul died, and his three sons, and all his house died together.

7 And when all the men of Israel that *were* in the valley saw that they fled, and that Saul and his sons were dead, then they forsook their cities, and fled: and the Philistines came and dwelt in them.

8 And it came to pass on the morrow, when the Philistines came to strip the slain, that they found Saul and his sons fallen in mount Gilboa.

9 And when they had stripped him, they took his head, and his armour, and sent into the land of the Philistines round about, to carry tidings unto their idols, and to the people.

10 And they put his armour in the house of their gods, and fastened his head in the temple of Dagon.

11 And when all Jabesh-gilead heard all that the Philistines had done to Saul,

12 They arose, all the valiant men, and took away the body of Saul, and the bodies of his sons, and brought them to Jabesh, and buried their bones under the oak in Jabesh, and fasted seven days.

13 So Saul died for his transgression which he committed against the LORD, *even* against the word of the LORD, which he kept not, and also for asking *counsel* of *one that had* a familiar spirit, to enquire *of it;*

10:13 Why Not Sin?
◄ Deuteronomy 32:51
Proverbs 11:19 ►

14 And enquired not of the LORD: therefore he slew him, and turned the kingdom
unto David the son of Jesse.

11
1 Then all Israel gathered themselves to
David unto Hebron, saying, Behold, we *are*
thy bone and thy flesh.
2 And moreover in time past, even when
Saul was king, thou *wast* he that leddest
out and broughtest in Israel: and the LORD
thy God said unto thee, Thou shalt feed
my people Israel, and thou shalt be ruler
over my people Israel, and thou shalt be
ruler over my people Israel.
3 Therefore came all the elders of Israel
to the king to Hebron; and David made a
covenant with them in Hebron before the
LORD; and they anointed David king over
Israel, according to the word of the LORD
by Samuel.
4 And David and all Israel went to Jerusalem, which *is* Jebus; where the Jebusites
were, the inhabitants of the land.
5 And the inhabitants of Jebus said to
David, Thou shalt not come hither. Nevertheless David took the castle of Zion,
which *is* the city of David.
6 And David said, Whosoever smiteth the
Jebusites first shall be chief and captain.
So Joab the son of Zeruiah went first up,
and was chief.
7 And David dwelt in the castle; therefore they called it the city of David.
8 And he built the city round about, even
from Millo round about: and Joab repaired
the rest of the city.
9 So David waxed greater and greater: for
the LORD of hosts *was* with him.
10 These also *are* the chief of the mighty
men whom David had, who strengthened
themselves with him in his kingdom, *and*
with all Israel, to make him king, according
to the word of the LORD concerning Israel.
11 And this *is* the number of the mighty
men whom David had; Jashobeam, and
Hachmonite, the chief of the captains: he
lifted up his spear against three hundred
slain *by him* at one time.
12 And after him *was* Eleazar the son of
Dodo, the Ahohite, who *was one* of the
three mighties.
13 He was with David at Pas-dammim,
and there the Philistines were gathered
together to battle, where was a parcel of
ground full of barley; and the people fled
from before the Philistines.
14 And they set themselves in the midst
of *that* parcel, and delivered it, and slew
the Philistines; and the LORD saved *them*
by a great deliverance.
15 Now three of the thirty captains went
down to the rock to David, into the cave
of Adullam; and the host of the Philistines
encamped in the valley of Rephaim.
16 And David *was* then in the hold, and
the Philistines' garrison *was* then at Bethlehem.
17 And David longed, and said, Oh that
one would give me drink of the water of
the well of Bethlehem, that *is* at the gate!
18 And the three brake through the host
of the Philistines, and drew water out of
the well of Bethlehem, that *was* by the gate,
and took *it,* and brought *it* to David: but
David would not drink *of* it, but poured it
out to the LORD,
19 And said, My God forbid it me, that I
should do this thing: shall I drink the
blood of these men that have put their lives
in jeopardy? for with *the jeopardy of* their
lives they brought it. Therefore he would
not drink it. These things did these three
mightiest.
20 And Abishai the brother of Joab, he
was chief of the three: for lifting up his
spear against three hundred, he slew *them,*
and had a name among the three.
21 Of the three, he was more honourable
than the two; for he was their captain:
howbeit he attained not to the *first* three.
22 Benaiah the son of Jehoiada, the son
of a valiant man of Kabzeel, who had done
many acts; he slew two lionlike men of
Moab: also he went down and slew a lion
in a pit in a snowy day.
23 And he slew an Egyptian, a man of
great stature, five cubits high; and in the
Egyptian's hand *was* a spear like a weaver's
beam; and he went down to him with a
staff, and plucked the spear out of the
Egyptian's hand, and slew him with his
own spear.
24 These *things* did Benaiah the son of
Jehoiada, and had the name among the
three mighties.
25 Behold, he was honourable among
the thirty, but attained not to the *first* three:
and David set him over his guard.
26 Also the valiant men of the armies
were, Asahel the brother of Joab, Elhanan
the son of Dodo of Bethlehem,

27 Shammoth the Harorite, Helez the Pelonite,

28 Ira the son of Ikkesh the Tekoite, Abiezer the Antothite,

29 Sibbecai the Hushathite, Ilai the Ahohite,

30 Maharai the Netophathite, Heled the son of Baanah the Netophathite,

31 Ithai the son of Ribai of Gibeah, *that pertained* to the children of Benjamin, Benaiah the Pirathonite,

32 Hurai of the brooks of Gaash, Abiel the Arbathite,

33 Azmaveth the Baharumite, Eliahba the Shaalbonite,

34 The sons of Hashem the Gizonite, Jonathan the son of Shage the Hararite,

35 Ahiam the son of Sacar the Hararite, Eliphal the son of Ur,

36 Hepher the Mecherathite, Ahijah the Pelonite,

37 Hezro the Carmelite, Naarai the son of Ezbai,

38 Joel the brother of Nathan, Mibhar the son of Haggeri,

39 Zelek the Ammonite, Naharai the Berothite, the armourbearer of Joab the son of Zeruiah,

40 Ira the Ithrite, Gareb the Ithrite,

41 Uriah the Hittite, Zabad the son of Ahlai,

42 Adina the son of Shiza the Reubenite, a captain of the Reubenites, and thirty with him,

43 Hanan the son of Maachah, and Joshaphat the Mithnite,

44 Uzzia the Ashterathite, Shama and Jehiel the sons of Hothan the Aroerite,

45 Jediael the son of Shimri, and Joha his brother, the Tizite,

46 Eliel the Mahavite, and Jeribai, and Joshaviah, the sons of Elnaam, and Ithmah the Moabite,

47 Eliel, and Obed, and Jasiel the Mesobaite.

12

1 Now these *are* they that came to David to Ziklag, while he yet kept himself close because of Saul the son of Kish: and they *were* among the mighty men, helpers of the war.

2 *They were* armed with bows, and could use both the right hand and the left in *hurling* stones and *shooting* arrows out of a bow, *even* of Saul's brethren of Benjamin.

3 The chief *was* Ahiezer, then Joash, the sons of Shemaah the Gibeathite; and Jeziel, and Pelet, the sons of Azmaveth; and Berachah, and Jehu the Antothite,

4 And Ismaiah the Gibeonite, a mighty man among the thirty, and over the thirty; and Jeremiah, and Jahaziel, and Johanan, and Josabad the Gederathite,

5 Eluzai, and Jerimoth, and Bealiah, and Shemariah, and Shephatiah the Haruphite,

6 Elkanah, and Jesiah, and Azareel, and Joezer, and Jashobeam, the Korhites,

7 And Joelah, and Zebadiah, the sons of Jeroham of Gedor.

8 And of the Gadites there separated themselves unto David into the hold to the wilderness men of might, *and* men of war *fit* for the battle, that could handle shield and buckler, whose faces *were like* the faces of lions, and *were* as swift as the roes upon the mountains;

9 Ezer the first, Obadiah the second, Eliab the third,

10 Mishmannah the fourth, Jeremiah the fifth,

11 Attai the sixth, Eliel the seventh,

12 Johanan the eighth, Elzabad the ninth,

13 Jeremiah the tenth, Machbanai the eleventh.

14 These *were* of the sons of Gad, captains of the host: one of the least *was* over an hundred, and the greatest over a thousand.

15 These *are* they that went over Jordan in the first month, when it had overflown all his banks; and they put to flight all *them* of the valleys, *both* toward the east, and toward the west.

16 And there came of the children of Benjamin and Judah to the hold unto David.

17 And David went out to meet them, and answered and said unto them, If ye be come peaceably unto me to help me, mine heart shall be knit unto you: but if *ye be come* to betray me to mine enemies, seeing *there is* no wrong in mine hands, the God of our fathers look *thereon,* and rebuke *it.*

18 Then the spirit came upon Amasai, *who was* chief of the captains, *and he said,* Thine *are we,* David, and on thy side, thou son of Jesse: peace, peace *be* unto thee, and peace *be* to thine helpers; for thy God helpeth thee. Then David received them, and made them captains of the band.

19 And there fell *some* of Manasseh to

David, when he came with the Philistines
against Saul to battle: but they helped
them not: for the lords of the Philistines
upon advisement sent him away, saying,
He will fall to his master Saul to *the jeop-*
ardy of our heads.
20 As he went to Ziklag, there fell to him
of Manasseh, Adnah, and Jozabad, and
Jediael, and Michael, and Jozabad, and
Elihu, and Zilthai, captains of the thousands that *were* of Manasseh.
21 And they helped David against the
band *of the rovers:* for they *were* all mighty
men of valour, and were captains in the
host.
22 For at *that* time day by day there came
to David to help him, until *it was* a great
host, like the host of God.
23 And these *are* the numbers of the
bands *that were* ready armed to the war,
and came to David to Hebron, to turn the
kingdom of Saul to him, according to the
word of the LORD.
24 The children of Judah that bare shield
and spear *were* six thousand and eight hundred, ready armed to the war.
25 Of the children of Simeon, mighty
men of valour for the war, seven thousand
and one hundred.
26 Of the children of Levi four thousand
and six hundred.
27 And Jehoiada *was* the leader of the
Aaronites, and with him *were* three thousand and seven hundred;
28 And Zadok, a young man mighty of
valour, and of his father's house twenty
and two captains.
29 And of the children of Benjamin, the
kindred of Saul, three thousand: for hitherto the greatest part of them had kept the
ward of the house of Saul.
30 And of the children of Ephraim twenty thousand and eight hundred, mighty
men of valour, famous throughout the
house of their fathers.
31 And of the half tribe of Manasseh eighteen thousand, which were expressed by
name, to come and make David king.
32 And of the children of Issachar, *which*
were men that had understanding of the
times, to know what Israel ought to do;
the heads of them *were* two hundred; and
all their brethren *were* at their commandment.
33 Of Zebulun, such as went forth to battle, expert in war,
with all instruments
of war, fifty thou-
sand, which could
keep rank: *they were*
not of double heart.

12:33 Double Life
◄ 2 Kings 17:33
Zephaniah 1:4-5 ►

34 And of Naphtali a thousand captains,
and with them with shield and spear thirty
and seven thousand.
35 And of the Danites expert in war twenty and eight thousand and six hundred.
36 And of Asher, such as went forth to
battle, expert in war, forty thousand.
37 And on the other side of Jordan, of
the Reubenites, and the Gadites, and of the
half tribe of Manasseh, with all manner of
instruments of war for the battle, an hundred and twenty thousand.
38 All these men
of war, that could
keep rank, came
with a perfect heart
to Hebron, to make
David king over all
Israel: and all the rest also of Israel *were* of
one heart to make David king.

12:38 Teamwork
◄ 2 Kings 6:1-3
Ezra 10:4 ►

39 And there they were with David three
days, eating and drinking: for their brethren had prepared for them.
40 Moreover they that were nigh them,
even unto Issachar and Zebulun and Naphtali, brought bread on asses, and on camels, and on mules, and on oxen, *and* meat,
meal, cakes of figs, and bunches of raisins,
and wine, and oil, and oxen, and sheep
abundantly: for *there was* joy in Israel.

13

1 And David consulted with the captains
of thousands and hundreds, *and* with every
leader.
2 And David said unto all the congregation of Israel, If *it seem* good unto you, and
that it be of the LORD our God, let us send
abroad unto our brethren every where, *that*
are left in all the land of Israel, and with
them *also* to the priests and Levites *which*
are in their cities *and* suburbs, that they
may gather themselves unto us:
3 And let us bring again the ark of our
God to us: for we enquired not at it in the
days of Saul.
4 And all the congregation said that they
would do so: for the thing was right in the
eyes of all the people.
5 So David gathered all Israel together,
from Shihor of Egypt even unto the enter-

ing of Hemath, to bring the ark of God from Kirjath-jearim.

6 And David went up, and all Israel, to Baalah, *that is,* to Kirjath-jearim, which *belonged* to Judah, to bring up thence the ark of God the LORD, that dwelleth *between* the cherubims, whose name is called *on it.*

7 And they carried the ark of God in a new cart out of the house of Abinadab: and Uzza and Ahio drave the cart.

8 And David and all Israel played before God with all *their* might, and with singing, and with harps, and with psalteries, and with timbrels, and with cymbals, and with trumpets.

9 And when they came unto the threshingfloor of Chidon, Uzza put forth his hand to hold the ark; for the oxen stumbled.

10 And the anger of the LORD was kindled against Uzza, and he smote him, because he put his hand to the ark: and there he died before God.

11 And David was displeased, because the LORD had made a breach upon Uzza: wherefore that place is called Perez-uzza to this day.

12 And David was afraid of God that day, saying, How shall I bring the ark of God *home* to me?

13 So David brought not the ark *home* to himself to the city of David, but carried it aside into the house of Obed-edom the Gittite.

14 And the ark of God remained with the family of Obed-edom in his house three months. And the LORD blessed the house of Obed-edom, and all that he had.

14

1 Now Hiram king of Tyre sent messengers to David, and timber of cedars, with masons and carpenters, to build him an house.

2 And David perceived that the LORD had confirmed him king over Israel, for his kingdom was lifted up on high, because of his people Israel.

3 And David took more wives at Jerusalem: and David begat more sons and daughters.

4 Now these *are* the names of *his* children which he had in Jerusalem; Shammua, and Shobab, Nathan, and Solomon,

5 And Ibhar, and Elishua, and Elpalet,

6 And Nogah, and Nepheg, and Japhia,

7 And Elishama, and Beeliada, and Eliphalet.

8 And when the Philistines heard that David was anointed king over all Israel, all the Philistines went up to seek David. And David heard *of it,* and went out against them.

9 And the Philistines came and spread themselves in the valley of Rephaim.

10 And David enquired of God, saying, Shall I go up against the Philistines? and wilt thou deliver them into mine hand? And the LORD said unto him, Go up; for I will deliver them into thine hand.

11 So they came up to Baal-perazim; and David smote them there. Then David said, God hath broken in upon mine enemies by mine hand like the breaking forth of waters: therefore they called the name of that place Baal-perazim.

12 And when they had left their gods there, David gave a commandment, and they were burned with fire.

13 And the Philistines yet again spread themselves abroad in the valley.

14 Therefore David enquired again of God; and God said unto him, Go not up after them; turn away from them, and come upon them over against the mulberry trees.

15 And it shall be, when thou shalt hear a sound of going in the tops of the mulberry trees, *that* then thou shalt go out to battle: for God is gone forth before thee to smite the host of the Philistines.

16 David therefore did as God commanded him: and they smote the host of the Philistines from Gibeon even to Gazer.

17 And the fame of David went out into all lands; and the LORD brought the fear of him upon all nations.

15

1 And *David* made him houses in the city of David, and prepared a place for the ark of God, and pitched for it a tent.

2 Then David said, None ought to carry the ark of God but the Levites: for them hath the LORD chosen to carry the ark of God, and to minister unto him for ever.

3 And David gathered all Israel together to Jerusalem, to bring up the ark of the LORD unto his place, which he had prepared for it.

4 And David assembled the children of Aaron, and the Levites:

5 Of the sons of Kohath; Uriel the chief, and his brethren an hundred and twenty:

6 Of the sons of Merari; Asaiah the

chief, and his brethren two hundred and twenty:

7 Of the sons of Gershom; Joel the chief, and his brethren an hundred and thirty:

8 Of the sons of Elizaphan; Shemaiah the chief, and his brethren two hundred:

9 Of the sons of Hebron; Eliel the chief, and his brethren fourscore:

10 Of the sons of Uzziel; Amminadab the chief, and his brethren an hundred and twelve.

11 And David called for Zadok and Abiathar the priests, and for the Levites, for Uriel, Asaiah, and Joel, Shemaiah, and Eliel, and Amminadab,

12 And said unto them, Ye *are* the chief of the fathers of the Levites: sanctify yourselves, *both* ye and your brethren, that ye may bring up the ark of the LORD God of Israel unto *the place that* I have prepared for it.

13 For because ye *did it* not at the first, the LORD our God made a breach upon us, for that we sought him not after the due order.

14 So the priests and the Levites sanctified themselves to bring up the ark of the LORD God of Israel.

15 And the children of the Levites bare the ark of God upon their shoulders with the staves thereon, as Moses commanded according to the word of the LORD.

16 And David spake to the chief of the Levites to appoint their brethren *to be* the singers with instruments of musick, psalteries and harps and cymbals, sounding, by lifting up the voice with joy.

17 So the Levites appointed Heman the son of Joel; and of his brethren, Asaph the son of Berechiah; and of the sons of Merari their brethren, Ethan the son of Kushaiah;

18 And with them their brethren of the second *degree,* Zechariah, Ben, and Jaaziel, and Shemiramoth, and Jehiel, and Unni, Eliab, and Benaiah, and Maaseiah, and Mattithiah, and Elipheleh, and Mikneiah, and Obed-edom, and Jeiel, the porters.

19 So the singers, Heman, Asaph, and Ethan, *were appointed* to sound with cymbals of brass;

20 And Zechariah, and Aziel, and Shemiramoth, and Jehiel, and Unni, and Eliab, and Maaseiah, and Benaiah, with psalteries on Alamoth;

21 And Mattithiah, and Elipheleh, and Mikneiah, and Obed-edom, and Jeiel, and Azaziah, with harps on the Sheminith to excel.

22 And Chenaniah, chief of the Levites, *was* for song: he instructed about the song, because he *was* skilful.

23 And Berechiah and Elkanah *were* doorkeepers for the ark.

24 And Shebaniah, and Jehoshaphat, and Nethaneel, and Amasai, and Zechariah, and Benaiah, and Eliezer, the priests, did blow with the trumpets before the ark of God: and Obed-edom and Jehiah *were* doorkeepers for the ark.

25 So David, and the elders of Israel, and the captains over thousands, went to bring up the ark of the covenant of the LORD out of the house of Obed-edom with joy.

26 And it came to pass, when God helped the Levites that bare the ark of the covenant of the LORD, that they offered seven bullocks and seven rams.

27 And David *was* clothed with a robe of fine linen, and all the Levites that bare the ark, and the singers, and Chenaniah the master of the song with the singers: David also *had* upon him an ephod of linen.

28 Thus all Israel brought up the ark of the covenant of the LORD with shouting, and with sound of the cornet, and with trumpets, and with cymbals, making a noise with psalteries and harps.

29 And it came to pass, *as* the ark of the covenant of the LORD came to the city of David, that Michal the daughter of Saul looking out at a window saw king David dancing and playing: and she despised him in her heart.

16

1 So they brought the ark of God, and set it in the midst of the tent that David had pitched for it: and they offered burnt sacrifices and peace offerings before God.

2 And when David had made an end of offering the burnt offerings and the peace offerings, he blessed the people in the name of the LORD.

3 And he dealt to every one of Israel, both man and woman, to every one a loaf of bread, and a good piece of flesh, and a flagon *of wine.*

4 And he appointed *certain* of the Levites to minister before the ark of the LORD, and to record, and to thank and praise the LORD God of Israel:

5 Asaph the chief, and next to him
Zechariah, Jeiel, and Shemiramoth, and
Jehiel, and Mattithiah, and Eliab, and Benaiah, and Obed-edom: and Jeiel with
psalteries and with harps; but Asaph made
a sound with cymbals;
6 Benaiah also and Jahaziel the priests
with trumpets continually before the ark
of the covenant of God.
7 Then on that day David delivered first
this psalm to thank the LORD into the hand
of Asaph and his brethren.
8 Give thanks
unto the LORD, call
upon his name,
make known his
deeds among the
people.

16:8 Your Testimony
◄ Psalm 107:2 ►

9 Sing unto him, sing psalms unto him,
talk ye of all his wondrous works.
10 Glory ye in his holy name: let the heart
of them rejoice that seek the LORD.
11 Seek the LORD
and his strength,
seek his face contin-
ually.
12 Remember his
marvellous works
that he hath done, his wonders, and the
judgments of his mouth;

16:11 Duty to Pray
◄ Hosea 14:2 ►

13 O ye seed of Israel his servant, ye children of Jacob, his chosen ones.
14 He *is* the LORD our God; his judgments
are in all the earth.
15 Be ye mindful always of his covenant;
the word *which* he commanded to a thousand generations;
16 *Even of the covenant* which he made
with Abraham, and of his oath unto Isaac;
17 And hath confirmed the same to Ja-
cob for a law, *and* to Israel *for* an everlasting covenant,
18 Saying, Unto thee will I give the land
of Canaan, the lot of your inheritance;
19 When ye were but few, even a few, and
strangers in it.
20 And *when* they went from nation to
nation, and from *one* kingdom to another
people;
21 He suffered no man to do them wrong:
yea, he reproved kings for their sakes,
22 *Saying,* Touch not mine anointed, and
do my prophets no harm.
23 Sing unto the LORD, all the earth; shew
forth from day to day his salvation.
24 Declare his glory among the heathen;
his marvellous works among all nations.
25 For great *is* the LORD, and greatly to
be praised: he also *is* to be feared above
all gods.
26 For all the gods of the people *are* idols:
but the LORD made the heavens.
27 Glory and honour *are* in his presence;
strength and gladness *are* in his place.
28 Give unto the LORD, ye kindreds of the
people, give unto the LORD glory and
strength.
29 Give unto the
LORD the glory *due*
unto his name:
bring an offering,
and come before
him: worship the
LORD in the beauty
of holiness.
30 Fear before
him, all the earth:
the world also shall
be stable, that it be
not moved.
31 Let the heavens
be glad, and let the
earth rejoice: and
let *men* say among
the nations, The
LORD reigneth.

16:29 Holiness
◄ Leviticus 19:2
Luke 1:74-75 ►

16:29 Worship
◄ 2 Kings 17:36
Psalm 29:2 ►

16:30 Fearing God
◄ Joshua 24:14
2 Chronicles 19:7 ►

32 Let the sea roar, and the fulness
thereof: let the fields rejoice, and all that
is therein.
33 Then shall the trees of the wood sing
out at the presence of the LORD, because
he cometh to judge the earth.
34 O give thanks unto the LORD; for *he is*
good; for his mercy *endureth* for ever.
35 And say ye, Save us, O God of our salvation, and gather us together, and deliver
us from the heathen, that we may give
thanks to thy holy name, *and* glory in thy
praise.
36 Blessed *be* the LORD God of Israel for
ever and ever. And all the people said,
Amen, and praised the LORD.
37 So he left there before the ark of the
covenant of the LORD Asaph and his brethren, to minister before the ark continually, as every day's work required:
38 And Obed-edom with their brethren,
threescore and eight; Obed-edom also the
son of Jeduthun and Hosah *to be* porters:
39 And Zadok the priest, and his brethren

the priests, before the tabernacle of the
LORD in the high place that *was* at Gibeon,
40 To offer burnt offerings unto the LORD
upon the altar of the burnt offering continually morning and evening, and *to do*
according to all that is written in the
law of the LORD, which he commanded
Israel;
41 And with them Heman and Jeduthun,
and the rest that were chosen, who were
expressed by name, to give thanks to the
LORD, because his mercy *endureth* for ever;
42 And with them Heman and Jeduthun
with trumpets and cymbals for those that
should make a sound, and with musical
instruments of God. And the sons of Jeduthun *were* porters.
43 And all the people departed every man
to his house: and David returned to bless
his house.

17 1 Now it came to pass, as David sat in
his house, that David said to Nathan the
prophet, Lo, I dwell in an house of cedars,
but the ark of the covenant of the LORD
remaineth under curtains.
2 Then Nathan said unto David, Do all
that *is* in thine heart; for God *is* with thee.
3 And it came to pass the same night, that
the word of God came to Nathan, saying,
4 Go and tell David my servant, Thus
saith the LORD, Thou shalt not build me
an house to dwell in:
5 For I have not dwelt in an house since
the day that I brought up Israel unto this
day; but have gone from tent to tent, and
from *one* tabernacle *to another.*
6 Wheresoever I have walked with all Israel, spake I a word to any of the judges of
Israel, whom I commanded to feed my
people, saying, Why have ye not built me
an house of cedars?
7 Now therefore thus shalt thou say unto
my servant David, Thus saith the LORD of
hosts, I took thee from the sheepcote, *even*
from following the sheep, that thou
shouldest be ruler over my people Israel:
8 And I have been with thee whithersoever thou hast walked, and have cut off
all thine enemies from before thee, and
have made thee a name like the name of
the great men that *are* in the earth.
9 Also I will ordain a place for my people Israel, and will plant them, and they
shall dwell in their place, and shall be
moved no more; neither shall the children
of wickedness waste them any more, as at
the beginning,
10 And since the time that I commanded
judges *to be* over my people Israel. Moreover I will subdue all thine enemies. Furthermore I tell thee that the LORD will
build thee an house.
11 And it shall come to pass, when thy
days be expired that thou must go *to be*
with thy fathers, that I will raise up thy
seed after thee, which shall be of thy sons;
and I will establish his kingdom.
12 He shall build me an house, and I will
stablish his throne for ever.
13 I will be his father, and he shall be my
son: and I will not take my mercy away
from him, as I took *it* from *him* that was
before thee:
14 But I will settle him in mine house
and in my kingdom for ever: and his
throne shall be established for evermore.
15 According to all these words, and according to all this vision, so did Nathan
speak unto David.
16 And David the king came and sat before the LORD, and said, Who *am* I, O LORD
God, and what *is* mine house, that thou
hast brought me hitherto?
17 And *yet* this was a small thing in thine
eyes, O God; for thou hast *also* spoken of
thy servant's house for a great while to
come, and hast regarded me according to
the estate of a man of high degree, O LORD
God.
18 What can David *speak* more to thee for
the honour of thy servant? for thou
knowest thy servant.
19 O LORD, for thy servant's sake, and according to thine own heart, hast thou done
all this greatness, in making known all
these great things.
20 O LORD, *there is*
none like thee, nei-
ther *is there any* God
beside thee, accord-
ing to all that we
have heard with
our ears.

17:20 Only One God
◄ 2 Samuel 7:22
Psalm 83:18 ►

21 And what one nation in the earth *is*
like thy people Israel, whom God went to
redeem *to be* his own people, to make thee
a name of greatness and terribleness, by
driving out nations from before thy people, whom thou hast redeemed out of
Egypt?

22For thy people Israel didst thou make
thine own people for ever; and thou, LORD,
becamest their God.
23Therefore now, LORD, let the thing that
thou hast spoken concerning thy servant
and concerning his house be established
for ever, and do as thou hast said.
24Let it even be established, that thy
name may be magnified for ever, saying,
The LORD of hosts *is* the God of Israel, *even*
a God to Israel: and *let* the house of David
thy servant *be* established before thee.
25For thou, O my God, hast told thy servant that thou wilt build him an house:
therefore thy servant hath found *in his heart*
to pray before thee.
26And now, LORD, thou art God, and
hast promised this goodness unto thy servant:
27Now therefore let it please thee to
bless the house of thy servant, that it may
be before thee for ever: for thou blessest,
O LORD, and *it shall be* blessed for ever.

18

1Now after this it came to pass, that
David smote the Philistines, and subdued
them, and took Gath and her towns out
of the hand of the Philistines.
2And he smote Moab; and the Moabites became David's servants, *and* brought
gifts.
3And David smote Hadarezer king of
Zobah unto Hamath, as he went to stablish
his dominion by the river Euphrates.
4And David took
from him a thou-
sand chariots, and
seven thousand
horsemen, and
twenty thousand
footmen: David also houghed all the chariot *horses,* but reserved of them an hundred chariots.

18:4 Cruelty to Animals
◄ 2 Samuel 8:4
Proverbs 12:10 ►

5And when the Syrians of Damascus
came to help Hadarezer king of Zobah,
David slew of the Syrians two and twenty
thousand men.
6Then David put *garrisons* in Syria-
damascus; and the Syrians became David's
servants, *and* brought gifts. Thus the LORD
preserved David whithersoever he went.
7And David took the shields of gold that
were on the servants of Hadarezer, and
brought them to Jerusalem.
8Likewise from Tibhath, and from
Chun, cities of Hadarezer, brought David
very much brass, wherewith Solomon
made the brasen sea, and the pillars, and
the vessels of brass.
9Now when Tou king of Hamath heard
how David had smitten all the host of
Hadarezer king of Zobah;
10He sent Hadoram his son to king David, to enquire of his welfare, and to con-
gratulate him, because he had fought
against Hadarezer, and smitten him; (for
Hadarezer had war with Tou;) and *with him*
all manner of vessels of gold and silver and
brass.
11Them also king David dedicated unto
the LORD, with the silver and the gold that
he brought from all *these* nations; from
Edom, and from Moab, and from the children of Ammon, and from the Philistines,
and from Amalek.
12Moreover Abishai the son of Zeruiah
slew of the Edomites in the valley of salt
eighteen thousand.
13And he put garrisons in Edom; and
all the Edomites became David's servants.
Thus the LORD preserved David whithersoever he went.
14So David reigned over all Israel, and
executed judgment and justice among all
his people.
15And Joab the son Zeruiah *was* over the
host; and Jehoshaphat the son of Ahilud,
recorder.
16And Zadok the son of Ahitub, and
Abimelech the son of Abiathar, *were* the
priests; and Shavsha was scribe;
17And Benaiah the son of Jehoiada *was*
over the Cherethites and the Pelethites;
and the sons of David *were* chief about the
king.

19

1Now it came to pass after this, that
Nahash the king of the children of Ammon died, and his son reigned in his stead.
2And David said, I will shew kindness
unto Hanun the son of Nahash, because
his father shewed kindness to me. And
David sent messengers to comfort him
concerning his father. So the servants of
David came into the land of the children
of Ammon to Hanun, to comfort him.
3But the princes of the children of Ammon said to Hanun, Thinkest thou that
David doth honour thy father, that he hath
sent comforters unto thee? are not his servants come unto thee for to search, and to
overthrow, and to spy out the land?

4 Wherefore Hanun took David's servants, and shaved them, and cut off their
garments in the midst hard by their buttocks, and sent them away.
5 Then there went *certain*, and told David how the men were served. And he sent
to meet them: for the men were greatly
ashamed. And the king said, Tarry at Jericho until your beards be grown, and *then*
return.
6 And when the children of Ammon saw
that they had made themselves odious to
David, Hanun and the children of Ammon
sent a thousand talents of silver to hire
them chariots and horsemen out of Mesopotamia, and out of Syria-maachah, and
out of Zobah.
7 So they hired thirty and two thousand
chariots, and the king of Maachah and his
people; who came and pitched before
Medeba. And the children of Ammon gathered themselves together from their cities,
and came to battle.
8 And when David heard *of it,* he sent
Joab, and all the host of the mighty men.
9 And the children of Ammon came out,
and put the battle in array before the gate
of the city: and the kings that were come
were by themselves in the field.
10 Now when Joab saw that the battle was
set against him before and behind, he
chose out of all the choice of Israel, and
put *them* in array against the Syrians.
11 And the rest of the people he delivered unto the hand of Abishai his brother,
and they set *themselves* in array against the
children of Ammon.
12 And he said, If the Syrians be too
strong for me, then thou shalt help me:
but if the children of Ammon be too strong
for thee, then I will help thee.
13 Be of good courage, and let us behave
ourselves valiantly for our people, and for
the cities of our God: and let the LORD do
that which is good in his sight.
14 So Joab and the people that *were* with
him drew nigh before the Syrians unto the
battle; and they fled before him.
15 And when the children of Ammon saw
that the Syrians were fled, they likewise
fled before Abishai his brother, and entered into the city. Then Joab came to Jerusalem.
16 And when the Syrians saw that they
were put to the worse before Israel, they
sent messengers, and drew forth the Syrians that *were* beyond the river: and Shophach the captain of the host of Hadarezer
went before them.
17 And it was told David; and he gathered all Israel, and passed over Jordan, and
came upon them, and set *the battle* in array against them. So when David had put
the battle in array against the Syrians, they
fought with him.
18 But the Syrians fled before Israel; and
David slew of the Syrians seven thousand
men which fought in chariots, and forty
thousand footmen, and killed Shophach
the captain of the host.
19 And when the servants of Hadarezer
saw that they were put to the worse before
Israel, they made peace with David, and
became his servants: neither would the
Syrians help the children of Ammon any
more.

20

1 And it came to pass, that after the year
was expired, at the time that kings go out
to battle, Joab led forth the power of the
army, and wasted the country of the children of Ammon, and came and besieged
Rabbah. But David tarried at Jerusalem.
And Joab smote Rabbah, and destroyed it.
2 And David took the crown of their king
from off his head, and found it to weigh a
talent of gold, and *there were* precious
stones in it; and it was set upon David's
head: and he brought also exceeding much
spoil out of the city.
3 And he brought out the people that
were in it, and cut *them* with saws, and with
harrows of iron, and with axes. Even so
dealt David with all the cities of the children of Ammon. And David and all the
people returned to Jerusalem.
4 And it came to pass after this, that there
arose war at Gezer with the Philistines; at
which time Sibbechai the Hushathite slew
Sippai, *that was* of the children of the giant: and they were subdued.
5 And there was war again with the
Philistines; and Elhanan the son of Jair
slew Lahmi the brother of Goliath the Gittite, whose spear staff *was* like a weaver's
beam.
6 And yet again there was war at Gath,
where was a man of *great* stature, whose
fingers and toes *were* four and twenty, six
on each hand, and six *on each foot:* and he
also was the son of the giant.

7 But when he defied Israel, Jonathan the
son of Shimea David's brother slew him.
8 These were born unto the giant in Gath;
and they fell by the hand of David, and by
the hand of his servants.

21

1 And Satan stood up against Israel, and
provoked David to number Israel.
2 And David said to Joab and to the rulers
of the people, Go, number Israel from Beer-
sheba even to Dan; and bring the number
of them to me, that I may know *it*.
3 And Joab answered, The LORD make his
people an hundred times so many more
as they *be*: but, my lord the king, *are* they
not all my lord's servants? why then doth
my lord require this thing? why will he be
a cause of trespass to Israel?
4 Nevertheless the king's word prevailed
against Joab. Wherefore Joab departed,
and went throughout all Israel, and came
to Jerusalem.
5 And Joab gave the sum of the number
of the people unto David. And all *they of*
Israel were a thousand thousand and an
hundred thousand men that drew sword:
and Judah *was* four hundred threescore
and ten thousand men that drew sword.
6 But Levi and Benjamin counted he not
among them: for the king's word was
abominable to Joab.
7 And God was displeased with this
thing; therefore he smote Israel.
8 And David said unto God, I have
sinned greatly, because I have done this
thing: but now, I beseech thee, do away
the iniquity of thy servant; for I have done
very foolishly.
9 And the LORD spake unto Gad, David's
seer, saying,
10 Go and tell David, saying, Thus saith
the LORD, I offer thee three *things*: choose
thee one of them, that I may do *it* unto
thee.
11 So Gad came to David, and said unto
him, Thus saith the LORD, Choose thee
12 Either three years' famine; or three
months to be destroyed before thy foes,
while that the sword of thine enemies
overtaketh *thee*; or else three days the
sword of the LORD, even the pestilence, in
the land, and the angel of the LORD destroying throughout all the coasts of Israel.
Now therefore advise thyself what word I
shall bring again to him that sent me.
13 And David said unto Gad, I am in a
great strait: let me fall now into the hand
of the LORD; for very great *are* his mercies:
but let me not fall into the hand of man.
14 So the LORD sent pestilence upon
Israel: and there fell of Israel seventy thousand men.
15 And God sent an angel unto Jerusalem to destroy it: and as he was destroying, the LORD beheld, and he repented him
of the evil, and said to the angel that destroyed, It is enough, stay now thine hand.
And the angel of the LORD stood by the
threshingfloor of Ornan the Jebusite.
16 And David lifted up his eyes, and saw
the angel of the LORD stand between the
earth and the heaven, having a drawn
sword in his hand stretched out over Jerusalem. Then David and the elders *of Israel,*
who were clothed in sackcloth, fell upon
their faces.
17 And David said
unto God, *Is it* not
I *that* commanded
the people to be
numbered? even I it
is that have sinned
and done evil in-
deed; but *as for*
these sheep, what
have they done? let
thine hand, I pray
thee, O LORD my
God, be on me, and on my father's house;
but not on thy people, that they should
be plagued.

21:17 Praying for Others
◄ 1 Kings 13:6
2 Chronicles 30:18 ►

21:17 Remorse
◄ Numbers 14:39
Matthew 26:75 ►

18 Then the angel of the LORD commanded Gad to say to David, that David should
go up, and set up an altar unto the LORD in
the threshingfloor of Ornan the Jebusite.
19 And David went up at the saying of
Gad, which he spake in the name of the
LORD.
20 And Ornan turned back, and saw the
angel; and his four sons with him hid
themselves. Now Ornan was threshing
wheat.
21 And as David came to Ornan, Ornan
looked and saw David, and went out of
the threshingfloor, and bowed himself to
David with *his* face to the ground.
22 Then David said to Ornan, Grant me
the place of *this* threshingfloor, that I may
build an altar therein unto the LORD: thou
shalt grant it me for the full price: that the
plague may be stayed from the people.

23 And Ornan said unto David, Take *it*
to thee, and let my lord the king do
that which is good in his eyes: lo,I give
thee the oxen *also* for burnt offerings, and
the threshing instruments for wood, and
the wheat for the meat offering; I give
it all.
24 And king David said to Ornan, Nay;
but I will verily buy it for the full price: for
I will not take *that* which *is* thine for the
LORD, nor offer burnt offerings without
cost.
25 So David gave to Ornan for the place
six hundred shekels of gold by weight.
26 And David built there an altar unto
the LORD, and offered burnt offerings and
peace offerings, and called upon the LORD;
and he answered him from heaven by fire
upon the altar of burnt offering.
27 And the LORD commanded the angel;
and he put up his sword again into the
sheath thereof.
28 At that time when David saw that the
LORD had answered him in the threshingfloor of Ornan the Jebusite, then he sacrificed there.
29 For the tabernacle of the LORD, which
Moses made in the wilderness, and the altar of the burnt offering, *were* at that season in the high place at Gibeon.
30 But David could not go before it to
enquire of God: for he was afraid because
of the sword of the angel of the LORD.

22

1 Then David said, This *is* the house of
the LORD God, and this *is* the altar of the
burnt offering for Israel.
2 And David commanded to gather together the strangers that *were* in the land
of Israel; and he set masons to hew
wrought stones to build the house of God.
3 And David prepared iron in abundance
for the nails for the doors of the gates, and
for the joinings; and brass in abundance
without weight;
4 Also cedar trees in abundance: for the
Zidonians and they of Tyre brought much
cedar wood to David.
5 And David said, Solomon my son *is*
young and tender, and the house *that is* to
be builded for the LORD *must be* exceeding
magnifical, of fame and of glory throughout all countries: I will *therefore* now make
preparation for it. So David prepared
abundantly before his death.
6 Then he called for Solomon his son,
and charged him to build an house for the
LORD God of Israel.
7 And David said to Solomon, My son,
as for me, it was in my mind to build an
house unto the name of the LORD my God:
8 But the word of the LORD came to me,
saying, Thou hast shed blood abundantly,
and hast made great wars: thou shalt not
build an house unto my name, because
thou hast shed much blood upon the earth
in my sight.
9 Behold, a son shall be born to thee,
who shall be a man of rest; and I will give
him rest from all his enemies round about:
for his name shall be Solomon, and I will
give peace and quietness unto Israel in his
days.
10 He shall build an house for my name;
and he shall be my son, and I *will be* his
father; and I will establish the throne of
his kingdom over Israel for ever.
11 Now, my son, the LORD be with thee;
and prosper thou, and build the house of
the LORD thy God, as he hath said of thee.
12 Only the LORD
give thee wisdom
and understanding,
and give thee charge
concerning Israel,
that thou mayest
keep the law of the LORD thy God.

22:12 Understanding
◄ Deuteronomy 4:6
Psalm 119:104 ►

13 Then shalt thou prosper, if thou takest
heed to fulfil the statutes and judgments
which the LORD charged Moses with concerning Israel: be strong, and of good courage; dread not, nor be dismayed.
14 Now, behold, in my trouble I have prepared for the house of the LORD an hundred thousand talents of gold, and a
thousand thousand talents of silver; and
of brass and iron without weight; for it is
in abundance: timber also and stone have
I prepared; and thou mayest add thereto.
15 Moreover *there are* workmen with thee
in abundance, hewers and workers of stone
and timber, and all manner of cunning
men for every manner of work.
16 Of the gold, the silver, and the brass,
and the iron, *there is* no number. Arise
therefore, and be doing, and the LORD be
with thee.
17 David also commanded all the princes
of Israel to help Solomon his son, *saying,*
18 *Is* not the LORD your God with you?
and hath he *not* given you rest on every

side? for he hath given the inhabitants of
the land into mine hand; and the land is
subdued before the LORD, and before his
people.
19Now set your heart and your soul to
seek the LORD your God; arise therefore,
and build ye the sanctuary of the LORD
God, to bring the ark of the covenant of
the LORD, and the holy vessels of God, into
the house that is to be built to the name
of the LORD.

23

1So when David was old and full of days,
he made Solomon his son king over Israel.
2And he gathered together all the princes
of Israel, with the priests and the Levites.
3Now the Levites were numbered from
the age of thirty years and upward: and
their number by their polls, man by man,
was thirty and eight thousand.
4Of which, twenty and four thousand
were to set forward the work of the house
of the LORD; and six thousand *were* officers and judges:
5Moreover four thousand *were* porters;
and four thousand praised the LORD with
the instruments which I made, *said David,*
to praise *therewith.*
6And David divided them into courses
among the sons of Levi, *namely,* Gershon,
Kohath, and Merari.
7Of the Gershonites *were,* Laadan, and
Shimei.
8The sons of Laadan; the chief *was* Jehiel, and Zetham, and Joel, three.
9The sons of Shimei; Shelomith, and
Haziel, and Haran, three. These *were* the
chief of the fathers of Laadan.
10And the sons of Shimei *were,* Jahath,
Zina, and Jeush, and Beriah. These four
were the sons of Shimei.
11And Jahath was the chief, and Zizah
the second: but Jeush and Beriah had not
many sons; therefore they were in one reckoning, according to *their* father's house.
12The sons of Kohath; Amram, Izhar,
Hebron, and Uzziel, four.
13The sons of Amram; Aaron and Moses: and Aaron was separated, that he
should sanctify the most holy things, he
and his sons for ever, to burn incense before the LORD, to minister unto him, and
to bless in his name for ever.
14Now *concerning* Moses the man of
God, his sons were named of the tribe of
Levi.
15The sons of Moses *were,* Gershom, and
Eliezer.
16Of the sons of Gershom, Shebuel *was*
the chief.
17And the sons of Eliezer *were,* Rehabiah the chief. And Eliezer had none other
sons; but the sons of Rehabiah were very
many.
18Of the sons of Izhar; Shelomith the
chief.
19Of the sons of Hebron; Jeriah the first,
Amariah the second, Jahaziel the third, and
Jekameam the fourth.
20Of the sons of Uzziel; Micah the first,
and Jesiah the second.
21The sons of Merari; Mahli, and Mushi. The sons of Mahli; Eleazar, and Kish.
22And Eleazar died, and had no sons,
but daughters: and their brethren the sons
of Kish took them.
23The sons of Mushi; Mahli, and Eder,
and Jeremoth, three.
24These *were* the sons of Levi after the
house of their fathers; *even* the chief of the
fathers, as they were counted by number
of names by their polls, that did the work
for the service of the house of the LORD,
from the age of twenty years and upward.
25For David said, The LORD God of Israel hath given rest unto his people, that
they may dwell in Jerusalem for ever:
26And also unto the Levites; they shall
no *more* carry the tabernacle, nor any vessels of it for the service thereof.
27For by the last words of David the Levites *were* numbered from twenty years old
and above:
28Because their office *was* to wait on the
sons of Aaron for the service of the house
of the LORD, in the courts, and in the chambers, and in the purifying of all holy things,
and the work of the service of the house
of God;
29Both for the shewbread, and for the
fine flour for meat offering, and for the
unleavened cakes, and for *that which is*
baked in the pan, and for that which is fried,
and for all manner of measure and size;
30And to stand every morning to thank
and praise the LORD, and likewise at even;
31And to offer all burnt sacrifices unto
the LORD in the sabbaths, in the new
moons, and on the set feasts, by number,
according to the order commanded unto
them, continually before the LORD:

32 And that they should keep the charge of the tabernacle of the congregation, and the charge of the holy *place*, and the charge of the sons of Aaron their brethren, in the service of the house of the LORD.

24

1 Now *these are* the divisions of the sons of Aaron. The sons of Aaron; Nadab, and Abihu, Eleazar, and Ithamar.

2 But Nadab and Abihu died before their father, and had no children: therefore Eleazar and Ithamar executed the priest's office.

3 And David distributed them, both Zadok of the sons of Eleazar, and Ahimelech of the sons of Ithamar, according to their offices in their service.

4 And there were more chief men found of the sons of Eleazar than of the sons of Ithamar; and *thus* were they divided. Among the sons of Eleazar *there were* sixteen chief men of the house of *their* fathers, and eight among the sons of Ithamar according to the house of their fathers.

5 Thus were they divided by lot, one sort with another; for the governors of the sanctuary, and governors *of the house* of God, were of the sons of Eleazar, and of the sons of Ithamar.

6 And Shemaiah the son of Nethaneel the scribe, *one* of the Levites, wrote them before the king, and the princes, and Zadok the priest, and Ahimelech the son of Abiathar, and *before* the chief of the fathers of the priests and Levites: one principal household being taken for Eleazar, and *one* taken for Ithamar.

7 Now the first lot came forth to Jehoiarib, the second to Jedaiah,

8 The third to Harim, the fourth to Seorim,

9 The fifth to Malchijah, the sixth to Mijamin,

10 The seventh to Hakkoz, the eighth to Abijah,

11 The ninth to Jeshua, the tenth to Shecaniah,

12 The eleventh to Eliashib, the twelfth to Jakim,

13 The thirteenth to Huppah, the fourteenth to Jeshebeab,

14 The fifteenth to Bilgah, the sixteenth to Immer,

15 The seventeenth to Hezir, the eighteenth to Aphses,

16 The nineteenth to Pethahiah, the twentieth to Jehezekel,

17 The one and twentieth to Jachin, the two and twentieth to Gamul,

18 The three and twentieth to Delaiah, the four and twentieth to Maaziah.

19 These *were* the orderings of them in their service to come into the house of the LORD, according to their manner, under Aaron their father, as the LORD God of Israel had commanded him.

20 And the rest of the sons of Levi *were these:* Of the sons of Amram; Shubael: of the sons of Shubael; Jehdeiah.

21 Concerning Rehabiah: of the sons of Rehabiah, the first *was* Isshiah.

22 Of the Izharites; Shelomoth: of the sons of Shelomoth; Jahath.

23 And the sons *of Hebron;* Jeriah *the first,* Amariah the second, Jahaziel the third, Jekameam the fourth.

24 *Of* the sons of Uzziel; Michah: of the sons of Michah; Shamir.

25 The brother of Michah *was* Isshiah: of the sons of Isshiah; Zechariah.

26 The sons of Merari *were* Mahli and Mushi: the sons of Jaaziah; Beno.

27 The sons of Merari by Jaaziah; Beno, and Shoham, and Zaccur, and Ibri.

28 Of Mahli *came* Eleazar, who had no sons.

29 Concerning Kish: the son of Kish *was* Jerahmeel.

30 The sons also of Mushi; Mahli, and Eder, and Jerimoth. These *were* the sons of the Levites after the house of their fathers.

31 These likewise cast lots over against their brethren the sons of Aaron in the presence of David the king, and Zadok, and Ahimelech, and the chief of the fathers of the priests and Levites, even the principal fathers over against their younger brethren.

25

1 Moreover David and the captains of the host separated to the service of the sons of Asaph, and of Heman, and of Jeduthun, who should prophesy with harps, with psalteries, and with cymbals: and the number of the workmen according to their service was:

2 Of the sons of Asaph; Zaccur, and Joseph, and Nethaniah, and Asarelah, the sons of Asaph under the hands of Asaph, which prophesied according to the order of the king.

3 Of Jeduthun: the sons of Jeduthun;
Gedaliah, and Zeri, and Jeshaiah, Hashabiah, and Mattithiah, six, under the hands
of their father Jeduthun, who prophesied
with a harp, to give thanks and to praise
the LORD.
4 Of Heman: the sons of Heman; Bukkiah, Mattaniah, Uzziel, Shebuel, and Jerimoth, Hananiah, Hanani, Eliathah,
Giddalti, and Romamti-ezer, Joshbekashah, Mallothi, Hothir, *and* Mahazioth:
5 All these *were* the sons of Heman the
king's seer in the words of God, to lift up
the horn. And God gave to Heman fourteen sons and three daughters.
6 All these *were* under the hands of their
father for song *in* the house of the LORD,
with cymbals, psalteries, and harps, for the
service of the house of God, according to
the king's order to Asaph, Jeduthun, and
Heman.
7 So the number of them, with their
brethren that were instructed in the songs
of the LORD, *even* all that were cunning,
was two hundred fourscore and eight.
8 And they cast lots, ward against *ward,*
as well the small as the great, the teacher
as the scholar.
9 Now the first lot came forth for Asaph
to Joseph: the second to Gedaliah, who
with his brethren and sons *were* twelve:
10 The third to Zaccur, *he,* his sons, and
his brethren, *were* twelve:
11 The fourth to Izri, *he,* his sons, and his
brethren, *were* twelve:
12 The fifth to Nethaniah, *he,* his sons,
and his brethren, *were* twelve:
13 The sixth to Bukkiah, *he,* his sons, and
his brethren, *were* twelve:
14 The seventh to Jesharelah, *he,* his sons,
and his brethren, *were* twelve:
15 The eighth to Jeshaiah, *he,* his sons,
and his brethren, *were* twelve:
16 The ninth to Mattaniah, *he,* his sons,
and his brethren, *were* twelve:
17 The tenth to Shimei, *he,* his sons, and
his brethren, *were* twelve:
18 The eleventh to Azareel, *he,* his sons,
and his brethren, *were* twelve:
19 The twelfth to Hashabiah, *he,* his sons,
and his brethren, *were* twelve:
20 The thirteenth to Shubael, *he,* his sons,
and his brethren, *were* twelve:
21 The fourteenth to Mattithiah, *he,* his
sons, and his brethren, *were* twelve:
22 The fifteenth to Jeremoth, *he,* his sons,
and his brethren, *were* twelve:
23 The sixteenth to Hananiah, *he,* his
sons, and his brethren, *were* twelve:
24 The seventeenth to Joshbekashah, *he,*
his sons, and his brethren, *were* twelve:
25 The eighteenth to Hanani, *he,* his sons,
and his brethren, *were* twelve:
26 The nineteenth to Mallothi, *he,* his
sons, and his brethren, *were* twelve:
27 The twentieth to Eliathah, *he,* his sons,
and his brethren, *were* twelve:
28 The one and twentieth to Hothir, *he,*
his sons, and his brethren, *were* twelve:
29 The two and twentieth to Giddalti, *he,*
his sons, and his brethren, *were* twelve:
30 The three and twentieth to Mahazioth,
he, his sons, and his brethren, *were* twelve:
31 The four and twentieth to Romamti-
ezer, *he,* his sons, and his brethren, *were*
twelve.

26

1 Concerning the divisions of the porters:
Of the Korhites *was* Meshelemiah the son
of Kore, of the sons of Asaph.
2 And the sons of Meshelemiah *were,*
Zechariah the firstborn, Jediael the second,
Zebadiah the third, Jathniel the fourth,
3 Elam the fifth, Jehohanan the sixth,
Elioenai the seventh.
4 Moreover the sons of Obed-edom *were,*
Shemaiah the firstborn, Jehozabad the second, Joah the third, and Sacar the fourth,
and Nethaneel the fifth,
5 Ammiel the sixth, Issachar the seventh,
Peulthai the eighth: for God blessed him.
6 Also unto Shemaiah his son were sons
born, that ruled throughout the house of
their father: for they *were* mighty men of
valour.
7 The sons of Shemaiah; Othni, and Re-
phael, and Obed, Elzabad, whose brethren
were strong men, Elihu, and Semachiah.
8 All these of the sons of Obed-edom:
they and their sons and their brethren, able
men for strength for the service, *were* threescore and two of Obed-edom.
9 And Meshelemiah had sons and brethren, strong men, eighteen.
10 Also Hosah, of the children of Merari, had sons; Simri the chief, (for *though*
he was not the firstborn, yet his father
made him the chief;)
11 Hilkiah the second, Tebaliah the third,
Zechariah the fourth: all the sons and
brethren of Hosah *were* thirteen.

12 Among these *were* the divisions of the porters, *even* among the chief men, *having* wards one against another, to minister in the house of the LORD.

13 And they cast lots, as well the small as the great, according to the house of their fathers, for every gate.

14 And the lot eastward fell to Shelemiah. Then for Zechariah his son, a wise counsellor, they cast lots; and his lot came out northward.

15 To Obed-edom southward; and to his sons the house of Asuppim.

16 To Shuppim and Hosah *the lot came forth* westward, with the gate Shallecheth, by the causeway of the going up, ward against ward.

17 Eastward *were* six Levites, northward four a day, southward four a day, and toward Asuppim two *and* two.

18 At Parbar westward, four at the causeway, *and* two at Parbar.

19 These *are* the divisions of the porters among the sons of Kore, and among the sons of Merari.

20 And of the Levites, Ahijah *was* over the treasures of the house of God, and over the treasures of the dedicated things.

21 *As concerning* the sons of Laadan; the sons of the Gershonite Laadan, chief fathers, *even* of Laadan the Gershonite, *were* Jehieli.

22 The sons of Jehieli; Zetham, and Joel his brother, *which were* over the treasures of the house of the LORD.

23 Of the Amramites, *and* the Izharites, the Hebronites, *and* the Uzzielites:

24 And Shebuel the son of Gershom, the son of Moses, *was* ruler of the treasures.

25 And his brethren by Eliezer; Rehabiah his son, and Jeshaiah his son, and Joram his son, and Zichri his son, and Shelomith his son.

26 Which Shelomith and his brethren *were* over all the treasures of the dedicated things, which David the king, and the chief fathers, the captains over thousands and hundreds, and the captains of the host, had dedicated.

27 Out of the spoils won in battles did they dedicate to maintain the house of the LORD.

28 And all that Samuel the seer, and Saul the son of Kish, and Abner the son of Ner, and Joab the son of Zeruiah, had dedicated; *and* whosoever had dedicated *any thing, it was* under the hand of Shelomith, and of his brethren.

29 Of the Izharites, Chenaniah and his sons *were* for the outward business over Israel, for officers and judges.

30 *And* of the Hebronites, Hashabiah and his brethren, men of valour, a thousand and seven hundred, *were* officers among them of Israel on this side Jordan westward in all the business of the LORD, and in the service of the king.

31 Among the Hebronites *was* Jerijah the chief, *even* among the Hebronites, according to the generations of his fathers. In the fortieth year of the reign of David they were sought for, and there were found among them mighty men of valour at Jazer of Gilead.

32 And his brethren, men of valour, *were* two thousand and seven hundred chief fathers, whom king David made rulers over the Reubenites, the Gadites, and the half tribe of Manasseh, for every matter pertaining to God, and affairs of the king.

27

1 Now the children of Israel after their number, *to wit,* the chief fathers and captains of thousands and hundreds, and their officers that served the king in any matter of the courses, which came in and went out month by month throughout all the months of the year, of every course *were* twenty and four thousand.

2 Over the first course for the first month *was* Jashobeam the son of Zabdiel: and in his course *were* twenty and four thousand.

3 Of the children of Perez *was* the chief of all the captains of the host for the first month.

4 And over the course of the second month *was* Dodai an Ahohite, and of his course *was* Mikloth also the ruler: in his course likewise *were* twenty and four thousand.

5 The third captain of the host for the third month *was* Benaiah the son of Jehoiada, a chief priest: and in his course *were* twenty and four thousand.

6 This *is that* Benaiah, *who was* mighty *among* the thirty, and above the thirty: and in his course *was* Ammizabad his son.

7 The fourth *captain* for the fourth month *was* Asahel the brother of Joab, and Zebadiah his son after him: and in his course *were* twenty and four thousand.

8 The fifth captain for the fifth month *was* Shamhuth the Izrahite: and in his course *were* twenty and four thousand.

9 The sixth *captain* for the sixth month *was* Ira the son of Ikkesh the Tekoite: and in his course *were* twenty and four thousand.

10 The seventh *captain* for the seventh month *was* Helez the Pelonite, of the children of Ephraim: and in his course *were* twenty and four thousand.

11 The eighth *captain* for the eighth month *was* Sibbecai the Hushathite, of the Zarhites: and in his course *were* twenty and four thousand.

12 The ninth *captain* for the ninth month *was* Abiezer the Anetothite, of the Benjamites: and in his course *were* twenty and four thousand.

13 The tenth *captain* for the tenth month *was* Maharai the Netophathite, of the Zarhites: and in his course *were* twenty and four thousand.

14 The eleventh *captain* for the eleventh month *was* Benaiah the Pirathonite, of the children of Ephraim: and in his course *were* twenty and four thousand.

15 The twelfth *captain* for the twelfth month *was* Heldai the Netophathite, of Othniel: and in his course *were* twenty and four thousand.

16 Furthermore over the tribes of Israel: the ruler of the Reubenites *was* Eliezer the son of Zichri: of the Simeonites, Shephatiah the son of Maachah:

17 Of the Levites, Hashabiah the son of Kemuel: of the Aaronites, Zadok:

18 Of Judah, Elihu, *one* of the brethren of David: of Issachar, Omri the son of Michael:

19 Of Zebulun, Ishmaiah the son of Obadiah: of Naphtali, Jerimoth the son of Azriel:

20 Of the children of Ephraim, Hoshea the son of Azaziah: of the half tribe of Manasseh, Joel the son of Pedaiah:

21 Of the half *tribe* of Manasseh in Gilead, Iddo the son of Zechariah: of Benjamin, Jaasiel the son of Abner:

22 Of Dan, Azareel the son of Jeroham. These *were* the princes of the tribes of Israel.

23 But David took not the number of them from twenty years old and under: because the LORD had said he would increase Israel like to the stars of the heavens.

24 Joab the son of Zeruiah began to number, but he finished not, because there fell wrath for it against Israel; neither was the number put in the account of the chronicles of king David.

25 And over the king's treasures *was* Azmaveth the son of Adiel: and over the storehouses in the fields, in the cities, and in the villages, and in the castles, *was* Jehonathan the son of Uzziah:

26 And over them that did the work of the field for tillage of the ground *was* Ezri the son of Chelub:

27 And over the vineyards was Shimei the Ramathite: over the increase of the vineyards for the wine cellars *was* Zabdi the Shiphmite:

28 And over the olive trees and the sycomore trees that *were* in the low plains *was* Baal-hanan the Gederite: and over the cellars of oil *was* Joash:

29 And over the herds that fed in Sharon *was* Shitrai the Sharonite: and over the herds *that were* in the valleys *was* Shaphat the son of Adlai:

30 Over the camels also *was* Obil the Ishmaelite: and over the asses *was* Jehdeiah the Meronothite:

31 And over the flocks *was* Jaziz the Hagerite. All these *were* the rulers of the substance which *was* king David's.

32 Also Jonathan David's uncle was a counsellor, a wise man, and a scribe: and Jehiel the son of Hachmoni *was* with the king's sons:

33 And Ahithophel *was* the king's counsellor: and Hushai the Archite *was* the king's companion:

34 And after Ahithophel *was* Jehoiada the son of Benaiah, and Abiathar: and the general of the king's army *was* Joab.

28

1 And David assembled all the princes of Israel, the princes of the tribes, and the captains of the companies that ministered to the king by course, and the captains over the thousands, and captains over the hundreds, and the stewards over all the substance and possession of the king, and of his sons, with the officers, and with the mighty men, and with all the valiant men, unto Jerusalem.

2 Then David the king stood up upon his feet, and said, Hear me, my brethren, and

my people: *As for me,* I *had* in mine heart to build an house of rest for the ark of the covenant of the LORD, and for the footstool of our God, and had made ready for the building:

3 But God said unto me, Thou shalt not build an house for my name, because thou *hast been* a man of war, and hast shed blood.

4 Howbeit the LORD God of Israel chose me before all the house of my father to be king over Israel for ever: for he hath chosen Judah *to be* the ruler; and of the house of Judah, the house of my father; and among the sons of my father he liked me to make *me* king over all Israel:

5 And of all my sons, (for the LORD hath given me many sons,) he hath chosen Solomon my son to sit upon the throne of the kingdom of the LORD over Israel.

6 And he said unto me, Solomon thy son, he shall build my house and my courts: for I have chosen him *to be* my son, and I will be his father.

7 Moreover I will establish his kingdom for ever, if he be constant to do my commandments and my judgments, as at this day.

8 Now therefore in the sight of all Israel the congregation of the LORD, and in the audience of our God, keep and seek for all the commandments of the LORD your God: that ye may possess this good land, and leave *it* for an inheritance for your children after you for ever.

9 And thou, Solomon my son, know thou the God of thy father, and serve him with a perfect heart and with a willing mind: for the LORD searcheth all hearts, and understandeth all the imaginations of the thoughts: if thou seek him, he will be found of thee; but if thou forsake him, he will cast thee off for ever.

10 Take heed now; for the LORD hath chosen thee to build an house for the sanctuary: be strong, and do *it.*

11 Then David gave to Solomon his son the pattern of the porch, and of the houses thereof, and of the treasuries thereof, and of the upper chambers thereof, and of the inner parlours thereof, and of the place of the mercy seat,

12 And the pattern of all that he had by the spirit, of the courts of the house of the LORD, and of all the chambers round about, of the treasuries of the house of God, and of the treasuries of the dedicated things:

13 Also for the courses of the priests and the Levites, and for all the work of the service of the house of the LORD, and for all the vessels of service in the house of the LORD.

14 *He gave* of gold by weight for *things* of gold, for all instruments of all manner of service; *silver also* for all instruments of silver by weight, for all instruments of every kind of service:

15 Even the weight for the candlesticks of gold, and for their lamps of gold, by weight for every candlestick, and for the lamps thereof: and for the candlesticks of silver by weight, *both* for the candlestick, and *also* for the lamps thereof, according to the use of every candlestick.

16 And by weight *he gave* gold for the tables of shewbread, for every table; and *likewise* silver for the tables of silver:

17 Also pure gold for the fleshhooks, and the bowls, and the cups: and for the golden basons *he gave gold* by weight for every bason; and *likewise silver* by weight for every bason of silver:

18 And for the altar of incense refined gold by weight; and gold for the pattern of the chariot of the cherubims, that spread out *their wings,* and covered the ark of the covenant of the LORD.

19 All *this, said David,* the LORD made me understand in writing by *his* hand upon me, *even* all the works of this pattern.

20 And David said to Solomon his son, Be strong and of good courage, and do *it:* fear not, nor be dismayed: for the LORD God, *even* my God, *will be* with thee; he will not fail thee, nor forsake thee, until thou hast finished all the work for the service of the house of the LORD.

21 And, behold, the courses of the priests and the Levites, *even they shall be with thee* for all the service of the house of God: and *there shall be* with thee for all manner of workmanship every willing skilful man, for any manner of service: also the princes and all the people *will be* wholly at thy commandment.

29

1 Furthermore David the king said unto all the congregation, Solomon my son, whom alone God hath chosen, *is yet* young and tender, and the work *is* great: for the palace *is* not for man, but for the LORD God.

2 Now I have prepared with all my might for the house of my God the gold for *things to be made* of gold, and the silver for *things* of silver, and the brass for *things* of brass, the iron for *things* of iron, and wood for *things* of wood; onyx stones, and *stones* to be set, glistering stones, and of divers colours, and all manner of precious stones, and marble stones in abundance.

3 Moreover, because I have set my affection to the house of my God, I have of mine own proper good, of gold and silver, *which* I have given to the house of my God, over and above all that I have prepared for the holy house,

29:3-4 Examples of Generosity
◄ Numbers 7:3
2 Chronicles 24:10 ►

4 *Even* three thousand talents of gold, of the gold of Ophir, and seven thousand talents of refined silver, to overlay the walls of the houses *withal:*

5 The gold for *things* of gold, and the silver for *things* of silver, and for all manner of work *to be made* by the hands of artificers. And who *then* is willing to consecrate his service this day unto the LORD?

29:5 Commitment
◄ Exodus 32:29
Proverbs 23:26 ►

6 Then the chief of the fathers and princes of the tribes of Israel, and the captains of thousands and of hundreds, with the rulers of the king's work, offered willingly,

7 And gave for the service of the house of God of gold five thousand talents and ten thousand drams, and of silver ten thousand talents, and of brass eighteen thousand talents, and one hundred thousand talents of iron.

8 And they with whom *precious* stones were found gave *them* to the treasure of the house of the LORD, by the hand of Jehiel the Gershonite.

9 Then the people rejoiced, for that they offered willingly, because with perfect heart they offered willingly to the LORD: and David the king also rejoiced with great joy.

29:9 Tithing
◄ 2 Samuel 8:10-11
2 Chronicles 15:18 ►

10 Wherefore David blessed the LORD before all the congregation: and David said, Blessed *be* thou, LORD God of Israel our father, for ever and ever.

29:10 Names of God
◄ 2 Samuel 22:2
Psalm 71:22 ►

11 Thine, O LORD, *is* the greatness, and the power, and the glory, and the victory, and the majesty: for all *that is* in the heaven and in the earth *is thine;* thine *is* the kingdom, O LORD, and thou art exalted as head above all.

29:10 Perfect Father
◄ Psalm 68:5 ►

12 Both riches and honour *come* of thee, and thou reignest over all; and in thine hand *is* power and might; and in thine hand *it is* to make great, and to give strength unto all.

29:12 God's Control
◄ Deuteronomy 4:39
Job 9:12 ►

29:12 God's Power
◄ 2 Chronicles 25:8 ►

13 Now therefore, our God, we thank thee, and praise thy glorious name.

14 But who *am* I, and what *is* my people, that we should be able to offer so willingly after this sort? for all things *come* of thee, and of thine own have we given thee.

29:12 Source of Wealth
◄ Deuteronomy 8:18
Ecclesiastes 5:19 ►

29:14 Earth
◄ Leviticus 25:23
Psalm 24:1 ►

15 For we *are* strangers before thee, and sojourners, as *were* all our fathers: our days on the earth *are* as a shadow, and *there is* none abiding.

29:15 Life Is Short
◄ Genesis 47:9
Job 7:6 ►

16 O LORD our God, all this store that we have prepared to build thee an house for thine holy name *cometh* of thine hand, and *is* all thine own.

17 I know also, my God, that thou triest the heart, and hast pleasure in uprightness. As for me, in the uprightness of mine heart I have willingly offered all these things: and now have I seen with joy thy people,

which are present here, to offer willingly
unto thee.
18O LORD God of Abraham, Isaac, and
of Israel, our fathers, keep this for ever in
the imagination of the thoughts of the
heart of thy people, and prepare their heart
unto thee:
19And give unto Solomon my son a perfect heart, to keep thy commandments, thy
testimonies, and thy statutes, and to do all
these things, and to build the palace, for
the which I have made provision.
20And David said to all the congregation, Now bless the LORD your God. And
all the congregation blessed the LORD God
of their fathers, and bowed down their
heads, and worshipped the LORD, and the
king.
21And they sacrificed sacrifices unto the
LORD, and offered burnt offerings unto the
LORD, on the morrow after that day, *even* a
thousand bullocks, a thousand rams, *and* a
thousand lambs, with their drink offerings,
and sacrifices in abundance for all Israel:
22And did eat and drink before the LORD
on that day with great gladness. And they
made Solomon the son of David king the
second time, and anointed *him* unto the
LORD *to be* the chief governor, and Zadok
to be priest.
23Then Solomon sat on the throne of
the LORD as king instead of David his father, and prospered; and all Israel obeyed
him.
24And all the princes, and the mighty
men, and all the sons likewise of king
David, submitted themselves unto Solomon the king.
25And the LORD magnified Solomon exceedingly in the sight of all Israel, and bestowed upon him *such* royal majesty as had
not been on any king before him in Israel.
26Thus David the son of Jesse reigned
over all Israel.
27And the time that he reigned over Israel *was* forty years; seven years reigned he
in Hebron, and thirty and three *years*
reigned he in Jerusalem.
28And he died in a good old age, full of
days, riches, and honour: and Solomon his
son reigned in his stead.
29Now the acts of David the king, first
and last, behold, they *are* written in the
book of Samuel the seer, and in the book
of Nathan the prophet, and in the book
of Gad the seer,
30With all his reign and his might, and
the times that went over him, and over Israel, and over all the kingdoms of the
countries.

2 Chronicles

AUTHOR
Probably Ezra the scribe

MAIN POINT
God wants to unify his people around worship of him and shows his standards in his dealings with the kings of Judah.

DATE WRITTEN
Approximately 430 B.C.

36 CHAPTERS

MAIN PEOPLE

Solomon, the queen of Sheba, Rehoboam, Asa, Jehoshaphat, Jehoram, Joash, Uzziah, Ahaz, Hezekiah, Manasseh, Josiah

SPECIAL FEATURES

- *Was originally one book with 1 Chronicles*
- *Provides a commentary on 1 and 2 Kings, emphasizing the history of faith instead of politics, especially in Judah*
- *Records the construction of the temple right down to the fine details*
- *Tells the story of Joash, one of the best kings of either kingdom, who became king at age seven*
- *Describes how Nebuchadnezzar conquered Judah, destroyed Jerusalem, and took the people of Israel captive to Babylon*
- *Ninth book of History*

HOW THE BOOK GOT ITS NAME

When Jerome translated the book from Hebrew into Latin, he proclaimed it "the chronicle of the whole of sacred history" (the Hebrew name means "journals").

1

1And Solomon the son of David was
strengthened in his kingdom, and the
LORD his God *was* with him, and magnified him exceedingly.
2Then Solomon spake unto all Israel, to
the captains of thousands and of hundreds, and to the judges, and to every governor in all Israel, the chief of the fathers.
3So Solomon, and all the congregation
with him, went to the high place that *was*
at Gibeon; for there was the tabernacle of
the congregation of God, which Moses the
servant of the LORD had made in the wilderness.
4But the ark of God had David brought
up from Kirjath-jearim to *the place which*
David had prepared for it: for he had
pitched a tent for it at Jerusalem.
5Moreover the brasen altar, that Bezaleel
the son of Uri, the son of Hur, had made,
he put before the tabernacle of the LORD:
and Solomon and the congregation sought
unto it.
6And Solomon went up thither to the

brasen altar before the LORD, which *was* at
the tabernacle of the congregation, and offered a thousand burnt offerings upon it.
7In that night did God appear unto Solomon, and said unto him, Ask what I shall
give thee.
8And Solomon said unto God, Thou
hast shewed great mercy unto David my
father, and hast made me to reign in his
stead.
9Now, O LORD God, let thy promise
unto David my father be established: for
thou hast made me king over a people like
the dust of the earth in multitude.
10Give me now
wisdom and knowl-
edge, that I may go
out and come in
before this people:
for who can judge
this thy people, *that is so* great?

1:10
Praying for Wisdom
◄ Psalm 90:12 ►

11And God said to Solomon, Because
this was in thine heart, and thou hast not
asked riches, wealth, or honour, nor the
life of thine enemies, neither yet hast asked
long life; but hast asked wisdom and
knowledge for thyself, that thou mayest
judge my people, over whom I have made
thee king:
12Wisdom and knowledge *is* granted
unto thee; and I will give thee riches, and
wealth, and honour, such as none of the
kings have had that *have been* before thee,
neither shall there any after thee have the
like.
13Then Solomon came *from his journey*
to the high place that *was* at Gibeon to Jerusalem, from before the tabernacle of the
congregation, and reigned over Israel.
14And Solomon gathered chariots and
horsemen: and he had a thousand and four
hundred chariots, and twelve thousand
horsemen, which he placed in the chariot
cities, and with the king at Jerusalem.
15And the king made silver and gold at
Jerusalem *as plenteous* as stones, and cedar
trees made he as the sycomore trees that
are in the vale for abundance.
16And Solomon had horses brought out
of Egypt, and linen yarn: the king's merchants received the linen yarn at a price.
17And they fetched up, and brought
forth out of Egypt a chariot for six hundred *shekels* of silver, and an horse for an
hundred and fifty: and so brought they out
horses for all the kings of the Hittites, and
for the kings of Syria, by their means.

2

1And Solomon determined to build an
house for the name of the LORD, and an
house for his kingdom.
2And Solomon told out threescore and
ten thousand men to bear burdens, and
fourscore thousand to hew in the mountain, and three thousand and six hundred
to oversee them.
3And Solomon sent to Huram the king
of Tyre, saying, As thou didst deal with
David my father, and didst send him cedars to build him an house to dwell
therein, *even so deal with me.*
4Behold, I build an house to the name
of the LORD my God, to dedicate *it* to him,
and to burn before him sweet incense, and
for the continual shewbread, and for the
burnt offerings morning and evening, on
the sabbaths, and on the new moons, and
on the solemn feasts of the LORD our God.
This *is an ordinance* for ever to Israel.
5And the house which I build *is* great:
for great *is* our God above all gods.
6But who is able to build him an house,
seeing the heaven and heaven of heavens
cannot contain him? who *am* I then, that I
should build him an house, save only to
burn sacrifice before him?
7Send me now therefore a man cunning
to work in gold, and in silver, and in brass,
and in iron, and in purple, and crimson,
and blue, and that can skill to grave with
the cunning men that *are* with me in Judah and in Jerusalem, whom David my
father did provide.
8Send me also cedar trees, fir trees, and
algum trees, out of Lebanon: for I know
that thy servants can skill to cut timber in
Lebanon; and, behold, my servants *shall
be* with thy servants,
9Even to prepare me timber in abundance: for the house which I am about to
build *shall be* wonderful great.
10And, behold, I will give to thy servants,
the hewers that cut timber, twenty thousand measures of beaten wheat, and twenty thousand measures of barley, and twenty
thousand baths of wine, and twenty thousand baths of oil.
11Then Huram the king of Tyre answered
in writing, which he sent to Solomon, Because the LORD hath loved his people, he
hath made thee king over them.

12 Huram said moreover, Blessed *be* the LORD God of Israel, that made heaven and earth, who hath given to David the king a wise son, endued with prudence and understanding, that might build an house for the LORD, and an house for his kingdom.

13 And now I have sent a cunning man, endued with understanding, of Huram my father's,

14 The son of a woman of the daughters of Dan, and his father *was* a man of Tyre, skilful to work in gold, and in silver, in brass, in iron, in stone, and in timber, in purple, in blue, and in fine linen, and in crimson; also to grave any manner of graving, and to find out every device which shall be put to him, with thy cunning men, and with the cunning men of my lord David thy father.

15 Now therefore the wheat, and the barley, the oil, and the wine, which my lord hath spoken of, let him send unto his servants:

16 And we will cut wood out of Lebanon, as much as thou shalt need: and we will bring it to thee in flotes by sea to Joppa; and thou shall carry it up to Jerusalem.

17 And Solomon numbered all the strangers that *were* in the land of Israel, after the numbering wherewith David his father had numbered them; and they were found an hundred and fifty thousand and three thousand and six hundred.

18 And he set threescore and ten thousand of them *to be* bearers of burdens, and fourscore thousand *to be* hewers in the mountain, and three thousand and six hundred overseers to set the people a work.

3

1 Then Solomon began to build the house of the LORD at Jerusalem in mount Moriah, where *the LORD* appeared unto David his father, in the place that David had prepared in the threshingfloor of Ornan the Jebusite.

2 And he began to build in the second *day* of the second month, in the fourth year of his reign.

3 Now these *are the things wherein* Solomon was instructed for the building of the house of God. The length by cubits after the first measure *was* threescore cubits, and the breadth twenty cubits.

4 And the porch that *was* in the front *of the house,* the length *of it was* according to the breadth of the house, twenty cubits, and the height *was* an hundred and twenty: and he overlaid it within with pure gold.

5 And the greater house he cieled with fir tree, which he overlaid with fine gold, and set thereon palm trees and chains.

6 And he garnished the house with precious stones for beauty: and the gold *was* gold of Parvaim.

7 He overlaid also the house, the beams, the posts, and the walls thereof, and the doors thereof, with gold; and graved cherubims on the walls.

8 And he made the most holy house, the length whereof *was* according to the breadth of the house, twenty cubits, and the breadth thereof twenty cubits: and he overlaid it with fine gold, *amounting* to six hundred talents.

9 And the weight of the nails *was* fifty shekels of gold. And he overlaid the upper chambers with gold.

10 And in the most holy house he made two cherubims of image work, and overlaid them with gold.

11 And the wings of the cherubims *were* twenty cubits long: one wing *of the one cherub was* five cubits, reaching to the wall of the house: and the other wing *was likewise* five cubits, reaching to the wing of the other cherub.

12 And *one* wing of the other cherub *was* five cubits, reaching to the wall of the house: and the other wing *was* five cubits *also,* joining to the wing of the other cherub.

13 The wings of these cherubims spread themselves forth twenty cubits: and they stood on their feet, and their faces *were* inward.

14 And he made the vail *of* blue, and purple, and crimson, and fine linen, and wrought cherubims thereon.

15 Also he made before the house two pillars of thirty and five cubits high, and the chapiter that *was* on the top of each of them *was* five cubits.

16 And he made chains, *as* in the oracle, and put *them* on the heads of the pillars; and made an hundred pomegranates, and put *them* on the chains.

17 And he reared up the pillars before the temple, one on the right hand, and the other on the left; and called the name of that on the right hand Jachin, and the name of that on the left Boaz.

4

1 Moreover he made an altar of brass,
twenty cubits the length thereof, and twenty cubits the breadth thereof, and ten cubits the height thereof.
2 Also he made a molten sea of ten cubits from brim to brim, round in compass,
and five cubits the height thereof; and a
line of thirty cubits did compass it round
about.
3 And under it *was* the similitude of oxen,
which did compass it round about: ten in
a cubit, compassing the sea round about.
Two rows of oxen *were* cast, when it was
cast.
4 It stood upon twelve oxen, three looking toward the north, and three looking
toward the west, and three looking toward
the south, and three looking toward the
east: and the sea *was set* above upon them,
and all their hinder parts *were* inward.
5 And the thickness of it *was* an handbreadth, and the brim of it like the work
of the brim of a cup, with flowers of lilies;
and it received and held three thousand
baths.
6 He made also ten lavers, and put five
on the right hand,and five on the left, to
wash in them: such things as they offered
for the burnt offering they washed in them;
but the sea *was* for the priests to wash in.
7 And he made ten candlesticks of gold
according to their form, and set *them* in
the temple, five on the right hand, and five
on the left.
8 He made also ten tables, and placed
them in the temple, five on the right side,
and five on the left. And he made an hundred basons of gold.
9 Furthermore he made the court of the
priests, and the great court, and doors for
the court, and overlaid the doors of them
with brass.
10 And he set the sea on the right side of
the east end, over against the south.
11 And Huram made the pots, and the
shovels, and the basons. And Huram finished the work that he was to make for
king Solomon for the house of God;
12 *To wit,* the two pillars, and the pommels, and the chapiters *which were* on the
top of the two pillars, and the two wreaths
to cover the two pommels of the chapiters
which *were* on the top of the pillars;
13 And four hundred pomegranates on
the two wreaths; two rows of pomegranates on each wreath, to cover the two pommels of the chapiters which *were* upon the
pillars.
14 He made also bases, and lavers made
he upon the bases;
15 One sea, and twelve oxen under it.
16 The pots also, and the shovels, and the
fleshhooks, and all their instruments, did
Huram his father make to king Solomon
for the house of the LORD of bright brass.
17 In the plain of Jordan did the king cast
them, in the clay ground between Succoth
and Zeredathah.
18 Thus Solomon made all these vessels
in great abundance: for the weight of the
brass could not be found out.
19 And Solomon made all the vessels that
were for the house of God, the golden altar
also, and the tables whereon the shewbread *was set;*
20 Moreover the candlesticks with their
lamps, that they should burn after the
manner before the oracle, of pure gold;
21 And the flowers, and the lamps, and
the tongs, *made he of* gold, *and* that perfect
gold;
22 And the snuffers, and the basons, and
the spoons, and the censers, *of* pure gold:
and the entry of the house, the inner doors
thereof for the most holy *place,* and the
doors of the house of the temple, *were of*
gold.

5

1 Thus all the work that Solomon made
for the house of the LORD was finished:
and Solomon brought in *all* the things that
David his father had dedicated; and the
silver, and the gold, and all the instruments, put he among the treasures of the
house of God.
2 Then Solomon assembled the elders of
Israel, and all the heads of the tribes, the
chief of the fathers of the children of Israel, unto Jerusalem, to bring up the ark
of the covenant of the LORD out of the city
of David, which *is* Zion.
3 Wherefore all the men of Israel assembled themselves unto the king in the feast
which *was* in the seventh month.
4 And all the elders of Israel came; and
the Levites took up the ark.
5 And they brought up the ark, and the
tabernacle of the congregation, and all
the holy vessels that *were* in the tabernacle, these did the priests *and* the Levites
bring up.

6 Also king Solomon, and all the congregation of Israel that were assembled
unto him before the ark, sacrificed sheep
and oxen, which could not be told nor
numbered for multitude.
7 And the priests brought in the ark of
the covenant of the LORD unto his place,
to the oracle of the house, into the most
holy *place, even* under the wings of the
cherubims:
8 For the cherubims spread forth *their*
wings over the place of the ark, and the
cherubims covered the ark and the staves
thereof above.
9 And they drew out the staves *of the ark,*
that the ends of the staves were seen from
the ark before the oracle; but they were not
seen without. And there it is unto this day.
10 *There was* nothing in the ark save the
two tables which Moses put *therein* at Horeb, when the LORD made *a covenant* with
the children of Israel, when they came out
of Egypt.
11 And it came to pass, when the priests
were come out of the holy *place:* (for all
the priests *that were* present were sanctified, *and* did not *then* wait by course:
12 Also the Levites *which were* the singers, all of them of Asaph, of Heman, of
Jeduthun, with their sons and their brethren, *being* arrayed in white linen, having
cymbals and psalteries and harps, stood
at the east end of the altar, and with them
an hundred and twenty priests sounding
with trumpets:)
13 It came even to
pass, as the trum-
peters and singers
were as one, to make
one sound to be
heard in praising
and thanking the LORD; and when they lifted up *their* voice with the trumpets and
cymbals and instruments of musick, and
praised the LORD, *saying,* For *he is* good;
for his mercy *endureth* for ever: that *then*
the house was filled with a cloud, *even* the
house of the LORD;
14 So that the priests could not stand
to minister by reason of the cloud: for the
glory of the LORD had filled the house
of God.

5:13-14
Christian Duties
◄ John 9:4 ►

6

1 Then said Solomon, The LORD hath
said that he would dwell in the thick darkness.
2 But I have built an house of habitation
for thee, and a place for thy dwelling for
ever.
3 And the king turned his face, and
blessed the whole congregation of Israel:
and all the congregation of Israel stood.
4 And he said, Blessed *be* the LORD God
of Israel, who hath with his hands fulfilled
that which he spake with his mouth to my
father David, saying,
5 Since the day that I brought forth my
people out of the land of Egypt I chose no
city among all the tribes of Israel to build
an house in, that my name might be there;
neither chose I any man to be a ruler over
my people Israel:
6 But I have chosen Jerusalem, that my
name might be there; and have chosen
David to be over my people Israel.
7 Now it was in the heart of David my
father to build an house for the name of
the LORD God of Israel.
8 But the LORD said to David my father,
Forasmuch as it was in thine heart to build
an house for my name, thou didst well in
that it was in thine heart:
9 Notwithstanding thou shalt not build
the house; but thy son which shall come
forth out of thy loins, he shall build the
house for my name.
10 The LORD therefore hath performed
his word that he hath spoken: for I am ris-
en up in the room of David my father, and
am set on the throne of Israel, as the LORD
promised, and have built the house for the
name of the LORD God of Israel.
11 And in it have I put the ark, wherein *is*
the covenant of the LORD, that he made
with the children of Israel.
12 And he stood before the altar of the
LORD in the presence of all the congregation of Israel, and spread forth his hands:
13 For Solomon had made a brasen scaf-
fold, of five cubits long, and five cubits
broad, and three cubits high, and had set
it in the midst of the court: and upon it he
stood, and kneeled down upon his knees
before all the congregation of Israel, and
spread forth his hands toward heaven,
14 And said, O LORD God of Israel, *there
is* no God like thee in the heaven, nor in
the earth; which keepest covenant, and
shewest mercy unto thy servants, that walk
before thee with all their hearts:
15 Thou which hast kept with thy servant

David my father that which thou hast
promised him; and spakest with thy
mouth, and hast fulfilled *it* with thine
hand, as *it is* this day.
16Now therefore, O LORD God of Israel,
keep with thy servant David my father that
which thou hast promised him, saying,
There shall not fail thee a man in my sight
to sit upon the throne of Israel; yet so that
thy children take heed to their way to walk
in my law, as thou hast walked before me.
17Now then, O LORD God of Israel, let
thy word be verified, which thou hast spoken unto thy servant David.
18But will God in very deed dwell with
men on the earth? behold, heaven and the
heaven of heavens cannot contain thee;
how much less this house which I have
built!
19Have respect therefore to the prayer
of thy servant, and to his supplication,
O LORD my God, to hearken unto the cry
and the prayer which thy servant prayeth
before thee:
20That thine eyes may be open upon this
house day and night, upon the place
whereof thou hast said that thou wouldest
put thy name there; to hearken unto the
prayer which thy servant prayeth toward
this place.
21Hearken therefore unto the supplications of thy servant, and of thy people Israel, which they shall make toward this
place: hear thou from thy dwelling place,
even from heaven; and when thou hearest,
forgive.
22If a man sin against his neighbour, and
an oath be laid upon him to make him
swear, and the oath come before thine altar in this house;
23Then hear thou from heaven, and do,
and judge thy servants, by requiting the
wicked, by recompensing his way upon his
own head; and by justifying the righteous,
by giving him according to his righteousness.
24And if thy people Israel be put to the
worse before the enemy, because they have
sinned against thee; and shall return and
confess thy name, and pray and make supplication before thee in this house;
25Then hear thou from the heavens, and
forgive the sin of thy people Israel, and
bring them again unto the land which thou
gavest to them and to their fathers.
26When the heaven is shut up, and there
is no rain, because they have sinned against
thee; *yet* if they pray toward this place, and
confess thy name, and turn from their sin,
when thou dost afflict them;
27Then hear thou from heaven, and forgive the sin of thy servants, and of thy people Israel, when thou hast taught them the
good way, wherein they should walk; and
send rain upon thy land, which thou hast
given unto thy people for an inheritance.
28If there be dearth in the land, if there
be pestilence, if there be blasting, or mildew, locusts, or caterpillers; if their enemies besiege them in the cities of their
land; whatsoever sore or whatsoever sickness *there be:*
29*Then* what prayer *or* what supplication
soever shall be made of any man, or of all
thy people Israel, when every one shall
know his own sore and his own grief, and
shall spread forth his hands in this house:
30Then hear thou from heaven thy
dwelling place, and forgive, and render
unto every man according unto all his
ways, whose heart thou knowest; (for thou
only knowest the hearts of the children of
men:)
31That they may fear thee, to walk in thy
ways, so long as they live in the land which
thou gavest unto our fathers.
32Moreover concerning the stranger,
which is not of thy people Israel, but is
come from a far country for thy great
name's sake, and thy mighty hand, and thy
stretched out arm; if they come and pray
in this house;
33Then hear thou from the heavens, *even*
from thy dwelling place, and do according to all that the stranger calleth to thee
for; that all people of the earth may know
thy name, and fear thee, as *doth* thy people Israel, and may know that this house
which I have built is called by thy name.
34If thy people go out to war against
their enemies by the way that thou shalt
send them, and they pray unto thee toward
this city which thou hast chosen, and the
house which I have built for thy name;
35Then hear thou from the heavens their
prayer and their supplication, and maintain their cause.
36If they sin against thee, (for *there is* no
man which sinneth not,) and thou be angry with them, and deliver them over be-

fore *their* enemies, and they carry them
away captives unto a land far off or near;
37 Yet *if* they bethink themselves in the
land whither they are carried captive, and
turn and pray unto thee in the land of their
captivity, saying, We have sinned, we have
done amiss, and have dealt wickedly;
38 If they return to thee with all their
heart and with all their soul in the land of
their captivity, whither they have carried
them captives, and pray toward their land,
which thou gavest unto their fathers, and
toward the city which thou hast chosen,
and toward the house which I have built
for thy name:
39 Then hear thou from the heavens, *even*
from thy dwelling place, their prayer and
their supplications, and maintain their
cause, and forgive thy people which have
sinned against thee.
40 Now, my God, let, I beseech thee,
thine eyes be open, and *let* thine ears *be*
attent unto the prayer *that is made* in this
place.
41 Now therefore arise, O LORD God, into
thy resting place, thou, and the ark of thy
strength: let thy priests, O LORD God, be
clothed with salvation, and let thy saints
rejoice in goodness.
42 O LORD God, turn not away the face
of thine anointed: remember the mercies
of David thy servant.

7

1 Now when Solomon had made an end
of praying, the fire came down from
heaven, and consumed the burnt offering
and the sacrifices; and the glory of the
LORD filled the house.
2 And the priests could not enter into the
house of the LORD, because the glory of
the LORD had filled the LORD'S house.
3 And when all the children of Israel saw
how the fire came down, and the glory of
the LORD upon the house, they bowed
themselves with their faces to the ground
upon the pavement, and worshipped, and
praised the LORD, *saying,* For *he is* good;
for his mercy *endureth* for ever.
4 Then the king and all the people offered sacrifices before the LORD.
5 And king Solomon offered a sacrifice
of twenty and two thousand oxen, and an
hundred and twenty thousand sheep: so
the king and all the people dedicated the
house of God.
6 And the priests waited on their offices:
the Levites also with instruments of musick
of the LORD, which David the king had
made to praise the LORD, because his mercy *endureth* for ever, when David praised
by their ministry; and the priests sounded
trumpets before them, and all Israel stood.
7 Moreover Solomon hallowed the middle of the court that *was* before the house
of the LORD: for there he offered burnt
offerings, and the fat of the peace offerings, because the brasen altar which Solomon had made was not able to receive the
burnt offerings, and the meat offerings,
and the fat.
8 Also at the same time Solomon kept
the feast seven days, and all Israel with
him, a very great congregation, from the
entering in of Hamath unto the river of
Egypt.
9 And in the eighth day they made a solemn assembly: for they kept the dedication of the altar seven days, and the feast
seven days.
10 And on the three and twentieth day
of the seventh month he sent the people
away into their tents, glad and merry in
heart for the goodness that the LORD had
shewed unto David, and to Solomon, and
to Israel his people.
11 Thus Solomon finished the house of
the LORD, and the king's house: and all that
came into Solomon's heart to make in the
house of the LORD, and in his own house,
he prosperously effected.
12 And the LORD appeared to Solomon
by night, and said unto him, I have heard
thy prayer, and have chosen this place to
myself for an house of sacrifice.
13 If I shut up heaven that there be no
rain, or if I command the locusts to devour the land, or if I send pestilence among
my people;
14 If my people,
which are called
by my name, shall
humble themselves,
and pray, and seek
my face, and turn
from their wicked ways; then will I hear
from heaven, and will forgive their sin, and
will heal their land.

7:14
How to Pray
◄ Isaiah 58:9 ►

15 Now mine eyes shall be open, and
mine ears attent unto the prayer *that is
made* in this place.
16 For now have I chosen and sanctified

this house, that my name may be there for ever: and mine eyes and mine heart shall be there perpetually.

17 And as for thee, if thou wilt walk before me, as David thy father walked, and do according to all that I have commanded thee, and shalt observe my statutes and my judgments;

18 Then will I stablish the throne of thy kingdom, according as I have covenanted with David thy father, saying, There shall not fail thee a man *to be* ruler in Israel.

19 But if ye turn away, and forsake my statutes and my commandments, which I have set before you, and shall go and serve other gods, and worship them;

20 Then will I pluck them up by the roots out of my land which I have given them; and this house, which I have sanctified for my name, will I cast out of my sight, and will make it *to be* a proverb and a byword among all nations.

21 And this house, which is high, shall be an astonishment to every one that passeth by it; so that he shall say, Why hath the LORD done thus unto this land, and unto this house?

22 And it shall be answered, Because they forsook the LORD God of their fathers, which brought them forth out of the land of Egypt, and laid hold on other gods, and worshipped them, and served them: therefore hath he brought all this evil upon them.

8

1 And it came to pass at the end of twenty years, wherein Solomon had built the house of the LORD, and his own house,

2 That the cities which Huram had restored to Solomon, Solomon built them, and caused the children of Israel to dwell there.

3 And Solomon went to Hamath-zobah, and prevailed against it.

4 And he built Tadmor in the wilderness, and all the store cities, which he built in Hamath.

5 Also he built Beth-horon the upper, and Beth-horon the nether, fenced cities, with walls, gates, and bars;

6 And Baalath, and all the store cities that Solomon had, and all the chariot cities, and the cities of the horsemen, and all that Solomon desired to build in Jerusalem, and in Lebanon, and throughout all the land of his dominion.

7 *As for* all the people *that were* left of the Hittites, and the Amorites, and the Perizzites, and the Hivites, and the Jebusites, which *were* not of Israel,

8 *But* of their children, who were left after them in the land, whom the children of Israel consumed not, them did Solomon make to pay tribute until this day.

9 But of the children of Israel did Solomon make no servants for his work; but they *were* men of war, and chief of his captains, and captains of his chariots and horsemen.

10 And these *were* the chief of king Solomon's officers, *even* two hundred and fifty, that bare rule over the people.

11 And Solomon brought up the daughter of Pharaoh out of the city of David unto the house that he had built for her: for he said, My wife shall not dwell in the house of David king of Israel, because *the places are* holy, whereunto the ark of the LORD hath come.

12 Then Solomon offered burnt offerings unto the LORD on the altar of the LORD, which he had built before the porch,

13 Even after a certain rate every day, offering according to the commandment of Moses, on the sabbaths, and on the new moons, and on the solemn feasts, three times in the year, *even* in the feast of unleavened bread, and in the feast of weeks, and in the feast of tabernacles.

14 And he appointed, according to the order of David his father, the courses of the priests to their service, and the Levites to their charges, to praise and minister before the priests, as the duty of every day required: the porters also by their courses at every gate: for so had David the man of God commanded.

15 And they departed not from the commandment of the king unto the priests and Levites concerning any matter, or concerning the treasures.

16 Now all the work of Solomon was prepared unto the day of the foundation of the house of the LORD, and until it was finished. *So* the house of the LORD was perfected.

17 Then went Solomon to Ezion-geber, and to Eloth, at the sea side in the land of Edom.

18 And Huram sent him by the hands of his servants ships, and servants that had

knowledge of the sea; and they went
with the servants of Solomon to Ophir,
and took thence four hundred and fifty
talents of gold, and brought *them* to king
Solomon.

9

1 And when the queen of Sheba heard
of the fame of Solomon, she came to prove
Solomon with hard questions at Jerusalem, with a very great company, and camels that bare spices, and gold in abundance,
and precious stones: and when she was
come to Solomon, she communed with
him of all that was in her heart.
2 And Solomon told her all her questions: and there was nothing hid from
Solomon which he told her not.
3 And when the queen of Sheba had seen
the wisdom of Solomon, and the house
that he had built,
4 And the meat of his table, and the sitting of his servants, and the attendance
of his ministers, and their apparel; his cupbearers also, and their apparel; and his
ascent by which he went up into the house
of the LORD; there was no more spirit
in her.
5 And she said to the king, *It was* a true
report which I heard in mine own land of
thine acts, and of thy wisdom:
6 Howbeit I believed not their words,
until I came, and mine eyes had seen *it:*
and, behold, the one half of the greatness
of thy wisdom was not told me: *for* thou
exceedest the fame that I heard.
7 Happy *are* thy men, and happy *are* these
thy servants, which stand continually before thee, and hear thy wisdom.
8 Blessed be the LORD thy God, which
delighted in thee to set thee on his throne,
to be king for the LORD thy God: because
thy God loved Israel, to establish them for
ever, therefore made he thee king over
them, to do judgment and justice.
9 And she gave the king an hundred and
twenty talents of gold, and of spices great
abundance, and precious stones: neither
was there any such spice as the queen of
Sheba gave king Solomon.
10 And the servants also of Huram, and
the servants of Solomon, which brought
gold from Ophir, brought algum trees and
precious stones.
11 And the king made *of* the algum trees
terraces to the house of the LORD, and to
the king's palace, and harps and psalteries
for singers: and there were none such seen
before in the land of Judah.
12 And king Solomon gave to the queen
of Sheba all her desire, whatsoever she
asked, beside *that* which she had brought
unto the king. So she turned, and went
away to her own land, she and her servants.
13 Now the weight of gold that came to
Solomon in one year was six hundred and
threescore and six talents of gold;
14 Beside *that which* chapmen and merchants brought. And all the kings of Arabia and governors of the country brought
gold and silver to Solomon.
15 And king Solomon made two hundred
targets of beaten gold: six hundred *shekels*
of beaten gold went to one target.
16 And three hundred shields *made he of*
beaten gold: three hundred *shekels* of gold
went to one shield. And the king put them
in the house of the forest of Lebanon.
17 Moreover the king made a great throne
of ivory, and overlaid it with pure gold.
18 And *there were* six steps to the throne,
with a footstool of gold, *which were* fastened to the throne, and stays on each side
of the sitting place, and two lions standing by the stays:
19 And twelve lions stood there on the
one side and on the other upon the six
steps. There was not the like made in any
kingdom.
20 And all the drinking vessels of king
Solomon *were of* gold, and all the vessels
of the house of the forest of Lebanon *were*
of pure gold: none *were of* silver; it was *not*
any thing accounted of in the days of Solomon.
21 For the king's ships went to Tarshish
with the servants of Huram: every three
years once came the ships of Tarshish
bringing gold, and silver, ivory, and apes,
and peacocks.
22 And king Solomon passed all the
kings of the earth in riches and wisdom.
23 And all the kings of the earth sought
the presence of Solomon, to hear his wisdom, that God had put in his heart.
24 And they brought every man his
present, vessels of silver, and vessels of
gold, and raiment, harness, and spices,
horses, and mules, a rate year by year.
25 And Solomon had four thousand
stalls for horses and chariots, and twelve
thousand horsemen; whom he bestowed

in the chariot cities, and with the king at Jerusalem.

26 And he reigned over all the kings from the river even unto the land of the Philistines, and to the border of Egypt.

27 And the king made silver in Jerusalem as stones, and cedar trees made he as the sycomore trees that *are* in the low plains in abundance.

28 And they brought unto Solomon horses out of Egypt, and out of all lands.

29 Now the rest of the acts of Solomon, first and last, *are* they not written in the book of Nathan the prophet, and in the prophecy of Ahijah the Shilonite, and in the visions of Iddo the seer against Jeroboam the son of Nebat?

30 And Solomon reigned in Jerusalem over all Israel forty years.

31 And Solomon slept with his fathers, and he was buried in the city of David his father: and Rehoboam his son reigned in his stead.

10

1 And Rehoboam went to Shechem: for to Shechem were all Israel come to make him king.

2 And it came to pass, when Jeroboam the son of Nebat, who *was* in Egypt, whither he had fled from the presence of Solomon the king, heard *it*, that Jeroboam returned out of Egypt.

3 And they sent and called him. So Jeroboam and all Israel came and spake to Rehoboam, saying,

4 Thy father made our yoke grievous: now therefore ease thou somewhat the grievous servitude of thy father, and his heavy yoke that he put upon us, and we will serve thee.

5 And he said unto them, Come again unto me after three days. And the people departed.

6 And king Rehoboam took counsel with the old men that had stood before Solomon his father while he yet lived, saying, What counsel give ye *me* to return answer to this people?

7 And they spake unto him, saying, If thou be kind to this people, and please them, and speak good words to them, they will be thy servants for ever.

8 But he forsook the counsel which the old men gave him, and took counsel with the young men that were brought up with him, that stood before him.

9 And he said unto them, What advice give ye that we may return answer to this people, which have spoken to me, saying, Ease somewhat the yoke that thy father did put upon us?

10 And the young men that were brought up with him spake unto him, saying, Thus shalt thou answer the people that spake unto thee, saying, Thy father made our yoke heavy, but make thou *it* somewhat lighter for us; thus shalt thou say unto them, My little *finger* shall be thicker than my father's loins.

11 For whereas my father put a heavy yoke upon you, I will put more to your yoke: my father chastised you with whips, but I *will chastise you* with scorpions.

12 So Jeroboam and all the people came to Rehoboam on the third day, as the king bade, saying, Come again to me on the third day.

13 And the king answered them roughly; and king Rehoboam forsook the counsel of the old men,

14 And answered them after the advice of the young men, saying, My father made your yoke heavy, but I will add thereto: my father chastised you with whips, but I *will chastise you* with scorpions.

15 So the king hearkened not unto the people: for the cause was of God, that the LORD might perform his word, which he spake by the hand of Ahijah the Shilonite to Jeroboam the son of Nebat.

16 And when all Israel *saw* that the king would not hearken unto them, the people answered the king, saying, What portion have we in David? and *we have* none inheritance in the son of Jesse: every man to your tents, O Israel: *and* now, David, see to thine own house. So all Israel went to their tents.

17 But *as for* the children of Israel that dwelt in the cities of Judah, Rehoboam reigned over them.

18 Then king Rehoboam sent Hadoram that *was* over the tribute; and the children of Israel stoned him with stones, that he died. But king Rehoboam made speed to get him up to *his* chariot, to flee to Jerusalem.

19 And Israel rebelled against the house of David unto this day.

11

1 And when Rehoboam was come to Jerusalem, he gathered of the house of Judah and Benjamin an hundred and four-

score thousand chosen *men*, which were
warriors, to fight against Israel, that he
might bring the kingdom again to Rehoboam.
2 But the word of the LORD came to Shemaiah the man of God, saying,
3 Speak unto Rehoboam the son of Solomon, king of Judah, and to all Israel in
Judah and Benjamin, saying,
4 Thus saith the LORD, Ye shall not go
up, nor fight against your brethren: return
every man to his house: for this thing is
done of me. And they obeyed the words
of the LORD, and returned from going
against Jeroboam.
5 And Rehoboam dwelt in Jerusalem,
and built cities for defence in Judah.
6 He built even Bethlehem, and Etam,
and Tekoa,
7 And Beth-zur, and Shoco, and Adullam,
8 And Gath, and Mareshah, and Ziph,
9 And Adoraim, and Lachish, and Azekah,
10 And Zorah, and Aijalon, and Hebron,
which *are* in Judah and in Benjamin fenced
cities.
11 And he fortified the strong holds, and
put captains in them, and store of victual,
and of oil and wine.
12 And in every several city *he put* shields
and spears, and made them exceeding
strong, having Judah and Benjamin on his
side.
13 And the priests and the Levites that
were in all Israel resorted to him out of all
their coasts.
14 For the Levites left their suburbs and
their possession, and came to Judah and
Jerusalem: for Jeroboam and his sons had
cast them off from executing the priest's
office unto the LORD:
15 And he ordained him priests for the
high places, and for the devils, and for the
calves which he had made.
16 And after them out of all the tribes of
Israel such as set their hearts to seek the
LORD God of Israel came to Jerusalem, to
sacrifice unto the LORD God of their fathers.
17 So they strengthened the kingdom of
Judah, and made Rehoboam the son of
Solomon strong, three years: for three years
they walked in the way of David and Solomon.
18 And Rehoboam took him Mahalath
the daughter of Jerimoth the son of David
to wife, *and* Abihail the daughter of Eliab
the son of Jesse;
19 Which bare him children; Jeush, and
Shamariah, and Zaham.
20 And after her he took Maachah the
daughter of Absalom; which bare him
Abijah, and Attai, and Ziza, and Shelomith.
21 And Rehoboam loved Maachah the
daughter of Absalom above all his wives
and his concubines: (for he took eighteen
wives, and threescore concubines; and
begat twenty and eight sons, and threescore daughters.)
22 And Rehoboam made Abijah the son
of Maachah the chief, *to be* ruler among
his brethren: for *he thought* to make him
king.
23 And he dealt wisely, and dispersed of
all his children throughout all the countries of Judah and Benjamin, unto every
fenced city: and he gave them victual in
abundance. And he desired many wives.

12

1 And it came to pass, when Rehoboam
had established the kingdom, and had
strengthened himself, he forsook the law
of the LORD, and all Israel with him.
2 And it came to pass, *that* in the fifth
year of king Rehoboam Shishak king of
Egypt came up against Jerusalem, because
they had transgressed against the LORD,
3 With twelve hundred chariots, and
threescore thousand horsemen: and the
people *were* without number that came
with him out of Egypt; the Lubim, the
Sukkiims, and the Ethiopians.
4 And he took the fenced cities which
pertained to Judah, and came to Jerusalem.
5 Then came Shemaiah the prophet to
Rehoboam, and *to* the princes of Judah,
that were gathered together to Jerusalem
because of Shishak, and said unto them,
Thus saith the LORD, Ye have forsaken me,
and therefore have I also left you in the
hand of Shishak.
6 Whereupon the princes of Israel and
the king humbled themselves; and they
said, The LORD *is* righteous.
7 And when the LORD saw that they humbled themselves, the word of the LORD
came to Shemaiah, saying, They have humbled themselves; *therefore* I will not destroy
them, but I will grant them some deliverance; and my wrath shall not be poured

out upon Jerusalem by the hand of Shishak.
8 Nevertheless they shall be his servants;
that they may know my service, and the
service of the kingdoms of the countries.
9 So Shishak king of Egypt came up
against Jerusalem, and took away the treasures of the house of the LORD, and the
treasures of the king's house; he took all:
he carried away also the shields of gold
which Solomon had made.
10 Instead of which king Rehoboam
made shields of brass, and committed *them*
to the hands of the chief of the guard, that
kept the entrance of the king's house.
11 And when the king entered into the
house of the LORD, the guard came and
fetched them, and brought them again into
the guard chamber.
12 And when he humbled himself, the
wrath of the LORD turned from him that
he would not destroy *him* altogether: and
also in Judah things went well.
13 So king Rehoboam strengthened himself in Jerusalem, and reigned: for Rehoboam *was* one and forty years old when
he began to reign, and he reigned seventeen years in Jerusalem, the city which the
LORD had chosen out of all the tribes of
Israel, to put his name there. And his
mother's name *was* Naamah an Ammonitess.
14 And he did evil, because he prepared
not his heart to seek the LORD.
15 Now the acts of Rehoboam, first and
last, *are* they not written in the book of
Shemaiah the prophet, and of Iddo the
seer concerning genealogies? And *there*
were wars between Rehoboam and Jeroboam continually.
16 And Rehoboam slept with his fathers,
and was buried in the city of David: and
Abijah his son reigned in his stead.

13

1 Now in the eighteenth year of king Jeroboam began Abijah to reign over Judah.
2 He reigned three years in Jerusalem. His
mother's name also *was* Michaiah the
daughter of Uriel of Gibeah. And there was
war between Abijah and Jeroboam.
3 And Abijah set the battle in array with
an army of valiant men of war, *even* four
hundred thousand chosen men: Jeroboam
also set the battle in array against him with
eight hundred thousand chosen men, *be-*
ing mighty men of valour.
4 And Abijah stood up upon mount
Zemaraim, which *is* in mount Ephraim,
and said, Hear me, thou Jeroboam, and
all Israel;
5 Ought ye not to know that the LORD
God of Israel gave the kingdom over Israel
to David for ever, *even* to him and to his
sons by a covenant of salt?
6 Yet Jeroboam the son of Nebat, the servant of Solomon the son of David, is risen
up, and hath rebelled against his lord.
7 And there are gathered unto him vain
men, the children of Belial, and have
strengthened themselves against Rehoboam the son of Solomon, when Rehoboam
was young and tenderhearted, and could
not withstand them.
8 And now ye think to withstand the
kingdom of the LORD in the hand of the
sons of David; and ye *be* a great multitude,
and *there are* with you golden calves, which
Jeroboam made you for gods.
9 Have ye not cast out the priests of the
LORD, the sons of Aaron, and the Levites,
and have made you priests after the manner of the nations of *other* lands? so that
whosoever cometh to consecrate himself
with a young bullock and seven rams, *the*
same may be a priest of *them that are* no
gods.
10 But as for us, the LORD *is* our God, and
we have not forsaken him; and the priests,
which minister unto the LORD, *are* the sons
of Aaron, and the Levites *wait* upon *their*
business:
11 And they burn unto the LORD every
morning and every evening burnt sacrifices
and sweet incense: the shewbread also *set*
they in order upon the pure table; and the
candlestick of gold with the lamps thereof,
to burn every evening: for we keep the
charge of the LORD our God; but ye have
forsaken him.
12 And, behold, God himself is with us
for *our* captain, and his priests with sounding trumpets to cry alarm against you.
O children of Israel, fight ye not against
the LORD God of your fathers; for ye shall
not prosper.
13 But Jeroboam caused an ambushment
to come about behind them: so they were
before Judah, and the ambushment *was*
behind them.
14 And when Judah looked back, behold,
the battle *was* before and behind: and they

cried unto the LORD, and the priests sounded with the trumpets.
15Then the men of Judah gave a shout:
and as the men of Judah shouted, it came
to pass, that God smote Jeroboam and all
Israel before Abijah and Judah.
16And the children of Israel fled before
Judah: and God delivered them into their
hand.
17And Abijah and his people slew them
with a great slaughter: so there fell down
slain of Israel five hundred thousand chosen men.
18Thus the children of Israel were
brought under at that time, and the children of Judah prevailed, because they relied upon the LORD God of their fathers.
19And Abijah pursued after Jeroboam,
and took cities from him, Bethel with the
towns thereof, and Jeshanah with the
towns thereof, and Ephrain with the towns
thereof.
20Neither did Jeroboam recover strength
again in the days of Abijah: and the LORD
struck him, and he died.
21But Abijah waxed mighty, and married
fourteen wives, and begat twenty and two
sons, and sixteen daughters.
22And the rest of the acts of Abijah, and
his ways, and his sayings, *are* written in the
story of the prophet Iddo.

14

1So Abijah slept with his fathers, and
they buried him in the city of David: and
Asa his son reigned in his stead. In his days
the land was quiet ten years.
2And Asa did *that which was* good and
right in the eyes of the LORD his God:
3For he took away the altars of the
strange *gods,* and the high places, and brake
down the images, and cut down the groves:
4And command-
ed Judah to seek the
LORD God of their
fathers, and to do
the law and the
commandment.

14:4 Seeking God
◄ Deuteronomy 4:29
Psalm 105:4 ►

5Also he took away out of all the cities
of Judah the high places and the images:
and the kingdom was quiet before him.
6And he built fenced cities in Judah: for
the land had rest, and he had no war in
those years; because the LORD had given
him rest.
7Therefore he said unto Judah, Let us
build these cities, and make about *them*
walls, and towers, gates, and bars, *while* the
land *is* yet before us; because we have
sought the LORD our God, we have sought
him, and he hath given us rest on every
side. So they built and prospered.
8And Asa had an army *of men* that bare
targets and spears, out of Judah three hundred thousand; and out of Benjamin, that
bare shields and drew bows, two hundred
and fourscore thousand: all these *were*
mighty men of valour.
9And there came out against them Zerah
the Ethiopian with an host of a thousand
thousand, and three hundred chariots; and
came unto Mareshah.
10Then Asa went out against him, and
they set the battle in array in the valley of
Zephathah at Mareshah.
11And Asa cried unto the LORD his God,
and said, LORD, *it is* nothing with thee to
help, whether with many, or with them
that have no power: help us, O LORD our
God; for we rest on thee, and in thy name
we go against this multitude. O LORD, thou
art our God; let not man prevail against
thee.
12So the LORD smote the Ethiopians before Asa and before Judah; and the Ethiopians fled.
13And Asa and the people that *were* with
him pursued them unto Gerar: and the
Ethiopians were overthrown, that they
could not recover themselves; for they were
destroyed before the LORD, and before his
host; and they carried away very much
spoil.
14And they smote all the cities round
about Gerar; for the fear of the LORD came
upon them: and they spoiled all the cities;
for there was exceeding much spoil in
them.
15They smote also the tents of cattle, and
carried away sheep and camels in abundance, and returned to Jerusalem.

15

1And the Spirit of God came upon Azariah the son of Oded:
2And he went out to meet Asa, and said
unto him, Hear ye me, Asa, and all Judah
and Benjamin; The LORD *is* with you, while
ye be with him; and if ye seek him, he will
be found of you; but if ye forsake him, he
will forsake you.
3Now for a long season Israel *hath been*
without the true God, and without a teaching priest, and without law.

4 But when they in their trouble did turn unto the LORD God of Israel, and sought him, he was found of them.

5 And in those times *there was* no peace to him that went out, nor to him that came in, but great vexations *were* upon all the inhabitants of the countries.

6 And nation was destroyed of nation, and city of city: for God did vex them with all adversity.

7 Be ye strong therefore, and let not your hands be weak: for your work shall be rewarded.

8 And when Asa heard these words, and the prophecy of Oded the prophet, he took courage, and put away the abominable idols out of all the land of Judah and Benjamin, and out of the cities which he had taken from mount Ephraim, and renewed the altar of the LORD, that *was* before the porch of the LORD.

9 And he gathered all Judah and Benjamin, and the strangers with them out of Ephraim and Manasseh, and out of Simeon: for they fell to him out of Israel in abundance, when they saw that the LORD his God *was* with him.

10 So they gathered themselves together at Jerusalem in the third month, in the fifteenth year of the reign of Asa.

11 And they offered unto the LORD the same time, of the spoil *which* they had brought, seven hundred oxen and seven thousand sheep.

12 And they entered into a covenant to seek the LORD God of their fathers with all their heart and with all their soul;

13 That whosoever would not seek the LORD God of Israel should be put to death, whether small or great, whether man or woman.

14 And they sware unto the LORD with a loud voice, and with shouting, and with trumpets, and with cornets.

15 And all Judah rejoiced at the oath: for they had sworn with all their heart, and sought him with their whole desire; and he was found of them: and the LORD gave them rest round about.

16 And also *concerning* Maachah the mother of Asa the king, he removed her from *being* queen, because she had made an idol in a grove: and Asa cut down her idol, and stamped *it,* and burnt *it* at the brook Kidron.

17 But the high places were not taken away out of Israel: nevertheless the heart of Asa was perfect all his days.

18 And he brought into the house of God the things that his father had dedicated, and that he himself had dedicated, silver, and gold, and vessels.

15:18 Tithing
◄ 1 Chronicles 29:9
Ezra 8:28 ►

19 And there was no *more* war unto the five and thirtieth year of the reign of Asa.

16

1 In the six and thirtieth year of the reign of Asa Baasha king of Israel came up against Judah, and built Ramah, to the intent that he might let none go out or come in to Asa king of Judah.

2 Then Asa brought out silver and gold out of the treasures of the house of the LORD and of the king's house, and sent to Ben-hadad king of Syria, that dwelt at Damascus, saying,

3 *There is* a league between me and thee, as *there was* between my father and thy father: behold, I have sent thee silver and gold; go, break thy league with Baasha king of Israel, that he may depart from me.

4 And Ben-hadad hearkened unto king Asa, and sent the captains of his armies against the cities of Israel; and they smote Ijon, and Dan, and Abel-maim, and all the store cities of Naphtali.

5 And it came to pass, when Baasha heard *it,* that he left off building of Ramah, and let his work cease.

6 Then Asa the king took all Judah; and they carried away the stones of Ramah, and the timber thereof, wherewith Baasha was building; and he built therewith Geba and Mizpah.

7 And at that time Hanani the seer came to Asa king of Judah, and said unto him, Because thou hast relied on the king of Syria, and not relied on the LORD thy God, therefore is the host of the king of Syria escaped out of thine hand.

8 Were not the Ethiopians and the Lubims a huge host, with very many chariots and horsemen? yet, because thou didst rely on the LORD, he delivered them into thine hand.

9 For the eyes of the LORD run to and fro throughout

16:9
Protection
◄ Psalm 34:7 ►

the whole earth, to shew himself strong in
the behalf of *them* whose heart *is* perfect
toward him. Herein thou hast done foolishly: therefore from henceforth thou shalt
have wars.
10 Then Asa was
wroth with the seer,
and put him in a
prison house; for *he*
was in a rage with
him because of this
thing. And Asa oppressed *some* of the
people the same time.

16:10 Mad
◄ 2 Kings 5:12
Esther 3:5 ►

11 And, behold, the acts of Asa, first and
last, lo, they *are* written in the book of the
kings of Judah and Israel.
12 And Asa in the
thirty and ninth
year of his reign was
diseased in his feet,
until his disease *was*
exceeding *great*: yet
in his disease he sought not to the LORD,
but to the physicians.

16:12 Only Human
◄ 1 Kings 22:43
Jonah 1:3 ►

13 And Asa slept with his fathers, and
died in the one and fortieth year of his
reign.
14 And they buried him in his own sepulchres, which he had made for himself
in the city of David, and laid him in the
bed which was filled with sweet odours
and divers kinds *of spices* prepared by the
apothecaries' art: and they made a very
great burning for him.

17

1 And Jehoshaphat his son reigned in his
stead, and strengthened himself against
Israel.
2 And he placed forces in all the fenced
cities of Judah, and set garrisons in the
land of Judah, and in the cities of Ephraim, which Asa his father had taken.
3 And the LORD was with Jehoshaphat,
because he walked in the first ways of his
father David, and sought not unto Baalim;
4 But sought to the *LORD* God of his father, and walked in his commandments,
and not after the doings of Israel.
5 Therefore the LORD stablished the kingdom in his hand; and all Judah brought
to Jehoshaphat presents; and he had riches
and honour in abundance.
6 And his heart was lifted up in the ways
of the LORD: moreover he took away the
high places and groves out of Judah.
7 Also in the third year of his reign he sent
to his princes, *even*
to Ben-hail, and to
Obadiah, and to
Zechariah, and
to Nethaneel, and
to Michaiah, to
teach in the cities of Judah.

17:7 Sunday School
◄ 2 Kings 17:28
Ezra 7:10 ►

8 And with them *he sent* Levites, *even* Shemaiah, and Nethaniah, and Zebadiah, and
Asahel, and Shemiramoth, and Jehonathan, and Adonijah, and Tobijah, and Tob-
adonijah, Levites; and with them Elishama
and Jehoram, priests.
9 And they taught in Judah, and *had* the
book of the law of the LORD with them,
and went about throughout all the cities
of Judah, and taught the people.
10 And the fear of the LORD fell upon all
the kingdoms of the lands that *were* round
about Judah, so that they made no war
against Jehoshaphat.
11 Also *some* of the Philistines brought
Jehoshaphat presents, and tribute silver;
and the Arabians brought him flocks,
seven thousand and seven hundred rams,
and seven thousand and seven hundred he
goats.
12 And Jehoshaphat waxed great exceedingly; and he built in Judah castles, and
cities of store.
13 And he had much business in the cities of Judah: and the men of war, mighty
men of valour, *were* in Jerusalem.
14 And these *are* the numbers of them
according to the house of their fathers: Of
Judah, the captains of thousands; Adnah
the chief, and with him mighty men of
valour three hundred thousand.
15 And next to him *was* Jehohanan the
captain, and with him two hundred and
fourscore thousand.
16 And next him *was* Amasiah the son of
Zichri, who willingly offered himself unto
the LORD; and with him two hundred
thousand mighty men of valour.
17 And of Benjamin; Eliada a mighty
man of valour, and with him armed men
with bow and shield two hundred thousand.
18 And next him *was* Jehozabad, and with
him an hundred and fourscore thousand
ready prepared for the war.
19 These waited on the king, beside *those*
whom the king put in the fenced cities
throughout all Judah.

18

1 Now Jehoshaphat had riches and
honour in abundance, and joined affinity
with Ahab.
2 And after *certain* years he went down
to Ahab to Samaria. And Ahab killed sheep
and oxen for him in abundance, and for
the people that *he had* with him, and persuaded him to go up *with him* to Ramoth-
gilead.
3 And Ahab king of Israel said unto Jehoshaphat king of Judah, Wilt thou go
with me to Ramoth-gilead? And he answered him, I *am* as thou *art,* and my people as thy people; and *we will be* with thee
in the war.
4 And Jehoshaphat said unto the king of
Israel, Enquire, I pray thee, at the word of
the LORD to day.
5 Therefore the king of Israel gathered
together of prophets four hundred men,
and said unto them, Shall we go to Ramoth-
gilead to battle, or shall I forbear? And they
said, Go up; for God will deliver *it* into
the king's hand.
6 But Jehoshaphat said, *Is there* not here
a prophet of the LORD besides, that we
might enquire of him?
7 And the king of Israel said unto Jehoshaphat, *There is* yet one man, by whom we
may enquire of the LORD: but I hate him;
for he never prophesied good unto me, but
always evil: the same *is* Micaiah the son of
Imla. And Jehoshaphat said, Let not the
king say so.
8 And the king of Israel called for one *of
his* officers, and said, Fetch quickly Micaiah the son of Imla.
9 And the king of Israel and Jehoshaphat
king of Judah sat either of them on his
throne, clothed in *their* robes, and they sat
in a void place at the entering in of the
gate of Samaria; and all the prophets
prophesied before them.
10 And Zedekiah the son of Chenaanah
had made him horns of iron, and said,
Thus saith the LORD, With these thou shalt
push Syria until they be consumed.
11 And all the prophets prophesied so,
saying, Go up to Ramoth-gilead, and prosper: for the LORD shall deliver *it* into the
hand of the king.
12 And the messenger that went to call
Micaiah spake to him, saying, Behold, the
words of the prophets *declare* good to the
king with one assent; let thy word therefore, I pray thee, be like one of theirs, and
speak thou good.
13 And Micaiah said, *As* the LORD liveth,
even what my God saith, that will I speak.
14 And when he was come to the king,
the king said unto him, Micaiah, shall we
go to Ramoth-gilead to battle, or shall I
forbear? And he said, Go ye up, and prosper, and they shall be delivered into your
hand.
15 And the king said to him, How many
times shall I adjure thee that thou say nothing but the truth to me in the name of the
LORD?
16 Then he said, I did see all Israel scattered upon the mountains, as sheep that
have no shepherd: and the LORD said,
These have no master; let them return *therefore* every man to his house in peace.
17 And the king of Israel said to Jehoshaphat, Did I not tell thee *that* he would
not prophesy good unto me, but evil?
18 Again he said, Therefore hear the word
of the LORD; I saw the LORD sitting upon
his throne, and all the host of heaven
standing on his right hand and *on* his left.
19 And the LORD said, Who shall entice
Ahab king of Israel, that he may go up and
fall at Ramoth-gilead? And one spake saying after this manner, and another saying
after that manner.
20 Then there came out a spirit, and
stood before the LORD, and said, I will
entice him. And the LORD said unto him,
Wherewith?
21 And he said, I will go out, and be a
lying spirit in the mouth of all his prophets. And *the LORD said,* Thou shalt entice
him, and thou shalt also prevail: go out,
and do *even* so.
22 Now therefore, behold, the LORD hath
put a lying spirit in the mouth of these thy
prophets, and the LORD hath spoken evil
against thee.
23 Then Zedekiah the son of Chenaanah
came near, and smote Micaiah upon the
cheek, and said, Which way went the Spirit of the LORD from me to speak unto thee?
24 And Micaiah said, Behold, thou shalt
see on that day when thou shalt go into
an inner chamber to hide thyself.
25 Then the king of Israel said, Take ye
Micaiah, and carry him back to Amon the
governor of the city, and to Joash the king's
son;

26 And say, Thus saith the king, Put this *fellow* in the prison, and feed him with bread of affliction and with water of affliction, until I return in peace.

27 And Micaiah said, If thou certainly return in peace, *then* hath not the LORD spoken by me. And he said, Hearken, all ye people.

28 So the king of Israel and Jehoshaphat the king of Judah went up to Ramoth-gilead.

29 And the king of Israel said unto Jehoshaphat, I will disguise myself, and will go to the battle; but put thou on thy robes. So the king of Israel disguised himself; and they went to the battle.

30 Now the king of Syria had commanded the captains of the chariots that *were* with him, saying, Fight ye not with small or great, save only with the king of Israel.

31 And it came to pass, when the captains of the chariots saw Jehoshaphat, that they said, It *is* the king of Israel. Therefore they compassed about him to fight: but Jehoshaphat cried out, and the LORD helped him; and God moved them *to depart* from him.

32 For it came to pass, that, when the captains of the chariots perceived that it was not the king of Israel, they turned back again from pursuing him.

33 And a *certain* man drew a bow at a venture, and smote the king of Israel between the joints of the harness: therefore he said to his chariot man, Turn thine hand, that thou mayest carry me out of the host; for I am wounded.

34 And the battle increased that day: howbeit the king of Israel stayed *himself* up in *his* chariot against the Syrians until the even: and about the time of the sun going down he died.

19

1 And Jehoshaphat the king of Judah returned to his house in peace to Jerusalem.

2 And Jehu the son of Hanani the seer went out to meet him, and said to king Jehoshaphat, Shouldest thou help the ungodly, and love them that hate the LORD? therefore is wrath upon thee from before the LORD.

3 Nevertheless there are good things found in thee, in that thou hast taken away the groves out of the land, and hast prepared thine heart to seek God.

4 And Jehoshaphat dwelt at Jerusalem: and he went out again through the people from Beer-sheba to mount Ephraim, and brought them back unto the LORD God of their fathers.

5 And he set judges in the land throughout all the fenced cities of Judah, city by city,

6 And said to the judges, Take heed what ye do: for ye judge not for man, but for the LORD, who *is* with you in the judgment.

19:6 Leaders Should...
◄ 2 Samuel 23:3
Psalm 2:10-11 ►

7 Wherefore now let the fear of the LORD be upon you; take heed and do *it:* for *there is* no iniquity with the LORD our God, nor respect of persons, nor taking of gifts.

19:7 Fearing God
◄ 1 Chronicles 16:30
Proverbs 3:7 ►

8 Moreover in Jerusalem did Jehoshaphat set of the Levites, and *of* the priests, and of the chief of the fathers of Israel, for the judgment of the LORD, and for controversies, when they returned to Jerusalem.

9 And he charged them, saying, Thus shall ye do in the fear of the LORD, faithfully, and with a perfect heart.

10 And what cause soever shall come to you of your brethren that dwell in their cities, between blood and blood, between law and commandment, statutes and judgments, ye shall even warn them that they trespass not against the LORD, and *so* wrath come upon you, and upon your brethren: this do, and ye shall not trespass.

11 And, behold, Amariah the chief priest *is* over you in all matters of the LORD; and Zebadiah the son of Ishmael, the ruler of the house of Judah, for all the king's matters: also the Levites *shall be* officers before you. Deal courageously, and the LORD shall be with the good.

20

1 It came to pass after this also, *that* the children of Moab, and the children of Ammon, and with them *other* beside the Ammonites, came against Jehoshaphat to battle.

2 Then there came some that told Jehoshaphat, saying, There cometh a great multitude against thee from beyond the sea on this side Syria; and, behold, they *be* Hazazon-tamar, which *is* En-gedi.

3 And Jehoshaphat feared, and set

himself to seek the LORD, and proclaimed a fast throughout all Judah.

4 And Judah gathered themselves together, to ask *help* of the LORD: even out of all the cities of Judah they came to seek the LORD.

5 And Jehoshaphat stood in the congregation of Judah and Jerusalem, in the house of the LORD, before the new court,

6 And said, O LORD God of our fathers, *art* not thou God in heaven? and rulest *not* thou over all the kingdoms of the heathen? and in thine hand *is there not* power and might, so that none is able to withstand thee?

7 *Art* not thou our God, *who* didst drive out the inhabitants of this land before thy people Israel, and gavest it to the seed of Abraham thy friend for ever?

20:7 God's Friends
◄ Deuteronomy 34:10
James 2:23 ►

8 And they dwelt therein, and have built thee a sanctuary therein for thy name, saying,

9 If, *when* evil cometh upon us, *as* the sword, judgment, or pestilence, or famine, we stand before this house, and in thy presence, (for thy name *is* in this house,) and cry unto thee in our affliction, then thou wilt hear and help.

10 And now, behold, the children of Ammon and Moab and mount Seir, whom thou wouldest not let Israel invade, when they came out of the land of Egypt, but they turned from them, and destroyed them not;

11 Behold, *I say, how* they reward us, to come to cast us out of thy possession, which thou hast given us to inherit.

12 O our God, wilt thou not judge them? for we have no might against this great company that cometh against us; neither know we what to do: but our eyes *are* upon thee.

20:12
God's Role
◄ Psalm 127:1 ►

13 And all Judah stood before the LORD, with their little ones, their wives, and their children.

14 Then upon Jahaziel the son of Zechariah, the son of Benaiah, the son of Jeiel, the son of Mattaniah, a Levite of the sons of Asaph, came the Spirit of the LORD in the midst of the congregation;

15 And he said, Hearken ye, all Judah, and ye inhabitants of Jerusalem, and thou king Jehoshaphat, Thus saith the LORD unto you, Be not afraid nor dismayed by reason of this great multitude; for the battle *is* not yours, but God's.

16 To morrow go ye down against them: behold, they come up by the cliff of Ziz; and ye shall find them at the end of the brook, before the wilderness of Jeruel.

17 Ye shall not *need* to fight in this *battle:* set yourselves, stand ye *still,* and see the salvation of the LORD with you, O Judah and Jerusalem: fear not, nor be dismayed; to morrow go out against them: for the LORD *will be* with you.

18 And Jehoshaphat bowed his head with *his* face to the ground: and all Judah and the inhabitants of Jerusalem fell before the LORD, worshipping the LORD.

19 And the Levites, of the children of the Kohathites, and of the children of the Korhites, stood up to praise the LORD God of Israel with a loud voice on high.

20 And they rose early in the morning, and went forth into the wilderness of Tekoa: and as they went forth, Jehoshaphat stood and said, Hear me, O Judah, and ye inhabitants of Jerusalem; Believe in the LORD your God, so shall ye be established; believe his prophets, so shall ye prosper.

20:20
Faith
◄ Mark 11:22 ►

21 And when he had consulted with the people, he appointed singers unto the LORD, and that should praise the beauty of holiness, as they went out before the army, and to say, Praise the LORD; for his mercy *endureth* for ever.

22 And when they began to sing and to praise, the LORD set ambushments against the children of Ammon, Moab, and mount Seir, which were come against Judah; and they were smitten.

23 For the children of Ammon and Moab stood up against the inhabitants of mount Seir, utterly to slay and destroy *them:* and when they had made an end of the inhabitants of Seir, every one helped to destroy another.

24 And when Judah came toward the

watch tower in the wilderness, they looked
unto the multitude, and, behold, they *were*
dead bodies fallen to the earth, and none
escaped.
25 And when Jehoshaphat and his people came to take away the spoil of them,
they found among them in abundance
both riches with the dead bodies, and precious jewels, which they stripped off for
themselves, more than they could carry
away: and they were three days in gathering of the spoil, it was so much.
26 And on the fourth day they assembled
themselves in the valley of Berachah; for
there they blessed the LORD: therefore the
name of the same place was called, The
valley of Berachah, unto this day.
27 Then they returned, every man of Judah and Jerusalem, and Jehoshaphat in the
forefront of them, to go again to Jerusalem with joy; for the LORD had made them
to rejoice over their enemies.
28 And they came to Jerusalem with psalteries and harps and trumpets unto the
house of the LORD.
29 And the fear of God was on all the
kingdoms of *those* countries, when they
had heard that the LORD fought against the
enemies of Israel.
30 So the realm of Jehoshaphat was quiet: for his God gave him rest round about.
31 And Jehoshaphat reigned over Judah:
he was thirty and five years old when he
began to reign, and he reigned twenty and
five years in Jerusalem. And his mother's
name *was* Azubah the daughter of Shilhi.
32 And he walked in the way of Asa his
father, and departed not from it, doing *that
which was* right in the sight of the LORD.
33 Howbeit the high places were not tak-
en away: for as yet the people had not prepared their hearts unto the God of their
fathers.
34 Now the rest of the acts of Jehoshaphat, first and last, behold, they *are* written in the book of Jehu the son of Hanani,
who *is* mentioned in the book of the kings
of Israel.
35 And after this did Jehoshaphat king
of Judah join himself with Ahaziah king
of Israel, who did very wickedly:
36 And he joined himself with him to
make ships to go to Tarshish: and they
made the ships in Ezion-gaber.
37 Then Eliezer the son of Dodavah of
Mareshah prophesied against Jehoshaphat, saying, Because thou hast joined thyself with Ahaziah, the LORD hath broken
thy works. And the ships were broken, that
they were not able to go to Tarshish.

21

1 Now Jehoshaphat slept with his fathers,
and was buried with his fathers in the city
of David. And Jehoram his son reigned in
his stead.
2 And he had brethren the sons of Jehoshaphat, Azariah, and Jehiel, and Zechariah, and Azariah, and Michael, and
Shephatiah: all these *were* the sons of
Jehoshaphat king of Israel.
3 And their father gave them great gifts
of silver, and of gold, and of precious
things, with fenced cities in Judah: but the
kingdom gave he to Jehoram; because he
was the firstborn.
4 Now when Jehoram was risen up to the
kingdom of his father, he strengthened
himself, and slew all his brethren with
the sword, and *divers* also of the princes of
Israel.
5 Jehoram *was* thirty and two years old
when he began to reign, and he reigned
eight years in Jerusalem.
6 And he walked in the way of the kings
of Israel, like as did the house of Ahab:
for he had the daughter of Ahab to wife:
and he wrought *that which was* evil in the
eyes of the LORD.
7 Howbeit the LORD would not destroy
the house of David, because of the covenant that he had made with David, and
as he promised to give a light to him and
to his sons for ever.
8 In his days the Edomites revolted from
under the dominion of Judah, and made
themselves a king.
9 Then Jehoram went forth with his
princes, and all his chariots with him: and
he rose up by night, and smote the Edomites which compassed him in, and the captains of the chariots.
10 So the Edomites revolted from under
the hand of Judah unto this day. The same
time *also* did Libnah revolt from under his
hand; because he had forsaken the LORD
God of his fathers.
11 Moreover he made high places in the
mountains of Judah, and caused the inhabitants of Jerusalem to commit fornication, and compelled Judah *thereto*.
12 And there came a writing to him from

Elijah the prophet, saying, Thus saith the LORD God of David thy father, Because thou hast not walked in the ways of Jehoshaphat thy father, nor in the ways of Asa king of Judah,

13 But hast walked in the way of the kings of Israel, and hast made Judah and the inhabitants of Jerusalem to go a whoring, like to the whoredoms of the house of Ahab, and also hast slain thy brethren of thy father's house, *which were* better than thyself:

14 Behold, with a great plague will the LORD smite thy people, and thy children, and thy wives, and all thy goods:

15 And thou *shalt have* great sickness by disease of thy bowels, until thy bowels fall out by reason of the sickness day by day.

16 Moreover the LORD stirred up against Jehoram the spirit of the Philistines, and of the Arabians, that *were* near the Ethiopians:

17 And they came up into Judah, and brake into it, and carried away all the substance that was found in the king's house, and his sons also, and his wives; so that there was never a son left him, save Jehoahaz, the youngest of his sons.

18 And after all this the LORD smote him in his bowels with an incurable disease.

19 And it came to pass, that in process of time, after the end of two years, his bowels fell out by reason of his sickness: so he died of sore diseases. And his people made no burning for him, like the burning of his fathers.

20 Thirty and two years old was he when he began to reign, and he reigned in Jerusalem eight years, and departed without being desired. Howbeit they buried him in the city of David, but not in the sepulchres of the kings.

22

1 And the inhabitants of Jerusalem made Ahaziah his youngest son king in his stead: for the band of men that came with the Arabians to the camp had slain all the eldest. So Ahaziah the son of Jehoram king of Judah reigned.

2 Forty and two years old *was* Ahaziah when he began to reign, and he reigned one year in Jerusalem. His mother's name also *was* Athaliah the daughter of Omri.

3 He also walked in the ways of the house of Ahab: for his mother was his counsellor to do wickedly.

4 Wherefore he did evil in the sight of the LORD like the house of Ahab: for they were his counsellors after the death of his father to his destruction.

5 He walked also after their counsel, and went with Jehoram the son of Ahab king of Israel to war against Hazael king of Syria at Ramoth-gilead: and the Syrians smote Joram.

6 And he returned to be healed in Jezreel because of the wounds which were given him at Ramah, when he fought with Hazael king of Syria. And Azariah the son of Jehoram king of Judah went down to see Jehoram the son of Ahab at Jezreel, because he was sick.

7 And the destruction of Ahaziah was of God by coming to Joram: for when he was come, he went out with Jehoram against Jehu the son of Nimshi, whom the LORD had anointed to cut off the house of Ahab.

8 And it came to pass, that, when Jehu was executing judgment upon the house of Ahab, and found the princes of Judah, and the sons of the brethren of Ahaziah, that ministered to Ahaziah, he slew them.

9 And he sought Ahaziah: and they caught him, (for he was hid in Samaria,) and brought him to Jehu: and when they had slain him, they buried him: Because, said they, he *is* the son of Jehoshaphat, who sought the LORD with all his heart. So the house of Ahaziah had no power to keep still the kingdom.

10 But when Athaliah the mother of Ahaziah saw that her son was dead, she arose and destroyed all the seed royal of the house of Judah.

11 But Jehoshabeath, the daughter of the king, took Joash the son of Ahaziah, and stole him from among the king's sons that were slain, and put him and his nurse in a bedchamber. So Jehoshabeath, the daughter of king Jehoram, the wife of Jehoiada the priest, (for she was the sister of Ahaziah,) hid him from Athaliah, so that she slew him not.

12 And he was with them hid in the house of God six years: and Athaliah reigned over the land.

23

1 And in the seventh year Jehoiada strengthened himself, and took the captains of hundreds, Azariah the son of Jeroham, and Ishmael the son of Jehohanan, and Azariah the son of Obed, and Maase-

iah the son of Adaiah, and Elishaphat the
son of Zichri, into covenant with him.
2 And they went about in Judah, and
gathered the Levites out of all the cities of
Judah, and the chief of the fathers of Israel, and they came to Jerusalem.
3 And all the congregation made a covenant with the king in the house of God.
And he said unto them, Behold, the king's
son shall reign, as the LORD hath said of
the sons of David.
4 This *is* the thing that ye shall do; A third
part of you entering on the sabbath, of the
priests and of the Levites, *shall be* porters
of the doors;
5 And a third part *shall be* at the king's
house; and a third part at the gate of the
foundation: and all the people *shall be* in
the courts of the house of the LORD.
6 But let none come into the house of
the LORD, save the priests, and they that
minister of the Levites; they shall go in,
for they *are* holy: but all the people shall
keep the watch of the LORD.
7 And the Levites shall compass the king
round about, every man with his weapons
in his hand; and whosoever *else* cometh
into the house, he shall be put to death:
but be ye with the king when he cometh
in, and when he goeth out.
8 So the Levites and all Judah did according to all things that Jehoiada the priest
had commanded, and took every man his
men that were to come in on the sabbath,
with them that were to go *out* on the sabbath: for Jehoiada the priest dismissed not
the courses.
9 Moreover Jehoiada the priest delivered
to the captains of hundreds spears, and
bucklers, and shields, that *had been* king
David's, which *were* in the house of God.
10 And he set all the people, every man
having his weapon in his hand, from the
right side of the temple to the left side of
the temple, along by the altar and the temple, by the king round about.
11 Then they brought out the king's son,
and put upon him the crown, and *gave him*
the testimony, and made him king. And
Jehoiada and his sons anointed him, and
said, God save the king.
12 Now when Athaliah heard the noise
of the people running and praising the
king, she came to the people into the
house of the LORD:

13 And she looked, and, behold, the king
stood at his pillar at the entering in, and
the princes and the trumpets by the king:
and all the people of the land rejoiced, and
sounded with trumpets, also the singers
with instruments of musick, and such as
taught to sing praise. Then Athaliah rent
her clothes, and said, Treason, Treason.
14 Then Jehoiada the priest brought out
the captains of hundreds that were set over
the host, and said unto them, Have her
forth of the ranges: and whoso followeth
her, let him be slain with the sword. For
the priest said, Slay her not in the house
of the LORD.
15 So they laid hands on her; and when
she was come to the entering of the horse
gate by the king's house, they slew her
there.
16 And Jehoiada made a covenant between him, and between all the people,
and between the king, that they should be
the LORD'S people.
17 Then all the people went to the house
of Baal, and brake it down, and brake his
altars and his images in pieces, and slew
Mattan the priest of Baal before the altars.
18 Also Jehoiada appointed the offices of
the house of the LORD by the hand of the
priests the Levites, whom David had distributed in the house of the LORD, to offer
the burnt offerings of the LORD, as *it is*
written in the law of Moses, with rejoicing
and with singing, *as it was ordained* by
David.
19 And he set the porters at the gates of
the house of the LORD, that none *which was*
unclean in any thing should enter in.
20 And he took the captains of hundreds,
and the nobles, and the governors of the
people, and all the people of the land, and
brought down the king from the house of
the LORD: and they came through the high
gate into the king's house, and set the king
upon the throne of the kingdom.
21 And all the people of the land rejoiced:
and the city was quiet, after that they had
slain Athaliah with the sword.

24

1 Joash *was* seven
years old when he
began to reign, and
he reigned forty
years in Jerusalem.
His mother's name
also *was* Zibiah of Beer-sheba.

24:1 Young Leaders
◄ 2 Samuel 5:4
2 Chronicles 34:1-3 ►

2 And Joash did *that which was* right in the sight of the LORD all the days of Jehoiada the priest.

24:1-2 Young Men
◄ 1 Samuel 17:37
2 Chronicles 34:1-3 ►

3 And Jehoiada took for him two wives; and he begat sons and daughters.

4 And it came to pass after this, *that* Joash was minded to repair the house of the LORD.

5 And he gathered together the priests and the Levites, and said to them, Go out unto the cities of Judah, and gather of all Israel money to repair the house of your God from year to year, and see that ye hasten the matter. Howbeit the Levites hastened *it* not.

24:5 Hurrying
◄ 2 Kings 4:29
2 Chronicles 35:21 ►

6 And the king called for Jehoiada the chief, and said unto him, Why hast thou not required of the Levites to bring in out of Judah and out of Jerusalem the collection, *according to the commandment* of Moses the servant of the LORD, and of the congregation of Israel, for the tabernacle of witness?

7 For the sons of Athaliah, that wicked woman, had broken up the house of God; and also all the dedicated things of the house of the LORD did they bestow upon Baalim.

8 And at the king's commandment they made a chest, and set it without at the gate of the house of the LORD.

9 And they made a proclamation through Judah and Jerusalem, to bring in to the LORD the collection *that* Moses the servant of God *laid* upon Israel in the wilderness.

10 And all the princes and all the people rejoiced, and brought in, and cast into the chest, until they had made an end.

24:10 Examples of Generosity
◄ 1 Chronicles 29:3-4
Ezra 1:6 ►

11 Now it came to pass, that at what time the chest was brought unto the king's office by the hand of the Levites, and when they saw that *there was* much money, the king's scribe and the high priest's officer came and emptied the chest, and took it, and carried it to his place again. Thus they did day by day, and gathered money in abundance.

12 And the king and Jehoiada gave it to such as did the work of the service of the house of the LORD, and hired masons and carpenters to repair the house of the LORD, and also such as wrought iron and brass to mend the house of the LORD.

13 So the workmen wrought, and the work was perfected by them, and they set the house of God in his state, and strengthened it.

14 And when they had finished *it,* they brought the rest of the money before the king and Jehoiada, whereof were made vessels for the house of the LORD, *even* vessels to minister, and to offer *withal,* and spoons, and vessels of gold and silver. And they offered burnt offerings in the house of the LORD continually all the days of Jehoiada.

15 But Jehoiada waxed old, and was full of days when he died; an hundred and thirty years old *was he* when he died.

16 And they buried him in the city of David among the kings, because he had done good in Israel, both toward God, and toward his house.

17 Now after the death of Jehoiada came the princes of Judah, and made obeisance to the king. Then the king hearkened unto them.

18 And they left the house of the LORD God of their fathers, and served groves and idols: and wrath came upon Judah and Jerusalem for this their trespass.

19 Yet he sent prophets to them, to bring them again unto the LORD; and they testified against them: but they would not give ear.

20 And the Spirit of God came upon Zechariah the son of Jehoiada the priest, which stood above the people, and said unto them, Thus saith God, Why transgress ye the commandments of the LORD, that ye cannot prosper? because ye have forsaken the LORD, he hath also forsaken you.

21 And they conspired against him, and stoned him with stones at the commandment of the king in the court of the house of the LORD.

22 Thus Joash the king remembered not the kindness

24:22 Unthankfulness to People
◄ 1 Samuel 25:21
Psalm 35:12 ►

which Jehoiada his father had done to
him, but slew his son. And when he died,
he said, The LORD look upon *it,* and require *it.*
23 And it came to pass at the end of the
year, *that* the host of Syria came up against
him: and they came to Judah and Jerusalem, and destroyed all the princes of the
people from among the people, and sent
all the spoil of them unto the king of Damascus.
24 For the army of the Syrians came with
a small company of men, and the LORD
delivered a very great host into their hand,
because they had forsaken the LORD God
of their fathers. So they executed judgment
against Joash.
25 And when they were departed from
him, (for they left him in great diseases,)
his own servants conspired against him for
the blood of the sons of Jehoiada the
priest, and slew him on his bed, and he
died: and they buried him in the city of
David, but they buried him not in the sepulchres of the kings.
26 And these are they that conspired
against him; Zabad the son of Shimeath
an Ammonitess, and Jehozabad the son of
Shimrith a Moabitess.
27 Now *concerning* his sons, and the greatness of the burdens *laid* upon him, and
the repairing of the house of God, behold,
they *are* written in the story of the book of
the kings. And Amaziah his son reigned
in his stead.

25

1 Amaziah *was* twenty and five years old
when he began to reign, and he reigned
twenty and nine years in Jerusalem. And
his mother's name *was* Jehoaddan of Jerusalem.
2 And he did *that which was* right in the
sight of the LORD, but not with a perfect
heart.
3 Now it came to pass, when the kingdom was established to him, that he slew
his servants that had killed the king his
father.
4 But he slew not their children, but *did*
as *it is* written in the law in the book of
Moses, where the LORD commanded,
saying, The fathers shall not die for the
children, neither shall the children die for
the fathers, but every man shall die for his
own sin.
5 Moreover Amaziah gathered Judah together, and made them captains over
thousands, and captains over hundreds, according to the houses of *their* fathers,
throughout all Judah and Benjamin: and
he numbered them from twenty years old
and above, and found them three hundred
thousand choice *men, able* to go forth to
war, that could handle spear and shield.
6 He hired also an hundred thousand
mighty men of valour out of Israel for an
hundred talents of silver.
7 But there came a man of God to him,
saying, O king, let not the army of Israel
go with thee; for the LORD *is* not with Israel,
to wit, with all the children of Ephraim.
8 But if thou wilt
go, do *it,* be strong
for the battle: God
shall make thee fall
before the enemy:
for God hath pow-
er to help, and to cast down.

25:8 God's Power
◄ 1 Chronicles 29:12
Job 26:12 ►

9 And Amaziah said to the man of God,
But what shall we do for the hundred talents which I have given to the army of Israel? And the man of God answered, The
LORD is able to give thee much more than
this.
10 Then Amaziah separated them, *to wit,*
the army that was come to him out of
Ephraim, to go home again: wherefore
their anger was greatly kindled against
Judah, and they returned home in great
anger.
11 And Amaziah strengthened himself,
and led forth his people, and went to the
valley of salt, and smote of the children of
Seir ten thousand.
12 And *other* ten thousand *left* alive did
the children of Judah carry away captive,
and brought them unto the top of the rock,
and cast them down from the top of the
rock, that they all were broken in pieces.
13 But the soldiers of the army which
Amaziah sent back, that they should not
go with him to battle, fell upon the cities
of Judah, from Samaria even unto Beth-
horon, and smote three thousand of them,
and took much spoil.
14 Now it came to pass, after that Amaziah was come from the slaughter of the
Edomites, that he brought the gods of the
children of Seir, and set them up *to be* his
gods, and bowed down himself before
them, and burned incense unto them.

15 Wherefore the anger of the LORD was kindled against Amaziah, and he sent unto him a prophet, which said unto him, Why hast thou sought after the gods of the people, which could not deliver their own people out of thine hand?

16 And it came to pass, as he talked with him, that *the king* said unto him, Art thou made of the king's counsel? forbear; why shouldest thou be smitten? Then the prophet forbare, and said, I know that God hath determined to destroy thee, because thou hast done this, and hast not hearkened unto my counsel.

17 Then Amaziah king of Judah took advice, and sent to Joash, the son of Jehoahaz, the son of Jehu, king of Israel, saying, Come, let us see one another in the face.

18 And Joash king of Israel sent to Amaziah king of Judah, saying, The thistle that *was* in Lebanon sent to the cedar that *was* in Lebanon, saying, Give thy daughter to my son to wife: and there passed by a wild beast that *was* in Lebanon, and trode down the thistle.

19 Thou sayest, Lo, thou hast smitten the Edomites; and thine heart lifteth thee up to boast: abide now at home; why shouldest thou meddle to *thine* hurt, that thou shouldest fall, *even* thou, and Judah with thee?

20 But Amaziah would not hear; for it *came* of God, that he might deliver them into the hand *of their enemies,* because they sought after the gods of Edom.

21 So Joash the king of Israel went up; and they saw one another in the face, *both* he and Amaziah king of Judah, at Beth-shemesh, which *belongeth* to Judah.

22 And Judah was put to the worse before Israel, and they fled every man to his tent.

23 And Joash the king of Israel took Amaziah king of Judah, the son of Joash, the son of Jehoahaz, at Beth-shemesh, and brought him to Jerusalem, and brake down the wall of Jerusalem from the gate of Ephraim to the corner gate, four hundred cubits.

24 And *he took* all the gold and the silver, and all the vessels that were found in the house of God with Obed-edom, and the treasures of the king's house, the hostages also, and returned to Samaria.

25 And Amaziah the son of Joash king of Judah lived after the death of Joash son of Jehoahaz king of Israel fifteen years.

26 Now the rest of the acts of Amaziah, first and last, behold, *are* they not written in the book of the kings of Judah and Israel?

27 Now after the time that Amaziah did turn away from following the LORD they made a conspiracy against him in Jerusalem; and he fled to Lachish: but they sent to Lachish after him, and slew him there.

28 And they brought him upon horses, and buried him with his fathers in the city of Judah.

26

1 Then all the people of Judah took Uzziah, who *was* sixteen years old, and made him king in the room of his father Amaziah.

2 He built Eloth, and restored it to Judah, after that the king slept with his fathers.

3 Sixteen years old *was* Uzziah when he began to reign, and he reigned fifty and two years in Jerusalem. His mother's name also *was* Jecoliah of Jerusalem.

4 And he did *that which was* right in the sight of the LORD, according to all that his father Amaziah did.

5 And he sought God in the days of Zechariah, who had understanding in the visions of God: and as long as he sought the LORD, God made him to prosper.

6 And he went forth and warred against the Philistines, and brake down the wall of Gath, and the wall of Jabneh, and the wall of Ashdod, and built cities about Ashdod, and among the Philistines.

7 And God helped him against the Philistines, and against the Arabians that dwelt in Gur-baal, and the Mehunims.

8 And the Ammonites gave gifts to Uzziah: and his name spread abroad *even* to the entering in of Egypt; for he strengthened *himself* exceedingly.

9 Moreover Uzziah built towers in Jerusalem at the corner gate, and at the valley gate, and at the turning *of the wall,* and fortified them.

10 Also he built towers in the desert, and digged many wells: for he had much cattle, both in the low country, and in the plains: husbandmen *also,* and vine dressers in the mountains, and in Carmel: for he loved husbandry.

11 Moreover Uzziah had an host of fighting men, that went out to war by bands, according to the number of their account

by the hand of Jeiel the scribe and Maaseiah the ruler, under the hand of Hananiah, *one* of the king's captains.
12 The whole number of the chief of the
fathers of the mighty men of valour *were*
two thousand and six hundred.
13 And under their hand *was* an army,
three hundred thousand and seven thousand and five hundred, that made war with
mighty power, to help the king against the
enemy.
14 And Uzziah prepared for them throughout all the host shields, and spears, and
helmets, and habergeons, and bows, and
slings *to cast* stones.
15 And he made in Jerusalem engines,
invented by cunning men, to be on the
towers and upon the bulwarks, to shoot
arrows and great stones withal. And his
name spread far abroad; for he was
marvellously helped, till he was strong.
16 But when he was strong, his heart was
lifted up to *his* destruction: for he transgressed against the LORD his God, and went
into the temple of the LORD to burn incense upon the altar of incense.
17 And Azariah the priest went in after
him, and with him fourscore priests of the
LORD, *that were* valiant men:
18 And they withstood Uzziah the king,
and said unto him, *It appertaineth* not unto
thee, Uzziah, to burn incense unto the
LORD, but to the priests the sons of Aaron,
that are consecrated to burn incense: go
out of the sanctuary; for thou hast trespassed; neither *shall it be* for thine honour
from the LORD God.
19 Then Uzziah was wroth, and *had* a
censer in his hand to burn incense: and
while he was wroth with the priests, the
leprosy even rose up in his forehead before the priests in the house of the LORD,
from beside the incense altar.
20 And Azariah the chief priest, and all
the priests, looked upon him, and, behold,
he *was* leprous in his forehead, and they
thrust him out from thence; yea, himself
hasted also to go out, because the LORD
had smitten him.
21 And Uzziah the king was a leper unto
the day of his death, and dwelt in a several house, *being* a leper; for he was cut off
from the house of the LORD: and Jotham
his son *was* over the king's house, judging
the people of the land.
22 Now the rest of the acts of Uzziah, first
and last, did Isaiah the prophet, the son
of Amoz, write.
23 So Uzziah slept with his fathers, and
they buried him with his fathers in the
field of the burial which *belonged* to the
kings; for they said, He *is* a leper: and Jotham his son reigned in his stead.

27

1 Jotham *was* twenty and five years old
when he began to reign, and he reigned
sixteen years in Jerusalem. His mother's
name also *was* Jerushah, the daughter of
Zadok.
2 And he did *that which was* right in the
sight of the LORD, according to all that his
father Uzziah did: howbeit he entered not
into the temple of the LORD. And the people did yet corruptly.
3 He built the high gate of the house of
the LORD, and on the wall of Ophel he
built much.
4 Moreover he built cities in the mountains of Judah, and in the forests he built
castles and towers.
5 He fought also with the king of the
Ammonites, and prevailed against them.
And the children of Ammon gave him the
same year an hundred talents of silver, and
ten thousand measures of wheat, and ten
thousand of barley. So much did the children of Ammon pay unto him, both the
second year, and the third.
6 So Jotham became mighty, because
he prepared his ways before the LORD
his God.
7 Now the rest of the acts of Jotham, and
all his wars, and his ways, lo, they *are* written in the book of the kings of Israel and
Judah.
8 He was five and twenty years old when
he began to reign, and reigned sixteen years
in Jerusalem.
9 And Jotham slept with his fathers, and
they buried him in the city of David: and
Ahaz his son reigned in his stead.

28

1 Ahaz *was* twenty years old when he
began to reign, and he reigned sixteen years
in Jerusalem: but he did not *that which was*
right in the sight of the LORD, like David
his father:
2 For he walked in the ways of the kings
of Israel, and made also molten images for
Baalim.
3 Moreover he burnt incense in the valley of the son of Hinnom, and burnt his

children in the fire, after the abominations of the heathen whom the LORD had cast out before the children of Israel.

4 He sacrificed also and burnt incense in the high places, and on the hills, and under every green tree.

5 Wherefore the LORD his God delivered him into the hand of the king of Syria; and they smote him, and carried away a great multitude of them captives, and brought *them* to Damascus. And he was also delivered into the hand of the king of Israel, who smote him with a great slaughter.

6 For Pekah the son of Remaliah slew in Judah an hundred and twenty thousand in one day, *which were* all valiant men; because they had forsaken the LORD God of their fathers.

7 And Zichri, a mighty man of Ephraim, slew Maaseiah the king's son, and Azrikam the governor of the house, and Elkanah *that was* next to the king.

8 And the children of Israel carried away captive of their brethren two hundred thousand, women, sons, and daughters, and took also away much spoil from them, and brought the spoil to Samaria.

28:9 Temper
◄ Daniel 3:19 ►

9 But a prophet of the LORD was there, whose name *was* Oded: and he went out before the host that came to Samaria, and said unto them, Behold, because the LORD God of your fathers was wroth with Judah, he hath delivered them into your hand, and ye have slain them in a rage *that* reacheth up unto heaven.

10 And now ye purpose to keep under the children of Judah and Jerusalem for bondmen and bondwomen unto you: *but are there* not with you, even with you, sins against the LORD your God?

11 Now hear me therefore, and deliver the captives again, which ye have taken captive of your brethren: for the fierce wrath of the LORD *is* upon you.

12 Then certain of the heads of the children of Ephraim, Azariah the son of Johanan, Berechiah the son of Meshillemoth, and Jehizkiah the son of Shallum, and Amasa the son of Hadlai, stood up against them that came from the war,

13 And said unto them, Ye shall not bring in the captives hither: for whereas we have offended against the LORD *already*, ye intend to add *more* to our sins and to our trespass: for our trespass is great, and *there is* fierce wrath against Israel.

14 So the armed men left the captives and the spoil before the princes and all the congregation.

15 And the men which were expressed by name rose up, and took the captives, and with the spoil clothed all that were naked among them, and arrayed them, and shod them, and gave them to eat and to drink, and anointed them, and carried all the feeble of them upon asses, and brought them to Jericho, the city of palm trees, to their brethren: then they returned to Samaria.

28:15 Compassion
◄ Exodus 2:6
Job 29:13 ►

28:15
Work that Helps Others
◄ Job 29:15-16 ►

16 At that time did king Ahaz send unto the kings of Assyria to help him.

17 For again the Edomites had come and smitten Judah, and carried away captives.

18 The Philistines also had invaded the cities of the low country, and of the south of Judah, and had taken Beth-shemesh, and Ajalon, and Gederoth, and Shocho with the villages thereof, and Timnah with the villages thereof, Gimzo also and the villages thereof: and they dwelt there.

19 For the LORD brought Judah low because of Ahaz king of Israel; for he made Judah naked, and transgressed sore against the LORD.

20 And Tilgath-pilneser king of Assyria came unto him, and distressed him, but strengthened him not.

21 For Ahaz took away a portion *out* of the house of the LORD, and *out* of the house of the king, and of the princes, and gave *it* unto the king of Assyria: but he helped him not.

22 And in the time of his distress did he trespass yet more against the LORD: this *is that* king Ahaz.

28:22 Stubborn People
◄ 2 Kings 17:14
2 Chronicles 33:23 ►

23 For he sacrificed unto the gods of Damascus, which smote him: and he said,

Because the gods of the kings of Syria help
them, *therefore* will I sacrifice to them, that
they may help me. But they were the ruin
of him, and of all Israel.
24 And Ahaz gathered together the vessels of the house of God, and cut in pieces
the vessels of the house of God, and shut
up the doors of the house of the LORD, and
he made him altars in every corner of Jerusalem.
25 And in every several city of Judah he
made high places to burn incense unto
other gods, and provoked to anger the
LORD God of his fathers.
26 Now the rest of his acts and of all his
ways, first and last, behold, they *are* written in the book of the kings of Judah and
Israel.
27 And Ahaz slept with his fathers, and
they buried him in the city, *even* in Jerusalem: but they brought him not into the
sepulchres of the kings of Israel: and Hezekiah his son reigned in his stead.

29

1 Hezekiah began to reign *when he was*
five and twenty years old, and he reigned
nine and twenty years in Jerusalem. And
his mother's name *was* Abijah, the daughter of Zechariah.
2 And he did *that which was* right in the
sight of the LORD, according to all that
David his father had done.
3 He in the first year of his reign, in the
first month, opened the doors of the house
of the LORD, and repaired them.
4 And he brought in the priests and the
Levites, and gathered them together into
the east street,
5 And said unto them, Hear me, ye Levites, sanctify now yourselves, and sanctify the house of the LORD God of your
fathers, and carry forth the filthiness out
of the holy *place.*
6 For our fathers have trespassed, and
done *that which was* evil in the eyes of the
LORD our God, and have forsaken him, and
have turned away their faces from the habitation of the LORD, and turned *their* backs.
7 Also they have shut up the doors of the
porch, and put out the lamps, and have
not burned incense nor offered burnt offerings in the holy *place* unto the God of
Israel.
8 Wherefore the wrath of the LORD was
upon Judah and Jerusalem, and he hath
delivered them to trouble, to astonishment, and to hissing, as ye see with your
eyes.
9 For, lo, our fathers have fallen by the
sword, and our sons and our daughters
and our wives *are* in captivity for this.
10 Now *it is* in mine heart to make a covenant with the LORD God of Israel, that
his fierce wrath may turn away from us.
11 My sons, be not now negligent: for the
LORD hath chosen you to stand before him,
to serve him, and that ye should minister
unto him, and burn incense.
12 Then the Levites arose, Mahath the son
of Amasai, and Joel the son of Azariah, of
the sons of the Kohathites: and of the sons
of Merari, Kish the son of Abdi, and Azariah the son of Jehalelel: and of the Gershonites; Joah the son of Zimmah, and
Eden the son of Joah:
13 And of the sons of Elizaphan; Shimri,
and Jeiel: and of the sons of Asaph; Zechariah, and Mattaniah:
14 And of the sons of Heman; Jehiel, and
Shimei: and of the sons of Jeduthun; Shemaiah, and Uzziel.
15 And they gathered their brethren, and
sanctified themselves, and came, according to the commandment of the king, by
the words of the LORD, to cleanse the house
of the LORD.
16 And the priests went into the inner
part of the house of the LORD, to cleanse
it, and brought out all the uncleanness that
they found in the temple of the LORD into
the court of the house of the LORD. And
the Levites took *it,* to carry *it* out abroad
into the brook Kidron.
17 Now they began on the first *day* of the
first month to sanctify, and on the eighth
day of the month came they to the porch
of the LORD: so they sanctified the house
of the LORD in eight days; and in the sixteenth day of the first month they made
an end.
18 Then they went in to Hezekiah the
king, and said, We have cleansed all the
house of the LORD, and the altar of burnt
offering, with all the vessels thereof, and
the shewbread table, with all the vessels
thereof.
19 Moreover all the vessels, which king
Ahaz in his reign did cast away in his transgression, have we prepared and sanctified,
and, behold, they *are* before the altar of
the LORD.

20 Then Hezekiah the king rose early, and gathered the rulers of the city, and went up to the house of the LORD.

29:20 Devotions
◄ 1 Samuel 1:19
Job 1:5 ►

21 And they brought seven bullocks, and seven rams, and seven lambs, and seven he goats, for a sin offering for the kingdom, and for the sanctuary, and for Judah. And he commanded the priests the sons of Aaron to offer *them* on the altar of the LORD.

22 So they killed the bullocks, and the priests received the blood, and sprinkled *it* on the altar: likewise, when they had killed the rams, they sprinkled the blood upon the altar: they killed also the lambs, and they sprinkled the blood upon the altar.

23 And they brought forth the he goats *for* the sin offering before the king and the congregation; and they laid their hands upon them:

24 And the priests killed them, and they made reconciliation with their blood upon the altar, to make an atonement for all Israel: for the king commanded *that* the burnt offering and the sin offering *should be made* for all Israel.

25 And he set the Levites in the house of the LORD with cymbals, with psalteries, and with harps, according to the commandment of David, and of Gad the king's seer, and Nathan the prophet: for *so was* the commandment of the LORD by his prophets.

26 And the Levites stood with the instruments of David, and the priests with the trumpets.

27 And Hezekiah commanded to offer the burnt offering upon the altar. And when the burnt offering began, the song of the LORD began *also* with the trumpets, and with the instruments *ordained* by David king of Israel.

28 And all the congregation worshipped, and the singers sang, and the trumpeters sounded: *and* all *this continued* until the burnt offering was finished.

29 And when they had made an end of offering, the king and all that were present with him bowed themselves, and worshipped.

30 Moreover Hezekiah the king and the princes commanded the Levites to sing praise unto the LORD with the words of David, and of Asaph the seer. And they sang praises with gladness, and they bowed their heads and worshipped.

31 Then Hezekiah answered and said, Now ye have consecrated yourselves unto the LORD, come near and bring sacrifices and thank offerings into the house of the LORD. And the congregation brought in sacrifices and thank offerings; and as many as were of a free heart burnt offerings.

32 And the number of the burnt offerings, which the congregation brought, was threescore and ten bullocks, an hundred rams, *and* two hundred lambs: all these *were* for a burnt offering to the LORD.

33 And the consecrated things *were* six hundred oxen and three thousand sheep.

34 But the priests were too few, so that they could not flay all the burnt offerings: wherefore their brethren the Levites did help them, till the work was ended, and until the *other* priests had sanctified themselves: for the Levites *were* more upright in heart to sanctify themselves than the priests.

35 And also the burnt offerings *were* in abundance, with the fat of the peace offerings, and the drink offerings for *every* burnt offering. So the service of the house of the LORD was set in order.

36 And Hezekiah rejoiced, and all the people, that God had prepared the people: for the thing was *done* suddenly.

30

1 And Hezekiah sent to all Israel and Judah, and wrote letters also to Ephraim and Manasseh, that they should come to the house of the LORD at Jerusalem, to keep the passover unto the LORD God of Israel.

30:1
Friends and Church
◄ Isaiah 2:3 ►

2 For the king had taken counsel, and his princes, and all the congregation in Jerusalem, to keep the passover in the second month.

3 For they could not keep it at that time, because the priests had not sanctified themselves sufficiently, neither had the people gathered themselves together to Jerusalem.

4 And the thing pleased the king and all the congregation.

5So they established a decree to make
proclamation throughout all Israel, from
Beer-sheba even to Dan, that they should
come to keep the passover unto the LORD
God of Israel at Jerusalem: for they had
not done *it* of a long *time in such sort* as it
was written.
6So the posts
went with the let-
ters from the king
and his princes
throughout all Is-
rael and Judah, and
according to the commandment of the
king, saying, Ye children of Israel, turn
again unto the LORD God of Abraham,
Isaac, and Israel, and he will return to the
remnant of you, that are escaped out of
the hand of the kings of Assyria.

30:6 Repent!
◄ 2 Kings 17:13
Proverbs 1:23 ►

7And be not ye like your fathers, and like
your brethren, which trespassed against
the LORD God of their fathers, *who* therefore gave them up to desolation, as ye see.
8Now be ye not stiffnecked, as your fathers *were, but* yield yourselves unto the
LORD, and enter into his sanctuary, which
he hath sanctified for ever: and serve the
LORD your God, that the fierceness of his
wrath may turn away from you.
9For if ye turn
again unto the
LORD, your breth-
ren and your chil-
dren *shall find*
compassion before
them that lead them captive, so that they
shall come again into this land: for the
LORD your God *is* gracious and merciful,
and will not turn away *his* face from you,
if ye return unto him.

30:9 Promise of Mercy
◄ 2 Samuel 22:26
Psalm 89:28 ►

10So the posts
passed from city to
city through the
country of Ephraim
and Manasseh even
unto Zebulun: but
they laughed them
to scorn, and
mocked them.
11Nevertheless
divers of Asher and
Manasseh and of
Zebulun humbled themselves, and came
to Jerusalem.

30:10 Mocking
◄ 2 Kings 2:23
2 Chronicles 36:16 ►

30:10
Rejecting God's Word
◄ 2 Chronicles 36:16 ►

12Also in Judah the hand of God was to
give them one heart to do the commandment of the king and of the princes, by
the word of the LORD.
13And there assembled at Jerusalem
much people to keep the feast of unleavened bread in the second month, a very
great congregation.
14And they arose and took away the altars that *were* in Jerusalem, and all the altars for incense took they away, and cast
them into the brook Kidron.
15Then they killed the passover on the
fourteenth *day* of the second month: and
the priests and the Levites were ashamed,
and sanctified themselves, and brought in
the burnt offerings into the house of the
LORD.
16And they stood in their place after
their manner, according to the law of Moses the man of God: the priests sprinkled
the blood, *which they received* of the hand
of the Levites.
17For *there were* many in the congregation that were not sanctified: therefore the
Levites had the charge of the killing of the
passovers for every one *that was* not clean,
to sanctify *them* unto the LORD.
18For a multi-
tude of the people,
even many of
Ephraim, and Ma-
nasseh, Issachar,
and Zebulun, had
not cleansed themselves, yet did they eat
the passover otherwise than it was written. But Hezekiah prayed for them, saying, The good LORD pardon every one

30:18
Praying for Others
◄ 1 Chronicles 21:17
Job 42:10 ►

19*That* prepareth his heart to seek God,
the LORD God of his fathers, though *he be*
not *cleansed* according to the purification
of the sanctuary.
20And the LORD hearkened to Hezekiah, and healed the people.
21And the chil-
dren of Israel that
were present at Je-
rusalem kept the
feast of unleavened
bread seven days
with great gladness: and the Levites and
the priests praised the LORD day by day,
singing with loud instruments unto the
LORD.

30:21
Gladness
◄ Nehemiah 8:17 ►

22And Hezekiah spake comfortably
unto all the Levites that taught the good

knowledge of the LORD: and they did eat
throughout the feast seven days, offering
peace offerings, and making confession to
the LORD God of their fathers.
23 And the whole assembly took counsel to keep other seven days: and they kept
other seven days with gladness.
24 For Hezekiah king of Judah did give
to the congregation a thousand bullocks
and seven thousand sheep; and the princes
gave to the congregation a thousand bullocks and ten thousand sheep: and a great
number of priests sanctified themselves.
25 And all the congregation of Judah,
with the priests and the Levites, and all the
congregation that came out of Israel, and
the strangers that came out of the land of
Israel, and that dwelt in Judah, rejoiced.
26 So there was great joy in Jerusalem:
for since the time of Solomon the son of
David king of Israel *there was* not the like
in Jerusalem.
27 Then the priests the Levites arose and
blessed the people: and their voice was
heard, and their prayer came *up* to his holy
dwelling place, *even* unto heaven.

31

1 Now when all this was finished, all Israel that were present went out to the cities of Judah, and brake the images in
pieces, and cut down the groves, and threw
down the high places and the altars out of
all Judah and Benjamin, in Ephraim also
and Manasseh, until they had utterly destroyed them all. Then all the children of
Israel returned, every man to his possession, into their own cities.
2 And Hezekiah appointed the courses
of the priests and the Levites after their
courses, every man according to his service, the priests and Levites for burnt offerings and for peace offerings, to minister,
and to give thanks, and to praise in the
gates of the tents of the LORD.
3 *He appointed* also the king's portion of
his substance for the burnt offerings, *to wit,*
for the morning and evening burnt offerings, and the burnt offerings for the sabbaths, and for the new moons, and for the
set feasts, as *it is* written in the law of the
LORD.
4 Moreover he commanded the people
that dwelt in Jerusalem to give the portion
of the priests and the Levites, that they
might be encouraged in the law of the
LORD.
5 And as soon as the commandment
came abroad, the children of Israel
brought in abundance the firstfruits of
corn, wine, and oil, and honey, and of all
the increase of the field; and the tithe of
all *things* brought they in abundantly.
6 And *concerning* the children of Israel
and Judah, that dwelt in the cities of Judah, they also brought in the tithe of oxen
and sheep, and the tithe of holy things
which were consecrated unto the LORD
their God, and laid *them* by heaps.
7 In the third month they began to lay
the foundation of the heaps, and finished
them in the seventh month.
8 And when Hezekiah and the princes
came and saw the heaps, they blessed the
LORD, and his people Israel.
9 Then Hezekiah questioned with the
priests and the Levites concerning the
heaps.
10 And Azariah the chief priest of the
house of Zadok answered him, and said,
Since *the people* began to bring the offerings into the house of the LORD, we have
had enough to eat, and have left plenty:
for the LORD hath blessed his people; and
that which is left *is* this great store.
11 Then Hezekiah commanded to prepare chambers in the house of the LORD;
and they prepared *them,*
12 And brought in the offerings and the
tithes and the dedicated *things* faithfully:
over which Cononiah the Levite *was* ruler,
and Shimei his brother *was* the next.
13 And Jehiel, and Azaziah, and Nahath,
and Asahel, and Jerimoth, and Jozabad,
and Eliel, and Ismachiah, and Mahath, and
Benaiah, *were* overseers under the hand of
Cononiah and Shimei his brother, at the
commandment of Hezekiah the king, and
Azariah the ruler of the house of God.
14 And Kore the son of Imnah the Levite,
the porter toward the east, *was* over the
freewill offerings of God, to distribute the
oblations of the LORD, and the most holy
things.
15 And next him *were* Eden, and Miniamin, and Jeshua, and Shemaiah, Amariah, and Shecaniah, in the cities of the
priests, in *their* set office, to give to their
brethren by courses, as well to the great as
to the small:
16 Beside their genealogy of males, from
three years old and upward, *even* unto

every one that entereth into the house of the LORD, his daily portion for their service in their charges according to their courses;

17 Both to the genealogy of the priests by the house of their fathers, and the Levites from twenty years old and upward, in their charges by their courses;

18 And to the genealogy of all their little ones, their wives, and their sons, and their daughters, through all the congregation: for in their set office they sanctified themselves in holiness:

19 Also of the sons of Aaron the priests, *which were* in the fields of the suburbs of their cities, in every several city, the men that were expressed by name, to give portions to all the males among the priests, and to all that were reckoned by genealogies among the Levites.

20 And thus did Hezekiah throughout all Judah, and wrought *that which was* good and right and truth before the LORD his God.

31:20
Who Is Religious?
◄ 1 Chronicles 4:10
Job 1:1 ►

21 And in every work that he began in the service of the house of God, and in the law, and in the commandments, to seek his God, he did *it* with all his heart, and prospered.

32

1 After these things, and the establishment thereof, Sennacherib king of Assyria came, and entered into Judah, and encamped against the fenced cities, and thought to win them for himself.

2 And when Hezekiah saw that Sennacherib was come, and that he was purposed to fight against Jerusalem,

3 He took counsel with his princes and his mighty men to stop the waters of the fountains which *were* without the city: and they did help him.

4 So there was gathered much people together, who stopped all the fountains, and the brook that ran through the midst of the land, saying, Why should the kings of Assyria come, and find much water?

5 Also he strengthened himself, and built up all the wall that was broken, and raised *it* up to the towers, and another wall without, and repaired Millo *in* the city of David, and made darts and shields in abundance.

6 And he set captains of war over the people, and gathered them together to him in the street of the gate of the city, and spake comfortably to them, saying,

7 Be strong and courageous, be not afraid nor dismayed for the king of Assyria, nor for all the multitude that *is* with him: for *there be* more with us than with him:

8 With him *is* an arm of flesh; but with us *is* the LORD our God to help us, and to fight our battles. And the people rested themselves upon the words of Hezekiah king of Judah.

9 After this did Sennacherib king of Assyria send his servants to Jerusalem, (but he *himself laid siege* against Lachish, and all his power with him,) unto Hezekiah king of Judah, and unto all Judah that *were* at Jerusalem, saying,

10 Thus saith Sennacherib king of Assyria, Whereon do ye trust, that ye abide in the siege in Jerusalem?

11 Doth not Hezekiah persuade you to give over yourselves to die by famine and by thirst, saying, The LORD our God shall deliver us out of the hand of the king of Assyria?

12 Hath not the same Hezekiah taken away his high places and his altars, and commanded Judah and Jerusalem, saying, Ye shall worship before one altar, and burn incense upon it?

13 Know ye not what I and my fathers have done unto all the people of *other* lands? were the gods of the nations of those lands any ways able to deliver their lands out of mine hand?

14 Who *was there* among all the gods of those nations that my fathers utterly destroyed, that could deliver his people out of mine hand, that your God should be able to deliver you out of mine hand?

15 Now therefore let not Hezekiah deceive you, nor persuade you on this manner, neither yet believe him: for no god of any nation or kingdom was able to deliver his people out of mine hand, and out of the hand of my fathers: how much less shall your God deliver you out of mine hand?

16 And his servants spake yet *more* against the LORD God, and against his servant Hezekiah.

17 He wrote also letters to rail on the LORD God of Israel, and to speak against

him, saying, As the gods of the nations of *other* lands have not delivered their people out of mine hand, so shall not the God of Hezekiah deliver his people out of mine hand.

18 Then they cried with a loud voice in the Jews' speech unto the people of Jerusalem that *were* on the wall, to affright them, and to trouble them; that they might take the city.

19 And they spake against the God of Jerusalem, as against the gods of the people of the earth, *which were* the work of the hands of man.

20 And for this *cause* Hezekiah the king, and the prophet Isaiah the son of Amoz, prayed and cried to heaven.

21 And the LORD sent an angel, which cut off all the mighty men of valour, and the leaders and captains in the camp of the king of Assyria. So he returned with shame of face to his own land. And when he was come into the house of his god, they that came forth of his own bowels slew him there with the sword.

22 Thus the LORD saved Hezekiah and the inhabitants of Jerusalem from the hand of Sennacherib the king of Assyria, and from the hand of all *other,* and guided them on every side.

23 And many brought gifts unto the LORD to Jerusalem, and presents to Hezekiah king of Judah: so that he was magnified in the sight of all nations from thenceforth.

24 In those days Hezekiah was sick to the death, and prayed unto the LORD: and he spake unto him, and he gave him a sign.

25 But Hezekiah rendered not again according to the benefit *done* unto him; for his heart was lifted up: therefore there was wrath upon him, and upon Judah and Jerusalem.

26 Notwithstanding Hezekiah humbled himself for the pride of his heart, *both* he and the inhabitants of Jerusalem, so that the wrath of the LORD came not upon them in the days of Hezekiah.

27 And Hezekiah had exceeding much riches and honour: and he made himself treasuries for silver, and for gold, and for precious stones, and for spices, and for shields, and for all manner of pleasant jewels;

28 Storehouses also for the increase of corn, and wine, and oil; and stalls for all manner of beasts, and cotes for flocks.

29 Moreover he provided him cities, and possessions of flocks and herds in abundance: for God had given him substance very much.

30 This same Hezekiah also stopped the upper watercourse of Gihon, and brought it straight down to the west side of the city of David. And Hezekiah prospered in all his works.

31 Howbeit in *the business of* the ambassadors of the princes of Babylon, who sent unto him to enquire of the wonder that was *done* in the land, God left him, to try him, that he might know all *that was* in his heart.

32 Now the rest of the acts of Hezekiah, and his goodness, behold, they *are* written in the vision of Isaiah the prophet, the son of Amoz, *and* in the book of the kings of Judah and Israel.

33 And Hezekiah slept with his fathers, and they buried him in the chiefest of the sepulchres of the sons of David: and all Judah and the inhabitants of Jerusalem did him honour at his death. And Manasseh his son reigned in his stead.

33

1 Manasseh *was* twelve years old when he began to reign, and he reigned fifty and five years in Jerusalem:

2 But did *that which was* evil in the sight of the LORD, like unto the abominations of the heathen, whom the LORD had cast out before the children of Israel.

3 For he built again the high places which Hezekiah his father had broken down, and he reared up altars for Baalim, and made groves, and worshipped all the host of heaven, and served them.

4 Also he built altars in the house of the LORD, whereof the LORD had said, In Jerusalem shall my name be for ever.

5 And he built altars for all the host of heaven in the two courts of the house of the LORD.

6 And he caused his children to pass through the fire in the valley of the son of Hinnom: also he observed times, and used enchantments, and used witchcraft, and dealt with a familiar spirit, and with wizards: he wrought much evil in the sight of the LORD, to provoke him to anger.

7 And he set a carved image, the idol which he had made, in the house of God, of which God had said to David and to

Solomon his son, In this house, and in Jerusalem, which I have chosen before all the tribes of Israel, will I put my name for ever:

8 Neither will I any more remove the foot of Israel from out of the land which I have appointed for your fathers; so that they will take heed to do all that I have commanded them, according to the whole law and the statutes and the ordinances by the hand of Moses.

9 So Manasseh made Judah and the inhabitants of Jerusalem to err, *and* to do worse than the heathen, whom the LORD had destroyed before the children of Israel.

10 And the LORD spake to Manasseh, and to his people: but they would not hearken.

11 Wherefore the LORD brought upon them the captains of the host of the king of Assyria, which took Manasseh among the thorns, and bound him with fetters, and carried him to Babylon.

12 And when he was in affliction, he besought the LORD his God, and humbled himself greatly before the God of his fathers,

13 And prayed unto him: and he was intreated of him, and heard his supplication, and brought him again to Jerusalem into his kingdom. Then Manasseh knew that the LORD he *was* God.

14 Now after this he built a wall without the city of David, on the west side of Gihon, in the valley, even to the entering in at the fish gate, and compassed about Ophel, and raised it up a very great height, and put captains of war in all the fenced cities of Judah.

15 And he took away the strange gods, and the idol out of the house of the LORD, and all the altars that he had built in the mount of the house of the LORD, and in Jerusalem, and cast *them* out of the city.

16 And he repaired the altar of the LORD, and sacrificed thereon peace offerings and thank offerings, and commanded Judah to serve the LORD God of Israel.

17 Nevertheless the people did sacrifice still in the high places, *yet* unto the LORD their God only.

18 Now the rest of the acts of Manasseh, and his prayer unto his God, and the words of the seers that spake to him in the name of the LORD God of Israel, behold, they *are written* in the book of the kings of Israel.

19 His prayer also, and *how God* was intreated of him, and all his sin, and his trespass, and the places wherein he built high places, and set up groves and graven images, before he was humbled: behold, they *are* written among the sayings of the seers.

20 So Manasseh slept with his fathers, and they buried him in his own house: and Amon his son reigned in his stead.

21 Amon *was* two and twenty years old when he began to reign, and reigned two years in Jerusalem.

22 But he did *that which was* evil in the sight of the LORD, as did Manasseh his father: for Amon sacrificed unto all the carved images which Manasseh his father had made, and served them;

23 And humbled not himself before the LORD, as Manasseh his father had humbled himself; but Amon trespassed more and more.

33:23 Stubborn People
◄ 2 Chronicles 28:22
Nehemiah 9:29 ►

24 And his servants conspired against him, and slew him in his own house.

25 But the people of the land slew all them that had conspired against king Amon; and the people of the land made Josiah his son king in his stead.

34

1 Josiah *was* eight years old when he began to reign, and he reigned in Jerusalem one and thirty years.

34:1-3 Young Leaders
◄ 2 Chronicles 24:1
Luke 3:23 ►

2 And he did *that which was* right in the sight of the LORD, and walked in the ways of David his father, and declined *neither* to the right hand, nor to the left.

34:1-3 Young Men
◄ 2 Chronicles 24:1-2
Psalm 71:5 ►

3 For in the eighth year of his reign, while he was yet young, he began to seek after the God of David his father: and in the twelfth year he began to purge Judah and Jerusalem from the high places, and the groves, and the carved images, and the molten images.

4 And they brake down the altars of Baalim in his presence; and the images, that *were* on high above them, he cut down; and the groves, and the carved images, and the molten images, he brake in pieces, and made dust *of them,* and strowed *it* upon the graves of them that had sacrificed unto them.

5 And he burnt the bones of the priests upon their altars, and cleansed Judah and Jerusalem.

6 And *so did he* in the cities of Manasseh, and Ephraim, and Simeon, even unto Naphtali, with their mattocks round about.

7 And when he had broken down the altars and the groves, and had beaten the graven images into powder, and cut down all the idols throughout all the land of Israel, he returned to Jerusalem.

8 Now in the eighteenth year of his reign, when he had purged the land, and the house, he sent Shaphan the son of Azaliah, and Maaseiah the governor of the city, and Joah the son of Joahaz the recorder, to repair the house of the LORD his God.

9 And when they came to Hilkiah the high priest, they delivered the money that was brought into the house of God, which the Levites that kept the doors had gathered of the hand of Manasseh and Ephraim, and of all the remnant of Israel, and of all Judah and Benjamin; and they returned to Jerusalem.

10 And they put *it* in the hand of the workmen that had the oversight of the house of the LORD, and they gave it to the workmen that wrought in the house of the LORD, to repair and amend the house:

11 Even to the artificers and builders gave they *it,* to buy hewn stone, and timber for couplings, and to floor the houses which the kings of Judah had destroyed.

12 And the men did the work faithfully: and the overseers of them *were* Jahath and Obadiah, the Levites, of the sons of Merari; and Zechariah and Meshullam, of the sons of the Kohathites, to set *it* forward; and *other of* the Levites, all that could skill of instruments of musick.

13 Also *they were* over the bearers of burdens, and *were* overseers of all that wrought the work in any manner of service: and of the Levites *there were* scribes, and officers, and porters.

14 And when they brought out the money that was brought into the house of the LORD, Hilkiah the priest found a book of the law of the LORD *given* by Moses.

15 And Hilkiah answered and said to Shaphan the scribe, I have found the book of the law in the house of the LORD. And Hilkiah delivered the book to Shaphan.

16 And Shaphan carried the book to the king, and brought the king word back again, saying, All that was committed to thy servants, they do *it.*

17 And they have gathered together the money that was found in the house of the LORD, and have delivered it into the hand of the overseers, and to the hand of the workmen.

18 Then Shaphan the scribe told the king, saying, Hilkiah the priest hath given me a book. And Shaphan read it before the king.

19 And it came to pass, when the king had heard the words of the law, that he rent his clothes.

20 And the king commanded Hilkiah, and Ahikam the son of Shaphan, and Abdon the son of Micah, and Shaphan the scribe, and Asaiah a servant of the king's, saying,

21 Go, enquire of the LORD for me, and for them that are left in Israel and in Judah, concerning the words of the book that is found: for great *is* the wrath of the LORD that is poured out upon us, because our fathers have not kept the word of the LORD, to do after all that is written in this book.

22 And Hilkiah, and *they* that the king *had appointed,* went to Huldah the prophetess, the wife of Shallum the son of Tikvath, the son of Hasrah, keeper of the wardrobe; (now she dwelt in Jerusalem in the college:) and they spake to her to that *effect.*

23 And she answered them, Thus saith the LORD God of Israel, Tell ye the man that sent you to me,

24 Thus saith the LORD, Behold, I will bring evil upon this place, and upon the inhabitants thereof, *even* all the curses that are written in the book which they have read before the king of Judah:

25 Because they have forsaken me, and have burned incense unto other gods, that they might provoke me to anger with all the works of their hands; therefore my

wrath shall be poured out upon this place,
and shall not be quenched.
26 And as for the king of Judah, who sent
you to enquire of the LORD, so shall ye say
unto him, Thus saith the LORD God of Israel *concerning* the words which thou hast
heard;
27 Because thine heart was tender, and
thou didst humble thyself before God,
when thou heardest his words against this
place, and against the inhabitants thereof,
and humbledst thyself before me, and
didst rend thy clothes, and weep before
me; I have even heard *thee* also, saith the
LORD.
28 Behold, I will gather thee to thy fathers, and thou shalt be gathered to thy
grave in peace, neither shall thine eyes see
all the evil that I will bring upon this place,
and upon the inhabitants of the same. So
they brought the king word again.
29 Then the king sent and gathered together all the elders of Judah and Jerusalem.
30 And the king went up into the house
of the LORD, and all the men of Judah, and
the inhabitants of Jerusalem, and the
priests, and the Levites, and all the people, great and small: and he read in their
ears all the words of the book of the covenant that was found in the house of the
LORD.
31 And the king stood in his place, and
made a covenant before the LORD, to walk
after the LORD, and to keep his commandments, and his testimonies, and his statutes, with all his heart, and with all his
soul, to perform the words of the covenant
which are written in this book.
32 And he caused all that were present
in Jerusalem and Benjamin to stand *to it.*
And the inhabitants of Jerusalem did according to the covenant of God, the God
of their fathers.
33 And Josiah took away all the abominations out of all the countries that *pertained* to the children of Israel, and made
all that were present in Israel to serve, *even*
to serve the LORD their God. *And* all his
days they departed not from following the
LORD, the God of their fathers.

35

1 Moreover Josiah kept a passover unto
the LORD in Jerusalem: and they killed the
passover on the fourteenth *day* of the first
month.
2 And he set the
priests in their
charges, and en-
couraged them to
the service of the
house of the LORD,

35:2 Encouraging People
◄ Exodus 14:13
Isaiah 41:13 ►

3 And said unto the Levites that taught
all Israel, which were holy unto the LORD,
Put the holy ark in the house which Solomon the son of David king of Israel did
build; *it shall* not *be* a burden upon *your*
shoulders: serve now the LORD your God,
and his people Israel,
4 And prepare *yourselves* by the houses
of your fathers, after your courses, according to the writing of David king of Israel,
and according to the writing of Solomon
his son.
5 And stand in the holy *place* according
to the divisions of the families of the fathers of your brethren the people, and *after* the division of the families of the
Levites.
6 So kill the passover, and sanctify yourselves, and prepare your brethren, that *they*
may do according to the word of the LORD
by the hand of Moses.
7 And Josiah gave to the people, of the
flock, lambs and kids, all for the passover
offerings, for all that were present, to the
number of thirty thousand, and three
thousand bullocks: these *were* of the king's
substance.
8 And his princes gave willingly unto the
people, to the priests, and to the Levites:
Hilkiah and Zechariah and Jehiel, rulers
of the house of God, gave unto the priests
for the passover offerings two thousand
and six hundred *small cattle,* and three
hundred oxen.
9 Conaniah also, and Shemaiah and
Nethaneel, his brethren, and Hashabiah
and Jeiel and Jozabad, chief of the Levites,
gave unto the Levites for passover offerings five thousand *small cattle,* and five
hundred oxen.
10 So the service was prepared, and the
priests stood in their place, and the Levites
in their courses, according to the king's
commandment.
11 And they killed the passover, and the
priests sprinkled *the blood* from their
hands, and the Levites flayed *them.*
12 And they removed the burnt offerings, that they might give according to the

divisions of the families of the people, to
offer unto the Lord, as *it is* written in the
book of Moses. And so *did they* with the
oxen.
13 And they roasted the passover with fire
according to the ordinance: but the *other*
holy *offerings* sod they in pots, and in caldrons, and in pans, and divided *them*
speedily among all the people.
14 And afterward they made ready for
themselves, and for the priests: because the
priests the sons of Aaron *were busied* in
offering of burnt offerings and the fat until night; therefore the Levites prepared for
themselves, and for the priests the sons of
Aaron.
15 And the singers the sons of Asaph *were*
in their place, according to the commandment of David, and Asaph, and Heman,
and Jeduthun the king's seer; and the porters *waited* at every gate; they might not
depart from their service; for their brethren the Levites prepared for them.
16 So all the service of the Lord was prepared the same day, to keep the passover,
and to offer burnt offerings upon the altar
of the Lord, according to the commandment of king Josiah.
17 And the children of Israel that were
present kept the passover at that time, and
the feast of unleavened bread seven days.
18 And there was no passover like to that
kept in Israel from the days of Samuel the
prophet; neither did all the kings of Israel
keep such a passover as Josiah kept, and
the priests, and the Levites, and all Judah
and Israel that were present, and the inhabitants of Jerusalem.
19 In the eighteenth year of the reign of
Josiah was this passover kept.
20 After all this, when Josiah had prepared
the temple, Necho king of Egypt came up
to fight against Charchemish by Euphrates: and Josiah went out against him.
21 But he sent am-
bassadors to him,
saying, What have I
to do with thee,
thou king of Judah?
I come not against
thee this day, but against the house wherewith I have war: for God commanded me
to make haste: forbear thee from *meddling
with* God, who *is* with me, that he destroy
thee not.

35:21 Hurrying
◄ 2 Chronicles 24:5
Psalm 119:60 ►

22 Nevertheless Josiah would not turn his
face from him, but disguised himself, that
he might fight with him, and hearkened
not unto the words of Necho from the
mouth of God, and came to fight in the
valley of Megiddo.
23 And the archers shot at king Josiah;
and the king said to his servants, Have me
away; for I am sore wounded.
24 His servants therefore took him out
of that chariot, and put him in the second
chariot that he had; and they brought him
to Jerusalem, and he died, and was buried
in *one of* the sepulchres of his fathers. And
all Judah and Jerusalem mourned for Josiah.
25 And Jeremiah lamented for Josiah:
and all the singing men and the singing
women spake of Josiah in their lamentations to this day, and made them an ordinance in Israel: and, behold, they *are*
written in the lamentations.
26 Now the rest of the acts of Josiah, and
his goodness, according to *that which was*
written in the law of the Lord,
27 And his deeds, first and last, behold,
they *are* written in the book of the kings
of Israel and Judah.

36

1 Then the people of the land took Jehoahaz the son of Josiah, and made him king
in his father's stead in Jerusalem.
2 Jehoahaz *was* twenty and three years
old when he began to reign, and he reigned
three months in Jerusalem.
3 And the king of Egypt put him down
at Jerusalem, and condemned the land in
an hundred talents of silver and a talent
of gold.
4 And the king of Egypt made Eliakim
his brother king over Judah and Jerusalem,
and turned his name to Jehoiakim. And
Necho took Jehoahaz his brother, and carried him to Egypt.
5 Jehoiakim *was* twenty and five years old
when he began to reign, and he reigned
eleven years in Jerusalem: and he did *that
which was* evil in the sight of the Lord
his God.
6 Against him came up Nebuchadnezzar
king of Babylon, and bound him in fetters, to carry him to Babylon.
7 Nebuchadnezzar also carried of the vessels of the house of the Lord to Babylon,
and put them in his temple at Babylon.
8 Now the rest of the acts of Jehoiakim,

and his abominations which he did, and
that which was found in him, behold, they
are written in the book of the kings of Israel and Judah: and Jehoiachin his son
reigned in his stead.
9 Jehoiachin *was* eight years old when he
began to reign, and he reigned three
months and ten days in Jerusalem: and he
did *that which was* evil in the sight of the
LORD.
10 And when the year was expired, king
Nebuchadnezzar sent, and brought him to
Babylon, with the goodly vessels of the
house of the LORD, and made Zedekiah his
brother king over Judah and Jerusalem.
11 Zedekiah *was* one and twenty years old
when he began to reign, and reigned elev-
en years in Jerusalem.
12 And he did *that which was* evil in the
sight of the LORD his God, *and* humbled
not himself before Jeremiah the prophet
speaking from the mouth of the LORD.
13 And he also rebelled against king Nebuchadnezzar, who had made him swear by
God: but he stiffened his neck, and hardened his heart from turning unto the LORD
God of Israel.
14 Moreover all the chief of the priests,
and the people, transgressed very much
after all the abominations of the heathen;
and polluted the house of the LORD which
he had hallowed in Jerusalem.
15 And the LORD God of their fathers sent
to them by his messengers, rising up
betimes, and sending; because he had
compassion on his people, and on his
dwelling place:
16 But they
mocked the mes-
sengers of God, and
despised his words,
and misused his
prophets, until the
wrath of the LORD arose against his people, till *there was* no
remedy.
17 Therefore he
brought upon them
the king of the
Chaldees, who slew
their young men with the sword in the
house of their sanctuary, and had no compassion upon young man or maiden, old
man, or him that stooped for age: he gave
them all into his hand.
18 And all the vessels of the house of
God, great and small, and the treasures of
the house of the LORD, and the treasures
of the king, and of his princes; all *these* he
brought to Babylon.
19 And they burnt the house of God, and
brake down the wall of Jerusalem, and
burnt all the palaces thereof with fire,
and destroyed all the goodly vessels
thereof.
20 And them that had escaped from the
sword carried he away to Babylon; where
they were servants to him and his sons
until the reign of the kingdom of Persia:
21 To fulfil the word of the LORD by the
mouth of Jeremiah, until the land had
enjoyed her sabbaths: *for* as long as she
lay desolate she kept sabbath, to fulfil
threescore and ten years.
22 Now in the first year of Cyrus king of
Persia, that the word of the LORD *spoken*
by the mouth of Jeremiah might be accomplished, the LORD stirred up the spirit of
Cyrus king of Persia, that he made a proclamation throughout all his kingdom, and
put it also in writing, saying,
23 Thus saith Cyrus king of Persia, All the
kingdoms of the earth hath the LORD God
of heaven given me; and he hath charged
me to build him an house in Jerusalem,
which *is* in Judah. Who *is there* among you
of all his people? The LORD his God *be* with
him, and let him go up.

36:16 Mocking
◄ 2 Chronicles 30:10
Nehemiah 4:1 ►

36:16
Rejecting God's Word
◄ 2 Chronicles 30:10
Psalm 50:17 ►

Ezra

AUTHOR
Probably Ezra the scribe

MAIN POINT
God is faithful and kept his promise to return his people to their land. He also rewards the faithfulness of his servants.

DATE WRITTEN
Approximately 450 B.C.

10 CHAPTERS

MAIN PEOPLE

Cyrus, Zerubbabel, Haggai, Zechariah, Darius, Artaxerxes I, Ezra

SPECIAL FEATURES

- *Was originally one book with Nehemiah*
- *Tells how Zerubbabel led a group of exiles back to Jerusalem and the people's wimpy response*
- *Describes Ezra's return to Jerusalem 80 years later . . . and the mess he found*
- *Inspires readers with Ezra's challenge to repent*
- *Tenth book of History*

HOW THE BOOK GOT ITS NAME

The book is a tribute to the priest and scribe Ezra, whose name means "help" and who helped call God's people back to faithfulness.

1 [1]Now in the first year of Cyrus king of
Persia, that the word of the LORD by the
mouth of Jeremiah might be fulfilled, the
LORD stirred up the spirit of Cyrus king of
Persia, that he made a proclamation
throughout all his kingdom, and *put it* also
in writing, saying,
[2]Thus saith Cyrus king of Persia, The
LORD God of heaven hath given me all the
kingdoms of the earth; and he hath
charged me to build him an house at Jerusalem, which *is* in Judah.
[3]Who *is there* among you of all his people? his God be with him, and let him go
up to Jerusalem, which *is* in Judah, and
build the house of the LORD God of Israel,
(he *is* the God,) which *is* in Jerusalem.
[4]And whosoever remaineth in any place
where he sojourneth, let the men of his
place help him with silver, and with gold,
and with goods, and with beasts, beside
the freewill offering for the house of God
that *is* in Jerusalem.
[5]Then rose up the chief of the fathers of
Judah and Benjamin, and the priests, and
the Levites, with all *them* whose spirit God
had raised, to go up to build the house of
the LORD which *is* in Jerusalem.
[6]And all they
that *were* about
them strengthened
their hands with
vessels of silver,
with gold, with

1:6
Examples of Generosity
◄ 2 Chronicles 24:10
Ezra 2:69 ►

goods, and with beasts, and with precious
things, beside all *that* was willingly offered.
7 Also Cyrus the king brought forth the
vessels of the house of the LORD, which
Nebuchadnezzar had brought forth out of
Jerusalem, and had put them in the house
of his gods;
8 Even those did Cyrus king of Persia
bring forth by the hand of Mithredath the
treasurer, and numbered them unto Sheshbazzar, the prince of Judah.
9 And this *is* the number of them: thirty
chargers of gold, a thousand chargers of
silver, nine and twenty knives,
10 Thirty basons of gold, silver basons of
a second *sort* four hundred and ten, *and*
other vessels a thousand.
11 All the vessels of gold and of silver *were*
five thousand and four hundred. All *these*
did Sheshbazzar bring up with *them of* the
captivity that were brought up from Babylon unto Jerusalem.

2

1 Now these *are* the children of the province that went up out of the captivity, of
those which had been carried away, whom
Nebuchadnezzar the king of Babylon had
carried away unto Babylon, and came
again unto Jerusalem and Judah, every one
unto his city;
2 Which came with Zerubbabel: Jeshua,
Nehemiah, Seraiah, Reelaiah, Mordecai,
Bilshan, Mizpar, Bigvai, Rehum, Baanah.
The number of the men of the people of
Israel:
3 The children of Parosh, two thousand
an hundred seventy and two.
4 The children of Shephatiah, three hundred seventy and two.
5 The children of Arah, seven hundred
seventy and five.
6 The children of Pahath-moab, of the
children of Jeshua *and* Joab, two thousand
eight hundred and twelve.
7 The children of Elam, a thousand two
hundred fifty and four.
8 The children of Zattu, nine hundred
forty and five.
9 The children of Zaccai, seven hundred
and threescore.
10 The children of Bani, six hundred forty and two.
11 The children of Bebai, six hundred
twenty and three.
12 The children of Azgad, a thousand two
hundred twenty and two.
13 The children of Adonikam, six hundred sixty and six.
14 The children of Bigvai, two thousand
fifty and six.
15 The children of Adin, four hundred
fifty and four.
16 The children of Ater of Hezekiah,
ninety and eight.
17 The children of Bezai, three hundred
twenty and three.
18 The children of Jorah, an hundred and
twelve.
19 The children of Hashum, two hundred
twenty and three.
20 The children of Gibbar, ninety and
five.
21 The children of Bethlehem, an hundred twenty and three.
22 The men of Netophah, fifty and six.
23 The men of Anathoth, an hundred
twenty and eight.
24 The children of Azmaveth, forty and
two.
25 The children of Kirjath-arim, Chephirah, and Beeroth, seven hundred and
forty and three.
26 The children of Ramah and Gaba, six
hundred twenty and one.
27 The men of Michmas, an hundred
twenty and two.
28 The men of Bethel and Ai, two hundred twenty and three.
29 The children of Nebo, fifty and two.
30 The children of Magbish, an hundred
fifty and six.
31 The children of the other Elam, a thousand two hundred fifty and four.
32 The children of Harim, three hundred
and twenty.
33 The children of Lod, Hadid, and Ono,
seven hundred twenty and five.
34 The children of Jericho, three hundred
forty and five.
35 The children of Senaah, three thousand and six hundred and thirty.
36 The priests: the children of Jedaiah, of
the house of Jeshua, nine hundred seventy and three.
37 The children of Immer, a thousand fifty and two.
38 The children of Pashur, a thousand
two hundred forty and seven.
39 The children of Harim, a thousand
and seventeen.
40 The Levites: the children of Jeshua and

Kadmiel, of the children of Hodaviah, seventy and four.
41 The singers: the children of Asaph, an
hundred twenty and eight.
42 The children of the porters: the children of Shallum, the children of Ater, the
children of Talmon, the children of Akkub,
the children of Hatita, the children of Shobai, *in* all an hundred thirty and nine.
43 The Nethinims: the children of Ziha,
the children of Hasupha, the children of
Tabbaoth,
44 The children of Keros, the children of
Siaha, the children of Padon,
45 The children of Lebanah, the children
of Hagabah, the children of Akkub,
46 The children of Hagab, the children
of Shalmai, the children of Hanan,
47 The children of Giddel, the children
of Gahar, the children of Reaiah,
48 The children of Rezin, the children of
Nekoda, the children of Gazzam,
49 The children of Uzza, the children of
Paseah, the children of Besai,
50 The children of Asnah, the children
of Mehunim, the children of Nephusim,
51 The children of Bakbuk, the children
of Hakupha, the children of Harhur,
52 The children of Bazluth, the children
of Mehida, the children of Harsha,
53 The children of Barkos, the children
of Sisera, the children of Thamah,
54 The children of Neziah, the children
of Hatipha.
55 The children of Solomon's servants:
the children of Sotai, the children of So-
phereth, the children of Peruda,
56 The children of Jaalah, the children of
Darkon, the children of Giddel,
57 The children of Shephatiah, the children of Hattil, the children of Pochereth
of Zebaim, the children of Ami.
58 All the Nethinims, and the children
of Solomon's servants, *were* three hundred
ninety and two.
59 And these *were* they which went up
from Tel-melah, Tel-harsa, Cherub, Addan,
and Immer: but they could not shew their
father's house, and their seed, whether they
were of Israel:
60 The children of Delaiah, the children
of Tobiah, the children of Nekoda, six
hundred fifty and two.
61 And of the children of the priests: the
children of Habaiah, the children of Koz,
the children of Barzillai; which took a wife
of the daughters of Barzillai the Gileadite,
and was called after their name:
62 These sought their register *among*
those that were reckoned by genealogy, but
they were not found: therefore were they,
as polluted, put from the priesthood.
63 And the Tirshatha said unto them, that
they should not eat of the most holy
things, till there stood up a priest with
Urim and with Thummim.
64 The whole congregation together *was*
forty and two thousand three hundred *and*
threescore,
65 Beside their servants and their maids,
of whom *there were* seven thousand three
hundred thirty and seven: and *there were*
among them two hundred singing men
and singing women.
66 Their horses *were* seven hundred thirty and six; their mules, two hundred forty
and five;
67 Their camels, four hundred thirty and
five; *their* asses, six thousand seven hundred and twenty.
68 And *some* of the chief of the fathers,
when they came to the house of the LORD
which *is* at Jerusalem, offered freely for the
house of God to set it up in his place:
69 They gave after
their ability unto
the treasure of the
work threescore
and one thousand
drams of gold, and
five thousand pound of silver, and one
hundred priests' garments.

2:69
Examples of Generosity
◄ Ezra 1:6
Ezra 8:25 ►

70 So the priests, and the Levites, and
some of the people, and the singers, and
the porters, and the Nethinims, dwelt in
their cities, and all Israel in their cities.

3

1 And when the seventh month was
come, and the children of Israel *were* in
the cities, the people gathered themselves
together as one man to Jerusalem.
2 Then stood up Jeshua the son of Jozadak, and his brethren the priests, and Zerubbabel the son of Shealtiel, and his
brethren, and builded the altar of the God
of Israel, to offer burnt offerings thereon,
as *it is* written in the law of Moses the man
of God.
3 And they set the altar upon his bases;
for fear *was* upon them because of the people of those countries: and they offered

burnt offerings thereon unto the LORD, *even* burnt offerings morning and evening.

4 They kept also the feast of tabernacles, as *it is* written, and *offered* the daily burnt offerings by number, according to the custom, as the duty of every day required;

5 And afterward *offered* the continual burnt offering, both of the new moons, and of all the set feasts of the LORD that were consecrated, and of every one that willingly offered a freewill offering unto the LORD.

6 From the first day of the seventh month began they to offer burnt offerings unto the LORD. But the foundation of the temple of the LORD was not *yet* laid.

7 They gave money also unto the masons, and to the carpenters; and meat, and drink, and oil, unto them of Zidon, and to them of Tyre, to bring cedar trees from Lebanon to the sea of Joppa, according to the grant that they had of Cyrus king of Persia.

8 Now in the second year of their coming unto the house of God at Jerusalem, in the second month, began Zerubbabel the son of Shealtiel, and Jeshua the son of Jozadak, and the remnant of their brethren the priests and the Levites, and all they that were come out of the captivity unto Jerusalem; and appointed the Levites, from twenty years old and upward, to set forward the work of the house of the LORD.

9 Then stood Jeshua *with* his sons and his brethren, Kadmiel and his sons, the sons of Judah, together, to set forward the workmen in the house of God: the sons of Henadad, *with* their sons and their brethren the Levites.

10 And when the builders laid the foundation of the temple of the LORD, they set the priests in their apparel with trumpets, and the Levites the sons of Asaph with cymbals, to praise the LORD, after the ordinance of David king of Israel.

11 And they sang together by course in praising and giving thanks unto the LORD; because *he is* good, for his mercy *endureth* for ever toward Israel. And all the people shouted with a great shout, when they praised the LORD, because the foundation of the house of the LORD was laid.

12 But many of the priests and Levites and chief of the fathers, *who were* ancient men, that had seen the first house, when the foundation of this house was laid before their eyes, wept with a loud voice; and many shouted aloud for joy:

13 So that the people could not discern the noise of the shout of joy from the noise of the weeping of the people: for the people shouted with a loud shout, and the noise was heard afar off.

4

1 Now when the adversaries of Judah and Benjamin heard that the children of the captivity builded the temple unto the LORD God of Israel;

2 Then they came to Zerubbabel, and to the chief of the fathers, and said unto them, Let us build with you: for we seek your God, as ye *do;* and we do sacrifice unto him since the days of Esar-haddon king of Assur, which brought us up hither.

3 But Zerubbabel, and Jeshua, and the rest of the chief of the fathers of Israel, said unto them, Ye have nothing to do with us to build an house unto our God; but we ourselves together will build unto the LORD God of Israel, as king Cyrus the king of Persia hath commanded us.

4 Then the people of the land weakened the hands of the people of Judah, and troubled them in building,

5 And hired counsellors against them, to frustrate their purpose, all the days of Cyrus king of Persia, even until the reign of Darius king of Persia.

6 And in the reign of Ahasuerus, in the beginning of his reign, wrote they *unto him* an accusation against the inhabitants of Judah and Jerusalem.

7 And in the days of Artaxerxes wrote Bishlam, Mithredath, Tabeel, and the rest of their companions, unto Artaxerxes king of Persia; and the writing of the letter *was* written in the Syrian tongue, and interpreted in the Syrian tongue.

8 Rehum the chancellor and Shimshai the scribe wrote a letter against Jerusalem to Artaxerxes the king in this sort:

9 Then *wrote* Rehum the chancellor, and Shimshai the scribe, and the rest of their companions; the Dinaites, the Apharsathchites, the Tarpelites, the Apharsites, the Archevites, the Babylonians, the Susanchites, the Dehavites, *and* the Elamites,

10 And the rest of the nations whom the great and noble Asnapper brought over, and set in the cities of Samaria, and the rest *that are* on this side the river, and at such a time.

11This *is* the copy of the letter that they sent unto him, *even* unto Artaxerxes the king; Thy servants the men on this side the river, and at such a time.

12Be it known unto the king, that the Jews which came up from thee to us are come unto Jerusalem, building the rebellious and the bad city, and have set up the walls *thereof*, and joined the foundations.

13Be it known now unto the king, that, if this city be builded, and the walls set up *again*, *then* will they not pay toll, tribute, and custom, and *so* thou shalt endamage the revenue of the kings.

14Now because we have maintenance from *the king's* palace, and it was not meet for us to see the king's dishonour, therefore have we sent and certified the king;

15That search may be made in the book of the records of thy fathers: so shalt thou find in the book of the records, and know that this city *is* a rebellious city, and hurtful unto kings and provinces, and that they have moved sedition within the same of old time: for which cause was this city destroyed.

16We certify the king that, if this city be builded *again*, and the walls thereof set up, by this means thou shalt have no portion on this side the river.

17*Then* sent the king an answer unto Rehum the chancellor, and *to* Shimshai the scribe, and *to* the rest of their companions that dwell in Samaria, and *unto* the rest beyond the river, Peace, and at such a time.

18The letter which ye sent unto us hath been plainly read before me.

19And I commanded, and search hath been made, and it is found that this city of old time hath made insurrection against kings, and *that* rebellion and sedition have been made therein.

20There have been mighty kings also over Jerusalem, which have ruled over all *countries* beyond the river; and toll, tribute, and custom, was paid unto them.

21Give ye now commandment to cause these men to cease, and that this city be not builded, until *another* commandment shall be given from me.

22Take heed now that ye fail not to do this: why should damage grow to the hurt of the kings?

23Now when the copy of king Artaxerxes' letter *was* read before Rehum, and Shimshai the scribe, and their companions, they went up in haste to Jerusalem unto the Jews, and made them to cease by force and power.

24Then ceased the work of the house of God which *is* at Jerusalem. So it ceased unto the second year of the reign of Darius king of Persia.

5

1Then the prophets, Haggai the prophet, and Zechariah the son of Iddo, prophesied unto the Jews that *were* in Judah and Jerusalem in the name of the God of Israel, *even* unto them.

2Then rose up Zerubbabel the son of Shealtiel, and Jeshua the son of Jozadak, and began to build the house of God which *is* at Jerusalem: and with them *were* the prophets of God helping them.

3At the same time came to them Tatnai, governor on this side the river, and Shethar-boznai, and their companions, and said thus unto them, Who hath commanded you to build this house, and to make up this wall?

4Then said we unto them after this manner, What are the names of the men that make this building?

5But the eye of their God was upon the elders of the Jews, that they could not cause them to cease, till the matter came to Darius: and then they returned answer by letter concerning this *matter*.

6The copy of the letter that Tatnai, governor on this side the river, and Shethar-boznai, and his companions the Apharsachites, which *were* on this side the river, sent unto Darius the king:

7They sent a letter unto him, wherein was written thus; Unto Darius the king, all peace.

8Be it known unto the king, that we went into the province of Judea, to the house of the great God, which is builded with great stones, and timber is laid in the walls, and this work goeth fast on, and prospereth in their hands.

9Then asked we those elders, *and* said unto them thus, Who commanded you to build this house, and to make up these walls?

10We asked their names also, to certify thee, that we might write the names of the men that *were* the chief of them.

11And thus they returned us answer, saying, We are the servants of the God of

heaven and earth, and build the house that
was builded these many years ago, which
a great king of Israel builded and set up.
12 But after that
our fathers had pro-
voked the God of
heaven unto wrath,
he gave them into
the hand of Nebu-
chadnezzar the king of Babylon, the Chaldean, who destroyed this house, and
carried the people away into Babylon.

5:12 Losers
◄ Deuteronomy 31:20
Psalm 78:40 ►

13 But in the first year of Cyrus the king
of Babylon *the same* king Cyrus made a
decree to build this house of God.
14 And the vessels also of gold and silver
of the house of God, which Nebuchadnezzar took out of the temple that *was* in
Jerusalem, and brought them into the temple of Babylon, those did Cyrus the king
take out of the temple of Babylon, and they
were delivered unto *one,* whose name *was*
Sheshbazzar, whom he had made governor;
15 And said unto him, Take these vessels,
go, carry them into the temple that *is* in
Jerusalem, and let the house of God be
builded in his place.
16 Then came the same Sheshbazzar, *and*
laid the foundation of the house of God
which *is* in Jerusalem: and since that time
even until now hath it been in building,
and *yet* it is not finished.
17 Now therefore, if *it seem* good to the
king, let there be search made in the king's
treasure house, which *is* there at Babylon,
whether it be *so,* that a decree was made of
Cyrus the king to build this house of God
at Jerusalem, and let the king send his pleasure to us concerning this matter.

6

1 Then Darius the king made a decree,
and search was made in the house of the
rolls, where the treasures were laid up in
Babylon.
2 And there was found at Achmetha, in
the palace that *is* in the province of the
Medes, a roll, and therein *was* a record thus
written:
3 In the first year of Cyrus the king *the
same* Cyrus the king made a decree *concerning* the house of God at Jerusalem, Let the
house be builded, the place where they
offered sacrifices, and let the foundations
thereof be strongly laid; the height thereof
threescore cubits, *and* the breadth thereof
threescore cubits;
4 *With* three rows of great stones, and a
row of new timber: and let the expences
be given out of the king's house:
5 And also let the golden and silver vessels of the house of God, which Nebuchadnezzar took forth out of the temple which
is at Jerusalem, and brought unto Babylon,
be restored, and brought again unto the
temple which *is* at Jerusalem, *every one*
to his place, and place *them* in the house
of God.
6 Now *therefore,* Tatnai, governor beyond
the river, Shethar-boznai, and your companions the Apharsachites, which *are* beyond the river, be ye far from thence:
7 Let the work of this house of God
alone; let the governor of the Jews and the
elders of the Jews build this house of God
in his place.
8 Moreover I make a decree what ye shall
do to the elders of these Jews for the building of this house of God: that of the king's
goods, *even* of the tribute beyond the river,
forthwith expences be given unto these
men, that they be not hindered.
9 And that which they have need of, both
young bullocks, and rams, and lambs, for
the burnt offerings of the God of heaven,
wheat, salt, wine, and oil, according to the
appointment of the priests which *are* at
Jerusalem, let it be given them day by day
without fail:
10 That they may offer sacrifices of sweet
savours unto the God of heaven, and pray
for the life of the king, and of his sons.
11 Also I have made a decree, that whosoever shall alter this word, let timber be
pulled down from his house, and being
set up, let him be hanged thereon; and let
his house be made a dunghill for this.
12 And the God that hath caused his
name to dwell there destroy all kings and
people, that shall put to their hand to alter *and* to destroy this house of God which
is at Jerusalem. I Darius have made a decree; let it be done with speed.
13 Then Tatnai, governor on this side the
river, Shethar-boznai, and their companions, according to that which Darius the
king had sent, so they did speedily.
14 And the elders of the Jews builded,
and they prospered through the prophesying of Haggai the prophet and Zechariah the son of Iddo. And they builded, and
finished *it,* according to the commandment

of the God of Israel, and according to the
commandment of Cyrus, and Darius, and
Artaxerxes king of Persia.
15 And this house was finished on the
third day of the month Adar, which was
in the sixth year of the reign of Darius the
king.
16 And the children of Israel, the priests,
and the Levites, and the rest of the children of the captivity, kept the dedication
of this house of God with joy,
17 And offered at the dedication of this
house of God an hundred bullocks, two
hundred rams, four hundred lambs; and
for a sin offering for all Israel, twelve he
goats, according to the number of the
tribes of Israel.
18 And they set the priests in their divisions, and the Levites in their courses, for
the service of God, which *is* at Jerusalem;
as it is written in the book of Moses.
19 And the children of the captivity kept
the passover upon the fourteenth *day* of
the first month.
20 For the priests and the Levites were
purified together, all of them *were* pure,
and killed the passover for all the children
of the captivity, and for their brethren the
priests, and for themselves.
21 And the children of Israel, which were
come again out of captivity, and all such
as had separated themselves unto them
from the filthiness of the heathen of
the land, to seek the LORD God of Israel,
did eat,
22 And kept the feast of unleavened
bread seven days with joy: for the LORD
had made them joyful, and turned the
heart of the king of Assyria unto them, to
strengthen their hands in the work of the
house of God, the God of Israel.

7

1 Now after these things, in the reign of
Artaxerxes king of Persia, Ezra the son of
Seraiah, the son of Azariah, the son of
Hilkiah,
2 The son of Shallum, the son of Zadok,
the son of Ahitub,
3 The son of Amariah, the son of Azariah, the son of Meraioth,
4 The son of Zerahiah, the son of Uzzi,
the son of Bukki,
5 The son of Abishua, the son of Phinehas, the son of Eleazar, the son of Aaron
the chief priest:
6 This Ezra went up from Babylon; and
he *was* a ready scribe in the law of Moses,
which the LORD God of Israel had given:
and the king granted him all his request,
according to the hand of the LORD his God
upon him.
7 And there went up *some* of the children
of Israel, and of the priests, and the Levites, and the singers, and the porters, and
the Nethinims, unto Jerusalem, in the seventh year of Artaxerxes the king.
8 And he came to Jerusalem in the fifth
month, which *was* in the seventh year of
the king.
9 For upon the first *day* of the first month
began he to go up from Babylon, and on
the first *day* of the fifth month came he to
Jerusalem, according to the good hand of
his God upon him.
10 For Ezra had
prepared his heart
to seek the law of
the LORD, and to do
it, and to teach in
Israel statutes and
judgments.

7:10 Sunday School
◄ 2 Chronicles 17:7
Nehemiah 8:7 ►

11 Now this *is* the copy of the letter that
the king Artaxerxes gave unto Ezra the
priest, the scribe, *even* a scribe of the words
of the commandments of the LORD, and
of his statutes to Israel.
12 Artaxerxes, king of kings, unto Ezra the
priest, a scribe of the law of the God of
heaven, perfect *peace*, and at such a time.
13 I make a decree, that all they of the
people of Israel, and *of* his priests and Levites, in my realm, which are minded of
their own freewill to go up to Jerusalem,
go with thee.
14 Forasmuch as thou art sent of the king,
and of his seven counsellors, to enquire
concerning Judah and Jerusalem, according to the law of thy God which *is* in thine
hand;
15 And to carry the silver and gold, which
the king and his counsellors have freely
offered unto the God of Israel, whose habitation *is* in Jerusalem,
16 And all the silver and gold that thou
canst find in all the province of Babylon,
with the freewill offering of the people,
and of the priests, offering willingly for the
house of their God which *is* in Jerusalem:
17 That thou mayest buy speedily with
this money bullocks, rams, lambs, with
their meat offerings and their drink offer-

ings, and offer them upon the altar of the
house of your God which *is* in Jerusalem.
18 And whatsoever shall seem good to
thee, and to thy brethren, to do with the
rest of the silver and the gold, that do after the will of your God.
19 The vessels also that are given thee for
the service of the house of thy God, *those*
deliver thou before the God of Jerusalem.
20 And whatsoever more shall be needful for the house of thy God, which thou
shalt have occasion to bestow, bestow *it*
out of the king's treasure house.
21 And I, *even* I Artaxerxes the king, do
make a decree to all the treasurers which
are beyond the river, that whatsoever Ezra
the priest, the scribe of the law of the God
of heaven, shall require of you, it be done
speedily,
22 Unto an hundred talents of silver, and
to an hundred measures of wheat, and to
an hundred baths of wine, and to an hundred baths of oil, and salt without prescrib-
ing *how much*.
23 Whatsoever is commanded by the
God of heaven, let it be diligently done
for the house of the God of heaven: for
why should there be wrath against the
realm of the king and his sons?
24 Also we certify you, that touching any
of the priests and Levites, singers, porters,
Nethinims, or ministers of this house of
God, it shall not be lawful to impose toll,
tribute, or custom, upon them.
25 And thou, Ezra, after the wisdom of
thy God, that *is* in thine hand, set magistrates and judges, which may judge all the
people that *are* beyond the river, all such
as know the laws of thy God; and teach ye
them that know *them* not.
26 And whosoever
will not do the law
of thy God, and
the law of the
king, let judgment
be executed speedi-
ly upon him,
whether *it be* unto
death, or to ban-
ishment, or to con-
fiscation of goods,
or to imprison-
ment.

7:26
Obeying the Law
◄ Proverbs 24:21 ►

7:26 Rebellion
◄ Deuteronomy 17:12
Ezra 10:8 ►

27 Blessed *be* the LORD God of our fathers, which hath put *such a thing* as this
in the king's heart, to beautify the house
of the LORD which *is* in Jerusalem:
28 And hath extended mercy unto me
before the king, and his counsellors, and
before all the king's mighty princes. And
I was strengthened as the hand of the
LORD my God *was* upon me, and I gathered together out of Israel chief men to go
up with me.

8

1 These *are* now the chief of their fathers,
and *this is* the genealogy of them that went
up with me from Babylon, in the reign of
Artaxerxes the king.
2 Of the sons of Phinehas; Gershom: of
the sons of Ithamar; Daniel: of the sons of
David; Hattush.
3 Of the sons of Shechaniah, of the sons
of Pharosh; Zechariah: and with him were
reckoned by genealogy of the males an
hundred and fifty.
4 Of the sons of Pahath-moab; Elihoenai
the son of Zerahiah, and with him two
hundred males.
5 Of the sons of Shechaniah; the son of
Jahaziel, and with him three hundred
males.
6 Of the sons also of Adin; Ebed the son
of Jonathan, and with him fifty males.
7 And of the sons of Elam; Jeshaiah the
son of Athaliah, and with him seventy
males.
8 And of the sons of Shephatiah; Zebadiah the son of Michael, and with him
fourscore males.
9 Of the sons of Joab; Obadiah the son
of Jehiel, and with him two hundred and
eighteen males.
10 And of the sons of Shelomith; the son
of Josiphiah, and with him an hundred
and threescore males.
11 And of the sons of Bebai; Zechariah
the son of Bebai, and with him twenty and
eight males.
12 And of the sons of Azgad; Johanan the
son of Hakkatan, and with him an hundred and ten males.
13 And of the last sons of Adonikam,
whose names *are* these, Eliphelet, Jeiel, and
Shemaiah, and with them threescore
males.
14 Of the sons also of Bigvai; Uthai, and
Zabbud, and with them seventy males.
15 And I gathered them together to the
river than runneth to Ahava; and there
abode we in tents three days: and I viewed

the people, and the priests, and found there none of the sons of Levi.

16 Then sent I for Eliezer, for Ariel, for Shemaiah, and for Elnathan, and for Jarib, and for Elnathan, and for Nathan, and for Zechariah, and for Meshullam, chief men; also for Joiarib, and for Elnathan, men of understanding.

17 And I sent them with commandment unto Iddo the chief at the place Casiphia, and I told them what they should say unto Iddo, *and* to his brethren the Nethinims, at the place Casiphia, that they should bring unto us ministers for the house of our God.

18 And by the good hand of our God upon us they brought us a man of understanding, of the sons of Mahli, the son of Levi, the son of Israel; and Sherebiah, with his sons and his brethren, eighteen;

19 And Hashabiah, and with him Jeshaiah of the sons of Merari, his brethren and their sons, twenty;

20 Also of the Nethinims, whom David and the princes had appointed for the service of the Levites, two hundred and twenty Nethinims: all of them were expressed by name.

21 Then I proclaimed a fast there, at the river of Ahava, that we might afflict ourselves before our God, to seek of him a right way for us, and for our little ones, and for all our substance.

8:21 Willingness to Learn
◄ Jeremiah 42:3 ►

22 For I was ashamed to require of the king a band of soldiers and horsemen to help us against the enemy in the way: because we had spoken unto the king, saying, The hand of our God *is* upon all them for good that seek him; but his power and his wrath *is* against all them that forsake him.

23 So we fasted and besought our God for this: and he was intreated of us.

24 Then I separated twelve of the chief of the priests, Sherebiah, Hashabiah, and ten of their brethren with them,

25 And weighed unto them the silver, and the gold, and the vessels, *even* the offering of the house of our God, which the king, and his counsellors, and his lords, and all Israel *there* present, had offered:

8:25 Examples of Generosity
◄ Ezra 2:69
Nehemiah 7:70 ►

26 I even weighed unto their hand six hundred and fifty talents of silver, and silver vessels an hundred talents, *and* of gold an hundred talents;

27 Also twenty basons of gold, of a thousand drams; and two vessels of fine copper, precious as gold.

28 And I said unto them, Ye *are* holy unto the LORD; the vessels *are* holy also; and the silver and the gold *are* a freewill offering unto the LORD God of your fathers.

8:28 Tithing
◄ 2 Chronicles 15:18
Proverbs 3:9 ►

29 Watch ye, and keep *them*, until ye weigh *them* before the chief of the priests and the Levites, and chief of the fathers of Israel, at Jerusalem, in the chambers of the house of the LORD.

30 So took the priests and the Levites the weight of the silver, and the gold, and the vessels, to bring *them* to Jerusalem unto the house of our God.

31 Then we departed from the river of Ahava on the twelfth *day* of the first month, to go unto Jerusalem: and the hand of our God was upon us, and he delivered us from the hand of the enemy, and of such as lay in wait by the way.

32 And we came to Jerusalem, and abode there three days.

33 Now on the fourth day was the silver and the gold and the vessels weighed in the house of our God by the hand of Meremoth the son of Uriah the priest; and with him *was* Eleazar the son of Phinehas; and with them *was* Jozabad the son of Jeshua, and Noadiah the son of Binnui, Levites;

34 By number *and* by weight of every one: and all the weight was written at that time.

35 *Also* the children of those that had been carried away, which were come out of the captivity, offered burnt offerings unto the God of Israel, twelve bullocks for all Israel, ninety and six rams, seventy and seven lambs, twelve he goats *for* a sin offering: all *this was* a burnt offering unto the LORD.

36 And they delivered the king's commissions unto the king's lieutenants, and to the governors on this side the river: and

they furthered the people, and the house
of God.

9 1 Now when these things were done, the
princes came to me, saying, The people of
Israel, and the priests, and the Levites, have
not separated themselves from the people
of the lands, *doing* according to their abominations, *even* of the Canaanites, the Hittites, the Perizzites, the Jebusites, the
Ammonites, the Moabites, the Egyptians,
and the Amorites.

2 For they have taken of their daughters
for themselves, and for their sons: so that
the holy seed have mingled themselves
with the people of *those* lands: yea, the
hand of the princes and rulers hath been
chief in this trespass.

3 And when I heard this thing, I rent my
garment and my mantle, and plucked off
the hair of my head and of my beard, and
sat down astonied.

4 Then were assembled unto me every
one that trembled at the words of the God
of Israel, because of the transgression of
those that had been carried away; and I
sat astonied until the evening sacrifice.

5 And at the evening sacrifice I arose up
from my heaviness; and having rent my
garment and my mantle, I fell upon my
knees, and spread out my hands unto the
LORD my God.

6 And said, O my
God, I am ashamed
and blush to lift up
my face to thee, my
God: for our iniqui-
ties are increased
over *our* head, and
our trespass is
grown up unto the
heavens.

7 Since the days of
our fathers *have* we
been in a great tres-
pass unto this day;
and for our iniqui-
ties have we, our
kings, *and* our
priests, been deliv-
ered into the hand
of the kings of the lands, to the sword, to
captivity, and to a spoil, and to confusion
of face, as *it is* this day.

9:6 Callousness
◄ Jeremiah 5:28 ►

9:6 Feeling Guilty
◄ Numbers 21:7
Psalm 40:12 ►

9:6 Guilty Conscience
◄ Exodus 9:27
Job 15:21 ►

8 And now for a little space grace hath
been *shewed* from the LORD our God, to
leave us a remnant to escape, and to give
us a nail in his holy place, that our God
may lighten our eyes, and give us a little
reviving in our bondage.

9 For we *were* bondmen; yet our God
hath not forsaken us in our bondage, but
hath extended mercy unto us in the sight
of the kings of Persia, to give us a reviving,
to set up the house of our God, and to repair the desolations thereof, and to give
us a wall in Judah and in Jerusalem.

10 And now, O our God, what shall we
say after this? for we have forsaken thy
commandments,

11 Which thou hast commanded by thy
servants the prophets, saying, The land,
unto which ye go to possess it, is an unclean land with the filthiness of the people of the lands, with their abominations,
which have filled it from one end to another with their uncleanness.

12 Now therefore give not your daughters unto their sons, neither take their
daughters unto your sons, nor seek their
peace or their wealth for ever: that ye may
be strong, and eat the good of the land,
and leave *it* for an inheritance to your children for ever.

13 And after all
that is come upon
us for our evil
deeds, and for our
great trespass, see-
ing that thou our
God hast punished us less than our iniquities *deserve,* and hast given us *such* deliverance as this;

9:13 Mercy from God
◄ Genesis 19:16
Nehemiah 9:17 ►

14 Should we again break thy commandments, and join in affinity with the people of these abominations? wouldest not
thou be angry with us till thou hadst consumed *us,* so that *there should be* no remnant nor escaping?

15 O LORD God of Israel, thou *art* righteous: for we remain yet escaped, as *it is*
this day: behold, we *are* before thee in our
trespasses: for we cannot stand before thee
because of this.

10 1 Now when Ezra had prayed, and when
he had confessed, weeping and casting
himself down before the house of God,
there assembled unto him out of Israel
a very great congregation of men and
women and children: for the people wept
very sore.

2 And Shechaniah the son of Jehiel, *one* of the sons of Elam, answered and said unto Ezra, We have trespassed against our God, and have taken strange wives of the people of the land: yet now there is hope in Israel concerning this thing.

3 Now therefore let us make a covenant with our God to put away all the wives, and such as are born of them, according to the counsel of my lord, and of those that tremble at the commandment of our God; and let it be done according to the law.

4 Arise; for *this* matter *belongeth* unto thee: we also *will be* with thee: be of good courage, and do *it*.

10:4 Teamwork
◄ 1 Chronicles 12:38
Nehemiah 4:16-17 ►

5 Then arose Ezra, and made the chief priests, the Levites, and all Israel, to swear that they should do according to this word. And they sware.

6 Then Ezra rose up from before the house of God, and went into the chamber of Johanan the son of Eliashib: and *when* he came thither, he did eat no bread, nor drink water: for he mourned because of the transgression of them that had been carried away.

7 And they made proclamation throughout Judah and Jerusalem unto all the children of the captivity, that they should gather themselves together unto Jerusalem;

8 And that whosoever would not come within three days, according to the counsel of the princes and the elders, all his substance should be forfeited, and himself separated from the congregation of those that had been carried away.

10:8 Rebellion
◄ Ezra 7:26
Romans 13:2 ►

9 Then all the men of Judah and Benjamin gathered themselves together unto Jerusalem within three days. It *was* the ninth month, on the twentieth *day* of the month; and all the people sat in the street of the house of God, trembling because of *this* matter, and for the great rain.

10 And Ezra the priest stood up, and said unto them, Ye have transgressed, and have taken strange wives, to increase the trespass of Israel.

11 Now therefore make confession unto the LORD God of your fathers, and do his pleasure: and separate yourselves from the people of the land, and from the strange wives.

10:11 Confession
◄ Numbers 5:7
Job 33:27 ►

12 Then all the congregation answered and said with a loud voice, As thou hast said, so must we do.

13 But the people *are* many, and *it is* a time of much rain, and we are not able to stand without, neither *is this* a work of one day or two: for we are many that have transgressed in this thing.

14 Let now our rulers of all the congregation stand, and let all them which have taken strange wives in our cities come at appointed times, and with them the elders of every city, and the judges thereof, until the fierce wrath of our God for this matter be turned from us.

15 Only Jonathan the son of Asahel and Jahaziah the son of Tikvah were employed about this *matter:* and Meshullam and Shabbethai the Levite helped them.

16 And the children of the captivity did so. And Ezra the priest, *with* certain chief of the fathers, after the house of their fathers, and all of them by *their* names, were separated, and sat down in the first day of the tenth month to examine the matter.

17 And they made an end with all the men that had taken strange wives by the first day of the first month.

18 And among the sons of the priests there were found that had taken strange wives: *namely,* of the sons of Jeshua the son of Jozadak, and his brethren; Maaseiah, and Eliezer, and Jarib, and Gedaliah.

19 And they gave their hands that they would put away their wives; and *being* guilty, *they offered* a ram of the flock for their trespass.

20 And of the sons of Immer; Hanani, and Zebadiah.

21 And of the sons of Harim; Maaseiah, and Elijah, and Shemaiah, and Jehiel, and Uzziah.

22 And of the sons of Pashur; Elioenai, Maaseiah, Ishmael, Nethaneel, Jozabad, and Elasah.

23 Also of the Levites; Jozabad, and Shimei, and Kelaiah, (the same *is* Kelita,) Pethahiah, Judah, and Eliezer.

24Of the singers also; Eliashib: and of the porters; Shallum, and Telem, and Uri.
25Moreover of Israel: of the sons of Parosh; Ramiah, and Jeziah, and Malchiah, and Miamin, and Eleazar, and Malchijah, and Benaiah.
26And of the sons of Elam; Mattaniah, Zechariah, and Jehiel, and Abdi, and Jeremoth, and Eliah.
27And of the sons of Zattu; Elioenai, Eliashib, Mattaniah, and Jeremoth, and Zabad, and Aziza.
28Of the sons also of Bebai; Jehohanan, Hananiah, Zabbai, *and* Athlai.
29And of the sons of Bani; Meshullam, Malluch, and Adaiah, Jashub, and Sheal, and Ramoth.
30And of the sons of Pahath-moab; Adna, and Chelal, Benaiah, Maaseiah, Mattaniah, Bezaleel, and Binnui, and Manasseh.
31And *of* the sons of Harim; Eliezer, Ishijah, Malchiah, Shemaiah, Shimeon,
32Benjamin, Malluch, *and* Shemariah.
33Of the sons of Hashum; Mattenai, Mattathah, Zabad, Eliphelet, Jeremai, Manasseh, *and* Shimei.
34Of the sons of Bani; Maadai, Amram, and Uel,
35Benaiah, Bedeiah, Chelluh,
36Vaniah, Meremoth, Eliashib,
37Mattaniah, Mattenai, and Jaasau,
38And Bani, and Binnui, Shimei,
39And Shelemiah, and Nathan, and Adaiah,
40Machnadebai, Shashai, Sharai,
41Azareel, and Shelemiah, Shemariah,
42Shallum, Amariah, *and* Joseph.
43Of the sons of Nebo; Jeiel, Mattithiah, Zabad, Zebina, Jadau, and Joel, Benaiah.
44All these had taken strange wives: and *some* of them had wives by whom they had children.

Nehemiah

AUTHOR
Probably Nehemiah, with Ezra as editor

MAIN POINT
God is out to renew and rebuild, whether the project be walls or a people's faith.

DATE WRITTEN
Approximately 445-432 B.C.

13 CHAPTERS

☐☐☐☐☐☐☐☐☐☐☐☐☐

MAIN PEOPLE

Nehemiah, Ezra, Sanballat, Tobiah

SPECIAL FEATURES

- *Was originally one book with Ezra*
- *Proves that the third time really can be the charm, when it comes to returning to Jerusalem*
- *Mentions Nehemiah's unusual occupation: sipping from the Persian king's cup to test for poison*
- *Describes the huge response to the discovery and reading of the long-lost laws of the Lord*
- *Shows what planning and prayer can do*
- *Eleventh book of History*

HOW THE BOOK GOT ITS NAME

The book of Nehemiah takes its name from the man who led the people of Israel in rebuilding the walls of Jerusalem.

1 1The words of Nehemiah the son of
Hachaliah. And it came to pass in the
month Chisleu, in the twentieth year, as I
was in Shushan the palace,
2That Hanani, one of my brethren,
came, he and *certain* men of Judah; and I
asked them concerning the Jews that had
escaped, which were left of the captivity,
and concerning Jerusalem.
3And they said unto me, The remnant
that are left of the captivity there in the
province *are* in great affliction and reproach: the wall of Jerusalem also *is* broken down, and the gates thereof are burned
with fire.
4And it came to pass, when I heard these
words, that I sat down and wept, and
mourned *certain* days, and fasted, and
prayed before the God of heaven,
5And said, I beseech thee, O LORD God
of heaven, the great and terrible God, that
keepeth covenant and mercy for them that
love him and observe his commandments:
6Let thine ear now be attentive, and
thine eyes open, that thou mayest hear the
prayer of thy servant, which I pray before
thee now, day and night, for the children
of Israel thy servants, and confess the sins
of the children of Israel, which we have
sinned against thee: both I and my father's
house have sinned.
7We have dealt very corruptly against

thee, and have not kept the commandments, nor the statutes, nor the judgments, which thou commandedst thy servant Moses.

8 Remember, I beseech thee, the word that thou commandedst thy servant Moses, saying, *If* ye transgress, I will scatter you abroad among the nations:

9 But *if* ye turn unto me, and keep my commandments, and do them; though there were of you cast out unto the uttermost part of the heaven, *yet* will I gather them from thence, and will bring them unto the place that I have chosen to set my name there.

10 Now these *are* thy servants and thy people, whom thou hast redeemed by thy great power, and by thy strong hand.

11 O Lord, I beseech thee, let now thine ear be attentive to the prayer of thy servant, and to the prayer of thy servants, who desire to fear thy name: and prosper, I pray thee, thy servant this day, and grant him mercy in the sight of this man. For I was the king's cupbearer.

2

1 And it came to pass in the month Nisan, in the twentieth year of Artaxerxes the king, *that* wine *was* before him: and I took up the wine, and gave *it* unto the king. Now I had not been *beforetime* sad in his presence.

2 Wherefore the king said unto me, Why *is* thy countenance sad, seeing thou *art* not sick? this *is* nothing *else* but sorrow of heart. Then I was very sore afraid,

3 And said unto the king, Let the king live for ever: why should not my countenance be sad, when the city, the place of my fathers' sepulchres, *lieth* waste, and the gates thereof are consumed with fire?

4 Then the king said unto me, For what dost thou make request? So I prayed to the God of heaven.

5 And I said unto the king, If it please the king, and if thy servant have found favour in thy sight, that thou wouldest send me unto Judah, unto the city of my fathers' sepulchres, that I may build it.

6 And the king said unto me, (the queen also sitting by him,) For how long shall thy journey be? and when wilt thou return? So it pleased the king to send me; and I set him a time.

7 Moreover I said unto the king, If it please the king, let letters be given me to the governors beyond the river, that they may convey me over till I come into Judah;

8 And a letter unto Asaph the keeper of the king's forest, that he may give me timber to make beams for the gates of the palace which *appertained* to the house, and for the wall of the city, and for the house that I shall enter into. And the king granted me, according to the good hand of my God upon me.

9 Then I came to the governors beyond the river, and gave them the king's letters. Now the king had sent captains of the army and horsemen with me.

10 When Sanballat the Horonite, and Tobiah the servant, the Ammonite, heard *of it*, it grieved them exceedingly that there was come a man to seek the welfare of the children of Israel.

11 So I came to Jerusalem, and was there three days.

12 And I arose in the night, I and some few men with me; neither told I *any* man what my God had put in my heart to do at Jerusalem: neither *was there any* beast with me, save the beast that I rode upon.

13 And I went out by night by the gate of the valley, even before the dragon well, and to the dung port, and viewed the walls of Jerusalem, which were broken down, and the gates thereof were consumed with fire.

14 Then I went on to the gate of the fountain, and to the king's pool: but *there was* no place for the beast *that was* under me to pass.

15 Then went I up in the night by the brook, and viewed the wall, and turned back, and entered by the gate of the valley, and *so* returned.

16 And the rulers knew not whither I went, or what I did; neither had I as yet told *it* to the Jews, nor to the priests, nor to the nobles, nor to the rulers, nor to the rest that did the work.

17 Then said I unto them, Ye see the distress that we *are* in, how Jerusalem *lieth* waste, and the gates thereof are burned with fire: come, and let us build up the wall of Jerusalem, that we be no more a reproach.

18 Then I told them of the hand of my God which was good upon me; as also the king's words that he had spoken unto me. And they said, Let us rise up and build. So

they strengthened their hands for *this* good *work.*

19 But when Sanballat the Horonite, and Tobiah the servant, the Ammonite, and Geshem the Arabian, heard *it,* they laughed us to scorn, and despised us, and said, What *is* this thing that ye do? will ye rebel against the king?

20 Then answered I them, and said unto them, The God of heaven, he will prosper us; therefore we his servants will arise and build: but ye have no portion, nor right, nor memorial, in Jerusalem.

3

1 Then Eliashib the high priest rose up with his brethren the priests, and they builded the sheep gate; they sanctified it, and set up the doors of it; even unto the tower of Meah they sanctified it, unto the tower of Hananeel.

2 And next unto him builded the men of Jericho. And next to them builded Zaccur the son of Imri.

3 But the fish gate did the sons of Hassenaah build, who *also* laid the beams thereof, and set up the doors thereof, the locks thereof, and the bars thereof.

4 And next unto them repaired Meremoth the son of Urijah, the son of Koz. And next unto them repaired Meshullam the son of Berechiah, the son of Meshezabeel. And next unto them repaired Zadok the son of Baana.

5 And next unto them the Tekoites repaired; but their nobles put not their necks to the work of their Lord.

6 Moreover the old gate repaired Jehoiada the son of Paseah, and Meshullam the son of Besodeiah; they laid the beams thereof, and set up the doors thereof, and the locks thereof, and the bars thereof.

7 And next unto them repaired Melatiah the Gibeonite, and Jadon the Meronothite, the men of Gibeon, and of Mizpah, unto the throne of the governor on this side the river.

8 Next unto him repaired Uzziel the son of Harhaiah, of the goldsmiths. Next unto him also repaired Hananiah the son of *one of* the apothecaries, and they fortified Jerusalem unto the broad wall.

9 And next unto them repaired Rephaiah the son of Hur, the ruler of the half part of Jerusalem.

10 And next unto them repaired Jedaiah the son of Harumaph, even over against his house. And next unto him repaired Hattush the son of Hashabniah.

11 Malchijah the son of Harim, and Hashub the son of Pahath-moab, repaired the other piece, and the tower of the furnaces.

12 And next unto him repaired Shallum the son of Halohesh, the ruler of the half part of Jerusalem, he and his daughters.

13 The valley gate repaired Hanun, and the inhabitants of Zanoah; they built it, and set up the doors thereof, the locks thereof, and the bars thereof, and a thousand cubits on the wall unto the dung gate.

14 But the dung gate repaired Malchiah the son of Rechab, the ruler of part of Beth-haccerem; he build it, and set up the doors thereof, the locks thereof, and the bars thereof.

15 But the gate of the fountain repaired Shallun the son of Col-hozeh, the ruler of part of Mizpah; he built it, and covered it, and set up the doors thereof, the locks thereof, and the bars thereof, and the wall of the pool of Siloah by the king's garden, and unto the stairs that go down from the city of David.

16 After him repaired Nehemiah the son of Azbuk, the ruler of the half part of Beth-zur, unto *the place* over against the sepulchres of David, and to the pool that was made, and unto the house of the mighty.

17 After him repaired the Levites, Rehum the son of Bani. Next unto him repaired Hashabiah, the ruler of the half part of Keilah, in his part.

18 After him repaired their brethren, Bavai the son of Henadad, the ruler of the half part of Keilah.

19 And next to him repaired Ezer the son of Jeshua, the ruler of Mizpah, another piece over against the going up to the armoury at the turning *of the wall.*

20 After him Baruch the son of Zabbai earnestly repaired the other piece, from the turning *of the wall* unto the door of the house of Eliashib the high priest.

21 After him repaired Meremoth the son of Urijah the son of Koz another piece, from the door of the house of Eliashib even to the end of the house of Eliashib.

22 And after him repaired the priests, the men of the plain.

23 After him repaired Benjamin and Hashub over against their house. After him

repaired Azariah the son of Maaseiah the son of Ananiah by his house.

24After him repaired Binnui the son of Henadad another piece, from the house of Azariah unto the turning *of the wall,* even unto the corner.

25Palal the son of Uzai, over against the turning *of the wall,* and the tower which lieth out from the king's high house, that *was* by the court of the prison. After him Pedaiah the son of Parosh.

26Moreover the Nethinims dwelt in Ophel, unto *the place* over against the water gate toward the east, and the tower that lieth out.

27After them the Tekoites repaired another piece, over against the great tower that lieth out, even unto the wall of Ophel.

28From above the horse gate repaired the priests, every one over against his house.

29After them repaired Zadok the son of Immer over against his house. After him repaired also Shemaiah the son of Shechaniah, the keeper of the east gate.

30After him repaired Hananiah the son of Shelemiah, and Hanun the sixth son of Zalaph, another piece. After him repaired Meshullam the son of Berechiah over against his chamber.

31After him repaired Malchiah the goldsmith's son unto the place of the Nethinims, and of the merchants, over against the gate Miphkad, and to the going up of the corner.

32And between the going up of the corner unto the sheep gate repaired the goldsmiths and the merchants.

4

1But it came to pass, that when Sanballat heard that we builded the wall, he was wroth, and took great indignation, and mocked the Jews.

4:1 Mocking
◄ 2 Chronicles 36:16
Psalm 22:7 ►

2And he spake before his brethren and the army of Samaria, and said, What do these feeble Jews? will they fortify themselves? will they sacrifice? will they make an end in a day? will they revive the stones out of the heaps of the rubbish which are burned?

3Now Tobiah the Ammonite *was* by him, and he said, Even that which they build, if a fox go up, he shall even break down their stone wall.

4Hear, O our God; for we are despised: and turn their reproach upon their own head, and give them for a prey in the land of captivity:

5And cover not their iniquity, and let not their sin be blotted out from before thee: for they have provoked *thee* to anger before the builders.

6So built we the wall; and all the wall was joined together unto the half thereof: for the people had a mind to work.

7But it came to pass, *that* when Sanballat, and Tobiah, and the Arabians, and the Ammonites, and the Ashdodites, heard that the walls of Jerusalem were made up, *and* that the breaches began to be stopped, then they were very wroth,

8And conspired all of them together to come *and* to fight against Jerusalem, and to hinder it.

9Nevertheless we made our prayer unto our God, and set a watch against them day and night, because of them.

10And Judah said, The strength of the bearers of burdens is decayed, and *there is* much rubbish; so that we are not able to build the wall.

11And our adversaries said, They shall not know, neither see, till we come in the midst among them, and slay them, and cause the work to cease.

12And it came to pass, that when the Jews which dwelt by them came, they said unto us ten times, From all places whence ye shall return unto us *they will be upon you.*

13Therefore set I in the lower places behind the wall, *and* on the higher places, I even set the people after their families with their swords, their spears, and their bows.

14And I looked, and rose up, and said unto the nobles, and to the rulers, and to the rest of the people, Be not ye afraid of them: remember the Lord, *which is* great and terrible, and fight for your brethren, your sons, and your daughters, your wives, and your houses.

4:14
Remember...
◄ Psalm 63:6 ►

15And it came to pass, when our enemies heard that it was known unto us, and God had brought their counsel to nought, that we returned all of us to the wall, every one unto his work.

16 And it came to pass from that time forth, *that* the half of my servants wrought in the work, and the other half of them held both the spears, the shields, and the bows, and the habergeons; and the rulers *were* behind all the house of Judah.

4:16-17 Teamwork
◄ Ezra 10:4
Matthew 18:19 ►

17 They which builded on the wall, and they that bare burdens, with those that laded, *every one* with one of his hands wrought in the work, and with the other *hand* held a weapon.

18 For the builders, every one had his sword girded by his side, and *so* builded. And he that sounded the trumpet *was* by me.

19 And I said unto the nobles, and to the rulers, and to the rest of the people, The work *is* great and large, and we are separated upon the wall, one far from another.

20 In what place *therefore* ye hear the sound of the trumpet, resort ye thither unto us: our God shall fight for us.

21 So we laboured in the work: and half of them held the spears from the rising of the morning till the stars appeared.

22 Likewise at the same time said I unto the people, Let every one with his servant lodge within Jerusalem, that in the night they may be a guard to us, and labour on the day.

23 So neither I, nor my brethren, nor my servants, nor the men of the guard which followed me, none of us put off our clothes, *saving that* every one put them off for washing.

5

1 And there was a great cry of the people and of their wives against their brethren the Jews.

2 For there were that said, We, our sons, and our daughters, *are* many: therefore we take up corn *for them,* that we may eat, and live.

3 *Some* also there were that said, We have mortgaged our lands, vineyards, and houses, that we might buy corn, because of the dearth.

4 There were also that said, We have borrowed money for the king's tribute, *and that upon* our lands and vineyards.

5 Yet now our flesh *is* as the flesh of our brethren, our children as their children: and, lo, we bring into bondage our sons and our daughters to be servants, and *some* of our daughters are brought unto bondage *already:* neither *is it* in our power *to redeem them;* for other men have our lands and vineyards.

6 And I was very angry when I heard their cry and these words.

5:6
Anger
◄ 1 Samuel 11:6 ►

7 Then I consulted with myself, and I rebuked the nobles, and the rulers, and said unto them, Ye exact usury, every one of his brother. And I set a great assembly against them.

8 And I said unto them, We after our ability have redeemed our brethren the Jews, which were sold unto the heathen; and will ye even sell your brethren? or shall they be sold unto us? Then held they their peace, and found nothing *to answer.*

9 Also I said, It *is* not good that ye do: ought ye not to walk in the fear of our God because of the reproach of the heathen our enemies?

5:9 Embarrassing God
◄ 2 Samuel 12:14
Ezekiel 36:20 ►

10 I likewise, *and* my brethren, and my servants, might exact of them money and corn: I pray you, let us leave off this usury.

11 Restore, I pray you, to them, even this day, their lands, their vineyards, their oliveyards, and their houses, also the hundredth *part* of the money, and of the corn, the wine, and the oil, that ye exact of them.

12 Then said they, We will restore *them,* and will require nothing of them; so will we do as thou sayest. Then I called the priests, and took an oath of them, that they should do according to this promise.

13 Also I shook my lap, and said, So God shake out every man from his house, and from his labour, that performeth not this promise, even thus be he shaken out, and emptied. And all the congregation said, Amen, and praised the LORD. And the people did according to this promise.

14 Moreover from the time that I was appointed to be their governor in the land of Judah, from the twentieth year even unto the two and thirtieth year of Artaxerxes the king, *that is,* twelve years, I and my brethren have not eaten the bread of the governor.

15 But the former governors that *had been*
before me were chargeable unto the people, and had taken of them bread and wine,
beside forty shekels of silver; yea, even their
servants bare rule over the people: but so
did not I, because of the fear of God.
16 Yea, also I continued in the work of
this wall, neither bought we any land: and
all my servants *were* gathered thither unto
the work.
17 Moreover *there were* at my table an
hundred and fifty of the Jews and rulers,
beside those that came unto us from
among the heathen that *are* about us.
18 Now *that* which was prepared *for me*
daily *was* one ox *and* six choice sheep; also
fowls were prepared for me, and once in
ten days store of all sorts of wine: yet for
all this required not I the bread of the governor, because the bondage was heavy
upon this people.
19 Think upon me, my God, for good,
according to all that I have done for this
people.

6

1 Now it came to pass, when Sanballat,
and Tobiah, and Geshem the Arabian, and
the rest of our enemies, heard that I had
builded the wall, and *that* there was no
breach left therein; (though at that time I
had not set up the doors upon the gates;)
2 That Sanballat and Geshem sent unto
me, saying, Come,
let us meet togeth-
er in *some one of* the
villages in the plain
of Ono. But they
thought to do me
mischief.

6:2 Mischief
◄ 1 Samuel 23:9
Job 15:35 ►

3 And I sent messengers unto them, saying, I *am* doing a great work, so that I cannot come down: why should the work
cease, whilst I leave it, and come down to
you?
4 Yet they sent unto me four times after
this sort; and I answered them after the
same manner.
5 Then sent Sanballat his servant unto me
in like manner the fifth time with an open
letter in his hand;
6 Wherein *was* written, It is reported
among the heathen, and Gashmu saith *it,*
that thou and the Jews think to rebel: for
which cause thou buildest the wall, that
thou mayest be their king, according to
these words.
7 And thou hast also appointed prophets to preach of thee at Jerusalem, saying,
There is a king in Judah: and now shall it
be reported to the king according to these
words. Come now therefore, and let us take
counsel together.
8 Then I sent unto him, saying, There are
no such things done as thou sayest, but
thou feignest them out of thine own heart.
9 For they all made us afraid, saying,
Their hands shall be weakened from the
work, that it be not done. Now therefore,
O God, strengthen my hands.
10 Afterward I came unto the house of
Shemaiah the son of Delaiah the son of
Mehetabeel, who *was* shut up; and he said,
Let us meet together in the house of God,
within the temple, and let us shut the
doors of the temple: for they will come to
slay thee; yea, in the night will they come
to slay thee.
11 And I said, Should such a man as I
flee? and who *is there,* that, *being* as I *am,*
would go into the temple to save his life? I
will not go in.
12 And, lo, I perceived that God had not
sent him; but that he pronounced this
prophecy against me: for Tobiah and Sanballat had hired him.
13 Therefore *was* he hired, that I should
be afraid, and do so, and sin, and *that* they
might have *matter* for an evil report, that
they might reproach me.
14 My God, think thou upon Tobiah and
Sanballat according to these their works,
and on the prophetess Noadiah, and the
rest of the prophets, that would have put
me in fear.
15 So the wall was finished in the twenty
and fifth *day* of *the month* Elul, in fifty and
two days.
16 And it came to pass, that when all our
enemies heard *thereof,* and all the heathen
that *were* about us saw *these things,* they
were much cast down in their own eyes:
for they perceived that this work was
wrought of our God.
17 Moreover in those days the nobles of
Judah sent many letters unto Tobiah, and
the letters of Tobiah came unto them.
18 For *there were* many in Judah sworn
unto him, because he *was* the son in law
of Shechaniah the son of Arah; and his son
Johanan had taken the daughter of Meshullam the son of Berechiah.

19 Also they reported his good deeds before me, and uttered my words to him. *And* Tobiah sent letters to put me in fear.

7

1 Now it came to pass, when the wall was built, and I had set up the doors, and the porters and the singers and the Levites were appointed,

2 That I gave my brother Hanani, and Hananiah the ruler of the palace, charge over Jerusalem: for he *was* a faithful man, and feared God above many.

3 And I said unto them, Let not the gates of Jerusalem be opened until the sun be hot; and while they stand by, let them shut the doors, and bar *them:* and appoint watches of the inhabitants of Jerusalem, every one in his watch, and every one *to be* over against his house.

4 Now the city *was* large and great: but the people *were* few therein, and the houses *were* not builded.

5 And my God put into mine heart to gather together the nobles, and the rulers, and the people, that they might be reckoned by genealogy. And I found a register of the genealogy of them which came up at the first, and found written therein,

6 These *are* the children of the province, that went up out of the captivity, of those that had been carried away, whom Nebuchadnezzar the king of Babylon had carried away, and came again to Jerusalem and to Judah, every one unto his city;

7 Who came with Zerubbabel, Jeshua, Nehemiah, Azariah, Raamiah, Nahamani, Mordecai, Bilshan, Mispereth, Bigvai, Nehum, Baanah. The number, *I say,* of the men of the people of Israel *was this;*

8 The children of Parosh, two thousand an hundred seventy and two.

9 The children of Shephatiah, three hundred seventy and two.

10 The children of Arah, six hundred fifty and two.

11 The children of Pahath-moab, of the children of Jeshua and Joab, two thousand and eight hundred *and* eighteen.

12 The children of Elam, a thousand two hundred fifty and four.

13 The children of Zattu, eight hundred forty and five.

14 The children of Zaccai, seven hundred and threescore.

15 The children of Binnui, six hundred forty and eight.

16 The children of Bebai, six hundred twenty and eight.

17 The children of Azgad, two thousand three hundred twenty and two.

18 The children of Adonikam, six hundred threescore and seven.

19 The children of Bigvai, two thousand threescore and seven.

20 The children of Adin, six hundred fifty and five.

21 The children of Ater of Hezekiah, ninety and eight.

22 The children of Hashum, three hundred twenty and eight.

23 The children of Bezai, three hundred twenty and four.

24 The children of Hariph, an hundred and twelve.

25 The children of Gibeon, ninety and five.

26 The men of Bethlehem and Netophah, an hundred fourscore and eight.

27 The men of Anathoth, an hundred twenty and eight.

28 The men of Beth-azmaveth, forty and two.

29 The men of Kirjath-jearim, Chephirah, and Beeroth, seven hundred forty and three.

30 The men of Ramah and Gaba, six hundred twenty and one.

31 The men of Michmas, an hundred and twenty and two.

32 The men of Bethel and Ai, an hundred twenty and three.

33 The men of the other Nebo, fifty and two.

34 The children of the other Elam, a thousand two hundred fifty and four.

35 The children of Harim, three hundred and twenty.

36 The children of Jericho, three hundred forty and five.

37 The children of Lod, Hadid, and Ono, seven hundred twenty and one.

38 The children of Senaah, three thousand nine hundred and thirty.

39 The priests: the children of Jedaiah, of the house of Jeshua, nine hundred seventy and three.

40 The children of Immer, a thousand fifty and two.

41 The children of Pashur, a thousand two hundred forty and seven.

42 The children of Harim, a thousand and seventeen.

43 The Levites: the children of Jeshua, of
Kadmiel, *and* of the children of Hodevah,
seventy and four.
44 The singers: the children of Asaph, an
hundred forty and eight.
45 The porters: the children of Shallum,
the children of Ater, the children of Talmon, the children of Akkub, the children
of Hatita, the children of Shobai, an hundred thirty and eight.
46 The Nethinims: the children of Ziha,
the children of Hashupha, the children of
Tabbaoth,
47 The children of Keros, the children of
Sia, the children of Padon,
48 The children of Lebana, the children
of Hagaba, the children of Shalmai,
49 The children of Hanan, the children
of Giddel, the children of Gahar,
50 The children of Reaiah, the children
of Rezin, the children of Nekoda,
51 The children of Gazzam, the children
of Uzza, the children of Phaseah,
52 The children of Besai, the children of
Meunim, the children of Nephishesim,
53 The children of Bakbuk, the children
of Hakupha, the children of Harhur,
54 The children of Bazlith, the children
of Mehida, the children of Harsha,
55 The children of Barkos, the children
of Sisera, the children of Tamah,
56 The children of Neziah, the children
of Hatipha.
57 The children of Solomon's servants:
the children of Sotai, the children of So-
phereth, the children of Perida,
58 The children of Jaala, the children of
Darkon, the children of Giddel,
59 The children of Shephatiah, the children of Hattil, the children of Pochereth
of Zebaim, the children of Amon.
60 All the Nethinims, and the children
of Solomon's servants, *were* three hundred
ninety and two.
61 And these *were* they which went up *also*
from Telmelah, Telharesha, Cherub, Ad-
don, and Immer: but they could not shew
their father's house, nor their seed, whether
they *were* of Israel.
62 The children of Delaiah, the children
of Tobiah, the children of Nekoda, six
hundred forty and two.
63 And of the priests: the children of
Habaiah, the children of Koz, the children
of Barzillai, which took *one* of the daughters of Barzillai the Gileadite to wife, and
was called after their name.
64 These sought their register *among*
those that were reckoned by genealogy, but
it was not found: therefore were they, as
polluted, put from the priesthood.
65 And the Tirshatha said unto them, that
they should not eat of the most holy
things, till there stood *up* a priest with
Urim and Thummim.
66 The whole congregation together *was*
forty and two thousand three hundred and
threescore,
67 Beside their manservants and their
maidservants, of whom *there were* seven
thousand three hundred thirty and seven:
and they had two hundred forty and five
singing men and singing women.
68 Their horses, seven hundred thirty and
six: their mules, two hundred forty and
five:
69 *Their* camels, four hundred thirty and
five: six thousand seven hundred and
twenty asses.
70 And some of
the chief of the fa-
thers gave unto the
work. The Tirshatha
gave to the treasure
a thousand drams
of gold, fifty basons, five hundred and thirty priests' garments.

7:70
Examples of Generosity
◄ Ezra 8:25
Luke 19:8 ►

71 And *some* of the chief of the fathers
gave to the treasure of the work twenty
thousand drams of gold, and two thousand and two hundred pounds of silver.
72 And *that* which the rest of the people
gave *was* twenty thousand drams of gold,
and two thousand pounds of silver, and
threescore and seven priests' garments.
73 So the priests, and the Levites, and the
porters, and the singers, and *some* of the
people, and the Nethinims, and all Israel,
dwelt in their cities; and when the seventh
month came, the children of Israel *were* in
their cities.

8

1 And all the people gathered themselves
together as one man into the street that
was before the water gate; and they spake
unto Ezra the scribe to bring the book of
the law of Moses, which the LORD had
commanded to Israel.
2 And Ezra the priest brought the law
before the congregation both of men
and women, and all that could hear with

understanding, upon the first day of the
seventh month.
3And he read therein before the street
that *was* before the water gate from the
morning until midday, before the men and
the women, and those that could understand; and the ears of all the people *were*
attentive unto the book of the law.
4And Ezra the scribe stood upon a pul-
pit of wood, which they had made for the
purpose; and beside him stood Mattithiah, and Shema, and Anaiah, and Urijah,
and Hilkiah, and Maaseiah, on his right
hand; and on his left hand, Pedaiah, and
Mishael, and Malchiah, and Hashum,
and Hashbadana, Zechariah, *and* Meshullam.
5And Ezra opened the book in the sight
of all the people; (for he was above all the
people;) and when he opened it, all the
people stood up:
6And Ezra blessed the LORD, the great
God. And all the people answered, Amen,
Amen, with lifting up their hands: and they
bowed their heads, and worshipped the
LORD with *their* faces to the ground.
7Also Jeshua, and
Bani, and Sherebi-
ah, Jamin, Akkub,
Shabbethai, Ho-
dijah, Maaseiah,
Kelita, Azariah, Joz-
abad, Hanan, Pelaiah, and the Levites,
caused the people to understand the law:
and the people *stood* in their place.

8:7 Sunday School
◄ Ezra 7:10
Matthew 5:2 ►

8So they read in the book in the law of
God distinctly, and gave the sense, and
caused *them* to understand the reading.
9And Nehemiah, which *is* the Tirshatha,
and Ezra the priest the scribe, and the Levites that taught the people, said unto all
the people, This day *is* holy unto the LORD
your God; mourn not, nor weep. For all
the people wept,
when they heard the
words of the law.
10Then he said
unto them, Go your
way, eat the fat, and
drink the sweet, and
send portions unto
them for whom
nothing is prepared:
for *this* day *is* holy
unto our Lord: nei-
ther be ye sorry; for the joy of the LORD is
your strength.

8:10 Giving
◄ Deuteronomy 15:12-14
Proverbs 25:21 ►

8:10 Joy
◄ Psalm 16:11 ►

11So the Levites stilled all the people,
saying, Hold your peace, for the day *is* holy;
neither be ye grieved.
12And all the people went their way to
eat, and to drink, and to send portions,
and to make great mirth, because they had
understood the words that were declared
unto them.
13And on the second day were gathered
together the chief of the fathers of all the
people, the priests, and the Levites, unto
Ezra the scribe, even to understand the
words of the law.
14And they found written in the law
which the LORD had commanded by Moses, that the children of Israel should dwell
in booths in the feast of the seventh
month:
15And that they should publish and proclaim in all their cities, and in Jerusalem,
saying, Go forth unto the mount, and fetch
olive branches, and pine branches, and
myrtle branches, and palm branches, and
branches of thick trees, to make booths,
as *it is* written.
16So the people went forth, and brought
them, and made themselves booths, every
one upon the roof of his house, and in
their courts, and in the courts of the house
of God, and in the street of the water gate,
and in the street of the gate of Ephraim.
17And all the
congregation of
them that were
come again out of
the captivity made
booths, and sat un-
der the booths: for since the days of Jeshua the son of Nun unto that day had not
the children of Israel done so. And there
was very great gladness.

8:17 Gladness
◄ 2 Chronicles 30:21
Psalm 4:7 ►

18Also day by day, from the first day unto
the last day, he read in the book of the law
of God. And they kept the feast seven days;
and on the eighth day *was*
a solemn assembly, according unto the
manner.

9

1Now in the twenty and fourth day of
this month the children of Israel were assembled with fasting, and with sack-
clothes, and earth upon them.
2And the seed of Israel separated themselves from all strangers, and stood and

confessed their sins, and the iniquities of their fathers.

3And they stood up in their place, and read in the book of the law of the LORD their God *one* fourth part of the day; and *another* fourth part they confessed, and worshipped the LORD their God.

4Then stood up upon the stairs, of the Levites, Jeshua, and Bani, Kadmiel, Shebaniah, Bunni, Sherebiah, Bani, *and* Chenani, and cried with a loud voice unto the LORD their God.

5Then the Levites, Jeshua, and Kadmiel, Bani, Hashabniah, Sherebiah, Hodijah, Shebaniah, *and* Pethahiah, said, Stand up *and* bless the LORD your God for ever and ever: and blessed be thy glorious name, which is exalted above all blessing and praise.

6Thou, *even* thou, *art* LORD alone; thou hast made heaven, the heaven of heavens, with all their host, the earth, and all *things* that *are* therein, the seas, and all that *is* therein, and thou preservest them all; and the host of heaven worshippeth thee.

9:6 Safety
◄ 2 Samuel 8:6
Psalm 31:23 ►

7Thou *art* the LORD the God, who didst choose Abram, and broughtest him forth out of Ur of the Chaldees, and gavest him the name of Abraham;

8And foundest his heart faithful before thee, and madest a covenant with him to give the land of the Canaanites, the Hittites, the Amorites, and the Perizzites, and the Jebusites, and the Girgashites, to give *it, I say,* to his seed, and hast performed thy words; for thou *art* righteous:

9And didst see the affliction of our fathers in Egypt, and heardest their cry by the Red sea;

10And shewedst signs and wonders upon Pharaoh, and on all his servants, and on all the people of his land: for thou knewest that they dealt proudly against them. So didst thou get thee a name, as *it is* this day.

11And thou didst divide the sea before them, so that they went through the midst of the sea on the dry land; and their persecutors thou threwest into the deeps, as a stone into the mighty waters.

12Moreover thou leddest them in the day by a cloudy pillar; and in the night by a pillar of fire, to give them light in the way wherein they should go.

13Thou camest down also upon mount Sinai, and spakest with them from heaven, and gavest them right judgments, and true laws, good statutes and commandments:

14And madest known unto them thy holy sabbath, and commandedst them precepts, statutes, and laws, by the hand of Moses thy servant:

15And gavest them bread from heaven for their hunger, and broughtest forth water for them out of the rock for their thirst, and promisedst them that they should go in to possess the land which thou hadst sworn to give them.

16But they and our fathers dealt proudly, and hardened their necks, and hearkened not to thy commandments,

17And refused to obey, neither were mindful of thy wonders that thou didst among them; but hardened their necks, and in their rebellion appointed a captain to return to their bondage: but thou *art* a God ready to pardon, gracious and merciful, slow to anger, and of great kindness, and forsookest them not.

9:17 Mercy from God
◄ Ezra 9:13
Nehemiah 9:31 ►

18Yea, when they had made them a molten calf, and said, This *is* thy God that brought thee up out of Egypt, and had wrought great provocations;

19Yet thou in thy manifold mercies forsookest them not in the wilderness: the pillar of the cloud departed not from them by day, to lead them in the way; neither the pillar of fire by night, to shew them light, and the way wherein they should go.

20Thou gavest also thy good spirit to instruct them, and withheldest not thy manna from their mouth, and gavest them water for their thirst.

9:20
God's Teaching
◄ Luke 12:12 ►

21Yea, forty years didst thou sustain them in the wilderness, *so that* they lacked nothing; their clothes waxed not old, and their feet swelled not.

22Moreover thou gavest them kingdoms and nations, and didst divide them into corners: so they possessed the land of

Sihon, and the land of the king of Heshbon, and the land of Og king of Bashan.
23 Their children also multipliedst thou
as the stars of heaven, and broughtest them
into the land, concerning which thou
hadst promised to their fathers, that they
should go in to possess *it*.
24 So the children went in and possessed
the land, and thou subduedst before them
the inhabitants of the land, the Canaanites, and gavest them into their hands, with
their kings, and the people of the land,
that they might do with them as they
would.
25 And they took strong cities, and a fat
land, and possessed houses full of all
goods, wells digged, vineyards, and
oliveyards, and fruit trees in abundance:
so they did eat, and were filled, and became fat, and delighted themselves in thy
great goodness.
26 Nevertheless
they were disobedi-
ent, and rebelled
against thee, and
cast thy law behind
their backs, and
slew thy prophets which testified against
them to turn them to thee, and they
wrought great provocations.

9:26 Gratitude
◄ Deuteronomy 32:6
Ezekiel 16:17-18 ►

27 Therefore thou deliveredst them into
the hand of their enemies, who vexed
them: and in the time of their trouble,
when they cried unto thee, thou heardest
them from heaven; and according to thy
manifold mercies thou gavest them saviours, who saved them out of the hand of
their enemies.
28 But after they had rest, they did evil
again before thee: therefore leftest thou
them in the hand of their enemies, so that
they had the dominion over them: yet
when they returned, and cried unto thee,
thou heardest *them* from heaven; and
many times didst thou deliver them according to thy mercies;
29 And testifiedst
against them, that
thou mightest bring
them again unto
thy law: yet they
dealt proudly, and
hearkened not unto thy commandments,
but sinned against thy judgments, (which
if a man do, he shall live in them;) and
withdrew the shoulder, and hardened their
neck, and would not hear.

9:29 Stubborn People
◄ 2 Chronicles 33:23
Jeremiah 6:15 ►

30 Yet many years didst thou forbear
them, and testifiedst against them by thy
spirit in thy prophets: yet would they not
give ear: therefore gavest thou them into
the hand of the people of the lands.
31 Nevertheless
for thy great mer-
cies' sake thou didst
not utterly con-
sume them, nor
forsake them; for
thou *art* a gracious and merciful God.

9:31 Mercy from God
◄ Nehemiah 9:17
Psalm 103:11 ►

32 Now therefore, our God, the great, the
mighty, and the terrible God, who keepest
covenant and mercy, let not all the trouble seem little before thee, that hath come
upon us, on our kings, on our princes,
and on our priests, and on our prophets,
and on our fathers, and on all thy people,
since the time of the kings of Assyria unto
this day.
33 Howbeit thou *art* just in all that is
brought upon us; for thou hast done right,
but we have done wickedly:
34 Neither have our kings, our princes,
our priests, nor our fathers, kept thy law,
nor hearkened unto thy commandments
and thy testimonies, wherewith thou didst
testify against them.
35 For they have not served thee in their
kingdom, and in thy great goodness that
thou gavest them, and in the large and fat
land which thou gavest before them, neither turned they from their wicked works.
36 Behold, we *are* servants this day, and
for the land that thou gavest unto our fathers to eat the fruit thereof and the good
thereof, behold, we *are* servants in it:
37 And it yieldeth much increase unto
the kings whom thou hast set over us because of our sins: also they have dominion over our bodies, and over our cattle,
at their pleasure, and we *are* in great distress.
38 And because of all this we make a sure
covenant, and write *it*; and our princes, Levites, *and* priests, seal *unto it*.

10

1 Now those that sealed *were*, Nehemiah, the Tirshatha, the son of Hachaliah,
and Zidkijah,
2 Seraiah, Azariah, Jeremiah,
3 Pashur, Amariah, Malchijah,
4 Hattush, Shebaniah, Malluch,

5 Harim, Meremoth, Obadiah,
6 Daniel, Ginnethon, Baruch,
7 Meshullam, Abijah, Mijamin,
8 Maaziah, Bilgai, Shemaiah: these *were* the priests.
9 And the Levites: both Jeshua the son of Azaniah, Binnui of the sons of Henadad, Kadmiel;
10 And their brethren, Shebaniah, Hodijah, Kelita, Pelaiah, Hanan,
11 Micha, Rehob, Hashabiah,
12 Zaccur, Sherebiah, Shebaniah,
13 Hodijah, Bani, Beninu.
14 The chief of the people; Parosh, Pahath-moab, Elam, Zatthu, Bani,
15 Bunni, Azgad, Bebai,
16 Adonijah, Bigvai, Adin,
17 Ater, Hizkijah, Azzur,
18 Hodijah, Hashum, Bezai,
19 Hariph, Anathoth, Nebai,
20 Magpiash, Meshullam, Hezir,
21 Meshezabeel, Zadok, Jaddua,
22 Pelatiah, Hanan, Anaiah,
23 Hoshea, Hananiah, Hashub,
24 Hallohesh, Pileha, Shobek,
25 Rehum, Hashabnah, Maaseiah,
26 And Ahijah, Hanan, Anan,
27 Malluch, Harim, Baanah.
28 And the rest of the people, the priests, the Levites, the porters, the singers, the Nethinims, and all they that had separated themselves from the people of the lands unto the law of God, their wives, their sons, and their daughters, every one having knowledge, and having understanding;
29 They clave to their brethren, their nobles, and entered into a curse, and into an oath, to walk in God's law, which was given by Moses the servant of God, and to observe and do all the commandments of the LORD our Lord, and his judgments and his statutes;
30 And that we would not give our daughters unto the people of the land, nor take their daughters for our sons:
31 And *if* the people of the land bring ware or any victuals on the sabbath day to sell, *that* we would not buy it of them on the sabbath, or on the holy day: and *that* we would leave the seventh year, and the exaction of every debt.
32 Also we made ordinances for us, to charge ourselves yearly with the third part of a shekel for the service of the house of our God;
33 For the shewbread, and for the continual meat offering, and for the continual burnt offering, of the sabbaths, of the new moons, for the set feasts, and for the holy *things,* and for the sin offerings to make an atonement for Israel, and *for* all the work of the house of our God.
34 And we cast the lots among the priests, the Levites, and the people, for the wood offering, to bring *it* into the house of our God, after the houses of our fathers, at times appointed year by year, to burn upon the altar of the LORD our God, as *it is* written in the law:
35 And to bring the firstfruits of our ground, and the firstfruits of all fruit of all trees, year by year, unto the house of the LORD:
36 Also the firstborn of our sons, and of our cattle, as *it is* written in the law, and the firstlings of our herds and of our flocks, to bring to the house of our God, unto the priests that minister in the house of our God:
37 And *that* we should bring the firstfruits of our dough, and our offerings, and the fruit of all manner of trees, of wine and of oil, unto the priests, to the chambers of the house of our God; and the tithes of our ground unto the Levites, that the same Levites might have the tithes in all the cities of our tillage.
38 And the priest the son of Aaron shall be with the Levites, when the Levites take tithes: and the Levites shall bring up the tithe of the tithes unto the house of our God, to the chambers, into the treasure house.
39 For the children of Israel and the children of Levi shall bring the offering of the corn, of the new wine, and the oil, unto the chambers, where *are* the vessels of the sanctuary, and the priests that minister, and the porters, and the singers: and we will not forsake the house of our God.

11

1 And the rulers of the people dwelt at Jerusalem: the rest of the people also cast lots, to bring one of ten to dwell in Jerusalem the holy city, and nine parts *to dwell* in *other* cities.
2 And the people blessed all the men, that willingly offered themselves to dwell at Jerusalem.

11:2
Willingness to Work
◄ Judges 8:25
Psalm 110:3 ►

3 Now these *are* the chief of the province
that dwelt in Jerusalem: but in the cities
of Judah dwelt every one in his possession
in their cities, *to wit*, Israel, the priests, and
the Levites, and the Nethinims, and the
children of Solomon's servants.
4 And at Jerusalem dwelt *certain* of the
children of Judah, and of the children of
Benjamin. Of the children of Judah; Atha-
iah the son of Uzziah, the son of Zechariah, the son of Amariah, the son of
Shephatiah, the son of Mahalaleel, of the
children of Perez;
5 And Maaseiah the son of Baruch, the
son of Col-hozeh, the son of Hazaiah, the
son of Adaiah, the son of Joiarib, the son
of Zechariah, the son of Shiloni.
6 All the sons of Perez that dwelt at Jerusalem *were* four hundred threescore and
eight valiant men.
7 And these *are* the sons of Benjamin;
Sallu the son of Meshullam, the son of
Joed, the son of Pedaiah, the son of Kolaiah, the son of Maaseiah, the son of Ithiel,
the son of Jesaiah.
8 And after him Gabbai, Sallai, nine hundred twenty and eight.
9 And Joel the son of Zichri *was* their
overseer: and Judah the son of Senuah *was*
second over the city.
10 Of the priests: Jedaiah the son of Joiarib, Jachin.
11 Seraiah the son of Hilkiah, the son of
Meshullam, the son of Zadok, the son of
Meraioth, the son of Ahitub, *was* the ruler
of the house of God.
12 And their brethren that did the work
of the house *were* eight hundred twenty
and two: and Adaiah the son of Jeroham,
the son of Pelaliah, the son of Amzi, the
son of Zechariah, the son of Pashur, the
son of Malchiah,
13 And his brethren, chief of the fathers,
two hundred forty and two: and Amashai
the son of Azareel, the son of Ahasai, the
son of Meshillemoth, the son of Immer,
14 And their brethren, mighty men of
valour, an hundred twenty and eight: and
their overseer *was* Zabdiel, the son of *one
of* the great men.
15 Also of the Levites: Shemaiah the son
of Hashub, the son of Azrikam, the son of
Hashabiah, the son of Bunni;
16 And Shabbethai and Jozabad, of the
chief of the Levites, *had* the oversight of
the outward business of the house of God.
17 And Mattaniah the son of Micha, the
son of Zabdi, the son of Asaph, *was* the
principal to begin the thanksgiving in
prayer: and Bakbukiah the second among
his brethren, and Abda the son of Shammua, the son of Galal, the son of Jeduthun.
18 All the Levites in the holy city *were* two
hundred fourscore and four.
19 Moreover the porters, Akkub, Talmon,
and their brethren that kept the gates, *were*
an hundred seventy and two.
20 And the residue of Israel, of the priests,
and the Levites, *were* in all the cities of Judah, every one in his inheritance.
21 But the Nethinims dwelt in Ophel:
and Ziha and Gispa *were* over the Nethinims.
22 The overseer also of the Levites at Jerusalem *was* Uzzi the son of Bani, the
son of Hashabiah, the son of Mattaniah,
the son of Micha. Of the sons of Asaph,
the singers *were* over the business of the
house of God.
23 For *it was* the king's commandment
concerning them, that a certain portion
should be for the singers, due for every day.
24 And Pethahiah the son of Meshezabeel, of the children of Zerah the son of
Judah, *was* at the king's hand in all matters concerning the people.
25 And for the villages, with their fields,
some of the children of Judah dwelt at
Kirjath-arba, and *in* the villages thereof,
and at Dibon, and *in* the villages thereof,
and at Jekabzeel, and *in* the villages
thereof,
26 And at Jeshua, and at Moladah, and
at Beth-phelet,
27 And at Hazar-shual, and at Beer-
sheba, and *in* the villages thereof,
28 And at Ziklag, and at Mekonah, and
in the villages thereof,
29 And at En-rimmon, and at Zareah, and
at Jarmuth,
30 Zanoah, Adullam, and *in* their villages, at Lachish, and the fields thereof, at
Azekah, and *in* the villages thereof. And
they dwelt from Beer-sheba unto the valley of Hinnom.
31 The children also of Benjamin from
Geba *dwelt* at Michmash, and Aija, and
Bethel, and *in* their villages,
32 *And* at Anathoth, Nob, Ananiah,
33 Hazor, Ramah, Gittaim,

34 Hadid, Zeboim, Neballat,

35 Lod, and Ono, the valley of craftsmen.

36 And of the Levites *were* divisions *in* Judah, *and* in Benjamin.

12

1 Now these *are* the priests and the Levites that went up with Zerubbabel the son of Shealtiel, and Jeshua: Seraiah, Jeremiah, Ezra,

2 Amariah, Malluch, Hattush,

3 Shechaniah, Rehum, Meremoth,

4 Iddo, Ginnetho, Abijah,

5 Miamin, Maadiah, Bilgah,

6 Shemaiah, and Joiarib, Jedaiah,

7 Sallu, Amok, Hilkiah, Jedaiah. These *were* the chief of the priests and of their brethren in the days of Jeshua.

8 Moreover the Levites: Jeshua, Binnui, Kadmiel, Sherebiah, Judah, *and* Mattaniah, *which was* over the thanksgiving, he and his brethren.

9 Also Bakbukiah and Unni, their brethren, *were* over against them in the watches.

10 And Jeshua begat Joiakim, Joiakim also begat Eliashib, and Eliashib begat Joiada,

11 And Joiada begat Jonathan, and Jonathan begat Jaddua.

12 And in the days of Joiakim were priests, the chief of the fathers: of Seraiah, Meraiah; of Jeremiah, Hananiah;

13 Of Ezra, Meshullam; of Amariah, Jehohanan;

14 Of Melicu, Jonathan; of Shebaniah, Joseph;

15 Of Harim, Adna; of Meraioth, Helkai;

16 Of Iddo, Zechariah; of Ginnethon, Meshullam;

17 Of Abijah, Zichri; of Miniamin, of Moadiah, Piltai;

18 Of Bilgah, Shammua; of Shemaiah, Jehonathan;

19 And of Joiarib, Mattenai; of Jedaiah, Uzzi;

20 Of Sallai, Kallai; of Amok, Eber;

21 Of Hilkiah, Hashabiah; of Jedaiah, Nethaneel.

22 The Levites in the days of Eliashib, Joiada, and Johanan, and Jaddua, *were* recorded chief of the fathers: also the priests, to the reign of Darius the Persian.

23 The sons of Levi, the chief of the fathers, *were* written in the book of the chronicles, even until the days of Johanan the son of Eliashib.

24 And the chief of the Levites: Hashabiah, Sherebiah, and Jeshua the son of Kadmiel, with their brethren over against them, to praise *and* to give thanks, according to the commandment of David the man of God, ward over against ward.

25 Mattaniah, and Bakbukiah, Obadiah, Meshullam, Talmon, Akkub, *were* porters keeping the ward at the thresholds of the gates.

26 These *were* in the days of Joiakim the son of Jeshua, the son of Jozadak, and in the days of Nehemiah the governor, and of Ezra the priest, the scribe.

27 And at the dedication of the wall of Jerusalem they sought the Levites out of all their places, to bring them to Jerusalem, to keep the dedication with gladness, both with thanksgivings, and with singing, *with* cymbals, psalteries, and with harps.

28 And the sons of the singers gathered themselves together, both out of the plain country round about Jerusalem, and from the villages of Netophathi;

29 Also from the house of Gilgal, and out of the fields of Geba and Azmaveth: for the singers had builded them villages round about Jerusalem.

30 And the priests and the Levites purified themselves, and purified the people, and the gates, and the wall.

31 Then I brought up the princes of Judah upon the wall, and appointed two great *companies of them that gave* thanks, *whereof one* went on the right hand upon the wall toward the dung gate:

32 And after them went Hoshaiah, and half of the princes of Judah,

33 And Azariah, Ezra, and Meshullam,

34 Judah, and Benjamin, and Shemaiah, and Jeremiah,

35 And *certain* of the priests' sons with trumpets; *namely,* Zechariah the son of Jonathan, the son of Shemaiah, the son of Mattaniah, the son of Michaiah, the son of Zaccur, the son of Asaph:

36 And his brethren, Shemaiah, and Azarael, Milalai, Gilalai, Maai, Nethaneel, and Judah, Hanani, with the musical instruments of David the man of God, and Ezra the scribe before them.

37 And at the fountain gate, which was over against them, they went up by the stairs of the city of David, at the going up of the wall, above the house of David, even unto the water gate eastward.

38And the other *company of them that gave*
thanks went over against *them,* and I after
them, and the half of the people upon the
wall, from beyond the tower of the furnaces even unto the broad wall;
39And from above the gate of Ephraim,
and above the old gate, and above the fish
gate, and the tower of Hananeel, and the
tower of Meah, even unto the sheep gate:
and they stood still in the prison gate.
40So stood the two *companies of them that*
gave thanks in the house of God, and I,
and the half of the rulers with me:
41And the priests; Eliakim, Maaseiah,
Miniamin, Michaiah, Elioenai, Zechariah,
and Hananiah, with trumpets;
42And Maaseiah, and Shemaiah, and
Eleazar, and Uzzi, and Jehohanan, and
Malchijah, and Elam, and Ezer. And the
singers sang loud, with Jezrahiah *their*
overseer.
43Also that day
they offered great
sacrifices, and re-
joiced: for God had
made them rejoice
with great joy: the
wives also and the children rejoiced: so
that the joy of Jerusalem was heard even
afar off.

12:43
Serving
◄ Psalm 40:8 ►

44And at that time were some appointed over the chambers for the treasures, for
the offerings, for the firstfruits, and for the
tithes, to gather into them out of the fields
of the cities the portions of the law for the
priests and Levites: for Judah rejoiced for
the priests and for the Levites that waited.
45And both the singers and the porters
kept the ward of their God, and the ward
of the purification, according to the commandment of David, *and* of Solomon
his son.
46For in the days of David and Asaph of
old *there were* chief of the singers, and songs
of praise and thanksgiving unto God.
47And all Israel in the days of Zerubbabel, and in the days of Nehemiah, gave
the portions of the singers and the porters, every day his portion: and they sanctified *holy things* unto the Levites; and the
Levites sanctified *them* unto the children
of Aaron.

13

1On that day they read in the book of
Moses in the audience of the people; and
therein was found written, that the Ammonite and the Moabite should not come
into the congregation of God for ever;
2Because they met not the children of
Israel with bread and with water, but hired
Balaam against them, that he should curse
them: howbeit our God turned the curse
into a blessing.
3Now it came to pass, when they had
heard the law, that they separated from
Israel all the mixed multitude.
4And before this, Eliashib the priest,
having the oversight of the chamber of the
house of our God, *was* allied unto Tobiah:
5And he had prepared for him a great
chamber, where aforetime they laid the
meat offerings, the frankincense, and the
vessels, and the tithes of the corn, the new
wine, and the oil, which was commanded
to be given to the Levites, and the singers,
and the porters; and the offerings of the
priests.
6But in all this *time* was not I at Jerusalem: for in the two and thirtieth year of
Artaxerxes king of Babylon came I unto the
king, and after certain days obtained I leave
of the king:
7And I came to Jerusalem, and understood of the evil that Eliashib did for Tobiah, in preparing him a chamber in the
courts of the house of God.
8And it grieved me sore: therefore I cast
forth all the household stuff of Tobiah out
of the chamber.
9Then I commanded, and they cleansed
the chambers: and thither brought I again
the vessels of the house of God, with the
meat offering and the frankincense.
10And I perceived that the portions of
the Levites had not been given *them:* for
the Levites and the singers, that did the
work, were fled every one to his field.
11Then contended I with the rulers, and
said, Why is the house of God forsaken?
And I gathered them together, and set them
in their place.
12Then brought all Judah the tithe of the
corn and the new wine and the oil unto
the treasuries.
13And I made treasurers over the treasuries, Shelemiah the priest, and Zadok the
scribe, and of the Levites, Pedaiah: and
next to them *was* Hanan the son of Zaccur, the son of Mattaniah: for they were
counted faithful, and their office *was* to
distribute unto their brethren.

14 Remember me, O my God, concerning this, and wipe not out my good deeds that I have done for the house of my God, and for the offices thereof.

15 In those days saw I in Judah *some* treading winepresses on the sabbath, and bringing in sheaves, and lading asses; as also wine, grapes, and figs, and all *manner of* burdens, which they brought into Jerusalem on the sabbath day: and I testified *against them* in the day wherein they sold victuals.

16 There dwelt men of Tyre also therein, which brought fish, and all manner of ware, and sold on the sabbath unto the children of Judah, and in Jerusalem.

17 Then I contended with the nobles of Judah, and said unto them, What evil thing *is* this that ye do, and profane the sabbath day?

18 Did not your fathers thus, and did not our God bring all this evil upon us, and upon this city? yet ye bring more wrath upon Israel by profaning the sabbath.

19 And it came to pass, that when the gates of Jerusalem began to be dark before the sabbath, I commanded that the gates should be shut, and charged that they should not be opened till after the sabbath: and *some* of my servants set I at the gates, *that* there should no burden be brought in on the sabbath day.

20 So the merchants and sellers of all kind of ware lodged without Jerusalem once or twice.

21 Then I testified against them, and said unto them, Why lodge ye about the wall? if ye do *so* again, I will lay hands on you. From that time forth came they no *more* on the sabbath.

22 And I commanded the Levites that they should cleanse themselves, and *that* they should come *and* keep the gates, to sanctify the sabbath day. Remember me, O my God, *concerning* this also, and spare me according to the greatness of thy mercy.

23 In those days also saw I Jews *that* had married wives of Ashdod, of Ammon, *and* of Moab:

24 And their children spake half in the speech of Ashdod, and could not speak in the Jews' language, but according to the language of each people.

25 And I contended with them, and cursed them, and smote certain of them, and plucked off their hair, and made them swear by God, *saying,* Ye shall not give your daughters unto their sons, nor take their daughters unto your sons, or for yourselves.

26 Did not Solomon king of Israel sin by these things? yet among many nations was there no king like him, who was beloved of his God, and God made him king over all Israel: nevertheless even him did outlandish women cause to sin.

27 Shall we then hearken unto you to do all this great evil, to transgress against our God in marrying strange wives?

28 And *one* of the sons of Joiada, the son of Eliashib the high priest, *was* son in law to Sanballat the Horonite: therefore I chased him from me.

29 Remember them, O my God, because they have defiled the priesthood, and the covenant of the priesthood, and of the Levites.

30 Thus cleansed I them from all strangers, and appointed the wards of the priests and the Levites, every one in his business;

31 And for the wood offering, at times appointed, and for the firstfruits. Remember me, O my God, for good.

Esther

AUTHOR
Unknown; possibly Mordecai, Ezra, or Nehemiah

MAIN POINT
God is in control and puts his people in the right place at the right time.

DATE WRITTEN
Approximately 483-471 B.C.

10 CHAPTERS
☐☐☐☐☐☐☐☐☐☐

MAIN PEOPLE

Esther, Mordecai, King Ahasuerus (Xerxes I), Haman

SPECIAL FEATURES

- *Tells a true story of faith in God without once mentioning God by name*
- *Describes the chances taken by a brave young Jewish woman who became queen of Persia*
- *Shows how the tables turned for a trickster named Haman*
- *Records the start of the Jewish feast of Purim, still celebrated today*
- *Twelfth book of History*

HOW THE BOOK GOT ITS NAME

One of only two books of the Bible named for a woman (the other is Ruth), the book of Esther tells about faith and courage.

1

1 Now it came to pass in the days of Ahasuerus, (this *is* Ahasuerus which reigned, from India even unto Ethiopia, *over* an hundred and seven and twenty provinces:)

2 *That* in those days, when the king Ahasuerus sat on the throne of his kingdom, which *was* in Shushan the palace,

3 In the third year of his reign, he made a feast unto all his princes and his servants; the power of Persia and Media, the nobles and princes of the provinces, *being* before him:

4 When he shewed the riches of his glorious kingdom and the honour of his excellent majesty many days, *even* an hundred and fourscore days.

> **1:4**
> **Showing Off Stuff**
> ◄ Esther 5:11 ►

5 And when these days were expired, the king made a feast unto all the people that were present in Shushan the palace, both unto great and small, seven days, in the court of the garden of the king's palace;

6 *Where were* white, green, and blue, *hangings,* fastened with cords of fine linen and purple to silver rings and pillars of marble: the beds *were of* gold and silver, upon a pavement of red, and blue, and white, and black, marble.

7 And they gave *them* drink in vessels of gold, (the vessels being diverse one from another,) and royal wine in abundance, according to the state of the king.

8 And the drinking *was* according to the law; none did compel: for so the king had appointed to all the officers of his house, that they should do according to every man's pleasure.

9 Also Vashti the queen made a feast for the women *in* the royal house which *belonged* to king Ahasuerus.

10 On the seventh day, when the heart of the king was merry with wine, he commanded Mehuman, Biztha, Harbona, Bigtha, and Abagtha, Zethar, and Carcas, the seven chamberlains that served in the presence of Ahasuerus the king,

11 To bring Vashti the queen before the king with the crown royal, to shew the people and the princes her beauty: for she *was* fair to look on.

12 But the queen Vashti refused to come at the king's commandment by *his* chamberlains: therefore was the king very wroth, and his anger burned in him.

13 Then the king said to the wise men, which knew the times, (for so *was* the king's manner toward all that knew law and judgment:

14 And the next unto him *was* Carshena, Shethar, Admatha, Tarshish, Meres, Marsena, *and* Memucan, the seven princes of Persia and Media, which saw the king's face, *and* which sat the first in the kingdom;)

15 What shall we do unto the queen Vashti according to law, because she hath not performed the commandment of the king Ahasuerus by the chamberlains?

16 And Memucan answered before the king and the princes, Vashti the queen hath not done wrong to the king only, but also to all the princes, and to all the people that *are* in all the provinces of the king Ahasuerus.

17 For *this* deed of the queen shall come abroad unto all women, so that they shall despise their husbands in their eyes, when it shall be reported, The king Ahasuerus commanded Vashti the queen to be brought in before him, but she came not.

18 *Likewise* shall the ladies of Persia and Media say this day unto all the king's princes, which have heard of the deed of the queen. Thus *shall there arise* too much contempt and wrath.

19 If it please the king, let there go a royal commandment from him, and let it be written among the laws of the Persians and the Medes, that it be not altered, That Vashti come no more before king Ahasuerus; and let the king give her royal estate unto another that is better than she.

20 And when the king's decree which he shall make shall be published throughout all his empire, (for it is great,) all the wives shall give to their husbands honour, both to great and small.

21 And the saying pleased the king and the princes; and the king did according to the word of Memucan:

22 For he sent letters into all the king's provinces, into every province according to the writing thereof, and to every people after their language, that every man should bear rule in his own house, and that *it* should be published according to the language of every people.

2

1 After these things, when the wrath of king Ahasuerus was appeased, he remembered Vashti, and what she had done, and what was decreed against her.

2 Then said the king's servants that ministered unto him, Let there be fair young virgins sought for the king:

3 And let the king appoint officers in all the provinces of his kingdom, that they may gather together all the fair young virgins unto Shushan the palace, to the house of the women unto the custody of Hege the king's chamberlain, keeper of the women; and let their things for purification be given *them:*

4 And let the maiden which pleaseth the king be queen instead of Vashti. And the thing pleased the king; and he did so.

5 *Now* in Shushan the palace there was a certain Jew, whose name *was* Mordecai, the son of Jair, the son of Shimei, the son of Kish, a Benjamite;

6 Who had been carried away from Jerusalem with the captivity which had been carried away with Jeconiah king of Judah, whom Nebuchadnezzar the king of Babylon had carried away.

7 And he brought up Hadassah, that *is,* Esther, his uncle's daughter: for she had neither father nor mother, and the maid *was* fair and beautiful; whom Mordecai, when her father and mother were dead, took for his own daughter.

8 So it came to pass, when the king's commandment and his decree was heard, and

when many maidens were gathered together unto Shushan the palace, to the custody of Hegai, that Esther was brought also unto the king's house, to the custody of Hegai, keeper of the women.

9And the maiden pleased him, and she obtained kindness of him; and he speedily gave her her things for purification, with such things as belonged to her, and seven maidens, *which were* meet to be given her, out of the king's house: and he preferred her and her maids unto the best *place* of the house of the women.

10Esther had not shewed her people nor her kindred: for Mordecai had charged her that she should not shew *it*.

11And Mordecai walked every day before the court of the women's house, to know how Esther did, and what should become of her.

2:11
Parents Care
◄ 2 Samuel 18:29 ►

12Now when every maid's turn was come to go in to king Ahasuerus, after that she had been twelve months, according to the manner of the women, (for so were the days of their purifications accomplished, *to wit*, six months with oil of myrrh, and six months with sweet odours, and with *other* things for the purifying of the women;)

13Then thus came *every* maiden unto the king; whatsoever she desired was given her to go with her out of the house of the women unto the king's house.

14In the evening she went, and on the morrow she returned into the second house of the women, to the custody of Shaashgaz, the king's chamberlain, which kept the concubines: she came in unto the king no more, except the king delighted in her, and that she were called by name.

15Now when the turn of Esther, the daughter of Abihail the uncle of Mordecai, who had taken her for his daughter, was come to go in unto the king, she required nothing but what Hegai the king's chamberlain, the keeper of the women, appointed. And Esther obtained favour in the sight of all them that looked upon her.

16So Esther was taken unto king Ahasuerus into his house royal in the tenth month, which *is* the month Tebeth, in the seventh year of his reign.

17And the king loved Esther above all the women, and she obtained grace and favour in his sight more than all the virgins; so that he set the royal crown upon her head, and made her queen instead of Vashti.

18Then the king made a great feast unto all his princes and his servants, *even* Esther's feast; and he made a release to the provinces, and gave gifts, according to the state of the king.

19And when the virgins were gathered together the second time, then Mordecai sat in the king's gate.

20Esther had not *yet* shewed her kindred nor her people; as Mordecai had charged her: for Esther did the commandment of Mordecai, like as when she was brought up with him.

21In those days, while Mordecai sat in the king's gate, two of the king's chamberlains, Bigthan and Teresh, of those which kept the door, were wroth, and sought to lay hand on the king Ahasuerus.

22And the thing was known to Mordecai, who told it unto Esther the queen; and Esther certified the king *thereof* in Mordecai's name.

23And when inquisition was made of the matter, it was found out; therefore they were both hanged on a tree: and it was written in the book of the chronicles before the king.

3

1After these things did king Ahasuerus promote Haman the son of Hammedatha the Agagite, and advanced him, and set his seat above all the princes that *were* with him.

2And all the king's servants, that *were* in the king's gate, bowed, and reverenced Haman: for the king had so commanded concerning him. But Mordecai bowed not, nor did *him* reverence.

3Then the king's servants, which *were* in the king's gate, said unto Mordecai, Why transgressest thou the king's commandment?

4Now it came to pass, when they spake daily unto him, and he hearkened not unto them, that they told Haman, to see whether Mordecai's matters would stand: for he had told them that he *was* a Jew.

5And when Haman saw that Mordecai bowed not, nor did him reverence, then was Haman full of wrath.

6 And he thought scorn to lay hands on Mordecai alone; for they had shewed him the people of Mordecai: wherefore Haman sought to destroy all the Jews that *were* throughout the whole kingdom of Ahasuerus, *even* the people of Mordecai.

3:5 Mad
◄ 2 Chronicles 16:10
Amos 1:11 ►

3:6
Examples of Revenge
◄ 1 Kings 22:27
Ezekiel 25:15 ►

7 In the first month, that *is,* the month Nisan, in the twelfth year of king Ahasuerus, they cast Pur, that *is,* the lot, before Haman from day to day, and from month to month, *to* the twelfth *month,* that *is,* the month Adar.

8 And Haman said unto king Ahasuerus, There is a certain people scattered abroad and dispersed among the people in all the provinces of thy kingdom; and their laws *are* diverse from all people; neither keep they the king's laws: therefore it *is* not for the king's profit to suffer them.

9 If it please the king, let it be written that they may be destroyed: and I will pay ten thousand talents of silver to the hands of those that have the charge of the business, to bring *it* into the king's treasuries.

10 And the king took his ring from his hand, and gave it unto Haman the son of Hammedatha the Agagite, the Jews' enemy.

11 And the king said unto Haman, The silver *is* given to thee, the people also, to do with them as it seemeth good to thee.

12 Then were the king's scribes called on the thirteenth day of the first month, and there was written according to all that Haman had commanded unto the king's lieutenants, and to the governors that *were* over every province, and to the rulers of every people of every province according to the writing thereof, and *to* every people after their language; in the name of king Ahasuerus was it written, and sealed with the king's ring.

13 And the letters were sent by posts into all the king's provinces, to destroy, to kill, and to cause to perish, all Jews, both young and old, little children and women, in one day, *even* upon the thirteenth *day* of the twelfth month, which *is* the month Adar, and *to take* the spoil of them for a prey.

14 The copy of the writing for a commandment to be given in every province was published unto all people, that they should be ready against that day.

15 The posts went out, being hastened by the king's commandment, and the decree was given in Shushan the palace. And the king and Haman sat down to drink; but the city Shushan was perplexed.

4

1 When Mordecai perceived all that was done, Mordecai rent his clothes, and put on sackcloth with ashes, and went out into the midst of the city, and cried with a loud and a bitter cry;

2 And came even before the king's gate: for none *might* enter into the king's gate clothed with sackcloth.

3 And in every province, whithersoever the king's commandment and his decree came, *there was* great mourning among the Jews, and fasting, and weeping, and wailing; and many lay in sackcloth and ashes.

4 So Esther's maids and her chamberlains came and told *it* her. Then was the queen exceedingly grieved; and she sent raiment to clothe Mordecai, and to take away his sackcloth from him: but he received *it* not.

5 Then called Esther for Hatach, *one* of the king's chamberlains, whom he had appointed to attend upon her, and gave him a commandment to Mordecai, to know what it *was,* and why it *was.*

6 So Hatach went forth to Mordecai unto the street of the city, which *was* before the king's gate.

7 And Mordecai told him of all that had happened unto him, and of the sum of the money that Haman had promised to pay to the king's treasuries for the Jews, to destroy them.

8 Also he gave him the copy of the writing of the decree that was given at Shushan to destroy them, to shew *it* unto Esther, and to declare *it* unto her, and to charge her that she should go in unto the king, to make supplication unto him, and to make request before him for her people.

9 And Hatach came and told Esther the words of Mordecai.

10 Again Esther spake unto Hatach, and gave him commandment unto Mordecai;

11 All the king's servants, and the people of the king's provinces, do know, that whosoever, whether man or woman, shall come unto the king into the inner court,

who is not called, *there is* one law of his to put *him* to death, except such to whom the king shall hold out the golden sceptre, that he may live: but I have not been called to come in unto the king these thirty days.

12 And they told to Mordecai Esther's words.

13 Then Mordecai commanded to answer Esther, Think not with thyself that thou shalt escape in the king's house, more than all the Jews.

14 For if thou altogether holdest thy peace at this time, *then* shall there enlargement and deliverance arise to the Jews from another place; but thou and thy father's house shall be destroyed: and who knoweth whether thou art come to the kingdom for *such* a time as this?

15 Then Esther bade *them* return Mordecai *this answer,*

16 Go, gather together all the Jews that are present in Shushan, and fast ye for me, and neither eat nor drink three days, night or day: I also and my maidens will fast likewise; and so will I go in unto the king, which *is* not according to the law: and if I perish, I perish.

4:16 Young Women
◄ Ruth 1:16
Mark 16:1 ►

17 So Mordecai went his way, and did according to all that Esther had commanded him.

5

1 Now it came to pass on the third day, that Esther put on *her* royal *apparel,* and stood in the inner court of the king's house, over against the king's house: and the king sat upon his royal throne in the royal house, over against the gate of the house.

2 And it was so, when the king saw Esther the queen standing in the court, *that* she obtained favour in his sight: and the king held out to Esther the golden sceptre that *was* in his hand. So Esther drew near, and touched the top of the sceptre.

3 Then said the king unto her, What wilt thou, queen Esther? and what *is* thy request? it shall be even given thee to the half of the kingdom.

4 And Esther answered, If *it seem* good unto the king, let the king and Haman come this day unto the banquet that I have prepared for him.

5 Then the king said, Cause Haman to make haste, that he may do as Esther hath said. So the king and Haman came to the banquet that Esther had prepared.

6 And the king said unto Esther at the banquet of wine, What *is* thy petition? and it shall be granted thee: and what *is* thy request? even to the half of the kingdom it shall be performed.

7 Then answered Esther, and said, My petition and my request *is;*

8 If I have found favour in the sight of the king, and if it please the king to grant my petition, and to perform my request, let the king and Haman come to the banquet that I shall prepare for them, and I will do to morrow as the king hath said.

9 Then went Haman forth that day joyful and with a glad heart: but when Haman saw Mordecai in the king's gate, that he stood not up, nor moved for him, he was full of indignation against Mordecai.

10 Nevertheless Haman refrained himself: and when he came home, he sent and called for his friends, and Zeresh his wife.

11 And Haman told them of the glory of his riches, and the multitude of his children, and all *the things* wherein the king had promoted him, and how he had advanced him above the princes and servants of the king.

5:11 Showing Off Stuff
◄ Esther 1:4
Isaiah 39:2 ►

12 Haman said moreover, Yea, Esther the queen did let no man come in with the king unto the banquet that she had prepared but myself; and to morrow am I invited unto her also with the king.

13 Yet all this availeth me nothing, so long as I see Mordecai the Jew sitting at the king's gate.

14 Then said Zeresh his wife and all his friends unto him, Let a gallows be made of fifty cubits high, and to morrow speak thou unto the king that Mordecai may be hanged thereon: then go thou in merrily with the king unto the banquet. And the thing pleased Haman; and he caused the gallows to be made.

6

1 On that night could not the king sleep, and he commanded to bring the book of records of the chronicles; and they were read before the king.

2 And it was found written, that Mordecai had told of Bigthana and Teresh, two

of the king's chamberlains, the keepers of
the door, who sought to lay hand on the
king Ahasuerus.
3And the king said, What honour and
dignity hath been done to Mordecai for
this? Then said the king's servants that
ministered unto him, There is nothing
done for him.
4And the king said, Who *is* in the court?
Now Haman was come into the outward
court of the king's house, to speak unto
the king to hang Mordecai on the gallows
that he had prepared for him.
5And the king's servants said unto him,
Behold, Haman standeth in the court. And
the king said, Let him come in.
6So Haman came in. And the king said
unto him, What shall be done unto the
man whom the king delighteth to honour?
Now Haman thought in his heart, To
whom would the king delight to do
honour more than to myself?
7And Haman answered the king, For the
man whom the king delighteth to honour,
8Let the royal apparel be brought which
the king *useth* to wear, and the horse that
the king rideth upon, and the crown royal
which is set upon his head:
9And let this apparel and horse be delivered to the hand of one of the king's
most noble princes, that they may array
the man *withal* whom the king delighteth
to honour, and bring him on horseback
through the street of the city, and proclaim
before him, Thus shall it be done to the
man whom the king delighteth to honour.
10Then the king said to Haman, Make
haste, *and* take the apparel and the horse,
as thou hast said, and do even so to
Mordecai the Jew, that sitteth at the king's
gate: let nothing fail of all that thou hast
spoken.
11Then took Haman the apparel and the
horse, and arrayed Mordecai, and brought
him on horseback through the street of the
city, and proclaimed before him, Thus
shall it be done unto the man whom the
king delighteth to honour.
12And Mordecai came again to the king's
gate. But Haman hasted to his house
mourning, and having his head covered.
13And Haman told Zeresh his wife and
all his friends every *thing* that had befallen
him. Then said his wise men and Zeresh
his wife unto him, If Mordecai *be* of the
seed of the Jews, before whom thou hast
begun to fall, thou shalt not prevail against
him, but shalt surely fall before him.
14And while they *were* yet talking with
him, came the king's chamberlains, and
hasted to bring Haman unto the banquet
that Esther had prepared.

7

1So the king and Haman came to banquet with Esther the queen.
2And the king said again unto Esther on
the second day at the banquet of wine,
What *is* thy petition, queen Esther? and it
shall be granted thee: and what *is* thy request? and it shall be performed, *even* to
the half of the kingdom.
3Then Esther the queen answered and
said, If I have found favour in thy sight, O
king, and if it please the king, let my life
be given me at my petition, and my people at my request:
4For we are sold, I and my people, to be
destroyed, to be slain, and to perish. But
if we had been sold for bondmen and
bondwomen, I had held my tongue, although the enemy could not countervail
the king's damage.
5Then the king Ahasuerus answered and
said unto Esther the queen, Who is he, and
where is he, that durst presume in his heart
to do so?
6And Esther said, The adversary and
enemy *is* this wicked Haman. Then Haman
was afraid before the king and the queen.
7And the king arising from the banquet
of wine in his wrath *went* into the palace
garden: and Haman stood up to make request for his life to Esther the queen; for
he saw that there was evil determined
against him by the king.
8Then the king returned out of the palace garden into the place of the banquet
of wine; and Haman was fallen upon the
bed whereon Esther *was*. Then said the
king, Will he force the queen also before
me in the house? As the word went out of
the king's mouth, they covered Haman's
face.
9And Harbonah, one of the chamberlains, said before the king, Behold also, the
gallows fifty cubits high, which Haman
had made for Mordecai, who had spoken
good for the king, standeth in the house
of Haman. Then the king said, Hang him
thereon.
10So they hanged Haman on the gallows

that he had prepared for Mordecai. Then was the king's wrath pacified.

8

1 On that day did the king Ahasuerus give the house of Haman the Jews' enemy unto Esther the queen. And Mordecai came before the king; for Esther had told what he *was* unto her.

2 And the king took off his ring, which he had taken from Haman, and gave it unto Mordecai. And Esther set Mordecai over the house of Haman.

3 And Esther spake yet again before the king, and fell down at his feet, and besought him with tears to put away the mischief of Haman the Agagite, and his device that he had devised against the Jews.

4 Then the king held out the golden sceptre toward Esther. So Esther arose, and stood before the king,

5 And said, If it please the king, and if I have found favour in his sight, and the thing *seem* right before the king, and I *be* pleasing in his eyes, let it be written to reverse the letters devised by Haman the son of Hammedatha the Agagite, which he wrote to destroy the Jews which *are* in all the king's provinces:

6 For how can I endure to see the evil that shall come unto my people? or how can I endure to see the destruction of my kindred?

7 Then the king Ahasuerus said unto Esther the queen and to Mordecai the Jew, Behold, I have given Esther the house of Haman, and him they have hanged upon the gallows, because he laid his hand upon the Jews.

8 Write ye also for the Jews, as it liketh you, in the king's name, and seal *it* with the king's ring: for the writing which is written in the king's name, and sealed with the king's ring, may no man reverse.

9 Then were the king's scribes called at that time in the third month, that *is,* the month Sivan, on the three and twentieth *day* thereof; and it was written according to all that Mordecai commanded unto the Jews, and to the lieutenants, and the deputies and rulers of the provinces which *are* from India unto Ethiopia, an hundred twenty and seven provinces, unto every province according to the writing thereof, and unto every people after their language, and to the Jews according to their writing, and according to their language.

10 And he wrote in the king Ahasuerus' name, and sealed *it* with the king's ring, and sent letters by posts on horseback, *and* riders on mules, camels, *and* young dromedaries:

11 Wherein the king granted the Jews which *were* in every city to gather themselves together, and to stand for their life, to destroy, to slay, and to cause to perish, all the power of the people and province that would assault them, *both* little ones and women, and *to take* the spoil of them for a prey,

12 Upon one day in all the provinces of king Ahasuerus, *namely,* upon the thirteenth *day* of the twelfth month, which *is* the month Adar.

13 The copy of the writing for a commandment to be given in every province *was* published unto all people, and that the Jews should be ready against that day to avenge themselves on their enemies.

14 *So* the posts that rode upon mules *and* camels went out, being hastened and pressed on by the king's commandment. And the decree was given at Shushan the palace.

15 And Mordecai went out from the presence of the king in royal apparel of blue and white, and with a great crown of gold, and with a garment of fine linen and purple: and the city of Shushan rejoiced and was glad.

16 The Jews had light, and gladness, and joy, and honour.

17 And in every province, and in every city, whithersoever the king's commandment and his decree came, the Jews had joy and gladness, a feast and a good day. And many of the people of the land became Jews; for the fear of the Jews fell upon them.

9

1 Now in the twelfth month, that *is,* the month Adar, on the thirteenth day of the same, when the king's commandment and his decree drew near to be put in execution, in the day that the enemies of the Jews hoped to have power over them, (though it was turned to the contrary, that the Jews had rule over them that hated them;)

2 The Jews gathered themselves together in their cities throughout all the provinces of the king Ahasuerus, to lay hand on such as sought their hurt: and no man could

withstand them; for the fear of them fell upon all people.

3 And all the rulers of the provinces, and the lieutenants, and the deputies, and officers of the king, helped the Jews; because the fear of Mordecai fell upon them.

4 For Mordecai *was* great in the king's house, and his fame went out throughout all the provinces: for this man Mordecai waxed greater and greater.

5 Thus the Jews smote all their enemies with the stroke of the sword, and slaughter, and destruction, and did what they would unto those that hated them.

6 And in Shushan the palace the Jews slew and destroyed five hundred men.

7 And Parshandatha, and Dalphon, and Aspatha,

8 And Poratha, and Adalia, and Aridatha,

9 And Parmashta, and Arisai, and Aridai, and Vajezatha,

10 The ten sons of Haman the son of Hammedatha, the enemy of the Jews, slew they; but on the spoil laid they not their hand.

11 On that day the number of those that were slain in Shushan the palace was brought before the king.

12 And the king said unto Esther the queen, The Jews have slain and destroyed five hundred men in Shushan the palace, and the ten sons of Haman; what have they done in the rest of the king's provinces? now what *is* thy petition? and it shall be granted thee: or what *is* thy request further? and it shall be done.

13 Then said Esther, If it please the king, let it be granted to the Jews which *are* in Shushan to do to morrow also according unto this day's decree, and let Haman's ten sons be hanged upon the gallows.

14 And the king commanded it so to be done: and the decree was given at Shushan; and they hanged Haman's ten sons.

15 For the Jews that *were* in Shushan gathered themselves together on the fourteenth day also of the month Adar, and slew three hundred men at Shushan; but on the prey they laid not their hand.

16 But the other Jews that *were* in the king's provinces gathered themselves together, and stood for their lives, and had rest from their enemies, and slew of their foes seventy and five thousand, but they laid not their hands on the prey,

17 On the thirteenth day of the month Adar; and on the fourteenth day of the same rested they, and made it a day of feasting and gladness.

18 But the Jews that *were* at Shushan assembled together on the thirteenth *day* thereof; and on the fourteenth thereof; and on the fifteenth *day* of the same they rested, and made it a day of feasting and gladness.

19 Therefore the Jews of the villages, that dwelt in the unwalled towns, made the fourteenth day of the month Adar *a day of* gladness and feasting, and a good day, and of sending portions one to another.

20 And Mordecai wrote these things, and sent letters unto all the Jews that *were* in all the provinces of the king Ahasuerus, *both* nigh and far,

21 To stablish *this* among them, that they should keep the fourteenth day of the month Adar, and the fifteenth day of the same, yearly,

22 As the days wherein the Jews rested from their enemies, and the month which was turned unto them from sorrow to joy, and from mourning into a good day: that they should make them days of feasting and joy, and of sending portions one to another, and gifts to the poor.

23 And the Jews undertook to do as they had begun, and as Mordecai had written unto them;

24 Because Haman the son of Hammedatha, the Agagite, the enemy of all the Jews, had devised against the Jews to destroy them, and had cast Pur, that *is*, the lot, to consume them, and to destroy them;

25 But when *Esther* came before the king, he commanded by letters that his wicked device, which he devised against the Jews, should return upon his own head, and that he and his sons should be hanged on the gallows.

26 Wherefore they called these days Purim after the name of Pur. Therefore for all the words of this letter, and *of that* which they had seen concerning this matter, and which had come unto them,

27 The Jews ordained, and took upon them, and upon their seed, and upon all such as joined themselves unto them, so as it should not fail, that they would keep these two days according to their writing,

and according to their *appointed* time every year;

28 And *that* these days *should be* remembered and kept throughout every generation, every family, every province, and every city; and *that* these days of Purim should not fail from among the Jews, nor the memorial of them perish from their seed.

29 Then Esther the queen, the daughter of Abihail, and Mordecai the Jew, wrote with all authority, to confirm this second letter of Purim.

30 And he sent the letters unto all the Jews, to the hundred twenty and seven provinces of the kingdom of Ahasuerus, *with* words of peace and truth,

31 To confirm these days of Purim in their times *appointed*, according as Mordecai the Jew and Esther the queen had enjoined them, and as they had decreed for themselves and for their seed, the matters of the fastings and their cry.

32 And the decree of Esther confirmed these matters of Purim; and it was written in the book.

10

1 And the king Ahasuerus laid a tribute upon the land, and *upon* the isles of the sea.

2 And all the acts of his power and of his might, and the declaration of the greatness of Mordecai, whereunto the king advanced him, *are* they not written in the book of the chronicles of the kings of Media and Persia?

3 For Mordecai the Jew *was* next unto king Ahasuerus, and great among the Jews, and accepted of the multitude of his brethren, seeking the wealth of his people, and speaking peace to all his seed.

Job

AUTHOR

Unknown; possibly Job, Moses, Solomon, or Elihu

MAIN POINT

Even righteous people suffer in this world, but God remains good and remains with us.

DATE WRITTEN

Unknown

42 CHAPTERS

MAIN PEOPLE

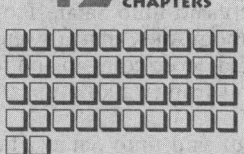

Job, Job's wife, Eliphaz the Temanite, Bildad the Shuhite, Zophar the Naamathite, Elihu the Buzite

SPECIAL FEATURES

- *Believed by many to be the oldest book in the Bible, describing events that happened in 2000-1800 B.C.*
- *Describes conversations between God and Satan*
- *Shows what is helpful (and what is not helpful) to say to a friend who is suffering*
- *Shows that a person's faith should be in God, not in things or people*
- *First book of Poetry*

HOW THE BOOK GOT ITS NAME

The book takes its name from the main person, Job, a name that has become a symbol of suffering and patience.

1 1There was a man in the land of Uz, whose name *was* Job; and that man was perfect and upright, and one that feared God, and eschewed evil.

1:1 Who Is Religious?
◄ 2 Chronicles 31:20
Daniel 6:10 ►

2And there were born unto him seven sons and three daughters.

3His substance also was seven thousand sheep, and three thousand camels, and five hundred yoke of oxen, and five hundred she asses, and a very great household; so that this man was the greatest of all the men of the east.

4And his sons went and feasted *in their* houses, every one his day; and sent and called for their three sisters to eat and to drink with them.

5And it was so, when the days of *their* feasting were gone about, that Job sent and sanctified them, and rose up early in the morning, and offered burnt offerings *according* to the number of them all: for Job said, It may be that my sons have sinned, and cursed God in their hearts. Thus did Job continually.

1:5 Devotions
◄ 2 Chronicles 29:20
Psalm 57:8 ►

6 Now there was a day when the sons of
God came to present themselves before the
LORD, and Satan came also among them.
7 And the LORD said unto Satan, Whence
comest thou? Then Satan answered the
LORD, and said, From going to and fro in
the earth, and from walking up and down
in it.
8 And the LORD said unto Satan, Hast
thou considered my servant Job, that *there*
is none like him in the earth, a perfect and
an upright man, one that feareth God, and
escheweth evil?
9 Then Satan answered the LORD, and
said, Doth Job fear God for nought?
10 Hast not thou made an hedge about
him, and about his house, and about all
that he hath on every side? thou hast
blessed the work of his hands, and his substance is increased in the land.
11 But put forth thine hand now, and
touch all that he hath, and he will curse
thee to thy face.
12 And the LORD
said unto Satan, Be-
hold, all that he
hath *is* in thy pow-
er; only upon him-
self put not forth
thine hand. So Sa-
tan went forth from
the presence of the
LORD.
13 And there was
a day when his sons
and his daughters *were* eating and drinking wine in their eldest brother's house:
14 And there came a messenger unto Job,
and said, The oxen were plowing, and the
asses feeding beside them:
15 And the Sabeans fell *upon them*, and
took them away; yea, they have slain the
servants with the edge of the sword; and I
only am escaped alone to tell thee.
16 While he *was* yet speaking, there came
also another, and said, The fire of God is
fallen from heaven, and hath burned up
the sheep, and the servants, and consumed
them; and I only am escaped alone to tell
thee.
17 While he *was* yet speaking, there came
also another, and said, The Chaldeans
made out three bands, and fell upon the
camels, and have carried them away, yea,
and slain the servants with the edge of the
sword; and I only am escaped alone to tell
thee.
18 While he *was* yet speaking, there came
also another, and said, Thy sons and thy
daughters *were* eating and drinking wine
in their eldest brother's house:
19 And, behold, there came a great wind
from the wilderness, and smote the four
corners of the house, and it fell upon the
young men, and they are dead; and I only
am escaped alone to tell thee.
20 Then Job arose,
and rent his man-
tle, and shaved his
head, and fell down
upon the ground,
and worshipped,
21 And said, Naked came I out of my
mother's womb, and naked shall I return
thither: the LORD gave, and the LORD hath
taken away; blessed be the name of the
LORD.
22 In all this Job sinned not, nor charged
God foolishly.

1:12
Satan's Power
◄ Luke 4:6 ►

1:12
Satan's Weakness
◄ Luke 10:19 ►

1:20 Grief
◄ 2 Samuel 18:33
Jeremiah 31:15 ►

2

1 Again there was a day when the sons
of God came to present themselves before
the LORD, and Satan came also among
them to present himself before the LORD.
2 And the LORD said unto Satan, From
whence comest thou? And Satan answered
the LORD, and said, From going to and fro
in the earth, and from walking up and
down in it.
3 And the LORD said unto Satan, Hast
thou considered my servant Job, that *there*
is none like him in the earth, a perfect and
an upright man, one that feareth God, and
escheweth evil? and still he holdeth fast
his integrity, although thou movedst me
against him, to destroy him without cause.
4 And Satan answered the LORD, and
said, Skin for skin, yea, all that a man hath
will he give for his life.
5 But put forth thine hand now, and
touch his bone and his flesh, and he will
curse thee to thy face.
6 And the LORD said unto Satan, Behold,
he *is* in thine hand; but save his life.
7 So went Satan forth from the presence
of the LORD, and smote Job with sore boils
from the sole of his foot unto his crown.
8 And he took him a potsherd to scrape
himself withal; and he sat down among
the ashes.
9 Then said his wife unto him, Dost thou

still retain thine integrity? curse God,
and die.
10 But he said unto her, Thou speakest
as one of the foolish women speaketh.
What? shall we receive good at the hand
of God, and shall we not receive evil? In
all this did not Job sin with his lips.
11 Now when Job's
three friends heard
of all this evil that
was come upon him,
they came every one
from his own place;
Eliphaz the Temanite, and Bildad the Shuhite, and Zophar the Naamathite: for they
had made an appointment together to come
to mourn with him and to comfort him.

> **2:11 Sick People**
> ◄ 2 Kings 13:14
> Matthew 25:36 ►

12 And when they lifted up their eyes afar
off, and knew him not, they lifted up their
voice, and wept; and they rent every one
his mantle, and sprinkled dust upon their
heads toward heaven.
13 So they sat down with him upon the
ground seven days and seven nights, and
none spake a word unto him: for they saw
that *his* grief was very great.

3

1 After this opened Job his mouth, and
cursed his day.
2 And Job spake, and said,
3 Let the day perish wherein I was born,
and the night *in which* it was said, There is
a man child conceived.
4 Let that day be darkness; let not God
regard it from above, neither let the light
shine upon it.
5 Let darkness and the shadow of death
stain it; let a cloud dwell upon it; let the
blackness of the day terrify it.
6 *As for* that night, let darkness seize upon
it; let it not be joined unto the days of the
year, let it not come into the number of
the months.
7 Lo, let that night be solitary, let no joyful voice come therein.
8 Let them curse it that curse the day, who
are ready to raise up their mourning.
9 Let the stars of the twilight thereof be
dark; let it look for light, but *have* none;
neither let it see the dawning of the day:
10 Because it shut not up the doors of my
mother's womb, nor hid sorrow from mine
eyes.
11 Why died I not from the womb? *why*
did I *not* give up the ghost when I came
out of the belly?
12 Why did the knees prevent me? or why
the breasts that I should suck?
13 For now should I have lain still and
been quiet, I should have slept: then had I
been at rest,
14 With kings and counsellors of the
earth, which built desolate places for
themselves;
15 Or with princes that had gold, who
filled their houses with silver:
16 Or as an hidden untimely birth I had
not been; as infants *which* never saw light.
17 There the wicked cease *from* troubling;
and there the weary be at rest.
18 *There* the prisoners rest together; they
hear not the voice of the oppressor.
19 The small and great are there; and the
servant *is* free from his master.
20 Wherefore is light given to him that is
in misery, and life unto the bitter *in* soul;
21 Which long for death, but it *cometh*
not; and dig for it more than for hid treasures;
22 Which rejoice exceedingly, *and* are
glad, when they can find the grave?
23 *Why is light given* to a man whose way
is hid, and whom God hath hedged in?
24 For my sighing cometh before I eat,
and my roarings are poured out like the
waters.
25 For the thing which I greatly feared is
come upon me, and that which I was afraid
of is come unto me.
26 I was not in safety, neither had I rest,
neither was I quiet; yet trouble came.

4

1 Then Eliphaz the Temanite answered
and said,
2 *If* we assay to commune with thee, wilt
thou be grieved? but who can withhold
himself from speaking?
3 Behold, thou hast instructed many, and
thou hast strengthened the weak hands.
4 Thy words have upholden him that was
falling, and thou hast strengthened the
feeble knees.
5 But now it is come upon thee, and thou
faintest; it toucheth thee, and thou art troubled.
6 *Is* not *this* thy fear, thy confidence, thy
hope, and the uprightness of thy ways?
7 Remember, I pray thee, who *ever* perished, being innocent? or where were the
righteous cut off?
8 Even as I have seen, they that plow iniquity, and sow wickedness, reap the same.

9 By the blast of God they perish, and by
the breath of his nostrils are they consumed.
10 The roaring of the lion, and the voice
of the fierce lion, and the teeth of the
young lions, are broken.
11 The old lion perisheth for lack of prey,
and the stout lion's whelps are scattered
abroad.
12 Now a thing was secretly brought to
me, and mine ear received a little thereof.
13 In thoughts from the visions of the
night, when deep sleep falleth on men,
14 Fear came upon me, and trembling,
which made all my bones to shake.
15 Then a spirit passed before my face;
the hair of my flesh stood up:
16 It stood still, but I could not discern
the form thereof: an image *was* before mine
eyes, *there was* silence, and I heard a voice,
saying,
17 Shall mortal man be more just than
God? shall a man be more pure than his
maker?
18 Behold, he put no trust in his servants;
and his angels he charged with folly:
19 How much less
in them that dwell
in houses of clay,
whose foundation
is in the dust, *which*
are crushed before
the moth?

4:19
Mortality
◄ Job 10:9 ►

20 They are destroyed from morning to
evening: they perish for ever without any
regarding *it.*
21 Doth not their excellency *which is* in
them go away? they die, even without wisdom.

5

1 Call now, if there be any that will answer thee; and to which of the saints wilt
thou turn?
2 For wrath killeth the foolish man, and
envy slayeth the silly one.
3 I have seen the foolish taking root: but
suddenly I cursed his habitation.
4 His children are far from safety, and
they are crushed in the gate, neither *is there*
any to deliver *them.*
5 Whose harvest the hungry eateth up,
and taketh it even out of the thorns, and
the robber swalloweth up their substance.
6 Although affliction cometh not forth
of the dust, neither doth trouble spring out
of the ground;
7 Yet man is born unto trouble, as the
sparks fly upward.
8 I would seek unto God, and unto God
would I commit my cause:
9 Which doeth great things and unsearchable; marvellous things without
number:
10 Who giveth rain upon the earth, and
sendeth waters upon the fields:
11 To set up on high those that be low;
that those which mourn may be exalted
to safety.
12 He disappointeth the devices of the
crafty, so that their hands cannot perform
their enterprise.
13 He taketh the wise in their own craftiness: and the counsel of the froward is carried headlong.
14 They meet with darkness in the daytime, and grope in the noonday as in the
night.
15 But he saveth
the poor from the
sword, from their
mouth, and from
the hand of the
mighty.

5:15
Promises to the Poor
◄ Psalm 12:5 ►

16 So the poor hath hope, and iniquity
stoppeth her mouth.
17 Behold, happy
is the man whom
God correcteth:
therefore despise
not thou the chas-
tening of the Al-
mighty:

5:17
Hardship
◄ Job 23:10 ►

18 For he maketh sore, and bindeth up:
he woundeth, and his hands make whole.
19 He shall deliv-
er thee in six trou-
bles: yea, in seven
there shall no evil
touch thee.
20 In famine he
shall redeem thee from death: and in war
from the power of the sword.

5:19
Evil Attacks
◄ Psalm 91:3 ►

21 Thou shalt be hid from the scourge of
the tongue: neither shalt thou be afraid of
destruction when it cometh.
22 At destruction and famine thou shalt
laugh: neither shalt thou be afraid of the
beasts of the earth.
23 For thou shalt be in league with the
stones of the field: and the beasts of the
field shall be at peace with thee.

24 And thou shalt know that thy tabernacle *shall be* in peace; and thou shalt visit
thy habitation, and shalt not sin.
25 Thou shalt know also that thy seed
shall be great, and thine offspring as the
grass of the earth.
26 Thou shalt come to *thy* grave in a full
age, like as a shock of corn cometh in in
his season.
27 Lo this, we have searched it, so it *is;*
hear it, and know thou *it* for thy good.

6

1 But Job answered and said,
2 O that my grief were throughly weighed,
and my calamity laid in the balances together!
3 For now it would be heavier than the
sand of the sea: therefore my words are
swallowed up.
4 For the arrows of the Almighty *are* within me, the poison whereof drinketh up my
spirit: the terrors of God do set themselves
in array against me.
5 Doth the wild ass bray when he hath
grass? or loweth the ox over his fodder?
6 Can that which is unsavoury be eaten
without salt? or is there *any* taste in the
white of an egg?
7 The things *that* my soul refused to
touch *are* as my sorrowful meat.
8 Oh that I might have my request; and
that God would grant *me* the thing that I
long for!
9 Even that it would please God to destroy me; that he would let loose his hand,
and cut me off!
10 Then should I yet have comfort; yea, I
would harden myself in sorrow: let him
not spare; for I have not concealed the
words of the Holy One.
11 What *is* my strength, that I should
hope? and what *is* mine end, that I should
prolong my life?
12 *Is* my strength the strength of stones?
or *is* my flesh of brass?
13 *Is* not my help in me? and is wisdom
driven quite from me?
14 To him that is afflicted pity *should be*
shewed from his friend; but he forsaketh
the fear of the Almighty.
15 My brethren have dealt deceitfully as
a brook, *and* as the stream of brooks they
pass away;
16 Which are blackish by reason of the
ice, *and* wherein the snow is hid:
17 What time they wax warm, they vanish: when it is hot, they are consumed out
of their place.
18 The paths of their way are turned
aside; they go to nothing, and perish.
19 The troops of Tema looked, the companies of Sheba waited for them.
20 They were confounded because they
had hoped; they came thither, and were
ashamed.
21 For now ye are no thing; ye see *my* casting down, and are afraid.
22 Did I say, Bring unto me? or, Give a
reward for me of your substance?
23 Or, Deliver me from the enemy's
hand? or, Redeem me from the hand of
the mighty?
24 Teach me, and I will hold my tongue:
and cause me to understand wherein I have
erred.
25 How forcible
are right words! but
what doth your ar-
guing reprove?
26 Do ye imagine
to reprove words,
and the speeches of one that is desperate,
which are as wind?
27 Yea, ye overwhelm the fatherless, and
ye dig *a pit* for your friend.
28 Now therefore be content, look upon
me; for *it is* evident unto you if I lie.
29 Return, I pray you, let it not be iniquity; yea, return again, my righteousness
is in it.
30 Is there iniquity in my tongue? cannot my taste discern perverse things?

6:25
Wise Words
◄ Proverbs 15:23 ►

7

1 *Is there* not an appointed time to man
upon earth? *are not* his days also like the
days of an hireling?
2 As a servant earnestly desireth the shadow, and as an hireling looketh for *the re-*
ward of his work:
3 So am I made to possess months of
vanity, and wearisome nights are appointed to me.
4 When I lie down, I say, When shall I
arise, and the night be gone? and I am full
of tossings to and fro unto the dawning of
the day.
5 My flesh is clothed with worms and
clods of dust; my skin is broken, and become loathsome.
6 My days are swifter than a weaver's
shuttle, and are spent without hope.
7 O remember that my life is wind: mine

Turn to the next page for more . . .

eye shall no more see good.

8 The eye of him that hath seen me shall see me no *more:* thine eyes *are* upon me, and I *am* not.

7:6 Life Is Short
◄ 1 Chronicles 29:15
Job 8:9 ►

9 *As* the cloud is consumed and vanisheth away: so he that goeth down to the grave shall come up no *more.*

10 He shall return no more to his house, neither shall his place know him any more.

11 Therefore I will not refrain my mouth; I will speak in the anguish of my spirit; I will complain in the bitterness of my soul.

12 *Am* I a sea, or a whale, that thou settest a watch over me?

13 When I say, My bed shall comfort me, my couch shall ease my complaint;

14 Then thou scarest me with dreams, and terrifiest me through visions:

15 So that my soul chooseth strangling, *and* death rather than my life.

16 I loathe *it;* I would not live alway: let me alone; for my days *are* vanity.

17 What *is* man, that thou shouldest magnify him? and that thou shouldest set thine heart upon him?

18 And *that* thou shouldest visit him every morning, *and* try him every moment?

19 How long wilt thou not depart from me, nor let me alone till I swallow down my spittle?

20 I have sinned; what shall I do unto thee, O thou preserver of men? why hast thou set me as a mark against thee, so that I am a burden to myself?

21 And why dost thou not pardon my transgression, and take away mine iniquity? for now shall I sleep in the dust; and thou shalt seek me in the morning, but I *shall* not *be.*

8

1 Then answered Bildad the Shuhite, and said,

2 How long wilt thou speak these *things?* and *how long shall* the words of thy mouth *be like* a strong wind?

3 Doth God pervert judgment? or doth the Almighty pervert justice?

4 If thy children have sinned against him, and he have cast them away for their transgression;

5 If thou wouldest seek unto God betimes, and make thy supplication to the Almighty;

6 If thou *wert* pure and upright; surely now he would awake for thee, and make the habitation of thy righteousness prosperous.

7 Though thy beginning was small, yet thy latter end should greatly increase.

8 For enquire, I pray thee, of the former age, and prepare thyself to the search of their fathers:

9 (For we *are but of* yesterday, and know nothing, because our days upon earth *are* a shadow:)

8:9
Ignorance
◄ Psalm 73:22 ►

8:9 Life Is Short
◄ Job 7:6
Job 9:25 ►

10 Shall not they teach thee, *and* tell thee, and utter words out of their heart?

11 Can the rush grow up without mire? can the flag grow without water?

12 Whilst it *is* yet in his greenness, *and* not cut down, it withereth before any *other* herb.

13 So *are* the paths of all that forget God; and the hypocrite's hope shall perish:

14 Whose hope shall be cut off, and whose trust *shall be* a spider's web.

15 He shall lean upon his house, but it shall not stand: he shall hold it fast, but it shall not endure.

16 He *is* green before the sun, and his branch shooteth forth in his garden.

17 His roots are wrapped about the heap, *and* seeth the place of stones.

18 If he destroy him from his place, then *it* shall deny him, *saying,* I have not seen thee.

19 Behold, this *is* the joy of his way, and out of the earth shall others grow.

20 Behold, God will not cast away a perfect *man,* neither will he help the evil doers:

21 Till he fill thy mouth with laughing, and thy lips with rejoicing.

22 They that hate thee shall be clothed with shame; and the dwelling place of the wicked shall come to nought.

9

1 Then Job answered and said,

2 I know *it is* so of a truth: but how should man be just with God?

3 If he will contend with him, he cannot answer him one of a thousand.

4 *He is* wise in heart, and mighty in

and they shall not escape, and their hope *shall be as* the giving up of the ghost.

11:20 Disappointment
◄ Deuteronomy 28:39
Job 20:18 ►

12

1 And Job answered and said,

2 No doubt but ye *are* the people, and wisdom shall die with you.

3 But I have understanding as well as you; I *am* not inferior to you: yea, who knoweth not such things as these?

4 I am *as* one mocked of his neighbour, who calleth upon God, and he answereth him: the just upright *man is* laughed to scorn.

5 He that is ready to slip with *his* feet *is as* a lamp despised in the thought of him that is at ease.

6 The tabernacles of robbers prosper, and they that provoke God are secure; into whose hand God bringeth *abundantly.*

12:6
Injustice
◄ Job 21:7 ►

12:6
Just You Wait
◄ Psalm 37:35 ►

7 But ask now the beasts, and they shall teach thee; and the fowls of the air, and they shall tell thee:

8 Or speak to the earth, and it shall teach thee: and the fishes of the sea shall declare unto thee.

9 Who knoweth not in all these that the hand of the LORD hath wrought this?

10 In whose hand *is* the soul of every living thing, and the breath of all mankind.

11 Doth not the ear try words? and the mouth taste his meat?

12 With the ancient *is* wisdom; and in length of days understanding.

13 With him *is* wisdom and strength, he hath counsel and understanding.

14 Behold, he breaketh down, and it cannot be built again: he shutteth up a man, and there can be no opening.

15 Behold, he withholdeth the waters, and they dry up: also he sendeth them out, and they overturn the earth.

16 With him *is* strength and wisdom: the deceived and the deceiver *are* his.

17 He leadeth counsellors away spoiled, and maketh the judges fools.

18 He looseth the bond of kings, and girdeth their loins with a girdle.

19 He leadeth princes away spoiled, and overthroweth the mighty.

20 He removeth away the speech of the trusty, and taketh away the understanding of the aged.

21 He poureth contempt upon princes, and weakeneth the strength of the mighty.

22 He discovereth deep things out of darkness, and bringeth out to light the shadow of death.

23 He increaseth the nations, and destroyeth them: he enlargeth the nations, and straiteneth them *again.*

24 He taketh away the heart of the chief of the people of the earth, and causeth them to wander in a wilderness *where there is* no way.

25 They grope in the dark without light, and he maketh them to stagger like *a* drunken *man.*

13

1 Lo, mine eye hath seen all *this,* mine ear hath heard and understood it.

2 What ye know, *the same* do I know also: I *am* not inferior unto you.

3 Surely I would speak to the Almighty, and I desire to reason with God.

4 But ye *are* forgers of lies, ye *are* all physicians of no value.

5 Oh that ye would altogether hold your peace! and it should be your wisdom.

6 Hear now my reasoning, and hearken to the pleadings of my lips.

7 Will ye speak wickedly for God? and talk deceitfully for him?

8 Will ye accept his person? will ye contend for God?

9 Is it good that he should search you out? or as one man mocketh another, do ye *so* mock him?

10 He will surely reprove you, if ye do secretly accept persons.

13:10 Favoritism
◄ Deuteronomy 1:17
Proverbs 24:23 ►

11 Shall not his excellency make you afraid? and his dread fall upon you?

12 Your remembrances *are* like unto ashes, your bodies to bodies of clay.

13 Hold your peace, let me alone, that I may speak, and let come on me what *will.*

14 Wherefore do I take my flesh in my teeth, and put my life in mine hand?

15 Though he slay me, yet will I trust in

him: but I will maintain mine own ways
before him.
16He also *shall be* my salvation: for an
hypocrite shall not come before him.
17Hear diligently my speech, and my
declaration with your ears.
18Behold now, I have ordered *my* cause;
I know that I shall be justified.
19Who *is* he *that* will plead with me? for
now, if I hold my tongue, I shall give up
the ghost.
20Only do not two *things* unto me: then
will I not hide myself from thee.
21Withdraw thine hand far from me: and
let not thy dread make me afraid.
22Then call thou, and I will answer: or
let me speak, and answer thou me.
23How many *are* mine iniquities and
sins? make me to know my transgression
and my sin.
24Wherefore hidest thou thy face, and
holdest me for thine enemy?
25Wilt thou break a leaf driven to and
fro? and wilt thou pursue the dry stubble?
26For thou writest
bitter things against
me, and makest me
to possess the iniq-
uities of my youth.
27Thou puttest
my feet also in the stocks, and lookest narrowly unto all my paths; thou settest a
print upon the heels of my feet.
28And he, as a rotten thing, consumeth,
as a garment that is moth eaten.

13:26
Results of Sin
◄ Job 20:11 ►

14 1Man *that is* born of a woman *is* of few
days, and full of trouble.
2He cometh forth
like a flower, and
is cut down: he
fleeth also as a
shadow, and con-
tinueth not.

14:2 Life Is Short
◄ Job 9:25
Psalm 39:5 ►

3And dost thou open thine eyes upon
such an one, and bringest me into judgment with thee?
4Who can bring a clean *thing* out of an
unclean? not one.
5Seeing his days *are* determined, the
number of his months *are* with thee, thou
hast appointed his bounds that he cannot
pass;
6Turn from him, that he may rest, till
he shall accomplish, as an hireling, his day.
7For there is hope of a tree, if it be cut
down, that it will sprout again, and that
the tender branch thereof will not cease.
8Though the root thereof wax old in the
earth, and the stock thereof die in the
ground;
9*Yet* through the scent of water it will
bud, and bring forth boughs like a plant.
10But man dieth, and wasteth away: yea,
man giveth up the ghost, and where *is* he?
11*As* the waters fail from the sea, and the
flood decayeth and drieth up:
12So man lieth down, and riseth not: till
the heavens *be* no more, they shall not
awake, nor be raised out of their sleep.
13Oh that thou wouldest hide me in the
grave, that thou wouldest keep me secret,
until thy wrath be past, that thou wouldest
appoint me a set time, and remember me!
14If a man die, shall he live *again*? all
the days of my appointed time will I wait,
till my change come.
15Thou shalt call, and I will answer thee:
thou wilt have a desire to the work of thine
hands.
16For now thou
numberest my steps:
dost thou not watch
over my sin?
17My transgres-
sion *is* sealed up in
a bag, and thou sewest up mine iniquity.

14:16 God Sees Sin
◄ Job 10:14
Jeremiah 2:22 ►

18And surely the mountain falling
cometh to nought, and the rock is removed
out of his place.
19The waters wear the stones: thou
washest away the things which grow *out*
of the dust of the earth; and thou destroyest the hope of man.
20Thou prevailest for ever against him,
and he passeth: thou changest his countenance, and sendest him away.
21His sons come to honour, and he
knoweth *it* not; and they are brought low,
but he perceiveth *it* not of them.
22But his flesh upon him shall have
pain, and his soul within him shall mourn.

15 1Then answered Eliphaz the Temanite,
and said,
2Should a wise man utter vain knowledge, and fill his
belly with the east
wind?
3Should he rea-
son with unprofit-
able talk? or with

15:3 Idle Talk
◄ Job 11:12
Proverbs 10:19 ►

speeches wherewith he can do no good?
4 Yea, thou castest off fear, and restrainest
prayer before God.
5 For thy mouth uttereth thine iniquity,
and thou choosest the tongue of the crafty.
6 Thine own mouth condemneth thee,
and not I: yea, thine own lips testify against
thee.
7 *Art* thou the first man *that* was born?
or wast thou made before the hills?
8 Hast thou heard the secret of God? and
dost thou restrain wisdom to thyself?
9 What knowest thou, that we know not?
what understandest thou, which *is* not in us?
10 With us *are* both the grayheaded and
very aged men, much elder than thy father.
11 *Are* the consolations of God small with
thee? is there any secret thing with thee?
12 Why doth thine heart carry thee away?
and what do thy eyes wink at,
13 That thou turnest thy spirit against
God, and lettest *such* words go out of thy
mouth?
14 What *is* man, that he should be clean?
and *he which is* born of a woman, that he
should be righteous?
15 Behold, he putteth no trust in his
saints; yea, the heavens are not clean in
his sight.
16 How much more abominable and
filthy *is* man, which drinketh iniquity like
water?
17 I will shew thee, hear me; and that
which I have seen I will declare;
18 Which wise men have told from their
fathers, and have not hid *it:*
19 Unto whom alone the earth was given,
and no stranger passed among them.
20 The wicked man travaileth with pain
all *his* days, and the number of years is hidden to the oppressor.
21 A dreadful
sound *is* in his ears:
in prosperity the
destroyer shall
come upon him.

15:21 Guilty Conscience
◄ Ezra 9:6
Psalm 40:12 ►

22 He believeth
not that he shall return out of darkness,
and he is waited for of the sword.
23 He wandereth abroad for bread, *saying,* Where *is it?* he knoweth that the day
of darkness is ready at his hand.
24 Trouble and anguish shall make him
afraid; they shall prevail against him, as a
king ready to the battle.
25 For he stretcheth out his hand against
God, and strengtheneth himself against
the Almighty.
26 He runneth upon him, *even* on *his*
neck, upon the thick bosses of his bucklers:
27 Because he covereth his face with his
fatness, and maketh collops of fat on *his*
flanks.
28 And he dwelleth in desolate cities, *and*
in houses which no man inhabiteth, which
are ready to become heaps.
29 He shall not be rich, neither shall his
substance continue, neither shall he prolong the perfection thereof upon the earth.
30 He shall not depart out of darkness;
the flame shall dry up his branches, and by
the breath of his mouth shall he go away.
31 Let not him that is deceived trust in
vanity: for vanity shall be his recompence.
32 It shall be accomplished before his
time, and his branch shall not be green.
33 He shall shake off his unripe grape as
the vine, and shall cast off his flower as
the olive.
34 For the congregation of hypocrites
shall be desolate, and fire shall consume
the tabernacles of bribery.
35 They conceive
mischief, and bring
forth vanity, and
their belly pre-
pareth deceit.

15:35 Mischief
◄ Nehemiah 6:2
Psalm 10:7 ►

16

1 Then Job an-
swered and said,
2 I have heard many such things: miserable comforters *are* ye all.
3 Shall vain words have an end? or what
emboldeneth thee that thou answerest?
4 I also could speak as ye *do:* if your soul
were in my soul's stead, I could heap up
words against you, and shake mine head
at you.
5 *But* I would strengthen you with my
mouth, and the moving of my lips should
asswage *your grief.*
6 Though I speak, my grief is not asswaged: and *though* I forbear, what am I
eased?
7 But now he hath made me weary: thou
hast made desolate all my company.
8 And thou hast filled me with wrinkles,
which is a witness *against me:* and my leanness rising up in me beareth witness to my
face.

9He teareth *me* in his wrath, who hateth
me: he gnasheth upon me with his teeth;
mine enemy sharpeneth his eyes upon me.
10They have gaped upon me with their
mouth; they have smitten me upon the
cheek reproachfully; they have gathered
themselves together against me.
11God hath delivered me to the ungodly, and turned me over into the hands of
the wicked.
12I was at ease, but he hath broken me
asunder: he hath also taken *me* by my neck,
and shaken me to pieces, and set me up
for his mark.
13His archers compass me round about,
he cleaveth my reins asunder, and doth not
spare; he poureth out my gall upon the
ground.
14He breaketh me with breach upon
breach, he runneth upon me like a giant.
15I have sewed sackcloth upon my skin,
and defiled my horn in the dust.
16My face is foul with weeping, and my
eyelids is the shadow of death;
17Not for *any* injustice in mine hands:
also my prayer *is* pure.
18O earth, cover not thou my blood, and
let my cry have no place.
19Also now, behold, my witness *is* in
heaven, and my record *is* on high.
20My friends
scorn me: *but* mine
eye poureth out
tears unto God.
21Oh that one
might plead for a
man with God, as a man *pleadeth* for his
neighbour!
22When a few years are come, then I
shall go the way *whence* I shall not return.

16:20
Whom Can You Trust?
◄ Job 19:19 ►

17

1My breath is corrupt, my days are extinct, the graves *are ready* for me.
2*Are there* not mockers with me? and
doth not mine eye continue in their provocation?
3Lay down now, put me in a surety
with thee; who *is* he *that* will strike hands
with me?
4For thou hast hid their heart from understanding: therefore shalt thou not exalt *them*.
5He that speaketh flattery to *his* friends,
even the eyes of his children shall fail.
6He hath made me also a byword of the
people; and aforetime I was as a tabret.
7Mine eye also is dim by reason of sorrow, and all my members *are* as a shadow.
8Upright *men* shall be astonied at this,
and the innocent shall stir up himself
against the hypocrite.
9The righteous
also shall hold on
his way, and he that
hath clean hands
shall be stronger
and stronger.
10But as for you
all, do ye return,
and come now: for
I cannot find *one*
wise *man* among
you.
11My days are past, my purposes are broken off, *even* the thoughts of my heart.
12They change the night into day: the
light *is* short because of darkness.
13If I wait, the grave *is* mine house: I have
made my bed in the darkness.
14I have said to corruption, Thou *art* my
father: to the worm, *Thou art* my mother,
and my sister.
15And where *is* now my hope? as for my
hope, who shall see it?
16They shall go down to the bars of the
pit, when *our* rest together *is* in the dust.

17:9
Determination
◄ John 15:9 ►

17:9
Making Progress
◄ Psalm 84:7 ►

18

1Then answered Bildad the Shuhite, and
said,
2How long *will it be ere* ye make an end
of words? mark, and afterwards we will
speak.
3Wherefore are we counted as beasts,
and reputed vile in your sight?
4He teareth himself in his anger: shall
the earth be forsaken for thee? and shall
the rock be removed out of his place?
5Yea, the light of the wicked shall be put
out, and the spark of his fire shall not
shine.
6The light shall be dark in his tabernacle, and his candle shall be put out with
him.
7The steps of his strength shall be straitened, and his own counsel shall cast him
down.
8For he is cast into a net by his own feet,
and he walketh upon a snare.
9The gin shall take *him* by the heel, *and*
the robber shall prevail against him.
10The snare *is* laid for him in the ground,
and a trap for him in the way.

11 Terrors shall make him afraid on every
side, and shall drive him to his feet.
12 His strength shall be hungerbitten,
and destruction *shall be* ready at his side.
13 It shall devour the strength of his skin:
even the firstborn of death shall devour his
strength.
14 His confidence shall be rooted out of
his tabernacle, and it shall bring him to
the king of terrors.
15 It shall dwell in his tabernacle, because
it is none of his: brimstone shall be scattered upon his habitation.
16 His roots shall be dried up beneath,
and above shall his branch be cut off.
17 His remembrance shall perish from
the earth, and he shall have no name in
the street.
18 He shall be driven from light into
darkness, and chased out of the world.
19 He shall neither have son nor nephew among his people, nor any remaining
in his dwellings.
20 They that come after *him* shall be
astonied at his day, as they that went before were affrighted.
21 Surely such *are* the dwellings of the
wicked, and this *is* the place *of him that*
knoweth not God.

19

1 Then Job answered and said,
2 How long will ye vex my soul, and
break me in pieces with words?
3 These ten times have ye reproached me:
ye are not ashamed *that* ye make yourselves
strange to me.
4 And be it indeed
that I have erred,
mine error remain-
eth with myself.
5 If indeed ye will
magnify *yourselves*
against me, and plead against me my reproach:

19:4 Blame
◄ Deuteronomy 24:16
Proverbs 9:12 ►

6 Know now that God hath overthrown
me, and hath compassed me with his
net.
7 Behold, I cry out of wrong, but I am
not heard: I cry aloud, but *there is* no judgment.
8 He hath fenced up my way that I cannot pass, and he hath set darkness in my
paths.
9 He hath stripped me of my glory, and
taken the crown *from* my head.
10 He hath destroyed me on every side,
and I am gone: and mine hope hath he
removed like a tree.
11 He hath also kindled his wrath against
me, and he counteth me unto him as *one
of* his enemies.
12 His troops come together, and raise
up their way against me, and encamp
round about my tabernacle.
13 He hath put my brethren far from me,
and mine acquaintance are verily estranged from me.
14 My kinsfolk have failed, and my familiar friends have forgotten me.
15 They that dwell in mine house, and
my maids, count me for a stranger: I am
an alien in their sight.
16 I called my servant, and he gave
me no answer; I intreated him with my
mouth.
17 My breath is strange to my wife,
though I intreated for the children's *sake*
of mine own body.
18 Yea, young children despised me; I
arose, and they spake against me.
19 All my inward
friends abhorred
me: and they whom
I loved are turned
against me.
20 My bone cleav-
eth to my skin and to my flesh, and I am
escaped with the skin of my teeth.

19:19
Whom Can You Trust?
◄ Job 16:20
Psalm 38:11 ►

21 Have pity upon me, have pity upon
me, O ye my friends; for the hand of God
hath touched me.
22 Why do ye persecute me as God, and
are not satisfied with my flesh?
23 Oh that my words were now written!
oh that they were printed in a book!
24 That they were graven with an iron
pen and lead in the rock for ever!
25 For I know *that* my redeemer liveth,
and *that* he shall stand at the latter *day*
upon the earth:
26 And *though* after my skin *worms* destroy
this *body*, yet in my flesh shall I see God:
27 Whom I shall see for myself, and mine
eyes shall behold, and not another; *though*
my reins be consumed within me.
28 But ye should say, Why persecute we
him, seeing the root of the matter is found
in me?
29 Be ye afraid of the sword: for wrath
bringeth the punishments of the sword, that
ye may know *there is* a judgment.

20

1 Then answered Zophar the Naamathite,
and said,
2 Therefore do my thoughts cause me to
answer, and for *this* I make haste.
3 I have heard the check of my reproach,
and the spirit of my understanding causeth
me to answer.
4 Knowest thou *not* this of old, since man
was placed upon earth,
5 That the triumphing of the
wicked *is* short, and
the joy of the hypocrite
but for a moment?

20:5
Happiness
◄ Proverbs 14:13 ►

6 Though his excellency mount up to the
heavens, and his head reach unto the
clouds;
7 *Yet* he shall perish for ever like his own
dung: they which have seen him shall say,
Where *is* he?
8 He shall fly away as a dream, and shall
not be found: yea, he shall be chased away
as a vision of the night.
9 The eye also *which* saw him shall *see*
him no more; neither shall his place any
more behold him.
10 His children shall seek to please the
poor, and his hands shall restore their
goods.
11 His bones are
full *of the sin* of his
youth, which shall
lie down with him
in the dust.

20:11 Results of Sin
◄ Job 13:26
Psalm 25:7 ►

12 Though wickedness
be sweet in his mouth, *though* he
hide it under his tongue;
13 *Though* he spare it, and forsake it not;
but keep it still within his mouth:
14 *Yet* his meat in his bowels is turned, *it*
is the gall of asps within him.
15 He hath swallowed down riches, and
he shall vomit them up again: God shall
cast them out of his belly.
16 He shall suck the poison of asps: the
viper's tongue shall slay him.
17 He shall not see the rivers, the floods,
the brooks of honey and butter.
18 That which he
laboured for shall
he restore, and shall
not swallow *it*
down: according to
his substance *shall*

20:18 Disappointment
◄ Job 11:20
Job 27:17 ►

the restitution *be*, and he shall not rejoice
therein.
19 Because he hath oppressed *and* hath
forsaken the poor; *because* he hath violently
taken away an house which he builded
not;
20 Surely he shall not feel quietness in
his belly, he shall not save of that which
he desired.
21 There shall none of his meat be left;
therefore shall no man look for his goods.
22 In the fulness of his sufficiency he
shall be in straits: every hand of the wicked
shall come upon him.
23 *When* he is about to fill his belly, *God*
shall cast the fury of his wrath upon him,
and shall rain *it* upon him while he is
eating.
24 He shall flee from the iron weapon,
and the bow of steel shall strike him
through.
25 It is drawn, and cometh out of the
body; yea, the glittering sword cometh out
of his gall: terrors *are* upon him.
26 All darkness *shall be* hid in his secret
places: a fire not blown shall consume
him; it shall go ill with him that is left in
his tabernacle.
27 The heaven shall reveal his iniquity;
and the earth shall rise up against him.
28 The increase of
his house shall depart,
and his goods
shall flow away in
the day of his
wrath.

20:28
Soon Gone
◄ Psalm 49:10 ►

29 This *is* the portion of a wicked man
from God, and the heritage appointed
unto him by God.

21

1 But Job answered and said,
2 Hear diligently my speech, and let this
be your consolations.
3 Suffer me that I may speak; and after
that I have spoken, mock on.
4 As for me, *is* my complaint to man? and
if *it were so*, why should not my spirit be
troubled?
5 Mark me, and be astonished, and lay
your hand upon *your* mouth.
6 Even when I
remember I am
afraid, and trembling
taketh hold
on my flesh.
7 Wherefore do

21:7 Injustice
◄ Job 12:6
Psalm 73:14 ►

the wicked live, become old, yea, are
mighty in power?
8 Their seed is established in their sight
with them, and their offspring before their
eyes.
9 Their houses *are* safe from fear, neither
is the rod of God upon them.
10 Their bull gendereth, and faileth not;
their cow calveth, and casteth not her calf.
11 They send forth their little ones like a
flock, and their children dance.
12 They take the timbrel and harp, and
rejoice at the sound of the organ.
13 They spend their days in wealth, and
in a moment go down to the grave.
14 Therefore they say unto God, Depart
from us; for we desire not the knowledge
of thy ways.
15 What *is* the Almighty, that we should
serve him? and what profit should we have,
if we pray unto him?
16 Lo, their good *is* not in their hand: the
counsel of the wicked is far from me.
17 How oft is the candle of the wicked
put out! and *how oft* cometh their destruction upon them! *God* distributeth sorrows
in his anger.
18 They are as stubble before the wind,
and as chaff that the storm carrieth away.
19 God layeth up his iniquity for his
children: he rewardeth him, and he shall
know *it*.
20 His eyes shall see his destruction, and
he shall drink of the wrath of the Almighty.
21 For what pleasure *hath* he in his house
after him, when the number of his months
is cut off in the midst?
22 Shall *any* teach God knowledge? seeing he judgeth those that are high.
23 One dieth in his full strength, being
wholly at ease and quiet.
24 His breasts are full of milk, and his
bones are moistened with marrow.
25 And another dieth in the bitterness of
his soul, and never eateth with pleasure.
26 They shall lie down alike in the dust,
and the worms shall cover them.
27 Behold, I know your thoughts, and the
devices *which* ye wrongfully imagine
against me.
28 For ye say, Where *is* the house of the
prince? and where *are* the dwelling places
of the wicked?
29 Have ye not asked them that go by the
way? and do ye not know their tokens,
30 That the wicked is reserved to the day
of destruction? they shall be brought forth
to the day of wrath.
31 Who shall declare his way to his face?
and who shall repay him *what* he hath
done?
32 Yet shall he be brought to the grave,
and shall remain in the tomb.
33 The clods of the valley shall be sweet
unto him, and every man shall draw after
him, as *there are* innumerable before him.
34 How then comfort ye me in vain, seeing in your answers there remaineth falsehood?

22

1 Then Eliphaz the Temanite answered
and said,
2 Can a man be profitable unto God, as
he that is wise may be profitable unto himself?
3 *Is it* any pleasure to the Almighty, that
thou art righteous? or *is it* gain *to him* that
thou makest thy ways perfect?
4 Will he reprove thee for fear of thee?
will he enter with thee into judgment?
5 *Is* not thy wickedness great? and thine
iniquities infinite?
6 For thou hast taken a pledge from thy
brother for nought, and stripped the naked of their clothing.
7 Thou hast not given water to the weary
to drink, and thou hast withholden bread
from the hungry.
8 But *as for* the mighty man, he had the
earth; and the honourable man dwelt in it.
9 Thou hast sent widows away empty,
and the arms of the fatherless have been
broken.
10 Therefore snares *are* round about thee,
and sudden fear troubleth thee;
11 Or darkness, *that* thou canst not see;
and abundance of waters cover thee.
12 *Is* not God in the height of heaven?
and behold the height of the stars, how
high they are!
13 And thou sayest, How doth God
know? can he judge through the dark
cloud?
14 Thick clouds *are* a covering to him,
that he seeth not; and he walketh in the
circuit of heaven.
15 Hast thou marked the old way which
wicked men have trodden?
16 Which were cut down out of time,
whose foundation was overflown with a
flood:

17 Which said unto God, Depart from us:
and what can the Almighty do for them?
18 Yet he filled their houses with good
things: but the counsel of the wicked is far
from me.
19 The righteous see *it,* and are glad: and
the innocent laugh them to scorn.
20 Whereas our substance is not cut
down, but the remnant of them the fire
consumeth.
21 Acquaint now
thyself with him,
and be at peace:
thereby good shall
come unto thee.

22:21
Seeking Peace
◄ Psalm 34:14 ►

22 Receive, I pray
thee, the law from his mouth, and lay up
his words in thine heart.
23 If thou return to the Almighty, thou
shalt be built up, thou shalt put away iniquity far from thy tabernacles.
24 Then shalt thou lay up gold as dust,
and the *gold* of Ophir as the stones of the
brooks.
25 Yea, the Almighty shall be thy defence,
and thou shalt have plenty of silver.
26 For then shalt thou have thy delight
in the Almighty, and shalt lift up thy face
unto God.
27 Thou shalt make thy prayer unto him,
and he shall hear thee, and thou shalt pay
thy vows.
28 Thou shalt also decree a thing, and it
shall be established unto thee: and the
light shall shine upon thy ways.
29 When *men* are cast down, then thou
shalt say, *There is* lifting up; and he shall
save the humble person.
30 He shall deliver the island of the innocent: and it is delivered by the pureness
of thine hands.

23

1 Then Job answered and said,
2 Even to day *is* my complaint bitter: my
stroke is heavier than my groaning.
3 Oh that I knew
where I might find
him! *that* I might
come *even* to his
seat!

23:3
Finding God
◄ Jeremiah 29:13 ►

4 I would order
my cause before him, and fill my mouth
with arguments.
5 I would know the words *which* he
would answer me, and understand what
he would say unto me.
6 Will he plead against me with *his* great
power? No; but he would put *strength*
in me.
7 There the righteous might dispute with
him; so should I be delivered for ever from
my judge.
8 Behold, I go forward, but he *is* not *there;*
and backward, but I cannot perceive him:
9 On the left hand, where he doth work,
but I cannot behold *him:* he hideth himself on the right hand, that I cannot
see *him:*
10 But he know-
eth the way that I
take: *when* he hath
tried me, I shall
come forth as gold.

23:10 Hardship
◄ Job 5:17
Psalm 119:67 ►

11 My foot hath
held his steps, his
way have I kept,
and not declined.
12 Neither have I
gone back from the
commandment of
his lips; I have esteemed the words of his
mouth more than my necessary *food.*

23:10
Pain
◄ Psalm 66:10 ►

13 But he *is* in one *mind,* and who can
turn him? and *what* his soul desireth, even
that he doeth.
14 For he performeth *the thing that is* appointed for me: and many such *things are*
with him.
15 Therefore am I troubled at his presence: when I consider, I am afraid of him.
16 For God maketh my heart soft, and
the Almighty troubleth me:
17 Because I was not cut off before the
darkness, *neither* hath he covered the darkness from my face.

24

1 Why, seeing times are not hidden from
the Almighty, do they that know him not
see his days?
2 *Some* remove
the landmarks; they
violently take away
flocks, and feed
thereof.

24:2 Violence
◄ Genesis 6:13
Psalm 55:9 ►

3 They drive away
the ass of the fatherless, they take the
widow's ox for a pledge.
4 They turn the needy out of the way:
the poor of the earth hide themselves together.
5 Behold, *as* wild asses in the desert, go
they forth to their work; rising betimes for

a prey: the wilderness *yieldeth* food for
them *and* for *their* children.
6 They reap *every one* his corn in the field:
and they gather the vintage of the wicked.
7 They cause the naked to lodge without
clothing, that *they have* no covering in the
cold.
8 They are wet with the showers of the
mountains, and embrace the rock for want
of a shelter.
9 They pluck the
fatherless from the
breast, and take a
pledge of the poor.
10 They cause *him*
to go naked with-
out clothing, and they take away the sheaf
from the hungry;
11 *Which* make oil within their walls, *and*
tread *their* winepresses, and suffer thirst.
12 Men groan from out of the city, and
the soul of the wounded crieth out: yet
God layeth not folly *to them.*
13 They are of those that rebel against the
light; they know not the ways thereof, nor
abide in the paths thereof.
14 The murderer rising with the light
killeth the poor and needy, and in the
night is as a thief.
15 The eye also of the adulterer waiteth
for the twilight, saying, No eye shall see
me: and disguiseth *his* face.
16 In the dark they dig through houses,
which they had marked for themselves in
the daytime: they know not the light.
17 For the morning *is* to them even as the
shadow of death: if *one* know *them, they
are in* the terrors of the shadow of death.
18 He *is* swift as the waters; their portion
is cursed in the earth: he beholdeth not
the way of the vineyards.
19 Drought and heat consume the snow
waters: *so doth* the grave *those which* have
sinned.
20 The womb shall forget him; the worm
shall feed sweetly on him; he shall be no
more remembered; and wickedness shall
be broken as a tree.
21 He evil entreateth the barren *that*
beareth not: and doeth not good to the
widow.
22 He draweth also the mighty with his
power: he riseth up, and no *man* is sure of
life.
23 *Though* it be given him *to be* in safety,
whereon he resteth; yet his eyes *are* upon
their ways.
24 They are exalted for a little while, but
are gone and brought low; they are taken
out of the way as all *other,* and cut off as
the tops of the ears of corn.
25 And if *it be* not *so* now, who will make
me a liar, and make my speech nothing
worth?

24:9
Cruelty
◄ Psalm 35:15 ►

25

1 Then answered Bildad the Shuhite, and
said,
2 Dominion and fear *are* with him, he
maketh peace in his high places.
3 Is there any number of his armies? and
upon whom doth not his light arise?
4 How then can man be justified with
God? or how can he be clean *that is* born
of a woman?
5 Behold even to the moon, and it
shineth not; yea, the stars are not pure in
his sight.
6 How much less man, *that is* a worm?
and the son of man, *which is* a worm?

26

1 But Job answered and said,
2 How hast thou helped *him that is* without power? *how* savest thou the arm *that
hath* no strength?
3 How hast thou counseled *him that hath*
no wisdom? and *how* hast thou plentifully declared the thing as it is?
4 To whom hast thou uttered words? and
whose spirit came from thee?
5 Dead *things* are formed from under the
waters, and the inhabitants thereof.
6 Hell *is* naked
before him, and de-
struction hath no
covering.
7 He stretcheth
out the north over
the empty place, *and* hangeth the earth
upon nothing.
8 He bindeth up the waters in his thick
clouds; and the cloud is not rent under
them.
9 He holdeth back the face of his throne,
and spreadeth his cloud upon it.
10 He hath compassed the waters with
bounds, until the day and night come to
an end.
11 The pillars of
heaven tremble and
are astonished at
his reproof.
12 He divideth

26:6
What God Knows
◄ Job 31:4 ►

26:12 God's Power
◄ 2 Chronicles 25:8
Psalm 62:11 ►

the sea with his power, and by his understanding he smiteth through the proud.

13 By his spirit he hath garnished the heavens; his hand hath formed the crooked serpent.

14 Lo, these *are* parts of his ways: but how little a portion is heard of him? but the thunder of his power who can understand?

27

1 Moreover Job continued his parable, and said,

2 *As* God liveth, *who* hath taken away my judgment; and the Almighty, *who* hath vexed my soul;

3 All the while my breath *is* in me, and the spirit of God *is* in my nostrils;

4 My lips shall not speak wickedness, nor my tongue utter deceit.

5 God forbid that I should justify you: till I die I will not remove mine integrity from me.

6 My righteousness I hold fast, and will not let it go: my heart shall not reproach *me* so long as I live.

7 Let mine enemy be as the wicked, and he that riseth up against me as the unrighteous.

8 For what *is* the hope of the hypocrite, though he hath gained, when God taketh away his soul?

9 Will God hear his cry when trouble cometh upon him?

10 Will he delight himself in the Almighty? will he always call upon God?

11 I will teach you by the hand of God: *that* which *is* with the Almighty will I not conceal.

12 Behold, all ye yourselves have seen *it;* why then are ye thus altogether vain?

13 This *is* the portion of a wicked man with God, and the heritage of oppressors, *which* they shall receive of the Almighty.

14 If his children be multiplied, *it is* for the sword: and his offspring shall not be satisfied with bread.

15 Those that remain of him shall be buried in death: and his widows shall not weep.

16 Though he heap up silver as the dust, and prepare raiment as the clay;

27:16-17 Hoarding
◄ Psalm 39:6 ►

17 He may prepare *it,* but the just shall put *it* on, and the innocent shall divide the silver.

18 He buildeth his house as a moth, and as a booth *that* the keeper maketh.

27:17 Disappointment
◄ Job 20:18
Proverbs 11:7 ►

19 The rich man shall lie down, but he shall not be gathered: he openeth his eyes, and he *is* not.

20 Terrors take hold on him as waters, a tempest stealeth him away in the night.

21 The east wind carrieth him away, and he departeth: and as a storm hurleth him out of his place.

22 For *God* shall cast upon him, and not spare: he would fain flee out of his hand.

23 *Men* shall clap their hands at him, and shall hiss him out of his place.

28

1 Surely there is a vein for the silver, and a place for gold *where* they fine *it.*

2 Iron is taken out of the earth, and brass *is* molten *out of* the stone.

3 He setteth an end to darkness, and searcheth out all perfection: the stones of darkness, and the shadow of death.

4 The flood breaketh out from the inhabitant; *even the waters* forgotten of the foot: they are dried up, they are gone away from men.

5 *As for* the earth, out of it cometh bread: and under it is turned up as it were fire.

6 The stones of it *are* the place of sapphires: and it hath dust of gold.

7 *There is* a path which no fowl knoweth, and which the vulture's eye hath not seen:

8 The lion's whelps have not trodden it, nor the fierce lion passed by it.

9 He putteth forth his hand upon the rock; he overturneth the mountains by the roots.

10 He cutteth out rivers among the rocks; and his eye seeth every precious thing.

11 He bindeth the floods from overflowing; and *the thing that is* hid bringeth he forth to light.

12 But where shall wisdom be found? and where *is* the place of understanding?

13 Man knoweth not the price thereof; neither is it found in the land of the living.

14 The depth saith, It *is* not in me: and the sea saith, *It is* not with me.

15 It cannot be gotten for gold, neither shall silver be weighed *for* the price thereof.

16 It cannot be valued with the gold of Ophir, with the precious onyx, or the sapphire.

17The gold and the crystal cannot equal it: and the exchange of it *shall not be for* jewels of fine gold.

18No mention shall be made of coral, or of pearls: for the price of wisdom *is* above rubies.

19The topaz of Ethiopia shall not equal it, neither shall it be valued with pure gold.

20Whence then cometh wisdom? and where *is* the place of understanding?

21Seeing it is hid from the eyes of all living, and kept close from the fowls of the air.

22Destruction and death say, We have heard the fame thereof with our ears.

23God understandeth the way thereof, and he knoweth the place thereof.

24For he looketh to the ends of the earth, *and* seeth under the whole heaven;

25To make the weight for the winds; and he weigheth the waters by measure.

26When he made a decree for the rain, and a way for the lightning of the thunder:

27Then did he see it, and declare it; he prepared it, yea, and searched it out.

28And unto man he said, Behold, the fear of the Lord, that *is* wisdom; and to depart from evil *is* understanding.

28:28
Stay Away!
◄ Psalm 34:14 ►

28:28
True Wisdom
◄ Job 32:7 ►

29

1Moreover Job continued his parable, and said,

2Oh that I were as *in* months past, as *in* the days *when* God preserved me;

3When his candle shined upon my head, *and when* by his light I walked *through* darkness;

4As I was in the days of my youth, when the secret of God *was* upon my tabernacle;

5When the Almighty *was* yet with me, *when* my children *were* about me;

6When I washed my steps with butter, and the rock poured me out rivers of oil;

7When I went out to the gate through the city, *when* I prepared my seat in the street!

8The young men saw me, and hid themselves: and the aged arose, *and* stood up.

9The princes refrained talking, and laid *their* hand on their mouth.

10The nobles held their peace, and their tongue cleaved to the roof of their mouth.

11When the ear heard *me,* then it blessed me; and when the eye saw *me,* it gave witness to me:

12Because I delivered the poor that cried, and the fatherless, and *him that had* none to help him.

13The blessing of him that was ready to perish came upon me: and I caused the widow's heart to sing for joy.

29:13 Compassion
◄ 2 Chronicles 28:15
Luke 10:33-34 ►

14I put on righteousness, and it clothed me: my judgment *was* as a robe and a diadem.

15I was eyes to the blind, and feet *was* I to the lame.

16I *was* a father to the poor: and the cause *which* I knew not I searched out.

29:15-16
Work that Helps Others
◄ 2 Chronicles 28:15
Proverbs 31:20 ►

17And I brake the jaws of the wicked, and plucked the spoil out of his teeth.

18Then I said, I shall die in my nest, and I shall multiply *my* days as the sand.

19My root *was* spread out by the waters, and the dew lay all night upon my branch.

20My glory *was* fresh in me, and my bow was renewed in my hand.

21Unto me *men* gave ear, and waited, and kept silence at my counsel.

22After my words they spake not again; and my speech dropped upon them.

23And they waited for me as for the rain; and they opened their mouth wide *as* for the latter rain.

24*If* I laughed on them, they believed *it* not; and the light of my countenance they cast not down.

25I chose out their way, and sat chief, and dwelt as a king in the army, as one *that* comforteth the mourners.

30

1But now *they that are* younger than I have me in derision, whose fathers I would have disdained to have set with the dogs of my flock.

30:1 Old People
◄ 2 Kings 2:23
Lamentations 5:12 ►

2Yea, whereto *might* the strength of their hands *profit* me, in whom old age was perished?

3 For want and famine *they were* solitary;
fleeing into the wilderness in former time
desolate and waste.
4 Who cut up mallows by the bushes, and
juniper roots *for* their meat.
5 They were driven forth from among
men, (they cried after them as *after* a thief;)
6 To dwell in the cliffs of the valleys, *in*
caves of the earth, and *in* the rocks.
7 Among the bushes they brayed; under
the nettles they were gathered together.
8 *They were* children of fools, yea, children of base men: they were viler than the
earth.
9 And now am I their song, yea, I am their
byword.
10 They abhor me, they flee far from me,
and spare not to spit in my face.
11 Because he hath loosed my cord, and
afflicted me, they have also let loose the
bridle before me.
12 Upon *my* right *hand* rise the youth;
they push away my feet, and they raise up
against me the ways of their destruction.
13 They mar my path, they set forward
my calamity, they have no helper.
14 They came *upon me* as a wide breaking in *of waters:* in the desolation they
rolled themselves *upon me.*
15 Terrors are turned upon me: they pursue my soul as the wind: and my welfare
passeth away as a cloud.
16 And now my soul is poured out upon
me; the days of affliction have taken hold
upon me.
17 My bones are pierced in me in the
night season: and my sinews take no rest.
18 By the great force *of my disease* is my
garment changed: it bindeth me about as
the collar of my coat.
19 He hath cast me into the mire, and I
am become like dust and ashes.
20 I cry unto thee, and thou dost not hear
me: I stand up, and thou regardest me *not.*
21 Thou art become cruel to me: with
thy strong hand thou opposest thyself
against me.
22 Thou liftest me up to the wind; thou
causest me to ride *upon it,* and dissolvest
my substance.
23 For I know *that*
thou wilt bring me
to death, and *to* the
house appointed
for all living.

30:23 Death
◄ 2 Samuel 14:14
Psalm 49:10 ►

24 Howbeit he will not stretch out *his*
hand to the grave, though they cry in his
destruction.
25 Did not I weep for him that was in
trouble? was *not* my soul grieved for the
poor?
26 When I looked for good, then evil
came *unto me:* and when I waited for light,
there came darkness.
27 My bowels boiled, and rested not: the
days of affliction prevented me.
28 I went mourning without the sun: I
stood up, *and* I cried in the congregation.
29 I am a brother to dragons, and a companion to owls.
30 My skin is black upon me, and my
bones are burned with heat.
31 My harp also is *turned* to mourning,
and my organ into the voice of them that
weep.

31

1 I made a covenant with mine eyes; why
then should I think upon a maid?
2 For what portion of God *is there* from
above? and *what* inheritance of the Almighty from on high?
3 *Is* not destruction to the wicked? and a
strange *punishment* to the workers of iniquity?
4 Doth not he see
my ways, and count
all my steps?
5 If I have walked
with vanity, or if my
foot hath hasted to
deceit;

31:4 What God Knows
◄ Job 26:6
Job 34:21 ►

6 Let me be weighed in an even balance,
that God may know mine integrity.
7 If my step hath turned out of the way,
and mine heart walked after mine eyes,
and if any blot hath cleaved to mine hands;
8 *Then* let me sow, and let another eat;
yea, let my offspring be rooted out.
9 If mine heart have been deceived by a
woman, or *if* I have laid wait at my
neighbour's door;
10 *Then* let my wife grind unto another,
and let others bow down upon her.
11 For this *is* an heinous crime; yea, it *is*
an iniquity *to be punished by* the judges.
12 For it *is* a fire *that* consumeth to destruction, and would root out all mine
increase.
13 If I did despise the cause of my manservant or of my maidservant, when they
contended with me;

14What then shall I do when God riseth
up? and when he visiteth, what shall I answer him?
15Did not he that made me in the womb
make him? and did not one fashion us in
the womb?
16If I have withheld the poor from *their*
desire, or have caused the eyes of the widow to fail;
17Or have eaten my morsel myself alone,
and the fatherless hath not eaten thereof;
18(For from my youth he was brought
up with me, as *with* a father, and I have
guided her from my mother's womb;)
19If I have seen any perish for want of
clothing, or any poor without covering;
20If his loins have not blessed me, and
if he were *not* warmed with the fleece of
my sheep;
21If I have lifted up my hand against the
fatherless, when I saw my help in the gate:
22*Then* let mine arm fall from my shoulder blade, and mine arm be broken from
the bone.
23For destruction *from* God *was* a terror
to me, and by reason of his highness I
could not endure.
24If I have made
gold my hope, or
have said to the fine
gold, *Thou art* my
confidence;

31:24-25, 28
Wealth
◄ Psalm 52:7 ►

25If I rejoiced be-
cause my wealth *was* great, and because
mine hand had gotten much;
26If I beheld the sun when it shined, or
the moon walking *in* brightness;
27And my heart hath been secretly enticed, or my mouth hath kissed my hand:
28This also *were* an iniquity *to be punished by* the judge: for I should have denied the God *that is* above.
29If I rejoiced at the destruction of him
that hated me, or lifted up myself when
evil found him:
30Neither have I suffered my mouth to
sin by wishing a curse to his soul.
31If the men of my tabernacle said not,
Oh that we had of his flesh! we cannot be
satisfied.
32The stranger did not lodge in the street:
but I opened my doors to the traveller.
33If I covered my transgressions as Adam,
by hiding mine iniquity in my bosom:
34Did I fear a great multitude, or did the
contempt of families terrify me, that I kept
silence, *and* went not out of the door?
35Oh that one would hear me! behold,
my desire *is, that* the Almighty would answer me, and *that* mine adversary had written a book.
36Surely I would take it upon my shoulder, *and* bind it *as* a crown to me.
37I would declare unto him the number of my steps; as a prince would I go near
unto him.
38If my land cry against me, or that the
furrows likewise thereof complain;
39If I have eaten the fruits thereof without money, or have caused the owners
thereof to lose their life:
40Let thistles grow instead of wheat, and
cockle instead of barley. The words of Job
are ended.

32

1So these three men ceased to answer
Job, because he *was* righteous in his own
eyes.
2Then was kindled the wrath of Elihu
the son of Barachel the Buzite, of the kindred of Ram: against Job was his wrath kindled, because he justified himself rather
than God.
3Also against his three friends was his
wrath kindled, because they had found no
answer, and *yet* had condemned Job.
4Now Elihu had waited till Job had spoken, because they *were* elder than he.
5When Elihu saw that *there was* no answer in the mouth of *these* three men, then
his wrath was kindled.
6And Elihu the
son of Barachel the
Buzite answered
and said, I *am*
young, and ye *are*
very old; wherefore
I was afraid, and durst not shew you mine
opinion.

32:6 Respecting Adults
◄ Leviticus 19:32
Proverbs 23:22 ►

7I said, Days
should speak, and
multitude of years
should teach wis-
dom.

32:7 True Wisdom
◄ Job 28:28
Psalm 111:10 ►

8But *there is* a
spirit in man: and
the inspiration of
the Almighty giveth
them understand-
ing.
9Great men are

32:8
Gifts from God
◄ Ecclesiastes 2:26 ►

not *always* wise: neither do the aged understand judgment.

10 Therefore I said, Hearken to me; I also will shew mine opinion.

11 Behold, I waited for your words; I gave ear to your reasons, whilst ye searched out what to say.

12 Yea, I attended unto you, and, behold, *there was* none of you that convinced Job, or that answered his words:

13 Lest ye should say, We have found out wisdom: God thrusteth him down, not man.

14 Now he hath not directed *his* words against me: neither will I answer him with your speeches.

15 They were amazed, they answered no more: they left off speaking.

16 When I had waited, (for they spake not, but stood still, *and* answered no more;)

17 *I said,* I will answer also my part, I also will shew mine opinion.

18 For I am full of matter, the spirit within me constraineth me.

19 Behold, my belly *is* as wine *which* hath no vent; it is ready to burst like new bottles.

20 I will speak, that I may be refreshed: I will open my lips and answer.

21 Let me not, I pray you, accept any man's person, neither let me give flattering titles unto man.

22 For I know not to give flattering titles; *in so doing* my maker would soon take me away.

33

1 Wherefore, Job, I pray thee, hear my speeches, and hearken to all my words.

2 Behold, now I have opened my mouth, my tongue hath spoken in my mouth.

3 My words *shall be of* the uprightness of my heart: and my lips shall utter knowledge clearly.

4 The Spirit of God hath made me, and the breath of the Almighty hath given me life.

5 If thou canst answer me, set *thy words* in order before me, stand up.

6 Behold, I *am* according to thy wish in God's stead: I also am formed out of the clay.

7 Behold, my terror shall not make thee afraid, neither shall my hand be heavy upon thee.

8 Surely thou hast spoken in mine hearing, and I have heard the voice of *thy* words, *saying,*

9 I am clean without transgression, I *am* innocent; neither *is there* iniquity in me.

10 Behold, he findeth occasions against me, he counteth me for his enemy,

11 He putteth my feet in the stocks, he marketh all my paths.

12 Behold, *in* this thou art not just: I will answer thee, that God is greater than man.

13 Why dost thou strive against him? for he giveth not account of any of his matters.

14 For God speaketh once, yea twice, *yet man* perceiveth it not.

15 In a dream, in a vision of the night, when deep sleep falleth upon men, in slumberings upon the bed;

16 Then he openeth the ears of men, and sealeth their instruction,

17 That he may withdraw man *from his* purpose, and hide pride from man.

18 He keepeth back his soul from the pit, and his life from perishing by the sword.

19 He is chastened also with pain upon his bed, and the multitude of his bones with strong *pain:*

20 So that his life abhorreth bread, and his soul dainty meat.

21 His flesh is consumed away, that it cannot be seen; and his bones *that* were not seen stick out.

22 Yea, his soul draweth near unto the grave, and his life to the destroyers.

23 If there be a messenger with him, an interpreter, one among a thousand, to shew unto man his uprightness:

24 Then he is gracious unto him, and saith, Deliver him from going down to the pit: I have found a ransom.

25 His flesh shall be fresher than a child's: he shall return to the days of his youth:

26 He shall pray unto God, and he will be favourable unto him: and he shall see his face with joy: for he will render unto man his righteousness.

27 He looketh upon men, and *if any* say, I have sinned, and perverted *that which was* right, and it profited me not;

33:27 Confession
◄ Ezra 10:11
Proverbs 28:13 ►

28 He will deliver his soul from going into the pit, and his life shall see the light.

29 Lo, all these *things* worketh God
oftentimes with man,
30 To bring back his soul from the pit,
to be enlightened with the light of the living.
31 Mark well, O Job, hearken unto me:
hold thy peace, and I will speak.
32 If thou hast any thing to say, answer
me: speak, for I desire to justify thee.
33 If not, hearken unto me: hold thy
peace, and I shall teach thee wisdom.

34

1 Furthermore Elihu answered and said,
2 Hear my words, O ye wise *men;* and
give ear unto me, ye that have knowledge.
3 For the ear trieth words, as the mouth
tasteth meat.
4 Let us choose to us judgment: let us
know among ourselves what *is* good.
5 For Job hath said, I am righteous: and
God hath taken away my judgment.
6 Should I lie against my right? my
wound *is* incurable without transgression.
7 What man *is* like Job, *who* drinketh up
scorning like water?
8 Which goeth in company with the
workers of iniquity, and walketh with
wicked men.
9 For he hath said, It profiteth a man
nothing that he should delight himself
with God.
10 Therefore hearken unto me, ye men
of understanding: far be it from God, *that
he should do* wickedness; and *from* the Almighty, *that he should commit* iniquity.
11 For the work of a man shall he render
unto him, and cause every man to find
according to *his* ways.
12 Yea, surely God will not do wickedly,
neither will the Almighty pervert judgment.
13 Who hath given him a charge over the
earth? or who hath disposed the whole
world?
14 If he set his heart upon man, *if* he gather unto himself his spirit and his breath;
15 All flesh shall perish together, and
man shall turn again unto dust.
16 If now *thou hast* understanding, hear
this: hearken to the voice of my words.
17 Shall even he that hateth right govern?
and wilt thou condemn him that is most
just?
18 *Is it fit* to say to a king, *Thou art* wicked? *and* to princes, *Ye are* ungodly?
19 *How much less to him* that accepteth not
the persons of princes, nor regardeth the
rich more than the poor? for they all *are*
the work of his hands.
20 In a moment shall they die, and the
people shall be troubled at midnight, and
pass away: and the mighty shall be taken
away without hand.
21 For his eyes *are*
upon the ways of
man, and he seeth
all his goings.

34:21 What God Knows
◄ Job 31:4
Psalm 147:5 ►

22 *There is* no
darkness, nor
shadow of death, where the workers of
iniquity may hide themselves.
23 For he will not lay upon man more
than right; that he should enter into judgment with God.
24 He shall break in pieces mighty men
without number, and set others in their
stead.
25 Therefore he knoweth their works, and
he overturneth *them* in the night, so that
they are destroyed.
26 He striketh them as wicked men in the
open sight of others;
27 Because they turned back from him,
and would not consider any of his ways:
28 So that they cause the cry of the poor
to come unto him, and he heareth the cry
of the afflicted.
29 When he giveth quietness, who then
can make trouble? and when he hideth *his*
face, who then can behold him? whether
it be done against a nation, or against a man
only:
30 That the hypocrite reign not, lest the
people be ensnared.
31 Surely it is meet to be said unto God,
I have borne *chastisement,* I will not offend
any more:
32 *That which* I see not teach thou me: if
I have done iniquity, I will do no more.
33 *Should it be* according to thy mind? he
will recompense it, whether thou refuse,
or whether thou choose; and not I: therefore speak what thou knowest.
34 Let men of understanding tell me, and
let a wise man hearken unto me.
35 Job hath spoken without knowledge,
and his words *were* without wisdom.
36 My desire *is that* Job may be tried unto
the end because of *his* answers for wicked
men.
37 For he addeth rebellion unto his sin,

he clappeth *his hands* among us, and multiplieth his words against God.

35

1 Elihu spake moreover, and said,

2 Thinkest thou this to be right, *that* thou saidst, My righteousness *is* more than God's?

35:2
Self-righteousness
◄ Job 9:20
Proverbs 12:15 ►

3 For thou saidst, What advantage will it be unto thee? *and,* What profit shall I have, *if I be cleansed* from my sin?

4 I will answer thee, and thy companions with thee.

5 Look unto the heavens, and see; and behold the clouds *which* are higher than thou.

6 If thou sinnest, what doest thou against him? or *if* thy transgressions be multiplied, what doest thou unto him?

7 If thou be righteous, what givest thou him? or what receiveth he of thine hand?

8 Thy wickedness *may hurt* a man as thou *art;* and thy righteousness *may profit* the son of man.

9 By reason of the multitude of oppressions they make *the oppressed* to cry: they cry out by reason of the arm of the mighty.

10 But none saith, Where *is* God my maker, who giveth songs in the night;

11 Who teacheth us more than the beasts of the earth, and maketh us wiser than the fowls of heaven?

12 There they cry, but none giveth answer, because of the pride of evil men.

13 Surely God will not hear vanity, neither will the Almighty regard it.

14 Although thou sayest thou shalt not see him, *yet* judgment *is* before him; therefore trust thou in him.

15 But now, because *it is* not *so,* he hath visited in his anger; yet he knoweth *it* not in great extremity:

16 Therefore doth Job open his mouth in vain; he multiplieth words without knowledge.

36

1 Elihu also proceeded, and said,

2 Suffer me a little, and I will shew thee that *I have* yet to speak on God's behalf.

3 I will fetch my knowledge from afar, and will ascribe righteousness to my Maker.

4 For truly my words *shall* not *be* false: he that is perfect in knowledge *is* with thee.

5 Behold, God *is* mighty, and despiseth not *any: he is* mighty in strength *and* wisdom.

6 He preserveth not the life of the wicked: but giveth right to the poor.

7 He withdraweth not his eyes from the righteous: but with kings *are they* on the throne; yea, he doth establish them for ever, and they are exalted.

36:7
Rewarded Goodness
◄ Psalm 34:15 ►

8 And if *they be* bound in fetters, *and* be holden in cords of affliction;

9 Then he sheweth them their work, and their transgressions that they have exceeded.

10 He openeth also their ear to discipline, and commandeth that they return from iniquity.

11 If they obey and serve *him,* they shall spend their days in prosperity, and their years in pleasures.

12 But if they obey not, they shall perish by the sword, and they shall die without knowledge.

13 But the hypocrites in heart heap up wrath: they cry not when he bindeth them.

14 They die in youth, and their life *is* among the unclean.

15 He delivereth the poor in his affliction, and openeth their ears in oppression.

16 Even so would he have removed thee out of the strait *into* a broad place, where *there is* no straitness; and that which *should be* set on thy table should be full of fatness.

17 But thou hast fulfilled the judgment of the wicked: judgment and justice take hold *on thee.*

18 Because *there is* wrath, *beware* lest he take thee away with *his* stroke: then a great ransom cannot deliver thee.

19 Will he esteem thy riches? *no,* not gold, nor all the forces of strength.

20 Desire not the night, when people are cut off in their place.

21 Take heed, regard not iniquity: for this hast thou chosen rather than affliction.

22 Behold, God exalteth by his power: who teacheth like him?

23 Who hath enjoined him his way? or who can say, Thou hast wrought iniquity?

24 Remember that thou magnify his work, which men behold.

25 Every man may see it; man may behold *it* afar off.
26 Behold, God *is* great, and we know *him*
not, neither can the number of his years
be searched out.
27 For he maketh small the drops of water: they pour down rain according to the
vapour thereof:
28 Which the clouds do drop *and* distil
upon man abundantly.
29 Also can *any* understand the spread-
ings of the clouds, *or* the noise of his tabernacle?
30 Behold, he spreadeth his light upon
it, and covereth the bottom of the sea.
31 For by them judgeth he the people; he
giveth meat in abundance.
32 With clouds he covereth the light; and
commandeth it *not to shine* by *the cloud* that
cometh betwixt.
33 The noise thereof sheweth concerning
it, the cattle also concerning the vapour.

37

1 At this also my heart trembleth, and is
moved out of his place.
2 Hear attentively the noise of his voice,
and the sound *that* goeth out of his mouth.
3 He directeth it under the whole heaven,
and his lightning unto the ends of the
earth.
4 After it a voice roareth: he thundereth
with the voice of his excellency; and he will
not stay them when his voice is heard.
5 God thundereth marvellously with his
voice; great things doeth he, which we cannot comprehend.
6 For he saith to the snow, Be thou *on*
the earth; likewise to the small rain, and
to the great rain of his strength.
7 He sealeth up the hand of every man;
that all men may know his work.
8 Then the beasts go into dens, and remain in their places.
9 Out of the south cometh the whirlwind: and cold out of the north.
10 By the breath of God frost is given: and
the breadth of the waters is straitened.
11 Also by watering he wearieth the thick
cloud: he scattereth his bright cloud:
12 And it is turned round about by his
counsels: that they may do whatsoever he
commandeth them upon the face of the
world in the earth.
13 He causeth it to come, whether for
correction, or for his land, or for mercy.
14 Hearken unto this, O Job: stand still,
and consider the wondrous works of God.
15 Dost thou know when God disposed
them, and caused the light of his cloud to
shine?
16 Dost thou know the balancings of the
clouds, the wondrous works of him which
is perfect in knowledge?
17 How thy garments *are* warm, when he
quieteth the earth by the south *wind?*
18 Hast thou with him spread out the sky,
which is strong, *and* as a molten looking
glass?
19 Teach us what we shall say unto him;
for we cannot order *our speech* by reason of
darkness.
20 Shall it be told him that I speak? if
a man speak, surely he shall be swallowed up.
21 And now *men* see not the bright light
which *is* in the clouds: but the wind
passeth, and cleanseth them.
22 Fair weather cometh out of the north:
with God *is* terrible majesty.
23 *Touching* the Almighty, we cannot find
him out: *he is* excellent in power, and in
judgment, and in plenty of justice: he will
not afflict.
24 Men do therefore fear him: he respecteth not any *that are* wise of heart.

38

1 Then the LORD answered Job out of the
whirlwind, and said,
2 Who *is* this that darkeneth counsel by
words without knowledge?
3 Gird up now thy loins like a man; for I
will demand of thee, and answer thou me.
4 Where wast thou when I laid the foundations of the earth? declare, if thou hast
understanding.
5 Who hath laid the measures thereof, if
thou knowest? or who hath stretched the
line upon it?
6 Whereupon are the foundations thereof fastened? or who laid the corner stone
thereof;
7 When the morning stars sang together,
and all the sons of God shouted for joy?
8 Or *who* shut up the sea with doors,
when it brake forth, *as if* it had issued out
of the womb?
9 When I made the cloud the garment
thereof, and thick darkness a swaddling-
band for it,
10 And brake up for it my decreed *place,*
and set bars and doors,
11 And said, Hitherto shalt thou come,

but no further: and here shall thy proud waves be stayed?

12 Hast thou commanded the morning since thy days; *and* caused the dayspring to know his place;

13 That it might take hold of the ends of the earth, that the wicked might be shaken out of it?

14 It is turned as clay *to* the seal; and they stand as a garment.

15 And from the wicked their light is withholden, and the high arm shall be broken.

16 Hast thou entered into the springs of the sea? or hast thou walked in the search of the depth?

17 Have the gates of death been opened unto thee? or hast thou seen the doors of the shadow of death?

18 Hast thou perceived the breadth of the earth? declare if thou knowest it all.

19 Where *is* the way *where* light dwelleth? and *as for* darkness, where *is* the place thereof,

20 That thou shouldest take it to the bound thereof, and that thou shouldest know the paths *to* the house thereof?

21 Knowest thou *it,* because thou wast then born? or *because* the number of thy days *is* great?

22 Hast thou entered into the treasures of the snow? or hast thou seen the treasures of the hail,

23 Which I have reserved against the time of trouble, against the day of battle and war?

24 By what way is the light parted, *which* scattereth the east wind upon the earth?

25 Who hath divided a watercourse for the overflowing of waters, or a way for the lightning of thunder;

26 To cause it to rain on the earth, *where* no man *is; on* the wilderness, wherein *there is* no man;

27 To satisfy the desolate and waste *ground;* and to cause the bud of the tender herb to spring forth?

28 Hath the rain a father? or who hath begotten the drops of dew?

29 Out of whose womb came the ice? and the hoary frost of heaven, who hath gendered it?

30 The waters are hid as *with* a stone, and the face of the deep is frozen.

31 Canst thou bind the sweet influences of Pleiades, or loose the bands of Orion?

32 Canst thou bring forth Mazzaroth in his season? or canst thou guide Arcturus with his sons?

33 Knowest thou the ordinances of heaven? canst thou set the dominion thereof in the earth?

34 Canst thou lift up thy voice to the clouds, that abundance of waters may cover thee?

35 Canst thou send lightnings, that they may go, and say unto thee, Here we *are?*

36 Who hath put wisdom in the inward parts? or who hath given understanding to the heart?

37 Who can number the clouds in wisdom? or who can stay the bottles of heaven,

38 When the dust groweth into hardness, and the clods cleave fast together?

39 Wilt thou hunt the prey for the lion? or fill the appetite of the young lions,

40 When they couch in *their* dens, *and* abide in the covert to lie in wait?

41 Who provideth for the raven his food? when his young ones cry unto God, they wander for lack of meat.

39

1 Knowest thou the time when the wild goats of the rock bring forth? *or* canst thou mark when the hinds do calve?

2 Canst thou number the months *that* they fulfil? or knowest thou the time when they bring forth?

3 They bow themselves, they bring forth their young ones, they cast out their sorrows.

4 Their young ones are in good liking, they grow up with corn; they go forth, and return not unto them.

5 Who hath sent out the wild ass free? or who hath loosed the bands of the wild ass?

6 Whose house I have made the wilderness, and the barren land his dwellings.

7 He scorneth the multitude of the city, neither regardeth he the crying of the driver.

8 The range of the mountains *is* his pasture, and he searcheth after every green thing.

9 Will the unicorn be willing to serve thee, or abide by thy crib?

10 Canst thou bind the unicorn with his band in the furrow? or will he harrow the valleys after thee?

11 Wilt thou trust him, because his

strength *is* great? or wilt thou leave thy
labour to him?
12 Wilt thou believe him, that he will
bring home thy seed, and gather *it into* thy
barn?
13 *Gavest thou* the goodly wings unto the
peacocks? or wings and feathers unto the
ostrich?
14 Which leaveth her eggs in the earth,
and warmeth them in dust,
15 And forgetteth that the foot may crush
them, or that the wild beast may break
them.
16 She is hardened against her young
ones, as though *they were* not hers: her
labour is in vain without fear;
17 Because God hath deprived her of wisdom, neither hath he imparted to her understanding.
18 What time she lifteth up herself on
high, she scorneth the horse and his rider.
19 Hath thou given the horse strength?
hast thou clothed his neck with thunder?
20 Canst thou make him afraid as a grasshopper? the glory of his nostrils *is* terrible.
21 He paweth in the valley, and rejoiceth
in *his* strength: he goeth on to meet the
armed men.
22 He mocketh at fear, and is not affrighted; neither turneth he back from the
sword.
23 The quiver rattleth against him, the
glittering spear and the shield.
24 He swalloweth the ground with fierceness and rage: neither believeth he that *it*
is the sound of the trumpet.
25 He saith among the trumpets, Ha, ha;
and he smelleth the battle afar off, the
thunder of the captains, and the shouting.
26 Doth the hawk fly by thy wisdom, *and*
stretch her wings toward the south?
27 Doth the eagle mount up at thy command, and make her nest on high?
28 She dwelleth and abideth on the rock,
upon the crag of the rock, and the strong
place.
29 From thence she seeketh the prey, *and*
her eyes behold afar off.
30 Her young ones also suck up blood:
and where the slain *are,* there *is* she.

40

1 Moreover the LORD answered Job, and
said,
2 Shall he that contendeth with the Almighty instruct *him?* he that reproveth
God, let him answer it.
3 Then Job answered the LORD, and said,
4 Behold, I am vile; what shall I answer
thee? I will lay mine hand upon my
mouth.
5 Once have I spoken; but I will not answer: yea, twice; but I will proceed no further.
6 Then answered the LORD unto Job out
of the whirlwind, and said,
7 Gird up thy loins now like a man: I will
demand of thee, and declare thou unto me.
8 Wilt thou also disannul my judgment?
wilt thou condemn me, that thou mayest
be righteous?
9 Hast thou an arm like God? or canst
thou thunder with a voice like him?
10 Deck thyself now *with* majesty and excellency; and array thyself with glory and
beauty.
11 Cast abroad the rage of thy wrath: and
behold every one *that is* proud, and abase
him.
12 Look on every one *that is* proud, *and*
bring him low; and tread down the wicked in their place.
13 Hide them in the dust together; *and*
bind their faces in secret.
14 Then will I also confess unto thee that
thine own right hand can save thee.
15 Behold now behemoth, which I made
with thee; he eateth grass as an ox.
16 Lo now, his strength *is* in his loins, and
his force *is* in the navel of his belly.
17 He moveth his tail like a cedar: the
sinews of his stones are wrapped together.
18 His bones *are as* strong pieces of brass;
his bones *are* like bars of iron.
19 He *is* the chief of the ways of God: he
that made him can make his sword to approach *unto him.*
20 Surely the mountains bring him forth
food, where all the beasts of the field play.
21 He lieth under the shady trees, in the
covert of the reed, and fens.
22 The shady trees cover him *with* their
shadow; the willows of the brook compass
him about.
23 Behold, he drinketh up a river, *and*
hasteth not: he trusteth that he can draw
up Jordan into his mouth.
24 He taketh it with his eyes: *his* nose
pierceth through snares.

41

1 Canst thou draw out leviathan with an
hook? or his tongue with a cord *which* thou
lettest down?

2 Canst thou put an hook into his nose? or bore his jaw through with a thorn?

3 Will he make many supplications unto thee? will he speak soft *words* unto thee?

4 Will he make a covenant with thee? wilt thou take him for a servant for ever?

5 Wilt thou play with him as *with* a bird? or wilt thou bind him for thy maidens?

6 Shall the companions make a banquet of him? shall they part him among the merchants?

7 Canst thou fill his skin with barbed irons? or his head with fish spears?

8 Lay thine hand upon him, remember the battle, do no more.

9 Behold, the hope of him is in vain: shall not *one* be cast down even at the sight of him?

10 None *is so* fierce that dare stir him up: who then is able to stand before me?

11 Who hath prevented me, that I should repay *him? whatsoever is* under the whole heaven is mine.

12 I will not conceal his parts, nor his power, nor his comely proportion.

13 Who can discover the face of his garment? *or* who can come *to him* with his double bridle?

14 Who can open the doors of his face? his teeth *are* terrible round about.

15 *His* scales *are his* pride, shut up together *as with* a close seal.

16 One is so near to another, that no air can come between them.

17 They are joined one to another, they stick together, that they cannot be sundered.

18 By his neesings a light doth shine, and his eyes *are* like the eyelids of the morning.

19 Out of his mouth go burning lamps, *and* sparks of fire leap out.

20 Out of his nostrils goeth smoke, as *out* of a seething pot or caldron.

21 His breath kindleth coals, and a flame goeth out of his mouth.

22 In his neck remaineth strength, and sorrow is turned into joy before him.

23 The flakes of his flesh are joined together: they are firm in themselves; they cannot be moved.

24 His heart is as firm as a stone; yea, as hard as a piece of the nether *millstone.*

25 When he raiseth up himself, the mighty are afraid: by reason of breakings they purify themselves.

26 The sword of him that layeth at him cannot hold: the spear, the dart, nor the habergeon.

27 He esteemeth iron as straw, *and* brass as rotten wood.

28 The arrow cannot make him flee: slingstones are turned with him into stubble.

29 Darts are counted as stubble: he laugheth at the shaking of a spear.

30 Sharp stones *are* under him: he spreadeth sharp pointed things upon the mire.

31 He maketh the deep to boil like a pot: he maketh the sea like a pot of ointment.

32 He maketh a path to shine after him; *one* would think the deep *to be* hoary.

33 Upon earth there is not his like, who is made without fear.

34 He beholdeth all high *things:* he *is* a king over all the children of pride.

42

1 Then Job answered the LORD, and said,

2 I know that thou canst do every *thing,* and *that* no thought can be withholden from thee.

42:2
All-powerful
◄ Psalm 115:3 ►

3 Who *is* he that hideth counsel without knowledge? therefore have I uttered that I understood not; things too wonderful for me, which I knew not.

4 Hear, I beseech thee, and I will speak: I will demand of thee, and declare thou unto me.

5 I have heard of thee by the hearing of the ear: but now mine eye seeth thee.

6 Wherefore I abhor *myself,* and repent in dust and ashes.

7 And it was *so,* that after the LORD had spoken these words unto Job, the LORD said to Eliphaz the Temanite, My wrath is kindled against thee, and against thy two friends: for ye have not spoken of me *the thing that is* right, as my servant Job *hath.*

8 Therefore take unto you now seven bullocks and seven rams, and go to my servant Job, and offer up for yourselves a burnt offering; and my servant Job shall pray for you: for him will I accept: lest I deal with you *after your* folly, in that ye have not spoken of me *the thing which is* right, like my servant Job.

9 So Eliphaz the Temanite and Bildad the

Shuhite *and* Zophar the Naamathite went, and did according as the LORD commanded them: the LORD also accepted Job.

42:9 Accepted by God
◄ 2 Samuel 24:23
Ezekiel 20:40 ►

10And the LORD turned the captivity of Job, when he prayed for his friends: also the LORD gave Job twice as much as he had before.

42:10
Praying for Others
◄ 2 Chronicles 30:18
Psalm 106:23 ►

11Then came there unto him all his brethren, and all his sisters, and all they that had been of his acquaintance before, and did eat bread with him in his house: and they bemoaned him, and comforted him over all the evil that the LORD had brought upon him: every man also gave him a piece of money, and every one an earring of gold.

12So the LORD blessed the latter end of Job more than his beginning: for he had fourteen thousand sheep, and six thousand camels, and a thousand yoke of oxen, and a thousand she asses.

13He had also seven sons and three daughters.

14And he called the name of the first, Jemima; and the name of the second, Kezia; and the name of the third, Keren-happuch.

15And in all the land were no women found *so* fair as the daughters of Job: and their father gave them inheritance among their brethren.

16After this lived Job an hundred and forty years, and saw his sons, and his sons' sons, *even* four generations.

17So Job died, *being* old and full of days.

Psalms

AUTHOR
David, Asaph, sons of Korah, Solomon, Heman, Ethan, Moses, and other unnamed folk

MAIN POINT
Poems and songs are important ways to talk to the Lord, whether to praise, confess, cry for help, or worship him.

DATE WRITTEN
1440-586 B.C.

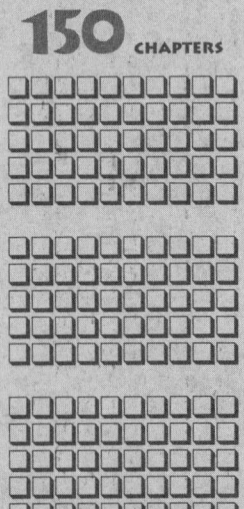

150 CHAPTERS

MAIN PEOPLE

David, Moses, other people of God

SPECIAL FEATURES

- *Is the longest book in the Bible*
- *Is the Bible's biggest collection of songs*
- *Is the Bible's most emotional book*
- *Organized into five books with different themes ranging from "Let us praise the LORD!" to "God, when are you going to smash our enemies?"*
- *Includes Psalm 119, which is not only a tribute to God's Word but also a Hebrew word puzzle*
- *Second book of Poetry*

HOW THE BOOK GOT ITS NAME

The word psalm means "sacred song" and reminds us that this collection of poetry was set to music.

Psalm 1

1 Blessed *is* the man that walketh not in the counsel of the ungodly, nor standeth in the way of sinners, nor sitteth in the seat of the scornful.

1:1 Bad Friends
◄ Exodus 34:12
Proverbs 1:15 ►

2 But his delight *is* in the law of the LORD; and in his law doth he meditate day and night.

3 And he shall be like a tree planted by the rivers of water, that bringeth forth his fruit in his season; his leaf also shall not wither; and whatsoever he doeth shall prosper.

4 The ungodly *are* not so: but *are* like the chaff which the wind driveth away.

5 Therefore the ungodly shall not stand in the judgment, nor sinners in the congregation of the righteous.

6 For the LORD knoweth the way of the righteous: but the way of the ungodly shall perish.

Psalm 2

1 Why do the heathen rage, and the people imagine a vain thing?

2 The kings of the earth set themselves, and the rulers take counsel together, against the LORD, and against his anointed, *saying,*

3 Let us break their bands asunder, and cast away their cords from us.

4 He that sitteth in the heavens shall laugh: the Lord shall have them in derision.

5 Then shall he speak unto them in his wrath, and vex them in his sore displeasure.

6 Yet have I set my king upon my holy hill of Zion.

2:6
Jesus the King
◄ Isaiah 9:7 ►

7 I will declare the decree: the LORD hath said unto me, Thou *art* my Son; this day have I begotten thee.

8 Ask of me, and I shall give *thee* the heathen *for* thine inheritance, and the uttermost parts of the earth *for* thy possession.

9 Thou shalt break them with a rod of iron; thou shalt dash them in pieces like a potter's vessel.

10 Be wise now therefore, O ye kings: be instructed, ye judges of the earth.

2:10-11
Leaders Should...
◄ 2 Chronicles 19:6
Proverbs 16:12 ►

11 Serve the LORD with fear, and rejoice with trembling.

12 Kiss the Son, lest he be angry, and ye perish *from* the way, when his wrath is kindled but a little. Blessed *are* all they that put their trust in him.

2:12 God's Anger
◄ 2 Kings 22:13
John 3:36 ►

Psalm 3

A Psalm of David, when he fled from Absalom his son.

1 LORD, how are they increased that trouble me! many *are* they that rise up against me.

2 Many *there be* which say of my soul, *There is* no help for him in God. Selah.

3 But thou, O LORD, *art* a shield for me; my glory, and the lifter up of mine head.

4 I cried unto the LORD with my voice, and he heard me out of his holy hill. Selah.

5 I laid me down and slept; I awaked; for the LORD sustained me.

6 I will not be afraid of ten thousands of people, that have set *themselves* against me round about.

7 Arise, O LORD; save me, O my God: for thou hast smitten all mine enemies *upon* the cheek bone; thou hast broken the teeth of the ungodly.

8 Salvation *belongeth* unto the LORD: thy blessing *is* upon thy people. Selah.

Psalm 4

To the chief Musician on Neginoth, A Psalm of David.

1 Hear me when I call, O God of my righteousness: thou hast enlarged me *when I was* in distress; have mercy upon me, and hear my prayer.

2 O ye sons of men, how long *will ye turn*

my glory into shame? *how long* will ye love
vanity, *and* seek after leasing? Selah.
3But know that the LORD hath set apart
him that is godly for himself: the LORD will
hear when I call unto him.
4Stand in awe,
and sin not: com-
mune with your
own heart upon
your bed, and be
still. Selah.

4:4 Respecting God
◄ Joshua 5:15
Psalm 33:8 ►

5Offer the sacrifices of righteousness,
and put your trust in the LORD.
6*There be* many that say, Who will shew
us *any* good? LORD, lift thou up the light
of thy countenance upon us.
7Thou hast put
gladness in my
heart, more than in
the time *that* their
corn and their wine
increased.

4:7 Gladness
◄ Nehemiah 8:17
Psalm 45:15 ►

8I will both lay me down in peace, and
sleep: for thou, LORD, only makest me
dwell in safety.

Psalm 5

To the chief Musician upon Nehiloth,
A Psalm of David.

1Give ear to my words, O LORD, consider my meditation.
2Hearken unto the voice of my cry, my
King, and my God: for unto thee will I
pray.
3My voice shalt
thou hear in the
morning, O LORD;
in the morning will
I direct *my prayer*
unto thee, and will
look up.

5:3 Praying
◄ Psalm 55:17 ►

4For thou *art* not a God that hath pleasure in wickedness: neither shall evil dwell
with thee.
5The foolish shall not stand in thy sight:
thou hatest all workers of iniquity.
6Thou shalt de-
stroy them that
speak leasing: the
LORD will abhor the
bloody and deceit-
ful man.

5:6 Lying
◄ Leviticus 19:11
Psalm 31:18 ►

7But as for me, I will come *into* thy house
in the multitude of thy mercy: *and* in thy
fear will I worship toward thy holy temple.
8Lead me, O LORD, in thy righteousness
because of mine enemies; make thy way
straight before my face.
9For *there is* no faithfulness in their
mouth; their inward part *is* very wickedness; their throat *is* an open sepulchre; they
flatter with their tongue.
10Destroy thou them, O God; let them
fall by their own counsels; cast them out
in the multitude of their transgressions; for
they have rebelled against thee.
11But let all those
that put their trust
in thee rejoice: let
them ever shout for
joy, because thou
defendest them: let
them also that love thy name be joyful in
thee.

5:11 Rejoicing
◄ Deuteronomy 16:11
Psalm 32:11 ►

12For thou, LORD, wilt bless the righteous; with favour wilt thou compass him
as *with* a shield.

Psalm 6

To the chief Musician on Neginoth upon
Sheminith, A Psalm of David.

1O LORD, rebuke me not in thine anger,
neither chasten me in thy hot displeasure.
2Have mercy
upon me, O LORD;
for I *am* weak:
O LORD, heal me;
for my bones are
vexed.

6:2 Praying for Mercy
◄ 1 Kings 8:30
Psalm 27:7 ►

3My soul is also sore vexed: but thou,
O LORD, how long?
4Return, O LORD, deliver my soul: oh
save me for thy mercies' sake.
5For in death *there is* no remembrance
of thee: in the grave who shall give thee
thanks?
6I am weary with my groaning; all the
night make I my bed to swim; I water my
couch with my tears.
7Mine eye is consumed because of grief;
it waxeth old because of all mine enemies.
8Depart from me, all ye workers of iniquity; for the LORD hath heard the voice
of my weeping.
9The LORD hath heard my supplication;
the LORD will receive my prayer.

10Let all mine enemies be ashamed and
sore vexed: let them return *and* be ashamed
suddenly.

Psalm 7

Shiggaion of David, which he sang
unto the LORD, concerning the words
of Cush the Benjamite.

1O LORD my God,
in thee do I put my
trust: save me from
all them that perse-
cute me, and deliv-
er me:

> **7:1**
> **Bullies**
> ◄ Psalm 31:15 ►

2Lest he tear my soul like a lion, rend-
ing *it* in pieces, while *there is* none to deliver.
3O LORD my God, if I have done this; if
there be iniquity in my hands;
4If I have rewarded evil unto him that
was at peace with me; (yea, I have delivered him that without cause is mine
enemy:)
5Let the enemy persecute my soul, and
take *it;* yea, let him tread down my life
upon the earth, and lay mine honour in
the dust. Selah.
6Arise, O LORD, in thine anger, lift up
thyself because of the rage of mine enemies: and awake for me *to* the judgment
that thou hast commanded.
7So shall the congregation of the people compass thee about: for their sakes
therefore return thou on high.
8The LORD shall judge the people: judge
me, O LORD, according to my righteousness, and according to mine integrity *that*
is in me.
9Oh let the wickedness of the wicked
come to an end; but establish the just: for
the righteous God
trieth the hearts and
reins.
10My defence *is*
of God, which
saveth the upright
in heart.
11God judgeth
the righteous, and
God is angry *with*
the wicked every day.
12If he turn not,
he will whet his sword; he hath bent his
bow, and made it ready.

> **7:10**
> **Why Do Right?**
> ◄ Psalm 32:11 ►

> **7:12 Warning!**
> ◄ 1 Kings 9:7
> Isaiah 14:23 ►

13He hath also prepared for him the instruments of death; he ordaineth his arrows against the persecutors.
14Behold, he travaileth with iniquity,
and hath conceived mischief, and brought
forth falsehood.
15He made a pit, and digged it, and is
fallen into the ditch *which* he made.
16His mischief shall return upon his
own head, and his violent dealing shall
come down upon his own pate.
17I will praise the LORD according to his
righteousness: and will sing praise to the
name of the LORD most high.

Psalm 8

To the chief Musician upon Gittith,
A Psalm of David.

1O LORD our Lord, how excellent *is* thy
name in all the earth! who hast set thy glory above the heavens.
2Out of the
mouth of babes
and sucklings hast
thou ordained
strength because of
thine enemies, that
thou mightest still the enemy and the
avenger.

> **8:2**
> **Weakness**
> ◄ 1 Corinthians 1:27 ►

3When I consider thy heavens, the work
of thy fingers, the moon and the stars,
which thou hast ordained;
4What is man, that thou art mindful of
him? and the son of man, that thou visitest
him?
5For thou hast made him a little lower
than the angels, and hast crowned him
with glory and honour.
6Thou madest
him to have domin-
ion over the works
of thy hands; thou
hast put all *things*
under his feet:

> **8:6 Animals vs. People**
> ◄ Genesis 1:28
> Psalm 82:6 ►

7All sheep and oxen, yea, and the beasts
of the field;
8The fowl of the air, and the fish of the
sea, *and whatsoever* passeth through the
paths of the seas.
9O LORD our Lord, how excellent *is* thy
name in all the earth!

Psalm 9

To the chief Musician upon Muthlabben, A Psalm of David.

1 I will praise *thee,* O LORD, with my whole heart; I will shew forth all thy marvellous works.

2 I will be glad and rejoice in thee: I will sing praise to thy name, O thou most High.

3 When mine enemies are turned back, they shall fall and perish at thy presence.

4 For thou hast maintained my right and my cause; thou satest in the throne judging right.

5 Thou hast rebuked the heathen, thou hast destroyed the wicked, thou hast put out their name for ever and ever.

6 O thou enemy, destructions are come to a perpetual end: and thou hast destroyed cities; their memorial is perished with them.

7 But the LORD shall endure for ever: he hath prepared his throne for judgment.

8 And he shall judge the world in righteousness, he shall minister judgment to the people in uprightness.

9 The LORD also will be a refuge for the oppressed, a refuge in times of trouble.

10 And they that know thy name will put their trust in thee: for thou, LORD, hast not forsaken them that seek thee.

11 Sing praises to the LORD, which dwelleth in Zion: declare among the people his doings.

9:11 Praising God
◄ Psalm 33:2 ►

12 When he maketh inquisition for blood, he remembereth them: he forgetteth not the cry of the humble.

13 Have mercy upon me, O LORD; consider my trouble *which I suffer* of them that hate me, thou that liftest me up from the gates of death:

14 That I may shew forth all thy praise in the gates of the daughter of Zion: I will rejoice in thy salvation.

15 The heathen are sunk down in the pit *that* they made: in the net which they hid is their own foot taken.

16 The LORD is known *by* the judgment *which* he executeth: the wicked is snared in the work of his own hands. Higgaion. Selah.

17 The wicked shall be turned into hell, *and* all the nations that forget God.

9:17 Don't Forget...
◄ Judges 8:34
Psalm 50:22 ►

18 For the needy shall not alway be forgotten: the expectation of the poor shall *not* perish for ever.

19 Arise, O LORD; let not man prevail: let the heathen be judged in thy sight.

20 Put them in fear, O LORD: *that* the nations may know themselves *to be but* men. Selah.

Psalm 10

1 Why standest thou afar off, O LORD? *why* hidest thou *thyself* in times of trouble?

2 The wicked in *his* pride doth persecute the poor: let them be taken in the devices that they have imagined.

10:2 Arrogance
◄ Psalm 73:6 ►

3 For the wicked boasteth of his heart's desire, and blesseth the covetous, *whom* the LORD abhorreth.

4 The wicked, through the pride of his countenance, will not seek *after God:* God *is* not in all his thoughts.

5 His ways are always grievous; thy judgments *are* far above out of his sight: *as for* all his enemies, he puffeth at them.

6 He hath said in his heart, I shall not be moved: for *I shall* never *be* in adversity.

7 His mouth is full of cursing and deceit and fraud: under his tongue *is* mischief and vanity.

10:7 Mischief
◄ Job 15:35
Psalm 36:4 ►

8 He sitteth in the lurking places of the villages: in the secret places doth he murder the innocent: his eyes are privily set against the poor.

9 He lieth in wait secretly as a lion in his den: he lieth in wait to catch the poor: he doth catch the poor, when he draweth him into his net.

10 He croucheth, *and* humbleth himself, that the poor may fall by his strong ones.

11 He hath said in his heart, God hath forgotten: he hideth his face; he will never see *it.*

12 Arise, O LORD; O God, lift up thine hand: forget not the humble.

13 Wherefore doth the wicked contemn God? he hath said in his heart, Thou wilt not require *it.*

14 Thou hast seen *it;* for thou beholdest mischief and spite, to requite *it* with thy hand: the poor committeth himself unto thee; thou art the helper of the fatherless.

> **10:14**
> **God's Care for Kids**
> ◄ Deuteronomy 10:18
> Psalm 68:5 ►

15 Break thou the arm of the wicked and the evil *man:* seek out his wickedness *till* thou find none.

16 The LORD *is* King for ever and ever: the heathen are perished out of his land.

17 LORD, thou hast heard the desire of the humble: thou wilt prepare their heart, thou wilt cause thine ear to hear:

18 To judge the fatherless and the oppressed, that the man of the earth may no more oppress.

Psalm 11

To the chief Musician, *A Psalm* of David.

1 In the LORD put I my trust: How say ye to my soul, Flee *as* a bird to your mountain?

2 For, lo, the wicked bend *their* bow, they make ready their arrow upon the string, that they may privily shoot at the upright in heart.

3 If the foundations be destroyed, what can the righteous do?

4 The LORD *is* in his holy temple, the LORD'S throne *is* in heaven: his eyes behold, his eyelids try, the children of men.

5 The LORD trieth the righteous: but the wicked and him that loveth violence his soul hateth.

6 Upon the wicked he shall rain snares, fire and brimstone, and an horrible tempest: *this shall be* the portion of their cup.

7 For the righteous LORD loveth righteousness; his countenance doth behold the upright.

Psalm 12

To the chief Musician upon Sheminith,
A Psalm of David.

1 Help, LORD; for the godly man ceaseth; for the faithful fail from among the children of men.

2 They speak vanity every one with his neighbour: *with* flattering lips *and* with a double heart do they speak.

3 The LORD shall cut off all flattering lips, *and* the tongue that speaketh proud things:

4 Who have said, With our tongue will we prevail; our lips *are* our own: who *is* lord over us?

5 For the oppression of the poor, for the sighing of the needy, now will I arise, saith the LORD; I will set *him* in safety *from him that* puffeth at him.

> **12:5**
> **Promises to the Poor**
> ◄ Job 5:15
> Psalm 14:6 ►

6 The words of the LORD *are* pure words: *as* silver tried in a furnace of earth, purified seven times.

7 Thou shalt keep them, O LORD, thou shalt preserve them from this generation for ever.

8 The wicked walk on every side, when the vilest men are exalted.

Psalm 13

To the chief Musician, A Psalm of David.

1 How long wilt thou forget me, O LORD? for ever? how long wilt thou hide thy face from me?

> **13:1**
> **Pray and Wait**
> ◄ Psalm 40:17 ►

2 How long shall I take counsel in my soul, *having* sorrow in my heart daily? how long shall mine enemy be exalted over me?

3 Consider *and* hear me, O LORD my God: lighten mine eyes, lest I sleep the *sleep of* death;

4 Lest mine enemy say, I have prevailed against him; *and* those that trouble me rejoice when I am moved.

5 But I have trusted in thy mercy; my heart shall rejoice in thy salvation.

6 I will sing unto the LORD, because he hath dealt bountifully with me.

Psalm 14

To the chief Musician, *A Psalm* of David.

1 The fool hath said in his heart, *There is* no God. They are corrupt, they have done abominable works, *there is* none that doeth good.

2 The LORD looked down from heaven upon the children of men, to see if there were any that did understand, *and* seek God.

3 They are all gone aside, they are *all* together become filthy: *there is* none that doeth good, no, not one.

14:3 Everyone Sins
◄ 1 Kings 8:46
Psalm 53:3 ►

4 Have all the workers of iniquity no knowledge? who eat up my people *as* they eat bread, and call not upon the LORD.

5 There were they in great fear: for God *is* in the generation of the righteous.

6 Ye have shamed the counsel of the poor, because the LORD *is* his refuge.

14:6 Promises to the Poor
◄ Psalm 12:5
Psalm 68:10 ►

7 Oh that the salvation of Israel *were come* out of Zion! when the LORD bringeth back the captivity of his people, Jacob shall rejoice, *and* Israel shall be glad.

Psalm 15

A Psalm of David.

1 LORD, who shall abide in thy tabernacle? who shall dwell in thy holy hill?

2 He that walketh uprightly, and worketh righteousness, and speaketh the truth in his heart.

3 *He that* backbiteth not with his tongue, nor doeth evil to his neighbour, nor taketh up a reproach against his neighbour.

4 In whose eyes a vile person is contemned; but he honoureth them that fear the LORD. *He that* sweareth to *his own* hurt, and changeth not.

5 *He that* putteth not out his money to usury, nor taketh reward against the innocent. He that doeth these *things* shall never be moved.

Psalm 16

Michtam of David.

1 Preserve me, O God: for in thee do I put my trust.

2 *O my soul,* thou hast said unto the LORD, Thou *art* my Lord: my goodness *extendeth* not to thee;

3 *But* to the saints that *are* in the earth, and *to* the excellent, in whom *is* all my delight.

4 Their sorrows shall be multiplied *that* hasten *after* another *god:* their drink offerings of blood will I not offer, nor take up their names into my lips.

5 The LORD *is* the portion of mine inheritance and of my cup: thou maintainest my lot.

6 The lines are fallen unto me in pleasant *places;* yea, I have a goodly heritage.

7 I will bless the LORD, who hath given me counsel: my reins also instruct me in the night seasons.

8 I have set the LORD always before me: because *he is* at my right hand, I shall not be moved.

9 Therefore my heart is glad, and my glory rejoiceth: my flesh also shall rest in hope.

10 For thou wilt not leave my soul in hell; neither wilt thou suffer thine Holy One to see corruption.

11 Thou wilt shew me the path of life: in thy presence *is* fulness of joy; at thy right hand *there are* pleasures for evermore.

16:11 Joy
◄ Nehemiah 8:10
Psalm 30:5 ►

16:11 Right Paths
◄ Psalm 23:3 ►

Psalm 17

A Prayer of David.

1 Hear the right, O LORD, attend unto my cry, give ear unto my prayer, *that goeth* not out of feigned lips.

2 Let my sentence come forth from thy presence; let thine eyes behold the things that are equal.

3 Thou hast proved mine heart;

17:3 Life Tests
◄ Daniel 12:10 ►

thou hast visited *me* in the night; thou hast
tried me, *and* shalt find nothing; I am purposed *that* my mouth shall not transgress.
4 Concerning the words of men, by the
word of thy lips I have kept *me from* the
paths of the destroyer.
5 Hold up my goings in thy paths, *that*
my footsteps slip not.
6 I have called upon thee, for thou wilt
hear me, O God: incline thine ear unto me,
and hear my speech.
7 Shew thy marvellous lovingkindness,
O thou that savest by thy right hand them
which put their trust *in thee* from those that
rise up *against them.*
8 Keep me as the apple of the eye, hide
me under the shadow of thy wings,
9 From the wicked that oppress me, *from*
my deadly enemies, *who* compass me
about.
10 They are inclosed in their own fat: with
their mouth they speak proudly.
11 They have now compassed us in our
steps: they have set their eyes bowing down
to the earth;
12 Like as a lion *that* is greedy of his prey,
and as it were a young lion lurking in secret places.
13 Arise, O LORD, disappoint him, cast
him down: deliver my soul from the wicked, *which is* thy sword:
14 From men *which are* thy hand, O LORD,
from men of the world, *which have* their
portion in *this* life, and whose belly thou
fillest with thy hid *treasure:* they are full of
children, and leave the rest of their *substance* to their babes.
15 As for me, I will
behold thy face in
righteousness: I
shall be satisfied,
when I awake, with
thy likeness.

17:15
Satisfaction
◄ Psalm 36:8 ►

Psalm 18

To the chief Musician, *A Psalm* of David, the servant of the LORD, who spake unto the LORD the words of this song in the day *that* the LORD delivered him from the hand of all his enemies, and from the hand of Saul: And he said,

1 I will love thee, O LORD, my strength.
2 The LORD *is* my rock, and my fortress,
and my deliverer; my God, my strength,
in whom I will trust; my buckler, and the
horn of my salvation, *and* my high tower.
3 I will call upon the LORD, *who is worthy*
to be praised: so shall I be saved from mine
enemies.
4 The sorrows of death compassed me,
and the floods of ungodly men made me
afraid.
5 The sorrows of hell compassed me
about: the snares of death prevented me.
6 In my distress I called upon the LORD,
and cried unto my God: he heard my voice
out of his temple, and my cry came before
him, *even* into his ears.
7 Then the earth shook and trembled; the
foundations also of the hills moved and
were shaken, because he was wroth.
8 There went up a smoke out of his nostrils, and fire out of his mouth devoured:
coals were kindled by it.
9 He bowed the heavens also, and came
down: and darkness *was* under his feet.
10 And he rode upon a cherub, and did
fly: yea, he did fly upon the wings of the
wind.
11 He made darkness his secret place; his
pavilion round about him *were* dark waters *and* thick clouds of the skies.
12 At the brightness *that was* before him
his thick clouds passed, hail *stones* and
coals of fire.
13 The LORD also thundered in the heavens, and the Highest gave his voice; hail
stones and coals of fire.
14 Yea, he sent out his arrows, and scattered them; and he shot out lightnings, and
discomfited them.
15 Then the channels of waters were seen,
and the foundations of the world were discovered at thy rebuke, O LORD, at the blast
of the breath of thy nostrils.
16 He sent from above, he took me, he
drew me out of many waters.
17 He delivered me from my strong
enemy, and from them which hated me:
for they were too strong for me.
18 They prevented me in the day of my
calamity: but the LORD was my stay.
19 He brought me forth also into a large
place; he delivered me, because he delighted in me.
20 The LORD rewarded me according to
my righteousness; according to the cleanness of my hands hath he recompensed me.

21 For I have kept the ways of the LORD, and have not wickedly departed from my God.

22 For all his judgments *were* before me, and I did not put away his statutes from me.

23 I was also upright before him, and I kept myself from mine iniquity.

24 Therefore hath the LORD recompensed me according to my righteousness, according to the cleanness of my hands in his eyesight.

25 With the merciful thou wilt shew thyself merciful; with an upright man thou wilt shew thyself upright;

26 With the pure thou wilt shew thyself pure; and with the froward thou wilt shew thyself froward.

27 For thou wilt save the afflicted people; but wilt bring down high looks.

28 For thou wilt light my candle: the LORD my God will enlighten my darkness.

29 For by thee I have run through a troop; and by my God have I leaped over a wall.

30 *As for* God, his way *is* perfect: the word of the LORD is tried: he *is* a buckler to all those that trust in him.

18:30 God's Perfection
◄ 2 Samuel 22:31
Ecclesiastes 3:14 ►

31 For who *is* God save the LORD? or who *is* a rock save our God?

18:30
God's Ways
◄ Isaiah 55:8-9 ►

32 *It is* God that girdeth me with strength, and maketh my way perfect.

33 He maketh my feet like hinds' *feet*, and setteth me upon my high places.

34 He teacheth my hands to war, so that a bow of steel is broken by mine arms.

35 Thou hast also given me the shield of thy salvation: and thy right hand hath holden me up, and thy gentleness hath made me great.

36 Thou hast enlarged my steps under me, that my feet did not slip.

37 I have pursued mine enemies, and overtaken them: neither did I turn again till they were consumed.

38 I have wounded them that they were not able to rise: they are fallen under my feet.

39 For thou hast girded me with strength unto the battle: thou hast subdued under me those that rose up against me.

40 Thou hast also given me the necks of mine enemies; that I might destroy them that hate me.

41 They cried, but *there was* none to save *them: even* unto the LORD, but he answered them not.

42 Then did I beat them small as the dust before the wind: I did cast them out as the dirt in the streets.

43 Thou hast delivered me from the strivings of the people; *and* thou hast made me the head of the heathen: a people *whom* I have not known shall serve me.

44 As soon as they hear of me, they shall obey me: the strangers shall submit themselves unto me.

45 The strangers shall fade away, and be afraid out of their close places.

46 The LORD liveth; and blessed *be* my rock; and let the God of my salvation be exalted.

47 *It is* God that avengeth me, and subdueth the people under me.

48 He delivereth me from mine enemies: yea, thou liftest me up above those that rise up against me: thou hast delivered me from the violent man.

49 Therefore will I give thanks unto thee, O LORD, among the heathen, and sing praises unto thy name.

50 Great deliverance giveth he to his king; and sheweth mercy to his anointed, to David, and to his seed for evermore.

Psalm 19

To the chief Musician, A Psalm of David.

1 The heavens declare the glory of God; and the firmament sheweth his handywork.

19:1
Nature Teaches Us
◄ Psalm 97:6 ►

2 Day unto day uttereth speech, and night unto night sheweth knowledge.

3 *There is* no speech nor language, *where* their voice is not heard.

4 Their line is gone out through all the earth, and their words to the end of the world. In them hath he set a tabernacle for the sun,

5 Which *is* as a bridegroom coming out

of his chamber, *and* rejoiceth as a strong man to run a race.

6 His going forth *is* from the end of the heaven, and his circuit unto the ends of it: and there is nothing hid from the heat thereof.

7 The law of the LORD *is* perfect, converting the soul: the testimony of the LORD *is* sure, making wise the simple.

8 The statutes of the LORD *are* right, rejoicing the heart: the commandment of the LORD *is* pure, enlightening the eyes.

19:8
The Bible as a Guide
◄ Psalm 119:105 ►

9 The fear of the LORD *is* clean, enduring for ever: the judgments of the LORD *are* true *and* righteous altogether.

10 More to be desired *are they* than gold, yea, than much fine gold: sweeter also than honey and the honeycomb.

11 Moreover by them is thy servant warned: *and* in keeping of them *there is* great reward.

12 Who can understand *his* errors? cleanse thou me from secret *faults.*

13 Keep back thy servant also from presumptuous *sins;* let them not have dominion over me: then shall I be upright, and I shall be innocent from the great transgression.

14 Let the words of my mouth, and the meditation of my heart, be acceptable in thy sight, O LORD, my strength, and my redeemer.

Psalm 20

To the chief Musician, A Psalm of David.

1 The LORD hear thee in the day of trouble; the name of the God of Jacob defend thee;

2 Send thee help from the sanctuary, and strengthen thee out of Zion;

3 Remember all thy offerings, and accept thy burnt sacrifice; Selah.

4 Grant thee according to thine own heart, and fulfil all thy counsel.

5 We will rejoice in thy salvation, and in the name of our God we will set up *our* banners: the LORD fulfil all thy petitions.

6 Now know I that the LORD saveth his anointed; he will hear him from his holy heaven with the saving strength of his right hand.

7 Some *trust* in chariots, and some in horses: but we will remember the name of the LORD our God.

8 They are brought down and fallen: but we are risen, and stand upright.

9 Save, LORD: let the king hear us when we call.

Psalm 21

To the chief Musician, A Psalm of David.

1 The king shall joy in thy strength, O LORD; and in thy salvation how greatly shall he rejoice!

2 Thou hast given him his heart's desire, and hast not withholden the request of his lips. Selah.

3 For thou preventest him with the blessings of goodness: thou settest a crown of pure gold on his head.

4 He asked life of thee, *and* thou gavest *it* him, *even* length of days for ever and ever.

5 His glory *is* great in thy salvation: honour and majesty hast thou laid upon him.

6 For thou hast made him most blessed for ever: thou hast made him exceeding glad with thy countenance.

7 For the king trusteth in the LORD, and through the mercy of the most High he shall not be moved.

8 Thine hand shall find out all thine enemies: thy right hand shall find out those that hate thee.

9 Thou shalt make them as a fiery oven in the time of thine anger: the LORD shall swallow them up in his wrath, and the fire shall devour them.

10 Their fruit shalt thou destroy from the earth, and their seed from among the children of men.

11 For they intended evil against thee: they imagined a mischievous device, *which* they are not able *to perform.*

12 Therefore shalt thou make them turn their back, *when* thou shalt make ready *thine arrows* upon thy strings against the face of them.

13 Be thou exalted, LORD, in thine own strength: *so* will we sing and praise thy power.

Psalm 22

To the chief Musician
upon Aijeleth Shahar,
A Psalm of David.

1 My God, my God, why hast thou forsaken me? *why art thou so* far from helping me, *and from* the words of my roaring?

2 O my God, I cry in the daytime, but thou hearest not; and in the night season, and am not silent.

3 But thou *art* holy, *O thou* that inhabitest the praises of Israel.

4 Our fathers trusted in thee: they trusted, and thou didst deliver them.

5 They cried unto thee, and were delivered: they trusted in thee, and were not confounded.

6 But I *am* a worm, and no man; a reproach of men, and despised of the people.

7 All they that see me laugh me to scorn: they shoot out the lip, they shake the head *saying*,

22:7 Mocking
< Nehemiah 4:1
Acts 2:13 >

8 He trusted on the LORD *that* he would deliver him: let him deliver him, seeing he delighted in him.

9 But thou *art* he that took me out of the womb: thou didst make me hope *when I was* upon my mother's breasts.

10 I was cast upon thee from the womb: thou *art* my God from my mother's belly.

11 Be not far from me; for trouble *is* near; for *there is* none to help.

12 Many bulls have compassed me: strong *bulls* of Bashan have beset me round.

13 They gaped upon me *with* their mouths, *as* a ravening and a roaring lion.

14 I am poured out like water, and all my bones are out of joint: my heart is like wax; it is melted in the midst of my bowels.

15 My strength is dried up like a potsherd; and my tongue cleaveth to my jaws; and thou hast brought me into the dust of death.

16 For dogs have compassed me: the assembly of the wicked have inclosed me: they pierced my hands and my feet.

17 I may tell all my bones: they look *and* stare upon me.

18 They part my garments among them, and cast lots upon my vesture.

19 But be not thou far from me, O LORD: O my strength, haste thee to help me.

20 Deliver my soul from the sword; my darling from the power of the dog.

21 Save me from the lion's mouth: for thou hast heard me from the horns of the unicorns.

22 I will declare thy name unto my brethren: in the midst of the congregation will I praise thee.

23 Ye that fear the LORD, praise him; all ye the seed of Jacob, glorify him; and fear him, all ye the seed of Israel.

24 For he hath not despised nor abhorred the affliction of the afflicted; neither hath he hid his face from him; but when he cried unto him, he heard.

25 My praise *shall be* of thee in the great congregation: I will pay my vows before them that fear him.

26 The meek shall eat and be satisfied: they shall praise the LORD that seek him: your heart shall live for ever.

22:26 Meekness
< Psalm 37:11 >

27 All the ends of the world shall remember and turn unto the LORD: and all the kindreds of the nations shall worship before thee.

28 For the kingdom *is* the LORD'S: and he *is* the governor among the nations.

29 All *they that be* fat upon earth shall eat and worship: all they that go down to the dust shall bow before him: and none can keep alive his own soul.

30 A seed shall serve him; it shall be accounted to the Lord for a generation.

31 They shall come, and shall declare his righteousness unto a people that shall be born, that he hath done *this*.

Psalm 23

A Psalm of David.

1 The LORD *is* my shepherd; I shall not want.

2 He maketh me to lie down in green pastures: he leadeth me beside the still waters.

23:2 God's Guidance
< Psalm 25:9 >

3 He restoreth my soul: he leadeth me in the paths of righteousness for his name's sake.

> **23:3 Right Paths**
> ◄ Psalm 16:11
> Psalm 25:10 ►

4 Yea, though I walk through the valley of the shadow of death, I will fear no evil: for thou *art* with me; thy rod and thy staff they comfort me.

5 Thou preparest a table before me in the presence of mine enemies: thou anointest my head with oil; my cup runneth over.

6 Surely goodness and mercy shall follow me all the days of my life: and I will dwell in the house of the LORD for ever.

Psalm 24

A Psalm of David.

1 The earth *is* the LORD'S, and the fulness thereof; the world, and they that dwell therein.

> **24:1 Earth**
> ◄ 1 Chronicles 29:14
> Psalm 50:10 ►

2 For he hath founded it upon the seas, and established it upon the floods.

3 Who shall ascend into the hill of the LORD? or who shall stand in his holy place?

> **24:3-4 God's Presence**
> ◄ Isaiah 26:2 ►

4 He that hath clean hands, and a pure heart; who hath not lifted up his soul unto vanity, nor sworn deceitfully.

5 He shall receive the blessing from the LORD, and righteousness from the God of his salvation.

6 This *is* the generation of them that seek him, that seek thy face, O Jacob. Selah.

7 Lift up your heads, O ye gates; and be ye lift up, ye everlasting doors; and the King of glory shall come in.

8 Who *is* this King of glory? The LORD strong and mighty, the LORD mighty in battle.

9 Lift up your heads, O ye gates; even lift *them* up, ye everlasting doors; and the King of glory shall come in.

10 Who is this King of glory? The LORD of hosts, he *is* the King of glory. Selah.

Psalm 25

A *Psalm* of David.

1 Unto thee, O LORD, do I lift up my soul.

2 O my God, I trust in thee: let me not be ashamed, let not mine enemies triumph over me.

3 Yea, let none that wait on thee be ashamed: let them be ashamed which transgress without cause.

4 Shew me thy ways, O LORD; teach me thy paths.

5 Lead me in thy truth, and teach me: for thou *art* the God of my salvation; on thee do I wait all the day.

> **25:5 Waiting for God**
> ◄ Psalm 27:14 ►

6 Remember, O LORD, thy tender mercies and thy lovingkindnesses; for they *have been* ever of old.

7 Remember not the sins of my youth, nor my transgressions: according to thy mercy remember thou me for thy goodness' sake, O LORD.

> **25:7 Results of Sin**
> ◄ Job 20:11
> Ecclesiastes 11:9 ►

8 Good and upright *is* the LORD: therefore will he teach sinners in the way.

9 The meek will he guide in judgment: and the meek will he teach his way.

> **25:9 God's Guidance**
> ◄ Psalm 23:2
> Psalm 32:8 ►

10 All the paths of the LORD *are* mercy and truth unto such as keep his covenant and his testimonies.

> **25:10 Right Paths**
> ◄ Psalm 23:3
> Psalm 119:35 ►

11 For thy name's sake, O LORD, pardon mine iniquity; for it *is* great.

12 What man *is* he that feareth the LORD? him shall he teach in the way *that* he shall choose.

> **25:12 God as Teacher**
> ◄ Deuteronomy 4:36
> Psalm 32:8 ►

13 His soul shall dwell at ease; and his seed shall inherit the earth.

> **25:12 Why Fear God?**
> ◄ 1 Samuel 12:14
> Psalm 31:19 ►

14 The secret of the LORD *is* with them
that fear him; and he will shew them his
covenant.
15 Mine eyes *are* ever toward the LORD;
for he shall pluck my feet out of the net.
16 Turn thee unto me, and have mercy
upon me; for I *am* desolate and afflicted.
17 The troubles of my heart are enlarged:
O bring thou me out of my distresses.
18 Look upon mine affliction and my
pain; and forgive all my sins.
19 Consider mine enemies; for they are
many; and they hate me with cruel hatred.
20 O keep my soul, and deliver me: let
me not be ashamed; for I put my trust in
thee.
21 Let integrity and uprightness preserve
me; for I wait on thee.
22 Redeem Israel, O God, out of all his
troubles.

Psalm 26

A Psalm of David.

1 Judge me, O LORD; for I have walked in
mine integrity: I have trusted also in the
LORD; *therefore* I shall not slide.
2 Examine me, O LORD, and prove me;
try my reins and my heart.
3 For thy lovingkindness *is* before mine
eyes: and I have walked in thy truth.
4 I have not sat with vain persons, neither will I go in with dissemblers.
5 I have hated the congregation of evildoers; and will not sit with the wicked.
6 I will wash mine hands in innocency:
so will I compass thine altar, O LORD:
7 That I may publish with the voice of
thanksgiving, and tell of all thy wondrous
works.
8 LORD, I have loved the habitation of thy
house, and the place where thine honour
dwelleth.
9 Gather not my soul with sinners, nor
my life with bloody men:
10 In whose hands
is mischief, and
their right hand is
full of bribes.
11 But as for me, I
will walk in mine
integrity: redeem me, and be merciful
unto me.

26:10 Bribery
◄ Exodus 23:8
Proverbs 17:23 ►

12 My foot standeth in an even place: in
the congregations will I bless the LORD.

Psalm 27

A Psalm of David.

1 The LORD *is* my light and my salvation;
whom shall I fear? the LORD *is* the strength
of my life; of whom shall I be afraid?
2 When the wicked, *even* mine enemies
and my foes, came upon me to eat up my
flesh, they stumbled and fell.
3 Though an host should encamp against
me, my heart shall not fear: though war
should rise against me, in this *will* I *be* confident.
4 One *thing* have I desired of the LORD,
that will I seek after; that I may dwell in
the house of the LORD all the days of my
life, to behold the beauty of the LORD, and
to enquire in his temple.
5 For in the time of trouble he shall hide
me in his pavilion: in the secret of his tabernacle shall he hide me; he shall set me
up upon a rock.
6 And now shall mine head be lifted up
above mine enemies round about me:
therefore will I offer in his tabernacle sacrifices of joy; I will sing, yea, I will sing
praises unto the LORD.
7 Hear, O LORD,
when I cry with my
voice: have mercy
also upon me, and
answer me.
8 *When thou saidst,*
Seek ye my face; my heart said unto thee,
Thy face, LORD, will I seek.

27:7 Praying for Mercy
◄ Psalm 6:2
Psalm 51:1 ►

9 Hide not thy face *far* from me; put not
thy servant away in anger: thou hast been
my help; leave me not, neither forsake me,
O God of my salvation.
10 When my father and my mother forsake me, then the LORD will take me up.
11 Teach me thy way, O LORD, and lead
me in a plain path, because of mine enemies.
12 Deliver me not
over unto the will
of mine enemies:
for false witnesses
are risen up against
me, and such as
breathe out cruelty.

27:12 Crime
◄ Genesis 49:5
Proverbs 11:17 ►

13*I had fainted,* unless I had believed to
see the goodness of the LORD in the land
of the living.
14Wait on the
LORD: be of good
courage, and he
shall strengthen
thine heart: wait, I
say, on the LORD.

27:14 Waiting for God
◄ Psalm 25:5
Psalm 62:5 ►

Psalm 28

A *Psalm* of David.

1Unto thee will I cry, O LORD my rock;
be not silent to me: lest, *if* thou be silent
to me, I become like them that go down
into the pit.
2Hear the voice of my supplications,
when I cry unto thee, when I lift up my
hands toward thy holy oracle.
3Draw me not away with the wicked,
and with the workers of iniquity, which
speak peace to their neighbours, but mischief *is* in their hearts.
4Give them according to their deeds, and
according to the wickedness of their
endeavours: give them after the work of
their hands; render to them their desert.
5Because they regard not the works of
the LORD, nor the operation of his hands,
he shall destroy them, and not build them
up.
6Blessed *be* the LORD, because he hath
heard the voice of my supplications.
7The LORD *is* my strength and my shield;
my heart trusted in him, and I am helped:
therefore my heart greatly rejoiceth; and
with my song will I praise him.
8The LORD *is* their
strength, and he *is*
the saving strength
of his anointed.
9Save thy people,
and bless thine in-
heritance: feed them also, and lift them
up for ever.

28:8 Finding Strength
◄ 2 Samuel 22:33
Psalm 46:1 ►

Psalm 29

A Psalm of David.

1Give unto the LORD, O ye mighty, give
unto the LORD glory and strength.
2Give unto the LORD the glory due unto
his name; worship
the LORD in the
beauty of holiness.
3The voice of the
LORD *is* upon the
waters: the God of
glory thundereth: the LORD *is* upon many
waters.

29:2 Worship
◄ 1 Chronicles 16:29
Psalm 95:6 ►

4The voice of the LORD *is* powerful; the
voice of the LORD *is* full of majesty.
5The voice of the LORD breaketh the cedars; yea, the LORD breaketh the cedars of
Lebanon.
6He maketh them also to skip like a calf;
Lebanon and Sirion like a young unicorn.
7The voice of the LORD divideth the
flames of fire.
8The voice of the LORD shaketh the wilderness; the LORD shaketh the wilderness
of Kadesh.
9The voice of the LORD maketh the hinds
to calve, and discovereth the forests: and
in his temple doth
every one speak of
his glory.
10The LORD sit-
teth upon the flood;
yea, the LORD sitteth
King for ever.
11The LORD will
give strength unto
his people; the
LORD will bless his
people with peace.

29:10 God's Control
◄ Job 9:12
Psalm 47:2 ►

29:11 Peace of Mind
◄ Psalm 119:165 ►

Psalm 30

A Psalm *and* Song *at* the dedication
of the house of David.

1I will extol thee, O LORD; for thou hast
lifted me up, and hast not made my foes
to rejoice over me.
2O LORD my God, I cried unto thee, and
thou hast healed me.
3O LORD, thou hast brought up my soul
from the grave: thou hast kept me alive,
that I should not go down to the pit.
4Sing unto the LORD, O ye saints of his,
and give thanks at
the remembrance
of his holiness.
5For his anger
endureth but a mo-
ment; in his favour

30:5 Joy
◄ Psalm 16:11
Psalm 89:16 ►

is life: weeping may endure for a night, but
joy *cometh* in the morning.
6 And in my prosperity I said, I shall
never be moved.
7 LORD, by thy favour thou hast made my
mountain to stand strong: thou didst hide
thy face, *and* I was troubled.
8 I cried to thee, O LORD; and unto the
LORD I made supplication.
9 What profit *is there* in my blood, when
I go down to the pit? Shall the dust praise
thee? shall it declare thy truth?
10 Hear, O LORD, and have mercy upon
me: LORD, be thou my helper.
11 Thou hast turned for me my mourning into dancing: thou hast put off my
sackcloth, and girded me with gladness;
12 To the end that *my* glory may sing
praise to thee, and not be silent. O LORD
my God, I will give thanks unto thee for
ever.

Psalm 31

To the chief Musician,
A Psalm of David.

1 In thee, O LORD, do I put my trust; let
me never be ashamed: deliver me in thy
righteousness.
2 Bow down thine ear to me; deliver me
speedily: be thou my strong rock, for an
house of defence to save me.
3 For thou *art* my rock and my fortress;
therefore for thy name's sake lead me, and
guide me.
4 Pull me out of the net that they have
laid privily for me: for thou *art* my
strength.
5 Into thine hand I commit my spirit:
thou hast redeemed me, O LORD God of
truth.
6 I have hated
them that regard
lying vanities: but I
trust in the LORD.
7 I will be glad
and rejoice in thy
mercy: for thou hast considered my trouble; thou hast known my soul in adversities;

31:6 Worshiping Things
◄ 1 Kings 16:13
Jeremiah 2:5 ►

8 And hast not shut me up into the hand
of the enemy: thou hast set my feet in a
large room.
9 Have mercy upon me, O LORD, for I am
in trouble: mine eye is consumed with
grief, *yea,* my soul and my belly.
10 For my life is
spent with grief,
and my years with
sighing: my strength
faileth because of
mine iniquity, and
my bones are consumed.

31:10 Unhappiness
◄ Job 10:1
Psalm 42:6 ►

11 I was a re-
proach among all
mine enemies, but
especially among
my neighbours,
and a fear to mine
acquaintance: they that did see me without fled from me.

31:11
Being Friendless
◄ Psalm 38:11 ►

12 I am forgotten as a dead man out of
mind: I am like a broken vessel.
13 For I have heard the slander of many:
fear *was* on every side: while they took
counsel together against me, they devised
to take away my life.
14 But I trusted in thee, O LORD: I said,
Thou *art* my God.
15 My times *are* in
thy hand: deliver
me from the hand
of mine enemies,
and from them that
persecute me.

31:15 Bullies
◄ Psalm 7:1
Psalm 119:86 ►

16 Make thy face to shine upon thy servant: save me for thy mercies' sake.
17 Let me not be ashamed, O LORD; for I
have called upon thee: let the wicked be
ashamed, *and* let them be silent in the
grave.
18 Let the lying lips
be put to silence;
which speak griev-
ous things proudly
and contemptuous-
ly against the righ-
teous.

31:18 Lying
◄ Psalm 5:6
Psalm 101:7 ►

19 *Oh* how great *is*
thy goodness, which
thou hast laid up
for them that fear
thee; *which* thou
hast wrought for them that trust in thee
before the sons of men!

31:19 Why Fear God?
◄ Psalm 25:12
Psalm 103:13 ►

20 Thou shalt hide them in the secret of
thy presence from the pride of man: thou
shalt keep them secretly in a pavilion from
the strife of tongues.

21 Blessed *be* the LORD: for he hath shewed me his marvellous kindness in a strong city.

22 For I said in my haste, I am cut off from before thine eyes: nevertheless thou heardest the voice of my supplications when I cried unto thee.

23 O love the LORD, all ye his saints: *for* the LORD preserveth the faithful, and plentifully rewardeth the proud doer.

31:23 Love for God
◄ Joshua 22:5
Matthew 22:37 ►

24 Be of good courage, and he shall strengthen your heart, all ye that hope in the LORD.

31:23 Safety
◄ Nehemiah 9:6
Psalm 37:28 ►

Psalm 32

A *Psalm* of David, Maschil.

1 Blessed *is he whose* transgression *is* forgiven, *whose* sin *is* covered.

2 Blessed *is* the man unto whom the LORD imputeth not iniquity, and in whose spirit *there is* no guile.

3 When I kept silence, my bones waxed old through my roaring all the day long.

32:3 Not Confessing
◄ Psalm 38:4 ►

4 For day and night thy hand was heavy upon me: my moisture is turned into the drought of summer. Selah.

5 I acknowledged my sin unto thee, and mine iniquity have I not hid. I said, I will confess my transgressions unto the LORD; and thou forgavest the iniquity of my sin. Selah.

6 For this shall every one that is godly pray unto thee in a time when thou mayest be found: surely in the floods of great waters they shall not come nigh unto him.

7 Thou *art* my hiding place; thou shalt preserve me from trouble; thou shalt compass me about with songs of deliverance. Selah.

32:8 God's Guidance
◄ Psalm 25:9
Psalm 48:14 ►

8 I will instruct thee and teach thee in the way which thou shalt go: I will guide thee with mine eye.

32:8 God as Teacher
◄ Psalm 25:12
Psalm 71:17 ►

9 Be ye not as the horse, *or* as the mule, *which* have no understanding: whose mouth must be held in with bit and bridle, lest they come near unto thee.

10 Many sorrows *shall be* to the wicked: but he that trusteth in the LORD, mercy shall compass him about.

32:11 Rejoicing
◄ Psalm 5:11
Zephaniah 3:14 ►

11 Be glad in the LORD, and rejoice, ye righteous: and shout for joy, all *ye that are* upright in heart.

32:11 Why Do Right?
◄ Psalm 7:10
Psalm 37:37 ►

Psalm 33

1 Rejoice in the LORD, O ye righteous: *for* praise is comely for the upright.

2 Praise the LORD with harp: sing unto him with the psaltery *and* an instrument of ten strings.

33:2 Praising God
◄ Psalm 9:11
Psalm 67:3 ►

3 Sing unto him a new song; play skilfully with a loud noise.

4 For the word of the LORD *is* right; and all his works *are done* in truth.

33:4 God's Word
◄ 2 Samuel 7:28
Psalm 146:6 ►

5 He loveth righteousness and judgment: the earth is full of the goodness of the LORD.

6 By the word of the LORD were the heavens made; and all the host of them by the breath of his mouth.

7 He gathereth the waters of the sea together as an heap: he layeth up the depth in storehouses.

8 Let all the earth fear the LORD: let all the inhabitants of the world stand in awe of him.

33:8 Respecting God
◄ Psalm 4:4
Psalm 89:7 ►

9 For he spake, and it was *done;* he commanded, and it stood fast.

10 The LORD bringeth the counsel of the heathen to nought: he maketh the devices of the people of none effect.

11 The counsel of the LORD standeth for ever, the thoughts of his heart to all generations.

12 Blessed *is* the nation whose God *is* the LORD: *and* the people *whom* he hath chosen for his own inheritance.

13 The LORD looketh from heaven; he beholdeth all the sons of men.

14 From the place of his habitation he looketh upon all the inhabitants of the earth.

15 He fashioneth their hearts alike; he considereth all their works.

16 There is no king saved by the multitude of an host: a mighty man is not delivered by much strength.

17 An horse *is* a vain thing for safety: neither shall he deliver *any* by his great strength.

18 Behold, the eye of the LORD *is* upon them that fear him, upon them that hope in his mercy;

19 To deliver their soul from death, and to keep them alive in famine.

20 Our soul waiteth for the LORD: he *is* our help and our shield.

33:20 Waiting
◄ Genesis 49:18
Psalm 37:7 ►

21 For our heart shall rejoice in him, because we have trusted in his holy name.

22 Let thy mercy, O LORD, be upon us, according as we hope in thee.

Psalm 34

A Psalm of David, when he changed his behaviour before Abimelech; who drove him away, and he departed.

1 I will bless the LORD at all times: his praise *shall* continually *be* in my mouth.

2 My soul shall make her boast in the LORD: the humble shall hear *thereof,* and be glad.

34:2
Boasting
◄ Psalm 44:8 ►

3 O magnify the LORD with me, and let us exalt his name together.

4 I sought the LORD, and he heard me, and delivered me from all my fears.

5 They looked unto him, and were lightened: and their faces were not ashamed.

6 This poor man cried, and the LORD heard *him,* and saved him out of all his troubles.

7 The angel of the LORD encampeth round about them that fear him, and delivereth them.

34:7 Protection
◄ 2 Chronicles 16:9
Psalm 41:2 ►

8 O taste and see that the LORD *is* good: blessed *is* the man *that* trusteth in him.

9 O fear the LORD, ye his saints: for *there is* no want to them that fear him.

10 The young lions do lack, and suffer hunger: but they that seek the LORD shall not want any good *thing.*

11 Come, ye children, hearken unto me: I will teach you the fear of the LORD.

12 What man *is he that* desireth life, *and* loveth *many* days, that he may see good?

34:14
Doing Good
◄ Psalm 37:3 ►

13 Keep thy tongue from evil, and thy lips from speaking guile.

14 Depart from evil, and do good; seek peace, and pursue it.

34:14 Seeking Peace
◄ Job 22:21
Isaiah 27:5 ►

15 The eyes of the LORD *are* upon the righteous, and his ears *are open* unto their cry.

34:14 Stay Away!
◄ Job 28:28
Psalm 97:10 ►

16 The face of the LORD *is* against them that do evil, to cut off the remembrance of them from the earth.

34:15
Rewarded Goodness
◄ Job 36:7
Psalm 37:25 ►

17 *The righteous* cry, and the LORD heareth, and delivereth them out of all their troubles.

34:16
Evildoers
◄ Psalm 37:9 ►

18 The LORD *is*

nigh unto them that are of a broken heart; and saveth such as be of a contrite spirit.

34:18
Feeling Sorry
◄ Psalm 51:17 ►

34:18
Repentance
◄ Jeremiah 3:22 ►

19 Many *are* the afflictions of the righteous: but the LORD delivereth him out of them all.

20 He keepeth all his bones: not one of them is broken.

21 Evil shall slay the wicked: and they that hate the righteous shall be desolate.

22 The LORD redeemeth the soul of his servants: and none of them that trust in him shall be desolate.

Psalm 35

A Psalm of David.

1 Plead *my cause,* O LORD, with them that strive with me: fight against them that fight against me.

2 Take hold of shield and buckler, and stand up for mine help.

3 Draw out also the spear, and stop *the way* against them that persecute me: say unto my soul, I *am* thy salvation.

4 Let them be confounded and put to shame that seek after my soul: let them be turned back and brought to confusion that devise my hurt.

5 Let them be as chaff before the wind: and let the angel of the LORD chase *them.*

6 Let their way be dark and slippery: and let the angel of the LORD persecute them.

7 For without cause have they hid for me their net *in* a pit, *which* without cause they have digged for my soul.

8 Let destruction come upon him at unawares; and let his net that he hath hid catch himself: into that very destruction let him fall.

9 And my soul shall be joyful in the LORD: it shall rejoice in his salvation.

10 All my bones shall say, LORD, who *is* like unto thee, which deliverest the poor from him that is too strong for him, yea, the poor and the needy from him that spoileth him?

11 False witnesses did rise up; they laid to my charge *things* that I knew not.

12 They rewarded me evil for good *to* the spoiling of my soul.

35:12 Unthankfulness to People
◄ 2 Chronicles 24:22
Ecclesiastes 9:15 ►

13 But as for me, when they were sick, my clothing *was* sackcloth: I humbled my soul with fasting; and my prayer returned into mine own bosom.

35:13 Nice
◄ 2 Kings 6:22
Luke 22:51 ►

14 I behaved myself as though *he had been* my friend *or* brother: I bowed down heavily, as one that mourneth *for his* mother.

15 But in mine adversity they rejoiced, and gathered themselves together: *yea,* the abjects gathered themselves together against me, and I knew *it* not; they did tear *me,* and ceased not:

35:15 Cruelty
◄ Job 24:9
Psalm 69:21 ►

16 With hypocritical mockers in feasts, they gnashed upon me with their teeth.

17 Lord, how long wilt thou look on? rescue my soul from their destructions, my darling from the lions.

18 I will give thee thanks in the great congregation: I will praise thee among much people.

19 Let not them that are mine enemies wrongfully rejoice over me: *neither* let them wink with the eye that hate me without a cause.

20 For they speak not peace: but they devise deceitful matters against *them that are* quiet in the land.

21 Yea, they opened their mouth wide against me, *and* said, Aha, aha, our eye hath seen *it.*

22 *This* thou hast seen, O LORD: keep not silence: O Lord, be not far from me.

23 Stir up thyself, and awake to my judgment, *even* unto my cause, my God and my Lord.

24 Judge me, O LORD my God, according to thy righteousness; and let them not rejoice over me.

25 Let them not say in their hearts, Ah, so would we have it: let them not say, We have swallowed him up.

26 Let them be ashamed and brought to confusion together that rejoice at mine

hurt: let them be clothed with shame and dishonour that magnify *themselves* against me.

27Let them shout for joy, and be glad, that favour my righteous cause: yea, let them say continually, Let the LORD be magnified, which hath pleasure in the prosperity of his servant.

28And my tongue shall speak of thy righteousness *and* of thy praise all the day long.

Psalm 36

To the chief Musician, *A Psalm* of David, the servant of the LORD.

1The transgression of the wicked saith within my heart, *that there is* no fear of God before his eyes.

2For he flattereth himself in his own eyes, until his iniquity be found to be hateful.

36:2
Lying to Yourself
◄ Isaiah 44:20 ►

3The words of his mouth *are* iniquity and deceit: he hath left off to be wise, *and* to do good.

36:3
Dishonest People
◄ Proverbs 12:5 ►

4He deviseth mischief upon his bed; he setteth himself in a way *that is* not good; he abhorreth not evil.

36:4 Mischief
◄ Psalm 10:7
Proverbs 4:16

5Thy mercy, O LORD, *is* in the heavens; *and* thy faithfulness *reacheth* unto the clouds.

6Thy righteousness *is* like the great mountains; thy judgments *are* a great deep: O LORD, thou preservest man and beast.

7How excellent *is* thy lovingkindness, O God! therefore the children of men put their trust under the shadow of thy wings.

8They shall be abundantly satisfied with the fatness of thy house; and thou shalt make them drink of the river of thy pleasures.

36:8 Satisfaction
◄ Psalm 17:15
Psalm 63:5 ►

9For with thee *is* the fountain of life: in thy light shall we see light.

10O continue thy lovingkindness unto them that know thee; and thy righteousness to the upright in heart.

11Let not the foot of pride come against me, and let not the hand of the wicked remove me.

12There are the workers of iniquity fallen: they are cast down, and shall not be able to rise.

Psalm 37

A Psalm of David.

1Fret not thyself because of evildoers, neither be thou envious against the workers of iniquity.

37:1
Envy
◄ Proverbs 3:31 ►

2For they shall soon be cut down like the grass, and wither as the green herb.

3Trust in the LORD, and do good; *so* shalt thou dwell in the land, and verily thou shalt be fed.

37:3 Doing Good
◄ Psalm 34:14
Psalm 37:27 ►

4Delight thyself also in the LORD; and he shall give thee the desires of thine heart.

37:3, 5
Trusting God
◄ Psalm 115:11 ►

5Commit thy way unto the LORD; trust also in him; and he shall bring *it* to pass.

6And he shall bring forth thy righteousness as the light, and thy judgment as the noonday.

7Rest in the LORD, and wait patiently for him: fret not thyself because of him who prospereth in his way, because of the man who bringeth wicked devices to pass.

37:7 Waiting
◄ Psalm 33:20
Psalm 40:1 ►

8Cease from anger, and forsake wrath: fret not thyself in any wise to do evil.

9For evildoers shall be cut off: but those that wait upon the LORD, they shall inherit the earth.

37:9 Evildoers
◄ Psalm 34:16
Psalm 94:16 ►

10For yet a little while, and the wicked

shall not *be:* yea, thou shalt diligently consider his place, and it *shall* not *be.*
11 But the meek
shall inherit the
earth; and shall de-
light themselves in
the abundance of
peace.

37:11 Meekness
◄ Psalm 22:26
Psalm 147:6 ►

12 The wicked plotteth against the just,
and gnasheth upon him with his teeth.
13 The Lord shall laugh at him: for he
seeth that his day is coming.
14 The wicked have drawn out the sword,
and have bent their bow, to cast down the
poor and needy, *and* to slay such as be of
upright conversation.
15 Their sword shall enter into their own
heart, and their bows shall be broken.
16 A little that a righteous man hath *is*
better than the riches of many wicked.
17 For the arms of the wicked shall be
broken: but the LORD upholdeth the righteous.
18 The LORD knoweth the days of the
upright: and their inheritance shall be for
ever.
19 They shall not be ashamed in the evil
time: and in the days of famine they shall
be satisfied.
20 But the wicked shall perish, and the
enemies of the LORD *shall be* as the fat of
lambs: they shall consume; into smoke
shall they consume away.
21 The wicked bor-
roweth, and payeth
not again: but the
righteous sheweth
mercy, and giveth.

37:21 Borrowing
◄ 2 Kings 6:5
Proverbs 22:7 ►

22 For *such as be*
blessed of him shall inherit the earth;
and *they that be* cursed of him shall be
cut off.
23 The steps of a *good* man are ordered
by the LORD: and he delighteth in his
way.
24 Though he fall, he shall not be utterly
cast down: for the LORD upholdeth *him
with* his hand.
25 I have been
young, and *now* am
old; yet have I not
seen the righteous
forsaken, nor his
seed begging bread.

37:25 Rewarded Goodness
◄ Psalm 34:15
Psalm 92:12 ►

26 *He is* ever merciful, and lendeth; and
his seed *is* blessed.

37:26 Sharing
◄ Deuteronomy 15:8
Psalm 112:5 ►

27 Depart from
evil, and do good;
and dwell for ever-
more.

37:27 Doing Good
◄ Psalm 37:3
Luke 6:35 ►

28 For the LORD
loveth judgment,
and forsaketh not
his saints; they are
preserved for ever:
but the seed of the
wicked shall be cut
off.

37:28 Safety
◄ Psalm 31:23
Psalm 146:9 ►

29 The righteous
shall inherit the
land, and dwell
therein for ever.
30 The mouth of
the righteous spea-
keth wisdom, and his tongue talketh of
judgment.
31 The law of his God *is* in his heart; none
of his steps shall slide.
32 The wicked watcheth the righteous,
and seeketh to slay him.
33 The LORD will not leave him in his
hand, nor condemn him when he is
judged.
34 Wait on the LORD, and keep his way,
and he shall exalt thee to inherit the land:
when the wicked are cut off, thou shalt
see *it.*
35 I have seen the
wicked in great
power, and spread-
ing himself like a
green bay tree.

37:35 Just You Wait
◄ Job 12:6
Psalm 73:3 ►

36 Yet he passed
away, and, lo, he *was* not: yea, I sought him,
but he could not be found.
37 Mark the per-
fect *man,* and be-
hold the upright:
for the end of *that*
man *is* peace.

37:37 Why Do Right?
◄ Psalm 32:11
Psalm 49:14 ►

38 But the trans-
gressors shall be destroyed together: the
end of the wicked shall be cut off.
39 But the salvation of the righteous *is*
of the LORD: *he is* their strength in the time
of trouble.
40 And the LORD shall help them and
deliver them: he shall deliver them from
the wicked, and save them, because they
trust in him.

Psalm 38

A Psalm of David,
to bring to remembrance.

1O LORD, rebuke me not in thy wrath: neither chasten me in thy hot displeasure.

2For thine arrows stick fast in me, and thy hand presseth me sore.

3*There is* no soundness in my flesh because of thine anger; neither *is there any* rest in my bones because of my sin.

4For mine iniquities are gone over mine head: as an heavy burden they are too heavy for me.

38:4 Not Confessing
◄ Psalm 32:3
Psalm 51:3 ►

5My wounds stink *and* are corrupt because of my foolishness.

6I am troubled; I am bowed down greatly; I go mourning all the day long.

7For my loins are filled with a loathsome *disease*: and *there is* no soundness in my flesh.

8I am feeble and sore broken: I have roared by reason of the disquietness of my heart.

9Lord, all my desire *is* before thee; and my groaning is not hid from thee.

10My heart panteth, my strength faileth me: as for the light of mine eyes, it also is gone from me.

38:10 Your Body
◄ 1 Samuel 20:3
Psalm 49:12 ►

11My lovers and my friends stand aloof from my sore; and my kinsmen stand afar off.

38:11 Being Friendless
◄ Psalm 31:11
Psalm 88:18 ►

12They also that seek after my life lay snares *for me:* and they that seek my hurt speak mischievous things, and imagine deceits all the day long.

38:11 Loneliness
◄ Psalm 102:7 ►

13But I, as a deaf *man,* heard not; and *I was* as a dumb man *that* openeth not his mouth.

38:11 Whom Can You Trust?
◄ Job 19:19
Micah 7:5 ►

14Thus I was as a man that heareth not, and in whose mouth *are* no reproofs.

15For in thee, O LORD, do I hope: thou wilt hear, O Lord my God.

16For I said, *Hear me,* lest *otherwise* they should rejoice over me: when my foot slippeth, they magnify *themselves* against me.

17For I *am* ready to halt, and my sorrow *is* continually before me.

18For I will declare mine iniquity; I will be sorry for my sin.

19But mine enemies *are* lively, *and* they are strong: and they that hate me wrongfully are multiplied.

20They also that render evil for good are mine adversaries; because I follow *the thing that* good *is.*

21Forsake me not, O LORD: O my God, be not far from me.

22Make haste to help me, O Lord my salvation.

Psalm 39

To the chief Musician, *even* to Jeduthun,
A Psalm of David.

1I said, I will take heed to my ways, that I sin not with my tongue: I will keep my mouth with a bridle, while the wicked is before me.

39:1 Pitfalls
◄ Deuteronomy 4:9
Matthew 26:41 ►

2I was dumb with silence, I held my peace, *even* from good; and my sorrow was stirred.

3My heart was hot within me, while I was musing the fire burned: *then* spake I with my tongue,

4LORD, make me to know mine end, and the measure of my days, what it *is; that* I may know how frail I *am.*

5Behold, thou hast made my days *as* an handbreadth; and mine age *is* as nothing before thee: verily every man at his best state *is* altogether vanity. Selah.

39:5 Life Is Short
◄ Job 14:2
Psalm 89:47 ►

39:6 Hoarding
◄ Job 27:16-17
Ecclesiastes 2:26 ►

6Surely every

man walketh in a vain shew: surely they
are disquieted in vain: he heapeth up
riches, and knoweth not who shall gather
them.
7 And now, Lord, what wait I for? my
hope *is* in thee.
8 Deliver me from all my transgressions:
make me not the reproach of the foolish.
9 I was dumb, I opened not my mouth;
because thou didst *it.*
10 Remove thy stroke away from me: I am
consumed by the blow of thine hand.
11 When thou with rebukes dost correct
man for iniquity, thou makest his beauty
to consume away like a moth: surely every
man *is* vanity. Selah.
12 Hear my prayer, O LORD, and give ear
unto my cry; hold not thy peace at my
tears: for I *am* a stranger with thee, *and* a
sojourner, as all my fathers *were.*
13 O spare me, that I may recover
strength, before I go hence, and be no
more.

Psalm 40

To the chief Musician,
A Psalm of David.

1 I waited patiently for the LORD; and
he inclined unto
me, and heard my
cry.

40:1 Waiting
◄ Psalm 37:7
Psalm 130:6 ►

2 He brought me
up also out of an horrible pit, out of the
miry clay, and set my feet upon a rock, *and*
established my goings.
3 And he hath put
a new song in my
mouth, *even* praise
unto our God:
many shall see *it,*
and fear, and shall
trust in the LORD.

40:3 New Life
◄ Ezekiel 11:19 ►

4 Blessed *is* that
man that maketh
the LORD his trust,
and respecteth not
the proud, nor such
as turn aside to lies.

40:4 Proud People
◄ Psalm 119:78 ►

5 Many, O LORD my God, *are* thy wonderful works *which* thou hast done, and thy
thoughts *which are* to us-ward: they cannot be reckoned up in order unto thee: *if* I
would declare and speak *of them,* they are
more than can be numbered.
6 Sacrifice and offering thou didst not
desire; mine ears hast thou opened: burnt
offering and sin offering hast thou not required.
7 Then said I, Lo, I come: in the volume
of the book *it is* written of me,
8 I delight to do
thy will, O my God:
yea, thy law *is* within my heart.

40:8 Serving
◄ Nehemiah 12:43
Psalm 100:2 ►

9 I have preached
righteousness in
the great congregation: lo, I have
not refrained my
lips, O LORD, thou
knowest.

40:8 Submitting to God
◄ Psalm 143:10 ►

10 I have not hid
thy righteousness within my heart; I have
declared thy faithfulness and thy salvation:
I have not concealed thy lovingkindness
and thy truth from the great congregation.
11 Withhold not thou thy tender mercies
from me, O LORD: let thy lovingkindness
and thy truth continually preserve me.
12 For innumerable evils have compassed me about:
mine iniquities
have taken hold
upon me, so that I
am not able to look
up; they are more
than the hairs of
mine head: therefore my heart faileth me.

40:12 Feeling Guilty
◄ Ezra 9:6
Daniel 5:6 ►

40:12 Guilty Conscience
◄ Job 15:21
Daniel 5:6 ►

13 Be pleased, O LORD, to deliver me:
O LORD, make haste to help me.
14 Let them be ashamed and confounded
together that seek after my soul to destroy
it; let them be driven backward and put to
shame that wish me evil.
15 Let them be desolate for a reward of
their shame that say unto me, Aha, aha.
16 Let all those that seek thee rejoice and
be glad in thee: let such as love thy salvation say continually, The LORD be
magnified.
17 But I *am* poor
and needy; *yet* the
Lord thinketh upon

40:17 Pray and Wait
◄ Psalm 13:1
Psalm 69:3 ►

me: thou *art* my help and my deliverer; make no tarrying, O my God.

Psalm 41

To the chief Musician, A Psalm of David.

1 Blessed *is* he that considereth the poor: the LORD will deliver him in time of trouble.

41:1 Kind to the Poor
◄ Deuteronomy 24:12
Proverbs 14:21 ►

2 The LORD will preserve him, and keep him alive; *and* he shall be blessed upon the earth: and thou wilt not deliver him unto the will of his enemies.

41:1 Promises to Givers
◄ Proverbs 3:9-10 ►

3 The LORD will strengthen him upon the bed of languishing: thou wilt make all his bed in his sickness.

41:2 Protection
◄ Psalm 34:7
Psalm 91:4 ►

4 I said, LORD, be merciful unto me: heal my soul; for I have sinned against thee.

41:3 Rewards
◄ Psalm 112:9 ►

5 Mine enemies speak evil of me, When shall he die, and his name perish?

6 And if he come to see *me,* he speaketh vanity: his heart gathereth iniquity to itself; *when* he goeth abroad, he telleth *it.*

7 All that hate me whisper together against me: against me do they devise my hurt.

8 An evil disease, *say they,* cleaveth fast unto him: and *now* that he lieth he shall rise up no more.

9 Yea, mine own familiar friend, in whom I trusted, which did eat of my bread, hath lifted up *his* heel against me.

10 But thou, O LORD, be merciful unto me, and raise me up, that I may requite them.

11 By this I know that thou favourest me, because mine enemy doth not triumph over me.

12 And as for me, thou upholdest me in mine integrity, and settest me before thy face for ever.

13 Blessed *be* the LORD God of Israel from everlasting, and to everlasting. Amen, and Amen.

Psalm 42

To the chief Musician, Maschil,
for the sons of Korah.

1 As the hart panteth after the water brooks, so panteth my soul after thee, O God.

2 My soul thirsteth for God, for the living God: when shall I come and appear before God?

42:2 Desire for God
◄ Psalm 63:1 ►

3 My tears have been my meat day and night, while they continually say unto me, Where *is* thy God?

4 When I remember these *things,* I pour out my soul in me: for I had gone with the multitude, I went with them to the house of God, with the voice of joy and praise, with a multitude that kept holyday.

5 Why art thou cast down, O my soul? and *why* art thou disquieted in me? hope thou in God: for I shall yet praise him *for* the help of his countenance.

6 O my God, my soul is cast down within me: therefore will I remember thee from the land of Jordan, and of the Hermonites, from the hill Mizar.

42:6 Unhappiness
◄ Psalm 31:10
Psalm 69:2 ►

7 Deep calleth unto deep at the noise of thy waterspouts: all thy waves and thy billows are gone over me.

8 *Yet* the LORD will command his lovingkindness in the daytime, and in the night his song *shall be* with me, *and* my prayer unto the God of my life.

9 I will say unto God my rock, Why hast thou forgotten me? why go I mourning because of the oppression of the enemy?

10 *As* with a sword in my bones, mine enemies reproach me; while they say daily unto me, Where *is* thy God?

11 Why art thou cast down, O my soul? and why art thou disquieted within me? hope thou in God: for I shall yet praise him, *who is* the health of my countenance, and my God.

Psalm 43

1Judge me, O God, and plead my cause against an ungodly nation: O deliver me from the deceitful and unjust man.

2For thou *art* the God of my strength: why dost thou cast me off? why go I mourning because of the oppression of the enemy?

3O send out thy light and thy truth: let them lead me; let them bring me unto thy holy hill, and to thy tabernacles.

4Then will I go unto the altar of God, unto God my exceeding joy: yea, upon the harp will I praise thee, O God my God.

5Why art thou cast down, O my soul? and why art thou disquieted within me? hope in God: for I shall yet praise him, *who is* the health of my countenance, and my God.

Psalm 44

To the chief Musician for the sons of Korah, Maschil.

1We have heard with our ears, O God, our fathers have told us, *what* work thou didst in their days, in the times of old.

2*How* thou didst drive out the heathen with thy hand, and plantedst them; *how* thou didst afflict the people, and cast them out.

3For they got not the land in possession by their own sword, neither did their own arm save them: but thy right hand, and thine arm, and the light of thy countenance, because thou hadst a favour unto them.

4Thou art my King, O God: command deliverances for Jacob.

5Through thee will we push down our enemies: through thy name will we tread them under that rise up against us.

6For I will not trust in my bow, neither shall my sword save me.

7But thou hast saved us from our enemies, and hast put them to shame that hated us.

8In God we boast all the day long, and praise thy name for ever. Selah.

9But thou hast cast off, and put us to shame; and goest not forth with our armies.

44:8 Boasting
◄ Psalm 34:2
Isaiah 45:25 ►

10Thou makest us to turn back from the enemy: and they which hate us spoil for themselves.

11Thou hast given us like sheep *appointed* for meat; and hast scattered us among the heathen.

12Thou sellest thy people for nought, and dost not increase *thy wealth* by their price.

13Thou makest us a reproach to our neighbours, a scorn and a derision to them that are round about us.

14Thou makest us a byword among the heathen, a shaking of the head among the people.

15My confusion *is* continually before me, and the shame of my face hath covered me,

16For the voice of him that reproacheth and blasphemeth; by reason of the enemy and avenger.

17All this is come upon us; yet have we not forgotten thee, neither have we dealt falsely in thy covenant.

18Our heart is not turned back, neither have our steps declined from thy way;

19Though thou hast sore broken us in the place of dragons, and covered us with the shadow of death.

20If we have forgotten the name of our God, or stretched out our hands to a strange god;

21Shall not God search this out? for he knoweth the secrets of the heart.

22Yea, for thy sake are we killed all the day long; we are counted as sheep for the slaughter.

23Awake, why sleepest thou, O Lord? arise, cast *us* not off for ever.

24Wherefore hidest thou thy face, *and* forgettest our affliction and our oppression?

25For our soul is bowed down to the dust: our belly cleaveth unto the earth.

26Arise for our help, and redeem us for thy mercies' sake.

Psalm 45

To the chief Musician upon Shoshannim, for the sons of Korah, Maschil, A Song of loves.

1My heart is inditing a good matter: I speak of the things which I have made touching the king: my tongue *is* the pen of a ready writer.

2Thou art fairer than the children of men: grace is poured into thy lips: therefore God hath blessed thee for ever.

3Gird thy sword upon *thy* thigh, O *most* mighty, with thy glory and thy majesty.

4And in thy majesty ride prosperously because of truth and meekness *and* righteousness; and thy right hand shall teach thee terrible things.

5Thine arrows *are* sharp in the heart of the king's enemies; *whereby* the people fall under thee.

6Thy throne, O God, *is* for ever and ever: the sceptre of thy kingdom *is* a right sceptre.

7Thou lovest righteousness, and hatest wickedness: therefore God, thy God, hath anointed thee with the oil of gladness above thy fellows.

8All thy garments *smell* of myrrh, and aloes, *and* cassia, out of the ivory palaces, whereby they have made thee glad.

9Kings' daughters *were* among thy honourable women: upon thy right hand did stand the queen in gold of Ophir.

10Hearken, O daughter, and consider, and incline thine ear; forget also thine own people, and thy father's house;

11So shall the king greatly desire thy beauty: for he *is* thy Lord; and worship thou him.

12And the daughter of Tyre *shall be there* with a gift; *even* the rich among the people shall intreat thy favour.

13The king's daughter *is* all glorious within: her clothing *is* of wrought gold.

14She shall be brought unto the king in raiment of needlework: the virgins her companions that follow her shall be brought unto thee.

15With gladness and rejoicing shall they be brought: they shall enter into the king's palace.

45:15 Gladness
◄ Psalm 4:7
Acts 2:46 ►

16Instead of thy fathers shall be thy children, whom thou mayest make princes in all the earth.

17I will make thy name to be remembered in all generations: therefore shall the people praise thee for ever and ever.

Psalm 46

To the chief Musician for the sons of Korah, A Song upon Alamoth.

1God *is* our refuge and strength, a very present help in trouble.

46:1 Finding Strength
◄ Psalm 28:8
Psalm 73:26 ►

2Therefore will not we fear, though the earth be removed, and though the mountains be carried into the midst of the sea;

3*Though* the waters thereof roar *and* be troubled, *though* the mountains shake with the swelling thereof. Selah.

4*There is* a river, the streams whereof shall make glad the city of God, the holy *place* of the tabernacles of the most High.

5God *is* in the midst of her; she shall not be moved: God shall help her, *and that* right early.

6The heathen raged, the kingdoms were moved: he uttered his voice, the earth melted.

7The LORD of hosts *is* with us; the God of Jacob *is* our refuge. Selah.

8Come, behold the works of the LORD, what desolations he hath made in the earth.

9He maketh wars to cease unto the end of the earth; he breaketh the bow, and cutteth the spear in sunder; he burneth the chariot in the fire.

10Be still, and know that I *am* God: I will be exalted among the heathen, I will be exalted in the earth.

11The LORD of hosts *is* with us; the God of Jacob *is* our refuge. Selah.

Psalm 47

To the chief Musician, A Psalm for the sons of Korah.

1O clap your hands, all ye people; shout unto God with the voice of triumph.

2For the LORD most high *is* terrible; *he is* a great King over all the earth.

47:2 God's Control
◄ Psalm 29:10
Psalm 83:18 ►

3He shall subdue

the people under us, and the nations under our feet.

4 He shall choose our inheritance for us, the excellency of Jacob whom he loved. Selah.

5 God is gone up with a shout, the LORD with the sound of a trumpet.

6 Sing praises to God, sing praises: sing praises unto our King, sing praises.

7 For God *is* the King of all the earth: sing ye praises with understanding.

8 God reigneth over the heathen: God sitteth upon the throne of his holiness.

9 The princes of the people are gathered together, *even* the people of the God of Abraham: for the shields of the earth *belong* unto God: he is greatly exalted.

Psalm 48

A Song *and* Psalm for the sons of Korah.

1 Great *is* the LORD, and greatly to be praised in the city of our God, *in* the mountain of his holiness.

2 Beautiful for situation, the joy of the whole earth, *is* mount Zion, *on* the sides of the north, the city of the great King.

3 God is known in her palaces for a refuge.

4 For, lo, the kings were assembled, they passed by together.

5 They saw *it, and* so they marvelled; they were troubled, *and* hasted away.

6 Fear took hold upon them there, *and* pain, as of a woman in travail.

7 Thou breakest the ships of Tarshish with an east wind.

8 As we have heard, so have we seen in the city of the LORD of hosts, in the city of our God: God will establish it for ever. Selah.

9 We have thought of thy lovingkindness, O God, in the midst of thy temple.

10 According to thy name, O God, so *is* thy praise unto the ends of the earth: thy right hand is full of righteousness.

48:9 Wise Thoughts
◄ Psalm 119:59 ►

11 Let mount Zion rejoice, let the daughters of Judah be glad, because of thy judgments.

12 Walk about Zion, and go round about her: tell the towers thereof.

13 Mark ye well her bulwarks, consider her palaces; that ye may tell *it* to the generation following.

14 For this God *is* our God for ever and ever: he will be our guide *even* unto death.

48:14 God's Guidance
◄ Psalm 32:8
Psalm 73:24 ►

Psalm 49

To the chief Musician,
A Psalm for the sons of Korah.

1 Hear this, all *ye* people; give ear, all *ye* inhabitants of the world:

2 Both low and high, rich and poor, together.

3 My mouth shall speak of wisdom; and the meditation of my heart *shall be* of understanding.

4 I will incline mine ear to a parable: I will open my dark saying upon the harp.

5 Wherefore should I fear in the days of evil, *when* the iniquity of my heels shall compass me about?

6 They that trust in their wealth, and boast themselves in the multitude of their riches;

7 None *of them* can by any means redeem his brother, nor give to God a ransom for him:

8 (For the redemption of their soul *is* precious, and it ceaseth for ever:)

9 That he should still live for ever, *and* not see corruption.

10 For he seeth *that* wise men die, likewise the fool and the brutish person perish, and leave their wealth to others.

49:10 Death
◄ Job 30:23
Psalm 89:48 ►

11 Their inward thought *is, that* their houses *shall continue* for ever, *and* their dwelling places to all generations; they call *their* lands after their own names.

49:10 Soon Gone
◄ Job 20:28
Proverbs 23:5 ►

49:11 Ambition
◄ 2 Kings 14:10
Isaiah 14:13 ►

12 Nevertheless man *being* in honour abideth

Turn to the next page for more . . .

not: he is like the beasts *that* perish.

13 This their way *is* their folly: yet their posterity approve their sayings. Selah.

14 Like sheep they are laid in the grave; death shall feed on them; and the upright shall have dominion over them in the morning; and their beauty shall consume in the grave from their dwelling.

49:12 Your Body
◄ Psalm 38:10
Psalm 78:39 ►

49:14 Why Do Right?
◄ Psalm 37:37
Psalm 64:10 ►

49:15 Resurrection
◄ Psalm 71:20 ►

15 But God will redeem my soul from the power of the grave: for he shall receive me. Selah.

16 Be not thou afraid when one is made rich, when the glory of his house is increased;

17 For when he dieth he shall carry nothing away: his glory shall not descend after him.

18 Though while he lived he blessed his soul: and *men* will praise thee, when thou doest well to thyself.

19 He shall go to the generation of his fathers; they shall never see light.

20 Man *that is* in honour, and understandeth not, is like the beasts *that* perish.

Psalm 50

A Psalm of Asaph.

1 The mighty God, *even* the LORD, hath spoken, and called the earth from the rising of the sun unto the going down thereof.

2 Out of Zion, the perfection of beauty, God hath shined.

3 Our God shall come, and shall not keep silence: a fire shall devour before him, and it shall be very tempestuous round about him.

4 He shall call to the heavens from above, and to the earth, that he may judge his people.

5 Gather my saints together unto me; those that have made a covenant with me by sacrifice.

6 And the heavens shall declare his righteousness: for God *is* judge himself. Selah.

7 Hear, O my people, and I will speak; O Israel, and I will testify against thee: I *am* God, *even* thy God.

8 I will not reprove thee for thy sacrifices or thy burnt offerings, *to have been* continually before me.

9 I will take no bullock out of thy house, *nor* he goats out of thy folds.

10 For every beast of the forest *is* mine, *and* the cattle upon a thousand hills.

50:10 Earth
◄ Psalm 24:1
Psalm 60:7 ►

11 I know all the fowls of the mountains: and the wild beasts of the field *are* mine.

12 If I were hungry, I would not tell thee: for the world *is* mine, and the fulness thereof.

13 Will I eat the flesh of bulls, or drink the blood of goats?

14 Offer unto God thanksgiving; and pay thy vows unto the most High:

15 And call upon me in the day of trouble: I will deliver thee, and thou shalt glorify me.

16 But unto the wicked God saith, What hast thou to do to declare my statutes, or *that* thou shouldest take my covenant in thy mouth?

17 Seeing thou hatest instruction, and castest my words behind thee.

18 When thou sawest a thief, then thou consentedst with him, and hast been partaker with adulterers.

50:17 Rejecting God's Word
◄ 2 Chronicles 36:16
Proverbs 1:7 ►

19 Thou givest thy mouth to evil, and thy tongue frameth deceit.

20 Thou sittest *and* speakest against thy brother; thou slanderest thine own mother's son.

21 These *things* hast thou done, and I kept silence; thou thoughtest that I was altogether *such an one* as thyself: *but* I will reprove thee, and set *them* in order before thine eyes.

22 Now consider this, ye that forget God, lest I tear *you* in pieces, and *there be* none to deliver.

50:22 Don't Forget...
◄ Psalm 9:17
Psalm 78:11 ►

23 Whoso offereth praise glorifieth me: and to him that ordereth *his* conversation *aright* will I shew the salvation of God.

Psalm 51

To the chief Musician, A Psalm of David, when Nathan the prophet came unto him, after he had gone in to Bathsheba.

1 Have mercy upon me, O God, according to thy lovingkindness: according unto the multitude of thy tender mercies blot out my transgressions.

51:1 Praying for Mercy
◄ Psalm 27:7
Psalm 85:7 ►

2 Wash me throughly from mine iniquity, and cleanse me from my sin.

3 For I acknowledge my transgressions: and my sin *is* ever before me.

51:3 Mistakes
◄ Deuteronomy 9:7
Psalm 137:1 ►

4 Against thee, thee only, have I sinned, and done *this* evil in thy sight: that thou mightest be justified when thou speakest, *and* be clear when thou judgest.

51:3 Not Confessing
◄ Psalm 38:4
Psalm 73:21 ►

5 Behold, I was shapen in iniquity; and in sin did my mother conceive me.

6 Behold, thou desirest truth in the inward parts: and in the hidden *part* thou shalt make me to know wisdom.

7 Purge me with hyssop, and I shall be clean: wash me, and I shall be whiter than snow.

8 Make me to hear joy and gladness; *that* the bones *which* thou hast broken may rejoice.

9 Hide thy face from my sins, and blot out all mine iniquities.

10 Create in me a clean heart, O God; and renew a right spirit within me.

11 Cast me not away from thy presence; and take not thy holy spirit from me.

51:10 New Person
◄ Isaiah 40:31 ►

12 Restore unto me the joy of thy salvation; and uphold me *with thy* free spirit.

13 *Then* will I teach transgressors thy ways; and sinners shall be converted unto thee.

14 Deliver me from bloodguiltiness, O God, thou God of my salvation: *and* my tongue shall sing aloud of thy righteousness.

15 O Lord, open thou my lips; and my mouth shall shew forth thy praise.

16 For thou desirest not sacrifice; else would I give *it:* thou delightest not in burnt offering.

17 The sacrifices of God *are* a broken spirit: a broken and a contrite heart, O God, thou wilt not despise.

51:17 Feeling Sorry
◄ Psalm 34:18
Isaiah 57:15 ►

18 Do good in thy good pleasure unto Zion: build thou the walls of Jerusalem.

19 Then shalt thou be pleased with the sacrifices of righteousness, with burnt offering and whole burnt offering: then shall they offer bullocks upon thine altar.

Psalm 52

To the chief Musician, Maschil, *A Psalm* of David, when Doeg the Edomite came and told Saul, and said unto him, David is come to the house of Ahimelech.

1 Why boastest thou thyself in mischief, O mighty man? the goodness of God *endureth* continually.

2 Thy tongue deviseth mischiefs; like a sharp rasor, working deceitfully.

3 Thou lovest evil more than good; *and* lying rather than to speak righteousness. Selah.

4 Thou lovest all devouring words, O *thou* deceitful tongue.

5 God shall likewise destroy thee for ever, he shall take thee away, and pluck thee out of *thy* dwelling place, and root thee out of the land of the living. Selah.

6 The righteous also shall see, and fear, and shall laugh at him:

7 Lo, *this is* the man *that* made not God his strength; but trusted in the abundance of his riches, *and* strengthened himself in his wickedness.

52:7 Wealth
◄ Job 31:24-25, 28
Proverbs 11:28 ►

8 But I *am* like a green olive tree in the

house of God: I trust in the mercy of God
for ever and ever.
9 I will praise thee for ever, because thou
hast done *it:* and I will wait on thy name;
for *it is* good before thy saints.

Psalm 53

To the chief Musician upon Mahalath,
Maschil, *A Psalm* of David.

1 The fool hath said in his heart, *There is*
no God. Corrupt are they, and have done
abominable iniquity: *there is* none that
doeth good.
2 God looked down from heaven upon
the children of men, to see if there were
any that did understand, that did seek God.
3 Every one of
them is gone back:
they are altogether
become filthy; *there*
is none that doeth
good, no, not one.

53:3 Everyone Sins
◄ Psalm 14:3
Psalm 130:3 ►

4 Have the work-
ers of iniquity no
knowledge? who
eat up my people
as they eat bread:
they have not called
upon God.

53:4 Not Praying
◄ Isaiah 43:22 ►

5 There were they
in great fear, *where*
no fear was: for God
hath scattered the
bones of him that
encampeth *against*
thee: thou hast put *them* to shame, because
God hath despised them.

53:5 Guilty Fear
◄ Leviticus 26:17
Proverbs 28:1 ►

6 Oh that the salvation of Israel *were come*
out of Zion! When God bringeth back the
captivity of his people, Jacob shall rejoice,
and Israel shall be glad.

Psalm 54

To the chief Musician on Neginoth, Maschil,
A Psalm of David, when the Ziphims
came and said to Saul, Doth not
David hide himself with us?

1 Save me, O God, by thy name, and
judge me by thy strength.
2 Hear my prayer, O God; give ear to the
words of my mouth.
3 For strangers are risen up against me,
and oppressors seek after my soul: they
have not set God before them. Selah.
4 Behold, God *is* mine helper: the Lord
is with them that uphold my soul.
5 He shall reward evil unto mine enemies: cut them off in thy truth.
6 I will freely sacrifice unto thee: I will
praise thy name, O LORD; for *it is* good.
7 For he hath delivered me out of all trouble: and mine eye hath seen *his desire* upon
mine enemies.

Psalm 55

To the chief Musician on Neginoth, Maschil,
A Psalm of David.

1 Give ear to my prayer, O God; and hide
not thyself from my supplication.
2 Attend unto me, and hear me: I mourn
in my complaint, and make a noise;
3 Because of the voice of the enemy, because of the oppression of the wicked: for
they cast iniquity upon me, and in wrath
they hate me.
4 My heart is sore pained within me: and
the terrors of death are fallen upon me.
5 Fearfulness and trembling are come
upon me, and horror hath overwhelmed
me.
6 And I said, Oh that I had wings like a
dove! *for then* would I fly away, and be at
rest.
7 Lo, *then* would I wander far off, *and* remain in the wilderness. Selah.
8 I would hasten my escape from the
windy storm *and* tempest.
9 Destroy, O Lord,
and divide their
tongues: for I have
seen violence and
strife in the city.

55:9 Violence
◄ Job 24:2
Psalm 73:6 ►

10 Day and night
they go about it upon the walls thereof:
mischief also and sorrow *are* in the midst
of it.
11 Wickedness *is* in the midst thereof:
deceit and guile depart not from her
streets.
12 For *it was* not an enemy *that* reproached me; then I could have borne *it:*
neither *was it* he that hated me *that* did
magnify *himself* against me; then I would
have hid myself from him:

13But *it was* thou, a man mine equal, my guide, and mine acquaintance.

14We took sweet counsel together, *and* walked unto the house of God in company.

15Let death seize upon them, *and* let them go down quick into hell: for wickedness is in their dwellings, *and* among them.

16As for me, I will call upon God; and the LORD shall save me.

17Evening, and morning, and at noon, will I pray, and cry aloud: and he shall hear my voice.

55:17 Praying
◄ Psalm 5:3
Psalm 119:147 ►

18He hath delivered my soul in peace from the battle *that was* against me: for there were many with me.

19God shall hear, and afflict them, even he that abideth of old. Selah. Because they have no changes, therefore they fear not God.

20He hath put forth his hands against such as be at peace with him: he hath broken his covenant.

21*The words* of his mouth were smoother than butter, but war *was* in his heart: his words were softer than oil, yet *were* they drawn swords.

22Cast thy burden upon the LORD, and he shall sustain thee: he shall never suffer the righteous to be moved.

23But thou, O God, shalt bring them down into the pit of destruction: bloody and deceitful men shall not live out half their days; but I will trust in thee.

Psalm 56

To the chief Musician upon Jonath-elem-rechokim, Michtam of David, when the Philistines took him in Gath.

1Be merciful unto me, O God: for man would swallow me up; he fighting daily oppresseth me.

2Mine enemies would daily swallow *me* up: for *they be* many that fight against me, O thou most High.

3What time I am afraid, I will trust in thee.

4In God I will praise his word, in God I have put my trust; I will not fear what flesh can do unto me.

5Every day they wrest my words: all their thoughts *are* against me for evil.

6They gather themselves together, they hide themselves, they mark my steps, when they wait for my soul.

7Shall they escape by iniquity? in *thine* anger cast down the people, O God.

8Thou tellest my wanderings: put thou my tears into thy bottle: *are they* not in thy book?

9When I cry *unto thee,* then shall mine enemies turn back: this I know; for God *is* for me.

10In God will I praise *his* word: in the LORD will I praise *his* word.

11In God have I put my trust: I will not be afraid what man can do unto me.

12Thy vows *are* upon me, O God: I will render praises unto thee.

13For thou hast delivered my soul from death: *wilt* not *thou deliver* my feet from falling, that I may walk before God in the light of the living?

Psalm 57

To the chief Musician, Al-taschith, Michtam of David, when he fled from Saul in the cave.

1Be merciful unto me, O God, be merciful unto me: for my soul trusteth in thee: yea, in the shadow of thy wings will I make my refuge, until *these* calamities be overpast.

2I will cry unto God most high; unto God that performeth *all things* for me.

3He shall send from heaven, and save *from* the reproach of him that would swallow me up. Selah. God shall send forth his mercy and his truth.

4My soul *is* among lions: *and* I lie *even among* them that are set on fire, *even* the sons of men, whose teeth *are* spears and arrows, and their tongue a sharp sword.

5Be thou exalted, O God, above the heavens; *let* thy glory *be* above all the earth.

6They have prepared a net for my steps; my soul is bowed down: they have digged a pit before me, into the midst whereof they are fallen *themselves.* Selah.

7My heart is fixed, O God, my heart is fixed: I will sing and give praise.

8 Awake up, my glory; awake, psaltery and harp: I *myself* will awake early.

57:8 Devotions
◄ Job 1:5
Psalm 119:147 ►

9 I will praise thee, O Lord, among the people: I will sing unto thee among the nations.

10 For thy mercy *is* great unto the heavens, and thy truth unto the clouds.

11 Be thou exalted, O God, above the heavens: *let* thy glory *be* above all the earth.

Psalm 58

To the chief Musician, Al-taschith,
Michtam of David.

1 Do ye indeed speak righteousness, O congregation? do ye judge uprightly, O ye sons of men?

2 Yea, in heart ye work wickedness; ye weigh the violence of your hands in the earth.

3 The wicked are estranged from the womb: they go astray as soon as they be born, speaking lies.

4 Their poison *is* like the poison of a serpent: *they are* like the deaf adder *that* stoppeth her ear;

5 Which will not hearken to the voice of charmers, charming never so wisely.

6 Break their teeth, O God, in their mouth: break out the great teeth of the young lions, O LORD.

7 Let them melt away as waters *which* run continually: *when* he bendeth *his bow to shoot* his arrows, let them be as cut in pieces.

8 As a snail *which* melteth, let *every one of them* pass away: *like* the untimely birth of a woman, *that* they may not see the sun.

9 Before your pots can feel the thorns, he shall take them away as with a whirlwind, both living, and in *his* wrath.

10 The righteous shall rejoice when he seeth the vengeance: he shall wash his feet in the blood of the wicked.

11 So that a man shall say, Verily *there is* a reward for the righteous: verily he is a God that judgeth in the earth.

58:11 God as Judge
◄ Genesis 18:25
Psalm 75:7 ►

Psalm 59

To the chief Musician, Al-taschith,
Michtam of David; when Saul sent,
and they watched the house to kill him.

1 Deliver me from mine enemies, O my God: defend me from them that rise up against me.

2 Deliver me from the workers of iniquity, and save me from bloody men.

3 For, lo, they lie in wait for my soul: the mighty are gathered against me; not *for* my transgression, nor *for* my sin, O LORD.

4 They run and prepare themselves without *my* fault: awake to help me, and behold.

5 Thou therefore, O LORD God of hosts, the God of Israel, awake to visit all the heathen: be not merciful to any wicked transgressors. Selah.

6 They return at evening: they make a noise like a dog, and go round about the city.

7 Behold, they belch out with their mouth: swords *are* in their lips: for who, *say they,* doth hear?

8 But thou, O LORD, shalt laugh at them; thou shalt have all the heathen in derision.

9 *Because of* his strength will I wait upon thee: for God *is* my defence.

10 The God of my mercy shall prevent me: God shall let me see *my desire* upon mine enemies.

11 Slay them not, lest my people forget: scatter them by thy power; and bring them down, O Lord our shield.

12 *For* the sin of their mouth *and* the words of their lips let them even be taken in their pride: and for cursing and lying *which* they speak.

13 Consume *them* in wrath, consume *them,* that they *may* not *be:* and let them know that God ruleth in Jacob unto the ends of the earth. Selah.

14 And at evening let them return; *and* let them make a noise like a dog, and go round about the city.

15 Let them wander up and down for meat, and grudge if they be not satisfied.

16 But I will sing of thy power; yea, I will sing aloud of thy mercy in the morning: for thou hast been my defence and refuge in the day of my trouble.

17 Unto thee, O my strength, will I sing:

for God *is* my defence, *and* the God of my
mercy.

Psalm 60

To the chief Musician upon Shushan-eduth,
Michtam of David, to teach; when he strove
with Aram-naharaim and with Aram-zobah,
when Joab returned, and smote of Edom
in the valley of salt twelve thousand.

1 O God, thou hast cast us off, thou hast
scattered us, thou hast been displeased; O
turn thyself to us again.
2 Thou hast made the earth to tremble;
thou hast broken it: heal the breaches
thereof; for it shaketh.
3 Thou hast shewed thy people hard
things: thou hast made us to drink the
wine of astonishment.
4 Thou hast given a banner to them that
fear thee, that it may be displayed because
of the truth. Selah.
5 That thy beloved may be delivered; save
with thy right hand, and hear me.
6 God hath spoken in his holiness; I will
rejoice, I will divide Shechem, and mete
out the valley of Succoth.
7 Gilead *is* mine,
and Manasseh *is*
mine; Ephraim also
is the strength of
mine head; Judah *is*
my lawgiver;

60:7 Earth
◄ Psalm 50:10
Psalm 89:11 ►

8 Moab *is* my washpot; over Edom will I
cast out my shoe: Philistia, triumph thou
because of me.
9 Who will bring me *into* the strong city?
who will lead me into Edom?
10 *Wilt* not thou, O God, *which* hadst cast
us off? and *thou,* O God, *which* didst not
go out with our armies?
11 Give us help from trouble: for vain *is*
the help of man.
12 Through God we shall do valiantly: for
he *it is that* shall tread down our enemies.

Psalm 61

To the chief Musician upon Neginah,
A Psalm of David.

1 Hear my cry, O God; attend unto my
prayer.
2 From the end of the earth will I cry unto
thee, when my heart is overwhelmed: lead
me to the rock *that* is higher than I.
3 For thou hast been a shelter for me, *and*
a strong tower from the enemy.
4 I will abide in thy tabernacle for ever: I
will trust in the covert of thy wings. Selah.
5 For thou, O God, hast heard my vows:
thou hast given *me* the heritage of those
that fear thy name.
6 Thou wilt prolong the king's life: *and*
his years as many generations.
7 He shall abide before God for ever:
O prepare mercy and truth, *which* may preserve him.
8 So will I sing praise unto thy name for
ever, that I may daily perform my vows.

Psalm 62

To the chief Musician, to Jeduthun,
A Psalm of David.

1 Truly my soul waiteth upon God: from
him *cometh* my salvation.
2 He only *is* my rock and my salvation;
he is my defence; I shall not be greatly
moved.
3 How long will ye imagine mischief
against a man? ye shall be slain all of you:
as a bowing wall *shall ye be, and as* a totter-
ing fence.
4 They only consult to cast *him* down
from his excellency: they delight in lies:
they bless with their mouth, but they curse
inwardly. Selah.
5 My soul, wait
thou only upon
God; for my expec-
tation *is* from him.
6 He only *is* my
rock and my salva-
tion: *he is* my defence; I shall not be moved.

62:5 Waiting for God
◄ Psalm 27:14
Psalm 123:2 ►

7 In God *is* my salvation and my glory:
the rock of my strength, *and* my refuge, *is*
in God.
8 Trust in him at all times; ye people,
pour out your heart before him: God *is* a
refuge for us. Selah.
9 Surely men of low degree *are* vanity, *and*
men of high degree
are a lie: to be laid
in the balance, they
are altogether *light-
er* than vanity.
10 Trust not in

62:10 Money's Dangers
◄ Deuteronomy 8:13-14
Proverbs 28:20 ►

oppression, and become not vain in robbery: if riches increase, set not your heart
upon them.
11God hath spo-
ken once; twice
have I heard this;
that power *belongeth*
unto God.

62:11 God's Power
◄ Job 26:12
Psalm 65:6 ►

12Also unto thee,
O Lord, *belongeth*
mercy: for thou ren-
derest to every man
according to his
work.

62:12 Actions Judged
◄ Proverbs 24:12 ►

Psalm 63

A Psalm of David, when he was
in the wilderness of Judah.

1O God, thou *art*
my God; early will
I seek thee: my soul
thirsteth for thee,
my flesh longeth
for thee in a dry and
thirsty land, where no water is;

63:1 Desire for God
◄ Psalm 42:2
Psalm 119:174 ►

2To see thy power and thy glory, so *as* I
have seen thee in the sanctuary.
3Because thy lovingkindness *is* better
than life, my lips shall praise thee.
4Thus will I bless thee while I live: I will
lift up my hands in thy name.
5My soul shall
be satisfied as *with*
marrow and fatness;
and my mouth shall
praise *thee* with joy-
ful lips:

63:5 Satisfaction
◄ Psalm 36:8
Psalm 103:5 ►

6When I remem-
ber thee upon my
bed, *and* meditate
on thee in the *night*
watches.

63:6 Remember...
◄ Nehemiah 4:14
Ecclesiastes 12:1 ►

7Because thou
hast been my help, therefore in the shadow of thy wings will I rejoice.
8My soul followeth hard after thee: thy
right hand upholdeth me.
9But those *that* seek my soul, to destroy
it, shall go into the lower parts of the earth.
10They shall fall by the sword: they shall
be a portion for foxes.
11But the king shall rejoice in God; every
one that sweareth
by him shall glory:
but the mouth of
them that speak lies
shall be stopped.

63:11 Liars
◄ Proverbs 19:5 ►

Psalm 64

To the chief Musician, A Psalm of David.

1Hear my voice, O God, in my prayer:
preserve my life from fear of the enemy.
2Hide me from the secret counsel of the
wicked; from the insurrection of the workers of iniquity:
3Who whet their tongue like a sword,
and bend *their bows to shoot* their arrows,
even bitter words:
4That they may shoot in secret at the
perfect: suddenly do they shoot at him,
and fear not.
5They encourage themselves *in* an evil
matter: they commune of laying snares
privily; they say, Who shall see them?
6They search out
iniquities; they ac-
complish a diligent
search: both the in-
ward *thought* of
every one *of them,*
and the heart, *is* deep.

64:6 Bad Thoughts
◄ Deuteronomy 15:9
Psalm 94:11 ►

7But God shall shoot at them *with* an
arrow; suddenly shall they be wounded.
8So they shall make their own tongue
to fall upon themselves: all that see them
shall flee away.
9And all men shall fear, and shall declare the work of God; for they shall wisely consider of his doing.
10The righteous
shall be glad in the
LORD, and shall
trust in him; and all
the upright in heart
shall glory.

64:10 Why Do Right?
◄ Psalm 49:14
Psalm 97:11 ►

Psalm 65

To the chief Musician,
A Psalm *and* Song of David.

1Praise waiteth for thee, O God, in Sion:
and unto thee shall the vow be performed.
2O thou that hearest prayer, unto thee
shall all flesh come.

3 Iniquities prevail against me: *as for* our
transgressions, thou shalt purge them
away.
4 Blessed *is the man whom* thou choosest,
and causest to approach *unto thee, that* he
may dwell in thy courts: we shall be satisfied with the goodness of thy house, *even*
of thy holy temple.
5 *By* terrible things in righteousness wilt
thou answer us, O God of our salvation;
who art the confidence of all the ends of
the earth, and of them that are afar off *upon*
the sea:
6 Which by his
strength setteth fast
the mountains; *being*
girded with power:
7 Which stilleth
the noise of the
seas, the noise of their waves, and the tumult of the people.

65:6 God's Power
◄ Psalm 62:11
Psalm 93:4 ►

8 They also that dwell in the uttermost
parts are afraid at thy tokens: thou makest
the outgoings of the morning and evening
to rejoice.
9 Thou visitest the
earth, and waterest
it: thou greatly en-
richest it with the
river of God, *which*
is full of water: thou
preparest them corn, when thou hast so
provided for it.

65:9 Blessings
◄ 1 Kings 3:13
Psalm 68:19 ►

10 Thou waterest the ridges thereof abundantly: thou settlest the furrows thereof:
thou makest it soft with showers: thou
blessest the springing thereof.
11 Thou crownest the year with thy goodness; and thy paths drop fatness.
12 They drop *upon* the pastures of the wilderness: and the little hills rejoice on every
side.
13 The pastures are
clothed with flocks;
the valleys also are
covered over with
corn; they shout for
joy, they also sing.

65:13 Nature's Praise
◄ Psalm 69:34 ►

Psalm 66

To the chief Musician, A Song *or* Psalm.

1 Make a joyful noise unto God, all ye
lands:
2 Sing forth the honour of his name:
make his praise glorious.
3 Say unto God, How terrible *art thou in*
thy works! through the greatness of thy
power shall thine enemies submit themselves unto thee.
4 All the earth shall worship thee, and
shall sing unto thee; they shall sing *to* thy
name. Selah.
5 Come and see the works of God: *he is*
terrible *in his* doing toward the children
of men.
6 He turned the sea into dry *land:* they
went through the flood on foot: there did
we rejoice in him.
7 He ruleth by his power for ever; his eyes
behold the nations: let not the rebellious
exalt themselves. Selah.
8 O bless our God, ye people, and make
the voice of his praise to be heard:
9 Which holdeth our soul in life, and
suffereth not our feet to be moved.
10 For thou,
O God, hast proved
us: thou hast tried
us, as silver is tried.
11 Thou brought-
est us into the net;
thou laidst affliction upon our loins.

66:10 Pain
◄ Job 23:10
Isaiah 48:10 ►

12 Thou hast caused men to ride over our
heads; we went through fire and through
water: but thou broughtest us out into a
wealthy *place.*
13 I will go into thy house with burnt offerings: I will pay thee my vows,
14 Which my lips have uttered, and
my mouth hath spoken, when I was in
trouble.
15 I will offer unto thee burnt sacrifices
of fatlings, with the incense of rams; I will
offer bullocks with goats. Selah.
16 Come *and* hear, all ye that fear God,
and I will declare what he hath done for
my soul.
17 I cried unto him with my mouth, and
he was extolled with my tongue.
18 If I regard iniq-
uity in my heart,
the Lord will not
hear *me:*
19 *But* verily God
hath heard *me;* he
hath attended to the voice of my prayer.

66:18 Unanswered Prayer
◄ 1 Samuel 28:6
Proverbs 1:28 ►

20 Blessed *be* God, which hath not turned
away my prayer, nor his mercy from me.

Psalm 67

To the chief Musician on Neginoth,
A Psalm *or* Song.

1 God be merciful unto us, and bless us; *and* cause his face to shine upon us; Selah.

2 That thy way may be known upon earth, thy saving health among all nations.

3 Let the people praise thee, O God; let all the people praise thee.

4 O let the nations be glad and sing for joy: for thou shalt judge the people righteously, and govern the nations upon earth. Selah.

67:3 Praising God
◄ Psalm 33:2
Isaiah 42:12 ►

5 Let the people praise thee, O God; let all the people praise thee.

6 *Then* shall the earth yield her increase; *and* God, *even* our own God, shall bless us.

7 God shall bless us; and all the ends of the earth shall fear him.

Psalm 68

To the chief Musician,
A Psalm *or* Song of David.

1 Let God arise, let his enemies be scattered: let them also that hate him flee before him.

2 As smoke is driven away, *so* drive *them* away: as wax melteth before the fire, *so* let the wicked perish at the presence of God.

3 But let the righteous be glad; let them rejoice before God: yea, let them exceedingly rejoice.

4 Sing unto God, sing praises to his name: extol him that rideth upon the heavens by his name JAH, and rejoice before him.

5 A father of the fatherless, and a judge of the widows, *is* God in his holy habitation.

68:5
God's Care for Kids
◄ Psalm 10:14
Psalm 146:9 ►

6 God setteth the solitary in families: he bringeth out those which are bound with chains: but the rebellious dwell in a dry *land.*

68:5 Perfect Father
◄ 1 Chronicles 29:10
Isaiah 63:16 ►

7 O God, when thou wentest forth before thy people, when thou didst march through the wilderness; Selah:

8 The earth shook, the heavens also dropped at the presence of God: *even* Sinai itself *was moved* at the presence of God, the God of Israel.

9 Thou, O God, didst send a plentiful rain, whereby thou didst confirm thine inheritance, when it was weary.

10 Thy congregation hath dwelt therein: thou, O God, hast prepared of thy goodness for the poor.

68:10
Promises to the Poor
◄ Psalm 14:6
Psalm 69:33 ►

11 The Lord gave the word: great *was* the company of those that published *it.*

12 Kings of armies did flee apace: and she that tarried at home divided the spoil.

13 Though ye have lien among the pots, *yet shall ye be as* the wings of a dove covered with silver, and her feathers with yellow gold.

14 When the Almighty scattered kings in it, it was *white* as snow in Salmon.

15 The hill of God *is as* the hill of Bashan; an high hill *as* the hill of Bashan.

16 Why leap ye, ye high hills? *this is* the hill *which* God desireth to dwell in; yea, the LORD will dwell *in it* for ever.

17 The chariots of God *are* twenty thousand, *even* thousands of angels: the Lord *is* among them, *as in* Sinai, in the holy *place.*

18 Thou hast ascended on high, thou hast led captivity captive: thou hast received gifts for men; yea, *for* the rebellious also, that the LORD God might dwell *among them.*

19 Blessed *be* the Lord, *who* daily loadeth us *with benefits, even* the God of our salvation. Selah.

68:19
Blessings
◄ Psalm 65:9 ►

20 *He that is* our God *is* the God of salvation; and unto God the Lord *belong* the issues from death.

21 But God shall wound the head of his enemies, *and* the hairy scalp of such an one as goeth on still in his trespasses.

22 The Lord said, I will bring again from Bashan, I will bring *my people* again from the depths of the sea:

23 That thy foot may be dipped in the

blood of *thine* enemies, *and* the tongue of
thy dogs in the same.
24 They have seen thy goings, O God;
even the goings of my God, my King, in
the sanctuary.
25 The singers went before, the players
on instruments *followed* after; among *them*
were the damsels playing with timbrels.
26 Bless ye God in the congregations, *even*
the Lord, from the fountain of Israel.
27 There *is* little Benjamin *with* their ruler, the princes of Judah *and* their council,
the princes of Zebulun, *and* the princes of
Naphtali.
28 Thy God hath commanded thy strength:
strengthen, O God, that which thou hast
wrought for us.
29 Because of thy temple at Jerusalem
shall kings bring presents unto thee.
30 Rebuke the company of spearmen, the
multitude of the bulls, with the calves of
the people, *till every one* submit himself
with pieces of silver: scatter thou the people *that* delight in war.
31 Princes shall come out of Egypt; Ethiopia shall soon stretch out her hands unto
God.
32 Sing unto God, ye kingdoms of the
earth; O sing praises unto the Lord; Selah:
33 To him that rideth upon the heavens
of heavens, *which were* of old; lo, he doth
send out his voice, *and that* a mighty voice.
34 Ascribe ye strength unto God: his excellency *is* over Israel, and his strength *is*
in the clouds.
35 O God, *thou art* terrible out of thy holy
places: the God of Israel *is* he that giveth
strength and power unto *his* people.
Blessed *be* God.

Psalm 69

To chief Musician upon Shoshannim,
A Psalm of David.

1 Save me, O God; for the waters are
come in unto *my* soul.
2 I sink in deep
mire, where *there is*
no standing: I am
come into deep wa-
ters, where the
floods overflow me.

69:2 Unhappiness
◄ Psalm 42:6
Psalm 73:16 ►

3 I am weary of my crying: my throat is
dried: mine eyes
fail while I wait for
my God.

69:3 Pray and Wait
◄ Psalm 40:17
Psalm 119:82 ►

4 They that hate
me without a cause
are more than the
hairs of mine head: they that would destroy me, *being* mine enemies wrongfully,
are mighty: then I restored *that* which I
took not away.
5 O God, thou knowest my foolishness;
and my sins are not hid from thee.
6 Let not them that wait on thee, O Lord
GOD of hosts, be ashamed for my sake: let
not those that seek thee be confounded
for my sake, O God of Israel.
7 Because for thy sake I have borne reproach; shame hath covered my face.
8 I am become a stranger unto my brethren, and an alien unto my mother's children.
9 For the zeal of
thine house hath
eaten me up; and
the reproaches of
them that re-
proached thee are
fallen upon me.

69:9
Why Jesus Died
◄ Isaiah 53:5 ►

10 When I wept, *and chastened* my soul
with fasting, that was to my reproach.
11 I made sackcloth also my garment; and
I became a proverb to them.
12 They that sit in the gate speak against
me; and I *was* the song of the drunkards.
13 But as for me, my prayer *is* unto thee,
O LORD, *in* an acceptable time: O God, in
the multitude of thy mercy hear me, in the
truth of thy salvation.
14 Deliver me out of the mire, and let me
not sink: let me be delivered from them
that hate me, and out of the deep waters.
15 Let not the waterflood overflow me,
neither let the deep swallow me up, and
let not the pit shut her mouth upon me.
16 Hear me, O LORD; for thy lovingkindness *is* good: turn unto me according
to the multitude of thy tender mercies.
17 And hide not thy face from thy servant; for I am in trouble: hear me speedily.
18 Draw nigh unto my soul, *and* redeem
it: deliver me because of mine enemies.
19 Thou hast known my reproach, and
my shame, and my dishonour: mine adversaries *are* all before thee.
20 Reproach hath broken my heart; and

I am full of heaviness: and I looked *for some* to take pity, but *there was* none; and for comforters, but I found none.

21They gave me also gall for my meat; and in my thirst they gave me vinegar to drink.

69:21 Cruelty
◄ Psalm 35:15
Proverbs 25:20 ►

22Let their table become a snare before them: and *that which should have been* for *their* welfare, *let it become* a trap.

23Let their eyes be darkened, that they see not; and make their loins continually to shake.

24Pour out thine indignation upon them, and let thy wrathful anger take hold of them.

25Let their habitation be desolate; *and* let none dwell in their tents.

26For they persecute *him* whom thou hast smitten; and they talk to the grief of those whom thou hast wounded.

27Add iniquity unto their iniquity: and let them not come into thy righteousness.

28Let them be blotted out of the book of the living, and not be written with the righteous.

29But I *am* poor and sorrowful: let thy salvation, O God, set me up on high.

30I will praise the name of God with a song, and will magnify him with thanksgiving.

31*This* also shall please the LORD better than an ox *or* bullock that hath horns and hoofs.

32The humble shall see *this, and* be glad: and your heart shall live that seek God.

33For the LORD heareth the poor, and despiseth not his prisoners.

69:33 Promises to the Poor
◄ Psalm 68:10
Psalm 109:31 ►

34Let the heaven and earth praise him, the seas, and every thing that moveth therein.

69:34 Nature's Praise
◄ Psalm 65:13
Psalm 98:8 ►

35For God will save Zion, and will build the cities of Judah: that they may dwell there, and have it in possession.

36The seed also of his servants shall inherit it: and they that love his name shall dwell therein.

Psalm 70

To the chief Musician, *A Psalm* of David, to bring to remembrance.

1*Make haste,* O God, to deliver me; make haste to help me, O LORD.

2Let them be ashamed and confounded that seek after my soul: let them be turned backward, and put to confusion, that desire my hurt.

3Let them be turned back for a reward of their shame that say, Aha, aha.

4Let all those that seek thee rejoice and be glad in thee: and let such as love thy salvation say continually, Let God be magnified.

5But I *am* poor and needy: make haste unto me, O God: thou *art* my help and my deliverer; O LORD, make no tarrying.

Psalm 71

1In thee, O LORD, do I put my trust: let me never be put to confusion.

2Deliver me in thy righteousness, and cause me to escape: incline thine ear unto me, and save me.

3Be thou my strong habitation, whereunto I may continually resort: thou hast given commandment to save me; for thou *art* my rock and my fortress.

4Deliver me, O my God, out of the hand of the wicked, out of the hand of the unrighteous and cruel man.

5For thou *art* my hope, O Lord GOD: *thou art* my trust from my youth.

71:5 Young Men
◄ 2 Chronicles 34:1-3
Luke 2:49 ►

6By thee have I been holden up from the womb: thou art he that took me out of my mother's bowels: my praise *shall be* continually of thee.

7I am as a wonder unto many; but thou *art* my strong refuge.

8Let my mouth be filled *with* thy praise *and with* thy honour all the day.

9Cast me not off in the time of old age; forsake me not when my strength faileth.

10For mine enemies speak against me; and they that lay wait for my soul take counsel together,

11Saying, God hath forsaken him: persecute and take him; for *there is* none to deliver *him.*

12 O God, be not far from me: O my God, make haste for my help.

13 Let them be confounded *and* consumed that are adversaries to my soul; let them be covered *with* reproach and dishonour that seek my hurt.

14 But I will hope continually, and will yet praise thee more and more.

15 My mouth shall shew forth thy righteousness *and* thy salvation all the day; for I know not the numbers *thereof.*

16 I will go in the strength of the Lord GOD: I will make mention of thy righteousness, *even* of thine only.

17 O God, thou hast taught me from my youth: and hitherto have I declared thy wondrous works.

71:17 God as Teacher
◄ Psalm 32:8
Psalm 94:10 ►

18 Now also when I am old and greyheaded, O God, forsake me not; until I have shewed thy strength unto *this* generation, *and* thy power to every one *that* is to come.

19 Thy righteousness also, O God, *is* very high, who hast done great things: O God, who *is* like unto thee!

20 *Thou,* which hast shewed me great and sore troubles, shalt quicken me again, and shalt bring me up again from the depths of the earth.

71:20 Resurrection
◄ Psalm 49:15
Hosea 13:14 ►

21 Thou shalt increase my greatness, and comfort me on every side.

71:21 God's Comfort
◄ Psalm 86:17 ►

22 I will also praise thee with the psaltery, *even* thy truth, O my God: unto thee will I sing with the harp, O thou Holy One of Israel.

71:22 Names of God
◄ 1 Chronicles 29:10
Matthew 6:9 ►

23 My lips shall greatly rejoice when I sing unto thee; and my soul, which thou hast redeemed.

24 My tongue also shall talk of thy righteousness all the day long: for they are confounded, for they are brought unto shame, that seek my hurt.

Psalm 72

A Psalm for Solomon.

1 Give the king thy judgments, O God, and thy righteousness unto the king's son.

2 He shall judge thy people with righteousness, and thy poor with judgment.

3 The mountains shall bring peace to the people, and the little hills, by righteousness.

4 He shall judge the poor of the people, he shall save the children of the needy, and shall break in pieces the oppressor.

5 They shall fear thee as long as the sun and moon endure, throughout all generations.

6 He shall come down like rain upon the mown grass: as showers *that* water the earth.

7 In his days shall the righteous flourish; and abundance of peace so long as the moon endureth.

8 He shall have dominion also from sea to sea, and from the river unto the ends of the earth.

9 They that dwell in the wilderness shall bow before him; and his enemies shall lick the dust.

10 The kings of Tarshish and of the isles shall bring presents: the kings of Sheba and Seba shall offer gifts.

11 Yea, all kings shall fall down before him: all nations shall serve him.

12 For he shall deliver the needy when he crieth; the poor also, and *him* that hath no helper.

13 He shall spare the poor and needy, and shall save the souls of the needy.

14 He shall redeem their soul from deceit and violence: and precious shall their blood be in his sight.

15 And he shall live, and to him shall be given of the gold of Sheba: prayer also shall be made for him continually; *and* daily shall he be praised.

16 There shall be an handful of corn in the earth upon the top of the mountains; the fruit thereof shall shake like Lebanon: and *they* of the city shall flourish like grass of the earth.

17 His name shall endure for ever: his name shall be continued as long as the sun: and *men* shall be blessed in him: all nations shall call him blessed.

18 Blessed *be* the LORD God, the God of
Israel, who only doeth wondrous things.
19 And blessed *be* his glorious name for
ever: and let the whole earth be filled *with*
his glory; Amen, and Amen.
20 The prayers of David the son of Jesse
are ended.

Psalm 73

A Psalm of Asaph.

1 Truly God *is* good to Israel, *even* to such
as are of a clean heart.
2 But as for me, my feet were almost
gone; my steps had well nigh slipped.
3 For I was envi-
ous at the foolish,
when I saw the
prosperity of the
wicked.

73:3 Just You Wait
◄ Psalm 37:35
Psalm 73:12 ►

4 For *there are* no
bands in their death: but their strength *is*
firm.
5 They *are* not in trouble *as other* men;
neither are they plagued like *other* men.
6 Therefore pride
compasseth them
about as a chain;
violence covereth
them *as* a garment.

73:6 Arrogance
◄ Psalm 10:2
Psalm 119:21 ►

7 Their eyes stand
out with fatness:
they have more
than heart could
wish.

73:6 Violence
◄ Psalm 55:9
Proverbs 4:17 ►

8 They are corrupt,
and speak wickedly
concerning oppression: they speak loftily.
9 They set their mouth against the heavens, and their tongue walketh through the
earth.
10 Therefore his people return hither: and
waters of a full *cup* are wrung out to them.
11 And they say, How doth God know?
and is there knowledge in the most High?
12 Behold, these
are the ungodly,
who prosper in the
world; they increase
in riches.

73:12 Just You Wait
◄ Psalm 73:3
Jeremiah 5:28 ►

13 Verily I have
cleansed my heart *in* vain, and washed my
hands in innocency.
14 For all the day long have I been
plagued, and chas-
tened every morn-
ing.

73:14 Injustice
◄ Job 21:7
Ecclesiastes 7:15 ►

15 If I say, I will
speak thus; behold,
I should offend
against the genera-
tion of thy children.
16 When I thought
to know this, it *was*
too painful for me;

73:16 Unhappiness
◄ Psalm 69:2
Psalm 137:1 ►

17 Until I went in-
to the sanctuary of God; *then* understood
I their end.
18 Surely thou
didst set them in
slippery places: thou
castedst them down
into destruction.

73:18 Wicked Insecurity
◄ Proverbs 23:34 ►

19 How are they
brought into desolation, as in a moment!
they are utterly consumed with terrors.
20 As a dream when *one* awaketh; *so,*
O Lord, when thou awakest, thou shalt despise their image.
21 Thus my heart
was grieved, and I
was pricked in my
reins.

73:21 Not Confessing
◄ Psalm 51:3
John 16:8 ►

22 So foolish *was*
I, and ignorant: I
was *as* a beast be-
fore thee.

73:22 Ignorance
◄ Job 8:9
Ecclesiastes 8:7 ►

23 Nevertheless I
am continually
with thee: thou hast
holden *me* by my
right hand.
24 Thou shalt
guide me with thy
counsel, and after-
ward receive me *to*
glory.

73:24 God's Guidance
◄ Psalm 48:14
Isaiah 30:21 ►

25 Whom have I
in heaven *but thee?* and *there is* none upon
earth *that* I desire beside thee.
26 My flesh and
my heart faileth: *but*
God *is* the strength
of my heart, and my
portion for ever.

73:26 Finding Strength
◄ Psalm 46:1
Psalm 81:1 ►

27 For, lo, they
that are far from thee shall perish: thou
hast destroyed all them that go a whoring
from thee.

28 But *it is* good for me to draw near to God: I have put my trust in the Lord GOD, that I may declare all thy works.

Psalm 74

Maschil of Asaph.

1 O God, why hast thou cast *us* off for ever? *why* doth thine anger smoke against the sheep of thy pasture?

2 Remember thy congregation, *which* thou hast purchased of old; the rod of thine inheritance, *which* thou hast redeemed; this mount Zion, wherein thou hast dwelt.

3 Lift up thy feet unto the perpetual desolations; *even* all *that* the enemy hath done wickedly in the sanctuary.

4 Thine enemies roar in the midst of thy congregations; they set up their ensigns *for* signs.

5 *A man* was famous according as he had lifted up axes upon the thick trees.

6 But now they break down the carved work thereof at once with axes and hammers.

7 They have cast fire into thy sanctuary, they have defiled *by casting down* the dwelling place of thy name to the ground.

8 They said in their hearts, Let us destroy them together: they have burned up all the synagogues of God in the land.

9 We see not our signs: *there is* no more any prophet: neither *is there* among us any that knoweth how long.

10 O God, how long shall the adversary reproach? shall the enemy blaspheme thy name for ever?

11 Why withdrawest thou thy hand, even thy right hand? pluck *it* out of thy bosom.

12 For God *is* my King of old, working salvation in the midst of the earth.

13 Thou didst divide the sea by thy strength: thou brakest the heads of the dragons in the waters.

14 Thou brakest the heads of leviathan in pieces, *and* gavest him *to be* meat to the people inhabiting the wilderness.

15 Thou didst cleave the fountain and the flood: thou driedst up mighty rivers.

16 The day *is* thine, the night also *is* thine: thou hast prepared the light and the sun.

17 Thou hast set all the borders of the earth: thou hast made summer and winter.

18 Remember this, *that* the enemy hath reproached, O LORD, and *that* the foolish people have blasphemed thy name.

19 O deliver not the soul of thy turtledove unto the multitude *of the wicked:* forget not the congregation of thy poor for ever.

20 Have respect unto the covenant: for the dark places of the earth are full of the habitations of cruelty.

21 O let not the oppressed return ashamed: let the poor and needy praise thy name.

22 Arise, O God, plead thine own cause: remember how the foolish man reproacheth thee daily.

23 Forget not the voice of thine enemies: the tumult of those that rise up against thee increaseth continually.

Psalm 75

To the chief Musician, Al-taschith,
A Psalm *or* Song of Asaph.

1 Unto thee, O God, do we give thanks, *unto thee* do we give thanks: for *that* thy name is near thy wondrous works declare.

2 When I shall receive the congregation I will judge uprightly.

3 The earth and all the inhabitants thereof are dissolved: I bear up the pillars of it. Selah.

4 I said unto the fools, Deal not foolishly: and to the wicked, Lift not up the horn:

5 Lift not up your horn on high: speak *not with* a stiff neck.

6 For promotion *cometh* neither from the east, nor from the west, nor from the south.

7 But God *is* the judge: he putteth down one, and setteth up another.

8 For in the hand of the LORD *there is* a cup, and the wine is red; it is full of mixture; and he poureth out of the same: but the dregs thereof, all the wicked of the earth shall wring *them* out, *and* drink *them.*

75:7 God as Judge
◄ Psalm 58:11
Psalm 96:13 ►

75:7 God at Work
◄ 1 Kings 14:7
Daniel 2:21 ►

9But I will declare for ever; I will sing
praises to the God of Jacob.
10All the horns of the wicked also will I
cut off; *but* the horns of the righteous shall
be exalted.

Psalm 76

To the chief Musician on Neginoth,
A Psalm *or* Song of Asaph.

1In Judah *is* God known: his name *is*
great in Israel.
2In Salem also is his tabernacle, and his
dwelling place in Zion.
3There brake he the arrows of the bow,
the shield, and the sword, and the battle.
Selah.
4Thou *art* more glorious *and* excellent
than the mountains of prey.
5The stouthearted are spoiled, they have
slept their sleep: and none of the men of
might have found their hands.
6At thy rebuke, O God of Jacob, both
the chariot and horse are cast into a dead
sleep.
7Thou, *even* thou, *art* to be feared: and
who may stand in thy sight when once
thou art angry?
8Thou didst cause judgment to be heard
from heaven; the earth feared, and was
still,
9When God arose to judgment, to save
all the meek of the earth. Selah.
10Surely the wrath of man shall praise
thee: the remainder of wrath shalt thou
restrain.
11Vow, and pay unto the LORD your God:
let all that be round about him bring
presents unto him that ought to be feared.
12He shall cut off the spirit of princes:
he is terrible to the kings of the earth.

Psalm 77

To the chief Musician, to Jeduthun,
A Psalm of Asaph.

1I cried unto God with my voice, *even*
unto God with my voice; and he gave ear
unto me.
2In the day of my trouble I sought the
Lord: my sore ran in the night, and ceased
not: my soul refused to be comforted.
3I remembered God, and was troubled:
I complained, and my spirit was overwhelmed. Selah.
4Thou holdest mine eyes waking: I am
so troubled that I cannot speak.
5I have considered the days of old, the
years of ancient times.
6I call to remembrance my song in the
night: I commune with mine own heart:
and my spirit made diligent search.
7Will the Lord cast off for ever? and will
he be favourable no more?
8Is his mercy clean gone for ever? doth
his promise fail for evermore?
9Hath God forgotten to be gracious?
hath he in anger shut up his tender mercies? Selah.
10And I said, This *is* my infirmity: *but I*
will remember the years of the right hand
of the most High.
11I will remember the works of the LORD:
surely I will remember thy wonders of old.
12I will meditate also of all thy work,
and talk of thy doings.
13Thy way, O God, *is* in the sanctuary:
who *is so* great a God as *our* God?
14Thou *art* the God that doest wonders:
thou hast declared thy strength among the
people.
15Thou hast with *thine* arm redeemed
thy people, the sons of Jacob and Joseph.
Selah.
16The waters saw thee, O God, the waters saw thee; they were afraid: the depths
also were troubled.
17The clouds poured out water: the skies
sent out a sound: thine arrows also went
abroad.
18The voice of thy thunder *was* in the
heaven: the lightnings lightened the world:
the earth trembled and shook.
19Thy way *is* in the sea, and thy path in
the great waters, and thy footsteps are not
known.
20Thou leddest thy people like a flock
by the hand of Moses and Aaron.

Psalm 78

Maschil of Asaph.

1Give ear, O my people, *to* my law: incline your ears to the words of my mouth.
2I will open my mouth in a parable: I
will utter dark sayings of old:

3 Which we have heard and known, and our fathers have told us.

4 We will not hide *them* from their children, shewing to the generation to come the praises of the LORD, and his strength, and his wonderful works that he hath done.

5 For he established a testimony in Jacob, and appointed a law in Israel, which he commanded our fathers, that they should make them known to their children:

6 That the generation to come might know *them, even* the children *which* should be born; *who* should arise and declare *them* to their children:

78:6 Instruction
◄ Deuteronomy 6:7
Ezekiel 44:23 ►

7 That they might set their hope in God, and not forget the works of God, but keep his commandments:

8 And might not be as their fathers, a stubborn and rebellious generation; a generation *that* set not their heart aright, and whose spirit was not stedfast with God.

9 The children of Ephraim, *being* armed, *and* carrying bows, turned back in the day of battle.

10 They kept not the covenant of God, and refused to walk in his law;

11 And forgat his works, and his wonders that he had shewed them.

78:11 Don't Forget...
◄ Psalm 50:22
Isaiah 17:10 ►

12 Marvellous things did he in the sight of their fathers, in the land of Egypt, *in* the field of Zoan.

13 He divided the sea, and caused them to pass through; and he made the waters to stand as an heap.

14 In the daytime also he led them with a cloud, and all the night with a light of fire.

15 He clave the rocks in the wilderness, and gave *them* drink as *out of* the great depths.

16 He brought streams also out of the rock, and caused waters to run down like rivers.

17 And they sinned yet more against him by provoking the most High in the wilderness.

18 And they tempted God in their heart by asking meat for their lust.

19 Yea, they spake against God; they said, Can God furnish a table in the wilderness?

20 Behold, he smote the rock, that the waters gushed out, and the streams overflowed; can he give bread also? can he provide flesh for his people?

21 Therefore the LORD heard *this,* and was wroth: so a fire was kindled against Jacob, and anger also came up against Israel;

22 Because they believed not in God, and trusted not in his salvation:

23 Though he had commanded the clouds from above, and opened the doors of heaven,

24 And had rained down manna upon them to eat, and had given them of the corn of heaven.

25 Man did eat angels' food: he sent them meat to the full.

26 He caused an east wind to blow in the heaven: and by his power he brought in the south wind.

27 He rained flesh also upon them as dust, and feathered fowls like as the sand of the sea:

28 And he let *it* fall in the midst of their camp, round about their habitations.

29 So they did eat, and were well filled: for he gave them their own desire;

30 They were not estranged from their lust. But while their meat *was* yet in their mouths,

31 The wrath of God came upon them, and slew the fattest of them, and smote down the chosen *men* of Israel.

32 For all this they sinned still, and believed not for his wondrous works.

33 Therefore their days did he consume in vanity, and their years in trouble.

34 When he slew them, then they sought him: and they returned and enquired early after God.

35 And they remembered that God *was* their rock, and the high God their redeemer.

36 Nevertheless they did flatter him with their mouth, and they lied unto him with their tongues.

37 For their heart was not right with him, neither were they stedfast in his covenant.

38 But he, *being* full of compassion, forgave *their* iniquity, and destroyed *them* not: yea, many a time turned he his anger away, and did not stir up all his wrath.

39 For he remembered that they *were but*

Turn to the next page for more . . .

flesh; a wind that passeth away, and cometh not again.

78:39 Your Body
◄ Psalm 49:12
Psalm 103:14 ►

40How oft did they provoke him in the wilderness, *and* grieve him in the desert!

78:40 Losers
◄ Ezra 5:12
Psalm 78:56 ►

41Yea, they turned back and tempted God, and limited the Holy One of Israel.

42They remembered not his hand, *nor* the day when he delivered them from the enemy.

43How he had wrought his signs in Egypt, and his wonders in the field of Zoan:

44And had turned their rivers into blood; and their floods, that they could not drink.

45He sent divers sorts of flies among them, which devoured them; and frogs, which destroyed them.

46He gave also their increase unto the caterpiller, and their labour unto the locust.

47He destroyed their vines with hail, and their sycomore trees with frost.

48He gave up their cattle also to the hail, and their flocks to hot thunderbolts.

49He cast upon them the fierceness of his anger, wrath, and indignation, and trouble, by sending evil angels *among them.*

50He made a way to his anger; he spared not their soul from death, but gave their life over to the pestilence;

51And smote all the firstborn in Egypt; the chief of *their* strength in the tabernacles of Ham:

52But made his own people to go forth like sheep, and guided them in the wilderness like a flock.

53And he led them on safely, so that they feared not: but the sea overwhelmed their enemies.

54And he brought them to the border of his sanctuary, *even to* this mountain, *which* his right hand had purchased.

55He cast out the heathen also before them, and divided them an inheritance by line, and made the tribes of Israel to dwell in their tents.

56Yet they tempted and provoked the most high God, and kept not his testimonies:

78:56 Losers
◄ Psalm 78:40
Psalm 106:7 ►

57But turned back, and dealt unfaithfully like their fathers: they were turned aside like a deceitful bow.

58For they provoked him to anger with their high places, and moved him to jealousy with their graven images.

59When God heard *this,* he was wroth, and greatly abhorred Israel:

60So that he forsook the tabernacle of Shiloh, the tent *which* he placed among men;

61And delivered his strength into captivity, and his glory into the enemy's hand.

62He gave his people over also unto the sword; and was wroth with his inheritance.

63The fire consumed their young men; and their maidens were not given to marriage.

64Their priests fell by the sword; and their widows made no lamentation.

65Then the Lord awaked as one out of sleep, *and* like a mighty man that shouteth by reason of wine.

66And he smote his enemies in the hinder parts: he put them to a perpetual reproach.

67Moreover he refused the tabernacle of Joseph, and chose not the tribe of Ephraim:

68But chose the tribe of Judah, the mount Zion which he loved.

69And he built his sanctuary like high *palaces,* like the earth which he hath established for ever.

70He chose David also his servant, and took him from the sheepfolds:

71From following the ewes great with young he brought him to feed Jacob his people, and Israel his inheritance.

72So he fed them according to the integrity of his heart; and guided them by the skilfulness of his hands.

Psalm 79

A Psalm of Asaph.

1O God, the heathen are come into thine inheritance; thy holy temple have they defiled; they have laid Jerusalem on heaps.

2 The dead bodies of thy servants have
they given *to be* meat unto the fowls of the
heaven, the flesh of thy saints unto the
beasts of the earth.
3 Their blood have they shed like water
round about Jerusalem; and *there was* none
to bury *them.*
4 We are become a reproach to our
neighbours, a scorn and derision to them
that are round about us.
5 How long, LORD? wilt thou be angry
for ever? shall thy jealousy burn like fire?
6 Pour out thy wrath upon the heathen
that have not known thee, and upon the
kingdoms that have not called upon thy
name.
7 For they have devoured Jacob, and laid
waste his dwelling place.
8 O remember not against us former iniquities: let thy tender mercies speedily
prevent us: for we are brought very low.
9 Help us, O God of our salvation, for
the glory of thy name: and deliver us, and
purge away our sins, for thy name's sake.
10 Wherefore should the heathen say,
Where *is* their God? let him be known
among the heathen in our sight *by* the re-
venging of the blood of thy servants *which
is* shed.
11 Let the sighing of the prisoner come
before thee; according to the greatness of
thy power preserve thou those that are
appointed to die;
12 And render unto our neighbours sevenfold into their bosom their reproach,
wherewith they have reproached thee,
O Lord.
13 So we thy people and sheep of thy pasture will give thee thanks for ever: we will
shew forth thy praise to all generations.

Psalm 80

To the chief Musician upon
Shoshannim-Eduth, A Psalm of Asaph.

1 Give ear, O Shepherd of Israel, thou
that leadest Joseph like a flock; thou that
dwellest *between* the cherubims, shine
forth.
2 Before Ephraim and Benjamin and
Manasseh stir up thy strength, and come
and save us.
3 Turn us again, O God, and cause thy
face to shine; and we shall be saved.
4 O LORD God of hosts, how long wilt
thou be angry against the prayer of thy
people?
5 Thou feedest them with the bread of
tears; and givest them tears to drink in great
measure.
6 Thou makest us a strife unto our
neighbours: and our enemies laugh among
themselves.
7 Turn us again, O God of hosts, and
cause thy face to shine; and we shall be
saved.
8 Thou hast brought a vine out of Egypt:
thou hast cast out the heathen, and planted it.
9 Thou preparedst *room* before it, and
didst cause it to take deep root, and it filled
the land.
10 The hills were covered with the shadow of it, and the boughs thereof *were like*
the goodly cedars.
11 She sent out her boughs unto the sea,
and her branches unto the river.
12 Why hast thou *then* broken down her
hedges, so that all they which pass by the
way do pluck her?
13 The boar out of the wood doth waste
it, and the wild beast of the field doth devour it.
14 Return, we beseech thee, O God of
hosts: look down from heaven, and behold, and visit this vine;
15 And the vineyard which thy right hand
hath planted, and the branch *that* thou
madest strong for thyself.
16 *It is* burned with fire, *it is* cut down:
they perish at the rebuke of thy countenance.
17 Let thy hand be upon the man of thy
right hand, upon the son of man *whom*
thou madest strong for thyself.
18 So will not we go back from thee:
quicken us, and we will call upon thy
name.
19 Turn us again, O LORD God of hosts,
cause thy face to shine; and we shall be
saved.

Psalm 81

To the chief Musician upon Gittith,
A Psalm of Asaph.

1 Sing aloud unto God our strength:
make a joyful noise unto the God of Jacob.

Turn to the next page for more . . .

2 Take a psalm, and bring hither the timbrel, the pleasant harp with the psaltery.

> **81:1 Finding Strength**
> ◄ Psalm 73:26
> Psalm 84:5 ►

3 Blow up the trumpet in the new moon, in the time appointed, on our solemn feast day.

4 For this *was* a statute for Israel, *and* a law of the God of Jacob.

5 This he ordained in Joseph *for* a testimony, when he went out through the land of Egypt: *where* I heard a language *that* I understood not.

6 I removed his shoulder from the burden: his hands were delivered from the pots.

7 Thou calledst in trouble, and I delivered thee; I answered thee in the secret place of thunder: I proved thee at the waters of Meribah. Selah.

8 Hear, O my people, and I will testify unto thee: O Israel, if thou wilt hearken unto me;

9 There shall no strange god be in thee; neither shalt thou worship any strange god.

10 I *am* the LORD thy God, which brought thee out of the land of Egypt: open thy mouth wide, and I will fill it.

11 But my people would not hearken to my voice; and Israel would none of me.

12 So I gave them up unto their own hearts' lust: *and* they walked in their own counsels.

13 Oh that my people had hearkened unto me, *and* Israel had walked in my ways!

14 I should soon have subdued their enemies, and turned my hand against their adversaries.

15 The haters of the LORD should have submitted themselves unto him: but their time should have endured for ever.

16 He should have fed them also with the finest of the wheat: and with honey out of the rock should I have satisfied thee.

> **81:16 Blessing**
> ◄ Exodus 23:25
> Isaiah 30:23 ►

Psalm 82

A Psalm of Asaph.

1 God standeth in the congregation of the mighty; he judgeth among the gods.

2 How long will ye judge unjustly, and accept the persons of the wicked? Selah.

> **82:2 Don't Be Unfair**
> ◄ Deuteronomy 24:17
> Proverbs 29:27 ►

3 Defend the poor and fatherless: do justice to the afflicted and needy.

> **82:3 Be Fair**
> ◄ Deuteronomy 16:20
> Proverbs 21:3 ►

4 Deliver the poor and needy: rid *them* out of the hand of the wicked.

> **82:3**
> **Fair to the Poor**
> ◄ Proverbs 21:13 ►

5 They know not, neither will they understand; they walk on in darkness: all the foundations of the earth are out of course.

6 I have said, Ye *are* gods; and all of you *are* children of the most High.

> **82:6 Animals vs. People**
> ◄ Psalm 8:6
> Matthew 6:26 ►

7 But ye shall die like men, and fall like one of the princes.

8 Arise, O God, judge the earth: for thou shalt inherit all nations.

Psalm 83

A Song *or* Psalm of Asaph.

1 Keep not thou silence, O God: hold not thy peace, and be not still, O God.

2 For, lo, thine enemies make a tumult: and they that hate thee have lifted up the head.

3 They have taken crafty counsel against thy people, and consulted against thy hidden ones.

4 They have said, Come, and let us cut them off from *being* a nation; that the name of Israel may be no more in remembrance.

5 For they have consulted together with one consent: they are confederate against thee:

6 The tabernacles of Edom, and the Ishmaelites; of Moab, and the Hagarenes;

7 Gebal, and Ammon, and Amalek; the Philistines with the inhabitants of Tyre;

8 Assur also is joined with them: they have holpen the children of Lot. Selah.

9 Do unto them as *unto* the Midianites;

as *to* Sisera, as *to* Jabin, at the brook of Kison:

10 *Which* perished at Endor: they became *as* dung for the earth.

11 Make their nobles like Oreb, and like Zeeb: yea, all their princes as Zebah, and as Zalmunna:

12 Who said, Let us take to ourselves the houses of God in possession.

13 O my God, make them like a wheel; as the stubble before the wind.

14 As the fire burneth a wood, and as the flame setteth the mountains on fire;

15 So persecute them with thy tempest, and make them afraid with thy storm.

16 Fill their faces with shame; that they may seek thy name, O LORD.

17 Let them be confounded and troubled for ever; yea, let them be put to shame, and perish:

83:18 God's Control
◄ Psalm 47:2
Psalm 93:1 ►

18 That *men* may know that thou, whose name alone *is* JEHOVAH, *art* the most high over all the earth.

83:18 Only One God
◄ 1 Chronicles 17:20
Psalm 86:10 ►

Psalm 84

To the chief Musician upon Gittith,
A Psalm for the sons of Korah.

1 How amiable *are* thy tabernacles, O LORD of hosts!

2 My soul longeth, yea, even fainteth for the courts of the LORD: my heart and my flesh crieth out for the living God.

3 Yea, the sparrow hath found an house, and the swallow a nest for herself, where she may lay her young, *even* thine altars, O LORD of hosts, my King, and my God.

4 Blessed *are* they that dwell in thy house: they will be still praising thee. Selah.

5 Blessed *is* the man whose strength *is* in thee; in whose heart *are* the ways *of them*.

84:5 Finding Strength
◄ Psalm 81:1
Psalm 89:21 ►

6 *Who* passing through the valley of Baca make it a well; the rain also filleth the pools.

7 They go from strength to strength, *every one of them* in Zion appeareth before God.

84:7 Making Progress
◄ Job 17:9
Psalm 92:12 ►

8 O LORD God of hosts, hear my prayer: give ear, O God of Jacob. Selah.

9 Behold, O God our shield, and look upon the face of thine anointed.

10 For a day in thy courts *is* better than a thousand. I had rather be a doorkeeper in the house of my God, than to dwell in the tents of wickedness.

11 For the LORD God *is* a sun and shield: the LORD will give grace and glory: no good *thing* will he withhold from them that walk uprightly.

12 O LORD of hosts, blessed *is* the man that trusteth in thee.

Psalm 85

To the chief Musician,
A Psalm for the sons of Korah.

1 LORD, thou hast been favourable unto thy land: thou hast brought back the captivity of Jacob.

2 Thou hast forgiven the iniquity of thy people, thou hast covered all their sin. Selah.

3 Thou hast taken away all thy wrath: thou hast turned *thyself* from the fierceness of thine anger.

4 Turn us, O God of our salvation, and cause thine anger toward us to cease.

5 Wilt thou be angry with us for ever? wilt thou draw out thine anger to all generations?

6 Wilt thou not revive us again: that thy people may rejoice in thee?

7 Shew us thy mercy, O LORD, and grant us thy salvation.

85:7 Praying for Mercy
◄ Psalm 51:1
Psalm 119:77 ►

8 I will hear what God the LORD will speak: for he will speak peace unto his people, and to his saints: but let them not turn again to folly.

9 Surely his salvation *is* nigh them that fear him; that glory may dwell in our land.

10 Mercy and truth are met together; righteousness and peace have kissed *each other*.

11 Truth shall spring out of the earth; and

righteousness shall look down from
heaven.
12Yea, the LORD shall give *that which is*
good; and our land shall yield her increase.
13Righteousness shall go before him;
and shall set *us* in the way of his steps.

Psalm 86

A Prayer of David.

1Bow down thine ear, O LORD, hear me:
for I *am* poor and needy.
2Preserve my soul; for I *am* holy: O thou
my God, save thy servant that trusteth in
thee.
3Be merciful unto me, O Lord: for I cry
unto thee daily.
4Rejoice the soul of thy servant: for unto
thee, O Lord, do I lift up my soul.
5For thou, Lord,
art good, and ready
to forgive; and plen-
teous in mercy unto
all them that call
upon thee.

86:5 God's Mercy
◄ 2 Samuel 24:14
Psalm 103:17 ►

6Give ear, O LORD, unto my prayer; and
attend to the voice of my supplications.
7In the day of my trouble I will call upon
thee: for thou wilt answer me.
8Among the gods *there is* none like unto
thee, O Lord; neither *are there any works*
like unto thy works.
9All nations whom thou hast made shall
come and worship before thee, O Lord;
and shall glorify thy name.
10For thou *art*
great, and doest
wondrous things:
thou *art* God alone.
11Teach me thy
way, O LORD; I will
walk in thy truth: unite my heart to fear
thy name.

86:10 Only One God
◄ Psalm 83:18
Isaiah 43:10 ►

12I will praise thee, O Lord my God, with
all my heart: and I will glorify thy name
for evermore.
13For great *is* thy mercy toward me: and
thou hast delivered my soul from the lowest hell.
14O God, the proud are risen against me,
and the assemblies of violent *men* have
sought after my soul; and have not set thee
before them.
15But thou, O Lord, *art* a God full of
compassion, and gracious, longsuffering,
and plenteous in mercy and truth.
16O turn unto me, and have mercy upon
me; give thy strength unto thy servant, and
save the son of thine handmaid.
17Shew me a to-
ken for good; that
they which hate me
may see *it*, and be
ashamed: because
thou, LORD, hast
holpen me, and comforted me.

86:17 God's Comfort
◄ Psalm 71:21
Isaiah 12:1 ►

Psalm 87

A Psalm *or* Song for the sons of Korah.

1His foundation *is* in the holy mountains.
2The LORD loveth the gates of Zion more
than all the dwellings of Jacob.
3Glorious things are spoken of thee,
O city of God. Selah.
4I will make mention of Rahab and Babylon to them that know me: behold Philistia, and Tyre, with Ethiopia; this *man* was
born there.
5And of Zion it shall be said, This and
that man was born in her: and the highest
himself shall establish her.
6The LORD shall count, when he writeth
up the people, *that* this *man* was born there.
Selah.
7As well the singers as the players on
instruments *shall be there:* all my springs
are in thee.

Psalm 88

A Song *or* Psalm for the sons of Korah,
to the chief Musician upon Mahalath
Leannoth, Maschil of Heman the Ezrahite.

1O LORD God of my salvation, I have
cried day *and* night before thee:
2Let my prayer come before thee: incline
thine ear unto my cry;
3For my soul is full of troubles: and my
life draweth nigh unto the grave.
4I am counted with them that go down
into the pit: I am as a man *that hath* no
strength:
5Free among the dead, like the slain that
lie in the grave, whom thou rememberest no
more: and they are cut off from thy hand.

6 Thou hast laid me in the lowest pit, in darkness, in the deeps.

7 Thy wrath lieth hard upon me, and thou hast afflicted *me* with all thy waves. Selah.

8 Thou hast put away mine acquaintance far from me; thou hast made me an abomination unto them: *I am* shut up, and I cannot come forth.

9 Mine eye mourneth by reason of affliction: LORD, I have called daily upon thee, I have stretched out my hands unto thee.

10 Wilt thou shew wonders to the dead? shall the dead arise *and* praise thee? Selah.

11 Shall thy lovingkindness be declared in the grave? *or* thy faithfulness in destruction?

12 Shall thy wonders be known in the dark? and thy righteousness in the land of forgetfulness?

13 But unto thee have I cried, O LORD; and in the morning shall my prayer prevent thee.

14 LORD, why castest thou off my soul? *why* hidest thou thy face from me?

15 I *am* afflicted and ready to die from *my* youth up: *while* I suffer thy terrors I am distracted.

16 Thy fierce wrath goeth over me; thy terrors have cut me off.

17 They came round about me daily like water; they compassed me about together.

18 Lover and friend hast thou put far from me, *and* mine acquaintance into darkness.

88:18 Being Friendless
◄ Psalm 38:11
Psalm 142:4 ►

Psalm 89

Maschil of Ethan the Ezrahite.

1 I will sing of the mercies of the LORD for ever: with my mouth will I make known thy faithfulness to all generations.

2 For I have said, Mercy shall be built up for ever: thy faithfulness shalt thou establish in the very heavens.

3 I have made a covenant with my chosen, I have sworn unto David my servant,

4 Thy seed will I establish for ever, and build up thy throne to all generations. Selah.

5 And the heavens shall praise thy wonders, O LORD: thy faithfulness also in the congregation of the saints.

6 For who in the heaven can be compared unto the LORD? *who* among the sons of the mighty can be likened unto the LORD?

7 God is greatly to be feared in the assembly of the saints, and to be had in reverence of all *them that are* about him.

89:7 Respecting God
◄ Psalm 33:8
Psalm 111:9 ►

8 O LORD God of hosts, who *is* a strong LORD like unto thee? or to thy faithfulness round about thee?

9 Thou rulest the raging of the sea: when the waves thereof arise, thou stillest them.

10 Thou hast broken Rahab in pieces, as one that is slain; thou hast scattered thine enemies with thy strong arm.

11 The heavens *are* thine, the earth also *is* thine: *as for* the world and the fulness thereof, thou hast founded them.

89:11 Earth
◄ Psalm 60:7
Haggai 2:8 ►

12 The north and the south thou hast created them: Tabor and Hermon shall rejoice in thy name.

13 Thou hast a mighty arm: strong is thy hand, *and* high is thy right hand.

14 Justice and judgment *are* the habitation of thy throne: mercy and truth shall go before thy face.

15 Blessed *is* the people that know the joyful sound: they shall walk, O LORD, in the light of thy countenance.

16 In thy name shall they rejoice all the day: and in thy righteousness shall they be exalted.

89:16 Joy
◄ Psalm 30:5
Psalm 126:5 ►

17 For thou *art* the glory of their strength: and in thy favour our horn shall be exalted.

18 For the LORD *is* our defence; and the Holy One of Israel *is* our king.

19 Then thou spakest in vision to thy holy one, and saidst, I have laid help upon *one that is* mighty; I have exalted *one* chosen out of the people.

20 I have found David my servant; with my holy oil have I anointed him:

21 With whom my hand shall be

Turn to the next page for more . . .

established: mine arm also shall strengthen him.

> **89:21**
> **Finding Strength**
> ◄ Psalm 84:5 ►

22 The enemy shall not exact upon him; nor the son of wickedness afflict him.

23 And I will beat down his foes before his face, and plague them that hate him.

24 But my faithfulness and my mercy *shall be* with him: and in my name shall his horn be exalted.

25 I will set his hand also in the sea, and his right hand in the rivers.

26 He shall cry unto me, Thou *art* my father, my God, and the rock of my salvation.

27 Also I will make him *my* firstborn, higher than the kings of the earth.

28 My mercy will I keep for him for evermore, and my covenant shall stand fast with him.

> **89:28**
> **Promise of Mercy**
> ◄ 2 Chronicles 30:9
> Psalm 103:8 ►

29 His seed also will I make *to endure* for ever, and his throne as the days of heaven.

30 If his children forsake my law, and walk not in my judgments;

31 If they break my statutes, and keep not my commandments;

32 Then will I visit their transgression with the rod, and their iniquity with stripes.

33 Nevertheless my lovingkindness will I not utterly take from him, nor suffer my faithfulness to fail.

34 My covenant will I not break, nor alter the thing that is gone out of my lips.

35 Once have I sworn by my holiness that I will not lie unto David.

36 His seed shall endure for ever, and his throne as the sun before me.

37 It shall be established for ever as the moon, and *as* a faithful witness in heaven. Selah.

38 But thou hast cast off and abhorred, thou hast been wroth with thine anointed.

39 Thou hast made void the covenant of thy servant: thou hast profaned his crown *by casting it* to the ground.

40 Thou hast broken down all his hedges; thou hast brought his strong holds to ruin.

41 All that pass by the way spoil him: he is a reproach to his neighbours.

42 Thou hast set up the right hand of his adversaries; thou hast made all his enemies to rejoice.

43 Thou hast also turned the edge of his sword, and hast not made him to stand in the battle.

44 Thou hast made his glory to cease, and cast his throne down to the ground.

45 The days of his youth hast thou shortened: thou hast covered him with shame. Selah.

46 How long, LORD? wilt thou hide thyself for ever? shall thy wrath burn like fire?

47 Remember how short my time is: wherefore hast thou made all men in vain?

> **89:47 Life Is Short**
> ◄ Psalm 39:5
> Psalm 90:9 ►

48 What man *is he that* liveth, and shall not see death? shall he deliver his soul from the hand of the grave? Selah.

> **89:48 Death**
> ◄ Psalm 49:10
> Ecclesiastes 3:19 ►

> **89:48 Mortality**
> ◄ Job 10:9
> Psalm 103:16 ►

49 Lord, where *are* thy former lovingkindnesses, *which* thou swarest unto David in thy truth?

50 Remember, Lord, the reproach of thy servants; *how* I do bear in my bosom *the reproach of* all the mighty people;

51 Wherewith thine enemies have reproached, O LORD; wherewith they have reproached the footsteps of thine anointed.

52 Blessed *be* the LORD for evermore. Amen, and Amen.

Psalm 90

A Prayer of Moses the man of God.

1 LORD, thou hast been our dwelling place in all generations.

2 Before the mountains were brought forth, or ever thou hadst formed the earth and the world, even from everlasting to everlasting, thou *art* God.

3 Thou turnest man to destruction; and sayest, Return, ye children of men.

4 For a thousand years in thy sight *are but* as yesterday when it is past, and *as* a watch in the night.

5 Thou carriest them away as with a

12Blessed *is* the man whom thou chastenest, O LORD, and teachest him out of thy law;

94:11 Bad Thoughts
◄ Psalm 64:6
Proverbs 15:26 ►

13That thou mayest give him rest from the days of adversity, until the pit be digged for the wicked.

94:12 Difficulties
◄ Deuteronomy 8:5
Proverbs 3:11-12 ►

14For the LORD will not cast off his people, neither will he forsake his inheritance.

15But judgment shall return unto righteousness: and all the upright in heart shall follow it.

16Who will rise up for me against the evildoers? *or* who will stand up for me against the workers of iniquity?

94:16 Evildoers
◄ Psalm 37:9
Psalm 119:115 ►

17Unless the LORD *had been* my help, my soul had almost dwelt in silence.

18When I said, My foot slippeth; thy mercy, O LORD, held me up.

19In the multitude of my thoughts within me thy comforts delight my soul.

20Shall the throne of iniquity have fellowship with thee, which frameth mischief by a law?

21They gather themselves together against the soul of the righteous, and condemn the innocent blood.

22But the LORD is my defence; and my God *is* the rock of my refuge.

23And he shall bring upon them their own iniquity, and shall cut them off in their own wickedness; *yea,* the LORD our God shall cut them off.

Psalm 95

1O come, let us sing unto the LORD: let us make a joyful noise to the rock of our salvation.

2Let us come before his presence with thanksgiving, and make a joyful noise unto him with psalms.

3For the LORD *is* a great God, and a great King above all gods.

4In his hand *are* the deep places of the earth: the strength of the hills *is* his also.

5The sea *is* his, and he made it: and his hands formed the dry *land.*

6O come, let us worship and bow down: let us kneel before the LORD our maker.

95:6 Worship
◄ Psalm 29:2
Psalm 96:9 ►

7For he *is* our God; and we *are* the people of his pasture, and the sheep of his hand. To day if ye will hear his voice,

8Harden not your heart, as in the provocation, *and* as *in* the day of temptation in the wilderness:

95:8
Hard-heart Aches
◄ Proverbs 28:14 ►

9When your fathers tempted me, proved me, and saw my work.

10Forty years long was I grieved with *this* generation, and said, It *is* a people that do err in their heart, and they have not known my ways:

11Unto whom I sware in my wrath that they should not enter into my rest.

Psalm 96

1O sing unto the LORD a new song: sing unto the LORD, all the earth.

2Sing unto the LORD, bless his name; shew forth his salvation from day to day.

3Declare his glory among the heathen, his wonders among all people.

4For the LORD *is* great, and greatly to be praised: he *is* to be feared above all gods.

5For all the gods of the nations *are* idols: but the LORD made the heavens.

6Honour and majesty *are* before him: strength and beauty *are* in his sanctuary.

96:9 Worship
◄ Psalm 95:6
Psalm 99:5 ►

7Give unto the LORD, O ye kindreds of the people, give unto the LORD glory and strength.

8Give unto the LORD the glory *due unto* his name: bring an offering, and come into his courts.

9O worship the LORD in the beauty of holiness: fear before him, all the earth.

10Say among the heathen *that* the LORD reigneth: the world also shall be established that it shall not be moved: he shall judge the people righteously.

11Let the heavens rejoice, and let the
earth be glad; let the sea roar, and the
fulness thereof.
12Let the field be joyful, and all that *is*
therein: then shall all the trees of the wood
rejoice
13Before the LORD: for he cometh, for
he cometh to judge
the earth: he shall
judge the world
with righteousness,
and the people with
his truth.

96:13 God as Judge
◄ Psalm 75:7
Ecclesiastes 3:17 ►

Psalm 97

1The LORD reigneth; let the earth rejoice;
let the multitude of isles be glad *thereof*.
2Clouds and darkness *are* round about
him: righteousness and judgment *are* the
habitation of his throne.
3A fire goeth before him, and burneth
up his enemies round about.
4His lightnings enlightened the world:
the earth saw, and trembled.
5The hills melted like wax at the presence of the LORD, at the presence of the
Lord of the whole earth.
6The heavens de-
clare his righteous-
ness, and all the
people see his glory.
7Confounded be
all they that serve
graven images, that boast themselves of
idols: worship him, all *ye* gods.

97:6 Nature Teaches Us
◄ Psalm 19:1
Acts 14:17 ►

8Zion heard, and was glad; and the
daughters of Judah rejoiced because of thy
judgments, O LORD.
9For thou, LORD, *art* high above all the
earth: thou art exalted far above all gods.
10Ye that love the
LORD, hate evil: he
preserveth the souls
of his saints; he
delivereth them out
of the hand of the
wicked.

97:10 Stay Away!
◄ Psalm 34:14
Proverbs 4:27 ►

11Light is sown
for the righteous,
and gladness for the
upright in heart.
12Rejoice in the
LORD, ye righteous; and give thanks at the
remembrance of his holiness.

97:11 Why Do Right?
◄ Psalm 64:10
Psalm 112:4 ►

Psalm 98

A Psalm.

1O sing unto the LORD a new song; for
he hath done marvellous things: his right
hand, and his holy arm, hath gotten him
the victory.
2The LORD hath made known his salvation: his righteousness hath he openly
shewed in the sight of the heathen.
3He hath remembered his mercy and his
truth toward the house of Israel: all the
ends of the earth have seen the salvation
of our God.
4Make a joyful noise unto the LORD, all
the earth: make a loud noise, and rejoice,
and sing praise.
5Sing unto the LORD with the harp; with
the harp, and the voice of a psalm.
6With trumpets and sound of cornet
make a joyful noise before the LORD, the
King.
7Let the sea roar, and the fulness thereof;
the world, and they that dwell therein.
8Let the floods
clap *their* hands: let
the hills be joyful
together
9Before the LORD;
for he cometh to
judge the earth: with righteousness shall
he judge the world, and the people with
equity.

98:8 Nature's Praise
◄ Psalm 69:34
Psalm 148:3 ►

Psalm 99

1The LORD reigneth; let the people tremble: he sitteth *between* the cherubims; let
the earth be moved.
2The LORD *is* great in Zion; and he *is* high
above all the people.
3Let them praise thy great and terrible
name; *for* it *is* holy.
4The king's strength also loveth judgment; thou dost establish equity, thou
executest judgment and righteousness in
Jacob.
5Exalt ye the
LORD our God, and
worship at his foot-
stool; *for* he *is* holy.
6Moses and
Aaron among his
priests, and Samuel among them that call

99:5 Worship
◄ Psalm 96:9
Zechariah 14:17 ►

upon his name; they called upon the LORD,
and he answered them.
7 He spake unto them in the cloudy pillar: they kept his testimonies, and the ordinance *that* he gave them.
8 Thou answeredst them, O LORD our
God: thou wast a God that forgavest them,
though thou tookest vengeance of their
inventions.
9 Exalt the LORD our God, and worship
at his holy hill; for the LORD our God *is*
holy.

Psalm 100

A Psalm of praise.

1 Make a joyful noise unto the LORD, all
ye lands.
2 Serve the LORD
with gladness: come
before his presence
with singing.
3 Know ye that the
LORD he *is* God: *it is*
he *that* hath made us, and not we ourselves;
we are his people, and the sheep of his pasture.

100:2 Serving
◄ Psalm 40:8
Psalm 126:5-6 ►

4 Enter into his
gates with thanks-
giving, *and* into his
courts with praise:
be thankful unto
him, *and* bless his
name.

100:4 Thankfulness
◄ Deuteronomy 8:10
Psalm 107:22 ►

5 For the LORD *is* good; his mercy *is* everlasting; and his truth *endureth* to all generations.

Psalm 101

A Psalm of David.

1 I will sing of mercy and judgment: unto
thee, O LORD, will I sing.
2 I will behave myself wisely in a perfect
way. O when wilt thou come unto me? I
will walk within my house with a perfect
heart.
3 I will set no wicked thing before mine
eyes: I hate the work of them that turn
aside; *it* shall not cleave to me.
4 A froward heart shall depart from me:
I will not know a wicked *person*.
5 Whoso privily slandereth his neighbour, him will I cut off: him that hath an
high look and a proud heart will not I
suffer.
6 Mine eyes *shall be* upon the faithful of
the land, that they may dwell with me:
he that walketh in a perfect way, he shall
serve me.
7 He that worketh
deceit shall not
dwell within my
house: he that tell-
eth lies shall not
tarry in my sight.

101:7 Lying
◄ Psalm 31:18
Psalm 120:2 ►

8 I will early destroy all the wicked of the
land; that I may cut off all wicked doers
from the city of the LORD.

Psalm 102

A Prayer of the afflicted, when he is
overwhelmed, and poureth out his
complaint before the LORD.

1 Hear my prayer, O LORD, and let my
cry come unto thee.
2 Hide not thy face from me in the day
when I am in trouble; incline thine ear
unto me: in the day *when* I call answer me
speedily.
3 For my days are consumed like smoke,
and my bones are burned as an hearth.
4 My heart is smitten, and withered like
grass; so that I forget to eat my bread.
5 By reason of the voice of my groaning
my bones cleave to my skin.
6 I am like a pelican of the wilderness:
I am like an owl of the desert.
7 I watch, and am
as a sparrow alone
upon the house top.
8 Mine enemies
reproach me all the
day; *and* they that
are mad against me are sworn against me.

102:7 Loneliness
◄ Psalm 38:11
John 16:32 ►

9 For I have eaten ashes like bread, and
mingled my drink with weeping,
10 Because of thine indignation and thy
wrath: for thou hast lifted me up, and cast
me down.
11 My days *are* like
a shadow that
declineth; and I am
withered like grass.
12 But thou,
O LORD, shalt

102:11 Life Is Short
◄ Psalm 90:9
Ecclesiastes 6:12 ►

endure for ever; and thy remembrance unto all generations.

13 Thou shalt arise, *and* have mercy upon Zion: for the time to favour her, yea, the set time, is come.

14 For thy servants take pleasure in her stones, and favour the dust thereof.

15 So the heathen shall fear the name of the LORD, and all the kings of the earth thy glory.

16 When the LORD shall build up Zion, he shall appear in his glory.

17 He will regard the prayer of the destitute, and not despise their prayer.

18 This shall be written for the generation to come: and the people which shall be created shall praise the LORD.

19 For he hath looked down from the height of his sanctuary; from heaven did the LORD behold the earth;

20 To hear the groaning of the prisoner; to loose those that are appointed to death;

21 To declare the name of the LORD in Zion, and his praise in Jerusalem;

22 When the people are gathered together, and the kingdoms, to serve the LORD.

23 He weakened my strength in the way; he shortened my days.

24 I said, O my God, take me not away in the midst of my days: thy years *are* throughout all generations.

25 Of old hast thou laid the foundation of the earth: and the heavens *are* the work of thy hands.

26 They shall perish, but thou shalt endure: yea, all of them shall wax old like a garment; as a vesture shalt thou change them, and they shall be changed:

27 But thou *art* the same, and thy years shall have no end.

28 The children of thy servants shall continue, and their seed shall be established before thee.

Psalm 103

A Psalm of David.

1 Bless the LORD, O my soul: and all that is within me, *bless* his holy name.

2 Bless the LORD, O my soul, and forget not all his benefits:

3 Who forgiveth all thine iniquities; who healeth all thy diseases;

4 Who redeemeth thy life from destruction; who crowneth thee with lovingkindness and tender mercies;

103:3 Forgiveness
◄ Leviticus 5:10
Psalm 130:4 ►

5 Who satisfieth thy mouth with good *things; so that* thy youth is renewed like the eagle's.

103:5 Satisfaction
◄ Psalm 63:5
Psalm 107:9 ►

6 The LORD executeth righteousness and judgment for all that are oppressed.

103:6 God's Justice
◄ Deuteronomy 32:4
Proverbs 16:11 ►

7 He made known his ways unto Moses, his acts unto the children of Israel.

8 The LORD *is* merciful and gracious, slow to anger, and plenteous in mercy.

103:8 Promise of Mercy
◄ Psalm 89:28
Isaiah 54:7 ►

9 He will not always chide: neither will he keep *his anger* for ever.

10 He hath not dealt with us after our sins; nor rewarded us according to our iniquities.

11 For as the heaven is high above the earth, *so* great is his mercy toward them that fear him.

103:11 Mercy from God
◄ Nehemiah 9:31 ►

12 As far as the east is from the west, *so* far hath he removed our transgressions from us.

13 Like as a father pitieth *his* children, *so* the LORD pitieth them that fear him.

103:13 Why Fear God?
◄ Psalm 31:19
Psalm 147:11 ►

14 For he knoweth our frame; he remembereth that we *are* dust.

103:14 Your Body
◄ Psalm 78:39
Psalm 141:7 ►

15 *As for* man, his days *are* as grass: as a flower of the field, so he flourisheth.

16 For the wind passeth over it, and it is gone; and the place thereof shall know it no more.

103:16 Mortality
◄ Psalm 89:48
Ecclesiastes 3:20 ►

17But the mercy of the LORD *is* from everlasting to everlasting upon them that fear him, and his righteousness unto children's children;

103:17 God's Mercy
◄ Psalm 86:5
Psalm 106:1 ►

18To such as keep his covenant, and to those that remember his commandments to do them.

19The LORD hath prepared his throne in the heavens; and his kingdom ruleth over all.

20Bless the LORD, ye his angels, that excel in strength, that do his commandments, hearkening unto the voice of his word.

21Bless ye the LORD, all *ye* his hosts; *ye* ministers of his, that do his pleasure.

22Bless the LORD, all his works in all places of his dominion: bless the LORD, O my soul.

Psalm 104

1Bless the LORD, O my soul. O LORD my God, thou art very great; thou art clothed with honour and majesty.

2Who coverest *thyself* with light as *with* a garment: who stretchest out the heavens like a curtain:

3Who layeth the beams of his chambers in the waters: who maketh the clouds his chariot: who walketh upon the wings of the wind:

4Who maketh his angels spirits; his ministers a flaming fire:

5*Who* laid the foundations of the earth, *that* it should not be removed for ever.

6Thou coveredst it with the deep as *with* a garment: the waters stood above the mountains.

7At thy rebuke they fled; at the voice of thy thunder they hasted away.

8They go up by the mountains; they go down by the valleys unto the place which thou hast founded for them.

9Thou hast set a bound that they may not pass over; that they turn not again to cover the earth.

10He sendeth the springs into the valleys, *which* run among the hills.

11They give drink to every beast of the field: the wild asses quench their thirst.

12By them shall the fowls of the heaven have their habitation, *which* sing among the branches.

13He watereth the hills from his chambers: the earth is satisfied with the fruit of thy works.

14He causeth the grass to grow for the cattle, and herb for the service of man: that he may bring forth food out of the earth;

15And wine *that* maketh glad the heart of man, *and* oil to make *his* face to shine, and bread *which* strengtheneth man's heart.

16The trees of the LORD are full *of sap;* the cedars of Lebanon, which he hath planted;

17Where the birds make their nests: *as for* the stork, the fir trees *are* her house.

18The high hills *are* a refuge for the wild goats; *and* the rocks for the conies.

19He appointed the moon for seasons: the sun knoweth his going down.

20Thou makest darkness, and it is night: wherein all the beasts of the forest do creep *forth.*

21The young lions roar after their prey, and seek their meat from God.

22The sun ariseth, they gather themselves together, and lay them down in their dens.

23Man goeth forth unto his work and to his labour until the evening.

24O LORD, how manifold are thy works! in wisdom hast thou made them all: the earth is full of thy riches.

25*So is* this great and wide sea, wherein *are* things creeping innumerable, both small and great beasts.

26There go the ships: *there is* that leviathan, *whom* thou hast made to play therein.

27These wait all upon thee; that thou mayest give *them* their meat in due season.

28*That* thou givest them they gather: thou openest thine hand, they are filled with good.

29Thou hidest thy face, they are troubled: thou takest away their breath, they die, and return to their dust.

30Thou sendest forth thy spirit, they are created: and thou renewest the face of the earth.

31The glory of the LORD shall endure for ever: the LORD shall rejoice in his works.

32He looketh on the earth, and it trembleth: he toucheth the hills, and they smoke.

33 I will sing unto the LORD as long as I
live: I will sing praise to my God while I
have my being.
34 My meditation of him shall be sweet:
I will be glad in the LORD.
35 Let the sinners be consumed out of
the earth, and let the wicked be no more.
Bless thou the LORD, O my soul. Praise ye
the LORD.

Psalm 105

1 O give thanks unto the LORD; call upon
his name: make known his deeds among
the people.
2 Sing unto him, sing psalms unto him:
talk ye of all his wondrous works.
3 Glory ye in his holy name: let the heart
of them rejoice that
seek the LORD.
4 Seek the LORD,
and his strength:
seek his face ever-
more.
5 Remember his
marvellous works that he hath done; his
wonders, and the judgments of his mouth;

105:4 Seeking God
◄ 2 Chronicles 14:4
Isaiah 55:6 ►

6 O ye seed of Abraham his servant, ye
children of Jacob his chosen.
7 He *is* the LORD our God: his judgments
are in all the earth.
8 He hath remembered his covenant for
ever, the word *which* he commanded to a
thousand generations.
9 Which *covenant* he made with Abraham, and his oath unto Isaac;
10 And confirmed the same unto Jacob
for a law, *and* to Israel *for* an everlasting
covenant:
11 Saying, Unto thee will I give the land
of Canaan, the lot of your inheritance:
12 When they were *but* a few men in
number; yea, very few, and strangers in it.
13 When they went from one nation to
another, from *one* kingdom to another
people;
14 He suffered no man to do them
wrong: yea, he reproved kings for their
sakes;
15 *Saying,* Touch not mine anointed, and
do my prophets no harm.
16 Moreover he called for a famine upon
the land: he brake the whole staff of bread.
17 He sent a man before them, *even* Joseph, *who* was sold for a servant:
18 Whose feet they hurt with fetters: he
was laid in iron:
19 Until the time that his word came: the
word of the LORD tried him.
20 The king sent and loosed him; *even* the
ruler of the people, and let him go free.
21 He made him lord of his house, and
ruler of all his substance:
22 To bind his princes at his pleasure; and
teach his senators wisdom.
23 Israel also came into Egypt; and Jacob
sojourned in the land of Ham.
24 And he increased his people greatly;
and made them stronger than their enemies.
25 He turned their heart to hate his people, to deal subtilly with his servants.
26 He sent Moses his servant; *and* Aaron
whom he had chosen.
27 They shewed his signs among them,
and wonders in the land of Ham.
28 He sent darkness, and made it dark;
and they rebelled not against his word.
29 He turned their waters into blood, and
slew their fish.
30 Their land brought forth frogs in
abundance, in the chambers of their kings.
31 He spake, and there came divers sorts
of flies, *and* lice in all their coasts.
32 He gave them hail for rain, *and* flaming fire in their land.
33 He smote their vines also and their fig
trees; and brake the trees of their coasts.
34 He spake, and the locusts came, and
caterpillers, and that without number,
35 And did eat up all the herbs in their
land, and devoured the fruit of their
ground.
36 He smote also all the firstborn in their
land, the chief of all their strength.
37 He brought them forth also with silver and gold: and *there was* not one feeble
person among their tribes.
38 Egypt was glad when they departed:
for the fear of them fell upon them.
39 He spread a cloud for a covering; and
fire to give light in the night.
40 *The people* asked, and he brought
quails, and satisfied them with the bread
of heaven.
41 He opened the rock, and the waters
gushed out; they ran in the dry places *like*
a river.
42 For he remembered his holy promise,
and Abraham his servant.

43 And he brought forth his people with joy, *and* his chosen with gladness:

44 And gave them the lands of the heathen: and they inherited the labour of the people;

45 That they might observe his statutes, and keep his laws. Praise ye the LORD.

Psalm 106

1 Praise ye the LORD. O give thanks unto the LORD; for *he is* good: for his mercy *endureth* for ever.

106:1 God's Mercy
◄ Psalm 103:17
Psalm 108:4 ►

2 Who can utter the mighty acts of the LORD? *who* can shew forth all his praise?

3 Blessed *are* they that keep judgment, *and* he that doeth righteousness at all times.

4 Remember me, O LORD, with the favour *that thou bearest unto* thy people: O visit me with thy salvation;

5 That I may see the good of thy chosen, that I may rejoice in the gladness of thy nation, that I may glory with thine inheritance.

6 We have sinned with our fathers, we have committed iniquity, we have done wickedly.

7 Our fathers understood not thy wonders in Egypt; they remembered not the multitude of thy mercies; but provoked *him* at the sea, *even* at the Red sea.

106:7 Losers
◄ Psalm 78:56
Isaiah 3:8 ►

8 Nevertheless he saved them for his name's sake, that he might make his mighty power to be known.

9 He rebuked the Red sea also, and it was dried up: so he led them through the depths, as through the wilderness.

10 And he saved them from the hand of him that hated *them,* and redeemed them from the hand of the enemy.

11 And the waters covered their enemies: there was not one of them left.

12 Then believed they his words; they sang his praise.

13 They soon forgat his works; they waited not for his counsel:

14 But lusted exceedingly in the wilderness, and tempted God in the desert.

15 And he gave them their request; but sent leanness into their soul.

16 They envied Moses also in the camp, *and* Aaron the saint of the LORD.

17 The earth opened and swallowed up Dathan, and covered the company of Abiram.

18 And a fire was kindled in their company; the flame burned up the wicked.

19 They made a calf in Horeb, and worshipped the molten image.

20 Thus they changed their glory into the similitude of an ox that eateth grass.

21 They forgat God their saviour, which had done great things in Egypt;

22 Wondrous works in the land of Ham, *and* terrible things by the Red sea.

23 Therefore he said that he would destroy them, had not Moses his chosen stood before him in the breach, to turn away his wrath, lest he should destroy *them.*

106:23 Praying for Others
◄ Job 42:10
Ephesians 1:16 ►

24 Yea, they despised the pleasant land, they believed not his word:

25 But murmured in their tents, *and* hearkened not unto the voice of the LORD.

26 Therefore he lifted up his hand against them, to overthrow them in the wilderness:

27 To overthrow their seed also among the nations, and to scatter them in the lands.

28 They joined themselves also unto Baal-peor, and ate the sacrifices of the dead.

29 Thus they provoked *him* to anger with their inventions: and the plague brake in upon them.

30 Then stood up Phinehas, and executed judgment: and *so* the plague was stayed.

31 And that was counted unto him for righteousness unto all generations for evermore.

32 They angered *him* also at the waters of strife, so that it went ill with Moses for their sakes:

33 Because they provoked his spirit, so that he spake unadvisedly with his lips.

34 They did not destroy the nations, concerning whom the LORD commanded them:

35 But were mingled among the heathen, and learned their works.

36 And they served their idols: which were a snare unto them.

37 Yea, they sacrificed their sons and their daughters unto devils,

38 And shed innocent blood, *even* the blood of their sons and of their daughters, whom they sacrificed unto the idols of Canaan: and the land was polluted with blood.

39 Thus were they defiled with their own works, and went a whoring with their own inventions.

40 Therefore was the wrath of the LORD kindled against his people, insomuch that he abhorred his own inheritance.

41 And he gave them into the hand of the heathen; and they that hated them ruled over them.

42 Their enemies also oppressed them, and they were brought into subjection under their hand.

43 Many times did he deliver them; but they provoked *him* with their counsel, and were brought low for their iniquity.

44 Nevertheless he regarded their affliction, when he heard their cry:

45 And he remembered for them his covenant, and repented according to the multitude of his mercies.

46 He made them also to be pitied of all those that carried them captives.

47 Save us, O LORD our God, and gather us from among the heathen, to give thanks unto thy holy name, *and* to triumph in thy praise.

48 Blessed *be* the Lord God of Israel from everlasting to everlasting: and let all the people say, Amen. Praise ye the LORD.

Psalm 107

1 O give thanks unto the LORD, for *he is* good: for his mercy *endureth* for ever.

2 Let the redeemed of the LORD say *so*, whom he hath redeemed from the hand of the enemy;

107:2 Your Testimony
◄ 1 Chronicles 16:8
Isaiah 12:4 ►

3 And gathered them out of the lands, from the east, and from the west, from the north, and from the south.

4 They wandered in the wilderness in a solitary way; they found no city to dwell in.

5 Hungry and thirsty, their soul fainted in them.

6 Then they cried unto the LORD in their trouble, *and* he delivered them out of their distresses.

7 And he led them forth by the right way, that they might go to a city of habitation.

8 Oh that *men* would praise the LORD *for* his goodness, and *for* his wonderful works to the children of men!

9 For he satisfieth the longing soul, and filleth the hungry soul with goodness.

107:9 Satisfaction
◄ Psalm 103:5
Isaiah 58:11 ►

10 Such as sit in darkness and in the shadow of death, *being* bound in affliction and iron;

11 Because they rebelled against the words of God, and contemned the counsel of the most High:

12 Therefore he brought down their heart with labour; they fell down, and *there was* none to help.

13 Then they cried unto the LORD in their trouble, *and* he saved them out of their distresses.

14 He brought them out of darkness and the shadow of death, and brake their bands in sunder.

15 Oh that *men* would praise the LORD *for* his goodness, and *for* his wonderful works to the children of men!

16 For he hath broken the gates of brass, and cut the bars of iron in sunder.

17 Fools because of their transgression, and because of their iniquities, are afflicted.

18 Their soul abhorreth all manner of meat; and they draw near unto the gates of death.

19 Then they cry unto the LORD in their trouble, *and* he saveth them out of their distresses.

20 He sent his word, and healed them, and delivered *them* from their destructions.

21 Oh that *men* would praise the LORD *for* his goodness, and *for* his wonderful works to the children of men!

107:22 Thankfulness
◄ Psalm 100:4
Colossians 1:12 ►

22 And let them sacrifice the sacri-

fices of thanksgiving, and declare his works with rejoicing.

23 They that go down to the sea in ships, that do business in great waters;

24 These see the works of the LORD, and his wonders in the deep.

25 For he commandeth, and raiseth the stormy wind, which lifteth up the waves thereof.

26 They mount up to the heaven, they go down again to the depths: their soul is melted because of trouble.

27 They reel to and fro, and stagger like a drunken man, and are at their wit's end.

28 Then they cry unto the LORD in their trouble, and he bringeth them out of their distresses.

29 He maketh the storm a calm, so that the waves thereof are still.

30 Then are they glad because they be quiet; so he bringeth them unto their desired haven.

31 Oh that *men* would praise the LORD *for* his goodness, and *for* his wonderful works to the children of men!

32 Let them exalt him also in the congregation of the people, and praise him in the assembly of the elders.

33 He turneth rivers into a wilderness, and the watersprings into dry ground;

34 A fruitful land into barrenness, for the wickedness of them that dwell therein.

35 He turneth the wilderness into a standing water, and dry ground into watersprings.

36 And there he maketh the hungry to dwell, that they may prepare a city for habitation;

37 And sow the fields, and plant vineyards, which may yield fruits of increase.

38 He blesseth them also, so that they are multiplied greatly; and suffereth not their cattle to decrease.

39 Again, they are minished and brought low through oppression, affliction, and sorrow.

40 He poureth contempt upon princes, and causeth them to wander in the wilderness, *where there is* no way.

41 Yet setteth he the poor on high from affliction, and maketh *him* families like a flock.

42 The righteous shall see *it*, and rejoice: and all iniquity shall stop her mouth.

43 Whoso *is* wise, and will observe these *things*, even they shall understand the lovingkindness of the LORD.

Psalm 108

A Song *or* Psalm of David.

1 O God, my heart is fixed; I will sing and give praise, even with my glory.

2 Awake, psaltery and harp: I *myself* will awake early.

3 I will praise thee, O LORD, among the people: and I will sing praises unto thee among the nations.

4 For thy mercy *is* great above the heavens: and thy truth *reacheth* unto the clouds.

108:4 God's Mercy
◄ Psalm 106:1
Psalm 119:64 ►

5 Be thou exalted, O God, above the heavens: and thy glory above all the earth;

6 That thy beloved may be delivered: save *with* thy right hand, and answer me.

7 God hath spoken in his holiness; I will rejoice, I will divide Shechem, and mete out the valley of Succoth.

8 Gilead *is* mine; Manasseh *is* mine; Ephraim also *is* the strength of mine head; Judah *is* my lawgiver;

9 Moab *is* my washpot; over Edom will I cast out my shoe; over Philistia will I triumph.

10 Who will bring me into the strong city? who will lead me into Edom?

11 *Wilt* not *thou,* O God, *who* hast cast us off? and wilt not thou, O God, go forth with our hosts?

12 Give us help from trouble: for vain *is* the help of man.

13 Through God we shall do valiantly: for he *it is that* shall tread down our enemies.

Psalm 109

To the chief Musician,
A Psalm of David.

1 Hold not thy peace, O God of my praise;

2 For the mouth of the wicked and the mouth of the deceitful are opened against me: they have spoken against me with a lying tongue.

3 They compassed me about also with

words of hatred; and fought against me
without a cause.
4For my love they are my adversaries: but
I *give myself unto* prayer.
5And they have rewarded me evil for
good, and hatred for my love.
6Set thou a wicked man over him: and
let Satan stand at his right hand.
7When he shall be judged, let him be
condemned: and let his prayer become
sin.
8Let his days be few; *and* let another take
his office.
9Let his children be fatherless, and his
wife a widow.
10Let his children be continually vaga-
bonds, and beg: let them seek *their bread*
also out of their desolate places.
11Let the extortioner catch all that he
hath; and let the strangers spoil his labour.
12Let there be none to extend mercy
unto him: neither let there be any to favour
his fatherless children.
13Let his posterity be cut off; *and* in the
generation following let their name be
blotted out.
14Let the iniquity of his fathers be remembered with the LORD; and let not the
sin of his mother be blotted out.
15Let them be before the LORD continually, that he may cut off the memory of
them from the earth.
16Because that he
remembered not
to shew mercy, but
persecuted the poor
and needy man,
that he might even
slay the broken in heart.

109:16
Mercy
◄ Proverbs 21:13 ►

17As he loved cursing, so let it come unto
him: as he delighted not in blessing, so let
it be far from him.
18As he clothed himself with cursing like
as with his garment, so let it come into his
bowels like water, and like oil into his
bones.
19Let it be unto him as the garment
which covereth him, and for a girdle wherewith he is girded continually.
20*Let* this *be* the reward of mine adversaries from the LORD, and of them that
speak evil against my soul.
21But do thou for me, O GOD the Lord,
for thy name's sake: because thy mercy *is*
good, deliver thou me.
22For I *am* poor and needy, and my heart
is wounded within me.
23I am gone like the shadow when it
declineth: I am tossed up and down as the
locust.
24My knees are weak through fasting;
and my flesh faileth of fatness.
25I became also a reproach unto them:
when they looked upon me they shaked
their heads.
26Help me, O LORD my God: O save me
according to thy mercy:
27That they may know that this *is* thy
hand; *that* thou, LORD, hast done it.
28Let them curse, but bless thou: when
they arise, let them be ashamed; but let
thy servant rejoice.
29Let mine adversaries be clothed with
shame, and let them cover themselves with
their own confusion, as with a mantle.
30I will greatly praise the LORD with my
mouth; yea, I will praise him among the
multitude.
31For he shall
stand at the right
hand of the poor, to
save *him* from those
that condemn his
soul.

109:31
Promises to the Poor
◄ Psalm 69:33
Psalm 140:12 ►

Psalm 110

A Psalm of David.

1The LORD said unto my Lord, Sit thou
at my right hand, until I make thine enemies thy footstool.
2The LORD shall send the rod of thy
strength out of Zion: rule thou in the midst
of thine enemies.
3Thy people *shall*
be willing in the day
of thy power, in the
beauties of holiness
from the womb of
the morning: thou
hast the dew of thy youth.

110:3
Willingness to Work
◄ Nehemiah 11:2
Isaiah 1:19 ►

4The LORD hath sworn, and will not repent, Thou *art* a priest for ever after the
order of Melchizedek.
5The Lord at thy right hand shall strike
through kings in the day of his wrath.
6He shall judge among the heathen, he
shall fill *the places* with the dead bodies; he
shall wound the heads over many countries.

7 He shall drink of the brook in the way: therefore shall he lift up the head.

Psalm 111

1 Praise ye the LORD. I will praise the LORD with *my* whole heart, in the assembly of the upright, and *in* the congregation.

2 The works of the LORD *are* great, sought out of all them that have pleasure therein.

3 His work *is* honourable and glorious: and his righteousness endureth for ever.

4 He hath made his wonderful works to be remembered: the LORD *is* gracious and full of compassion.

5 He hath given meat unto them that fear him: he will ever be mindful of his covenant.

6 He hath shewed his people the power of his works, that he may give them the heritage of the heathen.

7 The works of his hands *are* verity and judgment; all his commandments *are* sure.

8 They stand fast for ever and ever, *and are* done in truth and uprightness.

9 He sent redemption unto his people: he hath commanded his covenant for ever: holy and reverend *is* his name.

> **111:9 Respecting God**
> ◄ Psalm 89:7
> Habakkuk 2:20 ►

10 The fear of the LORD *is* the beginning of wisdom: a good understanding have all they that do *his commandments:* his praise endureth for ever.

> **111:10 True Wisdom**
> ◄ Job 32:7
> Proverbs 1:20 ►

Psalm 112

1 Praise ye the LORD. Blessed *is* the man *that* feareth the LORD, *that* delighteth greatly in his commandments.

2 His seed shall be mighty upon earth: the generation of the upright shall be blessed.

3 Wealth and riches *shall be* in his house: and his righteousness endureth for ever.

> **112:4 Why Do Right?**
> ◄ Psalm 97:11
> Proverbs 2:7 ►

4 Unto the upright there ariseth light in the darkness: *he is* gracious, and full of compassion, and righteous.

5 A good man sheweth favour, and lendeth: he will guide his affairs with discretion.

> **112:5 Sharing**
> ◄ Psalm 37:26
> Matthew 5:42 ►

6 Surely he shall not be moved for ever: the righteous shall be in everlasting remembrance.

7 He shall not be afraid of evil tidings: his heart is fixed, trusting in the LORD.

> **112:7 Security**
> ◄ Psalm 91:5
> Psalm 125:1 ►

8 His heart *is* established, he shall not be afraid, until he see *his desire* upon his enemies.

9 He hath dispersed, he hath given to the poor; his righteousness endureth for ever; his horn shall be exalted with honour.

> **112:9 Rewards**
> ◄ Psalm 41:3
> Proverbs 11:17 ►

10 The wicked shall see *it*, and be grieved; he shall gnash with his teeth, and melt away: the desire of the wicked shall perish.

Psalm 113

1 Praise ye the LORD. Praise, O ye servants of the LORD, praise the name of the LORD.

2 Blessed be the name of the LORD from this time forth and for evermore.

3 From the rising of the sun unto the going down of the same the LORD'S name *is* to be praised.

4 The LORD *is* high above all nations, *and* his glory above the heavens.

5 Who *is* like unto the LORD our God, who dwelleth on high,

6 Who humbleth *himself* to behold *the things that are* in heaven, and in the earth!

7 He raiseth up the poor out of the dust, *and* lifteth the needy out of the dunghill;

8 That he may set *him* with princes, *even* with the princes of his people.

9 He maketh the barren woman to keep house, *and to be* a joyful mother of children. Praise ye the LORD.

Psalm 114

1 When Israel went out of Egypt, the house of Jacob from a people of strange language;

2 Judah was his sanctuary, *and* Israel his dominion.

3 The sea saw *it,* and fled: Jordan was driven back.

4 The mountains skipped like rams, *and* the little hills like lambs.

5 What *ailed* thee, O thou sea, that thou fleddest? thou Jordan, *that* thou wast driven back?

6 Ye mountains, *that* ye skipped like rams; *and* ye little hills, like lambs?

7 Tremble, thou earth, at the presence of the Lord, at the presence of the God of Jacob;

8 Which turned the rock *into* a standing water, the flint into a fountain of waters.

Psalm 115

1 Not unto us, O LORD, not unto us, but unto thy name give glory, for thy mercy, *and* for thy truth's sake.

2 Wherefore should the heathen say, Where *is* now their God?

3 But our God *is* in the heavens: he hath done whatsoever he hath pleased.

115:3 All-powerful
◄ Job 42:2
Psalm 135:6 ►

4 Their idols *are* silver and gold, the work of men's hands.

5 They have mouths, but they speak not: eyes have they, but they see not:

6 They have ears, but they hear not: noses have they, but they smell not:

7 They have hands, but they handle not: feet have they, but they walk not: neither speak they through their throat.

8 They that make them are like unto them; *so is* every one that trusteth in them.

9 O Israel, trust thou in the LORD: he *is* their help and their shield.

10 O house of Aaron, trust in the LORD: he *is* their help and their shield.

11 Ye that fear the LORD, trust in the LORD: he *is* their help and their shield.

115:11 Trusting God
◄ Psalm 37:3, 5
Psalm 118:8 ►

12 The LORD hath been mindful of us: he will bless *us;* he will bless the house of Israel; he will bless the house of Aaron.

115:12
God's Care for You
◄ Matthew 6:32 ►

13 He will bless them that fear the LORD, *both* small and great.

14 The LORD shall increase you more and more, you and your children.

15 Ye *are* blessed of the LORD which made heaven and earth.

16 The heaven, *even* the heavens, *are* the LORD'S: but the earth hath he given to the children of men.

17 The dead praise not the LORD, neither any that go down into silence.

18 But we will bless the LORD from this time forth and for evermore. Praise the LORD.

Psalm 116

1 I love the LORD, because he hath heard my voice *and* my supplications.

2 Because he hath inclined his ear unto me, therefore will I call upon *him* as long as I live.

3 The sorrows of death compassed me, and the pains of hell gat hold upon me: I found trouble and sorrow.

4 Then called I upon the name of the LORD; O LORD, I beseech thee, deliver my soul.

5 Gracious *is* the LORD, and righteous; yea, our God *is* merciful.

6 The LORD preserveth the simple: I was brought low, and he helped me.

7 Return unto thy rest, O my soul; for the LORD hath dealt bountifully with thee.

8 For thou hast delivered my soul from death, mine eyes from tears, *and* my feet from falling.

116:8 Evil Attacks
◄ Psalm 91:3
Isaiah 46:4 ►

9 I will walk before the LORD in the land of the living.

10 I believed, therefore have I spoken: I was greatly afflicted:

11 I said in my haste, All men *are* liars.

12 What shall I render unto the LORD *for* all his benefits toward me?

13 I will take the cup of salvation, and call upon the name of the LORD.

14 I will pay my vows unto the LORD now in the presence of all his people.

15 Precious in the sight of the LORD *is* the death of his saints.

16 O LORD, truly I *am* thy servant; I *am* thy servant, *and* the son of thine handmaid: thou hast loosed my bonds.

17 I will offer to thee the sacrifice of thanksgiving, and will call upon the name of the LORD.

18 I will pay my vows unto the LORD now in the presence of all his people,

19 In the courts of the LORD'S house, in the midst of thee, O Jerusalem. Praise ye the LORD.

Psalm 117

1 O praise the LORD, all ye nations: praise him, all ye people.

2 For his merciful kindness is great toward us: and the truth of the LORD *endureth* for ever. Praise ye the LORD.

Psalm 118

1 O give thanks unto the LORD; for *he is* good: because his mercy *endureth* for ever.

2 Let Israel now say, that his mercy *endureth* for ever.

3 Let the house of Aaron now say, that his mercy *endureth* for ever.

4 Let them now that fear the LORD say, that his mercy *endureth* for ever.

5 I called upon the LORD in distress: the LORD answered me, *and set me* in a large place.

6 The LORD *is* on my side; I will not fear: what can man do unto me?

7 The LORD taketh my part with them that help me: therefore shall I see *my desire* upon them that hate me.

8 *It is* better to trust in the LORD than to put confidence in man.

118:8 Trusting God
◄ Psalm 115:11
Proverbs 3:5 ►

9 *It is* better to trust in the LORD than to put confidence in princes.

118:9
Trusting in People
◄ Psalm 146:3 ►

10 All nations compassed me about: but in the name of the LORD will I destroy them.

11 They compassed me about; yea, they compassed me about: but in the name of the LORD I will destroy them.

12 They compassed me about like bees; they are quenched as the fire of thorns: for in the name of the LORD I will destroy them.

13 Thou hast thrust sore at me that I might fall: but the LORD helped me.

14 The LORD *is* my strength and song, and is become my salvation.

15 The voice of rejoicing and salvation *is* in the tabernacles of the righteous: the right hand of the LORD doeth valiantly.

16 The right hand of the LORD is exalted: the right hand of the LORD doeth valiantly.

17 I shall not die, but live, and declare the works of the LORD.

18 The LORD hath chastened me sore: but he hath not given me over unto death.

19 Open to me the gates of righteousness: I will go into them, *and* I will praise the LORD:

20 This gate of the LORD, into which the righteous shall enter.

21 I will praise thee: for thou hast heard me, and art become my salvation.

22 The stone *which* the builders refused is become the head *stone* of the corner.

118:22
The Ultimate
◄ Matthew 21:42 ►

23 This is the LORD'S doing; it *is* marvellous in our eyes.

24 This *is* the day *which* the LORD hath made; we will rejoice and be glad in it.

25 Save now, I beseech thee, O LORD: O LORD, I beseech thee, send now prosperity.

26 Blessed *be* he that cometh in the name of the LORD: we have blessed you out of the house of the LORD.

27 God *is* the LORD, which hath shewed us light: bind the sacrifice with cords, *even* unto the horns of the altar.

28 Thou *art* my God, and I will praise thee: *thou art* my God, I will exalt thee.

29 O give thanks unto the LORD; for *he is* good: for his mercy *endureth* for ever.

Psalm 119

ALEPH.

1 Blessed *are* the undefiled in the way, who walk in the law of the LORD.

2 Blessed *are* they that keep his testimonies, *and that* seek him with the whole
heart.
3 They also do no iniquity: they walk in
his ways.
4 Thou hast commanded *us* to keep thy
precepts diligently.
5 O that my ways were directed to keep
thy statutes!
6 Then shall I not be ashamed, when I
have respect unto all thy commandments.
7 I will praise thee with uprightness of
heart, when I shall have learned thy righteous judgments.
8 I will keep thy statutes: O forsake me
not utterly.

BETH.

9 Wherewithal
shall a young man
cleanse his way? by
taking heed *thereto*
according to thy
word.

119:9
For Kids Only
◄ Proverbs 20:29 ►

10 With my whole
heart have I sought
thee: O let me not
wander from thy
commandments.

119:9
Purity
◄ John 15:3 ►

11 Thy word have
I hid in mine heart, that I might not sin
against thee.
12 Blessed *art* thou, O LORD: teach me thy
statutes.
13 With my lips have I declared all the
judgments of thy mouth.
14 I have rejoiced in the way of thy testimonies, as *much as* in all riches.
15 I will meditate in thy precepts, and
have respect unto thy ways.
16 I will delight myself in thy statutes: I
will not forget thy word.

GIMEL.

17 Deal bountifully with thy servant, *that*
I may live, and keep thy word.
18 Open thou mine eyes, that I may behold wondrous things out of thy law.
19 I *am* a stranger in the earth: hide not
thy commandments from me.
20 My soul breaketh for the longing *that*
it hath unto thy judgments at all times.
21 Thou hast rebuked the proud *that are*
cursed, which do
err from thy com-
mandments.

119:21 Arrogance
◄ Psalm 73:6
Proverbs 6:17 ►

22 Remove from
me reproach and
contempt; for I
have kept thy testimonies.
23 Princes also did sit *and* speak against
me: *but* thy servant did meditate in thy statutes.
24 Thy testimonies also *are* my delight
and my counsellors.

DALETH.

25 My soul cleaveth unto the dust:
quicken thou me according to thy word.
26 I have declared my ways, and thou
heardest me: teach me thy statutes.
27 Make me to understand the way of thy
precepts: so shall I talk of thy wondrous
works.
28 My soul melteth for heaviness:
strengthen thou me according unto thy
word.
29 Remove from me the way of lying: and
grant me thy law graciously.
30 I have chosen the way of truth: thy
judgments have I laid *before me.*
31 I have stuck unto thy testimonies:
O LORD, put me not to shame.
32 I will run the way of thy commandments, when thou shalt enlarge my heart.

HE.

33 Teach me, O LORD, the way of thy statutes; and I shall keep it *unto* the end.
34 Give me understanding, and I shall
keep thy law; yea, I shall observe it with
my whole heart.
35 Make me to go
in the path of thy
commandments;
for therein do I de-
light.

119:35 Right Paths
◄ Psalm 25:10
Proverbs 2:9 ►

36 Incline my
heart unto thy testimonies, and not to covetousness.
37 Turn away mine eyes from beholding
vanity; *and* quicken thou me in thy way.
38 Stablish thy word unto thy servant,
who *is devoted* to thy fear.
39 Turn away my reproach which I fear:
for thy judgments *are* good.
40 Behold, I have longed after thy precepts: quicken me in thy righteousness.

VAU.

41 Let thy mercies come also unto me, O LORD, *even* thy salvation, according to thy word.

42 So shall I have wherewith to answer him that reproacheth me: for I trust in thy word.

43 And take not the word of truth utterly out of my mouth; for I have hoped in thy judgments.

44 So shall I keep thy law continually for ever and ever.

45 And I will walk at liberty: for I seek thy precepts.

46 I will speak of thy testimonies also before kings, and will not be ashamed.

47 And I will delight myself in thy commandments, which I have loved.

48 My hands also will I lift up unto thy commandments, which I have loved; and I will meditate in thy statutes.

ZAIN.

49 Remember the word unto thy servant, upon which thou hast caused me to hope.

50 This *is* my comfort in my affliction: for thy word hath quickened me.

51 The proud have had me greatly in derision: *yet* have I not declined from thy law.

52 I remembered thy judgments of old, O LORD; and have comforted myself.

53 Horror hath taken hold upon me because of the wicked that forsake thy law.

54 Thy statutes have been my songs in the house of my pilgrimage.

55 I have remembered thy name, O LORD, in the night, and have kept thy law.

56 This I had, because I kept thy precepts.

CHETH.

57 *Thou art* my portion, O LORD: I have said that I would keep thy words.

58 I intreated thy favour with *my* whole heart: be merciful unto me according to thy word.

59 I thought on my ways, and turned my feet unto thy testimonies.

60 I made haste, and delayed not to keep thy commandments.

119:59 Wise Thoughts
◄ Psalm 48:9
Proverbs 12:5 ►

119:60 Hurrying
◄ 2 Chronicles 35:21
Zechariah 8:21 ►

61 The bands of the wicked have robbed me: *but* I have not forgotten thy law.

62 At midnight I will rise to give thanks unto thee because of thy righteous judgments.

63 I *am* a companion of all *them* that fear thee, and of them that keep thy precepts.

64 The earth, O LORD, is full of thy mercy: teach me thy statutes.

119:64 God's Mercy
◄ Psalm 108:4
Lamentations 3:22-23 ►

TETH.

65 Thou hast dealt well with thy servant, O LORD, according unto thy word.

66 Teach me good judgment and knowledge: for I have believed thy commandments.

67 Before I was afflicted I went astray: but now have I kept thy word.

68 Thou *art* good, and doest good; teach me thy statutes.

119:67 Hardship
◄ Job 23:10
2 Corinthians 4:17 ►

69 The proud have forged a lie against me: *but* I will keep thy precepts with *my* whole heart.

70 Their heart is as fat as grease; *but* I delight in thy law.

71 *It is* good for me that I have been afflicted; that I might learn thy statutes.

72 The law of thy mouth *is* better unto me than thousands of gold and silver.

119:71 Lessons of Life
◄ Isaiah 1:16-17 ►

119:72 Valuing the Bible
◄ Psalm 119:127 ►

JOD.

73 Thy hands have made me and fashioned me: give me understanding, that I may learn thy commandments.

74 They that fear thee will be glad when they see me; because I have hoped in thy word.

75 I know, O LORD, that thy judgments *are* right, and *that* thou in faithfulness hast afflicted me.

76 Let, I pray thee, thy merciful kindness

be for my comfort, according to thy word unto thy servant.

77 Let thy tender mercies come unto me, that I may live: for thy law *is* my delight.

119:77 Praying for Mercy
◄ Psalm 85:7
Psalm 123:3 ►

78 Let the proud be ashamed; for they dealt perversely with me without a cause: *but* I will meditate in thy precepts.

119:78 Proud People
◄ Psalm 40:4
Psalm 119:85 ►

79 Let those that fear thee turn unto me, and those that have known thy testimonies.

80 Let my heart be sound in thy statutes; that I be not ashamed.

CAPH.

81 My soul fainteth for thy salvation: *but* I hope in thy word.

82 Mine eyes fail for thy word, saying, When wilt thou comfort me?

119:82 Pray and Wait
◄ Psalm 69:3
John 11:6 ►

83 For I am become like a bottle in the smoke; *yet* do I not forget thy statutes.

84 How many *are* the days of thy servant? when wilt thou execute judgment on them that persecute me?

85 The proud have digged pits for me, which *are* not after thy law.

119:85 Proud People
◄ Psalm 119:78
Psalm 123:4 ►

86 All thy commandments *are* faithful: they persecute me wrongfully; help thou me.

119:86 Bullies
◄ Psalm 31:15
Psalm 119:157 ►

87 They had almost consumed me upon earth; but I forsook not thy precepts.

88 Quicken me after thy lovingkindness; so shall I keep the testimony of thy mouth.

LAMED.

89 For ever, O LORD, thy word is settled in heaven.

90 Thy faithfulness *is* unto all generations: thou hast established the earth, and it abideth.

91 They continue this day according to thine ordinances: for all *are* thy servants.

92 Unless thy law *had been* my delights, I should then have perished in mine affliction.

93 I will never forget thy precepts: for with them thou hast quickened me.

94 I *am* thine, save me; for I have sought thy precepts.

95 The wicked have waited for me to destroy me: *but* I will consider thy testimonies.

96 I have seen an end of all perfection: *but* thy commandment *is* exceeding broad.

MEM.

97 O how love I thy law! it *is* my meditation all the day.

98 Thou through thy commandments hast made me wiser than mine enemies: for they *are* ever with me.

99 I have more understanding than all my teachers: for thy testimonies *are* my meditation.

100 I understand more than the ancients, because I keep thy precepts.

101 I have refrained my feet from every evil way, that I might keep thy word.

102 I have not departed from thy judgments: for thou hast taught me.

103 How sweet are thy words unto my taste! *yea, sweeter* than honey to my mouth!

104 Through thy precepts I get understanding: therefore I hate every false way.

119:104 Understanding
◄ 1 Chronicles 22:12
Proverbs 2:6 ►

NUN.

105 Thy word *is* a lamp unto my feet, and a light unto my path.

119:105 The Bible as a Guide
◄ Psalm 19:8
Psalm 119:130 ►

106 I have sworn, and I will perform *it,* that I will keep thy righteous judgments.

107 I am afflicted very much: quicken me, O LORD, according unto thy word.

108 Accept, I beseech thee, the freewill offerings of my mouth, O LORD, and teach me thy judgments.

109 My soul *is* continually in my hand:
yet do I not forget thy law.
110 The wicked have laid a snare for me:
yet I erred not from thy precepts.
111 Thy testimonies have I taken as an
heritage for ever: for they *are* the rejoicing
of my heart.
112 I have inclined mine heart to perform
thy statutes alway, *even unto* the end.

SAMECH.

113 I hate *vain* thoughts: but thy law do I
love.
114 Thou *art* my hiding place and my
shield: I hope in thy word.
115 Depart from
me, ye evildoers: for
I will keep the com-
mandments of my
God.
116 Uphold me ac-
cording unto thy word, that I may live: and
let me not be ashamed of my hope.

119:115 Evildoers
◄ Psalm 94:16
Isaiah 9:17 ►

117 Hold thou me up, and I shall be safe:
and I will have respect unto thy statutes
continually.
118 Thou hast trodden down all them
that err from thy statutes: for their deceit
is falsehood.
119 Thou puttest away all the wicked of
the earth *like* dross: therefore I love thy testimonies.
120 My flesh trembleth for fear of thee;
and I am afraid of thy judgments.

AIN.

121 I have done judgment and justice:
leave me not to mine oppressors.
122 Be surety for thy servant for good: let
not the proud oppress me.
123 Mine eyes fail for thy salvation, and
for the word of thy righteousness.
124 Deal with thy servant according unto
thy mercy, and teach me thy statutes.
125 I *am* thy servant; give me understanding, that I may know thy testimonies.
126 *It is* time for *thee,* LORD, to work: *for*
they have made void thy law.
127 Therefore I
love thy command-
ments above gold;
yea, above fine
gold.
128 Therefore I es-
teem all *thy* precepts *concerning* all *things*
to be right; *and* I hate every false way.

119:127
Valuing the Bible
◄ Psalm 119:72
Psalm 119:162 ►

PE.

129 Thy testimonies *are* wonderful: therefore doth my soul keep them.
130 The entrance
of thy words giveth
light; it giveth un-
derstanding unto
the simple.
131 I opened my
mouth, and panted: for I longed for thy
commandments.

119:130
The Bible as a Guide
◄ Psalm 119:105
Proverbs 6:23 ►

132 Look thou upon me, and be merciful unto me, as thou usest to do unto those
that love thy name.
133 Order my steps in thy word: and let
not any iniquity have dominion over me.
134 Deliver me from the oppression of
man: so will I keep thy precepts.
135 Make thy face to shine upon thy servant; and teach me thy statutes.
136 Rivers of waters run down mine eyes,
because they keep not thy law.

TZADDI.

137 Righteous *art* thou, O LORD, and upright *are* thy judgments.
138 Thy testimonies *that* thou hast commanded *are* righteous and very faithful.
139 My zeal hath consumed me, because
mine enemies have forgotten thy words.
140 Thy word *is* very pure: therefore thy
servant loveth it.
141 I *am* small and despised: *yet* do not I
forget thy precepts.
142 Thy righteousness *is* an everlasting
righteousness, and thy law *is* the truth.
143 Trouble and anguish have taken hold
on me: *yet* thy commandments *are* my delights.
144 The righteousness of thy testimonies
is everlasting: give me understanding, and
I shall live.

KOPH.

145 I cried with *my* whole heart; hear me,
O LORD: I will keep thy statutes.
146 I cried unto
thee; save me, and I
shall keep thy tes-
timonies.
147 I prevented
the dawning of the

119:147 Devotions
◄ Psalm 57:8
Mark 1:35 ►

Turn to the next page for more . . .

morning, and cried: I hoped in thy word.

> **119:147 Praying**
> ◄ Psalm 55:17
> Zechariah 8:21 ►

148 Mine eyes prevent the *night* watches, that I might meditate in thy word.

149 Hear my voice according unto thy lovingkindness: O LORD, quicken me according to thy judgment.

150 They draw nigh that follow after mischief: they are far from thy law.

151 Thou *art* near, O LORD; and all thy commandments *are* truth.

152 Concerning thy testimonies, I have known of old that thou hast founded them for ever.

RESH.

153 Consider mine affliction, and deliver me: for I do not forget thy law.

154 Plead my cause, and deliver me: quicken me according to thy word.

155 Salvation *is* far from the wicked: for they seek not thy statutes.

156 Great *are* thy tender mercies, O LORD: quicken me according to thy judgments.

157 Many *are* my persecutors and mine enemies; *yet* do I not decline from thy testimonies.

> **119:157 Bullies**
> ◄ Psalm 119:86
> Psalm 119:161 ►

158 I beheld the transgressors, and was grieved; because they kept not thy word.

159 Consider how I love thy precepts: quicken me, O LORD, according to thy lovingkindness.

160 Thy word *is* true *from* the beginning: and every one of thy righteous judgments *endureth* for ever.

SCHIN.

161 Princes have persecuted me without a cause: but my heart standeth in awe of thy word.

> **119:161 Bullies**
> ◄ Psalm 119:157
> Psalm 143:3 ►

162 I rejoice at thy word, as one that findeth great spoil.

> **119:162 Valuing the Bible**
> ◄ Psalm 119:127
> Proverbs 23:23 ►

163 I hate and abhor lying: *but* thy law do I love.

164 Seven times a day do I praise thee because of thy righteous judgments.

165 Great peace have they which love thy law: and nothing shall offend them.

> **119:165 Peace of Mind**
> ◄ Psalm 29:11
> Proverbs 3:17 ►

166 LORD, I have hoped for thy salvation, and done thy commandments.

167 My soul hath kept thy testimonies; and I love them exceedingly.

168 I have kept thy precepts and thy testimonies: for all my ways *are* before thee.

TAU.

169 Let my cry come near before thee, O LORD: give me understanding according to thy word.

170 Let my supplication come before thee: deliver me according to thy word.

171 My lips shall utter praise, when thou hast taught me thy statutes.

172 My tongue shall speak of thy word: for all thy commandments *are* righteousness.

173 Let thine hand help me; for I have chosen thy precepts.

174 I have longed for thy salvation, O LORD; and thy law *is* my delight.

> **119:174 Desire for God**
> ◄ Psalm 63:1
> Psalm 143:6 ►

175 Let my soul live, and it shall praise thee; and let thy judgments help me.

176 I have gone astray like a lost sheep; seek thy servant; for I do not forget thy commandments.

Psalm 120

A Song of degrees.

1 In my distress I cried unto the LORD, and he heard me.

2 Deliver my soul, O LORD, from lying lips, *and* from a deceitful tongue.

> **120:2 Lying**
> ◄ Psalm 101:7
> Proverbs 12:22 ►

3 What shall be given unto thee? or what shall be done unto thee, thou false tongue?

4 Sharp arrows of the mighty, with coals of juniper.

5 Woe is me, that I sojourn in Mesech, *that* I dwell in the tents of Kedar!

6 My soul hath long dwelt with him that hateth peace.

7 I *am for* peace: but when I speak, they *are* for war.

Psalm 121

A Song of degrees.

1 I will lift up mine eyes unto the hills, from whence cometh my help.

2 My help *cometh* from the LORD, which made heaven and earth.

3 He will not suffer thy foot to be moved: he that keepeth thee will not slumber.

4 Behold, he that keepeth Israel shall neither slumber nor sleep.

5 The LORD *is* thy keeper: the LORD *is* thy shade upon thy right hand.

6 The sun shall not smite thee by day, nor the moon by night.

7 The LORD shall preserve thee from all evil: he shall preserve thy soul.

8 The LORD shall preserve thy going out and thy coming in from this time forth, and even for evermore.

Psalm 122

A Song of degrees of David.

1 I was glad when they said unto me, Let us go into the house of the LORD.

2 Our feet shall stand within thy gates, O Jerusalem.

3 Jerusalem is builded as a city that is compact together:

4 Whither the tribes go up, the tribes of the LORD, unto the testimony of Israel, to give thanks unto the name of the LORD.

5 For there are set thrones of judgment, the thrones of the house of David.

6 Pray for the peace of Jerusalem: they shall prosper that love thee.

7 Peace be within thy walls, *and* prosperity within thy palaces.

8 For my brethren and companions' sakes, I will now say, Peace *be* within thee.

9 Because of the house of the LORD our God I will seek thy good.

Psalm 123

A Song of degrees.

1 Unto thee lift I up mine eyes, O thou that dwellest in the heavens.

2 Behold, as the eyes of servants *look* unto the hand of their masters, *and* as the eyes of a maiden unto the hand of her mistress; so our eyes *wait* upon the LORD our God, until that he have mercy upon us.

3 Have mercy upon us, O LORD, have mercy upon us: for we are exceedingly filled with contempt.

4 Our soul is exceedingly filled with the scorning of those that are at ease, *and* with the contempt of the proud.

> **123:2 Waiting for God**
> ◄ Psalm 62:5
> Proverbs 20:22 ►

> **123:3 Praying for Mercy**
> ◄ Psalm 119:77
> Daniel 9:16 ►

> **123:4 Apathy**
> ◄ Isaiah 32:9 ►

> **123:4 Proud People**
> ◄ Psalm 119:85
> Psalm 138:6 ►

Psalm 124

A Song of degrees of David.

1 If *it had* not *been* the LORD who was on our side, now may Israel say;

2 If *it had* not *been* the LORD who was on our side, when men rose up against us:

3 Then they had swallowed us up quick, when their wrath was kindled against us:

4 Then the waters had overwhelmed us, the stream had gone over our soul:

5 Then the proud waters had gone over our soul.

6 Blessed *be* the LORD, who hath not given us *as* a prey to their teeth.

7 Our soul is escaped as a bird out of the snare of the fowlers: the snare is broken, and we are escaped.

8 Our help *is* in the name of the LORD, who made heaven and earth.

Psalm 125

A Song of degrees.

1They that trust in the LORD *shall be* as mount Zion, *which* cannot be removed, *but* abideth for ever.

125:1 Security
◄ Psalm 112:7
Proverbs 1:33 ►

2As the mountains *are* round about Jerusalem, so the LORD *is* round about his people from henceforth even for ever.

125:2 Protection
◄ Psalm 91:4
Zechariah 2:5 ►

3For the rod of the wicked shall not rest upon the lot of the righteous; lest the righteous put forth their hands unto iniquity.

4Do good, O LORD, unto *those that be* good, and to *them that are* upright in their hearts.

5As for such as turn aside unto their crooked ways, the LORD shall lead them forth with the workers of iniquity: *but* peace *shall be* upon Israel.

Psalm 126

A Song of degrees.

1When the LORD turned again the captivity of Zion, we were like them that dream.

2Then was our mouth filled with laughter, and our tongue with singing: then said they among the heathen, The LORD hath done great things for them.

3The LORD hath done great things for us; *whereof* we are glad.

4Turn again our captivity, O LORD, as the streams in the south.

5They that sow in tears shall reap in joy.

126:5 Joy
◄ Psalm 89:16
Psalm 132:16 ►

6He that goeth forth and weepeth, bearing precious seed, shall doubtless come again with rejoicing, bringing his sheaves *with him.*

126:5-6 Serving
◄ Psalm 100:2
Luke 10:17 ►

Psalm 127

A Song of degrees for Solomon.

1Except the LORD build the house, they labour in vain that build it: except the LORD keep the city, the watchman waketh *but* in vain.

127:1 God's Role
◄ 2 Chronicles 20:12
Jeremiah 10:23 ►

2*It is* vain for you to rise up early, to sit up late, to eat the bread of sorrows: *for* so he giveth his beloved sleep.

127:2 Worry
◄ Matthew 6:25 ►

3Lo, children *are* an heritage of the LORD: *and* the fruit of the womb *is his* reward.

4As arrows *are* in the hand of a mighty man; so *are* children of the youth.

5Happy *is* the man that hath his quiver full of them: they shall not be ashamed, but they shall speak with the enemies in the gate.

Psalm 128

A Song of degrees.

1Blessed *is* every one that feareth the LORD; that walketh in his ways.

2For thou shalt eat the labour of thine hands: happy *shalt* thou *be,* and *it shall be* well with thee.

128:2 Source of Happiness
◄ Psalm 144:15 ►

3Thy wife *shall be* as a fruitful vine by the sides of thine house: thy children like olive plants round about thy table.

4Behold, that thus shall the man be blessed that feareth the LORD.

5The LORD shall bless thee out of Zion: and thou shalt see the good of Jerusalem all the days of thy life.

6Yea, thou shalt see thy children's children, *and* peace upon Israel.

Psalm 129

A Song of degrees.

1Many a time have they afflicted me from my youth, may Israel now say:

2Many a time have they afflicted me from my youth: yet they have not prevailed against me.

3The plowers plowed upon my back: they made long their furrows.

4The LORD *is* righteous: he hath cut asunder the cords of the wicked.

5Let them all be confounded and turned back that hate Zion.

6Let them be as the grass *upon* the housetops, which withereth afore it groweth up:

7Wherewith the mower filleth not his hand; nor he that bindeth sheaves his bosom.

8Neither do they which go by say, The blessing of the LORD *be* upon you: we bless you in the name of the LORD.

Psalm 130

A Song of degrees.

1Out of the depths have I cried unto thee, O LORD.

2Lord, hear my voice: let thine ears be attentive to the voice of my supplications.

3If thou, LORD, shouldest mark iniquities, O Lord, who shall stand?

130:3 Everyone Sins
◄ Psalm 53:3
Proverbs 20:9 ►

4But *there is* forgiveness with thee, that thou mayest be feared.

130:4 Forgiveness
◄ Psalm 103:3
Ezekiel 18:22 ►

5I wait for the LORD, my soul doth wait, and in his word do I hope.

6My soul *waiteth* for the Lord more than they that watch for the morning: *I say, more than* they that watch for the morning.

130:6 Waiting
◄ Psalm 40:1
Isaiah 25:9 ►

7Let Israel hope in the LORD: for with the LORD *there is* mercy, and with him *is* plenteous redemption.

8And he shall redeem Israel from all his iniquities.

Psalm 131

A Song of degrees of David.

1LORD, my heart is not haughty, nor mine eyes lofty: neither do I exercise myself in great matters, or in things too high for me.

2Surely I have behaved and quieted myself, as a child that is weaned of his mother: my soul *is* even as a weaned child.

3Let Israel hope in the LORD from henceforth and for ever.

Psalm 132

A Song of degrees.

1LORD, remember David, *and* all his afflictions:

2How he sware unto the LORD, *and* vowed unto the mighty *God* of Jacob;

3Surely I will not come into the tabernacle of my house, nor go up into my bed;

4I will not give sleep to mine eyes, *or* slumber to mine eyelids,

5Until I find out a place for the LORD, an habitation for the mighty *God* of Jacob.

6Lo, we heard of it at Ephratah: we found it in the fields of the wood.

7We will go into his tabernacles: we will worship at his footstool.

8Arise, O LORD, into thy rest; thou, and the ark of thy strength.

9Let thy priests be clothed with righteousness; and let thy saints shout for joy.

10For thy servant David's sake turn not away the face of thine anointed.

11The LORD hath sworn *in* truth unto David; he will not turn from it; Of the fruit of thy body will I set upon thy throne.

12If thy children will keep my covenant and my testimony that I shall teach them, their children shall also sit upon thy throne for evermore.

13For the LORD hath chosen Zion; he hath desired *it* for his habitation.

14This *is* my rest for ever: here will I dwell; for I have desired it.

15I will abundantly bless her provision: I will satisfy her poor with bread.

132:16 Joy
◄ Psalm 126:5
Isaiah 12:3 ►

16I will also

clothe her priests with salvation: and her saints shall shout aloud for joy.

17 There will I make the horn of David to bud: I have ordained a lamp for mine anointed.

18 His enemies will I clothe with shame: but upon himself shall his crown flourish.

Psalm 133

A Song of degrees of David.

1 Behold, how good and how pleasant *it is* for brethren to dwell together in unity!

2 *It is* like the precious ointment upon the head, that ran down upon the beard, *even* Aaron's beard: that went down to the skirts of his garments;

3 As the dew of Hermon, *and as the dew* that descended upon the mountains of Zion: for there the LORD commanded the blessing, *even* life for evermore.

Psalm 134

A Song of degrees.

1 Behold, bless ye the LORD, all *ye* servants of the LORD, which by night stand in the house of the LORD.

2 Lift up your hands *in* the sanctuary, and bless the LORD.

3 The LORD that made heaven and earth bless thee out of Zion.

Psalm 135

1 Praise ye the LORD. Praise ye the name of the LORD; praise *him*, O ye servants of the LORD.

2 Ye that stand in the house of the LORD, in the courts of the house of our God,

3 Praise the LORD; for the LORD *is* good: sing praises unto his name; for *it is* pleasant.

4 For the LORD hath chosen Jacob unto himself, *and* Israel for his peculiar treasure.

5 For I know that the LORD *is* great, and *that* our Lord *is* above all gods.

6 Whatsoever the LORD pleased, *that* did he in heaven, and in earth, in the seas, and all deep places.

135:6 All-powerful
◄ Psalm 115:3
Isaiah 43:13 ►

135:6 God's Control
◄ Psalm 93:1
Daniel 2:20 ►

7 He causeth the vapours to ascend from the ends of the earth; he maketh lightnings for the rain; he bringeth the wind out of his treasuries.

8 Who smote the firstborn of Egypt, both of man and beast.

9 *Who* sent tokens and wonders into the midst of thee, O Egypt, upon Pharaoh, and upon all his servants.

10 Who smote great nations, and slew mighty kings;

11 Sihon king of the Amorites, and Og king of Bashan, and all the kingdoms of Canaan:

12 And gave their land *for* an heritage, an heritage unto Israel his people.

13 Thy name, O LORD, *endureth* for ever; *and* thy memorial, O LORD, throughout all generations.

14 For the LORD will judge his people, and he will repent himself concerning his servants.

15 The idols of the heathen *are* silver and gold, the work of men's hands.

16 They have mouths, but they speak not; eyes have they, but they see not;

17 They have ears, but they hear not; neither is there *any* breath in their mouths.

18 They that make them are like unto them: *so is* every one that trusteth in them.

19 Bless the LORD, O house of Israel: bless the LORD, O house of Aaron:

20 Bless the LORD, O house of Levi: ye that fear the LORD, bless the LORD.

21 Blessed be the LORD out of Zion, which dwelleth at Jerusalem. Praise ye the LORD.

Psalm 136

1 O give thanks unto the LORD; for *he is* good: for his mercy *endureth* for ever.

2 O give thanks unto the God of gods: for his mercy *endureth* for ever.

3 O give thanks to the Lord of lords: for his mercy *endureth* for ever.

4 To him who alone doeth great wonders: for his mercy *endureth* for ever.

5 To him that by wisdom made the heavens: for his mercy *endureth* for ever.

6 To him that stretched out the earth

above the waters: for his mercy *endureth* for ever.

7To him that made great lights: for his mercy *endureth* for ever:

8The sun to rule by day: for his mercy *endureth* for ever:

9The moon and stars to rule by night: for his mercy *endureth* for ever.

10To him that smote Egypt in their firstborn: for his mercy *endureth* for ever:

11And brought out Israel from among them: for his mercy *endureth* for ever:

12With a strong hand, and with a stretched out arm: for his mercy *endureth* for ever.

13To him which divided the Red sea into parts: for his mercy *endureth* for ever:

14And made Israel to pass through the midst of it: for his mercy *endureth* for ever:

15But overthrew Pharaoh and his host in the Red sea: for his mercy *endureth* for ever.

16To him which led his people through the wilderness: for his mercy *endureth* for ever.

17To him which smote great kings: for his mercy *endureth* for ever:

18And slew famous kings: for his mercy *endureth* for ever:

19Sihon king of the Amorites: for his mercy *endureth* for ever:

20And Og the king of Bashan: for his mercy *endureth* for ever:

21And gave their land for an heritage: for his mercy *endureth* for ever:

22*Even* an heritage unto Israel his servant: for his mercy *endureth* for ever.

23Who remembered us in our low estate: for his mercy *endureth* for ever:

24And hath redeemed us from our enemies: for his mercy *endureth* for ever.

25Who giveth food to all flesh: for his mercy *endureth* for ever.

26O give thanks unto the God of heaven: for his mercy *endureth* for ever.

Psalm 137

1By the rivers of Babylon, there we sat down, yea, we wept, when we remembered Zion.

137:1 Mistakes
◄ Psalm 51:3
Mark 14:72 ►

2We hanged our harps upon the willows in the midst thereof.

137:1 Unhappiness
◄ Psalm 73:16
Jeremiah 15:10 ►

3For there they that carried us away captive required of us a song; and they that wasted us *required of us* mirth, *saying,* Sing us *one* of the songs of Zion.

4How shall we sing the LORD'S song in a strange land?

5If I forget thee, O Jerusalem, let my right hand forget *her cunning.*

6If I do not remember thee, let my tongue cleave to the roof of my mouth; if I prefer not Jerusalem above my chief joy.

7Remember, O LORD, the children of Edom in the day of Jerusalem; who said, Rase *it,* rase *it, even* to the foundation thereof.

8O daughter of Babylon, who art to be destroyed; happy *shall he be,* that rewardeth thee as thou hast served us.

9Happy *shall he be,* that taketh and dasheth thy little ones against the stones.

Psalm 138

A Psalm of David.

1I will praise thee with my whole heart: before the gods will I sing praise unto thee.

2I will worship toward thy holy temple, and praise thy name for thy lovingkindness and for thy truth: for thou hast magnified thy word above all thy name.

3In the day when I cried thou answeredst me, *and* strengthenedst me *with* strength in my soul.

4All the kings of the earth shall praise thee, O LORD, when they hear the words of thy mouth.

5Yea, they shall sing in the ways of the LORD: for great *is* the glory of the LORD.

6Though the LORD *be* high, yet hath he respect unto the lowly: but the proud he knoweth afar off.

138:6 Proud People
◄ Psalm 123:4
Malachi 3:15 ►

7Though I walk in the midst of trouble, thou wilt revive me: thou shalt stretch forth thine hand against the wrath of mine enemies, and thy right hand shall save me.

8The LORD will perfect *that which*

concerneth me: thy mercy, O LORD, *endureth* for ever: forsake not the works of thine own hands.

Psalm 139

To the chief Musician, A Psalm of David.

1O LORD, thou hast searched me, and known *me.*

2Thou knowest my downsitting and mine uprising, thou understandest my thought afar off.

3Thou compassest my path and my lying down, and art acquainted *with* all my ways.

4For *there is* not a word in my tongue, *but,* lo, O LORD, thou knowest it altogether.

5Thou hast beset me behind and before, and laid thine hand upon me.

6*Such* knowledge *is* too wonderful for me; it is high, I cannot *attain* unto it.

7Whither shall I go from thy spirit? or whither shall I flee from thy presence?

8If I ascend up into heaven, thou *art* there: if I make my bed in hell, behold, thou *art there.*

139:8 Where Is God?
◄ Deuteronomy 4:39
Proverbs 15:3 ►

9*If* I take the wings of the morning, *and* dwell in the uttermost parts of the sea;

10Even there shall thy hand lead me, and thy right hand shall hold me.

11If I say, Surely the darkness shall cover me; even the night shall be light about me.

12Yea, the darkness hideth not from thee; but the night shineth as the day: the darkness and the light *are* both alike *to thee.*

13For thou hast possessed my reins: thou hast covered me in my mother's womb.

14I will praise thee; for I am fearfully *and* wonderfully made: marvellous *are* thy works; and *that* my soul knoweth right well.

15My substance was not hid from thee, when I was made in secret, *and* curiously wrought in the lowest parts of the earth.

16Thine eyes did see my substance, yet being unperfect; and in thy book all *my members* were written, *which* in continuance were fashioned, when *as yet there was* none of them.

17How precious also are thy thoughts unto me, O God! how great is the sum of them!

18*If* I should count them, they are more in number than the sand: when I awake, I am still with thee.

19Surely thou wilt slay the wicked, O God: depart from me therefore, ye bloody men.

20For they speak against thee wickedly, *and* thine enemies take *thy name* in vain.

21Do not I hate them, O LORD, that hate thee? and am not I grieved with those that rise up against thee?

22I hate them with perfect hatred: I count them mine enemies.

23Search me, O God, and know my heart: try me, and know my thoughts:

24And see if *there be any* wicked way in me, and lead me in the way everlasting.

Psalm 140

To the chief Musician, A Psalm of David.

1Deliver me, O LORD, from the evil man: preserve me from the violent man;

2Which imagine mischiefs in *their* heart; continually are they gathered together *for* war.

3They have sharpened their tongues like a serpent; adders' poison *is* under their lips. Selah.

4Keep me, O LORD, from the hands of the wicked; preserve me from the violent man; who have purposed to overthrow my goings.

5The proud have hid a snare for me, and cords; they have spread a net by the wayside; they have set gins for me. Selah.

6I said unto the LORD, Thou *art* my God: hear the voice of my supplications, O LORD.

7O GOD the Lord, the strength of my salvation, thou hast covered my head in the day of battle.

8Grant not, O LORD, the desires of the wicked: further not his wicked device; *lest* they exalt themselves. Selah.

9*As for* the head of those that compass me about, let the mischief of their own lips cover them.

10Let burning coals fall upon them: let them be cast into the fire; into deep pits, that they rise not up again.

11 Let not an evil speaker be established in the earth: evil shall hunt the violent man to overthrow *him*.

12 I know that the LORD will maintain the cause of the afflicted, *and* the right of the poor.

> **140:12**
> **Promises to the Poor**
> ◄ Psalm 109:31
> Isaiah 11:4 ►

13 Surely the righteous shall give thanks unto thy name: the upright shall dwell in thy presence.

Psalm 141

A Psalm of David.

1 LORD, I cry unto thee: make haste unto me; give ear unto my voice, when I cry unto thee.

2 Let my prayer be set forth before thee *as* incense; *and* the lifting up of my hands *as* the evening sacrifice.

3 Set a watch, O LORD, before my mouth; keep the door of my lips.

4 Incline not my heart to *any* evil thing, to practise wicked works with men that work iniquity: and let me not eat of their dainties.

5 Let the righteous smite me; *it shall be* a kindness: and let him reprove me; *it shall be* an excellent oil, *which* shall not break my head: for yet my prayer also *shall be* in their calamities.

> **141:5**
> **Taking Advice**
> ◄ Proverbs 15:5 ►

6 When their judges are overthrown in stony places, they shall hear my words; for they are sweet.

7 Our bones are scattered at the grave's mouth, as when one cutteth and cleaveth *wood* upon the earth.

> **141:7 Your Body**
> ◄ Psalm 103:14
> Isaiah 2:22 ►

8 But mine eyes *are* unto thee, O GOD the Lord: in thee is my trust; leave not my soul destitute.

9 Keep me from the snares *which* they have laid for me, and the gins of the workers of iniquity.

10 Let the wicked fall into their own nets, whilst that I withal escape.

Psalm 142

Maschil of David; A Prayer when he was in the cave.

1 I cried unto the LORD with my voice; with my voice unto the LORD did I make my supplication.

2 I poured out my complaint before him; I shewed before him my trouble.

3 When my spirit was overwhelmed within me, then thou knewest my path. In the way wherein I walked have they privily laid a snare for me.

4 I looked on *my* right hand, and beheld, but *there was* no man that would know me: refuge failed me; no man cared for my soul.

> **142:4 Being Friendless**
> ◄ Psalm 88:18
> Mark 14:48 ►

5 I cried unto thee, O LORD: I said, Thou *art* my refuge *and* my portion in the land of the living.

6 Attend unto my cry; for I am brought very low: deliver me from my persecutors; for they are stronger than I.

7 Bring my soul out of prison, that I may praise thy name: the righteous shall compass me about; for thou shalt deal bountifully with me.

Psalm 143

A Psalm of David.

1 Hear my prayer, O LORD, give ear to my supplications: in thy faithfulness answer me, *and* in thy righteousness.

2 And enter not into judgment with thy servant: for in thy sight shall no man living be justified.

3 For the enemy hath persecuted my soul; he hath smitten my life down to the ground; he hath made me to dwell in darkness, as those that have been long dead.

> **143:3 Bullies**
> ◄ Psalm 119:161
> Jeremiah 15:15 ►

4 Therefore is my spirit overwhelmed within me; my heart within me is desolate.

5 I remember the days of old; I meditate on all thy works; I muse on the work of thy hands.

6 I stretch forth
my hands unto
thee: my soul *thirst-*
eth after thee, as a
thirsty land. Selah.

143:6 Desire for God
◄ Psalm 119:174
Amos 8:11 ►

7 Hear me speed-
ily, O LORD: my spirit faileth: hide not thy
face from me, lest I be like unto them that
go down into the pit.
8 Cause me to hear thy lovingkindness
in the morning; for in thee do I trust: cause
me to know the way wherein I should
walk; for I lift up my soul unto thee.
9 Deliver me, O LORD, from mine enemies: I flee unto thee to hide me.
10 Teach me to do
thy will; for thou *art*
my God: thy spirit
is good; lead me
into the land of up-
rightness.

143:10
Submitting to God
◄ Psalm 40:8
Matthew 6:10 ►

11 Quicken me, O LORD, for thy name's
sake: for thy righteousness' sake bring my
soul out of trouble.
12 And of thy mercy cut off mine enemies, and destroy all them that afflict my
soul: for I *am* thy servant.

Psalm 144

A Psalm of David.

1 Blessed *be* the LORD my strength, which
teacheth my hands to war, *and* my fingers
to fight:
2 My goodness, and my fortress; my high
tower, and my deliverer; my shield, and *he*
in whom I trust; who subdueth my people under me.
3 LORD, what *is* man, that thou takest
knowledge of him! *or* the son of man, that
thou makest account of him!
4 Man is like to vanity: his days *are* as a
shadow that passeth away.
5 Bow thy heavens, O LORD, and come
down: touch the mountains, and they shall
smoke.
6 Cast forth lightning, and scatter them:
shoot out thine arrows, and destroy them.
7 Send thine hand from above; rid me,
and deliver me out of great waters, from
the hand of strange children;
8 Whose mouth speaketh vanity, and
their right hand *is* a right hand of falsehood.
9 I will sing a new song unto thee, O God:
upon a psaltery *and* an instrument of ten
strings will I sing praises unto thee.
10 *It is he* that giveth salvation unto kings:
who delivereth David his servant from the
hurtful sword.
11 Rid me, and deliver me from the hand
of strange children, whose mouth speaketh
vanity, and their right hand *is* a right hand
of falsehood:
12 That our sons *may be* as plants grown
up in their youth; *that* our daughters *may*
be as corner stones, polished *after* the similitude of a palace:
13 *That* our garners *may be* full, afford-
ing all manner of store: *that* our sheep may
bring forth thousands and ten thousands
in our streets:
14 *That* our oxen *may be* strong to labour;
that there be no breaking in, nor going out;
that *there be* no complaining in our streets.
15 Happy *is that*
people, that is in
such a case: *yea,*
happy *is that* peo-
ple, whose God *is*
the LORD.

144:15
Source of Happiness
◄ Psalm 128:2
Proverbs 3:18 ►

Psalm 145

David's *Psalm* of praise.

1 I will extol thee, my God, O king; and I
will bless thy name for ever and ever.
2 Every day will I bless thee; and I will
praise thy name for ever and ever.
3 Great *is* the LORD, and greatly to be
praised; and his greatness *is* unsearchable.
4 One generation shall praise thy works
to another, and shall declare thy mighty
acts.
5 I will speak of the glorious honour of
thy majesty, and of thy wondrous works.
6 And *men* shall speak of the might of
thy terrible acts: and I will declare thy
greatness.
7 They shall abundantly utter the memory of thy great goodness, and shall sing
of thy righteousness.
8 The LORD *is* gracious, and full of compassion; slow to anger, and of great mercy.
9 The LORD *is* good to all: and his tender
mercies *are* over all his works.
10 All thy works shall praise thee,
O LORD; and thy saints shall bless thee.

11 They shall speak of the glory of thy kingdom, and talk of thy power;

12 To make known to the sons of men his mighty acts, and the glorious majesty of his kingdom.

13 Thy kingdom *is* an everlasting kingdom, and thy dominion *endureth* throughout all generations.

14 The LORD upholdeth all that fall, and raiseth up all *those that be* bowed down.

15 The eyes of all wait upon thee; and thou givest them their meat in due season.

16 Thou openest thine hand, and satisfiest the desire of every living thing.

17 The LORD *is* righteous in all his ways, and holy in all his works.

18 The LORD *is* nigh unto all them that call upon him, to all that call upon him in truth.

19 He will fulfil the desire of them that fear him: he also will hear their cry, and will save them.

20 The LORD preserveth all them that love him: but all the wicked will he destroy.

21 My mouth shall speak the praise of the LORD: and let all flesh bless his holy name for ever and ever.

Psalm 146

1 Praise ye the LORD. Praise the LORD, O my soul.

2 While I live will I praise the LORD: I will sing praises unto my God while I have any being.

3 Put not your trust in princes, *nor* in the son of man, in whom *there is* no help.

146:3 Trusting in People
◄ Psalm 118:9
Isaiah 2:22 ►

4 His breath goeth forth, he returneth to his earth; in that very day his thoughts perish.

5 Happy *is he* that *hath* the God of Jacob for his help, whose hope *is* in the LORD his God:

6 Which made heaven, and earth, the sea, and all that therein *is*: which keepeth truth for ever:

146:6 God's Word
◄ Psalm 33:4
Isaiah 65:16 ►

7 Which executeth judgment for the oppressed: which giveth food to the hungry. The LORD looseth the prisoners:

8 The LORD openeth *the eyes of* the blind: the LORD raiseth them that are bowed down: the LORD loveth the righteous:

146:8 God's Love
◄ Deuteronomy 7:8
Jeremiah 31:3 ►

9 The LORD preserveth the strangers; he relieveth the fatherless and widow: but the way of the wicked he turneth upside down.

146:9 God's Care for Kids
◄ Psalm 68:5
Proverbs 15:25 ►

146:9 Safety
◄ Psalm 37:28
Proverbs 2:8 ►

10 The LORD shall reign for ever, *even* thy God, O Zion, unto all generations. Praise ye the LORD.

Psalm 147

1 Praise ye the LORD: for *it is* good to sing praises unto our God; for *it is* pleasant; *and* praise is comely.

2 The LORD doth build up Jerusalem: he gathereth together the outcasts of Israel.

3 He healeth the broken in heart, and bindeth up their wounds.

4 He telleth the number of the stars; he calleth them all by *their* names.

5 Great *is* our Lord, and of great power: his understanding *is* infinite.

147:5 What God Knows
◄ Job 34:21
Hebrews 4:13 ►

6 The LORD lifteth up the meek: he casteth the wicked down to the ground.

147:6 Meekness
◄ Psalm 37:11
Psalm 149:4 ►

7 Sing unto the LORD with thanksgiving; sing praise upon the harp unto our God:

8 Who covereth the heaven with clouds, who prepareth rain for the earth, who maketh grass to grow upon the mountains.

9 He giveth to the beast his food, *and* to the young ravens which cry.

10 He delighteth not in the strength of the horse: he taketh not pleasure in the legs of a man.

11 The LORD taketh pleasure in them that fear him, in those that hope in his mercy.

Turn to the next page for more . . .

12 Praise the
LORD, O Jerusalem;
praise thy God,
O Zion.
13 For he hath
strengthened the
bars of thy gates; he hath blessed thy children within thee.
14 He maketh peace *in* thy borders, *and*
filleth thee with the finest of the wheat.
15 He sendeth forth his commandment
upon earth: his word runneth very swiftly.
16 He giveth snow like wool: he scattereth the hoar frost like ashes.
17 He casteth forth his ice like morsels:
who can stand before his cold?
18 He sendeth out his word, and melteth
them: he causeth his wind to blow, *and*
the waters flow.
19 He sheweth his word unto Jacob, his
statutes and his judgments unto Israel.
20 He hath not dealt so with any nation:
and *as for his* judgments, they have not
known them. Praise ye the LORD.

147:11 Why Fear God?
◄ Psalm 103:13
Proverbs 1:7 ►

Psalm 148

1 Praise ye the LORD. Praise ye the LORD
from the heavens: praise him in the heights.
2 Praise ye him, all his angels: praise ye
him, all his hosts.
3 Praise ye him,
sun and moon:
praise him, all ye
stars of light.
4 Praise him, ye
heavens of heavens,
and ye waters that *be* above the heavens.
5 Let them praise the name of the LORD:
for he commanded, and they were created.
6 He hath also stablished them for ever
and ever: he hath made a decree which
shall not pass.
7 Praise the LORD from the earth, ye dragons, and all deeps:
8 Fire, and hail; snow, and vapours;
stormy wind fulfilling his word:
9 Mountains, and all hills; fruitful trees,
and all cedars:
10 Beasts, and all cattle; creeping things,
and flying fowl:
11 Kings of the earth, and all people;
princes, and all judges of the earth:
12 Both young men, and maidens; old
men, and children:
13 Let them praise the name of the LORD:
for his name alone is excellent; his glory *is*
above the earth and heaven.
14 He also exalteth the horn of his people, the praise of all his saints; *even* of the
children of Israel, a people near unto him.
Praise ye the LORD.

148:3 Nature's Praise
◄ Psalm 98:8
Isaiah 44:23 ►

Psalm 149

1 Praise ye the LORD. Sing unto the LORD
a new song, *and* his praise in the congregation of saints.
2 Let Israel rejoice in him that made him:
let the children of Zion be joyful in their
King.
3 Let them praise his name in the dance:
let them sing praises unto him with the
timbrel and harp.
4 For the LORD
taketh pleasure in
his people: he will
beautify the meek
with salvation.
5 Let the saints be
joyful in glory: let
them sing aloud upon their beds.
6 *Let* the high *praises* of God *be* in their
mouth, and a twoedged sword in their
hand;
7 To execute vengeance upon the heathen, *and* punishments upon the people;
8 To bind their kings with chains, and
their nobles with fetters of iron;
9 To execute upon them the judgment
written: this honour have all his saints.
Praise ye the LORD.

149:4 Meekness
◄ Psalm 147:6
Isaiah 11:4 ►

Psalm 150

1 Praise ye the LORD. Praise God in his
sanctuary: praise him in the firmament of
his power.
2 Praise him for his mighty acts: praise
him according to his excellent greatness.
3 Praise him with the sound of the trumpet: praise him with the psaltery and harp.
4 Praise him with the timbrel and dance:
praise him with stringed instruments and
organs.
5 Praise him upon the loud cymbals:
praise him upon the high sounding cymbals.
6 Let every thing that hath breath praise
the LORD. Praise ye the LORD.

Proverbs

AUTHOR
Mostly Solomon

MAIN POINT
God wants us to live godly and healthy lives.

DATE WRITTEN
Early in Solomon's reign, which began in 970 B.C.

31 CHAPTERS

MAIN PEOPLE

Because it is a book of wise sayings, there are no named characters.

SPECIAL FEATURES

- *Read by many people one proverb per day every month, since it has 31 chapters*
- *Starts right out with a collection of wisdom for young people (chapters 1-9)*
- *Concludes with right-on advice for anyone wanting to be a leader (chapters 25-31)*
- *Shows that Solomon started out completely on God's track but then got derailed and didn't follow his own advice*
- *Third book of Poetry*

HOW THE BOOK GOT ITS NAME

The term proverb comes from a Hebrew word that means "to rule or govern." Each proverb is a short sentence that governs or rules our lives, so this book is a treasure chest of advice.

1
1The proverbs of Solomon the son of
David, king of Israel;
2To know wisdom and instruction; to
perceive the words of understanding;
3To receive the instruction of wisdom,
justice, and judgment, and equity;
4To give subtilty to the simple, to the
young man knowledge and discretion.
5A wise *man* will hear, and will increase
learning; and a man of understanding shall
attain unto wise counsels:
6To understand a proverb, and the interpretation; the words of the wise, and
their dark sayings.
7The fear of the
LORD *is* the begin-
ning of knowledge:
but fools despise
wisdom and in-
struction.
8My son, hear
the instruction of
thy father, and for-
sake not the law of
thy mother:
9For they *shall be*
an ornament of grace unto thy head, and
chains about thy neck.

1:7 Rejecting God's Word
◄ Psalm 50:17
Proverbs 1:22 ►

1:7 Why Fear God?
◄ Psalm 147:11
Isaiah 50:10 ►

Turn to the next page for more . . .

10 My son, if sin-
ners entice thee,
consent thou not.
11 If they say,
Come with us, let
us lay wait for
blood, let us lurk
privily for the inno-
cent without cause:
12 Let us swallow
them up alive as the
grave; and whole, as
those that go down into the pit:
13 We shall find all precious substance,
we shall fill our houses with spoil:
14 Cast in thy lot among us; let us all have
one purse:
15 My son, walk
not thou in the way
with them; refrain
thy foot from their
path:
16 For their feet
run to evil, and
make haste to shed
blood.
17 Surely in vain
the net is spread in
the sight of any
bird.
18 And they lay
wait for their *own*
blood; they lurk
privily for their *own*
lives.
19 So *are* the ways
of every one that is
greedy of gain;
which taketh away
the life of the own-
ers thereof.
20 Wisdom crieth
without; she utter-
eth her voice in the
streets:
21 She crieth in
the chief place of
concourse, in the
openings of the
gates: in the city she
uttereth her words,
saying,
22 How long, ye
simple ones, will ye
love simplicity? and the scorners delight

1:8
Parents
◄ Proverbs 6:23 ►

1:10
Saying No
◄ Proverbs 4:14 ►

1:15 Bad Friends
◄ Psalm 1:1
Proverbs 4:14 ►

1:16
Bad People
◄ Proverbs 4:16 ►

1:19
Greed
◄ Ecclesiastes 5:10 ►

1:20 True Wisdom
◄ Psalm 111:10
Proverbs 4:7 ►

1:22
Naiveté
◄ Proverbs 7:7 ►

1:22
Rejecting God's Word
◄ Proverbs 1:7
Proverbs 5:12 ►

in their scorning, and fools hate knowledge?
23 Turn you at my
reproof: behold, I
will pour out my
spirit unto you, I
will make known
my words unto
you.
24 Because I have
called, and ye re-
fused; I have
stretched out my
hand, and no man
regarded;
25 But ye have set at nought all my counsel, and would none of my reproof:
26 I also will laugh at your calamity; I
will mock when your fear cometh;
27 When your fear cometh as desolation,
and your destruction cometh as a whirlwind; when distress and anguish cometh
upon you.
28 Then shall they
call upon me, but I
will not answer;
they shall seek me
early, but they shall
not find me:
29 For that they hated knowledge, and
did not choose the fear of the LORD:
30 They would none of my counsel: they
despised all my reproof.
31 Therefore shall they eat of the fruit of
their own way, and be filled with their own
devices.
32 For the turning
away of the simple
shall slay them, and
the prosperity of
fools shall destroy
them.
33 But whoso
hearkeneth unto
me shall dwell safe-
ly, and shall be qui-
et from fear of evil.

1:23 Repent!
◄ 2 Chronicles 30:6
Isaiah 22:12 ►

1:24 Hard-hearted
◄ Leviticus 26:23
Ecclesiastes 8:11 ►

1:28 Unanswered Prayer
◄ Psalm 66:18
Proverbs 21:13 ►

1:32 Success
◄ Deuteronomy 32:15
Proverbs 30:9 ►

1:33 Security
◄ Psalm 125:1
Proverbs 3:24 ►

2

1 My son, if thou
wilt receive my words, and hide my commandments with thee;
2 So that thou incline thine ear unto
wisdom, *and* apply thine heart to understanding;
3 Yea, if thou criest after knowledge, *and*
liftest up thy voice for understanding;

4If thou seekest her as silver, and searchest for her as *for* hid treasures;

2:3 Praying for Wisdom
◄ Psalm 90:12
Ephesians 1:17 ►

5Then shalt thou understand the fear of the LORD, and find the knowledge of God.

2:6
Getting Wisdom
◄ Ecclesiastes 2:26 ►

6For the LORD giveth wisdom: out of his mouth *cometh* knowledge and understanding.

2:6 Understanding
◄ Psalm 119:104
Proverbs 8:14 ►

7He layeth up sound wisdom for the righteous: *he is* a buckler to them that walk uprightly.

8He keepeth the paths of judgment, and preserveth the way of his saints.

2:7 Why Do Right?
◄ Psalm 112:4
Proverbs 2:21 ►

9Then shalt thou understand righteousness, and judgment, and equity; *yea,* every good path.

2:8 Safety
◄ Psalm 146:9
Isaiah 49:8 ►

10When wisdom entereth into thine heart, and knowledge is pleasant unto thy soul;

2:9 Right Paths
◄ Psalm 119:35
Proverbs 4:11 ►

11Discretion shall preserve thee, understanding shall keep thee:

12To deliver thee from the way of the evil *man,* from the man that speaketh froward things;

2:11 Discretion
◄ Genesis 41:39
Proverbs 5:2 ►

13Who leave the paths of uprightness, to walk in the ways of darkness;

14Who rejoice to do evil, *and* delight in the frowardness of the wicked;

15Whose ways *are* crooked, and *they* froward in their paths:

16To deliver thee from the strange woman, *even* from the stranger *which* flattereth with her words;

17Which forsaketh the guide of her youth, and forgetteth the covenant of her God.

18For her house inclineth unto death, and her paths unto the dead.

19None that go unto her return again, neither take they hold of the paths of life.

20That thou mayest walk in the way of good *men,* and keep the paths of the righteous.

21For the upright shall dwell in the land, and the perfect shall remain in it.

2:21 Why Do Right?
◄ Proverbs 2:7
Proverbs 10:9 ►

22But the wicked shall be cut off from the earth, and the transgressors shall be rooted out of it.

3

1My son, forget not my law; but let thine heart keep my commandments:

2For length of days, and long life, and peace, shall they add to thee.

3Let not mercy and truth forsake thee: bind them about thy neck; write them upon the table of thine heart:

3:3
Showing Mercy
◄ Proverbs 11:17 ►

4So shall thou find favour and good understanding in the sight of God and man.

3:5 Trusting God
◄ Psalm 118:8
Isaiah 26:4 ►

5Trust in the LORD with all thine heart; and lean not unto thine own understanding.

3:7
Conceit
◄ Proverbs 26:5 ►

6In all thy ways acknowledge him, and he shall direct thy paths.

3:7 Fearing God
◄ 2 Chronicles 19:7
Ecclesiastes 12:13 ►

7Be not wise in thine own eyes: fear the LORD, and depart from evil.

8It shall be health to thy navel, and marrow to thy bones.

3:9 Tithing
◄ Ezra 8:28
Micah 4:13 ►

9Honour the LORD with thy substance, and with the firstfruits of all thine increase:

3:9-10
Promises to Givers
◄ Psalm 41:1
Proverbs 11:25 ►

10So shall thy

barns be filled with plenty, and thy presses
shall burst out with new wine.
11 My son, despise
not the chastening
of the LORD; neither
be weary of his cor-
rection:
12 For whom the
LORD loveth he correcteth; even as a father
the son *in whom* he delighteth.

3:11-12 Difficulties
◀ Psalm 94:12
John 15:2 ▶

13 Happy *is* the man *that* findeth wisdom, and the man *that* getteth understanding.
14 For the merchandise of it *is* better than
the merchandise of silver, and the gain
thereof than fine gold.
15 She *is* more precious than rubies: and
all the things thou canst desire are not to
be compared unto her.
16 Length of days *is* in her right hand;
and in her left hand riches and honour.
17 Her ways *are*
ways of pleasant-
ness, and all her
paths *are* peace.
18 She *is* a tree of
life to them that lay
hold upon her: and
happy *is every one*
that retaineth her.
19 The LORD by
wisdom hath
founded the earth;
by understanding hath he established the
heavens.

3:17 Peace of Mind
◀ Psalm 119:165
Isaiah 26:3 ▶

3:18
Source of Happiness
◀ Psalm 144:15
Proverbs 14:21 ▶

20 By his knowledge the depths are
broken up, and the clouds drop down
the dew.
21 My son, let not them depart from thine
eyes: keep sound wisdom and discretion:
22 So shall they be life unto thy soul, and
grace to thy neck.
23 Then shalt thou walk in thy way safely, and thy foot shall not stumble.
24 When thou
liest down, thou
shalt not be afraid:
yea, thou shalt lie
down, and thy sleep
shall be sweet.

3:24 Security
◀ Proverbs 1:33
Isaiah 33:16 ▶

25 Be not afraid of sudden fear, neither
of the desolation of the wicked, when it
cometh.
26 For the LORD shall be thy confidence,
and shall keep thy foot from being taken.
27 Withhold not good from them to
whom it is due, when it is in the power of
thine hand to do *it*.
28 Say not unto thy neighbour, Go, and
come again, and to morrow I will give;
when thou hast it by thee.
29 Devise not evil against thy neighbour,
seeing he dwelleth securely by thee.
30 Strive not with
a man without
cause, if he have
done thee no harm.
31 Envy thou not
the oppressor, and
choose none of his
ways.
32 For the froward
is abomination to
the LORD: but his
secret *is* with the
righteous.
33 The curse of
the LORD *is* in the
house of the wick-
ed: but he blesseth
the habitation of
the just.

3:30
Arguing
◀ Proverbs 17:14 ▶

3:31 Envy
◀ Psalm 37:1
Proverbs 14:30 ▶

3:32
Rewarded Goodness
◀ Psalm 92:12
Proverbs 4:18 ▶

34 Surely he scorneth the scorners: but
he giveth grace unto the lowly.
35 The wise shall inherit glory: but shame
shall be the promotion of fools.

4

1 Hear, ye children, the instruction of a
father, and attend to know understanding.
2 For I give you good doctrine, forsake
ye not my law.
3 For I was my father's son, tender and
only *beloved* in the sight of my mother.
4 He taught me also, and said unto me,
Let thine heart retain my words: keep my
commandments, and live.
5 Get wisdom, get understanding: forget
it not; neither decline from the words of
my mouth.
6 Forsake her not, and she shall preserve
thee: love her, and she shall keep thee.
7 Wisdom *is* the
principal thing;
therefore get wis-
dom: and with all
thy getting get un-
derstanding.

4:7 True Wisdom
◀ Proverbs 1:20
Proverbs 9:1 ▶

8 Exalt her, and she shall promote thee:
she shall bring thee to honour, when thou
dost embrace her.
9 She shall give to thine head an orna-

ment of grace: a
crown of glory shall
she deliver to thee.
10 Hear, O my
son, and receive my
sayings; and the
years of thy life
shall be many.
11 I have taught
thee in the way of
wisdom; I have l
ed thee in right
paths.
12 When thou
goest, thy steps
shall not be strait-
ened; and when
thou runnest, thou
shalt not stumble.
13 Take fast hold
of instruction; let
her not go: keep her;
for she *is* thy life.
14 Enter not into
the path of the
wicked, and go not
in the way of evil
men.
15 Avoid it, pass
not by it, turn from
it, and pass away.
16 For they sleep
not, except they
have done mischief;
and their sleep is
taken away, unless
they cause *some* to
fall.
17 For they eat the
bread of wicked-
ness, and drink the
wine of violence.
18 But the path of
the just *is* as the
shining light, that
shineth more and
more unto the per-
fect day.
19 The way of the
wicked *is* as dark-
ness: they know
not at what they
stumble.
20 My son, attend
to my words; in-

4:11 Right Paths
◄ Proverbs 2:9
Proverbs 4:18 ►

4:14 Bad Friends
◄ Proverbs 1:15
Proverbs 22:24 ►

4:14 Saying No
◄ Proverbs 1:10
Luke 21:34 ►

4:15 Argument Avoidance
◄ Romans 16:17 ►

4:16 Bad People
◄ Proverbs 1:16
Proverbs 6:18 ►

4:16 Mischief
◄ Psalm 36:4
Proverbs 6:14 ►

4:17 Violence
◄ Psalm 73:6
Isaiah 59:6 ►

4:18 Making Progress
◄ Psalm 92:12
2 Corinthians 3:18 ►

4:18 Rewarded Goodness
◄ Proverbs 3:32
Proverbs 12:13 ►

cline thine ear unto
my sayings.
21 Let them not
depart from thine
eyes; keep them in
the midst of thine
heart.
22 For they *are* life unto those that find
them, and health to all their flesh.
23 Keep thy heart
with all diligence;
for out of it *are* the
issues of life.
24 Put away from
thee a froward
mouth, and per-
verse lips put far
from thee.
25 Let thine eyes
look right on, and
let thine eyelids
look straight before
thee.
26 Ponder the
path of thy feet,
and let all thy ways
be established.
27 Turn not to the
right hand nor to the left: remove thy foot
from evil.

5

1 My son, attend unto my wisdom, *and*
bow thine ear to my understanding:
2 That thou may-
est regard discre-
tion, and *that* thy
lips may keep
knowledge.
3 For the lips of a
strange woman drop *as* an honeycomb,
and her mouth *is* smoother than oil:
4 But her end is bitter as wormwood,
sharp as a twoedged sword.
5 Her feet go down to death; her steps
take hold on hell.
6 Lest thou shouldest ponder the path of
life, her ways are moveable, *that* thou canst
not know *them.*
7 Hear me now therefore, O ye children,
and depart not from the words of my
mouth.
8 Remove thy way far from her, and come
not nigh the door of her house:
9 Lest thou give thine honour unto others, and thy years unto the cruel:
10 Lest strangers be filled with thy

4:18 Right Paths
◄ Proverbs 4:11
Isaiah 2:3 ►

4:23 Heart
◄ Proverbs 23:7 ►

4:27 One Goal
◄ Joshua 1:7
Ezekiel 1:12 ►

4:27 Stay Away!
◄ Psalm 97:10
Proverbs 14:16 ►

5:2 Discretion
◄ Proverbs 2:11
Isaiah 28:26 ►

wealth; and thy labours *be* in the house of
a stranger;
11And thou mourn at the last, when thy
flesh and thy body are consumed,
12And say, How
have I hated in-
struction, and my
heart despised re-
proof;
13And have not
obeyed the voice of my teachers, nor inclined mine ear to them that instructed
me!
14I was almost in all evil in the midst of
the congregation and assembly.
15Drink waters out of thine own cistern,
and running waters out of thine own well.
16Let thy fountains be dispersed abroad,
and rivers of waters in the streets.
17Let them be only thine own, and not
strangers' with thee.
18Let thy fountain be blessed: and rejoice with the wife of thy youth.
19*Let her be as* the loving hind and pleasant roe; let her breasts satisfy thee at all
times; and be thou ravished always with
her love.
20And why wilt thou, my son, be ravished with a strange woman, and embrace
the bosom of a stranger?
21For the ways of man *are* before the eyes
of the LORD, and he pondereth all his goings.
22His own iniq-
uities shall take the
wicked himself,
and he shall be
holden with the
cords of his sins.
23He shall die without instruction; and
in the greatness of his folly he shall go
astray.

5:12
Rejecting God's Word
◄ Proverbs 1:22 ►

5:22
Bad Habits
◄ John 8:34 ►

6

1My son, if thou be surety for thy
friend, *if* thou hast stricken thy hand with
a stranger,
2Thou art snared with the words of thy
mouth, thou art taken with the words of
thy mouth.
3Do this now, my son, deliver thyself,
when thou art come into the hand of thy
friend; go, humble thyself, and make sure
thy friend.
4Give not sleep to thine eyes, nor slumber to thine eyelids.
5Deliver thyself as a roe from the hand
of the hunter, and as
a bird from the
hand of the fowler.
6Go to the ant,
thou sluggard; con-
sider her ways, and
be wise:
7Which having
no guide, overseer,
or ruler,
8Provideth her
meat in the sum-
mer, *and* gathereth
her food in the har-
vest.
9How long wilt
thou sleep, O slug-
gard? when wilt
thou arise out of thy sleep?
10*Yet* a little sleep, a little slumber, a little folding of the hands to sleep:
11So shall thy poverty come as one that
travelleth, and thy want as an armed man.
12A naughty person, a wicked man,
walketh with a froward mouth.
13He winketh with his eyes, he speaketh
with his feet, he teacheth with his fingers;
14Frowardness *is*
in his heart, he
deviseth mischief
continually; he
soweth discord.
15Therefore shall
his calamity come
suddenly; suddenly
shall he be broken
without remedy.
16These six *things*
doth the LORD hate:
yea, seven *are* an
abomination unto
him:
17A proud look,
a lying tongue, and
hands that shed in-
nocent blood,
18An heart that
deviseth wicked
imaginations, feet
that be swift in run-
ning to mischief,
19A false witness
that speaketh lies, and he that soweth discord among brethren.
20My son, keep thy father's command-

6:4
Sleep
◄ Proverbs 6:9-10 ►

6:6
Lazy People
◄ Proverbs 13:4 ►

6:9-10 Sleep
◄ Proverbs 6:4
Proverbs 10:5 ►

6:14 Mischief
◄ Proverbs 4:16
Proverbs 24:2 ►

6:17 Arrogance
◄ Psalm 119:21
Proverbs 11:2 ►

6:18 Bad People
◄ Proverbs 4:16
Isaiah 59:7 ►

6:19 Hurtful Lying
◄ Deuteronomy 19:16
Proverbs 12:17 ►

ment, and forsake not the law of thy mother:

21Bind them continually upon thine heart, *and* tie them about thy neck.

22When thou goest, it shall lead thee; when thou sleepest, it shall keep thee; and *when* thou awakest, it shall talk with thee.

23For the commandment *is* a lamp; and the law *is* light; and reproofs of instruction *are* the way of life:

6:23 Parents
◄ Proverbs 1:8
Proverbs 12:1 ►

24To keep thee from the evil woman, from the flattery of the tongue of a strange woman.

6:23 The Bible as a Guide
◄ Psalm 119:130
2 Peter 1:19 ►

25Lust not after her beauty in thine heart; neither let her take thee with her eyelids.

26For by means of a whorish woman *a man is brought* to a piece of bread: and the adulteress will hunt for the precious life.

27Can a man take fire in his bosom, and his clothes not be burned?

28Can one go upon hot coals, and his feet not be burned?

29So he that goeth in to his neighbour's wife; whosoever toucheth her shall not be innocent.

30*Men* do not despise a thief, if he steal to satisfy his soul when he is hungry;

31But *if* he be found, he shall restore sevenfold; he shall give all the substance of his house.

32*But* whoso committeth adultery with a woman lacketh understanding: he *that* doeth it destroyeth his own soul.

33A wound and dishonour shall he get; and his reproach shall not be wiped away.

6:33 Sin Hurts
◄ Proverbs 23:29 ►

34For jealousy *is* the rage of a man: therefore he will not spare in the day of vengeance.

35He will not regard any ransom; neither will he rest content, though thou givest many gifts.

7

1My son, keep my words, and lay up my commandments with thee.

2Keep my commandments, and live; and my law as the apple of thine eye.

3Bind them upon thy fingers, write them upon the table of thine heart.

4Say unto wisdom, Thou *art* my sister; and call understanding *thy* kinswoman:

5That they may keep thee from the strange woman, from the stranger *which* flattereth with her words.

6For at the window of my house I looked through my casement,

7And beheld among the simple ones, I discerned among the youths, a young man void of understanding,

7:7 Naiveté
◄ Proverbs 1:22
Proverbs 8:5 ►

8Passing through the street near her corner; and he went the way to her house,

9In the twilight, in the evening, in the black and dark night:

10And, behold, there met him a woman *with* the attire of an harlot, and subtil of heart.

11(She *is* loud and stubborn; her feet abide not in her house:

12Now *is she* without, now in the streets, and lieth in wait at every corner.)

13So she caught him, and kissed him, *and* with an impudent face said unto him,

14*I have* peace offerings with me; this day have I payed my vows.

15Therefore came I forth to meet thee, diligently to seek thy face, and I have found thee.

16I have decked my bed with coverings of tapestry, with carved *works,* with fine linen of Egypt.

17I have perfumed my bed with myrrh, aloes, and cinnamon.

18Come, let us take our fill of love until the morning: let us solace ourselves with loves.

19For the goodman *is* not at home, he is gone a long journey:

20He hath taken a bag of money with him, *and* will come home at the day appointed.

21With her much fair speech she caused him to yield, with the flattering of her lips she forced him.

22He goeth after her straightway, as an ox goeth to the slaughter, or as a fool to the correction of the stocks;

23Till a dart strike through his liver; as a bird hasteth to the snare, and knoweth not that it *is* for his life.

24 Hearken unto me now therefore, O ye
children, and attend to the words of my
mouth.
25 Let not thine heart decline to her ways,
go not astray in her paths.
26 For she hath cast down many wounded: yea, many strong *men* have been slain
by her.
27 Her house *is* the way to hell, going
down to the chambers of death.

8

1 Doth not wisdom cry? and understanding put forth her voice?
2 She standeth in the top of high places,
by the way in the places of the paths.
3 She crieth at the gates, at the entry of
the city, at the coming in at the doors.
4 Unto you, O men, I call; and my voice
is to the sons of man.
5 O ye simple, un-
derstand wisdom:
and, ye fools, be ye
of an understand-
ing heart.
6 Hear; for I will
speak of excellent things; and the opening
of my lips *shall be* right things.

8:5 Naiveté
◄ Proverbs 7:7
Proverbs 14:15 ►

7 For my mouth shall speak truth; and
wickedness *is* an abomination to my lips.
8 All the words of my mouth *are* in righteousness; *there is* nothing froward or perverse in them.
9 They *are* all plain to him that understandeth, and right to them that find
knowledge.
10 Receive my instruction, and not silver;
and knowledge rather than choice gold.
11 For wisdom *is* better than rubies; and
all the things that may be desired are not
to be compared to it.
12 I wisdom dwell with prudence, and
find out knowledge of witty inventions.
13 The fear of the LORD *is* to hate evil:
pride, and arrogancy, and the evil way, and
the froward mouth, do I hate.
14 Counsel *is*
mine, and sound
wisdom: I *am* un-
derstanding; I have
strength.
15 By me kings
reign, and princes decree justice.

8:14 Understanding
◄ Proverbs 2:6
Proverbs 11:12 ►

16 By me princes rule, and nobles, *even*
all the judges of the earth.
17 I love them that love me; and those
that seek me early shall find me.
18 Riches and
honour *are* with
me; *yea*, durable
riches and righ-
teousness.
19 My fruit *is* bet-
ter than gold, yea, than fine gold; and my
revenue than choice silver.

8:18
Invisible Wealth
◄ Proverbs 10:22 ►

20 I lead in the way of righteousness, in
the midst of the paths of judgment:
21 That I may cause those that love me
to inherit substance; and I will fill their
treasures.
22 The LORD possessed me in the beginning of his way, before his works of old.
23 I was set up from everlasting, from the
beginning, or ever the earth was.
24 When *there were* no depths, I was
brought forth; when *there were* no fountains abounding with water.
25 Before the mountains were settled,
before the hills was I brought forth:
26 While as yet he had not made the
earth, nor the fields, nor the highest part
of the dust of the world.
27 When he prepared the heavens, I *was*
there: when he set a compass upon the face
of the depth:
28 When he established the clouds
above: when he strengthened the fountains
of the deep:
29 When he gave to the sea his decree,
that the waters should not pass his commandment: when he appointed the foundations of the earth:
30 Then I was by him, *as* one brought up
with him: and I was daily *his* delight, rejoicing always before him;
31 Rejoicing in the habitable part of his
earth; and my delights *were* with the sons
of men.
32 Now therefore hearken unto me, O ye
children: for blessed *are they that* keep my
ways.
33 Hear instruction, and be wise, and refuse it not.
34 Blessed *is* the man that heareth me,
watching daily at my gates, waiting at the
posts of my doors.
35 For whoso
findeth me findeth
life, and shall ob-
tain favour of the
LORD.
36 But he that

8:36 Spiritual Death
◄ Genesis 2:17
Ezekiel 18:20 ►

sinneth against me wrongeth his own soul:
all they that hate me love death.

9

1 Wisdom hath
builded her house,
she hath hewn out
her seven pillars:
2 She hath killed
her beasts; she hath
mingled her wine; she hath also furnished
her table.

> **9:1 True Wisdom**
> ◄ Proverbs 4:7
> Hosea 14:9 ►

3 She hath sent forth her maidens: she
crieth upon the highest places of the city,
4 Whoso *is* simple, let him turn in hither:
as for him that wanteth understanding, she
saith to him,
5 Come, eat of my bread, and drink of
the wine *which* I have mingled.
6 Forsake the foolish, and live; and go in
the way of understanding.
7 He that reproveth a scorner getteth to
himself shame: and he that rebuketh a
wicked *man getteth* himself a blot.
8 Reprove not a scorner, lest he hate thee:
rebuke a wise man, and he will love thee.
9 Give *instruction* to a wise *man,* and he
will be yet wiser: teach a just *man,* and he
will increase in learning.
10 The fear of the LORD *is* the beginning
of wisdom: and the knowledge of the holy
is understanding.
11 For by me thy days shall be multiplied,
and the years of thy life shall be increased.
12 If thou be wise,
thou shalt be wise
for thyself: but *if*
thou scornest, thou
alone shalt bear *it.*
13 A foolish wom-
an *is* clamorous: *she is* simple, and knoweth
nothing.

> **9:12 Blame**
> ◄ Job 19:4
> Jeremiah 31:30 ►

14 For she sitteth at the door of her house,
on a seat in the high places of the city,
15 To call passengers who go right on
their ways:
16 Whoso *is* simple, let him turn in
hither: and *as for* him that wanteth understanding, she saith to him,
17 Stolen waters are sweet, and bread *eat-
en* in secret is pleasant.
18 But he knoweth not that the dead *are*
there; *and that* her guests *are* in the depths
of hell.

10

1 The proverbs of Solomon. A wise son
maketh a glad father: but a foolish son *is*
the heaviness of his mother.
2 Treasures of wickedness profit nothing:
but righteousness delivereth from death.
3 The LORD will not suffer the soul of the
righteous to famish: but he casteth away
the substance of the wicked.
4 He becometh
poor that dealeth
with a slack hand:
but the hand of the
diligent maketh
rich.

> **10:4 Diligence**
> ◄ Proverbs 13:4 ►

5 He that gath-
ereth in summer *is*
a wise son: *but* he
that sleepeth in har-
vest *is* a son that
causeth shame.

> **10:5 Sleep**
> ◄ Proverbs 6:9-10
> Proverbs 19:15 ►

6 Blessings *are* upon the head of the just:
but violence covereth the mouth of the
wicked.
7 The memory of the just *is* blessed: but
the name of the wicked shall rot.
8 The wise in heart will receive commandments: but a prating fool shall fall.
9 He that walketh
uprightly walketh
surely: but he that
perverteth his ways
shall be known.
10 He that wink-
eth with the eye causeth sorrow: but a prating fool shall fall.

> **10:9 Why Do Right?**
> ◄ Proverbs 2:21
> Proverbs 14:11 ►

11 The mouth of a righteous *man is* a well
of life: but violence covereth the mouth
of the wicked.
12 Hatred stirreth
up strifes: but love
covereth all sins.
13 In the lips of
him that hath un-
derstanding wis-
dom is found: but a rod *is* for the back of
him that is void of understanding.

> **10:12 Hate**
> ◄ Leviticus 19:17
> Proverbs 15:17 ►

14 Wise *men* lay up knowledge: but the
mouth of the foolish *is* near destruction.
15 The rich man's wealth *is* his strong city:
the destruction of the poor *is* their poverty.
16 The labour of the righteous *tendeth* to
life: the fruit of the wicked to sin.
17 He *is in* the way of life that keepeth
instruction: but he that refuseth reproof
erreth.
18 He that hideth hatred *with* lying lips,
and he that uttereth a slander, *is* a fool.
19 In the multitude of words there

Turn to the next page for more . . .

wanteth not sin: but he that refraineth his lips *is* wise.

> **10:19 Idle Talk**
> ◄ Job 15:3
> Proverbs 14:23 ►

20 The tongue of the just *is as* choice silver: the heart of the wicked *is* little worth.

21 The lips of the righteous feed many: but fools die for want of wisdom.

22 The blessing of the LORD, it maketh rich, and he addeth no sorrow with it.

> **10:22 Invisible Wealth**
> ◄ Proverbs 8:18
> Proverbs 13:7 ►

23 *It is* as sport to a fool to do mischief: but a man of understanding hath wisdom.

24 The fear of the wicked, it shall come upon him: but the desire of the righteous shall be granted.

25 As the whirlwind passeth, so *is* the wicked no *more:* but the righteous *is* an everlasting foundation.

26 As vinegar to the teeth, and as smoke to the eyes, so *is* the sluggard to them that send him.

27 The fear of the LORD prolongeth days: but the years of the wicked shall be shortened.

28 The hope of the righteous *shall be* gladness: but the expectation of the wicked shall perish.

29 The way of the LORD *is* strength to the upright: but destruction *shall be* to the workers of iniquity.

30 The righteous shall never be removed: but the wicked shall not inhabit the earth.

31 The mouth of the just bringeth forth wisdom: but the froward tongue shall be cut out.

32 The lips of the righteous know what is acceptable: but the mouth of the wicked *speaketh* frowardness.

11

1 A false balance *is* abomination to the LORD: but a just weight *is* his delight.

> **11:2 Arrogance**
> ◄ Proverbs 6:17
> Proverbs 13:10 ►

2 *When* pride cometh, then cometh shame: but with the lowly *is* wisdom.

> **11:3 Used to Sin**
> ◄ Proverbs 12:8 ►

3 The integrity of the upright shall guide them: but the perverseness of transgressors shall destroy them.

4 Riches profit not in the day of wrath: but righteousness delivereth from death.

> **11:4 Money's Limits**
> ◄ Ecclesiastes 6:2 ►

5 The righteousness of the perfect shall direct his way: but the wicked shall fall by his own wickedness.

6 The righteousness of the upright shall deliver them: but transgressors shall be taken in *their own* naughtiness.

7 When a wicked man dieth, *his* expectation shall perish: and the hope of unjust *men* perisheth.

> **11:7 Disappointment**
> ◄ Job 27:17
> Isaiah 17:11 ►

8 The righteous is delivered out of trouble, and the wicked cometh in his stead.

9 An hypocrite with *his* mouth destroyeth his neighbour: but through knowledge shall the just be delivered.

10 When it goeth well with the righteous, the city rejoiceth: and when the wicked perish, *there is* shouting.

> **11:11 Better Neighborhoods**
> ◄ Proverbs 14:34 ►

11 By the blessing of the upright the city is exalted: but it is overthrown by the mouth of the wicked.

> **11:12 Understanding**
> ◄ Proverbs 8:14
> Proverbs 13:15 ►

12 He that is void of wisdom despiseth his neighbour: but a man of understanding holdeth his peace.

> **11:13 Gossiping**
> ◄ Leviticus 19:16
> Proverbs 17:9 ►

13 A talebearer revealeth secrets: but he that is of a faithful spirit concealeth the matter.

> **11:14 Advice**
> ◄ Proverbs 12:15 ►

14 Where no counsel *is*, the people fall: but in the multitude of counsellors *there is* safety.

> **11:14 Getting Opinions**
> ◄ Proverbs 15:22 ►

15 He that is

surety for a stranger shall smart *for it:* and he that hateth suretiship is sure.

16A gracious woman retaineth honour: and strong *men* retain riches.

17The merciful man doeth good to his own soul: but *he that is* cruel troubleth his own flesh.

11:17 Crime
◄ Psalm 27:12 ►

18The wicked worketh a deceitful work: but to him that soweth righteousness *shall be* a sure reward.

11:17 Rewards
◄ Psalm 112:9
Proverbs 14:31 ►

19As righteousness *tendeth* to life: so he that pursueth evil *pursueth it* to his own death.

11:17 Showing Mercy
◄ Proverbs 3:3
Hosea 12:6 ►

20They that are of a froward heart *are* abomination to the LORD: but *such as are* upright in *their* way *are* his delight.

11:19 Why Not Sin?
◄ 1 Chronicles 10:13
Ezekiel 18:4 ►

21*Though* hand *join* in hand, the wicked shall not be unpunished: but the seed of the righteous shall be delivered.

22*As* a jewel of gold in a swine's snout, *so is* a fair woman which is without discretion.

23The desire of the righteous *is* only good: *but* the expectation of the wicked *is* wrath.

24There is that scattereth, and yet increaseth; and *there is* that withholdeth more than is meet, but *it tendeth* to poverty.

11:24 Being Stingy
◄ Proverbs 21:13 ►

25The liberal soul shall be made fat: and he that watereth shall be watered also himself.

11:25 Promises to Givers
◄ Proverbs 3:9-10
Proverbs 22:9 ►

26He that withholdeth corn, the people shall curse him: but blessing *shall be* upon the head of him that selleth *it*.

27He that diligently seeketh good procureth favour: but he that seeketh mischief, it shall come unto him.

28He that trusteth in his riches shall fall: but the righteous shall flourish as a branch.

11:28 Wealth
◄ Psalm 52:7
Proverbs 18:11 ►

29He that troubleth his own house shall inherit the wind: and the fool *shall be* servant to the wise of heart.

30The fruit of the righteous *is* a tree of life; and he that winneth souls *is* wise.

31Behold, the righteous shall be recompensed in the earth: much more the wicked and the sinner.

12

1Whoso loveth instruction loveth knowledge: but he that hateth reproof *is* brutish.

12:1 Parents
◄ Proverbs 6:23
Ecclesiastes 12:11 ►

2A good *man* obtaineth favour of the LORD: but a man of wicked devices will he condemn.

3A man shall not be established by wickedness: but the root of the righteous shall not be moved.

4A virtuous woman *is* a crown to her husband: but she that maketh ashamed *is* as rottenness in his bones.

5The thoughts of the righteous *are* right: *but* the counsels of the wicked *are* deceit.

12:5 Dishonest People
◄ Psalm 36:3
Proverbs 27:6 ►

6The words of the wicked *are* to lie in wait for blood: but the mouth of the upright shall deliver them.

12:5 Wise Thoughts
◄ Psalm 119:59
Proverbs 21:5 ►

7The wicked are overthrown, and *are* not: but the house of the righteous shall stand.

12:8 Used to Sin
◄ Proverbs 11:3
Proverbs 15:4 ►

8A man shall be commended according to his wisdom: but he that is of a perverse heart shall be despised.

9*He that is* despised, and hath a servant, *is* better than he that honoureth himself, and lacketh bread.

10A righteous *man* regardeth the life of his beast: but the tender mercies of the wicked *are* cruel.

Turn to the next page for more . . .

11He that tilleth his land shall be satisfied with bread: but he that followeth vain *persons is* void of understanding.

12:10 Cruelty to Animals
◄ 1 Chronicles 18:4 ►

12The wicked desireth the net of evil *men:* but the root of the righteous yieldeth *fruit.*

12:13 Rewarded Goodness
◄ Proverbs 4:18
Proverbs 20:7 ►

13The wicked is snared by the transgression of *his* lips: but the just shall come out of trouble.

14A man shall be satisfied with good by the fruit of *his* mouth: and the recompense of a man's hands shall be rendered unto him.

15The way of a fool *is* right in his own eyes: but he that hearkeneth unto counsel *is* wise.

12:15 Advice
◄ Proverbs 11:14
Proverbs 13:10 ►

16A fool's wrath is presently known: but a prudent *man* covereth shame.

12:15 Self-righteousness
◄ Job 35:2
Proverbs 16:2 ►

17*He that* speaketh truth sheweth forth righteousness: but a false witness deceit.

12:17 Hurtful Lying
◄ Proverbs 6:19
Proverbs 19:9 ►

18There is that speaketh like the piercings of a sword: but the tongue of the wise *is* health.

19The lip of truth shall be established for ever: but a lying tongue *is* but for a moment.

12:19 Honesty
◄ Zephaniah 3:13 ►

20Deceit *is* in the heart of them that imagine evil: but to the counsellors of peace *is* joy.

12:20 Peacemaking
◄ Matthew 5:9 ►

21There shall no evil happen to the just: but the wicked shall be filled with mischief.

22Lying lips *are* abomination to the LORD: but they that deal truly *are* his delight.

23A prudent man concealeth knowledge: but the heart of fools proclaimeth foolishness.

12:22 Lying
◄ Psalm 120:2
Proverbs 19:9 ►

24The hand of the diligent shall bear rule: but the slothful shall be under tribute.

25Heaviness in the heart of man maketh it stoop: but a good word maketh it glad.

26The righteous *is* more excellent than his neighbour: but the way of the wicked seduceth them.

27The slothful *man* roasteth not that which he took in hunting: but the substance of a diligent man *is* precious.

12:27 Waste
◄ Proverbs 18:9 ►

28In the way of righteousness *is* life; and *in* the pathway *thereof there is* no death.

13

1A wise son *heareth* his father's instruction: but a scorner heareth not rebuke.

2A man shall eat good by the fruit of *his* mouth: but the soul of the transgressors *shall eat* violence.

3He that keepeth his mouth keepeth his life: *but* he that openeth wide his lips shall have destruction.

4The soul of the sluggard desireth, and *hath* nothing: but the soul of the diligent shall be made fat.

13:4 Diligence
◄ Proverbs 10:4
Proverbs 22:29 ►

5A righteous *man* hateth lying: but a wicked *man* is loathsome, and cometh to shame.

13:4 Lazy People
◄ Proverbs 6:6
Proverbs 15:19 ►

6Righteousness keepeth *him that is* upright in the way: but wickedness overthroweth the sinner.

13:7 Invisible Wealth
◄ Proverbs 10:22
Ephesians 1:18 ►

7There is that maketh himself rich, yet *hath* nothing: *there is* that maketh himself poor, yet *hath* great riches.

8The ransom of a man's life *are* his riches: but the poor heareth not rebuke.

9The light of the righteous rejoiceth: but the lamp of the wicked shall be put out.

10 Only by pride cometh contention: but with the well advised *is* wisdom.

11 Wealth *gotten* by vanity shall be diminished: but he that gathereth by labour shall increase.

12 Hope deferred maketh the heart sick: but *when* the desire cometh, *it is* a tree of life.

13 Whoso despiseth the word shall be destroyed: but he that feareth the commandment shall be rewarded.

13:10 Advice
◀ Proverbs 12:15
Proverbs 15:22 ▶

13:10 Arrogance
◀ Proverbs 11:2
Proverbs 16:18 ▶

13:11 Working Hard
◀ Leviticus 23:3
Proverbs 14:23 ▶

14 The law of the wise *is* a fountain of life, to depart from the snares of death.

15 Good understanding giveth favour: but the way of transgressors *is* hard.

16 Every prudent *man* dealeth with knowledge: but a fool layeth open *his* folly.

13:15 Understanding
◀ Proverbs 11:12
Proverbs 14:29 ▶

17 A wicked messenger falleth into mischief: but a faithful ambassador *is* health.

18 Poverty and shame *shall be to* him that refuseth instruction: but he that regardeth reproof shall be honoured.

19 The desire accomplished is sweet to the soul: but *it is* abomination to fools to depart from evil.

20 He that walketh with wise *men* shall be wise: but a companion of fools shall be destroyed.

21 Evil pursueth sinners: but to the righteous good shall be repaid.

22 A good *man* leaveth an inheritance to his children's children: and the wealth of the sinner *is* laid up for the just.

23 Much food *is in* the tillage of the poor: but there is *that is* destroyed for want of judgment.

24 He that spareth his rod hateth his son: but he that loveth him chasteneth him betimes.

13:24 Discipline
◀ Proverbs 19:18 ▶

25 The righteous eateth to the satisfying of his soul: but the belly of the wicked shall want.

14

1 Every wise woman buildeth her house: but the foolish plucketh it down with her hands.

2 He that walketh in his uprightness feareth the LORD: but *he that is* perverse in his ways despiseth him.

3 In the mouth of the foolish *is* a rod of pride: but the lips of the wise shall preserve them.

4 Where no oxen *are*, the crib *is* clean: but much increase *is* by the strength of the ox.

5 A faithful witness will not lie: but a false witness will utter lies.

6 A scorner seeketh wisdom, and *findeth it* not: but knowledge *is* easy unto him that understandeth.

7 Go from the presence of a foolish man, when thou perceivest not *in him* the lips of knowledge.

8 The wisdom of the prudent *is* to understand his way: but the folly of fools *is* deceit.

9 Fools make a mock at sin: but among the righteous *there is* favour.

10 The heart knoweth his own bitterness; and a stranger doth not intermeddle with his joy.

11 The house of the wicked shall be overthrown: but the tabernacle of the upright shall flourish.

12 There is a way which seemeth right unto a man, but the end thereof *are* the ways of death.

13 Even in laughter the heart is sorrowful; and the end of that mirth *is* heaviness.

14 The backslider in heart shall be filled with his own ways: and a good man *shall be satisfied* from himself.

15 The simple

14:11 Why Do Right?
◀ Proverbs 10:9
Proverbs 28:6 ▶

14:13 Happiness
◀ Job 20:5
Ecclesiastes 2:10 ▶

14:13 Laughter
◀ Ecclesiastes 2:2 ▶

14:15 Naiveté
◀ Proverbs 8:5
Proverbs 22:3 ▶

believeth every word: but the prudent *man* looketh well to his going.

16A wise *man* feareth, and departeth from evil: but the fool rageth, and is confident.

14:16 Stay Away!
◄ Proverbs 4:27
Zechariah 7:10 ►

17*He that is* soon angry dealeth foolishly: and a man of wicked devices is hated.

18The simple inherit folly: but the prudent are crowned with knowledge.

19The evil bow before the good; and the wicked at the gates of the righteous.

20The poor is hated even of his own neighbour: but the rich *hath* many friends.

21He that despiseth his neighbour sinneth: but he that hath mercy on the poor, happy *is* he.

14:21 Kind to the Poor
◄ Psalm 41:1
Proverbs 19:17 ►

22Do they not err that devise evil? but mercy and truth *shall be* to them that devise good.

14:21 Source of Happiness
◄ Proverbs 3:18
Proverbs 16:20 ►

23In all labour there is profit: but the talk of the lips *tendeth* only to penury.

14:23 Idle Talk
◄ Proverbs 10:19
Proverbs 29:11 ►

24The crown of the wise is their riches: *but* the foolishness of fools *is* folly.

14:23 Working Hard
◄ Proverbs 13:11
Ecclesiastes 9:10 ►

25A true witness delivereth souls: but a deceitful *witness* speaketh lies.

26In the fear of the LORD *is* strong confidence: and his children shall have a place of refuge.

27The fear of the LORD *is* a fountain of life, to depart from the snares of death.

28In the multitude of people *is* the king's honour: but in the want of people *is* the destruction of the prince.

29*He that is* slow to wrath *is* of great understanding: but *he that is* hasty of spirit exalteth folly.

14:29 Understanding
◄ Proverbs 13:15
Proverbs 17:27 ►

30A sound heart *is* the life of the flesh: but envy the rottenness of the bones.

14:30 Envy
◄ Proverbs 3:31
Proverbs 23:17 ►

31He that oppresseth the poor reproacheth his Maker: but he that honoureth him hath mercy on the poor.

14:31 Rewards
◄ Proverbs 11:17
Isaiah 58:10 ►

32The wicked is driven away in his wickedness: but the righteous hath hope in his death.

33Wisdom resteth in the heart of him that hath understanding: but *that which is* in the midst of fools is made known.

34Righteousness exalteth a nation: but sin *is* a reproach to any people.

14:34 Better Neighborhoods
◄ Proverbs 11:11
Proverbs 16:12 ►

35The king's favour *is* toward a wise servant: but his wrath is *against* him that causeth shame.

15

1A soft answer turneth away wrath: but grievous words stir up anger.

2The tongue of the wise useth knowledge aright: but the mouth of fools poureth out foolishness.

3The eyes of the LORD *are* in every place, beholding the evil and the good.

15:3 Where Is God?
◄ Psalm 139:8
Isaiah 66:1 ►

4A wholesome tongue *is* a tree of life: but perverseness therein *is* a breach in the spirit.

15:4 Used to Sin
◄ Proverbs 12:8
Proverbs 28:6 ►

5A fool despiseth his father's instruction: but he that regardeth reproof is prudent.

15:5 Taking Advice
◄ Psalm 141:5
Proverbs 17:10 ►

6In the house of the righteous *is* much treasure: but in the revenues of the wicked is trouble.

7The lips of the wise disperse knowledge: but the heart of the foolish *doeth* not so.

8The sacrifice of the wicked *is* an abomination to the LORD: but the prayer of the upright *is* his delight.

9 The way of the wicked *is* an abomination unto the LORD: but he loveth him that followeth after righteousness.

10 Correction *is* grievous unto him that forsaketh the way: *and* he that hateth reproof shall die.

11 Hell and destruction *are* before the LORD: how much more then the hearts of the children of men?

12 A scorner loveth not one that reproveth him: neither will he go unto the wise.

13 A merry heart maketh a cheerful countenance: but by sorrow of the heart the spirit is broken.

14 The heart of him that hath understanding seeketh knowledge: but the mouth of fools feedeth on foolishness.

15 All the days of the afflicted *are* evil: but he that is of a merry heart *hath* a continual feast.

16 Better *is* little with the fear of the LORD than great treasure and trouble therewith.

15:16 Contentment
◄ Luke 3:14 ►

17 Better *is* a dinner of herbs where love is, than a stalled ox and hatred therewith.

15:17 Hate
◄ Proverbs 10:12
1 John 2:9 ►

18 A wrathful man stirreth up strife: but *he that is* slow to anger appeaseth strife.

19 The way of the slothful *man is* as an hedge of thorns: but the way of the righteous *is* made plain.

15:19 Lazy People
◄ Proverbs 13:4
Proverbs 19:24 ►

20 A wise son maketh a glad father: but a foolish man despiseth his mother.

21 Folly *is* joy to *him that is* destitute of wisdom: but a man of understanding walketh uprightly.

15:22 Advice
◄ Proverbs 13:10
Proverbs 20:18 ►

22 Without counsel purposes are disappointed: but in the multitude of counsellors they are established.

15:22 Getting Opinions
◄ Proverbs 11:14
Proverbs 24:6 ►

23 A man hath joy by the answer of his mouth: and a word *spoken* in due season, how good *is it!*

15:23 Wise Words
◄ Job 6:25
Proverbs 16:24 ►

24 The way of life *is* above to the wise, that he may depart from hell beneath.

25 The LORD will destroy the house of the proud: but he will establish the border of the widow.

15:25 God's Care for Kids
◄ Psalm 146:9
Jeremiah 49:11 ►

26 The thoughts of the wicked *are* an abomination to the LORD: but *the words* of the pure *are* pleasant words.

15:26 Bad Thoughts
◄ Psalm 94:11
Proverbs 23:7 ►

27 He that is greedy of gain troubleth his own house; but he that hateth gifts shall live.

28 The heart of the righteous studieth to answer: but the mouth of the wicked poureth out evil things.

29 The LORD *is* far from the wicked: but he heareth the prayer of the righteous.

30 The light of the eyes rejoiceth the heart: *and* a good report maketh the bones fat.

31 The ear that heareth the reproof of life abideth among the wise.

32 He that refuseth instruction despiseth his own soul: but he that heareth reproof getteth understanding.

33 The fear of the LORD *is* the instruction of wisdom; and before honour *is* humility.

16

1 The preparations of the heart in man, and the answer of the tongue, *is* from the LORD.

2 All the ways of a man *are* clean in his own eyes; but the LORD weigheth the spirits.

16:2 Self-righteousness
◄ Proverbs 12:15
Proverbs 20:6 ►

3 Commit thy works unto the LORD, and thy thoughts shall be established.

4 The LORD hath made all *things* for himself: yea, even the wicked for the day of evil.

5 Every one *that is* proud in heart *is* an abomination to the LORD: *though* hand *join* in hand, he shall not be unpunished.

6 By mercy and truth iniquity is purged: and by the fear of the LORD *men* depart from evil.

7 When a man's ways please the LORD, he maketh even his enemies to be at peace with him.

16:7
Pleasing God
◄ Matthew 3:17 ►

8 Better *is* a little with righteousness than great revenues without right.

16:8
Getting Ahead
◄ Proverbs 21:6 ►

9 A man's heart deviseth his way: but the LORD directeth his steps.

10 A divine sentence *is* in the lips of the king: his mouth transgresseth not in judgment.

11 A just weight and balance *are* the LORD'S: all the weights of the bag *are* his work.

16:11 God's Justice
◄ Psalm 103:6
Isaiah 45:21 ►

12 *It is* an abomination to kings to commit wickedness: for the throne is established by righteousness.

16:12
Better Neighborhoods
◄ Proverbs 14:34
Proverbs 25:5 ►

13 Righteous lips *are* the delight of kings; and they love him that speaketh right.

16:12 Leaders Should...
◄ Psalm 2:10-11
Proverbs 20:28 ►

14 The wrath of a king *is as* messengers of death: but a wise man will pacify it.

15 In the light of the king's countenance *is* life; and his favour *is* as a cloud of the latter rain.

16 How much better *is it* to get wisdom than gold! and to get understanding rather to be chosen than silver!

17 The highway of the upright *is* to depart from evil: he that keepeth his way preserveth his soul.

18 Pride *goeth* before destruction, and an haughty spirit before a fall.

16:18 Arrogance
◄ Proverbs 13:10
Proverbs 21:4 ►

19 Better *it is to be* of an humble spirit with the lowly, than to divide the spoil with the proud.

20 He that handleth a matter wisely shall find good: and whoso trusteth in the LORD, happy *is* he.

16:20
Source of Happiness
◄ Proverbs 14:21
Proverbs 28:14 ►

21 The wise in heart shall be called prudent: and the sweetness of the lips increaseth learning.

22 Understanding *is* a wellspring of life unto him that hath it: but the instruction of fools *is* folly.

23 The heart of the wise teacheth his mouth, and addeth learning to his lips.

24 Pleasant words *are as* an honeycomb, sweet to the soul, and health to the bones.

16:24 Wise Words
◄ Proverbs 15:23
Proverbs 25:11 ►

25 There is a way that seemeth right unto a man, but the end thereof *are* the ways of death.

26 He that laboureth laboureth for himself; for his mouth craveth it of him.

27 An ungodly man diggeth up evil: and in his lips *there is* as a burning fire.

28 A froward man soweth strife: and a whisperer separateth chief friends.

29 A violent man enticeth his neighbour, and leadeth him into the way *that is* not good.

30 He shutteth his eyes to devise froward things: moving his lips he bringeth evil to pass.

31 The hoary head *is* a crown of glory, *if* it be found in the way of righteousness.

32 *He that is* slow to anger *is* better than the mighty; and he that ruleth his spirit than he that taketh a city.

16:32
Self-control
◄ Proverbs 25:28 ►

33 The lot is cast into the lap; but the whole disposing thereof *is* of the LORD.

17

1 Better *is* a dry morsel, and quietness therewith, than an house full of sacrifices *with* strife.

2 A wise servant shall have rule over a son that causeth shame, and shall have part of the inheritance among the brethren.

3 The fining pot *is* for silver, and the furnace for gold: but the LORD trieth the hearts.

4 A wicked doer giveth heed to false lips; *and* a liar giveth ear to a naughty tongue.

5Whoso mocketh the poor reproacheth his Maker: *and* he that is glad at calamities shall not be unpunished.

17:5 Mockers
◄ Proverbs 30:17 ►

6Children's children *are* the crown of old men; and the glory of children *are* their fathers.

7Excellent speech becometh not a fool: much less do lying lips a prince.

8A gift *is as* a precious stone in the eyes of him that hath it: whithersoever it turneth, it prospereth.

9He that covereth a transgression seeketh love; but he that repeateth a matter separateth *very* friends.

17:9 Gossiping
◄ Proverbs 11:13
Proverbs 18:8 ►

10A reproof entereth more into a wise man than an hundred stripes into a fool.

17:10 Taking Advice
◄ Proverbs 15:5
Proverbs 25:12 ►

11An evil *man* seeketh only rebellion: therefore a cruel messenger shall be sent against him.

12Let a bear robbed of her whelps meet a man, rather than a fool in his folly.

13Whoso rewardeth evil for good, evil shall not depart from his house.

14The beginning of strife *is as* when one letteth out water: therefore leave off contention, before it be meddled with.

17:14 Arguing
◄ Proverbs 3:30
Proverbs 20:3 ►

15He that justifieth the wicked, and he that condemneth the just, even they both *are* abomination to the LORD.

17:15 Excusing Sin
◄ Proverbs 24:24 ►

16Wherefore *is there* a price in the hand of a fool to get wisdom, seeing *he hath* no heart *to it?*

17A friend loveth at all times, and a brother is born for adversity.

17:17 Friendship
◄ Proverbs 18:24 ►

18A man void of understanding striketh hands, *and* becometh surety in the presence of his friend.

19He loveth transgression that loveth strife: *and* he that exalteth his gate seeketh destruction.

20He that hath a froward heart findeth no good: and he that hath a perverse tongue falleth into mischief.

21He that begetteth a fool *doeth it* to his sorrow: and the father of a fool hath no joy.

22A merry heart doeth good *like* a medicine: but a broken spirit drieth the bones.

23A wicked *man* taketh a gift out of the bosom to pervert the ways of judgment.

17:23 Bribery
◄ Psalm 26:10
Isaiah 1:23 ►

24Wisdom *is* before him that hath understanding; but the eyes of a fool *are* in the ends of the earth.

25A foolish son *is* a grief to his father, and bitterness to her that bare him.

26Also to punish the just *is* not good, *nor* to strike princes for equity.

27He that hath knowledge spareth his words: *and* a man of understanding is of an excellent spirit.

17:27 Talking
◄ Matthew 5:37 ►

28Even a fool, when he holdeth his peace, is counted wise: *and* he that shutteth his lips *is esteemed* a man of understanding.

17:27 Understanding
◄ Proverbs 14:29
2 Timothy 2:7 ►

18

1Through desire a man, having separated himself, seeketh *and* intermeddleth with all wisdom.

2A fool hath no delight in understanding, but that his heart may discover itself.

3When the wicked cometh, *then* cometh also contempt, and with ignominy reproach.

4The words of a man's mouth *are as* deep waters, *and* the wellspring of wisdom *as* a flowing brook.

5*It is* not good to accept the person of the wicked, to overthrow the righteous in judgment.

6A fool's lips enter into contention, and his mouth calleth for strokes.

7 A fool's mouth *is* his destruction, and his lips *are* the snare of his soul.

8 The words of a talebearer *are* as wounds, and they go down into the innermost parts of the belly.

> **18:8 Gossiping**
> ◄ Proverbs 17:9
> Proverbs 20:19 ►

9 He also that is slothful in his work is brother to him that is a great waster.

> **18:9 Laziness**
> ◄ Proverbs 24:30-31 ►

10 The name of the LORD *is* a strong tower: the righteous runneth into it, and is safe.

> **18:9 Waste**
> ◄ Proverbs 12:27
> Proverbs 29:3 ►

11 The rich man's wealth *is* his strong city, and as an high wall in his own conceit.

> **18:11 Wealth**
> ◄ Proverbs 11:28
> Mark 10:24 ►

12 Before destruction the heart of man is haughty, and before honour *is* humility.

13 He that answereth a matter before he heareth *it,* it *is* folly and shame unto him.

14 The spirit of a man will sustain his infirmity; but a wounded spirit who can bear?

15 The heart of the prudent getteth knowledge; and the ear of the wise seeketh knowledge.

16 A man's gift maketh room for him, and bringeth him before great men.

17 *He that is* first in his own cause *seemeth* just; but his neighbour cometh and searcheth him.

18 The lot causeth contentions to cease, and parteth between the mighty.

19 A brother offended *is harder to be won* than a strong city: and *their* contentions *are* like the bars of a castle.

> **18:19 Fighting**
> ◄ Genesis 21:10
> Proverbs 19:13 ►

20 A man's belly shall be satisfied with the fruit of his mouth; *and* with the increase of his lips shall he be filled.

21 Death and life *are* in the power of the tongue: and they that love it shall eat the fruit thereof.

22 *Whoso* findeth a wife findeth a good *thing,* and obtaineth favour of the LORD.

23 The poor useth intreaties; but the rich answereth roughly.

24 A man *that hath* friends must shew himself friendly: and there is a friend *that* sticketh closer than a brother.

> **18:24 Friendship**
> ◄ Proverbs 17:17
> Proverbs 27:10 ►

19

1 Better *is* the poor that walketh in his integrity, than *he that is* perverse in his lips, and is a fool.

2 Also, *that* the soul *be* without knowledge, *it is* not good; and he that hasteth with *his* feet sinneth.

> **19:2 Being Hasty**
> ◄ Proverbs 21:5 ►

3 The foolishness of man perverteth his way: and his heart fretteth against the LORD.

4 Wealth maketh many friends; but the poor is separated from his neighbour.

5 A false witness shall not be unpunished, and *he that* speaketh lies shall not escape.

> **19:5 Liars**
> ◄ Psalm 63:11
> Proverbs 19:9 ►

6 Many will intreat the favour of the prince: and every man *is* a friend to him that giveth gifts.

7 All the brethren of the poor do hate him: how much more do his friends go far from him? he pursueth *them with* words, *yet* they *are* wanting *to him.*

8 He that getteth wisdom loveth his own soul: he that keepeth understanding shall find good.

> **19:9 Hurtful Lying**
> ◄ Proverbs 12:17
> Proverbs 24:28 ►

9 A false witness shall not be unpunished, and *he that* speaketh lies shall perish.

> **19:9 Liars**
> ◄ Proverbs 19:5
> Isaiah 44:25 ►

10 Delight is not seemly for a fool; much less for a servant to have rule over princes.

> **19:9 Lying**
> ◄ Proverbs 12:22
> Proverbs 21:6 ►

11 The discretion of a man deferreth

his anger; and *it is* his glory to pass over a transgression.

12 The king's wrath *is* as the roaring of a lion; but his favour *is* as dew upon the grass.

13 A foolish son *is* the calamity of his father: and the contentions of a wife *are* a continual dropping.

19:13 Fighting
◄ Proverbs 18:19
Proverbs 21:9 ►

14 House and riches *are* the inheritance of fathers and a prudent wife *is* from the LORD.

19:15 Sleep
◄ Proverbs 10:5
Proverbs 20:13 ►

15 Slothfulness casteth into a deep sleep; and an idle soul shall suffer hunger.

16 He that keepeth the commandment keepeth his own soul; *but* he that despiseth his ways shall die.

17 He that hath pity upon the poor lendeth unto the LORD; and that which he hath given will he pay him again.

19:17 Kind to the Poor
◄ Proverbs 14:21
Proverbs 28:27 ►

18 Chasten thy son while there is hope, and let not thy soul spare for his crying.

19:18 Discipline
◄ Proverbs 13:24
Proverbs 22:15 ►

19 A man of great wrath shall suffer punishment: for if thou deliver *him,* yet thou must do it again.

20 Hear counsel, and receive instruction, that thou mayest be wise in thy latter end.

21 *There are* many devices in a man's heart; nevertheless the counsel of the LORD, that shall stand.

19:21 Planning
◄ Genesis 11:4
Jeremiah 22:13-14 ►

22 The desire of a man *is* his kindness: and a poor man *is* better than a liar.

23 The fear of the LORD *tendeth* to life: and *he that hath it* shall abide satisfied; he shall not be visited with evil.

24 A slothful *man* hideth his hand in *his* bosom, and will not so much as bring it to his mouth again.

19:24 Lazy People
◄ Proverbs 15:19
Proverbs 20:4 ►

25 Smite a scorner, and the simple will beware: and reprove one that hath understanding, *and* he will understand knowledge.

26 He that wasteth *his* father, *and* chaseth away *his* mother, *is* a son that causeth shame, and bringeth reproach.

27 Cease, my son, to hear the instruction *that causeth* to err from the words of knowledge.

28 An ungodly witness scorneth judgment: and the mouth of the wicked devoureth iniquity.

29 Judgments are prepared for scorners, and stripes for the back of fools.

20

1 Wine *is* a mocker, strong drink *is* raging: and whosoever is deceived thereby is not wise.

20:1 Drinking Too Much
◄ Proverbs 21:17 ►

2 The fear of a king *is* as the roaring of a lion: *whoso* provoketh him to anger sinneth *against* his own soul.

20:1 Getting Drunk
◄ Deuteronomy 21:20
Proverbs 23:20 ►

3 *It is* an honour for a man to cease from strife: but every fool will be meddling.

20:3 Arguing
◄ Proverbs 17:14
Proverbs 25:8 ►

4 The sluggard will not plow by reason of the cold; *therefore* shall he beg in harvest, and *have* nothing.

20:4 Lazy People
◄ Proverbs 19:24
Proverbs 21:25 ►

5 Counsel in the heart of man *is like* deep water; but a man of understanding will draw it out.

6 Most men will proclaim every one his own goodness: but a faithful man who can find?

20:6 Self-righteousness
◄ Proverbs 16:2
Proverbs 21:2 ►

7 The just *man* walketh in his integrity: his children *are* blessed after him.

20:7 Rewarded Goodness
◄ Proverbs 12:13
Isaiah 3:10 ►

8 A king that sitteth in the throne of judgment scattereth away all evil with his eyes.

9 Who can say, I have made my heart clean, I am pure from my sin?

20:9 Everyone Sins
◄ Psalm 130:3
Ecclesiastes 7:20 ►

10 Divers weights, *and* divers measures, both of them *are* alike abomination to the LORD.

11 Even a child is known by his doings, whether his work *be* pure, and whether *it be* right.

12 The hearing ear, and the seeing eye, the LORD hath made even both of them.

13 Love not sleep, lest thou come to poverty; open thine eyes, *and* thou shalt be satisfied with bread.

20:13 Sleep
◄ Proverbs 19:15
Proverbs 23:21 ►

14 *It is* naught, *it is* naught, saith the buyer: but when he is gone his way, then he boasteth.

15 There is gold, and a multitude of rubies: but the lips of knowledge *are* a precious jewel.

16 Take his garment that is surety *for* a stranger: and take a pledge of him for a strange woman.

17 Bread of deceit *is* sweet to a man; but afterwards his mouth shall be filled with gravel.

18 *Every* purpose is established by counsel: and with good advice make war.

20:18 Advice
◄ Proverbs 15:22 ►

19 He that goeth about *as* a talebearer revealeth secrets: therefore meddle not with him that flattereth with his lips.

20:19 Gossiping
◄ Proverbs 18:8
Proverbs 26:20 ►

20 Whoso curseth his father or his mother, his lamp shall be put out in obscure darkness.

21 An inheritance *may be* gotten hastily at the beginning; but the end thereof shall not be blessed.

22 Say not thou, I will recompense evil; *but* wait on the LORD, and he shall save thee.

20:22 Revenge
◄ Leviticus 19:18
Proverbs 24:29 ►

20:22 Waiting for God
◄ Psalm 123:2
Isaiah 8:17 ►

23 Divers weights *are* an abomination unto the LORD; and a false balance *is* not good.

24 Man's goings *are* of the LORD; how can a man then understand his own way?

25 *It is* a snare to the man *who* devoureth *that which is* holy, and after vows to make enquiry.

26 A wise king scattereth the wicked, and bringeth the wheel over them.

27 The spirit of man *is* the candle of the LORD, searching all the inward parts of the belly.

28 Mercy and truth preserve the king: and his throne is upholden by mercy.

20:28 Leaders Should...
◄ Proverbs 16:12
Proverbs 29:4 ►

29 The glory of young men *is* their strength: and the beauty of old men *is* the grey head.

20:29 For Kids Only
◄ Psalm 119:9
Ecclesiastes 11:9 ►

30 The blueness of a wound cleanseth away evil: so *do* stripes the inward parts of the belly.

21

1 The king's heart *is* in the hand of the LORD, *as* the rivers of water: he turneth it whithersoever he will.

21:2 Self-righteousness
◄ Proverbs 20:6
Proverbs 30:12 ►

2 Every way of a man *is* right in his own eyes: but the LORD pondereth the hearts.

21:3 Be Fair
◄ Psalm 82:3
Isaiah 56:1 ►

3 To do justice and judgment *is* more acceptable to the LORD than sacrifice.

21:4 Arrogance
◄ Proverbs 16:18
Hosea 7:10 ►

4 An high look, and a proud heart, *and* the plowing of the wicked, *is* sin.

5 The thoughts of the diligent *tend* only to plenteousness; but of every

21:5 Being Hasty
◄ Proverbs 19:2
Proverbs 29:20 ►

one *that is* hasty only to want.

6 The getting of treasures by a lying tongue *is* a vanity tossed to and fro of them that seek death.

7 The robbery of the wicked shall destroy them; because they refuse to do judgment.

8 The way of man *is* froward and strange: but *as for* the pure, his work *is* right.

9 *It is* better to dwell in a corner of the housetop, than with a brawling woman in a wide house.

10 The soul of the wicked desireth evil: his neighbour findeth no favour in his eyes.

11 When the scorner is punished, the simple is made wise: and when the wise is instructed, he receiveth knowledge.

12 The righteous *man* wisely considereth the house of the wicked: *but God* overthroweth the wicked for *their* wickedness.

13 Whoso stoppeth his ears at the cry of the poor, he also shall cry himself, but shall not be heard.

21:5 Wise Thoughts
◄ Proverbs 12:5
Romans 12:3 ►

21:6 Getting Ahead
◄ Proverbs 16:8
Proverbs 22:16 ►

21:6 Lying
◄ Proverbs 19:9
Colossians 3:9 ►

21:9 Fighting
◄ Proverbs 19:13
Proverbs 21:19 ►

21:13 Being Stingy
◄ Proverbs 11:24
Proverbs 28:27 ►

21:13 Fair to the Poor
◄ Psalm 82:3
Proverbs 29:14 ►

21:13 Mercy
◄ Psalm 109:16
Ezekiel 34:4 ►

21:13 Unanswered Prayer
◄ Proverbs 1:28
Proverbs 28:9 ►

14 A gift in secret pacifieth anger: and a reward in the bosom strong wrath.

15 *It is* joy to the just to do judgment: but destruction *shall be* to the workers of iniquity.

16 The man that wandereth out of the way of understanding shall remain in the congregation of the dead.

17 He that loveth pleasure *shall be* a poor man: he that loveth wine and oil shall not be rich.

18 The wicked *shall be* a ransom for the righteous, and the transgressor for the upright.

19 *It is* better to dwell in the wilderness, than with a contentious and an angry woman.

20 *There is* treasure to be desired and oil in the dwelling of the wise; but a foolish man spendeth it up.

21 He that followeth after righteousness and mercy findeth life, righteousness, and honour.

22 A wise *man* scaleth the city of the mighty, and casteth down the strength of the confidence thereof.

23 Whoso keepeth his mouth and his tongue keepeth his soul from troubles.

24 Proud *and* haughty scorner *is* his name, who dealeth in proud wrath.

25 The desire of the slothful killeth him; for his hands refuse to labour.

26 He coveteth greedily all the day long: but the righteous giveth and spareth not.

27 The sacrifice of the wicked *is* abomination: how much more, *when* he bringeth it with a wicked mind?

28 A false witness shall perish: but the man that heareth speaketh constantly.

29 A wicked man hardeneth his face: but *as for* the upright, he directeth his way.

30 *There is* no wisdom nor understanding nor counsel against the LORD.

31 The horse *is* prepared against the day of battle: but safety *is* of the LORD.

21:17 Drinking Too Much
◄ Proverbs 20:1
Proverbs 23:31 ►

21:17 Luxury
◄ Isaiah 22:13 ►

21:19 Fighting
◄ Proverbs 21:9
Proverbs 27:15 ►

21:20 Being Frugal
◄ Genesis 41:35-36
John 6:12 ►

21:25 Lazy People
◄ Proverbs 20:4
Proverbs 26:16 ►

22

1 A *good* name *is* rather to be chosen than great riches, *and* loving favour rather than silver and gold.

2 The rich and poor meet together: the LORD *is* the maker of them all.

22:2 Equality
◄ Matthew 23:8 ►

3 A prudent *man* foreseeth the evil, and hideth himself: but the simple pass on, and are punished.

22:2 Family
◄ Malachi 2:10 ►

4 By humility *and* the fear of the LORD *are* riches, and honour, and life.

22:3 Naiveté
◄ Proverbs 14:15
Hosea 7:11 ►

5 Thorns *and* snares *are* in the way of the froward: he that doth keep his soul shall be far from them.

6 Train up a child in the way he should go: and when he is old, he will not depart from it.

7 The rich ruleth over the poor, and the borrower *is* servant to the lender.

22:7 Borrowing
◄ Psalm 37:21
Matthew 5:42 ►

8 He that soweth iniquity shall reap vanity: and the rod of his anger shall fail.

22:9 Promises to Givers
◄ Proverbs 11:25
Proverbs 28:27 ►

9 He that hath a bountiful eye shall be blessed; for he giveth of his bread to the poor.

10 Cast out the scorner, and contention shall go out; yea, strife and reproach shall cease.

11 He that loveth pureness of heart, *for* the grace of his lips the king *shall be* his friend.

12 The eyes of the LORD preserve knowledge, and he overthroweth the words of the transgressor.

13 The slothful *man* saith, *There is* a lion without, I shall be slain in the streets.

14 The mouth of strange women *is* a deep pit: he that is abhorred of the LORD shall fall therein.

15 Foolishness *is* bound in the heart of a child; *but* the rod of correction shall drive it far from him.

22:15 Discipline
◄ Proverbs 19:18
Proverbs 23:13 ►

22:15 Growing Up
◄ Jeremiah 4:22 ►

16 He that oppresseth the poor to increase his *riches*, *and* he that giveth to the rich, *shall* surely *come* to want.

22:16 Getting Ahead
◄ Proverbs 21:6
Proverbs 28:8 ►

17 Bow down thine ear, and hear the words of the wise, and apply thine heart unto my knowledge.

18 For *it is* a pleasant thing if thou keep them within thee; they shall withal be fitted in thy lips.

19 That thy trust may be in the LORD, I have made known to thee this day, even to thee.

20 Have not I written to thee excellent things in counsels and knowledge,

21 That I might make thee know the certainty of the words of truth; that thou mightest answer the words of truth to them that send unto thee?

22 Rob not the poor, because he *is* poor: neither oppress the afflicted in the gate:

23 For the LORD will plead their cause, and spoil the soul of those that spoiled them.

24 Make no friendship with an angry man; and with a furious man thou shalt not go:

22:24 Bad Friends
◄ Proverbs 4:14
Proverbs 23:6 ►

25 Lest thou learn his ways, and get a snare to thy soul.

22:24-25 Bad Examples
◄ Deuteronomy 18:9
Ezekiel 20:18 ►

26 Be not thou *one* of them that strike hands, *or* of them that are sureties for debts.

27 If thou hast nothing to pay, why should he take away thy bed from under thee?

28 Remove not the ancient landmark, which thy fathers have set.

22:29 Diligence
◄ Proverbs 13:4
Romans 12:8 ►

29 Seest thou a

man diligent in his business? he shall stand before kings; he shall not stand before mean *men.*

23

1 When thou sittest to eat with a ruler, consider diligently what *is* before thee:

2 And put a knife to thy throat, if thou *be* a man given to appetite.

3 Be not desirous of his dainties: for they *are* deceitful meat.

4 Labour not to be rich: cease from thine own wisdom.

5 Wilt thou set thine eyes upon that which is not? for *riches* certainly make themselves wings; they fly away as an eagle toward heaven.

6 Eat thou not the bread of *him that hath* an evil eye, neither desire thou his dainty meats:

7 For as he thinketh in his heart, so *is* he: Eat and drink, saith he to thee; but his heart *is* not with thee.

8 The morsel *which* thou hast eaten shalt thou vomit up, and lose thy sweet words.

9 Speak not in the ears of a fool: for he will despise the wisdom of thy words.

10 Remove not the old landmark; and enter not into the fields of the fatherless:

11 For their redeemer *is* mighty; he shall plead their cause with thee.

12 Apply thine heart unto instruction, and thine ears to the words of knowledge.

13 Withhold not correction from the child: for *if* thou beatest him with the rod, he shall not die.

14 Thou shalt beat him with the rod, and shalt deliver his soul from hell.

15 My son, if thine heart be wise, my heart shall rejoice, even mine.

16 Yea, my reins shall rejoice, when thy lips speak right things.

17 Let not thine heart envy sinners: but *be thou* in the fear of the LORD all the day long.

18 For surely there is an end; and thine expectation shall not be cut off.

19 Hear thou, my son, and be wise, and guide thine heart in the way.

20 Be not among winebibbers; among riotous eaters of flesh:

21 For the drunkard and the glutton shall come to poverty: and drowsiness shall clothe *a man* with rags.

22 Hearken unto thy father that begat thee, and despise not thy mother when she is old.

23 Buy the truth, and sell *it* not; *also* wisdom, and instruction, and understanding.

24 The father of the righteous shall greatly rejoice: and he that begetteth a wise *child* shall have joy of him.

25 Thy father and thy mother shall be

23:1-2 Restraint
◄ Proverbs 23:20 ►

23:5 Soon Gone
◄ Psalm 49:10
Proverbs 27:24 ►

23:6 Bad Friends
◄ Proverbs 22:24
Proverbs 24:1 ►

23:7 Bad Thoughts
◄ Proverbs 15:26
Proverbs 24:9 ►

23:7 Heart
◄ Proverbs 4:23
Matthew 6:18 ►

23:7 Hypocrisy
◄ Proverbs 26:25 ►

23:10 Kind to the Needy
◄ Deuteronomy 26:12
Isaiah 1:17 ►

23:13 Discipline
◄ Proverbs 22:15 ►

23:17 Envy
◄ Proverbs 14:30
Proverbs 24:1 ►

23:20 Getting Drunk
◄ Proverbs 20:1
Proverbs 23:29-31 ►

23:20 Moderation
◄ Proverbs 28:7 ►

23:20 Restraint
◄ Proverbs 23:1-2
Proverbs 25:16 ►

23:21 Sleep
◄ Proverbs 20:13 ►

23:22 Respecting Adults
◄ Job 32:6
1 Timothy 5:1-2 ►

23:23 Valuing the Bible
◄ Psalm 119:162 ►

glad, and she that bare thee shall rejoice.

26 My son, give me thine heart, and let thine eyes observe my ways.

23:26 Commitment
◄ 1 Chronicles 29:5
Romans 12:1 ►

27 For a whore *is* a deep ditch; and a strange woman *is* a narrow pit.

28 She also lieth in wait as *for* a prey, and increaseth the transgressors among men.

23:29 Sin Hurts
◄ Proverbs 6:33
Isaiah 1:6 ►

29 Who hath woe? who hath sorrow? who hath contentions? who hath babbling? who hath wounds without cause? who hath redness of eyes?

23:29-31 Getting Drunk
◄ Proverbs 23:20
Ecclesiastes 10:17 ►

30 They that tarry long at the wine; they that go to seek mixed wine.

23:31 Drinking
◄ Judges 13:4
Proverbs 31:4 ►

31 Look not thou upon the wine when it is red, when it giveth his colour in the cup, *when* it moveth itself aright.

23:31 Drinking Too Much
◄ Proverbs 21:17
Proverbs 31:4 ►

32 At the last it biteth like a serpent, and stingeth like an adder.

23:34 Wicked Insecurity
◄ Psalm 73:18
Isaiah 30:13 ►

33 Thine eyes shall behold strange women, and thine heart shall utter perverse things.

34 Yea, thou shalt be as he that lieth down in the midst of the sea, or as he that lieth upon the top of a mast.

35 They have stricken me, *shalt thou say, and* I was not sick; they have beaten me, *and* I felt *it* not: when shall I awake? I will seek it yet again.

24:1 Bad Friends
◄ Proverbs 23:6
1 Corinthians 5:9 ►

24

1 Be not thou envious against evil men, neither desire to be with them.

24:1 Envy
◄ Proverbs 23:17
Romans 13:13 ►

2 For their heart studieth destruction, and their lips talk of mischief.

24:2 Mischief
◄ Proverbs 6:14
Acts 13:10 ►

3 Through wisdom is an house builded; and by understanding it is established:

4 And by knowledge shall the chambers be filled with all precious and pleasant riches.

5 A wise man *is* strong; yea, a man of knowledge increaseth strength.

6 For by wise counsel thou shalt make thy war: and in multitude of counsellors *there is* safety.

24:6 Getting Opinions
◄ Proverbs 15:22 ►

7 Wisdom *is* too high for a fool: he openeth not his mouth in the gate.

8 He that deviseth to do evil shall be called a mischievous person.

9 The thought of foolishness *is* sin: and the scorner *is* an abomination to men.

24:9 Bad Thoughts
◄ Proverbs 23:7
Isaiah 66:18 ►

10 *If* thou faint in the day of adversity, thy strength *is* small.

11 If thou forbear to deliver *them that are* drawn unto death, and *those that are* ready to be slain;

12 If thou sayest, Behold, we knew it not; doth not he that pondereth the heart consider *it?* and he that keepeth thy soul, doth *not* he know *it?* and shall *not* he render to *every* man according to his works?

24:12 Actions Judged
◄ Psalm 62:12
Jeremiah 17:10 ►

13 My son, eat thou honey, because *it is* good; and the honeycomb, *which is* sweet to thy taste:

14 So *shall* the knowledge of wisdom *be* unto thy soul: when thou hast found *it*, then there shall be a reward, and thy expectation shall not be cut off.

15 Lay not wait, O wicked *man*, against the dwelling of the righteous; spoil not his resting place:

16 For a just *man* falleth seven times, and riseth up again: but the wicked shall fall into mischief.

[17]Rejoice not when thine enemy falleth, and let not thine heart be glad when he stumbleth:

24:17 Loving Enemies
◄ Exodus 23:4
Proverbs 25:21-22 ►

[18]Lest the LORD see *it,* and it displease him, and he turn away his wrath from him.

[19]Fret not thyself because of evil *men,* neither be thou envious at the wicked;

[20]For there shall be no reward to the evil *man;* the candle of the wicked shall be put out.

[21]My son, fear thou the LORD and the king: *and* meddle not with them that are given to change:

24:21 Obeying the Law
◄ Ezra 7:26
Ecclesiastes 8:2 ►

[22]For their calamity shall rise suddenly; and who knoweth the ruin of them both?

[23]These *things* also *belong* to the wise. *It is* not good to have respect of persons in judgment.

24:23 Favoritism
◄ Job 13:10
Malachi 2:9 ►

[24]He that saith unto the wicked, Thou *art* righteous; him shall the people curse, nations shall abhor him:

24:24 Excusing Sin
◄ Proverbs 17:15
Proverbs 28:4 ►

[25]But to them that rebuke *him* shall be delight, and a good blessing shall come upon them.

[26]*Every man* shall kiss *his* lips that giveth a right answer.

[27]Prepare thy work without, and make it fit for thyself in the field; and afterwards build thine house.

[28]Be not a witness against thy neighbour without cause; and deceive *not* with thy lips.

24:28 Hurtful Lying
◄ Proverbs 19:9
Proverbs 25:18 ►

[29]Say not, I will do so to him as he hath done to me: I will render to the man according to his work.

24:29 Revenge
◄ Proverbs 20:22
Matthew 5:39 ►

[30]I went by the field of the slothful, and by the vineyard of the man void of understanding;

[31]And, lo, it was all grown over with thorns, *and* nettles had covered the face thereof, and the stone wall thereof was broken down.

24:30-31 Laziness
◄ Proverbs 18:9
Ecclesiastes 10:18 ►

[32]Then I saw, *and* considered *it* well: I looked upon *it, and* received instruction.

[33]*Yet* a little sleep, a little slumber, a little folding of the hands to sleep:

[34]So shall thy poverty come as one that travelleth; and thy want as an armed man.

25

[1]These *are* also proverbs of Solomon, which the men of Hezekiah king of Judah copied out.

[2]*It is* the glory of God to conceal a thing: but the honour of kings *is* to search out a matter.

[3]The heaven for height, and the earth for depth, and the heart of kings *is* unsearchable.

[4]Take away the dross from the silver, and there shall come forth a vessel for the finer.

[5]Take away the wicked *from* before the king, and his throne shall be established in righteousness.

25:5 Better Neighborhoods
◄ Proverbs 16:12
Proverbs 28:2 ►

[6]Put not forth thyself in the presence of the king, and stand not in the place of great *men:*

[7]For better *it is* that it be said unto thee, Come up hither; than that thou shouldest be put lower in the presence of the prince whom thine eyes have seen.

[8]Go not forth hastily to strive, lest *thou know not* what to do in the end thereof, when thy neighbour hath put thee to shame.

25:8 Arguing
◄ Proverbs 20:3
Proverbs 26:17 ►

[9]Debate thy cause with thy neighbour *himself;* and discover not a secret to another:

25:8 Suing People
◄ Matthew 5:25 ►

[10]Lest he that heareth *it* put thee to shame, and thine infamy turn not away.

[11]A word fitly spoken *is like* apples of gold in pictures of silver.

Turn to the next page for more . . .

12 *As* an earring of gold, and an ornament of fine gold, *so is* a wise reprover upon an obedient ear.

25:11 Wise Words
◄ Proverbs 16:24
Ecclesiastes 9:17 ►

13 As the cold of snow in the time of harvest, *so is* a faithful messenger to them that send him: for he refresheth the soul of his masters.

25:12 Taking Advice
◄ Proverbs 17:10
Proverbs 27:5 ►

14 Whoso boasteth himself of a false gift *is like* clouds and wind without rain.

15 By long forbearing is a prince persuaded, and a soft tongue breaketh the bone.

16 Hast thou found honey? eat so much as is sufficient for thee, lest thou be filled therewith, and vomit it.

25:16 Restraint
◄ Proverbs 23:20
Luke 12:22 ►

17 Withdraw thy foot from thy neighbour's house; lest he be weary of thee, and *so* hate thee.

25:18 Hurtful Lying
◄ Proverbs 24:28
Matthew 19:18 ►

18 A man that beareth false witness against his neighbour *is* a maul, and a sword, and a sharp arrow.

25:20 Cruelty
◄ Psalm 69:21
Proverbs 28:3 ►

19 Confidence in an unfaithful man in time of trouble *is like* a broken tooth, and a foot out of joint.

25:21 Giving
◄ Nehemiah 8:10
Ecclesiastes 11:1 ►

20 *As* he that taketh away a garment in cold weather, *and as* vinegar upon nitre, so *is* he that singeth songs to an heavy heart.

25:21 Vengeance
◄ Exodus 23:5
Luke 6:27 ►

21 If thine enemy be hungry, give him bread to eat; and if he be thirsty, give him water to drink:

22 For thou shalt heap coals of fire upon his head, and the LORD shall reward thee.

25:21-22 Loving Enemies
◄ Proverbs 24:17
Matthew 5:44 ►

23 The north wind driveth away rain: so *doth* an angry countenance a backbiting tongue.

24 *It is* better to dwell in the corner of the housetop, than with a brawling woman and in a wide house.

25 *As* cold waters to a thirsty soul, so *is* good news from a far country.

26 A righteous man falling down before the wicked *is as* a troubled fountain, and a corrupt spring.

27 *It is* not good to eat much honey: so *for men* to search their own glory *is not* glory.

28 He that *hath* no rule over his own spirit *is like* a city *that is* broken down, *and* without walls.

25:28 Self-control
◄ Proverbs 16:32
Acts 24:25 ►

26

1 As snow in summer, and as rain in harvest, so honour is not seemly for a fool.

2 As the bird by wandering, as the swallow by flying, so the curse causeless shall not come.

3 A whip for the horse, a bridle for the ass, and a rod for the fool's back.

4 Answer not a fool according to his folly, lest thou also be like unto him.

5 Answer a fool according to his folly, lest he be wise in his own conceit.

26:5 Conceit
◄ Proverbs 3:7
Proverbs 26:12 ►

6 He that sendeth a message by the hand of a fool cutteth off the feet, *and* drinketh damage.

7 The legs of the lame are not equal: so *is* a parable in the mouth of fools.

8 As he that bindeth a stone in a sling, so *is* he that giveth honour to a fool.

9 *As* a thorn goeth up into the hand of a drunkard, so *is* a parable in the mouth of fools.

10 The great *God* that formed all *things* both rewardeth the fool, and rewardeth transgressors.

11 As a dog returneth to his vomit, *so* a fool returneth to his folly.

12 Seest thou a man wise in his

26:12 Conceit
◄ Proverbs 26:5
Isaiah 5:21 ►

own conceit? *there is* more hope of a fool than of him.

13The slothful *man* saith, *There is* a lion in the way; a lion *is* in the streets.

14*As* the door turneth upon his hinges, so *doth* the slothful upon his bed.

15The slothful hideth his hand in *his* bosom; it grieveth him to bring it again to his mouth.

16The sluggard *is* wiser in his own conceit than seven men that can render a reason.

> **26:16**
> **Lazy People**
> ◄ Proverbs 21:25 ►

17He that passeth by, *and* meddleth with strife *belonging* not to him, *is like* one that taketh a dog by the ears.

> **26:17 Arguing**
> ◄ Proverbs 25:8
> Philippians 2:3 ►

18As a mad *man* who casteth firebrands, arrows, and death,

19So *is* the man *that* deceiveth his neighbour, and saith, Am not I in sport?

> **26:19**
> **Teasing and Joking**
> ◄ Ephesians 5:4 ►

20Where no wood is, *there* the fire goeth out: so where *there is* no talebearer, the strife ceaseth.

> **26:20**
> **Gossiping**
> ◄ Proverbs 20:19 ►

21*As* coals *are* to burning coals, and wood to fire; so *is* a contentious man to kindle strife.

22The words of a talebearer *are* as wounds, and they go down into the innermost parts of the belly.

23Burning lips and a wicked heart *are like* a potsherd covered with silver dross.

24He that hateth dissembleth with his lips, and layeth up deceit within him;

25When he speaketh fair, believe him not: for *there are* seven abominations in his heart.

> **26:25 Hypocrisy**
> ◄ Proverbs 23:7
> Matthew 23:28 ►

26*Whose* hatred is covered by deceit, his wickedness shall be shewed before the *whole* congregation.

27Whoso diggeth a pit shall fall therein: and he that rolleth a stone, it will return upon him.

28A lying tongue hateth *those that are* afflicted by it; and a flattering mouth worketh ruin.

27

1Boast not thyself of to morrow; for thou knowest not what a day may bring forth.

> **27:1**
> **The Future**
> ◄ Ecclesiastes 3:22 ►

2Let another man praise thee, and not thine own mouth; a stranger, and not thine own lips.

3A stone *is* heavy, and the sand weighty; but a fool's wrath *is* heavier than them both.

4Wrath *is* cruel, and anger *is* outrageous; but who *is* able to stand before envy?

5Open rebuke *is* better than secret love.

> **27:5 Taking Advice**
> ◄ Proverbs 25:12
> Proverbs 29:15 ►

6Faithful *are* the wounds of a friend; but the kisses of an enemy *are* deceitful.

> **27:6**
> **"Dangerous Kisses"**
> ◄ 2 Samuel 20:9
> Mark 14:45 ►

7The full soul loatheth an honeycomb; but to the hungry soul every bitter thing is sweet.

8As a bird that wandereth from her nest, so *is* a man that wandereth from his place.

> **27:6 Dishonest People**
> ◄ Proverbs 12:5
> Jeremiah 5:27 ►

9Ointment and perfume rejoice the heart: so *doth* the sweetness of a man's friend by hearty counsel.

10Thine own friend, and thy father's friend, forsake not; neither go into thy brother's house in the day of thy calamity: *for* better *is* a neighbour *that is* near than a brother far off.

> **27:10 Friendship**
> ◄ Proverbs 18:24
> Proverbs 27:17 ►

11My son, be wise, and make my heart glad, that I may answer him that reproacheth me.

12A prudent *man* foreseeth the evil, *and* hideth himself; *but* the simple pass on, *and* are punished.

13Take his garment that is surety for a stranger, and take a pledge of him for a strange woman.

14He that blesseth his friend with a loud voice, rising early in the morning, it shall be counted a curse to him.

15A continual dropping in a very rainy day and a contentious woman are alike.

27:15 Fighting
◄ Proverbs 21:19 ►

16Whosoever hideth her hideth the wind, and the ointment of his right hand, *which* bewrayeth *itself*.

17Iron sharpeneth iron; so a man sharpeneth the countenance of his friend.

27:17 Friendship
◄ Proverbs 27:10
Ecclesiastes 4:9-10 ►

18Whoso keepeth the fig tree shall eat the fruit thereof: so he that waiteth on his master shall be honoured.

19As in water face *answereth* to face, so the heart of man to man.

20Hell and destruction are never full; so the eyes of man are never satisfied.

21*As* the fining pot for silver, and the furnace for gold; so *is* a man to his praise.

22Though thou shouldest bray a fool in a mortar among wheat with a pestle, *yet* will not his foolishness depart from him.

23Be thou diligent to know the state of thy flocks, *and* look well to thy herds.

24For riches *are* not for ever: and doth the crown *endure* to every generation?

27:24 Soon Gone
◄ Proverbs 23:5
Ecclesiastes 2:18 ►

25The hay appeareth, and the tender grass sheweth itself, and herbs of the mountains are gathered.

26The lambs *are* for thy clothing, and the goats *are* the price of the field.

27And *thou shalt have* goats' milk enough for thy food, for the food of thy household, and *for* the maintenance for thy maidens.

28

1The wicked flee when no man pursueth: but the righteous are bold as a lion.

28:1 Guilty Fear
◄ Psalm 53:5
Isaiah 2:19 ►

2For the transgression of a land many *are* the princes thereof: but by a man of understanding *and* knowledge the state *thereof* shall be prolonged.

28:2 Better Neighborhoods
◄ Proverbs 25:5
Proverbs 29:4 ►

3A poor man that oppresseth the poor *is like* a sweeping rain which leaveth no food.

28:3 Cruelty
◄ Proverbs 25:20
Amos 1:11 ►

4They that forsake the law praise the wicked: but such as keep the law contend with them.

28:4 Excusing Sin
◄ Proverbs 24:24
Isaiah 5:20 ►

5Evil men understand not judgment: but they that seek the LORD understand all *things*.

28:6 Used to Sin
◄ Proverbs 15:4
Ezekiel 9:9 ►

6Better *is* the poor that walketh in his uprightness, than *he that is* perverse *in his* ways, though he *be* rich.

28:6 Why Do Right?
◄ Proverbs 14:11 ►

7Whoso keepeth the law *is* a wise son: but he that is a companion of riotous *men* shameth his father.

28:7 Moderation
◄ Proverbs 23:20
Daniel 5:1 ►

8He that by usury and unjust gain increaseth his substance, he shall gather it for him that will pity the poor.

28:8 Getting Ahead
◄ Proverbs 22:16
Jeremiah 17:11 ►

9He that turneth away his ear from hearing the law, even his prayer *shall be* abomination.

28:9 Unanswered Prayer
◄ Proverbs 21:13
Isaiah 1:15 ►

10Whoso causeth the righteous to go astray in an evil way, he shall fall himself into his own pit: but the upright shall have good *things* in possession.

11The rich man *is* wise in his own conceit; but the poor that hath understand-

ing searcheth him
out.
12When righ-
teous *men* do re-
joice, *there is* great
glory: but when the
wicked rise, a man
is hidden.
13He that cov-
ereth his sins shall
not prosper: but
whoso confesseth
and forsaketh *them*
shall have mercy.
14Happy *is* the
man that feareth
alway: but he that
hardeneth his heart
shall fall into mis-
chief.
15*As* a roaring
lion, and a ranging
bear; *so is* a wicked
ruler over the poor
people.
16The prince that wanteth understanding *is* also a great oppressor: *but* he that
hateth covetousness shall prolong *his* days.
17A man that doeth violence to the
blood of *any* person shall flee to the pit;
let no man stay him.
18Whoso walketh uprightly shall be
saved: but *he that is* perverse *in his* ways
shall fall at once.
19He that tilleth his land shall have plenty of bread: but he that followeth after vain
persons shall have poverty enough.
20A faithful man
shall abound with
blessings: but he
that maketh haste
to be rich shall not
be innocent.
21To have respect of persons *is* not good:
for for a piece of bread *that* man will transgress.
22He that hasteth to be rich *hath* an evil
eye, and considereth not that poverty shall
come upon him.
23He that rebuketh a man afterwards
shall find more favour than he that
flattereth with the tongue.
24Whoso robbeth his father or his mother, and saith, *It is* no transgression; the
same *is* the companion of a destroyer.

28:13 Confession
◄ Job 33:27
Jeremiah 3:13 ►

28:13 Starting Over
◄ Job 11:14
Isaiah 55:7 ►

28:14 Hard-heart Aches
◄ Psalm 95:8
Proverbs 29:1 ►

28:14
Source of Happiness
◄ Proverbs 16:20
Proverbs 29:18 ►

28:20 Money's Dangers
◄ Psalm 62:10
Matthew 19:23 ►

25He that is of a proud heart stirreth up
strife: but he that putteth his trust in the
LORD shall be made fat.
26He that trust-
eth in his own heart
is a fool: but whoso
walketh wisely, he
shall be delivered.
27He that giveth
unto the poor shall
not lack: but he that
hideth his eyes
shall have many a
curse.
28When the
wicked rise, men
hide themselves:
but when they per-
ish, the righteous
increase.

29

1He, that being
often reproved
hardeneth *his* neck,
shall suddenly be
destroyed, and that
without remedy.
2When the righ-
teous are in author-
ity, the people
rejoice: but when
the wicked beareth
rule, the people
mourn.
3Whoso loveth
wisdom rejoiceth
his father: but he
that keepeth com-
pany with harlots
spendeth *his* sub-
stance.
4The king by
judgment estab-
lisheth the land:
but he that re-
ceiveth gifts over-
throweth it.
5A man that
flattereth his neigh-
bour spreadeth a
net for his feet.
6In the transgres-
sion of an evil man
there is a snare: but
the righteous doth sing and rejoice.
7The righteous considereth the cause of

28:26
Self-confidence
◄ Isaiah 47:8 ►

28:27 Being Stingy
◄ Proverbs 21:13
Ecclesiastes 5:13 ►

28:27 Kind to the Poor
◄ Proverbs 19:17
Matthew 19:21 ►

28:27
Promises to Givers
◄ Proverbs 22:9
Ecclesiastes 11:1 ►

29:1 Hard-heart Aches
◄ Proverbs 28:14
Isaiah 42:25 ►

29:3 Waste
◄ Proverbs 18:9
Luke 15:13 ►

29:4
Better Neighborhoods
◄ Proverbs 28:2
Proverbs 29:14 ►

29:4 Leaders Should...
◄ Proverbs 20:28
Proverbs 29:14 ►

the poor: *but* the wicked regardeth not to know *it.*

8 Scornful men bring a city into a snare: but wise *men* turn away wrath.

9 *If* a wise man contendeth with a foolish man, whether he rage or laugh, *there is* no rest.

10 The bloodthirsty hate the upright: but the just seek his soul.

11 A fool uttereth all his mind: but a wise *man* keepeth it in till afterwards.

29:11 Idle Talk
◄ Proverbs 14:23
Ecclesiastes 5:3 ►

12 If a ruler hearken to lies, all his servants *are* wicked.

13 The poor and the deceitful man meet together: the LORD lighteneth both their eyes.

29:14
Better Neighborhoods
◄ Proverbs 29:4
Isaiah 16:5 ►

14 The king that faithfully judgeth the poor, his throne shall be established for ever.

29:14 Fair to the Poor
◄ Proverbs 21:13
Jeremiah 22:16 ►

15 The rod and reproof give wisdom: but a child left *to himself* bringeth his mother to shame.

29:14
Leaders Should...
◄ Proverbs 29:4 ►

16 When the wicked are multiplied, transgression increaseth: but the righteous shall see their fall.

29:15 Taking Advice
◄ Proverbs 27:5
Ecclesiastes 7:5 ►

17 Correct thy son, and he shall give thee rest; yea, he shall give delight unto thy soul.

29:18
Source of Happiness
◄ Proverbs 28:14
John 13:17 ►

18 Where *there is* no vision, the people perish: but he that keepeth the law, happy *is* he.

19 A servant will not be corrected by words: for though he understand he will not answer.

29:20 Being Hasty
◄ Proverbs 21:5
Ecclesiastes 5:2 ►

20 Seest thou a man *that is* hasty in his words? *there is* more hope of a fool than of him.

21 He that delicately bringeth up his servant from a child shall have him become *his* son at the length.

22 An angry man stirreth up strife, and a furious man aboundeth in transgression.

23 A man's pride shall bring him low: but honour shall uphold the humble in spirit.

24 Whoso is partner with a thief hateth his own soul: he heareth cursing, and bewrayeth *it* not.

25 The fear of man bringeth a snare: but whoso putteth his trust in the LORD shall be safe.

26 Many seek the ruler's favour; but *every* man's judgment *cometh* from the LORD.

27 An unjust man *is* an abomination to the just: and *he that is* upright in the way *is* abomination to the wicked.

29:27 Don't Be Unfair
◄ Psalm 82:2
Proverbs 31:4-5 ►

30

1 The words of Agur the son of Jakeh, *even* the prophecy: the man spake unto Ithiel, even unto Ithiel and Ucal,

2 Surely I *am* more brutish than *any* man, and have not the understanding of a man.

3 I neither learned wisdom, nor have the knowledge of the holy.

4 Who hath ascended up into heaven, or descended? who hath gathered the wind in his fists? who hath bound the waters in a garment? who hath established all the ends of the earth? what *is* his name, and what *is* his son's name, if thou canst tell?

5 Every word of God *is* pure: he *is* a shield unto them that put their trust in him.

6 Add thou not unto his words, lest he reprove thee, and thou be found a liar.

7 Two *things* have I required of thee; deny me *them* not before I die:

8 Remove far from me vanity and lies: give me neither poverty nor riches; feed me with food convenient for me:

9 Lest I be full, and deny *thee,* and say, Who *is* the LORD? or lest I be poor, and steal, and take the name of my God *in vain.*

30:9
Success
◄ Proverbs 1:32 ►

10 Accuse not a servant unto his master, lest he curse thee, and thou be found guilty.

11 *There is* a generation *that* curseth their father, and doth not bless their mother.

12 *There is* a generation *that are* pure in

their own eyes, and
yet is not washed
from their filthi-
ness.
13*There is* a gen-
eration, O how
lofty are their eyes! and their eyelids are
lifted up.

30:12
Self-righteousness
◄ Proverbs 21:2
Jeremiah 2:35 ►

14*There is* a generation, whose teeth *are*
as swords, and their jaw teeth *as* knives, to
devour the poor from off the earth, and
the needy from *among* men.
15The horseleach hath two daughters,
crying, Give, give. There are three *things that*
are never satisfied, *yea,* four *things* say not,
It is enough:
16The grave; and the barren womb; the
earth *that* is not filled with water; and the
fire *that* saith not, *It is* enough.
17The eye *that*
mocketh at *his* fa-
ther, and despiseth
to obey *his* mother,
the ravens of the
valley shall pick it
out, and the young eagles shall eat it.

30:17 Mockers
◄ Proverbs 17:5
Isaiah 57:4 ►

18There be three *things which* are too
wonderful for me, yea, four which I know
not:
19The way of an eagle in the air; the way
of a serpent upon a rock; the way of a ship
in the midst of the sea; and the way of a
man with a maid.
20Such *is* the way of an adulterous woman; she eateth, and wipeth her mouth, and
saith, I have done no wickedness.
21For three *things* the earth is disquieted,
and for four *which* it cannot bear:
22For a servant when he reigneth; and a
fool when he is filled with meat;
23For an odious *woman* when she is married; and an handmaid that is heir to her
mistress.
24There be four *things which are* little
upon the earth, but they *are* exceeding wise:
25The ants *are* a people not strong, yet
they prepare their meat in the summer;
26The conies *are but* a feeble folk, yet
make they their houses in the rocks;
27The locusts have no king, yet go they
forth all of them by bands;
28The spider taketh hold with her hands,
and is in kings' palaces.
29There be three *things* which go well,
yea, four are comely in going:
30A lion *which is* strongest among beasts,
and turneth not away for any;
31A greyhound; an he goat also; and a
king, against whom *there is* no rising up.
32If thou hast done foolishly in lifting
up thyself, or if thou hast thought evil, *lay*
thine hand upon thy mouth.
33Surely the churning of milk bringeth
forth butter, and the wringing of the nose
bringeth forth blood: so the forcing of
wrath bringeth forth strife.

31

1The words of king Lemuel, the prophecy that his mother taught him.
2What, my son? and what, the son
of my womb? and what, the son of my
vows?
3Give not thy strength unto women, nor
thy ways to that which destroyeth kings.
4*It is* not for
kings, O Lemuel, *it*
is not for kings to
drink wine; nor
for princes strong
drink:

31:4 Drinking
◄ Proverbs 23:31
Jeremiah 35:6 ►

5Lest they drink,
and forget the law,
and pervert the
judgment of any of
the afflicted.

31:4 Drinking Too Much
◄ Proverbs 23:31
Isaiah 5:11 ►

6Give strong
drink unto him
that is ready to per-
ish, and wine unto
those that be of
heavy hearts.
7Let him drink,
and forget his pov-
erty, and remember his misery no more.

31:4-5 Don't Be Unfair
◄ Proverbs 29:27
Ecclesiastes 3:16 ►

8Open thy mouth for the dumb in the
cause of all such as are appointed to destruction.
9Open thy mouth, judge righteously,
and plead the cause of the poor and needy.
10Who can find a virtuous woman? for
her price *is* far above rubies.
11The heart of her husband doth safely
trust in her, so that he shall have no need
of spoil.
12She will do him good and not evil all
the days of her life.
13She seeketh wool, and flax, and
worketh willingly with her hands.
14She is like the merchants' ships; she
bringeth her food from afar.
15She riseth also while it is yet night,

and giveth meat to her household, and a
portion to her maidens.
16She considereth a field, and buyeth it:
with the fruit of her hands she planteth a
vineyard.
17She girdeth her loins with strength,
and strengtheneth her arms.
18She perceiveth that her merchandise *is* good: her candle goeth not out by
night.
19She layeth her hands to the spindle,
and her hands hold the distaff.
20She stretcheth
out her hand to the
poor; yea, she
reacheth forth her
hands to the needy.
21She is not
afraid of the snow
for her household:
for all her house-
hold *are* clothed
with scarlet.
22She maketh
herself coverings of tapestry; her clothing
is silk and purple.
23Her husband is known in the gates,
when he sitteth among the elders of the
land.
24She maketh fine linen, and selleth *it;*
and delivereth girdles unto the merchant.
25Strength and honour *are* her clothing;
and she shall rejoice in time to come.
26She openeth her mouth with wisdom;
and in her tongue *is* the law of kindness.
27She looketh well to the ways of her
household, and eateth not the bread of
idleness.
28Her children arise up, and call her
blessed; her husband *also,* and he praiseth
her.
29Many daughters have done virtuously,
but thou excellest them all.
30Favour *is* deceitful, and beauty *is* vain:
but a woman *that* feareth the LORD, she
shall be praised.
31Give her of the fruit of her hands; and
let her own works praise her in the gates.

31:20 Generosity
◄ Deuteronomy 15:7
Matthew 6:1 ►

31:20 Work that Helps Others
◄ Job 29:15-16
Isaiah 21:14 ►

Ecclesiastes

AUTHOR
Solomon

MAIN POINT
Life makes no sense apart from God, as Solomon learned by bitter experience and told us here.

DATE WRITTEN
Late in Solomon's reign, probably about 935 B.C.

12 CHAPTERS

MAIN PEOPLE

Because it is a book of observations and wisdom, there are no named characters.

SPECIAL FEATURES

- *Includes the famous refrain "Nothing is new on earth."*
- *Usually considered the most pessimistic book of the Bible*
- *Says there's a right time for everything (chapter 3)*
- *Concludes with a verse that countless students have tried to use as an excuse to get out of homework (12:12)*
- *Fourth book of Poetry*

HOW THE BOOK GOT ITS NAME

The word ecclesiastes comes from a Greek word meaning "a member of the assembly" and has come to refer to a preacher, since the book is like a sermon.

1

1 The words of the Preacher, the son of
David, king in Jerusalem.
2 Vanity of vanities, saith the Preacher,
vanity of vanities; all *is* vanity.
3 What profit hath a man of all his labour
which he taketh under the sun?
4 *One* generation passeth away, and *an-*
other generation cometh: but the earth
abideth for ever.
5 The sun also ariseth, and the sun goeth
down, and hasteth to his place where he
arose.
6 The wind goeth toward the south, and
turneth about unto the north; it whirleth
about continually, and the wind returneth
again according to his circuits.
7 All the rivers run into the sea; yet the
sea *is* not full; unto the place from whence
the rivers come, thither they return again.
8 All things *are*
full of labour; man
cannot utter *it:* the
eye is not satisfied
with seeing, nor
the ear filled with
hearing.

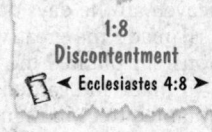

1:8
Discontentment
◄ Ecclesiastes 4:8 ►

9 The thing that hath been, it *is that*
which shall be; and that which is done *is*
that which shall be done: and *there is* no
new *thing* under the sun.
10 Is there *any* thing whereof it may be
said, See, this *is* new? it hath been already
of old time, which was before us.
11 *There is* no remembrance of former

things; neither shall there be *any* remembrance of *things* that are to come with *those* that shall come after.

12 I the Preacher was king over Israel in Jerusalem.

13 And I gave my heart to seek and search out by wisdom concerning all *things* that are done under heaven: this sore travail hath God given to the sons of man to be exercised therewith.

14 I have seen all the works that are done under the sun; and, behold, all *is* vanity and vexation of spirit.

15 *That which is* crooked cannot be made straight: and that which is wanting cannot be numbered.

16 I communed with mine own heart, saying, Lo, I am come to great estate, and have gotten more wisdom than all *they* that have been before me in Jerusalem: yea, my heart had great experience of wisdom and knowledge.

17 And I gave my heart to know wisdom, and to know madness and folly: I perceived that this also is vexation of spirit.

18 For in much wisdom *is* much grief: and he that increaseth knowledge increaseth sorrow.

2

1 I said in mine heart, Go to now, I will prove thee with mirth, therefore enjoy pleasure: and, behold, this also *is* vanity.

2 I said of laughter, *It is* mad: and of mirth, What doeth it?

2:2 Laughter
◄ Proverbs 14:13
Ecclesiastes 7:3 ►

3 I sought in mine heart to give myself unto wine, yet acquainting mine heart with wisdom; and to lay hold on folly, till I might see what *was* that good for the sons of men, which they should do under the heaven all the days of their life.

4 I made me great works; I builded me houses; I planted me vineyards:

5 I made me gardens and orchards, and I planted trees in them of all *kind of* fruits:

6 I made me pools of water, to water therewith the wood that bringeth forth trees:

7 I got *me* servants and maidens, and had servants born in my house; also I had great possessions of great and small cattle above all that were in Jerusalem before me:

8 I gathered me also silver and gold, and the peculiar treasure of kings and of the provinces: I gat me men singers and women singers, and the delights of the sons of men, *as* musical instruments, and that of all sorts.

9 So I was great, and increased more than all that were before me in Jerusalem: also my wisdom remained with me.

10 And whatsoever mine eyes desired I kept not from them, I withheld not my heart from any joy; for my heart rejoiced in all my labour: and this was my portion of all my labour.

2:10 Happiness
◄ Proverbs 14:13
Ecclesiastes 7:6 ►

11 Then I looked on all the works that my hands had wrought, and on the labour that I had laboured to do: and, behold, all *was* vanity and vexation of spirit, and *there was* no profit under the sun.

12 And I turned myself to behold wisdom, and madness, and folly: for what *can* the man *do* that cometh after the king? *even* that which hath been already done.

13 Then I saw that wisdom excelleth folly, as far as light excelleth darkness.

14 The wise man's eyes *are* in his head; but the fool walketh in darkness: and I myself perceived also that one event happeneth to them all.

15 Then said I in my heart, As it happeneth to the fool, so it happeneth even to me; and why was I then more wise? Then I said in my heart, that this also *is* vanity.

16 For *there is* no remembrance of the wise more than of the fool for ever; seeing that which now *is* in the days to come shall all be forgotten. And how dieth the wise *man?* as the fool.

17 Therefore I hated life; because the work that is wrought under the sun is grievous unto me: for all *is* vanity and vexation of spirit.

18 Yea, I hated all my labour which I had taken under the sun: because I should leave it unto the man that shall be after me.

2:18 Soon Gone
◄ Proverbs 27:24
Ecclesiastes 2:26 ►

19 And who knoweth whether he shall be a wise *man* or a fool? yet shall he have rule over all my labour wherein I have laboured, and wherein I have shewed myself wise under the sun. This *is* also vanity.

20 Therefore I went about to cause my heart to despair of all the labour which I took under the sun.

21 For there is a man whose labour *is* in wisdom, and in knowledge, and in equity; yet to a man that hath not laboured therein shall he leave it *for* his portion. This also *is* vanity and a great evil.

22 For what hath man of all his labour, and of the vexation of his heart, wherein he hath laboured under the sun?

23 For all his days *are* sorrows, and his travail grief; yea, his heart taketh not rest in the night. This is also vanity.

24 *There is* nothing better for a man, *than* that he should eat and drink, and *that* he should make his soul enjoy good in his labour. This also I saw, that it *was* from the hand of God.

25 For who can eat, or who else can hasten *hereunto,* more than I?

26 For *God* giveth to a man that *is* good in his sight wisdom, and knowledge, and joy: but to the sinner he giveth travail, to gather and to heap up, that he may give to *him that is* good before God. This also *is* vanity and vexation of spirit.

2:26 Getting Wisdom
◄ Proverbs 2:6
Daniel 2:21 ►

2:26 Gifts from God
◄ Job 32:8
Isaiah 50:4 ►

2:26 Hoarding
◄ Psalm 39:6
Ezekiel 28:4 ►

2:26 Soon Gone
◄ Ecclesiastes 2:18
Jeremiah 17:11 ►

3

1 To every *thing there is* a season, and a time to every purpose under the heaven:

2 A time to be born, and a time to die; a time to plant, and a time to pluck up *that which is* planted;

3 A time to kill, and a time to heal; a time to break down, and a time to build up;

4 A time to weep, and a time to laugh; a time to mourn, and a time to dance;

5 A time to cast away stones, and a time to gather stones together; a time to embrace, and a time to refrain from embracing;

6 A time to get, and a time to lose; a time to keep, and a time to cast away;

7 A time to rend, and a time to sew; a time to keep silence, and a time to speak;

3:7 Being Quiet
◄ Joshua 6:10
Amos 5:13 ►

8 A time to love, and a time to hate; a time of war, and a time of peace.

9 What profit hath he that worketh in that wherein he laboureth?

10 I have seen the travail, which God hath given to the sons of men to be exercised in it.

11 He hath made every *thing* beautiful in his time: also he hath set the world in their heart, so that no man can find out the work that God maketh from the beginning to the end.

12 I know that *there is* no good in them, but for *a man* to rejoice, and to do good in his life.

13 And also that every man should eat and drink, and enjoy the good of all his labour, it *is* the gift of God.

14 I know that, whatsoever God doeth, it shall be for ever: nothing can be put to it, nor any thing taken from it: and God doeth *it,* that *men* should fear before him.

3:14 God's Perfection
◄ Psalm 18:30
Matthew 5:48 ►

15 That which hath been is now; and that which is to be hath already been; and God requireth that which is past.

16 And moreover I saw under the sun the place of judgment, *that* wickedness *was* there; and the place of righteousness, *that* iniquity *was* there.

3:16 Don't Be Unfair
◄ Proverbs 31:4-5
Luke 16:10 ►

17 I said in mine heart, God shall judge the righteous and the wicked: for *there is* a time there for every purpose and for every work.

3:17 God as Judge
◄ Psalm 96:13
Hebrews 12:23 ►

18 I said in mine heart concerning the estate of the sons of men, that God might manifest them, and that they might see that they themselves are beasts.

19 For that which befalleth the sons of men befalleth beasts; even one thing

Turn to the next page for more . . .

befalleth them: as
the one dieth, so
dieth the other; yea,
they have all one
breath; so that a
man hath no pre-
eminence above a
beast: for all *is*
vanity.

3:19 Death
◄ Psalm 89:48
Ecclesiastes 8:8 ►

3:20 Mortality
◄ Psalm 103:16
1 Corinthians 15:53 ►

20All go unto one
place; all are of the
dust, and all turn to
dust again.
21Who knoweth the spirit of man that
goeth upward, and the spirit of the beast
that goeth downward to the earth?
22Wherefore I
perceive that *there is*
nothing better, than
that a man should
rejoice in his own
works; for that *is* his
portion: for who shall bring him to see
what shall be after him?

3:22 The Future
◄ Proverbs 27:1
Ecclesiastes 6:12 ►

4

1So I returned, and considered all the
oppressions that are done under the sun:
and behold the tears of *such as were* oppressed, and they had no comforter; and
on the side of their oppressors *there was*
power; but they had no comforter.
2Wherefore I praised the dead which are
already dead more than the living which
are yet alive.
3Yea, better *is he* than both they, which
hath not yet been, who hath not seen the
evil work that is done under the sun.
4Again, I considered all travail, and every
right work, that for this a man is envied of
his neighbour. This *is* also vanity and vexation of spirit.
5The fool foldeth his hands together,
and eateth his own flesh.
6Better *is* an handful *with* quietness, than
both the hands full *with* travail and vexation of spirit.
7Then I returned, and I saw vanity under the sun.
8There is one
alone, and *there is*
not a second; yea,
he hath neither
child nor brother:
yet *is there* no end of
all his labour; neither is his eye satisfied
with riches; neither *saith he,* For whom do
I labour, and bereave my soul of good?
This *is* also vanity, yea, it *is* a sore travail.

4:8 Discontentment
◄ Ecclesiastes 1:8
Ecclesiastes 5:10 ►

9Two *are* better
than one; because
they have a good
reward for their
labour.
10For if they fall,
the one will lift up his fellow: but woe to
him *that is* alone when he falleth; for *he*
hath not another to help him up.

4:9-10 Friendship
◄ Proverbs 27:17
John 15:13-14 ►

11Again, if two lie together, then they
have heat: but how can one be warm *alone?*
12And if one prevail against him, two
shall withstand him; and a threefold cord
is not quickly broken.
13Better *is* a poor and a wise child than
an old and foolish king, who will no more
be admonished.
14For out of prison he cometh to reign;
whereas also *he that is* born in his kingdom becometh poor.
15I considered all the living which walk
under the sun, with the second child that
shall stand up in his stead.
16*There is* no end of all the people, *even*
of all that have been before them: they also
that come after shall not rejoice in him.
Surely this also *is* vanity and vexation of
spirit.

5

1Keep thy foot when thou goest to the
house of God, and be more ready to hear,
than to give the sacrifice of fools: for they
consider not that they do evil.
2Be not rash with
thy mouth, and let
not thine heart be
hasty to utter *any*
thing before God:
for God *is* in
heaven, and thou
upon earth: there-
fore let thy words
be few.

5:2 Being Hasty
◄ Proverbs 29:20
Acts 19:36 ►

5:3 Idle Talk
◄ Proverbs 29:11
Ecclesiastes 10:13 ►

3For a dream
cometh through
the multitude of business; and a fool's
voice *is known* by multitude of words.
4When thou vowest a vow unto God,
defer not to pay it; for *he hath* no pleasure
in fools: pay that which thou hast vowed.
5Better *is it* that thou shouldest not vow,
than that thou shouldest vow and not pay.
6Suffer not thy mouth to cause thy flesh
to sin; neither say thou before the angel,

that it *was* an error: wherefore should God be angry at thy voice, and destroy the work of thine hands?

7 For in the multitude of dreams and many words *there are* also *divers* vanities: but fear thou God.

8 If thou seest the oppression of the poor, and violent perverting of judgment and justice in a province, marvel not at the matter: for *he that is* higher than the highest regardeth; and *there be* higher than they.

9 Moreover the profit of the earth is for all: the king *himself* is served by the field.

10 He that loveth silver shall not be satisfied with silver; nor he that loveth abundance with increase: this *is* also vanity.

5:10 Discontentment
◄ Ecclesiastes 4:8
Ecclesiastes 6:7 ►

11 When goods increase, they are increased that eat them: and what good *is there* to the owners thereof, saving the beholding *of them* with their eyes?

5:10 Greed
◄ Proverbs 1:19
Habakkuk 2:9-10 ►

12 The sleep of a labouring man *is* sweet, whether he eat little or much: but the abundance of the rich will not suffer him to sleep.

13 There is a sore evil *which* I have seen under the sun, *namely,* riches kept for the owners thereof to their hurt.

5:13 Being Stingy
◄ Proverbs 28:27
Isaiah 43:23 ►

14 But those riches perish by evil travail: and he begetteth a son, and *there is* nothing in his hand.

15 As he came forth of his mother's womb, naked shall he return to go as he came, and shall take nothing of his labour, which he may carry away in his hand.

16 And this also *is* a sore evil, *that* in all points as he came, so shall he go: and what profit hath he that hath laboured for the wind?

17 All his days also he eateth in darkness, and *he hath* much sorrow and wrath with his sickness.

18 Behold *that* which I have seen: *it is* good and comely *for one* to eat and to drink, and to enjoy the good of all his labour that he taketh under the sun all the days of his life, which God giveth him: for it *is* his portion.

19 Every man also to whom God hath given riches and wealth, and hath given him power to eat thereof, and to take his portion, and to rejoice in his labour; this *is* the gift of God.

5:19 Source of Wealth
◄ 1 Chronicles 29:12
Hosea 2:8 ►

20 For he shall not much remember the days of his life; because God answereth *him* in the joy of his heart.

6

1 There is an evil which I have seen under the sun, and it *is* common among men:

2 A man to whom God hath given riches, wealth, and honour, so that he wanteth nothing for his soul of all that he desireth, yet God giveth him not power to eat thereof, but a stranger eateth it: this *is* vanity, and it *is* an evil disease.

6:2 Money's Limits
◄ Proverbs 11:4
Zephaniah 1:18 ►

3 If a man beget an hundred *children,* and live many years, so that the days of his years be many, and his soul be not filled with good, and also *that* he have no burial; I say, *that* an untimely birth *is* better than he.

4 For he cometh in with vanity, and departeth in darkness, and his name shall be covered with darkness.

5 Moreover he hath not seen the sun, nor known *any thing:* this hath more rest than the other.

6 Yea, though he live a thousand years twice *told,* yet hath he seen no good: do not all go to one place?

7 All the labour of man *is* for his mouth, and yet the appetite is not filled.

6:7 Discontentment
◄ Ecclesiastes 5:10
Isaiah 29:8 ►

8 For what hath the wise more than the fool? what hath the poor, that knoweth to walk before the living?

9 Better *is* the sight of the eyes than the wandering of the desire: this *is* also vanity and vexation of spirit.

10 That which hath been is named already, and it is known that it *is* man: neither may he contend with him that is mightier than he.

11 Seeing there be many things that increase vanity, what *is* man the better?

12 For who knoweth what *is* good for man in *this* life, all the days of his vain life which he spendeth as a shadow? for who can tell a man what shall be after him under the sun?

6:12 The Future
◄ Ecclesiastes 3:22
Ecclesiastes 8:7 ►

6:12 Life Is Short
◄ Psalm 102:11
Isaiah 38:12 ►

7

1 A good name *is* better than precious ointment; and the day of death than the day of one's birth.

2 *It is* better to go to the house of mourning, than to go to the house of feasting: for that *is* the end of all men; and the living will lay *it* to his heart.

3 Sorrow *is* better than laughter: for by the sadness of the countenance the heart is made better.

7:3 Laughter
◄ Ecclesiastes 2:2
Ecclesiastes 7:6 ►

4 The heart of the wise *is* in the house of mourning; but the heart of fools *is* in the house of mirth.

7:5 Taking Advice
◄ Proverbs 29:15
Hebrews 12:5 ►

5 *It is* better to hear the rebuke of the wise, than for a man to hear the song of fools.

7:6 Happiness
◄ Ecclesiastes 2:10
Isaiah 16:10 ►

6 For as the crackling of thorns under a pot, so *is* the laughter of the fool: this also *is* vanity.

7:6 Laughter
◄ Ecclesiastes 7:3
Luke 6:25 ►

7 Surely oppression maketh a wise man mad; and a gift destroyeth the heart.

8 Better *is* the end of a thing than the beginning thereof: *and* the patient in spirit *is* better than the proud in spirit.

7:8 Quitting
◄ Luke 21:19 ►

9 Be not hasty in thy spirit to be angry: for anger resteth in the bosom of fools.

10 Say not thou, What is *the cause* that the former days were better than these? for thou dost not enquire wisely concerning this.

11 Wisdom *is* good with an inheritance: and *by it there is* profit to them that see the sun.

12 For wisdom *is* a defence, *and* money *is* a defence: but the excellency of knowledge *is, that* wisdom giveth life to them that have it.

13 Consider the work of God: for who can make *that* straight, which he hath made crooked?

14 In the day of prosperity be joyful, but in the day of adversity consider: God also hath set the one over against the other, to the end that man should find nothing after him.

15 All *things* have I seen in the days of my vanity: there is a just *man* that perisheth in his righteousness, and there is a wicked *man* that prolongeth *his life* in his wickedness.

7:15 Injustice
◄ Psalm 73:14
Ecclesiastes 9:2 ►

16 Be not righteous over much; neither make thyself over wise: why shouldest thou destroy thyself?

17 Be not over much wicked, neither be thou foolish: why shouldest thou die before thy time?

18 *It is* good that thou shouldest take hold of this; yea, also from this withdraw not thine hand: for he that feareth God shall come forth of them all.

19 Wisdom strengtheneth the wise more than ten mighty *men* which are in the city.

20 For *there is* not a just man upon earth, that doeth good, and sinneth not.

7:20 Everyone Sins
◄ Proverbs 20:9
Isaiah 53:6 ►

21 Also take no heed unto all words that are spoken; lest thou hear thy servant curse thee:

22 For oftentimes also thine own heart knoweth that thou thyself likewise hast cursed others.

23 All this have I proved by wisdom: I said, I will be wise; but it *was* far from me.

24 That which is far off, and exceeding deep, who can find it out?

25 I applied mine heart to know, and to search, and to seek out wisdom, and the

reason *of things,* and to know the wickedness of folly, even of foolishness *and* madness:
26And I find more bitter than death the
woman, whose heart *is* snares and nets, *and*
her hands *as* bands: whoso pleaseth God
shall escape from her; but the sinner shall
be taken by her.
27Behold, this have I found, saith the
preacher, *counting* one by one, to find out
the account:
28Which yet my soul seeketh, but I find
not: one man among a thousand have I
found; but a woman among all those have
I not found.
29Lo, this only have I found, that God
hath made man upright; but they have
sought out many inventions.

8

1Who *is* as the wise *man?* and who
knoweth the interpretation of a thing? a
man's wisdom maketh his face to shine,
and the boldness of his face shall be
changed.
2I *counsel thee* to
keep the king's
commandment,
and *that* in regard of
the oath of God.

8:2 Obeying the Law
◄ Proverbs 24:21
Matthew 17:27 ►

3Be not hasty to
go out of his sight: stand not in an evil
thing; for he doeth whatsoever pleaseth
him.
4Where the word of a king *is, there is*
power: and who may say unto him, What
doest thou?
5Whoso keepeth the commandment
shall feel no evil thing: and a wise man's
heart discerneth
both time and judg-
ment.

8:7 The Future
◄ Ecclesiastes 6:12
Ecclesiastes 9:12 ►

6Because to every
purpose there is
time and judgment,
therefore the misery
of man *is* great
upon him.

8:7 Ignorance
◄ Psalm 73:22
Ecclesiastes 9:12 ►

7For he knoweth
not that which shall
be: for who can tell
him when it shall
be?

8:8 Death
◄ Ecclesiastes 3:19
Romans 5:12 ►

8*There is* no man
that hath power
over the spirit to re-
tain the spirit; nei-
ther *hath he* power
in the day of death:
and *there is* no dis-
charge in *that* war;
neither shall wick-
edness deliver
those that are given to it.

8:8 Sinner Beware
◄ Deuteronomy 32:32
Ecclesiastes 12:14 ►

9All this have I seen, and applied my
heart unto every work that is done under
the sun: *there is* a time wherein one man
ruleth over another to his own hurt.
10And so I saw the wicked buried, who
had come and gone from the place of the
holy, and they were forgotten in the city
where they had so done: this *is* also vanity.
11Because sen-
tence against an evil
work is not execut-
ed speedily, there-
fore the heart of the
sons of men is fully
set in them to do
evil.

8:11 Hard-hearted
◄ Proverbs 1:24
Jeremiah 7:13 ►

12Though a sin-
ner do evil an hun-
dred times, and his
days be prolonged,
yet surely I know that it shall be well with
them that fear God, which fear before him:

8:11 Source of Evil
◄ Ecclesiastes 9:3 ►

13But it shall not be well with the wicked, neither shall he prolong *his* days, *which
are* as a shadow; because he feareth not
before God.
14There is a vanity which is done upon
the earth; that there be just *men,* unto
whom it happeneth according to the work
of the wicked; again, there be wicked *men,*
to whom it happeneth according to the
work of the righteous: I said that this also
is vanity.
15Then I commended mirth, because a
man hath no better thing under the sun,
than to eat, and to drink, and to be merry:
for that shall abide with him of his labour
the days of his life, which God giveth him
under the sun.
16When I applied mine heart to know
wisdom, and to see the business that is
done upon the earth: (for also *there is that*
neither day nor night seeth sleep with his
eyes:)
17Then I beheld all the work of God, that
a man cannot find out the work that is
done under the sun: because though a man

labour to seek *it* out, yet he shall not find *it;* yea further; though a wise *man* think to know *it,* yet shall he not be able to find *it.*

9

1 For all this I considered in my heart even to declare all this, that the righteous, and the wise, and their works, *are* in the hand of God: no man knoweth either love or hatred *by* all *that is* before them.

2 All *things come* alike to all: *there is* one event to the righteous, and to the wicked; to the good and to the clean, and to the unclean; to him that sacrificeth, and to him that sacrificeth not: as *is* the good, so *is* the sinner; *and* he that sweareth, as *he* that feareth an oath.

> **9:2 Injustice**
> ◄ Ecclesiastes 7:15
> Jeremiah 12:1 ►

3 This *is* an evil among all *things* that are done under the sun, that *there is* one event unto all: yea, also the heart of the sons of men is full of evil, and madness *is* in their heart while they live, and after that *they go* to the dead.

> **9:3 Blinded by Sin**
> ◄ Daniel 4:33-34 ►

> **9:3 Source of Evil**
> ◄ Ecclesiastes 8:11
> Jeremiah 17:9 ►

4 For to him that is joined to all the living there is hope: for a living dog is better than a dead lion.

5 For the living know that they shall die: but the dead know not any thing, neither have they any more a reward; for the memory of them is forgotten.

6 Also their love, and their hatred, and their envy, is now perished; neither have they any more a portion for ever in any *thing* that is done under the sun.

7 Go thy way, eat thy bread with joy, and drink thy wine with a merry heart; for God now accepteth thy works.

8 Let thy garments be always white; and let thy head lack no ointment.

9 Live joyfully with the wife whom thou lovest all the days of the life of thy vanity, which he hath given thee under the sun, all the days of thy vanity: for that *is* thy portion in *this* life, and in thy labour which thou takest under the sun.

10 Whatsoever thy hand findeth to do, do *it* with thy might; for *there is* no work, nor device, nor knowledge, nor wisdom, in the grave, whither thou goest.

> **9:10 Working Hard**
> ◄ Proverbs 14:23
> Ephesians 4:28 ►

11 I returned, and saw under the sun, that the race *is* not to the swift, nor the battle to the strong, neither yet bread to the wise, nor yet riches to men of understanding, nor yet favour to men of skill; but time and chance happeneth to them all.

12 For man also knoweth not his time: as the fishes that are taken in an evil net, and as the birds that are caught in the snare; so *are* the sons of men snared in an evil time, when it falleth suddenly upon them.

> **9:12 The Future**
> ◄ Ecclesiastes 8:7
> Ecclesiastes 10:14 ►

> **9:12 Ignorance**
> ◄ Ecclesiastes 8:7
> Ecclesiastes 11:5 ►

13 This wisdom have I seen also under the sun, and it *seemed* great unto me:

14 *There was* a little city, and few men within it; and there came a great king against it, and besieged it, and built great bulwarks against it:

15 Now there was found in it a poor wise man, and he by his wisdom delivered the city; yet no man remembered that same poor man.

> **9:15 Unthankfulness to People**
> ◄ Psalm 35:12
> Jeremiah 18:20 ►

16 Then said I, Wisdom *is* better than strength: nevertheless the poor man's wisdom *is* despised, and his words are not heard.

17 The words of wise *men are* heard in quiet more than the cry of him that ruleth among fools.

> **9:17 Wise Words**
> ◄ Proverbs 25:11
> Ecclesiastes 10:12 ►

18 Wisdom *is* better than weapons of war: but one sinner destroyeth much good.

10

1 Dead flies cause the ointment of the apothecary to send forth a stinking savour: *so doth* a little folly him that is in reputation for wisdom *and* honour.

2 A wise man's heart *is* at his right hand; but a fool's heart at his left.

3 Yea also, when he that is a fool walketh

by the way, his wisdom faileth *him,* and
he saith to every one *that* he *is* a fool.
4If the spirit of
the ruler rise up
against thee, leave
not thy place; for
yielding pacifieth
great offences.

10:4
Peace
◄ Romans 12:18 ►

5There is an evil *which* I have seen under the sun, as an error *which* proceedeth
from the ruler:
6Folly is set in great dignity, and the rich
sit in low place.
7I have seen servants upon horses, and
princes walking as servants upon the earth.
8He that diggeth a pit shall fall into it;
and whoso breaketh an hedge, a serpent
shall bite him.
9Whoso removeth stones shall be hurt
therewith; *and* he that cleaveth wood shall
be endangered thereby.
10If the iron be blunt, and he do not
whet the edge, then must he put to more
strength: but wisdom *is* profitable to direct.
11Surely the serpent will bite without
enchantment; and a babbler is no better.
12The words of a
wise man's mouth
are gracious; but the
lips of a fool will
swallow up him-
self.

10:12 Wise Words
◄ Ecclesiastes 9:17
Ecclesiastes 12:11 ►

13The beginning
of the words of his
mouth *is* foolish-
ness: and the end of
his talk *is* mischie-
vous madness.

10:13 Idle Talk
◄ Ecclesiastes 5:3
Ezekiel 36:3 ►

14A fool also is
full of words: a man
cannot tell what
shall be; and what
shall be after him,
who can tell him?

10:14 The Future
◄ Ecclesiastes 9:12
Ecclesiastes 11:2 ►

15The labour of the foolish wearieth
every one of them, because he knoweth not
how to go to the city.
16Woe to thee, O land, when thy king *is*
a child, and thy
princes eat in the
morning!
17Blessed *art*
thou, O land, when
thy king *is* the son
of nobles, and thy princes eat in due season, for strength, and not for drunkenness!

10:17 Getting Drunk
◄ Proverbs 23:29-31
Isaiah 5:11 ►

18By much sloth-
fulness the build-
ing decayeth; and
through idleness of
the hands the house
droppeth through.

10:18 Laziness
◄ Proverbs 24:30-31
2 Thessalonians 3:11 ►

19A feast is made
for laughter, and
wine maketh merry:
but money answer-
eth all *things.*

10:20
Cursing
◄ Luke 6:28 ►

20Curse not the
king, no not in thy
thought; and curse
not the rich in thy
bedchamber: for a
bird of the air shall
carry the voice, and
that which hath
wings shall tell the
matter.

10:20 Rulers
◄ 1 Samuel 24:6
Acts 23:5 ►

11

1Cast thy bread
upon the waters:
for thou shalt find
it after many days.

11:1 Giving
◄ Proverbs 25:21
Isaiah 58:7 ►

2Give a portion
to seven, and also
to eight; for thou
knowest not what
evil shall be upon
the earth.

11:1 Promises to Givers
◄ Proverbs 28:27
Isaiah 58:10 ►

3If the clouds be
full of rain, they
empty *themselves*
upon the earth: and
if the tree fall to-
ward the south, or
toward the north, in the place where the
tree falleth, there it shall be.

11:2 The Future
◄ Ecclesiastes 10:14
Matthew 24:43 ►

4He that observeth the wind shall not
sow; and he that regardeth the clouds shall
not reap.
5As thou know-
est not what *is* the
way of the spirit,
nor how the bones
do grow in the
womb of her that is
with child: even so thou knowest not the
works of God who maketh all.

11:5 Ignorance
◄ Ecclesiastes 9:12
John 3:8 ►

6In the morning sow thy seed, and in
the evening withhold not thine hand: for
thou knowest not whether shall prosper,

either this or that, or whether they both *shall be* alike good.

7 Truly the light *is* sweet, and a pleasant *thing it is* for the eyes to behold the sun:

8 But if a man live many years, *and* rejoice in them all; yet let him remember the days of darkness; for they shall be many. All that cometh *is* vanity.

9 Rejoice, O young man, in thy youth; and let thy heart cheer thee in the days of thy youth, and walk in the ways of thine heart, and in the sight of thine eyes: but know thou, that for all these *things* God will bring thee into judgment.

> **11:9 For Kids Only**
> ◄ Proverbs 20:29
> Lamentations 3:27 ►

> **11:9 Results of Sin**
> ◄ Psalm 25:7
> Jeremiah 3:25 ►

10 Therefore remove sorrow from thy heart, and put away evil from thy flesh: for childhood and youth *are* vanity.

12

1 Remember now thy Creator in the days of thy youth, while the evil days come not, nor the years draw nigh, when thou shalt say, I have no pleasure in them;

> **12:1 Remember...**
> ◄ Psalm 63:6
> Jonah 2:7 ►

> **12:1 Time**
> ◄ Psalm 90:12
> 1 Corinthians 7:29-31 ►

2 While the sun, or the light, or the moon, or the stars, be not darkened, nor the clouds return after the rain:

3 In the day when the keepers of the house shall tremble, and the strong men shall bow themselves, and the grinders cease because they are few, and those that look out of the windows be darkened,

4 And the doors shall be shut in the streets, when the sound of the grinding is low, and he shall rise up at the voice of the bird, and all the daughters of musick shall be brought low;

5 Also *when* they shall be afraid of *that which is* high, and fears *shall be* in the way, and the almond tree shall flourish, and the grasshopper shall be a burden, and desire shall fail: because man goeth to his long home, and the mourners go about the streets:

6 Or ever the silver cord be loosed, or the golden bowl be broken, or the pitcher be broken at the fountain, or the wheel broken at the cistern.

7 Then shall the dust return to the earth as it was: and the spirit shall return unto God who gave it.

8 Vanity of vanities, saith the preacher; all *is* vanity.

9 And moreover, because the preacher was wise, he still taught the people knowledge; yea, he gave good heed, and sought out, *and* set in order many proverbs.

10 The preacher sought to find out acceptable words: and *that which was* written *was* upright, *even* words of truth.

11 The words of the wise *are* as goads, and as nails fastened *by* the masters of assemblies, *which* are given from one shepherd.

> **12:11 Parents**
> ◄ Proverbs 12:1 ►

> **12:11 Wise Words**
> ◄ Ecclesiastes 10:12
> Isaiah 50:4 ►

12 And further, by these, my son, be admonished: of making many books *there is* no end; and much study *is* a weariness of the flesh.

13 Let us hear the conclusion of the whole matter: Fear God, and keep his commandments: for this *is* the whole *duty* of man.

> **12:13 Fearing God**
> ◄ Proverbs 3:7
> Isaiah 8:13 ►

> **12:13 Religious People**
> ◄ Deuteronomy 10:12
> Hosea 6:6 ►

14 For God shall bring every work into judgment, with every secret thing, whether *it be* good, or whether *it be* evil.

> **12:14 Sinner Beware**
> ◄ Ecclesiastes 8:8
> Matthew 25:31-33 ►

Song of Solomon

AUTHOR
Solomon

MAIN POINT
Marriage is good, and husbands and wives should love each other.

DATE WRITTEN
Probably early in Solomon's reign, which began in 970 B.C.

8 CHAPTERS
☐☐☐☐☐☐☐☐

MAIN PEOPLE

Solomon, his wife (a Shulamite woman), young women of Jerusalem

SPECIAL FEATURES

✖ *Includes the Bible's most direct statements about sex*

✖ *Provides a picture of God's love for his people*

✖ *Celebrates marriage*

✖ *Praises the power of love*

✖ *Fifth book of Poetry*

HOW THE BOOK GOT ITS NAME

The book is a wedding love song; it is sometimes called the Song of Solomon because Solomon wrote it.

1
1The song of songs, which *is* Solomon's.
2Let him kiss me with the kisses of his
mouth: for thy love *is* better than wine.
3Because of the savour of thy good ointments thy name *is as* ointment poured
forth, therefore do the virgins love thee.
4Draw me, we will run after thee: the
king hath brought me into his chambers:
we will be glad and rejoice in thee, we will
remember thy love more than wine: the
upright love thee.
5I *am* black, but comely, O ye daughters
of Jerusalem, as the tents of Kedar, as the
curtains of Solomon.
6Look not upon me, because I *am* black,
because the sun hath looked upon me: my
mother's children were angry with me; they
made me the keeper of the vineyards; *but*
mine own vineyard have I not kept.
7Tell me, O thou whom my soul loveth,
where thou feedest, where thou makest *thy*
flock to rest at noon: for why should I be
as one that turneth aside by the flocks of
thy companions?
8If thou know not, O thou fairest among
women, go thy way forth by the footsteps
of the flock, and feed thy kids beside the
shepherds' tents.
9I have compared thee, O my love, to a
company of horses in Pharaoh's chariots.
10Thy cheeks are comely with rows *of*
jewels, thy neck with chains *of gold*.
11We will make thee borders of gold with
studs of silver.

12 While the king *sitteth* at his table, my spikenard sendeth forth the smell thereof.

13 A bundle of myrrh *is* my wellbeloved unto me; he shall lie all night betwixt my breasts.

14 My beloved *is* unto me *as* a cluster of camphire in the vineyards of En-gedi.

15 Behold, thou *art* fair, my love; behold, thou *art* fair; thou *hast* doves' eyes.

16 Behold, thou *art* fair, my beloved, yea, pleasant: also our bed *is* green.

17 The beams of our house *are* cedar, *and* our rafters of fir.

2

1 I *am* the rose of Sharon, *and* the lily of the valleys.

2 As the lily among thorns, so *is* my love among the daughters.

3 As the apple tree among the trees of the wood, so *is* my beloved among the sons. I sat down under his shadow with great delight, and his fruit *was* sweet to my taste.

4 He brought me to the banqueting house, and his banner over me *was* love.

5 Stay me with flagons, comfort me with apples: for I *am* sick of love.

6 His left hand *is* under my head, and his right hand doth embrace me.

7 I charge you, O ye daughters of Jerusalem, by the roes, and by the hinds of the field, that ye stir not up, nor awake *my* love, till he please.

8 The voice of my beloved! behold, he cometh leaping upon the mountains, skipping upon the hills.

9 My beloved is like a roe or a young hart: behold, he standeth behind our wall, he looketh forth at the windows, shewing himself through the lattice.

10 My beloved spake, and said unto me, Rise up, my love, my fair one, and come away.

11 For, lo, the winter is past, the rain is over *and* gone;

12 The flowers appear on the earth; the time of the singing *of birds* is come, and the voice of the turtle is heard in our land;

13 The fig tree putteth forth her green figs, and the vines *with* the tender grape give a *good* smell. Arise, my love, my fair one, and come away.

14 O my dove, *that art* in the clefts of the rock, in the secret *places* of the stairs, let me see thy countenance, let me hear thy voice; for sweet *is* thy voice, and thy countenance *is* comely.

15 Take us the foxes, the little foxes, that spoil the vines: for our vines *have* tender grapes.

16 My beloved *is* mine, and I *am* his: he feedeth among the lilies.

17 Until the day break, and the shadows flee away, turn, my beloved, and be thou like a roe or a young hart upon the mountains of Bether.

3

1 By night on my bed I sought him whom my soul loveth: I sought him, but I found him not.

2 I will rise now, and go about the city in the streets, and in the broad ways I will seek him whom my soul loveth: I sought him, but I found him not.

3 The watchmen that go about the city found me: *to whom I said,* Saw ye him whom my soul loveth?

4 *It was* but a little that I passed from them, but I found him whom my soul loveth: I held him, and would not let him go, until I had brought him into my mother's house, and into the chamber of her that conceived me.

5 I charge you, O ye daughters of Jerusalem, by the roes, and by the hinds of the field, that ye stir not up, nor awake *my* love, till he please.

6 Who *is* this that cometh out of the wilderness like pillars of smoke, perfumed with myrrh and frankincense, with all powders of the merchant?

7 Behold his bed, which *is* Solomon's; threescore valiant men *are* about it, of the valiant of Israel.

8 They all hold swords, *being* expert in war: every man *hath* his sword upon his thigh because of fear in the night.

9 King Solomon made himself a chariot of the wood of Lebanon.

10 He made the pillars thereof *of* silver, the bottom thereof *of* gold, the covering of it *of* purple, the midst thereof being paved *with* love, for the daughters of Jerusalem.

11 Go forth, O ye daughters of Zion, and behold king Solomon with the crown wherewith his mother crowned him in the day of his espousals, and in the day of the gladness of his heart.

4

1 Behold, thou *art* fair, my love; behold, thou *art* fair; thou *hast* doves' eyes within thy locks: thy hair *is* as a flock of goats, that appear from mount Gilead.

2Thy teeth *are* like a flock *of sheep that*
are even shorn, which came up from the
washing; whereof every one bear twins,
and none *is* barren among them.
3Thy lips *are* like a thread of scarlet, and
thy speech *is* comely: thy temples *are*
like a piece of a pomegranate within thy
locks.
4Thy neck *is* like the tower of David
builded for an armoury, whereon there
hang a thousand bucklers, all shields of
mighty men.
5Thy two breasts *are* like two young roes
that are twins, which feed among the
lilies.
6Until the day break, and the shadows
flee away, I will get me to the mountain of
myrrh, and to the hill of frankincense.
7Thou *art* all fair, my love; *there is* no
spot in thee.
8Come with me from Lebanon, *my*
spouse, with me from Lebanon: look from
the top of Amana, from the top of Shenir
and Hermon, from the lions' dens, from
the mountains of the leopards.
9Thou hast ravished my heart, my sister, *my* spouse; thou hast ravished my heart
with one of thine eyes, with one chain of
thy neck.
10How fair is thy love, my sister, *my*
spouse! how much better is thy love than
wine! and the smell of thine ointments
than all spices!
11Thy lips, O *my* spouse, drop *as* the honeycomb: honey and milk *are* under thy
tongue; and the smell of thy garments *is*
like the smell of Lebanon.
12A garden inclosed *is* my sister, *my*
spouse; a spring shut up, a fountain sealed.
13Thy plants *are* an orchard of pomegranates, with pleasant fruits; camphire,
with spikenard,
14Spikenard and saffron; calamus and
cinnamon, with all trees of frankincense;
myrrh and aloes, with all the chief spices:
15A fountain of gardens, a well of living
waters, and streams from Lebanon.
16Awake, O north wind; and come, thou
south; blow upon my garden, *that* the
spices thereof may flow out. Let my beloved come into his garden, and eat his
pleasant fruits.

5

1I am come into my garden, my sister,
my spouse: I have gathered my myrrh with
my spice; I have eaten my honeycomb with
my honey; I have drunk my wine with my
milk: eat, O friends; drink, yea, drink abundantly, O beloved.
2I sleep, but my heart waketh: *it is* the
voice of my beloved that knocketh, *saying,*
Open to me, my sister, my love, my dove,
my undefiled: for my head is filled with
dew, *and* my locks with the drops of the
night.
3I have put off my coat; how shall I put
it on? I have washed my feet; how shall I
defile them?
4My beloved put in his hand by the hole
of the door, and my bowels were moved
for him.
5I rose up to open to my beloved; and
my hands dropped *with* myrrh, and my fingers *with* sweet smelling myrrh, upon the
handles of the lock.
6I opened to my beloved; but my beloved had withdrawn himself, *and* was
gone: my soul failed when he spake: I
sought him, but I could not find him;
I called him, but he gave me no answer.
7The watchmen that went about the city
found me, they smote me, they wounded
me; the keepers of the walls took away my
veil from me.
8I charge you, O daughters of Jerusalem,
if ye find my beloved, that ye tell him, that
I *am* sick of love.
9What *is* thy beloved more than *another*
beloved, O thou fairest among women?
what *is* thy beloved more than *another* beloved, that thou dost so charge us?
10My beloved *is* white and ruddy, the
chiefest among ten thousand.
11His head *is as* the most fine gold, his
locks *are* bushy, *and* black as a raven.
12His eyes *are* as *the eyes* of doves by the
rivers of waters, washed with milk, *and*
fitly set.
13His cheeks *are* as a bed of spices, *as*
sweet flowers: his lips *like* lilies, dropping
sweet smelling myrrh.
14His hands *are as* gold rings set with
the beryl: his belly *is as* bright ivory overlaid *with* sapphires.
15His legs *are as* pillars of marble, set
upon sockets of fine gold: his countenance
is as Lebanon, excellent as the cedars.
16His mouth *is* most sweet: yea, he *is*
altogether lovely. This *is* my beloved, and
this *is* my friend, O daughters of Jerusalem.

6

1 Whither is thy beloved gone, O thou fairest among women? whither is thy beloved turned aside? that we may seek him with thee.

2 My beloved is gone down into his garden, to the beds of spices, to feed in the gardens, and to gather lilies.

3 I *am* my beloved's, and my beloved *is* mine: he feedeth among the lilies.

4 Thou *art* beautiful, O my love, as Tirzah, comely as Jerusalem, terrible as *an army* with banners.

5 Turn away thine eyes from me, for they have overcome me: thy hair *is* as a flock of goats that appear from Gilead.

6 Thy teeth *are* as a flock of sheep which go up from the washing, whereof every one beareth twins, and *there is* not one barren among them.

7 As a piece of a pomegranate *are* thy temples within thy locks.

8 There are threescore queens, and fourscore concubines, and virgins without number.

9 My dove, my undefiled is *but* one; she *is* the *only* one of her mother, she *is* the choice *one* of her that bare her. The daughters saw her, and blessed her; *yea*, the queens and the concubines, and they praised her.

10 Who *is* she *that* looketh forth as the morning, fair as the moon, clear as the sun, *and* terrible as *an army* with banners?

11 I went down into the garden of nuts to see the fruits of the valley, *and* to see whether the vine flourished, *and* the pomegranates budded.

12 Or ever I was aware, my soul made me *like* the chariots of Amminadib.

13 Return, return, O Shulamite; return, return, that we may look upon thee. What will ye see in the Shulamite? As it were the company of two armies.

7

1 How beautiful are thy feet with shoes, O prince's daughter! the joints of thy thighs *are* like jewels, the work of the hands of a cunning workman.

2 Thy navel *is like* a round goblet, *which* wanteth not liquor: thy belly *is like* an heap of wheat set about with lilies.

3 Thy two breasts *are* like two young roes *that are* twins.

4 Thy neck *is* as a tower of ivory; thine eyes *like* the fishpools in Heshbon, by the gate of Bath-rabbim: thy nose *is* as the tower of Lebanon which looketh toward Damascus.

5 Thine head upon thee *is* like Carmel, and the hair of thine head like purple; the king *is* held in the galleries.

6 How fair and how pleasant art thou, O love, for delights!

7 This thy stature is like to a palm tree, and thy breasts to clusters *of grapes*.

8 I said, I will go up to the palm tree, I will take hold of the boughs thereof: now also thy breasts shall be as clusters of the vine, and the smell of thy nose like apples;

9 And the roof of thy mouth like the best wine for my beloved, that goeth *down* sweetly, causing the lips of those that are asleep to speak.

10 I *am* my beloved's, and his desire *is* toward me.

11 Come, my beloved, let us go forth into the field; let us lodge in the villages.

12 Let us get up early to the vineyards; let us see if the vine flourish, *whether* the tender grape appear, *and* the pomegranates bud forth: there will I give thee my loves.

13 The mandrakes give a smell, and at our gates *are* all manner of pleasant *fruits*, new and old, *which* I have laid up for thee, O my beloved.

8

1 O that thou *wert* as my brother, that sucked the breasts of my mother! *when* I should find thee without, I would kiss thee; yea, I should not be despised.

2 I would lead thee, *and* bring thee into my mother's house, *who* would instruct me: I would cause thee to drink of spiced wine of the juice of my pomegranate.

3 His left hand *should be* under my head, and his right hand should embrace me.

4 I charge you, O daughters of Jerusalem, that ye stir not up, nor awake *my* love, until he please.

5 Who *is* this that cometh up from the wilderness, leaning upon her beloved? I raised thee up under the apple tree: there thy mother brought thee forth: there she brought thee forth *that* bare thee.

6 Set me as a seal upon thine heart, as a seal upon thine arm: for love *is* strong as death; jealousy *is* cruel as the grave: the coals thereof *are* coals of fire, *which hath* a most vehement flame.

7 Many waters cannot quench love, nei-

ther can the floods drown it: if *a* man
would give all the substance of his house
for love, it would utterly be contemned.
8We have a little sister, and she hath no
breasts: what shall we do for our sister in
the day when she shall be spoken for?
9If she *be* a wall, we will build upon her
a palace of silver: and if she *be* a door, we
will inclose her with boards of cedar.
10I *am* a wall, and my breasts like towers: then was I in his eyes as one that found
favour.
11Solomon had a vineyard at Baal-
hamon; he let out the vineyard unto keepers; every one for the fruit thereof was to
bring a thousand *pieces* of silver.
12My vineyard, which *is* mine, *is* before
me: thou, O Solomon, *must have* a thousand, and those that keep the fruit thereof
two hundred.
13Thou that dwellest in the gardens, the
companions hearken to thy voice: cause
me to hear *it*.
14Make haste, my beloved, and be thou
like to a roe or to a young hart upon the
mountains of spices.

Isaiah

AUTHOR
Isaiah the prophet

MAIN POINT
Judah must repent and get ready for the Messiah whom God is sending to save them.

DATE WRITTEN
Chapters 1-39, approximately 700 B.C.; chapters 40-66, approximately 681 B.C., near the end of Isaiah's life

66 CHAPTERS

MAIN PEOPLE

Isaiah and his two sons Shear-Jashub and Maher-Shalal-Hash-Baz

SPECIAL FEATURES

- *Has some chapters on judgment and some on hope*
- *Includes one of the most vivid scenes in the Bible, featuring six-winged creatures (chapter 6)*
- *Has some famous prophecies about the coming Messiah, Jesus (chapters 9, 11, 53)*
- *Predicts some events that happened in Isaiah's lifetime and some that have not happened yet*
- *First book of the Major Prophets*

HOW THE BOOK GOT ITS NAME

The author and main person of the book is Isaiah, often considered the greatest prophet.

1
1The vision of Isaiah the son of Amoz,
which he saw concerning Judah and Jerusalem in the days of Uzziah, Jotham, Ahaz,
and Hezekiah, kings of Judah.
2Hear, O heavens, and give ear, O earth:
for the LORD hath spoken, I have nourished
and brought up children, and they have
rebelled against me.
3The ox knoweth his owner, and the ass
his master's crib: *but* Israel doth not know,
my people doth not consider.
4Ah sinful nation, a people laden with
iniquity, a seed of evildoers, children that
are corrupters: they have forsaken the
LORD, they have provoked the Holy One
of Israel unto anger, they are gone away
backward.
5Why should ye be stricken any more?
ye will revolt more
and more: the whole
head is sick, and the
whole heart faint.
6From the sole of
the foot even unto

1:5
Refusing Correction
◄ Isaiah 9:13 ►

the head *there is*
no soundness in it;
but wounds, and
bruises, and putri-
fying sores: they
have not been
closed, neither bound up, neither molli-
fied with ointment.

1:6 Sin Hurts
◄ Proverbs 23:29
Jeremiah 30:12 ►

7 Your country *is* desolate, your cities *are*
burned with fire: your land, strangers devour it in your presence, and *it is* desolate,
as overthrown by strangers.
8 And the daughter of Zion is left as a
cottage in a vineyard, as a lodge in a garden of cucumbers, as a besieged city.
9 Except the LORD of hosts had left unto
us a very small remnant, we should have
been as Sodom, *and* we should have been
like unto Gomorrah.
10 Hear the word of the LORD, ye rulers
of Sodom; give ear unto the law of our
God, ye people of Gomorrah.
11 To what purpose *is* the multitude of
your sacrifices unto me? saith the LORD: I
am full of the burnt offerings of rams, and
the fat of fed beasts; and I delight not in
the blood of bullocks, or of lambs, or of
he goats.
12 When ye come to appear before me,
who hath required this at your hand, to
tread my courts?
13 Bring no more vain oblations; incense
is an abomination unto me; the new
moons and sabbaths, the calling of assemblies, I cannot away with; *it is* iniquity, even
the solemn meeting.
14 Your new moons and your appointed
feasts my soul hateth: they are a trouble
unto me; I am weary to bear *them*.
15 And when ye
spread forth your
hands, I will hide
mine eyes from
you: yea, when ye
make many prayers,
I will not hear: your hands are full of
blood.

1:15 Unanswered Prayer
◄ Proverbs 28:9
Isaiah 59:2 ►

16 Wash you,
make you clean;
put away the evil of
your doings from
before mine eyes;
cease to do evil;

1:16-17 Lessons of Life
◄ Psalm 119:71
Matthew 11:29 ►

17 Learn to do well; seek judgment, relieve the oppressed, judge the fatherless,
plead for the
widow.

1:17 Kind to the Needy
◄ Proverbs 23:10
Jeremiah 22:3 ►

18 Come now,
and let us reason
together, saith the
LORD: though your
sins be as scarlet, they shall be as white as
snow; though they be red like crimson,
they shall be as wool.
19 If ye be willing
and obedient, ye
shall eat the good
of the land:
20 But if ye refuse
and rebel, ye shall
be devoured with the sword: for the mouth
of the LORD hath spoken *it*.

1:19 Willingness to Work
◄ Psalm 110:3
2 Corinthians 8:3 ►

21 How is the faithful city become an
harlot! it was full of judgment; righteousness lodged in it; but now murderers.
22 Thy silver is become dross, thy wine
mixed with water:
23 Thy princes
are rebellious, and
companions of
thieves: every one
loveth gifts, and
followeth after re-
wards: they judge not the fatherless, neither doth the cause of the widow come
unto them.

1:23 Bribery
◄ Proverbs 17:23
Isaiah 5:23 ►

24 Therefore saith the Lord, the LORD of
hosts, the mighty One of Israel, Ah, I will
ease me of mine adversaries, and avenge
me of mine enemies:
25 And I will turn my hand upon thee,
and purely purge away thy dross, and take
away all thy tin:
26 And I will restore thy judges as at the
first, and thy counsellors as at the beginning: afterward thou shalt be called, The
city of righteousness, the faithful city.
27 Zion shall be redeemed with judgment, and her converts with righteousness.
28 And the destruction of the transgressors and of the sinners *shall be* together,
and they that forsake the LORD shall be
consumed.
29 For they shall be ashamed of the oaks
which ye have desired, and ye shall be confounded for the gardens that ye have chosen.
30 For ye shall be as an oak whose leaf
fadeth, and as a garden that hath no
water.

31And the strong shall be as tow, and the
maker of it as a spark, and they shall both
burn together, and none shall quench *them*.

2

1The word that Isaiah the son of Amoz
saw concerning Judah and Jerusalem.
2And it shall come to pass in the last
days, *that* the mountain of the LORD'S
house shall be established in the top
of the mountains, and shall be exalted
above the hills; and all nations shall flow
unto it.
3And many peo-
ple shall go and say,
Come ye, and let us
go up to the moun-
tain of the LORD, to
the house of the
God of Jacob; and
he will teach us of
his ways, and we
will walk in his
paths: for out of
Zion shall go forth
the law, and the
word of the LORD
from Jerusalem.
4And he shall
judge among the
nations, and shall
rebuke many people: and they shall beat
their swords into plowshares, and their
spears into pruninghooks: nation shall not
lift up sword against nation, neither shall
they learn war any more.

2:3 Friends and Church
◄ 2 Chronicles 30:1
Jeremiah 31:6 ►

2:3 God as Teacher
◄ Psalm 94:10
Isaiah 28:26 ►

2:3 Right Paths
◄ Proverbs 4:18
Isaiah 26:7 ►

5O house of Jacob, come ye, and let us
walk in the light of the LORD.
6Therefore thou hast forsaken thy people the house of Jacob, because they be
replenished from the east, and *are* soothsayers like the Philistines, and they please
themselves in the children of strangers.
7Their land also is full of silver and gold,
neither *is there any* end of their treasures;
their land is also full of horses, neither *is*
there any end of their chariots:
8Their land also is full of idols; they
worship the work of their own hands, that
which their own fingers have made:
9And the mean man boweth down, and
the great man humbleth himself: therefore
forgive them not.
10Enter into the rock, and hide thee in
the dust, for fear of the LORD, and for the
glory of his majesty.
11The lofty looks of man shall be humbled, and the haughtiness of men shall be
bowed down, and the LORD alone shall be
exalted in that day.
12For the day of the LORD of hosts *shall*
be upon every *one that is* proud and lofty,
and upon every *one that is* lifted up; and
he shall be brought low:
13And upon all the cedars of Lebanon,
that are high and lifted up, and upon all
the oaks of Bashan,
14And upon all the high mountains, and
upon all the hills *that are* lifted up,
15And upon every high tower, and upon
every fenced wall,
16And upon all the ships of Tarshish,
and upon all pleasant pictures.
17And the loftiness of man shall be
bowed down, and the haughtiness of men
shall be made low: and the LORD alone
shall be exalted in that day.
18And the idols he shall utterly abolish.
19And they shall
go into the holes of
the rocks, and into
the caves of the
earth, for fear of
the LORD, and for
the glory of his majesty, when he ariseth
to shake terribly the earth.

2:19 Guilty Fear
◄ Proverbs 28:1
Isaiah 24:17 ►

20In that day a man shall cast his idols
of silver, and his idols of gold, which they
made *each one* for himself to worship, to
the moles and to the bats;
21To go into the clefts of the rocks, and
into the tops of the ragged rocks, for fear
of the LORD, and for the glory of his majesty, when he ariseth to shake terribly the
earth.
22Cease ye from
man, whose breath
is in his nostrils: for
wherein is he to be
accounted of?

2:22 Trusting in People
◄ Psalm 146:3
Isaiah 30:2 ►

3

1For, behold, the
Lord, the LORD of
hosts, doth take
away from Jerusa-
lem and from Ju-
dah the stay and the
staff, the whole stay
of bread, and the whole stay of water,
2The mighty man, and the man of war,
the judge, and the prophet, and the prudent, and the ancient,
3The captain of fifty, and the honourable

2:22 Your Body
◄ Psalm 141:7
Isaiah 40:6 ►

man, and the counsellor, and the cunning artificer, and the eloquent orator.

4And I will give children *to be* their princes, and babes shall rule over them.

5And the people shall be oppressed, every one by another, and every one by his neighbour: the child shall behave himself proudly against the ancient, and the base against the honourable.

6When a man shall take hold of his brother of the house of his father, *saying,* Thou hast clothing, be thou our ruler, and *let* this ruin *be* under thy hand:

7In that day shall he swear, saying, I will not be an healer; for in my house *is* neither bread nor clothing: make me not a ruler of the people.

8For Jerusalem is ruined, and Judah is fallen: because their tongue and their doings *are* against the LORD, to provoke the eyes of his glory.

3:8 Losers
◄ Psalm 106:7
Ezekiel 8:3 ►

9The shew of their countenance doth witness against them; and they declare their sin as Sodom, they hide *it* not. Woe unto their soul! for they have rewarded evil unto themselves.

10Say ye to the righteous, that *it shall be* well *with him:* for they shall eat the fruit of their doings.

3:10 Rewarded Goodness
◄ Proverbs 20:7
Matthew 13:43 ►

11Woe unto the wicked! *it shall be* ill *with him:* for the reward of his hands shall be given him.

12*As for* my people, children *are* their oppressors, and women rule over them. O my people, they which lead thee cause *thee* to err, and destroy the way of thy paths.

13The LORD standeth up to plead, and standeth to judge the people.

14The LORD will enter into judgment with the ancients of his people, and the princes thereof: for ye have eaten up the vineyard; the spoil of the poor *is* in your houses.

15What mean ye *that* ye beat my people to pieces, and grind the faces of the poor? saith the LORD GOD of hosts.

16Moreover the LORD saith, Because the daughters of Zion are haughty, and walk with stretched forth necks and wanton eyes, walking and mincing *as* they go, and making a tinkling with their feet:

17Therefore the LORD will smite with a scab the crown of the head of the daughters of Zion, and the LORD will discover their secret parts.

18In that day the Lord will take away the bravery of *their* tinkling ornaments *about their feet,* and *their* cauls, and *their* round tires like the moon,

19The chains, and the bracelets, and the mufflers,

20The bonnets, and the ornaments of the legs, and the headbands, and the tablets, and the earrings,

21The rings, and nose jewels,

22The changeable suits of apparel, and the mantles, and the wimples, and the crisping pins,

23The glasses, and the fine linen, and the hoods, and the vails.

24And it shall come to pass, *that* instead of sweet smell there shall be stink; and instead of a girdle a rent; and instead of well set hair baldness; and instead of a stomacher a girding of sackcloth; *and* burning instead of beauty.

25Thy men shall fall by the sword, and thy mighty in the war.

26And her gates shall lament and mourn; and she *being* desolate shall sit upon the ground.

4

1And in that day seven women shall take hold of one man, saying, We will eat our own bread, and wear our own apparel: only let us be called by thy name, to take away our reproach.

2In that day shall the branch of the LORD be beautiful and glorious, and the fruit of the earth *shall be* excellent and comely for them that are escaped of Israel.

3And it shall come to pass, *that he that is* left in Zion, and *he that* remaineth in Jerusalem, shall be called holy, *even* every one that is written among the living in Jerusalem:

4When the Lord shall have washed away the filth of the daughters of Zion, and shall have purged the blood of Jerusalem from the midst thereof by the spirit of judgment, and by the spirit of burning.

5And the LORD will create upon every dwelling place of mount Zion, and upon her assemblies, a cloud and smoke by day, and the shining of a flaming fire by

night: for upon all the glory *shall be* a defence.
6 And there shall be a tabernacle for a
shadow in the daytime from the heat, and
for a place of refuge, and for a covert from
storm and from rain.

5

1 Now will I sing to my wellbeloved a
song of my beloved touching his vineyard.
My wellbeloved hath a vineyard in a very
fruitful hill:
2 And he fenced it, and gathered out
the stones thereof, and planted it with the
choicest vine, and built a tower in the
midst of it, and also made a winepress
therein: and he looked that it should bring
forth grapes, and it brought forth wild
grapes.
3 And now, O inhabitants of Jerusalem,
and men of Judah, judge, I pray you, betwixt me and my vineyard.
4 What could have been done more to
my vineyard, that I have not done in it?
wherefore, when I looked that it should
bring forth grapes, brought it forth wild
grapes?
5 And now go to; I will tell you what I
will do to my vineyard: I will take away
the hedge thereof, and it shall be eaten up;
and break down the wall thereof, and it
shall be trodden down:
6 And I will lay it waste: it shall not be
pruned, nor digged; but there shall come
up briers and thorns: I will also command
the clouds that they rain no rain upon it.
7 For the vineyard of the LORD of hosts *is*
the house of Israel, and the men of Judah
his pleasant plant: and he looked for judgment, but behold oppression; for righteousness, but behold a cry.
8 Woe unto them that join house to
house, *that* lay field to field, till *there be* no
place, that they may be placed alone in the
midst of the earth!
9 In mine ears *said* the LORD of hosts, Of
a truth many houses shall be desolate, *even*
great and fair, without inhabitant.
10 Yea, ten acres of vineyard shall yield
one bath, and the seed of an homer shall
yield an ephah.
11 Woe unto them
that rise up early in
the morning, *that*
they may follow
strong drink; that
continue until
night, *till* wine in-
flame them!

5:11 Drinking Too Much
◄ Proverbs 31:4
Isaiah 28:1 ►

5:11 Getting Drunk
◄ Ecclesiastes 10:17
Isaiah 28:1 ►

12 And the harp,
and the viol, the
tabret, and pipe,
and wine, are in
their feasts: but they regard not the work
of the LORD, neither consider the operation of his hands.
13 Therefore my people are gone into
captivity, because *they have* no knowledge:
and their honourable men *are* famished,
and their multitude dried up with thirst.
14 Therefore hell hath enlarged herself,
and opened her mouth without measure:
and their glory, and their multitude, and
their pomp, and he that rejoiceth, shall
descend into it.
15 And the mean man shall be brought
down, and the mighty man shall be humbled, and the eyes of the lofty shall be
humbled:
16 But the LORD of hosts shall be exalted
in judgment, and God that is holy shall
be sanctified in righteousness.
17 Then shall the lambs feed after their
manner, and the waste places of the fat
ones shall strangers eat.
18 Woe unto them that draw iniquity
with cords of vanity, and sin as it were with
a cart rope:
19 That say, Let him make speed, *and* hasten his work, that we may see *it*: and let
the counsel of the Holy One of Israel draw
nigh and come, that we may know *it!*
20 Woe unto
them that call evil
good, and good
evil; that put dark-
ness for light, and
light for darkness;
that put bitter for sweet, and sweet for
bitter!

5:20 Excusing Sin
◄ Proverbs 28:4
Ezekiel 13:22 ►

21 Woe unto *them*
that are wise in their
own eyes, and pru-
dent in their own
sight!

5:21 Conceit
◄ Proverbs 26:12
Romans 12:16 ►

22 Woe unto *them*
that are mighty to
drink wine, and
men of strength
to mingle strong
drink:
23 Which justify

5:23 Bribery
◄ Isaiah 1:23
Isaiah 33:15 ►

the wicked for reward, and take away the righteousness of the righteous from him!

24 Therefore as the fire devoureth the stubble, and the flame consumeth the chaff, *so* their root shall be as rottenness, and their blossom shall go up as dust: because they have cast away the law of the LORD of hosts, and despised the word of the Holy One of Israel.

25 Therefore is the anger of the LORD kindled against his people, and he hath stretched forth his hand against them, and hath smitten them: and the hills did tremble, and their carcases *were* torn in the midst of the streets. For all this his anger is not turned away, but his hand *is* stretched out still.

26 And he will lift up an ensign to the nations from far, and will hiss unto them from the end of the earth: and, behold, they shall come with speed swiftly:

27 None shall be weary nor stumble among them; none shall slumber nor sleep; neither shall the girdle of their loins be loosed, nor the latchet of their shoes be broken:

28 Whose arrows *are* sharp, and all their bows bent, their horses' hoofs shall be counted like flint, and their wheels like a whirlwind:

29 Their roaring *shall be* like a lion, they shall roar like young lions: yea, they shall roar, and lay hold of the prey, and shall carry *it* away safe, and none shall deliver *it*.

30 And in that day they shall roar against them like the roaring of the sea: and if *one* look unto the land, behold darkness *and* sorrow, and the light is darkened in the heavens thereof.

6 1 In the year that king Uzziah died I saw also the Lord sitting upon a throne, high and lifted up, and his train filled the temple.

2 Above it stood the seraphims: each one had six wings; with twain he covered his face, and with twain he covered his feet, and with twain he did fly.

3 And one cried unto another, and said, Holy, holy, holy, *is* the LORD of hosts: the whole earth *is* full of his glory.

4 And the posts of the door moved at the voice of him that cried, and the house was filled with smoke.

5 Then said I, Woe *is* me! for I am undone; because I *am* a man of unclean lips, and I dwell in the midst of a people of unclean lips: for mine eyes have seen the King, the LORD of hosts.

6 Then flew one of the seraphims unto me, having a live coal in his hand, *which* he had taken with the tongs from off the altar:

7 And he laid *it* upon my mouth, and said, Lo, this hath touched thy lips; and thine iniquity is taken away, and thy sin purged.

8 Also I heard the voice of the Lord, saying, Whom shall I send, and who will go for us? Then said I, Here *am* I; send me.

9 And he said, Go, and tell this people, Hear ye indeed, but understand not; and see ye indeed, but perceive not.

10 Make the heart of this people fat, and make their ears heavy, and shut their eyes; lest they see with their eyes, and hear with their ears, and understand with their heart, and convert, and be healed.

11 Then said I, Lord, how long? And he answered, Until the cities be wasted without inhabitant, and the houses without man, and the land be utterly desolate,

12 And the LORD have removed men far away, and *there be* a great forsaking in the midst of the land.

13 But yet in it *shall be* a tenth, and *it* shall return, and shall be eaten: as a teil tree, and as an oak, whose substance is in them, when they cast *their leaves: so* the holy seed *shall be* the substance thereof.

7 1 And it came to pass in the days of Ahaz the son of Jotham, the son of Uzziah, king of Judah, *that* Rezin the king of Syria, and Pekah the son of Remaliah, king of Israel, went up toward Jerusalem to war against it, but could not prevail against it.

2 And it was told the house of David, saying, Syria is confederate with Ephraim. And his heart was moved, and the heart of his people, as the trees of the wood are moved with the wind.

3 Then said the LORD unto Isaiah, Go forth now to meet Ahaz, thou, and Shear-jashub thy son, at the end of the conduit of the upper pool in the highway of the fuller's field;

4 And say unto him, Take heed, and be quiet; fear not, neither be fainthearted for the two tails of these smoking firebrands, for the fierce anger of Rezin with Syria, and of the son of Remaliah.

5 Because Syria, Ephraim, and the son of
Remaliah, have taken evil counsel against
thee, saying,
6 Let us go up against Judah, and vex it,
and let us make a breach therein for us,
and set a king in the midst of it, *even* the
son of Tabeal:
7 Thus saith the Lord GOD, It shall not
stand, neither shall it come to pass.
8 For the head of Syria *is* Damascus, and
the head of Damascus *is* Rezin; and within threescore and five years shall Ephraim
be broken, that it be not a people.
9 And the head of Ephraim *is* Samaria,
and the head of Samaria *is* Remaliah's son.
If ye will not believe, surely ye shall not be
established.
10 Moreover the LORD spake again unto
Ahaz, saying,
11 Ask thee a sign of the LORD thy God;
ask it either in the depth, or in the height
above.
12 But Ahaz said, I will not ask, neither
will I tempt the LORD.
13 And he said, Hear ye now, O house of
David; *Is it* a small thing for you to weary
men, but will ye weary my God also?
14 Therefore the
Lord himself shall
give you a sign; Be-
hold, a virgin shall
conceive, and bear a
son, and shall call
his name Immanuel.

7:14
Christmas
◄ Isaiah 9:6 ►

15 Butter and honey shall he eat, that he
may know to refuse the evil, and choose
the good.
16 For before the child shall know to refuse the evil, and choose the good, the land
that thou abhorrest shall be forsaken of
both her kings.
17 The LORD shall bring upon thee, and
upon thy people, and upon thy father's
house, days that have not come, from the
day that Ephraim departed from Judah;
even the king of Assyria.
18 And it shall come to pass in that day,
that the LORD shall hiss for the fly that *is*
in the uttermost part of the rivers of
Egypt, and for the bee that *is* in the land
of Assyria.
19 And they shall come, and shall rest all
of them in the desolate valleys, and in the
holes of the rocks, and upon all thorns,
and upon all bushes.
20 In the same day shall the Lord shave
with a razor that is hired, *namely*, by them
beyond the river, by the king of Assyria,
the head, and the hair of the feet: and it
shall also consume the beard.
21 And it shall come to pass in that day,
that a man shall nourish a young cow, and
two sheep;
22 And it shall come to pass, for the
abundance of milk *that* they shall give he
shall eat butter: for butter and honey shall
every one eat that is left in the land.
23 And it shall come to pass in that day,
that every place shall be, where there were
a thousand vines at a thousand silverlings,
it shall *even* be for briers and thorns.
24 With arrows and with bows shall *men*
come thither; because all the land shall
become briers and thorns.
25 And *on* all hills that shall be digged
with the mattock, there shall not come
thither the fear of briers and thorns: but it
shall be for the sending forth of oxen, and
for the treading of lesser cattle.

8

1 Moreover the LORD said unto me, Take
thee a great roll, and write in it with a man's
pen concerning Maher-shalal-hash-baz.
2 And I took unto me faithful witnesses
to record, Uriah the priest, and Zechariah
the son of Jeberechiah.
3 And I went unto the prophetess; and
she conceived, and bare a son. Then said
the LORD to me, Call his name Maher-
shalal-hash-baz.
4 For before the child shall have knowledge to cry, My father, and my mother, the
riches of Damascus and the spoil of Samaria shall be taken away before the king
of Assyria.
5 The LORD spake also unto me again,
saying,
6 Forasmuch as this people refuseth the
waters of Shiloah that go softly, and rejoice in Rezin and Remaliah's son;
7 Now therefore, behold, the Lord
bringeth up upon them the waters of the
river, strong and many, *even* the king of
Assyria, and all his glory: and he shall
come up over all his channels, and go over
all his banks:
8 And he shall pass through Judah; he
shall overflow and go over, he shall reach
even to the neck; and the stretching out of
his wings shall fill the breadth of thy land,
O Immanuel.

9 Associate yourselves, O ye people, and ye shall be broken in pieces; and give ear, all ye of far countries: gird yourselves, and ye shall be broken in pieces; gird yourselves, and ye shall be broken in pieces.

10 Take counsel together, and it shall come to nought; speak the word, and it shall not stand: for God *is* with us.

11 For the LORD spake thus to me with a strong hand, and instructed me that I should not walk in the way of this people, saying,

12 Say ye not, A confederacy, to all *them to* whom this people shall say, A confederacy; neither fear ye their fear, nor be afraid.

13 Sanctify the LORD of hosts himself; and *let* him *be* your fear, and *let* him *be* your dread.

8:13 Fearing God
◄ Ecclesiastes 12:13
Matthew 10:28 ►

14 And he shall be for a sanctuary; but for a stone of stumbling and for a rock of offence to both the houses of Israel, for a gin and for a snare to the inhabitants of Jerusalem.

15 And many among them shall stumble, and fall, and be broken, and be snared, and be taken.

16 Bind up the testimony, seal the law among my disciples.

17 And I will wait upon the LORD, that hideth his face from the house of Jacob, and I will look for him.

8:17 Waiting for God
◄ Proverbs 20:22
Isaiah 40:31 ►

18 Behold, I and the children whom the LORD hath given me *are* for signs and for wonders in Israel from the LORD of hosts, which dwelleth in mount Zion.

19 And when they shall say unto you, Seek unto them that have familiar spirits, and unto wizards that peep, and that mutter: should not a people seek unto their God? for the living to the dead?

20 To the law and to the testimony: if they speak not according to this word, *it is* because *there is* no light in them.

21 And they shall pass through it, hardly bestead and hungry: and it shall come to pass, that when they shall be hungry, they shall fret themselves, and curse their king and their God, and look upward.

22 And they shall look unto the earth; and behold trouble and darkness, dimness of anguish; and *they shall be* driven to darkness.

9

1 Nevertheless the dimness *shall* not *be* such as *was* in her vexation, when at the first he lightly afflicted the land of Zebulun and the land of Naphtali, and afterward did more grievously afflict *her by* the way of the sea, beyond Jordan, in Galilee of the nations.

2 The people that walked in darkness have seen a great light: they that dwell in the land of the shadow of death, upon them hath the light shined.

3 Thou hast multiplied the nation, *and* not increased the joy: they joy before thee according to the joy in harvest, *and* as *men* rejoice when they divide the spoil.

4 For thou hast broken the yoke of his burden, and the staff of his shoulder, the rod of his oppressor, as in the day of Midian.

5 For every battle of the warrior *is* with confused noise, and garments rolled in blood; but *this* shall be with burning *and* fuel of fire.

6 For unto us a child is born, unto us a son is given: and the government shall be upon his shoulder: and his name shall be called Wonderful, Counsellor, The mighty God, The everlasting Father, The Prince of Peace.

9:6 Christmas
◄ Isaiah 7:14
Luke 1:31 ►

7 Of the increase of *his* government and peace *there shall be* no end, upon the throne of David, and upon his kingdom, to order it, and to establish it with judgment and with justice from henceforth even for ever. The zeal of the LORD of hosts will perform this.

9:7 Jesus the King
◄ Psalm 2:6
Isaiah 32:1 ►

8 The Lord sent a word into Jacob, and it hath lighted upon Israel.

9 And all the people shall know, *even* Ephraim and the inhabitant of Samaria, that say in the pride and stoutness of heart,

10 The bricks are fallen down, but we will build with hewn stones: the sycomores are cut down, but we will change *them into* cedars.

11 Therefore the LORD shall set up the

adversaries of Rezin against him, and join
his enemies together;
12 The Syrians before, and the Philistines
behind; and they shall devour Israel with
open mouth. For all this his anger is not
turned away, but his hand *is* stretched out
still.
13 For the people
turneth not unto
him that smiteth
them, neither do
they seek the LORD
of hosts.

> **9:13**
> **Refusing Correction**
> ◄ Isaiah 1:5
> Isaiah 42:25 ►

14 Therefore the LORD will cut off from
Israel head and tail, branch and rush, in
one day.
15 The ancient and honourable, he *is* the
head; and the prophet that teacheth lies,
he *is* the tail.
16 For the leaders of this people cause
them to err; and *they that are* led of them
are destroyed.
17 Therefore the
Lord shall have no
joy in their young
men, neither shall
have mercy on their
fatherless and wid-
ows: for every one *is* an hypocrite and an
evildoer, and every mouth speaketh folly.
For all this his anger is not turned away,
but his hand *is* stretched out still.

> **9:17 Evildoers**
> ◄ Psalm 119:115
> Isaiah 14:20 ►

18 For wickedness burneth as the fire: it
shall devour the briers and thorns, and
shall kindle in the thickets of the forest,
and they shall mount up *like* the lifting up
of smoke.
19 Through the wrath of the LORD of
hosts is the land darkened, and the people shall be as the fuel of the fire: no man
shall spare his brother.
20 And he shall snatch on the right hand,
and be hungry; and he shall eat on the left
hand, and they shall not be satisfied: they
shall eat every man the flesh of his own
arm:
21 Manasseh, Ephraim; and Ephraim,
Manasseh: *and* they together *shall be*
against Judah. For all this his anger is not
turned away, but his hand *is* stretched out
still.

10

1 Woe unto them that decree unrighteous
decrees, and that write grievousness *which*
they have prescribed;
2 To turn aside the needy from judgment,
and to take away the right from the
poor of my people, that widows may be
their prey, and *that* they may rob the fatherless!
3 And what will ye do in the day of visitation, and in the desolation *which* shall
come from far? to whom will ye flee for
help? and where will ye leave your glory?
4 Without me they shall bow down
under the prisoners, and they shall fall under the slain. For all this his anger is not
turned away, but his hand *is* stretched out
still.
5 O Assyrian, the rod of mine anger, and
the staff in their hand is mine indignation.
6 I will send him against an hypocritical
nation, and against the people of my wrath
will I give him a charge, to take the spoil,
and to take the prey, and to tread them
down like the mire of the streets.
7 Howbeit he meaneth not so, neither
doth his heart think so; but *it is* in his heart
to destroy and cut off nations not a few.
8 For he saith, *Are* not my princes altogether kings?
9 *Is* not Calno as Carchemish? *is* not Hamath as Arpad? *is* not Samaria as Damascus?
10 As my hand hath found the kingdoms
of the idols, and whose graven images did
excel them of Jerusalem and of Samaria;
11 Shall I not, as I have done unto Samaria and her idols, so do to Jerusalem
and her idols?
12 Wherefore it shall come to pass, *that*
when the Lord hath performed his whole
work upon mount Zion and on Jerusalem,
I will punish the fruit of the stout heart of
the king of Assyria, and the glory of his
high looks.
13 For he saith, By the strength of my
hand I have done *it,* and by my wisdom;
for I am prudent: and I have removed the
bounds of the people, and have robbed
their treasures, and I have put down the
inhabitants like a valiant *man:*
14 And my hand hath found as a nest the
riches of the people: and as one gathereth
eggs *that are* left, have I gathered all the
earth; and there was none that moved the
wing, or opened the mouth, or peeped.
15 Shall the axe boast itself against him
that heweth therewith? *or* shall the saw
magnify itself against him that shaketh it?
as if the rod should shake *itself* against

them that lift it up, *or* as if the staff should
lift up *itself, as if it were* no wood.
16 Therefore shall the Lord, the Lord of
hosts, send among his fat ones leanness;
and under his glory he shall kindle a burning like the burning of a fire.
17 And the light of Israel shall be for a
fire, and his Holy One for a flame: and it
shall burn and devour his thorns and his
briers in one day;
18 And shall consume the glory of his
forest, and of his fruitful field, both soul
and body: and they shall be as when a
standardbearer fainteth.
19 And the rest of the trees of his forest
shall be few, that a child may write them.
20 And it shall come to pass in that day,
that the remnant of Israel, and such as are
escaped of the house of Jacob, shall no
more again stay upon him that smote
them; but shall stay upon the LORD, the
Holy One of Israel, in truth.
21 The remnant shall return, *even* the
remnant of Jacob, unto the mighty God.
22 For though thy people Israel be as the
sand of the sea, *yet* a remnant of them shall
return: the consumption decreed shall
overflow with righteousness.
23 For the Lord GOD of hosts shall make
a consumption, even determined, in the
midst of all the land.
24 Therefore thus saith the Lord GOD of
hosts, O my people that dwellest in Zion,
be not afraid of the Assyrian: he shall smite
thee with a rod, and shall lift up his staff
against thee, after the manner of Egypt.
25 For yet a very little while, and the indignation shall cease, and mine anger in
their destruction.
26 And the LORD of hosts shall stir up a
scourge for him according to the slaughter of Midian at the rock of Oreb: and *as*
his rod *was* upon the sea, so shall he lift it
up after the manner of Egypt.
27 And it shall come to pass in that day,
that his burden shall be taken away from
off thy shoulder, and his yoke from off thy
neck, and the yoke shall be destroyed because of the anointing.
28 He is come to Aiath, he is passed to
Migron; at Michmash he hath laid up his
carriages:
29 They are gone over the passage: they
have taken up their lodging at Geba; Ramah is afraid; Gibeah of Saul is fled.
30 Lift up thy voice, O daughter of Gallim: cause it to be heard unto Laish, O poor
Anathoth.
31 Madmenah is removed; the inhabitants of Gebim gather themselves to flee.
32 As yet shall he remain at Nob that day:
he shall shake his hand *against* the mount
of the daughter of Zion, the hill of Jerusalem.
33 Behold, the Lord, the LORD of hosts,
shall lop the bough with terror: and the
high ones of stature *shall be* hewn down,
and the haughty shall be humbled.
34 And he shall cut down the thickets of
the forest with iron, and Lebanon shall fall
by a mighty one.

11

1 And there shall come forth a rod out
of the stem of Jesse, and a Branch shall
grow out of his roots:
2 And the spirit of the LORD shall rest
upon him, the spirit of wisdom and understanding, the spirit of counsel and
might, the spirit of knowledge and of the
fear of the LORD;
3 And shall make him of quick understanding in the fear of the LORD: and he
shall not judge after the sight of his eyes,
neither reprove after the hearing of his ears:
4 But with righ-
teousness shall he
judge the poor, and
reprove with equity
for the meek of the
earth: and he shall
smite the earth with
the rod of his
mouth, and with
the breath of his
lips shall he slay the
wicked.

11:4 Meekness
◄ Psalm 149:4
Isaiah 29:19 ►

11:4
Promises to the Poor
◄ Psalm 140:12
Isaiah 25:4 ►

5 And righteousness shall be the girdle
of his loins, and faithfulness the girdle of
his reins.
6 The wolf also shall dwell with the lamb,
and the leopard shall lie down with the
kid; and the calf and the young lion and
the fatling together; and a little child shall
lead them.
7 And the cow and the bear shall feed;
their young ones shall lie down together:
and the lion shall eat straw like the ox.
8 And the sucking child shall play on the
hole of the asp, and the weaned child shall
put his hand on the cockatrice' den.
9 They shall not hurt nor destroy in all

my holy mountain: for the earth shall be
full of the knowledge of the LORD, as the
waters cover the sea.
10And in that day there shall be a root
of Jesse, which shall stand for an ensign
of the people; to it shall the Gentiles seek:
and his rest shall be glorious.
11And it shall come to pass in that day,
that the Lord shall set his hand again the
second time to recover the remnant of his
people, which shall be left, from Assyria,
and from Egypt, and from Pathros, and
from Cush, and from Elam, and from Shinar, and from Hamath, and from the islands of the sea.
12And he shall set up an ensign for the
nations, and shall assemble the outcasts
of Israel, and gather together the dispersed
of Judah from the four corners of the earth.
13The envy also of Ephraim shall depart,
and the adversaries of Judah shall be cut
off: Ephraim shall not envy Judah, and
Judah shall not vex Ephraim.
14But they shall fly upon the shoulders
of the Philistines toward the west; they shall
spoil them of the east together: they shall
lay their hand upon Edom and Moab; and
the children of Ammon shall obey them.
15And the LORD shall utterly destroy the
tongue of the Egyptian sea; and with his
mighty wind shall he shake his hand over
the river, and shall smite it in the seven
streams, and make *men* go over dryshod.
16And there shall be an highway for the
remnant of his people, which shall be left,
from Assyria; like as it was to Israel in the
day that he came up out of the land of
Egypt.

12

1And in that day
thou shalt say,
O LORD, I will
praise thee: though
thou wast angry with
me, thine anger is
turned away, and thou comfortedst me.

12:1 God's Comfort
◄ Psalm 86:17
Isaiah 51:3 ►

2Behold, God *is* my salvation; I will trust,
and not be afraid: for the LORD JEHOVAH
is my strength and *my* song; he also is become my salvation.
3Therefore with
joy shall ye draw
water out of the
wells of salvation.

12:3 Joy
◄ Psalm 132:16
Isaiah 35:10 ►

4And in that day
shall ye say, Praise
the LORD, call upon
his name, declare
his doings among
the people, make
mention that his
name is exalted.

12:4 Your Testimony
◄ Psalm 107:2
Isaiah 62:6 ►

5Sing unto the LORD; for he hath done
excellent things: this *is* known in all the
earth.
6Cry out and shout, thou inhabitant of
Zion: for great *is* the Holy One of Israel in
the midst of thee.

13

1The burden of Babylon, which Isaiah
the son of Amoz did see.
2Lift ye up a banner upon the high
mountain, exalt the voice unto them,
shake the hand, that they may go into the
gates of the nobles.
3I have commanded my sanctified ones,
I have also called my mighty ones for mine
anger, *even* them that rejoice in my highness.
4The noise of a multitude in the mountains, like as of a great people; a tumultuous noise of the kingdoms of nations
gathered together: the LORD of hosts
mustereth the host of the battle.
5They come from a far country, from the
end of heaven, *even* the LORD, and the
weapons of his indignation, to destroy
the whole land.
6Howl ye; for the day of the LORD *is* at
hand; it shall come as a destruction from
the Almighty.
7Therefore shall all hands be faint, and
every man's heart shall melt:
8And they shall be afraid: pangs and
sorrows shall take hold of them; they shall
be in pain as a woman that travaileth: they
shall be amazed one at another; their faces
shall be as flames.
9Behold, the day of the LORD cometh,
cruel both with wrath and fierce anger, to
lay the land desolate: and he shall destroy
the sinners thereof out of it.
10For the stars of heaven and the con-
stellations thereof shall not give their light:
the sun shall be darkened in his going
forth, and the moon shall not cause her
light to shine.
11And I will punish the world for *their*
evil, and the wicked for their iniquity; and
I will cause the arrogancy of the proud to
cease, and will lay low the haughtiness of
the terrible.

12 I will make a man more precious than
fine gold; even a man than the golden
wedge of Ophir.
13 Therefore I will shake the heavens, and
the earth shall remove out of her place, in
the wrath of the LORD of hosts, and in the
day of his fierce anger.
14 And it shall be as the chased roe, and
as a sheep that no man taketh up: they
shall every man turn to his own people,
and flee every one into his own land.
15 Every one that is found shall be thrust
through; and every one that is joined *unto*
them shall fall by the sword.
16 Their children also shall be dashed to
pieces before their eyes; their houses shall
be spoiled, and their wives ravished.
17 Behold, I will stir up the Medes against
them, which shall not regard silver; and *as*
for gold, they shall not delight in it.
18 *Their* bows also shall dash the young
men to pieces; and they shall have no pity
on the fruit of the womb; their eye shall
not spare children.
19 And Babylon, the glory of kingdoms,
the beauty of the Chaldees' excellency,
shall be as when God overthrew Sodom
and Gomorrah.
20 It shall never be inhabited, neither
shall it be dwelt in from generation to generation: neither shall the Arabian pitch tent
there; neither shall the shepherds make
their fold there.
21 But wild beasts of the desert shall lie
there; and their houses shall be full of
doleful creatures; and owls shall dwell
there, and satyrs shall dance there.
22 And the wild beasts of the islands shall
cry in their desolate houses, and dragons
in *their* pleasant palaces: and her time *is*
near to come, and her days shall not be
prolonged.

14

1 For the LORD will have mercy on Jacob,
and will yet choose Israel, and set them in
their own land: and the strangers shall be
joined with them, and they shall cleave to
the house of Jacob.
2 And the people shall take them, and
bring them to their place: and the house
of Israel shall possess them in the land of
the LORD for servants and handmaids: and
they shall take them captives, whose captives they were; and they shall rule over
their oppressors.
3 And it shall come to pass in the day
that the LORD shall give thee rest from thy
sorrow, and from thy fear, and from the
hard bondage wherein thou wast made to
serve,
4 That thou shalt take up this proverb
against the king of Babylon, and say, How
hath the oppressor ceased! the golden city
ceased!
5 The LORD hath broken the staff of the
wicked, *and* the sceptre of the rulers.
6 He who smote the people in wrath with
a continual stroke, he that ruled the nations in anger, is persecuted, *and* none
hindereth.
7 The whole earth is at rest, *and* is quiet:
they break forth into singing.
8 Yea, the fir trees rejoice at thee, *and* the
cedars of Lebanon, *saying,* Since thou art
laid down, no feller is come up against us.
9 Hell from beneath is moved for thee
to meet *thee* at thy coming: it stirreth up
the dead for thee, *even* all the chief ones of
the earth; it hath raised up from their
thrones all the kings of the nations.
10 All they shall speak and say unto thee,
Art thou also become weak as we? art thou
become like unto us?
11 Thy pomp is brought down to the
grave, *and* the noise of thy viols: the worm
is spread under thee, and the worms cover
thee.
12 How art thou fallen from heaven,
O Lucifer, son of the morning! *how* art thou
cut down to the ground, which didst
weaken the nations!
13 For thou hast
said in thine heart,
I will ascend into
heaven, I will exalt
my throne above
the stars of God: I
will sit also upon the mount of the congregation, in the sides of the north:

14:13 Ambition
◄ Psalm 49:11
Isaiah 22:16 ►

14 I will ascend above the heights of the
clouds; I will be like the most High.
15 Yet thou shalt be brought down to
hell, to the sides of the pit.
16 They that see thee shall narrowly look
upon thee, *and* consider thee, *saying, Is* this
the man that made the earth to tremble,
that did shake kingdoms;
17 *That* made the world as a wilderness,
and destroyed the cities thereof; *that*
opened not the house of his prisoners?
18 All the kings of the nations, *even* all

of them, lie in glory, every one in his own
house.
19But thou art cast out of thy grave like
an abominable branch, *and as* the raiment
of those that are slain, thrust through with
a sword, that go down to the stones of the
pit; as a carcase trodden under feet.
20Thou shalt not
be joined with
them in burial, be-
cause thou hast de-
stroyed thy land,
and slain thy peo-
ple: the seed of evildoers shall never be
renowned.

14:20 Evildoers
◄ Isaiah 9:17
Isaiah 31:2 ►

21Prepare slaughter for his children for
the iniquity of their fathers; that they do
not rise, nor possess the land, nor fill the
face of the world with cities.
22For I will rise up against them, saith
the LORD of hosts, and cut off from Babylon the name, and remnant, and son, and
nephew, saith the LORD.
23I will also
make it a posses-
sion for the bittern,
and pools of water:
and I will sweep it
with the besom of
destruction, saith the LORD of hosts.

14:23 Warning!
◄ Psalm 7:12
Isaiah 66:4 ►

24The LORD of hosts hath sworn, saying,
Surely as I have thought, so shall it come
to pass; and as I have purposed, *so* shall it
stand:
25That I will break the Assyrian in my
land, and upon my mountains tread him
under foot: then shall his yoke depart from
off them, and his burden depart from off
their shoulders.
26This *is* the purpose that is purposed
upon the whole earth: and this *is* the
hand that is stretched out upon all the
nations.
27For the LORD of hosts hath purposed,
and who shall disannul *it?* and his hand *is*
stretched out, and who shall turn it back?
28In the year that king Ahaz died was
this burden.
29Rejoice not thou, whole Palestina, because the rod of him that smote thee is
broken: for out of the serpent's root shall
come forth a cockatrice, and his fruit *shall
be* a fiery flying serpent.
30And the firstborn of the poor shall
feed, and the needy shall lie down in safety: and I will kill thy root with famine, and
he shall slay thy remnant.
31Howl, O gate; cry, O city; thou, whole
Palestina, *art* dissolved: for there shall
come from the north a smoke, and none
shall be alone in his appointed times.
32What shall *one* then answer the messengers of the nation? That the LORD hath
founded Zion, and the poor of his people
shall trust in it.

15

1The burden of Moab. Because in the
night Ar of Moab is laid waste, *and* brought
to silence; because in the night Kir of Moab
is laid waste, *and* brought to silence;
2He is gone up to Bajith, and to Dibon,
the high places, to weep: Moab shall howl
over Nebo, and over Medeba: on all their
heads *shall be* baldness, *and* every beard
cut off.
3In their streets they shall gird themselves with sackcloth: on the tops of their
houses, and in their streets, every one shall
howl, weeping abundantly.
4And Heshbon shall cry, and Elealeh:
their voice shall be heard *even* unto Jahaz:
therefore the armed soldiers of Moab shall
cry out; his life shall be grievous unto him.
5My heart shall cry out for Moab; his
fugitives *shall flee* unto Zoar, an heifer of
three years old: for by the mounting up of
Luhith with weeping shall they go it up;
for in the way of Horonaim they shall raise
up a cry of destruction.
6For the waters of Nimrim shall be desolate: for the hay is withered away, the
grass faileth, there is no green thing.
7Therefore the abundance they have gotten, and that which they have laid up,
shall they carry away to the brook of the
willows.
8For the cry is gone round about the
borders of Moab; the howling thereof unto
Eglaim, and the howling thereof unto Beer-
elim.
9For the waters of Dimon shall be full
of blood: for I will bring more upon Dimon, lions upon him that escapeth of
Moab, and upon the remnant of the land.

16

1Send ye the lamb to the ruler of the
land from Sela to the wilderness, unto the
mount of the daughter of Zion.
2For it shall be, *that,* as a wandering bird
cast out of the nest, so the daughters of
Moab shall be at the fords of Arnon.
3Take counsel, execute judgment; make

thy shadow as the night in the midst of
the noonday; hide the outcasts; bewray not
him that wandereth.
4 Let mine outcasts dwell with thee,
Moab; be thou a covert to them from the
face of the spoiler: for the extortioner is at
an end, the spoiler ceaseth, the oppressors
are consumed out of the land.
5 And in mercy
shall the throne be
established: and he
shall sit upon it in
truth in the taber-
nacle of David,
judging, and seeking judgment, and hasting righteousness.

16:5
Better Neighborhoods
◄ Proverbs 29:14
Isaiah 32:16 ►

6 We have heard of the pride of Moab;
he is very proud: *even* of his haughtiness,
and his pride, and his wrath: *but* his lies
shall not *be* so.
7 Therefore shall Moab howl for Moab,
every one shall howl: for the foundations
of Kir-hareseth shall ye mourn; surely *they*
are stricken.
8 For the fields of Heshbon languish, *and*
the vine of Sibmah: the lords of the heathen have broken down the principal
plants thereof, they are come *even* unto Jazer, they wandered *through* the wilderness:
her branches are stretched out, they are
gone over the sea.
9 Therefore I will bewail with the weeping of Jazer the vine of Sibmah: I will water thee with my tears, O Heshbon, and
Elealeh: for the shouting for thy summer
fruits and for thy harvest is fallen.
10 And gladness is
taken away, and joy
out of the plentiful
field; and in the
vineyards there
shall be no singing,
neither shall there be shouting: the tread-
ers shall tread out no wine in *their* presses;
I have made *their vintage* shouting to cease.

16:10 Happiness
◄ Ecclesiastes 7:6
James 4:9 ►

11 Wherefore my bowels shall sound like
an harp for Moab, and mine inward parts
for Kir-haresh.
12 And it shall come to pass, when it is
seen that Moab is weary on the high place,
that he shall come to his sanctuary to pray;
but he shall not prevail.
13 This *is* the word that the LORD hath
spoken concerning Moab since that time.
14 But now the LORD hath spoken, saying, Within three years, as the years of an
hireling, and the glory of Moab shall be
contemned, with all that great multitude;
and the remnant *shall be* very small *and*
feeble.
1 The burden of Damascus. Behold, Damascus is taken away from *being* a city, and
it shall be a ruinous heap.
2 The cities of Aroer *are* forsaken: they
shall be for flocks, which shall lie down,
and none shall make *them* afraid.
3 The fortress also shall cease from
Ephraim, and the kingdom from Damascus, and the remnant of Syria: they shall
be as the glory of the children of Israel,
saith the LORD of hosts.
4 And in that day it shall come to pass,
that the glory of Jacob shall be made thin,
and the fatness of his flesh shall wax lean.
5 And it shall be as when the harvestman
gathereth the corn, and reapeth the ears
with his arm; and it shall be as he that
gathereth ears in the valley of Rephaim.
6 Yet gleaning grapes shall be left in it,
as the shaking of an olive tree, two *or* three
berries in the top of the uppermost bough,
four *or* five in the outmost fruitful branches
thereof, saith the LORD God of Israel.
7 At that day shall a man look to his
Maker, and his eyes shall have respect to
the Holy One of Israel.
8 And he shall not look to the altars, the
work of his hands, neither shall respect *that*
which his fingers have made, either the
groves, or the images.
9 In that day shall his strong cities be as
a forsaken bough, and an uppermost
branch, which they left because of the children of Israel: and there shall be desolation.
10 Because thou
hast forgotten the
God of thy salva-
tion, and hast not
been mindful of
the rock of thy
strength, therefore shalt thou plant pleasant plants, and shalt set it with strange
slips:

17:10 Don't Forget...
◄ Psalm 78:11
Isaiah 51:13 ►

11 In the day shalt
thou make thy
plant to grow, and
in the morning
shalt thou make thy
seed to flourish: *but*

17:11 Disappointment
◄ Proverbs 11:7
Jeremiah 8:15 ►

the harvest *shall be* a heap in the day of
grief and of desperate sorrow.
12 Woe to the multitude of many people, *which* make a noise like the noise of
the seas; and to the rushing of nations, *that*
make a rushing like the rushing of mighty
waters!
13 The nations shall rush like the rushing of many waters: but *God* shall rebuke
them, and they shall flee far off, and shall
be chased as the chaff of the mountains
before the wind, and like a rolling thing
before the whirlwind.
14 And behold at eveningtide trouble;
and before the morning he *is* not. This *is*
the portion of them that spoil us, and the
lot of them that rob us.

18

1 Woe to the land shadowing with wings,
which *is* beyond the rivers of Ethiopia:
2 That sendeth ambassadors by the sea,
even in vessels of bulrushes upon the waters, *saying,* Go, ye swift messengers, to a
nation scattered and peeled, to a people
terrible from their beginning hitherto; a
nation meted out and trodden down,
whose land the rivers have spoiled!
3 All ye inhabitants of the world, and
dwellers on the earth, see ye, when he
lifteth up an ensign on the mountains; and
when he bloweth a trumpet, hear ye.
4 For so the LORD said unto me, I will take
my rest, and I will consider in my dwelling place like a clear heat upon herbs, *and*
like a cloud of dew in the heat of harvest.
5 For afore the harvest, when the bud is
perfect, and the sour grape is ripening in
the flower, he shall both cut off the sprigs
with pruninghooks, and take away *and* cut
down the branches.
6 They shall be left together unto the
fowls of the mountains, and to the beasts
of the earth: and the fowls shall summer
upon them, and all the beasts of the earth
shall winter upon them.
7 In that time shall the present be
brought unto the LORD of hosts of a people scattered and peeled, and from a people terrible from their beginning hitherto;
a nation meted out and trodden under
foot, whose land the rivers have spoiled,
to the place of the name of the LORD of
hosts, the mount Zion.

19

1 The burden of Egypt. Behold, the LORD
rideth upon a swift cloud, and shall come
into Egypt: and the idols of Egypt shall be
moved at his presence, and the heart of
Egypt shall melt in the midst of it.
2 And I will set the Egyptians against the
Egyptians: and they shall fight every one
against his brother, and every one against
his neighbour; city against city, *and* kingdom against kingdom.
3 And the spirit of Egypt shall fail in the
midst thereof; and I will destroy the counsel thereof: and they shall seek to the idols,
and to the charmers, and to them that have
familiar spirits, and to the wizards.
4 And the Egyptians will I give over into
the hand of a cruel lord; and a fierce king
shall rule over them, saith the Lord, the
LORD of hosts.
5 And the waters shall fail from the sea,
and the river shall be wasted and dried up.
6 And they shall turn the rivers far away;
and the brooks of defence shall be emptied and dried up: the reeds and flags shall
wither.
7 The paper reeds by the brooks, by the
mouth of the brooks, and every thing sown
by the brooks, shall wither, be driven away,
and be no *more.*
8 The fishers also shall mourn, and all
they that cast angle into the brooks shall
lament, and they that spread nets upon the
waters shall languish.
9 Moreover they that work in fine flax,
and they that weave networks, shall be
confounded.
10 And they shall be broken in the purposes thereof, all that make sluices *and*
ponds for fish.
11 Surely the princes of Zoan *are* fools,
the counsel of the wise counsellors of
Pharaoh is become brutish: how say ye
unto Pharaoh, I *am* the son of the wise,
the son of ancient kings?
12 Where *are* they? where *are* thy wise
men? and let them tell thee now, and let
them know what the LORD of hosts hath
purposed upon Egypt.
13 The princes of Zoan are become fools,
the princes of Noph are deceived; they have
also seduced Egypt, *even they that are* the
stay of the tribes thereof.
14 The LORD hath mingled a perverse
spirit in the midst thereof: and they
have caused Egypt to err in every work
thereof, as a drunken *man* staggereth in his
vomit.
15 Neither shall there be *any* work for

Egypt, which the head or tail, branch or
rush, may do.
16 In that day shall Egypt be like unto
women: and it shall be afraid and fear because of the shaking of the hand of the
LORD of hosts, which he shaketh over it.
17 And the land of Judah shall be a terror
unto Egypt, every one that maketh mention thereof shall be afraid in himself, because of the counsel of the LORD of hosts,
which he hath determined against it.
18 In that day shall five cities in the land
of Egypt speak the language of Canaan,
and swear to the LORD of hosts; one shall
be called, The city of destruction.
19 In that day shall there be an altar to
the LORD in the midst of the land of Egypt,
and a pillar at the border thereof to the
LORD.
20 And it shall be for a sign and for a witness unto the LORD of hosts in the land of
Egypt: for they shall cry unto the LORD
because of the oppressors, and he shall
send them a saviour, and a great one, and
he shall deliver them.
21 And the LORD shall be known to Egypt,
and the Egyptians shall know the LORD in
that day, and shall do sacrifice and oblation; yea, they shall vow a vow unto the
LORD, and perform *it*.
22 And the LORD shall smite Egypt: he
shall smite and heal *it:* and they shall return *even* to the LORD, and he shall be
intreated of them, and shall heal them.
23 In that day shall there be a highway
out of Egypt to Assyria, and the Assyrian
shall come into Egypt, and the Egyptian
into Assyria, and the Egyptians shall serve
with the Assyrians.
24 In that day shall Israel be the third
with Egypt and with Assyria, *even* a blessing in the midst of the land:
25 Whom the LORD of hosts shall bless,
saying, Blessed *be* Egypt my people, and
Assyria the work of my hands, and Israel
mine inheritance.

20

1 In the year that Tartan came unto Ashdod, (when Sargon the king of Assyria sent
him,) and fought against Ashdod, and
took it;
2 At the same time spake the LORD by Isaiah the son of Amoz, saying, Go and loose
the sackcloth from off thy loins, and put
off thy shoe from thy foot. And he did so,
walking naked and barefoot.
3 And the LORD said, Like as my servant
Isaiah hath walked naked and barefoot
three years *for* a sign and wonder upon
Egypt and upon Ethiopia;
4 So shall the king of Assyria lead away
the Egyptians prisoners, and the Ethiopians captives, young and old, naked and
barefoot, even with *their* buttocks uncovered, to the shame of Egypt.
5 And they shall be afraid and ashamed
of Ethiopia their expectation, and of Egypt
their glory.
6 And the inhabitant of this isle shall say
in that day, Behold, such *is* our expectation, whither we flee for help to be delivered from the king of Assyria: and how
shall we escape?

21

1 The burden of the desert of the sea. As
whirlwinds in the south pass through; *so*
it cometh from the desert, from a terrible
land.
2 A grievous vision is declared unto me;
the treacherous dealer dealeth treacherously, and the spoiler spoileth. Go up, O Elam:
besiege, O Media; all the sighing thereof
have I made to cease.
3 Therefore are my loins filled with pain:
pangs have taken hold upon me, as the
pangs of a woman that travaileth: I was
bowed down at the hearing *of it;* I was dismayed at the seeing *of it.*
4 My heart panted, fearfulness affrighted
me: the night of my pleasure hath he
turned into fear unto me.
5 Prepare the table, watch in the watchtower, eat, drink: arise, ye princes, *and*
anoint the shield.
6 For thus hath the Lord said unto me,
Go, set a watchman, let him declare what
he seeth.
7 And he saw a chariot *with* a couple of
horsemen, a chariot of asses, *and* a chariot
of camels; and he hearkened diligently
with much heed:
8 And he cried, A lion: My lord, I stand
continually upon the watchtower in the
daytime, and I am set in my ward whole
nights:
9 And, behold, here cometh a chariot of
men, *with* a couple of horsemen. And he
answered and said, Babylon is fallen, is
fallen; and all the graven images of her
gods he hath broken unto the ground.
10 O my threshing, and the corn of my
floor: that which I have heard of the LORD

of hosts, the God of Israel, have I declared unto you.

11 The burden of Dumah. He calleth to me out of Seir, Watchman, what of the night? Watchman, what of the night?

12 The watchman said, The morning cometh, and also the night: if ye will enquire, enquire ye: return, come.

13 The burden upon Arabia. In the forest in Arabia shall ye lodge, O ye travelling companies of Dedanim.

14 The inhabitants of the land of Tema brought water to him that was thirsty, they prevented with their bread him that fled.

> **21:14**
> **Work that Helps Others**
> ◄ Proverbs 31:20
> Isaiah 50:4 ►

15 For they fled from the swords, from the drawn sword, and from the bent bow, and from the grievousness of war.

16 For thus hath the Lord said unto me, Within a year, according to the years of an hireling, and all the glory of Kedar shall fail:

17 And the residue of the number of archers, the mighty men of the children of Kedar, shall be diminished: for the LORD God of Israel hath spoken *it*.

22

1 The burden of the valley of vision. What aileth thee now, that thou art wholly gone up to the housetops?

2 Thou that art full of stirs, a tumultuous city, a joyous city: thy slain *men are* not slain with the sword, nor dead in battle.

3 All thy rulers are fled together, they are bound by the archers: all that are found in thee are bound together, *which* have fled from far.

4 Therefore said I, Look away from me; I will weep bitterly, labour not to comfort me, because of the spoiling of the daughter of my people.

5 For *it is* a day of trouble, and of treading down, and of perplexity by the Lord GOD of hosts in the valley of vision, breaking down the walls, and of crying to the mountains.

6 And Elam bare the quiver with chariots of men *and* horsemen, and Kir uncovered the shield.

7 And it shall come to pass, *that* thy choicest valleys shall be full of chariots, and the horsemen shall set themselves in array at the gate.

8 And he discovered the covering of Judah, and thou didst look in that day to the armour of the house of the forest.

9 Ye have seen also the breaches of the city of David, that they are many: and ye gathered together the waters of the lower pool.

10 And ye have numbered the houses of Jerusalem, and the houses have ye broken down to fortify the wall.

11 Ye made also a ditch between the two walls for the water of the old pool: but ye have not looked unto the maker thereof, neither had respect unto him that fashioned it long ago.

12 And in that day did the Lord GOD of hosts call to weeping, and to mourning, and to baldness, and to girding with sackcloth:

> **22:12 Repent!**
> ◄ Proverbs 1:23
> Jeremiah 25:5 ►

13 And behold joy and gladness, slaying oxen, and killing sheep, eating flesh, and drinking wine: let us eat and drink; for to morrow we shall die.

> **22:13 Luxury**
> ◄ Proverbs 21:17
> Isaiah 47:8-9 ►

14 And it was revealed in mine ears by the LORD of hosts, Surely this iniquity shall not be purged from you till ye die, saith the Lord GOD of hosts.

15 Thus saith the Lord GOD of hosts, Go, get thee unto this treasurer, *even* unto Shebna, which *is* over the house, *and say,*

16 What hast thou here? and whom hast thou here, that thou hast hewed thee out a sepulchre here, *as* he that heweth him out a sepulchre on high, *and* that graveth an habitation for himself in a rock?

> **22:16 Ambition**
> ◄ Isaiah 14:13
> Habakkuk 2:5 ►

17 Behold, the LORD will carry thee away with a mighty captivity, and will surely cover thee.

18 He will surely violently turn and toss thee *like* a ball into a large country: there shalt thou die, and there the chariots of thy glory *shall be* the shame of thy lord's house.

19 And I will drive thee from thy station, and from thy state shall he pull thee down.

and the Lord GOD will wipe away tears from off all faces; and the rebuke of his people shall he take away from off all the earth: for the LORD hath spoken *it*.

9 And it shall be said in that day, Lo, this *is* our God; we have waited for him, and he will save us: this *is* the LORD; we have waited for him, we will be glad and rejoice in his salvation.

25:9 Waiting
◄ Psalm 130:6
Isaiah 26:8 ►

10 For in this mountain shall the hand of the LORD rest, and Moab shall be trodden down under him, even as straw is trodden down for the dunghill.

11 And he shall spread forth his hands in the midst of them, as he that swimmeth spreadeth forth *his hands* to swim: and he shall bring down their pride together with the spoils of their hands.

12 And the fortress of the high fort of thy walls shall he bring down, lay low, *and* bring to the ground, *even* to the dust.

26

1 In that day shall this song be sung in the land of Judah; We have a strong city; salvation will *God* appoint *for* walls and bulwarks.

2 Open ye the gates, that the righteous nation which keepeth the truth may enter in.

26:2 God's Presence
◄ Psalm 24:3-4
John 10:9 ►

3 Thou wilt keep *him* in perfect peace, *whose* mind *is* stayed *on thee:* because he trusteth in thee.

26:3 Peace of Mind
◄ Proverbs 3:17
Isaiah 48:18 ►

4 Trust ye in the LORD for ever: for in the LORD JEHOVAH *is* everlasting strength:

26:4 Trusting God
◄ Proverbs 3:5
Isaiah 50:10 ►

5 For he bringeth down them that dwell on high; the lofty city, he layeth it low; he layeth it low, *even* to the ground; he bringeth it *even* to the dust.

6 The foot shall tread it down, *even* the feet of the poor, *and* the steps of the needy.

26:7 Right Paths
◄ Isaiah 2:3
Hebrews 12:13 ►

7 The way of the just *is* uprightness: thou, most upright, dost weigh the path of the just.

8 Yea, in the way of thy judgments, O LORD, have we waited for thee; the desire of *our* soul *is* to thy name, and to the remembrance of thee.

26:8 Waiting
◄ Isaiah 25:9
Isaiah 33:2 ►

9 With my soul have I desired thee in the night; yea, with my spirit within me will I seek thee early: for when thy judgments *are* in the earth, the inhabitants of the world will learn righteousness.

10 Let favour be shewed to the wicked, *yet* will he not learn righteousness: in the land of uprightness will he deal unjustly, and will not behold the majesty of the LORD.

11 LORD, *when* thy hand is lifted up, they will not see: *but* they shall see, and be ashamed for *their* envy at the people; yea, the fire of thine enemies shall devour them.

12 LORD, thou wilt ordain peace for us: for thou also hast wrought all our works in us.

13 O LORD our God, *other* lords besides thee have had dominion over us: *but* by thee only will we make mention of thy name.

14 *They are* dead, they shall not live; *they are* deceased, they shall not rise: therefore hast thou visited and destroyed them, and made all their memory to perish.

15 Thou hast increased the nation, O LORD, thou hast increased the nation: thou art glorified: thou hadst removed *it* far *unto* all the ends of the earth.

16 LORD, in trouble have they visited thee, they poured out a prayer *when* thy chastening *was* upon them.

17 Like as a woman with child, *that* draweth near the time of her delivery, is in pain, *and* crieth out in her pangs; so have we been in thy sight, O LORD.

18 We have been with child, we have been in pain, we have as it were brought forth wind; we have not wrought any deliverance in the earth; neither have the inhabitants of the world fallen.

19 Thy dead *men* shall live, *together with* my dead body shall they arise. Awake and sing, ye that dwell in dust: for thy dew *is as* the dew of herbs, and the earth shall cast out the dead.

20 Come, my people, enter thou into thy chambers, and shut thy doors about thee: hide thyself as it were for a little moment, until the indignation be overpast.

21 For, behold, the LORD cometh out of his place to punish the inhabitants of the earth for their iniquity: the earth also shall disclose her blood, and shall no more cover her slain.

27

1 In that day the LORD with his sore and great and strong sword shall punish leviathan the piercing serpent, even leviathan that crooked serpent; and he shall slay the dragon that *is* in the sea.

2 In that day sing ye unto her, A vineyard of red wine.

3 I the LORD do keep it; I will water it every moment: lest *any* hurt it, I will keep it night and day.

4 Fury *is* not in me: who would set the briers *and* thorns against me in battle? I would go through them, I would burn them together.

5 Or let him take hold of my strength, *that* he may make peace with me; *and* he shall make peace with me.

> **27:5 Seeking Peace**
> ◄ Psalm 34:14
> Colossians 3:15 ►

6 He shall cause them that come of Jacob to take root: Israel shall blossom and bud, and fill the face of the world with fruit.

7 Hath he smitten him, as he smote those that smote him? *or* is he slain according to the slaughter of them that are slain by him?

8 In measure, when it shooteth forth, thou wilt debate with it: he stayeth his rough wind in the day of the east wind.

9 By this therefore shall the iniquity of Jacob be purged; and this is all the fruit to take away his sin; when he maketh all the stones of the altar as chalkstones that are beaten in sunder, the groves and images shall not stand up.

10 Yet the defenced city *shall be* desolate, *and* the habitation forsaken, and left like a wilderness: there shall the calf feed, and there shall he lie down, and consume the branches thereof.

11 When the boughs thereof are withered, they shall be broken off: the women come, *and* set them on fire: for it *is* a people of no understanding: therefore he that made them will not have mercy on them, and he that formed them will shew them no favour.

12 And it shall come to pass in that day, *that* the LORD shall beat off from the channel of the river unto the stream of Egypt, and ye shall be gathered one by one, O ye children of Israel.

13 And it shall come to pass in that day, *that* the great trumpet shall be blown, and they shall come which were ready to perish in the land of Assyria, and the outcasts in the land of Egypt, and shall worship the LORD in the holy mount at Jerusalem.

28

1 Woe to the crown of pride, to the drunkards of Ephraim, whose glorious beauty *is* a fading flower, which *are* on the head of the fat valleys of them that are overcome with wine!

> **28:1 Drinking Too Much**
> ◄ Isaiah 5:11
> Isaiah 28:7 ►

> **28:1 Getting Drunk**
> ◄ Isaiah 5:11
> Nahum 1:10 ►

2 Behold, the Lord hath a mighty and strong one, *which* as a tempest of hail *and* a destroying storm, as a flood of mighty waters overflowing, shall cast down to the earth with the hand.

3 The crown of pride, the drunkards of Ephraim, shall be trodden under feet:

4 And the glorious beauty, which *is* on the head of the fat valley, shall be a fading flower, *and* as the hasty fruit before the summer; which *when* he that looketh upon it seeth, while it is yet in his hand he eateth it up.

5 In that day shall the LORD of hosts be for a crown of glory, and for a diadem of beauty, unto the residue of his people,

6 And for a spirit of judgment to him that sitteth in judgment, and for strength to them that turn the battle to the gate.

7 But they also have erred through wine, and through strong drink are out of the way; the priest and the prophet have erred through strong drink, they are swallowed up of wine, they are out of the way through strong drink; they err in vision, they stumble *in* judgment.

> **28:7 Drinking Too Much**
> ◄ Isaiah 28:1
> Isaiah 56:12 ►

8For all tables are full of vomit *and*
filthiness, *so that there is* no place *clean.*
9Whom shall he teach knowledge? and
whom shall he make to understand doctrine? *them that are* weaned from the milk,
and drawn from the breasts.
10For precept *must be* upon precept, precept upon precept; line upon line, line
upon line; here a little, *and* there a little:
11For with stammering lips and another
tongue will he speak to this people.
12To whom he said, This *is* the rest *where-*
with ye may cause the weary to rest; and
this *is* the refreshing: yet they would not
hear.
13But the word of the LORD was unto
them precept upon precept, precept upon
precept; line upon line, line upon line;
here a little, *and* there a little; that they
might go, and fall backward, and be broken, and snared, and taken.
14Wherefore hear
the word of the
LORD, ye scornful
men, that rule this
people which *is* in
Jerusalem.

28:14 Sin (Warnings)
◄ 1 Samuel 12:15
Jeremiah 13:16 ►

15Because ye have said, We have made a
covenant with death, and with hell are we
at agreement; when the overflowing
scourge shall pass through, it shall not
come unto us: for we have made lies our
refuge, and under falsehood have we hid
ourselves:
16Therefore thus
saith the Lord GOD,
Behold, I lay in
Zion for a founda-
tion a stone, a tried
stone, a precious
corner *stone,* a sure
foundation: he that believeth shall not
make haste.

28:16 Believer Be Glad
◄ 1 Kings 8:56
Matthew 10:42 ►

17Judgment also will I lay to the line,
and righteousness to the plummet: and the
hail shall sweep away the refuge of lies,
and the waters shall overflow the hiding
place.
18And your covenant with death shall
be disannulled, and your agreement with
hell shall not stand; when the overflowing scourge shall pass through, then ye
shall be trodden down by it.
19From the time that it goeth forth it
shall take you: for morning by morning
shall it pass over, by day and by night: and
it shall be a vexation only *to* understand
the report.
20For the bed is shorter than that *a man*
can stretch himself *on it:* and the covering
narrower than that he can wrap himself
in it.
21For the LORD shall rise up as *in* mount
Perazim, he shall be wroth as *in* the valley
of Gibeon, that he may do his work, his
strange work; and bring to pass his act, his
strange act.
22Now therefore be ye not mockers, lest
your bands be made strong: for I have
heard from the Lord GOD of hosts a consumption, even determined upon the
whole earth.
23Give ye ear, and hear my voice; hearken, and hear my speech.
24Doth the plowman plow all day to
sow? doth he open and break the clods of
his ground?
25When he hath made plain the face
thereof, doth he not cast abroad the fitches,
and scatter the cummin, and cast in the
principal wheat and the appointed barley
and rie in their place?
26For his God
doth instruct him
to discretion, *and*
doth teach him.
27For the fitches
are not threshed
with a threshing in-
strument, neither is
a cart wheel turned
about upon the
cummin; but the
fitches are beaten
out with a staff, and the cummin with a
rod.

28:26 Discretion
◄ Proverbs 5:2
Mark 12:34 ►

28:26 God as Teacher
◄ Isaiah 2:3
Isaiah 48:17 ►

28Bread *corn* is bruised; because he will
not ever be threshing it, nor break *it with*
the wheel of his cart, nor bruise it *with* his
horsemen.
29This also cometh forth from the LORD
of hosts, *which* is wonderful in counsel, *and*
excellent in working.

29

1Woe to Ariel, to Ariel, the city *where*
David dwelt! add ye year to year; let them
kill sacrifices.
2Yet I will distress Ariel, and there shall
be heaviness and sorrow: and it shall be
unto me as Ariel.
3And I will camp against thee round

about, and will lay siege against thee with
a mount, and I will raise forts against thee.
4And thou shalt be brought down, *and*
shalt speak out of the ground, and thy
speech shall be low out of the dust, and
thy voice shall be, as of one that hath a
familiar spirit, out of the ground, and thy
speech shall whisper out of the dust.
5Moreover the multitude of thy strangers shall be like small dust, and the multitude of the terrible ones *shall be* as chaff
that passeth away: yea, it shall be at an
instant suddenly.
6Thou shalt be visited of the LORD of
hosts with thunder, and with earthquake,
and great noise, with storm and tempest,
and the flame of devouring fire.
7And the multitude of all the nations
that fight against Ariel, even all that fight
against her and her munition, and that
distress her, shall be as a dream of a night
vision.
8It shall even be
as when an hungry
man dreameth, and,
behold, he eateth;
but he awaketh,
and his soul is emp-
ty: or as when a thirsty man dreameth, and,
behold, he drinketh; but he awaketh, and,
behold, *he is* faint, and his soul hath appetite: so shall the multitude of all the
nations be, that fight against mount Zion.

29:8 Discontentment
◄ Ecclesiastes 6:7
Isaiah 55:2 ►

9Stay yourselves, and wonder; cry ye out,
and cry: they are drunken, but not with
wine; they stagger, but not with strong
drink.
10For the LORD hath poured out upon
you the spirit of deep sleep, and hath
closed your eyes: the prophets and your
rulers, the seers hath he covered.
11And the vision of all is become unto
you as the words of a book that is sealed,
which *men* deliver to one that is learned,
saying, Read this, I pray thee: and he saith,
I cannot; for it *is* sealed:
12And the book is delivered to him that
is not learned, saying, Read this, I pray
thee: and he saith, I am not learned.
13Wherefore the Lord said, Forasmuch
as this people draw near *me* with their
mouth, and with their lips do honour me,
but have removed their heart far from me,
and their fear toward me is taught by the
precept of men:
14Therefore, behold, I will proceed to do
a marvellous work among this people, *even*
a marvellous work and a wonder: for the
wisdom of their wise *men* shall perish, and
the understanding of their prudent *men*
shall be hid.
15Woe unto them that seek deep to hide
their counsel from the LORD, and their
works are in the dark, and they say, Who
seeth us? and who knoweth us?
16Surely your turning of things upside
down shall be esteemed as the potter's clay:
for shall the work say of him that made it,
He made me not? or shall the thing framed
say of him that framed it, He had no understanding?
17*Is* it not yet a very little while, and Lebanon shall be turned into a fruitful field,
and the fruitful field shall be esteemed as
a forest?
18And in that day shall the deaf hear the
words of the book, and the eyes of the
blind shall see out of obscurity, and out
of darkness.
19The meek also
shall increase *their*
joy in the LORD,
and the poor
among men shall
rejoice in the Holy
One of Israel.

29:19 Meekness
◄ Isaiah 11:4
Matthew 5:5 ►

20For the terrible one is brought to
nought, and the scorner is consumed, and
all that watch for iniquity are cut off:
21That make a man an offender for a
word, and lay a snare for him that
reproveth in the gate, and turn aside the
just for a thing of nought.
22Therefore thus saith the LORD, who
redeemed Abraham, concerning the house
of Jacob, Jacob shall not now be ashamed,
neither shall his face now wax pale.
23But when he seeth his children, the
work of mine hands, in the midst of him,
they shall sanctify my name, and sanctify
the Holy One of Jacob, and shall fear the
God of Israel.
24They also that erred in spirit shall
come to understanding, and they that
murmured shall learn doctrine.

30

1Woe to the rebellious children, saith
the LORD, that take counsel, but not of me;
and that cover with a covering, but not of
my spirit, that they may add sin to sin:
2That walk to go down into Egypt, and

have not asked at my mouth; to strengthen themselves in the strength of Pharaoh, and to trust in the shadow of Egypt!

30:2 Trusting in People
◄ Isaiah 2:22
Isaiah 31:1-3 ►

3 Therefore shall the strength of Pharaoh be your shame, and the trust in the shadow of Egypt *your* confusion.

4 For his princes were at Zoan, and his ambassadors came to Hanes.

5 They were all ashamed of a people *that* could not profit them, nor be an help nor profit, but a shame, and also a reproach.

6 The burden of the beasts of the south: into the land of trouble and anguish, from whence *come* the young and old lion, the viper and fiery flying serpent, they will carry their riches upon the shoulders of young asses, and their treasures upon the bunches of camels, to a people *that* shall not profit *them*.

7 For the Egyptians shall help in vain, and to no purpose: therefore have I cried concerning this, Their strength *is* to sit still.

8 Now go, write it before them in a table, and note it in a book, that it may be for the time to come for ever and ever:

9 That this *is* a rebellious people, lying children, children *that* will not hear the law of the LORD:

10 Which say to the seers, See not; and to the prophets, Prophesy not unto us right things, speak unto us smooth things, prophesy deceits:

11 Get you out of the way, turn aside out of the path, cause the Holy One of Israel to cease from before us.

12 Wherefore thus saith the Holy One of Israel, Because ye despise this word, and trust in oppression and perverseness, and stay thereon:

13 Therefore this iniquity shall be to you as a breach ready to fall, swelling out in a high wall, whose breaking cometh suddenly at an instant.

30:13 Wicked Insecurity
◄ Proverbs 23:34
Jeremiah 13:16 ►

14 And he shall break it as the breaking of the potters' vessel that is broken in pieces; he shall not spare: so that there shall not be found in the bursting of it a sherd to take fire from the hearth, or to take water *withal* out of the pit.

15 For thus saith the Lord GOD, the Holy One of Israel; In returning and rest shall ye be saved; in quietness and in confidence shall be your strength: and ye would not.

16 But ye said, No; for we will flee upon horses; therefore shall ye flee: and, We will ride upon the swift; therefore shall they that pursue you be swift.

17 One thousand *shall flee* at the rebuke of one; at the rebuke of five shall ye flee: till ye be left as a beacon upon the top of a mountain, and as an ensign on an hill.

18 And therefore will the LORD wait, that he may be gracious unto you, and therefore will he be exalted, that he may have mercy upon you: for the LORD *is* a God of judgment: blessed *are* all they that wait for him.

19 For the people shall dwell in Zion at Jerusalem: thou shalt weep no more: he will be very gracious unto thee at the voice of thy cry; when he shall hear it, he will answer thee.

20 And *though* the Lord give you the bread of adversity, and the water of affliction, yet shall not thy teachers be removed into a corner any more, but thine eyes shall see thy teachers:

21 And thine ears shall hear a word behind thee, saying, This *is* the way, walk ye in it, when ye turn to the right hand, and when ye turn to the left.

30:21 God's Guidance
◄ Psalm 73:24
Isaiah 42:16 ►

22 Ye shall defile also the covering of thy graven images of silver, and the ornament of thy molten images of gold: thou shalt cast them away as a menstruous cloth; thou shalt say unto it, Get thee hence.

23 Then shall he give the rain of thy seed, that thou shalt sow the ground withal; and bread of the increase of the earth, and it shall be fat and plenteous: in that day shall thy cattle feed in large pastures.

30:23 Blessing
◄ Psalm 81:16
Amos 9:13 ►

24 The oxen likewise and the young asses that ear the ground shall eat clean provender, which hath been winnowed with the shovel and with the fan.

25 And there shall be upon every high
mountain, and upon every high hill, rivers *and* streams of waters in the day of the
great slaughter, when the towers fall.
26 Moreover the light of the moon shall
be as the light of the sun, and the light of
the sun shall be sevenfold, as the light of
seven days, in the day that the LORD
bindeth up the breach of his people, and
healeth the stroke of their wound.
27 Behold, the name of the LORD cometh
from far, burning *with* his anger, and the
burden *thereof is* heavy: his lips are full of
indignation, and his tongue as a devouring fire:
28 And his breath, as an overflowing
stream, shall reach to the midst of the neck,
to sift the nations with the sieve of vanity:
and *there shall be* a bridle in the jaws of the
people, causing *them* to err.
29 Ye shall have a song, as in the night
when a holy solemnity is kept; and gladness of heart, as when one goeth with a
pipe to come into the mountain of the
LORD, to the mighty One of Israel.
30 And the LORD shall cause his glorious
voice to be heard, and shall shew the light-
ing down of his arm, with the indignation
of *his* anger, and *with* the flame of a devouring fire, *with* scattering, and tempest,
and hailstones.
31 For through the voice of the LORD shall
the Assyrian be beaten down, *which* smote
with a rod.
32 And *in* every place where the grounded
staff shall pass, which the LORD shall lay
upon him, *it* shall be with tabrets and
harps: and in battles of shaking will he
fight with it.
33 For Tophet *is* ordained of old; yea, for
the king it is prepared; he hath made *it*
deep and large: the pile thereof *is* fire and
much wood; the breath of the LORD, like a
stream of brimstone, doth kindle it.

31

1 Woe to them
that go down to
Egypt for help; and
stay on horses, and
trust in chariots,
because *they are*
many; and in horsemen, because they are
very strong; but they look not unto
the Holy One of Israel, neither seek the
LORD!
2 Yet he also *is* wise, and will bring evil,
and will not call
back his words: but
will arise against
the house of the
evildoers, and
against the help of
them that work iniquity.
3 Now the Egyptians *are* men, and not
God; and their horses flesh, and not spirit. When the LORD shall stretch out his
hand, both he that helpeth shall fall, and
he that is holpen shall fall down, and they
all shall fail together.
4 For thus hath the LORD spoken unto
me, Like as the lion and the young lion
roaring on his prey, when a multitude of
shepherds is called forth against him, *he*
will not be afraid of their voice, nor abase
himself for the noise of them: so shall the
LORD of hosts come down to fight for
mount Zion, and for the hill thereof.
5 As birds flying, so will the LORD of
hosts defend Jerusalem; defending also he
will deliver *it; and* passing over he will preserve *it*.
6 Turn ye unto *him from* whom the children of Israel have deeply revolted.
7 For in that day every man shall cast
away his idols of silver, and his idols of
gold, which your own hands have made
unto you *for* a sin.
8 Then shall the Assyrian fall with the
sword, not of a mighty man; and the
sword, not of a mean man, shall devour
him: but he shall flee from the sword, and
his young men shall be discomfited.
9 And he shall pass over to his strong
hold for fear, and his princes shall be afraid
of the ensign, saith the LORD, whose fire *is*
in Zion, and his furnace in Jerusalem.

31:1-3
Trusting in People
◄ Isaiah 30:2
Isaiah 36:6 ►

31:2
Evildoers
◄ Isaiah 14:20 ►

32

1 Behold, a king
shall reign in righ-
teousness, and
princes shall rule in
judgment.
2 And a man shall
be as an hiding place from the wind, and
a covert from the tempest; as rivers of water in a dry place, as the shadow of a great
rock in a weary land.
3 And the eyes of them that see shall not
be dim, and the ears of them that hear shall
hearken.
4 The heart also of the rash shall understand knowledge, and the tongue of

32:1 Jesus the King
◄ Isaiah 9:7
Jeremiah 23:5 ►

the stammerers shall be ready to speak plainly.

5 The vile person shall be no more called liberal, nor the churl said *to be* bountiful.

6 For the vile person will speak villany, and his heart will work iniquity, to practise hypocrisy, and to utter error against the LORD, to make empty the soul of the hungry, and he will cause the drink of the thirsty to fail.

7 The instruments also of the churl *are* evil: he deviseth wicked devices to destroy the poor with lying words, even when the needy speaketh right.

8 But the liberal deviseth liberal things; and by liberal things shall he stand.

9 Rise up, ye women that are at ease; hear my voice, ye careless daughters; give ear unto my speech.

32:9 Apathy
◄ Psalm 123:4
Isaiah 47:8 ►

10 Many days and years shall ye be troubled, ye careless women: for the vintage shall fail, the gathering shall not come.

11 Tremble, ye women that are at ease; be troubled, ye careless ones: strip you, and make you bare, and gird *sackcloth* upon *your* loins.

12 They shall lament for the teats, for the pleasant fields, for the fruitful vine.

13 Upon the land of my people shall come up thorns *and* briers; yea, upon all the houses of joy *in* the joyous city:

14 Because the palaces shall be forsaken; the multitude of the city shall be left; the forts and towers shall be for dens for ever, a joy of wild asses, a pasture of flocks;

15 Until the spirit be poured upon us from on high, and the wilderness be a fruitful field, and the fruitful field be counted for a forest.

16 Then judgment shall dwell in the wilderness, and righteousness remain in the fruitful field.

32:16
Better Neighborhoods
◄ Isaiah 16:5
Isaiah 33:5 ►

17 And the work of righteousness shall be peace; and the effect of righteousness quietness and assurance for ever.

18 And my people shall dwell in a peaceable habitation, and in sure dwellings, and in quiet resting places;

19 When it shall hail, coming down on the forest; and the city shall be low in a low place.

20 Blessed *are* ye that sow beside all waters, that send forth *thither* the feet of the ox and the ass.

33

1 Woe to thee that spoilest, and thou *wast* not spoiled; and dealest treacherously, and they dealt not treacherously with thee! when thou shalt cease to spoil, thou shalt be spoiled; *and* when thou shalt make an end to deal treacherously, they shall deal treacherously with thee.

2 O LORD, be gracious unto us; we have waited for thee: be thou their arm every morning, our salvation also in the time of trouble.

33:2 Waiting
◄ Isaiah 26:8
Lamentations 3:25 ►

3 At the noise of the tumult the people fled; at the lifting up of thyself the nations were scattered.

4 And your spoil shall be gathered *like* the gathering of the caterpiller: as the running to and fro of locusts shall he run upon them.

5 The LORD is exalted; for he dwelleth on high: he hath filled Zion with judgment and righteousness.

33:5
Better Neighborhoods
◄ Isaiah 32:16
Isaiah 54:14 ►

6 And wisdom and knowledge shall be the stability of thy times, *and* strength of salvation: the fear of the LORD *is* his treasure.

7 Behold, their valiant ones shall cry without: the ambassadors of peace shall weep bitterly.

8 The highways lie waste, the wayfaring man ceaseth: he hath broken the covenant, he hath despised the cities, he regardeth no man.

9 The earth mourneth *and* languisheth: Lebanon is ashamed *and* hewn down: Sharon is like a wilderness; and Bashan and Carmel shake off *their fruits.*

10 Now will I rise, saith the LORD; now will I be exalted; now will I lift up myself.

11 Ye shall conceive chaff, ye shall bring forth stubble: your breath, *as* fire, shall devour you.

12 And the people shall be *as* the burnings of lime: *as* thorns cut up shall they be burned in the fire.

13 Hear, ye *that are* far off, what I have done; and, ye *that are* near, acknowledge my might.

14 The sinners in Zion are afraid; fearfulness hath surprised the hypocrites. Who among us shall dwell with the devouring fire? who among us shall dwell with everlasting burnings?

33:14 Guilty Fear
◄ Isaiah 24:17
Isaiah 66:4 ►

15 He that walketh righteously, and speaketh uprightly; he that despiseth the gain of oppressions, that shaketh his hands from holding of bribes, that stoppeth his ears from hearing of blood, and shutteth his eyes from seeing evil;

33:15 Bribery
◄ Isaiah 5:23
Amos 5:12 ►

16 He shall dwell on high: his place of defence *shall be* the munitions of rocks: bread shall be given him; his waters *shall be* sure.

33:16 Good Rewarded
◄ Psalm 91:14
Isaiah 58:14 ►

33:16 Security
◄ Proverbs 3:24
Isaiah 43:2 ►

17 Thine eyes shall see the king in his beauty: they shall behold the land that is very far off.

18 Thine heart shall meditate terror. Where *is* the scribe? where *is* the receiver? where *is* he that counted the towers?

19 Thou shalt not see a fierce people, a people of a deeper speech than thou canst perceive; of a stammering tongue, *that thou canst* not understand.

20 Look upon Zion, the city of our solemnities: thine eyes shall see Jerusalem a quiet habitation, a tabernacle *that* shall not be taken down; not one of the stakes thereof shall ever be removed, neither shall any of the cords thereof be broken.

21 But there the glorious LORD *will be* unto us a place of broad rivers *and* streams; wherein shall go no galley with oars, neither shall gallant ship pass thereby.

22 For the LORD *is* our judge, the LORD *is* our lawgiver, the LORD *is* our king; he will save us.

23 Thy tacklings are loosed; they could not well strengthen their mast, they could not spread the sail: then is the prey of a great spoil divided; the lame take the prey.

24 And the inhabitant shall not say, I am sick: the people that dwell therein *shall be* forgiven *their* iniquity.

34

1 Come near, ye nations, to hear; and hearken, ye people: let the earth hear, and all that is therein; the world, and all things that come forth of it.

2 For the indignation of the LORD *is* upon all nations, and *his* fury upon all their armies: he hath utterly destroyed them, he hath delivered them to the slaughter.

3 Their slain also shall be cast out, and their stink shall come up out of their carcases, and the mountains shall be melted with their blood.

4 And all the host of heaven shall be dissolved, and the heavens shall be rolled together as a scroll: and all their host shall fall down, as the leaf falleth off from the vine, and as a falling *fig* from the fig tree.

5 For my sword shall be bathed in heaven: behold, it shall come down upon Idumea, and upon the people of my curse, to judgment.

6 The sword of the LORD is filled with blood, it is made fat with fatness, *and* with the blood of lambs and goats, with the fat of the kidneys of rams: for the LORD hath a sacrifice in Bozrah, and a great slaughter in the land of Idumea.

7 And the unicorns shall come down with them, and the bullocks with the bulls; and their land shall be soaked with blood, and their dust made fat with fatness.

8 For *it is* the day of the LORD'S vengeance, *and* the year of recompences for the controversy of Zion.

9 And the streams thereof shall be turned into pitch, and the dust thereof into brimstone, and the land thereof shall become burning pitch.

10 It shall not be quenched night nor day; the smoke thereof shall go up for ever: from generation to generation it shall lie waste; none shall pass through it for ever and ever.

11 But the cormorant and the bittern shall possess it; the owl also and the raven shall dwell in it: and he shall stretch out upon it the line of confusion, and the stones of emptiness.

12 They shall call the nobles thereof to

the kingdom, but none *shall be* there, and all her princes shall be nothing.

13 And thorns shall come up in her palaces, nettles and brambles in the fortresses thereof: and it shall be an habitation of dragons, *and* a court for owls.

14 The wild beasts of the desert shall also meet with the wild beasts of the island, and the satyr shall cry to his fellow; the screech owl also shall rest there, and find for herself a place of rest.

15 There shall the great owl make her nest, and lay, and hatch, and gather under her shadow: there shall the vultures also be gathered, every one with her mate.

16 Seek ye out of the book of the LORD, and read: no one of these shall fail, none shall want her mate: for my mouth it hath commanded, and his spirit it hath gathered them.

34:16 Reading the Bible
◄ Deuteronomy 17:19
John 5:39 ►

17 And he hath cast the lot for them, and his hand hath divided it unto them by line: they shall possess it for ever, from generation to generation shall they dwell therein.

35

1 The wilderness and the solitary place shall be glad for them; and the desert shall rejoice, and blossom as the rose.

2 It shall blossom abundantly, and rejoice even with joy and singing: the glory of Lebanon shall be given unto it, the excellency of Carmel and Sharon, they shall see the glory of the LORD, *and* the excellency of our God.

3 Strengthen ye the weak hands, and confirm the feeble knees.

4 Say to them *that are* of a fearful heart, Be strong, fear not: behold, your God will come *with* vengeance, *even* God *with* a recompence; he will come and save you.

5 Then the eyes of the blind shall be opened, and the ears of the deaf shall be unstopped.

6 Then shall the lame *man* leap as an hart, and the tongue of the dumb sing: for in the wilderness shall waters break out, and streams in the desert.

7 And the parched ground shall become a pool, and the thirsty land springs of water: in the habitation of dragons, where each lay, *shall be* grass with reeds and rushes.

8 And an highway shall be there, and a way, and it shall be called The way of holiness; the unclean shall not pass over it; but it *shall be* for those: the wayfaring men, though fools, shall not err *therein*.

9 No lion shall be there, nor *any* ravenous beast shall go up thereon, it shall not be found there; but the redeemed shall walk *there*:

10 And the ransomed of the LORD shall return, and come to Zion with songs and everlasting joy upon their heads: they shall obtain joy and gladness, and sorrow and sighing shall flee away.

35:10 Joy
◄ Isaiah 12:3
Luke 2:10 ►

36

1 Now it came to pass in the fourteenth year of king Hezekiah, *that* Sennacherib king of Assyria came up against all the defenced cities of Judah, and took them.

2 And the king of Assyria sent Rabshakeh from Lachish to Jerusalem unto king Hezekiah with a great army. And he stood by the conduit of the upper pool in the highway of the fuller's field.

3 Then came forth unto him Eliakim, Hilkiah's son, which was over the house, and Shebna the scribe, and Joah, Asaph's son, the recorder.

4 And Rabshakeh said unto them, Say ye now to Hezekiah, Thus saith the great king, the king of Assyria, What confidence *is* this wherein thou trustest?

5 I say, *sayest thou*, (but *they are but* vain words) *I have* counsel and strength for war: now on whom dost thou trust, that thou rebellest against me?

6 Lo, thou trustest in the staff of this broken reed, on Egypt; whereon if a man lean, it will go into his hand, and pierce it: so *is* Pharaoh king of Egypt to all that trust in him.

36:6 Trusting in People
◄ Isaiah 31:1-3
Jeremiah 17:5 ►

7 But if thou say to me, We trust in the LORD our God: *is it* not he, whose high places and whose altars Hezekiah hath taken away, and said to Judah and to Jerusalem, Ye shall worship before this altar?

8 Now therefore give pledges, I pray thee, to my master the king of Assyria, and I will give thee two thousand horses, if thou be able on thy part to set riders upon them.

9 How then wilt thou turn away the face

of one captain of the least of my master's servants, and put thy trust on Egypt for chariots and for horsemen?

10 And am I now come up without the LORD against this land to destroy it? the LORD said unto me, Go up against this land, and destroy it.

11 Then said Eliakim and Shebna and Joah unto Rabshakeh, Speak, I pray thee, unto thy servants in the Syrian language; for we understand *it:* and speak not to us in the Jews' language, in the ears of the people that *are* on the wall.

12 But Rabshakeh said, Hath my master sent me to thy master and to thee to speak these words? *hath he* not *sent me* to the men that sit upon the wall, that they may eat their own dung, and drink their own piss with you?

13 Then Rabshakeh stood, and cried with a loud voice in the Jews' language, and said, Hear ye the words of the great king, the king of Assyria.

14 Thus saith the king, Let not Hezekiah deceive you: for he shall not be able to deliver you.

15 Neither let Hezekiah make you trust in the LORD, saying, The LORD will surely deliver us: this city shall not be delivered into the hand of the king of Assyria.

16 Hearken not to Hezekiah: for thus saith the king of Assyria, Make *an agreement* with me *by* a present, and come out to me: and eat ye every one of his vine, and every one of his fig tree, and drink ye every one the waters of his own cistern;

17 Until I come and take you away to a land like your own land, a land of corn and wine, a land of bread and vineyards.

18 *Beware* lest Hezekiah persuade you, saying, The LORD will deliver us. Hath any of the gods of the nations delivered his land out of the hand of the king of Assyria?

19 Where *are* the gods of Hamath and Arphad? where *are* the gods of Sepharvaim? and have they delivered Samaria out of my hand?

20 Who *are they* among all the gods of these lands, that have delivered their land out of my hand, that the LORD should deliver Jerusalem out of my hand?

21 But they held their peace, and answered him not a word: for the king's commandment was, saying, Answer him not.

22 Then came Eliakim, the son of Hilkiah, that *was* over the household, and Shebna the scribe, and Joah, the son of Asaph, the recorder, to Hezekiah with *their* clothes rent, and told him the words of Rabshakeh.

37

1 And it came to pass, when king Hezekiah heard *it,* that he rent his clothes, and covered himself with sackcloth, and went into the house of the LORD.

2 And he sent Eliakim, who *was* over the household, and Shebna the scribe, and the elders of the priests covered with sackcloth, unto Isaiah the prophet the son of Amoz.

3 And they said unto him, Thus saith Hezekiah, This day *is* a day of trouble, and of rebuke, and of blasphemy: for the children are come to the birth, and *there is* not strength to bring forth.

4 It may be the LORD thy God will hear the words of Rabshakeh, whom the king of Assyria his master hath sent to reproach the living God, and will reprove the words which the LORD thy God hath heard: wherefore lift up *thy* prayer for the remnant that is left.

5 So the servants of king Hezekiah came to Isaiah.

6 And Isaiah said unto them, Thus shall ye say unto your master, Thus saith the LORD, Be not afraid of the words that thou hast heard, wherewith the servants of the king of Assyria have blasphemed me.

7 Behold, I will send a blast upon him, and he shall hear a rumour, and return to his own land; and I will cause him to fall by the sword in his own land.

8 So Rabshakeh returned, and found the king of Assyria warring against Libnah: for he had heard that he was departed from Lachish.

9 And he heard say concerning Tirhakah king of Ethiopia, He is come forth to make war with thee. And when he heard *it,* he sent messengers to Hezekiah, saying,

10 Thus shall ye speak to Hezekiah king of Judah, saying, Let not thy God, in whom thou trustest, deceive thee, saying, Jerusalem shall not be given into the hand of the king of Assyria.

11 Behold, thou hast heard what the kings of Assyria have done to all lands by destroying them utterly; and shalt thou be delivered?

12 Have the gods of the nations delivered them which my fathers have destroyed, *as*

Gozan, and Haran, and Rezeph, and the children of Eden which *were* in Telassar?

13 Where *is* the king of Hamath, and the king of Arphad, and the king of the city of Sepharvaim, Hena, and Ivah?

14 And Hezekiah received the letter from the hand of the messengers, and read it: and Hezekiah went up unto the house of the LORD, and spread it before the LORD.

15 And Hezekiah prayed unto the LORD, saying,

16 O LORD of hosts, God of Israel, that dwellest *between* the cherubims, thou *art* the God, *even* thou alone, of all the kingdoms of the earth: thou hast made heaven and earth.

17 Incline thine ear, O LORD, and hear; open thine eyes, O LORD, and see: and hear all the words of Sennacherib, which hath sent to reproach the living God.

18 Of a truth, LORD, the kings of Assyria have laid waste all the nations, and their countries,

19 And have cast their gods into the fire: for they *were* no gods, but the work of men's hands, wood and stone: therefore they have destroyed them.

20 Now therefore, O LORD our God, save us from his hand, that all the kingdoms of the earth may know that thou *art* the LORD, *even* thou only.

21 Then Isaiah the son of Amoz sent unto Hezekiah, saying, Thus saith the LORD God of Israel, Whereas thou hast prayed to me against Sennacherib king of Assyria:

22 This *is* the word which the LORD hath spoken concerning him; The virgin, the daughter of Zion, hath despised thee, *and* laughed thee to scorn; the daughter of Jerusalem hath shaken her head at thee.

23 Whom hast thou reproached and blasphemed? and against whom hast thou exalted *thy* voice, and lifted up thine eyes on high? *even* against the Holy One of Israel.

24 By thy servants hast thou reproached the Lord, and hast said, By the multitude of my chariots am I come up to the height of the mountains, to the sides of Lebanon; and I will cut down the tall cedars thereof, *and* the choice fir trees thereof: and I will enter into the height of his border, *and* the forest of his Carmel.

25 I have digged, and drunk water; and with the sole of my feet have I dried up all the rivers of the besieged places.

26 Hast thou not heard long ago, *how* I have done it; *and* of ancient times, that I have formed it? now have I brought it to pass, that thou shouldest be to lay waste defenced cities *into* ruinous heaps.

27 Therefore their inhabitants *were* of small power, they were dismayed and confounded: they were *as* the grass of the field, and *as* the green herb, *as* the grass on the housetops, and *as corn* blasted before it be grown up.

28 But I know thy abode, and thy going out, and thy coming in, and thy rage against me.

29 Because thy rage against me, and thy tumult, is come up into mine ears, therefore will I put my hook in thy nose, and my bridle in thy lips, and I will turn thee back by the way by which thou camest.

30 And this *shall be* a sign unto thee, Ye shall eat *this* year such as groweth of itself; and the second year that which springeth of the same: and in the third year sow ye, and reap, and plant vineyards, and eat the fruit thereof.

31 And the remnant that is escaped of the house of Judah shall again take root downward, and bear fruit upward:

32 For out of Jerusalem shall go forth a remnant, and they that escape out of mount Zion: the zeal of the LORD of hosts shall do this.

33 Therefore thus saith the LORD concerning the king of Assyria, He shall not come into this city, nor shoot an arrow there nor come before it with shields, nor cast a bank against it.

34 By the way that he came, by the same shall he return, and shall not come into this city, saith the LORD.

35 For I will defend this city to save it for mine own sake, and for my servant David's sake.

36 Then the angel of the LORD went forth, and smote in the camp of the Assyrians a hundred and fourscore and five thousand: and when they arose early in the morning, behold, they *were* all dead corpses.

37 So Sennacherib king of Assyria departed, and went and returned, and dwelt at Nineveh.

38 And it came to pass, as he was worshipping in the house of Nisroch his god, that Adrammelech and Sharezer his sons smote him with the sword; and they

escaped into the land of Armenia: and Esar-haddon his son reigned in his stead.

38

1 In those days was Hezekiah sick unto death. And Isaiah the prophet the son of Amoz came unto him, and said unto him, Thus saith the LORD, Set thine house in order: for thou shalt die, and not live.

2 Then Hezekiah turned his face toward the wall, and prayed unto the LORD,

3 And said, Remember now, O LORD, I beseech thee, how I have walked before thee in truth and with a perfect heart, and have done *that which is* good in thy sight. And Hezekiah wept sore.

4 Then came the word of the LORD to Isaiah, saying,

5 Go, and say to Hezekiah, Thus saith the LORD, the God of David thy father, I have heard thy prayer, I have seen thy tears: behold, I will add unto thy days fifteen years.

6 And I will deliver thee and this city out of the hand of the king of Assyria: and I will defend this city.

7 And this *shall be* a sign unto thee from the LORD, that the LORD will do this thing that he hath spoken;

8 Behold, I will bring again the shadow of the degrees, which is gone down in the sun dial of Ahaz, ten degrees backward. So the sun returned ten degrees, by which degrees it was gone down.

9 The writing of Hezekiah king of Judah, when he had been sick, and was recovered of his sickness:

10 I said in the cutting off of my days, I shall go to the gates of the grave: I am deprived of the residue of my years.

11 I said, I shall not see the LORD, *even* the LORD, in the land of the living: I shall behold man no more with the inhabitants of the world.

12 Mine age is departed, and is removed from me as a shepherd's tent: I have cut off like a weaver my life: he will cut me off with pining sickness: from day *even* to night wilt thou make an end of me.

38:12 Life Is Short
◄ Ecclesiastes 6:12
James 4:14 ►

13 I reckoned till morning, *that,* as a lion, so will he break all my bones: from day *even* to night wilt thou make an end of me.

14 Like a crane *or* a swallow, so did I chatter: I did mourn as a dove: mine eyes fail *with looking* upward: O LORD, I am oppressed; undertake for me.

15 What shall I say? he hath both spoken unto me, and himself hath done *it:* I shall go softly all my years in the bitterness of my soul.

16 O Lord, by these *things men* live, and in all these *things is* the life of my spirit: so wilt thou recover me, and make me to live.

17 Behold, for peace I had great bitterness: but thou hast in love to my soul *delivered it* from the pit of corruption: for thou hast cast all my sins behind thy back.

18 For the grave cannot praise thee, death can *not* celebrate thee: they that go down into the pit cannot hope for thy truth.

19 The living, the living, he shall praise thee, as I *do* this day: the father to the children shall make known thy truth.

20 The LORD *was ready* to save me: therefore we will sing my songs to the stringed instruments all the days of our life in the house of the LORD.

21 For Isaiah had said, Let them take a lump of figs, and lay *it* for a plaister upon the boil, and he shall recover.

22 Hezekiah also had said, What *is* the sign that I shall go up to the house of the LORD?

39

1 At that time Merodach-baladan, the son of Baladan, king of Babylon, sent letters and a present to Hezekiah: for he had heard that he had been sick, and was recovered.

2 And Hezekiah was glad of them, and shewed them the house of his precious things, the silver, and the gold, and the spices, and the precious ointment, and all the house of his armour, and all that was found in his treasures: there was nothing in his house, nor in all his dominion, that Hezekiah shewed them not.

39:2 Showing Off Stuff
◄ Esther 5:11
Luke 20:46 ►

3 Then came Isaiah the prophet unto king Hezekiah, and said unto him, What said these men? and from whence came they unto thee? And Hezekiah said, They are come from a far country unto me, *even* from Babylon.

4 Then said he, What have they seen in thine house? And Hezekiah answered, All that *is* in mine house have they seen: there

is nothing among my treasures that I have
not shewed them.
5 Then said Isaiah to Hezekiah, Hear the
word of the LORD of hosts:
6 Behold, the days come, that all that *is*
in thine house, and *that* which thy fathers
have laid up in store until this day, shall
be carried to Babylon: nothing shall be left,
saith the LORD.
7 And of thy sons that shall issue from
thee, which thou shalt beget, shall they
take away; and they shall be eunuchs in
the palace of the king of Babylon.
8 Then said Hezekiah to Isaiah, Good *is*
the word of the LORD which thou hast spoken. He said moreover, For there shall be
peace and truth in my days.

40

1 Comfort ye,
comfort ye my peo-
ple, saith your God.
2 Speak ye com-
fortably to Jerusa-
lem, and cry unto
her, that her warfare is accomplished, that
her iniquity is pardoned: for she hath received of the LORD'S hand double for all
her sins.

40:1
Comforting Others
◄ 1 Corinthians 14:3 ►

3 The voice of him that crieth in the wilderness, Prepare ye the way of the LORD,
make straight in the desert a highway for
our God.
4 Every valley shall be exalted, and every
mountain and hill shall be made low: and
the crooked shall be made straight, and
the rough places plain:
5 And the glory of the LORD shall be revealed, and all flesh shall see *it* together:
for the mouth of the LORD hath spoken *it*.
6 The voice said,
Cry. And he said,
What shall I cry? All
flesh *is* grass, and
all the goodliness
thereof *is* as the
flower of the field:

40:6 Your Body
◄ Isaiah 2:22
Isaiah 64:6 ►

7 The grass withereth, the flower fadeth:
because the spirit of the LORD bloweth
upon it: surely the people *is* grass.
8 The grass withereth, the flower fadeth:
but the word of our God shall stand for
ever.
9 O Zion, that bringest good tidings, get
thee up into the high mountain; O Jerusalem, that bringest good tidings, lift up thy
voice with strength; lift *it* up, be not afraid;
say unto the cities of Judah, Behold your
God!
10 Behold, the Lord GOD will come with
strong *hand*, and his arm shall rule for him:
behold, his reward *is* with him, and his
work before him.
11 He shall feed his flock like a shepherd:
he shall gather the lambs with his arm, and
carry *them* in his bosom, *and* shall gently
lead those that are with young.
12 Who hath measured the waters in the
hollow of his hand, and meted out heav-
en with the span, and comprehended the
dust of the earth in a measure, and weighed
the mountains in scales, and the hills in a
balance?
13 Who hath directed the Spirit of the
LORD, or *being* his counsellor hath taught
him?
14 With whom took he counsel, and *who*
instructed him, and taught him in the path
of judgment, and taught him knowledge,
and shewed to him the way of understanding?
15 Behold, the nations *are* as a drop of a
bucket, and are counted as the small dust
of the balance: behold, he taketh up the
isles as a very little thing.
16 And Lebanon *is* not sufficient to burn,
nor the beasts thereof sufficient for a burnt
offering.
17 All nations before him *are* as nothing;
and they are counted to him less than
nothing, and vanity.
18 To whom then will ye liken God?
or what likeness will ye compare unto
him?
19 The workman melteth a graven image,
and the goldsmith spreadeth it over with
gold, and casteth silver chains.
20 He that *is* so impoverished that he
hath no oblation chooseth a tree *that* will
not rot; he seeketh unto him a cunning
workman to prepare a graven image, *that*
shall not be moved.
21 Have ye not known? have ye not
heard? hath it not been told you from the
beginning? have ye not understood from
the foundations of the earth?
22 *It is* he that sitteth upon the circle of
the earth, and the inhabitants thereof *are*
as grasshoppers; that stretcheth out the
heavens as a curtain, and spreadeth them
out as a tent to dwell in:
23 That bringeth the princes to nothing;

he maketh the judges of the earth as
vanity.
24 Yea, they shall not be planted; yea,
they shall not be sown: yea, their stock
shall not take root in the earth: and he
shall also blow upon them, and they shall
wither, and the whirlwind shall take them
away as stubble.
25 To whom then will ye liken me, or
shall I be equal? saith the Holy One.
26 Lift up your eyes on high, and behold
who hath created these *things,* that bringeth
out their host by number: he calleth them
all by names by the greatness of his might,
for that *he is* strong in power; not one
faileth.
27 Why sayest thou, O Jacob, and
speakest, O Israel, My way is hid from the
LORD, and my judgment is passed over
from my God?
28 Hast thou not known? hast thou not
heard, *that* the everlasting God, the LORD,
the Creator of the ends of the earth,
fainteth not, neither is weary? *there is* no
searching of his understanding.
29 He giveth power to the faint; and to
them that have no might he increaseth
strength.
30 Even the youths shall faint and be
weary, and the young men shall utterly fall:
31 But they that
wait upon the LORD
shall renew *their*
strength; they shall
mount up with
wings as eagles;
they shall run, and
not be weary; *and*
they shall walk, and
not faint.

40:31 New Person
◄ Psalm 51:10
Isaiah 41:1 ►

40:31 Waiting for God
◄ Isaiah 8:17
Hosea 12:6 ►

41

1 Keep silence be-
fore me, O islands;
and let the people
renew *their* strength:
let them come near;
then let them
speak: let us come
near together to
judgment.

41:1 New Person
◄ Isaiah 40:31
Romans 12:2 ►

2 Who raised up the righteous *man* from
the east, called him to his foot, gave the
nations before him, and made *him* rule
over kings? he gave *them* as the dust to his
sword, *and* as driven stubble to his bow.
3 He pursued them, *and* passed safely;
even by the way *that* he had not gone with
his feet.
4 Who hath wrought and done *it,* calling the generations from the beginning?
I the LORD, the first, and with the last; I
am he.
5 The isles saw *it,* and feared; the ends of
the earth were afraid, drew near, and came.
6 They helped every one his neighbour;
and *every one* said to his brother, Be of good
courage.
7 So the carpenter encouraged the goldsmith, *and* he that smootheth *with* the
hammer him that smote the anvil, saying,
It is ready for the sodering: and he fastened
it with nails, *that* it should not be moved.
8 But thou, Israel, *art* my servant, Jacob
whom I have chosen, the seed of Abraham
my friend.
9 *Thou* whom I have taken from the ends
of the earth, and called thee from the chief
men thereof, and said unto thee, Thou *art*
my servant; I have chosen thee, and not
cast thee away.
10 Fear thou not; for I *am* with thee: be
not dismayed; for I *am* thy God: I will
strengthen thee; yea, I will help thee; yea,
I will uphold thee with the right hand of
my righteousness.
11 Behold, all they that were incensed
against thee shall be ashamed and confounded: they shall be as nothing; and they
that strive with thee shall perish.
12 Thou shalt seek them, and shalt not
find them, *even* them that contended with
thee: they that war against thee shall be as
nothing, and as a thing of nought.
13 For I the LORD
thy God will hold
thy right hand, say-
ing unto thee, Fear
not; I will help thee.

41:13 Encouraging People
◄ 2 Chronicles 35:2
Matthew 9:2 ►

14 Fear not, thou
worm Jacob, *and* ye men of Israel; I will
help thee, saith the LORD, and thy redeemer, the Holy One of Israel.
15 Behold, I will make thee a new sharp
threshing instrument having teeth: thou
shalt thresh the mountains, and beat *them*
small, and shalt make the hills as chaff.
16 Thou shalt fan them, and the wind
shall carry them away, and the whirlwind
shall scatter them: and thou shalt rejoice
in the LORD, *and* shalt glory in the Holy
One of Israel.

17*When* the poor and needy seek water, and *there is* none, *and* their tongue faileth for thirst, I the LORD will hear them, *I* the God of Israel will not forsake them.

41:17 Answers to Prayer
◄ Psalm 91:15
Isaiah 58:9 ►

41:17 Promises to the Poor
◄ Isaiah 25:4
James 2:5 ►

18I will open rivers in high places, and fountains in the midst of the valleys: I will make the wilderness a pool of water, and the dry land springs of water.

19I will plant in the wilderness the cedar, the shittah tree, and the myrtle, and the oil tree; I will set in the desert the fir tree, *and* the pine, and the box tree together:

20That they may see, and know, and consider, and understand together, that the hand of the LORD hath done this, and the Holy One of Israel hath created it.

21Produce your cause, saith the LORD; bring forth your strong *reasons,* saith the King of Jacob.

22Let them bring *them* forth, and shew us what shall happen: let them shew the former things, what they *be,* that we may consider them, and know the latter end of them; or declare us things for to come.

23Shew the things that are to come hereafter, that we may know that ye *are* gods: yea, do good, or do evil, that we may be dismayed, and behold *it* together.

24Behold, ye *are* of nothing, and your work of nought: an abomination *is he that* chooseth you.

25I have raised up *one* from the north, and he shall come: from the rising of the sun shall he call upon my name: and he shall come upon princes as *upon* morter, and as the potter treadeth clay.

26Who hath declared from the beginning, that we may know? and beforetime, that we may say, *He is* righteous? yea, *there is* none that sheweth, yea, *there is* none that declareth, yea, *there is* none that heareth your words.

27The first *shall say* to Zion, Behold, behold them: and I will give to Jerusalem one that bringeth good tidings.

28For I beheld, and *there was* no man; even among them, and *there was* no counsellor, that, when I asked of them, could answer a word.

29Behold, they *are* all vanity; their works *are* nothing: their molten images *are* wind and confusion.

42

1Behold my servant, whom I uphold; mine elect, *in whom* my soul delighteth; I have put my spirit upon him: he shall bring forth judgment to the Gentiles.

2He shall not cry, nor lift up, nor cause his voice to be heard in the street.

3A bruised reed shall he not break, and the smoking flax shall he not quench: he shall bring forth judgment unto truth.

4He shall not fail nor be discouraged, till he have set judgment in the earth: and the isles shall wait for his law.

5Thus saith God the LORD, he that created the heavens, and stretched them out; he that spread forth the earth, and that which cometh out of it; he that giveth breath unto the people upon it, and spirit to them that walk therein:

6I the LORD have called thee in righteousness, and will hold thine hand, and will keep thee, and give thee for a covenant of the people, for a light of the Gentiles;

7To open the blind eyes, to bring out the prisoners from the prison, *and* them that sit in darkness out of the prison house.

8I *am* the LORD: that *is* my name: and my glory will I not give to another, neither my praise to graven images.

9Behold, the former things are come to pass, and new things do I declare: before they spring forth I tell you of them.

10Sing unto the LORD a new song, *and* his praise from the end of the earth, ye that go down to the sea, and all that is therein; the isles, and the inhabitants thereof.

11Let the wilderness and the cities thereof lift up *their voice,* the villages *that* Kedar doth inhabit: let the inhabitants of the rock sing, let them shout from the top of the mountains.

12Let them give glory unto the LORD, and declare his praise in the islands.

42:12 Praising God
◄ Psalm 67:3
Hebrews 13:15 ►

13The LORD shall go forth as a mighty man, he shall stir up jealousy like a man of war: he shall cry, yea, roar; he shall prevail against his enemies.

14 I have long time holden my peace; I have been still, *and* refrained myself: *now* will I cry like a travailing woman; I will destroy and devour at once.

15 I will make waste mountains and hills, and dry up all their herbs; and I will make the rivers islands, and I will dry up the pools.

16 And I will bring the blind by a way *that* they knew not; I will lead them in paths *that* they have not known: I will make darkness light before them, and crooked things straight. These things will I do unto them, and not forsake them.

42:16 God's Guidance
◄ Isaiah 30:21
Isaiah 48:17 ►

17 They shall be turned back, they shall be greatly ashamed, that trust in graven images, that say to the molten images, Ye *are* our gods.

18 Hear, ye deaf; and look, ye blind, that ye may see.

19 Who *is* blind, but my servant? or deaf, as my messenger *that* I sent? who *is* blind as *he that is* perfect, and blind as the LORD'S servant?

20 Seeing many things, but thou observest not; opening the ears, but he heareth not.

21 The LORD is well pleased for his righteousness' sake; he will magnify the law, and make *it* honourable.

22 But this *is* a people robbed and spoiled; *they are* all of them snared in holes, and they are hid in prison houses: they are for a prey, and none delivereth; for a spoil, and none saith, Restore.

23 Who among you will give ear to this? *who* will hearken and hear for the time to come?

24 Who gave Jacob for a spoil, and Israel to the robbers? did not the LORD, he against whom we have sinned? for they would not walk in his ways, neither were they obedient unto his law.

42:25 Hard-heart Aches
◄ Proverbs 29:1
Romans 2:5 ►

42:25 Refusing Correction
◄ Isaiah 9:13
Jeremiah 2:30 ►

25 Therefore he hath poured upon him the fury of his anger, and the strength of battle: and it hath set him on fire round about, yet he knew not; and it burned him, yet he laid *it* not to heart.

43

1 But now thus saith the LORD that created thee, O Jacob, and he that formed thee, O Israel, Fear not: for I have redeemed thee, I have called *thee* by thy name; thou *art* mine.

43:1 Adopted by God
◄ Deuteronomy 14:2
Isaiah 63:16 ►

2 When thou passest through the waters, I *will be* with thee; and through the rivers, they shall not overflow thee: when thou walkest through the fire, thou shalt not be burned; neither shall the flame kindle upon thee.

43:2 Security
◄ Isaiah 33:16
Hebrews 13:6 ►

3 For I *am* the LORD thy God, the Holy One of Israel, thy Saviour: I gave Egypt *for* thy ransom, Ethiopia and Seba for thee.

4 Since thou wast precious in my sight, thou hast been honourable, and I have loved thee: therefore will I give men for thee, and people for thy life.

5 Fear not: for I *am* with thee: I will bring thy seed from the east, and gather thee from the west;

6 I will say to the north, Give up; and to the south, Keep not back: bring my sons from far, and my daughters from the ends of the earth;

7 *Even* every one that is called by my name: for I have created him for my glory, I have formed him; yea, I have made him.

8 Bring forth the blind people that have eyes, and the deaf that have ears.

9 Let all the nations be gathered together, and let the people be assembled: who among them can declare this, and shew us former things? let them bring forth their witnesses, that they may be justified: or let them hear, and say, *It is* truth.

43:10 Only One God
◄ Psalm 86:10
Isaiah 44:6 ►

10 Ye *are* my witnesses, saith the LORD, and my servant whom I have chosen: that ye may

43:10 Witnessing
◄ John 15:27 ►

know and believe me, and understand that I *am* he: before me there was no God formed, neither shall there be after me.

11 I, *even* I, *am* the LORD; and beside me *there is* no saviour.

12 I have declared, and have saved, and I have shewed, when *there was* no strange *god* among you: therefore ye *are* my witnesses, saith the LORD, that I *am* God.

13 Yea, before the day *was* I *am* he; and *there is* none that can deliver out of my hand: I will work, and who shall let it?

43:13 All-powerful
◄ Psalm 135:6
Habakkuk 3:6 ►

14 Thus saith the LORD, your redeemer, the Holy One of Israel; For your sake I have sent to Babylon, and have brought down all their nobles, and the Chaldeans, whose cry *is* in the ships.

15 I *am* the LORD, your Holy One, the creator of Israel, your King.

16 Thus saith the LORD, which maketh a way in the sea, and a path in the mighty waters;

17 Which bringeth forth the chariot and horse, the army and the power; they shall lie down together, they shall not rise: they are extinct, they are quenched as tow.

18 Remember ye not the former things, neither consider the things of old.

19 Behold, I will do a new thing; now it shall spring forth; shall ye not know it? I will even make a way in the wilderness, *and* rivers in the desert.

20 The beast of the field shall honour me, the dragons and the owls: because I give waters in the wilderness, *and* rivers in the desert, to give drink to my people, my chosen.

21 This people have I formed for myself; they shall shew forth my praise.

22 But thou hast not called upon me, O Jacob; but thou hast been weary of me, O Israel.

43:22 Not Praying
◄ Psalm 53:4
Isaiah 64:7 ►

23 Thou hast not brought me the small cattle of thy burnt offerings; neither hast thou honoured me with thy sacrifices. I have not caused thee to serve with an offering, nor wearied thee with incense.

43:23 Being Stingy
◄ Ecclesiastes 5:13
Malachi 3:8 ►

24 Thou hast bought me no sweet cane with money, neither hast thou filled me with the fat of thy sacrifices: but thou hast made me to serve with thy sins, thou hast wearied me with thine iniquities.

43:24 Saying Thank You
◄ Luke 17:18 ►

25 I, *even* I, *am* he that blotteth out thy transgressions for mine own sake, and will not remember thy sins.

43:25 God's Forgiveness
◄ Isaiah 44:22 ►

26 Put me in remembrance: let us plead together: declare thou, that thou mayest be justified.

27 Thy first father hath sinned, and thy teachers have transgressed against me.

28 Therefore I have profaned the princes of the sanctuary, and have given Jacob to the curse, and Israel to reproaches.

44

1 Yet now hear, O Jacob my servant; and Israel, whom I have chosen:

2 Thus saith the LORD that made thee, and formed thee from the womb, *which* will help thee; Fear not, O Jacob, my servant; and thou, Jesurun, whom I have chosen.

3 For I will pour water upon him that is thirsty, and floods upon the dry ground: I will pour my spirit upon thy seed, and my blessing upon thine offspring:

4 And they shall spring up *as* among the grass, as willows by the water courses.

5 One shall say, I *am* the LORD'S; and another shall call *himself* by the name of Jacob; and another shall subscribe *with* his hand unto the LORD, and surname *himself* by the name of Israel.

6 Thus saith the LORD the King of Israel, and his redeemer the LORD of hosts; I *am* the first, and I *am* the last; and beside me *there is* no God.

44:6 Only One God
◄ Isaiah 43:10
Isaiah 45:18 ►

7 And who, as I, shall call, and shall declare it, and set it in order for me, since I appointed the ancient people? and the things that are coming, and shall come, let them shew unto them.

8 Fear ye not, neither be afraid: have not I told thee from that time, and have declared *it?* ye *are* even my witnesses. Is there a God beside me? yea, *there is* no God; I know not *any.*

9 They that make a graven image *are* all of them vanity; and their delectable things shall not profit; and they *are* their own witnesses; they see not, nor know; that they may be ashamed.

10 Who hath formed a god, or molten a graven image *that* is profitable for nothing?

11 Behold, all his fellows shall be ashamed: and the workmen, they *are* of men: let them all be gathered together, let them stand up; *yet* they shall fear, *and* they shall be ashamed together.

12 The smith with the tongs both worketh in the coals, and fashioneth it with hammers, and worketh it with the strength of his arms: yea, he is hungry, and his strength faileth: he drinketh no water, and is faint.

13 The carpenter stretcheth out *his* rule; he marketh it out with a line; he fitteth it with planes, and he marketh it out with the compass, and maketh it after the figure of a man, according to the beauty of a man; that it may remain in the house.

14 He heweth him down cedars, and taketh the cypress and the oak, which he strengtheneth for himself among the trees of the forest: he planteth an ash, and the rain doth nourish *it.*

15 Then shall it be for a man to burn: for he will take thereof, and warm himself; yea, he kindleth *it,* and baketh bread; yea, he maketh a god, and worshippeth *it;* he maketh it a graven image, and falleth down thereto.

16 He burneth part thereof in the fire; with part thereof he eateth flesh; he roasteth roast, and is satisfied: yea, he warmeth *himself,* and saith, Aha, I am warm, I have seen the fire:

17 And the residue thereof he maketh a god, *even* his graven image: he falleth down unto it, and worshippeth *it,* and prayeth unto it, and saith, Deliver me; for thou *art* my god.

18 They have not known nor understood: for he hath shut their eyes, that they cannot see; *and* their hearts, that they cannot understand.

19 And none considereth in his heart, neither *is there* knowledge nor understanding to say, I have burned part of it in the fire; yea, also I have baked bread upon the coals thereof; I have roasted flesh, and eaten *it:* and shall I make the residue thereof an abomination? shall I fall down to the stock of a tree?

20 He feedeth on ashes: a deceived heart hath turned him aside, that he cannot deliver his soul, nor say, *Is there* not a lie in my right hand?

44:20
Lying to Yourself
◄ Psalm 36:2
Galatians 6:3 ►

21 Remember these, O Jacob and Israel; for thou *art* my servant: I have formed thee; thou *art* my servant: O Israel, thou shalt not be forgotten of me.

22 I have blotted out, as a thick cloud, thy transgressions, and, as a cloud, thy sins: return unto me; for I have redeemed thee.

44:22
God's Forgiveness
◄ Isaiah 43:25
Isaiah 55:7 ►

23 Sing, O ye heavens; for the LORD hath done *it:* shout, ye lower parts of the earth: break forth into singing, ye mountains, O forest, and every tree therein: for the LORD hath redeemed Jacob, and glorified himself in Israel.

44:23 Nature's Praise
◄ Psalm 148:3
Isaiah 49:13 ►

24 Thus saith the LORD, thy redeemer, and he that formed thee from the womb, I *am* the LORD that maketh all *things;* that stretcheth forth the heavens alone; that spreadeth abroad the earth by myself;

25 That frustrateth the tokens of the liars, and maketh diviners mad; that turneth wise *men* backward, and maketh their knowledge foolish;

44:25
Being Smart
◄ 1 Corinthians 8:2 ►

26 That confirmeth the word of his servant, and performeth the counsel of his messengers; that saith to Jerusalem, Thou shalt be inhabited; and

44:25 Liars
◄ Proverbs 19:9
Revelation 21:8 ►

to the cities of Judah, Ye shall be built, and I will raise up the decayed places thereof:

27 That saith to the deep, Be dry, and I will dry up thy rivers:

28 That saith of Cyrus, *He is* my shepherd, and shall perform all my pleasure: even saying to Jerusalem, Thou shalt be built; and to the temple, Thy foundation shall be laid.

45

1 Thus saith the LORD to his anointed, to Cyrus, whose right hand I have holden, to subdue nations before him; and I will loose the loins of kings, to open before him the two leaved gates; and the gates shall not be shut;

2 I will go before thee, and make the crooked places straight: I will break in pieces the gates of brass, and cut in sunder the bars of iron:

3 And I will give thee the treasures of darkness, and hidden riches of secret places, that thou mayest know that I, the LORD, which call *thee* by thy name, *am* the God of Israel.

4 For Jacob my servant's sake, and Israel mine elect, I have even called thee by thy name: I have surnamed thee, though thou hast not known me.

5 I *am* the LORD, and *there is* none else, *there is* no God beside me: I girded thee, though thou hast not known me:

6 That they may know from the rising of the sun, and from the west, that *there is* none beside me. I *am* the LORD, and *there is* none else.

7 I form the light, and create darkness: I make peace, and create evil: I the LORD do all these *things.*

8 Drop down, ye heavens, from above, and let the skies pour down righteousness: let the earth open, and let them bring forth salvation, and let righteousness spring up together; I the LORD have created it.

9 Woe unto him that striveth with his Maker! *Let* the potsherd *strive* with the potsherds of the earth. Shall the clay say to him that fashioneth it, What makest thou? or thy work, He hath no hands?

10 Woe unto him that saith unto *his* father, What begettest thou? or to the woman, What hast thou brought forth?

11 Thus saith the LORD, the Holy One of Israel, and his Maker, Ask me of things to come concerning my sons, and concerning the work of my hands command ye me.

12 I have made the earth, and created man upon it: I, *even* my hands, have stretched out the heavens, and all their host have I commanded.

13 I have raised him up in righteousness, and I will direct all his ways: he shall build my city, and he shall let go my captives, not for price nor reward, saith the LORD of hosts.

14 Thus saith the LORD, The labour of Egypt, and merchandise of Ethiopia and of the Sabeans, men of stature, shall come over unto thee, and they shall be thine: they shall come after thee; in chains they shall come over, and they shall fall down unto thee, they shall make supplication unto thee, *saying,* Surely God *is* in thee; and *there is* none else, *there is* no God.

15 Verily thou *art* a God that hidest thyself, O God of Israel, the Saviour.

16 They shall be ashamed, and also confounded, all of them: they shall go to confusion together *that are* makers of idols.

17 *But* Israel shall be saved in the LORD with an everlasting salvation: ye shall not be ashamed nor confounded world without end.

18 For thus saith the LORD that created the heavens; God himself that formed the earth and made it; he hath established it, he created it not in vain, he formed it to be inhabited: I *am* the LORD; and *there is* none else.

45:18 Only One God
◄ Isaiah 44:6
Mark 12:29 ►

19 I have not spoken in secret, in a dark place of the earth: I said not unto the seed of Jacob, Seek ye me in vain: I the LORD speak righteousness, I declare things that are right.

20 Assemble yourselves and come; draw near together, ye *that are* escaped of the nations: they have no knowledge that set up the wood of their graven image, and pray unto a god *that* cannot save.

21 Tell ye, and bring *them* near; yea, let them take counsel together: who hath declared this from ancient time? *who* hath told it from that time? *have*

45:21 God's Justice
◄ Proverbs 16:11
Zephaniah 3:5 ►

not I the LORD? and *there is* no God else
beside me; a just God and a Saviour; *there*
is none beside me.
22Look unto me,
and be ye saved, all
the ends of the
earth: for I *am* God,
and *there is* none
else.

45:22
God Calls You
◄ Isaiah 55:1 ►

23I have sworn by myself, the word is
gone out of my mouth *in* righteousness, and shall not return, That unto me
every knee shall bow, every tongue shall
swear.
24Surely, shall *one* say, in the LORD have
I righteousness and strength: *even* to him
shall *men* come; and all that are incensed
against him shall be ashamed.
25In the LORD
shall all the seed of
Israel be justified,
and shall glory.

45:25 Boasting
◄ Psalm 44:8
Jeremiah 9:24 ►

46

1Bel boweth
down, Nebo stoop-
eth, their idols were upon the beasts, and
upon the cattle: your carriages *were* heavy
loaden; *they are* a burden to the weary *beast.*
2They stoop, they bow down together;
they could not deliver the burden, but
themselves are gone into captivity.
3Hearken unto me, O house of Jacob,
and all the remnant of the house of Israel,
which are borne *by me* from the belly,
which are carried from the womb:
4And *even* to *your*
old age I *am* he; and
even to hoar hairs
will I carry *you:* I
have made, and I
will bear; even I will
carry, and will deliver *you.*

46:4 Evil Attacks
◄ Psalm 116:8
1 Corinthians 10:13 ►

5To whom will ye liken me, and make
me equal, and compare me, that we may
be like?
6They lavish gold out of the bag, and
weigh silver in the balance, *and* hire a goldsmith; and he maketh it a god: they fall
down, yea, they worship.
7They bear him upon the shoulder, they
carry him, and set him in his place, and
he standeth; from his place shall he not
remove: yea, *one* shall cry unto him, yet
can he not answer, nor save him out of his
trouble.
8Remember this, and shew yourselves
men: bring *it* again to mind, O ye transgressors.
9Remember the former things of old: for
I *am* God, and *there is* none else; *I am* God,
and *there is* none like me,
10Declaring the end from the beginning,
and from ancient times *the things* that are
not *yet* done, saying, My counsel shall
stand, and I will do all my pleasure:
11Calling a ravenous bird from the east,
the man that executeth my counsel from a
far country: yea, I have spoken *it,* I will
also bring it to pass; I have purposed *it,* I
will also do it.
12Hearken unto me, ye stouthearted,
that *are* far from righteousness:
13I bring near my righteousness; it shall
not be far off, and my salvation shall not
tarry: and I will place salvation in Zion for
Israel my glory.

47

1Come down, and sit in the dust, O virgin daughter of Babylon, sit on the ground:
there is no throne, O daughter of the
Chaldeans: for thou shalt no more be
called tender and delicate.
2Take the millstones, and grind meal:
uncover thy locks, make bare the leg, uncover the thigh, pass over the rivers.
3Thy nakedness shall be uncovered, yea,
thy shame shall be seen: I will take vengeance, and I will not meet *thee as* a man.
4*As for* our redeemer, the LORD of hosts
is his name, the Holy One of Israel.
5Sit thou silent, and get thee into darkness, O daughter of the Chaldeans: for
thou shalt no more be called, The lady of
kingdoms.
6I was wroth with my people, I have
polluted mine inheritance, and given them
into thine hand: thou didst shew them no
mercy; upon the ancient hast thou very
heavily laid thy yoke.
7And thou saidst, I shall be a lady for
ever: *so* that thou
didst not lay these
things to thy heart,
neither didst re-
member the latter
end of it.

47:8 Apathy
◄ Isaiah 32:9
Isaiah 64:7 ►

8Therefore hear
now this, *thou that*
art given to plea-
sures, that dwellest
carelessly, that say-
est in thine heart, I

47:8 Self-confidence
◄ Proverbs 28:26
Hosea 10:13 ►

am, and none else beside me; I shall not sit *as* a widow, neither shall I know the loss of children:

47:8-9 Luxury
◄ Isaiah 22:13
Luke 8:14 ►

9 But these two *things* shall come to thee in a moment in one day, the loss of children, and widowhood: they shall come upon thee in their perfection for the multitude of thy sorceries, *and* for the great abundance of thine enchantments.

10 For thou hast trusted in thy wickedness: thou hast said, None seeth me. Thy wisdom and thy knowledge, it hath perverted thee; and thou hast said in thine heart, I *am,* and none else beside me.

11 Therefore shall evil come upon thee; thou shalt not know from whence it riseth: and mischief shall fall upon thee; thou shalt not be able to put if off: and desolation shall come upon thee suddenly, *which* thou shalt not know.

12 Stand now with thine enchantments, and with the multitude of thy sorceries, wherein thou hast laboured from thy youth; if so be thou shalt be able to profit, if so be thou mayest prevail.

13 Thou art wearied in the multitude of thy counsels. Let now the astrologers, the stargazers, the monthly prognosticators, stand up, and save thee from *these things* that shall come upon thee.

14 Behold, they shall be as stubble; the fire shall burn them; they shall not deliver themselves from the power of the flame: *there shall* not *be* a coal to warm at, *nor* fire to sit before it.

15 Thus shall they be unto thee with whom thou hast laboured, *even* thy merchants, from thy youth: they shall wander every one to his quarter; none shall save thee.

48

1 Hear ye this, O house of Jacob, which are called by the name of Israel, and are come forth out of the waters of Judah, which swear by the name of the LORD, and make mention of the God of Israel, *but* not in truth, nor in righteousness.

2 For they call themselves of the holy city, and stay themselves upon the God of Israel; The LORD of hosts *is* his name.

3 I have declared the former things from the beginning; and they went forth out of my mouth, and I shewed them; I did *them* suddenly, and they came to pass.

4 Because I knew that thou *art* obstinate, and thy neck *is* an iron sinew, and thy brow brass;

5 I have even from the beginning declared *it* to thee; before it came to pass I shewed *it* thee: lest thou shouldest say, Mine idol hath done them, and my graven image, and my molten image, hath commanded them.

6 Thou hast heard, see all this; and will not ye declare *it?* I have shewed thee new things from this time, even hidden things, and thou didst not know them.

7 They are created now, and not from the beginning; even before the day when thou heardest them not; lest thou shouldest say, Behold, I knew them.

8 Yea, thou heardest not; yea, thou knewest not; yea, from that time *that* thine ear was not opened: for I knew that thou wouldest deal very treacherously, and wast called a transgressor from the womb.

9 For my name's sake will I defer mine anger, and for my praise will I refrain for thee, that I cut thee not off.

48:9 God's Patience
◄ Numbers 14:18
Ezekiel 20:17 ►

10 Behold, I have refined thee, but not with silver; I have chosen thee in the furnace of affliction.

48:10 Pain
◄ Psalm 66:10
Malachi 3:3 ►

11 For mine own sake, *even* for mine own sake, will I do *it:* for how should *my name* be polluted? and I will not give my glory unto another.

12 Hearken unto me, O Jacob and Israel, my called; I *am* he; I *am* the first, I also *am* the last.

13 Mine hand also hath laid the foundation of the earth, and my right hand hath spanned the heavens: *when* I call unto them, they stand up together.

14 All ye, assemble yourselves, and hear; which among them hath declared these *things?* The LORD hath loved him: he will do his pleasure on Babylon, and his arm *shall be on* the Chaldeans.

15 I, *even* I, have spoken; yea, I have called him: I have brought him, and he shall make his way prosperous.

16 Come ye near unto me, hear ye this; I have not spoken in secret from the

beginning; from the time that it was, there *am* I: and now the Lord GOD, and his Spirit, hath sent me.

17 Thus saith the LORD, thy Redeemer, the Holy One of Israel; I *am* the LORD thy God which teacheth thee to profit, which leadeth thee by the way *that* thou shouldest go.

48:17 God's Guidance
◄ Isaiah 42:16
Luke 1:79 ►

48:17 God as Teacher
◄ Isaiah 28:26
Isaiah 54:13 ►

18 O that thou hadst hearkened to my commandments! then had thy peace been as a river, and thy righteousness as the waves of the sea:

48:18 Peace of Mind
◄ Isaiah 26:3
Isaiah 54:13 ►

19 Thy seed also had been as the sand, and the offspring of thy bowels like the gravel thereof; his name should not have been cut off nor destroyed from before me.

20 Go ye forth of Babylon, flee ye from the Chaldeans, with a voice of singing declare ye, tell this, utter it *even* to the end of the earth; say ye, The LORD hath redeemed his servant Jacob.

21 And they thirsted not *when* he led them through the deserts: he caused the waters to flow out of the rock for them: he clave the rock also, and the waters gushed out.

22 *There is* no peace, saith the LORD, unto the wicked.

49

1 Listen, O isles, unto me; and hearken, ye people, from far; The LORD hath called me from the womb; from the bowels of my mother hath he made mention of my name.

2 And he hath made my mouth like a sharp sword; in the shadow of his hand hath he hid me, and made me a polished shaft; in his quiver hath he hid me;

3 And said unto me, Thou *art* my servant, O Israel, in whom I will be glorified.

4 Then I said, I have laboured in vain, I have spent my strength for nought, and in vain: *yet* surely my judgment *is* with the LORD, and my work with my God.

5 And now, saith the LORD that formed me from the womb *to be* his servant, to bring Jacob again to him, Though Israel be not gathered, yet shall I be glorious in the eyes of the LORD, and my God shall be my strength.

6 And he said, It is a light thing that thou shouldest be my servant to raise up the tribes of Jacob, and to restore the preserved of Israel: I will also give thee for a light to the Gentiles, that thou mayest be my salvation unto the end of the earth.

7 Thus saith the LORD, the Redeemer of Israel, *and* his Holy One, to him whom man despiseth, to him whom the nation abhorreth, to a servant of rulers, Kings shall see and arise, princes also shall worship, because of the LORD that is faithful, *and* the Holy One of Israel, and he shall choose thee.

8 Thus saith the LORD, In an acceptable time have I heard thee, and in a day of salvation have I helped thee: and I will preserve thee, and give thee for a covenant of the people, to establish the earth, to cause to inherit the desolate heritages;

49:8 Safety
◄ Proverbs 2:8
2 Timothy 4:18 ►

9 That thou mayest say to the prisoners, Go forth; to them that *are* in darkness, Shew yourselves. They shall feed in the ways, and their pastures *shall be* in all high places.

10 They shall not hunger nor thirst; neither shall the heat nor sun smite them: for he that hath mercy on them shall lead them, even by the springs of water shall he guide them.

11 And I will make all my mountains a way, and my highways shall be exalted.

12 Behold, these shall come from far: and, lo, these from the north and from the west; and these from the land of Sinim.

13 Sing, O heavens; and be joyful, O earth; and break forth into singing, O mountains: for the LORD hath comforted his people, and will have mercy upon his afflicted.

49:13 Nature's Praise
◄ Isaiah 44:23
Isaiah 55:12 ►

14 But Zion said, The LORD hath forsaken me, and my Lord hath forgotten me.

15 Can a woman forget her sucking child, that she should not have compassion on the son of her womb? yea, they may forget, yet will I not forget thee.

16 Behold, I have graven thee upon the
palms of *my* hands; thy walls *are* continually before me.
17 Thy children shall make haste; thy
destroyers and they that made thee waste
shall go forth of thee.
18 Lift up thine eyes round about, and
behold: all these gather themselves together, *and* come to thee. *As* I live, saith the
LORD, thou shalt surely clothe thee with
them all, as with an ornament, and bind
them *on thee,* as a bride *doeth.*
19 For thy waste and thy desolate places,
and the land of thy destruction, shall even
now be too narrow by reason of the inhabitants, and they that swallowed thee up
shall be far away.
20 The children which thou shalt have,
after thou hast lost the other, shall
say again in thine ears, The place *is* too
strait for me: give place to me that I may
dwell.
21 Then shalt thou say in thine heart,
Who hath begotten me these, seeing I have
lost my children, and am desolate, a captive, and removing to and fro? and who
hath brought up these? Behold, I was left
alone; these, where *had* they *been?*
22 Thus saith the Lord GOD, Behold, I
will lift up mine hand to the Gentiles, and
set up my standard to the people: and they
shall bring thy sons in *their* arms, and thy
daughters shall be carried upon *their*
shoulders.
23 And kings shall be thy nursing fathers,
and their queens thy nursing mothers: they
shall bow down to thee with *their* face toward the earth, and lick up the dust of thy
feet; and thou shalt know that I *am* the
LORD: for they shall not be ashamed that
wait for me.
24 Shall the prey be taken from the
mighty, or the lawful captive delivered?
25 But thus saith the LORD, Even the captives of the mighty shall be taken away, and
the prey of the terrible shall be delivered:
for I will contend with him that contendeth with thee, and I will save thy children.
26 And I will feed them that oppress thee
with their own flesh; and they shall be
drunken with their own blood, as with
sweet wine: and all flesh shall know that I
the LORD *am* thy Saviour and thy Redeemer, the mighty One of Jacob.

50

1 Thus saith the LORD, Where *is* the bill
of your mother's divorcement, whom I
have put away? or which of my creditors *is*
it to whom I have sold you? Behold, for
your iniquities have ye sold yourselves, and
for your transgressions is your mother put
away.
2 Wherefore, when I came, *was there* no
man? when I called, *was there* none to answer? Is my hand shortened at all, that it
cannot redeem? or have I no power to deliver? behold, at my rebuke I dry up the
sea, I make the rivers a wilderness: their
fish stinketh, because *there is* no water, and
dieth for thirst.
3 I clothe the heavens with blackness,
and I make sackcloth their covering.
4 The Lord GOD
hath given me the
tongue of the
learned, that I
should know how
to speak a word in
season to *him that is*
weary: he wakeneth
morning by morn-
ing, he wakeneth
mine ear to hear as
the learned.
5 The Lord GOD
hath opened mine
ear, and I was not
rebellious, neither
turned away back.
6 I gave my back
to the smiters, and
my cheeks to them that plucked off the
hair: I hid not my face from shame and
spitting.
7 For the Lord GOD will help me; therefore shall I not be confounded: therefore
have I set my face like a flint, and I know
that I shall not be ashamed.
8 *He is* near that justifieth me; who will
contend with me? let us stand together:
who *is* mine adversary? let him come near
to me.
9 Behold, the
Lord GOD will help
me; who *is* he *that*
shall condemn me?
lo, they all shall
wax old as a gar-
ment; the moth shall eat them up.
10 Who *is* among you that feareth the

50:4 Gifts from God
◄ Ecclesiastes 2:26
Matthew 9:8 ►

50:4
Wise Words
◄ Ecclesiastes 12:11 ►

50:4
Work that Helps Others
◄ Isaiah 21:14
Matthew 25:35 ►

50:9
No Condemnation
◄ Luke 6:37 ►

Turn to the next page for more . . .

LORD, that obeyeth the voice of his servant, that walketh *in* darkness, and hath no light? let him trust in the name of the LORD, and stay upon his God.

50:10 Trusting God
◄ Isaiah 26:4 ►

50:10 Why Fear God?
◄ Proverbs 1:7
Malachi 3:16 ►

11 Behold, all ye that kindle a fire, that compass *yourselves* about with sparks: walk in the light of your fire, and in the sparks *that ye* have kindled. This shall ye have of mine hand; ye shall lie down in sorrow.

51

1 Hearken to me, ye that follow after righteousness, ye that seek the LORD: look unto the rock *whence* ye are hewn, and to the hole of the pit *whence* ye are digged.

2 Look unto Abraham your father, and unto Sarah *that* bare you: for I called him alone, and blessed him, and increased him.

3 For the LORD shall comfort Zion: he will comfort all her waste places; and he will make her wilderness like Eden, and her desert like the garden of the LORD; joy and gladness shall be found therein, thanksgiving, and the voice of melody.

51:3 God's Comfort
◄ Isaiah 12:1
Isaiah 51:12 ►

4 Hearken unto me, my people; and give ear unto me, O my nation: for a law shall proceed from me, and I will make my judgment to rest for a light of the people.

5 My righteousness *is* near; my salvation is gone forth, and mine arms shall judge the people; the isles shall wait upon me, and on mine arm shall they trust.

6 Lift up your eyes to the heavens, and look upon the earth beneath: for the heavens shall vanish away like smoke, and the earth shall wax old like a garment, and they that dwell therein shall die in like manner: but my salvation shall be for ever, and my righteousness shall not be abolished.

7 Hearken unto me, ye that know righteousness, the people in whose heart *is* my law; fear ye not the reproach of men, neither be ye afraid of their revilings.

8 For the moth shall eat them up like a garment, and the worm shall eat them like wool: but my righteousness shall be for ever, and my salvation from generation to generation.

9 Awake, awake, put on strength, O arm of the LORD; awake, as in the ancient days, in the generations of old. *Art* thou not it that hath cut Rahab, *and* wounded the dragon?

10 *Art* thou not it which hath dried the sea, the waters of the great deep; that hath made the depths of the sea a way for the ransomed to pass over?

11 Therefore the redeemed of the LORD shall return, and come with singing unto Zion; and everlasting joy *shall be* upon their head: they shall obtain gladness and joy; *and* sorrow and mourning shall flee away.

12 I, *even* I, *am* he that comforteth you: who *art* thou, that thou shouldest be afraid of a man *that* shall die, and of the son of man *which* shall be made as grass;

51:12 God's Comfort
◄ Isaiah 51:3
Isaiah 66:13 ►

13 And forgettest the LORD thy maker, that hath stretched forth the heavens, and laid the foundations of the earth; and hast feared continually every day because of the fury of the oppressor, as if he were ready to destroy? and where *is* the fury of the oppressor?

51:13 Don't Forget...
◄ Isaiah 17:10
Jeremiah 3:21 ►

14 The captive exile hasteneth that he may be loosed, and that he should not die in the pit, nor that his bread should fail.

15 But I *am* the LORD thy God, that divided the sea, whose waves roared: The LORD of hosts *is* his name.

16 And I have put my words in thy mouth, and I have covered thee in the shadow of mine hand, that I may plant the heavens, and lay the foundations of the earth, and say unto Zion, Thou *art* my people.

17 Awake, awake, stand up, O Jerusalem, which hast drunk at the hand of the LORD the cup of his fury; thou hast drunken the dregs of the cup of trembling, *and* wrung *them* out.

18 *There is* none to guide her among all the sons *whom* she hath brought forth; neither *is there any* that taketh her by

the hand of all the sons *that* she hath brought up.

19 These two *things* are come unto thee; who shall be sorry for thee? desolation, and destruction, and the famine, and the sword: by whom shall I comfort thee?

20 Thy sons have fainted, they lie at the head of all the streets, as a wild bull in a net: they are full of the fury of the LORD, the rebuke of thy God.

21 Therefore hear now this, thou afflicted, and drunken, but not with wine:

22 Thus saith thy Lord the LORD, and thy God *that* pleadeth the cause of his people, Behold, I have taken out of thine hand the cup of trembling, *even* the dregs of the cup of my fury; thou shalt no more drink it again:

23 But I will put it into the hand of them that afflict thee; which have said to thy soul, Bow down, that we may go over: and thou hast laid thy body as the ground, and as the street, to them that went over.

52

1 Awake, awake; put on thy strength, O Zion; put on thy beautiful garments, O Jerusalem, the holy city: for henceforth there shall no more come into thee the uncircumcised and the unclean.

2 Shake thyself from the dust; arise, *and* sit down, O Jerusalem: loose thyself from the bands of thy neck, O captive daughter of Zion.

3 For thus saith the LORD, Ye have sold yourselves for nought; and ye shall be redeemed without money.

4 For thus saith the Lord GOD, My people went down aforetime into Egypt to sojourn there; and the Assyrian oppressed them without cause.

5 Now therefore, what have I here, saith the LORD, that my people is taken away for nought? they that rule over them make them to howl, saith the LORD; and my name continually every day *is* blasphemed.

6 Therefore my people shall know my name: therefore *they shall know* in that day that I *am* he that doth speak: behold, *it is* I.

7 How beautiful upon the mountains are the feet of him that bringeth good tidings, that publisheth peace; that bringeth good tidings of good, that publisheth salvation; that saith unto Zion, Thy God reigneth!

8 Thy watchmen shall lift up the voice; with the voice together shall they sing: for they shall see eye to eye, when the LORD shall bring again Zion.

9 Break forth into joy, sing together, ye waste places of Jerusalem: for the LORD hath comforted his people, he hath redeemed Jerusalem.

10 The LORD hath made bare his holy arm in the eyes of all the nations; and all the ends of the earth shall see the salvation of our God.

11 Depart ye, depart ye, go ye out from thence, touch no unclean *thing;* go ye out of the midst of her; be ye clean, that bear the vessels of the LORD.

12 For ye shall not go out with haste, nor go by flight: for the LORD will go before you; and the God of Israel *will be* your rereward.

13 Behold, my servant shall deal prudently, he shall be exalted and extolled, and be very high.

14 As many were astonied at thee; his visage was so marred more than any man, and his form more than the sons of men:

15 So shall he sprinkle many nations; the kings shall shut their mouths at him: for *that* which had not been told them shall they see; and *that* which they had not heard shall they consider.

53

1 Who hath believed our report? and to whom is the arm of the LORD revealed?

2 For he shall grow up before him as a tender plant, and as a root out of a dry ground: he hath no form nor comeliness; and when we shall see him, *there is* no beauty that we should desire him.

3 He is despised and rejected of men; a man of sorrows, and acquainted with grief: and we hid as it were *our* faces from him; he was despised, and we esteemed him not.

4 Surely he hath borne our griefs, and carried our sorrows: yet we did esteem him stricken, smitten of God, and afflicted.

5 But he *was* wounded for our transgressions, *he was* bruised for our iniquities: the chastisement of our peace *was* upon him; and with his stripes we are healed.

6 All we like sheep have gone

53:5 Why Jesus Died

◄ Psalm 69:9

2 Corinthians 5:21 ►

53:6 Everyone Sins

◄ Ecclesiastes 7:20

Isaiah 64:6 ►

astray; we have turned every one to his own
way; and the LORD hath laid on him the
iniquity of us all.
7He was op-
pressed, and he
was afflicted, yet
he opened not his
mouth: he is
brought as a lamb
to the slaughter, and as a sheep before her
shearers is dumb, so he openeth not his
mouth.

> 53:7
> Jesus the Lamb
> ◄ John 1:29 ►

8He was taken from prison and from
judgment: and who shall declare his generation? for he was cut off out of the land
of the living: for the transgression of my
people was he stricken.
9And he made his grave with the wicked, and with the rich in his death; because
he had done no violence, neither *was any*
deceit in his mouth.
10Yet it pleased the LORD to bruise him;
he hath put *him* to grief: when thou shalt
make his soul an offering for sin, he shall
see *his* seed, he shall prolong *his* days, and
the pleasure of the LORD shall prosper in
his hand.
11He shall see of the travail of his soul,
and shall be satisfied: by his knowledge
shall my righteous servant justify many;
for he shall bear their iniquities.
12Therefore will I
divide him *a portion*
with the great, and
he shall divide the
spoil with the
strong; because he
hath poured out his soul unto death: and
he was numbered with the transgressors;
and he bare the sin of many, and made
intercession for the transgressors.

> 53:12
> What Jesus Did
> ◄ Hebrews 9:28 ►

54

1Sing, O barren, thou *that* didst not bear;
break forth into singing, and cry aloud,
thou *that* didst not travail with child: for
more *are* the children of the desolate than
the children of the married wife, saith the
LORD.
2Enlarge the place of thy tent, and let
them stretch forth the curtains of thine
habitations: spare not, lengthen thy cords,
and strengthen thy stakes;
3For thou shalt break forth on the right
hand and on the left; and thy seed shall
inherit the Gentiles, and make the desolate cities to be inhabited.
4Fear not; for thou shalt not be
ashamed: neither be thou confounded; for
thou shalt not be put to shame: for thou
shalt forget the shame of thy youth, and
shalt not remember the reproach of thy
widowhood any more.
5For thy Maker *is* thine husband; the
LORD of hosts *is* his name; and thy Redeemer the Holy One of Israel; The God of the
whole earth shall he be called.
6For the LORD hath called thee as a woman forsaken and grieved in spirit, and a
wife of youth, when thou wast refused,
saith thy God.
7For a small mo-
ment have I forsak-
en thee; but with
great mercies will I
gather thee.
8In a little wrath
I hid my face from thee for a moment; but
with everlasting kindness will I have mercy on thee, saith the LORD thy Redeemer.

> 54:7 Promise of Mercy
> ◄ Psalm 103:8
> Isaiah 55:7 ►

9For this *is as* the waters of Noah unto
me: for *as* I have sworn that the waters of
Noah should no more go over the earth;
so have I sworn that I would not be wroth
with thee, nor rebuke thee.
10For the mountains shall depart, and
the hills be removed; but my kindness
shall not depart from thee, neither shall
the covenant of my peace be removed,
saith the LORD that hath mercy on thee.
11O thou afflicted, tossed with tempest,
and not comforted, behold, I will lay thy
stones with fair colors, and lay thy foundations with sapphires.
12And I will
make thy windows
of agates, and thy
gates of carbuncles,
and all thy borders
of pleasant stones.
13And all thy
children *shall be*
taught of the LORD;
and great *shall be*
the peace of thy
children.
14In righteous-
ness shalt thou be
established: thou
shalt be far from
oppression; for
thou shalt not fear:

> 54:13 God as Teacher
> ◄ Isaiah 48:17
> Jeremiah 32:33 ►

> 54:13 Peace of Mind
> ◄ Isaiah 48:18
> Ezekiel 34:25 ►

> 54:14
> Better Neighborhoods
> ◄ Isaiah 33:5 ►

and from terror; for it shall not come near
thee.
15 Behold, they shall surely gather together, *but* not by me: whosoever shall
gather together against thee shall fall for
thy sake.
16 Behold, I have created the smith that
bloweth the coals in the fire, and that
bringeth forth an instrument for his work;
and I have created the waster to destroy.
17 No weapon that is formed against thee
shall prosper; and every tongue *that* shall
rise against thee in judgment thou shalt
condemn. This *is* the heritage of the servants of the LORD, and their righteousness
is of me, saith the LORD.

55

1 Ho, every one
that thirsteth, come
ye to the waters,
and he that hath no
money; come ye,
buy, and eat; yea,

> **55:1 God Calls You**
> ◄ Isaiah 45:22
> Matthew 22:9 ►

come, buy wine and milk without money
and without price.
2 Wherefore do ye
spend money for
that which is not
bread? and your
labour for *that
which* satisfieth not?

> **55:2 Discontentment**
> ◄ Isaiah 29:8
> Isaiah 65:13 ►

hearken diligently unto me, and eat ye *that
which is* good, and let your soul delight itself in fatness.
3 Incline your ear, and come unto me:
hear, and your soul shall live; and I will
make an everlasting covenant with you,
even the sure mercies of David.
4 Behold, I have given him *for* a witness
to the people, a leader and commander to
the people.
5 Behold, thou shalt call a nation *that*
thou knowest not, and nations *that* knew
not thee shall run unto thee because of the
LORD thy God, and
for the Holy One of
Israel; for he hath
glorified thee.

> **55:6 Seeking God**
> ◄ Psalm 105:4
> Jeremiah 29:13 ►

6 Seek ye the
LORD while he may
be found, call ye
upon him while he
is near:
7 Let the wicked
forsake his way, and
the unrighteous

> **55:7 God's Forgiveness**
> ◄ Isaiah 44:22
> Jeremiah 5:1 ►

man his thoughts:
and let him return
unto the LORD, and
he will have mercy
upon him; and to
our God, for he will
abundantly par-
don.

> **55:7 Promise of Mercy**
> ◄ Isaiah 54:7
> Jeremiah 3:12 ►

8 For my thoughts
are not your
thoughts, neither
are your ways my
ways, saith the
LORD.

> **55:7 Starting Over**
> ◄ Proverbs 28:13
> Ephesians 4:22 ►

9 For *as* the heav-
ens are higher than
the earth, so are my
ways higher than
your ways, and my thoughts than your
thoughts.

> **55:8-9 God's Ways**
> ◄ Psalm 18:30
> Hosea 14:9 ►

10 For as the rain cometh down, and the
snow from heaven, and returneth not
thither, but watereth the earth, and maketh
it bring forth and bud, that it may give seed
to the sower, and bread to the eater:
11 So shall my word be that goeth forth
out of my mouth: it shall not return unto
me void, but it shall accomplish that
which I please, and it shall prosper *in the
thing* whereto I sent it.
12 For ye shall go
out with joy, and be
led forth with
peace: the moun-
tains and the hills
shall break forth
before you into singing, and all the trees
of the field shall clap *their* hands.

> **55:12 Nature's Praise**
> ◄ Isaiah 49:13 ►

13 Instead of the thorn shall come up the
fir tree, and instead of the brier shall come
up the myrtle tree: and it shall be to the
LORD for a name, for an everlasting sign
that shall not be cut off.

56

1 Thus saith the
LORD, Keep ye judg-
ment, and do
justice: for my sal-
vation *is* near to
come, and my righ-
teousness to be revealed.

> **56:1 Be Fair**
> ◄ Proverbs 21:3
> Romans 13:7 ►

2 Blessed *is* the man *that* doeth this, and
the son of man *that* layeth hold on it; that
keepeth the sabbath from polluting it, and
keepeth his hand from doing any evil.
3 Neither let the son of the stranger, that

hath joined himself to the LORD, speak, saying, The LORD hath utterly separated me from his people: neither let the eunuch say, Behold, I *am* a dry tree.

4 For thus saith the LORD unto the eunuchs that keep my sabbaths, and choose *the things* that please me, and take hold of my covenant;

56:4-5
Invisible Gifts
◄ Jeremiah 24:7 ►

5 Even unto them will I give in mine house and within my walls a place and a name better than of sons and of daughters: I will give them an everlasting name, that shall not be cut off.

6 Also the sons of the stranger, that join themselves to the LORD, to serve him, and to love the name of the LORD, to be his servants, every one that keepeth the sabbath from polluting it, and taketh hold of my covenant;

7 Even them will I bring to my holy mountain, and make them joyful in my house of prayer: their burnt offerings and their sacrifices *shall be* accepted upon mine altar; for mine house shall be called an house of prayer for all people.

8 The Lord GOD which gathereth the outcasts of Israel saith, Yet will I gather *others* to him, beside those that are gathered unto him.

9 All ye beasts of the field, come to devour, *yea,* all ye beasts in the forest.

10 His watchmen *are* blind: they are all ignorant, they *are* all dumb dogs, they cannot bark; sleeping, lying down, loving to slumber.

11 Yea, *they are* greedy dogs *which* can never have enough, and they *are* shepherds *that* cannot understand: they all look to their own way, every one for his gain, from his quarter.

12 Come ye, *say they,* I will fetch wine, and we will fill ourselves with strong drink; and to morrow shall be as this day, *and* much more abundant.

56:12
Drinking Too Much
◄ Isaiah 28:7
Hosea 4:11 ►

57

1 The righteous perisheth, and no man layeth *it* to heart: and merciful men *are* taken away, none considering that the righteous is taken away from the evil *to come.*

2 He shall enter into peace: they shall rest in their beds, *each one* walking *in* his uprightness.

3 But draw near hither, ye sons of the sorceress, the seed of the adulterer and the whore.

4 Against whom do ye sport yourselves? against whom make ye a wide mouth, *and* draw out the tongue? *are* ye not children of transgression, a seed of falsehood,

57:4 Mockers
◄ Proverbs 30:17
Jude 18 ►

5 Enflaming yourselves with idols under every green tree, slaying the children in the valleys under the clifts of the rocks?

6 Among the smooth *stones* of the stream *is* thy portion; they, they *are* thy lot: even to them hast thou poured a drink offering, thou hast offered a meat offering. Should I receive comfort in these?

7 Upon a lofty and high mountain hast thou set thy bed: even thither wentest thou up to offer sacrifice.

8 Behind the doors also and the posts hast thou set up thy remembrance: for thou hast discovered *thyself to another* than me, and art gone up; thou hast enlarged thy bed, and made thee *a covenant* with them; thou lovedst their bed where thou sawest *it.*

9 And thou wentest to the king with ointment, and didst increase thy perfumes, and didst send thy messengers far off, and didst debase *thyself even* unto hell.

10 Thou art wearied in the greatness of thy way; *yet* saidst thou not, There is no hope: thou hast found the life of thine hand; therefore thou wast not grieved.

11 And of whom hast thou been afraid or feared, that thou hast lied, and hast not remembered me, nor laid *it* to thy heart? have not I held my peace even of old, and thou fearest me not?

12 I will declare thy righteousness, and thy works; for they shall not profit thee.

13 When thou criest, let thy companies deliver thee; but the wind shall carry them all away; vanity shall take *them:* but he that putteth his trust in me shall possess the land, and shall inherit my holy mountain;

14 And shall say, Cast ye up, cast ye up, prepare the way, take up the stumblingblock out of the way of my people.

15For thus saith the high and lofty One that inhabiteth eternity, whose name *is* Holy; I dwell in the high and holy *place,* with him also *that is* of a contrite and humble spirit, to revive the spirit of the humble, and to revive the heart of the contrite ones.

57:15 Feeling Sorry
◄ Psalm 51:17
Isaiah 66:2 ►

16For I will not contend for ever, neither will I be always wroth: for the spirit should fail before me, and the souls *which* I have made.

17For the iniquity of his covetousness was I wroth, and smote him: I hid me, and was wroth, and he went on frowardly in the way of his heart.

18I have seen his ways, and will heal him: I will lead him also, and restore comforts unto him and to his mourners.

19I create the fruit of the lips; Peace, peace to *him that is* far off, and to *him that is* near, saith the LORD; and I will heal him.

20But the wicked *are* like the troubled sea, when it cannot rest, whose waters cast up mire and dirt.

21*There is* no peace, saith my God, to the wicked.

58

1Cry aloud, spare not, lift up thy voice like a trumpet, and shew my people their transgression, and the house of Jacob their sins.

2Yet they seek me daily, and delight to know my ways, as a nation that did righteousness, and forsook not the ordinance of their God: they ask of me the ordinances of justice; they take delight in approaching to God.

3Wherefore have we fasted, *say they,* and thou seest not? *wherefore* have we afflicted our soul, and thou takest no knowledge? Behold, in the day of your fast ye find pleasure, and exact all your labours.

4Behold, ye fast for strife and debate, and to smite with the fist of wickedness: ye shall not fast as *ye do this* day, to make your voice to be heard on high.

5Is it such a fast that I have chosen? a day for a man to afflict his soul? *is it* to bow down his head as a bulrush, and to spread sackcloth and ashes *under him?* wilt thou call this a fast, and an acceptable day to the LORD?

6*Is* not this the fast that I have chosen? to loose the bands of wickedness, to undo the heavy burdens, and to let the oppressed go free, and that ye break every yoke?

7*Is it* not to deal thy bread to the hungry, and that thou bring the poor that are cast out to thy house? when thou seest the naked, that thou cover him; and that thou hide not thyself from thine own flesh?

58:7 Giving
◄ Ecclesiastes 11:1
Matthew 5:42 ►

58:7 Sympathy
◄ Acts 20:35 ►

8Then shall thy light break forth as the morning, and thine health shall spring forth speedily: and thy righteousness shall go before thee; the glory of the LORD shall be thy rereward.

9Then shalt thou call, and the LORD shall answer; thou shalt cry, and he shall say, Here I *am.* If thou take away from the midst of thee the yoke, the putting forth of the finger, and speaking vanity;

58:9 Answers to Prayer
◄ Isaiah 41:17
Isaiah 65:24 ►

58:9 How to Pray
◄ 2 Chronicles 7:14
Jeremiah 29:13 ►

10And *if* thou draw out thy soul to the hungry, and satisfy the afflicted soul; then shall thy light rise in obscurity, and thy darkness *be* as the noonday:

58:10 Promises to Givers
◄ Ecclesiastes 11:1
Luke 6:38 ►

58:10 Rewards
◄ Proverbs 14:31
Daniel 4:27 ►

11And the LORD shall guide thee continually, and satisfy thy soul in drought, and make fat thy bones: and thou shalt be like a watered garden, and like a spring of water, whose waters fail not.

58:11 Satisfaction
◄ Psalm 107:9
Jeremiah 31:14 ►

12And *they that shall be* of thee shall build the old waste places: thou shalt raise up the foundations of many generations; and thou shalt be called, The repairer of the breach, The restorer of paths to dwell in.

13 If thou turn away thy foot from the sabbath, *from* doing thy pleasure on my holy day; and call the sabbath a delight, the holy of the LORD, honourable; and shalt honour him, not doing thine own ways, nor finding thine own pleasure, nor speaking *thine own* words:

14 Then shalt thou delight thyself in the LORD; and I will cause thee to ride upon the high places of the earth, and feed thee with the heritage of Jacob thy father: for the mouth of the LORD hath spoken *it*.

58:14 Good Rewarded
◄ Isaiah 33:16
Daniel 12:3 ►

59

1 Behold, the LORD'S hand is not shortened, that it cannot save; neither his ear heavy, that it cannot hear:

2 But your iniquities have separated between you and your God, and your sins have hid *his* face from you, that he will not hear.

59:2 Unanswered Prayer
◄ Isaiah 1:15
Micah 3:4 ►

3 For your hands are defiled with blood, and your fingers with iniquity; your lips have spoken lies, your tongue hath muttered perverseness.

4 None calleth for justice, nor *any* pleadeth for truth: they trust in vanity, and speak lies; they conceive mischief, and bring forth iniquity.

5 They hatch cockatrice' eggs, and weave the spider's web: he that eateth of their eggs dieth, and that which is crushed breaketh out into a viper.

6 Their webs shall not become garments, neither shall they cover themselves with their works: their works *are* works of iniquity, and the act of violence *is* in their hands.

59:6 Violence
◄ Proverbs 4:17
Jeremiah 6:7 ►

7 Their feet run to evil, and they make haste to shed innocent blood: their thoughts *are* thoughts of iniquity; wasting and destruction *are* in their paths.

59:7 Bad People
◄ Proverbs 6:18
Micah 2:1 ►

8 The way of peace they know not; and *there is* no judgment in their goings: they have made them crooked paths: whosoever goeth therein shall not know peace.

9 Therefore is judgment far from us, neither doth justice overtake us: we wait for light, but behold obscurity; for brightness, *but* we walk in darkness.

10 We grope for the wall like the blind, and we grope as if *we had* no eyes: we stumble at noonday as in the night; *we are* in desolate places as dead *men*.

11 We roar all like bears, and mourn sore like doves: we look for judgment, but *there is* none; for salvation, *but* it is far off from us.

12 For our transgressions are multiplied before thee, and our sins testify against us: for our transgressions *are* with us; and *as for* our iniquities, we know them;

13 In transgressing and lying against the LORD, and departing away from our God, speaking oppression and revolt, conceiving and uttering from the heart words of falsehood.

14 And judgment is turned away backward, and justice standeth afar off: for truth is fallen in the street, and equity cannot enter.

15 Yea, truth faileth; and he *that* departeth from evil maketh himself a prey: and the LORD saw *it*, and it displeased him that *there was* no judgment.

16 And he saw that *there was* no man, and wondered that *there was* no intercessor: therefore his arm brought salvation unto him; and his righteousness, it sustained him.

59:16
Our Savior
◄ John 3:14-15 ►

17 For he put on righteousness as a breastplate, and an helmet of salvation upon his head; and he put on the garments of vengeance *for* clothing, and was clad with zeal as a cloke.

18 According to *their* deeds, accordingly he will repay, fury to his adversaries, recompence to his enemies; to the islands he will repay recompence.

19 So shall they fear the name of the LORD from the west, and his glory from the rising of the sun. When the enemy shall come in like a flood, the Spirit of the LORD shall lift up a standard against him.

20 And the Redeemer shall come to Zion, and unto them that turn from transgression in Jacob, saith the LORD.

21 As for me, this *is* my covenant with them, saith the LORD; My spirit that *is* upon thee, and my words which I have put in thy mouth, shall not depart out of thy mouth, nor out of the mouth of thy seed, nor out of the mouth of thy seed's seed, saith the LORD, from henceforth and for ever.

60

1 Arise, shine; for thy light is come, and the glory of the LORD is risen upon thee.

2 For, behold, the darkness shall cover the earth, and gross darkness the people: but the LORD shall arise upon thee, and his glory shall be seen upon thee.

3 And the Gentiles shall come to thy light, and kings to the brightness of thy rising.

4 Lift up thine eyes round about, and see: all they gather themselves together, they come to thee: thy sons shall come from far, and thy daughters shall be nursed at *thy* side.

5 Then thou shalt see, and flow together, and thine heart shall fear, and be enlarged; because the abundance of the sea shall be converted unto thee, the forces of the Gentiles shall come unto thee.

6 The multitude of camels shall cover thee, the dromedaries of Midian and Ephah; all they from Sheba shall come: they shall bring gold and incense; and they shall shew forth the praises of the LORD.

7 All the flocks of Kedar shall be gathered together unto thee, the rams of Nebaioth shall minister unto thee: they shall come up with acceptance on mine altar, and I will glorify the house of my glory.

8 Who *are* these *that* fly as a cloud, and as the doves to their windows?

9 Surely the isles shall wait for me, and the ships of Tarshish first, to bring thy sons from far, their silver and their gold with them, unto the name of the LORD thy God, and to the Holy One of Israel, because he hath glorified thee.

10 And the sons of strangers shall build up thy walls, and their kings shall minister unto thee: for in my wrath I smote thee, but in my favour have I had mercy on thee.

11 Therefore thy gates shall be open continually; they shall not be shut day nor night; that *men* may bring unto thee the forces of the Gentiles, and *that* their kings *may be* brought.

12 For the nation and kingdom that will not serve thee shall perish; yea, *those* nations shall be utterly wasted.

13 The glory of Lebanon shall come unto thee, the fir tree, the pine tree, and the box together, to beautify the place of my sanctuary; and I will make the place of my feet glorious.

14 The sons also of them that afflicted thee shall come bending unto thee; and all they that despised thee shall bow themselves down at the soles of thy feet; and they shall call thee, The city of the LORD, The Zion of the Holy One of Israel.

15 Whereas thou hast been forsaken and hated, so that no man went through *thee,* I will make thee an eternal excellency, a joy of many generations.

16 Thou shalt also suck the milk of the Gentiles, and shalt suck the breast of kings: and thou shalt know that I the LORD *am* thy Saviour and thy Redeemer, the mighty One of Jacob.

17 For brass I will bring gold, and for iron I will bring silver, and for wood brass, and for stones iron: I will also make thy officers peace, and thine exactors righteousness.

18 Violence shall no more be heard in thy land, wasting nor destruction within thy borders; but thou shalt call thy walls Salvation, and thy gates Praise.

19 The sun shall be no more thy light by day; neither for brightness shall the moon give light unto thee: but the LORD shall be unto thee an everlasting light, and thy God thy glory.

20 Thy sun shall no more go down; neither shall thy moon withdraw itself: for the LORD shall be thine everlasting light, and the days of thy mourning shall be ended.

21 Thy people also *shall be* all righteous: they shall inherit the land for ever, the branch of my planting, the work of my hands, that I may be glorified.

22 A little one shall become a thousand, and a small one a strong nation: I the LORD will hasten it in his time.

61

1 The Spirit of the Lord GOD *is* upon me; because the LORD hath anointed me to preach good tidings unto the meek; he hath sent me to bind up the brokenhearted, to proclaim liberty to the captives, and

the opening of the prison to *them that are* bound;

2 To proclaim the acceptable year of the LORD, and the day of vengeance of our God; to comfort all that mourn;

3 To appoint unto them that mourn in Zion, to give unto them beauty for ashes, the oil of joy for mourning, the garment of praise for the spirit of heaviness; that they might be called trees of righteousness, the planting of the LORD, that he might be glorified.

4 And they shall build the old wastes, they shall raise up the former desolations, and they shall repair the waste cities, the desolations of many generations.

5 And strangers shall stand and feed your flocks, and the sons of the alien *shall be* your plowmen and your vinedressers.

6 But ye shall be named the Priests of the LORD: *men* shall call you the Ministers of our God: ye shall eat the riches of the Gentiles, and in their glory shall ye boast yourselves.

7 For your shame *ye shall have* double; and *for* confusion they shall rejoice in their portion: therefore in their land they shall possess the double: everlasting joy shall be unto them.

8 For I the LORD love judgment, I hate robbery for burnt offering; and I will direct their work in truth, and I will make an everlasting covenant with them.

9 And their seed shall be known among the Gentiles, and their offspring among the people: all that see them shall acknowledge them, that they *are* the seed *which* the LORD hath blessed.

10 I will greatly rejoice in the LORD, my soul shall be joyful in my God; for he hath clothed me with the garments of salvation, he hath covered me with the robe of righteousness, as a bridegroom decketh *himself* with ornaments, and as a bride adorneth *herself* with her jewels.

11 For as the earth bringeth forth her bud, and as the garden causeth the things that are sown in it to spring forth; so the Lord GOD will cause righteousness and praise to spring forth before all the nations.

62

1 For Zion's sake will I not hold my peace, and for Jerusalem's sake I will not rest, until the righteousness thereof go forth as brightness, and the salvation thereof as a lamp *that* burneth.

2 And the Gentiles shall see thy righteousness, and all kings thy glory: and thou shalt be called by a new name, which the mouth of the LORD shall name.

3 Thou shalt also be a crown of glory in the hand of the LORD, and a royal diadem in the hand of thy God.

4 Thou shalt no more be termed Forsaken; neither shall thy land any more be termed Desolate: but thou shalt be called Hephzi-bah, and thy land Beulah: for the LORD delighteth in thee, and thy land shall be married.

5 For *as* a young man marrieth a virgin, *so* shall thy sons marry thee: and *as* the bridegroom rejoiceth over the bride, *so* shall thy God rejoice over thee.

6 I have set watchmen upon thy walls, O Jerusalem, *which* shall never hold their peace day nor night: ye that make mention of the LORD, keep not silence,

62:6 Your Testimony
◄ Isaiah 12:4
Jeremiah 51:10 ►

7 And give him no rest, till he establish, and till he make Jerusalem a praise in the earth.

8 The LORD hath sworn by his right hand, and by the arm of his strength, Surely I will no more give thy corn *to be* meat for thine enemies; and the sons of the stranger shall not drink thy wine, for the which thou hast laboured:

9 But they that have gathered it shall eat it, and praise the LORD; and they that have brought it together shall drink it in the courts of my holiness.

10 Go through, go through the gates; prepare ye the way of the people; cast up, cast up the highways; gather out the stones; lift up a standard for the people.

11 Behold, the LORD hath proclaimed unto the end of the world, Say ye to the daughter of Zion, Behold, thy salvation cometh; behold, his reward *is* with him, and his work before him.

12 And they shall call them, The holy people, The redeemed of the LORD: and thou shalt be called, Sought out, A city not forsaken.

63

1 Who *is* this that cometh from Edom, with dyed garments from Bozrah? this *that is* glorious in his apparel, travelling in the greatness of his strength? I that speak in righteousness, mighty to save.

earth shall swear by the God of truth; because the former troubles are forgotten, and because they are hid from mine eyes.

17 For, behold, I create new heavens and a new earth: and the former shall not be remembered, nor come into mind.

18 But be ye glad and rejoice for ever *in that* which I create: for, behold, I create Jerusalem a rejoicing, and her people a joy.

19 And I will rejoice in Jerusalem, and joy in my people: and the voice of weeping shall be no more heard in her, nor the voice of crying.

20 There shall be no more thence an infant of days, nor an old man that hath not filled his days: for the child shall die an hundred years old; but the sinner *being* an hundred years old shall be accursed.

21 And they shall build houses, and inhabit *them;* and they shall plant vineyards, and eat the fruit of them.

22 They shall not build, and another inhabit; they shall not plant, and another eat: for as the days of a tree *are* the days of my people, and mine elect shall long enjoy the work of their hands.

23 They shall not labour in vain, nor bring forth for trouble; for they *are* the seed of the blessed of the LORD, and their offspring with them.

24 And it shall come to pass, that before they call, I will answer; and while they are yet speaking, I will hear.

65:24 Answers to Prayer
◄ Isaiah 58:9
Jeremiah 33:3 ►

25 The wolf and the lamb shall feed together, and the lion shall eat straw like the bullock: and dust *shall be* the serpent's meat. They shall not hurt nor destroy in all my holy mountain, saith the LORD.

66

1 Thus saith the LORD, The heaven *is* my throne, and the earth *is* my footstool: where *is* the house that ye build unto me? and where *is* the place of my rest?

66:1 Where Is God?
◄ Proverbs 15:3
Jeremiah 23:24 ►

2 For all those *things* hath mine hand made, and all those *things* have been, saith the LORD: but to this *man* will I look, *even* to *him that is* poor and of a contrite spirit, and trembleth at my word.

66:2 Feeling Sorry
◄ Isaiah 57:15
Joel 2:13 ►

3 He that killeth an ox *is as if* he slew a man; he that sacrificeth a lamb, *as if* he cut off a dog's neck; he that offereth an oblation, *as if he offered* swine's blood; he that burneth incense, *as if* he blessed an idol. Yea, they have chosen their own ways, and their soul delighteth in their abominations.

4 I also will choose their delusions, and will bring their fears upon them; because when I called, none did answer; when I spake, they did not hear: but they did evil before mine eyes, and chose *that* in which I delighted not.

66:4 Guilty Fear
◄ Isaiah 33:14
Daniel 5:6 ►

66:4 Warning!
◄ Isaiah 14:23
Malachi 3:5 ►

5 Hear the word of the LORD, ye that tremble at his word; your brethren that hated you, that cast you out for my name's sake, said, Let the LORD be glorified: but he shall appear to your joy, and they shall be ashamed.

6 A voice of noise from the city, a voice from the temple, a voice of the LORD that rendereth recompence to his enemies.

7 Before she travailed, she brought forth; before her pain came, she was delivered of a man child.

8 Who hath heard such a thing? who hath seen such things? Shall the earth be made to bring forth in one day? *or* shall a nation be born at once? for as soon as Zion travailed, she brought forth her children.

9 Shall I bring to the birth, and not cause to bring forth? saith the LORD: shall I cause to bring forth, and shut *the womb?* saith thy God.

10 Rejoice ye with Jerusalem, and be glad with her, all ye that love her: rejoice for joy with her, all ye that mourn for her:

11 That ye may suck, and be satisfied with the breasts of her consolations; that ye may milk out, and be delighted with the abundance of her glory.

12 For thus saith the LORD, Behold, I will extend peace to her like a river, and the glory of the Gentiles like a flowing stream:

then shall ye suck, ye shall be borne upon
her sides, and be dandled upon *her* knees.
13As one whom
his mother com-
forteth, so will I
comfort you; and ye
shall be comforted
in Jerusalem.

66:13 God's Comfort
◄ Isaiah 51:12
2 Corinthians 1:3 ►

14And when ye see *this,* your heart shall
rejoice, and your bones shall flourish like
an herb: and the hand of the LORD shall
be known toward his servants, and *his* indignation toward his enemies.
15For, behold, the LORD will come with
fire, and with his chariots like a whirlwind,
to render his anger with fury, and his rebuke with flames of fire.
16For by fire and by his sword will the
LORD plead with all flesh: and the slain of
the LORD shall be many.
17They that sanctify themselves, and
purify themselves in the gardens behind
one *tree* in the midst, eating swine's flesh,
and the abomination, and the mouse, shall
be consumed together, saith the LORD.
18For I *know* their
works and their
thoughts: it shall
come, that I will
gather all nations
and tongues; and
they shall come, and see my glory.

66:18 Bad Thoughts
◄ Proverbs 24:9
Jeremiah 4:14 ►

19And I will set a sign among them, and
I will send those that escape of them unto
the nations, *to* Tarshish, Pul, and Lud, that
draw the bow, *to* Tubal, and Javan, *to* the
isles afar off, that have not heard my
fame, neither have seen my glory; and
they shall declare my glory among the
Gentiles.
20And they shall bring all your brethren
for an offering unto the LORD out of all
nations upon horses, and in chariots, and
in litters, and upon mules, and upon swift
beasts, to my holy mountain Jerusalem,
saith the LORD, as the children of Israel
bring an offering in a clean vessel into the
house of the LORD.
21And I will also take of them for priests
and for Levites, saith the LORD.
22For as the new heavens and the new
earth, which I will make, shall remain before me, saith the LORD, so shall your seed
and your name remain.
23And it shall come to pass, *that* from
one new moon to another, and from one
sabbath to another, shall all flesh come to
worship before me, saith the LORD.
24And they shall go forth, and look
upon the carcases of the men that have
transgressed against me: for their worm
shall not die, neither shall their fire be
quenched; and they shall be an abhorring
unto all flesh.

Jeremiah

AUTHOR
Jeremiah the prophet

MAIN POINT
God will not put up with wickedness and false worship. His people must turn from sin and run back to him.

DATE WRITTEN
Approximately 627-586 B.C.

52 CHAPTERS

MAIN PEOPLE

Jeremiah, Judah's last kings (Josiah, Jehoahaz, Jehoiakim, Jehoiachin, Zedekiah), Baruch, Ebed-melech, King Nebuchadnezzar, the family of Recab

SPECIAL FEATURES

* *Can be read alongside the historical events recorded in 2 Kings*
* *Describes the abuse that Jeremiah suffered and the terrible destruction of Jerusalem*
* *Uses pottery as a symbol*
* *Points out the good example set by the family of Recab, a family most people had never heard of*
* *Second book of the Major Prophets*

HOW THE BOOK GOT ITS NAME

The author and main person of the book is Jeremiah, a prophet who endured great hardships yet was faithful to his calling from God.

1
1 The words of Jeremiah the son of Hilkiah, of the priests that *were* in Anathoth
in the land of Benjamin:
2 To whom the word of the LORD came
in the days of Josiah the son of Amon king
of Judah, in the thirteenth year of his reign.
3 It came also in the days of Jehoiakim
the son of Josiah king of Judah, unto the
end of the eleventh year of Zedekiah the
son of Josiah king of Judah, unto the carrying away of Jerusalem captive in the fifth
month.
4 Then the word of the LORD came unto
me, saying,
5 Before I formed thee in the belly I knew
thee; and before thou camest forth out of
the womb I sanctified thee, *and* I ordained
thee a prophet unto the nations.
6 Then said I, Ah, Lord GOD! behold, I
cannot speak: for I *am* a child.
7 But the LORD said unto me, Say not,
I *am* a child: for thou shalt go to all that I
shall send thee, and whatsoever I command thee thou shalt speak.
8 Be not afraid of their faces: for I *am* with
thee to deliver thee, saith the LORD.
9 Then the LORD put forth his hand, and
touched my mouth. And the LORD said

unto me, Behold, I have put my words in
thy mouth.
10 See, I have this day set thee over the
nations and over the kingdoms, to root
out, and to pull down, and to destroy, and
to throw down, to build, and to plant.
11 Moreover the word of the LORD came
unto me, saying, Jeremiah, what seest
thou? And I said, I see a rod of an almond
tree.
12 Then said the LORD unto me, Thou
hast well seen: for I will hasten my word
to perform it.
13 And the word of the LORD came unto
me the second time, saying, What seest
thou? And I said, I see a seething pot; and
the face thereof *is* toward the north.
14 Then the LORD said unto me, Out of
the north an evil shall break forth upon
all the inhabitants of the land.
15 For, lo, I will call all the families of
the kingdoms of the north, saith the LORD;
and they shall come, and they shall set
every one his throne at the entering of the
gates of Jerusalem, and against all the walls
thereof round about, and against all the
cities of Judah.
16 And I will utter my judgments against
them touching all their wickedness, who
have forsaken me, and have burned incense unto other gods, and worshipped the
works of their own hands.
17 Thou therefore gird up thy loins, and
arise, and speak unto them all that I command thee: be not dismayed at their faces,
lest I confound thee before them.
18 For, behold, I have made thee this day
a defenced city, and an iron pillar, and
brasen walls against the whole land,
against the kings of Judah, against the
princes thereof, against the priests thereof,
and against the people of the land.
19 And they shall fight against thee; but
they shall not prevail against thee; for I
am with thee, saith the LORD, to deliver
thee.

2

1 Moreover the word of the LORD came
to me, saying,
2 Go and cry in the ears of Jerusalem,
saying, Thus saith the LORD; I remember
thee, the kindness of thy youth, the love
of thine espousals, when thou wentest after me in the wilderness, in a land *that was*
not sown.
3 Israel *was* holiness unto the LORD, *and*
the firstfruits of his increase: all that devour him shall offend; evil shall come
upon them, saith the LORD.
4 Hear ye the word of the LORD, O house
of Jacob, and all the families of the house
of Israel:
5 Thus saith the
LORD, What iniqui-
ty have your fathers
found in me, that
they are gone far
from me, and have
walked after vanity, and are become vain?

2:5 Worshiping Things
◄ Psalm 31:6
Jeremiah 10:8 ►

6 Neither said they, Where *is* the LORD
that brought us up out of the land of Egypt,
that led us through the wilderness, through
a land of deserts and of pits, through a land
of drought, and of the shadow of death,
through a land that no man passed
through, and where no man dwelt?
7 And I brought you into a plentiful
country, to eat the fruit thereof and the
goodness thereof; but when ye entered, ye
defiled my land, and made mine heritage
an abomination.
8 The priests said not, Where *is* the LORD?
and they that handle the law knew me not:
the pastors also transgressed against me,
and the prophets prophesied by Baal, and
walked after *things that* do not profit.
9 Wherefore I will yet plead with you,
saith the LORD, and with your children's
children will I plead.
10 For pass over the isles of Chittim, and
see; and send unto Kedar, and consider
diligently, and see if there be such a thing.
11 Hath a nation changed *their* gods,
which *are* yet no gods? but my people have
changed their glory for *that which* doth not
profit.
12 Be astonished, O ye heavens, at this,
and be horribly afraid, be ye very desolate,
saith the LORD.
13 For my people have committed two
evils; they have forsaken me the fountain
of living waters, *and* hewed them out cisterns, broken cisterns, that can hold no
water.
14 *Is* Israel a servant? *is* he a homeborn
slave? why is he spoiled?
15 The young lions roared upon him, *and*
yelled, and they made his land waste: his
cities are burned without inhabitant.
16 Also the children of Noph and Tahapa-
nes have broken the crown of thy head.

17 Hast thou not procured this unto thyself, in that thou hast forsaken the LORD thy God, when he led thee by the way?

18 And now what hast thou to do in the way of Egypt, to drink the waters of Sihor? or what hast thou to do in the way of Assyria, to drink the waters of the river?

19 Thine own wickedness shall correct thee, and thy backslidings shall reprove thee: know therefore and see that *it is* an evil *thing* and bitter, that thou hast forsaken the LORD thy God, and that my fear *is* not in thee, saith the Lord GOD of hosts.

20 For of old time I have broken thy yoke, *and* burst thy bands; and thou saidst, I will not transgress; when upon every high hill and under every green tree thou wanderest, playing the harlot.

21 Yet I had planted thee a noble vine, wholly a right seed: how then art thou turned into the degenerate plant of a strange vine unto me?

22 For though thou wash thee with nitre, and take thee much sope, *yet* thine iniquity is marked before me, saith the Lord GOD.

2:22 God Sees Sin
◄ Job 14:16
Jeremiah 16:17 ►

23 How canst thou say, I am not polluted, I have not gone after Baalim? see thy way in the valley, know what thou hast done: *thou art* a swift dromedary traversing her ways;

24 A wild ass used to the wilderness, *that* snuffeth up the wind at her pleasure; in her occasion who can turn her away? all they that seek her will not weary themselves; in her month they shall find her.

25 Withhold thy foot from being unshod, and thy throat from thirst: but thou saidst, There is no hope: no; for I have loved strangers, and after them will I go.

26 As the thief is ashamed when he is found, so is the house of Israel ashamed; they, their kings, their princes, and their priests, and their prophets,

27 Saying to a stock, Thou *art* my father; and to a stone, Thou hast brought me forth: for they have turned *their* back unto me, and not *their* face: but in the time of their trouble they will say, Arise, and save us.

28 But where *are* thy gods that thou hast made thee? let them arise, if they can save thee in the time of thy trouble: for *according to* the number of thy cities are thy gods, O Judah.

29 Wherefore will ye plead with me? ye all have transgressed against me, saith the LORD.

30 In vain have I smitten your children; they received no correction: your own sword hath devoured your prophets, like a destroying lion.

2:30 Refusing Correction
◄ Isaiah 42:25
Jeremiah 5:3 ►

31 O generation, see ye the word of the LORD. Have I been a wilderness unto Israel? a land of darkness? wherefore say my people, We are lords; we will come no more unto thee?

32 Can a maid forget her ornaments, *or* a bride her attire? yet my people have forgotten me days without number.

33 Why trimmest thou thy way to seek love? therefore hast thou also taught the wicked ones thy ways.

34 Also in thy skirts is found the blood of the souls of the poor innocents: I have not found it by secret search, but upon all these.

35 Yet thou sayest, Because I am innocent, surely his anger shall turn from me. Behold, I will plead with thee, because thou sayest, I have not sinned.

2:35 Self-righteousness
◄ Proverbs 30:12
2 Corinthians 10:12 ►

36 Why gaddest thou about so much to change thy way? thou also shalt be ashamed of Egypt, as thou wast ashamed of Assyria.

37 Yea, thou shalt go forth from him, and thine hands upon thine head: for the LORD hath rejected thy confidences, and thou shalt not prosper in them.

3

1 They say, If a man put away his wife, and she go from him, and become another man's, shall he return unto her again? shall not that land be greatly polluted? but thou hast played the harlot with many lovers; yet return again to me, saith the LORD.

2 Lift up thine eyes unto the high places, and see where thou hast not been lien with. In the ways hast thou sat for them, as the Arabian in the wilderness; and thou hast polluted the land with thy whoredoms and with thy wickedness.

3 Therefore the showers have been

withholden, and there hath been no latter
rain; and thou hadst a whore's forehead,
thou refusedst to be ashamed.
4 Wilt thou not from this time cry unto
me, My father, thou *art* the guide of my
youth?
5 Will he reserve *his anger* for ever? will
he keep *it* to the end? Behold, thou hast
spoken and done evil things as thou
couldest.
6 The LORD said also unto me in the days
of Josiah the king, Hast thou seen *that*
which backsliding Israel hath done? she
is gone up upon every high mountain and
under every green tree, and there hath
played the harlot.
7 And I said after she had done all these
things, Turn thou unto me. But she returned
not. And her treacherous sister Judah
saw *it*.
8 And I saw, when for all the causes
whereby backsliding Israel committed
adultery I had put her away, and given her
a bill of divorce; yet her treacherous sister
Judah feared not, but went and played the
harlot also.
9 And it came to pass through the lightness of her whoredom, that she defiled the
land, and committed adultery with stones
and with stocks.
10 And yet for all this her treacherous sister Judah hath not turned unto me with
her whole heart, but feignedly, saith the
LORD.
11 And the LORD said unto me, The backsliding Israel hath justified herself more
than treacherous Judah.
12 Go and pro-
claim these words
toward the north,
and say, Return,
thou backsliding Is-
rael, saith the LORD;
and I will not cause mine anger to fall upon
you: for I *am* merciful, saith the LORD, *and*
I will not keep *anger* for ever.

3:12
Promise of Mercy
◄ Isaiah 55:7 ►

13 Only acknowl-
edge thine iniquity,
that thou hast
transgressed against
the LORD thy God,
and hast scattered
thy ways to the strangers under every green
tree, and ye have not obeyed my voice,
saith the LORD.

3:13 Confession
◄ Proverbs 28:13
1 John 1:9 ►

14 Turn, O backsliding children, saith the
LORD; for I am married unto you: and I
will take you one of a city, and two of a
family, and I will bring you to Zion:
15 And I will give you pastors according
to mine heart, which shall feed you with
knowledge and understanding.
16 And it shall come to pass, when ye be
multiplied and increased in the land, in
those days, saith the LORD, they shall say
no more, The ark of the covenant of the
LORD: neither shall it come to mind: neither shall they remember it; neither shall
they visit *it*; neither shall *that* be done any
more.
17 At that time they shall call Jerusalem
the throne of the LORD; and all the nations
shall be gathered unto it, to the name of
the LORD, to Jerusalem: neither shall they
walk any more after the imagination of
their evil heart.
18 In those days the house of Judah shall
walk with the house of Israel, and they
shall come together out of the land of the
north to the land that I have given for an
inheritance unto your fathers.
19 But I said, How shall I put thee among
the children, and give thee a pleasant land,
a goodly heritage of the hosts of nations?
and I said, Thou shalt call me, My father;
and shalt not turn away from me.
20 Surely *as* a wife treacherously departeth from her husband, so have ye dealt
treacherously with me, O house of Israel,
saith the LORD.
21 A voice was
heard upon the
high places, weep-
ing *and* supplica-
tions of the chil-
dren of Israel: for
they have perverted their way, *and* they
have forgotten the LORD their God.

3:21 Don't Forget...
◄ Isaiah 51:13
Hebrews 2:1 ►

22 Return, ye
backsliding chil-
dren, *and* I will heal
your backslidings.
Behold, we come
unto thee; for thou
art the LORD our God.

3:22 Repentance
◄ Psalm 34:18
Joel 2:13 ►

23 Truly in vain *is salvation hoped for* from
the hills, *and from* the multitude of mountains: truly in the LORD our God *is* the salvation of Israel.
24 For shame hath devoured the labour

of our fathers from our youth; their flocks and their herds, their sons and their daughters.

25 We lie down in our shame, and our confusion covereth us: for we have sinned against the LORD our God, we and our fathers, from our youth even unto this day, and have not obeyed the voice of the LORD our God.

3:25 Results of Sin
◄ Ecclesiastes 11:9
Jeremiah 32:30 ►

4

1 If thou wilt return, O Israel, saith the LORD, return unto me: and if thou wilt put away thine abominations out of my sight, then shalt thou not remove.

2 And thou shalt swear, The LORD liveth, in truth, in judgment, and in righteousness; and the nations shall bless themselves in him, and in him shall they glory.

3 For thus saith the LORD to the men of Judah and Jerusalem, Break up your fallow ground, and sow not among thorns.

4 Circumcise yourselves to the LORD, and take away the foreskins of your heart, ye men of Judah and inhabitants of Jerusalem: lest my fury come forth like fire, and burn that none can quench *it*, because of the evil of your doings.

5 Declare ye in Judah, and publish in Jerusalem; and say, Blow ye the trumpet in the land: cry, gather together, and say, Assemble yourselves, and let us go into the defenced cities.

6 Set up the standard toward Zion: retire, stay not: for I will bring evil from the north, and a great destruction.

7 The lion is come up from his thicket, and the destroyer of the Gentiles is on his way; he is gone forth from his place to make thy land desolate; *and* thy cities shall be laid waste, without an inhabitant.

8 For this gird you with sackcloth, lament and howl: for the fierce anger of the LORD is not turned back from us.

9 And it shall come to pass at that day, saith the LORD, *that* the heart of the king shall perish, and the heart of the princes; and the prie sts shall be astonished, and the prophets shall wonder.

10 Then said I, Ah, Lord GOD! surely thou hast greatly deceived this people and Jerusalem, saying, Ye shall have peace; whereas the sword reacheth unto the soul.

11 At that time shall it be said to this people and to Jerusalem, A dry wind of the high places in the wilderness toward the daughter of my people, not to fan, nor to cleanse,

12 *Even* a full wind from those *places* shall come unto me: now also will I give sentence against them.

13 Behold, he shall come up as clouds, and his chariots *shall be* as a whirlwind: his horses are swifter than eagles. Woe unto us! for we are spoiled.

14 O Jerusalem, wash thine heart from wickedness, that thou mayest be saved. How long shall thy vain thoughts lodge within thee?

4:14 Bad Thoughts
◄ Isaiah 66:18
Matthew 9:4 ►

15 For a voice declareth from Dan, and publisheth affliction from mount Ephraim.

16 Make ye mention to the nations; behold, publish against Jerusalem, *that* watchers come from a far country, and give out their voice against the cities of Judah.

17 As keepers of a field, are they against her round about; because she hath been rebellious against me, saith the LORD.

18 Thy way and thy doings have procured these *things* unto thee; this *is* thy wickedness, because it is bitter, because it reacheth unto thine heart.

19 My bowels, my bowels! I am pained at my very heart; my heart maketh a noise in me; I cannot hold my peace, because thou hast heard, O my soul, the sound of the trump, the alarm of war.

20 Destruction upon destruction is cried; for the whole land is spoiled: suddenly are my tents spoiled, *and* my curtains in a moment.

21 How long shall I see the standard, *and* hear the sound of the trumpet?

22 For my people *is* foolish, they have not known me; they *are* sottish children, and they have none understanding: they *are* wise to do evil, but to do good they have no knowledge.

4:22 Growing Up
◄ Proverbs 22:15
1 Corinthians 13:11 ►

23 I beheld the earth, and, lo, *it was* without form, and void; and the heavens, and they *had* no light.

24 I beheld the mountains, and, lo, they

trembled, and all the hills moved lightly.
25 I beheld, and, lo, *there was* no man,
and all the birds of the heavens were fled.
26 I beheld, and, lo, the fruitful place *was*
a wilderness, and all the cities thereof were
broken down at the presence of the LORD,
and by his fierce anger.
27 For thus hath the LORD said, The
whole land shall be desolate; yet will I not
make a full end.
28 For this shall the earth mourn, and the
heavens above be black: because I have
spoken *it*, I have purposed *it*, and will not
repent, neither will I turn back from it.
29 The whole city shall flee for the noise
of the horsemen and bowmen; they shall
go into thickets, and climb up upon the
rocks: every city *shall be* forsaken, and not
a man dwell therein.
30 And *when* thou *art* spoiled, what wilt
thou do? Though thou clothest thyself
with crimson, though thou deckest thee
with ornaments of gold, though thou
rentest thy face with painting, in vain shalt
thou make thyself fair; *thy* lovers will despise thee, they will seek thy life.
31 For I have heard a voice as of a woman in travail, *and* the anguish as of her that
bringeth forth her first child, the voice of
the daughter of Zion, *that* bewaileth herself, *that* spreadeth her hands, *saying*, Woe
is me now! for my soul is wearied because
of murderers.

5

1 Run ye to and
fro through the
streets of Jerusalem,
and see now, and
know, and seek in
the broad places
thereof, if ye can find a man, if there be
any that executeth judgment, that seeketh
the truth; and I will pardon it.

5:1 God's Forgiveness
◄ Isaiah 55:7
Jeremiah 31:34 ►

2 And though they say, The LORD liveth;
surely they swear falsely.
3 O LORD, *are* not
thine eyes upon the
truth? thou hast
stricken them, but
they have not
grieved; thou hast
consumed them, *but* they have refused to
receive correction: they have made their
faces harder than a rock; they have refused
to return.

5:3 Refusing Correction
◄ Jeremiah 2:30
Amos 4:9 ►

4 Therefore I said, Surely these *are* poor;
they are foolish: for
they know not the
way of the LORD,
nor the judgment of
their God.

5:4
Poverty
◄ Matthew 18:23-25 ►

5 I will get me
unto the great men, and will speak unto
them; for they have known the way of the
LORD, *and* the judgment of their God: but
these have altogether broken the yoke, *and*
burst the bonds.
6 Wherefore a lion out of the forest shall
slay them, *and* a wolf of the evenings shall
spoil them, a leopard shall watch over their
cities: every one that goeth out thence shall
be torn in pieces: because their transgressions are many, *and* their backslidings are
increased.
7 How shall I pardon thee for this? thy
children have forsaken me, and sworn by
them that are no gods: when I had fed them
to the full, they then committed adultery,
and assembled themselves by troops in the
harlots' houses.
8 They were *as* fed horses in the morning: every one neighed after his
neighbour's wife.
9 Shall I not visit for these *things?* saith
the LORD: and shall not my soul be
avenged on such a nation as this?
10 Go ye up upon her walls, and destroy;
but make not a full end: take away her
battlements; for they *are* not the LORD'S.
11 For the house of Israel and the house
of Judah have dealt very treacherously
against me, saith the LORD.
12 They have belied the LORD, and
said, *It is* not he; neither shall evil come
upon us; neither shall we see sword nor
famine:
13 And the prophets shall become wind,
and the word *is* not in them: thus shall it
be done unto them.
14 Wherefore thus
saith the LORD God
of hosts, Because ye
speak this word, be-
hold, I will make
my words in thy
mouth fire, and this people wood, and it
shall devour them.

5:14
Power of the Bible
◄ Jeremiah 23:29 ►

15 Lo, I will bring a nation upon you
from far, O house of Israel, saith the LORD:
it *is* a mighty nation, it *is* an ancient nation, a nation whose language thou

knowest not, neither understandest what
they say.
16 Their quiver *is* as an open sepulchre,
they *are* all mighty men.
17 And they shall eat up thine harvest,
and thy bread, *which* thy sons and thy
daughters should eat: they shall eat up thy
flocks and thine herds: they shall eat up
thy vines and thy fig trees: they shall im-
poverish thy fenced cities, wherein thou
trustedst, with the sword.
18 Nevertheless in those days, saith the
LORD, I will not make a full end with you.
19 And it shall come to pass, when ye
shall say, Wherefore doeth the LORD our
God all these *things* unto us? then shalt
thou answer them, Like as ye have forsak-
en me, and served strange gods in your
land, so shall ye serve strangers in a land
that is not yours.
20 Declare this in the house of Jacob, and
publish it in Judah, saying,
21 Hear now this, O foolish people, and
without understanding; which have eyes,
and see not; which have ears, and hear not:
22 Fear ye not me? saith the LORD: will
ye not tremble at my presence, which have
placed the sand *for* the bound of the sea
by a perpetual decree, that it cannot pass
it: and though the waves thereof toss themselves, yet can they not prevail; though they
roar, yet can they not pass over it?
23 But this people hath a revolting and a
rebellious heart; they are revolted and
gone.
24 Neither say they in their heart, Let us
now fear the LORD our God, that giveth
rain, both the former and the latter, in his
season: he reserveth unto us the appointed weeks of the harvest.
25 Your iniquities have turned away these
things, and your sins have withholden good
things from you.
26 For among my people are found wicked *men:* they lay wait, as he that setteth
snares; they set a trap, they catch men.
27 As a cage is full
of birds, so *are* their
houses full of de-
ceit: therefore they
are become great,
and waxen rich.

5:27 Dishonest People
◄ Proverbs 27:6
Mark 7:22 ►

28 They are waxen fat, they shine: yea,
they overpass the deeds of the wicked: they
judge not the cause, the cause of the fatherless, yet they
prosper; and the
right of the needy
do they not judge.
29 Shall I not vis-
it for these *things?*
saith the LORD:
shall not my soul
be avenged on such
a nation as this?
30 A wonderful
and horrible thing
is committed in the land;

5:28 Callousness
◄ Ezra 9:6
Matthew 12:45 ►

5:28 Just You Wait
◄ Psalm 73:12
Jeremiah 12:1 ►

31 The prophets prophesy falsely, and the
priests bear rule by their means; and my
people love *to have it* so: and what will ye
do in the end thereof?

6

1 O ye children of Benjamin, gather yourselves to flee out of the midst of Jerusalem, and blow the trumpet in Tekoa, and
set up a sign of fire in Beth-haccerem: for
evil appeareth out of the north, and great
destruction.
2 I have likened the daughter of Zion to
a comely and delicate *woman.*
3 The shepherds with their flocks shall
come unto her; they shall pitch *their* tents
against her round about; they shall feed
every one in his place.
4 Prepare ye war against her; arise, and
let us go up at noon. Woe unto us! for the
day goeth away, for the shadows of the
evening are stretched out.
5 Arise, and let us go by night, and let us
destroy her palaces.
6 For thus hath the LORD of hosts said,
Hew ye down trees, and cast a mount
against Jerusalem: this *is* the city to be visited; she *is* wholly oppression in the midst
of her.
7 As a fountain
casteth out her wa-
ters, so she casteth
out her wickedness:
violence and spoil
is heard in her; be-
fore me continual-
ly *is* grief and wounds.

6:7 Violence
◄ Isaiah 59:6
Ezekiel 8:17 ►

8 Be thou instructed, O Jerusalem, lest
my soul depart from thee; lest I make thee
desolate, a land not inhabited.
9 Thus saith the LORD of hosts, They shall
throughly glean the remnant of Israel as
a vine: turn back thine hand as a grape-
gatherer into the baskets.

10 To whom shall I speak, and give warning, that they may hear? behold, their ear *is* uncircumcised, and they cannot hearken: behold, the word of the LORD is unto them a reproach; they have no delight in it.

11 Therefore I am full of the fury of the LORD; I am weary with holding in: I will pour it out upon the children abroad, and upon the assembly of young men together: for even the husband with the wife shall be taken, the aged with *him that is* full of days.

12 And their houses shall be turned unto others, *with their* fields and wives together: for I will stretch out my hand upon the inhabitants of the land, saith the LORD.

13 For from the least of them even unto the greatest of them every one *is* given to covetousness; and from the prophet even unto the priest every one dealeth falsely.

14 They have healed also the hurt *of the daughter* of my people slightly, saying, Peace, peace; when *there is* no peace.

15 Were they ashamed when they had committed abomination? nay, they were not at all ashamed, neither could they blush: therefore they shall fall among them that fall: at the time *that* I visit them they shall be cast down, saith the LORD.

6:15 Stubborn People
◄ Nehemiah 9:29
Daniel 9:13 ►

16 Thus saith the LORD, Stand ye in the ways, and see, and ask for the old paths, where *is* the good way, and walk therein, and ye shall find rest for your souls. But they said, We will not walk *therein*.

17 Also I set watchmen over you, *saying*, Hearken to the sound of the trumpet. But they said, We will not hearken.

18 Therefore hear, ye nations, and know, O congregation, what *is* among them.

19 Hear, O earth: behold, I will bring evil upon this people, *even* the fruit of their thoughts, because they have not hearkened unto my words, nor to my law, but rejected it.

20 To what purpose cometh there to me incense from Sheba, and the sweet cane from a far country? your burnt offerings *are* not acceptable, nor your sacrifices sweet unto me.

21 Therefore thus saith the LORD, Behold, I will lay stumblingblocks before this people, and the fathers and the sons together shall fall upon them; the neighbour and his friend shall perish.

22 Thus saith the LORD, Behold, a people cometh from the north country, and a great nation shall be raised from the sides of the earth.

23 They shall lay hold on bow and spear; they *are* cruel, and have no mercy; their voice roareth like the sea; and they ride upon horses, set in array as men for war against thee, O daughter of Zion.

24 We have heard the fame thereof: our hands wax feeble: anguish hath taken hold of us, *and* pain, as of a woman in travail.

25 Go not forth into the field, nor walk by the way; for the sword of the enemy *and* fear *is* on every side.

26 O daughter of my people, gird *thee* with sackcloth, and wallow thyself in ashes: make thee mourning, *as for* an only son, most bitter lamentation: for the spoiler shall suddenly come upon us.

27 I have set thee *for* a tower *and* a fortress among my people, that thou mayest know and try their way.

28 They *are* all grievous revolters, walking with slanders: *they are* brass and iron; they *are* all corrupters.

29 The bellows are burned, the lead is consumed of the fire; the founder melteth in vain: for the wicked are not plucked away.

30 Reprobate silver shall *men* call them, because the LORD hath rejected them.

7

1 The word that came to Jeremiah from the LORD, saying,

2 Stand in the gate of the LORD'S house, and proclaim there this word, and say, Hear the word of the LORD, all *ye of* Judah, that enter in at these gates to worship the LORD.

3 Thus saith the LORD of hosts, the God of Israel, Amend your ways and your doings, and I will cause you to dwell in this place.

4 Trust ye not in lying words, saying, The temple of the LORD, The temple of the LORD, The temple of the LORD, *are* these.

5 For if ye throughly amend your ways and your doings; if ye throughly execute judgment between a man and his neighbour;

6 *If* ye oppress not the stranger, the fa-

therless, and the
widow, and shed
not innocent blood
in this place, nei-
ther walk after
other gods to your
hurt:

7:6 New Kids
◄ Deuteronomy 31:12
Matthew 25:35 ►

7 Then will I cause you to dwell in this
place, in the land that I gave to your fathers, for ever and ever.
8 Behold, ye trust in lying words, that
cannot profit.
9 Will ye steal, murder, and commit adultery, and swear falsely, and burn incense
unto Baal, and walk after other gods whom
ye know not;
10 And come and stand before me in this
house, which is called by my name, and
say, We are delivered to do all these abominations?
11 Is this house, which is called by my
name, become a den of robbers in your
eyes? Behold, *even* I have seen *it,* saith the
LORD.
12 But go ye now unto my place which
was in Shiloh, where I set my name at the
first, and see what I did to it for the wickedness of my people Israel.
13 And now, be-
cause ye have done
all these works,
saith the LORD, and
I spake unto you,
rising up early and
speaking, but ye heard not; and I called
you, but ye answered not;

7:13 Hard-hearted
◄ Ecclesiastes 8:11
Hosea 7:10 ►

14 Therefore will I do unto *this* house,
which is called by my name, wherein ye
trust, and unto the place which I gave to
you and to your fathers, as I have done to
Shiloh.
15 And I will cast you out of my sight, as
I have cast out all your brethren, *even* the
whole seed of Ephraim.
16 Therefore pray not thou for this people, neither lift up cry nor prayer for them,
neither make intercession to me: for I will
not hear thee.
17 Seest thou not what they do in the
cities of Judah and in the streets of Jerusalem?
18 The children gather wood, and the fathers kindle the fire, and the women knead
their dough, to make cakes to the queen
of heaven, and to pour out drink offerings
unto other gods, that they may provoke
me to anger.
19 Do they provoke me to anger? saith
the LORD: *do they* not *provoke* themselves
to the confusion of their own faces?
20 Therefore thus saith the Lord GOD;
Behold, mine anger and my fury shall be
poured out upon this place, upon man,
and upon beast, and upon the trees of the
field, and upon the fruit of the ground;
and it shall burn, and shall not be
quenched.
21 Thus saith the LORD of hosts, the God
of Israel; Put your burnt offerings unto
your sacrifices, and eat flesh.
22 For I spake not unto your fathers, nor
commanded them in the day that I
brought them out of the land of Egypt,
concerning burnt offerings or sacrifices:
23 But this thing
commanded I
them, saying, Obey
my voice, and I will
be your God, and
ye shall be my peo-
ple: and walk ye in all the ways that I have
commanded you, that it may be well unto
you.

7:23 Obeying God
◄ 1 Samuel 15:22
Matthew 7:21 ►

24 But they hearkened not, nor inclined
their ear, but walked in the counsels *and*
in the imagination of their evil heart, and
went backward, and not forward.
25 Since the day that your fathers came
forth out of the land of Egypt unto this
day I have even sent unto you all my servants the prophets, daily rising up early
and sending *them:*
26 Yet they hearkened not unto me, nor
inclined their ear, but hardened their neck:
they did worse than their fathers.
27 Therefore thou shalt speak all these
words unto them; but they will not hearken to thee: thou shalt also call unto them;
but they will not answer thee.
28 But thou shalt say unto them, This *is*
a nation that obeyeth not the voice of the
LORD their God, nor receiveth correction:
truth is perished, and is cut off from their
mouth.
29 Cut off thine hair, *O Jerusalem,* and
cast *it* away, and take up a lamentation on
high places; for the LORD hath rejected and
forsaken the generation of his wrath.
30 For the children of Judah have done
evil in my sight, saith the LORD: they have

set their abominations in the house which
is called by my name, to pollute it.
31 And they have built the high places of
Tophet, which *is* in the valley of the son of
Hinnom, to burn their sons and their
daughters in the fire; which I commanded
them not, neither came it into my heart.
32 Therefore, behold, the days come,
saith the LORD, that it shall no more be
called Tophet, nor the valley of the son of
Hinnom, but the valley of slaughter: for
they shall bury in Tophet, till there be no
place.
33 And the carcases of this people shall
be meat for the fowls of the heaven, and
for the beasts of the earth; and none shall
fray *them* away.
34 Then will I cause to cease from the cities of Judah, and from the streets of Jerusalem, the voice of mirth, and the voice of
gladness, the voice of the bridegroom, and
the voice of the bride: for the land shall
be desolate.

8

1 At that time, saith the LORD, they shall
bring out the bones of the kings of Judah,
and the bones of his princes, and the bones
of the priests, and the bones of the prophets, and the bones of the inhabitants of
Jerusalem, out of their graves:
2 And they shall spread them before the
sun, and the moon, and all the host of
heaven, whom they have loved, and whom
they have served, and after whom they
have walked, and whom they have sought,
and whom they have worshipped: they
shall not be gathered, nor be buried; they
shall be for dung upon the face of the
earth.
3 And death shall be chosen rather than
life by all the residue of them that remain
of this evil family, which remain in all the
places whither I have driven them, saith
the LORD of hosts.
4 Moreover thou shalt say unto them,
Thus saith the LORD; Shall they fall, and
not arise? shall he turn away, and not return?
5 Why *then* is this people of Jerusalem
slidden back by a perpetual backsliding?
they hold fast deceit, they refuse to return.
6 I hearkened and heard, *but* they spake
not aright: no man repented him of his
wickedness, saying, What have I done?
every one turned to his course, as the horse
rusheth into the battle.
7 Yea, the stork in the heaven knoweth
her appointed times; and the turtle and
the crane and the swallow observe the time
of their coming; but my people know not
the judgment of the LORD.
8 How do ye say, We *are* wise, and the
law of the LORD *is* with us? Lo, certainly in
vain made he *it*; the pen of the scribes *is* in
vain.
9 The wise *men* are ashamed, they are
dismayed and taken: lo, they have rejected the word of the LORD; and what wisdom *is* in them?
10 Therefore will I give their wives unto
others, *and* their fields to them that shall
inherit *them*: for every one from the least
even unto the greatest is given to covetousness, from the prophet even unto the
priest every one dealeth falsely.
11 For they have healed the hurt of the
daughter of my people slightly, saying,
Peace, peace; when *there is* no peace.
12 Were they ashamed when they had
committed abomination? nay, they were
not at all ashamed, neither could they
blush: therefore shall they fall among them
that fall: in the time of their visitation they
shall be cast down, saith the LORD.
13 I will surely consume them, saith the
LORD: *there shall be* no grapes on the vine,
nor figs on the fig tree, and the leaf shall
fade; and *the things that* I have given them
shall pass away from them.
14 Why do we sit still? assemble yourselves, and let us enter into the defenced
cities, and let us be silent there: for the
LORD our God hath put us to silence, and
given us water of gall to drink, because we
have sinned against the LORD.
15 We looked for
peace, but no good
came; and for a time
of health, and be-
hold trouble!

8:15 Disappointment
◄ Isaiah 17:11
Jeremiah 14:19 ►

16 The snorting of
his horses was heard from Dan: the whole
land trembled at the sound of the neigh-
ing of his strong ones; for they are come,
and have devoured the land, and all that
is in it; the city, and those that dwell
therein.
17 For, behold, I will send serpents,
cockatrices, among you, which *will* not *be*
charmed, and they shall bite you, saith the
LORD.

18 *When* I would comfort myself against sorrow, my heart *is* faint in me.

19 Behold the voice of the cry of the daughter of my people because of them that dwell in a far country: *Is* not the LORD in Zion? *is* not her king in her? Why have they provoked me to anger with their graven images, *and* with strange vanities?

20 The harvest is past, the summer is ended, and we are not saved.

21 For the hurt of the daughter of my people am I hurt; I am black; astonishment hath taken hold on me.

22 *Is there* no balm in Gilead; *is there* no physician there? why then is not the health of the daughter of my people recovered?

9

1 Oh that my head were waters, and mine eyes a fountain of tears, that I might weep day and night for the slain of the daughter of my people!

2 Oh that I had in the wilderness a lodging place of wayfaring men; that I might leave my people, and go from them! for they *be* all adulterers, an assembly of treacherous men.

3 And they bend their tongues *like* their bow *for* lies: but they are not valiant for the truth upon the earth; for they proceed from evil to evil, and they know not me, saith the LORD.

4 Take ye heed every one of his neighbour, and trust ye not in any brother: for every brother will utterly supplant, and every neighbour will walk with slanders.

5 And they will deceive every one his neighbour, and will not speak the truth: they have taught their tongue to speak lies, *and* weary themselves to commit iniquity.

6 Thine habitation *is* in the midst of deceit; through deceit they refuse to know me, saith the LORD.

7 Therefore thus saith the LORD of hosts, Behold, I will melt them, and try them; for how shall I do for the daughter of my people?

8 Their tongue *is as* an arrow shot out; it speaketh deceit: *one* speaketh peaceably to his neighbour with his mouth, but in heart he layeth his wait.

9 Shall I not visit them for these *things?* saith the LORD: shall not my soul be avenged on such a nation as this?

10 For the mountains will I take up a weeping and wailing, and for the habitations of the wilderness a lamentation, because they are burned up, so that none can pass through *them;* neither can *men* hear the voice of the cattle; both the fowl of the heavens and the beast are fled; they are gone.

11 And I will make Jerusalem heaps, *and* a den of dragons; and I will make the cities of Judah desolate, without an inhabitant.

12 Who *is* the wise man, that may understand this? and *who is he* to whom the mouth of the LORD hath spoken, that he may declare it, for what the land perisheth *and* is burned up like a wilderness, that none passeth through?

13 And the LORD saith, Because they have forsaken my law which I set before them, and have not obeyed my voice, neither walked therein;

14 But have walked after the imagination of their own heart, and after Baalim, which their fathers taught them:

15 Therefore thus saith the LORD of hosts, the God of Israel; Behold, I will feed them, *even* this people, with wormwood, and give them water of gall to drink.

16 I will scatter them also among the heathen, whom neither they nor their fathers have known: and I will send a sword after them, till I have consumed them.

17 Thus saith the LORD of hosts, Consider ye, and call for the mourning women, that they may come; and send for cunning *women,* that they may come:

18 And let them make haste, and take up a wailing for us, that our eyes may run down with tears, and our eyelids gush out with waters.

19 For a voice of wailing is heard out of Zion, How are we spoiled! we are greatly confounded, because we have forsaken the land, because our dwellings have cast *us* out.

20 Yet hear the word of the LORD, O ye women, and let your ear receive the word of his mouth, and teach your daughters wailing, and every one her neighbour lamentation.

21 For death is come up into our windows, *and* is entered into our palaces, to cut off the children from without, *and* the young men from the streets.

22 Speak, Thus saith the LORD, Even the carcases of men shall fall as dung upon the open field, and as the handful after

the harvestman, and none shall gather *them.*

23 Thus saith the LORD, Let not the wise *man* glory in his wisdom, neither let the mighty *man* glory in his might, let not the rich *man* glory in his riches:

24 But let him that glorieth glory in this, that he understandeth and knoweth me, that I *am* the LORD which exercise lovingkindness, judgment, and righteousness, in the earth: for in these *things* I delight, saith the LORD.

9:24 Boasting
◄ Isaiah 45:25
Romans 2:17 ►

25 Behold, the days come, saith the LORD, that I will punish all *them which are* circumcised with the uncircumcised;

26 Egypt, and Judah, and Edom, and the children of Ammon, and Moab, and all *that are* in the utmost corners, that dwell in the wilderness: for all *these* nations *are* uncircumcised, and all the house of Israel *are* uncircumcised in the heart.

10

1 Hear ye the word which the LORD speaketh unto you, O house of Israel:

2 Thus saith the LORD, Learn not the way of the heathen, and be not dismayed at the signs of heaven; for the heathen are dismayed at them.

10:2 Superstition
◄ 1 Kings 20:23
Jeremiah 44:18 ►

3 For the customs of the people *are* vain: for *one* cutteth a tree out of the forest, the work of the hands of the workman, with the axe.

4 They deck it with silver and with gold; they fasten it with nails and with hammers, that it move not.

5 They *are* upright as the palm tree, but speak not: they must needs be borne, because they cannot go. Be not afraid of them; for they cannot do evil, neither also *is it* in them to do good.

6 Forasmuch as *there is* none like unto thee, O LORD; thou *art* great, and thy name *is* great in might.

7 Who would not fear thee, O King of nations? for to thee doth it appertain: forasmuch as among all the wise *men* of the nations, and in all their kingdoms, *there is* none like unto thee.

8 But they are altogether brutish and foolish: the stock *is* a doctrine of vanities.

9 Silver spread into plates is brought from Tarshish, and gold from Uphaz, the work of the workman, and of the hands of the founder: blue and purple *is* their clothing: they *are* all the work of cunning *men.*

10:8 Worshiping Things
◄ Jeremiah 2:5
Jeremiah 16:19 ►

10 But the LORD *is* the true God, he *is* the living God, and an everlasting king: at his wrath the earth shall tremble, and the nations shall not be able to abide his indignation.

11 Thus shall ye say unto them, The gods that have not made the heavens and the earth, *even* they shall perish from the earth, and from under these heavens.

12 He hath made the earth by his power, he hath established the world by his wisdom, and hath stretched out the heavens by his discretion.

13 When he uttereth his voice, *there is* a multitude of waters in the heavens, and he causeth the vapors to ascend from the ends of the earth; he maketh lightnings with rain, and bringeth forth the wind out of his treasures.

14 Every man is brutish in *his* knowledge: every founder is confounded by the graven image: for his molten image is falsehood, and *there is* no breath in them.

15 They *are* vanity, *and* the work of errors: in the time of their visitation they shall perish.

16 The portion of Jacob *is* not like them: for he *is* the former of all *things;* and Israel *is* the rod of his inheritance: The LORD of hosts *is* his name.

17 Gather up thy wares out of the land, O inhabitant of the fortress.

18 For thus saith the LORD, Behold, I will sling out the inhabitants of the land at this once, and will distress them, that they may find *it so.*

19 Woe is me for my hurt! my wound is grievous: but I said, Truly this *is* a grief, and I must bear it.

20 My tabernacle is spoiled, and all my cords are broken: my children are gone forth of me, and they *are* not: *there is* none to stretch forth my tent any more, and to set up my curtains.

21 For the pastors are become brutish, and have not sought the LORD: therefore

they shall not prosper, and all their flocks shall be scattered.

10:21 Not Praying
◄ Isaiah 64:7
Daniel 9:13 ►

22 Behold, the noise of the bruit is come, and a great commotion out of the north country, to make the cities of Judah desolate, *and* a den of dragons.

23 O LORD, I know that the way of man *is* not in himself: *it is* not in man that walketh to direct his steps.

10:23 God's Role
◄ Psalm 127:1
John 3:27 ►

24 O LORD, correct me, but with judgment; not in thine anger, lest thou bring me to nothing.

25 Pour out thy fury upon the heathen that know thee not, and upon the families that call not on thy name: for they have eaten up Jacob, and devoured him, and consumed him, and have made his habitation desolate.

11

1 The word that came to Jeremiah from the LORD, saying,

2 Hear ye the words of this covenant, and speak unto the men of Judah, and to the inhabitants of Jerusalem;

3 And say thou unto them, Thus saith the LORD God of Israel; Cursed *be* the man that obeyeth not the words of this covenant,

4 Which I commanded your fathers in the day *that* I brought them forth out of the land of Egypt, from the iron furnace, saying, Obey my voice, and do them, according to all which I command you: so shall ye be my people, and I will be your God:

5 That I may perform the oath which I have sworn unto your fathers, to give them a land flowing with milk and honey, as *it is* this day. Then answered I, and said, So be it, O LORD.

6 Then the LORD said unto me, Proclaim all these words in the cities of Judah, and in the streets of Jerusalem, saying, Hear ye the words of this covenant, and do them.

7 For I earnestly protested unto your fathers in the day *that* I brought them up out of the land of Egypt, *even* unto this day, rising early and protesting, saying, Obey my voice.

8 Yet they obeyed not, nor inclined their ear, but walked every one in the imagination of their evil heart: therefore I will bring upon them all the words of this covenant, which I commanded *them* to do; but they did *them* not.

9 And the LORD said unto me, A conspiracy is found among the men of Judah, and among the inhabitants of Jerusalem.

10 They are turned back to the iniquities of their forefathers, which refused to hear my words; and they went after other gods to serve them: the house of Israel and the house of Judah have broken my covenant which I made with their fathers.

11 Therefore thus saith the LORD, Behold, I will bring evil upon them, which they shall not be able to escape; and though they shall cry unto me, I will not hearken unto them.

12 Then shall the cities of Judah and inhabitants of Jerusalem go, and cry unto the gods unto whom they offer incense: but they shall not save them at all in the time of their trouble.

13 For *according to* the number of thy cities were thy gods, O Judah; and *according to* the number of the streets of Jerusalem have ye set up altars to *that* shameful thing, *even* altars to burn incense unto Baal.

14 Therefore pray not thou for this people, neither lift up a cry or prayer for them: for I will not hear *them* in the time that they cry unto me for their trouble.

15 What hath my beloved to do in mine house, *seeing* she hath wrought lewdness with many, and the holy flesh is passed from thee? when thou doest evil, then thou rejoicest.

16 The LORD called thy name, A green olive tree, fair, *and* of goodly fruit: with the noise of a great tumult he hath kindled fire upon it, and the branches of it are broken.

17 For the LORD of hosts, that planted thee, hath pronounced evil against thee, for the evil of the house of Israel and of the house of Judah, which they have done against themselves to provoke me to anger in offering incense unto Baal.

18 And the LORD hath given me knowledge *of it,* and I know *it:* then thou shewedst me their doings.

19 But I *was* like a lamb *or* an ox *that* is brought to the slaughter; and I knew not that they had devised devices against me, *saying,* Let us destroy the tree with the fruit

thereof, and let us cut him off from the
land of the living, that his name may be
no more remembered.
20 But, O LORD of hosts, that judgest righteously, that triest the reins and the heart,
let me see thy vengeance on them: for unto
thee have I revealed my cause.
21 Therefore thus saith the LORD of the
men of Anathoth, that seek thy life, saying, Prophesy not in the name of the LORD,
that thou die not by our hand:
22 Therefore thus saith the LORD of hosts,
Behold, I will punish them: the young men
shall die by the sword; their sons and their
daughters shall die by famine:
23 And there shall be no remnant of them:
for I will bring evil upon the men of Anathoth, *even* the year of their visitation.

12

1 Righteous *art*
thou, O LORD, when
I plead with thee:
yet let me talk with
thee of *thy* judg-
ments: Wherefore
doth the way of the
wicked prosper?
wherefore are all
they happy that
deal very treacher-
ously?

12:1 Injustice
◄ Ecclesiastes 9:2
Ezekiel 18:25 ►

12:1
Just You Wait
◄ Jeremiah 5:28 ►

2 Thou hast planted them, yea, they have
taken root: they grow, yea, they bring forth
fruit: thou *art* near in their mouth, and far
from their reins.
3 But thou, O LORD, knowest me: thou
hast seen me, and tried mine heart toward
thee: pull them out like sheep for the
slaughter, and prepare them for the day of
slaughter.
4 How long shall the land mourn, and
the herbs of every field wither, for the wickedness of them that dwell therein? the
beasts are consumed, and the birds; because
they said, He shall not see our last end.
5 If thou hast run with the footmen, and
they have wearied thee, then how canst
thou contend with horses? and *if* in the
land of peace, *wherein* thou trustedst, *they
wearied thee,* then how wilt thou do in the
swelling of Jordan?
6 For even thy brethren, and the house
of thy father, even they have dealt treacherously with thee; yea, they have called a
multitude after thee: believe them not,
though they speak fair words unto thee.
7 I have forsaken mine house, I have left
mine heritage; I have given the dearly beloved of my soul into the hand of her enemies.
8 Mine heritage is unto me as a lion in
the forest; it crieth out against me: therefore have I hated it.
9 Mine heritage *is* unto me *as* a speckled
bird, the birds round about *are* against her;
come ye, assemble all the beasts of the
field, come to devour.
10 Many pastors have destroyed my vineyard, they have trodden my portion under
foot, they have made my pleasant portion
a desolate wilderness.
11 They have made it desolate, *and being*
desolate it mourneth unto me; the whole
land is made desolate, because no man
layeth *it* to heart.
12 The spoilers are come upon all high
places through the wilderness: for the
sword of the LORD shall devour from the
one end of the land even to the *other* end
of the land: no flesh shall have peace.
13 They have sown wheat, but shall reap
thorns: they have put themselves to pain,
but shall not profit: and they shall be
ashamed of your revenues because of the
fierce anger of the LORD.
14 Thus saith the LORD against all mine
evil neighbours, that touch the inheritance
which I have caused my people Israel to
inherit; Behold, I will pluck them out of
their land, and pluck out the house of Judah from among them.
15 And it shall come to pass, after that I
have plucked them out I will return, and
have compassion on them, and will bring
them again, every man to his heritage, and
every man to his land.
16 And it shall come to pass, if they will
diligently learn the ways of my people, to
swear by my name, The LORD liveth; as they
taught my people to swear by Baal; then
shall they be built in the midst of my
people.
17 But if they will
not obey, I will ut-
terly pluck up and
destroy that nation,
saith the LORD.

12:17 Ouch!
◄ 1 Kings 13:21
Ephesians 5:6 ►

13

1 Thus saith the
LORD unto me, Go and get thee a linen
girdle, and put it upon thy loins, and put
it not in water.

2So I got a girdle according to the word
of the LORD, and put *it* on my loins.
3And the word of the LORD came unto
me the second time, saying,
4Take the girdle that thou hast got,
which *is* upon thy loins, and arise, go to
Euphrates, and hide it there in a hole of
the rock.
5So I went, and hid it by Euphrates, as
the LORD commanded me.
6And it came to pass after many days,
that the LORD said unto me, Arise, go to
Euphrates, and take the girdle from thence,
which I commanded thee to hide there.
7Then I went to Euphrates, and digged,
and took the girdle from the place where I
had hid it: and, behold, the girdle was
marred, it was profitable for nothing.
8Then the word of the LORD came unto
me, saying,
9Thus saith the LORD, After this manner
will I mar the pride of Judah, and the great
pride of Jerusalem.
10This evil people, which refuse to hear
my words, which walk in the imagination
of their heart, and walk after other gods,
to serve them, and to worship them, shall
even be as this girdle, which is good for
nothing.
11For as the girdle cleaveth to the loins
of a man, so have I caused to cleave unto
me the whole house of Israel and the
whole house of Judah, saith the LORD; that
they might be unto me for a people, and
for a name, and for a praise, and for a glory: but they would not hear.
12Therefore thou shalt speak unto them
this word; Thus saith the LORD God of Israel, Every bottle shall be filled with wine:
and they shall say unto thee, Do we not
certainly know that every bottle shall be
filled with wine?
13Then shalt thou say unto them, Thus
saith the LORD, Behold, I will fill all the
inhabitants of this land, even the kings that
sit upon David's throne, and the priests,
and the prophets, and all the inhabitants
of Jerusalem, with drunkenness.
14And I will dash them one against another, even the fathers and the sons together, saith the LORD: I will not pity, nor spare,
nor have mercy, but destroy them.
15Hear ye, and give ear; be not proud:
for the LORD hath spoken.
16Give glory to the LORD your God,
before he cause
darkness, and be-
fore your feet stum-
ble upon the dark
mountains, and,
while ye look for
light, he turn it into
the shadow of
death, *and* make *it*
gross darkness.
17But if ye will
not hear it, my soul
shall weep in secret places for *your* pride;
and mine eye shall weep sore, and run
down with tears, because the LORD'S flock
is carried away captive.
18Say unto the king and to the queen,
Humble yourselves, sit down: for your
principalities shall come down, *even* the
crown of your glory.
19The cities of the south shall be shut
up, and none shall open *them:* Judah shall
be carried away captive all of it, it shall be
wholly carried away captive.
20Lift up your eyes, and behold them
that come from the north: where *is* the
flock *that* was given thee, thy beautiful
flock?
21What wilt thou say when he shall
punish thee? for thou hast taught them *to
be* captains, *and* as chief over thee: shall
not sorrows take thee, as a woman in
travail?
22And if thou say in thine heart, Wherefore come these things upon me? For the
greatness of thine iniquity are thy skirts
discovered, *and* thy heels made bare.
23Can the Ethiopian change his skin, or
the leopard his spots? *then* may ye also do
good, that are accustomed to do evil.
24Therefore will I scatter them as the
stubble that passeth away by the wind of
the wilderness.
25This *is* thy lot, the portion of thy measures from me, saith the LORD; because
thou hast forgotten me, and trusted in
falsehood.
26Therefore will I discover thy skirts
upon thy face, that thy shame may appear.
27I have seen thine adulteries, and thy
neighings, the lewdness of thy whoredom,
and thine abominations on the hills in
the fields. Woe unto thee, O Jerusalem!
wilt thou not be made clean? when *shall it*
once *be?*

13:16 Sin (Warnings)
◄ Isaiah 28:14
Jonah 3:4 ►

13:16 Wicked Insecurity
◄ Isaiah 30:13
Jeremiah 23:12 ►

14

1 The word of the LORD that came to Jeremiah concerning the dearth.
2 Judah mourneth, and the gates thereof
languish; they are black unto the ground;
and the cry of Jerusalem is gone up.
3 And their nobles have sent their little
ones to the waters: they came to the pits,
and found no water; they returned with
their vessels empty; they were ashamed
and confounded, and covered their heads.
4 Because the ground is chapt, for there
was no rain in the earth, the plowmen were
ashamed, they covered their heads.
5 Yea, the hind also calved in the field,
and forsook *it,* because there was no grass.
6 And the wild asses did stand in the high
places, they snuffed up the wind like dragons; their eyes did fail, because *there was*
no grass.
7 O LORD, though our iniquities testify
against us, do thou *it* for thy name's sake:
for our backslidings are many; we have
sinned against thee.
8 O the hope of Israel, the saviour thereof
in time of trouble, why shouldest thou be
as a stranger in the land, and as a wayfaring man *that* turneth aside to tarry for a
night?
9 Why shouldest thou be as a man
astonied, as a mighty man *that* cannot
save? yet thou, O LORD, *art* in the midst of
us, and we are called by thy name; leave
us not.
10 Thus saith the LORD unto this people,
Thus have they loved to wander, they have
not refrained their feet, therefore the LORD
doth not accept them; he will now remember their iniquity, and visit their sins.
11 Then said the LORD unto me, Pray not
for this people for *their* good.
12 When they fast, I will not hear their
cry; and when they offer burnt offering and
an oblation, I will not accept them: but I
will consume them by the sword, and by
the famine, and by the pestilence.
13 Then said I, Ah, Lord GOD! behold,
the prophets say unto them, Ye shall not
see the sword, neither shall ye have famine; but I will give you assured peace in
this place.
14 Then the LORD said unto me, The
prophets prophesy lies in my name: I sent
them not, neither have I commanded
them, neither spake unto them: they
prophesy unto you a false vision and divination, and a thing of nought, and the
deceit of their heart.
15 Therefore thus saith the LORD concerning the prophets that prophesy in my
name, and I sent them not, yet they say,
Sword and famine shall not be in this land;
By sword and famine shall those prophets
be consumed.
16 And the people to whom they prophesy shall be cast out in the streets of Jerusalem because of the famine and the
sword; and they shall have none to bury
them, them, their wives, nor their sons, nor
their daughters: for I will pour their wickedness upon them.
17 Therefore thou shalt say this word
unto them; Let mine eyes run down with
tears night and day, and let them not cease:
for the virgin daughter of my people is
broken with a great breach, with a very
grievous blow.
18 If I go forth into the field, then behold the slain with the sword! and if I enter into the city, then behold them that are
sick with famine! yea, both the prophet
and the priest go about into a land that
they know not.
19 Hast thou ut-
terly rejected Ju-
dah? hath thy soul
lothed Zion? why
hast thou smitten
us, and *there is* no
healing for us? we looked for peace, and
there is no good; and for the time of healing, and behold trouble!

14:19 Disappointment
◄ Jeremiah 8:15
Amos 5:11 ►

20 We acknowledge, O LORD, our wickedness, *and* the iniquity of our fathers: for
we have sinned against thee.
21 Do not abhor *us,* for thy name's sake,
do not disgrace the throne of thy glory:
remember, break not thy covenant with us.
22 Are there *any* among the vanities of the
Gentiles that can cause rain? or can the heavens give showers? *art* not thou he, O LORD
our God? therefore we will wait upon thee:
for thou hast made all these *things.*

15

1 Then said the LORD unto me, Though
Moses and Samuel stood before me, *yet* my
mind *could* not *be* toward this people: cast
them out of my sight, and let them go forth.
2 And it shall come to pass, if they say
unto thee, Whither shall we go forth? then
thou shalt tell them, Thus saith the LORD;
Such as *are* for death, to death; and such

as *are* for the sword, to the sword; and
such as *are* for the famine, to the famine;
and such as *are* for the captivity, to the captivity.
3And I will appoint over them four
kinds, saith the LORD: the sword to slay,
and the dogs to tear, and the fowls of the
heaven, and the beasts of the earth, to devour and destroy.
4And I will cause them to be removed
into all kingdoms of the earth, because of
Manasseh the son of Hezekiah king of Judah, for *that* which he did in Jerusalem.
5For who shall have pity upon thee,
O Jerusalem? or who shall bemoan thee? or
who shall go aside to ask how thou doest?
6Thou hast forsaken me, saith the LORD,
thou art gone backward: therefore will I
stretch out my hand against thee, and destroy thee; I am weary with repenting.
7And I will fan them with a fan in the
gates of the land; I will bereave *them* of
children, I will destroy my people, *since*
they return not from their ways.
8Their widows are increased to me above
the sand of the seas: I have brought upon
them against the mother of the young men
a spoiler at noonday: I have caused *him* to
fall upon it suddenly, and terrors upon the
city.
9She that hath borne seven languisheth:
she hath given up the ghost; her sun is
gone down while *it was* yet day: she hath
been ashamed and confounded: and the
residue of them will I deliver to the sword
before their enemies, saith the LORD.
10Woe is me, my
mother, that thou
hast borne me a
man of strife and a
man of contention
to the whole earth!
I have neither lent on usury, nor men have
lent to me on usury; *yet* every one of them
doth curse me.

15:10 Unhappiness
◄ Psalm 137:1
Micah 7:1 ►

11The LORD said, Verily it shall be well
with thy remnant; verily I will cause the
enemy to entreat thee *well* in the time of
evil and in the time of affliction.
12Shall iron break the northern iron and
the steel?
13Thy substance and thy treasures will I
give to the spoil without price, and *that*
for all thy sins, even in all thy borders.
14And I will make *thee* to pass with thine
enemies into a land *which* thou knowest
not: for a fire is kindled in mine anger,
which shall burn upon you.
15O LORD, thou
knowest: remember
me, and visit me,
and revenge me of
my persecutors;
take me not away in
thy longsuffering: know that for thy sake I
have suffered rebuke.

15:15 Bullies
◄ Psalm 143:3
Lamentations 5:5 ►

16Thy words were found, and I did eat
them; and thy word was unto me the joy
and rejoicing of mine heart: for I am called
by thy name, O LORD God of hosts.
17I sat not in the assembly of the mockers, nor rejoiced; I sat alone because of thy
hand: for thou hast filled me with indignation.
18Why is my pain perpetual, and my
wound incurable, *which* refuseth to be
healed? wilt thou be altogether unto me
as a liar, *and as* waters *that* fail?
19Therefore thus saith the LORD, If thou
return, then will I bring thee again, *and*
thou shalt stand before me: and if thou
take forth the precious from the vile, thou
shalt be as my mouth: let them return unto
thee; but return not thou unto them.
20And I will make thee unto this people
a fenced brasen wall: and they shall fight
against thee, but they shall not prevail
against thee: for I *am* with thee to save thee
and to deliver thee, saith the LORD.
21And I will deliver thee out of the hand
of the wicked, and I will redeem thee out
of the hand of the terrible.

16

1The word of the LORD came also unto
me, saying,
2Thou shalt not take thee a wife, neither shalt thou have sons or daughters in
this place.
3For thus saith the LORD concerning the
sons and concerning the daughters that are
born in this place, and concerning their
mothers that bare them, and concerning
their fathers that begat them in this land;
4They shall die of grievous deaths; they
shall not be lamented; neither shall they
be buried; *but* they shall be as dung upon
the face of the earth: and they shall be consumed by the sword, and by famine; and
their carcases shall be meat for the fowls
of heaven, and for the beasts of the earth.
5For thus saith the LORD, Enter not into

the house of mourning, neither go to lament nor bemoan them: for I have taken
away my peace from this people, saith the
LORD, *even* lovingkindness and mercies.
6 Both the great and the small shall die
in this land: they shall not be buried, neither shall *men* lament for them, nor cut
themselves, nor make themselves bald for
them:
7 Neither shall *men* tear *themselves* for
them in mourning, to comfort them for
the dead; neither shall *men* give them the
cup of consolation to drink for their father or for their mother.
8 Thou shalt not also go into the house
of feasting, to sit with them to eat and to
drink.
9 For thus saith the LORD of hosts, the
God of Israel; Behold, I will cause to cease
out of this place in your eyes, and in your
days, the voice of mirth, and the voice of
gladness, the voice of the bridegroom, and
the voice of the bride.
10 And it shall come to pass, when thou
shalt shew this people all these words, and
they shall say unto thee, Wherefore hath
the LORD pronounced all this great evil
against us? or what *is* our iniquity? or what
is our sin that we have committed against
the LORD our God?
11 Then shalt thou say unto them, Because your fathers have forsaken me, saith
the LORD, and have walked after other
gods, and have served them, and have
worshipped them, and have forsaken me,
and have not kept my law;
12 And ye have done worse than your fathers; for, behold, ye walk every one after
the imagination of his evil heart, that they
may not hearken unto me:
13 Therefore will I cast you out of this
land into a land that ye know not, *neither*
ye nor your fathers; and there shall ye serve
other gods day and night; where I will not
shew you favour.
14 Therefore, behold, the days come,
saith the LORD, that it shall no more be
said, The LORD liveth, that brought up the
children of Israel out of the land of Egypt;
15 But, The LORD liveth, that brought up
the children of Israel from the land of the
north, and from all the lands whither he
had driven them: and I will bring them
again into their land that I gave unto their
fathers.
16 Behold, I will send for many fishers,
saith the LORD, and they shall fish them;
and after will I send for many hunters, and
they shall hunt them from every mountain, and from every hill, and out of the
holes of the rocks.
17 For mine eyes
are upon all their
ways: they are not
hid from my face,
neither is their iniq-
uity hid from mine
eyes.

16:17 God Sees Sin
◄ Jeremiah 2:22
Ezekiel 11:5 ►

18 And first I will recompense their iniquity and their sin double; because they
have defiled my land, they have filled mine
inheritance with the carcases of their detestable and abominable things.
19 O LORD, my
strength, and my
fortress, and my ref-
uge in the day of
affliction, the Gen-
tiles shall come
unto thee from the ends of the earth, and
shall say, Surely our fathers have inherited
lies, vanity, and *things* wherein *there is* no
profit.

16:19 Worshiping Things
◄ Jeremiah 10:8
Jonah 2:8 ►

20 Shall a man make gods unto himself,
and they *are* no gods?
21 Therefore, behold, I will this once
cause them to know, I will cause them to
know mine hand and my might; and they
shall know that my name *is* The LORD.

17

1 The sin of Judah *is* written with a pen
of iron, *and* with the point of a diamond:
it is graven upon the table of their heart,
and upon the horns of your altars;
2 Whilst their children remember their
altars and their groves by the green trees
upon the high hills.
3 O my mountain in the field, I will give
thy substance *and* all thy treasures to the
spoil, *and* thy high places for sin, throughout all thy borders.
4 And thou, even thyself, shalt discon-
tinue from thine heritage that I gave thee;
and I will cause thee to serve thine enemies in the land which thou knowest not:
for ye have kindled
a fire in mine anger,
which shall burn for
ever.
5 Thus saith the
LORD; Cursed *be* the

17:5 Trusting in People
◄ Isaiah 36:6
Hosea 5:13 ►

man that trusteth in man, and maketh flesh his arm, and whose heart departeth from the LORD.

6For he shall be like the heath in the desert, and shall not see when good cometh; but shall inhabit the parched places in the wilderness, *in* a salt land and not inhabited.

7Blessed *is* the man that trusteth in the LORD, and whose hope the LORD is.

8For he shall be as a tree planted by the waters, and *that* spreadeth out her roots by the river, and shall not see when heat cometh, but her leaf shall be green; and shall not be careful in the year of drought, neither shall cease from yielding fruit.

9The heart *is* deceitful above all *things,* and desperately wicked: who can know it?

17:9 Source of Evil
◄ Ecclesiastes 9:3
Matthew 23:25 ►

10I the LORD search the heart, *I* try the reins, even to give every man according to his ways, *and* according to the fruit of his doings.

17:10 Actions Judged
◄ Proverbs 24:12
Jeremiah 32:19 ►

11As the partridge sitteth *on eggs,* and hatcheth *them* not; *so* he that getteth riches, and not by right, shall leave them in the midst of his days, and at his end shall be a fool.

17:11 Getting Ahead
◄ Proverbs 28:8
Jeremiah 22:13 ►

17:11 Soon Gone
◄ Ecclesiastes 2:26
1 Timothy 6:7 ►

12A glorious high throne from the beginning *is* the place of our sanctuary.

13O LORD, the hope of Israel, all that forsake thee shall be ashamed, *and* they that depart from me shall be written in the earth, because they have forsaken the LORD, the fountain of living waters.

14Heal me, O LORD, and I shall be healed; save me, and I shall be saved: for thou *art* my praise.

15Behold, they say unto me, Where *is* the word of the LORD? let it come now.

16As for me, I have not hastened from *being* a pastor to follow thee: neither have I desired the woeful day; thou knowest: that which came out of my lips was *right* before thee.

17Be not a terror unto me: thou *art* my hope in the day of evil.

18Let them be confounded that persecute me, but let not me be confounded: let them be dismayed, but let not me be dismayed: bring upon them the day of evil, and destroy them with double destruction.

19Thus said the LORD unto me; Go and stand in the gate of the children of the people, whereby the kings of Judah come in, and by the which they go out, and in all the gates of Jerusalem;

20And say unto them, Hear ye the word of the LORD, ye kings of Judah, and all Judah, and all the inhabitants of Jerusalem, that enter in by these gates:

21Thus saith the LORD; Take heed to yourselves, and bear no burden on the sabbath day, nor bring *it* in by the gates of Jerusalem;

22Neither carry forth a burden out of your houses on the sabbath day, neither do ye any work, but hallow ye the sabbath day, as I commanded your fathers.

23But they obeyed not, neither inclined their ear, but made their neck stiff, that they might not hear, nor receive instruction.

24And it shall come to pass, if ye diligently hearken unto me, saith the LORD, to bring in no burden through the gates of this city on the sabbath day, but hallow the sabbath day, to do no work therein;

25Then shall there enter into the gates of this city kings and princes sitting upon the throne of David, riding in chariots and on horses, they, and their princes, the men of Judah, and the inhabitants of Jerusalem: and this city shall remain for ever.

26And they shall come from the cities of Judah, and from the places about Jerusalem, and from the land of Benjamin, and from the plain, and from the mountains, and from the south, bringing burnt offerings, and sacrifices, and meat offerings, and incense, and bringing sacrifices of praise, unto the house of the LORD.

27But if ye will not hearken unto me to hallow the sabbath day, and not to bear a burden, even entering in at the gates of Jerusalem on the sabbath day; then will I kindle a fire in the gates thereof, and it shall devour the palaces of Jerusalem, and it shall not be quenched.

18

1 The word which came to Jeremiah from the LORD, saying,

2 Arise, and go down to the potter's house, and there I will cause thee to hear my words.

3 Then I went down to the potter's house, and, behold, he wrought a work on the wheels.

4 And the vessel that he made of clay was marred in the hand of the potter: so he made it again another vessel, as seemed good to the potter to make *it.*

5 Then the word of the LORD came to me, saying,

6 O house of Israel, cannot I do with you as this potter? saith the LORD. Behold, as the clay *is* in the potter's hand, so *are* ye in mine hand, O house of Israel.

7 *At what* instant I shall speak concerning a nation, and concerning a kingdom, to pluck up, and to pull down, and to destroy *it;*

8 If that nation, against whom I have pronounced, turn from their evil, I will repent of the evil that I thought to do unto them.

9 And *at what* instant I shall speak concerning a nation, and concerning a kingdom, to build and to plant *it;*

10 If it do evil in my sight, that it obey not my voice, then I will repent of the good, wherewith I said I would benefit them.

11 Now therefore go to, speak to the men of Judah, and to the inhabitants of Jerusalem, saying, Thus saith the LORD; Behold, I frame evil against you, and devise a device against you: return ye now every one from his evil way, and make your ways and your doings good.

12 And they said, There is no hope: but we will walk after our own devices, and we will every one do the imagination of his evil heart.

13 Therefore thus saith the LORD; Ask ye now among the heathen, who hath heard such things: the virgin of Israel hath done a very horrible thing.

14 Will *a man* leave the snow of Lebanon *which cometh* from the rock of the field? *or* shall the cold flowing waters that come from another place be forsaken?

15 Because my people hath forgotten me, they have burned incense to vanity, and they have caused them to stumble in their ways *from* the ancient paths, to walk in paths, *in* a way not cast up;

16 To make their land desolate, *and* a perpetual hissing; every one that passeth thereby shall be astonished, and wag his head.

17 I will scatter them as with an east wind before the enemy; I will shew them the back, and not the face, in the day of their calamity.

18 Then said they, Come, and let us devise devices against Jeremiah; for the law shall not perish from the priest, nor counsel from the wise, nor the word from the prophet. Come, and let us smite him with the tongue, and let us not give heed to any of his words.

19 Give heed to me, O LORD, and hearken to the voice of them that contend with me.

20 Shall evil be recompensed for good? for they have digged a pit for my soul. Remember that I stood before thee to speak good for them, *and* to turn away thy wrath from them.

18:20
Unthankfulness to People
◄ Ecclesiastes 9:15 ►

21 Therefore deliver up their children to the famine, and pour out their *blood* by the force of the sword; and let their wives be bereaved of their children, and *be* widows; and let their men be put to death; *let* their young men *be* slain by the sword in battle.

22 Let a cry be heard from their houses, when thou shalt bring a troop suddenly upon them: for they have digged a pit to take me, and hid snares for my feet.

23 Yet, LORD, thou knowest all their counsel against me to slay *me:* forgive not their iniquity, neither blot out their sin from thy sight, but let them be overthrown before thee; deal *thus* with them in the time of thine anger.

19

1 Thus saith the LORD, Go and get a potter's earthen bottle, and *take* of the ancients of the people, and of the ancients of the priests;

2 And go forth unto the valley of the son of Hinnom, which *is* by the entry of the east gate, and proclaim there the words that I shall tell thee,

3 And say, Hear ye the word of the LORD, O kings of Judah, and inhabitants of Jerusalem; Thus saith the LORD of hosts, the

God of Israel; Behold, I will bring evil upon this place, the which whosoever heareth, his ears shall tingle.

4 Because they have forsaken me, and have estranged this place, and have burned incense in it unto other gods, whom neither they nor their fathers have known, nor the kings of Judah, and have filled this place with the blood of innocents;

5 They have built also the high places of Baal, to burn their sons with fire *for* burnt offerings unto Baal, which I commanded not, nor spake *it,* neither came *it* into my mind:

6 Therefore, behold, the days come, saith the LORD, that this place shall no more be called Tophet, nor The valley of the son of Hinnom, but The valley of slaughter.

7 And I will make void the counsel of Judah and Jerusalem in this place; and I will cause them to fall by the sword before their enemies, and by the hands of them that seek their lives: and their carcases will I give to be meat for the fowls of the heaven, and for the beasts of the earth.

8 And I will make this city desolate, and an hissing; every one that passeth thereby shall be astonished and hiss because of all the plagues thereof.

9 And I will cause them to eat the flesh of their sons and the flesh of their daughters, and they shall eat every one the flesh of his friend in the siege and straitness, wherewith their enemies, and they that seek their lives, shall straiten them.

10 Then shalt thou break the bottle in the sight of the men that go with thee,

11 And shalt say unto them, Thus saith the LORD of hosts; Even so will I break this people and this city, as *one* breaketh a potter's vessel, that cannot be made whole again: and they shall bury *them* in Tophet, till *there be* no place to bury.

12 Thus will I do unto this place, saith the LORD, and to the inhabitants thereof, and *even* make this city as Tophet:

13 And the houses of Jerusalem, and the houses of the kings of Judah, shall be defiled as the place of Tophet, because of all the houses upon whose roofs they have burned incense unto all the host of heaven, and have poured out drink offerings unto other gods.

14 Then came Jeremiah from Tophet, whither the LORD had sent him to prophesy; and he stood in the court of the LORD'S house; and said to all the people,

15 Thus saith the LORD of hosts, the God of Israel; Behold, I will bring upon this city and upon all her towns all the evil that I have pronounced against it, because they have hardened their necks, that they might not hear my words.

20

1 Now Pashur the son of Immer the priest, who *was* also chief governor in the house of the LORD, heard that Jeremiah prophesied these things.

2 Then Pashur smote Jeremiah the prophet, and put him in the stocks that *were* in the high gate of Benjamin, which *was* by the house of the LORD.

3 And it came to pass on the morrow, that Pashur brought forth Jeremiah out of the stocks. Then said Jeremiah unto him, The LORD hath not called thy name Pashur, but Magor-missabib.

4 For thus saith the LORD, Behold, I will make thee a terror to thyself, and to all thy friends: and they shall fall by the sword of their enemies, and thine eyes shall behold *it:* and I will give all Judah into the hand of the king of Babylon, and he shall carry them captive into Babylon, and shall slay them with the sword.

5 Moreover I will deliver all the strength of this city, and all the labours thereof, and all the precious things thereof, and all the treasures of the kings of Judah will I give into the hand of their enemies, which shall spoil them, and take them, and carry them to Babylon.

6 And thou, Pashur, and all that dwell in thine house shall go into captivity: and thou shalt come to Babylon, and there thou shalt die, and shalt be buried there, thou, and all thy friends, to whom thou hast prophesied lies.

7 O LORD, thou hast deceived me, and I was deceived: thou art stronger than I, and hast prevailed: I am in derision daily, every one mocketh me.

8 For since I spake, I cried out, I cried violence and spoil; because the word of the LORD was made a reproach unto me, and a derision, daily.

9 Then I said, I will not make mention of him, nor speak any more in his name. But *his word* was in mine heart as a burning fire shut up in my bones, and I was weary with forbearing, and I could not *stay.*

10For I heard the defaming of many, fear
on every side. Report, *say they,* and we will
report it. All my familiars watched for my
halting, *saying,* Peradventure he will be
enticed, and we shall prevail against him,
and we shall take our revenge on him.
11But the LORD *is* with me as a mighty
terrible one: therefore my persecutors shall
stumble, and they shall not prevail: they
shall be greatly ashamed; for they shall not
prosper: *their* everlasting confusion shall
never be forgotten.
12But, O LORD of hosts, that triest the
righteous, *and* seest the reins and the heart,
let me see thy vengeance on them: for unto
thee have I opened my cause.
13Sing unto the LORD, praise ye the
LORD: for he hath delivered the soul of the
poor from the hand of evildoers.
14Cursed *be* the day wherein I was born:
let not the day wherein my mother bare
me be blessed.
15Cursed *be* the man who brought tidings to my father, saying, A man child is
born unto thee; making him very glad.
16And let that man be as the cities which
the LORD overthrew, and repented not: and
let him hear the cry in the morning, and
the shouting at noontide;
17Because he slew me not from the
womb; or that my mother might have been
my grave, and her womb *to be* always great
with me.
18Wherefore came I forth out of the
womb to see labour and sorrow, that my
days should be consumed with shame?

21

1The word which came unto Jeremiah
from the LORD, when king Zedekiah sent
unto him Pashur the son of Melchiah, and
Zephaniah the son of Maaseiah the priest,
saying,
2Enquire, I pray thee, of the LORD for us;
for Nebuchadrezzar king of Babylon maketh war against us; if so be that the LORD
will deal with us according to all his wondrous works, that he may go up from us.
3Then said Jeremiah unto them, Thus
shall ye say to Zedekiah:
4Thus saith the LORD God of Israel; Behold, I will turn back the weapons of war
that *are* in your hands, wherewith ye fight
against the king of Babylon, and against
the Chaldeans, which besiege you without the walls, and I will assemble them
into the midst of this city.
5And I myself will fight against you with
an outstretched hand and with a strong
arm, even in anger, and in fury, and in great
wrath.
6And I will smite the inhabitants of this
city, both man and beast: they shall die of
a great pestilence.
7And afterward, saith the LORD, I will
deliver Zedekiah king of Judah, and his
servants, and the people, and such as are
left in this city from the pestilence, from
the sword, and from the famine, into the
hand of Nebuchadrezzar king of Babylon,
and into the hand of their enemies, and
into the hand of those that seek their life:
and he shall smite them with the edge of
the sword; he shall not spare them, neither have pity, nor have mercy.
8And unto this people thou shalt say,
Thus saith the LORD; Behold, I set before
you the way of life, and the way of death.
9He that abideth in this city shall die by
the sword, and by the famine, and by the
pestilence: but he that goeth out, and
falleth to the Chaldeans that besiege you,
he shall live, and his life shall be unto him
for a prey.
10For I have set my face against this city
for evil, and not for good, saith the LORD:
it shall be given into the hand of the king
of Babylon, and he shall burn it with fire.
11And touching the house of the king of
Judah, *say,* Hear ye the word of the LORD;
12O house of David, thus saith the LORD;
Execute judgment in the morning, and
deliver *him that is* spoiled out of the hand
of the oppressor, lest my fury go out like
fire, and burn that none can quench *it,*
because of the evil of your doings.
13Behold, I *am* against thee, O inhabitant of the valley, *and* rock of the plain,
saith the LORD; which say, Who shall come
down against us? or who shall enter into
our habitations?
14But I will punish you according to the
fruit of your doings, saith the LORD: and I
will kindle a fire in the forest thereof, and
it shall devour all things round about it.

22

1Thus saith the LORD; Go down to the
house of the king of Judah, and speak there
this word,
2And say, Hear the word of the LORD,
O king of Judah, that sittest upon the
throne of David, thou, and thy servants,
and thy people that enter in by these gates:

3 Thus saith the
LORD; Execute ye
judgment and righ-
teousness, and de-
liver the spoiled out
of the hand of the
oppressor: and do no wrong, do no violence to the stranger, the fatherless, nor the
widow, neither shed innocent blood in this
place.

22:3 Kind to the Needy
◄ Isaiah 1:17
James 1:27 ►

4 For if ye do this thing indeed, then shall
there enter in by the gates of this house
kings sitting upon the throne of David, riding in chariots and on horses, he, and his
servants, and his people.
5 But if ye will not hear these words, I
swear by myself, saith the LORD, that this
house shall become a desolation.
6 For thus saith the LORD unto the king's
house of Judah; Thou *art* Gilead unto me,
and the head of Lebanon: *yet* surely I will
make thee a wilderness, *and* cities *which*
are not inhabited.
7 And I will prepare destroyers against
thee, every one with his weapons: and they
shall cut down thy choice cedars, and cast
them into the fire.
8 And many nations shall pass by this
city, and they shall say every man to his
neighbour, Wherefore hath the LORD done
thus unto this great city?
9 Then they shall answer, Because they
have forsaken the covenant of the LORD
their God, and worshipped other gods, and
served them.
10 Weep ye not for the dead, neither bemoan him: *but* weep sore for him that
goeth away: for he shall return no more,
nor see his native country.
11 For thus saith the LORD touching Shallum the son of Josiah king of Judah, which
reigned instead of Josiah his father, which
went forth out of this place; He shall not
return thither any
more:
12 But he shall die
in the place whither
they have led him
captive, and shall
see this land no
more.

22:13 Getting Ahead
◄ Jeremiah 17:11
Ezekiel 22:13 ►

13 Woe unto him
that buildeth his
house by unrigh-
teousness, and his
chambers by wrong; *that* useth his
neighbour's service without wages, and
giveth him not for his work;

22:13-14 Planning
◄ Proverbs 19:21
Luke 12:18 ►

14 That saith, I will build me a wide
house and large chambers, and cutteth
him out windows; and *it is* cieled with cedar, and painted with vermilion.
15 Shalt thou reign, because thou clos-
est *thyself* in cedar? did not thy father eat
and drink, and do judgment and justice,
and then *it was* well with him?
16 He judged the
cause of the poor
and needy; then *it*
was well *with him*:
was not this to
know me? saith the
LORD.

22:16
Fair to the Poor
◄ Proverbs 29:14 ►

17 But thine eyes and thine heart *are* not
but for thy covetousness, and for to shed
innocent blood, and for oppression, and
for violence, to do *it*.
18 Therefore thus saith the LORD concerning Jehoiakim the son of Josiah king of
Judah; They shall not lament for him, *say-*
ing, Ah my brother! or, Ah sister! they shall
not lament for him, *saying*, Ah lord! or,
Ah his glory!
19 He shall be buried with the burial of
an ass, drawn and cast forth beyond the
gates of Jerusalem.
20 Go up to Lebanon, and cry; and lift
up thy voice in Bashan, and cry from the
passages: for all thy lovers are destroyed.
21 I spake unto thee in thy prosperity; *but*
thou saidst, I will not hear. This *hath been*
thy manner from thy youth, that thou
obeyedst not my voice.
22 The wind shall eat up all thy pastors,
and thy lovers shall go into captivity: surely
then shalt thou be ashamed and confounded for all thy wickedness.
23 O inhabitant of Lebanon, that makest
thy nest in the cedars, how gracious shalt
thou be when pangs come upon thee, the
pain as of a woman in travail!
24 *As* I live, saith the LORD, though
Coniah the son of Jehoiakim king of Judah were the signet upon my right hand,
yet would I pluck thee thence;
25 And I will give thee into the hand of
them that seek thy life, and into the hand
of them whose face thou fearest, even into
the hand of Nebuchadrezzar king of Babylon, and into the hand of the Chaldeans.

26 And I will cast thee out, and thy mother that bare thee, into another country, where ye were not born; and there shall ye die.

27 But to the land whereunto they desire to return, thither shall they not return.

28 *Is* this man Coniah a despised broken idol? *is he* a vessel wherein *is* no pleasure? wherefore are they cast out, he and his seed, and are cast into a land which they know not?

29 O earth, earth, earth, hear the word of the LORD.

30 Thus saith the LORD, Write ye this man childless, a man *that* shall not prosper in his days: for no man of his seed shall prosper, sitting upon the throne of David, and ruling any more in Judah.

23

1 Woe be unto the pastors that destroy and scatter the sheep of my pasture! saith the LORD.

2 Therefore thus saith the LORD God of Israel against the pastors that feed my people; Ye have scattered my flock, and driven them away, and have not visited them: behold, I will visit upon you the evil of your doings, saith the LORD.

3 And I will gather the remnant of my flock out of all countries whither I have driven them, and will bring them again to their folds; and they shall be fruitful and increase.

4 And I will set up shepherds over them which shall feed them: and they shall fear no more, nor be dismayed, neither shall they be lacking, saith the LORD.

5 Behold, the days come, saith the LORD, that I will raise unto David a righteous Branch, and a King shall reign and prosper, and shall execute judgment and justice in the earth.

23:5 Jesus the King
◄ Isaiah 32:1
Daniel 7:14 ►

6 In his days Judah shall be saved, and Israel shall dwell safely: and this *is* his name whereby he shall be called, THE LORD OUR RIGHTEOUSNESS.

7 Therefore, behold, the days come, saith the LORD, that they shall no more say, The LORD liveth, which brought up the children of Israel out of the land of Egypt;

8 But, The LORD liveth, which brought up and which led the seed of the house of Israel out of the north country, and from all countries whither I had driven them; and they shall dwell in their own land.

9 Mine heart within me is broken because of the prophets; all my bones shake; I am like a drunken man, and like a man whom wine hath overcome, because of the LORD, and because of the words of his holiness.

10 For the land is full of adulterers; for because of swearing the land mourneth; the pleasant places of the wilderness are dried up, and their course is evil, and their force *is* not right.

11 For both prophet and priest are profane; yea, in my house have I found their wickedness, saith the LORD.

12 Wherefore their way shall be unto them as slippery *ways* in the darkness: they shall be driven on, and fall therein: for I will bring evil upon them, *even* the year of their visitation, saith the LORD.

23:12 Wicked Insecurity
◄ Jeremiah 13:16
Ezekiel 13:10-11 ►

13 And I have seen folly in the prophets of Samaria; they prophesied in Baal, and caused my people Israel to err.

14 I have seen also in the prophets of Jerusalem an horrible thing: they commit adultery, and walk in lies: they strengthen also the hands of evildoers, that none doth return from his wickedness: they are all of them unto me as Sodom, and the inhabitants thereof as Gomorrah.

15 Therefore thus saith the LORD of hosts concerning the prophets; Behold, I will feed them with wormwood, and make them drink the water of gall: for from the prophets of Jerusalem is profaneness gone forth into all the land.

16 Thus saith the LORD of hosts, Hearken not unto the words of the prophets that prophesy unto you: they make you vain: they speak a vision of their own heart, *and* not out of the mouth of the LORD.

17 They say still unto them that despise me, The LORD hath said, Ye shall have peace; and they say unto every one that walketh after the imagination of his own heart, No evil shall come upon you.

18 For who hath stood in the counsel of the LORD, and hath perceived and heard his word? who hath marked his word, and heard *it?*

19 Behold, a whirlwind of the LORD is
gone forth in fury, even a grievous whirlwind: it shall fall grievously upon the head
of the wicked.
20 The anger of the LORD shall not return,
until he have executed, and till he have
performed the thoughts of his heart: in the
latter days ye shall consider it perfectly.
21 I have not sent these prophets, yet they
ran: I have not spoken to them, yet they
prophesied.
22 But if they had stood in my counsel,
and had caused my people to hear my
words, then they should have turned them
from their evil way, and from the evil of
their doings.
23 *Am* I a God at hand, saith the LORD,
and not a God afar off?
24 Can any hide
himself in secret
places that I shall
not see him? saith
the LORD. Do not I
fill heaven and
earth? saith the LORD.

23:24 Where Is God?
◄ Isaiah 66:1
Acts 17:27 ►

25 I have heard what the prophets said,
that prophesy lies in my name, saying, I
have dreamed, I have dreamed.
26 How long shall *this* be in the heart of
the prophets that prophesy lies? yea, *they
are* prophets of the deceit of their own
heart;
27 Which think to cause my people to
forget my name by their dreams which they
tell every man to his neighbour, as their
fathers have forgotten my name for Baal.
28 The prophet that hath a dream, let him
tell a dream; and he that hath my word,
let him speak my word faithfully. What *is*
the chaff to the wheat? saith the LORD.
29 *Is* not my word
like as a fire? saith
the LORD; and like
a hammer *that*
breaketh the rock in
pieces?

23:29
Power of the Bible
◄ Jeremiah 5:14
Ezekiel 37:7 ►

30 Therefore, behold, I *am* against the
prophets, saith the LORD, that steal my
words every one from his neighbour.
31 Behold, I *am* against the prophets,
saith the LORD, that use their tongues, and
say, He saith.
32 Behold, I *am* against them that prophesy false dreams, saith the LORD, and do
tell them, and cause my people to err by
their lies, and by their lightness; yet I sent
them not, nor commanded them: therefore they shall not profit this people at all,
saith the LORD.
33 And when this people, or the prophet, or a priest, shall ask thee, saying, What
is the burden of the LORD? thou shalt then
say unto them, What burden? I will even
forsake you, saith the LORD.
34 And *as for* the prophet, and the priest,
and the people, that shall say, The burden
of the LORD, I will even punish that man
and his house.
35 Thus shall ye say every one to his
neighbour, and every one to his brother,
What hath the LORD answered? and, What
hath the LORD spoken?
36 And the burden of the LORD shall ye
mention no more: for every man's word
shall be his burden; for ye have perverted
the words of the living God, of the LORD
of hosts our God.
37 Thus shalt thou say to the prophet,
What hath the LORD answered thee? and,
What hath the LORD spoken?
38 But since ye say, The burden of the
LORD; therefore thus saith the LORD; Because ye say this word, The burden of the
LORD, and I have sent unto you, saying, Ye
shall not say, The burden of the LORD;
39 Therefore, behold, I, even I, will utterly forget you, and I will forsake you, and
the city that I gave you and your fathers,
and cast you out of my presence:
40 And I will bring an everlasting reproach upon you, and a perpetual shame,
which shall not be forgotten.

24

1 The LORD shewed me, and, behold, two
baskets of figs *were* set before the temple
of the LORD, after that Nebuchadrezzar
king of Babylon had carried away captive
Jeconiah the son of Jehoiakim king of Judah, and the princes of Judah, with the
carpenters and smiths, from Jerusalem,
and had brought them to Babylon.
2 One basket *had* very good figs, *even* like
the figs *that are* first ripe: and the other
basket *had* very naughty figs, which could
not be eaten, they were so bad.
3 Then said the LORD unto me, What
seest thou, Jeremiah? And I said, Figs; the
good figs, very good; and the evil, very evil,
that cannot be eaten, they are so evil.
4 Again the word of the LORD came unto
me, saying,

5 Thus saith the LORD, the God of Israel; Like these good figs, so will I acknowledge them that are carried away captive of Judah, whom I have sent out of this place into the land of the Chaldeans for *their* good.

6 For I will set mine eyes upon them for good, and I will bring them again to this land: and I will build them, and not pull *them* down; and I will plant them, and not pluck *them* up.

7 And I will give them an heart to know me, that I *am* the LORD: and they shall be my people, and I will be their God: for they shall return unto me with their whole heart.

24:7 Invisible Gifts
◄ Isaiah 56:4-5
Ezekiel 11:19 ►

8 And as the evil figs, which cannot be eaten, they are so evil; surely thus saith the LORD, So will I give Zedekiah the king of Judah, and his princes, and the residue of Jerusalem, that remain in this land, and them that dwell in the land of Egypt:

9 And I will deliver them to be removed into all the kingdoms of the earth for *their* hurt, *to be* a reproach and a proverb, a taunt and a curse, in all places whither I shall drive them.

10 And I will send the sword, the famine, and the pestilence, among them, till they be consumed from off the land that I gave unto them and to their fathers.

25

1 The word that came to Jeremiah concerning all the people of Judah in the fourth year of Jehoiakim the son of Josiah king of Judah, that *was* the first year of Nebuchadrezzar king of Babylon;

2 The which Jeremiah the prophet spake unto all the people of Judah, and to all the inhabitants of Jerusalem, saying,

3 From the thirteenth year of Josiah the son of Amon king of Judah, even unto this day, that *is* the three and twentieth year, the word of the LORD hath come unto me, and I have spoken unto you, rising early and speaking; but ye have not hearkened.

4 And the LORD hath sent unto you all his servants the prophets, rising early and sending *them;* but ye have not hearkened, nor inclined your ear to hear.

5 They said, Turn ye again now every one from his evil way, and from the evil of your doings, and dwell in the land that the LORD hath given unto you and to your fathers for ever and ever:

25:5 Repent!
◄ Isaiah 22:12
Ezekiel 14:6 ►

6 And go not after other gods to serve them, and to worship them, and provoke me not to anger with the works of your hands; and I will do you no hurt.

7 Yet ye have not hearkened unto me, saith the LORD; that ye might provoke me to anger with the works of your hands to your own hurt.

8 Therefore thus saith the LORD of hosts; Because ye have not heard my words,

9 Behold, I will send and take all the families of the north, saith the LORD, and Nebuchadrezzar the king of Babylon, my servant, and will bring them against this land, and against the inhabitants thereof, and against all these nations round about, and will utterly destroy them, and make them an astonishment, and an hissing, and perpetual desolations.

10 Moreover I will take from them the voice of mirth, and the voice of gladness, the voice of the bridegroom, and the voice of the bride, the sound of the millstones, and the light of the candle.

11 And this whole land shall be a desolation, *and* an astonishment; and these nations shall serve the king of Babylon seventy years.

12 And it shall come to pass, when seventy years are accomplished, *that* I will punish the king of Babylon, and that nation, saith the LORD, for their iniquity, and the land of the Chaldeans, and will make it perpetual desolations.

13 And I will bring upon that land all my words which I have pronounced against it, *even* all that is written in this book, which Jeremiah hath prophesied against all the nations.

14 For many nations and great kings shall serve themselves of them also: and I will recompense them according to their deeds, and according to the works of their own hands.

15 For thus saith the LORD God of Israel unto me; Take the wine cup of this fury at my hand, and cause all the nations, to whom I send thee, to drink it.

16 And they shall drink, and be moved,

and be mad, because of the sword that I
will send among them.
17 Then took I the cup at the LORD'S
hand, and made all the nations to drink,
unto whom the LORD had sent me:
18 *To wit,* Jerusalem, and the cities of Judah, and the kings thereof, and the princes
thereof, to make them a desolation, an
astonishment, an hissing, and a curse; as
it is this day;
19 Pharaoh king of Egypt, and his servants, and his princes, and all his people;
20 And all the mingled people, and all
the kings of the land of Uz, and all the
kings of the land of the Philistines, and
Ashkelon, and Azzah, and Ekron, and the
remnant of Ashdod,
21 Edom, and Moab, and the children of
Ammon,
22 And all the kings of Tyrus, and all the
kings of Zidon, and the kings of the isles
which *are* beyond the sea,
23 Dedan, and Tema, and Buz, and all
that are in the utmost corners,
24 And all the kings of Arabia, and all
the kings of the mingled people that dwell
in the desert,
25 And all the kings of Zimri, and all the
kings of Elam, and all the kings of the
Medes,
26 And all the kings of the north, far and
near, one with another, and all the kingdoms of the world, which *are* upon the face
of the earth: and the king of Sheshach shall
drink after them.
27 Therefore thou shalt say unto them,
Thus saith the LORD of hosts, the God of
Israel; Drink ye, and be drunken, and spue,
and fall, and rise no more, because of the
sword which I will send among you.
28 And it shall be, if they refuse to take
the cup at thine hand to drink, then shalt
thou say unto them, Thus saith the LORD
of hosts; Ye shall certainly drink.
29 For, lo, I begin to bring evil on the city
which is called by my name, and should
ye be utterly unpunished? Ye shall not be
unpunished: for I will call for a sword
upon all the inhabitants of the earth, saith
the LORD of hosts.
30 Therefore prophesy thou against them
all these words, and say unto them, The
LORD shall roar from on high, and utter
his voice from his holy habitation; he shall
mightily roar upon his habitation; he shall
give a shout, as they that tread *the grapes,*
against all the inhabitants of the earth.
31 A noise shall come *even* to the ends of
the earth; for the LORD hath a controversy
with the nations, he will plead with all
flesh; he will give them *that are* wicked to
the sword, saith the LORD.
32 Thus saith the LORD of hosts, Behold,
evil shall go forth from nation to nation,
and a great whirlwind shall be raised up
from the coasts of the earth.
33 And the slain of the LORD shall be at
that day from *one* end of the earth even
unto the *other* end of the earth: they shall
not be lamented, neither gathered, nor
buried; they shall be dung upon the
ground.
34 Howl, ye shepherds, and cry; and wallow yourselves *in the ashes,* ye principal of
the flock: for the days of your slaughter
and of your dispersions are accomplished;
and ye shall fall like a pleasant vessel.
35 And the shepherds shall have no way
to flee, nor the principal of the flock to
escape.
36 A voice of the cry of the shepherds,
and an howling of the principal of the
flock, *shall be heard:* for the LORD hath
spoiled their pasture.
37 And the peaceable habitations are cut
down because of the fierce anger of the
LORD.
38 He hath forsaken his covert, as the
lion: for their land is desolate because of
the fierceness of the oppressor, and because of his fierce anger.

26

1 In the beginning of the reign of Jehoiakim the son of Josiah king of Judah came
this word from the LORD, saying,
2 Thus saith the LORD; Stand in the court
of the LORD'S house, and speak unto all
the cities of Judah, which come to worship in the LORD'S house, all the words that
I command thee to speak unto them; diminish not a word:
3 If so be they will hearken, and turn
every man from his evil way, that I may
repent me of the evil, which I purpose to
do unto them because of the evil of their
doings.
4 And thou shalt say unto them, Thus
saith the LORD; If ye will not hearken to
me, to walk in my law, which I have set
before you,
5 To hearken to the words of my servants

the prophets, whom I sent unto you, both rising up early, and sending *them*, but ye have not hearkened;

6 Then will I make this house like Shiloh, and will make this city a curse to all the nations of the earth.

7 So the priests and the prophets and all the people heard Jeremiah speaking these words in the house of the LORD.

8 Now it came to pass, when Jeremiah had made an end of speaking all that the LORD had commanded *him* to speak unto all the people, that the priests and the prophets and all the people took him, saying, Thou shalt surely die.

9 Why hast thou prophesied in the name of the LORD, saying, This house shall be like Shiloh, and this city shall be desolate without an inhabitant? And all the people were gathered against Jeremiah in the house of the LORD.

10 When the princes of Judah heard these things, then they came up from the king's house unto the house of the LORD, and sat down in the entry of the new gate of the LORD'S *house*.

11 Then spake the priests and the prophets unto the princes and to all the people, saying, This man *is* worthy to die; for he hath prophesied against this city, as ye have heard with your ears.

12 Then spake Jeremiah unto all the princes and to all the people, saying, The LORD sent me to prophesy against this house and against this city all the words that ye have heard.

13 Therefore now amend your ways and your doings, and obey the voice of the LORD your God; and the LORD will repent him of the evil that he hath pronounced against you.

14 As for me, behold, I *am* in your hand: do with me as seemeth good and meet unto you.

15 But know ye for certain, that if ye put me to death, ye shall surely bring innocent blood upon yourselves, and upon this city, and upon the inhabitants thereof: for of a truth the LORD hath sent me unto you to speak all these words in your ears.

16 Then said the princes and all the people unto the priests and to the prophets; This man *is* not worthy to die: for he hath spoken to us in the name of the LORD our God.

17 Then rose up certain of the elders of the land, and spake to all the assembly of the people, saying,

18 Micah the Morasthite prophesied in the days of Hezekiah king of Judah, and spake to all the people of Judah, saying, Thus saith the LORD of hosts; Zion shall be plowed *like* a field, and Jerusalem shall become heaps, and the mountain of the house as the high places of a forest.

19 Did Hezekiah king of Judah and all Judah put him at all to death? did he not fear the LORD, and besought the LORD, and the LORD repented him of the evil which he had pronounced against them? Thus might we procure great evil against our souls.

20 And there was also a man that prophesied in the name of the LORD, Urijah the son of Shemaiah of Kirjath-jearim, who prophesied against this city and against this land according to all the words of Jeremiah:

21 And when Jehoiakim the king, with all his mighty men, and all the princes, heard his words, the king sought to put him to death: but when Urijah heard it, he was afraid, and fled, and went into Egypt;

22 And Jehoiakim the king sent men into Egypt, *namely*, Elnathan the son of Achbor, and *certain* men with him into Egypt.

23 And they fetched forth Urijah out of Egypt, and brought him unto Jehoiakim the king; who slew him with the sword, and cast his dead body into the graves of the common people.

24 Nevertheless the hand of Ahikam the son of Shaphan was with Jeremiah, that they should not give him into the hand of the people to put him to death.

27

1 In the beginning of the reign of Jehoiakim the son of Josiah king of Judah came this word unto Jeremiah from the LORD, saying,

2 Thus saith the LORD to me; Make thee bonds and yokes, and put them upon thy neck,

3 And send them to the king of Edom, and to the king of Moab, and to the king of the Ammonites, and to the king of Tyrus, and to the king of Zidon, by the hand of the messengers which come to Jerusalem unto Zedekiah king of Judah;

4 And command them to say unto their

masters, Thus saith the LORD of hosts, the
God of Israel; Thus shall ye say unto your
masters;
5 I have made the earth, the man and the
beast that *are* upon the ground, by my great
power and by my outstretched arm, and
have given it unto whom it seemed meet
unto me.
6 And now have I given all these lands
into the hand of Nebuchadnezzar the king
of Babylon, my servant; and the beasts of
the field have I given him also to serve him.
7 And all nations shall serve him, and his
son, and his son's son, until the very time
of his land come: and then many nations
and great kings shall serve themselves
of him.
8 And it shall come to pass, *that* the nation and kingdom which will not serve the
same Nebuchadnezzar the king of Babylon, and that will not put their neck under the yoke of the king of Babylon, that
nation will I punish, saith the LORD, with
the sword, and with the famine, and with
the pestilence, until I have consumed them
by his hand.
9 Therefore hearken not ye to your
prophets, nor to your diviners, nor to your
dreamers, nor to your enchanters, nor to
your sorcerers, which speak unto you, saying, Ye shall not serve the king of Babylon:
10 For they prophesy a lie unto you, to
remove you far from your land; and that
I should drive you out, and ye should
perish.
11 But the nations that bring their neck
under the yoke of the king of Babylon, and
serve him, those will I let remain still in
their own land, saith the LORD; and they
shall till it, and dwell therein.
12 I spake also to Zedekiah king of Judah according to all these words, saying,
Bring your necks under the yoke of the king
of Babylon, and serve him and his people,
and live.
13 Why will ye die, thou and thy people,
by the sword, by the famine, and by the
pestilence, as the LORD hath spoken against
the nation that will not serve the king of
Babylon?
14 Therefore hearken not unto the words
of the prophets that speak unto you, saying, Ye shall not serve the king of Babylon:
for they prophesy a lie unto you.
15 For I have not sent them, saith the
LORD, yet they prophesy a lie in my name;
that I might drive you out, and that ye
might perish, ye, and the prophets that
prophesy unto you.
16 Also I spake to the priests and to all
this people, saying, Thus saith the LORD;
Hearken not to the words of your prophets that prophesy unto you, saying, Behold,
the vessels of the LORD'S house shall now
shortly be brought again from Babylon: for
they prophesy a lie unto you.
17 Hearken not unto them; serve the king
of Babylon, and live: wherefore should this
city be laid waste?
18 But if they *be* prophets, and if the word
of the LORD be with them, let them now
make intercession to the LORD of hosts, that
the vessels which are left in the house of
the LORD, and *in* the house of the king of
Judah, and at Jerusalem, go not to Babylon.
19 For thus saith the LORD of hosts concerning the pillars, and concerning the sea,
and concerning the bases, and concerning
the residue of the vessels that remain in
this city,
20 Which Nebuchadnezzar king of Babylon took not, when he carried away captive Jeconiah the son of Jehoiakim king of
Judah from Jerusalem to Babylon, and all
the nobles of Judah and Jerusalem;
21 Yea, thus saith the LORD of hosts, the
God of Israel, concerning the vessels that
remain *in* the house of the LORD, and *in*
the house of the king of Judah and of Jerusalem;
22 They shall be carried to Babylon, and
there shall they be until the day that I visit
them, saith the LORD; then will I bring
them up, and restore them to this place.

28

1 And it came to pass the same year, in
the beginning of the reign of Zedekiah king
of Judah, in the fourth year, *and* in the fifth
month, *that* Hananiah the son of Azur the
prophet, which *was* of Gibeon, spake unto
me in the house of the LORD, in the presence of the priests and of all the people,
saying,
2 Thus speaketh the LORD of hosts, the
God of Israel, saying, I have broken the
yoke of the king of Babylon.
3 Within two full years will I bring again
into this place all the vessels of the LORD'S
house, that Nebuchadnezzar king of Babylon took away from this place, and carried them to Babylon:

4 And I will bring again to this place Jeconiah the son of Jehoiakim king of Judah, with all the captives of Judah, that went into Babylon, saith the LORD: for I will break the yoke of the king of Babylon.

5 Then the prophet Jeremiah said unto the prophet Hananiah in the presence of the priests, and in the presence of all the people that stood in the house of the LORD,

6 Even the prophet Jeremiah said, Amen: the LORD do so: the LORD perform thy words which thou hast prophesied, to bring again the vessels of the LORD'S house, and all that is carried away captive, from Babylon into this place.

7 Nevertheless hear thou now this word that I speak in thine ears, and in the ears of all the people;

8 The prophets that have been before me and before thee of old prophesied both against many countries, and against great kingdoms, of war, and of evil, and of pestilence.

9 The prophet which prophesieth of peace, when the word of the prophet shall come to pass, *then* shall the prophet be known, that the LORD hath truly sent him.

10 Then Hananiah the prophet took the yoke from off the prophet Jeremiah's neck, and brake it.

11 And Hananiah spake in the presence of all the people, saying, Thus saith the LORD; Even so will I break the yoke of Nebuchadnezzar king of Babylon from the neck of all nations within the space of two full years. And the prophet Jeremiah went his way.

12 Then the word of the LORD came unto Jeremiah *the prophet,* after that Hananiah the prophet had broken the yoke from off the neck of the prophet Jeremiah, saying,

13 Go and tell Hananiah, saying, Thus saith the LORD; Thou hast broken the yokes of wood; but thou shalt make for them yokes of iron.

14 For thus saith the LORD of hosts, the God of Israel; I have put a yoke of iron upon the neck of all these nations, that they may serve Nebuchadnezzar king of Babylon; and they shall serve him: and I have given him the beasts of the field also.

15 Then said the prophet Jeremiah unto Hananiah the prophet, Hear now, Hananiah; The LORD hath not sent thee; but thou makest this people to trust in a lie.

16 Therefore thus saith the LORD; Behold, I will cast thee from off the face of the earth: this year thou shalt die, because thou hast taught rebellion against the LORD.

17 So Hananiah the prophet died the same year in the seventh month.

29

1 Now these *are* the words of the letter that Jeremiah the prophet sent from Jerusalem unto the residue of the elders which were carried away captives, and to the priests, and to the prophets, and to all the people whom Nebuchadnezzar had carried away captive from Jerusalem to Babylon;

2 (After that Jeconiah the king, and the queen, and the eunuchs, the princes of Judah and Jerusalem, and the carpenters, and the smiths, were departed from Jerusalem;)

3 By the hand of Elasah the son of Shaphan, and Gemariah the son of Hilkiah, (whom Zedekiah king of Judah sent unto Babylon to Nebuchadnezzar king of Babylon) saying,

4 Thus saith the LORD of hosts, the God of Israel, unto all that are carried away captives, whom I have caused to be carried away from Jerusalem unto Babylon;

5 Build ye houses, and dwell *in them;* and plant gardens, and eat the fruit of them;

6 Take ye wives, and beget sons and daughters; and take wives for your sons, and give your daughters to husbands, that they may bear sons and daughters; that ye may be increased there, and not diminished.

7 And seek the peace of the city whither I have caused you to be carried away captives, and pray unto the LORD for it: for in the peace thereof shall ye have peace.

8 For thus saith the LORD of hosts, the God of Israel; Let not your prophets and your diviners, that *be* in the midst of you, deceive you, neither hearken to your dreams which ye cause to be dreamed.

9 For they prophesy falsely unto you in my name: I have not sent them, saith the LORD.

10 For thus saith the LORD, That after seventy years be accomplished at Babylon I will visit you, and perform my good word toward you, in causing you to return to this place.

11 For I know the thoughts that I think toward you, saith the LORD, thoughts of

peace, and not of evil, to give you an expected end.
12 Then shall ye call upon me, and ye
shall go and pray unto me, and I will hearken unto you.
13 And ye shall
seek me, and find
me, when ye shall
search for me with
all your heart.
14 And I will be
found of you, saith
the LORD: and I will
turn away your cap-
tivity, and I will
gather you from all
the nations, and
from all the places
whither I have driv-
en you, saith the
LORD; and I will
bring you again into
the place whence I
caused you to be carried away captive.

29:13 Finding God
◄ Job 23:3
Hosea 6:3 ►

29:13 How to Pray
◄ Isaiah 58:9
Mark 11:24 ►

29:13 Seeking God
◄ Isaiah 55:6
Hosea 10:12 ►

15 Because ye have said, The LORD hath
raised us up prophets in Babylon;
16 *Know* that thus saith the LORD of the
king that sitteth upon the throne of David, and of all the people that dwelleth in
this city, *and* of your brethren that are not
gone forth with you into captivity;
17 Thus saith the LORD of hosts; Behold,
I will send upon them the sword, the famine, and the pestilence, and will make
them like vile figs, that cannot be eaten,
they are so evil.
18 And I will persecute them with the
sword, with the famine, and with the pestilence, and will deliver them to be removed to all the kingdoms of the earth, to
be a curse, and an astonishment, and an
hissing, and a reproach, among all the
nations whither I have driven them:
19 Because they have not hearkened to
my words, saith the LORD, which I sent
unto them by my servants the prophets,
rising up early and sending *them;* but ye
would not hear, saith the LORD.
20 Hear ye therefore the word of the
LORD, all ye of the captivity, whom I have
sent from Jerusalem to Babylon:
21 Thus saith the LORD of hosts, the God
of Israel, of Ahab the son of Kolaiah, and
of Zedekiah the son of Maaseiah, which
prophesy a lie unto you in my name; Behold, I will deliver them into the hand of
Nebuchadrezzar king of Babylon; and he
shall slay them before your eyes;
22 And of them shall be taken up a curse
by all the captivity of Judah which *are* in
Babylon, saying, The LORD make thee like
Zedekiah and like Ahab, whom the king
of Babylon roasted in the fire;
23 Because they have committed villany
in Israel, and have committed adultery
with their neighbours' wives, and have
spoken lying words in my name, which I
have not commanded them; even I know,
and *am* a witness, saith the LORD.
24 *Thus* shalt thou also speak to Shemaiah the Nehelamite, saying,
25 Thus speaketh the LORD of hosts, the
God of Israel, saying, Because thou hast
sent letters in thy name unto all the people that *are* at Jerusalem, and to Zephaniah the son of Maaseiah the priest, and to
all the priests, saying,
26 The LORD hath made thee priest in the
stead of Jehoiada the priest, that ye should
be officers in the house of the LORD, for
every man *that is* mad, and maketh himself a prophet, that thou shouldest put him
in prison, and in the stocks.
27 Now therefore why hast thou not reproved Jeremiah of Anathoth, which
maketh himself a prophet to you?
28 For therefore he sent unto us *in* Babylon, saying, This *captivity is* long: build ye
houses, and dwell *in them;* and plant gardens, and eat the fruit of them.
29 And Zephaniah the priest read this letter in the ears of Jeremiah the prophet.
30 Then came the word of the LORD unto
Jeremiah, saying,
31 Send to all them of the captivity, saying, Thus saith the LORD concerning Shemaiah the Nehelamite; Because that
Shemaiah hath prophesied unto you, and
I sent him not, and he caused you to trust
in a lie:
32 Therefore thus saith the LORD; Behold,
I will punish Shemaiah the Nehelamite,
and his seed: he shall not have a man to
dwell among this people; neither shall he
behold the good that I will do for my people, saith the LORD; because he hath taught
rebellion against the LORD.

30

1 The word that came to Jeremiah from
the LORD, saying,
2 Thus speaketh the LORD God of Israel,

saying, Write thee all the words that I have spoken unto thee in a book.

3 For, lo, the days come, saith the LORD, that I will bring again the captivity of my people Israel and Judah, saith the LORD: and I will cause them to return to the land that I gave to their fathers, and they shall possess it.

4 And these *are* the words that the LORD spake concerning Israel and concerning Judah.

5 For thus saith the LORD; We have heard a voice of trembling, of fear, and not of peace.

6 Ask ye now, and see whether a man doth travail with child? wherefore do I see every man with his hands on his loins, as a woman in travail, and all faces are turned into paleness?

7 Alas! for that day *is* great, so that none *is* like it: it *is* even the time of Jacob's trouble; but he shall be saved out of it.

8 For it shall come to pass in that day, saith the LORD of hosts, *that* I will break his yoke from off thy neck, and will burst thy bonds, and strangers shall no more serve themselves of him:

9 But they shall serve the LORD their God, and David their king, whom I will raise up unto them.

10 Therefore fear thou not, O my servant Jacob, saith the LORD; neither be dismayed, O Israel: for, lo, I will save thee from afar, and thy seed from the land of their captivity; and Jacob shall return, and shall be in rest, and be quiet, and none shall make *him* afraid.

11 For I *am* with thee, saith the LORD, to save thee: though I make a full end of all nations whither I have scattered thee, yet will I not make a full end of thee: but I will correct thee in measure, and will not leave thee altogether unpunished.

12 For thus saith the LORD, Thy bruise *is* incurable, *and* thy wound *is* grievous.

30:12 Sin Hurts
◄ Isaiah 1:6
Micah 1:9 ►

13 *There is* none to plead thy cause, that thou mayest be bound up: thou hast no healing medicines.

14 All thy lovers have forgotten thee; they seek thee not; for I have wounded thee with the wound of an enemy, with the chastisement of a cruel one, for the multitude of thine iniquity; *because* thy sins were increased.

15 Why criest thou for thine affliction? thy sorrow *is* incurable for the multitude of thine iniquity: *because* thy sins were increased, I have done these things unto thee.

16 Therefore all they that devour thee shall be devoured; and all thine adversaries, every one of them, shall go into captivity; and they that spoil thee shall be a spoil, and all that prey upon thee will I give for a prey.

17 For I will restore health unto thee, and I will heal thee of thy wounds, saith the LORD; because they called thee an Outcast, *saying,* This *is* Zion, whom no man seeketh after.

18 Thus saith the LORD; Behold, I will bring again the captivity of Jacob's tents, and have mercy on his dwellingplaces; and the city shall be builded upon her own heap, and the palace shall remain after the manner thereof.

19 And out of them shall proceed thanksgiving and the voice of them that make merry: and I will multiply them, and they shall not be few; I will also glorify them, and they shall not be small.

20 Their children also shall be as aforetime, and their congregation shall be established before me, and I will punish all that oppress them.

21 And their nobles shall be of themselves, and their governor shall proceed from the midst of them; and I will cause him to draw near, and he shall approach unto me: for who *is* this that engaged his heart to approach unto me? saith the LORD.

22 And ye shall be my people, and I will be your God.

23 Behold, the whirlwind of the LORD goeth forth with fury, a continuing whirlwind: it shall fall with pain upon the head of the wicked.

24 The fierce anger of the LORD shall not return, until he have done *it,* and until he have performed the intents of his heart: in the latter days ye shall consider it.

31

1 At the same time, saith the LORD, will I be the God of all the families of Israel, and they shall be my people.

2 Thus saith the LORD, The people *which were* left of the sword found grace in the wilderness; *even* Israel, when I went to cause him to rest.

3 The LORD hath appeared of old unto me, *saying,* Yea, I have loved thee with an everlasting love: therefore with lovingkindness have I drawn thee.

> **31:3 God's Love**
> ◄ Psalm 146:8
> John 3:16 ►

4 Again I will build thee, and thou shalt be built, O virgin of Israel: thou shalt again be adorned with thy tabrets, and shalt go forth in the dances of them that make merry.

5 Thou shalt yet plant vines upon the mountains of Samaria: the planters shall plant, and shall eat *them* as common things.

6 For there shall be a day, *that* the watchmen upon the mount Ephraim shall cry, Arise ye, and let us go up to Zion unto the LORD our God.

> **31:6 Friends and Church**
> ◄ Isaiah 2:3
> Zechariah 8:21 ►

7 For thus saith the LORD; Sing with gladness for Jacob, and shout among the chief of the nations: publish ye, praise ye, and say, O LORD, save thy people, the remnant of Israel.

8 Behold, I will bring them from the north country, and gather them from the coasts of the earth, *and* with them the blind and the lame, the woman with child and her that travaileth with child together: a great company shall return thither.

9 They shall come with weeping, and with supplications will I lead them: I will cause them to walk by the rivers of waters in a straight way, wherein they shall not stumble: for I am a father to Israel, and Ephraim *is* my firstborn.

10 Hear the word of the LORD, O ye nations, and declare *it* in the isles afar off, and say, He that scattered Israel will gather him, and keep him, as a shepherd *doth* his flock.

11 For the LORD hath redeemed Jacob, and ransomed him from the hand of *him that was* stronger than he.

12 Therefore they shall come and sing in the height of Zion, and shall flow together to the goodness of the LORD, for wheat, and for wine, and for oil, and for the young of the flock and of the herd: and their soul shall be as a watered garden; and they shall not sorrow any more at all.

13 Then shall the virgin rejoice in the dance, both young men and old together: for I will turn their mourning into joy, and will comfort them, and make them rejoice from their sorrow.

14 And I will satiate the soul of the priests with fatness, and my people shall be satisfied with my goodness, saith the LORD.

> **31:14 Satisfaction**
> ◄ Isaiah 58:11 ►

15 Thus saith the LORD; A voice was heard in Ramah, lamentation, *and* bitter weeping; Rahel weeping for her children refused to be comforted for her children, because they *were* not.

> **31:15 Grief**
> ◄ Job 1:20
> John 11:33 ►

16 Thus saith the LORD; Refrain thy voice from weeping, and thine eyes from tears: for thy work shall be rewarded, saith the LORD; and they shall come again from the land of the enemy.

17 And there is hope in thine end, saith the LORD, that thy children shall come again to their own border.

18 I have surely heard Ephraim bemoaning himself *thus;* Thou hast chastised me, and I was chastised, as a bullock unaccustomed *to the yoke:* turn thou me, and I shall be turned; for thou *art* the LORD my God.

19 Surely after that I was turned, I repented; and after that I was instructed, I smote upon *my* thigh: I was ashamed, yea, even confounded, because I did bear the reproach of my youth.

20 *Is* Ephraim my dear son? *is he* a pleasant child? for since I spake against him, I do earnestly remember him still: therefore my bowels are troubled for him; I will surely have mercy upon him, saith the LORD.

21 Set thee up waymarks, make thee high heaps: set thine heart toward the highway, *even* the way *which* thou wentest: turn again, O virgin of Israel, turn again to these thy cities.

22 How long wilt thou go about, O thou backsliding daughter? for the LORD hath created a new thing in the earth, A woman shall compass a man.

23 Thus saith the LORD of hosts, the God of Israel; As yet they shall use this speech in the land of Judah and in the cities

thereof, when I shall bring again their captivity; The LORD bless thee, O habitation
of justice, *and* mountain of holiness.
24 And there shall dwell in Judah itself,
and in all the cities thereof together, husbandmen, and they *that* go forth with
flocks.
25 For I have satiated the weary soul, and
I have replenished every sorrowful soul.
26 Upon this I awaked, and beheld; and
my sleep was sweet unto me.
27 Behold, the days come, saith the LORD,
that I will sow the house of Israel and the
house of Judah with the seed of man, and
with the seed of beast.
28 And it shall come to pass, *that* like as I
have watched over them, to pluck up, and
to break down, and to throw down, and to
destroy, and to afflict; so will I watch over
them, to build, and to plant, saith the LORD.
29 In those days they shall say no more,
The fathers have eaten a sour grape, and
the children's teeth are set on edge.
30 But every one
shall die for his
own iniquity: every
man that eateth the
sour grape, his teeth
shall be set on edge.

31:30 Blame
◄ Proverbs 9:12
Ezekiel 18:20 ►

31 Behold, the days come, saith the LORD,
that I will make a new covenant with the
house of Israel, and with the house of
Judah:
32 Not according to the covenant that I
made with their fathers in the day *that* I
took them by the hand to bring them out
of the land of Egypt; which my covenant
they brake, although I was an husband
unto them, saith the LORD:
33 But this *shall be* the covenant that I will
make with the house of Israel; After those
days, saith the LORD, I will put my law in
their inward parts, and write it in their
hearts; and will be their God, and they
shall be my people.
34 And they shall
teach no more every
man his neighbour,
and every man his
brother, saying,
Know the LORD: for
they shall all know me, from the least of
them unto the greatest of them, saith the
LORD; for I will forgive their iniquity, and
I will remember their sin no more.

31:34 God's Forgiveness
◄ Jeremiah 5:1
Jeremiah 33:8 ►

35 Thus saith the LORD, which giveth the
sun for a light by day, *and* the ordinances
of the moon and of the stars for a light by
night, which divideth the sea when the
waves thereof roar; The LORD of hosts *is*
his name:
36 If those ordinances depart from before
me, saith the LORD, *then* the seed of Israel
also shall cease from being a nation before me for ever.
37 Thus saith the LORD; If heaven above
can be measured, and the foundations of
the earth searched out beneath, I will also
cast off all the seed of Israel for all that
they have done, saith the LORD.
38 Behold, the days come, saith the LORD,
that the city shall be built to the LORD from
the tower of Hananeel unto the gate of the
corner.
39 And the measuring line shall yet go
forth over against it upon the hill Gareb,
and shall compass about to Goath.
40 And the whole valley of the dead bodies, and of the ashes, and all the fields unto
the brook of Kidron, unto the corner of
the horse gate toward the east, *shall be* holy
unto the LORD; it shall not be plucked up,
nor thrown down any more for ever.

32

1 The word that came to Jeremiah from
the LORD in the tenth year of Zedekiah king
of Judah, which *was* the eighteenth year of
Nebuchadrezzar.
2 For then the king of Babylon's army
besieged Jerusalem: and Jeremiah the
prophet was shut up in the court of the
prison, which *was* in the king of Judah's
house.
3 For Zedekiah king of Judah had shut
him up, saying, Wherefore dost thou
prophesy, and say, Thus saith the LORD,
Behold, I will give this city into the
hand of the king of Babylon, and he shall
take it;
4 And Zedekiah king of Judah shall not
escape out of the hand of the Chaldeans,
but shall surely be delivered into the hand
of the king of Babylon, and shall speak
with him mouth to mouth, and his eyes
shall behold his eyes;
5 And he shall lead Zedekiah to Babylon,
and there shall he be until I visit him, saith
the LORD: though ye fight with the Chaldeans, ye shall not prosper?
6 And Jeremiah said, The word of the
LORD came unto me, saying,

7 Behold, Hanameel the son of Shallum
thine uncle shall come unto thee, saying,
Buy thee my field that *is* in Anathoth: for
the right of redemption *is* thine to buy *it.*
8 So Hanameel mine uncle's son came
to me in the court of the prison according
to the word of the LORD, and said unto
me, Buy my field, I pray thee, that *is* in
Anathoth, which *is* in the country of Benjamin: for the right of inheritance *is* thine,
and the redemption *is* thine; buy *it* for thyself. Then I knew that this *was* the word of
the LORD.
9 And I bought the field of Hanameel my
uncle's son, that *was* in Anathoth, and
weighed him the money, *even* seventeen
shekels of silver.
10 And I subscribed the evidence, and
sealed *it,* and took witnesses, and weighed
him the money in the balances.
11 So I took the evidence of the purchase,
both that which was sealed *according* to the
law and custom, and that which was open:
12 And I gave the evidence of the purchase unto Baruch the son of Neriah, the
son of Maaseiah, in the sight of Hanameel
mine uncle's *son,* and in the presence of
the witnesses that subscribed the book of
the purchase, before all the Jews that sat
in the court of the prison.
13 And I charged Baruch before them,
saying,
14 Thus saith the LORD of hosts, the God
of Israel; Take these evidences, this evidence of the purchase, both which is
sealed, and this evidence which is open;
and put them in an earthen vessel, that
they may continue many days.
15 For thus saith the LORD of hosts, the
God of Israel; Houses and fields and vineyards shall be possessed again in this land.
16 Now when I had delivered the evidence of the purchase unto Baruch the son
of Neriah, I prayed unto the LORD, saying,
17 Ah Lord GOD! behold, thou hast made
the heaven and the earth by thy great power and stretched out arm, *and* there is nothing too hard for thee:
18 Thou shewest lovingkindness unto
thousands, and recompensest the iniquity of the fathers into the bosom of their
children after them: the Great, the Mighty
God, the LORD of hosts, *is* his name,
19 Great in counsel, and mighty in work:
for thine eyes *are* open upon all the ways
of the sons of men:
to give every one ac-
cording to his ways,
and according to
the fruit of his do-
ings:

32:19 Actions Judged
◄ Jeremiah 17:10
Ezekiel 18:30 ►

20 Which hast set
signs and wonders
in the land of
Egypt, *even* unto
this day, and in Is-
rael, and among
other men; and hast made thee a name, as
at this day;

32:30
Results of Sin
◄ Jeremiah 3:25 ►

21 And hast brought forth thy people Israel out of the land of Egypt with signs,
and with wonders, and with a strong hand,
and with a stretched out arm, and with
great terror;
22 And hast given them this land, which
thou didst swear to their fathers to give
them, a land flowing with milk and
honey;
23 And they came in, and possessed it;
but they obeyed not thy voice, neither
walked in thy law; they have done nothing of all that thou commandedst them to
do: therefore thou hast caused all this evil
to come upon them:
24 Behold the mounts, they are come
unto the city to take it; and the city is giv-
en into the hand of the Chaldeans, that
fight against it, because of the sword, and
of the famine, and of the pestilence: and
what thou hast spoken is come to pass;
and, behold, thou seest *it.*
25 And thou hast said unto me, O Lord
GOD, Buy thee the field for money, and
take witnesses; for the city is given into the
hand of the Chaldeans.
26 Then came the word of the LORD unto
Jeremiah, saying,
27 Behold, I *am* the LORD, the God of all
flesh: is there any thing too hard for me?
28 Therefore thus saith the LORD; Behold,
I will give this city into the hand of the
Chaldeans, and into the hand of
Nebuchadrezzar king of Babylon, and he
shall take it:
29 And the Chaldeans, that fight against
this city, shall come and set fire on this
city, and burn it with the houses, upon
whose roofs they have offered incense unto
Baal, and poured out drink offerings unto
other gods, to provoke me to anger.

30For the children of Israel and the children of Judah have only done evil before
me from their youth: for the children of
Israel have only provoked me to anger with
the work of their hands, saith the LORD.
31For this city hath been to me *as* a provocation of mine anger and of my fury from
the day that they built it even unto this
day; that I should remove it from before
my face,
32Because of all the evil of the children
of Israel and of the children of Judah,
which they have done to provoke me to
anger, they, their kings, their princes, their
priests, and their prophets, and the men
of Judah, and the inhabitants of Jerusalem.
33And they have
turned unto me the
back, and not the
face: though I
taught them, rising
up early and teach-
ing *them*, yet they have not hearkened to
receive instruction.

32:33 God as Teacher
◄ Isaiah 54:13
Micah 4:2 ►

34But they set their abominations in the
house, which is called by my name, to defile it.
35And they built the high places of Baal,
which *are* in the valley of the son of Hinnom, to cause their sons and their daughters to pass through *the fire* unto Molech;
which I commanded them not, neither
came it into my mind, that they should
do this abomination, to cause Judah to sin.
36And now therefore thus saith the
LORD, the God of Israel, concerning this
city, whereof ye say, It shall be delivered
into the hand of the king of Babylon by
the sword, and by the famine, and by the
pestilence;
37Behold, I will gather them out of all
countries, whither I have driven them in
mine anger, and in my fury, and in great
wrath; and I will bring them again unto
this place, and I will cause them to dwell
safely:
38And they shall be my people, and I
will be their God:
39And I will give them one heart, and
one way, that they may fear me for ever,
for the good of them, and of their children after them:
40And I will make an everlasting covenant with them, that I will not turn away
from them, to do them good; but I will
put my fear in their hearts, that they shall
not depart from me.
41Yea, I will rejoice over them to do them
good, and I will plant them in this land
assuredly with my whole heart and with
my whole soul.
42For thus saith the LORD; Like as I have
brought all this great evil upon this people, so will I bring upon them all the good
that I have promised them.
43And fields shall be bought in this land,
whereof ye say, *It is* desolate without man
or beast; it is given into the hand of the
Chaldeans.
44Men shall buy fields for money, and
subscribe evidences, and seal *them*, and
take witnesses in the land of Benjamin,
and in the places about Jerusalem, and in
the cities of Judah, and in the cities of the
mountains, and in the cities of the valley,
and in the cities of the south: for I will
cause their captivity to return, saith the
LORD.

33

1Moreover the word of the LORD came
unto Jeremiah the second time, while he
was yet shut up in the court of the prison,
saying,
2Thus saith the LORD the maker thereof,
the LORD that formed it, to establish it; the
LORD *is* his name;
3Call unto me,
and I will answer
thee, and shew thee
great and mighty
things, which thou
knowest not.

33:3 Answers to Prayer
◄ Isaiah 65:24
Zechariah 13:9 ►

4For thus saith the LORD, the God of Israel, concerning the houses of this city, and
concerning the houses of the kings of Judah, which are thrown down by the
mounts, and by the sword;
5They come to fight with the Chaldeans, but *it is* fill them with the dead bodies of men, whom I have slain in mine
anger and in my fury, and for all whose
wickedness I have hid my face from this
city.
6Behold, I will bring it health and cure,
and I will cure them, and will reveal unto
them the abundance of peace and truth.
7And I will cause the captivity of Judah
and the captivity of Israel to return, and
will build them, as at the first.
8And I will cleanse them from all their
iniquity, whereby they have sinned against

me; and I will par-
don all their iniqui-
ties, whereby they
have sinned, and
whereby they have
transgressed against
me.

33:8 God's Forgiveness
◄ Jeremiah 31:34
Ezekiel 36:25 ►

9 And it shall be to me a name of joy, a
praise and an honour before all the nations of the earth, which shall hear all
the good that I do unto them: and they
shall fear and tremble for all the goodness
and for all the prosperity that I procure
unto it.
10 Thus saith the LORD; Again there shall
be heard in this place, which ye say *shall
be* desolate without man and without
beast, *even* in the cities of Judah, and in
the streets of Jerusalem, that are desolate,
without man, and without inhabitant, and
without beast,
11 The voice of joy, and the voice of gladness, the voice of the bridegroom, and the
voice of the bride, the voice of them that
shall say, Praise the LORD of hosts: for the
LORD *is* good; for his mercy *endureth* for
ever: *and* of them that shall bring the sacrifice of praise into the house of the LORD.
For I will cause to return the captivity of
the land, as at the first, saith the LORD.
12 Thus saith the LORD of hosts; Again
in this place, which is desolate without
man and without beast, and in all the cities thereof, shall be an habitation of shepherds causing *their* flocks to lie down.
13 In the cities of the mountains, in the
cities of the vale, and in the cities of the
south, and in the land of Benjamin, and
in the places about Jerusalem, and in the
cities of Judah, shall the flocks pass again
under the hands of him that telleth *them*,
saith the LORD.
14 Behold, the days come, saith the LORD,
that I will perform that good thing which
I have promised unto the house of Israel
and to the house of Judah.
15 In those days, and at that time, will I
cause the Branch of righteousness to grow
up unto David; and he shall execute judgment and righteousness in the land.
16 In those days shall Judah be saved, and
Jerusalem shall dwell safely: and this *is the
name* wherewith she shall be called, The
LORD our righteousness.
17 For thus saith the LORD; David shall
never want a man to sit upon the throne
of the house of Israel;
18 Neither shall the priests the Levites
want a man before me to offer burnt offerings, and to kindle meat offerings, and
to do sacrifice continually.
19 And the word of the LORD came unto
Jeremiah, saying,
20 Thus saith the LORD; If ye can break
my covenant of the day, and my covenant
of the night, and that there should not be
day and night in their season;
21 *Then* may also my covenant be broken with David my servant, that he should
not have a son to reign upon his throne;
and with the Levites the priests, my ministers.
22 As the host of heaven cannot be numbered, neither the sand of the sea measured: so will I multiply the seed of David
my servant, and the Levites that minister
unto me.
23 Moreover the word of the LORD came
to Jeremiah, saying,
24 Considerest thou not what this people have spoken, saying, The two families
which the LORD hath chosen, he hath even
cast them off? thus they have despised my
people, that they should be no more a
nation before them.
25 Thus saith the LORD; If my covenant
be not with day and night, *and if* I have
not appointed the ordinances of heaven
and earth;
26 Then will I cast away the seed of Jacob, and David my servant, so that I will
not take *any* of his seed *to be* rulers over
the seed of Abraham, Isaac, and Jacob: for
I will cause their captivity to return, and
have mercy on them.

34

1 The word which came unto Jeremiah
from the LORD, when Nebuchadnezzar
king of Babylon, and all his army, and all
the kingdoms of the earth of his dominion, and all the people, fought against Jerusalem, and against all the cities thereof,
saying,
2 Thus saith the LORD, the God of Israel;
Go and speak to Zedekiah king of Judah,
and tell him, Thus saith the LORD; Behold,
I will give this city into the hand of the
king of Babylon, and he shall burn it with
fire:
3 And thou shalt not escape out of his
hand, but shalt surely be taken, and

delivered into his hand; and thine eyes shall behold the eyes of the king of Babylon, and he shall speak with thee mouth to mouth, and thou shalt go to Babylon.

4 Yet hear the word of the LORD, O Zedekiah king of Judah; Thus saith the LORD of thee, Thou shalt not die by the sword:

5 *But* thou shalt die in peace: and with the burnings of thy fathers, the former kings which were before thee, so shall they burn *odours* for thee; and they will lament thee, *saying,* Ah lord! for I have pronounced the word, saith the LORD.

6 Then Jeremiah the prophet spake all these words unto Zedekiah king of Judah in Jerusalem,

7 When the king of Babylon's army fought against Jerusalem, and against all the cities of Judah that were left, against Lachish, and against Azekah: for these defenced cities remained of the cities of Judah.

8 *This is* the word that came unto Jeremiah from the LORD, after that the king Zedekiah had made a covenant with all the people which *were* at Jerusalem, to proclaim liberty unto them;

9 That every man should let his manservant, and every man his maidservant, *being* an Hebrew or an Hebrewess, go free; that none should serve himself of them, *to wit,* of a Jew his brother.

10 Now when all the princes, and all the people, which had entered into the covenant, heard that every one should let his manservant, and every one his maidservant, go free, that none should serve themselves of them any more, then they obeyed, and let *them* go.

11 But afterward they turned, and caused the servants and the handmaids, whom they had let go free, to return, and brought them into subjection for servants and for handmaids.

12 Therefore the word of the LORD came to Jeremiah from the LORD, saying,

13 Thus saith the LORD, the God of Israel; I made a covenant with your fathers in the day that I brought them forth out of the land of Egypt, out of the house of bondmen, saying,

14 At the end of seven years let ye go every man his brother an Hebrew, which hath been sold unto thee; and when he hath served thee six years, thou shalt let him go free from thee: but your fathers hearkened not unto me, neither inclined their ear.

15 And ye were now turned, and had done right in my sight, in proclaiming liberty every man to his neighbour; and ye had made a covenant before me in the house which is called by my name:

16 But ye turned and polluted my name, and caused every man his servant, and every man his handmaid, whom ye had set at liberty at their pleasure, to return, and brought them into subjection, to be unto you for servants and for handmaids.

17 Therefore thus saith the LORD; Ye have not hearkened unto me, in proclaiming liberty, every one to his brother, and every man to his neighbour: behold, I proclaim a liberty for you, saith the LORD, to the sword, to the pestilence, and to the famine; and I will make you to be removed into all the kingdoms of the earth.

18 And I will give the men that have transgressed my covenant, which have not performed the words of the covenant which they had made before me, when they cut the calf in twain, and passed between the parts thereof,

19 The princes of Judah, and the princes of Jerusalem, the eunuchs, and the priests, and all the people of the land, which passed between the parts of the calf;

20 I will even give them into the hand of their enemies, and into the hand of them that seek their life: and their dead bodies shall be for meat unto the fowls of the heaven, and to the beasts of the earth.

21 And Zedekiah king of Judah and his princes will I give into the hand of their enemies, and into the hand of them that seek their life, and into the hand of the king of Babylon's army, which are gone up from you.

22 Behold, I will command, saith the LORD, and cause them to return to this city; and they shall fight against it, and take it, and burn it with fire: and I will make the cities of Judah a desolation without an inhabitant.

35

1 The word which came unto Jeremiah from the LORD in the days of Jehoiakim the son of Josiah king of Judah, saying,

2 Go unto the house of the Rechabites, and speak unto them, and bring them into the house of the LORD, into one of

the chambers, and give them wine to
drink.
3 Then I took Jaazaniah the son of Jeremiah, the son of Habaziniah, and his
brethren, and all his sons, and the whole
house of the Rechabites;
4 And I brought them into the house of
the LORD, into the chamber of the sons of
Hanan, the son of Igdaliah, a man of God,
which *was* by the chamber of the princes,
which *was* above the chamber of Maaseiah
the son of Shallum, the keeper of the door:
5 And I set before the sons of the house
of the Rechabites pots full of wine, and
cups, and I said unto them, Drink ye wine.
6 But they said,
We will drink no
wine: for Jonadab
the son of Rechab
our father com-
manded us, saying,
Ye shall drink no wine, *neither* ye, nor your
sons for ever:

35:6 Drinking
◄ Proverbs 31:4
Daniel 1:8 ►

7 Neither shall ye build house, nor sow
seed, nor plant vineyard, nor have *any:* but
all your days ye shall dwell in tents; that
ye may live many days in the land where
ye *be* strangers.
8 Thus have we obeyed the voice of Jonadab the son of Rechab our father in all
that he hath charged us, to drink no wine
all our days, we, our wives, our sons, nor
our daughters;
9 Nor to build houses for us to dwell in:
neither have we vineyard, nor field, nor
seed:
10 But we have dwelt in tents, and have
obeyed, and done according to all that
Jonadab our father commanded us.
11 But it came to pass, when Nebuchadrezzar king of Babylon came up into the
land, that we said, Come, and let us go to
Jerusalem for fear of the army of the
Chaldeans, and for fear of the army of the
Syrians: so we dwell at Jerusalem.
12 Then came the word of the LORD unto
Jeremiah, saying,
13 Thus saith the LORD of hosts, the God
of Israel; Go and tell the men of Judah and
the inhabitants of Jerusalem, Will ye not
receive instruction to hearken to my
words? saith the LORD.
14 The words of Jonadab the son of
Rechab, that he commanded his sons not
to drink wine, are performed; for unto this
day they drink none, but obey their father's
commandment: notwithstanding I have
spoken unto you, rising early and speaking; but ye hearkened not unto me.
15 I have sent also
unto you all my ser-
vants the prophets,
rising up early and
sending *them*, say-
ing, Return ye now
every man from his evil way, and amend
your doings, and go not after other gods
to serve them, and ye shall dwell in the
land which I have given to you and to your
fathers: but ye have not inclined your ear,
nor hearkened unto me.

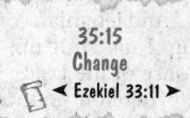

35:15
Change
◄ Ezekiel 33:11 ►

16 Because the sons of Jonadab the son
of Rechab have performed the commandment of their father, which he commanded them; but this people hath not
hearkened unto me:
17 Therefore thus saith the LORD God of
hosts, the God of Israel; Behold, I will
bring upon Judah and upon all the inhabitants of Jerusalem all the evil that I have
pronounced against them: because I have
spoken unto them, but they have not
heard; and I have called unto them, but
they have not answered.
18 And Jeremiah said unto the house of
the Rechabites, Thus saith the LORD of
hosts, the God of Israel; Because ye have
obeyed the commandment of Jonadab
your father, and kept all his precepts, and
done according unto all that he hath commanded you:
19 Therefore thus saith the LORD of hosts,
the God of Israel; Jonadab the son of
Rechab shall not want a man to stand before me for ever.

36

1 And it came to pass in the fourth year
of Jehoiakim the son of Josiah king of Judah, *that* this word came unto Jeremiah
from the LORD, saying,
2 Take thee a roll of a book, and write
therein all the words that I have spoken
unto thee against Israel, and against Judah,
and against all the nations, from the day I
spake unto thee, from the days of Josiah,
even into this day.
3 It may be that the house of Judah will
hear all the evil which I purpose to do unto
them; that they may return every man from
his evil way; that I may forgive their iniquity and their sin.

4Then Jeremiah called Baruch the son of Neriah: and Baruch wrote from the mouth of Jeremiah all the words of the LORD, which he had spoken unto him, upon a roll of a book.

5And Jeremiah commanded Baruch, saying, I *am* shut up; I cannot go into the house of the LORD:

6Therefore go thou, and read in the roll, which thou hast written from my mouth, the words of the LORD in the ears of the people in the LORD'S house upon the fasting day: and also thou shalt read them in the ears of all Judah that come out of their cities.

7It may be they will present their supplication before the LORD, and will return every one from his evil way: for great *is* the anger and the fury that the LORD hath pronounced against this people.

8And Baruch the son of Neriah did according to all that Jeremiah the prophet commanded him, reading in the book the words of the LORD in the LORD'S house.

9And it came to pass in the fifth year of Jehoiakim the son of Josiah king of Judah, in the ninth month, *that* they proclaimed a fast before the LORD to all the people in Jerusalem, and to all the people that came from the cities of Judah unto Jerusalem.

10Then read Baruch in the book the words of Jeremiah in the house of the LORD, in the chamber of Gemariah the son of Shaphan the scribe, in the higher court, at the entry of the new gate of the LORD'S house, in the ears of all the people.

11When Michaiah the son of Gemariah, the son of Shaphan, had heard out of the book all the words of the LORD,

12Then he went down into the king's house, into the scribe's chamber: and, lo, all the princes sat there, *even* Elishama the scribe, and Delaiah the son of Shemaiah, and Elnathan the son of Achbor, and Gemariah the son of Shaphan, and Zedekiah the son of Hananiah, and all the princes.

13Then Michaiah declared unto them all the words that he had heard, when Baruch read the book in the ears of the people.

14Therefore all the princes sent Jehudi the son of Nethaniah, the son of Shelemiah, the son of Cushi, unto Baruch, saying, Take in thine hand the roll wherein thou hast read in the ears of the people, and come. So Baruch the son of Neriah took the roll in his hand, and came unto them.

15And they said unto him, Sit down now, and read it in our ears. So Baruch read *it* in their ears.

16Now it came to pass, when they had heard all the words, they were afraid both one and other, and said unto Baruch, We will surely tell the king of all these words.

17And they asked Baruch, saying, Tell us now, How didst thou write all these words at his mouth?

18Then Baruch answered them, He pronounced all these words unto me with his mouth, and I wrote *them* with ink in the book.

19Then said the princes unto Baruch, Go, hide thee, thou and Jeremiah; and let no man know where ye be.

20And they went in to the king into the court, but they laid up the roll in the chamber of Elishama the scribe, and told all the words in the ears of the king.

21So the king sent Jehudi to fetch the roll: and he took it out of Elishama the scribe's chamber. And Jehudi read it in the ears of the king, and in the ears of all the princes which stood beside the king.

22Now the king sat in the winterhouse in the ninth month: and *there was a fire* on the hearth burning before him.

23And it came to pass, *that* when Jehudi had read three or four leaves, he cut it with the penknife, and cast *it* into the fire that *was* on the hearth, until all the roll was consumed in the fire that *was* on the hearth.

24Yet they were not afraid, nor rent their garments, *neither* the king, nor any of his servants that heard all these words.

25Nevertheless Elnathan and Delaiah and Gemariah had made intercession to the king that he would not burn the roll: but he would not hear them.

26But the king commanded Jerahmeel the son of Hammelech, and Seraiah the son of Azriel, and Shelemiah the son of Abdeel, to take Baruch the scribe and Jeremiah the prophet: but the LORD hid them.

27Then the word of the LORD came to Jeremiah, after that the king had burned the roll, and the words which Baruch wrote at the mouth of Jeremiah, saying,

28Take thee again another roll, and write in it all the former words that were in the first roll, which Jehoiakim the king of Judah hath burned.

29 And thou shalt say to Jehoiakim the king of Judah, Thus saith the LORD; Thou hast burned this roll, saying, Why hast thou written therein, saying, The king of Babylon shall certainly come and destroy this land, and shall cause to cease from thence man and beast?

30 Therefore thus saith the LORD of Jehoiakim king of Judah; He shall have none to sit upon the throne of David: and his dead body shall be cast out in the day to the heat, and in the night to the frost.

31 And I will punish him and his seed and his servants for their iniquity; and I will bring upon them, and upon the inhabitants of Jerusalem, and upon the men of Judah, all the evil that I have pronounced against them; but they hearkened not.

32 Then took Jeremiah another roll, and gave it to Baruch the scribe, the son of Neriah; who wrote therein from the mouth of Jeremiah all the words of the book which Jehoiakim king of Judah had burned in the fire: and there were added besides unto them many like words.

37

1 And king Zedekiah the son of Josiah reigned instead of Coniah the son of Jehoiakim, whom Nebuchadrezzar king of Babylon made king in the land of Judah.

2 But neither he, nor his servants, nor the people of the land, did hearken unto the words of the LORD, which he spake by the prophet Jeremiah.

3 And Zedekiah the king sent Jehucal the son of Shelemiah and Zephaniah the son of Maaseiah the priest to the prophet Jeremiah, saying, Pray now unto the LORD our God for us.

4 Now Jeremiah came in and went out among the people: for they had not put him into prison.

5 Then Pharaoh's army was come forth out of Egypt: and when the Chaldeans that besieged Jerusalem heard tidings of them, they departed from Jerusalem.

6 Then came the word of the LORD unto the prophet Jeremiah, saying,

7 Thus saith the LORD, the God of Israel; Thus shall ye say to the king of Judah, that sent you unto me to enquire of me; Behold, Pharaoh's army, which is come forth to help you, shall return to Egypt into their own land.

8 And the Chaldeans shall come again, and fight against this city, and take it, and burn it with fire.

9 Thus saith the LORD; Deceive not yourselves, saying, The Chaldeans shall surely depart from us: for they shall not depart.

10 For though ye had smitten the whole army of the Chaldeans that fight against you, and there remained *but* wounded men among them, *yet* should they rise up every man in his tent, and burn this city with fire.

11 And it came to pass, that when the army of the Chaldeans was broken up from Jerusalem for fear of Pharaoh's army,

12 Then Jeremiah went forth out of Jerusalem to go into the land of Benjamin, to separate himself thence in the midst of the people.

13 And when he was in the gate of Benjamin, a captain of the ward *was* there, whose name *was* Irijah, the son of Shelemiah, the son of Hananiah; and he took Jeremiah the prophet, saying, Thou fallest away to the Chaldeans.

14 Then said Jeremiah, *It is* false; I fall not away to the Chaldeans. But he hearkened not to him: so Irijah took Jeremiah, and brought him to the princes.

15 Wherefore the princes were wroth with Jeremiah, and smote him, and put him in prison in the house of Jonathan the scribe: for they had made that the prison.

16 When Jeremiah was entered into the dungeon, and into the cabins, and Jeremiah had remained there many days;

17 Then Zedekiah the king sent, and took him out: and the king asked him secretly in his house, and said, Is there *any* word from the LORD? And Jeremiah said, There is: for, said he, thou shalt be delivered into the hand of the king of Babylon.

18 Moreover Jeremiah said unto king Zedekiah, What have I offended against thee, or against thy servants, or against this people, that ye have put me in prison?

19 Where *are* now your prophets which prophesied unto you, saying, The king of Babylon shall not come against you, nor against this land?

20 Therefore hear now, I pray thee, O my lord the king: let my supplication, I pray thee, be accepted before thee; that thou cause me not to return to the house of Jonathan the scribe, lest I die there.

21 Then Zedekiah the king commanded that they should commit Jeremiah into the court of the prison, and that they should give him daily a piece of bread out of the bakers' street, until all the bread in the city were spent. Thus Jeremiah remained in the court of the prison.

38

1 Then Shephatiah the son of Mattan, and Gedaliah the son of Pashur, and Jucal the son of Shelemiah, and Pashur the son of Malchiah, heard the words that Jeremiah had spoken unto all the people, saying,

2 Thus saith the LORD, He that remaineth in this city shall die by the sword, by the famine, and by the pestilence: but he that goeth forth to the Chaldeans shall live; for he shall have his life for a prey, and shall live.

3 Thus saith the LORD, This city shall surely be given into the hand of the king of Babylon's army, which shall take it.

4 Therefore the princes said unto the king, We beseech thee, let this man be put to death: for thus he weakeneth the hands of the men of war that remain in this city, and the hands of all the people, in speaking such words unto them: for this man seeketh not the welfare of this people, but the hurt.

5 Then Zedekiah the king said, Behold, he *is* in your hand: for the king *is* not *he that* can do *any* thing against you.

6 Then took they Jeremiah, and cast him into the dungeon of Malchiah the son of Hammelech, that *was* in the court of the prison: and they let down Jeremiah with cords. And in the dungeon *there was* no water, but mire: so Jeremiah sunk in the mire.

7 Now when Ebed-melech the Ethiopian, one of the eunuchs which was in the king's house, heard that they had put Jeremiah in the dungeon; the king then sitting in the gate of Benjamin;

8 Ebed-melech went forth out of the king's house, and spake to the king, saying,

9 My lord the king, these men have done evil in all that they have done to Jeremiah the prophet, whom they have cast into the dungeon; and he is like to die for hunger in the place where he is: for *there is* no more bread in the city.

38:9 Helping Friends
◄ 1 Samuel 25:24
Philemon 1:10 ►

10 Then the king commanded Ebed-melech the Ethiopian, saying, Take from hence thirty men with thee, and take up Jeremiah the prophet out of the dungeon, before he die.

11 So Ebed-melech took the men with him, and went into the house of the king under the treasury, and took thence old cast clouts and old rotten rags, and let them down by cords into the dungeon to Jeremiah.

12 And Ebed-melech the Ethiopian said unto Jeremiah, Put now *these* old cast clouts and rotten rags under thine armholes under the cords. And Jeremiah did so.

13 So they drew up Jeremiah with cords, and took him up out of the dungeon: and Jeremiah remained in the court of the prison.

14 Then Zedekiah the king sent, and took Jeremiah the prophet unto him into the third entry that *is* in the house of the LORD: and the king said unto Jeremiah, I will ask thee a thing; hide nothing from me.

15 Then Jeremiah said unto Zedekiah, If I declare *it* unto thee, wilt thou not surely put me to death? and if I give thee counsel, wilt thou not hearken unto me?

16 So Zedekiah the king sware secretly unto Jeremiah, saying, *As* the LORD liveth, that made us this soul, I will not put thee to death, neither will I give thee into the hand of these men that seek thy life.

17 Then said Jeremiah unto Zedekiah, Thus saith the LORD, the God of hosts, the God of Israel; If thou wilt assuredly go forth unto the king of Babylon's princes, then thy soul shall live, and this city shall not be burned with fire; and thou shalt live, and thine house:

18 But if thou wilt not go forth to the king of Babylon's princes, then shall this city be given into the hand of the Chaldeans, and they shall burn it with fire, and thou shalt not escape out of their hand.

19 And Zedekiah the king said unto Jeremiah, I am afraid of the Jews that are fallen to the Chaldeans, lest they deliver me into their hand, and they mock me.

20 But Jeremiah said, They shall not deliver *thee*. Obey, I beseech thee, the voice of the LORD, which I speak unto thee: so it

shall be well unto thee, and thy soul shall live.

21 But if thou refuse to go forth, this *is* the word that the LORD hath shewed me:

22 And, behold, all the women that are left in the king of Judah's house *shall be* brought forth to the king of Babylon's princes, and those *women* shall say, Thy friends have set thee on, and have prevailed against thee: thy feet are sunk in the mire, *and* they are turned away back.

23 So they shall bring out all thy wives and thy children to the Chaldeans: and thou shalt not escape out of their hand, but shalt be taken by the hand of the king of Babylon: and thou shalt cause this city to be burned with fire.

24 Then said Zedekiah unto Jeremiah, Let no man know of these words, and thou shalt not die.

25 But if the princes hear that I have talked with thee, and they come unto thee, and say unto thee, Declare unto us now what thou hast said unto the king, hide it not from us, and we will not put thee to death; also what the king said unto thee:

26 Then thou shalt say unto them, I presented my supplication before the king, that he would not cause me to return to Jonathan's house, to die there.

27 Then came all the princes unto Jeremiah, and asked him: and he told them according to all these words that the king had commanded. So they left off speaking with him; for the matter was not perceived.

28 So Jeremiah abode in the court of the prison until the day that Jerusalem was taken: and he was *there* when Jerusalem was taken.

39

1 In the ninth year of Zedekiah king of Judah, in the tenth month, came Nebuchadrezzar king of Babylon and all his army against Jerusalem, and they besieged it.

2 *And* in the eleventh year of Zedekiah, in the fourth month, the ninth *day* of the month, the city was broken up.

3 And all the princes of the king of Babylon came in, and sat in the middle gate, *even* Nergal-sharezer, Samgar-nebo, Sarsechim, Rab-saris, Nergal-sharezer, Rabmag, with all the residue of the princes of the king of Babylon.

4 And it came to pass, *that* when Zedekiah the king of Judah saw them, and all the men of war, then they fled, and went forth out of the city by night, by the way of the king's garden, by the gate betwixt the two walls: and he went out the way of the plain.

5 But the Chaldeans' army pursued after them, and overtook Zedekiah in the plains of Jericho: and when they had taken him, they brought him up to Nebuchadnezzar king of Babylon to Riblah in the land of Hamath, where he gave judgment upon him.

6 Then the king of Babylon slew the sons of Zedekiah in Riblah before his eyes: also the king of Babylon slew all the nobles of Judah.

7 Moreover he put out Zedekiah's eyes, and bound him with chains, to carry him to Babylon.

8 And the Chaldeans burned the king's house, and the houses of the people, with fire, and brake down the walls of Jerusalem.

9 Then Nebuzar-adan the captain of the guard carried away captive into Babylon the remnant of the people that remained in the city, and those that fell away, that fell to him, with the rest of the people that remained.

10 But Nebuzar-adan the captain of the guard left of the poor of the people, which had nothing, in the land of Judah, and gave them vineyards and fields at the same time.

11 Now Nebuchadrezzar king of Babylon gave charge concerning Jeremiah to Nebuzar-adan the captain of the guard, saying,

12 Take him, and look well to him, and do him no harm; but do unto him even as he shall say unto thee.

13 So Nebuzar-adan the captain of the guard sent, and Nebushasban, Rab-saris, and Nergal-sharezer, Rab-mag, and all the king of Babylon's princes;

14 Even they sent, and took Jeremiah out of the court of the prison, and committed him unto Gedaliah the son of Ahikam the son of Shaphan, that he should carry him home: so he dwelt among the people.

15 Now the word of the LORD came unto Jeremiah, while he was shut up in the court of the prison, saying,

16 Go and speak to Ebed-melech the Ethiopian, saying, Thus saith the LORD of hosts, the God of Israel; Behold, I will

bring my words upon this city for evil, and not for good; and they shall be *accomplished* in that day before thee.

17 But I will deliver thee in that day, saith the LORD: and thou shalt not be given into the hand of the men of whom thou *art* afraid.

18 For I will surely deliver thee, and thou shalt not fall by the sword, but thy life shall be for a prey unto thee: because thou hast put thy trust in me, saith the LORD.

40

1 The word that came to Jeremiah from the LORD, after that Nebuzar-adan the captain of the guard had let him go from Ramah, when he had taken him being bound in chains among all that were carried away captive of Jerusalem and Judah, which were carried away captive unto Babylon.

2 And the captain of the guard took Jeremiah, and said unto him, The LORD thy God hath pronounced this evil upon this place.

3 Now the LORD hath brought *it*, and done according as he hath said: because ye have sinned against the LORD, and have not obeyed his voice, therefore this thing is come upon you.

4 And now, behold, I loose thee this day from the chains which *were* upon thine hand. If it seem good unto thee to come with me into Babylon, come; and I will look well unto thee: but if it seem ill unto thee to come with me into Babylon, forbear: behold, all the land *is* before thee: whither it seemeth good and convenient for thee to go, thither go.

5 Now while he was not yet gone back, *he said,* Go back also to Gedaliah the son of Ahikam the son of Shaphan, whom the king of Babylon hath made governor over the cities of Judah, and dwell with him among the people: or go wheresoever it seemeth convenient unto thee to go. So the captain of the guard gave him victuals and a reward, and let him go.

6 Then went Jeremiah unto Gedaliah the son of Ahikam to Mizpah; and dwelt with him among the people that were left in the land.

7 Now when all the captains of the forces which *were* in the fields, *even* they and their men, heard that the king of Babylon had made Gedaliah the son of Ahikam governor in the land, and had committed unto him men, and women, and children, and of the poor of the land, of them that were not carried away captive to Babylon;

8 Then they came to Gedaliah to Mizpah, even Ishmael the son of Nethaniah, and Johanan and Jonathan the sons of Kareah, and Seraiah the son of Tanhumeth, and the sons of Ephai the Netophathite, and Jezaniah the son of a Maachathite, they and their men.

9 And Gedaliah the son of Ahikam the son of Shaphan sware unto them and to their men, saying, Fear not to serve the Chaldeans: dwell in the land, and serve the king of Babylon, and it shall be well with you.

10 As for me, behold, I will dwell at Mizpah to serve the Chaldeans, which will come unto us: but ye, gather ye wine, and summer fruits, and oil, and put *them* in your vessels, and dwell in your cities that ye have taken.

11 Likewise when all the Jews that *were* in Moab, and among the Ammonites, and in Edom, and that *were* in all the countries, heard that the king of Babylon had left a remnant of Judah, and that he had set over them Gedaliah the son of Ahikam the son of Shaphan;

12 Even all the Jews returned out of all places whither they were driven, and came to the land of Judah, to Gedaliah, unto Mizpah, and gathered wine and summer fruits very much.

13 Moreover Johanan the son of Kareah, and all the captains of the forces that *were* in the fields, came to Gedaliah to Mizpah,

14 And said unto him, Dost thou certainly know that Baalis the king of the Ammonites hath sent Ishmael the son of Nethaniah to slay thee? But Gedaliah the son of Ahikam believed them not.

15 Then Johanan the son of Kareah spake to Gedaliah in Mizpah secretly, saying, Let me go, I pray thee, and I will slay Ishmael the son of Nethaniah, and no man shall know *it:* wherefore should he slay thee, that all the Jews which are gathered unto thee should be scattered, and the remnant in Judah perish?

16 But Gedaliah the son of Ahikam said unto Johanan the son of Kareah, Thou shalt not do this thing: for thou speakest falsely of Ishmael.

41

1 Now it came to pass in the seventh month, *that* Ishmael the son of Nethaniah the son of Elishama, of the seed royal, and the princes of the king, even ten men with him, came unto Gedaliah the son of Ahikam to Mizpah; and there they did eat bread together in Mizpah.

2 Then arose Ishmael the son of Nethaniah, and the ten men that were with him, and smote Gedaliah the son of Ahikam the son of Shaphan with the sword, and slew him, whom the king of Babylon had made governor over the land.

3 Ishmael also slew all the Jews that were with him, *even* with Gedaliah, at Mizpah, and the Chaldeans that were found there, *and* the men of war.

4 And it came to pass the second day after he had slain Gedaliah, and no man knew *it,*

5 That there came certain from Shechem, from Shiloh, and from Samaria, *even* fourscore men, having their beards shaven, and their clothes rent, and having cut themselves, with offerings and incense in their hand, to bring *them* to the house of the LORD.

6 And Ishmael the son of Nethaniah went forth from Mizpah to meet them, weeping all along as he went: and it came to pass, as he met them, he said unto them, Come to Gedaliah the son of Ahikam.

7 And it was *so,* when they came into the midst of the city, that Ishmael the son of Nethaniah slew them, *and cast them* into the midst of the pit, he, and the men that *were* with him.

8 But ten men were found among them that said unto Ishmael, Slay us not: for we have treasures in the field, of wheat, and of barley, and of oil, and of honey. So he forbare, and slew them not among their brethren.

9 Now the pit wherein Ishmael had cast all the dead bodies of the men, whom he had slain because of Gedaliah, *was* it which Asa the king had made for fear of Baasha king of Israel: *and* Ishmael the son of Nethaniah filled it with *them that were* slain.

10 Then Ishmael carried away captive all the residue of the people that *were* in Mizpah, *even* the king's daughters, and all the people that remained in Mizpah, whom Nebuzar-adan the captain of the guard had committed to Gedaliah the son of Ahikam: and Ishmael the son of Nethaniah carried them away captive, and departed to go over to the Ammonites.

11 But when Johanan the son of Kareah, and all the captains of the forces that *were* with him, heard of all the evil that Ishmael the son of Nethaniah had done,

12 Then they took all the men, and went to fight with Ishmael the son of Nethaniah, and found him by the great waters that *are* in Gibeon.

13 Now it came to pass, *that* when all the people which *were* with Ishmael saw Johanan the son of Kareah, and all the captains of the forces that *were* with him, then they were glad.

14 So all the people that Ishmael had carried away captive from Mizpah cast about and returned, and went unto Johanan the son of Kareah.

15 But Ishmael the son of Nethaniah escaped from Johanan with eight men, and went to the Ammonites.

16 Then took Johanan the son of Kareah, and all the captains of the forces that *were* with him, all the remnant of the people whom he had recovered from Ishmael the son of Nethaniah, from Mizpah, after *that* he had slain Gedaliah the son of Ahikam, *even* mighty men of war, and the women, and the children, and the eunuchs, whom he had brought again from Gibeon:

17 And they departed, and dwelt in the habitation of Chimham, which is by Bethlehem, to go to enter into Egypt,

18 Because of the Chaldeans: for they were afraid of them, because Ishmael the son of Nethaniah had slain Gedaliah the son of Ahikam, whom the king of Babylon made governor in the land.

42

1 Then all the captains of the forces, and Johanan the son of Kareah, and Jezaniah the son of Hoshaiah, and all the people from the least even unto the greatest, came near,

2 And said unto Jeremiah the prophet, Let, we beseech thee, our supplication be accepted before thee, and pray for us unto the LORD thy God, *even* for all this remnant; (for we are left *but* a few of many, as thine eyes do behold us:)

3 That the LORD thy God may shew us the way wherein we may walk, and the thing that we may do.

Turn to the next page for more . . .

42:3
Willingness to Learn
◄ Ezra 8:21
Matthew 18:3 ►

4 Then Jeremiah the prophet said unto them, I have heard *you;* behold, I will pray unto the LORD your God according to your words; and it shall come to pass, *that* whatsoever thing the LORD shall answer you, I will declare *it* unto you; I will keep nothing back from you.

5 Then they said to Jeremiah, The LORD be a true and faithful witness between us, if we do not even according to all things for the which the LORD thy God shall send thee to us.

6 Whether *it be* good, or whether *it be* evil, we will obey the voice of the LORD our God, to whom we send thee; that it may be well with us, when we obey the voice of the LORD our God.

7 And it came to pass after ten days, that the word of the LORD came unto Jeremiah.

8 Then called he Johanan the son of Kareah, and all the captains of the forces which *were* with him, and all the people from the least even to the greatest,

9 And said unto them, Thus saith the LORD, the God of Israel, unto whom ye sent me to present your supplication before him;

10 If ye will still abide in this land, then will I build you, and not pull *you* down, and I will plant you, and not pluck *you* up: for I repent me of the evil that I have done unto you.

11 Be not afraid of the king of Babylon, of whom ye are afraid; be not afraid of him, saith the LORD: for I *am* with you to save you, and to deliver you from his hand.

12 And I will shew mercies unto you, that he may have mercy upon you, and cause you to return to your own land.

13 But if ye say, We will not dwell in this land, neither obey the voice of the LORD your God,

14 Saying, No; but we will go into the land of Egypt, where we shall see no war, nor hear the sound of the trumpet, nor have hunger of bread; and there will we dwell:

15 And now therefore hear the word of the LORD, ye remnant of Judah; Thus saith the LORD of hosts, the God of Israel; If ye wholly set your faces to enter into Egypt, and go to sojourn there;

16 Then it shall come to pass, *that* the sword, which ye feared, shall overtake you there in the land of Egypt, and the famine, whereof ye were afraid, shall follow close after you there in Egypt; and there ye shall die.

17 So shall it be with all the men that set their faces to go into Egypt to sojourn there; they shall die by the sword, by the famine, and by the pestilence: and none of them shall remain or escape from the evil that I will bring upon them.

18 For thus saith the LORD of hosts, the God of Israel; As mine anger and my fury hath been poured forth upon the inhabitants of Jerusalem; so shall my fury be poured forth upon you, when ye shall enter into Egypt: and ye shall be an execration, and an astonishment, and a curse, and a reproach; and ye shall see this place no more.

19 The LORD hath said concerning you, O ye remnant of Judah; Go ye not into Egypt: know certainly that I have admonished you this day.

20 For ye dissembled in your hearts, when ye sent me unto the LORD your God, saying, Pray for us unto the LORD our God; and according unto all that the LORD our God shall say, so declare unto us, and we will do *it.*

21 And *now* I have this day declared *it* to you; but ye have not obeyed the voice of the LORD your God, nor any *thing* for the which he hath sent me unto you.

22 Now therefore know certainly that ye shall die by the sword, by the famine, and by the pestilence, in the place whither ye desire to go *and* to sojourn.

43

1 And it came to pass, *that* when Jeremiah had made an end of speaking unto all the people all the words of the LORD their God, for which the LORD their God had sent him to them, *even* all these words,

2 Then spake Azariah the son of Hoshaiah, and Johanan the son of Kareah, and all the proud men, saying unto Jeremiah, Thou speakest falsely: the LORD our God hath not sent thee to say, Go not into Egypt to sojourn there:

3 But Baruch the son of Neriah setteth thee on against us, for to deliver us into the hand of the Chaldeans, that they might put us to death, and carry us away captives into Babylon.

4So Johanan the son of Kareah, and all
the captains of the forces, and all the people, obeyed not the voice of the LORD, to
dwell in the land of Judah.
5But Johanan the son of Kareah, and all
the captains of the forces, took all the remnant of Judah, that were returned from all
nations, whither they had been driven, to
dwell in the land of Judah;
6*Even* men, and women, and children,
and the king's daughters, and every person that Nebuzar-adan the captain of the
guard had left with Gedaliah the son of
Ahikam the son of Shaphan, and Jeremiah the prophet, and Baruch the son of
Neriah.
7So they came into the land of Egypt:
for they obeyed not the voice of the LORD:
thus came they *even* to Tahpanhes.
8Then came the word of the LORD unto
Jeremiah in Tahpanhes, saying,
9Take great stones in thine hand, and
hide them in the clay in the brickkiln,
which *is* at the entry of Pharaoh's house
in Tahpanhes, in the sight of the men of
Judah;
10And say unto them, Thus saith the
LORD of hosts, the God of Israel; Behold, I
will send and take Nebuchadrezzar the
king of Babylon, my servant, and will set
his throne upon these stones that I have
hid; and he shall spread his royal pavilion
over them.
11And when he cometh, he shall smite
the land of Egypt, *and deliver* such *as are*
for death to death; and such *as are* for captivity to captivity; and such *as are* for the
sword to the sword.
12And I will kindle a fire in the houses
of the gods of Egypt; and he shall burn
them, and carry them away captives: and
he shall array himself with the land of
Egypt, as a shepherd putteth on his garment; and he shall go forth from thence
in peace.
13He shall break also the images of Beth-
shemesh, that *is* in the land of Egypt; and
the houses of the gods of the Egyptians
shall he burn with fire.

44

1The word that came to Jeremiah concerning all the Jews which dwell in the land
of Egypt, which dwell at Migdol, and at
Tahpanhes, and at Noph, and in the country of Pathros, saying,
2Thus saith the LORD of hosts, the God
of Israel; Ye have seen all the evil that I
have brought upon Jerusalem, and upon
all the cities of Judah; and, behold, this
day they *are* a desolation, and no man
dwelleth therein,
3Because of their wickedness which they
have committed to provoke me to anger,
in that they went to burn incense, *and* to
serve other gods, whom they knew not,
neither they, ye, nor your fathers.
4Howbeit I sent unto you all my servants
the prophets, rising early and sending
them, saying, Oh, do not this abominable
thing that I hate.
5But they hearkened not, nor inclined
their ear to turn from their wickedness, to
burn no incense unto other gods.
6Wherefore my fury and mine anger was
poured forth, and was kindled in the cities of Judah and in the streets of Jerusalem; and they are wasted *and* desolate, as
at this day.
7Therefore now thus saith the LORD, the
God of hosts, the God of Israel; Wherefore commit ye *this* great evil against your
souls, to cut off from you man and woman, child and suckling, out of Judah, to
leave you none to remain;
8In that ye provoke me unto wrath with
the works of your hands, burning incense
unto other gods in the land of Egypt,
whither ye be gone to dwell, that ye might
cut yourselves off, and that ye might be a
curse and a reproach among all the nations
of the earth?
9Have ye forgotten the wickedness of
your fathers, and the wickedness of the
kings of Judah, and the wickedness of their
wives, and your own wickedness, and the
wickedness of your wives, which they have
committed in the land of Judah, and in
the streets of Jerusalem?
10They are not humbled *even* unto this
day, neither have they feared, nor walked
in my law, nor in my statutes, that I set
before you and before your fathers.
11Therefore thus saith the LORD of hosts,
the God of Israel; Behold, I will set my face
against you for evil, and to cut off all Judah.
12And I will take the remnant of Judah,
that have set their faces to go into the land
of Egypt to sojourn there, and they shall
all be consumed, *and* fall in the land of
Egypt; they shall *even* be consumed by the

sword *and* by the famine: they shall die, from the least even unto the greatest, by the sword and by the famine: and they shall be an execration, *and* an astonishment, and a curse, and a reproach.

13 For I will punish them that dwell in the land of Egypt, as I have punished Jerusalem, by the sword, by the famine, and by the pestilence:

14 So that none of the remnant of Judah, which are gone into the land of Egypt to sojourn there, shall escape or remain, that they should return into the land of Judah, to the which they have a desire to return to dwell there: for none shall return but such as shall escape.

15 Then all the men which knew that their wives had burned incense unto other gods, and all the women that stood by, a great multitude, even all the people that dwelt in the land of Egypt, in Pathros, answered Jeremiah, saying,

16 *As for* the word that thou hast spoken unto us in the name of the LORD, we will not hearken unto thee.

17 But we will certainly do whatsoever thing goeth forth out of our own mouth, to burn incense unto the queen of heaven, and to pour out drink offerings unto her, as we have done, we, and our fathers, our kings, and our princes, in the cities of Judah, and in the streets of Jerusalem: for *then* had we plenty of victuals, and were well, and saw no evil.

18 But since we left off to burn incense to the queen of heaven, and to pour out drink offerings unto her, we have wanted all *things*, and have been consumed by the sword and by the famine.

44:18 Superstition
◄ Jeremiah 10:2
Matthew 14:2 ►

19 And when we burned incense to the queen of heaven, and poured out drink offerings unto her, did we make her cakes to worship her, and pour out drink offerings unto her, without our men?

20 Then Jeremiah said unto all the people, to the men, and to the women, and to all the people which had given him *that* answer, saying,

21 The incense that ye burned in the cities of Judah, and in the streets of Jerusalem, ye, and your fathers, your kings, and your princes, and the people of the land, did not the LORD remember them, and came it *not* into his mind?

22 So that the LORD could no longer bear, because of the evil of your doings, *and* because of the abominations which ye have committed; therefore is your land a desolation, and an astonishment, and a curse, without an inhabitant, as at this day.

23 Because ye have burned incense, and because ye have sinned against the LORD, and have not obeyed the voice of the LORD, nor walked in his law, nor in his statutes, nor in his testimonies; therefore this evil is happened unto you, as at this day.

24 Moreover Jeremiah said unto all the people, and to all the women, Hear the word of the LORD, all Judah that *are* in the land of Egypt:

25 Thus saith the LORD of hosts, the God of Israel, saying; Ye and your wives have both spoken with your mouths, and fulfilled with your hand, saying, We will surely perform our vows that we have vowed, to burn incense to the queen of heaven, and to pour out drink offerings unto her: ye will surely accomplish your vows, and surely perform your vows.

26 Therefore hear ye the word of the LORD, all Judah that dwell in the land of Egypt; Behold, I have sworn by my great name, saith the LORD, that my name shall no more be named in the mouth of any man of Judah in all the land of Egypt, saying, The Lord GOD liveth.

27 Behold, I will watch over them for evil, and not for good: and all the men of Judah that *are* in the land of Egypt shall be consumed by the sword and by the famine, until there be an end of them.

28 Yet a small number that escape the sword shall return out of the land of Egypt into the land of Judah, and all the remnant of Judah, that are gone into the land of Egypt to sojourn there, shall know whose words shall stand, mine, or theirs.

29 And this *shall be* a sign unto you, saith the LORD, that I will punish you in this place, that ye may know that my words shall surely stand against you for evil:

30 Thus saith the LORD; Behold, I will give Pharaoh-hophra king of Egypt into the hand of his enemies, and into the hand of them that seek his life; as I gave Zedekiah king of Judah into the hand of Neb-

uchadrezzar king of Babylon, his enemy,
and that sought his life.

45 1The word that Jeremiah the prophet
spake unto Baruch the son of Neriah, when
he had written these words in a book at
the mouth of Jeremiah, in the fourth year
of Jehoiakim the son of Josiah king of Judah, saying,
2Thus saith the LORD, the God of Israel,
unto thee, O Baruch;
3Thou didst say, Woe is me now! for the
LORD hath added grief to my sorrow; I
fainted in my sighing, and I find no rest.
4Thus shalt thou say unto him, The
LORD saith thus; Behold, *that* which I have
built will I break down, and that which I
have planted I will pluck up, even this
whole land.
5And seekest thou great things for thyself? seek *them* not: for, behold, I will bring
evil upon all flesh, saith the LORD: but thy
life will I give unto thee for a prey in all
places whither thou goest.

46 1The word of the LORD which came to
Jeremiah the prophet against the Gentiles;
2Against Egypt, against the army of
Pharaoh-necho king of Egypt, which was
by the river Euphrates in Carchemish,
which Nebuchadrezzar king of Babylon
smote in the fourth year of Jehoiakim the
son of Josiah king of Judah.
3Order ye the buckler and shield, and
draw near to battle.
4Harness the horses; and get up, ye
horsemen, and stand forth with *your* helmets; furbish the spears, *and* put on the
brigandines.
5Wherefore have I seen them dismayed
and turned away back? and their mighty
ones are beaten down, and are fled apace,
and look not back: *for* fear *was* round
about, saith the LORD.
6Let not the swift flee away, nor the
mighty man escape; they shall stumble,
and fall toward the north by the river Euphrates.
7Who *is* this *that* cometh up as a flood,
whose waters are moved as the rivers?
8Egypt riseth up like a flood, and *his*
waters are moved like the rivers; and he
saith, I will go up, *and* will cover the earth;
I will destroy the city and the inhabitants
thereof.
9Come up, ye horses; and rage, ye chariots; and let the mighty men come forth;
the Ethiopians and the Libyans, that handle the shield; and the Lydians, that handle *and* bend the bow.
10For this *is* the day of the Lord GOD of
hosts, a day of vengeance, that he may
avenge him of his adversaries: and the
sword shall devour, and it shall be satiate
and made drunk with their blood: for the
Lord GOD of hosts hath a sacrifice in the
north country by the river Euphrates.
11Go up into Gilead, and take balm,
O virgin, the daughter of Egypt: in vain
shalt thou use many medicines; *for* thou
shalt not be cured.
12The nations have heard of thy shame,
and thy cry hath filled the land: for the
mighty man hath stumbled against the
mighty, *and* they are fallen both together.
13The word that the LORD spake to Jeremiah the prophet, how Nebuchadrezzar
king of Babylon should come *and* smite
the land of Egypt.
14Declare ye in Egypt, and publish in
Migdol, and publish in Noph and in Tahpanhes: say ye, Stand fast, and prepare
thee; for the sword shall devour round
about thee.
15Why are thy valiant *men* swept away?
they stood not, because the LORD did drive
them.
16He made many to fall, yea, one fell
upon another: and they said, Arise, and
let us go again to our own people, and to
the land of our nativity, from the oppressing sword.
17They did cry there, Pharaoh king of
Egypt *is but* a noise; he hath passed the
time appointed.
18*As* I live, saith the King, whose name
is the LORD of hosts, Surely as Tabor *is*
among the mountains, and as Carmel by
the sea, *so* shall he come.
19O thou daughter dwelling in Egypt,
furnish thyself to go into captivity: for
Noph shall be waste and desolate without
an inhabitant.
20Egypt *is like* a very fair heifer, *but* destruction cometh; it cometh out of the
north.
21Also her hired men *are* in the midst of
her like fatted bullocks; for they also are
turned back, *and* are fled away together:
they did not stand, because the day of their
calamity was come upon them, *and* the
time of their visitation.

22 The voice thereof shall go like a serpent; for they shall march with an army,
and come against her with axes, as hewers
of wood.
23 They shall cut down her forest, saith
the LORD, though it cannot be searched;
because they are more than the grasshoppers, and *are* innumerable.
24 The daughter of Egypt shall be confounded; she shall be delivered into the
hand of the people of the north.
25 The LORD of hosts, the God of Israel,
saith; Behold, I will punish the multitude
of No, and Pharaoh, and Egypt, with their
gods, and their kings; even Pharaoh, and
all them that trust in him:
26 And I will deliver them into the hand
of those that seek their lives, and into the
hand of Nebuchadrezzar king of Babylon,
and into the hand of his servants: and afterward it shall be inhabited, as in the days
of old, saith the LORD.
27 But fear not thou, O my servant Jacob, and be not dismayed, O Israel: for,
behold, I will save thee from afar off, and
thy seed from the land of their captivity;
and Jacob shall return, and be in rest and
at ease, and none shall make *him* afraid.
28 Fear thou not, O Jacob my servant,
saith the LORD: for I *am* with thee; for I
will make a full end of all the nations
whither I have driven thee: but I will not
make a full end of thee, but correct thee in
measure; yet will I not leave thee wholly
unpunished.

47

1 The word of the LORD that came to Jeremiah the prophet against the Philistines,
before that Pharaoh smote Gaza.
2 Thus saith the LORD; Behold, waters rise
up out of the north, and shall be an overflowing flood, and shall overflow the land,
and all that is therein; the city, and them
that dwell therein: then the men shall cry,
and all the inhabitants of the land shall
howl.
3 At the noise of the stamping of the
hoofs of his strong *horses,* at the rushing
of his chariots, *and at* the rumbling of his
wheels, the fathers shall not look back to
their children for feebleness of hands;
4 Because of the day that cometh to spoil
all the Philistines, *and* to cut off from Tyrus
and Zidon every helper that remaineth: for
the LORD will spoil the Philistines, the remnant of the country of Caphtor.
5 Baldness is come upon Gaza; Ashkelon is cut off *with* the remnant of their valley: how long wilt thou cut thyself?
6 O thou sword of the LORD, how long
will it be ere thou be quiet? put up thyself
into thy scabbard, rest, and be still.
7 How can it be quiet, seeing the LORD
hath given it a charge against Ashkelon,
and against the sea shore? there hath he
appointed it.

48

1 Against Moab thus saith the LORD of
hosts, the God of Israel; Woe unto Nebo!
for it is spoiled: Kiriathaim is confounded
and taken: Misgab is confounded and dismayed.
2 *There shall be* no more praise of Moab:
in Heshbon they have devised evil against
it; come, and let us cut it off from *being* a
nation. Also thou shalt be cut down,
O Madmen; the sword shall pursue thee.
3 A voice of crying *shall be* from Horonaim, spoiling and great destruction.
4 Moab is destroyed; her little ones have
caused a cry to be heard.
5 For in the going up of Luhith continual weeping shall go up; for in the going
down of Horonaim the enemies have
heard a cry of destruction.
6 Flee, save your lives, and be like the
heath in the wilderness.
7 For because thou hast trusted in thy
works and in thy treasures, thou shalt also
be taken: and Chemosh shall go forth into
captivity *with* his priests and his princes
together.
8 And the spoiler shall come upon every
city, and no city shall escape: the valley also
shall perish, and the plain shall be destroyed, as the LORD hath spoken.
9 Give wings unto Moab, that it may
flee and get away: for the cities thereof
shall be desolate, without any to dwell
therein.
10 Cursed *be* he that doeth the work of
the LORD deceitfully, and cursed *be* he that
keepeth back his sword from blood.
11 Moab hath been at ease from his
youth, and he hath settled on his lees, and
hath not been emptied from vessel to vessel, neither hath he gone into captivity:
therefore his taste remained in him, and
his scent is not changed.
12 Therefore, behold, the days come,
saith the LORD, that I will send unto him
wanderers, that shall cause him to wan-

der, and shall empty his vessels, and break their bottles.

13 And Moab shall be ashamed of Chemosh, as the house of Israel was ashamed of Bethel their confidence.

14 How say ye, We *are* mighty and strong men for the war?

15 Moab is spoiled, and gone up *out of* her cities, and his chosen young men are gone down to the slaughter, saith the King, whose name *is* the LORD of hosts.

16 The calamity of Moab *is* near to come, and his affliction hasteth fast.

17 All ye that are about him, bemoan him; and all ye that know his name, say, How is the strong staff broken, *and* the beautiful rod!

18 Thou daughter that dost inhabit Dibon, come down from *thy* glory, and sit in thirst; for the spoiler of Moab shall come upon thee, *and* he shall destroy thy strong holds.

19 O inhabitant of Aroer, stand by the way, and espy; ask him that fleeth, and her that escapeth, *and* say, What is done?

20 Moab is confounded; for it is broken down: howl and cry; and tell ye it in Arnon, that Moab is spoiled,

21 And judgment is come upon the plain country; upon Holon, and upon Jahazah, and upon Mephaath,

22 And upon Dibon, and upon Nebo, and upon Beth-diblathaim,

23 And upon Kiriathaim, and upon Beth-gamul, and upon Beth-meon,

24 And upon Kerioth, and upon Bozrah, and upon all the cities of the land of Moab, far or near.

25 The horn of Moab is cut off, and his arm is broken, saith the LORD.

26 Make ye him drunken: for he magnified *himself* against the LORD: Moab also shall wallow in his vomit, and he also shall be in derision.

27 For was not Israel a derision unto thee? was he found among thieves? for since thou spakest of him, thou skippedst for joy.

28 O ye that dwell in Moab, leave the cities, and dwell in the rock, and be like the dove *that* maketh her nest in the sides of the hole's mouth.

29 We have heard the pride of Moab, (he is exceeding proud) his loftiness, and his arrogancy, and his pride, and the haughtiness of his heart.

30 I know his wrath, saith the LORD; but *it shall* not *be* so; his lies shall not so effect *it*.

31 Therefore will I howl for Moab, and I will cry out for all Moab; *mine heart* shall mourn for the men of Kir-heres.

32 O vine of Sibmah, I will weep for thee with the weeping of Jazer: thy plants are gone over the sea, they reach *even* to the sea of Jazer: the spoiler is fallen upon thy summer fruits and upon thy vintage.

33 And joy and gladness is taken from the plentiful field, and from the land of Moab; and I have caused wine to fail from the winepresses: none shall tread with shouting; *their* shouting *shall be* no shouting.

34 From the cry of Heshbon *even* unto Elealeh, *and even* unto Jahaz, have they uttered their voice, from Zoar *even* unto Horonaim, *as* an heifer of three years old: for the waters also of Nimrim shall be desolate.

35 Moreover I will cause to cease in Moab, saith the LORD, him that offereth in the high places, and him that burneth incense to his gods.

36 Therefore mine heart shall sound for Moab like pipes, and mine heart shall sound like pipes for the men of Kir-heres: because the riches *that* he hath gotten are perished.

37 For every head *shall be* bald, and every beard clipped: upon all the hands *shall be* cuttings, and upon the loins sackcloth.

38 *There shall be* lamentation generally upon all the housetops of Moab, and in the streets thereof: for I have broken Moab like a vessel wherein *is* no pleasure, saith the LORD.

39 They shall howl, *saying*, How is it broken down! how hath Moab turned the back with shame! so shall Moab be a derision and a dismaying to all them about him.

40 For thus saith the LORD; Behold, he shall fly as an eagle, and shall spread his wings over Moab.

41 Kerioth is taken, and the strong holds are surprised, and the mighty men's hearts in Moab at that day shall be as the heart of a woman in her pangs.

42 And Moab shall be destroyed from *being* a people, because he hath magnified *himself* against the LORD.

43 Fear, and the pit, and the snare, *shall be* upon thee, O inhabitant of Moab, saith the LORD.

44 He that fleeth from the fear shall fall into the pit; and he that getteth up out of the pit shall be taken in the snare: for I will bring upon it, *even* upon Moab, the year of their visitation, saith the LORD.

45 They that fled stood under the shadow of Heshbon because of the force: but a fire shall come forth out of Heshbon, and a flame from the midst of Sihon, and shall devour the corner of Moab, and the crown of the head of the tumultuous ones.

46 Woe be unto thee, O Moab! the people of Chemosh perisheth: for thy sons are taken captives, and thy daughters captives.

47 Yet will I bring again the captivity of Moab in the latter days, saith the LORD. Thus far *is* the judgment of Moab.

49

1 Concerning the Ammonites, thus saith the LORD; Hath Israel no sons? hath he no heir? why *then* doth their king inherit Gad, and his people dwell in his cities?

2 Therefore, behold, the days come, saith the LORD, that I will cause an alarm of war to be heard in Rabbah of the Ammonites; and it shall be a desolate heap, and her daughters shall be burned with fire: then shall Israel be heir unto them that were his heirs, saith the LORD.

3 Howl, O Heshbon, for Ai is spoiled: cry, ye daughters of Rabbah, gird you with sackcloth; lament, and run to and fro by the hedges; for their king shall go into captivity, *and* his priests and his princes together.

4 Wherefore gloriest thou in the valleys, thy flowing valley, O backsliding daughter? that trusted in her treasures, *saying,* Who shall come unto me?

5 Behold, I will bring a fear upon thee, saith the Lord GOD of hosts, from all those that be about thee; and ye shall be driven out every man right forth; and none shall gather up him that wandereth.

6 And afterward I will bring again the captivity of the children of Ammon, saith the LORD.

7 Concerning Edom, thus saith the LORD of hosts; *Is* wisdom no more in Teman? is counsel perished from the prudent? is their wisdom vanished?

8 Flee ye, turn back, dwell deep, O inhabitants of Dedan; for I will bring the calamity of Esau upon him, the time *that* I will visit him.

9 If grapegatherers come to thee, would they not leave *some* gleaning grapes? if thieves by night, they will destroy till they have enough.

10 But I have made Esau bare, I have uncovered his secret places, and he shall not be able to hide himself: his seed is spoiled, and his brethren, and his neighbours, and he *is* not.

11 Leave thy fatherless children, I will preserve *them* alive; and let thy widows trust in me.

49:11
God's Care for Kids
◄ Proverbs 15:25
Hosea 14:3 ►

12 For thus saith the LORD; Behold, they whose judgment *was* not to drink of the cup have assuredly drunken; and *art* thou he *that* shall altogether go unpunished? thou shalt not go unpunished, but thou shalt surely drink *of it*.

13 For I have sworn by myself, saith the LORD, that Bozrah shall become a desolation, a reproach, a waste, and a curse; and all the cities thereof shall be perpetual wastes.

14 I have heard a rumour from the LORD, and an ambassador is sent unto the heathen, *saying,* Gather ye together, and come against her, and rise up to the battle.

15 For, lo, I will make thee small among the heathen, *and* despised among men.

16 Thy terribleness hath deceived thee, *and* the pride of thine heart, O thou that dwellest in the clefts of the rock, that holdest the height of the hill: though thou shouldest make thy nest as high as the eagle, I will bring thee down from thence, saith the LORD.

17 Also Edom shall be a desolation: every one that goeth by it shall be astonished, and shall hiss at all the plagues thereof.

18 As in the overthrow of Sodom and Gomorrah and the neighbour *cities* thereof, saith the LORD, no man shall abide there, neither shall a son of man dwell in it.

19 Behold, he shall come up like a lion from the swelling of Jordan against the habitation of the strong: but I will suddenly make him run away from her: and who *is* a chosen *man, that* I may appoint over her? for who *is* like me? and who will

appoint me the time? and who *is* that shepherd that will stand before me?

20 Therefore hear the counsel of the LORD, that he hath taken against Edom; and his purposes, that he hath purposed against the inhabitants of Teman: Surely the least of the flock shall draw them out: surely he shall make their habitations desolate with them.

21 The earth is moved at the noise of their fall, at the cry the noise thereof was heard in the Red sea.

22 Behold, he shall come up and fly as the eagle, and spread his wings over Bozrah: and at that day shall the heart of the mighty men of Edom be as the heart of a woman in her pangs.

23 Concerning Damascus. Hamath is confounded, and Arpad: for they have heard evil tidings: they are fainthearted; *there is* sorrow on the sea; it cannot be quiet.

24 Damascus is waxed feeble, *and* turneth herself to flee, and fear hath seized on *her*: anguish and sorrows have taken her, as a woman in travail.

25 How is the city of praise not left, the city of my joy!

26 Therefore her young men shall fall in her streets, and all the men of war shall be cut off in that day, saith the LORD of hosts.

27 And I will kindle a fire in the wall of Damascus, and it shall consume the palaces of Ben-hadad.

28 Concerning Kedar, and concerning the kingdoms of Hazor, which Nebuchadrezzar king of Babylon shall smite, thus saith the LORD; Arise ye, go up to Kedar, and spoil the men of the east.

29 Their tents and their flocks shall they take away: they shall take to themselves their curtains, and all their vessels, and their camels; and they shall cry unto them, Fear *is* on every side.

30 Flee, get you far off, dwell deep, O ye inhabitants of Hazor, saith the LORD; for Nebuchadrezzar king of Babylon hath taken counsel against you, and hath conceived a purpose against you.

31 Arise, get you up unto the wealthy nation, that dwelleth without care, saith the LORD, which have neither gates nor bars, *which* dwell alone.

32 And their camels shall be a booty, and the multitude of their cattle a spoil: and I will scatter into all winds them *that are* in the utmost corners; and I will bring their calamity from all sides thereof, saith the LORD.

33 And Hazor shall be a dwelling for dragons, *and* a desolation for ever: there shall no man abide there, nor *any* son of man dwell in it.

34 The word of the LORD that came to Jeremiah the prophet against Elam in the beginning of the reign of Zedekiah king of Judah, saying,

35 Thus saith the LORD of hosts; Behold, I will break the bow of Elam, the chief of their might.

36 And upon Elam will I bring the four winds from the four quarters of heaven, and will scatter them toward all those winds; and there shall be no nation whither the outcasts of Elam shall not come.

37 For I will cause Elam to be dismayed before their enemies, and before them that seek their life: and I will bring evil upon them *even* my fierce anger, saith the LORD; and I will send the sword after them, till I have consumed them:

38 And I will set my throne in Elam, and will destroy from thence the king and the princes, saith the LORD.

39 But it shall come to pass in the latter days, *that* I will bring again the captivity of Elam, saith the LORD.

50

1 The word that the LORD spake against Babylon *and* against the land of the Chaldeans by Jeremiah the prophet.

2 Declare ye among the nations, and publish, and set up a standard; publish, *and* conceal not: say, Babylon is taken, Bel is confounded, Merodach is broken in pieces; her idols are confounded, her images are broken in pieces.

3 For out of the north there cometh up a nation against her, which shall make her land desolate, and none shall dwell therein: they shall remove, they shall depart, both man and beast.

4 In those days, and in that time, saith the LORD, the children of Israel shall come, they and the children of Judah together, going and weeping: they shall go, and seek the LORD their God.

5 They shall ask the way to Zion with their faces thitherward, *saying*, Come, and let us join ourselves to the LORD in a

perpetual covenant *that* shall not be forgotten.
6 My people hath been lost sheep: their
shepherds have caused them to go astray,
they have turned them away *on* the mountains: they have gone from mountain to
hill, they have forgotten their restingplace.
7 All that found them have devoured
them: and their adversaries said, We offend
not, because they have sinned against the
LORD, the habitation of justice, even the
LORD, the hope of their fathers.
8 Remove out of the midst of Babylon,
and go forth out of the land of the Chaldeans, and be as the he goats before the
flocks.
9 For, lo, I will raise and cause to come
up against Babylon an assembly of great
nations from the north country: and they
shall set themselves in array against her;
from thence she shall be taken: their arrows *shall be* as of a mighty expert man;
none shall return in vain.
10 And Chaldea shall be a spoil: all that
spoil her shall be satisfied, saith the LORD.
11 Because ye were glad, because ye rejoiced, O ye destroyers of mine heritage,
because ye are grown fat as the heifer at
grass, and bellow as bulls;
12 Your mother shall be sore confounded; she that bare you shall be
ashamed: behold, the hindermost of the
nations *shall be* a wilderness, a dry land,
and a desert.
13 Because of the wrath of the LORD it
shall not be inhabited, but it shall be wholly desolate: every one that goeth by Babylon shall be astonished, and hiss at all
her plagues.
14 Put yourselves in array against Babylon round about: all ye that bend the bow,
shoot at her, spare no arrows: for she hath
sinned against the LORD.
15 Shout against her round about: she
hath given her hand: her foundations are
fallen, her walls are thrown down: for it *is*
the vengeance of the LORD: take vengeance
upon her; as she hath done, do unto her.
16 Cut off the sower from Babylon, and
him that handleth the sickle in the time
of harvest: for fear of the oppressing sword
they shall turn every one to his people, and
they shall flee every one to his own land.
17 Israel *is* a scattered sheep; the lions
have driven *him* away: first the king of Assyria hath devoured him; and last this
Nebuchadrezzar king of Babylon hath broken his bones.
18 Therefore thus saith the LORD of hosts,
the God of Israel; Behold, I will punish
the king of Babylon and his land, as I have
punished the king of Assyria.
19 And I will bring Israel again to his
habitation, and he shall feed on Carmel
and Bashan, and his soul shall be satisfied upon mount Ephraim and Gilead.
20 In those days, and in that time, saith
the LORD, the iniquity of Israel shall be
sought for, and *there shall be* none; and the
sins of Judah, and they shall not be found:
for I will pardon them whom I reserve.
21 Go up against the land of Merathaim,
even against it, and against the inhabitants
of Pekod: waste and utterly destroy after
them, saith the LORD, and do according to
all that I have commanded thee.
22 A sound of battle *is* in the land, and
of great destruction.
23 How is the hammer of the whole earth
cut asunder and broken! how is Babylon
become a desolation among the nations!
24 I have laid a snare for thee, and thou
art also taken, O Babylon, and thou wast
not aware: thou art found, and also caught,
because thou hast striven against the LORD.
25 The LORD hath opened his armoury,
and hath brought forth the weapons of
his indignation: for this *is* the work of the
Lord GOD of hosts in the land of the Chaldeans.
26 Come against her from the utmost
border, open her storehouses: cast her up
as heaps, and destroy her utterly: let nothing of her be left.
27 Slay all her bullocks; let them go down
to the slaughter: woe unto them! for their
day is come, the time of their visitation.
28 The voice of them that flee and escape
out of the land of Babylon, to declare in
Zion the vengeance of the LORD our God,
the vengeance of his temple.
29 Call together the archers against Babylon: all ye that bend the bow, camp
against it round about; let none thereof
escape: recompense her according to her
work; according to all that she hath done,
do unto her: for she hath been proud
against the LORD, against the Holy One of
Israel.
30 Therefore shall her young men fall in

the streets, and all her men of war shall be cut off in that day, saith the LORD.

31 Behold, I *am* against thee, *O thou* most proud, saith the Lord GOD of hosts: for thy day is come, the time *that* I will visit thee.

32 And the most proud shall stumble and fall, and none shall raise him up: and I will kindle a fire in his cities, and it shall devour all round about him.

33 Thus saith the LORD of hosts; The children of Israel and the children of Judah *were* oppressed together: and all that took them captives held them fast; they refused to let them go.

34 Their Redeemer *is* strong; the LORD of hosts *is* his name: he shall throughly plead their cause, that he may give rest to the land, and disquiet the inhabitants of Babylon.

35 A sword *is* upon the Chaldeans, saith the LORD, and upon the inhabitants of Babylon, and upon her princes, and upon her wise *men*.

36 A sword *is* upon the liars; and they shall dote: a sword *is* upon her mighty men; and they shall be dismayed.

37 A sword *is* upon their horses, and upon their chariots, and upon all the mingled people that *are* in the midst of her; and they shall become as women: a sword *is* upon her treasures; and they shall be robbed.

38 A drought *is* upon her waters; and they shall be dried up: for it *is* the land of graven images, and they are mad upon *their* idols.

39 Therefore the wild beasts of the desert with the wild beasts of the islands shall dwell *there,* and the owls shall dwell therein: and it shall be no more inhabited for ever; neither shall it be dwelt in from generation to generation.

40 As God overthrew Sodom and Gomorrah and the neighbour *cities* thereof, saith the LORD; *so* shall no man abide there, neither shall any son of man dwell therein.

41 Behold, a people shall come from the north, and a great nation, and many kings shall be raised up from the coasts of the earth.

42 They shall hold the bow and the lance: they *are* cruel, and will not shew mercy: their voice shall roar like the sea, and they shall ride upon horses, *every one* put in array, like a man to the battle, against thee, O daughter of Babylon.

43 The king of Babylon hath heard the report of them, and his hands waxed feeble: anguish took hold of him, *and* pangs as of a woman in travail.

44 Behold, he shall come up like a lion from the swelling of Jordan unto the habitation of the strong: but I will make them suddenly run away from her: and who *is* a chosen *man, that* I may appoint over her? for who *is* like me? and who will appoint me the time? and who *is* that shepherd that will stand before me?

45 Therefore hear ye the counsel of the LORD, that he hath taken against Babylon; and his purposes, that he hath purposed against the land of the Chaldeans: Surely the least of the flock shall draw them out: surely he shall make *their* habitation desolate with them.

46 At the noise of the taking of Babylon the earth is moved, and the cry is heard among the nations.

51

1 Thus saith the LORD; Behold, I will raise up against Babylon, and against them that dwell in the midst of them that rise up against me, a destroying wind;

2 And will send unto Babylon fanners, that shall fan her, and shall empty her land: for in the day of trouble they shall be against her round about.

3 Against *him that* bendeth let the archer bend his bow, and against *him that* lifteth himself up in his brigandine: and spare ye not her young men; destroy ye utterly all her host.

4 Thus the slain shall fall in the land of the Chaldeans, and *they that are* thrust through in her streets.

5 For Israel *hath* not *been* forsaken, nor Judah of his God, of the LORD of hosts; though their land was filled with sin against the Holy One of Israel.

6 Flee out of the midst of Babylon, and deliver every man his soul: be not cut off in her iniquity; for this *is* the time of the LORD'S vengeance; he will render unto her a recompence.

7 Babylon *hath been* a golden cup in the LORD'S hand, that made all the earth drunken: the nations have drunken of her wine; therefore the nations are mad.

8 Babylon is suddenly fallen and destroyed: howl for her; take balm for her pain, if so she may be healed.

9 We would have healed Babylon, but she

is not healed: forsake her, and let us go every one into his own country: for her judgment reacheth unto heaven, and is lifted up *even* to the skies.

10 The LORD hath brought forth our righteousness: come, and let us declare in Zion the work of the LORD our God.

51:10 Your Testimony
◄ Isaiah 62:6
Mark 5:18-19 ►

11 Make bright the arrows; gather the shields: the LORD hath raised up the spirit of the kings of the Medes: for his device *is* against Babylon, to destroy it; because it *is* the vengeance of the LORD, the vengeance of his temple.

12 Set up the standard upon the walls of Babylon, make the watch strong, set up the watchmen, prepare the ambushes: for the LORD hath both devised and done that which he spake against the inhabitants of Babylon.

13 O thou that dwellest upon many waters, abundant in treasures, thine end is come, *and* the measure of thy covetousness.

14 The LORD of hosts hath sworn by himself, *saying*, Surely I will fill thee with men, as with caterpillers; and they shall lift up a shout against thee.

15 He hath made the earth by his power, he hath established the world by his wisdom, and hath stretched out the heaven by his understanding.

16 When he uttereth *his* voice, *there is* a multitude of waters in the heavens; and he causeth the vapors to ascend from the ends of the earth: he maketh lightnings with rain, and bringeth forth the wind out of his treasures.

17 Every man is brutish by *his* knowledge; every founder is confounded by the graven image: for his molten image *is* falsehood, and *there is* no breath in them.

18 They *are* vanity, the work of errors: in the time of their visitation they shall perish.

19 The portion of Jacob *is* not like them; for he *is* the former of all things: and *Israel* *is* the rod of his inheritance: the LORD of hosts is his name.

20 Thou *art* my battle axe *and* weapons of war: for with thee will I break in pieces the nations, and with thee will I destroy kingdoms;

21 And with thee will I break in pieces the horse and his rider; and with thee will I break in pieces the chariot and his rider;

22 With thee also will I break in pieces man and woman; and with thee will I break in pieces old and young; and with thee will I break in pieces the young man and the maid;

23 I will also break in pieces with thee the shepherd and his flock; and with thee will I break in pieces the husbandman and his yoke of oxen; and with thee will I break in pieces captains and rulers.

24 And I will render unto Babylon and to all the inhabitants of Chaldea all their evil that they have done in Zion in your sight, saith the LORD.

25 Behold, I *am* against thee, O destroying mountain, saith the LORD, which destroyest all the earth: and I will stretch out mine hand upon thee, and roll thee down from the rocks, and will make thee a burnt mountain.

26 And they shall not take of thee a stone for a corner, nor a stone for foundations; but thou shalt be desolate for ever, saith the LORD.

27 Set ye up a standard in the land, blow the trumpet among the nations, prepare the nations against her, call together against her the kingdoms of Ararat, Minni, and Ashchenaz; appoint a captain against her; cause the horses to come up as the rough caterpillers.

28 Prepare against her the nations with the kings of the Medes, the captains thereof, and all the rulers thereof, and all the land of his dominion.

29 And the land shall tremble and sorrow: for every purpose of the LORD shall be performed against Babylon, to make the land of Babylon a desolation without an inhabitant.

30 The mighty men of Babylon have forborn to fight, they have remained in *their* holds: their might hath failed; they became as women: they have burned her dwellingplaces; her bars are broken.

51:30 Cost of Sin
◄ 1 Samuel 17:24
Mark 9:18 ►

31 One post shall run to meet another, and one messenger to meet another, to

shew the king of Babylon that his city is
taken at *one* end,
32And that the passages are stopped, and
the reeds they have burned with fire, and
the men of war are affrighted.
33For thus saith the LORD of hosts, the
God of Israel; The daughter of Babylon *is*
like a threshingfloor, *it is* time to thresh
her: yet a little while, and the time of her
harvest shall come.
34Nebuchadrezzar the king of Babylon
hath devoured me, he hath crushed me,
he hath made me an empty vessel, he hath
swallowed me up like a dragon, he hath
filled his belly with my delicates, he
hath cast me out.
35The violence done to me and to my
flesh *be* upon Babylon, shall the inhabitant of Zion say; and my blood upon the
inhabitants of Chaldea, shall Jerusalem
say.
36Therefore thus saith the LORD; Behold,
I will plead thy cause, and take vengeance
for thee; and I will dry up her sea, and
make her springs dry.
37And Babylon shall become heaps, a
dwelling place for dragons, an astonishment, and an hissing, without an inhabitant.
38They shall roar together like lions:
they shall yell as lions' whelps.
39In their heat I will make their feasts,
and I will make them drunken, that they
may rejoice, and sleep a perpetual sleep,
and not wake, saith the LORD.
40I will bring them down like lambs to
the slaughter, like rams with he goats.
41How is Sheshach taken! and how is
the praise of the whole earth surprised!
how is Babylon become an astonishment
among the nations!
42The sea is come up upon Babylon: she
is covered with the multitude of the waves
thereof.
43Her cities are a desolation, a dry land,
and a wilderness, a land wherein no man
dwelleth, neither doth *any* son of man pass
thereby.
44And I will punish Bel in Babylon, and
I will bring forth out of his mouth that
which he hath swallowed up: and the
nations shall not flow together any more
unto him: yea, the wall of Babylon shall
fall.
45My people, go ye out of the midst of
her, and deliver ye every man his soul from
the fierce anger of the LORD.
46And lest your heart faint, and ye fear
for the rumour that shall be heard in the
land; a rumour shall both come *one* year,
and after that in *another* year *shall come* a
rumour, and violence in the land, ruler
against ruler.
47Therefore, behold, the days come, that
I will do judgment upon the graven images of Babylon: and her whole land shall
be confounded, and all her slain shall fall
in the midst of her.
48Then the heaven and the earth, and
all that *is* therein, shall sing for Babylon:
for the spoilers shall come unto her from
the north, saith the LORD.
49As Babylon *hath caused* the slain of
Israel to fall, so at Babylon shall fall the
slain of all the earth.
50Ye that have escaped the sword, go
away, stand not still: remember the LORD
afar off, and let Jerusalem come into your
mind.
51We are confounded, because we have
heard reproach: shame hath covered our
faces: for strangers are come into the sanctuaries of the LORD'S house.
52Wherefore, behold, the days come,
saith the LORD, that I will do judgment
upon her graven images: and through all
her land the wounded shall groan.
53Though Babylon should mount up to
heaven, and though she should fortify the
height of her strength, *yet* from me shall
spoilers come unto her, saith the LORD.
54A sound of a cry *cometh* from Babylon,
and great destruction from the land of the
Chaldeans:
55Because the LORD hath spoiled Babylon, and destroyed out of her the great
voice; when her waves do roar like great
waters, a noise of their voice is uttered:
56Because the spoiler is come upon her,
even upon Babylon, and her mighty men
are taken, every one of their bows is broken: for the LORD God of recompences
shall surely requite.
57And I will make drunk her princes,
and her wise *men*, her captains, and her
rulers, and her mighty men: and they shall
sleep a perpetual sleep, and not wake, saith
the King, whose name *is* the LORD of hosts.
58Thus saith the LORD of hosts; The
broad walls of Babylon shall be utterly

broken, and her high gates shall be burned with fire; and the people shall labour in vain, and the folk in the fire, and they shall be weary.

59 The word which Jeremiah the prophet commanded Seraiah the son of Neriah, the son of Maaseiah, when he went with Zedekiah the king of Judah into Babylon in the fourth year of his reign. And *this* Seraiah *was* a quiet prince.

60 So Jeremiah wrote in a book all the evil that should come upon Babylon, *even* all these words that are written against Babylon.

61 And Jeremiah said to Seraiah, When thou comest to Babylon, and shalt see, and shalt read all these words;

62 Then shalt thou say, O LORD, thou hast spoken against this place, to cut it off, that none shall remain in it, neither man nor beast, but that it shall be desolate for ever.

63 And it shall be, when thou hast made an end of reading this book, *that* thou shalt bind a stone to it, and cast it into the midst of Euphrates:

64 And thou shalt say, Thus shall Babylon sink, and shall not rise from the evil that I will bring upon her: and they shall be weary. Thus far *are* the words of Jeremiah.

52

1 Zedekiah *was* one and twenty years old when he began to reign, and he reigned eleven years in Jerusalem. And his mother's name *was* Hamutal the daughter of Jeremiah of Libnah.

2 And he did *that which was* evil in the eyes of the LORD, according to all that Jehoiakim had done.

3 For through the anger of the LORD it came to pass in Jerusalem and Judah, till he had cast them out from his presence, that Zedekiah rebelled against the king of Babylon.

4 And it came to pass in the ninth year of his reign, in the tenth month, in the tenth *day* of the month, *that* Nebuchadrezzar king of Babylon came, he and all his army, against Jerusalem, and pitched against it, and built forts against it round about.

5 So the city was besieged unto the eleventh year of king Zedekiah.

6 And in the fourth month, in the ninth *day* of the month, the famine was sore in the city, so that there was no bread for the people of the land.

7 Then the city was broken up, and all the men of war fled, and went forth out of the city by night by the way of the gate between the two walls, which *was* by the king's garden; (now the Chaldeans *were* by the city round about:) and they went by the way of the plain.

8 But the army of the Chaldeans pursued after the king, and overtook Zedekiah in the plains of Jericho; and all his army was scattered from him.

9 Then they took the king, and carried him up unto the king of Babylon to Riblah in the land of Hamath; where he gave judgment upon him.

10 And the king of Babylon slew the sons of Zedekiah before his eyes: he slew also all the princes of Judah in Riblah.

11 Then he put out the eyes of Zedekiah; and the king of Babylon bound him in chains, and carried him to Babylon, and put him in prison till the day of his death.

12 Now in the fifth month, in the tenth *day* of the month, which *was* the nineteenth year of Nebuchadrezzar king of Babylon, came Nebuzar-adan, captain of the guard, *which* served the king of Babylon, into Jerusalem,

13 And burned the house of the LORD, and the king's house; and all the houses of Jerusalem, and all the houses of the great *men*, burned he with fire:

14 And all the army of the Chaldeans, that *were* with the captain of the guard, brake down all the walls of Jerusalem round about.

15 Then Nebuzar-adan the captain of the guard carried away captive *certain* of the poor of the people, and the residue of the people that remained in the city, and those that fell away, that fell to the king of Babylon, and the rest of the multitude.

16 But Nebuzar-adan the captain of the guard left *certain* of the poor of the land for vinedressers and for husbandmen.

17 Also the pillars of brass that *were* in the house of the LORD, and the bases, and the brasen sea that *was* in the house of the LORD, the Chaldeans brake, and carried all the brass of them to Babylon.

18 The caldrons also, and the shovels, and the snuffers, and the bowls, and the spoons, and all the vessels of brass wherewith they ministered, took they away.

19 And the basons, and the firepans, and

the bowls, and the caldrons, and the
candlesticks, and the spoons, and the cups;
that which *was* of gold *in* gold, and *that*
which *was* of silver *in* silver, took the captain of the guard away.
20The two pillars, one sea, and twelve
brasen bulls that *were* under the bases,
which king Solomon had made in the
house of the LORD: the brass of all these
vessels was without weight.
21And *concerning* the pillars, the height
of one pillar *was* eighteen cubits; and a fil-
let of twelve cubits did compass it; and the
thickness thereof *was* four fingers: *it was*
hollow.
22And a chapiter of brass *was* upon it;
and the height of one chapiter *was* five
cubits, with network and pomegranates
upon the chapiters round about, all *of*
brass. The second pillar also and the pomegranates *were* like unto these.
23And there were ninety and six pomegranates on a side; *and* all the pomegranates upon the network *were* an hundred
round about.
24And the captain of the guard took Seraiah the chief priest, and Zephaniah the
second priest, and the three keepers of the
door:
25He took also out of the city an eunuch,
which had the charge of the men of war;
and seven men of them that were near the
king's person, which were found in the
city; and the principal scribe of the host,
who mustered the people of the land; and
threescore men of the people of the land,
that were found in the midst of the city.
26So Nebuzar-adan the captain of the
guard took them, and brought them to the
king of Babylon to Riblah.
27And the king of Babylon smote them,
and put them to death in Riblah in the
land of Hamath. Thus Judah was carried
away captive out of his own land.
28This *is* the people whom Nebuchadrezzar carried away captive: in the seventh
year three thousand Jews and three and
twenty:
29In the eighteenth year of Nebuchadrezzar he carried away captive from Jerusalem eight hundred thirty and two
persons:
30In the three and twentieth year of
Nebuchadrezzar Nebuzar-adan the captain
of the guard carried away captive of the
Jews seven hundred forty and five persons:
all the persons *were* four thousand and six
hundred.
31And it came to pass in the seven and
thirtieth year of the captivity of Jehoiachin
king of Judah, in the twelfth month, in the
five and twentieth *day* of the month, *that*
Evil-merodach king of Babylon in the *first*
year of his reign lifted up the head of Jehoiachin king of Judah, and brought him
forth out of prison,
32And spake kindly unto him, and set
his throne above the throne of the kings
that *were* with him in Babylon,
33And changed his prison garments: and
he did continually eat bread before him
all the days of his life.
34And *for* his diet, there was a continual
diet given him of the king of Babylon, every day a portion until the day of his death,
all the days of his life.

Lamentations

AUTHOR
Jeremiah the prophet

MAIN POINT
Disobedience is a sure path to disaster, bringing suffering to God's people and to God himself.

DATE WRITTEN
586 B.C., soon after the fall of Jerusalem

5 CHAPTERS

MAIN PEOPLE

Jeremiah, the people of Jerusalem

SPECIAL FEATURES

- *Was written in the style of ancient Jewish funeral songs and is a sad song for a once-great city*
- *Talks a lot about crying, yet has a strong message of hope*
- *Describes how God used Babylon, despite its own sin, to judge the people of Judah*
- *Third book of the Major Prophets*

HOW THE BOOK GOT ITS NAME

A lament is an expression of grief, protest, complaint, or prayer for rescue. This book includes all of those pieces.

1
1How doth the city sit solitary, *that was*
full of people *how* is she become as a widow she *that was* great among the nations,
and princess among the provinces, *how* is
she become tributary
2She weepeth sore in the night, and her
tears *are* on her cheeks: among all her lovers she hath none to comfort *her:* all her
friends have dealt treacherously with her,
they are become her enemies.
3Judah is gone into captivity because of
affliction, and because of great servitude:
she dwelleth among the heathen, she
findeth no rest: all her persecutors overtook her between the straits.
4The ways of Zion do mourn, because
none come to the solemn feasts: all her
gates are desolate: her priests sigh, her virgins are afflicted, and she *is* in bitterness.
5Her adversaries are the chief, her enemies prosper; for the LORD hath afflicted
her for the multitude of her transgressions:
her children are gone into captivity before
the enemy.
6And from the daughter of Zion all her
beauty is departed: her princes are become
like harts *that* find no pasture, and they are
gone without strength before the pursuer.
7Jerusalem remembered in the days of
her affliction and of her miseries all her
pleasant things that she had in the days of
old, when her people fell into the hand of
the enemy, and none did help her: the
adversaries saw her, *and* did mock at her
sabbaths.
8Jerusalem hath grievously sinned;
therefore she is removed: all that honoured
her despise her, because they have seen her

nakedness: yea, she sigheth, and turneth
backward.
9Her filthiness *is* in her skirts; she
remembereth not her last end; therefore
she came down wonderfully: she had no
comforter. O LORD, behold my affliction:
for the enemy hath magnified *himself.*
10The adversary hath spread out his
hand upon all her pleasant things: for she
hath seen *that* the heathen entered into her
sanctuary, whom thou didst command *that*
they should not enter into thy congregation.
11All her people sigh, they seek bread;
they have given their pleasant things for
meat to relieve the soul: see, O LORD, and
consider; for I am become vile.
12*Is it* nothing to you, all ye that pass
by? behold, and see if there be any sorrow
like unto my sorrow, which is done unto
me, wherewith the LORD hath afflicted *me*
in the day of his fierce anger.
13From above hath he sent fire into my
bones, and it prevaileth against them: he
hath spread a net for my feet, he hath
turned me back: he hath made me desolate *and* faint all the day.
14The yoke of my transgressions is
bound by his hand: they are wreathed, *and*
come up upon my neck: he hath made my
strength to fall, the Lord hath delivered me
into *their* hands, *from whom* I am not able
to rise up.
15The Lord hath trodden under foot all
my mighty *men* in the midst of me: he hath
called an assembly against me to crush my
young men: the Lord hath trodden the
virgin, the daughter of Judah, *as* in a winepress.
16For these *things* I weep; mine eye, mine
eye runneth down with water, because the
comforter that should relieve my soul is
far from me: my children are desolate, because the enemy prevailed.
17Zion spreadeth forth her hands, *and*
there is none to comfort her: the LORD hath
commanded concerning Jacob, *that* his adversaries *should be* round about him: Jerusalem is as a menstruous woman among
them.
18The LORD is righteous; for I have rebelled against his commandment: hear, I
pray you, all people, and behold my sorrow: my virgins and my young men are
gone into captivity.
19I called for my lovers, *but* they deceived
me: my priests and mine elders gave up
the ghost in the city, while they sought
their meat to relieve their souls.
20Behold, O LORD; for I *am* in distress:
my bowels are troubled; mine heart is
turned within me; for I have grievously
rebelled: abroad the sword bereaveth, at
home *there is* as death.
21They have heard that I sigh: *there is*
none to comfort me: all mine enemies
have heard of my trouble; they are glad
that thou hast done *it:* thou wilt bring the
day *that* thou hast called, and they shall
be like unto me.
22Let all their wickedness come before
thee; and do unto them, as thou hast done
unto me for all my transgressions: for my
sighs *are* many, and my heart *is* faint.

2

1How hath the Lord covered the daughter of Zion with a cloud in his anger, *and*
cast down from heaven unto the earth the
beauty of Israel, and remembered not his
footstool in the day of his anger!
2The Lord hath swallowed up all the
habitations of Jacob, and hath not pitied:
he hath thrown down in his wrath the
strong holds of the daughter of Judah; he
hath brought *them* down to the ground:
he hath polluted the kingdom and the
princes thereof.
3He hath cut off in *his* fierce anger all
the horn of Israel: he hath drawn back his
right hand from before the enemy, and he
burned against Jacob like a flaming fire,
which devoureth round about.
4He hath bent his bow like an enemy:
he stood with his right hand as an adversary, and slew all *that were* pleasant to the
eye in the tabernacle of the daughter of
Zion: he poured out his fury like fire.
5The Lord was as an enemy: he hath
swallowed up Israel, he hath swallowed up
all her palaces: he hath destroyed his
strong holds, and hath increased in the
daughter of Judah mourning and lamentation.
6And he hath violently taken away his
tabernacle, as *if it were of* a garden: he hath
destroyed his places of the assembly: the
LORD hath caused the solemn feasts and
sabbaths to be forgotten in Zion, and hath
despised in the indignation of his anger
the king and the priest.
7The Lord hath cast off his altar, he hath

abhorred his sanctuary, he hath given up into the hand of the enemy the walls of her palaces; they have made a noise in the house of the LORD, as in the day of a solemn feast.

8 The LORD hath purposed to destroy the wall of the daughter of Zion: he hath stretched out a line, he hath not withdrawn his hand from destroying: therefore he made the rampart and the wall to lament; they languished together.

9 Her gates are sunk into the ground; he hath destroyed and broken her bars: her king and her princes *are* among the Gentiles: the law *is* no *more;* her prophets also find no vision from the LORD.

10 The elders of the daughter of Zion sit upon the ground, *and* keep silence: they have cast up dust upon their heads; they have girded themselves with sackcloth: the virgins of Jerusalem hang down their heads to the ground.

11 Mine eyes do fail with tears, my bowels are troubled, my liver is poured upon the earth, for the destruction of the daughter of my people; because the children and the sucklings swoon in the streets of the city.

12 They say to their mothers, Where *is* corn and wine? when they swooned as the wounded in the streets of the city, when their soul was poured out into their mothers' bosom.

13 What thing shall I take to witness for thee? what thing shall I liken to thee, O daughter of Jerusalem? what shall I equal to thee, that I may comfort thee, O virgin daughter of Zion? for thy breach *is* great like the sea: who can heal thee?

14 Thy prophets have seen vain and foolish things for thee: and they have not discovered thine iniquity, to turn away thy captivity; but have seen for thee false burdens and causes of banishment.

15 All that pass by clap *their* hands at thee; they hiss and wag their head at the daughter of Jerusalem, *saying, Is* this the city that *men* call The perfection of beauty, The joy of the whole earth?

16 All thine enemies have opened their mouth against thee: they hiss and gnash the teeth: they say, We have swallowed *her* up: certainly this *is* the day that we looked for; we have found, we have seen *it.*

17 The LORD hath done *that* which he had devised; he hath fulfilled his word that he had commanded in the days of old: he hath thrown down, and hath not pitied: and he hath caused *thine* enemy to rejoice over thee, he hath set up the horn of thine adversaries.

18 Their heart cried unto the Lord, O wall of the daughter of Zion, let tears run down like a river day and night: give thyself no rest; let not the apple of thine eye cease.

19 Arise, cry out in the night: in the beginning of the watches pour out thine heart like water before the face of the Lord: lift up thy hands toward him for the life of thy young children, that faint for hunger in the top of every street.

20 Behold, O LORD, and consider to whom thou hast done this. Shall the women eat their fruit, *and* children of a span long? shall the priest and the prophet be slain in the sanctuary of the Lord?

21 The young and the old lie on the ground in the streets: my virgins and my young men are fallen by the sword; thou hast slain *them* in the day of thine anger; thou hast killed, *and* not pitied.

22 Thou hast called as in a solemn day my terrors round about, so that in the day of the LORD'S anger none escaped nor remained: those that I have swaddled and brought up hath mine enemy consumed.

3

1 I *am* the man *that* hath seen affliction by the rod of his wrath.

2 He hath led me, and brought *me into* darkness, but not *into* light.

3 Surely against me is he turned; he turneth his hand *against me* all the day.

4 My flesh and my skin hath he made old; he hath broken my bones.

5 He hath builded against me, and compassed *me* with gall and travail.

6 He hath set me in dark places, as *they that be* dead of old.

7 He hath hedged me about, that I cannot get out: he hath made my chain heavy.

8 Also when I cry and shout, he shutteth out my prayer.

9 He hath inclosed my ways with hewn stone, he hath made my paths crooked.

10 He *was* unto me *as* a bear lying in wait, *and as* a lion in secret places.

11 He hath turned aside my ways, and pulled me in pieces: he hath made me desolate.

12He hath bent his bow, and set me as a mark for the arrow.

13He hath caused the arrows of his quiver to enter into my reins.

14I was a derision to all my people; *and* their song all the day.

15He hath filled me with bitterness, he hath made me drunken with wormwood.

16He hath also broken my teeth with gravel stones, he hath covered me with ashes.

17And thou hast removed my soul far off from peace: I forgat prosperity.

18And I said, My strength and my hope is perished from the LORD:

19Remembering mine affliction and my misery, the wormwood and the gall.

20My soul hath *them* still in remembrance, and is humbled in me.

21This I recall to my mind, therefore have I hope.

22*It is of* the LORD'S mercies that we are not consumed, because his compassions fail not.

3:22-23 God's Mercy
◄ Psalm 119:64
Joel 2:13 ►

23*They are* new every morning: great *is* thy faithfulness.

24The LORD *is* my portion, saith my soul; therefore will I hope in him.

25The LORD *is* good unto them that wait for him, to the soul *that* seeketh him.

3:25 Waiting
◄ Isaiah 33:2
Luke 2:25 ►

26*It is* good that *a man* should both hope and quietly wait for the salvation of the LORD.

27*It is* good for a man that he bear the yoke in his youth.

3:27 For Kids Only
◄ Ecclesiastes 11:9
1 Timothy 4:12 ►

28He sitteth alone and keepeth silence, because he hath borne *it* upon him.

29He putteth his mouth in the dust; if so be there may be hope.

30He giveth *his* cheek to him that smiteth him: he is filled full with reproach.

31For the Lord will not cast off for ever:

32But though he cause grief, yet will he have compassion according to the multitude of his mercies.

33For he doth not afflict willingly nor grieve the children of men.

34To crush under his feet all the prisoners of the earth,

35To turn aside the right of a man before the face of the most High,

36To subvert a man in his cause, the Lord approveth not.

37Who *is* he *that* saith, and it cometh to pass, *when* the Lord commandeth *it* not?

38Out of the mouth of the most High proceedeth not evil and good?

39Wherefore doth a living man complain, a man for the punishment of his sins?

40Let us search and try our ways, and turn again to the LORD.

3:40 Self-examination
◄ Matthew 7:5 ►

41Let us lift up our heart with *our* hands unto God in the heavens.

42We have transgressed and have rebelled: thou hast not pardoned.

43Thou hast covered with anger, and persecuted us: thou hast slain, thou hast not pitied.

44Thou hast covered thyself with a cloud, that *our* prayer should not pass through.

45Thou hast made us *as* the offscouring and refuse in the midst of the people.

46All our enemies have opened their mouths against us.

47Fear and a snare is come upon us, desolation and destruction.

48Mine eye runneth down with rivers of water for the destruction of the daughter of my people.

49Mine eye trickleth down, and ceaseth not, without any intermission,

50Till the LORD look down, and behold from heaven.

51Mine eye affecteth mine heart because of all the daughters of my city.

52Mine enemies chased me sore, like a bird, without cause.

53They have cut off my life in the dungeon, and cast a stone upon me.

54Waters flowed over mine head; *then* I said, I am cut off.

55I called upon thy name, O LORD, out of the low dungeon.

56Thou hast heard my voice: hide not thine ear at my breathing, at my cry.

57 Thou drewest near in the day *that* I
called upon thee: thou saidst, Fear not.
58 O Lord, thou hast pleaded the causes
of my soul; thou hast redeemed my life.
59 O LORD, thou hast seen my wrong:
judge thou my cause.
60 Thou hast seen all their vengeance *and*
all their imaginations against me.
61 Thou hast heard their reproach,
O LORD, *and* all their imaginations against
me;
62 The lips of those that rose up against
me, and their device against me all the
day.
63 Behold their sitting down, and their
rising up; I *am* their musick.
64 Render unto them a recompence,
O LORD, according to the work of their
hands.
65 Give them sorrow of heart, thy curse
unto them.
66 Persecute and destroy them in anger
from under the heavens of the LORD.

4

1 How is the gold become dim! *how* is
the most fine gold changed! the stones of
the sanctuary are poured out in the top of
every street.
2 The precious sons of Zion, comparable
to fine gold, how are they esteemed as
earthen pitchers, the work of the hands of
the potter!
3 Even the sea monsters draw out the
breast, they give suck to their young ones:
the daughter of my people *is become* cruel,
like the ostriches in the wilderness.
4 The tongue of the sucking child cleaveth
to the roof of his mouth for thirst: the
young children ask bread, *and* no man
breaketh *it* unto them.
5 They that did feed delicately are desolate in the streets: they that were brought
up in scarlet embrace dunghills.
6 For the punishment of the iniquity of
the daughter of my people is greater than
the punishment of the sin of Sodom, that
was overthrown as in a moment, and no
hands stayed on her.
7 Her Nazarites were purer than snow,
they were whiter than milk, they were
more ruddy in body than rubies, their
polishing *was* of sapphire:
8 Their visage is blacker than a coal; they
are not known in the streets: their skin
cleaveth to their bones; it is withered, it is
become like a stick.
9 *They that be* slain with the sword are
better than *they that be* slain with hunger:
for these pine away, stricken through for
want of the fruits of the field.
10 The hands of the pitiful women have
sodden their own children: they were their
meat in the destruction of the daughter of
my people.
11 The LORD hath accomplished his fury;
he hath poured out his fierce anger, and
hath kindled a fire in Zion, and it hath
devoured the foundations thereof.
12 The kings of the earth, and all the inhabitants of the world, would not have
believed that the adversary and the enemy
should have entered into the gates of Jerusalem.
13 For the sins of her prophets, *and* the
iniquities of her priests, that have shed the
blood of the just in the midst of her,
14 They have wandered *as* blind *men* in
the streets, they have polluted themselves
with blood, so that men could not touch
their garments.
15 They cried unto them, Depart ye; *it is*
unclean; depart, depart, touch not: when
they fled away and wandered, they said
among the heathen, They shall no more
sojourn *there.*
16 The anger of the LORD hath divided
them; he will no more regard them: they
respected not the persons of the priests,
they favoured not the elders.
17 As for us, our eyes as yet failed for our
vain help: in our watching we have watched
for a nation *that* could not save *us.*
18 They hunt our steps, that we cannot
go in our streets: our end is near, our days
are fulfilled; for our end is come.
19 Our persecutors are swifter than the
eagles of the heaven: they pursued us upon
the mountains, they laid wait for us in the
wilderness.
20 The breath of our nostrils, the anointed of the LORD, was taken in their pits, of
whom we said, Under his shadow we shall
live among the heathen.
21 Rejoice and be glad, O daughter of
Edom, that dwellest in the land of Uz; the
cup also shall pass through unto thee: thou
shalt be drunken, and shalt make thyself
naked.
22 The punishment of thine iniquity is
accomplished, O daughter of Zion; he will
no more carry thee away into captivity: he

will visit thine iniquity, O daughter of Edom; he will discover thy sins.

5

1 Remember, O LORD, what is come upon us: consider, and behold our reproach.

2 Our inheritance is turned to strangers, our houses to aliens.

3 We are orphans and fatherless, our mothers *are* as widows.

4 We have drunken our water for money; our wood is sold unto us.

5 Our necks *are* under persecution: we labour, *and* have no rest.

5:5
Bullies
◄ Jeremiah 15:15 ►

6 We have given the hand *to* the Egyptians, *and to* the Assyrians, to be satisfied with bread.

7 Our fathers have sinned, *and are* not; and we have borne their iniquities.

8 Servants have ruled over us: *there is* none that doth deliver *us* out of their hand.

9 We gat our bread with *the peril of* our lives because of the sword of the wilderness.

10 Our skin was black like an oven because of the terrible famine.

11 They ravished the women in Zion, *and* the maids in the cities of Judah.

12 Princes are hanged up by their hand: the faces of elders were not honoured.

5:12
Old People
◄ Job 30:1 ►

13 They took the young men to grind, and the children fell under the wood.

14 The elders have ceased from the gate, the young men from their musick.

15 The joy of our heart is ceased; our dance is turned into mourning.

16 The crown is fallen *from* our head: woe unto us, that we have sinned!

17 For this our heart is faint; for these *things* our eyes are dim.

18 Because of the mountain of Zion, which is desolate, the foxes walk upon it.

19 Thou, O LORD, remainest for ever; thy throne from generation to generation.

20 Wherefore dost thou forget us for ever, *and* forsake us so long time?

21 Turn thou us unto thee, O LORD, and we shall be turned; renew our days as of old.

22 But thou hast utterly rejected us; thou art very wroth against us.

Ezekiel

AUTHOR
Ezekiel the prophet

MAIN POINT
God judges his own people and all the nations, but he will eventually provide the way of salvation.

DATE WRITTEN
Approximately 571 B.C.

48 CHAPTERS

MAIN PEOPLE

Ezekiel, Israel's leaders, Ezekiel's wife, King Nebuchadnezzar, "the Prince"

SPECIAL FEATURES

- *Describes Ezekiel's wild vision when God called him to be a messenger*
- *Tells how Ezekiel communicated his messages as a street preacher in Babylon*
- *Speaks of replacing the sinner's "heart of stone" with a "heart of flesh"*
- *Tells all about the amazing deeds that God asked Ezekiel to do, including lying on his side for 390 days*
- *Fourth book of the Major Prophets*

HOW THE BOOK GOT ITS NAME

The author and main person of the book is Ezekiel, a prophet to the people of Judah who were taken captive to Babylonia.

1

1 Now it came to pass in the thirtieth
year, in the fourth *month,* in the fifth *day*
of the month, as I *was* among the captives
by the river of Chebar, *that* the heavens
were opened, and I saw visions of God.
2 In the fifth *day* of the month, which
was the fifth year of king Jehoiachin's captivity,
3 The word of the LORD came expressly
unto Ezekiel the priest, the son of Buzi, in
the land of the Chaldeans by the river
Chebar; and the hand of the LORD was
there upon him.
4 And I looked, and, behold, a whirlwind
came out of the north, a great cloud, and
a fire infolding itself, and a brightness *was*
about it, and out of the midst thereof as
the colour of amber, out of the midst of
the fire.
5 Also out of the midst thereof *came* the
likeness of four living creatures. And this
was their appearance; they had the likeness
of a man.
6 And every one had four faces, and every one had four wings.
7 And their feet *were* straight feet; and the
sole of their feet *was* like the sole of a calf's
foot: and they sparkled like the colour of
burnished brass.
8 And *they had* the hands of a man under their wings on their four sides; and
they four had their faces and their wings.

9 Their wings *were* joined one to another; they turned not when they went; they went every one straight forward.

10 As for the likeness of their faces, they four had the face of a man, and the face of a lion, on the right side: and they four had the face of an ox on the left side; they four also had the face of an eagle.

11 Thus *were* their faces: and their wings *were* stretched upward; two *wings* of every one *were* joined one to another, and two covered their bodies.

12 And they went every one straight forward: whither the spirit was to go, they went; *and* they turned not when they went.

1:12 One Goal
◄ Proverbs 4:27
Luke 9:62 ►

13 As for the likeness of the living creatures, their appearance *was* like burning coals of fire, *and* like the appearance of lamps: it went up and down among the living creatures; and the fire was bright, and out of the fire went forth lightning.

14 And the living creatures ran and returned as the appearance of a flash of lightning.

15 Now as I beheld the living creatures, behold one wheel upon the earth by the living creatures, with his four faces.

16 The appearance of the wheels and their work *was* like unto the colour of a beryl: and they four had one likeness: and their appearance and their work *was* as it were a wheel in the middle of a wheel.

17 When they went, they went upon their four sides: *and* they turned not when they went.

18 As for their rings, they were so high that they were dreadful; and their rings *were* full of eyes round about them four.

19 And when the living creatures went, the wheels went by them: and when the living creatures were lifted up from the earth, the wheels were lifted up.

20 Whithersoever the spirit was to go, they went, thither *was their* spirit to go; and the wheels were lifted up over against them: for the spirit of the living creature *was* in the wheels.

21 When those went, *these* went; and when those stood, *these* stood; and when those were lifted up from the earth, the wheels were lifted up over against them: for the spirit of the living creature *was* in the wheels.

22 And the likeness of the firmament upon the heads of the living creature *was* as the colour of the terrible crystal, stretched forth over their heads above.

23 And under the firmament *were* their wings straight, the one toward the other: every one had two, which covered on this side, and every one had two, which covered on that side, their bodies.

24 And when they went, I heard the noise of their wings, like the noise of great waters, as the voice of the Almighty, the voice of speech, as the noise of an host: when they stood, they let down their wings.

25 And there was a voice from the firmament that *was* over their heads, when they stood, *and* had let down their wings.

26 And above the firmament that *was* over their heads *was* the likeness of a throne, as the appearance of a sapphire stone: and upon the likeness of the throne *was* the likeness as the appearance of a man above upon it.

27 And I saw as the colour of amber, as the appearance of fire round about within it, from the appearance of his loins even upward, and from the appearance of his loins even downward, I saw as it were the appearance of fire, and it had brightness round about.

28 As the appearance of the bow that is in the cloud in the day of rain, so *was* the appearance of the brightness round about. This *was* the appearance of the likeness of the glory of the LORD. And when I saw *it*, I fell upon my face, and I heard a voice of one that spake.

2

1 And he said unto me, Son of man, stand upon thy feet, and I will speak unto thee.

2 And the spirit entered into me when he spake unto me, and set me upon my feet, that I heard him that spake unto me.

3 And he said unto me, Son of man, I send thee to the children of Israel, to a rebellious nation that hath rebelled against me: they and their fathers have transgressed against me, *even* unto this very day.

4 For *they are* impudent children and stiffhearted. I do send thee unto them; and thou shalt say unto them, Thus saith the Lord GOD.

5 And they, whether they will hear, or

whether they will forbear, (for they *are* a rebellious house,) yet shall know that there hath been a prophet among them.

6And thou, son of man, be not afraid of them, neither be afraid of their words, though briers and thorns *be* with thee, and thou dost dwell among scorpions: be not afraid of their words, nor be dismayed at their looks, though they *be* a rebellious house.

7And thou shalt speak my words unto them, whether they will hear, or whether they will forbear: for they *are* most rebellious.

8But thou, son of man, hear what I say unto thee; Be not thou rebellious like that rebellious house: open thy mouth, and eat that I give thee.

9And when I looked, behold, an hand *was* sent unto me; and, lo, a roll of a book *was* therein;

10And he spread it before me; and it *was* written within and without: and *there was* written therein lamentations, and mourning, and woe.

3

1Moreover he said unto me, Son of man, eat that thou findest; eat this roll, and go speak unto the house of Israel.

2So I opened my mouth, and he caused me to eat that roll.

3And he said unto me, Son of man, cause thy belly to eat, and fill thy bowels with this roll that I give thee. Then did I eat *it;* and it was in my mouth as honey for sweetness.

4And he said unto me, Son of man, go, get thee unto the house of Israel, and speak with my words unto them.

5For thou *art* not sent to a people of a strange speech and of an hard language, *but* to the house of Israel;

6Not to many people of a strange speech and of an hard language, whose words thou canst not understand. Surely, had I sent thee to them, they would have hearkened unto thee.

7But the house of Israel will not hearken unto thee; for they will not hearken unto me: for all the house of Israel *are* impudent and hardhearted.

8Behold, I have made thy face strong against their faces, and thy forehead strong against their foreheads.

9As an adamant harder than flint have I made thy forehead: fear them not, neither be dismayed at their looks, though they *be* a rebellious house.

10Moreover he said unto me, Son of man, all my words that I shall speak unto thee receive in thine heart, and hear with thine ears.

11And go, get thee to them of the captivity, unto the children of thy people, and speak unto them, and tell them, Thus saith the Lord GOD; whether they will hear, or whether they will forbear.

12Then the spirit took me up, and I heard behind me a voice of a great rushing, *saying,* Blessed *be* the glory of the LORD from his place.

13*I heard* also the noise of the wings of the living creatures that touched one another, and the noise of the wheels over against them, and a noise of a great rushing.

14So the spirit lifted me up, and took me away, and I went in bitterness, in the heat of my spirit; but the hand of the LORD was strong upon me.

15Then I came to them of the captivity at Tel-abib, that dwelt by the river of Chebar, and I sat where they sat, and remained there astonished among them seven days.

16And it came to pass at the end of seven days, that the word of the LORD came unto me, saying,

17Son of man, I have made thee a watchman unto the house of Israel: therefore hear the word at my mouth, and give them warning from me.

18When I say unto the wicked, Thou shalt surely die; and thou givest him not warning, nor speakest to warn the wicked from his wicked way, to save his life; the same wicked *man* shall die in his iniquity; but his blood will I require at thine hand.

19Yet if thou warn the wicked, and he turn not from his wickedness, nor from his wicked way, he shall die in his iniquity; but thou hast delivered thy soul.

20Again, When a righteous *man* doth turn from his righteousness, and commit iniquity, and I lay a stumblingblock before him, he shall die: because thou hast not given him warning, he shall die in his sin, and his righteousness which he hath done shall not be remembered; but his blood will I require at thine hand.

21Nevertheless if thou warn the righ-

teous *man,* that the righteous sin not, and
he doth not sin, he shall surely live, because he is warned; also thou hast delivered thy soul.
22And the hand of the LORD was there
upon me; and he said unto me, Arise, go
forth into the plain, and I will there talk
with thee.
23Then I arose, and went forth into the
plain: and, behold, the glory of the LORD
stood there, as the glory which I saw by
the river of Chebar: and I fell on my face.
24Then the spirit entered into me, and
set me upon my feet, and spake with me,
and said unto me, Go, shut thyself within
thine house.
25But thou, O son of man, behold, they
shall put bands upon thee, and shall bind
thee with them, and thou shalt not go out
among them:
26And I will make thy tongue cleave to
the roof of thy mouth, that thou shalt be
dumb, and shalt not be to them a reprover:
for they *are* a rebellious house.
27But when I speak with thee, I will open
thy mouth, and thou shalt say unto them,
Thus saith the Lord GOD; He that heareth,
let him hear; and he that forbeareth, let
him forbear: for they *are* a rebellious
house.

4
1Thou also, son of man, take thee a tile,
and lay it before thee, and pourtray upon
it the city, *even* Jerusalem:
2And lay siege against it, and build a fort
against it, and cast a mount against it; set
the camp also against it, and set *battering*
rams against it round about.
3Moreover take thou unto thee an iron
pan, and set it *for* a wall of iron between
thee and the city: and set thy face against
it, and it shall be besieged, and thou shalt
lay siege against it. This *shall be* a sign to
the house of Israel.
4Lie thou also upon thy left side, and
lay the iniquity of the house of Israel upon
it: *according* to the number of the days that
thou shalt lie upon it thou shalt bear their
iniquity.
5For I have laid upon thee the years of
their iniquity, according to the number of
the days, three hundred and ninety days:
so shalt thou bear the iniquity of the house
of Israel.
6And when thou hast accomplished
them, lie again on thy right side, and thou
shalt bear the iniquity of the house of Judah forty days: I have appointed thee each
day for a year.
7Therefore thou shalt set thy face toward
the siege of Jerusalem, and thine arm *shall*
be uncovered, and thou shalt prophesy
against it.
8And, behold, I will lay bands upon
thee, and thou shalt not turn thee from
one side to another, till thou hast ended
the days of thy siege.
9Take thou also unto thee wheat, and
barley, and beans, and lentiles, and mil-
let, and fitches, and put them in one vessel, and make thee bread thereof, *according*
to the number of the days that thou shalt
lie upon thy side, three hundred and ninety days shalt thou eat thereof.
10And thy meat which thou shalt eat
shall be by weight, twenty shekels a day:
from time to time shalt thou eat it.
11Thou shalt drink also water by measure, the sixth part of an hin: from time to
time shalt thou drink.
12And thou shalt eat it *as* barley cakes,
and thou shalt bake it with dung that
cometh out of man, in their sight.
13And the LORD said, Even thus shall the
children of Israel eat their defiled bread
among the Gentiles, whither I will drive
them.
14Then said I, Ah Lord GOD! behold, my
soul hath not been polluted: for from my
youth up even till now have I not eaten of
that which dieth of itself, or is torn in
pieces; neither came there abominable
flesh into my mouth.
15Then he said unto me, Lo, I have giv-
en thee cow's dung for man's dung, and
thou shalt prepare thy bread therewith.
16Moreover he said unto me, Son of
man, behold, I will break the staff of bread
in Jerusalem: and they shall eat bread by
weight, and with care; and they shall drink
water by measure, and with astonishment:
17That they may want bread and water,
and be astonied one with another, and
consume away for their iniquity.

5
1And thou, son of man, take thee a sharp
knife, take thee a barber's razor, and cause
it to pass upon thine head and upon thy
beard: then take thee balances to weigh,
and divide the *hair.*
2Thou shalt burn with fire a third part
in the midst of the city, when the days of

the siege are fulfilled: and thou shalt take
a third part, *and* smite about it with a knife:
and a third part thou shalt scatter in the
wind; and I will draw out a sword after
them.
3 Thou shalt also take thereof a few in
number, and bind them in thy skirts.
4 Then take of them again, and cast them
into the midst of the fire, and burn them
in the fire; *for* thereof shall a fire come forth
into all the house of Israel.
5 Thus saith the Lord GOD; This *is* Jerusalem: I have set it in the midst of the
nations and countries *that are* round
about her.
6 And she hath changed my judgments
into wickedness more than the nations,
and my statutes more than the countries
that *are* round about her: for they have refused my judgments and my statutes, they
have not walked in them.
7 Therefore thus saith the Lord GOD; Because ye multiplied more than the nations
that *are* round about you, *and* have not
walked in my statutes, neither have kept
my judgments, neither have done according to the judgments of the nations that
are round about you;
8 Therefore thus saith the Lord GOD; Behold, I, even I, *am* against thee, and will
execute judgments in the midst of thee in
the sight of the nations.
9 And I will do in thee that which I have
not done, and whereunto I will not do any
more the like, because of all thine abominations.
10 Therefore the fathers shall eat the sons
in the midst of thee, and the sons shall eat
their fathers; and I will execute judgments
in thee, and the whole remnant of thee will
I scatter into all the winds.
11 Wherefore, *as* I live, saith the Lord
GOD; Surely, because thou hast defiled my
sanctuary with all thy detestable things,
and with all thine abominations, therefore
will I also diminish *thee;* neither shall mine
eye spare, neither will I have any pity.
12 A third part of thee shall die with the
pestilence, and with famine shall they be
consumed in the midst of thee: and a third
part shall fall by the sword round about
thee and I will scatter a third part into all
the winds, and I will draw out a sword after them.
13 Thus shall mine anger be accomplished, and I will cause my fury to rest
upon them, and I will be comforted: and
they shall know that I the LORD have spoken *it* in my zeal, when I have accomplished my fury in them.
14 Moreover I will make thee waste, and
a reproach among the nations that *are*
round about thee, in the sight of all that
pass by.
15 So it shall be a reproach and a taunt,
an instruction and an astonishment unto
the nations that *are* round about thee,
when I shall execute judgments in thee in
anger and in fury and in furious rebukes. I
the LORD have spoken *it.*
16 When I shall send upon them the evil
arrows of famine, which shall be for *their*
destruction, *and* which I will send to destroy you: and I will increase the famine
upon you, and will break your staff of
bread:
17 So will I send upon you famine and
evil beasts, and they shall bereave thee; and
pestilence and blood shall pass through
thee; and I will bring the sword upon thee.
I the LORD have spoken *it.*

6

1 And the word of the LORD came unto
me, saying,
2 Son of man, set thy face toward the
mountains of Israel, and prophesy against
them,
3 And say, Ye mountains of Israel, hear
the word of the Lord GOD; Thus saith the
Lord GOD to the mountains, and to the
hills, to the rivers, and to the valleys; Behold, I, *even* I, will bring a sword upon you,
and I will destroy your high places.
4 And your altars shall be desolate, and
your images shall be broken: and I will cast
down your slain *men* before your idols.
5 And I will lay the dead carcases of the
children of Israel before their idols; and I
will scatter your bones round about your
altars.
6 In all your dwellingplaces the cities
shall be laid waste, and the high places
shall be desolate; that your altars may be
laid waste and made desolate, and your
idols may be broken and cease, and your
images may be cut down, and your works
may be abolished.
7 And the slain shall fall in the midst of
you, and ye shall know that I *am* the LORD.
8 Yet will I leave a remnant, that ye may
have *some* that shall escape the sword

among the nations, when ye shall be scattered through the countries.
9 And they that escape of you shall remember me among the nations whither
they shall be carried captives, because I am
broken with their whorish heart, which
hath departed from me, and with their
eyes, which go a whoring after their idols:
and they shall lothe themselves for the
evils which they have committed in all
their abominations.
10 And they shall know that I *am* the
LORD, *and that* I have not said in vain that
I would do this evil unto them.
11 Thus saith the Lord GOD; Smite with
thine hand, and stamp with thy foot, and
say, Alas for all the evil abominations of
the house of Israel! for they shall fall by
the sword, by the famine, and by the pestilence.
12 He that is far off shall die of the pestilence; and he that is near shall fall by the
sword; and he that remaineth and is besieged shall die by the famine: thus will I
accomplish my fury upon them.
13 Then shall ye know that I *am* the LORD,
when their slain *men* shall be among their
idols round about their altars, upon every
high hill, in all the tops of the mountains,
and under every green tree, and under every thick oak, the place where they did offer sweet savour to all their idols.
14 So will I stretch out my hand upon
them, and make the land desolate, yea,
more desolate than the wilderness toward
Diblath, in all their habitations: and they
shall know that I *am* the LORD.

7

1 Moreover the word of the LORD came
unto me, saying,
2 Also, thou son of man, thus saith the
Lord GOD unto the land of Israel; An end,
the end is come upon the four corners of
the land.
3 Now *is* the end *come* upon thee, and I
will send mine anger upon thee, and will
judge thee according to thy ways, and will
recompense upon thee all thine abominations.
4 And mine eye shall not spare thee, neither will I have pity: but I will recompense
thy ways upon thee, and thine abominations shall be in the midst of thee: and ye
shall know that I *am* the LORD.
5 Thus saith the Lord GOD; An evil, an
only evil, behold, is come.
6 An end is come, the end is come: it
watcheth for thee; behold, it is come.
7 The morning is come unto thee, O thou
that dwellest in the land: the time is come,
the day of trouble *is* near, and not the
sounding again of the mountains.
8 Now will I shortly pour out my fury
upon thee, and accomplish mine anger
upon thee: and I will judge thee according to thy ways, and will recompense thee
for all thine abominations.
9 And mine eye shall not spare, neither
will I have pity: I will recompense thee
according to thy ways and thine abominations *that* are in the midst of thee; and
ye shall know that I *am* the LORD that
smiteth.
10 Behold the day, behold, it is come: the
morning is gone forth; the rod hath blos-
somed, pride hath budded.
11 Violence is risen up into a rod of wickedness: none of them *shall remain,* nor of
their multitude, nor of any of theirs: neither *shall there be* wailing for them.
12 The time is come, the day draweth
near: let not the buyer rejoice, nor the seller
mourn: for wrath *is* upon all the multitude
thereof.
13 For the seller shall not return to that
which is sold, although they were yet alive:
for the vision *is* touching the whole multitude thereof, *which* shall not return; neither shall any strengthen himself in the
iniquity of his life.
14 They have blown the trumpet, even to
make all ready; but none goeth to the battle: for my wrath *is* upon all the multitude
thereof.
15 The sword *is* without, and the pestilence and the famine within: he that *is* in
the field shall die with the sword; and he
that *is* in the city, famine and pestilence
shall devour him.
16 But they that escape of them shall escape, and shall be on the mountains like
doves of the valleys, all of them mourning, every one for his iniquity.
17 All hands shall be feeble, and all knees
shall be weak *as* water.
18 They shall also gird *themselves* with
sackcloth, and horror shall cover them;
and shame *shall be* upon all faces, and
baldness upon all their heads.
19 They shall cast their silver in the
streets, and their gold shall be removed:

their silver and their gold shall not be able to deliver them in the day of the wrath of the LORD: they shall not satisfy their souls, neither fill their bowels: because it is the stumblingblock of their iniquity.

20 As for the beauty of his ornament, he set it in majesty: but they made the images of their abominations *and* of their detestable things therein: therefore have I set it far from them.

21 And I will give it into the hands of the strangers for a prey, and to the wicked of the earth for a spoil; and they shall pollute it.

22 My face will I turn also from them, and they shall pollute my secret *place:* for the robbers shall enter into it, and defile it.

23 Make a chain: for the land is full of bloody crimes, and the city is full of violence.

24 Wherefore I will bring the worst of the heathen, and they shall possess their houses: I will also make the pomp of the strong to cease; and their holy places shall be defiled.

25 Destruction cometh; and they shall seek peace, and *there shall be* none.

26 Mischief shall come upon mischief, and rumour shall be upon rumour; then shall they seek a vision of the prophet; but the law shall perish from the priest, and counsel from the ancients.

27 The king shall mourn, and the prince shall be clothed with desolation, and the hands of the people of the land shall be troubled: I will do unto them after their way, and according to their deserts will I judge them; and they shall know that I *am* the LORD.

8

1 And it came to pass in the sixth year, in the sixth *month,* in the fifth *day* of the month, *as* I sat in mine house, and the elders of Judah sat before me, that the hand of the Lord GOD fell there upon me.

2 Then I beheld, and lo a likeness as the appearance of fire: from the appearance of his loins even downward, fire; and from his loins even upward, as the appearance of brightness, as the colour of amber.

3 And he put forth the form of an hand, and took me by a lock of mine head; and the spirit lifted me up between the earth and the heaven, and brought me in the visions of God to Jerusalem, to the door of the inner gate that looketh toward the north; where *was* the seat of the image of jealousy, which provoketh to jealousy.

8:3 Losers
◄ Isaiah 3:8
Hebrews 3:16 ►

4 And, behold, the glory of the God of Israel *was* there, according to the vision that I saw in the plain.

5 Then said he unto me, Son of man, lift up thine eyes now the way toward the north. So I lifted up mine eyes the way toward the north, and behold northward at the gate of the altar this image of jealousy in the entry.

6 He said furthermore unto me, Son of man, seest thou what they do? *even* the great abominations that the house of Israel committeth here, that I should go far off from my sanctuary? but turn thee yet again, *and* thou shalt see greater abominations.

7 And he brought me to the door of the court; and when I looked, behold a hole in the wall.

8 Then said he unto me, Son of man, dig now in the wall: and when I had digged in the wall, behold a door.

9 And he said unto me, Go in, and behold the wicked abominations that they do here.

10 So I went in and saw; and behold every form of creeping things, and abominable beasts, and all the idols of the house of Israel, pourtrayed upon the wall round about.

11 And there stood before them seventy men of the ancients of the house of Israel, and in the midst of them stood Jaazaniah the son of Shaphan, with every man his censer in his hand; and a thick cloud of incense went up.

12 Then said he unto me, Son of man, hast thou seen what the ancients of the house of Israel do in the dark, every man in the chambers of his imagery? for they say, The LORD seeth us not; the LORD hath forsaken the earth.

13 He said also unto me, Turn thee yet again, *and* thou shalt see greater abominations that they do.

14 Then he brought me to the door of the gate of the LORD'S house which *was* toward the north; and, behold, there sat women weeping for Tammuz.

15 Then said he unto me, Hast thou seen
this, O son of man? turn thee yet again,
and thou shalt see greater abominations
than these.
16 And he brought me into the inner
court of the LORD'S house, and, behold, at
the door of the temple of the LORD, between the porch and the altar, *were* about
five and twenty men, with their backs toward the temple of the LORD, and their
faces toward the east; and they worshipped
the sun toward the east.
17 Then he said
unto me, Hast thou
seen *this,* O son of
man? Is it a light
thing to the house
of Judah that they
commit the abominations which they
commit here? for they have filled the land
with violence, and have returned to provoke me to anger: and, lo, they put the
branch to their nose.

8:17 Violence
◄ Jeremiah 6:7
Amos 3:10 ►

18 Therefore will I also deal in fury: mine
eye shall not spare, neither will I have pity:
and though they cry in mine ears with a
loud voice, *yet* will I not hear them.

9

1 He cried also in mine ears with a loud
voice, saying, Cause them that have charge
over the city to draw near, even every man
with his destroying weapon in his hand.
2 And, behold, six men came from the
way of the higher gate, which lieth toward
the north, and every man a slaughter weapon in his hand; and one man among them
was clothed with linen, with a writer's
inkhorn by his side: and they went in, and
stood beside the brasen altar.
3 And the glory of the God of Israel was
gone up from the cherub, whereupon he
was, to the threshold of the house. And he
called to the man clothed with linen,
which *had* the writer's inkhorn by his side;
4 And the LORD said unto him, Go
through the midst of the city, through the
midst of Jerusalem, and set a mark upon
the foreheads of the men that sigh and that
cry for all the abominations that be done
in the midst thereof.
5 And to the others he said in mine hearing, Go ye after him through the city, and
smite: let not your eye spare, neither have
ye pity:
6 Slay utterly old *and* young, both maids,
and little children, and women: but come
not near any man upon whom *is* the mark;
and begin at my sanctuary. Then they began at the ancient men which *were* before
the house.
7 And he said unto them, Defile the
house, and fill the courts with the slain:
go ye forth. And they went forth, and slew
in the city.
8 And it came to pass, while they were
slaying them, and I was left, that I fell upon
my face, and cried, and said, Ah Lord GOD!
wilt thou destroy all the residue of Israel
in thy pouring out of thy fury upon Jerusalem?
9 Then said he
unto me, The iniq-
uity of the house of
Israel and Judah *is*
exceeding great,
and the land is full
of blood, and the city full of perverseness:
for they say, The LORD hath forsaken the
earth, and the LORD seeth not.

9:9 Used to Sin
◄ Proverbs 28:6
Matthew 17:17 ►

10 And as for me also, mine eye shall not
spare, neither will I have pity, *but* I will
recompense their way upon their head.
11 And, behold, the man clothed with
linen, which *had* the inkhorn by his side,
reported the matter, saying, I have done as
thou hast commanded me.

10

1 Then I looked, and, behold, in the firmament that was above the head of the
cherubims there appeared over them as it
were a sapphire stone, as the appearance
of the likeness of a throne.
2 And he spake unto the man clothed
with linen, and said, Go in between the
wheels, *even* under the cherub, and fill
thine hand with coals of fire from between
the cherubims, and scatter *them* over the
city. And he went in in my sight.
3 Now the cherubims stood on the right
side of the house, when the man went in;
and the cloud filled the inner court.
4 Then the glory of the LORD went up
from the cherub, *and stood* over the threshold of the house; and the house was filled
with the cloud, and the court was full of
the brightness of the LORD'S glory.
5 And the sound of the cherubims' wings
was heard *even* to the outer court, as the
voice of the Almighty God when he
speaketh.
6 And it came to pass, *that* when he had
commanded the man clothed with linen,

saying, Take fire from between the wheels,
from between the cherubims; then he went
in, and stood beside the wheels.
7 And *one* cherub stretched forth his
hand from between the cherubims unto
the fire that *was* between the cherubims,
and took *thereof,* and put *it* into the hands
of *him that was* clothed with linen: who
took *it,* and went out.
8 And there appeared in the cherubims
the form of a man's hand under their
wings.
9 And when I looked, behold the four
wheels by the cherubims, one wheel by
one cherub, and another wheel by another
cherub: and the appearance of the wheels
was as the colour of a beryl stone.
10 And *as for* their appearances, they four
had one likeness, as if a wheel had been
in the midst of a wheel.
11 When they went, they went upon their
four sides; they turned not as they went,
but to the place whither the head looked
they followed it; they turned not as they
went.
12 And their whole body, and their backs,
and their hands, and their wings, and the
wheels, *were* full of eyes round about, *even*
the wheels that they four had.
13 As for the wheels, it was cried unto
them in my hearing, O wheel.
14 And every one had four faces: the first
face *was* the face of a cherub, and the second face *was* the face of a man, and the
third the face of a lion, and the fourth the
face of an eagle.
15 And the cherubims were lifted up. This
is the living creature that I saw by the river
of Chebar.
16 And when the cherubims went, the
wheels went by them: and when the
cherubims lifted up their wings to mount
up from the earth, the same wheels also
turned not from beside them.
17 When they stood, *these* stood; and
when they were lifted up, *these* lifted up
themselves *also:* for the spirit of the living
creature *was* in them.
18 Then the glory of the LORD departed
from off the threshold of the house, and
stood over the cherubims.
19 And the cherubims lifted up their
wings, and mounted up from the earth in
my sight: when they went out, the wheels
also *were* beside them, and *every one* stood
at the door of the east gate of the LORD'S
house; and the glory of the God of Israel
was over them above.
20 This *is* the living creature that I saw
under the God of Israel by the river of
Chebar; and I knew that they *were* the
cherubims.
21 Every one had four faces apiece, and
every one four wings; and the likeness of
the hands of a man *was* under their wings.
22 And the likeness of their faces *was* the
same faces which I saw by the river of
Chebar, their appearances and themselves:
they went every one straight forward.

11

1 Moreover the spirit lifted me up, and
brought me unto the east gate of the
LORD'S house, which looketh eastward:
and behold at the door of the gate five and
twenty men; among whom I saw Jaazaniah the son of Azur, and Pelatiah the son
of Benaiah, the princes of the people.
2 Then said he unto me, Son of man,
these *are* the men that devise mischief, and
give wicked counsel in this city:
3 Which say, *It is* not near; let us build
houses: this *city is* the caldron, and we *be*
the flesh.
4 Therefore prophesy against them,
prophesy, O son of man.
5 And the Spirit of
the LORD fell upon
me, and said unto
me, Speak; Thus
saith the LORD;
Thus have ye said,
O house of Israel: for I know the things that
come into your mind, *every one of* them.

11:5 God Sees Sin
◄ Jeremiah 16:17
Hosea 7:2 ►

6 Ye have multiplied your slain in this
city, and ye have filled the streets thereof
with the slain.
7 Therefore thus saith the Lord GOD;
Your slain whom ye have laid in the midst
of it, they *are* the flesh, and this *city is* the
caldron: but I will bring you forth out of
the midst of it.
8 Ye have feared the sword; and I will
bring a sword upon you, saith the Lord
GOD.
9 And I will bring you out of the midst
thereof, and deliver you into the hands of
strangers, and will execute judgments
among you.
10 Ye shall fall by the sword; I will judge
you in the border of Israel; and ye shall
know that I *am* the LORD.

11 This *city* shall not be your caldron,
neither shall ye be the flesh in the midst
thereof; *but* I will judge you in the border
of Israel:
12 And ye shall know that I *am* the LORD:
for ye have not walked in my statutes, neither executed my judgments, but have
done after the manners of the heathen that
are round about you.
13 And it came to pass, when I prophesied, that Pelatiah the son of Benaiah died.
Then fell I down upon my face, and cried
with a loud voice, and said, Ah Lord GOD!
wilt thou make a full end of the remnant
of Israel?
14 Again the word of the LORD came unto
me, saying,
15 Son of man, thy brethren, *even* thy
brethren, the men of thy kindred, and all
the house of Israel wholly, *are* they unto
whom the inhabitants of Jerusalem have
said, Get you far from the LORD: unto us is
this land given in possession.
16 Therefore say, Thus saith the Lord
GOD; Although I have cast them far off
among the heathen, and although I have
scattered them among the countries, yet
will I be to them as a little sanctuary in
the countries where they shall come.
17 Therefore say, Thus saith the Lord
GOD; I will even gather you from the people, and assemble you out of the countries
where ye have been scattered, and I will
give you the land of Israel.
18 And they shall come thither, and they
shall take away all the detestable things
thereof and all the abominations thereof
from thence.
19 And I will give
them one heart,
and I will put a new
spirit within you;
and I will take the
stony heart out of
their flesh, and will
give them an heart
of flesh:
20 That they may
walk in my statutes,
and keep mine or-
dinances, and do them: and they shall be
my people, and I will be their God.
21 But *as for them* whose heart walketh
after the heart of their detestable things
and their abominations, I will recompense
their way upon their own heads, saith the
Lord GOD.
22 Then did the cherubims lift up their
wings, and the wheels beside them; and
the glory of the God of Israel *was* over them
above.
23 And the glory of the LORD went up
from the midst of the city, and stood upon
the mountain which *is* on the east side of
the city.
24 Afterwards the spirit took me up, and
brought me in a vision by the Spirit of God
into Chaldea, to them of the captivity.
So the vision that I had seen went up
from me.
25 Then I spake unto them of the captivity all the things that the LORD had
shewed me.

11:19 Invisible Gifts
◄ Jeremiah 24:7
Matthew 11:28 ►

11:19 New Life
◄ Psalm 40:3
Romans 6:4 ►

12

1 The word of the LORD also came unto
me, saying,
2 Son of man, thou dwellest in the midst
of a rebellious house, which have eyes to
see, and see not; they have ears to hear,
and hear not: for they *are* a rebellious
house.
3 Therefore, thou son of man, prepare
thee stuff for removing, and remove by day
in their sight; and thou shalt remove from
thy place to another place in their sight: it
may be they will consider, though they *be*
a rebellious house.
4 Then shalt thou bring forth thy stuff
by day in their sight, as stuff for removing: and thou shalt go forth at even in their
sight, as they that go forth into captivity.
5 Dig thou through the wall in their sight,
and carry out thereby.
6 In their sight shalt thou bear *it* upon
thy shoulders, *and* carry *it* forth in the twilight: thou shalt cover thy face, that thou
see not the ground: for I have set thee *for* a
sign unto the house of Israel.
7 And I did so as I was commanded: I
brought forth my stuff by day, as stuff for
captivity, and in the even I digged through
the wall with mine hand; I brought *it* forth
in the twilight, *and* I bare *it* upon *my* shoulder in their sight.
8 And in the morning came the word of
the LORD unto me, saying,
9 Son of man, hath not the house of Israel, the rebellious house, said unto thee,
What doest thou?
10 Say thou unto them, Thus saith the
Lord GOD; This burden *concerneth* the

prince in Jerusalem, and all the house of Israel that *are* among them.

11 Say, I *am* your sign: like as I have done, so shall it be done unto them: they shall remove *and* go into captivity.

12 And the prince that *is* among them shall bear upon *his* shoulder in the twilight, and shall go forth: they shall dig through the wall to carry out thereby: he shall cover his face, that he see not the ground with *his* eyes.

13 My net also will I spread upon him, and he shall be taken in my snare: and I will bring him to Babylon *to* the land of the Chaldeans; yet shall he not see it, though he shall die there.

14 And I will scatter toward every wind all that *are* about him to help him, and all his bands; and I will draw out the sword after them.

15 And they shall know that I *am* the LORD, when I shall scatter them among the nations, and disperse them in the countries.

16 But I will leave a few men of them from the sword, from the famine, and from the pestilence; that they may declare all their abominations among the heathen whither they come; and they shall know that I *am* the LORD.

17 Moreover the word of the LORD came to me, saying,

18 Son of man, eat thy bread with quaking, and drink thy water with trembling and with carefulness;

19 And say unto the people of the land, Thus saith the Lord GOD of the inhabitants of Jerusalem, *and* of the land of Israel; They shall eat their bread with carefulness, and drink their water with astonishment, that her land may be desolate from all that is therein, because of the violence of all them that dwell therein.

20 And the cities that are inhabited shall be laid waste, and the land shall be desolate; and ye shall know that I *am* the LORD.

21 And the word of the LORD came unto me, saying,

22 Son of man, what *is* that proverb *that* ye have in the land of Israel, saying, The days are prolonged, and every vision faileth?

23 Tell them therefore, Thus saith the Lord GOD; I will make this proverb to cease, and they shall no more use it as a proverb in Israel; but say unto them, The days are at hand, and the effect of every vision.

24 For there shall be no more any vain vision nor flattering divination within the house of Israel.

25 For I *am* the LORD: I will speak, and the word that I shall speak shall come to pass; it shall be no more prolonged: for in your days, O rebellious house, will I say the word, and will perform it, saith the Lord GOD.

26 Again the word of the LORD came to me, saying,

27 Son of man, behold, *they of* the house of Israel say, The vision that he seeth *is* for many days *to come,* and he prophesieth of the times *that are* far off.

28 Therefore say unto them, Thus saith the Lord GOD; There shall none of my words be prolonged any more, but the word which I have spoken shall be done, saith the Lord GOD.

13

1 And the word of the LORD came unto me, saying,

2 Son of man, prophesy against the prophets of Israel that prophesy, and say thou unto them that prophesy out of their own hearts, Hear ye the word of the LORD;

3 Thus saith the Lord GOD; Woe unto the foolish prophets, that follow their own spirit, and have seen nothing!

4 O Israel, thy prophets are like the foxes in the deserts.

5 Ye have not gone up into the gaps, neither made up the hedge for the house of Israel to stand in the battle in the day of the LORD.

6 They have seen vanity and lying divination, saying, The LORD saith: and the LORD hath not sent them: and they have made *others* to hope that they would confirm the word.

7 Have ye not seen a vain vision, and have ye not spoken a lying divination, whereas ye say, The LORD saith *it;* albeit I have not spoken?

8 Therefore thus saith the Lord GOD; Because ye have spoken vanity, and seen lies, therefore, behold, I *am* against you, saith the Lord GOD.

9 And mine hand shall be upon the prophets that see vanity, and that divine lies: they shall not be in the assembly of my people, neither shall they be written

in the writing of the house of Israel, neither shall they enter into the land of
Israel; and ye shall know that I *am* the Lord
GOD.
10 Because, even
because they have
seduced my people,
saying, Peace; and
there was no peace;
and one built up a
wall, and, lo, others daubed it with
untempered *morter:*

13:10-11
Wicked Insecurity
◄ Jeremiah 23:12
Matthew 7:26-27 ►

11 Say unto them which daub it with
untempered *morter,* that it shall fall: there
shall be an overflowing shower; and ye,
O great hailstones, shall fall; and a stormy
wind shall rend *it.*
12 Lo, when the wall is fallen, shall it not
be said unto you, Where *is* the daubing
wherewith ye have daubed *it?*
13 Therefore thus saith the Lord GOD; I
will even rend *it* with a stormy wind in
my fury; and there shall be an overflowing shower in mine anger, and great hailstones in *my* fury to consume *it.*
14 So will I break down the wall that ye
have daubed with untempered *morter,* and
bring it down to the ground, so that the
foundation thereof shall be discovered,
and it shall fall, and ye shall be consumed
in the midst thereof: and ye shall know
that I *am* the LORD.
15 Thus will I accomplish my wrath upon
the wall, and upon them that have daubed
it with untempered *morter,* and will say
unto you, The wall *is* no *more,* neither they
that daubed it;
16 *To wit,* the prophets of Israel which
prophesy concerning Jerusalem, and
which see visions of peace for her, and *there*
is no peace, saith the Lord GOD.
17 Likewise, thou son of man, set thy face
against the daughters of thy people, which
prophesy out of their own heart; and
prophesy thou against them,
18 And say, Thus saith the Lord GOD; Woe
to the *women* that sew pillows to all armholes, and make kerchiefs upon the head
of every stature to hunt souls! Will ye hunt
the souls of my people, and will ye save
the souls alive *that come* unto you?
19 And will ye pollute me among my
people for handfuls of barley and for
pieces of bread, to slay the souls that
should not die, and to save the souls alive
that should not live, by your lying to my
people that hear *your* lies?
20 Wherefore thus saith the Lord GOD;
Behold, I *am* against your pillows, wherewith ye there hunt the souls to make *them*
fly, and I will tear them from your arms,
and will let the souls go, *even* the souls
that ye hunt to make *them* fly.
21 Your kerchiefs also will I tear, and
deliver my people out of your hand, and
they shall be no more in your hand to be
hunted; and ye shall know that I *am* the
LORD.
22 Because with
lies ye have made
the heart of the
righteous sad,
whom I have not
made sad; and
strengthened the hands of the wicked, that
he should not return from his wicked way,
by promising him life:

13:22 Excusing Sin
◄ Isaiah 5:20
Malachi 2:17 ►

23 Therefore ye shall see no more vanity,
nor divine divinations: for I will deliver
my people out of your hand: and ye shall
know that I *am* the LORD.

14

1 Then came certain of the elders of Israel unto me, and sat before me.
2 And the word of the LORD came unto
me, saying,
3 Son of man, these men have set up
their idols in their heart, and put the
stumblingblock of their iniquity before
their face: should I be enquired of at all
by them?
4 Therefore speak unto them, and say
unto them, Thus saith the Lord GOD; Every man of the house of Israel that setteth
up his idols in his heart, and putteth the
stumblingblock of his iniquity before his
face, and cometh to the prophet; I the LORD
will answer him that cometh according to
the multitude of his idols;
5 That I may take the house of Israel in
their own heart, because they are all estranged from me through their idols.
6 Therefore say
unto the house of
Israel, Thus saith
the Lord GOD; Re-
pent, and turn *your-*
selves from your
idols; and turn away your faces from all
your abominations.

14:6 Repent!
◄ Jeremiah 25:5
Ezekiel 18:31 ►

7 For every one of the house of Israel, or

of the stranger that sojourneth in Israel,
which separateth himself from me, and
setteth up his idols in his heart, and
putteth the stumblingblock of his iniquity
before his face, and cometh to a prophet
to enquire of him concerning me; I the
LORD will answer him by myself:
8 And I will set my face against that man,
and will make him a sign and a proverb,
and I will cut him off from the midst of
my people; and ye shall know that I *am*
the LORD.
9 And if the prophet be deceived when
he hath spoken a thing, I the LORD have
deceived that prophet, and I will stretch
out my hand upon him, and will destroy
him from the midst of my people Israel.
10 And they shall bear the punishment
of their iniquity: the punishment of the
prophet shall be even as the punishment
of him that seeketh *unto him;*
11 That the house of Israel may go no
more astray from me, neither be polluted
any more with all their transgressions; but
that they may be my people, and I may be
their God, saith the Lord GOD.
12 The word of the LORD came again to
me, saying,
13 Son of man, when the land sinneth
against me by trespassing grievously, then
will I stretch out mine hand upon it, and
will break the staff of the bread thereof,
and will send famine upon it, and will cut
off man and beast from it:
14 Though these three men, Noah, Daniel, and Job, were in it, they should deliver
but their own souls by their righteousness,
saith the Lord GOD.
15 If I cause noisome beasts to pass
through the land, and they spoil it, so that
it be desolate, that no man may pass
through because of the beasts:
16 *Though* these three men *were* in it, *as* I
live, saith the Lord GOD, they shall deliver
neither sons nor daughters; they only shall
be delivered, but the land shall be desolate.
17 Or *if* I bring a sword upon that land,
and say, Sword, go through the land; so
that I cut off man and beast from it:
18 Though these three men *were* in it, *as*
I live, saith the Lord GOD, they shall deliver neither sons nor daughters, but they
only shall be delivered themselves.
19 Or *if* I send a pestilence into that land,
and pour out my fury upon it in blood, to
cut off from it man and beast:
20 Though Noah, Daniel, and Job, *were*
in it, *as* I live, saith the Lord GOD, they
shall deliver neither son nor daughter; they
shall *but* deliver their own souls by their
righteousness.
21 For thus saith the Lord GOD; How
much more when I send my four sore judgments upon Jerusalem, the sword, and the
famine, and the noisome beast, and the
pestilence, to cut off from it man and
beast?
22 Yet, behold, therein shall be left a remnant that shall be brought forth, *both* sons
and daughters: behold, they shall come
forth unto you, and ye shall see their way
and their doings: and ye shall be comforted concerning the evil that I have brought
upon Jerusalem, *even* concerning all that I
have brought upon it.
23 And they shall comfort you, when ye
see their ways and their doings: and ye
shall know that I have not done without
cause all that I have done in it, saith the
Lord GOD.

15

1 And the word of the LORD came unto
me, saying,
2 Son of man, What is the vine tree more
than any tree, *or than* a branch which is
among the trees of the forest?
3 Shall wood be taken thereof to do any
work? or will *men* take a pin of it to hang
any vessel thereon?
4 Behold, it is cast into the fire for fuel;
the fire devoureth both the ends of it, and
the midst of it is burned. Is it meet for *any*
work?
5 Behold, when it was whole, it was meet
for no work: how much less shall it be
meet yet for *any* work, when the fire hath
devoured it, and it is burned?
6 Therefore thus saith the Lord GOD;
As the vine tree among the trees of the
forest, which I have given to the fire for
fuel, so will I give the inhabitants of Jerusalem.
7 And I will set my face against them;
they shall go out from *one* fire, and *another*
fire shall devour them; and ye shall know
that I *am* the LORD, when I set my face
against them.
8 And I will make the land desolate, because they have committed a trespass, saith
the Lord GOD.

16

1 Again the word of the LORD came unto me, saying,

2 Son of man, cause Jerusalem to know her abominations,

3 And say, Thus saith the Lord GOD unto Jerusalem; Thy birth and thy nativity *is* of the land of Canaan; thy father *was* an Amorite, and thy mother an Hittite.

4 And *as for* thy nativity, in the day thou wast born thy navel was not cut, neither wast thou washed in water to supple *thee;* thou wast not salted at all, nor swaddled at all.

5 None eye pitied thee, to do any of these unto thee, to have compassion upon thee; but thou wast cast out in the open field, to the lothing of thy person, in the day that thou wast born.

6 And when I passed by thee, and saw thee polluted in thine own blood, I said unto thee *when thou wast* in thy blood, Live; yea, I said unto thee *when thou wast* in thy blood, Live.

7 I have caused thee to multiply as the bud of the field, and thou hast increased and waxen great, and thou art come to excellent ornaments: *thy* breasts are fashioned, and thine hair is grown, whereas thou *wast* naked and bare.

8 Now when I passed by thee, and looked upon thee, behold, thy time *was* the time of love; and I spread my skirt over thee, and covered thy nakedness: yea, I sware unto thee, and entered into a covenant with thee, saith the Lord GOD, and thou becamest mine.

16:8 Adopted by God
◄ Isaiah 63:16
Hosea 11:1 ►

9 Then washed I thee with water; yea, I throughly washed away thy blood from thee, and I anointed thee with oil.

10 I clothed thee also with broidered work, and shod thee with badgers' skin, and I girded thee about with fine linen, and I covered thee with silk.

11 I decked thee also with ornaments, and I put bracelets upon thy hands, and a chain on thy neck.

12 And I put a jewel on thy forehead, and earrings in thine ears, and a beautiful crown upon thine head.

13 Thus wast thou decked with gold and silver; and thy raiment *was of* fine linen, and silk, and broidered work; thou didst eat fine flour, and honey, and oil: and thou wast exceeding beautiful, and thou didst prosper into a kingdom.

14 And thy renown went forth among the heathen for thy beauty: for it *was* perfect through my comeliness, which I had put upon thee, saith the Lord GOD.

15 But thou didst trust in thine own beauty, and playedst the harlot because of thy renown, and pouredst out thy fornications on every one that passed by; his it was.

16 And of thy garments thou didst take, and deckedst thy high places with divers colours, and playedst the harlot thereupon: *the like things* shall not come, neither shall it be *so.*

16:17-18 Gratitude
◄ Nehemiah 9:26
Luke 17:17-18 ►

17 Thou hast also taken thy fair jewels of my gold and of my silver, which I had given thee, and madest to thyself images of men, and didst commit whoredom with them,

18 And tookest thy broidered garments, and coveredst them: and thou hast set mine oil and mine incense before them.

19 My meat also which I gave thee, fine flour, and oil, and honey, *wherewith* I fed thee, thou hast even set it before them for a sweet savour: and *thus* it was, saith the Lord GOD.

20 Moreover thou hast taken thy sons and thy daughters, whom thou hast borne unto me, and these hast thou sacrificed unto them to be devoured. *Is this* of thy whoredoms a small matter,

21 That thou hast slain my children, and delivered them to cause them to pass through *the fire* for them?

22 And in all thine abominations and thy whoredoms thou hast not remembered the days of thy youth, when thou wast naked and bare, *and* wast polluted in thy blood.

23 And it came to pass after all thy wickedness, (woe, woe unto thee! saith the Lord GOD;)

24 *That* thou hast also built unto thee an eminent place, and hast made thee an high place in every street.

25 Thou hast built thy high place at every head of the way, and hast made thy beauty to be abhorred, and hast opened

thy feet to every one that passed by, and
multiplied thy whoredoms.
26 Thou hast also committed fornication
with the Egyptians thy neighbours, great
of flesh; and hast increased thy whoredoms, to provoke me to anger.
27 Behold, therefore I have stretched out
my hand over thee, and have diminished
thine ordinary *food,* and delivered thee
unto the will of them that hate thee, the
daughters of the Philistines, which are
ashamed of thy lewd way.
28 Thou hast played the whore also with
the Assyrians, because thou wast unsatia-
ble; yea, thou hast played the harlot with
them, and yet couldest not be satisfied.
29 Thou hast moreover multiplied thy
fornication in the land of Canaan unto
Chaldea; and yet thou wast not satisfied
herewith.
30 How weak is thine heart, saith the
Lord GOD, seeing thou doest all these
things, the work of an imperious whorish
woman;
31 In that thou buildest thine eminent
place in the head of every way, and makest
thine high place in every street; and hast
not been as an harlot, in that thou scornest
hire;
32 *But as* a wife that committeth adultery,
which taketh strangers instead of her husband!
33 They give gifts to all whores: but thou
givest thy gifts to all thy lovers, and hirest
them, that they may come unto thee on
every side for thy whoredom.
34 And the contrary is in thee from *other*
women in thy whoredoms, whereas none
followeth thee to commit whoredoms: and
in that thou givest a reward, and no reward is given unto thee, therefore thou art
contrary.
35 Wherefore, O harlot, hear the word of
the LORD:
36 Thus saith the Lord GOD; Because thy
filthiness was poured out, and thy nakedness discovered through thy whoredoms
with thy lovers, and with all the idols of
thy abominations, and by the blood of thy
children, which thou didst give unto them;
37 Behold, therefore I will gather all thy
lovers, with whom thou hast taken pleasure, and all *them* that thou hast loved,
with all *them* that thou hast hated; I will
even gather them round about against
thee, and will discover thy nakedness unto
them, that they may see all thy nakedness.
38 And I will judge thee, as women that
break wedlock and shed blood are judged;
and I will give thee blood in fury and
jealousy.
39 And I will also give thee into their
hand, and they shall throw down thine
eminent place, and shall break down thy
high places: they shall strip thee also of
thy clothes, and shall take thy fair jewels,
and leave thee naked and bare.
40 They shall also bring up a company
against thee, and they shall stone thee with
stones, and thrust thee through with their
swords.
41 And they shall burn thine houses with
fire, and execute judgments upon thee in
the sight of many women: and I will cause
thee to cease from playing the harlot, and
thou also shalt give no hire any more.
42 So will I make my fury toward thee to
rest, and my jealousy shall depart from
thee, and I will be quiet, and will be no
more angry.
43 Because thou hast not remembered
the days of thy youth, but hast fretted me
in all these *things;* behold, therefore I also
will recompense thy way upon *thine* head,
saith the Lord GOD: and thou shalt not
commit this lewdness above all thine
abominations.
44 Behold, every one that useth proverbs
shall use *this* proverb against thee, saying,
As is the mother, *so is* her daughter.
45 Thou *art* thy mother's daughter, that
lotheth her husband and her children; and
thou *art* the sister of thy sisters, which
lothed their husbands and their children:
your mother *was* an Hittite, and your father an Amorite.
46 And thine elder sister *is* Samaria, she
and her daughters that dwell at thy left
hand: and thy younger sister, that dwelleth
at thy right hand, *is* Sodom and her daughters.
47 Yet hast thou not walked after their
ways, nor done after their abominations:
but, as *if that were* a very little *thing,* thou
wast corrupted more than they in all thy
ways.
48 *As* I live, saith the Lord GOD, Sodom
thy sister hath not done, she nor her
daughters, as thou hast done, thou and thy
daughters.

49 Behold, this was the iniquity of thy
sister Sodom, pride, fulness of bread, and
abundance of idleness was in her and in
her daughters, neither did she strengthen
the hand of the poor and needy.
50 And they were haughty, and committed abomination before me: therefore I
took them away as I saw *good*.
51 Neither hath Samaria committed half
of thy sins; but thou hast multiplied thine
abominations more than they, and hast
justified thy sisters in all thine abominations which thou hast done.
52 Thou also, which hast judged thy sisters, bear thine own shame for thy sins that
thou hast committed more abominable
than they: they are more righteous than
thou: yea, be thou confounded also, and
bear thy shame, in that thou hast justified
thy sisters.
53 When I shall bring again their captivity, the captivity of Sodom and her daughters, and the captivity of Samaria and her
daughters, then *will I bring again* the captivity of thy captives in the midst of them:
54 That thou mayest bear thine own
shame, and mayest be confounded in all
that thou hast done, in that thou art a comfort unto them.
55 When thy sisters, Sodom and her
daughters, shall return to their former estate, and Samaria and her daughters shall
return to their former estate, then thou and
thy daughters shall return to your former
estate.
56 For thy sister Sodom was not mentioned by thy mouth in the day of thy
pride,
57 Before thy wickedness was discovered,
as at the time of *thy* reproach of the daughters of Syria, and all *that are* round about
her, the daughters of the Philistines, which
despise thee round about.
58 Thou hast borne thy lewdness and
thine abominations, saith the LORD.
59 For thus saith the Lord GOD; I will
even deal with thee as thou hast done,
which hast despised the oath in breaking
the covenant.
60 Nevertheless I will remember my covenant with thee in the days of thy youth,
and I will establish unto thee an everlasting covenant.
61 Then thou shalt remember thy ways,
and be ashamed, when thou shalt receive
thy sisters, thine elder and thy younger:
and I will give them unto thee for daughters, but not by thy covenant.
62 And I will establish my covenant with
thee; and thou shalt know that I *am* the
LORD:
63 That thou mayest remember, and be
confounded, and never open thy mouth
any more because of thy shame, when I
am pacified toward thee for all that thou
hast done, saith the Lord GOD.

17

1 And the word of the LORD came unto
me, saying,
2 Son of man, put forth a riddle, and
speak a parable unto the house of Israel;
3 And say, Thus saith the Lord GOD; A
great eagle with great wings, longwinged,
full of feathers, which had divers colours,
came unto Lebanon, and took the highest
branch of the cedar:
4 He cropped off the top of his young
twigs, and carried it into a land of traffick;
he set it in a city of merchants.
5 He took also of the seed of the land,
and planted it in a fruitful field; he placed
it by great waters, *and* set it *as* a willow tree.
6 And it grew, and became a spreading
vine of low stature, whose branches turned
toward him, and the roots thereof were
under him: so it became a vine, and
brought forth branches, and shot forth
sprigs.
7 There was also another great eagle with
great wings and many feathers: and, behold, this vine did bend her roots toward
him, and shot forth her branches toward
him, that he might water it by the furrows
of her plantation.
8 It was planted in a good soil by great
waters, that it might bring forth branches,
and that it might bear fruit, that it might
be a goodly vine.
9 Say thou, Thus saith the Lord GOD;
Shall it prosper? shall he not pull up the
roots thereof, and cut off the fruit thereof,
that it wither? it shall wither in all the
leaves of her spring, even without great
power or many people to pluck it up by
the roots thereof.
10 Yea, behold, *being* planted, shall it
prosper? shall it not utterly wither, when
the east wind toucheth it? it shall wither
in the furrows where it grew.
11 Moreover the word of the LORD came
unto me, saying,

12 Say now to the rebellious house, Know
ye not what these *things mean*? tell *them*,
Behold, the king of Babylon is come to
Jerusalem, and hath taken the king thereof,
and the princes thereof, and led them with
him to Babylon;
13 And hath taken of the king's seed, and
made a covenant with him, and hath tak-
en an oath of him: he hath also taken the
mighty of the land:
14 That the kingdom might be base, that
it might not lift itself up, *but* that by keeping of his covenant it might stand.
15 But he rebelled against him in sending his ambassadors into Egypt, that they
might give him horses and much people.
Shall he prosper? shall he escape that
doeth such *things*? or shall he break the
covenant, and be delivered?
16 As I live, saith the Lord GOD, surely in
the place *where* the king *dwelleth* that made
him king, whose oath he despised, and
whose covenant he brake, *even* with him
in the midst of Babylon he shall die.
17 Neither shall Pharaoh with *his* mighty
army and great company make for him in
the war, by casting up mounts, and building forts, to cut off many persons:
18 Seeing he despised the oath by breaking the covenant, when, lo, he had given
his hand, and hath done all these *things*,
he shall not escape.
19 Therefore thus saith the Lord GOD; *As*
I live, surely mine oath that he hath despised, and my covenant that he hath broken, even it will I recompense upon his
own head.
20 And I will spread my net upon him,
and he shall be taken in my snare, and I
will bring him to Babylon, and will plead
with him there for his trespass that he hath
trespassed against me.
21 And all his fugitives with all his bands
shall fall by the sword, and they that remain shall be scattered toward all winds:
and ye shall know that I the LORD have
spoken *it*.
22 Thus saith the Lord GOD; I will also
take of the highest branch of the high cedar, and will set *it*; I will crop off from the
top of his young twigs a tender one, and
will plant *it* upon an high mountain and
eminent:
23 In the mountain of the height of Israel will I plant it: and it shall bring forth
boughs, and bear fruit, and be a goodly
cedar: and under it shall dwell all fowl of
every wing; in the shadow of the branches
thereof shall they dwell.
24 And all the trees of the field shall
know that I the LORD have brought down
the high tree, have exalted the low tree,
have dried up the green tree, and have
made the dry tree to flourish: I the LORD
have brought down the high tree, have exalted the low tree, have dried up the green
tree, and have made the dry tree to flourish: I the LORD have spoken and have
done *it*.

18

1 The word of the LORD came unto me
again, saying,
2 What mean ye, that ye use this proverb
concerning the land of Israel, saying, The
fathers have eaten sour grapes, and the
children's teeth are set on edge?
3 *As* I live, saith the Lord GOD, ye shall
not have *occasion* any more to use this proverb in Israel.
4 Behold, all
souls are mine; as
the soul of the fa-
ther, so also the
soul of the son is
mine: the soul that
sinneth, it shall die.

18:4 Why Not Sin?
◄ Proverbs 11:19
Romans 5:12 ►

5 But if a man be just, and do that which
is lawful and right,
6 *And* hath not eaten upon the mountains, neither hath lifted up his eyes to
the idols of the house of Israel, neither
hath defiled his neighbour's wife, neither
hath come near to a menstruous woman,
7 And hath not oppressed any, *but* hath
restored to the debtor his pledge, hath
spoiled none by violence, hath given his
bread to the hungry, and hath covered the
naked with a garment;
8 He *that* hath not given forth upon usury, neither hath taken any increase, *that*
hath withdrawn his hand from iniquity,
hath executed true judgment between man
and man,
9 Hath walked in my statutes, and hath
kept my judgments, to deal truly; he *is* just,
he shall surely live, saith the Lord GOD.
10 If he beget a son *that is* a robber, a
shedder of blood, and *that* doeth the like
to *any* one of these *things*,
11 And that doeth not any of those
duties, but even hath eaten upon the

mountains, and defiled his neighbour's
wife,
12 Hath oppressed the poor and needy,
hath spoiled by violence, hath not restored
the pledge, and hath lifted up his eyes to
the idols, hath committed abomination,
13 Hath given forth upon usury, and hath
taken increase: shall he then live? he shall
not live: he hath done all these abominations; he shall surely die; his blood shall
be upon him.
14 Now, lo, *if* he beget a son, that seeth
all his father's sins which he hath done,
and considereth, and doeth not such like,
15 *That* hath not eaten upon the mountains, neither hath lifted up his eyes to the
idols of the house of Israel, hath not defiled his neighbour's wife,
16 Neither hath oppressed any, hath not
withholden the pledge, neither hath
spoiled by violence, *but* hath given his
bread to the hungry, and hath covered the
naked with a garment,
17 *That* hath taken off his hand from the
poor, *that* hath not received usury nor increase, hath executed my judgments, hath
walked in my statutes; he shall not die for
the iniquity of his father, he shall surely
live.
18 *As for* his father, because he cruelly
oppressed, spoiled his brother by violence,
and did *that* which *is* not good among
his people, lo, even he shall die in his
iniquity.
19 Yet say ye, Why? doth not the son bear
the iniquity of the father? When the son
hath done that which is lawful and right,
and hath kept all my statutes, and hath
done them, he shall surely live.
20 The soul that
sinneth, it shall die.
The son shall not
bear the iniquity of
the father, neither
shall the father bear
the iniquity of the
son: the righteous-
ness of the righ-
teous shall be upon
him, and the wick-
edness of the wick-
ed shall be upon him.

18:20 Blame
◄ Jeremiah 31:30
Romans 14:4 ►

18:20 Spiritual Death
◄ Proverbs 8:36
Romans 6:23 ►

21 But if the wicked will turn from all his
sins that he hath committed, and keep all
my statutes, and do that which is lawful
and right, he shall surely live, he shall not
die.
22 All his trans-
gressions that he
hath committed,
they shall not be
mentioned unto
him: in his righ-
teousness that he hath done he shall live.

18:22 Forgiveness
◄ Psalm 130:4
Matthew 6:14 ►

23 Have I any pleasure at all that the
wicked should die? saith the Lord GOD:
and not that he should return from his
ways, and live?
24 But when the righteous turneth away
from his righteousness, and committeth iniquity, *and* doeth according to all the abominations that the wicked *man* doeth, shall
he live? All his righteousness that he hath
done shall not be mentioned: in his trespass that he hath trespassed, and in his sin
that he hath sinned, in them shall he die.
25 Yet ye say, The
way of the Lord is
not equal. Hear
now, O house of Is-
rael; Is not my way
equal? are not your
ways unequal?

18:25 Injustice
◄ Jeremiah 12:1
Habakkuk 1:2 ►

26 When a righteous *man* turneth away
from his righteousness, and committeth
iniquity, and dieth in them; for his iniquity that he hath done shall he die.
27 Again, when the wicked *man* turneth
away from his wickedness that he hath
committed, and doeth that which is lawful and right, he shall save his soul alive.
28 Because he considereth, and turneth
away from all his transgressions that he
hath committed, he shall surely live, he
shall not die.
29 Yet saith the house of Israel, The way
of the Lord is not equal. O house of Israel, are not my ways equal? are not your
ways unequal?
30 Therefore I will
judge you, O house
of Israel, every one
according to his
ways, saith the Lord
GOD. Repent, and
turn *yourselves* from all your transgressions;
so iniquity shall not be your ruin.

18:30 Actions Judged
◄ Jeremiah 32:19
Matthew 16:27 ►

31 Cast away from you all your transgressions, whereby ye have transgressed;
and make you a new heart and a new

Turn to the next page for more . . .

spirit: for why will
ye die, O house of
Israel?
32 For I have no
pleasure in the
death of him that
dieth, saith the Lord GOD: wherefore turn
yourselves, and live ye.

18:31 Repent!
◄ Ezekiel 14:6
Ezekiel 33:11 ►

19

1 Moreover take thou up a lamentation
for the princes of Israel,
2 And say, What *is* thy mother? A lioness:
she lay down among lions, she nourished
her whelps among young lions.
3 And she brought up one of her whelps:
it became a young lion, and it learned to
catch the prey; it devoured men.
4 The nations also heard of him; he was
taken in their pit, and they brought him
with chains unto the land of Egypt.
5 Now when she saw that she had waited, *and* her hope was lost, then she took
another of her whelps, *and* made him a
young lion.
6 And he went up and down among the
lions, he became a young lion, and learned
to catch the prey, *and* devoured men.
7 And he knew their desolate palaces,
and he laid waste their cities; and the land
was desolate, and the fulness thereof, by
the noise of his roaring.
8 Then the nations set against him on
every side from the provinces, and spread
their net over him: he was taken in their
pit.
9 And they put him in ward in chains,
and brought him to the king of Babylon:
they brought him into holds, that his voice
should no more be heard upon the mountains of Israel.
10 Thy mother *is* like a vine in thy blood,
planted by the waters: she was fruitful and
full of branches by reason of many waters.
11 And she had strong rods for the
sceptres of them that bare rule, and her
stature was exalted among the thick
branches, and she appeared in her height
with the multitude of her branches.
12 But she was plucked up in fury, she
was cast down to the ground, and the east
wind dried up her fruit: her strong rods
were broken and withered; the fire consumed them.
13 And now she *is* planted in the wilderness, in a dry and thirsty ground.
14 And fire is gone out of a rod of her
branches, *which* hath devoured her fruit,
so that she hath no strong rod *to be* a
sceptre to rule. This *is* a lamentation, and
shall be for a lamentation.

20

1 And it came to pass in the seventh year,
in the fifth *month,* the tenth *day* of the
month, *that* certain of the elders of Israel
came to enquire of the LORD, and sat before me.
2 Then came the word of the LORD unto
me, saying,
3 Son of man, speak unto the elders of
Israel, and say unto them, Thus saith the
Lord GOD; Are ye come to enquire of me?
As I live, saith the Lord GOD, I will not be
enquired of by you.
4 Wilt thou judge them, son of man, wilt
thou judge *them?* cause them to know the
abominations of their fathers:
5 And say unto them, Thus saith the Lord
GOD; In the day when I chose Israel, and
lifted up mine hand unto the seed of the
house of Jacob, and made myself known
unto them in the land of Egypt, when I
lifted up mine hand unto them, saying, I
am the LORD your God;
6 In the day *that* I lifted up mine hand
unto them, to bring them forth of the land
of Egypt into a land that I had espied for
them, flowing with milk and honey, which
is the glory of all lands:
7 Then said I unto them, Cast ye away
every man the abominations of his eyes,
and defile not yourselves with the idols of
Egypt: I *am* the LORD your God.
8 But they rebelled against me, and
would not hearken unto me: they did not
every man cast away the abominations of
their eyes, neither did they forsake the idols
of Egypt: then I said, I will pour out my
fury upon them to accomplish my anger
against them in the midst of the land of
Egypt.
9 But I wrought for my name's sake, that
it should not be polluted before the heathen, among whom they *were,* in whose
sight I made myself known unto them, in
bringing them forth out of the land of
Egypt.
10 Wherefore I caused them to go forth
out of the land of Egypt, and brought them
into the wilderness.
11 And I gave them my statutes, and
shewed them my judgments, which *if* a
man do, he shall even live in them.

ter; it is furbished that it may glitter: should
we then make mirth? it contemneth the
rod of my son, *as* every tree.
11And he hath given it to be furbished,
that it may be handled: this sword is sharpened, and it is furbished, to give it into
the hand of the slayer.
12Cry and howl, son of man: for it shall
be upon my people, it *shall be* upon all the
princes of Israel: terrors by reason of the
sword shall be upon my people: smite
therefore upon *thy* thigh.
13Because *it is* a trial, and what if *the
sword* contemn even the rod? it shall be
no *more,* saith the Lord GOD.
14Thou therefore, son of man, prophesy, and smite *thine* hands together, and let
the sword be doubled the third time, the
sword of the slain: it *is* the sword of the
great *men that are* slain, which entereth into
their privy chambers.
15I have set the point of the sword
against all their gates, that *their* heart may
faint, and *their* ruins be multiplied: ah! *it
is* made bright, *it is* wrapped up for the
slaughter.
16Go thee one way or other, *either* on
the right hand, *or* on the left, whithersoever
thy face *is* set.
17I will also smite mine hands together,
and I will cause my fury to rest: I the LORD
have said *it.*
18The word of the LORD came unto me
again, saying,
19Also, thou son of man, appoint thee
two ways, that the sword of the king of
Babylon may come: both twain shall come
forth out of one land: and choose thou a
place, choose *it* at the head of the way to
the city.
20Appoint a way, that the sword may
come to Rabbath of the Ammonites, and
to Judah in Jerusalem the defenced.
21For the king of Babylon stood at the
parting of the way, at the head of the two
ways, to use divination: he made *his* arrows bright, he consulted with images, he
looked in the liver.
22At his right hand was the divination
for Jerusalem, to appoint captains, to open
the mouth in the slaughter, to lift up the
voice with shouting, to appoint *battering*
rams against the gates, to cast a mount,
and to build a fort.
23And it shall be unto them as a false
divination in their sight, to them that have
sworn oaths: but he will call to remembrance the iniquity, that they may be
taken.
24Therefore thus saith the Lord GOD;
Because ye have made your iniquity to be
remembered, in that your transgressions
are discovered, so that in all your doings
your sins do appear; because, *I say,* that ye
are come to remembrance, ye shall be tak-
en with the hand.
25And thou, profane wicked prince of
Israel, whose day is come, when iniquity
shall have an end,
26Thus saith the Lord GOD; Remove the
diadem, and take off the crown: this *shall*
not *be* the same: exalt *him that is* low, and
abase *him that is* high.
27I will overturn, overturn, overturn, it:
and it shall be no *more,* until he come
whose right it is; and I will give it *him.*
28And thou, son of man, prophesy and
say, Thus saith the Lord GOD concerning
the Ammonites, and concerning their reproach; even say thou, The sword, the
sword *is* drawn: for the slaughter *it is* furbished, to consume because of the glittering:
29Whiles they see vanity unto thee,
whiles they divine a lie unto thee, to bring
thee upon the necks of *them that are* slain,
of the wicked, whose day is come, when
their iniquity *shall have* an end.
30Shall I cause *it* to return into his
sheath? I will judge thee in the place where
thou wast created, in the land of thy nativity.
31And I will pour out mine indignation
upon thee, I will blow against thee in the
fire of my wrath, and deliver thee into the
hand of brutish men, *and* skilful to destroy.
32Thou shalt be for fuel to the fire; thy
blood shall be in the midst of the land;
thou shalt be no *more* remembered: for I
the LORD have spoken *it.*

22

1Moreover the word of the LORD came
unto me, saying,
2Now, thou son of man, wilt thou judge,
wilt thou judge the bloody city? yea, thou
shalt shew her all her abominations.
3Then say thou, Thus saith the Lord
GOD, The city sheddeth blood in the midst
of it, that her time may come, and maketh
idols against herself to defile herself.
4Thou art become guilty in thy blood

that thou hast shed; and hast defiled thyself in thine idols which thou hast made;
and thou hast caused thy days to draw
near, and art come *even* unto thy years:
therefore have I made thee a reproach unto
the heathen, and a mocking to all countries.
5 *Those that be* near, and *those that be* far
from thee, shall mock thee, *which art* infa-
mous *and* much vexed.
6 Behold, the princes of Israel, every one
were in thee to their power to shed blood.
7 In thee have they set light by father and
mother: in the midst of thee have they
dealt by oppression with the stranger: in
thee have they vexed the fatherless and the
widow.
8 Thou hast despised mine holy things,
and hast profaned my sabbaths.
9 In thee are men that carry tales to shed
blood: and in thee they eat upon the
mountains: in the midst of thee they commit lewdness.
10 In thee have they discovered their fathers' nakedness: in thee have they humbled her that was set apart for pollution.
11 And one hath committed abomination with his neighbour's wife; and another hath lewdly defiled his daughter in
law; and another in thee hath humbled his
sister, his father's daughter.
12 In thee have they taken gifts to shed
blood; thou hast taken usury and increase,
and thou hast greedily gained of thy
neighbours by extortion, and hast forgotten me, saith the Lord GOD.
13 Behold, there-
fore I have smitten
mine hand at thy
dishonest gain
which thou hast
made, and at thy
blood which hath been in the midst of thee.

22:13 Getting Ahead
◄ Jeremiah 22:13
James 5:4 ►

14 Can thine heart endure, or can thine
hands be strong, in the days that I shall
deal with thee? I the LORD have spoken *it*,
and will do *it*.
15 And I will scatter thee among the heathen, and disperse thee in the countries,
and will consume thy filthiness out of thee.
16 And thou shalt take thine inheritance
in thyself in the sight of the heathen, and
thou shalt know that I *am* the LORD.
17 And the word of the LORD came unto
me, saying,
18 Son of man, the house of Israel is to
me become dross: all they *are* brass, and
tin, and iron, and lead, in the midst of the
furnace; they are *even* the dross of silver.
19 Therefore thus saith the Lord GOD;
Because ye are all become dross, behold,
therefore I will gather you into the midst
of Jerusalem.
20 *As* they gather silver, and brass, and
iron, and lead, and tin, into the midst of
the furnace, to blow the fire upon it, to
melt *it*; so will I gather *you* in mine anger
and in my fury, and I will leave *you there*,
and melt you.
21 Yea, I will gather you, and blow upon
you in the fire of my wrath, and ye shall
be melted in the midst thereof.
22 As silver is melted in the midst of the
furnace, so shall ye be melted in the midst
thereof; and ye shall know that I the LORD
have poured out my fury upon you.
23 And the word of the LORD came unto
me, saying,
24 Son of man, say unto her, Thou *art*
the land that is not cleansed, nor rained
upon in the day of indignation.
25 *There is* a conspiracy of her prophets
in the midst thereof, like a roaring lion
ravening the prey; they have devoured
souls; they have taken the treasure and
precious things; they have made her many
widows in the midst thereof.
26 Her priests have violated my law, and
have profaned mine holy things: they have
put no difference between the holy and
profane, neither have they shewed *difference* between the unclean and the clean,
and have hid their eyes from my sabbaths,
and I am profaned among them.
27 Her princes in the midst thereof *are*
like wolves ravening the prey, to shed
blood, *and* to destroy souls, to get dishonest gain.
28 And her prophets have daubed them
with untempered *morter*, seeing vanity, and
divining lies unto them, saying, Thus saith
the Lord GOD, when the LORD hath not
spoken.
29 The people of the land have used oppression, and exercised robbery, and have
vexed the poor and needy: yea, they have
oppressed the stranger wrongfully.
30 And I sought for a man among them,
that should make up the hedge, and
stand in the gap before me for the land,

that I should not destroy it: but I found none.

31 Therefore have I poured out mine indignation upon them; I have consumed them with the fire of my wrath: their own way have I recompensed upon their heads, saith the Lord GOD.

23

1 The word of the LORD came again unto me, saying,

2 Son of man, there were two women, the daughters of one mother:

3 And they committed whoredoms in Egypt; they committed whoredoms in their youth: there were their breasts pressed, and there they bruised the teats of their virginity.

4 And the names of them *were* Aholah the elder, and Aholibah her sister: and they were mine, and they bare sons and daughters. Thus *were* their names; Samaria *is* Aholah, and Jerusalem Aholibah.

5 And Aholah played the harlot when she was mine; and she doted on her lovers, on the Assyrians *her* neighbours,

6 *Which were* clothed with blue, captains and rulers, all of them desirable young men, horsemen riding upon horses.

7 Thus she committed her whoredoms with them, with all them *that were* the chosen men of Assyria, and with all on whom she doted: with all their idols she defiled herself.

8 Neither left she her whoredoms *brought* from Egypt: for in her youth they lay with her, and they bruised the breasts of her virginity, and poured their whoredom upon her.

9 Wherefore I have delivered her into the hand of her lovers, into the hand of the Assyrians, upon whom she doted.

10 These discovered her nakedness: they took her sons and her daughters, and slew her with the sword: and she became famous among women; for they had executed judgment upon her.

11 And when her sister Aholibah saw *this*, she was more corrupt in her inordinate love than she, and in her whoredoms more than her sister in *her* whoredoms.

12 She doted upon the Assyrians *her* neighbours, captains and rulers clothed most gorgeously, horsemen riding upon horses, all of them desirable young men.

13 Then I saw that she was defiled, *that* they *took* both one way,

14 And *that* she increased her whoredoms: for when she saw men pourtrayed upon the wall, the images of the Chaldeans pourtrayed with vermilion,

15 Girded with girdles upon their loins, exceeding in dyed attire upon their heads, all of them princes to look to, after the manner of the Babylonians of Chaldea, the land of their nativity:

16 And as soon as she saw them with her eyes, she doted upon them, and sent messengers unto them into Chaldea.

17 And the Babylonians came to her into the bed of love, and they defiled her with their whoredom, and she was polluted with them, and her mind was alienated from them.

18 So she discovered her whoredoms, and discovered her nakedness: then my mind was alienated from her, like as my mind was alienated from her sister.

19 Yet she multiplied her whoredoms, in calling to remembrance the days of her youth, wherein she had played the harlot in the land of Egypt.

20 For she doted upon their paramours, whose flesh *is as* the flesh of asses, and whose issue *is like* the issue of horses.

21 Thus thou calledst to remembrance the lewdness of thy youth, in bruising thy teats by the Egyptians for the paps of thy youth.

22 Therefore, O Aholibah, thus saith the Lord GOD; Behold, I will raise up thy lovers against thee, from whom thy mind is alienated, and I will bring them against thee on every side;

23 The Babylonians, and all the Chaldeans, Pekod, and Shoa, and Koa, *and* all the Assyrians with them: all of them desirable young men, captains and rulers, great lords and renowned, all of them riding upon horses.

24 And they shall come against thee with chariots, wagons, and wheels, and with an assembly of people, *which* shall set against thee buckler and shield and helmet round about: and I will set judgment before them, and they shall judge thee according to their judgments.

25 And I will set my jealousy against thee, and they shall deal furiously with thee: they shall take away thy nose and thine ears; and thy remnant shall fall by the sword: they shall take thy sons and thy

daughters; and thy residue shall be devoured by the fire.

26 They shall also strip thee out of thy clothes, and take away thy fair jewels.

27 Thus will I make thy lewdness to cease from thee, and thy whoredom *brought* from the land of Egypt: so that thou shalt not lift up thine eyes unto them, nor remember Egypt any more.

28 For thus saith the Lord GOD; Behold, I will deliver thee into the hand *of them* whom thou hatest, into the hand *of them* from whom thy mind is alienated:

29 And they shall deal with thee hatefully, and shall take away all thy labour, and shall leave thee naked and bare: and the nakedness of thy whoredoms shall be discovered, both thy lewdness and thy whoredoms.

30 I will do these *things* unto thee, because thou hast gone a whoring after the heathen, *and* because thou art polluted with their idols.

31 Thou hast walked in the way of thy sister; therefore will I give her cup into thine hand.

32 Thus saith the Lord GOD; Thou shalt drink of thy sister's cup deep and large: thou shalt be laughed to scorn and had in derision; it containeth much.

33 Thou shalt be filled with drunkenness and sorrow, with the cup of astonishment and desolation, with the cup of thy sister Samaria.

34 Thou shalt even drink it and suck *it* out, and thou shalt break the sherds thereof, and pluck off thine own breasts: for I have spoken *it*, saith the Lord GOD.

35 Therefore thus saith the Lord GOD; Because thou hast forgotten me, and cast me behind thy back, therefore bear thou also thy lewdness and thy whoredoms.

36 The LORD said moreover unto me; Son of man, wilt thou judge Aholah and Aholibah? yea, declare unto them their abominations;

37 That they have committed adultery, and blood *is* in their hands, and with their idols have they committed adultery, and have also caused their sons, whom they bare unto me, to pass for them through *the fire*, to devour *them*.

38 Moreover this they have done unto me: they have defiled my sanctuary in the same day, and have profaned my sabbaths.

39 For when they had slain their children to their idols, then they came the same day into my sanctuary to profane it; and, lo, thus have they done in the midst of mine house.

40 And furthermore, that ye have sent for men to come from far, unto whom a messenger *was* sent; and, lo, they came: for whom thou didst wash thyself, paintedst thy eyes, and deckedst thyself with ornaments,

41 And satest upon a stately bed, and a table prepared before it, whereupon thou hast set mine incense and mine oil.

42 And a voice of a multitude being at ease *was* with her: and with the men of the common sort *were* brought Sabeans from the wilderness, which put bracelets upon their hands, and beautiful crowns upon their heads.

43 Then said I unto *her that was* old in adulteries, Will they now commit whoredoms with her, and she *with them?*

44 Yet they went in unto her, as they go in unto a woman that playeth the harlot: so went they in unto Aholah and unto Aholibah, the lewd women.

45 And the righteous men, they shall judge them after the manner of adulteresses, and after the manner of women that shed blood; because they *are* adulteresses, and blood *is* in their hands.

46 For thus saith the Lord GOD; I will bring up a company upon them, and will give them to be removed and spoiled.

47 And the company shall stone them with stones, and dispatch them with their swords; they shall slay their sons and their daughters, and burn up their houses with fire.

48 Thus will I cause lewdness to cease out of the land, that all women may be taught not to do after your lewdness.

49 And they shall recompense your lewdness upon you, and ye shall bear the sins of your idols: and ye shall know that I *am* the Lord GOD.

24

1 Again in the ninth year, in the tenth month, in the tenth *day* of the month, the word of the LORD came unto me, saying,

2 Son of man, write thee the name of the day, *even* of this same day: the king of Babylon set himself against Jerusalem this same day.

3And utter a parable unto the rebellious
house, and say unto them, Thus saith the
Lord GOD; Set on a pot, set *it* on, and also
pour water into it:
4Gather the pieces thereof into it, *even*
every good piece, the thigh, and the shoulder; fill *it* with the choice bones.
5Take the choice of the flock, and burn
also the bones under it, *and* make it boil
well, and let them seethe the bones of it
therein.
6Wherefore thus saith the Lord GOD;
Woe to the bloody city, to the pot whose
scum is therein, and whose scum *is* not
gone out of it! bring it out piece by piece;
let no lot fall up on it.
7For her blood is in the midst of her;
she set it upon the top of a rock; she
poured it not upon the ground, to cover it
with dust;
8That it might cause fury to come up to
take vengeance; I have set her blood upon
the top of a rock, that it should not be
covered.
9Therefore thus saith the Lord GOD; Woe
to the bloody city! I will even make the
pile for fire great.
10Heap on wood, kindle the fire, consume the flesh, and spice it well, and let
the bones be burned.
11Then set it empty upon the coals
thereof, that the brass of it may be hot,
and may burn, and *that* the filthiness of it
may be molten in it, *that* the scum of it
may be consumed.
12She hath wearied *herself* with lies, and
her great scum went not forth out of her:
her scum *shall be* in the fire.
13In thy filthiness *is* lewdness: because I
have purged thee, and thou wast not
purged, thou shalt not be purged from thy
filthiness any more, till I have caused my
fury to rest upon thee.
14I the LORD have spoken *it:* it shall
come to pass, and I will do *it;* I will not go
back, neither will I spare, neither will I repent; according to thy ways, and according to thy doings, shall they judge thee,
saith the Lord GOD.
15Also the word of the LORD came unto
me, saying,
16Son of man, behold, I take away from
thee the desire of thine eyes with a stroke:
yet neither shalt thou mourn nor weep,
neither shall thy tears run down.
17Forbear to cry, make no mourning for
the dead, bind the tire of thine head upon
thee, and put on thy shoes upon thy feet,
and cover not *thy* lips, and eat not the
bread of men.
18So I spake unto the people in the
morning: and at even my wife died; and I
did in the morning as I was commanded.
19And the people said unto me, Wilt
thou not tell us what these *things are* to us,
that thou doest *so?*
20Then I answered them, The word of
the LORD came unto me, saying,
21Speak unto the house of Israel, Thus
saith the Lord GOD; Behold, I will profane
my sanctuary, the excellency of your
strength, the desire of your eyes, and that
which your soul pitieth; and your sons and
your daughters whom ye have left shall fall
by the sword.
22And ye shall do as I have done: ye shall
not cover *your* lips, nor eat the bread of
men.
23And your tires *shall be* upon your
heads, and your shoes upon your feet: ye
shall not mourn nor weep; but ye shall
pine away for your iniquities, and mourn
one toward another.
24Thus Ezekiel is unto you a sign: according to all that he hath done shall ye
do: and when this cometh, ye shall know
that I *am* the Lord GOD.
25Also, thou son of man, *shall it* not *be*
in the day when I take from them their
strength, the joy of their glory, the desire
of their eyes, and that whereupon they set
their minds, their sons and their daughters,
26*That* he that escapeth in that day shall
come unto thee, to cause *thee* to hear *it*
with *thine* ears?
27In that day shall thy mouth be opened
to him which is escaped, and thou shalt
speak, and be no more dumb: and thou
shalt be a sign unto them; and they shall
know that I *am* the LORD.

25

1The word of the LORD came again unto
me, saying,
2Son of man, set thy face against the
Ammonites, and prophesy against them;
3And say unto the Ammonites, Hear the
word of the Lord GOD; Thus saith the Lord
GOD; Because thou saidst, Aha, against
my sanctuary, when it was profaned; and
against the land of Israel, when it was

desolate; and against the house of Judah,
when they went into captivity;
4Behold, therefore I will deliver thee to
the men of the east for a possession, and
they shall set their palaces in thee, and
make their dwellings in thee: they shall eat
thy fruit, and they shall drink thy milk.
5And I will make Rabbah a stable for
camels, and the Ammonites a couching
place for flocks: and ye shall know that I
am the LORD.
6For thus saith the Lord GOD; Because
thou hast clapped *thine* hands, and
stamped with the feet, and rejoiced in
heart with all thy despite against the land
of Israel;
7Behold, therefore I will stretch out
mine hand upon thee, and will deliver thee
for a spoil to the heathen; and I will cut
thee off from the people, and I will cause
thee to perish out of the countries: I will
destroy thee; and thou shalt know that I
am the LORD.
8Thus saith the Lord GOD; Because that
Moab and Seir do say, Behold, the house
of Judah *is* like unto all the heathen;
9Therefore, behold, I will open the side
of Moab from the cities, from his cities
which are on his frontiers, the glory of the
country, Beth-jeshimoth, Baal-meon, and
Kiriathaim,
10Unto the men of the east with the
Ammonites, and will give them in possession, that the Ammonites may not be remembered among the nations.
11And I will execute judgments upon
Moab; and they shall know that I *am* the
LORD.
12Thus saith the Lord GOD; Because that
Edom hath dealt against the house of Judah by taking vengeance, and hath greatly
offended, and revenged himself upon
them;
13Therefore thus saith the Lord GOD; I
will also stretch out mine hand upon
Edom, and will cut off man and beast from
it; and I will make it desolate from Teman;
and they of Dedan shall fall by the sword.
14And I will lay my vengeance upon
Edom by the hand of my people Israel: and
they shall do in Edom according to mine
anger and according to my fury; and they
shall know my vengeance, saith the Lord
GOD.
15Thus saith the Lord GOD; Because the
Philistines have
dealt by revenge,
and have taken ven-
geance with a de-
spiteful heart, to
destroy *it* for the
old hatred;

25:15
Examples of Revenge
◄ Esther 3:6
Matthew 14:8 ►

16Therefore thus saith the Lord GOD;
Behold, I will stretch out mine hand upon
the Philistines, and I will cut off the
Cherethims, and destroy the remnant of
the sea coast.
17And I will execute great vengeance
upon them with furious rebukes; and they
shall know that I *am* the LORD, when I shall
lay my vengeance upon them.

26

1And it came to pass in the eleventh year,
in the first *day* of the month, *that* the word
of the LORD came unto me, saying,
2Son of man, because that Tyrus hath
said against Jerusalem, Aha, she is broken
that was the gates of the people: she is
turned unto me: I shall be replenished, *now*
she is laid waste:
3Therefore thus saith the Lord GOD; Behold, I *am* against thee, O Tyrus, and will
cause many nations to come up against
thee, as the sea causeth his waves to
come up.
4And they shall destroy the walls of
Tyrus, and break down her towers: I will
also scrape her dust from her, and make
her like the top of a rock.
5It shall be *a place for* the spreading of
nets in the midst of the sea: for I have spoken *it*, saith the Lord GOD: and it shall
become a spoil to the nations.
6And her daughters which *are* in the field
shall be slain by the sword; and they shall
know that I *am* the LORD.
7For thus saith the Lord GOD; Behold, I
will bring upon Tyrus Nebuchadrezzar
king of Babylon, a king of kings, from the
north, with horses, and with chariots, and
with horsemen, and companies, and much
people.
8He shall slay with the sword thy daughters in the field: and he shall make a fort
against thee, and cast a mount against thee,
and lift up the buckler against thee.
9And he shall set engines of war against
thy walls, and with his axes he shall break
down thy towers.
10By reason of the abundance of his
horses their dust shall cover thee: thy walls

shall shake at the noise of the horsemen,
and of the wheels, and of the chariots,
when he shall enter into thy gates, as men
enter into a city wherein is made a breach.
11 With the hoofs of his horses shall he
tread down all thy streets: he shall slay thy
people by the sword, and thy strong garrisons shall go down to the ground.
12 And they shall make a spoil of thy
riches, and make a prey of thy merchandise: and they shall break down thy walls,
and destroy thy pleasant houses: and they
shall lay thy stones and thy timber and thy
dust in the midst of the water.
13 And I will cause the noise of thy songs
to cease; and the sound of thy harps shall
be no more heard.
14 And I will make thee like the top of a
rock: thou shalt be *a place* to spread nets
upon; thou shalt be built no more: for I
the LORD have spoken *it,* saith the Lord
GOD.
15 Thus saith the Lord GOD to Tyrus;
Shall not the isles shake at the sound of
thy fall, when the wounded cry, when the
slaughter is made in the midst of thee?
16 Then all the princes of the sea shall
come down from their thrones, and lay
away their robes, and put off their broidered garments: they shall clothe themselves with trembling; they shall sit upon
the ground, and shall tremble at *every*
moment, and be astonished at thee.
17 And they shall take up a lamentation
for thee, and say to thee, How art thou
destroyed, *that wast* inhabited of sea-
faring men, the renowned city, which wast
strong in the sea, she and her inhabitants,
which cause their terror *to be* on all that
haunt it!
18 Now shall the isles tremble in the day
of thy fall; yea, the isles that *are* in the sea
shall be troubled at thy departure.
19 For thus saith the Lord GOD; When I
shall make thee a desolate city, like the cities that are not inhabited; when I shall
bring up the deep upon thee, and great
waters shall cover thee;
20 When I shall bring thee down with
them that descend into the pit, with the
people of old time, and shall set thee in
the low parts of the earth, in places desolate of old, with them that go down to the
pit, that thou be not inhabited; and I shall
set glory in the land of the living;
21 I will make thee a terror, and thou *shalt
be* no *more:* though thou be sought for, yet
shalt thou never be found again, saith the
Lord GOD.

27

1 The word of the LORD came again unto
me, saying,
2 Now, thou son of man, take up a lamentation for Tyrus;
3 And say unto Tyrus, O thou that art
situate at the entry of the sea, *which art* a
merchant of the people for many isles,
Thus saith the Lord GOD; O Tyrus, thou
hast said, I *am* of perfect beauty.
4 Thy borders *are* in the midst of the seas,
thy builders have perfected thy beauty.
5 They have made all thy *ship* boards of
fir trees of Senir: they have taken cedars
from Lebanon to make masts for thee.
6 *Of* the oaks of Bashan have they made
thine oars; the company of the Ashurites
have made thy benches *of* ivory, *brought* out
of the isles of Chittim.
7 Fine linen with broidered work from
Egypt was that which thou spreadest forth
to be thy sail; blue and purple from the
isles of Elishah was that which covered
thee.
8 The inhabitants of Zidon and Arvad
were thy mariners: thy wise *men,* O Tyrus,
that were in thee, were thy pilots.
9 The ancients of Gebal and the wise *men*
thereof were in thee thy calkers: all the
ships of the sea with their mariners were
in thee to occupy thy merchandise.
10 They of Persia and of Lud and of Phut
were in thine army, thy men of war: they
hanged the shield and helmet in thee; they
set forth thy comeliness.
11 The men of Arvad with thine army *were*
upon thy walls round about, and the
Gammadims were in thy towers: they
hanged their shields upon thy walls round
about; they have made thy beauty perfect.
12 Tarshish *was* thy merchant by reason
of the multitude of all *kind of* riches; with
silver, iron, tin, and lead, they traded in
thy fairs.
13 Javan, Tubal, and Meshech, they *were*
thy merchants: they traded the persons of
men and vessels of brass in thy market.
14 They of the house of Togarmah traded in thy fairs with horses and horsemen
and mules.
15 The men of Dedan *were* thy merchants;
many isles *were* the merchandise of thine

hand: they brought thee *for* a present horns
of ivory and ebony.
16 Syria *was* thy merchant by reason of
the multitude of the wares of thy making:
they occupied in thy fairs with emeralds,
purple, and broidered work, and fine lin-
en, and coral, and agate.
17 Judah, and the land of Israel, they *were*
thy merchants: they traded in thy market
wheat of Minnith, and Pannag, and honey, and oil, and balm.
18 Damascus *was* thy merchant in the
multitude of the wares of thy making, for
the multitude of all riches; in the wine of
Helbon, and white wool.
19 Dan also and Javan going to and fro
occupied in thy fairs: bright iron, cassia,
and calamus, were in thy market.
20 Dedan *was* thy merchant in precious
clothes for chariots.
21 Arabia, and all the princes of Kedar,
they occupied with thee in lambs, and rams,
and goats: in these *were they* thy merchants.
22 The merchants of Sheba and Raamah,
they *were* thy merchants: they occupied in
thy fairs with chief of all spices, and with
all precious stones, and gold.
23 Haran, and Canneh, and Eden, the
merchants of Sheba, Asshur, *and* Chilmad,
were thy merchants.
24 These *were* thy merchants in all sorts
of things, in blue clothes, and broidered
work, and in chests of rich apparel, bound
with cords, and made of cedar, among thy
merchandise.
25 The ships of Tarshish did sing of thee
in thy market: and thou wast replenished,
and made very glorious in the midst of the
seas.
26 Thy rowers have brought thee into
great waters: the east wind hath broken
thee in the midst of the seas.
27 Thy riches, and thy fairs, thy merchandise, thy mariners, and thy pilots, thy calkers, and the occupiers of thy merchandise,
and all thy men of war, that *are* in thee,
and in all thy company which *is* in the
midst of thee, shall fall into the midst of
the seas in the day of thy ruin.
28 The suburbs shall shake at the sound
of the cry of thy pilots.
29 And all that handle the oar, the mariners, *and* all the pilots of the sea, shall
come down from their ships, they shall
stand upon the land;
30 And shall cause their voice to be heard
against thee, and shall cry bitterly, and
shall cast up dust upon their heads, they
shall wallow themselves in the ashes:
31 And they shall make themselves utterly bald for thee, and gird them with sackcloth, and they shall weep for thee with
bitterness of heart *and* bitter wailing.
32 And in their wailing they shall take
up a lamentation for thee, and lament over
thee, *saying,* What *city is* like Tyrus, like the
destroyed in the midst of the sea?
33 When thy wares went forth out of the
seas, thou filledst many people; thou didst
enrich the kings of the earth with the multitude of thy riches and of thy merchandise.
34 In the time *when* thou shalt be broken by the seas in the depths of the waters
thy merchandise and all thy company in
the midst of thee shall fall.
35 All the inhabitants of the isles shall
be astonished at thee, and their kings shall
be sore afraid, they shall be troubled in
their countenance.
36 The merchants among the people shall
hiss at thee; thou *shalt be* a terror, and never shalt be any more.

28

1 The word of the LORD came again unto
me, saying,
2 Son of man, say unto the prince of
Tyrus, Thus saith the Lord GOD; Because
thine heart *is* lifted up, and thou hast said,
I *am* a God, I sit *in* the seat of God, in the
midst of the seas; yet thou *art* a man, and
not God, though thou set thine heart as
the heart of God:
3 Behold, thou *art* wiser than Daniel;
there is no secret that they can hide from
thee:
4 With thy wis-
dom and with
thine understand-
ing thou hast got-
ten thee riches, and
hast gotten gold
and silver into thy treasures:

28:4 Hoarding
◄ Ecclesiastes 2:26
Matthew 6:19 ►

5 By thy great wisdom *and* by thy traffick
hast thou increased thy riches, and thine
heart is lifted up because of thy riches:
6 Therefore thus saith the Lord GOD; Because thou hast set thine heart as the heart
of God;
7 Behold, therefore I will bring strangers
upon thee, the terrible of the nations: and

they shall draw their swords against the beauty of thy wisdom, and they shall defile thy brightness.

8 They shall bring thee down to the pit, and thou shalt die the deaths of *them that are* slain in the midst of the seas.

9 Wilt thou yet say before him that slayeth thee, I *am* God? but thou *shalt be* a man, and no God, in the hand of him that slayeth thee.

10 Thou shalt die the deaths of the uncircumcised by the hand of strangers: for I have spoken *it,* saith the Lord GOD.

11 Moreover the word of the LORD came unto me, saying,

12 Son of man, take up a lamentation upon the king of Tyrus, and say unto him, Thus saith the Lord GOD; Thou sealest up the sum, full of wisdom, and perfect in beauty.

13 Thou hast been in Eden the garden of God; every precious stone *was* thy covering, the sardius, topaz, and the diamond, the beryl, the onyx, and the jasper, the sapphire, the emerald, and the carbuncle, and gold: the workmanship of thy tabrets and of thy pipes was prepared in thee in the day that thou wast created.

14 Thou *art* the anointed cherub that covereth; and I have set thee *so:* thou wast upon the holy mountain of God; thou hast walked up and down in the midst of the stones of fire.

15 Thou *wast* perfect in thy ways from the day that thou wast created, till iniquity was found in thee.

16 By the multitude of thy merchandise they have filled the midst of thee with violence, and thou hast sinned: therefore I will cast thee as profane out of the mountain of God: and I will destroy thee, O covering cherub, from the midst of the stones of fire.

17 Thine heart was lifted up because of thy beauty, thou hast corrupted thy wisdom by reason of thy brightness: I will cast thee to the ground, I will lay thee before kings, that they may behold thee.

18 Thou hast defiled thy sanctuaries by the multitude of thine iniquities, by the iniquity of thy traffick; therefore will I bring forth a fire from the midst of thee, it shall devour thee, and I will bring thee to ashes upon the earth in the sight of all them that behold thee.

19 All they that know thee among the people shall be astonished at thee: thou shalt be a terror, and never *shalt* thou *be* any more.

20 Again the word of the LORD came unto me, saying,

21 Son of man, set thy face against Zidon, and prophesy against it,

22 And say, Thus saith the Lord GOD; Behold, I *am* against thee, O Zidon; and I will be glorified in the midst of thee: and they shall know that I *am* the LORD, when I shall have executed judgments in her, and shall be sanctified in her.

23 For I will send into her pestilence, and blood into her street; and the wounded shall be judged in the midst of her by the sword upon her on every side; and they shall know that I *am* the LORD.

24 And there shall be no more a pricking brier unto the house of Israel, nor *any* grieving thorn of all *that are* round about them, that despised them; and they shall know that I *am* the Lord GOD.

25 Thus saith the Lord GOD; When I shall have gathered the house of Israel from the people among whom they are scattered, and shall be sanctified in them in the sight of the heathen, then shall they dwell in their land that I have given to my servant Jacob.

26 And they shall dwell safely therein, and shall build houses, and plant vineyards; yea, they shall dwell with confidence, when I have executed judgments upon all those that despise them round about them; and they shall know that I *am* the LORD their God.

29

1 In the tenth year, in the tenth *month,* in the twelfth *day* of the month, the word of the LORD came unto me, saying,

2 Son of man, set thy face against Pharaoh king of Egypt, and prophesy against him, and against all Egypt:

3 Speak, and say, Thus saith the Lord GOD; Behold, I *am* against thee, Pharaoh king of Egypt, the great dragon that lieth in the midst of his rivers, which hath said, My river *is* mine own, and I have made *it* for myself.

4 But I will put hooks in thy jaws, and I will cause the fish of thy rivers to stick unto thy scales, and I will bring thee up out of the midst of thy rivers, and all the fish of thy rivers shall stick unto thy scales.

5 And I will leave thee *thrown* into the wilderness, thee and all the fish of thy rivers: thou shalt fall upon the open fields; thou shalt not be brought together, nor gathered: I have given thee for meat to the beasts of the field and to the fowls of the heaven.

6 And all the inhabitants of Egypt shall know that I *am* the LORD, because they have been a staff of reed to the house of Israel.

7 When they took hold of thee by thy hand, thou didst break, and rend all their shoulder: and when they leaned upon thee, thou brakest, and madest all their loins to be at a stand.

8 Therefore thus saith the Lord GOD; Behold, I will bring a sword upon thee, and cut off man and beast out of thee.

9 And the land of Egypt shall be desolate and waste; and they shall know that I *am* the LORD: because he hath said, The river *is* mine, and I have made *it*.

10 Behold, therefore I *am* against thee, and against thy rivers, and I will make the land of Egypt utterly waste *and* desolate, from the tower of Syene even unto the border of Ethiopia.

11 No foot of man shall pass through it, nor foot of beast shall pass through it, neither shall it be inhabited forty years.

12 And I will make the land of Egypt desolate in the midst of the countries *that are* desolate, and her cities among the cities *that are* laid waste shall be desolate forty years: and I will scatter the Egyptians among the nations, and will disperse them through the countries.

13 Yet thus saith the Lord GOD; At the end of forty years will I gather the Egyptians from the people whither they were scattered:

14 And I will bring again the captivity of Egypt, and will cause them to return *into* the land of Pathros, into the land of their habitation; and they shall be there a base kingdom.

15 It shall be the basest of the kingdoms; neither shall it exalt itself any more above the nations: for I will diminish them, that they shall no more rule over the nations.

16 And it shall be no more the confidence of the house of Israel, which bringeth *their* iniquity to remembrance, when they shall look after them: but they shall know that I *am* the Lord GOD.

17 And it came to pass in the seven and twentieth year, in the first *month,* in the first *day* of the month, the word of the LORD came unto me, saying,

18 Son of man, Nebuchadrezzar king of Babylon caused his army to serve a great service against Tyrus: every head *was* made bald, and every shoulder *was* peeled: yet had he no wages, nor his army, for Tyrus, for the service that he had served against it:

19 Therefore thus saith the Lord GOD; Behold, I will give the land of Egypt unto Nebuchadrezzar king of Babylon; and he shall take her multitude, and take her spoil, and take her prey; and it shall be the wages for his army.

20 I have given him the land of Egypt *for* his labour wherewith he served against it, because they wrought for me, saith the Lord GOD.

21 In that day will I cause the horn of the house of Israel to bud forth, and I will give thee the opening of the mouth in the midst of them; and they shall know that I *am* the LORD.

30

1 The word of the LORD came again unto me, saying,

2 Son of man, prophesy and say, Thus saith the Lord GOD; Howl ye, Woe worth the day

3 For the day *is* near, even the day of the LORD *is* near, a cloudy day; it shall be the time of the heathen.

4 And the sword shall come upon Egypt, and great pain shall be in Ethiopia, when the slain shall fall in Egypt, and they shall take away her multitude, and her foundations shall be broken down.

5 Ethiopia, and Libya, and Lydia, and all the mingled people, and Chub, and the men of the land that is in league, shall fall with them by the sword.

6 Thus saith the LORD; They also that uphold Egypt shall fall; and the pride of her power shall come down: from the tower of Syene shall they fall in it by the sword, saith the Lord GOD.

7 And they shall be desolate in the midst of the countries *that are* desolate, and her cities shall be in the midst of the cities *that are* wasted.

8 And they shall know that I *am* the LORD,

when I have set a fire in Egypt, and *when*
all her helpers shall be destroyed.
9 In that day shall messengers go forth
from me in ships to make the careless Ethiopians afraid, and great pain shall come
upon them, as in the day of Egypt: for, lo,
it cometh.
10 Thus saith the Lord GOD; I will also
make the multitude of Egypt to cease by
the hand of Nebuchadrezzar king of Babylon.
11 He and his people with him, the terrible of the nations, shall be brought to destroy the land: and they shall draw their
swords against Egypt, and fill the land with
the slain.
12 And I will make the rivers dry, and sell
the land into the hand of the wicked: and
I will make the land waste, and all that is
therein, by the hand of strangers: I the
LORD have spoken *it*.
13 Thus saith the Lord GOD; I will also
destroy the idols, and I will cause *their*
images to cease out of Noph; and there
shall be no more a prince of the land of
Egypt: and I will put a fear in the land of
Egypt.
14 And I will make Pathros desolate, and
will set fire in Zoan, and will execute judgments in No.
15 And I will pour my fury upon Sin, the
strength of Egypt; and I will cut off the
multitude of No.
16 And I will set fire in Egypt: Sin shall
have great pain, and No shall be rent asunder, and Noph *shall have* distresses daily.
17 The young men of Aven and of Pi-
beseth shall fall by the sword: and these
cities shall go into captivity.
18 At Tehaphnehes also the day shall be
darkened, when I shall break there the
yokes of Egypt: and the pomp of her
strength shall cease in her: as for her, a
cloud shall cover her, and her daughters
shall go into captivity.
19 Thus will I execute judgments in
Egypt: and they shall know that I *am* the
LORD.
20 And it came to pass in the eleventh
year, in the first *month*, in the seventh *day*
of the month, *that* the word of the LORD
came unto me, saying,
21 Son of man, I have broken the arm of
Pharaoh king of Egypt; and, lo, it shall not
be bound up to be healed, to put a roller
to bind it, to make it strong to hold the
sword.
22 Therefore thus saith the Lord GOD;
Behold, I *am* against Pharaoh king of
Egypt, and will break his arms, the strong,
and that which was broken; and I will
cause the sword to fall out of his hand.
23 And I will scatter the Egyptians among
the nations, and will disperse them
through the countries.
24 And I will strengthen the arms of the
king of Babylon, and put my sword in his
hand: but I will break Pharaoh's arms, and
he shall groan before him with the
groanings of a deadly wounded *man*.
25 But I will strengthen the arms of the
king of Babylon, and the arms of Pharaoh
shall fall down; and they shall know that I
am the LORD, when I shall put my sword
into the hand of the king of Babylon, and
he shall stretch it out upon the land of
Egypt.
26 And I will scatter the Egyptians among
the nations, and disperse them among the
countries; and they shall know that I *am*
the LORD.

31

1 And it came to pass in the eleventh year,
in the third *month*, in the first *day* of the
month, *that* the word of the LORD came
unto me, saying,
2 Son of man, speak unto Pharaoh king
of Egypt, and to his multitude; Whom art
thou like in thy greatness?
3 Behold, the Assyrian *was* a cedar in Lebanon with fair branches, and with a shadowing shroud, and of an high stature; and
his top was among the thick boughs.
4 The waters made him great, the deep
set him up on high with her rivers running round about his plants, and sent out
her little rivers unto all the trees of the
field.
5 Therefore his height was exalted above
all the trees of the field, and his boughs
were multiplied, and his branches became
long because of the multitude of waters,
when he shot forth.
6 All the fowls of heaven made their nests
in his boughs, and under his branches did
all the beasts of the field bring forth their
young, and under his shadow dwelt all
great nations.
7 Thus was he fair in his greatness, in the
length of his branches: for his root was by
great waters.

8 The cedars in the garden of God could not hide him: the fir trees were not like his boughs, and the chesnut trees were not like his branches; nor any tree in the garden of God was like unto him in his beauty.

9 I have made him fair by the multitude of his branches: so that all the trees of Eden, that *were* in the garden of God, envied him.

10 Therefore thus saith the Lord GOD; Because thou hast lifted up thyself in height, and he hath shot up his top among the thick boughs, and his heart is lifted up in his height;

11 I have therefore delivered him into the hand of the mighty one of the heathen; he shall surely deal with him: I have driven him out for his wickedness.

12 And strangers, the terrible of the nations, have cut him off, and have left him: upon the mountains and in all the valleys his branches are fallen, and his boughs are broken by all the rivers of the land; and all the people of the earth are gone down from his shadow, and have left him.

13 Upon his ruin shall all the fowls of the heaven remain, and all the beasts of the field shall be upon his branches:

14 To the end that none of all the trees by the waters exalt themselves for their height, neither shoot up their top among the thick boughs, neither their trees stand up in their height, all that drink water: for they are all delivered unto death, to the nether parts of the earth, in the midst of the children of men, with them that go down to the pit.

15 Thus saith the Lord GOD; In the day when he went down to the grave I caused a mourning: I covered the deep for him, and I restrained the floods thereof, and the great waters were stayed: and I caused Lebanon to mourn for him, and all the trees of the field fainted for him.

16 I made the nations to shake at the sound of his fall, when I cast him down to hell with them that descend into the pit: and all the trees of Eden, the choice and best of Lebanon, all that drink water, shall be comforted in the nether parts of the earth.

17 They also went down into hell with him unto *them that be* slain with the sword; and *they that were* his arm, *that* dwelt under his shadow in the midst of the heathen.

18 To whom art thou thus like in glory and in greatness among the trees of Eden? yet shalt thou be brought down with the trees of Eden unto the nether parts of the earth: thou shalt lie in the midst of the uncircumcised with *them that be* slain by the sword. This *is* Pharaoh and all his multitude, saith the Lord GOD.

32

1 And it came to pass in the twelfth year, in the twelfth month, in the first *day* of the month, *that* the word of the LORD came unto me, saying,

2 Son of man, take up a lamentation for Pharaoh king of Egypt, and say unto him, Thou art like a young lion of the nations, and thou *art* as a whale in the seas: and thou camest forth with thy rivers, and troubledst the waters with thy feet, and fouledst their rivers.

3 Thus saith the Lord GOD; I will therefore spread out my net over thee with a company of many people; and they shall bring thee up in my net.

4 Then will I leave thee upon the land, I will cast thee forth upon the open field, and will cause all the fowls of the heaven to remain upon thee, and I will fill the beasts of the whole earth with thee.

5 And I will lay thy flesh upon the mountains, and fill the valleys with thy height.

6 I will also water with thy blood the land wherein thou swimmest, *even* to the mountains; and the rivers shall be full of thee.

7 And when I shall put thee out, I will cover the heaven, and make the stars thereof dark; I will cover the sun with a cloud, and the moon shall not give her light.

8 All the bright lights of heaven will I make dark over thee, and set darkness upon thy land, saith the Lord GOD.

9 I will also vex the hearts of many people, when I shall bring thy destruction among the nations, into the countries which thou hast not known.

10 Yea, I will make many people amazed at thee, and their kings shall be horribly afraid for thee, when I shall brandish my sword before them; and they shall tremble at *every* moment, every man for his own life, in the day of thy fall.

11 For thus saith the Lord GOD; The

sword of the king of Babylon shall come upon thee.

12 By the swords of the mighty will I cause thy multitude to fall, the terrible of the nations, all of them: and they shall spoil the pomp of Egypt, and all the multitude thereof shall be destroyed.

13 I will destroy also all the beasts thereof from beside the great waters; neither shall the foot of man trouble them any more, nor the hoofs of beasts trouble them.

14 Then will I make their waters deep, and cause their rivers to run like oil, saith the Lord GOD.

15 When I shall make the land of Egypt desolate, and the country shall be destitute of that whereof it was full, when I shall smite all them that dwell therein, then shall they know that I *am* the LORD.

16 This *is* the lamentation wherewith they shall lament her: the daughters of the nations shall lament her: they shall lament for her, *even* for Egypt, and for all her multitude, saith the Lord GOD.

17 It came to pass also in the twelfth year, in the fifteenth *day* of the month, *that* the word of the LORD came unto me, saying,

18 Son of man, wail for the multitude of Egypt, and cast them down, *even* her, and the daughters of the famous nations, unto the nether parts of the earth, with them that go down into the pit.

19 Whom dost thou pass in beauty? go down, and be thou laid with the uncircumcised.

20 They shall fall in the midst of *them that are* slain by the sword: she is delivered to the sword: draw her and all her multitudes.

21 The strong among the mighty shall speak to him out of the midst of hell with them that help him: they are gone down, they lie uncircumcised, slain by the sword.

22 Asshur *is* there and all her company: his graves *are* about him: all of them slain, fallen by the sword:

23 Whose graves are set in the sides of the pit, and her company is round about her grave: all of them slain, fallen by the sword, which caused terror in the land of the living.

24 There *is* Elam and all her multitude round about her grave, all of them slain, fallen by the sword, which are gone down uncircumcised into the nether parts of the earth, which caused their terror in the land of the living; yet have they borne their shame with them that go down to the pit.

25 They have set her a bed in the midst of the slain with all her multitude: her graves *are* round about him: all of them uncircumcised, slain by the sword: though their terror was caused in the land of the living, yet have they borne their shame with them that go down to the pit: he is put in the midst of *them that be* slain.

26 There *is* Meshech, Tubal, and all her multitude: her graves *are* round about him: all of them uncircumcised, slain by the sword, though they caused their terror in the land of the living.

27 And they shall not lie with the mighty *that are* fallen of the uncircumcised, which are gone down to hell with their weapons of war: and they have laid their swords under their heads, but their iniquities shall be upon their bones, though *they were* the terror of the mighty in the land of the living.

28 Yea, thou shalt be broken in the midst of the uncircumcised, and shalt lie with *them that are* slain with the sword.

29 There *is* Edom, her kings, and all her princes, which with their might are laid by *them that were* slain by the sword: they shall lie with the uncircumcised, and with them that go down to the pit.

30 There *be* the princes of the north, all of them, and all the Zidonians, which are gone down with the slain; with their terror they are ashamed of their might; and they lie uncircumcised with *them that be* slain by the sword, and bear their shame with them that go down to the pit.

31 Pharaoh shall see them, and shall be comforted over all his multitude, *even* Pharaoh and all his army slain by the sword, saith the Lord GOD.

32 For I have caused my terror in the land of the living: and he shall be laid in the midst of the uncircumcised with *them that are* slain with the sword, *even* Pharaoh and all his multitude, saith the Lord GOD.

33

1 Again the word of the LORD came unto me, saying,

2 Son of man, speak to the children of thy people, and say unto them, When I bring the sword upon a land, if the people of the land take a man of their coasts, and set him for their watchman:

3 If when he seeth the sword come upon

the land, he blow the trumpet, and warn
the people;
4 Then whosoever heareth the sound of
the trumpet, and taketh not warning; if the
sword come, and take him away, his blood
shall be upon his own head.
5 He heard the sound of the trumpet, and
took not warning; his blood shall be upon
him. But he that taketh warning shall deliver his soul.
6 But if the watchman see the sword
come, and blow not the trumpet, and the
people be not warned; if the sword come,
and take *any* person from among them, he
is taken away in his iniquity; but his blood
will I require at the watchman's hand.
7 So thou, O son of man, I have set thee
a watchman unto the house of Israel; therefore thou shalt hear the word at my mouth,
and warn them from me.
8 When I say unto the wicked, O wicked
man, thou shalt surely die; if thou dost not
speak to warn the wicked from his way,
that wicked *man* shall die in his iniquity;
but his blood will I require at thine hand.
9 Nevertheless, if
thou warn the wick-
ed of his way to
turn from it; if he
do not turn from
his way, he shall die
in his iniquity; but thou hast delivered thy
soul.

33:9
Salvation
◄ Luke 14:18 ►

10 Therefore, O thou son of man, speak
unto the house of Israel; Thus ye speak,
saying, If our transgressions and our sins
be upon us, and we pine away in them,
how should we then live?
11 Say unto them,
As I live, saith the
Lord GOD, I have
no pleasure in the
death of the wick-
ed; but that the
wicked turn from
his way and live:
turn ye, turn ye
from your evil
ways; for why will
ye die, O house of
Israel?

33:11 Change
◄ Jeremiah 35:15
Hosea 6:1 ►

33:11 Repent!
◄ Ezekiel 18:31
Daniel 4:27 ►

12 Therefore, thou son of man, say unto
the children of thy people, The righteousness of the righteous shall not deliver him
in the day of his transgression: as for the
wickedness of the wicked, he shall not fall
thereby in the day that he turneth from
his wickedness; neither shall the righteous
be able to live for his *righteousness* in the
day that he sinneth.
13 When I shall say to the righteous, *that*
he shall surely live; if he trust to his own
righteousness, and commit iniquity, all his
righteousnesses shall not be remembered;
but for his iniquity that he hath committed, he shall die for it.
14 Again, when I say unto the wicked,
Thou shalt surely die; if he turn from his
sin, and do that which is lawful and right;
15 *If* the wicked restore the pledge, give
again that he had robbed, walk in the statutes of life, without committing iniquity;
he shall surely live, he shall not die.
16 None of his sins that he hath committed shall be mentioned unto him: he hath
done that which is lawful and right; he
shall surely live.
17 Yet the children of thy people say, The
way of the Lord is not equal: but as for
them, their way is not equal.
18 When the righteous turneth from his
righteousness, and committeth iniquity, he
shall even die thereby.
19 But if the wicked turn from his wickedness, and do that which is lawful and
right, he shall live thereby.
20 Yet ye say, The way of the Lord is not
equal. O ye house of Israel, I will judge
you every one after his ways.
21 And it came to pass in the twelfth year
of our captivity, in the tenth *month,* in the
fifth *day* of the month, *that* one that had
escaped out of Jerusalem came unto me,
saying, The city is smitten.
22 Now the hand of the LORD was upon
me in the evening, afore he that was escaped came; and had opened my mouth,
until he came to me in the morning; and
my mouth was opened, and I was no more
dumb.
23 Then the word of the LORD came unto
me, saying,
24 Son of man, they that inhabit those
wastes of the land of Israel speak, saying,
Abraham was one, and he inherited the
land: but we *are* many; the land is given
us for inheritance.
25 Wherefore say unto them, Thus saith
the Lord GOD; Ye eat with the blood, and
lift up your eyes toward your idols, and

shed blood: and shall ye possess the land?
26 Ye stand upon your sword, ye work
abomination, and ye defile every one his
neighbour's wife: and shall ye possess the
land?
27 Say thou thus unto them, Thus saith
the Lord GOD; *As* I live, surely they that
are in the wastes shall fall by the sword,
and him that *is* in the open field will I give
to the beasts to be devoured, and they that
be in the forts and in the caves shall die of
the pestilence.
28 For I will lay the land most desolate,
and the pomp of her strength shall cease;
and the mountains of Israel shall be desolate, that none shall pass through.
29 Then shall they know that I *am* the
LORD, when I have laid the land most desolate because of all their abominations
which they have committed.
30 Also, thou son of man, the children
of thy people still are talking against thee
by the walls and in the doors of the houses,
and speak one to another, every one to his
brother, saying, Come, I pray you, and hear
what is the word that cometh forth from
the LORD.
31 And they come unto thee as the people cometh, and they sit before thee *as* my
people, and they hear thy words, but they
will not do them: for with their mouth
they shew much love, *but* their heart goeth
after their covetousness.
32 And, lo, thou
art unto them as a
very lovely song of
one that hath a
pleasant voice, and
can play well on an
instrument: for they hear thy words, but
they do them not.

33:32
Listening and Doing
◄ Matthew 7:26 ►

33 And when this cometh to pass, (lo, it
will come,) then shall they know that a
prophet hath been among them.

34

1 And the word of the LORD came unto
me, saying,
2 Son of man, prophesy against the shepherds of Israel, prophesy, and say unto
them, Thus saith the Lord GOD unto the
shepherds; Woe *be* to the shepherds of Israel that do feed themselves! should not
the shepherds feed the flocks?
3 Ye eat the fat, and ye clothe you with
the wool, ye kill them that are fed: *but* ye
feed not the flock.
4 The diseased
have ye not
strengthened, nei-
ther have ye healed
that which was sick,
neither have ye
bound up *that which was* broken, neither
have ye brought again that which was driv-
en away, neither have ye sought that which
was lost; but with force and with cruelty
have ye ruled them.

34:4 Mercy
◄ Proverbs 21:13
Zechariah 11:16 ►

5 And they were scattered, because *there
is* no shepherd: and they became meat to
all the beasts of the field, when they were
scattered.
6 My sheep wandered through all the
mountains, and upon every high hill: yea,
my flock was scattered upon all the face of
the earth, and none did search or seek *after them.*
7 Therefore, ye shepherds, hear the word
of the LORD;
8 *As* I live, saith the Lord GOD, surely
because my flock became a prey, and my
flock became meat to every beast of the
field, because *there was* no shepherd, neither did my shepherds search for my flock,
but the shepherds fed themselves, and fed
not my flock;
9 Therefore, O ye shepherds, hear the
word of the LORD;
10 Thus saith the Lord GOD; Behold, I *am*
against the shepherds; and I will require
my flock at their hand, and cause them to
cease from feeding the flock; neither shall
the shepherds feed themselves any more;
for I will deliver my flock from their
mouth, that they may not be meat for
them.
11 For thus saith the Lord GOD; Behold,
I, *even* I, will both search my sheep, and
seek them out.
12 As a shepherd seeketh out his flock in
the day that he is among his sheep *that are*
scattered; so will I seek out my sheep, and
will deliver them out of all places where
they have been scattered in the cloudy and
dark day.
13 And I will bring them out from the
people, and gather them from the countries, and will bring them to their own
land, and feed them upon the mountains
of Israel by the rivers, and in all the inhabited places of the country.
14 I will feed them in a good pasture, and

upon the high mountains of Israel shall their fold be: there shall they lie in a good fold, and *in* a fat pasture shall they feed upon the mountains of Israel.

15 I will feed my flock, and I will cause them to lie down, saith the Lord GOD.

16 I will seek that which was lost, and bring again that which was driven away, and will bind up *that which was* broken, and will strengthen that which was sick: but I will destroy the fat and the strong; I will feed them with judgment.

17 And *as for* you, O my flock, thus saith the Lord GOD; Behold, I judge between cattle and cattle, between the rams and the he goats.

18 *Seemeth it* a small thing unto you to have eaten up the good pasture, but ye must tread down with your feet the residue of your pastures? and to have drunk of the deep waters, but ye must foul the residue with your feet?

19 And *as for* my flock, they eat that which ye have trodden with your feet; and they drink that which ye have fouled with your feet.

20 Therefore thus saith the Lord GOD unto them; Behold, I, *even* I, will judge between the fat cattle and between the lean cattle.

21 Because ye have thrust with side and with shoulder, and pushed all the diseased with your horns, till ye have scattered them abroad;

22 Therefore will I save my flock, and they shall no more be a prey; and I will judge between cattle and cattle.

23 And I will set up one shepherd over them, and he shall feed them, *even* my servant David; he shall feed them, and he shall be their shepherd.

24 And I the LORD will be their God, and my servant David a prince among them; I the LORD have spoken *it*.

25 And I will make with them a covenant of peace, and will cause the evil beasts to cease out of the land: and they shall dwell safely in the wilderness, and sleep in the woods.

34:25 Peace of Mind
◄ Isaiah 54:13
John 14:27 ►

26 And I will make them and the places round about my hill a blessing; and I will cause the shower to come down in his season; there shall be showers of blessing.

27 And the tree of the field shall yield her fruit, and the earth shall yield her increase, and they shall be safe in their land, and shall know that I *am* the LORD, when I have broken the bands of their yoke, and delivered them out of the hand of those that served themselves of them.

28 And they shall no more be a prey to the heathen, neither shall the beast of the land devour them; but they shall dwell safely, and none shall make *them* afraid.

29 And I will raise up for them a plant of renown, and they shall be no more consumed with hunger in the land, neither bear the shame of the heathen any more.

30 Thus shall they know that I the LORD their God *am* with them, and *that* they, *even* the house of Israel, *are* my people, saith the Lord GOD.

31 And ye my flock, the flock of my pasture, *are* men, *and* I *am* your God, saith the Lord GOD.

35

1 Moreover the word of the LORD came unto me, saying,

2 Son of man, set thy face against mount Seir, and prophesy against it,

3 And say unto it, Thus saith the Lord GOD; Behold, O mount Seir, I *am* against thee, and I will stretch out mine hand against thee, and I will make thee most desolate.

4 I will lay thy cities waste, and thou shalt be desolate, and thou shalt know that I *am* the LORD.

5 Because thou hast had a perpetual hatred, and hast shed *the blood of* the children of Israel by the force of the sword in the time of their calamity, in the time *that their* iniquity *had* an end:

6 Therefore, *as* I live, saith the Lord GOD, I will prepare thee unto blood, and blood shall pursue thee: sith thou hast not hated blood, even blood shall pursue thee.

7 Thus will I make mount Seir most desolate, and cut off from it him that passeth out and him that returneth.

8 And I will fill his mountains with his slain *men:* in thy hills, and in thy valleys, and in all thy rivers, shall they fall that are slain with the sword.

9 I will make thee perpetual desolations, and thy cities shall not return: and ye shall know that I *am* the LORD.

10 Because thou hast said, These two na-

tions and these two countries shall be
mine, and we will possess it; whereas the
LORD was there:
11 Therefore, *as* I live, saith the Lord GOD,
I will even do according to thine anger, and
according to thine envy which thou hast
used out of thy hatred against them; and I
will make myself known among them,
when I have judged thee.
12 And thou shalt know that I *am* the
LORD, *and that* I have heard all thy blasphemies which thou hast spoken against
the mountains of Israel, saying, They are
laid desolate, they are given us to consume.
13 Thus with your mouth ye have boasted against me, and have multiplied your
words against me: I have heard *them*.
14 Thus saith the Lord GOD; When the
whole earth rejoiceth, I will make thee
desolate.
15 As thou didst rejoice at the inheritance
of the house of Israel, because it was desolate, so will I do unto thee: thou shalt be
desolate, O mount Seir, and all Idumea,
even all of it: and they shall know that I
am the LORD.

36

1 Also, thou son of man, prophesy unto
the mountains of Israel, and say, Ye mountains of Israel, hear the word of the LORD:
2 Thus saith the Lord GOD; Because the
enemy hath said against you, Aha, even the
ancient high places are ours in possession:
3 Therefore
prophesy and say,
Thus saith the Lord
GOD; Because they
have made *you* des-
olate, and swal-
lowed you up on every side, that ye might
be a possession unto the residue of the
heathen, and ye are taken up in the lips of
talkers, and *are* an infamy of the people:

36:3 Idle Talk
◄ Ecclesiastes 10:13
Titus 1:10 ►

4 Therefore, ye mountains of Israel, hear
the word of the Lord GOD; Thus saith the
Lord GOD to the mountains, and to the
hills, to the rivers, and to the valleys, to
the desolate wastes, and to the cities that
are forsaken, which became a prey and
derision to the residue of the heathen that
are round about;
5 Therefore thus saith the Lord GOD;
Surely in the fire of my jealousy have I spoken against the residue of the heathen, and
against all Idumea, which have appointed
my land into their possession with the joy
of all *their* heart, with despiteful minds, to
cast it out for a prey.
6 Prophesy therefore concerning the land
of Israel, and say unto the mountains, and
to the hills, to the rivers, and to the valleys, Thus saith the Lord GOD; Behold, I
have spoken in my jealousy and in my fury,
because ye have borne the shame of the
heathen:
7 Therefore thus saith the Lord GOD; I
have lifted up mine hand, Surely the heathen that *are* about you, they shall bear
their shame.
8 But ye, O mountains of Israel, ye shall
shoot forth your branches, and yield your
fruit to my people of Israel; for they are at
hand to come.
9 For, behold, I *am* for you, and I will
turn unto you, and ye shall be tilled and
sown:
10 And I will multiply men upon you, all
the house of Israel, *even* all of it: and the
cities shall be inhabited, and the wastes
shall be builded:
11 And I will multiply upon you man and
beast; and they shall increase and bring
fruit: and I will settle you after your old
estates, and will do better *unto you* than at
your beginnings: and ye shall know that I
am the LORD.
12 Yea, I will cause men to walk upon
you, *even* my people Israel; and they shall
possess thee, and thou shalt be their inheritance, and thou shalt no more henceforth bereave them *of men*.
13 Thus saith the Lord GOD; Because they
say unto you, Thou *land* devourest up men,
and hast bereaved thy nations;
14 Therefore thou shalt devour men no
more, neither bereave thy nations any
more, saith the Lord GOD.
15 Neither will I cause *men* to hear in thee
the shame of the heathen any more, neither shalt thou bear the reproach of the
people any more, neither shalt thou cause
thy nations to fall any more, saith the Lord
GOD.
16 Moreover the word of the LORD came
unto me, saying,
17 Son of man, when the house of Israel
dwelt in their own land, they defiled it by
their own way and by their doings: their
way was before me as the uncleanness of a
removed woman.
18 Wherefore I poured my fury upon

them for the blood that they had shed upon the land, and for their idols *wherewith* they had polluted it:

19And I scattered them among the heathen, and they were dispersed through the countries: according to their way and according to their doings I judged them.

20And when they entered unto the heathen, whither they went, they profaned my holy name, when they said to them, These *are* the people of the LORD, and are gone forth out of his land.

36:20
Embarrassing God
◄ Nehemiah 5:9
Romans 2:23-24 ►

21But I had pity for mine holy name, which the house of Israel had profaned among the heathen, whither they went.

22Therefore say unto the house of Israel, Thus saith the Lord GOD; I do not *this* for your sakes, O house of Israel, but for mine holy name's sake, which ye have profaned among the heathen, whither ye went.

23And I will sanctify my great name, which was profaned among the heathen, which ye have profaned in the midst of them; and the heathen shall know that I *am* the LORD, saith the Lord GOD, when I shall be sanctified in you before their eyes.

24For I will take you from among the heathen, and gather you out of all countries, and will bring you into your own land.

25Then will I sprinkle clean water upon you, and ye shall be clean: from all your filthiness, and from all your idols, will I cleanse you.

36:25 God's Forgiveness
◄ Jeremiah 33:8
Micah 7:18 ►

26A new heart also will I give you, and a new spirit will I put within you: and I will take away the stony heart out of your flesh, and I will give you an heart of flesh.

27And I will put my spirit within you, and cause you to walk in my statutes, and ye shall keep my judgments, and do *them.*

36:27
The Spirit in You
◄ John 14:17 ►

28And ye shall dwell in the land that I gave to your fathers; and ye shall be my people, and I will be your God.

29I will also save you from all your uncleannesses: and I will call for the corn, and will increase it, and lay no famine upon you.

30And I will multiply the fruit of the tree, and the increase of the field, that ye shall receive no more reproach of famine among the heathen.

31Then shall ye remember your own evil ways, and your doings that *were* not good, and shall lothe yourselves in your own sight for your iniquities and for your abominations.

32Not for your sakes do I *this,* saith the Lord GOD, be it known unto you: be ashamed and confounded for your own ways, O house of Israel.

33Thus saith the Lord GOD; In the day that I shall have cleansed you from all your iniquities I will also cause *you* to dwell in the cities, and the wastes shall be builded.

34And the desolate land shall be tilled, whereas it lay desolate in the sight of all that passed by.

35And they shall say, This land that was desolate is become like the garden of Eden; and the waste and desolate and ruined cities *are become* fenced, *and* are inhabited.

36Then the heathen that are left round about you shall know that I the LORD build the ruined *places, and* plant that that was desolate: I the LORD have spoken *it,* and I will do *it.*

37Thus saith the Lord GOD; I will yet *for* this be enquired of by the house of Israel, to do *it* for them; I will increase them with men like a flock.

38As the holy flock, as the flock of Jerusalem in her solemn feasts; so shall the waste cities be filled with flocks of men: and they shall know that I *am* the LORD.

37

1The hand of the LORD was upon me, and carried me out in the spirit of the LORD, and set me down in the midst of the valley which *was* full of bones,

2And caused me to pass by them round about: and, behold, *there were* very many in the open valley; and, lo, *they were* very dry.

3And he said unto me, Son of man, can these bones live? And I answered, O Lord GOD, thou knowest.

4Again he said unto me, Prophesy upon these bones, and say unto them, O ye dry bones, hear the word of the LORD.

5 Thus saith the Lord GOD unto these
bones; Behold, I will cause breath to enter
into you, and ye shall live:
6 And I will lay sinews upon you, and
will bring up flesh upon you, and cover
you with skin, and put breath in you, and
ye shall live; and ye shall know that I *am*
the LORD.
7 So I prophesied
as I was command-
ed: and as I proph-
esied, there was a
noise, and behold a
shaking, and the
bones came together, bone to his bone.

37:7 Power of the Bible
◄ Jeremiah 23:29
Romans 1:16 ►

8 And when I beheld, lo, the sinews and
the flesh came up upon them, and the skin
covered them above: but *there was* no
breath in them.
9 Then said he unto me, Prophesy unto
the wind, prophesy, son of man, and say
to the wind, Thus saith the Lord GOD;
Come from the four winds, O breath, and
breathe upon these slain, that they may
live.
10 So I prophesied as he commanded me,
and the breath came into them, and they
lived, and stood up upon their feet, an
exceeding great army.
11 Then he said unto me, Son of man,
these bones are the whole house of Israel:
behold, they say, Our bones are dried,
and our hope is lost: we are cut off for our
parts.
12 Therefore prophesy and say unto
them, Thus saith the Lord GOD; Behold,
O my people, I will open your graves, and
cause you to come up out of your graves,
and bring you into the land of Israel.
13 And ye shall know that I *am* the LORD,
when I have opened your graves, O my
people, and brought you up out of your
graves,
14 And shall put my spirit in you, and ye
shall live, and I shall place you in your own
land: then shall ye know that I the LORD
have spoken *it,* and performed *it,* saith the
LORD.
15 The word of the LORD came again unto
me, saying,
16 Moreover, thou son of man, take thee
one stick, and write upon it, For Judah,
and for the children of Israel his companions: then take another stick, and write
upon it, For Joseph, the stick of Ephraim,
and *for* all the house of Israel his companions:
17 And join them one to another into
one stick; and they shall become one in
thine hand.
18 And when the children of thy people
shall speak unto thee, saying, Wilt thou
not shew us what thou *meanest* by these?
19 Say unto them, Thus saith the Lord
GOD; Behold, I will take the stick of Joseph, which *is* in the hand of Ephraim, and
the tribes of Israel his fellows, and will put
them with him, *even* with the stick of Judah, and make them one stick, and they
shall be one in mine hand.
20 And the sticks whereon thou writest
shall be in thine hand before their eyes.
21 And say unto them, Thus saith the
Lord GOD; Behold, I will take the children
of Israel from among the heathen, whither
they be gone, and will gather them on every side, and bring them into their own
land:
22 And I will make them one nation in
the land upon the mountains of Israel; and
one king shall be king to them all: and they
shall be no more two nations, neither shall
they be divided into two kingdoms any
more at all:
23 Neither shall they defile themselves
any more with their idols, nor with their
detestable things, nor with any of their
transgressions: but I will save them out of
all their dwellingplaces, wherein they have
sinned, and will cleanse them: so shall they
be my people, and I will be their God.
24 And David my servant *shall be* king
over them; and they all shall have one
shepherd: they shall also walk in my judgments, and observe my statutes, and do
them.
25 And they shall dwell in the land that I
have given unto Jacob my servant, wherein
your fathers have dwelt; and they shall
dwell therein, *even* they, and their children,
and their children's children for ever: and
my servant David *shall be* their prince for
ever.
26 Moreover I will make a covenant of
peace with them; it shall be an everlasting
covenant with them: and I will place
them, and multiply them, and will set my
sanctuary in the midst of them for evermore.
27 My tabernacle also shall be with them:

yea, I will be their God, and they shall be my people.

[28]And the heathen shall know that I the LORD do sanctify Israel, when my sanctuary shall be in the midst of them for evermore.

38

[1]And the word of the LORD came unto me, saying,

[2]Son of man, set thy face against Gog, the land of Magog, the chief prince of Meshech and Tubal, and prophesy against him,

[3]And say, Thus saith the Lord GOD; Behold I *am* against thee, O Gog, the chief prince of Meshech and Tubal:

[4]And I will turn thee back, and put hooks into thy jaws, and I will bring thee forth, and all thine army, horses and horsemen, all of them clothed with all sorts *of armour, even* a great company *with* bucklers and shields, all of them handling swords:

[5]Persia, Ethiopia, and Libya with them; all of them with shield and helmet:

[6]Gomer, and all his bands; the house of Togarmah of the north quarters, and all his bands: *and* many people with thee.

[7]Be thou prepared, and prepare for thyself, thou, and all thy company that are assembled unto thee, and be thou a guard unto them.

[8]After many days thou shalt be visited: in the latter years thou shalt come into the land *that is* brought back from the sword, *and is* gathered out of many people, against the mountains of Israel, which have been always waste: but it is brought forth out of the nations, and they shall dwell safely all of them.

[9]Thou shalt ascend and come like a storm, thou shalt be like a cloud to cover the land, thou, and all thy bands, and many people with thee.

[10]Thus saith the Lord GOD; It shall also come to pass, *that* at the same time shall things come into thy mind, and thou shalt think an evil thought:

[11]And thou shalt say, I will go up to the land of unwalled villages; I will go to them that are at rest, that dwell safely, all of them dwelling without walls, and having neither bars nor gates,

[12]To take a spoil, and to take a prey; to turn thine hand upon the desolate places *that are now* inhabited, and upon the people *that are* gathered out of the nations, which have gotten cattle and goods, that dwell in the midst of the land.

[13]Sheba, and Dedan, and the merchants of Tarshish, with all the young lions thereof, shall say unto thee, Art thou come to take a spoil? hast thou gathered thy company to take a prey? to carry away silver and gold, to take away cattle and goods, to take a great spoil?

[14]Therefore, son of man, prophesy and say unto Gog, Thus saith the Lord GOD; In that day when my people of Israel dwelleth safely, shalt thou not know *it*?

[15]And thou shalt come from thy place out of the north parts, thou, and many people with thee, all of them riding upon horses, a great company, and a mighty army:

[16]And thou shalt come up against my people of Israel, as a cloud to cover the land; it shall be in the latter days, and I will bring thee against my land, that the heathen may know me, when I shall be sanctified in thee, O Gog, before their eyes.

[17]Thus saith the Lord GOD; *Art* thou he of whom I have spoken in old time by my servants the prophets of Israel, which prophesied in those days *many* years that I would bring thee against them?

[18]And it shall come to pass at the same time when Gog shall come against the land of Israel, saith the Lord GOD, *that* my fury shall come up in my face.

[19]For in my jealousy *and* in the fire of my wrath have I spoken, Surely in that day there shall be a great shaking in the land of Israel;

[20]So that the fishes of the sea, and the fowls of the heaven, and the beasts of the field, and all creeping things that creep upon the earth, and all the men that *are* upon the face of the earth, shall shake at my presence, and the mountains shall be thrown down, and the steep places shall fall, and every wall shall fall to the ground.

[21]And I will call for a sword against him throughout all my mountains, saith the Lord GOD: every man's sword shall be against his brother.

[22]And I will plead against him with pestilence and with blood; and I will rain upon him, and upon his bands, and upon the many people that *are* with him, an

overflowing rain, and great hailstones, fire, and brimstone.

23 Thus will I magnify myself, and sanctify myself; and I will be known in the eyes of many nations, and they shall know that I *am* the LORD.

39

1 Therefore, thou son of man, prophesy against Gog, and say, Thus saith the Lord GOD; Behold, I *am* against thee, O Gog, the chief prince of Meshech and Tubal:

2 And I will turn thee back, and leave but the sixth part of thee, and will cause thee to come up from the north parts, and will bring thee upon the mountains of Israel:

3 And I will smite thy bow out of thy left hand, and will cause thine arrows to fall out of thy right hand.

4 Thou shalt fall upon the mountains of Israel, thou, and all thy bands, and the people that *is* with thee: I will give thee unto the ravenous birds of every sort, and *to* the beasts of the field to be devoured.

5 Thou shalt fall upon the open field: for I have spoken *it*, saith the Lord GOD.

6 And I will send a fire on Magog, and among them that dwell carelessly in the isles: and they shall know that I *am* the LORD.

7 So will I make my holy name known in the midst of my people Israel; and I will not *let them* pollute my holy name any more: and the heathen shall know that I *am* the LORD, the Holy One in Israel.

8 Behold, it is come, and it is done, saith the Lord GOD; this *is* the day whereof I have spoken.

9 And they that dwell in the cities of Israel shall go forth, and shall set on fire and burn the weapons, both the shields and the bucklers, the bows and the arrows, and the handstaves, and the spears, and they shall burn them with fire seven years:

10 So that they shall take no wood out of the field, neither cut down *any* out of the forests; for they shall burn the weapons with fire: and they shall spoil those that spoiled them, and rob those that robbed them, saith the Lord GOD.

11 And it shall come to pass in that day, *that* I will give unto Gog a place there of graves in Israel, the valley of the passengers on the east of the sea: and it shall stop the *noses* of the passengers: and there shall they bury Gog and all his multitude: and they shall call *it* The valley of Hamon-gog.

12 And seven months shall the house of Israel be burying of them, that they may cleanse the land.

13 Yea, all the people of the land shall bury *them*; and it shall be to them a renown the day that I shall be glorified, saith the Lord GOD.

14 And they shall sever out men of continual employment, passing through the land to bury with the passengers those that remain upon the face of the earth, to cleanse it: after the end of seven months shall they search.

15 And the passengers *that* pass through the land, when *any* seeth a man's bone, then shall he set up a sign by it, till the buriers have buried it in the valley of Hamon-gog.

16 And also the name of the city *shall be* Hamonah. Thus shall they cleanse the land.

17 And, thou son of man, thus saith the Lord GOD; Speak unto every feathered fowl, and to every beast of the field, Assemble yourselves, and come; gather yourselves on every side to my sacrifice that I do sacrifice for you, *even* a great sacrifice upon the mountains of Israel, that ye may eat flesh, and drink blood.

18 Ye shall eat the flesh of the mighty, and drink the blood of the princes of the earth, of rams, of lambs, and of goats, of bullocks, all of them fatlings of Bashan.

19 And ye shall eat fat till ye be full, and drink blood till ye be drunken, of my sacrifice which I have sacrificed for you.

20 Thus ye shall be filled at my table with horses and chariots, with mighty men, and with all men of war, saith the Lord GOD.

21 And I will set my glory among the heathen, and all the heathen shall see my judgment that I have executed, and my hand that I have laid upon them.

22 So the house of Israel shall know that I *am* the LORD their God from that day and forward.

23 And the heathen shall know that the house of Israel went into captivity for their iniquity: because they trespassed against me, therefore hid I my face from them, and gave them into the hand of their enemies: so fell they all by the sword.

24 According to their uncleanness and according to their transgressions have I

done unto them, and hid my face from
them.
25 Therefore thus saith the Lord GOD;
Now will I bring again the captivity of Jacob, and have mercy upon the whole
house of Israel, and will be jealous for my
holy name;
26 After that they have borne their shame,
and all their trespasses whereby they have
trespassed against me, when they dwelt
safely in their land, and none made *them*
afraid.
27 When I have brought them again from
the people, and gathered them out of their
enemies' lands, and am sanctified in them
in the sight of many nations;
28 Then shall they know that I *am* the
LORD their God, which caused them to be
led into captivity among the heathen: but
I have gathered them unto their own land,
and have left none of them any more there.
29 Neither will I hide my face any more
from them: for I have poured out my spirit upon the house of Israel, saith the Lord
GOD.

40

1 In the five and twentieth year of our
captivity, in the beginning of the year, in
the tenth *day* of the month, in the fourteenth year after that the city was smitten,
in the selfsame day the hand of the LORD
was upon me, and brought me thither.
2 In the visions of God brought he me
into the land of Israel, and set me upon a
very high mountain, by which *was* as the
frame of a city on the south.
3 And he brought me thither, and, behold, *there was* a man, whose appearance
was like the appearance of brass, with a
line of flax in his hand, and a measuring
reed; and he stood in the gate.
4 And the man said unto me, Son of man,
behold with thine eyes, and hear with
thine ears, and set thine heart upon all that
I shall shew thee; for to the intent that I
might shew *them* unto thee *art* thou
brought hither: declare all that thou seest
to the house of Israel.
5 And behold a wall on the outside of
the house round about, and in the man's
hand a measuring reed of six cubits *long*
by the cubit and an hand breadth: so he
measured the breadth of the building, one
reed; and the height, one reed.
6 Then came he unto the gate which
looketh toward the east, and went up the
stairs thereof, and measured the threshold
of the gate, *which was* one reed broad; and
the other threshold *of the gate, which was*
one reed broad.
7 And *every* little chamber *was* one reed
long, and one reed broad; and between the
little chambers *were* five cubits; and
the threshold of the gate by the porch of
the gate within *was* one reed.
8 He measured also the porch of the gate
within, one reed.
9 Then measured he the porch of the
gate, eight cubits; and the posts thereof,
two cubits; and the porch of the gate *was*
inward.
10 And the little chambers of the gate
eastward *were* three on this side, and three
on that side; they three *were* of one measure: and the posts had one measure on
this side and on that side.
11 And he measured the breadth of the
entry of the gate, ten cubits; *and* the length
of the gate, thirteen cubits.
12 The space also before the little chambers *was* one cubit *on this side,* and the space
was one cubit on that side: and the little
chambers *were* six cubits on this side, and
six cubits on that side.
13 He measured then the gate from the
roof of *one* little chamber to the roof of
another: the breadth *was* five and twenty
cubits, door against door.
14 He made also posts of threescore cubits, even unto the post of the court round
about the gate.
15 And from the face of the gate of the
entrance unto the face of the porch of the
inner gate *were* fifty cubits.
16 And *there were* narrow windows to the
little chambers, and to their posts within
the gate round about, and likewise to the
arches: and windows *were* round about
inward: and upon *each* post *were* palm
trees.
17 Then brought he me into the outward
court, and, lo, *there were* chambers, and a
pavement made for the court round about:
thirty chambers *were* upon the pavement.
18 And the pavement by the side of the
gates over against the length of the gates
was the lower pavement.
19 Then he measured the breadth from
the forefront of the lower gate unto the
forefront of the inner court without, an
hundred cubits eastward and northward.

20 And the gate of the outward court that looked toward the north, he measured the length thereof, and the breadth thereof.

21 And the little chambers thereof *were* three on this side and three on that side; and the posts thereof and the arches thereof were after the measure of the first gate: the length thereof *was* fifty cubits, and the breadth five and twenty cubits.

22 And their windows, and their arches, and their palm trees, *were* after the measure of the gate that looketh toward the east; and they went up unto it by seven steps; and the arches thereof *were* before them.

23 And the gate of the inner court *was* over against the gate toward the north, and toward the east; and he measured from gate to gate an hundred cubits.

24 After that he brought me toward the south, and behold a gate toward the south: and he measured the posts thereof and the arches thereof according to these measures.

25 And *there were* windows in it and in the arches thereof round about, like those windows: the length *was* fifty cubits, and the breadth five and twenty cubits.

26 And *there were* seven steps to go up to it, and the arches thereof *were* before them: and it had palm trees, one on this side, and another on that side, upon the posts thereof.

27 And *there was* a gate in the inner court toward the south: and he measured from gate to gate toward the south an hundred cubits.

28 And he brought me to the inner court by the south gate: and he measured the south gate according to these measures;

29 And the little chambers thereof, and the posts thereof, and the arches thereof, according to these measures: and *there were* windows in it and in the arches thereof round about: *it was* fifty cubits long, and five and twenty cubits broad.

30 And the arches round about *were* five and twenty cubits long, and five cubits broad.

31 And the arches thereof *were* toward the utter court; and palm trees *were* upon the posts thereof: and the going up to it *had* eight steps.

32 And he brought me into the inner court toward the east: and he measured the gate according to these measures.

33 And the little chambers thereof, and the posts thereof, and the arches thereof, *were* according to these measures: and *there were* windows therein and in the arches thereof round about: *it was* fifty cubits long, and five and twenty cubits broad.

34 And the arches thereof *were* toward the outward court; and palm trees *were* upon the posts thereof, on this side, and on that side: and the going up to it *had* eight steps.

35 And he brought me to the north gate, and measured *it* according to these measures;

36 The little chambers thereof, the posts thereof, and the arches thereof, and the windows to it round about: the length *was* fifty cubits, and the breadth five and twenty cubits.

37 And the posts thereof *were* toward the utter court; and palm trees *were* upon the posts thereof, on this side, and on that side: and the going up to it *had* eight steps.

38 And the chambers and the entries thereof *were* by the posts of the gates, where they washed the burnt offering.

39 And in the porch of the gate *were* two tables on this side, and two tables on that side, to slay thereon the burnt offering and the sin offering and the trespass offering.

40 And at the side without, as one goeth up to the entry of the north gate, *were* two tables; and on the other side, which *was* at the porch of the gate, *were* two tables.

41 Four tables *were* on this side, and four tables on that side, by the side of the gate; eight tables, whereupon they slew *their sacrifices.*

42 And the four tables *were* of hewn stone for the burnt offering, of a cubit and an half long, and a cubit and an half broad, and one cubit high: whereupon also they laid the instruments wherewith they slew the burnt offering and the sacrifice.

43 And within *were* hooks, an hand broad, fastened round about: and upon the tables *was* the flesh of the offering.

44 And without the inner gate *were* the chambers of the singers in the inner court, which *was* at the side of the north gate; and their prospect *was* toward the south: one at the side of the east gate *having* the prospect toward the north.

45 And he said unto me, This chamber, whose prospect *is* toward the south, *is* for

the priests, the keepers of the charge of the
house.
46 And the chamber whose prospect *is*
toward the north *is* for the priests, the keepers of the charge of the altar: these *are* the
sons of Zadok among the sons of Levi,
which come near to the LORD to minister
unto him.
47 So he measured the court, an hundred
cubits long, and an hundred cubits broad,
foursquare; and the altar *that was* before
the house.
48 And he brought me to the porch of
the house, and measured *each* post of the
porch, five cubits on this side, and five
cubits on that side: and the breadth of the
gate *was* three cubits on this side, and three
cubits on that side.
49 The length of the porch *was* twenty
cubits, and the breadth eleven cubits; and
he brought me by the steps whereby they
went up to it: and *there were* pillars by the
posts, one on this side, and another on that
side.

41

1 Afterward he brought me to the temple, and measured the posts, six cubits
broad on the one side, and six cubits broad
on the other side, *which was* the breadth
of the tabernacle.
2 And the breadth of the door *was* ten
cubits; and the sides of the door *were* five
cubits on the one side, and five cubits on
the other side: and he measured the length
thereof, forty cubits: and the breadth,
twenty cubits.
3 Then went he inward, and measured
the post of the door, two cubits; and the
door, six cubits; and the breadth of the
door, seven cubits.
4 So he measured the length thereof,
twenty cubits; and the breadth, twenty
cubits, before the temple: and he said unto
me, This *is* the most holy *place*.
5 After he measured the wall of the
house, six cubits; and the breadth of *every*
side chamber, four cubits, round about the
house on every side.
6 And the side chambers *were* three, one
over another, and thirty in order; and they
entered into the wall which *was* of the
house for the side chambers round about,
that they might have hold, but they had
not hold in the wall of the house.
7 And *there was* an enlarging, and a winding about still upward to the side chambers: for the winding about of the house
went still upward round about the house:
therefore the breadth of the house *was still*
upward, and so increased *from* the lowest
chamber to the highest by the midst.
8 I saw also the height of the house round
about: the foundations of the side chambers *were* a full reed of six great cubits.
9 The thickness of the wall, which *was*
for the side chamber without, *was* five cubits: and *that* which *was* left *was* the place
of the side chambers that *were* within.
10 And between the chambers *was* the
wideness of twenty cubits round about the
house on every side.
11 And the doors of the side chambers
were toward *the place that was* left, one door
toward the north, and another door toward the south: and the breadth of the
place that was left *was* five cubits round
about.
12 Now the building that *was* before the
separate place at the end toward the west
was seventy cubits broad; and the wall of
the building *was* five cubits thick round
about, and the length thereof ninety cubits.
13 So he measured the house, an hundred cubits long; and the separate place,
and the building, with the walls thereof,
an hundred cubits long;
14 Also the breadth of the face of the
house, and of the separate place toward
the east, an hundred cubits.
15 And he measured the length of the
building over against the separate place
which *was* behind it, and the galleries
thereof on the one side and on the other
side, an hundred cubits, with the inner
temple, and the porches of the court;
16 The door posts, and the narrow windows, and the galleries round about on
their three stories, over against the door,
cieled with wood round about, and from
the ground up to the windows, and the
windows *were* covered;
17 To that above the door, even unto the
inner house, and without, and by all the
wall round about within and without, by
measure.
18 And *it was* made with cherubims and
palm trees, so that a palm tree *was* between
a cherub and a cherub; and *every* cherub
had two faces;
19 So that the face of a man *was* toward

the palm tree on the one side, and the face of a young lion toward the palm tree on the other side: *it was* made through all the house round about.

20 From the ground unto above the door *were* cherubims and palm trees made, and *on* the wall of the temple.

21 The posts of the temple *were* squared, *and* the face of the sanctuary; the appearance *of the one* as the appearance *of the other.*

22 The altar of wood *was* three cubits high, and the length thereof two cubits; and the corners thereof, and the length thereof, and the walls thereof, *were* of wood: and he said unto me, This *is* the table that *is* before the LORD.

23 And the temple and the sanctuary had two doors.

24 And the doors had two leaves *apiece,* two turning leaves; two *leaves* for the one door, and two leaves for the other *door.*

25 And *there were* made on them, on the doors of the temple, cherubims and palm trees, like as *were* made upon the walls; and *there were* thick planks upon the face of the porch without.

26 And *there were* narrow windows and palm trees on the one side and on the other side, on the sides of the porch, and *upon* the side chambers of the house, and thick planks.

42

1 Then he brought me forth into the utter court, the way toward the north: and he brought me into the chamber that *was* over against the separate place, and which *was* before the building toward the north.

2 Before the length of an hundred cubits *was* the north door, and the breadth *was* fifty cubits.

3 Over against the twenty *cubits* which *were* for the inner court, and over against the pavement which *was* for the utter court, *was* gallery against gallery in three *stories.*

4 And before the chambers *was* a walk of ten cubits breadth inward, a way of one cubit; and their doors toward the north.

5 Now the upper chambers *were* shorter: for the galleries were higher than these, than the lower, and than the middlemost of the building.

6 For they *were* in three *stories,* but had not pillars as the pillars of the courts: therefore *the building* was straitened more than the lowest and the middlemost from the ground.

7 And the wall that *was* without over against the chambers, toward the utter court on the forepart of the chambers, the length thereof *was* fifty cubits.

8 For the length of the chambers that *were* in the utter court *was* fifty cubits: and, lo, before the temple *were* an hundred cubits.

9 And from under these chambers *was* the entry on the east side, as one goeth into them from the utter court.

10 The chambers *were* in the thickness of the wall of the court toward the east, over against the separate place, and over against the building.

11 And the way before them *was* like the appearance of the chambers which *were* toward the north, as long as they, *and* as broad as they: and all their goings out *were* both according to their fashions, and according to their doors.

12 And according to the doors of the chambers that *were* toward the south *was* a door in the head of the way, *even* the way directly before the wall toward the east, as one entereth into them.

13 Then said he unto me, The north chambers *and* the south chambers, which *are* before the separate place, they *be* holy chambers, where the priests that approach unto the LORD shall eat the most holy things: there shall they lay the most holy things, and the meat offering, and the sin offering, and the trespass offering; for the place *is* holy.

14 When the priests enter therein, then shall they not go out of the holy *place* into the utter court, but there they shall lay their garments wherein they minister; for they *are* holy; and shall put on other garments, and shall approach to *those things* which *are* for the people.

15 Now when he had made an end of measuring the inner house, he brought me forth toward the gate whose prospect *is* toward the east, and measured it round about.

16 He measured the east side with the measuring reed, five hundred reeds, with the measuring reed round about.

17 He measured the north side, five hundred reeds, with the measuring reed round about.

18 He measured the south side, five hundred reeds, with the measuring reed.

19 He turned about to the west side, *and* measured five hundred reeds with the measuring reed.

20 He measured it by the four sides: it had a wall round about, five hundred *reeds* long, and five hundred broad, to make a separation between the sanctuary and the profane place.

43

1 Afterward he brought me to the gate, *even* the gate that looketh toward the east:

2 And, behold, the glory of the God of Israel came from the way of the east: and his voice *was* like a noise of many waters: and the earth shined with his glory.

3 And *it was* according to the appearance of the vision which I saw, *even* according to the vision that I saw when I came to destroy the city: and the visions *were* like the vision that I saw by the river Chebar; and I fell upon my face.

4 And the glory of the LORD came into the house by the way of the gate whose prospect *is* toward the east.

5 So the spirit took me up, and brought me into the inner court; and, behold, the glory of the LORD filled the house.

6 And I heard *him* speaking unto me out of the house; and the man stood by me.

7 And he said unto me, Son of man, the place of my throne, and the place of the soles of my feet, where I will dwell in the midst of the children of Israel for ever, and my holy name, shall the house of Israel no more defile, *neither* they, nor their kings, by their whoredom, nor by the carcases of their kings in their high places.

8 In their setting of their threshold by my thresholds, and their post by my posts, and the wall between me and them, they have even defiled my holy name by their abominations that they have committed: wherefore I have consumed them in mine anger.

9 Now let them put away their whoredom, and the carcases of their kings, far from me, and I will dwell in the midst of them for ever.

10 Thou son of man, shew the house to the house of Israel, that they may be ashamed of their iniquities: and let them measure the pattern.

11 And if they be ashamed of all that they have done, shew them the form of the house, and the fashion thereof, and the goings out thereof, and the comings in thereof, and all the forms thereof, and all the ordinances thereof, and all the forms thereof, and all the laws thereof: and write *it* in their sight, that they may keep the whole form thereof, and all the ordinances thereof, and do them.

12 This *is* the law of the house; Upon the top of the mountain the whole limit thereof round about *shall be* most holy. Behold, this *is* the law of the house.

13 And these *are* the measures of the altar after the cubits: The cubit *is* a cubit and an hand breadth; even the bottom *shall be* a cubit, and the breadth a cubit, and the border thereof by the edge thereof round about *shall be* a span: and this *shall be* the higher place of the altar.

14 And from the bottom *upon* the ground *even* to the lower settle *shall be* two cubits, and the breadth one cubit; and from the lesser settle *even* to the greater settle *shall be* four cubits, and the breadth *one* cubit.

15 So the altar *shall be* four cubits; and from the altar and upward *shall be* four horns.

16 And the altar *shall be* twelve *cubits* long, twelve broad, square in the four squares thereof.

17 And the settle *shall be* fourteen *cubits* long and fourteen broad in the four squares thereof; and the border about it *shall be* half a cubit; and the bottom thereof *shall be* a cubit about; and his stairs shall look toward the east.

18 And he said unto me, Son of man, thus saith the Lord GOD; These *are* the ordinances of the altar in the day when they shall make it, to offer burnt offerings thereon, and to sprinkle blood thereon.

19 And thou shalt give to the priests the Levites that be of the seed of Zadok, which approach unto me, to minister unto me, saith the Lord GOD, a young bullock for a sin offering.

20 And thou shalt take of the blood thereof, and put *it* on the four horns of it, and on the four corners of the settle, and upon the border round about: thus shalt thou cleanse and purge it.

21 Thou shalt take the bullock also of the sin offering, and he shall burn it in the appointed place of the house, without the sanctuary.

22 And on the second day thou shalt of-

fer a kid of the goats without blemish for a sin offering; and they shall cleanse the altar, as they did cleanse *it* with the bullock.

23 When thou hast made an end of cleansing *it,* thou shalt offer a young bullock without blemish, and a ram out of the flock without blemish.

24 And thou shalt offer them before the LORD, and the priests shall cast salt upon them, and they shall offer them up *for* a burnt offering unto the LORD.

25 Seven days shalt thou prepare every day a goat *for* a sin offering: they shall also prepare a young bullock, and a ram out of the flock, without blemish.

26 Seven days shall they purge the altar and purify it; and they shall consecrate themselves.

27 And when these days are expired, it shall be, *that* upon the eighth day, and *so* forward, the priests shall make your burnt offerings upon the altar, and your peace offerings; and I will accept you, saith the Lord GOD.

43:27 Accepted by God
◄ Ezekiel 20:40
Acts 10:35 ►

44

1 Then he brought me back the way of the gate of the outward sanctuary which looketh toward the east; and it *was* shut.

2 Then said the LORD unto me; This gate shall be shut, it shall not be opened, and no man shall enter in by it; because the LORD, the God of Israel, hath entered in by it, therefore it shall be shut.

3 *It is* for the prince; the prince, he shall sit in it to eat bread before the LORD; he shall enter by the way of the porch of *that* gate, and shall go out by the way of the same.

4 Then brought he me the way of the north gate before the house: and I looked, and, behold, the glory of the LORD filled the house of the LORD: and I fell upon my face.

5 And the LORD said unto me, Son of man, mark well, and behold with thine eyes, and hear with thine ears all that I say unto thee concerning all the ordinances of the house of the LORD, and all the laws thereof; and mark well the entering in of the house, with every going forth of the sanctuary.

6 And thou shalt say to the rebellious, *even* to the house of Israel, Thus saith the Lord GOD; O ye house of Israel, let it suffice you of all your abominations,

7 In that ye have brought *into my sanctuary* strangers, uncircumcised in heart, and uncircumcised in flesh, to be in my sanctuary, to pollute it, *even* my house, when ye offer my bread, the fat and the blood, and they have broken my covenant because of all your abominations.

8 And ye have not kept the charge of mine holy things: but ye have set keepers of my charge in my sanctuary for yourselves.

9 Thus saith the Lord GOD; No stranger, uncircumcised in heart, nor uncircumcised in flesh, shall enter into my sanctuary, of any stranger that *is* among the children of Israel.

10 And the Levites that are gone away far from me, when Israel went astray, which went astray away from me after their idols; they shall even bear their iniquity.

11 Yet they shall be ministers in my sanctuary, *having* charge at the gates of the house, and ministering to the house: they shall slay the burnt offering and the sacrifice for the people, and they shall stand before them to minister unto them.

12 Because they ministered unto them before their idols, and caused the house of Israel to fall into iniquity; therefore have I lifted up mine hand against them, saith the Lord GOD, and they shall bear their iniquity.

13 And they shall not come near unto me, to do the office of a priest unto me, nor to come near to any of my holy things, in the most holy *place:* but they shall bear their shame, and their abominations which they have committed.

14 But I will make them keepers of the charge of the house, for all the service thereof, and for all that shall be done therein.

15 But the priests the Levites, the sons of Zadok, that kept the charge of my sanctuary when the children of Israel went astray from me, they shall come near to me to minister unto me, and they shall stand before me to offer unto me the fat and the blood, saith the Lord GOD:

16 They shall enter into my sanctuary, and they shall come near to my table, to minister unto me, and they shall keep my charge.

17 And it shall come to pass, *that* when they enter in at the gates of the inner court, they shall be clothed with linen garments; and no wool shall come upon them, whiles they minister in the gates of the inner court, and within.

18 They shall have linen bonnets upon their heads, and shall have linen breeches upon their loins; they shall not gird *themselves* with any thing that causeth sweat.

19 And when they go forth into the utter court, *even* into the utter court to the people, they shall put off their garments wherein they ministered, and lay them in the holy chambers, and they shall put on other garments; and they shall not sanctify the people with their garments.

20 Neither shall they shave their heads, nor suffer their locks to grow long; they shall only poll their heads.

21 Neither shall any priest drink wine, when they enter into the inner court.

22 Neither shall they take for their wives a widow, nor her that is put away: but they shall take maidens of the seed of the house of Israel, or a widow that had a priest before.

23 And they shall teach my people *the difference* between the holy and profane, and cause them to discern between the unclean and the clean.

44:23 Instruction
◄ Psalm 78:6
Colossians 3:16 ►

24 And in controversy they shall stand in judgment; *and* they shall judge it according to my judgments: and they shall keep my laws and my statutes in all mine assemblies; and they shall hallow my sabbaths.

25 And they shall come at no dead person to defile themselves: but for father, or for mother, or for son, or for daughter, for brother, or for sister that hath had no husband, they may defile themselves.

26 And after he is cleansed, they shall reckon unto him seven days.

27 And in the day that he goeth into the sanctuary, unto the inner court, to minister in the sanctuary, he shall offer his sin offering, saith the Lord GOD.

28 And it shall be unto them for an inheritance: I *am* their inheritance: and ye shall give them no possession in Israel: I *am* their possession.

29 They shall eat the meat offering, and the sin offering, and the trespass offering; and every dedicated thing in Israel shall be theirs.

30 And the first of all the firstfruits of all *things,* and every oblation of all, of every *sort* of your oblations, shall be the priest's: ye shall also give unto the priest the first of your dough, that he may cause the blessing to rest in thine house.

31 The priests shall not eat of any thing that is dead of itself, or torn, whether it be fowl or beast.

45

1 Moreover, when ye shall divide by lot the land for inheritance, ye shall offer an oblation unto the LORD, an holy portion of the land: the length *shall be* the length of five and twenty thousand *reeds,* and the breadth *shall be* ten thousand. This *shall be* holy in all the borders thereof round about.

2 Of this there shall be for the sanctuary five hundred *in length,* with five hundred *in breadth,* square round about; and fifty cubits round about for the suburbs thereof.

3 And of this measure shalt thou measure the length of five and twenty thousand, and the breadth of ten thousand: and in it shall be the sanctuary *and* the most holy *place.*

4 The holy *portion* of the land shall be for the priests the ministers of the sanctuary, which shall come near to minister unto the LORD: and it shall be a place for their houses, and an holy place for the sanctuary.

5 And the five and twenty thousand of length, and the ten thousand of breadth, shall also the Levites, the ministers of the house, have for themselves, for a possession for twenty chambers.

6 And ye shall appoint the possession of the city five thousand broad, and five and twenty thousand long, over against the oblation of the holy *portion:* it shall be for the whole house of Israel.

7 And *a portion shall be* for the prince on the one side and on the other side of the oblation of the holy *portion,* and of the possession of the city, before the oblation of the holy *portion,* and before the possession of the city, from the west side westward, and from the east side eastward: and the length *shall be* over against one of the

portions, from the west border unto the
east border.
8 In the land shall be his possession in
Israel: and my princes shall no more oppress my people; and *the rest of* the land
shall they give to the house of Israel according to their tribes.
9 Thus saith the Lord GOD; Let it suffice
you, O princes of Israel: remove violence
and spoil, and execute judgment and justice, take away your exactions from my
people, saith the Lord GOD.
10 Ye shall have just balances, and a just
ephah, and a just bath. I
11 The ephah and the bath shall be of one
measure, that the bath may contain the
tenth part of an homer, and the ephah the
tenth part of an homer: the measure
thereof shall be after the homer.
12 And the shekel *shall be* twenty gerahs:
twenty shekels, five and twenty shekels,
fifteen shekels, shall be your maneh.
13 This *is* the oblation that ye shall offer;
the sixth part of an ephah of an homer of
wheat, and ye shall give the sixth part of
an ephah of an homer of barley:
14 Concerning the ordinance of oil, the
bath of oil, *ye shall offer* the tenth part of a
bath out of the cor, *which is* an homer of
ten baths; for ten baths *are* an homer:
15 And one lamb out of the flock, out of
two hundred, out of the fat pastures of Israel; for a meat offering, and for a burnt
offering, and for peace offerings, to make
reconciliation for them, saith the Lord GOD.
16 All the people of the land shall give
this oblation for the prince in Israel.
17 And it shall be the prince's part *to give*
burnt offerings, and meat offerings, and
drink offerings, in the feasts, and in the
new moons, and in the sabbaths, in all
solemnities of the house of Israel: he shall
prepare the sin offering, and the meat offering, and the burnt offering, and the
peace offerings, to make reconciliation for
the house of Israel.
18 Thus saith the Lord GOD; In the first
month, in the first *day* of the month, thou
shalt take a young bullock without blemish, and cleanse the sanctuary:
19 And the priest shall take of the blood
of the sin offering, and put *it* upon the
posts of the house, and upon the four corners of the settle of the altar, and upon
the posts of the gate of the inner court.
20 And so thou shalt do the seventh *day*
of the month for every one that erreth, and
for *him that is* simple: so shall ye reconcile
the house.
21 In the first *month,* in the fourteenth day
of the month, ye shall have the passover, a
feast of seven days; unleavened bread shall
be eaten.
22 And upon that day shall the prince
prepare for himself and for all the people
of the land a bullock *for* a sin offering.
23 And seven days of the feast he shall
prepare a burnt offering to the LORD, sev-
en bullocks and seven rams without blemish daily the seven days; and a kid of the
goats daily *for* a sin offering.
24 And he shall prepare a meat offering
of an ephah for a bullock, and an ephah
for a ram, and an hin of oil for an ephah.
25 In the seventh *month,* in the fifteenth
day of the month, shall he do the like in
the feast of the seven days, according to
the sin offering, according to the burnt
offering, and according to the meat offering, and according to the oil.

46

1 Thus saith the Lord GOD; The gate of
the inner court that looketh toward the
east shall be shut the six working days; but
on the sabbath it shall be opened, and in
the day of the new moon it shall be
opened.
2 And the prince shall enter by the way
of the porch of *that* gate without, and shall
stand by the post of the gate, and the
priests shall prepare his burnt offering and
his peace offerings, and he shall worship
at the threshold of the gate: then he shall
go forth; but the gate shall not be shut until
the evening.
3 Likewise the people of the land shall
worship at the door of this gate before the
LORD in the sabbaths and in the new
moons.
4 And the burnt offering that the prince
shall offer unto the LORD in the sabbath
day *shall be* six lambs without blemish, and
a ram without blemish.
5 And the meat offering *shall be* an ephah
for a ram, and the meat offering for the
lambs as he shall be able to give, and an
hin of oil to an ephah.
6 And in the day of the new moon *it shall
be* a young bullock without blemish, and
six lambs, and a ram: they shall be without blemish.

7 And he shall prepare a meat offering,
an ephah for a bullock, and an ephah for
a ram, and for the lambs according as his
hand shall attain unto, and an hin of oil
to an ephah.
8 And when the prince shall enter, he
shall go in by the way of the porch of *that*
gate, and he shall go forth by the way
thereof.
9 But when the people of the land shall
come before the LORD in the solemn feasts,
he that entereth in by the way of the north
gate to worship shall go out by the way of
the south gate; and he that entereth by the
way of the south gate shall go forth by the
way of the north gate: he shall not return
by the way of the gate whereby he came
in, but shall go forth over against it.
10 And the prince in the midst of them,
when they go in, shall go in; and when
they go forth, shall go forth.
11 And in the feasts and in the solemnities the meat offering shall be an ephah to
a bullock, and ephah to a ram, and to the
lambs as he is able to give, and an hin of
oil to an ephah.
12 Now when the prince shall prepare a
voluntary burnt offering or peace offerings
voluntarily unto the LORD, *one* shall then
open him the gate that looketh toward the
east, and he shall prepare his burnt offering and his peace offerings, as he did on
the sabbath day: then he shall go forth;
and after his going forth *one* shall shut the
gate.
13 Thou shalt daily prepare a burnt offering unto the LORD *of* a lamb of the first
year without blemish: thou shalt prepare
it every morning.
14 And thou shalt prepare a meat offering for it every morning, the sixth part of
an ephah, and the third part of an hin of
oil, to temper with the fine flour; a meat
offering continually by a perpetual ordinance unto the LORD.
15 Thus shall they prepare the lamb, and
the meat offering, and the oil, every morning *for* a continual burnt offering.
16 Thus saith the Lord GOD; If the prince
give a gift unto any of his sons, the inheritance thereof shall be his sons'; it *shall be*
their possession by inheritance.
17 But if he give a gift of his inheritance
to one of his servants, then it shall be his
to the year of liberty; after it shall return
to the prince: but his inheritance shall be
his sons' for them.
18 Moreover the prince shall not take of
the people's inheritance by oppression, to
thrust them out of their possession; *but* he
shall give his sons inheritance out of his
own possession: that my people be not
scattered every man from his possession.
19 After he brought me through the entry, which *was* at the side of the gate, into
the holy chambers of the priests, which
looked toward the north: and, behold,
there *was* a place on the two sides westward.
20 Then said he unto me, This *is* the place
where the priests shall boil the trespass
offering and the sin offering, where they
shall bake the meat offering; that they bear
them not out into the utter court, to sanctify the people.
21 Then he brought me forth into the
utter court, and caused me to pass by the
four corners of the court; and, behold, in
every corner of the court *there was* a court.
22 In the four corners of the court *there*
were courts joined of forty *cubits* long and
thirty broad: these four corners *were* of one
measure.
23 And *there was* a row *of building* round
about in them, round about them four,
and *it was* made with boiling places under
the rows round about.
24 Then said he unto me, These *are* the
places of them that boil, where the ministers of the house shall boil the sacrifice of
the people.

47

1 Afterward he brought me again unto
the door of the house; and, behold, waters issued out from under the threshold
of the house eastward: for the forefront of
the house *stood toward* the east, and the
waters came down from under from the
right side of the house, at the south *side* of
the altar.
2 Then brought he me out of the way of
the gate northward, and led me about the
way without unto the utter gate by the way
that looketh eastward; and, behold, there
ran out waters on the right side.
3 And when the man that had the line in
his hand went forth eastward, he measured
a thousand cubits, and he brought me
through the waters; the waters *were* to the
ancles.
4 Again he measured a thousand, and

brought me through the waters; the waters *were* to the knees. Again he measured
a thousand, and brought me through; the
waters *were* to the loins.
5 Afterward he measured a thousand; *and*
it was a river that I could not pass over: for
the waters were risen, waters to swim in, a
river that could not be passed over.
6 And he said unto me, Son of man, hast
thou seen *this*? Then he brought me, and
caused me to return to the brink of the
river.
7 Now when I had returned, behold, at
the bank of the river *were* very many trees
on the one side and on the other.
8 Then said he unto me, These waters issue out toward the east country, and go
down into the desert, and go into the sea:
which being brought forth into the sea, the
waters shall be healed.
9 And it shall come to pass, *that* every
thing that liveth, which moveth, whithersoever the rivers shall come, shall live: and
there shall be a very great multitude of fish,
because these waters shall come thither:
for they shall be healed; and every thing
shall live whither the river cometh.
10 And it shall come to pass, *that* the fishers shall stand upon it from En-gedi even
unto En-eglaim; they shall be a *place* to
spread forth nets; their fish shall be according to their kinds, as the fish of the great
sea, exceeding many.
11 But the miry places thereof and the
marishes thereof shall not be healed; they
shall be given to salt.
12 And by the river upon the bank
thereof, on this side and on that side, shall
grow all trees for meat, whose leaf shall
not fade, neither shall the fruit thereof be
consumed: it shall bring forth new fruit
according to his months, because their
waters they issued out of the sanctuary:
and the fruit thereof shall be for meat, and
the leaf thereof for medicine.
13 Thus saith the Lord GOD; This *shall be*
the border, whereby ye shall inherit the
land according to the twelve tribes of Israel: Joseph *shall have two* portions.
14 And ye shall inherit it, one as well as
another: *concerning* the which I lifted up
mine hand to give it unto your fathers: and
this land shall fall unto you for inheritance.
15 And this *shall be* the border of the
land toward the north side, from the great
sea, the way of Hethlon, as men go to Zedad;
16 Hamath, Berothah, Sibraim, which *is*
between the border of Damascus and the
border of Hamath; Hazar-hatticon, which
is by the coast of Hauran.
17 And the border from the sea shall be
Hazar-enan, the border of Damascus, and
the north northward, and the border of
Hamath. And *this is* the north side.
18 And the east side ye shall measure
from Hauran, and from Damascus, and
from Gilead, and from the land of Israel
by Jordan, from the border unto the east
sea. And *this is* the east side.
19 And the south side southward, from
Tamar *even* to the waters of strife *in* Kadesh, the river to the great sea. And *this is*
the south side southward.
20 The west side also *shall be* the great sea
from the border, till a man come over
against Hamath. This *is* the west side.
21 So shall ye divide this land unto you
according to the tribes of Israel.
22 And it shall come to pass, *that* ye shall
divide it by lot for an inheritance unto you,
and to the strangers that sojourn among
you, which shall beget children among
you: and they shall be unto you as born in
the country among the children of Israel;
they shall have inheritance with you
among the tribes of Israel.
23 And it shall come to pass, *that* in what
tribe the stranger sojourneth, there shall
ye give *him* his inheritance, saith the Lord
GOD.

48

1 Now these *are* the names of the tribes.
From the north end to the coast of the
way of Hethlon, as one goeth to Hamath,
Hazar-enan, the border of Damascus
northward, to the coast of Hamath; for
these are his sides east *and* west; a *portion*
for Dan.
2 And by the border of Dan, from the east
side unto the west side, a *portion for* Asher.
3 And by the border of Asher, from the
east side even unto the west side, a *portion*
for Naphtali.
4 And by the border of Naphtali, from
the east side unto the west side, a *portion*
for Manasseh.
5 And by the border of Manasseh, from
the east side unto the west side, a *portion*
for Ephraim.

6 And by the border of Ephraim, from
the east side even unto the west side, a *portion for* Reuben.
7 And by the border of Reuben, from the
east side unto the west side, a *portion for*
Judah.
8 And by the border of Judah, from the
east side unto the west side, shall be the
offering which ye shall offer of five and
twenty thousand *reeds in* breadth, and *in*
length as one of the *other* parts, from the
east side unto the west side: and the sanctuary shall be in the midst of it.
9 The oblation that ye shall offer unto
the LORD *shall be* of five and twenty thousand in length, and of ten thousand in
breadth.
10 And for them, *even* for the priests, shall
be *this* holy oblation; toward the north five
and twenty thousand *in length,* and toward
the west ten thousand in breadth, and toward the east ten thousand in breadth, and
toward the south five and twenty thousand
in length: and the sanctuary of the LORD
shall be in the midst thereof.
11 *It shall be* for the priests that are sanctified of the sons of Zadok; which have
kept my charge, which went not astray
when the children of Israel went astray, as
the Levites went astray.
12 And *this* oblation of the land that is
offered shall be unto them a thing most
holy by the border of the Levites.
13 And over against the border of the
priests the Levites *shall have* five and twenty thousand in length, and ten thousand
in breadth: all the length *shall be* five and
twenty thousand, and the breadth ten
thousand.
14 And they shall not sell of it, neither
exchange, nor alienate the firstfruits of the
land: for *it is* holy unto the LORD.
15 And the five thousand, that are left in
the breadth over against the five and twenty thousand, shall be a profane *place* for
the city, for dwelling, and for suburbs: and
the city shall be in the midst thereof.
16 And these *shall be* the measures
thereof; the north side four thousand and
five hundred, and the south side four
thousand and five hundred, and on the
east side four thousand and five hundred,
and the west side four thousand and five
hundred.
17 And the suburbs of the city shall be
toward the north two hundred and fifty,
and toward the south two hundred and
fifty, and toward the east two hundred
and fifty, and toward the west two hundred and fifty.
18 And the residue in length over against
the oblation of the holy *portion shall be* ten
thousand eastward, and ten thousand
westward: and it shall be over against the
oblation of the holy *portion;* and the increase thereof shall be for food unto them
that serve the city.
19 And they that serve the city shall serve
it out of all the tribes of Israel.
20 All the oblation *shall be* five and twenty
thousand by five and twenty thousand: ye
shall offer the holy oblation foursquare,
with the possession of the city.
21 And the residue *shall be* for the prince,
on the one side and on the other of the
holy oblation, and of the possession of the
city, over against the five and twenty thousand of the oblation toward the east border, and westward over against the five and
twenty thousand toward the west border,
over against the portions for the prince:
and it shall be the holy oblation; and the
sanctuary of the house *shall be* in the midst
thereof.
22 Moreover from the possession of the
Levites, and from the possession of the city,
being in the midst *of that* which is the
prince's, between the border of Judah and
the border of Benjamin, shall be for the
prince.
23 As for the rest of the tribes, from the
east side unto the west side, Benjamin *shall
have* a *portion.*
24 And by the border of Benjamin, from
the east side unto the west side, Simeon
shall have a *portion.*
25 And by the border of Simeon, from
the east side unto the west side, Issachar a
portion.
26 And by the border of Issachar, from
the east side unto the west side, Zebulun a
portion.
27 And by the border of Zebulun, from
the east side unto the west side, Gad a *portion.*
28 And by the border of Gad, at the south
side southward, the border shall be even
from Tamar *unto* the waters of strife *in*
Kadesh, *and* to the river toward the great
sea.

29 This *is* the land which ye shall divide by lot unto the tribes of Israel for inheritance, and these *are* their portions, saith the Lord GOD.

30 And these *are* the goings out of the city on the north side, four thousand and five hundred measures.

31 And the gates of the city *shall be* after the names of the tribes of Israel: three gates northward; one gate of Reuben, one gate of Judah, one gate of Levi.

32 And at the east side four thousand and five hundred: and three gates; and one gate of Joseph, one gate of Benjamin, one gate of Dan.

33 And at the south side four thousand and five hundred measures: and three gates; one gate of Simeon, one gate of Issachar, one gate of Zebulun.

34 At the west side four thousand and five hundred, *with* their three gates; one gate of Gad, one gate of Asher, one gate of Naphtali.

35 *It was* round about eighteen thousand *measures:* and the name of the city from *that* day *shall be,* The LORD *is* there.

Daniel

AUTHOR
Daniel

MAIN POINT
It is possible to remain faithful to God in very difficult situations, and he who is in control of heaven and earth will help us when we try.

DATE WRITTEN
Approximately 535 B.C.

12 CHAPTERS

MAIN PEOPLE

Daniel, Nebuchadnezzar, Shadrach, Meshach, Abednego, Belshazzar, Darius

SPECIAL FEATURES

- *Describes how Daniel and three other young Hebrews in the king's service stood up for what was right*
- *Includes one of the hottest stories in the Bible—Daniel's three friends in the fiery furnace*
- *Also tells the famous story of Daniel in the Lion's den*
- *Tells the story of real handwriting on the wall*
- *Tells about Daniel's dreams and visions of the future, including a prediction about the Messiah, Jesus*
- *Fifth book of the Major Prophets*

HOW THE BOOK GOT ITS NAME

The author and main person of this book of prophecy is Daniel, a shining example of faith in God no matter how tough things get.

1
1In the third year of the reign of Jehoiakim king of Judah came Nebuchadnezzar
king of Babylon unto Jerusalem, and besieged it.
2And the Lord gave Jehoiakim king of
Judah into his hand, with part of the vessels of the house of God: which he carried
into the land of Shinar to the house of his
god; and he brought the vessels into the
treasure house of his god.
3And the king spake unto Ashpenaz the
master of his eunuchs, that he should bring
certain of the children of Israel, and of the
king's seed, and of the princes;
4Children in whom *was* no blemish, but
well favoured, and skilful in all wisdom,
and cunning in knowledge, and understanding science, and such as *had* ability
in them to stand in the king's palace, and
whom they might teach the learning and
the tongue of the Chaldeans.
5And the king appointed them a daily
provision of the king's meat, and of the
wine which he drank: so nourishing them
three years, that at the end thereof they
might stand before the king.
6Now among these were of the children
of Judah, Daniel, Hananiah, Mishael, and
Azariah:
7Unto whom the prince of the eunuchs

gave names: for he gave unto Daniel *the*
name of Belteshazzar; and to Hananiah, of
Shadrach; and to Mishael, of Meshach; and
to Azariah, of Abed-nego.
8 But Daniel pur-
posed in his heart
that he would not
defile himself with
the portion of the
king's meat, nor
with the wine which he drank: therefore
he requested of the prince of the eunuchs
that he might not defile himself.

1:8 Drinking
◄ Jeremiah 35:6
Daniel 10:3 ►

9 Now God had brought Daniel into
favour and tender love with the prince of
the eunuchs.
10 And the prince of the eunuchs said
unto Daniel, I fear my lord the king, who
hath appointed your meat and your drink:
for why should he see your faces worse liking than the children which *are* of your
sort? then shall ye make *me* endanger my
head to the king.
11 Then said Daniel to Melzar, whom the
prince of the eunuchs had set over Daniel,
Hananiah, Mishael, and Azariah,
12 Prove thy servants, I beseech thee, ten
days; and let them give us pulse to eat, and
water to drink.
13 Then let our countenances be looked
upon before thee, and the countenance of
the children that eat of the portion of the
king's meat: and as thou seest, deal with
thy servants.
14 So he consented to them in this matter, and proved them ten days.
15 And at the end of ten days their countenances appeared fairer and fatter in flesh
than all the children which did eat the
portion of the king's meat.
16 Thus Melzar took away the portion of
their meat, and the wine that they should
drink; and gave them pulse.
17 As for these
four children, God
gave them knowl-
edge and skill in all
learning and wis-
dom: and Daniel
had understanding in all visions and
dreams.

1:17
Study
◄ Acts 7:22 ►

18 Now at the end of the days that the
king had said he should bring them in,
then the prince of the eunuchs brought
them in before Nebuchadnezzar.
19 And the king communed with them;
and among them all was found none like
Daniel, Hananiah, Mishael, and Azariah:
therefore stood they before the king.
20 And in all matters of wisdom *and* understanding, that the king enquired of
them, he found them ten times better than
all the magicians *and* astrologers that *were*
in all his realm.
21 And Daniel continued *even* unto the
first year of king Cyrus.

2
1 And in the second year of the reign
of Nebuchadnezzar Nebuchadnezzar
dreamed dreams, wherewith his spirit was
troubled, and his sleep brake from him.
2 Then the king commanded to call the
magicians, and the astrologers, and the
sorcerers, and the Chaldeans, for to shew
the king his dreams. So they came and
stood before the king.
3 And the king said unto them, I have
dreamed a dream, and my spirit was troubled to know the dream.
4 Then spake the Chaldeans to the king
in Syriack, O king, live for ever: tell thy
servants the dream, and we will shew the
interpretation.
5 The king answered and said to the
Chaldeans, The thing is gone from me: if
ye will not make known unto me the
dream, with the interpretation thereof, ye
shall be cut in pieces, and your houses
shall be made a dunghill.
6 But if ye shew the dream, and the interpretation thereof, ye shall receive of me
gifts and rewards and great honour: therefore shew me the dream, and the interpretation thereof.
7 They answered again and said, Let the
king tell his servants the dream, and we
will shew the interpretation of it.
8 The king answered and said, I know of
certainty that ye would gain the time, because ye see the thing is gone from me.
9 But if ye will not make known unto me
the dream, *there is but* one decree for you:
for ye have prepared lying and corrupt
words to speak before me, till the time be
changed: therefore tell me the dream, and
I shall know that ye can shew me the interpretation thereof.
10 The Chaldeans answered before the
king, and said, There is not a man upon
the earth that can shew the king's matter:
therefore *there is* no king, lord, nor ruler,

that asked such things at any magician, or astrologer, or Chaldean.

11 And *it is* a rare thing that the king requireth, and there is none other that can shew it before the king, except the gods, whose dwelling is not with flesh.

12 For this cause the king was angry and very furious, and commanded to destroy all the wise *men* of Babylon.

13 And the decree went forth that the wise *men* should be slain; and they sought Daniel and his fellows to be slain.

14 Then Daniel answered with counsel and wisdom to Arioch the captain of the king's guard, which was gone forth to slay the wise *men* of Babylon:

15 He answered and said to Arioch the king's captain, Why *is* the decree *so* hasty from the king? Then Arioch made the thing known to Daniel.

16 Then Daniel went in, and desired of the king that he would give him time, and that he would shew the king the interpretation.

17 Then Daniel went to his house, and made the thing known to Hananiah, Mishael, and Azariah, his companions:

18 That they would desire mercies of the God of heaven concerning this secret; that Daniel and his fellows should not perish with the rest of the wise *men* of Babylon.

19 Then was the secret revealed unto Daniel in a night vision. Then Daniel blessed the God of heaven.

20 Daniel answered and said, Blessed be the name of God for ever and ever: for wisdom and might are his:

21 And he changeth the times and the seasons: he removeth kings, and setteth up kings: he giveth wisdom unto the wise, and knowledge to them that know understanding:

22 He revealeth the deep and secret things: he knoweth what *is* in the darkness, and the light dwelleth with him.

2:20 God's Control
◄ Psalm 135:6
Daniel 4:35 ►

2:21 Getting Wisdom
◄ Ecclesiastes 2:26
Luke 21:15 ►

2:21 God at Work
◄ Psalm 75:7 ►

23 I thank thee, and praise thee, O thou God of my fathers, who hast given me wisdom and might, and hast made known unto me now what we desired of thee: for thou hast *now* made known unto us the king's matter.

24 Therefore Daniel went in unto Arioch, whom the king had ordained to destroy the wise *men* of Babylon: he went and said thus unto him; Destroy not the wise *men* of Babylon: bring me in before the king, and I will shew unto the king the interpretation.

25 Then Arioch brought in Daniel before the king in haste and said thus unto him, I have found a man of the captives of Judah, that will make known unto the king the interpretation.

26 The king answered and said to Daniel, whose name *was* Belteshazzar, Art thou able to make known unto me the dream which I have seen, and the interpretation thereof?

27 Daniel answered in the presence of the king, and said, The secret which the king hath demanded cannot the wise *men,* the astrologers, the magicians, the soothsayers, shew unto the king;

28 But there is a God in heaven that revealeth secrets, and maketh known to the king Nebuchadnezzar what shall be in the latter days. Thy dream, and the visions of thy head upon thy bed, are these;

29 As for thee, O king, thy thoughts came *into thy mind* upon thy bed, what should come to pass hereafter: and he that revealeth secrets maketh known to thee what shall come to pass.

30 But as for me, this secret is not revealed to me for *any* wisdom that I have more than any living, but for *their* sakes that shall make known the interpretation to the king, and that thou mightest know the thoughts of thy heart.

31 Thou, O king, sawest, and behold a great image. This great image, whose brightness *was* excellent, stood before thee; and the form thereof *was* terrible.

32 This image's head *was* of fine gold, his breast and his arms of silver, his belly and his thighs of brass,

33 His legs of iron, his feet part of iron and part of clay.

34 Thou sawest till that a stone was cut out without hands, which smote the im-

age upon his feet *that were* of iron and clay,
and brake them to pieces.
35Then was the iron, the clay, the brass,
the silver, and the gold, broken to pieces
together, and became like the chaff of the
summer threshingfloors; and the wind
carried them away, that no place was found
for them: and the stone that smote the
image became a great mountain, and filled
the whole earth.
36This *is* the dream; and we will tell the
interpretation thereof before the king.
37Thou, O king, *art* a king of kings: for
the God of heaven hath given thee a kingdom, power, and strength, and glory.
38And wheresoever the children of men
dwell, the beasts of the field and the fowls
of the heaven hath he given into thine
hand, and hath made thee ruler over them
all. Thou *art* this head of gold.
39And after thee shall arise another kingdom inferior to thee, and another third
kingdom of brass, which shall bear rule
over all the earth.
40And the fourth kingdom shall be
strong as iron: forasmuch as iron breaketh
in pieces and subdueth all *things:* and as
iron that breaketh all these, shall it break
in pieces and bruise.
41And whereas thou sawest the feet and
toes, part of potters' clay, and part of iron,
the kingdom shall be divided; but there
shall be in it of the strength of the iron,
forasmuch as thou sawest the iron mixed
with miry clay.
42And *as* the toes of the feet *were* part of
iron, and part of clay, so the kingdom shall
be partly strong, and partly broken.
43And whereas thou sawest iron mixed
with miry clay, they shall mingle themselves with the seed of men: but they shall
not cleave one to another, even as iron is
not mixed with clay.
44And in the days of these kings shall
the God of heaven set up a kingdom,
which shall never be destroyed: and the
kingdom shall not be left to other people,
but it shall break in pieces and consume
all these kingdoms, and it shall stand for
ever.
45Forasmuch as thou sawest that the
stone was cut out of the mountain without hands, and that it brake in pieces the
iron, the brass, the clay, the silver, and the
gold; the great God hath made known to
the king what shall come to pass hereafter: and the dream *is* certain, and the interpretation thereof sure.
46Then the king Nebuchadnezzar fell
upon his face, and worshipped Daniel, and
commanded that they should offer an
oblation and sweet odours unto him.
47The king answered unto Daniel, and
said, Of a truth *it is,* that your God *is* a
God of gods, and a Lord of kings, and a
revealer of secrets, seeing thou couldst reveal this secret.
48Then the king made Daniel a great
man, and gave him many great gifts, and
made him ruler over the whole province
of Babylon, and chief of the governors over
all the wise *men* of Babylon.
49Then Daniel requested of the king,
and he set Shadrach, Meshach, and Abed-
nego, over the affairs of the province of
Babylon: but Daniel *sat* in the gate of the
king.

3

1Nebuchadnezzar the king made an
image of gold, whose height *was* threescore
cubits, *and* the breadth thereof six cubits:
he set it up in the plain of Dura, in the
province of Babylon.
2Then Nebuchadnezzar the king sent to
gather together the princes, the governors,
and the captains, the judges, the treasurers, the counsellors, the sheriffs, and all
the rulers of the provinces, to come to the
dedication of the image which Nebuchadnezzar the king had set up.
3Then the princes, the governors, and
captains, the judges, the treasurers, the
counsellors, the sheriffs, and all the rulers
of the provinces, were gathered together
unto the dedication of the image that Nebuchadnezzar the king had set up; and they
stood before the image that Nebuchadnezzar had set up.
4Then an herald cried aloud, To you it
is commanded, O people, nations, and
languages,
5*That* at what time ye hear the sound of
the cornet, flute, harp, sackbut, psaltery,
dulcimer, and all kinds of musick, ye fall
down and worship the golden image that
Nebuchadnezzar the king hath set up:
6And whoso falleth not down and
worshippeth shall the same hour be cast
into the midst of a burning fiery furnace.
7Therefore at that time, when all the
people heard the sound of the cornet, flute,

harp, sackbut, psaltery, and all kinds of
musick, all the people, the nations, and
the languages, fell down *and* worshipped
the golden image that Nebuchadnezzar the
king had set up.
8 Wherefore at that time certain Chaldeans came near, and accused the Jews.
9 They spake and said to the king Nebuchadnezzar, O king, live for ever.
10 Thou, O king, hast made a decree, that
every man that shall hear the sound of the
cornet, flute, harp, sackbut, psaltery, and
dulcimer, and all kinds of musick, shall
fall down and worship the golden image:
11 And whoso falleth not down and
worshippeth, *that* he should be cast into
the midst of a burning fiery furnace.
12 There are certain Jews whom thou hast
set over the affairs of the province of Babylon, Shadrach, Meshach, and Abed-nego;
these men, O king, have not regarded thee:
they serve not thy gods, nor worship the
golden image which thou hast set up.
13 Then Nebuchadnezzar in *his* rage and
fury commanded to bring Shadrach, Meshach, and Abed-nego. Then they brought
these men before the king.
14 Nebuchadnezzar spake and said unto
them, *Is it* true, O Shadrach, Meshach, and
Abed-nego, do not ye serve my gods, nor
worship the golden image which I have
set up?
15 Now if ye be ready that at what time
ye hear the sound of the cornet, flute, harp,
sackbut, psaltery, and dulcimer, and all
kinds of musick, ye fall down and worship
the image which I have made; *well:* but if
ye worship not, ye shall be cast the same
hour into the midst of a burning fiery furnace; and who *is* that God that shall deliver you out of my hands?
16 Shadrach, Meshach, and Abed-nego,
answered and said to the king, O Nebuchadnezzar, we *are* not careful to answer
thee in this matter.
17 If it be *so,* our God whom we serve is
able to deliver us from the burning fiery
furnace, and he will deliver *us* out of thine
hand, O king.
18 But if not, be it known unto thee,
O king, that we will not serve thy gods, nor
worship the golden image which thou hast
set up.
19 Then was Nebuchadnezzar full of fury,
and the form of his visage was changed
against Shadrach,
Meshach, and
Abed-nego: *there-*
fore he spake, and
commanded that
they should heat
the furnace one seven times more than it
was wont to be heated.

3:19 Temper
◄ 2 Chronicles 28:9
John 10:31 ►

20 And he commanded the most mighty
men that *were* in his army to bind Shadrach, Meshach, and Abed-nego, *and* to
cast *them* into the burning fiery furnace.
21 Then these men were bound in their
coats, their hosen, and their hats, and their
other garments, and were cast into the
midst of the burning fiery furnace.
22 Therefore because the king's commandment was urgent, and the furnace
exceeding hot, the flame of the fire slew
those men that took up Shadrach, Meshach, and Abed-nego.
23 And these three men, Shadrach,
Meshach, and Abed-nego, fell down
bound into the midst of the burning fiery
furnace.
24 Then Nebuchadnezzar the king was
astonied, and rose up in haste, *and* spake,
and said unto his counsellors, Did not we
cast three men bound into the midst of
the fire? They answered and said unto the
king, True, O king.
25 He answered and said, Lo, I see four
men loose, walking in the midst of the fire,
and they have no hurt; and the form of
the fourth is like the Son of God.
26 Then Nebuchadnezzar came near to
the mouth of the burning fiery furnace, *and*
spake, and said, Shadrach, Meshach, and
Abed-nego, ye servants of the most high
God, come forth, and come *hither.* Then
Shadrach, Meshach, and Abed-nego, came
forth of the midst of the fire.
27 And the princes, governors, and captains, and the king's counsellors, being
gathered together, saw these men, upon
whose bodies the fire had no power, nor
was an hair of their head singed, neither
were their coats changed, nor the smell of
fire had passed on them.
28 *Then* Nebuchadnezzar spake, and said,
Blessed *be* the God of Shadrach, Meshach,
and Abed-nego, who hath sent his angel,
and delivered his servants that trusted in
him, and have changed the king's word,
and yielded their bodies, that they might

not serve nor worship any god, except their own God.

29 Therefore I make a decree, That every people, nation, and language, which speak any thing amiss against the God of Shadrach, Meshach, and Abed-nego, shall be cut in pieces, and their houses shall be made a dunghill: because there is no other God that can deliver after this sort.

30 Then the king promoted Shadrach, Meshach, and Abed-nego, in the province of Babylon.

4

1 Nebuchadnezzar the king, unto all people, nations, and languages, that dwell in all the earth; Peace be multiplied unto you.

2 I thought it good to shew the signs and wonders that the high God hath wrought toward me.

3 How great *are* his signs! and how mighty *are* his wonders! his kingdom *is* an everlasting kingdom, and his dominion *is* from generation to generation.

4 I Nebuchadnezzar was at rest in mine house, and flourishing in my palace:

5 I saw a dream which made me afraid, and the thoughts upon my bed and the visions of my head troubled me.

6 Therefore made I a decree to bring in all the wise *men* of Babylon before me, that they might make known unto me the interpretation of the dream.

7 Then came in the magicians, the astrologers, the Chaldeans, and the soothsayers: and I told the dream before them; but they did not make known unto me the interpretation thereof.

8 But at the last Daniel came in before me, whose name *was* Belteshazzar, according to the name of my god, and in whom *is* the spirit of the holy gods: and before him I told the dream, *saying,*

9 O Belteshazzar, master of the magicians, because I know that the spirit of the holy gods *is* in thee, and no secret troubleth thee, tell me the visions of my dream that I have seen, and the interpretation thereof.

10 Thus *were* the visions of mine head in my bed; I saw, and behold a tree in the midst of the earth, and the height thereof *was* great.

11 The tree grew, and was strong, and the height thereof reached unto heaven, and the sight thereof to the end of all the earth:

12 The leaves thereof *were* fair, and the fruit thereof much, and in it *was* meat for all: the beasts of the field had shadow under it, and the fowls of the heaven dwelt in the boughs thereof, and all flesh was fed of it.

13 I saw in the visions of my head upon my bed, and, behold, a watcher and an holy one came down from heaven;

14 He cried aloud, and said thus, Hew down the tree, and cut off his branches, shake off his leaves, and scatter his fruit: let the beasts get away from under it, and the fowls from his branches:

15 Nevertheless leave the stump of his roots in the earth, even with a band of iron and brass, in the tender grass of the field; and let it be wet with the dew of heaven, and *let* his portion *be* with the beasts in the grass of the earth:

16 Let his heart be changed from man's, and let a beast's heart be given unto him; and let seven times pass over him.

17 This matter *is* by the decree of the watchers, and the demand by the word of the holy ones: to the intent that the living may know that the most High ruleth in the kingdom of men, and giveth it to whomsoever he will, and setteth up over it the basest of men.

18 This dream I king Nebuchadnezzar have seen. Now thou, O Belteshazzar, declare the interpretation thereof, forasmuch as all the wise *men* of my kingdom are not able to make known unto me the interpretation: but thou *art* able; for the spirit of the holy gods *is* in thee.

19 Then Daniel, whose name *was* Belteshazzar, was astonied for one hour, and his thoughts troubled him. The king spake, and said, Belteshazzar, let not the dream, or the interpretation thereof, trouble thee. Belteshazzar answered and said, My lord, the dream *be* to them that hate thee, and the interpretation thereof to thine enemies.

20 The tree that thou sawest, which grew, and was strong, whose height reached unto the heaven, and the sight thereof to all the earth;

21 Whose leaves *were* fair, and the fruit thereof much, and in it *was* meat for all; under which the beasts of the field dwelt, and upon whose branches the fowls of the heaven had their habitation:

22 It *is* thou, O king, that art grown and become strong: for thy greatness is grown,

and reacheth unto heaven, and thy dominion to the end of the earth.

23 And whereas the king saw a watcher and an holy one coming down from heaven, and saying, Hew the tree down, and destroy it; yet leave the stump of the roots thereof in the earth, even with a band of iron and brass, in the tender grass of the field; and let it be wet with the dew of heaven, and *let* his portion *be* with the beasts of the field, till seven times pass over him;

24 This *is* the interpretation, O king, and this *is* the decree of the most High, which is come upon my lord the king:

25 That they shall drive thee from men, and thy dwelling shall be with the beasts of the field, and they shall make thee to eat grass as oxen, and they shall wet thee with the dew of heaven, and seven times shall pass over thee, till thou know that the most High ruleth in the kingdom of men, and giveth it to whomsoever he will.

26 And whereas they commanded to leave the stump of the tree roots; thy kingdom shall be sure unto thee, after that thou shalt have known that the heavens do rule.

27 Wherefore, O king, let my counsel be acceptable unto thee, and break off thy sins by righteousness, and thine iniquities by shewing mercy to the poor; if it may be a lengthening of thy tranquility.

4:27 Repent!
◄ Ezekiel 33:11
Hosea 14:2 ►

4:27 Rewards
◄ Isaiah 58:10
Matthew 5:7 ►

4:27 Righteousness
◄ Hosea 10:12 ►

28 All this came upon the king Nebuchadnezzar.

29 At the end of twelve months he walked in the palace of the kingdom of Babylon.

30 The king spake, and said, Is not this great Babylon, that I have built for the house of the kingdom by the might of my power, and for the honour of my majesty?

31 While the word *was* in the king's mouth, there fell a voice from heaven, *saying,* O king Nebuchadnezzar, to thee it is spoken; The kingdom is departed from thee.

32 And they shall drive thee from men, and thy dwelling *shall be* with the beasts of the field: they shall make thee to eat grass as oxen, and seven times shall pass over thee, until thou know that the most High ruleth in the kingdom of men, and giveth it to whomsoever he will.

33 The same hour was the thing fulfilled upon Nebuchadnezzar: and he was driven from men, and did eat grass as oxen, and his body was wet with the dew of heaven, till his hairs were grown like eagles' *feathers,* and his nails like birds' *claws.*

4:33-34 Blinded by Sin
◄ Ecclesiastes 9:3
Luke 15:17 ►

34 And at the end of the days I Nebuchadnezzar lifted up mine eyes unto heaven, and mine understanding returned unto me, and I blessed the most High, and I praised and honoured him that liveth for ever, whose dominion *is* an everlasting dominion, and his kingdom *is* from generation to generation:

35 And all the inhabitants of the earth *are* reputed as nothing: and he doeth according to his will in the army of heaven, and *among* the inhabitants of the earth: and none can stay his hand, or say unto him, What doest thou?

4:35 God's Control
◄ Daniel 2:20
Matthew 6:13 ►

36 At the same time my reason returned unto me; and for the glory of my kingdom, mine honour and brightness returned unto me; and my counsellors and my lords sought unto me; and I was established in my kingdom, and excellent majesty was added unto me.

37 Now I Nebuchadnezzar praise and extol and honour the King of heaven, all whose works *are* truth, and his ways judgment: and those that walk in pride he is able to abase.

5

1 Belshazzar the king made a great feast to a thousand of his lords, and drank wine before the thousand.

5:1 Moderation
◄ Proverbs 28:7
Luke 15:13 ►

2 Belshazzar, whiles he tasted the wine, commanded to bring the golden and silver vessels which his father Nebuchadnezzar had taken out of the temple which *was*

in Jerusalem; that the king, and his princes,
his wives, and his concubines, might drink
therein.
3 Then they brought the golden vessels
that were taken out of the temple of the
house of God which *was* at Jerusalem; and
the king, and his princes, his wives, and
his concubines, drank in them.
4 They drank wine, and praised the gods
of gold, and of silver, of brass, of iron, of
wood, and of stone.
5 In the same hour came forth fingers of
a man's hand, and wrote over against the
candlestick upon the plaister of the wall
of the king's palace: and the king saw the
part of the hand that wrote.
6 Then the king's
countenance was
changed, and his
thoughts troubled
him, so that the
joints of his loins
were loosed, and his
knees smote one
against another.
7 The king cried
aloud to bring in
the astrologers, the
Chaldeans, and the
soothsayers. *And*
the king spake, and
said to the wise *men*
of Babylon, Whoso-
ever shall read this
writing, and shew me the interpretation
thereof, shall be clothed with scarlet, and
have a chain of gold about his neck, and
shall be the third ruler in the kingdom.

5:6 Feeling Guilty
◄ Psalm 40:12
John 8:9 ►

5:6 Guilty Conscience
◄ Psalm 40:12
John 8:9 ►

5:6 Guilty Fear
◄ Isaiah 66:4
Micah 7:17 ►

8 Then came in all the king's wise *men:*
but they could not read the writing, nor
make known to the king the interpretation
thereof.
9 Then was king Belshazzar greatly troubled, and his countenance was changed in
him, and his lords were astonied.
10 *Now* the queen, by reason of the words
of the king and his lords, came into the
banquet house: *and* the queen spake and
said, O king, live for ever: let not thy
thoughts trouble thee, nor let thy countenance be changed:
11 There is a man in thy kingdom, in
whom *is* the spirit of the holy gods; and
in the days of thy father light and understanding and wisdom, like the wisdom of
the gods, was found in him; whom the
king Nebuchadnezzar thy father, the king,
I say, thy father, made master of the magicians, astrologers, Chaldeans, *and* soothsayers;
12 Forasmuch as an excellent spirit, and
knowledge, and understanding, interpret-
ing of dreams, and shewing of hard sentences, and dissolving of doubts, were
found in the same Daniel, whom the
king named Belteshazzar: now let Daniel
be called, and he will shew the interpretation.
13 Then was Daniel brought in before the
king. *And* the king spake and said unto
Daniel, *Art* thou that Daniel, which *art* of
the children of the captivity of Judah,
whom the king my father brought out of
Jewry?
14 I have even heard of thee, that the spirit of the gods *is* in thee, and *that* light and
understanding and excellent wisdom is
found in thee.
15 And now the wise *men,* the astrologers, have been brought in before me, that
they should read this writing, and make
known unto me the interpretation thereof:
but they could not shew the interpretation
of the thing:
16 And I have heard of thee, that thou
canst make interpretations, and dissolve
doubts: now if thou canst read the writing, and make known to me the interpretation thereof, thou shalt be clothed with
scarlet, and *have* a chain of gold about thy
neck, and shalt be the third ruler in the
kingdom.
17 Then Daniel
answered and said
before the king, Let
thy gifts be to thy-
self, and give thy
rewards to another;
yet I will read the writing unto the king,
and make known to him the interpretation.

5:17 Unselfishness
◄ 2 Samuel 23:17
Romans 15:3 ►

18 O thou king, the most high God gave
Nebuchadnezzar thy father a kingdom,
and majesty, and glory, and honour:
19 And for the majesty that he gave him,
all people, nations, and languages, trembled and feared before him: whom he
would he slew; and whom he would he
kept alive; and whom he would he set up;
and whom he would he put down.

20 But when his heart was lifted up, and his mind hardened in pride, he was deposed from his kingly throne, and they took his glory from him:

21 And he was driven from the sons of men; and his heart was made like the beasts, and his dwelling *was* with the wild asses: they fed him with grass like oxen, and his body was wet with the dew of heaven; till he knew that the most high God ruled in the kingdom of men, and *that* he appointeth over it whomsoever he will.

22 And thou his son, O Belshazzar, hast not humbled thine heart, though thou knewest all this;

23 But hast lifted up thyself against the Lord of heaven; and they have brought the vessels of his house before thee, and thou, and thy lords, thy wives, and thy concubines, have drunk wine in them; and thou hast praised the gods of silver, and gold, of brass, iron, wood, and stone, which see not, nor hear, nor know: and the God in whose hand thy breath *is,* and whose *are* all thy ways, hast thou not glorified:

24 Then was the part of the hand sent from him; and this writing was written.

25 And this *is* the writing that was written, MENE, MENE, TEKEL, UPHARSIN.

26 This *is* the interpretation of the thing: MENE; God hath numbered thy kingdom, and finished it.

27 TEKEL; Thou art weighed in the balances, and art found wanting.

28 PERES; Thy kingdom is divided, and given to the Medes and Persians.

29 Then commanded Belshazzar, and they clothed Daniel with scarlet, and *put* a chain of gold about his neck, and made a proclamation concerning him, that he should be the third ruler in the kingdom.

30 In that night was Belshazzar the king of the Chaldeans slain.

31 And Darius the Median took the kingdom, *being* about threescore and two years old.

6

1 It pleased Darius to set over the kingdom an hundred and twenty princes, which should be over the whole kingdom;

2 And over these three presidents; of whom Daniel *was* first: that the princes might give accounts unto them, and the king should have no damage.

3 Then this Daniel was preferred above the presidents and princes, because an excellent spirit *was* in him; and the king thought to set him over the whole realm.

4 Then the presidents and princes sought to find occasion against Daniel concerning the kingdom; but they could find none occasion nor fault; forasmuch as he *was* faithful, neither was there any error or fault found in him.

5 Then said these men, We shall not find any occasion against this Daniel, except we find *it* against him concerning the law of his God.

6 Then these presidents and princes assembled together to the king, and said thus unto him, King Darius, live for ever.

7 All the presidents of the kingdom, the governors, and the princes, the counsellors, and the captains, have consulted together to establish a royal statute, and to make a firm decree, that whosoever shall ask a petition of any God or man for thirty days, save of thee, O king, he shall be cast into the den of lions.

8 Now, O king, establish the decree, and sign the writing, that it be not changed, according to the law of the Medes and Persians, which altereth not.

9 Wherefore king Darius signed the writing and the decree.

10 Now when Daniel knew that the writing was signed, he went into his house; and his windows being open in his chamber toward Jerusalem, he kneeled upon his knees three times a day, and prayed, and gave thanks before his God, as he did aforetime.

6:10 Praying Alone
◄ 1 Kings 17:19-20
Matthew 6:6 ►

6:10 Who Is Religious?
◄ Job 1:1
Luke 2:25 ►

11 Then these men assembled, and found Daniel praying and making supplication before his God.

12 Then they came near, and spake before the king concerning the king's decree; Hast thou not signed a decree, that every man that shall ask *a petition* of any God or man within thirty days, save of thee, O king, shall be cast into the den of lions? The king answered and said, The thing *is*

true, according to the law of the Medes and Persians, which altereth not.

13 Then answered they and said before the king, That Daniel, which *is* of the children of the captivity of Judah, regardeth not thee, O king, nor the decree that thou hast signed, but maketh his petition three times a day.

14 Then the king, when he heard *these* words, was sore displeased with himself, and set *his* heart on Daniel to deliver him: and he laboured till the going down of the sun to deliver him.

15 Then these men assembled unto the king, and said unto the king, Know, O king, that the law of the Medes and Persians *is*, That no decree nor statute which the king establisheth may be changed.

16 Then the king commanded, and they brought Daniel, and cast *him* into the den of lions. *Now* the king spake and said unto Daniel, Thy God whom thou servest continually, he will deliver thee.

17 And a stone was brought and laid upon the mouth of the den; and the king sealed it with his own signet, and with the signet of his lords; that the purpose might not be changed concerning Daniel.

18 Then the king went to his palace, and passed the night fasting: neither were instruments of musick brought before him: and his sleep went from him.

19 Then the king arose very early in the morning, and went in haste unto the den of lions.

20 And when he came to the den, he cried with a lamentable voice unto Daniel: *and* the king spake and said to Daniel, O Daniel, servant of the living God, is thy God, whom thou servest continually, able to deliver thee from the lions?

21 Then said Daniel unto the king, O king, live for ever.

22 My God hath sent his angel, and hath shut the lions' mouths, that they have not hurt me: forasmuch as before him innocency was found in me; and also before thee, O king, have I done no hurt.

6:22 Angels
◄ Psalm 91:11
Acts 12:7 ►

23 Then was the king exceeding glad for him, and commanded that they should take Daniel up out of the den. So Daniel was taken up out of the den, and no manner of hurt was found upon him, because he believed in his God.

24 And the king commanded, and they brought those men which had accused Daniel, and they cast *them* into the den of lions, them, their children, and their wives; and the lions had the mastery of them, and brake all their bones in pieces or ever they came at the bottom of the den.

25 Then king Darius wrote unto all people, nations, and languages, that dwell in all the earth; Peace be multiplied unto you.

26 I make a decree, That in every dominion of my kingdom men tremble and fear before the God of Daniel: for he is the living God, and stedfast for ever, and his kingdom *that* which shall not be destroyed, and his dominion *shall be even* unto the end.

27 He delivereth and rescueth, and he worketh signs and wonders in heaven and in earth, who hath delivered Daniel from the power of the lions.

28 So this Daniel prospered in the reign of Darius, and in the reign of Cyrus the Persian.

7

1 In the first year of Belshazzar king of Babylon Daniel had a dream and visions of his head upon his bed: then he wrote the dream, *and* told the sum of the matters.

2 Daniel spake and said, I saw in my vision by night, and, behold, the four winds of the heaven strove upon the great sea.

3 And four great beasts came up from the sea, diverse one from another.

4 The first *was* like a lion, and had eagle's wings: I beheld till the wings thereof were plucked, and it was lifted up from the earth, and made stand upon the feet as a man, and a man's heart was given to it.

5 And behold another beast, a second, like to a bear, and it raised up itself on one side, and *it had* three ribs in the mouth of it between the teeth of it: and they said thus unto it, Arise, devour much flesh.

6 After this I beheld, and lo another, like a leopard, which had upon the back of it four wings of a fowl; the beast had also four heads; and dominion was given to it.

7 After this I saw in the night visions, and behold a fourth beast, dreadful and terrible, and strong exceedingly; and it had great iron teeth: it devoured and brake in pieces, and stamped the residue with the

feet of it: and it *was* diverse from all the
beasts that *were* before it; and it had ten
horns.
8 I considered the horns, and, behold,
there came up among them another little
horn, before whom there were three of the
first horns plucked up by the roots: and,
behold, in this horn *were* eyes like the eyes
of man, and a mouth speaking great things.
9 I beheld till the thrones were cast down,
and the Ancient of days did sit, whose garment *was* white as snow, and the hair of
his head like the pure wool: his throne *was*
like the fiery flame, *and* his wheels *as* burning fire.
10 A fiery stream issued and came forth
from before him: thousand thousands
ministered unto him, and ten thousand
times ten thousand stood before him: the
judgment was set, and the books were
opened.
11 I beheld then because of the voice of
the great words which the horn spake: I
beheld *even* till the beast was slain, and
his body destroyed, and given to the burning flame.
12 As concerning the rest of the beasts,
they had their dominion taken away: yet
their lives were prolonged for a season and
time.
13 I saw in the night visions, and, behold,
one like the Son of man came with the
clouds of heaven, and came to the Ancient
of days, and they brought him near before
him.
14 And there was
given him domin-
ion, and glory, and
a kingdom, that all
people, nations,
and languages,
should serve him: his dominion *is* an everlasting dominion, which shall not pass
away, and his kingdom *that* which shall
not be destroyed.

7:14 Jesus the King
◄ Jeremiah 23:5
Zechariah 9:9 ►

15 I Daniel was grieved in my spirit in
the midst of *my* body, and the visions of
my head troubled me.
16 I came near unto one of them that
stood by, and asked him the truth of all
this. So he told me, and made me know
the interpretation of the things.
17 These great beasts, which are four, *are*
four kings, *which* shall arise out of the
earth.
18 But the saints of the most High shall
take the kingdom, and possess the kingdom for ever, even for ever and ever.
19 Then I would know the truth of the
fourth beast, which was diverse from all
the others, exceeding dreadful, whose teeth
were of iron, and his nails *of* brass; *which*
devoured, brake in pieces, and stamped the
residue with his feet;
20 And of the ten horns that *were* in his
head, and *of* the other which came up, and
before whom three fell; even *of* that horn
that had eyes, and a mouth that spake very
great things, whose look *was* more stout
than his fellows.
21 I beheld, and the same horn made war
with the saints, and prevailed against
them;
22 Until the Ancient of days came, and
judgment was given to the saints of the
most High; and the time came that the
saints possessed the kingdom.
23 Thus he said, The fourth beast shall
be the fourth kingdom upon earth, which
shall be diverse from all kingdoms, and
shall devour the whole earth, and shall
tread it down, and break it in pieces.
24 And the ten horns out of this kingdom *are* ten kings *that* shall arise: and another shall rise after them; and he shall be
diverse from the first, and he shall subdue
three kings.
25 And he shall speak *great* words against
the most High, and shall wear out the
saints of the most High, and think to
change times and laws: and they shall be
given into his hand until a time and times
and the dividing of time.
26 But the judgment shall sit, and they
shall take away his dominion, to consume
and to destroy *it* unto the end.
27 And the kingdom and dominion, and
the greatness of the kingdom under the
whole heaven, shall be given to the people of the saints of the most High, whose
kingdom *is* an everlasting kingdom, and
all dominions shall serve and obey him.
28 Hitherto *is* the end of the matter. As
for me Daniel, my cogitations much troubled me, and my countenance changed in
me: but I kept the matter in my heart.

8

1 In the third year of the reign of king
Belshazzar a vision appeared unto me, *even*
unto me Daniel, after that which appeared
unto me at the first.

2 And I saw in a vision; and it came to pass, when I saw, that I *was* at Shushan *in* the palace, which *is* in the province of Elam; and I saw in a vision, and I was by the river of Ulai.

3 Then I lifted up mine eyes, and saw, and, behold, there stood before the river a ram which had *two* horns: and the *two* horns *were* high; but one *was* higher than the other, and the higher came up last.

4 I saw the ram pushing westward, and northward, and southward; so that no beasts might stand before him, neither *was there any* that could deliver out of his hand; but he did according to his will, and became great.

5 And as I was considering, behold, an he goat came from the west on the face of the whole earth, and touched not the ground: and the goat *had* a notable horn between his eyes.

6 And he came to the ram that had *two* horns, which I had seen standing before the river, and ran unto him in the fury of his power.

7 And I saw him come close unto the ram, and he was moved with choler against him, and smote the ram, and brake his two horns: and there was no power in the ram to stand before him, but he cast him down to the ground, and stamped upon him: and there was none that could deliver the ram out of his hand.

8 Therefore the he goat waxed very great: and when he was strong, the great horn was broken; and for it came up four notable ones toward the four winds of heaven.

9 And out of one of them came forth a little horn, which waxed exceeding great, toward the south, and toward the east, and toward the pleasant *land*.

10 And it waxed great, *even* to the host of heaven; and it cast down *some* of the host and of the stars to the ground, and stamped upon them.

11 Yea, he magnified *himself* even to the prince of the host, and by him the daily *sacrifice* was taken away, and the place of his sanctuary was cast down.

12 And an host was given *him* against the daily *sacrifice* by reason of transgression, and it cast down the truth to the ground; and it practised, and prospered.

13 Then I heard one saint speaking, and another saint said unto that certain *saint* which spake, How long *shall be* the vision *concerning* the daily *sacrifice*, and the transgression of desolation, to give both the sanctuary and the host to be trodden under foot?

14 And he said unto me, Unto two thousand and three hundred days; then shall the sanctuary be cleansed.

15 And it came to pass, when I, *even* I Daniel, had seen the vision, and sought for the meaning, then, behold, there stood before me as the appearance of a man.

16 And I heard a man's voice between *the banks of* Ulai, which called, and said, Gabriel, make this *man* to understand the vision.

17 So he came near where I stood: and when he came, I was afraid, and fell upon my face: but he said unto me, Understand, O son of man: for at the time of the end *shall be* the vision.

18 Now as he was speaking with me, I was in a deep sleep on my face toward the ground: but he touched me, and set me upright.

19 And he said, Behold, I will make thee know what shall be in the last end of the indignation: for at the time appointed the end *shall be*.

20 The ram which thou sawest having *two* horns *are* the kings of Media and Persia.

21 And the rough goat *is* the king of Grecia: and the great horn that *is* between his eyes *is* the first king.

22 Now that being broken, whereas four stood up for it, four kingdoms shall stand up out of the nation, but not in his power.

23 And in the latter time of their kingdom, when the transgressors are come to the full, a king of fierce countenance, and understanding dark sentences, shall stand up.

24 And his power shall be mighty, but not by his own power: and he shall destroy wonderfully, and shall prosper, and practise, and shall destroy the mighty and the holy people.

25 And through his policy also he shall cause craft to prosper in his hand; and he shall magnify *himself* in his heart, and by peace shall destroy many: he shall also stand up against the Prince of princes; but he shall be broken without hand.

26 And the vision of the evening and the morning which was told *is* true: wherefore

shut thou up the vision; for it *shall be* for many days.

27 And I Daniel fainted, and was sick *certain* days; afterward I rose up, and did the king's business; and I was astonished at the vision, but none understood *it*.

9

1 In the first year of Darius the son of Ahasuerus, of the seed of the Medes, which was made king over the realm of the Chaldeans;

2 In the first year of his reign I Daniel understood by books the number of the years, whereof the word of the LORD came to Jeremiah the prophet, that he would accomplish seventy years in the desolations of Jerusalem.

3 And I set my face unto the Lord God, to seek by prayer and supplications, with fasting, and sackcloth, and ashes:

4 And I prayed unto the LORD my God, and made my confession, and said, O Lord, the great and dreadful God, keeping the covenant and mercy to them that love him, and to them that keep his commandments;

5 We have sinned, and have committed iniquity, and have done wickedly, and have rebelled, even by departing from thy precepts and from thy judgments:

6 Neither have we hearkened unto thy servants the prophets, which spake in thy name to our kings, our princes, and our fathers, and to all the people of the land.

7 O Lord, righteousness *belongeth* unto thee, but unto us confusion of faces, as at this day; to the men of Judah, and to the inhabitants of Jerusalem, and unto all Israel, *that are* near, and *that are* far off, through all the countries whither thou hast driven them, because of their trespass that they have trespassed against thee.

8 O Lord, to us *belongeth* confusion of face, to our kings, to our princes, and to our fathers, because we have sinned against thee.

9 To the Lord our God *belong* mercies and forgivenesses, though we have rebelled against him;

10 Neither have we obeyed the voice of the LORD our God, to walk in his laws, which he set before us by his servants the prophets.

11 Yea, all Israel have transgressed thy law, even by departing, that they might not obey thy voice; therefore the curse is poured upon us, and the oath that *is* written in the law of Moses the servant of God, because we have sinned against him.

12 And he hath confirmed his words, which he spake against us, and against our judges that judged us, by bringing upon us a great evil: for under the whole heaven hath not been done as hath been done upon Jerusalem.

13 As *it is* written in the law of Moses, all this evil is come upon us: yet made we not our prayer before the LORD our God, that we might turn from our iniquities, and understand thy truth.

9:13 Not Praying
◄ Jeremiah 10:21
Hosea 7:7 ►

9:13 Stubborn People
◄ Jeremiah 6:15
Luke 16:31 ►

14 Therefore hath the LORD watched upon the evil, and brought it upon us: for the LORD our God *is* righteous in all his works which he doeth: for we obeyed not his voice.

15 And now, O Lord our God, that hast brought thy people forth out of the land of Egypt with a mighty hand, and hast gotten thee renown, as at this day; we have sinned, we have done wickedly.

16 O Lord, according to all thy righteousness, I beseech thee, let thine anger and thy fury be turned away from thy city Jerusalem, thy holy mountain: because for our sins, and for the iniquities of our fathers, Jerusalem and thy people *are become* a reproach to all *that are* about us.

9:16 Praying for Mercy
◄ Psalm 123:3
Habakkuk 3:2 ►

17 Now therefore, O our God, hear the prayer of thy servant, and his supplications, and cause thy face to shine upon thy sanctuary that is desolate, for the Lord's sake.

18 O my God, incline thine ear, and hear; open thine eyes, and behold our desolations, and the city which is called by thy name: for we do not present our supplications before thee for our righteousnesses, but for thy great mercies.

19 O Lord, hear; O Lord, forgive; O Lord, hearken and do; defer not, for thine own sake, O my God: for thy city and thy people are called by thy name.

20 And whiles I *was* speaking, and praying, and confessing my sin and the sin of my people Israel, and presenting my supplication before the LORD my God for the holy mountain of my God;

21 Yea, whiles I *was* speaking in prayer, even the man Gabriel, whom I had seen in the vision at the beginning, being caused to fly swiftly, touched me about the time of the evening oblation.

22 And he informed *me,* and talked with me, and said, O Daniel, I am now come forth to give thee skill and understanding.

23 At the beginning of thy supplications the commandment came forth, and I am come to shew *thee;* for thou *art* greatly beloved: therefore understand the matter, and consider the vision.

24 Seventy weeks are determined upon thy people and upon thy holy city, to finish the transgression, and to make an end of sins, and to make reconciliation for iniquity, and to bring in everlasting righteousness, and to seal up the vision and prophecy, and to anoint the most Holy.

25 Know therefore and understand, *that* from the going forth of the commandment to restore and to build Jerusalem unto the Messiah the Prince *shall be* seven weeks, and threescore and two weeks: the street shall be built again, and the wall, even in troublous times.

26 And after threescore and two weeks shall Messiah be cut off, but not for himself: and the people of the prince that shall come shall destroy the city and the sanctuary; and the end thereof *shall be* with a flood, and unto the end of the war desolations are determined.

27 And he shall confirm the covenant with many for one week: and in the midst of the week he shall cause the sacrifice and the oblation to cease, and for the overspreading of abominations he shall make *it* desolate, even until the consummation, and that determined shall be poured upon the desolate.

10

1 In the third year of Cyrus king of Persia a thing was revealed unto Daniel, whose name was called Belteshazzar; and the thing *was* true, but the time appointed *was* long: and he understood the thing, and had understanding of the vision.

2 In those days I Daniel was mourning three full weeks.

3 I ate no pleasant bread, neither came flesh nor wine in my mouth, neither did I anoint myself at all, till three whole weeks were fulfilled.

10:3 Drinking
◄ Daniel 1:8
Matthew 11:18 ►

4 And in the four and twentieth day of the first month, as I was by the side of the great river, which *is* Hiddekel;

5 Then I lifted up mine eyes, and looked, and behold a certain man clothed in linen, whose loins *were* girded with fine gold of Uphaz:

6 His body also *was* like the beryl, and his face as the appearance of lightning, and his eyes as lamps of fire, and his arms and his feet like in colour to polished brass, and the voice of his words like the voice of a multitude.

7 And I Daniel alone saw the vision: for the men that were with me saw not the vision; but a great quaking fell upon them, so that they fled to hide themselves.

8 Therefore I was left alone, and saw this great vision, and there remained no strength in me: for my comeliness was turned in me into corruption, and I retained no strength.

9 Yet heard I the voice of his words: and when I heard the voice of his words, then was I in a deep sleep on my face, and my face toward the ground.

10 And, behold, an hand touched me, which set me upon my knees and *upon* the palms of my hands.

11 And he said unto me, O Daniel, a man greatly beloved, understand the words that I speak unto thee, and stand upright: for unto thee am I now sent. And when he had spoken this word unto me, I stood trembling.

12 Then said he unto me, Fear not, Daniel: for from the first day that thou didst set thine heart to understand, and to chasten thyself before thy God, thy words were heard, and I am come for thy words.

13 But the prince of the kingdom of Persia withstood me one and twenty days: but, lo, Michael, one of the chief princes, came to help me; and I remained there with the kings of Persia.

14 Now I am come to make thee understand what shall befall thy people in the

latter days: for yet the vision *is* for *many*
days.
15 And when he had spoken such words
unto me, I set my face toward the ground,
and I became dumb.
16 And, behold, *one* like the similitude
of the sons of men touched my lips: then I
opened my mouth, and spake, and said
unto him that stood before me, O my lord,
by the vision my sorrows are turned upon
me, and I have retained no strength.
17 For how can the servant of this my lord
talk with this my lord? for as for me,
straightway there remained no strength in
me, neither is there breath left in me.
18 Then there came again and touched
me *one* like the appearance of a man, and
he strengthened me,
19 And said, O man greatly beloved, fear
not: peace *be* unto thee, be strong, yea, be
strong. And when he had spoken unto me,
I was strengthened, and said, Let my lord
speak; for thou hast strengthened me.
20 Then said he, Knowest thou wherefore
I come unto thee? and now will I return to
fight with the prince of Persia: and when I
am gone forth, lo, the prince of Grecia
shall come.
21 But I will shew thee that which is
noted in the scripture of truth: and *there is*
none that holdeth with me in these things,
but Michael your prince.

11

1 Also I in the first year of Darius the
Mede, *even* I, stood to confirm and to
strengthen him.
2 And now will I shew thee the truth.
Behold, there shall stand up yet three kings
in Persia; and the fourth shall be far richer
than *they* all: and by his strength through
his riches he shall stir up all against the
realm of Grecia.
3 And a mighty king shall stand up, that
shall rule with great dominion, and do
according to his will.
4 And when he shall stand up, his kingdom shall be broken, and shall be divided toward the four winds of heaven; and
not to his posterity, nor according to his
dominion which he ruled: for his kingdom
shall be plucked up, even for others beside those.
5 And the king of the south shall be
strong, and *one* of his princes; and he shall
be strong above him, and have dominion;
his dominion *shall be* a great dominion.
6 And in the end of years they shall join
themselves together; for the king's daughter of the south shall come to the king of
the north to make an agreement: but she
shall not retain the power of the arm; neither shall he stand, nor his arm: but she
shall be given up, and they that brought
her, and he that begat her, and he that
strengthened her in *these* times.
7 But out of a branch of her roots shall
one stand up in his estate, which shall come
with an army, and shall enter into the fortress of the king of the north, and shall
deal against them, and shall prevail:
8 And shall also carry captives into Egypt
their gods, with their princes, *and* with
their precious vessels of silver and of gold;
and he shall continue *more* years than the
king of the north.
9 So the king of the south shall come into
his kingdom, and shall return into his own
land.
10 But his sons shall be stirred up, and
shall assemble a multitude of great forces:
and *one* shall certainly come, and overflow,
and pass through: then shall he return, and
be stirred up, *even* to his fortress.
11 And the king of the south shall be
moved with choler, and shall come forth
and fight with him, *even* with the king of
the north: and he shall set forth a great
multitude; but the multitude shall be giv-
en into his hand.
12 *And* when he hath taken away the
multitude, his heart shall be lifted up; and
he shall cast down *many* ten thousands:
but he shall not be strengthened *by it.*
13 For the king of the north shall return,
and shall set forth a multitude greater than
the former, and shall certainly come after
certain years with a great army and with
much riches.
14 And in those times there shall many
stand up against the king of the south: also
the robbers of thy people shall exalt themselves to establish the vision; but they shall
fall.
15 So the king of the north shall come,
and cast up a mount, and take the most
fenced cities: and the arms of the south
shall not withstand, neither his chosen
people, neither *shall there be any* strength
to withstand.
16 But he that cometh against him shall
do according to his own will, and none

shall stand before him: and he shall stand in the glorious land, which by his hand shall be consumed.

17 He shall also set his face to enter with the strength of his whole kingdom, and upright ones with him; thus shall he do: and he shall give him the daughter of women, corrupting her: but she shall not stand *on his side,* neither be for him.

18 After this shall he turn his face unto the isles, and shall take many: but a prince for his own behalf shall cause the reproach offered by him to cease; without his own reproach he shall cause *it* to turn upon him.

19 Then he shall turn his face toward the fort of his own land: but he shall stumble and fall, and not be found.

20 Then shall stand up in his estate a raiser of taxes *in* the glory of the kingdom: but within few days he shall be destroyed, neither in anger, nor in battle.

21 And in his estate shall stand up a vile person, to whom they shall not give the honour of the kingdom: but he shall come in peaceably, and obtain the kingdom by flatteries.

22 And with the arms of a flood shall they be overflown from before him, and shall be broken; yea, also the prince of the covenant.

23 And after the league *made* with him he shall work deceitfully: for he shall come up, and shall become strong with a small people.

24 He shall enter peaceably even upon the fattest places of the province; and he shall do *that* which his fathers have not done, nor his fathers' fathers; he shall scatter among them the prey, and spoil, and riches: *yea,* and he shall forecast his devices against the strong holds, even for a time.

25 And he shall stir up his power and his courage against the king of the south with a great army; and the king of the south shall be stirred up to battle with a very great and mighty army; but he shall not stand: for they shall forecast devices against him.

26 Yea, they that feed of the portion of his meat shall destroy him, and his army shall overflow: and many shall fall down slain.

27 And both these kings' hearts *shall be* to do mischief, and they shall speak lies at one table; but it shall not prosper: for yet the end *shall be* at the time appointed.

28 Then shall he return into his land with great riches; and his heart *shall be* against the holy covenant; and he shall do *exploits,* and return to his own land.

29 At the time appointed he shall return, and come toward the south; but it shall not be as the former, or as the latter.

30 For the ships of Chittim shall come against him: therefore he shall be grieved, and return, and have indignation against the holy covenant: so shall he do; he shall even return, and have intelligence with them that forsake the holy covenant.

31 And arms shall stand on his part, and they shall pollute the sanctuary of strength, and shall take away the daily *sacrifice,* and they shall place the abomination that maketh desolate.

32 And such as do wickedly against the covenant shall he corrupt by flatteries: but the people that do know their God shall be strong, and do *exploits.*

33 And they that understand among the people shall instruct many: yet they shall fall by the sword, and by flame, by captivity, and by spoil, *many* days.

34 Now when they shall fall, they shall be holpen with a little help: but many shall cleave to them with flatteries.

35 And *some* of them of understanding shall fall, to try them, and to purge, and to make *them* white, *even* to the time of the end: because *it is* yet for a time appointed.

36 And the king shall do according to his will; and he shall exalt himself, and magnify himself above every god, and shall speak marvellous things against the God of gods, and shall prosper till the indignation be accomplished: for that that is determined shall be done.

37 Neither shall he regard the God of his fathers, nor the desire of women, nor regard any god: for he shall magnify himself above all.

38 But in his estate shall he honour the God of forces: and a god whom his fathers knew not shall he honour with gold, and silver, and with precious stones, and pleasant things.

39 Thus shall he do in the most strong holds with a strange god, whom he shall acknowledge *and* increase with glory: and he shall cause them to rule over many, and shall divide the land for gain.

40 And at the time of the end shall the

king of the south push at him: and the king
of the north shall come against him like a
whirlwind, with chariots, and with horsemen, and with many ships; and he shall
enter into the countries, and shall overflow and pass over.
41 He shall enter also into the glorious
land, and many *countries* shall be overthrown: but these shall escape out of his
hand, *even* Edom, and Moab, and the chief
of the children of Ammon.
42 He shall stretch forth his hand also
upon the countries: and the land of Egypt
shall not escape.
43 But he shall have power over the treasures of gold and of silver, and over all the
precious things of Egypt: and the Libyans
and the Ethiopians *shall be* at his steps.
44 But tidings out of the east and out of
the north shall trouble him: therefore he
shall go forth with great fury to destroy,
and utterly to make away many.
45 And he shall plant the tabernacles of
his palace between the seas in the glorious holy mountain; yet he shall come to
his end, and none shall help him.

12

1 And at that time shall Michael stand
up, the great prince which standeth for the
children of thy people: and there shall be
a time of trouble, such as never was since
there was a nation *even* to that same time:
and at that time thy
people shall be de-
livered, every one
that shall be found
written in the book.
2 And many of
them that sleep in
the dust of the earth
shall awake, some
to everlasting life,
and some to shame
and everlasting con-
tempt.
3 And they that be
wise shall shine as
the brightness of
the firmament; and
they that turn many to righteousness as
the stars for ever and ever.
4 But thou, O Daniel, shut up the words,
and seal the book, *even* to the time of the
end: many shall run to and fro, and knowledge shall be increased.
5 Then I Daniel looked, and, behold,
there stood other two, the one on this side
of the bank of the river, and the other on
that side of the bank of the river.
6 And *one* said to the man clothed in lin-
en, which *was* upon the waters of the river,
How long *shall it be to* the end of these
wonders?
7 And I heard the man clothed in linen,
which *was* upon the waters of the river,
when he held up his right hand and his
left hand unto heaven, and sware by him
that liveth for ever that *it shall be* for a time,
times, and an half; and when he shall have
accomplished to scatter the power of the
holy people, all these *things* shall be finished.
8 And I heard, but I understood not: then
said I, O my Lord, what *shall be* the end of
these *things?*
9 And he said, Go thy way, Daniel: for
the words *are* closed up and sealed till the
time of the end.
10 Many shall be
purified, and made
white, and tried;
but the wicked
shall do wickedly:
and none of the
wicked shall understand; but the wise shall
understand.
11 And from the time *that* the daily *sacrifice* shall be taken away, and the abomination that maketh desolate set up, *there shall
be* a thousand two hundred and ninety
days.
12 Blessed *is* he that waiteth, and cometh
to the thousand three hundred and five
and thirty days.
13 But go thou thy way till the end *be:*
for thou shalt rest, and stand in thy lot at
the end of the days.

12:2
Life After Death
◄ John 5:28-29 ►

12:3 Good Rewarded
◄ Isaiah 58:14
Habakkuk 3:19 ►

12:3
Goodness Rewarded
◄ Matthew 10:42 ►

12:10 Life Tests
◄ Psalm 17:3
Zechariah 13:9 ►

Hosea

AUTHOR

Hosea the prophet

MAIN POINT

God loves his people even when they sin and are unfaithful to him. He will welcome back those who repent.

DATE WRITTEN

Approximately 715 B.C.

14 CHAPTERS

☐☐☐☐☐☐☐☐☐☐ ☐☐☐☐

MAIN PEOPLE

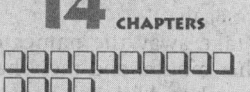

Hosea, Gomer, their children

SPECIAL FEATURES

- *Describes how God commanded Hosea to marry a woman certain to be unfaithful to him, in order to convince Israel of their unfaithfulness to God*
- *Tells how Hosea and Gomer's children got such strange names*
- *Tells how God is like a husband, father, lion, she-bear, and more*
- *Shows how Israel is like a wife, sick person, grapevine, olive tree, woman in labor, and smoke*
- *First book of the Minor Prophets*

HOW THE BOOK GOT ITS NAME

The name Hosea means "salvation," the very message that the prophet brought to Israel in several vivid ways.

1

1 The word of the LORD that came unto Hosea, the son of Beeri, in the days of Uzziah, Jotham, Ahaz, *and* Hezekiah, kings of Judah, and in the days of Jeroboam the son of Joash, king of Israel.

2 The beginning of the word of the LORD by Hosea. And the LORD said to Hosea, Go, take unto thee a wife of whoredoms and children of whoredoms: for the land hath committed great whoredom, *departing* from the LORD.

3 So he went and took Gomer the daughter of Diblaim; which conceived, and bare him a son.

4 And the LORD said unto him, Call his name Jezreel; for yet a little *while,* and I will avenge the blood of Jezreel upon the house of Jehu, and will cause to cease the kingdom of the house of Israel.

5 And it shall come to pass at that day, that I will break the bow of Israel in the valley of Jezreel.

6 And she conceived again, and bare a daughter. And *God* said unto him, Call her name Lo-ruhamah: for I will no more have mercy upon the house of Israel; but I will utterly take them away.

7 But I will have mercy upon the house of Judah, and will save them by the LORD their God, and will not save them by bow, nor by sword, nor by battle, by horses, nor by horsemen.

8 Now when she had weaned Lo-ruhamah, she conceived, and bare a son.

9 Then said *God,* Call his name Lo-ammi: for ye *are* not my people, and I will not be your *God.*

10 Yet the number of the children of Israel shall be as the sand of the sea, which cannot be measured nor numbered; and it shall come to pass, *that* in the place where it was said unto them, Ye *are* not my people, *there* it shall be said unto them, *Ye are* the sons of the living God.

11 Then shall the children of Judah and the children of Israel be gathered together, and appoint themselves one head, and they shall come up out of the land: for great *shall be* the day of Jezreel.

2

1 Say ye unto your brethren, Ammi; and to your sisters, Ru-hamah.

2 Plead with your mother, plead: for she *is* not my wife, neither *am* I her husband: let her therefore put away her whoredoms out of her sight, and her adulteries from between her breasts;

3 Lest I strip her naked, and set her as in the day that she was born, and make her as a wilderness, and set her like a dry land, and slay her with thirst.

4 And I will not have mercy upon her children; for they *be* the children of whoredoms.

5 For their mother hath played the harlot: she that conceived them hath done shamefully: for she said, I will go after my lovers, that give *me* my bread and my water, my wool and my flax, mine oil and my drink.

6 Therefore, behold, I will hedge up thy way with thorns, and make a wall, that she shall not find her paths.

7 And she shall follow after her lovers, but she shall not overtake them; and she shall seek them, but shall not find *them:* then shall she say, I will go and return to my first husband; for then *was it* better with me than now.

8 For she did not know that I gave her corn, and wine, and oil, and multiplied her silver and gold, *which* they prepared for Baal.

2:8
Source of Wealth
◄ Ecclesiastes 5:19 ►

9 Therefore will I return, and take away my corn in the time thereof, and my wine in the season thereof, and will recover my wool and my flax *given* to cover her nakedness.

10 And now will I discover her lewdness in the sight of her lovers, and none shall deliver her out of mine hand.

11 I will also cause all her mirth to cease, her feast days, her new moons, and her sabbaths, and all her solemn feasts.

12 And I will destroy her vines and her fig trees, whereof she hath said, These *are* my rewards that my lovers have given me: and I will make them a forest, and the beasts of the field shall eat them.

13 And I will visit upon her the days of Baalim, wherein she burned incense to them, and she decked herself with her earrings and her jewels, and she went after her lovers, and forgat me, saith the LORD.

14 Therefore, behold, I will allure her, and bring her into the wilderness, and speak comfortably unto her.

15 And I will give her her vineyards from thence, and the valley of Achor for a door of hope: and she shall sing there, as in the days of her youth, and as in the day when she came up out of the land of Egypt.

16 And it shall be at that day, saith the LORD, *that* thou shalt call me Ishi; and shalt call me no more Baali.

17 For I will take away the names of Baalim out of her mouth, and they shall no more be remembered by their name.

18 And in that day will I make a covenant for them with the beasts of the field, and with the fowls of heaven, and *with* the creeping things of the ground: and I will break the bow and the sword and the battle out of the earth, and will make them to lie down safely.

19 And I will betroth thee unto me for ever; yea, I will betroth thee unto me in righteousness, and in judgment, and in lovingkindness, and in mercies.

20 I will even betroth thee unto me in faithfulness: and thou shalt know the LORD.

21 And it shall come to pass in that day, I will hear, saith the LORD, I will hear the heavens, and they shall hear the earth;

22 And the earth shall hear the corn, and the wine, and the oil; and they shall hear Jezreel.

23 And I will sow her unto me in the

earth; and I will have mercy upon her that
had not obtained mercy; and I will say to
them which were not my people, Thou *art*
my people; and they shall say, *Thou art* my
God.

3

1 Then said the LORD unto me, Go yet,
love a woman beloved of *her* friend, yet
an adulteress, according to the love of the
LORD toward the children of Israel, who
look to other gods, and love flagons of
wine.
2 So I bought her to me for fifteen *pieces*
of silver, and *for* an homer of barley, and
an half homer of barley:
3 And I said unto her, Thou shalt abide
for me many days; thou shalt not play the
harlot, and thou shalt not be for *another*
man: so *will* I also *be* for thee.
4 For the children of Israel shall abide
many days without a king, and without a
prince, and without a sacrifice, and without an image, and without an ephod, and
without teraphim:
5 Afterward shall the children of Israel
return, and seek the LORD their God, and
David their king; and shall fear the LORD
and his goodness in the latter days.

4

1 Hear the word of the LORD, ye children
of Israel: for the LORD hath a controversy
with the inhabitants of the land, because
there is no truth, nor mercy, nor knowledge of God in the land.
2 By swearing, and lying, and killing, and
stealing, and committing adultery, they
break out, and blood toucheth blood.
3 Therefore shall the land mourn, and
every one that dwelleth therein shall languish, with the beasts of the field, and with
the fowls of heaven; yea, the fishes of the
sea also shall be taken away.
4 Yet let no man strive, nor reprove another: for thy people *are* as they that strive
with the priest.
5 Therefore shalt thou fall in the day, and
the prophet also shall fall with thee in the
night, and I will destroy thy mother.
6 My people are destroyed for lack of
knowledge: because thou hast rejected
knowledge, I will also reject thee, that thou
shalt be no priest to me: seeing thou hast
forgotten the law of thy God, I will also
forget thy children.
7 As they were increased, so they sinned
against me: *therefore* will I change their glory into shame.
8 They eat up the sin of my people, and
they set their heart on their iniquity.
9 And there shall be, like people, like
priest: and I will punish them for their
ways, and reward them their doings.
10 For they shall eat, and not have
enough: they shall commit whoredom,
and shall not increase: because they have
left off to take heed to the LORD.
11 Whoredom
and wine and new
wine take away the
heart.
12 My people ask
counsel at their
stocks, and their staff declareth unto them:
for the spirit of whoredoms hath caused
them to err, and they have gone a whoring
from under their God.

> **4:11 Drinking Too Much**
> ◄ Isaiah 56:12
> Habakkuk 2:5 ►

13 They sacrifice upon the tops of the
mountains, and burn incense upon the
hills, under oaks and poplars and elms,
because the shadow thereof *is* good: therefore your daughters shall commit whoredom, and your spouses shall commit
adultery.
14 I will not punish your daughters when
they commit whoredom, nor your spouses
when they commit adultery: for themselves are separated with whores, and they
sacrifice with harlots: therefore the people *that* doth not understand shall fall.
15 Though thou, Israel, play the harlot,
yet let not Judah offend; and come not ye
unto Gilgal, neither go ye up to Beth-aven,
nor swear, The LORD liveth.
16 For Israel slideth back as a backsliding heifer: now the LORD will feed them as
a lamb in a large place.
17 Ephraim *is* joined to idols: let him
alone.
18 Their drink is sour: they have committed whoredom continually: her rulers *with*
shame do love, Give ye.
19 The wind hath bound her up in her
wings, and they shall be ashamed because
of their sacrifices.

5

1 Hear ye this, O priests; and hearken, ye
house of Israel; and give ye ear, O house
of the king; for judgment *is* toward you,
because ye have been a snare on Mizpah,
and a net spread upon Tabor.
2 And the revolters are profound to make
slaughter, though I *have been* a rebuker of
them all.

3 I know Ephraim, and Israel is not hid from me: for now, O Ephraim, thou committest whoredom, *and* Israel is defiled.

4 They will not frame their doings to turn unto their God: for the spirit of whoredoms *is* in the midst of them, and they have not known the LORD.

5 And the pride of Israel doth testify to his face: therefore shall Israel and Ephraim fall in their iniquity; Judah also shall fall with them.

6 They shall go with their flocks and with their herds to seek the LORD; but they shall not find *him;* he hath withdrawn himself from them.

7 They have dealt treacherously against the LORD: for they have begotten strange children: now shall a month devour them with their portions.

8 Blow ye the cornet in Gibeah, *and* the trumpet in Ramah: cry aloud *at* Beth-aven, after thee, O Benjamin.

9 Ephraim shall be desolate in the day of rebuke: among the tribes of Israel have I made known that which shall surely be.

10 The princes of Judah were like them that remove the bound: *therefore* I will pour out my wrath upon them like water.

11 Ephraim *is* oppressed *and* broken in judgment, because he willingly walked after the commandment.

12 Therefore *will* I *be* unto Ephraim as a moth, and to the house of Judah as rottenness.

13 When Ephraim saw his sickness, and Judah *saw* his wound, then went Ephraim to the Assyrian, and sent to king Jareb: yet could he not heal you, nor cure you of your wound.

5:13 Trusting in People
◄ Jeremiah 17:5 ►

14 For I *will be* unto Ephraim as a lion, and as a young lion to the house of Judah: I, *even* I, will tear and go away; I will take away, and none shall rescue *him.*

15 I will go *and* return to my place, till they acknowledge their offence, and seek my face: in their affliction they will seek me early.

6

1 Come, and let us return unto the LORD: for he hath torn, and he will heal us; he hath smitten, and he will bind us up.

6:1 Change
◄ Ezekiel 33:11
Matthew 22:3 ►

2 After two days will he revive us: in the third day he will raise us up, and we shall live in his sight.

3 Then shall we know, *if* we follow on to know the LORD: his going forth is prepared as the morning; and he shall come unto us as the rain, as the latter *and* former rain unto the earth.

6:3 Finding God
◄ Jeremiah 29:13
Acts 17:27 ►

4 O Ephraim, what shall I do unto thee? O Judah, what shall I do unto thee? for your goodness *is* as a morning cloud, and as the early dew it goeth away.

5 Therefore have I hewed *them* by the prophets; I have slain them by the words of my mouth: and thy judgments *are as* the light *that* goeth forth.

6 For I desired mercy, and not sacrifice; and the knowledge of God more than burnt offerings.

6:6 Religious People
◄ Ecclesiastes 12:13
Micah 6:8 ►

7 But they like men have transgressed the covenant: there have they dealt treacherously against me.

8 Gilead *is* a city of them that work iniquity, *and is* polluted with blood.

9 And as troops of robbers wait for a man, *so* the company of priests murder in the way by consent: for they commit lewdness.

10 I have seen an horrible thing in the house of Israel: there *is* the whoredom of Ephraim, Israel is defiled.

11 Also, O Judah, he hath set an harvest for thee, when I returned the captivity of my people.

7

1 When I would have healed Israel, then the iniquity of Ephraim was discovered, and the wickedness of Samaria: for they commit falsehood; and the thief cometh in, *and* the troop of robbers spoileth without.

2 And they consider not in their hearts *that* I remember all their wickedness: now their own doings have beset them about; they are before my face.

7:2 God Sees Sin
◄ Ezekiel 11:5
Amos 5:12 ►

3They make the king glad with their
wickedness, and the princes with their lies.
4They *are* all adulterers, as an oven heated by the baker, *who* ceaseth from raising
after he hath kneaded the dough, until it
be leavened.
5In the day of our king the princes have
made *him* sick with bottles of wine; he
stretched out his hand with scorners.
6For they have made ready their heart
like an oven, whiles they lie in wait: their
baker sleepeth all the night; in the morning it burneth as a flaming fire.
7They are all hot
as an oven, and
have devoured their
judges; all their
kings are fallen:
there is none among
them that calleth unto me.

7:7 Not Praying
◄ Daniel 9:13
Zephaniah 1:6 ►

8Ephraim, he hath mixed himself
among the people; Ephraim is a cake not
turned.
9Strangers have devoured his strength,
and he knoweth *it* not: yea, gray hairs are
here and there upon him, yet he knoweth
not.
10And the pride
of Israel testifieth to
his face: and they do
not return to the
LORD their God, nor
seek him for all this.
11Ephraim also is
like a silly dove
without heart: they
call to Egypt, they
go to Assyria.
12When they shall
go, I will spread my
net upon them; I
will bring them
down as the fowls
of the heaven; I will
chastise them, as
their congregation hath heard.

7:10 Arrogance
◄ Proverbs 21:4
Habakkuk 2:4 ►

7:10 Hard-hearted
◄ Jeremiah 7:13
Amos 4:6 ►

7:11 Naiveté
◄ Proverbs 22:3 ►

13Woe unto them! for they have fled
from me: destruction unto them! because
they have transgressed against me: though
I have redeemed them, yet they have spoken lies against me.
14And they have not cried unto me with
their heart, when they howled upon their
beds: they assemble themselves for corn
and wine, *and* they rebel against me.
15Though I have bound *and* strengthened their arms, yet do they imagine mischief against me.
16They return, *but* not to the most High:
they are like a deceitful bow: their princes
shall fall by the sword for the rage of their
tongue: this *shall be* their derision in the
land of Egypt.

8

1*Set* the trumpet to thy mouth. *He shall
come* as an eagle against the house of the
LORD, because they have transgressed my
covenant, and trespassed against my law.
2Israel shall cry unto me, My God, we
know thee.
3Israel hath cast off *the thing that is* good:
the enemy shall pursue him.
4They have set up kings, but not by me:
they have made princes, and I knew *it*
not: of their silver and their gold have
they made them idols, that they may be
cut off.
5Thy calf, O Samaria, hath cast *thee* off;
mine anger is kindled against them: how
long *will it be* ere they attain to innocency?
6For from Israel *was* it also: the workman made it; therefore it *is* not God: but
the calf of Samaria shall be broken in
pieces.
7For they have sown the wind, and they
shall reap the whirlwind: it hath no stalk:
the bud shall yield no meal: if so be it yield,
the strangers shall swallow it up.
8Israel is swallowed up: now shall they
be among the Gentiles as a vessel wherein
is no pleasure.
9For they are gone up to Assyria, a wild
ass alone by himself: Ephraim hath hired
lovers.
10Yea, though they have hired among
the nations, now will I gather them, and
they shall sorrow a little for the burden of
the king of princes.
11Because Ephraim hath made many altars to sin, altars shall be unto him to sin.
12I have written to him the great things
of my law, *but* they were counted as a
strange thing.
13They sacrifice flesh *for* the sacrifices of
mine offerings, and eat *it; but* the LORD
accepteth them not; now will he remember their iniquity, and visit their sins: they
shall return to Egypt.
14For Israel hath forgotten his Maker,
and buildeth temples; and Judah hath
multiplied fenced cities: but I will send a

fire upon his cities, and it shall devour the palaces thereof.

9

1 Rejoice not, O Israel, for joy, as *other* people: for thou hast gone a whoring from thy God, thou hast loved a reward upon every cornfloor.

2 The floor and the winepress shall not feed them, and the new wine shall fail in her.

3 They shall not dwell in the LORD'S land; but Ephraim shall return to Egypt, and they shall eat unclean *things* in Assyria.

4 They shall not offer wine *offerings* to the LORD, neither shall they be pleasing unto him: their sacrifices *shall be* unto them as the bread of mourners; all that eat thereof shall be polluted: for their bread for their soul shall not come into the house of the LORD.

5 What will ye do in the solemn day, and in the day of the feast of the LORD?

6 For, lo, they are gone because of destruction: Egypt shall gather them up, Memphis shall bury them: the pleasant *places* for their silver, nettles shall possess them: thorns *shall be* in their tabernacles.

7 The days of visitation are come, the days of recompence are come; Israel shall know *it:* the prophet *is* a fool, the spiritual man *is* mad, for the multitude of thine iniquity, and the great hatred.

8 The watchman of Ephraim *was* with my God: *but* the prophet *is* a snare of a fowler in all his ways, *and* hatred in the house of his God.

9 They have deeply corrupted *themselves,* as in the days of Gibeah: *therefore* he will remember their iniquity, he will visit their sins.

10 I found Israel like grapes in the wilderness; I saw your fathers as the firstripe in the fig tree at her first time: *but* they went to Baal-peor, and separated themselves unto *that* shame; and *their* abominations were according as they loved.

11 *As for* Ephraim, their glory shall fly away like a bird, from the birth, and from the womb, and from the conception.

12 Though they bring up their children, yet will I bereave them, *that there shall* not *be* a man *left:* yea, woe also to them when I depart from them!

13 Ephraim, as I saw Tyrus, *is* planted in a pleasant place: but Ephraim shall bring forth his children to the murderer.

14 Give them, O LORD: what wilt thou give? give them a miscarrying womb and dry breasts.

15 All their wickedness *is* in Gilgal: for there I hated them: for the wickedness of their doings I will drive them out of mine house, I will love them no more: all their princes *are* revolters.

16 Ephraim is smitten, their root is dried up, they shall bear no fruit: yea, though they bring forth, yet will I slay *even* the beloved *fruit* of their womb.

17 My God will cast them away, because they did not hearken unto him: and they shall be wanderers among the nations.

10

1 Israel *is* an empty vine, he bringeth forth fruit unto himself: according to the multitude of his fruit he hath increased the altars; according to the goodness of his land they have made goodly images.

2 Their heart is divided; now shall they be found faulty: he shall break down their altars, he shall spoil their images.

10:2 The Time Is Now
◄ 2 Kings 17:41
Matthew 6:24 ►

3 For now they shall say, We have no king, because we feared not the LORD; what then should a king do to us?

4 They have spoken words, swearing falsely in making a covenant: thus judgment springeth up as hemlock in the furrows of the field.

5 The inhabitants of Samaria shall fear because of the calves of Beth-aven: for the people thereof shall mourn over it, and the priests thereof *that* rejoiced on it, for the glory thereof, because it is departed from it.

6 It shall be also carried unto Assyria *for* a present to king Jareb: Ephraim shall receive shame, and Israel shall be ashamed of his own counsel.

7 *As for* Samaria, her king is cut off as the foam upon the water.

8 The high places also of Aven, the sin of Israel, shall be destroyed: the thorn and the thistle shall come up on their altars; and they shall say to the mountains, Cover us; and to the hills, Fall on us.

9 O Israel, thou hast sinned from the days of Gibeah: there they stood: the battle in Gibeah against the children of iniquity did not overtake them.

10*It is* in my desire that I should chastise them; and the people shall be gathered against them, when they shall bind
themselves in their two furrows.
11And Ephraim *is as* an heifer *that is*
taught, *and* loveth to tread out *the corn;* but
I passed over upon her fair neck: I will
make Ephraim to ride; Judah shall plow,
and Jacob shall break his clods.
12Sow to your-
selves in righteous-
ness, reap in mercy;
break up your fal-
low ground: for *it*
is time to seek the
LORD, till he come
and rain righteous-
ness upon you.
13Ye have plowed
wickedness, ye have
reaped iniquity; ye
have eaten the fruit
of lies: because
thou didst trust in
thy way, in the mul-
titude of thy mighty
men.
14Therefore shall
a tumult arise among thy people, and all
thy fortresses shall be spoiled, as Shalman
spoiled Beth-arbel in the day of battle: the
mother was dashed in pieces upon *her*
children.
15So shall Bethel do unto you because
of your great wickedness: in a morning
shall the king of Israel utterly be cut off.

> **10:12 Righteousness**
> ◄ Daniel 4:27
> Matthew 5:20 ►

> **10:12 Seeking God**
> ◄ Jeremiah 29:13
> Amos 5:4 ►

> **10:13 Self-confidence**
> ◄ Isaiah 47:8
> Obadiah 1:3 ►

11

1When Israel *was*
a child, then I loved
him, and called my
son out of Egypt.
2As they called
them, so they went
from them: they sacrificed unto Baalim,
and burned incense to graven images.
3I taught Ephraim also to go, taking
them by their arms; but they knew not that
I healed them.
4I drew them with cords of a man, with
bands of love: and I was to them as they
that take off the yoke on their jaws, and I
laid meat unto them.
5He shall not return into the land of
Egypt, but the Assyrian shall be his king,
because they refused to return.
6And the sword shall abide on his
cities, and shall consume his branches,
and devour *them*, because of their own
counsels.
7And my people are bent to backsliding
from me: though they called them to the
most High, none at all would exalt *him*.
8How shall I give thee up, Ephraim? *how*
shall I deliver thee, Israel? how shall I make
thee as Admah? *how* shall I set thee as Zeboim? mine heart is turned within me, my
repentings are kindled together.
9I will not execute the fierceness of mine
anger, I will not return to destroy Ephraim: for I *am* God, and not man; the Holy
One in the midst of thee: and I will not
enter into the city.
10They shall walk after the LORD: he shall
roar like a lion: when he shall roar, then
the children shall tremble from the west.
11They shall tremble as a bird out of
Egypt, and as a dove out of the land of
Assyria: and I will place them in their
houses, saith the LORD.
12Ephraim compasseth me about with
lies, and the house of Israel with deceit:
but Judah yet ruleth with God, and is faithful with the saints.

> **11:1 Adopted by God**
> ◄ Ezekiel 16:8
> John 1:12 ►

12

1Ephraim feedeth on wind, and followeth after the east wind: he daily
increaseth lies and desolation; and they do
make a covenant with the Assyrians, and
oil is carried into Egypt.
2The LORD hath also a controversy with
Judah, and will punish Jacob according to
his ways; according to his doings will he
recompense him.
3He took his brother by the heel in the
womb, and by his strength he had power
with God:
4Yea, he had power over the angel, and
prevailed: he wept, and made supplication
unto him: he found him *in* Bethel, and
there he spake with us;
5Even the LORD
God of hosts; the
LORD *is* his memo-
rial.
6Therefore turn
thou to thy God:
keep mercy and
judgment, and wait
on thy God contin-
ually.
7*He is* a mer-
chant, the balances

> **12:6 Showing Mercy**
> ◄ Proverbs 11:17
> Micah 6:8 ►

> **12:6**
> **Waiting for God**
> ◄ Isaiah 40:31 ►

of deceit *are* in his hand: he loveth to oppress.

8 And Ephraim said, Yet I am become rich, I have found me out substance: *in* all my labours they shall find none iniquity in me that *were* sin.

9 And I *that am* the LORD thy God from the land of Egypt will yet make thee to dwell in tabernacles, as in the days of the solemn feast.

10 I have also spoken by the prophets, and I have multiplied visions, and used similitudes, by the ministry of the prophets.

11 *Is there* iniquity *in* Gilead? surely they are vanity: they sacrifice bullocks in Gilgal; yea, their altars *are* as heaps in the furrows of the fields.

12 And Jacob fled into the country of Syria, and Israel served for a wife, and for a wife he kept *sheep*.

13 And by a prophet the LORD brought Israel out of Egypt, and by a prophet was he preserved.

14 Ephraim provoked *him* to anger most bitterly: therefore shall he leave his blood upon him, and his reproach shall his Lord return unto him.

13

1 When Ephraim spake trembling, he exalted himself in Israel; but when he offended in Baal, he died.

2 And now they sin more and more, and have made them molten images of their silver, *and* idols according to their own understanding, all of it the work of the craftsmen: they say of them, Let the men that sacrifice kiss the calves.

3 Therefore they shall be as the morning cloud, and as the early dew that passeth away, as the chaff *that* is driven with the whirlwind out of the floor, and as the smoke out of the chimney.

4 Yet I *am* the LORD thy God from the land of Egypt, and thou shalt know no god but me: for *there is* no saviour beside me.

5 I did know thee in the wilderness, in the land of great drought.

6 According to their pasture, so were they filled; they were filled, and their heart was exalted; therefore have they forgotten me.

7 Therefore I will be unto them as a lion: as a leopard by the way will I observe *them*:

8 I will meet them as a bear *that is* bereaved *of her whelps*, and will rend the caul of their heart, and there will I devour them like a lion: the wild beast shall tear them.

9 O Israel, thou hast destroyed thyself; but in me *is* thine help.

10 I will be thy king: where *is any other* that may save thee in all thy cities? and thy judges of whom thou saidst, Give me a king and princes?

11 I gave thee a king in mine anger, and took *him* away in my wrath.

12 The iniquity of Ephraim *is* bound up; his sin *is* hid.

13 The sorrows of a travailing woman shall come upon him: he *is* an unwise son; for he should not stay long in *the place of* the breaking forth of children.

14 I will ransom them from the power of the grave; I will redeem them from death: O death, I will be thy plagues; O grave, I will be thy destruction: repentance shall be hid from mine eyes.

13:14 Resurrection
◄ Psalm 71:20
John 5:25 ►

15 Though he be fruitful among *his* brethren, an east wind shall come, the wind of the LORD shall come up from the wilderness, and his spring shall become dry, and his fountain shall be dried up: he shall spoil the treasure of all pleasant vessels.

16 Samaria shall become desolate; for she hath rebelled against her God: they shall fall by the sword: their infants shall be dashed in pieces, and their women with child shall be ripped up.

14

1 O Israel, return unto the LORD thy God; for thou hast fallen by thine iniquity.

14:2 Duty to Pray
◄ 1 Chronicles 16:11
Matthew 7:7 ►

2 Take with you words, and turn to the LORD: say unto him, Take away all iniquity, and receive *us* graciously: so will we render the calves of our lips.

14:2 Repent!
◄ Daniel 4:27
Joel 2:12 ►

3 Asshur shall not save us; we will not ride upon horses: neither will we say any more to the

14:3
God's Care for Kids
◄ Jeremiah 49:11 ►

work of our hands, *Ye are* our gods: for in
thee the fatherless findeth mercy.
4 I will heal their backsliding, I will love
them freely: for mine anger is turned away
from him.
5 I will be as the dew unto Israel: he shall
grow as the lily, and cast forth his roots as
Lebanon.
6 His branches shall spread, and his
beauty shall be as the olive tree, and his
smell as Lebanon.
7 They that dwell under his shadow shall
return; they shall revive *as* the corn, and
grow as the vine: the scent thereof *shall be*
as the wine of Lebanon.
8 Ephraim *shall say,* What have I to do
any more with idols? I have heard *him,* and
observed him: I *am* like a green fir tree.
From me is thy fruit found.
9 Who *is* wise,
and he shall understand these *things?*
prudent, and he
shall know them?
for the ways of the
LORD *are* right, and
the just shall walk
in them: but the
transgressors shall
fall therein.

14:9 God's Ways
◄ Isaiah 55:8-9
Habakkuk 3:6 ►

14:9 True Wisdom
◄ Proverbs 9:1
Matthew 7:24 ►

Joel

AUTHOR
Joel the prophet

MAIN POINT
God is powerful and holy, and he will judge sin on the day of the Lord. Repent, therefore, and return to him.

DATE WRITTEN
Probably 835-796 B.C

3 CHAPTERS

❑❑❑

MAIN PEOPLE

Joel, the people of Judah

SPECIAL FEATURES

- *Is one of the shortest books of the Bible yet one of its most powerful*
- *Predicts an awful plague of locusts*
- *Promises that the Holy Spirit will be with God's people*
- *Second book of the Minor Prophets*

HOW THE BOOK GOT ITS NAME

The author and main person, Joel, was a prophet to the southern kingdom, Judah.

1

1 The word of the LORD that came to Joel
the son of Pethuel.
2 Hear this, ye old men, and give ear, all
ye inhabitants of the land. Hath this been
in your days, or even in the days of your
fathers?
3 Tell ye your children of it, and *let* your
children *tell* their children, and their children another generation.
4 That which the palmerworm hath left
hath the locust eaten; and that which the
locust hath left hath the cankerworm eat-
en; and that which the cankerworm hath
left hath the caterpiller eaten.
5 Awake, ye drunkards, and weep; and
howl, all ye drinkers of wine, because of
the new wine; for it is cut off from your
mouth.
6 For a nation is come up upon my land,
strong, and without number, whose teeth
are the teeth of a lion, and he hath the
cheek teeth of a great lion.
7 He hath laid my vine waste, and barked
my fig tree: he hath made it clean bare,
and cast *it* away; the branches thereof are
made white.
8 Lament like a virgin girded with sackcloth for the husband of her youth.
9 The meat offering and the drink offering is cut off from the house of the LORD;
the priests, the LORD'S ministers, mourn.
10 The field is wasted, the land mourneth;
for the corn is wasted: the new wine is
dried up, the oil languisheth.
11 Be ye ashamed, O ye husbandmen;
howl, O ye vinedressers, for the wheat and
for the barley; because the harvest of the
field is perished.
12 The vine is dried up, and the fig tree
languisheth; the pomegranate tree, the
palm tree also, and the apple tree, *even*
all the trees of the field, are withered: because joy is withered away from the sons
of men.

13 Gird yourselves, and lament, ye
priests: howl, ye ministers of the altar:
come, lie all night in sackcloth, ye ministers of my God: for the meat offering and
the drink offering is withholden from the
house of your God.
14 Sanctify ye a fast, call a solemn assembly, gather the elders *and* all the inhabitants of the land *into* the house of the LORD
your God, and cry unto the LORD,
15 Alas for the day! for the day of the
LORD *is* at hand, and as a destruction from
the Almighty shall it come.
16 Is not the meat cut off before our eyes,
yea, joy and gladness from the house of
our God?
17 The seed is rotten under their clods,
the garners are laid desolate, the barns are
broken down; for the corn is withered.
18 How do the beasts groan! the herds
of cattle are perplexed, because they have
no pasture; yea, the flocks of sheep are
made desolate.
19 O LORD, to thee will I cry: for the fire
hath devoured the pastures of the wilderness, and the flame hath burned all the
trees of the field.
20 The beasts of the field cry also unto
thee: for the rivers of waters are dried up,
and the fire hath devoured the pastures of
the wilderness.

2

1 Blow ye the trumpet in Zion, and
sound an alarm in my holy mountain: let
all the inhabitants of the land tremble: for
the day of the LORD cometh, for *it is* nigh
at hand;
2 A day of darkness and of gloominess,
a day of clouds and of thick darkness, as
the morning spread upon the mountains:
a great people and a strong; there hath not
been ever the like, neither shall be any
more after it, *even* to the years of many
generations.
3 A fire devoureth before them; and behind them a flame burneth: the land *is* as
the garden of Eden before them, and behind them a desolate wilderness; yea, and
nothing shall escape them.
4 The appearance of them *is* as the appearance of horses; and as horsemen, so
shall they run.
5 Like the noise of chariots on the tops
of mountains shall they leap, like the noise
of a flame of fire that devoureth the stubble, as a strong people set in battle array.
6 Before their face the people shall be
much pained: all faces shall gather blackness.
7 They shall run like mighty men; they
shall climb the wall like men of war; and
they shall march every one on his ways,
and they shall not break their ranks:
8 Neither shall one thrust another; they
shall walk every one in his path: and *when*
they fall upon the sword, they shall not
be wounded.
9 They shall run to and fro in the city;
they shall run upon the wall, they shall
climb up upon the houses; they shall enter in at the windows like a thief.
10 The earth shall quake before them; the
heavens shall tremble: the sun and the
moon shall be dark, and the stars shall
withdraw their shining:
11 And the LORD shall utter his voice before his army: for his camp *is* very great:
for *he is* strong that executeth his word:
for the day of the LORD *is* great and very
terrible; and who can abide it?
12 Therefore also
now, saith the
LORD, turn ye *even*
to me with all your
heart, and with fast-
ing, and with
weeping, and with
mourning:
13 And rend your
heart, and not your
garments, and turn
unto the LORD your
God: for he *is* gra-
cious and merciful,
slow to anger, and
of great kindness,
and repenteth him
of the evil.
14 Who knoweth
if he will return and
repent, and leave a
blessing behind
him; *even* a meat
offering and a drink
offering unto the
LORD your God?
15 Blow the trumpet in Zion, sanctify a
fast, call a solemn assembly:
16 Gather the people, sanctify the congregation, assemble the elders, gather the
children, and those that suck the breasts:

2:12 Repent!
◄ Hosea 14:2
Malachi 3:7 ►

2:13 Feeling Sorry
◄ Isaiah 66:2
Zechariah 12:10 ►

2:13 God's Mercy
◄ Lamentations 3:22-23
Micah 7:18 ►

2:13 Repentance
◄ Jeremiah 3:22
Micah 7:18 ►

let the bridegroom go forth of his chamber, and the bride out of her closet.
17Let the priests, the ministers of the
LORD, weep between the porch and the
altar, and let them say, Spare thy people,
O LORD, and give not thine heritage to reproach, that the heathen should rule over
them: wherefore should they say among
the people, Where *is* their God?
18Then will the LORD be jealous for his
land, and pity his people.
19Yea, the LORD will answer and say unto
his people, Behold, I will send you corn,
and wine, and oil, and ye shall be satisfied therewith: and I will no more make
you a reproach among the heathen:
20But I will remove far off from you the
northern *army*, and will drive him into a
land barren and desolate, with his face
toward the east sea, and his hinder part
toward the utmost sea, and his stink shall
come up, and his ill savour shall come up,
because he hath done great things.
21Fear not, O land; be glad and rejoice:
for the LORD will do great things.
22Be not afraid, ye beasts of the field:
for the pastures of the wilderness do
spring, for the tree beareth her fruit, the
fig tree and the vine do yield their strength.
23Be glad then, ye children of Zion, and
rejoice in the LORD your God: for he hath
given you the former rain moderately, and
he will cause to come down for you the
rain, the former rain, and the latter rain in
the first *month*.
24And the floors shall be full of wheat,
and the fats shall overflow with wine
and oil.
25And I will restore to you the years that
the locust hath eaten, the cankerworm, and
the caterpiller, and the palmerworm, my
great army which I sent among you.
26And ye shall eat in plenty, and be satisfied, and praise the name of the LORD
your God, that hath dealt wondrously
with you: and my people shall never be
ashamed.
27And ye shall know that I *am* in the
midst of Israel, and *that* I *am* the LORD your
God, and none else: and my people shall
never be ashamed.
28And it shall come to pass afterward,
that I will pour out my spirit upon all flesh;
and your sons and your daughters shall
prophesy, your old men shall dream
dreams, your young men shall see visions:
29And also upon the servants and upon
the handmaids in those days will I pour
out my spirit.
30And I will shew wonders in the heavens and in the earth, blood, and fire, and
pillars of smoke.
31The sun shall be turned into darkness,
and the moon into blood, before the great
and the terrible day of the LORD come.
32And it shall come to pass, *that* whosoever shall call on the name of the LORD
shall be delivered: for in mount Zion and
in Jerusalem shall be deliverance, as the
LORD hath said, and in the remnant whom
the LORD shall call.

3

1For, behold, in those days, and in that
time, when I shall bring again the captivity of Judah and Jerusalem,
2I will also gather all nations, and will
bring them down into the valley of Jehoshaphat, and will plead with them there for
my people and *for* my heritage Israel,
whom they have scattered among the nations, and parted my land.
3And they have cast lots for my people;
and have given a boy for an harlot, and
sold a girl for wine, that they might
drink.
4Yea, and what have ye to do with me,
O Tyre, and Zidon, and all the coasts of
Palestine? will ye render me a recompence?
and if ye recompense me, swiftly *and*
speedily will I return your recompence
upon your own head;
5Because ye have taken my silver and my
gold, and have carried into your temples
my goodly pleasant things:
6The children also of Judah and the children of Jerusalem have ye sold unto the
Grecians, that ye might remove them far
from their border.
7Behold, I will raise them out of the
place whither ye have sold them, and will
return your recompence upon your own
head:
8And I will sell your sons and your
daughters into the hand of the children of
Judah, and they shall sell them to the Sabeans, to a people far off: for the LORD hath
spoken *it*.
9Proclaim ye this among the Gentiles;
Prepare war, wake up the mighty men, let
all the men of war draw near; let them
come up:

10 Beat your plowshares into swords, and your pruninghooks into spears: let the weak say, I *am* strong.

11 Assemble yourselves, and come, all ye heathen, and gather yourselves together round about: thither cause thy mighty ones to come down, O LORD.

12 Let the heathen be wakened, and come up to the valley of Jehoshaphat: for there will I sit to judge all the heathen round about.

13 Put ye in the sickle, for the harvest is ripe: come, get you down; for the press is full, the fats overflow; for their wickedness *is* great.

14 Multitudes, multitudes in the valley of decision: for the day of the LORD *is* near in the valley of decision.

15 The sun and the moon shall be darkened, and the stars shall withdraw their shining.

16 The LORD also shall roar out of Zion, and utter his voice from Jerusalem; and the heavens and the earth shall shake: but the LORD *will be* the hope of his people, and the strength of the children of Israel.

17 So shall ye know that I *am* the LORD your God dwelling in Zion, my holy mountain: then shall Jerusalem be holy, and there shall no strangers pass through her any more.

18 And it shall come to pass in that day, *that* the mountains shall drop down new wine, and the hills shall flow with milk, and all the rivers of Judah shall flow with waters, and a fountain shall come forth of the house of the LORD, and shall water the valley of Shittim.

19 Egypt shall be a desolation, and Edom shall be a desolate wilderness, for the violence *against* the children of Judah, because they have shed innocent blood in their land.

20 But Judah shall dwell for ever, and Jerusalem from generation to generation.

21 For I will cleanse their blood *that* I have not cleansed: for the LORD dwelleth in Zion.

Amos

AUTHOR
Amos the prophet

MAIN POINT
God was fed up with Israel's love for false gods, cruelty to the poor, and lazy attitude toward obeying God.

DATE WRITTEN
Probably about 760-750 B.C.

9 CHAPTERS

MAIN PEOPLE

Amos, Amaziah, Jeroboam II

SPECIAL FEATURES

- *Is one of the strongest statements that God punishes sin, just as he should*
- *Describes Amos's remarkable visions of judgment*
- *Shows the prophet's great courage in speaking strongly to the religious leaders of his day*
- *Third book of the Minor Prophets*

HOW THE BOOK GOT ITS NAME

The name Amos means "burden" or "burden bearer." The prophet certainly carried a heavy burden: God's message to Israel.

1 1The words of Amos, who was among
the herdmen of Tekoa, which he saw concerning Israel in the days of Uzziah king
of Judah, and in the days of Jeroboam the
son of Joash king of Israel, two years before the earthquake.
2And he said, The LORD will roar from
Zion, and utter his voice from Jerusalem;
and the habitations of the shepherds shall
mourn, and the top of Carmel shall wither.
3Thus saith the LORD; For three transgressions of Damascus, and for four, I will
not turn away *the punishment* thereof; because they have threshed Gilead with
threshing instruments of iron:
4But I will send a fire into the house of
Hazael, which shall devour the palaces of
Ben-hadad.
5I will break also the bar of Damascus,
and cut off the inhabitant from the plain
of Aven, and him that holdeth the sceptre
from the house of Eden: and the people
of Syria shall go into captivity unto Kir,
saith the LORD.
6Thus saith the LORD; For three transgressions of Gaza, and for four, I will not
turn away *the punishment* thereof; because
they carried away captive the whole captivity, to deliver *them* up to Edom:
7But I will send a fire on the wall of
Gaza, which shall devour the palaces
thereof:
8And I will cut off the inhabitant from
Ashdod, and him that holdeth the sceptre
from Ashkelon, and I will turn mine hand
against Ekron: and the remnant of the

Philistines shall perish, saith the Lord GOD.

9 Thus saith the LORD; For three transgressions of Tyrus, and for four, I will not turn away *the punishment* thereof; because they delivered up the whole captivity to Edom, and remembered not the brotherly covenant:

10 But I will send a fire on the wall of Tyrus, which shall devour the palaces thereof.

11 Thus saith the LORD; For three transgressions of Edom, and for four, I will not turn away *the punishment* thereof; because he did pursue his brother with the sword, and did cast off all pity, and his anger did tear perpetually, and he kept his wrath for ever:

1:11 Cruelty
◄ Proverbs 28:3
Matthew 18:30 ►

1:11 Mad
◄ Esther 3:5
Luke 4:28 ►

12 But I will send a fire upon Teman, which shall devour the palaces of Bozrah.

13 Thus saith the LORD; For three transgressions of the children of Ammon, and for four, I will not turn away *the punishment* thereof; because they have ripped up the women with child of Gilead, that they might enlarge their border:

14 But I will kindle a fire in the wall of Rabbah, and it shall devour the palaces thereof, with shouting in the day of battle, with a tempest in the day of the whirlwind:

15 And their king shall go into captivity, he and his princes together, saith the LORD.

2

1 Thus saith the LORD; For three transgressions of Moab, and for four, I will not turn away *the punishment* thereof; because he burned the bones of the king of Edom into lime:

2 But I will send a fire upon Moab, and it shall devour the palaces of Kirioth: and Moab shall die with tumult, with shouting, *and* with the sound of the trumpet:

3 And I will cut off the judge from the midst thereof, and will slay all the princes thereof with him, saith the LORD.

4 Thus saith the LORD; For three transgressions of Judah, and for four, I will not turn away *the punishment* thereof; because they have despised the law of the LORD, and have not kept his commandments, and their lies caused them to err, after the which their fathers have walked:

5 But I will send a fire upon Judah, and it shall devour the palaces of Jerusalem.

6 Thus saith the LORD; For three transgressions of Israel, and for four, I will not turn away *the punishment* thereof; because they sold the righteous for silver, and the poor for a pair of shoes;

7 That pant after the dust of the earth on the head of the poor, and turn aside the way of the meek: and a man and his father will go in unto the *same* maid, to profane my holy name:

8 And they lay *themselves* down upon clothes laid to pledge by every altar, and they drink the wine of the condemned *in* the house of their god.

9 Yet destroyed I the Amorite before them, whose height *was* like the height of the cedars, and he *was* strong as the oaks; yet I destroyed his fruit from above, and his roots from beneath.

10 Also I brought you up from the land of Egypt, and led you forty years through the wilderness, to possess the land of the Amorite.

11 And I raised up of your sons for prophets, and of your young men for Nazarites. *Is it* not even thus, O ye children of Israel? saith the LORD.

12 But ye gave the Nazarites wine to drink; and commanded the prophets, saying, Prophesy not.

13 Behold, I am pressed under you, as a cart is pressed *that is* full of sheaves.

14 Therefore the flight shall perish from the swift, and the strong shall not strengthen his force, neither shall the mighty deliver himself:

15 Neither shall he stand that handleth the bow; and *he that is* swift of foot shall not deliver *himself:* neither shall he that rideth the horse deliver himself.

16 And *he that is* courageous among the mighty shall flee away naked in that day, saith the LORD.

3

1 Hear this word that the LORD hath spoken against you, O children of Israel, against the whole family which I brought up from the land of Egypt, saying,

2 You only have I known of all the families of the earth: therefore I will punish you for all your iniquities.

3 Can two walk together, except they be agreed?

4 Will a lion roar in the forest, when he hath no prey? will a young lion cry out of his den, if he have taken nothing?

5 Can a bird fall in a snare upon the earth, where no gin *is* for him? shall *one* take up a snare from the earth, and have taken nothing at all?

6 Shall a trumpet be blown in the city, and the people not be afraid? shall there be evil in a city, and the LORD hath not done *it?*

7 Surely the Lord GOD will do nothing, but he revealeth his secret unto his servants the prophets.

8 The lion hath roared, who will not fear? the Lord GOD hath spoken, who can but prophesy?

9 Publish in the palaces at Ashdod, and in the palaces in the land of Egypt, and say, Assemble yourselves upon the mountains of Samaria, and behold the great tumults in the midst thereof, and the oppressed in the midst thereof.

10 For they know not to do right, saith the LORD, who store up violence and robbery in their palaces.

3:10 Violence
◄ Ezekiel 8:17
Micah 2:2 ►

11 Therefore thus saith the Lord GOD; An adversary *there shall be* even round about the land; and he shall bring down thy strength from thee, and thy palaces shall be spoiled.

12 Thus saith the LORD; As the shepherd taketh out of the mouth of the lion two legs, or a piece of an ear; so shall the children of Israel be taken out that dwell in Samaria in the corner of a bed, and in Damascus *in* a couch.

13 Hear ye, and testify in the house of Jacob, saith the Lord GOD, the God of hosts,

14 That in the day that I shall visit the transgressions of Israel upon him I will also visit the altars of Bethel: and the horns of the altar shall be cut off, and fall to the ground.

15 And I will smite the winter house with the summer house; and the houses of ivory shall perish, and the great houses shall have an end, saith the LORD.

4

1 Hear this word, ye kine of Bashan, that *are* in the mountain of Samaria, which oppress the poor, which crush the needy, which say to their masters, Bring, and let us drink.

2 The Lord GOD hath sworn by his holiness, that, lo, the days shall come upon you, that he will take you away with hooks, and your posterity with fishhooks.

3 And ye shall go out at the breaches, every *cow at that which is* before her; and ye shall cast *them* into the palace, saith the LORD.

4 Come to Bethel, and transgress; at Gilgal multiply transgression; and bring your sacrifices every morning, *and* your tithes after three years:

5 And offer a sacrifice of thanksgiving with leaven, and proclaim *and* publish the free offerings: for this liketh you, O ye children of Israel, saith the Lord GOD.

6 And I also have given you cleanness of teeth in all your cities, and want of bread in all your places: yet have ye not returned unto me, saith the LORD.

4:6 Hard-hearted
◄ Hosea 7:10
Haggai 2:17 ►

7 And also I have withholden the rain from you, when *there were* yet three months to the harvest: and I caused it to rain upon one city, and caused it not to rain upon another city: one piece was rained upon, and the piece whereupon it rained not withered.

8 So two *or* three cities wandered unto one city, to drink water; but they were not satisfied: yet have ye not returned unto me, saith the LORD.

9 I have smitten you with blasting and mildew: when your gardens and your vineyards and your fig trees and your olive trees increased, the palmerworm devoured *them:* yet have ye not returned unto me, saith the LORD.

4:9 Refusing Correction
◄ Jeremiah 5:3
Zephaniah 3:7 ►

10 I have sent among you the pestilence after the manner of Egypt: your young men have I slain with the sword, and have taken away your horses; and I have made the stink of your camps to come up unto your nostrils: yet have ye not returned unto me, saith the LORD.

11 I have overthrown *some* of you, as God overthrew Sodom and Gomorrah, and ye were as a firebrand plucked out of the

burning: yet have ye not returned unto me, saith the LORD.

12 Therefore thus will I do unto thee, O Israel: *and* because I will do this unto thee, prepare to meet thy God, O Israel.

4:12
Ready for the Future
◄ 2 Kings 20:1
Matthew 24:44 ►

13 For, lo, he that formeth the mountains, and createth the wind, and declareth unto man what *is* his thought, that maketh the morning darkness, and treadeth upon the high places of the earth, The LORD, The God of hosts, *is* his name.

5

1 Hear ye this word which I take up against you, *even* a lamentation, O house of Israel.

2 The virgin of Israel is fallen; she shall no more rise: she is forsaken upon her land; *there is* none to raise her up.

3 For thus saith the Lord GOD; The city that went out *by* a thousand shall leave an hundred, and that which went forth *by* an hundred shall leave ten, to the house of Israel.

4 For thus saith the LORD unto the house of Israel, Seek ye me, and ye shall live:

5:4 Seeking God
◄ Hosea 10:12
Zephaniah 2:3 ►

5 But seek not Bethel, nor enter into Gilgal, and pass not to Beer-sheba: for Gilgal shall surely go into captivity, and Bethel shall come to nought.

6 Seek the LORD, and ye shall live; lest he break out like fire in the house of Joseph, and devour *it*, and *there be* none to quench *it* in Bethel.

7 Ye who turn judgment to wormwood, and leave off righteousness in the earth,

8 *Seek him* that maketh the seven stars and Orion, and turneth the shadow of death into the morning, and maketh the day dark with night: that calleth for the waters of the sea, and poureth them out upon the face of the earth: The LORD *is* his name:

9 That strengtheneth the spoiled against the strong, so that the spoiled shall come against the fortress.

10 They hate him that rebuketh in the gate, and they abhor him that speaketh uprightly.

11 Forasmuch therefore as your treading *is* upon the poor, and ye take from him burdens of wheat: ye have built houses of hewn stone, but ye shall not dwell in them; ye have planted pleasant vineyards, but ye shall not drink wine of them.

5:11 Disappointment
◄ Jeremiah 14:19
Micah 6:15 ►

12 For I know your manifold transgressions and your mighty sins: they afflict the just, they take a bribe, and they turn aside the poor in the gate *from their right*.

5:12
Bribery
◄ Isaiah 33:15 ►

5:12
God Sees Sin
◄ Hosea 7:2 ►

13 Therefore the prudent shall keep silence in that time; for it *is* an evil time.

5:13 Being Quiet
◄ Ecclesiastes 3:7
Habakkuk 2:20 ►

14 Seek good, and not evil, that ye may live: and so the LORD, the God of hosts, shall be with you, as ye have spoken.

15 Hate the evil, and love the good, and establish judgment in the gate: it may be that the LORD God of hosts will be gracious unto the remnant of Joseph.

16 Therefore the LORD, the God of hosts, the Lord, saith thus; Wailing *shall be* in all streets; and they shall say in all the highways, Alas! alas! and they shall call the husbandman to mourning, and such as are skilful of lamentation to wailing.

17 And in all vineyards *shall be* wailing: for I will pass through thee, saith the LORD.

18 Woe unto you that desire the day of the LORD! to what end *is* it for you? the day of the LORD *is* darkness, and not light.

19 As if a man did flee from a lion, and a bear met him; or went into the house, and leaned his hand on the wall, and a serpent bit him.

20 *Shall* not the day of the LORD *be* darkness, and not light? even very dark, and no brightness in it?

21 I hate, I despise your feast days, and I will not smell in your solemn assemblies.

22 Though ye offer me burnt offerings and your meat offerings, I will not accept

them: neither will I regard the peace offerings of your fat beasts.
23 Take thou away from me the noise of
thy songs; for I will not hear the melody
of thy viols.
24 But let judgment run down as waters,
and righteousness as a mighty stream.
25 Have ye offered unto me sacrifices and
offerings in the wilderness forty years,
O house of Israel?
26 But ye have borne the tabernacle of
your Moloch and Chiun your images, the
star of your god, which ye made to yourselves.
27 Therefore will I cause you to go into
captivity beyond Damascus, saith the
LORD, whose name *is* The God of hosts.

6

1 Woe to them
that are at ease in
Zion, and trust in
the mountain of Sa-
maria, *which are*
named chief of the
nations, to whom the house of Israel came!

6:1 Apathy
◄ Isaiah 64:7
Zephaniah 1:12 ►

2 Pass ye unto Calneh, and see; and from
thence go ye to Hamath the great: then go
down to Gath of the Philistines: *be they*
better than these kingdoms? or their border greater than your border?
3 Ye that put far away the evil day, and
cause the seat of violence to come near;
4 That lie upon beds of ivory, and stretch
themselves upon their couches, and eat the
lambs out of the flock, and the calves out
of the midst of the stall;
5 That chant to the sound of the viol, *and*
invent to themselves instruments of
musick, like David;
6 That drink wine in bowls, and anoint
themselves with the chief ointments: but
they are not grieved for the affliction of
Joseph.
7 Therefore now shall they go captive
with the first that go captive, and the banquet of them that stretched themselves
shall be removed.
8 The Lord GOD hath sworn by himself,
saith the LORD the God of hosts, I abhor
the excellency of Jacob, and hate his palaces: therefore will I deliver up the city with
all that is therein.
9 And it shall come to pass, if there
remain ten men in one house, that they
shall die.
10 And a man's uncle shall take him up,
and he that burneth him, to bring out the
bones out of the house, and shall say unto
him that *is* by the sides of the house, *Is
there* yet *any* with thee? and he shall say,
No. Then shall he say, Hold thy tongue:
for we may not make mention of the name
of the LORD.
11 For, behold, the LORD commandeth,
and he will smite the great house with
breaches, and the little house with clefts.
12 Shall horses run upon the rock? will
one plow *there* with oxen? for ye have
turned judgment into gall, and the fruit of
righteousness into hemlock:
13 Ye which rejoice in a thing of nought,
which say, Have we not taken to us horns
by our own strength?
14 But, behold, I will raise up against you
a nation, O house of Israel, saith the LORD
the God of hosts; and they shall afflict you
from the entering in of Hemath unto the
river of the wilderness.

7

1 Thus hath the Lord GOD shewed unto
me; and, behold, he formed grasshoppers
in the beginning of the shooting up of the
latter growth; and, lo, *it was* the latter
growth after the king's mowings.
2 And it came to pass, *that* when they had
made an end of eating the grass of the land,
then I said, O Lord GOD, forgive, I beseech
thee: by whom shall Jacob arise? for he *is*
small.
3 The LORD repented for this: It shall not
be, saith the LORD.
4 Thus hath the Lord GOD shewed unto
me: and, behold, the Lord GOD called to
contend by fire, and it devoured the great
deep, and did eat up a part.
5 Then said I, O Lord GOD, cease, I beseech thee: by whom shall Jacob arise? for
he *is* small.
6 The LORD repented for this: This also
shall not be, saith the Lord GOD.
7 Thus he shewed me: and, behold, the
Lord stood upon a wall *made* by a plumbline, with a plumbline in his hand.
8 And the LORD said unto me, Amos,
what seest thou? And I said, A plumbline.
Then said the Lord, Behold, I will set a
plumbline in the midst of my people Israel: I will not again pass by them any more:
9 And the high places of Isaac shall be
desolate, and the sanctuaries of Israel shall
be laid waste; and I will rise against the
house of Jeroboam with the sword.

10Then Amaziah the priest of Bethel sent
to Jeroboam king of Israel, saying, Amos
hath conspired against thee in the midst
of the house of Israel: the land is not able
to bear all his words.
11For thus Amos saith, Jeroboam shall
die by the sword, and Israel shall surely
be led away captive out of their own land.
12Also Amaziah said unto Amos, O thou
seer, go, flee thee away into the land of
Judah, and there eat bread, and prophesy
there:
13But prophesy not again any more at
Bethel: for it *is* the king's chapel, and it *is*
the king's court.
14Then answered Amos, and said to
Amaziah, I *was* no prophet, neither *was* I a
prophet's son; but I *was* an herdman, and
a gatherer of sycomore fruit:
15And the LORD took me as I followed
the flock, and the LORD said unto me, Go,
prophesy unto my people Israel.
16Now therefore hear thou the word of
the LORD: Thou sayest, Prophesy not
against Israel, and drop not *thy word*
against the house of Isaac.
17Therefore thus saith the LORD; Thy
wife shall be an harlot in the city, and thy
sons and thy daughters shall fall by the
sword, and thy land shall be divided by
line; and thou shalt die in a polluted land:
and Israel shall surely go into captivity
forth of his land.

8

1Thus hath the Lord GOD shewed unto
me: and behold a basket of summer fruit.
2And he said, Amos, what seest thou?
And I said, A basket of summer fruit. Then
said the LORD unto me, The end is come
upon my people of Israel; I will not again
pass by them any more.
3And the songs of the temple shall be
howlings in that day, saith the Lord GOD:
there shall be many dead bodies in every
place; they shall cast *them* forth with silence.
4Hear this, O ye that swallow up the
needy, even to make the poor of the land
to fail,
5Saying, When will the new moon be
gone, that we may sell corn? and the sabbath, that we may set forth wheat, making
the ephah small, and the shekel great, and
falsifying the balances by deceit?
6That we may buy the poor for silver,
and the needy for a pair of shoes; *yea,* and
sell the refuse of the wheat?
7The LORD hath sworn by the excellency of Jacob, Surely I will never forget any
of their works.
8Shall not the land tremble for this, and
every one mourn that dwelleth therein?
and it shall rise up wholly as a flood; and
it shall be cast out and drowned, as *by* the
flood of Egypt.
9And it shall come to pass in that day,
saith the Lord GOD, that I will cause the
sun to go down at noon, and I will darken
the earth in the clear day:
10And I will turn your feasts into mourning, and all your songs into lamentation;
and I will bring up sackcloth upon all
loins, and baldness upon every head; and
I will make it as the mourning of an only
son, and the end thereof as a bitter day.
11Behold, the
days come, saith
the Lord GOD, that
I will send a famine
in the land, not a
famine of bread,
nor a thirst for water, but of hearing the
words of the LORD:

8:11
Desire for God
◄ Psalm 143:6 ►

12And they shall wander from sea to sea,
and from the north even to the east, they
shall run to and fro to seek the word of
the LORD, and shall not find *it.*
13In that day shall the fair virgins and
young men faint for thirst.
14They that swear by the sin of Samaria,
and say, Thy god, O Dan, liveth; and, The
manner of Beer-sheba liveth; even they
shall fall, and never rise up again.

9

1I saw the LORD standing upon the altar: and he said, Smite the lintel of the
door, that the posts may shake: and cut
them in the head, all of them; and I will
slay the last of them with the sword: he
that fleeth of them shall not flee away, and
he that escapeth of them shall not be delivered.
2Though they dig into hell, thence shall
mine hand take them; though they climb
up to heaven, thence will I bring them
down:
3And though they hide themselves in the
top of Carmel, I will search and take them
out thence; and though they be hid from
my sight in the bottom of the sea, thence
will I command the serpent, and he shall
bite them:
4And though they go into captivity

before their enemies, thence will I command the sword, and it shall slay them: and I will set mine eyes upon them for evil, and not for good.

5 And the Lord GOD of hosts *is* he that toucheth the land, and it shall melt, and all that dwell therein shall mourn: and it shall rise up wholly like a flood; and shall be drowned, as *by* the flood of Egypt.

6 *It is* he that buildeth his stories in the heaven, and hath founded his troop in the earth; he that calleth for the waters of the sea, and poureth them out upon the face of the earth: The LORD *is* his name.

7 *Are* ye not as children of the Ethiopians unto me, O children of Israel? saith the LORD. Have not I brought up Israel out of the land of Egypt? and the Philistines from Caphtor, and the Syrians from Kir?

8 Behold, the eyes of the Lord GOD *are* upon the sinful kingdom, and I will destroy it from off the face of the earth; saving that I will not utterly destroy the house of Jacob, saith the LORD.

9 For, lo, I will command, and I will sift the house of Israel among all nations, like as *corn* is sifted in a sieve, yet shall not the least grain fall upon the earth.

10 All the sinners of my people shall die by the sword, which say, The evil shall not overtake nor prevent us.

11 In that day will I raise up the tabernacle of David that is fallen, and close up the breaches thereof; and I will raise up his ruins, and I will build it as in the days of old:

12 That they may possess the remnant of Edom, and of all the heathen, which are called by my name, saith the LORD that doeth this.

13 Behold, the days come, saith the LORD, that the plowman shall overtake the reaper, and the treader of grapes him that soweth seed; and the mountains shall drop sweet wine, and all the hills shall melt.

9:13 Blessing
◄ Isaiah 30:23
Malachi 3:10 ►

14 And I will bring again the captivity of my people of Israel, and they shall build the waste cities, and inhabit *them;* and they shall plant vineyards, and drink the wine thereof; they shall also make gardens, and eat the fruit of them.

15 And I will plant them upon their land, and they shall no more be pulled up out of their land which I have given them, saith the LORD thy God.

Obadiah

AUTHOR
Obadiah the prophet

MAIN POINT
God judges those who hurt his people.

DATE WRITTEN
Possibly during Jehoram's reign in Judah, 853-841 B.C.

1 CHAPTER
❑

MAIN PEOPLE

The Edomites

SPECIAL FEATURES

- *Is one of the shortest books of the Bible*
- *Takes the form of poetry, a song of doom*
- *Fourth book of the Minor Prophets*

HOW THE BOOK GOT ITS NAME

The name Obadiah means "servant of the Lord" or "worshiper of Jehovah"—both meanings apply to this prophet.

1The vision of Obadiah. Thus saith the
Lord GOD concerning Edom; We have
heard a rumour from the LORD, and an
ambassador is sent among the heathen,
Arise ye, and let us rise up against her in
battle.
2Behold, I have made thee small among
the heathen: thou art greatly despised.
3The pride of
thine heart hath de-
ceived thee, thou
that dwellest in the
clefts of the rock,
whose habitation *is*
high; that saith in his heart, Who shall
bring me down to the ground?

1:3 Self-confidence
◄ Hosea 10:13
Matthew 26:33 ►

4Though thou exalt *thyself* as the eagle,
and though thou set thy nest among the
stars, thence will I bring thee down, saith
the LORD.
5If thieves came to thee, if robbers by
night, (how art thou cut off!) would they
not have stolen till they had enough? if
the grapegatherers came to thee, would
they not leave *some* grapes?
6How are *the things* of Esau searched out!
how are his hidden things sought up!
7All the men of thy confederacy have
brought thee *even* to the border: the men
that were at peace with thee have deceived
thee, *and* prevailed against thee; *they that
eat* thy bread have laid a wound under
thee: *there is* none understanding in him.
8Shall I not in that day, saith the LORD,
even destroy the wise *men* out of Edom,
and understanding out of the mount of
Esau?
9And thy mighty *men*, O Teman, shall
be dismayed, to the end that every one of
the mount of Esau may be cut off by
slaughter.
10For *thy* violence against thy brother
Jacob shame shall cover thee, and thou
shalt be cut off for ever.
11In the day that thou stoodest on the
other side, in the day that the strangers

carried away captive his forces, and foreigners entered into his gates, and cast lots upon Jerusalem, even thou *wast* as one of them.

12 But thou shouldest not have looked on the day of thy brother in the day that he became a stranger; neither shouldest thou have rejoiced over the children of Judah in the day of their destruction; neither shouldest thou have spoken proudly in the day of distress.

13 Thou shouldest not have entered into the gate of my people in the day of their calamity; yea, thou shouldest not have looked on their affliction in the day of their calamity, nor have laid *hands* on their substance in the day of their calamity;

14 Neither shouldest thou have stood in the crossway, to cut off those of his that did escape; neither shouldest thou have delivered up those of his that did remain in the day of distress.

15 For the day of the LORD *is* near upon all the heathen: as thou hast done, it shall be done unto thee: thy reward shall return upon thine own head.

16 For as ye have drunk upon my holy mountain, *so* shall all the heathen drink continually, yea, they shall drink, and they shall swallow down, and they shall be as though they had not been.

17 But upon mount Zion shall be deliverance, and there shall be holiness; and the house of Jacob shall possess their possessions.

18 And the house of Jacob shall be a fire, and the house of Joseph a flame, and the house of Esau for stubble, and they shall kindle in them, and devour them; and there shall not be *any* remaining of the house of Esau; for the LORD hath spoken *it*.

19 And *they of* the south shall possess the mount of Esau; and *they of* the plain the Philistines: and they shall possess the fields of Ephraim, and the fields of Samaria: and Benjamin *shall possess* Gilead.

20 And the captivity of this host of the children of Israel *shall possess* that of the Canaanites, *even* unto Zarephath; and the captivity of Jerusalem, which *is* in Sepharad, shall possess the cities of the south.

21 And saviours shall come up on mount Zion to judge the mount of Esau; and the kingdom shall be the LORD'S.

Jonah

AUTHOR
Jonah the prophet

MAIN POINT
God expects obedience from his people, especially when they know that he offers forgiveness to all people everywhere.

DATE WRITTEN
Approximately 785-760 B.C.

4 CHAPTERS
□□□□

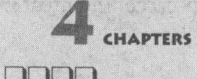

MAIN PEOPLE
Jonah, the boat's captain and crew, people of Nineveh

SPECIAL FEATURES
- *Is considered a book of prophecy but tells mainly about the prophet rather than his messages*
- *Tells the famous account of the disobedient prophet who was rescued from drowning by a huge fish sent by God*
- *Includes the shameful account of Jonah's angry response when the people of Nineveh repented*
- *Was mentioned by Jesus as a picture of his death and resurrection*
- *Fifth book of the Minor Prophets*

HOW THE BOOK GOT ITS NAME
The book of Jonah takes its name from the book's main person—the reluctant prophet Jonah.

1

1Now the word of the LORD came unto
Jonah the son of Amittai, saying,
2Arise, go to Nineveh, that great city, and
cry against it; for their wickedness is come
up before me.
3But Jonah rose
up to flee unto Tar-
shish from the pres-
ence of the LORD,
and went down to
Joppa; and he
found a ship going to Tarshish: so he paid
the fare thereof, and went down into it, to
go with them unto Tarshish from the presence of the LORD.
4But the LORD sent out a great wind into
the sea, and there was a mighty tempest in
the sea, so that the ship was like to be
broken.

1:3 Only Human
◄ 2 Chronicles 16:12
Luke 9:54 ►

5Then the mariners were afraid, and
cried every man unto his god, and cast
forth the wares that *were* in the ship into
the sea, to lighten *it* of them. But Jonah
was gone down into the sides of the ship;
and he lay, and was fast asleep.
6So the shipmaster came to him, and
said unto him, What meanest thou,
O sleeper? arise, call upon thy God, if so
be that God will think upon us, that we
perish not.
7And they said every one to his fellow,
Come, and let us cast lots, that we may
know for whose cause this evil *is* upon us.
So they cast lots, and the lot fell upon
Jonah.
8Then said they unto him, Tell us, we
pray thee, for whose cause this evil *is* upon
us; What *is* thine occupation? and whence

comest thou? what *is* thy country? and of what people *art* thou?

9 And he said unto them, I *am* an Hebrew; and I fear the LORD, the God of heaven, which hath made the sea and the dry *land*.

10 Then were the men exceedingly afraid, and said unto him, Why hast thou done this? For the men knew that he fled from the presence of the LORD, because he had told them.

11 Then said they unto him, What shall we do unto thee, that the sea may be calm unto us? for the sea wrought, and was tempestuous.

12 And he said unto them, Take me up, and cast me forth into the sea; so shall the sea be calm unto you: for I know that for my sake this great tempest *is* upon you.

13 Nevertheless the men rowed hard to bring *it* to the land; but they could not: for the sea wrought, and was tempestuous against them.

14 Wherefore they cried unto the LORD, and said, We beseech thee, O LORD, we beseech thee, let us not perish for this man's life, and lay not upon us innocent blood: for thou, O LORD, hast done as it pleased thee.

15 So they took up Jonah, and cast him forth into the sea: and the sea ceased from her raging.

16 Then the men feared the LORD exceedingly, and offered a sacrifice unto the LORD, and made vows.

17 Now the LORD had prepared a great fish to swallow up Jonah. And Jonah was in the belly of the fish three days and three nights.

2

1 Then Jonah prayed unto the LORD his God out of the fish's belly,

2 And said, I cried by reason of mine affliction unto the LORD, and he heard me; out of the belly of hell cried I, *and* thou heardest my voice.

3 For thou hadst cast me into the deep, in the midst of the seas; and the floods compassed me about: all thy billows and thy waves passed over me.

4 Then I said, I am cast out of thy sight; yet I will look again toward thy holy temple.

5 The waters compassed me about, *even* to the soul: the depth closed me round about, the weeds were wrapped about my head.

6 I went down to the bottoms of the mountains; the earth with her bars *was* about me for ever: yet hast thou brought up my life from corruption, O LORD my God.

7 When my soul fainted within me I remembered the LORD: and my prayer came in unto thee, into thine holy temple.

2:7 Remember...
◄ Ecclesiastes 12:1
Zechariah 10:9 ►

8 They that observe lying vanities forsake their own mercy.

2:8 Worshiping Things
◄ Jeremiah 16:19
Acts 14:15 ►

9 But I will sacrifice unto thee with the voice of thanksgiving; I will pay *that* that I have vowed. Salvation *is* of the LORD.

10 And the LORD spake unto the fish, and it vomited out Jonah upon the dry *land*.

3

1 And the word of the LORD came unto Jonah the second time, saying,

2 Arise, go unto Nineveh, that great city, and preach unto it the preaching that I bid thee.

3 So Jonah arose, and went unto Nineveh, according to the word of the LORD. Now Nineveh was an exceeding great city of three days' journey.

4 And Jonah began to enter into the city a day's journey, and he cried, and said, Yet forty days, and Nineveh shall be overthrown.

3:4 Sin (Warnings)
◄ Jeremiah 13:16
Hebrews 12:25 ►

5 So the people of Nineveh believed God, and proclaimed a fast, and put on sackcloth, from the greatest of them even to the least of them.

6 For word came unto the king of Nineveh, and he arose from his throne, and he laid his robe from him, and covered *him* with sackcloth, and sat in ashes.

7 And he caused *it* to be proclaimed and published through Nineveh by the decree of the king and his nobles, saying, Let neither man nor beast, herd nor flock, taste any thing: let them not feed, nor drink water:

8 But let man and beast be covered with sackcloth, and cry mightily unto God: yea, let them turn every one from his evil way,

and from the violence that *is* in their
hands.
9 Who can tell *if* God will turn and repent, and turn away from his fierce anger,
that we perish not?
10 And God saw their works, that they
turned from their evil way; and God repented of the evil, that he had said that he
would do unto them; and he did *it* not.

4

1 But it displeased Jonah exceedingly,
and he was very angry.
2 And he prayed unto the LORD, and said,
I pray thee, O LORD, *was* not this my saying, when I was yet in my country? Therefore I fled before unto Tarshish: for I knew
that thou *art* a gracious God, and merciful, slow to anger, and of great kindness,
and repentest thee of the evil.
3 Therefore now, O LORD, take, I beseech
thee, my life from me; for *it is* better for
me to die than to live.
4 Then said the LORD, Doest thou well
to be angry?
5 So Jonah went out of the city, and sat
on the east side of the city, and there made
him a booth, and sat under it in the shadow, till he might see what would become
of the city.
6 And the LORD God prepared a gourd,
and made *it* to come up over Jonah, that it
might be a shadow over his head, to deliver him from his grief. So Jonah was exceeding glad of the gourd.
7 But God prepared a worm when the
morning rose the next day, and it smote
the gourd that it withered.
8 And it came to
pass, when the sun
did arise, that God
prepared a vehe-
ment east wind;
and the sun beat
upon the head of Jonah, that he fainted,
and wished in himself to die, and said, *It
is* better for me to die than to live.

4:8-9 Impatience
◄ 2 Kings 5:11-12
Matthew 15:23 ►

9 And God said to Jonah, Doest thou well
to be angry for the gourd? And he said, I
do well to be angry, *even* unto death.
10 Then said the LORD, Thou hast had
pity on the gourd, for the which thou hast
not laboured, neither madest it grow;
which came up in a night, and perished in
a night:
11 And should not I spare Nineveh, that
great city, wherein are more than sixscore
thousand persons that cannot discern between their right hand and their left hand;
and *also* much cattle?

Micah

AUTHOR
Micah the prophet

MAIN POINT
Don't be fooled: God's judgment is coming, so the time to repent is now.

DATE WRITTEN
Possibly during the period 742-687 B.C., the reigns of Jotham, Ahaz, and Hezekiah

7 CHAPTERS

MAIN PEOPLE

The people of Samaria and Jerusalem

SPECIAL FEATURES

- *Presents God's message in classic Hebrew poetry*
- *Is organized in three parts, each beginning with "Hear" or "Listen" and ending with a promise from God*
- *Includes many prophecies about Jesus the Messiah*
- *Sixth book of the Minor Prophets*

HOW THE BOOK GOT ITS NAME

The author of the book, Micah, brought God's message to both Israel and Judah.

Chapter 1

1 The word of the LORD that came to Micah the Morasthite in the days of Jotham,
Ahaz, *and* Hezekiah, kings of Judah, which
he saw concerning Samaria and Jerusalem.
2 Hear, all ye people; hearken, O earth,
and all that therein is: and let the Lord GOD
be witness against you, the Lord from his
holy temple.
3 For, behold, the LORD cometh forth out
of his place, and will come down, and
tread upon the high places of the earth.
4 And the mountains shall be molten
under him, and the valleys shall be cleft,
as wax before the fire, *and* as the waters
that are poured down a steep place.
5 For the transgression of Jacob *is* all this,
and for the sins of the house of Israel. What
is the transgression of Jacob? *is it* not Samaria? and what *are* the high places of Judah? *are they* not Jerusalem?
6 Therefore I will make Samaria as an
heap of the field, *and* as plantings of a vineyard: and I will pour down the stones
thereof into the valley, and I will discover
the foundations thereof.
7 And all the graven images thereof shall
be beaten to pieces, and all the hires
thereof shall be burned with the fire, and
all the idols thereof will I lay desolate: for
she gathered *it* of the hire of an harlot, and
they shall return to the hire of an harlot.
8 Therefore I will wail and howl, I will

go stripped and naked: I will make a wailing like the dragons, and mourning as the
owls.
9 For her wound *is*
incurable; for it is
come unto Judah;
he is come unto the
gate of my people,
even to Jerusalem.

1:9
Sin Hurts
◄ Jeremiah 30:12 ►

10 Declare ye *it* not at Gath, weep ye not
at all: in the house of Aphrah roll thyself
in the dust.
11 Pass ye away, thou inhabitant of
Saphir, having thy shame naked: the inhabitant of Zaanan came not forth in the
mourning of Beth-ezel; he shall receive of
you his standing.
12 For the inhabitant of Maroth waited
carefully for good: but evil came down
from the LORD unto the gate of Jerusalem.
13 O thou inhabitant of Lachish, bind
the chariot to the swift beast: she *is* the beginning of the sin to the daughter of Zion:
for the transgressions of Israel were found
in thee.
14 Therefore shalt thou give presents to
Moresheth-gath: the houses of Achzib *shall*
be a lie to the kings of Israel.
15 Yet will I bring an heir unto thee,
O inhabitant of Mareshah: he shall come
unto Adullam the glory of Israel.
16 Make thee bald, and poll thee for thy
delicate children; enlarge thy baldness as
the eagle; for they are gone into captivity
from thee.

2

1 Woe to them
that devise iniquity,
and work evil upon
their beds! when
the morning is
light, they practise
it, because it is in
the power of their
hand.
2 And they covet
fields, and take
them by violence;
and houses, and take *them* away: so they
oppress a man and his house, even a man
and his heritage.

2:1 Bad People
◄ Isaiah 59:7
Romans 3:15 ►

2:2 Violence
◄ Amos 3:10
Micah 6:12 ►

3 Therefore thus saith the LORD; Behold,
against this family do I devise an evil, from
which ye shall not remove your necks; neither shall ye go haughtily: for this time *is*
evil.
4 In that day shall *one* take up a parable
against you, and lament with a doleful
lamentation, *and* say, We be utterly spoiled:
he hath changed the portion of my people: how hath he removed *it* from me!
turning away he hath divided our fields.
5 Therefore thou shalt have none that
shall cast a cord by lot in the congregation
of the LORD.
6 Prophesy ye not, *say they to them that*
prophesy: they shall not prophesy to them,
that they shall not take shame.
7 O *thou that art* named the house of Jacob, is the spirit of the LORD straitened?
are these his doings? do not my words do
good to him that walketh uprightly?
8 Even of late my people is risen up as
an enemy: ye pull off the robe with the
garment from them that pass by securely
as men averse from war.
9 The women of my people have ye cast
out from their pleasant houses; from their
children have ye taken away my glory for
ever.
10 Arise ye, and depart; for this *is* not *your*
rest: because it is polluted, it shall destroy
you, even with a sore destruction.
11 If a man walking in the spirit and falsehood do lie, *saying*, I will prophesy unto
thee of wine and of strong drink; he shall
even be the prophet of this people.
12 I will surely assemble, O Jacob, all of
thee; I will surely gather the remnant of
Israel; I will put them together as the sheep
of Bozrah, as the flock in the midst of their
fold: they shall make great noise by reason of *the multitude of* men.
13 The breaker is come up before them:
they have broken up, and have passed
through the gate, and are gone out by it:
and their king shall pass before them, and
the LORD on the head of them.

3

1 And I said, Hear, I pray you, O heads
of Jacob, and ye princes of the house of
Israel; *Is it* not for you to know judgment?
2 Who hate the good, and love the evil;
who pluck off their skin from off them,
and their flesh from off their bones;
3 Who also eat the flesh of my people,
and flay their skin from off them; and they
break their bones, and chop them in
pieces, as for the pot, and as flesh within
the caldron.
4 Then shall they cry unto the LORD, but
he will not hear them: he will even hide

Turn to the next page for more . . .

his face from them at that time, as they have behaved themselves ill in their doings.

> **3:4 Unanswered Prayer**
> ◄ Isaiah 59:2
> Zechariah 7:13 ►

5Thus saith the LORD concerning the prophets that make my people err, that bite with their teeth, and cry, Peace; and he that putteth not into their mouths, they even prepare war against him.

6Therefore night *shall be* unto you, that ye shall not have a vision; and it shall be dark unto you, that ye shall not divine; and the sun shall go down over the prophets, and the day shall be dark over them.

7Then shall the seers be ashamed, and the diviners confounded: yea, they shall all cover their lips; for *there is* no answer of God.

8But truly I am full of power by the spirit of the LORD, and of judgment, and of might, to declare unto Jacob his transgression, and to Israel his sin.

> **3:8 The Holy Spirit**
> ◄ Zechariah 4:6 ►

9Hear this, I pray you, ye heads of the house of Jacob, and princes of the house of Israel, that abhor judgment, and pervert all equity.

10They build up Zion with blood, and Jerusalem with iniquity.

11The heads thereof judge for reward, and the priests thereof teach for hire, and the prophets thereof divine for money: yet will they lean upon the LORD, and say, *Is* not the LORD among us? none evil can come upon us.

12Therefore shall Zion for your sake be plowed *as* a field, and Jerusalem shall become heaps, and the mountain of the house as the high places of the forest.

4

1But in the last days it shall come to pass, *that* the mountain of the house of the LORD shall be established in the top of the mountains, and it shall be exalted above the hills; and people shall flow unto it.

2And many nations shall come, and say, Come, and let us go up to the mountain of the LORD, and to the house of the God of Jacob; and he will teach us of his ways, and we will walk in his paths: for the law shall go forth of Zion, and the word of the LORD from Jerusalem.

> **4:2 God as Teacher**
> ◄ Jeremiah 32:33 ►

3And he shall judge among many people, and rebuke strong nations afar off; and they shall beat their swords into plowshares, and their spears into pruninghooks: nation shall not lift up a sword against nation, neither shall they learn war any more.

4But they shall sit every man under his vine and under his fig tree; and none shall make *them* afraid: for the mouth of the LORD of hosts hath spoken *it*.

5For all people will walk every one in the name of his god, and we will walk in the name of the LORD our God for ever and ever.

> **4:5 Walking with God**
> ◄ 2 Kings 23:3
> Malachi 2:6 ►

6In that day, saith the LORD, will I assemble her that halteth, and I will gather her that is driven out, and her that I have afflicted;

7And I will make her that halted a remnant, and her that was cast far off a strong nation: and the LORD shall reign over them in mount Zion from henceforth, even for ever.

8And thou, O tower of the flock, the strong hold of the daughter of Zion, unto thee shall it come, even the first dominion; the kingdom shall come to the daughter of Jerusalem.

9Now why dost thou cry out aloud? *is there* no king in thee? is thy counsellor perished? for pangs have taken thee as a woman in travail.

10Be in pain, and labour to bring forth, O daughter of Zion, like a woman in travail: for now shalt thou go forth out of the city, and thou shalt dwell in the field, and thou shalt go *even* to Babylon; there shalt thou be delivered; there the LORD shall redeem thee from the hand of thine enemies.

11Now also many nations are gathered against thee, that say, Let her be defiled, and let our eye look upon Zion.

12But they know not the thoughts of the LORD, neither understand they his counsel: for he shall gather them as the sheaves into the floor.

13Arise and thresh, O daughter of Zion:

for I will make
thine horn iron,
and I will make thy
hoofs brass: and
thou shalt beat in
pieces many peo-
ple: and I will consecrate their gain unto
the LORD, and their substance unto the
Lord of the whole earth.

4:13
Tithing
◄ Proverbs 3:9 ►

5

1 Now gather thyself in troops, O daughter of troops: he hath laid siege against us:
they shall smite the judge of Israel with a
rod upon the cheek.
2 But thou, Bethlehem Ephratah, *though*
thou be little among the thousands of Judah, *yet* out of thee shall he come forth
unto me *that is* to be ruler in Israel; whose
goings forth *have been* from of old, from
everlasting.
3 Therefore will he give them up, until
the time *that* she which travaileth hath
brought forth: then the remnant of his
brethren shall return unto the children of
Israel.
4 And he shall stand and feed in the
strength of the LORD, in the majesty of the
name of the LORD his God; and they shall
abide: for now shall he be great unto the
ends of the earth.
5 And this *man* shall be the peace, when
the Assyrian shall come into our land: and
when he shall tread in our palaces, then
shall we raise against him seven shepherds,
and eight principal men.
6 And they shall waste the land of Assyria with the sword, and the land of Nimrod in the entrances thereof: thus shall
he deliver *us* from the Assyrian, when he
cometh into our land, and when he
treadeth within our borders.
7 And the remnant of Jacob shall be in
the midst of many people as a dew from
the LORD, as the showers upon the grass,
that tarrieth not for man, nor waiteth for
the sons of men.
8 And the remnant of Jacob shall be
among the Gentiles in the midst of many
people as a lion among the beasts of the
forest, as a young lion among the flocks
of sheep: who, if he go through, both
treadeth down, and teareth in pieces, and
none can deliver.
9 Thine hand shall be lifted up upon
thine adversaries, and all thine enemies
shall be cut off.
10 And it shall come to pass in that day,
saith the LORD, that I will cut off thy horses
out of the midst of thee, and I will destroy
thy chariots:
11 And I will cut off the cities of thy land,
and throw down all thy strong holds:
12 And I will cut off witchcrafts out of
thine hand; and thou shalt have no *more*
soothsayers:
13 Thy graven images also will I cut off,
and thy standing images out of the midst
of thee; and thou shalt no more worship
the work of thine hands.
14 And I will pluck up thy groves out of
the midst of thee: so will I destroy thy
cities.
15 And I will execute vengeance in anger
and fury upon the heathen, such as they
have not heard.

6

1 Hear ye now what the LORD saith; Arise,
contend thou before the mountains, and
let the hills hear thy voice.
2 Hear ye, O mountains, the LORD'S controversy, and ye strong foundations of the
earth: for the LORD hath a controversy with
his people, and he will plead with Israel.
3 O my people, what have I done unto
thee? and wherein have I wearied thee?
testify against me.
4 For I brought thee up out of the land
of Egypt, and redeemed thee out of the
house of servants; and I sent before thee
Moses, Aaron, and Miriam.
5 O my people, remember now what Balak king of Moab consulted, and what Balaam the son of Beor answered him from
Shittim unto Gilgal; that ye may know the
righteousness of the LORD.
6 Wherewith shall I come before the
LORD, *and* bow myself before the high
God? shall I come before him with burnt
offerings, with calves of a year old?
7 Will the LORD be pleased with thousands of rams, *or*
with ten thousands
of rivers of oil?
shall I give my first-
born *for* my trans-
gression, the fruit
of my body *for* the
sin of my soul?
8 He hath shewed
thee, O man, what
is good; and what
doth the LORD

6:8 Religious People
◄ Hosea 6:6
Mark 12:33 ►

6:8 Showing Mercy
◄ Hosea 12:6
Matthew 5:7 ►

require of thee, but to do justly, and to love
mercy, and to walk humbly with thy God?
9The LORD'S voice crieth unto the city,
and *the man of* wisdom shall see thy name:
hear ye the rod, and who hath appointed it.
10Are there yet the treasures of wickedness in the house of the wicked, and the
scant measure *that is* abominable?
11Shall I count *them* pure with the wicked balances, and with the bag of deceitful
weights?
12For the rich
men thereof are full
of violence, and the
inhabitants thereof
have spoken lies,
and their tongue *is*
deceitful in their mouth.

6:12
Violence
◄ Micah 2:2 ►

13Therefore also will I make *thee* sick in
smiting thee, in making *thee* desolate because of thy sins.
14Thou shalt eat, but not be satisfied;
and thy casting down *shall be* in the midst
of thee; and thou shalt take hold, but shalt
not deliver; and *that* which thou deliverest
will I give up to the sword.
15Thou shalt sow,
but thou shalt not
reap; thou shalt
tread the olives, but
thou shalt not
anoint thee with
oil; and sweet wine, but shalt not drink
wine.

6:15 Disappointment
◄ Amos 5:11
Zephaniah 1:13 ►

16For the statutes of Omri are kept, and
all the works of the house of Ahab, and ye
walk in their counsels; that I should make
thee a desolation, and the inhabitants
thereof an hissing: therefore ye shall bear
the reproach of my people.

7
1Woe is me! for I
am as when they
have gathered the
summer fruits, as
the grapegleanings
of the vintage: *there*
is no cluster to eat:
my soul desired the
firstripe fruit.
2The good *man* is
perished out of the
earth: and *there is*
none upright among men: they all lie in
wait for blood; they hunt every man his
brother with a net.

7:1 Unhappiness
◄ Jeremiah 15:10
Luke 24:17 ►

7:2 Everyone Sins
◄ Isaiah 64:6
Romans 3:23 ►

3That they may do evil with both hands
earnestly, the prince asketh, and the judge
asketh for a reward; and the great *man*, he
uttereth his mischievous desire: so they
wrap it up.
4The best of them *is* as a brier: the most
upright *is sharper* than a thorn hedge: the
day of thy watchmen *and* thy visitation
cometh; now shall be their perplexity.
5Trust ye not in a
friend, put ye not
confidence in a
guide: keep the
doors of thy mouth
from her that lieth
in thy bosom.

7:5
Whom Can You Trust?
◄ Psalm 38:11
Matthew 26:56 ►

6For the son dishonoureth the father, the
daughter riseth up against her mother, the
daughter in law against her mother in law;
a man's enemies *are* the men of his own
house.
7Therefore I will look unto the LORD; I
will wait for the God of my salvation: my
God will hear me.
8Rejoice not against me, O mine enemy:
when I fall, I shall arise; when I sit in darkness, the LORD *shall be* a light unto me.
9I will bear the indignation of the LORD,
because I have sinned against him, until
he plead my cause, and execute judgment
for me: he will bring me forth to the light,
and I shall behold his righteousness.
10Then *she that is* mine enemy shall see
it, and shame shall cover her which said
unto me, Where is the LORD thy God? mine
eyes shall behold her: now shall she be
trodden down as the mire of the streets.
11*In* the day that thy walls are to be built,
in that day shall the decree be far removed.
12*In* that day *also* he shall come even to
thee from Assyria, and *from* the fortified
cities, and from the fortress even to the
river, and from sea to sea, and *from* mountain to mountain.
13Notwithstanding the land shall be
desolate because of them that dwell
therein, for the fruit of their doings.
14Feed thy people with thy rod, the flock
of thine heritage, which dwell solitarily *in*
the wood, in the midst of Carmel: let them
feed *in* Bashan and Gilead, as in the days
of old.
15According to the days of thy coming
out of the land of Egypt will I shew unto
him marvellous *things*.

16The nations shall see and be confounded at all their might: they shall lay
their hand upon *their* mouth, their ears
shall be deaf.
17They shall lick
the dust like a ser-
pent, they shall
move out of their
holes like worms of
the earth: they shall
be afraid of the
LORD our God, and
shall fear because of
thee.
18Who *is* a God
like unto thee, that
pardoneth iniquity, and passeth by the
transgression of the
remnant of his her-
itage? he retaineth
not his anger for
ever, because he
delighteth *in* mercy.
19He will turn
again, he will have
compassion upon
us; he will subdue
our iniquities; and
thou wilt cast all
their sins into the depths of the sea.
20Thou wilt perform the truth to Jacob,
and the mercy to Abraham, which thou
hast sworn unto our fathers from the days
of old.

7:17 Guilty Fear
◄ Daniel 5:6
Hebrews 10:27 ►

7:18 God's Forgiveness
◄ Ezekiel 36:25
Hebrews 8:12 ►

7:18 God's Mercy
◄ Joel 2:13
Luke 1:50 ►

7:18 Repentance
◄ Joel 2:13
Luke 6:21 ►

Nahum

AUTHOR
Nahum the prophet

MAIN POINT
"The Lord punishes his enemies" (1:2)

DATE WRITTEN
Probably between 663 and 654 B.C.

3 CHAPTERS

❑❑❑

MAIN PEOPLE

The people of Assyria and Judah

SPECIAL FEATURES

- *Has a message for Nineveh (capital city of Assyria) 100 years after Jonah preached there*
- *Was directed to the greatest military power in the world at the time: Assyria*
- *Shows that human power is useless against God*
- *Seventh book of the Minor Prophets*

HOW THE BOOK GOT ITS NAME

The author of the book, Nahum, spoke clearly to the capital city of Assyria.

1

1 The burden of Nineveh. The book of
the vision of Nahum the Elkoshite.
2 God *is* jealous, and the LORD revengeth;
the LORD revengeth, and *is* furious; the
LORD will take vengeance on his adversaries, and he reserveth *wrath* for his enemies.
3 The LORD *is* slow to anger, and great in
power, and will not
at all acquit *the*
wicked: the LORD
hath his way in the
whirlwind and in
the storm, and the
clouds *are* the dust of his feet.

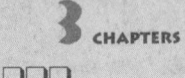

1:3 God's Power
◄ Psalm 93:4
Romans 16:25 ►

4 He rebuketh the sea, and maketh it dry,
and drieth up all the rivers: Bashan languisheth, and Carmel, and the flower of
Lebanon languisheth.
5 The mountains quake at him, and the
hills melt, and the earth is burned at his
presence, yea, the world, and all that dwell
therein.
6 Who can stand before his indignation?
and who can abide in the fierceness of his
anger? his fury is poured out like fire, and
the rocks are thrown down by him.
7 The LORD *is* good, a strong hold in the
day of trouble; and he knoweth them that
trust in him.
8 But with an overrunning flood he will
make an utter end of the place thereof, and
darkness shall pursue his enemies.
9 What do ye imagine against the LORD?
he will make an utter end: affliction shall
not rise up the second time.
10 For while *they*
be folden together
as thorns, and while
they are drunken
as drunkards, they
shall be devoured
as stubble fully dry.

1:10 Getting Drunk
◄ Isaiah 28:1
Habakkuk 2:15 ►

11 There is *one* come out of thee, that
imagineth evil against the LORD, a wicked
counsellor.
12 Thus saith the LORD: Though *they be*

quiet, and likewise many, yet thus shall they be cut down, when he shall pass through. Though I have afflicted thee, I will afflict thee no more.

13 For now will I break his yoke from off thee, and will burst thy bonds in sunder.

14 And the LORD hath given a commandment concerning thee, *that* no more of thy name be sown: out of the house of thy gods will I cut off the graven image and the molten image: I will make thy grave; for thou art vile.

15 Behold upon the mountains the feet of him that bringeth good tidings, that publisheth peace! O Judah, keep thy solemn feasts, perform thy vows: for the wicked shall no more pass through thee; he is utterly cut off.

2

1 He that dasheth in pieces is come up before thy face: keep the munition, watch the way, make *thy* loins strong, fortify *thy* power mightily.

2 For the LORD hath turned away the excellency of Jacob, as the excellency of Israel: for the emptiers have emptied them out, and marred their vine branches.

3 The shield of his mighty men is made red, the valiant men *are* in scarlet: the chariots *shall be* with flaming torches in the day of his preparation, and the fir trees shall be terribly shaken.

4 The chariots shall rage in the streets, they shall justle one against another in the broad ways: they shall seem like torches, they shall run like the lightnings.

5 He shall recount his worthies: they shall stumble in their walk; they shall make haste to the wall thereof, and the defence shall be prepared.

6 The gates of the rivers shall be opened, and the palace shall be dissolved.

7 And Huzzab shall be led away captive, she shall be brought up, and her maids shall lead *her* as with the voice of doves, tabering upon their breasts.

8 But Nineveh *is* of old like a pool of water: yet they shall flee away. Stand, stand, *shall they cry;* but none shall look back.

9 Take ye the spoil of silver, take the spoil of gold: for *there is* none end of the store *and* glory out of all the pleasant furniture.

10 She is empty, and void, and waste: and the heart melteth, and the knees smite together, and much pain *is* in all loins, and the faces of them all gather blackness.

11 Where *is* the dwelling of the lions, and the feeding place of the young lions, where the lion, *even* the old lion, walked, *and* the lion's whelp, and none made *them* afraid?

12 The lion did tear in pieces enough for his whelps, and strangled for his lionesses, and filled his holes with prey, and his dens with ravin.

13 Behold, I *am* against thee, saith the LORD of hosts, and I will burn her chariots in the smoke, and the sword shall devour thy young lions: and I will cut off thy prey from the earth, and the voice of thy messengers shall no more be heard.

3

1 Woe to the bloody city! it is all full of lies *and* robbery; the prey departeth not;

2 The noise of a whip, and the noise of the rattling of the wheels, and of the pransing horses, and of the jumping chariots.

3 The horseman lifteth up both the bright sword and the glittering spear: and *there is* a multitude of slain, and a great number of carcases; and *there is* none end of *their* corpses; they stumble upon their corpses:

4 Because of the multitude of the whoredoms of the wellfavoured harlot, the mistress of witchcrafts, that selleth nations through her whoredoms, and families through her witchcrafts.

5 Behold, I *am* against thee, saith the LORD of hosts; and I will discover thy skirts upon thy face, and I will shew the nations thy nakedness, and the kingdoms thy shame.

6 And I will cast abominable filth upon thee, and make thee vile, and will set thee as a gazingstock.

7 And it shall come to pass, *that* all they that look upon thee shall flee from thee, and say, Nineveh is laid waste: who will bemoan her? whence shall I seek comforters for thee?

8 Art thou better than populous No, that was situate among the rivers, *that had* the waters round about it, whose rampart *was* the sea, *and* her wall *was* from the sea?

9 Ethiopia and Egypt *were* her strength, and *it was* infinite; Put and Lubim were thy helpers.

10 Yet *was* she carried away, she went into captivity: her young children also were dashed in pieces at the top of all the streets: and they cast lots for her honourable men,

and all her great men were bound in chains.

11 Thou also shalt be drunken: thou shalt be hid, thou also shalt seek strength because of the enemy.

12 All thy strong holds *shall be like* fig trees with the firstripe figs: if they be shaken, they shall even fall into the mouth of the eater.

13 Behold, thy people in the midst of thee *are* women: the gates of thy land shall be set wide open unto thine enemies: the fire shall devour thy bars.

14 Draw thee waters for the siege, fortify thy strong holds: go into clay, and tread the morter, make strong the brickkiln.

15 There shall the fire devour thee; the sword shall cut thee off, it shall eat thee up like the cankerworm: make thyself many as the cankerworm, make thyself many as the locusts.

16 Thou hast multiplied thy merchants above the stars of heaven: the cankerworm spoileth, and fleeth away.

17 Thy crowned *are* as the locusts, and thy captains as the great grasshoppers, which camp in the hedges in the cold day, *but* when the sun ariseth they flee away, and their place is not known where they *are.*

18 Thy shepherds slumber, O king of Assyria: thy nobles shall dwell *in the dust:* thy people is scattered upon the mountains, and no man gathereth *them.*

19 *There is* no healing of thy bruise; thy wound is grievous: all that hear the bruit of thee shall clap the hands over thee: for upon whom hath not thy wickedness passed continually?

Habakkuk

AUTHOR
Habakkuk the prophet

MAIN POINT
Sometimes it looks as if evil is winning, but God is still in control of the world.

DATE WRITTEN
Between 612 and 589 B.C.

3 CHAPTERS

❑❑❑

MAIN PEOPLE

Habakkuk, the Chaldeans (also known as Babylonians)

SPECIAL FEATURES

- *Expresses Habakkuk's honest questions to God*
- *Is presented as a series of questions and answers*
- *Includes the powerful words: "I am in my holy temple. Let the whole earth be silent in front of me" (2:20).*
- *Eighth book of the Minor Prophets*

HOW THE BOOK GOT ITS NAME

The author, Habakkuk, presented God's message to Judah and God's people everywhere.

1 1The burden which Habakkuk the
prophet did see.
2O LORD, how
long shall I cry, and
thou wilt not hear!
even cry out unto
thee *of* violence,
and thou wilt not
save!

1:2 Injustice
◄ Ezekiel 18:25
Matthew 20:12 ►

3Why dost thou shew me iniquity, and
cause *me* to behold grievance? for spoiling and violence *are* before me: and there
are *that* raise up strife and contention.
4Therefore the law is slacked, and judgment doth never go forth: for the wicked
doth compass about the righteous; therefore wrong judgment proceedeth.
5Behold ye among the heathen, and regard, and wonder marvellously: for *I* will
work a work in your days, *which* ye will
not believe, though it be told *you*.
6For, lo, I raise up the Chaldeans, *that*
bitter and hasty nation, which shall march
through the breadth of the land, to possess the dwellingplaces *that are* not theirs.
7They *are* terrible and dreadful: their
judgment and their dignity shall proceed
of themselves.
8Their horses also are swifter than the
leopards, and are more fierce than the evening wolves: and their horsemen shall
spread themselves, and their horsemen
shall come from far; they shall fly as the
eagle *that* hasteth to eat.
9They shall come all for violence: their
faces shall sup up *as* the east wind, and
they shall gather the captivity as the sand.
10And they shall scoff at the kings, and
the princes shall be a scorn unto them: they
shall deride every strong hold; for they
shall heap dust, and take it.
11Then shall *his* mind change, and he
shall pass over, and offend, *imputing* this
his power unto his god.

12*Art* thou not from everlasting, O LORD
my God, mine Holy One? We shall not die.
O LORD, thou hast ordained them for judgment; and, O mighty God, thou hast established them for correction.
13*Thou art* of purer eyes than to behold
evil, and canst not look on iniquity: wherefore lookest thou upon them that deal
treacherously, *and* holdest thy tongue
when the wicked devoureth *the man that is*
more righteous than he?
14And makest men as the fishes of the
sea, as the creeping things, *that have* no
ruler over them?
15They take up all of them with the angle, they catch them in their net, and gather them in their drag: therefore they rejoice
and are glad.
16Therefore they sacrifice unto their net,
and burn incense unto their drag; because
by them their portion *is* fat, and their meat
plenteous.
17Shall they therefore empty their net,
and not spare continually to slay the nations?

2

1I will stand upon my watch, and set me
upon the tower, and will watch to see what
he will say unto me, and what I shall answer when I am reproved.
2And the LORD answered me, and said,
Write the vision,
and make *it* plain
upon tables, that
he may run that
readeth it.
3For the vision *is*
yet for an appoint-
ed time, but at the
end it shall speak,
and not lie: though
it tarry, wait for it;
because it will sure-
ly come, it will not
tarry.
4Behold, his soul
which is lifted up is
not upright in him:
but the just shall
live by his faith.
5Yea also, be-
cause he transgres-
seth by wine, *he is* a
proud man, neither
keepeth at home,
who enlargeth his
desire as hell, and *is* as death, and cannot
be satisfied, but gathereth unto him all
nations, and heapeth unto him all people:
6Shall not all these take up a parable
against him, and a taunting proverb against
him, and say, Woe to him that increaseth
that which is not his! how long? and to him
that ladeth himself with thick clay!
7Shall they not rise up suddenly that
shall bite thee, and awake that shall vex
thee, and thou shalt be for booties unto
them?
8Because thou hast spoiled many nations, all the remnant of the people shall
spoil thee; because of men's blood, and
for the violence of the land, of the city, and
of all that dwell therein.
9Woe to him that
coveteth an evil
covetousness to his
house, that he may
set his nest on high,
that he may be de-
livered from the power of evil!
10Thou hast consulted shame to thy
house by cutting off many people, and hast
sinned *against* thy soul.
11For the stone shall cry out of the wall,
and the beam out of the timber shall answer it.
12Woe to him that buildeth a town with
blood, and stablisheth a city by iniquity!
13Behold, *is it* not of the LORD of hosts
that the people shall labour in the very fire,
and the people shall weary themselves for
very vanity?
14For the earth shall be filled with the
knowledge of the glory of the LORD, as the
waters cover the sea.
15Woe unto him
that giveth his
neighbour drink,
that puttest thy
bottle to *him*, and
makest *him* drunk-
en also, that thou mayest look on their nakedness!
16Thou art filled with shame for glory:
drink thou also, and let thy foreskin be
uncovered: the cup of the LORD's right
hand shall be turned unto thee, and
shameful spewing *shall be* on thy glory.
17For the violence of Lebanon shall cover thee, and the spoil of beasts, *which* made
them afraid, because of men's blood, and

2:4 Arrogance
◄ Hosea 7:10
1 John 2:16 ►

2:4 Justification by Faith
◄ Romans 4:3 ►

2:5 Ambition
◄ Isaiah 22:16
Matthew 20:21 ►

2:5 Drinking Too Much
◄ Hosea 4:11
Ephesians 5:18 ►

2:9-10 Greed
◄ Ecclesiastes 5:10
Matthew 27:5 ►

2:15 Getting Drunk
◄ Nahum 1:10
Luke 21:34 ►

for the violence of the land, of the city, and of all that dwell therein.

18 What profiteth the graven image that the maker thereof hath graven it; the molten image, and a teacher of lies, that the maker of his work trusteth therein, to make dumb idols?

19 Woe unto him that saith to the wood, Awake; to the dumb stone, Arise, it shall teach! Behold, it *is* laid over with gold and silver, and *there is* no breath at all in the midst of it.

20 But the LORD *is* in his holy temple: let all the earth keep silence before him.

2:20 Being Quiet
◄ Amos 5:13
Zephaniah 1:7 ►

2:20 Respecting God
◄ Psalm 111:9 ►

3

1 A prayer of Habakkuk the prophet upon Shigionoth.

2 O LORD, I have heard thy speech, *and* was afraid: O LORD, revive thy work in the midst of the years, in the midst of the years make known; in wrath remember mercy.

3:2 Praying for Mercy
◄ Daniel 9:16
Luke 18:13 ►

3 God came from Teman, and the Holy One from mount Paran. Selah. His glory covered the heavens, and the earth was full of his praise.

4 And *his* brightness was as the light; he had horns *coming* out of his hand: and there *was* the hiding of his power.

5 Before him went the pestilence, and burning coals went forth at his feet.

6 He stood, and measured the earth: he beheld, and drove asunder the nations; and the everlasting mountains were scattered, the perpetual hills did bow: his ways *are* everlasting.

3:6 All-powerful
◄ Isaiah 43:13
Matthew 19:26 ►

3:6 God's Ways
◄ Hosea 14:9
Romans 11:33 ►

7 I saw the tents of Cushan in affliction: *and* the curtains of the land of Midian did tremble.

8 Was the LORD displeased against the rivers? *was* thine anger against the rivers? *was* thy wrath against the sea, that thou didst ride upon thine horses *and* thy chariots of salvation?

9 Thy bow was made quite naked, *according* to the oaths of the tribes, *even thy* word. Selah. Thou didst cleave the earth with rivers.

10 The mountains saw thee, *and* they trembled: the overflowing of the water passed by: the deep uttered his voice, *and* lifted up his hands on high.

11 The sun *and* moon stood still in their habitation: at the light of thine arrows they went, *and* at the shining of thy glittering spear.

12 Thou didst march through the land in indignation, thou didst thresh the heathen in anger.

13 Thou wentest forth for the salvation of thy people, *even* for salvation with thine anointed; thou woundedst the head out of the house of the wicked, by discovering the foundation unto the neck. Selah.

14 Thou didst strike through with his staves the head of his villages: they came out as a whirlwind to scatter me: their rejoicing *was* as to devour the poor secretly.

15 Thou didst walk through the sea with thine horses, *through* the heap of great waters.

16 When I heard, my belly trembled; my lips quivered at the voice: rottenness entered into my bones, and I trembled in myself, that I might rest in the day of trouble: when he cometh up unto the people, he will invade them with his troops.

17 Although the fig tree shall not blossom, neither *shall* fruit *be* in the vines; the labour of the olive shall fail, and the fields shall yield no meat; the flock shall be cut off from the fold, and *there shall be* no herd in the stalls:

3:17-18 Positive Attitude
◄ Acts 5:41 ►

18 Yet I will rejoice in the LORD, I will joy in the God of my salvation.

19 The LORD God *is* my strength, and he will make my feet like hinds' *feet*, and he will make me to walk upon mine high places. To the chief singer on my stringed instruments.

3:19 Good Rewarded
◄ Daniel 12:3
Matthew 19:28 ►

Zephaniah

AUTHOR
Zephaniah the prophet

MAIN POINT
Wake up! Get serious about God and show your love for him!

DATE WRITTEN
Probably between 640 and 621 B.C.

3 CHAPTERS

MAIN PEOPLE

The people of Judah

SPECIAL FEATURES

- *Tells about different days to come, both good and bad*
- *Includes a reference to the Fish Gate*
- *Is set against the background of King Josiah's good efforts toward reform*
- *Ninth book of the Minor Prophets*

HOW THE BOOK GOT ITS NAME

The author, Zephaniah, brings hope as well as challenge to the people of Judah.

1
1The word of the LORD which came unto
Zephaniah the son of Cushi, the son of Gedaliah, the son of Amariah, the son of Hiz-
kiah, in the days of Josiah the son of Amon,
king of Judah.
2I will utterly consume all *things* from
off the land, saith the LORD.
3I will consume man and beast; I will
consume the fowls of the heaven, and the
fishes of the sea, and the stumblingblocks
with the wicked; and I will cut off man
from off the land, saith the LORD.
4I will also
stretch out mine
hand upon Judah,
and upon all the
inhabitants of Jeru-
salem; and I will cut
off the remnant of Baal from this place,
and the name of the Chemarims with the
priests;

1:4-5 Double Life
◄ 1 Chronicles 12:33
Luke 16:13 ►

5And them that worship the host of
heaven upon the housetops; and them that
worship *and* that swear by the LORD, and
that swear by Malcham;
6And them that
are turned back
from the LORD; and
those that have not
sought the LORD,
nor enquired for
him.

1:6 Not Praying
◄ Hosea 7:7
James 4:2 ►

7Hold thy peace
at the presence of
the Lord GOD: for
the day of the LORD
is at hand: for the
LORD hath prepared a sacrifice, he hath bid
his guests.

1:7 Being Quiet
◄ Habakkuk 2:20
Zechariah 2:13 ►

8And it shall come to pass in the day of
the LORD'S sacrifice, that I will punish the
princes, and the king's children, and all
such as are clothed with strange apparel.
9In the same day also will I punish all

those that leap on the threshold, which
fill their masters' houses with violence and
deceit.
10 And it shall come to pass in that day,
saith the LORD, *that there shall be* the noise
of a cry from the fish gate, and an howling
from the second, and a great crashing from
the hills.
11 Howl, ye inhabitants of Maktesh, for
all the merchant people are cut down; all
they that bear silver are cut off.
12 And it shall
come to pass at that
time, *that* I will
search Jerusalem
with candles, and
punish the men
that are settled on their lees: that say in
their heart, The LORD will not do good,
neither will he do evil.

1:12 Apathy
◄ Amos 6:1
Matthew 22:5 ►

13 Therefore their
goods shall become
a booty, and their
houses a desola-
tion: they shall
also build houses,
but not inhabit *them;* and they shall
plant vineyards, but not drink the wine
thereof.

1:13 Disappointment
◄ Micah 6:15 ►

14 The great day of the LORD *is* near, *it is*
near, and hasteth greatly, *even* the voice of
the day of the LORD: the mighty man shall
cry there bitterly.
15 That day *is* a day of wrath, a day of
trouble and distress, a day of wasteness and
desolation, a day of darkness and gloominess, a day of clouds and thick darkness,
16 A day of the trumpet and alarm
against the fenced cities, and against the
high towers.
17 And I will bring distress upon men,
that they shall walk like blind men, because they have sinned against the LORD:
and their blood shall be poured out as
dust, and their flesh as the dung.
18 Neither their
silver nor their gold
shall be able to de-
liver them in the
day of the LORD'S
wrath; but the
whole land shall be devoured by the fire
of his jealousy: for he shall make even a
speedy riddance of all them that dwell in
the land.

1:18 Money's Limits
◄ Ecclesiastes 6:2
Revelation 18:17 ►

2

1 Gather yourselves together, yea, gather
together, O nation not desired;
2 Before the decree bring forth, *before* the
day pass as the chaff, before the fierce anger of the LORD come upon you, before
the day of the LORD'S anger come upon
you.
3 Seek ye the
LORD, all ye meek
of the earth, which
have wrought his
judgment; seek
righteousness, seek
meekness: it may be ye shall be hid in the
day of the LORD'S anger.

2:3 Seeking God
◄ Amos 5:4
Matthew 6:33 ►

4 For Gaza shall be forsaken, and Ashkelon a desolation: they shall drive out Ashdod at the noonday, and Ekron shall be
rooted up.
5 Woe unto the inhabitants of the sea
coast, the nation of the Cherethites! the
word of the LORD *is* against you; O Canaan,
the land of the Philistines, I will even destroy thee, that there shall be no inhabitant.
6 And the sea coast shall be dwellings
and cottages for shepherds, and folds for
flocks.
7 And the coast shall be for the remnant
of the house of Judah; they shall feed thereupon: in the houses of Ashkelon shall they
lie down in the evening: for the LORD their
God shall visit them, and turn away their
captivity.
8 I have heard the reproach of Moab, and
the revilings of the children of Ammon,
whereby they have reproached my people,
and magnified *themselves* against their
border.
9 Therefore *as* I live, saith the LORD of
hosts, the God of Israel, Surely Moab shall
be as Sodom, and the children of Ammon
as Gomorrah, *even* the breeding of nettles,
and saltpits, and a perpetual desolation:
the residue of my people shall spoil them,
and the remnant of my people shall possess them.
10 This shall they have for their pride,
because they have reproached and magnified *themselves* against the people of the
LORD of hosts.
11 The LORD *will be* terrible unto them:
for he will famish all the gods of the earth;
and *men* shall worship him, every one from
his place, *even* all the isles of the heathen.

12Ye Ethiopians also, ye *shall be* slain by my sword.

13And he will stretch out his hand against the north, and destroy Assyria; and will make Nineveh a desolation, *and* dry like a wilderness.

14And flocks shall lie down in the midst of her, all the beasts of the nations: both the cormorant and the bittern shall lodge in the upper lintels of it; *their* voice shall sing in the windows; desolation *shall be* in the thresholds: for he shall uncover the cedar work.

15This *is* the rejoicing city that dwelt carelessly, that said in her heart, I *am,* and *there is* none beside me: how is she become a desolation, a place for beasts to lie down in! every one that passeth by her shall hiss, *and* wag his hand.

3

1Woe to her that is filthy and polluted, to the oppressing city!

2She obeyed not the voice; she received not correction; she trusted not in the LORD; she drew not near to her God.

3Her princes within her *are* roaring lions; her judges *are* evening wolves; they gnaw not the bones till the morrow.

4Her prophets *are* light *and* treacherous persons: her priests have polluted the sanctuary, they have done violence to the law.

5The just LORD *is* in the midst thereof; he will not do iniquity: every morning doth he bring his judgment to light, he faileth not; but the unjust knoweth no shame.

3:5 God's Justice
◄ Isaiah 45:21
John 5:30 ►

6I have cut off the nations: their towers are desolate; I made their streets waste, that none passeth by: their cities are destroyed, so that there is no man, that there is none inhabitant.

7I said, Surely thou wilt fear me, thou wilt receive instruction; so their dwelling should not be cut off, howsoever I punished them: but they rose early, *and* corrupted all their doings.

3:7 Refusing Correction
◄ Amos 4:9
Hebrews 12:5 ►

8Therefore wait ye upon me, saith the LORD, until the day that I rise up to the prey: for my determination *is* to gather the nations, that I may assemble the kingdoms, to pour upon them mine indignation, *even* all my fierce anger: for all the earth shall be devoured with the fire of my jealousy.

9For then will I turn to the people a pure language, that they may all call upon the name of the LORD, to serve him with one consent.

10From beyond the rivers of Ethiopia my suppliants, *even* the daughter of my dispersed, shall bring mine offering.

11In that day shalt thou not be ashamed for all thy doings, wherein thou hast transgressed against me: for then I will take away out of the midst of thee them that rejoice in thy pride, and thou shalt no more be haughty because of my holy mountain.

12I will also leave in the midst of thee an afflicted and poor people, and they shall trust in the name of the LORD.

13The remnant of Israel shall not do iniquity, nor speak lies; neither shall a deceitful tongue be found in their mouth: for they shall feed and lie down, and none shall make *them* afraid.

3:13 Honesty
◄ Proverbs 12:19
Zechariah 8:16 ►

14Sing, O daughter of Zion; shout, O Israel; be glad and rejoice with all the heart, O daughter of Jerusalem.

3:14 Rejoicing
◄ Psalm 32:11
Zechariah 9:9 ►

15The LORD hath taken away thy judgments, he hath cast out thine enemy: the king of Israel, *even* the LORD, *is* in the midst of thee: thou shalt not see evil any more.

16In that day it shall be said to Jerusalem, Fear thou not: *and to* Zion, Let not thine hands be slack.

17The LORD thy God in the midst of thee *is* mighty; he will save, he will rejoice over thee with joy; he will rest in his love, he will joy over thee with singing.

18I will gather *them that are* sorrowful for the solemn assembly, *who* are of thee, *to whom* the reproach of it *was* a burden.

19Behold, at that time I will undo all that afflict thee: and I will save her that halteth, and gather her that was driven out; and I will get them praise and fame in every land where they have been put to shame.

20At that time will I bring you *again*,
even in the time that I gather you: for I
will make you a name and a praise among
all people of the earth, when I turn back
your captivity before your eyes, saith the
Lord.

Haggai

AUTHOR
Haggai the prophet

MAIN POINT
God wants his people to rebuild the temple in Jerusalem because he is worthy of worship.

DATE WRITTEN
520 B.C.

2 CHAPTERS

❑❑

MAIN PEOPLE

Haggai, Zerubbabel, Joshua the high priest

SPECIAL FEATURES

- *Packs a lot of challenge and promise into two short chapters*
- *Shows how important the temple was to God*
- *Explains why it is so important to give*
- *Tenth book of the Minor Prophets*

HOW THE BOOK GOT ITS NAME

The author, Haggai, had a clear message for God's people in Jerusalem and those in exile from the city.

1
1 In the second year of Darius the king,
in the sixth month, in the first day of the
month, came the word of the LORD by
Haggai the prophet unto Zerubbabel the
son of Shealtiel, governor of Judah, and
to Joshua the son of Josedech, the high
priest, saying,
2 Thus speaketh the LORD of hosts, saying, This people say, The time is not come,
the time that the LORD'S house should be
built.
3 Then came the word of the LORD by
Haggai the prophet, saying,
4 *Is it* time for you, O ye, to dwell in your
cieled houses, and this house *lie* waste?
5 Now therefore thus saith the LORD of
hosts; Consider your ways.
6 Ye have sown much, and bring in little; ye eat, but ye have not enough; ye
drink, but ye are not filled with drink; ye
clothe you, but there is none warm; and
he that earneth wages earneth wages *to put
it* into a bag with holes.
7 Thus saith the LORD of hosts; Consider
your ways.
8 Go up to the mountain, and bring
wood, and build the house; and I will take
pleasure in it, and I will be glorified, saith
the LORD.
9 Ye looked for much, and, lo, *it came* to
little; and when ye brought *it* home, I did
blow upon it. Why? saith the LORD of
hosts. Because of mine house that *is* waste,
and ye run every man unto his own house.
10 Therefore the heaven over you is stayed
from dew, and the earth is stayed *from* her
fruit.
11 And I called for a drought upon the
land, and upon the mountains, and upon
the corn, and upon the new wine, and
upon the oil, and upon *that* which the
ground bringeth forth, and upon men, and
upon cattle, and upon all the labour of the
hands.
12 Then Zerubbabel the son of Shealtiel,
and Joshua the son of Josedech, the high

priest, with all the remnant of the people, obeyed the voice of the LORD their God, and the words of Haggai the prophet, as the LORD their God had sent him, and the people did fear before the LORD.

13 Then spake Haggai the LORD'S messenger in the LORD'S message unto the people, saying, I *am* with you, saith the LORD.

14 And the LORD stirred up the spirit of Zerubbabel the son of Shealtiel, governor of Judah, and the spirit of Joshua the son of Josedech, the high priest, and the spirit of all the remnant of the people; and they came and did work in the house of the LORD of hosts, their God,

15 In the four and twentieth day of the sixth month, in the second year of Darius the king.

2

1 In the seventh *month,* in the one and twentieth *day* of the month, came the word of the LORD by the prophet Haggai, saying,

2 Speak now to Zerubbabel the son of Shealtiel, governor of Judah, and to Joshua the son of Josedech, the high priest, and to the residue of the people, saying,

3 Who *is* left among you that saw this house in her first glory? and how do ye see it now? *is it* not in your eyes in comparison of it as nothing?

4 Yet now be strong, O Zerubbabel, saith the LORD; and be strong, O Joshua, son of Josedech, the high priest; and be strong, all ye people of the land, saith the LORD, and work: for *I am* with you, saith the LORD of hosts:

5 *According to* the word that I covenanted with you when ye came out of Egypt, so my spirit remaineth among you: fear ye not.

6 For thus saith the LORD of hosts; Yet once, it *is* a little while, and I will shake the heavens, and the earth, and the sea, and the dry *land;*

7 And I will shake all nations, and the desire of all nations shall come: and I will fill this house with glory, saith the LORD of hosts.

8 The silver *is* mine, and the gold *is* mine, saith the LORD of hosts.

2:8
Earth
◄ Psalm 89:11 ►

9 The glory of this latter house shall be greater than of the former, saith the LORD of hosts: and in this place will I give peace, saith the LORD of hosts.

10 In the four and twentieth *day* of the ninth *month,* in the second year of Darius, came the word of the LORD by Haggai the prophet, saying,

11 Thus saith the LORD of hosts; Ask now the priests *concerning* the law, saying,

12 If one bear holy flesh in the skirt of his garment, and with his skirt do touch bread, or pottage, or wine, or oil, or any meat, shall it be holy? And the priests answered and said, No.

13 Then said Haggai, If *one that is* unclean by a dead body touch any of these, shall it be unclean? And the priests answered and said, It shall be unclean.

14 Then answered Haggai, and said, So *is* this people, and so *is* this nation before me, saith the LORD; and so *is* every work of their hands; and that which they offer there *is* unclean.

15 And now, I pray you, consider from this day and upward, from before a stone was laid upon a stone in the temple of the LORD:

16 Since those *days* were, when *one* came to an heap of twenty *measures,* there were *but* ten: when *one* came to the pressfat for to draw out fifty *vessels* out of the press, there were *but* twenty.

17 I smote you with blasting and with mildew and with hail in all the labours of your hands; yet ye *turned* not to me, saith the LORD.

2:17 Hard-hearted
◄ Amos 4:6
Matthew 11:20 ►

18 Consider now from this day and upward, from the four and twentieth day of the ninth *month, even* from the day that the foundation of the LORD'S temple was laid, consider *it.*

19 Is the seed yet in the barn? yea, as yet the vine, and the fig tree, and the pomegranate, and the olive tree, hath not brought forth: from this day will I bless *you.*

20 And again the word of the LORD came unto Haggai in the four and twentieth *day* of the month, saying,

21 Speak to Zerubbabel, governor of Judah, saying, I will shake the heavens and the earth;

22 And I will overthrow the throne of kingdoms, and I will destroy the strength

of the kingdoms of the heathen; and I will overthrow the chariots, and those that ride in them; and the horses and their riders shall come down, every one by the sword of his brother.

23In that day, saith the LORD of hosts,
will I take thee, O Zerubbabel, my servant, the son of Shealtiel, saith the LORD, and will make thee as a signet: for I have chosen thee, saith the LORD of hosts.

Zechariah

AUTHOR
Zechariah the prophet

MAIN POINT
God offers hope, for he will save his people through the Messiah who is to come.

DATE WRITTEN
Approximately 520-518 B.C. (chapters 1-8), 480 B.C. (chapters 9-14)

14 CHAPTERS

MAIN PEOPLE

Zerubbabel, Joshua the high priest

SPECIAL FEATURES

- *Describes Zechariah's many unusual visions, including a flying scroll and chariots*
- *Includes the prophet's big push to keep up the work on the temple*
- *Provides a lot of detail about the coming Messiah*
- *Eleventh book of the Minor Prophets*

HOW THE BOOK GOT ITS NAME

Zechariah was a prophet who communicated God's message to those who had returned to Jerusalem from captivity in Babylon.

1

1In the eighth month, in the second year
of Darius, came the word of the LORD unto
Zechariah, the son of Berechiah, the son
of Iddo the prophet, saying,
2The LORD hath been sore displeased
with your fathers.
3Therefore say thou unto them, Thus
saith the LORD of hosts; Turn ye unto me,
saith the LORD of hosts, and I will turn
unto you, saith the LORD of hosts.
4Be ye not as your fathers, unto whom
the former prophets have cried, saying,
Thus saith the LORD of hosts; Turn ye now
from your evil ways, and *from* your evil doings: but they did not hear, nor hearken
unto me, saith the LORD.
5Your fathers, where *are* they? and the
prophets, do they live for ever?
6But my words and my statutes, which I
commanded my servants the prophets, did
they not take hold of your fathers? and
they returned and said, Like as the LORD
of hosts thought to do unto us, according
to our ways, and according to our doings,
so hath he dealt with us.
7Upon the four and twentieth day of the
eleventh month, which *is* the month Sebat,
in the second year of Darius, came the
word of the LORD unto Zechariah, the son
of Berechiah, the son of Iddo the prophet,
saying,
8I saw by night, and behold a man riding

upon a red horse, and he stood among the
myrtle trees that *were* in the bottom; and
behind him *were there* red horses, speckled, and white.
9Then said I, O my lord, what *are* these?
And the angel that talked with me said
unto me, I will shew thee what these *be.*
10And the man that stood among the
myrtle trees answered and said, These *are*
they whom the LORD hath sent to walk to
and fro through the earth.
11And they answered the angel of the
LORD that stood among the myrtle trees,
and said, We have walked to and fro
through the earth, and, behold, all the
earth sitteth still, and is at rest.
12Then the angel of the LORD answered
and said, O LORD of hosts, how long wilt
thou not have mercy on Jerusalem and on
the cities of Judah, against which thou hast
had indignation these threescore and ten
years?
13And the LORD answered the angel that
talked with me *with* good words *and* comfortable words.
14So the angel that communed with me
said unto me, Cry thou, saying, Thus saith
the LORD of hosts; I am jealous for Jerusalem and for Zion with a great jealousy.
15And I am very sore displeased with the
heathen *that are* at ease: for I was but a
little displeased, and they helped forward
the affliction.
16Therefore thus saith the LORD; I am
returned to Jerusalem with mercies: my
house shall be built in it, saith the LORD
of hosts, and a line shall be stretched forth
upon Jerusalem.
17Cry yet, saying, Thus saith the LORD
of hosts; My cities through prosperity shall
yet be spread abroad; and the LORD shall
yet comfort Zion, and shall yet choose Jerusalem.
18Then lifted I up mine eyes, and saw,
and behold four horns.
19And I said unto the angel that talked
with me, What *be* these? And he answered
me, These *are* the horns which have scattered Judah, Israel, and Jerusalem.
20And the LORD shewed me four carpenters.
21Then said I, What come these to do?
And he spake, saying, These *are* the horns
which have scattered Judah, so that no
man did lift up his head: but these are
come to fray them, to cast out the horns
of the Gentiles, which lifted up *their* horn
over the land of Judah to scatter it.

2

1I lifted up mine eyes again, and looked,
and behold a man with a measuring line
in his hand.
2Then said I, Whither goest thou? And
he said unto me, To measure Jerusalem,
to see what *is* the breadth thereof, and what
is the length thereof.
3And, behold, the angel that talked with
me went forth, and another angel went out
to meet him,
4And said unto him, Run, speak to this
young man, saying, Jerusalem shall be inhabited *as* towns without walls for the
multitude of men and cattle therein:
5For I, saith the
LORD, will be unto
her a wall of fire
round about, and
will be the glory in
the midst of her.

2:5 Protection
◄ Psalm 125:2
Luke 21:18 ►

6Ho, ho, *come forth,* and flee from the
land of the north, saith the LORD: for I have
spread you abroad as the four winds of the
heaven, saith the LORD.
7Deliver thyself, O Zion, that dwellest
with the daughter of Babylon.
8For thus saith the LORD of hosts; After
the glory hath he sent me unto the nations
which spoiled you: for he that toucheth
you toucheth the apple of his eye.
9For, behold, I will shake mine hand
upon them, and they shall be a spoil to
their servants: and ye shall know that the
LORD of hosts hath sent me.
10Sing and rejoice, O daughter of Zion:
for, lo, I come, and I will dwell in the midst
of thee, saith the LORD.
11And many nations shall be joined to
the LORD in that day, and shall be my people: and I will dwell in the midst of thee,
and thou shalt know that the LORD of hosts
hath sent me unto thee.
12And the LORD shall inherit Judah his
portion in the holy land, and shall choose
Jerusalem again.
13Be silent, O all flesh, before the LORD:
for he is raised up
out of his holy
habitation.

2:13
Being Quiet
◄ Zephaniah 1:7 ►

3

1And he shewed
me Joshua the high
priest standing be-

fore the angel of the LORD, and Satan
standing at his right hand to resist him.
2And the LORD said unto Satan, The
LORD rebuke thee, O Satan; even the LORD
that hath chosen Jerusalem rebuke thee: *is*
not this a brand plucked out of the fire?
3Now Joshua was clothed with filthy
garments, and stood before the angel.
4And he answered and spake unto those
that stood before him, saying, Take away
the filthy garments from him. And unto
him he said, Behold, I have caused thine
iniquity to pass from thee, and I will clothe
thee with change of raiment.
5And I said, Let them set a fair mitre upon
his head. So they set a fair mitre upon his
head, and clothed him with garments. And
the angel of the LORD stood by.
6And the angel of the LORD protested
unto Joshua, saying,
7Thus saith the LORD of hosts; If thou
wilt walk in my ways, and if thou wilt keep
my charge, then thou shalt also judge my
house, and shalt also keep my courts, and
I will give thee places to walk among these
that stand by.
8Hear now, O Joshua the high priest,
thou, and thy fellows that sit before thee:
for they *are* men wondered at: for, behold,
I will bring forth my servant the BRANCH.
9For behold the stone that I have laid
before Joshua; upon one stone *shall be*
seven eyes: behold, I will engrave the graving thereof, saith the LORD of hosts, and I
will remove the iniquity of that land in
one day.
10In that day, saith the LORD of hosts,
shall ye call every man his neighbour under the vine and under the fig tree.

4

1And the angel that talked with me came
again, and waked me, as a man that is
wakened out of his sleep,
2And said unto me, What seest thou?
And I said, I have looked, and behold a
candlestick all *of* gold, with a bowl upon
the top of it, and his seven lamps thereon,
and seven pipes to the seven lamps, which
are upon the top thereof:
3And two olive trees by it, one upon the
right *side* of the bowl, and the other upon
the left *side* thereof.
4So I answered and spake to the angel
that talked with me, saying, What *are* these,
my lord?
5Then the angel that talked with me answered and said unto me, Knowest thou
not what these be? And I said, No, my lord.
6Then he answered and spake
unto me, saying,
This *is* the word of
the LORD unto Zerubbabel, saying,
Not by might, nor by power, but by my
spirit, saith the LORD of hosts.

4:6 The Holy Spirit
◄ Micah 3:8
Luke 4:14 ►

7Who *art* thou, O great mountain? before Zerubbabel *thou shalt become* a plain:
and he shall bring forth the headstone
thereof with shoutings, *crying*, Grace, grace
unto it.
8Moreover the word of the LORD came
unto me, saying,
9The hands of Zerubbabel have laid the
foundation of this house; his hands shall
also finish it; and thou shalt know that the
LORD of hosts hath sent me unto you.
10For who hath despised the day of
small things? for they shall rejoice, and
shall see the plummet in the hand of Zerubbabel *with* those seven; they *are* the eyes
of the LORD, which run to and fro through
the whole earth.
11Then answered I, and said unto him,
What *are* these two olive trees upon the
right *side* of the candlestick and upon the
left *side* thereof?
12And I answered again, and said unto
him, What *be these* two olive branches
which through the two golden pipes empty the golden *oil* out of themselves?
13And he answered me and said, Knowest thou not what these *be?* And I said, No,
my lord.
14Then said he, These *are* the two anointed ones, that stand by the LORD of the
whole earth.

5

1Then I turned, and lifted up mine eyes,
and looked, and behold a flying roll.
2And he said unto me, What seest thou?
And I answered, I see a flying roll; the
length thereof *is* twenty cubits, and the
breadth thereof ten cubits.
3Then said he
unto me, This *is* the
curse that goeth
forth over the face
of the whole earth:
for every one that
stealeth shall be cut off *as* on this side according to it; and every one that sweareth

5:3 Stealing
◄ Deuteronomy 23:24
Matthew 19:18 ►

shall be cut off *as* on that side according
to it.
4I will bring it
forth, saith the
LORD of hosts, and
it shall enter into
the house of the
thief, and into the
house of him that sweareth falsely by my
name: and it shall remain in the midst of
his house, and shall consume it with the
timber thereof and the stones thereof.

5:4 Perjury
◄ Leviticus 19:12
Malachi 3:5 ►

5Then the angel that talked with me
went forth, and said unto me, Lift up now
thine eyes, and see what *is* this that goeth
forth.
6And I said, What *is* it? And he said, This
is an ephah that goeth forth. He said moreover, This *is* their resemblance through all
the earth.
7And, behold, there was lifted up a talent of lead: and this *is* a woman that sitteth
in the midst of the ephah.
8And he said, This *is* wickedness. And
he cast it into the midst of the ephah; and
he cast the weight of lead upon the mouth
thereof.
9Then lifted I up mine eyes, and looked,
and, behold, there came out two women,
and the wind *was* in their wings; for they
had wings like the wings of a stork: and
they lifted up the ephah between the earth
and the heaven.
10Then said I to the angel that talked
with me, Whither do these bear the
ephah?
11And he said unto me, To build it an
house in the land of Shinar: and it shall
be established, and set there upon her own
base.

6

1And I turned, and lifted up mine eyes,
and looked, and, behold, there came four
chariots out from between two mountains;
and the mountains *were* mountains of
brass.
2In the first chariot *were* red horses; and
in the second chariot black horses;
3And in the third chariot white horses;
and in the fourth chariot grisled and bay
horses.
4Then I answered and said unto the angel that talked with me, What *are* these,
my lord?
5And the angel answered and said unto
me, These *are* the four spirits of the heavens, which go forth from standing before
the Lord of all the earth.
6The black horses which *are* therein go
forth into the north country; and the white
go forth after them; and the grisled go forth
toward the south country.
7And the bay went forth, and sought to
go that they might walk to and fro through
the earth: and he said, Get you hence, walk
to and fro through the earth. So they
walked to and fro through the earth.
8Then cried he upon me, and spake unto
me, saying, Behold, these that go toward
the north country have quieted my spirit
in the north country.
9And the word of the LORD came unto
me, saying,
10Take of *them of* the captivity, *even* of
Heldai, of Tobijah, and of Jedaiah, which
are come from Babylon, and come thou
the same day, and go into the house of
Josiah the son of Zephaniah;
11Then take silver and gold, and make
crowns, and set *them* upon the head of
Joshua the son of Josedech, the high priest;
12And speak unto him, saying, Thus
speaketh the LORD of hosts, saying, Behold
the man whose name *is* The BRANCH; and
he shall grow up out of his place, and he
shall build the temple of the LORD:
13Even he shall build the temple of the
LORD; and he shall bear the glory, and shall
sit and rule upon his throne; and he shall
be a priest upon his throne: and the counsel of peace shall be between them both.
14And the crowns shall be to Helem, and
to Tobijah, and to Jedaiah, and to Hen the
son of Zephaniah, for a memorial in the
temple of the LORD.
15And they *that are* far off shall come
and build in the temple of the LORD, and
ye shall know that the LORD of hosts hath
sent me unto you. And *this* shall come to
pass, if ye will diligently obey the voice of
the LORD your God.

7

1And it came to pass in the fourth year
of king Darius, *that* the word of the LORD
came unto Zechariah in the fourth *day* of
the ninth month, *even* in Chisleu;
2When they had sent unto the house of
God Sherezer and Regem-melech, and
their men, to pray before the LORD,
3*And* to speak unto the priests which
were in the house of the LORD of hosts, and
to the prophets, saying, Should I weep in

the fifth month, separating myself, as I
have done these so many years?
4 Then came the word of the LORD of
hosts unto me, saying,
5 Speak unto all the people of the land,
and to the priests, saying, When ye fasted
and mourned in the fifth and seventh
month, even those seventy years, did ye at
all fast unto me, *even* to me?
6 And when ye did eat, and when ye did
drink, did not ye eat *for yourselves,* and
drink *for yourselves?*
7 *Should ye* not *hear* the words which the
LORD hath cried by the former prophets,
when Jerusalem was inhabited and in
prosperity, and the cities thereof round
about her, when *men* inhabited the south
and the plain?
8 And the word of the LORD came unto
Zechariah, saying,
9 Thus speaketh the LORD of hosts, saying, Execute true judgment, and shew mercy and compassions every man to his
brother:
10 And oppress
not the widow, nor
the fatherless, the
stranger, nor the
poor; and let none
of you imagine evil
against his brother in your heart.

7:10 Stay Away!
◄ Proverbs 14:16
Romans 12:9 ►

11 But they refused to hearken, and
pulled away the shoulder, and stopped
their ears, that they should not hear.
12 Yea, they made their hearts *as* an adamant stone, lest they should hear the law,
and the words which the LORD of hosts
hath sent in his spirit by the former prophets: therefore came a great wrath from the
LORD of hosts.
13 Therefore it is
come to pass, *that*
as he cried, and
they would not
hear; so they cried,
and I would not
hear, saith the LORD of hosts:

7:13 Unanswered Prayer
◄ Micah 3:4
James 1:6-7 ►

14 But I scattered them with a whirlwind
among all the nations whom they knew
not. Thus the land was desolate after them,
that no man passed through nor returned:
for they laid the pleasant land desolate.

8

1 Again the word of the LORD of hosts
came *to me,* saying,
2 Thus saith the LORD of hosts; I was jealous for Zion with great jealousy, and I was
jealous for her with great fury.
3 Thus saith the LORD; I am returned unto
Zion, and will dwell in the midst of Jerusalem: and Jerusalem shall be called a city
of truth; and the mountain of the LORD of
hosts the holy mountain.
4 Thus saith the LORD of hosts; There
shall yet old men and old women dwell
in the streets of Jerusalem, and every man
with his staff in his hand for very age.
5 And the streets of the city shall be full
of boys and girls playing in the streets
thereof.
6 Thus saith the LORD of hosts; If it be
marvellous in the eyes of the remnant of
this people in these days, should it also be
marvellous in mine eyes? saith the LORD
of hosts.
7 Thus saith the LORD of hosts; Behold, I
will save my people from the east country,
and from the west country;
8 And I will bring them, and they shall
dwell in the midst of Jerusalem: and they
shall be my people, and I will be their God,
in truth and in righteousness.
9 Thus saith the LORD of hosts; Let your
hands be strong, ye that hear in these days
these words by the mouth of the prophets, which *were* in the day *that* the foundation of the house of the LORD of hosts was
laid, that the temple might be built.
10 For before these days there was no hire
for man, nor any hire for beast; neither *was
there any* peace to him that went out or
came in because of the affliction: for I set
all men every one against his neighbour.
11 But now I *will* not *be* unto the residue
of this people as in the former days, saith
the LORD of hosts.
12 For the seed *shall be* prosperous; the
vine shall give her fruit, and the ground
shall give her increase, and the heavens
shall give their dew; and I will cause the
remnant of this people to possess all these
things.
13 And it shall come to pass, *that* as ye
were a curse among the heathen, O house
of Judah, and house of Israel; so will I save
you, and ye shall be a blessing: fear not,
but let your hands be strong.
14 For thus saith the LORD of hosts; As I
thought to punish you, when your fathers
provoked me to wrath, saith the LORD of
hosts, and I repented not:

15 So again have I thought in these days
to do well unto Jerusalem and to the house
of Judah: fear ye
not.
16 These *are* the
things that ye shall
do; Speak ye every
man the truth to his
neighbour; execute
the judgment of truth and peace in your
gates:

8:16 Honesty
◄ Zephaniah 3:13
Malachi 2:6 ►

17 And let none of you imagine evil in
your hearts against his neighbour; and love
no false oath: for all these *are things* that I
hate, saith the LORD.
18 And the word of the LORD of hosts
came unto me, saying,
19 Thus saith the LORD of hosts; The fast
of the fourth *month,* and the fast of the
fifth, and the fast of the seventh, and the
fast of the tenth, shall be to the house of
Judah joy and gladness, and cheerful feasts;
therefore love the truth and peace.
20 Thus saith the LORD of hosts; *It shall*
yet *come to pass,* that there shall come people, and the inhabitants of many cities:
21 And the inhab-
itants of one *city*
shall go to another,
saying, Let us go
speedily to pray be-
fore the LORD, and
to seek the LORD of
hosts: I will go also.
22 Yea, many peo-
ple and strong na-
tions shall come to
seek the LORD of
hosts in Jerusalem,
and to pray before
the LORD.
23 Thus saith the
LORD of hosts; In
those days *it shall*
come to pass, that ten
men shall take hold out of all languages
of the nations, even shall take hold of the
skirt of him that is a Jew, saying, We will
go with you: for we have heard *that* God *is*
with you.

8:21
Friends and Church
◄ Jeremiah 31:6 ►

8:21 Hurrying
◄ Psalm 119:60
Matthew 28:7 ►

8:21 Praying
◄ Psalm 119:147
Luke 2:37 ►

9

1 The burden of the word of the LORD in
the land of Hadrach, and Damascus *shall*
be the rest thereof: when the eyes of man,
as of all the tribes of Israel, *shall be* toward
the LORD.
2 And Hamath also shall border thereby;
Tyrus, and Zidon, though it be very wise.
3 And Tyrus did build herself a strong
hold, and heaped up silver as the dust, and
fine gold as the mire of the streets.
4 Behold, the Lord will cast her out, and
he will smite her power in the sea; and she
shall be devoured with fire.
5 Ashkelon shall see *it,* and fear; Gaza also
shall see it, and be very sorrowful, and Ekron; for her expectation shall be ashamed;
and the king shall perish from Gaza, and
Ashkelon shall not be inhabited.
6 And a bastard shall dwell in Ashdod,
and I will cut off the pride of the Philistines.
7 And I will take away his blood out of
his mouth, and his abominations from
between his teeth: but he that remaineth,
even he, *shall be* for our God, and he shall
be as a governor in Judah, and Ekron as a
Jebusite.
8 And I will encamp about mine house
because of the army, because of him that
passeth by, and because of him that
returneth: and no oppressor shall pass
through them any more: for now have I
seen with mine eyes.
9 Rejoice greatly,
O daughter of Zion;
shout, O daughter
of Jerusalem: be-
hold, thy King
cometh unto thee:
he *is* just, and hav-
ing salvation; low-
ly, and riding upon
an ass, and upon a
colt the foal of an
ass.

9:9 Jesus the King
◄ Daniel 7:14
Matthew 2:2 ►

9:9 Rejoicing
◄ Zephaniah 3:14
Luke 10:20 ►

10 And I will cut off the chariot from
Ephraim, and the horse from Jerusalem,
and the battle bow shall be cut off: and he
shall speak peace unto the heathen: and
his dominion *shall be* from sea *even* to sea,
and from river *even* to the ends of the earth.
11 As for thee also, by the blood of thy
covenant I have sent forth thy prisoners
out of the pit wherein *is* no water.
12 Turn you to the strong hold, ye prisoners of hope: even to day do I declare
that I will render double unto thee;
13 When I have bent Judah for me, filled
the bow with Ephraim, and raised up thy
sons, O Zion, against thy sons, O Greece,

and made thee as the sword of a mighty man.

[14]And the LORD shall be seen over them, and his arrow shall go forth as the lightning: and the LORD GOD shall blow the trumpet, and shall go with whirlwinds of the south.

[15]The LORD of hosts shall defend them; and they shall devour, and subdue with sling stones; and they shall drink, *and* make a noise as through wine; and they shall be filled like bowls, *and* as the corners of the altar.

[16]And the LORD their God shall save them in that day as the flock of his people: for they *shall be as* the stones of a crown, lifted up as an ensign upon his land.

[17]For how great *is* his goodness, and how great *is* his beauty! corn shall make the young men cheerful, and new wine the maids.

10

[1]Ask ye of the LORD rain in the time of the latter rain; *so* the LORD shall make bright clouds, and give them showers of rain, to every one grass in the field.

[2]For the idols have spoken vanity, and the diviners have seen a lie, and have told false dreams; they comfort in vain: therefore they went their way as a flock, they were troubled, because *there was* no shepherd.

[3]Mine anger was kindled against the shepherds, and I punished the goats: for the LORD of hosts hath visited his flock the house of Judah, and hath made them as his goodly horse in the battle.

[4]Out of him came forth the corner, out of him the nail, out of him the battle bow, out of him every oppressor together.

[5]And they shall be as mighty *men*, which tread down *their enemies* in the mire of the streets in the battle: and they shall fight, because the LORD *is* with them, and the riders on horses shall be confounded.

[6]And I will strengthen the house of Judah, and I will save the house of Joseph, and I will bring them again to place them; for I have mercy upon them: and they shall be as though I had not cast them off: for I *am* the LORD their God, and will hear them.

[7]And *they of* Ephraim shall be like a mighty *man*, and their heart shall rejoice as through wine: yea, their children shall see *it*, and be glad; their heart shall rejoice in the LORD.

[8]I will hiss for them, and gather them; for I have redeemed them: and they shall increase as they have increased.

[9]And I will sow them among the people: and they shall remember me in far countries; and they shall live with their children, and turn again.

10:9
Remember...
Jonah 2:7

[10]I will bring them again also out of the land of Egypt, and gather them out of Assyria; and I will bring them into the land of Gilead and Lebanon; and *place* shall not be found for them.

[11]And he shall pass through the sea with affliction, and shall smite the waves in the sea, and all the deeps of the river shall dry up: and the pride of Assyria shall be brought down, and the sceptre of Egypt shall depart away.

[12]And I will strengthen them in the LORD; and they shall walk up and down in his name, saith the LORD.

11

[1]Open thy doors, O Lebanon, that the fire may devour thy cedars.

[2]Howl, fir tree; for the cedar is fallen; because the mighty are spoiled: howl, O ye oaks of Bashan; for the forest of the vintage is come down.

[3]*There is* a voice of the howling of the shepherds; for their glory is spoiled: a voice of the roaring of young lions; for the pride of Jordan is spoiled.

[4]Thus saith the LORD my God; Feed the flock of the slaughter;

[5]Whose possessors slay them, and hold themselves not guilty: and they that sell them say, Blessed *be* the LORD; for I am rich: and their own shepherds pity them not.

[6]For I will no more pity the inhabitants of the land, saith the LORD: but, lo, I will deliver the men every one into his neighbour's hand, and into the hand of his king: and they shall smite the land, and out of their hand I will not deliver *them*.

[7]And I will feed the flock of slaughter, *even* you, O poor of the flock. And I took unto me two staves; the one I called Beauty, and the other I called Bands; and I fed the flock.

[8]Three shepherds also I cut off in one

month; and my soul lothed them, and their soul also abhorred me.

9 Then said I, I will not feed you: that that dieth, let it die; and that that is to be cut off, let it be cut off; and let the rest eat every one the flesh of another.

10 And I took my staff, *even* Beauty, and cut it asunder, that I might break my covenant which I had made with all the people.

11 And it was broken in that day: and so the poor of the flock that waited upon me knew that it *was* the word of the LORD.

12 And I said unto them, If ye think good, give *me* my price; and if not, forbear. So they weighed for my price thirty *pieces* of silver.

13 And the LORD said unto me, Cast it unto the potter: a goodly price that I was prised at of them. And I took the thirty *pieces* of silver, and cast them to the potter in the house of the LORD.

14 Then I cut asunder mine other staff, *even* Bands, that I might break the brotherhood between Judah and Israel.

15 And the LORD said unto me, Take unto thee yet the instruments of a foolish shepherd.

16 For, lo, I will raise up a shepherd in the land, *which* shall not visit those that be cut off, neither shall seek the young one, nor heal that that is broken, nor feed that that standeth still: but he shall eat the flesh of the fat, and tear their claws in pieces.

11:16 Mercy
◄ Ezekiel 34:4
Matthew 25:43 ►

17 Woe to the idol shepherd that leaveth the flock! the sword *shall be* upon his arm, and upon his right eye: his arm shall be clean dried up, and his right eye shall be utterly darkened.

12

1 The burden of the word of the LORD for Israel, saith the LORD, which stretcheth forth the heavens, and layeth the foundation of the earth, and formeth the spirit of man within him.

2 Behold, I will make Jerusalem a cup of trembling unto all the people round about, when they shall be in the siege both against Judah *and* against Jerusalem.

3 And in that day will I make Jerusalem a burdensome stone for all people: all that burden themselves with it shall be cut in pieces, though all the people of the earth be gathered together against it.

4 In that day, saith the LORD, I will smite every horse with astonishment, and his rider with madness: and I will open mine eyes upon the house of Judah, and will smite every horse of the people with blindness.

5 And the governors of Judah shall say in their heart, The inhabitants of Jerusalem *shall be* my strength in the LORD of hosts their God.

6 In that day will I make the governors of Judah like an hearth of fire among the wood, and like a torch of fire in a sheaf; and they shall devour all the people round about, on the right hand and on the left: and Jerusalem shall be inhabited again in her own place, *even* in Jerusalem.

7 The LORD also shall save the tents of Judah first, that the glory of the house of David and the glory of the inhabitants of Jerusalem do not magnify *themselves* against Judah.

8 In that day shall the LORD defend the inhabitants of Jerusalem; and he that is feeble among them at that day shall be as David; and the house of David *shall be* as God, as the angel of the LORD before them.

9 And it shall come to pass in that day, *that* I will seek to destroy all the nations that come against Jerusalem.

10 And I will pour upon the house of David, and upon the inhabitants of Jerusalem, the spirit of grace and of supplications: and they shall look upon me whom they have pierced, and they shall mourn for him, as one mourneth for *his* only *son,* and shall be in bitterness for him, as one that is in bitterness for *his* firstborn.

12:10 Feeling Sorry
◄ Joel 2:13
2 Corinthians 7:10 ►

11 In that day shall there be a great mourning in Jerusalem, as the mourning of Hadadrimmon in the valley of Megiddon.

12 And the land shall mourn, every family apart; the family of the house of David apart, and their wives apart; the family of the house of Nathan apart, and their wives apart;

13 The family of the house of Levi apart, and their wives apart; the family of Shimei apart, and their wives apart;

14 All the families that remain, every family apart, and their wives apart.

13

1In that day there shall be a fountain
opened to the house of David and to the
inhabitants of Jerusalem for sin and for
uncleanness.
2And it shall come to pass in that day,
saith the LORD of hosts, *that* I will cut off
the names of the idols out of the land, and
they shall no more be remembered: and
also I will cause the prophets and the unclean spirit to pass out of the land.
3And it shall come to pass, *that* when
any shall yet prophesy, then his father and
his mother that begat him shall say unto
him, Thou shalt not live; for thou speakest
lies in the name of the LORD: and his father and his mother that begat him shall
thrust him through when he prophesieth.
4And it shall come to pass in that day,
that the prophets shall be ashamed every
one of his vision, when he hath prophesied; neither shall they wear a rough garment to deceive:
5But he shall say, I *am* no prophet, I *am*
an husbandman; for man taught me to
keep cattle from my youth.
6And *one* shall say unto him, What *are*
these wounds in thine hands? Then he
shall answer, *Those* with which I was
wounded *in* the house of my friends.
7Awake, O sword, against my shepherd,
and against the man *that is* my fellow, saith
the LORD of hosts: smite the shepherd, and
the sheep shall be scattered: and I will turn
mine hand upon the little ones.
8And it shall come to pass, *that* in all
the land, saith the LORD, two parts therein
shall be cut off *and* die; but the third shall
be left therein.
9And I will bring
the third part
through the fire,
and will refine
them as silver is re-
fined, and will try
them as gold is
tried: they shall call
on my name, and I
will hear them: I
will say, It *is* my
people: and they
shall say, The LORD
is my God.

13:9 Answers to Prayer
◄ Jeremiah 33:3
Luke 11:9 ►

13:9 Life Tests
◄ Daniel 12:10
Malachi 3:3 ►

14

1Behold, the day of the LORD cometh,
and thy spoil shall be divided in the midst
of thee.
2For I will gather all nations against Jerusalem to battle; and the city shall be tak-
en, and the houses rifled, and the women
ravished; and half of the city shall go forth
into captivity, and the residue of the people shall not be cut off from the city.
3Then shall the LORD go forth, and fight
against those nations, as when he fought
in the day of battle.
4And his feet shall stand in that day
upon the mount of Olives, which *is* before Jerusalem on the east, and the mount
of Olives shall cleave in the midst thereof
toward the east and toward the west, *and*
there shall be a very great valley; and half
of the mountain shall remove toward the
north, and half of it toward the south.
5And ye shall flee *to* the valley of the
mountains; for the valley of the mountains
shall reach unto Azal: yea, ye shall flee, like
as ye fled from before the earthquake in
the days of Uzziah king of Judah: and the
LORD my God shall come, *and* all the saints
with thee.
6And it shall come to pass in that day,
that the light shall not be clear, *nor* dark:
7But it shall be one day which shall be
known to the LORD, not day, nor night: but
it shall come to pass, *that* at evening time
it shall be light.
8And it shall be in that day, *that* living
waters shall go out from Jerusalem; half
of them toward the former sea, and half
of them toward the hinder sea: in summer
and in winter shall it be.
9And the LORD shall be king over all the
earth: in that day shall there be one LORD,
and his name one.
10All the land shall be turned as a plain
from Geba to Rimmon south of Jerusalem:
and it shall be lifted up, and inhabited in
her place, from Benjamin's gate unto the
place of the first gate, unto the corner gate,
and *from* the tower of Hananeel unto the
king's winepresses.
11And *men* shall dwell in it, and there
shall be no more utter destruction; but Jerusalem shall be safely inhabited.
12And this shall be the plague wherewith the LORD will smite all the people that
have fought against Jerusalem; Their flesh
shall consume away while they stand upon
their feet, and their eyes shall consume
away in their holes, and their tongue shall
consume away in their mouth.

13 And it shall come to pass in that day, *that* a great tumult from the LORD shall be among them; and they shall lay hold every one on the hand of his neighbour, and his hand shall rise up against the hand of his neighbour.

14 And Judah also shall fight at Jerusalem; and the wealth of all the heathen round about shall be gathered together, gold, and silver, and apparel, in great abundance.

15 And so shall be the plague of the horse, of the mule, of the camel, and of the ass, and of all the beasts that shall be in these tents, as this plague.

16 And it shall come to pass, *that* every one that is left of all the nations which came against Jerusalem shall even go up from year to year to worship the King, the LORD of hosts, and to keep the feast of tabernacles.

17 And it shall be, *that* whoso will not come up of *all* the families of the earth unto Jerusalem to worship the King, the LORD of hosts, even upon them shall be no rain.

14:17 Worship
◄ Psalm 99:5
Matthew 4:10 ►

18 And if the family of Egypt go not up, and come not, that *have* no *rain;* there shall be the plague, wherewith the LORD will smite the heathen that come not up to keep the feast of tabernacles.

19 This shall be the punishment of Egypt, and the punishment of all nations that come not up to keep the feast of tabernacles.

20 In that day shall there be upon the bells of the horses, HOLINESS UNTO THE LORD; and the pots in the LORD'S house shall be like the bowls before the altar.

21 Yea, every pot in Jerusalem and in Judah shall be holiness unto the LORD of hosts: and all they that sacrifice shall come and take of them, and seethe therein: and in that day there shall be no more the Canaanite in the house of the LORD of hosts.

Malachi

AUTHOR
Malachi the prophet

MAIN POINT
God wants his people to face up to their sins and get back to a right relationship with him.

DATE WRITTEN
Approximately 430 B.C.

4 CHAPTERS

MAIN PEOPLE
Malachi, the priests

SPECIAL FEATURES
- *Uses a lot of questions—from God as well as from his people*
- *Does not allow for any excuses from the priests*
- *Applauds the faithful few of Malachi's generation (and ours)*
- *Twelfth book of the Minor Prophets*

HOW THE BOOK GOT ITS NAME
The author of the book, Malachi, was a prophet to the people of Jerusalem.

1 1The burden of the word of the LORD to
Israel by Malachi.
2I have loved you, saith the LORD. Yet ye
say, Wherein hast thou loved us? *Was* not
Esau Jacob's brother? saith the LORD: yet I
loved Jacob,
3And I hated Esau, and laid his mountains and his heritage waste for the dragons of the wilderness.
4Whereas Edom saith, We are impoverished, but we will return and build the desolate places; thus saith the LORD of hosts, They shall build, but I will throw down; and they shall call them, The border of wickedness, and, The people against whom the LORD hath indignation for ever.
5And your eyes shall see, and ye shall say, The LORD will be magnified from the border of Israel.
6A son honoureth *his* father, and a ser-
vant his master: if then I *be* a father, where
is mine honour? and if I *be* a master, where *is* my fear? saith the LORD of hosts unto you, O priests, that despise my name. And ye say, Wherein have we despised thy name?
7Ye offer polluted bread upon mine altar; and ye say, Wherein have we polluted thee? In that ye say, The table of the LORD *is* contemptible.
8And if ye offer the blind for sacrifice, *is it* not evil? and if ye offer the lame and sick, *is it* not evil? offer it now unto thy governor; will he be pleased with thee, or accept thy person? saith the LORD of hosts.
9And now, I pray you, beseech God that he will be gracious unto us: this hath been by your means: will he regard your persons? saith the LORD of hosts.
10Who *is there* even among you that would shut the doors *for nought*? neither do ye kindle *fire* on mine altar for nought.

I have no pleasure in you, saith the LORD
of hosts, neither will I accept an offering
at your hand.
11 For from the rising of the sun even
unto the going down of the same my name
shall be great among the Gentiles; and in
every place incense *shall be* offered unto
my name, and a pure offering: for my name
shall be great among the heathen, saith the
LORD of hosts.
12 But ye have profaned it, in that ye say,
The table of the LORD *is* polluted; and the
fruit thereof, *even* his meat, *is* contemptible.
13 Ye said also, Behold, what a weariness
is it! and ye have snuffed at it, saith the
LORD of hosts; and ye brought *that which
was* torn, and the lame, and the sick; thus
ye brought an offering: should I accept this
of your hand? saith the LORD.
14 But cursed *be* the deceiver, which hath
in his flock a male, and voweth, and
sacrificeth unto the LORD a corrupt thing:
for I *am* a great King, saith the LORD of
hosts, and my name *is* dreadful among the
heathen.

2

1 And now, O ye priests, this commandment *is* for you.
2 If ye will not hear, and if ye will not lay
it to heart, to give glory unto my name,
saith the LORD of hosts, I will even send a
curse upon you, and I will curse your blessings: yea, I have cursed them already, because ye do not lay *it* to heart.
3 Behold, I will corrupt your seed, and
spread dung upon your faces, *even* the
dung of your solemn feasts; and *one* shall
take you away with it.
4 And ye shall know that I have sent this
commandment unto you, that my covenant might be with Levi, saith the LORD
of hosts.
5 My covenant was with him of life and
peace; and I gave
them to him *for* the
fear wherewith he
feared me, and was
afraid before my
name.

2:6 Honesty
◄ Zechariah 8:16
2 Corinthians 12:6 ►

6 The law of truth
was in his mouth,
and iniquity was
not found in his
lips: he walked with
me in peace and

2:6 Walking with God
◄ Micah 4:5
Revelation 3:4 ►

equity, and did turn many away from iniquity.
7 For the priest's lips should keep knowledge, and they should seek the law at his
mouth: for he *is* the messenger of the LORD
of hosts.
8 But ye are departed out of the way; ye
have caused many to stumble at the law;
ye have corrupted the covenant of Levi,
saith the LORD of hosts.
9 Therefore have I
also made you con-
temptible and base
before all the peo-
ple, according as ye
have not kept my
ways, but have been partial in the law.

2:9 Favoritism
◄ Proverbs 24:23
1 Timothy 5:21 ►

10 Have we not all
one father? hath
not one God creat-
ed us? why do we
deal treacherously
every man against
his brother, by profaning the covenant of
our fathers?

2:10 Family
◄ Proverbs 22:2
Mark 3:34 ►

11 Judah hath dealt treacherously, and an
abomination is committed in Israel and
in Jerusalem; for Judah hath profaned the
holiness of the LORD which he loved, and
hath married the daughter of a strange god.
12 The LORD will cut off the man that
doeth this, the master and the scholar, out
of the tabernacles of Jacob, and him that
offereth an offering unto the LORD of hosts.
13 And this have ye done again, covering
the altar of the LORD with tears, with weeping, and with crying out, insomuch that
he regardeth not the offering any more, or
receiveth *it* with good will at your hand.
14 Yet ye say, Wherefore? Because the
LORD hath been witness between thee and
the wife of thy youth, against whom thou
hast dealt treacherously: yet *is* she thy companion, and the wife of thy covenant.
15 And did not he make one? Yet had he
the residue of the spirit. And wherefore
one? That he might seek a godly seed.
Therefore take heed to your spirit, and let
none deal treacherously against the wife
of his youth.
16 For the LORD, the God of Israel, saith
that he hateth putting away: for *one*
covereth violence with his garment, saith
the LORD of hosts: therefore take heed to
your spirit, that ye deal not treacherously.

17 Ye have wearied the LORD with your words. Yet ye say, Wherein have we wearied *him?* When ye say, Every one that doeth evil *is* good in the sight of the LORD, and he delighteth in them; or, Where *is* the God of judgment?

> **2:17 Excusing Sin**
> ◄ Ezekiel 13:22
> Romans 1:32 ►

3

1 Behold, I will send my messenger, and he shall prepare the way before me: and the Lord, whom ye seek, shall suddenly come to his temple, even the messenger of the covenant, whom ye delight in: behold, he shall come, saith the LORD of hosts.

2 But who may abide the day of his coming? and who shall stand when he appeareth? for he *is* like a refiner's fire, and like fullers' sope:

3 And he shall sit *as* a refiner and purifier of silver: and he shall purify the sons of Levi, and purge them as gold and silver, that they may offer unto the LORD an offering in righteousness.

> **3:3 Life Tests**
> ◄ Zechariah 13:9
> Luke 6:48 ►

> **3:3 Pain**
> ◄ Isaiah 48:10
> 1 Peter 1:7 ►

4 Then shall the offering of Judah and Jerusalem be pleasant unto the LORD, as in the days of old, and as in former years.

5 And I will come near to you to judgment; and I will be a swift witness against the sorcerers, and against the adulterers, and against false swearers, and against those that oppress the hireling in *his* wages, the widow, and the fatherless, and that turn aside the stranger *from his right,* and fear not me, saith the LORD of hosts.

> **3:5 Perjury**
> ◄ Zechariah 5:4
> 1 Timothy 1:10 ►

> **3:5 Warning!**
> ◄ Isaiah 66:4 ►

6 For I *am* the LORD, I change not; therefore ye sons of Jacob are not consumed.

7 Even from the days of your fathers ye are gone away from mine ordinances, and have not kept *them.* Return unto me, and I will return unto you, saith the LORD of hosts. But ye said, Wherein shall we return?

> **3:7 Repent!**
> ◄ Joel 2:12
> Matthew 3:2 ►

8 Will a man rob God? Yet ye have robbed me. But ye say, Wherein have we robbed thee? In tithes and offerings.

> **3:8 Being Stingy**
> ◄ Isaiah 43:23
> Matthew 26:7-8 ►

9 Ye *are* cursed with a curse: for ye have robbed me, *even* this whole nation.

10 Bring ye all the tithes into the storehouse, that there may be meat in mine house, and prove me now herewith, saith the LORD of hosts, if I will not open you the windows of heaven, and pour you out a blessing, that *there shall* not *be room* enough *to receive it.*

> **3:10 Blessing**
> ◄ Amos 9:13
> Matthew 6:33 ►

11 And I will rebuke the devourer for your sakes, and he shall not destroy the fruits of your ground; neither shall your vine cast her fruit before the time in the field, saith the LORD of hosts.

12 And all nations shall call you blessed: for ye shall be a delightsome land, saith the LORD of hosts.

13 Your words have been stout against me, saith the LORD. Yet ye say, What have we spoken *so much* against thee?

14 Ye have said, It *is* vain to serve God: and what profit *is it* that we have kept his ordinance, and that we have walked mournfully before the LORD of hosts?

15 And now we call the proud happy; yea, they that work wickedness are set up; yea, *they that* tempt God are even delivered.

> **3:15 Proud People**
> ◄ Psalm 138:6
> Malachi 4:1 ►

16 Then they that feared the LORD spake often one to another: and the LORD hearkened, and heard *it,* and a book of remembrance was written before him for them that feared the LORD, and that thought upon his name.

> **3:16 Why Fear God?**
> ◄ Isaiah 50:10
> Luke 1:50 ►

17 And they shall be mine, saith the LORD

of hosts, in that day when I make up my
jewels; and I will spare them, as a man
spareth his own son that serveth him.
18 Then shall ye return, and discern between the righteous and the wicked, between him that serveth God and him that
serveth him not.

4

1 For, behold, the
day cometh, that
shall burn as an
oven; and all the
proud, yea, and all
that do wickedly,
shall be stubble: and the day that cometh
shall burn them up, saith the LORD of
hosts, that it shall leave them neither root
nor branch.
2 But unto you that fear my name shall
the Sun of righteousness arise with healing in his wings; and ye shall go forth, and
grow up as calves of the stall.
3 And ye shall tread down the wicked;
for they shall be ashes under the soles of
your feet in the day that I shall do *this,* saith
the LORD of hosts.
4 Remember ye the law of Moses my servant, which I commanded unto him in
Horeb for all Israel, *with* the statutes and
judgments.
5 Behold, I will send you Elijah the
prophet before the coming of the great and
dreadful day of the LORD:
6 And he shall turn the heart of the fathers to the children, and the heart of the
children to their fathers, lest I come and
smite the earth with a curse.

4:1 Proud People
◄ Malachi 3:15
1 Timothy 6:4 ►

New Testament

6 Blessed *are* they which do hunger and thirst after righteousness: for they shall be filled.

7 Blessed *are* the merciful: for they shall obtain mercy.

8 Blessed *are* the pure in heart: for they shall see God.

9 Blessed *are* the peacemakers: for they shall be called the children of God.

10 Blessed *are* they which are persecuted for righteousness' sake: for theirs is the kingdom of heaven.

11 Blessed are ye, when *men* shall revile you, and persecute *you,* and shall say all manner of evil against you falsely, for my sake.

12 Rejoice, and be exceeding glad: for great *is* your reward in heaven: for so persecuted they the prophets which were before you.

5:5
Meekness
◄ Isaiah 29:19 ►

5:7 Rewards
◄ Daniel 4:27
Matthew 6:14 ►

5:7 Showing Mercy
◄ Micah 6:8
Luke 6:36 ►

5:9 Peacemaking
◄ Proverbs 12:20
Romans 14:19 ►

5:11-12
Suffering Rewarded
◄ Romans 8:17 ►

13 Ye are the salt of the earth: but if the salt have lost his savour, wherewith shall it be salted? it is thenceforth good for nothing, but to be cast out, and to be trodden under foot of men.

14 Ye are the light of the world. A city that is set on an hill cannot be hid.

15 Neither do men light a candle, and put it under a bushel, but on a candlestick; and it giveth light unto all that are in the house.

16 Let your light so shine before men, that they may see your good works, and glorify your Father which is in heaven.

5:16
Good Works
◄ Colossians 1:10 ►

17 Think not that I am come to destroy the law, or the prophets: I am not come to destroy, but to fulfil.

18 For verily I say unto you, Till heaven and earth pass, one jot or one tittle shall in no wise pass from the law, till all be fulfilled.

19 Whosoever therefore shall break one of these least commandments, and shall teach men so, he shall be called the least in the kingdom of heaven: but whosoever shall do and teach *them,* the same shall be called great in the kingdom of heaven.

20 For I say unto you, That except your righteousness shall exceed *the righteousness* of the scribes and Pharisees, ye shall in no case enter into the kingdom of heaven.

5:20 Righteousness
◄ Hosea 10:12
Acts 24:25 ►

21 Ye have heard that it was said by them of old time, Thou shalt not kill; and whosoever shall kill shall be in danger of the judgment:

22 But I say unto you, That whosoever is angry with his brother without a cause shall be in danger of the judgment: and whosoever shall say to his brother, Raca, shall be in danger of the council: but whosoever shall say, Thou fool, shall be in danger of hell fire.

23 Therefore if thou bring thy gift to the altar, and there rememberest that thy brother hath ought against thee;

24 Leave there thy gift before the altar, and go thy way; first be reconciled to thy brother, and then come and offer thy gift.

25 Agree with thine adversary quickly, whiles thou art in the way with him; lest at any time the adversary deliver thee to the judge, and the judge deliver thee to the officer, and thou be cast into prison.

5:25 Suing People
◄ Proverbs 25:8
Matthew 5:40 ►

26 Verily I say unto thee, Thou shalt by no means come out thence, till thou hast paid the uttermost farthing.

27 Ye have heard that it was said by them of old time, Thou shalt not commit adultery:

28 But I say unto you, That whosoever looketh on a woman to lust after her hath committed adultery with her already in his heart.

29 And if thy right eye offend thee, pluck it out, and cast *it* from thee: for it is profitable for thee that one of thy members

should perish, and not *that* thy whole body should be cast into hell.

30 And if thy right hand offend thee, cut if off, and cast *it* from thee: for it is profitable for thee that one of thy members should perish, and not *that* thy whole body should be cast into hell.

31 It hath been said, Whosoever shall put away his wife, let him give her a writing of divorcement:

32 But I say unto you, That whosoever shall put away his wife, saving for the cause of fornication, causeth her to commit adultery: and whosoever shall marry her that is divorced committeth adultery.

33 Again, ye have heard that it hath been said by them of old time, Thou shalt not forswear thyself, but shalt perform unto the Lord thine oaths:

34 But I say unto you, Swear not at all; neither by heaven; for it is God's throne:

35 Nor by the earth; for it is his footstool: neither by Jerusalem; for it is the city of the great King.

36 Neither shalt thou swear by thy head, because thou canst not make one hair white or black.

37 But let your communication be, Yea, yea; Nay, nay: for whatsoever is more than these cometh of evil.

38 Ye have heard that it hath been said, An eye for an eye, and a tooth for a tooth:

39 But I say unto you, That ye resist not evil: but whosoever shall smite thee on thy right cheek, turn to him the other also.

40 And if any man will sue thee at the law, and take away thy coat, let him have *thy* cloke also.

41 And whosoever shall compel thee to go a mile, go with him twain.

42 Give to him that asketh thee, and from him that would borrow of thee turn not thou away.

43 Ye have heard that it hath been said, Thou shalt love thy neighbour, and hate thine enemy.

44 But I say unto you, Love your enemies, bless them that curse you, do good to them that hate you, and pray for them which despitefully use you, and persecute you;

45 That ye may be the children of your Father which is in heaven: for he maketh his sun to rise on the evil and on the good, and sendeth rain on the just and on the unjust.

46 For if ye love them which love you, what reward have ye? do not even the publicans the same?

47 And if ye salute your brethren only, what do ye more *than others?* do not even the publicans so?

48 Be ye therefore perfect, even as your Father which is in heaven is perfect.

6

1 Take heed that ye do not your alms before men, to be seen of them: otherwise ye have no

5:34 Swearing
< Leviticus 19:12
James 5:12 >

5:37 Talking
< Proverbs 17:27
Colossians 4:6 >

5:39 Revenge
< Proverbs 24:29
Romans 12:17 >

5:40 Suing People
< Matthew 5:25
1 Corinthians 6:1 >

5:42 Borrowing
< Proverbs 22:7 >

5:42 Giving
< Isaiah 58:7
Luke 3:11 >

5:42 How to Give
< Deuteronomy 16:17
Matthew 6:3 >

5:42 Sharing
< Psalm 112:5
Luke 6:35 >

5:44 Enemies
< Luke 23:34 >

5:44 Loving Enemies
< Proverbs 25:21-22
Romans 12:20 >

5:48 God's Perfection
< Ecclesiastes 3:14 >

5:48 Perfection
< 1 Kings 8:61
2 Corinthians 13:11 >

6:1 Generosity
< Proverbs 31:20
Matthew 19:21 >

6:1 Watch Out!
< Matthew 18:10 >

reward of your Father which is in heaven.
2Therefore when
thou doest *thine*
alms, do not sound
a trumpet before
thee, as the hypo-
crites do in the syn-
agogues and in the
streets, that they
may have glory of
men. Verily I say
unto you, They
have their reward.
3But when thou
doest alms, let not
thy left hand know
what thy right hand
doeth:
4That thine alms
may be in secret: and thy Father which
seeth in secret himself shall reward thee
openly.
5And when thou prayest, thou shalt not
be as the hypocrites *are:* for they love to
pray standing in the synagogues and in the
corners of the streets, that they may be seen
of men. Verily I say unto you, They have
their reward.
6But thou, when
thou prayest, enter
into thy closet, and
when thou hast
shut thy door, pray
to thy Father which
is in secret; and thy Father which seeth in
secret shall reward thee openly.
7But when ye pray, use not vain repeti-
tions, as the heathen *do:* for they think that
they shall be heard for their much speaking.
8Be not ye therefore like unto them: for
your Father knoweth what things ye have
need of, before ye ask him.
9After this man-
ner therefore pray
ye: Our Father
which art in heav-
en, Hallowed be thy
name.
10Thy kingdom
come. Thy will be
done in earth, as *it*
is in heaven.
11Give us this day
our daily bread.
12And forgive us
our debts, as we for-
give our debtors.
13And lead us
not into tempta-
tion, but deliver us
from evil: For thine
is the kingdom,
and the power, and
the glory, for ever.
Amen.
14For if ye forgive
men their tres-
passes, your heav-
enly Father will
also forgive you:
15But if ye forgive
not men their tres-
passes, neither will
your Father forgive
your trespasses.
16Moreover when
ye fast, be not, as
the hypocrites, of a
sad countenance:
for they disfigure
their faces, that
they may appear
unto men to fast.
Verily I say unto
you, They have
their reward.
17But thou, when
thou fastest, anoint
thine head, and
wash thy face;
18That thou ap-
pear not unto men
to fast, but unto thy
Father which is in
secret: and thy Fa-
ther, which seeth in
secret, shall reward
thee openly.
19Lay not up for
yourselves treasures
upon earth, where
moth and rust
doth corrupt, and
where thieves break
through and steal:
20But lay up for
yourselves treasures
in heaven, where
neither moth nor

6:2 Phonies
◄ Matthew 6:16 ►

6:2, 5 Showing Off
◄ 2 Kings 10:16
Matthew 6:16 ►

6:3 How to Give
◄ Matthew 5:42
Matthew 10:8 ►

6:6 Praying Alone
◄ Daniel 6:10
Acts 10:9 ►

6:9 Names of God
◄ Psalm 71:22
Matthew 6:26 ►

6:9 Perfect Father
◄ Isaiah 64:8
Matthew 7:11 ►

6:10 Submitting to God
◄ Psalm 143:10
Matthew 12:50 ►

6:13 God's Control
◄ Daniel 4:35
Acts 17:24 ►

6:14 Forgiveness
◄ Ezekiel 18:22
Mark 3:28 ►

6:14 Rewards
◄ Matthew 5:7
Matthew 25:40 ►

6:15 No Mercy
◄ Matthew 18:28 ►

6:16 Phonies
◄ Matthew 6:2
Matthew 12:2 ►

6:16 Showing Off
◄ Matthew 6:2, 5
Matthew 23:5 ►

6:18 Heart
◄ Proverbs 23:7
Matthew 15:18 ►

6:19 Hoarding
◄ Ezekiel 28:4
Luke 12:21 ►

rust doth corrupt, and where thieves do
not break through nor steal:
21 For where your treasure is, there will
your heart be also.
22 The light of the body is the eye: if
therefore thine eye be single, thy whole
body shall be full of light.
23 But if thine eye be evil, thy whole body
shall be full of darkness. If therefore the
light that is in thee be darkness, how great
is that darkness!
24 No man can
serve two masters:
for either he will
hate the one, and
love the other; or
else he will hold to
the one, and de-
spise the other. Ye
cannot serve God
and mammon.

> **6:24 The Time Is Now**
> ◄ Hosea 10:2
> Luke 9:62 ►

> **6:25 Worry**
> ◄ Psalm 127:2
> Matthew 13:22 ►

25 Therefore I say
unto you, Take no
thought for your
life, what ye shall eat, or what ye shall
drink; nor yet for your body, what ye shall
put on. Is not the life more than meat, and
the body than raiment?
26 Behold the
fowls of the air: for
they sow not, nei-
ther do they reap,
nor gather into
barns; yet your
heavenly Father
feedeth them. Are
ye not much better
than they?

> **6:26 Animals vs. People**
> ◄ Psalm 82:6
> Matthew 12:12 ►

> **6:26 Names of God**
> ◄ Matthew 6:9
> James 1:17 ►

27 Which of you
by taking thought
can add one cubit unto his stature?
28 And why take ye thought for raiment?
Consider the lilies of the field, how
they grow; they toil not, neither do they
spin:
29 And yet I say unto you, That even Solomon in all his glory was not arrayed like
one of these.
30 Wherefore, if God so clothe the grass
of the field, which to day is, and to morrow is cast into the oven, *shall he* not much
more *clothe* you, O ye of little faith?
31 Therefore take no thought, saying,
What shall we eat? or, What shall we drink?
or, Wherewithal shall we be clothed?
32 (For after all
these things do the
Gentiles seek:) for
your heavenly Fa-
ther knoweth that
ye have need of all
these things.

> **6:32 God's Care for You**
> ◄ Psalm 115:12
> Luke 12:7 ►

33 But seek ye first
the kingdom of
God, and his righ-
teousness; and all
these things shall
be added unto you.

> **6:33 Blessing**
> ◄ Malachi 3:10 ►

> **6:33 Job One**
> ◄ Joshua 24:15
> John 4:34 ►

34 Take therefore
no thought for the
morrow: for the
morrow shall take
thought for the
things of itself. Suf-
ficient unto the day
is the evil thereof.

> **6:33 Seeking God**
> ◄ Zephaniah 2:3
> Luke 11:10 ►

7

1 Judge not, that
ye be not judged.
2 For with what
judgment ye judge,
ye shall be judged: and with what measure ye mete, it shall be measured to you
again.
3 And why beholdest thou the mote that
is in thy brother's eye, but considerest not
the beam that is in thine own eye?
4 Or how wilt thou say to thy brother,
Let me pull out the mote out of thine eye;
and, behold, a beam *is* in thine own eye?
5 Thou hypocrite,
first cast out the
beam out of thine
own eye; and then
shalt thou see clear-
ly to cast out the
mote out of thy brother's eye.

> **7:5 Self-examination**
> ◄ Lamentations 3:40
> 1 Corinthians 11:28 ►

6 Give not that which is holy unto the
dogs, neither cast ye your pearls before
swine, lest they trample them under their
feet, and turn again and rend you.
7 Ask, and it shall
be given you; seek,
and ye shall find;
knock, and it shall
be opened unto
you:

> **7:7 Duty to Pray**
> ◄ Hosea 14:2
> Matthew 26:41 ►

8 For every one that asketh receiveth; and
he that seeketh findeth; and to him that
knocketh it shall be opened.
9 Or what man is there of you, whom if

his son ask bread, will he give him a stone?

10Or if he ask a fish, will he give him a serpent?

11If ye then, being evil, know how to give good gifts unto your children, how much more shall your Father which is in heaven give good things to them that ask him?

> **7:11 Perfect Father**
> ◄ Matthew 6:9
> Romans 8:15 ►

12Therefore all things whatsoever ye would that men should do to you, do ye even so to them: for this is the law and the prophets.

> **7:12 Golden Rule**
> ◄ Luke 6:31 ►

13Enter ye in at the strait gate: for wide *is* the gate, and broad *is* the way, that leadeth to destruction, and many there be which go in thereat:

14Because strait *is* the gate, and narrow *is* the way, which leadeth unto life, and few there be that find it.

15Beware of false prophets, which come to you in sheep's clothing, but inwardly they are ravening wolves.

16Ye shall know them by their fruits. Do men gather grapes of thorns, or figs of thistles?

17Even so every good tree bringeth forth good fruit; but a corrupt tree bringeth forth evil fruit.

18A good tree cannot bring forth evil fruit, neither *can* a corrupt tree bring forth good fruit.

19Every tree that bringeth not forth good fruit is hewn down, and cast into the fire.

20Wherefore by their fruits ye shall know them.

21Not every one that saith unto me, Lord, Lord, shall enter into the kingdom of heaven; but he that doeth the will of my Father which is in heaven.

> **7:21 Obeying God**
> ◄ Jeremiah 7:23
> Luke 8:21 ►

22Many will say to me in that day, Lord, Lord, have we not prophesied in thy name? and in thy name have cast out devils? and in thy name done many wonderful works?

23And then will I profess unto them, I never knew you: depart from me, ye that work iniquity.

24Therefore whosoever heareth these sayings of mine, and doeth them, I will liken him unto a wise man, which built his house upon a rock:

> **7:24 Obeying Christ**
> ◄ Matthew 4:20
> Matthew 9:9 ►

> **7:24 True Wisdom**
> ◄ Hosea 14:9
> 1 Corinthians 2:6 ►

25And the rain descended, and the floods came, and the winds blew, and beat upon that house; and it fell not: for it was founded upon a rock.

26And every one that heareth these sayings of mine, and doeth them not, shall be likened unto a foolish man, which built his house upon the sand:

> **7:26 Listening and Doing**
> ◄ Ezekiel 33:32
> Matthew 13:19 ►

> **7:26-27 Wicked Insecurity**
> ◄ Ezekiel 13:10-11 ►

27And the rain descended, and the floods came, and the winds blew, and beat upon that house; and it fell: and great was the fall of it.

28And it came to pass, when Jesus had ended these sayings, the people were astonished at his doctrine:

29For he taught them as *one* having authority, and not as the scribes.

> **7:29 The Teacher**
> ◄ Matthew 5:2
> Mark 6:34 ►

8

1When he was come down from the mountain, great multitudes followed him.

2And, behold, there came a leper and worshipped him, saying, Lord, if thou wilt, thou canst make me clean.

3And Jesus put forth *his* hand, and touched him, saying, I will; be thou clean. And immediately his leprosy was cleansed.

4And Jesus saith unto him, See thou tell no man; but go thy way, shew thyself to the priest, and offer the gift that Moses commanded, for a testimony unto them.

5And when Jesus was entered into Capernaum, there came unto him a centurion, beseeching him,

6 And saying, Lord, my servant lieth at home sick of the palsy, grievously tormented.

7 And Jesus saith unto him, I will come and heal him.

8 The centurion answered and said, Lord, I am not worthy that thou shouldest come under my roof: but speak the word only, and my servant shall be healed.

9 For I am a man under authority, having soldiers under me: and I say to this *man,* Go, and he goeth; and to another, Come, and he cometh; and to my servant, Do this, and he doeth *it.*

10 When Jesus heard *it,* he marvelled, and said to them that followed, Verily I say unto you, I have not found so great faith, no, not in Israel.

11 And I say unto you, That many shall come from the east and west, and shall sit down with Abraham, and Isaac, and Jacob, in the kingdom of heaven.

12 But the children of the kingdom shall be cast out into outer darkness: there shall be weeping and gnashing of teeth.

13 And Jesus said unto the centurion, Go thy way; and as thou hast believed, so be it done unto thee. And his servant was healed in the selfsame hour.

14 And when Jesus was come into Peter's house, he saw his wife's mother laid, and sick of a fever.

15 And he touched her hand, and the fever left her: and she arose, and ministered unto them.

16 When the even was come, they brought unto him many that were possessed with devils: and he cast out the spirits with *his* word, and healed all that were sick:

8:16 Help!
◄ Matthew 4:24
Matthew 9:32 ►

17 That it might be fulfilled which was spoken by Esaias the prophet, saying, Himself took our infirmities, and bare *our* sicknesses.

18 Now when Jesus saw great multitudes about him, he gave commandment to depart unto the other side.

19 And a certain scribe came, and said unto him, Master, I will follow thee whithersoever thou goest.

20 And Jesus saith unto him, The foxes have holes, and the birds of the air *have* nests; but the Son of man hath not where to lay *his* head.

21 And another of his disciples said unto him, Lord, suffer me first to go and bury my father.

8:21 Procrastination
◄ Genesis 19:16
Luke 9:61 ►

22 But Jesus said unto him, Follow me; and let the dead bury their dead.

23 And when he was entered into a ship, his disciples followed him.

24 And, behold, there arose a great tempest in the sea, insomuch that the ship was covered with the waves: but he was asleep.

25 And his disciples came to *him,* and awoke him, saying, Lord, save us: we perish.

26 And he saith unto them, Why are ye fearful, O ye of little faith? Then he arose, and rebuked the winds and the sea; and there was a great calm.

27 But the men marvelled, saying, What manner of man is this, that even the winds and the sea obey him!

28 And when he was come to the other side into the country of the Gergesenes, there met him two possessed with devils, coming out of the tombs, exceeding fierce, so that no man might pass by that way.

29 And, behold, they cried out, saying, What have we to do with thee, Jesus, thou Son of God? art thou come hither to torment us before the time?

30 And there was a good way off from them an herd of many swine feeding.

31 So the devils besought him, saying, If thou cast us out, suffer us to go away into the herd of swine.

32 And he said unto them, Go. And when they were come out, they went into the herd of swine: and, behold, the whole herd of swine ran violently down a steep place into the sea, and perished in the waters.

33 And they that kept them fled, and went their ways into the city, and told every thing, and what was befallen to the possessed of the devils.

34 And, behold, the whole city came out to meet Jesus: and when they saw him, they besought *him* that he would depart out of their coasts.

9

1 And he entered into a ship, and passed over, and came into his own city.

2 And, behold, they brought to him a

man sick of the palsy, lying on a bed: and Jesus seeing their faith said unto the sick of the palsy; Son, be of good cheer; thy sins be forgiven thee.

9:2 Encouraging People
◄ Isaiah 41:13
Matthew 14:27 ►

3 And, behold, certain of the scribes said within themselves, This *man* blasphemeth.

4 And Jesus knowing their thoughts said, Wherefore think ye evil in your hearts?

9:4 Bad Thoughts
◄ Jeremiah 4:14
Matthew 15:19 ►

5 For whether is easier, to say, *Thy* sins be forgiven thee; or to say, Arise, and walk?

6 But that ye may know that the Son of man hath power on earth to forgive sins, (then saith he to the sick of the palsy,) Arise, take up thy bed, and go unto thine house.

7 And he arose, and departed to his house.

8 But when the multitudes saw *it,* they marvelled, and glorified God, which had given such power unto men.

9:8 Gifts from God
◄ Isaiah 50:4
Matthew 25:15 ►

9 And as Jesus passed forth from thence, he saw a man, named Matthew, sitting at the receipt of custom: and he saith unto him, Follow me. And he arose, and followed him.

9:9 Obeying Christ
◄ Matthew 7:24
Matthew 21:6 ►

10 And it came to pass, as Jesus sat at meat in the house, behold, many publicans and sinners came and sat down with him and his disciples.

9:10 Accepting People
◄ Mark 9:38 ►

11 And when the Pharisees saw *it,* they said unto his disciples, Why eateth your Master with publicans and sinners?

12 But when Jesus heard *that,* he said unto them, They that be whole need not a physician, but they that are sick.

13 But go ye and learn what *that* meaneth, I will have mercy, and not sacrifice: for I am not come to call the righteous, but sinners to repentance.

14 Then came to him the disciples of John, saying, Why do we and the Pharisees fast oft, but thy disciples fast not?

15 And Jesus said unto them, Can the children of the bridechamber mourn, as long as the bridegroom is with them? but the days will come, when the bridegroom shall be taken from them, and then shall they fast.

16 No man putteth a piece of new cloth unto an old garment, for that which is put in to fill it up taketh from the garment, and the rent is made worse.

17 Neither do men put new wine into old bottles: else the bottles break, and the wine runneth out, and the bottles perish: but they put new wine into new bottles, and both are preserved.

18 While he spake these things unto them, behold, there came a certain ruler, and worshipped him, saying, My daughter is even now dead: but come and lay thy hand upon her, and she shall live.

19 And Jesus arose, and followed him, and *so did* his disciples.

20 And, behold, a woman, which was diseased with an issue of blood twelve years, came behind *him,* and touched the hem of his garment:

21 For she said within herself, If I may but touch his garment, I shall be whole.

22 But Jesus turned him about, and when he saw her, he said, Daughter, be of good comfort; thy faith hath made thee whole. And the woman was made whole from that hour.

23 And when Jesus came into the ruler's house, and saw the minstrels and the people making a noise,

24 He said unto them, Give place: for the maid is not dead, but sleepeth. And they laughed him to scorn.

25 But when the people were put forth, he went in, and took her by the hand, and the maid arose.

26 And the fame hereof went abroad into all that land.

27 And when Jesus departed thence, two blind men followed him, crying, and saying, *Thou* Son of David, have mercy on us.

28 And when he was come into the house, the blind men came to him: and Jesus saith unto them, Believe ye that I am able to do this? They said unto him, Yea, Lord.

29Then touched he their eyes, saying,
According to your faith be it unto you.
30And their eyes were opened; and Jesus
straitly charged them, saying, See *that* no
man know *it*.
31But they, when they were departed,
spread abroad his fame in all that country.
32As they went
out, behold, they
brought to him a
dumb man pos-
sessed with a devil.
33And when the
devil was cast out, the dumb spake: and
the multitudes marvelled, saying, It was
never so seen in Israel.

9:32 Help!
◄ Matthew 8:16
Mark 9:17-20 ►

34But the Pharisees said, He casteth out
devils through the prince of the devils.
35And Jesus went about all the cities and
villages, teaching in their synagogues, and
preaching the gospel of the kingdom, and
healing every sickness and every disease
among the people.
36But when he saw the multitudes, he
was moved with compassion on them,
because they fainted, and were scattered
abroad, as sheep having no shepherd.
37Then saith he unto his disciples, The
harvest truly *is* plenteous, but the labourers
are few;
38Pray ye therefore the Lord of the harvest, that he will send forth labourers into
his harvest.

10

1And when he had called unto *him* his
twelve disciples, he gave them power
against unclean spirits, to cast them out,
and to heal all manner of sickness and all
manner of disease.
2Now the names of the twelve apostles
are these; The first, Simon, who is called
Peter, and Andrew his brother; James *the*
son of Zebedee, and John his brother;
3Philip, and Bartholomew; Thomas, and
Matthew the publican; James *the son* of
Alphaeus, and Lebbaeus, whose surname
was Thaddaeus;
4Simon the Canaanite, and Judas Iscariot, who also betrayed him.
5These twelve Jesus sent forth, and commanded them, saying, Go not into the way
of the Gentiles, and into *any* city of the
Samaritans enter ye not:
6But go rather to the lost sheep of the
house of Israel.
7And as ye go, preach, saying, The kingdom of heaven is at hand.
8Heal the sick,
cleanse the lepers,
raise the dead, cast
out devils: freely ye
have received, free-
ly give.

10:8 How to Give
◄ Matthew 6:3
Luke 6:38 ►

9Provide neither gold, nor silver, nor
brass in your purses,
10Nor scrip for *your* journey, neither two
coats, neither shoes, nor yet staves: for the
workman is worthy of his meat.
11And into whatsoever city or town ye
shall enter, enquire who in it is worthy;
and there abide till ye go thence.
12And when ye come into an house, salute it.
13And if the house be worthy, let your
peace come upon it: but if it be not worthy, let your peace return to you.
14And whosoever shall not receive you,
nor hear your words, when ye depart out
of that house or city, shake off the dust of
your feet.
15Verily I say unto you, It shall be more
tolerable for the land of Sodom and
Gomorrha in the day of judgment, than
for that city.
16Behold, I send you forth as sheep in
the midst of wolves: be ye therefore wise
as serpents, and harmless as doves.
17But beware of
men: for they will
deliver you up to
the councils, and
they will scourge
you in their syna-
gogues;

10:17
Expecting Pain
◄ Matthew 24:9 ►

18And ye shall be brought before governors and kings for my sake, for a testimony against them and the Gentiles.
19But when they deliver you up, take no
thought how or what ye shall speak: for it
shall be given you in that same hour what
ye shall speak.
20For it is not ye that speak, but the Spirit
of your Father which speaketh in you.
21And the brother shall deliver up the
brother to death, and the father the child:
and the children shall rise up against *their*
parents, and cause them to be put to death.
22And ye shall be hated of all *men* for
my name's sake: but he that endureth to
the end shall be saved.

23 But when they persecute you in this city, flee ye into another: for verily I say unto you, Ye shall not have gone over the cities of Israel, till the Son of man be come.

10:22
Endurance
◄ Mark 13:13 ►

10:22
How to Be Saved
◄ Romans 10:9 ►

24 The disciple is not above *his* master, nor the servant above his lord.

25 It is enough for the disciple that he be as his master, and the servant as his lord. If they have called the master of the house Beelzebub, how much more *shall they call* them of his household?

26 Fear them not therefore: for there is nothing covered, that shall not be revealed; and hid, that shall not be known.

27 What I tell you in darkness, *that* speak ye in light: and what ye hear in the ear, *that* preach ye upon the housetops.

28 And fear not them which kill the body, but are not able to kill the soul: but rather fear him which is able to destroy both soul and body in hell.

10:28 Fearing God
◄ Isaiah 8:13
Luke 23:40 ►

29 Are not two sparrows sold for a farthing? and one of them shall not fall on the ground without your Father.

30 But the very hairs of your head are all numbered.

31 Fear ye not therefore, ye are of more value than many sparrows.

32 Whosoever therefore shall confess me before men, him will I confess also before my Father which is in heaven.

33 But whosoever shall deny me before men, him will I also deny before my Father which is in heaven.

34 Think not that I am come to send peace on earth: I came not to send peace, but a sword.

35 For I am come to set a man at variance against his father, and the daughter against her mother, and the daughter in law against her mother in law.

36 And a man's foes *shall be* they of his own household.

37 He that loveth father or mother more than me is not worthy of me: and he that loveth son or daughter more than me is not worthy of me.

10:37
Who Deserves Christ?
◄ Matthew 22:8 ►

38 And he that taketh not his cross, and followeth after me, is not worthy of me.

39 He that findeth his life shall lose it: and he that loseth his life for my sake shall find it.

40 He that receiveth you receiveth me, and he that receiveth me receiveth him that sent me.

41 He that receiveth a prophet in the name of a prophet shall receive a prophet's reward; and he that receiveth a righteous man in the name of a righteous man shall receive a righteous man's reward.

42 And whosoever shall give to drink unto one of these little ones a cup of cold *water* only in the name of a disciple, verily I say unto you, he shall in no wise lose his reward.

10:42 Believer Be Glad
◄ Isaiah 28:16
John 6:37 ►

10:42 Goodness Rewarded
◄ Daniel 12:3
Matthew 25:23 ►

10:42
Humility
◄ John 12:3 ►

11

1 And it came to pass, when Jesus had made an end of commanding his twelve disciples, he departed thence to teach and to preach in their cities.

2 Now when John had heard in the prison the works of Christ, he sent two of his disciples,

3 And said unto him, Art thou he that should come, or do we look for another?

4 Jesus answered and said unto them, Go and shew John again those things which ye do hear and see:

5 The blind receive their sight, and the lame walk, the lepers are cleansed, and the deaf hear, the dead are raised up, and the poor have the gospel preached to them.

6 And blessed is *he,* whosoever shall not be offended in me.

7 And as they departed, Jesus began to say unto the multitudes concerning John, What went ye out into the wilderness to see? A reed shaken with the wind?

8 But what went ye out for to see? A man clothed in soft raiment? behold, they that wear soft *clothing* are in kings' houses.

9 But what went ye out for to see? A prophet? yea, I say unto you, and more than a prophet.

10 For this is *he*, of whom it is written, Behold, I send my messenger before thy face, which shall prepare thy way before thee.

11 Verily I say unto you, Among them that are born of women there hath not risen a greater than John the Baptist: notwithstanding he that is least in the kingdom of heaven is greater than he.

12 And from the days of John the Baptist until now the kingdom of heaven suffereth violence, and the violent take it by force.

13 For all the prophets and the law prophesied until John.

14 And if ye will receive *it*, this is Elias, which was for to come.

15 He that hath ears to hear, let him hear.

16 But whereunto shall I liken this generation? It is like unto children sitting in the markets, and calling unto their fellows,

17 And saying, We have piped unto you, and ye have not danced; we have mourned unto you, and ye have not lamented.

18 For John came neither eating nor drinking, and they say, He hath a devil.

11:18 Drinking
◄ Daniel 10:3
Luke 1:15 ►

19 The Son of man came eating and drinking, and they say, Behold a man gluttonous, and a winebibber, a friend of publicans and sinners. But wisdom is justified of her children.

11:19 Friend of Jesus
◄ Luke 7:39 ►

20 Then began he to upbraid the cities wherein most of his mighty works were done, because they repented not:

11:20 Hard-hearted
◄ Haggai 2:17 ►

21 Woe unto thee, Chorazin! woe unto thee, Bethsaida! for if the mighty works, which were done in you, had been done in Tyre and Sidon, they would have repented long ago in sackcloth and ashes.

22 But I say unto you, It shall be more tolerable for Tyre and Sidon at the day of judgment, than for you.

23 And thou, Capernaum, which art exalted unto heaven, shalt be brought down to hell: for if the mighty works, which have been done in thee, had been done in Sodom, it would have remained until this day.

24 But I say unto you, That it shall be more tolerable for the land of Sodom in the day of judgment, than for thee.

25 At that time Jesus answered and said, I thank thee, O Father, Lord of heaven and earth, because thou hast hid these things from the wise and prudent, and hast revealed them unto babes.

26 Even so, Father: for so it seemed good in thy sight.

27 All things are delivered unto me of my Father: and no man knoweth the Son, but the Father; neither knoweth any man the Father, save the Son, and *he* to whomsoever the Son will reveal *him*.

28 Come unto me, all *ye* that labour and are heavy laden, and I will give you rest.

11:28 Invisible Gifts
◄ Ezekiel 11:19
Luke 11:13 ►

29 Take my yoke upon you, and learn of me; for I am meek and lowly in heart: and ye shall find rest unto your souls.

11:29 Lessons of Life
◄ Isaiah 1:16-17
John 6:45 ►

30 For my yoke *is* easy, and my burden is light.

12

1 At that time Jesus went on the sabbath day through the corn; and his disciples were an hungred, and began to pluck the ears of corn, and to eat.

2 But when the Pharisees saw *it*, they said unto him, Behold, thy disciples do that which is not lawful to do upon the sabbath day.

12:2 Phonies
◄ Matthew 6:16
Matthew 23:4 ►

3 But he said unto them, Have ye not read what David did, when he was an hungred, and they that were with him;

4 How he entered into the house of God, and did eat the shewbread, which was not lawful for him to eat, neither for them which were with him, but only for the priests?

5 Or have ye not read in the law, how
that on the sabbath days the priests in the
temple profane the sabbath, and are
blameless?
6 But I say unto you, That in this place is
one greater than the temple.
7 But if ye had known what *this* meaneth,
I will have mercy, and not sacrifice, ye
would not have condemned the guiltless.
8 For the Son of man is Lord even of the
sabbath day.
9 And when he
was departed thence,
he went into their
synagogue:
10 And, behold,
there was a man
which had *his* hand withered. And they
asked him, saying, Is it lawful to heal on
the sabbath days? that they might accuse
him.

> **12:9**
> **Going to Church**
> ◄ Mark 1:21 ►

11 And he said unto them, What man
shall there be among you, that shall have
one sheep, and if it fall into a pit on the
sabbath day, will he not lay hold on it, and
lift *it* out?
12 How much
then is a man bet-
ter than a sheep?
Wherefore it is law-
ful to do well on the
sabbath days.

> **12:12**
> **Animals vs. People**
> ◄ Matthew 6:26 ►

13 Then saith he to the man, Stretch forth
thine hand. And he stretched *it* forth; and
it was restored whole, like as the other.
14 Then the Pharisees went out, and held
a council against him, how they might
destroy him.
15 But when Jesus knew *it*, he withdrew
himself from thence: and great multitudes
followed him, and he healed them all;
16 And charged them that they should
not make him known:
17 That it might be fulfilled which was
spoken by Esaias the prophet, saying,
18 Behold my servant, whom I have
chosen; my beloved, in whom my soul is
well pleased: I will put my spirit upon him,
and he shall shew judgment to the Gentiles.
19 He shall not strive, nor cry; neither
shall any man hear his voice in the streets.
20 A bruised reed shall he not break, and
smoking flax shall he not quench, till he
send forth judgment unto victory.
21 And in his name shall the Gentiles
trust.
22 Then was brought unto him one possessed with a devil, blind, and dumb: and
he healed him, insomuch that the blind
and dumb both spake and saw.
23 And all the people were amazed, and
said, Is not this the son of David?
24 But when the Pharisees heard *it*, they
said, This *fellow* doth not cast out devils,
but by Beelzebub the prince of the devils.
25 And Jesus knew their thoughts, and
said unto them, Every kingdom divided
against itself is brought to desolation; and
every city or house divided against itself
shall not stand:
26 And if Satan cast out Satan, he is divided against himself; how shall then his
kingdom stand?
27 And if I by Beelzebub cast out devils,
by whom do your children cast *them* out?
therefore they shall be your judges.
28 But if I cast out devils by the Spirit of
God, then the kingdom of God is come
unto you.
29 Or else how can one enter into a
strong man's house, and spoil his goods,
except he first bind the strong man? and
then he will spoil his house.
30 He that is not with me is against me;
and he that gathereth not with me
scattereth abroad.
31 Wherefore I say unto you, All manner
of sin and blasphemy shall be forgiven
unto men: but the blasphemy *against* the
Holy Ghost shall not be forgiven unto men.
32 And whosoever speaketh a word
against the Son of man, it shall be forgiv-
en him: but whosoever speaketh against
the Holy Ghost, it shall not be forgiven
him, neither in this world, neither in the
world to come.
33 Either make the tree good, and his
fruit good; or else make the tree corrupt,
and his fruit corrupt: for the tree is known
by *his* fruit.
34 O generation of vipers, how can ye,
being evil, speak good things? for out of
the abundance of the heart the mouth
speaketh.
35 A good man out of the good treasure
of the heart bringeth forth good things:
and an evil man out of the evil treasure
bringeth forth evil things.
36 But I say unto you, That every idle

word that men
shall speak, they
shall give account
thereof in the day of
judgment.
37For by thy
words thou shalt be justified, and by thy
words thou shalt be condemned.

12:36
Getting Caught
◄ Matthew 18:23 ►

38Then certain of the scribes and of the
Pharisees answered, saying, Master, we
would see a sign from thee.
39But he answered and said unto them,
An evil and adulterous generation seeketh
after a sign; and there shall no sign be
given to it, but the sign of the prophet
Jonas:
40For as Jonas was three days and three
nights in the whale's belly; so shall the Son
of man be three days and three nights in
the heart of the earth.
41The men of Nineveh shall rise in judgment with this generation, and shall condemn it: because they repented at the
preaching of Jonas; and, behold, a greater
than Jonas *is* here.
42The queen of the south shall rise up
in the judgment with this generation, and
shall condemn it: for she came from the
uttermost parts of the earth to hear the
wisdom of Solomon; and, behold, a greater than Solomon *is* here.
43When the unclean spirit is gone out
of a man, he walketh through dry places,
seeking rest, and findeth none.
44Then he saith, I will return into my
house from whence I came out; and when
he is come, he findeth *it* empty, swept, and
garnished.
45Then goeth he,
and taketh with
himself seven other
spirits more wicked
than himself, and
they enter in and
dwell there: and the
last *state* of that
man is worse than
the first. Even so
shall it be also unto
this wicked genera-
tion.

12:45 Callousness
◄ Jeremiah 5:28
Matthew 13:15 ►

12:45
Demons
◄ Mark 1:26 ►

46While he yet talked to the people, behold, *his* mother and his brethren stood
without, desiring to speak with him.
47Then one said unto him, Behold, thy
mother and thy brethren stand without,
desiring to speak with thee.
48But he answered and said unto him
that told him, Who is my mother? and
who are my brethren?
49And he stretched forth his hand toward his disciples, and said, Behold my
mother and my brethren!
50For whosoever
shall do the will of
my Father which is
in heaven, the same
is my brother, and
sister, and mother.

12:50
Submitting to God
◄ Matthew 6:10
Matthew 26:42 ►

13

1The same day went Jesus out of the
house, and sat by the sea side.
2And great multitudes were gathered
together unto him, so that he went into a
ship, and sat; and the whole multitude
stood on the shore.
3And he spake many things unto them
in parables, saying, Behold, a sower went
forth to sow;
4And when he sowed, some *seeds* fell by
the way side, and the fowls came and devoured them up:
5Some fell upon stony places, where
they had not much earth: and forthwith
they sprung up, because they had no deep-
ness of earth:
6And when the sun was up, they were
scorched; and because they had no root,
they withered away.
7And some fell among thorns; and the
thorns sprung up, and choked them:
8But other fell into good ground, and
brought forth fruit, some an hundredfold,
some sixtyfold, some thirtyfold.
9Who hath ears to hear, let him hear.
10And the disciples came, and said unto
him, Why speakest thou unto them in parables?
11He answered and said unto them, Because it is given unto you to know the
mysteries of the kingdom of heaven, but
to them it is not given.
12For whosoever hath, to him shall be
given, and he shall have more abundance:
but whosoever hath not, from him shall
be taken away even that he hath.
13Therefore speak I to them in parables:
because they seeing see not; and hearing
they hear not, neither do they understand.
14And in them is fulfilled the prophecy
of Esaias, which saith, By hearing ye shall

hear, and shall not understand; and seeing ye shall see, and shall not perceive:

15For this people's heart is waxed gross, and *their* ears are dull of hearing, and their eyes they have closed; lest at any time they should see with *their* eyes, and hear with *their* ears, and should understand with *their* heart, and should be converted, and I should heal them.

13:15 Callousness
◄ Matthew 12:45
Matthew 26:74 ►

16But blessed *are* your eyes, for they see: and your ears, for they hear.

17For verily I say unto you, That many prophets and righteous *men* have desired to see *those things* which ye see, and have not seen *them;* and to hear *those things* which ye hear, and have not heard *them.*

18Hear ye therefore the parable of the sower.

19When any one heareth the word of the kingdom, and understandeth *it* not, then cometh the wicked *one,* and catcheth away that which was sown in his heart. This is he which received seed by the way side.

13:19 Listening and Doing
◄ Matthew 7:26
Luke 16:31 ►

20But he that received the seed into stony places, the same is he that heareth the word, and anon with joy receiveth it;

21Yet hath he not root in himself, but dureth for a while: for when tribulation or persecution ariseth because of the word, by and by he is offended.

22He also that received seed among the thorns is he that heareth the word; and the care of this world, and the deceitfulness of riches, choke the word, and he becometh unfruitful.

13:22 Worry
◄ Matthew 6:25
Luke 10:41 ►

23But he that received seed into the good ground is he that heareth the word, and understandeth *it;* which also beareth fruit, and bringeth forth, some an hundredfold, some sixty, some thirty.

13:23 Accepting God's Word
◄ Luke 10:38-39 ►

24Another parable put he forth unto them, saying, The kingdom of heaven is likened unto a man which sowed good seed in his field:

25But while men slept, his enemy came and sowed tares among the wheat, and went his way.

26But when the blade was sprung up, and brought forth fruit, then appeared the tares also.

27So the servants of the householder came and said unto him, Sir, didst not thou sow good seed in thy field? from whence then hath it tares?

28He said unto them, An enemy hath done this. The servants said unto him, Wilt thou then that we go and gather them up?

29But he said, Nay; lest while ye gather up the tares, ye root up also the wheat with them.

30Let both grow together until the harvest: and in the time of harvest I will say to the reapers, Gather ye together first the tares, and bind them in bundles to burn them: but gather the wheat into my barn.

31Another parable put he forth unto them, saying, The kingdom of heaven is like to a grain of mustard seed, which a man took, and sowed in his field:

32Which indeed is the least of all seeds: but when it is grown, it is the greatest among herbs, and becometh a tree, so that the birds of the air come and lodge in the branches thereof.

33Another parable spake he unto them; The kingdom of heaven is like unto leaven, which a woman took, and hid in three measures of meal, till the whole was leavened.

34All these things spake Jesus unto the multitude in parables; and without a parable spake he not unto them:

35That it might be fulfilled which was spoken by the prophet, saying, I will open my mouth in parables; I will utter things which have been kept secret from the foundation of the world.

36Then Jesus sent the multitude away, and went into the house: and his disciples came unto him, saying, Declare unto us the parable of the tares of the field.

13:36 Learning from Jesus
◄ Mark 4:10 ►

37He answered and said unto them, He
that soweth the good seed is the Son of
man;
38The field is the world; the good seed
are the children of the kingdom; but the
tares are the children of the wicked *one*;
39The enemy that sowed them is the
devil; the harvest is the end of the world;
and the reapers are the angels.
40As therefore the tares are gathered and
burned in the fire; so shall it be in the end
of this world.
41The Son of man shall send forth his
angels, and they shall gather out of his
kingdom all things that offend, and them
which do iniquity;
42And shall cast them into a furnace of
fire: there shall be wailing and gnashing
of teeth.
43Then shall the
righteous shine
forth as the sun in
the kingdom of
their Father. Who
hath ears to hear, let
him hear.

13:43
Rewarded Goodness
◄ Isaiah 3:10 ►

44Again, the kingdom of heaven is like
unto treasure hid in a field; the which
when a man hath found, he hideth, and
for joy thereof goeth and selleth all that
he hath, and buyeth that field.
45Again, the kingdom of heaven is like
unto a merchant man, seeking goodly
pearls:
46Who, when he had found one pearl
of great price, went and sold all that he
had, and bought it.
47Again, the kingdom of heaven is like
unto a net, that was cast into the sea, and
gathered of every kind:
48Which, when it was full, they drew to
shore, and sat down, and gathered the
good into vessels, but cast the bad away.
49So shall it be at the end of the world:
the angels shall come forth, and sever the
wicked from among the just,
50And shall cast them into the furnace
of fire: there shall be wailing and gnashing of teeth.
51Jesus saith unto them, Have ye understood all these things? They say unto him,
Yea, Lord.
52Then said he unto them, Therefore
every scribe *which is* instructed unto the
kingdom of heaven is like unto a man *that*
is an householder, which bringeth forth
out of his treasure *things* new and old.
53And it came to pass, *that* when Jesus
had finished these parables, he departed
thence.
54And when he was come into his own
country, he taught them in their synagogue, insomuch that they were astonished, and said, Whence hath this *man* this
wisdom, and *these* mighty works?
55Is not this the carpenter's son? is not
his mother called Mary? and his brethren,
James, and Joses, and Simon, and Judas?
56And his sisters, are they not all with
us? Whence then hath this *man* all these
things?
57And they were offended in him. But
Jesus said unto them, A prophet is not
without honour, save in his own country,
and in his own house.
58And he did not many mighty works
there because of their unbelief.

14

1At that time Herod the tetrarch heard
of the fame of Jesus,
2And said unto
his servants, This is
John the Baptist; he
is risen from the
dead; and therefore
mighty works do
shew forth themselves in him.

14:2 Superstition
◄ Jeremiah 44:18
Acts 12:15 ►

3For Herod had laid hold on John, and
bound him, and put *him* in prison for
Herodias' sake, his brother Philip's wife.
4For John said unto him, It is not lawful for thee to have her.
5And when he
would have put
him to death, he
feared the multi-
tude, because they
counted him as a
prophet.

14:5 The Crowd
◄ 1 Samuel 15:24
John 7:13 ►

6But when Herod's birthday was kept,
the daughter of Herodias danced before
them, and pleased Herod.
7Whereupon he promised with an oath
to give her whatsoever she would ask.
8And she, being
before instructed of
her mother, said,
Give me here John
Baptist's head in a
charger.

14:8 Examples of Revenge
◄ Ezekiel 25:15
Luke 4:29 ►

9And the king was sorry: nevertheless for

the oath's sake, and them which sat with him at meat, he commanded *it* to be given *her.*

10And he sent, and beheaded John in the prison.

11And his head was brought in a charger, and given to the damsel: and she brought *it* to her mother.

12And his disciples came, and took up the body, and buried it, and went and told Jesus.

13When Jesus heard *of it,* he departed thence by ship into a desert place apart: and when the people had heard *thereof,* they followed him on foot out of the cities.

14And Jesus went forth, and saw a great multitude, and was moved with compassion toward them, and he healed their sick.

15And when it was evening, his disciples came to him, saying, This is a desert place, and the time is now past; send the multitude away, that they may go into the villages, and buy themselves victuals.

16But Jesus said unto them, They need not depart; give ye them to eat.

17And they say unto him, We have here but five loaves, and two fishes.

18He said, Bring them hither to me.

19And he commanded the multitude to sit down on the grass, and took the five loaves, and the two fishes, and looking up to heaven, he blessed, and brake, and gave the loaves to *his* disciples, and the disciples to the multitude.

20And they did all eat, and were filled: and they took up of the fragments that remained twelve baskets full.

21And they that had eaten were about five thousand men, beside women and children.

22And straightway Jesus constrained his disciples to get into a ship, and to go before him unto the other side, while he sent the multitudes away.

23And when he had sent the multitudes away, he went up into a mountain apart to pray: and when the evening was come, he was there alone.

24But the ship was now in the midst of the sea, tossed with waves: for the wind was contrary.

25And in the fourth watch of the night Jesus went unto them, walking on the sea.

26And when the disciples saw him walking on the sea, they were troubled, saying, It is a spirit; and they cried out for fear.

27But straightway Jesus spake unto them, saying, Be of good cheer; it is I; be not afraid.

14:27
Encouraging People
◄ Matthew 9:2
Matthew 17:7 ►

28And Peter answered him and said, Lord, if it be thou, bid me come unto thee on the water.

29And he said, Come. And when Peter was come down out of the ship, he walked on the water, to go to Jesus.

30But when he saw the wind boisterous, he was afraid; and beginning to sink, he cried, saying, Lord, save me.

31And immediately Jesus stretched forth *his* hand, and caught him, and said unto him, O thou of little faith, wherefore didst thou doubt?

32And when they were come into the ship, the wind ceased.

33Then they that were in the ship came and worshipped him, saying, Of a truth thou art the Son of God.

34And when they were gone over, they came into the land of Gennesaret.

35And when the men of that place had knowledge of him, they sent out into all that country round about, and brought unto him all that were diseased;

36And besought him that they might only touch the hem of his garment: and as many as touched were made perfectly whole.

15

1Then came to Jesus scribes and Pharisees, which were of Jerusalem, saying,

2Why do thy disciples transgress the tradition of the elders? for they wash not their hands when they eat bread.

3But he answered and said unto them, Why do ye also transgress the commandment of God by your tradition?

4For God commanded, saying, Honour thy father and mother: and, He that curseth father or mother, let him die the death.

5But ye say, Whosoever shall say to *his* father or *his* mother, *It is* a gift, by whatsoever thou mightest be profited by me;

6And honour not his father or his mother, *he shall be free.* Thus have ye made the commandment of God of none effect by your tradition.

7*Ye* hypocrites, well did Esaias prophesy of you, saying,

8 This people draweth nigh unto me with their mouth, and honoureth me with *their* lips; but their heart is far from me.

9 But in vain they do worship me, teaching *for* doctrines the commandments of men.

10 And he called the multitude, and said unto them, Hear, and understand:

11 Not that which goeth into the mouth defileth a man; but that which cometh out of the mouth, this defileth a man.

12 Then came his disciples, and said unto him, Knowest thou that the Pharisees were offended, after they heard this saying?

13 But he answered and said, Every plant, which my heavenly Father hath not planted, shall be rooted up.

14 Let them alone: they be blind leaders of the blind. And if the blind lead the blind, both shall fall into the ditch.

15 Then answered Peter and said unto him, Declare unto us this parable.

16 And Jesus said, Are ye also yet without understanding?

17 Do not ye yet understand, that whatsoever entereth in at the mouth goeth into the belly, and is cast out into the draught?

18 But those things which proceed out of the mouth come forth from the heart; and they defile the man.

15:18 Heart
◄ Matthew 6:18
Luke 6:45 ►

19 For out of the heart proceed evil thoughts, murders, adulteries, fornications, thefts, false witness, blasphemies:

15:19 Bad Thoughts
◄ Matthew 9:4 ►

20 These are *the things* which defile a man: but to eat with unwashen hands defileth not a man.

21 Then Jesus went thence, and departed into the coasts of Tyre and Sidon.

22 And, behold, a woman of Canaan came out of the same coasts, and cried unto him, saying, Have mercy on me, O Lord, *thou* Son of David; my daughter is grievously vexed with a devil.

23 But he answered her not a word. And his disciples came and besought him, saying, Send her away; for she crieth after us.

15:23 Faith Tested
◄ Mark 5:35 ►

15:23 Impatience
◄ Jonah 4:8-9
Luke 9:54 ►

24 But he answered and said, I am not sent but unto the lost sheep of the house of Israel.

25 Then came she and worshipped him, saying, Lord, help me.

15:23 Not Caring
◄ Genesis 4:9
Matthew 27:42 ►

26 But he answered and said, It is not meet to take the children's bread, and to cast *it* to dogs.

27 And she said, Truth, Lord: yet the dogs eat of the crumbs which fall from their masters' table.

28 Then Jesus answered and said unto her, O woman, great *is* thy faith: be it unto thee even as thou wilt. And her daughter was made whole from that very hour.

29 And Jesus departed from thence, and came nigh unto the sea of Galilee; and went up into a mountain, and sat down there.

30 And great multitudes came unto him, having with them *those that were* lame, blind, dumb, maimed, and many others, and cast them down at Jesus' feet; and he healed them:

31 Insomuch that the multitude wondered, when they saw the dumb to speak, the maimed to be whole, the lame to walk, and the blind to see: and they glorified the God of Israel.

32 Then Jesus called his disciples *unto him,* and said, I have compassion on the multitude, because they continue with me now three days, and have nothing to eat: and I will not send them away fasting, lest they faint in the way.

33 And his disciples say unto him, Whence should we have so much bread in the wilderness, as to fill so great a multitude?

34 And Jesus saith unto them, How many loaves have ye? And they said, Seven, and a few little fishes.

35 And he commanded the multitude to sit down on the ground.

36 And he took the seven loaves and the fishes, and gave thanks, and brake *them,*

and gave to his disciples, and the disciples
to the multitude.
37 And they did all eat, and were filled:
and they took up of the broken *meat* that
was left seven baskets full.
38 And they that did eat were four thousand men, beside women and children.
39 And he sent away the multitude, and
took ship, and came into the coasts of
Magdala.

16

1 The Pharisees also with the Sadducees
came, and tempting desired him that he
would shew them a sign from heaven.
2 He answered and said unto them,
When it is evening, ye say, *It will be* fair
weather: for the sky is red.
3 And in the morning, *It will be* foul
weather to day: for the sky is red and
lowring. O *ye* hypocrites, ye can discern the
face of the sky; but can ye not *discern* the
signs of the times?
4 A wicked and adulterous generation
seeketh after a sign; and there shall no sign
be given unto it, but the sign of the prophet
Jonas. And he left them, and departed.
5 And when his disciples were come to
the other side, they had forgotten to take
bread.
6 Then Jesus said unto them, Take heed
and beware of the leaven of the Pharisees
and of the Sadducees.
7 And they reasoned among themselves,
saying, *It is* because we have taken no
bread.
8 *Which* when Jesus perceived, he said
unto them, O ye of little faith, why reason
ye among yourselves, because ye have
brought no bread?
9 Do ye not yet understand, neither
remember the five loaves of the five
thousand, and how many baskets ye took
up?
10 Neither the seven loaves of the four
thousand, and how many baskets ye took
up?
11 How is it that ye do not understand
that I spake *it* not to you concerning bread,
that ye should beware of the leaven of the
Pharisees and of the Sadducees?
12 Then understood they how that he
bade *them* not beware of the leaven of
bread, but of the doctrine of the Pharisees
and of the Sadducees.
13 When Jesus came into the coasts of
Caesarea Philippi, he asked his disciples,
saying, Whom do men say that I the Son
of man am?
14 And they said, Some *say that thou art*
John the Baptist: some, Elias; and others,
Jeremias, or one of the prophets.
15 He saith unto them, But whom say ye
that I am?
16 And Simon Peter answered and said,
Thou art the Christ, the Son of the living
God.
17 And Jesus answered and said unto
him, Blessed art thou, Simon Barjona: for
flesh and blood hath not revealed *it* unto
thee, but my Father which is in heaven.
18 And I say also unto thee, That thou
art Peter, and upon this rock I will build
my church; and the gates of hell shall not
prevail against it.
19 And I will give unto thee the keys of
the kingdom of heaven: and whatsoever
thou shalt bind on earth shall be bound
in heaven: and whatsoever thou shalt loose
on earth shall be loosed in heaven.
20 Then charged he his disciples that they
should tell no man that he was Jesus the
Christ.
21 From that time forth began Jesus to
shew unto his disciples, how that he must
go unto Jerusalem, and suffer many things
of the elders and chief priests and scribes,
and be killed, and be raised again the third
day.
22 Then Peter took him, and began to
rebuke him, saying, Be it far from thee,
Lord: this shall not be unto thee.
23 But he turned, and said unto Peter,
Get thee behind me, Satan: thou art an offence unto me: for thou savourest not the
things that be of God, but those that be of
men.
24 Then said Jesus
unto his disciples,
If any *man* will
come after me, let
him deny himself,
and take up his
cross, and follow me.

16:24
Controlling Yourself
◄ Luke 14:26-27 ►

25 For whosoever will save his life shall
lose it: and whosoever will lose his life for
my sake shall find it.
26 For what is a man profited, if he shall
gain the whole world, and lose his own
soul? or what shall a man give in exchange
for his soul?
27 For the Son of man shall come in the

Turn to the next page for more . . .

glory of his Father with his angels; and then he shall reward every man according to his works.

16:27 Actions Judged
◄ Ezekiel 18:30
Romans 2:6 ►

28Verily I say unto you, There be some standing here, which shall not taste of death, till they see the Son of man coming in his kingdom.

16:27
Jesus' Return: Why?
◄ Matthew 25:31-32 ►

17

1And after six days Jesus taketh Peter, James, and John his brother, and bringeth them up into an high mountain apart,

2And was transfigured before them: and his face did shine as the sun, and his raiment was white as the light.

3And, behold, there appeared unto them Moses and Elias talking with him.

4Then answered Peter, and said unto Jesus, Lord, it is good for us to be here: if thou wilt, let us make here three tabernacles; one for thee, and one for Moses, and one for Elias.

5While he yet spake, behold, a bright cloud overshadowed them: and behold a voice out of the cloud, which said, This is my beloved Son, in whom I am well pleased; hear ye him.

6And when the disciples heard *it*, they fell on their face, and were sore afraid.

7And Jesus came and touched them, and said, Arise, and be not afraid.

17:7 Encouraging People
◄ Matthew 14:27
Mark 16:6 ►

8And when they had lifted up their eyes, they saw no man, save Jesus only.

9And as they came down from the mountain, Jesus charged them, saying, Tell the vision to no man, until the Son of man be risen again from the dead.

10And his disciples asked him, saying, Why then say the scribes that Elias must first come?

11And Jesus answered and said unto them, Elias truly shall first come, and restore all things.

12But I say unto you, That Elias is come already, and they knew him not, but have done unto him whatsoever they listed. Likewise shall also the Son of man suffer of them.

13Then the disciples understood that he spake unto them of John the Baptist.

14And when they were come to the multitude, there came to him a *certain* man, kneeling down to him, and saying,

15Lord, have mercy on my son: for he is lunatick, and sore vexed: for ofttimes he falleth into the fire, and oft into the water.

16And I brought him to thy disciples, and they could not cure him.

17Then Jesus answered and said, O faithless and perverse generation, how long shall I be with you? how long shall I suffer you? bring him hither to me.

17:17 Used to Sin
◄ Ezekiel 9:9
1 Timothy 6:5 ►

18And Jesus rebuked the devil; and he departed out of him: and the child was cured from that very hour.

19Then came the disciples to Jesus apart, and said, Why could not we cast him out?

20And Jesus said unto them, Because of your unbelief: for verily I say unto you, If ye have faith as a grain of mustard seed, ye shall say unto this mountain, Remove hence to yonder place; and it shall remove; and nothing shall be impossible unto you.

21Howbeit this kind goeth not out but by prayer and fasting.

22And while they abode in Galilee, Jesus said unto them, The Son of man shall be betrayed into the hands of men:

23And they shall kill him, and the third day he shall be raised again. And they were exceeding sorry.

24And when they were come to Capernaum, they that received tribute *money* came to Peter, and said, Doth not your master pay tribute?

25He saith, Yes. And when he was come into the house, Jesus prevented him, saying, What thinkest thou, Simon? of whom do the kings of the earth take custom or tribute? of their own children, or of strangers?

26Peter saith unto him, Of strangers. Jesus saith unto him, Then are the children free.

27Notwithstanding, lest we should offend them, go thou to the sea, and cast an hook, and take up the fish that

17:27 Obeying the Law
◄ Ecclesiastes 8:2
Matthew 22:21 ►

first cometh up; and when thou hast
opened his mouth, thou shalt find a piece
of money: that take, and give unto them
for me and thee.

18

1 At the same time came the disciples
unto Jesus, saying, Who is the greatest in
the kingdom of heaven?
2 And Jesus called a little child unto him,
and set him in the midst of them,
3 And said, Verily
I say unto you, Ex-
cept ye be convert-
ed, and become as
little children, ye
shall not enter into
the kingdom of heaven.

> **18:3 Willingness to Learn**
> ◄ Jeremiah 42:3
> Luke 11:1 ►

4 Whosoever therefore shall humble
himself as this little child, the same is
greatest in the kingdom of heaven.
5 And whoso shall receive one such little child in my name receiveth me.
6 But whoso shall offend one of these little ones which believe in me, it were better for him that a millstone were hanged
about his neck, and *that* he were drowned
in the depth of the sea.
7 Woe unto the world because of offences! for it must needs be that offences
come; but woe to that man by whom the
offence cometh!
8 Wherefore if thy hand or thy foot offend thee, cut them off, and cast *them* from
thee: it is better for thee to enter into life
halt or maimed, rather than having two
hands or two feet to be cast into everlasting fire.
9 And if thine eye offend thee, pluck it
out, and cast *it* from thee: it is better for
thee to enter into life with one eye, rather
than having two eyes to be cast into hell
fire.
10 Take heed that
ye despise not one
of these little ones;
for I say unto you,
That in heaven their
angels do always
behold the face of my Father which is in
heaven.

> **18:10 Watch Out!**
> ◄ Matthew 6:1
> Matthew 24:4 ►

11 For the Son of man is come to save
that which was lost.
12 How think ye? if a man have an hundred sheep, and one of them be gone
astray, doth he not leave the ninety
and nine, and goeth into the mountains,
and seeketh that which is gone astray?
13 And if so be that he find it, verily I say
unto you, he rejoiceth more of that *sheep*,
than of the ninety and nine which went
not astray.
14 Even so it is not the will of your Father which is in heaven, that one of these
little ones should perish.
15 Moreover if thy brother shall trespass
against thee, go and tell him his fault between thee and him alone: if he shall hear
thee, thou hast gained thy brother.
16 But if he will not hear *thee, then* take
with thee one or two more, that in the
mouth of two or three witnesses every
word may be established.
17 And if he shall neglect to hear them,
tell *it* unto the church: but if he neglect to
hear the church, let him be unto thee as
an heathen man and a publican.
18 Verily I say unto you, Whatsoever ye
shall bind on earth shall be bound in heav-
en: and whatsoever ye shall loose on earth
shall be loosed in heaven.
19 Again I say
unto you, That if
two of you shall
agree on earth as
touching any thing
that they shall ask,
it shall be done for them of my Father
which is in heaven.

> **18:19 Teamwork**
> ◄ Nehemiah 4:16-17
> Mark 2:3 ►

20 For where two or three are gathered
together in my name, there am I in the
midst of them.
21 Then came Peter to him, and said,
Lord, how oft shall my brother sin against
me, and I forgive him? till seven times?
22 Jesus saith unto him, I say not unto
thee, Until seven times: but, Until seventy
times seven.
23 Therefore is the
kingdom of heaven
likened unto a cer-
tain king, which
would take account
of his servants.

> **18:23 Getting Caught**
> ◄ Matthew 12:36
> Matthew 21:34 ►

24 And when he
had begun to
reckon, one was
brought unto him,
which owed him
ten thousand tal-
ents.

> **18:23-25 Poverty**
> ◄ Jeremiah 5:4
> Luke 15:14 ►

25 But forasmuch as he had not to pay,

his lord commanded him to be sold, and his wife, and children, and all that he had, and payment to be made.

26 The servant therefore fell down, and worshipped him, saying, Lord, have patience with me, and I will pay thee all.

27 Then the lord of that servant was moved with compassion, and loosed him, and forgave him the debt.

28 But the same servant went out, and found one of his fellowservants, which owed him an hundred pence: and he laid hands on him, and took *him* by the throat, saying, Pay me that thou owest.

18:28 No Mercy
◄ Matthew 6:15
Matthew 18:35 ►

29 And his fellowservant fell down at his feet, and besought him, saying, Have patience with me, and I will pay thee all.

30 And he would not: but went and cast him into prison, till he should pay the debt.

18:30 Cruelty
◄ Amos 1:11
Luke 10:32 ►

31 So when his fellowservants saw what was done, they were very sorry, and came and told unto their lord all that was done.

32 Then his lord, after that he had called him, said unto him, O thou wicked servant, I forgave thee all that debt, because thou desiredst me:

33 Shouldest not thou also have had compassion on thy fellowservant, even as I had pity on thee?

34 And his lord was wroth, and delivered him to the tormentors, till he should pay all that was due unto him.

35 So likewise shall my heavenly Father do also unto you, if ye from your hearts forgive not every one his brother their trespasses.

18:35 No Mercy
◄ Matthew 18:28
Romans 1:31 ►

19

1 And it came to pass, *that* when Jesus had finished these sayings, he departed from Galilee, and came into the coasts of Judaea beyond Jordan;

2 And great multitudes followed him; and he healed them there.

3 The Pharisees also came unto him, tempting him, and saying unto him, Is it lawful for a man to put away his wife for every cause?

4 And he answered and said unto them, Have ye not read, that he which made *them* at the beginning made them male and female,

5 And said, For this cause shall a man leave father and mother, and shall cleave to his wife: and they twain shall be one flesh?

6 Wherefore they are no more twain, but one flesh. What therefore God hath joined together, let not man put asunder.

7 They say unto him, Why did Moses then command to give a writing of divorcement, and to put her away?

8 He saith unto them, Moses because of the hardness of your hearts suffered you to put away your wives: but from the beginning it was not so.

9 And I say unto you, Whosoever shall put away his wife, except *it be* for fornication, and shall marry another, committeth adultery: and whoso marrieth her which is put away doth commit adultery.

10 His disciples say unto him, If the case of the man be so with *his* wife, it is not good to marry.

11 But he said unto them, All *men* cannot receive this saying, save *they* to whom it is given.

12 For there are some eunuchs, which were so born from *their* mother's womb: and there are some eunuchs, which were made eunuchs of men: and there be eunuchs, which have made themselves eunuchs for the kingdom of heaven's sake. He that is able to receive *it*, let him receive *it*.

13 Then were there brought unto him little children, that he should put *his* hands on them, and pray: and the disciples rebuked them.

14 But Jesus said, Suffer little children, and forbid them not, to come unto me: for of such is the kingdom of heaven.

15 And he laid *his* hands on them, and departed thence.

16 And, behold, one came and said unto him, Good Master, what good thing shall I do, that I may have eternal life?

17 And he said unto him, Why callest thou me good? *there is* none good but one, *that is*, God: but if thou wilt enter into life, keep the commandments.

18He saith unto him, Which? Jesus said, Thou shalt do no murder, Thou shalt not commit adultery, Thou shalt not steal, Thou shalt not bear false witness,

19:18 Hurtful Lying
◄ Proverbs 25:18 ►

19:18 Stealing
◄ Zechariah 5:3
Romans 13:9 ►

19Honour thy father and *thy* mother: and, Thou shalt love thy neighbour as thyself.

20The young man saith unto him, All these things have I kept from my youth up: what lack I yet?

21Jesus said unto him, If thou wilt be perfect, go *and* sell that thou hast, and give to the poor, and thou shalt have treasure in heaven: and come *and* follow me.

19:21 Generosity
◄ Matthew 6:1
Luke 11:41 ►

19:21 Kind to the Poor
◄ Proverbs 28:27
Galatians 2:10 ►

22But when the young man heard that saying, he went away sorrowful: for he had great possessions.

19:21 Sacrifice
◄ Matthew 19:29 ►

23Then said Jesus unto his disciples, Verily I say unto you, That a rich man shall hardly enter into the kingdom of heaven.

19:23 Money's Dangers
◄ Proverbs 28:20
Mark 4:19 ►

24And again I say unto you, It is easier for a camel to go through the eye of a needle, than for a rich man to enter into the kingdom of God.

25When his disciples heard *it,* they were exceedingly amazed, saying, Who then can be saved?

26But Jesus beheld *them,* and said unto them, With men this is impossible; but with God all things are possible.

19:26 All-powerful
◄ Habakkuk 3:6
Mark 14:36 ►

27Then answered Peter and said unto him, Behold, we have forsaken all, and followed thee; what shall we have therefore?

28And Jesus said unto them, Verily I say unto you, That ye which have followed me, in the regeneration when the Son of man shall sit in the throne of his glory, ye also shall sit upon twelve thrones, judging the twelve tribes of Israel.

19:28 Good Rewarded
◄ Habakkuk 3:19
Luke 19:17 ►

29And every one that hath forsaken houses, or brethren, or sisters, or father, or mother, or wife, or children, or lands, for my name's sake, shall receive an hundredfold, and shall inherit everlasting life.

19:29 Sacrifice
◄ Matthew 19:21
Mark 8:35 ►

30But many *that are* first shall be last; and the last *shall be* first.

20

1For the kingdom of heaven is like unto a man *that is* an householder, which went out early in the morning to hire labourers into his vineyard.

2And when he had agreed with the labourers for a penny a day, he sent them into his vineyard.

3And he went out about the third hour, and saw others standing idle in the marketplace,

4And said unto them; Go ye also into the vineyard, and whatsoever is right I will give you. And they went their way.

5Again he went out about the sixth and ninth hour, and did likewise.

6And about the eleventh hour he went out, and found others standing idle, and saith unto them, Why stand ye here all the day idle?

7They say unto him, Because no man hath hired us. He saith unto them, Go ye also into the vineyard; and whatsoever is right, *that* shall ye receive.

8So when even was come, the lord of the vineyard saith unto his steward, Call the labourers, and give them *their* hire, beginning from the last unto the first.

9And when they came that *were hired* about the eleventh hour, they received every man a penny.

10But when the first came, they supposed

that they should have received more; and
they likewise received every man a penny.
11 And when they had received *it*, they
murmured against the goodman of the
house,
12 Saying, These
last have wrought
but one hour, and
thou hast made
them equal unto us,
which have borne
the burden and heat of the day.

20:12 Injustice
◄ Habakkuk 1:2
Romans 9:14 ►

13 But he answered one of them, and
said, Friend, I do thee no wrong: didst not
thou agree with me for a penny?
14 Take *that* thine *is*, and go thy way: I
will give unto this last, even as unto thee.
15 Is it not lawful for me to do what I
will with mine own? Is thine eye evil, because I am good?
16 So the last shall be first, and the first
last: for many be called, but few chosen.
17 And Jesus going up to Jerusalem took
the twelve disciples apart in the way, and
said unto them,
18 Behold, we go up to Jerusalem; and
the Son of man shall be betrayed unto the
chief priests and unto the scribes, and they
shall condemn him to death,
19 And shall deliver him to the Gentiles
to mock, and to scourge, and to crucify
him: and the third day he shall rise again.
20 Then came to him the mother of Zebedee's children with her sons, worshipping
him, and desiring a certain thing of him.
21 And he said
unto her, What wilt
thou? She saith
unto him, Grant
that these my two
sons may sit, the
one on thy right hand, and the other on
the left, in thy kingdom.

20:21 Ambition
◄ Habakkuk 2:5
Luke 11:43 ►

22 But Jesus answered and said, Ye know
not what ye ask. Are ye able to drink of
the cup that I shall drink of, and to be baptized with the baptism that I am baptized
with? They say unto him, We are able.
23 And he saith unto them, Ye shall drink
indeed of my cup, and be baptized with
the baptism that I am baptized with: but
to sit on my right hand, and on my left, is
not mine to give, but *it shall be given to them*
for whom it is prepared of my Father.
24 And when the ten heard *it*, they were
moved with indignation against the two
brethren.
25 But Jesus called them *unto him*, and
said, Ye know that the princes of the Gentiles exercise dominion over them, and
they that are great exercise authority upon
them.
26 But it shall not be so among you: but
whosoever will be great among you, let
him be your minister;
27 And whosoever will be chief among
you, let him be your servant:
28 Even as the Son of man came not to
be ministered unto, but to minister, and
to give his life a ransom for many.
29 And as they departed from Jericho, a
great multitude followed him.
30 And, behold, two blind men sitting by
the way side, when they heard that Jesus
passed by, cried out, saying, Have mercy
on us, O Lord, *thou* Son of David.
31 And the multitude rebuked them, because they should hold their peace: but
they cried the more, saying, Have mercy
on us, O Lord, *thou* Son of David.
32 And Jesus stood still, and called them,
and said, What will ye that I shall do unto
you?
33 They say unto him, Lord, that our eyes
may be opened.
34 So Jesus had compassion *on them*, and
touched their eyes: and immediately their
eyes received sight, and they followed him.

21

1 And when they drew nigh unto Jerusalem, and were come to Bethphage, unto
the mount of Olives, then sent Jesus two
disciples,
2 Saying unto them, Go into the village
over against you, and straightway ye shall
find an ass tied, and a colt with her: loose
them, and bring *them* unto me.
3 And if any *man* say ought unto you, ye
shall say, The Lord hath need of them; and
straightway he will send them.
4 All this was done, that it might be fulfilled which was spoken by the prophet,
saying,
5 Tell ye the
daughter of Sion,
Behold, thy King
cometh unto thee,
meek, and sitting
upon an ass, and a
colt the foal of an ass.

21:5 Jesus the King
◄ Matthew 2:2
Matthew 25:34 ►

6 And the disciples went, and did as

Jesus commanded them,

7 And brought the ass, and the colt, and put on them their clothes, and they set *him* thereon.

21:6 Obeying Christ
◄ Matthew 9:9
Matthew 26:19 ►

8 And a very great multitude spread their garments in the way; others cut down branches from the trees, and strawed *them* in the way.

9 And the multitudes that went before, and that followed, cried, saying, Hosanna to the Son of David: Blessed *is* he that cometh in the name of the Lord; Hosanna in the highest.

10 And when he was come into Jerusalem, all the city was moved, saying, Who is this?

11 And the multitude said, This is Jesus the prophet of Nazareth of Galilee.

12 And Jesus went into the temple of God, and cast out all them that sold and bought in the temple, and overthrew the tables of the moneychangers, and the seats of them that sold doves,

13 And said unto them, It is written, My house shall be called the house of prayer; but ye have made it a den of thieves.

14 And the blind and the lame came to him in the temple; and he healed them.

15 And when the chief priests and scribes saw the wonderful things that he did, and the children crying in the temple, and saying, Hosanna to the Son of David; they were sore displeased,

16 And said unto him, Hearest thou what these say? And Jesus saith unto them, Yea; have ye never read, Out of the mouth of babes and sucklings thou hast perfected praise?

17 And he left them, and went out of the city into Bethany; and he lodged there.

18 Now in the morning as he returned into the city, he hungered.

19 And when he saw a fig tree in the way, he came to it, and found nothing thereon, but leaves only, and said unto it, Let no fruit grow on thee henceforward for ever. And presently the fig tree withered away.

20 And when the disciples saw *it,* they marvelled, saying, How soon is the fig tree withered away!

21 Jesus answered and said unto them, Verily I say unto you, If ye have faith, and doubt not, ye shall not only do this *which is done* to the fig tree, but also if ye shall say unto this mountain, Be thou removed, and be thou cast into the sea; it shall be done.

22 And all things, whatsoever ye shall ask in prayer, believing, ye shall receive.

21:22
Benefits of Faith
◄ John 1:12 ►

23 And when he was come into the temple, the chief priests and the elders of the people came unto him as he was teaching, and said, By what authority doest thou these things? and who gave thee this authority?

21:22
Prayer
◄ John 14:13 ►

24 And Jesus answered and said unto them, I also will ask you one thing, which if ye tell me, I in like wise will tell you by what authority I do these things.

25 The baptism of John, whence was it? from heaven, or of men? And they reasoned with themselves, saying, If we shall say, From heaven; he will say unto us, Why did ye not then believe him?

26 But if we shall say, Of men; we fear the people; for all hold John as a prophet.

27 And they answered Jesus, and said, We cannot tell. And he said unto them, Neither tell I you by what authority I do these things.

28 But what think ye? A *certain* man had two sons; and he came to the first, and said, Son, go work to day in my vineyard.

29 He answered and said, I will not: but afterward he repented, and went.

30 And he came to the second, and said likewise. And he answered and said, I *go,* sir: and went not.

31 Whether of them twain did the will of *his* father? They say unto him, The first. Jesus saith unto them, Verily I say unto you, That the publicans and the harlots go into the kingdom of God before you.

32 For John came unto you in the way of righteousness, and ye believed him not: but the publicans and the harlots believed him: and ye, when ye had seen *it,* repented not afterward, that ye might believe him.

33 Hear another parable: There was a certain householder, which planted a

vineyard, and hedged it round about, and
digged a winepress in it, and built a tower,
and let it out to husbandmen, and went
into a far country:
34 And when the
time of the fruit
drew near, he sent
his servants to the
husbandmen, that
they might receive
the fruits of it.

21:34 Getting Caught
◄ Matthew 18:23
Matthew 25:19 ►

35 And the husbandmen took his servants, and beat one, and killed another,
and stoned another.
36 Again, he sent other servants more
than the first: and they did unto them likewise.
37 But last of all he sent unto them his
son, saying, They will reverence my son.
38 But when the husbandmen saw the
son, they said among themselves, This is
the heir; come, let us kill him, and let us
seize on his inheritance.
39 And they caught him, and cast *him* out
of the vineyard, and slew *him*.
40 When the lord therefore of the vineyard cometh, what will he do unto those
husbandmen?
41 They say unto him, He will miserably
destroy those wicked men, and will let out
his vineyard unto other husbandmen,
which shall render him the fruits in their
seasons.
42 Jesus saith unto
them, Did ye never
read in the scrip-
tures, The stone
which the builders
rejected, the same is
become the head of the corner: this is the
Lord's doing, and it is marvellous in our
eyes?

21:42 The Ultimate
◄ Psalm 118:22
Acts 4:11 ►

43 Therefore say I unto you, The kingdom
of God shall be taken from you, and given
to a nation bringing forth the fruits
thereof.
44 And whosoever shall fall on this stone
shall be broken: but on whomsoever it
shall fall, it will grind him to powder.
45 And when the chief priests and Pharisees had heard his parables, they perceived that he spake of them.
46 But when they sought to lay hands on
him, they feared the multitude, because
they took him for a prophet.

22

1 And Jesus answered and spake unto
them again by parables, and said,
2 The kingdom of heaven is like unto a
certain king, which made a marriage for
his son,
3 And sent forth
his servants to call
them that were bid-
den to the wedding:
and they would not
come.

22:3 Change
◄ Hosea 6:1
Luke 14:17 ►

4 Again, he sent forth other servants, saying, Tell them which are bidden, Behold, I
have prepared my dinner: my oxen and *my*
fatlings *are* killed, and all things *are* ready:
come unto the marriage.
5 But they made
light of *it*, and went
their ways, one to
his farm, another to
his merchandise:
6 And the rem-
nant took his ser-
vants, and entreated *them* spitefully, and
slew *them*.

22:5 Apathy
◄ Zephaniah 1:12
Matthew 24:12 ►

7 But when the king heard *thereof*, he was
wroth: and he sent forth his armies, and
destroyed those murderers, and burned up
their city.
8 Then saith he to
his servants, The
wedding is ready,
but they which
were bidden were
not worthy.

22:8 Who Deserves Christ?
◄ Matthew 10:37
Acts 13:46 ►

9 Go ye therefore
into the highways,
and as many as ye
shall find, bid to
the marriage.
10 So those ser-
vants went out into
the highways, and gathered together all as
many as they found, both bad and good:
and the wedding was furnished with
guests.

22:9 God Calls You
◄ Isaiah 55:1
John 7:37 ►

11 And when the king came in to see the
guests, he saw there a man which had not
on a wedding garment:
12 And he saith unto him, Friend, how
camest thou in hither not having a wedding garment? And he was speechless.
13 Then said the king to the servants,
Bind him hand and foot, and take him
away, and cast *him* into outer darkness;

there shall be weeping and gnashing of
teeth.
14 For many are called, but few *are*
chosen.
15 Then went the Pharisees, and took
counsel how they might entangle him in
his talk.
16 And they sent out unto him their disciples with the Herodians, saying, Master,
we know that thou art true, and teachest
the way of God in truth, neither carest thou
for any *man:* for thou regardest not the
person of men.
17 Tell us therefore, What thinkest thou?
Is it lawful to give tribute unto Caesar, or
not?
18 But Jesus perceived their wickedness, and said, Why tempt ye me, *ye* hypocrites?
19 Shew me the tribute money. And they
brought unto him a penny.
20 And he saith unto them, Whose *is* this
image and superscription?
21 They say unto
him, Caesar's. Then
saith he unto them,
Render therefore
unto Caesar the
things which are
Caesar's; and unto God the things that are
God's.

22:21 Obeying the Law
◄ Matthew 17:27
Romans 13:1 ►

22 When they had heard *these words,* they
marvelled, and left him, and went their
way.
23 The same day came to him the Sadducees, which say that there is no resurrection, and asked him,
24 Saying, Master, Moses said, If a man
die, having no children, his brother shall
marry his wife, and raise up seed unto his
brother.
25 Now there were with us seven brethren: and the first, when he had married a
wife, deceased, and, having no issue, left
his wife unto his brother:
26 Likewise the second also, and the
third, unto the seventh.
27 And last of all the woman died also.
28 Therefore in the resurrection whose
wife shall she be of the seven? for they all
had her.
29 Jesus answered and said unto them,
Ye do err, not knowing the scriptures, nor
the power of God.
30 For in the resurrection they neither
marry, nor are given in marriage, but are
as the angels of God in heaven.
31 But as touching the resurrection of the
dead, have ye not read that which was spoken unto you by God, saying,
32 I am the God of Abraham, and the
God of Isaac, and the God of Jacob? God
is not the God of the dead, but of the living.
33 And when the multitude heard *this,*
they were astonished at his doctrine.
34 But when the Pharisees had heard that
he had put the Sadducees to silence, they
were gathered together.
35 Then one of them, *which was* a lawyer,
asked *him a question,* tempting him, and
saying,
36 Master, which *is* the great commandment in the law?
37 Jesus said unto
him, Thou shalt
love the Lord thy
God with all thy
heart, and with all
thy soul, and with
all thy mind.

22:37 Love for God
◄ Psalm 31:23
2 Thessalonians 3:5 ►

38 This is the first and great commandment.
39 And the sec-
ond *is* like unto it,
Thou shalt love thy
neighbour as thy-
self.
40 On these two
commandments hang all the law and the
prophets.

22:39 Loving Others
◄ Deuteronomy 10:19
John 13:35 ►

41 While the Pharisees were gathered together, Jesus asked them,
42 Saying, What think ye of Christ?
whose son is he? They say unto him, *The*
Son of David.
43 He saith unto them, How then doth
David in spirit call him Lord, saying,
44 The LORD said unto my Lord, Sit thou
on my right hand, till I make thine enemies thy footstool?
45 If David then call him Lord, how is
he his son?
46 And no man was able to answer him
a word, neither durst any *man* from that
day forth ask him any more *questions.*

23

1 Then spake Jesus to the multitude, and
to his disciples,
2 Saying, The scribes and the Pharisees
sit in Moses' seat:

3 All therefore whatsoever they bid you observe, *that* observe and do; but do not ye after their works: for they say, and do not.

4 For they bind heavy burdens and grievous to be borne, and lay *them* on men's shoulders; but they *themselves* will not move them with one of their fingers.

23:4 Phonies
◄ Matthew 12:2
Matthew 23:13 ►

5 But all their works they do for to be seen of men: they make broad their phylacteries, and enlarge the borders of their garments,

23:5 Showing Off
◄ Matthew 6:16
Luke 18:12 ►

6 And love the uppermost rooms at feasts, and the chief seats in the synagogues,

7 And greetings in the markets, and to be called of men, Rabbi, Rabbi.

8 But be not ye called Rabbi: for one is your Master, *even* Christ; and all ye are brethren.

23:8 Equality
◄ Proverbs 22:2
Acts 10:28 ►

9 And call no *man* your father upon the earth: for one is your Father, which is in heaven.

10 Neither be ye called masters: for one is your Master, *even* Christ.

11 But he that is greatest among you shall be your servant.

12 And whosoever shall exalt himself shall be abased; and he that shall humble himself shall be exalted.

13 But woe unto you, scribes and Pharisees, hypocrites! for ye shut up the kingdom of heaven against men: for ye neither go in *yourselves,* neither suffer ye them that are entering to go in.

23:13 Phonies
◄ Matthew 23:4
Matthew 23:23 ►

14 Woe unto you, scribes and Pharisees, hypocrites! for ye devour widows' houses, and for a pretence make long prayer: therefore ye shall receive the greater damnation.

15 Woe unto you, scribes and Pharisees, hypocrites! for ye compass sea and land to make one proselyte, and when he is made, ye make him twofold more the child of hell than yourselves.

16 Woe unto you, *ye* blind guides, which say, Whosoever shall swear by the temple, it is nothing; but whosoever shall swear by the gold of the temple, he is a debtor!

17 *Ye* fools and blind: for whether is greater, the gold, or the temple that sanctifieth the gold?

18 And, Whosoever shall swear by the altar, it is nothing; but whosoever sweareth by the gift that is upon it, he is guilty.

19 *Ye* fools and blind: for whether *is* greater, the gift, or the altar that sanctifieth the gift?

20 Whoso therefore shall swear by the altar, sweareth by it, and by all things thereon.

21 And whoso shall swear by the temple, sweareth by it, and by him that dwelleth therein.

22 And he that shall swear by heaven, sweareth by the throne of God, and by him that sitteth thereon.

23 Woe unto you, scribes and Pharisees, hypocrites! for ye pay tithe of mint and anise and cummin, and have omitted the weightier *matters* of the law, judgment, mercy, and faith: these ought ye to have done, and not to leave the other undone.

23:23 Phonies
◄ Matthew 23:13
Matthew 23:27 ►

24 *Ye* blind guides, which strain at a gnat, and swallow a camel.

25 Woe unto you, scribes and Pharisees, hypocrites! for ye make clean the outside of the cup and of the platter, but within they are full of extortion and excess.

23:25 Source of Evil
◄ Jeremiah 17:9
Mark 7:21 ►

26 *Thou* blind Pharisee, cleanse first that *which is* within the cup and platter, that the outside of them may be clean also.

23:27 Good Looks
◄ 1 Samuel 16:7
John 7:24 ►

27 Woe unto you, scribes and Pharisees, hypocrites! for ye are like unto whited sepulchres,

23:27 Phonies
◄ Matthew 23:23
James 1:26 ►

which indeed appear beautiful outward, but are within full of dead *men's* bones, and of all uncleanness.

28 Even so ye also outwardly appear righteous unto men, but within ye are full of hypocrisy and iniquity.

23:28 Hypocrisy
◄ Proverbs 26:25
Luke 12:1 ►

29 Woe unto you, scribes and Pharisees, hypocrites! because ye build the tombs of the prophets, and garnish the sepulchres of the righteous,

30 And say, If we had been in the days of our fathers, we would not have been partakers with them in the blood of the prophets.

31 Wherefore ye be witnesses unto yourselves, that ye are the children of them which killed the prophets.

32 Fill ye up then the measure of your fathers.

33 *Ye* serpents, *ye* generation of vipers, how can ye escape the damnation of hell?

23:33 Telling the Truth
◄ Matthew 3:7
Acts 7:52 ►

34 Wherefore, behold, I send unto you prophets, and wise men, and scribes: and *some* of them ye shall kill and crucify; and *some* of them shall ye scourge in your synagogues, and persecute *them* from city to city:

35 That upon you may come all the righteous blood shed upon the earth, from the blood of righteous Abel unto the blood of Zacharias son of Barachias, whom ye slew between the temple and the altar.

36 Verily I say unto you, All these things shall come upon this generation.

37 O Jerusalem, Jerusalem, *thou* that killest the prophets, and stonest them which are sent unto thee, how often would I have gathered thy children together, even as a hen gathereth her chickens under *her* wings, and ye would not!

38 Behold, your house is left unto you desolate.

39 For I say unto you, Ye shall not see me henceforth, till ye shall say, Blessed *is* he that cometh in the name of the Lord.

24

1 And Jesus went out, and departed from the temple: and his disciples came to *him* for to shew him the buildings of the temple.

2 And Jesus said unto them, See ye not all these things? verily I say unto you, There shall not be left here one stone upon another, that shall not be thrown down.

3 And as he sat upon the mount of Olives, the disciples came unto him privately, saying, Tell us, when shall these things be? and what *shall be* the sign of thy coming, and of the end of the world?

4 And Jesus answered and said unto them, Take heed that no man deceive you.

24:4 Deception
◄ 1 Corinthians 6:9 ►

5 For many shall come in my name, saying, I am Christ; and shall deceive many.

24:4 Watch Out!
◄ Matthew 18:10
Mark 4:24 ►

6 And ye shall hear of wars and rumours of wars: see that ye be not troubled: for all *these things* must come to pass, but the end is not yet.

7 For nation shall rise against nation, and kingdom against kingdom: and there shall be famines, and pestilences, and earthquakes, in divers places.

8 All these *are* the beginning of sorrows.

9 Then shall they deliver you up to be afflicted, and shall kill you: and ye shall be hated of all nations for my name's sake.

24:9 Expecting Pain
◄ Matthew 10:17
Luke 21:12 ►

10 And then shall many be offended, and shall betray one another, and shall hate one another.

11 And many false prophets shall rise, and shall deceive many.

12 And because iniquity shall abound, the love of many shall wax cold.

24:12 Apathy
◄ Matthew 22:5 ►

13 But he that shall endure unto the end, the same shall be saved.

14 And this gospel of the kingdom shall be preached in all the world for a witness unto all nations; and then shall the end come.

15 When ye therefore shall see the abomination of desolation, spoken of by

Daniel the prophet, stand in the holy place, (whoso readeth, let him understand:)

16 Then let them which be in Judaea flee into the mountains:

17 Let him which is on the housetop not come down to take any thing out of his house:

18 Neither let him which is in the field return back to take his clothes.

19 And woe unto them that are with child, and to them that give suck in those days!

20 But pray ye that your flight be not in the winter, neither on the sabbath day:

21 For then shall be great tribulation, such as was not since the beginning of the world to this time, no, nor ever shall be.

> **24:21 Suffering**
> ◄ Deuteronomy 4:30
> John 16:33 ►

22 And except those days should be shortened, there should no flesh be saved: but for the elect's sake those days shall be shortened.

23 Then if any man shall say unto you, Lo, here *is* Christ, or there; believe *it* not.

24 For there shall arise false Christs, and false prophets, and shall shew great signs and wonders; insomuch that, if *it were* possible, they shall deceive the very elect.

25 Behold, I have told you before.

26 Wherefore if they shall say unto you, Behold, *he is* in the desert; go not forth: behold, he is in the secret chambers; believe *it* not.

27 For as the lightning cometh out of the east, and shineth even unto the west; so shall also the coming of the Son of man be.

> **24:27 Jesus' Return: When?**
> ◄ Matthew 24:36 ►

28 For wheresoever the carcase is, there will the eagles be gathered together.

29 Immediately after the tribulation of those days shall the sun be darkened, and the moon shall not give her light, and the stars shall fall from heaven, and the powers of the heavens shall be shaken:

30 And then shall appear the sign of the Son of man in heaven: and then shall all the tribes of the earth mourn, and they shall see the Son of man coming in the clouds of heaven with power and great glory.

> **24:30 Bad News**
> ◄ Mark 8:38 ►

31 And he shall send his angels with a great sound of a trumpet, and they shall gather together his elect from the four winds, from one end of heaven to the other.

32 Now learn a parable of the fig tree; When his branch is yet tender, and putteth forth leaves, ye know that summer is nigh:

33 So likewise ye, when ye shall see all these things, know that it is near, *even* at the doors.

34 Verily I say unto you, This generation shall not pass, till all these things be fulfilled.

35 Heaven and earth shall pass away, but my words shall not pass away.

36 But of that day and hour knoweth no *man*, no, not the angels of heaven, but my Father only.

> **24:36 Jesus' Return: When?**
> ◄ Matthew 24:27
> Luke 12:40 ►

37 But as the days of Noe *were*, so shall also the coming of the Son of man be.

38 For as in the days that were before the flood they were eating and drinking, marrying and giving in marriage, until the day that Noe entered into the ark,

39 And knew not until the flood came, and took them all away; so shall also the coming of the Son of man be.

40 Then shall two be in the field; the one shall be taken, and the other left.

41 Two *women shall be* grinding at the mill; the one shall be taken, and the other left.

42 Watch therefore: for ye know not what hour your Lord doth come.

43 But know this, that if the goodman of the house had known in what watch the thief would come, he would have watched, and would not have suffered his house to be broken up.

> **24:43 The Future**
> ◄ Ecclesiastes 11:2
> Acts 20:22 ►

44 Therefore be ye

> **24:44 Ready for the Future**
> ◄ Amos 4:12
> Matthew 25:10 ►

also ready: for in such an hour as ye think not the Son of man cometh.

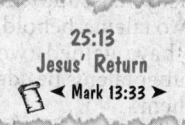

24:44 Watching for Jesus' Return
◄ Luke 19:13 ►

45 Who then is a faithful and wise servant, whom his lord hath made ruler over his household, to give them meat in due season?

46 Blessed *is* that servant, whom his lord when he cometh shall find so doing.

47 Verily I say unto you, That he shall make him ruler over all his goods.

48 But and if that evil servant shall say in his heart, My lord delayeth his coming;

49 And shall begin to smite *his* fellowservants, and to eat and drink with the drunken;

50 The lord of that servant shall come in a day when he looketh not for *him,* and in an hour that he is not aware of,

51 And shall cut him asunder, and appoint *him* his portion with the hypocrites: there shall be weeping and gnashing of teeth.

25

1 Then shall the kingdom of heaven be likened unto ten virgins, which took their lamps, and went forth to meet the bridegroom.

2 And five of them were wise, and five *were* foolish.

3 They that *were* foolish took their lamps, and took no oil with them:

4 But the wise took oil in their vessels with their lamps.

5 While the bridegroom tarried, they all slumbered and slept.

6 And at midnight there was a cry made, Behold, the bridegroom cometh; go ye out to meet him.

7 Then all those virgins arose, and trimmed their lamps.

8 And the foolish said unto the wise, Give us of your oil; for our lamps are gone out.

9 But the wise answered, saying, *Not so;* lest there be not enough for us and you: but go ye rather to them that sell, and buy for yourselves.

10 And while they went to buy, the bridegroom came; and they that were ready went in with him to the marriage: and the door was shut.

25:10 Ready for the Future
◄ Matthew 24:44
Mark 13:35 ►

11 Afterward came also the other virgins, saying, Lord, Lord, open to us.

12 But he answered and said, Verily I say unto you, I know you not.

13 Watch therefore, for ye know neither the day nor the hour wherein the Son of man cometh.

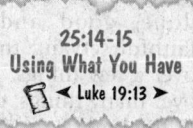

25:13 Jesus' Return
◄ Mark 13:33 ►

14 For *the kingdom of heaven is* as a man travelling into a far country, *who* called his own servants, and delivered unto them his goods.

25:14-15 Using What You Have
◄ Luke 19:13 ►

15 And unto one he gave five talents, to another two, and to another one; to every man according to his several ability; and straightway took his journey.

25:15 Church
◄ Romans 12:6

25:15 Gifts from God
◄ Matthew 9:8
Luke 11:9 ►

16 Then he that had received the five talents went and traded with the same, and made *them* other five talents.

17 And likewise he that *had received* two, he also gained other two.

18 But he that had received one went and digged in the earth, and hid his lord's money.

19 After a long time the lord of those servants cometh, and reckoneth with them.

25:19 Getting Caught
◄ Matthew 21:34
Luke 12:20 ►

20 And so he that had received five talents came and brought other five talents, saying, Lord, thou deliveredst unto me five talents: behold, I have gained beside them five talents more.

25:20 Talents
◄ 1 Timothy 4:7 ►

21 His lord said unto him, Well done, *thou* good and faithful servant: thou hast been faithful over a few things, I will make thee ruler over many things: enter thou into the joy of thy lord.

22 He also that had received two talents came and said, Lord, thou deliveredst unto me two talents: behold, I have gained two other talents beside them.

25:22-23
Work
◄ Mark 14:8 ►

25:23 Goodness Rewarded
◄ Matthew 10:42
Matthew 25:34 ►

23 His lord said unto him, Well done, good and faithful servant; thou hast been faithful over a few things, I will make thee ruler over many things: enter thou into the joy of thy lord.

24 Then he which had received the one talent came and said, Lord, I knew thee that thou art an hard man, reaping where thou hast not sown, and gathering where thou hast not strawed:

25 And I was afraid, and went and hid thy talent in the earth: lo, *there* thou hast *that is* thine.

26 His lord answered and said unto him, *Thou* wicked and slothful servant, thou knewest that I reap where I sowed not, and gather where I have not strawed:

27 Thou oughtest therefore to have put my money to the exchangers, and *then* at my coming I should have received mine own with usury.

28 Take therefore the talent from him, and give *it* unto him which hath ten talents.

29 For unto every one that hath shall be given, and he shall have abundance: but from him that hath not shall be taken away even that which he hath.

30 And cast ye the unprofitable servant into outer darkness: there shall be weeping and gnashing of teeth.

31 When the Son of man shall come in his glory, and all the holy angels with him, then shall he sit upon the throne of his glory:

25:31-32 Jesus' Return: Why?
◄ Matthew 16:27
1 Corinthians 4:5 ►

25:31-33
Sinner Beware
◄ Ecclesiastes 12:14
2 Thessalonians 1:9 ►

32 And before him shall be gathered all nations: and he shall separate them one from another, as a shepherd divideth *his* sheep from the goats:

25:32
Christ as Judge
◄ John 5:22 ►

33 And he shall set the sheep on his right hand, but the goats on the left.

34 Then shall the King say unto them on his right hand, Come, ye blessed of my Father, inherit the kingdom prepared for you from the foundation of the world:

25:34 Goodness Rewarded
◄ Matthew 25:23
Mark 9:41 ►

25:34 Jesus the King
◄ Matthew 21:5
Luke 1:33 ►

35 For I was an hungred, and ye gave me meat: I was thirsty, and ye gave me drink: I was a stranger, and ye took me in:

25:35
New Kids
◄ Jeremiah 7:6 ►

36 Naked, and ye clothed me: I was sick, and ye visited me: I was in prison, and ye came unto me.

25:35 Work that Helps Others
◄ Isaiah 50:4
Luke 10:34 ►

37 Then shall the righteous answer him, saying, Lord, when saw we thee an hungred, and fed *thee*? or thirsty, and gave *thee* drink?

25:35-36
Helping Weak People
◄ Acts 20:35 ►

38 When saw we thee a stranger, and took *thee* in? or naked, and clothed *thee*?

25:36 Sick People
◄ Job 2:11
James 5:14 ►

39 Or when saw we thee sick, or in prison, and came unto thee?

40 And the King shall answer and say unto them, Verily I say unto you, Inasmuch as ye have done *it* unto one of the least of these my brethren, ye have done *it* unto me.

25:40 Rewards
◄ Matthew 6:14
Luke 6:38 ►

41 Then shall he say also unto them on the left hand, Depart from me, ye cursed,

into everlasting fire, prepared for the devil and his angels:
42 For I was an hungred, and ye gave me
no meat: I was thirsty, and ye gave me no
drink:
43 I was a strang-
er, and ye took me
not in: naked, and
ye clothed me not:
sick, and in prison,
and ye visited me
not.

> **25:43 Mercy**
> ◄ Zechariah 11:16
> Luke 16:20-21 ►

44 Then shall they also answer him, saying, Lord, when saw we thee an hungred,
or athirst, or a stranger, or naked, or sick,
or in prison, and did not minister unto
thee?
45 Then shall he answer them, saying,
Verily I say unto you, Inasmuch as ye did
it not to one of the least of these, ye did *it*
not to me.
46 And these shall go away into everlasting punishment: but the righteous into life
eternal.

26

1 And it came to pass, when Jesus had
finished all these sayings, he said unto his
disciples,
2 Ye know that after two days is *the feast
of* the passover, and the Son of man is betrayed to be crucified.
3 Then assembled together the chief
priests, and the scribes, and the elders of
the people, unto the palace of the high
priest, who was called Caiaphas,
4 And consulted that they might take
Jesus by subtilty, and kill *him*.
5 But they said, Not on the feast *day*, lest
there be an uproar among the people.
6 Now when Jesus was in Bethany, in the
house of Simon the leper,
7 There came un-
to him a woman
having an alabaster
box of very pre-
cious ointment,
and poured it on
his head, as he sat *at meat*.

> **26:7-8 Being Stingy**
> ◄ Malachi 3:8
> John 12:5 ►

8 But when his disciples saw *it*, they had
indignation, saying, To what purpose *is*
this waste?
9 For this ointment might have been sold
for much, and given to the poor.
10 When Jesus understood *it*, he said unto
them, Why trouble ye the woman? for she
hath wrought a good work upon me.
11 For ye have the poor always with you;
but me ye have not always.
12 For in that she hath poured this ointment on my body, she did *it* for my
burial.
13 Verily I say unto you, Wheresoever this
gospel shall be preached in the whole
world, *there* shall also this, that this woman hath done, be told for a memorial of
her.
14 Then one of the twelve, called Judas
Iscariot, went unto the chief priests,
15 And said *unto them*, What will ye give
me, and I will deliver him unto you? And
they covenanted with him for thirty pieces
of silver.
16 And from that time he sought opportunity to betray him.
17 Now the first *day* of the *feast of* unleavened bread the disciples came to Jesus,
saying unto him, Where wilt thou that we
prepare for thee to eat the passover?
18 And he said, Go into the city to such
a man, and say unto him, The Master saith,
My time is at hand; I will keep the passover at thy house with my disciples.
19 And the disci-
ples did as Jesus
had appointed
them; and they
made ready the
passover.

> **26:19 Obeying Christ**
> ◄ Matthew 21:6
> Luke 5:5 ►

20 Now when the even was come, he sat
down with the twelve.
21 And as they did eat, he said, Verily I
say unto you, that one of you shall betray
me.
22 And they were exceeding sorrowful,
and began every one of them to say unto
him, Lord, is it I?
23 And he answered and said, He that
dippeth *his* hand with me in the dish, the
same shall betray me.
24 The Son of man goeth as it is written
of him: but woe unto that man by whom
the Son of man is betrayed! it had been
good for that man if he had not been born.
25 Then Judas, which betrayed him, answered and said, Master, is it I? He said
unto him, Thou hast said.
26 And as they were eating, Jesus took
bread, and blessed *it*, and brake *it*, and gave
it to the disciples, and said, Take, eat; this
is my body.
27 And he took the cup, and gave thanks,

and gave *it* to them, saying, Drink ye all
of it;
28 For this is my
blood of the new
testament, which is
shed for many for
the remission of
sins.

26:28 Forgiveness of Sin
◄ Luke 3:3 ►

29 But I say unto you, I will not drink
henceforth of this fruit of the vine, until
that day when I drink it new with you in
my Father's kingdom.
30 And when they had sung an hymn,
they went out into the mount of Olives.
31 Then saith Jesus unto them, All ye shall
be offended because of me this night: for
it is written, I will smite the shepherd, and
the sheep of the flock shall be scattered
abroad.
32 But after I am risen again, I will go
before you into Galilee.
33 Peter answered
and said unto him,
Though all *men*
shall be offended
because of thee, *yet*
will I never be of-
fended.

26:33 Self-confidence
◄ Obadiah 1:3
Luke 18:9 ►

34 Jesus said unto him, Verily I say unto
thee, That this night, before the cock crow,
thou shalt deny me thrice.
35 Peter said unto him, Though I should
die with thee, yet will I not deny thee. Likewise also said all the disciples.
36 Then cometh Jesus with them unto a
place called Gethsemane, and saith unto
the disciples, Sit ye here, while I go and
pray yonder.
37 And he took with him Peter and the
two sons of Zebedee, and began to be sorrowful and very heavy.
38 Then saith he unto them, My soul is
exceeding sorrowful, even unto death: tarry
ye here, and watch with me.
39 And he went a little farther, and fell
on his face, and prayed, saying, O my Father, if it be possible, let this cup pass from
me: nevertheless not as I will, but as thou
wilt.
40 And he cometh unto the disciples, and
findeth them asleep, and saith unto Peter,
What, could ye not watch with me one
hour?
41 Watch and pray, that ye enter not into
temptation: the spirit indeed *is* willing,
but the flesh *is*
weak.
42 He went away
again the second
time, and prayed,
saying, O my Fa-
ther, if this cup may
not pass away from
me, except I drink
it, thy will be done.
43 And he came
and found them
asleep again: for
their eyes were
heavy.
44 And he left
them, and went
away again, and
prayed the third
time, saying the same words.

26:41 Duty to Pray
◄ Matthew 7:7
Luke 18:1 ►

26:41 Pitfalls
◄ Psalm 39:1
Acts 20:31 ►

26:42 Submitting to God
◄ Matthew 12:50
John 5:30 ►

45 Then cometh he to his disciples, and
saith unto them, Sleep on now, and take
your rest: behold, the hour is at hand, and
the Son of man is betrayed into the hands
of sinners.
46 Rise, let us be going: behold, he is at
hand that doth betray me.
47 And while he yet spake, lo, Judas, one
of the twelve, came, and with him a great
multitude with swords and staves, from the
chief priests and elders of the people.
48 Now he that betrayed him gave them
a sign, saying, Whomsoever I shall kiss,
that same is he: hold him fast.
49 And forthwith he came to Jesus, and
said, Hail, master; and kissed him.
50 And Jesus said unto him, Friend,
wherefore art thou come? Then came they,
and laid hands on Jesus, and took him.
51 And, behold, one of them which were
with Jesus stretched out *his* hand, and drew
his sword, and struck a servant of the high
priest's, and smote off his ear.
52 Then said Jesus unto him, Put up
again thy sword into his place: for all they
that take the sword shall perish with the
sword.
53 Thinkest thou that I cannot now pray
to my Father, and he shall presently give
me more than twelve legions of angels?
54 But how then shall the scriptures be
fulfilled, that thus it must be?
55 In that same hour said Jesus to the
multitudes, Are ye come out as against a
thief with swords and staves for to take me?

I sat daily with you teaching in the temple, and ye laid no hold on me.
56 But all this was done, that the scriptures of the prophets might be fulfilled. Then all the disciples forsook him, and fled.

26:56 Whom Can You Trust?
◄ Micah 7:5
John 16:32 ►

57 And they that had laid hold on Jesus led *him* away to Caiaphas the high priest, where the scribes and the elders were assembled.
58 But Peter followed him afar off unto the high priest's palace, and went in, and sat with the servants, to see the end.
59 Now the chief priests, and elders, and all the council, sought false witness against Jesus, to put him to death;
60 But found none: yea, though many false witnesses came, *yet* found they none. At the last came two false witnesses,
61 And said, This *fellow* said, I am able to destroy the temple of God, and to build it in three days.
62 And the high priest arose, and said unto him, Answerest thou nothing? what *is it which* these witness against thee?
63 But Jesus held his peace. And the high priest answered and said unto him, I adjure thee by the living God, that thou tell us whether thou be the Christ, the Son of God.
64 Jesus saith unto him, Thou hast said: nevertheless I say unto you, Hereafter shall ye see the Son of man sitting on the right hand of power, and coming in the clouds of heaven.

26:64 Second Coming
◄ Mark 14:62 ►

65 Then the high priest rent his clothes, saying, He hath spoken blasphemy; what further need have we of witnesses? behold, now ye have heard his blasphemy.
66 What think ye? They answered and said, He is guilty of death.
67 Then did they spit in his face, and buffeted him; and others smote *him* with the palms of their hands,
68 Saying, Prophesy unto us, thou Christ, Who is he that smote thee?
69 Now Peter sat without in the palace: and a damsel came unto him, saying, Thou also wast with Jesus of Galilee.
70 But he denied before *them* all, saying, I know not what thou sayest.
71 And when he was gone out into the porch, another *maid* saw him, and said unto them that were there, This *fellow* was also with Jesus of Nazareth.
72 And again he denied with an oath, I do not know the man.
73 And after a while came unto *him* they that stood by, and said to Peter, Surely thou also art *one* of them; for thy speech bewrayeth thee.
74 Then began he to curse and to swear, *saying*, I know not the man. And immediately the cock crew.

26:74 Callousness
◄ Matthew 13:15
2 Timothy 3:13 ►

75 And Peter remembered the word of Jesus, which said unto him, Before the cock crow, thou shalt deny me thrice. And he went out, and wept bitterly.

26:75 Remorse
◄ 1 Chronicles 21:17
Matthew 27:3, 5 ►

27

1 When the morning was come, all the chief priests and elders of the people took counsel against Jesus to put him to death:
2 And when they had bound him, they led *him* away, and delivered him to Pontius Pilate the governor.
3 Then Judas, which had betrayeth him, when he saw that he was condemned, repented himself, and brought again the thirty pieces of silver to the chief priests and elders,

27:3, 5 Remorse
◄ Matthew 26:75
Hebrews 12:16-17 ►

4 Saying, I have sinned in that I have betrayed the innocent blood. And they said, What *is that* to us? see thou *to that.*
5 And he cast down the pieces of silver in the temple, and departed, and went and hanged himself.

27:5 Greed
◄ Habakkuk 2:9-10
1 Timothy 6:9 ►

6 And the chief priests took the silver pieces, and said, It is not lawful for to put them into the treasury, because it is the price of blood.
7 And they took counsel, and bought

with them the potter's field, to bury
strangers in.
8 Wherefore that field was called, The
field of blood, unto this day.
9 Then was fulfilled that which was spoken by Jeremy the prophet, saying, And
they took the thirty pieces of silver, the
price of him that was valued, whom they
of the children of Israel did value;
10 And gave them for the potter's field,
as the Lord appointed me.
11 And Jesus stood before the governor:
and the governor asked him, saying, Art
thou the King of the Jews? And Jesus said
unto him, Thou sayest.
12 And when he was accused of the chief
priests and elders, he answered nothing.
13 Then said Pilate unto him, Hearest
thou not how many things they witness
against thee?
14 And he answered him to never a word;
insomuch that the governor marvelled
greatly.
15 Now at *that* feast the governor was
wont to release unto the people a prisoner, whom they would.
16 And they had then a notable prisoner, called Barabbas.
17 Therefore
when they were
gathered together,
Pilate said unto
them, Whom will
ye that I release
unto you? Barabbas, or Jesus which is
called Christ?

27:17 Following God
◄ 1 Kings 18:21
Mark 10:21 ►

18 For he knew that for envy they had
delivered him.
19 When he was set down on the judgment seat, his wife sent unto him, saying,
Have thou nothing to do with that just
man: for I have suffered many things this
day in a dream because of him.
20 But the chief priests and elders persuaded the multitude that they should ask
Barabbas, and destroy Jesus.
21 The governor answered and said unto
them, Whether of the twain will ye that I
release unto you? They said, Barabbas.
22 Pilate saith unto them, What shall I do
then with Jesus which is called Christ? *They*
all say unto him, Let him be crucified.
23 And the governor said, Why, what evil
hath he done? But they cried out the more,
saying, Let him be crucified.
24 When Pilate
saw that he could
prevail nothing,
but *that* rather a tu-
mult was made, he
took water, and
washed *his* hands before the multitude,
saying, I am innocent of the blood of this
just person: see ye *to it*.

27:24
"It's Her Fault!"
◄ 1 Samuel 15:21 ►

25 Then answered all the people, and
said, His blood *be* on us, and on our children.
26 Then released he Barabbas unto them:
and when he had scourged Jesus, he delivered *him* to be crucified.
27 Then the soldiers of the governor took
Jesus into the common hall, and gathered
unto him the whole band *of soldiers*.
28 And they stripped him, and put on
him a scarlet robe.
29 And when they had platted a crown
of thorns, they put *it* upon his head, and a
reed in his right hand: and they bowed the
knee before him, and mocked him, saying, Hail, King of the Jews!
30 And they spit upon him, and took the
reed, and smote him on the head.
31 And after that they had mocked him,
they took the robe off from him, and put
his own raiment on him, and led him away
to crucify *him*.
32 And as they came out, they found a
man of Cyrene, Simon by name: him they
compelled to bear his cross.
33 And when they were come unto a
place called Golgotha, that is to say, a place
of a skull,
34 They gave him vinegar to drink mingled with gall: and when he had tasted
thereof, he would not drink.
35 And they crucified him, and parted his
garments, casting lots: that it might be fulfilled which was spoken by the prophet,
They parted my garments among them,
and upon my vesture did they cast lots.
36 And sitting down they watched him
there;
37 And set up over his head his accusation written, THIS IS JESUS THE KING OF
THE JEWS.
38 Then were there two thieves crucified
with him, one on the right hand, and another on the left.
39 And they that passed by reviled him,
wagging their heads,

[40]And saying, Thou that destroyest the
temple, and buildest *it* in three days, save
thyself. If thou be the Son of God, come
down from the cross.
[41]Likewise also the chief priests mocking *him,* with the scribes and elders, said,
[42]He saved oth-
ers; himself he can-
not save. If he be
the King of Israel,
let him now come
down from the
cross, and we will believe him.

27:42 Not Caring
◄ Matthew 15:23
Luke 10:31-32 ►

[43]He trusted in God; let him deliver him
now, if he will have him: for he said, I am
the Son of God.
[44]The thieves also, which were crucified
with him, cast the same in his teeth.
[45]Now from the sixth hour there was
darkness over all the land unto the ninth
hour.
[46]And about the ninth hour Jesus cried
with a loud voice, saying, Eli, Eli, lama
sabachthani? that is to say, My God, my
God, why hast thou forsaken me?
[47]Some of them that stood there, when
they heard *that,* said, This *man* calleth for
Elias.
[48]And straightway one of them ran, and
took a spunge, and filled *it* with vinegar,
and put *it* on a reed, and gave him to drink.
[49]The rest said, Let be, let us see whether Elias will come to save him.
[50]Jesus, when he had cried again with a
loud voice, yielded up the ghost.
[51]And, behold, the veil of the temple was
rent in twain from the top to the bottom;
and the earth did quake, and the rocks
rent;
[52]And the graves were opened; and
many bodies of the saints which slept
arose,
[53]And came out of the graves after his
resurrection, and went into the holy city,
and appeared unto many.
[54]Now when the centurion, and they
that were with him, watching Jesus, saw
the earthquake, and those things that were
done, they feared greatly, saying, Truly this
was the Son of God.
[55]And many women were there beholding afar off, which followed Jesus from
Galilee, ministering unto him:
[56]Among which was Mary Magdalene,
and Mary the mother of James and Joses,
and the mother of
Zebedee's children.
[57]When the even
was come, there
came a rich man of
Arimathaea, named
Joseph, who also himself was Jesus' disciple:

27:55-56 Being a Friend
◄ 2 Kings 2:2
Matthew 28:1 ►

[58]He went to Pilate, and begged the
body of Jesus. Then Pilate commanded the
body to be delivered.
[59]And when Joseph had taken the body,
he wrapped it in a clean linen cloth,
[60]And laid it in his own new tomb,
which he had hewn out in the rock: and
he rolled a great stone to the door of the
sepulchre, and departed.
[61]And there was Mary Magdalene, and
the other Mary, sitting over against the sepulchre.
[62]Now the next day, that followed the
day of the preparation, the chief priests
and Pharisees came together unto Pilate,
[63]Saying, Sir, we remember that that deceiver said, while he was yet alive, After
three days I will rise again.
[64]Command therefore that the sepulchre be made sure until the third day, lest
his disciples come by night, and steal him
away, and say unto the people, He is risen
from the dead: so the last error shall be
worse than the first.
[65]Pilate said unto them, Ye have a watch:
go your way, make *it* as sure as ye can.
[66]So they went, and made the sepulchre
sure, sealing the stone, and setting a watch.

28

[1]In the end of the
sabbath, as it began
to dawn toward the
first *day* of the
week, came Mary
Magdalene and the
other Mary to see the sepulchre.

28:1 Being a Friend
◄ Matthew 27:55-56
John 11:16 ►

[2]And, behold, there was a great earthquake: for the angel of the Lord descended from heaven, and came and rolled back
the stone from the door, and sat upon it.
[3]His countenance was like lightning,
and his raiment white as snow:
[4]And for fear of him the keepers did
shake, and became as dead *men.*
[5]And the angel answered and said unto
the women, Fear not ye: for I know that ye
seek Jesus, which was crucified.
[6]He is not here: for he is risen, as he

said. Come, see the place where the Lord lay.

7 And go quickly, and tell his disciples that he is risen from the dead; and, behold, he goeth before you into Galilee; there shall ye see him: lo, I have told you.

28:7 Hurrying
◄ Zechariah 8:21
Luke 10:4 ►

8 And they departed quickly from the sepulchre with fear and great joy; and did run to bring his disciples word.

9 And as they went to tell his disciples, behold, Jesus met them, saying, All hail. And they came and held him by the feet, and worshipped him.

10 Then said Jesus unto them, Be not afraid: go tell my brethren that they go into Galilee, and there shall they see me.

11 Now when they were going, behold, some of the watch came into the city, and shewed unto the chief priests all the things that were done.

12 And when they were assembled with the elders, and had taken counsel, they gave large money unto the soldiers,

13 Saying, Say ye, His disciples came by night, and stole him *away* while we slept.

14 And if this come to the governor's ears, we will persuade him, and secure you.

15 So they took the money, and did as they were taught: and this saying is commonly reported among the Jews until this day.

16 Then the eleven disciples went away into Galilee, into a mountain where Jesus had appointed them.

17 And when they saw him, they worshipped him: but some doubted.

18 And Jesus came and spake unto them, saying, All power is given unto me in heaven and in earth.

19 Go ye therefore, and teach all nations, baptizing them in the name of the Father, and of the Son, and of the Holy Ghost:

28:19
Baptism
◄ Mark 16:16 ►

20 Teaching them to observe all things whatsoever I have commanded you: and, lo, I am with you alway, *even* unto the end of the world. Amen.

Mark

AUTHOR

Mark, a young man who worked with the apostle Paul

MAIN POINT

Everyone needs to hear the facts of Jesus' life, ministry, death, and resurrection, because Jesus is the Savior.

DATE WRITTEN

Between A.D. 55 and 65

16 CHAPTERS

MAIN PEOPLE

Jesus, the disciples, Pilate, the Jewish religious leaders

SPECIAL FEATURES

- *Presents the facts of Jesus' adult life and ministry in a straightforward style, much like a newspaper*
- *Shows that Jesus is a man of action, not just words, by recording more of his miracles than his teachings*
- *Describes Jesus' identity as both servant and Savior in fast-paced detail*
- *Was written to urge the Christians in Rome to continue in their faith, that their belief in Jesus was good*
- *Second of the four Gospels*

HOW THE BOOK GOT ITS NAME

Gospel means "good news"; this book contains the good news about Jesus as recorded by Mark, a co-worker of the apostle Paul

1 1The beginning of the gospel of Jesus
Christ, the Son of God;
2As it is written in the prophets, Behold,
I send my messenger before thy face, which
shall prepare thy way before thee.
3The voice of one crying in the wilderness, Prepare ye the way of the Lord, make
his paths straight.
4John did baptize in the wilderness, and
preach the baptism of repentance for the
remission of sins.
5And there went out unto him all the
land of Judaea, and they of Jerusalem, and
were all baptized of him in the river of Jordan, confessing their sins.
6And John was clothed with camel's
hair, and with a girdle of a skin about his
loins; and he did eat locusts and wild
honey;
7And preached, saying, There cometh
one mightier than I after me, the latchet
of whose shoes I am not worthy to stoop
down and unloose.
8I indeed have baptized you with water:
but he shall baptize you with the Holy
Ghost.
9And it came to pass in those days, that
Jesus came from Nazareth of Galilee, and
was baptized of John in Jordan.
10And straightway coming up out of the
water, he saw the heavens opened, and the
Spirit like a dove descending upon him:

11 And there came a voice from heaven, *saying,* Thou art my beloved Son, in whom I am well pleased.

12 And immediately the Spirit driveth him into the wilderness.

13 And he was there in the wilderness forty days, tempted of Satan; and was with the wild beasts; and the angels ministered unto him.

14 Now after that John was put in prison, Jesus came into Galilee, preaching the gospel of the kingdom of God,

15 And saying, The time is fulfilled, and the kingdom of God is at hand: repent ye, and believe the gospel.

16 Now as he walked by the sea of Galilee, he saw Simon and Andrew his brother casting a net into the sea: for they were fishers.

17 And Jesus said unto them, Come ye after me, and I will make you to become fishers of men.

18 And straightway they forsook their nets, and followed him.

1:18 Serving Quickly
◄ 1 Kings 19:20
Luke 4:39 ►

19 And when he had gone a little farther thence, he saw James the *son* of Zebedee, and John his brother, who also were in the ship mending their nets.

20 And straightway he called them: and they left their father Zebedee in the ship with the hired servants, and went after him.

21 And they went into Capernaum; and straightway on the sabbath day he entered into the synagogue, and taught.

1:21 Going to Church
◄ Matthew 12:9
Luke 4:16 ►

22 And they were astonished at his doctrine: for he taught them as one that had authority, and not as the scribes.

23 And there was in their synagogue a man with an unclean spirit; and he cried out,

24 Saying, Let *us* alone; what have we to do with thee, thou Jesus of Nazareth? art thou come to destroy us? I know thee who thou art, the Holy One of God.

25 And Jesus rebuked him, saying, Hold thy peace, and come out of him.

26 And when the unclean spirit had torn him, and cried with a loud voice, he came out of him.

1:26 Demons
◄ Matthew 12:45
Mark 5:9 ►

27 And they were all amazed, insomuch that they questioned among themselves, saying, What thing is this? what new doctrine *is* this? for with authority commandeth he even the unclean spirits, and they do obey him.

28 And immediately his fame spread abroad throughout all the region round about Galilee.

29 And forthwith, when they were come out of the synagogue, they entered into the house of Simon and Andrew, with James and John.

30 But Simon's wife's mother lay sick of a fever, and anon they tell him of her.

31 And he came and took her by the hand, and lifted her up; and immediately the fever left her, and she ministered unto them.

32 And at even, when the sun did set, they brought unto him all that were diseased, and them that were possessed with devils.

33 And all the city was gathered together at the door.

34 And he healed many that were sick of divers diseases, and cast out many devils; and suffered not the devils to speak, because they knew him.

35 And in the morning, rising up a great while before day, he went out, and departed into a solitary place, and there prayed.

1:35 Devotions
◄ Psalm 119:147 ►

36 And Simon and they that were with him followed after him.

37 And when they had found him, they said unto him, All *men* seek for thee.

38 And he said unto them, Let us go into the next towns, that I may preach there also: for therefore came I forth.

39 And he preached in their synagogues throughout all Galilee, and cast out devils.

40 And there came a leper to him, beseeching him, and kneeling down to him, and saying unto him, If thou wilt, thou canst make me clean.

41 And Jesus, moved with compassion, put forth *his* hand, and touched him, and

saith unto him, I will; be thou clean.

42 And as soon as he had spoken, immediately the leprosy departed from him, and he was cleansed.

> **1:41 God's Response**
> ◄ Mark 2:5 ►

43 And he straitly charged him, and forthwith sent him away;

44 And saith unto him, See thou say nothing to any man: but go thy way, shew thyself to the priest, and offer for thy cleansing those things which Moses commanded, for a testimony unto them.

45 But he went out, and began to publish *it* much, and to blaze abroad the matter, insomuch that Jesus could no more openly enter into the city, but was without in desert places: and they came to him from every quarter.

2

1 And again he entered into Capernaum, after *some* days; and it was noised that he was in the house.

2 And straightway many were gathered together, insomuch that there was no room to receive *them,* no, not so much as about the door: and he preached the word unto them.

3 And they come unto him, bringing one sick of the palsy, which was borne of four.

> **2:3 Teamwork**
> ◄ Matthew 18:19
> Mark 6:7 ►

4 And when they could not come nigh unto him for the press, they uncovered the roof where he was: and when they had broken *it* up, they let down the bed wherein the sick of the palsy lay.

5 When Jesus saw their faith, he said unto the sick of the palsy, Son, thy sins be forgiven thee.

> **2:5 God's Response**
> ◄ Mark 1:41
> Mark 5:34 ►

6 But there were certain of the scribes sitting there, and reasoning in their hearts,

7 Why doth this *man* thus speak blasphemies? who can forgive sins but God only?

8 And immediately when Jesus perceived in his spirit that they so reasoned within themselves, he said unto them, Why reason ye these things in your hearts?

9 Whether is it easier to say to the sick of the palsy, *Thy* sins be forgiven thee; or to say, Arise, and take up thy bed, and walk?

10 But that ye may know that the Son of man hath power on earth to forgive sins, (he saith to the sick of the palsy,)

11 I say unto thee, Arise, and take up thy bed, and go thy way into thine house.

12 And immediately he arose, took up the bed, and went forth before them all; insomuch that they were all amazed, and glorified God, saying, We never saw it on this fashion.

13 And he went forth again by the sea side; and all the multitude resorted unto him, and he taught them.

14 And as he passed by, he saw Levi the *son* of Alphaeus sitting at the receipt of custom, and said unto him, Follow me. And he arose and followed him.

15 And it came to pass, that, as Jesus sat at meat in his house, many publicans and sinners sat also together with Jesus and his disciples: for there were many, and they followed him.

16 And when the scribes and Pharisees saw him eat with publicans and sinners, they said unto his disciples, How is it that he eateth and drinketh with publicans and sinners?

17 When Jesus heard *it,* he saith unto them, They that are whole have no need of the physician, but they that are sick: I came not to call the righteous, but sinners to repentance.

18 And the disciples of John and of the Pharisees used to fast: and they come and say unto him, Why do the disciples of John and of the Pharisees fast, but thy disciples fast not?

19 And Jesus said unto them, Can the children of the bridechamber fast, while the bridegroom is with them? as long as they have the bridegroom with them, they cannot fast.

20 But the days will come, when the bridegroom shall be taken away from them, and then shall they fast in those days.

21 No man also seweth a piece of new cloth on an old garment: else the new piece that filled it up taketh away from the old, and the rent is made worse.

22 And no man putteth new wine into old bottles: else the new wine doth burst the bottles, and the wine is spilled, and the bottles will be marred: but new wine must be put into new bottles.

23 And it came to pass, that he went
through the corn fields on the sabbath day;
and his disciples began, as they went, to
pluck the ears of corn.
24 And the Phari-
sees said unto him,
Behold, why do
they on the sabbath
day that which is
not lawful?

2:24
Legalism
◄ Luke 6:2 ►

25 And he said unto them, Have ye never read what David did, when he had need,
and was an hungred, he, and they that were
with him?
26 How he went into the house of God
in the days of Abiathar the high priest, and
did eat the shewbread, which is not lawful to eat but for the priests, and gave also
to them which were with him?
27 And he said unto them, The sabbath
was made for man, and not man for the
sabbath:
28 Therefore the Son of man is Lord also
of the sabbath.

3

1 And he entered again into the synagogue; and there was a man there which
had a withered hand.
2 And they watched him, whether he
would heal him on the sabbath day; that
they might accuse him.
3 And he saith unto the man which had
the withered hand, Stand forth.
4 And he saith unto them, Is it lawful to
do good on the sabbath days, or to do evil?
to save life, or to kill? But they held their
peace.
5 And when he had looked round about
on them with anger, being grieved for the
hardness of their hearts, he saith unto the
man, Stretch forth thine hand. And he
stretched *it* out: and his hand was restored
whole as the other.
6 And the Pharisees went forth, and
straightway took counsel with the Herodians against him, how they might destroy
him.
7 But Jesus withdrew himself with his
disciples to the sea: and a great multitude
from Galilee followed him, and from
Judaea,
8 And from Jerusalem, and from Idu-
maea, and *from* beyond Jordan; and they
about Tyre and Sidon, a great multitude,
when they had heard what great things he
did, came unto him.
9 And he spake to his disciples, that a
small ship should wait on him because of
the multitude, lest they should throng him.
10 For he had healed many; insomuch
that they pressed upon him for to touch
him, as many as had plagues.
11 And unclean spirits, when they saw
him, fell down before him, and cried, saying, Thou art the Son of God.
12 And he straitly charged them that they
should not make him known.
13 And he goeth up into a mountain, and
calleth *unto him* whom he would: and they
came unto him.
14 And he ordained twelve, that they
should be with him, and that he might
send them forth to preach,
15 And to have power to heal sicknesses,
and to cast out devils:
16 And Simon he surnamed Peter;
17 And James the *son* of Zebedee, and
John the brother of James; and he surnamed them Boanerges, which is, The sons
of thunder:
18 And Andrew, and Philip, and Bartholomew, and Matthew, and Thomas, and
James the *son* of Alphaeus, and Thaddaeus, and Simon the Canaanite,
19 And Judas Iscariot, which also betrayed him: and they went into an house.
20 And the multitude cometh together
again, so that they could not so much as
eat bread.
21 And when his friends heard *of it*, they
went out to lay hold on him: for they said,
He is beside himself.
22 And the scribes which came down
from Jerusalem said, He hath Beelzebub,
and by the prince of the devils casteth he
out devils.
23 And he called them *unto him*, and said
unto them in parables, How can Satan cast
out Satan?
24 And if a kingdom be divided against
itself, that kingdom cannot stand.
25 And if a house be divided against itself, that house cannot stand.
26 And if Satan rise up against himself,
and be divided, he cannot stand, but hath
an end.
27 No man can enter into a strong man's
house, and spoil his goods, except he will
first bind the strong man; and then he will
spoil his house.
28 Verily I say unto you, All sins shall be

forgiven unto the
sons of men, and
blasphemies where-
with soever they
shall blaspheme:

3:28 Forgiveness
◄ Matthew 6:14
Acts 5:31 ►

29But he that
shall blaspheme against the Holy Ghost
hath never forgiveness, but is in danger of
eternal damnation:

30Because they said, He hath an unclean
spirit.

31There came then his brethren and his
mother, and, standing without, sent unto
him, calling him.

32And the multitude sat about him, and
they said unto him, Behold, thy mother
and thy brethren without seek for thee.

33And he an-
swered them, say-
ing, Who is my
mother, or my
brethren?

3:34 Family
◄ Malachi 2:10
Acts 17:26 ►

34And he looked
round about on them which sat about
him, and said, Behold my mother and my
brethren!

35For whosoever shall do the will of
God, the same is my brother, and my sister, and mother.

4

1And he began again to teach by the sea
side: and there was gathered unto him a
great multitude, so that he entered into a
ship, and sat in the sea; and the whole
multitude was by the sea on the land.

2And he taught them many things by parables, and said unto them in his doctrine,

3Hearken; Behold, there went out a sower to sow:

4And it came to pass, as he sowed, some
fell by the way side, and the fowls of the
air came and devoured it up.

5And some fell on stony ground, where
it had not much earth; and immediately it
sprang up, because it had no depth of
earth:

6But when the sun was up, it was
scorched; and because it had no root, it
withered away.

7And some fell among thorns, and the
thorns grew up, and choked it, and it yielded no fruit.

8And other fell on good ground, and did
yield fruit that sprang up and increased;
and brought forth, some thirty, and some
sixty, and some an hundred.

9And he said unto them, He that hath
ears to hear, let him hear.

10And when he
was alone, they that
were about him
with the twelve
asked of him the
parable.

4:10
Learning from Jesus
◄ Matthew 13:36
Mark 7:17 ►

11And he said unto them, Unto you it is
given to know the mystery of the kingdom
of God: but unto them that are without,
all *these* things are done in parables:

12That seeing they may see, and not perceive; and hearing they may hear, and not
understand; lest at any time they should
be converted, and *their* sins should be forgiven them.

13And he said unto them, Know ye not
this parable? and how then will ye know
all parables?

14The sower soweth the word.

15And these are they by the way side,
where the word is sown; but when they
have heard, Satan cometh immediately,
and taketh away the word that was sown
in their hearts.

16And these are they likewise which are
sown on stony ground; who, when they
have heard the word, immediately receive
it with gladness;

17And have no root in themselves, and
so endure but for a time: afterward, when
affliction or persecution ariseth for the
word's sake, immediately they are offended.

18And these are they which are sown
among thorns; such as hear the word,

19And the cares
of this world, and
the deceitfulness of
riches, and the lusts
of other things en-
tering in, choke the
word, and it becometh unfruitful.

4:19 Money's Dangers
◄ Matthew 19:23
1 Timothy 6:9 ►

20And these are they which are sown on
good ground; such as hear the word, and
receive *it*, and bring forth fruit, some
thirtyfold, some sixty, and some an hundred.

21And he said unto them, Is a candle
brought to be put under a bushel, or under a bed? and not to be set on a candlestick?

22For there is nothing hid, which shall
not be manifested; neither was any thing

kept secret, but that it should come abroad.

23 If any man have ears to hear, let him hear.

24 And he said unto them, Take heed what ye hear: with what measure ye mete, it shall be measured to you: and unto you that hear shall more be given.

4:24 Watch Out!
◄ Matthew 24:4
Mark 13:9 ►

25 For he that hath, to him shall be given: and he that hath not, from him shall be taken even that which he hath.

26 And he said, So is the kingdom of God, as if a man should cast seed into the ground;

27 And should sleep, and rise night and day, and the seed should spring and grow up, he knoweth not how.

28 For the earth bringeth forth fruit of herself; first the blade, then the ear, after that the full corn in the ear.

29 But when the fruit is brought forth, immediately he putteth in the sickle, because the harvest is come.

30 And he said, Whereunto shall we liken the kingdom of God? or with what comparison shall we compare it?

31 *It is* like a grain of mustard seed, which, when it is sown in the earth, is less than all the seeds that be in the earth:

32 But when it is sown, it groweth up, and becometh greater than all herbs, and shooteth out great branches; so that the fowls of the air may lodge under the shadow of it.

33 And with many such parables spake he the word unto them, as they were able to hear *it*.

34 But without a parable spake he not unto them: and when they were alone, he expounded all things to his disciples.

35 And the same day, when the even was come, he saith unto them, Let us pass over unto the other side.

36 And when they had sent away the multitude, they took him even as he was in the ship. And there were also with him other little ships.

37 And there arose a great storm of wind, and the waves beat into the ship, so that it was now full.

38 And he was in the hinder part of the ship, asleep on a pillow: and they awake him, and say unto him, Master, carest thou not that we perish?

39 And he arose, and rebuked the wind, and said unto the sea, Peace, be still. And the wind ceased, and there was a great calm.

40 And he said unto them, Why are ye so fearful? how is it that ye have no faith?

41 And they feared exceedingly, and said one to another, What manner of man is this, that even the wind and the sea obey him?

5

1 And they came over unto the other side of the sea, into the country of the Gadarenes.

2 And when he was come out of the ship, immediately there met him out of the tombs a man with an unclean spirit,

3 Who had *his* dwelling among the tombs; and no man could bind him, no, not with chains:

4 Because that he had been often bound with fetters and chains, and the chains had been plucked asunder by him, and the fetters broken in pieces: neither could any *man* tame him.

5 And always, night and day, he was in the mountains, and in the tombs, crying, and cutting himself with stones.

6 But when he saw Jesus afar off, he ran and worshipped him,

7 And cried with a loud voice, and said, What have I to do with thee, Jesus, *thou* Son of the most high God? I adjure thee by God, that thou torment me not.

8 For he said unto him, Come out of the man, *thou* unclean spirit.

9 And he asked him, What *is* thy name? And he answered, saying, My name *is* Legion: for we are many.

5:9 Demons
◄ Mark 1:26
Mark 7:30 ►

10 And he besought him much that he would not send them away out of the country.

11 Now there was there nigh unto the mountains a great herd of swine feeding.

12 And all the devils besought him, saying, Send us into the swine, that we may enter into them.

13 And forthwith Jesus gave them leave. And the unclean spirits went out, and entered into the swine: and the herd ran vio-

lently down a steep place into the sea,
(they were about two thousand;) and were
choked in the sea.
14And they that fed the swine fled, and
told *it* in the city, and in the country. And
they went out to see what it was that was
done.
15And they come to Jesus, and see him
that was possessed with the devil, and had
the legion, sitting, and clothed, and in his
right mind: and they were afraid.
16And they that saw *it* told them how it
befell to him that was possessed with the
devil, and *also* concerning the swine.
17And they began to pray him to depart
out of their coasts.
18And when he
was come into the
ship, he that had
been possessed
with the devil
prayed him that he
might be with him.
19Howbeit Jesus
suffered him not,
but saith unto
him, Go home to
thy friends, and tell
them how great
things the Lord hath done for thee, and
hath had compassion on thee.
20And he departed, and began to publish in Decapolis how great things Jesus
had done for him: and all *men* did marvel.
21And when Jesus was passed over again
by ship unto the other side, much people
gathered unto him: and he was nigh unto
the sea.
22And, behold, there cometh one of the
rulers of the synagogue, Jairus by name;
and when he saw him, he fell at his feet,
23And besought him greatly, saying, My
little daughter lieth at the point of death:
I pray thee, come and lay thy hands on her,
that she may be healed; and she shall live.
24And *Jesus* went with him; and much
people followed him, and thronged him.
25And a certain woman, which had an
issue of blood twelve years,
26And had suffered many things of
many physicians, and had spent all that
she had, and was nothing bettered, but
rather grew worse,
27When she had heard of Jesus, came in
the press behind, and touched his garment.

5:18-19 Your Testimony
◄ Jeremiah 51:10
Acts 1:8 ►

5:19
Helping at Home
◄ 1 Timothy 5:4 ►

28For she said, If I may touch but his
clothes, I shall be whole.
29And straightway the fountain of her
blood was dried up; and she felt in *her*
body that she was healed of that plague.
30And Jesus, immediately knowing in
himself that virtue had gone out of him,
turned him about in the press, and said,
Who touched my clothes?
31And his disciples said unto him, Thou
seest the multitude thronging thee, and
sayest thou, Who touched me?
32And he looked round about to see her
that had done this thing.
33But the woman fearing and trembling,
knowing what was done in her, came and
fell down before him, and told him all the
truth.
34And he said
unto her, Daughter,
thy faith hath
made thee whole;
go in peace, and
be whole of thy
plague.
35While he yet
spake, there came
from the ruler of
the synagogue's
house certain which
said, Thy daughter
is dead: why troublest thou the Master any
further?
36As soon as Jesus heard the word that
was spoken, he saith unto the ruler of the
synagogue, Be not afraid, only believe.
37And he suffered no man to follow
him, save Peter, and James, and John the
brother of James.
38And he cometh to the house of the
ruler of the synagogue, and seeth the
tumult, and them that wept and wailed
greatly.
39And when he was come in, he saith
unto them, Why make ye this ado, and
weep? the damsel is not dead, but sleepeth.
40And they laughed him to scorn. But
when he had put them all out, he taketh
the father and the mother of the damsel,
and them that were with him, and entereth
in where the damsel was lying.
41And he took the damsel by the hand,
and said unto her, Talitha cumi; which is,
being interpreted, Damsel, I say unto thee,
arise.

5:34 God's Response
◄ Mark 2:5
Mark 7:29 ►

5:35 Faith Tested
◄ Matthew 15:23
Mark 10:13 ►

42 And straightway the damsel arose, and walked; for she was *of the age* of twelve years. And they were astonished with a great astonishment.

43 And he charged them straitly that no man should know it; and commanded that something should be given her to eat.

6

1 And he went out from thence, and came into his own country; and his disciples follow him.

2 And when the sabbath day was come, he began to teach in the synagogue: and many hearing *him* were astonished, saying, From whence hath this *man* these things? and what wisdom *is* this which is given unto him, that even such mighty works are wrought by his hands?

3 Is not this the carpenter, the son of Mary, the brother of James, and Joses, and of Juda, and Simon? and are not his sisters here with us? And they were offended at him.

4 But Jesus said unto them, A prophet is not without honour, but in his own country, and among his own kin, and in his own house.

5 And he could there do no mighty work, save that he laid his hands upon a few sick folk, and healed *them.*

6 And he marvelled because of their unbelief. And he went round about the villages, teaching.

7 And he called *unto him* the twelve, and began to send them forth by two and two; and gave them power over unclean spirits;

6:7 Teamwork
◄ Mark 2:3
Philippians 1:27 ►

8 And commanded them that they should take nothing for *their* journey, save a staff only; no scrip, no bread, no money in *their* purse:

9 But *be* shod with sandals; and not put on two coats.

10 And he said unto them, In what place soever ye enter into an house, there abide till ye depart from that place.

11 And whosoever shall not receive you, nor hear you, when ye depart thence, shake off the dust under your feet for a testimony against them. Verily I say unto you, It shall be more tolerable for Sodom and Gomorrha in the day of judgment, than for that city.

12 And they went out, and preached that men should repent.

13 And they cast out many devils, and anointed with oil many that were sick, and healed *them.*

14 And king Herod heard *of him;* (for his name was spread abroad:) and he said, That John the Baptist was risen from the dead, and therefore mighty works do shew forth themselves in him.

15 Others said, That it is Elias. And others said, That it is a prophet, or as one of the prophets.

16 But when Herod heard *thereof,* he said, It is John, whom I beheaded: he is risen from the dead.

17 For Herod himself had sent forth and laid hold upon John, and bound him in prison for Herodias' sake, his brother Philip's wife: for he had married her.

18 For John had said unto Herod, It is not lawful for thee to have thy brother's wife.

19 Therefore Herodias had a quarrel against him, and would have killed him; but she could not:

20 For Herod feared John, knowing that he was a just man and an holy, and observed him; and when he heard him, he did many things, and heard him gladly.

21 And when a convenient day was come, that Herod on his birthday made a supper to his lords, high captains, and chief *estates* of Galilee;

22 And when the daughter of the said Herodias came in, and danced, and pleased Herod and them that sat with him, the king said unto the damsel, Ask of me whatsoever thou wilt, and I will give *it* thee.

23 And he sware unto her, Whatsoever thou shalt ask of me, I will give *it* thee, unto the half of my kingdom.

6:23 Foolish Promises
◄ Joshua 9:19
Acts 23:21 ►

24 And she went forth, and said unto her mother, What shall I ask? And she said, The head of John the Baptist.

25 And she came in straightway with haste unto the king, and asked, saying, I will that thou give me by and by in a charger the head of John the Baptist.

26 And the king was exceeding sorry; *yet* for his oath's sake, and for their sakes which sat with him, he would not reject her.

27 And immediately the king sent an executioner, and commanded his head to be brought: and he went and beheaded him in the prison,

28 And brought his head in a charger, and gave it to the damsel: and the damsel gave it to her mother.

29 And when his disciples heard *of it,* they came and took up his corpse, and laid it in a tomb.

30 And the apostles gathered themselves together unto Jesus, and told him all things, both what they had done, and what they had taught.

31 And he said unto them, Come ye yourselves apart into a desert place, and rest a while: for there were many coming and going, and they had no leisure so much as to eat.

6:31
Rest
◄ Leviticus 23:3 ►

32 And they departed into a desert place by ship privately.

33 And the people saw them departing, and many knew him, and ran afoot thither out of all cities, and outwent them, and came together unto him.

34 And Jesus, when he came out, saw much people, and was moved with compassion toward them, because they were as sheep not having a shepherd: and he began to teach them many things.

6:34 The Teacher
◄ Matthew 7:29
Luke 4:15 ►

35 And when the day was now far spent, his disciples came unto him, and said, This is a desert place, and now the time *is* far passed:

36 Send them away, that they may go into the country round about, and into the villages, and buy themselves bread: for they have nothing to eat.

37 He answered and said unto them, Give ye them to eat. And they say unto him, Shall we go and buy two hundred pennyworth of bread, and give them to eat?

38 He saith unto them, How many loaves have ye? go and see. And when they knew, they say, Five, and two fishes.

39 And he commanded them to make all sit down by companies upon the green grass.

40 And they sat down in ranks, by hundreds, and by fifties.

41 And when he had taken the five loaves and the two fishes, he looked up to heaven, and blessed, and brake the loaves, and gave *them* to his disciples to set before them; and the two fishes divided he among them all.

42 And they did all eat, and were filled.

43 And they took up twelve baskets full of the fragments, and of the fishes.

44 And they that did eat of the loaves were about five thousand men.

45 And straightway he constrained his disciples to get into the ship, and to go to the other side before unto Bethsaida, while he sent away the people.

46 And when he had sent them away, he departed into a mountain to pray.

47 And when even was come, the ship was in the midst of the sea, and he alone on the land.

48 And he saw them toiling in rowing; for the wind was contrary unto them: and about the fourth watch of the night he cometh unto them, walking upon the sea, and would have passed by them.

49 But when they saw him walking upon the sea, they supposed it had been a spirit, and cried out:

50 For they all saw him, and were troubled. And immediately he talked with them, and saith unto them, Be of good cheer: it is I; be not afraid.

51 And he went up unto them into the ship; and the wind ceased: and they were sore amazed in themselves beyond measure, and wondered.

52 For they considered not *the miracle* of the loaves: for their heart was hardened.

53 And when they had passed over, they came into the land of Gennesaret, and drew to the shore.

54 And when they were come out of the ship, straightway they knew him,

55 And ran through that whole region round about, and began to carry about in beds those that were sick, where they heard he was.

56 And whithersoever he entered, into villages, or cities, or country, they laid the sick in the streets, and besought him that they might touch if it were but the border of his garment: and as many as touched him were made whole.

7

1 Then came together unto him the Pharisees, and certain of the scribes, which came from Jerusalem.

2 And when they saw some of his disciples eat bread with defiled, that is to say, with unwashen, hands, they found fault.

3 For the Pharisees, and all the Jews, except they wash *their* hands oft, eat not, holding the tradition of the elders.

4 And *when they come* from the market, except they wash, they eat not. And many other things there be, which they have received to hold, *as* the washing of cups, and pots, brasen vessels, and of tables.

5 Then the Pharisees and scribes asked him, Why walk not thy disciples according to the tradition of the elders, but eat bread with unwashen hands?

6 He answered and said unto them, Well hath Esaias prophesied of you hypocrites, as it is written, This people honoureth me with *their* lips, but their heart is far from me.

7 Howbeit in vain do they worship me, teaching *for* doctrines the commandments of men.

8 For laying aside the commandment of God, ye hold the tradition of men, *as* the washing of pots and cups: and many other such like things ye do.

9 And he said unto them, Full well ye reject the commandment of God, that ye may keep your own tradition.

10 For Moses said, Honour thy father and thy mother; and, Whoso curseth father or mother, let him die the death:

11 But ye say, If a man shall say to his father or mother, *It is* Corban, that is to say, a gift, by whatsoever thou mightest be profited by me; *he shall be free.*

12 And ye suffer him no more to do ought for his father or his mother;

13 Making the word of God of none effect through your tradition, which ye have delivered: and many such like things do ye.

14 And when he had called all the people *unto him,* he said unto them, Hearken unto me every one *of you,* and understand:

15 There is nothing from without a man, that entering into him can defile him: but the things which come out of him, those are they that defile the man.

16 If any man have ears to hear, let him hear.

17 And when he was entered into the house from the people, his disciples asked him concerning the parable.

7:17
Learning from Jesus
◄ Mark 4:10
Mark 9:11 ►

18 And he saith unto them, Are ye so without understanding also? Do ye not perceive, that whatsoever thing from without entereth into the man, *it* cannot defile him;

19 Because it entereth not into his heart, but into the belly, and goeth out into the draught, purging all meats?

20 And he said, That which cometh out of the man, that defileth the man.

21 For from within, out of the heart of men, proceed evil thoughts, adulteries, fornications, murders,

7:21 Source of Evil
◄ Matthew 23:25
Hebrews 3:12 ►

22 Thefts, covetousness, wickedness, deceit, lasciviousness, an evil eye, blasphemy, pride, foolishness:

7:22
Dishonest People
◄ Jeremiah 5:27 ►

23 All these evil things come from within, and defile the man.

24 And from thence he arose, and went into the borders of Tyre and Sidon, and entered into an house, and would have no man know *it:* but he could not be hid.

25 For a *certain* woman, whose young daughter had an unclean spirit, heard of him, and came and fell at his feet:

26 The woman was a Greek, a Syrophenician by nation; and she besought him that he would cast forth the devil out of her daughter.

27 But Jesus said unto her, Let the children first be filled: for it is not meet to take the children's bread, and to cast *it* unto the dogs.

28 And she answered and said unto him, Yes, Lord: yet the dogs under the table eat of the children's crumbs.

29 And he said unto her, For this saying go thy way; the devil is gone out of thy daughter.

7:29 God's Response
◄ Mark 5:34
Mark 10:52 ►

30 And when she was come to her house, she found the devil gone out, and

her daughter laid upon the bed.

7:30 Demons
◄ Mark 5:9
Mark 9:17 ►

31 And again, departing from the coasts of Tyre and Sidon, he came unto the sea of Galilee, through the midst of the coasts of Decapolis.

32 And they bring unto him one that was deaf, and had an impediment in his speech; and they beseech him to put his hand upon him.

33 And he took him aside from the multitude, and put his fingers into his ears, and he spit, and touched his tongue;

34 And looking up to heaven, he sighed, and saith unto him, Ephphatha, that is, Be opened.

35 And straightway his ears were opened, and the string of his tongue was loosed, and he spake plain.

36 And he charged them that they should tell no man: but the more he charged them, so much the more a great deal they published *it;*

37 And were beyond measure astonished, saying, He hath done all things well: he maketh both the deaf to hear, and the dumb to speak.

8

1 In those days the multitude being very great, and having nothing to eat, Jesus called his disciples *unto him,* and saith unto them,

2 I have compassion on the multitude, because they have now been with me three days, and have nothing to eat:

3 And if I send them away fasting to their own houses, they will faint by the way: for divers of them came from far.

4 And his disciples answered him, From whence can a man satisfy these *men* with bread here in the wilderness?

5 And he asked them, How many loaves have ye? And they said, Seven.

6 And he commanded the people to sit down on the ground: and he took the seven loaves, and gave thanks, and brake, and gave to his disciples to set before *them;* and they did set *them* before the people.

7 And they had a few small fishes: and he blessed, and commanded to set them also before *them.*

8 So they did eat, and were filled: and they took up of the broken *meat* that was left seven baskets.

9 And they that had eaten were about four thousand: and he sent them away.

10 And straightway he entered into a ship with his disciples, and came into the parts of Dalmanutha.

11 And the Pharisees came forth, and began to question with him, seeking of him a sign from heaven, tempting him.

12 And he sighed deeply in his spirit, and saith, Why doth this generation seek after a sign? verily I say unto you, There shall no sign be given unto this generation.

13 And he left them, and entering into the ship again departed to the other side.

14 Now *the disciples* had forgotten to take bread, neither had they in the ship with them more than one loaf.

15 And he charged them, saying, Take heed, beware of the leaven of the Pharisees, and *of* the leaven of Herod.

16 And they reasoned among themselves, saying, *It is* because we have no bread.

17 And when Jesus knew *it,* he saith unto them, Why reason ye, because ye have no bread? perceive ye not yet, neither understand? have ye your heart yet hardened?

18 Having eyes, see ye not? and having ears, hear ye not? and do ye not remember?

19 When I brake the five loaves among five thousand, how many baskets full of fragments took ye up? They say unto him, Twelve.

20 And when the seven among four thousand, how many baskets full of fragments took ye up? And they said, Seven.

21 And he said unto them, How is it that ye do not understand?

22 And he cometh to Bethsaida; and they bring a blind man unto him, and besought him to touch him.

23 And he took the blind man by the hand, and led him out of the town; and when he had spit on his eyes, and put his hands upon him, he asked him if he saw ought.

24 And he looked up, and said, I see men as trees, walking.

25 After that he put *his* hands again upon his eyes, and made him look up: and he was restored, and saw every man clearly.

26 And he sent him away to his house, saying, Neither go into the town, nor tell *it* to any in the town.

27 And Jesus went out, and his disciples,

into the towns of Caesarea Philippi: and by the way he asked his disciples, saying unto them, Whom do men say that I am?

28 And they answered, John the Baptist: but some *say,* Elias; and others, One of the prophets.

29 And he saith unto them, But whom say ye that I am? And Peter answereth and saith unto him, Thou art the Christ.

30 And he charged them that they should tell no man of him.

31 And he began to teach them, that the Son of man must suffer many things, and be rejected of the elders, and *of* the chief priests, and scribes, and be killed, and after three days rise again.

32 And he spake that saying openly. And Peter took him, and began to rebuke him.

33 But when he had turned about and looked on his disciples, he rebuked Peter, saying, Get thee behind me, Satan: for thou savourest not the things that be of God, but the things that be of men.

34 And when he had called the people *unto him* with his disciples also, he said unto them, Whosoever will come after me, let him deny himself, and take up his cross, and follow me.

35 For whosoever will save his life shall lose it; but whosoever shall lose his life for my sake and the gospel's, the same shall save it.

8:35 Sacrifice
◄ Matthew 19:29
Mark 9:35 ►

36 For what shall it profit a man, if he shall gain the whole world, and lose his own soul?

37 Or what shall a man give in exchange for his soul?

38 Whosoever therefore shall be ashamed of me and of my words in this adulterous and sinful generation; of him also shall the Son of man be ashamed, when he cometh in the glory of his Father with the holy angels.

8:38 Bad News
◄ Matthew 24:30
Luke 21:26 ►

9

1 And he said unto them, Verily I say unto you, That there be some of them that stand here, which shall not taste of death, till they have seen the kingdom of God come with power.

2 And after six days Jesus taketh *with him* Peter, and James, and John, and leadeth them up into an high mountain apart by themselves: and he was transfigured before them.

3 And his raiment became shining, exceeding white as snow; so as no fuller on earth can white them.

4 And there appeared unto them Elias with Moses: and they were talking with Jesus.

5 And Peter answered and said to Jesus, Master, it is good for us to be here: and let us make three tabernacles; one for thee, and one for Moses, and one for Elias.

6 For he wist not what to say; for they were sore afraid.

7 And there was a cloud that overshadowed them: and a voice came out of the cloud, saying, This is my beloved Son: hear him.

8 And suddenly, when they had looked round about, they saw no man any more, save Jesus only with themselves.

9 And as they came down from the mountain, he charged them that they should tell no man what things they had seen, till the Son of man were risen from the dead.

10 And they kept that saying with themselves, questioning one with another what the rising from the dead should mean.

11 And they asked him, saying, Why say the scribes that Elias must first come?

9:11 Learning from Jesus
◄ Mark 7:17
Mark 9:28 ►

12 And he answered and told them, Elias verily cometh first, and restoreth all things; and how it is written of the Son of man, that he must suffer many things, and be set at nought.

13 But I say unto you, That Elias is indeed come, and they have done unto him whatsoever they listed, as it is written of him.

14 And when he came to *his* disciples, he saw a great multitude about them, and the scribes questioning with them.

15 And straightway all the people, when they beheld him, were greatly amazed, and running to *him* saluted him.

16 And he asked the scribes, What question ye with them?

17 And one of the multitude answered and said, Master, I have brought unto thee

my son, which hath a dumb spirit;

18 And wheresoever he taketh him, he teareth him: and he foameth, and gnasheth with his teeth, and pineth away: and I spake to thy disciples that they should cast him out; and they could not.

9:17 Demons
◄ Mark 7:30
Mark 16:9 ►

9:17-20 Help!
◄ Matthew 9:32
Luke 5:18-19 ►

9:18 Cost of Sin
◄ Jeremiah 51:30
John 15:5 ►

19 He answereth him, and saith, O faithless generation, how long shall I be with you? how long shall I suffer you? bring him unto me.

20 And they brought him unto him: and when he saw him, straightway the spirit tare him; and he fell on the ground, and wallowed foaming.

21 And he asked his father, How long is it ago since this came unto him? And he said, Of a child.

22 And ofttimes it hath cast him into the fire, and into the waters, to destroy him: but if thou canst do any thing, have compassion on us, and help us.

23 Jesus said unto him, If thou canst believe, all things *are* possible to him that believeth.

24 And straightway the father of the child cried out, and said with tears, Lord, I believe; help thou mine unbelief.

25 When Jesus saw that the people came running together, he rebuked the foul spirit, saying unto him, *Thou* dumb and deaf spirit, I charge thee, come out of him, and enter no more into him.

26 And *the spirit* cried, and rent him sore, and came out of him: and he was as one dead; insomuch that many said, He is dead.

27 But Jesus took him by the hand, and lifted him up; and he arose.

28 And when he was come into the house, his disciples asked him privately, Why could not we cast him out?

9:28
Learning from Jesus
◄ Mark 9:11
Mark 10:10 ►

29 And he said unto them, This kind can come forth by nothing, but by prayer and fasting.

30 And they departed thence, and passed through Galilee; and he would not that any man should know *it*.

31 For he taught his disciples, and said unto them, The Son of man is delivered into the hands of men, and they shall kill him; and after that he is killed, he shall rise the third day.

32 But they understood not that saying, and were afraid to ask him.

33 And he came to Capernaum: and being in the house he asked them, What was it that ye disputed among yourselves by the way?

34 But they held their peace: for by the way they had disputed among themselves, who *should be* the greatest.

35 And he sat down, and called the twelve, and saith unto them, If any man desire to be first, *the same* shall be last of all, and servant of all.

9:35 Sacrifice
◄ Mark 8:35
John 12:24 ►

36 And he took a child, and set him in the midst of them: and when he had taken him in his arms, he said unto them,

37 Whosoever shall receive one of such children in my name, receiveth me: and whosoever shall receive me, receiveth not me, but him that sent me.

38 And John answered him, saying, Master, we saw one casting out devils in thy name, and he followeth not us: and we forbad him, because he followeth not us.

9:38 Accepting People
◄ Matthew 9:10
Mark 9:39 ►

39 But Jesus said, Forbid him not: for there is no man which shall do a miracle in my name, that can lightly speak evil of me.

9:39 Accepting People
◄ Mark 9:38
Luke 9:49-50 ►

40 For he that is not against us is on our part.

41 For whosoever shall give you a cup of water to drink in my name, because ye belong to Christ,

9:41
Goodness Rewarded
◄ Matthew 25:34
Luke 6:35 ►

verily I say unto you, he shall not lose his
reward.
42 And whosoever shall offend one of
these little ones that believe in me, it is
better for him that a millstone were hanged
about his neck, and he were cast into
the sea.
43 And if thy hand offend thee, cut it off:
it is better for thee to enter into life
maimed, than having two hands to go into
hell, into the fire that never shall be
quenched:
44 Where their worm dieth not, and the
fire is not quenched.
45 And if thy foot offend thee, cut it off:
it is better for thee to enter halt into life,
than having two feet to be cast into hell,
into the fire that never shall be quenched:
46 Where their worm dieth not, and the
fire is not quenched.
47 And if thine eye offend thee, pluck it
out: it is better for thee to enter into the
kingdom of God with one eye, than having two eyes to be cast into hell fire:
48 Where their worm dieth not, and the
fire is not quenched.
49 For every one shall be salted with fire,
and every sacrifice shall be salted with salt.
50 Salt *is* good: but if the salt have lost
his saltness, wherewith will ye season it?
Have salt in yourselves, and have peace one
with another.

10

1 And he arose from thence, and cometh
into the coasts of Judaea by the farther side
of Jordan: and the people resort unto him
again; and, as he was wont, he taught them
again.
2 And the Pharisees came to him, and
asked him, Is it lawful for a man to put
away *his* wife? tempting him.
3 And he answered and said unto them,
What did Moses command you?
4 And they said, Moses suffered to write
a bill of divorcement, and to put *her* away.
5 And Jesus answered and said unto
them, For the hardness of your heart he
wrote you this precept.
6 But from the beginning of the creation
God made them male and female.
7 For this cause shall a man leave his father and mother, and cleave to his wife;
8 And they twain shall be one flesh: so
then they are no more twain, but one flesh.
9 What therefore God hath joined together, let not man put asunder.
10 And in the
house his disciples
asked him again of
the same *matter*.
11 And he saith
unto them, Whoso-
ever shall put away his wife, and marry another, committeth adultery against her.

10:10
Learning from Jesus
◄ Mark 9:28
Mark 13:4 ►

12 And if a woman shall put away her
husband, and be married to another, she
committeth adultery.
13 And they
brought young
children to him,
that he should
touch them: and *his*
disciples rebuked
those that brought *them*.

10:13 Faith Tested
◄ Mark 5:35
Luke 5:18-19 ►

14 But when Jesus saw *it*, he was much
displeased, and said unto them, Suffer the
little children to come unto me, and forbid them not: for of such is the kingdom
of God.
15 Verily I say unto you, Whosoever shall
not receive the kingdom of God as a little
child, he shall not enter therein.
16 And he took them up in his arms, put
his hands upon them, and blessed them.
17 And when he was gone forth into the
way, there came one running, and kneeled
to him, and asked him, Good Master, what
shall I do that I may inherit eternal life?
18 And Jesus said unto him, Why callest
thou me good? *there is* none good but one,
that is, God.
19 Thou knowest the commandments,
Do not commit adultery, Do not kill, Do
not steal, Do not bear false witness, Defraud not, Honour thy father and mother.
20 And he answered and said unto him,
Master, all these have I observed from my
youth.
21 Then Jesus be-
holding him loved
him, and said unto
him, One thing
thou lackest: go thy
way, sell whatso-
ever thou hast, and give to the poor, and
thou shalt have treasure in heaven: and
come, take up the cross, and follow me.

10:21 Following God
◄ Matthew 27:17
Luke 16:13 ►

22 And he was sad at that saying, and
went away grieved: for he had great possessions.
23 And Jesus looked round about, and

saith unto his disciples, How hardly shall
they that have riches enter into the kingdom of God!
24 And the disci-
ples were aston-
ished at his words.
But Jesus answereth
again, and saith
unto them, Chil-
dren, how hard is it for them that trust in
riches to enter into the kingdom of God!

10:24 Wealth
◄ Proverbs 18:11
Luke 12:19-20 ►

25 It is easier for a camel to go through
the eye of a needle, than for a rich man to
enter into the kingdom of God.
26 And they were astonished out of measure, saying among themselves, Who then
can be saved?
27 And Jesus looking upon them saith,
With men *it is* impossible, but not with
God: for with God all things are possible.
28 Then Peter be-
gan to say unto
him, Lo, we have
left all, and have
followed thee.

10:28
This for That
◄ Luke 5:11 ►

29 And Jesus an-
swered and said, Verily I say unto you,
There is no man that hath left house, or
brethren, or sisters, or father, or mother,
or wife, or children, or lands, for my sake,
and the gospel's,
30 But he shall receive an hundredfold
now in this time, houses, and brethren,
and sisters, and mothers, and children, and
lands, with persecutions; and in the world
to come eternal life.
31 But many *that are* first shall be last;
and the last first.
32 And they were in the way going up to
Jerusalem; and Jesus went before them:
and they were amazed; and as they followed, they were afraid. And he took again
the twelve, and began to tell them what
things should happen unto him,
33 *Saying,* Behold, we go up to Jerusalem;
and the Son of man shall be delivered unto
the chief priests, and unto the scribes; and
they shall condemn him to death, and
shall deliver him to the Gentiles:
34 And they shall mock him, and shall
scourge him, and shall spit upon him, and
shall kill him: and the third day he shall
rise again.
35 And James and John, the sons of Zebedee, come unto him, saying, Master, we
would that thou
shouldest do for us
whatsoever we shall
desire.
36 And he said
unto them, What
would ye that I should do for you?

10:35-37 Giving In
◄ 1 Kings 11:4
2 Peter 2:20 ►

37 They said unto him, Grant unto us
that we may sit, one on thy right hand,
and the other on thy left hand, in thy glory.
38 But Jesus said unto them, Ye know not
what ye ask: can ye drink of the cup that I
drink of? and be baptized with the baptism that I am baptized with?
39 And they said unto him, We can. And
Jesus said unto them, Ye shall indeed drink
of the cup that I drink of; and with the
baptism that I am baptized withal shall ye
be baptized:
40 But to sit on my right hand and on
my left hand is not mine to give; but *it
shall be given to them* for whom it is prepared.
41 And when the ten heard *it,* they began to be much displeased with James and
John.
42 But Jesus called them *to him,* and saith
unto them, Ye know that they which are
accounted to rule over the Gentiles exercise lordship over them; and their great
ones exercise authority upon them.
43 But so shall it
not be among you:
but whosoever will
be great among
you, shall be your
minister:

10:43-44
Serving People
◄ Luke 10:36-37 ►

44 And whosoever of you will be the
chiefest, shall be servant of all.
45 For even the Son of man came not to
be ministered unto, but to minister, and
to give his life a ransom for many.
46 And they came to Jericho: and as he
went out of Jericho with his disciples and
a great number of people, blind Bartimae-
us, the son of Timaeus, sat by the highway
side begging.
47 And when he heard that it was Jesus
of Nazareth, he began to cry out, and say,
Jesus, *thou* Son of David, have mercy
on me.
48 And many charged him that he should
hold his peace: but he cried the more a
great deal, *Thou* Son of David, have mercy
on me.

49 And Jesus stood still, and commanded him to be called. And they call the blind
man, saying unto him, Be of good comfort, rise; he calleth thee.
50 And he, casting away his garment,
rose, and came to Jesus.
51 And Jesus answered and said unto
him, What wilt thou that I should do unto
thee? The blind man said unto him, Lord,
that I might receive my sight.
52 And Jesus said
unto him, Go thy
way; thy faith hath
made thee whole.
And immediately
he received his
sight, and followed Jesus in the way.

10:52 God's Response
◄ Mark 7:29
Luke 7:10 ►

11

1 And when they came nigh to Jerusalem, unto Bethphage and Bethany, at the
mount of Olives, he sendeth forth two of
his disciples,
2 And saith unto them, Go your way into
the village over against you: and as soon
as ye be entered into it, ye shall find a colt
tied, whereon never man sat; loose him,
and bring *him*.
3 And if any man say unto you, Why do
ye this? say ye that the Lord hath need of
him; and straightway he will send him
hither.
4 And they went their way, and found
the colt tied by the door without in a
place where two ways met; and they loose
him.
5 And certain of them that stood there
said unto them, What do ye, loosing the
colt?
6 And they said unto them even as Jesus
had commanded: and they let them go.
7 And they brought the colt to Jesus, and
cast their garments on him; and he sat
upon him.
8 And many spread their garments in the
way: and others cut down branches off the
trees, and strawed *them* in the way.
9 And they that went before, and they
that followed, cried, saying, Hosanna;
Blessed *is* he that cometh in the name of
the Lord:
10 Blessed *be* the kingdom of our father
David, that cometh in the name of the
Lord: Hosanna in the highest.
11 And Jesus entered into Jerusalem, and
into the temple: and when he had looked
round about upon all things, and now the
eventide was come, he went out unto Bethany with the twelve.
12 And on the morrow, when they were
come from Bethany, he was hungry:
13 And seeing a fig tree afar off having
leaves, he came, if haply he might find any
thing thereon: and when he came to it, he
found nothing but leaves; for the time of
figs was not *yet*.
14 And Jesus answered and said unto it,
No man eat fruit of thee hereafter for ever.
And his disciples heard *it*.
15 And they come to Jerusalem: and Jesus
went into the temple, and began to cast
out them that sold and bought in the temple, and overthrew the tables of the
moneychangers, and the seats of them that
sold doves;
16 And would not suffer that any man
should carry *any* vessel through the
temple.
17 And he taught, saying unto them, Is it
not written, My house shall be called of
all nations the house of prayer? but ye have
made it a den of thieves.
18 And the scribes and chief priests heard
it, and sought how they might destroy him:
for they feared him, because all the people was astonished at his doctrine.
19 And when even was come, he went out
of the city.
20 And in the morning, as they passed by,
they saw the fig tree dried up from the roots.
21 And Peter calling to remembrance
saith unto him, Master, behold, the fig tree
which thou cursedst is withered away.
22 And Jesus an-
swering saith unto
them, Have faith in
God.

11:22 Faith
◄ 2 Chronicles 20:20
Luke 8:50 ►

23 For verily I say
unto you, That who-
soever shall say unto this mountain, Be
thou removed, and be thou cast into the
sea; and shall not doubt in his heart, but
shall believe that those things which he
saith shall come to pass; he shall have
whatsoever he saith.
24 Therefore I say
unto you, What
things soever ye
desire, when ye
pray, believe that
ye receive *them*, and
ye shall have *them*.

11:24 How to Pray
◄ Jeremiah 29:13
James 5:16 ►

11:25
Forgiving Others
◄ Luke 11:4 ►

25And when ye
stand praying, for-
give, if ye have
ought against any:
that your Father
also which is in
heaven may forgive you your trespasses.
26But if ye do not forgive, neither will
your Father which is in heaven forgive your
trespasses.
27And they come again to Jerusalem:
and as he was walking in the temple, there
come to him the chief priests, and the
scribes, and the elders,
28And say unto him, By what authority
doest thou these things? and who gave thee
this authority to do these things?
29And Jesus answered and said unto
them, I will also ask of you one question,
and answer me, and I will tell you by what
authority I do these things.
30The baptism of John, was *it* from heav-
en, or of men? answer me.
31And they reasoned with themselves,
saying, If we shall say, From heaven; he
will say, Why then did ye not believe him?
32But if we shall say, Of men; they feared
the people: for all *men* counted John, that
he was a prophet indeed.
33And they answered and said unto
Jesus, We cannot tell. And Jesus answering
saith unto them, Neither do I tell you by
what authority I do these things.

12

1And he began to speak unto them by
parables. A *certain* man planted a vineyard,
and set an hedge about *it*, and digged *a
place for* the winefat, and built a tower, and
let it out to husbandmen, and went into a
far country.
2And at the season he sent to the husbandmen a servant, that he might receive
from the husbandmen of the fruit of the
vineyard.
3And they caught *him*, and beat him,
and sent *him* away empty.
4And again he sent unto them another
servant; and at him they cast stones, and
wounded *him* in the head, and sent *him*
away shamefully handled.
5And again he sent another; and him
they killed, and many others; beating
some, and killing some.
6Having yet therefore one son, his
wellbeloved, he sent him also last unto
them, saying, They will reverence my son.
7But those husbandmen said among
themselves, This is the heir; come, let us
kill him, and the inheritance shall be
ours.
8And they took him, and killed *him*, and
cast *him* out of the vineyard.
9What shall therefore the lord of the
vineyard do? he will come and destroy the
husbandmen, and will give the vineyard
unto others.
10And have ye not read this scripture;
The stone which the builders rejected is
become the head of the corner:
11This was the Lord's doing, and it is
marvellous in our eyes?
12And they sought to lay hold on him,
but feared the people: for they knew that
he had spoken the parable against them:
and they left him, and went their way.
13And they send unto him certain of the
Pharisees and of the Herodians, to catch
him in *his* words.
14And when they were come, they say
unto him, Master, we know that thou art
true, and carest for no man: for thou
regardest not the person of men, but
teachest the way of God in truth: Is it lawful to give tribute to Caesar, or not?
15Shall we give, or shall we not give? But
he, knowing their hypocrisy, said unto
them, Why tempt ye me? bring me a penny, that I may see *it*.
16And they brought *it*. And he saith unto
them, Whose *is* this image and superscription? And they said unto him, Caesar's.
17And Jesus answering said unto them,
Render to Caesar the things that are
Caesar's, and to God the things that are
God's. And they marvelled at him.
18Then come unto him the Sadducees,
which say there is no resurrection; and they
asked him, saying,
19Master, Moses wrote unto us, If a
man's brother die, and leave *his* wife *behind him*, and leave no children, that his
brother should take his wife, and raise up
seed unto his brother.
20Now there were seven brethren: and
the first took a wife, and dying left no seed.
21And the second took her, and died,
neither left he any seed: and the third likewise.
22And the seven had her, and left no
seed: last of all the woman died also.
23In the resurrection therefore, when

they shall rise, whose wife shall she be of
them? for the seven had her to wife.
24And Jesus answering said unto them,
Do ye not therefore err, because ye know
not the scriptures, neither the power of
God?
25For when they shall rise from the dead,
they neither marry, nor are given in marriage; but are as the angels which are in
heaven.
26And as touching the dead, that they
rise: have ye not read in the book of Moses, how in the bush God spake unto him,
saying, I *am* the God of Abraham, and the
God of Isaac, and the God of Jacob?
27He is not the God of the dead, but the
God of the living: ye therefore do greatly
err.
28And one of the scribes came, and having heard them reasoning together, and
perceiving that he had answered them well,
asked him, Which is the first commandment of all?
29And Jesus an-
swered him, The
first of all the com-
mandments *is*,
Hear, O Israel; The
Lord our God is
one Lord:

12:29 Only One God
◄ Isaiah 45:18
1 Corinthians 8:4 ►

30And thou shalt love the Lord thy God
with all thy heart, and with all thy soul,
and with all thy mind, and with all thy
strength: this *is* the first commandment.
31And the second
is like, *namely* this,
Thou shalt love thy
neighbour as thy-
self. There is none
other command-
ment greater than these.

12:31 Neighbors
◄ Leviticus 19:18
Romans 13:10 ►

32And the scribe said unto him, Well,
Master, thou hast said the truth: for there
is one God; and there is none other but he:
33And to love
him with all the
heart, and with all
the understanding,
and with all the
soul, and with all
the strength, and to love *his* neighbour as
himself, is more than all whole burnt offerings and sacrifices.

12:33 Religious People
◄ Micah 6:8
Romans 13:10 ►

34And when Jesus saw that he answered
discreetly, he said unto him, Thou art not
far from the king-
dom of God. And
no man after that
durst ask him *any*
question.

12:34
Discretion
◄ Isaiah 28:26 ►

35And Jesus an-
swered and said, while he taught in the
temple, How say the scribes that Christ is
the Son of David?
36For David himself said by the Holy
Ghost, The Lord said to my Lord, Sit thou
on my right hand, till I make thine enemies thy footstool.
37David therefore himself calleth him
Lord; and whence is he *then* his son? And
the common people heard him gladly.
38And he said unto them in his doctrine,
Beware of the scribes, which love to go in
long clothing, and *love* salutations in the
marketplaces,
39And the chief seats in the synagogues,
and the uppermost rooms at feasts:
40Which devour widows' houses, and
for a pretence make long prayers: these
shall receive greater damnation.
41And Jesus sat over against the treasury,
and beheld how the people cast money
into the treasury: and many that were rich
cast in much.
42And there came a certain poor widow, and she threw in two mites, which
make a farthing.
43And he called *unto him* his disciples,
and saith unto them, Verily I say unto you,
That this poor widow hath cast more in,
than all they which have cast into the treasury:
44For all *they* did cast in of their abundance; but she of her want did cast in all
that she had, *even* all her living.

13

1And as he went out of the temple, one
of his disciples saith unto him, Master, see
what manner of stones and what buildings *are here!*
2And Jesus answering said unto him,
Seest thou these great buildings? there
shall not be left one stone upon another,
that shall not be thrown down.
3And as he sat upon the mount of Olives over against the
temple, Peter and
James and John
and Andrew asked
him privately,
4Tell us, when

13:4
Learning from Jesus
◄ Mark 10:10
Luke 3:12 ►

shall these things be? and what *shall be* the
sign when all these things shall be fulfilled?
5 And Jesus answering them began to say,
Take heed lest any *man* deceive you:
6 For many shall come in my name, saying, I am *Christ;* and shall deceive many.
7 And when ye shall hear of wars and
rumours of wars, be ye not troubled: for
such things must needs be; but the end *shall*
not *be* yet.
8 For nation shall rise against nation, and
kingdom against kingdom: and there shall
be earthquakes in divers places, and there
shall be famines and troubles: these *are* the
beginnings of sorrows.
9 But take heed to
yourselves: for they
shall deliver you up
to councils; and in
the synagogues ye
shall be beaten: and
ye shall be brought before rulers and kings
for my sake, for a testimony against them.

13:9 Watch Out!
◄ Mark 4:24
Mark 13:33 ►

10 And the gospel must first be published
among all nations.
11 But when they shall lead *you,* and deliver you up, take no thought beforehand
what ye shall speak, neither do ye premedi-
tate: but whatsoever shall be given you in
that hour, that speak ye: for it is not ye
that speak, but the Holy Ghost.
12 Now the brother shall betray the
brother to death, and the father the son;
and children shall rise up against *their* parents, and shall cause them to be put to
death.
13 And ye shall be
hated of all *men* for
my name's sake:
but he that shall
endure unto the
end, the same shall
be saved.

13:13 Endurance
◄ Matthew 10:22
Hebrews 12:7 ►

14 But when ye shall see the abomination of desolation, spoken of by Daniel
the prophet, standing where it ought not,
(let him that readeth understand,) then let
them that be in Judaea flee to the mountains:
15 And let him that is on the housetop
not go down into the house, neither enter
therein, to take any thing out of his house:
16 And let him that is in the field not turn
back again for to take up his garment.
17 But woe to them that are with child,
and to them that give suck in those days!
18 And pray ye that your flight be not in
the winter.
19 For *in* those days shall be affliction,
such as was not from the beginning of the
creation which God created unto this time,
neither shall be.
20 And except that the Lord had shortened those days, no flesh should be saved:
but for the elect's sake, whom he hath chosen, he hath shortened the days.
21 And then if any man shall say to you,
Lo, here *is* Christ; or, lo, *he is* there; believe *him* not:
22 For false Christs and false prophets
shall rise, and shall shew signs and wonders, to seduce, if *it were* possible, even the
elect.
23 But take ye heed: behold, I have foretold you all things.
24 But in those days, after that tribulation, the sun shall be darkened, and the
moon shall not give her light,
25 And the stars of heaven shall fall, and
the powers that are in heaven shall be
shaken.
26 And then shall they see the Son of man
coming in the clouds with great power and
glory.
27 And then shall he send his angels, and
shall gather together his elect from the four
winds, from the uttermost part of the earth
to the uttermost part of heaven.
28 Now learn a parable of the fig tree;
When her branch is yet tender, and putteth
forth leaves, ye know that summer is near:
29 So ye in like manner, when ye shall
see these things come to pass, know that
it is nigh, *even* at the doors.
30 Verily I say unto you, that this generation shall not pass, till all these things be
done.
31 Heaven and
earth shall pass
away: but my words
shall not pass away.
32 But of that
day and *that* hour
knoweth no man,
no, not the angels
which are in heav-
en, neither the Son,
but the Father.
33 Take ye heed,

13:33 Jesus' Return
◄ Matthew 25:13
Luke 12:37 ►

13:33 Watch Out!
◄ Mark 13:9
Luke 8:18 ►

watch and pray: for ye know not when the time is.

34 *For the Son of man is* as a man taking a far journey, who left his house, and gave authority to his servants, and to every man his work, and commanded the porter to watch.

35 Watch ye therefore: for ye know not when the master of the house cometh, at even, or at midnight, or at the cockcrowing, or in the morning:

13:35
Ready for the Future
◄ Matthew 25:10
Luke 12:35-36 ►

36 Lest coming suddenly he find you sleeping.

37 And what I say unto you I say unto all, Watch.

14

1 After two days was *the feast of* the passover, and of unleavened bread: and the chief priests and the scribes sought how they might take him by craft, and put *him* to death.

2 But they said, Not on the feast *day,* lest there be an uproar of the people.

3 And being in Bethany in the house of Simon the leper, as he sat at meat, there came a woman having an alabaster box of ointment of spikenard very precious; and she brake the box, and poured *it* on his head.

4 And there were some that had indignation within themselves, and said, Why was this waste of the ointment made?

5 For it might have been sold for more than three hundred pence, and have been given to the poor. And they murmured against her.

6 And Jesus said, Let her alone; why trouble ye her? she hath wrought a good work on me.

7 For ye have the poor with you always, and whensoever ye will ye may do them good: but me ye have not always.

8 She hath done what she could: she is come aforehand to anoint my body to the burying.

14:8 Work
◄ Matthew 25:22-23
Luke 12:48 ►

9 Verily I say unto you, Wheresoever this gospel shall be preached throughout the whole world, *this* also that she hath done shall be spoken of for a memorial of her.

10 And Judas Iscariot, one of the twelve, went unto the chief priests, to betray him unto them.

11 And when they heard *it,* they were glad, and promised to give him money. And he sought how he might conveniently betray him.

12 And the first day of unleavened bread, when they killed the passover, his disciples said unto him, Where wilt thou that we go and prepare that thou mayest eat the passover?

13 And he sendeth forth two of his disciples, and saith unto them, Go ye into the city, and there shall meet you a man bearing a pitcher of water: follow him.

14 And wheresoever he shall go in, say ye to the goodman of the house, The Master saith, Where is the guestchamber, where I shall eat the passover with my disciples?

15 And he will shew you a large upper room furnished *and* prepared: there make ready for us.

16 And his disciples went forth, and came into the city, and found as he had said unto them: and they made ready the passover.

17 And in the evening he cometh with the twelve.

18 And as they sat and did eat, Jesus said, Verily I say unto you, One of you which eateth with me shall betray me.

19 And they began to be sorrowful, and to say unto him one by one, *Is* it I? and another *said, Is* it I?

20 And he answered and said unto them, *It is* one of the twelve, that dippeth with me in the dish.

21 The Son of man indeed goeth, as it is written of him: but woe to that man by whom the Son of man is betrayed! good were it for that man if he had never been born.

22 And as they did eat, Jesus took bread, and blessed, and brake *it,* and gave to them, and said, Take, eat: this is my body.

23 And he took the cup, and when he had given thanks, he gave *it* to them: and they all drank of it.

24 And he said unto them, This is my blood of the new testament, which is shed for many.

25 Verily I say unto you, I will drink no more of the fruit of the vine, until that day that I drink it new in the kingdom of God.

26 And when they had sung an hymn, they went out into the mount of Olives.

27 And Jesus saith unto them, All ye shall be offended because of me this night: for it is written, I will smite the shepherd, and the sheep shall be scattered.

28 But after that I am risen, I will go before you into Galilee.

29 But Peter said unto him, Although all shall be offended, yet *will* not I.

30 And Jesus saith unto him, Verily I say unto thee, That this day, *even* in this night, before the cock crow twice, thou shalt deny me thrice.

31 But he spake the more vehemently, If I should die with thee, I will not deny thee in any wise. Likewise also said they all.

32 And they came to a place which was named Gethsemane: and he saith to his disciples, Sit ye here, while I shall pray.

33 And he taketh with him Peter and James and John, and began to be sore amazed, and to be very heavy;

34 And saith unto them, My soul is exceeding sorrowful unto death: tarry ye here, and watch.

35 And he went forward a little, and fell on the ground, and prayed that, if it were possible, the hour might pass from him.

36 And he said, Abba, Father, all things *are* possible unto thee; take away this cup from me: nevertheless not what I will, but what thou wilt.

14:36 All-powerful
◄ Matthew 19:26
Luke 1:37 ►

37 And he cometh, and findeth them sleeping, and saith unto Peter, Simon, sleepest thou? couldest not thou watch one hour?

38 Watch ye and pray, lest ye enter into temptation. The spirit truly *is* ready, but the flesh *is* weak.

39 And again he went away, and prayed, and spake the same words.

40 And when he returned, he found them asleep again, (for their eyes were heavy,) neither wist they what to answer him.

41 And he cometh the third time, and saith unto them, Sleep on now, and take *your* rest: it is enough, the hour is come; behold, the Son of man is betrayed into the hands of sinners.

42 Rise up, let us go; lo, he that betrayeth me is at hand.

43 And immediately, while he yet spake, cometh Judas, one of the twelve, and with him a great multitude with swords and staves, from the chief priest and the scribes and the elders.

44 And he that betrayed him had given them a token, saying, Whomsoever I shall kiss, that same is he; take him, and lead *him* away safely.

45 And as soon as he was come, he goeth straightway to him, and saith, Master, master; and kissed him.

14:45
"Dangerous Kisses"
◄ Proverbs 27:6 ►

46 And they laid their hands on him, and took him.

47 And one of them that stood by drew a sword, and smote a servant of the high priest, and cut off his ear.

48 And Jesus answered and said unto them, Are ye come out, as against a thief, with swords and *with* staves to take me?

14:48 Being Friendless
◄ Psalm 142:4
Mark 14:50 ►

49 I was daily with you in the temple teaching, and ye took me not: but the scriptures must be fulfilled.

50 And they all forsook him, and fled.

51 And there followed him a certain young man, having a linen cloth cast about *his* naked *body;* and the young men laid hold on him:

14:50 Being Friendless
◄ Mark 14:48
Luke 15:16 ►

52 And he left the linen cloth, and fled from them naked.

53 And they led Jesus away to the high priest: and with him were assembled all the chief priests and the elders and the scribes.

54 And Peter followed him afar off, even into the palace of the high priest: and he sat with the servants, and warmed himself at the fire.

55 And the chief priests and all the council sought for witness against Jesus to put him to death; and found none.

56 For many bare false witness against him, but their witness agreed not together.

57 And there arose certain, and bare false witness against him, saying,

58 We heard him say, I will destroy this temple that is made with hands, and

within three days I will build another
made without hands.
59 But neither so did their witness agree
together.
60 And the high priest stood up in the
midst, and asked Jesus, saying, Answerest
thou nothing? what *is it which* these witness against thee?
61 But he held his peace, and answered
nothing. Again the high priest asked him,
and said unto him, Art thou the Christ,
the Son of the Blessed?
62 And Jesus said,
I am: and ye shall
see the Son of man
sitting on the right
hand of power, and
coming in the
clouds of heaven.

14:62 Second Coming
◄ Matthew 26:64
Luke 21:27 ►

63 Then the high priest rent his clothes,
and saith, What need we any further witnesses?
64 Ye have heard the blasphemy: what
think ye? And they all condemned him to
be guilty of death.
65 And some began to spit on him, and
to cover his face, and to buffet him, and
to say unto him, Prophesy: and the servants did strike him with the palms of their
hands.
66 And as Peter was beneath in the palace, there cometh one of the maids of the
high priest:
67 And when she saw Peter warming
himself, she looked upon him, and
said, And thou also wast with Jesus of Nazareth.
68 But he denied, saying, I know not,
neither understand I what thou sayest. And
he went out into the porch; and the cock
crew.
69 And a maid saw him again, and began to say to them that stood by, This is
one of them.
70 And he denied it again. And a little
after, they that stood by said again to Peter, Surely thou art *one* of them: for thou
art a Galilaean, and thy speech agreeth
thereto.
71 But he began to
curse and to swear,
saying, I know not
this man of whom
ye speak.
72 And the second

14:72 Mistakes
◄ Psalm 137:1
Luke 16:25 ►

time the cock crew. And Peter called to
mind the word that Jesus said unto him,
Before the cock crow twice, thou shalt deny
me thrice. And when he thought thereon,
he wept.

15

1 And straightway in the morning the
chief priests held a consultation with the
elders and scribes and the whole council,
and bound Jesus, and carried *him* away,
and delivered *him* to Pilate.
2 And Pilate asked him, Art thou the King
of the Jews? And he answering said unto
him, Thou sayest *it*.
3 And the chief priests accused him of
many things: but he answered nothing.
4 And Pilate asked him again, saying,
Answerest thou nothing? behold how
many things they witness against thee.
5 But Jesus yet answered nothing; so that
Pilate marvelled.
6 Now at *that* feast he released unto them
one prisoner, whomsoever they desired.
7 And there was *one* named Barabbas,
which lay bound with them that had made
insurrection with him, who had committed murder in the insurrection.
8 And the multitude crying aloud began
to desire *him to do* as he had ever done unto
them.
9 But Pilate answered them, saying, Will
ye that I release unto you the King of the
Jews?
10 For he knew that the chief priests had
delivered him for envy.
11 But the chief priests moved the people, that he should rather release Barabbas unto them.
12 And Pilate answered and said again
unto them, What will ye then that I shall
do *unto him* whom ye call the King of the
Jews?
13 And they cried out again, Crucify him.
14 Then Pilate said unto them, Why, what
evil hath he done? And they cried out the
more exceedingly, Crucify him.
15 And *so* Pilate, willing to content the
people, released Barabbas unto them, and
delivered Jesus, when he had scourged *him*,
to be crucified.
16 And the soldiers led him away into the
hall, called Praetorium; and they call together the whole band.
17 And they clothed him with purple,
and platted a crown of thorns, and put it
about his *head*,

18 And began to salute him, Hail, King of the Jews!

19 And they smote him on the head with a reed, and did spit upon him, and bowing *their* knees worshipped him.

20 And when they had mocked him, they took off the purple from him, and put his own clothes on him, and led him out to crucify him.

21 And they compel one Simon a Cyrenian, who passed by, coming out of the country, the father of Alexander and Rufus, to bear his cross.

22 And they bring him unto the place Golgotha, which is, being interpreted, The place of a skull.

23 And they gave him to drink wine mingled with myrrh: but he received *it* not.

24 And when they had crucified him, they parted his garments, casting lots upon them, what every man should take.

25 And it was the third hour, and they crucified him.

26 And the superscription of his accusation was written over, THE KING OF THE JEWS.

27 And with him they crucify two thieves; the one on his right hand, and the other on his left.

28 And the scripture was fulfilled, which saith, And he was numbered with the transgressors.

29 And they that passed by railed on him, wagging their heads, and saying, Ah, thou that destroyest the temple, and buildest *it* in three days,

30 Save thyself, and come down from the cross.

31 Likewise also the chief priests mocking said among themselves with the scribes, He saved others; himself he cannot save.

32 Let Christ the King of Israel descend now from the cross, that we may see and believe. And they that were crucified with him reviled him.

33 And when the sixth hour was come, there was darkness over the whole land until the ninth hour.

34 And at the ninth hour Jesus cried with a loud voice, saying, Eloi, Eloi, lama sabachthani? which is, being interpreted, My God, my God, why hast thou forsaken me?

35 And some of them that stood by, when they heard *it*, said, Behold, he calleth Elias.

36 And one ran and filled a spunge full of vinegar, and put *it* on a reed, and gave him to drink, saying, Let alone; let us see whether Elias will come to take him down.

37 And Jesus cried with a loud voice, and gave up the ghost.

38 And the veil of the temple was rent in twain from the top to the bottom.

39 And when the centurion, which stood over against him, saw that he so cried out, and gave up the ghost, he said, Truly this man was the Son of God.

40 There were also women looking on afar off: among whom was Mary Magdalene, and Mary the mother of James the less and of Joses, and Salome;

41 (Who also, when he was in Galilee, followed him, and ministered unto him;) and many other women which came up with him unto Jerusalem.

42 And now when the even was come, because it was the preparation, that is, the day before the sabbath,

43 Joseph of Arimathaea, an honourable counsellor, which also waited for the kingdom of God, came, and went in boldly unto Pilate, and craved the body of Jesus.

44 And Pilate marvelled if he were already dead: and calling *unto him* the centurion, he asked him whether he had been any while dead.

45 And when he knew *it* of the centurion, he gave the body to Joseph.

46 And he bought fine linen, and took him down, and wrapped him in the linen, and laid him in a sepulchre which was hewn out of a rock, and rolled a stone unto the door of the sepulchre.

47 And Mary Magdalene and Mary *the mother* of Joses beheld where he was laid.

16

1 And when the sabbath was past, Mary Magdalene, and Mary the *mother* of James, and Salome, had bought sweet spices, that they might come and anoint him.

16:1 Young Women
◄ Esther 4:16
Luke 1:38 ►

2 And very early in the morning the first *day* of the week, they came unto the sepulchre at the rising of the sun.

3 And they said among themselves, Who shall roll us away the stone from the door of the sepulchre?

4 And when they looked, they saw that

the stone was rolled away: for it was very great.

5 And entering into the sepulchre, they saw a young man sitting on the right side, clothed in a long white garment; and they were affrighted.

6 And he saith unto them, Be not affrighted: Ye seek Jesus of Nazareth, which was crucified: he is risen; he is not here: behold the place where they laid him.

16:6
Encouraging People
◄ Matthew 17:7
Acts 23:11 ►

7 But go your way, tell his disciples and Peter that he goeth before you into Galilee: there shall ye see him, as he said unto you.

8 And they went out quickly, and fled from the sepulchre; for they trembled and were amazed: neither said they any thing to any *man;* for they were afraid.

9 Now when *Jesus* was risen early the first *day* of the week, he appeared first to Mary Magdalene, out of whom he had cast seven devils.

16:9 Demons
◄ Mark 9:17
Luke 10:19 ►

10 *And* she went and told them that had been with him, as they mourned and wept.

11 And they, when they had heard that he was alive, and had been seen of her, believed not.

12 After that he appeared in another form unto two of them, as they walked, and went into the country.

13 And they went and told *it* unto the residue: neither believed they them.

14 Afterward he appeared unto the eleven as they sat at meat, and upbraided them with their unbelief and hardness of heart, because they believed not them which had seen him after he was risen.

15 And he said unto them, Go ye into all the world, and preach the gospel to every creature.

16 He that believeth and is baptized shall be saved; but he that believeth not shall be damned.

16:16 Baptism
◄ Matthew 28:19
John 3:5 ►

17 And these signs shall follow them that believe; In my name shall they cast out devils; they shall speak with new tongues;

18 They shall take up serpents; and if they drink any deadly thing, it shall not hurt them; they shall lay hands on the sick, and they shall recover.

19 So then after the Lord had spoken unto them, he was received up into heaven, and sat on the right hand of God.

20 And they went forth, and preached every where, the Lord working with *them,* and confirming the word with signs following. Amen.

16:20
Working with God
◄ 1 Samuel 14:45
1 Corinthians 3:9 ►

Luke

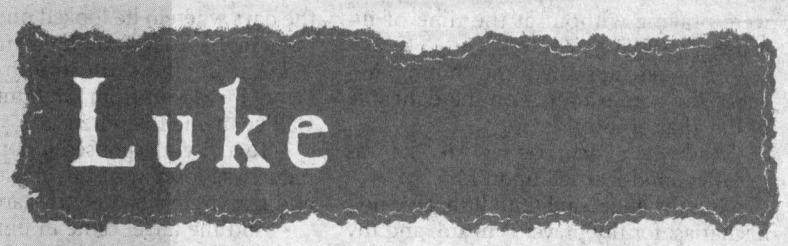

AUTHOR
Luke, a doctor and Gentile Christian

MAIN POINT
Lovers of God, discover the good news about Jesus, who is the Son of God and Son of Man.

DATE WRITTEN
Approximately A.D. 60

24 CHAPTERS

MAIN PEOPLE

Jesus, Elizabeth, Zechariah, John the Baptist, Mary, the disciples, Herod the Great, Pilate, Mary Magdalene

SPECIAL FEATURES

- *Is the most complete Gospel of the four (Matthew, Mark, Luke, John); most of the information in 9:51—18:35 is not found in any other Gospel*
- *Shows Luke's educated eye for detail in its description of people, illnesses, and miracles*
- *Gives an important place to women in this account of Jesus' life*
- *Was written by the author of Acts; the two books fit together*
- *Third of the four Gospels*

HOW THE BOOK GOT ITS NAME

Gospel means "good news"; this book contains the good news about Jesus as recorded by Luke.

1
1 Forasmuch as many have taken in hand
to set forth in order a declaration of those
things which are most surely believed
among us,
2 Even as they delivered them unto us,
which from the beginning were eyewitnesses, and ministers of the word;
3 It seemed good to me also, having had
perfect understanding of all things from
the very first, to write unto thee in order,
most excellent Theophilus,
4 That thou mightest know the certainty
of those things, wherein thou hast been
instructed.
5 There was in the days of Herod, the
king of Judaea, a certain priest named
Zacharias, of the course of Abia: and his
wife *was* of the daughters of Aaron, and
her name *was* Elisabeth.
6 And they were both righteous before
God, walking in all the commandments
and ordinances of the Lord blameless.
7 And they had no child, because that
Elisabeth was barren, and they both were
now well stricken in years.
8 And it came to pass, that while he executed the priest's office before God in the
order of his course,
9 According to the custom of the priest's
office, his lot was to burn incense when
he went into the temple of the Lord.
10 And the whole multitude of the people

were praying without at the time of incense.

11 And there appeared unto him an angel of the Lord standing on the right side of the altar of incense.

12 And when Zacharias saw *him,* he was troubled, and fear fell upon him.

13 But the angel said unto him, Fear not, Zacharias: for thy prayer is heard; and thy wife Elisabeth shall bear thee a son, and thou shalt call his name John.

14 And thou shalt have joy and gladness; and many shall rejoice at his birth.

15 For he shall be great in the sight of the Lord, and shall drink neither wine nor strong drink; and he shall be filled with the Holy Ghost, even from his mother's womb.

1:15 Drinking
◄ Matthew 11:18
Romans 14:21 ►

16 And many of the children of Israel shall he turn to the Lord their God.

17 And he shall go before him in the spirit and power of Elias, to turn the hearts of the fathers to the children, and the disobedient to the wisdom of the just; to make ready a people prepared for the Lord.

18 And Zacharias said unto the angel, Whereby shall I know this? for I am an old man, and my wife well stricken in years.

19 And the angel answering said unto him, I am Gabriel, that stand in the presence of God; and am sent to speak unto thee, and to shew thee these glad tidings.

20 And, behold, thou shalt be dumb, and not able to speak, until the day that these things shall be performed, because thou believest not my words, which shall be fulfilled in their season.

21 And the people waited for Zacharias, and marvelled that he tarried so long in the temple.

22 And when he came out, he could not speak unto them: and they perceived that he had seen a vision in the temple: for he beckoned unto them, and remained speechless.

23 And it came to pass, that, as soon as the days of his ministration were accomplished, he departed to his own house.

24 And after those days his wife Elisabeth conceived, and hid herself five months, saying,

25 Thus hath the Lord dealt with me in the days wherein he looked on *me,* to take away my reproach among men.

26 And in the sixth month the angel Gabriel was sent from God unto a city of Galilee, named Nazareth,

27 To a virgin espoused to a man whose name was Joseph, of the house of David; and the virgin's name *was* Mary.

28 And the angel came in unto her, and said, Hail, *thou that art* highly favoured, the Lord *is* with thee: blessed *art* thou among women.

29 And when she saw *him,* she was troubled at his saying, and cast in her mind what manner of salutation this should be.

30 And the angel said unto her, Fear not, Mary: for thou hast found favour with God.

31 And, behold, thou shalt conceive in thy womb, and bring forth a son, and shalt call his name JESUS.

1:31 Christmas
◄ Isaiah 9:6
John 1:14 ►

32 He shall be great, and shall be called the Son of the Highest: and the Lord God shall give unto him the throne of his father David:

33 And he shall reign over the house of Jacob for ever; and of his kingdom there shall be no end.

1:33 Jesus the King
◄ Matthew 25:34
John 1:49 ►

34 Then said Mary unto the angel, How shall this be, seeing I know not a man?

35 And the angel answered and said unto her, The Holy Ghost shall come upon thee, and the power of the Highest shall overshadow thee: therefore also that holy thing which shall be born of thee shall be called the Son of God.

36 And, behold, thy cousin Elisabeth, she hath also conceived a son in her old age: and this is the sixth month with her, who was called barren.

37 For with God nothing shall be impossible.

1:37 All-powerful
◄ Mark 14:36
Revelation 19:6 ►

38 And Mary said,

1:38 Young Women
◄ Mark 16:1
Luke 10:39 ►

the consolation of
Israel: and the Holy
Ghost was upon
him.
26 And it was re-
vealed unto him by
the Holy Ghost,
that he should not
see death, before he
had seen the Lord's
Christ.
27 And he came
by the Spirit into
the temple: and when the parents brought
in the child Jesus, to do for him after the
custom of the law,
28 Then took he him up in his arms, and
blessed God, and said,
29 Lord, now lettest thou thy servant depart in peace, according to thy word:
30 For mine eyes
have seen thy salva-
tion,
31 Which thou
hast prepared be-
fore the face of all
people;
32 A light to lighten the Gentiles, and the
glory of thy people Israel.
33 And Joseph and his mother marvelled
at those things which were spoken of him.
34 And Simeon blessed them, and said
unto Mary his mother, Behold, this *child*
is set for the fall and rising again of many
in Israel; and for a sign which shall be spoken against;
35 (Yea, a sword shall pierce through thy
own soul also,) that the thoughts of many
hearts may be revealed.
36 And there was one Anna, a prophetess, the daughter of Phanuel, of the tribe
of Aser: she was of a great age, and had
lived with an hus-
band seven years
from her virginity;
37 And she *was* a
widow of about
fourscore and four
years, which depart-
ed not from the
temple, but served
God with fastings
and prayers night
and day.
38 And she com-
ing in that instant gave thanks likewise
unto the Lord, and spake of him to all
them that looked for redemption in Jerusalem.
39 And when they had performed all
things according to the law of the Lord,
they returned into Galilee, to their own city
Nazareth.
40 And the child grew, and waxed strong
in spirit, filled with wisdom: and the grace
of God was upon him.
41 Now his parents went to Jerusalem
every year at the feast of the passover.
42 And when he was twelve years old,
they went up to Jerusalem after the custom of the feast.
43 And when they had fulfilled the days,
as they returned, the child Jesus tarried
behind in Jerusalem; and Joseph and his
mother knew not *of it.*
44 But they, supposing him to have been
in the company, went a day's journey; and
they sought him among *their* kinsfolk and
acquaintance.
45 And when they found him not, they
turned back again to Jerusalem, seeking
him.
46 And it came to pass, that after three
days they found him in the temple, sitting
in the midst of the doctors, both hearing
them, and asking them questions.
47 And all that heard him were astonished at his understanding and answers.
48 And when they saw him, they were
amazed: and his mother said unto him,
Son, why hast thou thus dealt with us?
behold, thy father and I have sought thee
sorrowing.
49 And he said
unto them, How is
it that ye sought
me? wist ye not that
I must be about my
Father's business?
50 And they understood not the saying
which he spake unto them.
51 And he went down with them, and
came to Nazareth, and was subject unto
them: but his mother kept all these sayings in her heart.
52 And Jesus increased in wisdom and
stature, and in favour with God and man.

3

1 Now in the fifteenth year of the reign
of Tiberius Caesar, Pontius Pilate being
governor of Judaea, and Herod being

2:25 Waiting
◄ Lamentations 3:25
Acts 1:4 ►

2:25 Who Is Religious?
◄ Daniel 6:10
Luke 2:37 ►

2:30 Only One Savior
◄ Luke 1:69
John 10:9 ►

2:37 Praying
◄ Zechariah 8:21
Acts 10:2 ►

2:37 Who Is Religious?
◄ Luke 2:25
John 1:47 ►

2:49 Young Men
◄ Psalm 71:5
2 Timothy 1:5 ►

tetrarch of Galilee, and his brother Philip
tetrarch of Ituraea and of the region of
Trachonitis, and Lysanias the tetrarch of
Abilene,
2 Annas and Caiaphas being the high
priests, the word of God came unto John
the son of Zacharias in the wilderness.
3 And he came
into all the country
about Jordan,
preaching the bap-
tism of repentance
for the remission of
sins;

3:3 Forgiveness of Sin
◄ Matthew 26:28
Luke 24:47 ►

4 As it is written in the book of the words
of Esaias the prophet, saying, The voice of
one crying in the wilderness, Prepare ye the
way of the Lord, make his paths straight.
5 Every valley shall be filled, and every
mountain and hill shall be brought low;
and the crooked shall be made straight,
and the rough ways *shall be* made smooth;
6 And all flesh
shall see the salva-
tion of God.
7 Then said he to
the multitude that
came forth to be
baptized of him, O generation of vipers,
who hath warned you to flee from the
wrath to come?

3:6 Salvation for Anyone
◄ Acts 2:21 ►

8 Bring forth therefore fruits worthy of
repentance, and begin not to say within
yourselves, We have Abraham to *our* father:
for I say unto you, That God is able of these
stones to raise up children unto Abraham.
9 And now also the axe is laid unto the
root of the trees: every tree therefore which
bringeth not forth good fruit is hewn
down, and cast into the fire.
10 And the people asked him, saying,
What shall we do then?
11 He answereth
and saith unto
them, He that hath
two coats, let him
impart to him that
hath none; and he
that hath meat, let him do likewise.

3:11 Giving
◄ Matthew 5:42
Luke 12:33 ►

12 Then came also
publicans to be
baptized, and said
unto him, Master,
what shall we do?
13 And he said
unto them, Exact no more than that which
is appointed you.

3:12 Learning from Jesus
◄ Mark 13:4
Luke 11:1 ►

14 And the sol-
diers likewise de-
manded of him,
saying, And what
shall we do? And he
said unto them, Do
violence to no man, neither accuse *any*
falsely; and be content with your wages.

3:14 Contentment
◄ Proverbs 15:16
Philippians 4:11 ►

15 And as the people were in expectation,
and all men mused in their hearts of John,
whether he were the Christ, or not;
16 John answered, saying unto *them* all,
I indeed baptize you with water; but one
mightier than I cometh, the latchet of
whose shoes I am not worthy to unloose:
he shall baptize you with the Holy Ghost
and with fire:
17 Whose fan *is* in his hand, and he will
throughly purge his floor, and will gather
the wheat into his garner; but the chaff he
will burn with fire unquenchable.
18 And many other things in his exhortation preached he unto the people.
19 But Herod the tetrarch, being reproved
by him for Herodias his brother Philip's
wife, and for all the evils which Herod had
done,
20 Added yet this above all, that he shut
up John in prison.
21 Now when all the people were baptized, it came to pass, that Jesus also being
baptized, and praying, the heaven was
opened,
22 And the Holy Ghost descended in a
bodily shape like a dove upon him, and a
voice came from heaven, which said, Thou
art my beloved Son; in thee I am well
pleased.
23 And Jesus him-
self began to be
about thirty years
of age, being (as
was supposed) the
son of Joseph,
which was *the son* of Heli,

3:23 Young Leaders
◄ 2 Chronicles 34:1, 3
Luke 18:18 ►

24 Which was *the son* of Matthat, which
was *the son* of Levi, which was *the son* of
Melchi, which was *the son* of Janna, which
was *the son* of Joseph,
25 Which was *the son* of Mattathias,
which was *the son* of Amos, which was *the*
son of Naum, which was *the son* of Esli,
which was *the son* of Nagge,

26 Which was *the son* of Maath, which was *the son* of Mattathias, which was *the son* of Semei, which was *the son* of Joseph, which was *the son* of Juda,

27 Which was *the son* of Joanna, which was *the son* of Rhesa, which was *the son* of Zorobabel, which was *the son* of Salathiel, which was *the son* of Neri,

28 Which was *the son* of Melchi, which was *the son* of Addi, which was *the son* of Cosam, which was *the son* of Elmodam, which was *the son* of Er,

29 Which was *the son* of Jose, which was *the son* of Eliezer, which was *the son* of Jorim, which was *the son* of Matthat, which was *the son* of Levi,

30 Which was *the son* of Simeon, which was *the son* of Juda, which was *the son* of Joseph, which was *the son* of Jonan, which was *the son* of Eliakim,

31 Which was *the son* of Melea, which was *the son* of Menan, which was *the son* of Mattatha, which was *the son* of Nathan, which was *the son* of David,

32 Which was *the son* of Jesse, which was *the son* of Obed, which was *the son* of Booz, which was *the son* of Salmon, which was *the son* of Naasson,

33 Which was *the son* of Aminadab, which was *the son* of Aram, which was *the son* of Esrom, which was *the son* of Phares, which was *the son* of Juda,

34 Which was *the son* of Jacob, which was *the son* of Isaac, which was *the son* of Abraham, which was *the son* of Thara, which was *the son* of Nachor,

35 Which was *the son* of Saruch, which was *the son* of Ragau, which was *the son* of Phalec, which was *the son* of Heber, which was *the son* of Sala,

36 Which was *the son* of Cainan, which was *the son* of Arphaxad, which was *the son* of Sem, which was *the son* of Noe, which was *the son* of Lamech,

37 Which was *the son* of Mathusala, which was *the son* of Enoch, which was *the son* of Jared, which was *the son* of Maleleel, which was *the son* of Cainan,

38 Which was *the son* of Enos, which was *the son* of Seth, which was *the son* of Adam, which was *the son* of God.

4

1 And Jesus being full of the Holy Ghost returned from Jordan, and was led by the Spirit into the wilderness,

2 Being forty days tempted of the devil. And in those days he did eat nothing: and when they were ended, he afterward hungered.

3 And the devil said unto him, If thou be the Son of God, command this stone that it be made bread.

4 And Jesus answered him, saying, It is written, That man shall not live by bread alone, but by every word of God.

5 And the devil, taking him up into an high mountain, shewed unto him all the kingdoms of the world in a moment of time.

6 And the devil said unto him, All this power will I give thee, and the glory of them: for that is delivered unto me; and to whomsoever I will I give it.

4:6 Satan's Power
◄ Job 1:12
Acts 26:18 ►

7 If thou therefore wilt worship me, all shall be thine.

8 And Jesus answered and said unto him, Get thee behind me, Satan: for it is written, Thou shalt worship the Lord thy God, and him only shalt thou serve.

9 And he brought him to Jerusalem, and set him on a pinnacle of the temple, and said unto him, If thou be the Son of God, cast thyself down from hence:

10 For it is written, He shall give his angels charge over thee, to keep thee:

11 And in *their* hands they shall bear thee up, lest at any time thou dash thy foot against a stone.

12 And Jesus answering said unto him, It is said, Thou shalt not tempt the Lord thy God.

4:13 Defeat of Satan
◄ Genesis 3:15
John 12:30-31 ►

13 And when the devil had ended all the temptation, he departed from him for a season.

4:14 The Holy Spirit
◄ Zechariah 4:6
Acts 1:8 ►

14 And Jesus returned in the power of the Spirit into Galilee: and there went out a fame of him through all the region round about.

4:15 The Teacher
◄ Mark 6:34
Luke 5:3 ►

15 And he taught

in their synagogues, being glorified of all.
16And he came to
Nazareth, where he
had been brought
up: and, as his cus-
tom was, he went
into the synagogue
on the sabbath day,
and stood up for to read.

4:16 Going to Church
◄ Mark 1:21
Acts 13:14 ►

17And there was delivered unto him the
book of the prophet Esaias. And when he
had opened the book, he found the place
where it was written,
18The Spirit of the Lord *is* upon me, because he hath anointed me to preach the
gospel to the poor; he hath sent me to heal
the brokenhearted, to preach deliverance
to the captives, and recovering of sight to
the blind, to set at liberty them that are
bruised,
19To preach the acceptable year of the
Lord.
20And he closed the book, and he gave
it again to the minister, and sat down. And
the eyes of all them that were in the synagogue were fastened on him.
21And he began to say unto them, This
day is this scripture fulfilled in your ears.
22And all bare him witness, and wondered at the gracious words which proceeded out of his mouth. And they said, Is
not this Joseph's son?
23And he said unto them, Ye will surely
say unto me this proverb, Physician, heal
thyself: whatsoever we have heard done in
Capernaum, do also here in thy country.
24And he said, Verily I say unto you, No
prophet is accepted in his own country.
25But I tell you of a truth, many widows
were in Israel in the days of Elias, when
the heaven was shut up three years and six
months, when great famine was throughout all the land;
26But unto none of them was Elias sent,
save unto Sarepta, *a city* of Sidon, unto a
woman *that was* a widow.
27And many lepers were in Israel in the
time of Eliseus the prophet; and none of
them was cleansed, saving Naaman the
Syrian.
28And all they
in the synagogue,
when they heard
these things, were
filled with wrath,

4:28 Mad
◄ Amos 1:11
Luke 6:11 ►

29And rose up,
and thrust him out
of the city, and led
him unto the brow
of the hill whereon
their city was built,
that they might cast him down headlong.

4:29 Examples of Revenge
◄ Matthew 14:8
Acts 5:33 ►

30But he passing through the midst of
them went his way,
31And came down to Capernaum, a city
of Galilee, and taught them on the sabbath days.
32And they were astonished at his doctrine: for his word was with power.
33And in the synagogue there was a man,
which had a spirit of an unclean devil, and
cried out with a loud voice,
34Saying, Let *us* alone; what have we to
do with thee, *thou* Jesus of Nazareth? art
thou come to destroy us? I know thee who
thou art; the Holy One of God.
35And Jesus rebuked him, saying, Hold
thy peace, and come out of him. And when
the devil had thrown him in the midst, he
came out of him, and hurt him not.
36And they were all amazed, and spake
among themselves, saying, What a word *is*
this! for with authority and power he
commandeth the unclean spirits, and they
come out.
37And the fame of him went out into
every place of the country round about.
38And he arose out of the synagogue,
and entered into Simon's house. And
Simon's wife's mother was taken with a
great fever; and they besought him for her.
39And he stood
over her, and re-
buked the fever;
and it left her: and
immediately she
arose and minis-
tered unto them.

4:39 Serving Quickly
◄ Mark 1:18
Luke 19:6 ►

40Now when the sun was setting, all they
that had any sick with divers diseases
brought them unto him; and he laid his
hands on every one of them, and healed
them.
41And devils also came out of many, crying out, and saying, Thou art Christ the
Son of God. And he rebuking *them* suffered
them not to speak: for they knew that he
was Christ.
42And when it was day, he departed and
went into a desert place: and the people

sought him, and came unto him, and
stayed him, that he should not depart from
them.
43 And he said unto them, I must preach
the kingdom of God to other cities also:
for therefore am I sent.
44 And he preached in the synagogues of
Galilee.

5

1 And it came to pass, that, as the people
pressed upon him to hear the word of God,
he stood by the lake of Gennesaret,
2 And saw two ships standing by the lake:
but the fishermen were gone out of them,
and were washing *their* nets.
3 And he entered
into one of the
ships, which was
Simon's, and prayed
him that he would
thrust out a little
from the land. And he sat down, and
taught the people out of the ship.

> **5:3 The Teacher**
> ◄ Luke 4:15
> John 3:2 ►

4 Now when he had left speaking, he said
unto Simon, Launch out into the deep, and
let down your nets for a draught.
5 And Simon an-
swering said unto
him, Master, we
have toiled all the
night, and have
taken nothing: nev-
ertheless at thy word I will let down the
net.

> **5:5 Obeying Christ**
> ◄ Matthew 26:19
> Luke 6:47 ►

6 And when they had this done, they inclosed a great multitude of fishes: and their
net brake.
7 And they beckoned unto *their* partners,
which were in the other ship, that they
should come and help them. And they
came, and filled both the ships, so that
they began to sink.
8 When Simon Peter saw *it*, he fell down
at Jesus' knees, saying, Depart from me;
for I am a sinful man, O Lord.
9 For he was astonished, and all that were
with him, at the draught of the fishes
which they had taken:
10 And so *was* also James, and John, the
sons of Zebedee, which were partners with
Simon. And Jesus
said unto Simon,
Fear not; from
henceforth thou
shalt catch men.

> **5:11 This for That**
> ◄ Mark 10:28
> Luke 5:27-28 ►

11 And when they
had brought their ships to land, they forsook all, and followed him.
12 And it came to pass, when he was in a
certain city, behold a man full of leprosy:
who seeing Jesus fell on *his* face, and besought him, saying, Lord, if thou wilt, thou
canst make me clean.
13 And he put forth *his* hand, and
touched him, saying, I will: be thou clean.
And immediately the leprosy departed
from him.
14 And he charged him to tell no man:
but go, and shew thyself to the priest, and
offer for thy cleansing, according as Moses commanded, for a testimony unto
them.
15 But so much the more went there a
fame abroad of him: and great multitudes
came together to hear, and to be healed
by him of their infirmities.
16 And he withdrew himself into the wilderness, and prayed.
17 And it came to pass on a certain day,
as he was teaching, that there were Pharisees and doctors of the law sitting by,
which were come out of every town of Galilee, and Judaea, and Jerusalem: and the
power of the Lord was *present* to heal them.
18 And, behold,
men brought in a
bed a man which
was taken with a
palsy: and they
sought *means* to
bring him in, and
to lay *him* before
him.
19 And when they
could not find by
what *way* they
might bring him in
because of the multitude, they went upon
the housetop, and let him down through
the tiling with *his* couch into the midst
before Jesus.

> **5:18-19 Faith Tested**
> ◄ Mark 10:13
> John 9:24 ►

> **5:18-19 Help!**
> ◄ Mark 9:17-20
> Luke 18:40 ►

20 And when he saw their faith, he said
unto him, Man, thy sins are forgiven thee.
21 And the scribes and the Pharisees began to reason, saying, Who is this which
speaketh blasphemies? Who can forgive
sins, but God alone?
22 But when Jesus perceived their
thoughts, he answering said unto them,
What reason ye in your hearts?
23 Whether is easier, to say, Thy sins be

forgiven thee; or to say, Rise up and walk?

24 But that ye may know that the Son of man hath power upon earth to forgive sins, (he said unto the sick of the palsy,) I say unto thee, Arise, and take up thy couch, and go into thine house.

25 And immediately he rose up before them, and took up that whereon he lay, and departed to his own house, glorifying God.

26 And they were all amazed, and they glorified God, and were filled with fear, saying, We have seen strange things to day.

27 And after these things he went forth, and saw a publican, named Levi, sitting at the receipt of custom: and he said unto him, Follow me.

5:27-28 This for That
◄ Luke 5:11
Luke 14:33 ►

28 And he left all, rose up, and followed him.

29 And Levi made him a great feast in his own house: and there was a great company of publicans and of others that sat down with them.

30 But their scribes and Pharisees murmured against his disciples, saying, Why do ye eat and drink with publicans and sinners?

31 And Jesus answering said unto them, They that are whole need not a physician; but they that are sick.

32 I came not to call the righteous, but sinners to repentance.

33 And they said unto him, Why do the disciples of John fast often, and make prayers, and likewise *the disciples* of the Pharisees; but thine eat and drink?

34 And he said unto them, Can ye make the children of the bridechamber fast, while the bridegroom is with them?

35 But the days will come, when the bridegroom shall be taken away from them, and then shall they fast in those days.

36 And he spake also a parable unto them; No man putteth a piece of a new garment upon an old; if otherwise, then both the new maketh a rent, and the piece that was *taken* out of the new agreeth not with the old.

37 And no man putteth new wine into old bottles; else the new wine will burst the bottles, and be spilled, and the bottles shall perish.

38 But new wine must be put into new bottles; and both are preserved.

39 No man also having drunk old *wine* straightway desireth new: for he saith, The old is better.

6

1 And it came to pass on the second sabbath after the first, that he went through the corn fields; and his disciples plucked the ears of corn, and did eat, rubbing *them* in *their* hands.

2 And certain of the Pharisees said unto them, Why do ye that which is not lawful to do on the sabbath days?

6:2 Legalism
◄ Mark 2:24
Luke 13:14 ►

3 And Jesus answering them said, Have ye not read so much as this, what David did, when himself was an hungred, and they which were with him;

4 How he went into the house of God, and did take and eat the shewbread, and gave also to them that were with him; which it is not lawful to eat but for the priests alone?

5 And he said unto them, That the Son of man is Lord also of the sabbath.

6 And it came to pass also on another sabbath, that he entered into the synagogue and taught: and there was a man whose right hand was withered.

7 And the scribes and Pharisees watched him, whether he would heal on the sabbath day; that they might find an accusation against him.

8 But he knew their thoughts, and said to the man which had the withered hand, Rise up, and stand forth in the midst. And he arose and stood forth.

9 Then said Jesus unto them, I will ask you one thing; Is it lawful on the sabbath days to do good, or to do evil? to save life, or to destroy *it*?

10 And looking round about upon them all, he said unto the man, Stretch forth thy hand. And he did so: and his hand was restored whole as the other.

11 And they were filled with madness; and communed one with another what they might do to Jesus.

6:11 Mad
◄ Luke 4:28
Acts 19:28 ►

12 And it came to pass in those days, that
he went out into a mountain to pray, and
continued all night in prayer to God.
13 And when it was day, he called *unto*
him his disciples: and of them he chose
twelve, whom also he named apostles;
14 Simon, (whom he also named Peter,)
and Andrew his brother, James and John,
Philip and Bartholomew,
15 Matthew and Thomas, James the *son*
of Alphaeus, and Simon called Zelotes,
16 And Judas *the brother* of James, and
Judas Iscariot, which also was the traitor.
17 And he came down with them, and
stood in the plain, and the company of
his disciples, and a great multitude of people out of all Judaea and Jerusalem, and
from the sea coast of Tyre and Sidon,
which came to hear him, and to be healed
of their diseases;
18 And they that were vexed with unclean
spirits: and they were healed.
19 And the whole multitude sought to
touch him: for there went virtue out of
him, and healed *them* all.
20 And he lifted up his eyes on his disciples, and said, Blessed *be ye* poor: for yours
is the kingdom of God.
21 Blessed *are ye*
that hunger now:
for ye shall be
filled. Blessed *are ye*
that weep now: for
ye shall laugh.

6:21 Repentance
◄ Micah 7:18
Luke 15:7 ►

22 Blessed are ye,
when men shall
hate you, and when
they shall separate
you *from their com-*
pany, and shall re-
proach *you,* and cast
out your name as evil, for the Son of man's
sake.

6:22
Why Suffer?
◄ 1 Timothy 4:10 ►

23 Rejoice ye in that day, and leap for joy:
for, behold, your reward *is* great in heav-
en: for in the like manner did their fathers
unto the prophets.
24 But woe unto you that are rich! for ye
have received your consolation.
25 Woe unto you
that are full! for ye
shall hunger. Woe
unto you that laugh
now! for ye shall
mourn and weep.

6:25 Laughter
◄ Ecclesiastes 7:6
James 4:9 ►

26 Woe unto you, when all men shall
speak well of you! for so did their fathers
to the false prophets.
27 But I say unto
you which hear,
Love your enemies,
do good to them
which hate you,

6:27 Vengeance
◄ Proverbs 25:21
Luke 6:35 ►

28 Bless them that
curse you, and pray
for them which de-
spitefully use you.
29 And unto him
that smiteth thee
on the *one* cheek
offer also the other;
and him that taketh away thy cloke forbid
not *to take thy* coat also.

6:28 Cursing
◄ Ecclesiastes 10:20
Romans 12:14 ►

30 Give to every man that asketh of thee;
and of him that taketh away thy goods ask
them not again.
31 And as ye
would that men
should do to you,
do ye also to them
likewise.

6:31
Golden Rule
◄ Matthew 7:12 ►

32 For if ye love
them which love you, what thank have ye?
for sinners also love those that love them.
33 And if ye do good to them which do
good to you, what
thank have ye? for
sinners also do
even the same.
34 And if ye lend
to them of whom ye
hope to receive,
what thank have
ye? for sinners also
lend to sinners, to
receive as much
again.

6:35 Doing Good
◄ Psalm 37:27
Romans 13:3 ►

6:35
Goodness Rewarded
◄ Mark 9:41
John 4:36 ►

35 But love ye
your enemies, and
do good, and lend,
hoping for nothing
again; and your re-
ward shall be great,
and ye shall be the
children of the
Highest: for he is
kind unto the
unthankful and *to*
the evil.
36 Be ye therefore

6:35
Sharing
◄ Matthew 5:42 ►

6:35 Vengeance
◄ Luke 6:27
Romans 12:20 ►

Turn to the next page for more . . .

merciful, as your Father also is merciful.

6:36 Showing Mercy
◄ Matthew 5:7
James 2:13 ►

37Judge not, and ye shall not be judged: condemn not, and ye shall not be condemned: forgive, and ye shall be forgiven:

6:37 No Condemnation
◄ Isaiah 50:9
John 3:18 ►

38Give, and it shall be given unto you; good measure, pressed down, and shaken together, and running over, shall men give into your bosom. For with the same measure that ye mete withal it shall be measured to you again.

6:38 How to Give
◄ Matthew 10:8
Luke 12:33 ►

6:38 Promises to Givers
◄ Isaiah 58:10
Luke 14:14 ►

39And he spake a parable unto them, Can the blind lead the blind? shall they not both fall into the ditch?

6:38 Rewards
◄ Matthew 25:40 ►

40The disciple is not above his master: but every one that is perfect shall be as his master.

41And why beholdest thou the mote that is in thy brother's eye, but perceivest not the beam that is in thine own eye?

42Either how canst thou say to thy brother, Brother, let me pull out the mote that is in thine eye, when thou thyself beholdest not the beam that is in thine own eye? Thou hypocrite, cast out first the beam out of thine own eye, and then shalt thou see clearly to pull out the mote that is in thy brother's eye.

43For a good tree bringeth not forth corrupt fruit; neither doth a corrupt tree bring forth good fruit.

44For every tree is known by his own fruit. For of thorns men do not gather figs, nor of a bramble bush gather they grapes.

6:45 Heart
◄ Matthew 15:18
Romans 10:10 ►

45A good man out of the good treasure of his heart bringeth forth that which is good; and an evil man out of the evil treasure of his heart bringeth forth that which is evil: for of the abundance of the heart his mouth speaketh.

46And why call ye me, Lord, Lord, and do not the things which I say?

47Whosoever cometh to me, and heareth my sayings, and doeth them, I will shew you to whom he is like:

6:47 Obeying Christ
◄ Luke 5:5
John 2:7 ►

48He is like a man which built an house, and digged deep, and laid the foundation on a rock: and when the flood arose, the stream beat vehemently upon that house, and could not shake it: for it was founded upon a rock.

6:48 Life Tests
◄ Malachi 3:3
1 Corinthians 3:13 ►

49But he that heareth, and doeth not, is like a man that without a foundation built an house upon the earth; against which the stream did beat vehemently, and immediately it fell; and the ruin of that house was great.

7

1Now when he had ended all his sayings in the audience of the people, he entered into Capernaum.

2And a certain centurion's servant, who was dear unto him, was sick, and ready to die.

3And when he heard of Jesus, he sent unto him the elders of the Jews, beseeching him that he would come and heal his servant.

4And when they came to Jesus, they besought him instantly, saying, That he was worthy for whom he should do this:

5For he loveth our nation, and he hath built us a synagogue.

6Then Jesus went with them. And when he was now not far from the house, the centurion sent friends to him, saying unto him, Lord, trouble not thyself: for I am not worthy that thou shouldest enter under my roof:

7Wherefore neither thought I myself worthy to come unto thee: but say in a word, and my servant shall be healed.

8For I also am a man set under authority, having under me soldiers, and I say unto one, Go, and he goeth; and to another,

Come, and he cometh; and to my servant, Do this, and he doeth *it.*

9When Jesus heard these things, he marvelled at him, and turned him about, and said unto the people that followed him, I say unto you, I have not found so great faith, no, not in Israel.

10And they that were sent, returning to the house, found the servant whole that had been sick.

7:10 God's Response
◄ Mark 10:52
Luke 17:14 ►

11And it came to pass the day after, that he went into a city called Nain; and many of his disciples went with him, and much people.

12Now when he came nigh to the gate of the city, behold, there was a dead man carried out, the only son of his mother, and she was a widow: and much people of the city was with her.

13And when the Lord saw her, he had compassion on her, and said unto her, Weep not.

14And he came and touched the bier: and they that bare *him* stood still. And he said, Young man, I say unto thee, Arise.

15And he that was dead sat up, and began to speak. And he delivered him to his mother.

16And there came a fear on all: and they glorified God, saying, That a great prophet is risen up among us; and, That God hath visited his people.

17And this rumour of him went forth throughout all Judaea, and throughout all the region round about.

18And the disciples of John shewed him of all these things.

19And John calling *unto him* two of his disciples sent *them* to Jesus, saying, Art thou he that should come? or look we for another?

20When the men were come unto him, they said, John Baptist hath sent us unto thee, saying, Art thou he that should come? or look we for another?

21And in that same hour he cured many of *their* infirmities and plagues, and of evil spirits; and unto many *that were* blind he gave sight.

22Then Jesus answering said unto them, Go your way, and tell John what things ye have seen and heard; how that the blind see, the lame walk, the lepers are cleansed, the deaf hear, the dead are raised, to the poor the gospel is preached.

23And blessed is *he,* whosoever shall not be offended in me.

24And when the messengers of John were departed, he began to speak unto the people concerning John, What went ye out into the wilderness for to see? A reed shaken with the wind?

25But what went ye out for to see? A man clothed in soft raiment? Behold, they which are gorgeously apparelled, and live delicately, are in kings' courts.

26But what went ye out for to see? A prophet? Yea, I say unto you, and much more than a prophet.

27This is *he,* of whom it is written, Behold, I send my messenger before thy face, which shall prepare thy way before thee.

28For I say unto you, Among those that are born of women there is not a greater prophet than John the Baptist: but he that is least in the kingdom of God is greater than he.

29And all the people that heard *him,* and the publicans, justified God, being baptized with the baptism of John.

30But the Pharisees and lawyers rejected the counsel of God against themselves, being not baptized of him.

31And the Lord said, Whereunto then shall I liken the men of this generation? and to what are they like?

32They are like unto children sitting in the marketplace, and calling one to another, and saying, We have piped unto you, and ye have not danced; we have mourned to you, and ye have not wept.

33For John the Baptist came neither eating bread nor drinking wine; and ye say, He hath a devil.

34The Son of man is come eating and drinking; and ye say, Behold a gluttonous man, and a winebibber, a friend of publicans and sinners!

35But wisdom is justified of all her children.

36And one of the Pharisees desired him that he would eat with him. And he went into the Pharisee's house, and sat down to meat.

37And, behold, a woman in the city, which was a sinner, when she knew that *Jesus* sat at meat in the Pharisee's house, brought an alabaster box of ointment,

38 And stood at his feet behind *him* weeping, and began to wash his feet with tears,
and did wipe *them* with the hairs of her
head, and kissed his feet, and anointed
them with the ointment.

39 Now when the
Pharisee which had
bidden him saw *it,*
he spake within
himself, saying,
This man, if he were
a prophet, would have known who and
what manner of woman *this is* that
toucheth him: for she is a sinner.

7:39 Friend of Jesus
◄ Matthew 11:19
Luke 19:7 ►

40 And Jesus answering said unto him,
Simon, I have somewhat to say unto thee.
And he saith, Master, say on.

41 There was a certain creditor which had
two debtors: the one owed five hundred
pence, and the other fifty.

42 And when they had nothing to pay, he
frankly forgave them both. Tell me therefore, which of them will love him most?

43 Simon answered and said, I suppose
that *he,* to whom he forgave most. And he
said unto him, Thou hast rightly judged.

44 And he turned to the woman, and said
unto Simon, Seest thou this woman? I
entered into thine house, thou gavest me
no water for my feet: but she hath washed
my feet with tears, and wiped *them* with
the hairs of her head.

45 Thou gavest me no kiss: but this woman since the time I came in hath not ceased
to kiss my feet.

46 My head with oil thou didst not
anoint: but this woman hath anointed my
feet with ointment.

47 Wherefore I say
unto thee, Her sins,
which are many, are
forgiven; for she
loved much: but to
whom little is for-
given, *the same* loveth little.

7:47
Loving Jesus
◄ John 11:16 ►

48 And he said unto her, Thy sins are forgiven.

49 And they that sat at meat with him
began to say within themselves, Who is
this that forgiveth sins also?

50 And he said to the woman, Thy faith
hath saved thee; go in peace.

8

1 And it came to pass afterward, that he
went throughout every city and village,
preaching and shewing the glad tidings of
the kingdom of God: and the twelve *were*
with him,

2 And certain women, which had been
healed of evil spirits and infirmities, Mary
called Magdalene, out of whom went sev-
en devils,

3 And Joanna the wife of Chuza Herod's
steward, and Susanna, and many others,
which ministered unto him of their substance.

4 And when much people were gathered
together, and were come to him out of
every city, he spake by a parable:

5 A sower went out to sow his seed: and
as he sowed, some fell by the way side; and
it was trodden down, and the fowls of the
air devoured it.

6 And some fell upon a rock; and as soon
as it was sprung up, it withered away, because it lacked moisture.

7 And some fell among thorns; and the
thorns sprang up with it, and choked it.

8 And other fell on good ground, and
sprang up, and bare fruit an hundredfold.
And when he had said these things, he
cried, He that hath ears to hear, let him
hear.

9 And his disciples asked him, saying,
What might this parable be?

10 And he said, Unto you it is given to
know the mysteries of the kingdom of
God: but to others in parables; that seeing
they might not see, and hearing they might
not understand.

11 Now the parable is this: The seed is
the word of God.

12 Those by the way side are they that
hear; then cometh the devil, and taketh
away the word out of their hearts, lest they
should believe and be saved.

13 They on the rock *are they,* which, when
they hear, receive the word with joy; and
these have no root, which for a while
believe, and in time of temptation fall
away.

14 And that which
fell among thorns
are they, which,
when they have
heard, go forth, and
are choked with
cares and riches and pleasures of *this* life,
and bring no fruit to perfection.

8:14 Luxury
◄ Isaiah 47:8-9
Luke 12:19 ►

15 But that on the good ground are they,
which in an honest and good heart, hav-

ing heard the word, keep *it,* and bring forth fruit with patience.

16 No man, when he hath lighted a candle, covereth it with a vessel, or putteth *it* under a bed; but setteth *it* on a candlestick, that they which enter in may see the light.

17 For nothing is secret, that shall not be made manifest; neither *any thing* hid, that shall not be known and come abroad.

18 Take heed therefore how ye hear: for whosoever hath, to him shall be given; and whosoever hath not, from him shall be taken even that which he seemeth to have.

8:18 Watch Out!
◄ Mark 13:33
Luke 11:35 ►

19 Then came to him *his* mother and his brethren, and could not come at him for the press.

20 And it was told him *by certain* which said, Thy mother and thy brethren stand without, desiring to see thee.

21 And he answered and said unto them, My mother and my brethren are these which hear the word of God, and do it.

8:21 Obeying God
◄ Matthew 7:21
Acts 5:29 ►

22 Now it came to pass on a certain day, that he went into a ship with his disciples: and he said unto them, Let us go over unto the other side of the lake. And they launched forth.

23 But as they sailed he fell asleep: and there came down a storm of wind on the lake; and they were filled *with water,* and were in jeopardy.

24 And they came to him, and awoke him, saying, Master, master, we perish. Then he arose, and rebuked the wind and the raging of the water: and they ceased, and there was a calm.

25 And he said unto them, Where is your faith? And they being afraid wondered, saying one to another, What manner of man is this! for he commandeth even the winds and water, and they obey him.

26 And they arrived at the country of the Gadarenes, which is over against Galilee.

27 And when he went forth to land, there met him out of the city a certain man, which had devils long time, and ware no clothes, neither abode in *any* house, but in the tombs.

28 When he saw Jesus, he cried out, and fell down before him, and with a loud voice said, What have I to do with thee, Jesus, *thou* Son of God most high? I beseech thee, torment me not.

29 (For he had commanded the unclean spirit to come out of the man. For oftentimes it had caught him: and he was kept bound with chains and in fetters; and he brake the bands, and was driven of the devil into the wilderness.)

30 And Jesus asked him, saying, What is thy name? And he said, Legion: because many devils were entered into him.

31 And they besought him that he would not command them to go out into the deep.

32 And there was there an herd of many swine feeding on the mountain: and they besought him that he would suffer them to enter into them. And he suffered them.

33 Then went the devils out of the man, and entered into the swine: and the herd ran violently down a steep place into the lake, and were choked.

34 When they that fed *them* saw what was done, they fled, and went and told *it* in the city and in the country.

35 Then they went out to see what was done; and came to Jesus, and found the man, out of whom the devils were departed, sitting at the feet of Jesus, clothed, and in his right mind: and they were afraid.

36 They also which saw *it* told them by what means he that was possessed of the devils was healed.

37 Then the whole multitude of the country of the Gadarenes round about besought him to depart from them; for they were taken with great fear: and he went up into the ship, and returned back again.

38 Now the man out of whom the devils were departed besought him that he might be with him: but Jesus sent him away, saying,

39 Return to thine own house, and shew how great things God hath done unto thee. And he went his way, and published throughout the whole city how great things Jesus had done unto him.

40 And it came to pass, that, when Jesus was returned, the people *gladly* received him: for they were all waiting for him.

41And, behold, there came a man named
Jairus, and he was a ruler of the synagogue:
and he fell down at Jesus' feet, and besought him that he would come into his
house:
42For he had one only daughter, about
twelve years of age, and she lay a dying.
But as he went the people thronged him.
43And a woman having an issue of
blood twelve years, which had spent all her
living upon physicians, neither could be
healed of any,
44Came behind *him*, and touched the
border of his garment: and immediately
her issue of blood stanched.
45And Jesus said, Who touched me?
When all denied, Peter and they that were
with him said, Master, the multitude
throng thee and press *thee*, and sayest thou,
Who touched me?
46And Jesus said, Somebody hath
touched me: for I perceive that virtue is
gone out of me.
47And when the woman saw that she
was not hid, she came trembling, and falling down before him, she declared unto
him before all the people for what cause
she had touched him and how she was
healed immediately.
48And he said unto her, Daughter, be of
good comfort: thy faith hath made thee
whole; go in peace.
49While he yet spake, there cometh one
from the ruler of the synagogue's *house*,
saying to him, Thy daughter is dead; trouble not the Master.
50But when Jesus
heard *it*, he an-
swered him, saying,
Fear not: believe
only, and she shall
be made whole.

8:50 Faith
◄ Mark 11:22
John 6:28-29 ►

51And when he came into the house, he
suffered no man to go in, save Peter, and
James, and John, and the father and the
mother of the maiden.
52And all wept, and bewailed her: but
he said, Weep not; she is not dead, but
sleepeth.
53And they laughed him to scorn, knowing that she was dead.
54And he put them all out, and took her
by the hand, and called, saying, Maid,
arise.
55And her spirit came again, and she
arose straightway: and he commanded to
give her meat.
56And her parents were astonished: but
he charged them that they should tell no
man what was done.

9

1Then he called his twelve disciples together, and gave them power and authority over all devils, and to cure diseases.
2And he sent them to preach the kingdom of God, and to heal the sick.
3And he said unto them, Take nothing
for *your* journey, neither staves, nor scrip,
neither bread, neither money; neither have
two coats apiece.
4And whatsoever house ye enter into,
there abide, and thence depart.
5And whosoever will not receive you,
when ye go out of that city, shake off the
very dust from your feet for a testimony
against them.
6And they departed, and went through
the towns, preaching the gospel, and healing every where.
7Now Herod the tetrarch heard of all
that was done by him: and he was perplexed, because that it was said of some,
that John was risen from the dead;
8And of some, that Elias had appeared;
and of others, that one of the old prophets was risen again.
9And Herod said, John have I beheaded: but who is this, of whom I hear such
things? And he desired to see him.
10And the apostles, when they were returned, told him all that they had done.
And he took them, and went aside privately into a desert place belonging to the city
called Bethsaida.
11And the people, when they knew *it*,
followed him: and he received them, and
spake unto them of the kingdom of
God, and healed them that had need of
healing.
12And when the day began to wear away,
then came the twelve, and said unto him,
Send the multitude away, that they may
go into the towns and country round
about, and lodge, and get victuals: for we
are here in a desert place.
13But he said unto them, Give ye them
to eat. And they said, We have no more
but five loaves and two fishes; except we
should go and buy meat for all this people.
14For they were about five thousand

men. And he said to his disciples, Make them sit down by fifties in a company.

15 And they did so, and made them all sit down.

16 Then he took the five loaves and the two fishes, and looking up to heaven, he blessed them, and brake, and gave to the disciples to set before the multitude.

17 And they did eat, and were all filled: and there was taken up of fragments that remained to them twelve baskets.

18 And it came to pass, as he was alone praying, his disciples were with him: and he asked them, saying, Whom say the people that I am?

19 They answering said, John the Baptist; but some *say*, Elias; and others *say*, that one of the old prophets is risen again.

20 He said unto them, But whom say ye that I am? Peter answering said, The Christ of God.

21 And he straitly charged them, and commanded *them* to tell no man that thing;

22 Saying, The Son of man must suffer many things, and be rejected of the elders and chief priests and scribes, and be slain, and be raised the third day.

23 And he said to *them* all, If any *man* will come after me, let him deny himself, and take up his cross daily, and follow me.

24 For whosoever will save his life shall lose it: but whosoever will lose his life for my sake, the same shall save it.

25 For what is a man advantaged, if he gain the whole world, and lose himself, or be cast away?

26 For whosoever shall be ashamed of me and of my words, of him shall the Son of man be ashamed, when he shall come in his own glory, and *in his* Father's, and of the holy angels.

27 But I tell you of a truth, there be some standing here, which shall not taste of death, till they see the kingdom of God.

28 And it came to pass about an eight days after these sayings, he took Peter and John and James, and went up into a mountain to pray.

29 And as he prayed, the fashion of his countenance was altered, and his raiment *was* white *and* glistering.

30 And, behold, there talked with him two men, which were Moses and Elias:

31 Who appeared in glory, and spake of his decease which he should accomplish at Jerusalem.

32 But Peter and they that were with him were heavy with sleep: and when they were awake, they saw his glory, and the two men that stood with him.

33 And it came to pass, as they departed from him, Peter said unto Jesus, Master, it is good for us to be here: and let us make three tabernacles; one for thee, and one for Moses, and one for Elias: not knowing what he said.

34 While he thus spake, there came a cloud, and overshadowed them: and they feared as they entered into the cloud.

35 And there came a voice out of the cloud, saying, This is my beloved Son: hear him.

36 And when the voice was past, Jesus was found alone. And they kept *it* close, and told no man in those days any of those things which they had seen.

37 And it came to pass, that on the next day, when they were come down from the hill, much people met him.

38 And, behold, a man of the company cried out, saying, Master, I beseech thee, look upon my son: for he is mine only child.

39 And, lo, a spirit taketh him, and he suddenly crieth out; and it teareth him that he foameth again, and bruising him hardly departeth from him.

40 And I besought thy disciples to cast him out; and they could not.

41 And Jesus answering said, O faithless and perverse generation, how long shall I be with you, and suffer you? Bring thy son hither.

42 And as he was yet a coming, the devil threw him down, and tare *him*. And Jesus rebuked the unclean spirit, and healed the child, and delivered him again to his father.

43 And they were all amazed at the mighty power of God. But while they wondered every one at all things which Jesus did, he said unto his disciples,

44 Let these sayings sink down into your ears: for the Son of man shall be delivered into the hands of men.

45 But they understood not this saying, and it was hid from them, that they perceived it not: and they feared to ask him of that saying.

46Then there arose a reasoning among
them, which of them should be greatest.
47And Jesus, perceiving the thought of
their heart, took a child, and set him by
him,
48And said unto them, Whosoever shall
receive this child in my name receiveth me:
and whosoever shall receive me receiveth
him that sent me: for he that is least among
you all, the same shall be great.
49And John answered and said, Master, we saw one casting out devils in thy name; and we forbad him, because he followeth not with us.

9:49-50 Accepting People
◄ Mark 9:39
Philippians 1:17-18 ►

50And Jesus said unto him, Forbid *him*
not: for he that is not against us is for us.
51And it came to pass, when the time
was come that he should be received up,
he stedfastly set his face to go to Jerusalem,
52And sent messengers before his face:
and they went, and entered into a village of the Samaritans, to make ready for him.

9:53 Cold Shoulder
◄ 1 Samuel 25:10 ►

53And they did not receive him, because his face was as though he would go to Jerusalem.

9:53 Different People
◄ John 4:9 ►

54And when his disciples James and John saw *this*, they said, Lord, wilt thou that we command fire to come down from heaven, and consume them, even as Elias did?

9:54 Impatience
◄ Matthew 15:23
Luke 10:40 ►

55But he turned, and rebuked them, and said, Ye know not what manner of spirit ye are of.

9:54 Only Human
◄ Jonah 1:3
Luke 22:24 ►

56For the Son of man is not come to destroy men's lives, but to save *them*. And they went to another village.

9:55 Examples of Mercy
◄ 2 Kings 6:22
John 8:7 ►

57And it came to
pass, that, as they went in the way, a certain *man* said unto him, Lord, I will follow thee whithersoever thou goest.
58And Jesus said unto him, Foxes have
holes, and birds of the air *have* nests; but
the Son of man hath not where to lay *his*
head.
59And he said unto another, Follow me.
But he said, Lord, suffer me first to go and
bury my father.
60Jesus said unto him, Let the dead bury
their dead: but go thou and preach the
kingdom of God.
61And another also said, Lord, I will follow thee; but let me first go bid them farewell, which are at home at my house.

9:61 Procrastination
◄ Matthew 8:21
Acts 17:32 ►

62And Jesus said unto him, No man, having put his hand to the plough, and looking back, is fit for the kingdom of God.

9:62 One Goal
◄ Ezekiel 1:12
Philippians 3:13 ►

9:62 The Time Is Now
◄ Matthew 6:24
James 1:8 ►

10

1After these things the Lord appointed other seventy also, and sent them two and two
before his face into every city and place,
whither he himself would come.
2Therefore said he unto them, The harvest truly *is* great, but the labourers *are* few:
pray ye therefore the Lord of the harvest,
that he would send forth labourers into
his harvest.
3Go your ways: behold, I send you forth
as lambs among wolves.
4Carry neither purse, nor scrip, nor shoes: and salute no man by the way.

10:4 Hurrying
◄ Matthew 28:7
Luke 14:21 ►

5And into whatsoever house ye enter, first say, Peace *be* to this house.
6And if the son of peace be there, your
peace shall rest upon it: if not, it shall turn
to you again.
7And in the same house remain, eating
and drinking such things as they give: for
the labourer is worthy of his hire. Go not
from house to house.

8 And into whatsoever city ye enter, and they receive you, eat such things as are set before you:

9 And heal the sick that are therein, and say unto them, The kingdom of God is come nigh unto you.

10 But into whatsoever city ye enter, and they receive you not, go your ways out into the streets of the same, and say,

11 Even the very dust of your city, which cleaveth on us, we do wipe off against you: notwithstanding be ye sure of this, that the kingdom of God is come nigh unto you.

12 But I say unto you, that it shall be more tolerable in that day for Sodom, than for that city.

13 Woe unto thee, Chorazin! woe unto thee, Bethsaida! for if the mighty works had been done in Tyre and Sidon, which have been done in you, they had a great while ago repented, sitting in sackcloth and ashes.

14 But it shall be more tolerable for Tyre and Sidon at the judgment, than for you.

15 And thou, Capernaum, which art exalted to heaven, shalt be thrust down to hell.

16 He that heareth you heareth me; and he that despiseth you despiseth me; and he that despiseth me despiseth him that sent me.

17 And the seventy returned again with joy, saying, Lord, even the devils are subject unto us through thy name.

10:17 Serving
◄ Psalm 126:5-6
John 4:36 ►

18 And he said unto them, I beheld Satan as lightning fall from heaven.

10:19 Demons
◄ Mark 16:9
Acts 8:7 ►

19 Behold, I give unto you power to tread on serpents and scorpions, and over all the power of the enemy: and nothing shall by any means hurt you.

10:19 Satan's Weakness
◄ Job 1:12
Romans 16:20 ►

10:19 Tempted by Satan
◄ Luke 22:31-32 ►

20 Notwithstanding in this rejoice not, that the spirits are subject unto you; but rather rejoice, because your names are written in heaven.

10:20 Rejoicing
◄ Zechariah 9:9
Romans 12:15 ►

21 In that hour Jesus rejoiced in spirit, and said, I thank thee, O Father, Lord of heaven and earth, that thou hast hid these things from the wise and prudent, and hast revealed them unto babes: even so, Father; for so it seemed good in thy sight.

10:21 Jesus' Joy
◄ Luke 15:5 ►

22 All things are delivered to me of my Father: and no man knoweth who the Son is, but the Father; and who the Father is, but the Son, and *he* to whom the Son will reveal *him*.

23 And he turned him unto *his* disciples, and said privately, Blessed *are* the eyes which see the things that ye see:

24 For I tell you, that many prophets and kings have desired to see those things which ye see, and have not seen *them;* and to hear those things which ye hear, and have not heard *them*.

25 And, behold, a certain lawyer stood up, and tempted him, saying, Master, what shall I do to inherit eternal life?

26 He said unto him, What is written in the law? how readest thou?

27 And he answering said, Thou shalt love the Lord thy God with all thy heart, and with all thy soul, and with all thy strength, and with all thy mind; and thy neighbour as thyself.

28 And he said unto him, Thou hast answered right: this do, and thou shalt live.

29 But he, willing to justify himself, said unto Jesus, And who is my neighbour?

30 And Jesus answering said, A certain *man* went down from Jerusalem to Jericho, and fell among thieves, which stripped him of his raiment, and wounded *him,* and departed, leaving *him* half dead.

31 And by chance there came down a certain priest that way: and when he saw him, he passed by on the other side.

10:31-32 Not Caring
◄ Matthew 27:42
Luke 18:4 ►

32And likewise a Levite, when he was at the place, came and looked *on him,* and passed by on the other side.

10:32
Cruelty
◄ Matthew 18:30 ►

33But a certain Samaritan, as he journeyed, came where he was: and when he saw him, he had compassion *on him,*

10:33-34 Compassion
◄ Job 29:13
Acts 16:33 ►

34And went to *him,* and bound up his wounds, pouring in oil and wine, and set him on his own beast, and brought him to an inn, and took care of him.

10:34
Work that Helps Others
◄ Matthew 25:35
1 Corinthians 16:15-16 ►

35And on the morrow when he departed, he took out two pence, and gave *them* to the host, and said unto him, Take care of him; and whatsoever thou spendest more, when I come again, I will repay thee.

36Which now of these three, thinkest thou, was neighbour unto him that fell among the thieves?

10:36-37
Serving People
◄ Mark 10:43-44
John 13:14 ►

37And he said, He that shewed mercy on him. Then said Jesus unto him, Go, and do thou likewise.

38Now it came to pass, as they went, that he entered into a certain village: and a certain woman named Martha received him into her house.

10:38-39
Accepting God's Word
◄ Matthew 13:23
Acts 2:41 ►

39And she had a sister called Mary, which also sat at Jesus' feet, and heard his word.

10:39 Young Women
◄ Luke 1:38
John 11:24 ►

40But Martha was cumbered about much serving, and came to him, and said, Lord, dost thou not care that my sister hath left me to serve alone? bid her therefore that she help me.

10:40
Impatience
◄ Luke 9:54 ►

41And Jesus answered and said unto her, Martha, Martha, thou art careful and troubled about many things:

10:41 Worry
◄ Matthew 13:22
Luke 12:29 ►

42But one thing is needful: and Mary hath chosen that good part, which shall not be taken away from her.

11

1And it came to pass, that, as he was praying in a certain place, when he ceased, one of his disciples said unto him, Lord, teach us to pray, as John also taught his disciples.

11:1
Learning from Jesus
◄ Luke 3:12
Luke 18:18 ►

11:1
Willingness to Learn
◄ Matthew 18:3
John 9:36 ►

2And he said unto them, When ye pray, say, Our Father which art in heaven, Hallowed be thy name. Thy kingdom come. Thy will be done, as in heaven, so in earth.

3Give us day by day our daily bread.

4And forgive us our sins; for we also forgive every one that is indebted to us. And lead us not into temptation; but deliver us from evil.

11:4 Forgiving Others
◄ Mark 11:25
Luke 17:4 ►

5And he said unto them, Which of you shall have a friend, and shall go unto him at midnight, and say unto him, Friend, lend me three loaves;

6For a friend of mine in his journey is come to me, and I have nothing to set before him?

7And he from within shall answer and say, Trouble me not: the door is now shut, and my children are with me in bed; I cannot rise and give thee.

8I say unto you, Though he will not rise and give him, because he is his friend, yet because of his importunity he will rise and give him as many as he needeth.

9And I say unto you, Ask, and it shall be given you; seek, and ye shall

11:9 Answers to Prayer
◄ Zechariah 13:9
John 14:14 ►

find; knock, and it
shall be opened
unto you.
10For every one
that asketh re-
ceiveth; and he that
seeketh findeth;
and to him that
knocketh it shall be
opened.

11:9 Gifts from God
◄ Matthew 25:15
John 3:27 ►

11:10 Seeking God
◄ Matthew 6:33
Acts 17:27 ►

11If a son shall
ask bread of any of
you that is a father,
will he give him a stone? or if *he ask* a fish,
will he for a fish give him a serpent?
12Or if he shall ask an egg, will he offer
him a scorpion?
13If ye then, be-
ing evil, know how
to give good gifts
unto your children:
how much more
shall *your* heavenly
Father give the Holy Spirit to them that
ask him?

11:13 Invisible Gifts
◄ Matthew 11:28
John 10:28 ►

14And he was casting out a devil, and it
was dumb. And it came to pass, when the
devil was gone out, the dumb spake; and
the people wondered.
15But some of them said, He casteth out
devils through Beelzebub the chief of the
devils.
16And others, tempting *him*, sought of
him a sign from heaven.
17But he, knowing their thoughts, said
unto them, Every kingdom divided against
itself is brought to desolation; and a house
divided against a house falleth.
18If Satan also be divided against himself, how shall his kingdom stand? because
ye say that I cast out devils through Beelzebub.
19And if I by Beelzebub cast out devils,
by whom do your sons cast *them* out?
therefore shall they be your judges.
20But if I with the finger of God cast out
devils, no doubt the kingdom of God is
come upon you.
21When a strong man armed keepeth his
palace, his goods are in peace:
22But when a stronger than he shall
come upon him, and overcome him, he
taketh from him all his armour wherein
he trusted, and divideth his spoils.
23He that is not with me is against me:
and he that gathereth not with me scattereth.
24When the unclean spirit is gone out
of a man, he walketh through dry places,
seeking rest; and finding none, he saith, I
will return unto my house whence I came
out.
25And when he cometh, he findeth *it*
swept and garnished.
26Then goeth he, and taketh *to him* sev-
en other spirits more wicked than himself;
and they enter in, and dwell there: and the
last *state* of that man is worse than the first.
27And it came to pass, as he spake these
things, a certain woman of the company
lifted up her voice, and said unto him,
Blessed *is* the womb that bare thee, and
the paps which thou hast sucked.
28But he said, Yea rather, blessed *are* they
that hear the word of God, and keep it.
29And when the people were gathered
thick together, he began to say, This is an
evil generation: they seek a sign; and there
shall no sign be given it, but the sign of
Jonas the prophet.
30For as Jonas was a sign unto the Nin-
evites, so shall also the Son of man be to
this generation.
31The queen of the south shall rise up
in the judgment with the men of this generation, and condemn them: for she came
from the utmost parts of the earth to hear
the wisdom of Solomon; and, behold, a
greater than Solomon *is* here.
32The men of Nineve shall rise up in the
judgment with this generation, and shall
condemn it: for they repented at the
preaching of Jonas; and, behold, a greater
than Jonas *is* here.
33No man, when he hath lighted a
candle, putteth *it* in a secret place, neither
under a bushel, but on a candlestick, that
they which come in may see the light.
34The light of the body is the eye: therefore when thine eye is single, thy whole
body also is full of light; but when *thine*
eye is evil, thy body also *is* full of darkness.
35Take heed
therefore that the
light which is in
thee be not dark-
ness.
36If thy whole
body therefore *be* full of light, having no

11:35 Watch Out!
◄ Luke 8:18
Luke 12:15 ►

part dark, the whole shall be full of light,
as when the bright shining of a candle doth
give thee light.
37 And as he spake, a certain Pharisee
besought him to dine with him: and he
went in, and sat down to meat.
38 And when the Pharisee saw *it*, he marvelled that he had not first washed before
dinner.
39 And the Lord said unto him, Now do
ye Pharisees make clean the outside of the
cup and the platter; but your inward part
is full of ravening and wickedness.
40 *Ye* fools, did not he that made that
which is without make that which is within also?
41 But rather give
alms of such things
as ye have; and, be-
hold, all things are
clean unto you.

11:41 Generosity
◄ Matthew 19:21
Luke 12:33 ►

42 But woe unto
you, Pharisees! for ye tithe mint and rue
and all manner of herbs, and pass over
judgment and the love of God: these ought
ye to have done, and not to leave the other undone.
43 Woe unto you,
Pharisees! for ye
love the uppermost
seats in the syna-
gogues, and greet-
ings in the markets.

11:43 Ambition
◄ Matthew 20:21
Luke 22:24 ►

44 Woe unto you, scribes and Pharisees,
hypocrites! for ye are as graves which appear not, and the men that walk over *them*
are not aware *of them*.
45 Then answered one of the lawyers, and
said unto him, Master, thus saying thou
reproachest us also.
46 And he said, Woe unto you also, *ye*
lawyers! for ye lade men with burdens
grievous to be borne, and ye yourselves
touch not the burdens with one of your
fingers.
47 Woe unto you! for ye build the sepulchres of the prophets, and your fathers
killed them.
48 Truly ye bear witness that ye allow the
deeds of your fathers: for they indeed killed
them, and ye build their sepulchres.
49 Therefore also said the wisdom of
God, I will send them prophets and apostles, and *some* of them they shall slay and
persecute:
50 That the blood of all the prophets,
which was shed from the foundation of
the world, may be required of this generation;
51 From the blood of Abel unto the
blood of Zacharias, which perished between the altar and the temple: verily I say
unto you, It shall be required of this generation.
52 Woe unto you, lawyers! for ye have
taken away the key of knowledge: ye entered not in yourselves, and them that were
entering in ye hindered.
53 And as he said these things unto them,
the scribes and the Pharisees began to urge
him vehemently, and to provoke him to
speak of many things:
54 Laying wait for him, and seeking to
catch something out of his mouth, that
they might accuse him.

12

1 In the mean
time, when there
were gathered to-
gether an innumer-
able multitude of
people, insomuch
that they trode one upon another, he began to say unto his disciples first of all,
Beware ye of the leaven of the Pharisees,
which is hypocrisy.

12:1 Hypocrisy
◄ Matthew 23:28
1 Timothy 4:2 ►

2 For there is nothing covered, that shall
not be revealed; neither hid, that shall not
be known.
3 Therefore whatsoever ye have spoken
in darkness shall be heard in the light; and
that which ye have spoken in the ear in
closets shall be proclaimed upon the
housetops.
4 And I say unto you my friends, Be not
afraid of them that kill the body, and after
that have no more that they can do.
5 But I will forewarn you whom ye shall
fear: Fear him, which after he hath killed
hath power to cast into hell; yea, I say unto
you, Fear him.
6 Are not five sparrows sold for two far-
things, and not one of them is forgotten
before God?
7 But even the
very hairs of your
head are all num-
bered. Fear not
therefore: ye are of
more value than
many sparrows.

12:7 God's Care for You
◄ Matthew 6:32
1 Peter 5:7 ►

8 Also I say unto you, Whosoever shall
confess me before men, him shall the Son
of man also confess before the angels
of God:
9 But he that denieth me before men
shall be denied before the angels of God.
10 And whosoever shall speak a word
against the Son of man, it shall be forgiv-
en him: but unto him that blasphemeth
against the Holy Ghost it shall not be forgiven.
11 And when they bring you unto the synagogues, and *unto* magistrates, and powers, take ye no thought how or what thing
ye shall answer, or what ye shall say:
12 For the Holy
Ghost shall teach
you in the same
hour what ye ought
to say.

12:12 God's Teaching
◄ Nehemiah 9:20
John 14:26 ►

13 And one of the
company said unto him, Master, speak to
my brother, that he divide the inheritance
with me.
14 And he said unto him, Man, who
made me a judge or a divider over you?
15 And he said
unto them, Take
heed, and beware
of covetousness: for
a man's life con-
sisteth not in the
abundance of the
things which he possesseth.

12:15 Watch Out!
◄ Luke 11:35
Luke 21:8 ►

16 And he spake a parable unto them,
saying, The ground of a certain rich man
brought forth plentifully:
17 And he thought
within himself, say-
ing, What shall I
do, because I have
no room where to
bestow my fruits?

12:18 Planning
◄ Jeremiah 22:13-14
James 4:13 ►

18 And he said,
This will I do: I will
pull down my
barns, and build
greater; and there
will I bestow all my
fruits and my
goods.

12:19 Luxury
◄ Luke 8:14
1 Timothy 5:6 ►

19 And I will say
to my soul, Soul,
thou hast much
goods laid up for
many years; take thine ease, eat, drink, *and*
be merry.

12:19-20 Wealth
◄ Mark 10:24
1 Timothy 6:17 ►

20 But God said
unto him, *Thou*
fool, this night thy
soul shall be re-
quired of thee: then
whose shall those
things be, which thou hast provided?

12:20 Getting Caught
◄ Matthew 25:19
Luke 12:48 ►

21 So *is* he that
layeth up treasure
for himself, and is
not rich toward
God.

12:21 Hoarding
◄ Matthew 6:19
James 5:3 ►

22 And he said
unto his disciples,
Therefore I say unto
you, Take no
thought for your
life, what ye shall
eat; neither for the
body, what ye shall put on.

12:22 Restraint
◄ Proverbs 25:16
Luke 21:34 ►

23 The life is more than meat, and the
body *is more* than raiment.
24 Consider the ravens: for they neither
sow nor reap; which neither have storehouse nor barn; and God feedeth them:
how much more are ye better than the
fowls?
25 And which of you with taking thought
can add to his stature one cubit?
26 If ye then be not able to do that thing
which is least, why take ye thought for the
rest?
27 Consider the lilies how they grow:
they toil not, they spin not; and yet I say
unto you, that Solomon in all his glory
was not arrayed like one of these.
28 If then God so clothe the grass, which
is to day in the field, and to morrow is
cast into the oven; how much more *will he*
clothe you, O ye of little faith?
29 And seek not
ye what ye shall eat,
or what ye shall
drink, neither be ye
of doubtful mind.

12:29 Worry
◄ Luke 10:41
Luke 21:34 ►

30 For all these
things do the nations of the world seek
after: and your Father knoweth that ye have
need of these things.
31 But rather seek ye the kingdom of
God; and all these things shall be added
unto you.
32 Fear not, little flock; for it is your

Father's good pleasure to give you the kingdom.

33 Sell that ye have, and give alms; provide yourselves bags which wax not old, a treasure in the heavens that faileth not, where no thief approacheth, neither moth corrupteth.

34 For where your treasure is, there will your heart be also.

35 Let your loins be girded about, and *your* lights burning;

36 And ye yourselves like unto men that wait for their lord, when he will return from the wedding; that when he cometh and knocketh, they may open unto him immediately.

37 Blessed *are* those servants, whom the lord when he cometh shall find watching: verily I say unto you, that he shall gird himself, and make them to sit down to meat, and will come forth and serve them.

38 And if he shall come in the second watch, or come in the third watch, and find *them* so, blessed are those servants.

39 And this know, that if the goodman of the house had known what hour the thief would come, he would have watched, and not have suffered his house to be broken through.

40 Be ye therefore ready also: for the Son of man cometh at an hour when ye think not.

41 Then Peter said unto him, Lord, speakest thou this parable unto us, or even to all?

42 And the Lord said, Who then is that faithful and wise steward, whom *his* lord shall make ruler over his household, to give *them their* portion of meat in due season?

43 Blessed *is* that servant, whom his lord when he cometh shall find so doing.

44 Of a truth I say unto you, that he will make him ruler over all that he hath.

45 But and if that servant say in his heart, My lord delayeth his coming; and shall begin to beat the menservants and maidens, and to eat and drink, and to be drunken;

46 The lord of that servant will come in a day when he looketh not for *him*, and at an hour when he is not aware, and will cut him in sunder, and will appoint him his portion with the unbelievers.

47 And that servant, which knew his lord's will, and prepared not *himself*, neither did according to his will, shall be beaten with many *stripes*.

48 But he that knew not, and did commit things worthy of stripes, shall be beaten with few *stripes*. For unto whomsoever much is given, of him shall be much required: and to whom men have committed much, of him they will ask the more.

49 I am come to send fire on the earth; and what will I if it be already kindled?

50 But I have a baptism to be baptized with; and how am I straitened till it be accomplished!

51 Suppose ye that I am come to give peace on earth? I tell you, Nay; but rather division:

52 For from henceforth there shall be five in one house divided, three against two, and two against three.

53 The father shall be divided against the son, and the son against the father; the mother against the daughter, and the

12:33 Generosity
◄ Luke 11:41
Luke 18:22 ►

12:33 Giving
◄ Luke 3:11
Acts 20:35 ►

12:33 How to Give
◄ Luke 6:38
Romans 12:8 ►

12:35-36 Ready for the Future
◄ Mark 13:35
Revelation 19:7 ►

12:37 Good News
◄ John 14:3 ►

12:37 Jesus' Return
◄ Mark 13:33
1 Thessalonians 5:5-6 ►

12:40 Jesus' Return: When?
◄ Matthew 24:36
1 Thessalonians 5:2 ►

12:48 Getting Caught
◄ Luke 12:20
Luke 19:15 ►

12:48 Unknown Sins
◄ Leviticus 5:17
Acts 3:17 ►

12:48 Work
◄ Mark 14:8
1 Peter 4:11 ►

daughter against the mother; the mother
in law against her daughter in law, and the
daughter in law against her mother in law.
54And he said also to the people, When
ye see a cloud rise out of the west, straightway ye say, There cometh a shower; and so
it is.
55And when *ye see* the south wind blow,
ye say, There will be heat; and it cometh
to pass.
56*Ye* hypocrites, ye can discern the face
of the sky and of the earth; but how is it
that ye do not discern this time?
57Yea, and why even of yourselves judge
ye not what is right?
58When thou goest with thine adversary
to the magistrate, *as thou art* in the way,
give diligence that thou mayest be delivered from him; lest he hale thee to the
judge, and the judge deliver thee to the
officer, and the officer cast thee into prison.
59I tell thee, thou shalt not depart
thence, till thou hast paid the very last
mite.

13

1There were present at that season some
that told him of the Galilaeans, whose
blood Pilate had mingled with their sacrifices.

13:2-3 Repent!
◄ Matthew 3:2
Acts 3:19 ►

2And Jesus an-
swering said unto
them, Suppose ye
that these Galilae-
ans were sinners
above all the Gali-
laeans, because they suffered such things?
3I tell you, Nay: but, except ye repent,
ye shall all likewise perish.
4Or those eighteen, upon whom the
tower in Siloam fell, and slew them, think
ye that they were sinners above all men
that dwelt in Jerusalem?
5I tell you, Nay: but, except ye repent,
ye shall all likewise perish.
6He spake also this parable; A certain
man had a fig tree planted in his vineyard;
and he came and sought fruit thereon, and
found none.
7Then said he unto the dresser of his
vineyard, Behold, these three years I come
seeking fruit on this fig tree, and find
none: cut it down; why cumbereth it the
ground?
8And he answering said unto him, Lord,
let it alone this year also, till I shall dig
about it, and dung *it:*
9And if it bear fruit, *well:* and if not, *then*
after that thou shalt cut it down.
10And he was teaching in one of the synagogues on the sabbath.

13:11 Feeling Helpless
◄ John 5:7 ►

11And, behold,
there was a woman
which had a spirit
of infirmity eigh-
teen years, and was
bowed together,
and could in no wise lift up *herself.*
12And when Jesus saw her, he called *her*
to him, and said unto her, Woman, thou
art loosed from thine infirmity.
13And he laid *his* hands on her: and immediately she was made straight, and glorified God.

13:14 Legalism
◄ Luke 6:2
John 5:10 ►

14And the ruler
of the synagogue
answered with in-
dignation, because
that Jesus had
healed on the sab-
bath day, and said unto the people, There
are six days in which men ought to work:
in them therefore come and be healed, and
not on the sabbath day.
15The Lord then answered him, and said,
Thou hypocrite, doth not each one of you
on the sabbath loose his ox or *his* ass from
the stall, and lead *him* away to watering?
16And ought not this woman, being a
daughter of Abraham, whom Satan hath
bound, lo, these eighteen years, be loosed
from this bond on the sabbath day?
17And when he had said these things,
all his adversaries were ashamed: and all
the people rejoiced for all the glorious
things that were done by him.
18Then said he, Unto what is the kingdom of God like? and whereunto shall I
resemble it?
19It is like a grain of mustard seed, which
a man took, and cast into his garden; and
it grew, and waxed a great tree; and the fowls
of the air lodged in the branches of it.
20And again he said, Whereunto shall I
liken the kingdom of God?
21It is like leaven, which a woman took
and hid in three measures of meal, till the
whole was leavened.
22And he went through the cities and
villages, teaching, and journeying toward
Jerusalem.
23Then said one unto him, Lord, are

there few that be saved? And he said unto them,

24 Strive to enter in at the strait gate: for many, I say unto you, will seek to enter in, and shall not be able.

25 When once the master of the house is risen up, and hath shut to the door, and ye begin to stand without, and to knock at the door, saying, Lord, Lord, open unto us; and he shall answer and say unto you, I know you not whence ye are:

26 Then shall ye begin to say, We have eaten and drunk in thy presence, and thou hast taught in our streets.

27 But he shall say, I tell you, I know you not whence ye are; depart from me, all *ye* workers of iniquity.

28 There shall be weeping and gnashing of teeth, when ye shall see Abraham, and Isaac, and Jacob, and all the prophets, in the kingdom of God, and you *yourselves* thrust out.

29 And they shall come from the east, and *from* the west, and from the north, and *from* the south, and shall sit down in the kingdom of God.

30 And, behold, there are last which shall be first, and there are first which shall be last.

31 The same day there came certain of the Pharisees, saying unto him, Get thee out, and depart hence: for Herod will kill thee.

32 And he said unto them, Go ye, and tell that fox, Behold, I cast out devils, and I do cures to day and to morrow, and the third *day* I shall be perfected.

33 Nevertheless I must walk to day, and to morrow, and the *day* following: for it cannot be that a prophet perish out of Jerusalem.

34 O Jerusalem, Jerusalem, which killest the prophets, and stonest them that are sent unto thee; how often would I have gathered thy children together, as a hen *doth gather* her brood under *her* wings, and ye would not!

35 Behold, your house is left unto you desolate: and verily I say unto you, Ye shall not see me, until *the time* come when ye shall say, Blessed *is* he that cometh in the name of the Lord.

14

1 And it came to pass, as he went into the house of one of the chief Pharisees to eat bread on the sabbath day, that they watched him.

2 And, behold, there was a certain man before him which had the dropsy.

3 And Jesus answering spake unto the lawyers and Pharisees, saying, Is it lawful to heal on the sabbath day?

4 And they held their peace. And he took *him*, and healed him, and let him go;

5 And answered them, saying, Which of you shall have an ass or an ox fallen into a pit, and will not straightway pull him out on the sabbath day?

14:5
Animals
◄ Deuteronomy 22:6 ►

6 And they could not answer him again to these things.

7 And he put forth a parable to those which were bidden, when he marked how they chose out the chief rooms; saying unto them,

8 When thou art bidden of any *man* to a wedding, sit not down in the highest room; lest a more honourable man than thou be bidden of him;

9 And he that bade thee and him come and say to thee, Give this man place; and thou begin with shame to take the lowest room.

10 But when thou art bidden, go and sit down in the lowest room; that when he that bade thee cometh, he may say unto thee, Friend, go up higher: then shalt thou have worship in the presence of them that sit at meat with thee.

11 For whosoever exalteth himself shall be abased; and he that humbleth himself shall be exalted.

12 Then said he also to him that bade him, When thou makest a dinner or a supper, call not thy friends, nor thy brethren, neither thy kinsmen, nor *thy* rich neighbours; lest they also bid thee again, and a recompence be made thee.

13 But when thou makest a feast, call the poor, the maimed, the lame, the blind:

14 And thou shalt be blessed; for they cannot recompense thee: for thou shalt be recompensed at the resurrection of the just.

14:14
Promises to Givers
◄ Luke 6:38
2 Corinthians 9:7 ►

15 And when one of them that sat at meat with him heard these things, he said unto

him, Blessed *is* he that shall eat bread in the kingdom of God.

16 Then said he unto him, A certain man made a great supper, and bade many:

17 And sent his servant at supper time to say to them that were bidden, Come; for all things are now ready.

14:17 Change
◄ Matthew 22:3
2 Corinthians 5:20 ►

18 And they all with one *consent* began to make excuse. The first said unto him, I have bought a piece of ground, and I must needs go and see it: I pray thee have me excused.

14:18 Salvation
◄ Ezekiel 33:9
Acts 24:25 ►

19 And another said, I have bought five yoke of oxen, and I go to prove them: I pray thee have me excused.

20 And another said, I have married a wife, and therefore I cannot come.

21 So that servant came, and shewed his lord these things. Then the master of the house being angry said to his servant, Go out quickly into the streets and lanes of the city, and bring in hither the poor, and the maimed, and the halt, and the blind.

14:21 Hurrying
◄ Luke 10:4 ►

22 And the servant said, Lord, it is done as thou hast commanded, and yet there is room.

23 And the lord said unto the servant, Go out into the highways and hedges, and compel *them* to come in, that my house may be filled.

24 For I say unto you, That none of those men which were bidden shall taste of my supper.

25 And there went great multitudes with him: and he turned, and said unto them,

26 If any *man* come to me, and hate not his father, and mother, and wife, and children, and brethren, and sisters, yea, and his own life also, he cannot be my disciple.

14:26-27 Controlling Yourself
◄ Matthew 16:24
Romans 8:13 ►

27 And whosoever doth not bear his cross, and come after me, cannot be my disciple.

28 For which of you, intending to build a tower, sitteth not down first, and counteth the cost, whether he have *sufficient* to finish *it*?

29 Lest haply, after he hath laid the foundation, and is not able to finish *it*, all that behold *it* begin to mock him,

30 Saying, This man began to build, and was not able to finish.

31 Or what king, going to make war against another king, sitteth not down first, and consulteth whether he be able with ten thousand to meet him that cometh against him with twenty thousand?

32 Or else, while the other is yet a great way off, he sendeth an ambassage, and desireth conditions of peace.

33 So likewise, whosoever he be of you that forsaketh not all that he hath, he cannot be my disciple.

14:33 This for That
◄ Luke 5:27-28
Luke 18:29-30 ►

34 Salt *is* good: but if the salt have lost his savour, wherewith shall it be seasoned?

35 It is neither fit for the land, nor yet for the dunghill; *but* men cast it out. He that hath ears to hear, let him hear.

15

1 Then drew near unto him all the publicans and sinners for to hear him.

2 And the Pharisees and scribes murmured, saying, This man receiveth sinners, and eateth with them.

3 And he spake this parable unto them, saying,

4 What man of you, having an hundred sheep, if he lose one of them, doth not leave the ninety and nine in the wilderness, and go after that which is lost, until he find it?

5 And when he hath found *it*, he layeth *it* on his shoulders, rejoicing.

15:5 Jesus' Joy
◄ Luke 10:21
John 15:11 ►

6 And when he cometh home, he calleth together *his* friends and neighbours, saying unto them, Rejoice with me; for I have found my sheep which was lost.

7 I say unto you, that likewise joy shall be in heaven over one sinner that repenteth, more

15:7 Repentance
◄ Luke 6:21
Acts 2:38 ►

than over ninety and nine just persons, which need no repentance.

8 Either what woman having ten pieces of silver, if she lose one piece, doth not light a candle, and sweep the house, and seek diligently till she find *it?*

9 And when she hath found *it,* she calleth *her* friends and *her* neighbours together, saying, Rejoice with me; for I have found the piece which I had lost.

10 Likewise, I say unto you, there is joy in the presence of the angels of God over one sinner that repenteth.

11 And he said, A certain man had two sons:

12 And the younger of them said to *his* father, Father, give me the portion of goods that falleth *to me.* And he divided unto them *his* living.

13 And not many days after the younger son gathered all together, and took his journey into a far country, and there wasted his substance with riotous living.

14 And when he had spent all, there arose a mighty famine in that land; and he began to be in want.

15 And he went and joined himself to a citizen of that country; and he sent him into his fields to feed swine.

16 And he would fain have filled his belly with the husks that the swine did eat: and no man gave unto him.

17 And when he came to himself, he said, How many hired servants of my father's have bread enough and to spare, and I perish with hunger!

18 I will arise and go to my father, and will say unto him, Father, I have sinned against heaven, and before thee,

19 And am no more worthy to be called thy son: make me as one of thy hired servants.

20 And he arose, and came to his father. But when he was yet a great way off, his father saw him, and had compassion, and ran, and fell on his neck, and kissed him.

21 And the son said unto him, Father, I have sinned against heaven, and in thy sight, and am no more worthy to be called thy son.

22 But the father said to his servants, Bring forth the best robe, and put *it* on him; and put a ring on his hand, and shoes on *his* feet:

23 And bring hither the fatted calf, and kill *it;* and let us eat, and be merry:

24 For this my son was dead, and is alive again; he was lost, and is found. And they began to be merry.

25 Now his elder son was in the field: and as he came and drew nigh to the house, he heard musick and dancing.

26 And he called one of the servants, and asked what these things meant.

27 And he said unto him, Thy brother is come; and thy father hath killed the fatted calf, because he hath received him safe and sound.

28 And he was angry, and would not go in: therefore came his father out, and intreated him.

29 And he answering said to *his* father, Lo, these many years do I serve thee, neither transgressed I at any time thy commandment: and yet thou never gavest me a kid, that I might make merry with my friends:

30 But as soon as this thy son was come, which hath devoured thy living with harlots, thou hast killed for him the fatted calf.

31 And he said unto him, Son, thou art ever with me, and all that I have is thine.

32 It was meet that we should make merry, and be glad: for this thy brother was dead, and is alive again; and was lost, and is found.

15:13 Moderation
◄ Daniel 5:1
Galatians 5:21 ►

15:13 Waste
◄ Proverbs 29:3
Luke 16:1 ►

15:14 Discontentment
◄ Isaiah 65:13
John 4:13 ►

15:14 Poverty
◄ Matthew 18:23-25
Ephesians 2:12 ►

15:16 Being Friendless
◄ Mark 14:50
Luke 16:20 ►

15:17 Blinded by Sin
◄ Daniel 4:33-34
Acts 7:54 ►

16

1 And he said also unto his disciples, There was a certain rich man, which had a steward; and

16:1 Waste
◄ Luke 15:13 ►

the same was accused unto him that he
had wasted his goods.
2 And he called him, and said unto him,
How is it that I hear this of thee? give an
account of thy stewardship; for thou
mayest be no longer steward.
3 Then the steward said within himself,
What shall I do? for my lord taketh away
from me the stewardship: I cannot dig; to
beg I am ashamed.
4 I am resolved what to do, that, when I
am put out of the stewardship, they may
receive me into their houses.
5 So he called every one of his lord's debtors *unto him,* and said unto the first, How
much owest thou unto my lord?
6 And he said, An hundred measures of
oil. And he said unto him, Take thy bill,
and sit down quickly, and write fifty.
7 Then said he to another, And how
much owest thou? And he said, An hundred measures of wheat. And he said unto
him, Take thy bill, and write fourscore.
8 And the lord commended the unjust
steward, because he had done wisely: for
the children of this world are in their generation wiser than the children of light.
9 And I say unto you, Make to yourselves
friends of the mammon of unrighteousness; that, when ye fail, they may receive
you into everlasting habitations.
10 He that is faith-
ful in that which is
least is faithful also
in much: and he
that is unjust in the
least is unjust also
in much.

16:10
Don't Be Unfair
◄ Ecclesiastes 3:16 ►

11 If therefore ye have not been faithful
in the unrighteous mammon, who will
commit to your trust the true *riches?*
12 And if ye have not been faithful in that
which is another man's, who shall give you
that which is your
own?
13 No servant can
serve two masters:
for either he will
hate the one, and
love the other; or
else he will hold to
the one, and de-
spise the other. Ye
cannot serve God
and mammon.

16:13 Double Life
◄ Zephaniah 1:4-5
1 Corinthians 10:21 ►

16:13 Following God
◄ Mark 10:21
John 6:67 ►

14 And the Pharisees also, who were covetous, heard all these things: and they derided him.
15 And he said unto them, Ye are they
which justify yourselves before men; but
God knoweth your hearts: for that which
is highly esteemed among men is abomination in the sight of God.
16 The law and the prophets *were* until
John: since that time the kingdom of God
is preached, and every man presseth into it.
17 And it is easier for heaven and earth
to pass, than one tittle of the law to fail.
18 Whosoever putteth away his wife, and
marrieth another, committeth adultery:
and whosoever marrieth her that is put
away from *her* husband committeth adultery.
19 There was a certain rich man, which
was clothed in purple and fine linen, and
fared sumptuously every day:
20 And there was
a certain beggar
named Lazarus,
which was laid at
his gate, full of
sores,
21 And desiring to
be fed with the
crumbs which fell
from the rich man's
table: moreover the
dogs came and
licked his sores.
22 And it came to
pass, that the beg-
gar died, and was
carried by the an-
gels into Abraham's
bosom: the rich
man also died, and was buried;

16:20 Being Friendless
◄ Luke 15:16
Luke 16:21 ►

16:20-21 Mercy
◄ Matthew 25:43
James 4:17 ►

16:21 Being Friendless
◄ Luke 16:20
John 5:7 ►

23 And in hell he lift up his eyes, being
in torments, and seeth Abraham afar off,
and Lazarus in his bosom.
24 And he cried and said, Father Abraham, have mercy on me, and send Lazarus, that he may dip the tip of his finger in
water, and cool my tongue; for I am tormented in this flame.
25 But Abraham
said, Son, remem-
ber that thou in
thy lifetime re-
ceivedst thy good
things, and likewise

16:25 Mistakes
◄ Mark 14:72
1 Corinthians 15:9 ►

Lazarus evil things: but now he is comforted, and thou art tormented.
26And beside all this, between us and
you there is a great gulf fixed: so that they
which would pass from hence to you cannot; neither can they pass to us, that *would
come* from thence.
27Then he said, I pray thee therefore, father, that thou wouldest send him to my
father's house:
28For I have five brethren; that he may
testify unto them, lest they also come into
this place of torment.
29Abraham saith unto him, They have
Moses and the prophets; let them hear
them.
30And he said, Nay, father Abraham: but
if one went unto them from the dead, they
will repent.
31And he said
unto him, If they
hear not Moses and
the prophets, nei-
ther will they be
persuaded, though
one rose from the
dead.

16:31 Listening and Doing
◄ Matthew 13:19
James 1:23-24 ►

16:31 Stubborn People
◄ Daniel 9:13
Revelation 9:21 ►

17

1Then said he
unto the disciples,
It is impossible but
that offences will
come: but woe *unto
him,* through whom they come!
2It were better for him that a millstone
were hanged about his neck, and he cast
into the sea, than that he should offend
one of these little ones.
3Take heed to yourselves: If thy brother
trespass against thee, rebuke him; and if
he repent, forgive him.
4And if he tres-
pass against thee
seven times in a
day, and seven
times in a day turn
again to thee, say-
ing, I repent; thou shalt forgive him.

17:4 Forgiving Others
◄ Luke 11:4
Ephesians 4:32 ►

5And the apostles said unto the Lord,
Increase our faith.
6And the Lord said, If ye had faith as a
grain of mustard seed, ye might say unto
this sycamine tree, Be thou plucked up by
the root, and be thou planted in the sea;
and it should obey you.
7But which of you, having a servant
plowing or feeding cattle, will say unto
him by and by, when he is come from the
field, Go and sit down to meat?
8And will not rather say unto him, Make
ready wherewith I may sup, and gird thyself, and serve me, till I have eaten and
drunken; and afterward thou shalt eat and
drink?
9Doth he thank that servant because he
did the things that were commanded him?
I trow not.
10So likewise ye, when ye shall have
done all those things which are commanded you, say, We are unprofitable servants:
we have done that which was our duty
to do.
11And it came to pass, as he went to Jerusalem, that he passed through the midst
of Samaria and Galilee.
12And as he entered into a certain village, there met him ten men that were lepers, which stood afar off:
13And they lifted up *their* voices, and
said, Jesus, Master, have mercy on us.
14And when he
saw *them,* he said
unto them, Go
shew yourselves
unto the priests.
And it came to pass,
that, as they went, they were cleansed.

17:14 God's Response
◄ Luke 7:10
John 4:51 ►

15And one of them, when he saw that
he was healed, turned back, and with a
loud voice glorified God,
16And fell down on *his* face at his feet,
giving him thanks: and he was a Samaritan.
17And Jesus an-
swering said, Were
there not ten
cleansed? but where
are the nine?
18There are not
found that returned
to give glory to
God, save this
stranger.
19And he said
unto him, Arise, go
thy way: thy faith hath made thee whole.

17:17-18 Gratitude
◄ Ezekiel 16:17-18
Romans 1:21 ►

17:18 Saying Thank You
◄ Isaiah 43:24
2 Timothy 3:2 ►

20And when he was demanded of the
Pharisees, when the kingdom of God
should come, he answered them and said,
The kingdom of God cometh not with ob-
servation:

21 Neither shall they say, Lo here! or, lo there! for, behold, the kingdom of God is within you.

22 And he said unto the disciples, The days will come, when ye shall desire to see one of the days of the Son of man, and ye shall not see *it*.

23 And they shall say to you, See here; or, see there: go not after *them*, nor follow *them*.

24 For as the lightning, that lighteneth out of the one *part* under heaven, shineth unto the other *part* under heaven; so shall also the Son of man be in his day.

25 But first must he suffer many things, and be rejected of this generation.

26 And as it was in the days of Noe, so shall it be also in the days of the Son of man.

27 They did eat, they drank, they married wives, they were given in marriage, until the day that Noe entered into the ark, and the flood came, and destroyed them all.

28 Likewise also as it was in the days of Lot; they did eat, they drank, they bought, they sold, they planted, they builded;

29 But the same day that Lot went out of Sodom it rained fire and brimstone from heaven, and destroyed *them* all.

30 Even thus shall it be in the day when the Son of man is revealed.

31 In that day, he which shall be upon the housetop, and his stuff in the house, let him not come down to take it away: and he that is in the field, let him likewise not return back.

32 Remember Lot's wife.

33 Whosoever shall seek to save his life shall lose it; and whosoever shall lose his life shall preserve it.

34 I tell you, in that night there shall be two *men* in one bed; the one shall be taken, and the other shall be left.

35 Two *women* shall be grinding together; the one shall be taken, and the other left.

36 Two *men* shall be in the field; the one shall be taken, and the other left.

37 And they answered and said unto him, Where, Lord? And he said unto them, Wheresoever the body *is*, thither will the eagles be gathered together.

18

1 And he spake a parable unto them *to this end*, that men ought always to pray, and not to faint;

2 Saying, There was in a city a judge, which feared not God, neither regarded man:

18:1 Duty to Pray
◄ Matthew 26:41
Luke 21:36 ►

3 And there was a widow in that city; and she came unto him, saying, Avenge me of mine adversary.

4 And he would not for a while: but afterward he said within himself, Though I fear not God, nor regard man;

18:4 Not Caring
◄ Luke 10:31-32
Luke 18:39 ►

5 Yet because this widow troubleth me, I will avenge her, lest by her continual coming she weary me.

6 And the Lord said, Hear what the unjust judge saith.

7 And shall not God avenge his own elect, which cry day and night unto him, though he bear long with them?

8 I tell you that he will avenge them speedily. Nevertheless when the Son of man cometh, shall he find faith on the earth?

9 And he spake this parable unto certain which trusted in themselves that they were righteous, and despised others:

18:9 Self-confidence
◄ Matthew 26:33
1 Corinthians 10:12 ►

10 Two men went up into the temple to pray; the one a Pharisee, and the other a publican.

11 The Pharisee stood and prayed thus with himself, God, I thank thee, that I am not as other men *are*, extortioners, unjust, adulterers, or even as this publican.

18:12 Earning Heaven
◄ Romans 9:32 ►

12 I fast twice in the week, I give tithes of all that I possess.

18:12 Showing Off
◄ Matthew 23:5 ►

13 And the publican, standing afar off, would not lift up so much as *his* eyes unto heaven,

18:13 Praying for Mercy
◄ Habakkuk 3:2 ►

but smote upon his breast, saying, God be merciful to me a sinner.

14 I tell you, this man went down to his house justified *rather* than the other: for every one that exalteth himself shall be abased; and he that humbleth himself shall be exalted.

15 And they brought unto him also infants, that he would touch them: but when *his* disciples saw *it,* they rebuked them.

16 But Jesus called them *unto him,* and said, Suffer little children to come unto me, and forbid them not: for of such is the kingdom of God.

17 Verily I say unto you, Whosoever shall not receive the kingdom of God as a little child shall in no wise enter therein.

18 And a certain ruler asked him, saying, Good Master, what shall I do to inherit eternal life?

18:18
Learning from Jesus
◄ Luke 11:1
John 6:28 ►

19 And Jesus said unto him, Why callest thou me good? none *is* good, save one, *that is,* God.

18:18 Young Leaders
◄ Luke 3:23
Acts 7:58 ►

20 Thou knowest the commandments, Do not commit adultery, Do not kill, Do not steal, Do not bear false witness, Honour thy father and thy mother.

21 And he said, All these have I kept from my youth up.

22 Now when Jesus heard these things, he said unto him, Yet lackest thou one thing: sell all that thou hast, and distribute unto the poor, and thou shalt have treasure in heaven: and come, follow me.

18:22 Generosity
◄ Luke 12:33
Luke 19:8 ►

23 And when he heard this, he was very sorrowful: for he was very rich.

24 And when Jesus saw that he was very sorrowful, he said, How hardly shall they that have riches enter into the kingdom of God!

25 For it is easier for a camel to go through a needle's eye, than for a rich man to enter into the kingdom of God.

26 And they that heard *it* said, Who then can be saved?

27 And he said, The things which are impossible with men are possible with God.

28 Then Peter said, Lo, we have left all, and followed thee.

29 And he said unto them, Verily I say unto you, There is no man that hath left house, or parents, or brethren, or wife, or children, for the kingdom of God's sake,

18:29-30 This for That
◄ Luke 14:33
Philippians 3:8 ►

30 Who shall not receive manifold more in this present time, and in the world to come life everlasting.

31 Then he took *unto him* the twelve, and said unto them, Behold, we go up to Jerusalem, and all things that are written by the prophets concerning the Son of man shall be accomplished.

32 For he shall be delivered unto the Gentiles, and shall be mocked, and spitefully entreated, and spitted on:

33 And they shall scourge *him,* and put him to death: and the third day he shall rise again.

34 And they understood none of these things: and this saying was hid from them, neither knew they the things which were spoken.

35 And it came to pass, that as he was come nigh unto Jericho, a certain blind man sat by the way side begging:

36 And hearing the multitude pass by, he asked what it meant.

37 And they told him, that Jesus of Nazareth passeth by.

38 And he cried, saying, Jesus, *thou* Son of David, have mercy on me.

39 And they which went before rebuked him, that he should hold his peace: but he cried so much the more, *Thou* Son of David, have mercy on me.

18:39 Not Caring
◄ Luke 18:4
James 2:16 ►

40 And Jesus stood, and commanded him to be brought unto him: and when he was come near, he asked him,

18:40 Help!
◄ Luke 5:18-19
John 1:41-42 ►

41 Saying, What wilt thou that I shall do unto thee? And he said, Lord, that I may receive my sight.

42 And Jesus said unto him, Receive thy
sight: thy faith hath saved thee.
43 And immediately he received his sight,
and followed him, glorifying God: and all
the people, when they saw *it*, gave praise
unto God.

19

1 And *Jesus* entered and passed through
Jericho.
2 And, behold, *there was* a man named
Zacchaeus, which was the chief among the
publicans, and he was rich.
3 And he sought to see Jesus who he was;
and could not for the press, because he was
little of stature.
4 And he ran before, and climbed up into
a sycomore tree to see him: for he was to
pass that *way*.
5 And when Jesus came to the place, he
looked up, and saw him, and said unto
him, Zacchaeus, make haste, and come
down; for to day I must abide at thy house.
6 And he made
haste, and came
down, and received
him joyfully.

19:6 Serving Quickly
◄ Luke 4:39
Acts 9:20 ►

7 And when they
saw *it*, they all mur-
mured, saying, That
he was gone to be
guest with a man
that is a sinner.

19:7 Friend of Jesus
◄ Luke 7:39
John 8:11 ►

8 And Zacchaeus
stood, and said
unto the Lord; Be-
hold, Lord, the half
of my goods I give
to the poor; and if I
have taken any
thing from any man
by false accusation,
I restore *him* four-
fold.

19:8 Examples of Generosity
◄ Nehemiah 7:70
Luke 21:1-4 ►

19:8 Generosity
◄ Luke 18:22
1 Corinthians 13:3 ►

9 And Jesus said
unto him, This day
is salvation come to
this house, forso-
much as he also is a son of Abraham.
10 For the Son of
man is come to seek
and to save that
which was lost.

19:10 Why Jesus Came
◄ Luke 2:11
John 3:17 ►

11 And as they
heard these things,
he added and spake a parable, because he
was nigh to Jerusalem, and because they
thought that the kingdom of God should
immediately appear.
12 He said therefore, A certain nobleman
went into a far country to receive for himself a kingdom, and to return.
13 And he called
his ten servants,
and delivered them
ten pounds, and
said unto them,
Occupy till I come.

19:13 Using What You Have
◄ Matthew 25:14-15
1 Corinthians 4:2 ►

14 But his citizens
hated him, and
sent a message
after him, saying,
We will not have
this *man* to reign
over us.

19:13 Watching for Jesus' Return
◄ Matthew 24:44
1 Corinthians 1:7 ►

15 And it came to
pass, that when he
was returned, hav-
ing received the
kingdom, then he
commanded these
servants to be called unto him, to whom
he had given the money, that he might
know how much every man had gained
by trading.

19:15 Getting Caught
◄ Luke 12:48
Romans 14:12 ►

16 Then came the first, saying, Lord, thy
pound hath gained ten pounds.
17 And he said
unto him, Well,
thou good servant:
because thou hast
been faithful in a
very little, have
thou authority over ten cities.

19:17 Good Rewarded
◄ Matthew 19:28
1 Corinthians 6:2 ►

18 And the second came, saying, Lord,
thy pound hath gained five pounds.
19 And he said likewise to him, Be thou
also over five cities.
20 And another came, saying, Lord, behold, *here is* thy pound, which I have kept
laid up in a napkin:
21 For I feared thee, because thou art an
austere man: thou takest up that thou
layedst not down, and reapest that thou
didst not sow.
22 And he saith unto him, Out of thine
own mouth will I judge thee, *thou* wicked
servant. Thou knewest that I was an austere man, taking up that I laid not down,
and reaping that I did not sow:
23 Wherefore then gavest not thou my
money into the bank, that at my coming I

might have required mine own with usury?

24 And he said unto them that stood by, Take from him the pound, and give *it* to him that hath ten pounds.

25 (And they said unto him, Lord, he hath ten pounds.)

26 For I say unto you, That unto every one which hath shall be given; and from him that hath not, even that he hath shall be taken away from him.

27 But those mine enemies, which would not that I should reign over them, bring hither, and slay *them* before me.

28 And when he had thus spoken, he went before, ascending up to Jerusalem.

29 And it came to pass, when he was come nigh to Bethphage and Bethany, at the mount called *the mount* of Olives, he sent two of his disciples,

30 Saying, Go ye into the village over against *you;* in the which at your entering ye shall find a colt tied, whereon yet never man sat: loose him, and bring *him hither.*

31 And if any man ask you, Why do ye loose *him?* thus shall ye say unto him, Because the Lord hath need of him.

32 And they that were sent went their way, and found even as he had said unto them.

33 And as they were loosing the colt, the owners thereof said unto them, Why loose ye the colt?

34 And they said, The Lord hath need of him.

35 And they brought him to Jesus: and they cast their garments upon the colt, and they set Jesus thereon.

36 And as he went, they spread their clothes in the way.

37 And when he was come nigh, even now at the descent of the mount of Olives, the whole multitude of the disciples began to rejoice and praise God with a loud voice for all the mighty works that they had seen;

38 Saying, Blessed *be* the King that cometh in the name of the Lord: peace in heaven, and glory in the highest.

39 And some of the Pharisees from among the multitude said unto him, Master, rebuke thy disciples.

40 And he answered and said unto them, I tell you that, if these should hold their peace, the stones would immediately cry out.

41 And when he was come near, he beheld the city, and wept over it,

42 Saying, If thou hadst known, even thou, at least in this thy day, the things *which belong* unto thy peace! but now they are hid from thine eyes.

43 For the days shall come upon thee, that thine enemies shall cast a trench about thee, and compass thee round, and keep thee in on every side,

44 And shall lay thee even with the ground, and thy children within thee; and they shall not leave in thee one stone upon another; because thou knewest not the time of thy visitation.

45 And he went into the temple, and began to cast out them that sold therein, and them that bought;

46 Saying unto them, It is written, My house is the house of prayer: but ye have made it a den of thieves.

47 And he taught daily in the temple. But the chief priests and the scribes and the chief of the people sought to destroy him,

48 And could not find what they might do: for all the people were very attentive to hear him.

20

1 And it came to pass, *that* on one of those days, as he taught the people in the temple, and preached the gospel, the chief priests and the scribes came upon *him* with the elders,

2 And spake unto him, saying, Tell us, by what authority doest thou these things? or who is he that gave thee this authority?

3 And he answered and said unto them, I will also ask you one thing; and answer me:

4 The baptism of John, was it from heaven, or of men?

5 And they reasoned with themselves, saying, If we shall say, From heaven; he will say, Why then believed ye him not?

6 But and if we say, Of men; all the people will stone us: for they be persuaded that John was a prophet.

7 And they answered, that they could not tell whence *it was.*

8 And Jesus said unto them, Neither tell I you by what authority I do these things.

9 Then began he to speak to the people this parable; A certain man planted a vineyard, and let it forth to husbandmen, and went into a far country for a long time.

10 And at the season he sent a servant to the husbandmen, that they should give

him of the fruit of the vineyard: but the
husbandmen beat him, and sent *him* away
empty.
11 And again he sent another servant: and
they beat him also, and entreated *him*
shamefully, and sent *him* away empty.
12 And again he sent a third: and they
wounded him also, and cast *him* out.
13 Then said the lord of the vineyard,
What shall I do? I will send my beloved
son: it may be they will reverence *him* when
they see him.
14 But when the husbandmen saw him,
they reasoned among themselves, saying,
This is the heir: come, let us kill him, that
the inheritance may be ours.
15 So they cast him out of the vineyard,
and killed *him*. What therefore shall the
lord of the vineyard do unto them?
16 He shall come and destroy these husbandmen, and shall give the vineyard to
others. And when they heard *it*, they said,
God forbid.
17 And he beheld them, and said, What
is this then that is written, The stone which
the builders rejected, the same is become
the head of the corner?
18 Whosoever shall fall upon that stone
shall be broken; but on whomsoever it
shall fall, it will grind him to powder.
19 And the chief priests and the scribes
the same hour sought to lay hands on him;
and they feared the people: for they perceived that he had spoken this parable
against them.
20 And they watched *him*, and sent forth
spies, which should feign themselves just
men, that they might take hold of his
words, that so they might deliver him unto
the power and authority of the governor.
21 And they asked him, saying, Master,
we know that thou sayest and teachest
rightly, neither acceptest thou the person
of any, but teachest the way of God truly:
22 Is it lawful for us to give tribute unto
Caesar, or no?
23 But he perceived their craftiness, and
said unto them, Why tempt ye me?
24 Shew me a penny. Whose image and
superscription hath it? They answered and
said, Caesar's.
25 And he said unto them, Render therefore unto Caesar the things which be
Caesar's, and unto God the things which
be God's.
26 And they could not take hold of his
words before the people: and they marvelled at his answer, and held their peace.
27 Then came to *him* certain of the Sadducees, which deny that there is any resurrection; and they asked him,
28 Saying, Master, Moses wrote unto us,
If any man's brother die, having a wife, and
he die without children, that his brother
should take his wife, and raise up seed
unto his brother.
29 There were therefore seven brethren:
and the first took a wife, and died without
children.
30 And the second took her to wife, and
he died childless.
31 And the third took her; and in like
manner the seven also: and they left no
children, and died.
32 Last of all the woman died also.
33 Therefore in the resurrection whose
wife of them is she? for seven had her to
wife.
34 And Jesus answering said unto them,
The children of this world marry, and are
given in marriage:
35 But they which shall be accounted
worthy to obtain that world, and the resurrection from the dead, neither marry, nor
are given in marriage:
36 Neither can
they die any more:
for they are equal
unto the angels;
and are the chil-
dren of God, being
the children of the resurrection.

20:36
Eternal Life
◄ John 6:50 ►

37 Now that the dead are raised, even
Moses shewed at the bush, when he calleth
the Lord the God of Abraham, and the God
of Isaac, and the God of Jacob.
38 For he is not a God of the dead, but
of the living: for all live unto him.
39 Then certain of the scribes answering
said, Master, thou hast well said.
40 And after that they durst not ask him
any *question at all*.
41 And he said unto them, How say they
that Christ is David's son?
42 And David himself saith in the book
of Psalms, The LORD said unto my Lord,
Sit thou on my right hand,
43 Till I make thine enemies thy footstool.
44 David therefore calleth him Lord, how
is he then his son?

45 Then in the audience of all the people he said unto his disciples,
46 Beware of the
scribes, which de-
sire to walk in long
robes, and love
greetings in the
markets, and the
highest seats in the synagogues, and the
chief rooms at feasts;

> **20:46**
> **Showing Off Stuff**
> ◄ Isaiah 39:2
> Acts 25:23 ►

47 Which devour widows' houses, and
for a shew make long prayers: the same
shall receive greater damnation.

21

1 And he looked up, and saw the rich
men casting their gifts into the treasury.
2 And he saw also a certain poor widow
casting in thither two mites.
3 And he said, Of a truth I say unto you,
that this poor widow hath cast in more
than they all:
4 For all these
have of their abun-
dance cast in unto
the offerings of
God: but she of her
penury hath cast in
all the living that she had.

> **21:1-4**
> **Examples of Generosity**
> ◄ Luke 19:8
> Acts 4:34-35 ►

5 And as some spake of the temple, how
it was adorned with goodly stones and
gifts, he said,
6 *As for* these things which ye behold, the
days will come, in the which there shall
not be left one stone upon another, that
shall not be thrown down.
7 And they asked him, saying, Master, but
when shall these things be? and what sign
will there be when these things shall come
to pass?
8 And he said,
Take heed that ye be
not deceived: for
many shall come in
my name, saying, I
am *Christ;* and the
time draweth near: go ye not therefore after them.

> **21:8 Watch Out!**
> ◄ Luke 12:15
> 1 Corinthians 3:10 ►

9 But when ye shall hear of wars and
commotions, be not terrified: for these
things must first come to pass; but the end
is not by and by.
10 Then said he unto them, Nation shall
rise against nation, and kingdom against
kingdom:
11 And great earthquakes shall be in
divers places, and famines, and pestilences;
and fearful sights and great signs shall
there be from heaven.
12 But before all
these, they shall lay
their hands on you,
and persecute *you,*
delivering *you* up to
the synagogues,
and into prisons, being brought before
kings and rulers for my name's sake.

> **21:12 Expecting Pain**
> ◄ Matthew 24:9
> John 15:20 ►

13 And it shall turn to you for a testimony.
14 Settle *it* therefore in your hearts, not
to meditate before what ye shall answer:
15 For I will give
you a mouth and
wisdom, which all
your adversaries
shall not be able to
gainsay nor resist.

> **21:15 Getting Wisdom**
> ◄ Daniel 2:21
> James 1:5 ►

16 And ye shall be betrayed both by parents, and brethren, and kinsfolks, and
friends; and *some* of you shall they cause
to be put to death.
17 And ye shall be hated of all *men* for
my name's sake.
18 But there shall
not an hair of your
head perish.
19 In your pa-
tience possess ye
your souls.

> **21:18**
> **Protection**
> ◄ Zechariah 2:5 ►

20 And when ye
shall see Jerusalem
compassed with ar-
mies, then know
that the desolation
thereof is nigh.

> **21:19 Quitting**
> ◄ Ecclesiastes 7:8
> Romans 12:12 ►

21 Then let them which are in Judaea flee
to the mountains; and let them which are
in the midst of it depart out; and let not
them that are in the countries enter there-
into.
22 For these be the days of vengeance,
that all things which are written may be
fulfilled.
23 But woe unto them that are with child,
and to them that give suck, in those days!
for there shall be great distress in the land,
and wrath upon this people.
24 And they shall fall by the edge of the
sword, and shall be led away captive into
all nations: and Jerusalem shall be trodden down of the Gentiles, until the times
of the Gentiles be fulfilled.

25 And there shall be signs in the sun,
and in the moon, and in the stars; and
upon the earth distress of nations, with
perplexity; the sea and the waves roaring;
26 Men's hearts
failing them for
fear, and for look-
ing after those
things which are
coming on the
earth: for the powers of heaven shall be
shaken.

21:26 Bad News
◄ Mark 8:38
2 Thessalonians 1:7-8 ►

27 And then shall
they see the Son of
man coming in a
cloud with power
and great glory.

21:27 Second Coming
◄ Mark 14:62
Acts 1:11 ►

28 And when
these things begin to come to pass, then
look up, and lift up your heads; for your
redemption draweth nigh.
29 And he spake to them a parable; Behold the fig tree, and all the trees;
30 When they now shoot forth, ye see and
know of your own selves that summer is
now nigh at hand.
31 So likewise ye, when ye see these
things come to pass, know ye that the kingdom of God is nigh at hand.
32 Verily I say unto you, This generation
shall not pass away,
till all be fulfilled.
33 Heaven and
earth shall pass
away: but my words
shall not pass away.
34 And take heed
to yourselves, lest
at any time your
hearts be over-
charged with sur-
feiting, and
drunkenness, and
cares of this life,
and *so* that day
come upon you un-
awares.
35 For as a snare
shall it come on all
them that dwell on
the face of the
whole earth.
36 Watch ye there-
fore, and pray al-
ways, that ye may
be accounted wor-
thy to escape all
these things that
shall come to pass,
and to stand before
the Son of man.

21:34 Getting Drunk
◄ Habakkuk 2:15
Romans 13:13 ►

21:34 Restraint
◄ Luke 12:22
1 Corinthians 9:27 ►

21:34 Saying No
◄ Proverbs 4:14
Romans 6:13 ►

21:34 Worry
◄ Luke 12:29
1 Corinthians 7:32 ►

21:36 Duty to Pray
◄ Luke 18:1
John 16:24 ►

37 And in the day time he was teaching
in the temple; and at night he went out,
and abode in the mount that is called *the
mount* of Olives.
38 And all the people came early in the
morning to him in the temple, for to hear
him.

22

1 Now the feast of unleavened bread
drew nigh, which is called the Passover.
2 And the chief priests and scribes sought
how they might kill him; for they feared
the people.
3 Then entered Satan into Judas surnamed Iscariot, being of the number of the
twelve.
4 And he went his way, and communed
with the chief priests and captains, how
he might betray him unto them.
5 And they were glad, and covenanted to
give him money.
6 And he promised, and sought opportunity to betray him unto them in the absence of the multitude.
7 Then came the day of unleavened
bread, when the passover must be killed.
8 And he sent Peter and John, saying, Go
and prepare us the passover, that we
may eat.
9 And they said unto him, Where wilt
thou that we prepare?
10 And he said unto them, Behold, when
ye are entered into the city, there shall a
man meet you, bearing a pitcher of water;
follow him into the house where he
entereth in.
11 And ye shall say unto the goodman of
the house, The Master saith unto thee,
Where is the guestchamber, where I shall
eat the passover with my disciples?
12 And he shall shew you a large upper
room furnished: there make ready.
13 And they went, and found as he had
said unto them: and they made ready the
passover.
14 And when the hour was come, he sat
down, and the twelve apostles with him.
15 And he said unto them, With desire I
have desired to eat this passover with you
before I suffer:

16 For I say unto you, I will not any more eat thereof, until it be fulfilled in the kingdom of God.

17 And he took the cup, and gave thanks, and said, Take this, and divide *it* among yourselves:

18 For I say unto you, I will not drink of the fruit of the vine, until the kingdom of God shall come.

19 And he took bread, and gave thanks, and brake *it,* and gave unto them, saying, This is my body which is given for you: this do in remembrance of me.

20 Likewise also the cup after supper, saying, This cup *is* the new testament in my blood, which is shed for you.

21 But, behold, the hand of him that betrayeth me *is* with me on the table.

22 And truly the Son of man goeth, as it was determined: but woe unto that man by whom he is betrayed!

23 And they began to enquire among themselves, which of them it was that should do this thing.

24 And there was also a strife among them, which of them should be accounted the greatest.

22:24 Ambition
◄ Luke 11:43
John 5:44 ►

22:24 Only Human
◄ Luke 9:54
Galatians 2:13 ►

25 And he said unto them, The kings of the Gentiles exercise lordship over them; and they that exercise authority upon them are called benefactors.

26 But ye *shall* not *be* so: but he that is greatest among you, let him be as the younger; and he that is chief, as he that doth serve.

27 For whether *is* greater, he that sitteth at meat, or he that serveth? *is* not he that sitteth at meat? but I am among you as he that serveth.

28 Ye are they which have continued with me in my temptations.

29 And I appoint unto you a kingdom, as my Father hath appointed unto me;

30 That ye may eat and drink at my table in my kingdom, and sit on thrones judging the twelve tribes of Israel.

31 And the Lord said, Simon, Simon, behold, Satan hath desired *to have* you, that he may sift *you* as wheat:

32 But I have prayed for thee, that thy faith fail not: and when thou art converted, strengthen thy brethren.

22:31-32 Tempted by Satan
◄ Luke 10:19
Romans 16:20 ►

33 And he said unto him, Lord, I am ready to go with thee, both into prison, and to death.

34 And he said, I tell thee, Peter, the cock shall not crow this day, before that thou shalt thrice deny that thou knowest me.

35 And he said unto them, When I sent you without purse, and scrip, and shoes, lacked ye any thing? And they said, Nothing.

36 Then said he unto them, But now, he that hath a purse, let him take *it,* and likewise *his* scrip: and he that hath no sword, let him sell his garment, and buy one.

37 For I say unto you, that this that is written must yet be accomplished in me, And he was reckoned among the transgressors: for the things concerning me have an end.

38 And they said, Lord, behold, here *are* two swords. And he said unto them, It is enough.

39 And he came out, and went, as he was wont, to the mount of Olives; and his disciples also followed him.

40 And when he was at the place, he said unto them, Pray that ye enter not into temptation.

41 And he was withdrawn from them about a stone's cast, and kneeled down, and prayed,

42 Saying, Father, if thou be willing, remove this cup from me: nevertheless not my will, but thine, be done.

43 And there appeared an angel unto him from heaven, strengthening him.

44 And being in an agony he prayed more earnestly: and his sweat was as it were great drops of blood falling down to the ground.

45 And when he rose up from prayer, and was come to his disciples, he found them sleeping for sorrow,

46 And said unto them, Why sleep ye? rise and pray, lest ye enter into temptation.

47 And while he yet spake, behold a multitude, and he that was called Judas, one of the twelve, went before them, and drew near unto Jesus to kiss him.

48 But Jesus said unto him, Judas,
betrayest thou the Son of man with a kiss?
49 When they which were about him saw
what would follow, they said unto him,
Lord, shall we smite with the sword?
50 And one of them smote the servant of
the high priest, and cut off his right ear.
51 And Jesus an-
swered and said,
Suffer ye thus far.
And he touched
his ear, and healed
him.

22:51 Nice
◄ Psalm 35:13
Luke 23:34 ►

52 Then Jesus said unto the chief priests,
and captains of the temple, and the elders,
which were come to him, Be ye come out,
as against a thief, with swords and staves?
53 When I was daily with you in the temple, ye stretched forth no hands against
me: but this is your hour, and the power
of darkness.
54 Then took they him, and led *him*, and
brought him into the high priest's house.
And Peter followed afar off.
55 And when they had kindled a fire in
the midst of the hall, and were set down
together, Peter sat down among them.
56 But a certain maid beheld him as he
sat by the fire, and earnestly looked upon
him, and said, This man was also with him.
57 And he denied him, saying, Woman,
I know him not.
58 And after a little while another saw
him, and said, Thou art also of them. And
Peter said, Man, I am not.
59 And about the space of one hour after
another confidently affirmed, saying, Of
a truth this *fellow* also was with him: for
he is a Galilaean.
60 And Peter said, Man, I know not what
thou sayest. And immediately, while he yet
spake, the cock crew.
61 And the Lord turned, and looked upon
Peter. And Peter remembered the word of
the Lord, how he had said unto him, Before the cock crow, thou shalt deny me
thrice.
62 And Peter went out, and wept bitterly.
63 And the men that held Jesus mocked
him, and smote *him*.
64 And when they had blindfolded him,
they struck him on the face, and asked him,
saying, Prophesy, who is it that smote thee?
65 And many other things blasphe-
mously spake they against him.
66 And as soon as it was day, the elders
of the people and the chief priests and the
scribes came together, and led him into
their council, saying,
67 Art thou the Christ? tell us. And he
said unto them, If I tell you, ye will not
believe:
68 And if I also ask *you*, ye will not answer me, nor let *me* go.
69 Hereafter shall the Son of man sit on
the right hand of the power of God.
70 Then said they all, Art thou then the
Son of God? And he said unto them, Ye
say that I am.
71 And they said, What need we any further witness? for we ourselves have heard
of his own mouth.

23

1 And the whole multitude of them
arose, and led him unto Pilate.
2 And they began to accuse him, saying,
We found this *fellow* perverting the nation,
and forbidding to give tribute to Caesar,
saying that he himself is Christ a King.
3 And Pilate asked him, saying, Art thou
the King of the Jews? And he answered him
and said, Thou sayest *it*.
4 Then said Pilate to the chief priests and
to the people, I find no fault in this man.
5 And they were the more fierce, saying,
He stirreth up the people, teaching
throughout all Jewry, beginning from Galilee to this place.
6 When Pilate heard of Galilee, he asked
whether the man were a Galilaean.
7 And as soon as he knew that he belonged unto Herod's jurisdiction, he sent
him to Herod, who himself also was at
Jerusalem at that time.
8 And when Herod saw Jesus, he was exceeding glad: for he was desirous to see
him of a long *season*, because he had heard
many things of him; and he hoped to have
seen some miracle done by him.
9 Then he questioned with him in many
words; but he answered him nothing.
10 And the chief priests and scribes stood
and vehemently accused him.
11 And Herod with his men of war set
him at nought, and mocked *him*, and arrayed him in a gorgeous robe, and sent him
again to Pilate.
12 And the same day Pilate and Herod
were made friends together: for before they
were at enmity between themselves.
13 And Pilate, when he had called

together the chief priests and the rulers and the people,

14Said unto them, Ye have brought this man unto me, as one that perverteth the people: and, behold, I, having examined *him* before you, have found no fault in this man touching those things whereof ye accuse him:

15No, nor yet Herod: for I sent you to him; and, lo, nothing worthy of death is done unto him.

16I will therefore chastise him, and release *him*.

17(For of necessity he must release one unto them at the feast.)

18And they cried out all at once, saying, Away with this *man*, and release unto us Barabbas:

19(Who for a certain sedition made in the city, and for murder, was cast into prison.)

20Pilate therefore, willing to release Jesus, spake again to them.

21But they cried, saying, Crucify *him*, crucify him.

22And he said unto them the third time, Why, what evil hath he done? I have found no cause of death in him: I will therefore chastise him, and let *him* go.

23And they were instant with loud voices, requiring that he might be crucified. And the voices of them and of the chief priests prevailed.

24And Pilate gave sentence that it should be as they required.

25And he released unto them him that for sedition and murder was cast into prison, whom they had desired; but he delivered Jesus to their will.

26And as they led him away, they laid hold upon one Simon, a Cyrenian, coming out of the country, and on him they laid the cross, that he might bear *it* after Jesus.

27And there followed him a great company of people, and of women, which also bewailed and lamented him.

28But Jesus turning unto them said, Daughters of Jerusalem, weep not for me, but weep for yourselves, and for your children.

29For, behold, the days are coming, in the which they shall say, Blessed *are* the barren, and the wombs that never bare, and the paps which never gave suck.

30Then shall they begin to say to the mountains, Fall on us; and to the hills, Cover us.

31For if they do these things in a green tree, what shall be done in the dry?

32And there were also two others, malefactors, led with him to be put to death.

33And when they were come to the place, which is called Calvary, there they crucified him, and the malefactors, one on the right hand, and the other on the left.

34Then said Jesus, Father, forgive them; for they know not what they do. And they parted his raiment, and cast lots.

23:34 Enemies
◄ Matthew 5:44
Acts 7:60 ►

23:34 Nice
◄ Luke 22:51
Acts 7:60 ►

35And the people stood beholding. And the rulers also with them derided *him*, saying, He saved others; let him save himself, if he be Christ, the chosen of God.

36And the soldiers also mocked him, coming to him, and offering him vinegar,

37And saying, If thou be the king of the Jews, save thyself.

38And a superscription also was written over him in letters of Greek, and Latin, and Hebrew, THIS IS THE KING OF THE JEWS.

39And one of the malefactors which were hanged railed on him, saying, If thou be Christ, save thyself and us.

40But the other answering rebuked him, saying, Dost not thou fear God, seeing thou art in the same condemnation?

23:40 Fearing God
◄ Matthew 10:28
Romans 11:20 ►

41And we indeed justly; for we receive the due reward of our deeds: but this man hath done nothing amiss.

42And he said unto Jesus, Lord, remember me when thou comest into thy kingdom.

43And Jesus said unto him, Verily I say unto thee, To day shalt thou be with me in paradise.

44And it was about the sixth hour, and there was a darkness over all the earth until the ninth hour.

45 And the sun was darkened, and the veil of the temple was rent in the midst.

46 And when Jesus had cried with a loud voice, he said, Father, into thy hands I commend my spirit: and having said thus, he gave up the ghost.

47 Now when the centurion saw what was done, he glorified God, saying, Certainly this was a righteous man.

48 And all the people that came together to that sight, beholding the things which were done, smote their breasts, and returned.

49 And all his acquaintance, and the women that followed him from Galilee, stood afar off, beholding these things.

50 And, behold, *there was* a man named Joseph, a counsellor; *and he was* a good man, and a just:

51 (The same had not consented to the counsel and deed of them;) *he was* of Arimathaea, a city of the Jews: who also himself waited for the kingdom of God.

52 This *man* went unto Pilate, and begged the body of Jesus.

53 And he took it down, and wrapped it in linen, and laid it in a sepulchre that was hewn in stone, wherein never man before was laid.

54 And that day was the preparation, and the sabbath drew on.

55 And the women also, which came with him from Galilee, followed after, and beheld the sepulchre, and how his body was laid.

56 And they returned, and prepared spices and ointments; and rested the sabbath day according to the commandment.

24

1 Now upon the first *day* of the week, very early in the morning, they came unto the sepulchre, bringing the spices which they had prepared, and certain *others* with them.

2 And they found the stone rolled away from the sepulchre.

3 And they entered in, and found not the body of the Lord Jesus.

4 And it came to pass, as they were much perplexed thereabout, behold, two men stood by them in shining garments:

5 And as they were afraid, and bowed down *their* faces to the earth, they said unto them, Why seek ye the living among the dead?

6 He is not here, but is risen: remember how he spake unto you when he was yet in Galilee,

7 Saying, The Son of man must be delivered into the hands of sinful men, and be crucified, and the third day rise again.

8 And they remembered his words,

9 And returned from the sepulchre, and told all these things unto the eleven, and to all the rest.

10 It was Mary Magdalene, and Joanna, and Mary *the mother* of James, and other *women that were* with them, which told these things unto the apostles.

11 And their words seemed to them as idle tales, and they believed them not.

12 Then arose Peter, and ran unto the sepulchre; and stooping down, he beheld the linen clothes laid by themselves, and departed, wondering in himself at that which was come to pass.

13 And, behold, two of them went that same day to a village called Emmaus, which was from Jerusalem *about* threescore furlongs.

14 And they talked together of all these things which had happened.

15 And it came to pass, that, while they communed *together* and reasoned, Jesus himself drew near, and went with them.

16 But their eyes were holden that they should not know him.

17 And he said unto them, What manner of communications *are* these that ye have one to another, as ye walk, and are sad?

24:17
Unhappiness
◄ Micah 7:1 ►

18 And the one of them, whose name was Cleopas, answering said unto him, Art thou only a stranger in Jerusalem, and hast not known the things which are come to pass there in these days?

19 And he said unto them, What things? And they said unto him, Concerning Jesus of Nazareth, which was a prophet mighty in deed and word before God and all the people:

20 And how the chief priests and our rulers delivered him to be condemned to death, and have crucified him.

21 But we trusted that it had been he which should have redeemed Israel: and beside all this, to day is the third day since these things were done.

22 Yea, and certain women also of our company made us astonished, which were early at the sepulchre;

23 And when they found not his body, they came, saying, that they had also seen a vision of angels, which said that he was alive.

24 And certain of them which were with us went to the sepulchre, and found *it* even so as the women had said: but him they saw not.

25 Then he said unto them, O fools, and slow of heart to believe all that the prophets have spoken:

26 Ought not Christ to have suffered these things, and to enter into his glory?

27 And beginning at Moses and all the prophets, he expounded unto them in all the scriptures the things concerning himself.

24:27 Sunday School
◄ Matthew 5:2
Acts 8:35 ►

28 And they drew nigh unto the village, whither they went: and he made as though he would have gone further.

29 But they constrained him, saying, Abide with us: for it is toward evening, and the day is far spent. And he went in to tarry with them.

30 And it came to pass, as he sat at meat with them, he took bread, and blessed *it*, and brake, and gave to them.

31 And their eyes were opened, and they knew him; and he vanished out of their sight.

32 And they said one to another, Did not our heart burn within us, while he talked with us by the way, and while he opened to us the scriptures?

33 And they rose up the same hour, and returned to Jerusalem, and found the eleven gathered together, and them that were with them,

34 Saying, The Lord is risen indeed, and hath appeared to Simon.

35 And they told what things *were done* in the way, and how he was known of them in breaking of bread.

36 And as they thus spake, Jesus himself stood in the midst of them, and saith unto them, Peace *be* unto you.

37 But they were terrified and affrighted, and supposed that they had seen a spirit.

38 And he said unto them, Why are ye troubled? and why do thoughts arise in your hearts?

39 Behold my hands and my feet, that it is I myself: handle me, and see; for a spirit hath not flesh and bones, as ye see me have.

40 And when he had thus spoken, he shewed them *his* hands and *his* feet.

41 And while they yet believed not for joy, and wondered, he said unto them, Have ye here any meat?

42 And they gave him a piece of a broiled fish, and of an honeycomb.

43 And he took *it*, and did eat before them.

44 And he said unto them, These *are* the words which I spake unto you, while I was yet with you, that all things must be fulfilled, which were written in the law of Moses, and *in* the prophets, and *in* the psalms, concerning me.

45 Then opened he their understanding, that they might understand the scriptures,

46 And said unto them, Thus it is written, and thus it behoved Christ to suffer, and to rise from the dead the third day:

47 And that repentance and remission of sins should be preached in his name among all nations, beginning at Jerusalem.

24:47
Forgiveness of Sin
◄ Luke 3:3
Acts 2:38 ►

48 And ye are witnesses of these things.

49 And, behold, I send the promise of my Father upon you: but tarry ye in the city of Jerusalem, until ye be endued with power from on high.

50 And he led them out as far as to Bethany, and he lifted up his hands, and blessed them.

51 And it came to pass, while he blessed them, he was parted from them, and carried up into heaven.

52 And they worshipped him, and returned to Jerusalem with great joy:

53 And were continually in the temple, praising and blessing God. Amen.

John

AUTHOR
John, one of Jesus' disciples

MAIN POINT
Jesus is the Son of God, and all who believe in him will have eternal life.

DATE WRITTEN
Probably A.D. 85-90

21 CHAPTERS

MAIN PEOPLE

Jesus, John the Baptist, the disciples, Mary, Martha, Lazarus, Mary (Jesus' mother), Pilate, Mary Magdalene

SPECIAL FEATURES

- *Opens with the dramatic explanation of Jesus' identity as the eternal Word*
- *Includes six miracles not found in the other Gospels*
- *Contains the most important verse in the Bible—John 3:16—which tells how to be saved from sin and go to heaven*
- *Describes what happened during the Last Supper in great detail—after all, John was right there*
- *Fourth of the four Gospels*

HOW THE BOOK GOT ITS NAME

Gospel means "good news"; this book contains the good news about Jesus as recorded by John.

1

1 In the beginning was the Word, and
the Word was with God, and the Word
was God.
2 The same was in the beginning with
God.
3 All things were made by him; and without
him was not any thing made that was
made.
4 In him was life; and the life was the
light of men.
5 And the light shineth in darkness; and
the darkness comprehended it not.
6 There was a man sent from God, whose
name *was* John.
7 The same came for a witness, to bear
witness of the Light, that all *men* through
him might believe.
8 He was not that Light, but *was sent* to
bear witness of that Light.
9 *That* was the true Light, which lighteth
every man that cometh into the world.
10 He was in the
world, and the
world was made by
him, and the world
knew him not.
11 He came unto
his own, and his
own received him
not.
12 But as many as
received him, to
them gave he power
to become the

1:12 Adopted by God
◄ Hosea 11:1
Romans 8:15 ►

1:12 Benefits of Faith
◄ Matthew 21:22
John 7:38 ►

sons of God, *even* to them that believe on
his name:
13 Which were born, not of blood, nor
of the will of the flesh, nor of the will of
man, but of God.
14 And the Word
was made flesh, and
dwelt among us,
(and we beheld his
glory, the glory as of
the only begotten
of the Father,) full of grace and truth.

1:14 Christmas
◄ Luke 1:31
Romans 8:3 ►

15 John bare witness of him, and cried,
saying, This was he of whom I spake, He
that cometh after me is preferred before
me: for he was before me.
16 And of his fulness have all we received,
and grace for grace.
17 For the law was given by Moses, *but*
grace and truth came by Jesus Christ.
18 No man hath seen God at any time;
the only begotten Son, which is in the
bosom of the Father, he hath declared *him.*
19 And this is the record of John, when
the Jews sent priests and Levites from Jerusalem to ask him, Who art thou?
20 And he confessed, and denied not; but
confessed, I am not the Christ.
21 And they asked him, What then? Art
thou Elias? And he saith, I am not. Art thou
that prophet? And he answered, No.
22 Then said they unto him, Who art
thou? that we may give an answer to them
that sent us. What sayest thou of thyself?
23 He said, I *am* the voice of one crying
in the wilderness, Make straight the way
of the Lord, as said the prophet Esaias.
24 And they which were sent were of the
Pharisees.
25 And they asked him, and said unto
him, Why baptizest thou then, if thou be
not that Christ, nor Elias, neither that
prophet?
26 John answered them, saying, I baptize
with water: but there standeth one among
you, whom ye know not;
27 He it is, who coming after me is preferred before me, whose shoe's latchet I am
not worthy to unloose.
28 These things
were done in Betha-
bara beyond Jor-
dan, where John
was baptizing.
29 The next day

1:29 Jesus the Lamb
◄ Isaiah 53:7
1 Corinthians 5:7 ►

John seeth Jesus coming unto him, and
saith, Behold the Lamb of God, which
taketh away the sin of the world.
30 This is he of whom I said, After me
cometh a man which is preferred before
me: for he was before me.
31 And I knew him not: but that he
should be made manifest to Israel, therefore am I come baptizing with water.
32 And John bare record, saying, I saw
the Spirit descending from heaven like a
dove, and it abode upon him.
33 And I knew him not: but he that sent
me to baptize with water, the same said
unto me, Upon whom thou shalt see the
Spirit descending, and remaining on him,
the same is he which baptizeth with the
Holy Ghost.
34 And I saw, and bare record that this is
the Son of God.
35 Again the next day after John stood,
and two of his disciples;
36 And looking upon Jesus as he walked,
he saith, Behold the Lamb of God!
37 And the two disciples heard him
speak, and they followed Jesus.
38 Then Jesus turned, and saw them following, and saith unto them, What seek
ye? They said unto him, Rabbi, (which is
to say, being interpreted, Master,) where
dwellest thou?
39 He saith unto them, Come and see.
They came and saw where he dwelt, and
abode with him that day: for it was about
the tenth hour.
40 One of the two which heard John
speak, and followed him, was Andrew, Simon Peter's brother.
41 He first findeth
his own brother Si-
mon, and saith
unto him, We have
found the Messias,
which is, being in-
terpreted, the Christ.

1:41-42 Help!
◄ Luke 18:40
John 1:45-46 ►

42 And he brought him to Jesus. And
when Jesus beheld him, he said, Thou art
Simon the son of Jona: thou shalt be called
Cephas, which is by interpretation, A
stone.
43 The day following Jesus would go
forth into Galilee, and findeth Philip, and
saith unto him, Follow me.
44 Now Philip was of Bethsaida, the city
of Andrew and Peter.

45Philip findeth Nathanael, and saith unto him, We have found him, of whom Moses in the law, and the prophets, did write, Jesus of Nazareth, the son of Joseph.

1:45-46 Help!
◄ John 1:41-42
John 8:3 ►

46And Nathanael said unto him, Can there any good thing come out of Nazareth? Philip saith unto him, Come and see.

47Jesus saw Nathanael coming to him, and saith of him, Behold an Israelite indeed, in whom is no guile!

1:47 Who Is Religious?
◄ Luke 2:37
John 8:29 ►

48Nathanael saith unto him, Whence knowest thou me? Jesus answered and said unto him, Before that Philip called thee, when thou wast under the fig tree, I saw thee.

49Nathanael answered and saith unto him, Rabbi, thou art the Son of God; thou art the King of Israel.

1:49 Jesus the King
◄ Luke 1:33
John 18:37 ►

50Jesus answered and said unto him, Because I said unto thee, I saw thee under the fig tree, believest thou? thou shalt see greater things than these.

51And he saith unto him, Verily, verily, I say unto you, Hereafter ye shall see heaven open, and the angels of God ascending and descending upon the Son of man.

2

1And the third day there was a marriage in Cana of Galilee; and the mother of Jesus was there:

2And both Jesus was called, and his disciples, to the marriage.

3And when they wanted wine, the mother of Jesus saith unto him, They have no wine.

4Jesus saith unto her, Woman, what have I to do with thee? mine hour is not yet come.

5His mother saith unto the servants, Whatsoever he saith unto you, do *it*.

6And there were set there six waterpots of stone, after the manner of the purifying of the Jews, containing two or three firkins apiece.

7Jesus saith unto them, Fill the waterpots with water. And they filled them up to the brim.

2:7 Obeying Christ
◄ Luke 6:47
John 11:29 ►

8And he saith unto them, Draw out now, and bear unto the governor of the feast. And they bare *it*.

9When the ruler of the feast had tasted the water that was made wine, and knew not whence it was: (but the servants which drew the water knew;) the governor of the feast called the bridegroom,

10And saith unto him, Every man at the beginning doth set forth good wine; and when men have well drunk, then that which is worse: *but* thou hast kept the good wine until now.

11This beginning of miracles did Jesus in Cana of Galilee, and manifested forth his glory; and his disciples believed on him.

12After this he went down to Capernaum, he, and his mother, and his brethren, and his disciples: and they continued there not many days.

13And the Jews' passover was at hand, and Jesus went up to Jerusalem,

14And found in the temple those that sold oxen and sheep and doves, and the changers of money sitting:

15And when he had made a scourge of small cords, he drove them all out of the temple, and the sheep, and the oxen; and poured out the changers' money, and overthrew the tables;

16And said unto them that sold doves, Take these things hence; make not my Father's house an house of merchandise.

17And his disciples remembered that it was written, The zeal of thine house hath eaten me up.

18Then answered the Jews and said unto him, What sign shewest thou unto us, seeing that thou doest these things?

19Jesus answered and said unto them, Destroy this temple, and in three days I will raise it up.

20Then said the Jews, Forty and six years was this temple in building, and wilt thou rear it up in three days?

21But he spake of the temple of his body.

22When therefore he was risen from the dead, his disciples remembered that he had said this unto them; and they believed

the scripture, and the word which Jesus
had said.
23Now when he was in Jerusalem at the
passover, in the feast *day*, many believed
in his name, when they saw the miracles
which he did.
24But Jesus did not commit himself unto
them, because he knew all *men*,
25And needed not that any should testify of man: for he knew what was in man.

3

1There was a man
of the Pharisees,
named Nicodemus,
a ruler of the Jews:

> **3:1-2**
> **Publicly Christian**
> ◄ John 7:13 ►

2The same came
to Jesus by night,
and said unto him,
Rabbi, we know that
thou art a teacher
come from God: for
no man can do
these miracles that
thou doest, except God be with him.

> **3:2 The Teacher**
> ◄ Luke 5:3
> John 7:14 ►

3Jesus answered and said unto him, Verily, verily, I say unto thee, Except a man be
born again, he cannot see the kingdom of
God.
4Nicodemus saith unto him, How can a
man be born when he is old? can he enter
the second time into his mother's womb,
and be born?
5Jesus answered,
Verily, verily, I say
unto thee, Except a
man be born of wa-
ter and *of* the Spir-
it, he cannot enter
into the kingdom of God.

> **3:5 Baptism**
> ◄ Mark 16:16
> Acts 2:38 ►

6That which is born of the flesh is flesh;
and that which is born of the Spirit is spirit.
7Marvel not that I said unto thee, Ye
must be born again.
8The wind blow-
eth where it listeth,
and thou hearest
the sound thereof,
but canst not tell
whence it cometh,
and whither it goeth: so is every one that
is born of the Spirit.

> **3:8**
> **Ignorance**
> ◄ Ecclesiastes 11:5 ►

9Nicodemus answered and said unto
him, How can these things be?
10Jesus answered and said unto him, Art
thou a master of Israel, and knowest not
these things?
11Verily, verily, I say unto thee, We speak
that we do know, and testify that we have
seen; and ye receive not our witness.
12If I have told you earthly things, and
ye believe not, how shall ye believe, if I
tell you *of* heavenly things?
13And no man
hath ascended up
to heaven, but he
that came down
from heaven, *even*
the Son of man
which is in heaven.

> **3:14-15 Our Savior**
> ◄ Isaiah 59:16
> John 6:35 ►

14And as Moses
lifted up the ser-
pent in the wilder-
ness, even so must
the Son of man be
lifted up:

> **3:15**
> **Salvation by Faith**
> ◄ John 3:36 ►

15That whoso-
ever believeth in
him should not
perish, but have
eternal life.

> **3:16**
> **A Great Gift**
> ◄ John 4:10 ►

16For God so
loved the world,
that he gave his
only begotten Son,
that whosoever
believeth in him
should not perish,
but have everlasting
life.

> **3:16 God's Love**
> ◄ Jeremiah 31:3
> John 16:27 ►

> **3:16**
> **Jesus**
> ◄ John 6:68 ►

17For God sent
not his Son into the
world to condemn
the world; but that
the world through
him might be
saved.

> **3:16**
> **Value of People**
> ◄ 1 Corinthians 6:20 ►

18He that belie-
veth on him is not
condemned: but he
that believeth not
is condemned al-
ready, because he
hath not believed
in the name of the
only begotten Son
of God.

> **3:17 Why Jesus Came**
> ◄ Luke 19:10
> Acts 5:31 ►

19And this is the
condemnation,
that light is come
into the world, and
men loved darkness

> **3:18 No Condemnation**
> ◄ Luke 6:37
> John 5:24 ►

rather than light, because their deeds were evil.

20 For every one that doeth evil hateth the light, neither cometh to the light, lest his deeds should be reproved.

21 But he that doeth truth cometh to the light, that his deeds may be made manifest, that they are wrought in God.

22 After these things came Jesus and his disciples into the land of Judaea; and there he tarried with them, and baptized.

23 And John also was baptizing in Aenon near to Salim, because there was much water there: and they came, and were baptized.

24 For John was not yet cast into prison.

25 Then there arose a question between *some* of John's disciples and the Jews about purifying.

26 And they came unto John, and said unto him, Rabbi, he that was with thee beyond Jordan, to whom thou barest witness, behold, the same baptizeth, and all *men* come to him.

27 John answered and said, A man can receive nothing, except it be given him from heaven.

3:27 Gifts from God
◄ Luke 11:9
1 Corinthians 4:7 ►

28 Ye yourselves bear me witness, that I said, I am not the Christ, but that I am sent before him.

3:27 God's Role
◄ Jeremiah 10:23
John 15:5 ►

29 He that hath the bride is the bridegroom: but the friend of the bridegroom, which standeth and heareth him, rejoiceth greatly because of the bridegroom's voice: this my joy therefore is fulfilled.

30 He must increase, but I *must* decrease.

31 He that cometh from above is above all: he that is of the earth is earthly, and speaketh of the earth: he that cometh from heaven is above all.

32 And what he hath seen and heard, that he testifieth; and no man receiveth his testimony.

33 He that hath received his testimony hath set to his seal that God is true.

34 For he whom God hath sent speaketh the words of God: for God giveth not the Spirit by measure *unto him*.

35 The Father loveth the Son, and hath given all things into his hand.

36 He that believeth on the Son hath everlasting life: and he that believeth not the Son shall not see life; but the wrath of God abideth on him.

3:36 God's Anger
◄ Psalm 2:12
Romans 1:18 ►

3:36 Salvation by Faith
◄ John 3:15
John 5:24 ►

4

1 When therefore the Lord knew how the Pharisees had heard that Jesus made and baptized more disciples than John,

2 (Though Jesus himself baptized not, but his disciples,)

3 He left Judaea, and departed again into Galilee.

4 And he must needs go through Samaria.

5 Then cometh he to a city of Samaria, which is called Sychar, near to the parcel of ground that Jacob gave to his son Joseph.

6 Now Jacob's well was there. Jesus therefore, being wearied with *his* journey, sat thus on the well: *and* it was about the sixth hour.

7 There cometh a woman of Samaria to draw water: Jesus saith unto her, Give me to drink.

8 (For his disciples were gone away unto the city to buy meat.)

9 Then saith the woman of Samaria unto him, How is it that thou, being a Jew, askest drink of me, which am a woman of Samaria? for the Jews have no dealings with the Samaritans.

4:9 Different People
◄ Luke 9:53
Acts 10:28 ►

10 Jesus answered and said unto her, If thou knewest the gift of God, and who it is that saith to thee, Give me to drink; thou wouldest have asked of him, and he would have given thee living water.

4:10 A Great Gift
◄ John 3:16
Romans 5:15 ►

11 The woman saith unto him, Sir, thou hast nothing to draw with, and the well is deep: from whence then hast thou that living water?

12 Art thou greater than our father Jacob, which gave us the well, and drank thereof himself, and his children, and his cattle?

13 Jesus answered and said unto her, Whosoever drinketh of this water shall thirst again:

4:13 Discontentment
◄ Luke 15:14
Revelation 18:14 ►

14 But whosoever drinketh of the water that I shall give him shall never thirst; but the water that I shall give him shall be in him a well of water springing up into everlasting life.

15 The woman saith unto him, Sir, give me this water, that I thirst not, neither come hither to draw.

16 Jesus saith unto her, Go, call thy husband, and come hither.

17 The woman answered and said, I have no husband. Jesus said unto her, Thou hast well said, I have no husband:

18 For thou hast had five husbands; and he whom thou now hast is not thy husband: in that saidst thou truly.

19 The woman saith unto him, Sir, I perceive that thou art a prophet.

20 Our fathers worshipped in this mountain; and ye say, that in Jerusalem is the place where men ought to worship.

21 Jesus saith unto her, Woman, believe me, the hour cometh, when ye shall neither in this mountain, nor yet at Jerusalem, worship the Father.

22 Ye worship ye know not what: we know what we worship: for salvation is of the Jews.

23 But the hour cometh, and now is, when the true worshippers shall worship the Father in spirit and in truth: for the Father seeketh such to worship him.

24 God *is* a Spirit: and they that worship him must worship *him* in spirit and in truth.

4:24 Worship
◄ Matthew 4:10
Revelation 14:7 ►

25 The woman saith unto him, I know that Messias cometh, which is called Christ: when he is come, he will tell us all things.

26 Jesus saith unto her, I that speak unto thee am *he*.

27 And upon this came his disciples, and marvelled that he talked with the woman: yet no man said, What seekest thou? or, Why talkest thou with her?

28 The woman then left her waterpot, and went her way into the city, and saith to the men,

29 Come, see a man, which told me all things that ever I did: is not this the Christ?

30 Then they went out of the city, and came unto him.

31 In the mean while his disciples prayed him, saying, Master, eat.

32 But he said unto them, I have meat to eat that ye know not of.

33 Therefore said the disciples one to another, Hath any man brought him *ought* to eat?

34 Jesus saith unto them, My meat is to do the will of him that sent me, and to finish his work.

4:34 Job One
◄ Matthew 6:33
John 17:4 ►

35 Say not ye, There are yet four months, and *then* cometh harvest? behold, I say unto you, Lift up your eyes, and look on the fields; for they are white already to harvest.

36 And he that reapeth receiveth wages, and gathereth fruit unto life eternal: that both he that soweth and he that reapeth may rejoice together.

4:36 Goodness Rewarded
◄ Luke 6:35
Romans 2:10 ►

4:36 Serving
◄ Luke 10:17
Acts 11:23 ►

37 And herein is that saying true, One soweth, and another reapeth.

38 I sent you to reap that whereon ye bestowed no labour: other men laboured, and ye are entered into their labours.

39 And many of the Samaritans of that city believed on him for the saying of the woman, which testified, He told me all that ever I did.

40 So when the Samaritans were come unto him, they besought him that he would tarry with them: and he abode there two days.

41 And many more believed because of his own word;

42 And said unto the woman, Now we believe, not because of thy saying: for we have heard *him* ourselves, and know that this is indeed the Christ, the Saviour of the world.

43 Now after two days he departed thence, and went into Galilee.

44 For Jesus himself testified, that a prophet hath no honour in his own country.

45 Then when he was come into Galilee, the Galilaeans received him, having seen all the things that he did at Jerusalem at the feast: for they also went unto the feast.

46 So Jesus came again into Cana of Galilee, where he made the water wine. And there was a certain nobleman, whose son was sick at Capernaum.

47 When he heard that Jesus was come out of Judaea into Galilee, he went unto him, and besought him that he would come down, and heal his son: for he was at the point of death.

48 Then said Jesus unto him, Except ye see signs and wonders, ye will not believe.

49 The nobleman saith unto him, Sir, come down ere my child die.

50 Jesus saith unto him, Go thy way; thy son liveth. And the man believed the word that Jesus had spoken unto him, and he went his way.

51 And as he was now going down, his servants met him, and told *him*, saying, Thy son liveth.

4:51 God's Response
◄ Luke 17:14
John 9:7 ►

52 Then enquired he of them the hour when he began to amend. And they said unto him, Yesterday at the seventh hour the fever left him.

53 So the father knew that *it was* at the same hour, in the which Jesus said unto him, Thy son liveth: and himself believed, and his whole house.

54 This *is* again the second miracle *that* Jesus did, when he was come out of Judaea into Galilee.

5

1 After this there was a feast of the Jews; and Jesus went up to Jerusalem.

2 Now there is at Jerusalem by the sheep *market* a pool, which is called in the Hebrew tongue Bethesda, having five porches.

3 In these lay a great multitude of impotent folk, of blind, halt, withered, waiting for the moving of the water.

4 For an angel went down at a certain season into the pool, and troubled the water: whosoever then first after the troubling of the water stepped in was made whole of whatsoever disease he had.

5 And a certain man was there, which had an infirmity thirty and eight years.

6 When Jesus saw him lie, and knew that he had been now a long time *in that case*, he saith unto him, Wilt thou be made whole?

7 The impotent man answered him, Sir, I have no man, when the water is troubled, to put me into the pool: but while I am coming, another steppeth down before me.

5:7 Being Friendless
◄ Luke 16:21 ►

5:7 Feeling Helpless
◄ Luke 13:11
John 6:44 ►

8 Jesus saith unto him, Rise, take up thy bed, and walk.

9 And immediately the man was made whole, and took up his bed, and walked: and on the same day was the sabbath.

10 The Jews therefore said unto him that was cured, It is the sabbath day: it is not lawful for thee to carry *thy* bed.

5:10 Legalism
◄ Luke 13:14
Acts 15:5 ►

11 He answered them, He that made me whole, the same said unto me, Take up thy bed, and walk.

12 Then asked they him, What man is that which said unto thee, Take up thy bed, and walk?

13 And he that was healed wist not who it was: for Jesus had conveyed himself away, a multitude being in *that* place.

14 Afterward Jesus findeth him in the temple, and said unto him, Behold, thou art made whole: sin no more, lest a worse thing come unto thee.

15 The man departed, and told the Jews that it was Jesus, which had made him whole.

16 And therefore did the Jews persecute Jesus, and sought to slay him, because he had done these things on the sabbath day.

17 But Jesus answered them, My Father worketh hitherto, and I work.

18 Therefore the Jews sought the more to kill him, because he not only had broken the sabbath, but said also that God was his Father, making himself equal with God.

19 Then answered Jesus and said unto
them, Verily, verily, I say unto you, The Son
can do nothing of himself, but what he
seeth the Father do: for what things soever
he doeth, these also doeth the Son likewise.
20 For the Father loveth the Son, and
sheweth him all things that himself doeth:
and he will shew him greater works than
these, that ye may marvel.
21 For as the Father raiseth up the dead,
and quickeneth *them;* even so the Son
quickeneth whom he will.
22 For the Father
judgeth no man,
but hath commit-
ted all judgment
unto the Son:
23 That all *men*
should honour the Son, even as they
honour the Father. He that honoureth not
the Son honoureth not the Father which
hath sent him.

5:22 Christ as Judge
◄ Matthew 25:32
Acts 10:42 ►

24 Verily, verily, I
say unto you, He
that heareth my
word, and believeth
on him that sent
me, hath everlast-
ing life, and shall
not come into con-
demnation; but is
passed from death
unto life.

5:24 No Condemnation
◄ John 3:18
Romans 8:1 ►

5:24 Salvation by Faith
◄ John 3:36
John 6:40 ►

25 Verily, verily, I
say unto you, The
hour is coming,
and now is, when
the dead shall hear
the voice of the Son
of God: and they
that hear shall live.

5:25 Resurrection
◄ Hosea 13:14
John 6:40 ►

26 For as the Father hath life in himself;
so hath he given to the Son to have life in
himself;
27 And hath given him authority to execute judgment also, because he is the Son
of man.
28 Marvel not at
this: for the hour is
coming, in the
which all that are in
the graves shall hear
his voice,
29 And shall come forth; they that have
done good, unto the resurrection of life;
and they that have done evil, unto the resurrection of damnation.

5:28-29
Life After Death
◄ Daniel 12:2
Acts 24:15 ►

30 I can of mine
own self do noth-
ing: as I hear, I
judge: and my judg-
ment is just; be-
cause I seek not
mine own will, but
the will of the Fa-
ther which hath
sent me.
31 If I bear witness
of myself, my wit-
ness is not true.

5:30 God's Justice
◄ Zephaniah 3:5
Romans 2:2 ►

5:30 Submitting to God
◄ Matthew 26:42
John 7:17 ►

32 There is another that beareth witness
of me; and I know that the witness which
he witnesseth of me is true.
33 Ye sent unto John, and he bare witness unto the truth.
34 But I receive not testimony from man:
but these things I say, that ye might be
saved.
35 He was a burning and a shining light:
and ye were willing for a season to rejoice
in his light.
36 But I have greater witness than *that* of
John: for the works which the Father hath
given me to finish, the same works that I
do, bear witness of me, that the Father hath
sent me.
37 And the Father himself, which hath
sent me, hath borne witness of me. Ye have
neither heard his voice at any time, nor
seen his shape.
38 And ye have not his word abiding in
you: for whom he hath sent, him ye believe not.
39 Search the scrip-
tures; for in them ye
think ye have eter-
nal life: and they
are they which tes-
tify of me.

5:39 Reading the Bible
◄ Isaiah 34:16
Acts 17:11 ►

40 And ye will not come to me, that ye
might have life.
41 I receive not honour from men.
42 But I know you, that ye have not the
love of God in you.
43 I am come in my Father's name, and
ye receive me not: if another shall come in
his own name, him ye will receive.
44 How can ye believe, which receive
honour one of another, and seek not the

honour that *cometh*
from God only?
45 Do not think
that I will accuse
you to the Father:
there is *one* that
accuseth you, *even* Moses, in whom ye
trust.

5:44 Ambition
◄ Luke 22:24
2 Thessalonians 2:4 ►

46 For had ye believed Moses, ye would
have believed me: for he wrote of me.
47 But if ye believe not his writings, how
shall ye believe my words?

6

1 After these things Jesus went over the
sea of Galilee, which is *the sea* of Tiberias.
2 And a great multitude followed him,
because they saw his miracles which he did
on them that were diseased.
3 And Jesus went up into a mountain,
and there he sat with his disciples.
4 And the passover, a feast of the Jews,
was nigh.
5 When Jesus then lifted up *his* eyes, and
saw a great company come unto him, he
saith unto Philip, Whence shall we buy
bread, that these may eat?
6 And this he said to prove him: for he
himself knew what he would do.
7 Philip answered him, Two hundred
pennyworth of bread is not sufficient for
them, that every one of them may take a
little.
8 One of his disciples, Andrew, Simon
Peter's brother, saith unto him,
9 There is a lad here, which hath five barley loaves, and two small fishes: but what
are they among so many?
10 And Jesus said, Make the men sit
down. Now there was much grass in the
place. So the men sat down, in number
about five thousand.
11 And Jesus took the loaves; and when
he had given thanks, he distributed to the
disciples, and the disciples to them that
were set down; and likewise of the fishes
as much as they would.
12 When they
were filled, he said
unto his disciples,
Gather up the frag-
ments that remain,
that nothing be
lost.

6:12
Being Frugal
◄ Proverbs 21:20 ►

13 Therefore they gathered *them* together, and filled twelve baskets with the fragments of the five barley loaves, which
remained over and above unto them that
had eaten.
14 Then those men, when they had seen
the miracle that Jesus did, said, This is of a
truth that prophet that should come into
the world.
15 When Jesus therefore perceived that
they would come and take him by force,
to make him a king, he departed again into
a mountain himself alone.
16 And when even was *now* come, his disciples went down unto the sea,
17 And entered into a ship, and went
over the sea toward Capernaum. And it
was now dark, and Jesus was not come to
them.
18 And the sea arose by reason of a great
wind that blew.
19 So when they had rowed about five
and twenty or thirty furlongs, they see Jesus
walking on the sea, and drawing nigh unto
the ship: and they were afraid.
20 But he saith unto them, It is I; be not
afraid.
21 Then they willingly received him into
the ship: and immediately the ship was at
the land whither they went.
22 The day following, when the people
which stood on the other side of the sea
saw that there was none other boat there,
save that one whereinto his disciples were
entered, and that Jesus went not with his
disciples into the boat, but *that* his disciples were gone away alone;
23 (Howbeit there came other boats from
Tiberias nigh unto the place where they
did eat bread, after that the Lord had giv-
en thanks:)
24 When the people therefore saw that
Jesus was not there, neither his disciples,
they also took shipping, and came to Capernaum, seeking for Jesus.
25 And when they had found him on the
other side of the sea, they said unto him,
Rabbi, when camest thou hither?
26 Jesus answered them and said, Verily,
verily, I say unto you, Ye seek me, not because ye saw the miracles, but because ye
did eat of the loaves, and were filled.
27 Labour not for
the meat which
perisheth, but for
that meat which
endureth unto ever-
lasting life, which

6:27 Things That Last
◄ 1 Kings 19:8
1 Corinthians 3:14 ►

the Son of man shall give unto you: for him hath God the Father sealed.

28 Then said they unto him, What shall we do, that we might work the works of God?

6:28 Learning from Jesus
◄ Luke 18:18 ►

29 Jesus answered and said unto them, This is the work of God, that ye believe on him whom he hath sent.

6:28-29 Faith
◄ Luke 8:50
John 20:27 ►

30 They said therefore unto him, What sign shewest thou then, that we may see, and believe thee? what dost thou work?

31 Our fathers did eat manna in the desert; as it is written, He gave them bread from heaven to eat.

32 Then Jesus said unto them, Verily, verily, I say unto you, Moses gave you not that bread from heaven; but my Father giveth you the true bread from heaven.

33 For the bread of God is he which cometh down from heaven, and giveth life unto the world.

34 Then said they unto him, Lord, evermore give us this bread.

35 And Jesus said unto them, I am the bread of life: he that cometh to me shall never hunger; and he that believeth on me shall never thirst.

6:35 Our Savior
◄ John 3:14-15
John 6:67-68 ►

36 But I said unto you, That ye also have seen me, and believe not.

37 All that the Father giveth me shall come to me; and him that cometh to me I will in no wise cast out.

6:37 Believer Be Glad
◄ Matthew 10:42
Romans 8:38-39 ►

38 For I came down from heaven, not to do mine own will, but the will of him that sent me.

39 And this is the Father's will which hath sent me, that of all which he hath given me I should lose nothing, but should raise it up again at the last day.

6:40 Resurrection
◄ John 5:25
John 11:25 ►

40 And this is the will of him that sent me, that every one which seeth the Son, and believeth on him, may have everlasting life: and I will raise him up at the last day.

6:40 Salvation by Faith
◄ John 5:24
John 11:25 ►

41 The Jews then murmured at him, because he said, I am the bread which came down from heaven.

42 And they said, Is not this Jesus, the son of Joseph, whose father and mother we know? how is it then that he saith, I came down from heaven?

43 Jesus therefore answered and said unto them, Murmur not among yourselves.

44 No man can come to me, except the Father which hath sent me draw him: and I will raise him up at the last day.

6:44 Feeling Helpless
◄ John 5:7
John 15:5 ►

45 It is written in the prophets, And they shall be all taught of God. Every man therefore that hath heard, and hath learned of the Father, cometh unto me.

6:45 Lessons of Life
◄ Matthew 11:29
Ephesians 4:20-23 ►

46 Not that any man hath seen the Father, save he which is of God, he hath seen the Father.

47 Verily, verily, I say unto you, He that believeth on me hath everlasting life.

48 I am that bread of life.

49 Your fathers did eat manna in the wilderness, and are dead.

50 This is the bread which cometh down from heaven, that a man may eat thereof, and not die.

6:50 Eternal Life
◄ Luke 20:36
John 8:51 ►

51 I am the living bread which came down from heaven: if any man eat of this bread, he shall live for ever: and the bread that I will give is my flesh, which I will give for the life of the world.

52 The Jews therefore strove among themselves, saying, How can this man give us *his* flesh to eat?

53 Then Jesus said unto them, Verily, verily, I say unto you, Except ye eat the flesh

of the Son of man, and drink his blood, ye have no life in you.

54 Whoso eateth my flesh, and drinketh my blood, hath eternal life; and I will raise him up at the last day.

55 For my flesh is meat indeed, and my blood is drink indeed.

56 He that eateth my flesh, and drinketh my blood, dwelleth in me, and I in him.

57 As the living Father hath sent me, and I live by the Father: so he that eateth me, even he shall live by me.

58 This is that bread which came down from heaven: not as your fathers did eat manna, and are dead: he that eateth of this bread shall live for ever.

59 These things said he in the synagogue, as he taught in Capernaum.

60 Many therefore of his disciples, when they had heard *this*, said, This is an hard saying; who can hear it?

61 When Jesus knew in himself that his disciples murmured at it, he said unto them, Doth this offend you?

62 *What* and if ye shall see the Son of man ascend up where he was before?

63 It is the spirit that quickeneth; the flesh profiteth nothing: the words that I speak unto you, *they* are spirit, and *they* are life.

64 But there are some of you that believe not. For Jesus knew from the beginning who they were that believed not, and who should betray him.

65 And he said, Therefore said I unto you, that no man can come unto me, except it were given unto him of my Father.

66 From that *time* many of his disciples went back, and walked no more with him.

67 Then said Jesus unto the twelve, Will ye also go away?

68 Then Simon Peter answered him, Lord, to whom shall we go? thou hast the words of eternal life.

69 And we believe and are sure that thou art that Christ, the Son of the living God.

6:67
Following God
◄ Luke 16:13 ►

6:67-68 Our Savior
◄ John 6:35
Acts 4:12 ►

6:68 Jesus
◄ John 3:16
John 8:24 ►

70 Jesus answered them, Have not I chosen you twelve, and one of you is a devil?

71 He spake of Judas Iscariot *the son* of Simon: for he it was that should betray him, being one of the twelve.

7

1 After these things Jesus walked in Galilee: for he would not walk in Jewry, because the Jews sought to kill him.

2 Now the Jews' feast of tabernacles was at hand.

3 His brethren therefore said unto him, Depart hence, and go into Judaea, that thy disciples also may see the works that thou doest.

4 For *there is* no man *that* doeth any thing in secret, and he himself seeketh to be known openly. If thou do these things, shew thyself to the world.

5 For neither did his brethren believe in him.

6 Then Jesus said unto them, My time is not yet come: but your time is alway ready.

7 The world cannot hate you; but me it hateth, because I testify of it, that the works thereof are evil.

8 Go ye up unto this feast: I go not up yet unto this feast; for my time is not yet full come.

9 When he had said these words unto them, he abode *still* in Galilee.

10 But when his brethren were gone up, then went he also up unto the feast, not openly, but as it were in secret.

11 Then the Jews sought him at the feast, and said, Where is he?

12 And there was much murmuring among the people concerning him: for some said, He is a good man: others said, Nay; but he deceiveth the people.

13 Howbeit no man spake openly of him for fear of the Jews.

14 Now about the midst of the feast Jesus went up into the temple, and taught.

15 And the Jews marvelled, saying,

7:13 Publicly Christian
◄ John 3:1-2
John 12:42 ►

7:13 The Crowd
◄ Matthew 14:5
Acts 12:3 ►

7:14 The Teacher
◄ John 3:2
John 8:2 ►

How knoweth this man letters, having never learned?

16 Jesus answered them, and said, My doctrine is not mine, but his that sent me.

17 If any man will do his will, he shall know of the doctrine, whether it be of God, or *whether* I speak of myself.

7:17 Submitting to God
◄ John 5:30
Acts 21:14 ►

18 He that speaketh of himself seeketh his own glory: but he that seeketh his glory that sent him, the same is true, and no unrighteousness is in him.

19 Did not Moses give you the law, and *yet* none of you keepeth the law? Why go ye about to kill me?

20 The people answered and said, Thou hast a devil: who goeth about to kill thee?

21 Jesus answered and said unto them, I have done one work, and ye all marvel.

22 Moses therefore gave unto you circumcision; (not because it is of Moses, but of the fathers;) and ye on the sabbath day circumcise a man.

23 If a man on the sabbath day receive circumcision, that the law of Moses should not be broken; are ye angry at me, because I have made a man every whit whole on the sabbath day?

24 Judge not according to the appearance, but judge righteous judgment.

7:24 Good Looks
◄ Matthew 23:27
2 Corinthians 5:12 ►

25 Then said some of them of Jerusalem, Is not this he, whom they seek to kill?

26 But, lo, he speaketh boldly, and they say nothing unto him. Do the rulers know indeed that this is the very Christ?

27 Howbeit we know this man whence he is: but when Christ cometh, no man knoweth whence he is.

28 Then cried Jesus in the temple as he taught, saying, Ye both know me, and ye know whence I am: and I am not come of myself, but he that sent me is true, whom ye know not.

29 But I know him: for I am from him, and he hath sent me.

30 Then they sought to take him: but no man laid hands on him, because his hour was not yet come.

31 And many of the people believed on him, and said, When Christ cometh, will he do more miracles than these which this *man* hath done?

32 The Pharisees heard that the people murmured such things concerning him; and the Pharisees and the chief priests sent officers to take him.

33 Then said Jesus unto them, Yet a little while am I with you, and *then* I go unto him that sent me.

34 Ye shall seek me, and shall not find *me:* and where I am, *thither* ye cannot come.

35 Then said the Jews among themselves, Whither will he go, that we shall not find him? will he go unto the dispersed among the Gentiles, and teach the Gentiles?

36 What *manner of* saying is this that he said, Ye shall seek me, and shall not find *me:* and where I am, *thither* ye cannot come?

37 In the last day, that great *day* of the feast, Jesus stood and cried, saying, If any man thirst, let him come unto me, and drink.

7:37 God Calls You
◄ Matthew 22:9
Romans 10:12 ►

38 He that believeth on me, as the scripture hath said, out of his belly shall flow rivers of living water.

7:38 Benefits of Faith
◄ John 1:12
John 14:12 ►

39 (But this spake he of the Spirit, which they that believe on him should receive: for the Holy Ghost was not yet *given;* because that Jesus was not yet glorified.)

40 Many of the people therefore, when they heard this saying, said, Of a truth this is the Prophet.

41 Others said, This is the Christ. But some said, Shall Christ come out of Galilee?

42 Hath not the scripture said, That Christ cometh of the seed of David, and out of the town of Bethlehem, where David was?

43 So there was a division among the people because of him.

44 And some of them would have taken him; but no man laid hands on him.

45 Then came the officers to the chief priests and Pharisees; and they said unto them, Why have ye not brought him?

46 The officers answered, Never man spake like this man.

47 Then answered them the Pharisees, Are ye also deceived?

48 Have any of the rulers or of the Pharisees believed on him?

49 But this people who knoweth not the law are cursed.

50 Nicodemus saith unto them, (he that came to Jesus by night, being one of them,)

51 Doth our law judge *any* man, before it hear him, and know what he doeth?

52 They answered and said unto him, Art thou also of Galilee? Search, and look: for out of Galilee ariseth no prophet.

53 And every man went unto his own house.

8

1 Jesus went unto the mount of Olives.

2 And early in the morning he came again into the temple, and all the people came unto him; and he sat down, and taught them.

8:2
The Teacher
◄ John 7:14 ►

3 And the scribes and Pharisees brought unto him a woman taken in adultery; and when they had set her in the midst,

8:3 Help!
◄ John 1:45-46
John 11:28 ►

4 They say unto him, Master, this woman was taken in adultery, in the very act.

5 Now Moses in the law commanded us, that such should be stoned: but what sayest thou?

6 This they said, tempting him, that they might have to accuse him. But Jesus stooped down, and with *his* finger wrote on the ground, *as though he heard them not.*

7 So when they continued asking him, he lifted up himself, and said unto them, He that is without sin among you, let him first cast a stone at her.

8:7
Examples of Mercy
◄ Luke 9:55 ►

8 And again he stooped down, and wrote on the ground.

9 And they which heard *it,* being convicted by *their own* conscience, went out one by one, beginning at the eldest, *even* unto the last: and Jesus was left alone, and the woman standing in the midst.

8:9
Feeling Guilty
◄ Daniel 5:6 ►

8:9
Guilty Conscience
◄ Daniel 5:6 ►

10 When Jesus had lifted up himself, and saw none but the woman, he said unto her, Woman, where are those thine accusers? hath no man condemned thee?

11 She said, No man, Lord. And Jesus said unto her, Neither do I condemn thee: go, and sin no more.

8:11 Friend of Jesus
◄ Luke 19:7
Romans 5:8 ►

12 Then spake Jesus again unto them, saying, I am the light of the world: he that followeth me shall not walk in darkness, but shall have the light of life.

13 The Pharisees therefore said unto him, Thou bearest record of thyself; thy record is not true.

14 Jesus answered and said unto them, Though I bear record of myself, *yet* my record is true: for I know whence I came, and whither I go; but ye cannot tell whence I come, and whither I go.

15 Ye judge after the flesh; I judge no man.

16 And yet if I judge, my judgment is true: for I am not alone, but I and the Father that sent me.

17 It is also written in your law, that the testimony of two men is true.

18 I am one that bear witness of myself, and the Father that sent me beareth witness of me.

19 Then said they unto him, Where is thy Father? Jesus answered, Ye neither know me, nor my Father: if ye had known me, ye should have known my Father also.

20 These words spake Jesus in the treasury, as he taught in the temple: and no man laid hands on him; for his hour was not yet come.

21 Then said Jesus again unto them, I go my way, and ye shall seek me, and shall die in your sins: whither I go, ye cannot come.

22 Then said the Jews, Will he kill himself? because he saith, Whither I go, ye cannot come.

23 And he said unto them, Ye are from beneath; I am from above: ye are of this world; I am not of this world.

24 I said therefore unto you, that ye shall

die in your sins: for
if ye believe not that
I am *he,* ye shall die
in your sins.
25Then said they
unto him, Who art
thou? And Jesus saith unto them, Even *the*
same that I said unto you from the beginning.

8:24 Jesus
◄ John 6:68
Acts 4:12 ►

26I have many things to say and to judge
of you: but he that sent me is true; and I
speak to the world those things which I
have heard of him.
27They understood not that he spake to
them of the Father.
28Then said Jesus unto them, When ye
have lifted up the Son of man, then shall
ye know that I am *he,* and *that* I do nothing of myself; but as my Father hath taught
me, I speak these things.
29And he that
sent me is with me:
the Father hath not
left me alone; for I
do always those
things that please
him.

8:29 Pleasing God
◄ Matthew 3:17
1 Thessalonians 2:4 ►

30As he spake
these words, many
believed on him.
31Then said Jesus
to those Jews which
believed on him, If ye continue in my
word, *then* are ye my disciples indeed;

8:29 Who Is Religious?
◄ John 1:47
Acts 10:2 ►

32And ye shall know the truth, and the
truth shall make you free.
33They answered him, We be Abraham's
seed, and were never in bondage to any man:
how sayest thou, Ye shall be made free?
34Jesus answered
them, Verily, verily,
I say unto you,
Whosoever com-
mitteth sin is the
servant of sin.

8:34 Bad Habits
◄ Proverbs 5:22
Acts 8:23 ►

35And the servant abideth not in the
house for ever: *but* the Son abideth ever.
36If the Son therefore shall make you
free, ye shall be free indeed.
37I know that ye are Abraham's seed; but
ye seek to kill me, because my word hath
no place in you.
38I speak that which I have seen with
my Father: and ye do that which ye have
seen with your father.
39They answered and said unto him,
Abraham is our father. Jesus saith unto
them, If ye were Abraham's children, ye
would do the works of Abraham.
40But now ye seek to kill me, a man that
hath told you the truth, which I have heard
of God: this did not Abraham.
41Ye do the deeds of your father. Then
said they to him, We be not born of fornication; we have one Father, *even* God.
42Jesus said unto them, If God were your
Father, ye would love me: for I proceeded
forth and came from God; neither came I
of myself, but he sent me.
43Why do ye not understand my speech?
even because ye cannot hear my word.
44Ye are of your father the devil, and the
lusts of *your* father ye will do. He was a
murderer from the beginning, and abode
not in the truth, because there is no truth
in him. When he speaketh a lie, he
speaketh of his own: for he is a liar, and
the father of it.
45And because I tell *you* the truth, ye believe me not.
46Which of you convinceth me of sin?
And if I say the truth, why do ye not believe me?
47He that is of God heareth God's words:
ye therefore hear *them* not, because ye are
not of God.
48Then answered the Jews, and said unto
him, Say we not well that thou art a Samaritan, and hast a devil?
49Jesus answered, I have not a devil; but
I honour my Father, and ye do dishonour
me.
50And I seek not mine own glory: there
is one that seeketh and judgeth.
51Verily, verily, I
say unto you, If a
man keep my say-
ing, he shall never
see death.
52Then said the
Jews unto him, Now we know that thou
hast a devil. Abraham is dead, and the
prophets; and thou sayest, If a man
keep my saying, he shall never taste of
death.

8:51 Eternal Life
◄ John 6:50
John 11:26 ►

53Art thou greater than our father Abraham, which is dead? and the prophets are
dead: whom makest thou thyself?
54Jesus answered, If I honour myself, my
honour is nothing: it is my Father that

might be fulfilled, which he spake, Lord,
who hath believed our report? and to
whom hath the arm of the Lord been revealed?
39 Therefore they could not believe, because that Esaias said again,
40 He hath blinded their eyes, and hardened their heart; that they should not see
with *their* eyes, nor understand with *their*
heart, and be converted, and I should heal
them.
41 These things
said Esaias, when
he saw his glory,
and spake of him.
42 Nevertheless
among the chief
rulers also many believed on him; but because of the Pharisees they did not confess *him*, lest they should be put out of the
synagogue:

12:42 Publicly Christian
◀ John 7:13
John 19:38 ▶

43 For they loved
the praise of men
more than the
praise of God.
44 Jesus cried and
said, He that believ-
eth on me, believeth not on me, but on
him that sent me.

12:43 Popularity
◀ Acts 12:1-3 ▶

45 And he that seeth me seeth him that
sent me.
46 I am come a
light into the world,
that whosoever be-
lieveth on me
should not abide in
darkness.

12:46 Salvation by Faith
◀ John 11:25
John 20:31 ▶

47 And if any man hear my words, and
believe not, I judge him not: for I came not
to judge the world, but to save the world.
48 He that rejecteth me, and receiveth not
my words, hath one that judgeth him: the
word that I have spoken, the same shall
judge him in the last day.
49 For I have not spoken of myself; but
the Father which sent me, he gave me a
commandment, what I should say, and
what I should speak.
50 And I know that his commandment
is life everlasting: whatsoever I speak therefore, even as the Father said unto me, so I
speak.

13

1 Now before the feast of the passover,
when Jesus knew that his hour was come
that he should depart out of this world
unto the Father,
having loved his
own which were in
the world, he loved
them unto the end.
2 And supper be-
ing ended, the devil having now put into
the heart of Judas Iscariot, Simon's *son*, to
betray him;

13:1 Being a Friend
◀ John 11:16
Romans 16:4 ▶

3 Jesus knowing that the Father had giv-
en all things into his hands, and that he
was come from God, and went to God;
4 He riseth from supper, and laid aside
his garments; and took a towel, and girded
himself.
5 After that he poureth water into a
bason, and began to wash the disciples'
feet, and to wipe *them* with the towel
wherewith he was girded.
6 Then cometh he to Simon Peter: and
Peter saith unto him, Lord, dost thou wash
my feet?
7 Jesus answered and said unto him,
What I do thou knowest not now; but thou
shalt know hereafter.
8 Peter saith unto him, Thou shalt never
wash my feet. Jesus answered him, If I wash
thee not, thou hast no part with me.
9 Simon Peter saith unto him, Lord, not
my feet only, but also *my* hands and *my*
head.
10 Jesus saith to him, He that is washed
needeth not save to wash *his* feet, but is
clean every whit: and ye are clean, but not
all.
11 For he knew who should betray him;
therefore said he, Ye are not all clean.
12 So after he had washed their feet, and
had taken his garments, and was set down
again, he said unto them, Know ye what I
have done to you?
13 Ye call me Master and Lord: and ye
say well; for so I am.
14 If I then, *your*
Lord and Master,
have washed your
feet; ye also ought
to wash one anoth-
er's feet.

13:14 Serving People
◀ Luke 10:36-37
John 21:16 ▶

15 For I have giv-
en you an example,
that ye should do as
I have done to you.
16 Verily, verily, I
say unto you, The

13:15 Free Samples
◀ 2 Thessalonians 3:9 ▶

servant is not greater than his lord; neither he that is sent greater than he that sent
him.
17 If ye know
these things, happy
are ye if ye do them.
18 I speak not of
you all: I know
whom I have cho-
sen: but that the scripture may be fulfilled,
He that eateth bread with me hath lifted
up his heel against me.

13:17 Source of Happiness
◄ Proverbs 29:18 ►

19 Now I tell you before it come, that,
when it is come to pass, ye may believe
that I am *he*.
20 Verily, verily, I say unto you, He that
receiveth whomsoever I send receiveth me;
and he that receiveth me receiveth him that
sent me.
21 When Jesus had thus said, he was troubled in spirit, and testified, and said, Verily, verily, I say unto you, that one of you
shall betray me.
22 Then the disciples looked one on another, doubting of whom he spake.
23 Now there was
leaning on Jesus'
bosom one of his
disciples, whom
Jesus loved.
24 Simon Peter
therefore beckoned to him, that he should
ask who it should be of whom he spake.

13:23 Jesus' Friends
◄ John 11:35-36
John 15:15 ►

25 He then lying on Jesus' breast saith
unto him, Lord, who is it?
26 Jesus answered, He it is, to whom I
shall give a sop, when I have dipped *it*.
And when he had dipped the sop, he gave
it to Judas Iscariot, *the son* of Simon.
27 And after the sop Satan entered into
him. Then said Jesus unto him, That thou
doest, do quickly.
28 Now no man at the table knew for
what intent he spake this unto him.
29 For some *of them* thought, because Judas had the bag, that Jesus had said unto
him, Buy *those things* that we have need of
against the feast; or, that he should give
something to the poor.
30 He then having received the sop went
immediately out: and it was night.
31 Therefore, when he was gone out, Jesus
said, Now is the Son of man glorified, and
God is glorified in him.
32 If God be glorified in him, God shall
also glorify him in himself, and shall
straightway glorify him.
33 Little children, yet a little while I am
with you. Ye shall seek me: and as I said
unto the Jews, Whither I go, ye cannot
come; so now I say to you.
34 A new commandment I give unto you,
That ye love one another; as I have loved
you, that ye also love one another.
35 By this shall all
men know that ye
are my disciples, if
ye have love one to
another.
36 Simon Peter
said unto him,
Lord, whither goest
thou? Jesus an-
swered him, Whith-
er I go, thou canst
not follow me now;
but thou shalt follow me afterwards.

13:35 Love
◄ John 21:16 ►

13:35 Loving Others
◄ Matthew 22:39
John 15:12 ►

37 Peter said unto him, Lord, why cannot I follow thee now? I will lay down my
life for thy sake.
38 Jesus answered him, Wilt thou lay
down thy life for my sake? Verily, verily, I
say unto thee, The cock shall not crow, till
thou hast denied me thrice.

14

1 Let not your heart be troubled: ye believe in God, believe also in me.
2 In my Father's house are many man-
sions: if *it were* not *so*, I would have told
you. I go to prepare a place for you.
3 And if I go and
prepare a place for
you, I will come
again, and receive
you unto myself;
that where I am,
there ye may be also.

14:3 Good News
◄ Luke 12:37
Philippians 3:20-21 ►

4 And whither I go ye know, and the way
ye know.
5 Thomas saith unto him, Lord, we know
not whither thou goest; and how can we
know the way?
6 Jesus saith unto him, I am the way, the
truth, and the life: no man cometh unto
the Father, but by me.
7 If ye had known me, ye should have
known my Father also: and from henceforth ye know him, and have seen him.
8 Philip saith unto him, Lord, shew us
the Father, and it sufficeth us.
9 Jesus saith unto him, Have I been so

long time with you, and yet hast thou not known me, Philip? he that hath seen me hath seen the Father; and how sayest thou *then*, Shew us the Father?

10 Believest thou not that I am in the Father, and the Father in me? the words that I speak unto you I speak not of myself: but the Father that dwelleth in me, he doeth the works.

11 Believe me that I *am* in the Father, and the Father in me: or else believe me for the very works' sake.

12 Verily, verily, I say unto you, He that believeth on me, the works that I do shall he do also; and greater *works* than these shall he do; because I go unto my Father.

14:12 Benefits of Faith
◄ John 7:38
Romans 10:11 ►

13 And whatsoever ye shall ask in my name, that will I do, that the Father may be glorified in the Son.

14:13 Prayer
◄ Matthew 21:22
John 15:7 ►

14 If ye shall ask any thing in my name, I will do *it*.

15 If ye love me, keep my commandments.

14:14 Answers to Prayer
◄ Luke 11:9
John 15:7 ►

16 And I will pray the Father, and he shall give you another Comforter, that he may abide with you for ever;

17 *Even* the Spirit of truth; whom the world cannot receive, because it seeth him not, neither knoweth him: but ye know him; for he dwelleth with you, and shall be in you.

14:17 The Spirit in You
◄ Ezekiel 36:27
Romans 8:9 ►

18 I will not leave you comfortless: I will come to you.

19 Yet a little while, and the world seeth me no more; but ye see me: because I live, ye shall live also.

20 At that day ye shall know that I *am* in my Father, and ye in me, and I in you.

14:20 Jesus' Home
◄ John 17:23 ►

21 He that hath my commandments, and keepeth them, he it is that loveth me: and he that loveth me shall be loved of my Father, and I will love him, and will manifest myself to him.

14:21 Obeying Christ
◄ John 11:29
John 21:6 ►

22 Judas saith unto him, not Iscariot, Lord, how is it that thou wilt manifest thyself unto us, and not unto the world?

23 Jesus answered and said unto him, If a man love me, he will keep my words: and my Father will love him, and we will come unto him, and make our abode with him.

24 He that loveth me not keepeth not my sayings: and the word which ye hear is not mine, but the Father's which sent me.

25 These things have I spoken unto you, being *yet* present with you.

26 But the Comforter, *which is* the Holy Ghost, whom the Father will send in my name, he shall teach you all things, and bring all things to your remembrance, whatsoever I have said unto you.

14:26 God's Teaching
◄ Luke 12:12
1 Corinthians 2:13 ►

27 Peace I leave with you, my peace I give unto you: not as the world giveth, give I unto you. Let not your heart be troubled, neither let it be afraid.

14:27 Peace of Mind
◄ Ezekiel 34:25
John 16:33 ►

28 Ye have heard how I said unto you, I go away, and come *again* unto you. If ye loved me, ye would rejoice, because I said, I go unto the Father: for my Father is greater than I.

29 And now I have told you before it come to pass, that, when it is come to pass, ye might believe.

30 Hereafter I will not talk much with you: for the prince of this world cometh, and hath nothing in me.

14:30 Defeat of Satan
◄ John 12:30-31
2 Thessalonians 2:8 ►

31 But that the world may know that I love the Father; and as the Father gave me commandment, even so I do. Arise, let us go hence.

15

1I am the true vine, and my Father is the
husbandman.
2Every branch in
me that beareth not
fruit he taketh
away: and every
branch that beareth
fruit, he purgeth it,
that it may bring forth more fruit.

15:2 Difficulties
◄ Proverbs 3:11-12
Revelation 3:19 ►

3Now ye are
clean through the
word which I have
spoken unto you.
4Abide in me,
and I in you. As the
branch cannot bear fruit of itself, except it
abide in the vine; no more can ye, except
ye abide in me.

15:3 Purity
◄ Psalm 119:9
John 17:17 ►

5I am the vine, ye
are the branches:
He that abideth in
me, and I in him,
the same bringeth
forth much fruit:
for without me ye
can do nothing.

15:5 Cost of Sin
◄ Mark 9:18 ►

6If a man abide
not in me, he is cast
forth as a branch,
and is withered;
and men gather
them, and cast *them*
into the fire, and
they are burned.

15:5 Feeling Helpless
◄ John 6:44
Acts 3:2 ►

15:5 God's Role
◄ John 3:27
2 Corinthians 3:5 ►

7If ye abide in
me, and my words
abide in you, ye
shall ask what ye
will, and it shall be
done unto you.
8Herein is my Fa-
ther glorified, that
ye bear much fruit;
so shall ye be my
disciples.

15:7 Answers to Prayer
◄ John 14:14
1 John 3:22 ►

15:7 Prayer
◄ John 14:13
Acts 16:25-26 ►

9As the Father
hath loved me, so
have I loved you:
continue ye in my
love.
10If ye keep my
commandments, ye
shall abide in my
love; even as I
have kept my Fa-
ther's commandments, and abide in his
love.

15:9 Determination
◄ Job 17:9
Acts 13:43 ►

11These things
have I spoken unto
you, that my joy
might remain in
you, and *that* your
joy might be full.

15:11 Jesus' Joy
◄ Luke 15:5
John 17:13 ►

12This is my com-
mandment, That ye
love one another, as
I have loved you.
13Greater love
hath no man than
this, that a man lay
down his life for his
friends.

15:11 Joy
◄ Luke 2:10
John 16:24 ►

15:12 Loving Others
◄ John 13:35
Romans 12:9 ►

14Ye are my
friends, if ye do
whatsoever I com-
mand you.
15Henceforth I
call you not ser-
vants; for the ser-
vant knoweth not
what his lord
doeth: but I have
called you friends;
for all things that I
have heard of my
Father I have made
known unto you.

15:13-14 Friendship
◄ Ecclesiastes 4:9-10
►

15:15 Jesus' Friends
◄ John 13:23 ►

16Ye have not
chosen me, but I have chosen you, and ordained you, that ye should go and bring
forth fruit, and *that* your fruit should remain: that whatsoever ye shall ask of the
Father in my name, he may give it you.
17These things I command you, that ye
love one another.
18If the world hate you, ye know that *it*
hated me before it hated you.
19If ye were of the world, the world
would love his own: but because ye are not
of the world, but I have chosen you out of
the world, therefore the world hateth you.
20Remember the
word that I said
unto you, The ser-
vant is not greater
than his lord. If they
have persecuted me,
they will also persecute you; if they have
kept my saying, they will keep yours also.
21But all these things will they do unto

15:20 Expecting Pain
◄ Luke 21:12
John 16:2 ►

you for my name's sake, because they know not him that sent me.

22 If I had not come and spoken unto them, they had not had sin: but now they have no cloke for their sin.

23 He that hateth me hateth my Father also.

24 If I had not done among them the works which none other man did, they had not had sin: but now have they both seen and hated both me and my Father.

25 But *this cometh to pass,* that the word might be fulfilled that is written in their law, They hated me without a cause.

26 But when the Comforter is come, whom I will send unto you from the Father, *even* the Spirit of truth, which proceedeth from the Father, he shall testify of me:

27 And ye also shall bear witness, because ye have been with me from the beginning.

15:27 Witnessing
◄ Isaiah 43:10
Acts 1:8 ►

16

1 These things have I spoken unto you, that ye should not be offended.

2 They shall put you out of the synagogues: yea, the time cometh, that whosoever killeth you will think that he doeth God service.

16:2 Expecting Pain
◄ John 15:20
2 Timothy 3:12 ►

3 And these things will they do unto you, because they have not known the Father, nor me.

4 But these things have I told you, that when the time shall come, ye may remember that I told you of them. And these things I said not unto you at the beginning, because I was with you.

5 But now I go my way to him that sent me; and none of you asketh me, Whither goest thou?

6 But because I have said these things unto you, sorrow hath filled your heart.

7 Nevertheless I tell you the truth; It is expedient for you that I go away: for if I go not away, the Comforter will not come unto you; but if I depart, I will send him unto you.

16:8 Not Confessing
◄ Psalm 73:21
Acts 2:37 ►

8 And when he is come, he will reprove the world of sin, and of righteousness, and of judgment:

9 Of sin, because they believe not on me;

10 Of righteousness, because I go to my Father, and ye see me no more;

11 Of judgment, because the prince of this world is judged.

12 I have yet many things to say unto you, but ye cannot bear them now.

13 Howbeit when he, the Spirit of truth, is come, he will guide you into all truth: for he shall not speak of himself; but whatsoever he shall hear, *that* shall he speak: and he will shew you things to come.

16:13 God's Guidance
◄ John 10:4 ►

16:13 Guidance
◄ Acts 8:39 ►

14 He shall glorify me: for he shall receive of mine, and shall shew *it* unto you.

15 All things that the Father hath are mine: therefore said I, that he shall take of mine, and shall shew *it* unto you.

16 A little while, and ye shall not see me: and again, a little while, and ye shall see me, because I go to the Father.

17 Then said *some* of his disciples among themselves, What is this that he saith unto us, A little while, and ye shall not see me: and again, a little while, and ye shall see me: and, Because I go to the Father?

18 They said therefore, What is this that he saith, A little while? we cannot tell what he saith.

19 Now Jesus knew that they were desirous to ask him, and said unto them, Do ye enquire among yourselves of that I said, A little while, and ye shall not see me: and again, a little while, and ye shall see me?

20 Verily, verily, I say unto you, That ye shall weep and lament, but the world shall rejoice: and ye shall be sorrowful, but your sorrow shall be turned into joy.

21 A woman when she is in travail hath sorrow, because her hour is come: but as soon as she is delivered of the child, she remembereth no more the anguish, for joy that a man is born into the world.

22 And ye now therefore have sorrow: but I will see you again, and your heart shall rejoice, and your joy no man taketh from you.

23 And in that day ye shall ask me nothing. Verily, verily, I say unto you, Whatsoever ye shall ask the Father in my name,
he will give *it* you.
24 Hitherto have
ye asked nothing in
my name: ask, and
ye shall receive, that
your joy may be
full.

16:24 Duty to Pray
◄ Luke 21:36
Ephesians 6:18 ►

25 These things
have I spoken unto
you in proverbs:
but the time
cometh, when I
shall no more speak
unto you in prov-
erbs, but I shall shew you plainly of the
Father.

16:24 Joy
◄ John 15:11
John 17:13 ►

26 At that day ye shall ask in my name:
and I say not unto you, that I will pray the
Father for you:
27 For the Father
himself loveth you,
because ye have
loved me, and have
believed that I came
out from God.

16:27 God's Love
◄ John 3:16
Romans 5:8 ►

28 I came forth from the Father, and am
come into the world: again, I leave the
world, and go to the Father.
29 His disciples said unto him, Lo, now
speakest thou plainly, and speakest no
proverb.
30 Now are we sure that thou knowest
all things, and needest not that any man
should ask thee: by this we believe that
thou camest forth
from God.
31 Jesus answered
them, Do ye now
believe?

16:32 Loneliness
◄ Psalm 102:7
2 Timothy 4:16 ►

32 Behold, the
hour cometh, yea,
is now come, that
ye shall be scat-
tered, every man to
his own, and shall
leave me alone: and
yet I am not alone,
because the Father
is with me.

16:32 Whom Can You Trust?
◄ Matthew 26:56
2 Timothy 1:15 ►

33 These things I
have spoken unto
you, that in me ye
might have peace.
In the world ye
shall have tribula-
tion: but be of good
cheer; I have over-
come the world.

16:33 Peace of Mind
◄ John 14:27
Philippians 4:7 ►

16:33 Suffering
◄ Matthew 24:21
Acts 14:22 ►

17

1 These words spake Jesus, and lifted up
his eyes to heaven, and said, Father, the
hour is come; glorify thy Son, that thy Son
also may glorify thee:
2 As thou hast given him power over all
flesh, that he should give eternal life to as
many as thou hast given him.
3 And this is life eternal, that they might
know thee the only true God, and Jesus
Christ, whom thou hast sent.
4 I have glorified
thee on the earth: I
have finished the
work which thou
gavest me to do.

17:4 Job One
◄ John 4:34
Acts 20:24 ►

5 And now, O Fa-
ther, glorify thou me with thine own self
with the glory which I had with thee before the world was.
6 I have manifested thy name unto the
men which thou gavest me out of the
world: thine they were, and thou gavest
them me; and they have kept thy word.
7 Now they have known that all things
whatsoever thou hast given me are of thee.
8 For I have given unto them the words
which thou gavest me; and they have received *them*, and have known surely that I
came out from thee, and they have believed
that thou didst send me.
9 I pray for them: I pray not for the world,
but for them which thou hast given me;
for they are thine.
10 And all mine are thine, and thine are
mine; and I am glorified in them.
11 And now I am no more in the world,
but these are in the world, and I come to
thee. Holy Father, keep through thine own
name those whom thou hast given me,
that they may be one, as we *are*.
12 While I was with them in the world, I
kept them in thy name: those that thou
gavest me I have kept, and none of them
is lost, but the son
of perdition; that
the scripture might
be fulfilled.
13 And now come
I to thee; and these

17:13 Jesus' Joy
◄ John 15:11
Hebrews 12:2 ►

things I speak in the
world, that they
might have my joy
fulfilled in them-
selves.

17:13 Joy
◄ John 16:24
Romans 14:17 ►

14I have given
them thy word; and the world hath hated
them, because they are not of the world,
even as I am not of the world.
15I pray not that thou shouldest take
them out of the world, but that thou
shouldest keep them from the evil.
16They are not of the world, even as I
am not of the world.
17Sanctify them
through thy truth:
thy word is truth.
18As thou hast
sent me into the
world, even so have
I also sent them into the world.

17:17 Purity
◄ John 15:3
Ephesians 5:26 ►

19And for their sakes I sanctify myself,
that they also might be sanctified through
the truth.
20Neither pray I for these alone, but for
them also which shall believe on me
through their word;
21That they all may be one; as thou, Father, *art* in me, and I in thee, that they also
may be one in us: that the world may believe that thou hast sent me.
22And the glory which thou gavest me I
have given them; that they may be one,
even as we are one:
23I in them, and
thou in me, that
they may be made
perfect in one; and
that the world may
know that thou
hast sent me, and hast loved them, as thou
hast loved me.

17:23 Jesus' Home
◄ John 14:20
Romans 8:10 ►

24Father, I will that they also, whom
thou hast given me, be with me where I
am; that they may behold my glory, which
thou hast given me: for thou lovedst me
before the foundation of the world.
25O righteous Father, the world hath
not known thee: but I have known thee,
and these have known that thou hast
sent me.
26And I have declared unto them thy
name, and will declare *it:* that the love
wherewith thou hast loved me may be in
them, and I in them.

18

1When Jesus had spoken these words,
he went forth with his disciples over the
brook Cedron, where was a garden, into
the which he entered, and his disciples.
2And Judas also, which betrayed him,
knew the place: for Jesus ofttimes resorted
thither with his disciples.
3Judas then, having received a band *of
men* and officers from the chief priests and
Pharisees, cometh thither with lanterns
and torches and weapons.
4Jesus therefore, knowing all things that
should come upon him, went forth, and
said unto them, Whom seek ye?
5They answered him, Jesus of Nazareth.
Jesus saith unto them, I am *he.* And Judas
also, which betrayed him, stood with
them.
6As soon then as he had said unto them,
I am *he,* they went backward, and fell to
the ground.
7Then asked he them again, Whom seek
ye? And they said, Jesus of Nazareth.
8Jesus answered, I have told you that I
am *he:* if therefore ye seek me, let these go
their way:
9That the saying might be fulfilled,
which he spake, Of them which thou
gavest me have I lost none.
10Then Simon Peter having a sword drew
it, and smote the high priest's servant, and
cut off his right ear. The servant's name was
Malchus.
11Then said Jesus unto Peter, Put up thy
sword into the sheath: the cup which my
Father hath given me, shall I not drink it?
12Then the band and the captain and
officers of the Jews took Jesus, and bound
him,
13And led him away to Annas first; for
he was father in law to Caiaphas, which
was the high priest that same year.
14Now Caiaphas was he, which gave
counsel to the Jews, that it was expedient
that one man should die for the people.
15And Simon Peter followed Jesus, and
so did another disciple: that disciple was
known unto the high priest, and went in
with Jesus into the palace of the high
priest.
16But Peter stood at the door without.
Then went out that other disciple, which
was known unto the high priest, and spake
unto her that kept the door, and brought
in Peter.

17 Then saith the damsel that kept the door unto Peter, Art not thou also *one* of this man's disciples? He saith, I am not.

18 And the servants and officers stood there, who had made a fire of coals; for it was cold: and they warmed themselves: and Peter stood with them, and warmed himself.

19 The high priest then asked Jesus of his disciples, and of his doctrine.

20 Jesus answered him, I spake openly to the world; I ever taught in the synagogue, and in the temple, whither the Jews always resort; and in secret have I said nothing.

21 Why askest thou me? ask them which heard me, what I have said unto them: behold, they know what I said.

22 And when he had thus spoken, one of the officers which stood by struck Jesus with the palm of his hand, saying, Answerest thou the high priest so?

23 Jesus answered him, If I have spoken evil, bear witness of the evil: but if well, why smitest thou me?

24 Now Annas had sent him bound unto Caiaphas the high priest.

25 And Simon Peter stood and warmed himself. They said therefore unto him, Art not thou also *one* of his disciples? He denied *it*, and said, I am not.

26 One of the servants of the high priest, being *his* kinsman whose ear Peter cut off, saith, Did not I see thee in the garden with him?

27 Peter then denied again: and immediately the cock crew.

28 Then led they Jesus from Caiaphas unto the hall of judgment: and it was early; and they themselves went not into the judgment hall, lest they should be defiled; but that they might eat the passover.

29 Pilate then went out unto them, and said, What accusation bring ye against this man?

30 They answered and said unto him, If he were not a malefactor, we would not have delivered him up unto thee.

31 Then said Pilate unto them, Take ye him, and judge him according to your law. The Jews therefore said unto him, It is not lawful for us to put any man to death:

32 That the saying of Jesus might be fulfilled, which he spake, signifying what death he should die.

33 Then Pilate entered into the judgment hall again, and called Jesus, and said unto him, Art thou the King of the Jews?

34 Jesus answered him, Sayest thou this thing of thyself, or did others tell it thee of me?

35 Pilate answered, Am I a Jew? Thine own nation and the chief priests have delivered thee unto me: what hast thou done?

36 Jesus answered, My kingdom is not of this world: if my kingdom were of this world, then would my servants fight, that I should not be delivered to the Jews: but now is my kingdom not from hence.

37 Pilate therefore said unto him, Art thou a king then? Jesus answered, Thou sayest that I am a king. To this end was I born, and for this cause came I into the world, that I should bear witness unto the truth. Every one that is of the truth heareth my voice.

18:37 Jesus the King
◄ John 1:49
1 Corinthians 15:25 ►

38 Pilate saith unto him, What is truth? And when he had said this, he went out again unto the Jews, and saith unto them, I find in him no fault *at all*.

39 But ye have a custom, that I should release unto you one at the passover: will ye therefore that I release unto you the King of the Jews?

40 Then cried they all again, saying, Not this man, but Barabbas. Now Barabbas was a robber.

19

1 Then Pilate therefore took Jesus, and scourged *him*.

2 And the soldiers platted a crown of thorns, and put *it* on his head, and they put on him a purple robe,

3 And said, Hail, King of the Jews! and they smote him with their hands.

4 Pilate therefore went forth again, and saith unto them, Behold, I bring him forth to you, that ye may know that I find no fault in him.

5 Then came Jesus forth, wearing the crown of thorns, and the purple robe. And *Pilate* saith unto them, Behold the man!

6 When the chief priests therefore and officers saw him, they cried out, saying, Crucify *him*, crucify *him*. Pilate saith unto them, Take ye him, and crucify *him*: for I find no fault in him.

7 The Jews answered him, We have a law,

and by our law he ought to die, because he made himself the Son of God.

8 When Pilate therefore heard that saying, he was the more afraid;

9 And went again into the judgment hall, and saith unto Jesus, Whence art thou? But Jesus gave him no answer.

10 Then saith Pilate unto him, Speakest thou not unto me? knowest thou not that I have power to crucify thee, and have power to release thee?

11 Jesus answered, Thou couldest have no power *at all* against me, except it were given thee from above: therefore he that delivered me unto thee hath the greater sin.

12 And from thenceforth Pilate sought to release him: but the Jews cried out, saying, If thou let this man go, thou art not Caesar's friend: whosoever maketh himself a king speaketh against Caesar.

13 When Pilate therefore heard that saying, he brought Jesus forth, and sat down in the judgment seat in a place that is called the Pavement, but in the Hebrew, Gabbatha.

14 And it was the preparation of the passover, and about the sixth hour: and he saith unto the Jews, Behold your King!

15 But they cried out, Away with *him,* away with *him,* crucify him. Pilate saith unto them, Shall I crucify your King? The chief priests answered, We have no king but Caesar.

19:15 Fanatics
◄ 1 Kings 18:28
Acts 7:57 ►

16 Then delivered he him therefore unto them to be crucified. And they took Jesus, and led *him* away.

17 And he bearing his cross went forth into a place called *the place* of a skull, which is called in the Hebrew Golgotha:

18 Where they crucified him, and two others with him, on either side one, and Jesus in the midst.

19 And Pilate wrote a title, and put *it* on the cross. And the writing was, JESUS of NAZARETH THE KING OF THE JEWS.

20 This title then read many of the Jews: for the place where Jesus was crucified was nigh to the city: and it was written in Hebrew, *and* Greek, *and* Latin.

21 Then said the chief priests of the Jews to Pilate, Write not, The King of the Jews; but that he said, I am King of the Jews.

22 Pilate answered, What I have written I have written.

23 Then the soldiers, when they had crucified Jesus, took his garments, and made four parts, to every soldier a part; and also *his* coat: now the coat was without seam, woven from the top throughout.

24 They said therefore among themselves, Let us not rend it, but cast lots for it, whose it shall be: that the scripture might be fulfilled, which saith, They parted my raiment among them, and for my vesture they did cast lots. These things therefore the soldiers did.

25 Now there stood by the cross of Jesus his mother, and his mother's sister, Mary the *wife* of Cleophas, and Mary Magdalene.

26 When Jesus therefore saw his mother, and the disciple standing by, whom he loved, he saith unto his mother, Woman, behold thy son!

27 Then saith he to the disciple, Behold thy mother! And from that hour that disciple took her unto his own *home.*

28 After this, Jesus knowing that all things were now accomplished, that the scripture might be fulfilled, saith, I thirst.

29 Now there was set a vessel full of vinegar: and they filled a spunge with vinegar, and put *it* upon hyssop, and put *it* to his mouth.

30 When Jesus therefore had received the vinegar, he said, It is finished: and he bowed his head, and gave up the ghost.

31 The Jews therefore, because it was the preparation, that the bodies should not remain upon the cross on the sabbath day, (for that sabbath day was an high day,) besought Pilate that their legs might be broken, and *that* they might be taken away.

32 Then came the soldiers, and brake the legs of the first, and of the other which was crucified with him.

33 But when they came to Jesus, and saw that he was dead already, they brake not his legs:

34 But one of the soldiers with a spear pierced his side, and forthwith came there out blood and water.

35 And he that saw *it* bare record, and his record is true: and he knoweth that he saith true, that ye might believe.

36 For these things were done, that the scripture should be fulfilled, A bone of him shall not be broken.

37 And again another scripture saith,
They shall look on him whom they
pierced.
38 And after this
Joseph of Ari-
mathaea, being a
disciple of Jesus, but
secretly for fear of
the Jews, besought
Pilate that he might take away the body of
Jesus: and Pilate gave *him* leave. He came
therefore, and took the body of Jesus.

19:38
Publicly Christian
◄ John 12:42 ►

39 And there came also Nicodemus,
which at the first came to Jesus by night,
and brought a mixture of myrrh and aloes, about an hundred pound *weight.*
40 Then took they the body of Jesus, and
wound it in linen clothes with the spices,
as the manner of the Jews is to bury.
41 Now in the place where he was crucified there was a garden; and in the garden
a new sepulchre, wherein was never man
yet laid.
42 There laid they Jesus therefore because
of the Jews' preparation *day;* for the sepulchre was nigh at hand.

20

1 The first *day* of the week cometh Mary
Magdalene early, when it was yet dark,
unto the sepulchre, and seeth the stone tak-
en away from the sepulchre.
2 Then she runneth, and cometh to Simon Peter, and to the other disciple, whom
Jesus loved, and saith unto them, They
have taken away the Lord out of the sepulchre, and we know not where they have
laid him.
3 Peter therefore went forth, and that other disciple, and came to the sepulchre.
4 So they ran both together: and the other disciple did outrun Peter, and came first
to the sepulchre.
5 And he stooping down, *and looking in,*
saw the linen clothes lying; yet went he
not in.
6 Then cometh Simon Peter following
him, and went into the sepulchre, and
seeth the linen clothes lie,
7 And the napkin, that was about his
head, not lying with the linen clothes, but
wrapped together in a place by itself.
8 Then went in also that other disciple,
which came first to the sepulchre, and he
saw, and believed.
9 For as yet they knew not the scripture,
that he must rise again from the dead.
10 Then the disciples went away again
unto their own home.
11 But Mary stood
without at the sep-
ulchre weeping:
and as she wept,
she stooped down,
and looked into the
sepulchre,
12 And seeth two
angels in white sit-
ting, the one at the
head, and the oth-
er at the feet, where
the body of Jesus had lain.

20:11 Grief
◄ John 11:33
Acts 9:39 ►

20:11 Loving Jesus
◄ John 12:3
John 21:16 ►

13 And they say unto her, Woman, why
weepest thou? She saith unto them, Because they have taken away my Lord, and
I know not where they have laid him.
14 And when she had thus said, she
turned herself back, and saw Jesus standing, and knew not that it was Jesus.
15 Jesus saith unto her, Woman, why
weepest thou? whom seekest thou? She,
supposing him to be the gardener, saith
unto him, Sir, if thou have borne him
hence, tell me where thou hast laid him,
and I will take him away.
16 Jesus saith unto her, Mary. She turned
herself, and saith unto him, Rabboni;
which is to say, Master.
17 Jesus saith unto her, Touch me not;
for I am not yet ascended to my Father:
but go to my brethren, and say unto them,
I ascend unto my Father, and your Father;
and *to* my God, and your God.
18 Mary Magdalene came and told the
disciples that she had seen the Lord, and
that he had spoken these things unto her.
19 Then the same day at evening, being
the first *day* of the week, when the doors
were shut where the disciples were assembled for fear of the Jews, came Jesus and
stood in the midst, and saith unto them,
Peace *be* unto you.
20 And when he had so said, he shewed
unto them *his* hands and his side. Then
were the disciples glad, when they saw the
Lord.
21 Then said Jesus to them again, Peace
be unto you: as *my* Father hath sent me,
even so send I you.
22 And when he had said this, he
breathed on *them,* and saith unto them,
Receive ye the Holy Ghost:

23 Whose soever sins ye remit, they are remitted unto them; *and* whose soever *sins* ye retain, they are retained.

24 But Thomas, one of the twelve, called Didymus, was not with them when Jesus came.

25 The other disciples therefore said unto him, We have seen the Lord. But he said unto them, Except I shall see in his hands the print of the nails, and put my finger into the print of the nails, and thrust my hand into his side, I will not believe.

26 And after eight days again his disciples were within, and Thomas with them: *then* came Jesus, the doors being shut, and stood in the midst, and said, Peace *be* unto you.

27 Then saith he to Thomas, Reach hither thy finger, and behold my hands; and reach hither thy hand, and thrust *it* into my side: and be not faithless, but believing.

20:27 Faith
◄ John 6:28-29
Ephesians 6:16 ►

28 And Thomas answered and said unto him, My Lord and my God.

29 Jesus saith unto him, Thomas, because thou hast seen me, thou hast believed: blessed *are* they that have not seen, and *yet* have believed.

30 And many other signs truly did Jesus in the presence of his disciples, which are not written in this book:

31 But these are written, that ye might believe that Jesus is the Christ, the Son of God; and that believing ye might have life through his name.

20:31 Salvation by Faith
◄ John 12:46
Acts 10:43 ►

20:31
Why the Bible?
◄ Romans 15:4 ►

21

1 After these things Jesus shewed himself again to the disciples at the sea of Tiberias; and on this wise shewed he *himself*.

2 There were together Simon Peter, and Thomas called Didymus, and Nathanael of Cana in Galilee, and the *sons* of Zebedee, and two other of his disciples.

3 Simon Peter saith unto them, I go a fishing. They say unto him, We also go with thee. They went forth, and entered into a ship immediately; and that night they caught nothing.

4 But when the morning was now come, Jesus stood on the shore: but the disciples knew not that it was Jesus.

5 Then Jesus saith unto them, Children, have ye any meat? They answered him, No.

6 And he said unto them, Cast the net on the right side of the ship, and ye shall find. They cast therefore, and now they were not able to draw it for the multitude of fishes.

21:6
Obeying Christ
◄ John 14:21 ►

7 Therefore that disciple whom Jesus loved saith unto Peter, It is the Lord. Now when Simon Peter heard that it was the Lord, he girt *his* fisher's coat *unto him*, (for he was naked,) and did cast himself into the sea.

8 And the other disciples came in a little ship; (for they were not far from land, but as it were two hundred cubits,) dragging the net with fishes.

9 As soon then as they were come to land, they saw a fire of coals there, and fish laid thereon, and bread.

10 Jesus saith unto them, Bring of the fish which ye have now caught.

11 Simon Peter went up, and drew the net to land full of great fishes, and hundred and fifty and three: and for all there were so many, yet was not the net broken.

12 Jesus saith unto them, Come *and* dine. And none of the disciples durst ask him, Who art thou? knowing that it was the Lord.

13 Jesus then cometh, and taketh bread, and giveth them, and fish likewise.

14 This is now the third time that Jesus shewed himself to his disciples, after that he was risen from the dead.

15 So when they had dined, Jesus saith to Simon Peter, Simon, *son* of Jonas, lovest thou me more than these? He saith unto him, Yea, Lord; thou knowest that I love thee. He saith unto him, Feed my lambs.

16 He saith to him again the second time, Simon, *son* of Jonas, lovest thou me? He saith unto him, Yea, Lord; thou knowest that I love thee. He saith

21:16 Love
◄ John 13:35
1 Corinthians 13:1 ►

Turn to the next page for more . . .

unto him, Feed my sheep.

17 He saith unto him the third time, Simon, *son* of Jonas, lovest thou me? Peter was grieved because he said unto him the third time, Lovest thou me? And he said unto him, Lord, thou knowest all things; thou knowest that I love thee. Jesus saith unto him, Feed my sheep.

21:16 Loving Jesus
◄ John 20:11
Acts 21:13 ►

21:16 Serving People
◄ John 13:14
Galatians 5:13 ►

18 Verily, verily, I say unto thee, When thou wast young, thou girdedst thyself, and walkedst whither thou wouldest: but when thou shalt be old, thou shalt stretch forth thy hands, and another shall gird thee, and carry *thee* whither thou wouldest not.

19 This spake he, signifying by what death he should glorify God. And when he had spoken this, he saith unto him, Follow me.

20 Then Peter, turning about, seeth the disciple whom Jesus loved following; which also leaned on his breast at supper, and said, Lord, which is he that betrayeth thee?

21 Peter seeing him saith to Jesus, Lord, and what *shall* this man *do*?

22 Jesus saith unto him, If I will that he tarry till I come, what *is that* to thee? follow thou me.

23 Then went this saying abroad among the brethren, that that disciple should not die: yet Jesus said not unto him, He shall not die; but, If I will that he tarry till I come, what *is that* to thee?

24 This is the disciple which testifieth of these things, and wrote these things: and we know that his testimony is true.

25 And there are also many other things which Jesus did, the which, if they should be written every one, I suppose that even the world itself could not contain the books that should be written. Amen.

Acts

AUTHOR
Luke, a doctor and Gentile Christian

MAIN POINT
The church began with the fire of the Holy Spirit, then spread throughout the world so that everyone can hear about Jesus.

DATE WRITTEN
Between A.D. 63 and 70

28 CHAPTERS

MAIN PEOPLE

Peter, John, James, Stephen, Philip, Paul, Barnabas, Cornelius, James (Jesus' brother), Timothy, Lydia, Silas, Titus, Apollos, Agabus, Ananias, Felix, Festus, Agrippa, Luke

SPECIAL FEATURES

- *Was written by a doctor who was eyewitness to many of the events—the details are sharp and many*
- *Shows how the Holy Spirit brought the message of Christ to people of every language*
- *Includes the story of the first Christian in Africa*
- *Describes how Saul, who hated Christians, turned into the great apostle Paul, Christianity's first missionary, as well as his four missionary journeys and earthquake adventure*
- *Tells of a shipwreck*
- *Tells how Christianity got started*
- *Sequel to the four Gospels*

HOW THE BOOK GOT ITS NAME

The acts of the apostles (the early church) and the acts of the Holy Spirit take center stage in this book.

1

1 The former treatise have I made,
O Theophilus, of all that Jesus began both
to do and teach,
2 Until the day in which he was taken
up, after that he through the Holy Ghost
had given commandments unto the apostles whom he had chosen:
3 To whom also he shewed himself alive
after his passion by many infallible proofs,
being seen of them forty days, and speaking of the things pertaining to the kingdom of God:
4 And, being as-
sembled together
with *them*, com-
manded them that
they should not de-
part from Jerusa-
lem, but wait for the promise of the Father,
which, *saith he*, ye have heard of me.

1:4
Waiting
◄ Luke 2:25 ►

5For John truly baptized with water; but ye shall be baptized with the Holy Ghost not many days hence.

6When they therefore were come together, they asked of him, saying, Lord, wilt thou at this time restore again the kingdom to Israel?

7And he said unto them, It is not for you to know the times or the seasons, which the Father hath put in his own power.

8But ye shall receive power, after that the Holy Ghost is come upon you: and ye shall be witnesses unto me both in Jerusalem, and in all Judaea, and in Samaria, and unto the uttermost part of the earth.

1:8 The Holy Spirit
◄ Luke 4:14
Acts 2:2 ►

1:8 Witnessing
◄ John 15:27
Acts 5:20-21 ►

1:8 Your Testimony
◄ Mark 5:18-19
Ephesians 5:19 ►

9And when he had spoken these things, while they beheld, he was taken up; and a cloud received him out of their sight.

10And while they looked stedfastly toward heaven as he went up, behold, two men stood by them in white apparel;

11Which also said, Ye men of Galilee, why stand ye gazing up into heaven? this same Jesus, which is taken up from you into heaven, shall so come in like manner as ye have seen him go into heaven.

1:11 Second Coming
◄ Luke 21:27
Hebrews 9:28 ►

12Then returned they unto Jerusalem from the mount called Olivet, which is from Jerusalem a sabbath day's journey.

13And when they were come in, they went up into an upper room, where abode both Peter, and James, and John, and Andrew, Philip, and Thomas, Bartholomew, and Matthew, James *the son* of Alphaeus, and Simon Zelotes, and Judas *the brother* of James.

14These all continued with one accord in prayer and supplication, with the women, and Mary the mother of Jesus, and with his brethren.

15And in those days Peter stood up in the midst of the disciples, and said, (the number of names together were about an hundred and twenty,)

16Men *and* brethren, this scripture must needs have been fulfilled, which the Holy Ghost by the mouth of David spake before concerning Judas, which was guide to them that took Jesus.

17For he was numbered with us, and had obtained part of this ministry.

18Now this man purchased a field with the reward of iniquity; and falling headlong, he burst asunder in the midst, and all his bowels gushed out.

19And it was known unto all the dwellers at Jerusalem; insomuch as that field is called in their proper tongue, Aceldama, that is to say, The field of blood.

20For it is written in the book of Psalms, Let his habitation be desolate, and let no man dwell therein: and his bishoprick let another take.

21Wherefore of these men which have companied with us all the time that the Lord Jesus went in and out among us,

22Beginning from the baptism of John, unto that same day that he was taken up from us, must one be ordained to be a witness with us of his resurrection.

23And they appointed two, Joseph called Barsabas, who was surnamed Justus, and Matthias.

24And they prayed, and said, Thou, Lord, which knowest the hearts of all *men*, shew whether of these two thou hast chosen,

25That he may take part of this ministry and apostleship, from which Judas by transgression fell, that he might go to his own place.

26And they gave forth their lots; and the lot fell upon Matthias; and he was numbered with the eleven apostles.

2

1And when the day of Pentecost was fully come, they were all with one accord in one place.

2And suddenly there came a sound from heaven as of a rushing mighty wind, and it filled all the house where they were sitting.

2:2 The Holy Spirit
◄ Acts 1:8
Acts 4:33 ►

3And there appeared unto them cloven

tongues like as of fire, and it sat upon each of them.

4And they were all filled with the Holy Ghost, and began to speak with other tongues, as the Spirit gave them utterance.

5And there were dwelling at Jerusalem Jews, devout men, out of every nation under heaven.

6Now when this was noised abroad, the multitude came together, and were confounded, because that every man heard them speak in his own language.

7And they were all amazed and marvelled, saying one to another, Behold, are not all these which speak Galilaeans?

8And how hear we every man in our own tongue, wherein we were born?

9Parthians, and Medes, and Elamites, and the dwellers in Mesopotamia, and in Judaea, and Cappadocia, in Pontus, and Asia,

10Phrygia, and Pamphylia, in Egypt, and in the parts of Libya about Cyrene, and strangers of Rome, Jews and proselytes,

11Cretes and Arabians, we do hear them speak in our tongues the wonderful works of God.

12And they were all amazed, and were in doubt, saying one to another, What meaneth this?

13Others mocking said, These men are full of new wine.

2:13 Mocking
◄ Psalm 22:7
Acts 17:32 ►

14But Peter, standing up with the eleven, lifted up his voice, and said unto them, Ye men of Judaea, and all *ye* that dwell at Jerusalem, be this known unto you, and hearken to my words:

15For these are not drunken, as ye suppose, seeing it is *but* the third hour of the day.

16But this is that which was spoken by the prophet Joel;

17And it shall come to pass in the last days, saith God,I will pour out of my Spirit upon all flesh: and your sons and your daughters shall prophesy, and your young men shall see visions, and your old men shall dream dreams:

18And on my servants and on my handmaidens I will pour out in those days of my Spirit; and they shall prophesy:

19And I will shew wonders in heaven above, and signs in the earth beneath; blood, and fire, and vapour of smoke:

20The sun shall be turned into darkness, and the moon into blood, before that great and notable day of the Lord come:

21And it shall come to pass, *that* whosoever shall call on the name of the Lord shall be saved.

2:21
Salvation for Anyone
◄ Luke 3:6
Romans 5:18 ►

22Ye men of Israel, hear these words; Jesus of Nazareth, a man approved of God among you by miracles and wonders and signs, which God did by him in the midst of you, as ye yourselves also know:

23Him, being delivered by the determinate counsel and foreknowledge of God, ye have taken, and by wicked hands have crucified and slain:

24Whom God hath raised up, having loosed the pains of death: because it was not possible that he should be holden of it.

25For David speaketh concerning him, I foresaw the Lord always before my face, for he is on my right hand, that I should not be moved:

26Therefore did my heart rejoice, and my tongue was glad; moreover also my flesh shall rest in hope:

27Because thou wilt not leave my soul in hell, neither wilt thou suffer thine Holy One to see corruption.

28Thou hast made known to me the ways of life; thou shalt make me full of joy with thy countenance.

29Men *and* brethren, let me freely speak unto you of the patriarch David, that he is both dead and buried, and his sepulchre is with us unto this day.

30Therefore being a prophet, and knowing that God had sworn with an oath to him, that of the fruit of his loins, according to the flesh, he would raise up Christ to sit on his throne;

31He seeing this before spake of the resurrection of Christ, that his soul was not left in hell, neither his flesh did see corruption.

32This Jesus hath God raised up, whereof we all are witnesses.

33Therefore being by the right hand of God exalted, and having received of the Father the promise of the Holy Ghost, he

hath shed forth this, which ye now see and
hear.
34 For David is not ascended into the
heavens: but he saith himself, The LORD
said unto my Lord, Sit thou on my right
hand,
35 Until I make thy foes thy footstool.
36 Therefore let all the house of Israel
know assuredly, that God hath made that
same Jesus, whom ye have crucified, both
Lord and Christ.
37 Now when they
heard *this,* they
were pricked in
their heart, and said
unto Peter and to
the rest of the apos-
tles, Men *and* breth-
ren, what shall we
do?
38 Then Peter said
unto them, Repent,
and be baptized ev-
ery one of you in
the name of Jesus
Christ for the remis-
sion of sins, and ye
shall receive the gift
of the Holy Ghost.
39 For the prom-
ise is unto you, and
to your children,
and to all that are
afar off, *even* as
many as the Lord
our God shall call.
40 And with many
other words did he
testify and exhort,
saying, Save your-
selves from this un-
toward generation.
41 Then they that
gladly received his
word were bap-
tized: and the same
day there were add-
ed *unto them* about
three thousand souls.
42 And they continued stedfastly in the
apostles' doctrine and fellowship, and in
breaking of bread, and in prayers.
43 And fear came upon every soul: and
many wonders and signs were done by the
apostles.

2:37 Not Confessing
◄ John 16:8
Acts 16:29 ►

2:37 Willingness to Learn
◄ John 9:36
Acts 8:31 ►

2:38 Baptism
◄ John 3:5
Acts 10:48 ►

2:38 Forgiveness of Sin
◄ Luke 24:47
Romans 3:25 ►

2:38 Repentance
◄ Luke 15:7
Acts 3:19 ►

2:41 Accepting God's Word
◄ Luke 10:38-39
Acts 17:11 ►

44 And all that believed were together,
and had all things common;
45 And sold their possessions and goods,
and parted them to all *men,* as every man
had need.
46 And they, con-
tinuing daily with
one accord in the
temple, and break-
ing bread from
house to house, did
eat their meat with gladness and singleness of heart,
47 Praising God, and having favour with
all the people. And the Lord added to the
church daily such as should be saved.

2:46 Gladness
◄ Psalm 45:15
Acts 11:23 ►

3

1 Now Peter and John went up together
into the temple at the hour of prayer, *being* the ninth *hour.*
2 And a certain
man lame from his
mother's womb
was carried, whom
they laid daily at
the gate of the tem-
ple which is called Beautiful, to ask alms
of them that entered into the temple;
3 Who seeing Peter and John about to
go into the temple asked an alms.
4 And Peter, fastening his eyes upon him
with John, said, Look on us.
5 And he gave heed unto them, expecting to receive something of them.
6 Then Peter said, Silver and gold have I
none; but such as I have give I thee: In the
name of Jesus Christ of Nazareth rise up
and walk.
7 And he took him by the right hand, and
lifted *him* up: and immediately his feet and
ancle bones received strength.
8 And he leaping up stood, and walked,
and entered with them into the temple,
walking, and leaping, and praising God.
9 And all the people saw him walking
and praising God:
10 And they knew that it was he which
sat for alms at the Beautiful gate of the temple: and they were filled with wonder and
amazement at that which had happened
unto him.
11 And as the lame man which was
healed held Peter and John, all the people
ran together unto them in the porch that
is called Solomon's, greatly wondering.
12 And when Peter saw *it,* he answered

3:2 Feeling Helpless
◄ John 15:5
Romans 5:6 ►

unto the people, Ye men of Israel, why marvel ye at this? or why look ye so earnestly on us, as though by our own power or holiness we had made this man to walk?

13 The God of Abraham, and of Isaac, and of Jacob, the God of our fathers, hath glorified his Son Jesus; whom ye delivered up, and denied him in the presence of Pilate, when he was determined to let *him* go.

14 But ye denied the Holy One and the Just, and desired a murderer to be granted unto you;

15 And killed the Prince of life, whom God hath raised from the dead; whereof we are witnesses.

16 And his name through faith in his name hath made this man strong, whom ye see and know: yea, the faith which is by him hath given him this perfect soundness in the presence of you all.

17 And now, brethren, I wot that through ignorance ye did *it,* as *did* also your rulers.

3:17 Unknown Sins
◄ Luke 12:48
1 Timothy 1:13 ►

18 But those things, which God before had shewed by the mouth of all his prophets, that Christ should suffer, he hath so fulfilled.

19 Repent ye therefore, and be converted, that your sins may be blotted out, when the times of refreshing shall come from the presence of the Lord;

3:19 Repent!
◄ Luke 13:2-3
Acts 8:22 ►

3:19 Repentance
◄ Acts 2:38 ►

20 And he shall send Jesus Christ, which before was preached unto you:

21 Whom the heaven must receive until the times of restitution of all things, which God hath spoken by the mouth of all his holy prophets since the world began.

22 For Moses truly said unto the fathers, A prophet shall the Lord your God raise up unto you of your brethren, like unto me; him shall ye hear in all things whatsoever he shall say unto you.

23 And it shall come to pass, *that* every soul, which will not hear that prophet, shall be destroyed from among the people.

24 Yea, and all the prophets from Samuel and those that follow after, as many as have spoken, have likewise foretold of these days.

25 Ye are the children of the prophets, and of the covenant which God made with our fathers, saying unto Abraham, And in thy seed shall all the kindreds of the earth be blessed.

26 Unto you first God, having raised up his Son Jesus, sent him to bless you, in turning away every one of you from his iniquities.

4

1 And as they spake unto the people, the priests, and the captain of the temple, and the Sadducees, came upon them,

2 Being grieved that they taught the people, and preached through Jesus the resurrection from the dead.

3 And they laid hands on them, and put *them* in hold unto the next day: for it was now eventide.

4 Howbeit many of them which heard the word believed; and the number of the men was about five thousand.

5 And it came to pass on the morrow, that their rulers, and elders, and scribes,

6 And Annas the high priest, and Caiaphas, and John, and Alexander, and as many as were of the kindred of the high priest, were gathered together at Jerusalem.

7 And when they had set them in the midst, they asked, By what power, or by what name, have ye done this?

8 Then Peter, filled with the Holy Ghost, said unto them, Ye rulers of the people, and elders of Israel,

9 If we this day be examined of the good deed done to the impotent man, by what means he is made whole;

10 Be it known unto you all, and to all the people of Israel, that by the name of Jesus Christ of Nazareth, whom ye crucified, whom God raised from the dead, *even* by him doth this man stand here before you whole.

4:11 The Ultimate
◄ Matthew 21:42
Ephesians 2:20 ►

11 This is the stone which was set at nought of you builders, which is become the head of the corner.

4:12 Jesus
◄ John 8:24
1 Corinthians 2:2 ►

12 Neither is there salvation in any other: for there is

Turn to the next page for more . . .

none other name
under heaven given
among men, where-
by we must be
saved.

4:12 Only One Savior
◄ John 10:9
Acts 15:11 ►

[13]Now when they
saw the boldness of
Peter and John, and
perceived that they
were unlearned and
ignorant men, they
marvelled; and they
took knowledge of them, that they had
been with Jesus.

4:12 Our Savior
◄ John 6:67-68
1 Corinthians 3:11 ►

[14]And beholding the man which was
healed standing with them, they could say
nothing against it.
[15]But when they had commanded them
to go aside out of the council, they conferred among themselves,
[16]Saying, What shall we do to these
men? for that indeed a notable miracle
hath been done by them *is* manifest to all
them that dwell in Jerusalem; and we cannot deny *it*.
[17]But that it spread no further among
the people, let us straitly threaten them,
that they speak henceforth to no man in
this name.
[18]And they called them, and commanded them not to speak at all nor teach in
the name of Jesus.
[19]But Peter and John answered and said
unto them, Whether it be right in the sight
of God to hearken unto you more than
unto God, judge ye.
[20]For we cannot but speak the things
which we have seen and heard.
[21]So when they had further threatened
them, they let them go, finding nothing
how they might punish them, because of
the people: for all *men* glorified God for
that which was done.
[22]For the man was above forty years old,
on whom this miracle of healing was
shewed.
[23]And being let go, they went to their
own company, and reported all that the
chief priests and elders had said unto
them.
[24]And when they heard that, they lifted
up their voice to God with one accord, and
said, Lord, thou *art* God, which hast made
heaven, and earth, and the sea, and all that
in them is:
[25]Who by the mouth of thy servant David hast said, Why did the heathen rage,
and the people imagine vain things?
[26]The kings of the earth stood up, and
the rulers were gathered together against
the Lord, and against his Christ.
[27]For of a truth against thy holy child
Jesus, whom thou hast anointed, both
Herod, and Pontius Pilate, with the Gentiles, and the people of Israel, were gathered together,
[28]For to do whatsoever thy hand and thy
counsel determined before to be done.
[29]And now, Lord, behold their threatenings: and grant unto thy servants, that
with all boldness they may speak thy word,
[30]By stretching forth thine hand to heal;
and that signs and wonders may be done
by the name of thy holy child Jesus.
[31]And when they had prayed, the place
was shaken where they were assembled
together; and they were all filled with the
Holy Ghost, and they spake the word of
God with boldness.
[32]And the multitude of them that believed were of one heart and of one soul:
neither said any *of them* that ought of the
things which he possessed was his own;
but they had all things common.
[33]And with great
power gave the
apostles witness of
the resurrection of
the Lord Jesus: and
great grace was
upon them all.

4:33 The Holy Spirit
◄ Acts 2:2
Acts 6:8 ►

[34]Neither was
there any among
them that lacked:
for as many as were
possessors of lands
or houses sold them, and brought the
prices of the things that were sold,

4:34-35 Examples of Generosity
◄ Luke 21:1-4
Acts 11:29 ►

[35]And laid *them* down at the apostles'
feet: and distribution was made unto every man according as he had need.
[36]And Joses, who by the apostles was
surnamed Barnabas, (which is, being interpreted, The son of consolation,) a Levite, *and* of the country of Cyprus,
[37]Having land, sold *it*, and brought the
money, and laid *it* at the apostles' feet.

5

[1]But a certain man named Ananias, with
Sapphira his wife, sold a possession,
[2]And kept back *part* of the price, his wife

also being privy *to it,* and brought a certain part, and laid *it* at the apostles' feet.

3 But Peter said, Ananias, why hath Satan filled thine heart to lie to the Holy Ghost, and to keep back *part* of the price of the land?

4 Whiles it remained, was it not thine own? and after it was sold, was it not in thine own power? why hast thou conceived this thing in thine heart? thou hast not lied unto men, but unto God.

5 And Ananias hearing these words fell down, and gave up the ghost: and great fear came on all them that heard these things.

6 And the young men arose, wound him up, and carried *him* out, and buried *him.*

7 And it was about the space of three hours after, when his wife, not knowing what was done, came in.

8 And Peter answered unto her, Tell me whether ye sold the land for so much? And she said, Yea, for so much.

9 Then Peter said unto her, How is it that ye have agreed together to tempt the Spirit of the Lord? behold, the feet of them which have buried thy husband *are* at the door, and shall carry thee out.

10 Then fell she down straightway at his feet, and yielded up the ghost: and the young men came in, and found her dead, and, carrying *her* forth, buried *her* by her husband.

11 And great fear came upon all the church, and upon as many as heard these things.

12 And by the hands of the apostles were many signs and wonders wrought among the people; (and they were all with one accord in Solomon's porch.

13 And of the rest durst no man join himself to them: but the people magnified them.

14 And believers were the more added to the Lord, multitudes both of men and women.)

15 Insomuch that they brought forth the sick into the streets, and laid *them* on beds and couches, that at the least the shadow of Peter passing by might overshadow some of them.

16 There came also a multitude *out* of the cities round about unto Jerusalem, bringing sick folks, and them which were vexed with unclean spirits: and they were healed every one.

17 Then the high priest rose up, and all they that were with him, (which is the sect of the Sadducees,) and were filled with indignation,

18 And laid their hands on the apostles, and put them in the common prison.

19 But the angel of the Lord by night opened the prison doors, and brought them forth, and said,

20 Go, stand and speak in the temple to the people all the words of this life.

5:20-21 Witnessing
◄ Acts 1:8
Acts 18:9-10 ►

21 And when they heard *that,* they entered into the temple early in the morning, and taught. But the high priest came, and they that were with him, and called the council together, and all the senate of the children of Israel and sent to the prison to have them brought.

22 But when the officers came, and found them not in the prison, they returned, and told,

23 Saying, The prison truly found we shut with all safety, and the keepers standing without before the doors: but when we had opened, we found no man within.

24 Now when the high priest and the captain of the temple and the chief priests heard these things, they doubted of them whereunto this would grow.

25 Then came one and told them, saying, Behold, the men whom ye put in prison are standing in the temple, and teaching the people.

26 Then went the captain with the officers, and brought them without violence: for they feared the people, lest they should have been stoned.

27 And when they had brought them, they set *them* before the council: and the high priest asked them,

28 Saying, Did not we straitly command you that ye should not teach in this name? and, behold, ye have filled Jerusalem with your doctrine, and intend to bring this man's blood upon us.

29 Then Peter and the *other* apostles answered and said, We ought to obey God rather than men.

5:29
Obeying God
◄ Luke 8:21 ►

30 The God of our fathers raised up

Jesus, whom ye slew and hanged on a tree.

31 Him hath God exalted with his right hand *to be* a Prince and a Saviour, for to give repentance to Israel, and forgiveness of sins.

> **5:31 Forgiveness**
> ◄ Mark 3:28
> Acts 13:38 ►

> **5:31 Why Jesus Came**
> ◄ John 3:17
> Acts 13:23 ►

32 And we are his witnesses of these things; and *so is* also the Holy Ghost, whom God hath given to them that obey him.

33 When they heard *that,* they were cut *to the heart,* and took counsel to slay them.

> **5:33 Examples of Revenge**
> ◄ Luke 4:29
> Acts 23:12 ►

34 Then stood there up one in the council, a Pharisee, named Gamaliel, a doctor of the law, had in reputation among all the people, and commanded to put the apostles forth a little space;

35 And said unto them, Ye men of Israel, take heed to yourselves what ye intend to do as touching these men.

36 For before these days rose up Theudas, boasting himself to be somebody; to whom a number of men, about four hundred, joined themselves: who was slain; and all, as many as obeyed him, were scattered, and brought to nought.

37 After this man rose up Judas of Galilee in the days of the taxing, and drew away much people after him: he also perished; and all, *even* as many as obeyed him, were dispersed.

38 And now I say unto you, Refrain from these men, and let them alone: for if this counsel or this work be of men, it will come to nought:

39 But if it be of God, ye cannot overthrow it; lest haply ye be found even to fight against God.

40 And to him they agreed: and when they had called the apostles, and beaten *them,* they commanded that they should not speak in the name of Jesus, and let them go.

> **5:41 Positive Attitude**
> ◄ Habakkuk 3:17-18
> Acts 16:23, 25 ►

41 And they departed from the presence of the council, rejoicing that they were counted worthy to suffer shame for his name.

> **5:41 Suffering for Jesus**
> ◄ Acts 9:16 ►

42 And daily in the temple, and in every house, they ceased not to teach and preach Jesus Christ.

6

1 And in those days, when the number of the disciples was multiplied, there arose a murmuring of the Grecians against the Hebrews, because their widows were neglected in the daily ministration.

2 Then the twelve called the multitude of the disciples *unto them,* and said, It is not reason that we should leave the word of God, and serve tables.

3 Wherefore, brethren, look ye out among you seven men of honest report, full of the Holy Ghost and wisdom, whom we may appoint over this business.

4 But we will give ourselves continually to prayer, and to the ministry of the word.

5 And the saying pleased the whole multitude: and they chose Stephen, a man full of faith and of the Holy Ghost, and Philip, and Prochorus, and Nicanor, and Timon, and Parmenas, and Nicolas a proselyte of Antioch:

6 Whom they set before the apostles: and when they had prayed, they laid *their* hands on them.

7 And the word of God increased; and the number of the disciples multiplied in Jerusalem greatly; and a great company of the priests were obedient to the faith.

8 And Stephen, full of faith and power, did great wonders and miracles among the people.

> **6:8 The Holy Spirit**
> ◄ Acts 4:33
> Acts 19:11-12 ►

9 Then there arose certain of *the synagogue,* which is called the synagogue of the Libertines, and Cyrenians, and Alexandrians, and of them of Cilicia and of Asia, disputing with Stephen.

10 And they were not able to resist the wisdom and the spirit by which he spake.

11 Then they suborned men, which said, We have heard him speak blasphemous words against Moses, and *against* God.

12 And they stirred up the people, and

the elders, and the scribes, and came upon
him, and caught him, and brought *him* to
the council,
13 And set up false witnesses, which said,
This man ceaseth not to speak blasphemous words against this holy place, and
the law:
14 For we have heard him say, that this
Jesus of Nazareth shall destroy this place,
and shall change the customs which Moses delivered us.
15 And all that sat in the council, looking stedfastly on him, saw his face as it
had been the face of an angel.
7 1 Then said the high priest, Are these
things so?
2 And he said, Men, brethren, and fathers, hearken; The God of glory appeared
unto our father Abraham, when he was in
Mesopotamia, before he dwelt in Charran,
3 And said unto him, Get thee out of thy
country, and from thy kindred, and come
into the land which I shall shew thee.
4 Then came he out of the land of the
Chaldaeans, and dwelt in Charran: and
from thence, when his father was dead, he
removed him into this land, wherein ye
now dwell.
5 And he gave him none inheritance in
it, no, not *so much as* to set his foot on: yet
he promised that he would give it to him
for a possession, and to his seed after him,
when *as yet* he had no child.
6 And God spake on this wise, That his
seed should sojourn in a strange land; and
that they should bring them into bondage, and entreat *them* evil four hundred
years.
7 And the nation to whom they shall be
in bondage will I judge, said God: and after that shall they come forth, and serve
me in this place.
8 And he gave him the covenant of circumcision: and so *Abraham* begat Isaac,
and circumcised him the eighth day; and
Isaac *begat* Jacob; and Jacob *begat* the
twelve patriarchs.
9 And the patriarchs, moved with envy,
sold Joseph into Egypt: but God was with
him,
10 And delivered him out of all his afflictions, and gave him favour and wisdom
in the sight of Pharaoh king of Egypt; and
he made him governor over Egypt and all
his house.
11 Now there came a dearth over all the
land of Egypt and Chanaan, and great affliction: and our fathers found no sustenance.
12 But when Jacob heard that there was
corn in Egypt, he sent out our fathers first.
13 And at the second *time* Joseph was
made known to his brethren; and Joseph's
kindred was made known unto Pharaoh.
14 Then sent Joseph, and called his father Jacob to *him,* and all his kindred,
threescore and fifteen souls.
15 So Jacob went down into Egypt, and
died, he, and our fathers,
16 And were carried over into Sychem,
and laid in the sepulchre that Abraham
bought for a sum of money of the sons of
Emmor *the father* of Sychem.
17 But when the time of the promise
drew nigh, which God had sworn to Abraham, the people grew and multiplied in
Egypt,
18 Till another king arose, which knew
not Joseph.
19 The same dealt subtilly with our kindred, and evil entreated our fathers, so that
they cast out their young children, to the
end they might not live.
20 In which time Moses was born, and
was exceeding fair, and nourished up in
his father's house three months:
21 And when he was cast out, Pharaoh's
daughter took him up, and nourished him
for her own son.
22 And Moses was
learned in all the
wisdom of the
Egyptians, and was
mighty in words
and in deeds.

7:22 Study
◄ Daniel 1:17
Acts 22:3 ►

23 And when he was full forty years old,
it came into his heart to visit his brethren
the children of Israel.
24 And seeing one *of them* suffer wrong,
he defended *him,* and avenged him that
was oppressed, and smote the Egyptian:
25 For he supposed his brethren would
have understood how that God by his
hand would deliver them: but they understood not.
26 And the next day he shewed himself
unto them as they strove, and would have
set them at one again, saying, Sirs, ye are
brethren; why do ye wrong one to another?
27 But he that did his neighbour wrong

thrust him away, saying, Who made thee a
ruler and a judge over us?
28 Wilt thou kill me, as thou diddest the
Egyptian yesterday?
29 Then fled Moses at this saying, and
was a stranger in the land of Madian,
where he begat two sons.
30 And when forty years were expired,
there appeared to him in the wilderness
of mount Sina an angel of the Lord in a
flame of fire in a bush.
31 When Moses saw *it,* he wondered at
the sight: and as he drew near to behold
it, the voice of the Lord came unto him,
32 *Saying,* I *am* the God of thy fathers,
the God of Abraham, and the God of Isaac,
and the God of Jacob. Then Moses trembled, and durst not behold.
33 Then said the Lord to him, Put off thy
shoes from thy feet: for the place where
thou standest is holy ground.
34 I have seen, I have seen the affliction
of my people which is in Egypt, and I have
heard their groaning, and am come down
to deliver them. And now come, I will send
thee into Egypt.
35 This Moses whom they refused, saying, Who made thee a ruler and a judge?
the same did God send *to be* a ruler and a
deliverer by the hand of the angel which
appeared to him in the bush.
36 He brought them out, after that he had
shewed wonders and signs in the land of
Egypt, and in the Red sea, and in the wilderness forty years.
37 This is that Moses, which said unto
the children of Israel, A prophet shall the
Lord your God raise up unto you of your
brethren, like unto me; him shall ye hear.
38 This is he, that was in the church in
the wilderness with the angel which spake
to him in the mount Sina, and *with* our
fathers: who received the lively oracles to
give unto us:
39 To whom our fathers would not obey,
but thrust *him* from them, and in their
hearts turned back again into Egypt,
40 Saying unto Aaron, Make us gods to
go before us: for *as for* this Moses, which
brought us out of the land of Egypt, we
wot not what is become of him.
41 And they made a calf in those days,
and offered sacrifice unto the idol, and
rejoiced in the works of their own hands.
42 Then God turned, and gave them up
to worship the host of heaven; as it is written in the book of the prophets, O ye
house of Israel, have ye offered to me slain
beasts and sacrifices *by the space of* forty
years in the wilderness?
43 Yea, ye took up the tabernacle of
Moloch, and the star of your god Rem-
phan, figures which ye made to worship
them: and I will carry you away beyond
Babylon.
44 Our fathers had the tabernacle of witness in the wilderness, as he had appointed, speaking unto Moses, that he should
make it according to the fashion that he
had seen.
45 Which also our fathers that came after brought in with Jesus into the possession of the Gentiles, whom God drave out
before the face of our fathers, unto the days
of David;
46 Who found favour before God, and
desired to find a tabernacle for the God of
Jacob.
47 But Solomon built him an house.
48 Howbeit the most High dwelleth not
in temples made with hands; as saith the
prophet,
49 Heaven *is* my throne, and earth *is* my
footstool: what house will ye build me?
saith the Lord: or what *is* the place of my
rest?
50 Hath not my hand made all these
things?
51 Ye stiffnecked and uncircumcised in
heart and ears, ye do always resist the Holy
Ghost: as your fathers *did,* so *do* ye.
52 Which of the
prophets have not
your fathers perse-
cuted? and they
have slain them
which shewed be-
fore of the coming of the Just One; of
whom ye have been now the betrayers and
murderers:

7:52 Telling the Truth
◄ Matthew 23:33
2 Corinthians 3:12 ►

53 Who have received the law by the dis-
position of angels, and have not kept *it.*
54 When they
heard these things,
they were cut to the
heart, and they
gnashed on him
with *their* teeth.

7:54 Blinded by Sin
◄ Luke 15:17
1 Corinthians 2:8 ►

55 But he, being full of the Holy Ghost,
looked up stedfastly into heaven, and saw

the glory of God, and Jesus standing on the right hand of God,

56And said, Behold, I see the heavens opened, and the Son of man standing on the right hand of God.

57Then they cried out with a loud voice, and stopped their ears, and ran upon him with one accord,

58And cast *him* out of the city, and stoned *him*: and the witnesses laid down their clothes at a young man's feet, whose name was Saul.

59And they stoned Stephen, calling upon *God*, and saying, Lord Jesus, receive my spirit.

60And he kneeled down, and cried with a loud voice, Lord, lay not this sin to their charge. And when he had said this, he fell asleep.

7:57 Fanatics
◄ John 19:15
Acts 9:1 ►

7:57 Temper
◄ John 10:31
Acts 22:23 ►

7:58 Young Leaders
◄ Luke 18:18
Acts 9:6 ►

7:60 Enemies
◄ Luke 23:34 ►

7:60 Nice
◄ Luke 23:34
1 Corinthians 4:12 ►

8

1And Saul was consenting unto his death. And at that time there was a great persecution against the church which was at Jerusalem; and they were all scattered abroad throughout the regions of Judaea and Samaria, except the apostles.

2And devout men carried Stephen *to his burial,* and made great lamentation over him.

3As for Saul, he made havock of the church, entering into every house, and haling men and women committed *them* to prison.

4Therefore they that were scattered abroad went every where preaching the word.

5Then Philip went down to the city of Samaria, and preached Christ unto them.

6And the people with one accord gave heed unto those things which Philip spake, hearing and seeing the miracles which he did.

7For unclean spirits, crying with loud voice, came out of many that were possessed *with them:* and many taken with palsies, and that were lame, were healed.

8:7 Demons
◄ Luke 10:19
Acts 19:13 ►

8And there was great joy in that city.

9But there was a certain man, called Simon, which beforetime in the same city used sorcery, and bewitched the people of Samaria, giving out that himself was some great one:

10To whom they all gave heed, from the least to the greatest, saying, This man is the great power of God.

11And to him they had regard, because that of long time he had bewitched them with sorceries.

12But when they believed Philip preaching the things concerning the kingdom of God, and the name of Jesus Christ, they were baptized, both men and women.

13Then Simon himself believed also: and when he was baptized, he continued with Philip, and wondered, beholding the miracles and signs which were done.

14Now when the apostles which were at Jerusalem heard that Samaria had received the word of God, they sent unto them Peter and John:

15Who, when they were come down, prayed for them, that they might receive the Holy Ghost:

16(For as yet he was fallen upon none of them: only they were baptized in the name of the Lord Jesus.)

17Then laid they *their* hands on them, and they received the Holy Ghost.

18And when Simon saw that through laying on of the apostles' hands the Holy Ghost was given, he offered them money,

19Saying, Give me also this power, that on whomsoever I lay hands, he may receive the Holy Ghost.

20But Peter said unto him, Thy money perish with thee, because thou hast thought that the gift of God may be purchased with money.

21Thou hast neither part nor lot in this matter: for thy heart is not right in the sight of God.

22Repent there-
fore of this thy
wickedness, and
pray God, if per-
haps the thought of
thine heart may be
forgiven thee.

8:22 Repent!
◄ Acts 3:19
Acts 17:30 ►

23For I perceive
that thou art in the
gall of bitterness,
and *in* the bond of
iniquity.

8:23 Bad Habits
◄ John 8:34
Romans 6:16 ►

24Then answered
Simon, and said, Pray ye to the Lord for
me, that none of these things which ye
have spoken come upon me.
25And they, when they had testified and
preached the word of the Lord, returned
to Jerusalem, and preached the gospel in
many villages of the Samaritans.
26And the angel of the Lord spake unto
Philip, saying, Arise, and go toward the
south unto the way that goeth down from
Jerusalem unto Gaza, which is desert.
27And he arose and went: and, behold,
a man of Ethiopia, an eunuch of great authority under Candace queen of the Ethiopians, who had the charge of all her
treasure, and had come to Jerusalem for
to worship,
28Was returning, and sitting in his chariot read Esaias the prophet.
29Then the Spirit said unto Philip, Go
near, and join thyself to this chariot.
30And Philip ran thither to *him,* and
heard him read the prophet Esaias, and
said, Understandest thou what thou
readest?
31And he said,
How can I, except
some man should
guide me? And he
desired Philip that
he would come up
and sit with him.

8:31 Willingness to Learn
◄ Acts 2:37
Acts 9:6 ►

32The place of the scripture which he
read was this, He was led as a sheep to the
slaughter; and like a lamb dumb before
his shearer, so opened he not his mouth:
33In his humiliation his judgment was
taken away: and who shall declare his
generation? for his life is taken from the
earth.
34And the eunuch answered Philip, and
said, I pray thee, of whom speaketh the
prophet this? of himself, or of some other
man?
35Then Philip
opened his mouth,
and began at the
same scripture, and
preached unto him
Jesus.

8:35 Sunday School
◄ Luke 24:27
Acts 18:26 ►

36And as they went on *their* way, they
came unto a certain water: and the eunuch
said, See, *here is* water; what doth hinder
me to be baptized?
37And Philip said, If thou believest with
all thine heart, thou mayest. And he answered and said, I believe that Jesus Christ
is the Son of God.
38And he commanded the chariot to
stand still: and they went down both into
the water, both Philip and the eunuch; and
he baptized him.
39And when they
were come up out
of the water, the
Spirit of the Lord
caught away Philip,
that the eunuch
saw him no more: and he went on his way
rejoicing.

8:39 Guidance
◄ John 16:13
Acts 10:19-20 ►

40But Philip was found at Azotus: and
passing through he preached in all the cities, till he came to Caesarea.

9

1And Saul, yet
breathing out
threatenings and
slaughter against
the disciples of the
Lord, went unto the
high priest,

9:1 Fanatics
◄ Acts 7:57
Acts 21:36 ►

2And desired of him letters to Damascus to the synagogues, that if he found any
of this way, whether they were men or
women, he might bring them bound unto
Jerusalem.
3And as he journeyed, he came near
Damascus: and suddenly there shined
round about him a light from heaven:
4And he fell to the earth, and heard a
voice saying unto him, Saul, Saul, why
persecutest thou me?
5And he said, Who art thou, Lord? And
the Lord said, I am Jesus whom thou
persecutest: *it is* hard for thee to kick
against the pricks.
6And he trembling and astonished said,
Lord, what wilt thou have me to do? And

the Lord *said* unto
him, Arise, and go
into the city, and it
shall be told thee
what thou must do.

> **9:6**
> **Willingness to Learn**
> ◄ Acts 8:31
> Acts 16:30 ►

7And the men
which journeyed
with him stood
speechless, hearing
a voice, but seeing
no man.

> **9:6 Young Leaders**
> ◄ Acts 7:58
> Acts 9:22 ►

8And Saul arose
from the earth; and when his eyes were
opened, he saw no man: but they led him
by the hand, and brought *him* into Damascus.
9And he was three days without sight,
and neither did eat nor drink.
10And there was a certain disciple at
Damascus, named Ananias; and to him
said the Lord in a vision, Ananias. And he
said, Behold, I *am here,* Lord.
11And the Lord *said* unto him, Arise, and
go into the street which is called Straight,
and enquire in the house of Judas for *one*
called Saul, of Tarsus: for, behold, he
prayeth,
12And hath seen in a vision a man
named Ananias coming in, and putting *his*
hand on him, that he might receive his
sight.
13Then Ananias answered, Lord, I have
heard by many of this man, how much evil
he hath done to thy saints at Jerusalem:
14And here he hath authority from the
chief priests to bind all that call on thy
name.
15But the Lord said unto him, Go thy
way: for he is a chosen vessel unto me, to
bear my name before the Gentiles, and
kings, and the children of Israel:
16For I will shew
him how great
things he must suf-
fer for my name's
sake.

> **9:16**
> **Suffering for Jesus**
> ◄ Acts 5:41
> Romans 8:17 ►

17And Ananias
went his way, and entered into the house;
and putting his hands on him said, Brother Saul, the Lord, *even* Jesus, that appeared
unto thee in the way as thou camest, hath
sent me, that thou mightest receive thy
sight, and be filled with the Holy Ghost.
18And immediately there fell from his
eyes as it had been scales: and he received
sight forthwith, and arose, and was baptized.
19And when he had received meat, he
was strengthened. Then was Saul certain
days with the disciples which were at Damascus.
20And straight-
way he preached
Christ in the syna-
gogues, that he is
the Son of God.

> **9:20 Serving Quickly**
> ◄ Luke 19:6
> Acts 10:29 ►

21But all that
heard *him* were amazed, and said; Is not
this he that destroyed them which called
on this name in Jerusalem, and came
hither for that intent, that he might bring
them bound unto the chief priests?
22But Saul in-
creased the more in
strength, and con-
founded the Jews
which dwelt at Da-
mascus, proving
that this is very Christ.

> **9:22**
> **Young Leaders**
> ◄ Acts 9:6 ►

23And after that many days were fulfilled, the Jews took counsel to kill him:
24But their laying await was known of
Saul. And they watched the gates day and
night to kill him.
25Then the disciples took him by night,
and let *him* down by the wall in a basket.
26And when Saul was come to Jerusalem, he assayed to join himself to the disciples: but they were all afraid of him, and
believed not that he was a disciple.
27But Barnabas took him, and brought
him to the apostles, and declared unto
them how he had seen the Lord in the way,
and that he had spoken to him, and how
he had preached boldly at Damascus in
the name of Jesus.
28And he was with them coming in and
going out at Jerusalem.
29And he spake boldly in the name of
the Lord Jesus, and disputed against the
Grecians: but they went about to slay him.
30*Which* when the brethren knew, they
brought him down to Caesarea, and sent
him forth to Tarsus.
31Then had the churches rest throughout all Judaea and Galilee and Samaria,
and were edified; and walking in the fear
of the Lord, and in the comfort of the Holy
Ghost, were multiplied.
32And it came to pass, as Peter passed

throughout all *quarters*, he came down also to the saints which dwelt at Lydda.

33 And there he found a certain man named Aeneas, which had kept his bed eight years, and was sick of the palsy.

34 And Peter said unto him, Aeneas, Jesus Christ maketh thee whole: arise, and make thy bed. And he arose immediately.

35 And all that dwelt at Lydda and Saron saw him, and turned to the Lord.

36 Now there was at Joppa a certain disciple named Tabitha, which by interpretation is called Dorcas: this woman was full of good works and almsdeeds which she did.

37 And it came to pass in those days, that she was sick, and died: whom when they had washed, they laid *her* in an upper chamber.

38 And forasmuch as Lydda was nigh to Joppa, and the disciples had heard that Peter was there, they sent unto him two men, desiring *him* that he would not delay to come to them.

39 Then Peter arose and went with them. When he was come, they brought him into the upper chamber: and all the widows stood by him weeping, and shewing the coats and garments which Dorcas made, while she was with them.

9:39 Grief
◄ John 20:11 ►

40 But Peter put them all forth, and kneeled down, and prayed; and turning *him* to the body said, Tabitha, arise. And she opened her eyes: and when she saw Peter, she sat up.

41 And he gave her *his* hand, and lifted her up, and when he had called the saints and widows, presented her alive.

42 And it was known throughout all Joppa; and many believed in the Lord.

43 And it came to pass, that he tarried many days in Joppa with one Simon a tanner.

10

1 There was a certain man in Caesarea called Cornelius, a centurion of the band called the Italian *band*,

2 A devout *man*, and one that feared God with all his house, which gave much alms to the people, and prayed to God alway.

10:2 Praying
◄ Luke 2:37
Acts 16:25 ►

10:2 Who Is Religious?
◄ John 8:29
Acts 11:24 ►

3 He saw in a vision evidently about the ninth hour of the day an angel of God coming in to him, and saying unto him, Cornelius.

4 And when he looked on him, he was afraid, and said, What is it, Lord? And he said unto him, Thy prayers and thine alms are come up for a memorial before God.

5 And now send men to Joppa, and call for *one* Simon, whose surname is Peter:

6 He lodgeth with one Simon a tanner, whose house is by the sea side: he shall tell thee what thou oughtest to do.

7 And when the angel which spake unto Cornelius was departed, he called two of his household servants, and a devout soldier of them that waited on him continually;

8 And when he had declared all *these* things unto them, he sent them to Joppa.

9 On the morrow, as they went on their journey, and drew nigh unto the city, Peter went up upon the housetop to pray about the sixth hour:

10:9 Praying Alone
◄ Matthew 6:6
Acts 10:30 ►

10 And he became very hungry, and would have eaten: but while they made ready, he fell into a trance,

11 And saw heaven opened, and a certain vessel descending unto him, as it had been a great sheet knit at the four corners, and let down to the earth:

12 Wherein were all manner of fourfooted beasts of the earth, and wild beasts, and creeping things, and fowls of the air.

13 And there came a voice to him, Rise, Peter; kill, and eat.

14 But Peter said, Not so, Lord; for I have never eaten any thing that is common or unclean.

15 And the voice *spake* unto him again the second time, What God hath cleansed, *that* call not thou common.

16 This was done thrice: and the vessel was received up again into heaven.

17 Now while Peter doubted in himself what this vision which he had seen should mean, behold, the men which were sent

from Cornelius had made enquiry for Simon's house, and stood before the gate,

18 And called, and asked whether Simon, which was surnamed Peter, were lodged there.

19 While Peter thought on the vision, the Spirit said unto him, Behold, three men seek thee.

10:19-20 Guidance
◄ Acts 8:39
Acts 13:2 ►

20 Arise therefore, and get thee down, and go with them, doubting nothing: for I have sent them.

21 Then Peter went down to the men which were sent unto him from Cornelius; and said, Behold, I am he whom ye seek: what *is* the cause wherefore ye are come?

22 And they said, Cornelius the centurion, a just man, and one that feareth God, and of good report among all the nation of the Jews, was warned from God by an holy angel to send for thee into his house, and to hear words of thee.

23 Then called he them in, and lodged *them.* And on the morrow Peter went away with them, and certain brethren from Joppa accompanied him.

24 And the morrow after they entered into Caesarea. And Cornelius waited for them, and had called together his kinsmen and near friends.

25 And as Peter was coming in, Cornelius met him, and fell down at his feet, and worshipped *him.*

26 But Peter took him up, saying, Stand up; I myself also am a man.

27 And as he talked with him, he went in, and found many that were come together.

28 And he said unto them, Ye know how that it is an unlawful thing for a man that is a Jew to keep company, or come unto one of another nation; but God hath shewed me that I should not call any man common or unclean.

10:28 Different People
◄ John 4:9
Acts 11:3 ►

10:28 Equality
◄ Matthew 23:8
Romans 10:12 ►

29 Therefore came I *unto you* without gainsaying, as soon as I was sent for: I ask therefore for what intent ye have sent for me?

10:29 Serving Quickly
◄ Acts 9:20
Acts 16:10 ►

30 And Cornelius said, Four days ago I was fasting until this hour; and at the ninth hour I prayed in my house, and, behold, a man stood before me in bright clothing,

10:30 Praying Alone
◄ Acts 10:9 ►

31 And said, Cornelius, thy prayer is heard, and thine alms are had in remembrance in the sight of God.

32 Send therefore to Joppa, and call hither Simon, whose surname is Peter; he is lodged in the house of *one* Simon a tanner by the sea side: who, when he cometh, shall speak unto thee.

33 Immediately therefore I sent to thee; and thou hast well done that thou art come. Now therefore are we all here present before God, to hear all things that are commanded thee of God.

34 Then Peter opened *his* mouth, and said, Of a truth I perceive that God is no respecter of persons:

35 But in every nation he that feareth him, and worketh righteousness, is accepted with him.

10:35 Accepted by God
◄ Ezekiel 43:27
2 Corinthians 5:9 ►

36 The word which *God* sent unto the children of Israel, preaching peace by Jesus Christ: (he is Lord of all:)

10:35 Why Fear God?
◄ Luke 1:50 ►

37 That word, *I say,* ye know, which was published throughout all Judaea, and began from Galilee, after the baptism which John preached;

38 How God anointed Jesus of Nazareth with the Holy Ghost and with power: who went about doing good, and healing all that were oppressed of the devil; for God was with him.

39 And we are witnesses of all things which he did both in the land of the Jews, and in Jerusalem; whom they slew and hanged on a tree:

40Him God raised up the third day, and shewed him openly;

41Not to all the people, but unto witnesses chosen before of God, *even* to us, who did eat and drink with him after he rose from the dead.

42And he commanded us to preach unto the people, and to testify that it is he which was ordained of God *to be* the Judge of quick and dead.

10:42 Christ as Judge
◄ John 5:22
Acts 17:31 ►

43To him give all the prophets witness, that through his name whosoever believeth in him shall receive remission of sins.

10:43 Salvation by Faith
◄ John 20:31
Acts 13:39 ►

44While Peter yet spake these words, the Holy Ghost fell on all them which heard the word.

45And they of the circumcision which believed were astonished, as many as came with Peter, because that on the Gentiles also was poured out the gift of the Holy Ghost.

46For they heard them speak with tongues, and magnify God. Then answered Peter,

47Can any man forbid water, that these should not be baptized, which have received the Holy Ghost as well as we?

48And he commanded them to be baptized in the name of the Lord. Then prayed they him to tarry certain days.

10:48 Baptism
◄ Acts 2:38
Acts 22:16 ►

11

1And the apostles and brethren that were in Judaea heard that the Gentiles had also received the word of God.

2And when Peter was come up to Jerusalem, they that were of the circumcision contended with him,

3Saying, Thou wentest in to men uncircumcised, and didst eat with them.

11:3 Different People
◄ Acts 10:28
Acts 19:34 ►

4But Peter rehearsed *the matter* from the beginning, and expounded *it* by order unto them, saying,

5I was in the city of Joppa praying: and in a trance I saw a vision, A certain vessel descend, as it had been a great sheet, let down from heaven by four corners; and it came even to me:

6Upon the which when I had fastened mine eyes, I considered, and saw fourfooted beasts of the earth, and wild beasts, and creeping things, and fowls of the air.

7And I heard a voice saying unto me, Arise, Peter; slay and eat.

8But I said, Not so, Lord: for nothing common or unclean hath at any time entered into my mouth.

9But the voice answered me again from heaven, What God hath cleansed, *that* call not thou common.

10And this was done three times: and all were drawn up again into heaven.

11And, behold, immediately there were three men already come unto the house where I was, sent from Caesarea unto me.

12And the spirit bade me go with them, nothing doubting. Moreover these six brethren accompanied me, and we entered into the man's house:

13And he shewed us how he had seen an angel in his house, which stood and said unto him, Send men to Joppa, and call for Simon, whose surname is Peter;

14Who shall tell thee words, whereby thou and all thy house shall be saved.

15And as I began to speak, the Holy Ghost fell on them, as on us at the beginning.

16Then remembered I the word of the Lord, how that he said, John indeed baptized with water; but ye shall be baptized with the Holy Ghost.

17Forasmuch then as God gave them the like gift as *he did* unto us, who believed on the Lord Jesus Christ; what was I, that I could withstand God?

18When they heard these things, they held their peace, and glorified God, saying, Then hath God also to the Gentiles granted repentance unto life.

19Now they which were scattered abroad upon the persecution that arose about Stephen travelled as far as Phenice, and Cyprus, and Antioch, preaching the word to none but unto the Jews only.

20And some of them were men of Cyprus and Cyrene, which, when they were come to Antioch, spake unto the Grecians, preaching the Lord Jesus.

21And the hand of the Lord was with them: and a great number believed, and turned unto the Lord.

22Then tidings of these things came unto the ears of the church which was in Jerusalem: and they sent forth Barnabas, that he should go as far as Antioch.

23Who, when he came, and had seen the grace of God, was glad, and exhorted them all, that with purpose of heart they would cleave unto the Lord.

11:23 Gladness
◄ Acts 2:46
Acts 14:17 ►

11:23 Serving
◄ John 4:36 ►

11:23 Standing Strong
◄ Job 11:14-15
1 Corinthians 15:58 ►

24For he was a good man, and full of the Holy Ghost and of faith: and much people was added unto the Lord.

25Then departed Barnabas to Tarsus, for to seek Saul:

26And when he had found him, he brought him unto Antioch. And it came to pass, that a whole year they assembled themselves with the church, and taught much people. And the disciples were called Christians first in Antioch.

11:24 Who Is Religious?
◄ Acts 10:2
Acts 22:12 ►

27And in these days came prophets from Jerusalem unto Antioch.

28And there stood up one of them named Agabus, and signified by the spirit that there should be great dearth throughout all the world: which came to pass in the days of Claudius Caesar.

29Then the disciples, every man according to his ability, determined to send relief unto the brethren which dwelt in Judaea:

11:29 Examples of Generosity
◄ Acts 4:34-35
2 Corinthians 8:2 ►

30Which also they did, and sent it to the elders by the hands of Barnabas and Saul.

12

1Now about that time Herod the king stretched forth *his* hands to vex certain of the church.

2And he killed James the brother of John with the sword.

12:1-3 Popularity
◄ John 12:43
Acts 24:27 ►

3And because he saw it pleased the Jews, he proceeded further to take Peter also. (Then were the days of unleavened bread.)

12:3 The Crowd
◄ John 7:13 ►

4And when he had apprehended him, he put *him* in prison, and delivered *him* to four quaternions of soldiers to keep him; intending after Easter to bring him forth to the people.

5Peter therefore was kept in prison: but prayer was made without ceasing of the church unto God for him.

6And when Herod would have brought him forth, the same night Peter was sleeping between two soldiers, bound with two chains: and the keepers before the door kept the prison.

7And, behold, the angel of the Lord came upon *him*, and a light shined in the prison: and he smote Peter on the side, and raised him up, saying, Arise up quickly. And his chains fell off from *his* hands.

12:7 Angels
◄ Daniel 6:22
Acts 27:23 ►

8And the angel said unto him, Gird thyself, and bind on thy sandals. And so he did. And he saith unto him, Cast thy garment about thee, and follow me.

9And he went out, and followed him; and wist not that it was true which was done by the angel; but thought he saw a vision.

10When they were past the first and the second ward, they came unto the iron gate that leadeth unto the city; which opened to them of his own accord: and they went out, and passed on through one street; and forthwith the angel departed from him.

11And when Peter was come to himself, he said, Now I know of a surety, that the Lord hath sent his angel, and hath delivered me out of the hand of Herod, and *from* all the expectation of the people of the Jews.

12And when he had considered *the thing*, he came to the house of Mary the mother of John, whose surname was Mark; where many were gathered together praying.

13 And as Peter knocked at the door of the gate, a damsel came to hearken, named Rhoda.

14 And when she knew Peter's voice, she opened not the gate for gladness, but ran in, and told how Peter stood before the gate.

15 And they said unto her, Thou art mad. But she constantly affirmed that it was even so. Then said they, It is his angel.

12:15 Superstition
◄ Matthew 14:2
Acts 14:11 ►

16 But Peter continued knocking: and when they had opened *the door,* and saw him, they were astonished.

17 But he, beckoning unto them with the hand to hold their peace, declared unto them how the Lord had brought him out of the prison. And he said, Go shew these things unto James, and to the brethren. And he departed, and went into another place.

18 Now as soon as it was day, there was no small stir among the soldiers, what was become of Peter.

19 And when Herod had sought for him, and found him not, he examined the keepers, and commanded that *they* should be put to death. And he went down from Judaea to Caesarea, and *there* abode.

20 And Herod was highly displeased with them of Tyre and Sidon: but they came with one accord to him, and, having made Blastus the king's chamberlain their friend, desired peace; because their country was nourished by the king's *country.*

21 And upon a set day Herod, arrayed in royal apparel, sat upon his throne, and made an oration unto them.

22 And the people gave a shout, *saying, It is* the voice of a god, and not of a man.

23 And immediately the angel of the Lord smote him, because he gave not God the glory: and he was eaten of worms, and gave up the ghost.

24 But the word of God grew and multiplied.

25 And Barnabas and Saul returned from Jerusalem, when they had fulfilled *their* ministry, and took with them John, whose surname was Mark.

13

1 Now there were in the church that was at Antioch certain prophets and teachers; as Barnabas, and Simeon that was called Niger, and Lucius of Cyrene, and Manaen, which had been brought up with Herod the tetrarch, and Saul.

2 As they ministered to the Lord, and fasted, the Holy Ghost said, Separate me Barnabas and Saul for the work whereunto I have called them.

13:2 Guidance
◄ Acts 10:19-20
Acts 16:6 ►

3 And when they had fasted and prayed, and laid *their* hands on them, they sent *them* away.

4 So they, being sent forth by the Holy Ghost, departed unto Seleucia; and from thence they sailed to Cyprus.

5 And when they were at Salamis, they preached the word of God in the synagogues of the Jews: and they had also John to *their* minister.

6 And when they had gone through the isle unto Paphos, they found a certain sorcerer, a false prophet, a Jew, whose name *was* Bar-jesus:

7 Which was with the deputy of the country, Sergius Paulus, a prudent man; who called for Barnabas and Saul, and desired to hear the word of God.

8 But Elymas the sorcerer (for so is his name by interpretation) withstood them, seeking to turn away the deputy from the faith.

9 Then Saul, (who also *is called* Paul,) filled with the Holy Ghost, set his eyes on him,

10 And said, O full of all subtilty and all mischief, *thou* child of the devil, *thou* enemy of all righteousness, wilt thou not cease to pervert the right ways of the Lord?

13:10 Mischief
◄ Proverbs 24:2 ►

11 And now, behold, the hand of the Lord *is* upon thee, and thou shalt be blind, not seeing the sun for a season. And immediately there fell on him a mist and a darkness; and he went about seeking some to lead him by the hand.

12 Then the deputy, when he saw what was done, believed, being astonished at the doctrine of the Lord.

13Now when Paul and his company loosed from Paphos, they came to Perga in Pamphylia: and John departing from them returned to Jerusalem.

14But when they departed from Perga, they came to Antioch in Pisidia, and went into the synagogue on the sabbath day, and sat down.

13:14 Going to Church
◄ Luke 4:16
Hebrews 10:25 ►

15And after the reading of the law and the prophets the rulers of the synagogue sent unto them, saying, *Ye* men *and* brethren, if ye have any word of exhortation for the people, say on.

16Then Paul stood up, and beckoning with *his* hand said, Men of Israel, and ye that fear God, give audience.

17The God of this people of Israel chose our fathers, and exalted the people when they dwelt as strangers in the land of Egypt, and with an high arm brought he them out of it.

18And about the time of forty years suffered he their manners in the wilderness.

19And when he had destroyed seven nations in the land of Chanaan, he divided their land to them by lot.

20And after that he gave *unto them* judges about the space of four hundred and fifty years, until Samuel the prophet.

21And afterward they desired a king: and God gave unto them Saul the son of Cis, a man of the tribe of Benjamin, by the space of forty years.

22And when he had removed him, he raised up unto them David to be their king; to whom also he gave testimony, and said, I have found David the *son* of Jesse, a man after mine own heart, which shall fulfil all my will.

23Of this man's seed hath God according to *his* promise raised unto Israel a Saviour, Jesus:

13:23 Why Jesus Came
◄ Acts 5:31
1 Timothy 1:15 ►

24When John had first preached before his coming the baptism of repentance to all the people of Israel.

25And as John fulfilled his course, he said, Whom think ye that I am? I am not *he.* But, behold, there cometh one after me, whose shoes of *his* feet I am not worthy to loose.

26Men *and* brethren, children of the stock of Abraham, and whosoever among you feareth God, to you is the word of this salvation sent.

27For they that dwell at Jerusalem, and their rulers, because they knew him not, nor yet the voices of the prophets which are read every sabbath day, they have fulfilled *them* in condemning *him.*

28And though they found no cause of death *in him,* yet desired they Pilate that he should be slain.

29And when they had fulfilled all that was written of him, they took *him* down from the tree, and laid *him* in a sepulchre.

30But God raised him from the dead:

31And he was seen many days of them which came up with him from Galilee to Jerusalem, who are his witnesses unto the people.

32And we declare unto you glad tidings, how that the promise which was made unto the fathers,

33God hath fulfilled the same unto us their children, in that he hath raised up Jesus again; as it is also written in the second psalm, Thou art my Son, this day have I begotten thee.

34And as concerning that he raised him up from the dead, *now* no more to return to corruption, he said on this wise, I will give you the sure mercies of David.

35Wherefore he saith also in another *psalm,* Thou shalt not suffer thine Holy One to see corruption.

36For David, after he had served his own generation by the will of God, fell on sleep, and was laid unto his fathers, and saw corruption:

37But he, whom God raised again, saw no corruption.

38Be it known unto you therefore, men *and* brethren, that through this man is preached unto you the forgiveness of sins:

13:38 Forgiveness
◄ Acts 5:31
Acts 26:18 ►

39And by him all that believe are justified from all things, from which ye could not be justified by the law of Moses.

13:39 Salvation by Faith
◄ Acts 10:43
Acts 16:31 ►

40 Beware therefore, lest that come upon
you, which is spoken of in the prophets;
41 Behold, ye despisers, and wonder, and
perish: for I work a work in your days, a
work which ye shall in no wise believe,
though a man declare it unto you.
42 And when the Jews were gone out of
the synagogue, the Gentiles besought that
these words might be preached to them
the next sabbath.
43 Now when the
congregation was
broken up, many of
the Jews and reli-
gious proselytes fol-
lowed Paul and
Barnabas: who, speaking to them, persuaded them to continue in the grace of God.

13:43 Determination
◄ John 15:9
Romans 2:7 ►

44 And the next sabbath day came almost
the whole city together to hear the word
of God.
45 But when the Jews saw the multitudes,
they were filled with envy, and spake
against those things which were spoken by
Paul, contradicting and blaspheming.
46 Then Paul and
Barnabas waxed
bold, and said, It
was necessary that
the word of God
should first have
been spoken to you: but seeing ye put it
from you, and judge yourselves unworthy
of everlasting life, lo, we turn to the Gentiles.

13:46
Who Deserves Christ?
◄ Matthew 22:8 ►

47 For so hath the Lord commanded us,
saying, I have set thee to be a light of the
Gentiles, that thou shouldest be for salvation unto the ends of the earth.
48 And when the Gentiles heard this, they
were glad, and glorified the word of the
Lord: and as many as were ordained to
eternal life believed.
49 And the word of the Lord was published throughout all the region.
50 But the Jews stirred up the devout and
honourable women, and the chief men of
the city, and raised persecution against
Paul and Barnabas, and expelled them out
of their coasts.
51 But they shook off the dust of their
feet against them, and came unto Iconium.
52 And the disciples were filled with joy,
and with the Holy Ghost.

14

1 And it came to pass in Iconium, that
they went both together into the synagogue of the Jews, and so spake, that a great
multitude both of the Jews and also of the
Greeks believed.
2 But the unbelieving Jews stirred up the
Gentiles, and made their minds evil affected against the brethren.
3 Long time therefore abode they speaking boldly in the Lord, which gave testimony unto the word of his grace, and
granted signs and wonders to be done by
their hands.
4 But the multitude of the city was divided: and part held with the Jews, and
part with the apostles.
5 And when there was an assault made
both of the Gentiles, and also of the Jews
with their rulers, to use *them* despitefully,
and to stone them,
6 They were ware of *it,* and fled unto Lystra and Derbe, cities of Lycaonia, and unto
the region that lieth round about:
7 And there they preached the gospel.
8 And there sat a certain man at Lystra,
impotent in his feet, being a cripple from
his mother's womb, who never had
walked:
9 The same heard
Paul speak: who
stedfastly behold-
ing him, and per-
ceiving that he had
faith to be healed,

14:9
God's Response
◄ John 9:7 ►

10 Said with a loud voice, Stand upright
on thy feet. And he leaped and walked.
11 And when the
people saw what
Paul had done, they
lifted up their
voices, saying in the
speech of Lycaonia,
The gods are come down to us in the likeness of men.

14:11 Superstition
◄ Acts 12:15
Acts 17:23 ►

12 And they called Barnabas, Jupiter; and
Paul, Mercurius, because he was the chief
speaker.
13 Then the priest of Jupiter, which was
before their city, brought oxen and gar-
lands unto the gates, and would have done
sacrifice with the people.
14 *Which* when the apostles, Barnabas
and Paul, heard *of,* they rent their clothes,
and ran in among the people, crying out,
15 And saying, Sirs, why do ye these

things? We also are
men of like pas-
sions with you, and
preach unto you
that ye should turn
from these vanities
unto the living God, which made heaven,
and earth, and the sea, and all things that
are therein:

> **14:15**
> **Worshiping Things**
> ◄ Jonah 2:8 ►

16 Who in times past suffered all nations
to walk in their own ways.
17 Nevertheless
he left not himself
without witness, in
that he did good,
and gave us rain
from heaven, and
fruitful seasons, fill-
ing our hearts with
food and gladness.

> **14:17**
> **Gladness**
> ◄ Acts 11:23 ►

> **14:17**
> **Nature Teaches Us**
> ◄ Psalm 97:6
> Romans 1:20 ►

18 And with these
sayings scarce re-
strained they the
people, that they had not done sacrifice
unto them.
19 And there came thither *certain* Jews
from Antioch and Iconium, who persuaded the people, and, having stoned Paul,
drew *him* out of the city, supposing he had
been dead.
20 Howbeit, as the disciples stood round
about him, he rose up, and came into the
city: and the next day he departed with
Barnabas to Derbe.
21 And when they had preached the gospel to that city, and had taught many, they
returned again to Lystra, and *to* Iconium,
and Antioch,
22 Confirming
the souls of the
disciples, *and* ex-
horting them to
continue in the
faith, and that we
must through much tribulation enter into
the kingdom of God.

> **14:22 Suffering**
> ◄ John 16:33
> Romans 5:3 ►

23 And when they had ordained them
elders in every church, and had prayed
with fasting, they commended them to the
Lord, on whom they believed.
24 And after they had passed throughout
Pisidia, they came to Pamphylia.
25 And when they had preached the word
in Perga, they went down into Attalia:
26 And thence sailed to Antioch, from
whence they had been recommended to
the grace of God for the work which they
fulfilled.
27 And when they were come, and had
gathered the church together, they rehearsed all that God had done with them,
and how he had opened the door of faith
unto the Gentiles.
28 And there they abode long time with
the disciples.

15

1 And certain men which came down
from Judaea taught the brethren, *and said,*
Except ye be circumcised after the manner
of Moses, ye cannot be saved.
2 When therefore Paul and Barnabas had
no small dissension and disputation with
them, they determined that Paul and Barnabas, and certain other of them, should
go up to Jerusalem unto the apostles and
elders about this question.
3 And being brought on their way by the
church, they passed through Phenice and
Samaria, declaring the conversion of the
Gentiles: and they caused great joy unto
all the brethren.
4 And when they were come to Jerusalem, they were received of the church, and
of the apostles and elders, and they declared all things that God had done with
them.
5 But there rose
up certain of the
sect of the Pharisees
which believed,
saying, That it was
needful to circum-
cise them, and to command *them* to keep
the law of Moses.

> **15:5 Legalism**
> ◄ John 5:10
> Acts 16:3 ►

6 And the apostles and elders came together for to consider of this matter.
7 And when there had been much disputing, Peter rose up, and said unto them,
Men *and* brethren, ye know how that a
good while ago God made choice among
us, that the Gentiles by my mouth should
hear the word of the gospel, and believe.
8 And God, which knoweth the hearts,
bare them witness, giving them the Holy
Ghost, even as *he did* unto us;
9 And put no difference between us and
them, purifying their hearts by faith.
10 Now therefore why tempt ye God, to
put a yoke upon the neck of the disciples,
which neither our fathers nor we were able
to bear?

11 But we believe
that through the
grace of the Lord
Jesus Christ we
shall be saved, even
as they.

15:11
Grace
◄ Romans 3:24 ►

15:11 Only One Savior
◄ Acts 4:12
Romans 5:9 ►

12 Then all the
multitude kept si-
lence, and gave au-
dience to Barnabas
and Paul, declaring
what miracles and
wonders God had wrought among the
Gentiles by them.
13 And after they had held their peace,
James answered, saying, Men *and* brethren, hearken unto me:
14 Simeon hath declared how God at the
first did visit the Gentiles, to take out of
them a people for his name.
15 And to this agree the words of the
prophets; as it is written,
16 After this I will return, and will build
again the tabernacle of David, which is
fallen down; and I will build again the
ruins thereof, and I will set it up:
17 That the residue of men might seek
after the Lord, and all the Gentiles, upon
whom my name is called, saith the Lord,
who doeth all these things.
18 Known unto God are all his works
from the beginning of the world.
19 Wherefore my sentence is, that we
trouble not them, which from among the
Gentiles are turned to God:
20 But that we write unto them, that they
abstain from pollutions of idols, and *from*
fornication, and *from* things strangled, and
from blood.
21 For Moses of old time hath in every
city them that preach him, being read in
the synagogues every sabbath day.
22 Then pleased it the apostles and elders, with the whole church, to send chosen men of their own company to Antioch
with Paul and Barnabas; *namely,* Judas surnamed Barsabas, and Silas, chief men
among the brethren:
23 And they wrote *letters* by them after
this manner; The apostles and elders and
brethren *send* greeting unto the brethren
which are of the Gentiles in Antioch and
Syria and Cilicia:
24 Forasmuch as we have heard, that certain which went out from us have troubled you with words, subverting your
souls, saying, *Ye must* be circumcised, and
keep the law: to whom we gave no *such*
commandment:
25 It seemed good unto us, being assembled with one accord, to send chosen men
unto you with our beloved Barnabas and
Paul,
26 Men that have hazarded their lives for
the name of our Lord Jesus Christ.
27 We have sent therefore Judas and Silas, who shall also tell *you* the same things
by mouth.
28 For it seemed good to the Holy Ghost,
and to us, to lay upon you no greater burden than these necessary things;
29 That ye abstain from meats offered to
idols, and from blood, and from things
strangled, and from fornication: from
which if ye keep yourselves, ye shall do
well. Fare ye well.
30 So when they were dismissed, they
came to Antioch: and when they had gathered the multitude together, they delivered
the epistle:
31 *Which* when they had read, they rejoiced for the consolation.
32 And Judas and Silas, being prophets also themselves, exhorted the brethren with many words, and confirmed
them.
33 And after they had tarried *there* a space,
they were let go in peace from the brethren unto the apostles.
34 Notwithstanding it pleased Silas to
abide there still.
35 Paul also and Barnabas continued in
Antioch, teaching and preaching the word
of the Lord, with many others also.
36 And some days after Paul said unto
Barnabas, Let us go again and visit our
brethren in every city where we have
preached the word of the Lord, *and see* how
they do.
37 And Barnabas determined to take with
them John, whose surname was Mark.
38 But Paul thought not good to take him
with them, who departed from them from
Pamphylia, and went not with them to the
work.
39 And the contention was so sharp between them, that they departed asunder
one from the other: and so Barnabas took
Mark, and sailed unto Cyprus;
40 And Paul chose Silas, and departed,

being recommended by the brethren unto
the grace of God.
41 And he went through Syria and Cilicia, confirming the churches.

16 1 Then came he to Derbe and Lystra: and,
behold, a certain disciple was there, named
Timotheus, the son of a certain woman,
which was a Jewess, and believed; but his
father *was* a Greek:
2 Which was well reported of by
the brethren that were at Lystra and Iconium.
3 Him would Paul
have to go forth
with him; and took
and circumcised
him because of the
Jews which were in
those quarters: for they knew all that his
father was a Greek.

> **16:3 Legalism**
> ◄ Acts 15:5
> Acts 21:20 ►

4 And as they went through the cities,
they delivered them the decrees for to keep,
that were ordained of the apostles and elders which were at Jerusalem.
5 And so were the churches established
in the faith, and increased in number daily.
6 Now when they
had gone throughout Phrygia and the
region of Galatia,
and were forbidden
of the Holy Ghost
to preach the word in Asia,

> **16:6 Guidance**
> ◄ Acts 13:2
> Romans 8:14 ►

7 After they were come to Mysia, they
assayed to go into Bithynia: but the Spirit
suffered them not.
8 And they passing by Mysia came down
to Troas.
9 And a vision appeared to Paul in the
night; There stood a man of Macedonia,
and prayed him, saying, Come over into
Macedonia, and help us.
10 And after he
had seen the vision,
immediately we endeavoured to go
into Macedonia, assuredly gathering
that the Lord had called us for to preach
the gospel unto them.

> **16:10 Serving Quickly**
> ◄ Acts 10:29 ►

11 Therefore loosing from Troas, we came
with a straight course to Samothracia, and
the next *day* to Neapolis;
12 And from thence to Philippi, which
is the chief city of that part of Macedonia,
and a colony: and we were in that city abiding certain days.
13 And on the sabbath we went out of
the city by a river side, where prayer was
wont to be made; and we sat down, and
spake unto the women which resorted
thither.
14 And a certain woman named Lydia, a
seller of purple, of the city of Thyatira,
which worshipped God, heard *us:* whose
heart the Lord opened, that she attended
unto the things which were spoken of Paul.
15 And when she was baptized, and her
household, she besought *us,* saying, If ye
have judged me to be faithful to the Lord,
come into my house, and abide *there.* And
she constrained us.
16 And it came to pass, as we went to
prayer, a certain damsel possessed with a
spirit of divination met us, which brought
her masters much gain by soothsaying:
17 The same followed Paul and us, and
cried, saying, These men are the servants
of the most high God, which shew unto
us the way of salvation.
18 And this did she many days. But Paul,
being grieved, turned and said to the spirit, I command thee in the name of Jesus
Christ to come out of her. And he came
out the same hour.
19 And when her masters saw that the
hope of their gains was gone, they caught
Paul and Silas, and drew *them* into the marketplace unto the rulers,
20 And brought them to the magistrates,
saying, These men, being Jews, do exceedingly trouble our city,
21 And teach customs, which are not lawful for us to receive, neither to observe,
being Romans.
22 And the multitude rose up together
against them: and the magistrates rent off
their clothes, and commanded to beat
them.
23 And when they
had laid many
stripes upon them,
they cast *them* into
prison, charging
the jailer to keep
them safely:

> **16:23, 25 Positive Attitude**
> ◄ Acts 5:41
> 2 Corinthians 6:10 ►

24 Who, having received such a charge,
thrust them into the inner prison, and
made their feet fast in the stocks.
25 And at midnight Paul and Silas

Turn to the next page for more . . .

prayed, and sang
praises unto God:
and the prisoners
heard them.
26And suddenly
there was a great
earthquake, so that
the foundations of
the prison were
shaken: and imme-
diately all the doors
were opened, and
every one's bands were loosed.

16:25 Praying
◄ Acts 10:2
1 Thessalonians 3:10 ►

16:25-26 Prayer
◄ John 15:7
James 5:18 ►

27And the keeper of the prison awaking
out of his sleep, and seeing the prison
doors open, he drew out his sword, and
would have killed himself, supposing that
the prisoners had been fled.
28But Paul cried with a loud voice, saying, Do thyself no harm: for we are all here.
29Then he called
for a light, and
sprang in, and came
trembling, and fell
down before Paul
and Silas,
30And brought
them out, and said,
Sirs, what must I do
to be saved?
31And they said,
Believe on the Lord
Jesus Christ, and
thou shalt be saved,
and thy house.
32And they spake
unto him the word
of the Lord, and to
all that were in his house.

16:29 Not Confessing
◄ Acts 2:37
Acts 24:25 ►

16:30 Willingness to Learn
◄ Acts 9:6 ►

16:31 Salvation by Faith
◄ Acts 13:39
Romans 9:33 ►

33And he took
them the same hour
of the night, and
washed *their* stripes;
and was baptized,
he and all his,
straightway.

16:33 Compassion
◄ Luke 10:33-34
Acts 28:2 ►

34And when he had brought them into
his house, he set meat before them, and
rejoiced, believing in God with all his
house.
35And when it was day, the magistrates
sent the serjeants, saying, Let those
men go.
36And the keeper of the prison told this
saying to Paul, The magistrates have sent
to let you go: now therefore depart, and
go in peace.
37But Paul said unto them, They have
beaten us openly uncondemned, being
Romans, and have cast *us* into prison; and
now do they thrust us out privily? nay verily; but let them come themselves and fetch
us out.
38And the serjeants told these words
unto the magistrates: and they feared,
when they heard that they were Romans.
39And they came and besought them,
and brought *them* out, and desired *them*
to depart out of the city.
40And they went out of the prison, and
entered into *the house of* Lydia and when
they had seen the brethren, they comforted them, and departed.

17

1Now when they had passed through
Amphipolis and Apollonia, they came to
Thessalonica, where was a synagogue of
the Jews:
2And Paul, as his manner was, went in
unto them, and three sabbath days reasoned with them out of the scriptures,
3Opening and alleging, that Christ must
needs have suffered, and risen again from
the dead; and that this Jesus, whom I
preach unto you, is Christ.
4And some of them believed, and con-
sorted with Paul and Silas; and of the devout Greeks a great multitude, and of the
chief women not a few.
5But the Jews which believed not, moved
with envy, took unto them certain lewd
fellows of the baser sort, and gathered
a company, and set all the city on an
uproar, and assaulted the house of Jason,
and sought to bring them out to the
people.
6And when they found them not, they
drew Jason and certain brethren unto the
rulers of the city, crying, These that have
turned the world upside down are come
hither also;
7Whom Jason hath received: and these
all do contrary to the decrees of Caesar,
saying that there is another king, *one* Jesus.
8And they troubled the people and the
rulers of the city, when they heard these
things.
9And when they had taken security of
Jason, and of the other, they let them go.
10And the brethren immediately sent
away Paul and Silas by night unto Berea:

who coming *thither* went into the synagogue of the Jews.
11These were
more noble than
those in Thessaloni-
ca, in that they
received the word
with all readiness of
mind, and searched
the scriptures daily,
whether those things
were so.
12Therefore
many of them be-
lieved; also of honourable women which
were Greeks, and of men, not a few.
13But when the Jews of Thessalonica had
knowledge that the word of God was
preached of Paul at Berea, they came
thither also, and stirred up the people.
14And then immediately the brethren
sent away Paul to go as it were to the
sea: but Silas and Timotheus abode there
still.
15And they that conducted Paul brought
him unto Athens: and receiving a commandment unto Silas and Timotheus for
to come to him with all speed, they departed.
16Now while Paul waited for them at
Athens, his spirit was stirred in him, when
he saw the city wholly given to idolatry.
17Therefore disputed he in the synagogue with the Jews, and with the devout
persons, and in the market daily with them
that met with him.
18Then certain philosophers of the Epi-
cureans, and of the Stoicks, encountered
him. And some said, What will this babbler say? other some, He seemeth to be a
setter forth of strange gods: because he
preached unto them Jesus, and the resurrection.
19And they took him, and brought him
unto Areopagus, saying, May we know
what this new doctrine, whereof thou
speakest, *is?*
20For thou bringest certain strange
things to our ears: we would know therefore what these things mean.
21(For all the Athenians and strangers
which were there spent their time in nothing else, but either to tell, or to hear some
new thing.)
22Then Paul stood in the midst of Mars'
hill, and said, *Ye* men of Athens, I perceive that in all things ye are too superstitious.
23For as I passed
by, and beheld your
devotions, I found
an altar with this
inscription, TO
THE UNKNOWN
GOD. Whom therefore ye ignorantly worship, him declare I unto you.
24God that made
the world and all
things therein, see-
ing that he is Lord
of heaven and
earth, dwelleth not
in temples made with hands;
25Neither is worshipped with men's
hands, as though he needed any thing,
seeing he giveth to all life, and breath, and
all things;
26And hath made
of one blood all na-
tions of men for to
dwell on all the face
of the earth, and
hath determined
the times before appointed, and the
bounds of their habitation;
27That they
should seek the
Lord, if haply they
might feel after
him, and find him,
though he be not
far from every one
of us:
28For in him we
live, and move, and
have our being; as
certain also of your
own poets have
said, For we are also
his offspring.
29Forasmuch
then as we are the
offspring of God,
we ought not to think that the Godhead is
like unto gold, or
silver, or stone,
graven by art and
man's device.
30And the times
of this ignorance

17:11 Accepting God's Word
◄ Acts 2:41
1 Thessalonians 2:13 ►

17:11 Reading the Bible
◄ John 5:39
Romans 15:4 ►

17:23 Superstition
◄ Acts 14:11
Acts 28:4 ►

17:24 God's Control
◄ Matthew 6:13
Romans 9:19 ►

17:26 Family
◄ Mark 3:34
Romans 14:13 ►

17:27 Finding God
◄ Hosea 6:3 ►

17:27 Seeking God
◄ Luke 11:10 ►

17:27 Where Is God?
◄ Jeremiah 23:24 ►

17:30 Repent!
◄ Acts 8:22
Acts 26:20 ►

God winked at; but now commandeth all
men every where to repent:
31 Because he
hath appointed a
day, in the which he
will judge the world
in righteousness by
that man whom he
hath ordained; *whereof* he hath given assurance unto all *men*, in that he hath raised
him from the dead.

17:31 Christ as Judge
◄ Acts 10:42
Romans 2:16 ►

32 And when they
heard of the resur-
rection of the dead,
some mocked: and
others said, We will
hear thee again of
this *matter*.

17:32 Mocking
◄ Acts 2:13
Hebrews 11:36 ►

33 So Paul de-
parted from among
them.
34 Howbeit cer-
tain men clave unto
him, and believed: among the which
was Dionysius the Areopagite, and a
woman named Damaris, and others with
them.

17:32 Procrastination
◄ Luke 9:61
Acts 24:25 ►

18

1 After these things Paul departed from
Athens, and came to Corinth;
2 And found a certain Jew named Aquila, born in Pontus, lately come from Italy,
with his wife Priscilla; (because that Claudius had commanded all Jews to depart
from Rome:) and came unto them.
3 And because he was of the same craft,
he abode with them, and wrought: for by
their occupation they were tentmakers.
4 And he reasoned in the synagogue every sabbath, and persuaded the Jews and
the Greeks.
5 And when Silas and Timotheus were
come from Macedonia, Paul was pressed
in the spirit, and testified to the Jews *that*
Jesus *was* Christ.
6 And when they opposed themselves,
and blasphemed, he shook *his* raiment,
and said unto them, Your blood *be* upon
your own heads; I *am* clean: from henceforth I will go unto the Gentiles.
7 And he departed thence, and entered
into a certain *man's* house, named Justus,
one that worshipped God, whose house
joined hard to the synagogue.
8 And Crispus, the chief ruler of the synagogue, believed on the Lord with all his
house; and many of the Corinthians hearing believed, and were baptized.
9 Then spake the
Lord to Paul in the
night by a vision,
Be not afraid, but
speak, and hold not
thy peace:

18:9-10 Witnessing
◄ Acts 5:20-21
Acts 22:14-15 ►

10 For I am with thee, and no man shall
set on thee to hurt thee: for I have much
people in this city.
11 And he continued *there* a year and six
months, teaching the word of God among
them.
12 And when Gallio was the deputy of
Achaia, the Jews made insurrection with
one accord against Paul, and brought him
to the judgment seat,
13 Saying, This *fellow* persuadeth men to
worship God contrary to the law.
14 And when Paul was now about to
open *his* mouth, Gallio said unto the Jews,
If it were a matter of wrong or wicked lewdness, O *ye* Jews, reason would that I should
bear with you:
15 But if it be a question of words and
names, and *of* your law, look ye *to it*; for I
will be no judge of such *matters*.
16 And he drave them from the judgment
seat.
17 Then all the Greeks took Sosthenes,
the chief ruler of the synagogue, and beat
him before the judgment seat. And Gallio
cared for none of those things.
18 And Paul *after this* tarried *there* yet a
good while, and then took his leave of the
brethren, and sailed thence into Syria, and
with him Priscilla and Aquila; having
shorn *his* head in Cenchrea: for he had a
vow.
19 And he came to Ephesus, and left
them there: but he himself entered into
the synagogue, and reasoned with the Jews.
20 When they desired *him* to tarry longer
time with them, he consented not;
21 But bade them farewell, saying, I must
by all means keep this feast that cometh
in Jerusalem: but I will return again unto
you, if God will. And he sailed from Ephesus.
22 And when he had landed at Caesarea,
and gone up, and saluted the church, he
went down to Antioch.
23 And after he had spent some time
there, he departed, and went over *all* the

country of Galatia and Phrygia in order,
strengthening all the disciples.
24And a certain Jew named Apollos,
born at Alexandria, an eloquent man, *and*
mighty in the scriptures, came to Ephesus.
25This man was instructed in the way of
the Lord; and being fervent in the spirit,
he spake and taught diligently the things
of the Lord, knowing only the baptism of
John.
26And he began
to speak boldly
in the synagogue:
whom when Aqui-
la and Priscilla had
heard, they took
him unto *them*, and expounded unto him
the way of God more perfectly.

18:26 Sunday School
◄ Acts 8:35
Acts 28:23 ►

27And when he was disposed to pass
into Achaia, the brethren wrote, exhorting
the disciples to receive him: who, when
he was come, helped them much which
had believed through grace:
28For he mightily convinced the Jews,
and that publickly, shewing by the scriptures that Jesus was Christ.

19

1And it came to pass, that, while Apollos was at Corinth, Paul having passed
through the upper coasts came to Ephesus: and finding certain disciples,
2He said unto them, Have ye received
the Holy Ghost since ye believed? And they
said unto him, We have not so much as
heard whether there be any Holy Ghost.
3And he said unto them, Unto what then
were ye baptized? And they said, Unto
John's baptism.
4Then said Paul, John verily baptized
with the baptism of repentance, saying
unto the people, that they should believe
on him which should come after him, that
is, on Christ Jesus.
5When they heard *this*, they were baptized in the name of the Lord Jesus.
6And when Paul had laid *his* hands upon
them, the Holy Ghost came on them; and
they spake with tongues, and prophesied.
7And all the men were about twelve.
8And he went into the synagogue, and
spake boldly for the space of three months,
disputing and persuading the things concerning the kingdom of God.
9But when divers were hardened, and
believed not, but spake evil of that way
before the multitude, he departed from
them, and separated the disciples, disputing daily in the school of one Tyrannus.
10And this continued by the space of two
years; so that all they which dwelt in Asia
heard the word of the Lord Jesus, both Jews
and Greeks.
11And God
wrought special
miracles by the
hands of Paul:
12So that from
his body were
brought unto the sick handkerchiefs or
aprons, and the diseases departed from
them, and the evil spirits went out of them.

19:11-12 The Holy Spirit
◄ Acts 6:8
1 Corinthians 2:4 ►

13Then certain of
the vagabond Jews,
exorcists, took up-
on them to call over
them which had
evil spirits the
name of the Lord Jesus, saying, We adjure
you by Jesus whom Paul preacheth.

19:13 Demons
◄ Acts 8:7
Ephesians 6:12 ►

14And there were seven sons of *one* Sce-
va, a Jew, *and* chief of the priests, which
did so.
15And the evil spirit answered and said,
Jesus I know, and Paul I know; but who
are ye?
16And the man in whom the evil spirit
was leaped on them, and overcame them,
and prevailed against them, so that they
fled out of that house naked and wounded.
17And this was known to all the Jews
and Greeks also dwelling at Ephesus; and
fear fell on them all, and the name of the
Lord Jesus was magnified.
18And many that believed came, and
confessed, and shewed their deeds.
19Many of them also which used curious arts brought their books together, and
burned them before all *men*: and they
counted the price of them, and found *it*
fifty thousand *pieces* of silver.
20So mightily grew the word of God and
prevailed.
21After these things were ended, Paul
purposed in the spirit, when he had passed
through Macedonia and Achaia, to go to
Jerusalem, saying, After I have been there,
I must also see Rome.
22So he sent into Macedonia two of
them that ministered unto him, Timotheus
and Erastus; but he himself stayed in Asia
for a season.

23And the same time there arose no small stir about that way.

24For a certain *man* named Demetrius, a silversmith, which made silver shrines for Diana, brought no small gain unto the craftsmen;

25Whom he called together with the workmen of like occupation, and said, Sirs, ye know that by this craft we have our wealth.

26Moreover ye see and hear, that not alone at Ephesus, but almost throughout all Asia, this Paul hath persuaded and turned away much people, saying that they be no gods, which are made with hands:

27So that not only this our craft is in danger to be set at nought; but also that the temple of the great goddess Diana should be despised, and her magnificence should be destroyed, whom all Asia and the world worshippeth.

28And when they heard *these sayings*, they were full of wrath, and cried out, saying, Great *is* Diana of the Ephesians.

19:28 Mad
◄ Luke 6:11
James 1:20 ►

29And the whole city was filled with confusion: and having caught Gaius and Aristarchus, men of Macedonia, Paul's companions in travel, they rushed with one accord into the theatre.

30And when Paul would have entered in unto the people, the disciples suffered him not.

31And certain of the chief of Asia, which were his friends, sent unto him, desiring *him* that he would not adventure himself into the theatre.

32Some therefore cried one thing, and some another: for the assembly was confused; and the more part knew not wherefore they were come together.

33And they drew Alexander out of the multitude, the Jews putting him forward. And Alexander beckoned with the hand, and would have made his defence unto the people.

34But when they knew that he was a Jew, all with one voice about the space of two hours cried out, Great *is* Diana of the Ephesians.

19:34 Different People
◄ Acts 11:3
Galatians 2:12 ►

35And when the townclerk had appeased the people, he said, *Ye* men of Ephesus, what man is there that knoweth not how that the city of the Ephesians is a worshipper of the great goddess Diana, and of the *image* which fell down from Jupiter?

36Seeing then that these things cannot be spoken against, ye ought to be quiet, and to do nothing rashly.

19:36
Being Hasty
◄ Ecclesiastes 5:2 ►

37For ye have brought hither these men, which are neither robbers of churches, nor yet blasphemers of your goddess.

38Wherefore if Demetrius, and the craftsmen which are with him, have a matter against any man, the law is open, and there are deputies: let them implead one another.

39But if ye enquire any thing concerning other matters, it shall be determined in a lawful assembly.

40For we are in danger to be called in question for this day's uproar, there being no cause whereby we may give an account of this concourse.

41And when he had thus spoken, he dismissed the assembly.

20

1And after the uproar was ceased, Paul called unto *him* the disciples, and embraced *them*, and departed for to go into Macedonia.

2And when he had gone over those parts, and had given them much exhortation, he came into Greece,

3And *there* abode three months. And when the Jews laid wait for him, as he was about to sail into Syria, he purposed to return through Macedonia.

4And there accompanied him into Asia Sopater of Berea; and of the Thessalonians, Aristarchus and Secundus; and Gaius of Derbe, and Timotheus; and of Asia, Tychicus and Trophimus.

5These going before tarried for us at Troas.

6And we sailed away from Philippi after the days of unleavened bread, and came unto them to Troas in five days; where we abode seven days.

7And upon the first *day* of the week, when the disciples came together to break bread, Paul preached unto them, ready to depart on the morrow; and continued his speech until midnight.

8 And there were many lights in the upper chamber, where they were gathered together.

9 And there sat in a window a certain young man named Eutychus, being fallen into a deep sleep: and as Paul was long preaching, he sunk down with sleep, and fell down from the third loft, and was taken up dead.

10 And Paul went down, and fell on him, and embracing *him* said, Trouble not yourselves; for his life is in him.

11 When he therefore was come up again, and had broken bread, and eaten, and talked a long while, even till break of day, so he departed.

12 And they brought the young man alive, and were not a little comforted.

13 And we went before to ship, and sailed unto Assos, there intending to take in Paul: for so had he appointed, minding himself to go afoot.

14 And when he met with us at Assos, we took him in, and came to Mitylene.

15 And we sailed thence, and came the next *day* over against Chios; and the next *day* we arrived at Samos, and tarried at Trogyllium; and the next *day* we came to Miletus.

16 For Paul had determined to sail by Ephesus, because he would not spend the time in Asia: for he hasted, if it were possible for him, to be at Jerusalem the day of Pentecost.

17 And from Miletus he sent to Ephesus, and called the elders of the church.

18 And when they were come to him, he said unto them, Ye know, from the first day that I came into Asia, after what manner I have been with you at all seasons,

20:18-19 Humility
◄ John 12:3 ►

19 Serving the Lord with all humility of mind, and with many tears, and temptations, which befell me by the lying in wait of the Jews:

20 *And* how I kept back nothing that was profitable *unto you,* but have shewed you, and have taught you publickly, and from house to house,

21 Testifying both to the Jews, and also to the Greeks, repentance toward God, and faith toward our Lord Jesus Christ.

22 And now, behold, I go bound in the spirit unto Jerusalem, not knowing the things that shall befall me there:

20:22 The Future
◄ Matthew 24:43
James 4:14 ►

23 Save that the Holy Ghost witnesseth in every city, saying that bonds and afflictions abide me.

24 But none of these things move me, neither count I my life dear unto myself, so that I might finish my course with joy, and the ministry, which I have received of the Lord Jesus, to testify the gospel of the grace of God.

20:24 Job One
◄ John 17:4
Philippians 3:13-14 ►

25 And now, behold, I know that ye all, among whom I have gone preaching the kingdom of God, shall see my face no more.

26 Wherefore I take you to record this day, that I *am* pure from the blood of all *men.*

27 For I have not shunned to declare unto you all the counsel of God.

28 Take heed therefore unto yourselves, and to all the flock, over the which the Holy Ghost hath made you overseers, to feed the church of God, which he hath purchased with his own blood.

29 For I know this, that after my departing shall grievous wolves enter in among you, not sparing the flock.

30 Also of your own selves shall men arise, speaking perverse things, to draw away disciples after them.

31 Therefore watch, and remember, that by the space of three years I ceased not to warn every one night and day with tears.

20:31 Caring for the Church
◄ 2 Corinthians 7:12 ►

32 And now, brethren, I commend you to God, and to the word of his grace, which is able to build you up, and to give you an inheritance among all them which are sanctified.

20:31 Pitfalls
◄ Matthew 26:41
1 Corinthians 10:12 ►

33 I have coveted no man's silver, or gold, or apparel.

34 Yea, ye yourselves know, that these hands have ministered unto my necessities, and to them that were with me.

35 I have shewed you all things, how that so labouring ye ought to support the weak, and to remember the words of the Lord Jesus, how he said, It is more blessed to give than to receive.

20:35 Giving
◄ Luke 12:33
Romans 12:13 ►

20:35 Helping Weak People
◄ Matthew 25:35-36
Romans 14:1 ►

36 And when he had thus spoken, he kneeled down, and prayed with them all.

20:35 Sympathy
◄ Isaiah 58:7
Romans 15:1 ►

37 And they all wept sore, and fell on Paul's neck, and kissed him,

38 Sorrowing most of all for the words which he spake, that they should see his face no more. And they accompanied him unto the ship.

20:38 Love for Friends
◄ 1 Samuel 18:3
Romans 16:4 ►

21

1 And it came to pass, that after we were gotten from them, and had launched, we came with a straight course unto Coos, and the *day* following unto Rhodes, and from thence unto Patara:

2 And finding a ship sailing over unto Phenicia, we went aboard, and set forth.

3 Now when we had discovered Cyprus, we left it on the left hand, and sailed into Syria, and landed at Tyre: for there the ship was to unlade her burden.

4 And finding disciples, we tarried there seven days: who said to Paul through the Spirit, that he should not go up to Jerusalem.

5 And when we had accomplished those days, we departed and went our way; and they all brought us on our way, with wives and children, till *we were* out of the city: and we kneeled down on the shore, and prayed.

6 And when we had taken our leave one of another, we took ship; and they returned home again.

7 And when we had finished *our* course from Tyre, we came to Ptolemais, and saluted the brethren, and abode with them one day.

8 And the next *day* we that were of Paul's company departed, and came unto Caesarea: and we entered into the house of Philip the evangelist, which was *one* of the seven; and abode with him.

9 And the same man had four daughters, virgins, which did prophesy.

21:9 Young Women
◄ John 12:3 ►

10 And as we tarried *there* many days, there came down from Judaea a certain prophet, named Agabus.

11 And when he was come unto us, he took Paul's girdle, and bound his own hands and feet, and said, Thus saith the Holy Ghost, So shall the Jews at Jerusalem bind the man that owneth this girdle, and shall deliver *him* into the hands of the Gentiles.

12 And when we heard these things, both we, and they of that place, besought him not to go up to Jerusalem.

13 Then Paul answered, What mean ye to weep and to break mine heart? for I am ready not to be bound only, but also to die at Jerusalem for the name of the Lord Jesus.

21:13 Loving Jesus
◄ John 21:16 ►

14 And when he would not be persuaded, we ceased, saying, The will of the Lord be done.

21:14 Submitting to God
◄ John 7:17
Romans 12:2 ►

15 And after those days we took up our carriages, and went up to Jerusalem.

16 There went with us also *certain* of the disciples of Caesarea, and brought with them one Mnason of Cyprus, an old disciple, with whom we should lodge.

17 And when we were come to Jerusalem, the brethren received us gladly.

18 And the *day* following Paul went in with us unto James; and all the elders were present.

19 And when he had saluted them, he declared particularly what things God had

wrought among the Gentiles by his ministry.

20 And when they heard *it,* they glorified the Lord, and said unto him, Thou seest, brother, how many thousands of Jews there are which believe; and they are all zealous of the law:

21:20 Legalism
◄ Acts 16:3
Acts 22:3 ►

21 And they are informed of thee, that thou teachest all the Jews which are among the Gentiles to forsake Moses, saying that they ought not to circumcise *their* children, neither to walk after the customs.

22 What is it therefore? the multitude must needs come together: for they will hear that thou art come.

23 Do therefore this that we say to thee: We have four men which have a vow on them;

24 Them take, and purify thyself with them, and be at charges with them, that they may shave *their* heads: and all may know that those things, whereof they were informed concerning thee, are nothing; but *that* thou thyself also walkest orderly, and keepest the law.

25 As touching the Gentiles which believe, we have written *and* concluded that they observe no such thing, save only that they keep themselves from *things* offered to idols, and from blood, and from strangled, and from fornication.

26 Then Paul took the men, and the next day purifying himself with them entered into the temple, to signify the accomplishment of the days of purification, until that an offering should be offered for every one of them.

27 And when the seven days were almost ended, the Jews which were of Asia, when they saw him in the temple, stirred up all the people, and laid hands on him,

28 Crying out, Men of Israel, help: This is the man, that teacheth all *men* every where against the people, and the law, and this place: and further brought Greeks also into the temple, and hath polluted this holy place.

29 (For they had seen before with him in the city Trophimus an Ephesian, whom they supposed that Paul had brought into the temple.)

30 And all the city was moved, and the people ran together: and they took Paul, and drew him out of the temple: and forthwith the doors were shut.

31 And as they went about to kill him, tidings came unto the chief captain of the band, that all Jerusalem was in an uproar.

32 Who immediately took soldiers and centurions, and ran down unto them: and when they saw the chief captain and the soldiers, they left beating of Paul.

33 Then the chief captain came near, and took him, and commanded *him* to be bound with two chains; and demanded who he was, and what he had done.

34 And some cried one thing, some another, among the multitude: and when he could not know the certainty for the tumult, he commanded him to be carried into the castle.

35 And when he came upon the stairs, so it was, that he was borne of the soldiers for the violence of the people.

36 For the multitude of the people followed after, crying, Away with him.

21:36 Fanatics
◄ Acts 9:1
Acts 22:23 ►

37 And as Paul was to be led into the castle, he said unto the chief captain, May I speak unto thee? Who said, Canst thou speak Greek?

38 Art not thou that Egyptian, which before these days madest an uproar, and leddest out into the wilderness four thousand men that were murderers?

39 But Paul said, I am a man *which am* a Jew of Tarsus, *a city* in Cilicia, a citizen of no mean city: and, I beseech thee, suffer me to speak unto the people.

40 And when he had given him licence, Paul stood on the stairs, and beckoned with the hand unto the people. And when there was made a great silence, he spake unto *them* in the Hebrew tongue, saying,

22

1 Men, brethren, and fathers, hear ye my defence *which I make* now unto you.

2 (And when they heard that he spake in the Hebrew tongue to them, they kept the more silence: and he saith,)

3 I am verily a man *which am* a Jew, born in Tarsus, *a city* in Cilicia, yet brought up in this city at the feet of

22:3 Legalism
◄ Acts 21:20
Romans 10:2 ►

Turn to the next page for more . . .

Gamaliel, *and*
taught according to
the perfect manner
of the law of the fa-
thers, and was zeal-
ous toward God, as
ye all are this day.

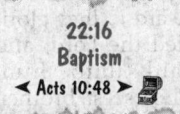

22:3
Study
◄ Acts 7:22 ►

4 And I persecuted this way unto the
death, binding and delivering into prisons
both men and women.
5 As also the high priest doth bear me
witness, and all the estate of the elders:
from whom also I received letters unto the
brethren, and went to Damascus, to bring
them which were there bound unto Jerusalem, for to be punished.
6 And it came to pass, that, as I made my
journey, and was come nigh unto Damascus about noon, suddenly there shone
from heaven a great light round about me.
7 And I fell unto the ground, and heard
a voice saying unto me, Saul, Saul, why
persecutest thou me?
8 And I answered, Who art thou, Lord?
And he said unto me, I am Jesus of Nazareth, whom thou persecutest.
9 And they that were with me saw indeed
the light, and were afraid; but they heard
not the voice of him that spake to me.
10 And I said, What shall I do, Lord? And
the Lord said unto me, Arise, and go into
Damascus; and there it shall be told thee
of all things which are appointed for thee
to do.
11 And when I could not see for the glory
of that light, being led by the hand of them
that were with me, I came into Damascus.
12 And one Ana-
nias, a devout man
according to the
law, having a good
report of all the
Jews which dwelt
there,

22:12
Who Is Religious?
◄ Acts 11:24
2 Timothy 1:5 ►

13 Came unto me, and stood, and said
unto me, Brother Saul, receive thy sight.
And the same hour I looked up upon him.
14 And he said,
The God of our fa-
thers hath chosen
thee, that thou
shouldest know his
will, and see that
Just One, and shouldest hear the voice of
his mouth.

22:14-15 Witnessing
◄ Acts 18:9-10
Titus 2:15 ►

15 For thou shalt be his witness unto all
men of what thou hast seen and heard.
16 And now why
tarriest thou? arise,
and be baptized,
and wash away thy
sins, calling on the
name of the Lord.

22:16
Baptism
◄ Acts 10:48 ►

17 And it came to pass, that, when I was
come again to Jerusalem, even while I
prayed in the temple, I was in a trance;
18 And saw him saying unto me, Make
haste, and get thee quickly out of Jerusalem: for they will not receive thy testimony concerning me.
19 And I said, Lord, they know that I im-
prisoned and beat in every synagogue
them that believed on thee:
20 And when the blood of thy martyr Stephen was shed, I also was standing by, and
consenting unto his death, and kept the
raiment of them that slew him.
21 And he said unto me, Depart: for I will
send thee far hence unto the Gentiles.
22 And they gave him audience unto this
word, and *then* lifted up their voices,
and said, Away with such a *fellow* from
the earth: for it is not fit that he should
live.
23 And as they
cried out, and cast
off *their* clothes,
and threw dust into
the air,

22:23
Fanatics
◄ Acts 21:36 ►

24 The chief cap-
tain commanded
him to be brought
into the castle, and
bade that he should
be examined by
scourging; that he
might know wherefore they cried so
against him.

22:23
Temper
◄ Acts 7:57 ►

25 And as they bound him with thongs,
Paul said unto the centurion that stood by,
Is it lawful for you to scourge a man that
is a Roman, and uncondemned?
26 When the centurion heard *that,* he
went and told the chief captain, saying,
Take heed what thou doest: for this man
is a Roman.
27 Then the chief captain came, and said
unto him, Tell me, art thou a Roman? He
said, Yea.
28 And the chief captain answered, With

a great sum obtained I this freedom. And
Paul said, But I was *free* born.
29 Then straightway they departed from
him which should have examined him:
and the chief captain also was afraid, after
he knew that he was a Roman, and because
he had bound him.
30 On the morrow, because he would
have known the certainty wherefore he was
accused of the Jews, he loosed him from
his bands, and commanded the chief
priests and all their council to appear, and
brought Paul down, and set him before
them.

23

1 And Paul, earnestly beholding the
council, said, Men *and* brethren, I have
lived in all good conscience before God
until this day.
2 And the high priest Ananias commanded them that stood by him to smite him
on the mouth.
3 Then said Paul unto him, God shall
smite thee, *thou* whited wall: for sittest
thou to judge me after the law, and
commandest me to be smitten contrary to
the law?
4 And they that stood by said, Revilest
thou God's high priest?
5 Then said Paul,
I wist not, brethren,
that he was the high
priest: for it is writ-
ten, Thou shalt not
speak evil of the rul-
er of thy people.

> **23:5 Rulers**
> ◄ Ecclesiastes 10:20
> Romans 13:1 ►

6 But when Paul perceived that the one
part were Sadducees, and the other Pharisees, he cried out in the council, Men *and*
brethren, I am a Pharisee, the son of a
Pharisee: of the hope and resurrection of
the dead I am called in question.
7 And when he had so said, there arose a
dissension between the Pharisees and the
Sadducees: and the multitude was divided.
8 For the Sadducees say that there is no
resurrection, neither angel, nor spirit: but
the Pharisees confess both.
9 And there arose a great cry: and the
scribes *that were* of the Pharisees' part
arose, and strove, saying, We find no evil
in this man: but if a spirit or an angel hath
spoken to him, let us not fight against God.
10 And when there arose a great dissension, the chief captain, fearing lest Paul
should have been pulled in pieces of them,
commanded the soldiers to go down, and
to take him by force from among them,
and to bring *him* into the castle.
11 And the night
following the Lord
stood by him, and
said, Be of good
cheer, Paul: for as
thou hast testified
of me in Jerusalem, so must thou bear witness also at Rome.

> **23:11**
> **Encouraging People**
> ◄ Mark 16:6
> Acts 27:22 ►

12 And when it
was day, certain of
the Jews banded to-
gether, and bound
themselves under a
curse, saying that
they would neither eat nor drink till they
had killed Paul.

> **23:12**
> **Examples of Revenge**
> ◄ Acts 5:33 ►

13 And they were more than forty which
had made this conspiracy.
14 And they came to the chief priests and
elders, and said, We have bound ourselves
under a great curse, that we will eat nothing until we have slain Paul.
15 Now therefore ye with the council signify to the chief captain that he bring him
down unto you to morrow, as though ye
would enquire something more perfectly
concerning him: and we, or ever he come
near, are ready to kill him.
16 And when Paul's sister's son heard of
their lying in wait, he went and entered
into the castle, and told Paul.
17 Then Paul called one of the centurions unto *him*, and said, Bring this young
man unto the chief captain: for he hath a
certain thing to tell him.
18 So he took him, and brought *him* to
the chief captain, and said, Paul the prisoner called me unto *him*, and prayed me
to bring this young man unto thee, who
hath something to say unto thee.
19 Then the chief captain took him by
the hand, and went *with him* aside privately, and asked *him*, What is that thou hast
to tell me?
20 And he said, The Jews have agreed to
desire thee that thou wouldest bring down
Paul to morrow into the council, as though
they would enquire somewhat of him
more perfectly.
21 But do not thou yield unto them: for
there lie in wait for him of them more than
forty men, which have bound themselves

Turn to the next page for more . . .

with an oath, that they will neither eat nor drink till they have killed him: and now are they ready, looking for a promise from thee.

23:21
Foolish Promises
◄ Mark 6:23 ►

22 So the chief captain *then* let the young man depart, and charged *him, See thou* tell no man that thou hast shewed these things to me.

23 And he called unto *him* two centurions, saying, Make ready two hundred soldiers to go to Caesarea, and horsemen threescore and ten, and spearmen two hundred, at the third hour of the night;

24 And provide *them* beasts, that they may set Paul on, and bring *him* safe unto Felix the governor.

25 And he wrote a letter after this manner:

26 Claudius Lysias unto the most excellent governor Felix *sendeth* greeting.

27 This man was taken of the Jews, and should have been killed of them: then came I with an army, and rescued him, having understood that he was a Roman.

28 And when I would have known the cause wherefore they accused him, I brought him forth into their council:

29 Whom I perceived to be accused of questions of their law, but to have nothing laid to his charge worthy of death or of bonds.

30 And when it was told me how that the Jews laid wait for the man, I sent straightway to thee, and gave commandment to his accusers also to say before thee what *they had* against him. Farewell.

31 Then the soldiers, as it was commanded them, took Paul, and brought *him* by night to Antipatris.

32 On the morrow they left the horsemen to go with him, and returned to the castle:

33 Who, when they came to Caesarea, and delivered the epistle to the governor, presented Paul also before him.

34 And when the governor had read *the letter,* he asked of what province he was. And when he understood that *he was* of Cilicia;

35 I will hear thee, said he, when thine accusers are also come. And he commanded him to be kept in Herod's judgment hall.

24

1 And after five days Ananias the high priest descended with the elders, and *with* a certain orator *named* Tertullus, who informed the governor against Paul.

2 And when he was called forth, Tertullus began to accuse *him,* saying, Seeing that by thee we enjoy great quietness, and that very worthy deeds are done unto this nation by thy providence,

3 We accept *it* always, and in all places, most noble Felix, with all thankfulness.

4 Notwithstanding, that I be not further tedious unto thee, I pray thee that thou wouldest hear us of thy clemency a few words.

5 For we have found this man *a* pestilent *fellow,* and a mover of sedition among all the Jews throughout the world, and a ringleader of the sect of the Nazarenes:

6 Who also hath gone about to profane the temple: whom we took, and would have judged according to our law.

7 But the chief captain Lysias came *upon us,* and with great violence took *him* away out of our hands,

8 Commanding his accusers to come unto thee: by examining of whom thyself mayest take knowledge of all these things, whereof we accuse him.

9 And the Jews also assented, saying that these things were so.

10 Then Paul, after that the governor had beckoned unto him to speak, answered, Forasmuch as I know that thou hast been of many years a judge unto this nation, I do the more cheerfully answer for myself:

11 Because that thou mayest understand, that there are yet but twelve days since I went up to Jerusalem for to worship.

12 And they neither found me in the temple disputing with any man, neither raising up the people, neither in the synagogues, nor in the city:

13 Neither can they prove the things whereof they now accuse me.

14 But this I confess unto thee, that after the way which they call heresy, so worship I the God of my fathers, believing all things which are written in the law and in the prophets:

15 And have hope toward God, which they themselves also allow, that there shall be a res-

24:15 Life After Death
◄ John 5:28-29
Revelation 20:13 ►

urrection of the dead, both of the just and unjust.

> **24:15 Resurrection**
> ◄ John 11:25
> 1 Corinthians 15:22 ►

16And herein do I exercise myself, to have always a conscience void of offence toward God, and *toward* men.

> **24:16 Clear Conscience**
> ◄ Romans 9:1 ►

17Now after many years I came to bring alms to my nation, and offerings.

18Whereupon certain Jews from Asia found me purified in the temple, neither with multitude, nor with tumult.

19Who ought to have been here before thee, and object, if they had ought against me.

20Or else let these same *here* say, if they have found any evil doing in me, while I stood before the council,

21Except it be for this one voice, that I cried standing among them, Touching the resurrection of the dead I am called in question by you this day.

22And when Felix heard these things, having more perfect knowledge of *that* way, he deferred them, and said, When Lysias the chief captain shall come down, I will know the uttermost of your matter.

23And he commanded a centurion to keep Paul, and to let *him* have liberty, and that he should forbid none of his acquaintance to minister or come unto him.

> **24:25 Not Confessing**
> ◄ Acts 16:29 ►

> **24:25 Procrastination**
> ◄ Acts 17:32 ►

24And after certain days, when Felix came with his wife Drusilla, which was a Jewess, he sent for Paul, and heard him concerning the faith in Christ.

> **24:25 Righteousness**
> ◄ Matthew 5:20
> 1 Corinthians 15:34 ►

25And as he reasoned of righteousness, temperance, and judgment to come Felix trembled, and answered, Go thy way for this time; when I have a convenient season, I will call for thee.

> **24:25 Salvation**
> ◄ Luke 14:18
> Acts 28:27 ►

> **24:25 Self-control**
> ◄ Proverbs 25:28
> Romans 6:12 ►

26He hoped also that money should have been given him of Paul, that he might loose him: wherefore he sent for him the oftener, and communed with him.

27But after two years Porcius Festus came into Felix' room: and Felix, willing to shew the Jews a pleasure, left Paul bound.

> **24:27 Popularity**
> ◄ Acts 12:1-3
> Acts 25:9 ►

25

1Now when Festus was come into the province, after three days he ascended from Caesarea to Jerusalem.

2Then the high priest and the chief of the Jews informed him against Paul, and besought him,

3And desired favour against him, that he would send for him to Jerusalem, laying wait in the way to kill him.

4But Festus answered, that Paul should be kept at Caesarea, and that he himself would depart shortly *thither*.

5Let them therefore, said he, which among you are able, go down with *me*, and accuse this man, if there be any wickedness in him.

6And when he had tarried among them more than ten days, he went down unto Caesarea; and the next day sitting on the judgment seat commanded Paul to be brought.

7And when he was come, the Jews which came down from Jerusalem stood round about, and laid many and grievous complaints against Paul, which they could not prove.

8While he answered for himself, Neither against the law of the Jews, neither against the temple, nor yet against Caesar, have I offended any thing at all.

9But Festus, willing to do the Jews a pleasure, answered Paul, and said, Wilt thou go up to Jerusalem, and there be judged of these things before me?

> **25:9 Popularity**
> ◄ Acts 24:27
> Ephesians 6:6 ►

10Then said Paul, I stand at Caesar's judgment seat, where I ought to be judged:

to the Jews have I done no wrong, as thou
very well knowest.
11For if I be an offender, or have committed any thing worthy of death, I refuse
not to die: but if there be none of these
things whereof these accuse me, no man
may deliver me unto them. I appeal unto
Caesar.
12Then Festus, when he had conferred
with the council, answered, Hast thou appealed unto Caesar? unto Caesar shalt
thou go.
13And after certain days king Agrippa
and Bernice came unto Caesarea to salute
Festus.
14And when they had been there many
days, Festus declared Paul's cause unto the
king, saying, There is a certain man left in
bonds by Felix:
15About whom, when I was at Jerusalem, the chief priests and the elders of the
Jews informed *me,* desiring *to have* judgment against him.
16To whom I answered, It is not the
manner of the Romans to deliver any man
to die, before that he which is accused have
the accusers face to face, and have licence
to answer for himself concerning the crime
laid against him.
17Therefore, when they were come
hither, without any delay on the morrow I
sat on the judgment seat, and commanded the man to be brought forth.
18Against whom when the accusers
stood up, they brought none accusation
of such things as I supposed:
19But had certain questions against him
of their own superstition, and of one Jesus,
which was dead, whom Paul affirmed to
be alive.
20And because I doubted of such manner of questions, I asked *him* whether he
would go to Jerusalem, and there be
judged of these matters.
21But when Paul had appealed to be reserved unto the hearing of Augustus, I
commanded him to be kept till I might
send him to Caesar.
22Then Agrippa said unto Festus, I
would also hear
the man myself. To
morrow, said he,
thou shalt hear
him.
23And on the

25:23
Showing Off Stuff
◄ Luke 20:46 ►

morrow, when Agrippa was come, and
Bernice, with great pomp, and was entered
into the place of hearing, with the chief
captains, and principal men of the city, at
Festus' commandment Paul was brought
forth.
24And Festus said, King Agrippa, and all
men which are here present with us, ye see
this man, about whom all the multitude
of the Jews have dealt with me, both at Jerusalem, and *also* here, crying that he ought
not to live any longer.
25But when I found that he had committed nothing worthy of death, and that
he himself hath appealed to Augustus, I
have determined to send him.
26Of whom I have no certain thing to
write unto my lord. Wherefore I have
brought him forth before you, and specially before thee, O king Agrippa, that,
after examination had, I might have somewhat to write.
27For it seemeth to me unreasonable to
send a prisoner, and not withal to signify
the crimes *laid* against him.

26

1Then Agrippa said unto Paul, Thou art
permitted to speak for thyself. Then Paul
stretched forth the hand, and answered for
himself:
2I think myself happy, king Agrippa,
because I shall answer for myself this day
before thee touching all the things whereof
I am accused of the Jews:
3Especially *because I know* thee to be expert in all customs and questions which
are among the Jews: wherefore I beseech
thee to hear me patiently.
4My manner of life from my youth,
which was at the first among mine own
nation at Jerusalem, know all the Jews;
5Which knew me from the beginning,
if they would testify, that after the most
straitest sect of our religion I lived a Pharisee.
6And now I stand and am judged for the
hope of the promise made of God unto
our fathers:
7Unto which *promise* our twelve tribes,
instantly serving *God* day and night, hope
to come. For which hope's sake, king Agrippa, I am accused of the Jews.
8Why should it be thought a thing incredible with you, that God should raise
the dead?
9I verily thought with myself, that I

ought to do many things contrary to the
name of Jesus of Nazareth.
10 Which thing I also did in Jerusalem:
and many of the saints did I shut up in
prison, having received authority from the
chief priests; and when they were put to
death, I gave my voice against *them*.
11 And I punished them oft in every synagogue, and compelled *them* to blaspheme; and being exceedingly mad against
them, I persecuted *them* even unto strange
cities.
12 Whereupon as I went to Damascus
with authority and commission from the
chief priests,
13 At midday, O king, I saw in the way a
light from heaven, above the brightness of
the sun, shining round about me and them
which journeyed with me.
14 And when we were all fallen to the
earth, I heard a voice speaking unto me,
and saying in the Hebrew tongue, Saul,
Saul, why persecutest thou me? *it is* hard
for thee to kick against the pricks.
15 And I said, Who art thou, Lord? And
he said, I am Jesus whom thou persecutest.
16 But rise, and stand upon thy feet: for I
have appeared unto thee for this purpose,
to make thee a minister and a witness both
of these things which thou hast seen, and
of those things in the which I will appear
unto thee;
17 Delivering thee from the people, and
from the Gentiles, unto whom now I send
thee,
18 To open their
eyes, *and* to turn
them from darkness
to light, and *from*
the power of Satan
unto God, that they
may receive forgive-
ness of sins, and
inheritance among
them which are
sanctified by faith
that is in me.

26:18 Forgiveness
◄ Acts 13:38
Ephesians 1:7 ►

26:18 Satan's Power
◄ Luke 4:6
2 Corinthians 4:3-4 ►

19 Whereupon, O king Agrippa, I was not
disobedient unto the heavenly vision:
20 But shewed
first unto them of
Damascus, and at
Jerusalem, and
throughout all the
coasts of Judaea,
and *then* to the Gentiles, that they should
repent and turn to God, and do works
meet for repentance.

26:20
Repent!
◄ Acts 17:30 ►

21 For these causes the Jews caught me
in the temple, and went about to kill *me*.
22 Having therefore obtained help of
God, I continue unto this day, witnessing
both to small and great, saying none other things than those which the prophets
and Moses did say should come:
23 That Christ should suffer, *and* that he
should be the first that should rise from
the dead, and should shew light unto the
people, and to the Gentiles.
24 And as he thus spake for himself, Festus said with a loud voice, Paul, thou art
beside thyself; much learning doth make
thee mad.
25 But he said, I am not mad, most noble Festus; but speak forth the words of
truth and soberness.
26 For the king knoweth of these things,
before whom also I speak freely: for I am
persuaded that none of these things are
hidden from him; for this thing was not
done in a corner.
27 King Agrippa, believest thou the
prophets? I know that thou believest.
28 Then Agrippa said unto Paul, Almost
thou persuadest me to be a Christian.
29 And Paul said, I would to God, that
not only thou, but also all that hear me
this day, were both almost, and altogether
such as I am, except these bonds.
30 And when he had thus spoken, the
king rose up, and the governor, and Bernice, and they that sat with them:
31 And when they were gone aside, they
talked between themselves, saying, This
man doeth nothing worthy of death or of
bonds.
32 Then said Agrippa unto Festus, This
man might have been set at liberty, if he
had not appealed unto Caesar.

27

1 And when it was determined that we
should sail into Italy, they delivered Paul
and certain other prisoners unto *one*
named Julius, a centurion of Augustus'
band.
2 And entering into a ship of Adramytti-
um, we launched, meaning to sail by the
coasts of Asia; *one* Aristarchus, a Macedo-
nian of Thessalonica, being with us.
3 And the next *day* we touched at Sidon.
And Julius courteously entreated Paul, and

gave *him* liberty to go unto his friends to
refresh himself.
4And when we had launched from
thence, we sailed under Cyprus, because
the winds were contrary.
5And when we had sailed over the sea
of Cilicia and Pamphylia, we came to
Myra, *a city* of Lycia.
6And there the centurion found a ship
of Alexandria sailing into Italy; and he put
us therein.
7And when we had sailed slowly many
days, and scarce were come over against
Cnidus, the wind not suffering us, we
sailed under Crete, over against Salmone;
8And, hardly passing it, came unto a
place which is called The fair havens; nigh
whereunto was the city *of* Lasea.
9Now when much time was spent, and
when sailing was now dangerous, because
the fast was now already past, Paul admonished *them*,
10And said unto them, Sirs, I perceive
that this voyage will be with hurt and
much damage, not only of the lading and
ship, but also of our lives.
11Nevertheless the centurion believed
the master and the owner of the ship, more
than those things which were spoken by
Paul.
12And because the haven was not com-
modious to winter in, the more part advised to depart thence also, if by any means
they might attain to Phenice, *and there* to
winter; *which is* an haven of Crete, and lieth
toward the south west and north west.
13And when the south wind blew softly,
supposing that they had obtained *their*
purpose, loosing *thence*, they sailed close
by Crete.
14But not long after there arose against
it a tempestuous wind, called Euroclydon.
15And when the ship was caught, and
could not bear up into the wind, we let
her drive.
16And running under a certain island
which is called Clauda, we had much work
to come by the boat:
17Which when they had taken up, they
used helps, undergirding the ship; and,
fearing lest they should fall into the quick-
sands, strake sail, and so were driven.
18And we being exceedingly tossed with
a tempest, the next *day* they lightened the
ship;
19And the third *day* we cast out with our
own hands the tackling of the ship.
20And when neither sun nor stars in
many days appeared, and no small tempest lay on *us*, all hope that we should be
saved was then taken away.
21But after long abstinence Paul stood
forth in the midst of them, and said, Sirs,
ye should have hearkened unto me, and
not have loosed from Crete, and to have
gained this harm and loss.
22And now I ex-
hort you to be of
good cheer: for
there shall be no
loss of *any man's* life
among you, but of
the ship.
23For there stood
by me this night
the angel of God,
whose I am, and
whom I serve,

27:22
Encouraging People
◄ Acts 23:11 ►

27:23 Angels
◄ Acts 12:7
Hebrews 1:14 ►

24Saying, Fear not, Paul; thou must be
brought before Caesar: and, lo, God hath
given thee all them that sail with thee.
25Wherefore, sirs, be of good cheer: for
I believe God, that it shall be even as it
was told me.
26Howbeit we must be cast upon a certain island.
27But when the fourteenth night was
come, as we were driven up and down in
Adria, about midnight the shipmen deemed
that they drew near to some country;
28And sounded, and found *it* twenty
fathoms: and when they had gone a little
further, they sounded again, and found *it*
fifteen fathoms.
29Then fearing lest we should have fall-
en upon rocks, they cast four anchors out
of the stern, and wished for the day.
30And as the shipmen were about to flee
out of the ship, when they had let down
the boat into the sea, under colour as
though they would have cast anchors out
of the foreship,
31Paul said to the centurion and to the
soldiers, Except these abide in the ship, ye
cannot be saved.
32Then the soldiers cut off the ropes of
the boat, and let her fall off.
33And while the day was coming on,
Paul besought *them* all to take meat, saying, This day is the fourteenth day that ye

have tarried and continued fasting, having taken nothing.
34 Wherefore I pray you to take *some*
meat: for this is for your health: for there
shall not an hair fall from the head of any
of you.
35 And when he had thus spoken, he
took bread, and gave thanks to God in
presence of them all: and when he had
broken *it,* he began to eat.
36 Then were they all of good cheer, and
they also took *some* meat.
37 And we were in all in the ship two
hundred threescore and sixteen souls.
38 And when they had eaten enough,
they lightened the ship, and cast out the
wheat into the sea.
39 And when it was day, they knew not
the land: but they discovered a certain
creek with a shore, into the which they
were minded, if it were possible, to thrust
in the ship.
40 And when they had taken up the anchors, they committed *themselves* unto the
sea, and loosed the rudder bands, and
hoisted up the mainsail to the wind, and
made toward shore.
41 And falling into a place where two seas
met, they ran the ship aground; and the
forepart stuck fast, and remained unmove-
able, but the hinder part was broken with
the violence of the waves.
42 And the soldiers' counsel was to kill
the prisoners, lest any of them should
swim out, and escape.
43 But the centurion, willing to save Paul,
kept them from *their* purpose; and commanded that they which could swim
should cast *themselves* first *into the sea,* and
get to land:
44 And the rest, some on boards, and
some on *broken pieces* of the ship. And so
it came to pass, that they escaped all safe
to land.

28

1 And when they were escaped, then they
knew that the island was called Melita.
2 And the barba-
rous people shewed
us no little kind-
ness: for they kin-
dled a fire, and
received us every
one, because of the present rain, and because of the cold.

28:2 Compassion
◄ Acts 16:33
Hebrews 10:34 ►

3 And when Paul had gathered a bundle
of sticks, and laid *them* on the fire, there
came a viper out of the heat, and fastened
on his hand.
4 And when the
barbarians saw the
venomous beast
hang on his hand,
they said among
themselves, No
doubt this man is a murderer, whom,
though he hath escaped the sea, yet vengeance suffereth not to live.

28:4
Superstition
◄ Acts 17:23 ►

5 And he shook off the beast into the fire,
and felt no harm.
6 Howbeit they looked when he should
have swollen, or fallen down dead suddenly: but after they had looked a great while,
and saw no harm come to him, they
changed their minds, and said that he was
a god.
7 In the same quarters were possessions
of the chief man of the island, whose name
was Publius; who received us, and lodged
us three days courteously.
8 And it came to pass, that the father of
Publius lay sick of a fever and of a bloody
flux: to whom Paul entered in, and prayed,
and laid his hands on him, and healed
him.
9 So when this was done, others also,
which had diseases in the island, came,
and were healed:
10 Who also ho-
noured us with
many honours; and
when we departed,
they laded *us* with
such things as were
necessary.

28:10
"Thank You"
◄ 2 Kings 4:13 ►

11 And after three
months we depart-
ed in a ship of Al-
exandria, which
had wintered in the
isle, whose sign was Castor and Pollux.

28:10
Respecting God's People
◄ Exodus 33:8
Philippians 2:29 ►

12 And landing at Syracuse, we tarried
there three days.
13 And from thence we fetched a compass, and came to Rhegium: and after one
day the south wind blew, and we came the
next day to Puteoli:
14 Where we found brethren, and were
desired to tarry with them seven days: and
so we went toward Rome.
15 And from thence, when the brethren

heard of us, they came to meet us as far as
Appii Forum, and The three taverns: whom
when Paul saw, he thanked God, and took
courage.
16 And when we came to Rome, the centurion delivered the prisoners to the captain of the guard: but Paul was suffered to
dwell by himself with a soldier that kept
him.
17 And it came to pass, that after three
days Paul called the chief of the Jews
together: and when they were come together, he said unto them, Men *and* brethren, though I have committed nothing
against the people, or customs of our
fathers, yet was I delivered prisoner
from Jerusalem into the hands of the Romans.
18 Who, when they had examined me,
would have let *me* go, because there was
no cause of death in me.
19 But when the Jews spake against *it,* I
was constrained to appeal unto Caesar; not
that I had ought to accuse my nation of.
20 For this cause therefore have I called
for you, to see *you,* and to speak with *you:*
because that for the hope of Israel I am
bound with this chain.
21 And they said unto him, We neither
received letters out of Judaea concerning
thee, neither any of the brethren that came
shewed or spake any harm of thee.
22 But we desire to hear of thee what thou
thinkest: for as concerning this sect, we
know that every
where it is spoken
against.
23 And when they
had appointed him
a day, there came
many to him into *his* lodging; to whom
he expounded and testified the kingdom
of God, persuading them concerning Jesus,
both out of the law of Moses, and *out
of* the prophets, from morning till evening.

28:23 Sunday School
◄ Acts 18:26 ►

24 And some believed the things which
were spoken, and some believed not.
25 And when they agreed not among
themselves, they departed, after that Paul
had spoken one word, Well spake the Holy
Ghost by Esaias the prophet unto our fathers,
26 Saying, Go unto this people, and say,
Hearing ye shall hear, and shall not understand; and seeing ye shall see, and not
perceive:
27 For the heart
of this people is
waxed gross, and
their ears are dull of
hearing, and their
eyes have they
closed; lest they should see with *their* eyes,
and hear with *their* ears, and understand
with *their* heart, and should be converted,
and I should heal them.

28:27 Salvation
◄ Acts 24:25
Hebrews 2:3 ►

28 Be it known therefore unto you, that
the salvation of God is sent unto the Gentiles, and *that* they will hear it.
29 And when he had said these words,
the Jews departed, and had great reasoning among themselves.
30 And Paul dwelt two whole years in his
own hired house, and received all that
came in unto him,
31 Preaching the kingdom of God, and
teaching those things which concern the
Lord Jesus Christ, with all confidence, no
man forbidding him.

Romans

AUTHOR
Paul the apostle

MAIN POINT
Jesus provided the way of salvation for all people, and those who put their faith in him can now live for him.

DATE WRITTEN
About A.D. 57

16 CHAPTERS

MAIN PEOPLE

Paul, Phoebe

SPECIAL FEATURES

- *Carefully explains how to be saved, yet has many touches of a personal letter*
- *Describes the change that occurs when Jesus moves into a person's life*
- *Expresses Paul's anguish over the hardness of many peoples' hearts to Jesus*
- *First of Paul's epistles*

HOW THE BOOK GOT ITS NAME

Paul was writing to Christians in Rome.

1

1Paul, a servant of Jesus Christ, called *to*
be an apostle, separated unto the gospel
of God,
2(Which he had promised afore by his
prophets in the holy scriptures,)
3Concerning his Son Jesus Christ our
Lord, which was made of the seed of David according to the flesh;
4And declared *to be* the Son of God with
power, according to the spirit of holiness,
by the resurrection from the dead:
5By whom we have received grace and
apostleship, for obedience to the faith
among all nations, for his name:
6Among whom are ye also the called of
Jesus Christ:
7To all that be in Rome, beloved of God,
called *to be* saints: Grace to you and peace
from God our Father, and the Lord Jesus
Christ.
8First, I thank my God through Jesus
Christ for you all, that your faith is spoken of throughout the whole world.
9For God is my witness, whom I serve
with my spirit in the gospel of his Son,
that without ceasing I make mention of
you always in my prayers;
10Making request, if by any means now
at length I might have a prosperous journey by the will of God to come unto you.
11For I long to see you, that I may impart unto you some spiritual gift, to the
end ye may be established;
12That is, that I may be comforted together with you by the mutual faith both
of you and me.

13 Now I would not have you ignorant,
brethren, that oftentimes I purposed to
come unto you, (but was let hitherto,) that
I might have some fruit among you also,
even as among other Gentiles.
14 I am debtor both to the Greeks, and
to the Barbarians; both to the wise, and to
the unwise.
15 So, as much as in me is, I am ready to
preach the gospel to you that are at Rome
also.
16 For I am not
ashamed of the gos-
pel of Christ: for it
is the power of God
unto salvation to
every one that be-
lieveth; to the Jew first, and also to the
Greek.

1:16 Power of the Bible
◄ Ezekiel 37:7
Ephesians 6:17 ►

17 For therein is the righteousness of God
revealed from faith to faith: as it is written, The just shall live by faith.
18 For the wrath
of God is revealed
from heaven against
all ungodliness and
unrighteousness of
men, who hold the
truth in unrighteousness;

1:18 God's Anger
◄ John 3:36
Romans 2:8 ►

19 Because that which may be known of
God is manifest in them; for God hath
shewed *it* unto them.
20 For the invisi-
ble things of him
from the creation of
the world are clear-
ly seen, being un-
derstood by the
things that are made, *even* his eternal power and Godhead; so that they are without
excuse:

1:20
Nature Teaches Us
◄ Acts 14:17 ►

21 Because that,
when they knew
God, they glorified
him not as God, nei-
ther were thankful;
but became vain in
their imaginations, and their foolish heart
was darkened.

1:21
Gratitude
◄ Luke 17:17-18 ►

22 Professing themselves to be wise, they
became fools,
23 And changed the glory of the uncor-
ruptible God into an image made like to
corruptible man, and to birds, and fourfooted beasts, and creeping things.
24 Wherefore God also gave them up to
uncleanness through the lusts of their own
hearts, to dishonour their own bodies between themselves:
25 Who changed the truth of God into a
lie, and worshipped and served the creature more than the Creator, who is blessed
for ever. Amen.
26 For this cause God gave them up unto
vile affections: for even their women did
change the natural use into that which is
against nature:
27 And likewise also the men, leaving the
natural use of the woman, burned in their
lust one toward another; men with men
working that which is unseemly, and receiving in themselves that recompence of
their error which was meet.
28 And even as
they did not like to
retain God in *their*
knowledge, God
gave them over to a
reprobate mind, to
do those things which are not convenient;

1:28
Brain Power
◄ Romans 8:7 ►

29 Being filled with all unrighteousness,
fornication, wickedness, covetousness, maliciousness; full of envy, murder, debate,
deceit, malignity; whisperers,
30 Backbiters, haters of God, despiteful,
proud, boasters, inventors of evil things,
disobedient to parents,
31 Without under-
standing, covenant-
breakers, without
natural affection,
implacable, unmer-
ciful:

1:31 No Mercy
◄ Matthew 18:35
James 2:13 ►

32 Who knowing
the judgment of
God, that they
which commit such
things are worthy of
death, not only do
the same, but have pleasure in them that
do them.

1:32
Excusing Sin
◄ Malachi 2:17 ►

2

1 Therefore thou art inexcusable, O man,
whosoever thou art that judgest: for wherein thou judgest another, thou condemnest
thyself; for thou
that judgest doest
the same things.
2 But we are sure
that the judgment
of God is according

2:2 God's Justice
◄ John 5:30
Revelation 15:3 ►

to truth against them which commit such things.

3 And thinkest thou this, O man, that judgest them which do such things, and doest the same, that thou shalt escape the judgment of God?

4 Or despisest thou the riches of his goodness and forbearance and longsuffering; not knowing that the goodness of God leadeth thee to repentance?

5 But after thy hardness and impenitent heart treasurest up unto thyself wrath against the day of wrath and revelation of the righteous judgment of God;

2:5 Hard-heart Aches
◄ Isaiah 42:25
Hebrews 3:13 ►

2:6 Actions Judged
◄ Matthew 16:27
2 Corinthians 5:10 ►

6 Who will render to every man according to his deeds:

7 To them who by patient continuance in well doing seek for glory and honour and immortality, eternal life:

2:7 Determination
◄ Acts 13:43
Galatians 6:9 ►

2:7 Eternal Life
◄ John 11:26
1 Corinthians 15:53 ►

8 But unto them that are contentious, and do not obey the truth, but obey unrighteousness, indignation and wrath,

2:8 God's Anger
◄ Romans 1:18
Ephesians 5:6 ►

9 Tribulation and anguish, upon every soul of man that doeth evil, of the Jew first, and also of the Gentile;

10 But glory, honour, and peace, to every man that worketh good, to the Jew first, and also to the Gentile:

2:10 Goodness Rewarded
◄ John 4:36
1 Corinthians 3:8 ►

11 For there is no respect of persons with God.

12 For as many as have sinned without law shall also perish without law: and as many as have sinned in the law shall be judged by the law;

13 (For not the hearers of the law *are* just before God, but the doers of the law shall be justified.

14 For when the Gentiles, which have not the law, do by nature the things contained in the law, these, having not the law, are a law unto themselves:

15 Which shew the work of the law written in their hearts, their conscience also bearing witness, and *their* thoughts the mean while accusing or else excusing one another;)

16 In the day when God shall judge the secrets of men by Jesus Christ according to my gospel.

2:16 Christ as Judge
◄ Acts 17:31
Romans 14:10 ►

17 Behold, thou art called a Jew, and restest in the law, and makest thy boast of God,

2:17 Boasting
◄ Jeremiah 9:24
1 Corinthians 1:31 ►

18 And knowest *his* will, and approvest the things that are more excellent, being instructed out of the law;

19 And art confident that thou thyself art a guide of the blind, a light of them which are in darkness,

20 An instructor of the foolish, a teacher of babes, which hast the form of knowledge and of the truth in the law.

21 Thou therefore which teachest another, teachest thou not thyself? thou that preachest a man should not steal, dost thou steal?

22 Thou that sayest a man should not commit adultery, dost thou commit adultery? thou that abhorrest idols, dost thou commit sacrilege?

23 Thou that makest thy boast of the law, through breaking the law dishonourest thou God?

2:23-24 Embarrassing God
◄ Ezekiel 36:20
2 Peter 2:2 ►

24 For the name of God is blasphemed among the Gentiles through you, as it is written.

25 For circumcision verily profiteth, if thou keep the law: but if thou be a breaker of the law, thy circumcision is made uncircumcision.

26 Therefore if the uncircumcision keep

the righteousness of the law, shall not his
uncircumcision be counted for circumcision?
27And shall not uncircumcision which
is by nature, if it fulfil the law, judge thee,
who by the letter and circumcision dost
transgress the law?
28For he is not a Jew, which is one outwardly; neither *is that* circumcision, which
is outward in the flesh:
29But he *is* a Jew, which is one inwardly;
and circumcision *is that* of the heart, in
the spirit, *and* not in the letter; whose
praise *is* not of men, but of God.

3

1What advantage then hath the Jew? or
what profit *is there* of circumcision?
2Much every way: chiefly, because that
unto them were committed the oracles
of God.
3For what if some did not believe? shall
their unbelief make the faith of God without effect?
4God forbid: yea,
let God be true, but
every man a liar; as
it is written, That
thou mightest be
justified in thy say-
ings, and mightest overcome when thou
art judged.

3:4 God's Word
◄ Isaiah 65:16
Titus 1:2 ►

5But if our unrighteousness commend
the righteousness of God, what shall we
say? *Is* God unrighteous who taketh vengeance? (I speak as a man)
6God forbid: for then how shall God
judge the world?
7For if the truth of God hath more
abounded through my lie unto his glory;
why yet am I also judged as a sinner?
8And not *rather,* (as we be slanderously
reported, and as some affirm that we say,)
Let us do evil, that good may come? whose
damnation is just.
9What then? are we better *than they?* No,
in no wise: for we have before proved
both Jews and Gentiles, that they are all
under sin;
10As it is written, There is none righteous, no, not one:
11There is none that understandeth,
there is none that seeketh after God.
12They are all gone out of the way, they
are together become unprofitable; there is
none that doeth good, no, not one.
13Their throat *is* an open sepulchre; with
their tongues they have used deceit; the
poison of asps *is* under their lips:
14Whose mouth *is* full of cursing and
bitterness:
15Their feet *are*
swift to shed blood:
16Destruction
and misery *are* in
their ways:
17And the way of
peace have they not known:

3:15 Bad People
◄ Micah 2:1
1 Peter 5:8 ►

18There is no fear of God before their
eyes.
19Now we know that what things soever
the law saith, it saith to them who are under the law: that every mouth may be
stopped, and all the world may become
guilty before God.
20Therefore by the deeds of the law there
shall no flesh be justified in his sight: for
by the law *is* the knowledge of sin.
21But now the righteousness of God
without the law is manifested, being witnessed by the law and the prophets;
22Even the righteousness of God *which
is* by faith of Jesus Christ unto all and upon
all them that believe: for there is no difference:
23For all have
sinned, and come
short of the glory of
God;
24Being justified
freely by his grace
through the re-
demption that is in
Christ Jesus:
25Whom God
hath set forth *to
be* a propitiation
through faith in his
blood, to declare
his righteousness
for the remission of
sins that are past,
through the for-
bearance of God;

3:23 Everyone Sins
◄ Micah 7:2
Galatians 3:22 ►

3:24 Grace
◄ Acts 15:11
Romans 5:15 ►

3:25 Forgiveness of Sin
◄ Acts 2:38
Hebrews 9:22 ►

26To declare, *I say,* at this time his
righteousness: that he might be just, and
the justifier of him which believeth in
Jesus.
27Where *is* boasting then? It is exclud-
ed. By what law? of works? Nay: but by
the law of faith.
28Therefore we conclude that a man is

justified by faith without the deeds of the
law.
29 *Is he* the God of the Jews only? *is he*
not also of the Gentiles? Yes, of the Gentiles also:
30 Seeing *it is* one God, which shall justify the circumcision by faith, and uncircumcision through faith.
31 Do we then make void the law through
faith? God forbid: yea, we establish the law.

4

1 What shall we say then that Abraham
our father, as pertaining to the flesh, hath
found?
2 For if Abraham were justified by works,
he hath *whereof* to glory; but not before
God.
3 For what saith
the scripture? Abra-
ham believed God,
and it was counted
unto him for righ-
teousness.

> **4:3**
> **Justification by Faith**
> ◄ Habakkuk 2:4
> Romans 5:1 ►

4 Now to him that worketh is the reward
not reckoned of grace, but of debt.
5 But to him that worketh not, but
believeth on him that justifieth the ungodly, his faith is counted for righteousness.
6 Even as David also describeth the
blessedness of the man, unto whom God
imputeth righteousness without works,
7 *Saying,* Blessed *are* they whose iniquities are forgiven, and whose sins are
covered.
8 Blessed *is* the man to whom the Lord
will not impute sin.
9 *Cometh* this blessedness then upon the
circumcision *only,* or upon the uncircumcision also? for we say that faith was reckoned to Abraham for righteousness.
10 How was it then reckoned? when he
was in circumcision, or in uncircumcision?
Not in circumcision, but in uncircumcision.
11 And he received the sign of circumcision, a seal of the righteousness of the faith
which *he had yet* being uncircumcised: that
he might be the father of all them that
believe, though they be not circumcised;
that righteousness might be imputed unto
them also:
12 And the father of circumcision to them
who are not of the circumcision only, but
who also walk in the steps of that faith of
our father Abraham, which *he had* being
yet uncircumcised.
13 For the promise, that he should be the
heir of the world, *was* not to Abraham, or
to his seed, through the law, but through
the righteousness of faith.
14 For if they which are of the law *be*
heirs, faith is made void, and the promise
made of none effect:
15 Because the law worketh wrath: for
where no law is, *there is* no transgression.
16 Therefore *it is* of faith, that *it might be*
by grace; to the end the promise might be
sure to all the seed; not to that only which
is of the law, but to that also which is of
the faith of Abraham; who is the father of
us all,
17 (As it is written, I have made thee a
father of many nations,) before him whom
he believed, *even* God, who quickeneth the
dead, and calleth those things which be
not as though they were.
18 Who against hope believed in hope,
that he might become the father of many
nations; according to that which was spoken, So shall thy seed be.
19 And being not weak in faith, he considered not his own body now dead, when
he was about an hundred years old, neither yet the deadness of Sarah's womb:
20 He staggered not at the promise of
God through unbelief; but was strong in
faith, giving glory to God;
21 And being ful-
ly persuaded that,
what he had prom-
ised, he was able
also to perform.
22 And therefore
it was imputed to him for righteousness.

> **4:21 God's Promises**
> ◄ 1 Kings 8:56
> 2 Corinthians 1:20 ►

23 Now it was not written for his sake
alone, that it was imputed to him;
24 But for us also, to whom it shall be
imputed, if we believe on him that raised
up Jesus our Lord from the dead;
25 Who was de-
livered for our of-
fences, and was
raised again for
our justification.

> **5:1**
> **Justification by Faith**
> ◄ Romans 4:3
> Galatians 3:6 ►

5

1 Therefore being
justified by faith,
we have peace with
God through our
Lord Jesus Christ:
2 By whom also
we have access by

> **5:2 God's Presence**
> ◄ John 10:9
> Ephesians 2:18 ►

faith into this grace wherein we stand, and
rejoice in hope of the glory of God.
3And not only *so,*
but we glory in
tribulations also:
knowing that tribu-
lation worketh pa-
tience;

5:3 Suffering
◄ Acts 14:22
1 Thessalonians 3:4 ►

4And patience, experience; and experience, hope:
5And hope maketh not ashamed; because the love of God is shed abroad in
our hearts by the Holy Ghost which is giv-
en unto us.
6For when we
were yet without
strength, in due
time Christ died for
the ungodly.

5:6 Feeling Helpless
◄ Acts 3:2
Romans 7:18 ►

7For scarcely for
a righteous man will one die: yet peradventure for a good man some would
even dare to die.
8But God com-
mendeth his love
toward us, in that,
while we were yet
sinners, Christ died
for us.

5:8 Friend of Jesus
◄ John 8:11
1 Timothy 1:15 ►

9Much more
then, being now
justified by his
blood, we shall be
saved from wrath
through him.

5:8 God's Love
◄ John 16:27
Ephesians 2:4-5 ►

10For if, when we
were enemies, we
were reconciled to
God by the death of
his Son, much
more, being recon-
ciled, we shall be saved by his life.

5:9 Only One Savior
◄ Acts 15:11
1 Thessalonians 5:9 ►

11And not only *so,* but we also joy in God
through our Lord
Jesus Christ, by
whom we have now
received the atone-
ment.

5:12 Death
◄ Ecclesiastes 8:8
Hebrews 9:27 ►

12Wherefore, as
by one man sin en-
tered into the world,
and death by sin;
and so death passed
upon all men, for
that all have sinned:

5:12 Why Not Sin?
◄ Ezekiel 18:4
Romans 6:23 ►

13(For until the law sin was in the world:
but sin is not imputed when there is no
law.
14Nevertheless death reigned from
Adam to Moses, even over them that had
not sinned after the similitude of Adam's
transgression, who is the figure of him that
was to come.
15But not as the
offence, so also *is*
the free gift. For
if through the
offence of one
many be dead,
much more the
grace of God, and
the gift by grace,
which is by one
man, Jesus Christ,
hath abounded
unto many.

5:15 A Great Gift
◄ John 4:10
Romans 6:23 ►

5:15 Grace
◄ Romans 3:24
Romans 11:6 ►

16And not as *it was* by one that sinned,
so is the gift: for the judgment *was* by one
to condemnation, but the free gift *is* of
many offences unto justification.
17For if by one man's offence death
reigned by one; much more they which
receive abundance of grace and of the gift
of righteousness shall reign in life by one,
Jesus Christ.)
18Therefore as by
the offence of one
judgment came upon
all men to condem-
nation; even so by
the righteousness of
one *the free gift came* upon all men unto
justification of life.

5:18 Salvation for Anyone
◄ Acts 2:21
Romans 10:13 ►

19For as by one man's disobedience
many were made sinners, so by the obedience of one shall many be made righteous.
20Moreover the law entered, that the
offence might abound. But where sin
abounded, grace did much more abound:
21That as sin hath reigned unto death,
even so might grace reign through righteousness unto eternal life by Jesus Christ
our Lord.

6

1What shall we
say then? Shall we
continue in sin,
that grace may
abound?
2God forbid.

6:2 Freedom
◄ Romans 6:7 ►

How shall we, that are dead to sin, live any
longer therein?
3 Know ye not, that so many of us as were
baptized into Jesus Christ were baptized
into his death?
4 Therefore we are
buried with him by
baptism into death:
that like as Christ
was raised up from
the dead by the
glory of the Father, even so we also should
walk in newness of life.

6:4 New Life
◄ Ezekiel 11:19
Romans 7:6 ►

5 For if we have been planted together
in the likeness of his death, we shall be
also *in the likeness* of *his* resurrection:
6 Knowing this,
that our old man is
crucified with *him*,
that the body of sin
might be destroyed,
that henceforth we
should not serve sin.

6:6
Old Life
◄ Ephesians 4:22 ►

7 For he that is
dead is freed from
sin.
8 Now if we be
dead with Christ,
we believe that we
shall also live with him:

6:7 Freedom
◄ Romans 6:2
Romans 6:11 ►

9 Knowing that Christ being raised from
the dead dieth no more; death hath no
more dominion over him.
10 For in that he died, he died unto sin
once: but in that he liveth, he liveth unto
God.
11 Likewise reck-
on ye also your-
selves to be dead
indeed unto sin,
but alive unto God
through Jesus Christ
our Lord.

6:11 Freedom
◄ Romans 6:7
Galatians 2:20 ►

12 Let not sin
therefore reign in
your mortal body,
that ye should obey
it in the lusts
thereof.

6:12 Self-control
◄ Acts 24:25
1 Corinthians 6:12 ►

13 Neither yield
ye your members *as*
instruments of un-
righteousness unto
sin: but yield your-
selves unto God, as

6:13 Saying No
◄ Luke 21:34
Ephesians 6:13 ►

those that are alive from the dead, and
your members *as* instruments of righteousness unto God.
14 For sin shall not have dominion over
you: for ye are not under the law, but under grace.
15 What then? shall we sin, because we
are not under the law, but under grace?
God forbid.
16 Know ye not,
that to whom ye
yield yourselves ser-
vants to obey, his
servants ye are to
whom ye obey;
whether of sin unto death, or of obedience unto righteousness?

6:16 Bad Habits
◄ Acts 8:23
Romans 7:23 ►

17 But God be thanked, that ye were the
servants of sin, but ye have obeyed from
the heart that form of doctrine which was
delivered you.
18 Being then made free from sin, ye became the servants of righteousness.
19 I speak after the manner of men because of the infirmity of your flesh: for as
ye have yielded your members servants to
uncleanness and to iniquity unto iniquity; even so now yield your members servants to righteousness unto holiness.
20 For when ye were the servants of sin,
ye were free from righteousness.
21 What fruit had ye then in those things
whereof ye are now ashamed? for the end
of those things *is* death.
22 But now being made free from sin,
and become servants to God, ye have your
fruit unto holiness, and the end everlasting life.
23 For the wages
of sin *is* death; but
the gift of God *is*
eternal life through
Jesus Christ our
Lord.

6:23 A Great Gift
◄ Romans 5:15
Romans 8:32 ►

7

1 Know ye not,
brethren, (for I
speak to them that
know the law,) how
that the law hath
dominion over a
man as long as he
liveth?
2 For the woman
which hath an hus-
band is bound by

6:23 Spiritual Death
◄ Ezekiel 18:20
Romans 8:6 ►

6:23
Why Not Sin?
◄ Romans 5:12 ►

the law to *her* husband so long as he liveth;
but if the husband be dead, she is loosed
from the law of *her* husband.
3 So then if, while *her* husband liveth,
she be married to another man, she shall
be called an adulteress: but if her husband
be dead, she is free from that law; so that
she is no adulteress, though she be married to another man.
4 Wherefore, my brethren, ye also are become dead to the law by the body of Christ;
that ye should be married to another, *even*
to him who is raised from the dead, that
we should bring forth fruit unto God.
5 For when we were in the flesh, the
motions of sins, which were by the law,
did work in our members to bring forth
fruit unto death.
6 But now we are
delivered from the
law, that being dead
wherein we were
held; that we
should serve in
newness of spirit, and not *in* the oldness
of the letter.

7:6 New Life
◄ Romans 6:4
2 Corinthians 5:17 ►

7 What shall we say then? *Is* the law sin?
God forbid. Nay, I had not known sin, but
by the law: for I had not known lust, except the law had said, Thou shalt not
covet.
8 But sin, taking occasion by the commandment, wrought in me all manner of
concupiscence. For without the law sin *was*
dead.
9 For I was alive without the law once:
but when the commandment came, sin
revived, and I died.
10 And the commandment, which *was*
ordained to life, I found *to be* unto death.
11 For sin, taking occasion by the commandment, deceived me, and by it slew *me*.
12 Wherefore the law *is* holy, and the
commandment holy, and just, and good.
13 Was then that which is good made
death unto me? God forbid. But sin, that
it might appear sin, working death in me
by that which is good; that sin by the
commandment might become exceeding
sinful.
14 For we know that the law is spiritual:
but I am carnal, sold under sin.
15 For that which I do I allow not: for
what I would, that do I not; but what I
hate, that do I.
16 If then I do that which I would not, I
consent unto the law that *it is* good.
17 Now then it is no more I that do it,
but sin that dwelleth in me.
18 For I know that
in me (that is, in
my flesh,) dwelleth
no good thing: for
to will is present
with me; but *how* to
perform that which is good I find not.

7:18 Feeling Helpless
◄ Romans 5:6 ►

19 For the good that I would I do not:
but the evil which I would not, that I do.
20 Now if I do that I would not, it is
no more I that do it, but sin that dwelleth
in me.
21 I find then a law, that, when I would
do good, evil is present with me.
22 For I delight in the law of God after
the inward man:
23 But I see an-
other law in my
members, warring
against the law of
my mind, and
bringing me into
captivity to the law of sin which is in my
members.

7:23 Bad Habits
◄ Romans 6:16
2 Timothy 2:26 ►

24 O wretched man that I am! who shall
deliver me from the body of this death?
25 I thank God through Jesus Christ our
Lord. So then with the mind I myself serve
the law of God; but with the flesh the law
of sin.

8

1 *There is* there-
fore now no con-
demnation to them
which are in Christ
Jesus, who walk not
after the flesh, but
after the Spirit.

8:1 No Condemnation
◄ John 5:24
Romans 8:34 ►

2 For the law of the Spirit of life in Christ
Jesus hath made me free from the law of
sin and death.
3 For what the law
could not do, in
that it was weak
through the flesh,
God sending his
own Son in the
likeness of sinful flesh, and for sin, condemned sin in the flesh:

8:3 Christmas
◄ John 1:14
Philippians 2:7 ►

4 That the righteousness of the law might
be fulfilled in us, who walk not after the
flesh, but after the Spirit.

5 For they that are after the flesh do mind the things of the flesh; but they that are after the Spirit the things of the Spirit.

6 For to be carnally minded *is* death; but to be spiritually minded *is* life and peace.

8:6 Spiritual Death
◄ Romans 6:23
James 1:15 ►

7 Because the carnal mind *is* enmity against God: for it is not subject to the law of God, neither indeed can be.

8:7 Brain Power
◄ Romans 1:28
Ephesians 4:17 ►

8 So then they that are in the flesh cannot please God.

9 But ye are not in the flesh, but in the Spirit, if so be that the Spirit of God dwell in you. Now if any man have not the Spirit of Christ, he is none of his.

8:9 The Spirit in You
◄ John 14:17
1 Corinthians 3:16 ►

10 And if Christ *be* in you, the body *is* dead because of sin; but the Spirit *is* life because of righteousness.

8:10 Jesus' Home
◄ John 17:23
Galatians 2:20 ►

11 But if the Spirit of him that raised up Jesus from the dead dwell in you, he that raised up Christ from the dead shall also quicken your mortal bodies by his Spirit that dwelleth in you.

8:13 Controlling Yourself
◄ Luke 14:26-27
Romans 15:1 ►

12 Therefore, brethren, we are debtors, not to the flesh, to live after the flesh.

8:14 Guidance
◄ Acts 16:6
Galatians 5:18 ►

13 For if ye live after the flesh, ye shall die: but if ye through the Spirit do mortify the deeds of the body, ye shall live.

8:15 Adopted by God
◄ John 1:12
2 Corinthians 6:18 ►

14 For as many as are led by the Spirit of God, they are the sons of God.

8:15 Perfect Father
◄ Matthew 7:11
1 Peter 1:17 ►

15 For ye have not received the spirit of bondage again to fear; but ye have received the Spirit of adoption, whereby we cry, Abba, Father.

16 The Spirit itself beareth witness with our spirit, that we are the children of God:

17 And if children, then heirs; heirs of God, and joint-heirs with Christ; if so be that we suffer with *him*, that we may be also glorified together.

8:17 Suffering for Jesus
◄ Acts 9:16
Romans 8:36 ►

8:17 Suffering Rewarded
◄ Matthew 5:11-12
2 Timothy 2:12 ►

18 For I reckon that the sufferings of this present time *are* not worthy *to be compared* with the glory which shall be revealed in us.

19 For the earnest expectation of the creature waiteth for the manifestation of the sons of God.

20 For the creature was made subject to vanity, not willingly, but by reason of him who hath subjected *the same* in hope,

21 Because the creature itself also shall be delivered from the bondage of corruption into the glorious liberty of the children of God.

22 For we know that the whole creation groaneth and travaileth in pain together until now.

23 And not only *they*, but ourselves also, which have the firstfruits of the Spirit, even we ourselves groan within ourselves, waiting for the adoption, *to wit*, the redemption of our body.

24 For we are saved by hope: but hope that is seen is not hope: for what a man seeth, why doth he yet hope for?

25 But if we hope for that we see not, *then* do we with patience wait for *it*.

26 Likewise the Spirit also helpeth our infirmities: for we know not what we should pray for as we ought: but the Spirit itself maketh intercession for us with groanings which cannot be uttered.

27 And he that searcheth the hearts knoweth what *is* the mind of the Spirit, because he maketh intercession for the saints according to *the will of* God.

28 And we know that all things work together for good to them that love God, to them who are the called according to *his* purpose.

29For whom he did foreknow, he also
did predestinate *to be* conformed to the
image of his Son, that he might be the firstborn among many brethren.
30Moreover whom he did predestinate,
them he also called: and whom he called,
them he also justified: and whom he justified, them he also glorified.
31What shall we then say to these things?
If God *be* for us, who *can be* against us?
32He that spared
not his own Son,
but delivered him
up for us all, how
shall he not with
him also freely give
us all things?

8:32 A Great Gift
◄ Romans 6:23
2 Corinthians 9:15 ►

33Who shall lay any thing to the charge
of God's elect? *It is* God that justifieth.
34Who *is* he that
condemneth? *It is*
Christ that died, yea
rather, that is risen
again, who is even
at the right hand of
God, who also maketh intercession for us.

8:34 No Condemnation
◄ Romans 8:1
1 John 3:21 ►

35Who shall separate us from the love
of Christ? *shall* tribulation, or distress, or
persecution, or famine, or nakedness, or
peril, or sword?
36As it is written,
For thy sake we are
killed all the day
long; we are ac-
counted as sheep
for the slaughter.

8:36 Suffering for Jesus
◄ Romans 8:17
2 Corinthians 1:7 ►

37Nay, in all these things we are more
than conquerors through him that
loved us.
38For I am per-
suaded, that neither
death, nor life, nor
angels, nor princi-
palities, nor pow-
ers, nor things
present, nor things to come,

8:38-39 Believer Be Glad
◄ John 6:37
2 Corinthians 5:1 ►

39Nor height, nor depth, nor any other
creature, shall be able to separate us from
the love of God, which is in Christ Jesus
our Lord.

9

1I say the truth in
Christ, I lie not, my
conscience also
bearing me witness
in the Holy Ghost,

9:1 Clear Conscience
◄ Acts 24:16
2 Corinthians 1:12 ►

2That I have great heaviness and continual sorrow in my heart.
3For I could wish that myself were accursed from Christ for my brethren, my
kinsmen according to the flesh:
4Who are Israelites; to whom *pertaineth*
the adoption, and the glory, and the covenants, and the giving of the law, and the
service *of God,* and the promises;
5Whose *are* the fathers, and of whom as
concerning the flesh Christ *came,* who is
over all, God blessed for ever. Amen.
6Not as though the word of God hath
taken none effect. For they *are* not all Israel, which are of Israel:
7Neither, because they are the seed of
Abraham, *are they* all children: but, In Isaac
shall thy seed be called.
8That is, They which are the children of
the flesh, these *are* not the children of God:
but the children of the promise are counted for the seed.
9For this *is* the word of promise, At this
time will I come, and Sarah shall have a
son.
10And not only *this;* but when Rebecca
also had conceived by one, *even* by our father Isaac;
11(For *the children* being not yet born,
neither having done any good or evil, that
the purpose of God according to election
might stand, not of works, but of him that
calleth;)
12It was said unto her, The elder shall
serve the younger.
13As it is written, Jacob have I loved, but
Esau have I hated.
14What shall we
say then? *Is there*
unrighteousness
with God? God
forbid.

9:14 Injustice
◄ Matthew 20:12 ►

15For he saith to
Moses, I will have mercy on whom I will
have mercy, and I will have compassion
on whom I will have compassion.
16So then *it is* not of him that willeth,
nor of him that runneth, but of God that
sheweth mercy.
17For the scripture saith unto Pharaoh,
Even for this same purpose have I raised
thee up, that I might shew my power in
thee, and that my name might be declared
throughout all the earth.
18Therefore hath he mercy on whom he

will *have mercy,* and whom he will he hardeneth.

19Thou wilt say then unto me, Why doth he yet find fault? For who hath resisted his will?

9:19
God's Control
◄ Acts 17:24 ►

20Nay but, O man, who art thou that repliest against God? Shall the thing formed say to him that formed *it,* Why hast thou made me thus?

21Hath not the potter power over the clay, of the same lump to make one vessel unto honour, and another unto dishonour?

22*What* if God, willing to shew *his* wrath, and to make his power known, endured with much longsuffering the vessels of wrath fitted to destruction:

9:22 God's Patience
◄ Ezekiel 20:17
1 Peter 3:20 ►

23And that he might make known the riches of his glory on the vessels of mercy, which he had afore prepared unto glory,

24Even us, whom he hath called, not of the Jews only, but also of the Gentiles?

25As he saith also in Osee, I will call them my people, which were not my people; and her beloved, which was not beloved.

26And it shall come to pass, *that* in the place where it was said unto them, Ye *are* not my people; there shall they be called the children of the living God.

27Esaias also crieth concerning Israel, Though the number of the children of Israel be as the sand of the sea, a remnant shall be saved:

28For he will finish the work, and cut *it* short in righteousness: because a short work will the Lord make upon the earth.

29And as Esaias said before, Except the Lord of Sabaoth had left us a seed, we had been as Sodoma, and been made like unto Gomorrha.

30What shall we say then? That the Gentiles, which followed not after righteousness, have attained to righteousness, even the righteousness which is of faith.

31But Israel, which followed after the law of righteousness, hath not attained to the law of righteousness.

32Wherefore? Because *they sought it* not by faith, but as it were by the works of the law. For they stumbled at that stumblingstone;

9:32 Earning Heaven
◄ Luke 18:12
Romans 10:3 ►

33As it is written, Behold, I lay in Sion a stumblingstone and rock of offence: and whosoever believeth on him shall not be ashamed.

9:33 Salvation by Faith
◄ Acts 16:31
Romans 10:9 ►

10

1Brethren, my heart's desire and prayer to God for Israel is, that they might be saved.

2For I bear them record that they have a zeal of God, but not according to knowledge.

10:2 Legalism
◄ Acts 22:3
Galatians 1:14 ►

3For they being ignorant of God's righteousness, and going about to establish their own righteousness, have not submitted themselves unto the righteousness of God.

10:3 Earning Heaven
◄ Romans 9:32
Galatians 3:10 ►

4For Christ *is* the end of the law for righteousness to every one that believeth.

5For Moses describeth the righteousness which is of the law, That the man which doeth those things shall live by them.

6But the righteousness which is of faith speaketh on this wise, Say not in thine heart, Who shall ascend into heaven? (that is, to bring Christ down *from above:*)

7Or, Who shall descend into the deep? (that is, to bring up Christ again from the dead.)

8But what saith it? The word is nigh thee, *even* in thy mouth, and in thy heart: that is, the word of faith, which we preach;

9That if thou shalt confess with thy mouth the Lord Jesus, and shalt believe in thine heart that God hath raised him from the dead, thou shalt be saved.

10:9 How to Be Saved
◄ Matthew 10:22
1 Corinthians 1:21 ►

10:9 Salvation by Faith
◄ Romans 9:33
2 Timothy 3:15 ►

10For with the

heart man believeth
unto righteousness;
and with the mouth
confession is made
unto salvation.
11For the scrip-
ture saith, Whoso-
ever believeth on
him shall not be
ashamed.
12For there is no
difference between
the Jew and the
Greek: for the same
Lord over all is rich
unto all that call
upon him.
13For whosoever
shall call upon the
name of the Lord
shall be saved.
14How then shall
they call on him in
whom they have
not believed? and
how shall they be-
lieve in him of
whom they have
not heard? and how
shall they hear
without a preacher?
15And how shall they preach, except
they be sent? as it is written, How beautiful are the feet of them that preach the
gospel of peace, and bring glad tidings of
good things!
16But they have not all obeyed the gospel. For Esaias saith, Lord, who hath believed our report?
17So then faith *cometh* by hearing, and
hearing by the word of God.
18But I say, Have they not heard? Yes verily, their sound went into all the earth, and
their words unto the ends of the world.
19But I say, Did not Israel know? First
Moses saith, I will provoke you to jealousy by *them that are* no people, *and* by a foolish nation I will anger you.
20But Esaias is very bold, and saith, I was
found of them that sought me not; I was
made manifest unto them that asked not
after me.
21But to Israel he saith, All day long I
have stretched forth my hands unto a disobedient and gainsaying people.

10:10
Heart
◄ Luke 6:45 ►

10:11 Benefits of Faith
◄ John 14:12
Colossians 1:23 ►

10:12 Equality
◄ Acts 10:28
Galatians 3:28 ►

10:12 God Calls You
◄ John 7:37
1 Timothy 2:4 ►

10:13
Salvation for Anyone
◄ Romans 5:18
1 Timothy 2:4 ►

11

1I say then, Hath God cast away his people? God forbid. For I also am an Israelite,
of the seed of Abraham, *of* the tribe of Benjamin.
2God hath not cast away his people
which he foreknew. Wot ye not what the
scripture saith of Elias? how he maketh
intercession to God against Israel, saying,
3Lord, they have killed thy prophets, and
digged down thine altars; and I am left
alone, and they seek my life.
4But what saith the answer of God unto
him? I have reserved to myself seven thousand men, who have not bowed the knee
to *the image of* Baal.
5Even so then at this present time also
there is a remnant according to the election of grace.
6And if by grace,
then *is it* no more of
works: otherwise
grace is no more
grace. But if *it be* of
works, then is it no
more grace: otherwise work is no more
work.
7What then? Israel hath not obtained
that which he seeketh for; but the election hath obtained it, and the rest were
blinded
8(According as it is written, God hath
given them the spirit of slumber, eyes that
they should not see, and ears that they
should not hear;) unto this day.
9And David saith, Let their table be
made a snare, and a trap, and a stumblingblock, and a recompence unto them:
10Let their eyes be darkened, that they
may not see, and bow down their back
alway.
11I say then, Have they stumbled that
they should fall? God forbid: but *rather*
through their fall salvation *is come* unto
the Gentiles, for to provoke them to jealousy.
12Now if the fall of them *be* the riches
of the world, and the diminishing of them
the riches of the Gentiles; how much more
their fulness?
13For I speak to you Gentiles, inasmuch
as I am the apostle of the Gentiles, I magnify mine office:
14If by any means I may provoke to
emulation *them which are* my flesh, and
might save some of them.

11:6 Grace
◄ Romans 5:15
Ephesians 2:5 ►

15 For if the casting away of them *be* the reconciling of the world, what *shall* the receiving *of them be,* but life from the dead?

16 For if the firstfruit *be* holy, the lump *is* also *holy:* and if the root *be* holy, so *are* the branches.

17 And if some of the branches be broken off, and thou, being a wild olive tree, wert graffed in among them, and with them partakest of the root and fatness of the olive tree;

18 Boast not against the branches. But if thou boast, thou bearest not the root, but the root thee.

19 Thou wilt say then, The branches were broken off, that I might be graffed in.

20 Well; because of unbelief they were broken off, and thou standest by faith. Be not highminded, but fear:

11:20 Fearing God
◄ Luke 23:40
1 Peter 1:17 ►

21 For if God spared not the natural branches, *take heed* lest he also spare not thee.

22 Behold therefore the goodness and severity of God: on them which fell, severity; but toward thee, goodness, if thou continue in *his* goodness: otherwise thou also shalt be cut off.

23 And they also, if they abide not still in unbelief, shall be graffed in: for God is able to graff them in again.

24 For if thou wert cut out of the olive tree which is wild by nature, and wert graffed contrary to nature into a good olive tree: how much more shall these, which be the natural *branches,* be graffed into their own olive tree?

25 For I would not, brethren, that ye should be ignorant of this mystery, lest ye should be wise in your own conceits; that blindness in part is happened to Israel, until the fulness of the Gentiles be come in.

26 And so all Israel shall be saved: as it is written, There shall come out of Sion the Deliverer, and shall turn away ungodliness from Jacob:

27 For this *is* my covenant unto them, when I shall take away their sins.

28 As concerning the gospel, *they are* enemies for your sakes: but as touching the election, *they are* beloved for the fathers' sakes.

29 For the gifts and calling of God *are* without repentance.

30 For as ye in times past have not believed God, yet have now obtained mercy through their unbelief:

31 Even so have these also now not believed, that through your mercy they also may obtain mercy.

32 For God hath concluded them all in unbelief, that he might have mercy upon all.

33 O the depth of the riches both of the wisdom and knowledge of God! how unsearchable *are* his judgments, and his ways past finding out!

11:33 God's Ways
◄ Habakkuk 3:6
Revelation 15:3 ►

34 For who hath known the mind of the Lord? or who hath been his counsellor?

35 Or who hath first given to him, and it shall be recompensed unto him again?

36 For of him, and through him, and to him, *are* all things: to whom *be* glory for ever. Amen.

12

1 I beseech you therefore, brethren, by the mercies of God, that ye present your bodies a living sacrifice, holy, acceptable unto God, *which is* your reasonable service.

12:1 Commitment
◄ Proverbs 23:26
2 Timothy 2:21 ►

2 And be not conformed to this world: but be ye transformed by the renewing of your mind, that ye may prove what *is* that good, and acceptable, and perfect, will of God.

12:2 New Person
◄ Isaiah 41:1
2 Corinthians 4:16 ►

12:2 Submitting to God
◄ Acts 21:14
Ephesians 6:6 ►

3 For I say, through the grace given unto me, to every man that is among you, not to think *of himself* more highly than he ought to think; but to think soberly, according as God hath dealt to every man the measure of faith.

12:3 Wise Thoughts
◄ Proverbs 21:5
Philippians 4:8 ►

4For as we have
many members in
one body, and all
members have not
the same office:
5So we, *being*
many, are one body
in Christ, and every
one members one
of another.
6Having then
gifts differing ac-
cording to the grace
that is given to us,
whether prophecy,
let us prophesy ac-
cording to the pro-
portion of faith;
7Or ministry, *let
us wait* on *our* min-
istering: or he that
teacheth, on teach-
ing;
8Or he that ex-
horteth, on exhor-
tation: he that
giveth, *let him do it*
with simplicity; he
that ruleth, with
diligence; he that
sheweth mercy,
with cheerfulness.
9*Let* love be with-
out dissimulation.
Abhor that which is
evil; cleave to that
which is good.
10*Be* kindly affec-
tioned one to an-
other with brotherly
love; in honour
preferring one an-
other;
11Not slothful in
business; fervent in
spirit; serving the
Lord;
12Rejoicing in
hope; patient in trib-
ulation; continuing
instant in prayer;
13Distributing to
the necessity of
saints; given to hos-
pitality.

12:5
God's Body
◄ 1 Corinthians 12:27 ►

12:6 Church
◄ Matthew 25:15
1 Corinthians 4:7 ►

12:8 Diligence
◄ Proverbs 22:29
Hebrews 6:11 ►

12:8 How to Give
◄ Luke 12:33
1 Corinthians 16:2 ►

12:9 Loving Others
◄ John 15:12
1 Thessalonians 3:12 ►

12:9 Stay Away!
◄ Zechariah 7:10
1 Corinthians 10:6 ►

12:10
Kindness
◄ 1 Corinthians 13:4 ►

12:12 Quitting
◄ Luke 21:19
1 Thessalonians 5:14 ►

12:13 Giving
◄ Acts 20:35
Galatians 6:10 ►

14Bless them
which persecute
you: bless, and
curse not.
15Rejoice with
them that do re-
joice, and weep
with them that
weep.
16*Be* of the same
mind one toward
another. Mind not
high things, but
condescend to men
of low estate. Be not
wise in your own
conceits.
17Recompense to
no man evil for
evil. Provide things
honest in the sight
of all men.
18If it be possi-
ble, as much as
lieth in you, live
peaceably with all
men.
19Dearly be-
loved, avenge not
yourselves, but *rath-
er* give place unto
wrath: for it is writ-
ten, Vengeance *is*
mine; I will repay,
saith the Lord.
20Therefore if
thine enemy hun-
ger, feed him; if he
thirst, give him
drink: for in so do-
ing thou shalt heap
coals of fire on his
head.
21Be not over-
come of evil, but
overcome evil with
good.

13

1Let every soul be
subject unto the
higher powers. For
there is no power
but of God: the
powers that be are
ordained of God.
2Whosoever

12:13
Hospitality
◄ 1 Timothy 3:2 ►

12:14 Cursing
◄ Luke 6:28
James 3:10 ►

12:15 Rejoicing
◄ Luke 10:20
Philippians 4:4 ►

12:16 Conceit
◄ Isaiah 5:21
1 Corinthians 8:2 ►

12:17 Revenge
◄ Matthew 5:39
1 Thessalonians 5:15 ►

12:18 Peace
◄ Ecclesiastes 10:4
Titus 1:6 ►

12:20
Loving Enemies
◄ Matthew 5:44 ►

12:20 Vengeance
◄ Luke 6:35
1 Thessalonians 5:15 ►

13:1 Obeying the Law
◄ Matthew 22:21
Titus 3:1 ►

therefore resisteth the power, resisteth the ordinance of God: and they that resist shall receive to themselves damnation.

13:1 Rulers
◄ Acts 23:5
1 Peter 2:17 ►

3For rulers are not a terror to good works, but to the evil. Wilt thou then not be afraid of the power? do that which is good, and thou shalt have praise of the same:

13:2 Rebellion
◄ Ezra 10:8
Jude 1:8 ►

4For he is the minister of God to thee for good. But if thou do that which is evil, be afraid; for he beareth not the sword in vain: for he is the minister of God, a revenger to *execute* wrath upon him that doeth evil.

13:3 Doing Good
◄ Luke 6:35
Galatians 6:10 ►

5Wherefore *ye* must needs be subject, not only for wrath, but also for conscience sake.

6For for this cause pay ye tribute also: for they are God's ministers, attending continually upon this very thing.

7Render therefore to all their dues: tribute to whom tribute *is due;* custom to whom custom; fear to whom fear; honour to whom honour.

13:7 Be Fair
◄ Isaiah 56:1
Colossians 4:1 ►

8Owe no man any thing, but to love one another: for he that loveth another hath fulfilled the law.

9For this, Thou shalt not commit adultery, Thou shalt not kill, Thou shalt not steal, Thou shalt not bear false witness, Thou shalt not covet; and if *there be* any other commandment, it is briefly comprehended in this saying, namely, Thou shalt love thy neighbour as thyself.

13:9 Stealing
◄ Matthew 19:18
Ephesians 4:28 ►

10Love worketh no ill to his neighbour: therefore love *is* the fulfilling of the law.

13:10 Neighbors
◄ Mark 12:31
Romans 15:1-2 ►

11And that, knowing the time, that now *it is* high time to awake out of sleep: for now *is* our salvation nearer than when we believed.

13:10 Religious People
◄ Mark 12:33
James 1:27 ►

12The night is far spent, the day is at hand: let us therefore cast off the works of darkness, and let us put on the armour of light.

13:12 Christian Duties
◄ John 9:4
Ephesians 5:8 ►

13Let us walk honestly, as in the day; not in rioting and drunkenness, not in chambering and wantonness, not in strife and envying.

13:13 Envy
◄ Proverbs 24:1
1 Corinthians 13:4 ►

13:13 Getting Drunk
◄ Luke 21:34
1 Corinthians 6:10 ►

14But put ye on the Lord Jesus Christ, and make not provision for the flesh, to *fulfil* the lusts *thereof.*

14

1Him that is weak in the faith receive ye, *but* not to doubtful disputations.

14:1 Helping Weak People
◄ Acts 20:35
Romans 15:1 ►

2For one believeth that he may eat all things: another, who is weak, eateth herbs.

3Let not him that eateth despise him that eateth not; and let not him which eateth not judge him that eateth: for God hath received him.

4Who art thou that judgest another man's servant? to his own master he standeth or falleth. Yea, he shall be holden up: for God is able to make him stand.

14:4 Blame
◄ Ezekiel 18:20
Galatians 6:5 ►

5One man esteemeth one day above another: another esteemeth every day *alike.* Let every man be fully persuaded in his own mind.

6He that regardeth the day, regardeth *it* unto the Lord; and he that regardeth not the day, to the Lord he doth not regard *it.* He that eateth, eateth to the Lord, for he

giveth God thanks; and he that eateth not,
to the Lord he eateth not, and giveth God
thanks.
7 For none of us liveth to himself, and
no man dieth to himself.
8 For whether we live, we live unto the
Lord; and whether we die, we die unto the
Lord: whether we live therefore, or die, we
are the Lord's.
9 For to this end Christ both died, and
rose, and revived, that he might be Lord
both of the dead and living.
10 But why dost
thou judge thy
brother? or why
dost thou set at
nought thy brother?
for we shall all
stand before the judgment seat of Christ.

14:10 Christ as Judge
◀ Romans 2:16
1 Corinthians 4:5 ▶

11 For it is written, *As* I live, saith the Lord,
every knee shall bow to me, and every
tongue shall confess to God.
12 So then every
one of us shall give
account of himself
to God.
13 Let us not
therefore judge one
another any more:
but judge this rath-
er, that no man put
a stumblingblock
or an occasion to
fall in *his* brother's
way.

14:12 Getting Caught
◀ Luke 19:15
1 Peter 4:4-5 ▶

14:13 Family
◀ Acts 17:26
1 Corinthians 8:13 ▶

14 I know, and am persuaded by the Lord
Jesus, that *there is* nothing unclean of itself: but to him that esteemeth any thing
to be unclean, to him *it is* unclean.
15 But if thy brother be grieved with *thy*
meat, now walkest thou not charitably.
Destroy not him with thy meat, for whom
Christ died.
16 Let not then your good be evil spoken of:
17 For the king-
dom of God is not
meat and drink; but
righteousness, and
peace, and joy in
the Holy Ghost.

14:17
Joy
◀ John 17:13 ▶

18 For he that in these things serveth
Christ *is* acceptable to God, and approved
of men.
19 Let us therefore follow after the things
which make for
peace, and things
wherewith one may
edify another.
20 For meat de-
stroy not the work
of God. All things
indeed *are* pure; but
it is evil for that
man who eateth
with offence.
21 *It is* good nei-
ther to eat flesh,
nor to drink wine,
nor *any thing*
whereby thy broth-
er stumbleth, or is
offended, or is
made weak.
22 Hast thou
faith? have *it* to thy-
self before God.
Happy *is* he that
condemneth not
himself in that
thing which he
alloweth.
23 And he that
doubteth is
damned if he eat,
because *he eateth*
not of faith: for
whatsoever *is* not of
faith is sin.

15

1 We then that are
strong ought to
bear the infirmities
of the weak, and
not to please our-
selves.
2 Let every one of
us please *his* neigh-
bour for *his* good to
edification.
3 For even Christ
pleased not him-
self; but, as it is
written, The re-
proaches of them
that reproached
thee fell on me.
4 For whatsoever
things were written
aforetime were
written for our

14:19
Peacemaking
◀ Matthew 5:9 ▶

14:21 Drinking
◀ Luke 1:15
1 Corinthians 8:13 ▶

15:1
Controlling Yourself
◀ Romans 8:13
Galatians 5:24 ▶

15:1
Helping Weak People
◀ Romans 14:1
1 Corinthians 8:11 ▶

15:1 Sympathy
◀ Acts 20:35
Galatians 6:2 ▶

15:1-2 Neighbors
◀ Romans 13:10
Galatians 5:14 ▶

15:3 Unselfishness
◀ Daniel 5:17
1 Corinthians 10:33 ▶

15:4
Reading the Bible
◀ Acts 17:11 ▶

15:4 Why the Bible?
◀ John 20:31
1 Corinthians 10:11 ▶

learning, that we through patience and
comfort of the scriptures might have hope.
5 Now the God of patience and consolation grant you to be likeminded one toward another according to Christ Jesus:
6 That ye may with one mind *and* one
mouth glorify God, even the Father of our
Lord Jesus Christ.
7 Wherefore receive ye one another, as
Christ also received us to the glory of God.
8 Now I say that Jesus Christ was a minister of the circumcision for the truth of
God, to confirm the promises *made* unto
the fathers:
9 And that the Gentiles might glorify
God for *his* mercy; as it is written, For this
cause I will confess to thee among the
Gentiles, and sing unto thy name.
10 And again he saith, Rejoice, ye Gentiles, with his people.
11 And again, Praise the Lord, all ye Gentiles; and laud him, all ye people.
12 And again, Esaias saith, There shall be
a root of Jesse, and he that shall rise to
reign over the Gentiles; in him shall the
Gentiles trust.
13 Now the God of hope fill you with all
joy and peace in believing, that ye may
abound in hope, through the power of the
Holy Ghost.
14 And I myself
also am persuaded
of you, my brethren,
that ye also are full
of goodness, filled
with all knowledge,
able also to admonish one another.

15:14
Giving Advice
◄ 1 Corinthians 4:14 ►

15 Nevertheless, brethren, I have written
the more boldly unto you in some sort, as
putting you in mind, because of the grace
that is given to me of God,
16 That I should be the minister of Jesus
Christ to the Gentiles, ministering the gospel of God, that the offering up of the Gentiles might be acceptable, being sanctified
by the Holy Ghost.
17 I have therefore whereof I may glory
through Jesus Christ in those things which
pertain to God.
18 For I will not dare to speak of any of
those things which Christ hath not
wrought by me, to make the Gentiles obedient, by word and deed,
19 Through mighty signs and wonders,
by the power of the Spirit of God; so that
from Jerusalem, and round about unto
Illyricum, I have fully preached the gospel
of Christ.
20 Yea, so have I strived to preach the gospel, not where Christ was named, lest I
should build upon another man's foundation:
21 But as it is written, To whom he was
not spoken of, they shall see: and they that
have not heard shall understand.
22 For which cause also I have been much
hindered from coming to you.
23 But now having no more place in
these parts, and having a great desire these
many years to come unto you;
24 Whensoever I take my journey into
Spain, I will come to you: for I trust to see
you in my journey, and to be brought on
my way thitherward by you, if first I be
somewhat filled with your *company*.
25 But now I go unto Jerusalem to minister unto the saints.
26 For it hath pleased them of Macedonia and Achaia to make a certain contri-
bution for the poor saints which are at
Jerusalem.
27 It hath pleased them verily; and their
debtors they are. For if the Gentiles have
been made partakers of their spiritual
things, their duty is also to minister unto
them in carnal things.
28 When therefore I have performed this,
and have sealed to them this fruit, I will
come by you into Spain.
29 And I am sure that, when I come unto
you, I shall come in the fulness of the blessing of the gospel of Christ.
30 Now I beseech you, brethren, for the
Lord Jesus Christ's sake, and for the love
of the Spirit, that ye strive together with
me in *your* prayers to God for me;
31 That I may be delivered from them that
do not believe in Judaea; and that my service which *I have* for Jerusalem may be
accepted of the saints;
32 That I may come unto you with joy
by the will of God, and may with you be
refreshed.
33 Now the God of peace *be* with you all.
Amen.

16

1 I commend unto you Phebe our sister,
which is a servant of the church which is
at Cenchrea:
2 That ye receive her in the Lord, as
becometh saints, and that ye assist her in

whatsoever business she hath need of you: for she hath been a succourer of many, and of myself also.

3 Greet Priscilla and Aquila my helpers in Christ Jesus:

4 Who have for my life laid down their own necks: unto whom not only I give thanks, but also all the churches of the Gentiles.

16:4 Being a Friend
◄ John 13:1
2 Timothy 1:16 ►

16:4 Love for Friends
◄ Acts 20:38
2 Corinthians 12:15 ►

5 Likewise *greet* the church that is in their house. Salute my wellbeloved Epaenetus, who is the firstfruits of Achaia unto Christ.

6 Greet Mary, who bestowed much labour on us.

7 Salute Andronicus and Junia, my kinsmen, and my fellowprisoners, who are of note among the apostles, who also were in Christ before me.

8 Greet Amplias my beloved in the Lord.

9 Salute Urbane, our helper in Christ, and Stachys my beloved.

10 Salute Apelles approved in Christ. Salute them which are of Aristobulus' *household.*

11 Salute Herodion my kinsman. Greet them that be of the *household* of Narcissus, which are in the Lord.

12 Salute Tryphena and Tryphosa, who labour in the Lord. Salute the beloved Persis, which laboured much in the Lord.

13 Salute Rufus chosen in the Lord, and his mother and mine.

14 Salute Asyncritus, Phlegon, Hermas, Patrobas, Hermes, and the brethren which are with them.

15 Salute Philologus, and Julia, Nereus, and his sister, and Olympas, and all the saints which are with them.

16 Salute one another with an holy kiss. The churches of Christ salute you.

17 Now I beseech you, brethren, mark them which cause divisions and offences contrary to the doctrine which ye have learned; and avoid them.

18 For they that are such serve not our Lord Jesus Christ, but their own belly; and by good words and fair speeches deceive the hearts of the simple.

16:17 Argument Avoidance
◄ Proverbs 4:15
1 Timothy 6:20 ►

19 For your obedience is come abroad unto all *men.* I am glad therefore on your behalf: but yet I would have you wise unto that which is good, and simple concerning evil.

20 And the God of peace shall bruise Satan under your feet shortly. The grace of our Lord Jesus Christ *be* with you. Amen.

16:20 Satan's Weakness
◄ Luke 10:19
1 Corinthians 10:13 ►

16:20 Tempted by Satan
◄ Luke 22:31-32
1 Corinthians 10:13 ►

21 Timotheus my workfellow, and Lucius, and Jason, and Sosipater, my kinsmen, salute you.

22 I Tertius, who wrote *this* epistle, salute you in the Lord.

23 Gaius mine host, and of the whole church, saluteth you. Erastus the chamberlain of the city saluteth you, and Quartus a brother.

24 The grace of our Lord Jesus Christ *be* with you all. Amen.

25 Now to him that is of power to stablish you according to my gospel, and the preaching of Jesus Christ, according to the revelation of the mystery, which was kept secret since the world began,

16:25 God's Power
◄ Nahum 1:3 ►

26 But now is made manifest, and by the scriptures of the prophets, according to the commandment of the everlasting God, made known to all nations for the obedience of faith:

27 To God only wise, *be* glory through Jesus Christ for ever. Amen.

1 Corinthians

AUTHOR
Paul the apostle

MAIN POINT
The church at Corinth had some big problems, so Paul set them straight.

DATE WRITTEN
About A.D. 55

16 CHAPTERS

MAIN PEOPLE

Paul, Timothy, members of Chloe's household

SPECIAL FEATURES

- *Speaks honestly about some serious problems in the church*
- *Teaches clearly and directly about spiritual gifts and how God uses all of his people, even the "little guys"*
- *Includes a wonderful tribute to love (chapter 13)*
- *Reveals the sure truth about the resurrection from the dead*
- *Second of Paul's epistles*

HOW THE BOOK GOT ITS NAME

The book is Paul's first letter to the Christians in Corinth.

1 1Paul, called *to be* an apostle of Jesus
Christ through the will of God, and Sosthenes *our* brother,
2Unto the church of God which is at
Corinth, to them that are sanctified in
Christ Jesus, called *to be* saints, with all that
in every place call upon the name of Jesus
Christ our Lord, both theirs and ours:
3Grace *be* unto you, and peace, from
God our Father, and *from* the Lord Jesus
Christ.
4I thank my God always on your behalf,
for the grace of God which is given you by
Jesus Christ;
5That in every thing ye are enriched by
him, in all utterance, and *in* all knowledge;
6Even as the testimony of Christ was
confirmed in you:
7So that ye come behind in no gift; waiting for the coming of our Lord Jesus Christ:
8Who shall also confirm you unto the
end, *that ye may be*
blameless in the
day of our Lord
Jesus Christ.
9God *is* faithful,
by whom ye were
called unto the fellowship of his Son Jesus
Christ our Lord.

1:7
Watching for Jesus' Return
◄ Luke 19:13
1 Corinthians 4:5 ►

10Now I beseech
you, brethren, by
the name of our
Lord Jesus Christ,
that ye all speak the
same thing, and
that there be no divisions among you; but
that ye be perfectly joined together in the
same mind and in the same judgment.
11For it hath been declared unto me of
you, my brethren, by them *which are of the
house* of Chloe, that there are contentions
among you.

1:10
Getting Along
◄ 2 Corinthians 13:11

12 Now this I say, that every one of you saith, I am of Paul; and I of Apollos; and I of Cephas; and I of Christ.

13 Is Christ divided? was Paul crucified for you? or were ye baptized in the name of Paul?

14 I thank God that I baptized none of you, but Crispus and Gaius;

15 Lest any should say that I had baptized in mine own name.

16 And I baptized also the household of Stephanas: besides, I know not whether I baptized any other.

17 For Christ sent me not to baptize, but to preach the gospel: not with wisdom of words, lest the cross of Christ should be made of none effect.

18 For the preaching of the cross is to them that perish foolishness; but unto us which are saved it is the power of God.

19 For it is written, I will destroy the wisdom of the wise, and will bring to nothing the understanding of the prudent.

20 Where *is* the wise? where *is* the scribe? where *is* the disputer of this world? hath not God made foolish the wisdom of this world?

21 For after that in the wisdom of God the world by wisdom knew not God, it pleased God by the foolishness of preaching to save them that believe.

1:21 How to Be Saved
< Romans 10:9
1 Corinthians 15:2 >

22 For the Jews require a sign, and the Greeks seek after wisdom:

23 But we preach Christ crucified, unto the Jews a stumblingblock, and unto the Greeks foolishness;

24 But unto them which are called, both Jews and Greeks, Christ the power of God, and the wisdom of God.

25 Because the foolishness of God is wiser than men; and the weakness of God is stronger than men.

26 For ye see your calling, brethren, how that not many wise men after the flesh, not many mighty, not many noble, *are called:*

27 But God hath chosen the foolish things of the world to confound the wise; and God hath chosen the weak things of the world to confound the things which are mighty;

1:27 Weakness
< Psalm 8:2
2 Corinthians 12:9-10 >

28 And base things of the world, and things which are despised, hath God chosen, *yea,* and things which are not, to bring to nought things that are:

29 That no flesh should glory in his presence.

30 But of him are ye in Christ Jesus, who of God is made unto us wisdom, and righteousness, and sanctification, and redemption:

31 That, according as it is written, He that glorieth, let him glory in the Lord.

1:31 Boasting
< Romans 2:17
2 Corinthians 10:17 >

2

1 And I, brethren, when I came to you, came not with excellency of speech or of wisdom, declaring unto you the testimony of God.

2 For I determined not to know any thing among you, save Jesus Christ, and him crucified.

2:2 Jesus
< Acts 4:12
1 Corinthians 3:11 >

3 And I was with you in weakness, and in fear, and in much trembling.

4 And my speech and my preaching *was* not with enticing words of man's wisdom, but in demonstration of the Spirit and of power:

2:4 The Holy Spirit
< Acts 19:11-12
Ephesians 3:16 >

5 That your faith should not stand in the wisdom of men, but in the power of God.

6 Howbeit we speak wisdom among them that are perfect: yet not the wisdom of this world, nor of the princes of this world, that come to nought:

2:6 True Wisdom
< Matthew 7:24
1 Corinthians 12:8 >

7 But we speak the wisdom of God in a mystery, *even* the hidden *wisdom,* which God ordained before the world unto our glory:

8 Which none of the princes of this world knew: for

2:8 Blinded by Sin
< Acts 7:54
2 Peter 2:16 >

had they known *it,* they would not have crucified the Lord of glory.

9 But as it is written, Eye hath not seen, nor ear heard, neither have entered into the heart of man, the things which God hath prepared for them that love him.

10 But God hath revealed *them* unto us by his Spirit: for the Spirit searcheth all things, yea, the deep things of God.

11 For what man knoweth the things of a man, save the spirit of man which is in him? even so the things of God knoweth no man, but the Spirit of God.

12 Now we have received, not the spirit of the world, but the spirit which is of God; that we might know the things that are freely given to us of God.

13 Which things also we speak, not in the words which man's wisdom teacheth, but which the Holy Ghost teacheth; comparing spiritual things with spiritual.

2:13 God's Teaching
◄ John 14:26
1 John 2:27 ►

14 But the natural man receiveth not the things of the Spirit of God: for they are foolishness unto him: neither can he know *them,* because they are spiritually discerned.

15 But he that is spiritual judgeth all things, yet he himself is judged of no man.

16 For who hath known the mind of the Lord, that he may instruct him? But we have the mind of Christ.

3

1 And I, brethren, could not speak unto you as unto spiritual, but as unto carnal, *even* as unto babes in Christ.

2 I have fed you with milk, and not with meat: for hitherto ye were not able *to bear it,* neither yet now are ye able.

3 For ye are yet carnal: for whereas *there is* among you envying, and strife, and divisions, are ye not carnal, and walk as men?

4 For while one saith, I am of Paul; and another, I *am* of Apollos; are ye not carnal?

5 Who then is Paul, and who *is* Apollos, but ministers by whom ye believed, even as the Lord gave to every man?

6 I have planted, Apollos watered; but God gave the increase.

7 So then neither is he that planteth any thing, neither he that watereth; but God that giveth the increase.

8 Now he that planteth and he that watereth are one: and every man shall receive his own reward according to his own labour.

3:8 Goodness Rewarded
◄ Romans 2:10
Ephesians 6:8 ►

9 For we are labourers together with God: ye are God's husbandry, *ye are* God's building.

3:9 Working with God
◄ Mark 16:20
2 Corinthians 6:1 ►

10 According to the grace of God which is given unto me, as a wise masterbuilder, I have laid the foundation, and another buildeth thereon. But let every man take heed how he buildeth thereupon.

3:10 Watch Out!
◄ Luke 21:8
1 Corinthians 10:12 ►

11 For other foundation can no man lay than that is laid, which is Jesus Christ.

3:11 Jesus
◄ 1 Corinthians 2:2 ►

12 Now if any man build upon this foundation gold, silver, precious stones, wood, hay, stubble;

3:11 Our Savior
◄ Acts 4:12 ►

13 Every man's work shall be made manifest: for the day shall declare it, because it shall be revealed by fire; and the fire shall try every man's work of what sort it is.

3:13 Life Tests
◄ Luke 6:48
James 1:12 ►

14 If any man's work abide which he hath built thereupon, he shall receive a reward.

3:14 Things That Last
◄ John 6:27
1 Corinthians 13:13 ►

15 If any man's work shall be burned, he shall suffer loss: but he himself shall be saved; yet so as by fire.

16 Know ye not that ye are the temple of God, and *that* the Spirit of God dwelleth in you?

3:16 The Spirit in You
◄ Romans 8:9
1 Corinthians 6:19 ►

17 If any man defile the temple of God, him shall God

destroy; for the temple of God is holy, which *temple* ye are.

18Let no man deceive himself. If any man among you seemeth to be wise in this world, let him become a fool, that he may be wise.

19For the wisdom of this world is foolishness with God. For it is written, He taketh the wise in their own craftiness.

20And again, The Lord knoweth the thoughts of the wise, that they are vain.

21Therefore let no man glory in men. For all things are yours;

22Whether Paul, or Apollos, or Cephas, or the world, or life, or death, or things present, or things to come; all are yours;

23And ye are Christ's; and Christ *is* God's.

4

1Let a man so account of us, as of the ministers of Christ, and stewards of the mysteries of God.

2Moreover it is required in stewards, that a man be found faithful.

> **4:2**
> **Using What You Have**
> ➤ Luke 19:13
> 1 Corinthians 6:20 ➤

3But with me it is a very small thing that I should be judged of you, or of man's judgment: yea, I judge not mine own self.

4For I know nothing by myself; yet am I not hereby justified: but he that judgeth me is the Lord.

5Therefore judge nothing before the time, until the Lord come, who both will bring to light the hidden things of darkness, and will make manifest the counsels of the hearts: and then shall every man have praise of God.

> **4:5 Christ as Judge**
> ➤ Romans 14:10
> 2 Timothy 4:1 ➤

> **4:5**
> **Jesus' Return: Why?**
> ➤ Matthew 25:31-32
> 2 Timothy 4:1 ➤

6And these things, brethren, I have in a figure transferred to myself and *to* Apollos for your sakes; that ye might learn in us not to think *of men* above that which is written, that no one of you be puffed up for one against another.

> **4:5**
> **Watching for Jesus' Return**
> ➤ 1 Corinthians 1:7
> 1 Thessalonians 5:23 ➤

7For who maketh thee to differ *from another?* and what hast thou that thou didst not receive? now if thou didst receive *it,* why dost thou glory, as if thou hadst not received *it?*

> **4:7 Church**
> ➤ Romans 12:6
> 1 Corinthians 12:4 ➤

> **4:7 Gifts from God**
> ➤ John 3:27
> James 1:5 ➤

8Now ye are full, now ye are rich, ye have reigned as kings without us: and I would to God ye did reign, that we also might reign with you.

9For I think that God hath set forth us the apostles last, as it were appointed to death: for we are made a spectacle unto the world, and to angels, and to men.

10We *are* fools for Christ's sake, but ye *are* wise in Christ; we *are* weak, but ye *are* strong; ye *are* honourable, but we *are* despised.

11Even unto this present hour we both hunger, and thirst, and are naked, and are buffeted, and have no certain dwellingplace;

12And labour, working with our own hands: being reviled, we bless; being persecuted, we suffer it:

> **4:12**
> **Nice**
> ➤ Acts 7:60 ➤

13Being defamed, we intreat: we are made as the filth of the world, *and are* the offscouring of all things unto this day.

14I write not these things to shame you, but as my beloved sons I warn *you.*

> **4:14 Giving Advice**
> ➤ Romans 15:14
> Ephesians 6:4 ➤

15For though ye have ten thousand instructers in Christ, yet *have ye* not many fathers: for in Christ Jesus I have begotten you through the gospel.

16Wherefore I beseech you, be ye followers of me.

17For this cause have I sent unto you Timotheus, who is my beloved son, and faithful in the Lord, who shall bring you into remembrance of my ways which be in Christ, as I teach every where in every church.

18Now some are puffed up, as though I would not come to you.

19But I will come to you shortly, if the

Lord will, and will know, not the speech of them which are puffed up, but the power.

[20]For the kingdom of God *is* not in word, but in power.

[21]What will ye? shall I come unto you with a rod, or in love, and *in* the spirit of meekness?

5

[1]It is reported commonly *that there is* fornication among you, and such fornication as is not so much as named among the Gentiles, that one should have his father's wife.

[2]And ye are puffed up, and have not rather mourned, that he that hath done this deed might be taken away from among you.

[3]For I verily, as absent in body, but present in spirit, have judged already, as though I were present, *concerning* him that hath so done this deed,

[4]In the name of our Lord Jesus Christ, when ye are gathered together, and my spirit, with the power of our Lord Jesus Christ,

[5]To deliver such an one unto Satan for the destruction of the flesh, that the spirit may be saved in the day of the Lord Jesus.

[6]Your glorying *is* not good. Know ye not that a little leaven leaveneth the whole lump?

[7]Purge out therefore the old leaven, that ye may be a new lump, as ye are unleavened. For even Christ our passover is sacrificed for us:

5:7 Jesus the Lamb
◄ John 1:29
1 Peter 1:19 ►

[8]Therefore let us keep the feast, not with old leaven, neither with the leaven of malice and wickedness; but with the unleavened *bread* of sincerity and truth.

5:8 Malice
◄ 1 Corinthians 14:20 ►

5:8 Sincerity
◄ Joshua 24:14
2 Corinthians 1:12 ►

[9]I wrote unto you in an epistle not to company with fornicators:

5:9 Bad Friends
◄ Proverbs 24:1
1 Corinthians 5:11 ►

[10]Yet not altogether with the fornicators of this world, or with the covetous, or extortioners, or with idolaters; for then must ye needs go out of the world.

[11]But now I have written unto you not to keep company, if any man that is called a brother be a fornicator, or covetous, or an idolater, or a railer, or a drunkard, or an extortioner; with such an one no not to eat.

5:11 Bad Friends
◄ 1 Corinthians 5:9
2 Corinthians 6:14 ►

[12]For what have I to do to judge them also that are without? do not ye judge them that are within?

[13]But them that are without God judgeth. Therefore put away from among yourselves that wicked person.

6

[1]Dare any of you, having a matter against another, go to law before the unjust, and not before the saints?

6:1 Suing People
◄ Matthew 5:40 ►

[2]Do ye not know that the saints shall judge the world? and if the world shall be judged by you, are ye unworthy to judge the smallest matters?

6:2 Good Rewarded
◄ Luke 19:17
Revelation 3:21 ►

[3]Know ye not that we shall judge angels? how much more things that pertain to this life?

[4]If then ye have judgments of things pertaining to this life, set them to judge who are least esteemed in the church.

[5]I speak to your shame. Is it so, that there is not a wise man among you? no, not one that shall be able to judge between his brethren?

[6]But brother goeth to law with brother, and that before the unbelievers.

[7]Now therefore there is utterly a fault among you, because ye go to law one with another. Why do ye not rather take wrong? why do ye not rather *suffer yourselves to* be defrauded?

[8]Nay, ye do wrong, and defraud, and that *your* brethren.

[9]Know ye not that the unrighteous shall not inherit the kingdom of God? Be not de-

6:9 Deception
◄ Matthew 24:4
1 Corinthians 15:33 ►

ceived: neither fornicators, nor idolaters,
nor adulterers, nor effeminate, nor abus-
ers of themselves with mankind,
[10]Nor thieves,
nor covetous, nor
drunkards, nor
revilers, nor extor-
tioners, shall in-
herit the kingdom
of God.

6:10 Getting Drunk
◄ Romans 13:13
Ephesians 5:18 ►

[11]And such were some of you: but ye are
washed, but ye are sanctified, but ye are
justified in the name of the Lord Jesus, and
by the Spirit of our God.
[12]All things are
lawful unto me, but
all things are not ex-
pedient: all things
are lawful for me,
but I will not be
brought under the power of any.

6:12 Self-control
◄ Romans 6:12
James 3:2 ►

[13]Meats for the belly, and the belly for
meats: but God shall destroy both it and
them. Now the body *is* not for fornication,
but for the Lord; and the Lord for the body.
[14]And God hath both raised up the
Lord, and will also raise up us by his own
power.
[15]Know ye not
that your bodies are
the members of
Christ? shall I then
take the members
of Christ, and make
them the members of an harlot? God forbid.

6:15 Hurting Yourself
◄ Leviticus 21:5
1 Thessalonians 5:23 ►

[16]What? know ye not that he which is
joined to an harlot is one body? for two,
saith he, shall be one flesh.
[17]But he that is joined unto the Lord is
one spirit.
[18]Flee fornication. Every sin that a man
doeth is without the body; but he that
committeth for-
nication sinneth
against his own
body.
[19]What? know ye
not that your body
is the temple of the
Holy Ghost *which is*
in you, which ye
have of God, and ye
are not your own?
[20]For ye are
bought with a
price: therefore glo-
rify God in your
body, and in your
spirit, which are
God's.

6:19 The Spirit in You
◄ 1 Corinthians 3:16
2 Timothy 1:14 ►

6:20
Using What You Have
◄ 1 Corinthians 4:2
Ephesians 6:7 ►

6:20 Value of People
◄ John 3:16
1 Peter 1:18-19 ►

7

[1]Now concerning the things whereof ye
wrote unto me: *It is* good for a man not to
touch a woman.
[2]Nevertheless, *to avoid* fornication, let
every man have his own wife, and let every woman have her own husband.
[3]Let the husband render unto the wife
due benevolence: and likewise also the
wife unto the husband.
[4]The wife hath not power of her own
body, but the husband: and likewise also
the husband hath not power of his own
body, but the wife.
[5]Defraud ye not one the other, except *it
be* with consent for a time, that ye may give
yourselves to fasting and prayer; and come
together again, that Satan tempt you not
for your incontinency.
[6]But I speak this by permission, *and* not
of commandment.
[7]For I would that all men were even as I
myself. But every man hath his proper gift
of God, one after this manner, and another
after that.
[8]I say therefore to the unmarried and
widows, It is good for them if they abide
even as I.
[9]But if they cannot contain, let them
marry: for it is better to marry than to burn.
[10]And unto the married I command, *yet*
not I, but the Lord, Let not the wife depart
from *her* husband:
[11]But and if she depart, let her remain
unmarried, or be reconciled to *her* husband: and let not the husband put away
his wife.
[12]But to the rest speak I, not the Lord: If
any brother hath a wife that believeth not,
and she be pleased to dwell with him, let
him not put her away.
[13]And the woman which hath an husband that believeth not, and if he be
pleased to dwell with her, let her not leave
him.
[14]For the unbelieving husband is sanctified by the wife, and the unbelieving wife
is sanctified by the husband: else were your
children unclean; but now are they holy.
[15]But if the unbelieving depart, let him

depart. A brother or a sister is not under bondage in such *cases:* but God hath called us to peace.

16 For what knowest thou, O wife, whether thou shalt save *thy* husband? or how knowest thou, O man, whether thou shalt save *thy* wife?

17 But as God hath distributed to every man, as the Lord hath called every one, so let him walk. And so ordain I in all churches.

18 Is any man called being circumcised? let him not become uncircumcised. Is any called in uncircumcision? let him not be circumcised.

19 Circumcision is nothing, and uncircumcision is nothing, but the keeping of the commandments of God.

20 Let every man abide in the same calling wherein he was called.

21 Art thou called *being* a servant? care not for it: but if thou mayest be made free, use *it* rather.

22 For he that is called in the Lord, *being* a servant, is the Lord's freeman: likewise also he that is called, *being* free, is Christ's servant.

7:22 Serving Jesus
◄ John 12:26
Ephesians 6:6 ►

23 Ye are bought with a price; be not ye the servants of men.

24 Brethren, let every man, wherein he is called, therein abide with God.

25 Now concerning virgins I have no commandment of the Lord: yet I give my judgment, as one that hath obtained mercy of the Lord to be faithful.

26 I suppose therefore that this is good for the present distress, *I say,* that *it is* good for a man so to be.

27 Art thou bound unto a wife? seek not to be loosed. Art thou loosed from a wife? seek not a wife.

28 But and if thou marry, thou hast not sinned; and if a virgin marry, she hath not sinned. Nevertheless such shall have trouble in the flesh: but I spare you.

29 But this I say, brethren, the time *is* short: it remaineth, that both they that have wives be as though they had none;

7:29, 31 Time
◄ Ecclesiastes 12:1
Ephesians 5:15-16 ►

30 And they that weep, as though they wept not; and they that rejoice, as though they rejoiced not; and they that buy, as though they possessed not;

31 And they that use this world, as not abusing *it:* for the fashion of this world passeth away.

32 But I would have you without carefulness. He that is unmarried careth for the things that belong to the Lord, how he may please the Lord:

7:32 Worry
◄ Luke 21:34
Philippians 4:6 ►

33 But he that is married careth for the things that are of the world, how he may please *his* wife.

34 There is difference *also* between a wife and a virgin. The unmarried woman careth for the things of the Lord, that she may be holy both in body and in spirit: but she that is married careth for the things of the world, how she may please *her* husband.

35 And this I speak for your own profit; not that I may cast a snare upon you, but for that which is comely, and that ye may attend upon the Lord without distraction.

36 But if any man think that he behaveth himself uncomely toward his virgin, if she pass the flower of *her* age, and need so require, let him do what he will, he sinneth not: let them marry.

37 Nevertheless he that standeth stedfast in his heart, having no necessity, but hath power over his own will, and hath so decreed in his heart that he will keep his virgin, doeth well.

38 So then he that giveth *her* in marriage doeth well; but he that giveth *her* not in marriage doeth better.

39 The wife is bound by the law as long as her husband liveth; but if her husband be dead, she is at liberty to be married to whom she will; only in the Lord.

40 But she is happier if she so abide, after my judgment: and I think also that I have the Spirit of God.

8

1 Now as touching things offered unto idols, we know that we all have knowledge. Knowledge puffeth up, but charity edifieth.

2 And if any man think that he knoweth any thing,

8:2 Being Smart
◄ Isaiah 44:25
1 Corinthians 13:8 ►

he knoweth nothing yet as he ought to know.

8:2 Conceit
◄ Romans 12:16
Galatians 6:3 ►

3 But if any man love God, the same is known of him.

4 As concerning therefore the eating of those things that are offered in sacrifice unto idols, we know that an idol *is* nothing in the world, and that *there is* none other God but one.

8:4 Only One God
◄ Mark 12:29
Ephesians 4:6 ►

5 For though there be that are called gods, whether in heaven or in earth, (as there be gods many, and lords many,)

6 But to us *there is but* one God, the Father, of whom *are* all things, and we in him; and one Lord Jesus Christ, by whom *are* all things, and we by him.

7 Howbeit *there is* not in every man that knowledge: for some with conscience of the idol unto this hour eat *it* as a thing offered unto an idol; and their conscience being weak is defiled.

8 But meat commendeth us not to God: for neither, if we eat, are we the better; neither, if we eat not, are we the worse.

9 But take heed lest by any means this liberty of yours become a stumblingblock to them that are weak.

8:9 Free to...
◄ Galatians 5:13 ►

10 For if any man see thee which hast knowledge sit at meat in the idol's temple, shall not the conscience of him which is weak be emboldened to eat those things which are offered to idols;

11 And through thy knowledge shall the weak brother perish, for whom Christ died?

8:11 Helping Weak People
◄ Romans 15:1
1 Corinthians 9:22 ►

12 But when ye sin so against the brethren, and wound their weak conscience, ye sin against Christ.

13 Wherefore, if meat make my brother to offend, I will eat no flesh while the world standeth, lest I make my brother to offend.

8:13 Drinking
◄ Romans 14:21 ►

8:13 Family
◄ Romans 14:13 ►

9

1 Am I not an apostle? am I not free? have I not seen Jesus Christ our Lord? are not ye my work in the Lord?

2 If I be not an apostle unto others, yet doubtless I am to you: for the seal of mine apostleship are ye in the Lord.

3 Mine answer to them that do examine me is this,

4 Have we not power to eat and to drink?

5 Have we not power to lead about a sister, a wife, as well as other apostles, and *as* the brethren of the Lord, and Cephas?

6 Or I only and Barnabas, have not we power to forbear working?

7 Who goeth a warfare any time at his own charges? who planteth a vineyard, and eateth not of the fruit thereof? or who feedeth a flock, and eateth not of the milk of the flock?

8 Say I these things as a man? or saith not the law the same also?

9 For it is written in the law of Moses, Thou shalt not muzzle the mouth of the ox that treadeth out the corn. Doth God take care for oxen?

10 Or saith he *it* altogether for our sakes? For our sakes, no doubt, *this* is written: that he that ploweth should plow in hope; and that he that thresheth in hope should be partaker of his hope.

11 If we have sown unto you spiritual things, *is it* a great thing if we shall reap your carnal things?

12 If others be partakers of *this* power over you, *are* not we rather? Nevertheless we have not used this power; but suffer all things, lest we should hinder the gospel of Christ.

13 Do ye not know that they which minister about holy things live *of the things* of the temple? and they which wait at the altar are partakers with the altar?

14 Even so hath the Lord ordained that they which preach the gospel should live of the gospel.

15 But I have used none of these things: neither have I written these things, that it should be so done unto me: for *it were* better for me to die, than that any man should make my glorying void.

16 For though I preach the gospel, I have

nothing to glory of: for necessity is laid
upon me; yea, woe is unto me, if I preach
not the gospel!
17 For if I do this
thing willingly, I
have a reward: but
if against my will, a
dispensation *of the*
gospel is committed
unto me.

9:17 The Gospel
◄ Galatians 2:7 ►

18 What is my reward then? *Verily* that,
when I preach the gospel, I may make the
gospel of Christ without charge, that I
abuse not my power in the gospel.
19 For though I be free from all *men*, yet
have I made myself servant unto all, that I
might gain the more.
20 And unto the Jews I became as a
Jew, that I might gain the Jews; to them
that are under the law, as under the law,
that I might gain them that are under the
law;
21 To them that are without law, as without law, (being not without law to God,
but under the law to Christ,) that I might
gain them that are without law.
22 To the weak
became I as weak,
that I might gain
the weak: I am
made all things to
all *men*, that I might
by all means save some.

9:22 Helping Weak People
◄ 1 Corinthians 8:11
1 Thessalonians 5:14 ►

23 And this I do for the gospel's sake, that
I might be partaker thereof with *you*.
24 Know ye not that they which run in a
race run all, but one receiveth the prize?
So run, that ye may obtain.
25 And every man that striveth for the
mastery is temperate in all things. Now
they *do it* to obtain a corruptible crown;
but we an incorruptible.
26 I therefore so run, not as uncertainly;
so fight I, not as one that beateth the air:
27 But I keep un-
der my body, and
bring *it* into subjec-
tion: lest that by
any means, when I
have preached to
others, I myself should be a castaway.

9:27 Restraint
◄ Luke 21:34 ►

10
1 Moreover, brethren, I would not that
ye should be ignorant, how that all our
fathers were under the cloud, and all
passed through the sea;
2 And were all baptized unto Moses in
the cloud and in the sea;
3 And did all eat the same spiritual meat;
4 And did all drink the same spiritual
drink: for they drank of that spiritual Rock
that followed them: and that Rock was
Christ.
5 But with many of them God was not
well pleased: for they were overthrown in
the wilderness.
6 Now these
things were our ex-
amples, to the in-
tent we should not
lust after evil
things, as they also
lusted.

10:6 Stay Away!
◄ Romans 12:9
1 Thessalonians 5:22 ►

7 Neither be ye idolaters, as *were* some
of them; as it is written, The people sat
down to eat and drink, and rose up to play.
8 Neither let us commit fornication, as
some of them committed, and fell in one
day three and twenty thousand.
9 Neither let us tempt Christ, as some of
them also tempted,
and were destroyed
of serpents.
10 Neither mur-
mur ye, as some of
them also mur-
mured, and were
destroyed of the
destroyer.
11 Now all these
things happened
unto them for en-
samples: and they
are written for our
admonition, upon
whom the ends
of the world are
come.
12 Wherefore let
him that thinketh
he standeth take
heed lest he fall.
13 There hath no
temptation taken
you but such as is
common to man:
but God *is* faithful,
who will not suffer
you to be tempted
above that ye are
able; but will with

10:11 Why the Bible?
◄ Romans 15:4
1 John 5:13 ►

10:12 Pitfalls
◄ Acts 20:31
1 Corinthians 16:13 ►

10:12 Self-confidence
◄ Luke 18:9 ►

10:12 Watch Out!
◄ 1 Corinthians 3:10
Colossians 4:17 ►

10:13 Evil Attacks
◄ Isaiah 46:4
2 Corinthians 1:10 ►

the temptation also
make a way to es-
cape, that ye may be
able to bear *it*.
14 Wherefore, my
dearly beloved, flee
from idolatry.
15 I speak as to
wise men; judge ye
what I say.
16 The cup of
blessing which we
bless, is it not the
communion of the
blood of Christ?
The bread which we
break, is it not the
communion of the
body of Christ?
17 For we *being* many are one bread, *and*
one body: for we are all partakers of that
one bread.
18 Behold Israel after the flesh: are not
they which eat of the sacrifices partakers
of the altar?
19 What say I then? that the idol is any
thing, or that which is offered in sacrifice
to idols is any thing?
20 But *I say*, that the things which the
Gentiles sacrifice, they sacrifice to devils,
and not to God: and I would not that ye
should have fellowship with devils.
21 Ye cannot drink
the cup of the Lord,
and the cup of dev-
ils: ye cannot be
partakers of the
Lord's table, and of
the table of devils.
22 Do we provoke
the Lord to jealou-
sy? are we stronger
than he?
23 All things are
lawful for me, but all things are not expedient: all things are lawful for me, but all
things edify not.
24 Let no man seek his own, but every
man another's *wealth*.
25 Whatsoever is sold in the shambles,
that eat, asking no question for conscience
sake:
26 For the earth *is* the Lord's, and the
fulness thereof.
27 If any of them that believe not bid you
to a feast, and ye be disposed to go; whatsoever is set before you, eat, asking no
question for conscience sake.
28 But if any man say unto you, This is
offered in sacrifice unto idols, eat not for
his sake that shewed it, and for conscience
sake: for the earth *is* the Lord's, and the
fulness thereof:
29 Conscience, I say, not thine own, but
of the other: for why is my liberty judged
of another *man's* conscience?
30 For if I by grace be a partaker, why am
I evil spoken of for that for which I give
thanks?
31 Whether therefore ye eat, or drink, or
whatsoever ye do, do all to the glory of
God.
32 Give none offence, neither to the Jews,
nor to the Gentiles, nor to the church of
God:
33 Even as I please
all *men* in all *things*,
not seeking mine
own profit, but the
profit of many, that
they may be saved.

11

1 Be ye followers of me, even as I also *am*
of Christ.
2 Now I praise you, brethren, that ye remember me in all things, and keep the
ordinances, as I delivered *them* to you.
3 But I would have you know, that the
head of every man is Christ; and the head
of the woman *is* the man; and the head of
Christ *is* God.
4 Every man praying or prophesying,
having *his* head covered, dishonoureth his
head.
5 But every woman that prayeth or
prophesieth with *her* head uncovered
dishonoureth her head: for that is even all
one as if she were shaven.
6 For if the woman be not covered, let
her also be shorn: but if it be a shame for
a woman to be shorn or shaven, let her be
covered.
7 For a man in-
deed ought not to
cover *his* head, for-
asmuch as he is the
image and glory of
God: but the wom-
an is the glory of the man.
8 For the man is not of the woman; but
the woman of the man.

10:13 Satan's Weakness
◄ Romans 16:20
James 4:7 ►

10:13 Temptation
◄ Hebrews 2:18 ►

10:13 Tempted by Satan
◄ Romans 16:20
Hebrews 2:18 ►

10:21 Double Life
◄ Luke 16:13
James 1:8 ►

10:22 God Is Jealous
◄ 1 Kings 14:22 ►

10:33 Unselfishness
◄ Romans 15:3
2 Corinthians 8:9 ►

11:7 Made in God's Image
◄ Genesis 9:6
James 3:9 ►

9Neither was the man created for the
woman; but the woman for the man.
10For this cause ought the woman to
have power on *her* head because of the
angels.
11Nevertheless neither is the man without the woman, neither the woman without the man, in the Lord.
12For as the woman *is* of the man, even
so *is* the man also by the woman; but all
things of god.
13Judge in yourselves: is it comely that
a woman pray unto God uncovered?
14Doth not even nature itself teach you,
that, if a man have long hair, it is a shame
unto him?
15But if a woman have long hair, it is a
glory to her: for *her* hair is given her for a
covering.
16But if any man seem to be contentious,
we have no such custom, neither the
churches of God.
17Now in this that I declare *unto you* I
praise *you* not, that ye come together not
for the better, but for the worse.
18For first of all, when ye come together
in the church, I hear that there be divisions
among you; and I partly believe it.
19For there must be also heresies among
you, that they which are approved may be
made manifest among you.
20When ye come together therefore into
one place, *this* is not to eat the Lord's
supper.
21For in eating every one taketh before
other his own supper: and one is hungry,
and another is drunken.
22What? have ye not houses to eat and
to drink in? or despise ye the church of
God, and shame them that have not? What
shall I say to you? shall I praise you in this?
I praise *you* not.
23For I have received of the Lord that
which also I delivered unto you, That the
Lord Jesus the *same* night in which he was
betrayed took bread:
24And when he had given thanks, he
brake *it*, and said, Take, eat: this is my body,
which is broken for you: this do in remembrance of me.
25After the same manner also *he took*
the cup, when he had supped, saying, This
cup is the new testament in my blood: this
do ye, as oft as ye drink *it*, in remembrance
of me.
26For as often as ye eat this bread, and
drink *this* cup, ye do shew the Lord's death
till he come.
27Wherefore whosoever shall eat this
bread, and drink *this* cup of the Lord, unworthily, shall be guilty of the body and
blood of the Lord.
28But let a man
examine himself,
and so let him eat
of *that* bread, and
drink of *that* cup.

11:28 Self-examination
◄ Matthew 7:5
2 Corinthians 13:5 ►

29For he that
eateth and drinketh unworthily, eateth and
drinketh damnation to himself, not dis-
cerning the Lord's body.
30For this cause many *are* weak and
sickly among you, and many sleep.
31For if we would judge ourselves, we
should not be judged.
32But when we are judged, we are chastened of the Lord, that we should not be
condemned with the world.
33Wherefore, my brethren, when ye
come together to eat, tarry one for another.
34And if any man hunger, let him eat at
home; that ye come not together unto condemnation. And the rest will I set in order
when I come.

12

1Now concerning spiritual *gifts*, brethren, I would not have you ignorant.
2Ye know that ye were Gentiles, carried
away unto these dumb idols, even as ye
were led.
3Wherefore I give you to understand,
that no man speaking by the Spirit of God
calleth Jesus accursed: and *that* no man can
say that Jesus is the Lord, but by the Holy
Ghost.
4Now there are
diversities of gifts,
but the same Spirit.
5And there are
differences of ad-
ministrations, but
the same Lord.

12:4 Church
◄ 1 Corinthians 4:7
Ephesians 4:11 ►

6And there are diversities of operations,
but it is the same God which worketh all
in all.
7But the mani-
festation of the
Spirit is given to
every man to profit
withal.
8For to one is

12:8 True Wisdom
◄ 1 Corinthians 2:6
2 Timothy 3:15 ►

given by the Spirit the word of wisdom; to
another the word of knowledge by the
same Spirit;
9 To another faith by the same Spirit; to
another the gifts of healing by the same
Spirit;
10 To another the working of miracles;
to another prophecy; to another discern-
ing of spirits; to another *divers* kinds of
tongues; to another the interpretation of
tongues:
11 But all these worketh that one and the
selfsame Spirit, dividing to every man sev-
erally as he will.
12 For as the body is one, and hath many
members, and all the members of that one
body, being many, are one body: so also *is*
Christ.
13 For by one Spirit are we all baptized
into one body, whether *we be* Jews or Gentiles, whether *we be* bond or free; and have
been all made to drink into one Spirit.
14 For the body is not one member, but
many.
15 If the foot shall say, Because I am not
the hand, I am not of the body; is it therefore not of the body?
16 And if the ear shall say, Because I am
not the eye, I am not of the body; is it therefore not of the body?
17 If the whole body *were* an eye, where
were the hearing? If the whole *were* hearing, where *were* the smelling?
18 But now hath God set the members
every one of them in the body, as it hath
pleased him.
19 And if they were all one member,
where *were* the body?
20 But now *are they* many members, yet
but one body.
21 And the eye cannot say unto the hand,
I have no need of thee: nor again the head
to the feet, I have no need of you.
22 Nay, much more those members of
the body, which seem to be more feeble,
are necessary:
23 And those *members* of the body, which
we think to be less honourable, upon these
we bestow more abundant honour; and
our uncomely *parts* have more abundant
comeliness.
24 For our comely *parts* have no need: but
God hath tempered the body together,
having given more abundant honour to
that *part* which lacked:
25 That there should be no schism in the
body; but *that* the members should have
the same care one for another.
26 And whether one member suffer, all
the members suffer with it; or one member be honoured, all the members rejoice
with it.
27 Now ye are the
body of Christ, and
members in par-
ticular.

12:27 God's Body
◄ Romans 12:5
Ephesians 1:23 ►

28 And God hath
set some in the
church, first apostles, secondarily prophets, thirdly teachers, after that miracles,
then gifts of healings, helps, governments,
diversities of tongues.
29 *Are* all apostles? *are* all prophets? *are*
all teachers? *are* all workers of miracles?
30 Have all the gifts of healing? do all
speak with tongues? do all interpret?
31 But covet earnestly the best gifts: and
yet shew I unto you a more excellent way.

13

1 Though I speak
with the tongues of
men and of angels,
and have not char-
ity, I am become *as*
sounding brass, or
a tinkling cymbal.

13:1 Love
◄ John 21:16
1 John 3:14 ►

2 And though I have *the gift of* prophecy,
and understand all mysteries, and all
knowledge; and though I have all faith, so
that I could remove mountains, and have
not charity, I am nothing.
3 And though I
bestow all my
goods to feed *the*
poor, and though I
give my body to
be burned, and
have not charity, it
profiteth me noth-
ing.

13:3 Generosity
◄ Luke 19:8 ►

4 Charity suf-
fereth long, *and* is
kind; charity envi-
eth not; charity
vaunteth not itself,
is not puffed up,

13:4 Envy
◄ Romans 13:13
Galatians 5:26 ►

13:4 Kindness
◄ Romans 12:10
Ephesians 4:32 ►

5 Doth not be-
have itself un-
seemly, seeketh not
her own, is not easily provoked, thinketh
no evil;

6 Rejoiceth not in iniquity, but rejoiceth
in the truth;
7 Beareth all
things, believeth
all things, hopeth
all things, endur-
eth all things.
8 Charity never
faileth: but wheth-
er *there be* prophe-
cies, they shall fail;
whether *there be*
tongues, they shall
cease; whether *there*
be knowledge, it shall vanish away.
9 For we know in part, and we prophesy
in part.
10 But when that which is perfect is come,
then that which is in part shall be done
away.
11 When I was a
child, I spake as a
child, I understood
as a child, I thought
as a child: but when
I became a man, I
put away childish things.
12 For now we see through a glass, darkly;
but then face to face: now I know in part;
but then shall I know even as also I am
known.
13 And now abid-
eth faith, hope,
charity, these three;
but the greatest of
these *is* charity.

13:7
Patience
◄ Ephesians 4:2 ►

13:8
Being Smart
◄ 1 Corinthians 8:2 ►

13:11
Growing Up
◄ Jeremiah 4:22 ►

13:13
Importance of Love
◄ Galatians 5:6 ►

14

1 Follow after
charity, and desire
spiritual *gifts*, but
rather that ye may
prophesy.
2 For he that speak-
eth in an *unknown*
tongue speaketh not unto men, but unto
God: for no man understandeth *him;* howbeit in the spirit he speaketh mysteries.
3 But he that pro-
phesieth speaketh
unto men *to* edi-
fication, and ex-
hortation, and
comfort.
4 He that speaketh in an *unknown* tongue
edifieth himself; but he that prophesieth
edifieth the church.

13:13 Things That Last
◄ 1 Corinthians 3:14
2 Corinthians 4:18 ►

14:3 Comforting Others
◄ Isaiah 40:1
1 Corinthians 14:31 ►

5 I would that ye all spake with tongues,
but rather that ye prophesied: for greater
is he that prophesieth than he that
speaketh with tongues, except he interpret,
that the church may receive edifying.
6 Now, brethren, if I come unto you
speaking with tongues, what shall I profit
you, except I shall speak to you either by
revelation, or by knowledge, or by prophesying, or by doctrine?
7 And even things without life giving
sound, whether pipe or harp, except they
give a distinction in the sounds, how shall
it be known what is piped or harped?
8 For if the trumpet give an uncertain
sound, who shall prepare himself to the
battle?
9 So likewise ye, except ye utter by the
tongue words easy to be understood, how
shall it be known what is spoken? for ye
shall speak into the air.
10 There are, it may be, so many kinds of
voices in the world, and none of them *is*
without signification.
11 Therefore if I know not the meaning
of the voice, I shall be unto him that
speaketh a barbarian, and he that speaketh
shall be a barbarian unto me.
12 Even so ye, forasmuch as ye are zealous of spiritual *gifts*, seek that ye may excel to the edifying of the church.
13 Wherefore let him that speaketh in an
unknown tongue pray that he may interpret.
14 For if I pray in an *unknown* tongue, my
spirit prayeth, but my understanding is
unfruitful.
15 What is it then? I will pray with the
spirit, and I will pray with the understanding also: I will sing with the spirit, and I
will sing with the understanding also.
16 Else when thou shalt bless with the
spirit, how shall he that occupieth the
room of the unlearned say Amen at thy
giving of thanks, seeing he understandeth
not what thou sayest?
17 For thou verily givest thanks well, but
the other is not edified.
18 I thank my God, I speak with tongues
more than ye all:
19 Yet in the church I had rather speak
five words with my understanding, that *by*
my voice I might teach others also, than ten
thousand words in an *unknown* tongue.
20 Brethren, be not children in

Turn to the next page for more . . .

understanding:
howbeit in malice
be ye children, but
in understanding
be men.

14:20 Malice
◄ 1 Corinthians 5:8
Ephesians 4:31 ►

21 In the law it is
written, With *men of* other tongues and
other lips will I speak unto this people;
and yet for all that will they not hear me,
saith the Lord.
22 Wherefore tongues are for a sign, not
to them that believe, but to them that believe not: but prophesying *serveth* not for
them that believe not, but for them which
believe.
23 If therefore the whole church be come
together into one place, and all speak with
tongues, and there come in *those that are*
unlearned, or unbelievers, will they not say
that ye are mad?
24 But if all prophesy, and there come in
one that believeth not, or *one* unlearned,
he is convinced of all, he is judged of all:
25 And thus are the secrets of his heart
made manifest; and so falling down on *his*
face he will worship God, and report that
God is in you of a truth.
26 How is it then, brethren? when ye
come together, every one of you hath a
psalm, hath a doctrine, hath a tongue, hath
a revelation, hath an interpretation. Let all
things be done unto edifying.
27 If any man speak in an *unknown*
tongue, *let it be* by two, or at the most *by*
three, and *that* by course; and let one interpret.
28 But if there be no interpreter, let him
keep silence in the church; and let him
speak to himself, and to God.
29 Let the prophets speak two or three,
and let the other judge.
30 If *any thing* be revealed to another that
sitteth by, let the first hold his peace.
31 For ye may all
prophesy one by
one, that all may
learn, and all may
be comforted.

14:31 Comforting Others
◄ 1 Corinthians 14:3
2 Corinthians 2:7 ►

32 And the spirits
of the prophets are subject to the
prophets.
33 For God is not *the author* of confusion,
but of peace, as in all churches of the saints.
34 Let your women keep silence in the
churches: for it is not permitted unto them
to speak; but *they are commanded* to be
under obedience, as also saith the law.
35 And if they will learn any thing, let
them ask their husbands at home: for it is
a shame for women to speak in the church.
36 What? came the word of God out from
you? or came it unto you only?
37 If any man think himself to be a
prophet, or spiritual, let him acknowledge
that the things that I write unto you are
the commandments of the Lord.
38 But if any man be ignorant, let him
be ignorant.
39 Wherefore, brethren, covet to prophesy, and forbid not to speak with tongues.
40 Let all things be done decently and in
order.

15

1 Moreover, brethren, I declare unto you
the gospel which I preached unto you,
which also ye have received, and wherein
ye stand;
2 By which also ye
are saved, if ye keep
in memory what I
preached unto you,
unless ye have be-
lieved in vain.

15:2 How to Be Saved
◄ 1 Corinthians 1:21
2 Timothy 3:15 ►

3 For I delivered
unto you first of all
that which I also
received, how that
Christ died for our
sins according to
the scriptures;

15:3
Who Can Be Saved?
◄ Galatians 1:4 ►

4 And that he was buried, and that he
rose again the third day according to the
scriptures:
5 And that he was seen of Cephas, then
of the twelve:
6 After that, he was seen of above five
hundred brethren at once; of whom the
greater part remain unto this present, but
some are fallen asleep.
7 After that, he was seen of James; then
of all the apostles.
8 And last of all he was seen of me also,
as of one born out of due time.
9 For I am the
least of the apos-
tles, that am not
meet to be called an
apostle, because I
persecuted the
church of God.

15:9
Mistakes
◄ Luke 16:25 ►

10 But by the grace of God I am what I

am: and his grace *which was bestowed* upon
me was not in vain; but I laboured more
abundantly than they all: yet not I, but the
grace of God which was with me.
11 Therefore whether *it were* I or they, so
we preach, and so ye believed.
12 Now if Christ be preached that he rose
from the dead, how say some among you
that there is no resurrection of the dead?
13 But if there be no resurrection of the
dead, then is Christ not risen:
14 And if Christ be not risen, then *is* our
preaching vain, and your faith *is* also vain.
15 Yea, and we are found false witnesses
of God; because we have testified of God
that he raised up Christ: whom he raised
not up, if so be that the dead rise not.
16 For if the dead rise not, then is not
Christ raised:
17 And if Christ be not raised, your faith
is vain; ye are yet in your sins.
18 Then they also which are fallen asleep
in Christ are perished.
19 If in this life only we have hope in
Christ, we are of all men most miserable.
20 But now is Christ risen from the dead,
and become the firstfruits of them that
slept.
21 For since by man *came* death, by man
came also the resurrection of the dead.
22 For as in Adam
all die, even so in
Christ shall all be
made alive.
23 But every man
in his own order:
Christ the firstfruits; afterward they that are
Christ's at his coming.

15:22 Resurrection
◄ Acts 24:15
2 Corinthians 4:14 ►

24 Then *cometh* the end, when he shall
have delivered up the kingdom to God,
even the Father; when he shall have put
down all rule and all authority and power.
25 For he must
reign, till he hath
put all enemies under his feet.
26 The last enemy
that shall be destroyed *is* death.

15:25 Jesus the King
◄ John 18:37 ►

27 For he hath put all things under his
feet. But when he saith, all things are put
under *him, it is* manifest that he is excepted,
which did put all things under him.
28 And when all things shall be subdued
unto him, then shall the Son also himself
be subject unto him that put all things
under him, that God may be all in all.
29 Else what shall they do which are baptized for the dead, if the dead rise not at
all? why are they then baptized for the
dead?
30 And why stand we in jeopardy every
hour?
31 I protest by your rejoicing which I have
in Christ Jesus our Lord, I die daily.
32 If after the manner of men I have
fought with beasts at Ephesus, what
advantageth it me, if the dead rise not? let
us eat and drink; for to morrow we die.
33 Be not deceived: evil communications
corrupt good manners.
34 Awake to righteousness, and sin
not; for some have
not the knowledge
of God: I speak *this*
to your shame.

15:33 Deception
◄ 1 Corinthians 6:9
Galatians 6:7 ►

15:34 Righteousness
◄ Acts 24:25
Ephesians 6:14 ►

35 But some *man*
will say, How are the dead raised up? and
with what body do they come?
36 *Thou* fool, that which thou sowest is
not quickened, except it die:
37 And that which thou sowest, thou
sowest not that body that shall be, but bare
grain, it may chance of wheat, or of some
other *grain:*
38 But God giveth it a body as it hath
pleased him, and to every seed his own
body.
39 All flesh *is* not the same flesh: but *there*
is one *kind of* flesh of men, another flesh
of beasts, another of fishes, *and* another
of birds.
40 *There are* also celestial bodies, and
bodies terrestrial: but the glory of the celestial *is* one, and the *glory* of the terrestrial *is* another.
41 *There is* one glory of the sun, and another glory of the moon, and another glory of the stars: for *one* star differeth from
another star in glory.
42 So also *is* the resurrection of the dead.
It is sown in corruption; it is raised in incorruption:
43 It is sown in dishonour; it is raised in
glory: it is sown in weakness; it is raised in
power:

44 It is sown a natural body; it is raised a
spiritual body. There is a natural body, and
there is a spiritual body.
45 And so it is written, The first man
Adam was made a living soul; the last
Adam *was made* a quickening spirit.
46 Howbeit that *was* not first which is
spiritual, but that which is natural; and
afterward that which is spiritual.
47 The first man *is* of the earth, earthy:
the second man *is* the Lord from heaven.
48 As *is* the earthy, such *are* they also that
are earthy: and as *is* the heavenly, such *are*
they also that are heavenly.
49 And as we have borne the image of
the earthy, we shall also bear the image of
the heavenly.
50 Now this I say, brethren, that flesh and
blood cannot inherit the kingdom of God;
neither doth corruption inherit incorruption.
51 Behold, I shew you a mystery; We shall
not all sleep, but we shall all be changed,
52 In a moment, in the twinkling of an
eye, at the last trump: for the trumpet shall
sound, and the dead shall be raised incorruptible, and we shall be changed.
53 For this cor-
ruptible must put
on incorruption,
and this mortal
must put on immor-
tality.

> **15:53 Eternal Life**
> ◄ Romans 2:7
> 2 Corinthians 5:1 ►

54 So when this
corruptible shall
have put on incor-
ruption, and this
mortal shall have
put on immortality,
then shall be brought to pass the saying
that is written, Death is swallowed up in
victory.

> **15:53 Mortality**
> ◄ Ecclesiastes 3:20
> 2 Corinthians 4:7 ►

55 O death, where *is* thy sting? O grave,
where *is* thy victory?
56 The sting of death *is* sin; and the
strength of sin *is* the law.
57 But thanks *be* to God, which giveth
us the victory through our Lord Jesus
Christ.
58 Therefore, my
beloved brethren,
be ye stedfast, un-
movable, always
abounding in the
work of the Lord,
forasmuch as ye know that your labour is
not in vain in the Lord.

> **15:58 Standing Strong**
> ◄ Acts 11:23
> Galatians 5:1 ►

16

1 Now concerning the collection for the
saints, as I have given order to the churches
of Galatia, even so do ye.
2 Upon the first
day of the week let
every one of you lay
by him in store, as
God hath prospered
him, that there be
no gatherings when I come.

> **16:2 How to Give**
> ◄ Romans 12:8
> 2 Corinthians 9:7 ►

3 And when I come, whomsoever ye shall
approve by *your* letters, them will I send to
bring your liberality unto Jerusalem.
4 And if it be meet that I go also, they
shall go with me.
5 Now I will come unto you, when I shall
pass through Macedonia: for I do pass
through Macedonia.
6 And it may be that I will abide, yea,
and winter with you, that ye may bring me
on my journey whithersoever I go.
7 For I will not see you now by the way;
but I trust to tarry a while with you, if the
Lord permit.
8 But I will tarry at Ephesus until Pentecost.
9 For a great door and effectual is opened
unto me, and *there are* many adversaries.
10 Now if Timotheus come, see that he
may be with you without fear: for he
worketh the work of the Lord, as I also *do*.
11 Let no man therefore despise him: but
conduct him forth in peace, that he may
come unto me: for I look for him with the
brethren.
12 As touching *our* brother Apollos, I
greatly desired him to come unto you with
the brethren: but his will was not at all to
come at this time; but he will come when
he shall have convenient time.
13 Watch ye,
stand fast in the
faith, quit you like
men, be strong.
14 Let all your
things be done with
charity.

> **16:13 Pitfalls**
> ◄ 1 Corinthians 10:12
> Colossians 4:2 ►

15 I beseech you,
brethren, (ye know
the house of Steph-
anas, that it is the
firstfruits of Achaia,
and *that* they have

> **16:15-16 Work that Helps Others**
> ◄ Luke 10:34
> 2 Corinthians 1:11 ►

addicted themselves to the ministry of the
saints,)
16That ye submit yourselves unto such,
and to every one that helpeth with *us*, and
laboureth.
17I am glad of the coming of Stephanas
and Fortunatus and Achaicus: for that
which was lacking on your part they have
supplied.
18For they have refreshed my spirit and
yours: therefore acknowledge ye them that
are such.
19The churches of Asia salute you. Aquila and Priscilla salute you much in
the Lord, with the church that is in their
house.
20All the brethren greet you. Greet ye
one another with an holy kiss.
21The salutation of *me* Paul with mine
own hand.
22If any man love not the Lord Jesus
Christ, let him be Anathema Maranatha.
23The grace of our Lord Jesus Christ *be*
with you.
24My love *be* with you all in Christ Jesus.
Amen.

2 Corinthians

AUTHOR
Paul the apostle

MAIN POINT
There's a difference between true ministers of the gospel and fake ones, and Paul has a message for the pretenders.

DATE WRITTEN
About A.D. 55-57

13 CHAPTERS

☐☐☐☐☐☐☐☐☐☐☐☐☐

MAIN PEOPLE

Paul, Timothy, Titus, false teachers

SPECIAL FEATURES

- *Is one of Paul's most personal letters, in which he talks a lot about himself*
- *Counters some hefty charges against Paul and his ministry*
- *Tells about the apostle's "thorn in the flesh"*
- *Third of Paul's epistles*

HOW THE BOOK GOT ITS NAME

The book is Paul's second letter to the Christians in Corinth.

1

1 Paul, an apostle of Jesus Christ by the
will of God, and Timothy *our* brother, unto
the church of God which is at Corinth,
with all the saints which are in all Achaia:
2 Grace be to you and peace from God
our Father, and *from* the Lord Jesus Christ.
3 Blessed *be* God,
even the Father of
our Lord Jesus
Christ, the Father of
mercies, and the
God of all comfort;

> **1:3 God's Comfort**
> ◄ Isaiah 66:13
> 2 Corinthians 7:6 ►

4 Who comforteth us in all our tribulation, that we may be able to comfort them
which are in any trouble, by the comfort
wherewith we ourselves are comforted of
God.
5 For as the sufferings of Christ abound
in us, so our consolation also aboundeth
by Christ.
6 And whether we be afflicted, *it is* for
your consolation and salvation, which is
effectual in the enduring of the same sufferings which we also suffer: or whether
we be comforted, *it is* for your consolation
and salvation.
7 And our hope of
you *is* stedfast,
knowing, that as ye
are partakers of the
sufferings, so *shall*
ye be also of the
consolation.

> **1:7 Suffering for Jesus**
> ◄ Romans 8:36
> 2 Corinthians 11:23 ►

8 For we would not, brethren, have you
ignorant of our trouble which came to us
in Asia, that we were pressed out of measure, above strength, insomuch that we de-
spaired even of life:
9 But we had the sentence of death in
ourselves, that we should not trust in

ourselves, but in God which raiseth the dead:

10 Who delivered us from so great a death, and doth deliver: in whom we trust that he will yet deliver *us;*

1:10 Evil Attacks
◄ 1 Corinthians 10:13
2 Timothy 4:18 ►

11 Ye also helping together by prayer for us, that for the gift *bestowed* upon us by the means of many persons thanks may be given by many on our behalf.

1:11 Work that Helps Others
◄ 1 Corinthians 16:15-16
Philippians 4:3 ►

12 For our rejoicing is this, the testimony of our conscience, that in simplicity and godly sincerity, not with fleshly wisdom, but by the grace of God, we have had our conversation in the world, and more abundantly to you-ward.

1:12 Clear Conscience
◄ Romans 9:1
1 Timothy 1:5 ►

1:12 Sincerity
◄ 1 Corinthians 5:8
2 Corinthians 2:17 ►

13 For we write none other things unto you, than what ye read or acknowledge; and I trust ye shall acknowledge even to the end;

14 As also ye have acknowledged us in part, that we are your rejoicing, even as ye also *are* ours in the day of the Lord Jesus.

15 And in this confidence I was minded to come unto you before, that ye might have a second benefit;

16 And to pass by you into Macedonia, and to come again out of Macedonia unto you, and of you to be brought on my way toward Judaea.

17 When I therefore was thus minded, did I use lightness? or the things that I purpose, do I purpose according to the flesh, that with me there should be yea yea, and nay nay?

18 But *as* God *is* true, our word toward you was not yea and nay.

19 For the Son of God, Jesus Christ, who was preached among you by us, *even* by me and Silvanus and Timotheus, was not yea and nay, but in him was yea.

20 For all the promises of God in him *are* yea, and in him Amen, unto the glory of God by us.

1:20 God's Promises
◄ Romans 4:21
2 Corinthians 7:1 ►

21 Now he which stablisheth us with you in Christ, and hath anointed us, *is* God;

22 Who hath also sealed us, and given the earnest of the Spirit in our hearts.

23 Moreover I call God for a record upon my soul, that to spare you I came not as yet unto Corinth.

24 Not for that we have dominion over your faith, but are helpers of your joy: for by faith ye stand.

2

1 But I determined this with myself, that I would not come again to you in heaviness.

2 For if I make you sorry, who is he then that maketh me glad, but the same which is made sorry by me?

3 And I wrote this same unto you, lest, when I came, I should have sorrow from them of whom I ought to rejoice; having confidence in you all, that my joy is *the joy* of you all.

4 For out of much affliction and anguish of heart I wrote unto you with many tears; not that ye should be grieved, but that ye might know the love which I have more abundantly unto you.

5 But if any have caused grief, he hath not grieved me, but in part: that I may not overcharge you all.

6 Sufficient to such a man *is* this punishment, which *was inflicted* of many.

7 So that contrariwise ye *ought* rather to forgive *him,* and comfort *him,* lest perhaps such a one should be swallowed up with overmuch sorrow.

2:7 Comforting Others
◄ 1 Corinthians 14:31
1 Thessalonians 4:18 ►

8 Wherefore I beseech you that ye would confirm *your* love toward him.

9 For to this end also did I write, that I might know the proof of you, whether ye be obedient in all things.

10 To whom ye forgive any thing, I *forgive* also: for if I forgave any thing, to whom I forgave *it,* for your sakes *forgave I it* in the person of Christ;

11 Lest Satan should get an advantage of us: for we are not ignorant of his devices.

12 Furthermore, when I came to Troas to

preach Christ's gospel, and a door was
opened unto me of the Lord,
13 I had no rest in
my spirit, because I
found not Titus my
brother: but taking
my leave of them, I
went from thence
into Macedonia.

2:13 Good Friends
◄ 1 Kings 5:1
Philippians 2:25 ►

14 Now thanks *be* unto God, which always causeth us to triumph in Christ, and
maketh manifest the savour of his knowledge by us in every place.
15 For we are unto God a sweet savour
of Christ, in them that are saved, and in
them that perish:
16 To the one *we are* the savour of death
unto death; and to the other the savour of
life unto life. And who *is* sufficient for
these things?
17 For we are not
as many, which cor-
rupt the word of
God: but as of sin-
cerity, but as of
God, in the sight of
God speak we in Christ.

2:17 Sincerity
◄ 2 Corinthians 1:12
Philippians 1:10 ►

3

1 Do we begin again to commend ourselves? or need we, as some *others,* epistles
of commendation to you, or *letters* of commendation from you?
2 Ye are our epistle written in our hearts,
known and read of all men:
3 *Forasmuch as ye are* manifestly declared
to be the epistle of Christ ministered by
us, written not with ink, but with the Spirit
of the living God; not in tables of stone,
but in fleshy tables of the heart.
4 And such trust have we through Christ
to God-ward:
5 Not that we are
sufficient of our-
selves to think any
thing as of our-
selves; but our suf-
ficiency *is* of God;

3:5
God's Role
◄ John 15:5 ►

6 Who also hath
made us able ministers of the new testament; not of the letter, but of the spirit:
for the letter killeth, but the spirit giveth
life.
7 But if the ministration of death, written *and* engraven in stones, was glorious,
so that the children of Israel could not
stedfastly behold the face of Moses for the
glory of his countenance; which *glory* was
to be done away:
8 How shall not the ministration of the
spirit be rather glorious?
9 For if the ministration of condemnation *be* glory, much more doth the ministration of righteousness exceed in glory.
10 For even that which was made glorious had no glory in this respect, by reason
of the glory that excelleth.
11 For if that which is done away *was* glorious, much more that which remaineth *is*
glorious.
12 Seeing then
that we have
such hope, we use
great plainness of
speech:

3:12 Telling the Truth
◄ Acts 7:52
Galatians 4:16 ►

13 And not as
Moses, *which* put a vail over his face, that
the children of Israel could not stedfastly
look to the end of that which is abolished:
14 But their minds were blinded: for until this day remaineth the same vail
untaken away in the reading of the old testament; which *vail* is done away in Christ.
15 But even unto this day, when Moses
is read, the vail is upon their heart.
16 Nevertheless when it shall turn to the
Lord, the vail shall be taken away.
17 Now the Lord is that Spirit: and where
the Spirit of the Lord *is,* there *is* liberty.
18 But we all, with
open face behold-
ing as in a glass the
glory of the Lord,
are changed into
the same image
from glory to glory, *even* as by the Spirit of
the Lord.

3:18 Making Progress
◄ Proverbs 4:18
1 Timothy 4:15 ►

4

1 Therefore seeing we have this ministry,
as we have received mercy, we faint not;
2 But have renounced the hidden things
of dishonesty, not walking in craftiness,
nor handling the word of God deceitfully;
but by manifestation of the truth com-
mending ourselves to every man's conscience in the sight of God.
3 But if our gospel
be hid, it is hid to
them that are lost:
4 In whom the
god of this world
hath blinded the
minds of them which believe not, lest the

4:3-4 Satan's Power
◄ Acts 26:18
Ephesians 6:12 ►

light of the glorious
gospel of Christ,
who is the image of
God, should shine
unto them.

4:4
God on Earth
◄ Philippians 2:6 ►

5 For we preach
not ourselves, but Christ Jesus the Lord;
and ourselves your servants for Jesus' sake.
6 For God, who commanded the light to
shine out of darkness, hath shined in our
hearts, to *give* the light of the knowledge
of the glory of God in the face of Jesus
Christ.
7 But we have this
treasure in earthen
vessels, that the ex-
cellency of the pow-
er may be of God,
and not of us.

4:7 Mortality
◄ 1 Corinthians 15:53
2 Corinthians 4:16 ►

8 *We are* troubled on every side, yet not
distressed; *we are* perplexed, but not in
despair;
9 Persecuted, but not forsaken; cast
down, but not destroyed;
10 Always bearing about in the body the
dying of the Lord Jesus, that the life also
of Jesus might be made manifest in our
body.
11 For we which live are alway delivered
unto death for Jesus' sake, that the life also
of Jesus might be made manifest in our
mortal flesh.
12 So then death worketh in us, but life
in you.
13 We having the same spirit of faith,
according as it is written, I believed, and
therefore have I spoken; we also believe,
and therefore speak;
14 Knowing that
he which raised up
the Lord Jesus shall
raise up us also by
Jesus, and shall
present *us* with you.

4:14 Resurrection
◄ 1 Corinthians 15:22
1 Thessalonians 4:16 ►

15 For all things
are for your sakes,
that the abundant
grace might through
the thanksgiving of
many redound to
the glory of God.

4:16 Mortality
◄ 2 Corinthians 4:7
2 Corinthians 5:1 ►

16 For which
cause we faint not;
but though our out-
ward man perish,

4:16 New Person
◄ Romans 12:2
Ephesians 4:23 ►

yet the inward *man* is renewed day by day.
17 For our light
affliction, which is
but for a moment,
worketh for us a far
more exceeding *and*
eternal weight of
glory;

4:17 Hardship
◄ Psalm 119:67
Hebrews 12:11 ►

18 While we look
not at the things
which are seen, but
at the things which
are not seen: for the
things which are seen *are* temporal; but the
things which are not seen *are* eternal.

4:18 Things That Last
◄ 1 Corinthians 13:13
Hebrews 12:27 ►

5

1 For we know
that if our earthly
house of *this* taber-
nacle were dis-
solved, we have a
building of God, an
house not made
with hands, eternal
in the heavens.

5:1 Believer Be Glad
◄ Romans 8:38-39
Hebrews 6:19 ►

5:1 Eternal Life
◄ 1 Corinthians 15:53
1 Thessalonians 4:17 ►

2 For in this we
groan, earnestly de-
siring to be clothed
upon with our
house which is
from heaven:
3 If so be that
being clothed we
shall not be found
naked.

5:1 Mortality
◄ 2 Corinthians 4:16
2 Corinthians 5:4 ►

4 For we that are
in *this* tabernacle
do groan, being
burdened: not for
that we would be
unclothed, but
clothed upon, that mortality might be
swallowed up of life.

5:4 Mortality
◄ 2 Corinthians 5:1
Hebrews 9:27 ►

5 Now he that hath wrought us for the
selfsame thing *is* God, who also hath
given unto us the earnest of the Spirit.
6 Therefore *we are* always confident,
knowing that, whilst we are at home in
the body, we are absent from the Lord:
7 (For we walk by faith, not by sight:)
8 We are confident, *I say,* and willing rather to be absent from the body, and to be
present with the Lord.
9 Wherefore we labour, that, whether
present or absent, we may be accepted of
him.

Turn to the next page for more . . .

10 For we must all appear before the judgment seat of Christ; that every one may receive the things *done* in *his* body, according to that he hath done, whether *it be* good or bad.

5:9 Accepted by God
◄ Acts 10:35
Ephesians 1:6 ►

5:10 Actions Judged
◄ Romans 2:6
1 Peter 1:17 ►

11 Knowing therefore the terror of the Lord, we persuade men; but we are made manifest unto God; and I trust also are made manifest in your consciences.

12 For we commend not ourselves again unto you, but give you occasion to glory on our behalf, that ye may have somewhat to *answer* them which glory in appearance, and not in heart.

5:12 Good Looks
◄ John 7:24
2 Corinthians 10:7 ►

13 For whether we be beside ourselves, *it is* to God: or whether we be sober, *it is* for your cause.

14 For the love of Christ constraineth us; because we thus judge, that if one died for all, then were all dead:

15 And *that* he died for all, that they which live should not henceforth live unto themselves, but unto him which died for them, and rose again.

16 Wherefore henceforth know we no man after the flesh: yea, though we have known Christ after the flesh, yet now henceforth know we *him* no more.

17 Therefore if any man *be* in Christ, *he is* a new creature: old things are passed away; behold, all things are become new.

5:17 New Life
◄ Romans 7:6
Galatians 6:15 ►

18 And all things *are* of God, who hath reconciled us to himself by Jesus Christ, and hath given to us the ministry of reconciliation;

19 To wit, that God was in Christ, reconciling the world unto himself, not imputing their trespasses unto them; and hath committed unto us the word of reconciliation.

20 Now then we are ambassadors for Christ, as though God did beseech *you* by us: we pray *you* in Christ's stead, be ye reconciled to God.

5:20 Change
◄ Luke 14:17
Revelation 3:20 ►

21 For he hath made him *to be* sin for us, who knew no sin; that we might be made the righteousness of God in him.

5:21 Why Jesus Died
◄ Isaiah 53:5
Galatians 3:13 ►

6

1 We then, *as* workers together *with him*, beseech *you* also that ye receive not the grace of God in vain.

6:1 Working with God
◄ 1 Corinthians 3:9 ►

2 (For he saith, I have heard thee in a time accepted, and in the day of salvation have I succoured thee: behold, now *is* the accepted time; behold, now *is* the day of salvation.)

3 Giving no offence in any thing, that the ministry be not blamed:

4 But in all *things* approving ourselves as the ministers of God, in much patience, in afflictions, in necessities, in distresses,

5 In stripes, in imprisonments, in tumults, in labours, in watchings, in fastings;

6 By pureness, by knowledge, by longsuffering, by kindness, by the Holy Ghost, by love unfeigned,

7 By the word of truth, by the power of God, by the armour of righteousness on the right hand and on the left,

8 By honour and dishonour, by evil report and good report: as deceivers, and *yet* true;

9 As unknown, and *yet* well known; as dying, and, behold, we live; as chastened, and not killed;

10 As sorrowful, yet alway rejoicing; as poor, yet making many rich; as having nothing, and *yet* possessing all things.

6:10 Positive Attitude
◄ Acts 16:23, 25
Hebrews 10:34 ►

11 O *ye* Corinthians, our mouth is open unto you, our heart is enlarged.

12 Ye are not straitened in us, but ye are straitened in your own bowels.

13 Now for a recompence in the same,

(I speak as unto *my* children,) be ye also
enlarged.
14 Be ye not un-
equally yoked to-
gether with unbe-
lievers: for what
fellowship hath
righteousness with
unrighteousness? and what communion
hath light with darkness?

> **6:14 Bad Friends**
> ◄ 1 Corinthians 5:11
> 2 John 1:10 ►

15 And what concord hath Christ with
Belial? or what part hath he that believeth
with an infidel?
16 And what agreement hath the temple
of God with idols? for ye are the temple of
the living God; as God hath said, I will
dwell in them, and walk in *them;* and I will
be their God, and they shall be my people.
17 Wherefore come out from among
them, and be ye separate, saith the Lord,
and touch not the unclean *thing;* and I will
receive you,
18 And will be a
Father unto you,
and ye shall be my
sons and daughters,
saith the Lord Al-
mighty.

> **6:18 Adopted by God**
> ◄ Romans 8:15
> Galatians 3:26 ►

7

1 Having there-
fore these promises,
dearly beloved, let
us cleanse ourselves
from all filthiness
of the flesh and
spirit, perfecting
holiness in the fear
of God.

> **7:1 God's Promises**
> ◄ 2 Corinthians 1:20
> 2 Peter 1:4 ►

> **7:1 Holiness**
> ◄ Luke 1:74-75
> Ephesians 4:24 ►

2 Receive us; we
have wronged no
man, we have cor-
rupted no man, we
have defrauded no man.
3 I speak not *this* to condemn *you:* for I
have said before, that ye are in our hearts
to die and live with *you.*
4 Great *is* my boldness of speech toward
you, great *is* my glorying of you: I am filled
with comfort, I am exceeding joyful in all
our tribulation.
5 For, when we were come into Macedonia, our flesh had no rest, but we were troubled on every side; without *were* fightings,
within *were* fears.
6 Nevertheless God, that comforteth
those that are cast down, comforted us
by the coming of
Titus;
7 And not by his
coming only, but
by the consolation
wherewith he was
comforted in you, when he told us your
earnest desire, your mourning, your fervent
mind toward me; so that I rejoiced the
more.

> **7:6 God's Comfort**
> ◄ 2 Corinthians 1:3 ►

8 For though I made you sorry with a letter, I do not repent, though I did repent:
for I perceive that the same epistle hath
made you sorry, though *it were* but for a
season.
9 Now I rejoice, not that ye were made
sorry, but that ye sorrowed to repentance:
for ye were made sorry after a godly manner, that ye might receive damage by us in
nothing.
10 For godly sor-
row worketh repen-
tance to salvation
not to be repented
of: but the sorrow
of the world wor-
keth death.

> **7:10 Feeling Sorry**
> ◄ Zechariah 12:10 ►

11 For behold this selfsame thing, that ye
sorrowed after a godly sort, what carefulness it wrought in you, yea, *what* clearing
of yourselves, yea, *what* indignation, yea,
what fear, yea, *what* vehement desire, yea,
what zeal, yea, *what* revenge! In all *things*
ye have approved yourselves to be clear in
this matter.
12 Wherefore,
though I wrote
unto you, *I did it*
not for his cause
that had done the
wrong, nor for his
cause that suffered wrong, but that our care
for you in the sight of God might appear
unto you.

> **7:12 Caring for the Church**
> ◄ Acts 20:31
> 2 Corinthians 11:28 ►

13 Therefore we were comforted in your
comfort: yea, and exceedingly the more
joyed we for the joy of Titus, because his
spirit was refreshed by you all.
14 For if I have boasted any thing to him
of you, I am not ashamed; but as we spake
all things to you in truth, even so our
boasting, which *I made* before Titus, is
found a truth.
15 And his inward affection is more abundant toward you, whilst he remembereth

the obedience of you all, how with fear
and trembling ye received him.
16I rejoice therefore that I have confidence in you in all *things.*

8

1Moreover, brethren, we do you to wit
of the grace of God bestowed on the
churches of Macedonia;
2How that in a
great trial of afflic-
tion the abundance
of their joy and
their deep poverty
abounded unto the
riches of their liberality.

8:2
Examples of Generosity
◄ Acts 11:29
Philippians 4:16 ►

3For to *their*
power, I bear
record, yea, and be-
yond *their* power
they were willing of
themselves;

8:3 Willingness to Work
◄ Isaiah 1:19
1 Thessalonians 2:8 ►

4Praying us with much intreaty that we
would receive the gift, and *take upon us* the
fellowship of the ministering to the saints.
5And *this they did,* not as we hoped, but
first gave their own selves to the Lord, and
unto us by the will of God.
6Insomuch that we desired Titus, that
as he had begun, so he would also finish
in you the same grace also.
7Therefore, as ye abound in every *thing,*
in faith, and utterance, and knowledge, and
in all diligence, and *in* your love to us, *see*
that ye abound in this grace also.
8I speak not by commandment, but by
occasion of the forwardness of others, and
to prove the sincerity of your love.
9For ye know the
grace of our Lord
Jesus Christ, that,
though he was rich,
yet for your sakes
he became poor,
that ye through his
poverty might be rich.

8:9 Unselfishness
◄ 1 Corinthians 10:33
2 Corinthians 12:5 ►

10And herein I give *my* advice: for this is
expedient for you, who have begun before,
not only to do, but also to be forward a
year ago.
11Now therefore perform the doing *of*
it; that as *there was* a readiness to will, so
there may be a performance also out of that
which ye have.
12For if there be first a willing mind, *it*
is accepted according to that a man hath,
and not according to that he hath not.
13For *I mean* not that other men be
eased, and ye burdened:
14But by an equality, *that* now at this
time your abundance *may be a supply* for
their want, that their abundance also may
be *a supply* for your want: that there may
be equality:
15As it is written, He that *had gathered*
much had nothing over; and he that *had*
gathered little had no lack.
16But thanks *be* to God, which put the
same earnest care into the heart of Titus
for you.
17For indeed he accepted the exhortation; but being more forward, of his own
accord he went unto you.
18And we have sent with him the brother, whose praise is in the gospel throughout all the churches;
19And not *that* only, but who was also
chosen of the churches to travel with us
with this grace, which is administered by
us to the glory of the same Lord, and *dec-*
laration of your ready mind:
20Avoiding this, that no man should
blame us in this abundance which is administered by us:
21Providing for honest things, not only
in the sight of the Lord, but also in the
sight of men.
22And we have sent with them our
brother, whom we have oftentimes proved
diligent in many things, but now much
more diligent, upon the great confidence
which *I have* in you.
23Whether *any do enquire* of Titus, *he is*
my partner and fellowhelper concerning
you: or our brethren *be enquired of, they*
are the messengers of the churches, *and* the
glory of Christ.
24Wherefore shew ye to them, and before the churches, the proof of your love,
and of our boasting on your behalf.

9

1For as touching the ministering to the
saints, it is superfluous for me to write to
you:
2For I know the forwardness of your
mind, for which I boast of you to them of
Macedonia, that Achaia was ready a year
ago; and your zeal hath provoked very
many.
3Yet have I sent the brethren, lest our
boasting of you should be in vain in this
behalf; that, as I said, ye may be ready:
4Lest haply if they of Macedonia come

with me, and find you unprepared, we
(that we say not, ye) should be ashamed
in this same confident boasting.
5Therefore I thought it necessary to exhort the brethren, that they would go before unto you, and make up beforehand
your bounty, whereof ye had notice before,
that the same might be ready, as *a matter*
of bounty, and not as *of* covetousness.
6But this *I say,* He which soweth sparingly shall reap also sparingly; and he
which soweth bountifully shall reap also
bountifully.
7Every man ac-
cording as he pur-
poseth in his heart,
so let him give; not
grudgingly, or of
necessity: for God
loveth a cheerful
giver.

9:7
How to Give
◄ 1 Corinthians 16:2 ►

8And God *is* able
to make all grace
abound toward
you; that ye, always
having all sufficiency in all *things,* may
abound to every good work:

9:7
Promises to Givers
◄ Luke 14:14 ►

9(As it is written, He hath dispersed
abroad; he hath given to the poor: his righteousness remaineth for ever.
10Now he that
ministereth seed to
the sower both
minister bread for
your food, and
multiply your seed
sown, and increase the fruits of your righteousness;)

9:10
Growing Spiritually
◄ Ephesians 4:15 ►

11Being enriched in every thing to all
bountifulness, which causeth through us
thanksgiving to God.
12For the administration of this service
not only supplieth the want of the saints,
but is abundant also by many thanksgivings unto God;
13Whiles by the experiment of this ministration they glorify God for your professed subjection into the gospel of Christ,
and for *your* liberal distribution unto them,
and unto all *men;*
14And by their prayer for you, which long
after you for the exceeding grace of God in
you.
15Thanks *be* unto God for his unspeakable gift.

10

1Now I Paul my-
self beseech you
by the meekness
and gentleness of
Christ, who in pres-
ence *am* base
among you, but being absent am bold toward you:

9:15 A Great Gift
◄ Romans 8:32
Ephesians 2:8 ►

2But I beseech *you,* that I may not be
bold when I am present with that confidence, wherewith I think to be bold against
some, which think of us as if we walked
according to the flesh.
3For though we walk in the flesh, we do
not war after the flesh:
4(For the weapons of our warfare *are* not
carnal, but mighty through God to the
pulling down of strong holds;)
5Casting down imaginations, and every
high thing that exalteth itself against the
knowledge of God, and bringing into captivity every thought to the obedience of
Christ;
6And having in a readiness to revenge
all disobedience, when your obedience is
fulfilled.
7Do ye look on
things after the out-
ward appearance? If
any man trust to
himself that he is
Christ's, let him of
himself think this again, that, as he *is*
Christ's, even so *are* we Christ's.

10:7 Good Looks
◄ 2 Corinthians 5:12
James 2:2-4 ►

8For though I should boast somewhat
more of our authority, which the Lord
hath given us for edification, and not
for your destruction, I should not be
ashamed:
9That I may not seem as if I would terrify you by letters.
10For *his* letters, say they, *are* weighty and
powerful; but *his* bodily presence *is* weak,
and *his* speech contemptible.
11Let such an one think this, that, such
as we are in word by letters when we are
absent, such *will we be* also in deed when
we are present.
12For we dare not
make ourselves of
the number, or
compare ourselves
with some that
commend them-
selves: but they measuring themselves by

10:12
Self-righteousness
◄ Jeremiah 2:35
Revelation 3:17 ►

themselves, and comparing themselves
among themselves, are not wise.
13 But we will not boast of things without *our* measure, but according to the
measure of the rule which God hath distributed to us, a measure to reach even
unto you.
14 For we stretch not ourselves beyond
our measure, as though we reached not unto
you: for we are come as far as to you also
in *preaching* the gospel of Christ:
15 Not boasting of things without *our*
measure, *that is,* of other men's labours;
but having hope, when your faith is increased, that we shall be enlarged by you
according to our rule abundantly,
16 To preach the gospel in the *regions*
beyond you, *and* not to boast in another
man's line of things made ready to our
hand.
17 But he that
glorieth, let him
glory in the Lord.
18 For not he that
commendeth him-
self is approved, but
whom the Lord commendeth.

10:17
Boasting
◄ 1 Corinthians 1:31 ►

11

1 Would to God ye could bear with me a
little in *my* folly: and indeed bear with me.
2 For I am jealous over you with godly
jealousy: for I have espoused you to one
husband, that I may present *you as* a chaste
virgin to Christ.
3 But I fear, lest by any means, as the serpent beguiled Eve through his subtilty, so
your minds should be corrupted from the
simplicity that is in Christ.
4 For if he that cometh preacheth another
Jesus, whom we have not preached, or *if*
ye receive another spirit, which ye have not
received, or another gospel, which ye have
not accepted, ye might well bear with *him.*
5 For I suppose I was not a whit behind
the very chiefest apostles.
6 But though *I be* rude in speech, yet not
in knowledge; but we have been throughly
made manifest among you in all things.
7 Have I committed an offence in abas-
ing myself that ye might be exalted, because I have preached to you the gospel of
God freely?
8 I robbed other churches, taking wages
of them, to do you service.
9 And when I was present with you, and
wanted, I was chargeable to no man: for
that which was lacking to me the brethren
which came from Macedonia supplied:
and in all *things* I have kept myself from
being burdensome unto you, and so will I
keep *myself.*
10 As the truth of Christ is in me, no man
shall stop me of this boasting in the regions of Achaia.
11 Wherefore? because I love you not?
God knoweth.
12 But what I do, that I will do, that I
may cut off occasion from them which
desire occasion; that wherein they glory,
they may be found even as we.
13 For such *are* false apostles, deceitful
workers, transforming themselves into the
apostles of Christ.
14 And no marvel; for Satan himself is
transformed into an angel of light.
15 Therefore *it is* no great thing if his
ministers also be transformed as the ministers of righteousness; whose end shall be
according to their works.
16 I say again, Let no man think me a
fool; if otherwise, yet as a fool receive me,
that I may boast myself a little.
17 That which I speak, I speak *it* not after
the Lord, but as it were foolishly, in this
confidence of boasting.
18 Seeing that many glory after the flesh,
I will glory also.
19 For ye suffer fools gladly, seeing ye
yourselves are wise.
20 For ye suffer, if a man bring you into
bondage, if a man devour *you,* if a man
take *of you,* if a man exalt himself, if a man
smite you on the face.
21 I speak as concerning reproach, as
though we had been weak. Howbeit
whereinsoever any is bold, (I speak foolishly,) I am bold also.
22 Are they Hebrews? so *am* I. Are they
Israelites? so *am* I. Are they the seed of
Abraham? so *am* I.
23 Are they minis-
ters of Christ? (I
speak as a fool) I *am*
more; in labours
more abundant, in
stripes above mea-
sure, in prisons more frequent, in deaths
oft.

11:23
Suffering for Jesus
◄ 2 Corinthians 1:7
Philippians 3:10 ►

24 Of the Jews five times received I forty
stripes save one.
25 Thrice was I beaten with rods, once

was I stoned, thrice I suffered shipwreck, a night and a day I have been in the deep;

26 *In* journeyings often, *in* perils of waters, *in* perils of robbers, *in* perils by *mine own* countrymen, *in* perils by the heathen, *in* perils in the city, *in* perils in the wilderness, *in* perils in the sea, *in* perils among false brethren;

27 In weariness and painfulness, in watchings often, in hunger and thirst, in fastings often, in cold and nakedness.

28 Beside those things that are without, that which cometh upon me daily, the care of all the churches.

> **11:28**
> **Caring for the Church**
> ◄ 2 Corinthians 7:12
> 2 Corinthians 12:20 ►

29 Who is weak, and I am not weak? who is offended, and I burn not?

30 If I must needs glory, I will glory of the things which concern mine infirmities.

31 The God and Father of our Lord Jesus Christ, which is blessed for evermore, knoweth that I lie not.

32 In Damascus the governor under Aretas the king kept the city of the Damascenes with a garrison, desirous to apprehend me:

33 And through a window in a basket was I let down by the wall, and escaped his hands.

12

1 It is not expedient for me doubtless to glory. I will come to visions and revelations of the Lord.

2 I knew a man in Christ above fourteen years ago, (whether in the body, I cannot tell; or whether out of the body, I cannot tell: God knoweth;) such an one caught up to the third heaven.

3 And I knew such a man, (whether in the body, or out of the body, I cannot tell: God knoweth;)

4 How that he was caught up into paradise, and heard unspeakable words, which it is not lawful for a man to utter.

> **12:5**
> **Unselfishness**
> ◄ 2 Corinthians 8:9 ►

5 Of such an one will I glory: yet of myself I will not glory, but in mine infirmities.

> **12:6 Honesty**
> ◄ Malachi 2:6
> Ephesians 4:25 ►

6 For though I would desire to glory, I shall not be a fool; for I will say the truth: but *now* I forbear, lest any man should think of me above that which he seeth me *to be,* or *that* he heareth of me.

7 And lest I should be exalted above measure through the abundance of the revelations, there was given to me a thorn in the flesh, the messenger of Satan to buffet me, lest I should be exalted above measure.

8 For this thing I besought the Lord thrice, that it might depart from me.

9 And he said unto me, My grace is sufficient for thee: for my strength is made perfect in weakness. Most gladly therefore will I rather glory in my infirmities, that the power of Christ may rest upon me.

> **12:9-10 Weakness**
> ◄ 1 Corinthians 1:27
> 2 Corinthians 13:4 ►

10 Therefore I take pleasure in infirmities, in reproaches, in necessities, in persecutions, in distresses for Christ's sake: for when I am weak, then am I strong.

11 I am become a fool in glorying; ye have compelled me: for I ought to have been commended of you: for in nothing am I behind the very chiefest apostles, though I be nothing.

12 Truly the signs of an apostle were wrought among you in all patience, in signs, and wonders, and mighty deeds.

13 For what is it wherein ye were inferior to other churches, except *it be* that I myself was not burdensome to you? forgive me this wrong.

14 Behold, the third time I am ready to come to you; and I will not be burdensome to you: for I seek not yours, but you: for the children ought not to lay up for the parents, but the parents for the children.

15 And I will very gladly spend and be spent for you; though the more abundantly I love you, the less I be loved.

> **12:15 Love for Friends**
> ◄ Romans 16:4
> Philippians 1:8 ►

16 But be it so, I did not burden you: nevertheless, being crafty, I caught you with guile.

17 Did I make a gain of you by any of them whom I sent unto you?

18 I desired Titus, and with *him* I sent a

brother. Did Titus make a gain of you?
walked we not in the same spirit? *walked*
we not in the same steps?
19Again, think ye that we excuse ourselves unto you? we speak before God in
Christ: but *we do* all things, dearly beloved,
for your edifying.
20For I fear, lest,
when I come, I shall
not find you such as
I would, and *that* I
shall be found unto
you such as ye
would not: lest *there be* debates, envyings,
wraths, strifes, backbitings, whisperings,
swellings, tumults:

12:20
Caring for the Church
◄ 2 Corinthians 11:28
Galatians 4:11 ►

21*And* lest, when I come again, my God
will humble me among you, and *that* I
shall bewail many which have sinned
already, and have not repented of the uncleanness and fornication and lasciviousness which they have committed.

13

1This *is* the third *time* I am coming to
you. In the mouth of two or three witnesses shall every word be established.
2I told you before, and foretell you, as if
I were present, the second time; and being
absent now I write to them which heretofore have sinned, and to all other, that, if I
come again, I will not spare:
3Since ye seek a proof of Christ speaking in me, which to you-ward is not weak,
but is mighty in you.
4For though he
was crucified
through weakness,
yet he liveth by the
power of God. For
we also are weak in
him, but we shall live with him by the
power of God toward you.

13:4 Weakness
◄ 2 Corinthians 12:9-10
Hebrews 11:33-34 ►

5Examine your-
selves, whether ye
be in the faith;
prove your own
selves. Know ye not
your own selves,
how that Jesus Christ is in you, except ye
be reprobates?

13:5 Self-examination
◄ 1 Corinthians 11:28
Galatians 6:4 ►

6But I trust that ye shall know that we
are not reprobates.
7Now I pray to God that ye do no evil;
not that we should appear approved, but
that ye should do that which is honest,
though we be as reprobates.
8For we can do nothing against the truth,
but for the truth.
9For we are glad, when we are weak, and
ye are strong: and this also we wish, *even*
your perfection.
10Therefore I write these things being
absent, lest being present I should use
sharpness, according to the power which
the Lord hath given me to edification, and
not to destruction.
11Finally, breth-
ren, farewell. Be
perfect, be of good
comfort, be of one
mind, live in peace;
and the God of love
and peace shall be
with you.

13:11 Getting Along
◄ 1 Corinthians 1:10
Ephesians 4:3 ►

13:11 Perfection
◄ Matthew 5:48
Ephesians 4:13 ►

12Greet one an-
other with an holy
kiss.
13All the saints
salute you.
14The grace of the Lord Jesus Christ,
and the love of God, and the communion of the Holy Ghost, *be* with you all.
Amen.

Galatians

AUTHOR
Paul the apostle

MAIN POINT
Christians do not have to obey Jewish law to have faith and freedom in following Christ.

DATE WRITTEN
About A.D. 49

6 CHAPTERS
☐☐☐☐☐☐

MAIN PEOPLE

Paul, Peter, Barnabas, Titus, Abraham, false teachers

SPECIAL FEATURES

- *Counters people who would lay lots of extra rules on new believers when all we need to do is follow Jesus*
- *Sheds some new light on Abraham's two sons*
- *Has a famous passage about our ugly sinful side versus the Holy Spirit in us*
- *Fourth of Paul's epistles*

HOW THE BOOK GOT ITS NAME

The book is Paul's letter to the Christians in Galatia.

1

1 Paul, an apostle, (not of men, neither
by man, but by Jesus Christ, and God the
Father, who raised him from the dead;)
2 And all the brethren which are with me,
unto the churches of Galatia:
3 Grace *be* to you and peace from God
the Father, and *from* our Lord Jesus Christ,
4 Who gave him-
self for our sins,
that he might de-
liver us from this
present evil world,
according to the
will of God and our Father:

1:4 Who Can Be Saved?
◄ 1 Corinthians 15:3
1 Peter 2:24 ►

5 To whom *be* glory for ever and ever.
Amen.
6 I marvel that ye are so soon removed
from him that called you into the grace of
Christ unto another gospel:
7 Which is not another; but there be
some that trouble you, and would pervert
the gospel of Christ.
8 But though we, or an angel from heav-
en, preach any other gospel unto you than
that which we have preached unto you, let
him be accursed.
9 As we said before, so say I now again,
If any *man* preach any other gospel unto
you than that ye have received, let him be
accursed.
10 For do I now persuade men, or God?
or do I seek to please men? for if I yet
pleased men, I should not be the servant
of Christ.
11 But I certify you, brethren, that the
gospel which was preached of me is not
after man.
12 For I neither received it of man, neither was I taught *it,* but by the revelation
of Jesus Christ.
13 For ye have heard of my conversation
in time past in the Jews' religion, how that
beyond measure I persecuted the church
of God, and wasted it:

14And profited in
the Jews' religion
above many my
equals in mine own
nation, being more
exceedingly zealous
of the traditions of my fathers.

> 1:14
> Legalism
> ◄ Romans 10:2 ►

15But when it pleased God, who separated me from my mother's womb, and
called *me* by his grace,
16To reveal his Son in me, that I might
preach him among the heathen; immediately I conferred not with flesh and blood:
17Neither went I up to Jerusalem to
them which were apostles before me; but
I went into Arabia, and returned again
unto Damascus.
18Then after three years I went up to Jerusalem to see Peter, and abode with him
fifteen days.
19But other of the apostles saw I none,
save James the Lord's brother.
20Now the things which I write unto
you, behold, before God, I lie not.
21Afterwards I came into the regions of
Syria and Cilicia;
22And was unknown by face unto the
churches of Judaea which were in Christ:
23But they had heard only, That he
which persecuted us in times past now
preacheth the faith which once he destroyed.
24And they glorified God in me.

2

1Then fourteen years after I went up
again to Jerusalem with Barnabas, and
took Titus with *me* also.
2And I went up by revelation, and communicated unto them that gospel which I
preach among the Gentiles, but privately
to them which were of reputation, lest by
any means I should run, or had run, in
vain.
3But neither Titus, who was with me,
being a Greek, was compelled to be circumcised:
4And that because of false brethren unawares brought in, who came in privily
to spy out our liberty which we have in
Christ Jesus, that they might bring us into
bondage:
5To whom we gave place by subjection,
no, not for an hour; that the truth of the
gospel might continue with you.
6But of these who seemed to be somewhat, (whatsoever they were, it maketh no
matter to me: God accepteth no man's
person:) for they who seemed *to be somewhat* in conference added nothing to me:
7But contrari-
wise, when they
saw that the gospel
of the uncircumci-
sion was commit-
ted unto me, as *the*
gospel of the circumcision *was* unto Peter;

> 2:7 The Gospel
> ◄ 1 Corinthians 9:17
> Colossians 1:25 ►

8(For he that wrought effectually in Peter to the apostleship of the circumcision,
the same was mighty in me toward the
Gentiles:)
9And when James, Cephas, and John,
who seemed to be pillars, perceived the
grace that was given unto me, they gave to
me and Barnabas the right hands of fellowship; that we *should go* unto the heathen, and they unto the circumcision.
10Only *they would*
that we should re-
member the poor;
the same which I
also was forward
to do.

> 2:10
> Kind to the Poor
> ◄ Matthew 19:21 ►

11But when Peter was come to Antioch,
I withstood him to the face, because he
was to be blamed.
12For before that
certain came from
James, he did eat
with the Gentiles:
but when they were
come, he withdrew
and separated himself, fearing them which
were of the circumcision.

> 2:12
> Different People
> ◄ Acts 19:34 ►

13And the other
Jews dissembled
likewise with him;
insomuch that Bar-
nabas also was car-
ried away with their
dissimulation.

> 2:13
> Only Human
> ◄ Luke 22:24 ►

14But when I saw that they walked not
uprightly according to the truth of the gospel, I said unto Peter before *them* all, If
thou, being a Jew, livest after the manner
of Gentiles, and not as do the Jews, why
compellest thou the Gentiles to live as do
the Jews?
15We *who are* Jews by nature, and not
sinners of the Gentiles,
16Knowing that a man is not justified
by the works of the law, but by the faith of

Jesus Christ, even we have believed in Jesus
Christ, that we might be justified by the
faith of Christ, and not by the works of
the law: for by the works of the law shall
no flesh be justified.
[17]But if, while we seek to be justified by
Christ, we ourselves also are found sinners,
is therefore Christ the minister of sin? God
forbid.
[18]For if I build again the things which I
destroyed, I make myself a transgressor.
[19]For I through the law am dead to the
law, that I might live unto God.
[20]I am crucified
with Christ: never-
theless I live; yet not
I, but Christ liveth
in me: and the life
which I now live in
the flesh I live by
the faith of the Son
of God, who loved
me, and gave him-
self for me.

2:20 Freedom
◄ Romans 6:11
Galatians 5:24 ►

2:20 Jesus' Home
◄ Romans 8:10
Ephesians 3:17-19 ►

[21]I do not frus-
trate the grace of God: for if righteousness
come by the law, then Christ is dead in vain.

3

[1]O foolish Galatians, who hath bewitched you, that ye should not obey the
truth, before whose eyes Jesus Christ hath
been evidently set forth, crucified among
you?
[2]This only would I learn of you, Received ye the Spirit by the works of the law,
or by the hearing of faith?
[3]Are ye so foolish? having begun in the
Spirit, are ye now made perfect by the
flesh?
[4]Have ye suffered so many things in
vain? if *it be* yet in vain.
[5]He therefore that ministereth to you the
Spirit, and worketh miracles among you,
doeth he it by the works of the law, or by
the hearing of faith?
[6]Even as Abra-
ham believed God,
and it was account-
ed to him for righ-
teousness.

3:6
Justification by Faith
◄ Romans 5:1
Philippians 3:9 ►

[7]Know ye there-
fore that they which are of faith, the same
are the children of Abraham.
[8]And the scripture, foreseeing that God
would justify the heathen through faith,
preached before the gospel unto Abraham,
saying, In thee shall all nations be blessed.
[9]So then they which be of faith are
blessed with faithful Abraham.
[10]For as many as
are of the works of
the law are under
the curse: for it is
written, Cursed *is*
every one that con-
tinueth not in all things which are written
in the book of the law to do them.

3:10
Earning Heaven
◄ Romans 10:3 ►

[11]But that no man is justified by the law
in the sight of God, *it is* evident: for, The
just shall live by faith.
[12]And the law is not of faith: but, The
man that doeth them shall live in them.
[13]Christ hath re-
deemed us from
the curse of the law,
being made a curse
for us: for it is writ-
ten, Cursed *is* every
one that hangeth on a tree:

3:13 Why Jesus Died
◄ 2 Corinthians 5:21
Hebrews 2:9 ►

[14]That the blessing of Abraham might
come on the Gentiles through Jesus Christ;
that we might receive the promise of the
Spirit through faith.
[15]Brethren, I speak after the manner of
men; Though *it be* but a man's covenant,
yet *if it be* confirmed, no man disannulleth,
or addeth thereto.
[16]Now to Abraham and his seed were
the promises made. He saith not, And to
seeds, as of many; but as of one, And to
thy seed, which is Christ.
[17]And this I say, *that* the covenant, that
was confirmed before of God in Christ, the
law, which was four hundred and thirty
years after, cannot disannul, that it should
make the promise of none effect.
[18]For if the inheritance *be* of the law, *it*
is no more of promise: but God gave *it* to
Abraham by promise.
[19]Wherefore then *serveth* the law? It was
added because of transgressions, till the
seed should come to whom the promise
was made; *and it was* ordained by angels
in the hand of a mediator.
[20]Now a mediator is not *a mediator* of
one, but God is one.
[21]*Is* the law then against the promises
of God? God forbid: for if there had been
a law given which could have given life,
verily righteousness should have been by
the law.

22 But the scripture hath concluded all under sin, that the promise by faith of Jesus Christ might be given to them that believe.

3:22 Everyone Sins
◄ Romans 3:23
1 John 1:8 ►

23 But before faith came, we were kept under the law, shut up unto the faith which should afterwards be revealed.

24 Wherefore the law was our schoolmaster *to bring us* unto Christ, that we might be justified by faith.

25 But after that faith is come, we are no longer under a schoolmaster.

26 For ye are all the children of God by faith in Christ Jesus.

3:26 Adopted by God
◄ 2 Corinthians 6:18
Galatians 4:5-6 ►

27 For as many of you as have been baptized into Christ have put on Christ.

28 There is neither Jew nor Greek, there is neither bond nor free, there is neither male nor female: for ye are all one in Christ Jesus.

3:28 Equality
◄ Romans 10:12
James 2:5 ►

29 And if ye *be* Christ's, then are ye Abraham's seed, and heirs according to the promise.

4

1 Now I say, *That* the heir, as long as he is a child, differeth nothing from a servant, though he be lord of all;

2 But is under tutors and governors until the time appointed of the father.

3 Even so we, when we were children, were in bondage under the elements of the world:

4 But when the fulness of the time was come, God sent forth his Son, made of a woman, made under the law,

5 To redeem them that were under the law, that we might receive the adoption of sons.

4:5-6 Adopted by God
◄ Galatians 3:26
Ephesians 1:5 ►

6 And because ye are sons, God hath sent forth the Spirit of his Son into your hearts, crying, Abba, Father.

7 Wherefore thou art no more a servant, but a son; and if a son, then an heir of God through Christ.

8 Howbeit then, when ye knew not God, ye did service unto them which by nature are no gods.

9 But now, after that ye have known God, or rather are known of God, how turn ye again to the weak and beggarly elements, whereunto ye desire again to be in bondage?

10 Ye observe days, and months, and times, and years.

11 I am afraid of you, lest I have bestowed upon you labour in vain.

4:11 Caring for the Church
◄ 2 Corinthians 12:20
1 Thessalonians 3:10 ►

12 Brethren, I beseech you, be as I *am;* for I *am* as ye *are:* ye have not injured me at all.

13 Ye know how through infirmity of the flesh I preached the gospel unto you at the first.

14 And my temptation which was in my flesh ye despised not, nor rejected; but received me as an angel of God, *even* as Christ Jesus.

15 Where is then the blessedness ye spake of? for I bear you record, that, if *it had been* possible, ye would have plucked out your own eyes, and have given them to me.

16 Am I therefore become your enemy, because I tell you the truth?

4:16 Telling the Truth
◄ 2 Corinthians 3:12 ►

17 They zealously affect you, *but* not well; yea, they would exclude you, that ye might affect them.

18 But *it is* good to be zealously affected always in *a* good *thing,* and not only when I am present with you.

19 My little children, of whom I travail in birth again until Christ be formed in you,

20 I desire to be present with you now, and to change my voice; for I stand in doubt of you.

21 Tell me, ye that desire to be under the law, do ye not hear the law?

22 For it is written, that Abraham had two sons, the one by a bondmaid, the other by a freewoman.

23 But he *who was* of the bondwoman was born after the flesh; but he of the freewoman *was* by promise.

24 Which things are an allegory: for these

are the two covenants; the one from the
mount Sinai, which gendereth to bondage,
which is Agar.
25 For this Agar is mount Sinai in Arabia,
and answereth to Jerusalem which now is,
and is in bondage with her children.
26 But Jerusalem which is above is free,
which is the mother of us all.
27 For it is written, Rejoice, *thou* barren
that bearest not; break forth and cry, thou
that travailest not: for the desolate hath
many more children than she which hath
an husband.
28 Now we, brethren, as Isaac was, are the
children of promise.
29 But as then he that was born after the
flesh persecuted him *that was born* after the
Spirit, even so *it is* now.
30 Nevertheless what saith the scripture?
Cast out the bondwoman and her son: for
the son of the bondwoman shall not be
heir with the son of the free woman.
31 So then, brethren, we are not children
of the bondwoman, but of the free.

5

1 Stand fast therefore in the liberty wherewith Christ hath made us free, and be not entangled again with the yoke of bondage.

5:1 Standing Strong
◄ 1 Corinthians 15:58
Ephesians 4:14 ►

2 Behold, I Paul say unto you, that if ye
be circumcised, Christ shall profit you
nothing.
3 For I testify again to every man that is
circumcised, that he is a debtor to do the
whole law.
4 Christ is become of no effect unto you,
whosoever of you are justified by the law;
ye are fallen from grace.
5 For we through the Spirit wait for the
hope of righteousness by faith.
6 For in Jesus Christ neither circumcision availeth any thing, nor uncircumcision; but faith which worketh by love.

5:6 Importance of Love
◄ 1 Corinthians 13:13
Galatians 5:22 ►

7 Ye did run well; who did hinder you
that ye should not obey the truth?
8 This persuasion *cometh* not of him that
calleth you.
9 A little leaven leaveneth the whole
lump.
10 I have confidence in you through the
Lord, that ye will be none otherwise minded: but he that troubleth you shall bear
his judgment, whosoever he be.
11 And I, brethren, if I yet preach circumcision, why do I yet suffer persecution?
then is the offence of the cross ceased.
12 I would they were even cut off which
trouble you.
13 For, brethren, ye have been called unto liberty; only *use* not liberty for an occasion to the flesh, but by love serve one another.

5:13 Free to...
◄ 1 Corinthians 8:9
1 Peter 2:16 ►

14 For all the law is fulfilled in one word, *even* in this; Thou shalt love thy neighbour as thyself.

5:13 Serving People
◄ John 21:16
Galatians 6:2 ►

15 But if ye bite and devour one another, take heed that ye be not consumed one of another.

5:14 Neighbors
◄ Romans 15:1-2
James 2:8 ►

16 *This* I say then, Walk in the Spirit, and
ye shall not fulfil the lust of the flesh.
17 For the flesh lusteth against the Spirit, and the Spirit against the flesh: and
these are contrary the one to the other: so
that ye cannot do the things that ye would.
18 But if ye be led of the Spirit, ye are not under the law.
19 Now the works of the flesh are manifest, which are *these;* Adultery, fornication, uncleanness, lasciviousness,

5:18 Guidance
◄ Romans 8:14 ►

20 Idolatry, witchcraft, hatred, variance,
emulations, wrath, strife, seditions, heresies,
21 Envyings, murders, drunkenness, revellings, and such like: of the which I tell you before, as I have also told *you* in time past, that they which do such things

5:21 Moderation
◄ Luke 15:13
Ephesians 5:18 ►

5:21 Parties
◄ 1 Samuel 30:16
1 Peter 4:3 ►

shall not inherit the kingdom of God.

22 But the fruit of the Spirit is love, joy, peace, longsuffering, gentleness, goodness, faith,

23 Meekness, temperance: against such there is no law.

24 And they that are Christ's have crucified the flesh with the affections and lusts.

25 If we live in the Spirit, let us also walk in the Spirit.

26 Let us not be desirous of vain glory, provoking one another, envying one another.

6

1 Brethren, if a man be overtaken in a fault, ye which are spiritual, restore such an one in the spirit of meekness; considering thyself, lest thou also be tempted.

2 Bear ye one another's burdens, and so fulfil the law of Christ.

3 For if a man think himself to be something, when he is nothing, he deceiveth himself.

4 But let every man prove his own work, and then shall he have rejoicing in himself alone, and not in another.

5 For every man shall bear his own burden.

6 Let him that is taught in the word communicate unto him that teacheth in all good things.

7 Be not deceived; God is not mocked: for whatsoever a man soweth, that shall he also reap.

8 For he that soweth to his flesh shall of the flesh reap corruption; but he that soweth to the Spirit shall of the Spirit reap life everlasting.

9 And let us not be weary in well doing: for in due season we shall reap, if we faint not.

10 As we have therefore opportunity, let us do good unto all *men*, especially unto them who are of the household of faith.

11 Ye see how large a letter I have written unto you with mine own hand.

12 As many as desire to make a fair shew in the flesh, they constrain you to be circumcised; only lest they should suffer persecution for the cross of Christ.

13 For neither they themselves who are circumcised keep the law; but desire to have you circumcised, that they may glory in your flesh.

14 But God forbid that I should glory, save in the cross of our Lord Jesus Christ, by whom the world is crucified unto me, and I unto the world.

15 For in Christ Jesus neither circumcision availeth any thing, nor uncircumcision, but a new creature.

5:22 Importance of Love
◄ Galatians 5:6
Ephesians 3:17-19 ►

5:24 Controlling Yourself
◄ Romans 15:1 ►

5:24 Freedom
◄ Galatians 2:20
Colossians 2:20 ►

5:26 Envy
◄ 1 Corinthians 13:4
James 3:14 ►

6:2 Serving People
◄ Galatians 5:13
Galatians 6:10 ►

6:2 Sympathy
◄ Romans 15:1
Hebrews 13:3 ►

6:3 Conceit
◄ 1 Corinthians 8:2 ►

6:3 Lying to Yourself
◄ Isaiah 44:20
James 1:22 ►

6:4 Self-examination
◄ 2 Corinthians 13:5 ►

6:5 Blame
◄ Romans 14:4 ►

6:7 Deception
◄ 1 Corinthians 15:33
Ephesians 5:6 ►

6:9 Determination
◄ Romans 2:7
2 Timothy 3:14 ►

6:10 Serving People
◄ Galatians 6:2 ►

6:10 Giving
◄ Romans 12:13
1 Timothy 6:18 ►

6:10 Doing Good
◄ Romans 13:3
1 Timothy 6:18 ►

6:15 New Life
◄ 2 Corinthians 5:17
Ephesians 2:15 ►

16And as many as walk according to this
rule, peace *be* on them, and mercy, and
upon the Israel of God.
17From henceforth let no man trouble
me: for I bear in my body the marks of the
Lord Jesus.
18Brethren, the grace of our Lord Jesus
Christ *be* with your spirit. Amen.

Ephesians

AUTHOR
Paul the apostle

MAIN POINT
Be encouraged with the fact that the church is the body of Christ.

DATE WRITTEN
About A.D. 60

6 CHAPTERS

MAIN PEOPLE

Paul, Tychicus

SPECIAL FEATURES

- *Divides neatly into two sections: the unity we have with God, and the unity we have with other Christians*
- *Says how the church works like a human body*
- *Has a well-known section on how marriages are meant to be*
- *Talks about warfare and tells how to fight*
- *Fifth of Paul's epistles*

HOW THE BOOK GOT ITS NAME

The book is Paul's letter to the Christians in Ephesus.

1

1 Paul, an apostle of Jesus Christ by the
will of God, to the saints which are at Ephesus, and to the faithful in Christ Jesus:
2 Grace *be* to you, and peace, from God
our Father, and *from* the Lord Jesus Christ.
3 Blessed *be* the God and Father of our
Lord Jesus Christ, who hath blessed us
with all spiritual blessings in heavenly
places in Christ:
4 According as he hath chosen us in him
before the foundation of the world, that
we should be holy and without blame before him in love:
5 Having predesti-
nated us unto the
adoption of chil-
dren by Jesus Christ
to himself, accord-
ing to the good
pleasure of his will,
6 To the praise of the glory of his grace,

> **1:5**
> **Adopted by God**
> ◄ Galatians 4:5-6 ►

wherein he hath
made us accepted
in the beloved.
7 In whom we
have redemption
through his blood,
the forgiveness of
sins, according to
the riches of his
grace;
8 Wherein he hath
abounded toward
us in all wisdom and prudence;
9 Having made known unto us the mystery of his will, according to his good pleasure which he hath purposed in himself:
10 That in the dispensation of the fulness
of times he might gather together in one
all things in Christ, both which are in heav-
en, and which are on earth; *even* in him:
11 In whom also we have obtained an

> **1:6**
> **Accepted by God**
> ◄ 2 Corinthians 5:9 ►

> **1:7 Forgiveness**
> ◄ Acts 26:18
> James 5:15 ►

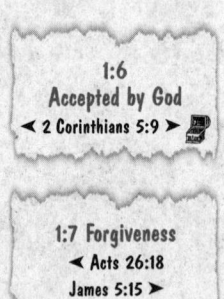

inheritance, being predestinated according to the purpose of him who worketh all things after the counsel of his own will:

12 That we should be to the praise of his glory, who first trusted in Christ.

13 In whom ye also *trusted*, after that ye heard the word of truth, the gospel of your salvation: in whom also after that ye believed, ye were sealed with that holy Spirit of promise,

14 Which is the earnest of our inheritance until the redemption of the purchased possession, unto the praise of his glory.

15 Wherefore I also, after I heard of your faith in the Lord Jesus, and love unto all the saints,

16 Cease not to give thanks for you, making mention of you in my prayers;

> **1:16 Praying for Others**
> ◄ Psalm 106:23 ►

17 That the God of our Lord Jesus Christ, the Father of glory, may give unto you the spirit of wisdom and revelation in the knowledge of him:

> **1:17 Praying for Wisdom**
> ◄ Proverbs 2:3
> Colossians 1:9 ►

18 The eyes of your understanding being enlightened; that ye may know what is the hope of his calling, and what the riches of the glory of his inheritance in the saints,

> **1:18 Invisible Wealth**
> ◄ Proverbs 13:7
> Ephesians 3:8 ►

19 And what *is* the exceeding greatness of his power to us-ward who believe, according to the working of his mighty power,

20 Which he wrought in Christ, when he raised him from the dead, and set *him* at his own right hand in the heavenly *places*,

21 Far above all principality, and power, and might, and dominion, and every name that is named, not only in this world, but also in that which is to come:

22 And hath put all *things* under his feet, and gave him *to be* the head over all *things* to the church,

23 Which is his body, the fulness of him that filleth all in all.

> **1:23 God's Body**
> ◄ 1 Corinthians 12:27
> Ephesians 4:12 ►

2

1 And you *hath he quickened*, who were dead in trespasses and sins;

2 Wherein in time past ye walked according to the course of this world, according to the prince of the power of the air, the spirit that now worketh in the children of disobedience:

3 Among whom also we all had our conversation in times past in the lusts of our flesh, fulfilling the desires of the flesh and of the mind; and were by nature the children of wrath, even as others.

4 But God, who is rich in mercy, for his great love wherewith he loved us,

> **2:4 God's Mercy**
> ◄ Luke 1:50
> Titus 3:5 ►

5 Even when we were dead in sins, hath quickened us together with Christ, (by grace ye are saved;)

> **2:4-5 God's Love**
> ◄ Romans 5:8
> 1 John 3:1 ►

6 And hath raised *us* up together, and made *us* sit together in heavenly *places* in Christ Jesus:

> **2:5 Grace**
> ◄ Romans 11:6
> Titus 2:11 ►

7 That in the ages to come he might shew the exceeding riches of his grace in *his* kindness toward us through Christ Jesus.

8 For by grace are ye saved through faith; and that not of yourselves: *it is* the gift of God:

> **2:8 A Great Gift**
> ◄ 2 Corinthians 9:15 ►

9 Not of works, lest any man should boast.

10 For we are his workmanship, created in Christ Jesus unto good works, which God hath before ordained that we should walk in them.

11 Wherefore remember, that ye *being* in time past Gentiles in the flesh, who are called Uncircumcision by that which is called the Circumcision in the flesh made by hands;

12 That at that time ye were without Christ, being aliens from the commonwealth of Israel, and strangers

> **2:12 Poverty**
> ◄ Luke 15:14
> Revelation 3:17 ►

from the covenants of promise, having no hope, and without God in the world:

13 But now in Christ Jesus ye who sometimes were far off are made nigh by the blood of Christ.

14 For he is our peace, who hath made both one, and hath broken down the middle wall of partition *between us;*

15 Having abolished in his flesh the enmity, *even* the law of commandments *contained* in ordinances; for to make in himself of twain one new man, *so* making peace;

> **2:15 New Life**
> ◄ Galatians 6:15
> Ephesians 4:24 ►

16 And that he might reconcile both unto God in one body by the cross, having slain the enmity thereby:

17 And came and preached peace to you which were afar off, and to them that were nigh.

18 For through him we both have access by one Spirit unto the Father.

> **2:18 God's Presence**
> ◄ Romans 5:2
> Ephesians 3:12 ►

19 Now therefore ye are no more strangers and foreigners, but fellowcitizens with the saints, and of the household of God;

20 And are built upon the foundation of the apostles and prophets, Jesus Christ himself being the chief corner *stone;*

> **2:20 The Ultimate**
> ◄ Acts 4:11
> 1 Peter 2:6 ►

21 In whom all the building fitly framed together groweth unto an holy temple in the Lord:

22 In whom ye also are builded together for an habitation of God through the Spirit.

3

1 For this cause I Paul, the prisoner of Jesus Christ for you Gentiles,

2 If ye have heard of the dispensation of the grace of God which is given me to youward:

3 How that by revelation he made known unto me the mystery; (as I wrote afore in few words,

4 Whereby, when ye read, ye may understand my knowledge in the mystery of Christ)

5 Which in other ages was not made known unto the sons of men, as it is now revealed unto his holy apostles and prophets by the Spirit;

6 That the Gentiles should be fellowheirs, and of the same body, and partakers of his promise in Christ by the gospel:

7 Whereof I was made a minister, according to the gift of the grace of God given unto me by the effectual working of his power.

8 Unto me, who am less than the least of all saints, is this grace given, that I should preach among the Gentiles the unsearchable riches of Christ;

> **3:8 Invisible Wealth**
> ◄ Ephesians 1:18
> Hebrews 11:26 ►

9 And to make all *men* see what *is* the fellowship of the mystery, which from the beginning of the world hath been hid in God, who created all things by Jesus Christ:

10 To the intent that now unto the principalities and powers in heavenly *places* might be known by the church the manifold wisdom of God,

11 According to the eternal purpose which he purposed in Christ Jesus our Lord:

12 In whom we have boldness and access with confidence by the faith of him.

> **3:12 Approaching God**
> ◄ 1 Timothy 3:13 ►

13 Wherefore I desire that ye faint not at my tribulations for you, which is your glory.

> **3:12 God's Presence**
> ◄ Ephesians 2:18
> Revelation 3:8 ►

14 For this cause I bow my knees unto the Father of our Lord Jesus Christ,

15 Of whom the whole family in heaven and earth is named,

16 That he would grant you, according to the riches of his glory, to be strengthened with might by his Spirit in the inner man;

> **3:16 The Holy Spirit**
> ◄ 1 Corinthians 2:4
> 1 Thessalonians 1:5 ►

17 That Christ may dwell in your hearts by faith; that ye, being rooted

> **3:17-19 Importance of Love**
> ◄ Galatians 5:22
> Ephesians 4:16 ►

and grounded in
love,
18 May be able to
comprehend with
all saints what *is*
the breadth, and
length, and depth, and height;
19 And to know the love of Christ, which
passeth knowledge, that ye might be filled
with all the fulness of God.
20 Now unto him that is able to do exceeding abundantly above all that we ask
or think, according to the power that
worketh in us,
21 Unto him *be* glory in the church by
Christ Jesus throughout all ages, world
without end. Amen.

3:17-19 Jesus' Home
◄ Galatians 2:20
Colossians 1:27 ►

4

1 I therefore, the prisoner of the Lord,
beseech you that ye walk worthy of the
vocation wherewith ye are called,
2 With all lowli-
ness and meekness,
with longsuffering,
forbearing one an-
other in love;
3 Endeavouring
to keep the unity of
the Spirit in the
bond of peace.
4 *There is* one
body, and one Spir-
it, even as ye are
called in one hope of your calling;
5 One Lord, one faith, one baptism,
6 One God and
Father of all, who *is*
above all, and
through all, and in
you all.
7 But unto every
one of us is given grace according to the
measure of the gift of Christ.
8 Wherefore he saith, When he ascended up on high, he led captivity captive, and
gave gifts unto men.
9 (Now that he ascended, what is it but
that he also descended first into the lower
parts of the earth?
10 He that descended is the same also
that ascended up
far above all heav-
ens, that he might
fill all things.)
11 And he gave
some, apostles; and
some, prophets; and some, evangelists; and
some, pastors and teachers;
12 For the perfect-
ing of the saints,
for the work of
the ministry, for
the edifying of the
body of Christ:
13 Till we all
come in the unity
of the faith, and of
the knowledge of
the Son of God,
unto a perfect man,
unto the measure of the stature of the
fulness of Christ:
14 That we *hence-
forth* be no more
children, tossed to
and fro, and carried
about with every
wind of doctrine,
by the sleight of men, *and* cunning craftiness, whereby they lie in wait to deceive;
15 But speaking
the truth in love,
may grow up into
him in all things,
which is the head,
even Christ:
16 From whom
the whole body
fitly joined togeth-
er and compacted
by that which every
joint supplieth, ac-
cording to the effectual working in the
measure of every part, maketh increase of
the body unto the edifying of itself in love.
17 This I say there-
fore, and testify in
the Lord, that ye
henceforth walk
not as other Gen-
tiles walk, in the
vanity of their mind,
18 Having the understanding darkened,
being alienated from the life of God
through the ignorance that is in them, because of the blindness of their heart:
19 Who being past feeling have given
themselves over unto lasciviousness, to
work all uncleanness with greediness.
20 But ye have not so learned Christ;
21 If so be that ye have heard him, and

4:2 Patience
◄ 1 Corinthians 13:7
Ephesians 6:9 ►

4:3 Getting Along
◄ 2 Corinthians 13:11
Philippians 1:27 ►

4:6 Only One God
◄ 1 Corinthians 8:4
1 Timothy 2:5 ►

4:11 Church
◄ 1 Corinthians 12:4 ►

4:12 God's Body
◄ Ephesians 1:23
Colossians 1:24 ►

4:13 Perfection
◄ 2 Corinthians 13:11
Philippians 3:15 ►

4:14 Standing Strong
◄ Galatians 5:1
Philippians 1:27 ►

4:15 Growing Spiritually
◄ 2 Corinthians 9:10
Colossians 1:10 ►

4:16 Importance of Love
◄ Ephesians 3:17-19
Ephesians 5:2 ►

4:17 Brain Power
◄ Romans 8:7
Colossians 1:21 ►

Turn to the next page for more . . .

have been taught by
him, as the truth is
in Jesus:
22That ye put off
concerning the for-
mer conversation
the old man, which
is corrupt according
to the deceitful
lusts;
23And be re-
newed in the spirit
of your mind;
24And that ye put
on the new man,
which after God is
created in righ-
teousness and true
holiness.
25Wherefore put-
ting away lying,
speak every man
truth with his
neighbour: for we
are members one of
another.
26Be ye angry,
and sin not: let not
the sun go down
upon your wrath:
27Neither give
place to the devil.
28Let him that
stole steal no more:
but rather let him
labour, working
with *his* hands the
thing which is
good, that he may
have to give to him
that needeth.
29Let no corrupt
communication
proceed out of your
mouth, but that
which is good to
the use of edifying,
that it may minister
grace unto the hear-
ers.
30And grieve not
the holy Spirit of
God, whereby ye
are sealed unto the
day of redemption.

4:20-23 Lessons of Life
◄ John 6:45
Philippians 4:11 ►

4:22 Old Life
◄ Romans 6:6
Colossians 3:9 ►

4:22 Starting Over
◄ Isaiah 55:7
Colossians 2:11 ►

4:23 New Person
◄ 2 Corinthians 4:16
Colossians 3:10 ►

4:24 Holiness
◄ 2 Corinthians 7:1
Hebrews 12:14 ►

4:24 New Life
◄ Ephesians 2:15
Colossians 3:10 ►

4:25 Honesty
◄ 2 Corinthians 12:6
Ephesians 6:14 ►

4:26-27 Resisting Satan
◄ Ephesians 6:11 ►

4:28 Stealing
◄ Romans 13:9
Titus 2:10 ►

31Let all bitter-
ness, and wrath,
and anger, and
clamour, and evil
speaking, be put
away from you,
with all malice:
32And be ye kind
one to another, ten-
derhearted, forgiv-
ing one another,
even as God for
Christ's sake hath
forgiven you.

5

1Be ye therefore
followers of God,
as dear children;
2And walk in
love, as Christ also
hath loved us, and
hath given himself
for us an offering
and a sacrifice to
God for a sweet-
smelling savour.
3But fornication,
and all unclean-
ness, or covetous-
ness, let it not
be once named
among you, as
becometh saints;
4Neither filthi-
ness, nor foolish
talking, nor jest-
ing, which are not
convenient: but
rather giving of
thanks.
5For this ye
know, that no
whoremonger, nor
unclean person,
nor covetous man,
who is an idolater,
hath any inheri-
tance in the king-
dom of Christ and
of God.
6Let no man de-
ceive you with vain
words: for because
of these things
cometh the wrath
of God upon the

4:28 Working Hard
◄ Ecclesiastes 9:10
1 Thessalonians 4:11 ►

4:31 Cruel Talk
◄ Titus 3:1-2 ►

4:31 Malice
◄ 1 Corinthians 14:20
Colossians 3:8 ►

4:32 Forgiving Others
◄ Luke 17:4
Colossians 3:13 ►

4:32 Kindness
◄ 1 Corinthians 13:4
Colossians 3:12 ►

5:2 Importance of Love
◄ Ephesians 4:16
Colossians 1:8 ►

5:4 Teasing and Joking
◄ Proverbs 26:19 ►

5:6 Deception
◄ Galatians 6:7
2 Thessalonians 2:3 ►

5:6 God's Anger
◄ Romans 2:8
1 Thessalonians 2:16 ►

children of disobe-
dience.
7 Be not ye there-
fore partakers with
them.
8 For ye were
sometimes dark-
ness, but now *are ye*
light in the Lord:
walk as children of
light:
9 (For the fruit of
the Spirit *is* in all goodness and righteousness and truth;)
10 Proving what is acceptable unto the
Lord.
11 And have no fellowship with the unfruitful works of darkness, but rather reprove *them*.
12 For it is a shame even to speak of those
things which are done of them in secret.
13 But all things that are reproved are
made manifest by the light: for whatsoever doth make manifest is light.
14 Wherefore he
saith, Awake thou
that sleepest, and
arise from the dead,
and Christ shall
give thee light.
15 See then that ye
walk circumspectly,
not as fools, but as
wise,
16 Redeeming the
time, because the
days are evil.
17 Wherefore be
ye not unwise, but
understanding
what the will of the
Lord *is*.
18 And be not
drunk with wine,
wherein is excess;
but be filled with
the Spirit;
19 Speaking to
yourselves in psalms
and hymns and
spiritual songs,
singing and making
melody in your
heart to the Lord;
20 Giving thanks

5:6 Ouch!
◄ Jeremiah 12:17
2 Thessalonians 1:8 ►

5:8 Christian Duties
◄ Romans 13:12
Philippians 2:15 ►

5:15-16 Time
◄ 1 Corinthians 7:29, 31
Colossians 4:5 ►

5:18 Drinking Too Much
◄ Habakkuk 2:5 ►

5:18 Getting Drunk
◄ 1 Corinthians 6:10
1 Thessalonians 5:7 ►

5:18 Moderation
◄ Galatians 5:21
1 Peter 4:3 ►

5:19 Your Testimony
◄ Acts 1:8
2 Timothy 1:8 ►

always for all things unto God and the
Father in the name of our Lord Jesus
Christ;
21 Submitting yourselves one to another
in the fear of God.
22 Wives, submit yourselves unto your
own husbands, as unto the Lord.
23 For the husband is the head of the
wife, even as Christ is the head of the
church: and he is the saviour of the body.
24 Therefore as the church is subject unto
Christ, so *let* the wives *be* to their own husbands in every thing.
25 Husbands, love your wives, even as
Christ also loved the church, and gave himself for it;
26 That he might
sanctify and cleanse
it with the washing
of water by the
word,
27 That he might
present it to himself a glorious church, not
having spot, or wrinkle, or any such thing;
but that it should be holy and without
blemish.
28 So ought men to love their wives as
their own bodies. He that loveth his wife
loveth himself.
29 For no man ever yet hated his own
flesh; but nourisheth and cherisheth it,
even as the Lord the church:
30 For we are members of his body, of
his flesh, and of his bones.
31 For this cause shall a man leave his
father and mother, and shall be joined
unto his wife, and they two shall be one
flesh.
32 This is a great mystery: but I speak concerning Christ and the church.
33 Nevertheless let every one of you in
particular so love his wife even as himself;
and the wife *see* that she reverence *her* husband.

5:26 Purity
◄ John 17:17
1 Peter 1:22 ►

6

1 Children, obey your parents in the
Lord: for this is right.
2 Honour thy father and mother; (which
is the first commandment with promise;)
3 That it may be well with thee, and thou
mayest live long on
the earth.
4 And, ye fathers,
provoke not your
children to wrath:
but bring them up

6:4 Giving Advice
◄ 1 Corinthians 4:14
Colossians 3:16 ►

in the nurture and admonition of the Lord.

5 Servants, be obedient to them that are *your* masters according to the flesh, with fear and trembling, in singleness of your heart, as unto Christ;

6 Not with eyeservice, as menpleasers; but as the servants of Christ, doing the will of God from the heart;

7 With good will doing service, as to the Lord, and not to men:

8 Knowing that whatsoever good thing any man doeth, the same shall he receive of the Lord, whether *he be* bond or free.

9 And, ye masters, do the same things unto them, forbearing threatening: knowing that your Master also is in heaven; neither is there respect of persons with him.

10 Finally, my brethren, be strong in the Lord, and in the power of his might.

11 Put on the whole armour of God, that ye may be able to stand against the wiles of the devil.

12 For we wrestle not against flesh and blood, but against principalities, against powers, against the rulers of the darkness of this world, against spiritual wickedness in high *places*.

13 Wherefore take unto you the whole armour of God, that ye may be able to withstand in the evil day, and having done all, to stand.

14 Stand therefore, having your loins girt about with truth, and having on the breastplate of righteousness;

15 And your feet shod with the preparation of the gospel of peace;

16 Above all, taking the shield of faith, wherewith ye shall be able to quench all the fiery darts of the wicked.

17 And take the helmet of salvation, and the sword of the Spirit, which is the word of God:

18 Praying always with all prayer and supplication in the Spirit, and watching thereunto with all perseverance and supplication for all saints;

19 And for me, that utterance may be given unto me, that I may open my mouth boldly, to make known the mystery of the gospel,

20 For which I am an ambassador in bonds: that therein I may speak boldly, as I ought to speak.

21 But that ye also may know my affairs, *and* how I do, Tychicus, a beloved brother and faithful minister in the Lord, shall make known to you all things:

22 Whom I have sent unto you for the

6:6 Popularity
◄ Acts 25:9
Colossians 3:22 ►

6:6 Serving Jesus
◄ 1 Corinthians 7:22
Philippians 1:1 ►

6:6 Submitting to God
◄ Romans 12:2
Hebrews 13:21 ►

6:7 Using What You Have
◄ 1 Corinthians 6:20
1 Timothy 6:20 ►

6:8 Goodness Rewarded
◄ 1 Corinthians 3:8
Colossians 3:24 ►

6:9 Patience
◄ Ephesians 4:2
Colossians 3:13 ►

6:11 Resisting Satan
◄ Ephesians 4:26-27
James 4:7 ►

6:12 Demons
◄ Acts 19:13
1 Timothy 4:1 ►

6:12 Satan's Power
◄ 2 Corinthians 4:3-4
2 Thessalonians 2:9 ►

6:13 Saying No
◄ Romans 6:13
2 Peter 3:17 ►

6:14 Honesty
◄ Ephesians 4:25 ►

6:14 Righteousness
◄ 1 Corinthians 15:34
Philippians 1:11 ►

6:16 Faith
◄ John 20:27
1 Thessalonians 5:8 ►

6:17 Power of the Bible
◄ Romans 1:16
Hebrews 4:12 ►

6:18 Duty to Pray
◄ John 16:24
Philippians 4:6 ►

same purpose, that ye might know our affairs, and *that* he might comfort your hearts.
23 Peace *be* to the brethren, and love with faith, from God the Father and the Lord Jesus Christ.
24 Grace *be* with all them that love our Lord Jesus Christ in sincerity. Amen.

Philippians

AUTHOR
Paul the apostle

MAIN POINT
Many things and people can make us happy, but only Jesus can give us true, deep-down joy.

DATE WRITTEN
About A.D. 61

4 CHAPTERS

☐☐☐☐

MAIN PEOPLE

Paul, Timothy, Epaphroditus, Euodia, Syntyche

SPECIAL FEATURES

- *Starts out as a thank-you note for the Philippians' gift to Paul*
- *Tells all about joy—yet it was written by a man in prison*
- *Gives practical advice on how to develop an attitude of gratitude and joy*
- *Sixth of Paul's epistles*

HOW THE BOOK GOT ITS NAME

The book is Paul's letter to the Christians in Philippi.

1

1 Paul and Timotheus, the servants of Jesus Christ, to all the saints in Christ Jesus which are at Philippi, with the bishops and deacons:

> **1:1 Serving Jesus**
> ◄ Ephesians 6:6
> Colossians 3:24 ►

2 Grace *be* unto you, and peace, from God our Father, and *from* the Lord Jesus Christ.

3 I thank my God upon every remembrance of you,

4 Always in every prayer of mine for you all making request with joy,

5 For your fellowship in the gospel from the first day until now;

6 Being confident of this very thing, that he which hath begun a good work in you will perform *it* until the day of Jesus Christ:

7 Even as it is meet for me to think this of you all, because I have you in my heart; inasmuch as both in my bonds, and in the defence and confirmation of the gospel, ye all are partakers of my grace.

8 For God is my record, how greatly I long after you all in the bowels of Jesus Christ.

> **1:8 Love for Friends**
> ◄ 2 Corinthians 12:15
> Philippians 4:1 ►

9 And this I pray, that your love may abound yet more and more in knowledge and *in* all judgment;

10 That ye may approve things that are excellent; that ye may be sincere and without offence till the day of Christ;

> **1:10 Sincerity**
> ◄ 2 Corinthians 2:17
> Titus 2:7 ►

11 Being filled with the fruits of righteousness, which are by Jesus Christ, unto the glory and praise of God.

> **1:11 Righteousness**
> ◄ Ephesians 6:14
> 1 Timothy 6:11 ►

12 But I would ye should understand, brethren, that the things *which happened*

unto me have fallen out rather unto the furtherance of the gospel;

13 So that my bonds in Christ are manifest in all the palace, and in all other *places;*

14 And many of the brethren in the Lord, waxing confident by my bonds, are much more bold to speak the word without fear.

15 Some indeed preach Christ even of envy and strife; and some also of good will:

16 The one preach Christ of contention, not sincerely, supposing to add affliction to my bonds:

17 But the other of love, knowing that I am set for the defence of the gospel.

> **1:17-18 Accepting People**
> ◄ Luke 9:49-50 ►

18 What then? notwithstanding, every way, whether in pretence, or in truth, Christ is preached; and I therein do rejoice, yea, and will rejoice.

19 For I know that this shall turn to my salvation through your prayer, and the supply of the Spirit of Jesus Christ,

20 According to my earnest expectation and *my* hope, that in nothing I shall be ashamed, but *that* with all boldness, as always, *so* now also Christ shall be magnified in my body, whether *it be* by life, or by death.

21 For to me to live *is* Christ, and to die *is* gain.

22 But if I live in the flesh, this *is* the fruit of my labour: yet what I shall choose I wot not.

23 For I am in a strait betwixt two, having a desire to depart, and to be with Christ; which is far better:

24 Nevertheless to abide in the flesh *is* more needful for you.

25 And having this confidence, I know that I shall abide and continue with you all for your furtherance and joy of faith;

26 That your rejoicing may be more abundant in Jesus Christ for me by my coming to you again.

> **1:27 Getting Along**
> ◄ Ephesians 4:3
> Philippians 4:2 ►

27 Only let your conversation be as it becometh the gospel of Christ: that whether I come and see you, or else be absent, I may hear of your affairs, that ye stand fast in one spirit, with one mind striving together for the faith of the gospel;

> **1:27 Living for God**
> ◄ 1 Thessalonians 4:12 ►

> **1:27 Standing Strong**
> ◄ Ephesians 4:14
> Philippians 4:1 ►

28 And in nothing terrified by your adversaries: which is to them an evident token of perdition, but to you of salvation, and that of God.

> **1:27 Teamwork**
> ◄ Mark 6:7 ►

29 For unto you it is given in the behalf of Christ, not only to believe on him, but also to suffer for his sake;

30 Having the same conflict which ye saw in me, and now hear *to be* in me.

2

1 If *there be* therefore any consolation in Christ, if any comfort of love, if any fellowship of the Spirit, if any bowels and mercies,

2 Fulfil ye my joy, that ye be likeminded, having the same love, *being* of one accord, of one mind.

3 *Let* nothing *be done* through strife or vainglory; but in lowliness of mind let each esteem other better than themselves.

> **2:3 Arguing**
> ◄ Proverbs 26:17
> 2 Timothy 2:14 ►

4 Look not every man on his own things, but every man also on the things of others.

5 Let this mind be in you, which was also in Christ Jesus:

6 Who, being in the form of God, thought it not robbery to be equal with God:

> **2:6 God on Earth**
> ◄ 2 Corinthians 4:4
> Colossians 1:15 ►

7 But made himself of no reputation, and took upon him the form of a servant, and was made in the likeness of men:

> **2:7 Christmas**
> ◄ Romans 8:3
> 1 Timothy 3:16 ►

8 And being found in fashion as a man, he humbled himself, and became obedient unto death, even the death of the cross.

9 Wherefore God also hath highly exalted him, and given him a name which is above every name:

10 That at the name of Jesus every knee
should bow, of *things* in heaven, and *things*
in earth, and *things* under the earth;
11 And *that* every tongue should confess
that Jesus Christ *is* Lord, to the glory of
God the Father.
12 Wherefore, my beloved, as ye have always obeyed, not as in my presence only,
but now much more in my absence, work
out your own salvation with fear and trembling.
13 For it is God which worketh in you
both to will and to do of *his* good pleasure.
14 Do all things without murmurings
and disputings:
15 That ye may be
blameless and
harmless, the sons
of God, without re-
buke, in the midst
of a crooked and
perverse nation, among whom ye shine as
lights in the world;

2:15 Christian Duties
◄ Ephesians 5:8
1 Thessalonians 5:5-6 ►

16 Holding forth the word of life; that
I may rejoice in the day of Christ, that I
have not run in vain, neither laboured in
vain.
17 Yea, and if I be offered upon the sacrifice and service of your faith, I joy, and
rejoice with you all.
18 For the same cause also do ye joy, and
rejoice with me.
19 But I trust in the Lord Jesus to send
Timotheus shortly unto you, that I also
may be of good comfort, when I know
your state.
20 For I have no man likeminded, who
will naturally care for your state.
21 For all seek their own, not the things
which are Jesus Christ's.
22 But ye know the proof of him, that, as
a son with the father, he hath served with
me in the gospel.
23 Him therefore I hope to send presently, so soon as I shall see how it will go
with me.
24 But I trust in the Lord that I also myself shall come shortly.
25 Yet I supposed
it necessary to send
to you Epaphrodi-
tus, my brother,
and companion in
labour, and fellow
soldier, but your messenger, and he that
ministered to my wants.

2:25 Good Friends
◄ 2 Corinthians 2:13
2 Timothy 1:16 ►

26 For he longed after you all, and was
full of heaviness, because that ye had heard
that he had been sick.
27 For indeed he was sick nigh unto
death: but God had mercy on him; and
not on him only, but on me also, lest I
should have sorrow upon sorrow.
28 I sent him therefore the more carefully, that, when ye see him again, ye
may rejoice, and that I may be the less sorrowful.
29 Receive him
therefore in the
Lord with all glad-
ness; and hold such
in reputation:
30 Because for the
work of Christ he was nigh unto death, not
regarding his life, to supply your lack of
service toward me.

2:29
Respecting God's People
◄ Acts 28:10
1 Thessalonians 5:12-13 ►

3

1 Finally, my brethren, rejoice in the
Lord. To write the same things to you, to
me indeed *is* not grievous, but for you *it is*
safe.
2 Beware of dogs, beware of evil workers, beware of the concision.
3 For we are the circumcision, which
worship God in the spirit, and rejoice in
Christ Jesus, and have no confidence in the
flesh.
4 Though I might also have confidence
in the flesh. If any other man thinketh that
he hath whereof he might trust in the flesh,
I more:
5 Circumcised the eighth day, of the stock
of Israel, *of* the tribe of Benjamin, an Hebrew of the Hebrews; as touching the law,
a Pharisee;
6 Concerning zeal, persecuting the
church; touching the righteousness which
is in the law, blameless.
7 But what things
were gain to me,
those I counted loss
for Christ.
8 Yea doubtless,
and I count all
things *but* loss for
the excellency of
the knowledge of
Christ Jesus my
Lord: for whom I
have suffered the

3:8
Sacrifice
◄ John 12:24 ►

3:8
This for That
◄ Luke 18:29-30 ►

loss of all things, and do count them *but* dung, that I may win Christ,

9And be found in him, not having mine own righteousness, which is of the law, but that which is through the faith of Christ, the righteousness which is of God by faith:

3:9 Justification by Faith
◄ Galatians 3:6
Hebrews 10:38 ►

10That I may know him, and the power of his resurrection, and the fellowship of his sufferings, being made conformable unto his death;

3:10 Suffering for Jesus
◄ 2 Corinthians 11:23
2 Timothy 2:12 ►

11If by any means I might attain unto the resurrection of the dead.

12Not as though I had already attained, either were already perfect: but I follow after, if that I may apprehend that for which also I am apprehended of Christ Jesus.

13Brethren, I count not myself to have apprehended: but *this* one thing *I do,* forgetting those things which are behind, and reaching forth unto those things which are before,

3:13 One Goal
◄ Luke 9:62 ►

3:13-14 Job One
◄ Acts 20:24 ►

14I press toward the mark for the prize of the high calling of God in Christ Jesus.

15Let us therefore, as many as be perfect, be thus minded: and if in any thing ye be otherwise minded, God shall reveal even this unto you.

3:15 Perfection
◄ Ephesians 4:13
Colossians 1:28 ►

16Nevertheless, whereto we have already attained, let us walk by the same rule, let us mind the same thing.

17Brethren, be followers together of me, and mark them which walk so as ye have us for an ensample.

18(For many walk, of whom I have told you often, and now tell you even weeping, *that they are* the enemies of the cross of Christ:

19Whose end *is* destruction, whose God *is their* belly, and *whose* glory *is* in their shame, who mind earthly things.)

20For our conversation is in heaven; from whence also we look for the Saviour, the Lord Jesus Christ:

21Who shall change our vile body, that it may be fashioned like unto his glorious body, according to the working whereby he is able even to subdue all things unto himself.

4

1Therefore, my brethren dearly beloved and longed for, my joy and crown, so stand fast in the Lord, *my* dearly beloved.

2I beseech Euodias, and beseech Syntyche, that they be of the same mind in the Lord.

3And I intreat thee also, true yokefellow, help those women which laboured with me in the gospel, with Clement also, and *with* other my fellowlabourers, whose names *are* in the book of life.

4Rejoice in the Lord alway: *and* again I say, Rejoice.

5Let your moderation be known unto all men. The Lord *is* at hand.

6Be careful for nothing; but in

3:20-21 Good News
◄ John 14:3
Colossians 3:4 ►

4:1 Love for Friends
◄ Philippians 1:8
2 Timothy 1:17 ►

4:1 Standing Strong
◄ Philippians 1:27
2 Thessalonians 2:2 ►

4:2 Getting Along
◄ Philippians 1:27
Colossians 2:2 ►

4:3 Work that Helps Others
◄ 2 Corinthians 1:11 ►

4:4 Rejoicing
◄ Romans 12:15
1 Thessalonians 5:16 ►

4:5 Ready for Jesus' Return
◄ Hebrews 10:37 ►

4:6 Duty to Pray
◄ Ephesians 6:18
Colossians 4:2 ►

4:6 Worry
◄ 1 Corinthians 7:32
1 Peter 5:7 ►

every thing by prayer and supplication with thanksgiving let your requests be made known unto God.

7 And the peace of God, which passeth all understanding, shall keep your hearts and minds through Christ Jesus.

4:7
Peace of Mind
➤ John 16:33 ➤

8 Finally, brethren, whatsoever things are true, whatsoever things *are* honest, whatsoever things *are* just, whatsoever things *are* pure, whatsoever things *are* lovely, whatsoever things *are* of good report; if *there be* any virtue, and if *there be* any praise, think on these things.

4:8
Wise Thoughts
➤ Romans 12:3 ➤

9 Those things, which ye have both learned, and received, and heard, and seen in me, do: and the God of peace shall be with you.

10 But I rejoiced in the Lord greatly, that now at the last your care of me hath flourished again; wherein ye were also careful, but ye lacked opportunity.

11 Not that I speak in respect of want: for I have learned, in whatsoever state I am, *therewith* to be content.

4:11 Contentment
➤ Luke 3:14
1 Timothy 6:6, 8 ➤

12 I know both how to be abased, and I know how to abound: every where and in all things I am instructed both to be full and to be hungry, both to abound and to suffer need.

4:11 Lessons of Life
➤ Ephesians 4:20-23
➤

13 I can do all things through Christ which strengtheneth me.

14 Notwithstanding ye have well done, that ye did communicate with my affliction.

15 Now ye Philippians know also, that in the beginning of the gospel, when I departed from Macedonia, no church communicated with me as concerning giving and receiving, but ye only.

16 For even in Thessalonica ye sent once and again unto my necessity.

4:16
Examples of Generosity
➤ 2 Corinthians 8:2 ➤

17 Not because I desire a gift: but I desire fruit that may abound to your account.

18 But I have all, and abound: I am full, having received of Epaphroditus the things *which were sent* from you, an odour of a sweet smell, a sacrifice acceptable, wellpleasing to God.

19 But my God shall supply all your need according to his riches in glory by Christ Jesus.

20 Now unto God and our Father *be* glory for ever and ever. Amen.

21 Salute every saint in Christ Jesus. The brethren which are with me greet you.

22 All the saints salute you, chiefly they that are of Caesar's household.

23 The grace of our Lord Jesus Christ *be* with you all. Amen.

Colossians

AUTHOR
Paul the apostle

MAIN POINT
Keep your faith in Jesus strong and growing, and correct any teaching that goes against the Bible.

DATE WRITTEN
About A.D. 60

4 CHAPTERS

MAIN PEOPLE

Paul, Timothy, Tychicus, Onesimus, Aristarchus, Mark, Epaphras

SPECIAL FEATURES

- *Teaches by example how you can pray for other Christians*
- *Shows how the church at Colosse had gotten mixed up but was not hopeless*
- *Gives a lot of tips for getting along with others and how to be a good worker*
- *Seventh of Paul's epistles*

HOW THE BOOK GOT ITS NAME

The book is Paul's letter to the Christians in Colosse.

1

1Paul, an apostle of Jesus Christ by the
will of God, and Timotheus *our* brother,
2To the saints and faithful brethren in
Christ which are at Colosse: Grace *be* unto
you, and peace, from God our Father and
the Lord Jesus Christ.
3We give thanks to God and the Father
of our Lord Jesus Christ, praying always
for you,
4Since we heard of your faith in Christ
Jesus, and of the love *which ye have* to all
the saints,
5For the hope which is laid up for you
in heaven, whereof ye heard before in the
word of the truth of the gospel;
6Which is come unto you, as *it is* in all
the world; and bringeth forth fruit, as *it*
doth also in you, since the day ye heard *of*
it, and knew the grace of God in truth:
7As ye also learned of Epaphras our dear
fellowservant, who is for you a faithful
minister of Christ;
8Who also declared unto us your love
in the Spirit.
9For this cause
we also, since the
day we heard *it,*
do not cease to
pray for you, and
to desire that ye
might be filled
with the knowl-
edge of his will
in all wisdom and
spiritual under-
standing;
10That ye might
walk worthy of the
Lord unto all pleas-
ing, being fruitful
in every good work,
and increasing in
the knowledge of
God;
11Strengthened
with all might,
according to his
glorious power,

1:8 Importance of Love
◄ Ephesians 5:2
Colossians 3:14 ►

1:9 Praying for Wisdom
◄ Ephesians 1:17
James 1:5 ►

1:10 Good Works
◄ Matthew 5:16
1 Timothy 6:18 ►

1:10 Growing Spiritually
◄ Ephesians 4:15
1 Thessalonians 3:12 ►

unto all patience and longsuffering with joyfulness;

12 Giving thanks unto the Father, which hath made us meet to be partakers of the inheritance of the saints in light:

> **1:12 Thankfulness**
> ◄ Psalm 107:22
> Colossians 2:7 ►

13 Who hath delivered us from the power of darkness, and hath translated *us* into the kingdom of his dear Son:

14 In whom we have redemption through his blood, *even* the forgiveness of sins:

15 Who is the image of the invisible God, the firstborn of every creature:

> **1:15 God on Earth**
> ◄ Philippians 2:6
> Hebrews 1:3 ►

16 For by him were all things created, that are in heaven, and that are in earth, visible and invisible, whether *they be* thrones, or dominions, or principalities, or powers: all things were created by him, and for him:

17 And he is before all things, and by him all things consist.

18 And he is the head of the body, the church: who is the beginning, the firstborn from the dead; that in all *things* he might have the preeminence.

19 For it pleased *the Father* that in him should all fulness dwell;

20 And, having made peace through the blood of his cross, by him to reconcile all things unto himself; by him, *I say*, whether *they be* things in earth, or things in heaven.

21 And you, that were sometime alienated and enemies in *your* mind by wicked works, yet now hath he reconciled

> **1:21 Brain Power**
> ◄ Ephesians 4:17
> Colossians 2:18 ►

22 In the body of his flesh through death, to present you holy and unblameable and unreproveable in his sight:

23 If ye continue in the faith grounded and settled, and *be* not moved away from the hope of the gospel, which ye have heard, *and* which was preached to every creature which is under heaven; whereof I Paul am made a minister;

> **1:23 Benefits of Faith**
> ◄ Romans 10:11
> Hebrews 4:3 ►

24 Who now rejoice in my sufferings for you, and fill up that which is behind of the afflictions of Christ in my flesh for his body's sake, which is the church:

> **1:24 God's Body**
> ◄ Ephesians 4:12
> Colossians 2:19 ►

25 Whereof I am made a minister, according to the dispensation of God which is given to me for you, to fulfil the word of God;

> **1:25 The Gospel**
> ◄ Galatians 2:7
> 1 Thessalonians 2:4 ►

26 *Even* the mystery which hath been hid from ages and from generations, but now is made manifest to his saints:

27 To whom God would make known what *is* the riches of the glory of this mystery among the Gentiles; which is Christ in you, the hope of glory:

> **1:27 Jesus' Home**
> ◄ Ephesians 3:17-19
> 1 John 3:24 ►

28 Whom we preach, warning every man, and teaching every man in all wisdom; that we may present every man perfect in Christ Jesus:

> **1:28 Perfection**
> ◄ Philippians 3:15
> 2 Timothy 3:17 ►

29 Whereunto I also labour, striving according to his working, which worketh in me mightily.

2

1 For I would that ye knew what great conflict I have for you, and *for* them at Laodicea, and *for* as many as have not seen my face in the flesh;

2 That their hearts might be comforted, being knit together in love, and unto all riches of the full assurance of understanding, to the acknowledgement of the mystery of God, and of the Father, and of Christ;

> **2:2 Getting Along**
> ◄ Philippians 4:2
> 1 Peter 3:8 ►

3 In whom are hid all the treasures of wisdom and knowledge.

4 And this I say, lest any man should beguile you with enticing words.

5For though I be absent in the flesh, yet
am I with you in the spirit, joying and beholding your order, and the stedfastness
of your faith in Christ.
6As ye have therefore received Christ
Jesus the Lord, *so* walk ye in him:
7Rooted and
built up in him,
and stablished in
the faith, as ye
have been taught,
abounding therein
with thanksgiving.

2:7 Thankfulness
◄ Colossians 1:12
Colossians 3:15 ►

8Beware lest any man spoil you through
philosophy and vain deceit, after the tradition of men, after the rudiments of the
world, and not after Christ.
9For in him dwelleth all the fulness of
the Godhead bodily.
10And ye are complete in him, which is
the head of all principality and power:
11In whom also
ye are circumcised
with the circumci-
sion made without
hands, in putting
off the body of the
sins of the flesh by the circumcision of
Christ:

2:11 Starting Over
◄ Ephesians 4:22
Hebrews 12:1 ►

12Buried with him in baptism, wherein
also ye are risen with *him* through the faith
of the operation of God, who hath raised
him from the dead.
13And you, being dead in your sins and
the uncircumcision of your flesh, hath he
quickened together with him, having forgiven you all trespasses;
14Blotting out the handwriting of ordinances that was against us, which was contrary to us, and took it out of the way,
nailing it to his cross;
15*And* having spoiled principalities and
powers, he made a shew of them openly,
triumphing over them in it.
16Let no man therefore judge you in
meat, or in drink, or in respect of an
holyday, or of the new moon, or of the
sabbath *days:*
17Which are a shadow of things to come;
but the body *is* of
Christ.
18Let no man be-
guile you of your re-
ward in a voluntary
humility and wor-
shipping of angels, intruding into those
things which he hath not seen, vainly
puffed up by his fleshly mind,

2:18 Brain Power
◄ Colossians 1:21
Titus 1:15 ►

19And not hold-
ing the Head, from
which all the body
by joints and bands
having nourish-
ment ministered,
and knit together, increaseth with the increase of God.

2:19 God's Body
◄ Colossians 1:24 ►

20Wherefore if ye
be dead with Christ
from the rudiments
of the world, why,
as though living in
the world, are ye
subject to ordinances,

2:20 Freedom
◄ Galatians 5:24
Colossians 3:3 ►

21(Touch not; taste not; handle not;
22Which all are to perish with the using;) after the commandments and doctrines of men?
23Which things have indeed a shew of
wisdom in will worship, and humility, and
neglecting of the body; not in any honour
to the satisfying of the flesh.

3

1If ye then be risen with Christ, seek
those things which are above, where Christ
sitteth on the right hand of God.
2Set your affection on things above, not
on things on the earth.
3For ye are dead,
and your life is hid
with Christ in God.
4When Christ,
who is our life, shall
appear, then shall
ye also appear with
him in glory.

3:3 Freedom
◄ Colossians 2:20
2 Timothy 2:11 ►

5Mortify there-
fore your members
which are upon the
earth; fornication,
uncleanness, inordinate affection, evil
concupiscence, and covetousness, which is
idolatry:

3:4 Good News
◄ Philippians 3:20-21
1 Thessalonians 3:13 ►

6For which things' sake the wrath of
God cometh on the children of disobedience:
7In the which ye
also walked some
time, when ye lived
in them.
8But now ye also
put off all these;

3:8 Malice
◄ Ephesians 4:31
1 Peter 2:1 ►

anger, wrath, mal-
ice, blasphemy,
filthy communica-
tion out of your
mouth.
9Lie not one to
another, seeing that
ye have put off the
old man with his
deeds;
10And have put
on the new *man*,
which is renewed in
knowledge after the
image of him that
created him:
11Where there is
neither Greek nor
Jew, circumcision
nor uncircumci-
sion, Barbarian,
Scythian, bond *nor*
free: but Christ *is*
all, and in all.
12Put on there-
fore, as the elect of
God, holy and be-
loved, bowels of
mercies, kindness,
humbleness of
mind, meekness,
longsuffering;
13Forbearing one
another, and forgiv-
ing one another, if
any man have a
quarrel against any:
even as Christ for-
gave you, so also
do ye.
14And above all
these things *put on*
charity, which is the
bond of perfect-
ness.
15And let the
peace of God rule
in your hearts, to
the which also ye
are called in one
body; and be ye
thankful.
16Let the word of
Christ dwell in you
richly in all wis-
dom; teaching and
admonishing one
another in psalms
and hymns and
spiritual songs,
singing with grace
in your hearts to
the Lord.
17And whatso-
ever ye do in word
or deed, *do* all in
the name of the
Lord Jesus, giving
thanks to God and
the Father by him.
18Wives, submit
yourselves unto
your own hus-
bands, as it is fit in the Lord.
19Husbands, love *your* wives, and be not
bitter against them.
20Children, obey *your* parents in all
things: for this is well pleasing unto the
Lord.
21Fathers, provoke not your children *to*
anger, lest they be discouraged.
22Servants, obey
in all things *your*
masters according
to the flesh; not
with eyeservice, as
menpleasers; but in
singleness of heart, fearing God:
23And whatsoever ye do, do *it* heartily,
as to the Lord, and not unto men;
24Knowing that
of the Lord ye shall
receive the reward
of the inheritance:
for ye serve the Lord
Christ.
25But he that
doeth wrong shall
receive for the
wrong which he
hath done: and
there is no respect
of persons.

4

1Masters, give
unto *your* servants
that which is just
and equal; know-
ing that ye also
have a Master in
heaven.

3:9 Lying
◄ Proverbs 21:6
Revelation 21:8 ►

3:9 Old Life
◄ Ephesians 4:22
1 Peter 4:3 ►

3:10 New Life
◄ Ephesians 4:24 ►

3:10 New Person
◄ Ephesians 4:23
Titus 3:5 ►

3:12 Kindness
◄ Ephesians 4:32
2 Peter 1:5-7 ►

3:13 Forgiving Others
◄ Ephesians 4:32 ►

3:13 Patience
◄ Ephesians 6:9 ►

3:14 Importance of Love
◄ Colossians 1:8
1 Timothy 6:11 ►

3:15 Seeking Peace
◄ Isaiah 27:5
1 Peter 3:11 ►

3:15 Thankfulness
◄ Colossians 2:7
1 Thessalonians 5:18 ►

3:16 Giving Advice
◄ Ephesians 6:4
1 Thessalonians 5:14 ►

3:16 Instruction
◄ Ezekiel 44:23
1 Timothy 4:11 ►

3:22 Popularity
◄ Ephesians 6:6 ►

3:24 Goodness Rewarded
◄ Ephesians 6:8 ►

3:24 Serving Jesus
◄ Philippians 1:1 ►

4:1 Be Fair
◄ Romans 13:7 ►

2 Continue in
prayer, and watch
in the same with
thanksgiving;
3 Withal praying
also for us, that
God would open
unto us a door of
utterance, to speak
the mystery of
Christ, for which I
am also in bonds:
4 That I may make
it manifest, as I
ought to speak.
5 Walk in wisdom
toward them that
are without, re-
deeming the time.
6 Let your speech
be alway with grace,
seasoned with salt,
that ye may know
how ye ought to
answer every man.
7 All my state shall Tychicus declare unto
you, *who is* a beloved brother, and a faithful minister and fellowservant in the Lord:
8 Whom I have sent unto you for the
same purpose, that he might know your
estate, and comfort your hearts;
9 With Onesimus, a faithful and beloved
brother, who is *one* of you. They shall make
known unto you all things which *are done*
here.

4:2 Duty to Pray
◄ Philippians 4:6
1 Thessalonians 5:17 ►

4:2 Pitfalls
◄ 1 Corinthians 16:13
1 Peter 5:8 ►

4:5 Time
◄ Ephesians 5:15-16
►

4:6 Talking
◄ Matthew 5:37
2 Timothy 1:13 ►

10 Aristarchus my fellowprisoner saluteth
you, and Marcus, sister's son to Barnabas,
(touching whom ye received commandments: if he come unto you, receive him;)
11 And Jesus, which is called Justus, who
are of the circumcision. These only *are my*
fellow workers unto the kingdom of God,
which have been a comfort unto me.
12 Epaphras, who is *one* of you, a servant
of Christ, saluteth you, always labouring
fervently for you in prayers, that ye may
stand perfect and complete in all the will
of God.
13 For I bear him record, that he hath a
great zeal for you, and them *that are* in
Laodicea, and them in Hierapolis.
14 Luke, the beloved physician, and Demas, greet you.
15 Salute the brethren which are in Laodicea, and Nymphas, and the church
which is in his house.
16 And when this epistle is read among
you, cause that it be read also in the church
of the Laodiceans; and that ye likewise read
the *epistle* from Laodicea.
17 And say to
Archippus, Take
heed to the minis-
try which thou hast
received in the
Lord, that thou ful-
fil it.
18 The salutation by the hand of me Paul.
Remember my bonds. Grace *be* with you.
Amen.

4:17 Watch Out!
◄ 1 Corinthians 10:12
1 Timothy 4:16 ►

1 Thessalonians

AUTHOR
Paul the apostle

MAIN POINT
Stay true to Jesus Christ, and remember that he will return again to earth.

DATE WRITTEN
About A.D. 51

5 CHAPTERS

MAIN PEOPLE

Paul, Timothy, Silas

SPECIAL FEATURES

- *Was written from Corinth and is one of Paul's earliest letters*
- *Reflects Timothy's good report on the Thessalonians*
- *Clears up some off-track ideas about Jesus' Second Coming*
- *Contains the famous "thief in the night" passage*
- *Eighth of Paul's epistles*

HOW THE BOOK GOT ITS NAME

The book is Paul's first letter to the Christians in Thessalonica.

1

1Paul, and Silvanus, and Timotheus,
unto the church of the Thessalonians
which is in God the Father and *in* the Lord
Jesus Christ: Grace *be* unto you, and peace,
from God our Father, and the Lord Jesus
Christ.
2We give thanks to God always for you
all, making mention of you in our prayers;
3Remembering without ceasing your
work of faith, and labour of love, and patience of hope in our Lord Jesus Christ, in
the sight of God and our Father;
4Knowing, brethren beloved, your election of God.
5For our gospel
came not unto you
in word only, but
also in power, and
in the Holy Ghost,
and in much assur-
ance; as ye know what manner of men we
were among you for your sake.

1:5 The Holy Spirit
◄ Ephesians 3:16
2 Timothy 1:7 ►

6And ye became followers of us, and of
the Lord, having received the word in much
affliction, with joy of the Holy Ghost:
7So that ye were ensamples to all that
believe in Macedonia and Achaia.
8For from you sounded out the word of
the Lord not only in Macedonia and Achaia, but also in every place your faith to
God-ward is spread abroad; so that we
need not to speak any thing.
9For they themselves shew of us what
manner of entering in we had unto you,
and how ye turned to God from idols to
serve the living and true God;
10And to wait for his Son from heaven,
whom he raised from the dead, *even* Jesus,
which delivered us from the wrath to
come.

2

1 For yourselves, brethren, know our entrance in unto you, that it was not in vain:
2 But even after that we had suffered before, and were shamefully entreated, as ye
know, at Philippi, we were bold in our God
to speak unto you the gospel of God with
much contention.
3 For our exhortation *was* not of deceit,
nor of uncleanness, nor in guile:
4 But as we were
allowed of God to
be put in trust with
the gospel, even so
we speak; not as
pleasing men, but
God, which trieth
our hearts.

2:4 Pleasing God
◄ John 8:29
1 Thessalonians 4:1 ►

2:4 The Gospel
◄ Colossians 1:25
1 Timothy 1:11 ►

5 For neither at
any time used we
flattering words, as
ye know, nor a
cloke of covetousness; God *is* witness:
6 Nor of men sought we glory, neither of
you, nor *yet* of others, when we might have
been burdensome, as the apostles of
Christ.
7 But we were
gentle among you,
even as a nurse
cherisheth her chil-
dren:

2:7
Gentleness
◄ 1 Timothy 3:3 ►

8 So being affec-
tionately desirous
of you, we were
willing to have im-
parted unto you,
not the gospel of
God only, but also
our own souls, because ye were dear
unto us.

2:8
Willingness to Work
◄ 2 Corinthians 8:3 ►

9 For ye remember, brethren, our labour
and travail: for labouring night and day,
because we would not be chargeable unto
any of you, we preached unto you the gospel of God.
10 Ye *are* witnesses, and God *also*, how
holily and justly and unblameably we behaved ourselves among you that believe:
11 As ye know how we exhorted and comforted and charged every one of you, as a
father *doth* his children,
12 That ye would walk worthy of God,
who hath called you unto his kingdom and
glory.
13 For this cause also thank we God without ceasing, be-
cause, when ye re-
ceived the word of
God which ye
heard of us, ye re-
ceived *it* not *as* the
word of men, but as it is in truth, the word
of God, which effectually worketh also in
you that believe.

2:13
Accepting God's Word
◄ Acts 17:11 ►

14 For ye, brethren, became followers of
the churches of God which in Judaea are
in Christ Jesus: for ye also have suffered
like things of your own countrymen, even
as they *have* of the Jews:
15 Who both killed the Lord Jesus, and
their own prophets, and have persecuted
us; and they please not God, and are contrary to all men:
16 Forbidding us
to speak to the Gen-
tiles that they might
be saved, to fill up
their sins alway: for
the wrath is come
upon them to the uttermost.

2:16
God's Anger
◄ Ephesians 5:6 ►

17 But we, brethren, being taken from
you for a short time in presence, not in
heart, endeavoured the more abundantly
to see your face with great desire.
18 Wherefore we would have come unto
you, even I Paul, once and again; but Satan hindered us.
19 For what *is* our hope, or joy, or crown
of rejoicing? *Are* not even ye in the presence of our Lord Jesus Christ at his coming?
20 For ye are our glory and joy.

3

1 Wherefore when we could no longer
forbear, we thought it good to be left at
Athens alone;
2 And sent Timotheus, our brother, and
minister of God, and our fellowlabourer
in the gospel of Christ, to establish you,
and to comfort you concerning your faith:
3 That no man should be moved by these
afflictions: for yourselves know that we are
appointed thereunto.
4 For verily, when
we were with you,
we told you before
that we should suf-
fer tribulation; even
as it came to pass,
and ye know.

3:4 Suffering
◄ Romans 5:3
Revelation 2:9 ►

5 For this cause, when I could no longer

forbear, I sent to know your faith, lest by
some means the tempter have tempted
you, and our labour be in vain.
6But now when Timotheus came from
you unto us, and brought us good tidings
of your faith and charity, and that ye have
good remembrance of us always, desiring
greatly to see us, as we also *to see* you:
7Therefore, brethren, we were comforted
over you in all our affliction and distress
by your faith:
8For now we live, if ye stand fast in the
Lord.
9For what thanks can we render to God
again for you, for all the joy wherewith we
joy for your sakes before our God;
10Night and day
praying exceedingly
that we might see
your face, and
might perfect that
which is lacking in
your faith?

3:10 Caring for the Church
◄ Galatians 4:11 ►

11Now God himself
and our Father,
and our Lord Jesus
Christ, direct our
way unto you.

3:10 Praying
◄ Acts 16:25
1 Timothy 5:5 ►

12And the Lord
make you to increase
and abound
in love one toward
another, and toward
all *men*, even
as we *do* toward
you:

3:12 Growing Spiritually
◄ Colossians 1:10
1 Thessalonians 4:10 ►

13To the end he
may stablish your
hearts unblameable
in holiness before
God, even our Father,
at the coming
of our Lord Jesus
Christ with all his
saints.

3:12 Loving Others
◄ Romans 12:9
Hebrews 13:1 ►

3:13 Good News
◄ Colossians 3:4
1 Thessalonians 4:16 ►

4

1Furthermore
then we beseech
you, brethren, and
exhort *you* by the
Lord Jesus, that as
ye have received of
us how ye ought
to walk and to
please God, *so* ye would abound more and
more.

4:1 Pleasing God
◄ 1 Thessalonians 2:4
Hebrews 11:5 ►

2For ye know what commandments we
gave you by the Lord Jesus.
3For this is the will of God, *even* your
sanctification, that ye should abstain from
fornication:
4That every one of you should know
how to possess his vessel in sanctification
and honour;
5Not in the lust of concupiscence, even
as the Gentiles which know not God:
6That no *man* go beyond and defraud
his brother in *any* matter: because that the
Lord *is* the avenger of all such, as we also
have forewarned you and testified.
7For God hath not called us unto uncleanness,
but unto holiness.
8He therefore that despiseth, despiseth
not man, but God, who hath also given
unto us his holy Spirit.
9But as touching brotherly love ye need
not that I write unto you: for ye yourselves
are taught of God to love one another.
10And indeed ye
do it toward all the
brethren which are
in all Macedonia:
but we beseech
you, brethren, that
ye increase more and more;

4:10 Growing Spiritually
◄ 1 Thessalonians 3:12
Hebrews 6:1 ►

11And that ye
study to be quiet,
and to do your own
business, and to
work with your
own hands, as we
commanded you;

4:11 Working Hard
◄ Ephesians 4:28
2 Thessalonians 3:12 ►

12That ye may
walk honestly toward
them that are
without, and *that* ye
may have lack of
nothing.

4:12 Living for God
◄ Philippians 1:27
1 Timothy 3:7 ►

13But I would not have you to be ignorant,
brethren, concerning them which are
asleep, that ye sorrow not, even as others
which have no hope.
14For if we believe that Jesus died and
rose again, even so them also which sleep
in Jesus will God bring with him.
15For this we say unto you by the word
of the Lord, that we which are alive *and*
remain unto the coming of the Lord shall
not prevent them which are asleep.
16For the Lord himself shall descend
from heaven with a shout, with the voice

of the archangel,
and with the trump
of God: and the
dead in Christ shall
rise first:
17 Then we which
are alive *and* remain
shall be caught up
together with them
in the clouds, to
meet the Lord in
the air: and so shall
we ever be with the
Lord.
18 Wherefore
comfort one an-
other with these
words.

Chapter 5

1 But of the times
and the seasons,
brethren, ye have
no need that I write
unto you.
2 For yourselves
know perfectly that
the day of the Lord
so cometh as a thief
in the night.
3 For when they
shall say, Peace and
safety; then sudden
destruction cometh
upon them, as tra-
vail upon a woman
with child; and they
shall not escape.
4 But ye, brethren,
are not in darkness,
that that day should
overtake you as a
thief.
5 Ye are all the
children of light,
and the children of
the day: we are not
of the night, nor of
darkness.
6 Therefore let us
not sleep, as *do* oth-
ers; but let us watch
and be sober.
7 For they that
sleep sleep in the
night; and they that
be drunken are

4:16 Good News
◄ 1 Thessalonians 3:13
1 Peter 5:4 ►

4:16 Resurrection
◄ 2 Corinthians 4:14 ►

4:17 Eternal Life
◄ 2 Corinthians 5:1
2 Timothy 1:10 ►

4:18 Comforting Others
◄ 2 Corinthians 2:7
1 Thessalonians 5:11 ►

5:2 Jesus' Return: When?
◄ Luke 12:40
Revelation 3:3 ►

5:5-6 Christian Duties
◄ Philippians 2:15 ►

5:5-6 Jesus' Return
◄ Luke 12:37
Revelation 3:11 ►

5:7 Getting Drunk
◄ Ephesians 5:18 ►

5:8 Faith
◄ Ephesians 6:16
1 Timothy 1:19 ►

drunken in the
night.
8 But let us, who
are of the day, be
sober, putting on
the breastplate of
faith and love;
and for an helmet,
the hope of salva-
tion.
9 For God hath
not appointed us to
wrath, but to ob-
tain salvation by
our Lord Jesus
Christ,
10 Who died for
us, that, whether we
wake or sleep, we
should live togeth-
er with him.
11 Wherefore
comfort yourselves
together, and edify
one another, even
as also ye do.
12 And we be-
seech you, breth-
ren, to know
them which labour
among you, and are
over you in the
Lord, and admon-
ish you;
13 And to esteem
them very highly in
love for their work's
sake. *And* be at
peace among your-
selves.
14 Now we exhort
you, brethren, warn
them that are un-
ruly, comfort the
feebleminded, sup-
port the weak, be
patient toward all
men.
15 See that none
render evil for evil
unto any *man;* but
ever follow that
which is good, both
among yourselves,
and to all *men*.

5:9 Only One Savior
◄ Romans 5:9
Hebrews 5:9 ►

5:11 Comforting Others
◄ 1 Thessalonians 4:18
1 Thessalonians 5:14 ►

5:12-13 Respecting God's People
◄ Philippians 2:29
1 Timothy 5:17 ►

5:14 Comforting Others
1 Thessalonians 5:11 ►

5:14 Giving Advice
◄ Colossians 3:16
2 Thessalonians 3:15 ►

5:14 Helping Weak People
◄ 1 Corinthians 9:22 ►

5:14 Quitting
◄ Romans 12:12
Titus 2:2 ►

5:15 Revenge
◄ Romans 12:17
1 Peter 3:9 ►

5:15 Vengeance
◄ Romans 12:20 ►

16 Rejoice ever-
more.
17 Pray without
ceasing.
18 In every thing
give thanks: for this
is the will of God in
Christ Jesus con-
cerning you.
19 Quench not
the Spirit.
20 Despise not
prophesyings.
21 Prove all things;
hold fast that which
is good.
22 Abstain from
all appearance of
evil.
23 And the very God of peace sanctify
you wholly; and *I pray God* your whole
spirit and soul and
body be preserved
blameless unto the
coming of our Lord
Jesus Christ.
24 Faithful *is* he
that calleth you,
who also will
do *it*.
25 Brethren, pray
for us.
26 Greet all the
brethren with an
holy kiss.
27 I charge you by
the Lord that this
epistle be read
unto all the holy
brethren.
28 The grace of our Lord Jesus Christ *be*
with you. Amen.

5:16 Rejoicing
◄ Philippians 4:4 ►

5:17 Duty to Pray
◄ Colossians 4:2
1 Timothy 2:8 ►

5:18 Thankfulness
◄ Colossians 3:15 ►

5:22 Stay Away!
◄ 1 Corinthians 10:6
1 Peter 3:11 ►

5:23 Hurting Yourself
◄ 1 Corinthians 6:15 ►

5:23 Watching for Jesus' Return
◄ 1 Corinthians 4:5
1 Timothy 6:14 ►

2 Thessalonians

AUTHOR
Paul the apostle

MAIN POINT
The return of Jesus is very important, so here is God's teaching once again.

DATE WRITTEN
About A.D. 51 or 52

3 CHAPTERS

❑❑❑

MAIN PEOPLE

Paul, Timothy, Silas

SPECIAL FEATURES

✱ *Shows how people can have trouble talking to each other*

✱ *Tells why Christ's return is no excuse for laziness*

✱ *Tells how the earth will disappear*

✱ *Ninth of Paul's epistles*

HOW THE BOOK GOT ITS NAME

The book is Paul's second letter to the Christians in Thessalonica.

1

1 Paul, and Silvanus, and Timotheus, unto the church of the Thessalonians in God our Father and the Lord Jesus Christ:

2 Grace unto you, and peace, from God our Father and the Lord Jesus Christ.

3 We are bound to thank God always for you, brethren, as it is meet, because that your faith groweth exceedingly, and the charity of every one of you all toward each other aboundeth;

4 So that we ourselves glory in you in the churches of God for your patience and faith in all your persecutions and tribulations that ye endure:

5 *Which is* a manifest token of the righteous judgment of God, that ye may be counted worthy of the kingdom of God, for which ye also suffer:

6 Seeing *it is* a righteous thing with God to recompense tribulation to them that trouble you;

7 And to you who are troubled rest with us, when the Lord Jesus shall be revealed from heaven with his mighty angels,

8 In flaming fire taking vengeance on them that know not God, and that obey not the gospel of our Lord Jesus Christ:

9 Who shall be punished with everlasting destruction from the presence of the Lord, and from the glory of his power;

10 When he shall come to be glorified in his saints, and to be admired in all them

1:7-8 Bad News
◄ Luke 21:26
Revelation 1:7 ►

1:8 Ouch!
◄ Ephesians 5:6
1 Timothy 1:9 ►

1:9 Sinner Beware
◄ Matthew 25:31-33
1 Timothy 6:7 ►

that believe (because our testimony among
you was believed) in that day.
11 Wherefore also we pray always for you,
that our God would count you worthy of
this calling, and fulfil all the good pleasure of *his* goodness, and the work of faith
with power:
12 That the name of our Lord Jesus Christ
may be glorified in you, and ye in him,
according to the grace of our God and the
Lord Jesus Christ.

2

1 Now we beseech you, brethren, by the
coming of our Lord Jesus Christ, and *by*
our gathering together unto him,
2 That ye be not
soon shaken in
mind, or be trou-
bled, neither by
spirit, nor by word,
nor by letter as
from us, as that the day of Christ is at hand.

2:2 Standing Strong
◄ Philippians 4:1
2 Thessalonians 2:15 ►

3 Let no man de-
ceive you by any
means: for *that day*
shall not come, ex-
cept there come a
falling away first,
and that man of sin be revealed, the son
of perdition;

2:3 Deception
◄ Ephesians 5:6
1 John 3:7 ►

4 Who opposeth
and exalteth him-
self above all that is
called God, or that
is worshipped; so
that he as God
sitteth in the temple of God, shewing himself that he is God.

2:4 Ambition
◄ John 5:44 ►

5 Remember ye not, that, when I was yet
with you, I told you these things?
6 And now ye know what withholdeth
that he might be revealed in his time.
7 For the mystery of iniquity doth already
work: only he who now letteth *will let,* until
he be taken out of
the way.
8 And then shall
that Wicked be re-
vealed, whom the
Lord shall consume
with the spirit of his
mouth, and shall
destroy with the
brightness of his
coming:
9 *Even him,* whose
coming is after the working of Satan with
all power and signs and lying wonders,
10 And with all deceivableness of unrighteousness in them that perish; because they
received not the love of the truth, that they
might be saved.
11 And for this cause God shall send them
strong delusion, that they should believe
a lie:
12 That they all might be damned who
believed not the truth, but had pleasure
in unrighteousness.
13 But we are bound to give thanks alway
to God for you, brethren beloved of the
Lord, because God hath from the beginning chosen you to salvation through sanctification of the Spirit and belief of the
truth:
14 Whereunto he called you by our gospel, to the obtaining of the glory of our
Lord Jesus Christ.
15 Therefore,
brethren, stand
fast, and hold the
traditions which ye
have been taught,
whether by word,
or our epistle.

2:8 Defeat of Satan
◄ John 14:30
Hebrews 2:14 ►

2:9 Satan's Power
◄ Ephesians 6:12
Hebrews 2:14 ►

2:15 Standing Strong
◄ 2 Thessalonians 2:2
1 Peter 5:9 ►

16 Now our Lord Jesus Christ himself,
and God, even our Father, which hath
loved us, and hath given *us* everlasting consolation and good hope through grace,
17 Comfort your hearts, and stablish you
in every good word and work.

3

1 Finally, brethren, pray for us, that the
word of the Lord may have *free* course, and
be glorified, even as *it is* with you:
2 And that we may be delivered from
unreasonable and wicked men: for all *men*
have not faith.
3 But the Lord is faithful, who shall
stablish you, and keep *you* from evil.
4 And we have confidence in the Lord
touching you, that ye both do and will do
the things which we command you.
5 And the Lord di-
rect your hearts
into the love of
God, and into the
patient waiting for
Christ.

3:5 Love for God
◄ Matthew 22:37
Jude 1:21 ►

6 Now we command you, brethren, in
the name of our Lord Jesus Christ, that
ye withdraw yourselves from every
brother that walketh disorderly, and not

after the tradition which he received of us.

7 For yourselves know how ye ought to follow us: for we behaved not ourselves disorderly among you;

8 Neither did we eat any man's bread for nought; but wrought with labour and travail night and day, that we might not be chargeable to any of you:

9 Not because we have not power, but to make ourselves an ensample unto you to follow us.

3:9 Free Samples
◄ John 13:15
1 Timothy 4:12 ►

10 For even when we were with you, this we commanded you, that if any would not work, neither should he eat.

11 For we hear that there are some which walk among you disorderly, working not at all, but are busybodies.

3:11 Boredom
◄ 1 Timothy 5:13 ►

12 Now them that are such we command and exhort by our Lord Jesus Christ, that with quietness they work, and eat their own bread.

3:11 Laziness
◄ Ecclesiastes 10:18
Hebrews 6:12 ►

13 But ye, brethren, be not weary in well doing.

3:12 Working Hard
◄ 1 Thessalonians 4:11
►

14 And if any man obey not our word by this epistle, note that man, and have no company with him, that he may be ashamed.

15 Yet count *him* not as an enemy, but admonish *him* as a brother.

3:15 Giving Advice
◄ 1 Thessalonians 5:14
Titus 3:10 ►

16 Now the Lord of peace himself give you peace always by all means. The Lord *be* with you all.

17 The salutation of Paul with mine own hand, which is the token in every epistle: so I write.

18 The grace of our Lord Jesus Christ *be* with you all. Amen.

1 Timothy

AUTHOR
Paul the apostle

MAIN POINT
Young leaders need to lead people God's way.

DATE WRITTEN
About A.D. 64

6 CHAPTERS
❑❑❑❑❑❑

MAIN PEOPLE

Paul, Timothy

SPECIAL FEATURES

- *Was written to a young man who was trying to be a good leader*
- *Spells out God's standards for leaders*
- *Reinforces God's desire for us to live by his standards*
- *Gives good advice about topics from worship to the treatment of groups in the church*
- *Tenth of Paul's epistles*

HOW THE BOOK GOT ITS NAME

The book is Paul's first letter of encouragement to young Timothy.

1

1Paul, an apostle of Jesus Christ by the
commandment of God our Saviour, and
Lord Jesus Christ, *which is* our hope;
2Unto Timothy, *my* own son in the faith:
Grace, mercy, *and* peace, from God our
Father and Jesus Christ our Lord.
3As I besought thee to abide still at Ephesus, when I went into Macedonia, that
thou mightest charge some that they teach
no other doctrine,
4Neither give heed to fables and endless genealogies, which minister questions,
rather than godly edifying which is in faith:
so do.
5Now the end of the commandment is
charity out of a
pure heart, and *of* a
good conscience,
and *of* faith un-
feigned:
6From which

1:5 Clear Conscience
◄ 2 Corinthians 1:12
1 Timothy 1:19 ►

some having swerved have turned aside
unto vain jangling;
7Desiring to be teachers of the law; understanding neither what they say, nor
whereof they affirm.
8But we know that the law *is* good, if a
man use it lawfully;
9Knowing this,
that the law is not
made for a righ-
teous man, but for
the lawless and dis-
obedient, for the
ungodly and for sinners, for unholy and
profane, for murderers of fathers and murderers of mothers,
for manslayers,
10For whore-
mongers, for them
that defile them-
selves with man-

1:9 Ouch!
◄ 2 Thessalonians 1:8
Hebrews 2:2-3 ►

1:10 Perjury
◄ Malachi 3:5 ►

kind, for menstealers, for liars, for perjured
persons, and if there be any other thing
that is contrary to sound doctrine;
11According to
the glorious gospel
of the blessed God,
which was commit-
ted to my trust.

> **1:11 The Gospel**
> ◄ 1 Thessalonians 2:4
> Titus 1:3 ►

12And I thank
Christ Jesus our Lord, who hath enabled
me, for that he counted me faithful, putting me into the ministry;
13Who was be-
fore a blasphemer,
and a persecutor,
and injurious: but I
obtained mercy, be-
cause I did *it* igno-
rantly in unbelief.

> **1:13 Unknown Sins**
> ◄ Acts 3:17 ►

14And the grace of our Lord was exceeding abundant with faith and love which is
in Christ Jesus.
15This *is* a faith-
ful saying, and
worthy of all accep-
tation, that Christ
Jesus came into the
world to save sin-
ners; of whom I am
chief.

> **1:15 Friend of Jesus**
> ◄ Romans 5:8 ►

16Howbeit for
this cause I ob-
tained mercy, that
in me first Jesus
Christ might shew forth all longsuffering,
for a pattern to them which should hereafter believe on him to life everlasting.

> **1:15 Why Jesus Came**
> ◄ Acts 13:23
> 2 Timothy 1:10 ►

17Now unto the King eternal, immor-
tal, invisible, the only wise God, *be* honour
and glory for ever and ever. Amen.
18This charge I commit unto thee, son
Timothy, according to the prophecies
which went before on thee, that thou by
them mightest war
a good warfare;
19Holding faith,
and a good con-
science; which
some having put
away concerning
faith have made
shipwreck:

> **1:19 Clear Conscience**
> ◄ 1 Timothy 1:5
> 1 Timothy 3:9 ►

20Of whom is
Hymenaeus and Al-
exander; whom I
have delivered unto Satan, that they may
learn not to blaspheme.

> **1:19 Faith**
> ◄ 1 Thessalonians 5:8
> 1 Timothy 6:12 ►

2

1I exhort therefore, that, first of all, supplications, prayers, intercessions, *and* giving of thanks, be made for all men;
2For kings, and *for* all that are in authority; that we may lead a quiet and peaceable life in all godliness and honesty.
3For this *is* good and acceptable in the
sight of God our Saviour;
4Who will have
all men to be saved,
and to come unto
the knowledge of
the truth.

> **2:4 God Calls You**
> ◄ Romans 10:12
> Revelation 22:17 ►

5For *there is* one
God, and one me-
diator between
God and men, the
man Christ Jesus;

> **2:4 Salvation for Anyone**
> ◄ Romans 10:13
> Titus 2:11-12 ►

6Who gave him-
self a ransom for
all, to be testified in
due time.
7Whereunto I am
ordained a preach-
er, and an apostle,
(I speak the truth in
Christ, *and* lie not;) a teacher of the Gentiles in faith and verity.

> **2:5 Only One God**
> ◄ Ephesians 4:6 ►

8I will therefore
that men pray every
where, lifting up
holy hands, with-
out wrath and
doubting.

> **2:8 Duty to Pray**
> ◄ 1 Thessalonians 5:17
> James 5:13 ►

9In like manner
also, that women
adorn themselves
in modest apparel,
with shamefaced-
ness and sobriety;
not with broided hair, or gold, or pearls,
or costly array;

> **2:9-10 Modesty**
> ◄ Genesis 24:65
> 1 Peter 3:1-2 ►

10But (which becometh women professing godliness) with good works.
11Let the woman learn in silence with
all subjection.
12But I suffer not a woman to teach, nor
to usurp authority over the man, but to be
in silence.
13For Adam was first formed, then Eve.
14And Adam was not deceived, but the
woman being deceived was in the transgression.

15 Notwithstanding she shall be saved in childbearing, if they continue in faith and charity and holiness with sobriety.

3

1 This *is* a true saying, If a man desire the office of a bishop, he desireth a good work.

2 A bishop then must be blameless, the husband of one wife, vigilant, sober, of good behaviour, given to hospitality, apt to teach;

3:2 Hospitality
◄ Romans 12:13
1 Timothy 5:10 ►

3 Not given to wine, no striker, not greedy of filthy lucre; but patient, not a brawler, not covetous;

3:3 Gentleness
◄ 1 Thessalonians 2:7
2 Timothy 2:24 ►

4 One that ruleth well his own house, having his children in subjection with all gravity;

5 (For if a man know not how to rule his own house, how shall he take care of the church of God?)

6 Not a novice, lest being lifted up with pride he fall into the condemnation of the devil.

7 Moreover he must have a good report of them which are without; lest he fall into reproach and the snare of the devil.

3:7 Living for God
◄ 1 Thessalonians 4:12
James 3:13 ►

8 Likewise *must* the deacons *be* grave, not doubletongued, not given to much wine, not greedy of filthy lucre;

9 Holding the mystery of the faith in a pure conscience.

3:9 Clear Conscience
◄ 1 Timothy 1:19
Hebrews 13:18 ►

10 And let these also first be proved; then let them use the office of a deacon, being *found* blameless.

11 Even so *must their* wives be grave, not slanderers, sober, faithful in all things.

12 Let the deacons be the husbands of one wife, ruling their children and their own houses well.

13 For they that have used the office of a deacon well purchase to themselves a good degree, and great boldness in the faith which is in Christ Jesus.

3:13 Approaching God
◄ Ephesians 3:12
Hebrews 4:16 ►

14 These things write I unto thee, hoping to come unto thee shortly:

15 But if I tarry long, that thou mayest know how thou oughtest to behave thyself in the house of God, which is the church of the living God, the pillar and ground of the truth.

16 And without controversy great is the mystery of godliness: God was manifest in the flesh, justified in the Spirit, seen of angels, preached unto the Gentiles, believed on in the world, received up into glory.

3:16 Christmas
◄ Philippians 2:7
1 John 4:2 ►

4

1 Now the Spirit speaketh expressly, that in the latter times some shall depart from the faith, giving heed to seducing spirits, and doctrines of devils;

4:1 Demons
◄ Ephesians 6:12
James 2:19 ►

2 Speaking lies in hypocrisy; having their conscience seared with a hot iron;

4:2 Hypocrisy
◄ Luke 12:1
Titus 1:16 ►

3 Forbidding to marry, *and commanding* to abstain from meats, which God hath created to be received with thanksgiving of them which believe and know the truth.

4 For every creature of God *is* good, and nothing to be refused, if it be received with thanksgiving:

5 For it is sanctified by the word of God and prayer.

6 If thou put the brethren in remembrance of these things, thou shalt be a good minister of Jesus Christ, nourished up in the words of faith and of good doctrine, whereunto thou hast attained.

7 But refuse profane and old wives' fables, and exercise thyself *rather* unto godliness.

4:7 Talents
◄ Matthew 25:20
1 Timothy 4:14 ►

8 For bodily exercise profiteth little: but godliness is profitable unto all things, having promise of the life that now is, and of that which is to come.

9 This *is* a faithful saying and worthy of all acceptation.

10 For therefore we both labour and suffer reproach, because we trust in the living God, who is the Saviour of all men, specially of those that believe.

> **4:10 Why Suffer?**
> ◄ Luke 6:22
> Hebrews 10:33 ►

11 These things command and teach.

> **4:11 Instruction**
> ◄ Colossians 3:16
> 2 Timothy 2:24 ►

12 Let no man despise thy youth; but be thou an example of the believers, in word, in conversation, in charity, in spirit, in faith, in purity.

> **4:12 For Kids Only**
> ◄ Lamentations 3:27
> Titus 2:6-7 ►

13 Till I come, give attendance to reading, to exhortation, to doctrine.

> **4:12 Free Samples**
> ◄ 2 Thessalonians 3:9
> Titus 2:7 ►

14 Neglect not the gift that is in thee, which was given thee by prophecy, with the laying on of the hands of the presbytery.

> **4:14 Talents**
> ◄ 1 Timothy 4:7
> 2 Timothy 1:6 ►

15 Meditate upon these things; give thyself wholly to them; that thy profiting may appear to all.

> **4:15 Making Progress**
> ◄ 2 Corinthians 3:18 ►

16 Take heed unto thyself, and unto the doctrine; continue in them: for in doing this thou shalt both save thyself, and them that hear thee.

> **4:16 Watch Out!**
> ◄ Colossians 4:17
> 2 Peter 1:19 ►

5

1 Rebuke not an elder, but intreat *him* as a father; *and* the younger men as brethren;

2 The elder women as mothers; the younger as sisters, with all purity.

> **5:1-2 Respecting Adults**
> ◄ Proverbs 23:22 ►

3 Honour widows that are widows indeed.

4 But if any widow have children or nephews, let them learn first to shew piety at home, and to requite their parents: for that is good and acceptable before God.

> **5:4 Helping at Home**
> ◄ Mark 5:19 ►

5 Now she that is a widow indeed, and desolate, trusteth in God, and continueth in supplications and prayers night and day.

> **5:5 Praying**
> ◄ 1 Thessalonians 3:10

6 But she that liveth in pleasure is dead while she liveth.

> **5:6 Luxury**
> ◄ Luke 12:19
> 2 Timothy 3:4 ►

7 And these things give in charge, that they may be blameless.

8 But if any provide not for his own, and specially for those of his own house, he hath denied the faith, and is worse than an infidel.

9 Let not a widow be taken into the number under threescore years old, having been the wife of one man,

10 Well reported of for good works; if she have brought up children, if she have lodged strangers, if she have washed the saints' feet, if she have relieved the afflicted, if she have diligently followed every good work.

> **5:10 Hospitality**
> ◄ 1 Timothy 3:2
> Titus 1:8 ►

11 But the younger widows refuse: for when they have begun to wax wanton against Christ, they will marry;

12 Having damnation, because they have cast off their first faith.

13 And withal they learn *to be* idle, wandering about from house to house; and not only idle, but tattlers also and busybodies, speaking things which they ought not.

> **5:13 Boredom**
> ◄ 2 Thessalonians 3:11
> 1 Peter 4:15 ►

14 I will therefore that the younger women marry, bear children, guide the house, give none occasion to the adversary to speak reproachfully.

15 For some are already turned aside after Satan.
16 If any man or woman that believeth
have widows, let them relieve them, and
let not the church be charged; that it may
relieve them that are widows indeed.
17 Let the elders
that rule well be
counted worthy of
double honour, es-
pecially they who
labour in the word
and doctrine.

5:17
Respecting God's People
◄ 1 Thessalonians 5:12-13
Hebrews 13:7 ►

18 For the scripture saith, Thou shalt not
muzzle the ox that treadeth out the corn.
And, The labourer *is* worthy of his reward.
19 Against an elder receive not an accusation, but before two or three witnesses.
20 Them that sin rebuke before all, that
others also may fear.
21 I charge *thee*
before God, and the
Lord Jesus Christ,
and the elect angels,
that thou observe
these things with-
out preferring one before another, doing
nothing by partiality.

5:21 Favoritism
◄ Malachi 2:9
James 2:4 ►

22 Lay hands suddenly on no man, neither be partaker of other men's sins: keep
thyself pure.
23 Drink no longer water, but use a little
wine for thy stomach's sake and thine often infirmities.
24 Some men's sins are open beforehand,
going before to judgment; and some *men*
they follow after.
25 Likewise also the good works *of some*
are manifest beforehand; and they that are
otherwise cannot be hid.

6

1 Let as many servants as are under the
yoke count their own masters worthy of
all honour, that the name of God and *his*
doctrine be not blasphemed.
2 And they that have believing masters,
let them not despise *them*, because they
are brethren; but rather do *them* service,
because they are faithful and beloved, partakers of the benefit. These things teach
and exhort.
3 If any man teach otherwise, and consent not to wholesome words, *even* the
words of our Lord Jesus Christ, and to the
doctrine which is according to godliness;
4 He is proud, knowing nothing, but
doting about ques-
tions and strifes of
words, whereof
cometh envy, strife,
railings, evil sur-
misings,
5 Perverse dis-
putings of men of
corrupt minds, and
destitute of the
truth, supposing
that gain is godli-
ness: from such
withdraw thyself.
6 But godliness
with contentment
is great gain.
7 For we brought
nothing into *this*
world, *and it is* cer-
tain we can carry
nothing out.
8 And having
food and raiment
let us be therewith
content.
9 But they that
will be rich fall into
temptation and a
snare, and *into*
many foolish and
hurtful lusts, which
drown men in de-
struction and perdi-
tion.
10 For the love of
money is the root
of all evil: which
while some coveted
after, they have
erred from the
faith, and pierced
themselves through
with many sorrows.
11 But thou, O
man of God, flee
these things; and
follow after righ-
teousness, godli-
ness, faith, love,
patience, meekness.
12 Fight the good
fight of faith, lay
hold on eternal life,
whereunto thou art

6:4 Proud People
◄ Malachi 4:1
James 4:6 ►

6:5
Used to Sin
◄ Matthew 17:17 ►

6:6, 8 Contentment
◄ Philippians 4:11
Hebrews 13:5 ►

6:7
Sinner Beware
◄ 2 Thessalonians 1:9

6:7
Soon Gone
◄ Jeremiah 17:11 ►

6:9 Greed
◄ Matthew 27:5
James 5:3 ►

6:9
Money's Dangers
◄ Mark 4:19 ►

6:11 Importance of Love
◄ Colossians 3:14
1 John 4:16 ►

6:11
Righteousness
◄ Philippians 1:11 ►

also called, and hast professed a good profession before many witnesses.

13 I give thee charge in the sight of God, who quickeneth all things, and *before* Christ Jesus, who before Pontius Pilate witnessed a good confession;

14 That thou keep *this* commandment without spot, unrebukeable, until the appearing of our Lord Jesus Christ:

15 Which in his times he shall shew, *who is* the blessed and only Potentate, the King of kings, and Lord of lords;

16 Who only hath immortality, dwelling in the light which no man can approach unto; whom no man hath seen, nor can see: to whom *be* honour and power everlasting. Amen.

17 Charge them that are rich in this world, that they be not highminded, nor trust in uncertain riches, but in the living God, who giveth us richly all things to enjoy;

18 That they do good, that they be rich in good works, ready to distribute, willing to communicate;

19 Laying up in store for themselves a good foundation against the time to come, that they may lay hold on eternal life.

20 O Timothy, keep that which is committed to thy trust, avoiding profane *and* vain babblings, and oppositions of science falsely so called:

21 Which some professing have erred concerning the faith. Grace *be* with thee. Amen.

6:12 Faith
◄ 1 Timothy 1:19
Hebrews 10:22 ►

6:14 Watching for Jesus' Return
◄ 1 Thessalonians 5:23
Titus 2:13 ►

6:17 Wealth
◄ Luke 12:19-20 ►

6:18 Doing Good
◄ Galatians 6:10
Hebrews 13:16 ►

6:18 Giving
◄ Galatians 6:10
Hebrews 13:16 ►

6:18 Good Works
◄ Colossians 1:10
Titus 2:7 ►

6:20 Argument Avoidance
◄ Romans 16:17
2 Timothy 2:16 ►

6:20 Using What You Have
◄ Ephesians 6:7
2 Timothy 1:14 ►

2 Timothy

AUTHOR
Paul the apostle

MAIN POINT
Here are final instructions to a young leader, spiritual father to son.

DATE WRITTEN
About A.D. 66 or 67

4 CHAPTERS

MAIN PEOPLE
Paul, Timothy, Luke, Mark

SPECIAL FEATURES
- *Is Paul's final letter to Timothy and reveals a lot about what's truly important to him*
- *Reveals Paul's loneliness*
- *Shows how a godly mother and grandmother can affect your life*
- *Includes many passages about Scripture's power in a person's life*
- *Eleventh of Paul's epistles*

HOW THE BOOK GOT ITS NAME
The book is Paul's second letter to Timothy.

1

1Paul, an apostle of Jesus Christ by the
will of God, according to the promise of
life which is in Christ Jesus,
2To Timothy, *my* dearly beloved son:
Grace, mercy, *and* peace, from God the
Father and Christ Jesus our Lord.
3I thank God, whom I serve from *my*
forefathers with pure conscience, that
without ceasing I have remembrance of
thee in my prayers night and day;
4Greatly desiring to see thee, being
mindful of thy tears, that I may be filled
with joy;
5When I call to
remembrance the
unfeigned faith that
is in thee, which
dwelt first in thy
grandmother Lois,
and thy mother Eu-
nice; and I am per-
suaded that in thee
also.
6Wherefore I put
thee in remem-
brance that thou
stir up the gift of
God, which is in
thee by the putting
on of my hands.
7For God hath
not given us the
spirit of fear; but of
power, and of love,
and of a sound
mind.
8Be not thou
therefore ashamed

1:5 Who Is Religious?
◄ Acts 22:12 ►

1:5 Young Men
◄ Luke 2:49
2 Timothy 3:15 ►

1:6 Talents
◄ 1 Timothy 4:14 ►

1:7 The Holy Spirit
◄ 1 Thessalonians 1:5 ►

of the testimony of
our Lord, nor of me
his prisoner: but be
thou partaker of the
afflictions of the
gospel according to
the power of God;
9Who hath saved us, and called *us* with
an holy calling, not according to our
works, but according to his own purpose
and grace, which was given us in Christ
Jesus before the world began,

1:8 Your Testimony
◄ Ephesians 5:19
1 Peter 3:15 ►

10But is now
made manifest by
the appearing of
our Saviour Jesus
Christ, who hath
abolished death,
and hath brought
life and immortali-
ty to light through
the gospel:
11Whereunto I
am appointed a
preacher, and an apostle, and a teacher of
the Gentiles.

1:10 Eternal Life
◄ 1 Thessalonians 4:17 ►

1:10 Why Jesus Came
◄ 1 Timothy 1:15
Hebrews 7:25 ►

12For the which cause I also suffer these
things: nevertheless I am not ashamed: for
I know whom I have believed, and am persuaded that he is able to keep that which I
have committed unto him against that day.
13Hold fast the
form of sound
words, which thou
hast heard of me, in
faith and love
which is in Christ
Jesus.
14That good
thing which was
committed unto
thee keep by the
Holy Ghost which
dwelleth in us.
15This thou
knowest, that all
they which are in
Asia be turned away
from me; of whom
are Phygellus and
Hermogenes.
16The Lord give
mercy unto the
house of Onesiph-
orus; for he oft re-

1:13 Talking
◄ Colossians 4:6
Titus 2:8 ►

1:14 The Spirit in You
◄ 1 Corinthians 6:19
1 John 2:27 ►

1:14
Using What You Have
◄ 1 Timothy 6:20
1 Peter 4:10 ►

1:15
Whom Can You Trust?
◄ John 16:32
2 Timothy 4:10 ►

freshed me, and
was not ashamed of
my chain:
17But, when he
was in Rome, he
sought me out very
diligently, and
found *me.*
18The Lord grant
unto him that he
may find mercy of
the Lord in that
day: and in how
many things he
ministered unto me
at Ephesus, thou
knowest very well.

1:16
Being a Friend
◄ Romans 16:4 ►

1:16
Good Friends
◄ Philippians 2:25 ►

1:17
Love for Friends
◄ Philippians 4:1 ►

2

1Thou therefore,
my son, be strong in the grace that is in
Christ Jesus.
2And the things that thou hast heard of
me among many witnesses, the same commit thou to faithful men, who shall be able
to teach others also.
3Thou therefore endure hardness, as a
good soldier of Jesus Christ.
4No man that warreth entangleth him-
self with the affairs of *this* life; that he may
please him who hath chosen him to be a
soldier.
5And if a man also strive for masteries,
yet is he not crowned, except he strive lawfully.
6The husbandman that laboureth must
be first partaker of the fruits.
7Consider what I
say; and the Lord
give thee under-
standing in all
things.
8Remember that
Jesus Christ of the seed of David was raised
from the dead according to my gospel:
9Wherein I suffer trouble, as an evil doer,
even unto bonds; but the word of God is
not bound.
10Therefore I endure all things for the
elect's sakes, that they may also obtain the
salvation which is in Christ Jesus with eternal glory.
11*It is* a faithful
saying: For if we be
dead with *him,* we
shall also live with
him:

2:7
Understanding
◄ Proverbs 17:27 ►

2:11 Freedom
◄ Colossians 3:3
1 Peter 2:24 ►

12 If we suffer, we shall also reign with *him:* if we deny *him,* he also will deny us:

2:12 Suffering for Jesus
◄ Philippians 3:10
Hebrews 11:25 ►

13 If we believe not, *yet* he abideth faithful: he cannot deny himself.

2:12 Suffering Rewarded
◄ Romans 8:17
Hebrews 10:34 ►

14 Of these things put *them* in remembrance, charging *them* before the Lord that they strive not about words to no profit, *but* to the subverting of the hearers.

2:14 Arguing
◄ Philippians 2:3
2 Timothy 2:24 ►

15 Study to shew thyself approved unto God, a workman that needeth not to be ashamed, rightly dividing the word of truth.

16 But shun profane *and* vain babblings: for they will increase unto more ungodliness.

2:16 Argument Avoidance
◄ 1 Timothy 6:20
2 Timothy 2:23 ►

17 And their word will eat as doth a canker: of whom is Hymenaeus and Philetus;

18 Who concerning the truth have erred, saying that the resurrection is past already; and overthrow the faith of some.

19 Nevertheless the foundation of God standeth sure, having this seal, The Lord knoweth them that are his. And, Let every one that nameth the name of Christ depart from iniquity.

20 But in a great house there are not only vessels of gold and of silver, but also of wood and of earth; and some to honour, and some to dishonour.

21 If a man therefore purge himself from these, he shall be a vessel unto honour, sanctified, and meet for the master's use, *and* prepared unto every good work.

2:21 Commitment
◄ Romans 12:1 ►

22 Flee also youthful lusts: but follow righteousness, faith, charity, peace, with them that call on the Lord out of a pure heart.

23 But foolish and unlearned questions avoid, knowing that they do gender strifes.

2:23 Argument Avoidance
◄ 2 Timothy 2:16
Titus 3:9 ►

24 And the servant of the Lord must not strive; but be gentle unto all *men,* apt to teach, patient,

2:24 Arguing
◄ 2 Timothy 2:14
James 3:14 ►

2:24 Gentleness
◄ 1 Timothy 3:3
Titus 3:2 ►

2:24 Instruction
◄ 1 Timothy 4:11 ►

25 In meekness instructing those that oppose themselves; if God peradventure will give them repentance to the acknowledging of the truth;

26 And *that* they may recover themselves out of the snare of the devil, who are taken captive by him at his will.

2:26 Bad Habits
◄ Romans 7:23
2 Peter 2:19 ►

3

1 This know also, that in the last days perilous times shall come.

2 For men shall be lovers of their own selves, covetous, boasters, proud, blasphemers, disobedient to parents, unthankful, unholy,

3:2 Saying Thank You
◄ Luke 17:18 ►

3 Without natural affection, trucebreakers, false accusers, incontinent, fierce, despisers of those that are good,

4 Traitors, heady, highminded, lovers of pleasures more than lovers of God;

3:4 Luxury
◄ 1 Timothy 5:6
Titus 3:3 ►

5 Having a form of godliness, but denying the power thereof: from such turn away.

6 For of this sort are they which creep into houses, and lead captive silly women laden with sins, led away with divers lusts,

7 Ever learning, and never able to come to the knowledge of the truth.

8 Now as Jannes and Jambres withstood Moses, so do these also resist the truth:

men of corrupt minds, reprobate concerning the faith.

9 But they shall proceed no further: for their folly shall be manifest unto all *men*, as theirs also was.

10 But thou hast fully known my doctrine, manner of life, purpose, faith, longsuffering, charity, patience,

11 Persecutions, afflictions, which came unto me at Antioch, at Iconium, at Lystra; what persecutions I endured: but out of *them* all the Lord delivered me.

12 Yea, and all that will live godly in Christ Jesus shall suffer persecution.

13 But evil men and seducers shall wax worse and worse, deceiving, and being deceived.

14 But continue thou in the things which thou hast learned and hast been assured of, knowing of whom thou hast learned *them*;

15 And that from a child thou hast known the holy scriptures, which are able to make thee wise unto salvation through faith which is in Christ Jesus.

16 All scripture *is* given by inspiration of God, and *is* profitable for doctrine, for reproof, for correction, for instruction in righteousness:

17 That the man of God may be perfect, throughly furnished unto all good works.

3:12 Expecting Pain
◄ John 16:2
Revelation 2:10 ►

3:13 Callousness
◄ Matthew 26:74
2 Peter 2:20 ►

3:14 Determination
◄ Galatians 6:9
Hebrews 12:1 ►

3:15 How to Be Saved
◄ 1 Corinthians 15:2
James 1:21 ►

3:15 Salvation by Faith
◄ Romans 10:9
1 John 5:1 ►

3:15 True Wisdom
◄ 1 Corinthians 12:8
James 3:17 ►

3:15
Young Men
◄ 2 Timothy 1:5 ►

3:17 Perfection
◄ Colossians 1:28
Hebrews 6:1 ►

4

1 I charge *thee* therefore before God, and the Lord Jesus Christ, who shall judge the quick and the dead at his appearing and his kingdom;

2 Preach the word; be instant in season, out of season; reprove, rebuke, exhort with all longsuffering and doctrine.

4:1 Christ as Judge
◄ 1 Corinthians 4:5
1 Peter 4:5 ►

4:1
Jesus' Return: Why?
◄ 1 Corinthians 4:5
Jude 1:14-15 ►

3 For the time will come when they will not endure sound doctrine; but after their own lusts shall they heap to themselves teachers, having itching ears;

4 And they shall turn away *their* ears from the truth, and shall be turned unto fables.

5 But watch thou in all things, endure afflictions, do the work of an evangelist, make full proof of thy ministry.

6 For I am now ready to be offered, and the time of my departure is at hand.

7 I have fought a good fight, I have finished *my* course, I have kept the faith:

8 Henceforth there is laid up for me a crown of righteousness, which the Lord, the righteous judge, shall give me at that day: and not to me only, but unto all them also that love his appearing.

9 Do thy diligence to come shortly unto me:

10 For Demas hath forsaken me, having loved this present world, and is departed unto Thessalonica; Crescens to Galatia, Titus unto Dalmatia.

4:10
Whom Can You Trust?
◄ 2 Timothy 1:15 ►

11 Only Luke is with me. Take Mark, and bring him with thee: for he is profitable to me for the ministry.

12 And Tychicus have I sent to Ephesus.

13 The cloke that I left at Troas with Carpus, when thou comest, bring *with thee*, and the books, *but* especially the parchments.

14 Alexander the coppersmith did me much evil: the Lord reward him according to his works:

15 Of whom be thou ware also; for he hath greatly withstood our words.

[16]At my first an-
swer no man stood
with me, but all
men forsook me: *I*
pray God that it may
not be laid to their
charge.

4:16
Loneliness
< John 16:32 >

[17]Notwithstanding the Lord stood with
me, and strengthened me; that by me the
preaching might be fully known, and *that*
all the Gentiles
might hear: and I
was delivered out of
the mouth of the
lion.
[18]And the Lord
shall deliver me
from every evil
work, and will pre-
serve *me* unto his
heavenly kingdom:
to whom *be* glory
for ever and ever. Amen.

4:18 Evil Attacks
< 2 Corinthians 1:10
Hebrews 2:15 >

4:18
Safety
< Isaiah 49:8 >

[19]Salute Prisca and Aquila, and the
household of Onesiphorus.
[20]Erastus abode at Corinth: but Trophimus have I left at Miletum sick.
[21]Do thy diligence to come before winter. Eubulus greeteth thee, and Pudens, and
Linus, and Claudia, and all the brethren.
[22]The Lord Jesus Christ *be* with thy spirit.
Grace *be* with you. Amen.

Titus

AUTHOR
Paul the apostle

MAIN POINT
Sound leadership principles must combine with spirituality to guide a church.

DATE WRITTEN
About A.D. 64

3 CHAPTERS

MAIN PEOPLE

Paul, Titus

SPECIAL FEATURES

- *Is brief but packed with information and advice*
- *Was written to Paul's special assistant on the island of Crete*
- *Convinces Titus and modern readers of the stupidity of arguing*
- *Reinforces God's desire for us to live by his standards*
- *Twelfth of Paul's epistles*

HOW THE BOOK GOT ITS NAME

The book is a letter from Paul to Titus, another young leader in the church.

1

1Paul, a servant of God, and an apostle
of Jesus Christ, according to the faith of
God's elect, and the acknowledging of the
truth which is after godliness;
2In hope of eternal life, which God, that cannot lie, promised before the world began;
3But hath in due times manifested his word through preaching, which is committed unto me according to the commandment of God our Saviour;
4To Titus, *mine* own son after the common faith: Grace, mercy, *and* peace, from God the Father and the Lord Jesus Christ our Saviour.
5For this cause left I thee in Crete, that
thou shouldest set in order the things that
are wanting, and ordain elders in every city,
as I had appointed thee:
6If any be blameless, the husband of one wife, having faithful children not accused of riot or unruly.
7For a bishop must be blameless, as the
steward of God; not selfwilled, not soon
angry, not given to wine, no striker, not
given to filthy lucre;
8But a lover of hospitality, a lover of good men, sober, just, holy, temperate;
9Holding fast the
faithful word as he hath been taught, that
he may be able by sound doctrine both to
exhort and to convince the gainsayers.

1:2 God's Word
◄ Romans 3:4
Hebrews 6:18 ►

1:3 The Gospel
◄ 1 Timothy 1:11 ►

1:6 Peace
◄ Romans 12:18
Hebrews 12:14 ►

1:8 Hospitality
◄ 1 Timothy 5:10
Hebrews 13:2 ►

[10]For there are
many unruly and
vain talkers and de-
ceivers, specially
they of the circum-
cision:

> **1:10**
> **Idle Talk**
> ◄ Ezekiel 36:3 ►

[11]Whose mouths must be stopped, who
subvert whole houses, teaching things
which they ought not, for filthy lucre's
sake.
[12]One of themselves, *even* a prophet of
their own, said, The Cretians *are* alway liars, evil beasts, slow bellies.
[13]This witness is true. Wherefore rebuke
them sharply, that they may be sound in
the faith;
[14]Not giving heed to Jewish fables, and
commandments of men, that turn from
the truth.
[15]Unto the pure
all things *are* pure:
but unto them that
are defiled and un-
believing *is* nothing
pure; but even their
mind and conscience is defiled.

> **1:15**
> **Brain Power**
> ◄ Colossians 2:18 ►

[16]They profess
that they know
God; but in works
they deny *him*, be-
ing abominable,
and disobedient,
and unto every good work reprobate.

> **1:16**
> **Hypocrisy**
> ◄ 1 Timothy 4:2 ►

2

[1]But speak thou the things which become sound doctrine:
[2]That the aged
men be sober,
grave, temperate,
sound in faith, in
charity, in patience.

> **2:2 Quitting**
> ◄ 1 Thessalonians 5:14
> Hebrews 10:36 ►

[3]The aged wom-
en likewise, that *they be* in behaviour as
becometh holiness, not false accusers, not
given to much wine, teachers of good
things;
[4]That they may teach the young women
to be sober, to love their husbands, to love
their children,
[5]*To be* discreet, chaste, keepers at home,
good, obedient to
their own hus-
bands, that the
word of God be not
blasphemed.
[6]Young men like-

> **2:6-7 For Kids Only**
> ◄ 1 Timothy 4:12
> 1 John 2:13-14 ►

wise exhort to be
sober minded.
[7]In all things
shewing thyself a
pattern of good
works: in doctrine
shewing uncor-
ruptness, gravity,
sincerity,
[8]Sound speech,
that cannot be con-
demned; that he
that is of the con-
trary part may be
ashamed, having
no evil thing to say
of you.
[9]*Exhort* servants
to be obedient unto
their own masters,
and to please *them*
well in all *things;*
not answering
again;
[10]Not purloin-
ing, but shewing all
good fidelity; that
they may adorn the
doctrine of God
our Saviour in all
things.
[11]For the grace of
God that bringeth
salvation hath ap-
peared to all men,
[12]Teaching us
that, denying un-
godliness and
worldly lusts, we
should live soberly,
righteously, and
godly, in this pre-
sent world;
[13]Looking for
that blessed hope,
and the glorious
appearing of the
great God and
our Saviour Jesus
Christ;
[14]Who gave him-
self for us, that he
might redeem us
from all iniquity,
and purify unto

> **2:7 Free Samples**
> ◄ 1 Timothy 4:12
> Hebrews 11:4 ►

> **2:7 Good Works**
> ◄ 1 Timothy 6:18
> Titus 2:14 ►

> **2:7 Sincerity**
> ◄ Philippians 1:10
> 1 John 3:18 ►

> **2:8 Talking**
> ◄ 2 Timothy 1:13
> James 3:2 ►

> **2:10 Stealing**
> ◄ Ephesians 4:28
> 1 Peter 4:15 ►

> **2:11 Grace**
> ◄ Ephesians 2:5
> Titus 3:7 ►

> **2:11-12**
> **Salvation for Anyone**
> ◄ 1 Timothy 2:4
> 2 Peter 3:9 ►

> **2:13**
> **Watching for Jesus' Return**
> ◄ 1 Timothy 6:14
> 1 John 2:28 ►

> **2:14 Good Works**
> ◄ Titus 2:7
> Titus 3:8 ►

himself a peculiar people, zealous of good works.

15 These things speak, and exhort, and rebuke with all authority. Let no man despise thee.

3

1 Put them in mind to be subject to principalities and powers, to obey magistrates, to be ready to every good work,

2 To speak evil of no man, to be no brawlers, *but* gentle, shewing all meekness unto all men.

3 For we ourselves also were sometimes foolish, disobedient, deceived, serving divers lusts and pleasures, living in malice and envy, hateful, *and* hating one another.

4 But after that the kindness and love of God our Saviour toward man appeared,

5 Not by works of righteousness which we have done, but according to his mercy he saved us, by the washing of regeneration, and renewing of the Holy Ghost;

6 Which he shed on us abundantly through Jesus Christ our Saviour;

7 That being justified by his grace, we should be made heirs according to the hope of eternal life.

8 *This is* a faithful saying, and these things I will that thou affirm constantly, that they which have believed in God might be careful to maintain good works. These things are good and profitable unto men.

9 But avoid foolish questions, and genealogies, and contentions, and strivings about the law; for they are unprofitable and vain.

10 A man that is an heretick after the first and second admonition reject;

11 Knowing that he that is such is subverted, and sinneth, being condemned of himself.

12 When I shall send Artemas unto thee, or Tychicus, be diligent to come unto me to Nicopolis: for I have determined there to winter.

13 Bring Zenas the lawyer and Apollos on their journey diligently, that nothing be wanting unto them.

14 And let ours also learn to maintain good works for necessary uses, that they be not unfruitful.

15 All that are with me salute thee. Greet them that love us in the faith. Grace *be* with you all. Amen.

2:15 Witnessing
◄ Acts 22:14-15 ►

3:1 Obeying the Law
◄ Romans 13:1
1 Peter 2:13-14 ►

3:1-2 Cruel Talk
◄ Ephesians 4:31
James 3:6 ►

3:2 Gentleness
◄ 2 Timothy 2:24
James 3:17 ►

3:3 Luxury
◄ 2 Timothy 3:4
James 5:5 ►

3:5 God's Mercy
◄ Ephesians 2:4 ►

3:5 New Person
◄ Colossians 3:10 ►

3:7 Grace
◄ Titus 2:11 ►

3:8 Good Works
◄ Titus 2:14
Hebrews 10:24 ►

3:9 Argument Avoidance
◄ 2 Timothy 2:23 ►

3:10 Giving Advice
◄ 2 Thessalonians 3:15 ►

Philemon

AUTHOR
Paul the apostle

MAIN POINT
Forgive others and accept brothers and sisters in Christ, no matter what their status or personality.

DATE WRITTEN
About A.D. 60

MAIN PEOPLE
Paul, Philemon, Onesimus

SPECIAL FEATURES

- *One of the shortest books in the Bible, it is a masterpiece of grace and tact*
- *Was written during Paul's first prison term in Rome*
- *Deals directly with slavery*
- *Thirteenth of Paul's epistles*

HOW THE BOOK GOT ITS NAME

The book is a letter from Paul to a man named Philemon and other leaders of the church at Colosse.

1 CHAPTER

☐

1Paul, a prisoner of Jesus Christ, and Timothy *our* brother, unto Philemon our dearly beloved, and fellowlabourer,

2And to *our* beloved Apphia, and Archippus our fellowsoldier, and to the church in thy house:

3Grace to you, and peace, from God our Father and the Lord Jesus Christ.

4I thank my God, making mention of thee always in my prayers,

5Hearing of thy love and faith, which thou hast toward the Lord Jesus, and toward all saints;

6That the communication of thy faith may become effectual by the acknowledging of every good thing which is in you in Christ Jesus.

7For we have great joy and consolation in thy love, because the bowels of the saints are refreshed by thee, brother.

8Wherefore, though I might be much bold in Christ to enjoin thee that which is convenient,

9Yet for love's sake I rather beseech *thee*, being such an one as Paul the aged, and now also a prisoner of Jesus Christ.

10I beseech thee for my son Onesimus, whom I have begotten in my bonds:

1:10 Helping Friends
◄ Jeremiah 38:9 ►

11Which in time past was to thee unprofitable, but now profitable to thee and to me:

12Whom I have sent again: thou therefore receive him, that is, mine own bowels:

13Whom I would have retained with me, that in thy stead he might have ministered unto me in the bonds of the gospel:

14But without thy mind would I do nothing; that thy benefit should not be as it were of necessity, but willingly.

15For perhaps he therefore departed for a season, that thou shouldest receive him for ever;

16 Not now as a servant, but above a servant, a brother beloved, specially to me,
but how much more unto thee, both in
the flesh, and in the Lord?
17 If thou count me therefore a partner,
receive him as myself.
18 If he hath wronged thee, or oweth *thee*
ought, put that on mine account;
19 I Paul have written *it* with mine own
hand, I will repay *it:* albeit I do not say to
thee how thou owest unto me even thine
own self besides.
20 Yea, brother, let me have joy of thee
in the Lord: refresh my bowels in the Lord.
21 Having confidence in thy obedience I
wrote unto thee, knowing that thou wilt
also do more than I say.
22 But withal prepare me also a lodging:
for I trust that through your prayers I shall
be given unto you.
23 There salute thee Epaphras, my fellowprisoner in Christ Jesus;
24 Marcus, Aristarchus, Demas, Lucas, my
fellowlabourers.
25 The grace of our Lord Jesus Christ *be*
with your spirit. Amen.

Hebrews

AUTHOR
Unknown; possibly Paul, Luke, Barnabas, Apollos, Silas, Philip, or Priscilla

MAIN POINT
Jesus Christ was and is greater than anyone or anything. He is more than worthy of our trust and faith.

DATE WRITTEN
Probably before the destruction of the temple in Jerusalem in A.D. 70

13 CHAPTERS

MAIN PEOPLE

Men and women of faith

SPECIAL FEATURES

- *Is a letter but takes the form of a sermon*
- *Reassures and challenges the Hebrew Christians, who were being harassed by both Jews and Romans to give up Christianity*
- *Includes an inspiring "Hall of Faith" section that describes people who believed God's promises over the centuries*
- *Describes what happens to those who refuse to listen to God*
- *First of the General epistles*

HOW THE BOOK GOT ITS NAME

The letter is addressed to Hebrew (Jewish) Christians.

1

1 God, who at sundry times and in divers
manners spake in time past unto the fathers by the prophets,
2 Hath in these last days spoken unto us
by *his* Son, whom he hath appointed heir of all things, by whom also he made the worlds;
3 Who being the brightness of *his* glory, and the express image of his person, and upholding all things by the word of his power, when he had by himself purged our sins, sat down on the right hand of the Majesty on high;

1:3
God on Earth
< Colossians 1:15 >

4 Being made so much better than the
angels, as he hath by inheritance obtained a more excellent name than they.
5 For unto which of the angels said he at
any time, Thou art my Son, this day have I begotten thee? And again, I will be to him a Father, and he shall be to me a Son?
6 And again, when he bringeth in the
firstbegotten into the world, he saith, And let all the angels of God worship him.
7 And of the angels he saith, Who maketh
his angels spirits, and his ministers a flame of fire.
8 But unto the Son *he saith,* Thy throne,
O God, *is* for ever and ever: a sceptre of righteousness *is* the sceptre of thy kingdom.

9Thou hast loved righteousness, and
hated iniquity; therefore God, *even* thy
God, hath anointed thee with the oil of
gladness above thy fellows.
10And, Thou, Lord, in the beginning hast
laid the foundation of the earth; and the
heavens are the works of thine hands:
11They shall perish; but thou remainest;
and they all shall wax old as doth a garment;
12And as a vesture shalt thou fold them
up, and they shall be changed: but thou
art the same, and thy years shall not fail.
13But to which of the angels said he at
any times, Sit on my right hand, until I
make thine enemies thy footstool?
14Are they not all
ministering spirits,
sent forth to minis-
ter for them who
shall be heirs of sal-
vation?

1:14
Angels
◄ Acts 27:23 ►

2

1Therefore we
ought to give the
more earnest heed
to the things which
we have heard, lest
at any time we
should let *them* slip.

2:1
Don't Forget...
◄ Jeremiah 3:21 ►

2For if the word
spoken by angels
was stedfast, and
every transgression
and disobedience
received a just rec-
ompence of reward;

2:2-3
Ouch!
◄ 1 Timothy 1:9 ►

3How shall we
escape, if we neglect
so great salvation;
which at the first
began to be spoken
by the Lord, and
was confirmed unto us by them that heard
him;

2:3 Salvation
◄ Acts 28:27
Hebrews 12:25 ►

4God also bearing *them* witness, both
with signs and wonders, and with divers
miracles, and gifts of the Holy Ghost, according to his own will?
5For unto the angels hath he not put in
subjection the world to come, whereof we
speak.
6But one in a certain place testified, saying, What is man, that thou art mindful of
him? or the son of man, that thou visitest
him?
7Thou madest him a little lower than the
angels; thou crownedst him with glory and
honour, and didst set him over the works
of thy hands:
8Thou hast put all things in subjection
under his feet. For in that he put all in subjection under him, he left nothing *that is*
not put under him. But now we see not
yet all things put under him.
9But we see Jesus,
who was made a lit-
tle lower than the
angels for the suf-
fering of death,
crowned with glory
and honour; that he by the grace of God
should taste death for every man.

2:9 Why Jesus Died
◄ Galatians 3:13
Hebrews 9:28 ►

10For it became him, for whom *are* all
things, and by whom *are* all things, in
bringing many sons unto glory, to make
the captain of their salvation perfect
through sufferings.
11For both he that sanctifieth and they
who are sanctified *are* all of one: for which
cause he is not ashamed to call them brethren,
12Saying, I will declare thy name unto
my brethren, in the midst of the church
will I sing praise unto thee.
13And again, I will put my trust in him.
And again, Behold I and the children
which God hath given me.
14Forasmuch
then as the children
are partakers of
flesh and blood, he
also himself like-
wise took part of
the same; that
through death he
might destroy him
that had the power
of death, that is, the
devil;

2:14 Defeat of Satan
◄ 2 Thessalonians 2:8
1 John 3:8 ►

2:14 Satan's Power
◄ 2 Thessalonians 2:9
►

15And deliver
them who through
fear of death were
all their lifetime
subject to bondage.
16For verily he
took not on *him the nature of* angels; but
he took on *him* the seed of Abraham.

2:15 Evil Attacks
◄ 2 Timothy 4:18
2 Peter 2:9 ►

17Wherefore in all things it behoved him
to be made like unto *his* brethren, that he
might be a merciful and faithful high priest

in things *pertaining* to God, to make reconciliation for the sins of the people.

18 For in that he himself hath suffered being tempted, he is able to succour them that are tempted.

> **2:18 Temptation**
> ◄ 1 Corinthians 10:13
> James 1:2-3 ►

3

1 Wherefore, holy brethren, partakers of the heavenly calling, consider the Apostle and High Priest of our profession, Christ Jesus;

> **2:18 Tempted by Satan**
> ◄ 1 Corinthians 10:13
> James 4:7 ►

2 Who was faithful to him that appointed him, as also Moses *was faithful* in all his house.

3 For this *man* was counted worthy of more glory than Moses, inasmuch as he who hath builded the house hath more honour than the house.

4 For every house is builded by some *man;* but he that built all things *is* God.

5 And Moses verily *was* faithful in all his house, as a servant, for a testimony of those things which were to be spoken after;

6 But Christ as a son over his own house; whose house are we, if we hold fast the confidence and the rejoicing of the hope firm unto the end.

7 Wherefore (as the Holy Ghost saith, To day if ye will hear his voice,

8 Harden not your hearts, as in the provocation, in the day of temptation in the wilderness:

9 When your fathers tempted me, proved me, and saw my works forty years.

10 Wherefore I was grieved with that generation, and said, They do alway err in *their* heart; and they have not known my ways.

11 So I sware in my wrath, They shall not enter into my rest.)

12 Take heed, brethren, lest there be in any of you an evil heart of unbelief, in departing from the living God.

> **3:12 Source of Evil**
> ◄ Mark 7:21
> 2 Peter 2:14 ►

13 But exhort one another daily, while it is called To day; lest any of you be hardened through the deceitfulness of sin.

> **3:13**
> **Hard-heart Aches**
> ◄ Romans 2:5 ►

14 For we are made partakers of Christ, if we hold the beginning of our confidence stedfast unto the end;

15 While it is said, To day if ye will hear his voice, harden not your hearts, as in the provocation.

16 For some, when they had heard, did provoke: howbeit not all that came out of Egypt by Moses.

> **3:16**
> **Losers**
> ◄ Ezekiel 8:3 ►

17 But with whom was he grieved forty years? *was it* not with them that had sinned, whose carcases fell in the wilderness?

18 And to whom sware he that they should not enter into his rest, but to them that believed not?

19 So we see that they could not enter in because of unbelief.

4

1 Let us therefore fear, lest, a promise being left *us* of entering into his rest, any of you should seem to come short of it.

2 For unto us was the gospel preached, as well as unto them: but the word preached did not profit them, not being mixed with faith in them that heard *it.*

3 For we which have believed do enter into rest, as he said, As I have sworn in my wrath, if they shall enter into my rest: although the works were finished from the foundation of the world.

> **4:3 Benefits of Faith**
> ◄ Colossians 1:23
> James 2:5 ►

4 For he spake in a certain place of the seventh *day* on this wise, And God did rest the seventh day from all his works.

5 And in this *place* again, If they shall enter into my rest.

6 Seeing therefore it remaineth that some must enter therein, and they to whom it was first preached entered not in because of unbelief:

7 Again, he limiteth a certain day, saying in David, To day, after so long a time; as it is said, To day if ye will hear his voice, harden not your hearts.

8 For if Jesus had given them rest, then would he not afterward have spoken of another day.

9 There remaineth therefore a rest to the people of God.

10 For he that is entered into his rest, he also hath ceased from his own works, as God *did* from his.

11 Let us labour therefore to enter into that rest, lest any man fall after the same example of unbelief.

4:11 Bad Examples
◄ Ezekiel 20:18
Hebrews 12:15 ►

12 For the word of God *is* quick, and powerful, and sharper than any twoedged sword, piercing even to the dividing asunder of soul and spirit, and of the joints and marrow, and *is* a discerner of the thoughts and intents of the heart.

4:12 Power of the Bible
◄ Ephesians 6:17 ►

13 Neither is there any creature that is not manifest in his sight: but all things *are* naked and opened unto the eyes of him with whom we have to do.

4:13 What God Knows
◄ Psalm 147:5
1 John 3:20 ►

14 Seeing then that we have a great high priest, that is passed into the heavens, Jesus the Son of God, let us hold fast *our* profession.

15 For we have not an high priest which cannot be touched with the feeling of our infirmities; but was in all points tempted like as *we are, yet* without sin.

16 Let us therefore come boldly unto the throne of grace, that we may obtain mercy, and find grace to help in time of need.

4:16 Approaching God
◄ 1 Timothy 3:13
Hebrews 10:19 ►

5

1 For every high priest taken from among men is ordained for men in things *pertaining* to God, that he may offer both gifts and sacrifices for sins:

2 Who can have compassion on the ignorant, and on them that are out of the way; for that he himself also is compassed with infirmity.

3 And by reason hereof he ought, as for the people, so also for himself, to offer for sins.

4 And no man taketh this honour unto himself, but he that is called of God, as *was* Aaron.

5 So also Christ glorified not himself to be made an high priest; but he that said unto him, Thou art my Son, to day have I begotten thee.

6 As he saith also in another *place,* Thou *art* a priest for ever after the order of Melchisedec.

7 Who in the days of his flesh, when he had offered up prayers and supplications with strong crying and tears unto him that was able to save him from death, and was heard in that he feared;

8 Though he were a Son, yet learned he obedience by the things which he suffered;

9 And being made perfect, he became the author of eternal salvation unto all them that obey him;

5:9 Only One Savior
◄ 1 Thessalonians 5:9
Hebrews 9:28 ►

10 Called of God an high priest after the order of Melchisedec.

11 Of whom we have many things to say, and hard to be uttered, seeing ye are dull of hearing.

12 For when for the time ye ought to be teachers, ye have need that one teach you again which *be* the first principles of the oracles of God; and are become such as have need of milk, and not of strong meat.

13 For every one that useth milk *is* unskilful in the word of righteousness: for he is a babe.

14 But strong meat belongeth to them that are of full age, *even* those who by reason of use have their senses exercised to discern both good and evil.

6

1 Therefore leaving the principles of the doctrine of Christ, let us go on unto perfection; not laying again the foundation of repentance from dead works, and of faith toward God,

6:1 Growing Spiritually
◄ 1 Thessalonians 4:10
1 Peter 2:2 ►

6:1 Perfection
◄ 2 Timothy 3:17
Hebrews 13:21 ►

2 Of the doctrine of baptisms, and of laying on of hands, and of resurrection of the dead, and of eternal judgment.

3 And this will we do, if God permit.

4 For *it is* impossible for those who were once enlightened, and have tasted of the heavenly gift, and were made partakers of the Holy Ghost,

5 And have tasted the good word of God, and the powers of the world to come,

6 If they shall fall away, to renew them again unto repentance; seeing they crucify to themselves the Son of God afresh, and put *him* to an open shame.

7 For the earth which drinketh in the rain that cometh oft upon it, and bringeth forth herbs meet for them by whom it is dressed, receiveth blessing from God:

8 But that which beareth thorns and briers *is* rejected, and *is* nigh unto cursing; whose end *is* to be burned.

9 But, beloved, we are persuaded better things of you, and things that accompany salvation, though we thus speak.

10 For God *is* not unrighteous to forget your work and labour of love, which ye have shewed toward his name, in that ye have ministered to the saints, and do minister.

11 And we desire that every one of you do shew the same diligence to the full assurance of hope unto the end:

6:11 Diligence
◄ Romans 12:8
2 Peter 1:10 ►

12 That ye be not slothful, but followers of them who through faith and patience inherit the promises.

6:12 Laziness
◄ 2 Thessalonians 3:11
►

13 For when God made promise to Abraham, because he could swear by no greater, he sware by himself,

14 Saying, Surely blessing I will bless thee, and multiplying I will multiply thee.

15 And so, after he had patiently endured, he obtained the promise.

16 For men verily swear by the greater: and an oath for confirmation *is* to them an end of all strife.

17 Wherein God, willing more abundantly to shew unto the heirs of promise the immutability of his counsel, confirmed *it* by an oath:

18 That by two immutable things, in which *it was* impossible for God to lie, we might have a strong consolation, who have fled for refuge to lay hold upon the hope set before us:

6:18 God's Word
◄ Titus 1:2 ►

19 Which *hope* we have as an anchor of the soul, both sure and stedfast, and which entereth into that within the veil;

6:19 Believer Be Glad
◄ 2 Corinthians 5:1 ►

20 Whither the forerunner is for us entered, *even* Jesus, made an high priest for ever after the order of Melchisedec.

7

1 For this Melchisedec, king of Salem, priest of the most high God, who met Abraham returning from the slaughter of the kings, and blessed him;

2 To whom also Abraham gave a tenth part of all; first being by interpretation King of righteousness, and after that also King of Salem, which is, King of peace;

3 Without father, without mother, without descent, having neither beginning of days, nor end of life; but made like unto the Son of God; abideth a priest continually.

4 Now consider how great this man *was,* unto whom even the patriarch Abraham gave the tenth of the spoils.

5 And verily they that are of the sons of Levi, who receive the office of the priesthood, have a commandment to take tithes of the people according to the law, that is, of their brethren, though they come out of the loins of Abraham:

6 But he whose descent is not counted from them received tithes of Abraham, and blessed him that had the promises.

7 And without all contradiction the less is blessed of the better.

8 And here men that die receive tithes; but there he *receiveth them,* of whom it is witnessed that he liveth.

9 And as I may so say, Levi also, who receiveth tithes, payed tithes in Abraham.

10 For he was yet in the loins of his father, when Melchisedec met him.

11 If therefore perfection were by the Levitical priesthood, (for under it the people received the law,) what further need *was there* that another priest should rise after the order of Melchisedec, and not be called after the order of Aaron?

12 For the priesthood being changed, there is made of necessity a change also of the law.

13 For he of whom these things are spo-

ken pertaineth to another tribe, of which
no man gave attendance at the altar.
14 For *it is* evident that our Lord sprang
out of Juda; of which tribe Moses spake
nothing concerning priesthood.
15 And it is yet far more evident: for that
after the similitude of Melchisedec there
ariseth another priest,
16 Who is made, not after the law of a
carnal commandment, but after the power of an endless life.
17 For he testifieth, Thou *art* a priest for
ever after the order of Melchisedec.
18 For there is verily a disannulling of the
commandment going before for the weakness and unprofitableness thereof.
19 For the law made nothing perfect, but
the bringing in of a better hope *did;* by the
which we draw nigh unto God.
20 And inasmuch as not without an oath
he was made priest:
21 (For those priests were made without
an oath; but this with an oath by him that
said unto him, The Lord sware and will
not repent, Thou *art* a priest for ever after
the order of Melchisedec:)
22 By so much was Jesus made a surety
of a better testament.
23 And they truly were many priests, because they were not suffered to continue
by reason of death:
24 But this *man,* because he continueth
ever, hath an unchangeable priesthood.
25 Wherefore he
is able also to save
them to the utter-
most that come
unto God by him,
seeing he ever liveth
to make intercession for them.

7:25 Why Jesus Came
◄ 2 Timothy 1:10
1 John 4:14 ►

26 For such an high priest became us, *who*
is holy, harmless, undefiled, separate
from sinners, and made higher than the
heavens;
27 Who needeth not daily, as those high
priests, to offer up sacrifice, first for his own
sins, and then for the people's: for this he
did once, when he offered up himself.
28 For the law maketh men high priests
which have infirmity; but the word of the
oath, which was since the law, *maketh* the
Son, who is consecrated for evermore.

8

1 Now of the things which we have
spoken *this is* the sum: We have such an
high priest, who is set on the right hand
of the throne of the Majesty in the
heavens;
2 A minister of the sanctuary, and of the
true tabernacle, which the Lord pitched,
and not man.
3 For every high priest is ordained to offer gifts and sacrifices: wherefore *it is* of
necessity that this man have somewhat
also to offer.
4 For if he were on earth, he should not
be a priest, seeing that there are priests that
offer gifts according to the law:
5 Who serve unto the example and shadow of heavenly things, as Moses was admonished of God when he was about to
make the tabernacle: for, See, saith he, *that*
thou make all things according to the pattern shewed to thee in the mount.
6 But now hath he obtained a more excellent ministry, by how much also he is
the mediator of a better covenant, which
was established upon better promises.
7 For if that first *covenant* had been faultless, then should no place have been
sought for the second.
8 For finding fault with them, he saith,
Behold, the days come, saith the Lord,
when I will make a new covenant with the
house of Israel and with the house of Judah:
9 Not according to the covenant that I
made with their fathers in the day when I
took them by the hand to lead them out
of the land of Egypt; because they continued not in my covenant, and I regarded
them not, saith the Lord.
10 For this *is* the covenant that I will make
with the house of Israel after those days,
saith the Lord; I will put my laws into their
mind, and write them in their hearts: and
I will be to them a God, and they shall be
to me a people:
11 And they shall not teach every man his
neighbour, and every man his brother, saying, Know the Lord: for all shall know me,
from the least to the greatest.
12 For I will be
merciful to their
unrighteousness,
and their sins and
their iniquities will
I remember no
more.

8:12 God's Forgiveness
◄ Micah 7:18
1 John 1:9 ►

13 In that he saith, A new *covenant,* he
hath made the first old. Now that which

decayeth and waxeth old *is* ready to vanish away.

9

1 Then verily the first *covenant* had also
ordinances of divine service, and a worldly sanctuary.
2 For there was a tabernacle made; the
first, wherein *was* the candlestick, and the
table, and the shewbread; which is called
the sanctuary.
3 And after the second veil, the tabernacle which is called the Holiest of all;
4 Which had the golden censer, and the
ark of the covenant overlaid round about
with gold, wherein *was* the golden pot that
had manna, and Aaron's rod that budded,
and the tables of the covenant;
5 And over it the cherubims of glory
shadowing the mercyseat; of which we cannot now speak particularly.
6 Now when these things were thus ordained, the priests went always into the
first tabernacle, accomplishing the service
of God.
7 But into the second *went* the high priest
alone once every year, not without blood,
which he offered for himself, and *for* the
errors of the people:
8 The Holy Ghost this signifying, that the
way into the holiest of all was not yet made
manifest, while as the first tabernacle was
yet standing:
9 Which *was* a figure for the time then
present, in which were offered both gifts
and sacrifices, that could not make him
that did the service perfect, as pertaining
to the conscience;
10 *Which stood* only in meats and drinks,
and divers washings, and carnal ordinances, imposed *on them* until the time of
reformation.
11 But Christ being come an high priest
of good things to come, by a greater and
more perfect tabernacle, not made with
hands, that is to say, not of this building;
12 Neither by the blood of goats and
calves, but by his own blood he entered in
once into the holy place, having obtained
eternal redemption *for us*.
13 For if the blood of bulls and of goats,
and the ashes of an heifer sprinkling the
unclean, sanctifieth to the purifying of the
flesh:
14 How much more shall the blood of
Christ, who through the eternal Spirit offered himself without spot to God, purge
your conscience from dead works to serve
the living God?
15 And for this cause he is the mediator
of the new testament, that by means of
death, for the redemption of the transgressions *that were* under the first testament,
they which are called might receive the
promise of eternal inheritance.
16 For where a testament *is*, there must
also of necessity be the death of the testator.
17 For a testament *is* of force after men
are dead: otherwise it is of no strength at
all while the testator liveth.
18 Whereupon neither the first *testament*
was dedicated without blood.
19 For when Moses had spoken every precept to all the people according to the law,
he took the blood of calves and of goats,
with water, and scarlet wool, and hyssop,
and sprinkled both the book, and all the
people,
20 Saying, This *is* the blood of the testament which God hath enjoined unto you.
21 Moreover he sprinkled with blood
both the tabernacle, and all the vessels of
the ministry.
22 And almost all
things are by the
law purged with
blood; and without
shedding of blood
is no remission.

9:22 Forgiveness of Sin
◄ Romans 3:25
Hebrews 10:18 ►

23 *It was* therefore necessary that the pat-
terns of things in the heavens should be
purified with these; but the heavenly
things themselves with better sacrifices
than these.
24 For Christ is not entered into the holy
places made with hands, *which are* the figures of the true; but into heaven itself, now
to appear in the presence of God for us:
25 Nor yet that he should offer himself
often, as the high priest entereth into the
holy place every year with blood of others;
26 For then must he often have suffered
since the foundation of the world: but now
once in the end of the world hath he appeared to put away
sin by the sacrifice
of himself.
27 And as it is ap-
pointed unto men
once to die, but af-

9:27
Death
◄ Romans 5:12 ►

7 By faith Noah, being warned of God of things not seen as yet, moved with fear, prepared an ark to the saving of his house; by the which he condemned the world, and became heir of the righteousness which is by faith.

8 By faith Abraham, when he was called to go out into a place which he should after receive for an inheritance, obeyed; and he went out, not knowing whither he went.

9 By faith he sojourned in the land of promise, as *in* a strange country, dwelling in tabernacles with Isaac and Jacob, the heirs with him of the same promise:

10 For he looked for a city which hath foundations, whose builder and maker *is* God.

11 Through faith also Sara herself received strength to conceive seed, and was delivered of a child when she was past age, because she judged him faithful who had promised.

12 Therefore sprang there even of one, and him as good as dead, *so many* as the stars of the sky in multitude, and as the sand which is by the sea shore innumerable.

13 These all died in faith, not having received the promises, but having seen them afar off, and were persuaded of *them,* and embraced *them,* and confessed that they were strangers and pilgrims on the earth.

14 For they that say such things declare plainly that they seek a country.

15 And truly, if they had been mindful of that *country* from whence they came out, they might have had opportunity to have returned.

16 But now they desire a better *country,* that is, an heavenly: wherefore God is not ashamed to be called their God: for he hath prepared for them a city.

17 By faith Abraham, when he was tried, offered up Isaac: and he that had received the promises offered up his only begotten *son,*

18 Of whom it was said, That in Isaac shall thy seed be called:

19 Accounting that God *was* able to raise *him* up, even from the dead; from whence also he received him in a figure.

20 By faith Isaac blessed Jacob and Esau concerning things to come.

21 By faith Jacob, when he was a dying, blessed both the sons of Joseph; and worshipped, *leaning* upon the top of his staff.

22 By faith Joseph, when he died, made mention of the departing of the children of Israel; and gave commandment concerning his bones.

23 By faith Moses, when he was born, was hid three months of his parents, because they saw *he was* a proper child; and they were not afraid of the king's commandment.

24 By faith Moses, when he was come to years, refused to be called the son of Pharaoh's daughter;

25 Choosing rather to suffer affliction with the people of God, than to enjoy the pleasures of sin for a season;

26 Esteeming the reproach of Christ greater riches than the treasures in Egypt: for he had respect unto the recompence of the reward.

27 By faith he forsook Egypt, not fearing the wrath of the king: for he endured, as seeing him who is invisible.

28 Through faith he kept the passover, and the sprinkling of blood, lest he that destroyed the firstborn should touch them.

11:25
Suffering for Jesus
◄ 2 Timothy 2:12
James 5:10 ►

11:26 Invisible Wealth
◄ Ephesians 3:8
James 2:5 ►

11:26
Suffering Rewarded
◄ Hebrews 10:34
Revelation 20:4 ►

11:26 Why Suffer?
◄ Hebrews 10:33
Hebrews 13:13 ►

29 By faith they passed through the Red sea as by dry *land:* which the Egyptians assaying to do were drowned.

30 By faith the walls of Jericho fell down, after they were compassed about seven days.

31 By faith the harlot Rahab perished not with them that believed not, when she had received the spies with peace.

32 And what shall I more say? for the time would fail me to tell of Gedeon, and *of* Barak, and *of* Samson, and *of* Jephthae; *of* David also, and Samuel, and *of* the prophets:

33 Who through faith subdued kingdoms,

wrought righteousness, obtained promises, stopped the mouths of lions,

> **11:33-34**
> **Weakness**
> ◄ 2 Corinthians 13:4 ►

34 Quenched the violence of fire, escaped the edge of the sword, out of weakness were made strong, waxed valiant in fight, turned to flight the armies of the aliens.

35 Women received their dead raised to life again: and others were tortured, not accepting deliverance; that they might obtain a better resurrection:

36 And others had trial of *cruel* mockings and scourgings, yea, moreover of bonds and imprisonment:

> **11:36**
> **Mocking**
> ◄ Acts 17:32 ►

37 They were stoned, they were sawn asunder, were tempted, were slain with the sword: they wandered about in sheepskins and goatskins; being destitute, afflicted, tormented;

38 (Of whom the world was not worthy:) they wandered in deserts, and *in* mountains, and *in* dens and caves of the earth.

39 And these all, having obtained a good report through faith, received not the promise:

40 God having provided some better thing for us, that they without us should not be made perfect.

12

1 Wherefore seeing we also are compassed about with so great a cloud of witnesses, let us lay aside every weight, and the sin which doth so easily beset *us*, and let us run with patience the race that is set before us,

> **12:1 Determination**
> ◄ 2 Timothy 3:14
> 1 Peter 1:13 ►

> **12:1 Starting Over**
> ◄ Colossians 2:11
> 1 Peter 2:11 ►

2 Looking unto Jesus the author and finisher of *our* faith; who for the joy that was set before him endured the cross, despising the shame, and is set down at the right hand of the throne of God.

> **12:2**
> **Jesus' Joy**
> ◄ John 17:13 ►

3 For consider him that endured such contradiction of sinners against himself, lest ye be wearied and faint in your minds.

4 Ye have not yet resisted unto blood, striving against sin.

5 And ye have forgotten the exhortation which speaketh unto you as unto children, My son, despise not thou the chastening of the Lord, nor faint when thou art rebuked of him:

> **12:5**
> **Refusing Correction**
> ◄ Zephaniah 3:7
> Revelation 16:11 ►

> **12:5**
> **Taking Advice**
> ◄ Ecclesiastes 7:5 ►

6 For whom the Lord loveth he chasteneth, and scourgeth every son whom he receiveth.

7 If ye endure chastening, God dealeth with you as with sons; for what son is he whom the father chasteneth not?

> **12:7 Endurance**
> ◄ Mark 13:13
> James 1:12 ►

8 But if ye be without chastisement, whereof all are partakers, then are ye bastards, and not sons.

9 Furthermore we have had fathers of our flesh which corrected *us*, and we gave *them* reverence: shall we not much rather be in subjection unto the Father of spirits, and live?

10 For they verily for a few days chastened *us* after their own pleasure; but he for *our* profit, that *we* might be partakers of his holiness.

11 Now no chastening for the present seemeth to be joyous, but grievous: nevertheless afterward it yieldeth the peaceable fruit of righteousness unto them which are exercised thereby.

> **12:11 Hardship**
> ◄ 2 Corinthians 4:17
> Revelation 7:14 ►

12 Wherefore lift up the hands which hang down, and the feeble knees;

13 And make straight paths for your feet, lest that which is lame be turned out of the way; but let it rather be healed.

> **12:13**
> **Right Paths**
> ◄ Isaiah 26:7 ►

14 Follow peace with all *men*, and holiness, without which no man shall see the Lord:

12:14 Holiness
◄ Ephesians 4:24
1 Peter 1:16 ►

15 Looking diligently lest any man fail of the grace of God; lest any root of bitterness springing up trouble *you*, and thereby many be defiled;

12:14 Peace
◄ Titus 1:6
James 3:17 ►

16 Lest there *be* any fornicator, or profane person, as Esau, who for one morsel of meat sold his birthright.

12:15 Bad Examples
◄ Hebrews 4:11
2 Peter 3:17 ►

17 For ye know how that afterward, when he would have inherited the blessing, he was rejected: for he found no place of repentance, though he sought it carefully with tears.

12:16-17 Remorse
◄ Matthew 27:3, 5 ►

18 For ye are not come unto the mount that might be touched, and that burned with fire, nor unto blackness, and darkness, and tempest,

19 And the sound of a trumpet, and the voice of words; which *voice* they that heard intreated that the word should not be spoken to them any more:

20 (For they could not endure that which was commanded, And if so much as a beast touch the mountain, it shall be stoned, or thrust through with a dart:

21 And so terrible was the sight, *that* Moses said, I exceedingly fear and quake:)

22 But ye are come unto mount Sion, and unto the city of the living God, the heavenly Jerusalem, and to an innumerable company of angels,

23 To the general assembly and church of the firstborn, which are written in heaven, and to God the Judge of all, and to the spirits of just men made perfect,

12:23 God as Judge
◄ Ecclesiastes 3:17
Revelation 18:8 ►

24 And to Jesus the mediator of the new covenant, and to the blood of sprinkling, that speaketh better things than *that of* Abel.

25 See that ye refuse not him that speaketh. For if they escaped not who refused him that spake on earth, much more *shall not* we *escape*, if we turn away from him that *speaketh* from heaven:

12:25 Salvation
◄ Hebrews 2:3 ►

12:25 Sin (Warnings)
◄ Jonah 3:4
2 Peter 3:17 ►

26 Whose voice then shook the earth: but now he hath promised, saying, Yet once more I shake not the earth only, but also heaven.

27 And this *word*, Yet once more, signifieth the removing of those things that are shaken, as of things that are made, that those things which cannot be shaken may remain.

12:27 Things That Last
◄ 2 Corinthians 4:18
1 Peter 1:25 ►

28 Wherefore we receiving a kingdom which cannot be moved, let us have grace, whereby we may serve God acceptably with reverence and godly fear:

29 For our God *is* a consuming fire.

13

1 Let brotherly love continue.

2 Be not forgetful to entertain strangers: for thereby some have entertained angels unawares.

13:1 Loving Others
◄ 1 Thessalonians 3:12
James 2:8 ►

3 Remember them that are in bonds, as bound with them; *and* them which suffer adversity, as being yourselves also in the body.

13:2 Hospitality
◄ Titus 1:8
1 Peter 4:9 ►

13:3 Sympathy
◄ Galatians 6:2
James 1:27 ►

4 Marriage *is* honourable in all, and the bed undefiled: but whoremongers and adulterers God will judge.

5 *Let your* conversation *be* without covetousness; *and be* content with such things as ye have: for he hath

13:5 Contentment
◄ 1 Timothy 6:6, 8 ►

said, I will never leave thee, nor forsake thee.

6So that we may boldly say, The Lord *is* my helper, and I will not fear what man shall do unto me.

13:6 Security
◄ Isaiah 43:2
1 Peter 3:13 ►

7Remember them which have the rule over you, who have spoken unto you the word of God: whose faith follow, considering the end of *their* conversation.

13:7 Respecting God's People
◄ 1 Timothy 5:17 ►

8Jesus Christ the same yesterday, and to day, and for ever.

9Be not carried about with divers and strange doctrines. For *it is* a good thing that the heart be established with grace; not with meats, which have not profited them that have been occupied therein.

10We have an altar, whereof they have no right to eat which serve the tabernacle.

11For the bodies of those beasts, whose blood is brought into the sanctuary by the high priest for sin, are burned without the camp.

12Wherefore Jesus also, that he might sanctify the people with his own blood, suffered without the gate.

13Let us go forth therefore unto him without the camp, bearing his reproach.

13:13 Why Suffer?
◄ Hebrews 11:26
1 Peter 4:14 ►

14For here have we no continuing city, but we seek one to come.

13:15 Praising God
◄ Isaiah 42:12
1 Peter 2:9 ►

15By him therefore let us offer the sacrifice of praise to God continually, that is, the fruit of *our* lips giving thanks to his name.

13:16 Doing Good
◄ 1 Timothy 6:18
James 4:17 ►

16But to do good and to communicate forget not: for with such sacrifices God is well pleased.

13:16 Giving
◄ 1 Timothy 6:18 ►

17Obey them that have the rule over you, and submit yourselves: for they watch for your souls, as they that must give account, that they may do it with joy, and not with grief: for that *is* unprofitable for you.

13:16 Pleasing God
◄ Hebrews 11:5
1 John 3:22 ►

18Pray for us: for we trust we have a good conscience, in all things willing to live honestly.

13:18 Clear Conscience
◄ 1 Timothy 3:9
1 Peter 3:16 ►

19But I beseech *you* the rather to do this, that I may be restored to you the sooner.

20Now the God of peace, that brought again from the dead our Lord Jesus, that great shepherd of the sheep, through the blood of the everlasting covenant,

21Make you perfect in every good work to do his will, working in you that which is wellpleasing in his sight, through Jesus Christ; to whom *be* glory for ever and ever. Amen.

13:21 Perfection
◄ Hebrews 6:1
James 1:4 ►

13:21 Submitting to God
◄ Ephesians 6:6
James 4:15 ►

22And I beseech you, brethren, suffer the word of exhortation: for I have written a letter unto you in few words.

23Know ye that *our* brother Timothy is set at liberty; with whom, if he come shortly, I will see you.

24Salute all them that have the rule over you, and all the saints. They of Italy salute you.

25Grace *be* with you all. Amen.

James

AUTHOR
James
(Jesus' half-brother)

MAIN POINT
The church must show its faith and its action; there is no place for hypocrisy in God's kingdom.

DATE WRITTEN
Probably A.D. 49

5 CHAPTERS

MAIN PEOPLE

None are mentioned by name

SPECIAL FEATURES

- *Is a how-to book on Christian living*
- *Includes a famous passage on faith versus works*
- *Compares the tongue to fire in vivid language*
- *Reveals God's rules on swearing*
- *Second of the General epistles*

HOW THE BOOK GOT ITS NAME

The letter is written by James to Jewish Christians specifically and to all Christians generally.

1 1James, a servant of God and of the Lord
Jesus Christ, to the twelve tribes which are
scattered abroad,
greeting.
2My brethren,
count it all joy
when ye fall into
divers temptations;
3Knowing *this*,
that the trying of
your faith worketh
patience.
4But let patience
have *her* perfect
work, that ye may
be perfect and en-
tire, wanting noth-
ing.
5If any of you
lack wisdom, let
him ask of God,
that giveth to all
men liberally, and
upbraideth not;
and it shall be giv-
en him.
6But let him ask
in faith, nothing
wavering. For he
that wavereth is like
a wave of the sea
driven with the
wind and tossed.
7For let not that
man think that he
shall receive any
thing of the Lord.
8A double mind-
ed man *is* unstable in all his ways.
9Let the brother of low degree rejoice

1:2-3 Temptation
◄ Hebrews 2:18
James 1:12 ►

1:4 Perfection
◄ Hebrews 13:21
1 Peter 5:10 ►

1:4 Quitting
◄ Hebrews 10:36
James 5:7 ►

1:5 Getting Wisdom
◄ Luke 21:15 ►

1:5 Gifts from God
◄ 1 Corinthians 4:7 ►

1:5 Praying for Wisdom
◄ Colossians 1:9 ►

Turn to the next page for more . . .

in that he is exalted:
10 But the rich, in
that he is made
low: because as
the flower of the
grass he shall pass
away.
11 For the sun is
no sooner risen
with a burning
heat, but it with-
ereth the grass, and
the flower thereof
falleth, and the
grace of the fashion
of it perisheth: so
also shall the rich
man fade away in
his ways.
12 Blessed *is* the
man that endureth
temptation: for
when he is tried, he
shall receive the
crown of life, which
the Lord hath
promised to them
that love him.
13 Let no man say
when he is tempt-
ed, I am tempted of
God: for God can-
not be tempted
with evil, neither
tempteth he any
man:
14 But every man
is tempted, when
he is drawn away of
his own lust, and
enticed.
15 Then when lust
hath conceived, it
bringeth forth sin:
and sin, when it is
finished, bringeth
forth death.
16 Do not err, my
beloved brethren.
17 Every good gift
and every perfect
gift is from above,
and cometh down
from the Father of
lights, with whom

1:5-6 Faith
◄ Hebrews 11:6
1 John 3:23 ►

1:6-7 Unanswered Prayer
◄ Zechariah 7:13
James 4:3 ►

1:8 Double Life
◄ 1 Corinthians 10:21
James 4:8 ►

1:8 The Time Is Now
◄ Luke 9:62
James 4:8 ►

1:12 Endurance
◄ Hebrews 12:7
James 5:11 ►

1:12 Life Tests
◄ 1 Corinthians 3:13 ►

1:12 Temptation
◄ James 1:2-3
2 Peter 2:9 ►

1:15 Spiritual Death
◄ Romans 8:6
James 5:20 ►

1:17 Names of God
◄ Matthew 6:26 ►

is no variableness, neither shadow of turning.
18 Of his own will begat he us with the
word of truth, that we should be a kind of
firstfruits of his creatures.
19 Wherefore, my beloved brethren, let
every man be swift to hear, slow to speak,
slow to wrath:
20 For the wrath
of man worketh not
the righteousness
of God.
21 Wherefore lay
apart all filthiness
and superfluity of
naughtiness, and
receive with meek-
ness the engrafted
word, which is able
to save your souls.
22 But be ye doers
of the word, and
not hearers only,
deceiving your own
selves.
23 For if any be a
hearer of the word,
and not a doer, he
is like unto a man
beholding his natu-
ral face in a glass:
24 For he behold-
eth himself, and
goeth his way, and straightway forgetteth
what manner of man he was.
25 But whoso looketh into the perfect law
of liberty, and continueth *therein*, he being not a forgetful
hearer, but a doer
of the work, this
man shall be
blessed in his deed.
26 If any man
among you seem
to be religious,
and bridleth not
his tongue, but
deceiveth his own
heart, this man's re-
ligion *is* vain.
27 Pure religion
and undefiled be-
fore God and the
Father is this, To
visit the fatherless

1:20 Mad
◄ Acts 19:28 ►

1:21 How to Be Saved
◄ 2 Timothy 3:15
2 Peter 1:10-11 ►

1:22 Lying to Yourself
◄ Galatians 6:3
James 1:26 ►

1:23-24 Listening and Doing
◄ Luke 16:31 ►

1:26 Lying to Yourself
◄ James 1:22
1 John 1:8 ►

1:26 Phonies
◄ Matthew 23:27 ►

1:27 Kind to the Needy
◄ Jeremiah 22:3 ►

and widows in their affliction, *and* to keep himself unspotted from the world.

2

1 My brethren, have not the faith of our Lord Jesus Christ, *the Lord* of glory, with respect of persons.

2 For if there come unto your assembly a man with a gold ring, in goodly apparel, and there come in also a poor man in vile raiment;

3 And ye have respect to him that weareth the gay clothing, and say unto him, Sit thou here in a good place; and say to the poor, Stand thou there, or sit here under my footstool:

4 Are ye not then partial in yourselves, and are become judges of evil thoughts?

5 Hearken, my beloved brethren, Hath not God chosen the poor of this world rich in faith, and heirs of the kingdom which he hath promised to them that love him?

6 But ye have despised the poor. Do not rich men oppress you, and draw you before the judgment seats?

7 Do not they blaspheme that worthy name by the which ye are called?

8 If ye fulfil the royal law according

1:27
Religious People
◄ Romans 13:10 ►

1:27
Sympathy
◄ Hebrews 13:3 ►

2:2-4
Good Looks
◄ 2 Corinthians 10:7 ►

2:4 Favoritism
◄ 1 Timothy 5:21
Jude 1:16 ►

2:5 Benefits of Faith
◄ Hebrews 4:3
1 Peter 2:6 ►

2:5
Equality
◄ Galatians 3:28 ►

2:5
Invisible Wealth
◄ Hebrews 11:26 ►

2:5
Promises to the Poor
◄ Isaiah 41:17 ►

2:8 Loving Others
◄ Hebrews 13:1
1 Peter 1:22 ►

to the scripture, Thou shalt love thy neighbour as thyself, ye do well:

9 But if ye have respect to persons, ye commit sin, and are convinced of the law as transgressors.

10 For whosoever shall keep the whole law, and yet offend in one *point,* he is guilty of all.

11 For he that said, Do not commit adultery, said also, Do not kill. Now if thou commit no adultery, yet if thou kill, thou art become a transgressor of the law.

12 So speak ye, and so do, as they that shall be judged by the law of liberty.

13 For he shall have judgment without mercy, that hath shewed no mercy; and mercy rejoiceth against judgment.

14 What *doth it* profit, my brethren, though a man say he hath faith, and have not works? can faith save him?

15 If a brother or sister be naked, and destitute of daily food,

16 And one of you say unto them, Depart in peace, be *ye* warmed and filled; notwithstanding ye give them not those things which are needful to the body; what *doth it* profit?

17 Even so faith, if it hath not works, is dead, being alone.

18 Yea, a man may say, Thou hast faith, and I have works: shew me thy faith without thy works, and I will shew thee my faith by my works.

19 Thou believest that there is one God; thou doest well: the devils also believe, and tremble.

2:8
Neighbors
◄ Galatians 5:14 ►

2:13
No Mercy
◄ Romans 1:31 ►

2:13
Showing Mercy
◄ Luke 6:36 ►

2:16
Not Caring
◄ Luke 18:39 ►

2:17-18 Good Works
◄ Hebrews 10:24
1 Peter 2:12 ►

2:19 Demons
◄ 1 Timothy 4:1
Revelation 16:14 ►

20 But wilt thou know, O vain man, that faith without works is dead?

21 Was not Abraham our father justified by works, when he had offered Isaac his son upon the altar?

22 Seest thou how faith wrought with his works, and by works was faith made perfect?

23 And the scripture was fulfilled which saith, Abraham believed God, and it was imputed unto him for righteousness: and he was called the Friend of God.

> **2:23 God's Friends**
> ◄ 2 Chronicles 20:7 ►

24 Ye see then how that by works a man is justified, and not by faith only.

25 Likewise also was not Rahab the harlot justified by works, when she had received the messengers, and had sent *them* out another way?

26 For as the body without the spirit is dead, so faith without works is dead also.

3

1 My brethren, be not many masters, knowing that we shall receive the greater condemnation.

2 For in many things we offend all. If any man offend not in word, the same *is* a perfect man, *and* able also to bridle the whole body.

> **3:2 Self-control**
> ◄ 1 Corinthians 6:12
> 2 Peter 1:5-7 ►

> **3:2 Talking**
> ◄ Titus 2:8 ►

3 Behold, we put bits in the horses' mouths, that they may obey us; and we turn about their whole body.

4 Behold also the ships, which though *they be* so great, and *are* driven of fierce winds, yet are they turned about with a very small helm, whithersoever the governor listeth.

5 Even so the tongue is a little member, and boasteth great things. Behold, how great a matter a little fire kindleth!

6 And the tongue *is* a fire, a world of iniquity: so is the tongue among our members, that it defileth the whole body, and setteth on fire the course of nature; and it is set on fire of hell.

> **3:6 Cruel Talk**
> ◄ Titus 3:1-2
> James 4:11 ►

7 For every kind of beasts, and of birds, and of serpents, and of things in the sea, is tamed, and hath been tamed of mankind:

8 But the tongue can no man tame; *it is* an unruly evil, full of deadly poison.

9 Therewith bless we God, even the Father; and therewith curse we men, which are made after the similitude of God.

> **3:9 Made in God's Image**
> ◄ 1 Corinthians 11:7 ►

10 Out of the same mouth proceedeth blessing and cursing. My brethren, these things ought not so to be.

> **3:10 Cursing**
> ◄ Romans 12:14 ►

11 Doth a fountain send forth at the same place sweet *water* and bitter?

12 Can the fig tree, my brethren, bear olive berries? either a vine, figs? so *can* no fountain both yield salt water and fresh.

> **3:13 Living for God**
> ◄ 1 Timothy 3:7
> 2 Peter 3:11 ►

13 Who *is* a wise man and endued with knowledge among you? let him shew out of a good conversation his works with meekness of wisdom.

> **3:14 Arguing**
> ◄ 2 Timothy 2:24 ►

14 But if ye have bitter envying and strife in your hearts, glory not, and lie not against the truth.

> **3:14 Envy**
> ◄ Galatians 5:26 ►

15 This wisdom descendeth not from above, but *is* earthly, sensual, devilish.

> **3:17 Gentleness**
> ◄ Titus 3:2 ►

16 For where envying and strife *is*, there *is* confusion and every evil work.

> **3:17 Peace**
> ◄ Hebrews 12:14 ►

17 But the wis-

dom that is from
above is first pure,
then peaceable,
gentle, *and* easy to
be intreated, full of
mercy and good
fruits, without partiality, and without hypocrisy.
18 And the fruit of righteousness is sown
in peace of them that make peace.

4

1 From whence *come* wars and fightings
among you? *come they* not hence, *even* of
your lusts that war in your members?
2 Ye lust, and have
not: ye kill, and de-
sire to have, and
cannot obtain: ye
fight and war, yet ye
have not, because
ye ask not.
3 Ye ask, and re-
ceive not, because
ye ask amiss, that ye
may consume *it*
upon your lusts.
4 Ye adulterers
and adulteresses,
know ye not that
the friendship of
the world is enmity
with God? whoso-
ever therefore will
be a friend of the
world is the enemy
of God.
5 Do ye think that
the scripture saith
in vain, The spirit
that dwelleth in us
lusteth to envy?
6 But he giveth
more grace. Where-
fore he saith, God
resisteth the proud,
but giveth grace
unto the humble.
7 Submit your-
selves therefore to
God. Resist the dev-
il, and he will flee
from you.
8 Draw nigh to
God, and he will
draw nigh to you.
Cleanse *your* hands,

3:17 True Wisdom
◄ 2 Timothy 3:15
1 John 2:20 ►

4:2
Not Praying
◄ Zephaniah 1:6 ►

4:3
Unanswered Prayer
◄ James 1:6-7 ►

4:6
Proud People
◄ 1 Timothy 6:4 ►

4:7 Resisting Satan
◄ Ephesians 6:11
1 Peter 5:8-9 ►

4:7 Satan's Weakness
◄ 1 Corinthians 10:13
Revelation 12:12 ►

4:7 Tempted by Satan
◄ Hebrews 2:18
1 John 4:4 ►

4:8
Double Life
◄ James 1:8 ►

ye sinners; and pu-
rify *your* hearts, *ye*
double minded.
9 Be afflicted, and
mourn, and weep:
let your laughter be
turned to mourn-
ing, and *your* joy to
heaviness.
10 Humble your-
selves in the sight of
the Lord, and he
shall lift you up.
11 Speak not evil
one of another,
brethren. He that
speaketh evil of
his brother, and
judgeth his brother,
speaketh evil of the
law, and judgeth
the law: but if thou
judge the law, thou
art not a doer of the
law, but a judge.
12 There is one lawgiver, who is able to
save and to destroy: who art thou that
judgest another?
13 Go to now, ye
that say, To day or
to morrow we will
go into such a city,
and continue there
a year, and buy and
sell, and get gain:
14 Whereas ye
know not what *shall*
be on the morrow.
For what *is* your
life? It is even
a vapour, that ap-
peareth for a little
time, and then
vanisheth away.
15 For that ye
ought to say, If the
Lord will, we shall
live, and do this, or
that.
16 But now ye
rejoice in your
boastings: all such
rejoicing is evil.
17 Therefore to him that knoweth to do
good, and doeth *it* not, to him it is sin.

4:8
The Time Is Now
◄ James 1:8 ►

4:9
Happiness
◄ Isaiah 16:10 ►

4:9
Laughter
◄ Luke 6:25 ►

4:11 Cruel Talk
◄ James 3:6
1 Peter 2:1 ►

4:13
Planning
◄ Luke 12:18 ►

4:14
The Future
◄ Acts 20:22 ►

4:14
Life Is Short
◄ Isaiah 38:12 ►

4:15 Submitting to God
◄ Hebrews 13:21
1 John 2:17 ►

Turn to the next page for more . . .

5

1 Go to now, *ye* rich men, weep and howl for your miseries that shall come upon *you*.

2 Your riches are corrupted, and your garments are motheaten.

3 Your gold and silver is cankered; and the rust of them shall be a witness against you, and shall eat your flesh as it were fire. Ye have heaped treasure together for the last days.

4 Behold, the hire of the labourers who have reaped down your fields, which is of you kept back by fraud, crieth: and the cries of them which have reaped are entered into the ears of the Lord of sabaoth.

5 Ye have lived in pleasure on the earth, and been wanton; ye have nourished your hearts, as in a day of slaughter.

6 Ye have condemned *and* killed the just; *and* he doth not resist you.

7 Be patient therefore, brethren, unto the coming of the Lord. Behold, the husbandman waiteth for the precious fruit of the earth, and hath long patience for it, until he receive the early and latter rain.

8 Be ye also patient; stablish your hearts: for the coming of the Lord draweth nigh.

9 Grudge not one against another, brethren, lest ye be condemned: behold, the judge standeth before the door.

10 Take, my brethren, the prophets, who have spoken in the name of the Lord, for an example of suffering affliction, and of patience.

11 Behold, we count them happy which endure. Ye have heard of the patience of Job, and have seen the end of the Lord; that the Lord is very pitiful, and of tender mercy.

12 But above all things, my brethren, swear not, neither by heaven, neither by the earth, neither by any other oath: but let your yea be yea; and *your* nay, nay; lest ye fall into condemnation.

13 Is any among you afflicted? let him pray. Is any merry? let him sing psalms.

14 Is any sick among you? let him call for the elders of the church; and let them pray over him, anointing him with oil in the name of the Lord:

15 And the prayer of faith shall save the sick, and the Lord shall raise him up; and if he have committed sins, they shall be forgiven him.

16 Confess *your*

4:17 Doing Good
◄ Hebrews 13:16
1 Peter 2:15 ►

4:17 Mercy
◄ Luke 16:20-21 ►

5:3 Greed
◄ 1 Timothy 6:9 ►

5:3 Hoarding
◄ Luke 12:21 ►

5:4 Getting Ahead
◄ Ezekiel 22:13 ►

5:5 Luxury
◄ Titus 3:3
2 Peter 2:13 ►

5:7 Pray and Wait
◄ John 11:21
2 Peter 3:9 ►

5:7 Quitting
◄ James 1:4
2 Peter 1:6 ►

5:8 Ready for Jesus' Return
◄ Hebrews 10:37
Revelation 3:11 ►

5:10 Free Samples
◄ Hebrews 11:4
1 Peter 2:21 ►

5:10 Suffering for Jesus
◄ Hebrews 11:25
1 Peter 2:20 ►

5:11 Endurance
◄ James 1:12
1 Peter 2:19 ►

5:12 Swearing
◄ Matthew 5:34 ►

5:13 Duty to Pray
◄ 1 Timothy 2:8 ►

5:14 Sick People
◄ Matthew 25:36 ►

5:15 Forgiveness
◄ Ephesians 1:7
1 John 1:9 ►

5:16 How to Pray
◄ Mark 11:24
1 John 3:22 ►

faults one to another, and pray one for
another, that ye may be healed. The effectual fervent prayer of a righteous man
availeth much.
17Elias was a man subject to like passions
as we are, and he prayed earnestly that it
might not rain: and
it rained not on the
earth by the space of
three years and six
months.
18And he prayed

5:18
Prayer
◄ Acts 16:25-26 ►

again, and the heaven gave rain, and the
earth brought forth her fruit.
19Brethren, if any of you do err from the
truth, and one convert him;
20Let him know,
that he which con-
verteth the sinner
from the error of
his way shall save a
soul from death,
and shall hide a
multitude of sins.

5:20 Spiritual Death
◄ James 1:15
Revelation 21:8 ►

1 Peter

AUTHOR
Peter the disciple

MAIN POINT
When you are going through hard times, God has not abandoned you. He still loves you and wants to comfort you.

DATE WRITTEN
About A.D. 62-64

5 CHAPTERS
❑❑❑❑❑

MAIN PEOPLE

Peter, Silvanus, Mark

SPECIAL FEATURES

- *Uses images given to Peter straight from Jesus, including stones and sheep*
- *Shows how Peter had grown in his faith from the scared disciple who denied he even knew Jesus*
- *Encourages and offers down-to-earth advice to people who are suffering*
- *Third of the General epistles*

HOW THE BOOK GOT ITS NAME

Peter, whose name is a pun on the Greek word for rock *(petra), was writing to Jewish Christians scattered throughout Asia Minor.*

1

1Peter, an apostle of Jesus Christ, to the
strangers scattered throughout Pontus,
Galatia, Cappadocia, Asia, and Bithynia,
2Elect according to the foreknowledge
of God the Father, through sanctification
of the Spirit, unto obedience and sprinkling of the blood of Jesus Christ: Grace
unto you, and peace, be multiplied.
3Blessed *be* the God and Father of our
Lord Jesus Christ, which according to his
abundant mercy hath begotten us again
unto a lively hope by the resurrection of
Jesus Christ from the dead,
4To an inheritance incorruptible, and
undefiled, and that fadeth not away, reserved in heaven for you,
5Who are kept by the power of God
through faith unto salvation ready to be
revealed in the last time.
6Wherein ye greatly rejoice, though now
for a season, if need be, ye are in heaviness through manifold temptations:
7That the trial of your faith, being much more precious than of gold that perisheth, though it be tried
with fire, might be found unto praise and
honour and glory at the appearing of Jesus
Christ:

1:7 Pain
◄ Malachi 3:3
1 Peter 4:12 ►

8Whom having not seen, ye love; in
whom, though now ye see *him* not, yet
believing, ye rejoice with joy unspeakable
and full of glory:
9Receiving the end of your faith, *even* the
salvation of *your* souls.
10Of which salvation the prophets have

enquired and searched diligently, who
prophesied of the grace *that should come*
unto you:
11Searching what, or what manner of
time the Spirit of Christ which was in them
did signify, when it testified beforehand
the sufferings of Christ, and the glory that
should follow.
12Unto whom it was revealed, that not
unto themselves, but unto us they did
minister the things, which are now reported unto you by them that have preached
the gospel unto you with the Holy Ghost
sent down from heaven; which things the
angels desire to look into.
13Wherefore gird up the loins of your
mind, be sober, and hope to the end for
the grace that is to
be brought unto
you at the revela-
tion of Jesus Christ;
14As obedient
children, not fash-
ioning yourselves
according to the
former lusts in your
ignorance:
15But as he which
hath called you is
holy, so be ye holy
in all manner of
conversation;
16Because it is
written, Be ye holy;
for I am holy.
17And if ye call
on the Father, who
without respect of
persons judgeth ac-
cording to every
man's work, pass
the time of your so-
journing *here* in
fear:
18Forasmuch as
ye know that ye
were not redeemed
with corruptible
things, *as* silver and
gold, from your
vain conversation
received by tradition
from your fathers;
19But with the
precious blood of

1:13 Determination
◄ Hebrews 12:1
Revelation 3:11 ►

1:16 Holiness
◄ Hebrews 12:14
2 Peter 3:11 ►

1:17 Actions Judged
◄ 2 Corinthians 5:10
Revelation 2:23 ►

1:17 Fearing God
◄ Romans 11:20
1 Peter 2:17 ►

1:17 Perfect Father
◄ Romans 8:15 ►

1:18-19 Value of People
◄ 1 Corinthians 6:20
Revelation 1:5 ►

Christ, as of a lamb
without blemish
and without spot:
20Who verily was
foreordained be-
fore the foundation
of the world, but was manifest in these last
times for you,
21Who by him do believe in God, that
raised him up from the dead, and gave him
glory; that your faith and hope might be
in God.
22Seeing ye have
purified your souls
in obeying the truth
through the Spirit
unto unfeigned
love of the brethren,
see that ye love one
another with a pure
heart fervently:
23Being born
again, not of cor-
ruptible seed, but
of incorruptible, by
the word of God,
which liveth and
abideth for ever.
24For all flesh *is*
as grass, and all the
glory of man as the
flower of grass. The
grass withereth, and
the flower thereof
falleth away:
25But the word of
the Lord endureth
for ever. And this
is the word which
by the gospel is
preached unto you.

2

1Wherefore lay-
ing aside all malice,
and all guile, and
hypocrisies, and
envies, and all evil
speakings,
2As newborn
babes, desire the
sincere milk of the
word, that ye may
grow thereby:
3If so be ye have
tasted that the Lord
is gracious.

1:19 Jesus the Lamb
◄ 1 Corinthians 5:7
Revelation 5:6 ►

1:22 Loving Others
◄ James 2:8
1 John 4:7 ►

1:22 Purity
◄ Ephesians 5:26 ►

1:24 Your Body
◄ Isaiah 64:6 ►

1:25 Things That Last
◄ Hebrews 12:27 ►

2:1 Cruel Talk
◄ James 4:11
1 Peter 3:10 ►

2:1 Malice
◄ Colossians 3:8 ►

2:2 Growing Spiritually
◄ Hebrews 6:1
2 Peter 1:5-6 ►

4 To whom coming, *as unto* a living stone, disallowed indeed of men, but chosen of God, *and* precious,

5 Ye also, as lively stones, are built up a spiritual house, an holy priesthood, to offer up spiritual sacrifices, acceptable to God by Jesus Christ.

6 Wherefore also it is contained in the scripture, Behold, I lay in Sion a chief corner stone, elect, precious: and he that believeth on him shall not be confounded.

2:6 Benefits of Faith
◄ James 2:5
1 John 5:14 ►

2:6
The Ultimate
◄ Ephesians 2:20 ►

7 Unto you therefore which believe *he is* precious: but unto them which be disobedient, the stone which the builders disallowed, the same is made the head of the corner,

8 And a stone of stumbling, and a rock of offence, *even to them* which stumble at the word, being disobedient: whereunto also they were appointed.

9 But ye *are* a chosen generation, a royal priesthood, an holy nation, a peculiar people; that ye should shew forth the praises of him who hath called you out of darkness into his marvellous light:

2:9
Praising God
◄ Hebrews 13:15 ►

10 Which in time past *were* not a people, but *are* now the people of God: which had not obtained mercy, but now have obtained mercy.

11 Dearly beloved, I beseech *you* as strangers and pilgrims, abstain from fleshly lusts, which war against the soul;

2:11
Starting Over
◄ Hebrews 12:1 ►

12 Having your conversation honest among the Gentiles: that, whereas they speak against you as evildoers, they may by *your* good works, which they shall behold, glorify God in the day of visitation.

2:12
Good Works
◄ James 2:17-18 ►

13 Submit yourselves to every ordinance of man for the Lord's sake: whether it be to the king, as supreme;

2:13-14
Obeying the Law
◄ Titus 3:1 ►

14 Or unto governors, as unto them that are sent by him for the punishment of evildoers, and for the praise of them that do well.

15 For so is the will of God, that with well doing ye may put to silence the ignorance of foolish men:

2:15 Doing Good
◄ James 4:17
1 Peter 3:11 ►

16 As free, and not using *your* liberty for a cloke of maliciousness, but as the servants of God.

2:16
Free to...
◄ Galatians 5:13 ►

17 Honour all *men*. Love the brotherhood. Fear God. Honour the king.

2:17 Fearing God
◄ 1 Peter 1:17
Revelation 14:7 ►

18 Servants, *be* subject to *your* masters with all fear; not only to the good and gentle, but also to the froward.

2:17 Rulers
◄ Romans 13:1
Jude 8 ►

19 For this *is* thankworthy, if a man for conscience toward God endure grief, suffering wrongfully.

2:19
Endurance
◄ James 5:11 ►

20 For what glory *is it*, if, when ye be buffeted for your faults, ye shall take it patiently? but if, when ye do well, and suffer *for it*, ye take it patiently, this *is* acceptable with God.

2:20
Suffering for Jesus
◄ James 5:10
1 Peter 3:14 ►

21 For even hereunto were ye called: because Christ also suffered for us, leaving us an example, that ye should follow his steps:

2:21
Free Samples
◄ James 5:10 ►

22Who did no sin, neither was guile found in his mouth:

23Who, when he was reviled, reviled not again; when he suffered, he threatened not; but committed *himself* to him that judgeth righteously:

24Who his own self bare our sins in his own body on the tree, that we, being dead to sins, should live unto righteousness: by whose stripes ye were healed.

25For ye were as sheep going astray; but are now returned unto the Shepherd and Bishop of your souls.

3

1Likewise, ye wives, *be* in subjection to your own husbands; that, if any obey not the word, they also may without the word be won by the conversation of the wives;

2While they behold your chaste conversation *coupled* with fear.

3Whose adorning let it not be that outward *adorning* of plaiting the hair, and of wearing of gold, or of putting on of apparel;

4But *let it be* the hidden man of the heart, in that which is not corruptible, *even the ornament* of a meek and quiet spirit, which is in the sight of God of great price.

5For after this manner in the old time the holy women also, who trusted in God, adorned themselves, being in subjection unto their own husbands:

6Even as Sarah obeyed Abraham, calling him lord: whose daughters ye are, as long as ye do well, and are not afraid with any amazement.

7Likewise, ye husbands, dwell with *them* according to knowledge, giving honour unto the wife, as unto the weaker vessel, and as being heirs together of the grace of life; that your prayers be not hindered.

8Finally, *be ye* all of one mind, having compassion one of another, love as brethren, *be* pitiful, *be* courteous:

9Not rendering evil for evil, or railing for railing: but contrariwise blessing; knowing that ye are thereunto called, that ye should inherit a blessing.

10For he that will love life, and see good days, let him refrain his tongue from evil, and his lips that they speak no guile:

11Let him eschew evil, and do good; let him seek peace, and ensue it.

12For the eyes of the Lord *are* over the righteous, and his ears *are open* unto their prayers: but the face of the Lord *is* against them that do evil.

13And who *is* he that will harm you, if ye be followers of that which is good?

14But and if ye suffer for righteousness' sake, happy *are ye:* and be not afraid of their terror, neither be troubled;

15But sanctify the Lord God in your hearts: and *be* ready always to *give* an answer to every

2:24 Freedom
◄ 2 Timothy 2:11 ►

2:24 What Jesus Did
◄ Hebrews 9:28
1 John 3:5 ►

2:24 Who Can Be Saved?
◄ Galatians 1:4
1 John 2:2 ►

2:24 Why Jesus Died
◄ Hebrews 9:28
1 Peter 3:18 ►

3:1-2 Modesty
◄ 1 Timothy 2:9-10 ►

3:8 Getting Along
◄ Colossians 2:2 ►

3:9 Revenge
◄ 1 Thessalonians 5:15 ►

3:10 Cruel Talk
◄ 1 Peter 2:1 ►

3:11 Doing Good
◄ 1 Peter 2:15
1 Peter 3:17 ►

3:11 Seeking Peace
◄ Colossians 3:15 ►

3:11 Stay Away!
◄ 1 Thessalonians 5:22 ►

3:13 Security
◄ Hebrews 13:6 ►

3:14 Suffering for Jesus
◄ 1 Peter 2:20
1 Peter 4:16 ►

3:15 Your Testimony
◄ 2 Timothy 1:8 ►

man that asketh you a reason of the hope
that is in you with meekness and fear:
16 Having a good
conscience; that,
whereas they speak
evil of you, as of
evildoers, they may
be ashamed that
falsely accuse your good conversation in
Christ.

> **3:16**
> **Clear Conscience**
> ◄ Hebrews 13:18 ►

17 For *it is* better,
if the will of God be
so, that ye suffer for
well doing, than for
evil doing.

> **3:17**
> **Doing Good**
> ◄ 1 Peter 3:11 ►

18 For Christ also
hath once suffered
for sins, the just for
the unjust, that he
might bring us to
God, being put to
death in the flesh,
but quickened by the Spirit:

> **3:18**
> **Why Jesus Died**
> ◄ 1 Peter 2:24 ►

19 By which also he went and preached
unto the spirits in prison;
20 Which some-
time were disobedi-
ent, when once the
longsuffering of
God waited in the
days of Noah, while
the ark was a preparing, wherein few, that
is, eight souls were saved by water.

> **3:20 God's Patience**
> ◄ Romans 9:22
> 2 Peter 3:9 ►

21 The like figure whereunto *even* baptism doth also now save us (not the putting away of the filth of the flesh, but the
answer of a good conscience toward God,)
by the resurrection of Jesus Christ:
22 Who is gone into heaven, and is on
the right hand of God; angels and author-
ities and powers being made subject unto
him.

4

1 Forasmuch then as Christ hath suffered
for us in the flesh, arm yourselves likewise
with the same mind: for he that hath suffered in the flesh hath ceased from sin;
2 That he no longer should live the rest
of *his* time in the flesh to the lusts of men,
but to the will of God.
3 For the time
past of *our* life may
suffice us to have
wrought the will of
the Gentiles, when
we walked in las-
civiousness, lusts,
excess of wine,
revellings, banquet-
ings, and abomin-
able idolatries:

> **4:3 Moderation**
> ◄ Ephesians 5:18
> 2 Peter 2:13 ►

> **4:3 Old Life**
> ◄ Colossians 3:9
> 2 Peter 1:9 ►

4 Wherein they
think it strange that
ye run not with
them to the same
excess of riot,
speaking evil of
you:

> **4:3**
> **Parties**
> ◄ Galatians 5:21 ►

5 Who shall give
account to him that
is ready to judge the
quick and the dead.

> **4:4-5**
> **Getting Caught**
> ◄ Romans 14:12 ►

6 For for this
cause was the gos-
pel preached also
to them that are
dead, that they
might be judged
according to men
in the flesh, but live
according to God
in the spirit.

> **4:5**
> **Christ as Judge**
> ◄ 2 Timothy 4:1 ►

7 But the end of all things is at hand: be
ye therefore sober, and watch unto prayer.
8 And above all things have fervent charity among yourselves: for charity shall cover the multitude of sins.
9 Use hospitality
one to another
without grudging.

> **4:9**
> **Hospitality**
> ◄ Hebrews 13:2 ►

10 As every man
hath received the
gift, *even so* minister
the same one to
another, as good
stewards of the
manifold grace of
God.

> **4:10**
> **Using What You Have**
> ◄ 2 Timothy 1:14 ►

11 If any man
speak, *let him speak*
as the oracles of
God; if any man
minister, *let him*
do it as of the
ability which God
giveth: that God in all things may be glorified through Jesus Christ, to whom be
praise and dominion for ever and ever.
Amen.

> **4:11**
> **Work**
> ◄ Luke 12:48 ►

12 Beloved, think it not strange concerning the fiery trial which is to try you,

as though some strange thing happened unto you:

13But rejoice, inasmuch as ye are partakers of Christ's sufferings; that, when his glory shall be revealed, ye may be glad also with exceeding joy.

14If ye be reproached for the name of Christ, happy *are ye;* for the spirit of glory and of God resteth upon you: on their part he is evil spoken of, but on your part he is glorified.

15But let none of you suffer as a murderer, or *as* a thief, or *as* an evildoer, or as a busybody in other men's matters.

16Yet if *any man suffer* as a Christian, let him not be ashamed; but let him glorify God on this behalf.

17For the time *is come* that judgment must begin at the house of God: and if *it* first *begin* at us, what shall the end *be* of them that obey not the gospel of God?

18And if the righteous scarcely be saved, where shall the ungodly and the sinner appear?

19Wherefore let them that suffer according to the will of God commit the keeping of their souls *to him* in well doing, as unto a faithful Creator.

5

1The elders which are among you I exhort, who am also an elder, and a witness of the sufferings of Christ, and also a partaker of the glory that shall be revealed:

2Feed the flock of God which is among you, taking the oversight *thereof,* not by constraint, but willingly; not for filthy lucre, but of a ready mind;

4:12
Pain
◄ 1 Peter 1:7 ►

4:12-13
Positive Attitude
◄ Hebrews 10:34 ►

4:14
Why Suffer?
◄ Hebrews 13:13 ►

4:15
Boredom
◄ 1 Timothy 5:13 ►

4:15
Stealing
◄ Titus 2:10 ►

4:16
Suffering for Jesus
◄ 1 Peter 3:14
1 Peter 5:10 ►

3Neither as being lords over *God's* heritage, but being ensamples to the flock.

4And when the chief Shepherd shall appear, ye shall receive a crown of glory that fadeth not away.

5Likewise, ye younger, submit yourselves unto the elder. Yea, all *of you* be subject one to another, and be clothed with humility: for God resisteth the proud, and giveth grace to the humble.

6Humble yourselves therefore under the mighty hand of God, that he may exalt you in due time:

7Casting all your care upon him; for he careth for you.

8Be sober, be vigilant; because your adversary the devil, as a roaring lion, walketh about, seeking whom he may devour:

9Whom resist stedfast in the faith, knowing that the same afflictions are accomplished in your brethren that are in the world.

10But the God of all grace, who hath called us unto his eternal glory by Christ Jesus, after that ye have suffered a while, make you perfect, stablish, strengthen, settle *you.*

5:4 Good News
◄ 1 Thessalonians 4:16
1 John 3:2 ►

5:7
God's Care for You
◄ Luke 12:7 ►

5:7
Worry
◄ Philippians 4:6 ►

5:8
Bad People
◄ Romans 3:15 ►

5:8 Pitfalls
◄ Colossians 4:2
Revelation 3:2 ►

5:8-9
Resisting Satan
◄ James 4:7 ►

5:9 Standing Strong
◄ 2 Thessalonians 2:15
2 Peter 3:17 ►

5:10
Perfection
◄ James 1:4 ►

5:10
Suffering for Jesus
◄ 1 Peter 4:16 ►

11To him *be* glory and dominion for ever
and ever. Amen.
12By Silvanus, a faithful brother unto
you, as I suppose, I have written briefly,
exhorting, and testifying that this is the
true grace of God wherein ye stand.

13The *church that is* at Babylon, elected
together with *you,* saluteth you; and *so doth*
Marcus my son.
14Greet ye one another with a kiss of
charity. Peace *be* with you all that are in
Christ Jesus. Amen.

2 Peter

AUTHOR
Peter the disciple

MAIN POINT
False teachers can spring up anywhere, so stay strong in the faith that you learned from the Bible.

DATE WRITTEN
About A.D. 67

3 CHAPTERS

MAIN PEOPLE

Peter, Paul

SPECIAL FEATURES

- *Refers to the time Peter saw Jesus transfigured on a mountain*
- *Provides solid ammunition against those who would attack the truth about Jesus*
- *Was the last book to be included in the official New Testament.*
- *Fourth of the General epistles*

HOW THE BOOK GOT ITS NAME

This is the second letter written by Peter.

1

1 Simon Peter, a servant and an apostle
of Jesus Christ, to them that have obtained
like precious faith with us through the
righteousness of God and our Saviour
Jesus Christ:
2 Grace and peace be multiplied unto
you through the knowledge of God, and
of Jesus our Lord,
3 According as his divine power hath giv-
en unto us all things that *pertain* unto life
and godliness, through the knowledge of
him that hath called us to glory and virtue:
4 Whereby are
given unto us ex-
ceeding great and
precious promises:
that by these ye
might be partakers
of the divine nature, having escaped the
corruption that is in the world through
lust.

1:4 God's Promises
◄ 2 Corinthians 7:1
1 John 2:25 ►

5 And beside this,
giving all diligence,
add to your faith
virtue; and to virtue
knowledge;
6 And to knowl-
edge temperance;
and to temperance
patience; and to
patience godliness;
7 And to godli-
ness brotherly
kindness; and to
brotherly kindness
charity.
8 For if these
things be in you,
and abound, they
make *you that ye shall* neither *be* barren nor
unfruitful in the knowledge of our Lord
Jesus Christ.

1:5-6
Growing Spiritually
◄ 1 Peter 2:2
2 Peter 3:18 ►

1:5-7
Kindness
◄ Colossians 3:12 ►

1:5-7
Self-control
◄ James 3:2 ►

Turn to the next page for more . . .

[9]But he that
lacketh these things
is blind, and cannot
see afar off, and
hath forgotten that
he was purged from
his old sins.
[10]Wherefore the
rather, brethren,
give diligence to
make your calling
and election sure:
for if ye do these
things, ye shall
never fall:
[11]For so an en-
trance shall be min-
istered unto you
abundantly into the
everlasting king-
dom of our Lord
and Saviour Jesus
Christ.
[12]Wherefore I
will not be negligent to put you always in
remembrance of these things, though ye
know *them,* and be established in the
present truth.
[13]Yea, I think it meet, as long as I am in
this tabernacle, to stir you up by putting
you in remembrance;
[14]Knowing that shortly I must put off
this my tabernacle, even as our Lord Jesus
Christ hath shewed me.
[15]Moreover I will endeavour that ye may
be able after my decease to have these
things always in remembrance.
[16]For we have not followed cunningly
devised fables, when we made known unto
you the power and coming of our Lord
Jesus Christ, but were eyewitnesses of his
majesty.
[17]For he received from God the Father
honour and glory, when there came such
a voice to him from the excellent glory,
This is my beloved Son, in whom I am well
pleased.
[18]And this voice which came from heav-
en we heard, when we were with him in
the holy mount.
[19]We have also a
more sure word of
prophecy; where-
unto ye do well that
ye take heed, as
unto a light that
shineth in a dark
place, until the day
dawn, and the day
star arise in your
hearts:
[20]Knowing this first, that no prophecy
of the scripture is of any private interpretation.
[21]For the prophecy came not in old time
by the will of man: but holy men of God
spake *as they were* moved by the Holy
Ghost.

1:6
Quitting
◄ James 5:7 ►

1:9
Old Life
◄ 1 Peter 4:3 ►

1:10 Diligence
◄ Hebrews 6:11
2 Peter 3:14 ►

1:10-11
How to Be Saved
◄ James 1:21
Revelation 22:14 ►

1:19
The Bible as a Guide
◄ Proverbs 6:23 ►

1:19
Watch Out!
◄ 1 Timothy 4:16 ►

2

[1]But there were false prophets also
among the people, even as there shall be
false teachers among you, who privily shall
bring in damnable heresies, even denying
the Lord that bought them, and bring
upon themselves swift destruction.
[2]And many shall
follow their perni-
cious ways; by rea-
son of whom the
way of truth shall
be evil spoken of.
[3]And through covetousness shall they
with feigned words make merchandise of
you: whose judgment now of a long time
lingereth not, and their damnation
slumbereth not.
[4]For if God spared not the angels that
sinned, but cast *them* down to hell, and
delivered *them* into chains of darkness, to
be reserved unto judgment;
[5]And spared not the old world, but
saved Noah the eighth *person,* a preacher
of righteousness, bringing in the flood
upon the world of the ungodly;
[6]And turning the cities of Sodom and
Gomorrah into ashes condemned *them*
with an overthrow, making *them* an
ensample unto those that after should live
ungodly;
[7]And delivered just Lot, vexed with the
filthy conversation of the wicked:
[8](For that righteous man dwelling
among them, in seeing and hearing, vexed
his righteous soul from day to day with
their unlawful deeds;)
[9]The Lord
knoweth how to
deliver the godly
out of temptations,
and to reserve the
unjust unto the day

2:2
Embarrassing God
◄ Romans 2:23-24 ►

2:9
Evil Attacks
◄ Hebrews 2:15 ►

of judgment to be
punished:
10But chiefly
them that walk after
the flesh in the lust
of uncleanness, and
despise government. Presumptuous *are*
they, selfwilled, they are not afraid to speak
evil of dignities.

> **2:9 Temptation**
> ◄ James 1:12
> Revelation 3:10 ►

11Whereas angels, which are greater in
power and might, bring not railing accusation against them before the Lord.
12But these, as natural brute beasts, made
to be taken and destroyed, speak evil of the
things that they understand not; and shall
utterly perish in their own corruption;
13And shall re-
ceive the reward of
unrighteousness, *as*
they that count it
pleasure to riot in
the daytime. Spots
they are and blem-
ishes, sporting
themselves with
their own deceiv-
ings while they
feast with you;

> **2:13 Luxury**
> ◄ James 5:5 ►

> **2:13 Moderation**
> ◄ 1 Peter 4:3 ►

14Having eyes
full of adultery, and
that cannot cease
from sin; beguiling
unstable souls: an
heart they have ex-
ercised with covetous practices; cursed
children:

> **2:14 Source of Evil**
> ◄ Hebrews 3:12 ►

15Which have forsaken the right way,
and are gone astray, following the way of
Balaam *the son* of Bosor, who loved the
wages of unrighteousness;
16But was re-
buked for his iniq-
uity: the dumb ass
speaking with
man's voice forbad
the madness of the
prophet.

> **2:16 Blinded by Sin**
> ◄ 1 Corinthians 2:8 ►

17These are wells without water, clouds
that are carried with a tempest; to whom
the mist of darkness is reserved for ever.
18For when they speak great swelling
words of vanity, they allure through the
lusts of the flesh, *through much* wantonness, those that were clean escaped from
them who live in error.
19While they
promise them liber-
ty, they themselves
are the servants of
corruption: for of
whom a man is
overcome, of the same is he brought in
bondage.

> **2:19 Bad Habits**
> ◄ 2 Timothy 2:26 ►

20For if after
they have escaped
the pollutions of the
world through the
knowledge of the
Lord and Saviour
Jesus Christ, they
are again entangled
therein, and over-
come, the latter end
is worse with them
than the beginning.

> **2:20 Callousness**
> ◄ 2 Timothy 3:13 ►

> **2:20 Giving In**
> ◄ Mark 10:35-37 ►

21For it had been better for them not to
have known the way of righteousness,
than, after they have known *it,* to turn from
the holy commandment delivered unto
them.
22But it is happened unto them according to the true proverb, The dog *is* turned
to his own vomit again; and the sow that
was washed to her wallowing in the mire.

3

1This second epistle, beloved, I now
write unto you; in *both* which I stir up your
pure minds by way of remembrance:
2That ye may be mindful of the words
which were spoken before by the holy
prophets, and of the commandment of us
the apostles of the Lord and Saviour:
3Knowing this first, that there shall come
in the last days scoffers, walking after their
own lusts,
4And saying, Where is the promise of
his coming? for since the fathers fell asleep,
all things continue as *they were* from the
beginning of the creation.
5For this they willingly are ignorant of,
that by the word of God the heavens were
of old, and the earth standing out of the
water and in the water:
6Whereby the world that then was, being overflowed with water, perished:
7But the heavens and the earth, which
are now, by the same word are kept in
store, reserved unto fire against the day of
judgment and perdition of ungodly men.
8But, beloved, be not ignorant of this
one thing, that one day *is* with the Lord as

a thousand years, and a thousand years as one day.

9 The Lord is not slack concerning his promise, as some men count slackness; but is longsuffering to us-ward, not willing that any should perish, but that all should come to repentance.

> **3:9**
> **God's Patience**
> ◄ 1 Peter 3:20 ►

> **3:9**
> **Pray and Wait**
> ◄ James 5:7 ►

> **3:9**
> **Salvation for Anyone**
> ◄ Titus 2:11-12 ►

10 But the day of the Lord will come as a thief in the night; in the which the heavens shall pass away with a great noise, and the elements shall melt with fervent heat, the earth also and the works that are therein shall be burned up.

> **3:10**
> **Second Coming**
> ◄ Hebrews 9:28 ►

11 *Seeing* then *that* all these things shall be dissolved, what manner *of persons* ought ye to be in *all* holy conversation and godliness,

> **3:11**
> **Holiness**
> ◄ 1 Peter 1:16 ►

> **3:11**
> **Living for God**
> ◄ James 3:13 ►

12 Looking for and hasting unto the coming of the day of God, wherein the heavens being on fire shall be dissolved, and the elements shall melt with fervent heat?

13 Nevertheless we, according to his promise, look for new heavens and a new earth, wherein dwelleth righteousness.

14 Wherefore, beloved, seeing that ye look for such things, be diligent that ye may be found of him in peace, without spot, and blameless.

> **3:14**
> **Diligence**
> ◄ 2 Peter 1:10 ►

15 And account *that* the longsuffering of our Lord *is* salvation; even as our beloved brother Paul also according to the wisdom given unto him hath written unto you;

16 As also in all *his* epistles, speaking in them of these things; in which are some things hard to be understood, which they that are unlearned and unstable wrest, as *they do* also the other scriptures, unto their own destruction.

> **3:17**
> **Bad Examples**
> ◄ Hebrews 12:15 ►

> **3:17**
> **Saying No**
> ◄ Ephesians 6:13 ►

17 Ye therefore, beloved, seeing ye know *these things* before, beware lest ye also, being led away with the error of the wicked, fall from your own stedfastness.

> **3:17**
> **Sin (Warnings)**
> ◄ Hebrews 12:25 ►

> **3:17**
> **Standing Strong**
> ◄ 1 Peter 5:9 ►

18 But grow in grace, and *in* the knowledge of our Lord and Saviour Jesus Christ. To him *be* glory both now and for ever. Amen.

> **3:18**
> **Growing Spiritually**
> ◄ 2 Peter 1:5-6 ►

1 John

AUTHOR
John the disciple

MAIN POINT
Here are the facts about Christianity; grow strong in your faith.

DATE WRITTEN
Probably between A.D. 85 and 90

5 CHAPTERS

MAIN PEOPLE
John, Jesus

SPECIAL FEATURES
- *Shows why John is called the apostle of love, for love is mentioned throughout the letter*
- *Uses brief statements and simple contrasts (light and darkness, love and fear, etc.) in a powerful way*
- *Encourages readers to be down-right bold in their prayers*
- *Fifth of the General epistles*

HOW THE BOOK GOT ITS NAME
The letter is the elderly disciple's first letter in the Bible, written to several churches.

1 1 That which was from the beginning,
which we have heard, which we have seen
with our eyes, which we have looked upon,
and our hands have handled, of the Word
of life;
2 (For the life was manifested, and we
have seen *it,* and bear witness, and shew
unto you that eternal life, which was with
the Father, and was manifested unto us;)
3 That which we have seen and heard
declare we unto you, that ye also may have
fellowship with us: and truly our fellowship *is* with the Father, and with his Son
Jesus Christ.
4 And these things write we unto you,
that your joy may be full.
5 This then is the message which we have
heard of him, and declare unto you, that
God is light, and in him is no darkness
at all.
6 If we say that we have fellowship with
him, and walk in darkness, we lie, and do
not the truth:
7 But if we walk in the light, as he is in
the light, we have
fellowship one
with another, and
the blood of Jesus
Christ his Son
cleanseth us from
all sin.
8 If we say that we
have no sin, we
deceive ourselves,
and the truth is not
in us.
9 If we confess our
sins, he is faithful
and just to forgive
us *our* sins, and to
cleanse us from all
unrighteousness.

1:8 Everyone Sins
◄ Galatians 3:22
1 John 5:19 ►

1:8 Lying to Yourself
◄ James 1:26
Revelation 3:17 ►

1:9 Confession
◄ Jeremiah 3:13 ►

10 If we say that we have not sinned, we make him a liar, and his word is not in us.

> **1:9**
> **Forgiveness**
> ◄ James 5:15 ►

2

1 My little children, these things write I unto you, that ye sin not. And if any man sin, we have an advocate with the Father, Jesus Christ the righteous:

> **1:9**
> **God's Forgiveness**
> ◄ Hebrews 8:12 ►

2 And he is the propitiation for our sins: and not for ours only, but also for *the sins of* the whole world.

> **2:2 Who Can Be Saved?**
> ◄ 1 Peter 2:24
> Revelation 1:5 ►

3 And hereby we do know that we know him, if we keep his commandments.

4 He that saith, I know him, and keepeth not his commandments, is a liar, and the truth is not in him.

5 But whoso keepeth his word, in him verily is the love of God perfected: hereby know we that we are in him.

6 He that saith he abideth in him ought himself also so to walk, even as he walked.

7 Brethren, I write no new commandment unto you, but an old commandment which ye had from the beginning. The old commandment is the word which ye have heard from the beginning.

8 Again, a new commandment I write unto you, which thing is true in him and in you: because the darkness is past, and the true light now shineth.

9 He that saith he is in the light, and hateth his brother, is in darkness even until now.

> **2:9 Hate**
> ◄ Proverbs 15:17
> 1 John 3:15 ►

10 He that loveth his brother abideth in the light, and there is none occasion of stumbling in him.

11 But he that hateth his brother is in darkness, and walketh in darkness, and knoweth not whither he goeth, because that darkness hath blinded his eyes.

12 I write unto you, little children, because your sins are forgiven you for his name's sake.

13 I write unto you, fathers, because ye have known him *that is* from the beginning. I write unto you, young men, because ye have overcome the wicked one. I write unto you, little children, because ye have known the Father.

> **2:13-14**
> **For Kids Only**
> ◄ Titus 2:6-7 ►

14 I have written unto you, fathers, because ye have known him *that is* from the beginning. I have written unto you, young men, because ye are strong, and the word of God abideth in you, and ye have overcome the wicked one.

15 Love not the world, neither the things *that are* in the world. If any man love the world, the love of the Father is not in him.

16 For all that *is* in the world, the lust of the flesh, and the lust of the eyes, and the pride of life, is not of the Father, but is of the world.

> **2:16**
> **Arrogance**
> ◄ Habakkuk 2:4 ►

17 And the world passeth away, and the lust thereof: but he that doeth the will of God abideth for ever.

> **2:17**
> **Submitting to God**
> ◄ James 4:15 ►

18 Little children, it is the last time: and as ye have heard that antichrist shall come, even now are there many antichrists; whereby we know that it is the last time.

> **2:18**
> **End Times**
> ◄ 1 John 4:3 ►

19 They went out from us, but they were not of us; for if they had been of us, they would *no doubt* have continued with us: but *they went out,* that they might be made manifest that they were not all of us.

20 But ye have an unction from the Holy One, and ye know all things.

> **2:20**
> **True Wisdom**
> ◄ James 3:17 ►

21 I have not written unto you because ye know not the truth, but because ye know it, and that no lie is of the truth.

22 Who is a liar but he that denieth that Jesus is the Christ? He is antichrist, that denieth the Father and the Son.

23 Whosoever denieth the Son, the same

hath not the Father: *(but) he that acknowledgeth the Son hath the Father also.*

24 Let that therefore abide in you, which ye have heard from the beginning. If that which ye have heard from the beginning shall remain in you, ye also shall continue in the Son, and in the Father.

25 And this is the promise that he hath promised us, *even* eternal life.

2:25
God's Promises
◄ 2 Peter 1:4 ►

26 These *things* have I written unto you concerning them that seduce you.

2:27
God's Teaching
◄ 1 Corinthians 2:13 ►

27 But the anointing which ye have received of him abideth in you, and ye need not that any man teach you: but as the same anointing teacheth you of all things, and is truth, and is no lie, and even as it hath taught you, ye shall abide in him.

2:27
The Spirit in You
◄ 2 Timothy 1:14 ►

28 And now, little children, abide in him; that, when he shall appear, we may have confidence, and not be ashamed before him at his coming.

2:28 Watching for Jesus' Return
◄ Titus 2:13 ►

29 If ye know that he is righteous, ye know that every one that doeth righteousness is born of him.

3

1 Behold, what manner of love the Father hath bestowed upon us, that we should be called the sons of God: therefore the world knoweth us not, because it knew him not.

3:1 God's Love
◄ Ephesians 2:4-5
1 John 4:9 ►

2 Beloved, now are we the sons of God, and it doth not yet appear what we shall be: but we know that, when he shall appear, we shall be like him; for we shall see him as he is.

3:2
Good News
◄ 1 Peter 5:4 ►

3 And every man that hath this hope in him purifieth himself, even as he is pure.

4 Whosoever committeth sin transgresseth also the law: for sin is the transgression of the law.

5 And ye know that he was manifested to take away our sins; and in him is no sin.

3:5
What Jesus Did
◄ 1 Peter 2:24 ►

6 Whosoever abideth in him sinneth not: whosoever sinneth hath not seen him, neither known him.

7 Little children, let no man deceive you: he that doeth righteousness is righteous, even as he is righteous.

3:7 Deception
◄ 2 Thessalonians 2:3 ►

8 He that committeth sin is of the devil; for the devil sinneth from the beginning. For this purpose the Son of God was manifested, that he might destroy the works of the devil.

3:8 Defeat of Satan
◄ Hebrews 2:14
Revelation 20:10 ►

9 Whosoever is born of God doth not commit sin; for his seed remaineth in him: and he cannot sin, because he is born of God.

10 In this the children of God are manifest, and the children of the devil: whosoever doeth not righteousness is not of God, neither he that loveth not his brother.

11 For this is the message that ye heard from the beginning, that we should love one another.

12 Not as Cain, *who* was of that wicked one, and slew his brother. And wherefore slew he him? Because his own works were evil, and his brother's righteous.

13 Marvel not, my brethren, if the world hate you.

14 We know that we have passed from death unto life, because we love the brethren. He that loveth not *his* brother abideth in death.

3:14 Love
◄ 1 Corinthians 13:1
1 John 4:20 ►

15 Whosoever hateth his brother is a murderer: and ye know that no

3:15 Hate
◄ 1 John 2:9
1 John 4:20 ►

murderer hath eternal life abiding in him.
16 Hereby perceive we the love *of God,*
because he laid down his life for us: and
we ought to lay down *our* lives for the
brethren.
17 But whoso hath this world's good, and
seeth his brother
have need, and
shutteth up his
bowels *of compas-*
sion from him, how
dwelleth the love of
God in him?

> **3:18 Sincerity**
> ◄ Titus 2:7 ►

18 My little chil-
dren, let us not love
in word, neither in
tongue; but in deed
and in truth.

> **3:20 What God Knows**
> ◄ Hebrews 4:13 ►

19 And hereby we
know that we are of
the truth, and shall
assure our hearts
before him.
20 For if our heart
condemn us, God is
greater than our
heart, and knoweth
all things.

> **3:21 No Condemnation**
> ◄ Romans 8:34 ►

21 Beloved, if our
heart condemn us
not, *then* have we
confidence toward
God.
22 And whatso-
ever we ask, we
receive of him, be-
cause we keep his
commandments,
and do those things
that are pleasing in
his sight.

> **3:22 Answers to Prayer**
> ◄ John 15:7 ►

> **3:22 How to Pray**
> ◄ James 5:16
> 1 John 5:14 ►

> **3:22 Pleasing God**
> ◄ Hebrews 13:16 ►

23 And this is his
commandment,
That we should be-
lieve on the name
of his Son Jesus
Christ, and love
one another, as he
gave us command-
ment.

> **3:23 Faith**
> ◄ James 1:5-6 ►

24 And he that
keepeth his com-
mandments
dwelleth in him,
and he in him. And
hereby we know that he abideth in us, by
the Spirit which he hath given us.

> **3:24 Jesus' Home**
> ◄ Colossians 1:27
> Revelation 3:20 ►

4

1 Beloved, believe not every spirit, but try
the spirits whether they are of God: because many false prophets are gone out
into the world.
2 Hereby know ye
the Spirit of God:
Every spirit that con-
fesseth that Jesus
Christ is come in
the flesh is of God:

> **4:2 Christmas**
> ◄ 1 Timothy 3:16 ►

3 And every spirit
that confesseth not
that Jesus Christ is
come in the flesh is
not of God: and
this is that *spirit* of
antichrist, whereof ye have heard that it
should come; and even now already is it
in the world.

> **4:3 End Times**
> ◄ 1 John 2:18
> 2 John 1:7 ►

4 Ye are of God,
little children, and
have overcome
them: because great-
er is he that is in
you, than he that is
in the world.

> **4:4 Tempted by Satan**
> ◄ James 4:7
> Revelation 3:10 ►

5 They are of the world: therefore speak
they of the world, and the world heareth
them.
6 We are of God: he that knoweth God
heareth us; he that is not of God heareth
not us. Hereby know we the spirit of truth,
and the spirit of error.
7 Beloved, let us
love one another: for
love is of God; and
every one that loveth
is born of God, and
knoweth God.

> **4:7 Loving Others**
> ◄ 1 Peter 1:22 ►

8 He that loveth not knoweth not God;
for God is love.
9 In this was manifested the love of God
toward us, because
that God sent his
only begotten Son
into the world,
that we might live
through him.

> **4:9 God's Love**
> ◄ 1 John 3:1
> 1 John 4:16 ►

10 Herein is love, not that we loved God,
but that he loved us, and sent his Son *to be*
the propitiation for our sins.
11 Beloved, if God so loved us, we ought
also to love one another.

12 No man hath seen God at any time. If we love one another, God dwelleth in us, and his love is perfected in us.

13 Hereby know we that we dwell in him, and he in us, because he hath given us of his Spirit.

14 And we have seen and do testify that the Father sent the Son *to be* the Saviour of the world.

4:14
Why Jesus Came
◄ Hebrews 7:25 ►

15 Whosoever shall confess that Jesus is the Son of God, God dwelleth in him, and he in God.

16 And we have known and believed the love that God hath to us. God is love; and he that dwelleth in love dwelleth in God, and God in him.

4:16
God's Love
◄ 1 John 4:9 ►

4:16
Importance of Love
◄ 1 Timothy 6:11 ►

17 Herein is our love made perfect, that we may have boldness in the day of judgment: because as he is, so are we in this world.

4:17
Approaching God
◄ Hebrews 10:19 ►

18 There is no fear in love; but perfect love casteth out fear: because fear hath torment. He that feareth is not made perfect in love.

19 We love him, because he first loved us.

20 If a man say, I love God, and hateth his brother, he is a liar: for he that loveth not his brother whom he hath seen, how can he love God whom he hath not seen?

4:20
Hate
◄ 1 John 3:15 ►

4:20
Love
◄ 1 John 3:14 ►

21 And this commandment have we from him, That he who loveth God love his brother also.

5

1 Whosoever believeth that Jesus is the Christ is born of God: and every one that loveth him that begat loveth him also that is begotten of him.

5:1
Salvation by Faith
◄ 2 Timothy 3:15 ►

2 By this we know that we love the children of God, when we love God, and keep his commandments.

3 For this is the love of God, that we keep his commandments: and his commandments are not grievous.

4 For whatsoever is born of God overcometh the world: and this is the victory that overcometh the world, *even* our faith.

5 Who is he that overcometh the world, but he that believeth that Jesus is the Son of God?

6 This is he that came by water and blood, *even* Jesus Christ; not by water only, but by water and blood. And it is the Spirit that beareth witness, because the Spirit is truth.

7 For there are three that bear record in heaven, the Father, the Word, and the Holy Ghost: and these three are one.

8 And there are three that bear witness in earth, the spirit, and the water, and the blood: and these three agree in one.

9 If we receive the witness of men, the witness of God is greater: for this is the witness of God which he hath testified of his Son.

10 He that believeth on the Son of God hath the witness in himself: he that believeth not God hath made him a liar; because he believeth not the record that God gave of his Son.

11 And this is the record, that God hath given to us eternal life, and this life is in his Son.

12 He that hath the Son hath life; *and* he that hath not the Son of God hath not life.

5:13
Why the Bible?
◄ 1 Corinthians 10:11 ►

13 These things have I written unto you that believe on the name of the Son of God; that ye may know that ye have eternal life, and that ye may believe on the name of the Son of God.

5:14
Benefits of Faith
◄ 1 Peter 2:6 ►

5:14
How to Pray
◄ 1 John 3:22 ►

14 And this is the

confidence that we have in him, that, if
we ask any thing according to his will, he
heareth us:
15 And if we know that he hear us, whatsoever we ask, we know that we have the
petitions that we desired of him.
16 If any man see his brother sin a sin
which is not unto death, he shall ask, and
he shall give him life for them that sin not
unto death. There is a sin unto death: I do
not say that he shall pray for it.
17 All unrighteousness is sin: and there
is a sin not unto death.
18 We know that whosoever is born of
God sinneth not; but he that is begotten
of God keepeth himself, and that wicked
one toucheth him not.
19 *And* we know
that we are of God,
and the whole
world lieth in wick-
edness.
20 And we know
that the Son of God is come, and hath
given us an understanding, that we may
know him that is true, and we are in him
that is true, *even* in his Son Jesus Christ.
This is the true God, and eternal life.
21 Little children, keep yourselves from
idols. Amen.

5:19
Everyone Sins
◄ 1 John 1:8 ►

2 John

AUTHOR
John the disciple

MAIN POINT
Truth and love matter more than anything else in the Christian walk.

DATE WRITTEN
About A.D. 90

1 CHAPTER

❑

MAIN PEOPLE

John, the elect lady, her children

SPECIAL FEATURES

- *Contains the message of the New Testament in a nutshell*
- *As one of the Bible's briefest books, proves the saying that good things come in small packages*
- *Tells us in no uncertain terms to love one another*
- *Sixth of the General epistles*

HOW THE BOOK GOT ITS NAME

This second letter from John was written to an unnamed woman or possibly to a church.

1 The elder unto the elect lady and her
children, whom I love in the truth; and
not I only, but also all they that have
known the truth;
2 For the truth's sake, which dwelleth in
us, and shall be with us for ever.
3 Grace be with you, mercy, *and* peace,
from God the Father, and from the Lord
Jesus Christ, the Son of the Father, in truth
and love.
4 I rejoiced greatly that I found of thy
children walking in truth, as we have received a commandment from the Father.
5 And now I beseech thee, lady, not as
though I wrote a new commandment unto
thee, but that which we had from the beginning, that we love one another.
6 And this is love, that we walk after his
commandments. This is the commandment, That, as ye have heard from the beginning, ye should walk in it.
7 For many de-
ceivers are entered
into the world, who
confess not that
Jesus Christ is come
in the flesh. This is
a deceiver and an antichrist.

1:7
End Times
◄ 1 John 4:3 ►

8 Look to yourselves, that we lose not
those things which we have wrought, but
that we receive a full reward.
9 Whosoever transgresseth, and abideth
not in the doctrine of Christ, hath not God.
He that abideth in the doctrine of Christ,
he hath both the Father and the Son.
10 If there come
any unto you, and
bring not this doc-
trine, receive him
not into *your* house,
neither bid him
God speed:

1:10
Bad Friends
◄ 2 Corinthians 6:14 ►

11For he that biddeth him God speed is partaker of his evil deeds.
12Having many things to write unto you, I would not *write* with paper and ink: but I trust to come unto you, and speak face to face, that our joy may be full.
13The children of thy elect sister greet thee. Amen.

3 John

AUTHOR
John the disciple

MAIN POINT
Be generous, be loving. Welcome people into your heart and into your home.

DATE WRITTEN
About A.D. 90

MAIN PEOPLE
John, Gaius, Diotrephes, Demetrius

SPECIAL FEATURES
- ✖ *Describes three lives to learn from—two by positive example, one by negative*
- ✖ *Convinces readers of the need to support and help Christian workers and missionaries*
- ✖ *Seventh of the General epistles*

HOW THE BOOK GOT ITS NAME
This third letter from John was written to Gaius, a Christian leader.

1 CHAPTER

❑

1The elder unto the wellbeloved Gaius,
whom I love in the truth.
2Beloved, I wish above all things that
thou mayest prosper and be in health, even
as thy soul prospereth.
3For I rejoiced greatly, when the brethren came and testified of the truth that is
in thee, even as thou walkest in the truth.
4I have no greater joy than to hear that
my children walk in truth.
5Beloved, thou doest faithfully whatsoever thou doest to the brethren, and to
strangers;
6Which have borne witness of thy charity before the church: whom if thou bring
forward on their journey after a godly sort,
thou shalt do well:
7Because that for his name's sake they
went forth, taking nothing of the Gentiles.
8We therefore ought to receive such, that
we might be fellowhelpers to the truth.
9I wrote unto the church: but Diotrephes, who loveth to have the preeminence
among them, receiveth us not.
10Wherefore, if I come, I will remember
his deeds which he doeth, prating against
us with malicious words: and not content
therewith, neither doth he himself receive
the brethren, and forbiddeth them that
would, and casteth *them* out of the church.
11Beloved, follow not that which is evil,
but that which is good. He that doeth good
is of God: but he that doeth evil hath not
seen God.
12Demetrius hath good report of all
men, and of the truth itself: yea, and we
also bear record; and ye know that our
record is true.
13I had many things to write, but I will
not with ink and pen write unto thee:
14But I trust I shall shortly see thee, and
we shall speak face to face. Peace *be* to thee.
Our friends salute thee. Greet the friends
by name.

Jude

AUTHOR
Jude, James's brother and Jesus' half-brother

MAIN POINT
Always be alert for false teaching and stay strong in your faith.

DATE WRITTEN
About A.D. 65

MAIN PEOPLE

Jude, James, Jesus

SPECIAL FEATURES

- *Talks about burglars to describe how false teachers trick people*
- *Refers to exciting characters from the Old Testament, including the archangel Michael*
- *Eighth of the General epistles*

HOW THE BOOK GOT ITS NAME

This brief letter was written by Jude to Jewish Christians specifically and all Christians generally.

1 CHAPTER

☐

1 Jude, the servant of Jesus Christ, and
brother of James, to them that are sanctified by God the Father, and preserved in
Jesus Christ, *and* called:
2 Mercy unto you, and peace, and love,
be multiplied.
3 Beloved, when I gave all diligence to
write unto you of the common salvation,
it was needful for me to write unto you,
and exhort *you* that ye should earnestly
contend for the faith which was once delivered unto the saints.
4 For there are certain men crept in unawares, who were before of old ordained
to this condemnation, ungodly men, turning the grace of our God into lasciviousness, and denying the only Lord God, and
our Lord Jesus Christ.
5 I will therefore put you in remembrance, though ye once knew this, how that
the Lord, having saved the people out of
the land of Egypt, afterward destroyed
them that believed not.
6 And the angels which kept not their
first estate, but left their own habitation,
he hath reserved in everlasting chains under darkness unto the judgment of the
great day.
7 Even as Sodom and Gomorrha, and the
cities about them in like manner, giving
themselves over to fornication, and going
after strange flesh, are set forth for an
example, suffering the vengeance of eternal fire.
8 Likewise also
these *filthy* dream-
ers defile the flesh,
despise dominion,
and speak evil of
dignities.
9 Yet Michael the
archangel, when
contending with
the devil he disput-
ed about the body
of Moses, durst not

1:8
Rebellion
◄ Romans 13:2 ►

1:8
Rulers
◄ 1 Peter 2:17 ►

bring against him a railing accusation, but
said, The Lord rebuke thee.
10But these speak evil of those things
which they know not: but what they know
naturally, as brute beasts, in those things
they corrupt themselves.
11Woe unto them! for they have gone in
the way of Cain, and ran greedily after the
error of Balaam for reward, and perished
in the gainsaying of Core.
12These are spots in your feasts of charity, when they feast with you, feeding
themselves without fear: clouds *they are*
without water, carried about of winds; trees
whose fruit withereth, without fruit, twice
dead, plucked up by the roots;
13Raging waves of the sea, foaming out
their own shame; wandering stars, to
whom is reserved the blackness of darkness for ever.
14And Enoch
also, the seventh
from Adam, proph-
esied of these, say-
ing, Behold, the
Lord cometh with
ten thousands of his saints,

1:14-15
Jesus' Return: Why?
◄ 2 Timothy 4:1 ►

15To execute judgment upon all, and to
convince all that are ungodly among them
of all their ungodly deeds which they
have ungodly committed, and of all
their hard *speeches*
which ungodly sin-
ners have spoken
against him.
16These are mur-
murers, complain-
ers, walking after their own lusts; and their
mouth speaketh great swelling *words,* having men's persons in admiration because
of advantage.

1:16
Favoritism
◄ James 2:4 ►

17But, beloved, remember ye the words
which were spoken before of the apostles
of our Lord Jesus Christ;
18How that they
told you there
should be mockers
in the last time,
who should walk
after their own un-
godly lusts.

1:18
Mockers
◄ Isaiah 57:4 ►

19These be they who separate themselves, sensual, having not the Spirit.
20But ye, beloved, building up yourselves on your most holy faith, praying in
the Holy Ghost,
21Keep your-
selves in the love of
God, looking for
the mercy of our
Lord Jesus Christ
unto eternal life.

1:21 Love for God
◄ 2 Thessalonians 3:5 ►

22And of some have compassion, making a difference:
23And others save with fear, pulling *them*
out of the fire; hating even the garment
spotted by the flesh.
24Now unto him that is able to keep you
from falling, and to present *you* faultless
before the presence of his glory with exceeding joy,
25To the only wise God our Saviour, *be*
glory and majesty, dominion and power,
both now and ever. Amen.

Revelation

AUTHOR
John the apostle

MAIN POINT
Be hopeful but be warned: Jesus is the Christ who reigns and will come again!

DATE WRITTEN
About A.D. 95

22 CHAPTERS

MAIN PEOPLE

John, Jesus

SPECIAL FEATURES

- *Opens with powerful letters to seven churches in Asia, which we can learn from today*
- *Features the scene of God on his heavenly throne, complete with crowns, lightning, winged creatures, and more*
- *Uses many prophecies from other parts of the Bible*
- *Tells of a grand white horse from heaven, whose rider's name is Faithful and True*
- *Describes what will happen to Satan*
- *Tells how the world will end (and begin again)*
- *Only book of Prophecy in the New Testament*

HOW THE BOOK GOT ITS NAME

The name revelation refers to the visions of the future that God revealed to John.

1
1 The Revelation of Jesus Christ, which
God gave unto him, to shew unto his servants things which must shortly come to
pass; and he sent and signified *it* by his
angel unto his servant John:
2 Who bare record of the word of God,
and of the testimony of Jesus Christ, and
of all things that he saw.
3 Blessed *is* he that readeth, and they that
hear the words of this prophecy, and keep
those things which are written therein: for
the time *is* at hand.
4 John to the seven churches which are
in Asia: Grace *be* unto you, and peace, from
him which is, and which was, and which
is to come; and from the seven Spirits
which are before his throne;
5 And from Jesus Christ, *who is* the faithful witness, *and* the first begotten of the
dead, and the prince of the kings of the

earth. Unto him
that loved us, and
washed us from our
sins in his own
blood,
6And hath made
us kings and priests
unto God and his
Father; to him *be*
glory and domin-
ion for ever and
ever. Amen.
7Behold, he
cometh with
clouds; and every
eye shall see him,
and they *also* which
pierced him: and
all kindreds of the
earth shall wail because of him. Even so,
Amen.

> **1:5**
> **Value of People**
> ◄ 1 Peter 1:18-19 ►

> **1:5**
> **Who Can Be Saved?**
> ◄ 1 John 2:2 ►

> **1:7**
> **Bad News**
> ◄ 2 Thessalonians 1:7-8

8I am Alpha and Omega, the beginning
and the ending, saith the Lord, which is,
and which was, and which is to come, the
Almighty.
9I John, who also am your brother, and
companion in tribulation, and in the kingdom and patience of Jesus Christ, was in
the isle that is called Patmos, for the word
of God, and for the testimony of Jesus
Christ.
10I was in the Spirit on the Lord's day,
and heard behind me a great voice, as of a
trumpet,
11Saying, I am Alpha and Omega, the
first and the last: and, What thou seest,
write in a book, and send *it* unto the sev-
en churches which are in Asia; unto Ephesus, and unto Smyrna, and unto Pergamos,
and unto Thyatira, and unto Sardis, and
unto Philadelphia, and unto Laodicea.
12And I turned to see the voice that
spake with me. And being turned, I saw
seven golden candlesticks;
13And in the midst of the seven candlesticks *one* like unto the Son of man, clothed
with a garment down to the foot, and girt
about the paps with a golden girdle.
14His head and *his* hairs *were* white like
wool, as white as snow; and his eyes *were*
as a flame of fire;
15And his feet like unto fine brass, as if
they burned in a furnace; and his voice as
the sound of many waters.
16And he had in his right hand seven
stars: and out of his mouth went a sharp
twoedged sword: and his countenance *was*
as the sun shineth in his strength.
17And when I saw him, I fell at his feet
as dead. And he laid his right hand upon
me, saying unto me, Fear not; I am the first
and the last:
18I *am* he that liveth, and was dead; and,
behold, I am alive for evermore, Amen;
and have the keys of hell and of death.
19Write the things which thou hast seen,
and the things which are, and the things
which shall be hereafter;
20The mystery of the seven stars which
thou sawest in my right hand, and the sev-
en golden candlesticks. The seven stars are
the angels of the seven churches: and the
seven candlesticks which thou sawest are
the seven churches.

2

1Unto the angel of the church of Ephesus write; These things saith he that
holdeth the seven stars in his right hand,
who walketh in the midst of the seven
golden candlesticks;
2I know thy works, and thy labour, and
thy patience, and how thou canst not bear
them which are evil: and thou hast tried
them which say they are apostles, and are
not, and hast found them liars:
3And hast borne, and hast patience, and
for my name's sake hast laboured, and hast
not fainted.
4Nevertheless I have *somewhat* against
thee, because thou hast left thy first love.
5Remember therefore from whence thou
art fallen, and repent, and do the first
works; or else I will come unto thee quickly, and will remove thy candlestick out of
his place, except thou repent.
6But this thou hast, that thou hatest the
deeds of the Nicolaitanes, which I also
hate.
7He that hath an ear, let him hear what
the Spirit saith unto the churches; To him
that overcometh will I give to eat of the
tree of life, which is in the midst of the
paradise of God.
8And unto the angel of the church in
Smyrna write; These things saith the first
and the last, which
was dead, and is
alive;
9I know thy
works, and tribula-
tion, and poverty,

> **2:9 Suffering**
> ◄ 1 Thessalonians 3:4
> Revelation 7:14 ►

(but thou art rich) and *I know* the blasphemy of them which say they are Jews, and are not, but *are* the synagogue of Satan.

10 Fear none of those things which thou shalt suffer: behold, the devil shall cast *some* of you into prison, that ye may be tried; and ye shall have tribulation ten days: be thou faithful unto death, and I will give thee a crown of life.

2:10
Expecting Pain
◄ 2 Timothy 3:12 ►

2:10
Invisible Gifts
◄ John 10:28 ►

11 He that hath an ear, let him hear what the Spirit saith unto the churches; He that overcometh shall not be hurt of the second death.

12 And to the angel of the church in Pergamos write; These things saith he which hath the sharp sword with two edges;

13 I know thy works, and where thou dwellest, *even* where Satan's seat *is*: and thou holdest fast my name, and hast not denied my faith, even in those days wherein Antipas *was* my faithful martyr, who was slain among you, where Satan dwelleth.

14 But I have a few things against thee, because thou hast there them that hold the doctrine of Balaam, who taught Balac to cast a stumblingblock before the children of Israel, to eat things sacrificed unto idols, and to commit fornication.

15 So hast thou also them that hold the doctrine of the Nicolaitanes, which thing I hate.

16 Repent; or else I will come unto thee quickly, and will fight against them with the sword of my mouth.

17 He that hath an ear, let him hear what the Spirit saith unto the churches; To him that overcometh will I give to eat of the hidden manna, and will give him a white stone, and in the stone a new name written, which no man knoweth saving he that receiveth *it*.

18 And unto the angel of the church in Thyatira write; These things saith the Son of God, who hath his eyes like unto a flame of fire, and his feet *are* like fine brass;

19 I know thy works, and charity, and service, and faith, and thy patience, and thy works; and the last *to be* more than the first.

20 Notwithstanding I have a few things against thee, because thou sufferest that woman Jezebel, which calleth herself a prophetess, to teach and to seduce my servants to commit fornication, and to eat things sacrificed unto idols.

21 And I gave her space to repent of her fornication; and she repented not.

22 Behold, I will cast her into a bed, and them that commit adultery with her into great tribulation, except they repent of their deeds.

23 And I will kill her children with death; and all the churches shall know that I am he which searcheth the reins and hearts: and I will give unto every one of you according to your works.

2:23
Actions Judged
◄ 1 Peter 1:17
Revelation 20:12 ►

24 But unto you I say, and unto the rest in Thyatira, as many as have not this doctrine, and which have not known the depths of Satan, as they speak; I will put upon you none other burden.

25 But that which ye have *already* hold fast till I come.

26 And he that overcometh, and keepeth my works unto the end, to him will I give power over the nations:

27 And he shall rule them with a rod of iron; as the vessels of a potter shall they be broken to shivers: even as I received of my Father.

28 And I will give him the morning star.

29 He that hath an ear, let him hear what the Spirit saith unto the churches.

3

1 And unto the angel of the church in Sardis write; These things saith he that hath the seven Spirits of God, and the seven stars; I know thy works, that thou hast a name that thou livest, and art dead.

2 Be watchful, and strengthen the things which remain, that are ready to die: for I have not found thy works perfect before God.

3:2
Pitfalls
◄ 1 Peter 5:8 ►

3 Remember therefore how thou hast received and heard, and hold fast, and repent. If therefore thou shalt not watch, I

will come on thee
as a thief, and thou
shalt not know
what hour I will
come upon thee.

> **3:3**
> **Jesus' Return: When?**
> ◄ 1 Thessalonians 5:2
> Revelation 16:15 ►

4Thou hast a few
names even in Sar-
dis which have not
defiled their gar-
ments; and they
shall walk with me
in white: for they
are worthy.

> **3:4**
> **Walking with God**
> ◄ Malachi 2:6 ►

5He that overcometh, the same shall be
clothed in white raiment; and I will not
blot out his name out of the book of life,
but I will confess his name before my Father, and before his angels.
6He that hath an ear, let him hear what
the Spirit saith unto the churches.
7And to the angel of the church in Philadelphia write; These things saith he that
is holy, he that is true, he that hath the key
of David, he that openeth, and no man
shutteth; and shutteth, and no man
openeth;
8I know thy
works: behold, I
have set before thee
an open door, and
no man can shut it:
for thou hast a lit-
tle strength, and hast kept my word, and
hast not denied my name.

> **3:8**
> **God's Presence**
> ◄ Ephesians 3:12 ►

9Behold, I will make them of the synagogue of Satan, which say they are Jews,
and are not, but do lie; behold, I will make
them to come and
worship before thy
feet, and to know
that I have loved
thee.

> **3:10**
> **Temptation**
> ◄ 2 Peter 2:9 ►

10Because thou
hast kept the word
of my patience, I
also will keep thee
from the hour of
temptation, which
shall come upon all
the world, to try
them that dwell
upon the earth.

> **3:10**
> **Tempted by Satan**
> ◄ 1 John 4:4
> Revelation 3:21 ►

11Behold, I come
quickly: hold that
fast which thou
hast, that no man
take thy crown.

> **3:11**
> **Determination**
> ◄ 1 Peter 1:13 ►

> **3:11 Jesus' Return**
> ◄ 1 Thessalonians 5:5-6
> Revelation 16:15 ►

12Him that
overcometh will I
make a pillar in the
temple of my God,
and he shall go no
more out: and I will
write upon him the
name of my God,
and the name of
the city of my God,
which is new Jerusalem, which cometh
down out of heaven from my God: and *I
will write upon him* my new name.

> **3:11**
> **Ready for Jesus' Return**
> ◄ James 5:8
> Revelation 22:20 ►

13He that hath an ear, let him hear what
the Spirit saith unto the churches.
14And unto the angel of the church of
the Laodiceans write; These things saith the
Amen, the faithful and true witness, the
beginning of the creation of God;
15I know thy works, that thou art neither cold nor hot: I would thou wert cold
or hot.
16So then because thou art lukewarm,
and neither cold nor hot, I will spue thee
out of my mouth.
17Because thou
sayest, I am rich,
and increased with
goods, and have
need of nothing;
and knowest not
that thou art
wretched, and mis-
erable, and poor,
and blind, and na-
ked:

> **3:17**
> **Self-righteousness**
> ◄ 2 Corinthians 10:12 ►

> **3:17**
> **Lying to Yourself**
> ◄ 1 John 1:8 ►

18I counsel thee
to buy of me gold
tried in the fire, that
thou mayest be
rich; and white
raiment, that thou
mayest be clothed,
and *that* the shame of thy nakedness do
not appear; and anoint thine eyes with
eyesalve, that thou mayest see.

> **3:17**
> **Poverty**
> ◄ Ephesians 2:12 ►

19As many as I
love, I rebuke and
chasten: be zealous
therefore, and re-
pent.
20Behold, I stand
at the door, and

> **3:19**
> **Difficulties**
> ◄ John 15:2 ►

knock: if any man
hear my voice, and
open the door, I
will come in to
him, and will sup
with him, and he
with me.
21 To him that
overcometh will I
grant to sit with me
in my throne, even
as I also overcame,
and am set down
with my Father in
his throne.
22 He that hath an
ear, let him hear
what the Spirit saith
unto the churches.

4

1 After this I
looked, and, behold,
a door *was*
opened in heaven:
and the first voice
which I heard *was* as it were of a trumpet
talking with me; which said, Come up
hither, and I will shew thee things which
must be hereafter.
2 And immediately I was in the spirit:
and, behold, a throne was set in heaven,
and *one* sat on the throne.
3 And he that sat was to look upon like a
jasper and a sardine stone: and *there was* a
rainbow round about the throne, in sight
like unto an emerald.
4 And round about the throne *were* four
and twenty seats: and upon the seats I saw
four and twenty elders sitting, clothed in
white raiment; and they had on their heads
crowns of gold.
5 And out of the throne proceeded lightnings
and thunderings and voices: and
there were seven lamps of fire burning before
the throne, which are the seven Spirits
of God.
6 And before the throne *there was* a sea
of glass like unto crystal: and in the midst
of the throne, and round about the throne,
were four beasts full of eyes before and
behind.
7 And the first beast *was* like a lion, and
the second beast like a calf, and the third
beast had a face as a man, and the fourth
beast *was* like a flying eagle.
8 And the four beasts had each of them
six wings about *him;* and *they were* full of
eyes within: and they rest not day and
night, saying, Holy, holy, holy, Lord God
Almighty, which was, and is, and is to
come.
9 And when those beasts give glory and
honour and thanks to him that sat on the
throne, who liveth for ever and ever,
10 The four and twenty elders fall down
before him that sat on the throne, and
worship him that liveth for ever and ever,
and cast their crowns before the throne,
saying,
11 Thou art worthy, O Lord, to receive
glory and honour and power: for thou hast
created all things, and for thy pleasure they
are and were created.

3:20 Change
◄ 2 Corinthians 5:20
►

3:20
Jesus' Home
◄ 1 John 3:24 ►

3:21 Good Rewarded
◄ 1 Corinthians 6:2
Revelation 5:10 ►

3:21
Tempted by Satan
◄ Revelation 3:10 ►

5

1 And I saw in the right hand of him that
sat on the throne a book written within
and on the backside, sealed with seven
seals.
2 And I saw a strong angel proclaiming
with a loud voice, Who is worthy to open
the book, and to loose the seals thereof?
3 And no man in heaven, nor in earth,
neither under the earth, was able to open
the book, neither to look thereon.
4 And I wept much, because no man was
found worthy to open and to read the
book, neither to look thereon.
5 And one of the elders saith unto me,
Weep not: behold, the Lion of the tribe of
Juda, the Root of David, hath prevailed to
open the book, and to loose the seven seals
thereof.
6 And I beheld,
and, lo, in the
midst of the throne
and of the four
beasts, and in the
midst of the elders,
stood a Lamb as it had been slain, having
seven horns and seven eyes, which are the
seven Spirits of God sent forth into all the
earth.
7 And he came and took the book out of
the right hand of him that sat upon the
throne.
8 And when he had taken the book, the
four beasts and four *and* twenty elders fell
down before the Lamb, having every one
of them harps, and golden vials full of
odours, which are the prayers of saints.
9 And they sung a new song, saying, Thou
art worthy to take the book, and to open

5:6 Jesus the Lamb
◄ 1 Peter 1:19
Revelation 6:1 ►

the seals thereof: for thou wast slain, and
hast redeemed us to God by thy blood out
of every kindred, and tongue, and people,
and nation;
10And hast made
us unto our God
kings and priests:
and we shall reign
on the earth.

5:10 Good Rewarded
◄ Revelation 3:21
Revelation 11:12 ►

11And I beheld,
and I heard the voice of many angels round
about the throne and the beasts and the
elders: and the number of them was ten
thousand times ten thousand, and thousands of thousands;
12Saying with a loud voice, Worthy is
the Lamb that was slain to receive power,
and riches, and wisdom, and strength, and
honour, and glory, and blessing.
13And every creature which is in heav-
en, and on the earth, and under the earth,
and such as are in the sea, and all that are
in them, heard I saying, Blessing, and
honour, and glory, and power, *be* unto him
that sitteth upon the throne, and unto the
Lamb for ever and ever.
14And the four beasts said, Amen. And
the four *and* twenty elders fell down and
worshipped him that liveth for ever and
ever.

6

1And I saw when
the Lamb opened
one of the seals,
and I heard, as it
were the noise of
thunder, one of the

6:1 Jesus the Lamb
◄ Revelation 5:6
Revelation 7:9 ►

four beasts saying, Come and see.
2And I saw, and behold a white horse:
and he that sat on him had a bow; and a
crown was given unto him: and he went
forth conquering, and to conquer.
3And when he had opened the second
seal, I heard the second beast say, Come
and see.
4And there went out another horse *that
was* red: and *power* was given to him that
sat thereon to take peace from the earth,
and that they should kill one another: and
there was given unto him a great sword.
5And when he had opened the third
seal, I heard the third beast say, Come and
see. And I beheld, and lo a black horse;
and he that sat on him had a pair of balances in his hand.
6And I heard a voice in the midst of the
four beasts say, A measure of wheat for a
penny, and three measures of barley for a
penny; and *see* thou hurt not the oil and
the wine.
7And when he had opened the fourth
seal, I heard the voice of the fourth beast
say, Come and see.
8And I looked, and behold a pale horse:
and his name that sat on him was Death,
and Hell followed with him. And power
was given unto them over the fourth part
of the earth, to kill with sword, and with
hunger, and with death, and with the
beasts of the earth.
9And when he had opened the fifth seal,
I saw under the altar the souls of them that
were slain for the word of God, and for
the testimony which they held:
10And they cried with a loud voice, saying, How long, O Lord, holy and true, dost
thou not judge and avenge our blood on
them that dwell on the earth?
11And white robes were given unto every one of them; and it was said unto them,
that they should rest yet for a little season,
until their fellowservants also and their
brethren, that should be killed as they *were*,
should be fulfilled.
12And I beheld when he had opened the
sixth seal, and, lo, there was a great earthquake; and the sun became black as sackcloth of hair, and the moon became as
blood;
13And the stars of heaven fell unto the
earth, even as a fig tree casteth her untimely
figs, when she is shaken of a mighty wind.
14And the heaven departed as a scroll
when it is rolled together; and every mountain and island were moved out of their
places.
15And the kings of the earth, and the
great men, and the rich men, and the chief
captains, and the mighty men, and every
bondman, and every free man, hid themselves in the dens and in the rocks of the
mountains;
16And said to the mountains and rocks,
Fall on us, and hide us from the face of
him that sitteth on the throne, and from
the wrath of the Lamb:
17For the great day of his wrath is come;
and who shall be able to stand?

7

1And after these things I saw four angels standing on the four corners of the
earth, holding the four winds of the earth,

that the wind should not blow on the
earth, nor on the sea, nor on any tree.
2 And I saw another angel ascending
from the east, having the seal of the living
God: and he cried with a loud voice to the
four angels, to whom it was given to hurt
the earth and the sea,
3 Saying, Hurt not the earth, neither the
sea, nor the trees, till we have sealed the
servants of our God in their foreheads.
4 And I heard the number of them which
were sealed: *and there were* sealed an hundred *and* forty *and* four thousand of all the
tribes of the children of Israel.
5 Of the tribe of Juda *were* sealed twelve
thousand. Of the tribe of Reuben *were*
sealed twelve thousand. Of the tribe of Gad
were sealed twelve thousand.
6 Of the tribe of Aser *were* sealed twelve
thousand. Of the tribe of Nepthalim *were*
sealed twelve thousand. Of the tribe of
Manasses *were* sealed twelve thousand.
7 Of the tribe of Simeon *were* sealed
twelve thousand. Of the tribe of Levi *were*
sealed twelve thousand. Of the tribe of Issachar *were* sealed twelve thousand.
8 Of the tribe of Zabulon *were* sealed
twelve thousand. Of the tribe of Joseph
were sealed twelve thousand. Of the tribe
of Benjamin *were* sealed twelve thousand.
9 After this I be-
held, and, lo, a
great multitude,
which no man
could number, of
all nations, and
kindreds, and people, and tongues, stood
before the throne, and before the Lamb,
clothed with white robes, and palms in
their hands;

7:9 Jesus the Lamb
◄ Revelation 6:1
Revelation 12:11 ►

10 And cried with a loud voice, saying,
Salvation to our God which sitteth upon
the throne, and unto the Lamb.
11 And all the angels stood round about
the throne, and *about* the elders and the
four beasts, and fell before the throne on
their faces, and worshipped God,
12 Saying, Amen: Blessing, and glory, and
wisdom, and thanksgiving, and honour,
and power, and might, *be* unto our God
for ever and ever. Amen.
13 And one of the elders answered, saying unto me, What are these which are arrayed in white robes? and whence came
they?
14 And I said unto
him, Sir, thou
knowest. And he
said to me, These
are they which
came out of great
tribulation, and
have washed their
robes, and made
them white in the
blood of the Lamb.
15 Therefore are
they before the throne of God, and serve
him day and night in his temple: and he
that sitteth on the throne shall dwell
among them.

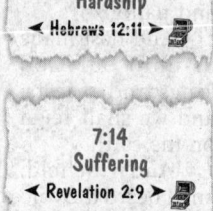

7:14
Hardship
◄ Hebrews 12:11 ►

7:14
Suffering
◄ Revelation 2:9 ►

16 They shall hunger no more, neither
thirst any more; neither shall the sun light
on them, nor any heat.
17 For the Lamb which is in the midst of
the throne shall feed them, and shall lead
them unto living fountains of waters: and
God shall wipe away all tears from their
eyes.

8

1 And when he had opened the seventh
seal, there was silence in heaven about the
space of half an hour.
2 And I saw the seven angels which stood
before God; and to them were given seven
trumpets.
3 And another angel came and stood at
the altar, having a golden censer; and there
was given unto him much incense, that he
should offer *it* with the prayers of all saints
upon the golden altar which was before
the throne.
4 And the smoke of the incense, *which
came* with the prayers of the saints, ascended up before God out of the angel's
hand.
5 And the angel took the censer, and
filled it with fire of the altar, and cast *it*
into the earth: and there were voices, and
thunderings, and lightnings, and an earthquake.
6 And the seven angels which had the
seven trumpets prepared themselves to
sound.
7 The first angel sounded, and there followed hail and fire mingled with blood,
and they were cast upon the earth: and the
third part of trees was burnt up, and all
green grass was burnt up.
8 And the second angel sounded, and as
it were a great mountain burning with fire

was cast into the sea: and the third part of
the sea became blood;
9And the third part of the creatures
which were in the sea, and had life, died;
and the third part of the ships were destroyed.
10And the third angel sounded, and
there fell a great star from heaven, burning as it were a lamp, and it fell upon the
third part of the rivers, and upon the fountains of waters;
11And the name of the star is called
Wormwood: and the third part of the waters became wormwood; and many men
died of the waters, because they were made
bitter.
12And the fourth angel sounded, and the
third part of the sun was smitten, and the
third part of the moon, and the third part
of the stars; so as the third part of them
was darkened, and the day shone not for a
third part of it, and the night likewise.
13And I beheld, and heard an angel flying through the midst of heaven, saying
with a loud voice, Woe, woe, woe, to the
inhabiters of the earth by reason of the
other voices of the trumpet of the three
angels, which are yet to sound!

9

1And the fifth angel sounded, and I saw
a star fall from heaven unto the earth: and
to him was given the key of the bottomless pit.
2And he opened the bottomless pit; and
there arose a smoke out of the pit, as the
smoke of a great furnace; and the sun and
the air were darkened by reason of the
smoke of the pit.
3And there came out of the smoke locusts upon the earth: and unto them was
given power, as the scorpions of the earth
have power.
4And it was commanded them that they
should not hurt the grass of the earth, neither any green thing, neither any tree; but
only those men which have not the seal of
God in their foreheads.
5And to them it was given that they
should not kill them, but that they should
be tormented five months: and their torment *was* as the torment of a scorpion,
when he striketh a man.
6And in those days shall men seek death,
and shall not find it; and shall desire to
die, and death shall flee from them.
7And the shapes of the locusts *were* like
unto horses prepared unto battle; and on
their heads *were* as it were crowns like gold,
and their faces *were* as the faces of men.
8And they had hair as the hair of wom-
en, and their teeth were as *the teeth* of lions.
9And they had breastplates, as it were
breastplates of iron; and the sound of their
wings *was* as the sound of chariots of many
horses running to battle.
10And they had tails like unto scorpions,
and there were stings in their tails: and their
power *was* to hurt men five months.
11And they had a king over them, *which*
is the angel of the bottomless pit, whose
name in the Hebrew tongue *is* Abaddon,
but in the Greek tongue hath *his* name
Apollyon.
12One woe is past; *and*, behold, there
come two woes more hereafter.
13And the sixth angel sounded, and I
heard a voice from the four horns of the
golden altar which is before God,
14Saying to the sixth angel which had
the trumpet, Loose the four angels which
are bound in the great river Euphrates.
15And the four angels were loosed,
which were prepared for an hour, and a
day, and a month, and a year, for to slay
the third part of men.
16And the number of the army of the
horsemen *were* two hundred thousand
thousand: and I heard the number of
them.
17And thus I saw the horses in the vision, and them that sat on them, having
breastplates of fire, and of jacinth, and
brimstone: and the heads of the horses
were as the heads of lions; and out of their
mouths issued fire and smoke and brimstone.
18By these three was the third part of
men killed, by the fire, and by the smoke,
and by the brimstone, which issued out of
their mouths.
19For their power is in their mouth, and
in their tails: for their tails *were* like unto
serpents, and had heads, and with them
they do hurt.
20And the rest of the men which were
not killed by these plagues yet repented
not of the works of their hands, that they
should not worship devils, and idols of
gold, and silver, and brass, and stone, and
of wood: which neither can see, nor hear,
nor walk:

21 Neither repent-
ed they of their
murders, nor of
their sorceries, nor
of their fornication,
nor of their thefts.

9:21
Stubborn People
< Luke 16:31 >

10

1 And I saw another mighty angel come
down from heaven, clothed with a cloud:
and a rainbow *was* upon his head, and his
face *was* as it were the sun, and his feet as
pillars of fire:
2 And he had in his hand a little book
open: and he set his right foot upon the
sea, and *his* left *foot* on the earth,
3 And cried with a loud voice, as *when* a
lion roareth: and when he had cried, sev-
en thunders uttered their voices.
4 And when the seven thunders had
uttered their voices, I was about to write:
and I heard a voice from heaven saying
unto me, Seal up those things which the
seven thunders uttered, and write them
not.
5 And the angel which I saw stand upon
the sea and upon the earth lifted up his
hand to heaven,
6 And sware by him that liveth for ever
and ever, who created heaven, and the
things that therein are, and the earth, and
the things that therein are, and the sea, and
the things which are therein, that there
should be time no longer:
7 But in the days of the voice of the seventh angel, when he shall begin to sound,
the mystery of God should be finished,
as he hath declared to his servants the
prophets.
8 And the voice which I heard from heav-
en spake unto me again, and said, Go *and*
take the little book which is open in the
hand of the angel which standeth upon
the sea and upon the earth.
9 And I went unto the angel, and
said unto him, Give me the little book.
And he said unto me, Take *it*, and eat
it up; and it shall make thy belly bitter,
but it shall be in thy mouth sweet as
honey.
10 And I took the little book out of the
angel's hand, and ate it up; and it was in
my mouth sweet as honey: and as soon as
I had eaten it, my belly was bitter.
11 And he said unto me, Thou must
prophesy again before many peoples, and
nations, and tongues, and kings.

11

1 And there was given me a reed like unto
a rod: and the angel stood, saying, Rise,
and measure the temple of God, and the
altar, and them that worship therein.
2 But the court which is without the temple leave out, and measure it not; for it is
given unto the Gentiles: and the holy city
shall they tread under foot forty *and* two
months.
3 And I will give *power* unto my two witnesses, and they shall prophesy a thousand
two hundred *and* threescore days, clothed
in sackcloth.
4 These are the two olive trees, and the
two candlesticks standing before the God
of the earth.
5 And if any man will hurt them, fire
proceedeth out of their mouth, and
devoureth their enemies: and if any man
will hurt them, he must in this manner be
killed.
6 These have power to shut heaven, that
it rain not in the days of their prophecy:
and have power over waters to turn them
to blood, and to smite the earth with all
plagues, as often as they will.
7 And when they shall have finished their
testimony, the beast that ascendeth out of
the bottomless pit shall make war against
them, and shall overcome them, and kill
them.
8 And their dead bodies *shall lie* in the
street of the great city, which spiritually is
called Sodom and Egypt, where also our
Lord was crucified.
9 And they of the people and kindreds
and tongues and nations shall see their
dead bodies three days and an half, and
shall not suffer their dead bodies to be put
in graves.
10 And they that dwell upon the earth
shall rejoice over them, and make merry,
and shall send gifts one to another; because these two prophets tormented them
that dwelt on the earth.
11 And after three days and an half the
Spirit of life from God entered into them,
and they stood upon their feet; and great
fear fell upon them which saw them.
12 And they heard
a great voice from
heaven saying unto
them, Come up
hither. And they as-
cended up to heav-

11:12
Good Rewarded
< Revelation 5:10 >

en in a cloud; and their enemies beheld
them.
13 And the same hour was there a great
earthquake, and the tenth part of the city
fell, and in the earthquake were slain of
men seven thousand: and the remnant
were affrighted, and gave glory to the God
of heaven.
14 The second woe is past; *and,* behold,
the third woe cometh quickly.
15 And the seventh angel sounded; and
there were great voices in heaven, saying,
The kingdoms of this world are become
the kingdoms of our Lord, and of his Christ;
and he shall reign for ever and ever.
16 And the four and twenty elders, which
sat before God on their seats, fell upon
their faces, and worshipped God,
17 Saying, We give thee thanks, O Lord
God Almighty, which art, and wast, and
art to come; because thou hast taken to
thee thy great power, and hast reigned.
18 And the nations were angry, and thy
wrath is come, and the time of the dead,
that they should be judged, and that thou
shouldest give reward unto thy servants the
prophets, and to the saints, and them that
fear thy name, small and great; and
shouldest destroy them which destroy the
earth.
19 And the temple of God was opened
in heaven, and there was seen in his temple the ark of his testament: and there were
lightnings, and voices, and thunderings,
and an earthquake, and great hail.

12

1 And there appeared a great wonder in
heaven; a woman clothed with the sun,
and the moon under her feet, and upon
her head a crown of twelve stars:
2 And she being with child cried, travailing in birth, and pained to be delivered.
3 And there appeared another wonder in
heaven; and behold a great red dragon,
having seven heads and ten horns, and
seven crowns upon his heads.
4 And his tail drew the third part of the
stars of heaven, and did cast them to
the earth: and the dragon stood before
the woman which was ready to be delivered, for to devour her child as soon as it
was born.
5 And she brought forth a man child,
who was to rule all nations with a rod of
iron: and her child was caught up unto
God, and *to* his throne.
6 And the woman fled into the wilderness, where she hath a place prepared of
God, that they should feed her there a
thousand two hundred *and* threescore
days.
7 And there was war in heaven: Michael
and his angels fought against the dragon;
and the dragon fought and his angels,
8 And prevailed not; neither was their
place found any more in heaven.
9 And the great dragon was cast out, that
old serpent, called the Devil, and Satan,
which deceiveth the whole world: he was
cast out into the earth, and his angels were
cast out with him.
10 And I heard a loud voice saying in
heaven, Now is come salvation, and
strength, and the kingdom of our God, and
the power of his Christ: for the accuser of
our brethren is cast down, which accused
them before our God day and night.
11 And they over-
came him by the
blood of the Lamb,
and by the word of
their testimony;
and they loved not
their lives unto the death.

12:11 Jesus the Lamb
◄ Revelation 7:9
Revelation 13:8 ►

12 Therefore re-
joice, *ye* heavens,
and ye that dwell
in them. Woe to
the inhabiters of
the earth and of the
sea! for the devil is come down unto you,
having great wrath, because he knoweth
that he hath but a short time.

12:12 Satan's Weakness
◄ James 4:7
Revelation 13:5 ►

13 And when the dragon saw that he was
cast unto the earth, he persecuted the
woman which brought forth the man *child.*
14 And to the woman were given two
wings of a great eagle, that she might fly
into the wilderness, into her place, where
she is nourished for a time, and times, and
half a time, from the face of the serpent.
15 And the serpent cast out of his mouth
water as a flood after the woman, that he
might cause her to be carried away of the
flood.
16 And the earth helped the woman, and
the earth opened her mouth, and swallowed up the flood which the dragon cast
out of his mouth.
17 And the dragon was wroth with the
woman, and went to make war with

the remnant of her seed, which keep the commandments of God, and have the testimony of Jesus Christ.

13

1 And I stood upon the sand of the sea, and saw a beast rise up out of the sea, having seven heads and ten horns, and upon his horns ten crowns, and upon his heads the name of blasphemy.

2 And the beast which I saw was like unto a leopard, and his feet were as *the feet* of a bear, and his mouth as the mouth of a lion: and the dragon gave him his power, and his seat, and great authority.

3 And I saw one of his heads as it were wounded to death; and his deadly wound was healed: and all the world wondered after the beast.

4 And they worshipped the dragon which gave power unto the beast: and they worshipped the beast, saying, Who *is* like unto the beast? who is able to make war with him?

5 And there was given unto him a mouth speaking great things and blasphemies; and power was given unto him to continue forty *and* two months.

13:5
Satan's Weakness
◄ Revelation 12:12 ►

6 And he opened his mouth in blasphemy against God, to blaspheme his name, and his tabernacle, and them that dwell in heaven.

7 And it was given unto him to make war with the saints, and to overcome them: and power was given him over all kindreds, and tongues, and nations.

8 And all that dwell upon the earth shall worship him, whose names are not written in the book of life of the Lamb slain from the foundation of the world.

13:8 Jesus the Lamb
◄ Revelation 12:11
Revelation 14:1 ►

9 If any man have an ear, let him hear.

10 He that leadeth into captivity shall go into captivity: he that killeth with the sword must be killed with the sword. Here is the patience and the faith of the saints.

11 And I beheld another beast coming up out of the earth; and he had two horns like a lamb, and he spake as a dragon.

12 And he exerciseth all the power of the first beast before him, and causeth the earth and them which dwell therein to worship the first beast, whose deadly wound was healed.

13 And he doeth great wonders, so that he maketh fire come down from heaven on the earth in the sight of men,

14 And deceiveth them that dwell on the earth by *the means of* those miracles which he had power to do in the sight of the beast; saying to them that dwell on the earth, that they should make an image to the beast, which had the wound by a sword, and did live.

15 And he had power to give life unto the image of the beast, that the image of the beast should both speak, and cause that as many as would not worship the image of the beast should be killed.

16 And he causeth all, both small and great, rich and poor, free and bond, to receive a mark in their right hand, or in their foreheads:

17 And that no man might buy or sell, save he that had the mark, or the name of the beast, or the number of his name.

18 Here is wisdom. Let him that hath understanding count the number of the beast: for it is the number of a man; and his number *is* Six hundred threescore *and* six.

14

1 And I looked, and, lo, a Lamb stood on the mount Sion, and with him an hundred forty *and* four thousand, having his Father's name written in their foreheads.

14:1 Jesus the Lamb
◄ Revelation 13:8
Revelation 15:3 ►

2 And I heard a voice from heaven, as the voice of many waters, and as the voice of a great thunder: and I heard the voice of harpers harping with their harps:

3 And they sung as it were a new song before the throne, and before the four beasts, and the elders: and no man could learn that song but the hundred *and* forty *and* four thousand, which were redeemed from the earth.

4 These are they which were not defiled with women; for they are virgins. These are they which follow the Lamb whithersoever he goeth. These were redeemed from among men, *being* the firstfruits unto God and to the Lamb.

5And in their mouth was found no guile:
for they are without fault before the throne
of God.
6And I saw another angel fly in the midst
of heaven, having the everlasting gospel
to preach unto them that dwell on the
earth, and to every nation, and kindred,
and tongue, and people,
7Saying with a
loud voice, Fear
God, and give glo-
ry to him; for the
hour of his judg-
ment is come: and
worship him that
made heaven, and
earth, and the sea,
and the fountains
of waters.
8And there fol-
lowed another angel, saying, Babylon is
fallen, is fallen, that great city, because she
made all nations drink of the wine of the
wrath of her fornication.
9And the third angel followed them, saying with a loud voice, If any man worship
the beast and his image, and receive *his*
mark in his forehead, or in his hand,
10The same shall drink of the wine of
the wrath of God, which is poured out
without mixture into the cup of his indignation; and he shall be tormented with fire
and brimstone in the presence of the holy
angels, and in the presence of the Lamb:
11And the smoke of their torment
ascendeth up for ever and ever: and they
have no rest day nor night, who worship
the beast and his image, and whosoever
receiveth the mark of his name.
12Here is the patience of the saints: here
are they that keep the commandments of
God, and the faith of Jesus.
13And I heard a voice from heaven saying unto me, Write, Blessed *are* the dead
which die in the Lord from henceforth: Yea,
saith the Spirit, that they may rest from their
labours; and their works do follow them.
14And I looked, and behold a white
cloud, and upon the cloud *one* sat like unto
the Son of man, having on his head a
golden crown, and in his hand a sharp
sickle.
15And another angel came out of the
temple, crying with a loud voice to him
that sat on the cloud, Thrust in thy
sickle, and reap: for the time is come for
thee to reap; for the harvest of the earth is
ripe.
16And he that sat on the cloud thrust in
his sickle on the earth; and the earth was
reaped.
17And another angel came out of the
temple which is in heaven, he also having
a sharp sickle.
18And another angel came out from the
altar, which had power over fire; and cried
with a loud cry to him that had the sharp
sickle, saying, Thrust in thy sharp sickle,
and gather the clusters of the vine of the
earth; for her grapes are fully ripe.
19And the angel thrust in his sickle into
the earth, and gathered the vine of the
earth, and cast *it* into the great winepress
of the wrath of God.
20And the winepress was trodden without the city, and blood came out of the
winepress, even unto the horse bridles, by
the space of a thousand *and* six hundred
furlongs.

14:7 Fearing God
◄ 1 Peter 2:17 ►

14:7 Worship
◄ John 4:24
Revelation 15:4 ►

15 1And I saw another sign in heaven, great
and marvellous, seven angels having the
seven last plagues; for in them is filled up
the wrath of God.
2And I saw as it were a sea of glass mingled with fire: and them that had gotten
the victory over the
beast, and over his
image, and over
his mark, *and* over
the number of his
name, stand on the
sea of glass, having
the harps of God.
3And they sing
the song of Moses
the servant of God,
and the song of the
Lamb, saying, Great
and marvellous *are*
thy works, Lord
God Almighty; just
and true *are* thy
ways, thou King of
saints.
4Who shall not
fear thee, O Lord,
and glorify thy
name? for *thou* only
art holy: for all na-
tions shall come

15:3 God's Justice
◄ Romans 2:2 ►

15:3 God's Ways
◄ Romans 11:33 ►

15:3 Jesus the Lamb
◄ Revelation 14:1
Revelation 17:14 ►

15:4 Worship
◄ Revelation 14:7
Revelation 19:10 ►

and worship before thee; for thy judgments are made manifest.

5 And after that I looked, and, behold, the temple of the tabernacle of the testimony in heaven was opened:

6 And the seven angels came out of the temple, having the seven plagues, clothed in pure and white linen, and having their breasts girded with golden girdles.

7 And one of the four beasts gave unto the seven angels seven golden vials full of the wrath of God, who liveth for ever and ever.

8 And the temple was filled with smoke from the glory of God, and from his power; and no man was able to enter into the temple, till the seven plagues of the seven angels were fulfilled.

16

1 And I heard a great voice out of the temple saying to the seven angels, Go your ways, and pour out the vials of the wrath of God upon the earth.

2 And the first went, and poured out his vial upon the earth; and there fell a noisome and grievous sore upon the men which had the mark of the beast, and *upon* them which worshipped his image.

3 And the second angel poured out his vial upon the sea; and it became as the blood of a dead *man:* and every living soul died in the sea.

4 And the third angel poured out his vial upon the rivers and fountains of waters; and they became blood.

5 And I heard the angel of the waters say, Thou art righteous, O Lord, which art, and wast, and shalt be, because thou hast judged thus.

6 For they have shed the blood of saints and prophets, and thou hast given them blood to drink; for they are worthy.

7 And I heard another out of the altar say, Even so, Lord God Almighty, true and righteous *are* thy judgments.

8 And the fourth angel poured out his vial upon the sun; and power was given unto him to scorch men with fire.

9 And men were scorched with great heat, and blasphemed the name of God, which hath power over these plagues: and they repented not to give him glory.

10 And the fifth angel poured out his vial upon the seat of the beast; and his kingdom was full of darkness; and they gnawed their tongues for pain,

11 And blasphemed the God of heaven because of their pains and their sores, and repented not of their deeds.

16:11
Refusing Correction
◄ Hebrews 12:5 ►

12 And the sixth angel poured out his vial upon the great river Euphrates; and the water thereof was dried up, that the way of the kings of the east might be prepared.

13 And I saw three unclean spirits like frogs *come* out of the mouth of the dragon, and out of the mouth of the beast, and out of the mouth of the false prophet.

14 For they are the spirits of devils, working miracles, *which* go forth unto the kings of the earth and of the whole world, to gather them to the battle of that great day of God Almighty.

16:14
Demons
◄ James 2:19 ►

15 Behold, I come as a thief. Blessed *is* he that watcheth, and keepeth his garments, lest he walk naked, and they see his shame.

16:15
Jesus' Return
◄ Revelation 3:11 ►

16 And he gathered them together into a place called in the Hebrew tongue Armageddon.

16:15
Jesus' Return: When?
◄ Revelation 3:3 ►

17 And the seventh angel poured out his vial into the air; and there came a great voice out of the temple of heaven, from the throne, saying, It is done.

18 And there were voices, and thunders, and lightnings; and there was a great earthquake, such as was not since men were upon the earth, so mighty an earthquake, *and* so great.

19 And the great city was divided into three parts, and the cities of the nations fell: and great Babylon came in remembrance before God, to give unto her the cup of the wine of the fierceness of his wrath.

20 And every island fled away, and the mountains were not found.

21 And there fell upon men a great hail out of heaven, *every stone* about the weight

of a talent: and men blasphemed God because of the plague of the hail; for the
plague thereof was exceeding great.

17

1And there came one of the seven angels which had the seven vials, and talked
with me, saying unto me, Come hither; I
will shew unto thee the judgment of
the great whore that sitteth upon many
waters:
2With whom the kings of the earth have
committed fornication, and the inhabitants of the earth have been made drunk
with the wine of her fornication.
3So he carried me away in the spirit into
the wilderness: and I saw a woman sit
upon a scarlet coloured beast, full of
names of blasphemy, having seven heads
and ten horns.
4And the woman was arrayed in purple
and scarlet colour, and decked with gold
and precious stones and pearls, having a
golden cup in her hand full of abominations and filthiness of her fornication:
5And upon her forehead *was* a name
written, MYSTERY, BABYLON THE GREAT,
THE MOTHER OF HARLOTS AND ABOM-
INATIONS OF THE EARTH.
6And I saw the woman drunken with the
blood of the saints, and with the blood of
the martyrs of Jesus: and when I saw her, I
wondered with great admiration.
7And the angel said unto me, Wherefore
didst thou marvel? I will tell thee the mystery of the woman, and of the beast that
carrieth her, which hath the seven heads
and ten horns.
8The beast that thou sawest was, and is
not; and shall ascend out of the bottomless pit, and go into perdition: and they
that dwell on the earth shall wonder,
whose names were not written in the book
of life from the foundation of the world,
when they behold the beast that was, and
is not, and yet is.
9And here *is* the mind which hath wisdom. The seven heads are seven mountains, on which the woman sitteth.
10And there are seven kings: five are fall-
en, and one is, *and* the other is not yet
come; and when he cometh, he must continue a short space.
11And the beast that was, and is not, even
he is the eighth, and is of the seven, and
goeth into perdition.
12And the ten horns which thou sawest
are ten kings, which have received no kingdom as yet; but receive power as kings one
hour with the beast.
13These have one mind, and shall give
their power and strength unto the beast.
14These shall
make war with the
Lamb, and the
Lamb shall over-
come them: for he
is Lord of lords, and
King of kings: and they that are with him
are called, and chosen, and faithful.

17:14 Jesus the Lamb
◄ Revelation 15:3
Revelation 19:9 ►

15And he saith unto me, The waters
which thou sawest, where the whore
sitteth, are peoples, and multitudes, and
nations, and tongues.
16And the ten horns which thou sawest
upon the beast, these shall hate the whore,
and shall make her desolate and naked,
and shall eat her flesh, and burn her with
fire.
17For God hath put in their hearts to
fulfil his will, and to agree, and give their
kingdom unto the beast, until the words
of God shall be fulfilled.
18And the woman which thou sawest is
that great city, which reigneth over the
kings of the earth.

18

1And after these things I saw another
angel come down from heaven, having
great power; and the earth was lightened
with his glory.
2And he cried mightily with a strong
voice, saying, Babylon the great is fallen,
is fallen, and is become the habitation of
devils, and the hold of every foul spirit,
and a cage of every unclean and hateful
bird.
3For all nations have drunk of the wine
of the wrath of her fornication, and the
kings of the earth have committed fornication with her, and the merchants of the
earth are waxed rich through the abundance of her delicacies.
4And I heard another voice from heav-
en, saying, Come out of her, my people,
that ye be not partakers of her sins, and
that ye receive not of her plagues.
5For her sins have reached unto heaven,
and God hath remembered her iniquities.
6Reward her even as she rewarded you,
and double unto her double according to
her works: in the cup which she hath filled
fill to her double.

7 How much she hath glorified herself, and lived deliciously, so much torment and sorrow give her: for she saith in her heart, I sit a queen, and am no widow, and shall see no sorrow.

8 Therefore shall her plagues come in one day, death, and mourning, and famine; and she shall be utterly burned with fire: for strong *is* the Lord God who judgeth her.

18:8 God as Judge
◄ Hebrews 12:23
Revelation 20:12 ►

9 And the kings of the earth, who have committed fornication and lived deliciously with her, shall bewail her, and lament for her, when they shall see the smoke of her burning,

10 Standing afar off for the fear of her torment, saying, Alas, alas, that great city Babylon, that mighty city! for in one hour is thy judgment come.

11 And the merchants of the earth shall weep and mourn over her; for no man buyeth their merchandise any more:

12 The merchandise of gold, and silver, and precious stones, and of pearls, and fine linen, and purple, and silk, and scarlet, and all thyine wood, and all manner vessels of ivory, and all manner vessels of most precious wood, and of brass, and iron, and marble,

13 And cinnamon, and odours, and ointments, and frankincense, and wine, and oil, and fine flour, and wheat, and beasts, and sheep, and horses, and chariots, and slaves, and souls of men.

14 And the fruits that thy soul lusted after are departed from thee, and all things which were dainty and goodly are departed from thee, and thou shalt find them no more at all.

18:14 Discontentment
◄ John 4:13 ►

15 The merchants of these things, which were made rich by her, shall stand afar off for the fear of her torment, weeping and wailing,

16 And saying, Alas, alas, that great city, that was clothed in fine linen, and purple, and scarlet, and decked with gold, and precious stones, and pearls!

17 For in one hour so great riches is come to nought. And every shipmaster, and all the company in ships, and sailors, and as many as trade by sea, stood afar off,

18:17 Money's Limits
◄ Zephaniah 1:18 ►

18 And cried when they saw the smoke of her burning, saying, What *city is* like unto this great city!

19 And they cast dust on their heads, and cried, weeping and wailing, saying, Alas, alas, that great city, wherein were made rich all that had ships in the sea by reason of her costliness! for in one hour is she made desolate.

20 Rejoice over her, *thou* heaven, and *ye* holy apostles and prophets; for God hath avenged you on her.

21 And a mighty angel took up a stone like a great millstone, and cast *it* into the sea, saying, Thus with violence shall that great city Babylon be thrown down, and shall be found no more at all.

22 And the voice of harpers, and musicians, and of pipers, and trumpeters, shall be heard no more at all in thee; and no craftsman, of whatsoever craft *he be,* shall be found any more in thee; and the sound of a millstone shall be heard no more at all in thee;

23 And the light of a candle shall shine no more at all in thee; and the voice of the bridegroom and of the bride shall be heard no more at all in thee: for thy merchants were the great men of the earth; for by thy sorceries were all nations deceived.

24 And in her was found the blood of prophets, and of saints, and of all that were slain upon the earth.

19

1 And after these things I heard a great voice of much people in heaven, saying, Alleluia; Salvation, and glory, and honour, and power, unto the Lord our God:

2 For true and righteous *are* his judgments: for he hath judged the great whore, which did corrupt the earth with her fornication, and hath avenged the blood of his servants at her hand.

3 And again they said, Alleluia. And her smoke rose up for ever and ever.

4 And the four and twenty elders and the four beasts fell down and worshipped God that sat on the throne, saying, Amen; Alleluia.

5 And a voice came out of the throne, saying, Praise our God, all ye his servants,

and ye that fear him, both small and great.
6And I heard as it
were the voice of a
great multitude,
and as the voice of
many waters, and as
the voice of mighty
thunderings, saying, Alleluia: for the Lord
God omnipotent reigneth.

> **19:6**
> **All-powerful**
> ◄ Luke 1:37 ►

7Let us be glad
and rejoice, and
give honour to him:
for the marriage of
the Lamb is come,
and his wife hath
made herself ready.

> **19:7**
> **Ready for the Future**
> ◄ Luke 12:35-36 ►

8And to her was granted that she should
be arrayed in fine linen, clean and white:
for the fine linen is the righteousness of
saints.
9And he saith
unto me, Write,
Blessed *are* they
which are called
unto the marriage
supper of the Lamb.
And he saith unto me, These are the true
sayings of God.

> **19:9 Jesus the Lamb**
> ◄ Revelation 17:14
> Revelation 21:22 ►

10And I fell at his
feet to worship
him. And he said
unto me, See *thou*
do it not: I am thy
fellowservant, and
of thy brethren that have the testimony of
Jesus: worship God: for the testimony of
Jesus is the spirit of prophecy.

> **19:10 Worship**
> ◄ Revelation 15:4
> Revelation 22:9 ►

11And I saw heaven opened, and behold
a white horse; and he that sat upon him
was called Faithful and True, and in righteousness he doth judge and make war.
12His eyes *were* as a flame of fire, and
on his head *were* many crowns; and he had
a name written, that no man knew, but he
himself.
13And he *was* clothed with a vesture
dipped in blood: and his name is called
The Word of God.
14And the armies *which were* in heaven
followed him upon white horses, clothed
in fine linen, white and clean.
15And out of his mouth goeth a sharp
sword, that with it he should smite the
nations: and he shall rule them with a rod
of iron: and he treadeth the winepress of
the fierceness and wrath of Almighty God.
16And he hath on *his* vesture and on his
thigh a name written, KING OF KINGS,
AND LORD OF LORDS.
17And I saw an angel standing in the
sun; and he cried with a loud voice,
saying to all the fowls that fly in the
midst of heaven, Come and gather yourselves together unto the supper of the great
God;
18That ye may eat the flesh of kings, and
the flesh of captains, and the flesh of
mighty men, and the flesh of horses, and
of them that sit on them, and the flesh of
all *men, both* free and bond, both small
and great.
19And I saw the beast, and the kings of
the earth, and their armies, gathered together to make war against him that sat
on the horse, and against his army.
20And the beast was taken, and with him
the false prophet that wrought miracles
before him, with which he deceived them
that had received the mark of the beast,
and them that worshipped his image.
These both were cast alive into a lake of
fire burning with brimstone.
21And the remnant were slain with the
sword of him that sat upon the horse,
which *sword* proceeded out of his mouth:
and all the fowls were filled with their
flesh.

20

1And I saw an angel come down from
heaven, having the key of the bottomless
pit and a great chain in his hand.
2And he laid hold on the dragon, that
old serpent, which is the Devil, and Satan,
and bound him a thousand years,
3And cast him into the bottomless pit,
and shut him up, and set a seal upon him,
that he should deceive the nations no
more, till the thousand years should be
fulfilled: and after that he must be loosed
a little season.
4And I saw
thrones, and they
sat upon them, and
judgment was given
unto them: and *I*
saw the souls of
them that were beheaded for the witness
of Jesus, and for the word of God, and
which had not worshipped the beast, neither his image, neither had received *his*
mark upon their foreheads, or in their

> **20:4**
> **Suffering Rewarded**
> ◄ Hebrews 11:26 ►

hands; and they lived and reigned with Christ a thousand years.

5 But the rest of the dead lived not again until the thousand years were finished. This *is* the first resurrection.

6 Blessed and holy *is* he that hath part in the first resurrection: on such the second death hath no power, but they shall be priests of God and of Christ, and shall reign with him a thousand years.

7 And when the thousand years are expired, Satan shall be loosed out of his prison,

8 And shall go out to deceive the nations which are in the four quarters of the earth, Gog and Magog, to gather them together to battle: the number of whom *is* as the sand of the sea.

9 And they went up on the breadth of the earth, and compassed the camp of the saints about, and the beloved city: and fire came down from God out of heaven, and devoured them.

10 And the devil that deceived them was cast into the lake of fire and brimstone, where the beast and the false prophet *are,* and shall be tormented day and night for ever and ever.

20:10
Defeat of Satan
◄ 1 John 3:8 ►

11 And I saw a great white throne, and him that sat on it, from whose face the earth and the heaven fled away; and there was found no place for them.

12 And I saw the dead, small and great, stand before God; and the books were opened: and another book was opened, which is *the book* of life: and the dead were judged out of those things which were written in the books, according to their works.

20:12 Actions Judged
◄ Revelation 2:23
Revelation 22:12 ►

20:12
God as Judge
◄ Revelation 18:8 ►

13 And the sea gave up the dead which were in it; and death and hell delivered up the dead which were in them: and they were judged every man according to their works.

20:13
Life After Death
◄ Acts 24:15 ►

14 And death and hell were cast into the lake of fire. This is the second death.

15 And whosoever was not found written in the book of life was cast into the lake of fire.

21

1 And I saw a new heaven and a new earth: for the first heaven and the first earth were passed away; and there was no more sea.

21:1, 4
Heaven
◄ Revelation 22:3, 5 ►

2 And I John saw the holy city, new Jerusalem, coming down from God out of heaven, prepared as a bride adorned for her husband.

3 And I heard a great voice out of heaven saying, Behold, the tabernacle of God *is* with men, and he will dwell with them, and they shall be his people, and God himself shall be with them, *and be* their God.

4 And God shall wipe away all tears from their eyes; and there shall be no more death, neither sorrow, nor crying, neither shall there be any more pain: for the former things are passed away.

5 And he that sat upon the throne said, Behold, I make all things new. And he said unto me, Write: for these words are true and faithful.

6 And he said unto me, It is done. I am Alpha and Omega, the beginning and the end. I will give unto him that is athirst of the fountain of the water of life freely.

7 He that overcometh shall inherit all things; and I will be his God, and he shall be my son.

21:8 Liars
◄ Isaiah 44:25
Revelation 22:15 ►

8 But the fearful, and unbelieving, and the abominable, and murderers, and whoremongers, and sorcerers, and idolaters, and all liars, shall have their part in the lake which burneth with fire and brimstone: which is the second death.

21:8
Lying
◄ Colossians 3:9 ►

21:8
Spiritual Death
◄ James 5:20 ►

9And there came unto me one of the
seven angels which had the seven vials full
of the seven last plagues, and talked with
me, saying, Come hither, I will shew thee
the bride, the Lamb's wife.
10And he carried me away in the spirit
to a great and high mountain, and shewed
me that great city, the holy Jerusalem, descending out of heaven from God,
11Having the glory of God: and her light
was like unto a stone most precious, even
like a jasper stone, clear as crystal;
12And had a wall great and high, *and*
had twelve gates, and at the gates twelve
angels, and names written thereon, which
are *the names* of the twelve tribes of the
children of Israel:
13On the east three gates; on the north
three gates; on the south three gates; and
on the west three gates.
14And the wall of the city had twelve
foundations, and in them the names of the
twelve apostles of the Lamb.
15And he that talked with me had a
golden reed to measure the city, and the
gates thereof, and the wall thereof.
16And the city lieth foursquare, and the
length is as large as the breadth: and he
measured the city with the reed, twelve
thousand furlongs. The length and the
breadth and the height of it are equal.
17And he measured the wall thereof, an
hundred *and* forty *and* four cubits, *according to* the measure of a man, that is, of the
angel.
18And the building of the wall of it was
of jasper: and the city *was* pure gold, like
unto clear glass.
19And the foundations of the wall of the
city *were* garnished with all manner of precious stones. The first foundation *was* jasper; the second, sapphire; the third, a
chalcedony; the fourth, an emerald;
20The fifth, sardonyx; the sixth, sardius;
the seventh, chrysolite; the eighth, beryl;
the ninth, a topaz; the tenth, a chryso-
prasus; the eleventh, a jacinth; the twelfth,
an amethyst.
21And the twelve gates *were* twelve
pearls; every several gate was of one pearl:
and the street of the city *was* pure gold, as
it were transparent glass.
22And I saw no temple therein: for the
Lord God Almighty and the Lamb are the
temple of it.
23And the city
had no need of the
sun, neither of the
moon, to shine in
it: for the glory of
God did lighten it,
and the Lamb *is* the light thereof.

21:22
Jesus the Lamb
◄ Revelation 19:9 ►

24And the nations of them which are
saved shall walk in the light of it: and the
kings of the earth do bring their glory and
honour into it.
25And the gates of it shall not be shut at
all by day: for there shall be no night there.
26And they shall bring the glory and
honour of the nations into it.
27And there shall in no wise enter into
it any thing that defileth, neither *whatsoever* worketh abomination, or *maketh* a lie:
but they which are written in the Lamb's
book of life.

22

1And he shewed me a pure river of water of life, clear as crystal, proceeding out
of the throne of God and of the Lamb.
2In the midst of the street of it, and on
either side of the river, *was there* the tree of
life, which bare twelve *manner of* fruits, *and*
yielded her fruit every month: and the
leaves of the tree *were* for the healing of
the nations.
3And there shall
be no more curse:
but the throne of
God and of the
Lamb shall be in it;
and his servants
shall serve him:

22:3, 5
Heaven
◄ Revelation 21:1, 4 ►

4And they shall see his face; and his
name *shall be* in their foreheads.
5And there shall be no night there; and
they need no candle, neither light of the
sun; for the Lord God giveth them light:
and they shall reign for ever and ever.
6And he said unto me, These sayings *are*
faithful and true: and the Lord God of the
holy prophets sent his angel to shew unto
his servants the things which must shortly
be done.
7Behold, I come quickly: blessed *is* he
that keepeth the sayings of the prophecy
of this book.
8And I John saw these things, and heard
them. And when I had heard and seen, I
fell down to worship before the feet of the
angel which shewed me these things.
9Then saith he unto me, See *thou do it*

Turn to the next page for more . . .

not: for I am thy
fellowservant, and
of thy brethren the
prophets, and of
them which keep
the sayings of this
book: worship God.

22:9
Worship
◄ Revelation 19:10 ►

10And he saith unto me, Seal not the sayings of the prophecy of this book: for the
time is at hand.
11He that is unjust, let him be unjust
still: and he which is filthy, let him be filthy
still: and he that is righteous, let him be
righteous still: and he that is holy, let him
be holy still.
12And, behold, I
come quickly; and
my reward *is* with
me, to give every
man according as
his work shall be.

22:12
Actions Judged
◄ Revelation 20:12 ►

13I am Alpha and Omega, the beginning
and the end, the
first and the last.
14Blessed *are* they
that do his com-
mandments, that
they may have right
to the tree of life,
and may enter in
through the gates
into the city.
15For without *are*
dogs, and sorcerers,

22:14
How to Be Saved
◄ 2 Peter 1:10-11 ►

22:15
Liars
◄ Revelation 21:8 ►

and whoremongers, and murderers, and
idolaters, and whosoever loveth and
maketh a lie.
16I Jesus have sent mine angel to testify
unto you these things in the churches. I
am the root and the offspring of David,
and the bright and morning star.
17And the Spirit
and the bride say,
Come. And let him
that heareth say,
Come. And let him
that is athirst come.
And whosoever will, let him take the water of life freely.

22:17
God Calls You
◄ 1 Timothy 2:4 ►

18For I testify unto every man that
heareth the words of the prophecy of this
book, If any man shall add unto these
things, God shall add unto him the plagues
that are written in this book:
19And if any man shall take away from
the words of the book of this prophecy,
God shall take away his part out of the
book of life, and out of the holy city, and
from the things which are written in this
book.
20He which tes-
tifieth these things
saith, Surely I come
quickly. Amen.
Even so, come, Lord
Jesus.

22:20
Ready for Jesus' Return
◄ Revelation 3:11 ►

21The grace of our Lord Jesus Christ *be*
with you all. Amen.

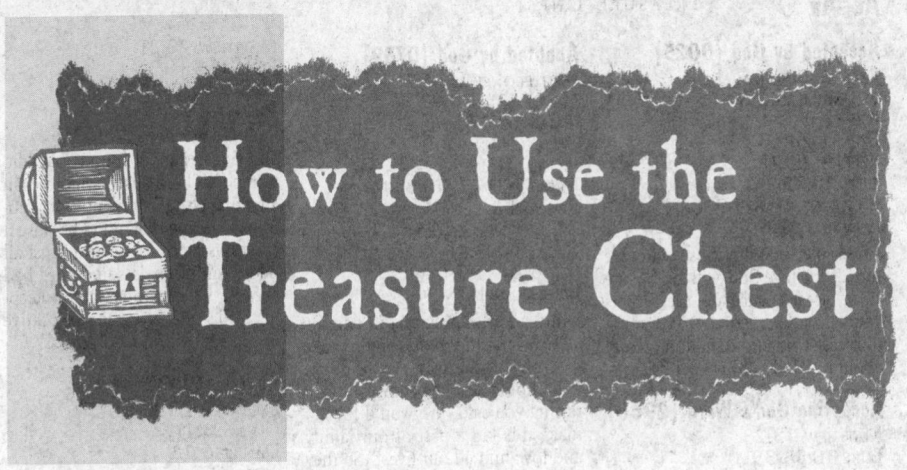

How to Use the Treasure Chest

Welcome to the Treasure Chest! Every treasure hunt in the *Treasure Study Bible* ends here. Whenever you come to the end of a hunt and see this symbol, come here—to the Treasure Chest.

Each Topical Entry has four parts: (1) the hunt's **title**, (2) the official Thompson Chain-Reference® **number**, (3) a list of the **verses** in that hunt, and (4) a short **summary** of what's in the hunt for you.

The **title** is the same one you will find in the Treasure Map and at every stop along that hunt.

The Thompson Chain-Reference® **number** is that hunt's official number. It's the same one you'll find in a Thompson Chain-Reference® Study Bible.

The list of **verses** shows you every stop in the hunt. They are listed in the order they appear in the Bible.

The **summary** tells you why that hunt is important. It spells out what the hunt is about and, briefly, how it can help you in your Christian life.

Remember, the Bible verses are the most important part. "For the word of God *is* quick, and powerful, and sharper than any twoedged sword, piercing even to the dividing asunder of soul and spirit, and of the joints and marrow, and *is* a discerner of the thoughts and intents of the heart." (Hebrews 4:12). Come to the Treasure Chest for some answers to your questions. Then go digging through the Bible for some more treasure!

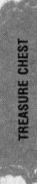

Accepted by God (0025)

Exodus 28:38
2 Samuel 24:23
Job 42:9
Ezekiel 20:40
Ezekiel 43:27
Acts 10:35
2 Corinthians 5:9
Ephesians 1:6

God is pleased with those who love him. If you love God, you can be sure he is pleased with you. He accepts your efforts to do good. Do your best to please God and then don't worry about it—God is your loving Father.

Accepting God's Word (2960)

Matthew 13:23
Luke 10:38-39
Acts 2:41
Acts 17:11
1 Thessalonians 2:13

These verses are about hearing God's Word. Many people hear it, but only some accept it. They listen closely and think about how it affects them. Whenever you hear God's truth, it's up to you to accept it.

Accepting People (4119)

Matthew 9:10
Mark 9:38
Mark 9:39
Luke 9:49-50
Philippians 1:17-18

Jesus' friends looked down on some people because they were different. But Jesus accepted all kinds of people, even people that no one else liked. Jesus loves everyone. Copy Jesus by being kind to everyone, even kids who are different from you.

Actions Judged (1353)

Psalm 62:12
Proverbs 24:12
Jeremiah 17:10
Jeremiah 32:19
Ezekiel 18:30
Matthew 16:27
Romans 2:6
2 Corinthians 5:10
1 Peter 1:17
Revelation 2:23
Revelation 20:12
Revelation 22:12

These verses are clear that one day God will judge us according to our actions. We can say good words, but if we treat other people badly it doesn't matter what we said. The best advice? Be kind and good to other people. Sooner or later you will have to give account of what you did.

Adopted by God (0739)

Deuteronomy 14:2
Isaiah 43:1
Isaiah 63:16
Ezekiel 16:8
Hosea 11:1
John 1:12
Romans 8:15
2 Corinthians 6:18
Galatians 3:26
Galatians 4:5-6
Ephesians 1:5

Being adopted means the parents who gave birth to you couldn't take care of you the way they thought they should. So the parents who are raising you said "We would love to make this kid a part of our family and love him all our lives!" So they did. It's really a wonderful thing. Christians are all adopted by God. He chooses to love us and give us a home in heaven. He loves you a lot.

Advice (0844)

Proverbs 11:14
Proverbs 12:15
Proverbs 13:10
Proverbs 15:22
Proverbs 20:18

It never hurts to ask for advice. If you have a tough problem to solve or decision to make, ask some other people what they think. They will often show you an option you didn't think about. They may even spare you from doing something foolish.

All-powerful (3809)

Job 42:2
Psalm 115:3
Psalm 135:6
Isaiah 43:13
Habakkuk 3:6
Matthew 19:26
Mark 14:36
Luke 1:37
Revelation 19:6

Nothing is impossible with God. God has more power than you can ever imagine. Your problems may seem massive to you, but they are easy for God to handle. Give your problems to him.

Ambition (3195)

Genesis 11:4
2 Samuel 15:1-2, 4
1 Kings 1:5
2 Kings 14:10
Psalm 49:11
Isaiah 14:13
Isaiah 22:16
Habakkuk 2:5
Matthew 20:21
Luke 11:43
Luke 22:24
John 5:44
2 Thessalonians 2:4

These verses show you people who wanted to be a success more than anything else. That's ambition. Ambition is sometimes good because it makes us reach for goals against all odds. Ambition is sometimes bad because we can forget about keeping God's rules along the way. Strive to succeed within God's rules.

Angels (0143)

Exodus 14:19
Psalm 91:11
Daniel 6:22
Acts 12:7
Acts 27:23
Hebrews 1:14

Angels are God's messengers and servants. They do more than just deliver messages. Their main job is to help people. They do whatever God tells them to do. Be glad God has done so much to get you through life.

Anger (3959)

Exodus 32:19
Leviticus 10:16
Numbers 16:15
Judges 14:19
1 Samuel 11:6
Nehemiah 5:6

Anger can be good. It's good to get angry at evil and at evil actions. God hates sin and so should you. The next time you get angry at evil, don't feel guilty—look for a way to do something about it.

Animals (4042)

Exodus 23:5
Deuteronomy 22:6
Luke 14:5

God created animals for people to enjoy. He also made us animal caretakers. He wants us to treat animals well. Don't be mean to animals. If you find a hurt animal, call a vet or someone else who can safely help it.

Animals vs. People (2240)

Genesis 1:28
Psalm 8:6
Psalm 82:6
Matthew 6:26
Matthew 12:12

These verses show that God values humans more than animals. He gave us the responsibility to care for the animals and the earth. We take care of the animals; God takes care of us. It's a good plan. How good a job are you doing?

Answers to Prayer (2819)

Psalm 91:15
Isaiah 41:17
Isaiah 58:9
Isaiah 65:24
Jeremiah 33:3
Zechariah 13:9
Luke 11:9
John 14:14
John 15:7
1 John 3:22

These verses are about God's response to your prayers. He doesn't always respond the way you think he will. But these verses tell you that he WILL respond. He doesn't forget.

Apathy (1083)

Psalm 123:4
Isaiah 32:9
Isaiah 47:8
Isaiah 64:7
Amos 6:1
Zephaniah 1:12
Matthew 22:5
Matthew 24:12

You just read about some people who stopped caring about God and the things that are important to him. They got comfortable with their lives and stopped listening to God. That's called apathy. It's dangerous. It doesn't please God. And it's a hard habit to break. Always have a tender heart.

Approaching God (0522)

Ephesians 3:12
1 Timothy 3:13
Hebrews 4:16
Hebrews 10:19
1 John 4:17

You can come to God—he won't yell at you. It's OK to pray whenever you want. God will listen.

Arguing (3732)

Proverbs 3:30
Proverbs 17:14
Proverbs 20:3
Proverbs 25:8
Proverbs 26:17
Philippians 2:3
2 Timothy 2:14
2 Timothy 2:24
James 3:14

Pointing a finger at other people's mistakes stirs up trouble. It's not your job to point out all the mistakes your friends make. It's better to stop arguing than to try to prove you are right. As much as you can, avoid arguments.

Argument Avoidance (1183)

Proverbs 4:15
Romans 16:17
1 Timothy 6:20
2 Timothy 2:16
2 Timothy 2:23
Titus 3:9

You just read about some things that God wants you to avoid—mostly, picking fights. God thinks you have better things to do with your time than fighting. Be easy to live with.

Arrogance (1722)

Psalm 10:2
Psalm 73:6
Psalm 119:21
Proverbs 6:17
Proverbs 11:2
Proverbs 13:10
Proverbs 16:18
Proverbs 21:4
Hosea 7:10
Habakkuk 2:4
1 John 2:16

Could you find one good word in these verses about pride? Pride brings out the worst in people. Don't let pride tell you you're better than others.

Bad Examples (1176)

Leviticus 20:23
Deuteronomy 18:9
Proverbs 22:24-25
Ezekiel 20:18
Hebrews 4:11
Hebrews 12:15
2 Peter 3:17

These verses are all warnings. They warn you to stay away from evil and from the people who do it. God gives us a lot of warnings about this. Over and over again he says to stay away from evil. It is very important to him. How about you?

Bad Friends (0276)

Exodus 23:2
Exodus 23:33
Exodus 34:12
Psalm 1:1
Proverbs 1:15
Proverbs 4:14
Proverbs 22:24
Proverbs 23:6
Proverbs 24:1
1 Corinthians 5:9
1 Corinthians 5:11
2 Corinthians 6:14
2 John 1:10

Bad kids make bad friends, and bad friends are bad to have. Don't make friends with kids who drag you down. Pick your friends carefully.

Bad Habits (2139)

Proverbs 5:22
John 8:34
Acts 8:23
Romans 6:16
Romans 7:23
2 Timothy 2:26
2 Peter 2:19

These verses talk about sin as if it's a jail we get locked into. That's because it is! Have you noticed how hard it is to stop sinning? That's why we need God's help every day. Don't be fooled into thinking you don't.

Bad News (1350)

Matthew 24:30
Mark 8:38
Luke 21:26
2 Thessalonians 1:7-8
Revelation 1:7

All our actions have results (consequences)—both good and bad. These verses are about that very thing. When Jesus comes again, each of us will see the consequences of our actions. Some of that will not be pleasant. That's why God's forgiveness is so important. Ask God to forgive you every time you need to.

Bad People (0031)

Proverbs 1:16
Proverbs 4:16
Proverbs 6:18
Isaiah 59:7
Micah 2:1
Romans 3:15
1 Peter 5:8

All the people in these verses did something bad. That's because some people like to do wrong. Watch out for people like that.

Bad Thoughts (2352)

Deuteronomy 15:9
Psalm 64:6
Psalm 94:11
Proverbs 15:26
Proverbs 23:7
Proverbs 24:9
Isaiah 66:18
Jeremiah 4:14
Matthew 9:4
Matthew 15:19

These verses reveal the problem with sinful thoughts. Our thoughts are important because our actions come out of them. Keep your thoughts pure and it will be LOADS easier to keep your actions pure.

Baptism (0756)
MATTHEW 28:19
MARK 16:16
JOHN 3:5
ACTS 2:38
ACTS 10:48
ACTS 22:16

God says baptism is important. It involves you and water and a minister. Baptism is a way of saying that you are going to follow God all your life. Ask someone at your church about baptism. They'll probably have something interesting to say.

Be Fair (1976)
DEUTERONOMY 16:20
PSALM 82:3
PROVERBS 21:3
ISAIAH 56:1
ROMANS 13:7
COLOSSIANS 4:1

In these verses God commands us to be fair to each other. We aren't perfect, so we'll never be completely fair. But we must try our best. Cheating someone just because you don't like him or her is not an option.

Being a Friend (1324)
RUTH 1:16
1 SAMUEL 20:17
2 KINGS 2:2
MATTHEW 27:55-56
MATTHEW 28:1
JOHN 11:16
JOHN 13:1
ROMANS 16:4
2 TIMOTHY 1:16

This Bible passage has examples of friends who stick together. Real friendship means you stick by your friends. You don't pull out over some little something. If your friends go through a hard time, be there for them if you can.

Being Friendless (1329)
PSALM 31:11
PSALM 38:11
PSALM 88:18
PSALM 142:4
MARK 14:48
MARK 14:50
LUKE 15:16
LUKE 16:20
LUKE 16:21
JOHN 5:7

These Bible verses are about people who didn't have any friends. As you can see, it is no fun not to have friends. If you know someone who has no friends, remember to help the person. If you have no friends, be friendly and then maybe you'll get some.

Being Frugal (1334)
GENESIS 41:35-36
PROVERBS 21:20
JOHN 6:12

In these verses these people had a lot of food sometimes and a little food at other times. Whenever they had plenty, they needed to save some for when they didn't. That's how you need to be with anything valuable, whether it's food, money, or other stuff. Don't use up all you have. Save some for another day when you will need it.

Being Hasty (2919)
PROVERBS 19:2
PROVERBS 21:5
PROVERBS 29:20
ECCLESIASTES 5:2
ACTS 19:36

These verses are about doing before thinking. They say that it's wise to think before doing something too quickly (if you can). Being hasty hurts more that it helps. Always take a moment to think through what you're about to do.

Being Quiet (3290)
JOSHUA 6:10
ECCLESIASTES 3:7
AMOS 5:13
HABAKKUK 2:20
ZEPHANIAH 1:7
ZECHARIAH 2:13

These verses say that there are times when you need to be quiet—absolutely quiet. If you are wise, you will learn to control the volume. Sometimes what you DON'T say matters more than what you DO say.

Being Smart (2021)
ISAIAH 44:25
1 CORINTHIANS 8:2
1 CORINTHIANS 13:8

From these verses we learn that we need to keep a level head about knowledge. For one thing, we can never know as much as God. And for another, brains don't make us wise. Go ahead and study, but don't get a big head about it. And don't worry if you're not Einstein. It's important to learn to love as well as think.

Being Stingy (2127)
PROVERBS 11:24
PROVERBS 21:13
PROVERBS 28:27
ECCLESIASTES 5:13
ISAIAH 43:23
MALACHI 3:8
MATTHEW 26:7-8
JOHN 12:5

These verses are about people who hold onto their stuff so tightly that they don't give much of anything. They're stingy. After a while, stingy people find that no one will give to them—including God. Stingy may be fun at first, but it gets real lonely real fast. God rewards generosity, not stinginess.

Believer Be Glad (3719)
1 KINGS 8:56
ISAIAH 28:16
MATTHEW 10:42
JOHN 6:37
ROMANS 8:38-39
2 CORINTHIANS 5:1
HEBREWS 6:19

These verses are meant to encourage you if you're a Christian. No matter how bad things get, you can always count on God. When all else fails, you can count on these three truths: (1) God keeps his promises, (2) God will always love you, (3) God has an awesome future planned for you.

Benefits of Faith (1208)
MATTHEW 21:22
JOHN 1:12
JOHN 7:38
JOHN 14:12
ROMANS 10:11
COLOSSIANS 1:23
HEBREWS 4:3
JAMES 2:5
1 PETER 2:6
1 JOHN 5:14

You just read about the good things that come from having faith. We don't believe in God in order to get good things, but because he is God and what he says is true. But having faith has good side effects, and the good side effects of faith are yours to enjoy.

Better Neighborhoods (2527)
PROVERBS 11:11
PROVERBS 14:34
PROVERBS 16:12
PROVERBS 25:5
PROVERBS 28:2
PROVERBS 29:4
PROVERBS 29:14
ISAIAH 16:5
ISAIAH 32:16
ISAIAH 33:5
ISAIAH 54:14

These verses are about people who

live righteously. The more people who live righteously in a town, the nicer the town is to live in. It's nicer for the town leaders because they don't have to worry about crime as much. And it's nicer for the people because they are safer. Obeying God makes life better for everyone. Do your part!

Blame (3453)
Deuteronomy 24:16
Job 19:4
Proverbs 9:12
Jeremiah 31:30
Ezekiel 18:20
Romans 14:4
Galatians 6:5

God holds each of us responsible for our own actions. No one else can take the rap for you when you mess up. So be careful how you live. Remember that you are responsible for everything you do, both good and bad.

Blessing (0481)
Exodus 23:25
Psalm 81:16
Isaiah 30:23
Amos 9:13
Malachi 3:10
Matthew 6:33

God wants to bless you. You don't have to bribe him—just ask.

Blessings (0480)
Genesis 24:35
2 Samuel 6:11
1 Kings 3:13
Psalm 65:9
Psalm 68:19

Good things come from God. Thank him!

Blinded by Sin (4171)
Ecclesiastes 9:3
Daniel 4:33-34
Luke 15:17
Acts 7:54
1 Corinthians 2:8
2 Peter 2:16

Nebuchadnezzar ate grass! Sin can drive people crazy. If you want to keep yourself from doing crazy things, obey God.

Boasting (0519)
Psalm 34:2
Psalm 44:8
Isaiah 45:25
Jeremiah 9:24
Romans 2:17
1 Corinthians 1:31
2 Corinthians 10:17

If you believe in Christ, you have it good. God has saved you from your sins and given you the Holy Spirit. Boast in what he has done.

Boredom (0033)
2 Thessalonians 3:11
1 Timothy 5:13
1 Peter 4:15

Do you have time on your hands? As these verses point out, it makes a difference what you do with it. Don't fiddle around doing nothing or go bugging other people. Find something useful to do.

Borrowing (0582)
Exodus 22:14
2 Kings 6:5
Psalm 37:21
Proverbs 22:7
Matthew 5:42

A borrower has a special responsibility. A good borrower returns whatever he or she borrows. Take good care of the stuff you borrow, and be sure to give it back.

Brain Power (2351)
Romans 1:28
Romans 8:7
Ephesians 4:17
Colossians 1:21
Colossians 2:18
Titus 1:15

These verses all talk about thoughts. What we DO grows out of what we THINK. Don't let your mind run wild. Keep your mind off of what is crude, dirty, and sinful. It makes a difference.

Bribery (2548)
Exodus 23:8
Psalm 26:10
Proverbs 17:23
Isaiah 1:23
Isaiah 5:23
Isaiah 33:15
Amos 5:12

These verses are about people who accept bribes. God hates bribery because it perverts justice. If the people who enforce the rules don't enforce the rules, who will enforce the rules? Do the right thing no matter what anyone offers you.

Bullies (3484)
Psalm 7:1
Psalm 31:15
Psalm 119:86
Psalm 119:157
Psalm 119:161
Psalm 143:3
Jeremiah 15:15
Lamentations 5:5

David and Jeremiah didn't deserve to be picked on by their enemies. But they didn't try to get revenge. They asked God for help. Don't try to get back at kids who hurt you. Call on God when you're hurting. Let God take care of you (and them) in the right way.

Callousness (4205)
Ezra 9:6
Jeremiah 5:28
Matthew 12:45
Matthew 13:15
Matthew 26:74
2 Timothy 3:13
2 Peter 2:20

God gave you a conscience to protect you from sin. When you know you have done something wrong, confess it! If you ignore your conscience again and again, soon you'll have a hard heart. And then you will have a pile of trouble!

Caring for Church (0732)
Acts 20:31
2 Corinthians 7:12
2 Corinthians 11:28
2 Corinthians 12:20
Galatians 4:11
1 Thessalonians 3:10

The apostle Paul knew what churches should be—a loving place of worship. Paul spent his time helping churches be that. You can help your church be what God wants by worshiping him there and loving the people around you. (You and Paul would have a lot in common then.)

Change (1789)
Jeremiah 35:15
Ezekiel 33:11
Hosea 6:1
Matthew 22:3
Luke 14:17
2 Corinthians 5:20
Revelation 3:20

In each of these verses God asks people to turn around—to change their ways from evil to good and live lives that please him. He is asking you that same. Will you do it?

Christ as Judge (1355)
Matthew 25:32
John 5:22
Acts 10:42
Acts 17:31
Romans 2:16
Romans 14:10
1 Corinthians 4:5

2 Timothy 4:1
1 Peter 4:5

One day Jesus will judge all of us. He will judge whether we obeyed him. You might look at people around you and think that you know whether they live for God or not, but only Jesus can really make that judgment. And when he is judging you, you won't be worrying about someone else. Don't be quick to judge others.

Christian Duties (2171)

2 Chronicles 5:13-14
John 9:4
Romans 13:12
Ephesians 5:8
Philippians 2:15
1 Thessalonians 5:5-6

These verses talk about some of your responsibilities in the family of God, such as worshiping and witnessing. The good news is that you don't have to wonder what you should do. God has told you in the Bible. The bad news is that some people still don't do it . Don't be one of those people—it just makes it harder on everyone else.

Christmas (0720)

Isaiah 7:14
Isaiah 9:6
Luke 1:31
John 1:14
Romans 8:3
Philippians 2:7
1 Timothy 3:16
1 John 4:2

God came to earth as a baby and grew up like you. He did this so that he could take the punishment for your sins. Thank you, God!

Church (0485)

Matthew 25:15
Romans 12:6
1 Corinthians 4:7
1 Corinthians 12:4
Ephesians 4:11

You have talents that are useful to others. You can let them go unused if you want to, but then they will just waste away. Meanwhile, your church needs those talents of yours. In fact, that's why you have them. Look for ways to help out at your church by doing what you do best.

Clear Conscience (0825)

Acts 24:16
Romans 9:1
2 Corinthians 1:12
1 Timothy 1:5
1 Timothy 1:19
1 Timothy 3:9
Hebrews 13:18
1 Peter 3:16

It's important to God that you have a clear conscience. When you know you haven't done anything wrong, you have a lot less to worry about. Try to make the right choices the first time.

Cold Shoulder (3401)

Numbers 20:18
Numbers 21:23
Deuteronomy 23:4
Judges 19:15
1 Samuel 25:10
Luke 9:53

Instead of welcoming strangers, some people ignore them or try to get rid of them. God wants you to reach out to kids you don't know. When you see a new kid at school, at church, or in the neighborhood, welcome him or her. You may make a new friend. You will certainly please God.

Comforting Others (0785)

Isaiah 40:1
1 Corinthians 14:3
1 Corinthians 14:31
2 Corinthians 2:7
1 Thessalonians 4:18
1 Thessalonians 5:11
1 Thessalonians 5:14

It's no fun to lose, fail, fall, get laughed at, or get hurt. So don't rub it in when someone else goes down. Show a little sympathy.

Commitment (3508)

Exodus 32:29
1 Chronicles 29:5
Proverbs 23:26
Romans 12:1
2 Timothy 2:21

God doesn't want part of you, he wants ALL of you. The more you give of yourself to God, the more he will be able to use you. Don't hold back. Give everything you are and everything you have to God. That's the kind of commitment God loves.

Compassion (3519)

Exodus 2:6
2 Chronicles 28:15
Job 29:13
Luke 10:33-34
Acts 16:33
Acts 28:2
Hebrews 10:34

Did the people in these verses just feel sorry for needy people? No, they helped them! Compassion is more than a feeling, it's an action. Give some of your time and energy to help kids who need help. That's compassion.

Conceit (1728)

Proverbs 3:7
Proverbs 26:5
Proverbs 26:12
Isaiah 5:21
Romans 12:16
1 Corinthians 8:2
Galatians 6:3

These verses are about conceit. The rule is this: "Don't be conceited." Know your bad points as well as your good. There is nothing wrong with being proud of a job well done. Just don't think it makes you especially wonderful. Everybody makes mistakes.

Confession (0816)

Leviticus 16:21
Leviticus 26:40
Numbers 5:7
Ezra 10:11
Job 33:27
Proverbs 28:13
Jeremiah 3:13
1 John 1:9

Boy, it's yucky sometimes to admit it when your wrong. But one of the best things about God is that as soon as you admit your sin, he forgives and forgets. Being forgiven is worth a little yuck, don't you think?

Contentment (0829)

Proverbs 15:16
Luke 3:14
Philippians 4:11
1 Timothy 6:6, 8
Hebrews 13:5

If you're always wanting more than what you have, you aren't content. It's OK to want things, but when you think, "If I just had THAT, then I'd be happy," you're not content anymore. Be happy with what you have. That's contentment.

Controlling Yourself (3205)

Matthew 16:24
Luke 14:26-27
Romans 8:13
Romans 15:1
Galatians 5:24

Following God means not following yourself. That's what these verses mean. You have to give up sin (which is hard) and obey God. Keep on. It's worth it.

Cost of Sin (3801)
LEVITICUS 26:37
DEUTERONOMY 28:32
JOSHUA 7:12
JUDGES 1:21
JUDGES 2:14
JUDGES 16:17
1 SAMUEL 17:24
JEREMIAH 51:30
MARK 9:18
JOHN 15:5

All the people in these verses were weak. Sin stole their courage and strength. Sin can make you weak and sickly. So try hard to stay away from sin. In the long run, it hurts.

Crime (2000)
GENESIS 49:5
PSALM 27:12
PROVERBS 11:17

The people described here were violent, cruel people. That means they enjoyed seeing other people hurt. God is never pleased with cruelty. Not on TV, not in the movies, not in your life. Another person's pain, in their bodies or their feelings, is not anything for you to enjoy.

The Crowd (2924)
1 SAMUEL 14:45
1 SAMUEL 15:24
MATTHEW 14:5
JOHN 7:13
ACTS 12:3

One of the most powerful forces on earth—for good and for bad—are crowds. Notice how crowds influenced events in each of the verses in this chain. If you have something important to say, say it to as many people as possible. But if the crowd is saying the wrong thing, don't listen no matter how many there are—or you may end up getting swept up in something bad.

Cruel Talk (3304)
EPHESIANS 4:31
TITUS 3:1-2
JAMES 3:6
JAMES 4:11
1 PETER 2:1
1 PETER 3:10

These verses are about making mean, angry, or cruel statements to people. God is against all of it. If you are angry, find a way to talk about it that doesn't hurt the people around you.

Cruelty (3520)
JOB 24:9
PSALM 35:15
PSALM 69:21
PROVERBS 25:20
PROVERBS 28:3
AMOS 1:11
MATTHEW 18:30
LUKE 10:32

The people in these verses were heartless. They showed no pity to people who were down. Don't follow their example. Be kind.

Cruelty to Animals (2002)
NUMBERS 22:27
2 SAMUEL 8:4
1 CHRONICLES 18:4
PROVERBS 12:10

These verses mention mistreatment of animals. God does not like it when animals are mistreated. Yes, it matters to him. Don't be cruel to an animal just because you are bigger or smarter.

Cursing (0479)
ECCLESIASTES 10:20
LUKE 6:28
ROMANS 12:14
JAMES 3:10

The mouth is for blessing, not cursing. That's the problem with name-calling. "Say something nice or say nothing at all."

"Dangerous Kisses" (3661)
2 SAMUEL 15:5
2 SAMUEL 20:9
PROVERBS 27:6
MARK 14:45

A kiss can be dangerous if it's from an enemy. Bad people sometimes act nice to hide their real motives. They may say nice words to you, but behind your back they are planning to hurt you. Don't believe everything people tell you. Don't trust everybody. Be careful about whom you trust.

Death (2158)
2 SAMUEL 14:14
JOB 30:23
PSALM 49:10
PSALM 89:48
ECCLESIASTES 3:19
ECCLESIASTES 8:8
ROMANS 5:12
HEBREWS 9:27

Death is not fun to talk about. But death is a part of life. People die. Animals die. Insects die. Because we know this, we try to make the most of our lives. Because we know everything dies someday, we follow God and hope to live with him in eternity.

Deception (1796)
MATTHEW 24:4
1 CORINTHIANS 6:9
1 CORINTHIANS 15:33
GALATIANS 6:7
EPHESIANS 5:6
2 THESSALONIANS 2:3
1 JOHN 3:7

You can find the same warning in all these verses: Don't be deceived. Some people will lie to you and try to get you to believe their lies. Don't be fooled. Even if you don't question them out loud, question them in your mind. And if their message doesn't match God's, don't believe it.

Defeat of Satan (3149)
GENESIS 3:15
LUKE 4:13
JOHN 12:30-31
JOHN 14:30
2 THESSALONIANS 2:8
HEBREWS 2:14
1 JOHN 3:8
REVELATION 20:10

These verses say that Jesus came to earth to take away Satan's power. Jesus did this when he died on the cross and then rose on the third day. When he comes back, Satan will be thrown into hell forever. You can look forward to that.

Demons (3156)
MATTHEW 12:45
MARK 1:26
MARK 5:9
MARK 7:30
MARK 9:17
MARK 16:9
LUKE 10:19
ACTS 8:7
ACTS 19:13
EPHESIANS 6:12
1 TIMOTHY 4:1
JAMES 2:19
REVELATION 16:14

These verses make it clear that demons are real. They have power in this world and can influence people. But they also don't have any power over God. God doesn't want you to be afraid of them, but to trust in him to protect you. Have faith in God and resist the devil, and you won't have to worry about demons.

Desire for God (0983)
PSALM 42:2
PSALM 63:1
PSALM 119:174
PSALM 143:6
AMOS 8:11

Have you ever seen a little kid get lost? He doesn't just want to find his mom a little bit. He wants to find her a WHOLE LOT. That's how we feel about God when we really love him. Worshiping him doesn't come hard for a person like that.

Determination (3441)

JOB 17:9
JOHN 15:9
ACTS 13:43
ROMANS 2:7
GALATIANS 6:9
2 TIMOTHY 3:14
HEBREWS 12:1
1 PETER 1:13
REVELATION 3:11

These verses explain how to persevere in your Christian life. Don't get tired of doing good. Don't give up yet—you can stay strong to the end!

Devotions (1002)

GENESIS 28:16
GENESIS 28:17-18
EXODUS 24:4
1 SAMUEL 1:19
2 CHRONICLES 29:20
JOB 1:5
PSALM 57:8
PSALM 119:147
MARK 1:35

Some of the people in these verses read God's word and prayed each morning. Spending time with God each morning is a good investment. It sets your mind on his word and invites him to guide you. It's an excellent way to get ready for the day ahead.

Different People (4083)

LUKE 9:53
JOHN 4:9
ACTS 10:28
ACTS 11:3
ACTS 19:34
GALATIANS 2:12

Some people think they are better than anyone who has a different color skin or speaks a different language. But just because a person is different doesn't mean he or she is not as good. Every person is made in God's image. Don't avoid kids who are different. Be friendly and kind to them.

Difficulties (0497)

DEUTERONOMY 8:5
PSALM 94:12
PROVERBS 3:11-12
JOHN 15:2
REVELATION 3:19

God has put you in a class with Teacher Experience. He lets you face difficulties in life because they are some of the best teachers you'll ever have. The next time something bad happens, remember that God is teaching you. Then look for the lessons.

Diligence (0564)

PROVERBS 10:4
PROVERBS 13:4
PROVERBS 22:29
ROMANS 12:8
HEBREWS 6:11
2 PETER 1:10
2 PETER 3:14

Why work? Because great rewards come to those who learn to sweat. Give it your best, and that's what you'll get.

Disappointment (1190)

DEUTERONOMY 28:39
JOB 11:20
JOB 20:18
JOB 27:17
PROVERBS 11:7
ISAIAH 17:11
JEREMIAH 8:15
JEREMIAH 14:19
AMOS 5:11
MICAH 6:15
ZEPHANIAH 1:13

In these verses, people were disappointed because they lived sinful lives. God saw their evil choices and withheld his blessing. Their hopes were dashed. Sometimes life will disappoint you no matter what you do. Don't bring it on yourself by rebelling against God and giving up his blessing on your life.

Discipline (1630)

PROVERBS 13:24
PROVERBS 19:18
PROVERBS 22:15
PROVERBS 23:13

God wants you to know right from wrong because he cares about you, so he gives parents the job of teaching you what they have learned. The quicker you learn, the less trouble you have as you grow up. Don't resent your parents for disciplining you. Their rules are what keep you from becoming a big friendless fool. Try hard to learn something every time you get in trouble. You'll soon be way ahead of your peers.

Discontentment (1121)

ECCLESIASTES 1:8
ECCLESIASTES 4:8
ECCLESIASTES 5:10
ECCLESIASTES 6:7
ISAIAH 29:8
ISAIAH 55:2
ISAIAH 65:13
LUKE 15:14
JOHN 4:13
REVELATION 18:14

Most of us always want more than we have. And the more we get, the more we want. But no amount of money or things makes us stop wanting more. We have to trust God to give us what we need because we can't trust ourselves to know when enough is enough.

Discretion (2916)

GENESIS 41:39
PROVERBS 2:11
PROVERBS 5:2
ISAIAH 28:26
MARK 12:34

These verses are about knowing what to say and when to say it. Just because you know what you are talking about doesn't mean you should talk. Sometimes not talking is the best thing to do. Sometimes you need to be careful how you say it. Ask God to teach you discretion—knowing how to say the right thing at the right time.

Dishonest People (3705)

PSALM 36:3
PROVERBS 12:5
PROVERBS 27:6
JEREMIAH 5:27
MARK 7:22

Some people are full of deceit. They will tell you anything just to get what they want. Dishonest people can really hurt you. Stay away from them as much as you can.

Doing Good (3905)

PSALM 34:14
PSALM 37:3
PSALM 37:27
LUKE 6:35
ROMANS 13:3
GALATIANS 6:10
1 TIMOTHY 6:18
HEBREWS 13:16
JAMES 4:17
1 PETER 2:15
1 PETER 3:11
1 PETER 3:17

Doing nice things for your friends is easy. Doing nice things for your enemies is hard. But a person who loves God is a full-time doer of good. God wants you to do good to ALL people, even the kids you don't like. Who is one kid you could do something nice for this week?

Don't Be Unfair (1982)

Deuteronomy 16:19
Deuteronomy 24:17
Psalm 82:2
Proverbs 29:27
Proverbs 31:4-5
Ecclesiastes 3:16
Luke 16:10

"Pick on someone your own size." People are sometimes dishonest and unfair to people who can't defend themselves. Remember, though, that God sees our hearts and judges us by our intentions as well as our actions. Never treat someone badly just because the person is weak or because you can get away with it. God doesn't like it.

Don't Forget... (3003)

Deuteronomy 4:9
Deuteronomy 6:10-12
Deuteronomy 8:11
Judges 8:34
Psalm 9:17
Psalm 50:22
Psalm 78:11
Isaiah 17:10
Isaiah 51:13
Jeremiah 3:21
Hebrews 2:1

You just read about people who forgot about God. They just went about their lives never thanking him for the things they have. Look around you. Everything you have comes from God. Don't forget him. Don't forget to thank him.

Double Life (3445)

2 Kings 17:33
1 Chronicles 12:33
Zephaniah 1:4-5
Luke 16:13
1 Corinthians 10:21
James 1:8
James 4:8

These verses explain that too many people try to lead double lives. They worship God on Sundays but worship themselves the rest of the week. The Bible says we can't have it both ways. Don't be wishy-washy about your faith. Live for God every day.

Drinking (3568)

Leviticus 10:9
Numbers 6:3
Deuteronomy 29:6
Judges 13:4
Proverbs 23:31
Proverbs 31:4
Jeremiah 35:6
Daniel 1:8
Daniel 10:3
Matthew 11:18
Luke 1:15
Romans 14:21
1 Corinthians 8:13

When God chose these people to do special jobs for him, he told them not to drink. Drinking can cause trouble. It is better not to drink at all than to risk blowing it because you drank too much. Just to be safe, don't drink.

Drinking Too Much (3575)

Proverbs 20:1
Proverbs 21:17
Proverbs 23:31
Proverbs 31:4
Isaiah 5:11
Isaiah 28:1
Isaiah 28:7
Isaiah 56:12
Hosea 4:11
Habakkuk 2:5
Ephesians 5:18

Alcoholic drinks such as beer and wine can affect people in bad ways. Drinking too much is foolish. Decide now never to drink too much. You will save yourself a lot of pain in the future.

Duty to Pray (2817)

1 Chronicles 16:11
Hosea 14:2
Matthew 7:7
Matthew 26:41
Luke 18:1
Luke 21:36
John 16:24
Ephesians 6:18
Philippians 4:6
Colossians 4:2
1 Thessalonians 5:17
1 Timothy 2:8
James 5:13

These verses tell us to communicate with God—not just when we need help and not just when we feel like it, but every day and whenever we need to. You don't have to go to a special place to pray or wait for a "prayer time." Talk to God throughout the day about all that's on your mind.

Earning Heaven (4120)

Luke 18:12
Romans 9:32
Romans 10:3
Galatians 3:10

No matter how good you are, you can't earn your way to heaven. Only Jesus can save you. Don't depend on your good deeds to save you. Depend on Jesus.

Earth (3455)

Exodus 19:5
Leviticus 25:23
1 Chronicles 29:14
Psalm 24:1
Psalm 50:10
Psalm 60:7
Psalm 89:11
Haggai 2:8

The earth belongs to God. We should treat it as an important and breakable gift from him. Take care of the world around you. Remember that God is the owner; we just live here.

Embarrassing God (2997)

2 Samuel 12:14
Nehemiah 5:9
Ezekiel 36:20
Romans 2:23-24
2 Peter 2:2

These verses are about people who make believing in God look like a foolish thing to do. How did they do it? They would obey God for a while and tell everyone else to, then they would stop. Then they would start again. Then they would stop. They made it look like believing in God is just a mood that comes and goes. You can do better than that.

Encouraging People (1019)

Exodus 14:13
2 Chronicles 35:2
Isaiah 41:13
Matthew 9:2
Matthew 14:27
Matthew 17:7
Mark 16:6
Acts 23:11
Acts 27:22

These verses show people encouraging other people. When you encourage someone you say something that helps the person feel better about his or her life. Jesus took time to encourage people by saying things like, "Don't be afraid. I'm here. . . ." You can encourage the people around you, too.

End Times (0196)

1 John 2:18
1 John 4:3
2 John 1:7

Don't be deceived. Not every "spiritual teacher" teaches the truth. Know the Bible so YOU don't fall for someone's tricks.

Endurance (3440)
MATTHEW 10:22
MARK 13:13
HEBREWS 12:7
JAMES 1:12
JAMES 5:11
1 PETER 2:19

A lot of people give up when hurts and disappointments come. But every hardship calls us to endure and keep trusting in God's good care. And God rewards those who do endure. No matter what happens, stay faithful to God.

Enemies (4082)
MATTHEW 5:44
LUKE 23:34
ACTS 7:60

Ouch! When someone picks on you, it's tempting to fight back. But God wants you to pray for those who hurt you, just like Jesus and Stephen did. Pray for kids who are mean. They need to change.

Envy (1137)
PSALM 37:1
PROVERBS 3:31
PROVERBS 14:30
PROVERBS 23:17
PROVERBS 24:1
ROMANS 13:13
1 CORINTHIANS 13:4
GALATIANS 5:26
JAMES 3:14

Sometimes we say "It's not fair!" when somebody gets something we didn't get. We wish we had been treated like they were, and we resent them for what they got. That's jealousy. Jealousy displeases God, makes us unhappy, and doesn't accomplish ANYTHING. When you feel jealous, try to remember that your turn will come.

Equality (2238)
PROVERBS 22:2
MATTHEW 23:8
ACTS 10:28
ROMANS 10:12
GALATIANS 3:28
JAMES 2:5

People have a way of putting other people in categories. Poor. Rich. Cool. Not cool. These verses say that God sees us all the same and gives us all the same opportunity to obey him. You are better than no one and no one is better than you. If God sees us all as equal, who are we to say otherwise?

Eternal Life (2405)
LUKE 20:36
JOHN 6:50
JOHN 8:51
JOHN 11:26
ROMANS 2:7
1 CORINTHIANS 15:53
2 CORINTHIANS 5:1
1 THESSALONIANS 4:17
2 TIMOTHY 1:10

The bad news is that our bodies die. The good news is that our spirits live forever. The best news is that through Jesus Christ we can live forever with a God who loves us and cares for us. Don't be afraid.

Everyone Sins (3340)
GENESIS 6:5
1 KINGS 8:46
PSALM 14:3
PSALM 53:3
PSALM 130:3
PROVERBS 20:9
ECCLESIASTES 7:20
ISAIAH 53:6
ISAIAH 64:6
MICAH 7:2
ROMANS 3:23
GALATIANS 3:22
1 JOHN 1:8
1 JOHN 5:19

These verses say over and over again that everyone sins. Everyone needs God's forgiveness. And everyone who wants to be forgiven and accepted by God must go to God and admit his or her sin. Admit your sinfulness to God.

Evil Attacks (0970)
JOB 5:19
PSALM 91:3
PSALM 116:8
ISAIAH 46:4
1 CORINTHIANS 10:13
2 CORINTHIANS 1:10
2 TIMOTHY 4:18
HEBREWS 2:15
2 PETER 2:9

Have you ever watched a play or a movie where the bad guys start to win and one of the good guys gets in danger and needs to be rescued? The person who rescues the good guy is called the hero. God is like that. He is the one who rescues you from every evil danger. Don't be afraid—God is the biggest hero of them all. Call on him for help.

Evildoers (1161)
PSALM 34:16
PSALM 37:9
PSALM 94:16
PSALM 119:115
ISAIAH 9:17
ISAIAH 14:20
ISAIAH 31:2

God has very definite feelings about evil. He wants no part of it, and he doesn't want you close to it. Be smart about this—if someone thinks doing evil or mean things is the greatest fun you can have, stay away.

Examples of Generosity (2115)
EXODUS 35:22
EXODUS 36:5
NUMBERS 7:3
1 CHRONICLES 29:3-4
2 CHRONICLES 24:10
EZRA 1:6
EZRA 2:69
EZRA 8:25
NEHEMIAH 7:70
LUKE 19:8
LUKE 21:1-4
ACTS 4:34-35
ACTS 11:29
2 CORINTHIANS 8:2
PHILIPPIANS 4:16

You just read about people who were generous—happy to give something to God or to someone else. They were generous in their actions and in their hearts. Generosity pleases God because he owns it all anyway, and he'll always make sure we have enough. Don't be stingy.

Examples of Mercy (2296)
1 SAMUEL 11:13
1 SAMUEL 26:9
2 SAMUEL 19:22
1 KINGS 1:52
2 KINGS 6:22
LUKE 9:55
JOHN 8:7

Each person in these verses had a reason to hurt someone else . . . and could have. But instead, all of them chose to be kind. That is mercy. Everyday you are around people whom you can hurt or help. God wants you to have mercy on them. Help them.

Examples of Revenge (2281)
1 KINGS 19:2
1 KINGS 22:27
ESTHER 3:6
EZEKIEL 25:15
MATTHEW 14:8
LUKE 4:29
ACTS 5:33
ACTS 23:12

These people got angry about something and made plans to get even. They thought they could take care of themselves by hurting other people. Don't take matters into your own hands. If you're in a bad situation, by all means get out of it. But let God take care of getting even.

Excusing Sin (2670)

PROVERBS 17:15
PROVERBS 24:24
PROVERBS 28:4
ISAIAH 5:20
EZEKIEL 13:22
MALACHI 2:17
ROMANS 1:32

These verses are about getting things backwards. They are about seeing sin and calling it something else so you can keep doing it. Be honest with yourself and with God—when you sin, don't pretend it's something else. Confess it to God.

Expecting Pain (3483)

MATTHEW 10:17
MATTHEW 24:9
LUKE 21:12
JOHN 15:20
JOHN 16:2
2 TIMOTHY 3:12
REVELATION 2:10

No one likes pain. But Jesus tells us to expect it. Don't try to get out of suffering for Jesus—some people just won't like you for it. And don't be scared of what other kids can do to you. Instead, look forward to what Jesus will give you.

Fair to the Poor (2801)

PSALM 82:3
PROVERBS 21:13
PROVERBS 29:14
JEREMIAH 22:16

These verses are about true heroes—people who defend the poor and the weak. People who have little have no power in this world. God loves it when you to make sure those people are treated fairly. Stick up for the little guy, and you're a real hero.

Faith (1202)

2 CHRONICLES 20:20
MARK 11:22
LUKE 8:50
JOHN 6:28-29
JOHN 20:27
EPHESIANS 6:16
1 THESSALONIANS 5:8
1 TIMOTHY 1:19
1 TIMOTHY 6:12
HEBREWS 10:22
HEBREWS 11:6
JAMES 1:5-6
1 JOHN 3:23

You just read about faith. Faith is believing in God—that he is there and that he cares about you. Faith is the greatest gift you can give God. Don't miss a chance to let God know you believe in him by telling him (praying) or showing him (obeying).

Faith Tested (1213)

MATTHEW 15:23
MARK 5:35
MARK 10:13
LUKE 5:18-19
JOHN 9:24
JOHN 11:3-6

These verses give examples of circumstances that test your faith. People get tired when they go through a lot of hard experiences. And it doesn't seem fair that people of faith should have to suffer. But part of having faith in God is knowing that he'll bring you through the hard times and your faith will be stronger. Whenever you go through these trying times, cling to God in faith.

Family (3393)

PROVERBS 22:2
MALACHI 2:10
MARK 3:34
ACTS 17:26
ROMANS 14:13
1 CORINTHIANS 8:13

You know that kid at school who really bugs you? Well, you should treat him as a brother. These verses tell us that everyone is part of the same family. God created every person. And all of God's people are part of God's family. Treat others as if they were part of your own family. In a very real way, they are.

Fanatics (1241)

1 KINGS 18:28
JOHN 19:15
ACTS 7:57
ACTS 9:1
ACTS 21:36
ACTS 22:23

The people described here went way overboard. They got very upset and didn't think clearly and made big mistakes because of it. Whenever you get in a frenzy, you make different choices than you would in a calm moment. Remember, your emotions tell you what you feel, not what to do.

Favoritism (1984)

LEVITICUS 19:15
DEUTERONOMY 1:17
JOB 13:10
PROVERBS 24:23
MALACHI 2:9
1 TIMOTHY 5:21
JAMES 2:4
JUDE 1:16

It's natural to like one person better than another. You might spend more time with that person or laugh more when you're together. That's not what these verses are talking about. These verses are talking about bending the rules for someone because you like the person. You have to do what is right whether you like the person or not.

Fearing God (3034)

DEUTERONOMY 10:12
DEUTERONOMY 13:4
JOSHUA 4:24
JOSHUA 24:14
1 CHRONICLES 16:30
2 CHRONICLES 19:7
PROVERBS 3:7
ECCLESIASTES 12:13
ISAIAH 8:13
MATTHEW 10:28
LUKE 23:40
ROMANS 11:20
1 PETER 1:17
1 PETER 2:17
REVELATION 14:7

These verses use the word fear. It's the kind of fear you feel when you go to the beach and feel the pounding surf. You tremble inside and respect the water because it is so much more powerful than you. God loves you very much, but he is a thousand times mightier than any pounding surf. Any normal kid would tremble just thinking about it.

Feeling Guilty (1763)

GENESIS 42:21
EXODUS 9:27
NUMBERS 21:7
EZRA 9:6
PSALM 40:12
DANIEL 5:6
JOHN 8:9

Someone in each of these verses felt guilty. You feel guilty whenever your conscience nags you about something you did wrong. And when that happens there's only one thing to do: confess your sin to God.

Feeling Helpless (3799)

LUKE 13:11
JOHN 5:7
JOHN 6:44
JOHN 15:5
ACTS 3:2
ROMANS 5:6

ROMANS 7:18

Jesus loves to help the helpless. You may not be sick or crippled. But you are helpless in another way—you can't save yourself from sin. Follow the example of the people in these verses. Go to Jesus for help.

Feeling Sorry (2712)

PSALM 34:18
PSALM 51:17
ISAIAH 57:15
ISAIAH 66:2
JOEL 2:13
ZECHARIAH 12:10
2 CORINTHIANS 7:10

These verses are about feeling bad about your sin. It's not bad to feel bad—it's good. It shows that you want to do the right thing. God loves that kind of attitude. Go to God, tell him how you feel, and think about this: "God is near to the broken-hearted."

Fighting (3733)

GENESIS 21:10
PROVERBS 18:19
PROVERBS 19:13
PROVERBS 21:9
PROVERBS 21:19
PROVERBS 27:15

Have you ever wished you could eat your words? Family conflicts can lead to ugly quarrels. You can say things you later wish you had not. When you have a problem with someone in your family, be careful what you say. Try to work things out without fighting.

Finding God (4100)

JOB 23:3
JEREMIAH 29:13
HOSEA 6:3
ACTS 17:27

Where is God? He is closer than you think. The Bible says he has left clues for us in nature, and we have the Bible itself for the details we can't find on our own. Seek God with all your heart and you will indeed find him.

Finding Strength (3806)

EXODUS 15:2
2 SAMUEL 22:33
PSALM 28:8
PSALM 46:1
PSALM 73:26
PSALM 81:1
PSALM 84:5
PSALM 89:21

God is stronger than the strongest person. He can protect you when you feel weak or vulnerable. If you depend only on your own strength or ability, what will you do when someone bigger comes along? Always pray that God will be your strength.

Following God (1793)

DEUTERONOMY 30:15
JOSHUA 24:15
RUTH 1:15
1 KINGS 18:21
MATTHEW 27:17
MARK 10:21
LUKE 16:13
JOHN 6:67

These verses are about choices. Everyday you choose to follow God, or you choose to follow something else. Not choosing at all is the same as choosing something else. Which will it be for you today?

Foolish Promises (2610)

GENESIS 25:33
JOSHUA 9:19
MARK 6:23
ACTS 23:21

These verses are about people who made promises too quickly and then later regretted it. It's like when you say, "If you let me go to this party, I'll do the dishes for a week!" Then the next week you wish you hadn't promised. The problem with foolish promises is if you keep them, you are unhappy and if you don't, you are undependable. You lose either way. Think before you promise.

For Kids Only (3964)

PSALM 119:9
PROVERBS 20:29
ECCLESIASTES 11:9
LAMENTATIONS 3:27
1 TIMOTHY 4:12
TITUS 2:6-7
1 JOHN 2:13-14

Some books are for "Adults Only." But the Bible has some advice meant just for kids. Each of these verses has a piece of it. Read verses like these for keys to being ahead of the game when you are young.

Forgiveness (1314)

LEVITICUS 5:10
PSALM 103:3
PSALM 130:4
EZEKIEL 18:22
MATTHEW 6:14
MARK 3:28
ACTS 5:31
ACTS 13:38
ACTS 26:18
EPHESIANS 1:7
JAMES 5:15
1 JOHN 1:9

These verses are about God's forgiveness. Of course, God cares whether you tried your best to obey him, but he will forgive you when you mess up too, if you ask him. That's a good deal. Don't you think so?

Forgiveness of Sin (3127)

MATTHEW 26:28
LUKE 3:3
LUKE 24:47
ACTS 2:38
ROMANS 3:25
HEBREWS 9:22
HEBREWS 10:18

These verses remind you that God really can forgive your sins. Before Christ died, forgiveness required a sacrifice. But Jesus was our once-for-all sacrifice. He died so we could be forgiven and our sins could be forgotten. Trust HIM to save you.

Forgiving Others (1315)

MARK 11:25
LUKE 11:4
LUKE 17:4
EPHESIANS 4:32
COLOSSIANS 3:13

These verses say clearly that God wants you to forgive other people. Why? Because God has forgiven you. He wants you to do the same for others. This doesn't mean you have to let people hurt you. But when they do, forgive them and don't take revenge.

Free Samples (1177)

JOHN 13:15
2 THESSALONIANS 3:9
1 TIMOTHY 4:12
TITUS 2:7
HEBREWS 11:4
JAMES 5:10
1 PETER 2:21

These verses are about examples. When someone is a good example he shows you through his life the way you want to live. Copying someone else's homework is not cool. But copying someone's good example is EXTRAORDINARILY cool. Look around and see what you can learn from others.

Free to... (2136)

1 CORINTHIANS 8:9
GALATIANS 5:13
1 PETER 2:16

These verses remind you that other people are always watching. Younger Christians will follow your example. Be extra careful to set a good one for them.

Freedom (3503)

Romans 6:2
Romans 6:7
Romans 6:11
Galatians 2:20
Galatians 5:24
Colossians 2:20
Colossians 3:3
2 Timothy 2:11
1 Peter 2:24

It's hard to stop doing all the things you used to do before you became a Christian. Old habits die hard. You can't do it alone. Only Jesus can help you get rid of those sinful desires. Depend on Jesus to free you from sin's hold.

Friend of Jesus (4104)

Matthew 11:19
Luke 7:39
Luke 19:7
John 8:11
Romans 5:8
1 Timothy 1:15

Losers, crooks, liars, cheaters—Jesus was friends with all of them. No one is too bad for him if they are willing to change. Jesus will always be your friend too, no matter what you were before, if you want to follow him. Don't worry about your past mistakes. Just go to your friend, Jesus.

Friends and Church (3924)

2 Chronicles 30:1
Isaiah 2:3
Jeremiah 31:6
Zechariah 8:21

People who love God invite their friends to worship him, too. They want the people they care about to know the God they care about. Church is a great place for your friends to meet God. Invite them!

Friendship (1322)

Proverbs 17:17
Proverbs 18:24
Proverbs 27:10
Proverbs 27:17
Ecclesiastes 4:9-10
John 15:13-14

You just read about being a good friend. Yes, God cares what kind of friend you are. He wants you to show love to your friends and be faithful to them. It pleases God when you are being a good friend.

The Future (2492)

Proverbs 27:1
Ecclesiastes 3:22
Ecclesiastes 6:12
Ecclesiastes 8:7
Ecclesiastes 9:12
Ecclesiastes 10:14
Ecclesiastes 11:2
Matthew 24:43
Acts 20:22
James 4:14

These verses are about seeing the future. YOU CAN'T! Since you can't know what is in the future, be glad that you know God will be there.

Generosity (2126)

Leviticus 25:35
Deuteronomy 15:7
Proverbs 31:20
Matthew 6:1
Matthew 19:21
Luke 11:41
Luke 12:33
Luke 18:22
Luke 19:8
1 Corinthians 13:3

These verses give guidelines for being generous. Generosity means giving more than is required. If you are naturally generous, that's great. If you aren't, practice. Generosity is something you can learn.

Gentleness (2276)

1 Thessalonians 2:7
1 Timothy 3:3
2 Timothy 2:24
Titus 3:2
James 3:17

The gentleness described in these verses is what you see in people who don't quarrel. They don't want to upset the people around them and they know when to stay calm. It's OK to yell loudly at a ball game, especially if your team is winning, but God wants you to be gentle with other people and their feelings. Learn when to tone it down.

Getting Ahead (0580)

Proverbs 16:8
Proverbs 21:6
Proverbs 22:16
Proverbs 28:8
Jeremiah 17:11
Jeremiah 22:13
Ezekiel 22:13
James 5:4

Sometime in your life you will try to earn something: money, grades, prizes, privileges. It may look like you can get more of these things by being unfair to other people. But if you do, you will lose the respect of others and the respect of God. The respect of others and the respect of God are worth more than money or grades, or prizes, or privileges. Remember to be a good person while you go for the gold.

Getting Along (3725)

1 Corinthians 1:10
2 Corinthians 13:11
Ephesians 4:3
Philippians 1:27
Philippians 4:2
Colossians 2:2
1 Peter 3:8

Live in harmony. You may not always agree with other Christians, but God wants you to get along with them. God's love can help you. Try your best to get along.

Getting Caught (3452)

Matthew 12:36
Matthew 18:23
Matthew 21:34
Matthew 25:19
Luke 12:20
Luke 12:48
Luke 19:15
Romans 14:12
1 Peter 4:4-5

Does it frustrate you to see kids get away with doing wrong? Other people may not notice them, but God sees it all. He holds all people accountable. Don't worry about what other kids get away with. They will have to answer to God someday, and they will not like it.

Getting Drunk (3571)

Deuteronomy 21:20
Proverbs 20:1
Proverbs 23:20
Proverbs 23:29-31
Ecclesiastes 10:17
Isaiah 5:11
Isaiah 28:1
Nahum 1:10
Habakkuk 2:15
Luke 21:34
Romans 13:13
1 Corinthians 6:10
Ephesians 5:18
1 Thessalonians 5:7

These verses are all about getting drunk. They don't have one good thing to say about it. God wants to protect you from the hurts that ruin people who get drunk. You can save yourself a lot of pain, sadness, fighting, sickness, and a few more troubles too gruesome to list. Just don't get drunk.

Getting Opinions (0848)

PROVERBS 11:14
PROVERBS 15:22
PROVERBS 24:6

It's good to ask one person for advice before you make a decision, but it's even better to ask several people. They won't all say the same thing and you can put their advice together like pieces of a puzzle. The more advice you get, the more you know about the problem. Ask two or three people if you can.

Getting Wisdom (3843)

PROVERBS 2:6
ECCLESIASTES 2:26
DANIEL 2:21
LUKE 21:15
JAMES 1:5

If you want to get wise, just ask God to make you wise. He promises to give wisdom to anyone who asks for it. Don't doubt it!

Gifts from God (4157)

JOB 32:8
ECCLESIASTES 2:26
ISAIAH 50:4
MATTHEW 9:8
MATTHEW 25:15
LUKE 11:9
JOHN 3:27
1 CORINTHIANS 4:7
JAMES 1:5

If you are a good student or a great soccer player, you have been given a gift. God has enabled you to perform well in that area. Thank him for the ways he has gifted you. Do not brag about it or show it off; just use it as well as you can.

Giving (2117)

DEUTERONOMY 15:12-14
NEHEMIAH 8:10
PROVERBS 25:21
ECCLESIASTES 11:1
ISAIAH 58:7
MATTHEW 5:42
LUKE 3:11
LUKE 12:33
ACTS 20:35
ROMANS 12:13
GALATIANS 6:10
1 TIMOTHY 6:18
HEBREWS 13:16

These verses are about giving to people. God hopes you can enjoy seeing other people use your stuff as much as you enjoy using it yourself. That doesn't mean you should give away everything you own. It does mean that if someone needs something and you have it, give it away if you can.

Giving Advice (0799)

ROMANS 15:14
1 CORINTHIANS 4:14
EPHESIANS 6:4
COLOSSIANS 3:16
1 THESSALONIANS 5:14
2 THESSALONIANS 3:15
TITUS 3:10

So you want to give advice? Say something nice and friendly. Don't make the person feel dumb.

Giving In (3588)

GENESIS 3:6
GENESIS 13:10-11, 13
GENESIS 25:29-30, 33
GENESIS 25:30
JOSHUA 7:21
JUDGES 14:17
JUDGES 16:17
1 SAMUEL 13:12
1 KINGS 11:1
1 KINGS 11:4
MARK 10:35-37
2 PETER 2:20

Sin looks good at first glance. Satan tempts us by showing us the fun side of sin. He makes it look harmless. But like eating a poisonous mushroom, sinning always has consequences that hurt. Don't give in to sin, no matter how good it looks.

Gladness (1936)

2 CHRONICLES 30:21
NEHEMIAH 8:17
PSALM 4:7
PSALM 45:15
ACTS 2:46
ACTS 11:23
ACTS 14:17

Gladness is like a smile inside of you. It is the happy feeling you get when life is going well. For the people in these verses, that meant that their crops were growing and their families were safe. It was also a time to stop and thank God for all that good stuff. Count your blessings.

God as Judge (1354)

GENESIS 18:25
PSALM 58:11
PSALM 75:7
PSALM 96:13
ECCLESIASTES 3:17
HEBREWS 12:23
REVELATION 18:8
REVELATION 20:12

Sometimes you see people who do wrong over and over again and don't get punished. Some people spend their whole lives not obeying God, and it seems like they don't get punished their whole life. These verses say clearly that there will come a day when God will judge sin. You take care of yourself and your own sin—confess it. God will take care of everyone else's.

God as Teacher (3556)

EXODUS 4:15
DEUTERONOMY 4:36
PSALM 25:12
PSALM 32:8
PSALM 71:17
PSALM 94:10
ISAIAH 2:3
ISAIAH 28:26
ISAIAH 48:17
ISAIAH 54:13
JEREMIAH 32:33
MICAH 4:2

God is our teacher and he is eager to teach us. Open the Bible and start reading. God will show you what is best if you will listen. Don't tune him out. Listen to his teaching.

God at Work (1166)

GENESIS 45:8
1 SAMUEL 2:7
2 SAMUEL 7:8
1 KINGS 14:7
PSALM 75:7
DANIEL 2:21

God does work in the world. People are not God's little puppets; we make choices on our own. But you can be sure that God is always at work, urging us all to go in the right direction.

God Calls You (1791)

ISAIAH 45:22
ISAIAH 55:1
MATTHEW 22:9
JOHN 7:37
ROMANS 10:12
1 TIMOTHY 2:4
REVELATION 22:17

In these verses God is inviting EVERYBODY to be his child. Nobody gets left out of this invitation. And he doesn't just sit and wait for you to come to him. He comes to you and invites you again and again and again and again. Have you answered his invitation?

God Is Jealous (1850)

EXODUS 20:5
EXODUS 34:14
DEUTERONOMY 4:24
DEUTERONOMY 29:20
JOSHUA 24:19

1 Kings 14:22
1 Corinthians 10:22

Let's say you have a friend who starts being friends with other people and you get jealous. That is not OK. Your friend is not yours to own, he is just your friend. He can do what he wants. But these verses say that God gets jealous when we let other things become more important than him. That is OK, because we aren't just his friends—we BELONG to him. We do what HE wants. Get it?

God on Earth (4044)

2 Corinthians 4:4
Philippians 2:6
Colossians 1:15
Hebrews 1:3

It's hard to imagine what God is like. Learning about Jesus can help. Jesus is God in the form of a man. If you want to get to know God better, get to know Jesus.

God Sees Sin (0804)

Job 10:14
Job 14:16
Jeremiah 2:22
Jeremiah 16:17
Ezekiel 11:5
Hosea 7:2
Amos 5:12

God sees everything we do. He knows everything we think. It is useless to try to hide anything from him. Go to God and admit anything wrong you've done. He already knows anyway, and he wants you to face it too.

God's Anger (3132)

2 Kings 22:13
Psalm 2:12
John 3:36
Romans 1:18
Romans 2:8
Ephesians 5:6
1 Thessalonians 2:16

These verses say that God does get angry with people who spend their whole lives in sin when they should be serving him. It's their stubborn rebellion that bothers him, not each individual mistake. God has infinite patience with anyone who tries to obey. Listen to God and try to live his way, and you'll never have to worry about angering God.

God's Body (0726)

Romans 12:5
1 Corinthians 12:27
Ephesians 1:23
Ephesians 4:12
Colossians 1:24
Colossians 2:19

The church is like God's body. Every member has a purpose. That means you have a purpose at your church too. See what you can do to help out.

God's Care for Kids (3830)

Deuteronomy 10:18
Psalm 10:14
Psalm 68:5
Psalm 146:9
Proverbs 15:25
Jeremiah 49:11
Hosea 14:3

God cares for the special needs of kids. He is a father to those who don't have one. He protects those who are in danger. He comforts those who are sad. Turn to God for whatever you need; he really does care for you.

God's Care for You (2911)

Psalm 115:12
Matthew 6:32
Luke 12:7
1 Peter 5:7

These verses all speak of God's care. You matter to God. He never forgets you or ignores you. Whenever you feel alone, remember that.

God's Comfort (0783)

Psalm 71:21
Psalm 86:17
Isaiah 12:1
Isaiah 51:3
Isaiah 51:12
Isaiah 66:13
2 Corinthians 1:3
2 Corinthians 7:6

God cares for you. Whenever you feel sad, he reaches out to comfort you. Remember that whenever troubles hit and get you down. Always tell your troubles to God.

God's Control (3415)

Deuteronomy 4:39
1 Chronicles 29:12
Job 9:12
Psalm 29:10
Psalm 47:2
Psalm 83:18
Psalm 93:1
Psalm 135:6
Daniel 2:20
Daniel 4:35
Matthew 6:13
Acts 17:24
Romans 9:19

Not only did God make the world, he keeps it going. He's in control of the laws that make the universe run. You may not always understand what God does, but that's OK—God is still in control. You need not worry that he can't handle your life.

God's Forgiveness (3125)

Isaiah 43:25
Isaiah 44:22
Isaiah 55:7
Jeremiah 5:1
Jeremiah 31:34
Jeremiah 33:8
Ezekiel 36:25
Micah 7:18
Hebrews 8:12
1 John 1:9

These verses say that God's forgiveness is a wonderful thing. You know how it is when someone is angry at you and keeps reminding you of it over and over again. God never does that. Our holy God makes a way for us to have our sin forgiven and forgotten. Take a minute to thank him for that.

God's Friends (1327)

Exodus 33:11
Numbers 12:8
Deuteronomy 34:10
2 Chronicles 20:7
James 2:23

These verses are about people who were "face to face" with God. That means they didn't hide who they were—they were completely honest with him. And even though they weren't perfect, God called them his friends. It is important to God that his friends be honest with him about everything.

God's Guidance (1465)

Psalm 23:2
Psalm 25:9
Psalm 32:8
Psalm 48:14
Psalm 73:24
Isaiah 30:21
Isaiah 42:16
Isaiah 48:17
Luke 1:79
John 10:4
John 16:13

These verses are about the ways God leads you. If you want to follow God, He'll find a way to show you what to do. Watch and listen for him—and most of all, obey what you know to be his will in the Bible.

God's Justice (1975)

Deuteronomy 32:4
Psalm 103:6
Proverbs 16:11

ISAIAH 45:21
ZEPHANIAH 3:5
JOHN 5:30
ROMANS 2:2
REVELATION 15:3

These verses say that God is the only one who can judge us fairly. He loves us all, so he doesn't judge us according to how we look or whether he likes us. God judges our actions and whether we obey him. He is the only fair judge there is, so let him do the judging.

God's Love (2206)

DEUTERONOMY 7:8
PSALM 146:8
JEREMIAH 31:3
JOHN 3:16
JOHN 16:27
ROMANS 5:8
EPHESIANS 2:4-5
1 JOHN 3:1
1 JOHN 4:9
1 JOHN 4:16

These verses explain how God loves you. For one, he thinks of you as his own child. For another, he sent Jesus to die for your sins. And finally, he's always with you so you're never alone.

God's Mercy (2297)

DEUTERONOMY 4:31
2 SAMUEL 24:14
PSALM 86:5
PSALM 103:17
PSALM 106:1
PSALM 108:4
PSALM 119:64
LAMENTATIONS 3:22-23
JOEL 2:13
MICAH 7:18
LUKE 1:50
EPHESIANS 2:4
TITUS 3:5

God is so powerful and perfect, and we are so sinful, that he has a right to punish us. He could get angry and hurt all of us. But these verses tell us that even though he COULD do that, he does not. He shows us love and kindness because he is merciful. And he asks you to do the same for the people around you, even your brothers and sisters.

God's Patience (2277)

NUMBERS 14:18
ISAIAH 48:9
EZEKIEL 20:17
ROMANS 9:22
1 PETER 3:20
2 PETER 3:9

These verses are about God's patience with people. As long as you are trying to do right, God doesn't get irritated or impatient with you. He is kind and gentle and patiently waiting to let you know how much he loves you.

God's Perfection (2730)

DEUTERONOMY 32:4
2 SAMUEL 22:31
PSALM 18:30
ECCLESIASTES 3:14
MATTHEW 5:48

These verses tell us one key fact about God: He is completely perfect and just. He doesn't mess up and he never gets anything wrong. That's why you can trust him. He won't let you down.

God's Power (3808)

1 CHRONICLES 29:12
2 CHRONICLES 25:8
JOB 26:12
PSALM 62:11
PSALM 65:6
PSALM 93:4
NAHUM 1:3
ROMANS 16:25

God has more power than anyone or anything. He is stronger than the biggest bully you'll ever meet. Ask God for strength. He has plenty to share.

God's Presence (0038)

PSALM 24:3-4
ISAIAH 26:2
JOHN 10:9
ROMANS 5:2
EPHESIANS 2:18
EPHESIANS 3:12
REVELATION 3:8

You have direct access to God through Jesus. You don't need a human priest to help you. And you don't have to beg, plead, or do God any favors before he'll listen. Just pray any time.

God's Promises (2878)

1 KINGS 8:56
ROMANS 4:21
2 CORINTHIANS 1:20
2 CORINTHIANS 7:1
2 PETER 1:4
1 JOHN 2:25

Did you know that God has made promises to you? As you can see from these verses, he surely has. And unlike human promises, he will keep every one. This is just one more reason you should trust him. Get to know these promises so you can be glad and not worry.

God's Response (1211)

MARK 1:41
MARK 2:5
MARK 5:34
MARK 7:29
MARK 10:52
LUKE 7:10
LUKE 17:14
JOHN 4:51
JOHN 9:7
ACTS 14:9

These verses tell about people who believed enough in God to ask for his help. When you ask for his help you show that you believe in him. And because you have faith that he can help you, he will.

God's Role (3798)

2 CHRONICLES 20:12
PSALM 127:1
JEREMIAH 10:23
JOHN 3:27
JOHN 15:5
2 CORINTHIANS 3:5

Some people think they're pretty clever. Guess what? They didn't get that way by accident. God controls all the circumstances of life, including the ones that make a person clever and successful. Be content with what you can do and thankful for it, and always pray for God's help. You depend on God for everything.

God's Teaching (1607)

NEHEMIAH 9:20
LUKE 12:12
JOHN 14:26
1 CORINTHIANS 2:13
1 JOHN 2:27

These verses are about the lessons you get from the Holy Spirit. The Holy Spirit teaches you about how to live for God. You didn't know you had your own tutor, did you? Learn to listen. Listen to learn.

God's Ways (4160)

PSALM 18:30
ISAIAH 55:8,9
HOSEA 14:9
HABAKKUK 3:6
ROMANS 11:33
REVELATION 15:3

These verses describe God's ways. We don't always understand God's ways because they are higher than ours. That is why we must trust him and do what he says, much the way a small child must trust his parents and do what they say. God knows what is best for you. Read the Bible to find out God's ways, and follow them.

God's Word (3700)

DEUTERONOMY 32:4
2 SAMUEL 7:28
PSALM 33:4
PSALM 146:6
ISAIAH 65:16
ROMANS 3:4
TITUS 1:2
HEBREWS 6:18

God always keeps his promises. You can trust God because he keeps his word. He has proven over and over again that his word is true. Don't doubt God's promises.

Going to Church (3523)

MATTHEW 12:9
MARK 1:21
LUKE 4:16
ACTS 13:14
HEBREWS 10:25

Sunday mornings see people going in all directions. Some folks sleep in; some read the paper; some watch TV; some go shopping; some go to church; others do their own thing. You can tell by reading these verses what Jesus and his disciples thought about it. Going to church is truly one of the most important things you can do as a Christian.

Golden Rule (1433)

MATTHEW 7:12
LUKE 6:31

These verses give you a good rule to live by: Treat people the way you want them to treat you. They won't always treat you the same way back, but that doesn't matter. You're only doing what God has done for you.

Good Friends (1323)

1 SAMUEL 18:1
1 SAMUEL 20:41
2 SAMUEL 1:26
2 SAMUEL 15:37
1 KINGS 5:1
2 CORINTHIANS 2:13
PHILIPPIANS 2:25
2 TIMOTHY 1:16

These people all had friends they liked and liked to be with. Friendships have been happening since the beginning of the world. The Bible has a lot to say about them. Don't take your friendships lightly.

Good Looks (0205)

1 SAMUEL 16:7
MATTHEW 23:27
JOHN 7:24
2 CORINTHIANS 5:12
2 CORINTHIANS 10:7
JAMES 2:2-4

Do good looks equal good kids? Maybe not. Good looks don't make good kids. Don't judge people by their appearance.

Good News (1349)

LUKE 12:37
JOHN 14:3
PHILIPPIANS 3:20-21
COLOSSIANS 3:4
1 THESSALONIANS 3:13
1 THESSALONIANS 4:16
1 PETER 5:4
1 JOHN 3:2

Each of these verses describes a reward that Christians will receive when Jesus comes back. These rewards will not be given to just anybody. Only those who believe in Christ and love him will be celebrating. And best of all, these rewards will never break, fade, or get lost.

Good Rewarded (1165)

PSALM 91:14
ISAIAH 33:16
ISAIAH 58:14
DANIEL 12:3
HABAKKUK 3:19
MATTHEW 19:28
LUKE 19:17
1 CORINTHIANS 6:2
REVELATION 3:21
REVELATION 5:10
REVELATION 11:12

God notices when you are trying to be who he wants you to be. Your efforts to obey him and to love people are like a grand show of friendship to him. He notices. And God will reward you in eternity, too.

Good Works (3902)

MATTHEW 5:16
COLOSSIANS 1:10
1 TIMOTHY 6:18
TITUS 2:7
TITUS 2:14
TITUS 3:8
HEBREWS 10:24
JAMES 2:17-18
1 PETER 2:12

Doing good works (1) pleases God, (2) sets an example for others, and (3) shows that your faith is real. It's not enough to say you believe in God. Prove it by doing good works for him.

Goodness Rewarded (1364)

DANIEL 12:3
MATTHEW 10:42
MATTHEW 25:23
MATTHEW 25:34
MARK 9:41
LUKE 6:35
JOHN 4:36
ROMANS 2:10
1 CORINTHIANS 3:8
EPHESIANS 6:8
COLOSSIANS 3:24

These verses are all about goodness: Good actions, good thoughts, good words, good intentions, and good motivations. God rewards them all because he wants us to be good people who love him and each other. Don't worry when it seems you try hard and no one notices. God never misses one good thing you do, and one day he will reward you.

The Gospel (3461)

1 CORINTHIANS 9:17
GALATIANS 2:7
COLOSSIANS 1:25
1 THESSALONIANS 2:4
1 TIMOTHY 1:11
TITUS 1:3

It is our job to spread the truth about Jesus. He wants us to share it with others. Don't keep the news all to yourself. Tell others what God has shown you.

Gossiping (3307)

LEVITICUS 19:16
PROVERBS 11:13
PROVERBS 17:9
PROVERBS 18:8
PROVERBS 20:19
PROVERBS 26:20

These verses are about gossip. People who gossip lose friends, make fights worse, and hurt innocent people. Don't gossip, period.

Grace (1447)

ACTS 15:11
ROMANS 3:24
ROMANS 5:15
ROMANS 11:6
EPHESIANS 2:5
TITUS 2:11
TITUS 3:7

These verses are about God's grace. If we had to become good to become God's children we would never become God's children. We aren't that good. Grace means that God forgives our sin because of HIS goodness, not our own. It's important that you do your best to obey God, but know that he loves you no matter what.

Gratitude (1458)
Deuteronomy 32:6
Nehemiah 9:26
Ezekiel 16:17-18
Luke 17:17-18
Romans 1:21

These verses are about people who should have been thankful and weren't. They got good things from God and then ignored him. Don't be one of those people! It's not a pretty sight. Whenever you feel grumpy, thank God for SOMETHING.

A Great Gift (3123)
John 3:16
John 4:10
Romans 5:15
Romans 6:23
Romans 8:32
2 Corinthians 9:15
Ephesians 2:8

Becoming a Christian is like receiving a gift. You don't pay for it. You don't work for it. You don't trade something for it. You just accept it. Of course, once you have the gift, God does want you to use it. But to get it you need only receive it.

Greed (4070)
Proverbs 1:19
Ecclesiastes 5:10
Habakkuk 2:9-10
Matthew 27:5
1 Timothy 6:9
James 5:3

"If I just had a little more. . . ." Don't waste your time wishing you had more stuff. Things can never make you happy. Soon after you get it, you just want more. Or it breaks. Instead of being greedy, be happy with what you have.

Grief (1948)
Genesis 23:2
Genesis 37:35
Genesis 42:38
Judges 21:2
Ruth 1:20
2 Samuel 18:33
Job 1:20
Jeremiah 31:15
John 11:33
John 20:11
Acts 9:39

These people felt grief. You feel grief whenever you lose something important to you, like when your grandfather dies or your favorite pet runs away. It's OK to grieve your loss. Go ahead and cry and feel sad. Eventually it won't hurt so bad.

Growing Spiritually (0995)
2 Corinthians 9:10
Ephesians 4:15
Colossians 1:10
1 Thessalonians 3:12
1 Thessalonians 4:10
Hebrews 6:1
1 Peter 2:2
2 Peter 1:5-6
2 Peter 3:18

Your body grows every year until it is finished. Then it stops. But your spirit doesn't work the same way. Your spirit grows a little each time you obey God and show love to people. Wouldn't it be a shame to have a grown-up body and a baby spirit?

Growing Up (4006)
Proverbs 22:15
Jeremiah 4:22
1 Corinthians 13:11

Growing up means more than getting taller. It means learning to make good choices. Your parents help you by giving you advice and making you face the consequences of your mistakes. Accept their advice and discipline as part of growing up.

Guidance (1611)
John 16:13
Acts 8:39
Acts 10:19-20
Acts 13:2
Acts 16:6
Romans 8:14
Galatians 5:18

These verses are about how the Holy Spirit helps you make decisions. Sometimes you can feel him guiding you one way or the other. Sometimes you just decide and trust him to lead you. Sometimes there is not a right or wrong choice, it's up to you. When a choice matters, trust him to help you make it.

The Guide (0419)
Psalm 19:8
Psalm 119:105
Psalm 119:130
Proverbs 6:23
2 Peter 1:19

God's word guides you. God's word points the way. Read the Bible and memorize key verses.

Guilty Conscience (0826)
Genesis 42:21
Exodus 9:27
Ezra 9:6
Job 15:21
Psalm 40:12
Daniel 5:6
John 8:9

These people knew they had done wrong and didn't know what to do. Life is no fun when you feel guilty. Don't let your sins pile up—go and say you're sorry to whoever you offended.

Guilty Fear (0856)
Genesis 3:8
Genesis 45:3
Leviticus 26:17
Psalm 53:5
Proverbs 28:1
Isaiah 2:19
Isaiah 24:17
Isaiah 33:14
Isaiah 66:4
Daniel 5:6
Micah 7:17
Hebrews 10:27

When people do wrong, they usually feel both guilty and afraid. They feel guilty for breaking the rules, and they feel afraid of getting caught. Then they can't have fun, because they're watching out for teachers or parents or police. Would you rather have a good time or a bad time? When you do something wrong, admit it. Life is no fun with guilty fear.

Happiness (1940)
Job 20:5
Proverbs 14:13
Ecclesiastes 2:10
Ecclesiastes 7:6
Isaiah 16:10
James 4:9

These verses are about happiness and how it changes. Life goes between happiness and unhappiness a lot. You need to know that you won't always be happy. Enjoy it when you can, but don't count on it to last forever. Only God lasts forever.

Hard-heart Aches (2716)
Psalm 95:8
Proverbs 28:14
Proverbs 29:1
Isaiah 42:25
Romans 2:5
Hebrews 3:13

Do you know the feeling when you know you should do something, but you don't want to? You feel that pull inside. These verses are about ignoring that feeling so long that you don't even notice it anymore. God talks to you sometimes through that feeling. If you ignore it, you won't hear him.

Hard-hearted (2713)

Leviticus 26:23
Proverbs 1:24
Ecclesiastes 8:11
Jeremiah 7:13
Hosea 7:10
Amos 4:6
Haggai 2:17
Matthew 11:20

These verses are about people who didn't care that they had displeased God. Their hearts were hard. When people's hearts are hard toward God, it leads to all kinds of trouble. Only a fool would want our mighty, loving God to be upset with him or her.

Hardship (0490)

Job 5:17
Job 23:10
Psalm 119:67
2 Corinthians 4:17
Hebrews 12:11
Revelation 7:14

Hardship can teach you a lot. "It makes you a better person." At pop quiz time ask: What can I learn from this?

Hate (2210)

Leviticus 19:17
Proverbs 10:12
Proverbs 15:17
1 John 2:9
1 John 3:15
1 John 4:20

These verses reveal God's attitude toward hate. When you hate someone you hope the worst happens to him or her. When you love someone you hope the best happens to him or her. God wants nothing to do with hate. And he doesn't want YOU using it on others either. A person might make you angry, but hating the person will only make things worse. Forgiveness is better.

Heart (4162)

Proverbs 4:23
Proverbs 23:7
Matthew 6:18
Matthew 15:18
Luke 6:45
Romans 10:10

Whatever is in your heart will come out in the way you talk and act. So the Bible tells you to guard your heart. That means you should carefully choose what you fall in love with. Don't get too attached to dirty jokes, racy TV shows, or angry music. Don't get to be close buddies with kids who drag you down. Fall in love with Jesus and his word.

Heaven (1359)

Revelation 21:1, 4
Revelation 22:3, 5

These verses are about the ways heaven will be different from earth, and it's all good news. All the very bad things that make earth a pain will be gone (hooray!). God has a place waiting for you where all badness is gone forever. Isn't that great?

Help! (4134)

Matthew 4:24
Matthew 8:16
Matthew 9:32
Mark 9:17-20
Luke 5:18-19
Luke 18:40
John 1:41-42
John 1:45-46
John 8:3
John 11:28
John 12:20-22

Jesus helped all kinds of people with all kinds of problems. No matter how big your problems seem, Jesus can help you too. Ask him for help and wisdom whenever you need it. And pray for other people too.

Helping at Home (4041)

Mark 5:19
1 Timothy 5:4

Chores, chores, chores. Helping around the house can be tiring. But God wants you to help your parents as much as you can. Doing your chores shows your parents and God that you love them. Do your best to help around the house.

Helping Friends (1784)

Genesis 37:21
Genesis 37:26
Genesis 44:33
1 Samuel 19:4
1 Samuel 25:24
Jeremiah 38:9
Philemon 1:10

The people in these verses stepped in to help a friend. They stepped in and spoke up in their friend's defense. We should all do that for our friends. Whenever your friend is in trouble, speak up in his or her defense. That's what good friends do for each other. (And you might need the same favor from your friend someday.)

Helping Weak People (1061)

Matthew 25:35-36
Acts 20:35
Romans 14:1
Romans 15:1
1 Corinthians 8:11
1 Corinthians 9:22
1 Thessalonians 5:14

One day you will meet someone who is weaker than you—maybe not in muscles, but in schoolwork, bravery, or some other way. These verses are very clear about how to treat those people—help them! Don't worry about who's watching or what people will think if they see you—help them! Help anyone who needs help because of a weakness. That's God's way.

Hoarding (2811)

Job 27:16-17
Psalm 39:6
Ecclesiastes 2:26
Ezekiel 28:4
Matthew 6:19
Luke 12:21
James 5:3

These verses are about hoarding money—saving up way more than you need and then just keeping it all to yourself. Some people spend their whole lives getting as much money as they can just to have as much money as they can. God says there are better ways to spend your time and energy. Having a lot of money won't do anything for you. Spend your time and energy doing God's work.

Holiness (1598)

Exodus 19:6
Leviticus 11:45
Leviticus 19:2
1 Chronicles 16:29
Luke 1:74-75
2 Corinthians 7:1
Ephesians 4:24
Hebrews 12:14
1 Peter 1:16
2 Peter 3:11

These verses are about being holy. God wants you to be holy. Holy doesn't mean fancy. It means totally committed to pleasing God. Go for it!

The Holy Spirit (3803)

Micah 3:8
Zechariah 4:6
Luke 4:14
Acts 1:8
Acts 2:2
Acts 4:33
Acts 6:8
Acts 19:11-12
1 Corinthians 2:4
Ephesians 3:16
1 Thessalonians 1:5
2 Timothy 1:7

Wow! The Holy Spirit gives people power to do amazing things! Do you want courage and strength to do great things for God? Depend on his Spirit.

Honesty (3701)
PROVERBS 12:19
ZEPHANIAH 3:13
ZECHARIAH 8:16
MALACHI 2:6
2 CORINTHIANS 12:6
EPHESIANS 4:25
EPHESIANS 6:14

God always tells the truth. He wants you to follow his example. Telling the truth shows you belong to him. And it's a sure way to build trust and friendship among others. Always strive to tell the truth.

Hospitality (3398)
ROMANS 12:13
1 TIMOTHY 3:2
1 TIMOTHY 5:10
TITUS 1:8
HEBREWS 13:2
1 PETER 4:9

Hospitality does not mean inviting kids over to show off your cool stuff. It means welcoming people and sharing what you have. Don't try to show off your stuff or try to keep it all to yourself. Just use it to make your friends and visitors feel at home.

How to Be Saved (3118)
MATTHEW 10:22
ROMANS 10:9
1 CORINTHIANS 1:21
1 CORINTHIANS 15:2
2 TIMOTHY 3:15
JAMES 1:21
2 PETER 1:10-11
REVELATION 22:14

These verses are about receiving God's forgiveness—becoming a Christian. When we place our faith in Christ, God forgives our sins. That's how we are saved.

How to Give (2121)
DEUTERONOMY 16:17
MATTHEW 5:42
MATTHEW 6:3
MATTHEW 10:8
LUKE 6:38
LUKE 12:33
ROMANS 12:8
1 CORINTHIANS 16:2
2 CORINTHIANS 9:7

These verses describe how you should give to God. Some have to do with attitude (cheerfully). Some have to do with timing (regularly). God doesn't want you to give just because you have to. God wants to see that you understand what giving is all about—showing love.

How to Pray (2824)
2 CHRONICLES 7:14
ISAIAH 58:9
JEREMIAH 29:13
MARK 11:24
JAMES 5:16
1 JOHN 3:22
1 JOHN 5:14

These verses tell you how God wants you to talk to him. God wants you to come to him sincerely, having made an honest effort to obey him. He wants this because you can hear him best when you come to him that way.

Humility (3897)
MATTHEW 10:42
JOHN 12:3
ACTS 20:18-19

We all want to look good. But when we serve God, we shouldn't care what others think of us. God loves humble service. Serve God without trying to impress others.

Hurrying (1498)
1 SAMUEL 21:8
2 KINGS 4:29
2 CHRONICLES 24:5
2 CHRONICLES 35:21
PSALM 119:60
ZECHARIAH 8:21
MATTHEW 28:7
LUKE 10:4
LUKE 14:21

Each of these people were supposed to hurry. Not all of them did. Hurrying isn't always good, but when you need to do it, DO IT! Sometimes there's no time to waste.

Hurtful Lying (3856)
EXODUS 20:16
EXODUS 23:1
DEUTERONOMY 19:16
PROVERBS 6:19
PROVERBS 12:17
PROVERBS 19:9
PROVERBS 24:28
PROVERBS 25:18
MATTHEW 19:18

Some kids like to make up stories and spread rumors about others. But lying for fun is not a harmless game. Lies hurt people. Don't spread rumors or lie about other kids.

Hurting Yourself (0521)
LEVITICUS 19:28
LEVITICUS 21:5
1 CORINTHIANS 6:15
1 THESSALONIANS 5:23

God created your body. In fact, he lives there. Treat it with respect.

Hypocrisy (2994)
PROVERBS 23:7
PROVERBS 26:25
MATTHEW 23:28
LUKE 12:1
1 TIMOTHY 4:2
TITUS 1:16

These verses are about people who say you should act one way, then they act completely differently. It's like lying with your life instead of your tongue. People don't like hypocrites. Neither does God. Don't be one.

Idle Talk (3306)
JOB 11:12
JOB 15:3
PROVERBS 10:19
PROVERBS 14:23
PROVERBS 29:11
ECCLESIASTES 5:3
ECCLESIASTES 10:13
EZEKIEL 36:3
TITUS 1:10

Yes, it's possible to talk too much. The person who watches what he says is wise. Don't babble; too many words will get you in trouble.

Ignorance (2036)
JOB 8:9
PSALM 73:22
ECCLESIASTES 8:7
ECCLESIASTES 9:12
ECCLESIASTES 11:5
JOHN 3:8

These verses are about the mysteries in life that we don't understand. We are ignorant of these things, not dumb. Ignorant just means we haven't learned something yet. You will never understand everything God does. Don't feel like you have to pretend to know something when you don't.

Impatience (2694)
NUMBERS 20:10
2 KINGS 5:11-12
JONAH 4:8-9
MATTHEW 15:23
LUKE 9:54
LUKE 10:40

Each of these people were impatient with someone. God knows that the people around you get on your nerves at times. That's why he tells you to WORK at patience. He knows it's hard work!

Importance of Love (2209)

1 Corinthians 13:13
Galatians 5:6
Galatians 5:22
Ephesians 3:17-19
Ephesians 4:16
Ephesians 5:2
Colossians 1:8
Colossians 3:14
1 Timothy 6:11
1 John 4:16

These verses all mention love as the most important trait you can have. Why is that? Because love includes all the other good traits in one way or another. If you love someone you will be truthful and kind; if you love someone you will be patient and forgiving. God knows that if you will be a loving person, all the other goodnesses will fall into place.

Injustice (1981)

Job 12:6
Job 21:7
Psalm 73:14
Ecclesiastes 7:15
Ecclesiastes 9:2
Jeremiah 12:1
Ezekiel 18:25
Habakkuk 1:2
Matthew 20:12
Romans 9:14

Someone in each of these verses thought God was unfair. Mostly they thought that because they saw people doing wrong but not being punished. Then they saw people doing right but having bad things happen to them. They needed to be more patient. Sometimes it takes years before a person faces the good or bad consequences of his or her actions. But one day, God's justice will respond.

Instruction (1782)

Leviticus 10:11
Deuteronomy 6:7
Psalm 78:6
Ezekiel 44:23
Colossians 3:16
1 Timothy 4:11
2 Timothy 2:24

It is the responsibility of your parents and their friends to teach you and your friends about God. These verses tell them that. This is how faith is passed down. If your parents try to teach you, listen. If they don't teach you, ask them questions. If they don't know the answers, find them together.

Invisible Gifts (0486)

Isaiah 56:4-5
Jeremiah 24:7
Ezekiel 11:19
Matthew 11:28
Luke 11:13
John 10:28
Revelation 2:10

Great character comes from God, not special parents. Why not ask him to give you these invisible gifts?

Invisible Wealth (2812)

Proverbs 8:18
Proverbs 10:22
Proverbs 13:7
Ephesians 1:18
Ephesians 3:8
Hebrews 11:26
James 2:5

These verses are about wealth you take with you when you die. The more deeply you know God now, the better you know him when you go to heaven. But also, the better you know God as you go through life, the happier and more secure you are. It's a great deal either way.

"It's Her Fault!" (3454)

Genesis 3:13
Genesis 16:5
Genesis 27:36
Exodus 32:22
1 Samuel 15:21
Matthew 27:24

Admitting our mistakes is hard, as the people in these verses found out. It's tempting to make excuses or accuse other people. Instead, we should admit our mistakes and not make excuses. Don't try to get away with sin. Face up to it and move on.

Jesus (4188)

John 3:16
John 6:68
John 8:24
Acts 4:12
1 Corinthians 2:2
1 Corinthians 3:11

Jesus is the ONLY one who can save you from your sins and give you eternal life. If you want to go to heaven, believe in Jesus.

Jesus' Friends (1326)

John 11:5
John 11:35-36
John 13:23
John 15:15

These verses are about Jesus and his friends. Jesus loved his friends and enjoyed being with them. He celebrated happy occasions with them but he also cried with them. Love your friends the way Jesus loved his.

Jesus' Home (3583)

John 14:20
John 17:23
Romans 8:10
Galatians 2:20
Ephesians 3:17-19
Colossians 1:27
1 John 3:24
Revelation 3:20

Jesus lives in the lives of believers. If you are a Christian, Jesus lives in you. If you aren't a Christian, he's a stranger. You need to invite Jesus into your life if you want him to live there. And then he will.

Jesus' Joy (1926)

Luke 10:21
Luke 15:5
John 15:11
John 17:13
Hebrews 12:2

Jesus had happy and sad days just like you do. What made him glad? These verses tell us that he found joy in obeying God and in the people who followed him. That means you are part of Jesus' joy. It also means he wants you to have joy. He wants to you to be glad that your life is a part of God's plan, the way his was.

Jesus' Return (3784)

Matthew 25:13
Mark 13:33
Luke 12:37
1 Thessalonians 5:5-6
Revelation 3:11
Revelation 16:15

The time of Jesus' return is a big mystery. No one knows when he will come back. Don't assume you can wait forever to get ready. Get ready now.

Jesus' Return: When? (1345)

Matthew 24:27
Matthew 24:36
Luke 12:40
1 Thessalonians 5:2
Revelation 3:3
Revelation 16:15

We don't know when Jesus will come again. No one knows. No one but God knows, and right now he's not telling. For now, obey God and love other people and let him take care of his schedule.

Jesus' Return: Why? (1347)

MATTHEW 16:27
MATTHEW 25:31-32
1 CORINTHIANS 4:5
2 TIMOTHY 4:1
JUDE 1:14-15

When Jesus comes back it will be to have a conversation with us about how we've spent our lives. Did we serve him? Were we kind to the people around us? We can choose now how that conversation will go. Live your life so that when you talk to God about it you'll both be smiling.

Jesus the King (3421)

PSALM 2:6
ISAIAH 9:7
ISAIAH 32:1
JEREMIAH 23:5
DANIEL 7:14
ZECHARIAH 9:9
MATTHEW 2:2
MATTHEW 21:5
MATTHEW 25:34
LUKE 1:33
JOHN 1:49
JOHN 18:37
1 CORINTHIANS 15:25

Close your eyes and imagine what it would be like for Jesus to be the king of the whole earth. He rules every country, every person, everywhere. What you imagine will one day happen. Jesus will rule over the whole world and fix all of our problems. When the world's problems get you down, look forward to that day.

Jesus the Lamb (3365)

ISAIAH 53:7
JOHN 1:29
1 CORINTHIANS 5:7
1 PETER 1:19
REVELATION 5:6
REVELATION 6:1
REVELATION 7:9
REVELATION 12:11
REVELATION 13:8
REVELATION 14:1
REVELATION 15:3
REVELATION 17:14
REVELATION 19:9
REVELATION 21:22

Long ago God's people sacrificed sheep, goats, and birds to pay for their sins. The animals took the person's place suffering the consequence that sin brings. But then Jesus became the Lamb of God who takes away the sin of the world. Now we no longer have to sacrifice for our sins. You can thank Jesus for being the Lamb who died for your sin.

Job One (4181)

JOSHUA 24:15
MATTHEW 6:33
JOHN 4:34
JOHN 17:4
ACTS 20:24
PHILIPPIANS 3:13,14

What are some of your goals? These verses explain some of God's goals for you. Together, they are your most important job in life; your number-one goal. Keep it on a poster. Don't forget it.

Joy (1928)

NEHEMIAH 8:10
PSALM 16:11
PSALM 30:5
PSALM 89:16
PSALM 126:5
PSALM 132:16
ISAIAH 12:3
ISAIAH 35:10
LUKE 2:10
JOHN 15:11
JOHN 16:24
JOHN 17:13
ROMANS 14:17

You can see from these verses that God has a lot to say about joy. He wants you to be joyful. He wants your friendship with him to bring you a lot of joy. You may not laugh all the time, but you can have joy inside knowing that God loves you and will never leave you.

Just You Wait (2897)

JOB 12:6
PSALM 37:35
PSALM 73:3
PSALM 73:12
JEREMIAH 5:28
JEREMIAH 12:1

For some people this is hard to take: Sometimes people who do wrong don't get punished and seem to get ahead. God says: Don't worry about them. Be who God wants you to be. God will deal with them.

Justification by Faith (1203)

HABAKKUK 2:4
ROMANS 4:3
ROMANS 5:1
GALATIANS 3:6
PHILIPPIANS 3:9
HEBREWS 10:38
HEBREWS 11:4

These verses describe what faith in God gives you. Believing in yourself only gives you conceit. Believing in God gives you confidence and also gives you righteousness. Your faith in Jesus' life and death lets you be with God and enjoy him even though you are a sinful person.

Kind to the Needy (3829)

EXODUS 22:22
DEUTERONOMY 14:29
DEUTERONOMY 24:17
DEUTERONOMY 26:12
PROVERBS 23:10
ISAIAH 1:17
JEREMIAH 22:3
JAMES 1:27

The Bible tells us to be kind to widows and orphans. Years ago, widows and orphans were quite defenseless and needed all the help they could get. Today, God wants us to care for anyone in need. You may not know an orphan, but you probably know someone who needs help. Be kind to that person.

Kind to the Poor (2802)

EXODUS 23:11
LEVITICUS 25:25
DEUTERONOMY 15:7
DEUTERONOMY 24:12
PSALM 41:1
PROVERBS 14:21
PROVERBS 19:17
PROVERBS 28:27
MATTHEW 19:21
GALATIANS 2:10

In these verses God commands us to be kind to the poor. It doesn't matter whether they "deserve it." Be generous and share, because when you do, you're sharing with the Lord.

Kindness (1998)

ROMANS 12:10
1 CORINTHIANS 13:4
EPHESIANS 4:32
COLOSSIANS 3:12
2 PETER 1:5-7

These verses are about love and kindness. We are most like God when we are kind to the people around us. Be kind to the person beside you now.

Laughter (1942)

PROVERBS 14:13
ECCLESIASTES 2:2
ECCLESIASTES 7:3
ECCLESIASTES 7:6
LUKE 6:25
JAMES 4:9

These verses are about laughing, but they aren't very funny. The only bad thing about laughing is that you stop sometimes. In life you will go through some times when you won't laugh very much. That is OK. You can always be sure that someday you'll laugh again.

Laziness (0581)

PROVERBS 18:9
PROVERBS 24:30-31
ECCLESIASTES 10:18
2 THESSALONIANS 3:11
HEBREWS 6:12

These people didn't do their chores. They were lazy. A lazy person avoids doing stuff just because he doesn't want to make the effort. It's better to take care of your responsibilities and THEN go have fun.

Lazy People (3384)

PROVERBS 6:6
PROVERBS 13:4
PROVERBS 15:19
PROVERBS 19:24
PROVERBS 20:4
PROVERBS 21:25
PROVERBS 26:16

Excuses, excuses, excuses! Lazy people waste a lot of time making excuses to get out of work. Instead, they should use that time to get their work done. Don't be a lazy person. Do your work without making excuses.

Leaders Should... (2541)

DEUTERONOMY 17:16
2 SAMUEL 23:3
2 CHRONICLES 19:6
PSALM 2:10-11
PROVERBS 16:12
PROVERBS 20:28
PROVERBS 29:4
PROVERBS 29:14

This is how leaders should act. "Leaders" means people like presidents, judges, mayors, college presidents, class presidents, kings, and anyone else who has authority over other people. People in authority are responsible to God to make the right decisions for the people they rule. It's a big responsibility. Pray for your leaders.

Learning from Jesus (2963)

MATTHEW 13:36
MARK 4:10
MARK 7:17
MARK 9:11
MARK 9:28
MARK 10:10
MARK 13:4
LUKE 3:12
LUKE 11:1
LUKE 18:18
JOHN 6:28

These people wanted Jesus to teach them. When Jesus was living on earth people asked him questions often. We can't ask Jesus questions in person, but we can go to the Bible and see how he answered those who did.

Legalism (2990)

MARK 2:24
LUKE 6:2
LUKE 13:14
JOHN 5:10
ACTS 15:5
ACTS 16:3
ACTS 21:20
ACTS 22:3
ROMANS 10:2
GALATIANS 1:14

These verses are about people who took great pride in rule-keeping. Now, many rules are good to keep and important to know. But these people measured everybody by their rulebook. In God's eyes we're all rule-breakers who need Christ's forgiveness, and no amount of rule-keeping can make us better than anyone else. So follow rules, but don't keep track of who's doing as well as you.

Lessons of Life (4179)

PSALM 119:71
ISAIAH 1:16-17
MATTHEW 11:29
JOHN 6:45
EPHESIANS 4:20-23
PHILIPPIANS 4:11

God is the best teacher you will ever have. He can teach you how to live rightly if you will just be teachable. If you want to learn the lessons God has for you, read the Bible often. Reflect on your experiences. Think about how God's word applies to you.

Liars (3703)

PSALM 63:11
PROVERBS 19:5
PROVERBS 19:9
ISAIAH 44:25
REVELATION 21:8
REVELATION 22:15

"Liar, liar, pants on fire!" Liars deserve more than a little teasing. God will punish people who lie all the time. Don't think you can get away with lying forever.

Life After Death (2416)

DANIEL 12:2
JOHN 5:28-29
ACTS 24:15
REVELATION 20:13

These verses say that when Jesus comes back everyone who has died will come back to life. Even if people have died already when Jesus returns, they will come back to life just as he did. Jesus will judge whether we believed in him or not. We won't be able to pretend we believed if we didn't. So don't start pretending now.

Life Is Short (2147)

GENESIS 47:9
1 CHRONICLES 29:15
JOB 7:6
JOB 8:9
JOB 9:25
JOB 14:2
PSALM 39:5
PSALM 89:47
PSALM 90:9
PSALM 102:11
ECCLESIASTES 6:12
ISAIAH 38:12
JAMES 4:14

Life probably doesn't seem short to you, does it? Christmas seems to take forever to get here. But as you get older life will go faster and faster. Just like these verses say, it will speed by. Use each day well.

Life Tests (2149)

PSALM 17:3
DANIEL 12:10
ZECHARIAH 13:9
MALACHI 3:3
LUKE 6:48
1 CORINTHIANS 3:13
JAMES 1:12

Every problem you face is a test: Will you trust in the Lord? How you respond to the problem will tell you the answer. Welcome every problem because it can make you stronger. It may not make you happy, but it will teach you something.

Listening and Doing (0943)

EZEKIEL 33:32
MATTHEW 7:26
MATTHEW 13:19
LUKE 16:31
JAMES 1:23-24

It is not enough to hear God's truth if you aren't going to obey God's truth. It is not enough just to hear what God wants you to do. You've got to do it, too.

Living for God (4014)

PHILIPPIANS 1:27
1 THESSALONIANS 4:12
1 TIMOTHY 3:7
JAMES 3:13
2 PETER 3:11

God's way is the best way. If you live the way God wants you to live, you will win the respect of others and feel good about yourself. Don't worry about what other kids are doing. Do what you know is right.

Loneliness (1331)

Psalm 38:11
Psalm 102:7
John 16:32
2 Timothy 4:16

The people in these verses were lonely. They had friends, but all their friends left. That will happen to you sometimes too. When it does, remember that God has not left you. Lonely is not forever.

Losers (2914)

Numbers 14:11
Numbers 14:23
Numbers 16:30
Deuteronomy 9:7
Deuteronomy 31:20
Ezra 5:12
Psalm 78:40
Psalm 78:56
Psalm 106:7
Isaiah 3:8
Ezekiel 8:3
Hebrews 3:16

These verses tell about people who irritated God. Why? Because they disobeyed, said they were sorry, disobeyed, said they were sorry, disobeyed, disobeyed, and disobeyed, till finally they only disobeyed and never said they were sorry. Keep your love for God. He won't have any reason to be angry with you then.

Love (4183)

John 13:35
John 21:16
1 Corinthians 13:1
1 John 3:14
1 John 4:20

Some kids aren't easy to love. But God says that you can't love him and hate someone else at the same time. A true test of your love for God is your love for others. Ask God to help you show love to the people around you.

Love for Friends (2202)

1 Samuel 18:3
Acts 20:38
Romans 16:4
2 Corinthians 12:15
Philippians 1:8
Philippians 4:1
2 Timothy 1:17

Friends are people who love and enjoy each other. Each of these verses is about friends who look out for each other and give things to each other. After all, if you can't love your friends, how will you show love to the new people you meet?

Love for God (2207)

Deuteronomy 6:5
Deuteronomy 10:12
Deuteronomy 11:1
Joshua 22:5
Psalm 31:23
Matthew 22:37
2 Thessalonians 3:5
Jude 1:21

In these verses you can see that God wants you to love him. When you love someone, how do you treat the person? You speak well of the person; you spend time with the person; you enjoy being with the person. That's what God wants too.

Loving Enemies (3395)

Exodus 23:4
Proverbs 24:17
Proverbs 25:21-22
Matthew 5:44
Romans 12:20

The secret to squashing your enemies is to be nice to them. That's right, be nice to them. They can't fight you if you don't fight back. Your kindness will be like "burning coals" on their head. It's better than an attack and more righteous, too.

Loving Jesus (2205)

Luke 7:47
John 11:16
John 12:3
John 20:11
John 21:16
Acts 21:13

Each of these people loved Jesus very much. They didn't just SAY they loved him, they SHOWED him that he was important to them. God mentioned these people in the Bible so that we would have examples to follow. Pay close attention to them.

Loving Others (2201)

Deuteronomy 10:19
Matthew 22:39
John 13:35
John 15:12
Romans 12:9
1 Thessalonians 3:12
Hebrews 13:1
James 2:8
1 Peter 1:22
1 John 4:7

The Bible says a lot about love. These verses are about love for other people. Loving people is what half of the Christian life is about. (Loving God is the other half.) You can't say you love God if you don't love people. They go together like fingers and thumbs.

Luxury (3200)

Proverbs 21:17
Isaiah 22:13
Isaiah 47:8-9
Luke 8:14
Luke 12:19
1 Timothy 5:6
2 Timothy 3:4
Titus 3:3
James 5:5
2 Peter 2:13

These verses are about filling your life with fun and pleasure—toys, parties, money, nice clothes, desserts, sleep. There is nothing wrong with enjoying yourself, just don't do it all the time or at all costs. Sometimes you should wait. Sometimes you should pass on the opportunity. Live for God, not for pleasure.

Lying (3702)

Leviticus 19:11
Psalm 5:6
Psalm 31:18
Psalm 101:7
Psalm 120:2
Proverbs 12:22
Proverbs 19:9
Proverbs 21:6
Colossians 3:9
Revelation 21:8

There's no getting around it. The Bible says, "Do not lie." Don't make up excuses or try to convince yourself that lying isn't bad. Lying is wrong. Don't do it!

Lying to Yourself (3196)

Psalm 36:2
Isaiah 44:20
Galatians 6:3
James 1:22
James 1:26
1 John 1:8
Revelation 3:17

These verses tell you what happens when you lie to yourself. If you do it long enough you'll start to believe your lies. You'll end up thinking you are better than you are. You'll stop asking for God's forgiveness. You'll come to believe you don't need God and that you don't sin. Admit the truth, even if it hurts!

Mad (3953)

Genesis 4:5
1 Samuel 18:8
2 Kings 5:12
2 Chronicles 16:10
Esther 3:5
Amos 1:11
Luke 4:28
Luke 6:11
Acts 19:28
James 1:20

"Be slow to grow angry." Lashing out in anger only makes conflicts worse. Whenever you feel angry, give yourself time to cool off before you do or say anything.

Made in God's Image (2239)

Genesis 1:26-27
Genesis 5:1
Genesis 9:6
1 Corinthians 11:7
James 3:9

God created us in his image, but that doesn't mean we LOOK like him. It does mean we have some of the same qualities that he has—we make choices, we love, we relate to others. We should remind each other a little bit of God and treat each other with respect. How are you doing on that?

Making Progress (0999)

Job 17:9
Psalm 84:7
Psalm 92:12
Proverbs 4:18
2 Corinthians 3:18
1 Timothy 4:15

You can't tell by looking in the mirror if your spirit has gotten stronger. The way you tell is by looking at how much more you obey God and how much better you treat other people. Is your spirit getting stronger?

Malice (2003)

1 Corinthians 5:8
1 Corinthians 14:20
Ephesians 4:31
Colossians 3:8
1 Peter 2:1

Each of these verses says plainly that it is not enough to avoid angry actions and violent behavior. Even your thoughts and intentions should be kind. It's hard to wish people well when you're angry with them, so keep asking for God's forgiveness and help until you can.

Meekness (2271)

Psalm 22:26
Psalm 37:11
Psalm 147:6
Psalm 149:4
Isaiah 11:4
Isaiah 29:19
Matthew 5:5

These verses are about how God looks out for people who are meek. A meek person is quiet and gentle. He or she doesn't say, "HEY! Everybody better be looking out for me!" God says there is good in being meek and that he will make sure meek people don't get lost along the way. You don't have to be loud and pushy. God will take care of you.

Mercy (1086)

Psalm 109:16
Proverbs 21:13
Ezekiel 34:4
Zechariah 11:16
Matthew 25:43
Luke 16:20-21
James 4:17

In each verse you just read somebody could have shown mercy but didn't. Mercy is being kind to someone that you don't HAVE to be kind to. God wants you to show mercy because he has shown mercy to you. Make a habit of showing mercy.

Mercy from God (2300)

Genesis 18:26
Genesis 19:16
Ezra 9:13
Nehemiah 9:17
Nehemiah 9:31
Psalm 103:11

These verses give examples of God showing mercy to people. God is not a hot-headed meany who gets angry over the least little offense. He is patient and kind, always looking for ways to teach and help you rather than punish you.

Mischief (2377)

1 Samuel 23:9
Nehemiah 6:2
Job 15:35
Psalm 10:7
Psalm 36:4
Proverbs 4:16
Proverbs 6:14
Proverbs 24:2
Acts 13:10

These verses are about people who enjoy making plans to deceive people. Sometimes they think up ways to get in trouble just because they are bored. But to God, sin is sin, whether you do it to be mean or to have fun. If getting in trouble is the best fun you can think of, you need to think a little harder.

Mistakes (4064)

Genesis 41:9
Deuteronomy 9:7
Psalm 51:3
Psalm 137:1
Mark 14:72
Luke 16:25
1 Corinthians 15:9

All the people in these verses felt bad about mistakes they made in the past. We all make mistakes. The good news is that mistakes can be good teachers. Instead of beating yourself up for the mistakes you've made, learn from them. Remember what went wrong before and do things differently next time.

Mockers (2393)

Proverbs 17:5
Proverbs 30:17
Isaiah 57:4
Jude 1:18

These verses are about people who make fun of just about everything. They don't take life or other people seriously. God is not pleased with these people. Don't be one of them.

Mocking (2394)

2 Kings 2:23
2 Chronicles 30:10
2 Chronicles 36:16
Nehemiah 4:1
Psalm 22:7
Acts 2:13
Acts 17:32
Hebrews 11:36

In each of these verses you see "mockers" making fun of people. No matter how clever they thought they were, they all showed contempt for people God loves. Never do that. Even if you disagree with someone or dislike someone, never make fun of the person. God doesn't like it.

Moderation (3574)

Proverbs 23:20
Proverbs 28:7
Daniel 5:1
Luke 15:13
Galatians 5:21
Ephesians 5:18
1 Peter 4:3
2 Peter 2:13

Ever heard of "too much of a good thing"? God wants us to enjoy good things, but overdoing it leads to trouble. These verses warn us not to drink too much wine, eat too much food, or waste too much money. When you are having fun, don't lose control. Know when to stop.

Modesty (3875)

Genesis 24:65
1 Timothy 2:9-10
1 Peter 3:1-2

These verses all say, "Dress modestly," which is an old way of saying, "Don't show off your looks." Your beauty should come from the inside, not from makeup and expensive clothes. The way you live is more important than what you wear or how beautiful you look. Dress to look nice, not to show off.

Money's Dangers (2806)

Deuteronomy 8:13-14
Psalm 62:10
Proverbs 28:20
Matthew 19:23
Mark 4:19
1 Timothy 6:9

These verses are about having plenty of money and having it easy in life. The problem with having all you want is that it distracts you from important things, such as God, other people's needs, and faith. You get used to it and soon want more and more. Enjoy your stuff, but don't trust it to make you a happy person. Only God can do that.

Money's Limits (2807)

Proverbs 11:4
Ecclesiastes 6:2
Zephaniah 1:18
Revelation 18:17

Sometimes we think that money can fix anything. These verses say that it can't. Some tragedies come no matter how much money you have, and no amount of money can fix them. That's why you shouldn't think too much of money—there are some things that only God can do.

Mortality (2403)

Job 4:19
Job 10:9
Psalm 89:48
Psalm 103:16
Ecclesiastes 3:20
1 Corinthians 15:53
2 Corinthians 4:7
2 Corinthians 4:16
2 Corinthians 5:1
2 Corinthians 5:4
Hebrews 9:27

These verses say that life as we know it doesn't last forever. One day our bodies will die and we won't live on earth anymore. But while we live in these bodies we choose where we will spend eternity—with God or without him. Make your choice now while you still can.

Naiveté (3854)

Proverbs 1:22
Proverbs 7:7
Proverbs 8:5
Proverbs 14:15
Proverbs 22:3
Hosea 7:11

Each of these verses warns you about being naive. A naive person believes way too much of what he or she hears. Just because a kid says his dad gave him a thousand dollars doesn't mean it's true. Keep your eyes wide open, be careful, and KNOW THE BIBLE. Some people will lie to you.

Names of God (3633)

Genesis 17:1
Genesis 18:25
Exodus 3:14
Exodus 6:3
Exodus 15:2
Deuteronomy 10:17
Deuteronomy 32:8
Deuteronomy 33:27
Joshua 3:10
1 Samuel 1:11
2 Samuel 22:2
1 Chronicles 29:10
Psalm 71:22
Matthew 6:9
Matthew 6:26
James 1:17

Who is god? He is a strong fortress. He is a loving father. He is a wonderful counselor. The Bible uses many names for God because only one won't do. Don't worry about which one is best. Just call him "Heavenly Father" and learn about him from the other ones that you find in the Bible.

Nature's Praise (2569)

Psalm 65:13
Psalm 69:34
Psalm 98:8
Psalm 148:3
Isaiah 44:23
Isaiah 49:13
Isaiah 55:12

These verses talk about mountains and valleys singing. Why? Because God is good! Nature praises God as flowers bloom, trees grow, wind blows, sun shines, rain falls. Let nature remind you of God's care for all his creation . . . including you. Take a lesson from nature and worship the Lord!

Nature Teaches Us (2498)

Psalm 19:1
Psalm 97:6
Acts 14:17
Romans 1:20

If you list all the people or things that tell you about God, these verses add one more to the list: nature. Nature shows you over and over again that God exists. The next time you walk out into the sunshine or the rain, or look up at the stars, let it remind you that God is walking with you.

Neighbors (3394)

Leviticus 19:18
Mark 12:31
Romans 13:10
Romans 15:1-2
Galatians 5:14
James 2:8

"Love your neighbor as yourself." You've heard this lots of times, but do you DO it? Think about how well you treat yourself. Now try to treat your parents, brothers, sisters, friends, classmates, teachers, and neighbors the same way.

New Kids (3396)

Exodus 22:21
Exodus 23:9
Leviticus 19:34
Leviticus 25:35
Numbers 35:15
Deuteronomy 10:19
Deuteronomy 27:19
Deuteronomy 31:12
Jeremiah 7:6
Matthew 25:35

Most kids are told, "Don't talk to strangers." That's a good rule to follow when dealing with adults. But these verses tell us to be kind to people we don't know. You can be kind to the kids you don't know very well. When you see a kid who needs help, see how you can help him or her.

New Life (2582)

Psalm 40:3
Ezekiel 11:19
Romans 6:4
Romans 7:6
2 Corinthians 5:17
Galatians 6:15
Ephesians 2:15
Ephesians 4:24
Colossians 3:10

These verses are about starting over. When we believe in Jesus and confess our sins to him it's like starting over clean and fresh. We get a wonderful new beginning. If you believe in Christ, never give up hope—he has made you all new.

New Person (2584)
PSALM 51:10
ISAIAH 40:31
ISAIAH 41:1
ROMANS 12:2
2 CORINTHIANS 4:16
EPHESIANS 4:23
COLOSSIANS 3:10
TITUS 3:5

These verses are about how God wants to change you—little by little from the inside out. The Holy Spirit lives inside you for just that purpose. Have you ever felt like quitting or giving up? Have confidence in the Lord. Let him change the way you think.

Nice (1436)
GENESIS 45:15
NUMBERS 12:13
1 SAMUEL 24:17
1 SAMUEL 26:11
2 KINGS 6:22
PSALM 35:13
LUKE 22:51
LUKE 23:34
ACTS 7:60
1 CORINTHIANS 4:12

Somebody was mean to each of the people in these verses. Instead of being mean back, these people acted kind. That is hard to do. But being mean back only makes both of you meaner. You don't have to let other people be mean to you—you can walk away and ignore them. But you have to choose. Do you want to be more like the mean person or more like God?

No Condemnation (3124)
ISAIAH 50:9
LUKE 6:37
JOHN 3:18
JOHN 5:24
ROMANS 8:1
ROMANS 8:34
1 JOHN 3:21

"Condemnation" is a big word about a simple idea: being guilty. A guilty person must be sentenced and punished for his crime. But Christians are no longer under God's sentence. So be glad: God doesn't condemn you if you know Jesus. And be sure not to condemn anyone else either: If you don't judge others, you won't be judged.

No Mercy (2302)
MATTHEW 6:15
MATTHEW 18:28
MATTHEW 18:35
ROMANS 1:31
JAMES 2:13

What happens to people who don't show mercy? These verses show you. They are the only people in danger of not receiving mercy from God. Don't be one of those people. Show mercy to others.

Not Caring (4163)
GENESIS 4:9
MATTHEW 15:23
MATTHEW 27:42
LUKE 10:31-32
LUKE 18:4
LUKE 18:39
JAMES 2:16

The people in these verses did not care about others. They ignored people in need when they could have helped. Don't be so heartless. If you see someone who needs help, do whatever you can for the person.

Not Confessing (1764)
PSALM 32:3
PSALM 38:4
PSALM 51:3
PSALM 73:21
JOHN 16:8
ACTS 2:37
ACTS 16:29
ACTS 24:25

Did you notice what happened to the people in these verses? They had piled up lots of sin. They were trying to ignore it rather than confess it to God. Confession cleans out the guilt and shame that comes from doing wrong. If you become aware of a sin, confess it. Let God take away your guilt.

Not Praying (1089)
PSALM 53:4
ISAIAH 43:22
ISAIAH 64:7
JEREMIAH 10:21
DANIEL 9:13
HOSEA 7:7
ZEPHANIAH 1:6
JAMES 4:2

God wants us to talk with him about our concerns, even though he already knows them. It's one of his ways of being with us. God misses us when we don't pray.

Obeying Christ (2619)
MATTHEW 4:20
MATTHEW 7:24
MATTHEW 9:9
MATTHEW 21:6
MATTHEW 26:19
LUKE 5:5
LUKE 6:47
JOHN 2:7
JOHN 11:29
JOHN 14:21
JOHN 21:6

Most of these verses are about people who obeyed Jesus when he lived on earth. They didn't question him. They obeyed him all the way, not just halfway. That's the way we all should do it.

Obeying God (2614)
DEUTERONOMY 26:16
DEUTERONOMY 32:46
JOSHUA 1:8
1 SAMUEL 15:22
JEREMIAH 7:23
MATTHEW 7:21
LUKE 8:21
ACTS 5:29

These verses are about choosing to obey God rather than someone else. This can be a hard choice if that someone is standing right in front of you and you have to say no right then and there. But if what the person asks means disobeying God, remember, You must obey God rather than people.

Obeying the Law (2525)
EZRA 7:26
PROVERBS 24:21
ECCLESIASTES 8:2
MATTHEW 17:27
MATTHEW 22:21
ROMANS 13:1
TITUS 3:1
1 PETER 2:13-14

You know God cares about whether or not you obey him. But does he care whether you obey the law? Speeding? Paying taxes? Staying out of locked houses? Leaving other people's property alone? According to these verses he cares very much. Obey the law.

Old Life (2642)
ROMANS 6:6
EPHESIANS 4:22
COLOSSIANS 3:9
1 PETER 4:3
2 PETER 1:9

You didn't become a DIFFERENT person when you became a Christian. You became a NEW person. God forgave all your sins, and you got to start over again. God doesn't want to change your whole personality. He made you and loves you the way you are. He just wants you to love him too.

Old People (3976)

2 Kings 2:23
Job 30:1
Lamentations 5:12

Some kids make fun of old people. They don't realize that people who are older have a lot to offer. Don't mock or ignore old people (as the people in these verses did). Instead, try to learn from them.

One Goal (3442)

Deuteronomy 5:32
Joshua 1:7
Proverbs 4:27
Ezekiel 1:12
Luke 9:62
Philippians 3:13

What do you live for? A lot of things fight for your attention: family, friends, school, sports, TV, clubs. It takes a lot of effort to stay focused on doing right. Don't let anything distract you from living God's way. Keep your eyes on pleasing God.

Only Human (2734)

Genesis 20:2
Numbers 20:12
1 Kings 3:3
1 Kings 22:43
2 Chronicles 16:12
Jonah 1:3
Luke 9:54
Luke 22:24
Galatians 2:13

You just read about some very good men who did some bad things. Even the people God uses in big ways sometimes make big mistakes. Don't be afraid of messing up. Only be afraid of not trying.

Only One God (2649)

Deuteronomy 4:35
Deuteronomy 6:4
Deuteronomy 32:39
2 Samuel 7:22
1 Chronicles 17:20
Psalm 83:18
Psalm 86:10
Isaiah 43:10
Isaiah 44:6
Isaiah 45:18
Mark 12:29
1 Corinthians 8:4
Ephesians 4:6
1 Timothy 2:5

These verses make it clear that there are no little gods, just one big one. That's why we don't just choose whom to serve or worship. There is only one God—the God you read about in the Bible. Worship him!

Only One Savior (3117)

Luke 1:69
Luke 2:30
John 10:9
Acts 4:12
Acts 15:11
Romans 5:9
1 Thessalonians 5:9
Hebrews 5:9
Hebrews 9:28

These verses explain that believing in Jesus is the only way to become a Christian. God sent Jesus to die for your sins because there is no one else who can do the job. And if you trust in him to save you, he will do it.

Ouch! (2620)

Deuteronomy 11:28
Deuteronomy 28:15
1 Samuel 12:15
1 Samuel 28:18
1 Kings 13:21
Jeremiah 12:17
Ephesians 5:6
2 Thessalonians 1:8
1 Timothy 1:9
Hebrews 2:2-3

These verses are about punishment for sin. Eventually sin will have some kind of bad result in your life. That's why God wants you to stay away from it. God, like a parent, lets you suffer the consequences of your sin, because he loves you and doesn't want you to do it again. The next time you suffer the consequences of what you did wrong, don't get angry. Learn something.

Our Savior (3368)

Isaiah 59:16
John 3:14-15
John 6:35
John 6:67-68
Acts 4:12
1 Corinthians 3:11

These verses tell us that Jesus does it all—he saves, helps, teaches, and gives eternal life. Jesus is the only Savior you will ever need. Don't depend on yourself or anyone else to save you from your sins.

Pain (0496)

Job 23:10
Psalm 66:10
Isaiah 48:10
Malachi 3:3
1 Peter 1:7
1 Peter 4:12

God uses hard times to teach us. "No pain, no gain," as some people say. Hard times can help you learn, so look for the lessons in every problem you face.

Parents (1778)

Proverbs 1:8
Proverbs 6:23
Proverbs 12:1
Ecclesiastes 12:11

God wants you to grow up to be wise. He does NOT want you to be a fool. That is why you have parents. In fact, these verses say that it's stupid not to listen to your mom and dad. They have loads of experience and they care about you too. Next time you feel like ignoring your mom or dad, look for the truth in what they say.

Parents Care (1642)

Genesis 37:14
1 Samuel 10:2
2 Samuel 18:29
Esther 2:11

The parents you just read about cared about their kids. They checked in on them to make sure they were OK. Your parents check in with you for the same reason. Don't push them away.

Parties (3408)

Exodus 32:6
Judges 9:27
Judges 16:25
1 Samuel 25:36
1 Samuel 30:16
Galatians 5:21
1 Peter 4:3

Parties can be fun, but they can also get out of control. A party should honor God just as much as anything else you do. It should not be used as an excuse to do something wrong in the name of fun. Whenever you go to a party, have fun without getting into trouble.

Patience (2275)

1 Corinthians 13:7
Ephesians 4:2
Ephesians 6:9
Colossians 3:13

These verses are about a special kind of patience—the kind of patience that still treats people with respect even after they have irritated you again and again and again. This kind of patience is particularly difficult with brothers and sisters. But if we are going to be loving people (as

God wants us to) we need this kind of patience.

Peace (3777)
ECCLESIASTES 10:4
ROMANS 12:18
TITUS 1:6
HEBREWS 12:14
JAMES 3:17

"I'm so angry at you!" When someone says this, it's tempting to strike back or accuse the person. But God wants you to live at peace with everyone. So take a deep breath and stay calm. Do whatever you can to explain your point of view and to work things out. Don't let little skirmishes turn into big wars.

Peace of Mind (3013)
PSALM 29:11
PSALM 119:165
PROVERBS 3:17
ISAIAH 26:3
ISAIAH 48:18
ISAIAH 54:13
EZEKIEL 34:25
JOHN 14:27
JOHN 16:33
PHILIPPIANS 4:7

These verses are about the kind of peace that comes from knowing that God will take care of you. Life will disappoint you; it will sometimes bother and disturb you. But you can know it will be all right eventually. That is peace. Take a deep breath and remember that God is on your side . . . and in control.

Peacemaking (3778)
PROVERBS 12:20
MATTHEW 5:9
ROMANS 14:19

God blesses people who make peace. Do you stir up trouble or do you try to make peace? Don't be a troublemaker. Go out of your way to keep the peace.

Perfect Father (1246)
1 CHRONICLES 29:10
PSALM 68:5
ISAIAH 63:16
ISAIAH 64:8
MATTHEW 6:9
MATTHEW 7:11
ROMANS 8:15
1 PETER 1:17

These verses tell you that God cares for you as if you were his very own kid—he is like all the best fathers in all the world rolled into one. God takes care of you, helps you feel good about yourself, and knows what's best for you. You can trust God to be a good dad.

Perfection (2729)
GENESIS 17:1
DEUTERONOMY 18:13
1 KINGS 8:61
MATTHEW 5:48
2 CORINTHIANS 13:11
EPHESIANS 4:13
PHILIPPIANS 3:15
COLOSSIANS 1:28
2 TIMOTHY 3:17
HEBREWS 6:1
HEBREWS 13:21
JAMES 1:4
1 PETER 5:10

These verses are about being perfect, complete, mature. God wants you to do your best to please him in every way. It's a goal he wants you to have. No, you can't be perfect. Sure, he'll forgive you if you sin. But that's no excuse not to try. Don't worry about whether you make it—just make it your goal.

Perjury (0871)
LEVITICUS 6:3
LEVITICUS 19:12
ZECHARIAH 5:4
MALACHI 3:5
1 TIMOTHY 1:10

When you swear to tell the truth you are saying, "With God watching, I declare that this is true." When you say that in court but don't tell the truth, you're not just telling a lie—you're breaking the law. And you are not just breaking a law made by people, you are breaking a law made by God. Never lie, especially in court.

Phonies (2750)
MATTHEW 6:2
MATTHEW 6:16
MATTHEW 12:2
MATTHEW 23:4
MATTHEW 23:13
MATTHEW 23:23
MATTHEW 23:27
JAMES 1:26

These verses are about people who say they love God but really don't. They do some good deeds, but they also do lots of bad ones. And their good deeds usually come from bad motives, such as the desire to show off. God isn't interested in people LOOKING like Christians, he's interested in people BEING Christians.

Pitfalls (3785)
DEUTERONOMY 4:9
PSALM 39:1
MATTHEW 26:41
ACTS 20:31
1 CORINTHIANS 10:12
1 CORINTHIANS 16:13
COLOSSIANS 4:2
1 PETER 5:8
REVELATION 3:2

Watch out. Sin is a real danger for everyone, even "good kids." Why? Because we're all weak in some ways. Sooner or later you will be tempted in your areas of weakness. Always be on guard and don't be smug. And use your best weapon—prayer.

Planning (2774)
GENESIS 11:4
PROVERBS 19:21
JEREMIAH 22:13-14
LUKE 12:18
JAMES 4:13

These verses are about making plans. It's OK to make plans. But remember, just because you make a plan doesn't mean you can always make it happen. Sometimes God's plan is different from yours. Don't be angry every time your plans get sidetracked. Be glad God has your life under control.

Pleasing God (1253)
PROVERBS 16:7
MATTHEW 3:17
JOHN 8:29
1 THESSALONIANS 2:4
1 THESSALONIANS 4:1
HEBREWS 11:5
HEBREWS 13:16
1 JOHN 3:22

These verses are about people who want to please God. Pleasing God should be more important to you than pleasing yourself or other people. Whenever you make a decision, aim to please God with your choice.

Popularity (2789)
JOHN 12:43
ACTS 12:1-3
ACTS 24:27
ACTS 25:9
EPHESIANS 6:6
COLOSSIANS 3:22

The people in these verses based their decisions on what other people wanted them to do. It's good to know what other people want, but you're going to make a bad decision if that's ALL you care about. Just ask King Herod.

Positive Attitude (1934)
HABAKKUK 3:17-18
ACTS 5:41

ACTS 16:23, 25
2 CORINTHIANS 6:10
HEBREWS 10:34
1 PETER 4:12-13

God always gives you a reason to be glad. Look for that reason the next time things go wrong. You can find it in these verses.

Poverty (2798)

JEREMIAH 5:4
MATTHEW 18:23-25
LUKE 15:14
EPHESIANS 2:12
REVELATION 3:17

The people in these verses were all poor, but their poverty had nothing to do with money. Some of them had a lot of money. But they were all poor in another way—they didn't have a relationship with God. Don't be fooled into thinking that money will make you rich. It won't.

Power of the Bible (0421)

JEREMIAH 5:14
JEREMIAH 23:29
EZEKIEL 37:7
ROMANS 1:16
EPHESIANS 6:17
HEBREWS 4:12

The Bible is a powerful book. When you read it, you get more than just a bit of information. God uses it to teach and change you. Make time for reading your Bible every day.

Praising God (1451)

PSALM 9:11
PSALM 33:2
PSALM 67:3
ISAIAH 42:12
HEBREWS 13:15
1 PETER 2:9

It feels good to be praised, doesn't it? To hear someone say nice things about you sends chills down your spine. These verses are about praising God. Sometimes it's good just to say how wonderful God is. How? Sing! Pray! Tell somebody else! God loves it.

Pray and Wait (3607)

PSALM 13:1
PSALM 40:17
PSALM 69:3
PSALM 119:82
JOHN 11:6
JOHN 11:21
JAMES 5:7
2 PETER 3:9

God doesn't like to see you suffer. He waits to answer your prayers until the best time. Meanwhile, have patience. Waiting for God's answers is good, because he knows the best timing for everything. Don't give up praying. Wait patiently for God's answers.

Prayer (4193)

MATTHEW 21:22
JOHN 14:13
JOHN 15:7
ACTS 16:25-26
JAMES 5:18

These verses tell us that prayer is powerful. God listens and cares about our cares. Be honest with him, thank and praise him, and trust him to answer.

Praying (1003)

PSALM 5:3
PSALM 55:17
PSALM 119:147
ZECHARIAH 8:21
LUKE 2:37
ACTS 10:2
ACTS 16:25
1 THESSALONIANS 3:10
1 TIMOTHY 5:5

Praying is not just talking to God. Praying is listening too. Listening to God means remembering he is with you all the time, like a friend. He'll find a way to tell you what you need to know—just don't forget he is there.

Praying Alone (2833)

DEUTERONOMY 9:25
1 SAMUEL 15:11
1 KINGS 17:19-20
DANIEL 6:10
MATTHEW 6:6
ACTS 10:9
ACTS 10:30

These people prayed when no one else heard them or even knew about it. That's OK, because God heard them. No one else has to know you're praying in order for your prayers to help. In fact, it's better that way—then God rewards you for what you do in secret.

Praying for Mercy (2301)

DEUTERONOMY 21:8
1 KINGS 8:30
PSALM 6:2
PSALM 27:7
PSALM 51:1
PSALM 85:7
PSALM 119:77
PSALM 123:3
DANIEL 9:16
HABAKKUK 3:2
LUKE 18:13

These people were asking God for mercy for them or their families, their towns, or their countries. God gives mercy because that is who he is. We ask for God's mercy, because we realize how many times we let him down, and we are AMAZED that he still is merciful. It's OK to ask God for mercy. It's even better to thank him for it.

Praying for Others (1785)

EXODUS 32:32
NUMBERS 12:13
NUMBERS 14:17
DEUTERONOMY 9:26
1 SAMUEL 7:5
1 KINGS 13:6
1 CHRONICLES 21:17
2 CHRONICLES 30:18
JOB 42:10
PSALM 106:23
EPHESIANS 1:16

These people were praying for others. They knew that God listens to these prayers and acts on them. Don't ever think your prayers won't make a difference. God hears them. Some problems have no other solution.

Praying for Wisdom (3841)

2 CHRONICLES 1:10
PSALM 90:12
PROVERBS 2:3
EPHESIANS 1:17
COLOSSIANS 1:9
JAMES 1:5

Lots of people have asked God for wisdom and gotten it. Don't be timid. God will give you wisdom, too. All you have to do is pray for it.

Procrastination (1500)

GENESIS 19:16
MATTHEW 8:21
LUKE 9:61
ACTS 17:32
ACTS 24:25

These people put off doing a lot of different things for a lot of different reasons. We do the same thing. Putting something off just makes your "Things To Do" list longer. That's no fun. Do the things you HAVE to do as soon as you can. Then you can do the things you WANT to do a lot longer.

Promise of Mercy (2299)

EXODUS 34:7
2 SAMUEL 22:26
2 CHRONICLES 30:9
PSALM 89:28
PSALM 103:8

ISAIAH 54:7
ISAIAH 55:7
JEREMIAH 3:12

These verses say that God is merciful. God promises he will be merciful when you go to him, no matter how many times you've come to him before. Don't put it off or be afraid.

Promises to Givers (2882)

PSALM 41:1
PROVERBS 3:9-10
PROVERBS 11:25
PROVERBS 22:9
PROVERBS 28:27
ECCLESIASTES 11:1
ISAIAH 58:10
LUKE 6:38
LUKE 14:14
2 CORINTHIANS 9:7

These verses are about a promise God makes to generous people: If you give, you will get. Though people may not give back to you, God will. Give willingly. God promises to reward you.

Promises to the Poor (2885)

JOB 5:15
PSALM 12:5
PSALM 14:6
PSALM 68:10
PSALM 69:33
PSALM 109:31
PSALM 140:12
ISAIAH 11:4
ISAIAH 25:4
ISAIAH 41:17
JAMES 2:5

These verses talk about promises God makes to the poor. Truly poor people aren't just poor in money, they are poor in options—that's why it's hard to stop being poor. God says he will look out for the poor and that we should too.

Protection (0364)

2 CHRONICLES 16:9
PSALM 34:7
PSALM 41:2
PSALM 91:4
PSALM 125:2
ZECHARIAH 2:5
LUKE 21:18

God really does look out for you. Ask him to guard your life every day. Then trust him to do so.

Proud People (1726)

PSALM 40:4
PSALM 119:78
PSALM 119:85
PSALM 123:4
PSALM 138:6
MALACHI 3:15
MALACHI 4:1
1 TIMOTHY 6:4
JAMES 4:6

All of these verses speak to the proud. They aren't very flattering, are they? God can't work with people like this. God opposes the proud, but blesses the humble.

Publicly Christian (1016)

JOHN 3:1-2
JOHN 7:13
JOHN 12:42
JOHN 19:38

These people all believed in Jesus but were afraid to admit it. They were afraid because they didn't know how other people would react. Admitting that you believe in Jesus can be hard. But whenever you get the chance, be honest about your beliefs.

Purity (0423)

PSALM 119:9
JOHN 15:3
JOHN 17:17
EPHESIANS 5:26
1 PETER 1:22

Do you ever feel dirty after doing something wrong? That is because sinning is like getting dirty. Obeying God's word makes you clean. Do what it says, and it will purify your life.

Quitting (2691)

ECCLESIASTES 7:8
LUKE 21:19
ROMANS 12:12
1 THESSALONIANS 5:14
TITUS 2:2
HEBREWS 10:36
JAMES 1:4
JAMES 5:7
2 PETER 1:6

These verses are about a kind of patience called perseverance. Perseverance means you stick to what you're doing. It means you don't give up just because you get tired or bored or discouraged. Being a Christian takes perseverance. Ask God to give you plenty.

Reading the Bible (0428)

DEUTERONOMY 17:19
ISAIAH 34:16
JOHN 5:39
ACTS 17:11
ROMANS 5:4

Read the Bible. Even if you can't understand it all, read it. Even if you don't have much time, read it. Even if you don't feel like it, read it. Everything written in the Bible is there to teach us.

Ready for Jesus' Return (1346)

PHILIPPIANS 4:5
HEBREWS 10:37
JAMES 5:8
REVELATION 3:11
REVELATION 22:20

Jesus is coming back and nobody knows when. EVERYONE will be surprised when it happens. Be ready today because it could be today.

Ready for the Future (2951)

2 KINGS 20:1
AMOS 4:12
MATTHEW 24:44
MATTHEW 25:10
MARK 13:35
LUKE 12:35-36
REVELATION 19:7

These verses are about being ready for big events—events like your death or Jesus' second coming. Be ready by staying close to God and loving the people around you. Make the most of your life and enjoy it.

Rebellion (2551)

DEUTERONOMY 17:12
EZRA 7:26
EZRA 10:8
ROMANS 13:2
JUDE 1:8

Can you accept someone else's authority? These verses are about people who will NOT accept someone else's authority—not human authority and not God's authority. There is not much hope for these people because they're in trouble with both God and the police. Do yourself a favor and honor God's choice of rulers.

Refusing Correction (2715)

ISAIAH 1:5
ISAIAH 9:13
ISAIAH 42:25
JEREMIAH 2:30
JEREMIAH 5:3
AMOS 4:9
ZEPHANIAH 3:7
HEBREWS 12:5
REVELATION 16:11

The people you just read about were being punished by God, because they had turned away from him. He was trying to get their attention, but they had turned away from God for so long that they just turned farther away. That is a sad way to live. Keep your heart turned toward God.

Rejecting God's Word (2967)
2 CHRONICLES 30:10
2 CHRONICLES 36:16
PSALM 50:17
PROVERBS 1:7
PROVERBS 1:22
PROVERBS 5:12

The people in these verses refused to listen to God and to God's people. And they didn't just say "No thank you." They were pushy about it. Be open. Be kind. Learn about God from people who know him.

Rejoicing (1932)
DEUTERONOMY 12:7
DEUTERONOMY 16:11
PSALM 5:11
PSALM 32:11
ZEPHANIAH 3:14
ZECHARIAH 9:9
LUKE 10:20
ROMANS 12:15
PHILIPPIANS 4:4
1 THESSALONIANS 5:16

Did those verses sound like commands to be happy? That's what they are! God knows there is at least one good thing in everyone's life. And he wants you to give up the grumps and the grumbles and teach yourself to celebrate the good things. And when YOU'VE got nothing to celebrate, you're to go find someone who does and celebrate with him or her.

Religious People (2985)
DEUTERONOMY 10:12
ECCLESIASTES 12:13
HOSEA 6:6
MICAH 6:8
MARK 12:33
ROMANS 13:10
JAMES 1:27

These verses are about what God wants us to do most of all. The list isn't long or complicated or even hard. But if you want to be religious, this is what you must do.

Remember... (2999)
NEHEMIAH 4:14
PSALM 63:6
ECCLESIASTES 12:1
JONAH 2:7
ZECHARIAH 10:9

These verses are about keeping God in mind as you go through your day. In the middle of school, work, or play, we can get so caught up in activity that we forget that God is with us. When we do that we lose touch with our most important help and guide. Remember God in everything you do. Remember: He is with you.

Remorse (1765)
NUMBERS 14:39
1 CHRONICLES 21:17
MATTHEW 26:75
MATTHEW 27:3, 5
HEBREWS 12:16-17

The people in these verses felt sorry. They felt remorse. When God convicts us of sin, we should feel sorry for what we've done. Never stop with feeling sorry, though. Do something to make it right.

Repent! (2706)
2 KINGS 17:13
2 CHRONICLES 30:6
PROVERBS 1:23
ISAIAH 22:12
JEREMIAH 25:5
EZEKIEL 14:6
EZEKIEL 18:31
EZEKIEL 33:11
DANIEL 4:27
HOSEA 14:2
JOEL 2:12
MALACHI 3:7
MATTHEW 3:2
LUKE 13:2-3
ACTS 3:19
ACTS 8:22
ACTS 17:30
ACTS 26:20

In each of these verses people are being told to repent. That means to quit sinning and start obeying. Repenting means being sorry and changing, not just SAYING you're sorry. You are never too young or too old to repent of your sins. God is always ready to forgive.

Repentance (2884)
PSALM 34:18
JEREMIAH 3:22
JOEL 2:13
MICAH 7:18
LUKE 6:21
LUKE 15:7
ACTS 2:38
ACTS 3:19

These verses are about people who repent of their sins. God is always glad to see you come to him and confess your sins. He isn't waiting to tell you off. You can go to him without fear!

Resisting Satan (3154)
EPHESIANS 4:26-27
EPHESIANS 6:11
JAMES 4:7
1 PETER 5:8-9

These verses tell us how to defeat Satan's power. They tell us to say no when Satan tempts us to do wrong. Stay close to God and RESIST when you feel drawn the wrong way.

Respecting Adults (3974)
LEVITICUS 19:32
JOB 32:6
PROVERBS 23:22
1 TIMOTHY 5:1-2

Respect your elders. Your parents and teachers deserve your respect. They know a lot more than you think. Don't act like you know everything. Listen to their advice.

Respecting God (3030)
EXODUS 3:5
JOSHUA 5:15
PSALM 4:4
PSALM 33:8
PSALM 89:7
PSALM 111:9
HABAKKUK 2:20

There is no other person or being like God. That is why he is called holy. That is why we treat him with respect. He is not an old man you get impatient with or a friend you play a joke on. God wants you to feel safe and happy with him because he loves you. But show him the respect he deserves.

Respecting God's People (3032)
EXODUS 33:8
ACTS 28:10
PHILIPPIANS 2:29
1 THESSALONIANS 5:12-13
1 TIMOTHY 5:17
HEBREWS 13:7

There are a lot of people who don't care about following God. That's why when you know people who work hard to follow God, like these verses say, you should respect them. Help them in any way you can. Let them teach you. Listen when they talk.

Rest (3010)
EXODUS 23:12
EXODUS 31:15
EXODUS 34:21
EXODUS 35:2
LEVITICUS 23:3
MARK 6:31

These verses TELL us to get some rest. God rested on the seventh day of creation, and he has asked us to do the same ever since. Don't overdo it. Leave time in your week and in your day to relax and refresh yourself. And when it's time to go to bed, GO TO BED!

Restraint (3207)

Proverbs 23:1-2
Proverbs 23:20
Proverbs 25:16
Luke 12:22
Luke 21:34
1 Corinthians 9:27

These verses are about having control of your appetites. It's OK for animals and bugs to indulge whatever urge comes along, but not for people. God wants you to live a balanced, self-controlled life. Put your urges in their place. Do whatever you SHOULD be doing and stop taking orders from your stomach.

Results of Sin (3975)

Job 13:26
Job 20:11
Psalm 25:7
Ecclesiastes 11:9
Jeremiah 3:25
Jeremiah 32:30

"I'm just a kid. Give me a break!" You may be young, but you still have to accept the consequences of your mistakes. Sin always hurts, no matter how old you are. Don't think you can get away with more because you are young.

Resurrection (2407)

Psalm 49:15
Psalm 71:20
Hosea 13:14
John 5:25
John 6:40
John 11:25
Acts 24:15
1 Corinthians 15:22
2 Corinthians 4:14
1 Thessalonians 4:16

What will God's people be in heaven? They won't be ghosts. They will be themselves, only better, because they'll never die again. Isn't that great?

Revenge (2279)

Leviticus 19:18
Proverbs 20:22
Proverbs 24:29
Matthew 5:39
Romans 12:17
1 Thessalonians 5:15
1 Peter 3:9

These verses are about you treating someone mean, because they treated you that way. If you just return mean for mean, then they'll just return mean back and it will go on and on and on. And it'll go on and on and on until the meanest kid wins. Let it stop with you. Treat people the way you WANT to be treated, not the way they treat you. That'll put a stop to the fighting and make the good guy the winner.

Rewarded Goodness (3054)

Job 36:7
Psalm 34:15
Psalm 37:25
Psalm 92:12
Proverbs 3:32
Proverbs 4:18
Proverbs 12:13
Proverbs 20:7
Isaiah 3:10
Matthew 13:43

If you've ever tried hard to be good, you know how hard it can be. And maybe you wondered, "Is it worth it?" These verses say YES. God always looks out for people who strive to please him—to be righteous. Do you strive to be righteous? You have God's attention.

Rewards (4086)

Psalm 41:3
Psalm 112:9
Proverbs 11:17
Proverbs 14:31
Isaiah 58:10
Daniel 4:27
Matthew 5:7
Matthew 6:14
Matthew 25:40
Luke 6:38

God is watching you. He wants to reward you for all the good deeds you do. God blesses people who are kind. Look for ways to help other kids, even if they can't pay you back. You'll get your reward from God.

Right Paths (2688)

Psalm 16:11
Psalm 23:3
Psalm 25:10
Psalm 119:35
Proverbs 2:9
Proverbs 4:11
Proverbs 4:18
Isaiah 2:3
Isaiah 26:7
Hebrews 12:13

These verses all talk about right paths. That means going through life the way you were created to do it. Obeying God each step of the way will smooth the road ahead for you.

Righteousness (3080)

Daniel 4:27
Hosea 10:12
Matthew 5:20
Acts 24:25
1 Corinthians 15:34
Ephesians 6:14
Philippians 1:11
1 Timothy 6:11

These verses tell it plainly, don't they? God wants you to stop sinning. Stop lying. Stop cheating. Stop being rude. Stop making fun of other people. God wants you to clean all that out of your life so there is more room for him in it. That's God's goal for you.

Rulers (2526)

Exodus 22:28
1 Samuel 24:6
Ecclesiastes 10:20
Acts 23:5
Romans 13:1
1 Peter 2:17
Jude 1:8

These verses are about people in authority like presidents, mayors, preachers, and city councils. God wants them to use their authority for good, not bad. God wants everyone else to respect their authority and obey them.

Sacrifice (4156)

Matthew 19:21
Matthew 19:29
Mark 8:35
Mark 9:35
John 12:24
Philippians 3:8

Jesus wants you to put him first in your life, no matter what it costs. Giving up your own needs to follow Jesus isn't easy, but it's worth it. Sacrifice your best for God, and he'll give you his best in return.

Safety (2913)

Deuteronomy 6:24
Joshua 24:17
2 Samuel 8:6
Nehemiah 9:6
Psalm 31:23
Psalm 37:28
Psalm 146:9
Proverbs 2:8
Isaiah 49:8
2 Timothy 4:18

These verses tell you that God watches over people who are faithful to him. Are you one of those people? Whenever you get in a tough situation, ask for God's help.

Salvation (1087)
EZEKIEL 33:9
LUKE 14:18
ACTS 24:25
ACTS 28:27
HEBREWS 2:3
HEBREWS 12:25

There are many reasons why people don't do the things they should—fear, neglect, laziness, ignorance. The people in these verses knew God, but they walked away from him. Don't walk away. Have faith in God to let him show you why being a Christian is worth the effort.

Salvation by Faith (1206)
JOHN 3:15
JOHN 3:36
JOHN 5:24
JOHN 6:40
JOHN 11:25
JOHN 12:46
JOHN 20:31
ACTS 10:43
ACTS 13:39
ACTS 16:31
ROMANS 9:33
ROMANS 10:9
2 TIMOTHY 3:15
1 JOHN 5:1

These verses are about believing in Jesus—believing that he died and that his death makes a way for you to live forever. Your body will die someday, but YOU will live on and on with him. That is a good thing. Believe and be glad.

Salvation for Anyone (3119)
LUKE 3:6
ACTS 2:21
ROMANS 5:18
ROMANS 10:13
1 TIMOTHY 2:4
TITUS 2:11-12
2 PETER 3:9

These verses are about who God wants to follow him—EVERYBODY! But not everybody will. You can be sure of one thing, though: no one who comes to God sincerely will be turned away. He doesn't play favorites.

Satan's Power (3150)
JOB 1:12
LUKE 4:6
ACTS 26:18
2 CORINTHIANS 4:3-4
EPHESIANS 6:12
2 THESSALONIANS 2:9
HEBREWS 2:14

These verses are about the power Satan has in the world. His main weapon is lying—he wants you to believe what is false so you won't follow God's Word. Satan really is up to no good. STAY AWAY FROM HIM! That means don't do occult things such as Ouija boards, tarot cards, fortune telling, and stuff like that.

Satan's Weakness (4199)
JOB 1:12
LUKE 10:19
ROMANS 16:20
1 CORINTHIANS 10:13
JAMES 4:7
REVELATION 12:12
REVELATION 13:5

Satan will try to tempt you to sin. But God is much stronger than Satan. The next time you feel tempted, remember that God is on your side. With his help, say no to temptation.

Satisfaction (0984)
PSALM 17:15
PSALM 36:8
PSALM 63:5
PSALM 103:5
PSALM 107:9
ISAIAH 58:11
JEREMIAH 31:14

All people have a lonely, empty place inside of them. That's why we make friends. But no matter how many friends you have, your lonely place never fills up all the way. God is the only one who is with you all the time and can fill up that lonely place.

Saying No (3590)
PROVERBS 1:10
PROVERBS 4:14
LUKE 21:34
ROMANS 6:13
EPHESIANS 6:13
2 PETER 3:17

"Everyone's doing it." "You won't get caught." People use many excuses for their sin. But an excuse is an excuse. Some people will say anything to get you to sin. Don't listen. It's OK to say no.

Saying Thank You (4116)
ISAIAH 43:24
LUKE 17:18
2 TIMOTHY 3:2

A lot of people forget to say thank-you to God. That makes him sad. God is so good to us that he deserves our thanks. Stop and think of what God has done for you. Then thank him!

Second Coming (1344)
MATTHEW 26:64
MARK 14:62
LUKE 21:27
ACTS 1:11
HEBREWS 9:28
2 PETER 3:10

These verses are about the next time Jesus will come to earth. The important thing about Jesus' second coming is not when or how he will come. The important thing is that he WILL come, and he wants you to be ready. Get Ready! How? By confessing your sin, obeying God, and loving other people TODAY.

Security (3174)
JOB 11:18
PSALM 91:5
PSALM 112:7
PSALM 125:1
PROVERBS 1:33
PROVERBS 3:24
ISAIAH 33:16
ISAIAH 43:2
HEBREWS 13:6
1 PETER 3:13

These verses are about trusting God to take care of you. You don't have to worry or be afraid. You can trust God to take care of you. Try to remember that God is in control of all that happens to you.

Seeking God (3191)
DEUTERONOMY 4:29
2 CHRONICLES 14:4
PSALM 105:4
ISAIAH 55:6
JEREMIAH 29:13
HOSEA 10:12
AMOS 5:4
ZEPHANIAH 2:3
MATTHEW 6:33
LUKE 11:10
ACTS 17:27

These verses tell you to work at knowing God more and loving him more. It won't happen if you don't try. It's not enough to do nothing, so pray, read your Bible, and do what he says!

Seeking Peace (3015)
JOB 22:21
PSALM 34:14
ISAIAH 27:5
COLOSSIANS 3:15
1 PETER 3:11

These verses are about helping yourself find peace. You don't do that by being deceitful and trying not to get caught. No peace there. You do it by trusting God, obeying him, and reminding yourself that he loves you and will take care of you.

Self-confidence (3188)
PROVERBS 28:26
ISAIAH 47:8
HOSEA 10:13
OBADIAH 1:3
MATTHEW 26:33
LUKE 18:9
1 CORINTHIANS 10:12

These verses are about thinking you can take care of yourself without God's help. Every person needs God. Be confident in him. Be grateful for the accomplishments he gives you.

Self-control (3569)
PROVERBS 16:32
PROVERBS 25:28
ACTS 24:25
ROMANS 6:12
1 CORINTHIANS 6:12
JAMES 3:2
2 PETER 1:5-7

People lose control in many ways. Some lose their temper; some eat nothing but junk food; others can't control their mouth. It's always better to have self-control. Controlling your desires saves you a lot of grief and honors God.

Self-examination (3197)
LAMENTATIONS 3:40
MATTHEW 7:5
1 CORINTHIANS 11:28
2 CORINTHIANS 13:5
GALATIANS 6:4

These verses tell you how to be honest with yourself. Are you pretending that one of your bad habits is not so bad? Do you need to apologize to someone, but you are putting it off? Ask yourself these hard questions before someone else does.

Self-righteousness (3219)
DEUTERONOMY 9:4
JOB 9:20
JOB 35:2
PROVERBS 12:15
PROVERBS 16:2
PROVERBS 20:6
PROVERBS 21:2
PROVERBS 30:12
JEREMIAH 2:35
2 CORINTHIANS 10:12
REVELATION 3:17

You just read about people who think they have no sin to repent of. They want everyone to believe that they have never done anything wrong, ever. But we all know better. Most of all, God knows better. Everybody has faults, so don't brag about how good you are.

Serving (3900)
NEHEMIAH 12:43
PSALM 40:8
PSALM 100:2
PSALM 126:5-6
LUKE 10:17
JOHN 4:36
ACTS 11:23

Serving God brings joy to people who love God. Even the worst jobs are no match for such willing, motivated workers. You do them because you want to, not because someone made you. Don't think of your daily chores as a pain; think of them as a way to serve God.

Serving Jesus (3895)
JOHN 12:26
1 CORINTHIANS 7:22
EPHESIANS 6:6
PHILIPPIANS 1:1
COLOSSIANS 3:24

Who's the boss? Jesus. It doesn't matter what anyone else thinks of your work, or whether they appreciate your efforts. You work for the Lord. Always do your best—not to impress others, but to serve Jesus well.

Serving People (3896)
MARK 10:43-44
LUKE 10:36-37
JOHN 13:14
JOHN 21:16
GALATIANS 5:13
GALATIANS 6:2
GALATIANS 6:10

Jesus washed his friends' dirty feet because he wanted to please his Father. Serving people isn't always fun or easy, but God loves it when we do it. Look for new ways to serve your family and friends. It may be hard work, but you'll please the Lord.

Serving Quickly (3899)
1 KINGS 19:20
MARK 1:18
LUKE 4:39
LUKE 19:6
ACTS 9:20
ACTS 10:29
ACTS 16:10

When God called these people to serve him, they obeyed him right away. God loves a quick response. God has called you to serve him, too. Don't wait for a convenient time—it will never come. Serve God as soon as you know how he wants you to serve.

Sharing (0583)
DEUTERONOMY 15:8
PSALM 37:26
PSALM 112:5
MATTHEW 5:42
LUKE 6:35

Sharing is hard. Sharing is noble. Sharing is worth it.

Showing Mercy (2298)
PROVERBS 3:3
PROVERBS 11:17
HOSEA 12:6
MICAH 6:8
MATTHEW 5:7
LUKE 6:36
JAMES 2:13

God wants you to ENJOY being good to other people because he's been good to you. These verses tell you to be merciful—that means to be kind whether someone deserves it or not. When you feel like being cruel, show mercy instead.

Showing Off (1026)
2 KINGS 10:16
MATTHEW 6:2, 5
MATTHEW 6:16
MATTHEW 23:5
LUKE 18:12

These verses are about people who show off how much they are doing for God. But the purpose of serving God is to draw attention to him, not yourself. If people see that you serve God, great! But don't show off or brag about it. Just serve God; he will reward you in due time.

Showing Off Stuff (1025)
ESTHER 1:4
ESTHER 5:11
ISAIAH 39:2
LUKE 20:46
ACTS 25:23

The people in these verses showed off their nice clothes, fancy belongings, and special privileges. They thought their nice things made them important. But having neat stuff doesn't make you any more important to God than you are with nothing. Don't forget that God looks at your intentions and the way you treat people, not how fancy your life is.

Sick People (3397)
2 KINGS 8:29
2 KINGS 13:14

Job 2:11
Matthew 25:36
James 5:14

Sick people need more than medicine. They need comfort from their friends. When someone you know gets sick, visit the person. Your friendly hello may help just as much as the medicine.

Sin (Warnings) (1795)

Genesis 19:17
Deuteronomy 29:20
Joshua 24:20
1 Samuel 12:15
Isaiah 28:14
Jeremiah 13:16
Jonah 3:4
Hebrews 12:25
2 Peter 3:17

These verses warn people who have ignored God time after time, day after day, month after month, year after year, decade after decade. They heard God's Word, but they wouldn't listen. Don't get used to sin and forget how much God hates it. Keep your heart tender toward God. Listen to him and obey.

Sin Hurts (0383)

Proverbs 6:33
Proverbs 23:29
Isaiah 1:6
Jeremiah 30:12
Micah 1:9

Sin hurts. Remember that next time you're tempted.

Sincerity (2987)

Joshua 24:14
1 Corinthians 5:8
2 Corinthians 1:12
2 Corinthians 2:17
Philippians 1:10
Titus 2:7
1 John 3:18

These verses are about sincerity—being honest about your thoughts and feelings. People like it when you are sincere because it means they can trust you. God is pleased when you are sincere because it means you are like him. Let people know that when you talk to them, you mean what you say.

Sinner Beware (3720)

Numbers 32:23
Deuteronomy 32:32
Ecclesiastes 8:8
Ecclesiastes 12:14
Matthew 25:31-33
2 Thessalonians 1:9
1 Timothy 6:7

It's a sure fact: God will punish sinners. In fact, the future is pretty rotten for people who persist in rebelling against God. If you want a better future, turn away from your sins, ask God for forgiveness, and do what he says.

Sleep (3377)

Proverbs 6:4
Proverbs 6:9-10
Proverbs 10:5
Proverbs 19:15
Proverbs 20:13
Proverbs 23:21

What does your mom have to do to get you out of bed in the morning? She shouldn't have to work too hard. The Bible warns us not to love sleep. Get the sleep you need, then get up!

Soon Gone (2809)

Job 20:28
Psalm 49:10
Proverbs 23:5
Proverbs 27:24
Ecclesiastes 2:18
Ecclesiastes 2:26
Jeremiah 17:11
1 Timothy 6:7

Now you know: Money is only for living on earth. When you leave for eternity, money won't have any place to go with you. You are permanent; money is not. Don't trust money to be with you always. That's God's job.

Source of Evil (1545)

Ecclesiastes 8:11
Ecclesiastes 9:3
Jeremiah 17:9
Matthew 23:25
Mark 7:21
Hebrews 3:12
2 Peter 2:14

Each of these verses talks about the source of evil inside us. We do wrong because it's inside us, a part of us. That's what people mean by "original sin." It doesn't mean that everyone always does evil things; it means you can't run from evil no matter how hard you try. The only way to get it out of you is to turn to Jesus for forgiveness and help. That's the good news—ask God to take away your sin, and he will.

Source of Happiness (1937)

Psalm 128:2
Psalm 144:15
Proverbs 3:18
Proverbs 14:21
Proverbs 16:20
Proverbs 28:14
Proverbs 29:18
John 13:17

If you read them closely, these verses tell you how to be happy. Happiness comes from obedience to God. That doesn't mean you're happy every minute when you obey God; it means you'll be happy a lot more.

Source of Wealth (2805)

Deuteronomy 8:18
1 Chronicles 29:12
Ecclesiastes 5:19
Hosea 2:8

These verses are about some of God's gifts to us. Being able to work to earn money to buy stuff you enjoy is a gift from God. Remember to thank God whenever somebody in your family gets a paycheck. It's a gift from God.

The Spirit in You (1602)

Ezekiel 36:27
John 14:17
Romans 8:9
1 Corinthians 3:16
1 Corinthians 6:19
2 Timothy 1:14
1 John 2:27

In one way or another these verses all say that God's Spirit lives in your spirit when you are a believer. That is a wonderful thing. God is with you and in you always and forever. Remember that the next time you feel scared, unimportant, or helpless.

Spiritual Death (2163)

Genesis 2:17
Proverbs 8:36
Ezekiel 18:20
Romans 6:23
Romans 8:6
James 1:15
James 5:20
Revelation 21:8

These verses say that your spirit can be either alive or dead. Your body may be alive, but your spirit is only alive if you have been "born again"—saved from your sins by faith in Christ. Otherwise, sin has killed your spirit and only God can raise it back to life. Trust in Christ.

Standing Strong (3438)

Joshua 23:7-8
1 Samuel 12:21
Job 11:14-15
Acts 11:23
1 Corinthians 15:58
Galatians 5:1
Ephesians 4:14
Philippians 1:27

Philippians 4:1
2 Thessalonians 2:2
2 Thessalonians 2:15
1 Peter 5:9
2 Peter 3:17

It's one thing to say, "I believe in Jesus." It's quite another to live for him your whole life. Jesus wants you to hold on to your faith as long as you live. When Jesus comes back, will he find you standing strong?

Starting Over (3346)

Job 11:14
Proverbs 28:13
Isaiah 55:7
Ephesians 4:22
Colossians 2:11
Hebrews 12:1
1 Peter 2:11

These verses say that you have better things to do with your life than sinning. Confess your sin to God and make up your mind to go his way. Replace every bad habit with something better. Stop the bad by starting the good.

Stay Away! (1798)

Job 28:28
Psalm 34:14
Psalm 97:10
Proverbs 4:27
Proverbs 14:16
Zechariah 7:10
Romans 12:9
1 Corinthians 10:6
1 Thessalonians 5:22
1 Peter 3:11

There's no mistaking these verses. God wants you to stay as far away from evil as you can. Don't see it. Don't hear it. Don't want it. And most of all, don't DO it. Get the picture?

Stealing (3447)

Exodus 20:15
Deuteronomy 23:24
Zechariah 5:3
Matthew 19:18
Romans 13:9
Ephesians 4:28
Titus 2:10
1 Peter 4:15

Stealing is a cop-out. People steal because they don't want to work for what they want. The Bible says that stealing is wrong. God wants you to work for what you want. Don't take the lazy way out by stealing.

Stubborn People (2714)

2 Kings 17:14
2 Chronicles 28:22
2 Chronicles 33:23
Nehemiah 9:29
Jeremiah 6:15
Daniel 9:13
Luke 16:31
Revelation 9:21

These people refused to tell God that they were sorry. They were determined to do their own thing, not God's. God won't MAKE you turn away from your sin. It's your choice. Have the courage to come to God with your sin and say you're sorry.

Study (2028)

Daniel 1:17
Acts 7:22
Acts 22:3

These people were well educated, and all of them were important leaders of God's people. Some folks will tell you that it's not important to learn. They think that because knowledge isn't EVERYTHING, it's therefore NOTHING. That's going too far. Learn all you can so you can serve God even better.

Submitting to God (3507)

Psalm 40:8
Psalm 143:10
Matthew 6:10
Matthew 12:50
Matthew 26:42
John 5:30
John 7:17
Acts 21:14
Romans 12:2
Ephesians 6:6
Hebrews 13:21
James 4:15
1 John 2:17

It's natural to want your own way. But God wants you to submit to his will. Don't be scared to give up what you want. Submitting to God is the best thing you can do for yourself.

Success (2898)

Deuteronomy 6:10-12
Deuteronomy 32:15
Proverbs 1:32
Proverbs 30:9

These verses are about the dangers you face when everything is going well. Danger? Yes. It's hard to remember that you need God when you have everything you need. Stay in touch with him no matter how well things are going. In the end, you depend on him anyway.

Suffering (0499)

Deuteronomy 4:30
Matthew 24:21
John 16:33
Acts 14:22
Romans 5:3
1 Thessalonians 3:4
Revelation 2:9
Revelation 7:14

Suffering is a part of life, even for people who love God, because of sin. Evil in the world brings suffering with it. But God cares about every hurt. Whenever you hurt, let God comfort you.

Suffering for Jesus (3474)

Acts 5:41
Acts 9:16
Romans 8:17
Romans 8:36
2 Corinthians 1:7
2 Corinthians 11:23
Philippians 3:10
2 Timothy 2:12
Hebrews 11:25
James 5:10
1 Peter 2:20
1 Peter 3:14
1 Peter 4:16
1 Peter 5:10

Many of Jesus' friends were beaten up and thrown into prison. Some were even killed. But they knew they were right, so they took it bravely. If you suffer a little for being a Christian, praise God as Jesus' friends did. You're in good company.

Suffering Rewarded (1365)

Matthew 5:11-12
Romans 8:17
2 Timothy 2:12
Hebrews 10:34
Hebrews 11:26
Revelation 20:4

These verses are about hard times and difficult situations. Life has them sometimes. God notices when we go through hard times, particularly when those hard times come because we serve him. He says, "Hold on. Be as strong as you can. I'll be waiting with better news when this is over."

Suing People (0870)

Proverbs 25:8
Matthew 5:25
Matthew 5:40
1 Corinthians 6:1

People sometimes sue each other when they cannot settle a disagreement. They take their fight to a court to have a judge decide who is right. God doesn't think that's very smart. He thinks we are smart when we talk to each other and listen to each other and find a way together to solve our problems. Whenever you have a fight, always try to work it out. It's not worth it to sue another person.

Sunday School (1779)

1 SAMUEL 9:27
2 KINGS 17:28
2 CHRONICLES 17:7
EZRA 7:10
NEHEMIAH 8:7
MATTHEW 5:2
LUKE 24:27
ACTS 8:35
ACTS 18:26
ACTS 28:23

Each of these people either taught or were taught spiritual skills. We can learn from other people how to be a better follower of Christ. Who gives you spiritual instruction? Listen to them carefully.

Superstition (2998)

1 SAMUEL 4:3
1 KINGS 20:23
JEREMIAH 10:2
JEREMIAH 44:18
MATTHEW 14:2
ACTS 12:15
ACTS 14:11
ACTS 17:23
ACTS 28:4

These verses are about superstition. Sometimes when life is hard to figure out, people will believe in magic to help them feel better. Maybe something bad happens on a certain day and they decide that that day is an unlucky day. Remember that the events in your life come from God. There's no such thing as luck.

Swearing (0475)

EXODUS 20:7
LEVITICUS 19:12
MATTHEW 5:34
JAMES 5:12

God doesn't like it when we use crude language. Don't swear.

Sympathy (3515)

ISAIAH 58:7
ACTS 20:35
ROMANS 15:1
GALATIANS 6:2
HEBREWS 13:3
JAMES 1:27

"Put yourself in his shoes." Sympathy is treating another person the way you would like to be treated if you were in his shoes. Try to think about how other kids feel. Give them the kind of help you would want in their situation.

Taking Advice (0795)

PSALM 141:5
PROVERBS 15:5
PROVERBS 17:10
PROVERBS 25:12
PROVERBS 27:5
PROVERBS 29:15
ECCLESIASTES 7:5
HEBREWS 12:5

Good advice can be painful to hear. But it comes from people who care. So if you want to learn, listen, listen, listen, even if it doesn't feel good.

Talents (4016)

MATTHEW 25:20
1 TIMOTHY 4:7
1 TIMOTHY 4:14
2 TIMOTHY 1:6

God gives all of us talents that we can use in serving him. It's your job to use the talents God has given you. Don't sit around doing nothing. Use your talents for God.

Talking (3295)

PROVERBS 17:27
MATTHEW 5:37
COLOSSIANS 4:6
2 TIMOTHY 1:13
TITUS 2:8
JAMES 3:2

These verses are about how we talk to other people. God cares about this because words are very powerful. Practice talking well—kindly, without gossip, only after you know what you're talking about, in turn, and so on. This will take practice, but it's well worth it.

The Teacher (3555)

MATTHEW 4:23
MATTHEW 5:2
MATTHEW 7:29
MARK 6:34
LUKE 4:15
LUKE 5:3
JOHN 3:2
JOHN 7:14
JOHN 8:2

Don't you wish you could have been there? Hearing Jesus teach must have been awesome! Jesus was the best teacher who ever lived. Many of his lessons are written in the Bible. Read them for yourself!

Teamwork (3728)

EXODUS 17:12
JUDGES 20:11
1 SAMUEL 14:6-7
2 KINGS 6:1-3
1 CHRONICLES 12:38
EZRA 10:4
NEHEMIAH 4:16-17
MATTHEW 18:19
MARK 2:3
MARK 6:7
PHILIPPIANS 1:27

All the people in these verses used teamwork. Teamwork is important. You can often do a lot more than you can alone if you work together with others. Don't try to do everything by yourself. Find others to help you.

Teasing and Joking (1890)

PROVERBS 26:19
EPHESIANS 5:4

There are two problems with joking around. First, too many times you are saying a serious thing and just hiding it behind a joke. That's like lying. Second, your words can get out of hand and hurt someone. Laughing is good. Lying is bad. Joking is fun. Hurting people is cruel. Be careful how you get your laughs. Get your laughs without hurting people.

Telling the Truth (4081)

MATTHEW 3:7
MATTHEW 23:33
ACTS 7:52
2 CORINTHIANS 3:12
GALATIANS 4:16

Jesus, Stephen, and Paul had the courage to tell the truth. Do you? Telling the truth is not always easy, but it is the right thing to do. Be bold about this. Tell the truth, even if it hurts.

Temper (3957)

2 CHRONICLES 28:9
DANIEL 3:19
JOHN 10:31
ACTS 7:57
ACTS 22:23

When you let your anger get out of control, you usually end up doing things you later regret. Don't lose your temper. When you feel angry, take a time out. Control your anger before it controls you.

Temptation (3586)

1 CORINTHIANS 10:13
HEBREWS 2:18
JAMES 1:2-3
JAMES 1:12
2 PETER 2:9
REVELATION 3:10

Saying no to temptation is sometimes hard, but it's never impossible. God always gives you a way out. He can help you resist temptation.

Whenever you feel tempted to do something wrong, ask God to help you find and take the escape route.

Tempted by Satan (2887)
LUKE 10:19
LUKE 22:31-32
ROMANS 16:20
1 CORINTHIANS 10:13
HEBREWS 2:18
JAMES 4:7
1 JOHN 4:4
REVELATION 3:10
REVELATION 3:21

These verses are about being tempted by Satan. This is what God says: (1) You have what it takes to say no. (2) Satan will leave you alone if you resist him. (3) One day God will punish Satan. Satan can't make you do anything. Don't think you have to do wrong. You can do the right thing.

"Thank You" (1450)
RUTH 2:10
1 SAMUEL 14:45
1 SAMUEL 15:6
2 SAMUEL 9:1
2 SAMUEL 10:2
1 KINGS 2:7
2 KINGS 4:13
ACTS 28:10

What did these people have in common? Someone had helped them. They were grateful. They wanted to do something to say thank you. We are the same way today, or at least we should be. When someone does something nice for you, thank the person.

Thankfulness (1455)
DEUTERONOMY 8:10
PSALM 100:4
PSALM 107:22
COLOSSIANS 1:12
COLOSSIANS 2:7
COLOSSIANS 3:15
1 THESSALONIANS 5:18

These verses are about thankfulness. Thankfulness is an action and an attitude (a way of thinking). Take time to thank God for the good things in your life. And instead of being grumpy, be happy for what you have.

Things That Last (3657)
1 KINGS 19:8
JOHN 6:27
1 CORINTHIANS 3:14
1 CORINTHIANS 13:13
2 CORINTHIANS 4:18
HEBREWS 12:27
1 PETER 1:25

God wants us to work for what will last. The deeds we do for God last forever—even if they're as small as sharing our stuff with others or doing the dishes for Mom. Make your life count. Do everything as a service to God.

This for That (3206)
MARK 10:28
LUKE 5:11
LUKE 5:27-28
LUKE 14:33
LUKE 18:29-30
PHILIPPIANS 3:8

These verses are about choosing a master. They say, "You have to serve somebody. Serve Jesus." You could choose not to follow Jesus because you don't want to give up anything to serve him, but then you'd have to give up him to serve whatever else you're serving. It's worth the sacrifice of a little "freedom" to serve the best master in the universe.

Time (3626)
PSALM 90:12
ECCLESIASTES 12:1
1 CORINTHIANS 7:29, 31
EPHESIANS 5:15-16
COLOSSIANS 4:5

Time is short. We need to make the most of the time we have. Don't wait until you get older to spend your time in a worthwhile manner. Now is the time to start using your time wisely.

The Time Is Now (3446)
1 KINGS 18:21
2 KINGS 17:41
HOSEA 10:2
MATTHEW 6:24
LUKE 9:62
JAMES 1:8
JAMES 4:8

Some people don't WANT to make up their minds about God, so they put it off. But remember that "not to decide is to decide." If you don't choose to follow God, you are choosing not to follow him. Make up your mind about God before it's too late.

Tithing (2120)
EXODUS 25:2
EXODUS 35:5
NUMBERS 31:50
2 SAMUEL 8:10-11
1 CHRONICLES 29:9
2 CHRONICLES 15:18
EZRA 8:28
PROVERBS 3:9
MICAH 4:13

God wants us to give some of what we have to him. It reminds us that God owns everything and will provide whatever we need. It also makes it possible for his work to get done—the work of telling everyone about his great love. Give what you can so you can be a part of God's work too.

True Wisdom (3840)
JOB 28:28
JOB 32:7
PSALM 111:10
PROVERBS 1:20
PROVERBS 4:7
PROVERBS 9:1
HOSEA 14:9
MATTHEW 7:24
1 CORINTHIANS 2:6
1 CORINTHIANS 12:8
2 TIMOTHY 3:15
JAMES 3:17
1 JOHN 2:20

God's wisdom is best. His word in the Bible gives you the best advice you'll ever get. Read his word and do what it says, and you will soon be wiser than ever.

Trusting God (1214)
PSALM 37:3, 5
PSALM 115:11
PSALM 118:8
PROVERBS 3:5
ISAIAH 26:4
ISAIAH 50:10

These verses are about trusting God. God will never let you down. You can trust him to take care of you and to help you. Give him the chance to come through.

Trusting in People (3184)
PSALM 118:9
PSALM 146:3
ISAIAH 2:22
ISAIAH 30:2
ISAIAH 31:1, 3
ISAIAH 36:6
JEREMIAH 17:5
HOSEA 5:13

These verses are about trusting people, rather than God, to take care of you. Yes, some people do help you and do favors for you, but they can't do everything for you all the time always just the way you need. They will let you down sometimes, because they're human just like you. But God will always be there for you. Put your trust in him.

The Ultimate (3179)
PSALM 118:22
MATTHEW 21:42

Acts 4:11
Ephesians 2:20
1 Peter 2:6

These verses are about a stone—the cornerstone. That's the stone that determines where the whole building will go. These verses say that Jesus is as important to us as that one stone is to the building. He'll help you know where to go and what to do. Read what he said and follow his example.

Unanswered Prayer (2820)

Deuteronomy 1:45
1 Samuel 14:37
1 Samuel 28:6
Psalm 66:18
Proverbs 1:28
Proverbs 21:13
Proverbs 28:9
Isaiah 1:15
Isaiah 59:2
Micah 3:4
Zechariah 7:13
James 1:6-7
James 4:3

The verses you just read are about times when God did not give people what they were praying for. That's because God wanted the people praying to do something else first—confess sin, stop being stubborn, or something like that. The next time you ask God for something, ask yourself: Am I doing my part?

Understanding (3848)

Deuteronomy 4:6
1 Chronicles 22:12
Psalm 119:104
Proverbs 2:6
Proverbs 8:14
Proverbs 11:12
Proverbs 13:15
Proverbs 14:29
Proverbs 17:27
2 Timothy 2:7

God's word gives understanding. Don't get it? Ask God to help you understand the issue better. He can help you learn and apply it to your life.

Unhappiness (0669)

Numbers 11:15
Joshua 7:7
1 Kings 19:4
Job 10:1
Psalm 31:10
Psalm 42:6
Psalm 69:2
Psalm 73:16
Psalm 137:1
Jeremiah 15:10
Micah 7:1
Luke 24:17

Sometimes you have a lot of bad days in a row and you feel sorry for yourself. These people did too. Knowing God doesn't mean bad days won't come. Knowing God means you are never alone, even on your worst day.

Unknown Sins (3357)

Leviticus 4:2
Leviticus 5:17
Luke 12:48
Acts 3:17
1 Timothy 1:13

Yes, it is possible to sin without knowing it. But these verses aren't meant to make you worry about every possible sin you could have done. Just ask God to show you how you've sinned. Then be quick to ask for forgiveness.

Unselfishness (3227)

Genesis 13:9
Genesis 14:23
Genesis 50:21
Numbers 11:29
1 Samuel 18:4
1 Samuel 23:17
2 Samuel 23:17
Daniel 5:17
Romans 15:3
1 Corinthians 10:33
2 Corinthians 8:9
2 Corinthians 12:5

These verses give you examples of people being unselfish. They were giving instead of getting. And they were enjoying it! Do something unselfish for someone else today.

Unthankfulness to People (1459)

Genesis 40:23
Numbers 16:13
Judges 8:35
Judges 9:18
1 Samuel 25:21
2 Chronicles 24:22
Psalm 35:12
Ecclesiastes 9:15
Jeremiah 18:20

In each of these verses someone was not grateful. How did they show it? Mostly by just forgetting. If a person does something nice for you, remember to thank the person.

Used to Sin (2745)

Proverbs 11:3
Proverbs 12:8
Proverbs 15:4
Proverbs 28:6
Ezekiel 9:9
Matthew 17:17
1 Timothy 6:5

These verses are about people who got so used to evil that it didn't bother them anymore. That is a sad and dangerous place to be. Every time you do something bad it makes you a weaker person. Stay away from every kind of evil.

Using What You Have (3451)

Matthew 25:14-15
Luke 19:13
1 Corinthians 4:2
1 Corinthians 6:20
Ephesians 6:7
1 Timothy 6:20
2 Timothy 1:14
1 Peter 4:10

God has given you a lot. You have skills and abilities that can be put to good use, and God wants you to use them. And you are responsible to use the gifts God has given you. Don't waste your time and talents. Use them!

Value of People (2243)

John 3:16
1 Corinthians 6:20
1 Peter 1:18-19
Revelation 1:5

These verses are about your worth to God. To God you are worth the life of his only Son, Jesus. You are certainly more important than money or things. That means you're WAY important!

Valuing the Bible (3697)

Psalm 119:72
Psalm 119:127
Psalm 119:162
Proverbs 23:23

These verses talk about the value of God's word. "Want to have real treasure?" they say, "Get some truth." The truth is worth more than gold. You can find the truth in the Bible. The Bible is a gold mine of truth worth treasuring.

Vengeance (1437)

Exodus 23:5
Proverbs 25:21
Luke 6:27
Luke 6:35
Romans 12:20
1 Thessalonians 5:15

Punch for punch, slap for slap? No! "Vengeance is mine," says the Lord. Do good to those who hurt you.

Violence (2547)
Genesis 6:13
Job 24:2
Psalm 55:9
Psalm 73:6
Proverbs 4:17
Isaiah 59:6
Jeremiah 6:7
Ezekiel 8:17
Amos 3:10
Micah 2:2
Micah 6:12

People have always been violent. It's neither a new problem nor a thing of the past. It breaks God's heart, too, and makes him angry. So let's protect each other and pray the way the Psalm writer did: "Lord, protect me from wicked people and make their lives miserable!" (Psalm 55:9).

Waiting (2693)
Genesis 49:18
Psalm 33:20
Psalm 37:7
Psalm 40:1
Psalm 130:6
Isaiah 25:9
Isaiah 26:8
Isaiah 33:2
Lamentations 3:25
Luke 2:25
Acts 1:4

These verses talk about sticking to God's schedule. Sometimes it seems as if God doesn't act quickly enough. But it's really just that we haven't waited long enough. Have faith. Wait a little longer. God has perfect timing.

Waiting for God (3762)
Psalm 25:5
Psalm 27:14
Psalm 62:5
Psalm 123:2
Proverbs 20:22
Isaiah 8:17
Isaiah 40:31
Hosea 12:6

"Wait for the Lord," these verses say. God does not do everything exactly when we think he should. He is wiser than we are. We need to wait patiently for him. So keep on waiting and trusting that he will do what is good in his own time. Don't ever give up on God.

Walking with God (1267)
Genesis 5:22-24
Genesis 6:9
2 Kings 23:3
Micah 4:5
Malachi 2:6
Revelation 3:4

All the people in these verses walked with God. Walking with God means living your life as if he is walking right beside you and pleasing him every step of the way. You can walk with God no matter how old you are. So, how about it? Are you living with God beside you all the time?

Warning! (3618)
Leviticus 26:16
Joshua 23:15
1 Samuel 12:25
1 Kings 9:7
Psalm 7:12
Isaiah 14:23
Isaiah 66:4
Malachi 3:5

These verses spell it out plainly: Evil people have a bleak future ahead of them. God promises to punish people who persist in doing evil. Take God's warnings seriously.

Waste (1335)
Proverbs 12:27
Proverbs 18:9
Proverbs 29:3
Luke 15:13
Luke 16:1

A lazy person is wasteful. He spends all his money, breaks all his stuff, and uses way more than he needs. Don't be wasteful.

Watch Out! (1799)
Matthew 6:1
Matthew 18:10
Matthew 24:4
Mark 4:24
Mark 13:9
Mark 13:33
Luke 8:18
Luke 11:35
Luke 12:15
Luke 21:8
1 Corinthians 3:10
1 Corinthians 10:12
Colossians 4:17
1 Timothy 4:16
2 Peter 1:19

These verses are caution signs. They say, "Watch out!" and "Danger ahead!" Some sins are like hidden traps, and it pays to know about them so you won't be so tempted to do them. Take a look at your life and listen to these warnings.

Watching for Jesus' Return (1348)
Matthew 24:44
Luke 19:13
1 Corinthians 1:7
1 Corinthians 4:5
1 Thessalonians 5:23
1 Timothy 6:14
Titus 2:13
1 John 2:28

Each verse you just read shows a way people either wait for Jesus' second coming or get ready for it. When you are at ball practice you don't need to stare at the clouds waiting for Jesus' second coming. You need to be playing ball! But the next time Jesus comes it will be a really big deal. God just wants you to look forward to actually SEEING him.

Weakness (3805)
Psalm 8:2
1 Corinthians 1:27
2 Corinthians 12:9-10
2 Corinthians 13:4
Hebrews 11:33-34

What a riddle! How can a weak person be strong? With God's help! God loves to work through weak people, because it shows his strength. Admit your weaknesses so God can show off his strength.

Wealth (3185)
Job 31:24-25, 28
Psalm 52:7
Proverbs 11:28
Proverbs 18:11
Mark 10:24
Luke 12:19-20
1 Timothy 6:17

These verses are about trusting in money and stuff instead of in God. No matter how much good stuff you have, you can never guarantee that you'll never lose it. Only God can guarantee your future. Don't worry if you don't have a lot. And if you do, don't get cocky about it.

What God Knows (3850)
Job 26:6
Job 31:4
Job 34:21
Psalm 147:5
Hebrews 4:13
1 John 3:20

God knows everything! When you feel sad or guilty, don't try to hide it from God. He knows all your problems and mistakes. And he still loves you! Go to God for help.

What Jesus Did (3362)
Isaiah 53:12
Hebrews 9:28
1 Peter 2:24
1 John 3:5

Do you feel guilty all the time, even after you have confessed your sins to God? You don't have to. Because Jesus died, you can be forgiven for EVERY wrong you ever did. Whenever you sin, ask God for forgiveness. Then stop feeling guilty.

Where Is God? (2645)

DEUTERONOMY 4:39
PSALM 139:8
PROVERBS 15:3
ISAIAH 66:1
JEREMIAH 23:24
ACTS 17:27

These verses remind us that God is everywhere. How can that be? It's impossible for us, but not for God. Always remember that God is never away from you. You can talk to him anytime you want—he'll be there listening.

Who Can Be Saved? (3359)

1 CORINTHIANS 15:3
GALATIANS 1:4
1 PETER 2:24
1 JOHN 2:2
REVELATION 1:5

No one is too bad for God. Everyone can be freed from sin because Jesus died for all people. No matter what you have done, go to Jesus. He can save you from your sins.

Who Deserves Christ? (3736)

MATTHEW 10:37
MATTHEW 22:8
ACTS 13:46

Some people think their family is more important than God. Others are too busy to bother with God. These people are not worthy of Christ. Only those who put Christ first deserve to be in his family. What place does Jesus have in your life?

Who Is Religious? (2986)

GENESIS 5:24
GENESIS 6:9
1 CHRONICLES 4:10
2 CHRONICLES 31:20
JOB 1:1
DANIEL 6:10
LUKE 2:25
LUKE 2:37
JOHN 1:47
JOHN 8:29
ACTS 10:2
ACTS 11:24
ACTS 22:12
2 TIMOTHY 1:5

The people described in these verses were all deeply religious. They cared a great deal about God and about pleasing him. Some of them were fishermen. Some were carpenters and tentmakers. Some were young and some were quite old. They are some of the best role models you'll ever find.

Whom Can You Trust? (1330)

JOB 16:20
JOB 19:19
PSALM 38:11
MICAH 7:5
MATTHEW 26:56
JOHN 16:32
2 TIMOTHY 1:15
2 TIMOTHY 4:10

You wouldn't want the friends you just read about, would you? False friends will always let you down, but even good friends sometimes do it. That's why the Bible tells us not to place all our trust in people—even in our friends. Some friends let you down because they're not really friends; others do it because they're only human and make a mistake. Don't expect your friends always to come through for you. Only God can be a perfect friend.

Why Do Right? (3737)

PSALM 7:10
PSALM 32:11
PSALM 37:37
PSALM 49:14
PSALM 64:10
PSALM 97:11
PSALM 112:4
PROVERBS 2:7
PROVERBS 2:21
PROVERBS 10:9
PROVERBS 14:11
PROVERBS 28:6

God blesses those who do what is right. Some sins may be fun for a little while. But God's way is best in the long run. If you want to enjoy God's blessings, always try to do what is right.

Why Fear God? (3035)

1 SAMUEL 12:14
PSALM 25:12
PSALM 31:19
PSALM 103:13
PSALM 147:11
PROVERBS 1:7
ISAIAH 50:10
MALACHI 3:16
LUKE 1:50
ACTS 10:35

These verses do say that there are benefits in fearing God. When you fear God that means you realize how big and powerful he is. But you don't have to be afraid that he will hurt you; he loves you more than you can possibly imagine. Respect God and his power the way you respect a mighty king.

Why Jesus Came (3360)

LUKE 2:11
LUKE 19:10
JOHN 3:17
ACTS 5:31
ACTS 13:23
1 TIMOTHY 1:15
2 TIMOTHY 1:10
HEBREWS 7:25
1 JOHN 4:14

Jesus had one reason to come to earth—us! He came to save us from our sins. That includes you. Have you asked Jesus to take away your sins? Have you thanked him for it?

Why Jesus Died (3361)

PSALM 69:9
ISAIAH 53:5
2 CORINTHIANS 5:21
GALATIANS 3:13
HEBREWS 2:9
HEBREWS 9:28
1 PETER 2:24
1 PETER 3:18

Without Jesus, we would be in BAD shape. We all deserve to die for our sins. Don't pay the price for your sins. Accept what Jesus has done for you—receive his gift of forgiveness and follow him always.

Why Not Sin? (3352)

GENESIS 2:17
GENESIS 3:19
DEUTERONOMY 32:51
1 CHRONICLES 10:13
PROVERBS 11:19
EZEKIEL 18:4
ROMANS 5:12
ROMANS 6:23

The verses you just read say more than, "do not sin." They tell you why not. Sin destroys. Sin eventually kills. And sin keeps you from knowing God is with you. That's three good reasons, huh?

Why Suffer? (3476)

LUKE 6:22
1 TIMOTHY 4:10
HEBREWS 10:33
HEBREWS 11:26
HEBREWS 13:13
1 PETER 4:14

It is not easy being a Christian. Other kids may make fun of you, insult you, or ignore you. People will hurt you. But suffering for Jesus is worth the pain because of the reward. Although Jesus says you will suffer, he promises to reward you. He will bless you. Ask Jesus to help you through it.

Why the Bible? (0424)
John 20:31
Romans 15:4
1 Corinthians 10:11
1 John 5:13

This isn't a book about small matters. It's a big book about big topics such as hope for the future, dangers to watch out for, and eternal life. That's why God gave us the Bible. It tells us everything we need to know about how to live, both now and forever. It has something for you today.

Wicked Insecurity (3180)
Psalm 73:18
Proverbs 23:34
Isaiah 30:13
Jeremiah 13:16
Jeremiah 23:12
Ezekiel 13:10-11
Matthew 7:26-27

These verses are about the horrible disadvantage you face when you live your life apart from God. In short, you risk suffering the consequences of sin. Those consequences are as real and painful as a broken family, a ruined future, and an incurable disease. Follow Jesus if you want less to worry about.

Willingness to Learn (2962)
Ezra 8:21
Jeremiah 42:3
Matthew 18:3
Luke 11:1
John 9:36
Acts 2:37
Acts 8:31
Acts 9:6
Acts 16:30

These verses are about people who wanted to learn about God so much that they ASKED someone to teach them. Don't be so busy telling people what you know about God that you don't have time to learn about God from them.

Willingness to Work (3892)
Judges 5:2
Judges 8:25
Nehemiah 11:2
Psalm 110:3
Isaiah 1:19
2 Corinthians 8:3
1 Thessalonians 2:8

God loves a willing worker. Don't make excuses or try to get out of your work. Get busy!

Wise Thoughts (2356)
Psalm 48:9
Psalm 119:59
Proverbs 12:5
Proverbs 21:5
Romans 12:3
Philippians 4:8

God is telling you in these verses to have wise thoughts. You don't have control over what pops into your mind, but you do have control over whether it stays there. And you have control over what you watch, read, and see. Fill your mind with what is good, pure, and pleasing to God. It will make you wise.

Wise Words (3297)
Job 6:25
Proverbs 15:23
Proverbs 16:24
Proverbs 25:11
Ecclesiastes 9:17
Ecclesiastes 10:12
Ecclesiastes 12:11
Isaiah 50:4

These verses are about the words you speak. The words you speak can make a big difference in the lives of people around you. Say constructive, encouraging words.

Witnessing (3603)
Isaiah 43:10
John 15:27
Acts 1:8
Acts 5:20-21
Acts 18:9-10
Acts 22:14-15
Titus 2:15

"You are my witnesses," said Jesus. That means God relies on you to tell others about him. You don't need to keep the good news to yourself. Share it!

Work (3890)
Matthew 25:22-23
Mark 14:8
Luke 12:48
1 Peter 4:11

Energy, talent, and time—God has given you all you need to get your work done. He will never give you an impossible job. So don't give up! Use your time well and your work will get done.

Work that Helps Others (3888)
2 Chronicles 28:15
Job 29:15-16
Proverbs 31:20
Isaiah 21:14
Isaiah 50:4
Matthew 25:35
Luke 10:34
1 Corinthians 16:15-16
2 Corinthians 1:11
Philippians 4:3

You can choose two kinds of work: (1) work that helps you or (2) work that helps others. God wants you to spend your time working to help others. Look for people who need help. Then do what you can to help them.

Working Hard (0605)
Genesis 2:15
Genesis 3:19
Leviticus 23:3
Proverbs 13:11
Proverbs 14:23
Ecclesiastes 9:10
Ephesians 4:28
1 Thessalonians 4:11
2 Thessalonians 3:12

God wants us to work and not sit around all the time. Right now for you, that probably means learning in school and being a helpful part of the family. Don't do either one halfway. God wants you to give your best whether you are cleaning your room, doing your homework, making your lunch, or doing your science project.

Working with God (3891)
1 Samuel 14:45
Mark 16:20
1 Corinthians 3:9
2 Corinthians 6:1

Too much work to do? Don't worry. God is with you. Don't try to do it all on your own. Ask God to help you get your work done.

Worry (3022)
Psalm 127:2
Matthew 6:25
Matthew 13:22
Luke 10:41
Luke 12:29
Luke 21:34
1 Corinthians 7:32
Philippians 4:6
1 Peter 5:7

These verses are about worry. Everyone has plenty to worry about—friends, school, clothes, mistakes, money, you name it. But worrying doesn't help, and God has it all under control anyway. Face trouble when it comes, but don't worry about it. God cares for you. Give your worries to him.

Worship (3921)
Deuteronomy 26:10
2 Kings 17:36
1 Chronicles 16:29
Psalm 29:2
Psalm 95:6
Psalm 96:9
Psalm 99:5
Zechariah 14:17
Matthew 4:10
John 4:24
Revelation 14:7
Revelation 15:4
Revelation 19:10
Revelation 22:9

"Worship the Lord." This is more than a good idea. It is a command. God wants you to worship him. And he deserves it. Give him the worship he deserves!

Worshiping Things (3748)
Deuteronomy 32:21
1 Kings 16:13
Psalm 31:6
Jeremiah 2:5
Jeremiah 10:8
Jeremiah 16:19
Jonah 2:8
Acts 14:15

These verses warn us not to worship "worthless idols." Anything that takes God's place in your life is an idol. Don't let anything become more important to you than God. Always put God first.

Young Leaders (3965)
Genesis 41:46
1 Samuel 17:33
2 Samuel 5:4
2 Chronicles 24:1
2 Chronicles 34:1,3
Luke 3:23
Luke 18:18
Acts 7:58
Acts 9:6
Acts 9:22

All of the people in these verses became leaders when they were young. God can use anyone, even a kid, to lead others. Don't think that you're too young for God to use you. Ask God to show you how you might be a leader.

Young Men (3966)
Genesis 41:38
Genesis 41:46
1 Samuel 2:26
1 Samuel 3:1
1 Samuel 17:33
1 Samuel 17:37
2 Chronicles 24:1-2
2 Chronicles 34:1-3
Psalm 71:5
Luke 2:49
2 Timothy 1:5
2 Timothy 3:15

"You're too young!" Have you ever heard that? God doesn't think you're too young to do important work for him. God can use you just as he used the young men in these verses. Don't wait until you've grown up to start living for God. Let God use you now.

Young Women (3968)
Judges 11:36
Ruth 1:16
Esther 4:16
Mark 16:1
Luke 1:38
Luke 10:39
John 11:24
John 12:3
Acts 21:9

The young women in these verses may have lived many years ago, but their examples show us how to live in any time of history. They were faithful, pure, loving, obedient, and caring. Ask God to help you develop these traits.

Your Body (3656)
1 Samuel 20:3
Psalm 38:10
Psalm 49:12
Psalm 78:39
Psalm 103:14
Psalm 141:7
Isaiah 2:22
Isaiah 40:6
Isaiah 64:6
1 Peter 1:24

Life is short! No matter how well we take care of ourselves, our bodies will get sick and die some day. Don't count on your body to last forever. And don't worry too much if it isn't perfect. It's only a temporary dwelling.

Your Testimony (3600)
1 Chronicles 16:8
Psalm 107:2
Isaiah 12:4
Isaiah 62:6
Jeremiah 51:10
Mark 5:18-19
Acts 1:8
Ephesians 5:19
2 Timothy 1:8
1 Peter 3:15

If you don't know how to tell your friends about Jesus, just tell them what God has done for you. Learn all you can to answer their questions. And always treat them with respect. Tell them what God has done for YOU, and leave the rest to God.

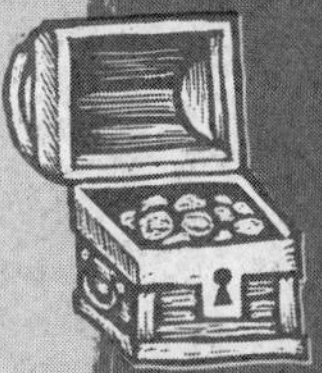

Daily Treasures from God—Note Pages

The Bible is a big book. That's good, because it means there's a lot there. God has told us a great deal. He's let us in on a lot of secrets.

You'll discover lots of secrets as you use the *Daily Treasures from God* pages that are in the front of this Bible. This reading plan will help you find answers to your questions. You'll want to be sure to write down the answers when you learn something new. It's harder to forget something after you've written it down.

The following pages provide the perfect place to take notes. Write down the answers you find. You'll be surprised at how much the Bible has to say to you!

January

ME

GOD

WORK

ADULTS

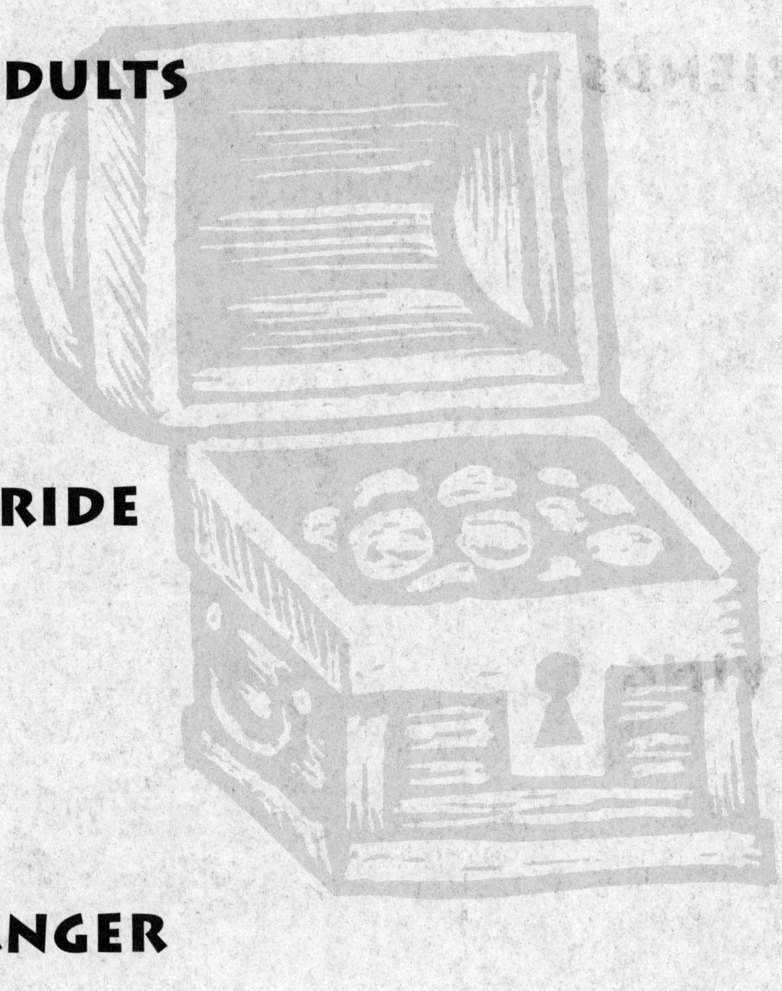

PRIDE

ANGER

February

FRIENDS

GIVING

SELF-CONFIDENCE

CHRISTIAN LIFE

March

BAD PEOPLE

ANGELS

DRINKING

ATTITUDES

BIBLE

PROBLEMS

WORSHIP

GOD'S WILL

April

DANGERS

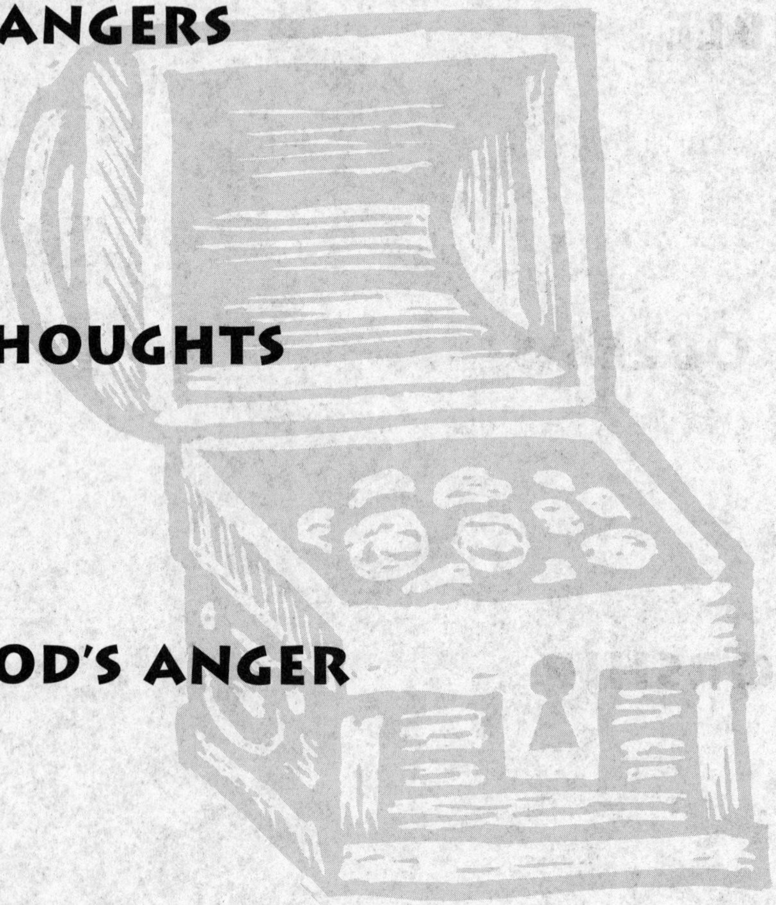

THOUGHTS

GOD'S ANGER

VALUE OF PEOPLE

PRIORITIES

MONEY

GROWING UP

July

TIME

FAMILY LIFE

FORGIVENESS

LYING

FUTURE

FAITH

SIN

FUN

August

JESUS

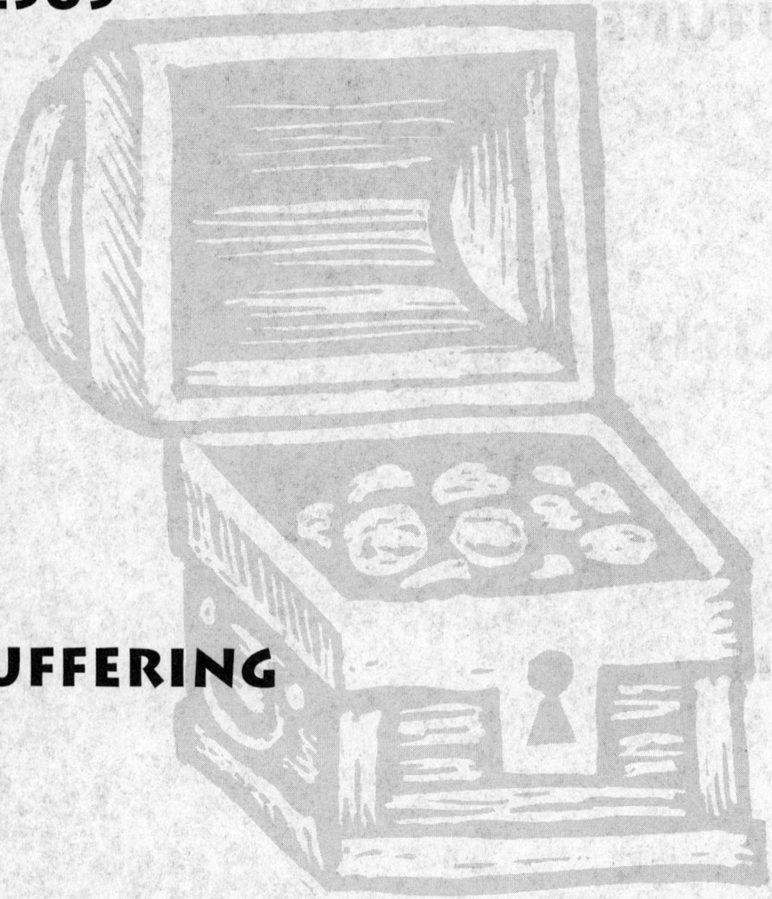

SUFFERING

PRAYER

September

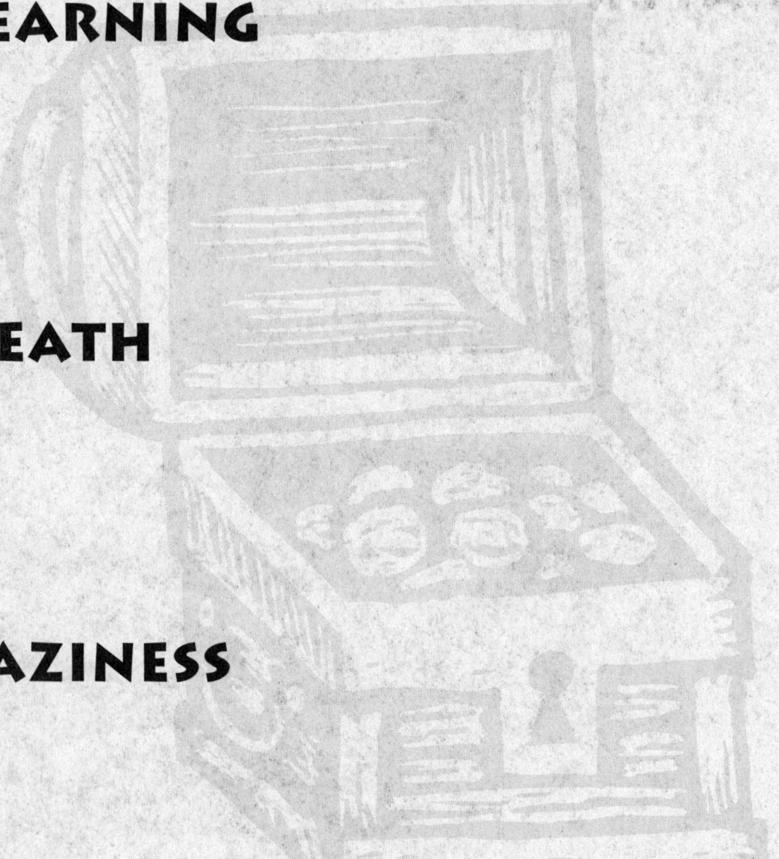

LEARNING

DEATH

LAZINESS

FEAR/COURAGE

REPENTANCE

FOOD

LEADERSHIP

WISDOM

October

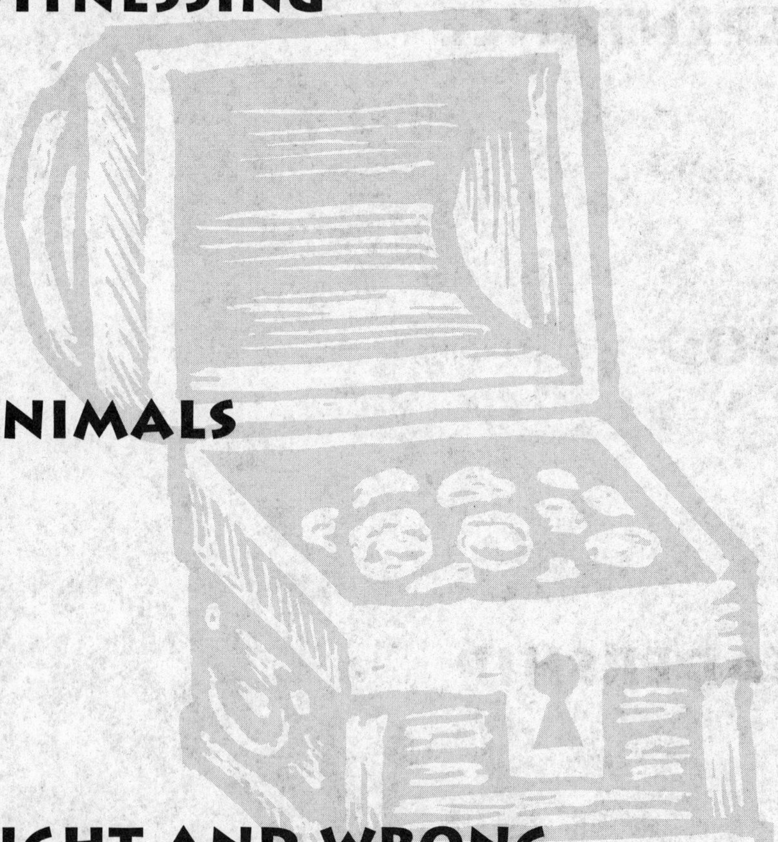

WITNESSING

ANIMALS

RIGHT AND WRONG

LIVING IN THE WORLD

FIGHTING

November

TRUSTING GOD

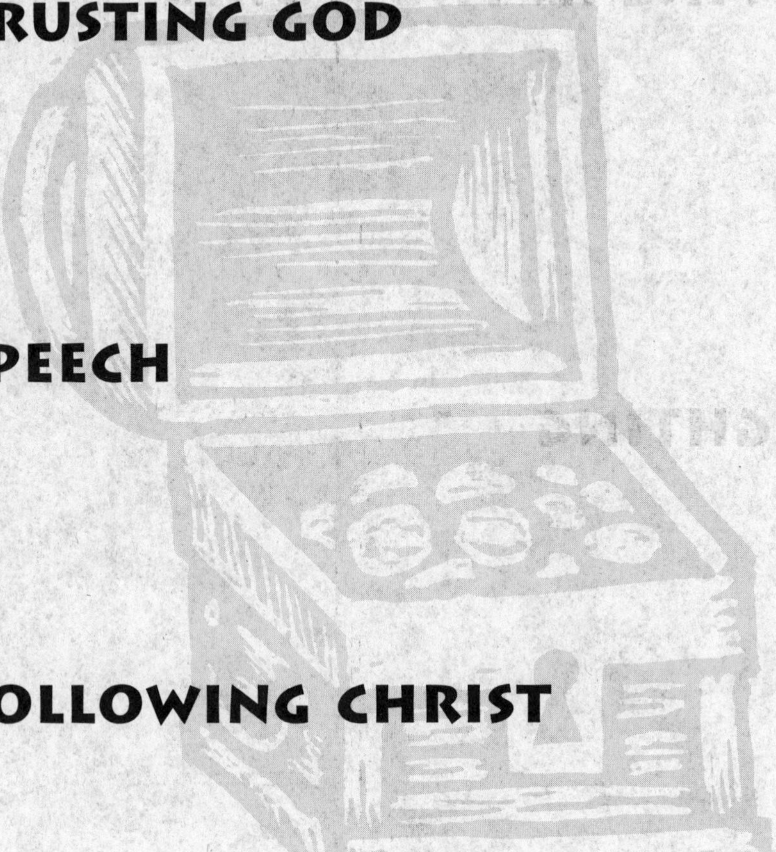

SPEECH

FOLLOWING CHRIST

CHURCH

JOKING AND TEASING

THANKFULNESS

ADVICE

December

THINGS

POOR PEOPLE

HAPPINESS

HELPING PEOPLE

RETURN OF CHRIST

FAILURE